CW00536790

AUTOCOURSE

GRAND PRIX
WHO'S WHO

4th EDITION

icon
PUBLISHING LIMITED

AUTOCOURSE
GRAND PRIX WHO'S WHO

4th EDITION

STEVE SMALL

First published in 1994 by Guinness Publishing
Second edition 1996 by Guinness Publishing
Third edition 2000 by Travel Publishing

Published in Great Britain by
Icon Publishing Limited
Regent Lodge, 4 Hanley Road
Malvern, Worcestershire, WR14 4PQ

www.autocourse.com

Publisher: Steve Small
Commercial director: Bryn Williams
Text editor: Ian Penberthy

Printed and bound in China through
World Print Limited
Hong Kong

DISTRIBUTORS
Gardners Books
1 Whittle Drive, Eastbourne,
East Sussex BN23 6QH
Tel: +44 (0)1323 521555
email: sales@gardners.com

Chaters Wholesale Ltd
25/26 Murrell Green Business Park,
Hook, Hampshire RG27 9GR
Telephone: +44 (0) 1256 765 443
Fax: +44 (0)1256 769 900
email: books@chaters.co.uk

NORTH AMERICA
Quayside Distribution Services
400 First Avenue North, Suite 300
Minneapolis, MN 55401 USA
Telephone: 612 344 8100
Fax: 612 344 8691

A catalogue record of this book is available from the
British Library

ISBN 978-1905334-69-8

ACKNOWLEDGEMENTS

MANY friends and colleagues gave their encouragement and assistance during the many years it took for this project to reach fruition initially and then again during the preparation of this fourth edition. I can truly say that without their help this volume would not have been so complete.

A number of people must be singled out for their sterling efforts on my behalf. Firstly, the late John Taylor, who was well known to serious followers of the sport for more than a decade as the statistical guru of the leading grand prix annual AUTOCOURSE. When I first discussed the idea for the first edition with him back in 1988, he willingly undertook the massive job of placing much of the contents of my reference folders on to a computer database, keeping his eagle eye open for the inevitable inaccuracies and omissions, and putting them right. Sadly, his early death from muscular dystrophy in 1991 meant that he did not see the finished article to which he had made such a major contribution. I was also fortunate indeed to enlist the help of the Autocourse house editor Peter Lovering. His skills and patience were stretched to the limit for the first three editions as he brought some semblance of literacy to the biographical pieces. This essential task has now been taken over with equal dedication by Ian Penberthy, who has become equally adept at putting to rights my wayward grammar!

Very special thanks go to Sir Jackie Stewart for so kindly contributing a foreword to this fourth edition. His deeds were indeed the stuff of legend, and he was one of the drivers of my youth who were an inspiration for this book.

Apart from the aforementioned, my gratitude goes to the following for their help, enthusiasm and forbearance over the years: Kathy Ager, Jean-Luc Alexandre, Simon Arron, Chris Bailey, Jeff Bloxham, Allen Brown, Mark Brown, Diana Burnett, Paul-Henri Cahier, Adriano Cimarosti, Donald Davidson, Paddy Driver, Simon Duncan, Peter J. Fox, Paul Fearnley, Soda Hayata, David Hayhoe, Alan Henry, Peter Higham, Neil Hodges, David Holland, Darrell Ingham, Roland J. Kraus, Christine Lalla, Hartmut Lehbrink, Richard Jenkins, Ian Marshall, Marius Matthee, Sir Stirling Moss, Wilfried Müller, Dave Nicholas, Doug Nye, Peter Nygaard, Edgardo Otero, Steven Palmer, Jimmy Piget, Ivan Ponting, Richard Poulter, Stuart Pringle, David Smith, Roger Smith, Nigel Snowdon, Keith and Mark Sutton, Steve Tee, Murray Walker, Ted Walker, Antonio Watson, Christian Weber, Bryn Williams and family, Jo Wright and Tim Wright and Kevin Wood. I apologise for any omissions here, which are entirely unintentional. In any case you know your help has been much appreciated.

I am also grateful for permission to reproduce photographs. The vast majority are from the amazing collection of LAT Photographic, with additional, but telling contributions from the Autocourse Archive, the Cahier Archive, Tony Crook, Ferret Fotographic, Graham Gauld, GP Photo, Maurice Louche, the Ludvigsen Library, Mercedes-Benz Archive, MPS (Motoring Press Service, Japan), Jürgen Nill, Yves Peyrouse, John Ross, Sutton Images, Roger Swann, Bob Tronolone and Christian Weber.

Efforts have been made to trace copyright holders of all photographs used in this book. I apologise for any omissions, which are unintentional, and would be pleased to include an appropriate acknowledgement in any subsequent edition.

ABOUT THE AUTHOR

MY earliest motorsport memory is of seeing some TV coverage of the 1961 British Grand Prix at Aintree. The circuit was only a few miles from my home and I was lucky enough to pay a visit to that year, but as luck would have it my big day out was for the Grand National and a different type of horse-power was on the agenda!

Nevertheless, I became a serious follower of motorsport by the mid-1960s, when the likes of Jim Clark, Graham Hill, Jochen Rindt and Jackie Stewart seemed to be racing almost every weekend across the many categories of the sport. It was then that I began compiling a motor sport library that eventually fuelled the ambition to produce the Grand Prix Who's Who.

Having gained a Dip. A.D. and M.A. in Graphic Design, I worked for more than a decade in advertising and design, before moving into the world of publishing. Since 1986, I have been the art editor, and now the publisher, of the prestigious motorsport annuals AUTOCOURSE and MOTOCOURSE, as well as many other acclaimed sporting titles.

The vast majority of photographs in this book have been provided from the AUTOCOURSE archive and the amazing LAT PHOTOGRAPHIC library.

LAT PHOTOGRAPHIC
www. latphoto.co.uk

Additional photographs from the following sources have helped immensely in bringing a freshness and vitality to the fourth edition.

CAHIER ARCHIVE
www.f1-photo.com
Bernoldi, Courage, de Portago, Eaton, Firman, Gendebien, Ickx, Mass, Patrese, Papis, Sala, Ayrton Senna, Stacey, Jackie Stewart, Stuck.

GETTY IMAGES
www.gettyimages.com
Ascari, Castellotti, Moss, Servoz-Gavin.

GRAND PRIX PHOTO
www.grandprixphoto.com
Baghetti, Cevert, Fangio, Frentzen, McLaren, Musso, Schell, Wacker.

PETER J.FOX PHOTOGRAPHY
www.peterjfox.com
Alguersuari, Alonso, Barrichello, Bourdais, Buemi, Button, Chandhok, Coulthard, d'Ambrosio, Davidson, de la Rosa, di Resta, Fisichella, Glock, Hülkenberg, Klien, Kobayashi, Kubica, Liuzzi, Massa, Kazuki Nakajima, Petrov, Nelson Piquet Jnr., Räikkönen, Nico Rosberg, Sato, Ralf Schumacher, Bruno Senna, Adrian Sutil, Jarno Truli, Webber, Markus Winkelhock, Wurz, Yamamoto.

HISPANIA RACING TEAM
Karthikeyan, Ricciardo.

LOTUS-RENAULT
Grosjean, Heidfeld.

RED BULL RACING
Title spread, Doornbos, Speed, Vettel.

SAUBER F1
Pérez.

SUTTON IMAGES
www.suttonimages.com
Adams, Amon, Botha, Brack, Brise, Cannon, Clark, Crawford, Gartner, Hahne, Hailwood, Graham Hill, Keizan, Kessel, Moreno, Morgan, Posey, Roos, Schuppan, Spence, Soler-Roig, Sullivan, Surtees, Aguri Suzuki, Toshio Suzuki, van Rooyen, von Opel, Dave Walker, Wilds.

FOREWORD by SIR JACKIE STEWART, OBE

FORMULA ONE Grand Prix racing and the FIA Formula One World Championship have come a long way. The first Grand Épreuve that counted for the 1950 World Championship started a magic carpet ride that has certainly seen its triumphs and sometimes its tragedies. Over more than 60 years, it has developed into a giant sport on a global basis.

I am old enough and lucky enough to have been able to take an interest in the sport from the very beginning. I was fortunate to have a big brother, eight years my senior, Jimmy Stewart, who took me to Silverstone when he drove for Ecurie Ecosse in the 1953 British Grand Prix. He was lying fifth, with ten laps to go, which meant that he was the leading British driver, until he went straight on at Copse Corner and badly damaged his Cooper Bristol, such that he had a DNF (Did Not Finish).

That weekend, however, I had the thrill of collecting some of the greatest names in the world of motorsport in my autograph book. I've still got it and it's one of my proudest possessions. For me, in those days as a wee boy, I could only have dreamed of playing a part in this fantastic sport, but remarkably that dream came true and I was able to make my mark on some of those 60-plus years of F1.

I was lucky to befriend a man called Fangio, who was my hero. One of the most important things in my life was to carry him to his last resting place. I was privileged to be driven by him and later the same day to drive the great man myself.

My first world championship grand prix was on New Year's Day in 1965, when I drove in the Grand Prix of South Africa in East London, managing to pick up a world championship point. It was a good year for me, and I managed to win a non-championship Formula 1 race, the Daily Express International Trophy at Silverstone, and then later in the season to win the Italian Grand Prix at Monza. I picked up enough points to end my rookie year in third place in the world championship, behind two great drivers: Jim Clark and Graham Hill.

Grand prix racing has changed enormously over the years. The technology over those six decades has constantly reached new heights and shapes, and there have been new ways of doing business and new financial benefits for drivers and teams alike. It has not been all sunshine, however; there have been quite a few showers, sometimes with very dark clouds that overshadowed our sport. Our safety record was abysmal for a period of time. Fortunately, that was corrected and today we have one of the best examples of risk management of any multi-national corporation, industry or sport.

I have seen a kaleidoscope of fantastically charismatic and skilled participants in the sport, not just the drivers, but the constructors, team owners, engineers, designers and aerodynamicists.

Television made F1 the world's largest broadcast sport. The whole world has become motorised and there is a distinct relationship, sometimes even a love affair, between man and machine; a large percentage of women drivers and car owners are also enthusiasts of the highest level of motorsport.

Formula One Grand Prix racing has focused the attention of the world on countries that few people even knew existed. It has projected those 'newly discovered' countries to hundreds of millions of people who watch the sport so passionately in today's high-definition, multi-camera analytical displays, becoming intoxicated by the sport, its colour, its glamour and its excitement.

Many people have played a part in making F1 what it is today, whether they be the car makers, the fuel and oil producers or the tyre manufacturers; not to mention the team owners or the multi-national sponsors who continue to project the sport commercially for the benefit of many.

There is the glamorous, global recognition of a name like Ferrari, established when the great Enzo Ferrari himself was leading his team and appearing from time to time at grands prix. Also Alfred Neubauer of Mercedes-Benz, Colin Chapman, John Cooper, Sir Alfred Owen, Frank Williams, Ken Tyrrell and Ron Dennis, and many more who have made it all happen in such a kaleidoscope of colour, motion, risk and reward.

Bernie Ecclestone must surely be recognised for bringing grand prix racing and its world championship to an extraordinarily high level in the business world, and for raising the game and the presentational skills that go along with F1, providing an example not only to other sports, but also to other industries and businesses.

The loss of life that we experienced for a while must be fully recognised, and those drivers who have paid the ultimate price have been deeply mourned over the years. We have lost so many wonderful and charismatic drivers. Fortunately, I have been truly blessed. I have never drawn blood from my body while driving a racing car, and I am still here, along with Stirling Moss, Tony Brooks, John Surtees and Jack Brabham. All of us of a certain age that allows us to have seen the sport from its very beginning; all of those 60-plus years.

Steve Small has produced a hugely informative publication, which marries a wealth of easy-to-use statistics with carefully researched biographies. Illustrated by a fascinating selection of contemporary photographs, this much enlarged fourth edition is undoubtedly the standard work of reference on grand prix drivers past and present, and it should find a place on the bookshelf of every motor racing enthusiast.

INTRODUCTION

THE first seeds of AUTOCOURSE GRAND PRIX WHO'S WHO were sown in the mid-1970s, when I began piecing together records of grand prix drivers' careers, not just in Formula 1, but in all other types of racing as well. My files began to multiply at a disconcerting rate as trivial and minor, seemingly irrelevant information about every driver was recorded. Even then, I had in mind a volume of this sort, but not perhaps of this magnitude or detail.

As time passed, I became increasingly aware of the need for such a book. There were few single sources of reference that enabled a reader to chart a driver's grand prix career, and even those were selective, usually concerning themselves merely with the upper strata, those who had scored championship points. It was this lack of completeness at even the most fundamental level that spurred me on. Through the 1980s, with the huge upsurge of statistical works on sport in general, I genuinely believed that someone must be about to publish a book of this sort – but still nothing was forthcoming. So, as outlined in the Acknowledgements, the first edition of the book took shape over a span of some five years, and the initial concept has not been altered fundamentally for this new and fully revised and enlarged fourth edition.

This is the first time the book has been compiled with the aid of the Internet and the instant access it provides to a plethora of websites, some of which are truly excellent, while many others frankly are a waste of time. Going online has been something of a double-edged sword. Simply checking a particular fact can be done in no time, but attempting to chase down a particular story can often lead one down many never-ending avenues, providing an amazing amount of material that is far too much to be used here. Thus I hope that this book prompts the reader to explore more deeply the story of a particular driver via both the print and online media.

Aside from the biographies, the raison d'être of this book is the unique statistical data, which is provided for every driver who has ever started a world championship grand prix since the inception of the drivers' championship in 1950, arranged alphabetically. Each driver's grand prix career is set out in chronological order on a race-by-race basis. Here you will find: the placing, the race, the circuit, the car number, the entrant, the tyre used, the car and engine, a commentary and a qualifying ranking from total entries. The last shows the qualifying position attained by each driver plus the total number of drivers entered for that particular race. These are not necessarily final starting positions, because drivers who failed to make the grid have their position shown between brackets in the place they should have occupied. This of course means that all slower drivers are moved one place down the order.

Since the third edition, the biographical details have also been expanded to include the driver's place of birth and death, and for this information I must thank both David Hayhoe and David Holland, who generously suggested I take advantage of the tireless research incorporated in their mammoth and highly recommended Grand Prix Data Book, last published in 2006.

As this work is focused on the drivers, I have steered clear of the minefield that is individual car chassis numbers; quite honestly, they have no place here, and would merely add to the clutter. What I have done, however, is to include additional lines where a driver competed in a different chassis/engine combination either in official practice or in the race itself: for example, Michele Alboreto in Austria in 1983 racing the Tyrrell 012, but practising in the 011 as well; or Peter Arundell at Brands Hatch in 1966 driving two Lotus 33s, one with a BRM engine and the other with a Climax. A word of warning regarding the race numbers: these are now allocated for a whole season, but this was not the case in earlier days. It was not uncommon for some Continental race organisers to change the numbers between practice and race, to try to defeat the wiles of pirate programme producers, so total accuracy in this respect is next to impossible. The same applies to the comment column. Published reasons for retirements and so forth often have proved to be contradictory, and sometimes teams were quite happy to give totally fictitious explanations for the failure of their cars in an attempt to disguise any weaknesses. Wherever possible, I have followed the most generally held views, but someone out there probably knows different.

I have concerned myself solely with the core statistics as described; there are other authors whose books compare and analyse racing data, and I am happy to leave that field in their most capable hands. At the end of each driver's entry, however, I have included a line giving details of his total starts, wins, pole positions, fastest laps and points scored. It should be noted that the recent changes to the number of points awarded for the first- to tenth-place finishers have made totals scored in earlier years meaningless for comparison purposes.

The vexed question of starts should be addressed here. For when does a driver 'start' a grand prix? To my mind, he does so only if he is on the grid when the flag drops or light goes green at the final start. If a driver failed to complete the parade lap, for instance (as was the case with Alain Prost at Imola in 1990), he cannot truly be said to have started the race. In the case of a restarted event, the restart is the only one that counts. By way of example, consider the British GP in 1986: poor Jacques Laffite certainly started the race, but it was declared null and void, and he was not present to take the restart. The different rules governing incidents of this sort over the years have led to inconsistencies that probably will never be resolved satisfactorily. I have decided, wherever applicable, to give two totals: the first being the true number of actual final race starts; and the second to include any incidents of the kind outlined.

TYRES

KEY FOR TYRES SHOWN IN STATISTICS

A: Avon
B: Bridgestone
C: Continental
D: Dunlop
E: Engelbert
F: Firestone
G: Goodyear
M: Michelin
P: Pirelli

SELECTED BIBLIOGRAPHY

YEARBOOKS, MAGAZINES & PERIODICALS

AUTOCAR & MOTOR
AUTOSPORT
GRAND PRIX INTERNATIONAL
MOTORING NEWS
MOTOR SPORT
ROAD & TRACK
GRAND PRIX YEAR
AUTOCOURSE
THE 'MOTOR' YEARBOOK 1948 to 1960
MARLBORO GRAND PRIX GUIDE 1972 to 1974
JOHN PLAYER MOTOR SPORT YEAR 1972 to 1976
INTERNATIONAL MOTOR RACING YEAR 1977 to 1978
MOTOR RACING AND RALLY DIRECTORY 1957
AUTOCOURSE CART OFFICIAL YEARBOOKS 1993 to 2005

DERRICK ALLSOP
THE BRITISH RACING HERO
FROM MOSS TO MANSELL
Magna Books

MICHAEL ARGETSINGER
WALT HANSGEN
David Bull Publishing

MICHAEL ARGETSINGER
MARK DONOHUE
David Bull Publishing

JOHN BLUNSDEN
FORMULA JUNIOR
MRP

KEN BRESLAUER
SEBRING
THE OFFICIAL HISTORY OF AMERICA'S GREAT SPORTS CAR RACE
David Bull Publishing

ADAM COOPER
PIERS COURAGE – *LAST OF THE GENTLEMAN RACERS*
Haynes Publishing

MICHAEL COOPER-EVANS
ROB WALKER
Hazleton Publishing

ROBERT CUTTER & BOB FENDELL
ENCYCLOPEDIA OF AUTO GREATS
Prentice Hall

ROBERT DALEY
THE CRUEL SPORT
Studio Vista

ROBERT DALEY
CARS AT SPEED
Foulis

LYLE KENYON ENGEL
JACKIE STEWART – *WORLD DRIVING CHAMPION*
Arco Publishing

EMERSON FITTIPALDI & ELIZABETH HAYWARD
FLYING ON THE GROUND
William Kimber

GRAHAM GAULD
FROM THE FELLS TO FERRARI –
THE OFFICIAL BIOGRAPHY OF CLIFF ALLISON
Veloce

GRAHAM GAULD
REG PARNELL
PSL

G. N. GEORGEANO (Ed)
ENCYCLOPEDIA OF MOTOR RACING
Ebury Press and Michael Joseph

MAURICE HAMILTON
BRITISH GRAND PRIX
Crowood Press

DAVID HAYHOE and DAVID HOLLAND
GRAND PRIX DATA BOOK 4
Haynes Publishing

ALAN HENRY
MARCH, THE GRAND PRIX & INDY CARS
Hazleton Publishing

ALAN HENRY
AUTOCOURSE 60 YEARS OF WORLD CHAMPIONSHIP GRAND PRIX MOTOR RACING
Icon Publishing Limited

PETER HIGHAM
INTERNATIONAL MOTOR RACING GUIDE
David Bull Publishing

INNES IRELAND
ALL ARMS AND ELBOWS
Transport Bookman

DENIS JENKINSON (Ed)
FANGIO
Michael Joseph

DENIS JENKINSON & CYRIL POSTHUMUS
VANWALL
Patrick Stephens

JENKINSON/ROEBUCK/HENRY/HAMILTON
THE GRAND PRIX DRIVERS
Hazleton Publishing

CHRIS JONES
ROAD RACE
George Allen & Unwin

MICHAEL KEYSER
THE SPEED MERCHANTS
Prentice Hall

GORDON KIRBY
EMERSON FITTIPALDI
Hazleton Publishing

HARTUT LEHBRINK
RACING FOR MERCEDES-BENZ –
A DICTIONARY OF THE 240 FASTEST DRIVERS OF MERCEDES-BENZ
Veloce

PETER MILLER
MEN AT THE WHEEL
Batsford

PETER MILLER
THE FAST ONES
Stanley Paul

GREG MILLS
FOR THE LOVE OF IT – *JOHN LOVE AND AN ERA OF SOUTHERN AFRICAN MOTORSPORT*
Ecurie Zoo

GREG MILLS
TONY MAGGS – *SOUTH AFRICA'S FORGOTTEN GRAND PRIX ACE*
Ecurie Zoo

GREG MILLS
PADDY – WHO?
Ecurie Zoo

CHRIS NIXON
RACING WITH THE DAVID BROWN ASTON MARTINS Vols 1 & 2
Transport Bookman

DOUG NYE
THE AUTOCOURSE HISTORY OF THE GRAND PRIX CAR 1945–65 & 1966–91
Hazleton Publishing

DOUG NYE
THEME LOTUS 1958–86
MRP

DOUG NYE
DINO – THE LITTLE FERRARI
Osprey

DOUG NYE
RACERS: *THE INSIDE STORY OF WILLIAMS GRAND PRIX ENGINEERING*
Osprey

DOUG NYE
COOPER CARS
Osprey

JIMMY PIGET
COMPANION TO FORMULA 1 REGISTER FACT BOOKS
Jimmy Piget

JIMMY PIGET
MEMENTO FOR GRAND PRIX, INDY CAR and OTHER MAJOR SINGLE SEATER RACES
Jimmy Piget

HEINZ PRÜLLER
JOCHEN RINDT
William Kimber

PETER REVSON & LEON MANDEL
SPEED WITH STYLE – *THE AUTOBIOGRAPHY OF PETER REVSON*
William Kimber

NIGEL ROEBUCK
GRAND PRIX GREATS
Patrick Stephens

Dr K. PAUL SHELDON with DUNCAN RABAGLIATI
A RECORD OF GRAND PRIX AND VOITURETTE RACING – Volumes 5, 6, 7 & 8
St Leonard's Press

IAN H. SMITH
THE STORY OF LOTUS – 1947–1960
THE BIRTH OF A LEGEND
MRP

ROGER SMITH
FORMULA 1 – ALL THE RACES
Haynes

JOHN SURTEES
JOHN SURTEES – WORLD CHAMPION
Hazleton Publishing

HANS TANNER & DOUG NYE
FERRARI – Fifth Edition
Haynes

JONATHAN THOMPSON with DUNCAN RABAGLIATI & Dr K. PAUL SHELDON
THE FORMULA ONE RECORD BOOK
Leslie Frewin

DAVID TREMAYNE
JOCHEN RINDT – UNCROWNED KING
Haynes Publishing

DAVID TREMAYNE
THE LOST GENERATION
Haynes Publishing

RECOMMENDED WEBSITES

OLD RACING CARS.COM
Allen Brown and Richard Jenkins
www.oldracingcars.com

RACING REFERENCE.INFO
www.racing-reference.info

FORMULA2 REGISTER
Stefan Örnerdal
www.formula2.net

DRIVER DATABASE
Andreas Åberg
www.driverdb.com
8W Who? What? Where? When? Why
forix.autosport.com

The 500 OWNERS ASSOCIATION
Neil Hodges
www.500race.org

RACING SPORTS CARS
www.racingsportscars.com

THE RACING LINE.NET
www.theracingline.net

WIKIPEDIA
THE FREE ENCYCLOPEDIA
en.wikipedia.org

AUTOCOURSE

GRAND PRIX WHO'S WHO

4th EDITION

FROM ABECASSIS TO ZUNINO

THE COMPLETE
GRAND PRIX
CAREER RECORD
OF EVERY DRIVER
TO HAVE STARTED
A WORLD
CHAMPIONSHIP RACE
1950-2011

GEORGE ABECASSIS

ENGLISH to the core, the jovial and fun loving George Abecassis possessed Latin looks due to a Portuguese heritage. He was car mad from an early age and having established himself in a successful garage business, George began racing in 1935 with a modified Austin Seven, but soon moved up to 'pukka' machinery in 1938, racing a single-seater Alta with great success, before crashing it badly at Albi just before the Second World Ward intervened and motor sporting activities ceased. George saw service in the RAF, flying bombers before eventually being shot down to become a prisoner of war.

As soon as hostilities were over, Abecassis was back on the circuits with his pre-war Alta, and in 1946 he joined forces with John Heath to buy a garage in Walton-on-Thames, Surrey. Soon the partners founded the HW Motors team to go motor racing

Initially George raced his faithful Alta, but 1947 saw him competing mainly in hill climbs and sprints in an ERA 2A and a Type 59 Bugatti. He did make a guest appearance, however, in the rear-engined D46 Cisitalia-Fiat at the Rome Grand Prix, where he took second place behind similarly mounted Piero Taruffi.

George began the 1948 season with a second place in the Jersey Road Race in a pre-war Maserati 6CM, but with very few events on home soil, he ventured on to the Continent with his GP Alta to take on the challenge of the daunting Bremgarten circuit, near Berne, in the European Grand Prix. It was a meeting marred by the deaths of three drivers, including Archille Varzi and Christian Kautz. In the race, George was lucky to escape unscathed when he was forced to avoid a spinning Talbot, leaving the road at high speed and running into a field.

Business commitments kept him largely away from the tracks the following year, but he was in the field for the second British Grand Prix held at Silverstone, where he took his GP Alta to a steady seventh place. George also entered the car in the French Grand Prix at Reims, but was forced to retire with a gearbox failure; subsequently he disposed of the troublesome machine in favour of the newly-built dual-purpose HWM-Alta.

Although the cars were capable of running to both Sports and Formula 2 regulations, Heath and Abecassis quickly dropped their plans to race at Le Mans, opting to run their nimble Alta-engined HWMs on a shoestring budget at home and abroad with the invaluable help of legendary mechanic and 'Mr Fixit' Alf Francis, who performed miracles with the underfinanced machines. Despite his ties with Heath, in the main Abecassis concentrated on sports cars, as the Formula 2 HWM-Altas where often rented out to paying drivers on the 'Continental Circus'. In the hands of Stirling Moss and Lance Macklin, these fast machines were the first to seriously challenge the Continental giants and brought much prestige to British motor sport, leading the way for the more successful Cooper, Connaught and Vanwall marques.

A casual invitation to race at Le Mans in 1950 with Lance Macklin brought fifth place overall and first place in the Index of Performance, and this led to George joining the works Aston Martin team between 1950 and '53. Results where often hard to come by, but he and Reg Parnell did finish second with the more competitive DB3S at the Sebring 12-hour race in 1953.

By 1954, the Formula 2 HWM single-seaters had become virtually redundant and the team concentrated on sports car racing with a potent Jaguar-engined HWM machine. George enjoyed some success, mainly in minor national events, until 1956, when John Heath was killed while participating in the Mille Miglia.

After marrying Angela, the daughter of Aston Martin owner Sir David Brown, that year, George ceased driving, quickly winding down the Walton team's racing activities by the end of the year. Thereafter, he concentrated on the successful garage business, which he ran for nearly three more decades.

ABECASSIS, George (GB) b 21/3/1913, Walton-on-Thames, Surrey – d 18/12/1991, Ibstone, nr High Wycombe, Buckinghamshire

	1951 Championship position: Unplaced							
	Race	Circuit	No	Entrant	Tyres	Capacity/Chassis/Engine	Comment	Q Pos/Entries
ret	SWISS GP	Bremgarten	12	HW Motors Ltd	D	2.0 HWM-Alta 4	*magneto*	20/21
	1952 Championship position: Unplaced							
ret	SWISS GP	Bremgarten	16	HW Motors Ltd	D	2.0 HWM-Alta 4	*hub shaft failure – crashed*	10/21

GP Starts: 2 GP Wins: 0 Pole positions: 0 Fastest laps: 0 Points: 0

KENNETH ACHESON

THE young Kenneth Acheson, from Cookstown Northern Ireland, no doubt was keen to emulate his father Harry's racing exploits, and he was quick enough on his first appearances in a competition car to convince his dad to purchase a Crosslé 32F to contest the 1977 Northern Ireland FF Championship. With the title duly delivered, the hitherto little-known Acheson moved across the water to race in no less than three FF1600 championships with a Royale RP24. Despite some early-season shunts that included a broken wrist, the shy Irishman proved almost unbeatable, prevailing in all three: the RAC

series, a tough Townsend Thoresen and a somewhat less-than-competitive BARC-backed Philips championship. In 56 starts, he scored an amazing 29 wins and 15 second places. In addition, Kenneth took 28 pole positions and undoubtedly was a deserving winner of the prestigious Grovewood Award.

A major step up to the British Formula 3 Championship in 1979 was hampered at first by a less-than-competitive Ralt, but a switch to a March saw him gradually become a contender for honours against the likes of Chico Serra, Mike Thackwell and Andrea de Cesaris. Although a victory eluded him in the Vandervell series, Acheson did score three non-championship wins for the tight-knit little team and proved he was well placed for honours in the 1980 season.

In the event, Kenneth was pipped to the title by Stefan Johansson, following a costly error in the final round at Thruxton. However, he had proved worthy of a place alongside his Swedish rival in the Toleman Formula Two team for 1981. A sound start to his season was halted after a collision with Michele Alboreto when challenging for the lead at Pau, which left him with a badly broken leg. Acheson bravely returned for the final round and grittily took a third place to remind everyone of his determination and talent.

A seat in a works Ralt-Honda could have been a springboard for F2 championship success, but in the event Acheson could only muster a somewhat disappointing seventh in the series. However, he did have the satisfaction of finishing ahead of his team leader, Jonathan Palmer. Looking for a more sympathetic environment for the 1983 season, the Irishman opted to join forces with Paul Owens, running a Maurer chassis with Heidegger power. Apart from a splendid second place at Pau, little was achieved and, not unnaturally, Acheson jumped at the chance to join the RAM team in Formula 1. His fruitless attempts to make an impression with the uncompetitive car, despite finally qualifying for the South African Grand Prix, proved to be a GP cul-de-sac, and his career momentum never recovered thereafter.

He had a one-off race in CART at the Meadowlands in 1984, but it led nowhere, and Kenneth cooled his heels until he was recalled to F1 duty mid-way through 1985. Manfred Winkelhock had been killed in a sports car race at Mosport Park and John MacDonald handed Acheson just three outings before the Skoal Bandit money ran out and his grand prix days were over.

Acheson opted to continue his racing career in Japan, where the burgeoning and well-paid sports car series provided him with an ideal opportunity to race competitively. He emerged as the 1987 joint All-Japan champion in a Porsche 962, thus paving the way for a place in the Sauber sports car team, the high point being a second place in the 1989 race, sharing with Mauro Baldi and Gianfranco Brancatelli. When the German team decided to opt for youth, Acheson was a casualty, but he was still in demand elsewhere, especially at the Sarthe classic, where subsequently he raced for Nissan, and then successfully for Jaguar and Toyota, placing third and second respectively in 1991 and 1992.

Kenneth made a final Le Mans appearance in 1995 with the Japanese-built SARD MC8R, and his final race came early the following year at Daytona. He was piloting a Lister-Storm GTL when a collision with a slower car resulted in a frightening 180mph accident. The Irishman suffered an eye injury and massive bruising, prompting his decision to retire from the sport.

ACHESON, Kenneth (GB) b 27/11/1957, Cookstown, Tyrone, Northern Ireland

1983 Championship position: Unplaced

	Race	Circuit	No	Entrant	Tyres	Capacity/Chassis/Engine	Comment	Q Pos/Entries
dnq	BRITISH GP	Silverstone	17	RAM Automotive Team March	P	3.0 RAM March 01-Cosworth V8		29/29
dnq	GERMAN GP	Hockenheim	17	RAM Automotive Team March	P	3.0 RAM March 01-Cosworth V8		27/29
dnq	AUSTRIAN GP	Österreichring	17	RAM Automotive Team March	P	3.0 RAM March 01-Cosworth V8		29/29
dnq	DUTCH GP	Zandvoort	17	RAM Automotive Team March	P	3.0 RAM March 01-Cosworth V8		29/29
dnq	ITALIAN GP	Monza	17	RAM Automotive Team March	P	3.0 RAM March 01-Cosworth V8		29/29
dnq	EUROPEAN GP	Brands Hatch	17	RAM Automotive Team March	P	3.0 RAM March 01-Cosworth V8		27/29
12	SOUTH AFRICAN GP	Kyalami	17	RAM Automotive Team March	P	3.0 RAM March 01-Cosworth V8	6 laps behind	24/26

1985 Championship position: Unplaced

	Race	Circuit	No	Entrant	Tyres	Capacity/Chassis/Engine	Comment	Q Pos/Entries
ret	AUSTRIAN GP	Österreichring	10	Skoal Bandit Formula 1 Team	P	1.5 t/c RAM 03-Hart 4	engine	23/27
dnq	DUTCH GP	Zandvoort	10	Skoal Bandit Formula 1 Team	P	1.5 t/c RAM 03-Hart 4		27/27
ret	ITALIAN GP	Monza	10	Skoal Bandit Formula 1 Team	P	1.5 t/c RAM 03-Hart 4	clutch	24/26

GP Starts: 3   GP Wins: 0   Pole positions: 0   Fastest laps: 0   Points: 0

PHILIPPE ADAMS

BEGINNING in karts in 1981, Philippe Adams' career developed steadily until he made an impression in the 1988 British Vauxhall Lotus series, finishing seventh overall in the championship, which boasted the likes of Allan McNish and Mika Häkkinen. The following year, he moved up to the British Formula 3 series, taking a single win at Brands Hatch and sixth place in the final standings with his Bowman Ralt. A second year in the category in 1990 saw Adams take sixth place overall yet again, and despite a couple of second-place finishes his points tally was way off those of the pacemakers, Häkkinen and Mika Salo.

For 1991, Philippe tried his luck in Japan, finishing 12th in the Formula 3 series, and also sampling both Formula Nippon and touring cars. His sojourn in the Far East clearly sharpened his skills, for a much more confident driver returned to British Formula 3 in 1992. The Belgian took three wins in his Ralt RT35 to cement his place as runner-up to runaway champion Gil de Ferran. Despite his success, Adams was forced to continue his career by stepping down to the Halfords British Formula 2 championship for 1993. Five wins in the ten-round series saw him emerge as the champion, although in truth his rivals were far from stellar.

Single-seaters seemed to be things of the past for Adams as he settled into competition in the Belgian Procar series with an Audi 80 Quattro. However, the opportunity to buy a drive for (reportedly) $500,000 in the then financially ailing Lotus team for the 1994 Belgian Grand Prix, replacing Alex Zanardi, proved irresistible. The wet conditions in practice caused the hapless driver to damage his car extensively, but he scraped on to the grid. In the race, more disappointment followed and he slid into retirement after numerous spins. He returned for just one more race, at Estoril (again taking Zanardi's seat), and despite the handicap of running an old Mugen engine, qualified and finished, albeit suffering with tired neck muscles. Subsequently, Philippe continued to race in touring cars successfully, taking an International Group N Series win with a BMW M3 at Magione in Italy in 1997. He also raced GT cars in Endurance events until 2000.

KURT ADOLFF

A FORMER paratrooper during the Second World War, Kurt Adolff had enjoyed competition on home soil driving Mercedes 170 saloons along with Fritz Riess and Karl Kling. However, his performances with the 2-litre Veritas RS sports between 1950 and 1952 brought him to the fore, his results including two third places at the Nürburgring.

In 1953, Kurt joined Ecurie Espadon (Team Swordfish), handling Swiss driver Rudi Fischer's T166 Ferrari. After bringing it home in a distant fourth place in the Eifelrennen, he retired the same car in that year's German Grand Prix. Subsequently, he occasionally competed in hill climbs with a Jaguar.

Adolff then concentrated on his family's successful textile business and later served as a consul to Chile.

ADAMS, Philippe (B) b 19/11/1969, Mouscron

1994 Championship position: Unplaced

	Race	Circuit	No	Entrant	Tyres	Capacity/Car/Engine	Comment	Q Pos/Entries
ret	BELGIAN GP	Spa	11	Team Lotus	G	3.5 Lotus 109-Mugen Honda V10	*spun off*	26/28
16	PORTUGUESE GP	Estoril	11	Team Lotus	G	3.5 Lotus 109-Mugen Honda V10	*4 laps behind*	25/28

GP Starts: 2   GP Wins: 0   Pole positions: 0   Fastest laps: 0   Points: 0

ADOLFF, Kurt (D) b 5/11/1921, Stuttgart – d 24/1/2012, Kreuth-am-Tegernsee

1953 Championship position: Unplaced

	Race	Circuit	No	Entrant	Tyres	Car/Engine	Comment	Q Pos/Entries
ret	GERMAN GP	Nürburgring	34	Ecurie Espadon	P	2.0 Ferrari 166 V12		27/35

GP Starts: 1   GP Wins: 0   Pole positions: 0   Fastest laps: 0   Points: 0

KURT AHRENS Jnr

PERHAPS Germany's most promising young driver of the early 1960s, Kurt Ahrens Jnr began racing in 1958, aged 18, driving an F3 Cooper. He was soon beating his father (a former 250cc German speedway champion and accomplished national car racer), notching up a dozen wins by the end of 1959. After a rather barren 1960 season with a Formula Junior Cooper, Kurt made amends the following year, defeating Gerhard Mitter to win the German Formula Junior championship, a feat that he repeated in 1963 after returning from a six-month suspension imposed by the ONS for disputing the official result of a race the previous year.

The acquisition of a Brabham in 1965 provided him with the opportunity to race in both F3 and F2, but his outings in the latter category were restricted by his commitments to his father's garage and scrap metal business. Nevertheless, he also found time to race the works Fiat-Abarth on occasion with success.

Backed by Caltex (who sponsored his only F1 ride in the German GP of that year), he enjoyed a full Formula 2 season in 1968, finishing second in the Eifelrennen, and third at both Jarama and Hockenheim, relishing the chance to compete with grand prix stars such as Jochen Rindt and Jackie Stewart.

Having previously stated his dislike of long-distance racing, it is perhaps surprising that Ahrens opted for this category in 1969, winning the Austrian GP with Jo Siffert in David Piper's Porsche 917. Racing a works Porsche, he proved a reliable partner for Vic Elford, the pair winning the Nürburgring 1000km in 1970, Kurt's final racing season before retirement to the family scrap business.

In recent years, Ahrens has been a regular visitor to historic racing festivals.

AHRENS Jnr, Kurt (D) b 19/4/1940, Braunschweig, nr Hanover

1966 Championship position: Unplaced

	Race	Circuit	No	Entrant	Tyres	Capacity/Car/Engine	Comment	Q Pos/Entries
ret	GERMAN GP (F2)	Nürburgring	25	Caltex Racing Team	D	1.0 Brabham BT18-Cosworth 4 F2	gearbox	22/30

1967 Championship position: Unplaced

	Race	Circuit	No	Entrant	Tyres	Capacity/Car/Engine	Comment	Q Pos/Entries
ret	GERMAN GP (F2)	Nürburgring	26	Ron Harris Racing Team	D	1.6 Protos-Cosworth 4 F2	split radiator	=21/25

1968 Championship position: Unplaced

	Race	Circuit	No	Entrant	Tyres	Capacity/Car/Engine	Comment	Q Pos/Entries
12	GERMAN GP	Nürburgring	17	Caltex Racing Team	D	3.0 Brabham BT24-Repco V8	3rd works car/1 lap behind	17/20

1969 Championship position: Unplaced

	Race	Circuit	No	Entrant	Tyres	Capacity/Car/Engine	Comment	Q Pos/Entries
7*	GERMAN GP (F2)	Nürburgring	20	Ahrens Racing Team	D	1.6 Brabham BT30-Cosworth 4 F2	*3rd in F2 class/1 lap behind	19/25

GP Starts: 4   GP Wins: 0   Pole positions: 0   Fastest laps: 0   Points: 0

ALBERS, Christijan (NL) b 16/4/1979, Eindhoven

2005 Championship position: 19th=   Wins: 0   Pole positions: 0   Fastest laps: 0   Points scored: 4

	Race	Circuit	No	Entrant	Tyres	Capacity/Chassis/Engine	Comment	Q Pos/Entries
ret	AUSTRALIAN GP	Melbourne	21	European Minardi Cosworth	B	3.0 Minardi PS04B-Cosworth V10	gearbox	17/20
13	MALAYSIAN GP	Sepang	21	European Minardi Cosworth	B	3.0 Minardi PS04B-Cosworth V10	lost bargeboard/4 laps behind	20/20
13	BAHRAIN GP	Sakhir Circuit	21	European Minardi Cosworth	B	3.0 Minardi PS04B-Cosworth V10	collision – new nose/4 laps behind	19/20
ret	SAN MARINO GP	Imola	21	European Minardi Cosworth	B	3.0 Minardi PS05-Cosworth V10	gearbox – fluid leak	20/20
ret	SPANISH GP	Barcelona	21	European Minardi Cosworth	B	3.0 Minardi PS05-Cosworth V10	gearbox	14/18
14	MONACO GP	Monte Carlo	21	European Minardi Cosworth	B	3.0 Minardi PS05-Cosworth V10	spun at Mirabeau/5 laps behind	14/18
17	EUROPEAN GP	Nürburgring	21	European Minardi Cosworth	B	3.0 Minardi PS05-Cosworth V10	2 laps behind	20/20
11	CANADIAN GP	Montreal	21	European Minardi Cosworth	B	3.0 Minardi PS05-Cosworth V10	3 laps behind	15/20
5	U S GP	Indianapolis	21	European Minardi Cosworth	B	3.0 Minardi PS05-Cosworth V10	1 lap behind	18/20
ret	FRENCH GP	Magny Cours	21	European Minardi Cosworth	B	3.0 Minardi PS05-Cosworth V10	puncture – spun off	20/20
18	BRITISH GP	Silverstone	21	European Minardi Cosworth	B	3.0 Minardi PS05-Cosworth V10	3 laps behind	18/20
13	GERMAN GP	Hockenheim	21	European Minardi Cosworth	B	3.0 Minardi PS05-Cosworth V10	2 laps behind	16/20
nc	HUNGARIAN GP	Hungaroring	21	European Minardi Cosworth	B	3.0 Minardi PS05-Cosworth V10	car damage & hydraulics/-11 laps	17/20
ret	TURKISH GP	Istanbul	21	European Minardi Cosworth	B	3.0 Minardi PS05-Cosworth V10	hydraulics	16/20
19	ITALIAN GP	Monza	21	European Minardi Cosworth	B	3.0 Minardi PS05-Cosworth V10	car damage/drive thru pen/-2 laps	20/20
12	BELGIAN GP	Spa	21	European Minardi Cosworth	B	3.0 Minardi PS05-Cosworth V10	started from pits/lost gears/-2 laps	18/20
14	BRAZILIAN GP	Interlagos	21	European Minardi Cosworth	B	3.0 Minardi PS05-Cosworth V10	2 laps behind	18/20
16	JAPANESE GP	Suzuka	21	European Minardi Cosworth	B	3.0 Minardi PS05-Cosworth V10	slow 2nd pit stop/4 laps behind	13/20
16/ret	CHINESE GP	Shanghai	21	European Minardi Cosworth	B	3.0 Minardi PS05-Cosworth V10	started from pitlane/loose wheel	18/20

2006 Championship position: Unplaced

	Race	Circuit	No	Entrant	Tyres	Capacity/Chassis/Engine	Comment	Q Pos/Entries
ret	BAHRAIN GP	Sakhir Circuit	19	MF1 Racing	B	2.4 Midland M16-Toyota V8	drive shaft	18/22
12	MALAYSIAN GP	Sepang	19	MF1 Racing	B	2.4 Midland M16-Toyota V8	2 laps behind	19/22
11	AUSTRALIAN GP	Melbourne	19	MF1 Racing	B	2.4 Midland M16-Toyota V8	1 lap behind	18/22
ret	SAN MARINO GP	Imola	19	MF1 Racing	B	2.4 Midland M16-Toyota V8	accident– hit by Ide	20/22

13	EUROPEAN GP	Nürburgring	19	MF1 Racing	B	2.4 Midland M16-Toyota V8	*1 lap behind*	18/22
ret	SPANISH GP	Barcelona	19	MF1 Racing	B	2.4 Midland M16-Toyota V8	*front wing – spun*	19/22
12	MONACO GP	Monte Carlo	19	MF1 Racing	B	2.4 Midland M16-Toyota V8	*1 lap behind*	17/22
15	BRITISH GP	Silverstone	19	MF1 Racing	B	2.4 Midland M16-Toyota V8	*1 lap behind*	18/22
ret	CANADIAN GP	Montreal	19	MF1 Racing	B	2.4 Midland M16-Toyota V8	*accident – hit by Monteiro/-lap 1*	20/22
ret	U S GP	Indianapolis	19	MF1 Racing	B	2.4 Midland M16-Toyota V8	*transmission*	14/22
15	FRENCH GP	Magny Cours	19	MF1 Racing	B	2.4 Midland M16-Toyota V8	*gearbox problems/2 laps behind*	16/22
dsq	GERMAN GP	Hockenheim	19	MF1 Racing	B	2.4 Midland M16-Toyota V8	*illegal rear wing*	18/22
10	HUNGARIAN GP	Hungaroring	19	MF1 Racing	B	2.4 Midland M16-Toyota V8	*3 laps behind*	21/22
ret	TURKISH GP	Istanbul	19	MF1 Racing	B	2.4 Midland M16-Toyota V8	*accident*	16/22
17	ITALIAN GP	Monza	19	Spyker MF1 Racing	B	2.4 Spyker M16-Toyota V8	*2 laps behind*	18/22
15	CHINESE GP	Shanghai Circuit	19	Spyker MF1 Racing	B	2.4 Spyker M16-Toyota V8	*3 laps behind*	19/22
ret	JAPANESE GP	Suzuka	19	Spyker MF1 Racing	B	2.4 Spyker M16-Toyota V8	*drive shaft/rear suspension*	16/22
14	BRAZILIAN GP	Interlagos	19	Spyker MF1 Racing	B	2.4 Spyker M16-Toyota V8	*1 lap behind*	18/22

2007 Championship position: Unplaced

ret	AUSTRALIAN GP	Melbourne	21	Etihad Aldar Spyker F1 Team	B	2.4 Spyker F8 VII-Ferrari V8	*accident*	22/22
ret	MALAYSIAN GP	Sepang	21	Etihad Aldar Spyker F1 Team	B	2.4 Spyker F8 VII-Ferrari V8	*transmission*	21/22
14	BAHRAIN GP	Sakhir Circuit	21	Etihad Aldar Spyker F1 Team	B	2.4 Spyker F8 VII-Ferrari V8	*2 laps behind*	22/22
14	SPANISH GP	Barcelona	21	Etihad Aldar Spyker F1 Team	B	2.4 Spyker F8 VII-Ferrari V8	*2 laps behind*	21/22
19/ret	MONACO GP	Monte Carlo	21	Etihad Aldar Spyker F1 Team	B	2.4 Spyker F8 VII-Ferrari V8	**no time set/drive shaft*	*22/22
ret	CANADIAN GP	Montreal	21	Etihad Aldar Spyker F1 Team	B	2.4 Spyker F8 VII-Ferrari V8	*accident/handling*	22/22
15	U S GP	Indianapolis	21	Etihad Aldar Spyker F1 Team	B	2.4 Spyker F8 VII-Ferrari V8	*3 laps behind*	22/22
ret	FRENCH GP	Magny Cours	21	Etihad Aldar Spyker F1 Team	B	2.4 Spyker F8 VII-Ferrari V8	*left pits with fuel hose attached*	21/22
15	BRITISH GP	Silverstone	21	Etihad Aldar Spyker F1 Team	B	2.4 Spyker F8 VII-Ferrari V8	*2 laps behind*	22/22

GP Starts: 46   GP Wins: 0   Pole positions: 0   Fastest laps: 0   Points: 4

CHRISTIJAN ALBERS

THE son of Dutch rallycross ace André Albers, Christijan soon made a name for himself in karts and Formula Ford, claiming both the Dutch and Belgian titles in 1997. A move up to the German F3 series in 1998 saw the youngster make his mark with wins at Norisring, and he emerged as a worthy champion the following season, taking six wins with Bertram Schafer's front-running team.

A step up to F3000 alongside Mark Webber in Paul Stoddart's European Aviation team proved a little too much, and Albers accepted an offer to join the DTM for 2001, albeit with a year-old Team Persson Mercedes. His performances included a fine second place at Magny-Cours and an end-of-season move to Keke Rosberg's team. Once again he impressed, and at the beginning of 2003 Albers suddenly found himself thrust into the full works car following the sudden retirement of Uwe Alzen.

Taking on the vastly experienced Berndt Schneider in equal machinery was certainly no easy task, but Albers carried the fight to him until the final race at Hockenheim, where a puncture halted his challenge for the title. Nevertheless, four wins and runner-up had cemented his reputation as a top-line driver in the category. Despite interest from both Jordan and Minardi, he continued in the DTM in 2004, scoring a brilliant win at Estoril, but eventually he had to settle for third overall in the final standings.

Albers grabbed the chance to step up to Formula 1 in 2005, joining Minardi. In truth, however, Paul Stoddart was running short of funds to keep the team afloat, and the lack of resources translated into issues of reliability. Even so, Albers finished 13 races. The highlight of his season came at the infamous massed withdrawal of the Michelin runners just before the start of the US Grand Prix, which gave him an unexpected opportunity to register his first world championship points, picking up fifth place in the six-car field. Christijan had showed more than enough promise to find a place with the Midland team, but his efforts brought no tangible success. Tenth in Hungary was the nearest he came to a points scoring finish, but the late-season purchase of the team by a consortium headed by Dutch car maker Spyker promised better days ahead.

Albers was promoted to de facto number one in the team, but soon began to struggle to match the pace of his rookie team-mate, Adrain Sutil. His tenure was on shaky ground following a disastrous gaffe at a pit stop during the French Grand Prix, where he drove off with a refuelling hose still attached to his car. Blithely trailing the offending attachment around part the Magny-Cours circuit merely worsened his cause. With his sponsorship money reportedly drying up, the Dutchman lost his place to Marcus Winkelhock, who was followed in short order by the well-funded Sakon Yamamoto.

His Formula 1 career at an end, Albers eventually found a way back into racing by returning to the DTM in 2008 with a two-year-old Audi for the Futurecom TME team. The Dutchman also retained his links with Colin Kolles by racing an LMP1 Audi at Le Mans in 2009 and 2010.

MICHELE ALBORETO

A SMOOTH and stylish driver without some of the more histrionic traits of his fellow countrymen, Michele Alboreto rose swiftly to the top. Backed by Paolo Pavanello, he was runner-up in the 1979 Italian F3 championship and became the 1980 European F3 champion after a season-long battle with Thierry Boutsen. This led to a drive for the Minardi F2 team in 1981, which yielded an end-of-season win at Misano. With the financial backing of Count Zanon, Michele had already leapt this career stepping-stone by gaining a place in the Tyrrell team after an impressive grand prix debut at Imola, which saw the curly-haired Italian smartly placed under a three-year contract.

The next two seasons were illuminated by wins at Las Vegas and Detroit, but the naturally aspirated Tyrrells were increasingly uncompetitive against the turbo onslaught, and it was no great surprise when Alboreto took up the offer of a Ferrari drive for 1984. After a promising start and a victory at Zolder in the Belgian GP, his season disintegrated amid a plague of engine failures, but a strong finish to the year bided well for 1985, which would be the high-water mark of his career. For much of the season, he held off the challenge of Alain Prost's McLaren, but the team lost momentum and Michele saw his title chance blighted by mechanical failure. Although three more years were spent at Maranello, somehow things were never the same. The arrival of Gerhard Berger in 1987 pushed the Italian to the margins and he opted out of the political turmoil that was Ferrari to return to Tyrrell for 1989.

It would be a brief reunion, with a splendid third in Mexico in the new Tyrrell 018 the highlight, before Michele split with the team after a sponsorship clash. Thereafter his career went into a swift decline in a succession of uncom-

petitive cars, which included the disastrously overweight Porsche-engined Footwork. An Indian summer in 1992 with some revitalised performances in the Footwork-Mugen restored his credibility, but the nadir of his Formula 1 career came with a move to the Lola Scuderia Italia team. The wretched Lola-Ferrari could well have brought Alboreto's tenure in grand prix racing to an end, but he found a berth with the restructured Minardi team in 1994. A single point at Monaco was garnered from a year that saw the team struggling to meet the technical changes demanded in the wake of the Senna tragedy. Increasingly disenchanted with his lot, especially after a fine levied as a result of the German Grand Prix first-lap crash, Alboreto finally bowed out of F1 at season's end.

With the enticing prospect of racing the Schübel-entered Alfa Romeo T155 in the high-profile DTM and ITC championships for 1995, Michele was looking forward to some competitive racing at last. Sadly, he rarely figured among the leading runners, finishing an anonymous year with just 22nd place in the DTM to show for his efforts.

Meanwhile, selective appearances with the Dick Simon Scandia Ferrari 333SP sports car, which included a second place at Sebring in 1996, paved the way for Alboreto to race in the newly formed IRL single-seater oval series. Michele was one of a handful of 'name' drivers contesting the 1996 championship, and he scored three top-six finishes in his five starts, although a chance of victory in the Indianapolis 500 ended with a gearbox failure. When sponsor Agip withdrew its support at the start of the 1997 season, Alboreto was left without a regular drive, but his luck was about to change at last. Rejoining Joest Racing for a second outing in their Porsche WSC95 prototype, Michele claimed an unexpected victory in the Le Mans 24-hour race partnered by Stefan Johansson and Tom Kristensen. Subsequently, he took a Joest Porsche LM1 to second place at Road Atlanta in 1998, and was part of Joest's squad handling the works backed 1999 Audi R8R challenger. His two races yielded a third place in the Sebring 12 Hours (with Johansson and Dindo Capello) and a fourth at Le Mans (with Laurent Aïello and Capello). In 2000, Michele won the Petit Le Mans, and took second at Sebring and third at Le Mans.

He began 2001 by winning the Sebring 12 Hours (again with Aïello and Capello), but tragically, a month later, he was killed while testing the Audi at the Lausitzring. The Italian suffered a puncture, which caused a tyre failure that resulted in air getting under his car and flipping it over the barriers into an earth bank. He died instantly when the car rebounded into the back of the crash barriers.

ALBORETO, Michele (I) b 23/12/1956, Milan – d 25/4/2001, Lausitz, nr Dresden, Germany

1981 Championship position: Unplaced

	Race	Circuit	No	Entrant	Tyres	Capacity/Car/Engine	Comment	Q Pos/Entries
ret	SAN MARINO GP	Imola	4	Team Tyrrell	M	3.0 Tyrrell 010-Cosworth V8	collision with Gabbiani	17/30
12	BELGIAN GP	Zolder	4	Team Tyrrell	M	3.0 Tyrrell 010-Cosworth V8	2 laps behind	19/31
ret	MONACO GP	Monte Carlo	4	Team Tyrrell	M	3.0 Tyrrell 010-Cosworth V8	spun – collision with Giacomelli	20/31
dnq	SPANISH GP	Jarama	4	Team Tyrrell	M	3.0 Tyrrell 010-Cosworth V8		25/30
16	FRENCH GP	Dijon	4	Team Tyrrell	M	3.0 Tyrrell 010-Cosworth V8	3 laps behind	23/29
ret	BRITISH GP	Silverstone	4	Team Tyrrell	M	3.0 Tyrrell 010-Cosworth V8	clutch	19/30
dnq	GERMAN GP	Hockenheim	4	Team Tyrrell	A	3.0 Tyrrell 010-Cosworth V8		29/30
ret	AUSTRIAN GP	Österreichring	4	Team Tyrrell	A	3.0 Tyrrell 010-Cosworth V8	engine	22/28
9/ret	DUTCH GP	Zandvoort	4	Team Tyrrell	A	3.0 Tyrrell 011-Cosworth V8	reserve starter/engine/-4 laps	25/30
ret	ITALIAN GP	Monza	4	Team Tyrrell	A	3.0 Tyrrell 011-Cosworth V8	hit Watson's wreckage	22/30
11	CANADIAN GP	Montreal	4	Team Tyrrell	A	3.0 Tyrrell 011-Cosworth V8	4 laps behind	22/30
13/ret	CAESARS PALACE GP	Las Vegas	4	Team Tyrrell	A	3.0 Tyrrell 011-Cosworth V8	electrical problems/-8 laps	17/30

1982 Championship position: 7th=   Wins: 1   Pole positions: 0   Fastest laps: 1   Points scored: 25

	Race	Circuit	No	Entrant	Tyres	Capacity/Car/Engine	Comment	Q Pos/Entries
7	SOUTH AFRICAN GP	Kyalami	3	Team Tyrrell	G	3.0 Tyrrell 011-Cosworth V8	1 lap behind	10/30
4*	BRAZILIAN GP	Rio	3	Team Tyrrell	G	3.0 Tyrrell 011-Cosworth V8	*1st & 2nd place cars dsq	13/31
4*	US GP WEST	Long Beach	3	Team Tyrrell	G	3.0 Tyrrell 011-Cosworth V8	*3rd place car disqualified	12/31
3	SAN MARINO GP	Imola	3	Team Tyrrell	G	3.0 Tyrrell 011-Cosworth V8		5/14
ret	BELGIAN GP	Zolder	3	Team Tyrrell	G	3.0 Tyrrell 011-Cosworth V8	engine	5/32
10/ret	MONACO GP	Monte Carlo	3	Team Tyrrell	G	3.0 Tyrrell 011-Cosworth V8	suspension/6 laps behind	9/31
ret	US GP (DETROIT)	Detroit	3	Team Tyrrell	G	3.0 Tyrrell 011-Cosworth V8	accident at chicane	16/28
ret	CANADIAN GP	Montreal	3	Team Tyrrell	G	3.0 Tyrrell 011-Cosworth V8	gearbox and fuel starvation	15/29
7	DUTCH GP	Zandvoort	3	Team Tyrrell	G	3.0 Tyrrell 011-Cosworth V8	1 lap behind	14/31
nc	BRITISH GP	Brands Hatch	3	Team Tyrrell	G	3.0 Tyrrell 011-Cosworth V8	handling problems/-32 laps	9/31
6	FRENCH GP	Paul Ricard	3	Team Tyrrell	G	3.0 Tyrrell 011-Cosworth V8		15/30
4	GERMAN GP	Hockenheim	3	Team Tyrrell	G	3.0 Tyrrell 011-Cosworth V8	1 lap behind	7/30
ret	AUSTRIAN GP	Österreichring	3	Team Tyrrell	G	3.0 Tyrrell 011-Cosworth V8	spun off	8/29
7	SWISS GP	Dijon	3	Team Tyrrell	G	3.0 Tyrrell 011-Cosworth V8	1 lap behind	12/29
5	ITALIAN GP	Monza	3	Team Tyrrell	G	3.0 Tyrrell 011-Cosworth V8	1 lap behind	11/30
1	CAESARS PALACE GP	Las Vegas	3	Team Tyrrell	G	3.0 Tyrrell 011-Cosworth V8	FL	3/30

1983 Championship position: 12th=   Wins: 1   Pole positions: 0   Fastest laps: 0   Points scored: 10

	Race	Circuit	No	Entrant	Tyres	Capacity/Car/Engine	Comment	Q Pos/Entries
ret	BRAZILIAN GP	Rio	3	Benetton Tyrrell Team	G	3.0 Tyrrell 011-Cosworth V8	incident with Baldi – oil cooler	11/27
9	US GP WEST	Long Beach	3	Benetton Tyrrell Team	G	3.0 Tyrrell 011-Cosworth V8	collision with Jarier/-2 laps	7/28
8	FRENCH GP	Paul Ricard	3	Benetton Tyrrell Team	G	3.0 Tyrrell 011-Cosworth V8	1 lap behind	15/29
ret	SAN MARINO GP	Imola	3	Benetton Tyrrell Team	G	3.0 Tyrrell 011-Cosworth V8	accident – collapsed suspension	13/28
ret	MONACO GP	Monte Carlo	3	Benetton Tyrrell Team	G	3.0 Tyrrell 011-Cosworth V8	collision with Mansell	11/28
14	BELGIAN GP	Spa	3	Benetton Tyrrell Team	G	3.0 Tyrrell 011-Cosworth V8	pit stop – gearbox/-2 laps	17/28
1	US GP (DETROIT)	Detroit	3	Benetton Tyrrell Team	G	3.0 Tyrrell 011-Cosworth V8		6/27
8	CANADIAN GP	Montreal	3	Benetton Tyrrell Team	G	3.0 Tyrrell 011-Cosworth V8	2 laps behind	17/28
13	BRITISH GP	Silverstone	3	Benetton Tyrrell Team	G	3.0 Tyrrell 011-Cosworth V8	2 laps behind	16/29
ret	GERMAN GP	Hockenheim	3	Benetton Tyrrell Team	G	3.0 Tyrrell 011-Cosworth V8	fuel pump drive	16/29
ret	AUSTRIAN GP	Österreichring	3	Benetton Tyrrell Team	G	3.0 Tyrrell 011-Cosworth V8	hit Johansson – spun off	18/29
dns	"	"	3	Benetton Tyrrell Team	G	3.0 Tyrrell 012-Cosworth V8	practiced only	– / –
6	DUTCH GP	Zandvoort	3	Benetton Tyrrell Team	G	3.0 Tyrrell 012-Cosworth V8	pit stop – fuel/1 lap behind	18/29
ret	ITALIAN GP	Monza	3	Benetton Tyrrell Team	G	3.0 Tyrrell 012-Cosworth V8	clutch	24/29
ret	EUROPEAN GP	Brands Hatch	3	Benetton Tyrrell Team	G	3.0 Tyrrell 012-Cosworth V8	engine	26/29
ret	SOUTH AFRICAN GP	Kyalami	3	Benetton Tyrrell Team	G	3.0 Tyrrell 012-Cosworth V8	engine	18/26

Driving his Tyrrell 011 to victory in the 1983 Detroit GP, Alboreto takes the last ever win for the V8 Ford-Cosworth DFV engine.

Alboreto moved to Ferrari in 1984, and this third place in Austria started a strong run towards the end of the year, leading to fourth place in the championship.

1984 Championship position: 4th   Wins: 1   Pole positions: 1   Fastest laps: 1   Points scored: 30.5

ret	BRAZILIAN GP	Rio	27	Scuderia Ferrari SpA SEFAC	G	1.5 t/c Ferrari 126C4 V6	brake caliper	2/27
11*/ret	SOUTH AFRICAN GP	Kyalami	27	Scuderia Ferrari SpA SEFAC	G	1.5 t/c Ferrari 126C4 V6	ignition/*11th place car dsq	10/27
1	BELGIAN GP	Zolder	27	Scuderia Ferrari SpA SEFAC	G	1.5 t/c Ferrari 126C4 V6		1/27
ret	SAN MARINO GP	Imola	27	Scuderia Ferrari SpA SEFAC	G	1.5 t/c Ferrari 126C4 V6	exhaust	13/28
ret	FRENCH GP	Dijon	27	Scuderia Ferrari SpA SEFAC	G	1.5 t/c Ferrari 126C4 V6	engine	10/27
6*	MONACO GP	Monte Carlo	27	Scuderia Ferrari SpA SEFAC	G	1.5 t/c Ferrari 126C4 V6	*3rd car dsq/half points/-1 lap	4/27
ret	CANADIAN GP	Montreal	27	Scuderia Ferrari SpA SEFAC	G	1.5 t/c Ferrari 126C4 V6	engine	6/26
ret	US GP (DETROIT)	Detroit	27	Scuderia Ferrari SpA SEFAC	G	1.5 t/c Ferrari 126C4 V6	engine	4/27
ret	US GP (DALLAS)	Dallas	27	Scuderia Ferrari SpA SEFAC	G	1.5 t/c Ferrari 126C4 V6	hit wall	9/27
5	BRITISH GP	Brands Hatch	27	Scuderia Ferrari SpA SEFAC	G	1.5 t/c Ferrari 126C4 V6	1 lap behind	9/27
ret	GERMAN GP	Hockenheim	27	Scuderia Ferrari SpA SEFAC	G	1.5 t/c Ferrari 126C4 V6	misfire	6/27
3	AUSTRIAN GP	Österreichring	27	Scuderia Ferrari SpA SEFAC	G	1.5 t/c Ferrari 126C4 V6		12/28
ret	DUTCH GP	Zandvoort	27	Scuderia Ferrari SpA SEFAC	G	1.5 t/c Ferrari 126C4 V6	engine	9/27
2	ITALIAN GP	Monza	27	Scuderia Ferrari SpA SEFAC	G	1.5 t/c Ferrari 126C4 V6		11/27
2	EUROPEAN GP	Nürburgring	27	Scuderia Ferrari SpA SEFAC	G	1.5 t/c Ferrari 126C4 V6	FL (shared with Piquet)	5/26
4	PORTUGUESE GP	Estoril	27	Scuderia Ferrari SpA SEFAC	G	1.5 t/c Ferrari 126C4 V6		8/27

1985 Championship position: 2nd   Wins: 2   Pole positions: 1   Fastest laps: 2   Points scored: 53

2	BRAZILIAN GP	Rio	27	Scuderia Ferrari SpA SEFAC	G	1.5 t/c Ferrari 156/85 V6		1/25
2	PORTUGUESE GP	Estoril	27	Scuderia Ferrari SpA SEFAC	G	1.5 t/c Ferrari 156/85 V6		5/26
ret	SAN MARINO GP	Imola	27	Scuderia Ferrari SpA SEFAC	G	1.5 t/c Ferrari 156/85 V6	electrics/FL	4/26
2	MONACO GP	Monte Carlo	27	Scuderia Ferrari SpA SEFAC	G	1.5 t/c Ferrari 156/85 V6	FL	3/26
1	CANADIAN GP	Montreal	27	Scuderia Ferrari SpA SEFAC	G	1.5 t/c Ferrari 156/85 V6		3/25
3	US GP (DETROIT)	Detroit	27	Scuderia Ferrari SpA SEFAC	G	1.5 t/c Ferrari 156/85 V6		3/25
ret	FRENCH GP	Paul Ricard	27	Scuderia Ferrari SpA SEFAC	G	1.5 t/c Ferrari 156/85 V6	turbo	3/26
2	BRITISH GP	Silverstone	27	Scuderia Ferrari SpA SEFAC	G	1.5 t/c Ferrari 156/85 V6	1 lap behind	6/26
1	GERMAN GP	Nürburgring	27	Scuderia Ferrari Spa SEFAC	G	1.5 t/c Ferrari 156/85 V6		8/27
3	AUSTRIAN GP	Österreichring	27	Scuderia Ferrari SpA SEFAC	G	1.5 t/c Ferrari 156/85 V6		9/27
4	DUTCH GP	Zandvoort	27	Scuderia Ferrari SpA SEFAC	G	1.5 t/c Ferrari 156/85 V6		16/27
13/ret	ITALIAN GP	Monza	27	Scuderia Ferrari SpA SEFAC	G	1.5 t/c Ferrari 156/85 V6	engine	7/26
ret	BELGIAN GP	Spa	27	Scuderia Ferrari SpA SEFAC	G	1.5 t/c Ferrari 156/85 V6	clutch	4/24
ret	EUROPEAN GP	Brands Hatch	27	Scuderia Ferrari SpA SEFAC	G	1.5 t/c Ferrari 156/85 V6	turbo	15/27
ret	SOUTH AFRICAN GP	Kyalami	27	Scuderia Ferrari SpA SEFAC	G	1.5 t/c Ferrari 156/85 V6	turbo	15/21
ret	AUSTRALIAN GP	Adelaide	27	Scuderia Ferrari SpA SEFAC	G	1.5 t/c Ferrari 156/85 V6	gear linkage	5/25

1986 Championship position: 8th=   Wins: 0   Pole positions: 0   Fastest laps: 0   Points scored: 14

ret	BRAZILIAN GP	Rio	27	Scuderia Ferrari SpA SEFAC	G	1.5 t/c Ferrari 156/85 V6	fuel pump	- / -
dns	"	"	27	Scuderia Ferrari SpA SEFAC	G	1.5 t/c Ferrari F1/86 V6	set grid time in this car	6/25
ret	SPANISH GP	Jerez	27	Scuderia Ferrari SpA SEFAC	G	1.5 t/c Ferrari F1/86 V6	wheel bearing	13/25
10/ret	SAN MARINO GP	Imola	27	Scuderia Ferrari SpA SEFAC	G	1.5 t/c Ferrari F1/86 V6	turbo/4 laps behind	5/26
ret	MONACO GP	Monte Carlo	27	Scuderia Ferrari SpA SEFAC	G	1.5 t/c Ferrari F1/86 V6	turbo	4/26
4	BELGIAN GP	Spa	27	Scuderia Ferrari SpA SEFAC	G	1.5 t/c Ferrari F1/86 V6		9/25
8	CANADIAN GP	Montreal	27	Scuderia Ferrari SpA SEFAC	G	1.5 t/c Ferrari F1/86 V6	spin – Johansson/1 lap behind	11/25
4	US GP (DETROIT)	Detroit	27	Scuderia Ferrari SpA SEFAC	G	1.5 t/c Ferrari F1/86 V6		11/26
8	FRENCH GP	Paul Ricard	27	Scuderia Ferrari SpA SEFAC	G	1.5 t/c Ferrari F1/86 V6	stalled on startline/-2 laps	6/26
ret	BRITISH GP	Brands Hatch	27	Scuderia Ferrari SpA SEFAC	G	1.5 t/c Ferrari F1/86 V6	turbo	12/26
ret	GERMAN GP	Hockenheim	27	Scuderia Ferrari SpA SEFAC	G	1.5 t/c Ferrari F1/86 V6	transmission	10/26
ret	HUNGARIAN GP	Hungaroring	27	Scuderia Ferrari SpA SEFAC	G	1.5 t/c Ferrari F1/86 V6	hit Warwick	15/26
2	AUSTRIAN GP	Österreichring	27	Scuderia Ferrari SpA SEFAC	G	1.5 t/c Ferrari F1/86 V6	1 lap behind	9/26
ret	ITALIAN GP	Monza	27	Scuderia Ferrari SpA SEFAC	G	1.5 t/c Ferrari F1/86 V6	engine	9/27
5	PORTUGUESE GP	Estoril	27	Scuderia Ferrari SpA SEFAC	G	1.5 t/c Ferrari F1/86 V6	1 lap behind	13/27
ret	MEXICAN GP	Mexico City	27	Scuderia Ferrari SpA SEFAC	G	1.5 t/c Ferrari F1/86 V6	turbo	12/26
ret	AUSTRALIAN GP	Adelaide	27	Scuderia Ferrari SpA SEFAC	G	1.5 t/c Ferrari F1/86 V6	hit from behind on grid	9/26

1987 Championship position: 7th   Wins: 0   Pole positions: 0   Fastest laps: 0   Points scored: 17

8/ret	BRAZILIAN GP	Rio	27	Scuderia Ferrari SpA SEFAC	G	1.5 t/c Ferrari F1/87 V6	spun off/3 laps behind	9/23

The end of an affair. The 1988 season saw Alboreto and Ferrari call an end to their five-year partnership. His second place at Monza (*left*) was his last podium for the team before he made a short-lived return to Tyrrell.

3	SAN MARINO GP	Imola	27	Scuderia Ferrari SpA SEFAC	G	1.5 t/c Ferrari F1/87 V6		7/27
ret	BELGIAN GP	Spa	27	Scuderia Ferrari SpA SEFAC	G	1.5 t/c Ferrari F1/87 V6	*transmission*	5/26
3	MONACO GP	Monte Carlo	27	Scuderia Ferrari SpA SEFAC	G	1.5 t/c Ferrari F1/87 V6		5/26
ret	US GP (DETROIT)	Detroit	27	Scuderia Ferrari SpA SEFAC	G	1.5 t/c Ferrari F1/87 V6	*gearbox*	7/26
ret	FRENCH GP	Paul Ricard	27	Scuderia Ferrari SpA SEFAC	G	1.5 t/c Ferrari F1/87 V6	*engine*	8/26
ret	BRITISH GP	Silverstone	27	Scuderia Ferrari SpA SEFAC	G	1.5 t/c Ferrari F1/87 V6	*rear suspension*	7/26
ret	GERMAN GP	Hockenheim	27	Scuderia Ferrari SpA SEFAC	G	1.5 t/c Ferrari F1/87 V6	*turbo*	5/26
ret	HUNGARIAN GP	Hungaroring	27	Scuderia Ferrari SpA SEFAC	G	1.5 t/c Ferrari F1/87 V6	*engine*	5/26
ret	AUSTRIAN GP	Österreichring	27	Scuderia Ferrari SpA SEFAC	G	1.5 t/c Ferrari F1/87 V6	*started from pits/turbo/exhaust*	6/26
ret	ITALIAN GP	Monza	27	Scuderia Ferrari SpA SEFAC	G	1.5 t/c Ferrari F1/87 V6	*turbo*	8/28
ret	PORTUGUESE GP	Estoril	27	Scuderia Ferrari SpA SEFAC	G	1.5 t/c Ferrari F1/87 V6	*gearbox*	6/27
15/ret	SPANISH GP	Jerez	27	Scuderia Ferrari SpA SEFAC	G	1.5 t/c Ferrari F1/87 V6	*engine/5 laps behind*	4/28
ret	MEXICAN GP	Mexico City	27	Scuderia Ferrari SpA SEFAC	G	1.5 t/c Ferrari F1/87 V6	*engine*	9/27
4	JAPANESE GP	Suzuka	27	Scuderia Ferrari SpA SEFAC	G	1.5 t/c Ferrari F1/87 V6		4/27
2*	AUSTRALIAN GP	Adelaide	27	Scuderia Ferrari SpA SEFAC	G	1.5 t/c Ferrari F1/87 V6	**2nd place car disqualified*	6/27

1988 Championship position: 5th Wins: 0 Pole positions: 0 Fastest laps: 1 Points scored: 24

5	BRAZILIAN GP	Rio	27	Scuderia Ferrari SpA SEFAC	G	1.5 t/c Ferrari F1/87/88C V6		6/31
18/ret	SAN MARINO GP	Imola	27	Scuderia Ferrari SpA SEFAC	G	1.5 t/c Ferrari F1/87/88C V6	*started from back/engine/-6 laps*	10/31
3	MONACO GP	Monte Carlo	27	Scuderia Ferrari SpA SEFAC	G	1.5 t/c Ferrari F1/87/88C V6		4/30
4	MEXICAN GP	Mexico City	27	Scuderia Ferrari SpA SEFAC	G	1.5 t/c Ferrari F1/87/88C V6	*1 lap behind*	5/30
ret	CANADIAN GP	Montreal	27	Scuderia Ferrari SpA SEFAC	G	1.5 t/c Ferrari F1/87/88C V6	*engine*	4/31
ret	US GP (DETROIT)	Detroit	27	Scuderia Ferrari SpA SEFAC	G	1.5 t/c Ferrari F1/87/88C V6	*accident*	3/31
3	FRENCH GP	Paul Ricard	27	Scuderia Ferrari SpA SEFAC	G	1.5 t/c Ferrari F1/87/88C V6		4/31
17/ret	BRITISH GP	Silverstone	27	Scuderia Ferrari SpA SEFAC	G	1.5 t/c Ferrari F1/87/88C V6	*out of fuel/3 laps behind*	2/31
4	GERMAN GP	Hockenheim	27	Scuderia Ferrari SpA SEFAC	G	1.5 t/c Ferrari F1/87/88C V6		4/31
ret	HUNGARIAN GP	Hungaroring	27	Scuderia Ferrari SpA SEFAC	G	1.5 t/c Ferrari F1/87/88C V6	*engine cut out*	15/31
ret	BELGIAN GP	Spa	27	Scuderia Ferrari SpA SEFAC	G	1.5 t/c Ferrari F1/87/88C V6	*engine*	4/31
2	ITALIAN GP	Monza	27	Scuderia Ferrari SpA SEFAC	G	1.5 t/c Ferrari F1/87/88C V6	*FL*	4/31
5	PORTUGUESE GP	Estoril	27	Scuderia Ferrari SpA SEFAC	G	1.5 t/c Ferrari F1/87/88C V6		7/31
ret	SPANISH GP	Jerez	27	Scuderia Ferrari SpA SEFAC	G	1.5 t/c Ferrari F1/87/88C V6	*engine*	10/31
11	JAPANESE GP	Suzuka	27	Scuderia Ferrari SpA SEFAC	G	1.5 t/c Ferrari F1/87/88C V6	*collision with Nannini/-1 lap*	9/31
ret	AUSTRALIAN GP	Adelaide	27	Scuderia Ferrari SpA SEFAC	G	1.5 t/c Ferrari F1/87/88C V6	*collision with Caffi on lap 1*	12/31

1989 Championship position: 11th= Wins: 0 Pole positions: 0 Fastest laps: 0 Points scored: 6

10	BRAZILIAN GP	Rio	4	Tyrrell Racing Organisation	G	3.5 Tyrrell 017B-Cosworth V8	*2 pit stops – gearbox/-2 laps*	20/38
dnq	SAN MARINO GP	Imola	4	Tyrrell Racing Organisation	G	3.5 Tyrrell 018-Cosworth V8		27/39
dnq	" "	"	4	Tyrrell Racing Organisation	G	3.5 Tyrrell 017B-Cosworth V8		– / –
5	MONACO GP	Monte Carlo	4	Tyrrell Racing Organisation	G	3.5 Tyrrell 018-Cosworth V8	*2 laps behind*	12/38
dns	"	"	4	Tyrrell Racing Organisation	G	3.5 Tyrrell 017B-Cosworth V8	*practice only*	– / –
3	MEXICAN GP	Mexico City	4	Tyrrell Racing Organisation	G	3.5 Tyrrell 018-Cosworth V8		7/39
ret	US GP (PHOENIX)	Phoenix	4	Tyrrell Racing Organisation	G	3.5 Tyrrell 018-Cosworth V8	*gearbox*	9/39
ret	CANADIAN GP	Montreal	4	Tyrrell Racing Organisation	G	3.5 Tyrrell 018-Cosworth V8	*electrics*	20/39
ret	GERMAN GP	Hockenheim	29	Equipe Larrousse	G	3.5 Lola LC89-Lamborghini V12	*electrics*	26/39
ret	HUNGARIAN GP	Hungaroring	29	Equipe Larrousse	G	3.5 Lola LC89-Lamborghini V12	*engine*	26/39
ret	BELGIAN GP	Spa	29	Equipe Larrousse	G	3.5 Lola LC89-Lamborghini V12	*collision with Patrese*	22/39
ret	ITALIAN GP	Monza	29	Equipe Larrousse	G	3.5 Lola LC89-Lamborghini V12	*engine*	13/39
11	PORTUGUESE GP	Estoril	29	Equipe Larrousse	G	3.5 Lola LC89-Lamborghini V12	*pit stop – tyres/2 laps behind*	21/39
dnpq	SPANISH GP	Jerez	29	Equipe Larrousse	G	3.5 Lola LC89-Lamborghini V12		33/38
dnq	JAPANESE GP	Suzuka	29	Equipe Larrousse	G	3.5 Lola LC89-Lamborghini V12		28/39
dnpq	AUSTRALIAN GP	Adelaide	29	Equipe Larrousse	G	3.5 Lola LC89-Lamborghini V12		32/39

1990 Championship position: Unplaced

10	US GP (PHOENIX)	Phoenix	9	Footwork Arrows Racing	G	3.5 Arrows A11B-Cosworth V8	*2 laps behind*	21/35
ret	BRAZILIAN GP	Interlagos	9	Footwork Arrows Racing	G	3.5 Arrows A11B-Cosworth V8	*handling – suspension*	23/35
dns	"	"	9	Footwork Arrows Racing	G	3.5 Arrows A11-Cosworth V8	*practice only*	– / –
dnq	SAN MARINO GP	Imola	9	Footwork Arrows Racing	G	3.5 Arrows A11B-Cosworth V8		29/34
dnq	MONACO GP	Monte Carlo	9	Footwork Arrows Racing	G	3.5 Arrows A11B-Cosworth V8		27/34
ret	CANADIAN GP	Montreal	9	Footwork Arrows Racing	G	3.5 Arrows A11B-Cosworth V8	*collision with Pirro*	14/35

17	MEXICAN GP	Mexico City	9	Footwork Arrows Racing	G	3.5 Arrows A11B-Cosworth V8	*power loss/3 laps behind*	17/35
10	FRENCH GP	Paul Ricard	9	Footwork Arrows Racing	G	3.5 Arrows A11B-Cosworth V8	*1 lap behind*	18/35
ret	BRITISH GP	Silverstone	9	Footwork Arrows Racing	G	3.5 Arrows A11B-Cosworth V8	*electrics*	25/35
ret	GERMAN GP	Hockenheim	9	Footwork Arrows Racing	G	3.5 Arrows A11B-Cosworth V8	*engine*	19/35
12	HUNGARIAN GP	Hungaroring	9	Footwork Arrows Racing	G	3.5 Arrows A11B-Cosworth V8	*pit stop – tyres/2 laps behind*	22/35
13	BELGIAN GP	Spa	9	Footwork Arrows Racing	G	3.5 Arrows A11B-Cosworth V8	*engine lost power/-1 lap*	26/33
12/ret	ITALIAN GP	Monza	9	Footwork Arrows Racing	G	3.5 Arrows A11B-Cosworth V8	*spun off/3 laps behind*	22/33
9	PORTUGUESE GP	Estoril	9	Footwork Arrows Racing	G	3.5 Arrows A11B-Cosworth V8	*1 lap behind*	19/33
10	SPANISH GP	Jerez	9	Footwork Arrows Racing	G	3.5 Arrows A11B-Cosworth V8	*2 laps behind*	26/33
ret	JAPANESE GP	Suzuka	9	Footwork Arrows Racing	G	3.5 Arrows A11B-Cosworth V8	*engine*	25/30
dnq	AUSTRALIAN GP	Adelaide	9	Footwork Arrows Racing	G	3.5 Arrows A11B-Cosworth V8		27/30

1991 Championship position: Unplaced

ret	US GP (PHOENIX)	Phoenix	9	Footwork Grand Prix International	G	3.5 Footwork A11C-Porsche V12	*gearbox*	25/34
dnq	BRAZILIAN GP	Interlagos	9	Footwork Grand Prix International	G	3.5 Footwork A11C-Porsche V12		29/34
dnq	SAN MARINO GP	Imola	9	Footwork Grand Prix International	G	3.5 Footwork A11C-Porsche V12		30/34
ret	MONACO GP	Monte Carlo	9	Footwork Grand Prix International	G	3.5 Footwork FA12-Porsche V12	*engine*	25/34
ret	CANADIAN GP	Montreal	9	Footwork Grand Prix International	G	3.5 Footwork FA12-Porsche V12	*engine*	21/34
ret	MEXICAN GP	Mexico City	9	Footwork Grand Prix International	G	3.5 Footwork FA12-Porsche V12	*started from pitlane/oil pressure*	26/34
ret	FRENCH GP	Magny Cours	9	Footwork Grand Prix International	G	3.5 Footwork FA12-Cosworth V8	*gearbox/transmission*	25/34
ret	BRITISH GP	Silverstone	9	Footwork Grand Prix International	G	3.5 Footwork FA12-Cosworth V8	*gearbox*	26/34
dnq	GERMAN GP	Hockenheim	9	Footwork Grand Prix International	G	3.5 Footwork FA12-Cosworth V8		27/34
dnq	HUNGARIAN GP	Hungaroring	9	Footwork Grand Prix International	G	3.5 Footwork FA12-Cosworth V8		28/34
dnpq	BELGIAN GP	Spa	9	Footwork Grand Prix International	G	3.5 Footwork FA12-Cosworth V8		31/34
dnq	ITALIAN GP	Monza	9	Footwork Grand Prix International	G	3.5 Footwork FA12-Cosworth V8		27/34
15	PORTUGUESE GP	Estoril	9	Footwork Grand Prix International	G	3.5 Footwork FA12-Cosworth V8	*3 laps behind*	24/34
ret	SPANISH GP	Barcelona	9	Footwork Grand Prix International	G	3.5 Footwork FA12-Cosworth V8	*engine*	24/33
dnq	JAPANESE GP	Suzuka	9	Footwork Grand Prix International	G	3.5 Footwork FA12-Cosworth V8		27/31
13	AUSTRALIAN GP	Adelaide	9	Footwork Grand Prix International	G	3.5 Footwork FA12-Cosworth V8	*wet race – stopped after 14 laps*	15/32

1992 Championship position: 10th   Wins: 0   Pole positions: 0   Fastest laps: 0   Points scored: 6

10	SOUTH AFRICAN GP	Kyalami	9	Footwork Grand Prix International	G	3.5 Footwork FA13-Mugen Honda V10	*gearbox trouble*	17/30
13	MEXICAN GP	Mexico City	9	Footwork Grand Prix International	G	3.5 Footwork FA13-Mugen Honda V10	*4 laps behind*	25/30
6	BRAZILIAN GP	Interlagos	9	Footwork Grand Prix International	G	3.5 Footwork FA13-Mugen Honda V10	*1 lap behind*	14/31
5	SPANISH GP	Barcelona	9	Footwork Grand Prix International	G	3.5 Footwork FA13-Mugen Honda V10	*1 lap behind*	16/32
5	SAN MARINO GP	Imola	9	Footwork Grand Prix International	G	3.5 Footwork FA13-Mugen Honda V10	*1 lap behind*	9/32
7	MONACO GP	Monte Carlo	9	Footwork Grand Prix International	G	3.5 Footwork FA13-Mugen Honda V10	*spin/1 lap behind*	11/32
7	CANADIAN GP	Montreal	9	Footwork Grand Prix International	G	3.5 Footwork FA13-Mugen Honda V10	*1 lap behind*	16/32
7*	FRENCH GP	Magny Cours	9	Footwork Grand Prix International	G	3.5 Footwork FA13-Mugen Honda V10	**aggregate of two parts/-1 lap*	14/30
7	BRITISH GP	Silverstone	9	Footwork Grand Prix International	G	3.5 Footwork FA13-Mugen Honda V10	*1 lap behind*	12/32
9	GERMAN GP	Hockenheim	9	Footwork Grand Prix International	G	3.5 Footwork FA13-Mugen Honda V10	*1 lap behind*	17/32
7	HUNGARIAN GP	Hungaroring	9	Footwork Grand Prix International	G	3.5 Footwork FA13-Mugen Honda V10	*spin/2 laps behind*	7/31
ret	BELGIAN GP	Spa	9	Footwork Grand Prix International	G	3.5 Footwork FA13-Mugen Honda V10	*gearbox*	14/30
7	ITALIAN GP	Monza	9	Footwork Grand Prix International	G	3.5 Footwork FA13-Mugen Honda V10	*1 lap behind*	16/28
6	PORTUGUESE GP	Estoril	9	Footwork Grand Prix International	G	3.5 Footwork FA13-Mugen Honda V10	*1 lap behind*	8/26
15	JAPANESE GP	Suzuka	9	Footwork Grand Prix International	G	3.5 Footwork FA13-Mugen Honda V10	*2 laps behind*	24/26
ret	AUSTRALIAN GP	Adelaide	9	Footwork Grand Prix International	G	3.5 Footwork FA13-Mugen Honda V10	*accident on lap 1*	11/26

1993 Championship position: Unplaced

ret	SOUTH AFRICAN GP	Kyalami	21	BMS Scuderia Italia SpA	G	3.5 Lola T93/30 BMS-Ferrari V12	*engine*	25/26
11	BRAZILIAN GP	Interlagos	21	BMS Scuderia Italia SpA	G	3.5 Lola T93/30 BMS-Ferrari V12	*3 laps behind*	25/26
11	EUROPEAN GP	Donington	21	BMS Scuderia Italia SpA	G	3.5 Lola T93/30 BMS-Ferrari V12	*6 laps behind*	24/26
dnq	SAN MARINO GP	Imola	21	BMS Scuderia Italia SpA	G	3.5 Lola T93/30 BMS-Ferrari V12		26/26
dnq	SPANISH GP	Barcelona	21	BMS Scuderia Italia SpA	G	3.5 Lola T93/30 BMS-Ferrari V12		26/26
ret	MONACO GP	Monte Carlo	21	BMS Scuderia Italia SpA	G	3.5 Lola T93/30 BMS-Ferrari V12	*gearbox*	24/26
dnq	CANADIAN GP	Montreal	21	BMS Scuderia Italia SpA	G	3.5 Lola T93/30 BMS-Ferrari V12		26/26
dnq	FRENCH GP	Magny Cours	21	BMS Scuderia Italia SpA	G	3.5 Lola T93/30 BMS-Ferrari V12		26/26
dnq	BRITISH GP	Silverstone	21	BMS Scuderia Italia SpA	G	3.5 Lola T93/30 BMS-Ferrari V12		26/26
16	GERMAN GP	Hockenheim	21	BMS Scuderia Italia SpA	G	3.5 Lola T93/30 BMS-Ferrari V12	*no clutch/2 laps behind*	26/26
ret	HUNGARIAN GP	Hungaroring	21	BMS Scuderia Italia SpA	G	3.5 Lola T93/30 BMS-Ferrari V12	*engine overheating*	25/26
14	BELGIAN GP	Spa	21	BMS Scuderia Italia SpA	G	3.5 Lola T93/30 BMS-Ferrari V12	*car handling badly/-3 laps*	25/26
ret	ITALIAN GP	Monza	21	BMS Scuderia Italia SpA	G	3.5 Lola T93/30 BMS-Ferrari V12	*suspension failure*	21/25
ret	PORTUGUESE GP	Estoril	21	BMS Scuderia Italia SpA	G	3.5 Lola T93/30 BMS-Ferrari V12	*gearbox/accident*	25/26

1994 Championship position: 24th   Wins: 0   Pole positions: 0   Fastest laps: 0   Points scored: 1

ret	BRAZILIAN GP	Interlagos	24	Minardi Scuderia Italia	G	3.5 Minardi M193B-Ford HB V8	*electrics*	22/28
ret	PACIFIC GP	T.I. Circuit	24	Minardi Scuderia Italia	G	3.5 Minardi M193B-Ford HB V8	*collision with Wendlinger*	15/28
ret	SAN MARINO GP	Imola	24	Minardi Scuderia Italia	G	3.5 Minardi M193B-Ford HB V8	*lost wheel while exiting pits*	15/28
6	MONACO GP	Monte Carlo	24	Minardi Scuderia Italia	G	3.5 Minardi M193B-Ford HB V8	*1 lap behind*	12/24
ret	SPANISH GP	Barcelona	24	Minardi Scuderia Italia	G	3.5 Minardi M193B-Ford HB V8	*engine*	14/27
11	CANADIAN GP	Montreal	24	Minardi Scuderia Italia	G	3.5 Minardi M194-Ford HB V8	*2 laps behind*	18/27
ret	FRENCH GP	Magny Cours	24	Minardi Scuderia Italia	G	3.5 Minardi M194-Ford HB V8	*engine*	21/28
ret	BRITISH GP	Silverstone	24	Minardi Scuderia Italia	G	3.5 Minardi M194-Ford HB V8	*engine*	17/28
ret	GERMAN GP	Hockenheim	24	Minardi Scuderia Italia	G	3.5 Minardi M194-Ford HB V8	*multiple accident at start*	23/28
7	HUNGARIAN GP	Hungaroring	24	Minardi Scuderia Italia	G	3.5 Minardi M194-Ford HB V8	*2 laps behind*	20/28
9*	BELGIAN GP	Spa	24	Minardi Scuderia Italia	G	3.5 Minardi M194-Ford HB V8	**1st place car dsq/1 lap behind*	18/28
ret	ITALIAN GP	Monza	24	Minardi Scuderia Italia	G	3.5 Minardi M194-Ford HB V8	*gearbox*	22/28
13	PORTUGUESE GP	Estoril	24	Minardi Scuderia Italia	G	3.5 Minardi M194-Ford HB V8	*2 laps behind*	19/28
14	EUROPEAN GP	Jerez	24	Minardi Scuderia Italia	G	3.5 Minardi M194-Ford HB V8	*2 laps behind*	20/28
ret	JAPANESE GP	Suzuka	24	Minardi Scuderia Italia	G	3.5 Minardi M194-Ford HB V8	*spun off*	21/28
ret	AUSTRALIAN GP	Adelaide	24	Minardi Scuderia Italia	G	3.5 Minardi M194-Ford HB V8	*accident*	16/28

GP Starts: 194   GP Wins: 5   Pole positions: 2   Fastest laps: 5 (1 shared)   Points: 186.50

JEAN ALESI

WHAT if Jean Alesi had taken up his Williams contract instead of joining Ferrari in 1991? Almost certainly the popular French driver would now be able to look back on more than just a single grand prix victory in what must be seen as a career that has failed to achieve anything like the success his natural talent demanded.

Jean, who was born in Avignon of Sicilian descent, demonstrated his ability early in his career when, in 1986, he shook the established order in French F3. Running his own Dallara-Alfa, he scored two race wins, on his way to the runner-up spot behind champion Yannick Dalmas. That this was achieved without the benefit of major sponsorship was not lost on the ORECA squad, who signed him up for 1987.

After a troublesome start, a change of chassis gave him the tools to take six successive wins and give the team its fifth consecutive French F3 title. Naturally, Alesi moved into the ORECA F3000 team for the following season, but the campaign proved to be a huge disappointment for all concerned, Jean being particularly unhappy at the lack of rapport on the engineering side of the team.

Alesi switched to Eddie Jordan's team, and the pair got on famously. Not only was the F3000 championship won – albeit narrowly from Érik Comas – but also Alesi stepped into the Tyrrell vacated by Michele Alboreto to score a sensational fourth place in the French Grand Prix on his F1 debut. An 18-month contract was quickly signed, and Alesi set about building a reputation as a fast and fearless racer intimidated by nobody – as Ayrton Senna would find at Phoenix and Gerhard Berger at Monaco in 1990 – but one who sometimes ran at the ragged edge or beyond, as at Monza, where he spun out in a fruitless attempt to match the pace of the McLarens.

Despite Alesi's flaws, Frank Williams decided he liked the Frenchman's style, and a contract was signed for him to race the Williams-Renault in 1991. After protracted negotiations, however, it was announced that he would be driving for Ferrari instead. Initially, Alesi found the going tough, his relative lack of experience proving a handicap in a difficult team environment. There were drives of brilliance in 1992 – at Barcelona and Magny-Cours, for example – but even more frustration in terms of solid results would follow in 1993.

Despite Ferrari's relative lack of success, Alesi signed for a further two years at Maranello, hoping the team's restructuring programme would bring him the success he craved. In the event, 1994 turned out to be a desperately disappointing year. His early season was disrupted by a back injury sustained in a testing accident. This caused him to miss two races, and his return to the wheel was punctuated by driver errors and engine failures. The Latin blood within him reached boiling point at Monza, where that elusive first grand prix win disappeared when his gearbox was damaged at a refuelling stop.

After 91 races, Jean's last year with the Prancing Horse finally brought an emotional and hugely popular win in Canada. Brilliant drives in Brazil and at the Nürburgring once again highlighted his mesmerising car control, but his volatility – surely such a factor in these performances – finally led him to fall out with Jean Todt. With the imminent arrival of Michael Schumacher, he lost little time in negotiating a seat at Benetton for 1996.

On paper, his chances of success were good, and a serious world championship bid lay in prospect. In the event, it was the usual cocktail of brilliance – at Monaco, where he could have won – mixed with an equal measure of stupidity, highlighted by needless shunts in Australia and Japan. The 1997 season saw much the same story and, despite some excellent drives – most notably at Monza – Alesi was left to contemplate a slide further down the grid after signing a two-year deal with Sauber.

Predictably, perhaps, the first season brought optimism and some sparkling performances, but the second yielded only mounting frustration at midfield obscurity followed by discord when the team failed to progress. To his credit, Alesi stuck out the rest of the season in his usual press-on style, but jumped at the opportunity to join friend and former Ferrari team-mate Alain Prost's team for 2000.

Partnered by rookie Nick Heidfeld, the Frenchman found that he had his work cut out to take the AP03 into the top ten, let alone close to victory. No points and his most frustrating season to date could have left Alesi contemplating retirement, but the born racer opted to stay put for 2001, and it was Heidfeld who left the Prost fold. Alesi continued to drive his heart out and, in pre-season testing, the AP04 absolutely flew. The situation during the year, however, was vastly different and the car struggled to repeat its earlier pace. It wasn't until the Monaco GP that he finally scored points, finishing in sixth, which was followed by fifth- and sixth-place finishes at the Canadian and German grands prix.

After Heinz-Harald Frentzen's sacking ahead of the latter event, Alesi was quickly linked to Jordan and, sensing the prospect of a far more competitive drive, he reached an agreement with Prost that saw his contract cancelled in favour of a seat swap with H-HF. Having joined Jordan, however, Alesi did not enjoy quite the success he was anticipating, and the Frenchman's last appearance in an F1 car, at Suzuka, was both short-lived and dramatic, as he was left with nowhere to turn when otherwise impressive rookie Kimi Räikkönen lost control of his Sauber.

Not long after confirming his retirement from Formula 1, Alesi was linked with Mercedes, not for an F1 ride, but to supplement its already strong line-up in the German DTM touring car series. A win in his maiden season (2002), at Donington Park, was followed by a repeat and further success at the Hockenheim season finale in 2003 – he finished fifth overall in both campaigns. Although 2004 proved a little less successful, Alesi continued as a key figure in Mercedes' plans for 2005, and he scored a splendid win at Hockenheim to reaffirm his place among the DTM front-runners. However, his exuberant driving style was often at odds with the meticulous technical nature of the formula, and much to his chagrin, Alesi found himself demoted into a year-old Persson Motorsports car for 2006.

Feeling snubbed at his treatment by Mercedes, Alesi decided to look for pastures new in racing. He became involved with Direxiv, a Japanese consortium planning to enter Formula 1 in partnership with a McLaren junior team, but in the event this came to nothing. In the meantime, he had found some racing action in 2008/09 in the Far and Middle Eastern Speedcar series, which reunited him in sporting combat with a number of ex-Formula 1 drivers, the Frenchman taking a total of four wins.

In 2010, Alesi joined Giancarlo Fisichella and Toni Villander to race a Ferrari 430GT for AF Corse in the Le Mans Series. The trio enjoyed a number of podium visits to take second place overall in the GT2 class.

Early in 2011, Alesi became an ambassador for Lotus Renault and was involved in the T125 F1-style race car, which can be bought for around US$1m, allowing those few with the wherewithal to indulge their F1 fantasy at the track of their choice.

Intriguingly, late in 2011, Alesi announced that he planned to enter the 2012 Indianapolis 500 in a Dallara with a Lotus-badged engine. At nearly 48 years of age, it seemed a brave move for the Frenchman, who was untried in the category. Whether it was just a PR stunt or a serious effort remained to be seen when this book went to press.

Jean was also reputed to be involved in the Indian-based Super Series, a one-make championship running prototype-style – but street-legal – Radical SR8 sports cars, which was planned for 2013.

Alesi is a wine connoisseur and has a vineyard near his hometown of Avignon, where he lives with his wife, Japanese model, actress, and pop singer Kumiko Goto, and their four children.

ALESI, Jean (F) b 11/6/1964, Montfavet, nr Avignon

1989 Championship position: 9th   Wins: 0   Pole positions: 0   Fastest laps: 0   Points scored: 8

	Race	Circuit	No	Entrant	Tyres	Capacity/Car/Engine	Comment	Q Pos/Entries
4	FRENCH GP	Paul Ricard	4	Tyrrell Racing Organisation	G	3.5 Tyrrell 018-Cosworth V8		16/39
ret	BRITISH GP	Silverstone	4	Tyrrell Racing Organisation	G	3.5 Tyrrell 018-Cosworth V8	spun off	22/39
10	GERMAN GP	Hockenheim	4	Tyrrell Racing Organisation	G	3.5 Tyrrell 018-Cosworth V8	spin-pit stop – tyres/-2 laps	10/39
9	HUNGARIAN GP	Hungaroring	4	Tyrrell Racing Organisation	G	3.5 Tyrrell 018-Cosworth V8	pit stop – tyres/1 lap behind	11/39
5	ITALIAN GP	Monza	4	Tyrrell Racing Organisation	G	3.5 Tyrrell 018-Cosworth V8	1 lap behind	10/39
4	SPANISH GP	Jerez	4	Tyrrell Racing Organisation	G	3.5 Tyrrell 018-Cosworth V8	pit stop – tyres/1 lap behind	9/38
ret	JAPANESE GP	Suzuka	4	Tyrrell Racing Organisation	G	3.5 Tyrrell 018-Cosworth V8	gearbox	18/39
ret	AUSTRALIAN GP	Adelaide	4	Tyrrell Racing Organisation	G	3.5 Tyrrell 018-Cosworth V8	electrics	15/39

1990 Championship position: 9th   Wins: 0   Pole positions: 0   Fastest laps: 0   Points scored: 13

	Race	Circuit	No	Entrant	Tyres	Capacity/Car/Engine	Comment	Q Pos/Entries
2	US GP (PHOENIX)	Phoenix	4	Tyrrell Racing Organisation	P	3.5 Tyrrell 018-Cosworth V8		4/35
7	BRAZILIAN GP	Interlagos	4	Tyrrell Racing Organisation	P	3.5 Tyrrell 019-Cosworth V8	collision with de Cesaris/-1 lap	7/35
6	SAN MARINO GP	Imola	4	Tyrrell Racing Organisation	P	3.5 Tyrrell 019-Cosworth V8	incident with Piquet/-1 lap	7/34
2	MONACO GP	Monte Carlo	4	Tyrrell Racing Organisation	P	3.5 Tyrrell 018-Cosworth V8		3/35
dns	"	" "	4	Tyrrell Racing Organisation	P	3.5 Tyrrell 019-Cosworth V8	practice only	– / –
ret	CANADIAN GP	Montreal	4	Tyrrell Racing Organisation	P	3.5 Tyrrell 019-Cosworth V8	spun off	8/35
7	MEXICAN GP	Mexico City	4	Tyrrell Racing Organisation	P	3.5 Tyrrell 019-Cosworth V8	misfire	6/35
ret	FRENCH GP	Paul Ricard	4	Tyrrell Racing Organisation	P	3.5 Tyrrell 019-Cosworth V8	differential	13/35
8	BRITISH GP	Silverstone	4	Tyrrell Racing Organisation	P	3.5 Tyrrell 019-Cosworth V8	pit stop – tyres/1 lap behind	6/35
11/ret	GERMAN GP	Hockenheim	4	Tyrrell Racing Organisation	P	3.5 Tyrrell 019-Cosworth V8	c.v. joint/5 laps behind	8/35
ret	HUNGARIAN GP	Hungaroring	4	Tyrrell Racing Organisation	P	3.5 Tyrrell 019-Cosworth V8	collision with Martini	6/35
8	BELGIAN GP	Spa	4	Tyrrell Racing Organisation	P	3.5 Tyrrell 019-Cosworth V8	pit stop – tyres/1 lap behind	9/33
ret	ITALIAN GP	Monza	4	Tyrrell Racing Organisation	P	3.5 Tyrrell 019-Cosworth V8	spun off	5/33
8	PORTUGUESE GP	Estoril	4	Tyrrell Racing Organisation	P	3.5 Tyrrell 019-Cosworth V8	1 lap behind	8/33
ret	SPANISH GP	Jerez	4	Tyrrell Racing Organisation	P	3.5 Tyrrell 019-Cosworth V8	bumped by Berger – puncture	4/33
dns	JAPANESE GP	Suzuka	4	Tyrrell Racing Organisation	P	3.5 Tyrrell 019-Cosworth V8	neck injury in practice	(7)/30
8	AUSTRALIAN GP	Adelaide	4	Tyrrell Racing Organisation	P	3.5 Tyrrell 019-Cosworth V8	1 lap behind	5/30

1991 Championship position: 7th   Wins: 0   Pole positions: 0   Fastest laps: 1   Points scored: 21

	Race	Circuit	No	Entrant	Tyres	Capacity/Car/Engine	Comment	Q Pos/Entries
12/ret	US GP (PHOENIX)	Phoenix	28	Scuderia Ferrari SpA	G	3.5 Fiat Ferrari 642 V12	gearbox/9 laps behind/FL	6/34
6	BRAZILIAN GP	Interlagos	28	Scuderia Ferrari SpA	G	3.5 Fiat Ferrari 642 V12		5/34
ret	SAN MARINO GP	Imola	28	Scuderia Ferrari SpA	G	3.5 Fiat Ferrari 642 V12	spun off	7/34
3	MONACO GP	Monte Carlo	28	Scuderia Ferrari SpA	G	3.5 Fiat Ferrari 642 V12		9/34
ret	CANADIAN GP	Montreal	28	Scuderia Ferrari SpA	G	3.5 Fiat Ferrari 642 V12	engine	7/34
ret	MEXICAN GP	Mexico City	28	Scuderia Ferrari SpA	G	3.5 Fiat Ferrari 642 V12	clutch	4/34
4	FRENCH GP	Magny Cours	28	Scuderia Ferrari SpA	G	3.5 Fiat Ferrari 643 V12		6/34
ret	BRITISH GP	Silverstone	28	Scuderia Ferrari SpA	G	3.5 Fiat Ferrari 643 V12	collision with Suzuki	6/34
3	GERMAN GP	Hockenheim	28	Scuderia Ferrari SpA	G	3.5 Fiat Ferrari 643 V12	ran without tyre change	6/34
5	HUNGARIAN GP	Hungaroring	28	Scuderia Ferrari SpA	G	3.5 Fiat Ferrari 643 V12		6/34
ret	BELGIAN GP	Spa	28	Scuderia Ferrari SpA	G	3.5 Fiat Ferrari 643 V12	engine	5/34
ret	ITALIAN GP	Monza	28	Scuderia Ferrari SpA	G	3.5 Fiat Ferrari 643 V12	engine	6/34
3	PORTUGUESE GP	Estoril	28	Scuderia Ferrari SpA	G	3.5 Fiat Ferrari 643 V12		6/34
4	SPANISH GP	Barcelona	28	Scuderia Ferrari SpA	G	3.5 Fiat Ferrari 643 V12		7/33
ret	JAPANESE GP	Suzuka	28	Scuderia Ferrari SpA	G	3.5 Fiat Ferrari 643 V12	engine	6/31
ret	AUSTRALIAN GP	Adelaide	28	Scuderia Ferrari SpA	G	3.5 Fiat Ferrari 643 V12	collision with Larini	7/31

1992 Championship position: 7th   Wins: 0   Pole positions: 0   Fastest laps: 0   Points scored: 18

	Race	Circuit	No	Entrant	Tyres	Capacity/Car/Engine	Comment	Q Pos/Entries
ret	SOUTH AFRICAN GP	Kyalami	27	Scuderia Ferrari SpA	G	3.5 Fiat Ferrari F92A V12	engine	5/30
ret	MEXICAN GP	Mexico City	27	Scuderia Ferrari SpA	G	3.5 Fiat Ferrari F92A V12	engine	10/30
4	BRAZILIAN GP	Interlagos	27	Scuderia Ferrari SpA	G	3.5 Fiat Ferrari F92A V12	1 lap behind	6/31
3	SPANISH GP	Barcelona	27	Scuderia Ferrari SpA	G	3.5 Fiat Ferrari F92A V12		8/32
ret	SAN MARINO GP	Imola	27	Scuderia Ferrari SpA	G	3.5 Fiat Ferrari F92A V12	collision with Berger	7/32
ret	MONACO GP	Monte Carlo	27	Scuderia Ferrari SpA	G	3.5 Fiat Ferrari F92A V12	gearbox	4/32
3	CANADIAN GP	Montreal	27	Scuderia Ferrari SpA	G	3.5 Fiat Ferrari F92A V12		8/32
ret	FRENCH GP	Magny Cours	27	Scuderia Ferrari SpA	G	3.5 Fiat Ferrari F92A V12	engine	6/30
ret	BRITISH GP	Silverstone	27	Scuderia Ferrari SpA	G	3.5 Fiat Ferrari F92A V12	fire extinguisher discharged	8/32
5	GERMAN GP	Hockenheim	27	Scuderia Ferrari SpA	G	3.5 Fiat Ferrari F92A V12		5/32
ret	HUNGARIAN GP	Hungaroring	27	Scuderia Ferrari SpA	G	3.5 Fiat Ferrari F92A V12	spun off	9/31
ret	BELGIAN GP	Spa	27	Scuderia Ferrari SpA	G	3.5 Fiat Ferrari F92AT V12	spun off	5/30
ret	ITALIAN GP	Monza	27	Scuderia Ferrari SpA	G	3.5 Fiat Ferrari F92AT V12	fuel pressure	3/28
ret	PORTUGUESE GP	Estoril	27	Scuderia Ferrari SpA	G	3.5 Fiat Ferrari F92AT V12	spun off	10/26
5	JAPANESE GP	Suzuka	27	Scuderia Ferrari SpA	G	3.5 Fiat Ferrari F92AT V12	1 lap behind	15/26
4	AUSTRALIAN GP	Adelaide	27	Scuderia Ferrari SpA	G	3.5 Fiat Ferrari F92AT V12	1 lap behind	6/26

1993 Championship position: 6th   Wins: 0   Pole positions: 0   Fastest laps: 0   Points scored: 16

	Race	Circuit	No	Entrant	Tyres	Capacity/Car/Engine	Comment	Q Pos/Entries
ret	SOUTH AFRICAN GP	Kyalami	27	Scuderia Ferrari SpA	G	3.5 Fiat Ferrari F93A V12	hydraulics	5/26
8	BRAZILIAN GP	Interlagos	27	Scuderia Ferrari SpA	G	3.5 Fiat Ferrari F93A V12	2 stop & go penalties/-1 lap-	9/26
ret	EUROPEAN GP	Donington	27	Scuderia Ferrari SpA	G	3.5 Fiat Ferrari F93A V12	active suspension system	9/26
ret	SAN MARINO GP	Imola	27	Scuderia Ferrari SpA	G	3.5 Fiat Ferrari F93A V12	clutch	9/26
ret	SPANISH GP	Barcelona	27	Scuderia Ferrari SpA	G	3.5 Fiat Ferrari F93A V12	engine	8/26
3	MONACO GP	Monte Carlo	27	Scuderia Ferrari SpA	G	3.5 Fiat Ferrari F93A V12	despite collision with Berger	5/26
ret	CANADIAN GP	Montreal	27	Scuderia Ferrari SpA	G	3.5 Fiat Ferrari F93A V12	engine	6/26
ret	FRENCH GP	Magny Cours	27	Scuderia Ferrari SpA	G	3.5 Fiat Ferrari F93A V12	engine	6/26
9	BRITISH GP	Silverstone	27	Scuderia Ferrari SpA	G	3.5 Fiat Ferrari F93A V12	1 lap behind	12/26
7	GERMAN GP	Hockenheim	27	Scuderia Ferrari SpA	G	3.5 Fiat Ferrari F93A V12	pit stop – loose bodywork	10/26
ret	HUNGARIAN GP	Hungaroring	27	Scuderia Ferrari SpA	G	3.5 Fiat Ferrari F93A V12	collision with Fittipaldi	8/26

ret	BELGIAN GP	Spa	27	Scuderia Ferrari SpA	G	3.5 Fiat Ferrari F93A V12	suspension	4/25
2	ITALIAN GP	Monza	27	Scuderia Ferrari SpA	G	3.5 Fiat Ferrari F93A V12		3/26
4	PORTUGUESE GP	Estoril	27	Scuderia Ferrari SpA	G	3.5 Fiat Ferrari F93A V12		5/26
ret	JAPANESE GP	Suzuka	27	Scuderia Ferrari SpA	G	3.5 Fiat Ferrari F93A V12	electrics	14/24
4	AUSTRALIAN GP	Adelaide	27	Scuderia Ferrari SpA	G	3.5 Fiat Ferrari F93A V12	1 lap behind	7/24

1994 Championship position: 5th   Wins: 0   Pole positions: 1   Fastest laps: 0   Points scored: 24

3	BRAZILIAN GP	Interlagos	27	Scuderia Ferrari SpA	G	3.5 Fiat Ferrari 412T1 V12	1 lap behind	3/28
5	MONACO GP	Monte Carlo	27	Scuderia Ferrari SpA	G	3.5 Fiat Ferrari 412T1 V12	collision with Brabham/-1 lap	5/24
4	SPANISH GP	Barcelona	27	Scuderia Ferrari SpA	G	3.5 Fiat Ferrari 412T1 V12	1 lap behind	6/27
3	CANADIAN GP	Montreal	27	Scuderia Ferrari SpA	G	3.5 Fiat Ferrari 412T1 V12		2/27
ret	FRENCH GP	Magny Cours	27	Scuderia Ferrari SpA	G	3.5 Fiat Ferrari 412T1B V12	spun – then hit Barrichello	4/28
2*	BRITISH GP	Silverstone	27	Scuderia Ferrari SpA	G	3.5 Fiat Ferrari 412T1B V12	*2nd place car disqualified	4/28
ret	GERMAN GP	Hockenheim	27	Scuderia Ferrari SpA	G	3.5 Fiat Ferrari 412T1B V12	electrics on lap 1	2/28
ret	HUNGARIAN GP	Hungaroring	27	Scuderia Ferrari SpA	G	3.5 Fiat Ferrari 412T1B V12	gearbox	13/28
ret	BELGIAN GP	Spa	27	Scuderia Ferrari SpA	G	3.5 Fiat Ferrari 412T1B V12	engine	5/28
ret	ITALIAN GP	Monza	27	Scuderia Ferrari SpA	G	3.5 Fiat Ferrari 412T1B V12	gearbox	1/28
ret	PORTUGUESE GP	Estoril	27	Scuderia Ferrari SpA	G	3.5 Fiat Ferrari 412T1B V12	collision with Brabham	5/28
10	EUROPEAN GP	Jerez	27	Scuderia Ferrari SpA	G	3.5 Fiat Ferrari 412T1B V12	1 lap behind	16/28
3	JAPANESE GP	Suzuka	27	Scuderia Ferrari SpA	G	3.5 Fiat Ferrari 412T1B V12		7/28
6	AUSTRALIAN GP	Adelaide	27	Scuderia Ferrari SpA	G	3.5 Fiat Ferrari 412T1B V12	1 lap behind	8/28

1995 Championship position: 5th   Wins: 1   Pole positions: 0   Fastest laps: 1   Points scored: 42

5	BRAZILIAN GP	Interlagos	27	Scuderia Ferrari SpA	G	3.0 Fiat Ferrari 412T2 V12	1 lap behind	6/26
2	ARGENTINE GP	Buenos Aires	27	Scuderia Ferrari SpA	G	3.0 Fiat Ferrari 412T2 V12		6/26
2	SAN MARINO GP	Imola	27	Scuderia Ferrari SpA	G	3.0 Fiat Ferrari 412T2 V12		5/26
ret	SPANISH GP	Barcelona	27	Scuderia Ferrari SpA	G	3.0 Fiat Ferrari 412T2 V12	engine	2/26
ret	MONACO GP	Monte Carlo	27	Scuderia Ferrari SpA	G	3.0 Fiat Ferrari 412T2 V12	accident/FL	5/26
1	CANADIAN GP	Montreal	27	Scuderia Ferrari SpA	G	3.0 Fiat Ferrari 412T2 V12		5/24
5	FRENCH GP	Magny Cours	27	Scuderia Ferrari SpA	G	3.0 Fiat Ferrari 412T2 V12		4/24
2	BRITISH GP	Silverstone	27	Scuderia Ferrari SpA	G	3.0 Fiat Ferrari 412T2 V12		6/24
ret	GERMAN GP	Hockenheim	27	Scuderia Ferrari SpA	G	3.0 Fiat Ferrari 412T2 V12	engine	10/24
ret	HUNGARIAN GP	Hungaroring	27	Scuderia Ferrari SpA	G	3.0 Fiat Ferrari 412T2 V12	engine	6/24
ret	BELGIAN GP	Spa	27	Scuderia Ferrari SpA	G	3.0 Fiat Ferrari 412T2 V12	suspension	2/24
ret	ITALIAN GP	Monza	27	Scuderia Ferrari SpA	G	3.0 Fiat Ferrari 412T2 V12	wheel bearing	5/24
5	PORTUGUESE GP	Estoril	27	Scuderia Ferrari SpA	G	3.0 Fiat Ferrari 412T2 V12		7/24
2	EUROPEAN GP	Nürburgring	27	Scuderia Ferrari SpA	G	3.0 Fiat Ferrari 412T2 V12		6/24
5	PACIFIC GP	T I. Circuit	27	Scuderia Ferrari SpA	G	3.0 Fiat Ferrari 412T2 V12	1 lap behind	4/24
ret	JAPANESE GP	Suzuka	27	Scuderia Ferrari SpA	G	3.0 Fiat Ferrari 412T2 V12	differential	2/24
ret	AUSTRALIAN GP	Adelaide	27	Scuderia Ferrari SpA	G	3.0 Fiat Ferrari 412T2 V12	collision with Schumacher	5/24

1996 Championship position: 4th   Wins: 0   Pole positions: 0   Fastest laps: 2   Points scored: 47

ret	AUSTRALIAN GP	Melbourne	3	Mild Seven Benetton Renault	G	3.0 Benetton 196-Renault V10	collision with Irvine	6/22
2	BRAZILIAN GP	Interlagos	3	Mild Seven Benetton Renault	G	3.0 Benetton 196-Renault V10		5/22
3	ARGENTINE GP	Buenos Aires	3	Mild Seven Benetton Renault	G	3.0 Benetton 196-Renault V10	FL	4/22
ret	EUROPEAN GP	Nürburgring	3	Mild Seven Benetton Renault	G	3.0 Benetton 196-Renault V10	collision with Salo, lap 1	4/22
6	SAN MARINO GP	Imola	3	Mild Seven Benetton Renault	G	3.0 Benetton 196-Renault V10	stop & go penalty/1 lap behind	5/22
ret	MONACO GP	Monte Carlo	3	Mild Seven Benetton Renault	G	3.0 Benetton 196-Renault V10	rear suspension – led race/FL	3/22
2	SPANISH GP	Barcelona	3	Mild Seven Benetton Renault	G	3.0 Benetton 196-Renault V10		4/22
3	CANADIAN GP	Montreal	3	Mild Seven Benetton Renault	G	3.0 Benetton 196-Renault V10		4/22
3	FRENCH GP	Magny Cours	3	Mild Seven Benetton Renault	G	3.0 Benetton 196-Renault V10		3/22
ret	BRITISH GP	Silverstone	3	Mild Seven Benetton Renault	G	3.0 Benetton 196-Renault V10	rear wheel bearing	5/22
2	GERMAN GP	Hockenheim	3	Mild Seven Benetton Renault	G	3.0 Benetton 196-Renault V10		5/20
3	HUNGARIAN GP	Hungaroring	3	Mild Seven Benetton Renault	G	3.0 Benetton 196-Renault V10		5/20
4	BELGIAN GP	Spa	3	Mild Seven Benetton Renault	G	3.0 Benetton 196-Renault V10		7/20
2	ITALIAN GP	Monza	3	Mild Seven Benetton Renault	G	3.0 Benetton 196-Renault V10		6/20
4	PORTUGUESE GP	Estoril	3	Mild Seven Benetton Renault	G	3.0 Benetton 196-Renault V10		3/20
ret	JAPANESE GP	Suzuka	3	Mild Seven Benetton Renault	G	3.0 Benetton 196-Renault V10	crashed on lap 1	9/20

1997 Championship position: 3rd=   Wins: 0   Pole positions: 1   Fastest laps: 0   Points scored: 36

ret	AUSTRALIAN GP	Melbourne	7	Mild Seven Benetton Renault	G	3.0 Benetton 197-Renault V10	ran out of fuel	8/24
6	BRAZILIAN GP	Interlagos	7	Mild Seven Benetton Renault	G	3.0 Benetton 197-Renault V10		6/22
7	ARGENTINE GP	Buenos Aires	7	Mild Seven Benetton Renault	G	3.0 Benetton 197-Renault V10		11/22
5	SAN MARINO GP	Imola	7	Mild Seven Benetton Renault	G	3.0 Benetton 197-Renault V10	1 lap behind	14/22
ret	MONACO GP	Monte Carlo	7	Mild Seven Benetton Renault	G	3.0 Benetton 197-Renault V10	spun and stalled	9/22
3	SPANISH GP	Barcelona	7	Mild Seven Benetton Renault	G	3.0 Benetton 197-Renault V10		4/22
2	CANADIAN GP	Montreal	7	Mild Seven Benetton Renault	G	3.0 Benetton 197-Renault V10		8/22
5	FRENCH GP	Magny Cours	7	Mild Seven Benetton Renault	G	3.0 Benetton 197-Renault V10		8/22
2	BRITISH GP	Silverstone	7	Mild Seven Benetton Renault	G	3.0 Benetton 197-Renault V10		11/22
6	GERMAN GP	Hockenheim	7	Mild Seven Benetton Renault	G	3.0 Benetton 197-Renault V10		6/22
11	HUNGARIAN GP	Hungaroring	7	Mild Seven Benetton Renault	G	3.0 Benetton 197-Renault V10	2 laps behind	9/22
8*	BELGIAN GP	Spa	7	Mild Seven Benetton Renault	G	3.0 Benetton 197-Renault V10	*3rd place car disqualified	2/22
2	ITALIAN GP	Monza	7	Mild Seven Benetton Renault	G	3.0 Benetton 197-Renault V10		1/22
ret	AUSTRIAN GP	A1-Ring	7	Mild Seven Benetton Renault	G	3.0 Benetton 197-Renault V10		15/22
2	LUXEMBOURG GP	Nürburgring	7	Mild Seven Benetton Renault	G	3.0 Benetton 197-Renault V10	collision with Irvine	10/22
5*	JAPANESE GP	Suzuka	7	Mild Seven Benetton Renault	G	3.0 Benetton 197-Renault V10	*4th place car disqualified	7/22
13	EUROPEAN GP	Jerez	7	Mild Seven Benetton Renault	G	3.0 Benetton 197-Renault V10	spin – 1 lap behind	10/22

1998 Championship position: 11th   Wins: 0   Pole positions: 0   Fastest laps: 0   Points scored: 9

ret	AUSTRALIAN GP	Melbourne	14	Red Bull Sauber Petronas	G	3.0 Sauber C17-Petronas V10	*engine*	12/22
9	BRAZILIAN GP	Interlagos	14	Red Bull Sauber Petronas	G	3.0 Sauber C17-Petronas V10	*1 lap behind*	15/22
5	ARGENTINE GP	Buenos Aires	14	Red Bull Sauber Petronas	G	3.0 Sauber C17-Petronas V10	*lost side winglet at pit stop*	11/22
6	SAN MARINO GP	Imola	14	Red Bull Sauber Petronas	G	3.0 Sauber C17-Petronas V10	*1 lap behind*	12/22
10	SPANISH GP	Barcelona	14	Red Bull Sauber Petronas	G	3.0 Sauber C17-Petronas V10	*2 laps behind*	14/22
ret/12	MONACO GP	Monte Carlo	14	Red Bull Sauber Petronas	G	3.0 Sauber C17-Petronas V10	*gearbox/6 laps behind*	11/22
ret	CANADIAN GP	Montreal	14	Red Bull Sauber Petronas	G	3.0 Sauber C17-Petronas V10	*collision on lap 1*	9/22
7th	FRENCH GP	Magny Cours	14	Red Bull Sauber Petronas	G	3.0 Sauber C17-Petronas V10	*minor collisions/1 lap behind*	11/22
ret	BRITISH GP	Silverstone	14	Red Bull Sauber Petronas	G	3.0 Sauber C17-Petronas V10	*electrics*	8/22
ret	AUSTRIAN GP	A1-Ring	14	Red Bull Sauber Petronas	G	3.0 Sauber C17-Petronas V10	*collision with Fisichella*	2/22
10	GERMAN GP	Hockenheim	14	Red Bull Sauber Petronas	G	3.0 Sauber C17-Petronas V10		11/22
7th	HUNGARIAN GP	Hungaroring	14	Red Bull Sauber Petronas	G	3.0 Sauber C17-Petronas V10	*1 lap behind*	11/22
3	BELGIAN GP	Spa	14	Red Bull Sauber Petronas	G	3.0 Sauber C17-Petronas V10		10/22
5	ITALIAN GP	Monza	14	Red Bull Sauber Petronas	G	3.0 Sauber C17-Petronas V10		8/22
10	LUXEMBOURG GP	Nürburgring	14	Red Bull Sauber Petronas	G	3.0 Sauber C17-Petronas V10	*1 lap behind*	11/22
7	JAPANESE GP	Suzuka	14	Red Bull Sauber Petronas	G	3.0 Sauber C17-Petronas V10		12/22

1999 Championship position: 15th=   Wins: 0   Pole positions: 0   Fastest laps: 0   Points scored: 2

ret	AUSTRALIAN GP	Melbourne	11	Red Bull Sauber Petronas	B	3.0 Sauber C18-Petronas V10	*gearbox on startline*	16/22
ret	BRAZILIAN GP	Interlagos	11	Red Bull Sauber Petronas	B	3.0 Sauber C18-Petronas V10	*gearbox*	14/22
6	SAN MARINO GP	Imola	11	Red Bull Sauber Petronas	B	3.0 Sauber C18-Petronas V10	*1 lap behind*	13/22
ret	MONACO GP	Monte Carlo	11	Red Bull Sauber Petronas	B	3.0 Sauber C18-Petronas V10	*hit wall*	14/22
ret	SPANISH GP	Barcelona	11	Red Bull Sauber Petronas	B	3.0 Sauber C18-Petronas V10	*transmission*	5/22
ret	CANADIAN GP	Montreal	11	Red Bull Sauber Petronas	B	3.0 Sauber C18-Petronas V10	*collision with Trulli*	8/22
ret	FRENCH GP	Magny Cours	11	Red Bull Sauber Petronas	B	3.0 Sauber C18-Petronas V10	*spun off*	2/22
14	BRITISH GP	Silverstone	11	Red Bull Sauber Petronas	B	3.0 Sauber C18-Petronas V10	*1 lap behind*	10/22
ret	AUSTRIAN GP	A1-Ring	11	Red Bull Sauber Petronas	B	3.0 Sauber C18-Petronas V10	*out of fuel*	17/22
8	GERMAN GP	Hockenheim	11	Red Bull Sauber Petronas	B	3.0 Sauber C18-Petronas V10		21/22
16	HUNGARIAN GP	Hungaroring	11	Red Bull Sauber Petronas	B	3.0 Sauber C18-Petronas V10	*fuel pressure/3 laps behind*	11/22
9	BELGIAN GP	Spa	11	Red Bull Sauber Petronas	B	3.0 Sauber C18-Petronas V10		16/22
9	ITALIAN GP	Monza	11	Red Bull Sauber Petronas	B	3.0 Sauber C18-Petronas V10		13/22
ret	EUROPEAN GP	Nürburgring	11	Red Bull Sauber Petronas	B	3.0 Sauber C18-Petronas V10	*driveshaft*	16/22
ret	MALAYSIAN GP	Sepang	11	Red Bull Sauber Petronas	B	3.0 Sauber C18-Petronas V10		15/22
6	JAPANESE GP	Suzuka	11	Red Bull Sauber Petronas	B	3.0 Sauber C18-Petronas V10	*1 lap behind*	10/22

2000 Championship position: Unplaced

ret	AUSTRALIAN GP	Melbourne	14	Gauloises Prost Renault	B	3.0 Prost AP03-Peugeot V10	*started from pitlane/hydraulics*	17/22
ret	BRAZILIAN GP	Interlagos	14	Gauloises Prost Renault	B	3.0 Prost AP03-Peugeot V10	*engine*	15/22
ret	SAN MARINO GP	Imola	14	Gauloises Prost Renault	B	3.0 Prost AP03-Peugeot V10	*hydraulics*	15/22
10	BRITISH GP	Silverstone	14	Gauloises Prost Renault	B	3.0 Prost AP03-Peugeot V10	*1 lap behind*	15/22
ret	SPANISH GP	Barcelona	14	Gauloises Prost Renault	B	3.0 Prost AP03-Peugeot V10	*collision with de la Rosa – lap 1*	18/22
9	EUROPEAN GP	Nürburgring	14	Gauloises Prost Renault	B	3.0 Prost AP03-Peugeot V10	*2 laps behind*	18/22
ret	MONACO GP	Monte Carlo	14	Gauloises Prost Renault	B	3.0 Prost AP03-Peugeot V10	*transmission*	7/22
ret	CANADIAN GP	Montreal	14	Gauloises Prost Renault	B	3.0 Prost AP03-Peugeot V10	*hydraulics*	17/22
14	FRENCH GP	Magny Cours	14	Gauloises Prost Renault	B	3.0 Prost AP03-Peugeot V10	*hit by Heidfeld/2 laps behind*	18/22
ret	AUSTRIAN GP	A1-Ring	14	Gauloises Prost Renault	B	3.0 Prost AP03-Peugeot V10	*collision with Heidfeld*	17/22
ret	GERMAN GP	Hockenheim	14	Gauloises Prost Renault	B	3.0 Prost AP03-Peugeot V10	*collision with Diniz*	20/22
ret	HUNGARIAN GP	Hungaroring	14	Gauloises Prost Renault	B	3.0 Prost AP03-Peugeot V10	*rear suspension/steering*	14/22
ret	BELGIAN GP	Spa	14	Gauloises Prost Renault	B	3.0 Prost AP03-Peugeot V10	*fuel pressure*	17/22
12	ITALIAN GP	Monza	14	Gauloises Prost Renault	B	3.0 Prost AP03-Peugeot V10	*2 laps behind*	19/22
ret	U S GP	Indianapolis	14	Gauloises Prost Renault	B	3.0 Prost AP03-Peugeot V10	*engine*	20/22
ret	JAPANESE GP	Suzuka	14	Gauloises Prost Renault	B	3.0 Prost AP03-Peugeot V10	*engine*	17/22
11	MALAYSIAN GP	Sepang	14	Gauloises Prost Renault	B	3.0 Prost AP03-Peugeot V10	*1 lap behind*	18/22

2001 Championship position: 14th=   Wins: 0   Pole positions: 0   Fastest laps: 0   Points scored: 5

9	AUSTRALIAN GP	Melbourne	22	Prost Acer	M	3.0 Prost AP04-Acer V10	*1 lap behind*	14/22
9	MALAYSIAN GP	Sepang	22	Prost Acer	M	3.0 Prost AP04-Acer V10	*1 lap behind*	13/22
8	BRAZILIAN GP	Interlagos	22	Prost Acer	M	3.0 Prost AP04-Acer V10	*1 lap behind*	15/22
9	SAN MARINO GP	Imola	22	Prost Acer	M	3.0 Prost AP04-Acer V10	*1 lap behind*	14/22
10	SPANISH GP	Barcelona	22	Prost Acer	M	3.0 Prost AP04-Acer V10	*1 lap behind*	15/22
10	AUSTRIAN GP	A1-Ring	22	Prost Acer	M	3.0 Prost AP04-Acer V10	*2 laps behind*	20/22
6	MONACO GP	Monte Carlo	22	Prost Acer	M	3.0 Prost AP04-Acer V10	*1 lap behind*	11/22
5	CANADIAN GP	Montreal	22	Prost Acer	M	3.0 Prost AP04-Acer V10		16/22
15/ret	EUROPEAN GP	Nürburgring	22	Prost Acer	M	3.0 Prost AP04-Acer V10	*spun off/3 laps behind*	14/22
12	FRANCE GP	Magny Cours	22	Prost Acer	M	3.0 Prost AP04-Acer V10	*2 laps behind*	19/22
11	BRITISH GP	Silverstone	22	Prost Acer	M	3.0 Prost AP04-Acer V10	*2 laps behind*	14/22
6	GERMAN GP	Hockenheim	22	Prost Acer	M	3.0 Prost AP04-Acer V10		14/22
10	HUNGARIAN GP	Hungaroring	12	Benson & Hedges Jordan Honda	B	3.0 Jordan EJ11-Honda V10	*2 laps behind*	12/22
6	BELGIAN GP	Spa	12	Benson & Hedges Jordan Honda	B	3.0 Jordan EJ11-Honda V10		13/22
8	ITALIAN GP	Monza	12	Benson & Hedges Jordan Honda	B	3.0 Jordan EJ11-Honda V10	*1 lap behind*	16/22
7	U S GP	Indianapolis	12	Benson & Hedges Jordan Honda	B	3.0 Jordan EJ11-Honda V10	*1 lap behind*	9/22
ret	JAPANESE GP	Suzuka	12	Benson & Hedges Jordan Honda	B	3.0 Jordan EJ11-Honda V10	*collision with Räikkönen*	11/22

GP Starts: 201   GP Wins: 1   Pole positions: 2   Fastest laps: 4   Points: 242

JAIME ALGUERSUARI

WHEN young Spaniard Jaime Alguersuari donned his helmet to take part in the 2008 Hungarian Grand Prix, he became the youngest ever driver to start a grand prix. At 19 years, 4 months and 3 days, he finally wrested that particular honour from Mike Thackwell.

Being fast-tracked into Formula 1 courtesy of his Red Bull patronage did not unduly faze the personable young man from Barcelona who, only a few months earlier, had been crowned the youngest ever British Formula 3 champion after defeating his Carlin team-mates, Brendan Hartley and Oliver Turvey, as well as the surprise package that was Sergio Pérez.

Alguersuari's rise to the top was remarkable, for he had only begun his competition career in the Italian Formula Junior series in 2005. The following year, he won the Italian Formula Renault winter series, and this set him up for the 2007 Formula Renault Italian season, where he finished a close second to his Epsilon Red Bull team-mate, Mika Mäki. Lurking in sixth place in the final standings was an Australian youngster by the name of Daniel Ricciardo...

Following his F3 success, Jaime stayed on with Carlin, but instead of a move to F3000, it was decided to run the champion in the World Series by Renault where, after a sluggish start, his results picked up to the point where he won in Portimao, just before his elevation to Formula 1.

With the very experienced Sébastien Bourdais perceived not to have matched his rookie team-mate, Sébastien Buemi, it was interesting to compare the fortunes of the inexperienced pair as they battled for supremacy at Toro Rosso. The 2010 season showed that they were well matched, Alguersuari looking a slightly more convincing performer, although Buemi edged his younger partner by just three points in the final ranking.

Deemed to have served his apprenticeship, Alguersuari came under pressure to deliver in 2011, and he responded well with some feisty drives. However, the shadow of Daniel Ricciardo was being cast behind him in an HRT in preparation for his elevation to Toro Rosso. Having out-scored Buemi, the Spaniard probably felt that he had done more than enough to retain his seat, so he must have been shocked when he was unceremoniously dropped from the Red Bull roster completely after the season was long finished. It was too late for the unfortunate youngster to look elsewhere for 2012, so he faced the prospect of concentrating on his other passion, music, while trying to prise open the Formula 1 door that had been so firmly slammed in his face.

ALGUERSUARI, Jaime (E) b 23/3/1990, Barcelona

2009 Unplaced

	Race	Circuit	No	Entrant	Tyres	Capacity/Car/Engine	Comment	Q Pos/Entries
15	HUNGARIAN GP	Hungaroring	11	Scuderia Toro Rosso	B	2.4 Toro Rosso STR4-Ferrari V8	1 lap behind	20/20
16	EUROPEAN GP	Valencia Street Circuit	11	Scuderia Toro Rosso	B	2.4 Toro Rosso STR4-Ferrari V8	1 lap behind	19/20
ret	BELGIAN GP	Spa	11	Scuderia Toro Rosso	B	2.4 Toro Rosso STR4-Ferrari V8	accident with Hamilton on lap 1	17/20
ret	ITALIAN GP	Monza	11	Scuderia Toro Rosso	B	2.4 Toro Rosso STR4-Ferrari V8	gearbox	20/20
ret	SINGAPORE GP	Marina Bay Circuit	11	Scuderia Toro Rosso	B	2.4 Toro Rosso STR4-Ferrari V8	brakes	17/20
ret	JAPANESE GP	Suzuka	11	Scuderia Toro Rosso	B	2.4 Toro Rosso STR4-Ferrari V8	accident	15/19
14	BRAZILIAN GP	Interlagos	11	Scuderia Toro Rosso	B	2.4 Toro Rosso STR4-Ferrari V8	1 lap behind	12/20
ret	ABU DHABI GP	Yas Marina Circuit	11	Scuderia Toro Rosso	B	2.4 Toro Rosso STR4-Ferrari V8	gearbox	15/20

2010 Championship position: 19th Wins: 0 Pole positions: 0 Fastest laps: 0 Points scored: 5

	Race	Circuit	No	Entrant	Tyres	Capacity/Car/Engine	Comment	Q Pos/Entries
13	BAHRAIN GP	Sakhir Circuit	17	Scuderia Toro Rosso	B	2.4 Toro Rosso STR5-Ferrari V8		18/24
11	AUSTRALIAN GP	Melbourne	17	Scuderia Toro Rosso	B	2.4 Toro Rosso STR5-Ferrari V8		17/24
9	MALAYSIAN GP	Sepang	17	Scuderia Toro Rosso	B	2.4 Toro Rosso STR5-Ferrari V8	first championship points	14/24
13	CHINESE GP	Shanghai Circuit	17	Scuderia Toro Rosso	B	2.4 Toro Rosso STR5-Ferrari V8	collision with Senna	12/24
10	SPANISH GP	Barcelona	17	Scuderia Toro Rosso	B	2.4 Toro Rosso STR5-Ferrari V8	collision–drive thru penalty/-1 lap	16/24
11	MONACO GP	Monte Carlo	17	Scuderia Toro Rosso	B	2.4 Toro Rosso STR5-Ferrari V8		17/24
12	TURKISH GP	Istanbul Park	17	Scuderia Toro Rosso	B	2.4 Toro Rosso STR5-Ferrari V8		16/24
12	CANADIAN GP	Montreal	17	Scuderia Toro Rosso	B	2.4 Toro Rosso STR5-Ferrari V8	1 lap behind	16/24
13	EUROPEAN GP	Valencia	17	Scuderia Toro Rosso	B	2.4 Toro Rosso STR5-Ferrari V8		17/24
ret	BRITISH GP	Silverstone	17	Scuderia Toro Rosso	B	2.4 Toro Rosso STR5-Ferrari V8	brakes	18/24
15	GERMAN GP	Hockenheim	17	Scuderia Toro Rosso	B	2.4 Toro Rosso STR5-Ferrari V8	hit Buemi–pit stop/1 lap behind	16/24
ret	HUNGARIAN GP	Hungaroring	17	Scuderia Toro Rosso	B	2.4 Toro Rosso STR5-Ferrari V8	blown engine	17/24
13	BELGIAN GP	Spa	17	Scuderia Toro Rosso	B	2.4 Toro Rosso STR5-Ferrari V8	cut chicane–20-sec time penalty	13/24
15	ITALIAN GP	Monza	17	Scuderia Toro Rosso	B	2.4 Toro Rosso STR5-Ferrari V8	1 lap behind	16/24
12	SINGAPORE GP	Marina Bay Circuit	17	Scuderia Toro Rosso	B	2.4 Toro Rosso STR5-Ferrari V8	1 lap behind	11/24
11	JAPANESE GP	Suzuka	17	Scuderia Toro Rosso	B	2.4 Toro Rosso STR5-Ferrari V8	pit stop–collision with Kobayashi	16/24
11	KOREAN GP	Yeongam	17	Scuderia Toro Rosso	B	2.4 Toro Rosso STR5-Ferrari V8		16/24
11	BRAZILIAN GP	Interlagos	17	Scuderia Toro Rosso	B	2.4 Toro Rosso STR5-Ferrari V8	1 lap behind	14/24
9	ABU DHABI GP	Yas Marina Circuit	17	Scuderia Toro Rosso	B	2.4 Toro Rosso STR5-Ferrari V8		17/24

2011		Championship position: 14th	Wins: 0	Pole positions: 0		Fastest laps: 0	Points scored: 26			
11	AUSTRALIAN GP	Melbourne	19	Scuderia Toro Rosso	P	2.4 Toro Rosso STR6-Ferrari V8		13th but 7 & 8th cars dsq/-1 lap	12/24
14	MALAYSIAN GP	Sepang	19	Scuderia Toro Rosso	P	2.4 Toro Rosso STR6-Ferrari V8		1 lap behind	13/24
ret	CHINESE GP	Shanghai Circuit	19	Scuderia Toro Rosso	P	2.4 Toro Rosso STR6-Ferrari V8		lost wheel after pit stop	7/24
16	TURKISH GP	Istanbul Park	19	Scuderia Toro Rosso	P	2.4 Toro Rosso STR6-Ferrari V8		major understeer/1 lap behind	17/24
16	SPANISH GP	Barcelona	19	Scuderia Toro Rosso	P	2.4 Toro Rosso STR6-Ferrari V8		2 laps behind	13/24
ret	MONACO GP	Monte Carlo	19	Scuderia Toro Rosso	P	2.4 Toro Rosso STR6-Ferrari V8		collision with Hamilton	20/24
8	CANADIAN GP	Montreal	19	Scuderia Toro Rosso	P	2.4 Toro Rosso STR6-Ferrari V8			18/24
8	EUROPEAN GP	Valencia	19	Scuderia Toro Rosso	P	2.4 Toro Rosso STR6-Ferrari V8		1 lap behind	18/24
10	BRITISH GP	Silverstone	19	Scuderia Toro Rosso	P	2.4 Toro Rosso STR6-Ferrari V8			18/24
12	GERMAN GP	Hockenheim	19	Scuderia Toro Rosso	P	2.4 Toro Rosso STR6-Ferrari V8		1 lap behind	17/24
10	HUNGARIAN GP	Hungaroring	19	Scuderia Toro Rosso	P	2.4 Toro Rosso STR6-Ferrari V8		1 lap behind	16/24
ret	BELGIAN GP	Spa	19	Scuderia Toro Rosso	P	2.4 Toro Rosso STR6-Ferrari V8		collision damage on lap 1	6/24
7	ITALIAN GP	Monza	19	Scuderia Toro Rosso	P	2.4 Toro Rosso STR6-Ferrari V8		1 lap behind	18/24
21/ret	SINGAPORE GP	Marina Bay Circuit	19	Scuderia Toro Rosso	P	2.4 Toro Rosso STR6-Ferrari V8		accident–hit wall/5 laps behind	16/24
15	JAPANESE GP	Suzuka	19	Scuderia Toro Rosso	P	2.4 Toro Rosso STR6-Ferrari V8			16/24
7	KOREAN GP	Yeongam	19	Scuderia Toro Rosso	P	2.4 Toro Rosso STR6-Ferrari V8			11/24
8	INDIAN GP	Buddh Circuit	19	Scuderia Toro Rosso	P	2.4 Toro Rosso STR6-Ferrari V8		1 lap behind	10/24
15	ABU DHABI GP	Yas Marina Circuit	19	Scuderia Toro Rosso	P	2.4 Toro Rosso STR6-Ferrari V8		20 sec pen–ignored blue flags	15/24
11	BRAZILIAN GP	Interlagos	19	Scuderia Toro Rosso	P	2.4 Toro Rosso STR6-Ferrari V8		1 lap behind	13/24

GP Starts: 46   GP Wins: 0   Pole positions: 0   Fastest laps: 0   Points: 31

PHILIPPE ALLIOT

A LATE starter in racing, Philippe Alliot tried his hand at the Motul racing school in 1975 and did well enough to embark on a season in Formule Renault in 1976, abandoning his studies in political science in the process.

Alliot spent two seasons in the shadow of one Alain Prost before clinching the Formule Renault title in 1978. The next four seasons were devoted to climbing the ladder in F3. He was third in the French championship in 1979 and spent three seasons contesting the European championship (finishing fifth, third, then fifth again) before a season in F2 in 1983, where he was always quick, but prone to error in the ORECA Martini. The highlight of his season came in sports cars however with a third place at Le Mans, sharing the Kremer Porsche with Mario and Michael Andretti.

Alliot moved up into the big league with the underpowered, underfinanced RAM-Hart, but his two seasons with the team were littered with shunts and no points were scored. So it was back to ORECA and F3000 for 1986, Alliot taking his March to victory at Spa, but then an opportunity to drive for Ligier arose after Jacques Laffite's accident at Brands Hatch. Philippe caused a stir by keeping pace with René Arnoux and scored a point in Mexico – which was enough to interest Larrousse, for whom he raced for the next three seasons. Then he returned to Ligier, where chassis of various appellations (JS33, JS33B and JS33C) were all subjected to a comprehensive crash-testing programme.

Thus it was surprising that he was invited to join Jean Todt's Peugeot sports car team for 1991/92. Paired with Mauro Baldi, he won three times (Suzuka '91, Donington and Magny-Cours '92) as the French manufacturer trampled all over the meagre opposition and the sports car championship headed for extinction. Far from being an endangered species, a more self-confident Alliot bounced back into Formula 1 for the third time at the age of 39 with Larrousse. At the behest of his former sports car entrant, Philippe was drafted into the McLaren-Peugeot squad for 1994, but his role was largely confined to testing, Ron Dennis preferring the talents of Martin Brundle. Eventually he did get one race – deputising for the suspended Häkkinen in Hungary – before reappearing for Larrousse, just once, at Spa. Realising that his days in grand prix racing were over, Alliot hit the French Supertourisme trail in 1995 with a works Peugeot.

In 1996, Philippe raced in the Le Mans 24-hours for Courage Competition, but the car was eliminated after a stuck throttle pitched it into the wall (with Alliot at the wheel) when holding fourth place.

Between 2000 and 2004, Philippe appeared in the FIA GT championship, mainly racing a Chrysler Viper GTS. More recently, he has run his own sports car team, entering and occasionally competing in a Ligier JS51 in the SPEED Euroseries, a multi-chassis platform that is seen as the final stepping stone to the Le Mans Series and 24-hour racing. The mini endurance sports car formula makes use of 2-litre Honda engines. He has also been seen behind the wheel of an AC Cobra in historic racing.

Back in 1995, Alliot and his brother Franck created a brand-new karting track, which operates under the name Karting Philippe Alliot, at Belleville-sur-Vie in the Vendée.

ALLIOT, Philippe (F) b 27/7/1954, Voves Eure et Loir, nr Chartres

1984 Championship position: Unplaced

	Race	Circuit	No	Entrant	Tyres	Capacity/Car/Engine	Comment	Q Pos/Entries
ret	BRAZILIAN GP	Rio	9	Skoal Bandit Formula 1 Team	P	1.5 t/c RAM 02-Hart 4	battery mounting	26/27
ret	SOUTH AFRICAN GP	Kyalami	9	Skoal Bandit Formula 1 Team	P	1.5 t/c RAM 02-Hart 4	water leak – engine	22/27
dnq	BELGIAN GP	Zolder	9	Skoal Bandit Formula 1 Team	P	1.5 t/c RAM 02-Hart 4		27/27
ret	SAN MARINO GP	Imola	9	Skoal Bandit Formula 1 Team	P	1.5 t/c RAM 02-Hart 4	engine	23/28
ret	FRENCH GP	Dijon	9	Skoal Bandit Formula 1 Team	P	1.5 t/c RAM 02-Hart 4	electrics	23/27
dnq	MONACO GP	Monte Carlo	9	Skoal Bandit Formula 1 Team	P	1.5 t/c RAM 02-Hart 4		27/27
10*	CANADIAN GP	Montreal	9	Skoal Bandit Formula 1 Team	P	1.5 t/c RAM 02-Hart 4	*10th place car dsq/-5 laps	26/26
ret	US GP (DETROIT)	Detroit	9	Skoal Bandit Formula 1 Team	P	1.5 t/c RAM 02-Hart 4	brakes – hit wall	20/27
dns	US GP (DALLAS)	Dallas	9	Skoal Bandit Formula 1 Team	P	1.5 t/c RAM 02-Hart 4	car damaged in practice	(24)/26
ret	BRITISH GP	Brands Hatch	9	Skoal Bandit Formula 1 Team	P	1.5 t/c RAM 02-Hart 4	accident – Johansson & Cheever	24/27
ret	GERMAN GP	Hockenheim	9	Skoal Bandit Formula 1 Team	P	1.5 t/c RAM 02-Hart 4	overheating	22/27
11	AUSTRIAN GP	Österreichring	9	Skoal Bandit Formula 1 Team	P	1.5 t/c RAM 02-Hart 4	3 laps behind	25/28
10*	DUTCH GP	Zandvoort	9	Skoal Bandit Formula 1 Team	P	1.5 t/c RAM 02-Hart 4	*8th & 9th cars dsq/-4 laps	26/27
ret	ITALIAN GP	Monza	9	Skoal Bandit Formula 1 Team	P	1.5 t/c RAM 02-Hart 4	electrics	23/27
ret	EUROPEAN GP	Nürburgring	9	Skoal Bandit Formula 1 Team	P	1.5 t/c RAM 02-Hart 4	turbo	25/26
ret	PORTUGUESE GP	Estoril	9	Skoal Bandit Formula 1 Team	P	1.5 t/c RAM 02-Hart 4	engine	27/27

1985 Championship position: Unplaced

	Race	Circuit	No	Entrant	Tyres	Capacity/Car/Engine	Comment	Q Pos/Entries
9	BRAZILIAN GP	Rio	10	Skoal Bandit Formula 1 Team	P	1.5 t/c RAM 03-Hart 4	3 laps behind	20/25
ret	PORTUGUESE GP	Estoril	10	Skoal Bandit Formula 1 Team	P	1.5 t/c RAM 03-Hart 4	spun off	20/26
ret	SAN MARINO GP	Imola	10	Skoal Bandit Formula 1 Team	P	1.5 t/c RAM 03-Hart 4	engine	21/26
dnq	MONACO GP	Monte Carlo	10	Skoal Bandit Formula 1 Team	P	1.5 t/c RAM 03-Hart 4		23/26
ret	CANADIAN GP	Montreal	10	Skoal Bandit Formula 1 Team	P	1.5 t/c RAM 03-Hart 4	accident	21/25
ret	US GP (DETROIT)	Detroit	10	Skoal Bandit Formula 1 Team	P	1.5 t/c RAM 03-Hart 4	accident with Brundle	23/25
ret	FRENCH GP	Paul Ricard	10	Skoal Bandit Formula 1 Team	P	1.5 t/c RAM 03-Hart 4	fuel pressure	23/26
ret	BRITISH GP	Silverstone	10	Skoal Bandit Formula 1 Team	P	1.5 t/c RAM 03-Hart 4	accident with Ghinzani	21/26
ret	GERMAN GP	Nürburgring	10	Skoal Bandit Formula 1 Team	P	1.5 t/c RAM 03-Hart 4	oil pressure	21/27
ret	AUSTRIAN GP	Österreichring	9	Skoal Bandit Formula 1 Team	P	1.5 t/c RAM 03-Hart 4	turbo	21/27
ret	DUTCH GP	Zandvoort	9	Skoal Bandit Formula 1 Team	P	1.5 t/c RAM 03-Hart 4	engine	25/27
ret	ITALIAN GP	Monza	9	Skoal Bandit Formula 1 Team	P	1.5 t/c RAM 03-Hart 4	turbo	26/26
ret	BELGIAN GP	Spa	9	Skoal Bandit Formula 1 Team	P	1.5 t/c RAM 03-Hart 4	accident	20/24
ret	EUROPEAN GP	Brands Hatch	9	Skoal Bandit Formula 1 Team	P	1.5 t/c RAM 03-Hart 4	engine	23/27

1986 Championship position: 18th= Wins: 0 Pole positions: 0 Fastest laps: 0 Points scored: 1

	Race	Circuit	No	Entrant	Tyres	Capacity/Car/Engine	Comment	Q Pos/Entries
ret	GERMAN GP	Hockenheim	26	Equipe Ligier	P	1.5 t/c Ligier JS27-Renault V6	engine	14/26
9	HUNGARIAN GP	Hungaroring	26	Equipe Ligier	P	1.5 t/c Ligier JS27-Renault V6	3 laps behind	12/26
ret	AUSTRIAN GP	Österreichring	26	Equipe Ligier	P	1.5 t/c Ligier JS27-Renault V6	engine	11/26
ret	ITALIAN GP	Monza	26	Equipe Ligier	P	1.5 t/c Ligier JS27-Renault V6	engine	14/27
ret	PORTUGUESE GP	Estoril	26	Equipe Ligier	P	1.5 t/c Ligier JS27-Renault V6	engine	11/27
6	MEXICAN GP	Mexico City	26	Equipe Ligier	P	1.5 t/c Ligier JS27-Renault V6	1 lap behind	10/26
8	AUSTRALIAN GP	Adelaide	26	Equipe Ligier	P	1.5 t/c Ligier JS27-Renault V6	3 laps behind	8/26

1987 Championship position: 16th= Wins: 0 Pole positions: 0 Fastest laps: 0 Points scored: 3

	Race	Circuit	No	Entrant	Tyres	Capacity/Car/Engine	Comment	Q Pos/Entries
10	SAN MARINO GP	Imola	30	Larrousse Calmels	G	3.5 Lola LC87-Cosworth V8	2nd non-turbo/3 laps behind	23/27
8	BELGIAN GP	Spa	30	Larrousse Calmels	G	3.5 Lola LC87-Cosworth V8	1st non-turbo/3 laps behind	22/26
ret	MONACO GP	Monte Carlo	30	Larrousse Calmels	G	3.5 Lola LC87-Cosworth V8	engine	18/26
ret	US GP (DETROIT)	Detroit	30	Larrousse Calmels	G	3.5 Lola LC87-Cosworth V8	collision with Arnoux	20/26
ret	FRENCH GP	Paul Ricard	30	Larrousse Calmels	G	3.5 Lola LC87-Cosworth V8	transmission	23/26
ret	BRITISH GP	Silverstone	30	Larrousse Calmels	G	3.5 Lola LC87-Cosworth V8	gearbox	22/26
6	GERMAN GP	Hockenheim	30	Larrousse Calmels	G	3.5 Lola LC87-Cosworth V8	3rd non-turbo/2 laps behind	21/26
ret	HUNGARIAN GP	Hungaroring	30	Larrousse Calmels	G	3.5 Lola LC87-Cosworth V8	spun off	15/26
12	AUSTRIAN GP	Österreichring	30	Larrousse Calmels	G	3.5 Lola LC87-Cosworth V8	2nd non-turbo/3 laps behind	22/26
ret	ITALIAN GP	Monza	30	Larrousse Calmels	G	3.5 Lola LC87-Cosworth V8	spun off	23/28
ret	PORTUGUESE GP	Estoril	30	Larrousse Calmels	G	3.5 Lola LC87-Cosworth V8	fuel pump	19/27
6	SPANISH GP	Jerez	30	Larrousse Calmels	G	3.5 Lola LC87-Cosworth V8	1st non-turbo/1 lap behind	17/28
6	MEXICAN GP	Mexico City	30	Larrousse Calmels	G	3.5 Lola LC87-Cosworth V8	1st non-turbo/3 laps behind	24/27
ret	JAPANESE GP	Suzuka	30	Larrousse Calmels	G	3.5 Lola LC87-Cosworth V8	startline accident	19/27
ret	AUSTRALIAN GP	Adelaide	30	Larrousse Calmels	G	3.5 Lola LC87-Cosworth V8	electrics	17/27

1988 Championship position: Unplaced

	Race	Circuit	No	Entrant	Tyres	Capacity/Car/Engine	Comment	Q Pos/Entries
ret	BRAZILIAN GP	Rio	30	Larrousse Calmels	G	3.5 Lola LC88-Cosworth V8	broken suspension – spun off	16/31
17	SAN MARINO GP	Imola	30	Larrousse Calmels	G	3.5 Lola LC88-Cosworth V8	pit stop – puncture/-3 laps	15/31
ret	MONACO GP	Monte Carlo	30	Larrousse Calmels	G	3.5 Lola LC88-Cosworth V8	collision with Patrese	13/30
ret	MEXICAN GP	Mexico City	30	Larrousse Calmels	G	3.5 Lola LC88-Cosworth V8	started from back/rear upright	13/30
10/ret	CANADIAN GP	Montreal	30	Larrousse Calmels	G	3.5 Lola LC88-Cosworth V8	engine cut out/3laps behind	17/31
ret	US GP (DETROIT)	Detroit	30	Larrousse Calmels	G	3.5 Lola LC88-Cosworth V8	gearbox	14/31
ret	FRENCH GP	Paul Ricard	30	Larrousse Calmels	G	3.5 Lola LC88-Cosworth V8	electrics	18/31
14	BRITISH GP	Silverstone	30	Larrousse Calmels	G	3.5 Lola LC88-Cosworth V8	2 laps behind	22/31
ret	GERMAN GP	Hockenheim	30	Larrousse Calmels	G	3.5 Lola LC88-Cosworth V8	spun off	20/31
12	HUNGARIAN GP	Hungaroring	30	Larrousse Calmels	G	3.5 Lola LC88-Cosworth V8	misfire/4 laps behind	20/31
9*	BELGIAN GP	Spa	30	Larrousse Calmels	G	3.5 Lola LC88-Cosworth V8	*3rd & 4th cars dsq/-1 lap	16/31
ret	ITALIAN GP	Monza	30	Larrousse Calmels	G	3.5 Lola LC88-Cosworth V8	engine	20/31
ret	PORTUGUESE GP	Estoril	30	Larrousse Calmels	G	3.5 Lola LC88-Cosworth V8	engine	20/31
14	SPANISH GP	Jerez	30	Larrousse Calmels	G	3.5 Lola LC88-Cosworth V8	wheel problem/3 laps behind	12/31
9	JAPANESE GP	Suzuka	30	Larrousse Calmels	G	3.5 Lola LC88-Cosworth V8	1 lap behind	19/31
10/ret	AUSTRALIAN GP	Adelaide	30	Larrousse Calmels	G	3.5 Lola LC88-Cosworth V8	out of fuel/7 laps behind	24/31

1989 Championship position: 26th= Wins: 0 Pole positions: 0 Fastest laps: 0 Points scored: 1

			No	Entrant	Tyres	Capacity/Car/Engine	Comment	Q Pos/Entries
12	BRAZILIAN GP	Rio	30	Larrousse Calmels	G	3.5 Lola LC88B-Lamborghini V12	3 laps behind	26/38
ret	SAN MARINO GP	Imola	30	Equipe Larrousse	G	3.5 Lola LC89-Lamborghini V12	engine – fuel injection	20/39
ret	MONACO GP	Monte Carlo	30	Equipe Larrousse	G	3.5 Lola LC89-Lamborghini V12	engine	17/38
nc	MEXICAN GP	Mexico City	30	Equipe Larrousse	G	3.5 Lola LC89-Lamborghini V12	accident damage – misfire/-41 laps	16/39
ret	US GP (PHOENIX)	Phoenix	30	Equipe Larrousse	G	3.5 Lola LC89-Lamborghini V12	spun off	12/39
ret	CANADIAN GP	Montreal	30	Equipe Larrousse	G	3.5 Lola LC89-Lamborghini V12	crashed	10/39
ret	FRENCH GP	Paul Ricard	30	Equipe Larrousse	G	3.5 Lola LC89-Lamborghini V12	engine	7/39
ret	BRITISH GP	Silverstone	30	Equipe Larrousse	G	3.5 Lola LC89-Lamborghini V12	engine	12/39
ret	GERMAN GP	Hockenheim	30	Equipe Larrousse	G	3.5 Lola LC89-Lamborghini V12	oil leak	15/39
dnpq	HUNGARIAN GP	Hungaroring	30	Equipe Larrousse	G	3.5 Lola LC89-Lamborghini V12		32/39
16/ret	BELGIAN GP	Spa	30	Equipe Larrousse	G	3.5 Lola LC89-Lamborghini V12	engine – oil pressure/-5 laps	11/39
ret	ITALIAN GP	Monza	30	Equipe Larrousse	G	3.5 Lola LC89-Lamborghini V12	throttle stuck – spun off	7/39
9	PORTUGUESE GP	Estoril	30	Equipe Larrousse	G	3.5 Lola LC89-Lamborghini V12	pit stop – tyres/1 lap behind	17/39
6	SPANISH GP	Jerez	30	Equipe Larrousse	G	3.5 Lola LC89-Lamborghini V12	pit stop – tyres/1 lap behind	5/38
ret	JAPANESE GP	Suzuka	30	Equipe Larrousse	G	3.5 Lola LC89-Lamborghini V12	engine	8/39
ret	AUSTRALIAN GP	Adelaide	30	Equipe Larrousse	G	3.5 Lola LC89-Lamborghini V12	collision with Berger	19/39

1990 Championship position: Unplaced

			No	Entrant	Tyres	Capacity/Car/Engine	Comment	Q Pos/Entries
excl	US GP (PHOENIX)	Phoenix	26	Ligier Gitanes	G	3.5 Ligier JS33B-Cosworth V8	dsq in practice – outside assist	(26)/35
12	BRAZILIAN GP	Interlagos	26	Ligier Gitanes	G	3.5 Ligier JS33B-Cosworth V8	3 laps behind	10/35
9	SAN MARINO GP	Imola	26	Ligier Gitanes	G	3.5 Ligier JS33B-Cosworth V8	pit stop – tyres/1 lap behind	17/34
dns	"	"	26	Ligier Gitanes	G	3.5 Ligier JS33-Cosworth V8	practice only	– / –
ret	MONACO GP	Monte Carlo	26	Ligier Gitanes	G	3.5 Ligier JS33B-Cosworth V8	gearbox	18/35
dns	"	" "	26	Ligier Gitanes	G	3.5 Ligier JS33-Cosworth V8	practice only	– / –
ret	CANADIAN GP	Montreal	26	Ligier Gitanes	G	3.5 Ligier JS33B-Cosworth V8	engine	17/35
18	MEXICAN GP	Mexico City	26	Ligier Gitanes	G	3.5 Ligier JS33B-Cosworth V8	pit stop – tyres/3 laps behind	22/35
dns	"	" "	26	Ligier Gitanes	G	3.5 Ligier JS33-Cosworth V8	practice only	– / –
9	FRENCH GP	Paul Ricard	26	Ligier Gitanes	G	3.5 Ligier JS33B-Cosworth V8	pit stop – tyres/1 lap behind	12/35
dns	"	" "	26	Ligier Gitanes	G	3.5 Ligier JS33-Cosworth V8	practice only	– / –
13	BRITISH GP	Silverstone	26	Ligier Gitanes	G	3.5 Ligier JS33B-Cosworth V8	3 laps behind	22/35
dns	"	"	26	Ligier Gitanes	G	3.5 Ligier JS33C-Cosworth V8	practice only	– / –
dsq	GERMAN GP	Hockenheim	26	Ligier Gitanes	G	3.5 Ligier JS33B-Cosworth V8	push start after startline accident	24/25
dns	"	"	26	Ligier Gitanes	G	3.5 Ligier JS33C-Cosworth V8	practice only	– / –
14	HUNGARIAN GP	Hungaroring	26	Ligier Gitanes	G	3.5 Ligier JS33B-Cosworth V8	pit stop/spin/3 laps behind	21/35
dnq	BELGIAN GP	Spa	26	Ligier Gitanes	G	3.5 Ligier JS33B-Cosworth V8		27/33
13	ITALIAN GP	Monza	26	Ligier Gitanes	G	3.5 Ligier JS33B-Cosworth V8	3 laps behind	20/33
ret	PORTUGUESE GP	Estoril	26	Ligier Gitanes	G	3.5 Ligier JS33B-Cosworth V8	collision with Mansell	21/33
ret	SPANISH GP	Jerez	26	Ligier Gitanes	G	3.5 Ligier JS33B-Cosworth V8	spun off	13/33
10	JAPANESE GP	Suzuka	26	Ligier Gitanes	G	3.5 Ligier JS33B-Cosworth V8	1 lap behind	21/30
11	AUSTRALIAN GP	Adelaide	26	Ligier Gitanes	G	3.5 Ligier JS33B-Cosworth V8	3 laps behind	19/30

1993 Championship position: 17th= Wins: 0 Pole positions: 0 Fastest laps: 0 Points scored: 2

			No	Entrant	Tyres	Capacity/Car/Engine	Comment	Q Pos/Entries
ret	SOUTH AFRICAN GP	Kyalami	19	Equipe Larrousse	G	3.5 Larrousse LH93-Lamborghini V12	spun off	11/26
7	BRAZILIAN GP	Interlagos	19	Equipe Larrousse	G	3.5 Larrousse LH93-Lamborghini V12	1 lap behind	11/26
ret	EUROPEAN GP	Donington	19	Equipe Larrousse	G	3.5 Larrousse LH93-Lamborghini V12	accident – hit by de Cesaris	15/26
5	SAN MARINO GP	Imola	19	Equipe Larrousse	G	3.5 Larrousse LH93-Lamborghini V12	2 laps behind	14/26
ret	SPANISH GP	Barcelona	19	Equipe Larrousse	G	3.5 Larrousse LH93-Lamborghini V12	gearbox	13/26
12	MONACO GP	Monte Carlo	19	Equipe Larrousse	G	3.5 Larrousse LH93-Lamborghini V12	3 laps behind	15/26
ret	CANADIAN GP	Montreal	19	Equipe Larrousse	G	3.5 Larrousse LH93-Lamborghini V12	gearbox	15/26
9	FRENCH GP	Magny Cours	19	Equipe Larrousse	G	3.5 Larrousse LH93-Lamborghini V12	2 laps behind	10/26
11	BRITISH GP	Silverstone	19	Equipe Larrousse	G	3.5 Larrousse LH93-Lamborghini V12	2 laps behind	24/26
12	GERMAN GP	Hockenheim	19	Equipe Larrousse	G	3.5 Larrousse LH93-Lamborghini V12	lost clutch/1 lap behind	23/26
8	HUNGARIAN GP	Hungaroring	19	Equipe Larrousse	G	3.5 Larrousse LH93-Lamborghini V12	early spin/2 laps behind	19/26
12	BELGIAN GP	Spa	19	Equipe Larrousse	G	3.5 Larrousse LH93-Lamborghini V12	2 laps behind	18/25
9	ITALIAN GP	Monza	19	Equipe Larrousse	G	3.5 Larrousse LH93-Lamborghini V12	collision at start/2 laps behind	16/26
10	PORTUGUESE GP	Estoril	19	Equipe Larrousse	G	3.5 Larrousse LH93-Lamborghini V12	lost clutch/2 laps behind	20/26

1994 Championship position: Unplaced

			No	Entrant	Tyres	Capacity/Car/Engine	Comment	Q Pos/Entries
ret	HUNGARIAN GP	Hungaroring	7	Marlboro McLaren Peugeot	G	3.5 McLaren MP4/9-Peugeot V10	engine	14/28
ret	BELGIAN GP	Spa	19	Tourtel Larrousse F1	G	3.5 Larrousse LH94-Ford HB V8	engine	19/28

GP Starts: 109 GP Wins: 0 Pole positions: 0 Fastest laps: 0 Points: 7

ALLISON, Cliff (GB) b 8/2/1932, Brough, Westmorland (now Cumbria) – d 7/4/2005, Brough, Cumbria

1958 Championship position: 14th= Wins: 0 Pole positions: 0 Fastest laps: 0 Points scored: 3

	Race	Circuit	No	Entrant	Tyres	Capacity/Car/Engine	Comment	Q Pos/Entries
6	MONACO GP	Monte Carlo	24	Team Lotus	D	2.0 Lotus 12-Climax 4	overheating/13 laps behind	13/28
6	DUTCH GP	Zandvoort	17	Team Lotus	D	2.2 Lotus 12-Climax 4	2 laps behind	11/17
4	BELGIAN GP	Spa	40	Team Lotus	D	2.2 Lotus 12-Climax 4	broken suspension on last lap	12/20
ret	FRENCH GP	Reims	26	Team Lotus	D	2.2 Lotus 12-Climax 4	engine	20/21
ret	BRITISH GP	Silverstone	17	Team Lotus	D	2.2 Lotus 12-Climax 4	oil pressure	5/21
dns	"	"	17	Team Lotus	D	2.2 Lotus 16-Climax 4	practice only	– / –
5/ret	GERMAN GP	Nürburgring	12	Team Lotus	D	2.0 Lotus 16-Climax 4	radiator/10th behind 5 F2 cars no points given/2 laps behind	24/26
dns	PORTUGUESE GP	Oporto	18	Team Lotus	D	2.0 Lotus 16-Climax 4	practice accident	13/15
ret	"	"	18	Scuderia Centro Sud/Team Lotus	D	2.5 Maserati 250F 6	team rented car/engine	– / –
7	ITALIAN GP	Monza	36	Team Lotus	D	1.5 Lotus 12-Climax 4	F2 car/9 laps behind	16/21
10	MOROCCAN GP	Casablanca	34	Team Lotus	D	2.0 Lotus 12-Climax 4	4 laps behind	16/25

1959 Championship position: 13th= Wins: 0 Pole positions: 0 Fastest laps: 0 Points scored: 2

			No	Entrant	Tyres	Capacity/Car/Engine	Comment	Q Pos/Entries
ret	MONACO GP	Monte Carlo	52	Scuderia Ferrari	D	1.5 Ferrari Dino 156 V6	collision with von Trips & Halford	15/24

9	DUTCH GP	Zandvoort	16	Scuderia Ferrari	D	2.4 Ferrari Dino 246 V6	poor handling/4 laps behind	15/15
ret	GERMAN GP	AVUS	17	Scuderia Ferrari	D	2.4 Ferrari Dino 246 V6	clutch in first heat/*10 sec pen*14/16	
5	ITALIAN GP	Monza	34	Scuderia Ferrari	D	2.4 Ferrari Dino 246 V6	1 lap behind	8/21
ret	US GP	Sebring	3	Scuderia Ferrari	D	2.4 Ferrari Dino 246 V6	clutch	7/19

1960 Championship position: 12th=   Wins: 0   Pole positions: 0   Fastest laps: 0   Points scored: 6

| 2 | ARGENTINE GP | Buenos Aires | 24 | Scuderia Ferrari | D | 2.4 Ferrari Dino 246 V6 | | 7/22 |
| dns | MONACO GP | Monte Carlo | 32 | Scuderia Ferrari | D | 2.4 Ferrari Dino 246 V6 | accident at chicane | 18/24 |

1961 Championship position: Unplaced

| 8 | MONACO GP | Monte Carlo | 32 | UDT-Laystall Racing Team | D | 1.5 Lotus 18-Climax 4 | | 15/21 |
| dnq | BELGIAN GP | Spa | 32 | UDT-Laystall Racing Team | D | 1.5 Lotus 18-Climax 4 | injured in practice crash | -/25 |

GP Starts: 16   GP Wins: 0   Pole positions: 0   Fastest laps: 0   Points: 11

CLIFF ALLISON

THE son of a garage owner from Brough, Westmoreland, Cliff Allison entered racing in 1951 with a diminutive F3 Cooper-JAP and progressed steadily in the formula, finishing to fourth in the 1955 championship. That year he also began racing works Lotus Eleven sports cars for Colin Chapman, culminating in an Index of Performance win with the little 750cc Lotus at Le Mans in 1957 – a season that also saw the Hornsey team move into single-seaters with the Lotus 12. It was here that Cliff showed his speed against such more established names as Jack Brabham and Roy Salvadori, although the car's woeful reliability limited his successes.

Ambitious plans were made for 1958, when Cliff and Graham Hill led the Lotus team in their world championship assault. The season began with a fine F2 class win at Silverstone, before his F1 debut at Monaco. Overheating problems forced Cliff to stop the car just short of the finish line, but he was able to push it home for a sixth-place classification.

He scored a fine fourth at Spa, finishing behind three cars, which it transpired would not have survived a further lap, and put up another tremendous performance in the German Grand Prix, when he drove a patched-up Lotus 16 that had been crashed in practice by Graham Hill. Cliff took the car from the back of the grid into fourth place before its repaired radiator sprang a leak, costing him a possible second-place finish. It remained one of his best ever drives in the Lotus, however. Later in the year, Allison was lucky to escape injury after a spectacular practice crash in Oporto wrote off his Lotus. He took up a vacant seat in the Centro Sud Maserati, the starting money being shared between the two concerns.

Allison produced another fine drive into seventh place at Monza, despite being forced to run the smaller F2-engined car in the race after his 2-litre unit blew during practice.

His efforts throughout the year did not go unnoticed, though, and on the recommendation of Mike Hawthorn, Cliff was invited by Ferrari for a test at Modena and then offered a works drive for 1959.

It was a big upheaval for Cliff, who was unwilling to uproot his wife and four young children from their home, so he began travelling back and forth between Brough and Maranello to embark on a solid first season, in which he was mainly employed in Ferrari's sports car programme. He showed his class on his debut by taking second place at a wet Sebring, following that with fifth at the Nürburgring and third at Goodwood. After elimination at Monaco, where he could not avoid the stationary Porsche of Wolfgang von Trips, Cliff was given a rather tired and underpowered F1 car for the Dutch Grand Prix. Then he had to wait until the German Grand Prix before another opportunity arose. Despite being handed a car with an engine that pulled fewer revs than those of his team-mates, Allison astounded everyone by setting the meeting's fastest practice lap. Sadly, as he was posted as reserve entry, he was pushed back down the grid; subsequently, he retired with a clutch problem.

The 1960 season began with success in Argentina, Cliff winning the 1000km for sports cars with Phil Hill and taking second place in the grand prix, despite running the entire race on one set of tyres, which were well worn at the finish. His upward career path came to a sudden halt at the next grand prix with a serious practice crash at Monaco. He had made an error by selecting the wrong gear and had been flung from the car. Unconscious for two weeks with rib and back injuries, in addition to a badly broken arm, he endured a slow recovery and his season was over.

A quiet and unassuming character, Allison nonetheless had confidence in his abilities, and before the accident at Monaco he had felt he was the equal of both his Ferrari team-mates, Phil Hill and von Trips, who would go on to contest the 1961 championship between them. Sadly, Cliff would not have the opportunity to prove his worth with the team, as Ferrari were unable to offer him anything more than selected sports car rides for that year.

Wanting to stay in F1, Cliff declined Ferrari's offer and threw in his lot with the newly formed British Racing Partnership to run their UDT Laystall team and drive the Lotus 18. He tried to regain his form in the many non-championship races held that year, and his results included a second place in the International Trophy, run to the 2.5-litre Inter-Continental Formula. For the Belgian Grand Prix, Cliff had to set a quicker practice time than team-mate Henry Taylor to claim the team's only available car for the race. However, disaster struck when he ran wide at Blanchimont and crashed heavily. He was thrown from the Lotus, breaking both legs. Reflecting on his luck to have survived two massive crashes in the space of just over a year, Cliff took the heartbreaking decision to retire from racing.

A BRILLIANTLY gifted man from Oviedo, Fernando Alonso single-handedly turned his country's passion for motorsport away from both rallying and motorcycle racing. Heroes such as Carlos Sainz, Ángel Nieto, Àlex Crivillé and Sete Gibernau were well and truly eclipsed for a whole new generation of Spanish fans who previously had viewed Formula 1 with mild disinterest.

Introduced to four wheels at the age of two, when his father built him a kart, Alonso established himself as a star of the future between the ages of 13 and 18, winning wherever he raced, from local festivals on home-made courses to regional and national championships the length and breadth of Spain. He also took his talents overseas, winning the world junior title in 1996 at the age of 15 and finishing second in the senior European championship two years later.

At the earliest opportunity, Alonso jumped straight into the Formula Nissan series, where he was under the guidance of former Minardi F1 pilot Adrian Campos. Incredibly, he won the title at his first attempt, with six wins, nine poles and eight fastest laps, attracting the attention of renowned driver manager Flavio Briatore. Having moved into the supporting FIA F3000 series for 2000, with the well-established Team Astromega, he experienced a difficult learning year among more seasoned drivers, which restricted his scoring opportunities. In dominating at the notorious Spa-Francorchamps circuit, however, he showed that here was a very special talent indeed. Confirmation of a management contract with Briatore quickly followed, and the Spaniard found himself being farmed out to Minardi, where he began his F1 career the following year, under the wing of Australian Paul Stoddart. Alonso flourished, easily out-performing his team-mates in both qualifying and races. Another year at the back of the grid would have served no useful purpose, so he spent the 2002 season testing for Renault and honing his talents in the knowledge that he would have a place in the team in 2003.

Fortunately, the Enstone team were about to enjoy a return to front-running form, and Alonso was able to take his first pole position and a podium finish only second time out, in Malaysia, and then, to great acclaim, second in his Spanish homeland. This would have been a highlight in itself, had it not been for the feat of Hungary where, still only 22, he dominated from pole, lapping champion-elect Michael Schumacher on the way to a crushing maiden win – then the youngest driver ever to stand on the top step in grand prix racing. Sixth in the championship with 55 points – 22 more than his more experienced team-mate, Jarno Trulli – merely underlined the Spaniard's huge talent.

Alonso remained with Renault in 2004 and, while unable to add a second victory to his tally, he scored points in 12 of the 18 races, ending the year with fourth place in the drivers' championship and another 59 points under his belt. Renault went into the 2005 season having marked themselves out as potential title contenders, and so it proved, Alonso taking a hat trick of wins in Malaysia, Bahrain and San Marino to stretch a commanding championship lead. This early-season form was maintained as the confident Spaniard added wins in the European and French grands prix to further strengthen his ambitions to become the sport's youngest ever world champion. Despite a late charge from Kimi Räikkönen, the amazing Alonso kept all his rivals at arm's length and capped the year with a dominant win in China to confirm that he always had the outright speed in reserve if needed.

Having secured his first world championship crown, Alonso proceeded to cause shock waves throughout Formula 1 when he announced that he had signed a contract to move to McLaren for 2007. This left him with the difficult task of maintaining his working relationship with the Renault team, who knew he would be leaving at the end of the season. In the event, a storming start to the year, which saw him win six of the first nine races, left little time for recriminations as both sides got on with the business

of wrapping up a second successive title. Just when everything seemed calm, however, Renault and Alonso hit choppy waters when their mass-damper suspension was first protested and then subsequently outlawed on appeal. This put them on the back foot as Michael Schumacher closed in relentlessly. Just when it seemed that the championship was slipping away, the German suffered a rare engine failure in his Ferrari in Japan and, with the Spaniard victorious, a second title was all but secured at the tender age of just 26.

However, Alonso's decision to switch from Renault to McLaren-Mercedes for the 2007 season would prove – in the short term at least –disastrous for him in terms of both prestige and fulfillment. Having arrived at Woking as the true heir apparent to the newly retired Schumacher, and armed with a three-year contract and number-one driver status, everything seemed set fair for further world championship winning successes. Instead, the Spaniard was caught in a maelstrom of drama and intrigue, much of which was of his own making.

The arrival of the brilliant, but inexperienced, Lewis Hamilton combined with the McLaren hierarchy's failure to impose team orders led to Alonso becoming an increasingly brooding and isolated figure within the team. The cut and thrust of the season's racing could have come straight from the pages of a far-fetched novel, with both Alonso and Hamilton scoring four wins apiece and amazingly ending the season on 109 points, just one adrift of the champion, Kimi Räikkönen. The Finn's late run to steal away the title merely underlined Alonso's assertion that not giving him the preferential treatment he felt his status merited had cost him a third world championship. He and McLaren quickly negotiated a divorce that saw the Spaniard return to Renault with his reputation seriously tarnished in the eyes of many Formula 1 fans.

Undoubtedly still a brilliant racing driver, Fernando was quite capable of sustaining a championship challenge against anybody given a competitive machine, but he started 2008 on the back foot, with a car that was off the pace. Previously accustomed to disputing podium positions, he soon found himself scratching around for the odd championship point. By mid-season, however, a tremendous amount of technical development work on the R28 had begun to pay dividends, and he would prove an inspirational figure in the team's return to form. A subsequently tarnished victory arrived in Singapore, courtesy of team-mate Nelsinho Piquet's deliberate crash to trigger a safety car period, and was followed by a well-taken win in Japan, which eventually brought him fifth place in the championship.

Rumours persisted that Alonso was looking towards a drive with Ferrari for 2010, but eventually he decided to stick with Renault in a season that saw him largely held in a holding pattern, without a car to trouble the leaders while waiting to descend on Maranello.

The de-motivated Kimi Räikkönen having departed from Ferrari, Alonso immediately set about raising the morale of a team badly in need of leadership. Usually in the wake of the faster Red Bull and McLaren cars, the Spaniard nevertheless used all his considerable racecraft to maximise every opportunity that came his way. In the end, despite taking five wins, the world championship slipped from his grasp in Abu Dhabi due to a huge strategic error on the part of his team that trapped him in midfield traffic.

It was a bitter blow for Alonso, who saw another championship slip from his grasp at the final hurdle. This time around, he hid his true feelings well and knuckled down to a second year of trying to build a platform from which the team could recapture the dominant form of the Schumacher years. In the end, 2011 provided just a solitary and unexpected victory at the British Grand Prix. In a season when everyone trailed in the slipstream of Sebastian Vettel, perhaps a truer picture of the outstanding performances he displayed emerges from the final statistics. Of the 19 races, he finished 18 in the points, and his only retirement was posted in Canada, after being spun out by Jenson Button.

ALONSO, Fernando (ESP) b 29/7/1981, Oviedo, Spain

2001 Championship position: Unplaced

	Race	Circuit	No	Entrant	Tyres	Capacity/Car/Engine	Comment	Q Pos/Entries
12	AUSTRALIAN GP	Melbourne	21	European Minardi F1	M	3.0 Minardi PS01-European V10	2 laps behind	19/22
13	MALAYSIAN GP	Sepang	21	European Minardi F1	M	3.0 Minardi PS01-European V10	3 laps behind	22/22
ret	BRAZILIAN GP	Interlagos	21	European Minardi F1	M	3.0 Minardi PS01-European V10	electronics	19/22
ret	SAN MARINO GP	Imola	21	European Minardi F1	M	3.0 Minardi PS01-European V10	accident	18/22
13	SPANISH GP	Barcelona	21	European Minardi F1	M	3.0 Minardi PS01-European V10	2 laps behind	18/22
ret	AUSTRIAN GP	A1-Ring	21	European Minardi F1	M	3.0 Minardi PS01-European V10	engine	18/22
ret	MONACO GP	Monte Carlo	21	European Minardi F1	M	3.0 Minardi PS01-European V10	gearbox	18/22
ret	CANADIAN GP	Montreal	21	European Minardi F1	M	3.0 Minardi PS01-European V10	*time disallowed/transmission	*21/22
14	EUROPEAN GP	Nürburgring	21	European Minardi F1	M	3.0 Minardi PS01-European V10	2 laps behind	21/22
17/ret	FRENCH GP	Magny Cours	21	European Minardi F1	M	3.0 Minardi PS01-European V10	engine/7 laps behind	21/22
16	BRITISH GP	Silverstone	21	European Minardi F1	M	3.0 Minardi PS01-European V10	3 laps behind	21/22
10	GERMAN GP	Hockenheim	21	European Minardi F1	M	3.0 Minardi PS01-European V10	1 lap behind	21/22
ret	HUNGARIAN GP	Hungaroring	21	European Minardi F1	M	3.0 Minardi PS01-European V10	spun off	18/22
ret/dns	BELGIAN GP	Spa	21	European Minardi F1	M	3.0 Minardi PS01-European V10	*outside 107%/gearbox in 1st race	*20/21
13	ITALIAN GP	Monza	21	European Minardi F1	M	3.0 Minardi PS01-European V10	2 laps behind	21/22
ret	U S GP	Indianapolis	21	European Minardi F1	M	3.0 Minardi PS01-European V10	driveshaft	17/22
11	JAPANESE GP	Suzuka	21	European Minardi F1	M	3.0 Minardi PS01-European V10	1 lap behind	18/22

2003 Championship position: 6th   Wins: 1   Pole positions: 2   Fastest laps: 1   Points scored: 55

	Race	Circuit	No	Entrant	Tyres	Capacity/Car/Engine	Comment	Q Pos/Entries
7	AUSTRALIAN GP	Melbourne	8	Mild Seven Renault F1 Team	M	3.0 Renault R23-V10	first championship points	10/20
3	MALAYSIAN GP	Sepang	8	Mild Seven Renault F1 Team	M	3.0 Renault R23-V10		1/20
3/ret	BRAZILIAN GP	Interlagos	8	Mild Seven Renault F1 Team	M	3.0 Renault R23-V10	accident, hit debris – race stopped	10/20
6	SAN MARINO GP	Imola	8	Mild Seven Renault F1 Team	M	3.0 Renault R23-V10		8/20
2	SPANISH GP	Barcelona	8	Mild Seven Renault F1 Team	M	3.0 Renault R23-V10		3/20
ret	AUSTRIAN GP	A1-Ring	8	Mild Seven Renault F1 Team	M	3.0 Renault R23-V10	engine	19/20
5	MONACO GP	Monte Carlo	8	Mild Seven Renault F1 Team	M	3.0 Renault R23-V10		8/19
4	CANADIAN GP	Montreal	8	Mild Seven Renault F1 Team	M	3.0 Renault R23-V10	FL	4/20
4	EUROPEAN GP	Nürburgring	8	Mild Seven Renault F1 Team	M	3.0 Renault R23-V10	contretemps with Coulthard	8/20
ret	FRENCH GP	Magny Cours	8	Mild Seven Renault F1 Team	M	3.0 Renault R23-V10	engine	7/20
ret	BRITISH GP	Silverstone	8	Mild Seven Renault F1 Team	M	3.0 Renault R23B-V10	electrics	8/20
4	GERMAN GP	Hockenheim	8	Mild Seven Renault F1 Team	M	3.0 Renault R23B-V10		8/20
1	HUNGARIAN GP	Hungaroring	8	Mild Seven Renault F1 Team	M	3.0 Renault R23B-V10	then youngest Grand Prix winner	1/20
8	ITALIAN GP	Monza	8	Mild Seven Renault F1 Team	M	3.0 Renault R23B-V10	collision – Verstappen/-1 lap	20/20
ret	U S GP	Indianapolis	8	Mild Seven Renault F1 Team	M	3.0 Renault R23B-V10	engine	6/20
ret	JAPANESE GP	Suzuka	8	Mild Seven Renault F1 Team	M	3.0 Renault R23B-V10	engine	5/20

2004 Championship position: 4th   Wins: 0   Pole positions: 1   Fastest laps: 0   Points scored: 59

	Race	Circuit	No	Entrant	Tyres	Capacity/Car/Engine	Comment	Q Pos/Entries
3	AUSTRALIAN GP	Melbourne	8	Mild Seven Renault F1 Team	M	3.0 Renault R24-V10		4/20
7	MALAYSIAN GP	Sepang	8	Mild Seven Renault F1 Team	M	3.0 Renault R24-V10	spun off in qualifying run	19/20
6	BAHRAIN GP	Sakhir Circuit	8	Mild Seven Renault F1 Team	M	3.0 Renault R24-V10	collision with Klien – pitstop	17/20
4	SAN MARINO GP	Imola	8	Mild Seven Renault F1 Team	M	3.0 Renault R24-V10	collision with Coulthard	6/20
4	SPANISH GP	Barcelona	8	Mild Seven Renault F1 Team	M	3.0 Renault R24-V10		8/20
ret	MONACO GP	Monte Carlo	8	Mild Seven Renault F1 Team	M	3.0 Renault R24-V10	crashed lapping R Schumacher	3/20
5	EUROPEAN GP	Nürburgring	8	Mild Seven Renault F1 Team	M	3.0 Renault R24-V10	steering rack problem	6/20
ret	CANADIAN GP	Montreal	8	Mild Seven Renault F1 Team	M	3.0 Renault R24-V10	driveshaft	5/20
ret	U S GP	Indianapolis	8	Mild Seven Renault F1 Team	M	3.0 Renault R24-V10	punctured tyre – accident	9/20
2	FRENCH GP	Magny Cours	8	Mild Seven Renault F1 Team	M	3.0 Renault R24-V10		1/20
10	BRITISH GP	Silverstone	8	Mild Seven Renault F1 Team	M	3.0 Renault R24-V10	*10 place drop – engine change	*16/20
3	GERMAN GP	Hockenheim	8	Mild Seven Renault F1 Team	M	3.0 Renault R24-V10	delayed after hitting debris	5/20
3	HUNGARIAN GP	Hungaroring	8	Mild Seven Renault F1 Team	M	3.0 Renault R24-V10		5/20
ret	BELGIAN GP	Spa	8	Mild Seven Renault F1 Team	M	3.0 Renault R24-V10	oil leak – spun out of lead	3/20
ret	ITALIAN GP	Monza	8	Mild Seven Renault F1 Team	M	3.0 Renault R24-V10	spun off	4/20
4	CHINESE GP	Shanghai	8	Mild Seven Renault F1 Team	M	3.0 Renault R24-V10		6/20
5	JAPANESE GP	Suzuka	8	Mild Seven Renault F1 Team	M	3.0 Renault R24-V10		11/20
4	BRAZILIAN GP	Interlagos	8	Mild Seven Renault F1 Team	M	3.0 Renault R24-V10	led race	9/20

2005 WORLD CHAMPION   Wins: 7   Pole positions: 6   Fastest laps: 2   Points scored: 133

	Race	Circuit	No	Entrant	Tyres	Capacity/Car/Engine	Comment	Q Pos/Entries
3	AUSTRALIAN GP	Melbourne	5	Mild Seven Renault F1 Team	M	3.0 Renault R25-Renault V10	great drive through the field/FL	13/20
1	MALAYSIAN GP	Sepang	5	Mild Seven Renault F1 Team	M	3.0 Renault R25-Renault V10		1/20
1	BAHRAIN GP	Sakhir Circuit	5	Mild Seven Renault F1 Team	M	3.0 Renault R25-Renault V10		1/20
1	SAN MARINO GP	Imola	5	Mild Seven Renault F1 Team	M	3.0 Renault R25-Renault V10	controlled race from front	2/20
2	SPANISH GP	Barcelona	5	Mild Seven Renault F1 Team	M	3.0 Renault R25-Renault V10		3/18
4	MONACO GP	Monte Carlo	5	Mild Seven Renault F1 Team	M	3.0 Renault R25-Renault V10	excessive tyre wear	2/18
1	EUROPEAN GP	Nürburgring	5	Mild Seven Renault F1 Team	M	3.0 Renault R25-Renault V10	FL	6/20
ret	CANADIAN GP	Montreal	5	Mild Seven Renault F1 Team	M	3.0 Renault R25-Renault V10	hit wall	3/20
dns*	U S GP	Indianapolis	5	Mild Seven Renault F1 Team	M	3.0 Renault R25-Renault V10	*withdrawn after parade lap	6/20
1	FRENCH GP	Magny Cours	5	Mild Seven Renault F1 Team	M	3.0 Renault R25-Renault V10		1/20
2	BRITISH GP	Silverstone	5	Mild Seven Renault F1 Team	M	3.0 Renault R25-Renault V10		1/20
1	GERMAN GP	Hockenheim	5	Mild Seven Renault F1 Team	M	3.0 Renault R25-Renault V10		3/20
11	HUNGARIAN GP	Hungaroring	5	Mild Seven Renault F1 Team	M	3.0 Renault R25-Renault V10	collision – new nose/1 lap behind	6/20
2	TURKISH GP	Istanbul	5	Mild Seven Renault F1 Team	M	3.0 Renault R25-Renault V10		3/20
2	ITALIAN GP	Monza	5	Mild Seven Renault F1 Team	M	3.0 Renault R25-Renault V10		3/20
2	BELGIAN GP	Spa	5	Mild Seven Renault F1 Team	M	3.0 Renault R25-Renault V10		5/20
3	BRAZILIAN GP	Interlagos	5	Mild Seven Renault F1 Team	M	3.0 Renault R25-Renault V10		1/20
3	JAPANESE GP	Suzuka	5	Mild Seven Renault F1 Team	M	3.0 Renault R25-Renault V10		16/20
1	CHINESE GP	Shanghai	5	Mild Seven Renault F1 Team	M	3.0 Renault R25-Renault V10		1/20

2006 WORLD CHAMPION   Wins: 7   Pole positions: 5   Fastest laps: 5   Points scored: 134

	Grand Prix	Circuit		Team		Engine	Notes	
1	BAHRAIN GP	Sakhir Circuit	1	Mild Seven Renault F1 Team	M	2.4 Renault R26-V8	*250th point scored*	4/22
2	MALAYSIAN GP	Sepang	1	Mild Seven Renault F1 Team	M	2.4 Renault R26-V8	*FL*	8/22
1	AUSTRALIAN GP	Melbourne	1	Mild Seven Renault F1 Team	M	2.4 Renault R26-V8		3/22
2	SAN MARINO GP	Imola	1	Mild Seven Renault F1 Team	M	2.4 Renault R26-V8	*FL*	5/22
2	EUROPEAN GP	Nürburgring	1	Mild Seven Renault F1 Team	M	2.4 Renault R26-V8		1/22
1	SPANISH GP	Barcelona	1	Mild Seven Renault F1 Team	M	2.4 Renault R26-V8		1/22
1	MONACO GP	Monte Carlo	1	Mild Seven Renault F1 Team	M	2.4 Renault R26-V8		2/22
1	BRITISH GP	Silverstone	1	Mild Seven Renault F1 Team	M	2.4 Renault R26-V8	*FL*	1/22
1	CANADIAN GP	Montreal	1	Mild Seven Renault F1 Team	M	2.4 Renault R26-V8		1/22
5	U S GP	Indianapolis	1	Mild Seven Renault F1 Team	M	2.4 Renault R26-V8		5/22
2	FRENCH GP	Magny Cours	1	Mild Seven Renault F1 Team	M	2.4 Renault R26-V8		3/22
5	GERMAN GP	Hockenheim	1	Mild Seven Renault F1 Team	M	2.4 Renault R26-V8	*blistered tyres*	7/22
ret	HUNGARIAN GP	Hungaroring	1	Mild Seven Renault F1 Team	M	2.4 Renault R26-V8	*loose wheel nut – spun off*	15/22
2	TURKISH GP	Istanbul	1	Mild Seven Renault F1 Team	M	2.4 Renault R26-V8		3/22
ret	ITALIAN GP	Monza	1	Mild Seven Renault F1 Team	M	2.4 Renault R26-V8	*engine*	10/22
2	CHINESE GP	Shanghai	1	Mild Seven Renault F1 Team	M	2.4 Renault R26-V8	*FL*	1/22
1	JAPANESE GP	Suzuka	1	Mild Seven Renault F1 Team	M	2.4 Renault R26-V8	*FL*	5/22
2	BRAZILIAN GP	Interlagos	1	Mild Seven Renault F1 Team	M	2.4 Renault R26-V8		4/22

2007   Championship position: 3rd   Wins: 4   Pole positions: 2   Fastest laps: 2   Points scored: 109

	Grand Prix	Circuit		Team		Engine	Notes	
2	AUSTRALIAN GP	Melbourne	1	Vodafone McLaren Mercedes	B	2.4 McLaren MP4/22-Mercedes V8		2/22
1	MALAYSIAN GP	Sepang	1	Vodafone McLaren Mercedes	B	2.4 McLaren MP4/22-Mercedes V8		2/22
5	BAHRAIN GP	Sakhir Circuit	1	Vodafone McLaren Mercedes	B	2.4 McLaren MP4/22-Mercedes V8	*unhappy with brakes*	4/22
3	SPANISH GP	Barcelona	1	Vodafone McLaren Mercedes	B	2.4 McLaren MP4/22-Mercedes V8		2/22
1	MONACO GP	Monte Carlo	1	Vodafone McLaren Mercedes	B	2.4 McLaren MP4/22-Mercedes V8	*FL*	1/22
7	CANADIAN GP	Montreal	1	Vodafone McLaren Mercedes	B	2.4 McLaren MP4/22-Mercedes V8	*stop & go pen – pitted under safety car*	2/22
2	U S GP	Indianapolis	1	Vodafone McLaren Mercedes	B	2.4 McLaren MP4/22-Mercedes V8		2/22
7	FRENCH GP	Magny Cours	1	Vodafone McLaren Mercedes	B	2.4 McLaren MP4/22-Mercedes V8	*gearbox failure in qualifying*	10/22
2	BRITISH GP	Silverstone	1	Vodafone McLaren Mercedes	B	2.4 McLaren MP4/22-Mercedes V8		3/22
1	EUROPEAN GP	Nürburgring	1	Vodafone McLaren Mercedes	B	2.4 McLaren MP4/22-Mercedes V8		2/22
4	HUNGARIAN GP	Hungaroring	1	Vodafone McLaren Mercedes	B	2.4 McLaren MP4/22-Mercedes V8	**five place grid penalty*	*1/22
3	TURKISH GP	Istanbul	1	Vodafone McLaren Mercedes	B	2.4 McLaren MP4/22-Mercedes V8		4/22
1	ITALIAN GP	Monza	1	Vodafone McLaren Mercedes	B	2.4 McLaren MP4/22-Mercedes V8	*FL*	1/22
3	BELGIAN GP	Spa	1	Vodafone McLaren Mercedes	B	2.4 McLaren MP4/22-Mercedes V8		3/22
ret	JAPANESE GP	Suzuka	1	Vodafone McLaren Mercedes	B	2.4 McLaren MP4/22-Mercedes V8	*crashed in rain*	2/22
2	CHINESE GP	Shanghai	1	Vodafone McLaren Mercedes	B	2.4 McLaren MP4/22-Mercedes V8		4/22
3	BRAZILIAN GP	Interlagos	1	Vodafone McLaren Mercedes	B	2.4 McLaren MP4/22-Mercedes V8		4/22

A breath of fresh air for the sport. Fernando Alonso took his Renault R25 to the championship in the 2005 Chinese Grand Prix, breaking the five-year stranglehold of Michael Schumacher and Ferrari.

2008 Championship position: 5th Wins: 2 Pole positions: 0 Fastest laps: 0 Points scored: 61

4	AUSTRALIAN GP	Melbourne	5	ING Renault F1 Team	B	2.4 Renault R28-V8		12/22
8	MALAYSIAN GP	Sepang	5	ING Renault F1 Team	B	2.4 Renault R28-V8		9/22
10	BAHRAIN GP	Sakhir Circuit	5	ING Renault F1 Team	B	2.4 Renault R28-V8		10/22
ret	SPANISH GP	Barcelona	5	ING Renault F1 Team	B	2.4 Renault R28-V8	engine	2/22
6	TURKISH GP	Istanbul	5	ING Renault F1 Team	B	2.4 Renault R28-V8		7/20
10	MONACO GP	Monte Carlo	5	ING Renault F1 Team	B	2.4 Renault R28-V8	pit stop – accident damage/-1 lap	7/20
ret	CANADIAN GP	Montreal	5	ING Renault F1 Team	B	2.4 Renault R28-V8	accident	4/20
8	FRENCH GP	Magny Cours	5	ING Renault F1 Team	B	2.4 Renault R28-V8	delayed by Fisichella	4/20
6	BRITISH GP	Silverstone	5	ING Renault F1 Team	B	2.4 Renault R28-V8		6/20
11	GERMAN GP	Hockenheim	5	ING Renault F1 Team	B	2.4 Renault R28-V8		5/20
4	HUNGARIAN GP	Hungaroring	5	ING Renault F1 Team	B	2.4 Renault R28-V8		7/20
ret	EUROPEAN GP	Valencia	5	ING Renault F1 Team	B	2.4 Renault R28-V8	accident damage on lap 1	12/20
4	BELGIAN GP	Spa	5	ING Renault F1 Team	B	2.4 Renault R28-V8		6/20
4	ITALIAN GP	Monza	5	ING Renault F1 Team	B	2.4 Renault R28-V8		8/20
1	SINGAPORE GP	Singapore Circuit	5	ING Renault F1 Team	B	2.4 Renault R28-V8	took advantage of Piquet 'crash'	15/20
1	JAPANESE GP	Suzuka	5	ING Renault F1 Team	B	2.4 Renault R28-V8		4/20
4	CHINESE GP	Shanghai	5	ING Renault F1 Team	B	2.4 Renault R28-V8		4/20
2	BRAZILIAN GP	Interlagos	5	ING Renault F1 Team	B	2.4 Renault R28-V8		6/20

2009 Championship position: 9th Wins: 0 Pole positions: 1 Fastest laps: 0 Points scored: 26

5*	AUSTRALIAN GP	Melbourne	7	ING Renault F1 Team	B	2.4 Renault R29-V8	*3rd place car disqualified	12/20
11	MALAYSIAN GP	Sepang	7	ING Renault F1 Team	B	2.4 Renault R29-V8	troubled by an ear infection	10/20
9	CHINESE GP	Shanghai	7	ING Renault F1 Team	B	2.4 Renault R29-V8	strategy affected by rain	2/20
8	BAHRAIN GP	Sakhir Circuit	7	ING Renault F1 Team	B	2.4 Renault R29-V8		7/20
5	SPANISH GP	Barcelona	7	ING Renault F1 Team	B	2.4 Renault R29-V8		8/20
7	MONACO GP	Monte Carlo	7	ING Renault F1 Team	B	2.4 Renault R29-V8		9/20
10	TURKISH GP	Istanbul	7	ING Renault F1 Team	B	2.4 Renault R29-V8	wrong tyre and fuel strategy	8/20
14	BRITISH GP	Silverstone	7	ING Renault F1 Team	B	2.4 Renault R29-V8	1 lap behind	10/20
7	GERMAN GP	Hockenheim	7	ING Renault F1 Team	B	2.4 Renault R29-V8	FL	12/20
ret	HUNGARIAN GP	Hungaroring	7	ING Renault F1 Team	B	2.4 Renault R29-V8	lost wheel at pitstop/fuel pump	1/20
6	EUROPEAN GP	Valencia	7	ING Renault F1 Team	B	2.4 Renault R29-V8		8/20
ret	BELGIAN GP	Spa	7	ING Renault F1 Team	B	2.4 Renault R29-V8	collision Sutil – wheel damage	13/20
5	ITALIAN GP	Monza	7	ING Renault F1 Team	B	2.4 Renault R29-V8	excellent drive	8/20
3	SINGAPORE GP	Singapore Circuit	7	Renault F1 Team	B	2.4 Renault R29-V8		6/20
10	JAPANESE GP	Suzuka	7	Renault F1 Team	B	2.4 Renault R29-V8		12/20
ret	BRAZILIAN GP	Interlagos	7	Renault F1 Team	B	2.4 Renault R29-V8	taken out by Sutil on lap 1	10/20
14	ABU DHABI GP	Yas Marina Circuit	7	Renault F1 Team	B	2.4 Renault R29-V8		16/20

2010 Championship position: 2nd Wins: 5 Pole positions: 2 Fastest laps: 5 Points scored: 252

1	BAHRAIN GP	Sakhir Circuit	8	Scuderia Ferrari Marlboro	B	2.4 Ferrari F10 V8	win in first race for Ferrari/FL	3/24
4	AUSTRALIAN GP	Melbourne	8	Scuderia Ferrari Marlboro	B	2.4 Ferrari F10 V8	delayed by spin on lap 1	3/24
13/ret	MALAYSIAN GP	Sepang	8	Scuderia Ferrari Marlboro	B	2.4 Ferrari F10 V8	engine/2 laps behind	19/24
4	CHINESE GP	Shanghai Circuit	8	Scuderia Ferrari Marlboro	B	2.4 Ferrari F10 V8	jump start – drive-through penalty	3/24
2	SPANISH GP	Barcelona	8	Scuderia Ferrari Marlboro	B	2.4 Ferrari F10 V8		4/24
6	MONACO GP	Monte Carlo	8	Scuderia Ferrari Marlboro	B	2.4 Ferrari F10 V8	practice crash – *no time set	*24/24
8	TURKISH GP	Istanbul Park	8	Scuderia Ferrari Marlboro	B	2.4 Ferrari F10 V8		12/24
3	CANADIAN GP	Montreal	8	Scuderia Ferrari Marlboro	B	2.4 Ferrari F10 V8		4/24
8	EUROPEAN GP	Valencia	8	Scuderia Ferrari Marlboro	B	2.4 Ferrari F10 V8		4/24
14	BRITISH GP	Silverstone	8	Scuderia Ferrari Marlboro	B	2.4 Ferrari F10 V8	drive-through penalty/FL	3/24
1	GERMAN GP	Hockenheim	8	Scuderia Ferrari Marlboro	B	2.4 Ferrari F10 V8	helped to win by Massa	2/24
2	HUNGARIAN GP	Hungaroring	8	Scuderia Ferrari Marlboro	B	2.4 Ferrari F10 V8		3/24
ret	BELGIAN GP	Spa	8	Scuderia Ferrari Marlboro	B	2.4 Ferrari F10 V8	crashed in heavy rain	10/24
1	ITALIAN GP	Monza	8	Scuderia Ferrari Marlboro	B	2.4 Ferrari F10 V8	FL	1/24
1	SINGAPORE GP	Marina Bay Circuit	8	Scuderia Ferrari Marlboro	B	2.4 Ferrari F10 V8	FL	1/24
3	JAPANESE GP	Suzuka	8	Scuderia Ferrari Marlboro	B	2.4 Ferrari F10 V8		5/24
1	KOREAN GP	Yeongam	8	Scuderia Ferrari Marlboro	B	2.4 Ferrari F10 V8	two part race/FL	3/24
3	BRAZILIAN GP	Interlagos	8	Scuderia Ferrari Marlboro	B	2.4 Ferrari F10 V8		5/24
7	ABU DHABI GP	Yas Marina Circuit	8	Scuderia Ferrari Marlboro	B	2.4 Ferrari F10 V8	compromised by pit stop strategy	3/24

2011 Championship position: 4th Wins: 1 Pole positions: 0 Fastest laps: 1 Points scored: 257

4	AUSTRALIAN GP	Melbourne	5	Scuderia Ferrari Marlboro	P	2.4 Ferrari F150th Italia V8		5/24
6	MALAYSIAN GP	Sepang	5	Scuderia Ferrari Marlboro	P	2.4 Ferrari F150th Italia V8	20-sec pen – collision with Hamilton	5/24
7	CHINESE GP	Shanghai Circuit	5	Scuderia Ferrari Marlboro	P	2.4 Ferrari F150th Italia V8		5/24
3	TURKISH GP	Istanbul Park	5	Scuderia Ferrari Marlboro	P	2.4 Ferrari F150th Italia V8		5/24
5	SPANISH GP	Barcelona	5	Scuderia Ferrari Marlboro	P	2.4 Ferrari F150th Italia V8	1 lap behind	4/24
2	MONACO GP	Monte Carlo	5	Scuderia Ferrari Marlboro	P	2.4 Ferrari F150th Italia V8		4/24
ret	CANADIAN GP	Montreal	5	Scuderia Ferrari Marlboro	P	2.4 Ferrari F150th Italia V8	collision with Button – spun off	2/24
2	EUROPEAN GP	Valencia	5	Scuderia Ferrari Marlboro	P	2.4 Ferrari F150th Italia V8		4/24
1	BRITISH GP	Silverstone	5	Scuderia Ferrari Marlboro	P	2.4 Ferrari F150th Italia V8	FL	3/24
2	GERMAN GP	Hockenheim	5	Scuderia Ferrari Marlboro	P	2.4 Ferrari F150th Italia V8		4/24
3	HUNGARIAN GP	Hungaroring	5	Scuderia Ferrari Marlboro	P	2.4 Ferrari F150th Italia V8		5/24
4	BELGIAN GP	Spa	5	Scuderia Ferrari Marlboro	P	2.4 Ferrari F150th Italia V8		8/24
3	ITALIAN GP	Monza	5	Scuderia Ferrari Marlboro	P	2.4 Ferrari F150th Italia V8		4/24
4	SINGAPORE GP	Marina Bay Circuit	5	Scuderia Ferrari Marlboro	P	2.4 Ferrari F150th Italia V8		5/24
2	JAPANESE GP	Suzuka	5	Scuderia Ferrari Marlboro	P	2.4 Ferrari F150th Italia V8		5/24
5	KOREAN GP	Yeongam	5	Scuderia Ferrari Marlboro	P	2.4 Ferrari F150th Italia V8		6/24
3	INDIAN GP	Buddh Circuit	5	Scuderia Ferrari Marlboro	P	2.4 Ferrari F150th Italia V8		4/24
2	ABU DHABI GP	Yas Marina Circuit	5	Scuderia Ferrari Marlboro	P	2.4 Ferrari F150th Italia V8		5/24
4	BRAZILIAN GP	Interlagos	5	Scuderia Ferrari Marlboro	P	2.4 Ferrari F150th Italia V8		5/24

GP Starts: 177 GP Wins: 27 Pole positions: 20 Fastest laps: 19 Points: 1086

CHRIS AMON

C HRIS AMON will always be best remembered as a notoriously unlucky driver who never managed to win a world championship grand prix, for whenever he seemed poised to triumph, dame fortune frowned and poor Chrissie was left to rue his unkind fate.

A New Zealand sheep farmer's son, Chris was racing a Maserati 250F by the age of 18, and he so impressed Reg Parnell in the 1962/63 winter series that he was invited to join the Parnell Grand Prix line-up at the tender age of 19. Amon learned quickly with the team, but the patron's untimely death was a big blow, and by 1965 Chris was spending most of his time with Bruce McLaren and his fledgling organisation, racing his big Elva sports cars. With Bruce busy running the operation, Chris undertook a large amount of testing for the team, and for Firestone, who were providing much needed income. A proposed 1966 grand prix season with McLaren failed to materialise due to a lack of engines, so it was more sports car racing in Britain and in the Can-Am series, topped by a wonderful win for Ford at Le Mans with Bruce, after deservedly beating the sister car of Denny Hulme and Ken Miles, despite the team attempting a 'dead-heat' finish.

Amon's successful season had been watched closely by Ferrari, who signed him for 1967. He got off to an encouraging start with wins in the Daytona 24-hours and Monza 1000km, but then came turmoil in the team. His new-found friend, Lorenzo Bandini, was killed at Monaco, Mike Parkes was injured at Spa and Ludovico Scarfiotti temporarily quit F1, putting a huge burden on Chris' shoulders, but he responded brilliantly with a string of great drives that continued into the following season. He came closest to a win in the 1968 British GP, where he had a classic battle with Jo Siffert. Ferrari quite possibly had the best chassis that year, but their advantage was negated by the large aerofoil wings run by their Cosworth-engined rivals, Lotus, McLaren and Matra.

The 1969 season started brightly, Chris taking a Dino 166 to the Tasman series and winning the championship, but the strain of the factory's huge racing programme was beginning to show, and Formula 1 suffered most. Frustrated, Chris jumped ship to drive the new works March in 1970, having been promised number-one status. He delivered a run of excellent early-season placings, including winning the International Trophy at Silverstone and then taking a superb second place to Pedro Rodriguez at Spa, followed by another second in the French Grand Prix at Clermont Ferrand. However the team's limitations soon became apparent, the car being fairly rudimentary and suffering from a lack of development due to limited financial support. Feeling somewhat misled over his status in the team, Chris signed a major two-year deal with the French Matra concern for 1971/72. A splendid aggregate win in the non-title Argentine GP bided well, only for luck to desert him at crucial times, most cruelly at Clermont Ferrand, where nobody could touch him until a puncture intervened, and then again at Monza, where he was forced to surrender the lead after losing his visor.

With Matra's withdrawal, Chris agreed to return to March for 1973, but a financial disagreement saw him sensationally sacked at the start of the year, to be replaced by Jean-Pierre Jarier. It was the start of a downward spiral in Formula 1 for the Kiwi, who became progressively dispirited as he saw his efforts go to waste, first at Tecno and then disastrously in 1974 with his own Amon project. Perhaps the most galling event for Amon during this period was his failure to take up an offer of a drive with Brabham, where his talents would surely have been rewarded with success.

Guest drives for Tyrrell (sadly ended when François Cevert was killed at Watkins Glen) and BRM (a team in steep and terminal decline) failed to ignite the latent spark.

He won a 1975 Tasman Cup race at Invercargill in a Talon F5000 car, but seemed washed up on the Formula 1 front. However, a chance meeting with Mo Nunn led to Chris accepting a drive in the Ensign late in 1975. Suddenly there was a sense of purpose for the driver, and in 1976 the old Amon was back, with a superb drive at Kyalami until a fuel problem halted his progress. The new MN176 was a cracking little chassis and Chris really flew, but unfortunately it was fragile, and after a couple of very lucky escapes when things broke he decided to get out in one piece. He refused to take the restart at the German Grand Prix after Niki Lauda's fiery accident, which led to an inevitable parting of the ways with Ensign. After being persuaded to join Walter Wolf's Williams team, he finally quit F1 for good after being T-boned in practice at Mosport.

Although he raced briefly for Wolf in Can-Am in 1977, he quit for good, claiming, "I'm just not enjoying this anymore."

"I was only 33, but I had been in it since I was 19 and I had had enough," he said. "I never got sick of the racing, but I got sick of the travelling, the restaurants, the hotels, the suitcases."

Married for the second time, he returned to New Zealand to tend the family farm. He did not sever his links with the world of motoring, however, and for many years was involved with Toyota, testing and advising on their road cars. In 2007, Amon lent his name to the Chris Amon International Scholarship to support Kiwi Toyota Racing Series champions in their quest to further their careers in International single-seater racing. He also participated in the design of his local Taupo Motorsport Circuit, which was used for a round of the now-defunct A1GP series in 2007.In January 2011, Chris, a modest soul, was honoured at the New Zealand Festival of Motoring at Hampton Downs for his massive contribution to the sport in his homeland.

AMON, Chris (NZ) b 20/7/1945, Palmerston North

1963 Championship position: Unplaced

	Race	Circuit	No	Entrant	Tyres	Capacity/Car/Engine	Comment	Q Pos/Entries
dns	MONACO GP	Monte Carlo	15	Reg Parnell (Racing)	D	1.5 Lola 4A-Climax V8	car driven by Trintignant	(15)/17
ret	BELGIAN GP	Spa	21	Reg Parnell (Racing)	D	1.5 Lola 4A-Climax V8	oil leak	15/20
ret	DUTCH GP	Zandvoort	10	Reg Parnell (Racing)	D	1.5 Lola 4A-Climax V8	water pump	12/19
dns	"	"	10T	Reg Parnell (Racing)	D	1.5 Lotus 24-Climax V8	practice only	– / –
7	FRENCH GP	Reims	30	Reg Parnell (Racing)	D	1.5 Lola 4A-Climax V8	2 laps behind	17/21
7	BRITISH GP	Silverstone	19	Reg Parnell (Racing)	D	1.5 Lola 4A-Climax V8	2 laps behind	14/23
ret	GERMAN GP	Nürburgring	21	Reg Parnell (Racing)	D	1.5 Lola 4A-Climax V8	crashed – broken steering	14/26
dns	ITALIAN GP	Monza	38	Reg Parnell (Racing)	D	1.5 Lola 4A-Climax V8	practice accident	(15)/28
ret	MEXICAN GP	Mexico City	18	Reg Parnell (Racing)	D	1.5 Lotus 24-BRM V8	gearbox	19/21

1964 Championship position: 16th=   Wins: 0   Pole positions: 0   Fastest laps: 0   Points scored: 2

	Race	Circuit	No	Entrant	Tyres	Capacity/Car/Engine	Comment	Q Pos/Entries
dnq	MONACO GP	Monte Carlo	17	Reg Parnell (Racing)	D	1.5 Lotus 25-BRM V8		18/20
5	DUTCH GP	Zandvoort	10	Reg Parnell (Racing)	D	1.5 Lotus 25-BRM V8	1 lap behind	13/18
ret	BELGIAN GP	Spa	27	Reg Parnell (Racing)	D	1.5 Lotus 25-BRM V8	engine – con-rod	11/20
10	FRENCH GP	Rouen	34	Reg Parnell (Racing)	D	1.5 Lotus 25-BRM V8	4 laps behind	14/17
ret	BRITISH GP	Brands Hatch	15	Reg Parnell (Racing)	D	1.5 Lotus 25-BRM V8	clutch	11/25
11/ret	GERMAN GP	Nürburgring	14	Reg Parnell (Racing)	D	1.5 Lotus 25-BRM V8	suspension/3 laps behind	9/24
ret	AUSTRIAN GP	Zeltweg	16	Reg Parnell (Racing)	D	1.5 Lotus 25-Climax V8	engine	17/20
ret	US GP	Watkins Glen	15	Reg Parnell (Racing)	D	1.5 Lotus 25-BRM V8	starter motor bolt	11/19
ret	MEXICAN GP	Mexico City	15	Reg Parnell (Racing)	D	1.5 Lotus 25-BRM V8	gearbox	12/19

1965 Championship position: Unplaced

	Race	Circuit	No	Entrant	Tyres	Capacity/Car/Engine	Comment	Q Pos/Entries
ret	FRENCH GP	Clermont Ferrand	24	Reg Parnell (Racing)	D	1.5 Lotus 25-BRM V8	fuel feed	8/17
dns	BRITISH GP	Silverstone	24	Ian Raby Racing	D	1.5 Brabham BT3-BRM V8	Raby drove car	– / –
ret	GERMAN GP	Nürburgring	19	Reg Parnell (Racing)	D	1.5 Lotus 25-BRM V8	electrics – ignition	16/22

1966 Championship position: Unplaced

	Race	Circuit	No	Entrant	Tyres	Capacity/Car/Engine	Comment	Q Pos/Entries
8	FRENCH GP	Reims	8	Cooper Car Co	D	3.0 Cooper T81-Maserati V12	loose hub nut/4 laps behind	7/17
dnq	ITALIAN GP	Monza	32	Chris Amon	–	2.0 Brabham BT11-BRM V8		22/22

1967 Championship position: 4th=   Wins: 0   Pole positions: 0   Fastest laps: 0   Points scored: 20

	Race	Circuit	No	Entrant	Tyres	Capacity/Car/Engine	Comment	Q Pos/Entries
3	MONACO GP	Monte Carlo	20	Scuderia Ferrari SpA SEFAC	F	3.0 Ferrari 312/67 V12	2 laps behind	15/18
4	DUTCH GP	Zandvoort	3	Scuderia Ferrari SpA SEFAC	F	3.0 Ferrari 312/67 V12		9/17
3	BELGIAN GP	Spa	1	Scuderia Ferrari SpA SEFAC	F	3.0 Ferrari 312/67 V12		=4/18
ret	FRENCH GP	Le Mans	2	Scuderia Ferrari SpA SEFAC	F	3.0 Ferrari 312/67 V12	throttle cable	7/15
3	BRITISH GP	Silverstone	8	Scuderia Ferrari SpA SEFAC	F	3.0 Ferrari 312/67 V12		6/21
3	GERMAN GP	Nürburgring	8	Scuderia Ferrari Spa SEFAC	F	3.0 Ferrari 312/67 V12		9/25
6	CANADIAN GP	Mosport Park	20	Scuderia Ferrari SpA SEFAC	F	3.0 Ferrari 312/67 V12	3 laps behind	4/19
7	ITALIAN GP	Monza	2	Scuderia Ferrari SpA SEFAC	F	3.0 Ferrari 312/67 V12	pit stop – handling/4 laps behind	4/18
ret	US GP	Watkins Glen	9	Scuderia Ferrari SpA SEFAC	F	3.0 Ferrari 312/67 V12	engine	4/18
9	MEXICAN GP	Mexico City	9	Scuderia Ferrari SpA SEFAC	F	3.0 Ferrari 312/67 V12	fuel feed problem/3 laps behind	2/19

1968 Championship position: 10   Wins: 0   Pole positions: 4   Fastest laps: 0   Points scored: 10

	Race	Circuit	No	Entrant	Tyres	Capacity/Car/Engine	Comment	Q Pos/Entries
4	SOUTH AFRICAN GP	Kyalami	8	Scuderia Ferrari SpA SEFAC	F	3.0 Ferrari 312/67 V12	pit stop – fuel/2 laps behind	8/23
ret	SPANISH GP	Jarama	19	Scuderia Ferrari SpA SEFAC	F	3.0 Ferrari 312/67/68 V12	fuel pump	1/14
ret	BELGIAN GP	Spa	22	Scuderia Ferrari SpA SEFAC	F	3.0 Ferrari 312/67/68 V12	stone holed radiator	1/18
6	DUTCH GP	Zandvoort	9	Scuderia Ferrari SpA SEFAC	F	3.0 Ferrari 312/68 V12	pit stop – tyres/5 laps behind	1/19
10	FRENCH GP	Rouen	24	Scuderia Ferrari SpA SEFAC	F	3.0 Ferrari 312/68 V12	engine and tyres/5 laps behind	5/18
2	BRITISH GP	Brands Hatch	5	Scuderia Ferrari SpA SEFAC	F	3.0 Ferrari 312/68 V12		3/20
ret	GERMAN GP	Nürburgring	8	Scuderia Ferrari SpA SEFAC	F	3.0 Ferrari 312/68 V12	spun off	2/20
ret	ITALIAN GP	Monza	9	Scuderia Ferrari SpA SEFAC	F	3.0 Ferrari 312/68 V12	spun off on oil	3/24
ret	CANADIAN GP	St Jovite	9	Scuderia Ferrari SpA SEFAC	F	3.0 Ferrari 312/68 V12	transmission	1/22
ret	US GP	Watkins Glen	6	Scuderia Ferrari SpA SEFAC	F	3.0 Ferrari 312/68 V12	water pipe	4/21
ret	MEXICAN GP	Mexico City	6	Scuderia Ferrari SpA SEFAC	F	3.0 Ferrari 312/68 V12	water pump drive – overheating	2/21

1969 Championship position: 12th   Wins: 0   Pole positions: 0   Fastest laps: 0   Points scored: 4

	Race	Circuit	No	Entrant	Tyres	Capacity/Car/Engine	Comment	Q Pos/Entries
ret	SOUTH AFRICAN GP	Kyalami	9	Scuderia Ferrari SpA SEFAC	F	3.0 Ferrari 312/69 V12	engine	5/18
ret	SPANISH GP	Montjuich Park	15	Scuderia Ferrari SpA SEFAC	F	3.0 Ferrari 312/69 V12	engine while leading race	2/14
ret	MONACO GP	Monte Carlo	11	Scuderia Ferrari SpA SEFAC	F	3.0 Ferrari 312/69 V12	differential	2/16
3	DUTCH GP	Zandvoort	8	Scuderia Ferrari SpA SEFAC	F	3.0 Ferrari 312/69 V12		4/15
ret	FRENCH GP	Clermont Ferrand	6	Scuderia Ferrari SpA SEFAC	F	3.0 Ferrari 312/69 V12	engine	6/13
ret	BRITISH GP	Silverstone	11	Scuderia Ferrari SpA SEFAC	F	3.0 Ferrari 312/69 V12	gearbox	5/17

1970 Championship position: 7th=   Wins: 0   Pole positions: 0   Fastest laps: 0   Points scored: 23

	Race	Circuit	No	Entrant	Tyres	Capacity/Car/Engine	Comment	Q Pos/Entries
ret	SOUTH AFRICAN GP	Kyalami	15	March Engineering	F	3.0 March 701-Cosworth V8	overheating	=1/24
ret	SPANISH GP	Jarama	9	March Engineering	F	3.0 March 701-Cosworth V8	engine/clutch	6/22
ret	MONACO GP	Monte Carlo	28	March Engineering	F	3.0 March 701-Cosworth V8	rear suspension bolt	2/21
2	BELGIAN GP	Spa	10	March Engineering	F	3.0 March 701-Cosworth V8	FL	3/18
ret	DUTCH GP	Zandvoort	8	March Engineering	F	3.0 March 701-Cosworth V8	clutch	4/24
2	FRENCH GP	Clermont Ferrand	14	March Engineering	F	3.0 March 701-Cosworth V8		3/23
5	BRITISH GP	Brands Hatch	16	March Engineering	F	3.0 March 701-Cosworth V8	1 lap behind	18/25
ret	GERMAN GP	Hockenheim	5	March Engineering	F	3.0 March 701-Cosworth V8	engine	6/25
8	AUSTRIAN GP	Österreichring	4	March Engineering	F	3.0 March 701-Cosworth V8	1 lap behind	6/24
7	ITALIAN GP	Monza	48	March Engineering	F	3.0 March 701-Cosworth V8	1 lap behind	21/27
3	CANADIAN GP	St Jovite	20	March Engineering	F	3.0 March 701-Cosworth V8		=5/20
5	US GP	Watkins Glen	12	March Engineering	F	3.0 March 701-Cosworth V8	pit stop – tyres/1 lap behind	5/27
4	MEXICAN GP	Mexico City	12	March Engineering	F	3.0 March 701-Cosworth V8		5/18

1971 Championship position: 9th=   Wins: 0   Pole positions: 1   Fastest laps: 0   Points scored: 9

	Race	Circuit	No	Entrant	Tyres	Capacity/Car/Engine	Comment	Q Pos/Entries
5	SOUTH AFRICAN GP	Kyalami	19	Equipe Matra Sports	G	3.0 Matra-Simca MS120B V12	1 lap behind	2/25

Kiwi battle. Amon in the Matra MS120B leads Howden Ganley's BRM in the 1971 Italian GP at Monza. Having qualified on pole, the unlucky New Zealander was robbed of a probable victory later in the race when he lost his visor, which caused him to drop to a sixth-place finish.

3	SPANISH GP	Montjuich Park	20	Equipe Matra Sports	G	3.0 Matra-Simca MS120B V12		=2/22
ret	MONACO GP	Monte Carlo	20	Equipe Matra Sports	G	3.0 Matra-Simca MS120B V12	cwp	=3/23
ret	DUTCH GP	Zandvoort	20	Equipe Matra Sports	G	3.0 Matra-Simca MS120B V12	spun off – damaged radiator	5/24
5	FRENCH GP	Paul Ricard	20	Equipe Matra Sports	G	3.0 Matra-Simca MS120B V12		9/24
ret	BRITISH GP	Silverstone	21	Equipe Matra Sports	G	3.0 Matra-Simca MS120B V12	dropped valve	9/24
ret	GERMAN GP	Nürburgring	10	Equipe Matra Sports	G	3.0 Matra-Simca MS120B V12	spun off – damaged suspension	16/23
6	ITALIAN GP	Monza	12	Equipe Matra Sports	G	3.0 Matra-Simca MS120B V12	lost visor while leading race	1/24
10	CANADIAN GP	Mosport Park	20	Equipe Matra Sports	G	3.0 Matra-Simca MS120B V12	3 laps behind	=4/27
12	US GP	Watkins Glen	11	Equipe Matra Sports	G	3.0 Matra-Simca MS120B V12	pit stop – tyres/2 laps behind	9/32

1972 Championship position: 9th=   Wins: 0   Pole positions: 1   Fastest laps: 2   Points scored: 12

ret/dns	ARGENTINE GP	Buenos Aires	16	Equipe Matra	G	3.0 Matra-Simca MS120C V12	gearbox on parade lap	(12)/22
15	SOUTH AFRICAN GP	Kyalami	15	Equipe Matra	G	3.0 Matra-Simca MS120C V12	2 pit stops – vibration/-3 laps	13/27
ret	SPANISH GP	Jarama	9	Equipe Matra	G	3.0 Matra-Simca MS120C V12	gearbox	6/26
6	MONACO GP	Monte Carlo	16	Equipe Matra	G	3.0 Matra-Simca MS120C V12	4 pit stops – goggles/-3 laps	=5/25
6	BELGIAN GP	Nivelles	5	Equipe Matra	G	3.0 Matra-Simca MS120C V12	fuel stop lay 3rd/FL/1 behind	13/26
3	FRENCH GP	Clermont Ferrand	9	Equipe Matra	G	3.0 Matra-Simca MS120D V12	pit stop – puncture/FL	1/29
4	BRITISH GP	Brands Hatch	17	Equipe Matra	G	3.0 Matra-Simca MS120C V12	1 lap behind	17/27
dns	"	"	17	Equipe Matra	G	3.0 Matra-Simca MS120D V12	practice only	– / –
15	GERMAN GP	Nürburgring	8	Equipe Matra	G	3.0 Matra-Simca MS120D V12	started late from pits/-1 lap	8/27
5	AUSTRIAN GP	Österreichring	10	Equipe Matra	G	3.0 Matra-Simca MS120D V12		6/26
dns	"	"	30T	Equipe Matra	G	3.0 Matra-Simca MS120C V12	practice only	– / –
ret	ITALIAN GP	Monza	20	Equipe Matra	G	3.0 Matra-Simca MS120D V12	brakes – worn pads	2/27
dns	"	"	20T	Equipe Matra	G	3.0 Matra-Simca MS120C V12	practice only	– / –
6	CANADIAN GP	Mosport Park	4	Equipe Matra	G	3.0 Matra-Simca MS120D V12	1 lap behind	10/25
15	US GP	Watkins Glen	18	Equipe Matra	G	3.0 Matra-Simca MS120D V12	started from back of grid/-2 laps	7/32

1973 Championship position: 19th=   Wins: 0   Pole positions: 0   Fastest laps: 0   Points scored: 1

6	BELGIAN GP	Zolder	22	Martini Racing Team	F	3.0 Tecno PA123 F12	3 laps behind	15/23
ret	MONACO GP	Monte Carlo	22	Martini Racing Team	F	3.0 Tecno PA123 F12	overheating	12/26
ret	BRITISH GP	Silverstone	22	Martini Racing Team	F	3.0 Tecno PA123 F12	fuel pressure	29/29
ret	DUTCH GP	Zandvoort	22	Martini Racing Team	F	3.0 Tecno PA123 F12	fuel pressure	19/24
dns	"	"	22T	Martini Racing Team	F	3.0 Tecno E731 F12	practice only	– / –
dns	AUSTRIAN GP	Österreichring	22	Martini Racing Team	F	3.0 Tecno PA123 F12	no race engine available	(23)/25
dns	"	"	22T	Martini Racing Team	F	3.0 Tecno E731 F12	no race engine available	– / –
10	CANADIAN GP	Mosport Park	29	Elf Team Tyrrell	G	3.0 Tyrrell 005-Cosworth V8	pit stop –tyres/3 laps behind	11/26
dns	US GP	Watkins Glen	29	Elf Team Tyrrell	G	3.0 Tyrrell 005-Cosworth V8	withdrawn after Cevert's death	(13)/28

1974 Championship position: Unplaced

ret	SPANISH GP	Jarama	30	Chris Amon Racing	F	3.0 Amon AF101-Cosworth V8	brakeshaft	24/28
dns	MONACO GP	Monte Carlo	30	Chris Amon Racing	F	3.0 Amon AF101-Cosworth V8	withdrawn – hub failure	(20)/28
dnq	GERMAN GP	Nürburgring	30	Chris Amon Racing	F	3.0 Amon AF101-Cosworth V8	driver unwell	31/32
dnq	ITALIAN GP	Monza	22	Chris Amon Racing	F	3.0 Amon AF101-Cosworth V8		30/31
nc	CANADIAN GP	Mosport Park	15	Team Motul BRM	F	3.0 BRM P201 V12	pit stop – misfire/-10 laps	25/30
9	US GP	Watkins Glen	15	Team Motul BRM	F	3.0 BRM P201 V12	2 laps behind	12/30

1975 Championship position: Unplaced

12	AUSTRIAN GP	Österreichring	31	HB Bewaking Team Ensign	G	3.0 Ensign N175-Cosworth V8	1 lap behind	24/30
12	ITALIAN GP	Monza	32	HB Bewaking Team Ensign	G	3.0 Ensign N175-Cosworth V8	misfire/4 laps behind	19/28

1976 Championship position: 18th   Wins: 0   Pole positions: 0   Fastest laps: 0   Points scored: 2

14	SOUTH AFRICAN GP	Kyalami	22	Team Ensign	G	3.0 Ensign N174-Cosworth V8	pit stop – fuel/2 laps behind	18/25
8	US GP WEST	Long Beach	22	Team Ensign	G	3.0 Ensign N174-Cosworth V8	pit stop – brakes/2 laps behind	17/27
5	SPANISH GP	Jarama	22	Team Ensign	G	3.0 Ensign N176-Cosworth V8	1 lap behind	10/30
ret	BELGIAN GP	Zolder	22	Team Ensign	G	3.0 Ensign N176-Cosworth V8	lost wheel – crashed	8/29
13	MONACO GP	Monte Carlo	22	Team Ensign	G	3.0 Ensign N176-Cosworth V8	painful wrist/4 laps behind	12/25
ret	SWEDISH GP	Anderstorp	22	Team Ensign	G	3.0 Ensign N176-Cosworth V8	suspension failure – crashed	3/27
ret	BRITISH GP	Brands Hatch	22	Team Ensign	G	3.0 Ensign N176-Cosworth V8	water leak	6/30
ret/dns	GERMAN GP	Nürburgring	22	Team Ensign	G	3.0 Ensign N176-Cosworth V8	driver withdrew after first start	17/28
dns	CANADIAN GP	Mosport Park	21	Walter Wolf Racing	G	3.0 Wolf Williams FW05-Cosworth V8	practice accident	(26)/27

GP Starts: 95 (97)   GP Wins: 0   Pole positions: 5   Fastest laps: 3   Points: 83

servedly awarded the Wolfgang von Trips Trophy for the best private entrant. Although the days of the independent were already numbered, Bob ploughed on, loyally supported by his French wife Marie-Edmée. His 1965 season was cut short after he wrote off his car in a practice accident at the Nürburgring, but this setback merely strengthened his resolve and he equipped his Brabham with an old Climax four-cylinder engine for the new 1966 3-litre formula.

Remarkably, Anderson returned to two-wheel competition briefly early in 1966. He had been asked by Yamaha to help sort out their troublesome 250cc RD05 machine, and he joined regular team riders Phil Read and Bill Ivy at Assen, taking an impressive fifth place in the wet conditions. A week later, he was back on four wheels at Reims for the French Grand Prix and heading for a certain fifth place until his transmission failed. Later, at Monza, he claimed sixth place, emulating John Surtees by scoring points in both the FIM motorcycle and the FIA F1 championships in the same year.

Once again, heroic performances gained placings that reflected the driver's skill and tenacity, but as the Cosworth era dawned even Bob was facing the stark reality that time was up for the impecunious privateer.

Testing his ancient Brabham on a wet track at Silverstone in preparation for the 1967 Canadian GP, he aquaplaned into a marshals' post, receiving severe throat and chest injuries. Poor Anderson had no chance of survival and eventually succumbed four hours later in Northampton hospital.

Seen as a lone wolf, Anderson would have loved to have been considered for a works drive, but while the grand prix circus wined and dined at the plushest of hotels on their travels, Bob was to be found resting his head in less-expensive establishments – if there was time for sleep at all, given his other duties as team manager, mechanic and public relations man.

Today, the occasionally abrasive Anderson is a forgotten figure, but those who knew him remember a man of remarkable integrity and indomitable spirit, who lived – and died – for his passion.

BOB ANDERSON

A TOUGH ex-motorcycle racer, Bob Anderson had tasted success in his two-wheel career before it had been ended by an injured back, and he switched to four-wheel competition at the relatively late age of 29 in 1961. He spent a season learning the ropes in Formula Junior for Lotus before buying the ex-Bowmaker Lola to have a crack at Formula 1 in 1963, competing in the many non-title races that abounded at the time. After a third place at Imola and a fourth at Syracuse, he won the Rome GP against fairly thin local opposition, quickly garnering the experience to compete full-time in the world championship in 1964.

Making the absolute most of a minute budget, he frequently out-drove more vaunted competitors with his Brabham and was de-

---

ANDERSON, Bob (GB) b 19/5/1931, Hendon, London – d 14/8/1967, Northampton

	1963 Championship position: Unplaced							
	Race	Circuit	No	Entrant	Tyres	Capacity/Car/Engine	Comment	Q Pos/Entries
12	BRITISH GP	Silverstone	22	DW Racing Enterprises	D	1.5 Lola 4-Climax V8	*7 laps behind*	16/23
12	ITALIAN GP	Monza	48	DW Racing Enterprises	D	1.5 Lola 4-Climax V8	*7 laps behind*	19/28
	1964 Championship position: 11th Wins: 0 Pole positions: 0 Fastest laps: 0 Points scored: 5							
7/ret	MONACO GP	Monte Carlo	16	DW Racing Enterprises	D	1.5 Brabham BT11-Climax V8	*gearbox mounting/-14 laps*	12/20
6	DUTCH GP	Zandvoort	34	DW Racing Enterprises	D	1.5 Brabham BT11-Climax V8	*2 laps behind*	11/18
dns	BELGIAN GP	Spa	18	DW Racing Enterprises	D	1.5 Brabham BT11-Climax V8	*ignition problems*	(19)/20
12	FRENCH GP	Rouen	32	DW Racing Enterprises	D	1.5 Brabham BT11-Climax V8	*7 laps behind*	15/17

	Race	Circuit	No	Entrant	Tyres	Capacity/Car/Engine	Comment	Q Pos/Entries
7	BRITISH GP	Brands Hatch	19	DW Racing Enterprises	D	1.5 Brabham BT11-Climax V8	2 laps behind	7/25
ret	GERMAN GP	Nürburgring	16	DW Racing Enterprises	D	1.5 Brabham BT11-Climax V8	suspension	15/24
3	AUSTRIAN GP	Zeltweg	22	DW Racing Enterprises	D	1.5 Brabham BT11-Climax V8	3 laps behind	14/20
11	ITALIAN GP	Monza	22	DW Racing Enterprises	D	1.5 Brabham BT11-Climax V8	3 laps behind	14/25

1965 Championship position: Unplaced

	Race	Circuit	No	Entrant	Tyres	Capacity/Car/Engine	Comment	Q Pos/Entries
nc	SOUTH AFRICAN GP	East London	14	DW Racing Enterprises	D	1.5 Brabham BT11-Climax V8	pit stops – brakes/-35 laps	12/25
9	MONACO GP	Monte Carlo	9	DW Racing Enterprises	D	1.5 Brabham BT11-Climax V8	pit stops/15 laps behind	9/17
dns	BELGIAN GP	Spa	24	DW Racing Enterprises	D	1.5 Brabham BT11-Climax V8	withdrawn after practice	(19)/21
9/ret	FRENCH GP	Clermont Ferrand	30	DW Racing Enterprises	D	1.5 Brabham BT11-Climax V8	spun off/6 laps behind	15/17
ret	BRITISH GP	Silverstone	18	DW Racing Enterprises	D	1.5 Brabham BT11-Climax V8	gearbox	17/23
ret	DUTCH GP	Zandvoort	36	DW Racing Enterprises	D	1.5 Brabham BT11-Climax V8	engine – overheating	16/17
dns	GERMAN GP	Nürburgring	18	DW Racing Enterprises	D	1.5 Brabham BT11-Climax V8	practice accident	(15)/22

1966 Championship position: 17th=   Wins: 0   Pole positions: 0   Fastest laps: 0   Points scored: 1

	Race	Circuit	No	Entrant	Tyres	Capacity/Car/Engine	Comment	Q Pos/Entries
ret	MONACO GP	Monte Carlo	15	DW Racing Enterprises	F	2.7 Brabham BT11-Climax 4	engine	8/16
7/ret	FRENCH GP	Reims	36	DW Racing Enterprises	F	2.7 Brabham BT11-Climax 4	transmission/4 laps behind	=12/17
nc	BRITISH GP	Brands Hatch	21	DW Racing Enterprises	F	2.7 Brabham BT11-Climax 4	pit stops – battery/-10 laps	10/20
ret	DUTCH GP	Zandvoort	34	DW Racing Enterprises	F	2.7 Brabham BT11-Climax 4	suspension	=15/18
ret	GERMAN GP	Nürburgring	19	DW Racing Enterprises	F	2.7 Brabham BT11-Climax 4	transmission	15/30
6	ITALIAN GP	Monza	40	DW Racing Enterprises	F	2.7 Brabham BT11-Climax 4	2 laps behind	15/22

1967 Championship position: 16th=   Wins: 0   Pole positions: 0   Fastest laps: 0   Points scored: 2

	Race	Circuit	No	Entrant	Tyres	Capacity/Car/Engine	Comment	Q Pos/Entries
5	SOUTH AFRICAN GP	Kyalami	14	DW Racing Enterprises	F	2.7 Brabham BT11-Climax 4	2 laps behind	10/18
dnq	MONACO GP	Monte Carlo	15	DW Racing Enterprises	F	2.7 Brabham BT11-Climax 4		14/18
9	DUTCH GP	Zandvoort	21	DW Racing Enterprises	F	2.7 Brabham BT11-Climax 4	4 laps behind	17/17
8	BELGIAN GP	Spa	19	DW Racing Enterprises	F	2.7 Brabham BT11-Climax 4	2 laps behind	17/18
ret	FRENCH GP	Le Mans	17	DW Racing Enterprises	D	2.7 Brabham BT11-Climax 4	ignition	14/15
ret	BRITISH GP	Silverstone	19	DW Racing Enterprises	F	2.7 Brabham BT11-Climax 4	engine	17/21

GP Starts: 25   GP Wins: 0   Pole positions: 0   Fastest laps: 0   Points: 8

CONNY ANDERSSON

THE likeable and humorous Conny Andersson spent his younger days as a top moto-cross rider in his native Sweden while also helping to run his father's garage dealership and, at the same time, raising a family of four daughters. This left little time to contemplate a racing career, until he was bitten by the bug after a visit to a racing school and a drive in a Formula Vee car at the Nürburgring.

By wheeling and dealing in second-hand cars, he scraped together enough cash to buy a Brabham BT21 and, at the relatively late age of 29, began his racing career.

Conny was trapped in F3 from 1970 to 1976 because he lacked the finance to move into higher spheres. But in his travels he acquitted himself well against the likes of James Hunt, Jody Scheckter, Jean-Pierre Jabouille and Jacques Laffite, who were all carving out top-line careers for themselves. In 1974, armed with a March-Toyota, he took six wins, four seconds and four thirds from 20 starts and began to be considered a serious prospect.

More success followed in 1975, despite the disappointment of a 'win' in the Monaco F3 race, which was taken away when he was penalised for jumping the start. This drive caught the eye of John Surtees, who gave him an end-of-season test in one of his F1 cars, but he failed to land a full-time ride for 1976, so it was back to the European championship, where he was particularly unlucky to be pipped to the title by Riccardo Patrese.

At the age of 36, his efforts finally brought Conny a one-off chance to drive a Surtees, in the Dutch Grand Prix that season. Then, unwilling to face a further year in Formula 3, he opted for another shot at F1 with the uncompetitive Stanley-BRM. He suffered a spate of engine failures and never got to grips with the chassis, so, wisely keeping what little was left of his racing budget, he called it a day.

ANDERSSON, Conny (S) b 28/12/1939, Alingsås

1976 Championship position: Unplaced

	Race	Circuit	No	Entrant	Tyres	Capacity/Car/Engine	Comment	Q Pos/Entries
ret	DUTCH GP	Zandvoort	18	Team Surtees	G	3.0 Surtees TS19-Cosworth V8	engine	26/27

1977 Championship position: Unplaced

	Race	Circuit	No	Entrant	Tyres	Capacity/Car/Engine	Comment	Q Pos/Entries
dnq	SPANISH GP	Jarama	35	Rotary Watches Stanley BRM	G	3.0 Stanley BRM P207 V12		31/31
dnq	BELGIAN GP	Zolder	35	Rotary Watches Stanley BRM	G	3.0 Stanley BRM P207 V12		29/32
dnq	SWEDISH GP	Anderstorp	35	Rotary Watches Stanley BRM	G	3.0 Stanley BRM P207 V12		30/31
dnq	FRENCH GP	Dijon	35	Rotary Watches Stanley BRM	G	3.0 Stanley BRM P207 V12		30/30

GP Starts: 1   GP Wins: 0   Pole positions: 0   Fastest laps: 0   Points: 0

MARIO ANDRETTI

OW many drivers in this book can you truly call 'legendary' – maybe a dozen – no more. Although Mario Andretti has 'only' a single world championship to his name, his charisma and racing exploits across the globe in many disciplines have placed him firmly in that exalted category.

Having arrived in the United States as the teenage son of poor Italian immigrants, Andretti went on to become one of America's greatest motor racing stars in a career that spanned more than 30 years – all of them spent racing competitively at the top level. His interest in motorsport was kindled as a boy in his native Italy and, as soon as he was old enough to race seriously, he set out with his twin brother, Aldo, on the US sprint and midget racing trail, taking his first notable win in 1962 at Teanack, New Jersey. He continued to win in this class until 1964, the season that also saw his USAC debut at Trenton, where he finished 11th and pocketed the princely sum of $526.90 for his day's work!

The following year, Mario recorded his first big race win in the Hoosier Grand Prix on the way to the first of his four USAC/Indy car titles. He also took third place (and Rookie of the Year) on his Indy 500 debut. At just 25 years of age, he was the sport's youngest champion, and he repeated the feat on the back of another eight victories.

Another major milestone in Andretti's career was passed in 1967, when he entered and won the Daytona 500, and took the first of his three victories in the Sebring 12-hour race, sharing a Ford GT40 with Bruce McLaren. Although he was runner-up in the USAC championship in both 1967 and 1968, he was considered the man to beat and only bad luck prevented him from retaining his crown.

Mario's fortune changed for the better in 1969, when he won his only Indianapolis 500 and also took an additional eight wins to convincingly wrap up a third USAC championship.

Andretti had visited Monza and had idolised Alberto Ascari in his youth, and he yearned for the chance to go grand prix racing. His opportunity came with Lotus late in the 1968 season, and the American caused a sensation by putting his car on pole for the US Grand Prix at Watkins Glen. His clashing USAC commitments limited his F1 appearances at this point – and chances of success – with both Lotus (1969) and March (1970), but he shone in sports cars, winning at Sebring and Watkins Glen for Ferrari in 1970, before achieving another personal dream by signing to race for the Scuderia in Formula 1 in 1971. His start could not have been better, for he won the South African Grand Prix, followed by the non-championship Questor Grand Prix in California. He was still splitting his season between USAC racing and his Ferrari F1 and sports car programme, the latter proving most successful in 1972, when he took four wins in the 312P with Jacky Ickx.

Mario largely concentrated on American racing in 1973 and '74, racing for Vel's Parnelli in F5000 and selected USAC events. He became the runner-up in both years and, in addition, made a successful return to dirt racing to take the USAC National Dirt Racing Championship with three wins in 1974.

It was win or bust for Mario in the 1975 US F5000 championship in Vel's Lola T332. Despite consistently being the fastest man in town, however, he still had to settle for second, behind Brian Redman. It was late that year when he debuted Parnelli's grand prix contender, and he campaigned the VPJ4 throughout 1975 (and briefly in 1976) without much success, before Parnelli suddenly withdrew from Formula 1, leaving him without a ride.

Having already tried the new Lotus 77 at the Brazilian Grand Prix, Mario was so spooked by the machine that he vowed never to drive it again. He was without a ride, however, and Colin Chapman persuaded the American that the car could be a winner. Together they set about reviving the famous marque's fortunes and, by the end of the 1976 season, they were back in the winner's circle after the American had taken the car to victory in the 1976 Japanese Grand Prix.

For 1977, the team introduced the 'ground-effect' type 78 car and, in terms of sheer speed, they were in the ascendancy. Mario took the car to four victories, but too many engine failures, coupled with some ill-advised tangles with opponents, left him only third in the final standings when he could have been the champion.

Andretti made no mistake the following year, however, especially when Lotus introduced their 79 car at Zolder. He trampled the opposition, and such was the black and gold car's dominance over the opposition that Mario put it on the front row of the grid for ten successive races, seven of them on pole. He and team-mate Ronnie Peterson were irresistible, and with Mario having taken six wins by the Dutch Grand Prix, the world championship was almost in reach. Sadly, what should have been a triumphant weekend for him at Monza was blackened by the death of the popular Swede following complications after his start-line crash.

However, Mario did win the world championship magnificently that year.

It was a different story in 1979, as Lotus got it badly wrong, bogged down in a technical mire. The over-ambitious car simply was not quick enough, despite Mario's perseverance. When he finished, the car was in the points more often than not, but compared to the previous year they were slim pickings indeed.

If Andretti had thought that things could not get much worse, he was in for a shock, because the 1980 season was indeed an 'annus horribilis'. The American scraped only a single point at the last race of the season. By then, he and Chapman had finally reached a parting of the ways, and lured perhaps by sentiment as much as anything, Mario joined Alfa Romeo for 1981.

It would become another disappointing season, however, largely due to the inadequacies of the car. Mario drove as well as ever, comfortably outclassing his young team-mate, Bruno Giacomelli, but decided to return to the States in 1982 to undertake a full Indy car schedule, rather than struggle with the latest 'ground-effect' cars, which he positively hated, considering them unsophisticated and without delicacy.

Mario's return with Patrick Racing was a success, even though a victory eluded him, for second places were enough to take him into third place in the championship, despite cutting short his schedule to take up an offer he couldn't refuse when Ferrari came calling. He had already taken a drive with Williams at Long Beach after the team had been left in the lurch by Carlos Reutemann's sudden retirement.

Putting a Ferrari on pole at Monza was the stuff of dreams, even if it was a slight let-down when he finished third, despite a sticking throttle. A final race on home soil brought down the curtain on a brilliant F1 career for the 42-year-old driver, who still had plenty of mileage left in him.

Thereafter, Mario concentrated on Indy car racing full time and soon took what would be his last Indy car crown in 1984. For another decade, however, revelling in the comforting surroundings of the superbly run Newman-Haas team, he remained capable of giving anyone a race on his day. By the end of his 'Arrivederci Mario' season in 1994, Andretti's Indy car record was staggering. A record total of 407 starts, 52 wins and 66 pole positions are testimony to the amazing and enduring talent of this legendary, yes say it again, legendary racing driver!

ANDRETTI, Mario (USA) b 28/2/1940, Montona, Italy (now Motorun, Croatia)

1968 Championship position: Unplaced

	Race	Circuit	No	Entrant	Tyres	Car/Engine	Comment	Q Pos/Entries
dns	ITALIAN GP	Monza	18	Gold Leaf Team Lotus	F	3.0 Lotus 49B-Cosworth V8	raced in USA within 24 hours	(11)/24
ret	US GP	Watkins Glen	12	Gold Leaf Team Lotus	F	3.0 Lotus 49B-Cosworth V8	clutch	1/21

1969 Championship position: Unplaced

	Race	Circuit	No	Entrant	Tyres	Car/Engine	Comment	Q Pos/Entries
ret	SOUTH AFRICAN GP	Kyalami	3	Gold Leaf Team Lotus	F	3.0 Lotus 49B-Cosworth V8	transmission	6/18
ret	GERMAN GP	Nürburgring	3	Gold Leaf Team Lotus	F	3.0 Lotus 63-Cosworth V8 (4WD)	accident – lost control of car	15/26
ret	US GP	Watkins Glen	9	Gold Leaf Team Lotus	F	3.0 Lotus 63-Cosworth V8 (4WD)	rear suspension damage	13/18

1970 Championship position: 15th= Wins: 0 Pole positions: 0 Fastest laps: 0 Points scored: 4

	Race	Circuit	No	Entrant	Tyres	Car/Engine	Comment	Q Pos/Entries
ret	SOUTH AFRICAN GP	Kyalami	8	STP Corporation	F	3.0 March 701-Cosworth V8	overheating	11/24
3	SPANISH GP	Jarama	18	STP Corporation	F	3.0 March 701-Cosworth V8	1 lap behind	19/22
ret	BRITISH GP	Brands Hatch	26	STP Corporation	F	3.0 March 701-Cosworth V8	rear suspension	9/25
ret	GERMAN GP	Hockenheim	11	STP Corporation	F	3.0 March 701-Cosworth V8	gear selection	9/25
ret	AUSTRIAN GP	Österreichring	5	STP Corporation	F	3.0 March 701-Cosworth V8	accident – jammed throttle	17/24

1971 Championship position: 8th Wins: 0 Pole positions: 0 Fastest laps: 1 Points scored: 12

	Race	Circuit	No	Entrant	Tyres	Car/Engine	Comment	Q Pos/Entries
1	SOUTH AFRICAN GP	Kyalami	6	Scuderia Ferrari SpA SEFAC	F	3.0 Ferrari 312B F12	FL	4/25
ret	SPANISH GP	Montjuich Park	6	Scuderia Ferrari SpA SEFAC	F	3.0 Ferrari 312B F12	fuel pump	8/22
dnq	MONACO GP	Monte Carlo	6	Scuderia Ferrari SpA SEFAC	F	3.0 Ferrari 312B F12	missed the only dry session	20/23
ret	DUTCH GP	Zandvoort	4	Scuderia Ferrari SpA SEFAC	F	3.0 Ferrari 312B F12	fuel pump	18/24
4	GERMAN GP	Nürburgring	5	Scuderia Ferrari SpA SEFAC	F	3.0 Ferrari 312B2 F12		11/23
13	CANADIAN GP	Mosport Park	6	Scuderia Ferrari SpA SEFAC	F	3.0 Ferrari 312B2 F12	pit stop – engine/4 laps behind	13/27
dns	US GP	Watkins Glen	6	Scuderia Ferrari SpA SEFAC	F	3.0 Ferrari 312B2 F12	practised, but went to USAC race	(6)/32

1972 Championship position: 12th= Wins: 0 Pole positions: 0 Fastest laps: 0 Points scored: 4

	Race	Circuit	No	Entrant	Tyres	Car/Engine	Comment	Q Pos/Entries
ret	ARGENTINE GP	Buenos Aires	10	Scuderia Ferrari SpA SEFAC	F	3.0 Ferrari 312B2 F12	engine – misfire	9/22
4	SOUTH AFRICAN GP	Kyalami	7	Scuderia Ferrari SpA SEFAC	F	3.0 Ferrari 312B2 F12		6/27
ret	SPANISH GP	Jarama	7	Scuderia Ferrari SpA SEFAC	F	3.0 Ferrari 312B2 F12	engine	5/26
7	ITALIAN GP	Monza	3	Scuderia Ferrari SpA SEFAC	F	3.0 Ferrari 312B2 F12	pit stop – wheel/1 lap behind	7/27
6	US GP	Watkins Glen	9	Scuderia Ferrari SpA SEFAC	F	3.0 Ferrari 312B2 F12	handling problems/-1 lap	10/32

1974 Championship position: Unplaced

	Race	Circuit	No	Entrant	Tyres	Car/Engine	Comment	Q Pos/Entries
7	CANADIAN GP	Mosport Park	55	Vel's Parnelli Jones Racing	F	3.0 Parnelli VPJ4-Cosworth V8	stalled at start/1 lap behind	16/30
dsq	US GP	Watkins Glen	55	Vel's Parnelli Jones Racing	F	3.0 Parnelli VPJ4-Cosworth V8	push start on grid	3/30

1975 Championship position: 14th Wins: 0 Pole positions: 0 Fastest laps: 1 Points scored: 5

	Race	Circuit	No	Entrant	Tyres	Car/Engine	Comment	Q Pos/Entries
ret	ARGENTINE GP	Buenos Aires	27	Vel's Parnelli Jones Racing	F	3.0 Parnelli VPJ4-Cosworth V8	driveshaft – c.v. joint	10/23
7	BRAZILIAN GP	Interlagos	27	Vel's Parnelli Jones Racing	G	3.0 Parnelli VPJ4-Cosworth V8		18/23
17/ret	SOUTH AFRICAN GP	Kyalami	27	Vel's Parnelli Jones Racing	G	3.0 Parnelli VPJ4-Cosworth V8	driveshaft – c.v. joint/-8 laps	6/28
ret	SPANISH GP	Montjuich Park	27	Vel's Parnelli Jones Racing	G	3.0 Parnelli VPJ4-Cosworth V8	broken suspension – accident/FL	4/26
ret	MONACO GP	Monte Carlo	27	Vel's Parnelli Jones Racing	G	3.0 Parnelli VPJ4-Cosworth V8	broken oil line – fire	13/26
4	SWEDISH GP	Anderstorp	27	Vel's Parnelli Jones Racing	G	3.0 Parnelli VPJ4-Cosworth V8		15/26
5	FRENCH GP	Paul Ricard	27	Vel's Parnelli Jones Racing	G	3.0 Parnelli VPJ4-Cosworth V8		=15/26
12	BRITISH GP	Silverstone	27	Vel's Parnelli Jones Racing	G	3.0 Parnelli VPJ4-Cosworth V8	collision – Jarier-pit stop/-2 laps	12/28
10/ret	GERMAN GP	Nürburgring	27	Vel's Parnelli Jones Racing	G	3.0 Parnelli VPJ4-Cosworth V8	broken wheel/fuel leak/-2 laps	13/26
ret	AUSTRIAN GP	Österreichring	27	Vel's Parnelli Jones Racing	G	3.0 Parnelli VPJ4-Cosworth V8	spun off	19/30
ret	ITALIAN GP	Monza	27	Vel's Parnelli Jones Racing	G	3.0 Parnelli VPJ4-Cosworth V8	multiple accident at chicane	15/28
ret	US GP	Watkins Glen	27	Vel's Parnelli Jones Racing	G	3.0 Parnelli VPJ4-Cosworth V8	suspension	5/24

1976 Championship position: 6th Wins: 1 Pole positions: 1 Fastest laps: 1 Points scored: 22

	Race	Circuit	No	Entrant	Tyres	Car/Engine	Comment	Q Pos/Entries
ret	BRAZILIAN GP	Interlagos	6	John Player Team Lotus	G	3.0 JPS Lotus 77-Cosworth V8	collision with Peterson	16/22
6	SOUTH AFRICAN GP	Kyalami	27	Vel's Parnelli Jones Racing	G	3.0 Parnelli VPJ4B-Cosworth V8	1 lap behind	13/25
ret	US GP WEST	Long Beach	27	Vel's Parnelli Jones Racing	G	3.0 Parnelli VPJ4B-Cosworth V8	water leak	15/27
ret	SPANISH GP	Jarama	5	John Player Team Lotus	G	3.0 JPS Lotus 77-Cosworth V8	gear selection	9/30
ret	BELGIAN GP	Zolder	5	John Player Team Lotus	G	3.0 JPS Lotus 77-Cosworth V8	driveshaft	11/29
ret	SWEDISH GP	Anderstorp	5	John Player Team Lotus	G	3.0 JPS Lotus 77-Cosworth V8	engine/FL	2/27
5	FRENCH GP	Paul Ricard	5	John Player Team Lotus	G	3.0 JPS Lotus 77-Cosworth V8		7/30
ret	BRITISH GP	Brands Hatch	5	John Player Team Lotus	G	3.0 JPS Lotus 77-Cosworth V8	engine	3/30
12	GERMAN GP	Nürburgring	5	John Player Team Lotus	G	3.0 JPS Lotus 77-Cosworth V8	pit stop – battery	12/28
5	AUSTRIAN GP	Österreichring	5	John Player Team Lotus	G	3.0 JPS Lotus 77-Cosworth V8		9/25
3	DUTCH GP	Zandvoort	5	John Player Team Lotus	G	3.0 JPS Lotus 77-Cosworth V8		6/27
ret	ITALIAN GP	Monza	5	John Player Team Lotus	G	3.0 JPS Lotus 77-Cosworth V8	collision with Stuck	14/29
3	CANADIAN GP	Mosport Park	5	John Player Team Lotus	G	3.0 JPS Lotus 77-Cosworth V8		5/27
ret	US GP EAST	Watkins Glen	5	John Player Team Lotus	G	3.0 JPS Lotus 77-Cosworth V8	hit kerb – damaged suspension	11/27
1	JAPANESE GP	Mount Fuji	5	John Player Team Lotus	G	3.0 JPS Lotus 77-Cosworth V8		1/27

1977 Championship position: 3rd Wins: 4 Pole positions: 7 Fastest laps: 4 Points scored: 47

	Race	Circuit	No	Entrant	Tyres	Car/Engine	Comment	Q Pos/Entries
5/ret	ARGENTINE GP	Buenos Aires	5	John Player Team Lotus	G	3.0 JPS Lotus 78-Cosworth V8	rear wheel bearing/2 laps behind	8/21
ret	BRAZILIAN GP	Interlagos	5	John Player Team Lotus	G	3.0 JPS Lotus 78-Cosworth V8	ignition	3/22
ret	SOUTH AFRICAN GP	Kyalami	5	John Player Team Lotus	G	3.0 JPS Lotus 78-Cosworth V8	collision Reutemann – suspension	6/23
1	US GP WEST	Long Beach	5	John Player Team Lotus	G	3.0 JPS Lotus 78-Cosworth V8		2/22
1	SPANISH GP	Jarama	5	John Player Team Lotus	G	3.0 JPS Lotus 78-Cosworth V8		1/31
5	MONACO GP	Monte Carlo	5	John Player Team Lotus	G	3.0 JPS Lotus 78-Cosworth V8		10/26
ret	BELGIAN GP	Zolder	5	John Player Team Lotus	G	3.0 JPS Lotus 78-Cosworth V8	hit Watson	1/32
6	SWEDISH GP	Anderstorp	5	John Player Team Lotus	G	3.0 JPS Lotus 78-Cosworth V8	pit stop – fuel/FL	1/31
1	FRENCH GP	Dijon	5	John Player Team Lotus	G	3.0 JPS Lotus 78-Cosworth V8	FL	1/30
14/ret	BRITISH GP	Silverstone	5	John Player Team Lotus	G	3.0 JPS Lotus 78-Cosworth V8	engine/6 laps behind	6/36
ret	GERMAN GP	Hockenheim	5	John Player Team Lotus	G	3.0 JPS Lotus 78-Cosworth V8	engine	7/30

ret	AUSTRIAN GP	Österreichring	5	John Player Team Lotus	G	3.0 JPS Lotus 78-Cosworth V8	engine	3/30
ret	DUTCH GP	Zandvoort	5	John Player Team Lotus	G	3.0 JPS Lotus 78-Cosworth V8	engine	1/34
1	ITALIAN GP	Monza	5	John Player Team Lotus	G	3.0 JPS Lotus 78-Cosworth V8	FL	4/34
2	US GP EAST	Watkins Glen	5	John Player Team Lotus	G	3.0 JPS Lotus 78-Cosworth V8		4/27
9/ret	CANADIAN GP	Mosport Park	5	John Player Team Lotus	G	3.0 JPS Lotus 78-Cosworth V8	engine/FL/3 laps behind	1/27
ret	JAPANESE GP	Mount Fuji	5	John Player Team Lotus	G	3.0 JPS Lotus 78-Cosworth V8	collision with Laffite	1/23

1978 WORLD CHAMPION Wins: 6 Pole positions: 8 Fastest laps: 3 Points scored: 64

1	ARGENTINE GP	Buenos Aires	5	John Player Team Lotus	G	3.0 JPS Lotus 78-Cosworth V8		1/27
4	BRAZILIAN GP	Rio	5	John Player Team Lotus	G	3.0 JPS Lotus 78-Cosworth V8		3/28
7	SOUTH AFRICAN GP	Kyalami	5	John Player Team Lotus	G	3.0 JPS Lotus 78-Cosworth V8	pit stop – fuel/FL/1 lap behind	2/30
2	US GP WEST	Long Beach	5	John Player Team Lotus	G	3.0 JPS Lotus 78-Cosworth V8		4/30
11	MONACO GP	Monte Carlo	5	John Player Team Lotus	G	3.0 JPS Lotus 78-Cosworth V8	pit stop – fuel gauge/-6 laps	4/30
1	BELGIAN GP	Zolder	5	John Player Team Lotus	G	3.0 JPS Lotus 78-Cosworth V8		1/30
1	SPANISH GP	Jarama	5	John Player Team Lotus	G	3.0 JPS Lotus 78-Cosworth V8	FL	1/29
ret	SWEDISH GP	Anderstorp	5	John Player Team Lotus	G	3.0 JPS Lotus 78-Cosworth V8	engine	1/27
1	FRENCH GP	Paul Ricard	5	John Player Team Lotus	G	3.0 JPS Lotus 78-Cosworth V8		2/29
ret	BRITISH GP	Brands Hatch	5	John Player Team Lotus	G	3.0 JPS Lotus 78-Cosworth V8	engine	2/30
1	GERMAN GP	Hockenheim	5	John Player Team Lotus	G	3.0 JPS Lotus 78-Cosworth V8		1/30
ret	AUSTRIAN GP	Österreichring	5	John Player Team Lotus	G	3.0 JPS Lotus 78-Cosworth V8	crashed – on lap 1	2/31
1	DUTCH GP	Zandvoort	5	John Player Team Lotus	G	3.0 JPS Lotus 78-Cosworth V8		1/33
6*	ITALIAN GP	Monza	5	John Player Team Lotus	G	3.0 JPS Lotus 78-Cosworth V8	*1st, but 1 min pen jump start/FL	1/32
ret	US GP EAST	Watkins Glen	5	John Player Team Lotus	G	3.0 JPS Lotus 78-Cosworth V8	engine	1/27
10	CANADIAN GP	Montreal	5	John Player Team Lotus	G	3.0 JPS Lotus 78-Cosworth V8	spin/1 lap behind	9/28

1979 Championship position: 10th= Wins: 0 Pole positions: 0 Fastest laps: 0 Points scored: 14

5	ARGENTINE GP	Buenos Aires	1	Martini Racing Team Lotus	G	3.0 Lotus 79-Cosworth V8	1 lap behind	7/26
ret	BRAZILIAN GP	Interlagos	1	Martini Racing Team Lotus	G	3.0 Lotus 79-Cosworth V8	fuel leak – fire	4/26
4	SOUTH AFRICAN GP	Kyalami	1	Martini Racing Team Lotus	G	3.0 Lotus 79-Cosworth V8		8/26
4	US GP WEST	Long Beach	1	Martini Racing Team Lotus	G	3.0 Lotus 79-Cosworth V8		6/26
3	SPANISH GP	Jarama	1	Martini Racing Team Lotus	G	3.0 Lotus 80-Cosworth V8		4/27
ret	BELGIAN GP	Zolder	1	Martini Racing Team Lotus	G	3.0 Lotus 79-Cosworth V8	brakes	5/28
dns	"	"	1	Martini Racing Team Lotus	G	3.0 Lotus 80-Cosworth V8	practice only	– / –
ret	MONACO GP	Monte Carlo	1	Martini Racing Team Lotus	G	3.0 Lotus 80-Cosworth V8	rear suspension	=13/25
ret	FRENCH GP	Dijon	1	Martini Racing Team Lotus	G	3.0 Lotus 80-Cosworth V8	brakes/suspension/flat tyre	12/27
ret	BRITISH GP	Silverstone	1	Martini Racing Team Lotus	G	3.0 Lotus 79-Cosworth V8	wheel bearing	9/26
ret	GERMAN GP	Hockenheim	1	Martini Racing Team Lotus	G	3.0 Lotus 79-Cosworth V8	driveshaft	11/26
ret	AUSTRIAN GP	Österreichring	1	Martini Racing Team Lotus	G	3.0 Lotus 79-Cosworth V8	clutch	16/26
ret	DUTCH GP	Zandvoort	1	Martini Racing Team Lotus	G	3.0 Lotus 79-Cosworth V8	rear suspension	17/26
5	ITALIAN GP	Monza	1	Martini Racing Team Lotus	G	3.0 Lotus 79-Cosworth V8		10/28
10/ret	CANADIAN GP	Montreal	1	Martini Racing Team Lotus	G	3.0 Lotus 79-Cosworth V8	out of fuel/6 laps behind	10/29
ret	US GP EAST	Watkins Glen	1	Martini Racing Team Lotus	G	3.0 Lotus 79-Cosworth V8	gearbox	17/30

1980 Championship position: 20th= Wins: 0 Pole positions: 0 Fastest laps: 0 Points scored: 1

ret	ARGENTINE GP	Buenos Aires	11	Team Essex Lotus	G	3.0 Lotus 81-Cosworth V8	fuel metering unit	6/28
ret	BRAZILIAN GP	Interlagos	11	Team Essex Lotus	G	3.0 Lotus 81-Cosworth V8	spun off	11/28
12	SOUTH AFRICAN GP	Kyalami	11	Team Essex Lotus	G	3.0 Lotus 81-Cosworth V8	broken exhaust/2 laps behind	15/28
ret	US GP WEST	Long Beach	11	Team Essex Lotus	G	3.0 Lotus 81-Cosworth V8	collision with Jarier	15/27
ret	BELGIAN GP	Zolder	11	Team Essex Lotus	G	3.0 Lotus 81-Cosworth V8	gear linkage	17/27
7	MONACO GP	Monte Carlo	11	Team Essex Lotus	G	3.0 Lotus 81-Cosworth V8	pit stop – gear linkage/-3 laps	19/27
ret	FRENCH GP	Paul Ricard	11	Team Essex Lotus	G	3.0 Lotus 81-Cosworth V8	gearbox	12/27
ret	BRITISH GP	Brands Hatch	11	Team Essex Lotus	G	3.0 Lotus 81-Cosworth V8	gearbox	9/27
7	GERMAN GP	Hockenheim	11	Team Essex Lotus	G	3.0 Lotus 81-Cosworth V8		9/26
ret	AUSTRIAN GP	Österreichring	11	Team Essex Lotus	G	3.0 Lotus 81-Cosworth V8	engine	17/25
8/ret	DUTCH GP	Zandvoort	11	Team Essex Lotus	G	3.0 Lotus 81-Cosworth V8	out of fuel/2 laps behind	10/28
ret	ITALIAN GP	Imola	11	Team Essex Lotus	G	3.0 Lotus 81-Cosworth V8	engine	10/28
ret	CANADIAN GP	Montreal	11	Team Essex Lotus	G	3.0 Lotus 81-Cosworth V8	engine	18/28
6	US GP EAST	Watkins Glen	11	Team Essex Lotus	G	3.0 Lotus 81-Cosworth V8	1 lap behind	11/27

1981 Championship position: 17th Wins: 0 Pole positions: 0 Fastest laps: 0 Points scored: 3

4	US GP WEST	Long Beach	22	Marlboro Team Alfa Romeo	M	3.0 Alfa Romeo 179C V12		6/29
ret	BRAZILIAN GP	Rio	22	Marlboro Team Alfa Romeo	M	3.0 Alfa Romeo 179C V12	collision at start	9/30
8	ARGENTINE GP	Buenos Aires	22	Marlboro Team Alfa Romeo	M	3.0 Alfa Romeo 179C V12	1 lap behind	17/29
ret	SAN MARINO GP	Imola	22	Marlboro Team Alfa Romeo	M	3.0 Alfa Romeo 179C V12	gearbox	12/30
10	BELGIAN GP	Zolder	22	Marlboro Team Alfa Romeo	M	3.0 Alfa Romeo 179C V12	misfire/1 lap behind	18/31
ret	MONACO GP	Monte Carlo	22	Marlboro Team Alfa Romeo	M	3.0 Alfa Romeo 179C V12	hit by de Cesaris	12/31
8	SPANISH GP	Jarama	22	Marlboro Team Alfa Romeo	M	3.0 Alfa Romeo 179C V12	hit by Piquet	8/30
8	FRENCH GP	Dijon	22	Marlboro Team Alfa Romeo	M	3.0 Alfa Romeo 179C V12	1 lap behind	10/29
ret	BRITISH GP	Silverstone	22	Marlboro Team Alfa Romeo	M	3.0 Alfa Romeo 179D V12	throttle linkage	11/30
9	GERMAN GP	Hockenheim	22	Marlboro Team Alfa Romeo	M	3.0 Alfa Romeo 179E V12	1 lap behind	12/30
ret	AUSTRIAN GP	Österreichring	22	Marlboro Team Alfa Romeo	M	3.0 Alfa Romeo 179E V12	engine	13/28
ret	DUTCH GP	Zandvoort	22	Marlboro Team Alfa Romeo	M	3.0 Alfa Romeo 179D V12	tyre failure –crashed	7/30
ret	ITALIAN GP	Monza	22	Marlboro Team Alfa Romeo	M	3.0 Alfa Romeo 179D V12	engine	13/30
7	CANADIAN GP	Montreal	22	Marlboro Team Alfa Romeo	M	3.0 Alfa Romeo 179D V12	1 lap behind	16/30
ret	CAESARS PALACE GP	Las Vegas	22	Marlboro Team Alfa Romeo	M	3.0 Alfa Romeo 179D V12	rear suspension	10/30

1982 Championship position: 19th Wins: 0 Pole positions: 0 Fastest laps: 0 Points scored: 4

ret	US GP WEST	Long Beach	5	TAG Williams Team	G	3.0 Williams FW07C-Cosworth V8	accident damage	14/31
3	ITALIAN GP	Monza	28	Scuderia Ferrari SpA SEFAC	G	1.5 t/c Ferrari 126C2 V6		1/30
ret	CAESARS PALACE GP	Las Vegas	28	Scuderia Ferrari SpA SEFAC	G	1.5 t/c Ferrari 126C2 V6	rear suspension	7/30

GP Starts: 128　GP Wins: 12　Pole positions: 18　Fastest laps: 10　Points: 180

MICHAEL ANDRETTI

THE son of the legendary Mario Andretti, Michael followed his father into racing in 1980, first in Formula Ford and then in Super Vee (winning the 1982 championship). He broke into Indy cars the following season, which also saw him co-drive with his father at Le Mans, where the pair finished third in a Porsche, also driven by Philippe Alliot.

Michael soon began to make a big impact on the Indy Car scene, scoring his first win at Long Beach in 1986. From that year through to 1992 – aside from a lean spell in 1988, when he was sixth overall – he always finished in the top three in the points standings, and 1991 proved to be a record-breaking season. His Newman-Haas Lola took eight wins, accumulating a record 234 points, and he posted single-season earnings of $2,461,734.

With this pedigree, the former Indy Car champion arrived in the high-profile world of Formula 1 with McLaren in 1993 carrying great expectations, only to be embroiled in a catalogue of collisions, spins and mechanical gremlins that seemed to sap his confidence visibly race by race. A lack of testing mileage, the FIA's rationing of practice laps and his unfamiliarity with the circuits all told against the pleasant American, who was under pressure to produce results.

Just as crucial, perhaps, was the difficulty he and his first wife, Sandy, experienced in coming to terms with the way of life in Europe, preferring to fly back to the States whenever possible. By September, he had had enough. Having attained a little credibility by finishing third in the Italian GP, the younger Andretti ended his unhappy sojourn in F1 and headed back home, buoyed by the prospect of returning to the familiarity of the Indy Car circuit for 1994 with a new challenger from Reynard.

Michael lost no time in resuming his winning ways at the season-opener at Surfers Paradise, but (despite another win in Toronto) he seemed ill at ease at Ganassi Racing, and it was no surprise when he returned to his spiritual home at Newman-Haas for 1995. In the increasingly competitive world of CART racing, Michael remained one of the series' outstanding drivers. Having remarried, he became the sport's elder statesman following the departure of his great rival, Al Unser Jnr, and continued to show the speed and commitment needed to compete at the sharp end of the grid. A switch to Team Green in 2001 saw a revitalised Andretti take third place in the CART series, and the following year he set a record benchmark of 42 CART wins before making a shock defection to the Indy Racing League.

For 2003, he formed Andretti Green Racing, hiring Dario Franchitti and Tony Kanaan to race in a three-car squad. Michael soon found the dual role of owner and driver too burdensome, and after another attempt at winning the Indy 500, (he once again held an early race lead before a broken throttle linkage put him out), he called time on his glittering driving career.

More success would come in his new role, however, and he watched his four-man squad, led by Kanaan, sweep to the 2004 IRL title and enjoyed the ultimate satisfaction of winning the Indy 500 at last (albeit as a team owner) when Dan Wheldon took a brilliant victory at the Brickyard in May 2005.

Another precocious Andretti talent has since appeared on the US scene in the form of Michael's son, Marco. The young charger was fast-tracked into the AGR team for 2006, and the chance to race alongside his son in the Indy 500 proved irresistible for Michael, who made one more attempt at the 'big prize' that had always eluded him.

In the event, it was Marco who nearly stole the show, being denied a sensational rookie win at the very last gasp by Sam Hornish Jr. Michael, who also had a real chance of victory, finished third, less than a second behind his teenage prodigy. After coming so close once again, Andretti returned to the Brickyard in 2007. Following a low-key finish of 13th place, however, he announced that this would be his last Indy 500 as a driver.

Andretti goes down in history as the driver who's led the most laps of the Indianapolis 500 (431) without winning the race. He competed in 16 500s and led the race nine times. For the record, he finished 2nd (1991), 3rd (2001 and 2006), 4th (1988), 5th (1984, 1990, 1991 and 1994) and 6th (1992).

In 2007, Dario Franchitti won a rain-shortened Indy 500 for the AGR and followed this with the IRL title, but since the Scot's departure, more recent seasons have been less successful, with Team Penske and Target Chip Ganassi Racing proving the dominant forces.

ANDRETTI, Michael (USA) b 5/10/1962, Bethlehem, Pennsylvania

1993 Championship position: 11th=   Wins: 0   Pole positions: 0   Fastest laps: 0   Points scored: 7

	Race	Circuit	No	Entrant	Tyres	Capacity/Car/Engine	Comment	Q Pos/Entries
ret	SOUTH AFRICAN GP	Kyalami	7	Marlboro McLaren	G	3.5 McLaren MP4/8-Ford HB V8	accident – ran into Warwick	9/26
ret	BRAZILIAN GP	Interlagos	7	Marlboro McLaren	G	3.5 McLaren MP4/8-Ford HB V8	accident with Berger at start	5/26
ret	EUROPEAN GP	Donington	7	Marlboro McLaren	G	3.5 McLaren MP4/8-Ford HB V8	collision Wendlinger – spun off	6/26
ret	SAN MARINO GP	Imola	7	Marlboro McLaren	G	3.5 McLaren MP4/8-Ford HB V8	spun off – brake trouble	6/26
5	SPANISH GP	Barcelona	7	Marlboro McLaren	G	3.5 McLaren MP4/8-Ford HB V8	1 lap behind	7/26
8	MONACO GP	Monte Carlo	7	Marlboro McLaren	G	3.5 McLaren MP4/8-Ford HB V8	early pit stop new nose/-2 laps	9/26
14	CANADIAN GP	Montreal	7	Marlboro McLaren	G	3.5 McLaren MP4/8-Ford HB V8	started late from pits/-3 laps	12/26
6	FRENCH GP	Magny Cours	7	Marlboro McLaren	G	3.5 McLaren MP4/8-Ford HB V8	1 lap behind	16/26
ret	BRITISH GP	Silverstone	7	Marlboro McLaren	G	3.5 McLaren MP4/8-Ford HB V8	spun off first corner	11/26
ret	GERMAN GP	Hockenheim	7	Marlboro McLaren	G	3.5 McLaren MP4/8-Ford HB V8	collision, Berger – bent steering	12/26
ret	HUNGARIAN GP	Hungaroring	7	Marlboro McLaren	G	3.5 McLaren MP4/8-Ford HB V8	throttle failure	11/26
8	BELGIAN GP	Spa	7	Marlboro McLaren	G	3.5 McLaren MP4/8-Ford HB V8	stalled at pit stop/1 lap behind	14/25
3	ITALIAN GP	Monza	7	Marlboro McLaren	G	3.5 McLaren MP4/8-Ford HB V8	despite early spin/1 lap behind	9/26

GP Starts: 13   GP Wins: 0   Pole positions: 0   Fastest laps: 0   Points: 7

APICELLA, Marco (I) b 7/10/1965, Bologna

1993 Championship position: Unplaced

	Race	Circuit	No	Entrant	Tyres	Capacity/Car/Engine	Comment	Q Pos/Entries
ret	ITALIAN GP	Monza	15	Sasol Jordan	G	3.5 Jordan 193-Hart V10	collision – suspension damage	23/26

GP Starts: 1   GP Wins: 0   Pole positions: 0   Fastest laps: 0   Points: 0

MARCO APICELLA

THIS diminutive Italian was a contemporary of Caffi, Tarquini, Larini and Barbazza in the national F3 series in 1984-85. He was certainly quick but also somewhat erratic, sampling three different chassis in 1985 and taking a couple of wins at Misano. In 1986 he was teamed with Larini in Enzo Coloni's Dallaras and the young hot-shots dominated proceedings, with Apicella taking the runner-up slot. If he felt something of a bridesmaid in that formula, it was as nothing to his experiences in the FIA F3000 championship, where he spent five seasons (1987-91) as 'the man most likely to' searching in vain for a win.

After testing for both Minardi and Modena Lamborghini, he joined the wave of Europeans invading the Japanese F3000 series in a bid to revive his career. Marco was a surprise choice for a one-off Jordan ride in the 1993 Italian Grand Prix, but his F1 career was one of the shortest ever, with the unlucky driver being eliminated in a first-lap mêlée.

Tangible success came at last for the Italian when he was crowned 1994 All-Japan F3000 champion driving for the Dome team. Although the following year, when he raced the 5-Zigen team's Reynard, proved less successful, Apicella continued competing in Formula Nippon, turning in some solid performances, whilst also testing the Dome F1 challenger which ultimately failed to make an appearance in the Grand Prix arena.

In 1999 he reappeared in Europe to take occasional drives in a Riley & Scott sports car, bagging a fourth place at Brno. His vast experience was also put to good use in the newly inaugurated Italian F3000 series, Marco winning rounds at both Vallelunga and Misano for Monaco Motorsport. But it was back to Japan for Apicella as the new millennium dawned to compete in the Japanese GT series firstly in a JLOC-Lamborghini and the TOMs-Toyota in 2003-04. He was still successfully competing in 2006 back with the JLOC squad in the GT300 class.

RENÉ ARNOUX

RENÉ ARNOUX'S early career was rich with promise. Winning the Shell Volant award set him on his way in Formule Renault, but René switched to Elf in 1974 when an opportunity arose to race their F2 car, taking fourth place at Nogaro on his debut. In 1975, he competed in Formula Super Renault, winning the championship, before undertaking a full season of Formula 2 with an Elf-backed works Martini-Renault.

He was the fastest man in the championship and came agonisingly close to taking it, scoring three wins (at Pau, Enna and Estoril) and six fastest laps, but eventually he lost out to Jean-Pierre Jabouille. Resolving to iron out the errors that had cost him so dearly in 1976, Arnoux was back the following season and again won three races (at Silverstone, Pau and Nogaro), deservedly taking the coveted title.

The little Martini team, which had enjoyed enviable success in the junior formulas for many years, ambitiously moved into Formula 1 for 1978, and Arnoux was naturally entrusted with their neat Cosworth-powered car, but the underfinanced project was doomed from the start, leaving the GP novice to scratch around for drives from mid-season. He did a couple of races for Surtees, who would have dearly loved to have got his hands on him earlier, for after running a string of second-raters, he could see gold here at last. However, René was destined for greater things, joining the Renault team for 1979.

Teamed with old rival Jabouille, the still shy newcomer began to assert himself from mid-season onwards, and looked a serious championship prospect at the start of 1980. Consecutive wins in Brazil and South Africa proved sadly illusory, but the game little Frenchman never gave up the struggle, although his car let him down repeatedly.

Unfortunately for Arnoux, his nemesis, in the shape of Alain Prost, joined the team for 1981, immediately pushing the unhappy incumbent to the margins. He bounced back in 1982, however, to something like his best, all but matching Prost's speed, but not his measured performances. When he won the French GP in defiance of team orders, it seemed that a split was inevitable, and sure enough, he moved on to Ferrari for 1983.

Driving in typically forceful style, Arnoux mounted a serious championship bid on the back of three mid-season wins, but eventually fell just short, finally ending up ten points adrift of the champion, Nelson Piquet.

In 1984, his performances became increasingly inconsistent and, despite an absolutely brilliant drive at Dallas, there were times when he seemed totally uninterested. It was a situation that could not last, and early in 1985 an 'amicable' separation was agreed. Joining Ligier for 1986, Arnoux showed brief flashes of his old form in the Renault-powered car, but when he voiced criticism in the press of the Alfa engine the team had arranged to use the following season, the Italian concern immediately terminated their involvement in the project. The team was then obliged to adapt their new design to accept the Megatron engine, and suffered the inevitable consequences. Things became even worse in 1988 with the totally disastrous JS31, which perhaps was one of the most evil-handling machines of recent times.

Although no longer a contender, Arnoux blithely drove on as if he were, but by now the summit of his ambitions was a desperate search for the championship point or two that would keep his team out of the pre-qualifying trap. His ever-increasing lack of track manners and general cussedness caused mounting consternation among his fellow drivers, and by the time he retired at the end of 1989, the halcyon days of the early 1980s were all but forgotten.

The Frenchman finally returned to the track in 1994, finishing 12th at Le Mans in a Dodge Viper. He was back in 1995 with a Ferrari 333SP, but much of his time was spent acting as a driver coach and adviser to wealthy Brazilian hopeful Pedro Diniz in his attempt to carve out a top-flight grand prix career, and acting as a grand prix pundit on Italian TV.

René also owns and runs four indoor karting tracks, where he hopes to unearth and nurture possible top-line French drivers of the future. On track, the popular Arnoux was an enthusiastic competitor in the short-lived Grand Prix Masters Series of 2006/07. Having been a regular visitor at historic events, he can often be seen demonstrating Alain Prost's 1983 F1 car at World Series by Renault events.

Fast and fearless, at his peak Arnoux was the equal of Didier Pironi, Jacques Laffite, Prost and Gilles Villeneuve, and in 1983 he very nearly became France's first world champion. His record of seven grand prix wins, 18 pole positions and 181 points puts him comfortably among the sport's higher echelons.

Arnoux's big break came in 1979, when he gained a works drive with Renault. He made an immediate impression with his forceful head-down driving style.

ARNOUX, René (F) b 4/7/1948, Pontcharra, nr Grenoble

1978 Championship position: Unplaced

	Race	Circuit	No	Entrant	Tyres	Capacity/Car/Engine	Comment	Q Pos/Entries
dnq	SOUTH AFRICAN GP	Kyalami	31	Automobiles Martini	G	3.0 Martini MK23-Cosworth V8		27/30
dnpq	MONACO GP	Monte Carlo	31	Automobiles Martini	G	3.0 Martini MK23-Cosworth V8		27/30
9	BELGIAN GP	Zolder	31	Automobiles Martini	G	3.0 Martini MK23-Cosworth V8	2 laps behind	19/30
14	FRENCH GP	Paul Ricard	31	Automobiles Martini	G	3.0 Martini MK23-Cosworth V8	1 lap behind	18/29
dnp	BRITISH GP	Brands Hatch	31	Automobiles Martini	G	3.0 Martini MK23-Cosworth V8	on reserve list-no practice allowed	-./-
dnpq	GERMAN GP	Hockenheim	31	Automobiles Martini	G	3.0 Martini MK23-Cosworth V8		=29/30
9	AUSTRIAN GP	Österreichring	31	Automobiles Martini	G	3.0 Martini MK23-Cosworth V8	2 laps behind	26/31
ret	DUTCH GP	Zandvoort	31	Automobiles Martini	G	3.0 Martini MK23-Cosworth V8	rear wing mounting	23/33
9	US GP EAST	Watkins Glen	18	Team Surtees	6	3.0 Surtees TS20-Cosworth V8	1 lap behind	21/27
ret	CANADIAN GP	Montreal	18	Team Surtees	6	3.0 Surtees TS20-Cosworth V8	oil pressure	16/28

1979 Championship position: 8th Wins: 0 Pole positions: 2 Fastest laps: 2 Points scored: 17

	Race	Circuit	No	Entrant	Tyres	Capacity/Car/Engine	Comment	Q Pos/Entries
dnq/ret	ARGENTINE GP	Buenos Aires	16	Equipe Renault Elf	M	.5 t/c Renault RS01 V6	dnq – started as 1st reserve/engine	25/26
ret	BRAZILIAN GP	Interlagos	16	Equipe Renault Elf	M	1.5 t/c Renault RS01 V6	spun off – could not restart	11/26
ret	SOUTH AFRICAN GP	Kyalami	16	Equipe Renault Elf	M	1.5 t/c Renault RS01 V6	burst tyre	10/26
dns	US GP WEST	Long Beach	16	Equipe Renault Elf	M	1.5 t/c Renault RS01 V6	c.v joint on race morning	(22)/
9	SPANISH GP	Jarama	16	Equipe Renault Elf	M	1.5 t/c Renault RS01 V6	1 lap behind	11/27
ret	BELGIAN GP	Zolder	16	Equipe Renault Elf	M	1.5 t/c Renault RS01 V6	no turbo boost	18/28
ret	MONACO GP	Monte Carlo	16	Equipe Renault Elf	M	1.5 t/c Renault RS10 V6	accident – damaged suspension	19/25
3	FRENCH GP	Dijon	16	Equipe Renault Elf	M	1.5 t/c Renault RS12 V6	FL	2/27
2	BRITISH GP	Silverstone	16	Equipe Renault Elf	M	1.5 t/c Renault RS12 V6		5/26
ret	GERMAN GP	Hockenheim	16	Equipe Renault Elf	M	1.5 t/c Renault RS12 V6	puncture	10/26
6	AUSTRIAN GP	Österreichring	16	Equipe Renault Elf	M	1.5 t/c Renault RS12 V6	pit stop –fuel/FL/1 lap behind	1/26
ret	DUTCH GP	Zandvoort	16	Equipe Renault Elf	M	1.5 t/c Renault RS12 V6	collision with Regazzoni	1/26
ret	ITALIAN GP	Monza	16	Equipe Renault Elf	M	1.5 t/c Renault RS12 V6	misfire	2/28
ret	CANADIAN GP	Montreal	16	Equipe Renault Elf	M	1.5 t/c Renault RS12 V6	accident with Stuck	8/29
2	US GP EAST	Watkins Glen	16	Equipe Renault Elf	M	1.5 t/c Renault RS12 V6		7/30

1980 Championship position: 6th Wins: 2 Pole positions: 3 Fastest laps: 4 Points scored: 29

	Race	Circuit	No	Entrant	Tyres	Capacity/Car/Engine	Comment	Q Pos/Entries
ret	ARGENTINE GP	Buenos Aires	16	Equipe Renault Elf	M	1.5 t/c Renault RE21 V6	suspension	19/28
1	BRAZILIAN GP	Interlagos	16	Equipe Renault Elf	M	1.5 t/c Renault RE21 V6	FL	6/28
1	SOUTH AFRICAN GP	Kyalami	16	Equipe Renault Elf	M	1.5 t/c Renault RE21 V6	FL	2/28
9	US GP WEST	Long Beach	16	Equipe Renault Elf	M	1.5 t/c Renault RE24 V6	brake problems/2 laps behind	2/27
4	BELGIAN GP	Zolder	16	Equipe Renault Elf	M	1.5 t/c Renault RE24 V6	1 lap behind	=5/27
ret	MONACO GP	Monte Carlo	16	Equipe Renault Elf	M	1.5 t/c Renault RE24 V6	accident with Patrese	20/27
5	FRENCH GP	Paul Ricard	16	Equipe Renault Elf	M	1.5 t/c Renault RE24 V6		=2/27
nc	BRITISH GP	Brands Hatch	16	Equipe Renault Elf	M	1.5 t/c Renault RE24 V6	pit stop – brakes/9 laps behind	16/27
ret	GERMAN GP	Hockenheim	16	Equipe Renault Elf	M	1.5 t/c Renault RE25 V6	engine – valve spring	3/26
9	AUSTRIAN GP	Österreichring	16	Equipe Renault Elf	M	1.5 t/c Renault RE25 V6	pit stops – tyres/FL/1 lap behind	1/25
2	DUTCH GP	Zandvoort	16	Equipe Renault Elf	M	1.5 t/c Renault RE25 V6	FL	1/28
10	ITALIAN GP	Imola	16	Equipe Renault Elf	M	1.5 t/c Renault RE25 V6	shock absorber/2 laps behind	1/28

Out front and in control. Arnoux, in the turbocharged Ferrari 126C3 V6, heads Andrea de Cesaris (22) and Nelson Piquet at the start of the 1983 German GP. The little Frenchman put in a determined title bid on the back of three mid-season wins, but eventually he lost out to Piquet.

ret	CANADIAN GP	Montreal	16	Equipe Renault Elf	M	1.5 t/c Renault RE25 V6	brakes/gearbox	23/28
7	US GP EAST	Watkins Glen	16	Equipe Renault Elf	M	1.5 t/c Renault RE25 V6	pit stop – tyres/1 lap behind	6/27

1981 Championship position: 9th= Wins: 0 Pole positions: 4 Fastest laps: 1 Points scored: 11

8	US GP WEST	Long Beach	16	Equipe Renault Elf	M	1.5 t/c Renault RE27B V6	3 laps behind	20/29
ret	BRAZILIAN GP	Rio	16	Equipe Renault Elf	M	1.5 t/c Renault RE27B V6	start line collision	8/30
5	ARGENTINE GP	Buenos Aires	16	Equipe Renault Elf	M	1.5 t/c Renault RE27B V6		5/29
8	SAN MARINO GP	Imola	16	Equipe Renault Elf	M	1.5 t/c Renault RE27B V6	1 lap behind	3/30
dnq	BELGIAN GP	Zolder	16	Equipe Renault Elf	M	1.5 t/c Renault RE30 V6		25/31
ret	MONACO GP	Monte Carlo	16	Equipe Renault Elf	M	1.5 t/c Renault RE27B V6	spun off	13/31
dns	"	"	16	Equipe Renault Elf	M	1.5 t/c Renault RE30 V6	damaged car in practice	– / –
ret	MONACO GP	Monte Carlo	16	Equipe Renault Elf	M	1.5 t/c Renault RE30 V6	spun off	13/31
9	SPANISH GP	Jarama	16	Equipe Renault Elf	M	1.5 t/c Renault RE30 V6		17/30
4	FRENCH GP	Dijon	16	Equipe Renault Elf	M	1.5 t/c Renault RE30 V6		1/29
9/ret	BRITISH GP	Silverstone	16	Equipe Renault Elf	M	1.5 t/c Renault RE30 V6	engine/FL/4 laps behind	1/30
13	GERMAN GP	Hockenheim	16	Equipe Renault Elf	M	1.5 t/c Renault RE30 V6	pit stop – split tyre/1 lap behind	2/30
2	AUSTRIAN GP	Österreichring	16	Equipe Renault Elf	M	1.5 t/c Renault RE30 V6		1/28
ret	DUTCH GP	Zandvoort	16	Equipe Renault Elf	M	1.5 t/c Renault RE30 V6	accident	2/30
ret	ITALIAN GP	Monza	16	Equipe Renault Elf	M	1.5 t/c Renault RE30 V6	crashed	1/30
ret	CANADIAN GP	Montreal	16	Equipe Renault Elf	M	1.5 t/c Renault RE30 V6	startline collision	8/30
ret	CAESARS PALACE GP	Las Vegas	16	Equipe Renault Elf	M	1.5 t/c Renault RE30 V6	electrics	13/30

1982 Championship position: 6th Wins: 2 Pole positions: 5 Fastest laps: 1 Points scored: 28

3	SOUTH AFRICAN GP	Kyalami	16	Equipe Renault Elf	M	1.5 t/c Renault RE30B V6		1/30
ret	BRAZILIAN GP	Rio	16	Equipe Renault Elf	M	1.5 t/c Renault RE30B V6	accident with Reutemann	4/31
ret	US GP WEST	Long Beach	16	Equipe Renault Elf	M	1.5 t/c Renault RE30B V6	hit by Giacomelli	3/31
ret	SAN MARINO GP	Imola	16	Equipe Renault Elf	M	1.5 t/c Renault RE30B V6	engine	1/14
ret	BELGIAN GP	Zolder	16	Equipe Renault Elf	M	1.5 t/c Renault RE30B V6	turbo compressor	2/32
ret	MONACO GP	Monte Carlo	16	Equipe Renault Elf	M	1.5 t/c Renault RE30B V6	spun off	1/31
10	US GP (DETROIT)	Detroit	16	Equipe Renault Elf	M	1.5 t/c Renault RE30B V6	3 laps behind	15/28
ret	CANADIAN GP	Montreal	16	Equipe Renault Elf	M	1.5 t/c Renault RE30B V6	spun off	2/29
ret	DUTCH GP	Zandvoort	16	Equipe Renault Elf	M	1.5 t/c Renault RE30B V6	suspension failure – crashed	1/31
ret	BRITISH GP	Brands Hatch	16	Equipe Renault Elf	M	1.5 t/c Renault RE30B V6	startline accident – hit by Patrese	6/30
1	FRENCH GP	Paul Ricard	16	Equipe Renault Elf	M	1.5 t/c Renault RE30B V6		1/30
2	GERMAN GP	Hockenheim	16	Equipe Renault Elf	M	1.5 t/c Renault RE30B V6		3/30
ret	AUSTRIAN GP	Österreichring	16	Equipe Renault Elf	M	1.5 t/c Renault RE30B V6	turbo	5/29
ret	SWISS GP	Dijon	16	Equipe Renault Elf	M	1.5 t/c Renault RE30B V6	fuel injection/5 laps behind	2/29
1	ITALIAN GP	Monza	16	Equipe Renault Elf	M	1.5 t/c Renault RE30B V6	FL	6/30
ret	CAESARS PALACE GP	Las Vegas	16	Equipe Renault Elf	M	1.5 t/c Renault RE30B V6	engine	2/30

1983 Championship position: 3rd Wins: 3 Pole positions: 4 Fastest laps: 2 Points scored: 49

10*	BRAZILIAN GP	Rio	28	Scuderia Ferrari SpA SEFAC	G	1.5 t/c Ferrari 126C2/B V6	*2nd place car disqualified/-1 lap	6/27
3	US GP WEST	Long Beach	28	Scuderia Ferrari SpA SEFAC	G	1.5 t/c Ferrari 126C2/B V6		2/28
7	FRENCH GP	Paul Ricard	28	Scuderia Ferrari SpA SEFAC	G	1.5 t/c Ferrari 126C2/B V6	1 lap behind	4/29
3	SAN MARINO GP	Imola	28	Scuderia Ferrari SpA SEFAC	G	1.5 t/c Ferrari 126C2/B V6	1 lap behind	1/28
ret	MONACO GP	Monte Carlo	28	Scuderia Ferrari SpA SEFAC	G	1.5 t/c Ferrari 126C2/B V6	hit barrier	2/28
ret	BELGIAN GP	Spa	28	Scuderia Ferrari SpA SEFAC	G	1.5 t/c Ferrari 126C2/B V6	engine	5/28
ret	US GP (DETROIT)	Detroit	28	Scuderia Ferrari SpA SEFAC	G	1.5 t/c Ferrari 126C2/B V6	electrics	1/27
1	CANADIAN GP	Montreal	28	Scuderia Ferrari SpA SEFAC	G	1.5 t/c Ferrari 126C2/B V6		1/28
5	BRITISH GP	Silverstone	28	Scuderia Ferrari SpA SEFAC	G	1.5 t/c Ferrari 126C3 V6		1/29
1	GERMAN GP	Hockenheim	28	Scuderia Ferrari SpA SEFAC	G	1.5 t/c Ferrari 126C3 V6	FL	2/29
2	AUSTRIAN GP	Österreichring	28	Scuderia Ferrari SpA SEFAC	G	1.5 t/c Ferrari 126C3 V6		2/29
1	DUTCH GP	Zandvoort	28	Scuderia Ferrari SpA SEFAC	G	1.5 t/c Ferrari 126C3 V6	FL	10/29
2	ITALIAN GP	Monza	28	Scuderia Ferrari SpA SEFAC	G	1.5 t/c Ferrari 126C3 V6		3/29
9	EUROPEAN GP	Brands Hatch	28	Scuderia Ferrari SpA SEFAC	G	1.5 t/c Ferrari 126C3 V6	spin/1 lap behind	5/29
ret	SOUTH AFRICAN GP	Kyalami	28	Scuderia Ferrari SpA SEFAC	G	1.5 t/c Ferrari 126C3 V6	engine	4/26

1984 Championship position: 6th Wins: 0 Pole positions: 0 Fastest laps: 2 Points scored: 27

ret	BRAZILIAN GP	Rio	28	Scuderia Ferrari SpA SEFAC	G	1.5 t/c Ferrari 126C4 V6	battery	10/27
ret	SOUTH AFRICAN GP	Kyalami	28	Scuderia Ferrari SpA SEFAC	G	1.5 t/c Ferrari 126C4 V6	fuel injection	15/27
3	BELGIAN GP	Zolder	28	Scuderia Ferrari SpA SEFAC	G	1.5 t/c Ferrari 126C4 V6	FL	2/27
2	SAN MARINO GP	Imola	28	Scuderia Ferrari SpA SEFAC	G	1.5 t/c Ferrari 126C4 V6		6/28
4	FRENCH GP	Dijon	28	Scuderia Ferrari SpA SEFAC	G	1.5 t/c Ferrari 126C4 V6		11/27
3*	MONACO GP	Monte Carlo	28	Scuderia Ferrari SpA SEFAC	G	1.5 t/c Ferrari 126C4 V6	*3rd place car dsq/half points	3/27
5	CANADIAN GP	Montreal	28	Scuderia Ferrari SpA SEFAC	G	1.5 t/c Ferrari 126C4 V6	pit stop – tyres/2 laps behind	5/26
ret	US GP (DETROIT)	Detroit	28	Scuderia Ferrari SpA SEFAC	G	1.5 t/c Ferrari 126C4 V6	spun off	15/27
2	US GP (DALLAS)	Dallas	28	Scuderia Ferrari SpA SEFAC	G	1.5 t/c Ferrari 126C4 V6	started from back of grid	4/27
6	BRITISH GP	Brands Hatch	28	Scuderia Ferrari SpA SEFAC	G	1.5 t/c Ferrari 126C4 V6	collision with de Cesaris/-1 lap	13/27
6	GERMAN GP	Hockenheim	28	Scuderia Ferrari SpA SEFAC	G	1.5 t/c Ferrari 126C4 V6	pit stop – tyres/1 lap behind	10/27
7	AUSTRIAN GP	Österreichring	28	Scuderia Ferrari SpA SEFAC	G	1.5 t/c Ferrari 126C4 V6	pit stop – tyres/1 lap behind	15/28
11*/ret	DUTCH GP	Zandvoort	28	Scuderia Ferrari SpA SEFAC	G	1.5 t/c Ferrari 126C4 V6	electrics/FL/*8th & 9th cars dsq	15/27
ret	ITALIAN GP	Monza	28	Scuderia Ferrari SpA SEFAC	G	1.5 t/c Ferrari 126C4 V6	gearbox	14/27
5	EUROPEAN GP	Nürburgring	28	Scuderia Ferrari SpA SEFAC	G	1.5 t/c Ferrari 126C4 V6		6/26
9	PORTUGUESE GP	Estoril	28	Scuderia Ferrari SpA SEFAC	G	1.5 t/c Ferrari 126C4 V6	1 lap behind	17/27

1985 Championship position: 17th= Wins: 0 Pole positions: 0 Fastest laps: 0 Points scored: 3

4	BRAZILIAN GP	Rio	28	Scuderia Ferrari SpA SEFAC	G	1.5 t/c Ferrari 156/85	1 lap behind	7/25

1986 Championship position: 8th= Wins: 0 Pole positions: 0 Fastest laps: 0 Points scored: 14

4	BRAZILIAN GP	Rio	25	Equipe Ligier	P	1.5 t/c Ligier JS27-Renault V6		4/25
ret	SPANISH GP	Jerez	25	Equipe Ligier	P	1.5 t/c Ligier JS27-Renault V6	driveshaft	6/25
ret	SAN MARINO GP	Imola	25	Equipe Ligier	P	1.5 t/c Ligier JS27-Renault V6	lost wheel	8/26
5	MONACO GP	Monte Carlo	25	Equipe Ligier	P	1.5 t/c Ligier JS27-Renault V6	1 lap behind	12/26

ret	BELGIAN GP	Spa	25	Equipe Ligier	P	1.5 t/c Ligier JS27-Renault V6	engine	7/25
6	CANADIAN GP	Montreal	25	Equipe Ligier	P	1.5 t/c Ligier JS27-Renault V6	1 lap behind	5/25
ret	US GP (DETROIT)	Detroit	25	Equipe Ligier	P	1.5 t/c Ligier JS27-Renault V6	hit wall & Boutsen – suspension	4/26
5	FRENCH GP	Paul Ricard	25	Equipe Ligier	P	1.5 t/c Ligier JS27-Renault V6	1 lap behind	4/26
4	BRITISH GP	Brands Hatch	25	Equipe Ligier	P	1.5 t/c Ligier JS27-Renault V6	2 laps behind	8/26
4	GERMAN GP	Hockenheim	25	Equipe Ligier	P	1.5 t/c Ligier JS27-Renault V6		8/26
ret	HUNGARIAN GP	Hungaroring	25	Equipe Ligier	P	1.5 t/c Ligier JS27-Renault V6	engine	9/26
10	AUSTRIAN GP	Österreichring	25	Equipe Ligier	P	1.5 t/c Ligier JS27-Renault V6	pit stop – misfire/5 laps behind	12/26
ret	ITALIAN GP	Monza	25	Equipe Ligie	P	1.5 t/c Ligier JS27-Renault V6	gearbox	11/27
7	PORTUGUESE GP	Estoril	25	Equipe Ligier	P	1.5 t/c Ligier JS27-Renault V6	1 lap behind	10/27
15/ret	MEXICAN GP	Mexico City	25	Equipe Ligier	P	1.5 t/c Ligier JS27-Renault V6	engine/5 laps behind	13/26
7	AUSTRALIAN GP	Adelaide	25	Equipe Ligier	P	1.5 t/c Ligier JS27-Renault V6	pit stop – puncture/-3 laps	5/26

1987 Championship position: 19th= Wins: 0 Pole positions: 0 Fastest laps: 0 Points scored: 1

dns	SAN MARINO GP	Imola	25	Ligier Loto	G	1.5 t/c Ligier JS29B-Megatron 4	suspension in a.m. warm-up	(14)/27
6	BELGIAN GP	Spa	25	Ligier Loto	G	1.5 t/c Ligier JS29B-Megatron 4	2 laps behind	16/26
11	MONACO GP	Monte Carlo	25	Ligier Loto	G	1.5 t/c Ligier JS29B-Megatron 4	4 laps behind	22/26
10	US GP (DETROIT)	Detroit	25	Ligier Loto	G	1.5 t/c Ligier JS29B-Megatron 4	3 laps behind	21/26
ret	FRENCH GP	Paul Ricard	25	Ligier Loto	G	1.5 t/c Ligier JS29C-Megatron 4	broken exhaust	13/26
ret	BRITISH GP	Silverstone	25	Ligier Loto	G	1.5 t/c Ligier JS29C-Megatron 4	electrics	16/26
ret	GERMAN GP	Hockenheim	25	Ligier Loto	G	1.5 t/c Ligier JS29C-Megatron 4	electrics	12/26
ret	HUNGARIAN GP	Hungaroring	25	Ligier Loto	G	1.5 t/c Ligier JS29C-Megatron 4	electrics	19/26
10	AUSTRIAN GP	Österreichring	25	Ligier Loto	G	1.5 t/c Ligier JS29C-Megatron 4	3 laps behind	16/26
10	ITALIAN GP	Monza	25	Ligier Loto	G	1.5 t/c Ligier JS29C-Megatron 4	2 laps behind	15/28
ret	PORTUGUESE GP	Estoril	25	Ligier Loto	G	1.5 t/c Ligier JS29C-Megatron 4	holed intercooler	18/27
ret	SPANISH GP	Jerez	25	Ligier Loto	G	1.5 t/c Ligier JS29C-Megatron 4	engine	14/28
ret	MEXICAN GP	Mexico City	25	Ligier Loto	G	1.5 t/c Ligier JS29C-Megatron 4	ignition	18/27
ret	JAPANESE GP	Suzuka	25	Ligier Loto	G	1.5 t/c Ligier JS29C-Megatron 4	out of fuel	18/27
ret	AUSTRALIAN GP	Adelaide	25	Ligier Loto	G	1.5 t/c Ligier JS29C-Megatron 4	electrics	20/27

1988 Championship position: Unplaced

ret	BRAZILIAN GP	Rio	25	Ligier Loto	G	3.5 Ligier JS31-Judd V8	clutch	18/31
dnq	SAN MARINO GP	Imola	25	Ligier Loto	G	3.5 Ligier JS31-Judd V8		29/31
ret	MONACO GP	Monte Carlo	25	Ligier Loto	G	3.5 Ligier JS31-Judd V8	started from pit lane/electrics	20/30
ret	MEXICAN GP	Mexico City	25	Ligier Loto	G	3.5 Ligier JS31-Judd V8	accident with Caffi	20/30
ret	CANADIAN GP	Montreal	25	Ligier Loto	G	3.5 Ligier JS31-Judd V8	gearbox	20/31
ret	US GP (DETROIT)	Detroit	25	Ligier Loto	G	3.5 Ligier JS31-Judd V8	engine	20/31
dnq	FRENCH GP	Paul Ricard	25	Ligier Loto	G	3.5 Ligier JS31-Judd V8		28/31
18	BRITISH GP	Silverstone	25	Ligier Loto	G	3.5 Ligier JS31-Judd V8	3 laps behind	25/31
17	GERMAN GP	Hockenheim	25	Ligier Loto	G	3.5 Ligier JS31-Judd V8	3 laps behind	17/31
ret	HUNGARIAN GP	Hungaroring	25	Ligier Loto	G	3.5 Ligier JS31-Judd V8	engine	25/31
ret	BELGIAN GP	Spa	25	Ligier Loto	G	3.5 Ligier JS31-Judd V8	accident with de Cesaris	17/31
13	ITALIAN GP	Monza	25	Ligier Loto	G	3.5 Ligier JS31-Judd V8	2 laps behind	24/31
10	PORTUGUESE GP	Estoril	25	Ligier Loto	G	3.5 Ligier JS31-Judd V8	2 laps behind	23/31
ret	SPANISH GP	Jerez	25	Ligier Loto	G	3.5 Ligier JS31-Judd V8	throttle jammed closed	19/31
17	JAPANESE GP	Suzuka	25	Ligier Loto	G	3.5 Ligier JS31-Judd V8	pit stop – tyres/3 laps behind	23/31
ret	AUSTRALIAN GP	Adelaide	25	Ligier Loto	G	3.5 Ligier JS31-Judd V8	accident with Berger	23/31

1989 Championship position: 23rd Wins: 0 Pole positions: 0 Fastest laps: 0 Points scored: 2

dnq	BRAZILIAN GP	Rio	25	Ligier Loto	G	3.5 Ligier JS33-Cosworth V8		28/38
dnq	SAN MARINO GP	Imola	25	Ligier Loto	G	3.5 Ligier JS33-Cosworth V8		28/39
12	MONACO GP	Monte Carlo	25	Ligier Loto	G	3.5 Ligier JS33-Cosworth V8	4 laps behind	21/38
14	MEXICAN GP	Mexico City	25	Ligier Loto	G	3.5 Ligier JS33-Cosworth V8	lost use of clutch/3 laps behind	25/39
dnq	US GP (PHOENIX)	Phoenix	25	Ligier Loto	G	3.5 Ligier JS33-Cosworth V8		29/39
5	CANADIAN GP	Montreal	25	Ligier Loto	G	3.5 Ligier JS33-Cosworth V8	1 lap behind	22/39
ret	FRENCH GP	Paul Ricard	25	Ligier Loto	G	3.5 Ligier JS33-Cosworth V8	gearbox	18/39
dnq	BRITISH GP	Silverstone	25	Ligier Loto	G	3.5 Ligier JS33-Cosworth V8		27/39
11	GERMAN GP	Hockenheim	25	Ligier Loto	G	3.5 Ligier JS33-Cosworth V8	gearbox problems/3 laps behind	23/39
dnq	HUNGARIAN GP	Hungaroring	25	Ligier Loto	G	3.5 Ligier JS33-Cosworth V8		27/39
ret	BELGIAN GP	Spa	25	Ligier Loto	G	3.5 Ligier JS33-Cosworth V8	collision with Alliot	17/39
9	ITALIAN GP	Monza	25	Ligier Loto	G	3.5 Ligier JS33-Cosworth V8	2 laps behind	23/39
13	PORTUGUESE GP	Estoril	25	Ligier Loto	G	3.5 Ligier JS33-Cosworth V8	2 laps behind	23/39
dnq	SPANISH GP	Jerez	25	Ligier Loto	G	3.5 Ligier JS33-Cosworth V8		27/38
dnq	JAPANESE GP	Suzuka	25	Ligier Loto	G	3.5 Ligier JS33-Cosworth V8		27/39
ret	AUSTRALIAN GP	Adelaide	25	Ligier Loto	G	3.5 Ligier JS33-Cosworth V8	collision with Cheever	26/39

GP Starts: 149 GP Wins: 7 Pole positions: 18 Fastest laps: 12 Points: 181

ARUNDELL, Peter (GB) b 8/11/1933, Ilford, Essex – d 16/6/2009, Fakenham, Norfolk

1963 Championship position: Unplaced

	Race	Circuit	No	Entrant	Tyres	Capacity/Car/Engine	Comment	Q Pos/Entries
dns	FRENCH GP	Reims	22	Team Lotus	D	1.5 Lotus 25-Climax V8	practised, but drove in FJ event	(16)/21

1964 Championship position: 8th= Wins: 0 Pole positions: 0 Fastest laps: 0 Points scored: 11

3	MONACO GP	Monte Carlo	11	Team Lotus	D	1.5 Lotus 25-Climax V8	3 laps behind	6/20
3	DUTCH GP	Zandvoort	20	Team Lotus	D	1.5 Lotus 25-Climax V8	1 lap behind	6/18
9	BELGIAN GP	Spa	24	Team Lotus	D	1.5 Lotus 25-Climax V8	pit stop – water/4 laps behind	4/20
4	FRENCH GP	Rouen	4	Team Lotus	D	1.5 Lotus 25-Climax V8		4/17

1966 Championship position: 17th= Wins: 0 Pole positions: 0 Fastest laps: 0 Points scored: 1

dns	BELGIAN GP	Spa	11	Team Lotus	F	3.0 Lotus 43-BRM H16	engine in practice	(18)/18
ret	FRENCH GP	Reims	4	Team Lotus	F	3.0 Lotus 43-BRM H16	gearbox	16/17

ret	BRITISH GP	Brands Hatch	2	Team Lotus	F	2.0 Lotus 33-BRM V8	gear linkage	20/20
dns	"	" "	1	Team Lotus	F	2.0 Lotus 33-Climax V8	practice only	– / –
ret	DUTCH GP	Zandvoort	8	Team Lotus	F	2.0 Lotus 33-BRM V8	ignition	=15/18
8*	GERMAN GP	Nürburgring	2	Team Lotus	F	2.0 Lotus 33-BRM V8	*12th after 4 F2 cars/-1 lap	18/30
8/ret	ITALIAN GP	Monza	24	Team Lotus	F	2.0 Lotus 33-BRM V8	engine/5 laps behind	13/22
6	US GP	Watkins Glen	2	Team Lotus	F	2.0 Lotus 33-Climax V8	no practice/spin – pit stop/-7 laps	– /19
dns	"	" "	2	Team Lotus	F	3.0 Lotus 43-BRM H16	no practice time recorded	– / –
7	MEXICAN GP	Mexico City	2	Team Lotus	F	2.0 Lotus 33-BRM V8	4 laps behind	18/19

GP Starts: 11   GP Wins: 0   Pole positions: 0   Fastest laps: 0   Points: 12

PETER ARUNDELL

THE sight of Peter Arundell's vermilion-red helmet at the front of an F1 grid should have been a regular one during the mid-1960s, but sadly grand prix racing saw the true driver on only four occasions before a massive accident in a Formula 2 race at Reims effectively ended his aspirations to emulate his team-mate, Jim Clark.

Arundell began his career with an MG TC in 1957, before going on to race a Lotus XI and then a Lola sports car, soon becoming the fastest private practitioner behind the works entries. Then when Peter won an end-of-season Junior race in the front-engined Elva-DKW, Colin Chapman was not slow to recognise the Essex man's potential and signed him for his Junior team in 1960, a season that, on occasion, saw him beat both his team-mates – Trevor Taylor and Jim Clark. As number two to Taylor during 1961, Peter maintained his progress, highlighted by winning the Monaco Junior race, and for 1962 he rightfully assumed the team leadership, dominating proceedings with some brilliant displays, taking 18 wins from 25 starts and easily claiming the BARC Junior championship.

In truth, he should have been promoted to Formula 1 at this stage, and certainly there would have been a drive for him elsewhere had he chosen to seek it. Instead he waited patiently for his opportunity, knowing that a better prospect than a Lotus would be hard to find. So it was more Formula Junior in 1963, with occasional F1 outings merely confirming his talent. A superb drive into second place at the Solitude GP was matched in the Mediterranean GP at Enna.

Arundell's fully deserved promotion finally came in 1964, and he began the season in tremendous style, his grand prix performances being backed by some equally impressive results in non-championship Formula 1 races. He was second in the News of the World Trophy at Goodwood, and third at both the Aintree 200 and the Syracuse GP (shared with Spence). In the newly inaugurated Formula 2, Peter was just as impressive, taking third place at Pau, second in the Grovewood Trophy at Mallory Park and fourth in the London Trophy before the fateful Reims race, when his spinning Lotus was hit broadside by Richie Ginther. The car was smashed into an earth bank and Arundell was hurled from the cockpit, suffering a broken arm, thigh and collarbone and severe concussion.

His rehabilitation was long and slow, but Chapman promised him a place in the team when fit, and he reappeared at the South African GP on New Year's Day in 1966, to take third place in the Lotus 33. Once the season got under way, Peter seemed a shadow of his former self, though, to be fair, the machinery at his disposal hardly gave him a chance to shine. Racing the works Formula 2 car brought only a second place at the Eifelrennen, so when Graham Hill was signed for 1967 Arundell was surplus to requirements.

Really, that was the end for Peter, although in 1968 he briefly raced an Alan Mann Escort, before a short spell with the McNamara F3 and Formula Vee projects in 1969.

After moving to Florida, he founded the software company Mystique, which made several controversial adult orientated computer games in the 1980s.

Serious illness brought about his return to the UK, and he made occasional appearances at historic festivals. But after a long period of ill health, he died on 16th June, 2009.

ALBERTO ASCARI

THE son of a famous racing driver – his father, Antonio, was killed at Montlhéry when the young Ascari was just seven years old – it was perhaps inevitable that Alberto should also follow a career in the sport. After racing Bianchi motorcycles from 1937, he drove the very first Ferrari T815 sports car in the 1940 Mille Miglia with his cousin, Minozzi, the pair leading their class before retirement.

The war soon brought racing to a halt in Italy, and it was 1947 before he was back in action. Second place in a little Cisitalia in a one-make race at Gezereh Island behind Franco Cortese brought him to the fore, and he was soon impressing with his speed behind the wheel of a Maserati 4CLT. His first major success was in a sports car race at Modena that year, and he benefited greatly from the tutelage of team-mate Luigi Villoresi, whom he beat to win the 1948 San Remo GP. He was second to his mentor in the British GP and even drove once for rivals Alfa Romeo, finishing third in the French GP at Reims.

After winning the 1949 Buenos Aires GP for Maserati, both Ascari and Villoresi left for Ferrari, where Alberto would enjoy spectacular success. In his first season, he won the Swiss, Italian and Perón GPs in the T125. In 1950, Alfa were back in competition with their 158s, and Ferrari concentrated mainly on Formula 2, winning a succession of races at Modena, Mons, Rome, Reims, Garda and the Nürburgring while their T375 F1 car was being developed. Ascari did take a second at Monaco, however, and at season's end won the Penya Rhin GP at Barcelona in the new 4.5-litre car.

In 1951, Ascari won two grands prix, the might of Alfa finally being beaten, but the championship went to Juan Fangio. With the change of formula restricting GP racing to 2-litre cars for 1952 and the Alfa team disbanded, Alberto was sitting pretty. His task in taking the championship was further eased by the absence of the injured Fangio, and missing the Swiss GP to compete at Indianapolis merely denied him the opportunity of a clean sweep, as the brilliant Italian surged to six championship victories, in addition to wins at Syracuse, Pau, Marseilles, Comminges and La Baule.

It was much the same in 1953, when he trampled on the opposition to take five more championship wins, adding victories at Pau and Bordeaux to his burgeoning tally. The run of success came to a halt with a move to Lancia for 1954, which left Ascari frustrated, as the car was delayed until the end of that year. He did win the Mille Miglia in a Lancia sports car and was allowed to appear as a guest driver for both Maserati and Ferrari, putting in a brilliant drive at Monza against the works Mercedes.

With the Lancias dominant at the start of 1955, Ascari led the Argentine GP until he lost control of the car on melting tar, won the non-championship Turin GP and Naples GP at Posillipo, and led at Pau before finishing fifth. At the Monaco GP, Alberto famously crashed his car into the harbour, emerging with facial injuries, but four days later he turned up unexpectedly at Monza to test a Ferrari sports car in preparation for the forthcoming Supercortemaggiore race. For some inexplicable reason, Ascari crashed the car, and he was thrown on to the track and killed instantly. While the Italian nation mourned the loss of its finest driver, Fangio is reported to have said, "I have lost my greatest opponent." Clearly this was true, but close scrutiny of their careers reveals that only rarely did they have the opportunity to race against each other in equally matched machinery.

Over the cobbles at Monza, a masterful Ascari heads for his sixth victory of the season, in the 1952 Italian Grand Prix.

ASCARI, Alberto (I) b 13/7/1918, Milan – d 26/5/1955, Monza Circuit

1950 Championship position: 5th Wins: 0 Pole positions: 0 Fastest laps: 0 Points scored: 11

	Race	Circuit	No	Entrant	Tyres	Capacity/Car/Engine	Comment	Q Pos/Entries
2	MONACO GP	Monte Carlo	40	Scuderia Ferrari	P	1.5 s/c Ferrari 125F1 V12	1 lap behind	7/21
ret	SWISS GP	Bremgarten	18	Scuderia Ferrari	P	1.5 s/c Ferrari 125F1 V12	scavenger pump	5/18
5	BELGIAN GP	Spa	4	Scuderia Ferrari	P	3.3 Ferrari 125/275F1 V12	1 lap behind	=7/14
dns	FRENCH GP	Reims	10	Scuderia Ferrari	P	3.3 Ferrari 125/275F1 V12	took part in F2 support race	– / –
ret	ITALIAN GP	Monza	16	Scuderia Ferrari	P	4.5 Ferrari 375F1 V12	engine	2/27
2*	"	"	48	Scuderia Ferrari	P	4.5 Ferrari 375F1 V12	*took over Serafini's car	– / –

1951 Championship position: 2nd Wins: 2 Pole positions: 2 Fastest laps: 0 Points scored: 28

	Race	Circuit	No	Entrant	Tyres	Capacity/Car/Engine	Comment	Q Pos/Entries
6	SWISS GP	Bremgarten	20	Scuderia Ferrari	P	4.5 Ferrari 375F1 V12	2 laps behind	7/21
2	BELGIAN GP	Spa	8	Scuderia Ferrari	P	4.5 Ferrari 375F1 V12		4/13
ret	FRENCH GP	Reims	12	Scuderia Ferrari	E	4.5 Ferrari 375F1 V12	gearbox	3/23
2*	"	"	14	Scuderia Ferrari	E/P	4.5 Ferrari 375F1 V12	*took over González's car	– / –
ret	BRITISH GP	Silverstone	11	Scuderia Ferrari	P	4.5 Ferrari 375F1 V12	gearbox	4/20
1	GERMAN GP	Nürburgring	71	Scuderia Ferrari	P	4.5 Ferrari 375F1 V12		1/23
1	ITALIAN GP	Monza	2	Scuderia Ferrari	P	4.5 Ferrari 375F1 V12		3/22
4	SPANISH GP	Pedralbes	2	Scuderia Ferrari	P	4.5 Ferrari 375F1 V12	tyre problems/2 laps behind	1/20

1952 WORLD CHAMPION Wins: 6 Pole positions: 5 Fastest laps: 6 (1 shared) Points scored: 53.5

	Race	Circuit	No	Entrant	Tyres	Capacity/Car/Engine	Comment	Q Pos/Entries
1	BELGIAN GP	Spa	4	Scuderia Ferrari	P	2.0 Ferrari 500 4	FL	1/22
1	FRENCH GP	Rouen	8	Scuderia Ferrari	P	2.0 Ferrari 500 4	FL	1/20
1	BRITISH GP	Silverstone	15	Scuderia Ferrari	P	2.0 Ferrari 500 4	FL	2/32
1	GERMAN GP	Nürburgring	101	Scuderia Ferrari	E	2.0 Ferrari 500 4	FL	1/32
1	DUTCH GP	Zandvoort	2	Scuderia Ferrari	P	2.0 Ferrari 500 4	FL	1/18
1	ITALIAN GP	Monza	12	Scuderia Ferrari	P	2.0 Ferrari 500 4	FL (shared with González)	1/35

1953 WORLD CHAMPION Wins: 5 Pole positions: 6 Fastest laps: 5 (2 shared) Points scored: 47

	Race	Circuit	No	Entrant	Tyres	Capacity/Car/Engine	Comment	Q Pos/Entries
1	ARGENTINE GP	Buenos Aires	10	Scuderia Ferrari	P	2.0 Ferrari 500 4	FL	1/16
1	DUTCH GP	Zandvoort	2	Scuderia Ferrari	P	2.0 Ferrari 500 4		1/20
1	BELGIAN GP	Spa	10	Scuderia Ferrari	P	2.0 Ferrari 500 4		2/22
4	FRENCH GP	Reims	10	Scuderia Ferrari	P	2.0 Ferrari 500 4	FL (shared with Fangio)	1/25
1	BRITISH GP	Silverstone	5	Scuderia Ferrari	P	2.0 Ferrari 500 4	FL (shared with González)	1/29
8*	GERMAN GP	Nürburgring	1	Scuderia Ferrari	P	2.0 Ferrari 500 4	lost wheel/*Villoresi took car/-1 lap	1/35
ret	"	"	4	Scuderia Ferrari	P	2.0 Ferrari 500 4	engine/took Villoresi's car/FL	– / –
1	SWISS GP	Bremgarten	46	Scuderia Ferrari	P	2.0 Ferrari 500 4	FL	2/23
ret	ITALIAN GP	Monza	4	Scuderia Ferrari	P	2.0 Ferrari 500 4	collision with Marimón	1/30

1954 Championship position: 25th Wins: 0 Pole positions: 0 Fastest laps: 2 (1 shared) Points scored: 1.14

	Race	Circuit	No	Entrant	Tyres	Capacity/Car/Engine	Comment	Q Pos/Entries
ret	FRENCH GP	Reims	10	Officine Alfieri Maserati	P	2.5 Maserati 250F 6	engine	3/22
ret	BRITISH GP	Silverstone	31	Officine Alfieri Maserati	P	2.5 Maserati 250F 6	con rod/FL (shared)	29/31
ret	"	"	32	Officine Alfieri Maserati	P	2.5 Maserati 250F 6	took Villoresi's car/con rod	– / –
ret	ITALIAN GP	Monza	34	Scuderia Ferrari	E	2.5 Ferrari 625 4	engine	2/21
ret	SPANISH GP	Pedralbes	34	Scuderia Lancia	P	2.5 Lancia D50 V8	clutch/FL	1/22

1955 Championship position: Unplaced

	Race	Circuit	No	Entrant	Tyres	Capacity/Car/Engine	Comment	Q Pos/Entries
ret	ARGENTINE GP	Buenos Aires	32	Scuderia Lancia	P	2.5 Lancia D50 V8	spun off on melting tar	3/22
ret	MONACO GP	Monte Carlo	26	Scuderia Lancia	P	2.5 Lancia D50 V8	crashed into harbour – unhurt	2/22

GP Starts: 31 GP Wins: 13 Pole positions: 14 Fastest laps: 13 Points: 140.64

ASHDOWN, Peter (GB) b 16/10/1934, Danbury, nr Chelmsford, Essex

1959 Championship position: Unplaced

	Race	Circuit	No	Entrant	Tyres	Capacity/Car/Engine	Comment	Q Pos/Entries
12	BRITISH GP (F2)	Aintree	52	Alan Brown Equipe	D	1.5 Cooper T45-Climax 4	3rd F2 car/6 laps behind	23/30

GP Starts: 1 GP Wins: 0 Pole positions: 0 Fastest laps: 0 Points: 0

PETER ASHDOWN

ALTHOUGH his sole grand prix appearance was in a Cooper, Peter Ashdown's reputation was built as a Lotus driver. Consistently high placings in the marque's early sports cars between 1955 and 1957 brought him a works drive, but a broken collarbone sustained in a crash at Rouen early in 1958 interrupted his season. Then, a chance meeting with Eric Broadley gave him a seat in the Lola Mk1 in 1959, when Peter drove some sparkling races in the excellent machine, becoming the man to beat in his class. He took a fine class win at Rouen and then won the Auvergne Trophy at Clermont-Ferrand, beating Behra's RS Porsche. His gift for handling small-capacity sports cars was further underlined by class wins in the Nürburgring 1000km in both 1960 and 1962.

Aside from his Aintree F1 appearance, there were no further opportunities to compete in grands prix, but Peter raced in Formula Junior, where he took second place behind Henry Taylor's Cooper at Monaco in 1960, but a poor 1961 season with the troublesome Mk3 Lola blunted his enthusiasm. After escaping a heavy crash at Silverstone in a Lotus 20, followed by few saloon car drives, this talented driver drifted into retirement.

IAN ASHLEY

ASHLEY raced extensively in Formula Ford, F3 and F5000 from 1967 to 1975, often showing great speed, but not always the ability to keep the car on the road. He owed his few opportunities at grand prix level mainly to his spirited performances in the big-engined F5000 cars. In 1972, he grabbed the opportunity to drive a decidedly elderly Lola T190 in which he harried competitors with much better equipment, but it was mid-way through the following year that a new and much more mature driver blossomed. After his Lola T330 had been sorted with the help of Frank Gardner, and previous engine maladies were eliminated, Ashley took a win at Jyllandsringen in Denmark and he became a serious front-runner.

Ian remained in the category for 1974, and in mid-season he took his Lola to the better-equipped ShellSport Team, which brought him a couple of wins – and the chance to drive the grand prix Token, previously handled by Tom Pryce and David Purley. Ashley did extremely well to qualify the car at the Nürburgring, and was running very well in the race before a puncture ruined things. More tyre and wheel problems afflicted his next race in Austria, and his loyal sponsors decided their driver would be better off elsewhere. They purchased a Brabham BT42, which turned out to be a real dog, and Ashley was left to rue his loyalty after previously turning down the offer of a drive with Surtees.

So in 1975 it was back to F5000, which was on its last legs as a series. The season started splendidly with him looking a good bet for championship honours, but another call to Formula 1 would undo all his good work. After reaching an agreement to drive for Williams at the German Grand Prix, Ian was also offered the chance to drive for Lotus in the same race. Although the latter offer was more promising, Ashley drove the Williams and it cost him dearly. A broken engine mounting pitched him into the Armco at 160mph, and a chipped ankle sidelined him from the race and a subsequent round of the Shellsport series. Not only had Ian's opportunity to race for Lotus evaporated, but also his F5000 championship bid faltered with a rash of engine problems. In the end, Ashley failed to show for the finale after splitting with long-time sponsor Richard Oaten.

For 1976, Ian signed up to drive the lamentable Stanley-BRM. The team did make the opening race in Brazil, but the engine lasted just two laps, and the whole operation went into limbo, leaving him without a drive of any description. He went back to Formula 3. Eventually, in mid-1977, he returned to Formula 1 with Hesketh, but it was another shambolic effort that gave the talented driver no real chance to succeed. It all ended disastrously for Ashley at Mosport, where another mechanical failure resulted in a huge shunt from which he was lucky to escape alive. He did receive serious leg injuries, however, from which he made a slow recovery

With racing off the menu, Ashley took up the same career as his father and became a pilot, eventually making a very good living flying Lear jets. His long-time friendship with Emerson Fittipaldi resulted in a return to the track in the IndyCar series. After a promising debut at the end of 1985, he eventually found a berth with Dick Simon in mid-1986. But once again it was something of a disaster, the car not being well prepared or competitive. A recurring story for the driver...

The itch to go racing remained, however, and after he tried his hand at racing motorcycles in America, he decided to compete in sidecar outfits in the European championships in 1990. Still looking trim and fit, subsequently he contested the fiercely competitive BTCC series in a Vauxhall Cavalier as a privateer in 1993. The thrill of danger and speed had obviously not deserted Ashley, who then returned to sidecars at world championship level before reverting to four-wheels once more in the TVR Tuscan series. He is still involved in the sport, mainly in historic racing as both a mechanic and driver.

ASHLEY, Ian (GB) b 26/10/1947, Wuppertal, Germany

	Race	Circuit	No	Entrant	Tyres	Capacity/Car/Engine	Comment	Q Pos/Entries
	1974 Championship position: Unplaced							
14	GERMAN GP	Nürburgring	32	Token Racing	F	3.0 Token RJ02-Cosworth V8	1 lap behind	26/32
nc	AUSTRIAN GP	Österreichring	35	Token Racing	F	3.0 Token RJ02-Cosworth V8	2 stops – wheel problems/-8 laps	25/31
dnq	CANADIAN GP	Mosport Park	42	Chequered Flag/Richard Oaten	G	3.0 Brabham BT42-Cosworth V8		30/30
dnq	US GP	Watkins Glen	42	Chequered Flag/Richard Oaten	G	3.0 Brabham BT42-Cosworth V8		29/30
	1975 Championship position: Unplaced							
dns	GERMAN GP	Nürburgring	20	Frank Williams Racing Cars	G	3.0 Williams FW03-Cosworth V8	practice accident – leg injuries	(20)/26
	1976 Championship position: Unplaced							
ret	BRAZILIAN GP	Interlagos	14	Stanley BRM	G	3.0 BRM P201B V12	oil pump	21/22
	1977 Championship position: Unplaced							
dnq	AUSTRIAN GP	Österreichring	39	Hesketh Racing	G	3.0 Hesketh 308E-Cosworth V8		28/30
dnq	DUTCH GP	Zandvoort	39	Hesketh Racing	G	3.0 Hesketh 308E-Cosworth V8		30/34
dnq	ITALIAN GP	Monza	25	Hesketh Racing	G	3.0 Hesketh 308E-Cosworth V8		30/34
17	US GP EAST	Watkins Glen	25	Hesketh Racing	G	3.0 Hesketh 308E-Cosworth V8	pit stop – wheel bearing/-4 laps	22/27
dns	CANADIAN GP	Mosport Park	25	Hesketh Racing	G	3.0 Hesketh 308E-Cosworth V8	injured in practice accident	(26)/27

GP Starts: 4   GP Wins: 0   Pole positions: 0   Fastest laps: 0   Points: 0

GERRY ASHMORE

FROM a motor racing family – his father Joe was a prominent post-war driver – Gerry Ashmore and his younger brother, Chris, were inevitably caught up in a motor racing environment. His father had long been a friend and racing cohort of Reg Parnell, and after cutting his teeth racing Jaguars, Gerry ambitiously joined forces with Parnell's son, Tim. They bought a pair of Lotus 18s and took in a plethora on minor races across the Continent in 1961.

By far his best result was second place in the Naples GP. It was held on the same day as the Monaco Grand Prix, so naturally the field was devoid of stellar drivers, but Ashmore impressed by taking pole position, ahead of Roy Salvadori and Italy's newest star, Giancarlo Baghetti. Although well behind Baghetti's Ferrari, Ashmore was still ahead of Lorenzo Bandini's Cooper-Maserati at the finish.

Gerry courted disaster on his next visit to Italy, however, crashing into the trees – luckily without long-term injury – on the first lap of the Italian GP in a separate accident to the one that killed Wolfgang von Trips and 15 spectators in the same race.

After a handful of unsuccessful races in 1962 (the Lotus now upgraded to 18/21 specification), Ashmore continued to make occasional appearances, such as in 1965 with the ex-David Prophet Lotus 30, and in 1970 driving a Lotus Elan 2+2.

BILL ASTON

THIS amateur racing enthusiast had served in the First World War and began his career on motorcycles before switching to four-wheel competition. In the late 1940s, Bill Aston was a front-runner with a 500cc Cooper-JAP in the extremely competitive Formula 3 class. As well as wins at home, he took a prestigious Continental victory at Brussels and placed second at Zandvoort in 1949. In 1951, his Cooper – now with an 1100cc engine – led the GP des Frontières at Chimay before the engine seized, but he did take a third place at Goodwood in the Lavant Cup, then a five-lap sprint race.

His business dealings as both civil engineer and fruit farmer no doubt helped finance his Aston-Butterworth Formula 2 single-seaters, which he ran with Robin Montgomerie-Charrington. Unfortunately, these small and beautifully bodied machines saw little success, being constantly afflicted by fuel system problems. Aston sensibly withdrew from the giddy heights of the grand prix world after this unsuccessful foray, but continued to enjoy racing at club events. In the late 1950s, he raced a Jaguar D-Type and Aston Martin DBR1, often winning his class. Even when he was well past 60 years of age, Bill continued to race (and win) with a Mini and the ex-Equipe Endeavour Jaguar 3.8 saloon.

ASHMORE, Gerry (GB) b 25/7/1936, West Bromwich, Staffordshire

1961 Championship position: Unplaced

	Race	Circuit	No	Entrant	Tyres	Capacity/Car/Engine	Comment	Q Pos/Entries
ret	BRITISH GP	Aintree	40	Gerry Ashmore	D	1.5 Lotus 18-Climax 4	ignition – misfire	26/30
16	GERMAN GP	Nürburgring	27	Gerry Ashmore	D	1.5 Lotus 18-Climax 4	2 laps behind	25/27
ret	ITALIAN GP	Monza	18	Gerry Ashmore	D	1.5 Lotus 18-Climax 4	accident on lap 1	25/33

1962 Championship position: Unplaced

	Race	Circuit	No	Entrant	Tyres	Capacity/Car/Engine	Comment	Q Pos/Entries
dnq	ITALIAN GP	Monza	52	Gerry Ashmore	D	1.5 Lotus 18/21-Climax 4		24/30

GP Starts: 3   GP Wins: 0   Pole positions: 0   Fastest laps: 0   Points: 0

ASTON, Bill (GB) b 29/3/1900, Stafford – d 4/3/1974, Lingfield, Surrey

1952 Championship position: Unplaced

	Race	Circuit	No	Entrant	Tyres	Capacity/Car/Engine	Comment	Q Pos/Entries
dns	BRITISH GP	Silverstone	2	W S Aston	D	2.0 Aston-Butterworth F4	too slow	30/32
ret	GERMAN GP	Nürburgring	114	W S Aston	D	2.0 Aston-Butterworth F4	oil pressure	21/32
dnq	ITALIAN GP	Monza	64	W S Aston	D	2.0 Aston-Butterworth F4		31/35

GP Starts: 1   GP Wins: 0   Pole positions: 0   Fastest laps: 0   Points: 0

RICHARD ATTWOOD

WHILE training as a trade apprentice at Jaguar, Richard Attwood made his competition debut in the 1960 season with a Triumph TR3, before joining the Midland Racing Partnership to race in Formula Junior, spending most of 1961 and 1962 at club level. In 1963, driving a Mk5A Lola-Ford, 'Dickie' shot to international prominence by winning the Monaco Formula Junior race, and his performances won him the first Grovewood Award and the princely sum of £500!

In 1964, Attwood was given a couple of chances in the works BRM, taking fourth in the non-championship News of the World Trophy at Goodwood, but failing to start in the experimental four-wheel-drive single-seater BRM P67 at the British Grand Prix.

Racing in the newly introduced Formula 2 for Midland Racing Partnership, he produced some excellent performances, most notably a win at Aspern in the Vienna GP and second place – behind Clark – at Pau, plus further runner-up spots in the Eifelrennen and at Albi. His all-round ability was now being recognised more widely,

and he became a founder member of the Ford sports-prototype team.

Joining Parnell Racing for 1965, Richard drove the team's none-too-quick Lotus 25-BRM to two points-scoring finishes, while in Formula 2 he was second again at Pau, and won the Rome GP at Vallelunga. His sports car career was now taking off, and he began what would be a long and successful partnership with David Piper, ending the season with a fantastic drive to win the Rand 9 Hours in Piper's Ferrari 365 P2.

Driving for BRM in the 1966 Tasman series, Attwood won the Gold Leaf Trophy race at Levin before another season of F2 and sports car events, which once again ended with a win at Kyalami in the Rand 9 Hours. Despite another successful Tasman interlude in New Zealand, where he took two second places and two thirds in four starts, Richard's only other single-seater drive in 1967 was a run in the works Cooper at Mosport, deputising for the injured Pedro Rodriguez.

When Mike Spence was so tragically killed at Indianapolis, early in 1968, Attwood was signed to replace him at BRM. His debut for the team at Monaco was stunning, 'Dickie' taking second place and fastest lap. Unfortunately, subsequent performances were not so impressive, and after the German GP he was released from his contract, returning to sports car racing.

In 1969, he was called back to F1 to try to reprise his Monaco performance for Lotus when Jochen Rindt was recovering from injuries received at Montjuich. Once again he showed his affinity with the streets of the principality by scoring a fine fourth place. Later in the season, he took Frank Williams' F2 Brabham to sixth (and second in class) in the German Grand Prix at the Nürburgring. That was also the year when he raced a factory Porsche for the first time, sharing a 908 Spyder with Elford to take second place in the BOAC 500 at Brands Hatch.

In 1970, he scored his greatest triumph, winning the Le Mans 24-hours race in a Porsche 917 with Hans Herrmann, and taking second place (also with the veteran German) at the Nürburgring 1000km. In 1971, Attwood's final racing year, he drove the John Wyer/Gulf Porsche, winning the Österreichring 1000km with Pedro Rodriguez, and finishing second at Le Mans with Herbert Müller.

Attwood retired at the end of the season for business reasons, but occasionally he was tempted back to the circuits in the 1980s, most notably at Le Mans in 1984, when he raced a Nimrod.

Now working for Porsche GB as an instructor and development adviser, Attwood's racing skills can still to be appreciated, as he is a popular competitor on the historic sports car scene, being a regular at Goodwood and many other high-profile events.

ATTWOOD, Richard (GB) b 4/4/1940, Wolverhampton, Staffordshire

1964 Championship position: Unplaced

	Race	Circuit	No	Entrant	Tyres	Capacity/Car/Engine	Comment	Q Pos/Entries
dns	BRITISH GP	Brands Hatch	21	Owen Racing Organisation	D	1.5 BRM P67 V8 4WD	car withdrawn	(24)/25

1964 Championship position: 14th= Wins: 0 Pole positions: 0 Fastest laps: 0 Points scored: 2

	Race	Circuit	No	Entrant	Tyres	Capacity/Car/Engine	Comment	Q Pos/Entries
ret	MONACO GP	Monte Carlo	15	Reg Parnell (Racing	D	1.5 Lotus 25-BRM V8	lost wheel	6/17
14/ret	BELGIAN GP	Spa	23	Reg Parnell (Racing)	D	1.5 Lotus 25-BRM V8	spun off in rain/6 laps behind	13/21
13	BRITISH GP	Silverstone	22	Reg Parnell (Racing)	D	1.5 Lotus 25-BRM V8	pit stops/17 laps behind	16/23
12	DUTCH GP	Zandvoort	34	Reg Parnell (Racing)	D	1.5 Lotus 25-BRM V8	3 laps behind	17/17
ret	GERMAN GP	Nürburgring	20	Reg Parnell (Racing)	D	1.5 Lotus 25-BRM V8	water hose leak	17/22
6	ITALIAN GP	Monza	40	Reg Parnell (Racing)	D	1.5 Lotus 25-BRM V8	1 lap behind	13/23
10	US GP	Watkins Glen	21	Reg Parnell (Racing)	D	1.5 Lotus 25-BRM V8	pit stop/9 laps behind	=16/18
6	MEXICAN GP	Mexico City	21	Reg Parnell (Racing)	D	1.5 Lotus 25-BRM V8	1 lap behind	17/18

1967 Championship position: Unplaced

	Race	Circuit	No	Entrant	Tyres	Capacity/Car/Engine	Comment	Q Pos/Entries
10	CANADIAN GP	Mosport Park	8	Cooper Car Co	F	3.0 Cooper T81B-Maserati V12	6 laps behind	14/19

1968 Championship position: 13th= Wins: 0 Pole positions: 0 Fastest laps: 1 Points scored: 6

	Race	Circuit	No	Entrant	Tyres	Capacity/Car/Engine	Comment	Q Pos/Entries
2	MONACO GP	Monte Carlo	15	Owen Racing Organisation	D	3.0 BRM P126 V12	FL	6/18
ret	BELGIAN GP	Spa	12	Owen Racing Organisation	D	3.0 BRM P126 V12	broken oil pipe	11/18
7	DUTCH GP	Zandvoort	16	Owen Racing Organisation	D	3.0 BRM P126 V12	5 laps behind	15/19
7	FRENCH GP	Rouen	22	Owen Racing Organisation	D	3.0 BRM P126 V12	pit stop – tyres/3 laps behind	=13/18
ret	BRITISH GP	Brands Hatch	11	Owen Racing Organisation	D	3.0 BRM P126 V12	radiator holed by stone	15/20
14	GERMAN GP	Nürburgring	11	Owen Racing Organisation	D	3.0 BRM P126 V12	1 lap behind	20/20

1969 Championship position: 13th= Wins: 0 Pole positions: 0 Fastest laps: 0 Points scored: 3

	Race	Circuit	No	Entrant	Tyres	Capacity/Car/Engine	Comment	Q Pos/Entries
4	MONACO GP	Monte Carlo	2	Gold Leaf Team Lotus	F	3.0 Lotus 49B-Cosworth V8		10/16
6*	GERMAN GP (F2)	Nürburgring	29	Frank Williams Racing Cars	D	1.6 Brabham BT30-Cosworth 4	2nd in F2 class/*no points scored	20/26

GP Starts: 17 GP Wins: 0 Pole positions: 0 Fastest laps: 1 Points: 11

BADOER, Luca (I) b 25/1/1971, Montebelluna, Treviso

1993 Championship position: Unplaced

	Race	Circuit	No	Entrant	Tyres	Capacity/Car/Engine	Comment	Q Pos/Entries
ret	SOUTH AFRICAN GP	Kyalami	22	BMS Scuderia Italia SpA	G	3.5 Lola T93/30 BMS-Ferrari V12	gearbox	26/26
12	BRAZILIAN GP	Interlagos	22	BMS Scuderia Italia SpA	G	3.5 Lola T93/30 BMS-Ferrari V12	pit stop – new nose/3 laps behind	21/26
dnq	EUROPEAN GP	Donington	22	BMS Scuderia Italia SpA	G	3.5 Lola T93/30 BMS-Ferrari V12		26/26
7	SAN MARINO GP	Imola	22	BMS Scuderia Italia SpA	G	3.5 Lola T93/30 BMS-Ferrari V12	3 laps behind	24/26
ret	SPANISH GP	Barcelona	22	BMS Scuderia Italia SpA	G	3.5 Lola T93/30 BMS-Ferrari V12	clutch	22/26
dnq	MONACO GP	Monte Carlo	22	BMS Scuderia Italia SpA	G	3.5 Lola T93/30 BMS-Ferrari V12		26/26
15	CANADIAN GP	Montreal	22	BMS Scuderia Italia SpA	G	3.5 Lola T93/30 BMS-Ferrari V12	4 laps behind	25/26
ret	FRENCH GP	Magny Cours	22	BMS Scuderia Italia SpA	G	3.5 Lola T93/30 BMS-Ferrari V12	suspension	22/26
ret	BRITISH GP	Silverstone	22	BMS Scuderia Italia SpA	G	3.5 Lola T93/30 BMS-Ferrari V12	engine – electrics	25/26
ret	GERMAN GP	Hockenheim	22	BMS Scuderia Italia SpA	G	3.5 Lola T93/30 BMS-Ferrari V12	suspension	25/26
ret	HUNGARIAN GP	Hungaroring	22	BMS Scuderia Italia SpA	G	3.5 Lola T93/30 BMS-Ferrari V12	spun off	26/26
13	BELGIAN GP	Spa	22	BMS Scuderia Italia SpA	G	3.5 Lola T93/30 BMS-Ferrari V12	2 laps behind	24/25
10	ITALIAN GP	Monza	22	BMS Scuderia Italia SpA	G	3.5 Lola T93/30 BMS-Ferrari V12	2 laps behind	25/26
14	PORTUGUESE GP	Estoril	22	BMS Scuderia Italia SpA	G	3.5 Lola T93/30 BMS-Ferrari V12	3 laps behind	26/26

1995 Championship position: Unplaced

	Race	Circuit	No	Entrant	Tyres	Capacity/Car/Engine	Comment	Q Pos/Entries
ret	BRAZILIAN GP	Interlagos	24	Minardi Scuderia Italia	G	3.0 Minardi M195-Ford EDM V8	gearbox	18/26
ret/dns	ARGENTINE GP	Buenos Aires	24	Minardi Scuderia Italia	G	3.0 Minardi M195-Ford EDM V8	accident at first start	(13)/26
14	SAN MARINO GP	Imola	24	Minardi Scuderia Italia	G	3.0 Minardi M195-Ford EDM V8	4 laps behind	20/26
ret	SPANISH GP	Barcelona	24	Minardi Scuderia Italia	G	3.0 Minardi M195-Ford EDM V8	gearbox	21/26
ret	MONACO GP	Monte Carlo	24	Minardi Scuderia Italia	G	3.0 Minardi M195-Ford EDM V8	suspension	16/26
8	CANADIAN GP	Montreal	24	Minardi Scuderia Italia	G	3.0 Minardi M195-Ford EDM V8	1 lap behind	19/24
13	FRENCH GP	Magny Cours	24	Minardi Scuderia Italia	G	3.0 Minardi M195-Ford EDM V8	3 laps behind	17/24
10	BRITISH GP	Silverstone	24	Minardi Scuderia Italia	G	3.0 Minardi M195-Ford EDM V8	1 lap behind	18/24
ret	GERMAN GP	Hockenheim	24	Minardi Scuderia Italia	G	3.0 Minardi M195-Ford EDM V8	gearbox	16/24
8	HUNGARIAN GP	Hungaroring	24	Minardi Scuderia Italia	G	3.0 Minardi M195-Ford EDM V8	2 laps behind	12/24
ret	BELGIAN GP	Spa	24	Minardi Scuderia Italia	G	3.0 Minardi M195-Ford EDM V8	spun off	19/24
ret	ITALIAN GP	Monza	24	Minardi Scuderia Italia	G	3.0 Minardi M195-Ford EDM V8	accident	18/24
14	PORTUGUESE GP	Estoril	24	Minardi Scuderia Italia	G	3.0 Minardi M195-Ford EDM V8	3 laps behind	18/24
11	EUROPEAN GP	Nürburgring	24	Minardi Scuderia Italia	G	3.0 Minardi M195-Ford EDM V8	3 laps behind	18/24
15	PACIFIC GP	T.I. Circuit	24	Minardi Scuderia Italia	G	3.0 Minardi M195-Ford EDM V8	3 laps behind	16/24
9	JAPANESE GP	Suzuka	24	Minardi Scuderia Italia	G	3.0 Minardi M195-Ford EDM V8	2 laps behind	18/24
dns	AUSTRALIAN GP	Adelaide	24	Minardi Scuderia Italia	G	3.0 Minardi M195-Ford EDM V8	electrical problem before start	(15)/24

1996 Championship position: Unplaced

	Race	Circuit	No	Entrant	Tyres	Capacity/Car/Engine	Comment	Q Pos/Entries
dnq	AUSTRALIAN GP	Melbourne	22	Forti Grand Prix	G	3.0 Forti FG01 95B-Ford Zetec R V8	not within 107% of pole	21/22
11	BRAZILIAN GP	Interlagos	22	Forti Grand Prix	G	3.0 Forti FG01 95B-Ford Zetec R V8	4 laps behind	19/22
ret	ARGENTINE GP	Buenos Aires	22	Forti Grand Prix	G	3.0 Forti FG01 95B-Ford Zetec R V8	accident – car overturned	21/22
dnq	EUROPEAN GP	Nürburgring	22	Forti Grand Prix	G	3.0 Forti FG01 95B-Ford Zetec R V8	not within 107% of pole	22/22
10	SAN MARINO GP	Imola	22	Forti Grand Prix	G	3.0 Forti FG03 97-Ford Zetec R V8	4 laps behind	21/22
ret	MONACO GP	Monte Carlo	22	Forti Grand Prix	G	3.0 Forti FG03 97-Ford Zetec R V8	collision with Villeneuve	21/22
dnq	SPANISH GP	Barcelona	22	Forti Grand Prix	G	3.0 Forti FG03-97 Ford Zetec R V8	not within 107% of pole	21/22
ret	CANADIAN GP	Montreal	22	Forti Grand Prix	G	3.0 Forti FG03 97-Ford Zetec R V8	gearbox	20/22
ret	FRENCH GP	Magny Cours	22	Forti Grand Prix	G	3.0 Forti FG03 97-Ford Zetec R V8	fuel pump	21/22
dnq	BRITISH GP	Silverstone	22	Forti Grand Prix	G	3.0 Forti FG03 97-Ford Zetec R V8	not within 107% of pole	22/22
dnp	GERMAN GP	Hockenheim	22	Forti Grand Prix	G	3.0 Forti FG03 97-Ford Zetec R V8	cars did not practice	– / –

1999 Championship position: Unplaced

ret	AUSTRALIAN GP	Melbourne	20	Fondmetal Minardi Ford	B	3.0 Minardi MO1-Ford Zetec R V10	gearbox		21/22
8	SAN MARINO GP	Imola	20	Fondmetal Minardi Ford	B	3.0 Minardi MO1-Ford Zetec R V10	3 laps behind		22/22
ret	MONACO GP	Monte Carlo	20	Fondmetal Minardi Ford	B	3.0 Minardi MO1-Ford Zetec R V10	gearbox		20/22
ret	SPANISH GP	Barcelona	20	Fondmetal Minardi Ford	B	3.0 Minardi MO1-Ford Zetec R V10	spun off		22/22
10	CANADIAN GP	Montreal	20	Fondmetal Minardi Ford	B	3.0 Minardi MO1-Ford Zetec R V10	1 lap behind		21/22
10	FRENCH GP	Magny Cours	20	Fondmetal Minardi Ford	B	3.0 Minardi MO1-Ford Zetec R V10	1 lap behind		20/22
ret	BRITISH GP	Silverstone	20	Fondmetal Minardi Ford	B	3.0 Minardi MO1-Ford Zetec R V10	gearbox		21/22
13	AUSTRIAN GP	A1-Ring	20	Fondmetal Minardi Ford	B	3.0 Minardi MO1-Ford Zetec R V10	3 laps behind		19/22
10	GERMAN GP	Hockenheim	20	Fondmetal Minardi Ford	B	3.0 Minardi MO1-Ford Zetec R V10	1 lap behind		19/22
14	HUNGARIAN GP	Hungaroring	20	Fondmetal Minardi Ford	B	3.0 Minardi MO1-Ford Zetec R V10	2 laps behind		19/22
ret	BELGIAN GP	Spa	20	Fondmetal Minardi Ford	B	3.0 Minardi MO1-Ford Zetec R V10	suspension		20/22
ret	ITALIAN GP	Monza	20	Fondmetal Minardi Ford	B	3.0 Minardi MO1-Ford Zetec R V10	hit by Takagi		19/22
ret	EUROPEAN GP	Nürburgring	20	Fondmetal Minardi Ford	B	3.0 Minardi MO1-Ford Zetec R V10	gearbox when fourth		19/22
ret	MALAYSIAN GP	Sepang	20	Fondmetal Minardi Ford	B	3.0 Minardi MO1-Ford Zetec R V10	overheating		21/22
ret	JAPANESE GP	Suzuka	20	Fondmetal Minardi Ford	B	3.0 Minardi MO1-Ford Zetec R V10	engine		22/22

2009 Championship position: Unplaced

17	EUROPEAN GP	Valencia	3	Scuderia Ferrari Marlboro	B	2.4 Ferrari F60 V8	hit by Grosjean – spin/-1 lap	20/20
14	BELGIAN GP	Spa	3	Scuderia Ferrari Marlboro	B	2.4 Ferrari F60 V8		13/20

GP Starts: 50 (49)   GP Wins: 0   Pole positions: 0   Fastest laps: 0   Points: 0

LUCA BADOER

LUCA BADOER was regarded as something of a prodigy when, aged only 19, he made his mark in Italian Formula 3 by winning the final round of the 1990 season, ahead of championship contenders Roberto Colciago and Alex Zanardi. Naturally all eyes were on the former Italian karting champion from Montebelluna in the following season and, after a quiet start in the early rounds, Luca reeled off four wins in a row amid growing acrimony as rival teams questioned the legality of his car. In fact, the last of these victories was wiped out due to the team running a non-scrutineered tyre; Badoer's season never recovered thereafter.

He had done enough, however, to move up to F3000 for 1992 and, at the wheel of the superbly engineered Team Crypton Reynard, Luca was a convincing champion, winning three of the early rounds and overcoming the effects of a nasty shunt at Spa to clinch the title with another victory at Nogaro.

Then the slightly built Badoer found himself pitched into the big time with the newly formed Lola Scuderia Italia team for 1993. The season was a fiasco, the car floundering at the back of the grid, and the only question to be answered at most of the early grands prix was which of the two unfortunate drivers – Luca or Michele Alboreto – would fail to qualify. With the team folding after the Portuguese Grand Prix, Badoer was left looking for a drive for 1994, and an unimpressive winter test for Benetton left him out in the cold.

Despite this setback, Badoer was back in business with Minardi the following season, but running customer Ford V8s meant the drivers were consigned to the grid's lower reaches and the pursuit of the occasional point. Luca managed to stay on board, however, while the veteran Pierluigi Martini was dropped mid-season. His replacement, the well-sponsored Pedro Lamy, proved evenly matched with the shy and quiet Milanese driver, and Badoer was forced to accept employment with fellow back-markers Forti Corse in 1996. It was a gamble that failed to pay off, as the struggling team had collapsed in financial ruin by mid-season, leaving Badoer largely unemployed (with the exception of a couple of sports car outings in a GT Lotus) over the next 18 months.

In 1998, he won the role of Ferrari test driver, which initially precluded any chance of a return to grand prix racing, but a year later he was allowed to rejoin the Minardi family to resurrect his grand prix career. It would be a season of huge disappointments for Luca, who suffered a broken wrist in a testing accident at Fiorano and then was devastated to be passed over by Ferrari after Michael Schumacher broke his leg at Silverstone.

To add to the driver's woes, a fourth place and three world championship points slipped away at the European Grand Prix when his Minardi's gearbox failed. Badoer, left in tears beside his stricken car, was one of the saddest sights of the 1999 season.

The Italian dutifully returned to his Ferrari test-driver role, which he held throughout the decade, clocking over 130,000 thousand kilometres in development work as the Scuderia exerted their crushing dominance on the sport between 2000 and 2004.

When Felipe Massa was sidelined following his accident at the Hungaroring in 2010, Luca was pitched into the action at the European Grand Prix. It was not too surprising that he struggled to get up to speed at Valencia, and he fared no better at Spa, where a spin in qualifying ruined his chances for the race. Formula 1 is a very unforgiving sport, and poor Badoer, despite support from some of his fellow drivers, received many negative press comments for his underwhelming performances. Ferrari quickly replaced him with Giancarlo Fisichella, and he reverted to his testing role until the end of the 2010 season.

In January, 2011 Badoer made a farewell appearance at a Ferrari press event held on the ice in Madonna di Campiglio. His F1 car fitted with special studded Pirelli tyres, Luca made a bizarre sight as he slithered slowly around the rink, making a good deal of noise, if nothing else.

GIANCARLO BAGHETTI

GIANCARLO BAGHETTI will for ever be known for his extraordinary feat of winning the very first world championship grand prix that he entered. In searing heat at Reims in 1961, the young Italian showed remarkable racecraft and composure as he took the sole surviving Ferrari to victory over the works Porsche driven by Dan Gurney. It was no fluke, for some weeks earlier Baghetti had done exactly the same thing in his first Formula 1 race at Syracuse, and he had followed that up with another victory, although the field at the Naples GP was weak and Giancarlo had an easy win. No other driver has ever won his first three Formula 1 races and probably none ever will, so Baghetti's place in motor racing folklore is secure.

From a wealthy family involved in the metal foundry business, Giancarlo began his racing career after he and his brother, Marco, borrowed their father's Alfa 1900TI and entered the 1958 Mille Miglia Rally without his knowledge. Only when the siblings returned having taken second place was their subterfuge revealed! Baghetti turned to sports car and Formula Junior racing over the next two years.

He took three wins in the tubby front-engined Dragada-Lancia to become the 1960 FJ champion, and was invited to join the Scuderia Sant Ambroeus team, who in turn were members of FISA (Federazione Italiane Scuderie Automobilistiche), a body that helped to promote young Italian racing talent, the ultimate aim being a place in the Ferrari Formula 1 team. Eventually, Baghetti was chosen and, as described, his early results were sensational, but his subsequent career never matched those dizzy heights. His next race, in the rain at Aintree, ended in a shunt, while Monza brought an engine failure, although he did set fastest lap. In 1962, the Ferrari team were left behind by the V8 opposition and, although Baghetti scored a few decent finishes in grands prix and a second place in the Mediterranean GP, he was being overshadowed by his old Junior rival, Lorenzo Bandini, although the pair shared a Ferrari 196 to take second place in the Targa Florio.

With Ferrari in a state of disarray by the end of the year, Baghetti made a disastrous move (with Phil Hill) to join Carlo Chiti's breakaway ATS organisation for 1963. After minimal testing, the cars were ill-prepared and frankly shoddy when they finally made their first appearance at the Belgian Grand Prix. Baghetti and Hill did the best they could with their hapless machines, which only managed to appear at five world championship events before the operation folded.

And there would be no real grand prix salvation in 1964, when Baghetti joined the Centro Sud team with their elderly BRMs. Apart from the satisfaction of beating Ludovico Scarfiotti's Ferrari at Monza, little was achieved, but his reputation gained him the occasional grand prix ride thereafter.

Baghetti could still be found in sports cars, taking a fine second place, with Jean Guichet, in the 1966 Targa Florio in a works Ferrari, and he was a regular in the European touring car championship with a Fiat Abarth. Surprisingly for one so famous, he was quite happy to drop down into the Italian F3 championship between 1967 and 1968, and he also took a Lancia Fulvia on the London–Sydney marathon, but was forced to abandon the effort when his passport and all his documents were stolen in Bombay.

His final race was the 1968 Targa Florio, where he shared a works Alfa Romeo T33 with Giampiero Biscaldi, taking sixth place.

The next two years were spent travelling and sailing his boat, before at the behest of his brother, he took up a new profession as photographer. Among his diverse assignments were shoots for Marlboro and Playboy. The lure of motorsport was never far away, however, and he became invoved in a new Italian magazine, Auto Oggi, as both a director and writer.

The lighthearted and fun loving Baghetti continued to enjoy his little slice of fame and certainly lived life to the full, until his early death from cancer at the age of 60.

BAGHETTI, Giancarlo (I) b 25/12/1934, Milan – d 27/11/1995, Milan

1961 Championship position: 9th   Wins: 0   Pole positions: 0   Fastest laps: 1   Points scored: 9

	Race	Circuit	No	Entrant	Tyres	Capacity/Car/Engine	Comment	Q Pos/Entries
1	FRENCH GP	Reims	50	FISA	D	1.5 Ferrari 156 V6	only driver to win his first ever GP	=12/26
ret	BRITISH GP	Aintree	58	Scuderia Sant Ambroeus	D	1.5 Ferrari 156 V6	crashed in rain	=18/30
ret	ITALIAN GP	Monza	32	Scuderia Sant Ambroeus	D	1.5 Ferrari 156 V6	engine/FL	6/33

1962 Championship position: 11th   Wins: 0   Pole positions: 0   Fastest laps: 0   Points scored: 5

	Race	Circuit	No	Entrant	Tyres	Capacity/Car/Engine	Comment	Q Pos/Entries
4	DUTCH GP	Zandvoort	2	Scuderia Ferrari SpA SEFAC	D	1.5 Ferrari 156 V6	1 lap behind	12/20
ret	BELGIAN GP	Spa	11	Scuderia Ferrari SpA SEFAC	D	1.5 Ferrari 156 V6	ignition	14/20
10	GERMAN GP	Nürburgring	2	Scuderia Ferrari SpA SEFAC	D	1.5 Ferrari 156 V6		13/30
5	ITALIAN GP	Monza	2	Scuderia Ferrari SpA SEFAC	D	1.5 Ferrari 156 V6		18/30

1963 Championship position: Unplaced

	Race	Circuit	No	Entrant	Tyres	Capacity/Car/Engine	Comment	Q Pos/Entries
ret	BELGIAN GP	Spa	27	Automobili Tourismo Sport	D	1.5 ATS 100 V8	gearbox	20/20
ret	DUTCH GP	Zandvoort	26	Automobili Tourismo Sport	D	1.5 ATS 100 V8	ignition	15/19
15	ITALIAN GP	Monza	14	Automobili Tourismo Sport	D	1.5 ATS 100 V8	pit stops/23 laps behind	25/28
ret	US GP	Watkins Glen	26	Automobili Tourismo Sport	D	1.5 ATS 100 V8	oil pump	20/21
ret	MEXICAN GP	Mexico City	26	Automobili Tourismo Sport	D	1.5 ATS 100 V8	carburation	21/21

1964 Championship position: Unplaced

	Race	Circuit	No	Entrant	Tyres	Capacity/Car/Engine	Comment	Q Pos/Entries
10	DUTCH GP	Zandvoort	32	Scuderia Centro Sud	D	1.5 BRM P57 V8	6 laps behind	16/18
8	BELGIAN GP	Spa	6	Scuderia Centro Sud	D	1.5 BRM P57 V8	1 lap behind	17/20
12	BRITISH GP	Brands Hatch	18	Scuderia Centro Sud	D	1.5 BRM P57 V8	4 laps behind	=21/25
ret	GERMAN GP	Nürburgring	18	Scuderia Centro Sud	D	1.5 BRM P57 V8	throttle linkage	21/24
7	AUSTRIAN GP	Zeltweg	18	Scuderia Centro Sud	D	1.5 BRM P57 V8	7 laps behind	15/20
8	ITALIAN GP	Monza	30	Scuderia Centro Sud	D	1.5 BRM P57 V8	1 lap behind	15/25

1965 Championship position: Unplaced

	Race	Circuit	No	Entrant	Tyres	Capacity/Car/Engine	Comment	Q Pos/Entries
ret	ITALIAN GP	Monza	10	Brabham Racing Organisation	D	1.5 Brabham BT7-Climax V8	engine – con rod	19/23

1966 Championship position: Unplaced

	Race	Circuit	No	Entrant	Tyres	Capacity/Car/Engine	Comment	Q Pos/Entries
nc	ITALIAN GP	Monza	44	Reg Parnell Racing Ltd	F	2.4 Ferrari 246 V6	loaned works car/pit stop/-9 laps	16/22
dns	"	"	44	Reg Parnell Racing Ltd	F	2.0 Lotus 25-BRM V8	engine in practice	– / –

1967 Championship position: Unplaced

	Race	Circuit	No	Entrant	Tyres	Capacity/Car/Engine	Comment	Q Pos/Entries
ret	ITALIAN GP	Monza	24	Team Lotus	F	3.0 Lotus 49-Cosworth V8	engine	17/18

GP Starts: 21   GP Wins: 1   Pole positions: 0   Fastest laps: 1   Points: 14

JULIAN BAILEY

THE determination with which Julian Bailey has pursued his career has enabled him to ride out innumerable financial crises as well as serious injuries sustained when a huge crash at Snetterton in 1980 left him with multiple fractures of his arm and leg. By the end of 1981, he was back in business and quicker than ever. Racing in FF1600 in 1982, he was involved in a season-long battle with Mauricio Gugelmin, which saw him lose out in the RAC championship, but gain some recompense by winning the prestigious Formula Ford Festival at Brands Hatch.

Julian's career then became bogged down for a number of seasons, which he spent scratching around in less-than-competitive cars, notably in F3. But he plugged on, waiting for a break, which finally came his way with a deal to race a Lola in Formula 3000 at the end of 1986. He took to the category and, with backing from Cavendish Finance, embarked on a full F3000 season in 1987. A superb win at Brands Hatch, his favourite circuit, provided the year's highlight, and the credibility from this win led to a seat at Tyrrell for 1988, but the 017 car fielded by the team that year was poor and his season was a complete washout.

After some excellent drives for the Nissan sports car team (including a third place at Donington in 1989), Julian scraped together enough cash to buy a ride with Lotus at the start of the 1991 season, but despite picking up a sixth place at Imola, he was dropped in favour of Johnny Herbert. Accepting that F1 would be for ever out of his reach, he concentrated on forging a career in the British touring car championship, enjoying the opportunity to race a works Toyota in 1993 alongside Will Hoy. Unlike some other notable grand prix refugees, however, Julian became a convincing performer in this type of racing, but rarely had the machinery to challenge for top BTCC honours.

Bailey found greater success with Toyota in South Africa during 1996 and 1997, before returning to sports cars to spearhead the Lister-Storm challenge in GT racing at home; he won the British championship in 1999 and the FIA GT title in 2000. He shared an MG Lola at Le Mans with Mark Blundell, before retiring from competition at the end of 2002 to concentrate on his various business interests. Recently, Julian and his wife, Debbie, have been guiding the career of his stepson, Jack Clarke, who thus far has graduated to the FIA Formula 2 championship.

BAILEY, Julian (GB) b 9/10/1961, Woolwich, London

1988 Championship position: Unplaced

	Race	Circuit	No	Entrant	Tyres	Capacity/Car/Engine	Comment	Q Pos/Entries
dnq	BRAZILIAN GP	Rio	4	Tyrrell Racing Organisation	G	3.5 Tyrrell 017-Cosworth V8		27/31
ret	SAN MARINO GP	Imola	4	Tyrrell Racing Organisation	G	3.5 Tyrrell 017-Cosworth V8	gearbox	21/31
dnq	MONACO GP	Monte Carlo	4	Tyrrell Racing Organisation	G	3.5 Tyrrell 017-Cosworth V8		30/30
dnq	MEXICAN GP	Mexico City	4	Tyrrell Racing Organisation	G	3.5 Tyrrell 017-Cosworth V8		29/30
ret	CANADIAN GP	Montreal	4	Tyrrell Racing Organisation	G	3.5 Tyrrell 017-Cosworth V8	collision with Sala on lap 1	23/31
9/ret	US GP (DETROIT)	Detroit	4	Tyrrell Racing Organisation	G	3.5 Tyrrell 017-Cosworth V8	hit wall/4 laps behind	23/31
dnq	FRENCH GP	Paul Ricard	4	Tyrrell Racing Organisation	G	3.5 Tyrrell 017-Cosworth V8		29/31
16	BRITISH GP	Silverstone	4	Tyrrell Racing Organisation	G	3.5 Tyrrell 017-Cosworth V8	2 laps behind	24/31
dnq	GERMAN GP	Hockenheim	4	Tyrrell Racing Organisation	G	3.5 Tyrrell 017-Cosworth V8		29/31
dnq	HUNGARIAN GP	Hungaroring	4	Tyrrell Racing Organisation	G	3.5 Tyrrell 017-Cosworth V8		29/31
dnq	BELGIAN GP	Spa	4	Tyrrell Racing Organisation	G	3.5 Tyrrell 017-Cosworth V8		30/31
12	ITALIAN GP	Monza	4	Tyrrell Racing Organisation	G	3.5 Tyrrell 017-Cosworth V8	2 laps behind	26/31
dnq	PORTUGUESE GP	Estoril	4	Tyrrell Racing Organisation	G	3.5 Tyrrell 017-Cosworth V8		27/31
dnq	SPANISH GP	Jerez	4	Tyrrell Racing Organisation	G	3.5 Tyrrell 017-Cosworth V8		29/31
14	JAPANESE GP	Suzuka	4	Tyrrell Racing Organisation	G	3.5 Tyrrell 017-Cosworth V8	2 laps behind	26/31
dnq	AUSTRALIAN GP	Adelaide	4	Tyrrell Racing Organisation	G	3.5 Tyrrell 017-Cosworth V8		28/31

1988 Championship position: 18th= Wins: 0 Pole positions: 0 Fastest laps: 0 Points scored: 1

	Race	Circuit	No	Entrant	Tyres	Capacity/Car/Engine	Comment	Q Pos/Entries
dnq	US GP (PHOENIX)	Phoenix	12	Team Lotus	G	3.5 Lotus 102B-Judd V8		30/34
dnq	BRAZILIAN GP	Interlagos	12	Team Lotus	G	3.5 Lotus 102B-Judd V8		30/34
6	SAN MARINO GP	Imola	12	Team Lotus	G	3.5 Lotus 102B-Judd V8	3 laps behind	26/34
dnq	MONACO GP	Monte Carlo	12	Team Lotus	G	3.5 Lotus 102B-Judd V8		28/34

GP Starts: 7 GP Wins: 0 Pole positions: 0 Fastest laps: 0 Points: 1

BALDI, Mauro (I) b 31/1/1954, Reggio-Emilia

1982 Championship position: 22nd= Wins: 0 Pole positions: 0 Fastest laps: 0 Points scored: 2

	Race	Circuit	No	Entrant	Tyres	Capacity/Car/Engine	Comment	Q Pos/Entries
dnq	SOUTH AFRICAN GP	Kyalami	30	Arrows Racing Team	P	3.0 Arrows A4-Cosworth V8		27/30
10*	BRAZILIAN GP	Rio	30	Arrows Racing Team	P	3.0 Arrows A4-Cosworth V8	*1st & 2nd cars dsq/-6 laps	19/31
dnq	US GP WEST	Long Beach	30	Arrows Racing Team	P	3.0 Arrows A4-Cosworth V8		30/31
ret	BELGIAN GP	Zolder	30	Arrows Racing Team	P	3.0 Arrows A4-Cosworth V8	throttle/spun off	28/32
dnq	MONACO GP	Monte Carlo	30	Arrows Racing Team	P	3.0 Arrows A4-Cosworth V8		21/31
ret	US GP (DETROIT)	Detroit	30	Arrows Racing Team	P	3.0 Arrows A4-Cosworth V8	hit Boesel on lap 1	24/28
8	CANADIAN GP	Montreal	30	Arrows Racing Team	P	3.0 Arrows A4-Cosworth V8	2 laps behind	17/29
6	DUTCH GP	Zandvoort	30	Arrows Racing Team	P	3.0 Arrows A4-Cosworth V8	1 lap behind	16/31
9	BRITISH GP	Brands Hatch	30	Arrows Racing Team	P	3.0 Arrows A4-Cosworth V8	2 laps behind	26/30
ret	FRENCH GP	Paul Ricard	30	Arrows Racing Team	P	3.0 Arrows A4-Cosworth V8	accident with Mass	25/30
ret	GERMAN GP	Hockenheim	30	Arrows Racing Team	P	3.0 Arrows A4-Cosworth V8	misfire	24/30
6	AUSTRIAN GP	Österreichring	30	Arrows Racing Team	P	3.0 Arrows A4-Cosworth V8	1 lap behind	23/29
dnq	SWISS GP	Dijon	30	Arrows Racing Team	P	3.0 Arrows A4-Cosworth V8		29/29
12	ITALIAN GP	Monza	30	Arrows Racing Team	P	3.0 Arrows A5-Cosworth V8	3 laps behind	24/30
11	CAESARS PALACE GP	Las Vegas	30	Arrows Racing Team	P	3.0 Arrows A4-Cosworth V8	3 laps behind	23/30

1983 Championship position: 16th Wins: 0 Pole positions: 0 Fastest laps: 0 Points scored: 3

	Race	Circuit	No	Entrant	Tyres	Capacity/Car/Engine	Comment	Q Pos/Entries
ret	BRAZILIAN GP	Rio	23	Marlboro Team Alfa Romeo	M	1.5 t/c Alfa Romeo 183T V8	collision damage	10/27
ret	US GP WEST	Long Beach	23	Marlboro Team Alfa Romeo	M	1.5 t/c Alfa Romeo 183T V8	accident	21/28
ret	FRENCH GP	Paul Ricard	23	Marlboro Team Alfa Romeo	M	1.5 t/c Alfa Romeo 183T V8	accident with Winkelhock	8/29
10/ret	SAN MARINO	Imola	23	Marlboro Team Alfa Romeo	M	1.5 t/c Alfa Romeo 183T V8	engine/3 laps behind	10/28
6	MONACO GP	Monte Carlo	23	Marlboro Team Alfa Romeo	M	1.5 t/c Alfa Romeo 183T V8	2 laps behind	13/28
ret	BELGIAN GP	Spa	23	Marlboro Team Alfa Romeo	M	1.5 t/c Alfa Romeo 183T V8	throttle linkage	12/28
12	US GP (DETROIT)	Detroit	23	Marlboro Team Alfa Romeo	M	1.5 t/c Alfa Romeo 183T V8	4 laps behind	25/27
10*	CANADIAN GP	Montreal	23	Marlboro Team Alfa Romeo	M	1.5 t/c Alfa Romeo 183T V8	*9th place car dsq/-3 laps	26/28
7	BRITISH GP	Silverstone	23	Marlboro Team Alfa Romeo	M	1.5 t/c Alfa Romeo 183T V8	1 lap behind	11/29
ret	GERMAN GP	Hockenheim	23	Marlboro Team Alfa Romeo	M	1.5 t/c Alfa Romeo 183T V8	engine	7/29
ret	AUSTRIAN GP	Österreichring	23	Marlboro Team Alfa Romeo	M	1.5 t/c Alfa Romeo 183T V8	engine	9/29
5	DUTCH GP	Zandvoort	23	Marlboro Team Alfa Romeo	M	1.5 t/c Alfa Romeo 183T V8		12/29
ret	ITALIAN GP	Monza	23	Marlboro Team Alfa Romeo	M	1.5 t/c Alfa Romeo 183T V8	turbo	10/29
ret	EUROPEAN GP	Brands Hatch	23	Marlboro Team Alfa Romeo	M	1.5 t/c Alfa Romeo 183T V8	clutch	15/29
ret	SOUTH AFRICAN GP	Kyalami	23	Marlboro Team Alfa Romeo	M	1.5 t/c Alfa Romeo 183T V8	engine	17/26

1984 Championship position: Unplaced

	Race	Circuit	No	Entrant	Tyres	Capacity/Car/Engine	Comment	Q Pos/Entries
ret	BRAZILIAN GP	Rio	21	Spirit Racing	P	1.5 t/c Spirit 101-Hart 4	distributor	24/27
8	SOUTH AFRICAN GP	Kyalami	21	Spirit Racing	P	1.5 t/c Spirit 101-Hart 4	tyre vibration/4 laps behind	20/27
ret	BELGIAN GP	Zolder	21	Spirit Racing	P	1.5 t/c Spirit 101-Hart 4	suspension	25/27
8*	SAN MARINO GP	Imola	21	Spirit Racing	P	1.5 t/c Spirit 101-Hart 4	*5th place car disqualified/-2 laps	24/28
ret	FRENCH GP	Dijon	21	Spirit Racing	P	1.5 t/c Spirit 101-Hart 4	engine	25/27
dnq	MONACO GP	Monte Carlo	21	Spirit Racing	P	1.5 t/c Spirit 101-Hart 4		26/27
8	EUROPEAN GP	Nürburgring	21	Spirit Racing	P	1.5 t/c Spirit 101-Hart 4	2 laps behind	24/26
15	PORTUGUESE GP	Estoril	21	Spirit Racing	P	1.5 t/c Spirit 101-Hart 4	4 laps behind	25/27

1985 Championship position: Unplaced

	Race	Circuit	No	Entrant	Tyres	Capacity/Car/Engine	Comment	Q Pos/Entries
ret	BRAZILIAN GP	Rio	21	Spirit Enterprises Ltd	P	1.5 t/c Spirit 101D-Hart 4	turbo/misfire	24/25
ret	PORTUGUESE GP	Estoril	21	Spirit Enterprises Ltd	P	1.5 t/c Spirit 101D-Hart 4	spun off	24/26
ret	SAN MARINO GP	Imola	21	Spirit Enterprises Ltd	P	1.5 t/c Spirit 101D-Hart 4	electrics	26/26

GP Starts: 36 GP Wins: 0 Pole positions: 0 Fastest laps: 0 Points: 5

MAURO BALDI

THIS Italian driver began racing in 1975 with a Renault 5, winning the Italian and European one-make championships and earning an F3 Ralt into the bargain. After finding his feet in 1978, Mauro Baldi was soon making his mark, finishing fourth in the 1979 European championship and third in the Italian series

Victory in the Monaco F3 race in 1980, by the huge margin of 47 seconds, was the platform from which Mauro began his domination of the formula. Armed with a March for the 1981 season, he trounced the opposition, recording eight wins and four second places in the 15-race European F3 series.

By-passing Formula 2, he secured a drive with Arrows for 1982 and did well enough in a difficult car, but when the opportunity arose to rejoin his former boss Paolo Pavanello in the reconstructed Alfa Romeo team, Mauro switched camps. However, the year disintegrated after political frictions had prompted the mid-season departure of designer Gérard Ducarouge. Unable to continue with the team for 1984 as a result of new sponsor Benetton's preference for Riccardo Patrese and Eddie Cheever, Mauro was left with no alternative but to race for the underfinanced Spirit outfit, and his F1 career eventually petered out.

Meanwhile Baldi had taken the opportunity to race sports cars for Martini Lancia, winning at Spa in 1985, and he quickly became one of prototype racing's most successful exponents, forging his reputation with privateer Porsches before becoming a key member of the Sauber-Mercedes factory-backed team. Mauro won at Jerez (with Jean-Louis Schlesser and Jochen Mass) and Spa (with Stefan Johansson), but Jaguar emerged as the championship winning team. In 1989, Baldi scored victories at Suzuka (with Schlesser), and Brands Hatch and Spa (both with Kenny Acheson) as the team saw off the challenge of the Joest Porsches.

With the C9 dominant in 1990, Mauro, was paired with Schlesser, and the experienced pair took six wins (at Suzuka, Monza, Dijon, Nürburgring, Donington and Montreal) from nine rounds, to win the drivers' championship just ahead of Mass.

In 1991, Baldi made the switch to Peugeot and immediately won the opening round at Suzuka (with Philippe Alliot), but failed to win elsewhere. The 1992 season was the final year for the ailing World Sportscar Championship, which shrank to just six rounds, leaving Peugeot to clean up. Baldi and Alliot won at Donington and the final round at Magny-Cours, but were overshadowed by their team-mates Derek Warwick and Yannick Dalmas.

In 1994, his major triumph came at Le Mans, where he shared the winning Porsche 962LM with Hurley Haywood and Dalmas. Mauro also briefly reappeared in single-seater competition, driving for Dale Coyne in an Indy Car race at Mid-Ohio.

In 1995, he was part of the Ferrari 333SP sports car attack in IMSA, taking fourth place at Sebring with Michele Alboreto and Eric van de Poele, but he suffered three indifferent seasons before enjoying welcome success with Gianpiero Moretti's Ferrari in 1998, when he shared in victories at Daytona, Sebring and Watkins Glen.

In 1999, Baldi joined Jean-Pierre Jabouille's team to race in the World Sports Car Cup, taking a win at Spa. He also drove for Dyson Racing in the USA, sharing the second-placed Ferrari 333SP with Didier Theys at Road Atlanta. In 2002, Baldi co-drove the winning Dallara-Judd in the Daytona 24-hour race, and his racing career continued until 2003: in the ALMS with a Riley & Scott, and in the GrandAm Series in a Doran-Dallara.

MARCEL BALSA

ONLY an enthusiastic French amateur, Marcel Balsa plugged away throughout the late 1940s and early 1950s with a BMW special, restricting himself in the main to events on home soil. He was a distant fourth in the Luxembourg GP in 1949 and third at Cadours the following year, an event overshadowed by the death of Raymond Sommer.

Balsa's machine was neither particularly speedy nor for that matter reliable, although he did scrape a sixth place at Cadours in 1952. On paper, his finest moment was winning the 1953 Coupe de Printemps at Montlhéry, but the quality of the opposition was meagre to say the least.

BALSA, Marcel (F) b 1/1/1909, Saint Frion – d 11/8/1984

	1952 Championship position: Unplaced							
	Race	Circuit	No	Entrant	Tyres	Capacity/Car/Engine	Comment	Q Pos/Entries
ret	GERMAN GP	Nürburgring	110	Marcel Balsa	–	2.0 BMW special 6		25/32
	GP Starts: 1 GP Wins: 0 Pole positions: 0 Fastest laps: 0 Points: 0							

WITH such a name, Lorenzo Bandini just had to be an Italian racing driver, although as a personality he didn't fit the stereotype, being calm, and possessed of an even temperament and a pleasant disposition Bandini worked as a garage mechanic for a Signor Freedi, who later became his father-in-law, before setting up on his own in Milan. Dreaming of nothing but racing, he worked assiduously, until beginning his racing career tentatively with Fiats and later a Lancia Appia Zagato, in which he won his class in the 1958 Mille Miglia. Later that year, he bought a Volpini Formula Junior and finished third on aggregate on his debut in the Sicilian Gold Cup at Syracuse.

Bandini began the 1959 season with his own machine, but was quickly taken into the works Stanguellini team, where he soon became a leading runner, winning the Liberty GP in Cuba at the beginning of 1960 and later taking the Pescara GP ahead of Denny Hulme. Already yearning for more powerful machinery, Lorenzo was fortunate to come under the wing of Signor Mimmo Dei of the Scuderia Centro Sud, who put him into his Formula 1 Cooper for 1961. An early-season third place at the Pau GP was a splendid start, but Bandini was soon overshadowed by Giancarlo Baghetti, who had been given the FISA-backed Ferrari in preference to him and was about to enjoy his brief spell of fame. Much was made in the press of the rivalry between the two young Italians, but in fact there was no friction, as they were good friends. Bandini raced on in the Cooper without much success, but took a superb win in the sports car Pescara GP before the season was out.

In 1962, Bandini was invited to join the Ferrari team at last, but it was a season of disarray at Maranello, with drivers chosen for races on a seemingly ad hoc basis. Nevertheless he finished a cool third at the Monaco GP, and in non-title races he took fifth place at Pau and a second at Naples, while he won the Mediterranean GP at Enna. Amazingly, he was dropped from the F1 team in favour of Willy Mairesse for 1963, so it was back to Centro Sud to race their newly acquired BRM while continuing in the Ferrari sports car squad. After a second place in the Targa Florio, Bandini shared a Ferrari 250P with Ludovico Scarfiotti to win Le Mans and later took second in the Reims 12-hours with John Surtees. This success stood him in good stead, and after Mairesse was injured, he returned to the fold.

Largely due to the efforts of Surtees, the team were on their way back, and in 1964 Bandini was the Englishman's number two, accepting his position stoically and scoring his first, and only, grand prix victory at the bumpy Zeltweg airfield circuit, when most of the more fancied runners failed to make it to the finish.

The final 1.5-litre season in 1965 was relatively uneventful and, although Bandini's position in the team remained the same, he was increasingly unhappy with the status quo, while relations with his team leader were becoming a little strained. In sports cars, Ferrari's programme was limited, but Lorenzo won the Targa Florio with Nino Vaccarella. The friction in the team continued into 1966, when Bandini drove the 2.4-litre Dino into second place at Monaco, even though Surtees wanted to race the car. The tense situation could not last, and when Surtees quit Maranello, Bandini suddenly found himself leading the team. A seemingly certain win in the French GP was lost when a throttle cable snapped, and Scarfiotti and Mike Parkes took the honours at the Italian Grand Prix at Monza when Bandini's Ferrari encountered fuel feed problems.

The 1967 season started well with victories in the Daytona 24-hours and Monza 1000km in a Ferrari 330P4, shared with Maranello newcomer Chris Amon. In F1, there was a second place in the Race of Champions at Brands Hatch, behind Gurney's Eagle. The next race in which he competed was his favourite, the Monaco Grand Prix. Qualifying second on the grid, Bandini led in the early stages before dropping behind Denny Hulme's Brabham. Late in the race, however, he made a final charge in a bid for victory. On the 82nd lap, he clipped the chicane entering the harbour front. His Ferrari vaulted the straw bales on the opposite side of the track and his left front suspension hit a lamp-post. Upon impact, the car cartwheeled and burst into flames as it landed upside down in the middle of the track.

The rescue crew was very slow to react, and the ill-fated driver, dreadfully burnt and injured, lay trapped for what seemed an eternity. Broken and charred, he was eventually dragged from the upturned wreck and rushed to hospital. There was no prospect of recovery for poor Bandini, though, and, mercifully perhaps, he passed away after clinging to life for three days.

Bandini took his only grand prix victory at the 1964 Austrian GP, after the more fancied runners had fallen by the wayside, victims of the rough concrete surface. The race was held on a temporary circuit marked out by straw bales, the organisers using the control tower seen in the background.

BANDINI, Lorenzo (I) b 21/12/1935, Barce, Cyrenaica, Libya – d 10/5/1967, Monte Carlo

1961 Championship position: Unplaced

	Race	Circuit	No	Entrant	Tyres	Capacity/Car/Engine	Comment	Q Pos/Entries
ret	BELGIAN GP	Spa	46	Scuderia Centro Sud	D	1.5 Cooper T53-Maserati 4	engine – oil pressure	17/25
12	BRITISH GP	Aintree	60	Scuderia Centro Sud	D	1.5 Cooper T53-Maserati 4	4 laps behind	21/30
ret	GERMAN GP	Nürburgring	32	Scuderia Centro Sud	D	1.5 Cooper T53-Maserati 4	engine	19/27
8	ITALIAN GP	Monza	62	Scuderia Centro Sud	D	1.5 Cooper T53-Maserati 4	2 laps behind	21/33

1962 Championship position: 12th= Wins: 0 Pole positions: 0 Fastest laps: 0 Points scored: 4

	Race	Circuit	No	Entrant	Tyres	Capacity/Car/Engine	Comment	Q Pos/Entries
3	MONACO GP	Monte Carlo	38	Scuderia Ferrari SpA SEFAC	D	1.5 Ferrari 156 V6		10/21
ret	GERMAN GP	Nürburgring	4	Scuderia Ferrari SpA SEFAC	D	1.5 Ferrari 156 V6	accident	18/30
8	ITALIAN GP	Monza	6	Scuderia Ferrari SpA SEFAC	D	1.5 Ferrari 156 V6	2 laps behind	17/30

1963 Championship position: 9th= Wins: 0 Pole positions: 0 Fastest laps: 0 Points scored: 6

	Race	Circuit	No	Entrant	Tyres	Capacity/Car/Engine	Comment	Q Pos/Entries
10	FRENCH GP	Reims	46	Scuderia Centro Sud	D	1.5 BRM P57 V8	8 laps behind	21/21
5	BRITISH GP	Silverstone	3	Scuderia Centro Sud	D	1.5 BRM P57 V8	1 lap behind	=7/23
ret	GERMAN GP	Nürburgring	15	Scuderia Centro Sud	D	1.5 BRM P57 V8	collision with Ireland	3/26
ret	ITALIAN GP	Monza	2	Scuderia Ferrari SpA SEFAC	D	1.5 Ferrari 156 V6	gearbox	6/28
5	US GP	Watkins Glen	24	Scuderia Ferrari SpA SEFAC	D	1.5 Ferrari 156 V6	4 laps behind	9/21
ret	MEXICAN GP	Mexico City	24	Scuderia Ferrari SpA SEFAC	D	1.5 Ferrari 156 V6	ignition	7/21
5	SOUTH AFRICAN GP	East London	4	Scuderia Ferrari SpA SEFAC	D	1.5 Ferrari 156 V6	1 lap behind	5/21

1964 Championship position: 4th= Wins: 1 Pole positions: 0 Fastest laps: 0 Points scored: 23

	Race	Circuit	No	Entrant	Tyres	Capacity/Car/Engine	Comment	Q Pos/Entries
10/ret	MONACO GP	Monte Carlo	20	Scuderia Ferrari SpA SEFAC	D	1.5 Ferrari 156 V6	gearbox/33 laps behind	7/20
ret	DUTCH GP	Zandvoort	4	Scuderia Ferrari SpA SEFAC	D	1.5 Ferrari 158 V8	fuel injection pump	10/18
dns	"	"	4	Scuderia Ferrari SpA SEFAC	D	1.5 Ferrari 158 V8	practice only	- / -
ret	BELGIAN GP	Spa	11	Scuderia Ferrari SpA SEFAC	D	1.5 Ferrari 158 V8	no oil	9/20
9	FRENCH GP	Rouen	26	Scuderia Ferrari SpA SEFAC	D	1.5 Ferrari 158 V8	2 laps behind	8/17
5	BRITISH GP	Brands Hatch	8	Scuderia Ferrari SpA SEFAC	D	1.5 Ferrari 156 V6	2 laps behind	=8/25
3	GERMAN GP	Nürburgring	8	Scuderia Ferrari SpA SEFAC	D	1.5 Ferrari 156 V6		4/24
1	AUSTRIAN GP	Zeltweg	8	Scuderia Ferrari SpA SEFAC	D	1.5 Ferrari 156 V6		7/20
3	ITALIAN GP	Monza	4	Scuderia Ferrari SpA SEFAC	D	1.5 Ferrari 158 V8	1 lap behind	7/25
dns	"	"	4	Scuderia Ferrari SpA SEFAC	D	1.5 Ferrari 156 V6	practice only	- / -
dns	"	"	4	Scuderia Ferrari Spa SEFAC	D	1.5 Ferrari 1512 F12	practice only	- / -
ret	US GP	Watkins Glen	8	North American Racing Team	D	1.5 Ferrari 1512 F12	engine	8/19
dns	"	" "	8	North American Racing Team	D	1.5 Ferrari 156 V6	practice only	- / -
3	MEXICAN GP	Mexico City	8	North American Racing Team	D	1.5 Ferrari 1512 F12		3/19

1965 Championship position: 6th Wins: 0 Pole positions: 0 Fastest laps: 0 Points scored: 13

	Race	Circuit	No	Entrant	Tyres	Capacity/Car/Engine	Comment	Q Pos/Entries
15/ret	SOUTH AFRICAN GP	East London	2	Scuderia Ferrari SpA SEFAC	D	1.5 Ferrari 1512 F12	ignition/19 laps behind	=6/25
2	MONACO GP	Monte Carlo	17	Scuderia Ferrari SpA SEFAC	D	1.5 Ferrari 1512 F12		4/17
9	BELGIAN GP	Spa	2	Scuderia Ferrari SpA SEFAC	D	1.5 Ferrari 1512 F12	2 laps behind	15/21
8/ret	FRENCH GP	Clermont Ferrand	4	Scuderia Ferrari SpA SEFAC	D	1.5 Ferrari 1512 F12	lost wheel – spun off/-3 laps	=3/17
ret	BRITISH GP	Silverstone	2	Scuderia Ferrari SpA SEFAC	D	1.5 Ferrari 158 V8	piston	=9/23
9	DUTCH GP	Zandvoort	4	Scuderia Ferrari SpA SEFAC	D	1.5 Ferrari 158 V8	1 lap behind	12/17
6	GERMAN GP	Nürburgring	8	Scuderia Ferrari SpA SEFAC	D	1.5 Ferrari 158 V8		7/22
4	ITALIAN GP	Monza	4	Scuderia Ferrari SpA SEFAC	D	1.5 Ferrari 1512 F12		5/23

The last ride. Bandini would lose his life in a fiery accident in the late stages of the 1967 Monaco Grand Prix while vainly chasing the Brabham of Denny Hulme. The Italian (left) leads John Surtees and Jochen Rindt around the hairpin where a temporary stand has been built on the site of the recently demolished railway station.

4	US GP	Watkins Glen	2	Scuderia Ferrari SpA SEFAC	D	1.5 Ferrari 1512 F12		1 lap behind	5/18
8	MEXICAN GP	Mexico City	2	Scuderia Ferrari SpA SEFAC	D	1.5 Ferrari 1512 F12		3 laps behind	7/18

1966 Championship position: 8th=   Wins: 0   Pole positions: 1   Fastest laps:2   Points scored: 12

2	MONACO GP	Monte Carlo	16	Scuderia Ferrari SpA SEFAC	F	2.4 Ferrari 246 V6	FL	5/16
dns	" " "		16T	Scuderia Ferrari SpA SEFAC	F	3.0 Ferrari 312/66 V12	practice only	– / –
3	BELGIAN GP	Spa	7	Scuderia Ferrari SpA SEFAC	D	2.4 Ferrari 246 V6	1 lap behind	5/18
nc	FRENCH GP	Reims	20	Scuderia Ferrari SpA SEFAC	F	3.0 Ferrari 312/66 V12	broken throttle cable/FL/-11 laps	1/17
6	DUTCH GP	Zandvoort	2	Scuderia Ferrari SpA SEFAC	F	3.0 Ferrari 312/66 V12	spin/3 laps behind	9/18
6	GERMAN GP	Nürburgring	9	Scuderia Ferrari SpA SEFAC	D	3.0 Ferrari 312/66 V12		6/30
ret	ITALIAN GP	Monza	2	Scuderia Ferrari SpA SEFAC	F	3.0 Ferrari 312/66 V12	ignition	5/22
ret	US GP	Watkins Glen	9	Scuderia Ferrari SpA SEFAC	F	3.0 Ferrari 312/66 V12	engine	3/19

1967 Championship position: Unplaced

ret	MONACO GP	Monte Carlo	18	Scuderia Ferrari SpA SEFAC	F	3.0 Ferrari 312/67 V12	fatal accident	2/18

GP Starts: 42   GP Wins: 1   Pole positions: 1   Fastest laps: 2   Points: 58

FABRIZIO BARBAZZA

FABRIZIO BARBAZZA earned a reputation as a wild, but fast driver in Italian F3, finishing third in the series with a Dallara-Alfa in 1985. Frustrated at the lack of opportunities in Europe, he took the unusual step of crossing the Atlantic to contest the newly created American Racing Series, which he promptly won. More success followed in 1987: filling a vacancy in Frank Arciero's Indy Car team, he took a splendid third place in the Indianapolis 500, earning the accolade of top rookie. He also finished 12th in the final points standings to claim the PPG Rookie of the Year Award.

Still intent on breaking into grand prix racing, Barbazza returned to Europe and scraped around in F3000 before finally securing an F1 drive in 1991, only to endure a dismal time fruitlessly attempting to qualify the AGS. Having found the finance to buy a seat in the Minardi team for 1993, he confirmed that he had plenty of ability, gaining two valuable sixth places for the team before making way for Pierluigi Martini at mid-season.

In 1995, Barbazza once again headed Stateside, but after finishing eighth in the Daytona 24-hours, he was seriously injured in a horrendous multiple accident at Road Atlanta, which destroyed his Ferrari 333SP. He then spent over a year recuperating before announcing his retirement from racing.

Subsequently, Barbazza became involved in the design and development of safety features for racing circuits, but in 2003 he moved to Cuba to run a fishing resort.

BARBAZZA, Fabrizio (I)   b 2/4/1963, Monza

1991 Championship position: Unplaced

	Race	Circuit	No	Entrant	Tyres	Capacity/Car/Engine	Comment	Q Pos/Entries
dnq	SAN MARINO GP	Imola	18	Automobiles Gonfaronaise Sportive	G	3.5 AGS JH25-Cosworth DFR V8		28/34
dnq	MONACO GP	Monaco	18	Automobiles Gonfaronaise Sportive	G	3.5 AGS JH25-Cosworth DFR V8		29/34
dnq	CANADIAN GP	Montreal	18	Automobiles Gonfaronaise Sportive	G	3.5 AGS JH25-Cosworth DFR V8		27/34
dnq	MEXICAN GP	Mexico City	18	Automobiles Gonfaronaise Sportive	G	3.5 AGS JH25-Cosworth DFR V8		30/34
dnq	FRENCH GP	Magny Cours	18	Automobiles Gonfaronaise Sportive	G	3.5 AGS JH25B-Cosworth DFR V8		28/34
dnq	BRITISH GP	Silverstone	18	Automobiles Gonfaronaise Sportive	G	3.5 AGS JH25B-Cosworth DFR V8		29/34
dnpq	GERMAN GP	Hockenheim	18	Automobiles Gonfaronaise Sportive	G	3.5 AGS JH25B-Cosworth DFR V8		33/34
dnpq	HUNGARIAN GP	Hungaroring	18	Automobiles Gonfaronaise Sportive	G	3.5 AGS JH25B-Cosworth DFR V8		33/34
dnpq	BELGIAN GP	Spa	18	Automobiles Gonfaronaise Sportive	G	3.5 AGS JH25B-Cosworth DFR V8		34/34
dnpq	ITALIAN GP	Monza	18	Automobiles Gonfaronaise Sportive	G	3.5 AGS JH25B-Cosworth DFR V8		31/34
dnpq	PORTUGUESE GP	Estoril	18	Automobiles Gonfaronaise Sportive	G	3.5 AGS JH27-Cosworth DFR V8		31/34
dnpq	SPANISH GP	Barcelona	18	Automobiles Gonfaronaise Sportive	G	3.5 AGS JH27-Cosworth DFR V8		32/33

1993 Championship position: 17th=   Wins: 0   Pole positions: 0   Fastest laps: 0   Points scored: 2

ret	SOUTH AFRICAN GP	Kyalami	24	Minardi Team	G	3.5 Minardi M193-Ford HB V8	accident – hit by Suzuki	24/26
ret	BRAZILIAN GP	Interlagos	24	Minardi Team	G	3.5 Minardi M193-Ford HB V8	collision with Brundle on lap 1	24/26
6	EUROPEAN GP	Donington	24	Minardi Team	G	3.5 Minardi M193-Ford HB V8	2 laps behind	20/26
6	SAN MARINO GP	Imola	24	Minardi Team	G	3.5 Minardi M193-Ford HB V8	2 laps behind	25/26
ret	SPANISH GP	Barcelona	24	Minardi Team	G	3.5 Minardi M193-Ford HB V8	spun off	25/26
11	MONACO GP	Monte Carlo	24	Minardi Team	G	3.5 Minardi M193-Ford HB V8	steering after collision/-3 laps	25/26
ret	CANADIAN GP	Montreal	24	Minardi Team	G	3.5 Minardi M193-Ford HB V8	gearbox	23/26
ret	FRENCH GP	Magny Cours	24	Minardi Team	G	3.5 Minardi M193-Ford HB V8	gearbox	24/26

GP Starts: 8   GP Wins: 0   Pole positions: 0   Fastest laps: 0   Points: 2

JOHN BARBER

JOHN BARBER, a Billingsgate fish merchant, went racing with a Cooper-JAP before purchasing a Formula 2 Cooper-Bristol Mk1 for the 1952 season. He won a minor Libre race at Snetterton, but crashed the car badly at season's end.

Barber ventured to Argentina at the start of 1953 and drove steadily to eighth in the championship grand prix, followed by a 12th place in the Buenos Aires Libre race. On his return to Britain, he briefly raced the flying saucer-shaped Golding-Cooper, which is believed to have been built on the frame of his damaged Mk1. It was while racing this car in the British Empire Trophy at the Isle of Man that he was innocently involved in the aftermath of a fatal accident that befell James Neilson. He soon dispensed with the car and was not seen in action again until a brief return to racing in 1955 with a Jaguar C-Type at national level.

SKIP BARBER

AFTER a little racing while studying English at Harvard University, Skip Barber became a three-time SCCA national champion when he competed in Formula Ford and FB during 1969 with a Caldwell, and 1970 with two different Tecnos.

This success persuaded a group of Philadelphia businessmen to fund his racing programme under the banner Gene Mason Racing, competing in the F5000 L & M Series. Barber was still relatively inexperienced, however, when he headed to Europe in 1971 to buy a March 711 (to replace his 701, which had been written off in an early-season crash), which he intended racing in the USA.

Before shipping the new car, however, he tackled a few grands prix – "keeping out of the way" – as well as the non-championship Jochen Rindt Memorial Trophy at Hockenheim, in which he managed a very worthy sixth place.

Back in America, Barber enjoyed some success with the car in Formula A in 1972, taking in the two F1 world championship races that year, before switching to GT machinery thereafter.

In 1975, he founded the Skip Barber School of High Performance Driving, quickly building it up to become one of the world's best-known racing schools. After renaming it the Skip Barber Racing School, initially in conjunction with Saab, he instigated the very successful single-seater Pro Series, known as the Barber-Dodge Pro Series in deference to its engine supplier. In 1999, he sold the business, which continues to thrive, with schools at Road Atlanta, Sebring, Road America, Laguna Seca and Lime Rock.

In the mid-1980s, Barber took an interest in Lime Rock circuit in Connecticut, and following the sale of the driving school he took full control of the picturesque track, which caters for all kinds of events, from Trans Am and ALMS to historics.

BARBER, John (GB) b 22/7/1929, Little Marlow, Buckinghamshire

1953	Championship position: Unplaced								
	Race	Circuit	No	Entrant	Tyres	Capacity/Car/Engine	Comment		Q Pos/Entries
8	ARGENTINE GP	Buenos Aires	22	Cooper/Frazer-Hartwell Syndicate	D	2.0 Cooper T23-Bristol 6	7 laps behind		16/16
	GP Starts: 1 GP Wins: 0 Pole positions: 0 Fastest laps: 0 Points: 0								

BARBER, John 'Skip' (USA) b 16/11/1936, Philadelphia, Pennsylvania

1971	Championship position: Unplaced							
	Race	Circuit	No	Entrant	Tyres	Capacity/Car/Engine	Comment	Q Pos/Entries
dnq	MONACO GP	Monte Carlo	28	Gene Mason Racing	F	3.0 March 711-Cosworth V8		23/23
nc	DUTCH GP	Zandvoort	22	Gene Mason Racing	F	3.0 March 711-Cosworth V8	10 laps behind	24/24
ret	CANADIAN GP	Mosport Park	33	Gene Mason Racing	F	3.0 March 711-Cosworth V8	oil pressure	24/27
nc	US GP	Watkins Glen	33	Gene Mason Racing	F	3.0 March 711-Cosworth V8	pit stop – gearbox/7 laps behind	27/32
1972	Championship position: Unplaced							
nc	CANADIAN GP	Mosport Park	33	Gene Mason Racing	G	3.0 March 711-Cosworth V8	pit stops – dirt in throttle/-56 laps	22/25
16	US GP	Watkins Glen	33	Gene Mason Racing	G	3.0 March 711-Cosworth V8	2 laps behind	20/32
	GP Starts: 5 GP Wins: 0 Pole positions: 0 Fastest laps: 0 Points: 0							

PAOLO BARILLA

THE wealthy scion of a family that owned a famous pasta company, Paolo Barilla began racing in karts, winning the 100cc Italian title in 1976, before graduating to the Italian F3 series, where he took third overall in 1981. This paved the way for him to join the Minardi Formula 2 team alongside another newcomer, Alessandro Nannini, in 1982. It was an unrewarding season for Paolo, who had to grapple with the team's mid-season engine and tyre problems as well as a super-quick team-mate. He failed to score any points, and Autosport unkindly described him as "The formula's most untidy driver."

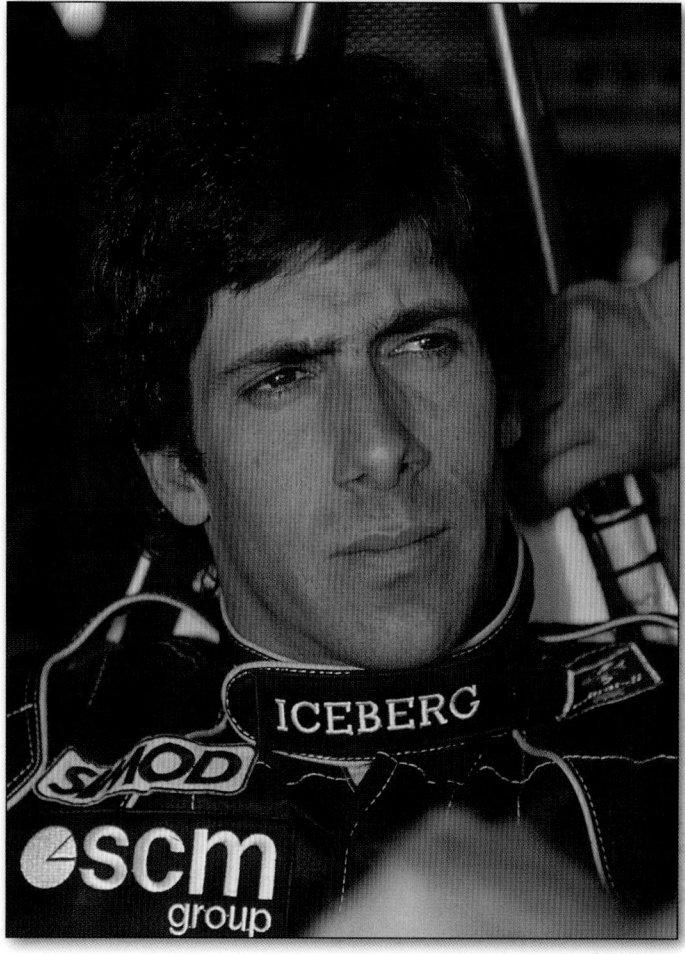

He began to make an impression and achieve international prominence in 1983 with a privately entered Lancia LC2. After some excellent performances, he was invited to join the works team the following season, when, despite the domination of the Porsche 956, Barilla still managed to claim second place at Kyalami (with Bob Wollek), third at Monza (with Mauro Baldi) and the Nürburgring (with Nannini), and fourth at Silverstone (again with Baldi).

His impressive performances led to a switch to the Joest Porsche team, and he drove immaculately to win the 1985 Le Mans 24-hours (with Klaus Ludwig and John Winter) and the 1986 Mount Fuji 1000km (with Piercarlo Ghinzani).

However, Paolo still yearned for success in single-seaters and he managed to secure a test driving role with Benetton, but spent two largely unproductive seasons attempting to get into F3000, switching from team to team in search of a competitive machine.

So it was back to Group C with Joest, where he gained a second place at Sebring in 1988 (with Winter) and a third in the Nürburgring 1000km (with Bob Wollek).

For 1989, Barilla went to Japan to compete in both their sports car and F3000 series, taking a win in the former category with a TOMS Toyota and a second place for Nakajima Racing at Nishinihon in the latter. This sole points scoring finish was good enough to place him tenth overall.

However, his knowledge of the Suzuka circuit and his friendship with Giancarlo Minardi provided him with the long-sought opportunity to make his grand prix debut – in place of the injured Pierluigi Martini – but his race was curtailed at the start with a broken clutch.

Paolo finally secured the number-two Minardi seat alongside Martini for the 1990 season. In truth, the M190 was something of a let-down compared to its fleet predecessor, but his performances in the car were lacklustre, and his place was taken over by Gianni Morbidelli before the 1990 season was out.

After a brief dalliance with sports cars in 1991, it was back to the family business for Paolo, where he worked alongside his brothers to learn all aspects of the burgeoning concern. He was briefly CEO and is now vice president.

For the eagle-eyed, the Barilla name continued to appear in racing circles throughout the 1990s, most notably on the helmet of Alex Zanardi.

BARILLA, Paolo (I) b 20/4/1961, Milan

	Race	Circuit	No	Entrant	Tyres	Capacity/Car/Engine	Comment	Q Pos/Entries
	1989 Championship position: Unplaced							
ret	JAPANESE GP	Suzuka	23	Minardi SpA	P	3.5 Minardi M189-Cosworth V8	clutch at start	19/39
	1990 Championship position: Unplaced							
ret	US GP (PHOENIX)	Phoenix	24	SCM Minardi Team	P	3.5 Minardi M189-Cosworth V8	driver cramp	14/35
ret	BRAZILIAN GP	Interlagos	24	SCM Minardi Team	P	3.5 Minardi M189-Cosworth V8	engine – valve	17/35
11	SAN MARINO GP	Imola	24	SCM Minardi Team	P	3.5 Minardi M190-Cosworth V8	spin/2 laps behind	27/34
dns	" "	"	24	SCM Minardi Team	P	3.5 Minardi M189-Cosworth V8	practice in this car only	– / –
ret	MONACO GP	Monte Carlo	24	SCM Minardi Team	P	3.5 Minardi M190-Cosworth V8	gearbox	19/35
dnq	CANADIAN GP	Montreal	24	SCM Minardi Team	P	3.5 Minardi M190-Cosworth V8		29/35
14	MEXICAN GP	Mexico City	24	SCM Minardi Team	P	3.5 Minardi M190-Cosworth V8	2 laps behind	16/35
dnq	FRENCH GP	Paul Ricard	24	SCM Minardi Team	P	3.5 Minardi M190-Cosworth V8		27/35
12	BRITISH GP	Silverstone	24	SCM Minardi Team	P	3.5 Minardi M190-Cosworth V8	2 laps behind	24/35
dnq	GERMAN GP	Hockenheim	24	SCM Minardi Team	P	3.5 Minardi M190-Cosworth V8		28/35
15	HUNGARIAN GP	Hungaroring	24	SCM Minardi Team	P	3.5 Minardi M190-Cosworth V8	3 laps behind	23/35
ret/dns	BELGIAN GP	Spa	24	SCM Minardi Team	P	3.5 Minardi M190-Cosworth V8	crashed at 2nd aborted start	25/33
dnq	ITALIAN GP	Monza	24	SCM Minardi Team	P	3.5 Minardi M190-Cosworth V8		28/33
dnq	PORTUGUESE GP	Estoril	24	SCM Minardi Team	P	3.5 Minardi M190-Cosworth V8		28/33
dnq	SPANISH GP	Jerez	24	SCM Minardi Team	P	3.5 Minardi M190-Cosworth V8		28/33

GP Starts: (8) 9   GP Wins: 0   Pole positions: 0   Fastest laps: 0   Points: 0

RUBENS BARRICHELLO

WHEN the curtain finally came down on Rubens Barrichello's illustrious Formula 1 career, the popular Brazilian had made a staggering total of 323 grand prix starts, with only Michael Schumacher on 287 within sight. His longevity in the sport's top echelon was such that the next active pursuer, Jenson Button, would need to race for another six seasons to overtake his amazing total.

Five times the Brazilian karting champion, 'Rubinho' arrived in Europe as a shy 17-year-old at the beginning of 1990, having contested only 11 Formula Ford races in his native country. He came to compete in the GM Lotus Euroseries and quickly became the season's front-runner, winning five rounds and the title. This triumph earned him a seat in West Surrey Racing's F3 team for 1991, and it was success again, as with four wins, he came through in a late-season surge to take the title ahead of close rival David Coulthard.

Already the subject of interest from Formula 1 teams, Barrichello took the next step up to F3000, where he became a consistent finisher, achieving third place in the final standings. That great talent spotter Eddie Jordan put his faith in the 21-year-old, who soon caused a stir with a stunning drive in the rain-soaked European GP at Donington, where he ran as high as second place until fuel pressure problems ended his race, although no doubt this performance reflected the benefit of traction control in the slippery conditions. He also outpaced the vastly experienced Ivan Capelli and Thierry Boutsen before the arrival of Eddie Irvine at Suzuka helped lift the team – and Barrichello – to a new level of performance.

Certainly Rubens started the 1994 season with real intent, before miraculously escaping serious injury in practice for the San Marino GP. The horrendous events of that weekend must have left him more traumatised than most as he struggled to come to terms with the loss of his friend and mentor, Ayrton Senna. Understandably, he took a little while to return to his best, and undoubtedly the joy of taking pole position at a rain-soaked Spa was the high point of his, and Jordan's, year.

Rumours abounded that Barrichello was a target for McLaren, but in the event he remained with Jordan for 1995, buoyed by the prospect of a works engine deal with Peugeot. Numerous excellent qualifying performances and second place in Canada showed what could be achieved, but a catalogue of mechanical failures cost the Brazilian and his team dear. The 1996 season soon produced the false dawn of a front-row start in Brazil, but after he slithered off the wet track in the race, his year slipped into a downward spiral and he never really regained his confidence.

Despite Barrichello's tender years, Jordan felt they could coax no more from the personable young driver, and an amicable parting led to him joining the newly formed Stewart Grand Prix team for 1997. The partnership proved productive, and his superb second place in the rain at Monaco gave credibility to both team and driver. While the following year was largely wasted in midfield obscurity, he emerged in 1999 as a much more mature performer. He ran at the front in a number of races and was rightly disappointed not to have given Stewart their first grand prix win, which fell to team-mate Johnny Herbert, who posted an unlikely victory at the Nürburgring.

Although Barrichello was slightly overshadowed by a resurgent Herbert towards the end of the year, he was still Ferrari's first choice to replace the departing Eddie Irvine for 2000. Being teamed with Michael Schumacher might not have been every driver's cup of tea, but he maintained that it was the best indicator of his own talent. The highlight of his first year with the Scuderia came at the German Grand Prix, where he finally ended his winless F1 career with a well-judged wet-weather success. Again paired with Schumacher for 2001, he showed well throughout the season, even

though a second career victory didn't come his way. His consistent finishes, however, were good enough for third overall in the championship.

Rubens finally won again in 2002. Indeed, the Brazilian took victory on four occasions and secured second overall in the drivers' championship, notching up 77 points, a good effort considering the team was effectively built around Schumacher. Barrichello played a supporting role once more in 2003, although he managed to knock up two more wins following impressive drives at Silverstone and Suzuka.

Barrichello's fifth season with the Scuderia found him again cast in a familiar supportive role and he helped ensure that Ferrari won the constructors' championship for the sixth year running. Although Schumacher naturally took much of the limelight, Rubens had a more than solid year, scoring points in 16 of the 18 races, including 14 podiums, two of which (in Italy and China) saw him on the top step.

In 2005, Rubens dutifully backed 'Schumi' once more. The Maranello team dropped the ball in a big way, however, leaving both drivers to struggle with recalcitrant machines. There was trouble brewing, and after Schumacher had enraged the normally placid Brazilian with his 'ungentlemanly' manoeuvres at both Monaco and Indianapolis, it seemed that Barrichello had had enough of stepping aside for his team-mate, and he set about finding a drive away from the team he had served so dutifully for six seasons.

Barrichello duly found a warm welcome at Honda as partner to Jenson Button in a strong driver line-up that proved an interesting match. At first, the Brazilian struggled to come to terms with the characteristics of the car. For the most part, he wore a somewhat non-plussed demeanor as the season slipped by and his contribution was largely overshadowed by Button's breakthrough win in Hungary, Honda taking fourth place in the constructors' standings.

For 2007, Honda produced a car so disappointing in performance that the team could only score six points, and all of this meagre haul came from the efforts of Jenson Button. Despite his illustrious career, the 35-year-old Brazilian could have been forgiven for thinking that his time was up after enduring a dreadful season and failing to score a single point. The following season was hardly an improvement, except at Silverstone, where an inspired tyre strategy brought an unexpected podium.

Salvation for Barrichello lay in the appointment of former Ferrari guru Ross Brawn who, having spent the season re-organising matters, had stepped into the breach when Honda pulled the plug on their programme. Picking up the pieces for 2009, the canny team principal already knew he had a special chassis, and when it was mated to a Mercedes engine, the Brawn GP001 hit the ground running and their rivals didn't know what had hit them. It was Jenson Button who made hay, but Barrichello was no slouch either, and his personal Indian summer yielded two more emotional wins, at Valencia and Monza.

There is no sentiment in Formula 1, however, and at the end of a fairytail season, the team passed to Mercedes, leaving the Brazilian to find a place with Williams and their new engine partner, Cosworth. Rubens took on the challenging task with relish, picking up points in nine races to take a more than respectable tenth place in the final points standings.

The following season, 2011, turned into something of a nightmare for all concerned at Williams, however, with an increasingly unhappy Barrichello salvaging two ninth places. To emphasise the team's unhappy situation, they also required two paying drivers on board for the 2011 season, and Rubens was unable to find the funding to keep his seat. With no suitable alternatives, he bade Formula 1 a fond farewell and set about forging a new career in Indy cars alongside his close friend, Tony Kanaan.

BARRICHELLO, Rubens (BR) b 23/5/1972, São Paulo

	Race	Circuit	No	Entrant	Tyres	Capacity/Car/Engine	Comment	Q Pos/Entries
1993	Championship position: 17th=		Wins: 0	Pole positions: 0		Fastest laps: 0	Points scored: 2	
ret	SOUTH AFRICAN GP	Kyalami	14	Sasol Jordan	G	3.5 Jordan 193-Hart V10	gearbox	14/26
ret	BRAZILIAN GP	Interlagos	14	Sasol Jordan	G	3.5 Jordan 193-Hart V10	gearbox hydraulics	14/26
10/ret	EUROPEAN GP	Donington	14	Sasol Jordan	G	3.5 Jordan 193-Hart V10	fuel pressure/5 laps behind	12/26
ret	SAN MARINO GP	Imola	14	Sasol Jordan	G	3.5 Jordan 193-Hart V10	spun off	13/26
12	SPANISH GP	Barcelona	14	Sasol Jordan	G	3.5 Jordan 193-Hart V10	pit stop – front wing flap/-3 laps	17/26
9	MONACO GP	Monte Carlo	14	Sasol Jordan	G	3.5 Jordan 193-Hart V10	2 laps behind	16/26
ret	CANADIAN GP	Montreal	14	Sasol Jordan	G	3.5 Jordan 193-Hart V10	electrical	14/26
7	FRENCH GP	Magny Cours	14	Sasol Jordan	G	3.5 Jordan 193-Hart V10	fading brakes/1 lap behind	8/26
10	BRITISH GP	Silverstone	14	Sasol Jordan	G	3.5 Jordan 193-Hart V10	1 lap behind	15/26
ret	GERMAN GP	Hockenheim	14	Sasol Jordan	G	3.5 Jordan 193-Hart V10	wheel bearing failure	17/26
ret	HUNGARIAN GP	Hungaroring	14	Sasol Jordan	G	3.5 Jordan 193-Hart V10	collision – Suzuki/lost wheel	16/26
ret	BELGIAN GP	Spa	14	Sasol Jordan	G	3.5 Jordan 193-Hart V10	wheel bearing failure	13/25
ret	ITALIAN GP	Monza	14	Sasol Jordan	G	3.5 Jordan 193-Hart V10	collision with Lehto on lap 1	19/26
13	PORTUGUESE GP	Estoril	14	Sasol Jordan	G	3.5 Jordan 193-Hart V10	pit stop – puncture/3 laps behind	15/26
5	JAPANESE GP	Suzuka	14	Sasol Jordan	G	3.5 Jordan 193-Hart V10		12/24
11	AUSTRALIAN GP	Adelaide	14	Sasol Jordan	G	3.5 Jordan 193-Hart V10	3 laps behind	13/24
1994	Championship position: 6th		Wins: 0	Pole positions: 1		Fastest laps: 0	Points scored: 19	
4	BRAZILIAN GP	Interlagos	14	Sasol Jordan	G	3.5 Jordan 194-Hart V10	1 lap behind	14/28
3	PACIFIC GP	T.I. Circuit	14	Sasol Jordan	G	3.5 Jordan 194-Hart V10	1 lap behind	8/28
dns	SAN MARINO GP	Imola	14	Sasol Jordan	G	3.5 Jordan 194-Hart V10	unfit – accident in practice	28/28
ret	MONACO GP	Monte Carlo	14	Sasol Jordan	G	3.5 Jordan 194-Hart V10	electrics	15/24
ret	SPANISH GP	Barcelona	14	Sasol Jordan	G	3.5 Jordan 194-Hart V10	gearbox	5/27
7	CANADIAN GP	Montreal	14	Sasol Jordan	G	3.5 Jordan 194-Hart V10	1 lap behind	6/27
ret	FRENCH GP	Magny Cours	14	Sasol Jordan	G	3.5 Jordan 194-Hart V10	taken off by Alesi	7/28
4*	BRITISH GP	Silverstone	14	Sasol Jordan	G	3.5 Jordan 194-Hart V10	*2nd car dsq/collision Häkkinen	6/28
ret	GERMAN GP	Hockenheim	14	Sasol Jordan	G	3.5 Jordan 194-Hart V10	multiple accident on lap 1	11/28
ret	HUNGARIAN GP	Hungaroring	14	Sasol Jordan	G	3.5 Jordan 194-Hart V10	accident with Irvine & Katayama	10/28
ret	BELGIAN GP	Spa	14	Sasol Jordan	G	3.5 Jordan 194-Hart V10	spun off	1/28
4	ITALIAN GP	Monza	14	Sasol Jordan	G	3.5 Jordan 194-Hart V10		16/28
4	PORTUGUESE GP	Estoril	14	Sasol Jordan	G	3.5 Jordan 194-Hart V10		8/28
12	EUROPEAN GP	Jerez	14	Sasol Jordan	G	3.5 Jordan 194-Hart V10	pit stop – puncture/1 lap behind	5/28
ret	JAPANESE GP	Suzuka	14	Sasol Jordan	G	3.5 Jordan 194-Hart V10	electrics	10/28
4	AUSTRALIAN GP	Adelaide	14	Sasol Jordan	G	3.5 Jordan 194-Hart V10		5/28
1995	Championship position: 11th		Wins: 0	Pole positions: 0		Fastest laps: 0	Points scored: 11	
ret	BRAZILIAN GP	Interlagos	14	Total Jordan Peugeot	G	3.0 Jordan 195-Peugeot V10	gearbox	16/26
ret	ARGENTINE GP	Buenos Aires	14	Total Jordan Peugeot	G	3.0 Jordan 195-Peugeot V10	started from pitlane/oil leak	10/26
ret	SAN MARINO GP	Imola	14	Total Jordan Peugeot	G	3.0 Jordan 195-Peugeot V10	gearbox	10/26
7	SPANISH GP	Barcelona	14	Total Jordan Peugeot	G	3.0 Jordan 195-Peugeot V10	1 lap behind	8/26
ret	MONACO GP	Monte Carlo	14	Total Jordan Peugeot	G	3.0 Jordan 195-Peugeot V10	throttle	11/26
2	CANADIAN GP	Montreal	14	Total Jordan Peugeot	G	3.0 Jordan 195-Peugeot V10		9/24
6	FRENCH GP	Magny Cours	14	Total Jordan Peugeot	G	3.0 Jordan 195-Peugeot V10	1 lap behind	5/24
11/ret	BRITISH GP	Silverstone	14	Total Jordan Peugeot	G	3.0 Jordan 195-Peugeot V10	collision with Blundell/-2 laps	9/24
ret	GERMAN GP	Hockenheim	14	Total Jordan Peugeot	G	3.0 Jordan 195-Peugeot V10	engine	5/24
7	HUNGARIAN GP	Hungaroring	14	Total Jordan Peugeot	G	3.0 Jordan 195-Peugeot V10	1 lap behind	14/24
6	BELGIAN GP	Spa	14	Total Jordan Peugeot	G	3.0 Jordan 195-Peugeot V10		12/24
ret	ITALIAN GP	Monza	14	Total Jordan Peugeot	G	3.0 Jordan 195-Peugeot V10	hydraulics	6/24
11	PORTUGUESE GP	Estoril	14	Total Jordan Peugeot	G	3.0 Jordan 195-Peugeot V10	1 lap behind	8/24
4	EUROPEAN GP	Nürburgring	14	Total Jordan Peugeot	G	3.0 Jordan 195-Peugeot V10	1 lap behind	11/24
ret	PACIFIC GP	T.I. Circuit	14	Total Jordan Peugeot	G	3.0 Jordan 195-Peugeot V10	engine	11/24
ret	JAPANESE GP	Suzuka	14	Total Jordan Peugeot	G	3.0 Jordan 195-Peugeot V10	spun off	10/24
ret	AUSTRALIAN GP	Adelaide	14	Total Jordan Peugeot	G	3.0 Jordan 195-Peugeot V10	understeer – accident	7/24
1996	Championship position: 8th		Wins: 0	Pole positions: 0		Fastest laps: 0	Points scored: 14	
ret	AUSTRALIAN GP	Melbourne	11	B & H Total Jordan Peugeot	G	3.0 Jordan 196-Peugeot V10	engine	8/22
ret	BRAZILIAN GP	Interlagos	11	B & H Total Jordan Peugeot	G	3.0 Jordan 196-Peugeot V10	spun off	2/22
4	ARGENTINE GP	Buenos Aires	11	B & H Total Jordan Peugeot	G	3.0 Jordan 196-Peugeot V10		6/22
5	EUROPEAN GP	Nürburgring	11	B & H Total Jordan Peugeot	G	3.0 Jordan 196-Peugeot V10		5/22
5	SAN MARINO GP	Imola	11	B & H Total Jordan Peugeot	G	3.0 Jordan 196-Peugeot V10	1 lap behind	9/22
ret	MONACO GP	Monte Carlo	11	B & H Total Jordan Peugeot	G	3.0 Jordan 196-Peugeot V10	spun off on lap 1	6/22
ret	SPANISH GP	Barcelona	11	B & H Total Jordan Peugeot	G	3.0 Jordan 196-Peugeot V10	clutch	7/22
ret	CANADIAN GP	Montreal	11	B & H Total Jordan Peugeot	G	3.0 Jordan 196-Peugeot V10	clutch	8/22
9	FRENCH GP	Magny Cours	11	B & H Total Jordan Peugeot	G	3.0 Jordan 196-Peugeot V10	1 lap behind	11/22
4	BRITISH GP	Silverstone	11	B & H Total Jordan Peugeot	G	3.0 Jordan 196-Peugeot V10		6/22
6	GERMAN GP	Hockenheim	11	B & H Total Jordan Peugeot	G	3.0 Jordan 196-Peugeot V10		9/20
6	HUNGARIAN GP	Hungaroring	11	B & H Total Jordan Peugeot	G	3.0 Jordan 196-Peugeot V10	1 lap behind	13/20
ret	BELGIAN GP	Spa	11	B & H Total Jordan Peugeot	G	3.0 Jordan 196-Peugeot V10	collision damage	10/20
5	ITALIAN GP	Monza	11	B & H Total Jordan Peugeot	G	3.0 Jordan 196-Peugeot V10		10/20
ret	PORTUGUESE GP	Estoril	11	B & H Total Jordan Peugeot	G	3.0 Jordan 196-Peugeot V10	spun off	9/20
9	JAPANESE GP	Suzuka	11	B & H Total Jordan Peugeot	G	3.0 Jordan 196-Peugeot V10		11/20
1997	Championship position: 13th		Wins: 0	Pole positions: 0		Fastest laps: 0	Points scored: 6	
ret	AUSTRALIAN GP	Melbourne	22	Stewart Ford	B	3.0 Stewart SF1-Ford Zetec-R V10	engine	11/22
ret	BRAZILIAN GP	Interlagos	22	Stewart Ford	B	3.0 Stewart SF1-Ford Zetec-R V10	broken suspension link	11/22
ret	ARGENTINE GP	Buenos Aires	22	Stewart Ford	B	3.0 Stewart SF1-Ford Zetec-R V10	hydraulics	5/22
ret	SAN MARINO GP	Imola	22	Stewart Ford	B	3.0 Stewart SF1-Ford Zetec-R V10	engine	13/22
2	MONACO GP	Monte Carlo	22	Stewart Ford	B	3.0 Stewart SF1-Ford Zetec-R V10		10/22
ret	SPANISH GP	Barcelona	22	Stewart Ford	B	3.0 Stewart SF1-Ford Zetec-R V10	engine	17/22
ret	CANADIAN GP	Montreal	22	Stewart Ford	B	3.0 Stewart SF1-Ford Zetec-R V10	gearbox	3/22

ret	FRENCH GP	Magny Cours	22	Stewart Ford	B	3.0 Stewart SF1-Ford Zetec-R V10	*engine*	13/22
ret	BRITISH GP	Silverstone	22	Stewart Ford	B	3.0 Stewart SF1-Ford Zetec-R V10	*engine*	22/22
ret	GERMAN GP	Hockenheim	22	Stewart Ford	B	3.0 Stewart SF1-Ford Zetec-R V10	*engine*	12/22
ret	HUNGARIAN GP	Hungaroring	22	Stewart Ford	B	3.0 Stewart SF1-Ford Zetec-R V10	*engine*	11/22
ret	BELGIAN GP	Spa	22	Stewart Ford	B	3.0 Stewart SF1-Ford Zetec-R V10	*spun off*	12/22
13	ITALIAN GP	Monza	22	Stewart Ford	B	3.0 Stewart SF1-Ford Zetec-R V10	*poor handling/1 lap behind*	11/22
ret	AUSTRIAN GP	A1-Ring	22	Stewart Ford	B	3.0 Stewart SF1-Ford Zetec-R V10	*crashed out*	5/22
ret	LUXEMBOURG GP	Nürburgring	22	Stewart Ford	B	3.0 Stewart SF1-Ford Zetec-R V10	*hydraulics*	9/22
ret	JAPANESE GP	Suzuka	22	Stewart Ford	B	3.0 Stewart SF1-Ford Zetec-R V10	*spun off*	12/22
ret	EUROPEAN GP	Jerez	22	Stewart Ford	B	3.0 Stewart SF1-Ford Zetec-R V10	*gearbox*	12/22

1998 Championship position: 12th   Wins: 0   Pole positions: 0   Fastest laps: 0   Points scored: 4

ret	AUSTRALIAN GP	Melbourne	10	Stewart Ford	B	3.0 Stewart SF2-Ford Zetec R V10	*gearbox failure on grid*	14/22
ret	BRAZILIAN GP	Interlagos	10	Stewart Ford	B	3.0 Stewart SF2-Ford Zetec R V10	*gearbox*	13/22
10	ARGENTINE GP	Buenos Aires	10	Stewart Ford	B	3.0 Stewart SF2-Ford Zetec R V10	*loose bodywork/2 laps behind*	14/22
ret	SAN MARINO GP	Imola	10	Stewart Ford	B	3.0 Stewart SF2-Ford Zetec R V10	*spun off after collision on lap 1*	17/22
5	SPANISH GP	Barcelona	10	Stewart Ford	B	3.0 Stewart SF2-Ford Zetec R V10	*1 lap behind*	9/22
ret	MONACO GP	Monte Carlo	10	Stewart Ford	B	3.0 Stewart SF2-Ford Zetec R V10	*suspension failure*	14/22
5	CANADIAN GP	Montreal	10	Stewart Ford	B	3.0 Stewart SF2-Ford Zetec R V10	*1 lap behind*	13/22
10	FRENCH GP	Magny Cours	10	Stewart Ford	B	3.0 Stewart SF2-Ford Zetec R V10	*handling problems/2 laps behind*	14/22
ret	BRITISH GP	Silverstone	10	Stewart Ford	B	3.0 Stewart SF2-Ford Zetec R V10	*spun off*	18/22
ret	AUSTRIAN GP	A1-Ring	10	Stewart Ford	B	3.0 Stewart SF2-Ford Zetec R V10	*brakes*	5/22
ret	GERMAN GP	Hockenheim	10	Stewart Ford	B	3.0 Stewart SF2-Ford Zetec R V10	*gearbox*	13/22
ret	HUNGARIAN GP	Hungaroring	10	Stewart Ford	B	3.0 Stewart SF2-Ford Zetec R V10	*gearbox*	14/22
ret/dns	BELGIAN GP	Spa	10	Stewart Ford	B	3.0 Stewart SF2-Ford Zetec R V10	*accident at first start*	14/22
10	ITALIAN GP	Monza	10	Stewart Ford	B	3.0 Stewart SF2-Ford Zetec R V10	*1 lap behind*	13/22
11	LUXEMBOURG GP	Nürburgring	10	Stewart Ford	B	3.0 Stewart SF2-Ford Zetec R V10	*2 laps behind*	12/22
ret	JAPANESE GP	Suzuka	10	Stewart Ford	B	3.0 Stewart SF2-Ford Zetec R V10	*differential*	16/22

1999 Championship position: 7th   Wins: 0   Pole positions: 1   Fastest laps: 0   Points scored: 21

5	AUSTRALIAN GP	Melbourne	16	Stewart Ford	B	3.0 Stewart SF3-Ford CR1 V10		4/22
ret	BRAZILIAN GP	Interlagos	16	Stewart Ford	B	3.0 Stewart SF3-Ford CR1 V100	*engine/led race*	3/22
3	SAN MARINO GP	Imola	16	Stewart Ford	B	3.0 Stewart SF3-Ford CR1 V10	*1 lap behind*	6/22
ret	MONACO GP	Monte Carlo	16	Stewart Ford	B	3.0 Stewart SF3-Ford CR1 V10	*suspension failure – accident*	5/22
dsq*	SPANISH GP	Barcelona	16	Stewart Ford	B	3.0 Stewart SF3-Ford CR1 V10	**illegal undertray/7th on road*	7/22
ret	CANADIAN GP	Montreal	16	Stewart Ford	B	3.0 Stewart SF3-Ford CR1 V10	*collision damage*	5/22
3	FRENCH GP	Magny Cours	16	Stewart Ford	B	3.0 Stewart SF3-Ford CR1 V10		1/22
8	BRITISH GP	Silverstone	16	Stewart Ford	B	3.0 Stewart SF3-Ford CR1 V10	*puncture*	7/22
ret	AUSTRIAN GP	A1-Ring	16	Stewart Ford	B	3.0 Stewart SF3-Ford CR1 V10	*engine*	5/22
ret	GERMAN GP	Hockenheim	16	Stewart Ford	B	3.0 Stewart SF3-Ford CR1 V10	*hydraulics*	6/22
5	HUNGARIAN GP	Hungaroring	16	Stewart Ford	B	3.0 Stewart SF3-Ford CR1 V10		8/22
10	BELGIAN GP	Spa	16	Stewart Ford	B	3.0 Stewart SF3-Ford CR1 V10	*lack of grip*	7/22
4	ITALIAN GP	Monza	16	Stewart Ford	B	3.0 Stewart SF3-Ford CR1 V10		7/22
3	EUROPEAN GP	Nürburgring	16	Stewart Ford	B	3.0 Stewart SF3-Ford CR1 V10		15/22
5	MALAYSIAN GP	Sepang	16	Stewart Ford	B	3.0 Stewart SF3-Ford CR1 V10		6/22
8	JAPANESE GP	Suzuka	16	Stewart Ford	B	3.0 Stewart SF3-Ford CR1 V10	*1 lap behind*	13/22

2000 Championship position: 4th   Wins: 1   Pole positions: 1   Fastest laps: 3   Points scored: 62

2	AUSTRALIAN GP	Melbourne	4	Scuderia Ferrari Marlboro	B	3.0 Ferrari F1-2000-V10	*FL*	4/22
ret	BRAZILIAN GP	Interlagos	4	Scuderia Ferrari Marlboro	B	3.0 Ferrari F1-2000-V10	*leaking hydraulics*	4/22
4	SAN MARINO GP	Imola	4	Scuderia Ferrari Marlboro	B	3.0 Ferrari F1-2000-V10	*loose seat belts/poor set-up*	4/22
ret	BRITISH GP	Silverstone	4	Scuderia Ferrari Marlboro	B	3.0 Ferrari F1-2000-V10	*leaking hydraulics/spin*	1/22
3	SPANISH GP	Barcelona	4	Scuderia Ferrari Marlboro	B	3.0 Ferrari F1-2000-V10		3/22
4	EUROPEAN GP	Nürburgring	4	Scuderia Ferrari Marlboro	B	3.0 Ferrari F1-2000-V10	*visibility/gearshift problems/-1 lap*	4/22
2	MONACO GP	Monte Carlo	4	Scuderia Ferrari Marlboro	B	3.0 Ferrari F1-2000-V10		6/22
2	CANADIAN GP	Montreal	4	Scuderia Ferrari Marlboro	B	3.0 Ferrari F1-2000-V10		3/22
3	FRENCH GP	Magny Cours	4	Scuderia Ferrari Marlboro	B	3.0 Ferrari F1-2000-V10	*slow 2nd pit stop/tyre problems*	3/22
3	AUSTRIAN GP	A1-Ring	4	Scuderia Ferrari Marlboro	B	3.0 Ferrari F1-2000-V10	*damage from lap 1 collison*	3/22
1	GERMAN GP	Hockenheim	4	Scuderia Ferrari Marlboro	B	3.0 Ferrari F1-2000-V10	*FL*	18/22
4	HUNGARIAN GP	Hungaroring	4	Scuderia Ferrari Marlboro	B	3.0 Ferrari F1-2000-V10		5/22
ret	BELGIAN GP	Spa	4	Scuderia Ferrari Marlboro	B	3.0 Ferrari F1-2000-V10	*fuel pressure/FL*	10/22
ret	ITALIAN GP	Monza	4	Scuderia Ferrari Marlboro	B	3.0 Ferrari F1-2000-V10	*multiple collision on lap 1*	2/22
2	U S GP	Indianapolis	4	Scuderia Ferrari Marlboro	B	3.0 Ferrari F1-2000-V10		4/22
4	JAPANESE GP	Suzuka	4	Scuderia Ferrari Marlboro	B	3.0 Ferrari F1-2000-V10		4/22
3	MALAYSIAN GP	Sepang	4	Scuderia Ferrari Marlboro	B	3.0 Ferrari F1-2000-V10		4/22

2001 Championship position: 3rd   Wins: 0   Pole positions: 0   Fastest laps: 0   Points scored: 56

3	AUSTRALIAN GP	Melbourne	2	Scuderia Ferrari Marlboro	B	3.0 Ferrari F2001-V10	*hit Frentzen, front wheel problem*	2/22
2	MALAYSIAN GP	Sepang	2	Scuderia Ferrari Marlboro	B	3.0 Ferrari F2001-V10		2/22
ret	BRAZILIAN GP	Interlagos	2	Scuderia Ferrari Marlboro	B	3.0 Ferrari F2001-V10	*ran into Ralf Schumacher*	6/22
3	SAN MARINO GP	Imola	2	Scuderia Ferrari Marlboro	B	3.0 Ferrari F2001-V10		6/22
ret	SPANISH GP	Barcelona	2	Scuderia Ferrari Marlboro	B	3.0 Ferrari F2001-V10	*broken rear suspension*	4/22
3	AUSTRIAN GP	A1-Ring	2	Scuderia Ferrari Marlboro	B	3.0 Ferrari F2001-V10	*let M Schumacher into 2nd place*	4/22
2	MONACO GP	Monte Carlo	2	Scuderia Ferrari Marlboro	B	3.0 Ferrari F2001-V10	*cramp due to pedal problems*	4/22
ret	CANADIAN GP	Montreal	2	Scuderia Ferrari Marlboro	B	3.0 Ferrari F2001-V10	*spun off avoiding Montoya*	5/22
5	EUROPEAN GP	Nürburgring	2	Scuderia Ferrari Marlboro	B	3.0 Ferrari F2001-V10		4/22
3	FRENCH GP	Magny Cours	2	Scuderia Ferrari Marlboro	B	3.0 Ferrari F2001-V10	*3 pit stop strategy*	8/22
3	BRITISH GP	Silverstone	2	Scuderia Ferrari Marlboro	B	3.0 Ferrari F2001-V10		6/22
2	GERMAN GP	Hockenheim	2	Scuderia Ferrari Marlboro	B	3.0 Ferrari F2001-V10		6/22
2	HUNGARIAN GP	Hungaroring	2	Scuderia Ferrari Marlboro	B	3.0 Ferrari F2001-V10		3/22
5	BELGIAN GP	Spa	2	Scuderia Ferrari Marlboro	B	3.0 Ferrari F2001-V10	*hit marker cone*	5/22
2	ITALIAN GP	Monza	2	Scuderia Ferrari Marlboro	B	3.0 Ferrari F2001-V10	*delayed at pit stop*	2/22
15/ret	U S GP	Indianapolis	2	Scuderia Ferrari Marlboro	B	3.0 Ferrari F2001-V10	*engine/2 laps behind*	5/22
5	JAPANESE GP	Suzuka	2	Scuderia Ferrari Marlboro	B	3.0 Ferrari F2001-V10		4/22

Barrichello leads the field at the start of the 2003 Japanese Grand Prix. This victory was one of nine during his six seasons at Maranello, which were largely spent playing a supporting role in the successful championship campaigns of Michael Schumacher.

2002 Championship position: 2nd   Wins: 4   Pole positions: 3   Fastest laps: 5   Points scored: 77

ret	AUSTRALIAN GP	Melbourne	2	Scuderia Ferrari Marlboro	B	3.0 Ferrari F2001-V10	hit by Ralf Schumacher at start	1/22
ret	MALAYSIAN GP	Sepang	2	Scuderia Ferrari Marlboro	B	3.0 Ferrari F2001-V10	engine	3/22
ret	BRAZILIAN GP	Interlagos	2	Scuderia Ferrari Marlboro	B	3.0 Ferrari F2001-V10	hydraulics/led race	8/22
2	SAN MARINO GP	Imola	2	Scuderia Ferrari Marlboro	B	3.0 Ferrari F2002-V10	FL	2/22
dns	SPANISH GP	Barcelona	2	Scuderia Ferrari Marlboro	B	3.0 Ferrari F2002-V10	gearbox failure on formation grid	2/21
2	AUSTRIAN GP	A1-Ring	2	Scuderia Ferrari Marlboro	B	3.0 Ferrari F2002-V10	let M Schumacher win on last lap	1/22
7	MONACO GP	Monte Carlo	2	Scuderia Ferrari Marlboro	B	3.0 Ferrari F2002-V10	stop-go pen/drive thru pen/FL	5/22
3	CANADIAN GP	Montreal	2	Scuderia Ferrari Marlboro	B	3.0 Ferrari F2002-V10		3/22
1	EUROPEAN GP	Nürburgring	2	Scuderia Ferrari Marlboro	B	3.0 Ferrari F2002-V10		4/22
2	BRITISH GP	Silverstone	2	Scuderia Ferrari Marlboro	B	3.0 Ferrari F2002-V10	started from back of grid/FL	2/22
dns	FRENCH GP	Magny Cours	2	Scuderia Ferrari Marlboro	B	3.0 Ferrari F2002-V10	electrics on formation grid	3/21
4	GERMAN GP	Hockenheim	2	Scuderia Ferrari Marlboro	B	3.0 Ferrari F2002-V10		3/22
1	HUNGARIAN GP	Hungaroring	2	Scuderia Ferrari Marlboro	B	3.0 Ferrari F2002-V10		1/20
2	BELGIAN GP	Spa	2	Scuderia Ferrari Marlboro	B	3.0 Ferrari F2002-V10		3/20
1	ITALIAN GP	Monza	2	Scuderia Ferrari Marlboro	B	3.0 Ferrari F2002-V10	FL	4/20
1	U S GP	Indianapolis	2	Scuderia Ferrari Marlboro	B	3.0 Ferrari F2002-V10	botched finish by M Schumacher/FL	2/20
2	JAPANESE GP	Suzuka	2	Scuderia Ferrari Marlboro	B	3.0 Ferrari F2002-V10		2/20

2003 Championship position: 4th   Wins: 2   Pole positions: 3   Fastest laps: 3   Points scored: 65

ret	AUSTRALIAN GP	Melbourne	2	Scuderia Ferrari Marlboro	B	3.0 Ferrari F2002-V10	crashed – HANS device problems	2/20
2	MALAYSIAN GP	Sepang	2	Scuderia Ferrari Marlboro	B	3.0 Ferrari F2002-V10	slight misfire	5/20
ret	BRAZILIAN GP	Interlagos	2	Scuderia Ferrari Marlboro	B	3.0 Ferrari F2002-V10	out of fuel when leading/FL	1/20
3	SAN MARINO GP	Imola	2	Scuderia Ferrari Marlboro	B	3.0 Ferrari F2002-V10		3/20
3	SPANISH GP	Barcelona	2	Scuderia Ferrari Marlboro	B	3.0 Ferrari F2003-GA V10	tyre problems/FL	2/20
3	AUSTRIAN GP	A1-Ring	2	Scuderia Ferrari Marlboro	B	3.0 Ferrari F2003-GA V10	delayed at first pit stop	5/20
8	MONACO GP	Monte Carlo	2	Scuderia Ferrari Marlboro	B	3.0 Ferrari F2003-GA V10		7/19
5	CANADIAN GP	Montreal	2	Scuderia Ferrari Marlboro	B	3.0 Ferrari F2003-GA V10		5/20
3	EUROPEAN GP	Nürburgring	2	Scuderia Ferrari Marlboro	B	3.0 Ferrari F2003-GA V10		5/20
7	FRENCH GP	Magny Cours	2	Scuderia Ferrari Marlboro	B	3.0 Ferrari F2003-GA V10	spun to tail of field on lap 1	8/20
1	BRITISH GP	Silverstone	2	Scuderia Ferrari Marlboro	B	3.0 Ferrari F2003-GA V10	FL	1/20
ret	GERMAN GP	Hockenheim	2	Scuderia Ferrari Marlboro	B	3.0 Ferrari F2003-GA V10	hit by Ralf Schumacher at start	2/20
ret	HUNGARIAN GP	Hungaroring	2	Scuderia Ferrari Marlboro	B	3.0 Ferrari F2003-GA V10	rear suspension failure	5/20
3	ITALIAN GP	Monza	2	Scuderia Ferrari Marlboro	B	3.0 Ferrari F2003-GA V10		3/20
ret	U S GP	Indianapolis	2	Scuderia Ferrari Marlboro	B	3.0 Ferrari F2003-GA V10	collision with Montoya	2/20
1	JAPANESE GP	Suzuka	2	Scuderia Ferrari Marlboro	B	3.0 Ferrari F2003-GA V10		1/20

2004 Championship position: 2nd   Wins: 2   Pole positions: 4   Fastest laps: 4   Points scored: 114

2	AUSTRALIAN GP	Melbourne	2	Scuderia Ferrari Marlboro	B	3.0 Ferrari F2004 V10	long brake pedal	2/20
4	MALAYSIAN GP	Sepang	2	Scuderia Ferrari Marlboro	B	3.0 Ferrari F2004 V10		3/20
2	BAHRAIN GP	Bahrain Circuit	2	Scuderia Ferrari Marlboro	B	3.0 Ferrari F2004 V10		2/20
6	SAN MARINO GP	Imola	2	Scuderia Ferrari Marlboro	B	3.0 Ferrari F2004 V10		4/20
2	SPANISH GP	Barcelona	2	Scuderia Ferrari Marlboro	B	3.0 Ferrari F2004 V10		5/20
3	MONACO GP	Monte Carlo	2	Scuderia Ferrari Marlboro	B	3.0 Ferrari F2004 V10	handling problems	6/20
2	EUROPEAN GP	Nürburgring	2	Scuderia Ferrari Marlboro	B	3.0 Ferrari F2004 V10	minor collision with Sato	7/20
2*	CANADIAN GP	Montreal	2	Scuderia Ferrari Marlboro	B	3.0 Ferrari F2004 V10	*2nd place car disqualified/FL	7/20
2	U S GP	Indianapolis	2	Scuderia Ferrari Marlboro	B	3.0 Ferrari F2004 V10	FL	1/20
3	FRENCH GP	Magny Cours	2	Scuderia Ferrari Marlboro	B	3.0 Ferrari F2004 V10	strong drive through field	10/20
3	BRITISH GP	Silverstone	2	Scuderia Ferrari Marlboro	B	3.0 Ferrari F2004 V10		2/20
12	GERMAN GP	Hockenheim	2	Scuderia Ferrari Marlboro	B	3.0 Ferrari F2004 V10	collision with Coulthard	7/20
2	HUNGARIAN GP	Hungaroring	2	Scuderia Ferrari Marlboro	B	3.0 Ferrari F2004 V10		2/20
3	BELGIAN GP	Spa	2	Scuderia Ferrari Marlboro	B	3.0 Ferrari F2004 V10	delayed by collision damage	6/20
1	ITALIAN GP	Monza	2	Scuderia Ferrari Marlboro	B	3.0 Ferrari F2004 V10	FL	1/20
1	CHINESE GP	Shanghai	2	Scuderia Ferrari Marlboro	B	3.0 Ferrari F2004 V10		1/20
ret	JAPANESE GP	Suzuka	2	Scuderia Ferrari Marlboro	B	3.0 Ferrari F2004 V10	collision with Coulthard/FL	15/20
3	BRAZILIAN GP	Interlagos	2	Scuderia Ferrari Marlboro	B	3.0 Ferrari F2004 V10	ran on intermediates at start	1/20

2005 Championship position: 8th   Wins: 0   Pole positions: 0   Fastest laps: 0   Points scored: 38

	GP	Circuit	No	Team	Tyre	Engine	Notes	
2	AUSTRALIAN GP	Melbourne	2	Scuderia Ferrari Marlboro	B	3.0 Ferrari F2004M-Ferrari V10	brake balance problem	11/20
ret	MALAYSIAN GP	Sepang	2	Scuderia Ferrari Marlboro	B	3.0 Ferrari F2004M-Ferrari V10	oversteer led to worn out tyres	12/20
9	BAHRAIN GP	Bahrain	2	Scuderia Ferrari Marlboro	B	3.0 Ferrari F2005-Ferrari V10	high tyre wear	15/20
ret	SAN MARINO GP	Imola	2	Scuderia Ferrari Marlboro	B	3.0 Ferrari F2005-Ferrari V10	electrics	9/20
9	SPANISH GP	Barcelona	2	Scuderia Ferrari Marlboro	B	3.0 Ferrari F2005-Ferrari V10	tyre problems/1 lap behind	16/18
8	MONACO GP	Monte Carlo	2	Scuderia Ferrari Marlboro	B	3.0 Ferrari F2005-Ferrari V10	stalled pit stop/also drive thru pen	10/18
3	EUROPEAN GP	Nürburgring	2	Scuderia Ferrari Marlboro	B	3.0 Ferrari F2005-Ferrari V10	three pit stop strategy	7/20
3	CANADIAN GP	Montreal	2	Scuderia Ferrari Marlboro	B	3.0 Ferrari F2005-Ferrari V10	no qualifying time set	20/20
2	U S GP	Indianapolis	2	Scuderia Ferrari Marlboro	B	3.0 Ferrari F2005-Ferrari V10		7/20
9	FRENCH GP	Magny Cours	2	Scuderia Ferrari Marlboro	B	3.0 Ferrari F2005-Ferrari V10	1 lap behind	5/20
7	BRITISH GP	Silverstone	2	Scuderia Ferrari Marlboro	B	3.0 Ferrari F2005-Ferrari V10	brake problems	6/20
10	GERMAN GP	Hockenheim	2	Scuderia Ferrari Marlboro	B	3.0 Ferrari F2005-Ferrari V10	poor grip/1 lap behind	15/20
10	HUNGARIAN GP	Hungaroring	2	Scuderia Ferrari Marlboro	B	3.0 Ferrari F2005-Ferrari V10	collision with Trulli/1 lap behind	7/20
10	TURKISH GP	Hungaroring	2	Scuderia Ferrari Marlboro	B	3.0 Ferrari F2005-Ferrari V10	tyre problems – no grip/-1 lap	11/20
12	ITALIAN GP	Monza	2	Scuderia Ferrari Marlboro	B	3.0 Ferrari F2005-Ferrari V10	puncture/1 lap behind	8/20
5	BELGIAN GP	Spa	2	Scuderia Ferrari Marlboro	B	3.0 Ferrari F2005-Ferrari V10		13/20
6	BRAZILIAN GP	Interlagos	2	Scuderia Ferrari Marlboro	B	3.0 Ferrari F2005-Ferrari V10		10/20
11	JAPANESE GP	Suzuka	2	Scuderia Ferrari Marlboro	B	3.0 Ferrari F2005-Ferrari V10	delayed by puncture	9/20
12	CHINESE GP	Shanghai	2	Scuderia Ferrari Marlboro	B	3.0 Ferrari F2005-Ferrari V10		8/20

2006 Championship position: 7th   Wins: 0   Pole positions: 0   Fastest laps: 0   Points scored: 30

	GP	Circuit	No	Team	Tyre	Engine	Notes	
15	BAHRAIN GP	Bahrain	11	Honda Racing F1 Team	M	2.4 Honda RA106-V8	1 lap behind	6/22
10	MALAYSIAN GP	Sepang	11	Honda Racing F1 Team	M	2.4 Honda RA106-V8	1 lap behind	12/22
7	AUSTRALIAN GP	Melbourne	11	Honda Racing F1 Team	M	2.4 Honda RA106-V8		17/22
10	SAN MARINO GP	Imola	11	Honda Racing F1 Team	M	2.4 Honda RA106-V8	fuel fill problem/rear brake trouble	3/22
5	EUROPEAN GP	Nürburgring	11	Honda Racing F1 Team	M	2.4 Honda RA106-V8	balance problems	4/22
7	SPANISH GP	Barcelona	11	Honda Racing F1 Team	M	2.4 Honda RA106-V8	severe understeer	5/22
4	MONACO GP	Monte Carlo	11	Honda Racing F1 Team	M	2.4 Honda RA106-V8	drive-thru pen – speeding in pitlane	7/22
10	BRITISH GP	Silverstone	11	Honda Racing F1 Team	M	2.4 Honda RA106-V8	poor handling/1 lap behind	6/22
ret	CANADIAN GP	Montreal	11	Honda Racing F1 Team	M	2.4 Honda RA106-V8	engine	9/22
6	U S GP	Indianapolis	11	Honda Racing F1 Team	M	2.4 Honda RA106-V8		4/22
ret	FRENCH GP	Magny Cours	11	Honda Racing F1 Team	M	2.4 Honda RA106-V8	engine	14/22
ret	GERMAN GP	Hockenheim	11	Honda Racing F1 Team	M	2.4 Honda RA106-V8	engine	6/22
4	HUNGARIAN GP	Hungaroring	11	Honda Racing F1 Team	M	2.4 Honda RA106-V8		3/22
8	TURKISH GP	Istanbul	11	Honda Racing F1 Team	M	2.4 Honda RA106-V8		14/22
6	ITALIAN GP	Monza	11	Honda Racing F1 Team	M	2.4 Honda RA106-V8		8/22
6	CHINESE GP	Shanghai	11	Honda Racing F1 Team	M	2.4 Honda RA106-V8		3/22
12	JAPANESE GP	Suzuka	11	Honda Racing F1 Team	M	2.4 Honda RA106-V8	1 lap behind	8/22
7	BRAZILIAN GP	Interlagos	11	Honda Racing F1 Team	M	2.4 Honda RA106-V8		5/22

2007 Championship position: Unplaced

	GP	Circuit	No	Team	Tyre	Engine	Notes	
11	AUSTRALIAN GP	Melbourne	8	Honda Racing F1 Team	B	2.4 Honda RA107-V8	held up by Button/1 lap behind	17/22
11	MALAYSIAN GP	Sepang	8	Honda Racing F1 Team	B	2.4 Honda RA107-V8	started from pitlane/1 lap behind	19/22
13	BAHRAIN GP	Sakhir Circuit	8	Honda Racing F1 Team	B	2.4 Honda RA107-V8	1 lap behind	15/22
10	SPANISH GP	Barcelona	8	Honda Racing F1 Team	B	2.4 Honda RA107-V8	1 lap behind	12/22
10	MONACO GP	Monte Carlo	8	Honda Racing F1 Team	B	2.4 Honda RA107-V8	1 lap behind	9/22
12	CANADIAN GP	Montreal	8	Honda Racing F1 Team	B	2.4 Honda RA107-V8		13/22
ret	U S GP	Indianapolis	8	Honda Racing F1 Team	B	2.4 Honda RA107-V8	accident/suspension damage	15/22
11	FRENCH GP	Magny Cours	8	Honda Racing F1 Team	B	2.4 Honda RA107-V8	braking problems/1 lap behind	13/22
9	BRITISH GP	Silverstone	8	Honda Racing F1 Team	B	2.4 Honda RA107-V8	one stop strategy/1 lap behind	14/22
11	EUROPEAN GP	Nürburgring	8	Honda Racing F1 Team	B	2.4 Honda RA107-V8	2 laps behind	18/22
18	HUNGARIAN GP	Hungaroring	8	Honda Racing F1 Team	B	2.4 Honda RA107-V8	1 lap behind	14/22
17	TURKISH GP	Istanbul	8	Honda Racing F1 Team	B	2.4 Honda RA107-V8	handling problems/1 lap behind	14/22
10	ITALIAN GP	Monza	8	Honda Racing F1 Team	B	2.4 Honda RA107-V8		12/22
13	BELGIAN GP	Spa	8	Honda Racing F1 Team	B	2.4 Honda RA107-V8	1 lap behind	18/22
10	JAPANESE GP	Suzuka	8	Honda Racing F1 Team	B	2.4 Honda RA107-V8		17/22
15	CHINESE GP	Shanghai	8	Honda Racing F1 Team	B	2.4 Honda RA107-V8	hit Davidson – spin /1 lap behind	17/22
ret	BRAZILIAN GP	Interlagos	8	Honda Racing F1 Team	B	2.4 Honda RA107-V8	engine	11/22

2008 Championship position: 14th   Wins: 0   Pole positions: 0   Fastest laps: 0   Points scored: 11

	GP	Circuit	No	Team	Tyre	Engine	Notes	
dsq*	AUSTRALIAN GP	Melbourne	17	Honda Racing F1 Team	B	2.4 Honda RA108-V8	6th*left pitlane against red light	11/22
13	MALAYSIAN GP	Sepang	17	Honda Racing F1 Team	B	2.4 Honda RA108-V8	drive-thru penalty/1 lap behind	14/22
11	BAHRAIN GP	Sakhir Circuit	17	Honda Racing F1 Team	B	2.4 Honda RA108-V8		12/22
ret	SPANISH GP	Barcelona	17	Honda Racing F1 Team	B	2.4 Honda RA108-V8	accident damage after pit collision	11/22
14	TURKISH GP	Istanbul	17	Honda Racing F1 Team	B	2.4 Honda RA108-V8	1 lap behind/record 257th event	12/20
6	MONACO GP	Monte Carlo	17	Honda Racing F1 Team	B	2.4 Honda RA108-V8		15/20
7	CANADIAN GP	Montreal	17	Honda Racing F1 Team	B	2.4 Honda RA108-V8		9/20
14	FRENCH GP	Magny Cours	17	Honda Racing F1 Team	B	2.4 Honda RA108-V8	poor handling/1 lap behind	18/20
3	BRITISH GP	Silverstone	17	Honda Racing F1 Team	B	2.4 Honda RA108-V8	great drive in wet despite pit delay	16/20
ret	GERMAN GP	Hockenheim	17	Honda Racing F1 Team	B	2.4 Honda RA108-V8	collision with Coulthard	18/20
16	HUNGARIAN GP	Hungaroring	17	Honda Racing F1 Team	B	2.4 Honda RA108-V8	2 laps behind	18/20
16	EUROPEAN GP	Valencia	17	Honda Racing F1 Team	B	2.4 Honda RA108-V8	1 lap behind	19/20
ret	BELGIAN GP	Spa	17	Honda Racing F1 Team	B	2.4 Honda RA108-V8	gearbox	16/20
17	ITALIAN GP	Monza	17	Honda Racing F1 Team	B	2.4 Honda RA108-V8	1 lap behind	16/20
ret	SINGAPORE GP	Singapore Circuit	17	Honda Racing F1 Team	B	2.4 Honda RA108-V8	electrics	18/20
13	JAPANESE GP	Suzuka	17	Honda Racing F1 Team	B	2.4 Honda RA108-V8	collision damage/1 lap behind	17/20
11	CHINESE GP	Shanghai	17	Honda Racing F1 Team	B	2.4 Honda RA108-V8		14/20
15	BRAZILIAN GP	Interlagos	17	Honda Racing F1 Team	B	2.4 Honda RA108-V8	1 lap behind	15/20

2009 Championship position: 3rd   Wins: 2   Pole positions: 1   Fastest laps: 2   Points scored: 77

	GP	Circuit	No	Team	Tyre	Engine	Notes	
2	AUSTRALIAN GP	Melbourne	23	Brawn GP Formula 1 Team	B	2.4 Brawn BGP001-Mercedes V8		2/20
5	MALAYSIAN GP	Sepang	23	Brawn GP Formula 1 Team	B	2.4 Brawn BGP001-Mercedes V8	rain shortened race	4/20

4	CHINESE GP	Sakhir Circuit	23	Brawn GP Formula 1 Team	B	2.4 Brawn BGP001-Mercedes V8	brake trouble/FL	4/20
5	BAHRAIN GP	Bahrain	23	Brawn GP Formula 1 Team	B	2.4 Brawn BGP001-Mercedes V8	ran 3 pit stop strategy	6/20
2	SPANISH GP	Barcelona	23	Brawn GP Formula 1 Team	B	2.4 Brawn BGP001-Mercedes V8	ran 3 pit stop strategy/FL	3/20
2	MONACO GP	Monte Carlo	23	Brawn GP Formula 1 Team	B	2.4 Brawn BGP001-Mercedes V8		3/20
ret	TURKISH GP	Istanbul	23	Brawn GP Formula 1 Team	B	2.4 Brawn BGP001-Mercedes V8	gearbox	3/20
3	BRITISH GP	Silverstone	23	Brawn GP Formula 1 Team	B	2.4 Brawn BGP001-Mercedes V8	fine drive despite back problems	2/20
6	GERMAN GP	Hockenheim	23	Brawn GP Formula 1 Team	B	2.4 Brawn BGP001-Mercedes V8	unhappy with his team's strategy	2/20
10	HUNGARIAN GP	Hungaroring	23	Brawn GP Formula 1 Team	B	2.4 Brawn BGP001-Mercedes V8	minor collision on lap 1	13/20
1	EUROPEAN GP	Valencia	23	Brawn GP Formula 1 Team	B	2.4 Brawn BGP001-Mercedes V8		3/20
7	BELGIAN GP	Spa	23	Brawn GP Formula 1 Team	B	2.4 Brawn BGP001-Mercedes V8	changed pit stop strategy	4/20
1	ITALIAN GP	Monza	23	Brawn GP Formula 1 Team	B	2.4 Brawn BGP001-Mercedes V8		5/20
6	SINGAPORE GP	Singapore Circuit	23	Brawn GP Formula 1 Team	B	2.4 Brawn BGP001-Mercedes V8		5/20
7	JAPANESE GP	Suzuka	23	Brawn GP Formula 1 Team	B	2.4 Brawn BGP001-Mercedes V8		5/20
8	BRAZILIAN GP	Interlagos	23	Brawn GP Formula 1 Team	B	2.4 Brawn BGP001-Mercedes V8	led race, later delayed by puncture	1/20
4	ABU DHABI GP	Yas Marina Circuit	23	Brawn GP Formula 1 Team	B	2.4 Brawn BGP001-Mercedes V8		4/20

2010 Championship position: 10th   Wins: 0   Pole positions: 0   Fastest laps: 0   Points scored: 47

10	BAHRAIN GP	Sakhir Circuit	9	AT&T Williams	B	2.4 Williams FW32 Cosworth V8		11/24
8	AUSTRALIAN GP	Melbourne	9	AT&T Williams	B	2.4 Williams FW32 Cosworth V8		8/24
12	MALAYSIAN GP	Sepang	9	AT&T Williams	B	2.4 Williams FW32 Cosworth V8	extra pit stop/1 lap behind	7/24
12	CHINESE GP	Shanghai Circuit	9	AT&T Williams	B	2.4 Williams FW32 Cosworth V8		11/24
9	SPANISH GP	Barcelona	9	AT&T Williams	B	2.4 Williams FW32 Cosworth V8		18/24
ret	MONACO GP	Monte Carlo	9	AT&T Williams	B	2.4 Williams FW32 Cosworth V8	accident – broken rear suspension	9/24
14	TURKISH GP	Istanbul Park	9	AT&T Williams	B	2.4 Williams FW32 Cosworth V8	1 lap behind	15/24
14	CANADIAN GP	Montreal	9	AT&T Williams	B	2.4 Williams FW32 Cosworth V8	1 lap behind	11/24
4	EUROPEAN GP	Valencia	9	AT&T Williams	B	2.4 Williams FW32 Cosworth V8	5-sec pen, speeding behind safetycar	9/24
5	BRITISH GP	Silverstone	9	AT&T Williams	B	2.4 Williams FW32 Cosworth V8		8/24
12	GERMAN GP	Hockenheim	9	AT&T Williams	B	2.4 Williams FW32 Cosworth V8	1 lap behind	8/24
10	HUNGARIAN GP	Hungaroring	9	AT&T Williams	B	2.4 Williams FW32 Cosworth V8	1 lap behind	12/24
ret	BELGIAN GP	Spa	9	AT&T Williams	B	2.4 Williams FW32 Cosworth V8	accident on lap 1 –hit Alonso	7/24
10	ITALIAN GP	Monza	9	AT&T Williams	B	2.4 Williams FW32 Cosworth V8	lap 1 collision with Buemi	10/24
6	SINGAPORE GP	Yas Marina Circuit	9	AT&T Williams	B	2.4 Williams FW32 Cosworth V8		6/24
9	JAPANESE GP	Suzuka	9	AT&T Williams	B	2.4 Williams FW32 Cosworth V8		8/24
7	KOREAN GP	Yeongam	9	AT&T Williams	B	2.4 Williams FW32 Cosworth V8		10/24
14	BRAZILIAN GP	Sao Paulo	9	AT&T Williams	B	2.4 Williams FW32 Cosworth V8	slow 1st stop/also puncture -1 lap	6/24

2011   Championship position: 17th   Wins: 0   Pole positions: 0   Fastest laps: 0   Points scored: 4

ret	AUSTRALIAN GP	Melbourne	11	AT&T Williams	P	2.4 Williams FW33-Cosworth V8	transmission	17/24
ret	MALAYSIAN GP	Sepang	11	AT&T Williams	P	2.4 Williams FW33-Cosworth V8	hydraulics/accident	15/24
13	CHINESE GP	Shanghai Circuit	11	AT&T Williams	P	2.4 Williams FW33-Cosworth V8		15/24
15	TURKISH GP	Istanbul Park	11	AT&T Williams	P	2.4 Williams FW33-Cosworth V8	balance/tyre wear/1 lap behind	11/24
17	SPANISH GP	Barcelona	11	AT&T Williams	P	2.4 Williams FW33-Cosworth V8	2 laps behind	19/24
9	MONACO GP	Monte Carlo	11	AT&T Williams	P	2.4 Williams FW33-Cosworth V8		12/24
9	CANADIAN GP	Montreal	11	AT&T Williams	P	2.4 Williams FW33-Cosworth V8		16/24
12	EUROPEAN GP	Valencia	11	AT&T Williams	P	2.4 Williams FW33-Cosworth V8	1 lap behind	13/24
13	BRITISH GP	Silverstone	11	AT&T Williams	P	2.4 Williams FW33-Cosworth V8	dry set up in wet/ 1 lap behind	15/24
ret	GERMAN GP	Hockenheim	11	AT&T Williams	P	2.4 Williams FW33-Cosworth V8	oil leak	14/24
13	HUNGARIAN GP	Hungaroring	11	AT&T Williams	P	2.4 Williams FW33-Cosworth V8	2 laps behind	15/24
16	BELGIAN GP	Spa	11	AT&T Williams	P	2.4 Williams FW33-Cosworth V8	collision–new front wing/-1 lap	14/24
12	ITALIAN GP	Monza	11	AT&T Williams	P	2.4 Williams FW33-Cosworth V8	1 lap behind	13/24
13	SINGAPORE GP	Marina Bay Circuit	11	AT&T Williams	P	2.4 Williams FW33-Cosworth V8	1 lap behind	12/24
17	JAPANESE GP	Suzuka	11	AT&T Williams	P	2.4 Williams FW33-Cosworth V8		13/24
12	KOREAN GP	Yeongam	11	AT&T Williams	P	2.4 Williams FW33-Cosworth V8		18/24
15	INDIAN GP	Buddh Circuit	11	AT&T Williams	P	2.4 Williams FW33-Cosworth V8	2 laps behind	16/24
12	ABU DHABI GP	Yas Marina Circuit	11	AT&T Williams	P	2.4 Williams FW33-Cosworth V8	1 lap behind/*no time set	24*/24
14	BRAZILIAN GP	São Paulo	11	AT&T Williams	P	2.4 Williams FW33-Cosworth V8	1 lap behind	12/24

GP Starts: 323 (326)   GP Wins: 11   Pole positions: 14   Fastest laps: 17   Points: 658

Surprise package. The splendid Brawn-Mercedes, employing the innovative double diffuser, stole a march on their rivals in 2009. While Jenson Button took the title, Rubens scored two race wins, including an emotional victory in the Italian GP at Monza, to complete a hat track of victories at the historic circuit.

EDGAR BARTH

A DISTINGUISHED pre-war motorcycle racer, Edgar Barth drove EMW sports cars between 1953 and 1956, and by winning his class in the 1956 Coupe de Paris at Montlhéry, he attracted the attention of the Porsche team.

After a successful class-winning debut for Porsche at the 1957 Nürburgring 1000km, Edgar and his family defected from East Germany. He then became a mainstay of the company's Formula 2, sports and hill-climb programme. He won the Targa Florio outright in 1959 (with Wolfgang Seidel) and was European mountain champion in 1959, 1963 and 1964, by which time he was already suffering from the cancer to which he succumbed, at the age of 48, in May, 1965.

Barth's son, Jürgen, also represented the Porsche factory team, winning the Le Mans 24-hours in 1977.

GIORGIO BASSI

H IS outing in Scuderia Centro Sud's elderly BRM was Giorgio Bassi's only single-seater appearance at top level, but this Milanese driver was a regular on his national scene.

In Formula 3, he drove a de Tomaso-Ford, his best finish being third at the closing race of the 1964 season at Monza, while the following year he shared the 1000cc ASA prototype with Giorgio Pianta to take a class win in the Targa Florio after finishing 17th overall.

ERWIN BAUER

A LTHOUGH Erwin Bauer's inclusion in this book is due to a single outing in the 1953 German Grand Prix, nevertheless he is of interest in that he provided one of Lotus' earliest Continental successes. When Colin Chapman was deemed too inexperienced by the organisers to tackle the Nürburgring 1000km in 1954, Erwin was brought in as a last-minute substitute for the Lotus creator and claimed fourth in the 1500cc class, ahead of some much more vaunted machinery, such as Porsches and Borgwards.

Bauer raced sports cars and saloons, and also rallied throughout the 1950s, sharing a Mercedes 220SE with Willi Heeks in 1956. In 1957, he teamed up with Gottfried Kochert in the Austrian's 2-litre Ferrari. Their partnership had a tragic ending at the 1958 Nürburgring 1000km, however, when Bauer, having claimed tenth place at the end of the race, failed to appreciate that he had finished. Racing on for one more lap, he slid wide while passing a slower car and crashed fatally into the trees that lined the mountain circuit.

BARTH, Edgar (D) b 26/1/1917, Herold-Erzegeberge – d 20/5/1965, Ludwigsburg, nr Stuttgart

	Race	Circuit	No	Entrant	Tyres	Capacity/Car/Engine	Comment	Q Pos/Entries
	1953 Championship position: Unplaced							
ret	GERMAN GP	Nürburgring	35	Rennkollektiv EMW	–	2.0 EMW 6	*exhaust*	24/35
	1957 Championship position: Unplaced							
12*	GERMAN GP (F2)	Nürburgring	21	Dr Ing F Porsche KG	–	1.5 Porsche 550RS F4 sports car	*1st in F2 class/1 lap behind*	12/24
	1958 Championship position: Unplaced							
6*	GERMAN GP (F2)	Nürburgring	21	Dr Ing F Porsche KG	–	1.5 Porsche RSK F4 sports car	*2nd in F2 class*	16/26
	1960 Championship position: Unplaced							
7	ITALIAN GP (F2)	Monza	24	Dr Ing F Porsche KG	D	1.5 Porsche 718 F4	*3 laps behind*	12/16
	1964 Championship position: Unplaced							
ret	GERMAN GP	Nürburgring	12	Rob Walker Racing Team	D	1.5 Cooper T66-Climax V8	*clutch*	20/24
	GP Starts: 5 GP Wins: 0 Pole positions: 0 Fastest laps: 0 Points: 0							

BASSI, Giorgio (I) b 20/1/1934, Milan

	Race	Circuit	No	Entrant	Tyres	Capacity/Car/Engine	Comment	Q Pos/Entries
	1965 Championship position: Unplaced							
ret	ITALIAN GP	Monza	52	Scuderia Centro Sud	D	1.5 BRM P57 V8	*engine*	22/23
	GP Starts: 1 GP Wins: 0 Pole positions: 0 Fastest laps: 0 Points: 0							

BAUER, Erwin (D) b 17/7/1912, Stuttgart – d 3/6/1958, Cologne

	Race	Circuit	No	Entrant	Tyres	Capacity/Car/Engine	Comment	Q Pos/Entries
	1953 Championship position: Unplaced							
ret	GERMAN GP	Nürburgring	31	Erwin Bauer	–	2.0 Veritas RS 6		33/35
	GP Starts: 1 GP Wins: 0 Pole positions: 0 Fastest laps: 0 Points: 0							

BAUMGARTNER, Zsolt (H) b 1/1/1981, Debrecen

	Race	Circuit	No	Entrant	Tyres	Capacity/Car/Engine	Comment	Q Pos/Entries
	2003 Championship position: Unplaced							
app	GERMAN GP	Hockenheim	36	Jordan Ford	B	3.0 Jordan EJ13-Ford Cosworth V10	*Friday test driver only*	– / –
ret	HUNGARIAN GP	Hungaroring	12	Jordan Ford	B	3.0 Jordan EJ13-Ford Cosworth V10	*engine*	19/20
11	ITALIAN GP	Monza	12	Jordan Ford	B	3.0 Jordan EJ13-Ford Cosworth V10	*2 laps behind*	18/20
	2004 Championship position: 20th Wins: 0 Pole positions: 0 Fastest laps: 0 Points scored: 1							
ret	AUSTRALIAN GP	Melbourne	20	European Minardi Cosworth	B	3.0 Minardi PS04B-Cosworth V10	*engine misfire – ECU failure*	17/20
16	MALAYSIAN GP	Sepang	20	European Minardi Cosworth	B	3.0 Minardi PS04B-Cosworth V10	*chassis imbalance/4 laps behind*	17/20
ret	BAHRAIN GP	Sakhir Circuit	20	European Minardi Cosworth	B	3.0 Minardi PS04B-Cosworth V10	*engine*	19/20
15	SAN MARINO GP	Imola	20	European Minardi Cosworth	B	3.0 Minardi PS04B-Cosworth V10	*4 laps behind*	18/20
ret	SPANISH GP	Barcelona	20	European Minardi Cosworth	B	3.0 Minardi PS04B-Cosworth V10	*spun off*	20/20
9	MONACO GP	Monte Carlo	20	European Minardi Cosworth	B	3.0 Minardi PS04B-Cosworth V10	*6 laps behind*	19/20
15	EUROPEAN GP	Nürburgring	20	European Minardi Cosworth	B	3.0 Minardi PS04B-Cosworth V10	*3 laps behind*	18/20
10*	CANADIAN GP	Montreal	20	European Minardi Cosworth	B	3.0 Minardi PS04B-Cosworth V10	*2nd, 5th, 8th, 10th cars dsq/-4 laps	18/20
8	US GP	Indianapolis	20	European Minardi Cosworth	B	3.0 Minardi PS04B-Cosworth V10	*3 laps behind*	19/20
ret	FRENCH GP	Magny Cours	20	European Minardi Cosworth	B	3.0 Minardi PS04B-Cosworth V10	*spun off*	20/20
ret	BRITISH GP	Silverstone	20	European Minardi Cosworth	B	3.0 Minardi PS04B-Cosworth V10	*engine*	19/20
16	GERMAN GP	Hockenheim	20	European Minardi Cosworth	B	3.0 Minardi PS04B-Cosworth V10	*4 laps behind*	20/20
15	HUNGARIAN GP	Hungaroring	20	European Minardi Cosworth	B	3.0 Minardi PS04B-Cosworth V10	*stalled at pit stop/5 laps behind*	18/20
ret	BELGIAN GP	Spa	20	European Minardi Cosworth	B	3.0 Minardi PS04B-Cosworth V10	*hit by Button's out of control car*	18/20
15	ITALIAN GP	Monza	20	European Minardi Cosworth	B	3.0 Minardi PS04B-Cosworth V10	*3 laps behind*	19/20
16	CHINESE GP	Shanghai	20	European Minardi Cosworth	B	3.0 Minardi PS04B-Cosworth V10	*3 laps behind*	17/20
ret	JAPANESE GP	Suzuka	20	European Minardi Cosworth	B	3.0 Minardi PS04B-Cosworth V10	*no time set/spun off*	*20/20
16	BRAZILIAN GP	Interlagos	20	European Minardi Cosworth	B	3.0 Minardi PS04B-Cosworth V10	*4 laps behind*	19/20

GP Starts: 20   GP Wins: 0   Pole positions: 0   Fastest laps: 0   Points: 1

ZSOLT BAUMGARTNER

ZSOLT who? That was the question most casual TV fans were asking as this little-known driver made his own piece of history at the 2003 Hungarian GP, becoming the first Magyar to race in modern Formula 1. Since then, however, Baumgartner has rarely made the motorsport headlines.

Aided by his father's connections with Renault in Hungary, Zsolt began in various junior series, winning the 2-litre Formula Renault German title in 1999, before struggling in both the German and Italian Formula 3 series in 2000 and 2001. Still impatient to progress, he made the jump into F3000 in the middle of the 2001 season with the Prost Junior team, before moving to reigning champions Nordic Racing for 2002. He scored only a single point, but fared slightly better the next year when he managed six points for Coloni.

Baumgartner had already joined Jordan as a test driver and was soon called into action at the aforementioned Hungaroring race when Ralph Firman had his accident. A second outing, at Monza, yielded 11th place before he returned to the sidelines again. For 2004, he joined Paul Stoddart's squad, surprising many people by generally out-performing his more highly rated team-mate, Gianmaria Bruni; he took a valuable world championship point with eighth place in the US Grand Prix. That was not enough to keep him on board for 2005, however, and his F1 dream was over. In 2007, he was briefly involved in Stoddart's Champ Car team, as reserve and test driver, but he never saw race action.

ÉLIE BAYOL

ÉLIE BAYOL built a reputation as a very quick driver in René Bonnet's 750cc Panhard during the 1951 season. For 1952, he ordered one of the latest OSCA F2 cars, but as this was not delivered until August, he was forced to make do in the meantime with a stripped sports model, which he drove to good effect, finishing fourth at Pau, fifth at Marseille and sixth at Modena. Then he raced the F2 car during the 1953 season, the undoubted highlight of which was an aggregate win in the Circuit du Lac at Aix-les-Bains.

Accepting an invitation to join the Gordini team for 1954, Bayol made a fine debut, taking fifth place in the Argentine GP, and he followed this with fourth at Pau and fifth at Bordeaux, where he blotted his copybook by ignoring repeated signals to pit and hand over his car to team leader Jean Behra. Gordini sacked him, but later he was forgiven and rejoined the team for 1955, only for his season to be curtailed after he sustained serious head injuries when he crashed the latest 3-litre Gordini in practice at Le Mans.

Thankfully Bayol made a full recovery and briefly reappeared on the circuits the following year, finishing sixth (with André Pilette) at Monaco and in the Reims 12-hours sports car race (with Hernando da Silva Ramos).

BAYOL, Élie (F) b 28/2/1914, Marseille – d 25/5/1995, La Ciotat

	Race	Circuit	No	Entrant	Tyres	Capacity/Car/Engine	Comment	Q Pos/Entries
	1952 Championship position: Unplaced							
ret	ITALIAN GP	Monza	34	Elie Bayol	–	2.0 OSCA 20 6	gearbox	10/35
	1953 Championship position: Unplaced							
ret	FRENCH GP	Reims	34	Elie Bayol	–	2.0 OSCA 20 6	mechanical	15/25
dns	SWISS GP	Berne	22	Elie Bayol	–	2.0 OSCA 20 6		– /23
ret	ITALIAN GP	Monza	34	OSCA Automobili	–	2.0 OSCA 20 6	mechanical	13/30
	1954 Championship position: 18th= Wins: 0 Pole positions: 0 Fastest laps: 0 Points scored: 2							
5	ARGENTINE GP	Buenos Aires	20	Equipe Gordini	E	2.5 Gordini Type 16 6	2 laps behind	15/18
	1955 Championship position: Unplaced							
ret	ARGENTINE GP	Buenos Aires	38	Equipe Gordini	E	2.5 Gordini Type 16 6	transmission	15/22
ret	MONACO GP	Monte Carlo	12	Equipe Gordini	E	2.5 Gordini Type 16 6	rear axle	16/22
	1955 Championship position: Unplaced							
6*	MONACO GP	Monte Carlo	4	Equipe Gordini	E	2.5 Gordini Type 32 8	*Pilette took over/12 laps behind	11/19

GP Starts: 7   GP Wins: 0   Pole positions: 0   Fastest laps: 0   Points: 2

BEAUMAN, Don (GB) b 26/7/1928 – d 9/7/1955, Rathnew, County Wicklow, Republic of Ireland

	Race	Circuit	No	Entrant	Tyres	Capacity/Car/Engine	Comment	Q Pos/Entries
	1954 Championship position: Unplaced							
11	BRITISH GP	Silverstone	25	Sir Jeremy Boles	D	2.0 Connaught A-Lea Francis 4	6 laps behind	17/31

GP Starts: 1   GP Wins: 0   Pole positions: 0   Fastest laps: 0   Points: 0

BECHEM, Karl-Günther (D) b 21/12/1921, Hagen – d 3/5/2011, Germany

	Race	Circuit	No	Entrant	Tyres	Capacity/Car/Engine	Comment	Q Pos/Entries
	1952 Championship position: Unplaced							
ret	GERMAN GP	Nürburgring	130	'Bernhard Nacke'	–	2.0 BMW-Eigenbau 6	used pseudonym of B Nacke	30/32
	1953 Championship position: Unplaced							
ret	GERMAN GP	Nürburgring	41	Gunther Bechem	–	2.0 AFM-BMW 6		30/35

GP Starts: 2   GP Wins: 0   Pole positions: 0   Fastest laps: 0   Points: 0

DON BEAUMANN

A POPULAR figure on the national scene, Don Beauman entered racing in 1950 with 500cc Coopers, before spending the 1953 season with the coveted pre-war TT Riley previously campaigned by his great chum, Mike Hawthorn.

Supported by Sir Jeremy Boles, Beauman intensified his racing activities in 1954 with an F2 Connaught, winning Formula Libre events at Oulton Park and Brands Hatch as well as taking a class win in an Aston Martin at Zandvoort.

The 1955 season saw the London hotelier claim third place in the Glover Trophy at Goodwood and compete in the Le Mans 24-hours in a works Jaguar. This shy and retiring figure, who had hopes of one day moving into grand prix racing, lost his life when he crashed his Connaught in the 1955 Leinster Trophy sports car race in Wicklow, Republic of Ireland.

KARL-GÜNTHER BECHEM

K ARL-GÜNTHER BECHEM raced a BMW sports car in 1950, but it seems his family were none too keen on him taking part in sporting competition. So, apparently, he entered the 1952 German Grand Prix under the pseudonym of 'Bernhard Nacke' to conceal his racing activities. Quite how he could have kept his secret if he had enjoyed any success it is hard to imagine!

By 1953, however, using his real name, Bechem had become heavily involved with the Borgward team and their neat 1500cc Rennsports. The season's highlight was a third place and class win in the Nürburgring 1000km, shared with Theo Helfrich.

The potent Borgward was certainly a match for the rival Porsche 550 sports, especially when fuel injection was installed. Bechem won the Eifel mountain meeting at the Nürburgring in May, 1954. At the end of that season, the team headed for Mexico to compete in the gruelling Carrera Panamericana road race. Early on, prospects for outright success looked bright when Günther took the lead. But, after surviving one off-road excursion, he crashed heavily at the end of the fourth leg of this 2000-mile marathon. The car was destroyed and poor Bechem seriously injured. Happily he made a complete recovery, but he never raced again.

JEAN BEHRA

HOW can a driver who never won a World Championship Grand Prix have left such a legacy? Even today those old enough to recall Behra remember the tiger, and those like me, too young to have seen him, are inspired by his mighty reputation and heroic deeds when, in the early fifties, he was cast as the perpetual underdog, battling for Gordini against the mighty works teams.

Behra took up the four-wheeled discipline after an immensely successful motor cycling career in which he was French champion three years running. Switching from his red bike to the French blue of Talbot, he placed sixth in the 1949 Coupe du Salon at Montlhéry, and then took part in the 1950 Monte Carlo Rally driving a Simca with Roger Loyer, another ex-motor cyclist who was later to race Gordinis. A month later Jean won a hill-climb in a borrowed Maserati four-cylinder, bringing him to the attention of Amédée Gordini. A drive in the 1950 Bol d'Or at St Germain convinced le patron that here was

a nugget that could be polished, and Behra was signed for the 1951 season, beginning his serious motor racing career at the age of 30. He finished third in his first race at Les Sables d'Olonne, and then did the same at Cadours.

It was 1952, however, when Behra became a national hero for his deeds not in championship Grands Prix, though he did superbly well to finish third at Bremgarten and fifth at the Nürburgring – circuits for the skilled and brave – but at the non-championship Reims GP. With Ascari hitherto virtually unbeatable, there was some surprise when Behra shot into an early lead, and this became mild consternation as the light-blue car held off the Ferrari challenge for lap after lap. Then came frenzied hysteria as the T500 suffered an engine failure, leaving Jean to cruise to a historic victory, much to the delight of the delirious French public. There were post-race mutterings about an oversize engine, but the result stood and Behra was for ever taken to the hearts of his countrymen.

He stayed with Gordini to the end of the 1954 season, suffering the heartbreaking succession of maladies that inevitably struck at the little underfinanced équipe, but when results were achieved the success was all the sweeter, as at Pau in 1954 when, after more than three hours' racing, Behra defeated the works Ferrari of Trintignant by a mere 60 yards.

After a test in a Maserati at Monza, where Ascari no less could only equal his time, Behra signed for the 1955 season and was immediately rewarded with non-championship wins at Pau and Bordeaux. Although he was out of luck in championship Grands Prix, Behra took sports car wins at Bari, Monza, the Nürburgring and Oporto in the 300TS, before a crash in the Tourist Trophy resulted in his ear being ground off – Jean subsequently receiving a plastic replacement. For 1956 he was relegated to the number two slot with the arrival of Stirling Moss, but this did not dampen his spirit; he merely raised his game to enjoy his best-ever championship year, even if that much sought first Grand Prix win still eluded him.

In 1957 he was cast as number two to Fangio, but still had his moments, none more memorable than the British GP when he left them all – Fangio, Hawthorn, Moss and Collins – in his wake until his Maserati's clutch failed. Perversely in non-title events his luck would hold, and he won the Pau, Modena and Moroccan GPs for Maserati, and the Caen GP and the International Trophy for BRM.

The following season, driving for BRM in F1 and for Porsche in sports cars and Formula 2, Behra had little luck with the cars from Bourne but won sports car races at AVUS and Rouen and took the Formula 2 honours at AVUS and in the Coupe de Vitesse at Reims. An offer to drive for a Ferrari team now bereft of Hawthorn, Collins and Musso in 1959 was too good to turn down, and the signs were encouraging when he won the Aintree 200 and finished second in the Syracuse GP after a spirited battle with Moss ended in a spin. Two sports car races for the Scuderia yielded a second place at Sebring with Allison and a third in the Nürburgring 1000 Km with Brooks, while he finished second in the Auvergne Trophy at Clermont Ferrand in his own Porsche. In championship Grands Prix, a great drive at Reims ended with engine failure. On pulling his stricken Ferrari into the pits, the frustration was too much for the little Frenchman, who was involved in a scuffle with team manager Tavoni which ended with Behra being shown the door. Running his own Porsches, he was entered for both the Grand Prix and the sports car race at AVUS, but in the rain-soaked support race he was killed instantly when he lost control on the slippery banking, crashed and was flung out of the car into a flag pole.

BEHRA, Jean (F) b 16/2/1921, Nice – d 1/8/1959, AVUS, Berlin, Germany

	Race	Circuit	No	Entrant	Tyres	Capacity/Car/Engine	Comment	Q Pos/Entries
	1951 Championship position: Unplaced							
ret	ITALIAN GP	Monza	50	Equipe Gordini	E	2.0 Gordini Type 15/i6 4	raced Trintignant's car – no practice	–/35
	1952 Championship position: 10th Wins: 0 Pole positions: 0 Fastest laps: 0 Points scored: 6							
3	SWISS GP	Bremgarten	6	Equipe Gordini	E	2.0 Gordini Type 16 6	1 lap behind	7/21
ret	BELGIAN GP	Spa	16	Equipe Gordini	E	2.0 Gordini Type 16 6	hit Taruffi's spinning car	5/22
7	FRENCH GP	Rouen	4	Equipe Gordini	E	2.0 Gordini Type 16 6	6 laps behind	4/20
5	GERMAN GP	Nürburgring	108	Equipe Gordini	E	2.0 Gordini Type 16 6	1 lap behind	11/32
ret	DUTCH GP	Zandvoort	8	Equipe Gordini	E	2.0 Gordini Type 16 6	carburettor	6/18
ret	ITALIAN GP	Monza	6	Equipe Gordini	E	2.0 Gordini Type 16 6	valve	11/35
	1953 Championship position: Unplaced							
6	ARGENTINE GP	Buenos Aires	30	Equipe Gordini	E	2.0 Gordini Type 16 6	3 laps behind	11/16
ret	BELGIAN GP	Spa	16	Equipe Gordini	E	2.0 Gordini Type 16 6	cylinder head gasket	14/22
10	FRENCH GP	Reims	2	Equipe Gordini	E	2.0 Gordini Type 16 6	5 laps behind	22/25
ret	BRITISH GP	Silverstone	30	Equipe Gordini	E	2.0 Gordini Type 16 6	fuel pump	22/29
ret	GERMAN GP	Nürburgring	9	Equipe Gordini	E	2.0 Gordini Type 16 6	gearbox	9/35
ret	SWISS GP	Bremgarten	6	Equipe Gordini	E	2.0 Gordini Type 16 6	oil pressure	12/23
	1954 Championship position: 21st Wins: 0 Pole positions: 0 Fastest laps: 1 (shared) Points scored: 0.14							
dsq*	ARGENTINE GP	Buenos Aires	18	Equipe Gordini	E	2.5 Gordini Type 16 6	*outside assistance after spin	17/18
ret	BELGIAN GP	Spa	12	Equipe Gordini	E	2.5 Gordini Type 16 6	rear suspension	7/15
6	FRENCH GP	Reims	24	Equipe Gordini	E	2.5 Gordini Type 16 6	5 laps behind	17/22
ret	BRITISH GP	Silverstone	17	Equipe Gordini	E	2.5 Gordini Type 16 6	rear suspension/FL (shared)	5/31
10	GERMAN GP	Nürburgring	9	Equipe Gordini	E	2.5 Gordini Type 16 6	2 laps behind	9/23
ret	SWISS GP	Bremgarten	10	Equipe Gordini	E	2.5 Gordini Type 16 6	clutch	14/16
ret	ITALIAN GP	Monza	44	Equipe Gordini	E	2.5 Gordini Type 16 6	engine	12/21
ret	SPANISH GP	Pedralbes	46	Equipe Gordini	E	2.5 Gordini Type 16 6	brakes	18/22
	1955 Championship position: 8th= Wins: 0 Pole positions: 0 Fastest laps: 0 Points scored: 6							
ret	ARGENTINE GP	Buenos Aires	16	Officine Alfieri Maserati	E	2.5 Maserati 250F 6	accident	4/22
ret	"	" "	20	Officine Alfieri Maserati	E	2.5 Maserati 250F 6	engine/Mantovani/Musso co-drove	– / –
6*	"	" "	28	Officine Alfieri Maserati	E	2.5 Maserati 250F 6	*took over Schell's car/-8 laps	– / –
3*	MONACO GP	Monte Carlo	34	Officine Alfieri Maserati	E	2.5 Maserati 250F 6	*Perdisa took over/1 lap behind	5/22
ret	"	" "	40	Officine Alfieri Maserati	E	2.5 Maserati 250F 6	took Perdisa's car/spun off	– / –
ret	BELGIAN GP	Spa	20	Officine Alfieri Maserati	E	2.5 Maserati 250F 6	spun off	5/14
5*	"	"	24	Officine Alfieri Maserati	E	2.5 Maserati 250F 6	*took over Mieres' car/1 lap behind	– / –
6	DUTCH GP	Zandvoort	14	Officine Alfieri Maserati	E	2.5 Maserati 250F 6	3 laps behind	6/16
ret	BRITISH GP	Aintree	2	Officine Alfieri Maserati	E	2.5 Maserati 250F 6	oil pipe	3/25
4	ITALIAN GP	Monza	36	Officine Alfieri Maserati	E	2.5 Maserati 250F 6		6/22
	1956 Championship position: 4th Wins: 0 Pole positions: 0 Fastest laps: 0 Points scored: 22							
2	ARGENTINE GP	Buenos Aires	4	Officine Alfieri Maserati	P	2.5 Maserati 250F 6		4/15
3	MONACO GP	Monte Carlo	30	Officine Alfieri Maserati	P	2.5 Maserati 250F 6	1 lap behind	4/19
7	BELGIAN GP	Spa	32	Officine Alfieri Maserati	P	2.5 Maserati 250F 6	engine problems/3 laps behind	4/16
3	FRENCH GP	Reims	4	Officine Alfieri Maserati	P	2.5 Maserati 250F 6		7/20
3	BRITISH GP	Silverstone	8	Officine Alfieri Maserati	P	2.5 Maserati 250F 6	2 laps behind	13/28
3	GERMAN GP	Nürburgring	6	Officine Alfieri Maserati	P	2.5 Maserati 250F 6		8/21
ret	ITALIAN GP	Monza	32	Officine Alfieri Maserati	P	2.5 Maserati 250F 6	magneto	5/26
ret	"	"	46	Officine Alfieri Maserati	P	2.5 Maserati 250F 6	took over Maglioli's car/steering	– / –
	1957 Championship position: 7th= Wins: 0 Pole positions: 0 Fastest laps: 0 Points scored: 8							
2	ARGENTINE GP	Buenos Aires	6	Officine Alfieri Maserati	P	2.5 Maserati 250F 6		3/16
6	FRENCH GP	Rouen	4	Officine Alfieri Maserati	P	2.5 Maserati 250F 6	pit stop – engine/8 laps behind	2/15
ret	BRITISH GP	Aintree	4	Officine Alfieri Maserati	P	2.5 Maserati 250F 6	clutch when leading	2/19
6	GERMAN GP	Nürburgring	2	Officine Alfieri Maserati	P	2.5 Maserati 250F 6		3/24
ret	PESCARA GP	Pescara	4	Officine Alfieri Maserati	P	2.5 Maserati 250F 6	oil pipe	4/16
ret	ITALIAN GP	Monza	6	Officine Alfieri Maserati	P	2.5 Maserati 250F V12	engine – overheating	5/19
	1958 Championship position: 10th= Wins: 0 Pole positions: 0 Fastest laps: 0 Points scored: 9							
5	ARGENTINE GP	Buenos Aires	4	Ken Kavanagh	P	2.5 Maserati 250F 6	2 laps behind	4/10
ret	MONACO GP	Monte Carlo	6	Owen Racing Organisation	D	2.5 BRM P25 4	brakes	2/28
3	DUTCH GP	Zandvoort	14	Owen Racing Organisation	D	2.5 BRM P25 4		4/17
ret	BELGIAN GP	Spa	8	Owen Racing Organisation	D	2.5 BRM P25 4	oil pressure	10/20
ret	FRENCH GP	Reims	14	Owen Racing Organisation	D	2.5 BRM P25 4	fuel pump	9/21
ret	BRITISH GP	Silverstone	19	Owen Racing Organisation	D	2.5 BRM P25 4	puncture – hit hare	8/21
ret	GERMAN GP	Nürburgring	5	Owen Racing Organisation	D	2.5 BRM P25 4	suspension	12/26
4	PORTUGUESE GP	Oporto	8	Owen Racing Organisation	D	2.5 BRM P25 4	1 lap behind	4/15
ret	ITALIAN GP	Monza	8	Owen Racing Organisation	D	2.5 BRM P25 4	brakes/clutch	8/21
ret	MOROCCAN GP	Casablanca	14	Owen Racing Organisation	D	2.5 BRM P25 4	engine	4/25
	1959 Championship position: 13th= Wins: 0 Pole positions: 0 Fastest laps: 0 Points scored: 2							
ret	MONACO GP	Monte Carlo	46	Scuderia Ferrari	D	2.4 Ferrari Dino 246 V6	engine	2/24
5	DUTCH GP	Zandvoort	1	Scuderia Ferrari	D	2.4 Ferrari Dino 246 V6	1 lap behind	4/15
ret	FRENCH GP	Reims	30	Scuderia Ferrari	D	2.4 Ferrari Dino 246 V6	engine	5/22
dns	GERMAN GP	AVUS	12	Jean Behra	D	1.5 Behra-Porsche F4	fatal accident in support race	–/16
	GP Starts: 53 GP Wins: 0 Pole positions: 0 Fastest laps: 1 (shared) Points: 53.14							

DEREK BELL

IT seems incomprehensible that a driver as talented as Derek Bell, when in his prime, only managed to start in nine world championship grand prix races. He seemed to be jinxed when it came to Formula 1 – always in the wrong car at the wrong time – and eventually he was passed over in favour of younger talent.

Tentatively entering the sport with a Lotus Seven in 1964, Bell soon moved into Formula 3, initially with a Lotus that was run – with the support of his step-father, 'Colonel Hender' – under the Church Farm Racing banner. It proved to be a character building couple of years for the driver, who realised that he needed the help of wiser and more experienced heads if his career was to progress. Thus he decided to team up with Peter Westbury, which put his career on a stable footing and brought promising results as well.

Despite a lack of funds, Bell and his step-father financed a season of Formula 2 in 1968 with a Brabham BT23, which brought him to the attention of Ferrari, who offered him a drive mid-way through the season. His debut for the Scuderia started badly, however, when he found himself in the midst of a huge pile-up in the F2 Monza Lottery GP. Fortunately he was exonerated from blame. Then he looked set to win at Zandvoort until his gearbox failed. Bell tasted grand prix racing in the scarlet cars and then enjoyed a trip down-under to contest the Tasman championship. Unfortunately, Ferrari withdrew from the bulk of their programme in mid-1969, leaving him without a drive, apart from a one-off outing in the 4WD McLaren.

To the rescue came Tom Wheatcroft, who, after financing a disastrous foray to the Tasman series, sponsored Derek in a full Formula 2 season in 1970. The campaign started well with a superb win in Barcelona, followed by second places at the Nürburgring and Zolder, but eventually Clay Regazzoni overhauled him in the race to be the European F2 champion. He was also invited by Jacques Swaters to drive a Ferrari 512 in the Spa 1000km – a race that would lay the foundations of his future sports car success – and scored his only world championship point with an appearance for Team Surtees at Watkins Glen. For 1971, Derek was paired with Jo Siffert in the Gulf/John Wyer Porsche, the team taking the sports car championship. Derek stayed with the team through the next three years, proving his worth as a top-drawer sports car driver, while his miscellaneous grand prix appearances with Tecno and Surtees proved eminently forgettable.

The 1975 season brought the first of his five Le Mans victories with Jacky Ickx in the Gulf and a successful championship campaign for Alfa Romeo – winning three times with Henri Pescarolo – in the T33. The next few seasons saw a globe-trotting Derek competing in F5000, G8, touring cars, Formula Atlantic, the World Championship of Makes events, etc, before joining the Rothmans Porsche factory squad, which would dominate sports car racing in the 1980s (Derek taking the drivers' championship – with Hans Stuck – in 1985 and 1986). In recognition of his many fine performances, Bell was awarded the MBE in 1986.

The 1990s saw Derek enjoying the cut and thrust of racing in IMSA. With a Nissan GTP, he took a splendid second place in the 1993 Sebring 12-hours and finished fourth in the GTP championship standings. After finishing sixth in the 1994 Le Mans 24-hours, he announced that he had driven in the French classic for the last time. But as he began his 32nd year in motorsport, the urge to race was still there. At Sebring, he shared the second-place Spice-Chevrolet with Andy Wallace and Jan Lammers, and, contrary to his earlier intentions, he was persuaded back to the Sarthe circuit once again, tempted by the chance of sharing a McLaren GTR with his son, Justin, and Wallace; the trio finished a fine third overall.

Although of an advanced age for a racing driver, Derek continued to race selectively, but now he spends more of his time in commentary and consultancy roles on both sides of the Atlantic, most notably for Porsche and Bentley.

BELL, Derek (GB) b 31/10/1941, Pinner, Middlesex

	Race	Circuit	No	Entrant	Tyres	Capacity/Car/Engine	Comment	Q Pos/Entries
	1968 Championship position: Unplaced							
ret	ITALIAN GP	Monza	7	Scuderia Ferrari SpA SEFAC	F	3.0 Ferrari 312/68 V12	*fuel metering unit*	8/24
ret	US GP	Watkins Glen	7	Scuderia Ferrari Spa SEFAC	F	3.0 Ferrari 312/68 V12	*engine*	15/21
	1969 Championship position: Unplaced							
ret	BRITISH GP	Silverstone	20	Bruce McLaren Motor Racing	G	3.0 McLaren M9A-Cosworth V8	*rear suspension*	15/17
	1970 Championship position: 22nd= Wins: 0 Pole positions: 0 Fastest laps: 0 Points scored: 1							
ret	BELGIAN GP	Spa	8	Tom Wheatcroft Racing	G	3.0 Brabham BT26A-Cosworth V8	*gear linkage*	15/18
6	US GP	Watkins Glen	18	Team Surtees	F	3.0 Surtees TS7-Cosworth V8	*1 lap behind*	13/27
	1971 Championship position: Unplaced							
ret	BRITISH GP	Silverstone	25	Team Surtees	F	3.0 Surtees TS9-Cosworth V8	*radius rod*	– / –
dns	"	"	25	Team Surtees	F	3.0 Surtees TS7-Cosworth V8	*qualified in this car*	23/24

1972 Championship position: Unplaced

dnq	FRENCH GP	Clermont Ferrand	21	Martini Racing Team	F	3.0 Tecno PA123 F12	chassis cracked	(28)/29
ret	GERMAN GP	Nürburgring	27	Martini Racing Team	F	3.0 Tecno PA123 F12	engine	25/27
dnq	ITALIAN GP	Monza	12	Martini Racing Team	F	3.0 Tecno PA123 F12		27/27
dns	CANADIAN GP	Mosport Park	31	Martini Racing Team	F	3.0 Tecno PA123 F12	accident in a.m.warm-up	(25)/25
ret	US GP	Watkins Glen	31	Martini Racing Team	F	3.0 Tecno PA123 F12	engine	30/32

1974 Championship position: Unplaced

dnq	BRITISH GP	Brands Hatch	*18	Bang & Olufsen Team Surtees	F	3.0 Surtees TS16-Cosworth V8	*also ran as 39 in 3rd practice	27/34
11	GERMAN GP	Nürburgring	18	Bang & Olufsen Team Surtees	F	3.0 Surtees TS16-Cosworth V8		25/32
dnq	AUSTRIAN GP	Österreichring	18	Team Surtees	F	3.0 Surtees TS16-Cosworth V8		28/31
dnq	ITALIAN GP	Monza	18	Team Surtees	F	3.0 Surtees TS16-Cosworth V8		28/31
dnq	CANADIAN GP	Mosport Park	18	Team Surtees	F	3.0 Surtees TS16-Cosworth V8		27/30

GP Starts: 9   GP Wins: 0   Pole positions: 0   Fastest laps: 0   Points: 1

STEFAN BELLOF

THOUGHT by many to be the great lost talent of the 1980s, Stefan Bellof's progress in motor sport was indeed sensational.

Already a karting multi-champion in his native Germany, Bellof took the national Formula Ford title at his first attempt, in 1980, adding the international German FF title the following year, which also saw his winning debut in Formula 3. Aboard a Ralt RT3 entered by Bertram Schafer, he won three races from just seven starts to finish third in the championship.

These exploits brought him to the attention of Willy Maurer, who, with the help of an engine deal from BMW's Dieter Stappert, made a place available for him in his Formula 2 team for 1982. He won first time out at Silverstone in the rain, after a battle with Frank Jelinski, following this up with a dominant win from pole position in round two at Hockenheim. Although he could not sustain this success, as various troubles blunted his challenge, he did record five fastest laps during the season.

Bellof chose to continue in F2 with Maurer in 1983, but the focus of his attention shifted with the offer of a works Porsche drive. Paired with experienced drivers Derek Bell and Jochen Mass, he took the car by the scruff of the neck and, with his aggressive point-and-squirt driving style, began to demolish lap records (and on occasion the car itself). Championship wins were chalked up at Silverstone, Mount Fuji and Kyalami. Bellof continued this success with Rothmans Porsche in 1984, winning six rounds (Monza, the Nürburgring, Spa, Imola, Mount Fuji and Sandown Park) and the endurance drivers' championship. He also found time to win the six-round German endurance championship in a Brun-entered Porsche.

Having reportedly turned down an offer from ATS to enter grands prix in 1983, Stefan had no qualms about joining the Tyrrell team for the following season. Despite the lack of a turbo engine, he was soon extracting the maximum from his car, and could well have won the rain-shortened Monaco GP if the race had been allowed to run longer. However, the punitive treatment meted out to the Tyrrell team after the Dutch GP brought an early end to his Formula 1 season, and all his efforts were declared null and void.

Bellof's last season dawned with the prospect of having to wait until mid-term for Renault turbo power, together with a one-race suspension (Brazil) after a dispute with the team. Despite this, Bellof still gave his all. It was such commitment, which some would say bordered on recklessness, that proved his undoing. He had switched to Walter Brun's team for sports car racing, and at the Spa 1000km he attempted an audacious overtaking manoeuvre on former team-mate Jacky Ickx at Eau Rouge. Their Porsches collided and poor Stefan perished as his car was destroyed against the barriers.

BELLOF, Stefan (D) b 20/11/1957, Giessen – d 1/9/1985, Spa-Francorchamps Circuit, Belgium

	Race	Circuit	No	Entrant	Tyres	Capacity/Car/Engine	Comment	Q Pos/Entries
	1984 Championship position: Unplaced (7 points scored disallowed by FIA)							
ret/dsq*	BRAZILIAN GP	Rio	4	Tyrrell Racing Organisation	G	3.0 Tyrrell 012-Cosworth V8	throttle cable/*dsq after appeal	23/27
ret/dsq*	SOUTH AFRICAN GP	Kyalami	4	Tyrrell Racing Organisation	G	3.0 Tyrrell 012-Cosworth V8	broken hub/*dsq after appeal	24/27
6/dsq*	BELGIAN GP	Zolder	4	Tyrrell Racing Organisation	G	3.0 Tyrrell 012-Cosworth V8	6th on road/*dsq after appeal	21/27
5/dsq*	SAN MARINO GP	Imola	4	Tyrrell Racing Organisation	G	3.0 Tyrrell 012-Cosworth V8	5th on road/*dsq after appeal	21/28
ret/dsq*	FRENCH GP	Dijon	4	Tyrrell Racing Organisation	G	3.0 Tyrrell 012-Cosworth V8	engine/*dsq after appeal	21/27
3/dsq*	MONACO GP	Monte Carlo	4	Tyrrell Racing Organisation	G	3.0 Tyrrell 012-Cosworth V8	3rd on road/*dsq after appeal	20/27
ret/dsq*	CANADIAN GP	Montreal	4	Tyrrell Racing Organisation	G	3.0 Tyrrell 012-Cosworth V8	driveshaft/*dsq after appeal	22/26
ret/dsq*	US GP (DETROIT)	Detroit	4	Tyrrell Racing Organisation	G	3.0 Tyrrell 012-Cosworth V8	accident/*dsq after appeal	16/27
ret/dsq*	US GP (DALLAS)	Dallas	4	Tyrrell Racing Organisation	G	3.0 Tyrrell 012-Cosworth V8	hit wall/*dsq after appeal	17/26
11/dsq*	BRITISH GP	Brands Hatch	4	Tyrrell Racing Organisation	G	3.0 Tyrrell 012-Cosworth V8	11th on road/*dsq after appeal	26/28
dsq*	AUSTRIAN GP	Österreichring	4	Tyrrell Racing Organisation	G	3.0 Tyrrell 012-Cosworth V8	*excl in practice/car underweight	28/28
9/dsq*	DUTCH GP	Zandvoort	4	Tyrrell Racing Organisation	G	3.0 Tyrrell 012-Cosworth V8	9th on road/*dsq after appeal	24/27
	1985 Championship position: 15th= Wins: 0 Pole positions: 0 Fastest laps: 0 Points scored: 4							
6	PORTUGUESE GP	Estoril	4	Tyrrell Racing Organisation	G	3.0 Tyrrell 012-Cosworth V8	2 laps behind	21/26
ret	SAN MARINO GP	Imola	4	Tyrrell Racing Organisation	G	3.0 Tyrrell 012-Cosworth V8	engine	24/26
dnq	MONACO GP	Monte Carlo	4	Tyrrell Racing Organisation	G	3.0 Tyrrell 012-Cosworth V8		22/26
11	CANADIAN GP	Montreal	4	Tyrrell Racing Organisation	G	3.0 Tyrrell 012-Cosworth V8	2 laps behind	23/25
4	US GP (DETROIT)	Detroit	4	Tyrrell Racing Organisation	G	3.0 Tyrrell 012-Cosworth V8		19/25
13	FRENCH GP	Paul Ricard	4	Tyrrell Racing Organisation	G	3.0 Tyrrell 012-Cosworth V8	3 laps behind	26/26
11	BRITISH GP	Silverstone	4	Tyrrell Racing Organisation	G	3.0 Tyrrell 012-Cosworth V8	6 laps behind	26/26
8	GERMAN GP	Nürburgring	3	Tyrrell Racing Organisation	G	1.5 t/c Tyrrell 014-Renault V6	1 lap behind	19/27
7/ret	AUSTRIAN GP	Österreichring	3	Tyrrell Racing Organisation	G	1.5 t/c Tyrrell 014-Renault V6	out of fuel/3 laps behind	22/27
ret	DUTCH GP	Zandvoort	4	Tyrrell Racing Organisation	G	1.5 t/c Tyrrell 014-Renault V6	engine	22/27

GP Starts: 20   GP Wins: 0   Pole positions: 0   Fastest laps: 0   Points: 4

BELMONDO Paul (F) b 23/4/1963, Boulogne-Billancourt, nr Paris

	Race	Circuit	No	Entrant	Tyres	Capacity/Car/Engine	Comment	Q Pos/Entries
	1992 Championship position: Unplaced							
dnq	SOUTH AFRICAN GP	Kyalami	17	March F1	G	3.5 March CG911-Ilmor V10		27/30
dnq	MEXICAN GP	Mexico City	17	March F1	G	3.5 March CG911-Ilmor V10		28/30
dnq	BRAZILIAN GP	Interlagos	17	March F1	G	3.5 March CG911-Ilmor V10		28/31
12	SPANISH GP	Barcelona	17	March F1	G	3.5 March CG911-Ilmor V10	4 laps behind	23/32
13	SAN MARINO GP	Imola	17	March F1	G	3.5 March CG911-Ilmor V10	3 laps behind	24/32
dnq	MONACO GP	Monte Carlo	17	March F1	G	3.5 March CG911-Ilmor V10		30/32
14	CANADIAN GP	Montreal	17	March F1	G	3.5 March CG911-Ilmor V10	5 laps behind	20/32
dnq	FRENCH GP	Magny Cours	17	March F1	G	3.5 March CG911-Ilmor V10		27/30
dnq	BRITISH GP	Silverstone	17	March F1	G	3.5 March CG911-Ilmor V10		28/32
13	GERMAN GP	Hockenheim	17	March F1	G	3.5 March CG911-Ilmor V10	1 lap behind	22/32
9	HUNGARIAN GP	Hungaroring	17	March F1	G	3.5 March CG911-Ilmor V10	3 laps behind	17/31
	1994 Championship position: Unplaced							
dnq	BRAZILIAN GP	Interlagos	33	Pacific Grand Prix	G	3.5 Pacific PR01-Ilmor V10	*no time set	*28/28
dnq	PACIFIC GP	T.I. Circuit	33	Pacific Grand Prix	G	3.5 Pacific PR01-Ilmor V10		27/28
dnq	SAN MARINO GP	Imola	33	Pacific Grand Prix	G	3.5 Pacific PR01-Ilmor V10		28/28
ret	MONACO GP	Monte Carlo	33	Pacific Grand Prix	G	3.5 Pacific PR01-Ilmor V10	driver fatigue	24/24
ret	SPANISH GP	Barcelona	33	Pacific Grand Prix	G	3.5 Pacific PR01-Ilmor V10	spun off on lap 2	26/27
dnq	CANADIAN GP	Montreal	33	Pacific Grand Prix	G	3.5 Pacific PR01-Ilmor V10		27/27
dnq	FRENCH GP	Magny Cours	33	Pacific Grand Prix	G	3.5 Pacific PR01-Ilmor V10		28/28
dnq	BRITISH GP	Silverstone	33	Pacific Grand Prix	G	3.5 Pacific PR01-Ilmor V10		28/28
dnq	GERMAN GP	Hockenheim	33	Pacific Grand Prix	G	3.5 Pacific PR01-Ilmor V10		27/28
dnq	HUNGARIAN GP	Hungaroring	33	Pacific Grand Prix	G	3.5 Pacific PR01-Ilmor V10		28/28
dnq	BELGIAN GP	Spa	33	Pacific Grand Prix	G	3.5 Pacific PR01-Ilmor V10		28/28
dnq	ITALIAN GP	Monza	33	Pacific Grand Prix	G	3.5 Pacific PR01-Ilmor V10		28/28
dnq	PORTUGUESE GP	Estoril	33	Pacific Grand Prix	G	3.5 Pacific PR01-Ilmor V10		28/28
dnq	EUROPEAN GP	Jerez	33	Pacific Grand Prix	G	3.5 Pacific PR01-Ilmor V10		28/28
dnq	JAPANESE GP	Suzuka	33	Pacific Grand Prix	G	3.5 Pacific PR01-Ilmor V10		28/28
dnq	AUSTRALIAN GP	Adelaide	33	Pacific Grand Prix	G	3.5 Pacific PR01-Ilmor V10		27/28

GP Starts: 7   GP Wins: 0   Pole positions: 0   Fastest laps: 0   Points: 0

BELSØ, Tom (DK) b 27/8/1942, Copenhagen

	Race	Circuit	No	Entrant	Tyres	Capacity/Car/Engine	Comment	Q Pos/Entries
	1973 Championship position: Unplaced							
dns	SWEDISH GP	Anderstorp	26	Frank Williams Racing Cars	F	3.0 Iso Marlboro 1R-Cosworth V8	practice only – Ganley raced car	(22)/22
	1974 Championship position: Unplaced							
ret	SOUTH AFRICAN GP	Kyalami	21	Frank Williams Racing Cars	F	3.0 Iso Marlboro FW01-Cosworth V8	clutch slip	27/27
dnq	SPANISH GP	Jarama	21	Frank Williams Racing Cars	F	3.0 Iso Marlboro FW02-Cosworth V8		28/28
8	SWEDISH GP	Anderstorp	21	Frank Williams Racing Cars	F	3.0 Iso Marlboro FW02-Cosworth V8	1 lap behind	21/28
dnq	BRITISH GP	Brands Hatch	21	Frank Williams Racing Cars	F	3.0 Iso Marlboro FW01-Cosworth V8		=28/34

GP Starts: 2   GP Wins: 0   Pole positions: 0   Fastest laps: 0   Points: 0

PAUL BELMONDO

BEING the son of one of France's most famous actors has probably done Belmondo no favours, but he has steadily plugged away at his chosen career, shrugging aside the jealous accusations that he was no more than a 'playboy racer.'

Certainly the winner of the 1982 Pilote Elf was something of an enigma during his years in French Formula 3 between 1983 and 1986, the young Belmondo putting in some useful performances without being quite on the pace of each new batch of hot-shots as they leap-frogged over him on their way up.

Eventually, in 1987, he followed more stellar talents into F3000 and scored a fifth place at Pau with a GBDA Lola, but nothing concrete was achieved during the next three seasons save a single sixth place in the Le Mans round in 1990. A disastrous 1991 season with the Apomatox team's Reynard was hardly ideal preparation for his unexpected elevation to the Grand Prix ranks, but he settled into the second March in the first half of 1992 surprisingly well – ironically his best performances for the team were at Hockenheim and the Hungaroring, his last two races before his money ran out. Charged with bringing the car home in one piece at all costs, Paul's sensible approach helped to keep the team afloat financially, and even his greatest detractors would admit that he had done a sound job in difficult circumstances. Just as it seemed that Paul would join the ranks of ex-Formula 1 driver's, he became part of the new Pacific Grand Prix team for 1994. Unfortunately, the car was never remotely competitive and his frustrating second spell in F1 was largely spent accumulating a string of non-qualifications along with team-mate Gachot.

Following his stab at F1, Belmondo turned his attentions to GT racing; initially he drove a Ferrari GT40 in 1996, before setting up his own team running Chrysler Vipers. The high point came late in 1999, when Paul won the FIA GT round at Homestead, beating the works cars. His Chrysler's were always serious competitors in the class until in 2004 he moved his squad into the Le Mans Endurance series to race his Belmondo Courage prototypes in the P2 class up until 2007.

Belmonda has made five appearances in Paris-Dakar in a Nissan, taking second in class in 2003. His most recent racing activity appears to be restricted to the Andros Ice Trophy .

In addition to some motorsport TV commentary, he has also followed his father into the acting profession and appeared in a number of French films since 2002. In 2009 Paul took to the stage in Paris and appeared in a light comedy.

TOM BELSØ

FOREVER being fatuously described as 'The smiling Dane' ill served this hard-working driver. After many years of endeavour he eventually became Denmark's first racing driver to compete in a World Championship Grand Prix and, more importantly, proved himself a formidable competitor in the early seventies in Formula 5000.

Originally a mechanic, his meticulous preparation was rewarded by the chance to race the Volvo on which he had worked. Tom was a winner first time out and by 1969, driving a Ford Escort, he was the Scandinavian saloon car champion. This success led to a test and subsequent drive in Formula Ford with Hawke in 1970.

Encouraged by his progress, Belsø sold his business interests and moved his family to England to compete in Formula Atlantic in 1971. He finished third in the championship with an old Brabham and then took the leap into Formula 2 for 1972. A fourth place at Albi was the best result in a season strewn with engine problems, but he caught the eye of Jackie Epstein, who signed him for his Shellsport F5000 team – for which he drove splendidly for three seasons. It was during this period that Frank Williams gave Tom his Grand Prix opportunities. Lack of finance curtailed his racing activities for 1976 but, irrepressible as ever, he was back for one more final tilt at F5000 in 1977 with John Jordan's Lola.

In 1982 Tom founded Belsø Foods, developing cereals, specialising in muesli for own label brands in supermakets in England and Scandinavia. His company was bought out in 2005 by Bokomo Foods, but he remained on board as a consultant. The Belsø name is still used exclusively in selected supermarkets in his native Denmark.

JEAN-PIERRE BELTOISE

LIKE Jean Behra, Jean-Pierre Beltoise was a French motorcycle champion, and he won 11 championships between 1961 and 1964 while working for the René Bonnet team as a mechanic. He made his four-wheel debut at Le Mans in 1963, winning the Index of Performance, but a year later his career was nearly ended when a horrendous accident at Reims left him with burns and multiple injuries, the most serious of which was a left arm so badly broken that its movement was permanently restricted. Nevertheless, he was back in 1965 racing the F3 Matra (the aerospace company having taken over the René Bonnet concern), and he scored a great first win for the marque at Reims. His pre-eminence in this formula was confirmed when he won the 1966 Monaco F3 race and all four rounds of the Argentinian Temporada series early in 1967. This success encouraged Matra to continue with their racing activities, and Beltoise was the spearhead of the team's Formula 2 programme from 1966, winning the F2 class of the German GP and later the European F2 championship for non-graded drivers in 1968, when he recorded victories at Hockenheim, Jarama and Zandvoort.

Although Beltoise contested a number of grands prix in a ballasted F2 Matra, he had to wait until early 1968 to get his hands on the team's raucous V12-engined F1 car, but he soon began to demonstrate its potential with a brilliant second place and fastest lap at Zandvoort. In 1969, he was placed in Ken Tyrrell's team as number two to Jackie Stewart while development work was undertaken on the V12 project, and he delivered seven points-scoring finishes. The following season, he raced the new Matra MS120-V12 and was unlucky not to win the French GP, a puncture having robbed him of the lead. Although he had done well enough on occasion, Matra signed Chris Amon for 1971, frustrating the Frenchman's F1 aspirations. It was not a happy season for Beltoise, who received a suspension when he was blamed for his involvement in the fatal accident that befell Ignazio Giunti in the Buenos Aires 1000km.

In 1972, Beltoise moved to BRM, where he soon enjoyed his day of days, winning the Monaco GP with a scintillating performance in pouring rain. Although a second place in the International Trophy and a win in the John Player Victory race at Brands Hatch merely disguised the team's imminent decline, Jean-Pierre stayed on until 1974, a fantastic drive to second place at Kyalami in the P201 being the only highlight of his final season with the team.

An established member of the Matra squad, Jean-Pierre enjoyed a tremendous year in sports car racing, winning four championship rounds (the Nürburgring, Watkins Glen, Paul Ricard and Brands Hatch), but at season's end he was looking for work on two fronts. With Matra out of endurance racing, he was forced to scratch around for drives, and the prospect of an F1 return with Ligier in 1976 evaporated when the seat went to Jacques Laffite. Jean-Pierre was involved with both the Ligier and Inaltera sports car projects before successfully switching to the French touring car scene, where he gained much enjoyment for many years. He also had the pleasure of helping the progress of his sons, Julien and Anthony, as they made their own racing careers.

BELTOISE, Jean-Pierre (F) b 26/4/1937, Paris

	Race	Circuit	No	Entrant	Tyres	Capacity/Car/Engine	Comment	Q Pos/Entries
	1966 Championship position: Unplaced							
8*	GERMAN GP (F2)	Nürburgring	34	Matra Sports	D	1.0 Matra MS5-Cosworth 4	*1st in F2 class/1 lap behind	19/30
	1967 Championship position: Unplaced							
dnq	MONACO GP	Monte Carlo	1	Matra Sports	D	1.6 Matra MS7-Cosworth 4 F2		17/18
7	US GP	Watkins Glen	22	Matra Sports	G	1.6 Matra MS7-Cosworth 4 F2	7 laps behind	18/18
7	MEXICAN GP	Mexico City	22	Matra Sports	G	1.6 Matra MS7-Cosworth 4 F2	2 laps behind	14/19
	1968 Championship position: 9th Wins: 0 Pole positions: 0 Fastest laps: 2 Points scored: 11							
6	SOUTH AFRICAN GP	Kyalami	21	Matra Sports	D	1.6 Matra MS7-Cosworth 4 F2	ballasted F2 car/3 laps behind	18/23
5	SPANISH GP	Jarama	6	Matra International	D	3.0 Matra MS10-Cosworth V8	2 pit stops – oil leak/FL/-9 laps	=4/14
ret	MONACO GP	Monte Carlo	1	Matra Sports	D	3.0 Matra MS11 V12	hit chicane – damaged suspension	8/18
8	BELGIAN GP	Spa	10	Matra Sports	D	3.0 Matra MS11 V12	pit stop – fuel/3 laps behind	13/18
2	DUTCH GP	Zandvoort	17	Matra Sports	D	3.0 Matra MS11 V12	pit stop – sand in throttle slides/FL	16/19
9	FRENCH GP	Rouen	6	Matra Sports	D	3.0 Matra MS11 V12	pit stop – tyres/4 laps behind	8/18
ret	BRITISH GP	Brands Hatch	18	Matra Sports	D	3.0 Matra MS11 V12	oil pressure	=13/18
ret	GERMAN GP	Nürburgring	12	Matra Sports	D	3.0 Matra MS11 V12	crashed	12/20
5	ITALIAN GP	Monza	6	Matra Sports	D	3.0 Matra MS11 V12	2 laps behind	19/24
ret	CANADIAN GP	St Jovite	18	Matra Sports	D	3.0 Matra MS11 V12	transmission	16/22
ret	US GP	Watkins Glen	21	Matra Sports	D	3.0 Matra MS11 V12	driveshaft	13/21
ret	MEXICAN GP	Mexico City	21	Matra Sports	D	3.0 Matra MS11 V12	rear suspension	13/21
	1969 Championship position: 5th Wins: 0 Pole positions: 0 Fastest laps: 1 Points scored: 21							
6	SOUTH AFRICAN GP	Kyalami	8	Matra International	D	3.0 Matra MS10-Cosworth V8	2 laps behind	=12/18
3	SPANISH GP	Montjuich Park	8	Matra International	D	3.0 Matra MS80-Cosworth V8	2 pit stops – gear linkage/-3 laps	12/14
ret	MONACO GP	Monte Carlo	8	Matra International	D	3.0 Matra MS80-Cosworth V8	universal joint	3/16
8	DUTCH GP	Zandvoort	5	Matra International	D	3.0 Matra MS80-Cosworth V8	3 laps behind	11/15
2	FRENCH GP	Clermont Ferrand	7	Matra International	D	3.0 Matra MS80-Cosworth V8		5/13
9	BRITISH GP	Silverstone (30)	4	Matra International	D	3.0 Matra MS84-Cosworth V8 4WD	6 laps behind	17/17
dns	"	"	4	Matra International	D	3.0 Matra MS80-Cosworth V8	practice only/Stewart in race	– / –
12/ret	GERMAN GP	Nürburgring	8	Matra International	D	3.0 Matra MS80-Cosworth V8	front upright/6th F1 car/-2 laps	10/26
3	ITALIAN GP	Monza	22	Matra International	D	3.0 Matra MS80-Cosworth V8	FL	6/15
4	CANADIAN GP	Mosport Park	18	Matra International	D	3.0 Matra MS80-Cosworth V8	1 lap behind	=2/20
ret	US GP	Watkins Glen	4	Matra International	D	3.0 Matra MS80-Cosworth V8	engine	7/18
5	MEXICAN GP	Mexico City	4	Matra International	D	3.0 Matra MS80-Cosworth V8		8/17
	1970 Championship position: 9th Wins: 0 Pole positions: 0 Fastest laps: 0 Points scored: 16							
4	SOUTH AFRICAN GP	Kyalami	3	Equipe Matra Elf	G	3.0 Matra-Simca MS120 V12		=7/24
ret	SPANISH GP	Jarama	4	Equipe Matra Elf	G	3.0 Matra-Simca MS120 V12	engine	4/22
ret	MONACO GP	Monte Carlo	8	Equipe Matra Elf	G	3.0 Matra-Simca MS120 V12	engine – cwp	6/21
3	BELGIAN GP	Spa	25	Equipe Matra Elf	G	3.0 Matra-Simca MS120 V12		11/18
5	DUTCH GP	Zandvoort	23	Equipe Matra Elf	G	3.0 Matra-Simca MS120 V12	1 lap behind	10/24
13/ret	FRENCH GP	Clermont Ferrand	21	Equipe Matra Elf	G	3.0 Matra-Simca MS120 V12	fuel pressure/3 laps behind	2/23
ret	BRITISH GP	Brands Hatch	7	Equipe Matra Elf	G	3.0 Matra-Simca MS120 V12	wheel bearing problem	11/25
ret	GERMAN GP	Hockenheim	8	Equipe Matra Elf	G	3.0 Matra-Simca MS120 V12	front suspension	23/25
6	AUSTRIAN GP	Österreichring	19	Equipe Matra Elf	G	3.0 Matra-Simca MS120 V12	pit stop – fuel/1 lap behind	=7/24
3	ITALIAN GP	Monza	40	Equipe Matra Elf	G	3.0 Matra-Simca MS120 V12		15/27
8	CANADIAN GP	St Jovite	23	Equipe Matra Elf	G	3.0 Matra-Simca MS120 V12	5 laps behind	13/20
ret	US GP	Watkins Glen	6	Equipe Matra Elf	G	3.0 Matra-Simca MS120 V12	handling	18/27
5	MEXICAN GP	Mexico City	6	Equipe Matra Elf	G	3.0 Matra-Simca MS120 V12		6/18
	1971 Championship position: 22nd Wins: 0 Pole positions: 0 Fastest laps: 0 Points scored: 1							
6	SPANISH GP	Montjuich Park	21	Equipe Matra Sports	G	3.0 Matra-Simca MS120B V12	1 lap behind	6/22
ret	MONACO GP	Monte Carlo	21	Equipe Matra Sports	G	3.0 Matra-Simca MS120B V12	cwp	7/23
9	DUTCH GP	Zandvoort	21	Equipe Matra Sports	G	3.0 Matra-Simca MS120B V12	5 laps behind	11/24
7	FRENCH GP	Paul Ricard	21	Equipe Matra Sports	G	3.0 Matra-Simca MS120B V12		8/24
7	BRITISH GP	Silverstone	22	Equipe Matra Sports	G	3.0 Matra-Simca MS120B V12	2 laps behind	15/24
ret	CANADIAN GP	Mosport Park	21	Equipe Matra Sports	G	3.0 Matra-Simca MS120B V12	hit guard rail	=11/27
8	US GP	Watkins Glen	12	Equipe Matra Sports	G	3.0 Matra-Simca MS120B V12	1 lap behind	11/32
	1972 Championship position: 11th Wins: 1 Pole positions: 0 Fastest laps: 1 Points scored: 9							
ret	SOUTH AFRICAN GP	Kyalami	10	Marlboro BRM	F	3.0 BRM P160B V12	engine	11/27
ret	SPANISH GP	Jarama	19	Marlboro BRM	F	3.0 BRM P160B V12	gear selection	7/26
dns	"	"	19T	Marlboro BRM	F	3.0 BRM P180 V12	practice only	– / –
1	MONACO GP	Monte Carlo	17	Marlboro BRM	F	3.0 BRM P160B V12	FL	4/25
ret	BELGIAN GP	Nivelles	23	Marlboro BRM	F	3.0 BRM P160B V12	overheating	6/26
15	FRENCH GP	Clermont Ferrand	5T	Marlboro BRM	F	3.0 BRM P160B V12	started from back/spin/-1 lap	– / –
dns	"	"	5	Marlboro BRM	F	3.0 BRM P160C V12	practice only	(14)/29
11	BRITISH GP	Brands Hatch	11	Marlboro BRM	F	3.0 BRM P160C V12	pit stop – puncture/6 laps behind	6/27
dns	"	"	43	Marlboro BRM	F	3.0 BRM P160B V12	practice only	– / –
9	GERMAN GP	Nürburgring	6	Marlboro BRM	F	3.0 BRM P160C V12	black flagged when 5th	13/27
8	AUSTRIAN GP	Österreichring	7	Marlboro BRM	F	3.0 BRM P160C V12		21/26
8	ITALIAN GP	Monza	21	Marlboro BRM	F	3.0 BRM P180 V12	1 lap behind	16/27
ret	CANADIAN GP	Mosport Park	14	Marlboro BRM	F	3.0 BRM P180 V12	oil cooler leak	=19/25
ret	US GP	Watkins Glen	17	Marlboro BRM	F	3.0 BRM P180 V12	ignition rotor	18/32
	1973 Championship position: 10th Wins: 0 Pole positions: 0 Fastest laps: 0 Points scored: 9							
ret	ARGENTINE GP	Buenos Aires	30	Marlboro BRM	F	3.0 BRM P160D V12	engine	7/19
ret	BRAZILIAN GP	Interlagos	15	Marlboro BRM	F	3.0 BRM P160D V12	electrics – damaged by stone	10/20
ret	SOUTH AFRICAN GP	Kyalami	16	Marlboro BRM	F	3.0 BRM P160D V12	clutch slip	7/25
5	SPANISH GP	Montjuich Park	15	Marlboro BRM	F	3.0 BRM P160E V12	1 lap behind	=9/22
ret	BELGIAN GP	Zolder	20	Marlboro BRM	F	3.0 BRM P160E V12	engine	5/23

	Race	Circuit	No	Entrant	Tyres	Capacity/Car/Engine	Comment	Q Pos/Entries
ret	MONACO GP	Monte Carlo	20	Marlboro BRM	F	3.0 BRM P160E V12	hit kerb and armco	11/26
ret	SWEDISH GP	Anderstorp	20	Marlboro BRM	F	3.0 BRM P160E V12	engine	9/22
11	FRENCH GP	Paul Ricard	20	Marlboro BRM	F	3.0 BRM P160E V12	1 lap behind	15/25
ret/dns	BRITISH GP	Silverstone	20	Marlboro BRM	F	3.0 BRM P160E V12	accident at 1st start/no restart	=16/29
5	DUTCH GP	Zandvoort	20	Marlboro BRM	F	3.0 BRM P160E V12		9/24
ret	GERMAN GP	Nürburgring	20	Marlboro BRM	F	3.0 BRM P160E V12	puncture/gearbox	9/23
5	AUSTRIAN GP	Österreichring	20	Marlboro BRM	F	3.0 BRM P160E V12		13/25
13	ITALIAN GP	Monza	20	Marlboro BRM	F	3.0 BRM P160E V12	pit stop – puncture/1 lap behind	13/25
4	CANADIAN GP	Mosport Park	20	Marlboro BRM	F	3.0 BRM P160E V12		16/26
9	US GP	Watkins Glen	20	Marlboro BRM	F	3.0 BRM P160E V12	pit stop/1 lap behind	15/28

1974 Championship position: 13th   Wins: 0   Pole positions: 0   Fastest laps: 0   Points scored: 10

	Race	Circuit	No	Entrant	Tyres	Capacity/Car/Engine	Comment	Q Pos/Entries
5	ARGENTINE GP	Buenos Aires	14	Team Motul BRM	F	3.0 BRM P160E V12		14/26
10	BRAZILIAN GP	Interlagos	14	Team Motul BRM	F	3.0 BRM P160E V12	1 lap behind	17/25
2	SOUTH AFRICAN GP	Kyalami	14	Team Motul BRM	F	3.0 BRM P201 V12		=11/27
ret	SPANISH GP	Jarama	14	Team Motul BRM	F	3.0 BRM P201 V12	engine	12/28
5	BELGIAN GP	Nivelles	14	Team Motul BRM	F	3.0 BRM P201 V12		7/32
ret	MONACO GP	Monte Carlo	14	Team Motul BRM	F	3.0 BRM P201 V12	collision with Hulme	=10/28
ret	SWEDISH GP	Anderstorp	14	Team Motul BRM	F	3.0 BRM P201 V12	engine	13/28
ret	DUTCH GP	Zandvoort	14	Team Motul BRM	F	3.0 BRM P201 V12	gearbox	16/27
10	FRENCH GP	Dijon	14	Team Motul BRM	F	3.0 BRM P201 V12	1 lap behind	17/30
12	BRITISH GP	Brands Hatch	14	Team Motul BRM	F	3.0 BRM P201 V12	pit stop – tyres/3 laps behind	23/34
ret	GERMAN GP	Nürburgring	14	Team Motul BRM	F	3.0 BRM P201 V12	accessory drive belt	15/32
ret	AUSTRIAN GP	Österreichring	14	Team Motul BRM	F	3.0 BRM P201 V12	engine	18/31
ret	ITALIAN GP	Monza	14	Team Motul BRM	F	3.0 BRM P201 V12	electrics	11/31
nc	CANADIAN GP	Mosport Park	14	Team Motul BRM	F	3.0 BRM P201 V12	pit stops – handling/-20 laps	17/30
dns	US GP	Watkins Glen	14	Team Motul BRM	F	3.0 BRM P201 V12	accident – broken bone in foot	30/30

GP Starts: 85 (86)   GP Wins: 1   Pole positions: 0   Fastest laps: 4   Points: 77

OLIVIER BERETTA

A MONÉGASQUE driver, Olivier Beretta began karting in 1983, scoring many wins before graduating to French F3 in 1989. In the following year, he began to cause a stir. Armed with a Dallara-Alfa, he took third place in the Monaco F3 race and then won at Pau before his season tailed off, although he still finished a creditable third in the overall standings. His 1991 campaign was less successful: a broken wrist in the Monaco F3 race hindered his progress; he also attempted to race his Ralt in both the French and British series, which dissipated his chances.

A move into F3000 in 1992 with Nelson Piquet's well-funded team saw disappointment for all concerned, Beretta making too many mistakes for comfort. A move to Forti Corse, however, brought immediate reward, as he won the 1993 season-opener from pole at Donington. Thereafter, he failed to make the podium and slipped down to finish sixth in the championship.

Olivier brought much-needed funds to the Larrousse team for 1994, and he was certainly not outclassed by his team-mate, Érik Comas. At Hockenheim, he came tantalisingly close to scoring a precious championship point, but after just one more race his sponsorship money ran out, and a succession of 'rent-a-drivers' were taken on to help the squad see out the season.

From 1996, Beretta rejuvinated his career in sports and GT racing, campaigning an ORECA Chrysler Viper with spectacular success. After the heartbreak of losing the GT2 title at the final round in 1997, he made no mistake the following year when paired with Pedro Lamy. The 1999 season saw Olivier and Karl Wendlinger crowned FIA GT champions as the Viper crushed the opposition. He also took the GTS class win at Le Mans, and it was more of the same in 2000, when this well-matched pair repeated their success.

After a couple of years of intermittent racing, Beretta was drawn back to the American Le Mans series, firstly in a JML Panoz and then in a Pratt & Miller Chevrolet. In 2004, he was teamed with Oliver Gavin and Jan Magnussen at Le Mans, the trio taking sixth overall, and Olivier notched his third GT1 class win. The following year, it was fifth overall and first in class again, and in 2006 the three drivers finished a superb fourth overall to claim a hat trick of class wins.

Beretta and Gavin were convincing champions in the GTS/GT1 class of the American Le Mans Series with their Corvette from 2005 to 2007, when the duo took a record nine wins from 11 starts. Indeed, the pair remained as GT-class contenders for the Corvette squad through until 2011, when Olivier was paired with Tommy Milner. In his final season with Chevrolet, the Monégasque scored a sixth class win (in the GTE-Pro class) at Le Mans.

With 41 wins in the ALMS, Beretta is the series' most successful competitor. In 2012, he fulfilled a boyhood dream of racing a Ferrari when he switched to the Risi Competizione squad, to begin a new chapter in his career.

BERETTA, Olivier (MC) b 23/11/1969, Monte Carlo

	Race	Circuit	No	Entrant	Tyres	Capacity/Car/Engine	Comment	Q Pos/Entries
	1994 Championship position: Unplaced							
ret	BRAZILIAN GP	Interlagos	19	Tourtel Larrousse F1	G	3.5 Larrousse LH94-Ford HB V8	spun – collision with Gachot	23/28
ret	PACIFIC GP	T.I. Circuit	19	Tourtel Larrousse F1	G	3.5 Larrousse LH94-Ford HB V8	electrics	21/28
ret	SAN MARINO GP	Imola	19	Tourtel Larrousse F1	G	3.5 Larrousse LH94-Ford HB V8	engine	23/28
8	MONACO GP	Monte Carlo	19	Tourtel Larrousse F1	G	3.5 Larrousse LH94-Ford HB V8	2 laps behind	18/24

	Race	Circuit	No	Entrant	Tyres	Capacity/Car/Engine	Comment	Q Pos/Entries
ret/dns	SPANISH GP	Barcelona	19	Tourtel Larrousse F1	G	3.5 Larrousse LH94-Ford HB V8	engine failure on parade lap	(17)/27
ret	CANADIAN GP	Montreal	19	Tourtel Larrousse F1	G	3.5 Larrousse LH94-Ford HB V8	engine	22/27
ret	FRENCH GP	Magny Cours	19	Tourtel Larrousse F1	G	3.5 Larrousse LH94-Ford HB V8	engine	25/28
14*	BRITISH GP	Silverstone	19	Tourtel Larrousse F1	G	3.5 Larrousse LH94-Ford HB V8	*2nd place car dsq/-2 laps	24/28
7	GERMAN GP	Hockenheim	19	Tourtel Larrousse F1	G	3.5 Larrousse LH94-Ford HB V8	1 lap behind	24/28
9	HUNGARIAN GP	Hungaroring	19	Tourtel Larrousse F1	G	3.5 Larrousse LH94-Ford HB V8	2 laps behind	25/28

GP Starts: 9 (10) GP Wins: 0 Pole positions: 0 Fastest laps: 0 Points: 0

ALLEN BERG

A STOCKY little Canadian driver, Allen Berg emerged from the 1982 North American Formula Atlantic series by way of the winter Pacific championship, which he won for New Zealand ex-racer Graeme Lawrence in a Ralt, to contest the 1983 British F3 championship. With no experience of this class of car or, naturally, the circuits, he did a good job in this formative season, especially after switching to the Eddie Jordan Racing team. This was the year when the Ayrton Senna/Martin Brundle axis dominated proceedings, but Allen regularly led the rest in pursuit of the star duo.

Having stayed with EJR, Berg had high hopes for success in 1984, but a season of mishaps and frustration saw him finish second in the standings to Johnny Dumfries. This left his career in something of a vacuum, and it was a surprise when he scraped together sufficient finance to take over the unwieldy Osella in mid-1986, after Christian Danner moved to Arrows. This was a year without the pressures of having to qualify, so at least Allen was able get some experience and racing mileage under his belt.

Berg then tried his hand at the German touring car championship with his own car in 1991, but in subsequent seasons he found a happy hunting ground down Mexico way. He was Formula 2 champion in 1993 and took third place overall in the well-funded 1995 Formula 3 series. In 2001, he was the PanAmerican IndyLights champion, and in 2002 he moved into the Toyota Atlantic series as a team owner.

GEORGES BERGER

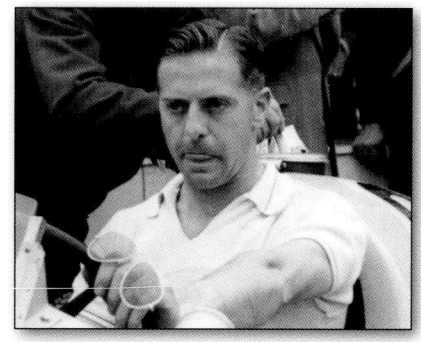

EARLY in his long career, Georges Berger raced a little Jicey-BMW, his best finish being third at Chimay in 1950. In 1953, he got his hands on a private Gordini, and then briefly became part of the works team early the following year, taking a Type 16 car to fourth in the non-championship race at Rouen.

Thereafter, Georges was a stalwart competitor in sports and GT racing, with machines such as a Maserati sports, an AC Bristol and a Ferrari 250GT. He often raced the last car with another ex-grand prix driver, André Simon. His greatest success, however, was winning the Tour de France rally with Willy Mairesse in 1960, again in a Ferrari.

In 1967, Berger was killed while taking part in the Marathon de la Route, an 84-hour endurance race at the Nürburgring, when he crashed his Porsche 911.

BERG, Allen (CDN) b 1/8/1961, Calgary, Alberta

	Race	Circuit	No	Entrant	Tyres	Capacity/Car/Engine	Comment	Q Pos/Entries
	1986 Championship position: Unplaced							
ret	US GP (DETROIT)	Detroit	22	Osella Squadra Corse	P	1.5 t/c Osella FA1F-Alfa Romeo V8	electrics	25/26
ret	FRENCH GP	Dijon	22	Osella Squadra Corse	P	1.5 t/c Osella FA1G-Alfa Romeo V8	turbo	26/26
ret/dns	BRITISH GP	Brands Hatch	22	Osella Squadra Corse	P	1.5 t/c Osella FA1H-Alfa Romeo V8	accident in first start	26/26
12	GERMAN GP	Hockenheim	22	Osella Squadra Corse	P	1.5 t/c Osella FA1F-Alfa Romeo V8	4 laps behind	26/26
ret	HUNGARIAN GP	Hungaroring	22	Osella Squadra Corse	P	1.5 t/c Osella FA1F-Alfa Romeo V8	turbo	26/26
ret	AUSTRIAN GP	Österreichring	22	Osella Squadra Corse	P	1.5 t/c Osella FA1F-Alfa Romeo V8	electrics	26/26
13	PORTUGUESE GP	Estoril	22	Osella Squadra Corse	P	1.5 t/c Osella FA1F-Alfa Romeo V8	7 laps behind	27/27
16	MEXICAN GP	Mexico City	22	Osella Squadra Corse	P	1.5 t/c Osella FA1F-Alfa Romeo V8	7 laps behind	26/26
nc	AUSTRALIAN GP	Adelaide	22	Osella Squadra Corse	P	1.5 t/c Osella FA1F-Alfa Romeo V8	started from pits/21 laps behind	26/26

GP Starts: 8 (9) GP Wins: 0 Pole positions: 0 Fastest laps: 0 Points: 0

BERGER, Georges (B) b 14/9/1918, Brussels – d 23/8/1967, Nürburgring, Germany

	Race	Circuit	No	Entrant	Tyres	Capacity/Car/Engine	Comment	Q Pos/Entries
	1953 Championship position: Unplaced							
ret	BELGIAN GP	Spa	34	Georges Berger	E	1.5 Simca Gordini Type 15 4	engine	20/22
	1954 Championship position: Unplaced							
ret	FRENCH GP	Reims	30	Georges Berger	E	1.5 Gordini Type 16 6	engine – valve	20/22

GP Starts: 2 GP Wins: 0 Pole positions: 0 Fastest laps: 0 Points: 0

GERHARD BERGER

WHEN Gerhard Berger finally hung up his helmet at the end of the 1997 season, he was really the last of the generation of superstars whose F1 careers dated back to the turbo era of the mid-1980s. Indeed he was somewhat unfortunate to have had to pit himself against such giants of the sport as Senna, Prost, Piquet and Mansell over an eight-season spell between 1986 and 1993, otherwise his tally of ten grand prix wins could easily have been much more.

With a limited racing background, first in Alfas and then in the German and European Formula 3 series, Berger had gained a reputation as a fast and safe driver who, above all, brought his car home to the finish when he breezed into the ATS team towards the end of 1984. His sixth place at Monza was sufficient indication that here was a rough diamond waiting to be polished, and even a close-season accident that left him with broken vertebrae in his neck was not enough to prevent him from lining up at the start of the 1985 season in the Arrows-BMW team. At first, he struggled somewhat alongside the quiet and talented Thierry Boutsen, but his aggressive driving style began to pay dividends in the second half of the season.

Benetton were running BMW engines in 1986, and Berger's connections with the German company helped him to a place in the team, but he soon proved the wisdom of his selection with some eye-catching drives, especially when the Pirelli tyres were working well. After disappointment in Austria, he gained his first grand prix win in Mexico and, on the not-too-distant horizon, a contract with Ferrari for 1987.

Despite a hesitant beginning, Gerhard's natural ebullience became quickly apparent and, after throwing away a victory in the Portuguese GP, he won the end-of-season Japanese and Australian races. In 1988, McLaren-Honda were utterly dominant, but Berger never gave up, and a lucky win at Monza was just reward for perhaps his best-ever year. However, his final season at Maranello was distinctly low-key. Psychologically outgunned by Mansell and striving to shake off the effects of a horrendous crash at Imola, he picked up a win at Estoril almost unnoticed before joining McLaren on a three-year contract to partner Senna.

Initially, it was a morale-sapping experience, as he struggled in his stellar team-mate's trail. He had difficulty fitting into the cockpit and sometimes was guilty of over-taxing his tyres, but gradually he got to grips with the situation at McLaren to become a perfect foil for Senna, both on and off the track. Grand prix wins came here and there; some were lucky and others well earned, with his final race for the team being perhaps his best, when his finely judged tactics brought him victory in Adelaide.

Enticed by a reputedly massive retainer, Gerhard rejoined Ferrari for 1993, but endured a pretty torrid year adapting to 'active' suspension, which obviously he disliked. Worryingly, he was involved in a number of alarming on-track incidents and claimed but a single podium finish. If he thought he could write it off as just a bad dream, then the start of the following year would become a nightmare. Second place in the Pacific GP showed that Ferrari were at last back on course towards winning again, but then came the deaths of his close friends, Roland Ratzenberger and Senna, at Imola. It must have been utterly devastating for Gerhard, who could easily have decided not to continue racing. However, after a week of soul searching, he carried on with the sport he loved so much. His subse-

quent win at Hockenheim ended a dry spell of nearly four years for Ferrari, and was welcomed by all followers of the sport.

As Ferrari continued their team restructuring in search of the holy grail of the world championship, Gerhard forged a good relationship with new team boss Jean Todt. He worked diligently and selflessly in Maranello's cause, and certainly the results achieved in 1995 did not reflect his true level of performance throughout the year. He could have won at Imola and Monza, but in the end had to be content with six third-place finishes. Gerhard has always been a team player, but he could have been excused for feeling unhappy at being pushed to the margins with the arrival of Michael Schumacher in 1996. Understandably, the chance to partner Jean Alesi once more, this time at Benetton, seemed like his best option. Berger faced a testing start to his Benetton career as he adapted to the nervous-handling car, but typically he worked tirelessly and was rewarded by a second place at Silverstone. It could have been even better at Hockenheim a fortnight later, when a blown engine robbed him of victory with only a couple of laps remaining.

What proved to be Gerhard's final season was blighted by a sinus problem that caused him to miss three races, followed by the death of his father in an air accident. That he came back to deliver a superb performance in winning the German Grand Prix showed his doubters that he could not be written off yet. However, at season's end he decided to call time on a career that had spanned 210 races to take up a position as head of motor sport with BMW as they prepared for a grand prix return in 2000.

After three exhausting years in the role, during which the Williams-BMW partnership had succeeded in it's goal of winning races, Gerhard decided to take a break from racing to pursue other business interests and spend more time in with his family.

However, the lure of racing was too great for Gerhard to resist, and at the end of 2005, after Red Bull's Dietrich Mateschitz acquired the Minardi team, Berger bought into the Faenza-based squad, subsequently renamed Scuderia Toro Rosso. With a wealth of experience behind him, the Austrian, along with Franz Tost, set about building up the squad within the inevitable financial constraints that restricted a team of it size.

The procurement of Ferrari power to replace V10 Cosworths in 2007 was a start, followed by the recruitment of respected engineer Giorgio Ascanelli. However, a major uplift came when Red Bull drafted the recently signed youngster Sebastian Vettel into the team at the Hungarian Grand Prix. At this stage, the philosophy had been that Red Bull were to win races, and Toro Rosso were to promote the brand and train young drivers – but on a limited budget.

In 2008, the remarkable Vettel delivered nine points scoring finishes, including of course a fairytale victory at Monza. This helped Toro Rosso to finished in sixth place in the constructors' championship, one place ahead of parent team Red Bull. In November of that year, Berger, acutely aware of the uphill struggle a team like Toro would face, decided to quit while he was ahead and sold his 50 per cent share in the team back to Mateschitz.

Despite persistent rumours of a possible return to F1, Berger, now living in Monte Carlo, seems happy to stay away from full-time involvement in the sport to which he has given so much.

BERGER, Gerhard (A) b 27/8/1959, Wörgl, nr Innsbruck

	Race	Circuit	No	Entrant	Tyres	Capacity/Car/Engine	Comment	Q Pos/Entries
1984	Championship position: Unplaced							
12/ret	AUSTRIAN GP	Österreichring	31	Team ATS	P	1.5 t/c ATS D7-BMW 4	*gearbox/3 laps behind*	20/28
6*	ITALIAN GP	Monza	31	Team ATS	P	1.5 t/c ATS D7-BMW 4	**not eligible for points/-2 laps*	20/27
ret	EUROPEAN GP	Nürburgring	31	Team ATS	P	1.5 t/c ATS D7-BMW 4	*accident with Surer*	18/26
13	PORTUGUESE GP	Estoril	14	Team ATS	P	1.5 t/c ATS D7-BMW 4	*2 laps behind*	23/27
1985	Championship position: 17th= Wins: 0 Pole positions: 0 Fastest laps: 0 Points scored: 3							
ret	BRAZILIAN GP	Rio	17	Barclay Arrows BMW	G	1.5 t/c Arrows A8-BMW 4	*suspension*	19/25
ret	PORTUGUESE GP	Estoril	17	Barclay Arrows BMW	G	1.5 t/c Arrows A8-BMW 4	*spun off*	17/26
ret	SAN MARINO GP	Imola	17	Barclay Arrows BMW	G	1.5 t/c Arrows A8-BMW 4	*electrics/engine*	10/26
ret	MONACO GP	Monte Carlo	17	Barclay Arrows BMW	G	1.5 t/c Arrows A8-BMW 4	*accident damage*	11/26
13	CANADIAN GP	Montreal	17	Barclay Arrows BMW	G	1.5 t/c Arrows A8-BMW 4	*3 laps behind*	12/25
11	US GP (DETROIT)	Detroit	17	Barclay Arrows BMW	G	1.5 t/c Arrows A8-BMW 4	*3 laps behind*	24/25
ret	FRENCH GP	Paul Ricard	17	Barclay Arrows BMW	G	1.5 t/c Arrows A8-BMW 4	*accident with Martini*	9/26
8	BRITISH GP	Silverstone	17	Barclay Arrows BMW	G	1.5 t/c Arrows A8-BMW 4	*2 laps behind*	17/26
7	GERMAN GP	Nürburgring	17	Barclay Arrows BMW	G	1.5 t/c Arrows A8-BMW 4	*1 lap behind*	17/27
ret	AUSTRIAN GP	Österreichring	17	Barclay Arrows BMW	G	1.5 t/c Arrows A8-BMW 4	*turbo*	17/27
9	DUTCH GP	Zandvoort	17	Barcaly Arrows BMW	G	1.5 t/c Arrows A8-BMW 4	*2 laps behind*	14/27
ret	ITALIAN GP	Monza	17	Barclay Arrows BMW	G	1.5 t/c Arrows A8-BMW 4	*engine*	11/26
7	BELGIAN GP	Spa	17	Barclay Arrows BMW	G	1.5 t/c Arrows A8-BMW 4	*1 lap behind*	8/24
10	EUROPEAN GP	Brands Hatch	17	Barclay Arrows BMW	G	1.5 t/c Arrows A8-BMW 4	*2 laps behind*	19/27
5	SOUTH AFRICAN GP	Kyalami	17	Barclay Arrows BMW	G	1.5 t/c Arrows A8-BMW 4	*1 lap behind*	11/21
6	AUSTRALIAN GP	Adelaide	17	Barclay Arrows BMW	G	1.5 t/c Arrows A8-BMW 4	*1 lap behind*	7/25
1986	Championship position: 7th Wins: 1 Pole positions: 0 Fastest laps: 2 Points scored: 17							
6	BRAZILIAN GP	Rio	20	Benetton Formula Ltd	P	1.5 t/c Benetton B186-BMW 4	*electrical problem/2 laps behind*	16/25
6	SPANISH GP	Jerez	20	Benetton Formula Ltd	P	1.5 t/c Benetton B186-BMW 4	*1 lap behind*	7/25
3	SAN MARINO GP	Imola	20	Benetton Formula Ltd	P	1.5 t/c Benetton B186-BMW 4	*1 lap behind*	9/26
ret	MONACO GP	Monte Carlo	20	Benetton Formula Ltd	P	1.5 t/c Benetton B186-BMW 4	*wheel drive pegs*	5/26
10	BELGIAN GP	Spa	20	Benetton Formula Ltd	P	1.5 t/c Benetton B186-BMW 4	*lost use of clutch/2 laps behind*	2/25
ret	CANADIAN GP	Montreal	20	Benetton Formula Ltd	P	1.5 t/c Benetton B186-BMW 4	*turbo boost*	7/25
ret	US GP (DETROIT)	Detroit	20	Benetton Formula Ltd	P	1.5 t/c Benetton B186-BMW 4	*engine cut out*	12/26
ret	FRENCH GP	Paul Ricard	20	Benetton Formula Ltd	P	1.5 t/c Benetton B186-BMW 4	*gearbox*	8/26
ret	BRITISH GP	Brands Hatch	20	Benetton Formula Ltd	P	1.5 t/c Benetton B186-BMW 4	*electrics*	4/26
10	GERMAN GP	Hockenheim	20	Benetton Formula Ltd	P	1.5 t/c Benetton B186-BMW 4	*2 laps behind/FL*	4/26
ret	HUNGARIAN GP	Hungaroring	20	Benetton Formula Ltd	P	1.5 t/c Benetton B186-BMW 4	*fuel leak/transmission*	11/26
7	AUSTRIAN GP	Österreichring	20	Benetton Formula Ltd	P	1.5 t/c Benetton B186-BMW 4	*pit stop – battery/FL/3 laps behind*	2/26
5	ITALIAN GP	Monza	20	Benetton Formula Ltd	P	1.5 t/c Benetton B186-BMW 4	*1 lap behind*	4/27
ret	PORTUGUESE GP	Estoril	20	Benetton Formula Ltd	P	1.5 t/c Benetton B186-BMW 4	*collision with Johansson – spun off*	4/27
1	MEXICAN GP	Mexico City	20	Benetton Formula Ltd	P	1.5 t/c Benetton B186-BMW 4		4/26
ret	AUSTRALIAN GP	Adelaide	20	Benetton Formula Ltd	P	1.5 t/c Benetton B186-BMW 4	*clutch/engine*	6/26
1987	Championship position: 5th Wins: 2 Pole positions: 3 Fastest laps: 3 Points scored: 36							
4	BRAZILIAN GP	Rio	28	Scuderia Ferrari SpA SEFAC	G	1.5 t/c Ferrari F1/87 V6		7/23
ret	SAN MARINO GP	Imola	28	Scuderia Ferrari SpA SEFAC	G	1.5 t/c Ferrari F1/87 V6	*electrics*	6/27
ret	BELGIAN GP	Spa	28	Scuderia Ferrari SpA SEFAC	G	1.5 t/c Ferrari F1/87 V6	*turbo*	4/26
4	MONACO GP	Monte Carlo	28	Scuderia Ferrari SpA SEFAC	G	1.5 t/c Ferrari F1/87 V6	*1 lap behind*	8/26
4	US GP (DETROIT)	Detroit	28	Scuderia Ferrari SpA SEFAC	G	1.5 t/c Ferrari F1/87 V6		12/26
ret	FRENCH GP	Paul Ricard	28	Scuderia Ferrari SpA SEFAC	G	1.5 t/c Ferrari F1/87 V6	*spun off – suspension*	6/26
ret	BRITISH GP	Silverstone	28	Scuderia Ferrari SpA SEFAC	G	1.5 t/c Ferrari F1/87 V6	*spun off*	8/26
ret	GERMAN GP	Hockenheim	28	Scuderia Ferrari SpA SEFAC	G	1.5 t/c Ferrari F1/87 V6	*turbo*	10/26
ret	HUNGARIAN GP	Hungaroring	28	Scuderia Ferrari SpA SEFAC	G	1.5 t/c Ferrari F1/87 V6	*differential*	2/26
ret	AUSTRIAN GP	Österreichring	28	Scuderia Ferrari SpA SEFAC	G	1.5 t/c Ferrari F1/87 V6	*turbo*	3/26
4	ITALIAN GP	Monza	28	Scuderia Ferrari SpA SEFAC	G	1.5 t/c Ferrari F1/87 V6		3/28
2	PORTUGUESE GP	Estoril	28	Scuderia Ferrari SpA SEFAC	G	1.5 t/c Ferrari F1/87 V6	*spin when leading/FL*	1/27

Driving for Benetton, Berger scored his first grand prix victory in the 1986 Mexican Grand Prix, where he used his Pirelli tyres to maximum advantage.

ret	SPANISH GP	Jerez	28	Scuderia Ferrari SpA SEFAC	G	1.5 t/c Ferrari F1/87 V6	smashed oil cooler/engine/FL	3/28
ret	MEXICAN GP	Mexico City	28	Scuderia Ferrari SpA SEFAC	G	1.5 t/c Ferrari F1/87 V6	engine	2/27
1	JAPANESE GP	Suzuka	28	Scuderia Ferrari SpA SEFAC	G	1.5 t/c Ferrari F1/87 V6		1/27
1	AUSTRALIAN GP	Adelaide	28	Scuderia Ferrari SpA SEFAC	G	1.5 t/c Ferrari F1/87 V6	FL	1/27

1988 Championship position: 3rd   Wins: 1   Pole positions: 1   Fastest laps: 2   Points scored: 41

2	BRAZILIAN GP	Rio	28	Scuderia Ferrari SpA SEFAC	G	1.5 t/c Ferrari F1/87/88C V6	FL	4/31
5	SAN MARINO GP	Imola	28	Scuderia Ferrari SpA SEFAC	G	1.5 t/c Ferrari F1/87/88C V6	power loss in engine/1 lap behind	5/31
2	MONACO GP	Monte Carlo	28	Scuderia Ferrari SpA SEFAC	G	1.5 t/c Ferrari F1/87/88C V6		3/30
3	MEXICAN GP	Mexico City	28	Scuderia Ferrari SpA SEFAC	G	1.5 t/c Ferrari F1/87/88C V6		3/30
ret	CANADIAN GP	Montreal	28	Scuderia Ferrari SpA SEFAC	G	1.5 t/c Ferrari F1/87/88C V6	electrics/engine	3/31
ret	US GP (DETROIT)	Detroit	28	Scuderia Ferrari SpA SEFAC	G	1.5 t/c Ferrari F1/87/88C V6	puncture	2/31
4	FRENCH GP	Paul Ricard	28	Scuderia Ferrari SpA SEFAC	G	1.5 t/c Ferrari F1/87/88C V6	1 lap behind	3/31
9	BRITISH GP	Silverstone	28	Scuderia Ferrari SpA SEFAC	G	1.5 t/c Ferrari F1/87/88C V6	low on fuel/1 lap behind	1/31
3	GERMAN GP	Hockenheim	28	Scuderia Ferrari SpA SEFAC	G	1.5 t/c Ferrari F1/87/88C V6		3/31
4	HUNGARIAN GP	Hungaroring	28	Scuderia Ferrari SpA SEFAC	G	1.5 t/c Ferrari F1/87/88C V6		9/31
ret	BELGIAN GP	Spa	28	Scuderia Ferrari SpA SEFAC	G	1.5 t/c Ferrari F1/87/88C V6	electrics/FL	3/31
1	ITALIAN GP	Monza	28	Scuderia Ferrari SpA SEFAC	G	1.5 t/c Ferrari F1/87/88C V6		3/31
ret	PORTUGUESE GP	Estoril	28	Scuderia Ferrari SpA SEFAC	G	1.5 t/c Ferrari F1/87/88C V6	spun off – fire extinguisher/FL	4/31
6	SPANISH GP	Jerez	28	Scuderia Ferrari SpA SEFAC	G	1.5 t/c Ferrari F1/87/88C V6	pit stop – tyres/low on fuel	8/31
4	JAPANESE GP	Suzuka	28	Scuderia Ferrari SpA SEFAC	G	1.5 t/c Ferrari F1/87/88C V6		3/31
ret	AUSTRALIAN GP	Adelaide	28	Scuderia Ferrari SpA SEFAC	G	1.5 t/c Ferrari F1/87/88C V6	accident with Arnoux	4/31

1989 Championship position: 7th   Wins: 1   Pole positions: 0   Fastest laps: 1   Points scored: 21

ret	BRAZILIAN GP	Rio	28	Scuderia Ferrari SpA SEFAC	G	3.5 Ferrari 640 V12	collision with Senna	3/38
ret	SAN MARINO GP	Imola	28	Scuderia Ferrari SpA SEFAC	G	3.5 Ferrari 640 V12	crashed at Tamburello	5/39
ret	MEXICAN GP	Mexico City	28	Scuderia Ferrari SpA SEFAC	G	3.5 Ferrari 640 V12	transmission	6/39
ret	US GP (PHOENIX)	Phoenix	28	Scuderia Ferrari SpA SEFAC	G	3.5 Ferrari 640 V12	alternator	8/39
ret	CANADIAN GP	Montreal	28	Scuderia Ferrari SpA SEFAC	G	3.5 Ferrari 640 V12	alternator belt	4/39
ret	FRENCH GP	Paul Ricard	28	Scuderia Ferrari SpA SEFAC	G	3.5 Ferrari 640 V12	gearbox oil leak	6/39
ret	BRITISH GP	Silverstone	28	Scuderia Ferrari SpA SEFAC	G	3.5 Ferrari 640 V12	gearbox	4/39
ret	GERMAN GP	Hockenheim	28	Scuderia Ferrari SpA SEFAC	G	3.5 Ferrari 640 V12	puncture – crashed	4/39
ret	HUNGARIAN GP	Hungaroring	28	Scuderia Ferrari SpA SEFAC	G	3.5 Ferrari 640 V12	gearbox	6/39
ret	BELGIAN GP	Spa	28	Scuderia Ferrari SpA SEFAC	G	3.5 Ferrari 640 V12	spun off	3/39
2	ITALIAN GP	Monza	28	Scuderia Ferrari SpA SEFAC	G	3.5 Ferrari 640 V12		2/39
1	PORTUGUESE GP	Estoril	28	Scuderia Ferrari SpA SEFAC	G	3.5 Ferrari 640 V12	FL	2/39
2	SPANISH GP	Jerez	28	Scuderia Ferrari SpA SEFAC	G	3.5 Ferrari 640 V12		2/38
ret	JAPANESE GP	Suzuka	28	Scuderia Ferrari SpA SEFAC	G	3.5 Ferrari 640 V12	gearbox electrics	3/39
ret	AUSTRALIAN GP	Adelaide	28	Scuderia Ferrari SpA SEFAC	G	3.5 Ferrari 640 V12	collision with Alliot	14/39

1990 Championship position: 3rd=   Wins: 0   Pole positions: 2   Fastest laps: 3   Points scored: 43

ret	US GP (PHOENIX)	Phoenix	28	Honda Marlboro McLaren	G	3.5 McLaren MP4/5B-Honda V10	led – spun – pit stop/clutch//FL	1/35
2	BRAZILIAN GP	Interlagos	28	Honda Marlboro McLaren	G	3.5 McLaren MP4/5B-Honda V10	pit stop – tyres/FL	2/35
2	SAN MARINO GP	Imola	28	Honda Marlboro McLaren	G	3.5 McLaren MP4/5B-Honda V10		2/34
3	MONACO GP	Monte Carlo	28	Honda Marlboro McLaren	G	3.5 McLaren MP4/5B-Honda V10		5/35
4	CANADIAN GP	Montreal	28	Honda Marlboro McLaren	G	3.5 McLaren MP4/5B-Honda V10	1 min penalty for jumped start/FL	2/35
3	MEXICAN GP	Mexico City	28	Honda Marlboro McLaren	G	3.5 McLaren MP4/5B-Honda V10	pit stop – tyres	1/35
5	FRENCH GP	Paul Ricard	28	Honda Marlboro McLaren	G	3.5 McLaren MP4/5B-Honda V10	pit stop – tyres/lost 1st gear	2/35
14/ret	BRITISH GP	Silverstone	28	Honda Marlboro McLaren	G	3.5 McLaren MP4/5B-Honda V10	throttle cable/4 laps behind	3/35
3	GERMAN GP	Hockenheim	28	Honda Marlboro McLaren	G	3.5 McLaren MP4/5B-Honda V10		2/35
16/ret	HUNGARIAN GP	Hungaroring	28	Honda Marlboro McLaren	G	3.5 McLaren MP4/5B-Honda V10	collision with Mansell/-5 laps	3/35
3	BELGIAN GP	Spa	28	Honda Marlboro McLaren	G	3.5 McLaren MP4/5B-Honda V10	pit stop – tyres	2/33
3	ITALIAN GP	Monza	28	Honda Marlboro McLaren	G	3.5 McLaren MP4/5B-Honda V10	pit stop – tyres/brake problems	3/33
4	PORTUGUESE GP	Estoril	28	Honda Marlboro McLaren	G	3.5 McLaren MP4/5B-Honda V10	pit stop – tyres	4/33
ret	SPANISH GP	Jerez	28	Honda Marlboro McLaren	G	3.5 McLaren MP4/5B-Honda V10	collision with Boutsen	5/33
ret	JAPANESE GP	Suzuka	28	Honda Marlboro McLaren	G	3.5 McLaren MP4/5B-Honda V10	spun off	4/30
4	AUSTRALIAN GP	Adelaide	28	Honda Marlboro McLaren	G	3.5 McLaren MP4/5B-Honda V10	pit stop – tyres/cramp problems	2/30

1991 Championship position: 4th   Wins: 1   Pole positions: 2   Fastest laps: 2   Points scored: 43

ret	US GP (PHOENIX)	Phoenix	2	Honda Marlboro McLaren	G	3.5 McLaren MP4/6-Honda V12	fuel pump	7/34
3	BRAZILIAN GP	Interlagos	2	Honda Marlboro McLaren	G	3.5 McLaren MP4/6-Honda V12		4/34
2	SAN MARINO GP	Imola	2	Honda Marlboro McLaren	G	3.5 McLaren MP4/6-Honda V12	FL	5/34
ret	MONACO GP	Monte Carlo	2	Honda Marlboro McLaren	G	3.5 McLaren MP4/6-Honda V12	crashed	6/34
ret	CANADIAN GP	Montreal	2	Honda Marlboro McLaren	G	3.5 McLaren MP4/6-Honda V12	electrics	6/34
ret	MEXICAN GP	Mexico City	2	Honda Marlboro McLaren	G	3.5 McLaren MP4/6-Honda V12	engine – overheating	5/34
ret	FRENCH GP	Magny Cours	2	Honda Marlboro McLaren	G	3.5 McLaren MP4/6-Honda V12	engine	5/34
2	BRITISH GP	Silverstone	2	Honda Marlboro McLaren	G	3.5 McLaren MP4/6-Honda V12	wheel vibration/pit stop – tyres	4/34
4	GERMAN GP	Hockenheim	2	Honda Marlboro McLaren	G	3.5 McLaren MP4/6-Honda V12		3/34
4	HUNGARIAN GP	Hungaroring	2	Honda Marlboro McLaren	G	3.5 McLaren MP4/6-Honda V12		5/34
2	BELGIAN GP	Spa	2	Honda Marlboro McLaren	G	3.5 McLaren MP4/6-Honda V12		4/34
4	ITALIAN GP	Monza	2	Honda Marlboro McLaren	G	3.5 McLaren MP4/6-Honda V12		3/34
ret	PORTUGUESE GP	Estoril	2	Honda Marlboro McLaren	G	3.5 McLaren MP4/6-Honda V12	engine	2/34
ret	SPANISH GP	Jerez	2	Honda Marlboro McLaren	G	3.5 McLaren MP4/6-Honda V12	engine – valve	1/33
1	JAPANESE GP	Suzuka	2	Honda Marlboro McLaren	G	3.5 McLaren MP4/6-Honda V12		1/31
3	AUSTRALIAN GP	Adelaide	2	Honda Marlboro McLaren	G	3.5 McLaren MP4/6-Honda V12	race abandoned – half points/FL	2/32

1992 Championship position: 5th   Wins: 2   Pole positions: 0   Fastest laps: 2   Points scored: 49

5	SOUTH AFRICAN GP	Kyalami	2	Honda Marlboro McLaren	G	3.5 McLaren MP4/6B-Honda V12		3/30
4	MEXICAN GP	Mexico City	2	Honda Marlboro McLaren	G	3.5 McLaren MP4/6B-Honda V12	FL	5/30
ret	BRAZILIAN GP	Interlagos	2	Honda Marlboro McLaren	G	3.5 McLaren MP4/7A-Honda V12	started from pit lane/overheating	4/31
dns	"		2	Honda Marlboro McLaren	G	3.5 McLaren MP4/6B-Honda V12	practice only	– / –
4	SPANISH GP	Barcelona	2	Honda Marlboro McLaren	G	3.5 McLaren MP4/7A-Honda V12		7/32
ret	SAN MARINO GP	Imola	2	Honda Marlboro McLaren	G	3.5 McLaren MP4/7A-Honda V12	collision Alesi	4/32

Gerhard gave McLaren a farewell victory in his final race for the team at the 1992 Australian Grand Prix, before returning to Ferrari to help spearhead a revival at Maranello.

ret	MONACO GP	Monte Carlo	2	Honda Marlboro McLaren	G	3.5 McLaren MP4/7A-Honda V12	gearbox	5/32
1	CANADIAN GP	Montreal	2	Honda Marlboro McLaren	G	3.5 McLaren MP4/7A-Honda V12	despite gearbox problems/FL	4/32
ret	FRENCH GP	Magny Cours	2	Honda Marlboro McLaren	G	3.5 McLaren MP4/7A-Honda V12	engine	4/30
5	BRITISH GP	Silverstone	2	Honda Marlboro McLaren	G	3.5 McLaren MP4/7A-Honda V12		5/32
ret	GERMAN GP	Hockenheim	2	Honda Marlboro McLaren	G	3.5 McLaren MP4/7A-Honda V12	2 pit stops/misfire	4/32
3	HUNGARIAN GP	Hungaroring	2	Honda Marlboro McLaren	G	3.5 McLaren MP4/7A-Honda V12		5/31
ret	BELGIAN GP	Spa	2	Honda Marlboro McLaren	G	3.5 McLaren MP4/7A-Honda V12	transmission failure at start	6/30
4	ITALIAN GP	Monza	2	Honda Marlboro McLaren	G	3.5 McLaren MP4/7A-Honda V12	started from pitlane/pit stop/tyres	5/28
2	PORTUGUESE GP	Estoril	2	Honda Marlboro McLaren	G	3.5 McLaren MP4/7A-Honda V12		4/26
2	JAPANESE GP	Suzuka	2	Honda Marlboro McLaren	G	3.5 McLaren MP4/7A-Honda V12		4/26
1	AUSTRALIAN GP	Adelaide	2	Honda Marlboro McLaren	G	3.5 McLaren MP4/7A-Honda V12	early tactical pit stop – tyres	4/26

1993 Championship position: 8th   Wins: 0   Pole positions: 0   Fastest laps: 0   Points scored: 12

6/ret	SOUTH AFRICAN GP	Kyalami	28	Scuderia Ferrari SpA	G	3.5 Fiat Ferrari F93A V12	engine/3 laps behind	15/26
ret	BRAZILIAN GP	Interlagos	28	Scuderia Ferrari SpA	G	3.5 Fiat Ferrari F93A V12	taken off by Andretti on lap 1	13/26
ret	EUROPEAN GP	Donington	28	Scuderia Ferrari SpA	G	3.5 Fiat Ferrari F93A V12	active system leakage	8/26
ret	SAN MARINO GP	Imola	28	Scuderia Ferrari SpA	G	3.5 Fiat Ferrari F93A V12	gearbox	8/26
6	SPANISH GP	Barcelona	28	Scuderia Ferrari SpA	G	3.5 Fiat Ferrari F93A V12	2 laps behind	11/26
14/ret	MONACO GP	Monte Carlo	28	Scuderia Ferrari SpA	G	3.5 Fiat Ferrari F93A V12	collision with Hill/8 laps behind	7/26
4	CANADIAN GP	Montreal	28	Scuderia Ferrari SpA	G	3.5 Fiat Ferrari F93A V12	1 lap behind	5/26
14	FRENCH GP	Magny Cours	28	Scuderia Ferrari SpA	G	3.5 Fiat Ferrari F93A V12	active system trouble/-2 laps	14/26
ret	BRITISH GP	Silverstone	28	Scuderia Ferrari SpA	G	3.5 Fiat Ferrari F93A V12	active system	13/26
6	GERMAN GP	Hockenheim	28	Scuderia Ferrari SpA	G	3.5 Fiat Ferrari F93A V12		9/26
3	HUNGARIAN GP	Hungaroring	28	Scuderia Ferrari SpA	G	3.5 Fiat Ferrari F93A V12		6/26
10/ret	BELGIAN GP	Spa	28	Scuderia Ferrari SpA	G	3.5 Fiat Ferrari F93A V12	collision – Brundle/2 laps behind	16/25
ret	ITALIAN GP	Monza	28	Scuderia Ferrari SpA	G	3.5 Fiat Ferrari F93A V12	active system	6/26
ret	PORTUGUESE GP	Estoril	28	Scuderia Ferrari SpA	G	3.5 Fiat Ferrari F93A V12	active system – spun exiting pit lane	8/26
ret	JAPANESE GP	Suzuka	28	Scuderia Ferrari SpA	G	3.5 Fiat Ferrari F93A V12	engine	5/24
5	AUSTRALIAN GP	Adelaide	28	Scuderia Ferrari SpA	G	3.5 Fiat Ferrari F93A V12	1 lap behind	6/24

1994 Championship position: 3rd   Wins: 1   Pole positions: 2   Fastest laps: 0   Points scored: 41

ret	BRAZILIAN GP	Interlagos	28	Scuderia Ferrari SpA	G	3.5 Fiat Ferrari 412T1 V12	engine – air valve leak	17/28
2	PACIFIC GP	T.I. Circuit	28	Scuderia Ferrari SpA	G	3.5 Fiat Ferrari 412T1 V12		5/28
ret	SAN MARINO GP	Imola	28	Scuderia Ferrari SpA	G	3.5 Fiat Ferrari 412T1 V12	led restarted race – later withdrew	3/28
3	MONACO GP	Monte Carlo	28	Scuderia Ferrari SpA	G	3.5 Fiat Ferrari 412T1 V12		3/24
ret	SPANISH GP	Barcelona	28	Scuderia Ferrari SpA	G	3.5 Fiat Ferrari 412T1 V12	gearbox	7/27
4	CANADIAN GP	Montreal	28	Scuderia Ferrari SpA	G	3.5 Fiat Ferrari 412T1 V12		3/27
3	FRENCH GP	Magny Cours	28	Scuderia Ferrari SpA	G	3.5 Fiat Ferrari 412T1B V12		5/28
ret	BRITISH GP	Silverstone	28	Scuderia Ferrari SpA	G	3.5 Fiat Ferrari 412T1B V12	engine	3/28
1	GERMAN GP	Hockenheim	28	Scuderia Ferrari SpA	G	3.5 Fiat Ferrari 412T1B V12		1/28
12/ret	HUNGARIAN GP	Hungaroring	28	Scuderia Ferrari SpA	G	3.5 Fiat Ferrari 412T1B V12	5 laps behind/engine	4/28
ret	BELGIAN GP	Spa	28	Scuderia Ferrari SpA	G	3.5 Fiat Ferrari 412T1B V12	engine	11/28
2	ITALIAN GP	Monza	28	Scuderia Ferrari SpA	G	3.5 Fiat Ferrari 412T1B V12		2/28
ret	PORTUGUESE GP	Estoril	28	Scuderia Ferrari SpA	G	3.5 Fiat Ferrari 412T1B V12	transmission	1/28
5	EUROPEAN GP	Jerez	28	Scuderia Ferrari SpA	G	3.5 Fiat Ferrari 412T1B V12	1 lap behind	6/28
ret	JAPANESE GP	Suzuka	28	Scuderia Ferrari SpA	G	3.5 Fiat Ferrari 412T1B V12	electrics	11/28
2	AUSTRALIAN GP	Adelaide	28	Scuderia Ferrari SpA	G	3.5 Fiat Ferrari 412T1B V12		11/28

1995 Championship position: 6th   Wins: 0   Pole positions: 1   Fastest laps: 2   Points scored: 31

3	BRAZILIAN GP	Interlagos	28	Scuderia Ferrari SpA	G	3.0 Fiat Ferrari 412T2 V12	1 lap behind	5/26
6	ARGENTINE GP	Buenos Aires	28	Scuderia Ferrari SpA	G	3.0 Fiat Ferrari 412T2 V12	long tyre stop/2 laps behind	8/26
3	SAN MARINO GP	Imola	28	Scuderia Ferrari SpA	G	3.0 Fiat Ferrari 412T2 V12	FL	2/26
3	SPANISH GP	Barcelona	28	Scuderia Ferrari SpA	G	3.0 Fiat Ferrari 412T2 V12		3/26
3	MONACO GP	Monte Carlo	28	Scuderia Ferrari SpA	G	3.0 Fiat Ferrari 412T2 V12		4/26

ret	CANADIAN GP	Montreal	28	Scuderia Ferrari SpA	G	3.0 Fiat Ferrari 412T2 V12	*collision with Brundle*	4/24
12	FRENCH GP	Magny Cours	28	Scuderia Ferrari SpA	G	3.0 Fiat Ferrari 412T2 V12	*long fuel stop/2 laps behind*	7/24
ret	BRITISH GP	Silverstone	28	Scuderia Ferrari SpA	G	3.0 Fiat Ferrari 412T2 V12	*loose wheel*	4/24
3	GERMAN GP	Hockenheim	28	Scuderia Ferrari SpA	G	3.0 Fiat Ferrari 412T2 V12		4/24
3	HUNGARIAN GP	Hungaroring	28	Scuderia Ferrari SpA	G	3.0 Fiat Ferrari 412T2 V12	*1 lap behind*	4/24
ret	BELGIAN GP	Spa	28	Scuderia Ferrari SpA	G	3.0 Fiat Ferrari 412T2 V12	*electrics*	1/24
ret	ITALIAN GP	Monza	28	Scuderia Ferrari SpA	G	3.0 Fiat Ferrari 412T2 V12	*suspension damage/FL*	3/24
4	PORTUGUESE GP	Estoril	28	Scuderia Ferrari SpA	G	3.0 Fiat Ferrari 412T2 V12		4/24
ret	EUROPEAN GP	Nürburgring	28	Scuderia Ferrari SpA	G	3.0 Fiat Ferrari 412T2 V12	*electrics*	4/24
4	PACIFIC GP	T.I. Circuit	28	Scuderia Ferrari SpA	G	3.0 Fiat Ferrari 412T2 V12	*1 lap behind*	5/24
ret	JAPANESE GP	Suzuka	28	Scuderia Ferrari SpA	G	3.0 Fiat Ferrari 412T2 V12	*electronic sensor*	5/24
ret	AUSTRALIAN GP	Adelaide	28	Scuderia Ferrari SpA	G	3.0 Fiat Ferrari 412T2 V12	*engine*	4/24

1996 Championship position: 6th   Wins: 0   Pole positions: 0   Fastest laps: 1   Points scored: 21

4	AUSTRALIAN GP	Melbourne	4	Mild Seven Benetton Renault	G	3.0 Benetton 196-Renault V10		7/22
ret	BRAZILIAN GP	Interlagos	4	Mild Seven Benetton Renault	G	3.0 Benetton 196-Renault V10	*gearbox hydraulics*	8/22
ret	ARGENTINE GP	Buenos Aires	4	Mild Seven Benetton Renault	G	3.0 Benetton 196-Renault V10	*rear suspension*	5/22
9	EUROPEAN GP	Nürburgring	4	Mild Seven Benetton Renault	G	3.0 Benetton 196-Renault V10	*brake problems at start*	8/22
3	SAN MARINO GP	Imola	4	Mild Seven Benetton Renault	G	3.0 Benetton 196-Renault V10		7/22
ret	MONACO GP	Monte Carlo	4	Mild Seven Benetton Renault	G	3.0 Benetton 196-Renault V10	*gearbox sensor*	4/22
ret	SPANISH GP	Barcelona	4	Mild Seven Benetton Renault	G	3.0 Benetton 196-Renault V10	*spun off*	5/22
ret	CANADIAN GP	Montreal	4	Mild Seven Benetton Renault	G	3.0 Benetton 196-Renault V10	*spun off*	7/22
4	FRENCH GP	Magny Cours	4	Mild Seven Benetton Renault	G	3.0 Benetton 196-Renault V10		4/22
2	BRITISH GP	Silverstone	4	Mild Seven Benetton Renault	G	3.0 Benetton 196-Renault V10		7/22
ret/13	GERMAN GP	Hockenheim	4	Mild Seven Benetton Renault	G	3.0 Benetton 196-Renault V10	*engine/led race*	2/20
ret	HUNGARIAN GP	Hungaroring	4	Mild Seven Benetton Renault	G	3.0 Benetton 196-Renault V10	*engine*	6/20
6	BELGIAN GP	Spa	4	Mild Seven Benetton Renault	G	3.0 Benetton 196-Renault V10	*spin/FL*	5/20
ret	ITALIAN GP	Monza	4	Mild Seven Benetton Renault	G	3.0 Benetton 196-Renault V10	*hydraulics*	8/20
6	PORTUGUESE GP	Estoril	4	Mild Seven Benetton Renault	G	3.0 Benetton 196-Renault V10	*collision with Irvine at finish*	5/20
4	JAPANESE GP	Suzuka	4	Mild Seven Benetton Renault	G	3.0 Benetton 196-Renault V10	*collision with Irvine*	4/20

1997 Championship position: 6th   Wins: 1   Pole positions: 1   Fastest laps: 2   Points scored: 27

4	AUSTRALIAN GP	Melbourne	8	Mild Seven Benetton Renault	G	3.0 Benetton B197-Renault V10		10/24
2	BRAZILIAN GP	Interlagos	8	Mild Seven Benetton Renault	G	3.0 Benetton B197-Renault V10		3/22
6	ARGENTINE GP	Buenos Aires	8	Mild Seven Benetton Renault	G	3.0 Benetton B197-Renault V10	*FL*	12/22
ret	SAN MARINO GP	Imola	8	Mild Seven Benetton Renault	G	3.0 Benetton B197-Renault V10	*spun off*	11/22
9	MONACO GP	Monte Carlo	8	Mild Seven Benetton Renault	G	3.0 Benetton B197-Renault V10	*pit stop – crash damage/-2 laps*	17/22
10	SPANISH GP	Barcelona	8	Mild Seven Benetton Renault	G	3.0 Benetton B197-Renault V10	*blistered tyres*	6/22
1	GERMAN GP	Hockenheim	8	Mild Seven Benetton Renault	G	3.0 Benetton B197-Renault V10	*FL*	1/22
8	HUNGARIAN GP	Hungaroring	8	Mild Seven Benetton Renault	G	3.0 Benetton B197-Renault V10		7/22
6*	BELGIAN GP	Spa	8	Mild Seven Benetton Renault	G	3.0 Benetton B197-Renault V10	**3rd place car disqualified*	15/22
7	ITALIAN GP	Monza	8	Mild Seven Benetton Renault	G	3.0 Benetton B197-Renault V10		7/22
10	AUSTRIAN GP	A1-Ring	8	Mild Seven Benetton Renault	G	3.0 Benetton B197-Renault V10	*started from pits/1 lap behind*	18/22
4	LUXEMBOURG GP	Nürburgring	8	Mild Seven Benetton Renault	G	3.0 Benetton B197-Renault V10		7/22
8	JAPANESE GP	Suzuka	8	Mild Seven Benetton Renault	G	3.0 Benetton B197-Renault V10		5/22
4*	EUROPEAN GP	Jerez	8	Mild Seven Benetton Renault	G	3.0 Benetton B197-Renault V10	**5th place car disqualified*	8/22

GP Starts: 210   GP Wins: 10   Pole positions: 12   Fastest laps: 21   Points: 385

Berger managed just a single win in his second spell at Ferrari, taking a totally dominant victory in the 1994 German Grand Prix at Hockenheim.

ÉRIC BERNARD

A FOUR-TIMES French karting champion, Éric Bernard showed immediate ability in a Winfield School competition (in which he beat Jean Alesi), his prize being a season in Formule Renault. Fifth place in the 1984 championship created the platform for a successful title bid the following season.

Although he had little money, Bernard decided to tackle the French F3 series. Running his own Martini-Alfa, he finished a creditable fifth, and armed with a Ralt for 1987 he ran old rival Alesi and his mighty ORECA team very close as the pair dominated proceedings

The backing of Winfield and Elf facilitated Bernard's step up into F3000, and after a false start with the works Ralt, he switched to Bromley Motorsport to kick-start his season. A fine second in the final round at Dijon led to a place in the DAMS Lola team for 1989. He won at Jerez, but was out of luck elsewhere and, compounding this with some unforced errors, could only finish a disappointed third in the championship. The year had its compensations, though, a couple of drives for Larrousse in mid-season paving the way for a full-time ride in 1990, with a magnificent fourth place in the British Grand Prix the

highlight of his first full season. The Larrousse team lost the use of Lamborghini engines in 1991, putting Éric into the also-ran category, and his season ended disastrously when he sustained a broken leg in a practice crash at the Japanese Grand Prix.

With the injury proving slow to heal, Bernard was sidelined for the following season, but he was not forgotten by his long-time sponsors Elf and became the Ligier team's test driver in 1993. Then the oil giant placed their faith in him for 1994, and Ligier gave him a contract for the season alongside newcomer Olivier Panis. Once the Briatore/Walkinshaw axis took control, however, the student remained in situ while the tutor, despite his third-place finish in the crash-decimated German GP, was dumped after the Portuguese race and replaced by Johnny Herbert. As some recompense, it was arranged for him to take the Englishman's place at Team Lotus for the European GP at Jerez, but after he finished in 18th place, three laps behind, his departure from the grand prix stage was barely noticed.

Éric followed many other unemployed grand prix drivers into the world of sports car racing. After contesting the Global GT series in a Ferrari, he moved to DAMS to help develop their front-engined Panoz-Ford. The 1997 season brought little but a spate of retirements, although in the following term he began an excellent partnership with David Brabham as the car became a contender for honours

Outright victories finally came in 1999, the Frenchman sharing wins at Portland, Road Atlanta, Donington, the Nürburgring and Kyalami with Brabham, Andy Wallace and Jean-Marc Gounon.

When General Motors decided to take on Audi with a Le Mans challenger, the Cadillac North Star LMP, in 2000, they lost little time in ensuring that they had Bernard's signature on a three-year contract. Despite some promise, ultimate success proved elusive, however, as the LMP900 prototype was unable to match the heavyweights of Audi and Panoz. Eventually the project was scrapped at the end of 2002, leaving Éric out of work.

Following this final stint in sports cars, he then became involved with the Paris-Dakar Rally, initially as boss of the KTM Gauloises bike team. In 2009, with the rally relocated to South America (running between Mar Del Plata and Lima), Bernard entered the gruelling event in a BMW, but was forced into retirement. Undaunted, he was back in 2012, but once again failed to make the finish.

Bernard is the godfather of the French F1 hopeful Charles Pic, who has graduated from GP2 and drives for the Marussia-Virgin team in 2012.

BERNARD, Éric (F) b 26/8/1964, Istres

	Race	Circuit	No	Entrant	Tyres	Capacity/Car/Engine	Comment	Q Pos/Entries
	1989 Championship position: Unplaced							
11/ret	FRENCH GP	Paul Ricard	29	Equipe Larrousse	G	3.5 Lola LC89-Lamborghini V12	engine/3 laps behind	15/39
ret	BRITISH GP	Silverstone	29	Equipe Larrousse	G	3.5 Lola LC89-Lamborghini V12	gearbox	13/39
	1990 Championship position: 13th Wins: 0 Pole positions: 0 Fastest laps: 0 Points scored: 5							
8	US GP (PHOENIX)	Phoenix	29	Espo Larrousse F1	G	3.5 Lola LC89-Lamborghini V12	spin/1 lap behind	15/35
ret	BRAZILIAN GP	Interlagos	29	Espo Larrousse F1	G	3.5 Lola LC89-Lamborghini V12	gearbox	11/35
13/ret	SAN MARINO GP	Imola	29	Espo Larrousse F1	G	3.5 Lola 90-Lamborghini V12	gearbox/5 laps behind	14/34
6	MONACO GP	Monte Carlo	29	Espo Larrousse F1	G	3.5 Lola 90-Lamborghini V12	2 laps behind	24/35
9	CANADIAN GP	Montreal	29	Espo Larrousse F1	G	3.5 Lola 90-Lamborghini V12	3 laps behind	23/35
ret	MEXICAN GP	Mexico City	29	Espo Larrousse F1	G	3.5 Lola 90-Lamborghini V12	brakes –spun off	26/35
8	FRENCH GP	Paul Ricard	29	Espo Larrousse F1	G	3.5 Lola 90-Lamborghini V12	pit stop – tyres/1 lap behind	11/35
4	BRITISH GP	Silverstone	29	Espo Larrousse F1	G	3.5 Lola 90-Lamborghini V12		8/35
ret	GERMAN GP	Hockenheim	29	Espo Larrousse F1	G	3.5 Lola 90-Lamborghini V12	fuel pressure	12/35
6	HUNGARIAN GP	Hungaroring	29	Espo Larrousse F1	G	3.5 Lola 90-Lamborghini V12	brake problems	12/35
9	BELGIAN GP	Spa	29	Espo Larrousse F1	G	3.5 Lola 90-Lamborghini V12	long pit stop – tyres/1 lap behind	15/33
ret	ITALIAN GP	Monza	29	Espo Larrousse F1	G	3.5 Lola 90-Lamborghini V12	clutch	13/33
ret	PORTUGUESE GP	Estoril	29	Espo Larrousse F1	G	3.5 Lola 90-Lamborghini V12	gearbox	10/33
ret	SPANISH GP	Jerez	29	Espo Larrousse F1	G	3.5 Lola 90-Lamborghini V12	gearbox	18/33
ret	JAPANESE GP	Suzuka	29	Espo Larrousse F1	G	3.5 Lola 90-Lamborghini V12	engine oil leak and fire	17/30
ret	AUSTRALIAN GP	Adelaide	29	Espo Larrousse F1	G	3.5 Lola 90-Lamborghini V12	gear selection	23/30
	1991 Championship position: 18th= Wins: 0 Pole positions: 0 Fastest laps: 0 Points scored: 1							
ret	US GP (PHOENIX)	Phoenix	29	Larrousse F1	G	3.5 Lola L91-Cosworth V8	engine	19/34
ret	BRAZILIAN GP	Interlagos	29	Larrousse F1	G	3.5 Lola L91-Cosworth V8	clutch	11/34
ret	SAN MARINO GP	Imola	29	Larrousse F1	G	3.5 Lola L91-Cosworth V8	engine – water leak	17/34
9	MONACO GP	Monte Carlo	29	Larrousse F1	G	3.5 Lola L91-Cosworth V8	2 laps behind	21/34
ret	CANADIAN GP	Montreal	29	Larrousse F1	G	3.5 Lola L91-Cosworth V8	gearbox	19/34
6	MEXICAN GP	Mexico City	29	Larrousse F1	G	3.5 Lola L91-Cosworth V8	1 lap behind	18/34
ret	FRENCH GP	Magny Cours	29	Larrousse F1	G	3.5 Lola L91-Cosworth V8	puncture	23/34
ret	BRITISH GP	Silverstone	29	Larrousse F1	G	3.5 Lola L91-Cosworth V8	gearbox	21/34
ret	GERMAN GP	Hockenheim	29	Larrousse F1	G	3.5 Lola L91-Cosworth V8	transmission	25/34
ret	HUNGARIAN GP	Hungaroring	29	Larrousse F1	G	3.5 Lola L91-Cosworth V8	engine	21/34
ret	BELGIAN GP	Spa	29	Larrousse F1	G	3.5 Lola L91-Cosworth V8	gearbox	20/34
ret	ITALIAN GP	Monza	29	Larrousse F1	G	3.5 Lola L91-Cosworth V8	engine	24/34
dnq	PORTUGUESE GP	Estoril	29	Larrousse F1	G	3.5 Lola L91-Cosworth V8	gearbox	27/34
ret	SPANISH GP	Barcelona	29	Larrousse F1	G	3.5 Lola L91-Cosworth V8	collision with Boutsen on lap 1	23/33
dnp	JAPANESE GP	Suzuka	29	Larrousse F1	G	3.5 Lola L91-Cosworth V8	free practice accident-broken leg	- / -
	1994 Championship position: 18th= Wins: 0 Pole positions: 0 Fastest laps: 0 Points scored: 4							
ret	BRAZILIAN GP	Interlagos	25	Ligier Gitanes Blondes	G	3.5 Ligier JS39B-Renault V10	multiple accident	20/28
10	PACIFIC GP	T.I. Circuit	25	Ligier Gitanes Blondes	G	3.5 Ligier JS39B-Renault V10	delayed fuel stop/5 laps behind	18/28
12	SAN MARINO GP	Imola	25	Ligier Gitanes Blondes	G	3.5 Ligier JS39B-Renault V10	3 laps behind	17/28
ret	MONACO GP	Monte Carlo	25	Ligier Gitanes Blondes	G	3.5 Ligier JS39B-Renault V10	spun off	21/24
8	SPANISH GP	Barcelona	25	Ligier Gitanes Blondes	G	3.5 Ligier JS39B-Renault V10	3 laps behind	20/27
13	CANADIAN GP	Montreal	25	Ligier Gitanes Blondes	G	3.5 Ligier JS39B-Renault V10	3 laps behind	24/27
ret	FRENCH GP	Magny Cours	25	Ligier Gitanes Blondes	G	3.5 Ligier JS39B-Renault V10	gearbox	15/28
13*	BRITISH GP	Silverstone	25	Ligier Gitanes Blondes	G	3.5 Ligier JS39B-Renault V10	*2nd place car dsq/2 laps behind	23/28
3	GERMAN GP	Hockenheim	25	Ligier Gitanes Blondes	G	3.5 Ligier JS39B-Renault V10		14/28
10	HUNGARIAN GP	Hungaroring	25	Ligier Gitanes Blondes	G	3.5 Ligier JS39B-Renault V10	2 laps behind	18/28
10*	BELGIAN GP	Spa	25	Ligier Gitanes Blondes	G	3.5 Ligier JS39B-Renault V10	*1st place car disqualified/-2 laps	16/28
7	ITALIAN GP	Monza	25	Ligier Gitanes Blondes	G	3.5 Ligier JS39B-Renault V10	1 lap behind	12/28
10	PORTUGUESE GP	Estoril	25	Ligier Gitanes Blondes	G	3.5 Ligier JS39B-Renault V10	1 lap behind	21/28
18	EUROPEAN GP	Jerez	11	Team Lotus	G	3.5 Lotus 109-Mugen Honda V10	3 laps behind	22/28

GP Starts: 45   GP Wins: 0   Pole positions: 0   Fastest laps: 0   Points: 10

BERNOLDI, Enrique (BR) b 19/10/1978, Curitiba

	Race	Circuit	No	Entrant	Tyres	Capacity/Car/Engine	Comment	Q Pos/Entries
	2001 Championship position: Unplaced							
ret	AUSTRALIAN GP	Melbourne	15	Orange Arrows Asiatech	B	3.0 Arrows A22-Asiatech V10	accident	18/22
ret	MALAYSIAN GP	Sepang	15	Orange Arrows Asiatech	B	3.0 Arrows A22-Asiatech V10	*times disallowed/spun off	*19/22
ret	BRAZILIAN GP	Interlagos	15	Orange Arrows Asiatech	B	3.0 Arrows A22-Asiatech V10	hydraulics	16/22
10	SAN MARINO GP	Imola	15	Orange Arrows Asiatech	B	3.0 Arrows A22-Asiatech V10	2 laps behind	16/22
ret	SPANISH GP	Barcelona	15	Orange Arrows Asiatech	B	3.0 Arrows A22-Asiatech V10	fuel pressure	16/22
ret	AUSTRIAN GP	A1-Ring	15	Orange Arrows Asiatech	B	3.0 Arrows A22-Asiatech V10	hydraulics	15/22
9	MONACO GP	Monte Carlo	15	Orange Arrows Asiatech	B	3.0 Arrows A22-Asiatech V10	frustrated Coulthard/-2 laps	20/22
ret	CANADIAN GP	Montreal	15	Orange Arrows Asiatech	B	3.0 Arrows A22-Asiatech V10	overheating	17/22
ret	EUROPEAN GP	Nürburgring	15	Orange Arrows Asiatech	B	3.0 Arrows A22-Asiatech V10	transmission	18/22
ret	FRENCH GP	Magny Cours	15	Orange Arrows Asiatech	B	3.0 Arrows A22-Asiatech V10	engine	20/22
ret	BRITISH GP	Silverstone	15	Orange Arrows Asiatech	B	3.0 Arrows A22-Asiatech V10	2 laps behind	20/22
8	GERMAN GP	Hockenheim	15	Orange Arrows Asiatech	B	3.0 Arrows A22-Asiatech V10	1 lap behind	19/22
ret	HUNGARIAN GP	Hungaroring	15	Orange Arrows Asiatech	B	3.0 Arrows A22-Asiatech V10	spun off	20/22
12	BELGIAN GP	Spa	15	Orange Arrows Asiatech	B	3.0 Arrows A22-Asiatech V10	*outside 107% time/-1 lap	*21/22
ret	ITALIAN GP	Monza	15	Orange Arrows Asiatech	B	3.0 Arrows A22-Asiatech V10	gearbox	18/22
13	UNITED STATES GP	Indianapolis	15	Orange Arrows Asiatech	B	3.0 Arrows A22-Asiatech V10	1 lap behind	19/22
14	JAPANESE GP	Suzuka	15	Orange Arrows Asiatech	B	3.0 Arrows A22-Asiatech V10	2 laps behind	20/22

	2002	Championship position: Unplaced							
dsq*	AUSTRALIAN GP	Melbourne	21	Orange Arrows	B	3.0 Arrows A23-Cosworth V10	*switched to spare car after 1st start	17/22
ret	MALAYSIAN GP	Sepang	21	Orange Arrows	B	3.0 Arrows A23-Cosworth V10	fuel pick-up	16/22
ret	BRAZILIAN GP	Interlagos	21	Orange Arrows	B	3.0 Arrows A23-Cosworth V10	rear track rod	21/22
ret	SAN MARINO GP	Imola	21	Orange Arrows	B	3.0 Arrows A23-Cosworth V10	engine	20/22
ret	SPANISH GP	Barcelona	21	Orange Arrows	B	3.0 Arrows A23-Cosworth V10	hydraulics	14/22
ret	AUSTRIAN GP	A1-Ring	21	Orange Arrows	B	3.0 Arrows A23-Cosworth V10	hit Frentzen – damaged suspension	12/22
12	MONACO GP	Monte Carlo	21	Orange Arrows	B	3.0 Arrows A23-Cosworth V10	2 laps behind	15/22
ret	CANADIAN GP	Montreal	21	Orange Arrows	B	3.0 Arrows A23-Cosworth V10	vibration	17/22
10	EUROPEAN GP	Nürburgring	21	Orange Arrows	B	3.0 Arrows A23-Cosworth V10	1 lap behind	21/22
ret	BRITISH GP	Silverstone	21	Orange Arrows	B	3.0 Arrows A23-Cosworth V10	driveshaft	18/22
ret	FRANCE GP	Magny Cours	21	Orange Arrows	B	3.0 Arrows A23-Cosworth V10	made only a token effort to qualify	21/21
ret	GERMAN GP	Hockenheim	21	Orange Arrows	B	3.0 Arrows A23-Cosworth V10	engine	18/22

GP Starts: 28   GP Wins: 0   Pole positions: 0   Fastest laps: 0   Points: 0

ENRIQUE BERNOLDI

MENTION Enrique Bernoldi, and inevitably most fans of F1 will only remember him for resolutely frustrating David Coulthard for 35 laps of the 2001 Monaco Grand Prix as the Scot tried to make his way through the field. Opinion was divided about the etiquette of the Arrows driver, but he was perfectly within his rights not to give his place away, and he showed a resolve that should be part of any driver's armour.

Bernoldi's early career was one of much promise, the youngster winning multiple kart titles in his native Brazil against such luminaries as Helio Castroneves and Tony Kanaan. Taking his first steps in Europe at the tender age of 16, he soon made a name for himself in 1997 by taking nine wins on his way to the European Formula Renault Championship.

Initially, his move to Formula 3 was delayed by injury caused in a road accident, and he took some time to find his form before a win at Spa. Good progress was made in 1998, when he took six wins to finish second in a three-way British F3 championship battle with fellow Brazilians Mario Haberfeld (the champion) and Luciano Burti (third).

With Red Bull backing, Bernoldi was given a berth in F3000 – where he produced a stirring drive from the back of the field to fifth at Hockenheim – and a role as test driver for Sauber.

His second year in the category should have produced two victories, but a puncture at Barcelona and a suspension failure at the Nürburgring, when he seemed well set, left the driver with only five points and 15th place in the final standings. A strong showing in winter testing for F3000 provided Enrique with the chance to show his pace, and Red Bull backed his place in the Arrows team for 2001.

It would be a tough season for the rookie, but he kept his head down and managed to out-qualify his experienced team-mate, Jos Verstappen, by 10–7, giving a good indication of his speed. He did enough to keep his seat for the following season, too, alongside Heinz-Harald Frentzen, but it would be a disaster for all concerned, Tom Walkinshaw's team finally collapsing in financial meltdown.

Determined to rebuild his reputation, Bernoldi opted to compete in the World Series by Nissan the following year, and he finished the season sixth in the drivers' championship, having taken wins at Valencia and Jarama.

He started the 2004 World Series with double-header wins at the Jarama opener, but failed to take a victory thereafter and could only finish third, behind champion Heikki Kovalainen and Tiago Monteiro.

Enrique secured a surprise return to F1 machinery with test-driver role for BAR in 2004, but after having barely raced in 2005, the Brazilian found a place in his homeland's stock car series for 2007. He was back on the international stage in 2008, however, joining Indycar team Conquest Racing to record a fine fifth place at St Petersburg, followed by a fourth at Long Beach. After this promising start, things went downhill and he struggled on the ovals, but he did post a 15th place in the Indy 500. A thumb injury ended his unhappy IRL season prematurely, and he returned to Brazil to stock cars and to briefly represent Flamengo in the Superleague single-seater formula.

Bernnoldi also moved into GT racing with a Chevrolet Corvette under the Sangari Team Brazil banner. He took a win (with Roberto Streit) at Paul Ricard, which no doubt helped to secure him a place in the crack Vitaphone Racing squad for 2010, to race their GT1 Maserati MC12. In the event, he scored a win on home soil at Interlagos, but could only finish 15th in the standings.

For 2011, Bernoldi switched to a Nissan GT-R with Sumo Power, but a string of fourth-place finishes was the best he could muster on his way to 12th in the standings, the identical JR Motorsports car of Michael Krumm and Lucas Luhr sweeping to the title.

MIKE BEUTTLER

BORN in Cairo in 1940 of English parents while his father was serving in the Army, Mike Beuttler became involved in motor racing immediately upon leaving school at the age of 16, assuming administrative duties with the Chequered Flag team. He had occasional chances to drive their front-engined Gemini car, but only when he struck out on his own – at the comparatively late age of 24 – with a Brabham F3 in club and Libre events did his racing career start in earnest.

With the backing of stockbroker colleagues Ralph Clarke and David Mordaunt – which would be so vital to his progress to Formula 1 – Beuttler moved into F3 for 1969 with encouraging results, given the calibre of opposition. Staying with the class for another season, he won three high-profile events, at Silverstone, Brands Hatch and Montlhéry, gaining third place in the Shellsport F3 championship and second place in that year's Grovewood Awards.

For 1971, Beuttler made ambitious plans to race a March 712. Alistair Guthrie joined the roster of backers, and with the factory 'overseeing' his efforts, he undertook a full European F2 series. However, it proved a bitter disappointment, the car beset by sundry maladies until the last round, when he won the Madunina GP at Vallelunga. March had also helped him into Formula 1, without any great success.

It was the same recipe for 1972, with the addition of another backer – Jack Durlacher – to help pay the bills, but no worthwhile results in grands prix. The most interesting aspect of the season, in fact, was the team's decision to adapt their 722 F2 car to accept the Cosworth engine. So much better was this machine's handling than that of the notorious 721X that the full-works cars were quickly consigned to history, and Ronnie Peterson and Niki Lauda found themselves the beneficiaries.

Beuttler and his partners gave it one more shot in 1973, starting the season with the old car, but he was no more competitive when the new March 731 finally arrived.

He called it quits and, after a single outing in the Brands Hatch 1000km in 1974, turned his back on racing and went into business. Later he moved to San Francisco, where he died, repotedly of AIDS, at the tragically young age of 45.

BEUTTLER, Mike (GB) b 13/8/1940, Cairo, Egypt – d 29/12/1988, San Francisco, California, USA

	Race	Circuit	No	Entrant	Tyres	Capacity/Car/Engine	Comment	Q Pos/Entries
	1971 Championship position: Unplaced							
ret	BRITISH GP	Silverstone	6	Clarke-Mordaunt-Guthrie Racing	F	3.0 March 711-Cosworth V8	oil pressure	20/24
dsq*	GERMAN GP	Nürburgring	28	Clarke-Mordaunt-Guthrie Racing	F	3.0 March 711-Cosworth V8	puncture – *wrong entry into pits	22/23
nc	AUSTRIAN GP	Österreichring	27	Clarke-Mordaunt-Guthrie Racing	F	3.0 March 711-Cosworth V8	pit stop – engine/7 laps behind	20/22
ret	ITALIAN GP	Monza	24	Clarke-Mordaunt-Guthrie Racing	F	3.0 March 711-Cosworth V8	engine	16/24
nc	CANADIAN GP	Mosport Park	19	STP March	F	3.0 March 711-Cosworth V8	pit stop/8 laps behind	22/27
	1972 Championship position: Unplaced							
dnq	SPANISH GP	Jarama	23	Clarke-Mordaunt-Guthrie Racing	F	3.0 March 721G-Cosworth V8		26/26
13	MONACO GP	Monte Carlo	5	Clarke-Mordaunt-Guthrie Racing	F	3.0 March 721G-Cosworth V8	4 laps behind	=22/25
ret	BELGIAN GP	Nivelles	14	Clarke-Mordaunt-Guthrie Racing	F	3.0 March 721G-Cosworth V8	driveshaft	22/26
ret	FRENCH GP	Clermont Ferrand	15	Clarke-Mordaunt-Guthrie Racing	F	3.0 March 721G-Cosworth V8	out of fuel	27/29
13	BRITISH GP	Brands Hatch	31	Clarke-Mordaunt-Guthrie Racing	F	3.0 March 721G-Cosworth V8	7 laps behind	23/27
8	GERMAN GP	Nürburgring	28	Clarke-Mordaunt-Guthrie Racing	F	3.0 March 721G-Cosworth V8		27/27
ret	AUSTRIAN GP	Österreichring	3	Clarke-Mordaunt-Guthrie Racing	F	3.0 March 721G-Cosworth V8	fuel metering unit	26/26
10	ITALIAN GP	Monza	16	Clarke-Mordaunt-Guthrie Racing	F	3.0 March 721G-Cosworth V8	1 lap behind	25/27
nc	CANADIAN GP	Mosport Park	27	Clarke-Mordaunt-Guthrie Racing	F	3.0 March 721G-Cosworth V8	spin – pit stop/21 laps behind	24/25
13	US GP	Watkins Glen	6	Clarke-Mordaunt-Guthrie Racing	F	3.0 March 721G-Cosworth V8	incident with Lauda/-2 laps	21/32
	1973 Championship position: Unplaced							
10/ret	ARGENTINE GP	Buenos Aires	22	Clarke-Mordaunt-Guthrie-Durlacher	G	3.0 March 721G-Cosworth V8	radius rod/6 laps behind	18/19
ret	BRAZILIAN GP	Interlagos	12	Clarke-Mordaunt-Guthrie-Durlacher	G	3.0 March 721G-Cosworth V8	overheating	19/20
nc	SOUTH AFRICAN GP	Kyalami	24	Clarke-Mordaunt-Guthrie-Durlacher	G	3.0 March 721G-Cosworth V8	pit stops/14 laps behind	23/25
7	SPANISH GP	Montjuich Park	12	Clarke-Mordaunt-Guthrie-Durlacher	G	3.0 March 731-Cosworth V8	1 lap behind	19/22
11/ret	BELGIAN GP	Zolder	15	Clarke-Mordaunt-Guthrie-Durlacher	G	3.0 March 731-Cosworth V8	spun off/7 laps behind	20/23
ret	MONACO GP	Monte Carlo	15	Clarke-Mordaunt-Guthrie-Durlacher	G	3.0 March 731-Cosworth V8	engine	21/26
8	SWEDISH GP	Anderstorp	15	Clarke-Mordaunt-Guthrie-Durlacher	G	3.0 March 731-Cosworth V8	3 laps behind	21/22
11	BRITISH GP	Silverstone	15	Clarke-Mordaunt-Guthrie-Durlacher	G	3.0 March 731-Cosworth V8	2 laps behind	=23/29
ret	DUTCH GP	Zandvoort	15	Clarke-Mordaunt-Guthrie-Durlacher	F	3.0 March 731-Cosworth V8	electrics	23/24
16	GERMAN GP	Nürburgring	15	Clarke-Mordaunt-Guthrie-Durlacher	F	3.0 March 731-Cosworth V8	1 lap behind	21/23
ret	AUSTRIAN GP	Österreichring	15	Clarke-Mordaunt-Guthrie-Durlacher	F	3.0 March 731-Cosworth V8	hit by Hailwood – broken oil cooler	11/25
ret	ITALIAN GP	Monza	15	Clarke-Mordaunt-Guthrie-Durlacher	F	3.0 March 731-Cosworth V8	broken gear lever	12/25
ret	CANADIAN GP	Mosport Park	15	Clarke-Mordaunt-Guthrie-Durlacher	F	3.0 March 731-Cosworth V8	engine	21/26
10	US GP	Watkins Glen	15	Clarke-Mordaunt-Guthrie-Durlacher	F	3.0 March 731-Cosworth V8	1 lap behind	27/28

GP Starts: 28   GP Wins: 0   Pole positions: 0   Fastest laps: 0   Points: 0

LUCIEN BIANCHI

BORN in Italy, Lucien Bianchi moved to Belgium as a child, when his father went to work as a racing mechanic for Johnny Claes. The young Bianchi nurtured hopes of a competition career, and in fact shared a Lancia with Claes in the 1955 Liège–Rome–Liège Rally, taking third place in what proved to be the terminally ill Claes' last event. Gradually Bianchi began to build his career in both sports cars and rallying, taking a class win with a Ferrari at Le Mans in 1957, and the first of three Tour de France rally wins (1957, 1958 and 1964).

Joining Equipe Nationale Belge, Lucien scored a third place at Pau in 1959, and a fourth the following year in the non-title South African GP. The Belgian team was hardly front rank, however, and most of his success during this period was in sports cars: he won the 1960 Paris 1000km with Olivier Gendebien in ENB's Ferrari, and the Sebring 12-hours and Angola GP in 1962.

Between 1963 and 1967, Formula 1 opportunities practically dried up, but Lucien busied himself in virtually every other form of competition – sports car and GT racing, Formula 2 (taking second on aggregate at Zolder in 1964) and Formula 3, as well as selected rallies. A reliable endurance racer, he became much in demand, driving works Porsches and Fords on occasion in addition to occupying his regular seat in the Equipe Nationale Belge, while the 1967 season saw him try his hand at the Indianapolis 500. Having comfortably posted a good qualifying time, he flew back to race in the Nürburgring 1000km for Porsche, but an electrical failure on the last lap cost him the race win and dropped him to fourth place. Afterwards he was given the news that he had been 'bumped' from the grid at Indy.

Bianchi found a regular grand prix drive at last in 1968, albeit in the fading Cooper team, and scored points in his first two races. However, he enjoyed his best ever sports car season, winning the Le Mans 24-hours with Pedro Rodriguez and the Watkins Glen 6-hours with Jacky Ickx for John Wyer, and taking the Circuit of Mugello in a works Alfa Romeo. At the end of the year, Bianchi took part in the London–Sydney Marathon, and his Citroën was in a seemingly unassailable lead, less than 100 miles from the finish, when it was involved in an accident with a non-competing vehicle while his co-driver, Jean-Claude Ogier, was at the wheel. Lucien was left suffering from a broken ankle and shock.

Having recovered from this crushing disappointment, Bianchi signed for Autodelta to race their Alfa T33s, but while practising at the Le Mans test weekend, he lost control on the Mulsanne Straight. The car veered across the track into a telegraph pole, disintegrated and burst into flames; the luckless Bianchi was killed instantly.

BIANCHI, Lucien (B) b 10/11/1934, Milan, Italy – d. 30/3/1969, Le Mans Circuit, France

	Race	Circuit	No	Entrant	Tyres	Capacity/Car/Engine	Comment	Q Pos/Entries
	1959 Championship position: Unplaced							
dnq	MONACO GP	Monte Carlo	10	Equipe Nationale Belge	D	1.5 Cooper T51-Climax 4 F2		19/24
	1960 Championship position: 19th= Wins: 0 Pole positions: 0 Fastest laps: 0 Points scored: 1							
6	BELGIAN GP	Spa	32	Equipe Nationale Belge	D	2.5 Cooper T51-Climax 4	pit stop – driveshaft/8 laps behind	15/18
ret	FRENCH GP	Reims	36	Fred Tuck Cars	D	2.5 Cooper T51-Climax 4	transmission	15/23
ret	BRITISH GP	Silverstone	24	Fred Tuck Cars	D	2.5 Cooper T51-Climax 4	engine	17/25
	1961 Championship position: Unplaced							
dnq	MONACO GP	Monte Carlo	10	Equipe Nationale Belge	D	1.5 Emeryson-Maserati 4		19/21
ret	BELGIAN GP	Spa	12	Equipe Nationale Belge	D	1.5 Lotus 18-Climax 4	hired Seidel's car for race/oil pipe	– /25
dns	"	"	12	Equipe Nationale Belge	D	1.5 Emeryson-Maserati 4	car uncompetitive	– / –
ret	FRENCH GP	Reims	28	UDT Laystall Racing Team	D	1.5 Lotus 18/21-Climax 4	overheating/clutch	19/26
ret	BRITISH GP	Aintree	32	UDT Laystall Racing Team	D	1.5 Lotus 18/21-Climax 4	gearbox	30/30
	1962 Championship position: Unplaced							
9	BELGIAN GP	Spa	19	Equipe Nationale Belge	D	1.5 Lotus 18/21-Climax 4	3 laps behind	18/20
16	GERMAN GP	Nürburgring	21	Equipe Nationale Belge	D	1.5 ENB-Maserati 4	1 lap behind	25/30
	1963 Championship position: Unplaced							
ret	BELGIAN GP	Spa	22	Reg Parnell (Racing)	D	1.5 Lola Mk4-Climax V8	accident in rain	16/20
	1965 Championship position: Unplaced							
12	BELGIAN GP	Spa	27	Scuderia Centro Sud	D	1.5 BRM P57 V8	3 laps behind	17/21
	1968 Championship position: Championship position: 17th= Wins: 0 Pole positions: 0 Fastest laps: 0 Points scored: 5							
3	MONACO GP	Monte Carlo	7	Cooper Car Co	F	3.0 Cooper T86B-BRM V12	4 laps behind	14/18
6	BELGIAN GP	Spa	15	Cooper Car Co	F	3.0 Cooper T86B-BRM V12	2 laps behind	12/18
ret	DUTCH GP	Zandvoort	14	Cooper Car Co	F	3.0 Cooper T86B-BRM V12	accident	18/19
ret	GERMAN GP	Nürburgring	19	Cooper Car Co	F	3.0 Cooper T86B-BRM V12	fuel leak	19/20
nc	CANADIAN GP	St Jovite	20	Cooper Car Co	F	3.0 Cooper T86B-BRM V12	pit stop – misfire/34 laps behind	19/22
ret	US GP	Watkins Glen	19	Cooper Car Co	F	3.0 Cooper T86B-BRM V12	clutch	20/21
ret	MEXICAN GP	Mexico City	19	Cooper Car Co	F	3.0 Cooper T86B-BRM V12	engine	21/21
	GP Starts: 17 GP Wins: 0 Pole positions: 0 Fastest laps: 0 Points: 6							

GINO BIANCO

GINO BIANCO was born in Milan and moved to Brazil when still a child, aged 12. He gained a foothold in motorsport as a mechanic, but soon began driving in local hill-climbs, where one of his best results came in the Gavea event of 1951 in a Maserati. With the patronage of Eitel Cantoni, he was one of the Escuderia Bandeirantes squad who ventured to Europe in 1952, but no finishes were recorded in any of the races in which he competed.

He returned to Brazil and raced in 1953 at national level, but little is known about his subsequent whereabouts or activities, even in his country of adoption.

HANS BINDER

WITH promising performances in Formula Ford and the Polifac German F3 championship behind him, Hans Binder, a protégé of Dr Helmut Marko entered Formula 2 in 1975 with a privateer March 752. He found the car a handful to drive and, although he finished second at the Salzburgring, an accident at Enna saw him switch to a works loaned Chevron for the last four races.

Binder found himself in the same position the following season; after the first five races of the F2 campaign with the troubled Osella team brought no reward, a deal was struck with Fred Opert, and Hans was back in a Chevron. Things improved rapidly, the Austrian taking fourth-place finishes in the final three races at Estoril, Nogaro and Hockenheim.

One-off drives for Ensign in Austria (replacing a disaffected Chris Amon) and for Wolf in Japan (in place of the injured Jacky Ickx and local driver Masami Kuwashima) whetted his appetite for 1977. With Team Surtees providing the bread and ATS-Penske the jam in his season, it would be charitable to say his performances were somewhat lacklustre, and in grand prix terms he was redundant.

BIANCO, Gino (I) b 22/7/1916, Milan, Italy – d 17/1/1983 Rio de Janeiro

	Race	Circuit	No	Entrant	Tyres	Capacity/Car/Engine	Comment	Q Pos/Entries
	1952 Championship position: Unplaced							
18	BRITISH GP	Silverstone	34	Escuderia Bandeirantes	P	2.0 Maserati A6GCM 6	8 laps behind	28/32
ret	GERMAN GP	Nürburgring	115	Escuderia Bandeirantes	P	2.0 Maserati A6GCM 6		16/32
ret	DUTCH GP	Zandvoort	18	Escuderia Bandeirantes	P	2.0 Maserati A6GCM 6	rear axle	12/18
ret	ITALIAN GP	Monza	46	Escuderia Bandeirantes	P	2.0 Maserati A6GCM 6	mechanical	24/35

GP Starts: 4   GP Wins: 0   Pole positions: 0   Fastest laps: 0   Points: 0

BINDER, Hans (A) b 12/6/1948, Zell am Ziller, nr Innsbruck

	Race	Circuit	No	Entrant	Tyres	Capacity/Car/Engine	Comment	Q Pos/Entries
	1976 Championship position: Unplaced							
ret	AUSTRIAN GP	Österreichring	22	Team Ensign	G	3.0 Ensign N176-Cosworth V8	throttle cable	19/25
ret	JAPANESE GP	Mount Fuji	21	Walter Wolf Racing	G	3.0 Wolf Williams FW05-Cosworth V8	wheel bearing	25/27
	1977 Championship position: Unplaced							
ret	ARGENTINE GP	Buenos Aires	18	Durex Team Surtees	G	3.0 Surtees TS19-Cosworth V8	damaged nose section	18/21
ret	BRAZILIAN GP	Interlagos	18	Durex Team Surtees	G	3.0 Surtees TS19-Cosworth V8	hit kerb – suspension damage	20/22
11	SOUTH AFRICAN GP	Kyalami	18	Durex Team Surtees	G	3.0 Surtees TS19-Cosworth V8	1 lap behind	19/23
11	US GP WEST	Long Beach	18	Durex Team Surtees	G	3.0 Surtees TS19-Cosworth V8	3 laps behind	19/22
9	SPANISH GP	Jarama	18	Durex Team Surtees	G	3.0 Surtees TS19-Cosworth V8	2 laps behind	20/31
ret	MONACO GP	Monte Carlo	18	Durex Team Surtees	G	3.0 Surtees TS19-Cosworth V8	fuel injection	19/26
12	AUSTRIAN GP	Österreichring	33	ATS Racing Team	G	3.0 Penske PC4-Cosworth V8	1 lap behind	19/30
8	DUTCH GP	Zandvoort	35	ATS Racing Team	G	3.0 Penske PC4-Cosworth V8	2 laps behind	18/34
dnq	ITALIAN GP	Monza	33	ATS Racing Team	G	3.0 Penske PC4-Cosworth V8		32/34
11	US GP EAST	Watkins Glen	18	Durex Team Surtees	G	3.0 Surtees TS19-Cosworth V8	2 laps behind	25/27
ret	CANADIAN GP	Mosport Park	18	Durex Team Surtees	G	3.0 Surtees TS19-Cosworth V8	collision with Keegan	24/27
ret	JAPANESE GP	Mount Fuji	18	Durex Team Surtees	G	3.0 Surtees TS19-Cosworth V8	collision with Takahara	21/23
	1978 Championship position: Unplaced							
dnq	AUSTRIAN GP	Österreichring	10	ATS Racing Team	G	3.0 ATS HS1-Cosworth V8		30/31

GP Starts: 13   GP Wins: 0   Pole positions: 0   Fastest laps: 0   Points: 0

CLEMENTE BIONDETTI

CLEMENTE BIONDETTI'S racing career began in 1923 on motorcycles, the Italian turning to cars in 1927. After early success in a Talbot, he joined the Maserati factory team in 1931, finishing third in both the Rome and French GPs.

His reputation really grew with Alfa Romeo, when he valiantly hung on to a trio of Mercedes in the Tripoli GP of 1937 as the rest of the field surrendered, before his engine blew. The 1938 season saw the first of his wins in the Mille Miglia, and he was at his peak as a driver as the Second World War broke out. Despite being 49 when racing resumed, he took a hat trick of wins (1947–49) in his beloved Mille Miglia and triumphed in the Tour of Sicily in both 1948 and 1949. His win in the rain-soaked 1947 race was quite brilliant. Minus two gears and suffering fuel feed problems with his Alfa Romeo, the veteran Italian beat the legendary Tazio Nuvolari into second place.

Eschewing the pure Ferrari sports cars that had brought him his other recent successes, Biondetti built a Ferrari-Jaguar hybrid that failed at the Italian GP in 1950 and disappointed elsewhere. Not surprisingly, he returned to the trusty steeds of the Prancing Horse, sharing Antonio Stagnoli's car to take third place in the 1952 Monaco Grand Prix, run that year for sports cars. The same year he was second in the Acerbo Cup, a 12-hour race at Pescara. For 1953, he raced the rival Lancia cars, but returned to the fold in 1954 – his final season – marking his last appearance in the Mille Miglia with a fourth place. Clemente had known that he had been suffering from cancer for several years and felt that to continue racing any longer could endanger others. A year later he was dead.

BIONDETTI, Clemente (I) b 18/8/1898, Buddusó, Sardinia – d 24/2/1955, Florence

	Race	Circuit	No	Entrant	Tyres	Capacity/Car/Engine	Comment	Q Pos/Entries
	1950 Championship position: Unplaced							
ret	ITALIAN GP	Monza	22	Clemente Biondetti	–	3.4 Ferrari 166S-Jaguar 6 (sports)	engine	25/27
	GP Starts: 1 GP Wins: 0 Pole positions: 0 Fastest laps: 0 Points: 0							

'BIRA, B' (Prince Birabongse) (T) b 15/7/1914, Bangkok – d 23/12/1985, Baron's Court, London, England

	Race	Circuit	No	Entrant	Tyres	Capacity/Car/Engine	Comment	Q Pos/Entries
	1950 Championship position: 6th Wins: 0 Pole positions: 0 Fastest laps: 0 Points scored: 5							
ret	BRITISH GP	Silverstone	21	Enrico Platé	P	1.5 s/c Maserati 4CLT/48 4	fuel feed	5/21
5	MONACO GP	Monte Carlo	50	Enrico Platé	P	1.5 s/c Maserati 4CLT/48 4	5 laps behind	15/21
4	SWISS GP	Bremgarten	30	Enrico Platé	P	1.5 s/c Maserati 4CLT/48 4	2 laps behind	8/18
ret	ITALIAN GP	Monza	30	Enrico Platé	P	1.5 s/c Maserati 4CLT/48 4	engine	15/27
	1951 Championship position: Unplaced							
ret	SPANISH GP	Pedralbes	18	'B Bira'	P	4.5 Maserati 4CLT/48-OSCA V12	engine on lap 1	19/20
	1952 Championship position: Unplaced							
ret	SWISS GP	Bremgarten	10	Equipe Gordini	E	1.5 Simca Gordini Type 15 4	engine	11/21
10	BELGIAN GP	Spa	20	Equipe Gordini	E	1.5 Simca Gordini Type 15 4	4 laps behind	18/22
ret	FRENCH GP	Rouen	6	Equipe Gordini	E	2.0 Gordini Type 16 6	rear axle	8/20
11	BRITISH GP	Silverstone	26	Equipe Gordini	E	2.0 Gordini Type 16 6	4 laps behind	10/32
	1953 Championship position: Unplaced							
ret	FRENCH GP	Reims	42	Connaught Engineering	D	2.0 Connaught A-Lea Francis 4	transmission	11/25
7	BRITISH GP	Silverstone	10	Connaught Engineering	D	2.0 Connaught A-Lea Francis 4	8 laps behind	19/29
ret	GERMAN GP	Nürburgring	14	Connaught Engineering	D	2.0 Connaught A-Lea Francis 4	engine	15/35
11	ITALIAN GP	Monza	44	Scuderia Milan	P	2.0 Maserati A6GCM 6	8 laps behind	23/30
	1954 Championship position: 14th Wins: 0 Pole positions: 0 Fastest laps: 0 Points scored: 3							
7	ARGENTINE GP	Buenos Aires	8	Officine Alfieri Maserati	P	2.5 Maserati A6GCM/250F 6	4 laps behind	10/18
6	BELGIAN GP	Spa	20	'B Bira'	P	2.5 Maserati 250F 6	1 lap behind	13/15
4	FRENCH GP	Reims	46	'B Bira'	P	2.5 Maserati 250F 6	1 lap behind	6/22
ret*	BRITISH GP	Silverstone	6	'B Bira'	P	2.5 Maserati 250F 6	*Flockhart took over – crashed	10/31
ret	GERMAN GP	Nürburgring	14	'B Bira'	P	2.5 Maserati 250F 6	steering	19/23
9	SPANISH GP	Pedralbes	18	'B Bira'	P	2.5 Maserati 250F 6	12 laps behind	15/22
	GP Starts: 19 GP Wins: 0 Pole positions: 0 Fastest laps: 0 Points: 8							

B 'BIRA'

PRINCE Birabongse Bhanuban of Siam (now Thailand) was the true title of this aristocrat, who had been educated at Eton and Cambridge before studying sculpture. In the mid-1930s, he lived in London under the care of his cousin, Prince Chula, who, after 'Bira' had tried his hand with a Riley Imp and an MG Magnette, gave him an ERA for his 21st birthday. Establishing the endearingly titled White Mouse Stable, 'Bira' won many races in a trio of ERAs in the immediate pre-war years, becoming one of the marque's most famous exponents. He also raced the ex-Whitney Straight Maserati and, less successfully, the ex-Richard Seaman Delage, and his outstanding performances were rewarded with the BRDC Road Racing Gold Star in 1936, 1937 and 1938.

After the war, 'Bira' was back in his ERA, but soon switched to Maserati, winning the 1947 GP des Frontières at Chimay. He continued to race in partnership with Chula until the end of the 1948 season, but meanwhile vhad entured out in an F2 Simca Gordini, winning a race at Skarpnack, Sweden.

Taking his Maserati San Remo into the Enrico Platé stable, 'Bira' had a busy year in 1949, which started with two fifths at Buenos Aires and a second to Juan Fangio at Mar del Plata. Then he returned to Europe and produced a run of excellent performances that brought second places at the Albi, French, San Remo and Rousillon grands prix, and third places in the Italian and Zandvoort GPs.

When the world championship was inaugurated in 1950, 'Bira' managed a fourth place at Bremgarten, but little else, as the cars were really outclassed. The following year, he put an OSCA V12 engine into the Maserati, but won only the five-lap Libre Richmond Trophy race at Goodwood. He continued to race the OSCA in Formula 1 races into 1952, but also handled the fast and fragile works Gordini. It was a frustrating time for the little prince, who seemed to lose interest after a long run of bad luck. Nevertheless he returned to the track occasionally in 1953 with the Connaught team until his own Maserati A6GCM was delivered late in the year. The acquisition of a true Maserati 250F early in 1954 seemed to whet 'Bira's' appetite for racing again and, in non-championship races, he won at Chimay and took second places at Rouen and Pescara, while in the French GP at Reims, he took his best championship placing for some years. Early in 1955, he scored his last win in the New Zealand GP at Ardmore, before returning to Europe to finish sixth at the Bordeaux GP and third in the International Trophy – his final race before his sudden decision to retire.

PABLO BIRGER

A VERSATILE driver who competed in his country's open-road Turismo Carretera events and also in selected single-seater races during the 1940s and 1950s, Pablo Birger arranged to drive a works Gordini in two consecutive Argentine Grands Prix. In the first of these, he was handed an old unsupercharged 1951 model that offered no threat to the powerful Ferraris and Maseratis.

Having qualified well for the 1955 race, he became involved in a five-car accident on the second lap when he collected Karl Kling's Mercedes, which was trying to avoid Jean Behra's car, which in turn was regaining the circuit after trying to overtake Harry Schell. Birger was forced into a spin and was hit by the Maserati of Carlos Menditeguy, forcing his immediate retirement.

Two weeks later, he took a 12th place on aggregate in the Formula Libre Buenos Aires City Grand Prix against largely the same opposition.

Birger died in a road accident in 1966, at the age of 42.

BIRGER, Pablo (RA) b 6/1/1924, Buenos Aires – d 9/3/1966, Buenos Aires

	Race	Circuit	No	Entrant		Tyres	Capacity/Car/Engine	Comment	Q Pos/Entries
	1953 Championship position: Unplaced								
ret	ARGENTINE GP	Buenos Aires	34	Equipe Gordini		E	1.5 Simca Gordini Type 15 4	*engine – cwp*	14/16
	1955 Championship position: Unplaced								
ret	ARGENTINE GP	Buenos Aires	40	Equipe Gordini		E	2.0 Gordini Type 16 6	*spun – hit by Menditéguy*	9/22
	GP Starts: 2 GP Wins: 0 Pole positions: 0 Fastest laps: 0 Points: 0								

HARRY BLANCHARD

H ARRY BLANCHARD was invited to race his Porsche RSK sports car in the inaugural US GP at Sebring to make up the numbers. He was a regular on the late-1950s American road racing scene, his best result being third place in the 1959 Watkins Glen GP, and was a class champion that year. However, Blanchard was fatally injured in the 1960 Buenos Aires 1000km when his Porsche crashed and overturned.

MICHAEL BLEEKEMOLEN

M ICHAEL BLEEKEMOLEN was a Dutch Formula Super Vee and Formula Ford driver who, due to his significant financial backing, found himself in a year-old, uncompetitive grand prix car in 1977, before he was really ready for the task. He was undeniably a quick driver in the lower formulas, but he needed much more experience to compete at grand prix level. To this end, he embarked on a full season of European F 3 in 1978, winning races and finishing a creditable fifth in the series. Again, with the help of his F & S Properties backing, he was turfed back into Formula 1 with ATS for another unsuccessful sortie at the top level, with a team that was constantly changing its drivers. After that, it was back to Formula 3, where he plugged away for another three seasons with some good finishes, but no victories.

The racer in him still remained, however, and for many seasons Michael was a competitor in various Renault one-make series. The owner of a highly successful racing school and several indoor karting tracks, he continued with outings in the German Porsche Carrera Cup, the Porsche Supercup, the Renault Clio Cup and the ADAC GT Masters. He also oversaw the racing exploits of his sons, Sebastiaan and Jeroen.

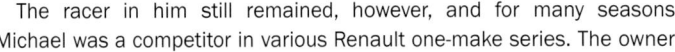

TREVOR BLOKDYK

A FORMER South African speedway champion, Trevor Blokdyk rode in Europe before returning home to compete on four wheels with a Ford-engined Type 52 Cooper in 1961. He proved to be an extremely fast and fearless competitor, and itched to return to Europe, which he did in 1962, to race in Formula Junior. Trevor did well (second at Nogaro and Caserta) until the money ran out, when he returned home to contest the South African championships – and his only grand prix – in the ex-John Love Cooper.

Blokdyk returned to Europe once more in 1965 to race in F3, where he was one of that season's star performers until a massive crash at Albi hospitalised him for three months with pelvic and leg injuries. He made his comeback at Rouen in 1966, finishing sixth, and continued to race in F3 in 1968 and early 1969, before returning to compete in South Africa. Extremely popular, and always ready with a smile, Trevor took up farming upon retirement, but died suddenly of a heart attack, aged just 59.

BLANCHARD, Harry (USA) b 30/6/1929, Burlington, Vermont – d 31/1/1960, Buenos Aires, Argentina

	Race	Circuit	No	Entrant	Tyres	Capacity/Car/Engine	Comment	Q Pos/Entries
	1959 Championship position: Unplaced							
7	US GP	Sebring	17	Blanchard Automobile Co	–	1.5 Porsche RSK F4 sports car	4 laps behind	16/19
	GP Starts: 1 GP Wins: 0 Pole positions: 0 Fastest laps: 0 Points: 0							

BLEEKEMOLEN, Michael (NL) b 2/10/1949

	1977	Championship position: Unplaced						
	Race	Circuit	No	Entrant	Tyres	Capacity/Car/Engine	Comment	Q Pos/Entries
dnq	DUTCH GP	Zandvoort	32	RAM Racing/F & S Properties	G	3.0 March 761-Cosworth V8		34/34
	1978	Championship position: Unplaced						
dnq	DUTCH GP	Zandvoort	10	F & S Properties/ATS Racing Team	G	3.0 ATS HS1-Cosworth V8		29/33
dnq	ITALIAN GP	Monza	9	F & S Properties/ATS Racing Team	G	3.0 ATS HS1-Cosworth V8		27/32
ret	US GP EAST	Watkins Glen	9	F & S Properties/ATS Racing Team	G	3.0 ATS HS1-Cosworth V8	oil pump leak	25/27
dnq	CANADIAN GP	Montreal	9	F & S Properties/ATS Racing Team	G	3.0 ATS HS1-Cosworth V8		28/28
	GP Starts: 1 GP Wins: 0 Pole positions: 0 Fastest laps: 0 Points: 0							

BLOKDYK, Trevor (ZA) b 30/11/1935, Krugersdorp, Transvaal – d 19/03/1995, Hekpoort, nr Krugersdorp

	1963	Championship position: Unplaced						
	Race	Circuit	No	Entrant	Tyres	Capacity/Car/Engine	Comment	Q Pos/Entries
12	SOUTH AFRICAN GP	East London	23	Scuderia Lupini	D	1.5 Cooper T51-Maserati 4	8 laps behind	19/21
	1965	Championship position: Unplaced						
dnq	SOUTH AFRICAN GP	East London	28	Trevor Blokdyk	D	1.5 Cooper T59-Ford 4		=21/25
	GP Starts: 1 GP Wins: 0 Pole positions: 0 Fastest laps: 0 Points: 0							

MARK BLUNDELL

MARK BLUNDELL is typical of a generation of British drivers, who have worked so hard to get into Formula 1 – a lot of talent, but not a lot of money. This former motocross rider had a quite remarkable first season in Formula Ford, winning 25 of his 70 races and receiving the 1984 Grovewood Award in recognition of this achievement.

The next two seasons were spent in FF1600 and FF2000, before Mark plunged straight into the F3000 championship for 1987 with an elderly Lola. Cracking drives in early-season races at Spa and Vallelunga brought him points scoring finishes and seemed to vindicate his decision to miss out on the traditional stepping-stone of Formula 3, especially when he was offered the works Lola for the 1988 F3000 season. Second place in the opening round at Jerez showed promise, but then the season slid away in a mire of development tweaks that saw the car engineered out of competitiveness.

In some ways, 1989 was a make-or-break year for Blundell in F3000. He moved to the Middlebridge team, and all the ingredients for success seemed to be there, but his season was ragged and he failed to make the top ten in the final points standings. Nevertheless, he must have shown something, because Nissan paired him with Julian Bailey in their rapid car to contest the endurance championship, and Williams signed him as a test driver for 1990.

It was a year well spent, as Mark familiarised himself with the intricacies of a Formula 1 car, but with no prospect of racing for the team in the immediate future, understandably he accepted an offer to join Brabham-Yamaha for 1991. Paired with the experienced Martin Brundle, he was certainly not overshadowed and scored his first championship point at Spa in the Belgian GP. However, the finances of the team were already parlous, and Blundell was reluctantly shown the door in favour of 'paying guests' at season's end.

The 1992 season was also spent on the F1 bench, acting as test driver for McLaren, but it brought an unexpected highlight when, in a one-off appearance for Peugeot, he won the Le Mans 24-hours with Derek Warwick and Yannick Dalmas. The well-funded, but under-achieving Ligier team had changed hands and, despite much criticism in the French press, new owner Cyril de Rouvre hired both Blundell and Brundle to revive their fortunes in 1993. Mark's superb third place in the opening race, followed by a fifth next time out in Brazil, bided well, but as the season wore on eyebrows were raised as the number of spins and incidents mounted, and suddenly he was facing an anxious winter, hoping to land a drive in 1994. In the event, he found a berth at Tyrrell, and his third place in Spain was a fillip for a team struggling to restore their fading credibility. Surprisingly, it was the hitherto unregarded Ukyo Katayama who took the eye as the year progressed, and once more Mark was seeking employment at season's end.

Luckily for him, Nigel Mansell's highly touted return to F1 with McLaren ended in farce, and the no-nonsense racer stepped up from the role of test driver, impressing everyone once more with his commitment. Although not far behind team-mate Häkkinen in terms of points, Blundell was perhaps always seen as a stop-gap until the arrival of David Coulthard. For 1996, he grabbed the opportunity to continue his racing career in Indy cars with PacWest after impressing in testing sessions.

It was a frightening baptism, Blundell surviving a monumental crash (after a brake failure on his car) in only his second outing at Rio, which sidelined him with a foot injury. Naturally it took some time for his confidence to return, but in 1997 success came in the form of three race wins (at Portland, Toronto and the 500-miler at Fontana). So outstanding were his performances that Mark appeared to be a serious championship contender for 1998, but the PacWest bubble had burst, and the hapless driver ended up a lowly equal 17th in the final points standings. His 1999 season was no better, interrupted as it was by a neck injury incurred in a testing accident that caused him to miss eight races. His woes continued into 2000. The PacWest Mercedes engines were underpowered and outgunned by the opposition, and through no fault of his own his CART career tailed away in something of a whimper.

His subsequent racing exploits were restricted to appearances at Le Mans, where he took second place in 2003 in a Bentley (with Johnny Herbert and David Brabham) and with the MG-Lola. He was also a regular member of ITV's grand prix punditry team. With the running of his sports management company, 2MB, taking up much of his time, he still managed to race occasionally, with an Audi R8 in the Total 24 Hours of Spa in 2010 and the 2011 Rolex 24-hour race at Daytona, where he took fourth with Martin Brundle. Mark announced his intention to return to the track full time in 2012, when he planned to contest the six-round Blancpain Endurance Series, in a GT3 McLaren MP4-12C.

BLUNDELL, Mark (GB) b 8/4/1966, Barnet, Hertfordshire

1991   Championship position: 18th=   Wins: 0   Pole positions: 0   Fastest laps: 0   Points scored: 1

	Race	Circuit	No	Entrant	Tyres	Capacity/Car/Engine	Comment	Q Pos/Entries
ret	US GP (PHOENIX)	Phoenix	8	Motor Racing Developments Ltd	P	3.5 Brabham BT59Y-Yamaha V12	spun off	24/34
ret	BRAZILIAN GP	Interlagos	8	Motor Racing Developments Ltd	P	3.5 Brabham BT59Y-Yamaha V12	engine	25/34
8	SAN MARINO GP	Imola	8	Motor Racing Developments Ltd	P	3.5 Brabham BT60Y-Yamaha V12	3 laps behind	23/34
ret	MONACO GP	Monte Carlo	8	Motor Racing Developments Ltd	P	3.5 Brabham BT60Y-Yamaha V12	crashed on Modena's oil	22/34
dnq	CANADIAN GP	Montreal	8	Motor Racing Developments Ltd	P	3.5 Brabham BT60Y-Yamaha V12		29/34
ret	MEXICAN GP	Mexico City	8	Motor Racing Developments Ltd	P	3.5 Brabham BT60Y-Yamaha V12	engine	12/34
ret	FRENCH GP	Magny Cours	8	Motor Racing Developments Ltd	P	3.5 Brabham BT60Y-Yamaha V12	accident – slid into pit wall	17/34
ret	BRITISH GP	Silverstone	8	Motor Racing Developments Ltd	P	3.5 Brabham BT60Y-Yamaha V12	engine	12/34
12	GERMAN GP	Hockenheim	8	Motor Racing Developments Ltd	P	3.5 Brabham BT60Y-Yamaha V12	2 laps behind	21/34
ret	HUNGARIAN GP	Hungaroring	8	Motor Racing Developments Ltd	P	3.5 Brabham BT60Y-Yamaha V12	spun off – stalled	20/34
6	BELGIAN GP	Spa	8	Motor Racing Developments Ltd	P	3.5 Brabham BT60Y-Yamaha V12		13/34
12	ITALIAN GP	Monza	8	Motor Racing Developments Ltd	P	3.5 Brabham BT60Y-Yamaha V12	1 lap behind	11/34
ret	PORTUGUESE GP	Estoril	8	Motor Racing Developments Ltd	P	3.5 Brabham BT60Y-Yamaha V12	rear suspension collapsed – spun	15/34
ret	SPANISH GP	Barcelona	8	Motor Racing Developments Ltd	P	3.5 Brabham BT60Y-Yamaha V12	engine	12/33
dnpq	JAPANESE GP	Suzuka	8	Motor Racing Developments Ltd	P	3.5 Brabham BT60Y-Yamaha V12		30/31
17	AUSTRALIAN GP	Adelaide	8	Motor Racing Developments Ltd	P	3.5 Brabham BT60Y-Yamaha V12	abandoned after 14 laps/-1 lap-	17/32

1993   Championship position: 10th   Wins: 0   Pole positions: 0   Fastest laps: 0   Points scored: 10

	Race	Circuit	No	Entrant	Tyres	Capacity/Car/Engine	Comment	Q Pos/Entries
3	SOUTH AFRICAN GP	Kyalami	26	Ligier Gitanes Blondes	G	3.5 Ligier JS39-Renault V10	1 lap behind	8/26
5	BRAZILIAN GP	Interlagos	26	Ligier Gitanes Blondes	G	3.5 Ligier JS39-Renault V10		10/26
ret	EUROPEAN GP	Donington	26	Ligier Gitanes Blondes	G	3.5 Ligier JS39-Renault V10	spun off	21/26
ret	SAN MARINO GP	Imola	26	Ligier Gitanes Blondes	G	3.5 Ligier JS39-Renault V10	spun off at first corner	7/26
7	SPANISH GP	Barcelona	26	Ligier Gitanes Blondes	G	3.5 Ligier JS39-Renault V10	2 laps behind	12/26
ret	MONACO GP	Monte Carlo	26	Ligier Gitanes Blondes	G	3.5 Ligier JS39-Renault V10	suspension	21/26
ret	CANADIAN GP	Montreal	26	Ligier Gitanes Blondes	G	3.5 Ligier JS39-Renault V10	spun off	9/26
ret	FRENCH GP	Magny Cours	26	Ligier Gitanes Blondes	G	3.5 Ligier JS39-Renault V10	collision with de Cesaris – spun off	4/26
7	BRITISH GP	Silverstone	26	Ligier Gitanes Blondes	G	3.5 Ligier JS39-Renault V10	spin/1 lap behind	9/26
3	GERMAN GP	Hockenheim	26	Ligier Gitanes Blondes	G	3.5 Ligier JS39-Renault V10		5/26
7	HUNGARIAN GP	Hungaroring	26	Ligier Gitanes Blondes	G	3.5 Ligier JS39-Renault V10	gear selection problems/-1 lap	12/26
11/ret	BELGIAN GP	Spa	26	Ligier Gitanes Blondes	G	3.5 Ligier JS39-Renault V10	taken off by Berger/2 laps behind	15/25
ret	ITALIAN GP	Monza	26	Ligier Gitanes Blondes	G	3.5 Ligier JS39-Renault V10	hit barrier – tyre damage	14/26
ret	PORTUGUESE GP	Estoril	26	Ligier Gitanes Blondes	G	3.5 Ligier JS39-Renault V10	collision witth Wendlinger	10/26
7	JAPANESE GP	Suzuka	26	Ligier Gitanes Blondes	G	3.5 Ligier JS39-Renault V10	brake and gearbox troubles	17/24
9	AUSTRALIAN GP	Adelaide	26	Ligier Gitanes Blondes	G	3.5 Ligier JS39-Renault V10	2 laps behind	14/24

1994   Championship position: 12   Wins: 0   Pole positions: 0   Fastest laps: 0   Points scored: 8

	Race	Circuit	No	Entrant	Tyres	Capacity/Car/Engine	Comment	Q Pos/Entries
ret	BRAZILIAN GP	Interlagos	4	Tyrrell	G	3.5 Tyrrell 022-Yamaha V10	accident – wheel failure	12/28
ret	PACIFIC GP	T.I. Circuit	4	Tyrrell	G	3.5 Tyrrell 022-Yamaha V10	hit by Comas – spun and stalled	12/28
9	SAN MARINO GP	Imola	4	Tyrrell	G	3.5 Tyrrell 022-Yamaha V10	2 laps behind	12/28
ret	MONACO GP	Monte Carlo	4	Tyrrell	G	3.5 Tyrrell 022-Yamaha V10	engine	10/24
3	SPANISH GP	Barcelona	4	Tyrrell	G	3.5 Tyrrell 022-Yamaha V10		11/27
10	CANADIAN GP	Montreal	4	Tyrrell	G	3.5 Tyrrell 022-Yamaha V10		13/27
10	FRENCH GP	Magny Cours	4	Tyrrell	G	3.5 Tyrrell 022-Yamaha V10	gearbox trouble/5 laps behind	17/28
ret	BRITISH GP	Silverstone	4	Tyrrell	G	3.5 Tyrrell 022-Yamaha V10	gearbox	11/28
ret	GERMAN GP	Hockenheim	4	Tyrrell	G	3.5 Tyrrell 022-Yamaha V10	multiple accident on lap 1	7/28
5	HUNGARIAN GP	Hungaroring	4	Tyrrell	G	3.5 Tyrrell 022-Yamaha V10	1 lap behind	11/28
5*	BELGIAN GP	Spa	4	Tyrrell	G	3.5 Tyrrell 022-Yamaha V10	*1st place car dsq/1 lap behind	12/28
ret	ITALIAN GP	Monza	4	Tyrrell	G	3.5 Tyrrell 022-Yamaha V10	brake trouble – spun out	21/28
ret	PORTUGUESE GP	Estoril	4	Tyrrell	G	3.5 Tyrrell 022-Yamaha V10	engine	12/28
13	EUROPEAN GP	Jerez	4	Tyrrell	G	3.5 Tyrrell 022-Yamaha V10	1 lap behind	14/28
ret	JAPANESE GP	Suzuka	4	Tyrrell	G	3.5 Tyrrell 022-Yamaha V10	electrics	13/28
ret	AUSTRALIAN GP	Adelaide	4	Tyrrell	G	3.5 Tyrrell 022-Yamaha V10	accident	13/28

1995   Championship position: 10th   Wins: 0   Pole positions: 0   Fastest laps: 0   Points scored: 13

	Race	Circuit	No	Entrant	Tyres	Capacity/Car/Engine	Comment	Q Pos/Entries
6	BRAZILIAN GP	Interlagos	7	Marlboro McLaren Mercedes	G	3.0 McLaren MP4/10-Mercedes V10	1 lap behind	9/26
ret	ARGENTINE GP	Buenos Aires	7	Marlboro McLaren Mercedes	G	3.0 McLaren MP4/10-Mercedes V10	engine	17/26
5	MONACO GP	Monte Carlo	7	Marlboro McLaren Mercedes	G	3.0 McLaren MP4/10B-Mercedes V10	1 lap behind	10/26
ret	CANADIAN GP	Montreal	7	Marlboro McLaren Mercedes	G	3.0 McLaren MP4/10B-Mercedes V10	engine	10/24
11	FRENCH GP	Magny Cours	7	Marlboro McLaren Mercedes	G	3.0 McLaren MP4/10B-Mercedes V10	2 laps behind	13/24
5	BRITISH GP	Silverstone	7	Marlboro McLaren Mercedes	G	3.0 McLaren MP4/10B-Mercedes V10	hit by Barrichello on last lap	10/24
ret	GERMAN GP	Hockenheim	7	Marlboro McLaren Mercedes	G	3.0 McLaren MP4/10B-Mercedes V10	engine	8/24
ret	HUNGARIAN GP	Hungaroring	7	Marlboro McLaren Mercedes	G	3.0 McLaren MP4/10B-Mercedes V10	engine	13/24
5	BELGIAN GP	Spa	7	Marlboro McLaren Mercedes	G	3.0 McLaren MP4/10B-Mercedes V10		6/24
4	ITALIAN GP	Monza	7	Marlboro McLaren Mercedes	G	3.0 McLaren MP4/10B-Mercedes V10		9/24
9	PORTUGUESE GP	Estoril	7	Marlboro McLaren Mercedes	G	3.0 McLaren MP4/10B/C-Mercedes V10	1 lap behind	– / –
dns	"	"	7	Marlboro McLaren Mercedes	G	3.0 McLaren MP4/10C-Mercedes V10	set grid time in this car	12/24
ret	EUROPEAN GP	Nürburgring	7	Marlboro McLaren Mercedes	G	3.0 McLaren MP4/10C-Mercedes V10	spun off	10/24
9	PACIFIC GP	T.I. Circuit	7	Marlboro McLaren Mercedes	G	3.0 McLaren MP4/10B-Mercedes V10	2 laps behind	10/24
7	JAPANESE GP	Suzuka	7	Marlboro McLaren Mercedes	G	3.0 McLaren MP4/10B-Mercedes V10	1 lap behind	24/24
4	AUSTRALIAN GP	Adelaide	7	Marlboro McLaren Mercedes	G	3.0 McLaren MP4/10B-Mercedes V10	2 laps behind	10/24

GP Starts: 61   GP Wins: 0   Pole positions: 0   Fastest laps: 0   Points: 32

RAUL BOESEL

ORIGINALLY Raul Boesel planned to follow the family tradition of show jumping, but utlimately he decided upon a motorsport career, despite initial opposition from his parents. After karting and saloon car success, he followed the well-trodden path of Brazilian hopefuls by heading for Europe with the aim of becoming the next Fittipaldi.

Never having driven a single-seater and with no English, Raul sensibly bought himself a drive with Van Diemen. Quickly learning from team-mates Roberto Moreno and Tommy Byrne, he finished runner-up in both Formula Ford championships in 1980, winning eight races. Opting for F3 for 1981, he enjoyed a remarkably consistent season, finishing in the points in 16 of the 20 rounds and winning three of them to take third place in the Marlboro championship.

Well funded after his success, Raul took his sponsorship money into F1 with the RAM March team, but it was a disastrous season. Things were not much better the following year, his F1 career effectively torpedoed as he struggled in a Ligier team then in steep decline.

Deciding to change course, Boesel headed off to the States and found a ride with Dick Simon's Indy Car team in 1985 and '86. After just missing out on a couple of good seats for 1987, he found himself a berth in the TWR Jaguar sports car team and enjoyed a highly successful season, winning the drivers' sports car title to raise his stature immensely.

Returning to Indy cars, Raul made little impression until 1993, when he enjoyed an excellent season with Simon. He posed a consistent threat to the elite, and was distinctly unlucky not to notch up a win. Unfortunately, he was not so competitive the following year, and a beautiful partnership ended in litigation as the Brazilian took his Duracell sponsorship to Rahal-Hogan. His new team, running a Lola-Mercedes combination, struggled, however, and it was often Boesel's car that hit problems.

For 1996, Raul opted to join forces with Barry Green's team – the reigning champions – with high hopes for an upturn in his fortunes. Sadly for the Brazilian, only fleeting glimpses of competitiveness were seen in a season plagued with engine and electrical maladies, and he took his substantial Brahma beer sponsorship to Patrick Racing for 1998. A late switch to Reynard chassis at the start of the season put the team on the pace and Raul posted some convincing performances, peaking with a pole position at Gateway. Unfortunately, the second half of the year saw a slump in the team's fortunes and Boesel was left without a CART ride at season's end.

The Brazilian decided to switch to the Indy Racing League for 1998, but the following two seasons brought only modest success. He briefly returned to the CART ranks in 1999 with Team KOOL Green at Miami (substituting for Paul Tracy), and with Dan Gurney's All American Racers at Chicago (where he scored a single point) and Laguna Seca. Raul also enjoyed a couple of sports car appearances in the DAMS Panoz, sharing third place at Mid-Ohio (with Bernard) and fifth at Watkins Glen (with Éric Bernard and Andy Wallace).

Boesel returned to Brazil to see out his racing days in the Stock Car Series and, in 2007, embarked on a new career as a DJ. He has since become one of Brazil's foremost exponents of house and techno music!

In 1987, the Autodromo Internacional de Pinhais, located in Raul's hometown of Curitiba, was renamed Circuito Raul Boesel in his honour.

BOESEL, Raul (BR) b 4/12/1957, Curitiba

	1982			Championship position: Unplaced					
	Race	Circuit	No	Entrant	Tyres	Capacity/Car/Engine	Comment		Q Pos/Entries
15	SOUTH AFRICAN GP	Kyalami	18	March Grand Prix Team	P	3.0 March 821-Cosworth V8	5 laps behind		21/30
ret	BRAZILIAN GP	Rio	18	Rothmans March Grand Prix Team	P	3.0 March 821-Cosworth V8	puncture – spun off		17/31
9*	US GP WEST	Long Beach	18	Rothmans March Grand Prix Team	P	3.0 March 821-Cosworth V8	*10th car disqualified/-5 laps		23/31
8	BELGIAN GP	Zolder	18	Rothmans March Grand Prix Team	P	3.0 March 821-Cosworth V8	4 laps behind		26/32
dnpq	MONACO GP	Monte Carlo	18	Rothmans March Grand Prix Team	A	3.0 March 821-Cosworth V8			29/31
ret	US GP (DETROIT)	Detroit	18	Rothmans March Grand Prix Team	A	3.0 March 821-Cosworth V8	hit by Baldi		21/28
ret	CANADIAN GP	Montreal	18	Rothmans March Grand Prix Team	A	3.0 March 821-Cosworth V8	engine		21/29
ret	DUTCH GP	Zandvoort	18	Rothmans March Grand Prix Team	A	3.0 March 821-Cosworth V8	engine		22/31
dnq	BRITISH GP	Brands Hatch	18	Rothmans March Grand Prix Team	A	3.0 March 821-Cosworth V8			30/30
dnq	FRENCH GP	Paul Ricard	18	Rothmans March Grand Prix Team	A	3.0 March 821-Cosworth V8			30/30
ret	GERMAN GP	Hockenheim	18	Rothmans March Grand Prix Team	A	3.0 March 821-Cosworth V8	puncture		25/30

dnq	AUSTRIAN GP	Österreichring	18	Rothmans March Grand Prix Team	A	3.0 March 821-Cosworth V8			27/29
ret	SWISS GP	Dijon	18	Rothmans March Grand Prix Team	A	3.0 March 821-Cosworth V8		gearbox oil leak	24/29
dnq	ITALIAN GP	Monza	18	Rothmans March Grand Prix Team	M	3.0 March 821-Cosworth V8			29/30
13	CAESARS PALACE GP	Las Vegas	18	Rothmans March Grand Prix Team	M	3.0 March 821-Cosworth V8		6 laps behind	24/30
	1983	Championship position: Unplaced							
ret	BRAZILIAN GP	Rio	26	Equipe Ligier Gitanes	M	3.0 Ligier JS21-Cosworth V8		electrics	17/27
7	US GP WEST	Long Beach	26	Equipe Ligier Gitanes	M	3.0 Ligier JS21-Cosworth V8		2 laps behind	26/28
ret	FRENCH GP	Paul Ricard	26	Equipe Ligier Gitanes	M	3.0 Ligier JS21-Cosworth V8		engine	25/29
9	SAN MARINO GP	Imola	26	Equipe Ligier Gitanes	M	3.0 Ligier JS21-Cosworth V8		2 laps behind	25/28
ret	MONACO GP	Monte Carlo	26	Equipe Ligier Gitanes	M	3.0 Ligier JS21-Cosworth V8		accident with Winkelhock	18/28
13	BELGIAN GP	Spa	26	Equipe Ligier Gitanes	M	3.0 Ligier JS21-Cosworth V8		1 lap behind	26/28
10	US GP (DETROIT)	Detroit	26	Equipe Ligier Gitanes	M	3.0 Ligier JS21-Cosworth V8		2 laps behind	23/27
ret	CANADIAN GP	Montreal	26	Equipe Ligier Gitanes	M	3.0 Ligier JS21-Cosworth V8		wheel bearing	24/28
ret	BRITISH GP	Silverstone	26	Equipe Ligier Gitanes	M	3.0 Ligier JS21-Cosworth V8		hydraulic suspension leak	22/29
ret	GERMAN GP	Hockenheim	26	Equipe Ligier Gitanes	M	3.0 Ligier JS21-Cosworth V8		engine	25/29
dnq	AUSTRIAN GP	Österreichring	26	Equipe Ligier Gitanes	M	3.0 Ligier JS21-Cosworth V8			27/29
10	DUTCH GP	Zandvoort	26	Equipe Ligier Gitanes	M	3.0 Ligier JS21-Cosworth V8		2 laps behind	24/29
dnq	ITALIAN GP	Monza	26	Equipe Ligier Gitanes	M	3.0 Ligier JS21-Cosworth V8			27/29
15	EUROPEAN GP	Brands Hatch	26	Equipe Ligier Gitanes	M	3.0 Ligier JS21-Cosworth V8		3 laps behind	23/29
nc	SOUTH AFRICAN GP	Kyalami	26	Equipe Ligier Gitanes	M	3.0 Ligier JS21-Cosworth V8		11 laps behind	23/26

GP Starts: 23　GP Wins: 0　Pole positions: 0　Fastest laps: 0　Points: 0

BOB BONDURANT

ORIGINALLY from Illinois, Bob Bondurant later moved to the West Coast, where he raced Triumphs and Corvettes with some success, although his big break came with the chance to race Carroll Shelby's hairy AC Cobra at Denver in 1963. A class win on his debut saw Bob signed full time for 1964 as the Shelby team headed for Europe to contest the classic long-distance events. His best result was a fourth place at Le Mans (with Dan Gurney) to win the GT class.

Bob had a hectic season in 1965, racing the Cobra and Ford GTs, in addition to a number of Formula 2 and Formula 3 outings. This led to an invitation to race the works Ferrari in place of the injured John Surtees at season's end.

Back in Europe for 1966, Bob raced for Bernard White's private team – picking up a fourth place at Monaco – in tandem with a freelance season of sports car rides, sharing Ferraris with Jochen Rindt, Mike Parkes and Masten Gregory, and taking a works Porsche to fourth place in the Nürburgring 1000km.

His career seemed to be over after a huge accident at Watkins Glen in 1967 prevented him from racing, but he made a successful comeback in Can-Am in 1970/71. Thereafter, he concentrated on his racing driver schools, but occasionally was tempted back behind the wheel in SCCA and NASCAR races.

BONDURANT, Bob (USA)　b 27/4/1933, Evanston, Illinois

	1965	Championship position: Unplaced							
	Race	Circuit	No	Entrant	Tyres	Capacity/Car/Engine	Comment		Q Pos/Entries
9	US GP	Watkins Glen	24	North American Racing Team	D	1.5 Ferrari 158 V8	4 laps behind		=13/18
ret	MEXICAN GP	Mexico City	22	Reg Parnell (Racing)	D	1.5 Lotus 33-BRM V8	rear suspension bolt		18/18
	1966	Championship position: 14th=　Wins: 0　Pole positions: 0　Fastest laps: 0　Points scored: 3							
4	MONACO GP	Monte Carlo	19	Team Chamaco Collect	G	2.0 BRM P261 V8	5 laps behind		16/16
ret	BELGIAN GP	Spa	(8) 24	Team Chamaco Collect	G	2.0 BRM P261 V8	also ran no 8 in practice/spun off		11/18
9	BRITISH GP	Brands Hatch	25	Team Chamaco Collect	G	2.0 BRM P261 V8	4 laps behind		14/20
ret	GERMAN GP	Nürburgring	14	Team Chamaco Collect	G	2.0 BRM P261 V8	engine		12/30
7	ITALIAN GP	Monza	48	Team Chamaco Collect	G	2.0 BRM P261 V8	3 laps behind		18/22
dsq*	US GP	Watkins Glen	16	Anglo American Racers	G	2.7 Eagle T1G-Climax 4	*push start		16/19
ret	MEXICAN GP	Mexico City	16	Anglo American Racers	G	3.0 Eagle T1G-Weslake V12	fuel feed		19/19
dns	"	" "	15	Anglo American Racers	G	2.7 Eagle T1G-Climax 4	practice only		– / –

GP Starts: 9　GP Wins: 0　Pole positions: 0　Fastest laps: 0　Points: 3

FELICE BONETTO

KNOWN as 'Il Pirata' (the pirate), Felice Bonetto was a fearless competitor who took no prisoners and was possessed of so much courage that some of his racing exploits placed him in the category of the foolhardy.

Bonetto was already well known in Italy in the late 1930s from his performances in his privately entered Alfa Romeo in the Mille Miglia, but he did not come to the fore internationally until the late 1940s, first with Cisitalia and then with Ferrari, for whom he scored second places in the Mille Miglia, and the Monza and Naples GPs in 1949.

The independently minded Felice campaigned the Maserati Milano and his own Alfa sports car to such effect that after winning the 1950 Oporto GP and leading the Mille Miglia in the Alfa, he was offered a works drive in 1951. He was very much the number three in the team, however, which did not go down too well, and he took the offer of a contract with Lancia to race their sports cars in 1952. This brought him perhaps his greatest triumph, in the Targa Florio.

Despite his age, Bonetto was more active than ever in 1953. Undertaking a full season of grands prix for the first time with the Maserati works team and racing sports cars again for Lancia, he won the Portuguese GP in Lisbon and placed third in the Mille Miglia before competing in the gruelling Carrera Panamericana. He lay in second place to Piero Taruffi when he was killed after skidding off the road and crashing into a lamp post in the village of Silao.

BONETTO, Felice (I) b 9/6/1903, Brescia – d 21/11/1953, Silao, Mexico

	1950	Championship position: 15th		Wins: 0	Pole positions: 0		Fastest laps: 0	Points scored: 2		
	Race	Circuit	No	Entrant	Tyres	Capacity/Car/Engine			Comment	Q Pos/Entries
5	SWISS GP	Bremgarten	34	Scuderia Milano	P	1.5 s/c Maserati Milano-Maserati 4			2 laps behind	12/18
ret	FRENCH GP	Reims	40	Scuderia Milano	P	1.5 s/c Maserati Milano-Maserati 4			engine	11/20
dns	ITALIAN GP	Monza	52	Scuderia Milano	P	1.5 s/c Maserati Milano-Speluzzi 4			withdrawn	(23)/27
	1951	Championship position: 7th		Wins: 0	Pole positions: 0		Fastest laps: 0	Points scored: 7		
4	BRITISH GP	Silverstone	4	Alfa Romeo SpA	P	1.5 s/c Alfa Romeo 159A 8			3 laps behind	7/20
ret	GERMAN GP	Nürburgring	77	Alfa Romeo SpA	P	1.5 s/c Alfa Romeo 159A 8			supercharger	10/23
3*	ITALIAN GP	Monza	40	Alfa Romeo SpA	P	1.5 s/c Alfa Romeo 159A 8			*Farina took over car/1 lap behind	7/22
5	SPANISH GP	Pedralbes	24	Alfa Romeo SpA	P	1.5 s/c Alfa Romeo 159M 8			2 laps behind	8/20
	1952	Championship position: 11th=		Wins: 0	Pole positions: 0		Fastest laps: 0	Points scored: 2		
dsq*	GERMAN GP	Nürburgring	105	Officine Alfieri Maserati	P	2.0 Maserati A6GCM 6			*push start after spin	10/32
5	ITALIAN GP	Monza	22	Officine Alfieri Maserati	P	2.0 Maserati A6GCM 6			1 lap behind	13/32
	1953	Championship position: 8th		Wins: 0	Pole positions: 0		Fastest laps: 0	Points scored: 6.5		
ret	ARGENTINE GP	Buenos Aires	6	Officine Alfieri Maserati	P	2.0 Maserati A6GCM 6			transmission	15/16
3*	DUTCH GP	Zandvoort	16	Officine Alfieri Maserati	P	2.0 Maserati A6GCM 6			*Gonzalez took over/1 lap behind	13/20
ret	FRENCH GP	Reims	24	Officine Alfieri Maserati	P	2.0 Maserati A6GCM 6			engine	2/25
6	BRITISH GP	Silverstone	25	Officine Alfieri Maserati	P	2.0 Maserati A6GCM 6			8 laps behind	16/29
4	GERMAN GP	Nürburgring	7	Officine Alfieri Maserati	P	2.0 Maserati A6GCM 6				7/35
ret*	SWISS GP	Bremgarten	30	Officine Alfieri Maserati	P	2.0 Maserati A6GCM 6			*Fangio took over/engine	10/23
4*	"	"	32	Officine Alfieri Maserati	P	2.0 Maserati A6GCM 6			*took Fangio's car/1 lap behind	– / –
ret	ITALIAN GP	Monza	52	Officine Alfieri Maserati	P	2.0 Maserati A6GCM 6			out of fuel	7/30
	GP Starts: 15	GP Wins: 0	Pole positions: 0	Fastest laps: 0	Points: 17.5					

JO BONNIER

FROM a comfortable background in Sweden, Jo Bonnier built a mighty reputation as an ice racer in the early 1950s with an Alfa Romeo Disco Volante, which led to him being appointed as a distributor for that marque in 1954. Moving into circuit racing the following year, he soon proved to be a front-runner in Scandinavia before venturing further afield in 1956 to race the GT Alfa, winning events at Aintree, AVUS and Castelfusano, and taking a class win at the Nürburgring 1000km with Mackay-Fraser. By now he had started to run Maserati sports cars, and in 1957 became involved with the works team, finishing third in the Swedish GP in a 300TS.

Although he had not really reached the front rank of drivers, Jo bought a Maserati 250F, which he raced in the 1957/58 seasons with only moderate results, the best being second

places at Syracuse and Caen against meagre opposition. At the tail end of 1958, he joined BRM and soon became the first driver to win a championship grand prix for Bourne when he won the 1959 Dutch GP. He stayed with BRM until the end of the 1960 season, but never came close to repeating his Zandvoort triumph, although he comfortably led the 1960 Argentine GP until his engine failed.

Having begun a successful association with Porsche in 1959, Bonnier took every opportunity to race for them again the following year, winning the Modena GP and taking a superb victory in the rain in the non-championship German GP in F2, and sharing the victorious RSK sports car with Hans Herrmann in the Targa Florio. With the Porsche team planning a grand prix assault in 1961, Bonnier – feeling his talents were being

overlooked at BRM – joined Dan Gurney to race the silver cars. After a winter interlude, which included taking a Yeoman Credit Cooper to victory in New Zealand at the Teretonga international and at Levin, the 1961 season started with a second place in Seidel's Lotus at Pau before Bonnier concentrated on his Porsche commitments. He made a promising beginning, with some good results in non-championship races, including second places at Solitude, Karlskoga and Modena, and thirds at Syracuse and Zeltweg. In grands prix, however, things were much tougher, and he was increasingly overshadowed by Gurney, especially in 1962, when he endured a fairly depressing time with the new Porsche 804 flat-eight; a second place at Solitude and a third at the Karlskoga GP were his only worthwhile results.

With Porsche withdrawing from Formula 1, Bonnier joined Rob Walker in 1963 and raced his privately entered cars for the next three seasons. When the mood took him, he could still be extremely quick, but by then he seemed more interested in his pivotal role as leader of the newly formed Grand Prix Drivers' Association. When Walker released him for 1966, Jo formed his own team, picking up occasional points racing a Cooper-Maserati and then a McLaren, as well as scrounging a few works drives, but he was really a shadow of his former self, especially in 1971, when he was very slow indeed.

If nothing else, Bonnier still enjoyed the life of a racing driver, and while the best days of his grand prix career were long past, he raced sports cars with great gusto. He shared a Chaparral with Phil Hill to win the Nürburgring 1000km in 1966, and raced his own and the Ecurie Filipinetti's Lola T70s with some minor success, but it was the acquisition of a 2-litre Lola in 1970 that seemingly re-awakened the racer that had for so long lain dormant. He won G5/6 races at both Silverstone and Jyllandsring, and took the European 2-litre championship with some terrific drives.

Although just past 40, Bonnier showed no sign of slackening his racing activities in 1971, and his lacklustre grand prix performances were thrown into sharp relief by more good results in the sports car categories, including a third in the Targa Florio with Richard Attwood, second place in the Auvergne Trophy and an outright win in the Barcelona 1000km with Ronnie Peterson. Retiring from Formula 1 at the end of the season, Bonnier raced on in a new Lola T280. However, at Le Mans in 1972, he was involved in a collision with a privateer Ferrari, and his yellow Lola was launched over the barriers into the trees. The man who had spent so much time crusading for circuit safety over the years had become another victim among a whole generation of racers who, sadly, paid the ultimate price.

BONNIER, Joakim (S) b 31/1/1930, Stockholm – d 11/6/1972, Le Mans Circuit, France

	Race	Circuit	No	Entrant	Tyres	Capacity/Car/Engine	Comment	Q Pos/Entries
	1956 Championship position: Unplaced							
ret	ITALIAN GP	Monza	34	Officine Alfieri Maserati	P	2.5 Maserati 250F 6	took over Villoresi's car/engine	– /26
	1957 Championship position: Unplaced							
7	ARGENTINE GP	Buenos Aires	24	Scuderia Centro Sud	P	2.5 Maserati 250F 6	5 laps behind	13/16
ret	BRITISH GP	Aintree	28	Jo Bonnier	P	2.5 Maserati 250F 6	transmission	17/19
ret	PESCARA GP	Pescara	16	Scuderia Centro Sud	P	2.5 Maserati 250F 6	overheating	9/16
ret	ITALIAN GP	Monza	24	Scuderia Centro Sud	P	2.5 Maserati 250F 6	overheating	13/19
	1958	Championship position: 14th=		Wins: 0	Pole positions: 0	Fastest laps: 0 Points scored: 3		
ret	MONACO GP	Monte Carlo	58	Jo Bonnier	P	2.5 Maserati 250F 6	accident	16/28
10	DUTCH GP	Zandvoort	11	Jo Bonnier	P	2.5 Maserati 250F 6	4 laps behind	15/17
9	BELGIAN GP	Spa	36	Jo Bonnier	P	2.5 Maserati 250F 6	2 laps behind	14/20
8	FRENCH GP	Reims	38	Giorgio Scarlatti	P	2.5 Maserati 250F 6	2 laps behind	16/21
ret	BRITISH GP	Silverstone	22	Jo Bonnier	P	2.5 Maserati 250F 6	gearbox	13/21
ret	GERMAN GP	Nürburgring	16	Scuderia Centro Sud	P	2.5 Maserati 250F 6	collision damage with Brabham	9/26
ret	PORTUGUESE GP	Oporto	32	Jo Bonnier	P	2.5 Maserati 250F 6	driver unwell	14/15
ret	ITALIAN GP	Monza	12	Owen Racing Organisation	D	2.5 BRM P25 4	transmission/fire	10/21
4	MOROCCAN GP	Casablanca	18	Owen Racing Organisation	D	2.5 BRM P25 4		8/25
	1959	Championship position: 8th=		Wins: 1	Pole positions: 1	Fastest laps: 0 Points scored: 10		
ret	MONACO GP	Monte Carlo	18	Owen Racing Organisation	D	2.5 BRM P25 4	brakes – accident	7/24
1	DUTCH GP	Zandvoort	7	Owen Racing Organisation	D	2.5 BRM P25 4		1/15
ret	FRENCH GP	Reims	4	Owen Racing Organisation	D	2.5 BRM P25 4	engine – head gasket	6/22
ret	BRITISH GP	Aintree	10	Owen Racing Organisation	D	2.5 BRM P25 4	throttle linkage	10/30
5 agg	GERMAN GP	AVUS	9	Owen Racing Organisation	D	2.5 BRM P25 4	7th heat 1/5th heat 2/-2 laps	7/16
ret	PORTUGUESE GP	Monsanto	7	Owen Racing Organisation	D	2.5 BRM P25 4	engine – fuel feed	5/16
8	ITALIAN GP	Monza	6	Owen Racing Organisation	D	2.5 BRM P25 4	2 laps behind	11/21
dns	“	“	6	Owen Racing Organisation	D	2.5 BRM P48 4	practice only	– / –
	1960	Championship position: 13th=		Wins: 0	Pole positions: 0	Fastest laps: 0 Points scored: 4		
7	ARGENTINE GP	Buenos Aires	40	Owen Racing Organisation	D	2.5 BRM P25 4	1 lap behind	5/22
5	MONACO GP	Monte Carlo	2	Owen Racing Organisation	D	2.5 BRM P48 4	pit stop – suspension/-17 laps	3/24
ret	DUTCH GP	Zandvoort	14	Owen Racing Organisation	D	2.5 BRM P48 4	engine – spun off on own oil	4/21
ret	BELGIAN GP	Spa	6	Owen Racing Organisation	D	2.5 BRM P48 4	engine	7/18
ret	FRENCH GP	Reims	8	Owen Racing Organisation	D	2.5 BRM P48 4	engine	8/23
ret	BRITISH GP	Silverstone	6	Owen Racing Organisation	D	2.5 BRM P48 4	rear suspension	4/25
ret	PORTUGUESE GP	Oporto	20	Owen Racing Organisation	D	2.5 BRM P48 4	engine	13/16
5	US GP	Riverside	15	Owen Racing Organisation	D	2.5 BRM P48 4	1 lap behind	4/23
	1961	Championship position: 13th=		Wins: 0	Pole positions: 0	Fastest laps: 0 Points scored: 3		
ret	MONACO GP	Monte Carlo	2	Porsche System Engineering	D	1.5 Porsche 787 F4	fuel injection	9/21
dns	“	“	2	Porsche System Engineering	D	1.5 Porsche 718 F4	practice only	– / –
11	DUTCH GP	Zandvoort	6	Porsche System Engineering	D	1.5 Porsche 787 F4	2 laps behind	12/17
7	BELGIAN GP	Spa	18	Porsche System Engineering	D	1.5 Porsche 718 F4		9/25
7	FRENCH GP	Reims	10	Porsche System Engineering	D	1.5 Porsche 718 F4		=12/26
5	BRITISH GP	Aintree	8	Porsche System Engineering	D	1.5 Porsche 718 F4		=1/30
ret	GERMAN GP	Nürburgring	8	Porsche System Engineering	D	1.5 Porsche 718 F4	engine	4/27
ret	ITALIAN GP	Monza	44	Porsche System Engineering	D	1.5 Porsche 718 F4	suspension	8/33
dns	“	“	44	Porsche System Engineering	D	1.5 Porsche 787 F4	practice only	– / –
6	US GP	Watkins Glen	11	Porsche System Engineering	D	1.5 Porsche 718 F4	2 laps behind	=9/19
	1962	Championship position: 14th		Wins: 0	Pole positions: 0	Fastest laps: 0 Points scored: 3		
7	DUTCH GP	Zandvoort	11	Porsche System Engineering	D	1.5 Porsche 804 F8	5 laps behind	13/20
5	MONACO GP	Monte Carlo	2	Porsche System Engineering	D	1.5 Porsche 718 F4	7 laps behind	18/21
10/ret	FRENCH GP	Rouen	32	Porsche System Engineering	D	1.5 Porsche 804 F8	gearbox/12 laps behind	9/17
ret	BRITISH GP	Aintree	10	Porsche System Engineering	D	1.5 Porsche 804 F8	engine – cwp	=7/21
7	GERMAN GP	Nürburgring	8	Porsche System Engineering	D	1.5 Porsche 804 F8		6/30
6	ITALIAN GP	Monza	18	Porsche System Engineering	D	1.5 Porsche 804 F8	1 lap behind	9/30
13	US GP	Watkins Glen	11	Porsche System Engineering	D	1.5 Porsche 804 F8	pit stops/21 laps behind	9/20
	1963	Championship position: 9th=		Wins: 0	Pole positions: 0	Fastest laps: 0 Points scored: 6		
7	MONACO GP	Monte Carlo	11	R R C Walker Racing Team	D	1.5 Cooper T60-Climax V8	6 laps behind	11/17
5	BELGIAN GP	Spa	12	R R C Walker Racing Team	D	1.5 Cooper T60-Climax V8	2 laps behind	=12/20
dns	“	“	12	R R C Walker Racing Team	D	1.5 Cooper T66-Climax V8	practice only – oil leak engine	– / –
11	DUTCH GP	Zandvoort	28	R R C Walker Racing Team	D	1.5 Cooper T60-Climax V8	pit stop – gearbox/24 laps behind	– / –
dns	“	“	28	R R C Walker Racing Team	D	1.5 Cooper T66-Climax V8	practice only – set grid time	8/19
nc	FRENCH GP	Reims	44	R R C Walker Racing Team	D	1.5 Cooper T60-Climax V8	ignition trouble/21 laps behind	11/21
dns	“	“	44	R R C Walker Racing Team	D	1.5 Cooper T66-Climax V8	practice only – engine problems	– / –
ret	BRITISH GP	Silverstone	14	R R C Walker Racing Team	D	1.5 Cooper T66-Climax V8	oil pressure	=10/23
6	GERMAN GP	Nürburgring	16	R R C Walker Racing Team	D	1.5 Cooper T66-Climax V8	1 lap behind	12/26
7	ITALIAN GP	Monza	58	R R C Walker Racing Team	D	1.5 Cooper T66-Climax V8	pit stop – fuel/2 laps behind	11/28
dns	“	“	58	R R C Walker Racing Team	D	1.5 Cooper T60-Climax V8	practice only	– / –
8	US GP	Watkins Glen	11	R R C Walker Racing Team	D	1.5 Cooper T66-Climax V8	pit stops/25 laps behind	12/21
5	MEXICAN GP	Mexico City	11	R R C Walker Racing Team	D	1.5 Cooper T66-Climax V8	3 laps behind	8/21
6	SOUTH AFRICAN GP	East London	12	R R C Walker Racing Team	D	1.5 Cooper T66-Climax V8	2 laps behind	11/21
	1964	Championship position: 15th		Wins: 0	Pole positions: 0	Fastest laps: 0 Points scored: 3		
5	MONACO GP	Monte Carlo	19	R R C Walker Racing Team	D	1.5 Cooper T66-Climax V8	4 laps behind	11/20

	Race	Circuit	No	Entrant	Tyres	Capacity/Car/Engine	Comment	Q Pos/Entries
9	DUTCH GP	Zandvoort	26	R R C Walker Racing Team	D	1.5 Brabham BT11-BRM V8	4 laps behind	12/18
dns	"	"	26T	R R C Walker Racing Team	D	1.5 Cooper T66-Climax V8	practice only	– / –
ret	BELGIAN GP	Spa	16	R R C Walker Racing Team	D	1.5 Brabham BT11-BRM V8	unwell after practice crash	14/20
dns	"	"	16	R R C Walker Racing Team	D	1.5 Cooper T66-Climax V8	practice only – crashed car	– / –
ret	BRITISH GP	Brands Hatch	16	R R C Walker Racing Team	D	1.5 Brabham BT11-BRM V8	brake pipe	=8/25
dns	"	"	16	R R C Walker Racing Team	D	1.5 Cooper T66-Climax V8	practice only	– / –
ret	GERMAN GP	Nürburgring	11	R R C Walker Racing Team	D	1.5 Brabham BT11-BRM V8	electrics	12/24
6	AUSTRIAN GP	Zeltweg	11	R R C Walker Racing Team	D	1.5 Brabham BT7-Climax V8	4 laps behind	10/20
12	ITALIAN GP	Monza	34	R R C Walker Racing Team	D	1.5 Brabham BT7-Climax V8	alternator problems/-4 laps	=12/25
ret	US GP	Watkins Glen	16	R R C Walker Racing Team	D	1.5 Brabham BT7-Climax V8	stub axle	9/19
ret	MEXICAN GP	Mexico City	16	R R C Walker Racing Team	D	1.5 Brabham BT7-Climax V8	wishbone	8/19
	1965	Championship position: Unplaced						
ret	SOUTH AFRICAN GP	East London	11	R R C Walker Racing Team	D	1.5 Brabham BT7-Climax V8	clutch	=6/25
7	MONACO GP	Monte Carlo	12	R R C Walker Racing Team	D	1.5 Brabham BT7-Climax V8	3 laps behind	=12/17
ret	BELGIAN GP	Spa	20	R R C Walker Racing Team	D	1.5 Brabham BT7-Climax V8	ignition	7/21
ret	FRENCH GP	Clermont Ferrand	34	R R C Walker Racing Team	D	1.5 Brabham BT7-Climax V8	alternator drive	=10/17
7	BRITISH GP	Silverstone	15	R R C Walker Racing Team	D	1.5 Brabham BT7-Climax V8	1 lap behind	14/23
ret	DUTCH GP	Zandvoort	26	R R C Walker Racing Team	D	1.5 Brabham BT7-Climax V8	valve spring	15/17
7	GERMAN GP	Nürburgring	16	R R C Walker Racing Team	D	1.5 Brabham BT7-Climax V8		9/22
7	ITALIAN GP	Monza	42	R R C Walker Racing Team	D	1.5 Brabham BT7-Climax V8	2 laps behind	14/23
8	US GP	Watkins Glen	15	R R C Walker Racing Team	D	1.5 Brabham BT7-Climax V8	3 laps behind	10/18
ret	MEXICAN GP	Mexico City	15	R R C Walker Racing Team	D	1.5 Brabham BT7-Climax V8	broken wishbone	12/18
	1966	Championship position: 17th= Wins: 0 Pole positions: 0 Fastest laps: 0 Points scored: 1						
nc	MONACO GP	Monte Carlo	18	Anglo-Suisse Racing Team	F	3.0 Cooper T81-Maserati V12	pit stops/27 laps behind	14/16
dns	" "	18T	Reg Parnell Racing Ltd	F	2.7 Lotus 25-Climax 4	practice only	– / –
ret	BELGIAN GP	Spa	20	Anglo-Suisse Racing Team	F	3.0 Cooper T81-Maserati V12	spun off in rain	6/18
nc	FRENCH GP	Reims	30	Brabham Racing Organisation	F	2.5 Brabham BT22-Climax 4	16 laps behind	17/17
dns	"	"	30	Anglo-Suisse Racing Team	D	3.0 Cooper T77-ATS V8	practice only/blown engine	– / –
ret	BRITISH GP	Brands Hatch	18	Anglo-Suisse Racing Team	F	1.5 Brabham BT7-Climax V8	car painted as a Ferrari/engine	15/20
7	DUTCH GP	Zandvoort	30	Anglo-Suisse Racing Team	F	3.0 Cooper T81-Maserati V12	6 laps behind	13/18
ret	GERMAN GP	Nürburgring	17	Anglo-Suisse Racing Team	F	3.0 Cooper T81-Maserati V12	clutch	13/30
ret	ITALIAN GP	Monza	38	Anglo-Suisse Racing Team	F	3.0 Cooper T81-Maserati V12	throttle linkage	12/22
nc	US GP	Watkins Glen	22	Anglo-Suisse Racing Team	F	3.0 Cooper T81-Maserati V12	pit stops/51 laps behind	15/19
6	MEXICAN GP	Mexico City	22	Anglo-Suisse Racing Team	F	3.0 Cooper T81-Maserati V12	2 laps behind	13/19
	1967	Championship position: 14th= Wins: 0 Pole positions: 0 Fastest laps: 0 Points scored: 3						
ret	SOUTH AFRICAN GP	Kyalami	15	Joakim Bonnier Racing Team	F	3.0 Cooper T81-Maserati V12	engine	12/18
ret	BELGIAN GP	Spa	39	Joakim Bonnier Racing Team	F	3.0 Cooper T81-Maserati V12	fuel feed	12/18
ret	BRITISH GP	Silverstone	23	Joakim Bonnier Racing Team	F	3.0 Cooper T81-Maserati V12	engine	19/21
5*	GERMAN GP	Nürburgring	16	Joakim Bonnier Racing Team	F	3.0 Cooper T81-Maserati V12	*6th on road behind an F2 car	=21/25
8	CANADIAN GP	Mosport Park	9	Joakim Bonnier Racing Team	F	3.0 Cooper T81-Maserati V12	5 laps behind	15/19
ret	ITALIAN GP	Monza	26	Joakim Bonnier Racing Team	F	3.0 Cooper T81-Maserati V12	overheating	14/18
6	US GP	Watkins Glen	16	Joakim Bonnier Racing Team	F	3.0 Cooper T81-Maserati V12	pit stop – wheel/7 laps behind	15/18
10	MEXICAN GP	Mexico City	16	Joakim Bonnier Racing Team	F	3.0 Cooper T81-Maserati V12	4 laps behind	17/19
	1968	Championship position: 21st= Wins: 0 Pole positions: 0 Fastest laps: 0 Points scored: 3						
ret	SOUTH AFRICAN GP	Kyalami	20	Joakim Bonnier Racing Team	F	3.0 Cooper T81-Maserati V12	lost rear wheel	19/23
dnq	MONACO GP	Monte Carlo	18	Joakim Bonnier Racing Team	G	3.0 McLaren M5A-BRM V12	not seeded	15/18
ret	BELGIAN GP	Spa	17	Joakim Bonnier Racing Team	G	3.0 McLaren M5A-BRM V12	wheel stud	16/18
8	DUTCH GP	Zandvoort	19	Joakim Bonnier Racing Team	G	3.0 McLaren M5A-BRM V12	8 laps behind	19/19
ret	BRITISH GP	Brands Hatch	23	Joakim Bonnier Racing Team	G	3.0 McLaren M5A-BRM V12	engine	20/20
6	ITALIAN GP	Monza	3	Joakim Bonnier Racing Team	G	3.0 McLaren M5A-BRM V12	4 laps behind	21/24
ret/dns	CANADIAN GP	St Jovite	22	Joakim Bonnier Racing Team	G	3.0 McLaren M5A-BRM V12	car would not start on grid	18/22
ret	US GP	Watkins Glen	17	Joakim Bonnier Racing Team	G	3.0 McLaren M5A-BRM V12	ignition trouble/4 laps behind	18/21
5	MEXICAN GP	Mexico City	17	Joakim Bonnier Racing Team	F	3.0 Honda RA301 V12	drove works spare car/-1 lap	18/21
dns	" "	17	Joakim Bonnier Racing Team	G	3.0 McLaren M5A-BRM V12	engine in practice	– / –
	1969	Championship position: Unplaced						
ret	BRITISH GP	Silverstone	18	Ecurie Bonnier/Gold Leaf Team Lotus	F	3.0 Lotus 63-Cosworth V8	engine	16/17
ret	GERMAN GP	Nürburgring	16	Ecurie Bonnier	F	3.0 Lotus 49B-Cosworth V8	fuel leak	23/26
	1970	Championship position: Unplaced						
dnq	ITALIAN GP	Monza	38	Ecurie Bonnier	G	3.0 McLaren M7C-Cosworth V8		24/27
ret	US GP	Watkins Glen	27	Ecurie Bonnier	G	3.0 McLaren M7C-Cosworth V8	water pipe	24/27
	1971	Championship position: Unplaced						
ret	SOUTH AFRICAN GP	Kyalami	23	Ecurie Bonnier	G	3.0 McLaren M7C-Cosworth V8	suspension	23/25
dnq	GERMAN GP	Nürburgring	27	Ecurie Bonnier	G	3.0 McLaren M7C-Cosworth V8		23/23
dns	AUSTRIAN GP	Österreichring	28	Ecurie Bonnier	G	3.0 McLaren M7C-Cosworth V8	fuel leak before start	(19)/22
10	ITALIAN GP	Monza	28	Ecurie Bonnier	G	3.0 McLaren M7C-Cosworth V8	4 laps behind	21/24
16/ret	US GP	Watkins Glen	29	Ecurie Bonnier	G	3.0 McLaren M7C-Cosworth V8	out of fuel/5 laps behind	31/32

GP Starts: 103 (104)   GP Wins: 1   Pole positions: 1   Fastest laps: 0   Points: 39

BONOMI, Roberto (RA) b 30/9/1919, Buenos Aires – d 10/1/1992, Buenos Aires

	Race	Circuit	No	Entrant	Tyres	Capacity/Car/Engine	Comment	Q Pos/Entries
	1960	Championship position: Unplaced						
11	ARGENTINE GP	Buenos Aires	4	Scuderia Centro Sud	D	2.5 Cooper T51-Maserati 4	4 laps behind	17/22

GP Starts: 1   GP Wins: 0   Pole positions: 0   Fastest laps: 0   Points: 0

ROBERTO BONOMI

ROBERTO BONOMI was a wealthy land owner who was the Argentine sports car champion of 1952 and 1953, racing Ferraris. His success continued into 1954 with a Ferrari 250MM Vignale, with which he scored wins in the Argentine 500-mile race, and events at Primavera, Costa Nera Lealtad and Mendoza. Thus he was regularly chosen to supplement the works teams in the annual Buenos Aires 1000km sports car race, placing fifth in 1957 in a Maserati 350S V12 with Luigi Piotti.

Then Roberto purchased a Maserati 300S, which he raced in sports car and Libre events between 1958 and 1961.

He hired a Cooper for his only grand prix appearance in 1960, also racing the same car in the Formule Libre Cordoba GP, before it was taken over by team-mate Carlos Menditeguy.

TOMMY 'SLIM' BORGUDD

TOMMY Borgudd began racing in Formula Ford and sports cars in his native Sweden between 1969 and 1973, but lack of finance forced him to fall back on his career as a jazz rock drummer (most famously in studio sessions with Abba). It was when he was working in New Orleans that he gained his nickname. After stepping in for a drummer called 'Memphis Slim', Borgudd was dubbed 'Little Slim'. Subsequently this was shortened to 'Slim' and it stuck, mainly because his subsequent pay-cheques were made out in this name and he had problems cashing them as his ID card showed his real name, Tommy!

After a few drives in 1976, Slim returned to the tracks on a more permanent basis the following year, and was soon performing heroics in both the Swedish and European F3 series with an outdated Ralt. Particularly impressive were his efforts in the European championship in 1979 when he finished third overall behind the dazzling Prost and experienced Bleekemolen despite having to miss races due to lack of money as the year wore on.

A planned season in Formula 2 in 1980 was aborted when the finance was not forthcoming, but Slim occasionally competed in a March in F3 while working on a deal that saw him join the ATS team in Grands Prix for 1981.

Sixth place – and a championship point – in the British Grand Prix was the high spot in a difficult season. Borgudd then began the next campaign with the Tyrrell team, but his money soon ran out and he was replaced by Brian Henton.

Between 1983 and 1985 he raced infrequently, appearing at Macau in 1984 (6th) and 1985 (11th) in F3 Ralt, as well as briefly trying his hand in three races in inaugural 1985 F3000 season in an outdated and unsuitable F1 Arrows A6.

'Slim', who went on to carve out a hugely successful, enjoyable – and profitable! – career as in truck racing. In 1986 and 1987, Borgudd was champion in Divisions 2 and 3 of the European Truck Racing Cup. He returned to the cars to contest the 1983 BTCC with a works Mazda Xedos, but this attractive car was never on the pace. It fared much better in the Nordic series the following year with Borguud taking the title. At the same time he returned Truck Racing and became Super Race Champion (in 1995) with a Mercedes-Benz 1834-S.

BORGUDD, Slim (Karl Edward Tommy Borguud) (S) b 25/11/1946, Borgholm, nr Kalmar

	1981	Championship position: 18=		Wins: 0	Pole positions: 0		Fastest laps: 0	Points scored: 1		
	Race	Circuit	No	Entrant	Tyres	Capacity/Car/Engine		Comment		Q Pos/Entries
13	SAN MARINO GP	Imola	10	Team ATS	M	3.0 ATS D4-Cosworth V8		pit stop – tyres/3 laps behind		24/30
dnq	BELGIAN GP	Zolder	9	Team ATS	M	3.0 ATS HGS1-Cosworth V8				27/31
dnpq	MONACO GP	Monte Carlo	10	Team ATS	M	3.0 ATS D4-Cosworth V8				27/31
dnq	SPANISH GP	Jarama	9	Team ATS	M	3.0 ATS HGS1-Cosworth V8				27/30
dnq	FRENCH GP	Dijon	9	Team ATS	M	3.0 ATS HGS1-Cosworth V8				27/29
6	BRITISH GP	Silverstone	9	Team ATS	A	3.0 ATS HGS1-Cosworth V8		1 lap behind		21/30
ret	GERMAN GP	Hockenheim	9	Team ATS	A	3.0 ATS HGS1-Cosworth V8		engine		20/30
ret	AUSTRIAN GP	Österreichring	9	Team ATS	A	3.0 ATS HGS1-Cosworth V8		brakes		21/28
10	DUTCH GP	Zandvoort	9	Team ATS	A	3.0 ATS HGS1-Cosworth V8		pit stop – tyres/4 laps behind		23/30
ret	ITALIAN GP	Monza	9	Team ATS	A	3.0 ATS HGS1-Cosworth V8		spun off		21/30
ret	CANADIAN GP	Montreal	9	Team ATS	A	3.0 ATS HGS1-Cosworth V8		spun off		21/30
dnq	CAESARS PALACE GP	Las Vegas	9	Team ATS	A	3.0 ATS HGS1-Cosworth V8				25/30
	1982	Championship position: Unplaced								
16	SOUTH AFRICAN GP	Kyalami	4	Team Tyrrell	G	3.0 Tyrrell 011-Cosworth V8		pit stop – tyres/5 laps behind		23/30
7*	BRAZILIAN GP	Rio	4	Team Tyrrell	G	3.0 Tyrrell 011-Cosworth V8		*1st & 2nd cars dsq/-2 laps		21/31
10*	US GP WEST	Long Beach	4	Team Tyrrell	G	3.0 Tyrrell 011-Cosworth V8		*3rd car dsq/collision/-7 laps		24/31
	GP Starts: 10	GP Wins: 0	Pole positions: 0		Fastest laps: 0	Points: 1				

LUKI BOTHA

LUKI BOTHA found success at national level in 1965 in sports cars, firstly in a Lotus 23, and then the following year, in a very competitive Porsche-engined Elva. Then he showed well on his single-seater debut in the end-of-season 1966 Rhodesian Grand Prix, bringing his Brabham BT11 home in second place, behind the visiting Bob Anderson's similar car. Less than three weeks later, he made his only appearance in a world championship grand prix at Kyalami, but spent many laps in the pits after engine problems at the the start.

For the home series, Botha soon took a step up in competitiveness after adding a Repco engine to his BT11; he finished third, behind Dave Charlton and John Love in the Rand Autumn Trophy at Kyalami. However, his inexperience was soon apparent and, though showing a fair turn of speed, he had a number of offs in the next few events. Sadly, he crashed again in the Taça Governo Geral de Moçambique (Governer General Cup) race in Lourenço Marques (now Maputo), Mozambique, his car killing at least seven young spectators who were in a run-off area; many others were hospitalized. Botha escaped personal injury and soon retired from competition.

Luki then worked in both civil engineering and farming, before returning to his hometown of Pretoria, where he became CEO of the Tswane Metropolitan Council.

BOTHA, Luki (ZA) b 16/1/1930, Pretoria – d 1/10/2006, Pretoria

1967 Championship position: Unplaced

	Race	Circuit	No	Entrant	Tyres	Capacity/Car/Engine	Comment	Q Pos/Entries
nc	SOUTH AFRICAN GP	Kyalami	20	Luki Botha	–	2.7 Brabham BT11-Climax 4	long pit stop/20 laps behind	17/18

GP Starts: 1　GP Wins: 0　Pole positions: 0　Fastest laps: 0　Points: 0

JEAN-CHRISTOPHE BOULLION

JEAN-CHRISTOPHE BOULLION, or 'Jules' as he is universally known, was always a man to watch. The 1990 French FF1600 champion soon began impressing in the French F3 championship with his style and speed. Fourth place in the 1992 series was a disappointment, though, and reflected the major chink in his armour, inconsistency. Nevertheless he moved up to F3000 with Apomatox and endured a character building year that yielded two second-place finishes. The shy and hitherto uncommunicative Frenchman really came of age in 1994, when a switch to DAMS saw him mount a thrilling late-season charge to win the last three races and snatch the title at the final round.

Given a testing contract with Williams for 1995, he was soon setting some impressive times and jumped at the chance to race for Sauber in place of the disappointing Karl Wendlinger. In view of his inexperience, Boullion did well to record two points-scoring finishes. On the debit side, however, he may have been pushing too hard, for there were perhaps too many spins.

His testing expertise was never in doubt, as he was capable of matching the times of Damon Hill. But questions still lingered over his qualities as a racer. Apart from the Renault Spyder series in 1997, Boullion had little opportunity to compete, accepting the task of shaking down the BAR team's first grand prix challenger in 1998, before returning to the Williams fold in 1999 to race their Renault Laguna in the BTCC series. Sadly, a single podium finish and tenth place overall were all the little Frenchman had to show for his efforts in this class.

Then Boullion successfully extended his career in sports prototypes, becoming an integral member of the Pescarolo Sport team. In 2005, teamed with Erik Comas and Emmanuel Collard, he took second place at Le Mans, thus preventing a 1-2-3 for the hitherto all-conquering Audi. More success followed in the Le Mans Endurance Series, the team taking the LMP1 crown in dramatic circumstances in Istanbul. Teamed with Emmanuel Collard, 'Jules' took the Pescarolo-Judd C60 to a thrilling win in atrocious wet conditions, just ahead of the title challenging ORECA Audi R8. That success was repeated in 2006, when the Pescarolo duo comfortably won all five rounds to share the title between them.

In 2007, Boullion took third for Pescarolo-Judd (with Collard and Romain Dumas) at Le Mans and was runner-up in the Le Mans Series. He finished second once more in 2009, before making a switch to Swiss Rebellion Racing to run their Lola-Toyota LMP1 petrol-driven prototypes. With co-driver Andrea Pillichi, he was second in the Le Mans Series in 2011, behind the Pescarolo team, but they did help Rebellion to take LMP1 team honours. For 2012, Boullion looked set to return to Pescarolo and link up once more with Collard.

BOULLION, Jean-Christophe b 27/12/1969, Saint Brieuc, nr Cote d'Amor

1995 Championship position: 16th   Wins: 0   Pole positions: 0   Fastest laps: 0   Points scored: 3

	Race	Circuit	No	Entrant	Tyres	Capacity/Car/Engine	Comment	Q Pos/Entries
8	MONACO GP	Monte Carlo	29	Red Bull Sauber Ford	G	3.0 Sauber C14-Ford Zetec-R V8	collision with Morbidelli/-4 laps	19/26
ret	CANADIAN GP	Montreal	29	Red Bull Sauber Ford	G	3.0 Sauber C14-Ford Zetec-R V8	spun off	18/24
ret	FRENCH GP	Magny Cours	29	Red Bull Sauber Ford	G	3.0 Sauber C14-Ford Zetec-R V8	gearbox	15/24
9	BRITISH GP	Silverstone	29	Red Bull Sauber Ford	G	3.0 Sauber C14-Ford Zetec-R V8	1 lap behind	16/24
5	GERMAN GP	Hockenheim	29	Red Bull Sauber Ford	G	3.0 Sauber C14-Ford Zetec-R V8	1 lap behind	14/24
10	HUNGARIAN GP	Hungaroring	29	Red Bull Sauber Ford	G	3.0 Sauber C14-Ford Zetec-R V8	3 laps behind	19/24
11	BELGIAN GP	Spa	29	Red Bull Sauber Ford	G	3.0 Sauber C14-Ford Zetec-R V8	1 lap behind	14/24
6	ITALIAN GP	Monza	29	Red Bull Sauber Ford	G	3.0 Sauber C14-Ford Zetec-R V8	started from pit lane/-1 lap	14/24
12	PORTUGUESE GP	Estoril	29	Red Bull Sauber Ford	G	3.0 Sauber C14-Ford Zetec-R V8	1 lap behind	14/24
ret	EUROPEAN GP	Nürburgring	29	Red Bull Sauber Ford	G	3.0 Sauber C14-Ford Zetec-R V8	spun off	13/24
ret	PACIFIC GP	T.I. Circuit	29	Red Bull Sauber Ford	G	3.0 Sauber C14-Ford Zetec-R V8	spun off	15/24

GP Starts: 11   GP Wins: 0   Pole positions: 0   Fastest laps: 0   Points: 3

BOURDAIS, Sébastien (F) b 28/2/1979, Le Mans

2008 Championship position: 17th   Wins: 0   Pole positions: 0   Fastest laps: 0   Points scored: 4

	Race	Circuit	No	Entrant	Tyres	Capacity/Car/Engine	Comment	Q Pos/Entries
7/ret	AUSTRALIAN GP	Melbourne	14	Scuderia Toro Rosso	B	2.4 Toro Rosso STR02B-Ferrari V8	transmission/3 laps behind	18/22
ret	MALAYSIAN GP	Sepang	14	Scuderia Toro Rosso	B	2.4 Toro Rosso STR02B-Ferrari V8	spun off on lap 1	19/22
15	BAHRAIN GP	Bahrain	14	Scuderia Toro Rosso	B	2.4 Toro Rosso STR02B-Ferrari V8	brake problems/1 lap behind	15/22
ret	SPANISH GP	Barcelona	14	Scuderia Toro Rosso	B	2.4 Toro Rosso STR02B-Ferrari V8	collision with Piquet	16/22
ret	TURKISH GP	Istanbul	14	Scuderia Toro Rosso	B	2.4 Toro Rosso STR02B-Ferrari V8	brake problems – spun out	18/20
ret	MONACO GP	Monte Carlo	14	Scuderia Toro Rosso	B	2.4 Toro Rosso STR03-Ferrari V8	accident	16/20
13	CANADIAN GP	Montreal	14	Scuderia Toro Rosso	B	2.4 Toro Rosso STR03-Ferrari V8	1 lap behind	16/20
17	FRENCH GP	Magny Cours	14	Scuderia Toro Rosso	B	2.4 Toro Rosso STR03-Ferrari V8	1 lap behind	14/20
11	BRITISH GP	Silverstone	14	Scuderia Toro Rosso	B	2.4 Toro Rosso STR03-Ferrari V8	1 lap behind	13/20
12	GERMAN GP	Hockenheim	14	Scuderia Toro Rosso	B	2.4 Toro Rosso STR03-Ferrari V8		15/20
18	HUNGARIAN GP	Hungaroring	14	Scuderia Toro Rosso	B	2.4 Toro Rosso STR03-Ferrari V8	delayed at pit stops/-3 laps	14/20
10	EUROPEAN GP	Valencia	14	Scuderia Toro Rosso	B	2.4 Toro Rosso STR03-Ferrari V8	collision damage with Heidfeld	10/20
7	BELGIAN GP	Spa	14	Scuderia Toro Rosso	B	2.4 Toro Rosso STR03-Ferrari V8	lay third on final lap	9/20
18	ITALIAN GP	Monza	14	Scuderia Toro Rosso	B	2.4 Toro Rosso STR03-Ferrari V8	stalled on grid – started from pitlane	4/20
12	SINGAPORE GP	Singapore Circuit	14	Scuderia Toro Rosso	B	2.4 Toro Rosso STR03-Ferrari V8		17/20
10*	JAPANESE GP	Suzuka	14	Scuderia Toro Rosso	B	2.4 Toro Rosso STR03-Ferrari V8	*6th on road - 25 sec penalty	10/20
13	CHINESE GP	Shanghai	14	Scuderia Toro Rosso	B	2.4 Toro Rosso STR03-Ferrari V8	hit Trulli – lost places	10/20
14	BRAZILIAN GP	Interlagos	14	Scuderia Toro Rosso	B	2.4 Toro Rosso STR03-Ferrari V8	1 lap behind	9/20

2009 Championship position: 19th   Wins: 0   Pole positions: 0   Fastest laps: 0   Points scored: 2

	Race	Circuit	No	Entrant	Tyres	Capacity/Car/Engine	Comment	Q Pos/Entries
8*	AUSTRALIAN GP	Melbourne	12	Scuderia Toro Rosso	B	2.4 Toro Rosso STR04-Ferrari V8	*3rd place car dsq	20/20
10	MALAYSIAN GP	Sepang	12	Scuderia Toro Rosso	B	2.4 Toro Rosso STR04-Ferrari V8	rain-shortened race	15/20
11	CHINESE GP	Shanghai	12	Scuderia Toro Rosso	B	2.4 Toro Rosso STR04-Ferrari V8		16/20
13	BAHRAIN GP	Bahrain	12	Scuderia Toro Rosso	B	2.4 Toro Rosso STR04-Ferrari V8		20/20
ret	SPANISH GP	Barcelona	12	Scuderia Toro Rosso	B	2.4 Toro Rosso STR04-Ferrari V8	hit team mate Buemi on lap 1	17/20
8	MONACO GP	Monte Carlo	12	Scuderia Toro Rosso	B	2.4 Toro Rosso STR04-Ferrari V8	good one-stop drive	14/20
18	TURKISH GP	Istanbul	12	Scuderia Toro Rosso	B	2.4 Toro Rosso STR04-Ferrari V8	1 lap behind	20/20
ret	BRITISH GP	Silverstone	12	Scuderia Toro Rosso	B	2.4 Toro Rosso STR04-Ferrari V8	collision – Kovalainen/engine	17/20
ret	GERMAN GP	Hockenheim	12	Scuderia Toro Rosso	B	2.4 Toro Rosso STR04-Ferrari V8	hydraulics	20/20

GP Starts: 27   GP Wins: 0   Pole positions: 0   Fastest laps: 0   Points: 6

Gerhard Berger (centre) must have been pleased to see his both his drivers in the points after the 2008 Belgian Grand Prix. Whilst Sebastian Vettel (right) looks happy enough with his fifth place, his Toro Rosso team mate Sébastien Bourdais looks slightly disappointed with his seventh place, having held third at the start of the final lap.

SÉBASTIEN BOURDAIS

IN today's world of Formula 1, drivers usually arrive in the top echelon by dint of success in the well-defined single-seat ladder system. Not so Sébastien Bourdais, who had to spend five years in the United States gaining the credentials to get his chance to race in F1. He probably thought the chance had passed him by back in 2002, when a possible drive with Arrows slipped away after the team went into liquidation.

The son of Patrick Bourdais, himself a keen rally and endurance racer, the young Sébastien soon began climbing through the junior national karting classes. Then success in Formula Renault paved the way to Formula 3, where he took eight wins on his way to the 1999 French championship. In the same year, he also emulated his father by making his debut at the Le Mans 24-hour race, driving a Porsche 911 in the GT2 class.

Bourdais now had his sights set firmly on Formula 1, and he took the step up to F3000 with Prost for the 2000 season. Faced with such tough competitors as Bruno Junqueira, Mark Webber and Fernando Alonso, he finished a solid ninth in the championship, with a best result of second place at Magny-Cours. The following season saw a switch to the DAMS team and an improvement to fourth place overall, a win at Silverstone being the highlight. Strengthening his title chances for 2002, he was lured to the crack Super Nova squad, and he was involved in a three-way title battle with Tomas Enge and Giorgio Pantano. After Enge's third place in the closing round at Monza, the title seemed to have gone the way of the Czech driver, but later he would have ten points deducted from his total after failing a drug test. This handed the championship to Bourdais in a somewhat unsatisfactory fashion, although with three wins and five pole positions in the first six races, he might well have expected to clinch the championship long before the Monza finale.

In the event, the F3000 crown did not prove the passport to a Formula 1 drive in 2003. Flavio Briatore blocked the Frenchman out of Renault and left him out on a limb in Europe, so he opted to take his chances in the CART (Champ Car) series, which had been rescued from the brink of collapse. Bourdais immediately gelled with the Newman-Haas team and he soon scored the first of three wins at Brands Hatch. He followed this with an even more impressive performance to take victory on the oval at Lausitz in Germany, and then picked up his third win on the wide open spaces of the airfield track at Cleveland. Fourth place in the final points standings saw him comfortably winning the Rookie of the Year honour and primed for an almost unprecedented spell of success.

In 2004, he began his domination of the Champ Car series, taking four successive championships and adding a further 28 wins (taking his final total to 31). That these had been achieved in just 73 starts showed his level of mastery. Despite his impressive record, though, Sébastien had little hope of breaking into Formula 1, until the US Grand Prix in 2006 and a meeting with Nicolas Todt. To Todt, he was the only current French driver possessing sufficient talent to represent his country at the highest level, and he set about securing the driver a place in grand prix racing.

Occasional sports car outings were also bringing rewards, such as a GT2 class win at Sebring in 2006 with the Panoz-Ford, and a year later second overall at Le Mans in the works Peugeot 908 HDi with Pedro Lamy and Stéphane Sarrazin.

True to his word, Todt secured Bourdais a test for Toro Rosso, and at the age of 29, the Frenchman finally found himself a berth in Formula 1 for 2008. But for a late-race engine failure, his grand prix debut in Australia could have provided a stunning fourth place. In the event, he was classified seventh, but he still joined a select band of drivers who have scored points on their debut. Thereafter, however, he struggled in the wake of his young team-mate, Sebastian Vettel, and became unhappy with the nervous characteristics of the car. It was only after mid-season, when changes were made to the STR03 chassis, that things began to pick up for him, and he became a more regular contender for Qualifying 3.

Bourdais was unlucky to end up with only seventh place at Spa, following a last-lap free-for-all in wet conditions, and more heartache came at Monza where, having qualified fourth, his car failed to start on the grid. This destroyed a great chance of a podium finish, and his meagre end-of-season points total of just four was poor reward for his efforts.

At the beginning of 2009, the jury seemed to be out on whether Bourdais deserved to retain his seat. However, with his new team-mate, the inexperienced Sébastien Buemi, scoring points from the outset, the Frenchman's sojourn in Formula 1 turned out to be disappointingly brief, as he fell out of favour and was replaced by unproven Jaime Alguersuari. After threatening legal action, he successfully negotiated a big pay-off from Toro Rosso and began rebuilding his career.

Bourdais proved his undoubted skill in the single-seater Superleague Formula by winning on his debut at Estoril and continued to add to his already impressive sports car racing pedigree. He took another second place for Peugeot at Le Mans in 2009 (with Stéphane Sarrazin and Franck Montagny), and in 2010 triumphed at Spa in the Le Mans Series (with Simon Pagenaud and Pedro Lamy). With the Peugeot, he was runner-up at the Circuit de la Sarthe once more in 2011, but he did win at Imola (with Anthony Davidson) and Silverstone (with Pagenaud). He also secured a return to Indy Car racing with Dayle Coyne on a truncated road-course-only schedule. Four sixth-place finishes enabled the French driver to set up a full-time return in 2012 with Lotus Dragon Racing.

In October 2011, as a guest driver, Bourdais showed his amazing versatility by sharing a Holden Commodore with Jamie Whincup to win the Gold Coast 600 in the Australian V8 Supercar class.

THIERRY BOUTSEN

WITH no family racing background, Thierry Boutsen went to the Pilette racing school, where he soon became a star pupil and set out on a Formula Ford career. In 1978, the young Belgian raced a Crosslé in the Benelux countries, winning 15 of his 18 races, which brought him to the attention of his boyhood idol, Jacky Ickx. With his help, Boutsen found a Formula 3 ride in 1979, but the season was fraught with troubles until a spectacular performance in the final round at Jarama, where he matched European champion Alain Prost. That one drive was enough to persuade the works Martini team to sign him in place of the little Frenchman, who was off to McLaren. The new season began well, with three wins in the first four races, but when March launched their new wing car, a depressed Boutsen was powerless to prevent himself from being overhauled by the determined Michele Alboreto.

Stepping up to Formula 2 with a works March in 1981, Boutsen was the surprise of the championship, winning races at the Nürburgring and Enna, and finishing runner-up in the point to Geoff Lees. Opting to race for Spirit in 1982 was something of a gamble that didn't quite come off, but his brilliant

wins at the Nürburgring, Enna and especially Spa marked him out as an immediate grand prix prospect. Thierry's hopes of racing the Spirit F1 car in 1983 were dashed when Johansson got the nod, but he managed to finance a ride with Arrows, with whom he would stay for three more seasons, quietly but impressively getting on with the job in hand. The car was never really competitive, but Boutsen was always a contender for points, and when Benetton signed him it was a long-overdue promotion.

Results in his first season with Benetton, 1987, were a mite disappointing, with niggling mechanical problems restricting the team's progress, while in 1988 his position was somewhat eroded by the arrival of the gregarious Alessandro Nannini, but Boutsen still finished third, behind the dominant McLarens on four occasions.

Joining Williams with Renault power for 1989 offered Thierry his big chance, but though he did little wrong – indeed he took two brilliant wins in torrential rain at Montreal and Adelaide – it seemed that he didn't quite fit the bill at Didcot, rather unfairly being compared with Nigel Mansell. In 1990, already feeling under-appreciated at Williams, he scored an absolutely superb win in the Hungarian GP, proving he had nerves of steel by fending off Ayrton Senna's late challenge, before he took the only feasible option open to him and signed a two-year deal with Ligier. Despite a massive budget, Ligier made a hash of things as usual, particularly in 1991, when Thierry just kept his head down, hoping things would improve. In fact they did somewhat the following season, when Renault engines became available, but such was the strained atmosphere within the team that at the end of the year the Belgian was probably glad to be out of it. Without a drive for 1993, he was soon called into the Jordan line-up, replacing the crestfallen Ivan Capelli. However, it was an undistinguished swansong, which came to a sad end when Boutsen retired from his farewell Formula 1 race at Spa on the first lap.

In 1994 and 1995, Thierry competed in the German Super Touring championship, but his Ford Mondeo was unable to challenge the dominance of Audi and BMW. On a wider stage, at Le Mans in 1995, he shared the sixth-place Kremer K8-Porsche with Hans Stuck and Christophe Bouchut. A return to sports cars and the sharp end of competition came in 1996, when Thierry was again paired with Stuck, in a works Porsche 911 GT1. After a second place at Le Mans, the experienced duo took end-of-season wins at Brands Hatch and Spa. Although eight top-six finishes were achieved the following year, no victories were forthcoming and both seasoned campaigners were dropped from the works squad.

Next Boutsen moved to the States in 1998 to race a Porsche 911 GT1 in selected US GT championship events, taking third and winning his class at Watkins Glen. He also drove Toyota's exciting Le Mans challenger, the GT-One. He was paired with Geoff Less and Ralf Kelleners, and the trio seemed set for a fairy-tail win until the car failed in the final hour.

Boutsen returned in 1999 for another outing in one of the potent Japanese machines, but the race ended in near disaster for the Belgian when his car was nudged into the barriers by a back-marker. Suffering from cracked vertebrae, he decided it was time to call it a day, retiring to spend more time with his second wife and young family, and to concentrate on building his thriving aviation business, Boutsen Aviation

Thierry Boutsen is still very active in motor racing through the Boutsen Energy Racing team, which aims to promote young talent in motorsport. The team competes in the Formula Le Mans class in the Le Mans Series, and also runs cars in Formula Renault and Eurocup Mégane Trophy.

BOUTSEN, Thierry (B) b 13/7/1957, Brussels

1983 Championship position: Unplaced

	Race	Circuit	No	Entrant	Tyres	Capacity/Car/Engine	Comment	Q Pos/Entries
ret	BELGIAN GP	Spa	30	Arrows Racing Team	G	3.0 Arrows A6-Cosworth V8	rear suspension	18/28
7	US GP (DETROIT)	Detroit	30	Arrows Racing Team	G	3.0 Arrows A6-Cosworth V8	1 lap behind	10/27
7	CANADIAN GP	Montreal	30	Arrows Racing Team	G	3.0 Arrows A6-Cosworth V8	1 lap behind	15/28
15	BRITISH GP	Silverstone	30	Arrows Racing Team	G	3.0 Arrows A6-Cosworth V8	2 laps behind	17/29
9*	GERMAN GP	Hockenheim	30	Arrows Racing Team	G	3.0 Arrows A6-Cosworth V8	*5th place car disqualified/-1 lap	14/29
13	AUSTRIAN GP	Österreichring	30	Arrows Racing Team	G	3.0 Arrows A6-Cosworth V8	pit stop – plugs/5 laps behind	19/29
14/ret	DUTCH GP	Zandvoort	30	Arrows Racing Team	G	3.0 Arrows A6-Cosworth V8	engine/4 laps behind	21/29
ret	ITALIAN GP	Monza	30	Arrows Racing Team	G	3.0 Arrows A6-Cosworth V8	engine	18/29
11	EUROPEAN GP	Brands Hatch	30	Arrows Racing Team	G	3.0 Arrows A6-Cosworth V8	1 lap behind	18/29
9	SOUTH AFRICAN GP	Kyalami	30	Arrows Racing Team	G	3.0 Arrows A6-Cosworth V8	3 laps behind	20/26

1984 Championship position: 14th=   Wins: 0   Pole positions: 0   Fastest laps: 0   Points scored: 5

	Race	Circuit	No	Entrant	Tyres	Capacity/Car/Engine	Comment	Q Pos/Entries
6*	BRAZILIAN GP	Rio	18	Barclay Nordica Arrows BMW	G	3.0 Arrows A6-Cosworth V8	*5th place car disqualified/-1 lap	21/27
12*	SOUTH AFRICAN GP	Kyalami	18	Barclay Nordica Arrows BMW	G	3.0 Arrows A6-Cosworth V8	*11th place car dsq/-5 laps	26/27
ret	BELGIAN GP	Zolder	18	Barclay Nordica Arrows BMW	G	1.5 t/c Arrows A7-BMW 4	misfire	17/27
5*	SAN MARINO GP	Imola	18	Barclay Nordica Arrows BMW	G	3.0 Arrows A6-Cosworth V8	*5th place car disqualified/-1 lap	20/28
11	FRENCH GP	Dijon	18	Barclay Nordica Arrows BMW	G	1.5 t/c Arrows A7-BMW 4	2 laps behind	14/27
dnq	MONACO GP	Monte Carlo	18	Barclay Nordica Arrows BMW	G	1.5 t/c Arrows A7-BMW 4		24/27
ret	CANADIAN GP	Montreal	18	Barclay Nordica Arrows BMW	G	1.5 t/c Arrows A7-BMW 4	engine	18/26
ret	US GP (DETROIT)	Detroit	18	Barclay Nordica Arrows BMW	G	1.5 t/c Arrows A7-BMW 4	engine	13/27
ret	US GP (DALLAS)	Dallas	18	Barclay Nordica Arrows BMW	G	1.5 t/c Arrows A7-BMW 4	hit wall	20/27
ret	BRITISH GP	Brands Hatch	18	Barclay Nordica Arrows BMW	G	1.5 t/c Arrows A7-BMW 4	electrics	12/27
ret	GERMAN GP	Hockenheim	18	Barclay Nordica Arrows BMW	G	1.5 t/c Arrows A7-BMW 4	oil pressure	15/27
5	AUSTRIAN GP	Österreichring	18	Barclay Nordica Arrows BMW	G	1.5 t/c Arrows A7-BMW 4	1 lap behind	17/28
ret	DUTCH GP	Zandvoort	18	Barclay Nordica Arrows BMW	G	1.5 t/c Arrows A7-BMW 4	accident with Arnoux	11/27
10	ITALIAN GP	Monza	18	Barclay Nordica Arrows BMW	G	1.5 t/c Arrows A7-BMW 4	2 pit stops/6 laps behind	19/27
9/ret	EUROPEAN GP	Nürburgring	18	Barclay Nordica Arrows BMW	G	1.5 t/c Arrows A7-BMW 4	electrics/3 laps behind	11/26
ret	PORTUGUESE GP	Estoril	18	Barclay Nordica Arrows BMW	G	1.5 t/c Arrows A7-BMW 4	driveshaft	18/27

1985 Championship position: 11th=   Wins: 0   Pole positions: 0   Fastest laps: 0   Points scored: 11

	Race	Circuit	No	Entrant	Tyres	Capacity/Car/Engine	Comment	Q Pos/Entries
11	BRAZILIAN GP	Rio	18	Barclay Arrows BMW	G	1.5 t/c Arrows A8-BMW 4	late start – fuel pressure/-4 laps	12/25
ret	PORTUGUESE GP	Estoril	18	Barclay Arrows BMW	G	1.5 t/c Arrows A8-BMW 4	electrics	16/26
2*	SAN MARINO GP	Imola	18	Barclay Arrows BMW	G	1.5 t/c Arrows A8-BMW 4	*1st place car disqualified/-1 lap	5/26
9	MONACO GP	Monte Carlo	18	Barclay Arrows BMW	G	1.5 t/c Arrows A8-BMW 4	2 laps behind	6/26
9	CANADIAN GP	Montreal	18	Barclay Arrows BMW	G	1.5 t/c Arrows A8-BMW 4	2 laps behind	7/25
7	US GP (DETROIT)	Detroit	18	Barclay Arrows BMW	G	1.5 t/c Arrows A8-BMW 4	1 lap behind	21/25
9	FRENCH GP	Paul Ricard	18	Barclay Arrows BMW	G	1.5 t/c Arrows A8-BMW 4	1 lap behind	12/26
ret	BRITISH GP	Silverstone	18	Barclay Arrows BMW	G	1.5 t/c Arrows A8-BMW 4	spun off	19/26
4	GERMAN GP	Nürburgring	18	Barclay Arrows BMW	G	1.5 t/c Arrows A8-BMW 4		15/27
8	AUSTRIAN GP	Österreichring	18	Barclay Arrows BMW	G	1.5 t/c Arrows A8-BMW 4	turbo boost problems/-3 laps	16/27
ret	DUTCH GP	Zandvoort	18	Barclay Arrows BMW	G	1.5 t/c Arrows A8-BMW 4	suspension	8/27
9	ITALIAN GP	Monza	18	Barclay Arrows BMW	G	1.5 t/c Arrows A8-BMW 4	1 lap behind	14/26
10/ret	BELGIAN GP	Spa	18	Barclay Arrows BMW	G	1.5 t/c Arrows A8-BMW 4	gearbox/3 laps behind	6/24
6	EUROPEAN GP	Brands Hatch	18	Barclay Arrows BMW	G	1.5 t/c Arrows A8-BMW 4	2 laps behind	12/27
6	SOUTH AFRICAN GP	Kyalami	18	Barclay Arrows BMW	G	1.5 t/c Arrows A8-BMW 4	1 lap behind	10/21
ret	AUSTRALIAN GP	Adelaide	18	Barclay Arrows BMW	G	1.5 t/c Arrows A8-BMW 4	oil leak	11/25

1986 Championship position: Unplaced

	Race	Circuit	No	Entrant	Tyres	Capacity/Car/Engine	Comment	Q Pos/Entries
ret	BRAZILIAN GP	Rio	18	Barclay Arrows BMW	G	1.5 t/c Arrows A8-BMW 4	broken exhaust	15/25
7	SPANISH GP	Jerez	18	Barclay Arrows BMW	G	1.5 t/c Arrows A8-BMW 4	4 laps behind	19/25
7	SAN MARINO GP	Imola	18	Barclay Arrows BMW	G	1.5 t/c Arrows A8-BMW 4	2 laps behind	12/26
8	MONACO GP	Monte Carlo	18	Barclay Arrows BMW	G	1.5 t/c Arrows A8-BMW 4	3 laps behind	14/26
ret	BELGIAN GP	Spa	18	Barclay Arrows BMW	G	1.5 t/c Arrows A8-BMW 4	electrics	14/25
ret	CANADIAN GP	Montreal	18	Barclay Arrows BMW	G	1.5 t/c Arrows A8-BMW 4	electrics	12/25
ret	US GP (DETROIT)	Detroit	18	Barclay Arrows BMW	G	1.5 t/c Arrows A8-BMW 4	accident – hit by Arnoux	13/26
nc	FRENCH GP	Paul Ricard	18	Barclay Arrows BMW	G	1.5 t/c Arrows A8-BMW 4	pit stops – bodywork/-13 laps	21/26
nc	BRITISH GP	Brands Hatch	18	Barclay Arrows BMW	G	1.5 t/c Arrows A8-BMW 4	pit stop – electrics/13 laps behind	13/26
ret	GERMAN GP	Hockenheim	18	Barclay Arrows BMW	G	1.5 t/c Arrows A9-BMW 4	turbo	21/26
ret	HUNGARIAN GP	Hungaroring	18	Barclay Arrows BMW	G	1.5 t/c Arrows A8-BMW 4	electrics	22/26
dns	“	“	18	Barclay Arrows BMW	G	1.5 t/c Arrows A9-BMW 4	practice only	– / –
ret	AUSTRIAN GP	Österreichring	18	Barclay Arrows BMW	G	1.5 t/c Arrows A9-BMW 4	turbo	18/26
dns	“	“	18	Barclay Arrows BMW	G	1.5 t/c Arrows A8-BMW 4	practice only	– / –
7	ITALIAN GP	Monza	18	Barclay Arrows BMW	G	1.5 t/c Arrows A8-BMW 4	2 laps behind	13/27
10	PORTUGUESE GP	Estoril	18	Barclay Arrows BMW	G	1.5 t/c Arrows A8-BMW 4	3 laps behind	21/27
7	MEXICAN GP	Mexico City	18	Barclay Arrows BMW	G	1.5 t/c Arrows A8-BMW 4	2 laps behind	21/26
ret	AUSTRALIAN GP	Adelaide	18	Barclay Arrows BMW	G	1.5 t/c Arrows A8-BMW 4	throttle spring	22/26

1987 Championship position: 8th   Wins: 0   Pole positions: 0   Fastest laps: 0   Points scored: 16

	Race	Circuit	No	Entrant	Tyres	Capacity/Car/Engine	Comment	Q Pos/Entries
5	BRAZILIAN GP	Rio	20	Benetton Formula Ltd	G	1.5 t/c Benetton B187-Cosworth V6	1 lap behind	6/23
ret	SAN MARINO GP	Imola	20	Benetton Formula Ltd	G	1.5 t/c Benetton B187-Cosworth V6	engine	12/27
ret	BELGIAN GP	Spa	20	Benetton Formula Ltd	G	1.5 t/c Benetton B187-Cosworth V6	driveshaft	7/26
ret	MONACO GP	Monte Carlo	20	Benetton Formula Ltd	G	1.5 t/c Benetton B187-Cosworth V6	driveshaft	9/26
ret	US GP (DETROIT)	Detroit	20	Benetton Formula Ltd	G	1.5 t/c Benetton B187-Cosworth V6	brake disc	4/26
ret	FRENCH GP	Paul Ricard	20	Benetton Formula Ltd	G	1.5 t/c Benetton B187-Cosworth V6	distributor drive	5/26
7	BRITISH GP	Silverstone	20	Benetton Formula Ltd	G	1.5 t/c Benetton B187-Cosworth V6	3 laps behind	5/26
ret	GERMAN GP	Hockenheim	20	Benetton Formula Ltd	G	1.5 t/c Benetton B187-Cosworth V6	engine	6/26
4	HUNGARIAN GP	Hungaroring	20	Benetton Formula Ltd	G	1.5 t/c Benetton B187-Cosworth V6	1 lap behind	7/26
4	AUSTRIAN GP	Österreichring	20	Benetton Formula Ltd	G	1.5 t/c Benetton B187-Cosworth V6	1 lap behind	4/26
5	ITALIAN GP	Monza	20	Benetton Formula Ltd	G	1.5 t/c Benetton B187-Cosworth V6		6/28
14	PORTUGUESE GP	Estoril	20	Benetton Formula Ltd	G	1.5 t/c Benetton B187-Cosworth V6	pit stop – engine/6 laps behind	9/27

16/ret	SPANISH GP	Jerez	20	Benetton Formula Ltd	G	1.5 t/c Benetton B187-Cosworth V6	spun off – brakes	8/28
ret	MEXICAN GP	Mexico City	20	Benetton Formula Ltd	G	1.5 t/c Benetton B187-Cosworth V6	electrics	4/27
5	JAPANESE GP	Suzuka	20	Benetton Formula Ltd	G	1.5 t/c Benetton B187-Cosworth V6		3/27
3*	AUSTRALIAN GP	Adelaide	20	Benetton Formula Ltd	G	1.5 t/c Benetton B187-Cosworth V6	*2nd place car disqualified/-1 lap	5/27

1988 Championship position: 4th   Wins: 0   Pole positions: 0   Fastest laps: 0   Points scored: 27

7	BRAZILIAN GP	Rio	20	Benetton Formula Ltd	G	3.5 Benetton B188-Cosworth V8	1 lap behind	7/31
4	SAN MARINO GP	Imola	20	Benetton Formula Ltd	G	3.5 Benetton B188-Cosworth V8	fractured exhaust/1 lap behind	8/31
8	MONACO GP	Monte Carlo	20	Benetton Formula Ltd	G	3.5 Benetton B188-Cosworth V8	2 laps behind	16/30
8	MEXICAN GP	Mexico City	20	Benetton Formula Ltd	G	3.5 Benetton B188-Cosworth V8	handling problems/3 laps behind	11/30
3	CANADIAN GP	Montreal	20	Benetton Formula Ltd	G	3.5 Benetton B188-Cosworth V8		7/31
3	US GP (DETROIT)	Detroit	20	Benetton Formula Ltd	G	3.5 Benetton B188-Cosworth V8	1 lap behind	5/31
ret	FRENCH GP	Paul Ricard	20	Benetton Formula Ltd	G	3.5 Benetton B188-Cosworth V8	electrics	5/31
ret	BRITISH GP	Silverstone	20	Benetton Formula Ltd	G	3.5 Benetton B188-Cosworth V8	driveshaft – c.v. joint	12/31
6	GERMAN GP	Hockenheim	20	Benetton Formula Ltd	G	3.5 Benetton B188-Cosworth V8	dry set up – wet race/1 lap behind	9/31
3	HUNGARIAN GP	Hungaroring	20	Benetton Formula Ltd	G	3.5 Benetton B188-Cosworth V8		3/31
dsq*	BELGIAN GP	Spa	20	Benetton Formula Ltd	G	3.5 Benetton B188-Cosworth V8	*3rd on the road/illegal fuel	6/31
6	ITALIAN GP	Monza	20	Benetton Formula Ltd	G	3.5 Benetton B188-Cosworth V8	misfire	8/31
3	PORTUGUESE GP	Estoril	20	Benetton Formula Ltd	G	3.5 Benetton B188-Cosworth V8		13/31
9	SPANISH GP	Jerez	20	Benetton Formula Ltd	G	3.5 Benetton B188-Cosworth V8	pit stop – replaced nose cone	4/31
3	JAPANESE GP	Suzuka	20	Benetton Formula Ltd	G	3.5 Benetton B188-Cosworth V8		10/31
5	AUSTRALIAN GP	Adelaide	20	Benetton Formula Ltd	G	3.5 Benetton B188-Cosworth V8	misfire/broken exhaust/-1 lap	10/31

1989 Championship position: 5th   Wins: 0   Pole positions: 0   Fastest laps: 0   Points scored: 37

ret	BRAZILIAN GP	Rio	5	Canon Williams Team	G	3.5 Williams FW12C-Renault V10	engine	4/38
4	SAN MARINO GP	Imola	5	Canon Williams Team	G	3.5 Williams FW12C-Renault V10	understeer/clutch/1 lap behind	6/39
10	MONACO GP	Monte Carlo	5	Canon Williams Team	G	3.5 Williams FW12C-Renault V10	pit stop – rear wing/3 laps behind	3/38
ret	MEXICAN GP	Mexico City	5	Canon Williams Team	G	3.5 Williams FW12C-Renault V10	electrics	8/39
6	US GP (PHOENIX)	Phoenix	5	Canon Williams Team	G	3.5 Williams FW12C-Renault V10	pit stop-puncture/1 lap behind	16/39
1	CANADIAN GP	Montreal	5	Canon Williams Team	G	3.5 Williams FW12C-Renault V10		6/39
ret	FRENCH GP	Paul Ricard	5	Canon Williams Team	G	3.5 Williams FW12C-Renault V10	gearbox	5/39
10	BRITISH GP	Silverstone	5	Canon Williams Team	G	3.5 Williams FW12C-Renault V10	clutch problems/2 laps behind	7/39
ret	GERMAN GP	Hockenheim	5	Canon Williams Team	G	3.5 Williams FW12C-Renault V10	collision with Pirro – spun off	6/39
3	HUNGARIAN GP	Hungaroring	5	Canon Williams Team	G	3.5 Williams FW12C-Renault V10		4/39
4	BELGIAN GP	Spa	5	Canon Williams Team	G	3.5 Williams FW12C-Renault V10		4/39
3	ITALIAN GP	Monza	5	Canon Williams Team	G	3.5 Williams FW12C-Renault V10		6/39
ret	PORTUGUESE GP	Estoril	5	Canon Williams Team	G	3.5 Williams FW13-Renault V10	overheating	8/39
ret	SPANISH GP	Jerez	5	Canon Williams Team	G	3.5 Williams FW13-Renault V10	fuel pressure – pump	22/38
3*	JAPANESE GP	Suzuka	5	Canon Williams Team	G	3.5 Williams FW13-Renault V10	*1st place car disqualified	7/39
1	AUSTRALIAN GP	Adelaide	5	Canon Williams Team	G	3.5 Williams FW13-Renault V10		5/39

1990 Championship position: 6th   Wins: 0   Pole positions: 1   Fastest laps: 1   Points scored: 34

3	US GP (PHOENIX)	Phoenix	5	Canon Williams Renault	G	3.5 Williams FW13B-Renault V10	engine cutting out	9/35
5	BRAZILIAN GP	Interlagos	5	Canon Williams Renault	G	3.5 Williams FW13B-Renault V10	long stop – tyres – nose/-1 lap	3/35
ret	SAN MARINO GP	Imola	5	Canon Williams Renault	G	3.5 Williams FW13B-Renault V10	missed gear – engine	4/34
4	MONACO GP	Monte Carlo	5	Canon Williams Renault	G	3.5 Williams FW13B-Renault V10	throttle problems/1 lap behind	6/35
ret	CANADIAN GP	Montreal	5	Canon Williams Renault	G	3.5 Williams FW13B-Renault V10	spun and collided with Larini	6/35
5	MEXICAN GP	Mexico City	5	Canon Williams Renault	G	3.5 Williams FW13B-Renault V10	brake problems	5/35
ret	FRENCH GP	Paul Ricard	5	Canon Williams Renault	G	3.5 Williams FW13B-Renault V10	engine	8/35
2	BRITISH GP	Silverstone	5	Canon Williams Renault	G	3.5 Williams FW13B-Renault V10	blistered tyres	4/35
6	GERMAN GP	Hockenheim	5	Canon Williams Renault	G	3.5 Williams FW13B-Renault V10	FL	6/35
1	HUNGARIAN GP	Hungaroring	5	Canon Williams Renault	G	3.5 Williams FW13B-Renault V10		1/35
ret	BELGIAN GP	Spa	5	Canon Williams Renault	G	3.5 Williams FW13B-Renault V10	transmission	4/33
ret	ITALIAN GP	Monza	5	Canon Williams Renault	G	3.5 Williams FW13B-Renault V10	suspension	6/33
ret	PORTUGUESE GP	Estoril	5	Canon Williams Renault	G	3.5 Williams FW13B-Renault V10	gearbox	7/33
4	SPANISH GP	Jerez	5	Canon Williams Renault	G	3.5 Williams FW13B-Renault V10	collision with Berger	7/33
5	JAPANESE GP	Suzuka	5	Canon Williams Renault	G	3.5 Williams FW13B-Renault V10	long pit stop – tyres	5/30
5	AUSTRALIAN GP	Adelaide	5	Canon Williams Renault	G	3.5 Williams FW13B-Renault V10	pit stop – tyres	9/30

1991 Championship position: Unplaced

ret	US GP (PHOENIX)	Phoenix	25	Ligier Gitanes	G	3.5 Ligier JS35-Lamborghini V12	electrics	20/34
10	BRAZILIAN GP	Interlagos	25	Ligier Gitanes	G	3.5 Ligier JS35-Lamborghini V12	3 laps behind	18/34
7	SAN MARINO GP	Imola	25	Ligier Gitanes	G	3.5 Ligier JS35-Lamborghini V12	cracked exhaust/3 laps behind	24/34

Boutsen led the 1990 Hungarian Grand Prix from start to finish in his Williams-Renault. Nannini's Benetton and Senna's McLaren follow, but the unlucky Italian was unceremoniously bundled out of the race by the Brazilian when well placed to win. Senna was just a few feet adrift of the Belgian at the finish.

7	MONACO GP	Monte Carlo	25	Ligier Gitanes	G	3.5 Ligier JS35-Lamborghini V12	2 laps behind	16/34
ret	CANADIAN GP	Montreal	25	Ligier Gitanes	G	3.5 Ligier JS35-Lamborghini V12	engine	16/34
8	MEXICAN GP	Mexico City	25	Ligier Gitanes	G	3.5 Ligier JS35-Lamborghini V12	2 laps behind	14/34
12	FRENCH GP	Magny Cours	25	Ligier Gitanes	G	3.5 Ligier JS35B-Lamborghini V12	3 laps behind	16/34
ret	BRITISH GP	Silverstone	25	Ligier Gitanes	G	3.5 Ligier JS35B-Lamborghini V12	engine	19/34
9	GERMAN GP	Hockenheim	25	Ligier Gitanes	G	3.5 Ligier JS35B-Lamborghini V12	1 lap behind	17/34
17/ret	HUNGARIAN GP	Hungaroring	25	Ligier Gitanes	G	3.5 Ligier JS35B-Lamborghini V12	engine/6 laps behind	19/34
11	BELGIAN GP	Spa	25	Ligier Gitanes	G	3.5 Ligier JS35B-Lamborghini V12	1 lap behind	18/34
ret	ITALIAN GP	Monza	25	Ligier Gitanes	G	3.5 Ligier JS35B-Lamborghini V12	spun off on lap 1	21/34
16	PORTUGUESE GP	Estoril	25	Ligier Gitanes	G	3.5 Ligier JS35B-Lamborghini V12	3 laps behind	20/34
ret	SPANISH GP	Barcelona	25	Ligier Gitanes	G	3.5 Ligier JS35B-Lamborghini V12	spun off on lap 1	26/33
9	JAPANESE GP	Suzuka	25	Ligier Gitanes	G	3.5 Ligier JS35B-Lamborghini V12	1 lap behind	17/31
ret	AUSTRALIAN GP	Adelaide	25	Ligier Gitanes	G	3.5 Ligier JS35B-Lamborghini V12	collision with Nakajima	20/32

1992 Championship position: 14th= Wins: 0 Pole positions: 0 Fastest laps: 0 Points scored: 2

ret	SOUTH AFRICAN GP	Kyalami	25	Ligier Gitanes Blondes	G	3.5 Ligier JS37-Renault V10	engine	14/30
10	MEXICAN GP	Mexico City	25	Ligier Gitanes Blondes	G	3.5 Ligier JS37-Renault V10	2 laps behind	22/30
ret	BRAZILIAN GP	Interlagos	25	Ligier Gitanes Blondes	G	3.5 Ligier JS37-Renault V10	collision with Comas	10/31
ret	SPANISH GP	Barcelona	25	Ligier Gitanes Blondes	G	3.5 Ligier JS37-Renault V10	engine	14/32
ret	SAN MARINO GP	Imola	25	Ligier Gitanes Blondes	G	3.5 Ligier JS37-Renault V10	fuel pump	10/32
12	MONACO GP	Monte Carlo	25	Ligier Gitanes Blondes	G	3.5 Ligier JS37-Renault V10	3 laps behind	22/32
10	CANADIAN GP	Montreal	25	Ligier Gitanes Blondes	G	3.5 Ligier JS37-Renault V10	2 laps behind	21/32
ret	FRENCH GP	Magny Cours	25	Ligier Gitanes Blondes	G	3.5 Ligier JS37-Renault V10	spun off	9/30
10	BRITISH GP	Silverstone	25	Ligier Gitanes Blondes	G	3.5 Ligier JS37-Renault V10	2 laps behind	13/32
7	GERMAN GP	Hockenheim	25	Ligier Gitanes Blondes	G	3.5 Ligier JS37-Renault V10		8/32
ret	HUNGARIAN GP	Hungaroring	25	Ligier Gitanes Blondes	G	3.5 Ligier JS37-Renault V10	collision with Comas on lap 1	8/31
ret	BELGIAN GP	Spa	25	Ligier Gitanes Blondes	G	3.5 Ligier JS37-Renault V10	crashed at Blanchimont	7/30
ret	ITALIAN GP	Monza	25	Ligier Gitanes Blondes	G	3.5 Ligier JS37-Renault V10	electrics	8/28
8	PORTUGUESE GP	Estoril	25	Ligier Gitanes Blondes	G	3.5 Ligier JS37-Renault V10	2 laps behind	11/26
ret	JAPANESE GP	Suzuka	25	Ligier Gitanes Blondes	G	3.5 Ligier JS37-Renault V10	gearbox	10/26
5	AUSTRALIAN GP	Adelaide	25	Ligier Gitanes Blondes	G	3.5 Ligier JS37-Renault V10	1 lap behind	22/26

1993 Championship position: Unplaced

ret	EUROPEAN GP	Donington	15	Sasol Jordan	G	3.5 Jordan 193-Hart V10	throttle problems	19/26
ret	SAN MARINO GP	Imola	15	Sasol Jordan	G	3.5 Jordan 193-Hart V10	gearbox hydraulic failure	19/26
11	SPANISH GP	Barcelona	15	Sasol Jordan	G	3.5 Jordan 193-Hart V10	throttle/fuel pressure/-3 laps	21/26
ret	MONACO GP	Monte Carlo	15	Sasol Jordan	G	3.5 Jordan 193-Hart V10	suspension	23/26
12	CANADIAN GP	Montreal	15	Sasol Jordan	G	3.5 Jordan 193-Hart V10	2 laps behind	24/26
11	FRENCH GP	Magny Cours	15	Sasol Jordan	G	3.5 Jordan 193-Hart V10	2 laps behind	20/26
ret	BRITISH GP	Silverstone	15	Sasol Jordan	G	3.5 Jordan 193-Hart V10	wheel bearing	23/26
13	GERMAN GP	Hockenheim	15	Sasol Jordan	G	3.5 Jordan 193-Hart V10	ran without tyre change	24/26
9	HUNGARIAN GP	Hungaroring	15	Sasol Jordan	G	3.5 Jordan 193-Hart V10	2 laps behind	24/26
ret	BELGIAN GP	Spa	15	Sasol Jordan	G	3.5 Jordan 193-Hart V10	gearbox on lap 1	20/25

GP Starts: 163   GP Wins: 3   Pole positions: 1   Fastest laps: 1   Points: 132

BRABHAM, David (AUS) b 5/9/1965, Wimbledon, London, England

1990 Championship position: Unplaced

	Race	Circuit	No	Entrant	Tyres	Capacity/Car/Engine	Comment	Q Pos/Entries
dnq	SAN MARINO GP	Imola	7	Motor Racing Developments	P	3.5 Brabham BT59-Judd V8		30/34
ret	MONACO GP	Monte Carlo	7	Motor Racing Developments	P	3.5 Brabham BT59-Judd V8	driveshaft – c.v. joint	25/35
dnq	CANADIAN GP	Montreal	7	Motor Racing Developments	P	3.5 Brabham BT59-Judd V8		30/35
ret	MEXICAN GP	Mexico City	7	Motor Racing Developments	P	3.5 Brabham BT59-Judd V8	electrics	21/35
15*	FRENCH GP	Paul Ricard	7	Motor Racing Developments	P	3.5 Brabham BT59-Judd V8	*15th place car dsq/-3 laps	25/35
dnq	BRITISH GP	Silverstone	7	Motor Racing Developments	P	3.5 Brabham BT59-Judd V8		28/35
ret	GERMAN GP	Hockenheim	7	Motor Racing Developments	P	3.5 Brabham BT59-Judd V8	engine	21/35
dnq	HUNGARIAN GP	Hungaroring	7	Motor Racing Developments	P	3.5 Brabham BT59-Judd V8		28/35
ret	BELGIAN GP	Spa	7	Motor Racing Developments	P	3.5 Brabham BT59-Judd V8	electrics	24/33
dnq	ITALIAN GP	Monza	7	Motor Racing Developments	P	3.5 Brabham BT59-Judd V8		29/33
ret	PORTUGUESE GP	Estoril	7	Motor Racing Developments	P	3.5 Brabham BT59-Judd V8	gearbox	26/33
dnq	SPANISH GP	Jerez	7	Motor Racing Developments	P	3.5 Brabham BT59-Judd V8		27/33
ret	JAPANESE GP	Suzuka	7	Motor Racing Developments	P	3.5 Brabham BT59-Judd V8	clutch	23/30
ret	AUSTRALIAN GP	Adelaide	7	Motor Racing Developments	P	3.5 Brabham BT59-Judd V8	spun off	25/30

1994 Championship position: Unplaced

12	BRAZILIAN GP	Interlagos	31	MTV Simtek Ford	G	3.5 Simtek S941-Ford HB V8	4 laps behind	26/28
ret	PACIFIC GP	T.I. Circuit	31	MTV Simtek Ford	G	3.5 Simtek S941-Ford HB V8	electrics	25/26
ret	SAN MARINO GP	Imola	31	MTV Simtek Ford	G	3.5 Simtek S941-Ford HB V8	accident after steering failure	24/28
ret	MONACO GP	Monte Carlo	31	MTV Simtek Ford	G	3.5 Simtek S941-Ford HB V8	broken suspension	22/24
10	SPANISH GP	Barcelona	31	MTV Simtek Ford	G	3.5 Simtek S941-Ford HB V8	4 laps behind	24/27
14	CANADIAN GP	Montreal	31	MTV Simtek Ford	G	3.5 Simtek S941-Ford HB V8	4 laps behind	25/27
ret	FRENCH GP	Magny Cours	31	MTV Simtek Ford	G	3.5 Simtek S941-Ford HB V8	gearbox	25/28
15*	BRITISH GP	Silverstone	31	MTV Simtek Ford	G	3.5 Simtek S941-Ford HB V8	*2nd place car dsq/-3 laps	25/28
ret	GERMAN GP	Hockenheim	31	MTV Simtek Ford	G	3.5 Simtek S941-Ford HB V8	clutch	25/28
11	HUNGARIAN GP	Hungaroring	31	MTV Simtek Ford	G	3.5 Simtek S941-Ford HB V8	3 laps behind	23/28
ret	BELGIAN GP	Spa	31	MTV Simtek Ford	G	3.5 Simtek S941-Ford HB V8	lost wheel after pit stop	21/28
ret	ITALIAN GP	Monza	31	MTV Simtek Ford	G	3.5 Simtek S941-Ford HB V8	brakes	26/28
ret	PORTUGUESE GP	Estoril	31	MTV Simtek Ford	G	3.5 Simtek S941-Ford HB V8	collision with Alesi	24/28
ret	EUROPEAN GP	Jerez	31	MTV Simtek Ford	G	3.5 Simtek S941-Ford HB V8	engine	25/28
12	JAPANESE GP	Suzuka	31	MTV Simtek Ford	G	3.5 Simtek S941-Ford HB V8	2 laps behind	24/28
ret	AUSTRALIAN GP	Adelaide	31	MTV Simtek Ford	G	3.5 Simtek S941-Ford HB V8	engine	24/28

GP Starts: 24   GP Wins: 0   Pole positions: 0   Fastest laps: 0   Points: 0

DAVID BRABHAM

THE youngest of the Brabham dynasty, David is the only one of three brothers to have emulated his father by starting in a world championship grand prix. Although he never matched the achievements of his legendary father, he did become one of the finest sports car drivers of his generation, with an outstanding cv crowned by an outright win at Le Mans in 2009.

A quick learner, David soon outgrew the Australian and New Zealand single-seater scene and headed first to the States to race in Formula Atlantic, then to England in 1988, initially to contest the Formula Vauxhall Lotus championship. This proved a backward step, but a switch to Class B of the Formula 3 series was an instant success, Brabham winning five times from just nine starts. Moving up to Class A with the Jewson-backed Bowman Ralt in 1989, he had a season-long battle for the F3 championship with Allan McNish, which was only resolved in David's favour on appeal the following February. With a win in the prestigious Macau F3 race, he seemed set for a year in F3000 with Middlebridge Racing, but unexpectedly this became a grand prix chance with the team when Gregor Foitek quit his seat after just two races of the 1990 season. Brabham applied himself sensibly and did as much as a novice could be expected to do in an uncompetitive car, but he was not retained at season's end.

Turning to sports cars, David drove for TWR Jaguar in 1991 (winning at the Nürburgring with Derek Warwick) and Toyota in 1992 while waiting for the opportunity to return to grand prix racing, which finally presented itself when the ambitious, but unproven Simtek team hired him to lead their Formula 1 assault in 1994. It was a character building year in which David was the team's mainstay, following the tragic death of team-mate Roland Ratzenberger. He had to cope with being paired with no fewer than four other drivers, and his determination and dedication in the face of adversity (which included a huge testing accident at Silverstone) were exemplary.

With Nick Wirth's fledgling outfit facing an uncertain future at the beginning of 1995, David amicably took his leave for the chance of a paid seat with BMW in the ever-growing BTCC. The aerodynamic regulations and rear-wheel-drive configuration of the 318i left him at a great disadvantage, but typically he got on with the job and was certainly not overshadowed by his much more experienced team-mate, multiple saloon champion Johnny Cecotto.

David understandably grabbed the chance to contest the 1996 All-Japan GT championship in McLaren F1 GTR and had the satisfaction of snatching the title from main rival Ralf Schumacher. At the end of the year, driving a BMW 320i, he joined brother Geoff to capture victory in the Bathurst 1000 after their team-mates were disqualifed.

His success in GT racing brought the opportunity to race a Panoz in 1997, and he quickly became a standard-bearer for the marque, putting in a succession of excellent performances over the next six seasons, which saw him become a regular contender for honours.

His disappointment must have been immense when he found himself pipped at the last in the 1999 American Le Mans Series by a team that had failed to register a single win, but had benefited from the idiosyncratic points system. A true gentleman, however, and one of motor racing's most sporting competitors, David was the first to congratulate the victors.

Brabham's skills and experience also saw him much in demand in top-line sports prototypes and GTs, as he worked first with the Bentley (taking second place at Le Mans with Johnny Herbert and Mark Blundell in 2003) and then the Prodrive Aston Martin, with which he was a double GTI class winner at Le Mans in 2007 and 2008, before his outright win the following year, when (with Alex Würz and Marc Gené) he gave Peugeot its win over Audi.

In 2007, David moved back into prototypes, being teamed with the experienced Stefan Johansson for the newly created Highcroft team, one of just three outfits running the Honda-engined Acura chassis. Four second-place finishes in 2008 were the springboard for championship success the following year, when he was teamed with Scott Sharp, the pair taking three wins on their way to the LMP1 title.

Running to LMP2 rules in 2010, The Patrón Highcroft Racing outfit scored another convincing championship win courtesy of David and his new driving partner, Simon Pagenaud. The pair took consecutive wins at Long Beach, Laguna Seca and Miller to underpin their success.

With Highcroft at the end of their programme and their future plans uncertain, David returned to GT racing In 2011, driving a Nissan GT-R with Sumo Power. He remained busier than ever for 2012, with plans to contest the Blancpain Endurance Series in a McLaren MP4-12C GT3 and to return to prototypes in the inaugural FIA World Endurance Championship, driving the Honda Performance Development ARX-03a for JRM, alongside team-mates Karun Chandhok and Peter Dumbreck.

SIR JACK BRABHAM, OBE

MUCH has been made of Sir Jack Brabham's achievement in becoming the only driver to win the world championship in a car of his own make. But that is only part of the story, for he was also the man who was largely responsible for developing the rear-engined Cooper, which changed the face of Formula 1 for ever; who went to Indianapolis in 1961 and shook the establishment; who built not only his own grand prix challenger, but also a succession of superb Formula 2 cars that allowed so many drivers to shine; and who was competitive to the end of his long career. Bowing out at the age of 44 in 1970, he could still show the youngsters a trick or two!

Jack had spent a number of years in the cut and thrust of midget racing on the cinder tracks of his native Australia, winning four successive titles between 1948 and 1951, before switching to hill-climbs, taking the championship in 1953. That season, Jack was bought a Cooper-Bristol, which was christened the RedeX Special, and he began to clean up with it. Eager to progress, however, he moved to England in 1955 and soon joined up with the Cooper team, making an early grand prix debut in the 'Bobtail' special. Although he drove a Maserati 250F in 1956, taking third places in the Aintree 200 and the Vanwall Trophy at Snetterton, he spent most of the season racing Cooper's 1500cc sports car while developing the Formula 2 car, which he would use to such great effect in 1957.

In 1958, Stirling Moss won the Argentine GP with Rob Walker's little Cooper, proving that the car could be a serious contender, and Jack persevered with the works machine, steadily honing the ground-breaking design on a race-by-race basis. He took occasional national wins, for example in the London Trophy and the Gold Cup, before the start of two golden years in 1959/60, when the Cooper proved, if not always unbeatable, at least very reliable, and Brabham won his first two championship titles, taking seven grand prix wins in the process. Other victories included the Brussels and Pau GPs in 1960, and the International Trophy in 1961, the year the team's fortunes began to slip.

In 1962, Jack branched out on his own, using a Lotus as a stop-gap while his first Brabham was completed. It was late in the season before the BT3 appeared, but this simple spaceframe car was very effective, soon taking world championship points and a second place in the non-title Mexican GP. For 1963, he signed Dan Gurney to drive for the team, and with such a fine driver on board he sometimes took a back seat, but his delight on the occasions when he beat the lanky Californian was obvious. Although he did not manage a championship win with his Brabham in the 1.5-litre formula, he scored a number of non-title victories, including races at Solitude and Zeltweg in 1963, and the International Trophy and Aintree 200 in 1964. In addition, he was very successful during the winter trips down-under for the Tasman series and in the newly introduced Formula 2, where he took four first places and two seconds in seven 1964 starts.

Brabham's finest season was 1966, when he won four championship grands prix with the ultra-reliable Repco-engined car to secure his third title, in addition to the F1 International Trophy and Gold Cup races, and no fewer than ten Formula 2 events in the Brabham-Honda. For 1967, reliability paid dividends once more: Jack took a couple of wins, but Denny Hulme won the title for Brabham before heading off to McLaren.

The Repco success was a minor miracle that couldn't last, and it didn't, with the four-cam 1968 engine a disastrous failure that blighted the season. Brabham switched to Ford power for 1969 and signed Jacky Ickx, but still won the International Trophy and had another crack at Indianapolis, which ended in retirement with ignition troubles.

In 1970, Jack's final year, he was quickly out of the traps with a runaway victory in South Africa, before enduring the heartache of losing a win at Monaco on the last corner when pressured into a mistake by Jochen Rindt. He also led the British GP until he ran out of fuel on the last lap, with Rindt once again the beneficiary. Brabham reflected that he should have won the championship that year, but retired mainly due to the pressure from his wife Betty, who had seen so many of his contemporaries perish.

Upon his retirement, Brabham sold up and walked away from racing, returning to Australia to spend more time on his other business interests, which included a farm and an engine company. But the sport would not let him go. Despite taking his three sons, Geoff, Gary and David, back to Australia, they all became successful drivers in their own right, and the 'old man' was often seen at the circuits, proffering his advice, no doubt, in his own inimitable and economical way.

He was a frequent visitor to historic festivals and drove with some verve, despite a nasty accident at the Goodwood Revival meeting in 2000, which put him in hospital.

By 2011, Brabham, the oldest surviving world champion, was no longer in good health, but he still managed to put in an appearance at Melbourne, as the old master of that select band of Australian drivers who have appeared in grand prix racing.

He was awarded the OBE following his third world championship in 1966 and was the first post-war racing driver to be knighted, receiving the honour in 1978 for services to motorsport. He has received several other honours, too, including the Australian Sports Medal and the Centenary Medal. In 2011, the suburb of Brabham in Perth, Western Australia, was named after him.

BRABHAM, Sir Jack (AUS) b 2/4/1926, Hurstville, nr Sydney

1955 Championship position: Unplaced

	Race	Circuit	No	Entrant	Tyres	Capacity/Car/Engine	Comment	Q Pos/Entries
ret	BRITISH GP	Aintree	40	Cooper Car Co	D	2.0 Cooper T40-Bristol 6	valve	25/25

1956 Championship position: Unplaced

	Race	Circuit	No	Entrant	Tyres	Capacity/Car/Engine	Comment	Q Pos/Entries
ret	BRITISH GP	Silverstone	30	Jack Brabham	D	2.5 Maserati 250F 6	engine	28/28

1957 Championship position: Unplaced

	Race	Circuit	No	Entrant	Tyres	Capacity/Car/Engine	Comment	Q Pos/Entries
6	MONACO GP	Monte Carlo	14	Cooper Car Co/R R C Walker	D	2.0 Cooper T43-Climax 4	out of fuel-pushed car home/-5 laps	15/21
ret	FRENCH GP	Rouen	22	Cooper Car Co	D	2.0 Cooper T43-Climax 4	hit straw bales	13/15
7	"	"	24	Cooper Car Co	D	1.5 Cooper T43-Climax 4	took over MacDowel's car/-9 laps	– / –
ret	BRITISH GP	Aintree	34	R R C Walker	D	2.0 Cooper T43-Climax 4	clutch	13/19
ret	GERMAN GP (F2)	Nürburgring	24	Cooper Car Co	D	1.5 Cooper T43-Climax 4	transmission	18/24
7	PESCARA GP	Pescara	24	Cooper Car Co	D	1.5 Cooper T43-Climax 4	pit stop – fuel/3 laps behind	16/16

1958 Championship position: 14th=   Wins: 0   Pole positions: 0   Fastest laps: 0   Points scored: 3

	Race	Circuit	No	Entrant	Tyres	Capacity/Car/Engine	Comment	Q Pos/Entries
4	MONACO GP	Monte Carlo	16	Cooper Car Co	D	2.2 Cooper T45-Climax 4	3 laps behind	3/28
8	DUTCH GP	Zandvoort	8	Cooper Car Co	D	2.0 Cooper T45-Climax 4	2 laps behind	5/17
ret	BELGIAN GP	Spa	22	Cooper Car Co	D	2.2 Cooper T45-Climax 4	overheating	8/20
6	FRENCH GP	Reims	22	Cooper Car Co	D	2.2 Cooper T45-Climax 4	1 lap behind	12/21
6	BRITISH GP	Silverstone	11	Cooper Car Co	D	2.0 Cooper T45-Climax 4		10/21
ret	GERMAN GP (F2)	Nürburgring	24	Cooper Car Co	D	1.5 Cooper T45-Climax 4	accident	10/26
7	PORTUGUESE GP	Oporto	14	Cooper Car Co	D	2.2 Cooper T45-Climax 4	2 laps behind	8/15
ret	ITALIAN GP	Monza	4	Cooper Car Co	D	2.0 Cooper T45-Climax 4	collision with Gendebien on lap 1	15/21
11*	MOROCCAN GP (F2)	Casablanca	50	Cooper Car Co	D	1.5 Cooper T45-Climax 4	*1st in F2 class/4 laps behind	19/25

1959 WORLD CHAMPION   Wins: 2   Pole positions: 1   Fastest laps: 1   Points scored: 34

	Race	Circuit	No	Entrant	Tyres	Capacity/Car/Engine	Comment	Q Pos/Entries
1	MONACO GP	Monte Carlo	24	Cooper Car Co	D	2.5 Cooper T51-Climax 4	FL	3/24
2	DUTCH GP	Zandvoort	8	Cooper Car Co	D	2.5 Cooper T51-Climax 4		2/15
3	FRENCH GP	Reims	8	Cooper Car Co	D	2.5 Cooper T51-Climax 4		2/22
1	BRITISH GP	Aintree	12	Cooper Car Co	D	2.5 Cooper T51-Climax 4		1/30
ret	GERMAN GP	AVUS	1	Cooper Car Co	D	2.5 Cooper T51-Climax 4	clutch – heat 1	4/16
ret	PORTUGUESE GP	Monsanto	1	Cooper Car Co	D	2.5 Cooper T51-Climax 4	accident with Cabral/hit straw bales	2/16
3	ITALIAN GP	Monza	12	Cooper Car Co	D	2.5 Cooper T51-Climax 4		3/21
4	US GP	Sebring	8	Cooper Car Co	D	2.5 Cooper T51-Climax 4	out of fuel/pushed car over line	2/19
dns	"	"	8	Cooper Car Co	D	2.5 Cooper T45-Climax 4	practice only	– / –

1960 WORLD CHAMPION   Wins: 5   Pole positions: 3   Fastest laps: 3 (1 shared)   Points scored: 43

	Race	Circuit	No	Entrant	Tyres	Capacity/Car/Engine	Comment	Q Pos/Entries
ret	ARGENTINE GP	Buenos Aires	18	Cooper Car Co	D	2.5 Cooper T51-Climax 4	engine	10/22
dsq	MONACO GP	Monte Carlo	8	Cooper Car Co	D	2.5 Cooper T53-Climax 4	outside assistance after spin	2/24
1	DUTCH GP	Zandvoort	11	Cooper Car Co	D	2.5 Cooper T53-Climax 4		2/21
1	BELGIAN GP	Spa	2	Cooper Car Co	D	2.5 Cooper T53-Climax 4	FL (shared with Ireland & G Hill)	1/18
1	FRENCH GP	Reims	16	Cooper Car Co	D	2.5 Cooper T53-Climax 4	FL	1/23
1	BRITISH GP	Silverstone	1	Cooper Car Co	D	2.5 Cooper T53-Climax 4		1/25
1	PORTUGUESE GP	Oporto	2	Cooper Car Co	D	2.5 Cooper T53-Climax 4		3/16
4	US GP	Riverside	2	Cooper Car Co	D	2.5 Cooper T53-Climax 4	FL/1 lap behind	2/23

1961 Championship position: 11th=   Wins: 0   Pole positions: 1   Fastest laps: 1   Points scored: 4

	Race	Circuit	No	Entrant	Tyres	Capacity/Car/Engine	Comment	Q Pos/Entries
ret	MONACO GP	Monte Carlo	24	Cooper Car Co	D	1.5 Cooper T55-Climax 4	ignition	21/21
6	DUTCH GP	Zandvoort	10	Cooper Car Co	D	1.5 Cooper T55-Climax 4		7/17

The rear-engined revolution pioneered by Brabham and Cooper in the late 1950s changed the face of racing forever. The Australian puts the light and nimble chassis to the test, as he probes the Cooper's limits of adhesion in the 1959 British Grand Prix at Aintree.

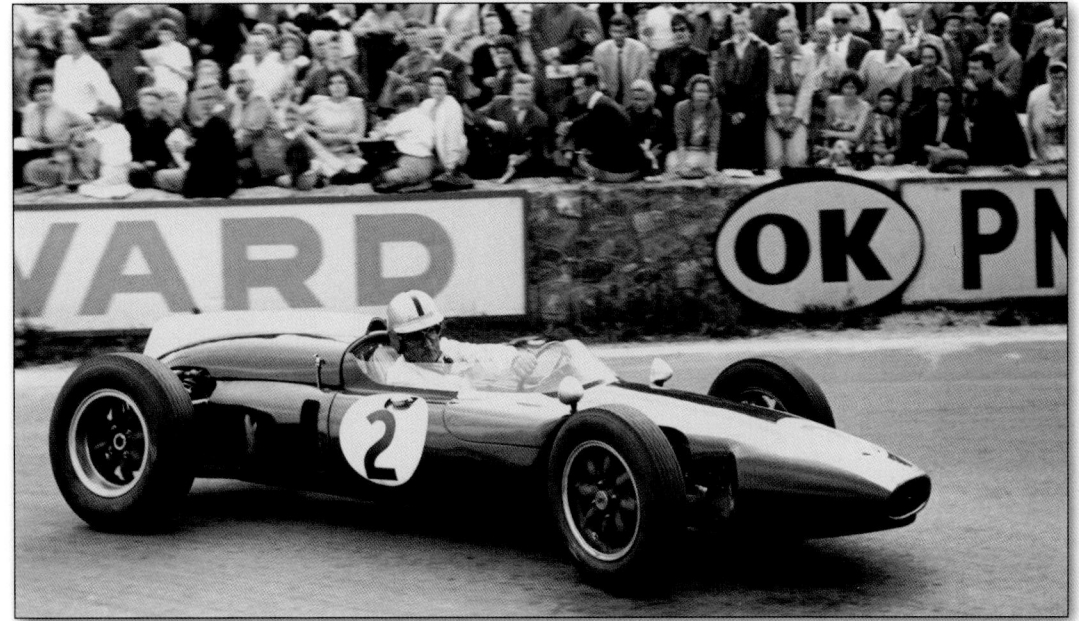

Cooper further refined their cars for 1960, and Brabham was unbeatable in the T53, producing a run of five consecutive wins. Pictured left, he rounds La Source on his way to the team's crushing 1-2 victory with Bruce McLaren in the Belgian Grand Prix.

ret	BELGIAN GP	Spa	28	Cooper Car Co	D	1.5 Cooper T55-Climax 4	engine	11/25
ret	FRENCH GP	Reims	2	Cooper Car Co	D	1.5 Cooper T55-Climax 4	oil pressure	14/26
4	BRITISH GP	Aintree	12	Cooper Car Co	D	1.5 Cooper T55-Climax 4		9/30
ret	GERMAN GP	Nürburgring	1	Cooper Car Co	D	1.5 Cooper T58-Climax V8	accident – throttle jammed	2/27
dns	"		1	Cooper Car Co	D	1.5 Cooper T55-Climax 4	practice only	- / -
ret	ITALIAN GP	Monza	10	Cooper Car Co	D	1.5 Cooper T58-Climax V8	overheating	10/33
dns	"	"	10	Cooper Car Co	D	1.5 Cooper T55-Climax 4	practice only	- / -
ret	US GP	Watkins Glen	1	Cooper Car Co	D	1.5 Cooper T58-Climax V8	overheating/FL	1/19
dns	"	" "	1	Cooper Car Co	D	1.5 Cooper T55-Climax 4	practice only	- / -

1962 Championship position: 9th   Wins: 0   Pole positions: 0   Fastest laps: 0   Points scored: 9

ret	DUTCH GP	Zandvoort	8	Brabham Racing Organisation	D	1.5 Lotus 24-Climax V8	accident	4/20
8/ret	MONACO GP	Monte Carlo	22	Brabham Racing Organisation	D	1.5 Lotus 24-Climax V8	spin – suspension	6/21
6	BELGIAN GP	Spa	15	Brabham Racing Organisation	D	1.5 Lotus 24-Climax V8	2 laps behind	15/20
ret	FRENCH GP	Rouen	26	Brabham Racing Organisation	D	1.5 Lotus 24-Climax V8	rear suspension	4/17
5	BRITISH GP	Aintree	30	Brabham Racing Organisation	D	1.5 Lotus 24-Climax V8	1 lap behind	9/21
ret	GERMAN GP	Nürburgring	16	Brabham Racing Organisation	D	1.5 Brabham BT3-Climax V8	throttle linkage	24/30
4	US GP	Watkins Glen	17	Brabham Racing Organisation	D	1.5 Brabham BT3-Climax V8	1 lap behind	=4/20
4	SOUTH AFRICAN GP	East London	10	Brabham Racing Organisation	D	1.5 Brabham BT3-Climax V8		3/17

1963   Championship position: 7th   Wins: 0   Pole positions: 0   Fastest laps: 0   Points scored: 14

9	MONACO GP	Monte Carlo	3	Brabham Racing Organisation	D	1.5 Lotus 25-Climax V8	borrowed car/pit stops/-23 laps	16/17
dns	"	" "	3	Brabham Racing Organisation	D	1.5 Brabham BT3-Climax V8	engine in practice	- / -
ret	BELGIAN GP	Spa	17	Brabham Racing Organisation	D	1.5 Brabham BT3-Climax V8	fuel injection pump	6/20
ret	DUTCH GP	Zandvoort	16	Brabham Racing Organisation	D	1.5 Brabham BT7-Climax V8	spin – chassis damage	4/19
4	FRENCH GP	Reims	6	Brabham Racing Organisation	D	1.5 Brabham BT7-Climax V8		=4/21
ret	BRITISH GP	Silverstone	8	Brabham Racing Organisation	D	1.5 Brabham BT7-Climax V8	engine	4/23
7	GERMAN GP	Nürburgring	9	Brabham Racing Organisation	D	1.5 Brabham BT7-Climax V8	pit stop/1 lap behind	8/26
5	ITALIAN GP	Monza	22	Brabham Racing Organisation	D	1.5 Brabham BT3-Climax V8	pit stop – fuel/2 laps behind	7/28
4	US GP	Watkins Glen	5	Brabham Racing Organisation	D	1.5 Brabham BT7-Climax V8	2 laps behind	5/21
2	MEXICAN GP	Mexico City	5	Brabham Racing Organisation	D	1.5 Brabham BT7-Climax V8		10/21
13/ret	SOUTH AFRICAN GP	East London	8	Brabham Racing Organisation	D	1.5 Brabham BT7-Climax V8	spin – split fuel tank/-15 laps	2/21

1964   Championship position: 8th=   Wins: 0   Pole positions: 0   Fastest laps: 1   Points scored: 11

ret	MONACO GP	Monte Carlo	5	Brabham Racing Organisation	D	1.5 Brabham BT7-Climax V8	fuel injection	2/20
ret	DUTCH GP	Zandvoort	14	Brabham Racing Organisation	D	1.5 Brabham BT7-Climax V8	ignition	7/18
3	BELGIAN GP	Spa	14	Brabham Racing Organisation	D	1.5 Brabham BT7-Climax V8		3/20
3	FRENCH GP	Rouen	20	Brabham Racing Organisation	D	1.5 Brabham BT7-Climax V8	FL	5/17
4	BRITISH GP	Brands Hatch	5	Brabham Racing Organisation	D	1.5 Brabham BT7-Climax V8	1 lap behind	4/25
12/ret	GERMAN GP	Nürburgring	6	Brabham Racing Organisation	D	1.5 Brabham BT11-Climax V8	engine – cwp	6/24
9	AUSTRIAN GP	Zeltweg	6	Brabham Racing Organisation	D	1.5 Brabham BT11-Climax V8	pit stop – fuel feed /-29 laps	6/20
ret	ITALIAN GP	Monza	14	Brabham Racing Organisation	D	1.5 Brabham BT11-Climax V8	engine – con rod	11/25
ret	US GP	Watkins Glen	5	Brabham Racing Organisation	D	1.5 Brabham BT11-Climax V8	engine	7/19
ret	MEXICAN GP	Mexico City	5	Brabham Racing Organisation	D	1.5 Brabham BT11-Climax V8	electrics	7/19

1965   Championship position: 10   Wins: 0   Pole positions: 0   Fastest laps: 0   Points scored: 9

8	SOUTH AFRICAN GP	East London	7	Brabham Racing Organisation	G	1.5 Brabham BT11-Climax V8	pit stop – battery/4 laps behind	=3/25
ret	MONACO GP	Monte Carlo	1	Brabham Racing Organisation	G	1.5 Brabham BT11-Climax V8	engine	2/17
4	BELGIAN GP	Spa	14	Brabham Racing Organisation	G	1.5 Brabham BT11-Climax V8	1 lap behind	10/21
dns	BRITISH GP	Silverstone	7 (8)	Brabham Racing Organisation	G	1.5 Brabham BT11-Climax V8	Gurney took over car for race	(8)/23
5	GERMAN GP	Nürburgring	4	Brabham Racing Organisation	G	1.5 Brabham BT11-Climax V8		14/22
3	US GP	Watkins Glen	7	Brabham Racing Organisation	G	1.5 Brabham BT11-Climax V8		7/18
ret	MEXICAN GP	Mexico City	7	Brabham Racing Organisation	G	1.5 Brabham BT11-Climax V8	oil leak	4/18

Life begins at 40. After five seasons without a grand prix win, Brabham bounced back in 1966 to take his third world championship. His decision to opt for simple and reliable Repco engines paid huge dividends in the new 3-litre formula, and a mid-season run of four straight wins guaranteed him the title. Pictured right, he leads team-mate Denny Hulme, Jim Clark's Lotus-Climax and Graham Hill's BRM in the 1966 Dutch GP.

1966 WORLD CHAMPION	Wins: 4	Pole positions: 3		Fastest laps: 1	Points scored: 45				
ret	MONACO GP	Monte Carlo	7	Brabham Racing Organisation	G	3.0 Brabham BT19-Repco V8	gearbox	=10/16
4	BELGIAN GP	Spa	3	Brabham Racing Organisation	G	3.0 Brabham BT19-Repco V8	2 laps behind	4/18
1	FRENCH GP	Reims	12	Brabham Racing Organisation	G	3.0 Brabham BT19-Repco V8		4/17
1	BRITISH GP	Brands Hatch	5	Brabham Racing Organisation	G	3.0 Brabham BT19-Repco V8	FL	1/20
1	DUTCH GP	Zandvoort	16	Brabham Racing Organisation	G	3.0 Brabham BT19-Repco V8		1/18
1	GERMAN GP	Nürburgring	3	Brabham Racing Organisation	G	3.0 Brabham BT19-Repco V8		5/30
ret	ITALIAN GP	Monza	10	Brabham Racing Organisation	G	3.0 Brabham BT19-Repco V8	oil leak	6/22
dns	"	"	10T	Brabham Racing Organisation	G	3.0 Brabham BT20-Repco V8	practice only	– / –
ret	US GP	Watkins Glen	5	Brabham Racing Organisation	G	3.0 Brabham BT20-Repco V8	engine	1/19
2	MEXICAN GP	Mexico City	5	Brabham Racing Organisation	G	3.0 Brabham BT20-Repco V8		4/19
1967 Championship position: 2nd		Wins: 2	Pole positions: 2		Fastest laps: 0	Points scored: 48			
6	SOUTH AFRICAN GP	Kyalami	1	Brabham Racing Organisation	G	3.0 Brabham BT20-Repco V8	pit stop – misfire/4 laps behind	1/18
ret	MONACO GP	Monte Carlo	8	Brabham Racing Organisation	G	3.0 Brabham BT19-Repco V8	engine	1/18
2	DUTCH GP	Zandvoort	1	Brabham Racing Organisation	G	3.0 Brabham BT19-Repco V8		3/17
dns	"	"	1	Brabham Racing Organisation	G	3.0 Brabham BT24-Repco V8	practice only	– / –
ret	BELGIAN GP	Spa	25	Brabham Racing Organisation	G	3.0 Brabham BT24-Repco V8	engine	7/18
1	FRENCH GP	Le Mans	3	Brabham Racing Organisation	G	3.0 Brabham BT24-Repco V8		2/15
4	BRITISH GP	Silverstone	1	Brabham Racing Organisation	G	3.0 Brabham BT24-Repco V8	wing mirrors fell off!	3/21
2	GERMAN GP	Nürburgring	1	Brabham Racing Organisation	G	3.0 Brabham BT24-Repco V8		8/25
1	CANADIAN GP	Mosport Park	1	Brabham Racing Organisation	G	3.0 Brabham BT24-Repco V8		7/19
2	ITALIAN GP	Monza	16	Brabham Racing Organisation	G	3.0 Brabham BT24-Repco V8		2/18
5	US GP	Watkins Glen	1	Brabham Racing Organisation	G	3.0 Brabham BT24-Repco V8	pit stop – puncture/4 laps behind	5/18
2	MEXICAN GP	Mexico City	1	Brabham Racing Organisation	G	3.0 Brabham BT24-Repco V8		5/19
1968 Championship position: 23rd=		Wins: 0	Pole positions: 0		Fastest laps: 0	Points scored: 2			
ret	SOUTH AFRICAN GP	Kyalami	2	Brabham Racing Organisation	G	3.0 Brabham BT24-Repco V8	valve spring	5/23
dns	SPANISH GP	Jarama	8	Brabham Racing Organisation	G	3.0 Brabham BT26-Repco V8	engine trouble in practice	(14)/14
ret	MONACO GP	Monte Carlo	2	Brabham Racing Organisation	G	3.0 Brabham BT26-Repco V8	rear radius arm	12/18
ret	BELGIAN GP	Spa	18	Brabham Racing Organisation	G	3.0 Brabham BT26-Repco V8	sticking throttle	18/18
ret	DUTCH GP	Zandvoort	5	Brabham Racing Organisation	G	3.0 Brabham BT26-Repco V8	spun off – could not restart	4/19
ret	FRENCH GP	Rouen	4	Brabham Racing Organisation	G	3.0 Brabham BT26-Repco V8	fuel pump	=13/18
ret	BRITISH GP	Brands Hatch	3	Brabham Racing Organisation	G	3.0 Brabham BT26-Repco V8	engine – camshaft	8/20
5	GERMAN GP	Nürburgring	4	Brabham Racing Organisation	G	3.0 Brabham BT26-Repco V8		15/20
ret	ITALIAN GP	Monza	10	Brabham Racing Organisation	G	3.0 Brabham BT26-Repco V8	oil pressure	17/24
ret	CANADIAN GP	St Jovite	5	Brabham Racing Organisation	G	3.0 Brabham BT26-Repco V8	wishbone mounting	=10/22
ret	US GP	Watkins Glen	3	Brabham Racing Organisation	G	3.0 Brabham BT26-Repco V8	cam follower	8/21
10/ret	MEXICAN GP	Mexico City	3	Brabham Racing Organisation	G	3.0 Brabham BT26-Repco V8	oil pressure/6 laps behind	8/21
1969 Championship position: 10th		Wins: 0	Pole positions: 2		Fastest laps: 1 (shared)	Points scored: 14			
ret	SOUTH AFRICAN GP	Kyalami	14	Motor Racing Developments	G	3.0 Brabham BT26A-Cosworth V8	lost rear wing	1/18

	Race	Circuit	No	Entrant	Tyres	Capacity/Car/Engine	Comment	Q Pos/Entries
ret	SPANISH GP	Montjuich Park	3	Motor Racing Developments	G	3.0 Brabham BT26A-Cosworth V8	engine	5/14
ret	MONACO GP	Monte Carlo	5	Motor Racing Developments	G	3.0 Brabham BT26A-Cosworth V8	accident with Surtees	=8/16
6	DUTCH GP	Zandvoort	11	Motor Racing Developments	G	3.0 Brabham BT26A-Cosworth V8		8/15
ret	ITALIAN GP	Monza	28	Motor Racing Developments	G	3.0 Brabham BT26A-Cosworth V8	oil leak – loose fuel pump	7/15
2	CANADIAN GP	Mosport Park	12	Motor Racing Developments	G	3.0 Brabham BT26A-Cosworth V8	FL (shared with Ickx)	=5/20
4	US GP	Watkins Glen	8	Motor Racing Developments	G	3.0 Brabham BT26A-Cosworth V8	pit stop – fuel/2 laps behind	10/18
3	MEXICAN GP	Mexico City	8	Motor Racing Developments	G	3.0 Brabham BT26A-Cosworth V8	engine problems	1/17

1970 Championship position: 5th=   Wins: 1   Pole positions: 1   Fastest laps: 4 (1 shared)   Points scored: 25

	Race	Circuit	No	Entrant	Tyres	Capacity/Car/Engine	Comment	Q Pos/Entries
1	SOUTH AFRICAN GP	Kyalami	12	Motor Racing Developments	G	3.0 Brabham BT33-Cosworth V8	FL (shared with Surtees)	3/24
ret	SPANISH GP	Jarama	7	Motor Racing Developments	G	3.0 Brabham BT33-Cosworth V8	engine/FL	1/22
2	MONACO GP	Monte Carlo	5	Motor Racing Developments	G	3.0 Brabham BT33-Cosworth V8	lost lead in last corner accident	4/21
ret	BELGIAN GP	Spa	18	Motor Racing Developments	G	3.0 Brabham BT33-Cosworth V8	flywheel and clutch	5/18
11	DUTCH GP	Zandvoort	18	Motor Racing Developments	G	3.0 Brabham BT33-Cosworth V8	2 pit stops – punctures/-4 laps	12/24
3	FRENCH GP	Clermont Ferrand	23	Motor Racing Developments	G	3.0 Brabham BT33-Cosworth V8	FL	5/23
2	BRITISH GP	Brands Hatch	17	Motor Racing Developments	G	3.0 Brabham BT33-Cosworth V8	out of fuel on last lap/FL	=1/25
ret	GERMAN GP	Hockenheim	3	Motor Racing Developments	G	3.0 Brabham BT33-Cosworth V8	split oil union	12/25
13	AUSTRIAN GP	Österreichring	10	Motor Racing Developments	G	3.0 Brabham BT33-Cosworth V8	pit stop – holed radiator/-4 laps	=7/24
ret	ITALIAN GP	Monza	44	Motor Racing Developments	G	3.0 Brabham BT33-Cosworth V8	accident when engine cut out	8/27
ret	CANADIAN GP	St Jovite	11	Motor Racing Developments	G	3.0 Brabham BT33-Cosworth V8	oil leak	19/20
10	US GP	Watkins Glen	15	Motor Racing Developments	G	3.0 Brabham BT33-Cosworth V8	3 laps behind	16/27
ret	MEXICAN GP	Mexico City	15	Motor Racing Developments	G	3.0 Brabham BT33-Cosworth V8	engine low oil pressure	4/18

GP Starts: 126   GP Wins: 14   Pole positions: 13   Fastest laps: 12   Points: 261

BILL BRACK

BILL BRACK was very much a leading light on the Canadian motor racing scene from the mid-1960s through to the late 1970s, who also made occasional racing forays abroad. His early career was spent successfully racing Mini Coopers, but after opening his own first car dealership, things developed rapidly. Bill became a Lotus distributor, which led to him getting hold of a potent twin-cam Lotus 47 sports car; then he went single-seater racing with a Lotus 41 Formula B car in 1967, winning the eastern championship

The following year, Brack used his connections with Lotus to ask Colin Chapman if he could drive one of his Lotus 49s in the St Jovite race. "If you don't ask, you don't get!"

The lure of $6,000 must have proved irresistible. Having never sat in a Formula 1 car before, Bill found himself rubbing shoulders with the stars and in a competitive machine. Later he would regret not having prepared well by testing the car in advance of the meeting. In the event, though, a driveshaft problem brought his grand prix debut to an early end.

Then Bill concentrated on the Formula A series, which was popular at the time, Initially he raced a modified ex-Indianapolis Lotus 42B, before switching to a newer Lola T140. In 1970, he acquired a Lotus 70, but largely played second fiddle to Eppie Wietzes' McLaren, before finally claiming a victory in the season finale at Mosport, which was the last hurrah for these big-engined cars in the Canadian championship.

Being a high-profile local driver brought Brack a couple more grand prix appearances with the BRM team at Mosport, which added interest for the spectators, but yielded little else. He did find success in the Formula B series, however, winning the championship in 1973 with an old Lotus 59/69. The following year, the venerable machine, now equipped with a BDA power plant, took the title in the newly introduced Formula Atlantic series. A switch to a Chevron chassis merely provided the Canadian with the wherewithal to win the Atlantic series once again in 1975. Despite intense competition from the likes of Bertil Ross, Gilles Villeneuve, Bobby Rahal, and Keke Rosberg, among many, Brack continued to be a competitive force in the series until 1979, when he stepped aside for Jacques (brother of Gilles) Villeneuve in 1979.

When his racing days ended, Brack opened a successful Chrysler dealership and supported his son, Kyle, who raced in the Formula BMW championship. He has also been heavily involved in the preservation of cars from the Formula Atlantic period, which are now a popular feature in historic events in North America.

BRACK, Bill (CDN) b 26/12/1935, Toronto

1968 Championship position: Unplaced

	Race	Circuit	No	Entrant	Tyres	Capacity/Car/Engine	Comment	Q Pos/Entries
ret	CANADIAN GP	St Jovite	27	Gold Leaf Team Lotus	F	3.0 Lotus 49B-Cosworth V8	driveshaft	=20/22

1969 Championship position: Unplaced

nc	CANADIAN GP	Mosport Park	16	Owen Racing Organisation	D	3.0 BRM P138 V12	10 laps behind	18/20

1972 Championship position: Unplaced

ret	CANADIAN GP	Mosport Park	17	Marlboro BRM	F	3.0 BRM P180 V12	spun and stalled	23/25

GP Starts: 3   GP Wins: 0   Pole positions: 0   Fastest laps: 0   Points: 0

VITTORIO BRAMBILLA

VITTORIO BRAMBILLA began racing motor-cycles as early as 1957, winning the 125cc Italian championship before turning to karting. He forsook his racing activities temporarily to tend the cars of his elder brother, Ernesto, before returning to two-wheel competition in 1968. The following year, he burst upon the Italian national scene in his F3 Birel, and his forceful driving style soon led to him being dubbed 'the Monza Gorilla', partly due to his burly physique.

Still relatively unknown, he moved into For-mula 2 in 1970 with a Brabham BT23, taking a second place at the Salzburgring, and he spent another two years jumping between F2 and F3, gaining numerous successes in the latter cat-egory, which culminated in him taking the Italian F3 title in 1972.

The 1973 season provided his big break-through. He had calmed his frenetic driving approach somewhat and, at the wheel of a well-sponsored March, he became a serious challenger for honours, looking particularly im-pressive as the season wore on, and taking wins at the Salzburgring and Albi.

Brambilla's sponsors, Beta Tools, were so delighted that they helped him secure a place in the March grand prix line-up for 1974. Join-ing the team two races into the season, he soon proved to be as quick as team-mate Hans Stuck, but the propensity to crash was still there. The following year was his best: he was much more consistent, qualified well and raced his heart out. In Sweden, he was stunningly fast in prac-tice and simply drove away from the field at the start until tyre trouble intervened, followed by driveshaft failure.

His moment came in Austria, however, where he scored the March factory team's first ever championship grand prix win in pouring rain at the Österreichring. It made no difference to the exuberant Italian that he had managed to dismantle the front of the car on the slowing-down lap – or that half-points were awarded, as the race had been ended prematurely with the chequered flag rather than being stopped and then restarted, as should have been the case. Max Mosley had read the rule book, and nobody could argue against him!

Unfortunately, 1976 saw a return to the bad habits of old, as in an effort to stay on the pace Brambilla indulged in a spate of chassis crunching, which must have driven the factory to distraction, such was the replacement tally. He scored only one points finish, but claimed second in the International Trophy at Silverstone and fourth in the Race of Champions at Brands Hatch.

However, the situation was redressed in 1977, when he took his Beta money to Surtees as number-one driver. He had a pretty good work-ing relationship with his demanding employer, and an excellent reliability record, although the car was just not quick enough for anything like outright success.

Nevertheless the partnership continued into 1978, with the new TS20 no more an effective challenger than its predecessor. At Monza, Vit-torio was involved in the start crash that claimed the life of Ronnie Peterson, suffering severe concussion that kept him out of the cockpit for almost a year, before Alfa Romeo (for whom he had won four rounds of the World Sports Car Championship in 1977 with their T33) brought him back for the last three races of the season. He made two more appearances for them in 1980, but it was painfully obvious that his days as a grand prix driver were over, although he did race the Osella sports car in a few rounds of the World Championship of Makes, before phasing himself out completely in 1981.

A decade later, Brambilla died, after suffering a heart attack while gardening at his home at Lesmo, near Milan.

BRAMBILLA, Vittorio (I) b 11/11/1937, Monza – d 26/05/2001, Camparada di Lesmo, Brianza

1974 Championship position: 18th   Wins: 0   Pole positions: 0   Fastest laps: 0   Points scored: 1

	Race	Circuit	No	Entrant	Tyres	Capacity/Car/Engine	Comment	Q Pos/Entries
10	SOUTH AFRICAN GP	Kyalami	10	Beta Tools/March Engineering	G	3.0 March 741-Cosworth V8	1 lap behind	19/27
dns	SPANISH GP	Jarama	10	Beta Tools/March Engineering	G	3.0 March 741-Cosworth V8	accident in practice	(10)/28
9	BELGIAN GP	Nivelles	10	Beta Tools/March Engineering	G	3.0 March 741-Cosworth V8	2 laps behind	31/32
ret	MONACO GP	Monte Carlo	10	Beta Tools/March Engineering	G	3.0 March 741-Cosworth V8	multiple accident lap 1	15/28
10/ret	SWEDISH GP	Anderstorp	10	Beta Tools/March Engineering	G	3.0 March 741-Cosworth V8	engine/2 laps behind	17/28
10	DUTCH GP	Zandvoort	10	Beta Tools/March Engineering	G	3.0 March 741-Cosworth V8	3 laps behind	15/27
11	FRENCH GP	Dijon	10	Beta Tools/March Engineering	G	3.0 March 741-Cosworth V8	1 lap behind	16/30
ret	BRITISH GP	Brands Hatch	10	Beta Tools/March Engineering	G	3.0 March 741-Cosworth V8	fuel pressure	=15/34
13	GERMAN GP	Nürburgring	10	Beta Tools/March Engineering	G	3.0 March 741-Cosworth V8		23/32
6	AUSTRIAN GP	Österreichring	10	Beta Tools/March Engineering	G	3.0 March 741-Cosworth V8		20/31
ret	ITALIAN GP	Monza	10	Beta Tools/March Engineering	G	3.0 March 741-Cosworth V8	crashed at chicane	13/31
dns	CANADIAN GP	Mosport Park	10	Beta Tools/March Engineering	G	3.0 March 741-Cosworth V8	accident in practice	29/30
ret	US GP	Watkins Glen	10	Beta Tools/March Engineering	G	3.0 March 741-Cosworth V8	fuel metering unit	25/30

1975 Championship position: 11th   Wins: 0   Pole positions: 1   Fastest laps: 1   Points scored: 6.5

	Race	Circuit	No	Entrant	Tyres	Capacity/Car/Engine	Comment	Q Pos/Entries
9	ARGENTINE GP	Buenos Aires	9	Beta Team March	G	3.0 March 741-Cosworth V8	1 lap behind	12/23
ret	BRAZILIAN GP	Interlagos	9	Beta Team March	G	3.0 March 741-Cosworth V8	engine	17/23
ret	SOUTH AFRICAN GP	Kyalami	9	Beta Team March	G	3.0 March 751-Cosworth V8	oil cooler leak	7/28
5*	SPANISH GP	Montjuich Park	9	Beta Team March	G	3.0 March 751-Cosworth V8	shortened race –*half points/-1 lap	5/26
ret	MONACO GP	Monte Carlo	9	Beta Team March	G	3.0 March 751-Cosworth V8	accident with Pryce	5/26
ret	BELGIAN GP	Zolder	9	Beta Team March	G	3.0 March 751-Cosworth V8	brakes	3/24
ret	SWEDISH GP	Anderstorp	9	Beta Team March	G	3.0 March 751-Cosworth V8	driveshaft	1/26
ret	DUTCH GP	Zandvoort	9	Beta Team March	G	3.0 March 751-Cosworth V8	collision with Depailler at start	11/25
ret	FRENCH GP	Paul Ricard	9	Beta Team March	G	3.0 March 751-Cosworth V8	rear damper	8/26
6	BRITISH GP	Silverstone	9	Beta Team March	G	3.0 March 751-Cosworth V8	1 lap behind	5/28
ret	GERMAN GP	Nürburgring	9	Beta Team March	G	3.0 March 751-Cosworth V8	puncture –suspension damage	11/26
1*	AUSTRIAN GP	Österreichring	9	Beta Team March	G	3.0 March 751-Cosworth V8	rain shortened race –*half points/FL	8/30
ret	ITALIAN GP	Monza	9	Beta Team March	G	3.0 March 751-Cosworth V8	clutch	9/28
7	US GP	Watkins Glen	9	Beta Team March	G	3.0 March 751-Cosworth V8		6/24

1976 Championship position: 19th=   Wins: 0   Pole positions: 0   Fastest laps: 0   Points scored: 1

	Race	Circuit	No	Entrant	Tyres	Capacity/Car/Engine	Comment	Q Pos/Entries
ret	BRAZILIAN GP	Interlagos	9	Beta Team March	G	3.0 March 761-Cosworth V8	oil leak	7/22
8	SOUTH AFRICAN GP	Kyalami	9	Beta Team March	G	3.0 March 761-Cosworth V8	1 lap behind	5/25
ret	US GP WEST	Long Beach	9	Beta Team March	G	3.0 March 761-Cosworth V8	collision with Reutemann	8/27
ret	SPANISH GP	Jarama	9	Beta Team March	G	3.0 March 761-Cosworth V8	accident – damaged suspension	6/30
ret	BELGIAN GP	Zolder	9	Beta Team March	G	3.0 March 761-Cosworth V8	driveshaft	5/29
ret	MONACO GP	Monte Carlo	9	Beta Team March	G	3.0 March 761-Cosworth V8	suspension	9/25
10	SWEDISH GP	Anderstorp	9	Beta Team March	G	3.0 March 761-Cosworth V8	spin/1 lap behind	15/27
ret	FRENCH GP	Paul Ricard	9	Beta Team March	G	3.0 March 761-Cosworth V8	engine – oil pressure	11/30
ret	BRITISH GP	Brands Hatch	9	Beta Team March	G	3.0 March 761-Cosworth V8	collision with Peterson	10/30
ret	GERMAN GP	Nürburgring	9	Beta Team March	G	3.0 March 761-Cosworth V8	brake failure	13/28
ret	AUSTRIAN GP	Österreichring	9	Beta Team March	G	3.0 March 761-Cosworth V8	collision with Fittipaldi	7/25
6	DUTCH GP	Zandvoort	9	Beta Team March	G	3.0 March 761-Cosworth V8		7/27
7	ITALIAN GP	Monza	9	Beta Team March	G	3.0 March 761-Cosworth V8		16/29
14	CANADIAN GP	Mosport Park	9	Beta Team March	G	3.0 March 761-Cosworth V8	1 lap behind	3/27
ret	US GP EAST	Watkins Glen	9	Beta Team March	G	3.0 March 761-Cosworth V8	burst tyre	4/27
ret	JAPANESE GP	Mount Fuji	9	Beta Team March	G	3.0 March 761-Cosworth V8	engine	8/27

Brambilla's only grand prix win came in the rain-shortened 1975 Austrian GP at the Österreichring. He drove a superb race in the torrential conditions before it was halted at just over half-distance. After taking the chequered flag, the exuberant Italian promptly lost control of his March and slithered into the Armco. Undeterred, he completed his slow-down lap with a slightly second-hand car.

1977 Championship position: 15th=   Wins: 0   Pole positions: 0   Fastest laps: 0   Points scored: 6

7/ret	ARGENTINE GP	Buenos Aires	19	Beta Team Surtees	G	3.0 Surtees TS19-Cosworth V8	fuel feed/5 laps behind	13/21
ret	BRAZILIAN GP	Interlagos	19	Beta Team Surtees	G	3.0 Surtees TS19-Cosworth V8	damaged radiator on kerb	11/22
7	SOUTH AFRICAN GP	Kyalami	19	Beta Team Surtees	G	3.0 Surtees TS19-Cosworth V8		14/23
ret	US GP WEST	Long Beach	19	Beta Team Surtees	G	3.0 Surtees TS19-Cosworth V8	collision with Mass	11/22
ret	SPANISH GP	Jarama	19	Beta Team Surtees	G	3.0 Surtees TS19-Cosworth V8	collision with Regazzoni	11/31
8	MONACO GP	Monte Carlo	19	Beta Team Surtees	G	3.0 Surtees TS19-Cosworth V8		14/26
4	BELGIAN GP	Zolder	19	Beta Team Surtees	G	3.0 Surtees TS19-Cosworth V8		12/32
ret	SWEDISH GP	Anderstorp	19	Beta Team Surtees	G	3.0 Surtees TS19-Cosworth V8	engine	13/31
13	FRENCH GP	Dijon	19	Beta Team Surtees	G	3.0 Surtees TS19-Cosworth V8	pit stop – tyres/3 laps behind	11/30
8	BRITISH GP	Silverstone	19	Beta Team Surtees	G	3.0 Surtees TS19-Cosworth V8	pit stop – puncture/1 lap behind	8/36
5	GERMAN GP	Hockenheim	19	Beta Team Surtees	G	3.0 Surtees TS19-Cosworth V8		10/30
15	AUSTRIAN GP	Österreichring	19	Beta Team Surtees	G	3.0 Surtees TS19-Cosworth V8	spin/2 laps behind	13/30
12/ret	DUTCH GP	Zandvoort	19	Beta Team Surtees	G	3.0 Surtees TS19-Cosworth V8	spun off	22/34
ret	ITALIAN GP	Monza	19	Beta Team Surtees	G	3.0 Surtees TS19-Cosworth V8	hit by Watson – radiator	10/34
19	US GP EAST	Watkins Glen	19	Beta Team Surtees	G	3.0 Surtees TS19-Cosworth V8	pit stop – collision damage/-5 laps	11/27
6/ret	CANADIAN GP	Mosport Park	19	Beta Team Surtees	G	3.0 Surtees TS19-Cosworth V8	crashed on oil/2 laps behind	15/27
8	JAPANESE GP	Mount Fuji	19	Beta Team Surtees	G	3.0 Surtees TS19-Cosworth V8	2 pit stops – plug leads/-2 laps	=8/23

1978 Championship position: 19th=   Wins: 0   Pole positions: 0   Fastest laps: 0   Points scored: 1

18	ARGENTINE GP	Buenos Aires	19	Beta Team Surtees	G	3.0 Surtees TS19-Cosworth V8	2 laps behind	12/27
dnq	BRAZILIAN GP	Rio	19	Beta Team Surtees	G	3.0 Surtees TS19-Cosworth V8		27/28
12	SOUTH AFRICAN GP	Kyalami	19	Beta Team Surtees	G	3.0 Surtees TS19-Cosworth V8	2 laps behind	19/30
ret	US GP WEST	Long Beach	19	Beta Team Surtees	G	3.0 Surtees TS19-Cosworth V8	engine – cwp	17/30
dnq	MONACO GP	Monte Carlo	19	Beta Team Surtees	G	3.0 Surtees TS20-Cosworth V8		24/30
dnq	"	"	19	Beta Team Surtees	G	3.0 Surtees TS19-Cosworth V8		-/-
13/ret	BELGIAN GP	Zolder	19	Beta Team Surtees	G	3.0 Surtees TS20-Cosworth V8	engine	12/30
7	SPANISH GP	Jarama	19	Beta Team Surtees	G	3.0 Surtees TS20-Cosworth V8	1 lap behind	16/29
ret	SWEDISH GP	Anderstorp	19	Beta Team Surtees	G	3.0 Surtees TS20-Cosworth V8	collision with Pironi – hit barrier	18/27
17	FRENCH GP	Paul Ricard	19	Beta Team Surtees	G	3.0 Surtees TS20-Cosworth V8	spin/2 laps behind	19/29
9	BRITISH GP	Brands Hatch	19	Beta Team Surtees	G	3.0 Surtees TS20-Cosworth V8	1 lap behind	25/30
ret	GERMAN GP	Hockenheim	19	Beta Team Surtees	G	3.0 Surtees TS20-Cosworth V8	fuel vaporisation	20/30
6	AUSTRIAN GP	Österreichring	19	Beta Team Surtees	G	3.0 Surtees TS20-Cosworth V8	1 lap behind	21/31
dsq	DUTCH GP	Zandvoort	19	Beta Team Surtees	G	3.0 Surtees TS20-Cosworth V8	push start after spin	22/33
ret/dns	ITALIAN GP	Monza	19	Beta Team Surtees	G	3.0 Surtees TS20-Cosworth V8	accident in first start	23/32

1979 Championship position: Unplaced

12	ITALIAN GP	Monza	36	Autodelta	G	3.0 Alfa Romeo 177 F12	1 lap behind	22/28
ret	CANADIAN GP	Montreal	36	Autodelta	G	3.0 Alfa Romeo 179 V12	fuel metering unit	18/29
dnq	US GP EAST	Watkins Glen	36	Autodelta	G	3.0 Alfa Romeo 179 V12		25/30

1980   Championship position: Unplaced

ret	DUTCH GP	Zandvoort	22	Marlboro Team Alfa Romeo	G	3.0 Alfa Romeo 179 V12	accident with Lees	22/28
ret	ITALIAN GP	Imola	22	Marlboro Team Alfa Romeo	G	3.0 Alfa Romeo 179 V12	spun off	19/28

GP Starts: 73 (74)   GP Wins: 1   Pole positions: 1   Fastest laps: 1   Points: 15.5

BRANCA, 'Toni' (Antonio) (CH) b 15/9/1916 – d 10/5/1985, Sierre

1950 Championship position: Unplaced

	Race	Circuit	No	Entrant	Tyres	Capacity/Car/Engine	Comment	Q Pos/Entries
11	SWISS GP	Bremgarten	40	Antonio Branca	P	1.5 s/c Maserati 4CL 4	7 laps behind	17/18
10	BELGIAN GP	Spa	30	Antonio Branca	P	1.5 s/c Maserati 4CL 4	6 laps behind	13/14

1951 Championship position: Unplaced

	Race	Circuit	No	Entrant	Tyres	Capacity/Car/Engine	Comment	Q Pos/Entries
ret	GERMAN GP	Nürburgring	92	Antonio Branca	P	1.5 s/c Maserati 4CLT/48-4	engine	17/23

GP Starts: 3   GP Wins: 0   Pole positions: 0   Fastest laps: 0   Points: 0

BRANDON, Eric (GB) b 18/7/1920, East London – d 8/8/1982, Gosport, Hampshire

1952 Championship position: Unplaced

	Race	Circuit	No	Entrant	Tyres	Capacity/Car/Engine	Comment	Q Pos/Entries
8	SWISS GP	Bremgarten	24	Ecurie Richmond	D	2.0 Cooper T20-Bristol 6	7 laps behind	17/21
9	BELGIAN GP	Spa	12	Ecurie Richmond	D	2.0 Cooper T20-Bristol 6	3 laps behind	12/22
20	BRITISH GP	Silverstone	10	Ecurie Richmond	D	2.0 Cooper T20-Bristol 6	9 laps behind	18/32
13	ITALIAN GP	Monza	36	Ecurie Richmond	D	2.0 Cooper T20-Bristol 6	7 laps behind	20/35

1954 Championship position: Unplaced

	Race	Circuit	No	Entrant	Tyres	Capacity/Car/Engine	Comment	Q Pos/Entries
ret	BRITISH GP	Silverstone	30	Ecurie Richmond	D	2.0 Cooper T23-Bristol 6	engine	25/31

GP Starts: 5   GP Wins: 0   Pole positions: 0   Fastest laps: 0   Points: 0

BRIDGER, Tommy (GB) b 24/6/1934, Welwyn, Hertfordshire – d 3/7/1991, Aboyne, Aberdeenshire, Scotland

1958 Championship position: Unplaced

	Race	Circuit	No	Entrant	Tyres	Capacity/Car/Engine	Comment	Q Pos/Entries
ret	MOROCCAN GP (F2)	Casablanca	56	British Racing Partnership	D	1.5 Cooper T45-Climax 4	accident	22/25

GP Starts: 1   GP Wins: 0   Pole positions: 0   Fastest laps: 0   Points: 0

TONI BRANCA

TONI BRANCA first appeared in 1947, when he raced a Maserati 4CLT, appearing in the Grand Prix d'Alsace at Strasbourg and the Comminges Grand Prix at St Gaudens without success. The following year, he placed fourth in the Grand Prix Suisse Oriental at Erlen, some three laps behind the winner, Toulo de Graffenried. In 1949, he took part in the Swiss Grand Prix at Bremgarten, finishing a distant 14th place, but fared better with eighth place in the lesser Lausanne Grand Prix held a month later.

Branca reportedly was bankrolled in his racing activities by an admiring Belgian countess, the Vicomtesse de Walkiers, who entered a Gordini for him to drive in the 1950 Jersey Road Race, where he managed 11th place.

He raced internationally for just a couple of seasons, usually at events in his native Switzerland, but sometimes further afield. The Formula 1 events were contested with a Maserati 4CLT, and Formula 2 races with a Type 15 Simca Gordini. Only occasionally did he mix it with the quick men – a front-row start at Geneva in 1950 saw him lead briefly – but he did get the occasional top-six finish in lesser races: third at Aix-les-Bains, fifth at Erlen in 1950 and another fifth at Naples in '51 with the Gordini. His best result with the Maserati was sixth in the 1951 Pescara Grand Prix. That season ended in a nasty crash at Goodwood, however, when he was unable to avoid the spinning ERA of Brian Shawe-Taylor. The British driver was seriously injured, while Branca was fortunate to escape with just mild concussion and a severe shaking.

Thereafter, Toni continued to compete, usually in hill-climbs, through to the mid-1950s with his Maser and later a Moretti.

ERIC BRANDON

A BOYHOOD friend of John Cooper, Eric Brandon not unnaturally became involved in racing from the early post-war days of the little Cooper 500cc cars, when he was instrumental in the early development of the company. By 1951, he was rightly regarded as one of the top drivers in the class, recording wins at home and abroad. He was crowned the first British National F3 champion ahead of his team-mate, Alan Brown; with the series sponsored by Autosport, he was the recipent of a winner's cheque for £150.

With Brown, he had already formed the Ecurie Richmond team, and the pair moved up to the new front-engined Cooper-Bristol cars built for the new Formula 2 rules in grands prix during 1952 and '53. Eric's best placing was a very distant fourth at a retirement-hit Syracuse GP in 1953.

Undaunted, Eric continued in his beloved F3, where he was always a front-runner, winning at Helsinki in both 1954 and 1955. He also joined a number of competitors who raced in the small-engined sports cars at the time, driving the 1100cc Halseylec-Climax (named after his electrical trading company), which he raced in 1955 and early 1956.

Thereafter, Eric transferred his interest from track to water and went racing hydroplanes.

TOMMY BRIDGER

TOMMY BRIDGER first entered racing with a Cooper-JAP in 1953 and, having been bitten by the bug, was back the following season, contesting minor events with a Kieft-Norton, which he continued to race through 1955. Armed with a competitive Cooper, he undertook a full season of F3 in both 1956 and 1957, enjoying some fantastic dices with 'the master', Jim Russell, usually emerging second best, but dogging his rival's footsteps race in and race out.

For 1958, Tommy tried his hand at Formula 2, finishing second on aggregate in the minor Crystal Palace Trophy race, and eighth in the Coupe de Vitesse at Reims. His only grand prix appearance, in Morocco, ended in a crash from which luckily he emerged shaken, but otherwise unharmed. He continued to race in F3, but was beaten for the national championship by Trevor Taylor.

Bridger returned to the circuits the following year, winning four races in his faithful Cooper-Norton. In 1960, he was due to drive a Britannia-Ford, but in the event it never raced. His swansong came when he handled a third works Lotus Formula Junior at the British Grand Prix. Given this competitive car, he comfortably held third place, albeit some 13 seconds behind his very fast team-mates, Trevor Taylor and Peter Arundell. Sadly, a spin at Beckett's ended his run, and thereafter he left competition to a new generation of young chargers.

TONY BRISE

AFTER Tony Brise had made his grand prix debut for Frank Williams and then been snapped up by Graham Hill to race for the Embassy Hill team, he was suddenly very hot property. Yet at the beginning of 1974, no one had been interested in securing the talents of the man who had just won the John Player F3 championship outright and, with Richard Robarts, was joint Lombard North Central champion. He lacked the necessary finance to secure a seat in the March team for a season of Formula 2 and, despite a second place in the F3 Monaco support race, thus was consigned to a season of racing in Formula Atlantic.

Having come from a motor sport family – his father John was a 500cc and stock car racer – it was natural that young Tony would involve himself in some way. He started racing karts from the age of eight, eventually becoming joint British karting champion in 1969. By then keen to try his hand at Formula Ford, but without the resources, he contented himself with karting until, late in 1970, the opportunity finally arose to drive an Elden – not the best of chassis, but at least it was a start. He raced the car in 1971, before replacing it with a more competitive Merlyn to finish his first full season as runner-up in the BOC Formula Ford championship.

Bernie Ecclestone had spotted Tony's talent and offered him a Brabham BT28 for 1972, but this car turned out to be uncompetitive, and only when he switched to a GRD did his fortunes improve. Mike Warner of GRD was another who wasn't slow to see Brise's talent, and he signed him for 1973 to replace poor Roger Williamson, who was bound for F1, where he was destined to meet his terrible fate at Zandvoort. As described earlier, Brise did the business, but only Teddy Savory was there to back him in 1974 with the Modus Atlantic drive.

Of Brise the grand prix driver, sadly, we were to see precious little, but at each of the ten grands prix he contested, be it in practice or the race itself, flashes of his brilliance were evident. His loss in the plane crash that also claimed the lives of Graham Hill and four members of the Hill team was a devastating blow for all followers of British motor racing, who felt they had lost a future world champion.

BRISE, Tony (GB) b 28/3/1952, Dartford, Kent – d 29/11/1975, Arkley, nr Barnet, Hertfordshire

1975 Championship position: 19th=   Wins: 0   Pole positions: 0   Fastest laps: 0   Points scored: 1

	Race	Circuit	No	Entrant	Tyres	Capacity/Car/Engine	Comment	Q Pos/Entries
7	SPANISH GP	Montjuich Park	21	Frank Williams Racing Cars	G	3.0 Williams FW03-Cosworth V8	hit by Pryce/2 laps behind	18/26
ret	BELGIAN GP	Zolder	23	Embassy Racing with Graham Hill	G	3.0 Hill GH1-Cosworth V8	engine	7/24
6	SWEDISH GP	Anderstorp	23	Embassy Racing with Graham Hill	G	3.0 Hill GH1-Cosworth V8	1 lap behind	17/26
7	DUTCH GP	Zandvoort	23	Embassy Racing with Graham Hill	G	3.0 Hill GH1-Cosworth V8	pit stop/1 lap behind	7/25
7	FRENCH GP	Paul Ricard	23	Embassy Racing with Graham Hill	G	3.0 Hill GH1-Cosworth V8		12/26
15/ret	BRITISH GP	Silverstone	23	Embassy Racing with Graham Hill	G	3.0 Hill GH1-Cosworth V8	crashed in rainstorm/-3 laps	13/28
ret	GERMAN GP	Nürburgring	23	Embassy Racing with Graham Hill	G	3.0 Hill GH1-Cosworth V8	crashed – suspension failure	17/26
15	AUSTRIAN GP	Österreichring	23	Embassy Racing with Graham Hill	G	3.0 Hill GH1-Cosworth V8	1 lap behind	16/30
ret	ITALIAN GP	Monza	23	Embassy Racing with Graham Hill	G	3.0 Hill GH1-Cosworth V8	multiple collision at chicane	6/28
ret	US GP	Watkins Glen	23	Embassy Racing with Graham Hill	G	3.0 Hill GH1-Cosworth V8	collision with Henton	17/24

GP Starts: 10   GP Wins: 0   Pole positions: 0   Fastest laps: 0   Points: 1

BRISTOW, Chris (GB) b 2/12/1937, South London – d 19/6/1960, Spa-Francorchamps Circuit, Belgium

1959 Championship position: Unplaced

	Race	Circuit	No	Entrant	Tyres	Capacity/Car/Engine	Comment	Q Pos/Entries
10*	BRITISH GP (F2)	Aintree	48	British Racing Partnership	D	1.5 Cooper T51-Borgward 4	*1st in F2 class/5 laps behind	16/30

1960 Championship position: Unplaced

	Race	Circuit	No	Entrant	Tyres	Capacity/Car/Engine	Comment	Q Pos/Entries
ret	MONACO GP	Monte Carlo	16	Yeoman Credit Racing Team	D	2.5 Cooper T51-Climax 4	gearbox	4/24
ret	DUTCH GP	Zandvoort	8	Yeoman Credit Racing Team	D	2.5 Cooper T51-Climax 4	engine	7/21
ret	BELGIAN GP	Spa	36	Yeoman Credit Racing Team	D	2.5 Cooper T51-Climax 4	fatal accident at Burnenville	9/18

GP Starts: 4   GP Wins: 0   Pole positions: 0   Fastest laps: 0   Points: 0

CHRIS BRISTOW

MANY felt that Chris Bristow had the ability to be a world champion, while his detractors maintained that he was too wild. Certainly he was very, very quick, but sadly we would never find out just how much he could have achieved.

With the support of his father, Chris entered racing in 1956 at the wheel of an MG Special, with which he scored an early win at Crystal Palace. Realising that he needed more competitive machinery than the special, he acquired an 1100cc Cooper sports car for 1957 and used it to win more than a dozen minor scratch and handicap events in a highly satisfying year.

For 1958, the Cooper was no longer eligible, so he purchased a very fast – but not so reliable – Elva, with which he traded places regularly with the more fashionable Lotus. His efforts brought him to the attention of the British Racing Partnership, who invited him to join them for 1959 to race their Formula 2 Cooper-Borgwards and Cooper-Monaco sports cars.

It was the John Davy Trophy at Brands Hatch that really brought him to the attention of the public, Bristow taking an aggregate win from Jack Brabham, Roy Salvadori and Bruce McLaren with an impressive display of speed coupled with a maturity that belied his inexperience.

For 1960, BRP – under the Yeoman Credit Racing Team banner – pinned their hopes on young Bristow and the experienced Harry Schell. When Schell was killed in practice for the International Trophy, Chris, something of loner, found himself paired with Tony Brooks. It would have been fascinating to measure his stature against a proven world-class pilot, but in the Belgian Grand Prix at Spa, while dicing with the Ferrari of the equally combative Willy Mairesse, he lost control of his Cooper, slid into some trackside fencing and was killed instantly in a gruesome accident.

PETER BROEKER

PETER BROEKER had been running his company, Stebro Automotive Manufacturing, since the late 1950s, specialising in stainless-steel free-flow exhaust systems. He went racing to publicise his products and was something of a mystery when he turned up at the 1963 US Grand Prix with his odd-looking little Stebro, powered by a beefed-up pushrod Ford motor. Qualifying some 15 seconds off the pole-position time, he annoyed all and sundry by leaving oil on the track; in the race, the Canadian circulated at the best pace he could manage to finish 22 laps adrift.

Seeking manufacturers of his exhaust systems, Peter brought an updated car to Europe in 1964 to compete in a trio of Formula 2 races, where it proved hopelessly uncompetitive, although he did manage to finish 12th on aggregate in the Berlin GP at AVUS (but too many laps adrift to be classified).

Broeker continued to race his Stebro on home soil over the next few seasons, before switching in 1969 to a Chevron, which brought him a number of top-six finishes in the Formula B category. He won a race in 1970 at Westwood and remained loyal to the marque as he graduated into Formula Atlantic in the mid-1970s.

BROEKER, Peter (CDN) b 15/5/1926, nr Stuttgart, Germany – d 4/11/1980, Ottowa, Ontario

1963 Championship position: Unplaced

	Race	Circuit	No	Entrant	Tyres	Capacity/Car/Engine	Comment	Q Pos/Entries
7	US GP	Watkins Glen	21	Canadian Stebro Racing	D	1.5 Stebro Mk1V-Ford 4	22 laps behind	21/21

GP Starts: 1   GP Wins: 0   Pole positions: 0   Fastest laps: 0   Points: 0

TONY BROOKS was still a dental student with little front-line experience when he shot to international prominence on the back of an absolutely stunning win at the Syracuse GP in the works Connaught in 1955. In only his second ever race abroad, the slightly built and reserved youngster trounced the works Maseratis and Gordinis, three times breaking the lap record and setting a best race lap some five seconds faster than his qualifying time. It had all seemed so easy, yet this was the first Continental win by a British car and driver since Henry Segrave had won at San Sebastian in 1924, so naturally the excitement it generated was immense. Few guessed that the floodgates would soon be opened, and that for British teams and drivers this was just the start.

After racing a Healey in 1952, Tony switched to a Frazer Nash, competing mainly in club events during the next two seasons – successfully, but largely unnoticed. It was not until the middle of the 1955 season that his career really took a step forward. Having raced Aston Martin's DB3S at Le Mans and Goodwood (where he shared third place with Peter Collins), he drove Riseley-Prichard's F2 Connaught in the Daily Telegraph Trophy at Aintree, finishing fourth, behind the Formula 1 cars of Mike Hawthorn, Harry Schell and Roy Salvadori. A win in the F2 class of the Avon Trophy at Castle Combe immediately preceded his momentous Syracuse victory, which of course made him a very hot property.

Signed by BRM for the 1956 season, he took second place in the Aintree 200 after being hampered by brake trouble, and then – the team having withdrawn after practice at Monaco – he prepared for his first championship grand prix start at Silverstone. It was nearly his last: when the throttle stuck at Abbey Curve, the car somersaulted, throwing out the driver, who was lucky to escape with a fractured jaw.

Joining Vanwall for 1957, Brooks soon displayed the smooth style and masterful car control that would bring him so much success over the next three seasons. After finishing second to Juan Fangio, no less, at Monaco, his season was hampered by the effects of a crash at Le Mans, which accounted for his handing his car to Stirling Moss at Aintree, where the British pair shared a momentous victory in their home grand prix. The following season saw Vanwall and Ferrari wage a ferocious battle for supremacy,

and although Hawthorn took the drivers' championship, Moss, Brooks and the ill-fated Stuart Lewis-Evans ensured the constructors' title came to Britain. Tony's three victories at the classic circuits of Spa, the Nürburgring and Monza spoke for themselves. Here was a driver of true world championship pedigree.

Unfortunately, Tony Vandervell withdrew from racing at the end of the year, and Brooks joined Ferrari to drive their front-engined 246 Dino. Again he put in some superb performances, finishing second at Monaco, despite physical sickness due to cockpit fumes, and giving wonderful demonstrations of high-speed artistry at Reims and AVUS. Ferrari did not enter his cars at Aintree, so Vandervell entered one of his Vanwalls especially for Brooks, but he retired with ignition trouble. But for a clutch failure at the start of the Italian GP, Tony may have been able to take the championship from Brabham's fleet little Cooper, but it was not to be.

With increasing business interests and recently married to an Italian girl, Pina, Tony stayed in England during 1960 and, after a Vanwall previously promised by Vandervell failed to materialise, took in a limited programme of events in the Yeoman Credit Cooper. The 1959 Type 51 car was certainly not particularly competitive, especially when Colin Chapman's Lotus 18 and then Cooper's works T53 'lowline' designs appeared and swamped the opposition. Nevertheless Tony continued to give his best, driving harder than ever in a fruitless attempt to make up for the car's lack of performance.

In 1961, he joined BRM alongside Graham Hill and once again endured the frustration of having to campaign an underpowered four-cylinder Climax engine against the might of Ferrari and their V6 'sharknose' cars. However, there were still glimpses of the Brooks of old (at Aintree, where he set the fastest lap in the rain, and a superb drive to third place in the US GP), after which he quietly retired to successfully develop his Weybridge garage business.

When he retired from the day-to-day running of the company, Tony had more time to give to the sport, and in the last decade he has been a welcome and popular celebrity guest at some of the many popular historic car events around the world.

Following Vanwall's withdrawal from racing at the end of 1958, Brooks joined Ferrari and lost no time in assuming the leadership of the team. His win in the broiling heat of the French Grand Prix was typical of his unflustered style.

BROOKS, Tony (GB) b 25/2/1932, Dukinfield, Cheshire

1956 Championship position: Unplaced

	Race	Circuit	No	Entrant	Tyres	Capacity/Car/Engine	Comment	Q Pos/Entries
dns	MONACO GP	Monte Carlo	12	Owen Racing Organisation	D	2.5 BRM P25 4	valve problems in practice	13/19
ret	BRITISH GP	Silverstone	24	Owen Racing Organisation	D	2.5 BRM P25 4	crashed – throttle stuck open	9/28

1957 Championship position: 5th   Wins: 0   Pole positions: 0   Fastest laps: 1   Points scored: 11

	Race	Circuit	No	Entrant	Tyres	Capacity/Car/Engine	Comment	Q Pos/Entries
2	MONACO GP	Monte Carlo	20	Vandervell Products	P	2.5 Vanwall 4		4/21
1*	BRITISH GP	Aintree	20	Vandervell Products	P	2.5 Vanwall 4	*Moss took over car	3/19
ret	"	"	18	Vandervell Products	P	2.5 Vanwall 4	took over Moss's car/engine	– / –
9	GERMAN GP	Nürburgring	11	Vandervell Products	P	2.5 Vanwall 4	road holding problems/-1 lap	5/24
ret	PESCARA GP	Pescara	28	Vandervell Products	P	2.5 Vanwall 4	engine	6/16
7	ITALIAN GP	Monza	22	Vandervell Products	P	2.5 Vanwall 4	pit stop – throttle/FL/-5 laps	3/19

1958 Championship position: 3rd   Wins: 3   Pole positions: 1   Fastest laps: 0   Points scored: 24

	Race	Circuit	No	Entrant	Tyres	Capacity/Car/Engine	Comment	Q Pos/Entries
ret	MONACO GP	Monte Carlo	30	Vandervell Products	D	2.5 Vanwall 4	spark plug	1/28
ret	DUTCH GP	Zandvoort	2	Vandervell Products	D	2.5 Vanwall 4	rear axle	3/17
1	BELGIAN GP	Spa	4	Vandervell Products	D	2.5 Vanwall 4		5/20
ret	FRENCH GP	Reims	10	Vandervell Products	D	2.5 Vanwall 4	gearbox	5/21
ret	"	"	12	Vandervell Products	D	2.5 Vanwall 4	engine/took over Lewis-Evans' car	– / –
7	BRITISH GP	Silverstone	8	Vandervell Products	D	2.5 Vanwall 4	1 lap behind	9/21
1	GERMAN GP	Nürburgring	8	Vandervell Products	D	2.5 Vanwall 4		2/26
ret	PORTUGUESE GP	Oporto	4	Vandervell Products	D	2.5 Vanwall 4	spun off	5/15
1	ITALIAN GP	Monza	28	Vandervell Products	D	2.5 Vanwall 4		2/21
ret	MOROCCAN GP	Casablanca	10	Vandervell Products	D	2.5 Vanwall 4	engine	7/25

1959 Championship position: 2nd   Wins: 2   Pole positions: 2   Fastest laps: 1   Points scored: 27

	Race	Circuit	No	Entrant	Tyres	Capacity/Car/Engine	Comment	Q Pos/Entries
2	MONACO GP	Monte Carlo	50	Scuderia Ferrari	D	2.4 Ferrari Dino 246 V6	physically sick during race	4/24
ret	DUTCH GP	Zandvoort	2	Scuderia Ferrari	D	2.4 Ferrari Dino 246 V6	oil leak	8/15
1	FRENCH GP	Reims	24	Scuderia Ferrari	D	2.4 Ferrari Dino 246 V6		1/22
ret	BRITISH GP	Aintree	20	Vandervell Products	D	2.5 Vanwall 4	misfire	17/30
1	GERMAN GP	AVUS	4	Scuderia Ferrari	D	2.4 Ferrari Dino 246 V6	1st both heats/FL (heat 1)	1/16
9	PORTUGUESE GP	Monsanto	14	Scuderia Ferrari	D	2.4 Ferrari Dino 246 V6	5 laps behind	10/16
ret	ITALIAN GP	Monza	30	Scuderia Ferrari	D	2.4 Ferrari Dino 246 V6	clutch failure at start	2/21
3	US GP	Sebring	2	Scuderia Ferrari	D	2.4 Ferrari Dino 246 V6	hit by von Trips – pit stop	4/19

1960 Championship position: 10th   Wins: 0   Pole positions: 0   Fastest laps: 0   Points scored: 7

	Race	Circuit	No	Entrant	Tyres	Capacity/Car/Engine	Comment	Q Pos/Entries
4	MONACO GP	Monte Carlo	18	Yeoman Credit Racing Team	D	2.5 Cooper T51-Climax 4	1 lap behind	3/24
ret	DUTCH GP	Zandvoort	9	Yeoman Credit Racing Team	D	2.5 Cooper T51-Climax 4	gearbox	10/21
ret	BELGIAN GP	Spa	38	Yeoman Credit Racing Team	D	2.5 Cooper T51-Climax 4	gearbox	2/18
ret	FRENCH GP	Reims	14	Vandervell Products	D	2.5 Vanwall VW11 4	transmission vibration	13/23
5	BRITISH GP	Silverstone	12	Yeoman Credit Racing Team	D	2.5 Cooper T51-Climax 4	1 lap behind	9/25
5	PORTUGUESE GP	Oporto	6	Yeoman Credit Racing Team	D	2.5 Cooper T51-Climax 4	6 laps behind	12/16
ret	US GP	Riverside	6	Yeoman Credit Racing Team	D	2.5 Cooper T51-Climax 4	spun off	9/23

1961 Championship position: 10th   Wins: 0   Pole positions: 0   Fastest laps: 1   Points scored: 6

	Race	Circuit	No	Entrant	Tyres	Capacity/Car/Engine	Comment	Q Pos/Entries
ret	MONACO GP	Monte Carlo	16	Owen Racing Organisation	D	1.5 BRM P48/57-Climax 4	valve	8/21
9	DUTCH GP	Zandvoort	5	Owen Racing Organisation	D	1.5 BRM P48/57-Climax 4	1 lap behind	8/17
13	BELGIAN GP	Spa	38	Owen Racing Organisation	D	1.5 BRM P48/57-Climax 4	pit stop – 6 laps behind	7/25
ret	FRENCH GP	Reims	24	Owen Racing Organisation	D	1.5 BRM P48/57-Climax 4	engine – overheating	11/26
9	BRITISH GP	Aintree	22	Owen Racing Organisation	D	1.5 BRM P48/57-Climax 4	FL	6/30
ret	GERMAN GP	Nürburgring	16	Owen Racing Organisation	D	1.5 BRM P48/57-Climax 4	engine	9/27
5	ITALIAN GP	Monza	26	Owen Racing Organisation	D	1.5 BRM P48/57-Climax 4		13/33
3	US GP	Watkins Glen	5	Owen Racing Organisation	D	1.5 BRM P48/57-Climax 4		=5/19

GP Starts: 38   GP Wins: 6 (1 shared)   Pole positions: 3   Fastest laps: 3   Points: 75

BROWN, Alan (GB) b 20/11/1919, Malton, Yorkshire – d 20/1/2004, Guildford, Surrey

1952 Championship position: 11th=   Wins: 0   Pole positions: 0   Fastest laps: 0   Points scored: 2

	Race	Circuit	No	Entrant	Tyres	Capacity/Car/Engine	Comment	Q Pos/Entries
5	SWISS GP	Bremgarten	26	Ecurie Richmond	D	2.0 Cooper T20-Bristol 6	3 laps behind	15/21
6	BELGIAN GP	Spa	10	Ecurie Richmond	D	2.0 Cooper T20-Bristol 6	2 laps behind	9/22
nc	BRITISH GP	Silverstone	11	Ecurie Richmond	D	2.0 Cooper T20-Bristol 6	16 laps behind	13/32
nc	ITALIAN GP	Monza	38	Ecurie Richmond	D	2.0 Cooper T20-Bristol 6	12 laps behind	21/35

1953 Championship position: Unplaced

	Race	Circuit	No	Entrant	Tyres	Capacity/Car/Engine	Comment	Q Pos/Entries
9	ARGENTINE GP	Buenos Aires	20	Cooper Car Co	D	2.0 Cooper T20-Bristol 6	hit spectator/10 laps behind	12/16
ret	BRITISH GP	Silverstone	19	R J Chase	D	2.0 Cooper T23-Bristol 6	fan belt	21/29
ret	GERMAN GP	Nürburgring	38	Equipe Anglaise	D	2.0 Cooper T23-Bristol 6	misfire – crashed	17/35
12	ITALIAN GP	Monza	46	Equipe Anglaise	D	2.0 Cooper T23-Bristol 6	10 laps behind	24/30

1954 Championship position: Unplaced

	Race	Circuit	No	Entrant	Tyres	Capacity/Car/Engine	Comment	Q Pos/Entries
dns	BRITISH GP	Silverstone	27	Equipe Anglaise	D	2.0 Cooper T23-Bristol 6		26/31

GP Starts: 8   GP Wins: 0   Pole positions: 0   Fastest laps: 0   Points: 2

BROWN, Warwick (AUS) b 24/12/1949, Sydney, New South Wales

1976 Championship position: Unplaced

	Race	Circuit	No	Entrant	Tyres	Capacity/Car/Engine	Comment	Q Pos/Entries
14	US GP EAST	Watkins Glen	21	Walter Wolf Racing	G	3.0 Wolf Williams FW05-Cosworth V8	5 laps behind	23/27

GP Starts: 1   GP Wins: 0   Pole positions: 0   Fastest laps: 0   Points: 0

ALAN BROWN

ALONG with his friend and team-mate, Eric Brandon, Alan Brown was a star of the 500cc champion-ships with his F3 Cooper, his personal highlight in this category being a win in the 1951 Luxembourg Grand Prix. For 1952, the pair raced their new F2 Cooper-Bristols under the Ecurie Richmond banner, but they were effectively works machines. Things started well when Brown scored two points on the car's Continental debut at Bremgarten, following this with two sixths, at the Monza Autodrome GP and the Belgian GP at Spa, but it was steadily overtaken by more sophisticated machinery, encouraging Alan to look elsewhere for racing success. He gave the prototype Vanwall its debut at the 1954 International Trophy and raced a Connaught at the same event a year later, but he concentrated on sports cars – Coopers and Connaughts from 1953 to 1955, and then a Jaguar D-Type in 1956, his last season of racing.

Brown went on to enter Formula 2 Coopers, giving rides to many aspiring racers, including Innes Ireland, Ken Tyrrell, Peter Ashdown and Mike Taylor.

WARWICK BROWN

A real tough nut – even by the standards of the Aussie school of hard knocks – Warwick Brown had plenty of guts and not a little ability, but apart from a single grand prix appearance, he had to content himself with a career in Australasia and North America. Early promise in 1972 with an elderly McLaren M10B encouraged Brown to buy a Lola T300 for the 1973 Tasman series. A third place at Levin and then second at Wigram proved that he was a real contender for championship honours, before disaster struck at Surfers Paradise. During the pre-race warm-up session, his Lola suffered a mechanical failure at over 130mph, leaving him hospitalised for three months with both legs fractured and back injuries. His season was emphatically over and his car totally destroyed. Unbowed, he limped back into action in 1974, with a new Lola T334, and was a popular winner of the final Tasman round at Adelaide.

Setting his sights on US F5000 later in the year, Brown enjoyed a successful foray, competing in three races and taking third place at Riverside to lay the groundwork for a return. He won the 1975 Tasman title, before heading Stateside again, where he competed in the UAC/SCCA F5000 series. Disadvantaged by running a Talon chassis against a whole fleet of Lolas, Brown nonetheless gained some pretty decent placings in his first year. Wisely he opted to join the Lola clan for 1976, where the competition was fierce. A third place at Watkins Glen and a fourth at Elkhart Lake were suddenly followed by the loss of his drive through his team's lack of finance. Fortunately, the chance of joining the crack VDS team in a third car put him back on track. Not only was Brown back in business, but also Chris Amon's practice accident for the Canadian Grand Prix gave him the unexpected opportunity to drive in the US Grand Prix a week later. Despite having no experience at this level, he out-qualified his team-mate Arturo Merzario and nursed the car to the finish, despite fading brakes, and losing third and fifth gears.

With F5000 collapsing in the USA at season's end, Brown began 1977 at home with a well-earned win in the four-race Rothman's International series. His year soon took a downturn, however, when the Lolas were morphed into their sports car guise for the CanAm series. A lurid practice accident at Laguna Seca left him with a broken ankle, and he took no further part in the series. Undaunted, Brown was back in action in 1978 to defend his Rothmans title down-under, making a clean sweep of all four rounds in the VDS Lola. Then, it was back to North America for a proper attack on the Can-Am championship, where he finished second to Alan Jones after a hard-fought championship battle.

Brown's chances of making it a hat-trick of Rothmans titles in 1979 effectively ended in a practice crash before the first race at Sandown Park, which put him in hospital with an ankle injury. He took an easy win in the final round at Oran Park, but his crown went to Larry Perkins. This proved to be his final victory, since he decided the time was right to retire from competition.

ADOLF BRUDES

A GERMAN nobleman, Adolf Brudes began his racing career on motorcycles, before turning to four wheels. His family owned a BMW dealership, and just before Italy entered the Second World War in 1940, he took third place in the Coppa Brescia in a BMW.

The war decimated everything he owned and he was virtually destitute after the cessation of hostilities. Finding work as a mechanic allowed him to resume his racing activities, occasionally taking the wheel of a Veritas – as in his appearance in the 1952 German GP – but mainly competing in a Borgward in events as diverse as the long-distance Buenos Aires 1000km, the Le Mans 24-hours, the Carrera Panamericana and speed record attempts at AVUS.

BRUDES von BRESLAU, Adolf (D) b Koutlin, nr Brelau (Wroclaw, PL) 15/10/1899 – d Bremen 5/11/1986

1952 Championship position: Unplaced

	Race	Circuit	No	Entrant	Tyres	Capacity/Car/Engine	Comment	Q Pos/Entries
ret	GERMAN GP	Nürburgring	126	Adolf Brudes	–	2.0 Veritas RS-6	engine	19/32

GP Starts: 1   GP Wins: 0   Pole positions: 0   Fastest laps: 0   Points: 0

IT must have been more than a little galling for Martin Brundle to see Ayrton Senna sweeping all before him in grand prix racing, for they were once very evenly matched in Formula 3. Martin may not have had the innate talent of the sadly deceased world champion, but in a truly competitive F1 car, he would surely have been a grand prix winner at the very least.

In 1983, Brundle started the F3 season buoyed by a strong finish to his first year in the series and ready to pit himself against Senna, the latest Formula Ford/FF2000 hotshot. Watching the Brazilian simply disappear into the distance to win no fewer than nine races would have broken the resolve of a lesser man, but in the second half of the season Martin staged a comeback. Winning six races, he fell just short in the chase for the Marlboro F3 title, but had given his career prospects a massive boost.

Joining Tyrrell in 1984, Martin finished fifth in his first race, and the nimble Cosworth-powered car was later in its element at Detroit, where he took a brilliant second place. Then came two blows to his progress. A practice crash at Dallas left him with broken ankles, ending his season, and, to add insult to injury, Tyrrell's points were later expunged due to the team's technical misdemeanours. Starting from scratch in 1985, he waited patiently for the Renault turbo engine, which by now was a long-overdue necessity for the team. Driving sensibly and displaying great car control, he did what he could with the equipment at his disposal, showing the odd flash of naked aggression, no doubt due to the frustration of being so far off the pace.

Reasoning that any move would be beneficial, Brundle opted to join Zakspeed in 1987, but, a gutsy fifth at Imola notwithstanding, it turned out to be a big mistake. Now four seasons into his grand prix career and seemingly no further forward than when he had started in Formula 1, he took the brave decision to join Jaguar for a season of sports car racing rather than just trail around at the tail-end of the grand prix pack. His courage was rewarded, the Norfolk man winning the World Sports Car drivers' title with victories at Jarama, Monza, Silverstone, Brands Hatch and Fuji. In tandem with this programme, he jetted back and forth across the Atlantic to compete for Jaguar in IMSA, sharing the winning car in the Daytona 24-hours.

A one-off drive for Williams at Spa kept Brundle in the picture, and for 1989 he joined the Brabham team as a much more confident and purposeful performer, putting the Judd-powered car in the points on three occasions. Unfortunately, the team was already suffering from financial strictures and, tiring of the uncertainty over Brabham's plans, Martin went back to Jaguar for the 1990 season, the highlight of which was, of course, the team's Le Mans victory, when he shared the winning car with John Nielsen and Price Cobb. Tempted by a package that included a Yamaha engine, he rejoined Brabham for 1991, but spent a generally frustrating season watching the stop-start development of a quite promising car gradually tail away.

By the end of the year, Brundle was glad to be able to look forward to a really good drive at last. Joining his old Jaguar boss Tom Walkinshaw at Benetton, he made a pretty disastrous start in the first four races, which in retrospect fatally damaged his long-term prospects with the team. From Imola onwards, he scored points in every round bar Canada (a race that he could well have won), and it was very hard on him indeed when he was dropped in favour of Ricardo Patrese. He moved to Ligier for 1993 and, after another tardy start to the season, helped bring about a welcome improvement in the team's fortunes, showing an application that had been sorely lacking there. His reward should have been the chance to carry on the good work in 1994, but in the end he successfully bided his time before grabbing the drive at McLaren vacated by Ayrton Senna.

Brundle's second place at Monaco was the high spot in a fraught season at Woking, the newly forged alliance with Peugeot doomed to last just 16 races. Honest, open and diligent, he would have loved to stay with the team for 1995, but in the end his seat went to Nigel Mansell as the McLaren looked for a star name. Brundle made a swift return to Ligier to work with Tom Walkinshaw once again, although the Mugen-Honda engine deal meant that he would only compete in 11 of the 17 races. He shone on the team's home track of Magny-Cours, hounding Coulthard's Williams to the finish line to claim fourth, and he picked up a place on the podium at Spa, but could achieve little else with a car that just wasn't quick enough.

The 1996 season saw Martin on the move once more, joining up again with Eddie Jordan, his old boss from the far-off F3 days of 1983. With Jordan needing to deliver the goods, it would be a tough year for the once happy-go-lucky team, who had by then become serious heavyweight underachievers. After miraculously emerging unscathed from a first-corner crash in the opening grand prix at Melbourne, Brundle struggled to come to terms with the car's set-up. By mid-season, things had improved, but crucially he and team-mate Rubens Barrichello had already lost the confidence of the team's management, and both were bundled out at season's end to make way for Giancarlo Fisichella and Ralf Schumacher.

With no further Formula 1 prospects, Martin took the opportunity to forge a brilliantly successful career as a TV commentator and assumed the role of adviser to David Coulthard. He kept his reflexes sharp by racing for Nissan and Toyota at Le Mans for three successive years between 1997 and 1999. He was back at the La Sarthe classic in 2001 with Bentley, but all four appearances ended in retirement.

In parallel with his TV commentating, Brundle continued to handle potent machinery on occasion, largely in demonstration roles, but the temptation to go racing again proved too strong to resist. In 2008, he took part in the Formula Palmer Audi series to briefly race against his son, Alex, who was a regular competitor.

Martin came out of retirement again to race in the 2011 Daytona 24-hours, sharing a Ford-powered Riley with Zak Brown, Mark Patterson, and former Ligier and Brabham team-mate Mark Blundell; the team finished fourth overall. He planned to return to Le Mans once again in 2012, to race alongside his son Alex in a Nissan LMP2.

Having initially started his TV commentating career with ITV in 1997, Brundle switched to the BBC in 2009. His pre-race grid walks soon became essential viewing as he hunted down drivers and VIPs alike in search of fascinating sound bites. With the BBC suddenly under pressure to cut costs and unable to continue paying for exclusive rights to Formula 1, he was head-hunted by Sky Sports to lead their 2012 line-up as they bring their comprehensive broadcasting package to the sport for the first time.

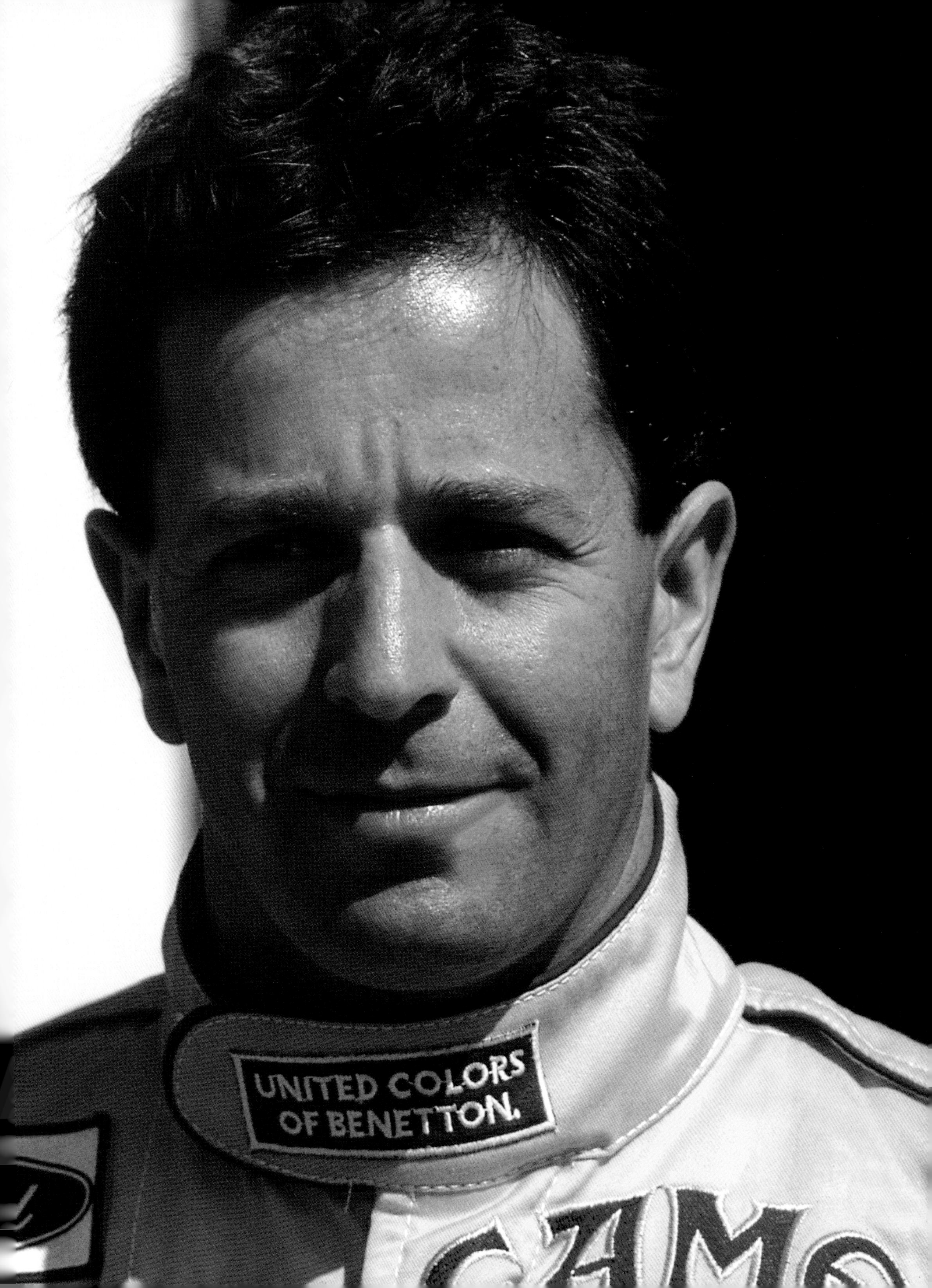
UNITED COLORS
OF BENETTON.

BRUNDLE, Martin (GB) b 1/6/1959, King's Lynn, Norfolk

1984 Championship position: Unplaced (2 points scored, but these were disallowed by FIA after the Tyrrell team were excluded for technical irregularities)

	Race	Circuit	No	Entrant	Tyres	Capacity/Car/Engine	Comment	Q Pos/Entries
5/dsq*	BRAZILIAN GP	Rio	3	Tyrrell Racing Organisation	G	3.0 Tyrrell 012-Cosworth V8	5th/*dsq after Dutch GP	19/27
11/dsq*	SOUTH AFRICAN GP	Kyalami	3	Tyrrell Racing Organisation	G	3.0 Tyrrell 012-Cosworth V8	11th/*dsq after Dutch GP	25/27
ret/dsq*	BELGIAN GP	Zolder	3	Tyrrell Racing Organisation	G	3.0 Tyrrell 012-Cosworth V8	lost wheel/*dsq after Dutch GP	22/27
11/dsq*	SAN MARINO GP	Imola	3	Tyrrell Racing Organisation	G	3.0 Tyrrell 012-Cosworth V8	11th/*dsq after Dutch GP	22/28
12/dsq*	FRENCH GP	Dijon	3	Tyrrell Racing Organisation	G	3.0 Tyrrell 012-Cosworth V8	12th/*dsq after Dutch GP	24/27
dnq	MONACO GP	Monte Carlo	3	Tyrrell Racing Organisation	G	3.0 Tyrrell 012-Cosworth V8	accident in practice	22/27
dsq*	CANADIAN GP	Montreal	3	Tyrrell Racing Organisation	G	3.0 Tyrrell 012-Cosworth V8	10th/*dsq after Dutch GP	21/26
dsq*	US GP (DETROIT)	Detroit	3	Tyrrell Racing Organisation	G	3.0 Tyrrell 012-Cosworth V8	2nd/*dsq after Dutch GP	11/27
dnq	US GP (DALLAS)	Dallas	3	Tyrrell Racing Organisation	G	3.0 Tyrrell 012-Cosworth V8	injured in practice accident	27/27

1985 Championship position: Unplaced

	Race	Circuit	No	Entrant	Tyres	Capacity/Car/Engine	Comment	Q Pos/Entries
8	BRAZILIAN GP	Rio	3	Tyrrell Racing Organisation	G	3.0 Tyrrell 012-Cosworth V8	3 laps behind	21/25
ret	PORTUGUESE GP	Estoril	3	Tyrrell Racing Organisation	G	3.0 Tyrrell 012-Cosworth V8	gear linkage	22/26
9	SAN MARINO GP	Imola	3	Tyrrell Racing Organisation	G	3.0 Tyrrell 012-Cosworth V8	4 laps behind	25/26
10	MONACO GP	Monte Carlo	3	Tyrrell Racing Organisation	G	3.0 Tyrrell 012-Cosworth V8	4 laps behind	18/26
12	CANADIAN GP	Montreal	3	Tyrrell Racing Organisation	G	3.0 Tyrrell 012-Cosworth V8	2 laps behind	24/25
ret	US GP (DETROIT)	Detroit	3	Tyrrell Racing Organisation	G	3.0 Tyrrell 012-Cosworth V8	accident with Alliot	18/25
ret	FRENCH GP	Paul Ricard	3	Tyrrell Racing Organisation	G	1.5 t/c Tyrrell 014-Renault V6	gearbox	21/26
7	BRITISH GP	Silverstone	3	Tyrrell Racing Organisation	G	1.5 t/c Tyrrell 014-Renault V6	started fom back of grid/-2 laps	20/26
10	GERMAN GP	Nürburgring	4	Tyrrell Racing Organisation	G	3.0 Tyrrell 012-Cosworth V8	4 laps behind	26/27
dnq	AUSTRIAN GP	Österreichring	4	Tyrrell Racing Organisation	G	3.0 Tyrrell 012-Cosworth V8		27/27
7	DUTCH GP	Zandvoort	3	Tyrrell Racing Organisation	G	1.5 t/c Tyrrell 014-Renault V6	1 lap behind	21/27
8	ITALIAN GP	Monza	3	Tyrrell Racing Organisation	G	1.5 t/c Tyrrell 014-Renault V6	1 lap behind	18/26
13	BELGIAN GP	Spa	3	Tyrrell Racing Organisation	G	1.5 t/c Tyrrell 014-Renault V6	5 laps behind	21/24
ret	EUROPEAN GP	Brands Hatch	3	Tyrrell Racing Organisation	G	1.5 t/c Tyrrell 014-Renault V6	water pipe	16/27
7	SOUTH AFRICAN GP	Kyalami	3	Tyrrell Racing Organisation	G	1.5 t/c Tyrrell 014-Renault V6	2 laps behind	17/21
nc	AUSTRALIAN GP	Adelaide	3	Tyrrell Racing Organisation	G	1.5 t/c Tyrrell 014-Renault V6	pit stop – electrics/33 laps behind	17/25

1986 Championship position: 11th   Wins: 0   Pole positions: 0   Fastest laps: 0   Points scored: 8

	Race	Circuit	No	Entrant	Tyres	Capacity/Car/Engine	Comment	Q Pos/Entries
5	BRAZILIAN GP	Rio	3	Data General Team Tyrrell	G	1.5 t/c Tyrrell 014-Renault V6	1 lap behind	17/25
dns	"	"	3	Data General Team Tyrrell	G	1.5 t/c Tyrrell 015-Renault V6	crashed in practice	– / -
ret	SPANISH GP	Jerez	3	Data General Team Tyrrell	G	1.5 t/c Tyrrell 014-Renault V6	engine – lost lubricant	12/25
8	SAN MARINO GP	Imola	3	Data General Team Tyrrell	G	1.5 t/c Tyrrell 014-Renault V6	race car/2 laps behind	– / -
dns	"	"	3	Data General Team Tyrrell	G	1.5 t/c Tyrrell 015-Renault V6	crashed car in warm up	13/26
ret	MONACO GP	Monte Carlo	3	Data General Team Tyrrell	G	1.5 t/c Tyrrell 015-Renault V6	accident with Tambay	10/26
ret	BELGIAN GP	Spa	3	Data General Team Tyrrell	G	1.5 t/c Tyrrell 015-Renault V6	gearbox	12/25
9	CANADIAN GP	Montreal	3	Data General Team Tyrrell	G	1.5 t/c Tyrrell 015-Renault V6	2 laps behind	19/25
ret	US GP (DETROIT)	Detroit	3	Data General Team Tyrrell	G	1.5 t/c Tyrrell 015-Renault V6	electrics	16/26
10	FRENCH GP	Paul Ricard	3	Data General Team Tyrrell	G	1.5 t/c Tyrrell 015-Renault V6	lost 4th gear/3 laps behind	15/26
5	BRITISH GP	Brands Hatch	3	Data General Team Tyrrell	G	1.5 t/c Tyrrell 015-Renault V6	3 laps behind	11/26
ret	GERMAN GP	Hockenheim	3	Data General Team Tyrrell	G	1.5 t/c Tyrrell 015-Renault V6	electrics	15/26
6	HUNGARIAN GP	Hungaroring	3	Data General Team Tyrrell	G	1.5 t/c Tyrrell 015-Renault V6	lost 4th gear/2 laps behind	16/26
ret	AUSTRIAN GP	Österreichring	3	Data General Team Tyrrell	G	1.5 t/c Tyrrell 015-Renault V6	turbo	17/26
10	ITALIAN GP	Monza	3	Data General Team Tyrrell	G	1.5 t/c Tyrrell 015-Renault V6	misfire/2 laps behind	20/27
ret	PORTUGUESE GP	Estoril	3	Data General Team Tyrrell	G	1.5 t/c Tyrrell 015-Renault V6	engine	19/27
11	MEXICAN GP	Mexico City	3	Data General Team Tyrrell	G	1.5 t/c Tyrrell 015-Renault V6	2 pit stops – tyres/3 laps behind	16/26
4	AUSTRALIAN GP	Adelaide	3	Data General Team Tyrrell	G	1.5 t/c Tyrrell 015-Renault V6	1 lap behind	16/26

1987 Championship position: 18th   Wins: 0   Pole positions: 0   Fastest laps: 0   Points scored: 2

	Race	Circuit	No	Entrant	Tyres	Capacity/Car/Engine	Comment	Q Pos/Entries
ret	BRAZILIAN GP	Rio	9	West Zakspeed Racing	G	1.5 t/c Zakspeed 861 4	turbo	19/23
5	SAN MARINO GP	Imola	9	West Zakspeed Racing	G	1.5 t/c Zakspeed 871 4	2 laps behind	16/27
ret	BELGIAN GP	Spa	9	West Zakspeed Racing	G	1.5 t/c Zakspeed 871 4	engine	18/26
7	MONACO GP	Monte Carlo	9	West Zakspeed Racing	G	1.5 t/c Zakspeed 871 4	2 laps behind	14/26
ret	US GP (DETROIT)	Detroit	9	West Zakspeed Racing	G	1.5 t/c Zakspeed 871 4	turbo	15/26
ret	FRENCH GP	Paul Ricard	9	West Zakspeed Racing	G	1.5 t/c Zakspeed 871 4	lost rear wheel	18/26
nc	BRITISH GP	Silverstone	9	West Zakspeed Racing	G	1.5 t/c Zakspeed 871 4	pit stop – electrics/-11 laps	17/26
nc	GERMAN GP	Hockenheim	9	West Zakspeed Racing	G	1.5 t/c Zakspeed 871 4	pit stops – electrics/-10 laps	19/26
ret	HUNGARIAN GP	Hungaroring	9	West Zakspeed Racing	G	1.5 t/c Zakspeed 871 4	turbo	22/26
dsq*	AUSTRIAN GP	Österreichring	9	West Zakspeed Racing	G	1.5 t/c Zakspeed 871 4	14th/*bodywork infringement	17/26
ret	ITALIAN GP	Monza	9	West Zakspeed Racing	G	1.5 t/c Zakspeed 871 4	gearbox	17/28
ret	PORTUGUESE GP	Estoril	9	West Zakspeed Racing	G	1.5 t/c Zakspeed 871 4	gearbox	17/27
11	SPANISH GP	Jerez	9	West Zakspeed Racing	G	1.5 t/c Zakspeed 871 4	2 laps behind	20/28
ret	MEXICAN GP	Mexico City	9	West Zakspeed Racing	G	1.5 t/c Zakspeed 871 4	turbo	13/27
ret	JAPANESE GP	Suzuka	9	West Zakspeed Racing	G	1.5 t/c Zakspeed 871 4	engine overheating	16/27
ret	AUSTRALIAN GP	Adelaide	9	West Zakspeed Racing	G	1.5 t/c Zakspeed 871 4	turbo and gear selection	16/27

1988 Championship position: Unplaced

	Race	Circuit	No	Entrant	Tyres	Capacity/Car/Engine	Comment	Q Pos/Entries
7*	BELGIAN GP	Spa	5	Canon Williams Team	G	3.5 Williams FW12-Judd V8	*3rd & 4th cars dsq/-1 lap	12/31

1989 Championship position: 16th=   Wins: 0   Pole positions: 0   Fastest laps: 0   Points scored: 4

	Race	Circuit	No	Entrant	Tyres	Capacity/Car/Engine	Comment	Q Pos/Entries
ret	BRAZILIAN GP	Rio	7	Motor Racing Developments	P	3.5 Brabham BT58-Judd V8	engine – wiring loom	13/38
ret	SAN MARINO GP	Imola	7	Motor Racing Developments	P	3.5 Brabham BT58-Judd V8	fuel pump	22/39
6	MONACO GP	Monte Carlo	7	Motor Racing Developments	P	3.5 Brabham BT58-Judd V8	pit stop when 3rd-battery/-2 laps	4/38
9	MEXICAN GP	Mexico City	7	Motor Racing Developments	P	3.5 Brabham BT58-Judd V8	1 lap behind	20/39
ret	US GP (PHOENIX)	Phoenix	7	Motor Racing Developments	P	3.5 Brabham BT58-Judd V8	brakes	5/39
dnpq	CANADIAN GP	Montreal	7	Motor Racing Developments	P	3.5 Brabham BT58-Judd V8		31/39
dnpq	FRENCH GP	Paul Ricard	7	Motor Racing Developments	P	3.5 Brabham BT58-Judd V8		32/39
ret	BRITISH GP	Silverstone	7	Motor Racing Developments	P	3.5 Brabham BT58-Judd V8	engine	20/39
8	GERMAN GP	Hockenheim	7	Motor Racing Developments	P	3.5 Brabham BT58-Judd V8	pit stop – slow puncture/-1 lap	12/39
12	HUNGARIAN GP	Hungaroring	7	Motor Racing Developments	P	3.5 Brabham BT58-Judd V8	hit Alesi and spun/-2 laps	15/39

ret	BELGIAN GP	Spa	7	Motor Racing Developments	P	3.5 Brabham BT58-Judd V8	*brakes*	20/39
6	ITALIAN GP	Monza	7	Motor Racing Developments	P	3.5 Brabham BT58-Judd V8	*1 lap behind*	12/39
8	PORTUGUESE GP	Estoril	7	Motor Racing Developments	P	3.5 Brabham BT58-Judd V8	*2 pit stops – tyres/1 lap behind*	10/39
ret	SPANISH GP	Jerez	7	Motor Racing Developments	P	3.5 Brabham BT58-Judd V8	*rear suspension – spun off*	8/38
5*	JAPANESE GP	Suzuka	7	Motor Racing Developments	P	3.5 Brabham BT58-Judd V8	**1st place car disqualified/-1 lap*	13/39
ret	AUSTRALIAN GP	Adelaide	7	Motor Racing Developments	P	3.5 Brabham BT58-Judd V8	*hit by Senna in rain*	12/39

1991 Championship position: 15th=   Wins: 0   Pole positions: 0   Fastest laps: 0   Points scored: 2

11	US GP (PHOENIX)	Phoenix	7	Motor Racing Developments Ltd	P	3.5 Brabham BT59Y-Yamaha V12	*8 laps behind*	12/34
12	BRAZILIAN GP	Interlagos	7	Motor Racing Developments Ltd	P	3.5 Brabham BT59Y-Yamaha V12	*4 laps behind*	26/34
11	SAN MARINO GP	Imola	7	Motor Racing Developments Ltd	P	3.5 Brabham BT60Y-Yamaha V12	*4 laps behind*	18/34
excl	MONACO GP	Monte Carlo	7	Motor Racing Developments Ltd	P	3.5 Brabham BT60Y-Yamaha V12	*missed weight check in practice*	27/34
ret	CANADIAN GP	Montreal	7	Motor Racing Developments Ltd	P	3.5 Brabham BT60Y-Yamaha V12	*engine*	20/34
ret	MEXICAN GP	Mexico City	7	Motor Racing Developments Ltd	P	3.5 Brabham BT60Y-Yamaha V12	*lost rear wheel*	17/34
ret	FRENCH GP	Magny Cours	7	Motor Racing Developments Ltd	P	3.5 Brabham BT60Y-Yamaha V12	*gearbox*	24/34
ret	BRITISH GP	Silverstone	7	Motor Racing Developments Ltd	P	3.5 Brabham BT60Y-Yamaha V12	*throttle cable*	14/34
11	GERMAN GP	Hockenheim	7	Motor Racing Developments Ltd	P	3.5 Brabham BT60Y-Yamaha V12	*2 laps behind*	15/34
ret	HUNGARIAN GP	Hungaroring	7	Motor Racing Developments Ltd	P	3.5 Brabham BT60Y-Yamaha V12	*foot cramp*	10/34
9	BELGIAN GP	Spa	7	Motor Racing Developments Ltd	P	3.5 Brabham BT60Y-Yamaha V12	*2 laps behind*	16/34
13	ITALIAN GP	Monza	7	Motor Racing Developments Ltd	P	3.5 Brabham BT60Y-Yamaha V12	*1 lap behind*	19/34
12	PORTUGUESE GP	Estoril	7	Motor Racing Developments Ltd	P	3.5 Brabham BT60Y-Yamaha V12	*2 laps behind*	19/34
10	SPANISH GP	Barcelona	7	Motor Racing Developments Ltd	P	3.5 Brabham BT60Y-Yamaha V12	*2 laps behind*	11/33
5	JAPANESE GP	Suzuka	7	Motor Racing Developments Ltd	P	3.5 Brabham BT60Y-Yamaha V12	*1 lap behind*	19/32
dnq	AUSTRALIAN GP	Adelaide	7	Motor Racing Developments Ltd	P	3.5 Brabham BT60Y-Yamaha V12		28/32

1992 Championship position: 6th   Wins: 0   Pole positions: 0   Fastest laps: 0   Points scored: 38

ret	SOUTH AFRICAN GP	Kyalami	20	Camel Benetton Ford	G	3.5 Benetton B191B-Ford HB V8	*spun – broke clutch restarting*	8/30
ret	MEXICAN GP	Mexico City	20	Camel Benetton Ford	G	3.5 Benetton B191B-Ford HB V8	*overheating*	4/30
ret	BRAZILIAN GP	Interlagos	20	Camel Benetton Ford	G	3.5 Benetton B191B-Ford HB V8	*collision with Alesi*	7/31
ret	SPANISH GP	Barcelona	20	Camel Benetton Ford	G	3.5 Benetton B192-Ford HB V8	*spun off*	6/32
4	SAN MARINO GP	Imola	20	Camel Benetton Ford	G	3.5 Benetton B192-Ford HB V8		6/32
5	MONACO GP	Monte Carlo	20	Camel Benetton Ford	G	3.5 Benetton B192-Ford HB V8		7/32
ret	CANADIAN GP	Montreal	20	Camel Benetton Ford	G	3.5 Benetton B192-Ford HB V8	*final drive*	7/32
3	FRENCH GP	Magny Cours	20	Camel Benetton Ford	G	3.5 Benetton B192-Ford HB V8		7/30
3	BRITISH GP	Silverstone	20	Camel Benetton Ford	G	3.5 Benetton B192-Ford HB V8		6/32
4	GERMAN GP	Hockenheim	20	Camel Benetton Ford	G	3.5 Benetton B192-Ford HB V8		9/32
5	HUNGARIAN GP	Hungaroring	20	Camel Benetton Ford	G	3.5 Benetton B192-Ford HB V8		6/31
4	BELGIAN GP	Spa	20	Camel Benetton Ford	G	3.5 Benetton B192-Ford HB V8		9/30
2	ITALIAN GP	Monza	20	Camel Benetton Ford	G	3.5 Benetton B192-Ford HB V8		9/28
4	PORTUGUESE GP	Estoril	20	Camel Benetton Ford	G	3.5 Benetton B192-Ford HB V8	*1 lap behind*	6/26
3	JAPANESE GP	Suzuka	20	Camel Benetton Ford	G	3.5 Benetton B192-Ford HB V8		13/26
3	AUSTRALIAN GP	Adelaide	20	Camel Benetton Ford	G	3.5 Benetton B192-Ford HB V8		8/26

1993 Championship position: 7th   Wins: 0   Pole positions: 0   Fastest laps: 0   Points scored: 13

ret	SOUTH AFRICAN GP	Kyalami	25	Ligier Gitanes Blondes	G	3.5 Ligier JS39-Renault V10	*spun off on oil*	12/26
ret	BRAZILIAN GP	Interlagos	25	Ligier Gitanes Blondes	G	3.5 Ligier JS39-Renault V10	*collision with Barbazza – spun off*	16/26
ret	EUROPEAN GP	Donington	25	Ligier Gitanes Blondes	G	3.5 Ligier JS39-Renault V10	*spun off and stalled*	22/26
3	SAN MARINO GP	Imola	25	Ligier Gitanes Blondes	G	3.5 Ligier JS39-Renault V10	*1 lap behind*	10/26
ret	SPANISH GP	Barcelona	25	Ligier Gitanes Blondes	G	3.5 Ligier JS39-Renault V10	*puncture – spun off*	18/26
6	MONACO GP	Monte Carlo	25	Ligier Gitanes Blondes	G	3.5 Ligier JS39-Renault V10	*collision – pit stop/2 laps behind*	13/26
5	CANADIAN GP	Montreal	25	Ligier Gitanes Blondes	G	3.5 Ligier JS39-Renault V10	*1 lap behind*	7/26
5	FRENCH GP	Magny Cours	25	Ligier Gitanes Blondes	G	3.5 Ligier JS39-Renault V10		3/26
14/ret	BRITISH GP	Silverstone	25	Ligier Gitanes Blondes	G	3.5 Ligier JS39-Renault V10	*gearbox/6 laps behind*	6/26
8	GERMAN GP	Hockenheim	25	Ligier Gitanes Blondes	G	3.5 Ligier JS39-Renault V10	*stop & go penalty/1 lap behind*	6/26
5	HUNGARIAN GP	Hungaroring	25	Ligier Gitanes Blondes	G	3.5 Ligier JS39-Renault V10	*collision with Berger/1 lap behind*	13/26
7	BELGIAN GP	Spa	25	Ligier Gitanes Blondes	G	3.5 Ligier JS39-Renault V10	*1 lap behind*	11/25
ret	ITALIAN GP	Monza	25	Ligier Gitanes Blondes	G	3.5 Ligier JS39-Renault V10	*taken off by Senna*	12/26
6	PORTUGUESE GP	Estoril	25	Ligier Gitanes Blondes	G	3.5 Ligier JS39-Renault V10	*1 lap behind*	11/26
9/ret	JAPANESE GP	Suzuka	25	Ligier Gitanes Blondes	G	3.5 Ligier JS39-Renault V10	*collision, Lehto – spun off/-2 laps*	15/24
6	AUSTRALIAN GP	Adelaide	25	Ligier Gitanes Blondes	G	3.5 Ligier JS39-Renault V10	*1 lap behind*	8/24

So near, yet so far. Brundle came close to winning the 1992 Canadian Grand Prix for Benetton, but was forced to retire with gearbox failure.

1994 Championship position: 7th   Wins: 0   Pole positions: 0   Fastest laps: 0   Points scored: 16

	Race	Circuit	No	Entrant	Tyres	Capacity/Car/Engine	Comment	Q Pos/Entries
ret	BRAZILIAN GP	Interlagos	8	Marlboro McLaren Peugeot	G	3.5 McLaren MP4/9-Peugeot V10	multiple accident	18/28
ret	PACIFIC GP	T.I. Circuit	8	Marlboro McLaren Peugeot	G	3.5 McLaren MP4/9-Peugeot V10	overheating	6/28
8	SAN MARINO GP	Imola	8	Marlboro McLaren Peugeot	G	3.5 McLaren MP4/9-Peugeot V10	1 lap behind	13/28
2	MONACO GP	Monte Carlo	8	Marlboro McLaren Peugeot	G	3.5 McLaren MP4/9-Peugeot V10		8/24
11/ret	SPANISH GP	Barcelona	8	Marlboro McLaren Peugeot	G	3.5 McLaren MP4/9-Peugeot V10	6 laps behind/transmission	8/27
ret	CANADIAN GP	Montreal	8	Marlboro McLaren Peugeot	G	3.5 McLaren MP4/9-Peugeot V10	electrics	12//27
ret	FRENCH GP	Magny Cours	8	Marlboro McLaren Peugeot	G	3.5 McLaren MP4/9-Peugeot V10	engine	12/28
ret	BRITISH GP	Silverstone	8	Marlboro McLaren Peugeot	G	3.5 McLaren MP4/9-Peugeot V10	engine at start	9/28
ret	GERMAN GP	Hockenheim	8	Marlboro McLaren Peugeot	G	3.5 McLaren MP4/9-Peugeot V10	engine	13/28
4/ret	HUNGARIAN GP	Hungaroring	8	Marlboro McLaren Peugeot	G	3.5 McLaren MP4/9-Peugeot V10	engine failure on last lap	6/28
ret	BELGIAN GP	Spa	8	Marlboro McLaren Peugeot	G	3.5 McLaren MP4/9-Peugeot V10	spun off	13/28
5	ITALIAN GP	Monza	8	Marlboro McLaren Peugeot	G	3.5 McLaren MP4/9-Peugeot V10		15/28
6	PORTUGUESE GP	Estoril	8	Marlboro McLaren Peugeot	G	3.5 McLaren MP4/9-Peugeot V10		7/28
ret	EUROPEAN GP	Jerez	8	Marlboro McLaren Peugeot	G	3.5 McLaren MP4/9-Peugeot V10	engine	15/28
ret	JAPANESE GP	Suzuka	8	Marlboro McLaren Peugeot	G	3.5 McLaren MP4/9-Peugeot V10	spun off and hit marshal	9/28
3	AUSTRALIAN GP	Adelaide	8	Marlboro McLaren Peugeot	G	3.5 McLaren MP4/9-Peugeot V10		9/28

1995 Championship position: 13th   Wins: 0   Pole positions: 0   Fastest laps: 0   Points scored: 7

	Race	Circuit	No	Entrant	Tyres	Capacity/Car/Engine	Comment	Q Pos/Entries
9	SPANISH GP	Barcelona	25	Ligier Gitanes Blondes	G	3.0 Ligier JS41-Mugen Honda V10	1 lap behind	11/26
ret	MONACO GP	Monte Carlo	25	Ligier Gitanes Blondes	G	3.0 Ligier JS41-Mugen Honda V10	spun off	8/26
ret	CANADIAN GP	Montreal	25	Ligier Gitanes Blondes	G	3.0 Ligier JS41-Mugen Honda V10	taken off by Berger	14/24
4	FRENCH GP	Magny Cours	25	Ligier Gitanes Blondes	G	3.0 Ligier JS41-Mugen Honda V10		9/24
ret	BRITISH GP	Silverstone	25	Ligier Gitanes Blondes	G	3.0 Ligier JS41-Mugen Honda V10	spun off	11/24
ret	HUNGARIAN GP	Hungaroring	25	Ligier Gitanes Blondes	G	3.0 Ligier JS41-Mugen Honda V10	engine	8/24
3	BELGIAN GP	Spa	25	Ligier Gitanes Blondes	G	3.0 Ligier JS41-Mugen Honda V10		13/24
ret	ITALIAN GP	Monza	25	Ligier Gitanes Blondes	G	3.0 Ligier JS41-Mugen Honda V10	puncture – suspension damage	11/24
8	PORTUGUESE GP	Estoril	25	Ligier Gitanes Blondes	G	3.0 Ligier JS41-Mugen Honda V10	1 lap behind	9/24
7	EUROPEAN GP	Nürburgring	25	Ligier Gitanes Blondes	G	3.0 Ligier JS41-Mugen Honda V10	2 laps behind	12/24
ret	AUSTRALIAN GP	Adelaide	25	Ligier Gitanes Blondes	G	3.0 Ligier JS41-Mugen Honda V10	spun off	11/24

1996 Championship position: 11th   Wins: 0   Pole positions: 0   Fastest laps: 0   Points scored: 8

	Race	Circuit	No	Entrant	Tyres	Capacity/Car/Engine	Comment	Q Pos/Entries
ret	AUSTRALIAN GP	Melbourne	12	B & H Total Jordan Peugeot	G	3.0 Jordan 196-Peugeot V10	started from pits, collision – Diniz	19/22
ret/12	BRAZILIAN GP	Interlagos	12	B & H Total Jordan Peugeot	G	3.0 Jordan 196-Peugeot V10	spun off/7 laps behind	6/22
ret	ARGENTINE GP	Buenos Aires	12	B & H Total Jordan Peugeot	G	3.0 Jordan 196-Peugeot V10	collision with Marques	15/22
6	EUROPEAN GP	Nürburgring	12	B & H Total Jordan Peugeot	G	3.0 Jordan 196-Peugeot V10		11/22
ret	SAN MARINO GP	Imola	12	B & H Total Jordan Peugeot	G	3.0 Jordan 196-Peugeot V10	spun off	12/22
ret	MONACO GP	Monte Carlo	12	B & H Total Jordan Peugeot	G	3.0 Jordan 196-Peugeot V10	spun off	16/22
ret	SPANISH GP	Barcelona	12	B & H Total Jordan Peugeot	G	3.0 Jordan 196-Peugeot V10	gearbox	15/22
6	CANADIAN GP	Montreal	12	B & H Total Jordan Peugeot	G	3.0 Jordan 196-Peugeot V10	collision with Lamy/1 lap behind	9/22
8	FRENCH GP	Magny Cours	12	B & H Total Jordan Peugeot	G	3.0 Jordan 196-Peugeot V10	excess understeer/1 lap behind	8/22
6	BRITISH GP	Silverstone	12	B & H Total Jordan Peugeot	G	3.0 Jordan 196-Peugeot V10	puncture/1 lap behind	8/22
10	GERMAN GP	Hockenheim	12	B & H Total Jordan Peugeot	G	3.0 Jordan 196-Peugeot V10	slow puncture/1 lap behind	10/20
ret	HUNGARIAN GP	Hungaroring	12	B & H Total Jordan Peugeot	G	3.0 Jordan 196-Peugeot V10	spun off – broken suspension	12/20
ret	BELGIAN GP	Spa	12	B & H Total Jordan Peugeot	G	3.0 Jordan 196-Peugeot V10	engine	8/20
4	ITALIAN GP	Monza	12	B & H Total Jordan Peugeot	G	3.0 Jordan 196-Peugeot V10		9/20
9	PORTUGUESE GP	Estoril	12	B & H Total Jordan Peugeot	G	3.0 Jordan 196-Peugeot V10	excessive tyre wear/1 lap behind	10/20
5	JAPANESE GP	Suzuka	12	B & H Total Jordan Peugeot	G	3.0 Jordan 196-Peugeot V10		10/20

GP Starts: 158   GP Wins: 0   Pole positions: 0   Fastest laps: 0   Points: 98

BRUNI, Gianmaria (I) b 30/5/1981, Rome

2003 Championship position: Unplaced

	Race	Circuit	No	Entrant	Tyres	Capacity/Car/Engine	Comment	Q Pos/Entries
app	GERMAN GP	Hockenheim	39	European Minardi Cosworth	B	3.0 Minardi PS03-Cosworth V10	Friday test driver only	-/-
app	HUNGARIAN GP	Hungaroring	39	European Minardi Cosworth	B	3.0 Minardi PS03-Cosworth V10	Friday test driver only	-/-
app	ITALIAN GP	Monza	39	European Minardi Cosworth	B	3.0 Minardi PS03-Cosworth V10	Friday test driver only	-/-
app	UNITED STATES GP	Indianapolis	39	European Minardi Cosworth	B	3.0 Minardi PS03-Cosworth V10	Friday test driver only	-/-
app	JAPANESE GP	Suzuka	39	European Minardi Cosworth	B	3.0 Minardi PS03-Cosworth V10	Friday test driver only	-/-

2004 Championship position: Unplaced

	Race	Circuit	No	Entrant	Tyres	Capacity/Car/Engine	Comment	Q Pos/Entries
nc	AUSTRALIAN GP	Melbourne	20	European Minardi Cosworth	B	3.0 Minardi PS04B-Cosworth V10	15 laps behind	20/20
14	MALAYSIAN GP	Sepang	20	European Minardi Cosworth	B	3.0 Minardi PS04B-Cosworth V10	3 laps behind	16/20
17	BAHRAIN GP	Sakhir Circuit	20	European Minardi Cosworth	B	3.0 Minardi PS04B-Cosworth V10	3 laps behind	18/20
ret	SAN MARINO GP	Imola	20	European Minardi Cosworth	B	3.0 Minardi PS04B-Cosworth V10	brake balance	17/20
ret	SPANISH GP	Barcelona	20	European Minardi Cosworth	B	3.0 Minardi PS04B-Cosworth V10	brake problems – spun out	18/20
ret	MONACO GP	Monte Carlo	20	European Minardi Cosworth	B	3.0 Minardi PS04B-Cosworth V10	gearbox	20/20
14	EUROPEAN GP	Nürburgring	20	European Minardi Cosworth	B	3.0 Minardi PS04B-Cosworth V10	*no time set/3 laps behind	*20/20
ret	CANADIAN GP	Montreal	20	European Minardi Cosworth	B	3.0 Minardi PS04B-Cosworth V10	*no time set/gearbox	*20/20
ret	UNITED STATES GP	Indianapolis	20	European Minardi Cosworth	B	3.0 Minardi PS04B-Cosworth V10	multiple collision on lap 1	18/20
18/ret	FRANCE GP	Magny Cours	20	European Minardi Cosworth	B	3.0 Minardi PS04B-Cosworth V10	gearbox oil leak/5 laps behind	19/20
16	BRITISH GP	Silverstone	20	European Minardi Cosworth	B	3.0 Minardi PS04B-Cosworth V10	4 laps behind	18/20
17	GERMAN GP	Hockenheim	20	European Minardi Cosworth	B	3.0 Minardi PS04B-Cosworth V10	4 laps behind	19/20
14	HUNGARIAN GP	Hungaroring	20	European Minardi Cosworth	B	3.0 Minardi PS04B-Cosworth V10	4 laps behind	19/20
ret	BELGIAN GP	Spa	20	European Minardi Cosworth	B	3.0 Minardi PS04B-Cosworth V10	accident damage – hit by Pantano	17/20
ret	ITALIAN GP	Monza	20	European Minardi Cosworth	B	3.0 Minardi PS04B-Cosworth V10	breathing problem after pit fire	20/20
ret	CHINESE GP	Shanghai	20	European Minardi Cosworth	B	3.0 Minardi PS04B-Cosworth V10	*no time set/lost front wheel	*20/20
16	JAPANESE GP	Suzuka	20	European Minardi Cosworth	B	3.0 Minardi PS04B-Cosworth V10	3 laps behind	18/20
17	BRAZILIAN GP	Interlagos	20	European Minardi Cosworth	B	3.0 Minardi PS04B-Cosworth V10	*no time set/4 laps behind	*20/20

GP Starts: 18   GP Wins: 0   Pole positions: 0   Fastest laps: 0   Points: 0

GIANMARIA BRUNI

ITALIAN driver Gianmaria Bruni began junior racing at his local track at the age of eight, progressing steadily through the feeder series and into karts before stepping into cars, opting for the Renault-powered Formula Campus series for 1997. This learning year paid dividends, as he returned the following season to take the title before moving up to the Formula Renault Euroseries, where he took on and beat the highly rated Antonio Pizzonia in the battle for the crown.

A move into British Formula 3 for 2000 with Fortec brought a satisfactory fifth in the standings, but no wins where achieved until the following year, when he improved his final position to fourth in a season dominated by Anthony Davidson and Takuma Sato.

Then Gianmaria was forced to step back to the Euro F3000 series, and in 2003 with the ADM team, he was a convincing front-runner, winning rounds at the Nürburgring, Magny-Cours and Donington, before abandoning his championship chances in favour of a test-driving role at Minardi.

Bruni's gamble was rewarded with a full-time race seat alongside Zsolt Baumgartner for 2004, but nothing of note was achieved by the Italian in an up-and-down campaign that began brightly enough, but was bogged down by a mid-season dip in form, which brought censure from team principal Paul Stoddart, who felt he wasn't trying hard enough.

Rather than continue the unequal struggle for 2005, Bruni made a bright start (including a win in Barcelona and a second place at Monaco) with Coloni, but the Italian jumped ship to join Durango and promptly disappeared towards the back end of the GP2 grid, slumping to an eventual tenth place in the final standings. He switched to newly formed Trident Racing for 2006 and soon scored a crushing victory at Imola. Another win came in mid-season at Hockenheim, but the headlines were made by 'young guns' Lewis Hamilton and Nelson Piquet Jr.

For 2007, the Italian chose to race in the GT2 class of the FIA GT Championship, sharing a Ferrari 430 with the experienced Stéphane Ortelli, the pair taking second place overall. The following year, Gianmaria was crowned GT2 champion (with Toni Villander), recording five victories and a class win at Le Mans (with Jaime Melo and Mika Salo).

He narrowly lost his crown in 2009, but took another three wins in the AF Corse machine. In 2010, Bruni (with Melo) competed very successfully in the USA in the ALMS, taking class wins with the 430 at Sebring, Utah and Mid-Ohio. Back in Europe, he also notched up a win at Silverstone. He found himself at the top of his class once more in 2011, sharing his Ferrari with Giancarlo Fisichella, the pair topping the final LM GTE-Pro class standings.

CLEMAR BUCCI

CLEMAR BUCCI forged his reputation in his native Argentina with a 4.5-litre Alfa Romeo, finishing third in the major Eva Perón Cup race in 1950. He continued to run this car in the early 1950s, but was also involved in trying to race the ill-fated Cisitalia-based Autoar. He took this futuristic rear-engined machine, developed with help from the Perónist government, to some fairly meaningless speed records in July, 1953, but it proved completely unraceworthy when it was driven briefly in practice at the 1954 Buenos Aires City GP. Bucci raced his trusty Alfa instead, but he was disqualified for not wearing a crash helmet!

Bucci travelled to Europe in mid-1954 to race for Gordini, but had little luck in his four championship races and fared no better in the three non-title events he contested, posting retirements at Pescara, Rouen and Caen.

He joined the works Maserati team for the 1955 Argentine GP, run in broiling heat, and then finished ninth in a 2.5-litre Ferrari sports car in the Formula Libre GP of Buenos Aires. This event held more interest for the locals than the championship race and drew a crowd estimated at 400,000. He was also invited to share a works Ferrari with Umberto Maglioli in that year's Buenos Aires 1000km, but the pair were disqualified after receiving outside assistance.

BUCCI, Clemar (RA) b 4/9/1920, Zenön Pereyra, Sante Fé – d 12/1/2011, Buenos Aires

	1954 Championship position: Unplaced								
	Race	Circuit	No	Entrant	Tyres	Capacity/Car/Engine	Comment		Q Pos/Entries
ret	BRITISH GP	Silverstone	18	Equipe Gordini	E	2.5 Gordini Type 16 6	crashed		13/31
ret	GERMAN GP	Nürburgring	11	Equipe Gordini	E	2.5 Gordini Type 16 6	lost wheel		16/23
ret	SWISS GP	Bremgarten	12	Equipe Gordini	E	2.5 Gordini Type 16 6	fuel pump on grid		10/15
ret	ITALIAN GP	Monza	46	Equipe Gordini	E	2.5 Gordini Type 16 6	transmission		17/21
	1955 Championship position: Unplaced								
ret	ARGENTINE GP	Buenos Aires	26	Officine Alfieri Maserati	P	2.5 Maserati 250F 6	fuel starvation/Schell/Menditéguy	20/22
	GP Starts: 5 GP Wins: 0 Pole positions: 0 Fastest laps: 0 Points: 0								

RONNIE BUCKNUM

ALTHOUGH Ronnie Bucknum had been competing very successfully in sports cars in the USA since 1956, his selection by Honda to spearhead their 1964 grand prix challenge was strange indeed. That said, he had plenty of experience handling such divers cars as a Porsche 356 Speedster, an Austin Healey 3000, an Alfa Romeo, a Ferrari 250GT and an AC Ace, with which he battled against a fleet of Corvettes. He also raced the famous Ol' Yaller Mk IX Ford V8.

His lack of international racing pedigree had its attractions for the secretive Japanese, since Ronnie could test and race the car without raising undue attention or expectations, and the opposition would never really know just how well it was progressing in that first season. After winning a GT race in Japan with a Honda S600, he was thrust into his first single-seat drive ever at the 1964 German Grand Prix. The novice did well just to survive a daunting debut at the Nürburgring, which ended when the car suffered a steering failure.

Two more races were safely completed before the team signed the vastly more experienced Richie Ginther to head their 1965 challenge and embarked on a winter of testing at Suzuka, during which the unlucky Bucknum again suffered a steering failure. He crashed and this time broke his leg. This set him back when the season began, and predictably he played second fiddle to his team-mate, although he did score points with a fifth place in Mexico as Ginther swept aside the opposition to record Honda's first grand prix win.

If nothing else, everybody now knew who Ronnie Bucknum was, and he was invited to join the Ford team for 1966, finishing third at Le Mans with Dick Hutcherson as the team's GT40s made a 1-2-3 clean sweep. Honda still thought well of their man, and as soon as two of their 3-litre cars were available he returned for the end-of-season American races, during which his car failed to perform.

Although this was his final bow in grands prix, in many ways Bucknum's career as a front-line racing driver was really just beginning. After more Ford sports cars and GT cars for Shelby in 1967, he went racing in Can-Am and USAC the following year. Driving for Dan Gurney's All-American Racers at the inaugural Michigan 250-miler in October, 1968, he won with the Eagle in only his second oval start. This victory was achieved amid much controversy, however, as initially the race was given to Bobby Unser. It transpired that the organiser's lap charts were array, and after an appeal by Mario Andretti against his championship rival, Unser, Bucknum was declared the winner, pocketing a cool $17,000 for his team.

In 1969, Bucknum signed for Roger Penske and raced the team's sports and Trans-Am cars, winning at Mid-Ohio and Kent in the latter category in a Chevrolet Camaro. In 1970, he teamed up with Sam Posey in the NART Ferrari in long-distance events, taking fourth place at Le Mans.

In 1971, he took the NART Ferrari 512S to second place in the Daytona 24-hour race (with Tony Adamowicz), by which time the Marine crew-cut had been replaced by collar-length hair and a beard!

Bucknum, who raced only intermittently thereafter, made his final racing appearances with a Ford Mustang at Daytona and Sebring in 1983. Later he suffered from diabetes and died at the comparatively young age of 57 in April, 1992.

Bucknum's son, Jeff, born in 1966, emulated his father by appearing in the Indy 500 on two occasions, but he has been more successful in the sports and GT categories.

BUCKNUM, Ronnie (USA) b 5/4/1936, Alhambra, California – d 23/4/1992, San Luis Obispo, California

1964 Championship position: Unplaced

	Race	Circuit	No	Entrant	Tyres	Capacity/Car/Engine	Comment	Q Pos/Entries
ret	GERMAN GP	Nürburgring	20	Honda R & D Co	D	1.5 Honda RA271 V12	*spun off*	22/24
ret	ITALIAN GP	Monza	28	Honda R & D Co	D	1.5 Honda RA271 V12	*brakes/oil leaks/overheating*	=9/25
ret	US GP	Watkins Glen	28	Honda R & D Co	D	1.5 Honda RA271 V12	*engine – head gasket*	14/19

1965 Championship position: 14th= Wins: 0 Pole positions: 0 Fastest laps: 0 Points scored: 2

	Race	Circuit	No	Entrant	Tyres	Capacity/Car/Engine	Comment	Q Pos/Entries
ret	MONACO GP	Monte Carlo	19	Honda R & D Co	G	1.5 Honda RA272 V12	*gear linkage*	=14/17
ret	BELGIAN GP	Spa	11	Honda R & D Co	G	1.5 Honda RA272 V12	*transmission*	11/21
ret	FRENCH GP	Clermont Ferrand	28	Honda R & D Co	G	1.5 Honda RA272 V12	*ignition*	16/17
ret	ITALIAN GP	Monza	22	Honda R & D Co	G	1.5 Honda RA272 V12	*engine*	6/23
13	US GP	Watkins Glen	12	Honda R & D Co	G	1.5 Honda RA272 V12	*pit stop/18 laps behind*	12/18
5	MEXICAN GP	Mexico City	12	Honda R & D Co	G	1.5 Honda RA272 V12	*1 lap behind*	10/18

1966 Championship position: Unplaced

	Race	Circuit	No	Entrant	Tyres	Capacity/Car/Engine	Comment	Q Pos/Entries
ret	US GP	Watkins Glen	14	Honda R & D Co	G	3.0 Honda RA273 V12	*transmission*	18/19
8	MEXICAN GP	Mexico City	14	Honda R & D Co	G	3.0 Honda RA273 V12	*pit stop – fire/5 laps behind*	14/19

GP Starts: 11 GP Wins: 0 Pole positions: 0 Fastest laps: 0 Points: 2

IVOR BUEB

A GARAGE owner from Cheltenham, Gloucestershire, Ivor Bueb began his career in 1952 with an Iota in 500cc racing, although he did not taste success until he got his hands on a Cooper for the 1954 season. He did so well, however, that he was invited to join the works team the following year, racing the 1100cc sports car in addition to his Formula 3 commitments. He was just pipped for the national championship by Jim Russell, but the high point of his season was his win at the tragic 1955 Le Mans race with Mike Hawthorn in the D-Type Jaguar.

Bueb cheerfully continued to race anything and everything that came his way, winning the Reims 12-hours for Jaguar (with Duncan Hamilton) in 1956 and repeating his Le Mans triumph with Hawthorn in 1957, a year that saw his Formula 1 debut for Connaught. He claimed fifth at Syracuse and third at Pau in the ageing car.

Although opportunities at grand prix level were limited to just six races, Ivor maintained his busy racing schedule in 1958, campaigning his own Lotus 12 in Formula 2, and driving for Ecurie Ecosse and Lister in sports cars. Teaming up with the ambitious British Racing Partnership for 1959, he was as competitive as ever with the team's Formula 2 Cooper-Borgward, but disaster struck when he overshot a fast bend at Gravenoire during the Auvergne Trophy race at Clermont Ferrand. Gravely injured, he died in hospital, and was the only driver to have lost his life at the mountain circuit.

BUEB, Ivor (GB) b 6/6/1923, East Ham, London – d 1/8/1959, Clermont-Ferrand, France

	Race	Circuit	No	Entrant	Tyres	Capacity/Car/Engine	Comment	Q Pos/Entries
	1957 Championship position: Unplaced							
ret	MONACO GP	Monte Carlo	12	Connaught Engineering	D	2.5 Connaught B-Alta 4	pit stop – exhaust/fuel tank	16/21
nc	BRITISH GP	Aintree	32	Gilby Engineering	D	2.5 Maserati 250F 6	19 laps behind	19/19
	1958 Championship position: Unplaced							
ret	BRITISH GP	Silverstone	15	B C Ecclestone	D	2.5 Connaught B-Alta 4	gearbox oil pump	17/21
11*/ret	GERMAN GP (F2)	Nürburgring	28	Ecurie Demi Litre	D	1.5 Lotus 12-Climax 4	oil pipe/*6th in F2 class/-21 laps	19/26
	1959 Championship position: Unplaced							
dnq	MONACO GP	Monte Carlo	34	British Racing Partnership	D	1.5 Cooper T51-Climax 4		17/24
13*	BRITISH GP (F2)	Aintree	46	British Racing Partnership	D	1.5 Cooper T51-Borgward 4	*4th in F2 class/6 laps behind	18/30

GP Starts: 5   GP Wins: 0   Pole positions: 0   Fastest laps: 0   Points: 0

BUEMI, Sébastien (CH) b 31/10/1988, Aigle

	Race	Circuit	No	Entrant	Tyres	Capacity/Car/Engine	Comment	Q Pos/Entries
	2009 Championship position: 16th Wins: 0 Pole positions: 0 Fastest laps: 0 Points scored: 6							
7	AUSTRALIAN GP	Melbourne	12	Scuderia Toro Rosso	B	2.4 Toro Rosso STR4-Ferrari V8	scored points on debut	16/20
16/ret	MALAYSIAN GP	Sepang	12	Scuderia Toro Rosso	B	2.4 Toro Rosso STR4-Ferrari V8	rain-shortened race – spun off	20/20
8	CHINESE GP	Shanghai	12	Scuderia Toro Rosso	B	2.4 Toro Rosso STR4-Ferrari V8		10/20
17	BAHRAIN GP	Sakhir Circuit	12	Scuderia Toro Rosso	B	2.4 Toro Rosso STR4-Ferrari V8	1 lap behind	17/20
ret	SPANISH GP	Barcelona	12	Scuderia Toro Rosso	B	2.4 Toro Rosso STR4-Ferrari V8	hit by Bourdais on lap 1	17/20
ret	MONACO GP	Monte Carlo	12	Scuderia Toro Rosso	B	2.4 Toro Rosso STR4-Ferrari V8	rammed Piquet – damaged car	11/20
15	TURKISH GP	Istanbul	12	Scuderia Toro Rosso	B	2.4 Toro Rosso STR4-Ferrari V8	1 lap behind	18/20
18	BRITISH GP	Silverstone	12	Scuderia Toro Rosso	B	2.4 Toro Rosso STR4-Ferrari V8	1 lap behind	20/20
16	GERMAN GP	Hockenheim	12	Scuderia Toro Rosso	B	2.4 Toro Rosso STR4-Ferrari V8		17/20
16	HUNGARIAN GP	Hungaroring	12	Scuderia Toro Rosso	B	2.4 Toro Rosso STR4-Ferrari V8	1 lap behind	11/20
ret	EUROPEAN GP	Valencia	12	Scuderia Toro Rosso	B	2.4 Toro Rosso STR4-Ferrari V8	brakes –accident	15/20
12	BELGIAN GP	Spa	12	Scuderia Toro Rosso	B	2.4 Toro Rosso STR4-Ferrari V8		16/20
13	ITALIAN GP	Monza	12	Scuderia Toro Rosso	B	2.4 Toro Rosso STR4-Ferrari V8	1 lap behind	19/20
ret	SINGAPORE GP	Singapore Circuit	12	Scuderia Toro Rosso	B	2.4 Toro Rosso STR4-Ferrari V8	gearbox	14/20
ret	JAPANESE GP	Suzuka	12	Scuderia Toro Rosso	B	2.4 Toro Rosso STR4-Ferrari V8	clutch	10/20
7	BRAZILIAN GP	Interlagos	12	Scuderia Toro Rosso	B	2.4 Toro Rosso STR4-Ferrari V8		6/20
8	ABU DHABI GP	Yas Marina Circuit	12	Scuderia Toro Rosso	B	2.4 Toro Rosso STR4-Ferrari V8		10/20
	2010 Championship position: 16th Wins: 0 Pole positions: 0 Fastest laps: 0 Points scored: 8							
16/ret	BAHRAIN GP	Sakhir Circuit	16	Scuderia Toro Rosso	B	2.4 Toro Rosso STR5-Ferrari V8	electrics/3 laps behind	15/24
ret	AUSTRALIAN GP	Melbourne	16	Scuderia Toro Rosso	B	2.4 Toro Rosso STR5-Ferrari V8	accident on lap 1	12/24
11	MALAYSIAN GP	Sepang	16	Scuderia Toro Rosso	B	2.4 Toro Rosso STR5-Ferrari V8	understeer from lap 1 contact	13/24
ret	CHINESE GP	Shanghai Circuit	16	Scuderia Toro Rosso	B	2.4 Toro Rosso STR5-Ferrari V8	hit by Liuzzi on lap 1	13/24
ret	SPANISH GP	Barcelona	16	Scuderia Toro Rosso	B	2.4 Toro Rosso STR5-Ferrari V8	hydraulics	15/24
10	MONACO GP	Monte Carlo	16	Scuderia Toro Rosso	B	2.4 Toro Rosso STR5-Ferrari V8		13/24
16	TURKISH GP	Istanbul Park	16	Scuderia Toro Rosso	B	2.4 Toro Rosso STR5-Ferrari V8	1 lap behind	14/24
8	CANADIAN GP	Montreal	16	Scuderia Toro Rosso	B	2.4 Toro Rosso STR5-Ferrari V8	3-stop strategy/1 lap behind	15/24
9*	EUROPEAN GP	Valencia	16	Scuderia Toro Rosso	B	2.4 Toro Rosso STR5-Ferrari V8	* 5 second post-race penalty	11/24
12	BRITISH GP	Silverstone	16	Scuderia Toro Rosso	B	2.4 Toro Rosso STR5-Ferrari V8		17/24
ret	GERMAN GP	Hockenheim	16	Scuderia Toro Rosso	B	2.4 Toro Rosso STR5-Ferrari V8	hit by Alguersuari on lap 1	16/24
12	HUNGARIAN GP	Hungaroring	16	Scuderia Toro Rosso	B	2.4 Toro Rosso STR5-Ferrari V8	1 lap behind	15/24
12	BELGIAN GP	Spa	16	Scuderia Toro Rosso	B	2.4 Toro Rosso STR5-Ferrari V8		15/24
11	ITALIAN GP	Monza	16	Scuderia Toro Rosso	B	2.4 Toro Rosso STR5-Ferrari V8		14/24

14	SINGAPORE GP	Marina Bay Circuit	16	Scuderia Toro Rosso	B	2.4 Toro Rosso STR5-Ferrari V8	*1 lap behind*	14/24
10	JAPANESE GP	Suzuka	16	Scuderia Toro Rosso	B	2.4 Toro Rosso STR5-Ferrari V8		18/24
ret	KOREAN GP	Yeongam	16	Scuderia Toro Rosso	B	2.4 Toro Rosso STR5-Ferrari V8	*crashed into Glock – accident*	17/24
13	BRAZILIAN GP	Interlagos	16	Scuderia Toro Rosso	B	2.4 Toro Rosso STR5-Ferrari V8	*5-place grid pen from Korea/-1 lap*	15/24
15	ABU DHABI GP	Yas Marina Circuit	16	Scuderia Toro Rosso	B	2.4 Toro Rosso STR5-Ferrari V8		18/24

2011 Championship position: 15th   Wins: 0   Pole positions: 0   Fastest laps: 0   Points scored: 15

8	AUSTRALIAN GP	Melbourne	18	Scuderia Toro Rosso	P	2.4 Toro Rosso STR6-Ferrari V8	*10th but 7 & 8th cars dsq/-1 lap*	10/24
13	MALAYSIAN GP	Sepang	18	Scuderia Toro Rosso	P	2.4 Toro Rosso STR6-Ferrari V8	*1 lap behind*	13/24
14	CHINESE GP	Shanghai Circuit	18	Scuderia Toro Rosso	P	2.4 Toro Rosso STR6-Ferrari V8		9/24
9	TURKISH GP	Istanbul Park	18	Scuderia Toro Rosso	P	2.4 Toro Rosso STR6-Ferrari V8		16/24
14	SPANISH GP	Barcelona	18	Scuderia Toro Rosso	P	2.4 Toro Rosso STR6-Ferrari V8	*1 lap behind*	11/24
10	MONACO GP	Monte Carlo	18	Scuderia Toro Rosso	P	2.4 Toro Rosso STR6-Ferrari V8	*1 lap behind*	17/24
10	CANADIAN GP	Montreal	18	Scuderia Toro Rosso	P	2.4 Toro Rosso STR6-Ferrari V8		15/24
13	EUROPEAN GP	Valencia	18	Scuderia Toro Rosso	P	2.4 Toro Rosso STR6-Ferrari V8	*1 lap behind*	17/24
ret	BRITISH GP	Silverstone	18	Scuderia Toro Rosso	P	2.4 Toro Rosso STR6-Ferrari V8	*hit by di Resta – tyre damage*	19/24
15	GERMAN GP	Hockenheim	18	Scuderia Toro Rosso	P	2.4 Toro Rosso STR6-Ferrari V8	*1 lap behind*	16/24
8	HUNGARIAN GP	Hungaroring	18	Scuderia Toro Rosso	P	2.4 Toro Rosso STR6-Ferrari V8	*1 lap behind*	18/24
ret	BELGIAN GP	Spa	18	Scuderia Toro Rosso	P	2.4 Toro Rosso STR6-Ferrari V8	*collision damage – hit by Perez*	11/24
10	ITALIAN GP	Monza	18	Scuderia Toro Rosso	P	2.4 Toro Rosso STR6-Ferrari V8	*1 lap behind*	16/24
12	SINGAPORE GP	Marina Bay Circuit	18	Scuderia Toro Rosso	P	2.4 Toro Rosso STR6-Ferrari V8	*1 lap behind*	14/24
ret	JAPANESE GP	Suzuka	18	Scuderia Toro Rosso	P	2.4 Toro Rosso STR6-Ferrari V8	*lost wheel after pitstop*	15/24
9	KOREAN GP	Yeongam	18	Scuderia Toro Rosso	P	2.4 Toro Rosso STR6-Ferrari V8		13/24
ret	INDIAN GP	Buddh Circuit	18	Scuderia Toro Rosso	P	2.4 Toro Rosso STR6-Ferrari V8	*engine*	9/24
ret	ABU DHABI GP	Yas Marina Circuit	18	Scuderia Toro Rosso	P	2.4 Toro Rosso STR6-Ferrari V8	*hydraulics*	13/24
12	BRAZILIAN GP	Interlagos	18	Scuderia Toro Rosso	P	2.4 Toro Rosso STR6-Ferrari V8	*1 lap behind*	14/24

GP Starts: 55   GP Wins: 0   Pole positions: 0   Fastest laps: 0   Points: 29

SÉBASTIEN BUEMI

SWISS driver Sébastien Buemi was fortunate to be part of the roster of Red Bull-backed junior drivers, but perhaps was a surprising choice to be given a seat in the Toro Rosso team for 2009, for in truth his performances in the GP2 class, though solid enough, where hardly earth shattering. Previously, he had made his way successfully through the various karting ranks, which had led to a move into German Formula BMW.

After a satisfactory third place overall in 2004 (behind winner Sebastian Vettel), Buemi made a real championship challenge in his second year, taking seven victories. His only rival was German hotshot Nico Hülkenberg, who eventually was awarded the crown after a tribunal had docked Buemi points for a driving infringement.

Sébastien then moved up to the German F3 Euroseries, driving the ubiquitous Mercedes-powered Dallara F305. The Swiss rookie claimed a single win at Oschersleben, but was a long way behind the title contenders, Vettel and Paul di Resta. However, he did make an impression in both the F3 Masters at Zandvoort, where he finished third, and at Macau, where he took fourth place.

Remaining in situ for 2007, Buemi was one of the title favourites, but despite three wins and regular podium visits, he was the 'bridesmaid' once more, as Romain Grosjean took the championship. It was a busy racing year for Sébastien, who took part in a total of 44 races. Despite his relative inexperience, he was also given a chance in mid-season to step up to the GP2 series with ART Grand Prix. In addition, he represented Switzerland in the A1GP series. Taking part in eight races, he recorded three fourth places, a fifth and a seventh to help his country to eighth place overall.

For 2008, Buemi switched to Team Trust Arden Racing and was swiftly in action in the newly created GP2 Asia Series. He recorded just one victory (at Sentul, Indonesia) in the ten-race series and had to be content with the runner-up position, once more behind Grosjean. In the GP2 series, he found the going somewhat tougher, managing just two Sprint race victories (Magny-Cours and Hungaroring) and three other podiums. Finishing sixth in the series hardly seemed to merit his swift elevation to the grand prix ranks, especially when the likes of Bruno Senna, Grosjean and Lucas di Grassi were still searching for a Formula 1 ride. He was given his big chance to make an impression in Formula 1, however, and took it with a points-scoring debut in Melbourne, and thereafter he generally out-performed his more experienced team-mate, Sébastien Bourdais. Given the machinery at his disposal, there was only so far that Buemi could expect to progress, so in reality his second year was spent locked in a battle for supremacy with his young team-mate, Jaime Alguersuari, but neither driver could muster much by way of points-scoring finishes.

In 2011, Buemi embarked upon a third season with the team, who supplied him with a neat car that ran well in race trim. This gave the Swiss driver a chance to steal points finishes in seven of the 19 races, but he looked less feisty than Alguersuari, and both drivers seemed content to drive within the limits of the car. Having given Sébastien three seasons to show his mettle, Red Bull and Helmut Marko decided that neither he – nor his team-mate – were going to progress any further, so both were ushered out of the door to make way for new talent who were thought to possess the same sort of hunger that had been shown by their star graduate, Sebastian Vettel. Buemi at least was kept on as a reserve driver for the Red Bull team, but he was also allowed to further his racing career on track by joining the Toyota sports car squad for 2012.

LUIZ PEREIRA BUENO

ALREADY twice the Brazilian touring car champion, Luiz Pereira Bueno was a very talented driver who, at the relatively late age of 30, travelled to Britain in 1969 to race in Formula Ford courtesy of a Brazilian government scheme. Racing under the SMART (Stirling Moss Automobile, Racing Team) banner with fellow countryman Ricardo Achcar, he started his campaign on the back foot, having arrived with the season already under way. Running a competitive Merlyn Mk11, however, he soon began to make his mark, finishing his debut season with six wins in addition to being well placed elsewhere. He opted to return to Brazil, however, and continue in his domestic racing series in 1970, rather than take up an offer to race an uncompetitive F5000 Leda in the UK.

The 1970 season opened with a five-race Brazilian FF series, which featured a large contingent of European stars. Bueno picked up a second place at Curitiba and a win on aggregate at Rio, where he beat Emerson Fittipaldi after a tremendous dice in the first heat. He finished fifth overall in the sometimes chaotic mini-championship, laying the groundwork for future Formula Ford success in Brazil.

Although Bueno was keen to take up the offer of a full-time return to Europe in 1971, he could not afford to do so and turned, instead, to sports cars, winning the 1972 Brazilian championship in a Porsche 908.

He did compete in the inaugural non-championship Brazilian GP in a works March 721 in 1972, finishing sixth, and the world championship race for Team Surtees a year later in an ageing car that was well off the pace; he struggled around to finish last. He made one further appearance in Europe that year, to participate in the 1000km of Osterreichring at Zeltweg. Unfortunately, his Porsche 908/3 was eliminated after a tangle with Helmut Marko's Ferrari.

In his homeland, however, Bueno continued to forge a long and successful career as both a driver and team owner, racing potent sports and touring cars in national championships. Luiz, who succumbed to lung cancer in 2011, is remembered fondly by those who worked with him as a kind and loyal man, with a tremendous wit and fine sense of humour. Despite his modest successes internationally, he certainly deserved his place among the giants of Brazilian motorsport.

BUENO, Luiz-Pereira (BR) b 16/01/1937, São Paulo – d 8/2/2011, Atibaia

1973 Championship position: Unplaced

	Race	Circuit	No	Entrant	Tyres	Capacity/Car/Engine	Comment	Q Pos/Entries
12	BRAZILIAN GP	Interlagos	23	Team Surtees	F	3.0 Surtees TS9B-Cosworth V8	pit stop – electrics/4 laps behind	20/20

GP Starts: 1   GP Wins: 0   Pole positions: 0   Fastest laps: 0   Points: 0

BURGESS, Ian (GB) b 6/7/1930, London

1958 Championship position: Unplaced

	Race	Circuit	No	Entrant	Tyres	Capacity/Car/Engine	Comment	Qual Pos/Entries
ret	BRITISH GP	Silverstone	12	Cooper Car Co	D	2.0 Cooper T45-Climax 4	clutch	16/21
7*	GERMAN GP (F2)	Nürburgring	26	High Efficiency Motors	D	1.5 Cooper T43-Climax 4 F2	*3rd in F2 class	14/26

1959 Championship position: Unplaced

ret	FRENCH GP	Reims	18	Scuderia Centro Sud	D	2.5 Cooper T51-Maserati 4	engine	19/22
ret	BRITISH GP	Aintree	22	Scuderia Centro Sud	D	2.5 Cooper T51-Maserati 4	gearbox	13/30
6	GERMAN GP	AVUS	18	Scuderia Centro Sud	D	2.5 Cooper T51-Maserati 4	9th heat 1/6th heat 2/-4 laps	15/16
14	ITALIAN GP	Monza	42	Scuderia Centro Sud	D	2.5 Cooper T51-Maserati 4	5 laps behind	16/21

1960 Championship position: Unplaced

dnq	MONACO GP	Monte Carlo	42	Scuderia Centro Sud	D	2.5 Cooper T51-Maserati 4		24/24
10	FRENCH GP	Reims	42	Scuderia Centro Sud	D	2.5 Cooper T51-Maserati 4	pit stop/14 laps behind	22/23
ret	BRITISH GP	Silverstone	17	Scuderia Centro Sud	D	2.5 Cooper T51-Maserati 4	engine	20/25
ret	US GP	Riverside	19	Scuderia Centro Sud	D	2.5 Cooper T51-Maserati 4	ignition	23/23

1961 Championship position: Unplaced

dns	DUTCH GP	Zandvoort	18	Camoradi International	D	1.5 Lotus 18-Climax 4	qualified but only a reserve entry	(15)/17
dns	BELGIAN GP	Spa	50	Camoradi International	D	1.5 Lotus 18-Climax 4	no starting money offered	22/25
14	FRENCH GP	Reims	38	Camoradi International	D	1.5 Lotus 18-Climax 4	pit stop/10 laps behind	24/26
14	BRITISH GP	Aintree	44	Camoradi International	D	1.5 Lotus 18-Climax 4	6 laps behind	25/30
12	GERMAN GP	Nürburgring	30	Camoradi International	D	1.5 Cooper T53-Climax 4	1 lap behind	24/27

1962 Championship position: Unplaced

12	BRITISH GP	Aintree	36	Anglo American Equipe	D	1.5 Cooper T53-Climax 4	4 laps behind	16/21
11	GERMAN GP	Nürburgring	25	Anglo American Equipe	D	1.5 Cooper T53-Climax 4		16/30
dnq	ITALIAN GP	Monza	62	Anglo American Equipe	D	1.5 Cooper T53-Climax 4		25/30

1963 Championship position: Unplaced

| ret | BRITISH GP | Silverstone | 16 | Scirocco-Powell (Racing Cars) | D | 1.5 Scirocco SP-BRM V8 | ignition | 20/23 |
| ret | GERMAN GP | Nürburgring | 24 | Scirocco-Powell (Racing Cars) | D | 1.5 Scirocco SP-BRM V8 | steering arm | 19/26 |

GP Starts: 16   GP Wins: 0   Pole positions: 0   Fastest laps: 0   Points: 0

IAN BURGESS

IAN BURGESS caused quite a stir when, in 1951, driving a works-loaned Cooper-Norton, he won the Eifelrennen 500cc race in the pouring rain at the Nürburgring, ahead of more seasoned practitioners Ken Wharton and Bill Whitehouse. He also scored a second place and set a lap record at Avus a few weeks later, but unfortunately he could not build on these successes. The next couple of seasons brought only moderate rewards. He raced a Kieft-Bristol sports car, and returned to the 500 class with both a Kieft and a Mackson in 1953.

It was only when he began working for the Cooper team at their Surbiton factory that his career started to prosper. Although employed in part to help run Cooper's racing drivers' school from Brands Hatch, Ian cajoled the management into letting him race their new Formula 2 cars.

Fourth place in the 1957 Gold Cup at Oulton Park led to a season in Tommy Atkins' similar car for 1958. A brilliant start to the year saw Ian win at Crystal Palace and Snetterton, and take fourth at both Montlhéry and Reims, until a broken leg sustained in a crash at AVUS curtailed his season.

Ian was back in 1959, driving for Atkins in F2 and also handling the Italian Scuderia Centro Sud team's Maserati-engined F1 Cooper, while a trip to New Zealand at the start of 1960 saw him win the Teretonga Trophy in Atkins' Cooper. For 1961, he became involved with the American Camoradi team, racing their Lotus 18, but with only moderate success at minor events.

He concentrated on the plethora of non-championship races in 1962, driving a Cooper for wealthy enthusiast Louise Bryden-Brown's Anglo-American Equipe. The chassis was a much modified Cooper T59 formula junior, and results were mixed to say the least. The car, which initially sported rear-mounted radiators and a pointed nose, was certainly a product of original thinking by mechanic-cum-designer Hugh Aiden-Jones, but by the end of the year it was racing conventionally once more with a single radiator behind a rather ugly chopped nose. Generally it proved reliable, if none too fast, and posted a few respectable finishes if the fields were depleted. He finished fifth in the Naples Grand Prix, and then in Scandinavia repeated the placings at Karlskoga and Roskildering.

For the 1963 season, Ian's last in racing, Aiden-Jones persuaded a wealthy young American, Hugh Powell, to bankroll a new team, using modified Emeryson Mk3s. The BRM-powered machine was handled initially by lead driver Tony Settember, and Burgess only came on board in mid-season, posting desultory results. The team was disbanded at the end of the year; it proved to be a dismal and costly exercise for all concerned.

His racing activities at an end, Burgess flitted around Europe and eventually found himself with a ten-year jail sentence for dealing in heroin. Currently in poor health, he now lives quietly in London.

BURTI, Luciano (BR) b 5/3/1975, São Paulo

2000 Championship position: Unplaced

	Race	Circuit	No	Entrant	Tyres	Capacity/Car/Engine	Comment	Q Pos/Entries
11	AUSTRIAN GP	A1-Ring	7	Jaguar Racing	B	3.0 Jaguar R1-Cosworth V10	started from pitlane	21/22

2001 Championship position: Unplaced

8	AUSTRALIAN GP	Melbourne	19	Jaguar Racing	M	3.0 Jaguar R2-Cosworth V10	1 lap behind	21/22
10	MALAYSIAN GP	Sepang	19	Jaguar Racing	M	3.0 Jaguar R2-Cosworth V10	1 lap behind	15/22
ret	BRAZILIAN GP	Interlagos	19	Jaguar Racing	M	3.0 Jaguar R2-Cosworth V10	engine – water seal	14/22
11	SAN MARINO GP	Imola	19	Jaguar Racing	M	3.0 Jaguar R2-Cosworth V10	2 laps behind	15/22
ret	SPANISH GP	Barcelona	23	Prost Acer	M	3.0 Prost AP04-Acer V10	1 lap behind	14/22
11	AUSTRIAN GP	A1-Ring	23	Prost Acer	M	3.0 Prost AP04-Acer V10	2 laps behind	17/22
ret	MONACO GP	Monte Carlo	23	Prost Acer	M	3.0 Prost AP04-Acer V10	slid off	21/22
8	CANADIAN GP	Montreal	23	Prost Acer	M	3.0 Prost AP04-Acer V10	1 lap behind	19/22
12	EUROPEAN GP	Nürburgring	23	Prost Acer	M	3.0 Prost AP04-Acer V10	2 laps behind	17/22
10	FRANCE GP	Magny Cours	23	Prost Acer	M	3.0 Prost AP04-Acer V10	1 lap behind	15/22
ret	BRITISH GP	Silverstone	23	Prost Acer	M	3.0 Prost AP04-Acer V10	engine	16/22
ret	GERMAN GP	Hockenheim	23	Prost Acer	M	3.0 Prost AP04-Acer V10	crash at 1st start/spun off	16/22
ret	HUNGARIAN GP	Hungaroring	23	Prost Acer	M	3.0 Prost AP04-Acer V10	spun off	19/22
ret/dns	BELGIAN GP	Spa	23	Prost Acer	M	3.0 Prost AP04-Acer V10	crash in 1st start/did not restart	18/22

GP Starts: 14 (15)   GP Wins: 0   Pole positions: 0   Fastest laps: 0   Points: 0

BUSSINELLO, Roberto (I) b 4/10/1927, Pistola – d 24/8/1999, Vicenza

1961 Championship position: Unplaced

	Race	Circuit	No	Entrant	Tyres	Capacity/Car/Engine	Comment	Qual Pos/Entries
ret	ITALIAN GP	Monza	54	Isobele de Tomaso	D	1.5 de Tomaso F1-OSCA 4	engine	24/33

1965 Championship position: Unplaced

dnq	GERMAN GP	Nürburgring	25	Scuderia Centro Sud	D	1.5 BRM P57 V8		21/22
13/ret	ITALIAN GP	Monza	50	Scuderia Centro Sud	D	1.5 BRM P57 V8	oil pressure/16 laps behind	21/23

GP Starts: 2   GP Wins: 0   Pole positions: 0   Fastest laps: 0   Points: 0

LUCIANO BURTI

LUCIANO BURTI was destined to be another of Formula 1's quickly forgotten talents, a young driver cast on to the grand prix scrapheap before he really had the chance to prove himself.

Like just about every other Brazilian, Burti began his career in karts, where he spent a few years developing before savouring his first taste of car racing by finishing as runner-up in the 1995 New Zealand Formula Ford series. Buoyed by his success, he moved to Europe in 1996. His first season yielded a hard-fought third in the Formula Vauxhall Junior series with Martin Donnelly Racing, while in the following year he claimed the Formula Vauxhall Winter Series title for Paul Stewart Racing. He also found time to return down-under to clinch the NZ Formula Ford title.

Graduating to Formula 3 in 1998, again with Paul Stewart Racing, Burti finished third overall in his debut season, with two wins, but, more importantly perhaps, the opportunity to try F1 power for the first time. He contested one of the strongest British F3 fields in years in 1999, eventually finishing second to Marc Hynes. It was cut-and-thrust racing that saw the Brazilian take five race wins to finish just ahead of another young talent by the name of Jenson Button.

Burti had shown enough to be kept on by new owners Ford when they bought the family-run operation and re-christened it Jaguar Racing for 2000. Initially he was given the test-driver role, but it led to an unexpected F1 debut when Eddie Irvine was ruled out of the Austrian Grand Prix at the A1-Ring. He kept his nose clean to race from the pit lane to 11th at the flag. Such was his promise in testing that the Brazilian started the 2001 season racing for Jaguar after Johnny Herbert slipped into F1 retirement. But he failed to convince the new management and, after only competing in four races, Pedro de la Rosa took over his Jaguar seat. He announced that he would be leaving the team to race for Prost, to replace Gaston Mazzacane. Despite the upheaval and obvious blow to his confidence, he settled in well with his new team, taking an eighth place in Canada to match the result he had recorded in Australia with Jaguar. After surviving unhurt in a massive crash at the start of the German Grand Prix, his season ended dramatically after a monumental Belgian GP shunt that left him unconscious and embedded in the tyre barrier above Eau Rouge. He was ruled out of the final three F1 races on doctors' orders. Indeed, such was the severity of his concussion, that he was told his racing career might well be over.

Burti regained his fitness, however, and took up the unexpected offer of acting as a test driver at Ferrari in 2002, but with Luca Badoer already in place, the Brazilian was handed the job of testing Bridgestone's race tyres – a role that saw him complete almost 100,000km. He continued his testing role with the Scuderia over the next couple of seasons, but the urge to pick up his racing career eventually led to a full-time return to Brazil to take part in the burgeoning Brazilian stock car series in 2005, when he took fifth place overall in a Chevrolet Astra. The next three seasons were spent running a VW Bora and then a Peugeot 307, but with little achieved by way of results. In 2009, a change of teams to Boettger Competições, running a Chevrolet Astra, brought a long awaited first win at Viamão. He switched teams once more in 2011, running a Peugeot for Itaipava Racing and gaining his second stock car win, with a 408 at Campo Grande in 2012.

In tandem with his racing activities, Burti also has a regular F1 commentating role for Globo TV Network on Brazilian TV, and he regularly lectures on building a successful business career.

ROBERTO BUSSINELLO

AN engineering graduate who began racing in 1958, Roberto Bussinello also worked as a development engineer and test driver for the de Tomaso team. He drove their F1 car on occasion, mainly in Italian events, taking fifth place in the Naples GP and fourth in the Coppa Italia of 1961.

In 1963, Bussinello moved to Alfa Romeo, again initially in a development role, but he was soon racing their lovely Giulietta GT car, finishing third in the 1964 Targa Florio and winning the Sandown Park six-hour race at season's end.

Roberto's handful of F1 sorties in the ageing Centro Sud BRM in 1965 yielded little, so it was back to Alfas and familiar territory, before acting as a team manager at Autodelta in 1968. In the early 1970s, he worked as an engineer on Herbert Müller's de Tomaso-Ford Pantera sports car.

JENSON BUTTON, MBE

To become a Formula 1 champion, or even an established front-line grand prix driver requires not only talent, but also more than a modicum of luck. Many a fine driver has seen his career prospects blunted by being in the wrong team at the wrong time and missed the chance to climb to the very top. Jenson Button seems to have led a charmed life in the Formula 1 game of snakes and ladders, however, climbing inexorably towards the top rung, when on more than one occasion it appeared that he was in danger of slithering off the board altogether.

Jenson's karting career began at the age of eight, and with the practical help of his father, John, he became the boy to beat in whatever class he contested from 1990 through to 1997. Much was expected when he switched to cars the following year, and he did not disappoint, taking nine wins on his way to the British FF championship at his first attempt. He also won the prestigious Formula Ford Festival, which earned him the 1998 McLaren Autosport Young Driver Award.

The 'Frome Flyer' was promoted to the British F3 series, where a pole position in his first race and a maiden victory in his third, at Thruxton, showed he had the speed to compete with more experienced competitors. He won two more races and finished third in the series, but already a run in a McLaren MP4/13 and then a test for Prost – where he outpaced Jean Alesi – had alerted Formula 1's talent spotters that he was someone special.

Suddenly Jenson was in Formula 1, with a seat at Williams, and at the tender age of 20, he found himself on the grid at Melbourne in March, 2000, where his dry wit, easy charm and calm demeanour stood him in good stead in front of the media hordes. His first season was quietly impressive, and he took eighth place in the final standings. Despite a five-year contract, he was always under pressure to perform in his rookie season, especially when Juan Pablo Montoya was confirmed for 2001, leading to Button being loaned to Benetton for a two-year period, a return to Grove being planned for 2003.

Jenson's first year at Benetton was character building, as his early golden promise seemed to be fading, with rumours that his recently acquired F1 lifestyle was deflecting him from focusing his efforts on mastering a recalcitrant car. With just two points scored, the season yielded little, but having retained the faith of Flavio Briatore for 2002, he was about to regain some career momentum as the Renault upsurge began. The first half of the year went well and he scored points on a regular basis, but in mid-season it was announced that he was to be replaced by test driver Fernando Alonso for 2003; almost inevitably came a dip in his performances.

Crucially for Button – and his career – David Richards of BAR Honda moved quickly to sign the 22-year-old, offering him the security of a two-year deal with a two-year option. Despite it being a difficult first year, Richards brought order to the previously somewhat unproductive regime, and Jenson quietly set about overshadowing his incumbent team-mate, Jacques Villeneuve. Before the end of the year, the out-of-favour Canadian had walked, leaving Button as the team's key driver for 2004.

At last BAR came up with an excellent car and Jenson blossomed with the BAR-Honda 006 at his disposal. Although never able to beat the Ferraris, he consistently carried the fight to Maranello, making ten visits to the podium in the process of scoring 85 points. A victory was tantalisingly close, Button finishing in second place on four occasions. The only shadow on the year was his ill-advised attempt to extricate himself from the team and sign for Williams-BMW in 2005. The matter was taken to the FIA Contract Recognition Board, who ruled in favour of BAR. Jenson reluctantly accepted the decision, but signed for the Williams team in 2006 in the belief that the partnership with BMW was his best chance of long-term success.

So for 2005, Button knuckled down at BAR, overcoming a sticky start to the year with the 007 car and its subsequent disqualification from the San Marino Grand Prix. His season only kicked in at the French Grand Prix, where fourth place started a splendidly consistent run of ten consecutive points-scoring finishes, but it was all overshadowed by his volte-face on his 2006 Williams contract. Frank Williams played hardball with the disaffected driver and eventually forced a heavy financial settlement from him to permit his release. However, Jenson and his advisors had the consolation of a five-year agreement with Honda, which was seen as more than adequate compensation.

Going into the 2006 season with no wins after 118 races had left Button looking like a man who might never win a grand prix, even more so after a disheartening run of unreliability and indifferent results. However, the weather would prove his greatest ally in his maiden victory at the Hungaroring, where heavy cloud and intermittent rain replaced the normal blazing August sunshine of Budapest. Driving beautifully in the difficult conditions, aided by his team's excellent strategy, he pulled off his first grand prix win while others foundered.

The breakthrough win certainly gave Button a new found confidence. In 2007, however, his ambitions were brought crashing to earth when the Honda RA107 proved to be an embarrassing failure. The inherent faults that the car possessed could not be ironed out and he was left struggling to scrape together just six points throughout a character-building year. With Lewis Hamilton having taken centre stage as Britain's latest championship hope, Jenson showed great maturity and not a little sardonic humour as once more he accepted his position as a midfield runner – at best. When the 2008 season got under way, Honda's 'Earthdreams' RA108 may as well have been an earthworks JCB as the shocking reality set in that things were only going to get worse for Jenson. Three points from a single sixth place found him in a salutary 18th (and last) place in the points table. That winter would be his lowest ebb; Honda having withdrawn from F1, he was faced with the very real prospect of no drive at all for 2009. Salvation was nigh, however, as Ross Brawn successfully negotiated to take control of the Brackley-based team and set about turning the F1 world on its head with the introduction of his Brawn BGP001. With the secret weapon of the double diffuser, Brawn had changed the F1 landscape at a stroke. Jenson went from also-ran to pace setter in one fell swoop, and boy did he make the most of his advantage.

Six wins in the first seven races left Jenson's opponents temporarily floored, and when they had recovered to claw back the Brawn's advantage, he used all his experience to manage the situation when things were not quite right with the car. His drive through the field to fifth place at Interlagos to take the championship showed just what a fine racer he can be when the odds are against him.

Having clinched the 2009 world championship, Jenson then stunned the F1 fraternity by joining the McLaren-Mercedes team to partner Lewis Hamilton. Many saw this move as sheer folly, suggesting that he might have bitten off more than he could chew in taking on arguably F1's fastest gun. Early-season victories in Melbourne and Shanghai, however, endorsed his brave decision to change teams and helped him get to grips with his new environment. Fifth place in the final rankings was a satisfactory first year, but better would follow in 2011, when once again he capitalised on any opportunity that came his way. He had the new MP4-26 set up to his liking, and even if he was never really a favourite for pole position, his ability to maximise everything in race situations stood him in good stead, rewarding him with three victories in a season that saw him gain the upper hand over his team-mate – no mean feat when that man was Lewis Hamilton.

To say that life is good for Button would be an understatement. With a new extended contract in his pocket and a team that is right behind him, he has earned his success, and there is no reason not to believe that another championship challenge is within his compass.

BUTTON, Jenson (F) b 19/1/1980, Frome, Somerset

2000 Championship position: 8th   Wins: 0   Pole positions: 0   Fastest laps: 0   Points scored: 12

	Race	Circuit	No	Entrant	Tyres	Capacity/Car/Engine	Comment	Q Pos/Entries
ret	AUSTRALIAN GP	Melbourne	10	BMW WilliamsF1 Team	B	3.0 Williams FW22-BMW V10	engine	21/22
6*	BRAZILIAN GP	Interlagos	10	BMW WilliamsF1 Team	B	3.0 Williams FW22-BMW V10	*2nd place car disqualified/-1 lap	9/22
ret	SAN MARINO GP	Imola	10	BMW WilliamsF1 Team	B	3.0 Williams FW22-BMW V10	engine	18/22
5	BRITISH GP	Silverstone	10	BMW WilliamsF1 Team	B	3.0 Williams FW22-BMW V10	broken exhaust	6/22
17/ret	SPANISH GP	Barcelona	10	BMW WilliamsF1 Team	B	3.0 Williams FW22-BMW V10	engine failure/4 laps behind	11/22
10/ret	EUROPEAN GP	Nürburgring	10	BMW WilliamsF1 Team	B	3.0 Williams FW22-BMW V10	electrics after collision/-5 laps	11/22
ret	MONACO GP	Monte Carlo	10	BMW WilliamsF1 Team	B	3.0 Williams FW22-BMW V10	started from pitlane/oil pressure	14/22
11	CANADIAN GP	Montreal	10	BMW WilliamsF1 Team	B	3.0 Williams FW22-BMW V10	1 lap behind	18/22
8	FRENCH GP	Magny Cours	10	BMW WilliamsF1 Team	B	3.0 Williams FW22-BMW V10	1 lap behind	10/22
5	AUSTRIAN GP	A1-Ring	10	BMW WilliamsF1 Team	B	3.0 Williams FW22-BMW V10	1 lap behind	18/22
4	GERMAN GP	Hockenheim	10	BMW WilliamsF1 Team	B	3.0 Williams FW22-BMW V10	started from back of grid	16/22
9	HUNGARIAN GP	Hungaroring	10	BMW WilliamsF1 Team	B	3.0 Williams FW22-BMW V10	throttle trouble/1 lap behind	8/22
5	BELGIAN GP	Spa	10	BMW WilliamsF1 Team	B	3.0 Williams FW22-BMW V10	collision with Trulli – heavy steering	3/22
ret	ITALIAN GP	Monza	10	BMW WilliamsF1 Team	B	3.0 Williams FW22-BMW V10	hit armco – suspension damage	12/22
ret	UNITED STATES GP	Indianapolis	10	BMW WilliamsF1 Team	B	3.0 Williams FW22-BMW V10	engine	6/22
5	JAPANESE GP	Suzuka	10	BMW WilliamsF1 Team	B	3.0 Williams FW22-BMW V10	1 lap behind	5/22
ret	MALAYSIAN GP	Sepang	10	BMW WilliamsF1 Team	B	3.0 Williams FW22-BMW V10	engine	16/22

2001 Championship position: 17th   Wins: 0   Pole positions: 0   Fastest laps: 0   Points scored: 2

	Race	Circuit	No	Entrant	Tyres	Capacity/Car/Engine	Comment	Q Pos/Entries
14/ret	AUSTRALIAN GP	Melbourne	8	Mild Seven Benetton Renault	M	3.0 Benetton B201-Renault V10	cracked exhaust – burnt electrics	16/22
11	MALAYSIAN GP	Sepang	8	Mild Seven Benetton Renault	M	3.0 Benetton B201-Renault V10	2 laps behind	17/22
10	BRAZILIAN GP	Interlagos	8	Mild Seven Benetton Renault	M	3.0 Benetton B201-Renault V10	7 laps behind	20/22
12	SAN MARINO GP	Imola	8	Mild Seven Benetton Renault	M	3.0 Benetton B201-Renault V10	refuelling delay/2 laps behind	21/22
15	SPANISH GP	Barcelona	8	Mild Seven Benetton Renault	M	3.0 Benetton B201-Renault V10	3 laps behind	21/22
ret	AUSTRIAN GP	A1-Ring	8	Mild Seven Benetton Renault	M	3.0 Benetton B201-Renault V10	engine	21/22
7	MONACO GP	Monte Carlo	8	Mild Seven Benetton Renault	M	3.0 Benetton B201-Renault V10	1 lap behind	17/22
ret	CANADIAN GP	Montreal	8	Mild Seven Benetton Renault	M	3.0 Benetton B201-Renault V10	oil leak	20/22
13	EUROPEAN GP	Nürburgring	8	Mild Seven Benetton Renault	M	3.0 Benetton B201-Renault V10	2 laps behind	20/22
16/ret	FRENCH GP	Magny Cours	8	Mild Seven Benetton Renault	M	3.0 Benetton B201-Renault V10	engine – spun off/4 laps behind	17/22
15	BRITISH GP	Silverstone	8	Mild Seven Benetton Renault	M	3.0 Benetton B201-Renault V10	2 laps behind	18/22
5	GERMAN GP	Hockenheim	8	Mild Seven Benetton Renault	M	3.0 Benetton B201-Renault V10		18/22
ret	HUNGARIAN GP	Hungaroring	8	Mild Seven Benetton Renault	M	3.0 Benetton B201-Renault V10	spun off	17/22
ret	BELGIAN GP	Spa	8	Mild Seven Benetton Renault	M	3.0 Benetton B201-Renault V10	hit marker cone – crashed out	15/22
ret	ITALIAN GP	Monza	8	Mild Seven Benetton Renault	M	3.0 Benetton B201-Renault V10	engine	11/22
9	UNITED STATES GP	Indianapolis	8	Mild Seven Benetton Renault	M	3.0 Benetton B201-Renault V10	1 lap behind	10/22
7	JAPANESE GP	Suzuka	8	Mild Seven Benetton Renault	M	3.0 Benetton B201-Renault V10		9/22

2002 Championship position: 7th   Wins: 0   Pole positions: 0   Fastest laps: 0   Points scored: 14

	Race	Circuit	No	Entrant	Tyres	Capacity/Car/Engine	Comment	Q Pos/Entries
ret	AUSTRALIAN GP	Melbourne	15	Mild Seven Renault F1 Team	M	3.0 Benetton R202-Renault V10	multiple accident at start	11/22
4	MALAYSIAN GP	Sepang	15	Mild Seven Renault F1 Team	M	3.0 Benetton R202-Renault V10	suspension problem when 3rd	8/22
4	BRAZILIAN GP	Interlagos	15	Mild Seven Renault F1 Team	M	3.0 Benetton R202-Renault V10		7/22
5	SAN MARINO GP	Imola	15	Mild Seven Renault F1 Team	M	3.0 Benetton R202-Renault V10		9/22
12/ret	SPANISH GP	Barcelona	15	Mild Seven Renault F1 Team	M	3.0 Benetton R202-Renault V10	hydraulics/5 laps behind	6/21
7	AUSTRIAN GP	A1-Ring	15	Mild Seven Renault F1 Team	M	3.0 Benetton R202-Renault V10		13/22
ret	MONACO GP	Monte Carlo	15	Mild Seven Renault F1 Team	M	3.0 Benetton R202-Renault V10	collision with Panis	8/22
15/ret	CANADIAN GP	Montreal	15	Mild Seven Renault F1 Team	M	3.0 Benetton R202-Renault V10	engine/5 laps behind	13/22
5	EUROPEAN GP	Nürburgring	15	Mild Seven Renault F1 Team	M	3.0 Benetton R202-Renault V10		8/22
12/ret	BRITISH GP	Silverstone	15	Mild Seven Renault F1 Team	M	3.0 Benetton R202-Renault V10	loose front wheel/6 laps behind	12/22
6	FRENCH GP	Magny Cours	15	Mild Seven Renault F1 Team	M	3.0 Benetton R202-Renault V10	1 lap behind	7/21
ret	GERMAN GP	Hockenheim	15	Mild Seven Renault F1 Team	M	3.0 Benetton R202-Renault V10	transmission	13/22
ret	HUNGARIAN GP	Hungaroring	15	Mild Seven Renault F1 Team	M	3.0 Benetton R202-Renault V10	spun off	9/20
ret	BELGIAN GP	Spa	15	Mild Seven Renault F1 Team	M	3.0 Benetton R202-Renault V10	engine	10/20
5	ITALIAN GP	Monza	15	Mild Seven Renault F1 Team	M	3.0 Benetton R202-Renault V10	imbalance problems	17/20
8	U S GP	Indianapolis	15	Mild Seven Renault F1 Team	M	3.0 Benetton R202-Renault V10	1 lap behind	14/20
6	JAPANESE GP	Suzuka	15	Mild Seven Renault F1 Team	M	3.0 Benetton R202-Renault V10	1 lap behind	10/20

2003 Championship position: 9th=   Wins: 0   Pole positions: 0   Fastest laps: 0   Points scored: 17

	Race	Circuit	No	Entrant	Tyres	Capacity/Car/Engine	Comment	Q Pos/Entries
10	AUSTRALIAN GP	Melbourne	17	Lucky Strike BAR Honda	B	3.0 BAR 005-Honda V10	held up behind Villeneuve at pit stop	8/20
7	MALAYSIAN GP	Sepang	17	Lucky Strike BAR Honda	B	3.0 BAR 005-Honda V10	handling/grip/1 lap behind	9/20
ret	BRAZILIAN GP	Interlagos	17	Lucky Strike BAR Honda	B	3.0 BAR 005-Honda V10	spun off	11/20
8	SAN MARINO GP	Imola	17	Lucky Strike BAR Honda	B	3.0 BAR 005-Honda V10	1 lap behind	9/20
9	SPANISH GP	Barcelona	17	Lucky Strike BAR Honda	B	3.0 BAR 005-Honda V10	collision damage/2 laps behind	5/20
4	AUSTRIAN GP	A1-Ring	17	Lucky Strike BAR Honda	B	3.0 BAR 005-Honda V10		7/20
dns	MONACO GP	Monte Carlo	17	Lucky Strike BAR Honda	B	3.0 BAR 005-Honda V10	accident in Saturday free practice	–/–
ret	CANADIAN GP	Montreal	17	Lucky Strike BAR Honda	B	3.0 BAR 005-Honda V10	gearbox	17/20
7	EUROPEAN GP	Nürburgring	17	Lucky Strike BAR Honda	B	3.0 BAR 005-Honda V10	oversteer	12/20
ret	FRENCH GP	Magny Cours	17	Lucky Strike BAR Honda	B	3.0 BAR 005-Honda V10	refuelling problem – out of fuel	14/20
8	BRITISH GP	Silverstone	17	Lucky Strike BAR Honda	B	3.0 BAR 005-Honda V10	great drive from back of grid	20/20
8	GERMAN GP	Hockenheim	17	Lucky Strike BAR Honda	B	3.0 BAR 005-Honda V10	locking differential/1 lap behind	17/20
10	HUNGARIAN GP	Hungaroring	17	Lucky Strike BAR Honda	B	3.0 BAR 005-Honda V10	1 lap behind	14/20
ret	ITALIAN GP	Monza	17	Lucky Strike BAR Honda	B	3.0 BAR 005-Honda V10	gearbox	7/20
ret	U S GP	Indianapolis	17	Lucky Strike BAR Honda	B	3.0 BAR 005-Honda V10	hydraulics	11/20
4	JAPANESE GP	Suzuka	17	Lucky Strike BAR Honda	B	3.0 BAR 005-Honda V10	briefly led race	9/20

2004 Championship position: 3rd   Wins: 0   Pole positions: 1   Fastest laps: 0   Points scored: 85

	Race	Circuit	No	Entrant	Tyres	Capacity/Car/Engine	Comment	Q Pos/Entries
6	AUSTRALIAN GP	Melbourne	9	Lucky Strike BAR Honda	M	3.0 BAR 006-Honda V10	delayed at 2nd pit stop	4/20
3	MALAYSIAN GP	Sepang	9	Lucky Strike BAR Honda	M	3.0 BAR 006-Honda V10	first podium	6/20
3	BAHRAIN GP	Sakhir Circuit	9	Lucky Strike BAR Honda	M	3.0 BAR 006-Honda V10		6/20
2	SAN MARINO GP	Imola	9	Lucky Strike BAR Honda	M	3.0 BAR 006-Honda V10	first pole position	1/20

8	SPANISH GP	Barcelona	9	Lucky Strike BAR Honda	M	3.0 BAR 006-Honda V10		14/20
2	MONACO GP	Monte Carlo	9	Lucky Strike BAR Honda	M	3.0 BAR 006-Honda V10		2/20
3	EUROPEAN GP	Nürburgring	9	Lucky Strike BAR Honda	M	3.0 BAR 006-Honda V10		5/20
3*	CANADIAN GP	Montreal	9	Lucky Strike BAR Honda	M	3.0 BAR 006-Honda V10	*2nd place car disqualified	2/20
ret	U S GP	Indianapolis	9	Lucky Strike BAR Honda	M	3.0 BAR 006-Honda V10	gearbox	4/20
5	FRENCH GP	Magny Cours	9	Lucky Strike BAR Honda	M	3.0 BAR 006-Honda V10		4/20
4	BRITISH GP	Silverstone	9	Lucky Strike BAR Honda	M	3.0 BAR 006-Honda V10		3/20
2	GERMAN GP	Hockenheim	9	Lucky Strike BAR Honda	M	3.0 BAR 006-Honda V10	*10 place penalty-engine change	*13/20
5	HUNGARIAN GP	Hungaroring	9	Lucky Strike BAR Honda	M	3.0 BAR 006-Honda V10		4/20
ret	BELGIAN GP	Spa	9	Lucky Strike BAR Honda	M	3.0 BAR 006-Honda V10	tyre failure – hit Baumgartner	12/20
3	ITALIAN GP	Monza	9	Lucky Strike BAR Honda	M	3.0 BAR 006-Honda V10		6/20
2	CHINESE GP	Shanghai	9	Lucky Strike BAR Honda	M	3.0 BAR 006-Honda V10		3/20
3	JAPANESE GP	Suzuka	9	Lucky Strike BAR Honda	M	3.0 BAR 006-Honda V10		5/20
ret	BRAZILIAN GP	Interlagos	9	Lucky Strike BAR Honda	M	3.0 BAR 006-Honda V10	engine	5/20

2005 Championship position: 9th   Wins: 0   Pole positions: 1   Fastest laps: 0   Points scored: 37

11	AUSTRALIAN GP	Melbourne	3	BAR Lucky Strike Honda	M	3.0 BAR 007-Honda V10	pitted on final lap/1 lap behind	8/20
ret	MALAYSIAN GP	Sepang	3	BAR Lucky Strike Honda	M	3.0 BAR 007-Honda V10	engine – oil leak	9/20
ret	BAHRAIN GP	Sakhir Circuit	3	BAR Lucky Strike Honda	M	3.0 BAR 007-Honda V10	transmission after pit stop	11/20
dsq	SAN MARINO GP	Imola	3	BAR Lucky Strike Honda	M	3.0 BAR 007-Honda V10	3rd on road. dsq – car underweight	3/20
10	EUROPEAN GP	Nürburgring	3	BAR Lucky Strike Honda	M	3.0 BAR 007-Honda V10	poor handling	13/20
ret	CANADIAN GP	Montreal	3	BAR Lucky Strike Honda	M	3.0 BAR 007-Honda V10	bounced of kerb – hit wall	1/20
dns*	U S GP	Indianapolis	3	BAR Lucky Strike Honda	M	3.0 BAR 007-Honda V10	*withdrawn after parade lap	3/20
4	FRENCH GP	Magny Cours	3	BAR Lucky Strike Honda	M	3.0 BAR 007-Honda V10	1 lap behind	7/20
5	BRITISH GP	Silverstone	3	BAR Lucky Strike Honda	M	3.0 BAR 007-Honda V10		3/20
3	GERMAN GP	Hockenheim	3	BAR Lucky Strike Honda	M	3.0 BAR 007-Honda V10		2/20
5	HUNGARIAN GP	Hungaroring	3	BAR Lucky Strike Honda	M	3.0 BAR 007-Honda V10	ran on harder compound tyres	8/20
5	TURKISH GP	Istanbul	3	BAR Lucky Strike Honda	M	3.0 BAR 007-Honda V10	good drive from low grid position	13/20
8	ITALIAN GP	Monza	3	BAR Lucky Strike Honda	M	3.0 BAR 007-Honda V10	refuelling delay/poor handling	4/20
3	BELGIAN GP	Spa	3	BAR Lucky Strike Honda	M	3.0 BAR 007-Honda V10	overcame poor handling	9/20
7	BRAZILIAN GP	Interlagos	3	BAR Lucky Strike Honda	M	3.0 BAR 007-Honda V10	graining tyres oversteer/-1 lap	4/20
5	JAPANESE GP	Suzuka	3	BAR Lucky Strike Honda	M	3.0 BAR 007-Honda V10	refuelling delays	2/20
8	CHINESE GP	Shanghai	3	BAR Lucky Strike Honda	M	3.0 BAR 007-Honda V10	poor handling	4/20

2006 Championship position: 6th   Wins: 1   Pole positions: 1   Fastest laps: 0   Points scored: 56

4	BAHRAIN GP	Sakhir Circuit	12	Lucky Strike Honda Racing F1 Team	M	2.4 Honda RA106-V8	bad start-clutch problems	3/22
3	MALAYSIAN GP	Sepang	12	Lucky Strike Honda Racing F1 Team	M	2.4 Honda RA106-V8	delayed by traffic	2/22
ret/10	AUSTRALIAN GP	Melbourne	12	Lucky Strike Honda Racing F1 Team	M	2.4 Honda RA106-V8	engine on last lap	1/22
7	SAN MARINO GP	Imola	12	Lucky Strike Honda Racing F1 Team	M	2.4 Honda RA106-V8	delayed at two pit stops	2/22
ret	EUROPEAN GP	Nürburgring	12	Lucky Strike Honda Racing F1 Team	M	2.4 Honda RA106-V8	engine	6/22
6	SPANISH GP	Barcelona	12	Lucky Strike Honda Racing F1 Team	M	2.4 Honda RA106-V8	understeer	8/22
11	MONACO GP	Monte Carlo	12	Lucky Strike Honda Racing F1 Team	M	2.4 Honda RA106-V8	oversteer	14/22
ret	BRITISH GP	Silverstone	12	Lucky Strike Honda Racing F1 Team	M	2.4 Honda RA106-V8	engine – oil leak	19/22
9	CANADIAN GP	Montreal	12	Lucky Strike Honda Racing F1 Team	M	2.4 Honda RA106-V8	low grip/1 lap behind	8/22
ret	U S GP	Indianapolis	12	Lucky Strike Honda Racing F1 Team	M	2.4 Honda RA106-V8	multiple collision – accident damage	7/22
ret	FRENCH GP	Magny Cours	12	Lucky Strike Honda Racing F1 Team	M	2.4 Honda RA106-V8	engine	19/22
4	GERMAN GP	Hockenheim	12	Lucky Strike Honda Racing F1 Team	M	2.4 Honda RA106-V8	electrical problems/tyre graining	4/22
1	HUNGARIAN GP	Hungaroring	12	Lucky Strike Honda Racing F1 Team	M	2.4 Honda RA106-V8	first Grand Prix win	4/22
4	TURKISH GP	Istanbul	12	Lucky Strike Honda Racing F1 Team	M	2.4 Honda RA106-V8		7/22
5	ITALIAN GP	Monza	12	Lucky Strike Honda Racing F1 Team	M	2.4 Honda RA106-V8		5/22
4	CHINESE GP	Shanghai	12	Lucky Strike Honda Racing F1 Team	M	2.4 Honda RA106-V8		4/22
4	JAPANESE GP	Suzuka	12	Lucky Strike Honda Racing F1 Team	M	2.4 Honda RA106-V8		7/22
3	BRAZILIAN GP	Interlagos	12	Lucky Strike Honda Racing F1 Team	M	2.4 Honda RA106-V8	great drive through the field	14/22

2007 Championship position: 15th   Wins: 0   Pole positions: 0   Fastest laps: 0   Points scored: 6

15	AUSTRALIAN GP	Melbourne	7	Honda Racing F1 Team	B	2.4 Honda RA107-V8	poor handling/1 lap behind	14/22
12	MALAYSIAN GP	Sepang	7	Honda Racing F1 Team	B	2.4 Honda RA107-V8	poor handling/1 lap behind	15/22
ret	BAHRAIN GP	Sakhir Circuit	7	Honda Racing F1 Team	B	2.4 Honda RA107-V8	collision with Coulthard on lap 1	16/22
12	SPANISH GP	Barcelona	7	Honda Racing F1 Team	B	2.4 Honda RA107-V8	collision – lost front wing/-1 lap	14/22
11	MONACO GP	Monte Carlo	7	Honda Racing F1 Team	B	2.4 Honda RA107-V8	1 lap behind	10/22
ret	CANADIAN GP	Montreal	7	Honda Racing F1 Team	B	2.4 Honda RA107-V8	gear selection on grid	15/22
12	U S GP	Indianapolis	7	Honda Racing F1 Team	B	2.4 Honda RA107-V8	1 lap behind	13/22
8	FRENCH GP	Magny Cours	7	Honda Racing F1 Team	B	2.4 Honda RA107-V8	much improved car performance	12/22
10	BRITISH GP	Silverstone	7	Honda Racing F1 Team	B	2.4 Honda RA107-V8	one-stop strategy/1 lap behind	18/22
ret	GERMAN GP	Hockenheim	7	Honda Racing F1 Team	B	2.4 Honda RA107-V8	crashed in heavy rain	18/22
ret	HUNGARIAN GP	Hungaroring	7	Honda Racing F1 Team	B	2.4 Honda RA107-V8	throttle sensor	17/22
13	TURKISH GP	Istanbul	7	Honda Racing F1 Team	B	2.4 Honda RA107-V8	1 lap behind	15/22
8	ITALIAN GP	Monza	7	Honda Racing F1 Team	B	2.4 Honda RA107-V8	understeer/flat-spotted tyre	10/22
ret	BELGIAN GP	Spa	7	Honda Racing F1 Team	B	2.4 Honda RA107-V8	hydraulics	14/22
11/ret	JAPANESE GP	Suzuka	7	Honda Racing F1 Team	B	2.4 Honda RA107-V8	taken out by Sato/1 lap behind	7/22
5	CHINESE GP	Shanghai	7	Honda Racing F1 Team	B	2.4 Honda RA107-V8		10/22
ret	BRAZILIAN GP	Interlagos	7	Honda Racing F1 Team	B	2.4 Honda RA107-V8	engine	16/22

2008 Championship position: 18th   Wins: 0   Pole positions: 0   Fastest laps: 0   Points scored: 3

ret	AUSTRALIAN GP	Melbourne	16	Honda Racing F1 Team	B	2.4 Honda RA108-V8	collison – Vettel on lap 1	13/22
10	MALAYSIAN GP	Sepang	16	Honda Racing F1 Team	B	2.4 Honda RA108-V8		11/22
ret	BAHRAIN GP	Sakhir Circuit	16	Honda Racing F1 Team	B	2.4 Honda RA108-V8	hit – Coulthard/accident damage	9/22
6	SPANISH GP	Barcelona	16	Honda Racing F1 Team	B	2.4 Honda RA108-V8		13/22
11	TURKISH GP	Istanbul	16	Honda Racing F1 Team	B	2.4 Honda RA108-V8	one-stop strategy – 1 lap behind	13/20
11	MONACO GP	Monte Carlo	16	Honda Racing F1 Team	B	2.4 Honda RA108-V8	pit stop – new front wing -1 lap	12/20
11	CANADIAN GP	Montreal	16	Honda Racing F1 Team	B	2.4 Honda RA108-V8		19/20
ret	FRENCH GP	Magny Cours	16	Honda Racing F1 Team	B	2.4 Honda RA108-V8	accident damage – car undriveable	17/20
ret	BRITISH GP	Silverstone	16	Honda Racing F1 Team	B	2.4 Honda RA108-V8	spun off	17/20

Everything fell into place for Jenson Button in 2009, when he found himself at the wheel of the Brawn-Mercedes. His path to the world championship was built on a scintillating start to the season that saw six victories in the first seven races. Pictured right, he heads for victory in the Spanish Grand Prix at Barcelona.

17	GERMAN GP	Hockenheim	16	Honda Racing F1 Team	B	2.4 Honda RA108-V8	extra pit stop/1 lap behind	14/20
12	HUNGARIAN GP	Hungaroring	16	Honda Racing F1 Team	B	2.4 Honda RA108-V8	1 lap behind	12/20
13	EUROPEAN GP	Valencia	16	Honda Racing F1 Team	B	2.4 Honda RA108-V8	one-stop strategy – 1 lap behind	16/20
15	BELGIAN GP	Spa	16	Honda Racing F1 Team	B	2.4 Honda RA108-V8	1 lap behind	17/20
15	ITALIAN GP	Monza	16	Honda Racing F1 Team	B	2.4 Honda RA108-V8		19/20
9	SINGAPORE GP	Singapore Circuit	16	Honda Racing F1 Team	B	2.4 Honda RA108-V8	lost time under safety car	12/20
14	JAPANESE GP	Suzuka	16	Honda Racing F1 Team	B	2.4 Honda RA108-V8	1 lap behind	18/20
16	CHINESE GP	Shanghai	16	Honda Racing F1 Team	B	2.4 Honda RA108-V8	understeer/1 lap behind	18/20
13	BRAZILIAN GP	Interlagos	16	Honda Racing F1 Team	B	2.4 Honda RA108-V8	1 lap behind	17/20

2009 WORLD CHAMPION　Wins: 6　Pole positions: 4　Fastest laps: 2　Points scored: 95

1	AUSTRALIAN GP	Melbourne	22	Brawn Grand Prix	B	2.4 Brawn BGP001-Mercedes V8	fairytale debut win for team	1/20
1	MALAYSIAN GP	Sepang	22	Brawn Grand Prix	B	2.4 Brawn BGP001-Mercedes V8	rain-shortened race/FL	1/20
3	CHINESE GP	Shanghai	22	Brawn Grand Prix	B	2.4 Brawn BGP001-Mercedes V8		5/20
1	BAHRAIN GP	Sakhir Circuit	22	Brawn Grand Prix	B	2.4 Brawn BGP001-Mercedes V8	despite overheated transformer	4/20
1	SPANISH GP	Barcelona	22	Brawn Grand Prix	B	2.4 Brawn BGP001-Mercedes V8		1/20
1	MONACO GP	Monte Carlo	22	Brawn Grand Prix	B	2.4 Brawn BGP001-Mercedes V8		1/20
1	TURKISH GP	Istanbul	22	Brawn Grand Prix	B	2.4 Brawn BGP001-Mercedes V8	FL	2/20
6	BRITISH GP	Silverstone	22	Brawn Grand Prix	B	2.4 Brawn BGP001-Mercedes V8	struggled with low tyre temperatures	6/20
5	GERMAN GP	Hockenheim	22	Brawn Grand Prix	B	2.4 Brawn BGP001-Mercedes V8	tyre problems	3/20
7	HUNGARIAN GP	Hungaroring	22	Brawn Grand Prix	B	2.4 Brawn BGP001-Mercedes V8	struggled with low tyre temperatures	8/20
7	EUROPEAN GP	Valencia	22	Brawn Grand Prix	B	2.4 Brawn BGP001-Mercedes V8	caught in traffic	5/20
ret	BELGIAN GP	Spa	22	Brawn Grand Prix	B	2.4 Brawn BGP001-Mercedes V8	collision with Grosjean on lap 1	14/20
2	ITALIAN GP	Monza	22	Brawn Grand Prix	B	2.4 Brawn BGP001-Mercedes V8	one-stop strategy	6/20
5	SINGAPORE GP	Singapore Circuit	22	Brawn Grand Prix	B	2.4 Brawn BGP001-Mercedes V8	brake troubles	12/20
8	JAPANESE GP	Suzuka	22	Brawn Grand Prix	B	2.4 Brawn BGP001-Mercedes V8		7/20
5	BRAZILIAN GP	Interlagos	22	Brawn Grand Prix	B	2.4 Brawn BGP001-Mercedes V8	great drive to clinch title	14/20
3	ABU DHABI GP	Yas Marina Circuit	22	Brawn Grand Prix	B	2.4 Brawn BGP001-Mercedes V8	good battle with Webber for 2nd	5/20

2010　Championship position: 5th　Wins: 2　Pole positions: 0　Fastest laps: 1　Points scored: 214

7	BAHRAIN GP	Sakhir Circuit	1	Vodafone McLaren Mercedes	B	2.4 McLaren MP4/25-Mercedes V8		4/24
1	AUSTRALIAN GP	Melbourne	1	Vodafone McLaren Mercedes	B	2.4 McLaren MP4/25-Mercedes V8	win in first race for McLaren	4/24
8	MALAYSIAN GP	Sepang	1	Vodafone McLaren Mercedes	B	2.4 McLaren MP4/25-Mercedes V8	engine	17/24
1	CHINESE GP	Shanghai Circuit	1	Vodafone McLaren Mercedes	B	2.4 McLaren MP4/25-Mercedes V8		5/24
5	SPANISH GP	Barcelona	1	Vodafone McLaren Mercedes	B	2.4 McLaren MP4/25-Mercedes V8	failed dash readout/tyre problems	5/24
ret	MONACO GP	Monte Carlo	1	Vodafone McLaren Mercedes	B	2.4 McLaren MP4/25-Mercedes V8	blocked sidepod – fire	8/24
2	TURKISH GP	Istanbul Park	1	Vodafone McLaren Mercedes	B	2.4 McLaren MP4/25-Mercedes V8		4/24
2	CANADIAN GP	Montreal	1	Vodafone McLaren Mercedes	B	2.4 McLaren MP4/25-Mercedes V8		5/24
3*	EUROPEAN GP	Valencia	1	Vodafone McLaren Mercedes	B	2.4 McLaren MP4/25-Mercedes V8	*5-sec pen, sped behind safetycar/FL	7/24
4	BRITISH GP	Silverstone	1	Vodafone McLaren Mercedes	B	2.4 McLaren MP4/25-Mercedes V8	good drive though field	14/24
5	GERMAN GP	Hockenheim	1	Vodafone McLaren Mercedes	B	2.4 McLaren MP4/25-Mercedes V8		5/24
8	HUNGARIAN GP	Hungaroring	1	Vodafone McLaren Mercedes	B	2.4 McLaren MP4/25-Mercedes V8	1 lap behind	11/24
ret	BELGIAN GP	Spa	1	Vodafone McLaren Mercedes	B	2.4 McLaren MP4/25-Mercedes V8	accident – taken out by Vettel	5/24
2	ITALIAN GP	Monza	1	Vodafone McLaren Mercedes	B	2.4 McLaren MP4/25-Mercedes V8	ran one-stop strategy	2/24
4	SINGAPORE GP	Marina Bay Circuit	1	Vodafone McLaren Mercedes	B	2.4 McLaren MP4/25-Mercedes V8		4/24
4	JAPANESE GP	Suzuka	1	Vodafone McLaren Mercedes	B	2.4 McLaren MP4/25-Mercedes V8	ran one-stop strategy	6/24
12	KOREAN GP	Yeongam	1	Vodafone McLaren Mercedes	B	2.4 McLaren MP4/25-Mercedes V8	tyre problems/spin	7/24
5	BRAZILIAN GP	Interlagos	1	Vodafone McLaren Mercedes	B	2.4 McLaren MP4/25-Mercedes V8		11/24
3	ABU DHABI GP	Yas Marina Circuit	1	Vodafone McLaren Mercedes	B	2.4 McLaren MP4/25-Mercedes V8		4/24

2011　Championship position: 2nd　Wins: 3　Pole positions: 0　Fastest laps: 3　Points scored: 270

6	AUSTRALIAN GP	Melbourne	4	Vodafone McLaren Mercedes	P	2.4 McLaren MP4/26-Mercedes V8	missed turn – drive-thru penalty	4/24
2	MALAYSIAN GP	Sepang	4	Vodafone McLaren Mercedes	P	2.4 McLaren MP4/26-Mercedes V8		4/24
4	CHINESE GP	Shanghai Circuit	4	Vodafone McLaren Mercedes	P	2.4 McLaren MP4/26-Mercedes V8		2/24

6	TURKISH GP	Istanbul Park	4	Vodafone McLaren Mercedes	P	2.4 McLaren MP4/26-Mercedes V8	*ran three-pit stop strategy*	6/24
3	SPANISH GP	Barcelona	4	Vodafone McLaren Mercedes	P	2.4 McLaren MP4/26-Mercedes V8	*poor start – ran three-stop strategy*	5/24
3	MONACO GP	Monte Carlo	4	Vodafone McLaren Mercedes	P	2.4 McLaren MP4/26-Mercedes V8		2/24
1	CANADIAN GP	Montreal	4	Vodafone McLaren Mercedes	P	2.4 McLaren MP4/26-Mercedes V8	*FL*	7/24
6	EUROPEAN GP	Valencia	4	Vodafone McLaren Mercedes	P	2.4 McLaren MP4/26-Mercedes V8	*lost use of KERS during race*	6/24
ret	BRITISH GP	Silverstone	4	Vodafone McLaren Mercedes	P	2.4 McLaren MP4/26-Mercedes V8	*lost wheel after pit stop*	19/24
ret	GERMAN GP	Hockenheim	4	Vodafone McLaren Mercedes	P	2.4 McLaren MP4/26-Mercedes V8	*hydraulics*	7/24
1	HUNGARIAN GP	Hungaroring	4	Vodafone McLaren Mercedes	P	2.4 McLaren MP4/26-Mercedes V8		3/24
3	BELGIAN GP	Spa	4	Vodafone McLaren Mercedes	P	2.4 McLaren MP4/26-Mercedes V8	*minor collision damage on lap 1*	13/24
2	ITALIAN GP	Monza	4	Vodafone McLaren Mercedes	P	2.4 McLaren MP4/26-Mercedes V8	*1 lap behind*	3/24
2	SINGAPORE GP	Marina Bay Circuit	4	Vodafone McLaren Mercedes	P	2.4 McLaren MP4/26-Mercedes V8		3/24
1	JAPANESE GP	Suzuka	4	Vodafone McLaren Mercedes	P	2.4 McLaren MP4/26-Mercedes V8	*FL*	2/24
4	KOREAN GP	Yeongam	4	Vodafone McLaren Mercedes	P	2.4 McLaren MP4/26-Mercedes V8		3/24
2	INDIAN GP	Buddh Circuit	4	Vodafone McLaren Mercedes	P	2.4 McLaren MP4/26-Mercedes V8		5/24
3	ABU DHABI GP	Yas Marina Circuit	4	Vodafone McLaren Mercedes	P	2.4 McLaren MP4/26-Mercedes V8	*lost use of KERS during race*	3/24
3	BRAZILIAN GP	Interlagos	4	Vodafone McLaren Mercedes	P	2.4 McLaren MP4/26-Mercedes V8		3/24

GP Starts: 208   GP Wins: 12   Pole positions: 7   Fastest laps: 6   Points: 811

TOMMY BYRNE

TOMMY BYRNE'S rise to the top was so rapid he was pitched into Formula 1 before he had completed his first season in Formula 3. He felt the opportunity of racing the Theodore was too good to miss, but the car was uncompetitive and he was never given a second chance at the top level.

After a little local rallying in a Mini, Tommy was really bitten by the motorsport bug after a visit to a racing school at Mondello Park. After some false starts, the young Irishman really started to blossom in 1978 in Formula Ford, and when he finally equipped himself with competitive machinery, a win was forthcoming. The following year proved to be disappointing, however, and it wasn't until 1980 that Byrne became a pace setter once more with his Van Diemen, finishing second in the Formula Ford Festival behind a dominant Roberto Moreno.

Without the budget to compete in Formula 3 for 1981, Bryne opted for FF2000, which proved an astute move: he not only swept to the championship, but this time also took victory at the Formula Ford Festival. This success brought him to the attention of the front-running Murray Taylor F3 team for 1982. Without sponsorship, he knew he had to get results or else he would be out on his ear. And he did just that, taking seven wins and the Marlboro Formula 3 title, despite missing rounds while pursuing a grand prix opportunity that came in mid-season.

Byrne did very well to qualify the Theodore for two races, but he returned to the job of clinching his F3 title, vowing not to try Formula 1 again unless he had a competitive car.

Tantalisingly, Tommy did get the chance to show his ability when he tested a McLaren F1 as reward for winning the Marlboro F3 crown. Despite setting some staggeringly quick times, he didn't shape up as a potential F1 champion in the eyes of Ron Dennis, who questioned whether the Irishman had sufficient desire and focus to make a long-term career in Formula 1.

So it was back to Formula 3 in Europe with Eddie Jordan for 1983, although Byrne was already eyeing up a potential move to the USA and the CART series. Two wins and a distant fourth place led nowhere, and the following year he had a final tilt at the European F3 crown with Gary Anderson's Anson team, finishing sixth overall.

Then Tommy decided to seek pastures new, so he headed off to America, where he was successful for more than a decade: he nearly took the ARS (later Indy Lights) series title in 1988 and was heartbroken again the following year when he lost out in the title battle at the season's final race. In 1990, he remained in situ, but a new kid on the block by the name of Paul Tracy blitzed the opposition, and the Irishman could only muster a single win. Despite his successes, the call for a CART ride never came and he remained marooned in the junior single-seat classes, including Mexican F3 before retiring at the end of 1992.

Since then, Byrne, still living in the USA, has passed on his considerable experience in both road and race driving as an instructor working out of his home in Florida and Mid-Ohio in the racing season.

BYRNE, Tommy (IRL) b 6/5/1958, Drogheda, Co Louth

1982 Championship position: Unplaced

	Race	Circuit	No	Entrant	Tyres	Capacity/Car/Engine	Comment	Qual Pos/Entries
dnq	GERMAN GP	Hockenheim	33	Theodore Racing Team	G	3.0 Theodore TY02-Cosworth V8		28/30
ret	AUSTRIAN GP	Österreichring	33	Theodore Racing Team	G	3.0 Theodore TY02-Cosworth V8	*spun off*	26/29
dnq	SWISS GP	Dijon	33	Theodore Racing Team	G	3.0 Theodore TY02-Cosworth V8		28/29
dnq	ITALIAN GP	Monza	33	Theodore Racing Team	G	3.0 Theodore TY02-Cosworth V8		30/30
ret	CAESARS PALACE GP	Las Vegas	33	Theodore Racing Team	G	3.0 Theodore TY02-Cosworth V8	*spun off*	26/30

GP Starts: 2   GP Wins: 0   Pole positions: 0   Fastest laps: 0   Points: 0

GUILIO CABIANCA

A VERY experienced and reliable sports car driver, Guilio Cabianca spent most of the 1950s pitting the works OSCA sports cars against more powerful opposition, regularly picking up class wins in classic events. He was seventh overall and first in class in the 1955 Targa Florio, and after a superb drive repeated the feat in the 1957 Mille Miglia with Louis Chiron (ninth overall). These performances led to his inclusion in the Ferrari sports car team for 1959 and 1960, when his best placing was fourth in the Targa Florio. He also took second place in the 1961 Mille Miglia in a Flammini Zagato. With the F2 OSCA, he finished third to Maurice Trintignant after taking an early lead in the 1958 Pau GP. Although his grand prix outings were few, he lay fifth in Jo Bonnier's Maserati in the 1958 Italian GP before engine trouble and scored points in the boycotted 1960 Italian GP for Scuderia Castellotti.

Cabianca lost his life testing one of Castellotti's Coopers at Modena in June 1961, when the throttle stuck open: the car ran through an open gateway into the street and crashed into a passing taxi, killing not only its driver, but also the three unfortunate occupants of the cab.

MARIO CABRAL

P ORTUGAL'S outstanding driver of the late 1950s, Mario 'Nicha' Cabral acquitted himself well in his first two grand prix outings. He did not pursue a full-time racing career, but made an impression on a visit to Brazil in late 1960 to win the Grande Premio do Rio de Janeiro at the Guanabara circuit in a 3-litre Maserati.

Back to F1 in Europe, he appeared in the 1961 Pau Grand Prix and was taken under the wing of Maurice Trintignant. The French veteran's intimate knowledge of the street track helped Mario to finish in a fine fourth place for Centro Sud, just behind his team-mate, Lorenzo Bandini. It was thought that both drivers were running oversized engines, at 2 litres rather than the then newly introduced mandatory 1.5 limit. Nobody seemed to object...

Cabral's racing activities were interrupted by national service (as a paratrooper in Angola), before he managed to return briefly to Formula 1 in 1963 with Centro Sud in their ageing Coopers. He qualified at Monza, but was asked to stand down by his team so that Giancarlo Baghetti could start in his troublesome ATS.

Mario made the grid for the 1964 Italian GP in the reworked, but still unsuccessful Derrington-Francis ATS. He was seriously injured, however, when he crashed in the 1965 F2 Rouen Grand Prix, resulting in a three-year absence from the circuits.

On his return in 1968, Cabral raced a variety of sports cars through to 1975, including David Piper's Porsche 917, in which he finished second at Villa Real in 1971. In 1973, he hired a works March for the F2 Estoril GP and performed very creditably to finish eighth on aggregate.

CABIANCA, Giulio (I) b 19/2/1923, Verona – d 15/6/1961, Modena Autodrome

1958 Championship position: Unplaced

	Race	Circuit	No	Entrant	Tyres	Capacity/Car/Engine	Comment	Qual Pos/Entries
dnq	MONACO GP	Monte Carlo	52	OSCA Automobili	–	1.5 OSCA 4 F2		25/28
ret	ITALIAN GP	Monza	22	Jo Bonnier	–	2.5 Maserati 250F 6	engine	20/21

1959 Championship position: Unplaced

	Race	Circuit	No	Entrant	Tyres	Capacity/Car/Engine	Comment	Qual Pos/Entries
15	ITALIAN GP	Monza	28	Ottorino Volonterio	D	2.5 Maserati 250F 6	pit stop/8 laps behind	21/21

1960 Championship position: 16th=   Wins: 0   Pole positions: 0   Fastest laps: 0   Points scored: 3

	Race	Circuit	No	Entrant	Tyres	Capacity/Car/Engine	Comment	Qual Pos/Entries
4	ITALIAN GP	Monza	2	Scuderia Castellotti	D	2.5 Cooper T51-Castellotti 4	2 laps behind	4/16

GP Starts: 3   GP Wins: 0   Pole positions: 0   Fastest laps: 0   Points: 3

CABRAL, Araújo Mário (P) b 15/1/1934 Cedofeita, Porto

1959 Championship position: Unplaced

	Race	Circuit	No	Entrant	Tyres	Chassis/Car/Engine	Comment	Qual Pos/Entries
10	PORTUGUESE GP	Monsanto	18	Scuderia Centro Sud	D	2.5 Cooper T51-Maserati 4	6 laps behind	14/16

1960 Championship position: Unplaced

	Race	Circuit	No	Entrant	Tyres	Chassis/Car/Engine	Comment	Qual Pos/Entries
ret	PORTUGUESE GP	Oporto	32	Scuderia Centro Sud	D	2.5 Cooper T51-Maserati 4	clutch/gearbox	15/16

1963 Championship position: Unplaced

	Race	Circuit	No	Entrant	Tyres	Chassis/Car/Engine	Comment	Qual Pos/Entries
ret	GERMAN GP	Nürburgring	22	Scuderia Centro Sud	D	1.5 Cooper T60-Climax V8	gearbox	20/26
dns	ITALIAN GP	Monza	64	Scuderia Centro Sud	D	1.5 Cooper T60-Climax V8	car withdrawn	21/28

1964 Championship position: Unplaced

	Race	Circuit	No	Entrant	Tyres	Chassis/Car/Engine	Comment	Qual Pos/Entries
ret	ITALIAN GP	Monza	50	Derrington-Francis Racing Team	D	1.5 D.F. ATS 100 V8	ignition	19/25

GP Starts: 4   GP Wins: 0   Pole positions: 0   Fastest laps: 0   Points: 0

ALEX CAFFI

WITH both of his uncles involved in motorsport, Alex Caffi always had a passion for speed. He began as a motocross racer in his teens and still indulges his two-wheel passion with Harley-Davidsons. He progressed to karting in 1980, moving smoothly up through Formula 4 and then the Fiat Abarth series, where he finished second in 1983. He was destined to be a perennial runner-up in Italian Formula 3, in 1984 and then 1985, when running a Coloni chassis probably cost him the title. However, he did take victory in the single-event European Cup at Paul Ricard in 1985 with a Dallara F385/Alfa.

For 1986, Caffi switched chassis again and ironically lost out to the Coloni stars Nicola Larini and Marco Apicella. At the same time, he completed his national service and his studies in accountancy, but none of these outside distractions halted his ambitions to graduate to F1.

Given a chance to race the unwieldy Osella at the Italian Grand Prix that season, Alex drove sensibly, kept out of the way and impressed everyone with his approach. This led to a full season with the team in 1987. The car was totally uncompetitive, but Caffi plugged away without complaint, quietly learning his trade while grateful for the chance to showcase his talents.

A move to the new Scuderia Italia Dallara team for 1988 brought some good performances in their neat little car, and with all his mechanics coming from his home town, Alex enjoyed the comfortable atmosphere. The following season he seemed to be a star in the making, qualifying in the top ten on six occasions and finishing a very impressive fourth at Monaco. Heartache came at Phoenix, though, where he lost a second place when his team-mate, Andrea de Cesaris, crassly elbowed him into the wall.

In retrospect, his move to the Arrows/Footwork operation proved to be a complete disaster. The 1990 season was spent marking time, and when the Porsche-engined car arrived it was hopelessly overweight and underpowered. A big practice shunt at Monaco shook him up, and things took a further dive when Alex was sidelined after a road accident that resulted in a broken jaw. The atmosphere in the team was not helped when he threatened legal action (successfully) to reclaim his seat (taken by Stefan Johansson) at Hockenheim.

A hot property barely two seasons earlier, now Caffi found that his career was on the skids, and after a brief flirtation with the hapless Andrea Moda team early in 1982, and a few races in Group C sports cars, he quit racing completely.

After a couple of years away, Alex returned to competition in the Italian and Spanish touring car championships with a works-backed Opel Vectra, which brought back his passion for racing. In 1998, he joined forces with Andrea Chiesa to successfully race a Riley & Scott sports car in the International Sports Racing Series, and he continued to impress in this discipline in 1999, both in Europe and in the USA, with his best results being third places in the FIA World Sports Car Cup at Spa (with Gianluca de Lorenzi) and Kyalami (with Nicola Larini). In addition, he took a fine sixth place at Le Mans in a Courage C52-Nissan prototype, sharing the driving duties with fellow F1 rejects Andrea Montermini and Domenico Schiattarella

From 2000, Caffi was a regular competitor in both the American Le Mans Series and the FIA GT Championship, but by 2004 he was only competing intermittently. He did return to Le Mans in both 2004 and 2007 (with his old cohort Chiesa), but failed to finish.

However, in 2006, Alex – paired with Denny Zardo – won the GT2 class of the Italian GT Championships (with six wins) in a Ferrari F430 GTC. He also made an impressive debut in the Grand Prix Masters event at a rain-soaked Silverstone, taking fifth place after virtually no practice time in the car. He has tried his hand at other forms of the sport, too, finishing 13th overall in the 2011 Monte Carlo Rally in a Skoda Fabia and entering the gruelling 2012 Dakar, where he was forced to retire his 4x4 Fiat after the third stage.

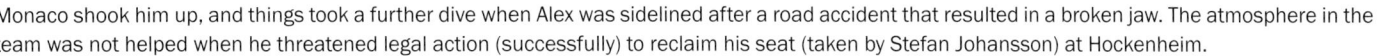

CAFFI, Alex (I) b 18/3/1964, Rovato, Brescia

	1986 Championship position: Unplaced							
	Race	Circuit	No	Entrant	Tyres	Capacity/Car/Engine	Comment	Qual Pos/Entries
11	ITALIAN GP	Monza	22	Osella Squadra Corse	P	1.5 t/c Osella FA1F-Alfa Romeo V8	6 laps behind	25/25
	1987 Championship position: Unplaced							
ret	BRAZILIAN GP	Rio	21	Osella Squadra Corse	G	1.5 t/c Osella FA1I-Alfa Romeo V8	driver exhaustion	21/23
12/ret	SAN MARINO GP	Imola	21	Osella Squadra Corse	G	1.5 t/c Osella FA1I-Alfa Romeo V8	out of fuel/5 laps behind	21/27
ret	BELGIAN GP	Spa	21	Osella Squadra Corse	G	1.5 t/c Osella FA1I-Alfa Romeo V8	engine	26/26
ret	MONACO GP	Monte Carlo	21	Osella Squadra Corse	G	1.5 t/c Osella FA1I-Alfa Romeo V8	electrics	16/26
ret	US GP (DETROIT)	Detroit	21	Osella Squadra Corse	G	1.5 t/c Osella FA1I-Alfa Romeo V8	gearbox	19/26
ret	FRENCH GP	Paul Ricard	21	Osella Squadra Corse	G	1.5 t/c Osella FA1I-Alfa Romeo V8	gearbox	20/26
ret	BRITISH GP	Silverstone	21	Osella Squadra Corse	G	1.5 t/c Osella FA1I-Alfa Romeo V8	engine	21/26
ret	GERMAN GP	Hockenheim	21	Osella Squadra Corse	G	1.5 t/c Osella FA1I-Alfa Romeo V8	engine	26/26
ret	HUNGARIAN GP	Hungaroring	21	Osella Squadra Corse	G	1.5 t/c Osella FA1I-Alfa Romeo V8	out of fuel	21/26
ret/dns*	AUSTRIAN GP	Österreichring	21	Osella Squadra Corse	G	1.5 t/c Osella FA1I-Alfa Romeo V8	*accident at 2nd start/electrics	21/26
ret	ITALIAN GP	Monza	21	Osella Squadra Corse	G	1.5 t/c Osella FA1I-Alfa Romeo V8	suspension	21/28
ret	PORTUGUESE GP	Estoril	21	Osella Squadra Corse	G	1.5 t/c Osella FA1I-Alfa Romeo V8	turbo	25/27
dnq	SPANISH GP	Jerez	21	Osella Squadra Corse	G	1.5 t/c Osella FA1I-Alfa Romeo V8		27/28
ret	MEXICAN GP	Mexico City	21	Osella Squadra Corse	G	1.5 t/c Osella FA1I-Alfa Romeo V8	engine	26/27
ret	JAPANESE GP	Suzuka	21	Osella Squadra Corse	G	1.5 t/c Osella FA1I-Alfa Romeo V8	out of fuel	24/27
dnq	AUSTRALIAN GP	Adelaide	21	Osella Squadra Corse	G	1.5 t/c Osella FA1I-Alfa Romeo V8		27/27

1988 Championship position: Unplaced

	Race	Circuit	No	Entrant	Tyres	Capacity/Car/Engine	Comment	Qual Pos/Entries
dnpq	BRAZILIAN GP	Rio	36	Scuderia Italia	G	3.5 Dallara 3087-Cosworth V8	F3000 car	31/31
ret	SAN MARINO GP	Imola	36	Scuderia Italia	G	3.5 Dallara 188-Cosworth V8	gearbox	24/31
ret	MONACO GP	Monte Carlo	36	Scuderia Italia	G	3.5 Dallara 188-Cosworth V8	hit by Capelli – spun off	17/30
ret	MEXICAN GP	Mexico City	36	Scuderia Italia	G	3.5 Dallara 188-Cosworth V8	brakes – accident	23/30
dnpq	CANADIAN GP	Montreal	36	Scuderia Italia	G	3.5 Dallara 188-Cosworth V8		31/31
8	US GP (DETROIT)	Detroit	36	Scuderia Italia	G	3.5 Dallara 188-Cosworth V8	cracked exhaust/2 laps behind	22/31
12	FRENCH GP	Paul Ricard	36	Scuderia Italia	G	3.5 Dallara 188-Cosworth V8	puncture/fuel problems/-2 laps	14/31
11	BRITISH GP	Silverstone	36	Scuderia Italia	G	3.5 Dallara 188-Cosworth V8	1 lap behind	21/31
15	GERMAN GP	Hockenheim	36	Scuderia Italia	G	3.5 Dallara 188-Cosworth V8	pit stop – puncture/2 laps behind	19/31
ret	HUNGARIAN GP	Hungaroring	36	Scuderia Italia	G	3.5 Dallara 188-Cosworth V8	engine	10/31
8*	BELGIAN GP	Spa	36	Scuderia Italia	G	3.5 Dallara 188-Cosworth V8	*3rd & 4th cars disqualified/-1 lap	15/31
ret	ITALIAN GP	Monza	36	Scuderia Italia	G	3.5 Dallara 188-Cosworth V8	electrics	21/31
7	PORTUGUESE GP	Estoril	36	Scuderia Italia	G	3.5 Dallara 188-Cosworth V8	broken exhaust/1 lap behind	17/31
10	SPANISH GP	Jerez	36	Scuderia Italia	G	3.5 Dallara 188-Cosworth V8	broken exhaust/1 lap behind	18/31
ret	JAPANESE GP	Suzuka	36	Scuderia Italia	G	3.5 Dallara 188-Cosworth V8	spun off	21/31
ret	AUSTRALIAN GP	Adelaide	36	Scuderia Italia	G	3.5 Dallara 188-Cosworth V8	clutch	11/31

1989 Championship position: 16th= Wins: 0 Pole positions: 0 Fastest laps: 0 Points scored: 4

	Race	Circuit	No	Entrant	Tyres	Capacity/Car/Engine	Comment	Qual Pos/Entries
dnpq	BRAZILIAN GP	Rio	21	Scuderia Italia	P	3.5 Dallara 189-Cosworth V8		31/38
7	SAN MARINO GP	Imola	21	Scuderia Italia	P	3.5 Dallara 189-Cosworth V8	pit stop – puncture/1 lap behind	9/39
4	MONACO GP	Monte Carlo	21	Scuderia Italia	P	3.5 Dallara 189-Cosworth V8	2 laps behind	9/38
13	MEXICAN GP	Mexico City	21	Scuderia Italia	P	3.5 Dallara 189-Cosworth V8	spin/tyre wear/2 laps behind	19/39
ret	US GP (PHOENIX)	Phoenix	21	Scuderia Italia	P	3.5 Dallara 189-Cosworth V8	hit by de Cesaris when 2nd	6/39
6	CANADIAN GP	Montreal	21	Scuderia Italia	P	3.5 Dallara 189-Cosworth V8	2 pit stops – tyres/2 spins/-2 laps	8/39
ret	FRENCH GP	Paul Ricard	21	Scuderia Italia	P	3.5 Dallara 189-Cosworth V8	clutch	26/39
dnpq	BRITISH GP	Silverstone	21	Scuderia Italia	P	3.5 Dallara 189-Cosworth V8		32/39
ret	GERMAN GP	Hockenheim	21	Scuderia Italia	P	3.5 Dallara 189-Cosworth V8	electrics	20/39
7	HUNGARIAN GP	Hungaroring	21	Scuderia Italia	P	3.5 Dallara 189-Cosworth V8		3/39
ret	BELGIAN GP	Spa	21	Scuderia Italia	P	3.5 Dallara 189-Cosworth V8	spun off	12/39
11/ret	ITALIAN GP	Monza	21	Scuderia Italia	P	3.5 Dallara 189-Cosworth V8	engine/6 laps behind	20/39
ret	PORTUGUESE GP	Estoril	21	Scuderia Italia	P	3.5 Dallara 189-Cosworth V8	collision with Piquet	7/39
ret	SPANISH GP	Jerez	21	Scuderia Italia	P	3.5 Dallara 189-Cosworth V8	engine	20/38
9*	JAPANESE GP	Suzuka	21	Scuderia Italia	P	3.5 Dallara 189-Cosworth V8	*1st place car disqualified/-1 lap	15/39
ret	AUSTRALIAN GP	Adelaide	21	Scuderia Italia	P	3.5 Dallara 189-Cosworth V8	spun off in rain	10/39

1990 Championship position: 16th= Wins: 0 Pole positions: 0 Fastest laps: 0 Points scored: 2

	Race	Circuit	No	Entrant	Tyres	Capacity/Car/Engine	Comment	Qual Pos/Entries
ret	BRAZILIAN GP	Interlagos	10	Footwork Arrows Racing	G	3.5 Arrows A11B-Cosworth V8	driver exhaustion	25/35
dnq	SAN MARINO GP	Imola	10	Footwork Arrows Racing	G	3.5 Arrows A11B-Cosworth V8		28/34
5	MONACO GP	Monte Carlo	10	Footwork Arrows Racing	G	3.5 Arrows A11B-Cosworth V8	tyre problems/2 laps behind	22/35
8	CANADIAN GP	Montreal	10	Footwork Arrows Racing	G	3.5 Arrows A11B-Cosworth V8	2 laps behind	26/35
dnq	MEXICAN GP	Mexico City	10	Footwork Arrows Racing	G	3.5 Arrows A11B-Cosworth V8		30/35
ret	FRENCH GP	Paul Ricard	10	Footwork Arrows Racing	G	3.5 Arrows A11B-Cosworth V8	rear suspension	22/35
7	BRITISH GP	Silverstone	10	Footwork Arrows Racing	G	3.5 Arrows A11B-Cosworth V8	1 lap behind	17/35
9	GERMAN GP	Hockenheim	10	Footwork Arrows Racing	G	3.5 Arrows A11B-Cosworth V8	1 lap behind	18/35
9	HUNGARIAN GP	Hungaroring	10	Footwork Arrows Racing	G	3.5 Arrows A11B-Cosworth V8	rev limiter problems/1 lap behind	26/35
10	BELGIAN GP	Spa	10	Footwork Arrows Racing	G	3.5 Arrows A11B-Cosworth V8	oversteer problems/1 lap behind	19/33
9	ITALIAN GP	Monza	10	Footwork Arrows Racing	G	3.5 Arrows A11B-Cosworth V8	pit stop – tyres/2 laps behind	21/33
13/ret	PORTUGUESE GP	Estoril	10	Footwork Arrows Racing	G	3.5 Arrows A11B-Cosworth V8	collision with Suzuki/3 laps behind	17/33
9	JAPANESE GP	Suzuka	10	Footwork Arrows Racing	G	3.5 Arrows A11B-Cosworth V8	pit stop – tyres/1 lap behind	24/30
dnq	AUSTRALIAN GP	Adelaide	10	Footwork Arrows Racing	G	3.5 Arrows A11B-Cosworth V8		29/30

1991 Championship position: Unplaced

	Race	Circuit	No	Entrant	Tyres	Capacity/Car/Engine	Comment	Qual Pos/Entries
dnq	US GP (PHOENIX)	Phoenix	10	Footwork Grand Prix International	G	3.5 Footwork A11C-Porsche V12		28/34
dnq	BRAZILIAN GP	Interlagos	10	Footwork Grand Prix International	G	3.5 Footwork A11C-Porsche V12		27/34
dnq	SAN MARINO GP	Imola	10	Footwork Grand Prix International	G	3.5 Footwork FA12-Porsche V12		29/34
dnq	MONACO GP	Monte Carlo	10	Footwork Grand Prix International	G	3.5 Footwork FA12-Porsche V12	accident in practice	30/34
dnpq	GERMAN GP	Hockenheim	10	Footwork Grand Prix International	G	3.5 Footwork FA12-Cosworth V8		32/34
dnpq	HUNGARIAN GP	Hungaroring	10	Footwork Grand Prix International	G	3.5 Footwork FA12-Cosworth V8		32/34
dnq	BELGIAN GP	Spa	10	Footwork Grand Prix International	G	3.5 Footwork FA12-Cosworth V8		29/34
dnpq	ITALIAN GP	Monza	10	Footwork Grand Prix International	G	3.5 Footwork FA12-Cosworth V8		33/34
dnpq	PORTUGUESE GP	Estoril	10	Footwork Grand Prix International	G	3.5 Footwork FA12-Cosworth V8		33/34
dnpq	SPANISH GP	Barcelona	10	Footwork Grand Prix International	G	3.5 Footwork FA12-Cosworth V8		31/33
10	JAPANESE GP	Suzuka	10	Footwork Grand Prix International	G	3.5 Footwork FA12-Cosworth V8	2 laps behind	26/31
15	AUSTRALIAN GP	Adelaide	10	Footwork Grand Prix International	G	3.5 Footwork FA12-Cosworth V8	rain shortened race/1 lap behind	23/32

1992 Championship position: Unplaced

	Race	Circuit	No	Entrant	Tyres	Capacity/Car/Engine	Comment	Qual Pos/Entries
dnp	SOUTH AFRICAN GP	Kyalami	34	Andrea Moda Formula	G	3.5 Coloni C4B-Judd V10	car ineligible – team excluded	– / –
dnp	MEXICAN GP	Mexico City	34	Andrea Moda Formula	G	3.5 Moda S921-Judd V10	cars arrived late – entry withdrawn	– / –

GP Starts: 56 GP Wins: 0 Pole positions: 0 Fastest laps: 0 Points: 6

CAMPBELL-JONES, John (GB) b 21/1/1930, Leatherhead, Surrey

1962 Championship position: Unplaced

	Race	Circuit	No	Entrant	Tyres	Capacity/Car/Engine	Comment	Qual Pos/Entries
11/ret	BELGIAN GP	Spa	4	Emeryson Cars	D	1.5 Lotus 18-Climax 4	borrowed car/gearbox/-16 laps	19/20
dns	"	"	4	Emeryson Cars	D	1.5 Emeryson 1006-Climax 4	practice only – broken gearbox	– / –

1963 Championship position: Unplaced

	Race	Circuit	No	Entrant	Tyres	Capacity/Car/Engine	Comment	Qual Pos/Entries
13	BRITISH GP	Silverstone	24	Tim Parnell	D	1.5 Lola 4-Climax V8	pit stop/8 laps behind	23/23

GP Starts: 2 GP Wins: 0 Pole positions: 0 Fastest laps: 0 Points: 0

JOHN CAMPBELL-JONES

JOHN CAMPBELL-JONES achieved some success in sports and GT cars between 1957 and 1961, mainly with a Lotus XI in which he took fourth in class at Vila Real in 1958. Then he bought a T45 Formula 2 Cooper to race at home and abroad, but usually could be found scratching around in minor F1 events.

He upgraded to a Cooper T51 for the 1961 season, his best placing being sixth at the London Trophy race at Crystal Palace, but his season was cut short by injury. He joined forces with Emeryson for his 1962 campaign, and the car brought little but a distant fifth place on aggregate in the Brussels GP and sixth in the Aintree 200. But that was better than anything his team-mate, Tony Settember, could achieve.

Under the wing of the Parnell stable in 1963, and despite having much better cars (Lotus 24-BRM V8 or a Lola 4-Climax V8), Campbell-Jones still could not make much headway, and he was not seen on the circuits again except for a surprise appearance in the 1966 Gold Cup at Oulton Park. He was disqualified from the event after his John Willment Automobiles BRP-Climax sprang an oil leak.

ADRIÁN CAMPOS

BEING the heir to a Spanish food conglomerate gave Adrián Campos the where-withal to go racing, and he funded the building of his own Formula 3 car, the Avidesa. In 1984, he moved up to the European F3 championship with a Ralt RT3, competing against such luminaries as Ivan Capelli, Johnny Dumfries, Gerhard Berger and Spanish compatriot Luis Perez Sala. Eventually the rookie finished 13th in the final standings.

Stepping into the German F3 series for 1985, Campos found this lower level of competition more suited to his abilities at the time, although he was only able to record a fairly distant third place in the final standings to Volker Weidler.

Without much of a track record – merely half a dozen F3000 races and just a single point scored at Jerez – during the 1986 season, Campos was a surprise choice for the second seat in the Minardi team for 1987. Although naturally overshadowed by his team-mate, Alessandro Nannini, he did better than many would have expected given his relative lack of experience. Despite a dismal run of non-finishes, the Spaniard was joined by Sala for 1988, but lost his seat to Pierluigi Martini after failing to qualify for three races in a row.

Despite initially having thoughts of retirement, Campos was soon back in action in the Spanish touring car championship. As this series grew in prominence, he became a leading player, winning the championship in 1994 with an Alfa 155. After some sports car action in a Ferrari 333SP, he retired at the end of 2007.

After setting up Adrián Campos Racing to contest the Spanish Open Fortuna by Nissan series, he had the immediate satisfaction in 1998 of helping the promising Marc Gené, not only to the title, but also to a grand prix seat at Minardi. Then he repeated the process in 1999 with an even greater talent, Fernando Alonso. Subsequently, Campos nurtured the career of this prodigious talent as he moved up into F3000 before coming under the management of Flavio Briatore.

Rumours of Adrián's involvement with Telefónica in a buy-out of Minardi came to nought, and instead he concentrated on single-seaters in Spain, eventually running in the Nissan World Series as well as the Spanish F3 championship. He ventured into GP2 in 2005, and eventually the team gained real success with Giorgio Pantano, Vitaly Petrov and Lucas di Grassi, all of whom won races, before he sold his interest to begin the process of forming an F1 team named Campos Meta. After struggling to find the necessary finances, however, he stepped aside to allow José Ramón Carabante to take control. Renamed Hispania Racing, the little Spanish team confounded expectations by taking to the tracks in 2010 and thus far surviving against the odds.

CAMPOS, Adrián (E) b 17/6/1960, Alcira, nr Valencia

1987 Championship position: Unplaced

	Race	Circuit	No	Entrant	Tyres	Capacity/Car/Engine	Comment	Qual Pos/Entries
dsq*	BRAZILIAN GP	Rio	23	Minardi Team	G	1.5 t/c Minardi M187-MM V6	*took incorrect starting procedure	16/23
ret	SAN MARINO GP	Imola	23	Minardi Team	G	1.5 t/c Minardi M187-MM V6	gearbox	18/27
ret/dns	BELGIAN GP	Spa	23	Minardi Team	G	1.5 t/c Minardi M187-MM V6	clutch at 1st start	19/26
dns	MONACO GP	Monte Carlo	23	Minardi Team	G	1.5 t/c Minardi M187-MM V6	accident in practice	(25)/26
ret	US GP (DETROIT)	Detroit	23	Minardi Team	G	1.5 t/c Minardi M187-MM V6	hit by Nakajima	25/26
ret	FRENCH GP	Paul Ricard	23	Minardi Team	G	1.5 t/c Minardi M187-MM V6	turbo	21/26
ret	BRITISH GP	Silverstone	23	Minardi Team	G	1.5 t/c Minardi M187-MM V6	fuel pump	20/26
ret	GERMAN GP	Hockenheim	23	Minardi Team	G	1.5 t/c Minardi M187-MM V6	engine	18/26
ret	HUNGARIAN GP	Hungaroring	23	Minardi Team	G	1.5 t/c Minardi M187-MM V6	spun off	24/26
ret	AUSTRIAN GP	Österreichring	23	Minardi Team	G	1.5 t/c Minardi M187-MM V6	electrics	19/26
ret	ITALIAN GP	Monza	23	Minardi Team	G	1.5 t/c Minardi M187-MM V6	engine – fuel filter fire	20/28

ret	PORTUGUESE GP	Estoril	23	Minardi Team	G	1.5 t/c Minardi M187-MM V6	started from pits/holed intercooler	20/27
14	SPANISH GP	Jerez	23	Minardi Team	G	1.5 t/c Minardi M187-MM V6	4 laps behind	24/28
ret	MEXICAN GP	Mexico City	23	Minardi Team	G	1.5 t/c Minardi M187-MM V6	gear linkage	19/27
ret	JAPANESE GP	Suzuka	23	Minardi Team	G	1.5 t/c Minardi M187-MM V6	engine	22/27
ret	AUSTRALIAN GP	Adelaide	23	Minardi Team	G	1.5 t/c Minardi M187-MM V6	gearbox	26/27

1988 Championship position: Unplaced

ret	BRAZILIAN GP	Rio	23	Lois Minardi Team	G	3.5 Minardi M188-Cosworth V8	rear wing mounting	23/31
16	SAN MARINO GP	Imola	23	Lois Minardi Team	G	3.5 Minardi M188-Cosworth V8	3 laps behind	22/31
dnq	MONACO GP	Monte Carlo	23	Lois Minardi Team	G	3.5 Minardi M188-Cosworth V8		29/30
dnq	MEXICAN GP	Mexico City	23	Lois Minardi Team	G	3.5 Minardi M188-Cosworth V8		30/30
dnq	CANADIAN GP	Montreal	23	Lois Minardi Team	G	3.5 Minardi M188-Cosworth V8		27/31

GP Starts: 16 (17) GP Wins: 0 Pole positions: 0 Fastest laps: 0 Points: 0

JOHN CANNON

A CANADIAN who had been born in Britain, John Cannon actually spent the early part of his career in California, where he began racing an Elva Courier in 1960. He drove a variety of powerful sports machines in the early 1960s before concentrating on the popular Can-Am series.

Although Cannon's car was somewhat outdated, he put up a number of fine performances, none better than in the wet at Laguna Seca in 1968, when he lapped the field to score an amazing win. This success led to a drive in Formula A in 1969 and an opportunity to drive single-seaters at last. He won three rounds and finished fourth in the championship. The next year, he took the SCCA Formula A title and then set about a completely new challenge, tackling the US GP in a BRM and the Questor GP in a March 701, as well as a full season in European F2, achieving moderate success.

It was back to the USA and the L & M F5000 series for 1972, although Cannon also drove in some British F5000 rounds and was right on the pace. Thereafter, he continued racing in the formula that had brought him so much success, spiced with occasional drives in USAC and Can-Am.

In 1999, he was killed in an accident while flying his ultra-light aircraft.

EITEL CANTONI

THIS veteran began racing in 1934, competing in open road events in Brazil, Uruguay and Argentina aboard modified touring cars. After the Second World War, he began racing single-seaters and took part in the Temporada series between 1948 and 1952 with a Maserati 4CLT.

His best placings were third in the 1949 rain-affected Buenos Aires Grand Prix II and sixth in the Rosario Grand Prix a week later.

After a fifth place in the 1952 Buenos Aires Grand Prix, despite being 46 years old, Cantoni joined the Brazilians Gino Bianco, Chico Landi and Alberto Crespo to race three of the new 2-litre Maserati A6GCMs. These cars were resplendent in buff and light blue paintwork, and entered under the Escuderia Bandeirantes banner. As well as his three world championship grand prix starts, he contested four other races in his brief Continental sojourn, yielding two finishes, a seventh in the Modena Grand Prix and a ninth in the AVUSrennen. Upon his return, he announced his retirement.

CANNON, John (CDN) b 21/6/1937, Hammersmith, London, England – 18/10/1999 nr Quemado, New Mexico, USA

1971 Championship position: Unplaced

	Race	Circuit	No	Entrant	Tyres	Capacity/Car/Engine	Comment	Q Pos/Entries
14	US GP	Watkins Glen	28	Yardley BRM	F	3.0 BRM P153 V12	3 laps behind	26/32

GP Starts: 1 GP Wins: 0 Pole positions: 0 Fastest laps: 0 Points: 0

CANTONI, Eitel (U) b Montevideo, 4/10/1996 – d 6/6/1997, Montevideo

1952 Championship position: Unplaced

	Race	Circuit	No	Entrant	Tyres	Capacity/Car/Engine	Comment	Q Pos/Entries
ret	BRITISH GP	Silverstone	35	Escuderia Bandeirantes	P	2.0 Maserati A6GCM 6	brakes on lap 1	27/32
ret	GERMAN GP	Nürburgring	116	Escuderia Bandeirantes	P	2.0 Maserati A6GCM 6	rear axle	26/32
11	ITALIAN GP	Monza	50	Escuderia Bandeirantes	P	2.0 Maserati A6GCM 6	5 laps behind	23/35

GP Starts: 3 GP Wins: 0 Pole positions: 0 Fastest laps: 0 Points: 0

IVAN CAPELLI

THE dividing line between success and failure in grand prix racing can be very narrow indeed, as the charming and popular Ivan Capelli has found to his cost. Having been perceived generally as being held back from the winner's circle only by the want of a top-flight car, the Italian's stock crashed with alarming rapidity when a golden opportunity with Ferrari turned sour.

Yet another ex-karting ace, Ivan went single-seater racing in 1982, taking sixth place in the Italian F3 championship. This brought him to the attention of Enzo Coloni, who quickly signed the Milanese to race his Ralt-Alfa. It was a stunning year for the team, with Capelli winning all but four of the series' 13 races to take the title by the staggering margin of 58 points. With Italy well and truly conquered, Coloni took his charge into the European arena, and once again he triumphed, although much less decisively. His European F3 championship was tainted with allegations regarding the car's legality and, as he acknowledged, he inherited a couple of lucky wins, including the prestigious Monaco race.

Then national service interrupted Ivan's racing progress, and when he entered the 1985 F3000 series at Vallelunga with a March, he immediately rolled it, almost to the point of destruction. Despite the most meagre of budgets, Capelli and his team did an outstanding job, and he won the Österreichring round to earn a couple of grand prix drives with Ken Tyrrell late in the season. Somewhat surprisingly, he was not on the F1 shopping list for 1986 and settled into another year of F3000 with the Genoa team, the mid-season arrival of Leyton House sponsorship giving the privateer outfit the boost it needed in its successful championship quest.

Capelli made another brief foray into Formula 1 with AGS, but long-term his future would lie wrapped in the comforting folds of the turquoise-blue Leyton House March Racing Team. In a sense, the team was Ivan's family: they believed in him and he reciprocated. Growing in stature, he had taken the car right to the front of the grid by the end of the 1988 season, and briefly led the Portuguese GP before taking a superb second place. This progress was temporarily halted in a disappointing year plagued by unreliability and the almost bewildering array of handling problems associated with the March CG891, but he bounced back the following year, finishing second to Prost at Paul Ricard and looking a potential winner at Silverstone until retirement. His final year with the team was spent embroiled in development of the new Ilmor V10, and it has to be said that some of his performances were less than convincing.

When the team's owner was arrested over financial irregularities in Japan, the future looked

bleak, but Capelli stood down from the two end-of-season races happy in the knowledge that he had a Ferrari contract in his pocket for 1992. However, it would be a season of almost unmitigated misery for poor Ivan, who failed to come to grips with the Ferrari F92A, a car that missed the boat on just about every count.

Before the season was out, Capelli found himself cast aside in favour of test driver Nicola Larini and his options appeared limited. To everyone's surprise, he was back on the grid at Kyalami with the Jordan team, reunited with his old boss from Leyton House/March, Ian Phillips. But it was a brief and unhappy sojourn for the Italian, who crashed very heavily in South Africa

and then failed to qualify at Interlagos before an amicable parting of the ways. Not yet 30, he was crushingly disappointed and came to the conclusion that he had no Formula 1 future at all.

Capelli picked up the pieces of his shattered career and joined the Nissan works team to race the 2-litre Primera in the German Super Touring championship in 1995 and 1996, but since then he has been an infrequent competitor, picking up occasional sports car drives to keep his hand in. His cheerful presence was not lost to F1, however, as subsequently he was able to maintain his involvement in grand prix racing by taking over a commentating role for Italian TV Rai 1.

CAPELLI, Ivan (I) b 24/5/1963, Milan

1985 Championship position: 17th= Wins: 0 Pole positions: 0 Fastest laps: 0 Points scored: 3

	Race	Circuit	No	Entrant	Tyres	Capacity/Car/Engine	Comment	Q Pos/Entries
ret	EUROPEAN GP	Brands Hatch	4	Tyrrell Racing Organisation	G	1.5 t/c Tyrrell 014-Renault V6	accident	24/27
4	AUSTRALIAN GP	Adelaide	4	Tyrrell Racing Organisation	G	1.5 t/c Tyrrell 014-Renault V6	1 lap behind	22/25

1986 Championship position: Unplaced

	Race	Circuit	No	Entrant	Tyres	Capacity/Car/Engine	Comment	Q Pos/Entries
ret	ITALIAN GP	Monza	31	Jolly Club SpA	P	1.5 t/c AGS JH21C-MM V6	puncture	25/27
ret	PORTUGUESE GP	Estoril	31	Jolly Club SpA	P	1.5 t/c AGS JH21C-MM V6	transmission	25/27

1987 Championship position: 19th= Wins: 0 Pole positions: 0 Fastest laps: 0 Points scored: 1

	Race	Circuit	No	Entrant	Tyres	Capacity/Car/Engine	Comment	Q Pos/Entries
dns	BRAZILIAN GP	Rio	16	Leyton House March Racing Team	G	3.5 March 87P-Cosworth V8	shortage of engine/ran F3000 car	23/23
ret	SAN MARINO GP	Imola	16	Leyton House March Racing Team	G	3.5 March 871-Cosworth V8	ignition	24/27
ret	BELGIAN GP	Spa	16	Leyton House March Racing Team	G	3.5 March 871-Cosworth V8	oil pressure	21/26
6*	MONACO GP	Monte Carlo	16	Leyton House March Racing Team	G	3.5 March 871-Cosworth V8	*2nd non-turbo/2 laps behind	19/26
ret	US GP (DETROIT)	Detroit	16	Leyton House March Racing Team	G	3.5 March 871-Cosworth V8	battery	22/26
ret	FRENCH GP	Paul Ricard	16	Leyton House March Racing Team	G	3.5 March 871-Cosworth V8	engine	22/26
ret	BRITISH GP	Silverstone	16	Leyton House March Racing Team	G	3.5 March 871-Cosworth V8	gearbox	25/26
ret	GERMAN GP	Hockenheim	16	Leyton House March Racing Team	G	3.5 March 871-Cosworth V8	started from pit lane/distributor	24/26
10*	HUNGARIAN GP	Hungaroring	16	Leyton House March Racing Team	G	3.5 March 871-Cosworth V8	*3rd non-turbo/2 laps behind	18/26
11*	AUSTRIAN GP	Österreichring	16	Leyton House March Racing Team	G	3.5 March 871-Cosworth V8	*1st non-turbo/3 laps behind	23/26
13*	ITALIAN GP	Monza	16	Leyton House March Racing Team	G	3.5 March 871-Cosworth V8	*2nd non-turbo/3 laps behind	25/28
9*	PORTUGUESE GP	Estoril	16	Leyton House March Racing Team	G	3.5 March 871-Cosworth V8	*1st non-turbo/3 laps behind	22/27
12*	SPANISH GP	Jerez	16	Leyton House March Racing Team	G	3.5 March 871-Cosworth V8	*3rd non-turbo/2 laps behind	19/28
ret	MEXICAN GP	Mexico City	16	Leyton House March Racing Team	G	3.5 March 871-Cosworth V8	engine	20/27
ret	JAPANESE GP	Suzuka	16	Leyton House March Racing Team	G	3.5 March 871-Cosworth V8	accident with Arnoux	21/27
ret	AUSTRALIAN GP	Adelaide	16	Leyton House March Racing Team	G	3.5 March 871-Cosworth V8	spun off	23/27

1988 Championship position: 7th= Wins: 0 Pole positions: 0 Fastest laps: 0 Points scored: 17

	Race	Circuit	No	Entrant	Tyres	Capacity/Car/Engine	Comment	Q Pos/Entries
ret	BRAZILIAN GP	Rio	16	Leyton House March Racing Team	G	3.5 March 881-Judd V8	started from pit lane/engine	9/31
ret	SAN MARINO GP	Imola	16	Leyton House March Racing Team	G	3.5 March 881-Judd V8	gearbox	9/31
10	MONACO GP	Monte Carlo	16	Leyton House March Racing Team	G	3.5 March 881-Judd V8	collision – Caffi-pit stop/-6 laps	22/30
16	MEXICAN GP	Mexico City	16	Leyton House March Racing Team	G	3.5 March 881-Judd V8	pit stop – gearbox/6 laps behind	10/30
5	CANADIAN GP	Montreal	16	Leyton House March Racing Team	G	3.5 March 881-Judd V8	severe understeer/1 lap behind	14/31
dns	US GP (DETROIT)	Detroit	16	Leyton House March Racing Team	G	3.5 March 881-Judd V8	accident in practice	(21)/31
9	FRENCH GP	Paul Ricard	16	Leyton House March Racing Team	G	3.5 March 881-Judd V8	1 lap behind	10/31
ret	BRITISH GP	Silverstone	16	Leyton House March Racing Team	G	3.5 March 881-Judd V8	electrics	6/31
5	GERMAN GP	Hockenheim	16	Leyton House March Racing Team	G	3.5 March 881-Judd V8		7/31
ret	HUNGARIAN GP	Hungaroring	16	Leyton House March Racing Team	G	3.5 March 881-Judd V8	misfire	4/31
3*	BELGIAN GP	Spa	16	Leyton House March Racing Team	G	3.5 March 881-Judd V8	*3rd & 4th place cars disqualified	14/31
5	ITALIAN GP	Monza	16	Leyton House March Racing Team	G	3.5 March 881-Judd V8		11/31
2	PORTUGUESE GP	Estoril	16	Leyton House March Racing Team	G	3.5 March 881-Judd V8		3/31
ret	SPANISH GP	Jerez	16	Leyton House March Racing Team	G	3.5 March 881-Judd V8	engine	6/31
ret	JAPANESE GP	Suzuka	16	Leyton House March Racing Team	G	3.5 March 881-Judd V8	electrics	4/31
6	AUSTRALIAN GP	Adelaide	16	Leyton House March Racing Team	G	3.5 March 881-Judd V8	pit stop – puncture/gearbox/-1 lap	9/31

1989 Championship position: Unplaced

	Race	Circuit	No	Entrant	Tyres	Capacity/Car/Engine	Comment	Q Pos/Entries
ret	BRAZILIAN GP	Rio	16	Leyton House March Racing Team	G	3.5 March 881-Judd V8	rear suspension	7/38
ret	SAN MARINO GP	Imola	16	Leyton House March Racing Team	G	3.5 March 881-Judd V8	spun off	13/39
11/ret	MONACO GP	Monte Carlo	16	Leyton House March Racing Team	G	3.5 March CG891-Judd V8	engine/4 laps behind	– / –
dns	"	" "	16	Leyton House March Racing Team	G	3.5 March 881-Judd V8	practice only – qualifying car	22/38
ret	MEXICAN GP	Mexico City	16	Leyton House March Racing Team	G	3.5 March CG891-Judd V8	driveshaft – c.v. joint	4/39
dns	"	" "	16	Leyton House March Racing Team	G	3.5 March 881-Judd V8	practice only	– / –
ret	US GP (PHOENIX)	Phoenix	16	Leyton House March Racing Team	G	3.5 March CG891-Judd V8	transmission	11/39
dns	"	" "	16	Leyton House March Racing Team	G	3.5 March 881-Judd V8	practice only	– / –
ret	CANADIAN GP	Montreal	16	Leyton House March Racing Team	G	3.5 March CG891-Judd V8	spun off	21/39
dns	"	" "	16	Leyton House March Racing Team	G	3.5 March 881-Judd V8	practice only	– / –
ret	FRENCH GP	Paul Ricard	16	Leyton House March Racing Team	G	3.5 March CG891-Judd V8	engine – electrics	12/39
ret	BRITISH GP	Silverstone	16	Leyton House March Racing Team	G	3.5 March CG891-Judd V8	transmission	8/39
ret	GERMAN GP	Hockenheim	16	Leyton House March Racing Team	G	3.5 March CG891-Judd V8	engine	22/39
ret	HUNGARIAN GP	Hungaroring	16	Leyton House March Racing Team	G	3.5 March CG891-Judd V8	transmission	14/39
12	BELGIAN GP	Spa	16	Leyton House March Racing Team	G	3.5 March CG891-Judd V8	1 lap behind	19/39
ret	ITALIAN GP	Monza	16	Leyton House March Racing Team	G	3.5 March CG891-Judd V8	engine	18/39
ret	PORTUGUESE GP	Estoril	16	Leyton House March Racing Team	G	3.5 March CG891-Judd V8	misfire	24/39
ret	SPANISH GP	Jerez	16	Leyton House March Racing Team	G	3.5 March CG891-Judd V8	transmission	19/38
ret	JAPANESE GP	Suzuka	16	Leyton House March Racing Team	G	3.5 March CG891-Judd V8	suspension	17/39
ret	AUSTRALIAN GP	Adelaide	16	Leyton House March Racing Team	G	3.5 March CG891-Judd V8	holed radiator	16/39

1990 Championship position: 10th= Wins: 0 Pole positions: 0 Fastest laps: 0 Points scored: 6

	Race	Circuit	No	Entrant	Tyres	Capacity/Car/Engine	Comment	Q Pos/Entries
ret	US GP (PHOENIX)	Phoenix	16	Leyton House Racing	G	3.5 Leyton House CG901-Judd V8	electrics	– / –
dns	"	"	16	Leyton House Racing	G	3.5 March CG891-Judd V8	practice only – qualifying car	27/35
dnq	BRAZILIAN GP	Interlagos	16	Leyton House Racing	G	3.5 Leyton House CG901-Judd V8		29/35
dnq	"	"	16	Leyton House Racing	G	3.5 March CG891-Judd V8		– / –
ret	SAN MARINO GP	Imola	16	Leyton House Racing	G	3.5 Leyton House CG901-Judd V8	hit by Nakajima	19/34
ret	MONACO GP	Monte Carlo	16	Leyton House Racing	G	3.5 Leyton House CG901-Judd V8	brakes	23/35
10	CANADIAN GP	Montreal	16	Leyton House Racing	G	3.5 Leyton House CG901-Judd V8	handling problems/3 laps behind	24/35
dnq	MEXICAN GP	Mexico City	16	Leyton House Racing	G	3.5 Leyton House CG901-Judd V8		28/35
2	FRENCH GP	Paul Ricard	16	Leyton House Racing	G	3.5 Leyton House CG901-Judd V8		7/35
ret	BRITISH GP	Silverstone	16	Leyton House Racing	G	3.5 Leyton House CG901-Judd V8	fuel line when 3rd	10/35
7	GERMAN GP	Hockenheim	16	Leyton House Racing	G	3.5 Leyton House CG901-Judd V8	lost 4th gear/1 lap behind	10/35
ret	HUNGARIAN GP	Hungaroring	16	Leyton House Racing	G	3.5 Leyton House CG901-Judd V8	gearbox	16/35
7	BELGIAN GP	Spa	16	Leyton House Racing	G	3.5 Leyton House CG901-Judd V8	broken exhaust/1 lap behind	12/33
ret	ITALIAN GP	Monza	16	Leyton House Racing	G	3.5 Leyton House CG901-Judd V8	engine cut out – fuel pump	16/33

	Race	Circuit	No	Entrant	Tyres	Capacity/Car/Engine	Comment	Q Pos/Entries
ret	PORTUGUESE GP	Estoril	16	Leyton House Racing	G	3.5 Leyton House CG901-Judd V8	engine	12/33
ret	SPANISH GP	Jerez	16	Leyton House Racing	G	3.5 Leyton House CG901-Judd V8	leg cramp	19/33
ret	JAPANESE GP	Suzuka	16	Leyton House Racing	G	3.5 Leyton House CG901-Judd V8	misfire – electrics	13/30
ret	AUSTRALIAN GP	Adelaide	16	Leyton House Racing	G	3.5 Leyton House CG901-Judd V8	sticking throttle	14/30

1991 Championship position: 18th= Wins: 0 Pole positions: 0 Fastest laps: 0 Points scored: 1

	Race	Circuit	No	Entrant	Tyres	Capacity/Car/Engine	Comment	Q Pos/Entries
ret	US GP (PHOENIX)	Phoenix	16	Leyton House Racing	G	3.5 Leyton House CG911-Ilmor V10	gearbox oil pump	18/34
ret	BRAZILIAN GP	Interlagos	16	Leyton House Racing	G	3.5 Leyton House CG911-Ilmor V10	engine	15/34
ret	SAN MARINO GP	Imola	16	Leyton House Racing	G	3.5 Leyton House CG911-Ilmor V10	spun off	22/34
ret	MONACO GP	Monte Carlo	16	Leyton House Racing	G	3.5 Leyton House CG911-Ilmor V10	leaking brake fluid	18/34
ret	CANADIAN GP	Montreal	16	Leyton House Racing	G	3.5 Leyton House CG911-Ilmor V10	engine	13/34
ret	MEXICAN GP	Mexico City	16	Leyton House Racing	G	3.5 Leyton House CG911-Ilmor V10	over-revved engine	22/34
ret	FRENCH GP	Magny Cours	16	Leyton House Racing	G	3.5 Leyton House CG911-Ilmor V10	spun avoiding Morbidelli	15/34
ret	BRITISH GP	Silverstone	16	Leyton House Racing	G	3.5 Leyton House CG911-Ilmor V10	selected wrong gear – spun off	16/34
ret	GERMAN GP	Hockenheim	16	Leyton House Racing	G	3.5 Leyton House CG911-Ilmor V10	engine – misfire	12/34
6	HUNGARIAN GP	Hungaroring	16	Leyton House Racing	G	3.5 Leyton House CG911-Ilmor V10	1 lap behind	9/34
ret	BELGIAN GP	Spa	16	Leyton House Racing	G	3.5 Leyton House CG911-Ilmor V10	engine	12/34
8	ITALIAN GP	Monza	16	Leyton House Racing	G	3.5 Leyton House CG911-Ilmor V10		12/34
17/ret	PORTUGUESE GP	Estoril	16	Leyton House Racing	G	3.5 Leyton House CG911-Ilmor V10	broken nose cone when 5th	9/34
ret	SPANISH GP	Barcelona	16	Leyton House Racing	G	3.5 Leyton House CG911-Ilmor V10	collision with Pirro	8/33

1992 Championship position: 12th= Wins: 0 Pole positions: 0 Fastest laps: 0 Points scored: 3

	Race	Circuit	No	Entrant	Tyres	Capacity/Car/Engine	Comment	Q Pos/Entries
ret	SOUTH AFRICAN GP	Kyalami	28	Scuderia Ferrari SpA	G	3.5 Fiat Ferrari F92A V12	engine	9/30
ret	MEXICAN GP	Mexico City	28	Scuderia Ferrari SpA	G	3.5 Fiat Ferrari F92A V12	startline collision	20/30
5	BRAZILIAN GP	Interlagos	28	Scuderia Ferrari SpA	G	3.5 Fiat Ferrari F92A V12	pit stop – tyres/1 lap behind	11/31
10/ret	SPANISH GP	Barcelona	28	Scuderia Ferrari SpA	G	3.5 Fiat Ferrari F92A V12	spun off	5/32
ret	SAN MARINO GP	Imola	28	Scuderia Ferrari SpA	G	3.5 Fiat Ferrari F92A V12	spun off	8/32
ret	MONACO GP	Monte Carlo	28	Scuderia Ferrari SpA	G	3.5 Fiat Ferrari F92A V12	spun off – wedged car on armco	8/32
ret	CANADIAN GP	Montreal	28	Scuderia Ferrari SpA	G	3.5 Fiat Ferrari F92A V12	crashed	9/32
ret	FRENCH GP	Magny Cours	28	Scuderia Ferrari SpA	G	3.5 Fiat Ferrari F92A V12	engine – electrics	8/30
9	BRITISH GP	Silverstone	28	Scuderia Ferrari SpA	G	3.5 Fiat Ferrari F92A V12	1 lap behind	14/32
ret	GERMAN GP	Hockenheim	28	Scuderia Ferrari SpA	G	3.5 Fiat Ferrari F92A V12	engine	12/32
6	HUNGARIAN GP	Hungaroring	28	Scuderia Ferrari SpA	G	3.5 Fiat Ferrari F92A V12	1 lap behind	10/31
ret	BELGIAN GP	Spa	28	Scuderia Ferrari SpA	G	3.5 Fiat Ferrari F92A V12	engine	12/30
ret	ITALIAN GP	Monza	28	Scuderia Ferrari SpA	G	3.5 Fiat Ferrari F92AT V12	spun off	7/28
ret	PORTUGUESE GP	Estoril	28	Scuderia Ferrari SpA	G	3.5 Fiat Ferrari F92AT V12	engine	16/26

1993 Championship position: Unplaced

	Race	Circuit	No	Entrant	Tyres	Capacity/Car/Engine	Comment	Q Pos/Entries
ret	SOUTH AFRICAN GP	Kyalami	15	Sasol Jordan	G	3.5 Jordan 193-Hart V10	crashed	18/26
dnq	BRAZILIAN GP	Interlagos	15	Sasol Jordan	G	3.5 Jordan 193-Hart V10		26/26

GP Starts: 93 GP Wins: 0 Pole positions: 0 Fastest laps: 0 Points: 31

PIERO CARINI

PIERO CARINI came to prominence in 1950, when he finished third in the F2 Modena GP with a sports OSCA. This car proved fast, but fragile in 1951, but he was invited to join Scuderia Marzotto for 1952 to race their Ferrari grand prix and sports cars. He did well enough to be signed by the works for 1953 as, in effect, a 'junior' driver, along with Umberto Maglioli. He was employed only occasionally and therefore decided to move to Alfa Romeo to race their very successful touring cars, scoring class wins in the 1954 Mille Miglia, Tour of Sicily and Dolomite Cup.

In 1955, he ventured abroad to score sports car wins in a Ferrari at Dakar and Caracas, Venezuela, as well as taking a class win in the Targa Florio in an OSCA with Giulio Cabianca.

Carini was competing in a 1500cc sports car race near Saint-Étienne in 1957 when his Ferrari Testa Rossa inexplicably crossed the central barrier and ploughed head-on into a similar car. He was killed instantly.

CARINI, Piero (I) b 6/3/1921, Genoa – d 30/5/1957, St Etienne, France

1952 Championship position: Unplaced

	Race	Circuit	No	Entrant	Tyres	Capacity/Car/Engine	Comment	Q Pos/Entries
ret	FRENCH GP	Rouen	40	Scuderia Marzotto	P	2.0 Ferrari 166 V12	head gasket	20/20
ret	GERMAN GP	Nürburgring	104	Scuderia Marzotto	P	2.0 Ferrari 166 V12	brakes	27/32

1953 Championship position: Unplaced

	Race	Circuit	No	Entrant	Tyres	Capacity/Car/Engine	Comment	Q Pos/Entries
ret	ITALIAN GP	Monza	12	Scuderia Ferrari	P	2.0 Ferrari 553 4	engine	20/30

GP Starts: 3 GP Wins: 0 Pole positions: 0 Fastest laps: 0 Points: 0

EUGENIO CASTELLOTTI

THE archetypal Italian racing driver of the 1950s, Eugenio Castellotti was dashing, handsome and very fast, but wild and erratic. He often charged into the lead at the start of a race, only to be overhauled as his tyres gave out or the car cried enough in response to the punishing treatment to which it had been subjected.

Having been presented with a Ferrari sports car by a local benefactor in 1950, when aged only 20, Eugenio entered the spotlight in 1952 with a win in the Portuguese GP, third place in the Bari GP and second in the Monaco GP (held for sports cars that year), as well as a class win in the Circuit of Sicily. The following season saw him claim the first of his three Italian mountain championships, win the Messina 10-hours in a Ferrari and finish third in the Carrera Panamericana in a Lancia.

Castellotti signed for Lancia for 1954, racing sports cars while waiting patiently for the chance to drive one of their much-anticipated grand prix cars. In fact, it was 1955 before he got his wish, making his grand prix debut at the Argentine GP, where he suffered from sunstroke in the intense heat and finally crashed the car. Back in Europe, however, he made amends, finishing fourth in the Turin GP, and second at Pau and – after Alberto Ascari crashed his car into the harbour – Monaco. Days later, Ascari was killed in a testing accident, and Castellotti led the team for one race, at Spa, before it was amalgamated with the Scuderia Ferrari, for whom he finished the season, taking third in the drivers' championship.

The 1956 season saw the Ferrari squad almost embarrassed by an over-supply of cars and drivers, which led to some friction within the team. This was particularly acute between Luigi Musso and Castellotti, the two Italians waging their own private duel in the Italian GP at Monza. By now, Eugenio was at his peak, particularly in sports cars. A stunning win in atrocious conditions in the Mille Miglia made up in part for his disappointment the previous year when he destroyed his tyres by racing too hard too early. Added to this was a victory in the Sebring 12-hours and second in the Nürburgring 1000km (both with Juan Fangio).

More sports car success lay ahead in 1957, when Eugenio shared the first and third cars in the Buenos Aires 1000km. On his return to Europe, he was recalled from a holiday to test the latest GP Ferrari at Modena. In wet conditions, the car crashed into a concrete barrier; 27-year-old Castellotti was hurled from the car and killed instantly.

CASTELLOTTI, Eugenio (I) b 10/10/1930, Lodi, Milan – d 14/3/1957, Modena Autodrome

1955 Championship position: 3rd Wins: 0 Pole positions: 1 Fastest laps: 0 Points scored: 12

	Race	Circuit	No	Entrant	Tyres	Capacity/Car/Engine	Comment	Q Pos/Entries
ret	ARGENTINE GP	Buenos Aires	36	Scuderia Lancia	P	2.5 Lancia D50 V8	*Villoresi also drove car/crashed*	12/22
2	MONACO GP	Monte Carlo	30	Scuderia Lancia	P	2.5 Lancia D50 V8	*pit stop – brakes*	4/22
ret	BELGIAN GP	Spa	30	Scuderia Lancia	P	2.5 Lancia D50 V8	*gearbox*	1/14
5	DUTCH GP	Zandvoort	6	Scuderia Ferrari	E	2.5 Ferrari 625 4	*3 laps behind*	9/16
dns	"	"	6	Scuderia Ferrari	E	2.5 Ferrari 625 4	*practice only*	- / -
ret	BRITISH GP	Aintree	20	Scuderia Ferrari	E	2.5 Ferrari 625 4	*transmission*	10/25
6*	"	"	16	Scuderia Ferrari	E	2.5 Ferrari 625 4	*took over Hawthorn's car/-3 laps*	- / -
3	ITALIAN GP	Monza	4	Scuderia Ferrari	E	2.5 Ferrari 555 4		4/22

1956 Championship position: 5th Wins: 0 Pole positions: 0 Fastest laps: 0 Points scored: 7.5

	Race	Circuit	No	Entrant	Tyres	Capacity/Car/Engine	Comment	Q Pos/Entries
ret	ARGENTINE GP	Buenos Aires	32	Scuderia Ferrari	E	2.5 Lancia-Ferrari D50 V8	*gearbox*	2/15
ret	MONACO GP	Monte Carlo	22	Scuderia Ferrari	E	2.5 Lancia-Ferrari D50 V8	*clutch*	3/19
4*	"	"	20	Scuderia Ferrari	E	2.5 Lancia-Ferrari D50 V8	*took over Fangio's car/-6 laps*	- / -
ret	BELGIAN GP	Spa	4	Scuderia Ferrari	E	2.5 Lancia-Ferrari D50 V8	*transmission*	5/16
2	FRENCH GP	Reims	12	Scuderia Ferrari	E	2.5 Lancia-Ferrari D50 V8		2/20
10*	BRITISH GP	Silverstone	3	Scuderia Ferrari	E	2.5 Lancia-Ferrari D50 V8	*de Portago took over car*	8/28
ret	GERMAN GP	Nürburgring	3	Scuderia Ferrari	E	2.5 Lancia-Ferrari D50 V8	*magneto*	3/21
ret	"	"	4	Scuderia Ferrari	E	2.5 Lancia-Ferrari D50 V8	*accident – took Musso's car*	- / -
ret	ITALIAN GP	Monza	24	Scuderia Ferrari	E	2.5 Lancia-Ferrari D50 V8	*tyres – accident*	2/26
8*	"	"	22	Scuderia Ferrari	E	2.5 Lancia-Ferrari D50 V8	*took Fangio's car/4 laps behind*	- / -

1957 Championship position: Unplaced

	Race	Circuit	No	Entrant	Tyres	Capacity/Car/Engine	Comment	Q Pos/Entries
ret	ARGENTINE GP	Buenos Aires	14	Scuderia Ferrari	E	2.5 Lancia-Ferrari D50A V8	*hub shaft – lost wheel*	4/16

GP Starts: 14 GP Wins: 0 Pole positions: 1 Fastest laps: 0 Points: 19.5

JOHNNY CECOTTO

THE son of an Italian immigrant, Johnny Cecotto began racing a 750cc Honda motorcycle in his native Venezuela in 1972. Soon outgrowing domestic competition, he made a dramatic European debut, scoring a 250/350cc double, then went on to take the 350cc title in his first season, becoming the youngest ever world champion. More bike successes followed – at 20, he was the youngest winner of the famous Daytona 200 – but a crash early in 1977 put him out of contention for the season. He came back to win the F750 title in 1978, but as Kenny Roberts' star rose, Cecotto's appetite for bike racing waned.

Cecotto made an inconclusive F2 debut in 1980, taking part in just three races, but he finally abandoned his bike career at the beginning of 1981. After a torrid first half of the season with Martini, he changed teams and, under the guidance of Markus Hotz, knuckled down to the job, swiftly becoming a top-six regular and scoring points in the last four races of the season. A hoped-for grand prix opportunity for 1982 failed to materialise, so he remained in F2 with a works March. He lost the championship to his teammate, Corrado Fabi, after the pair had finished the season level on points and Cecotto had been forced to drop his worst score from his total. Nevertheless he had made the transition from two wheels to four brilliantly, and this time there was a seat for him in Formula 1.

Johnny's first grand prix season in the Theodore produced little save a welcome sixth place at Long Beach, so he moved to Toleman to partner F1 newcomer Ayrton Senna in 1984. He spent the first half of the season somewhat in the Brazilian's shadow, until a very heavy crash in practice for the British Grand Prix left him hospitalised with serious leg and ankle injuries. It would be the end of his Formula 1 ambitions.

Upon recovery, Cecotto forged a successful new career in the flourishing touring car scene. Driving for BMW, he won the 1989 Italian championship and quickly became one of the Munich concern's favoured sons. He competed in the German, British and Italian series during the 1990s and was one of the undoubted stars of this class of racing. Even at the age of 42, he proved a match for Laurent Aïello and his Peugeot when his Schnizter BMW 320i snatched the 1998 German Super Touring title at the last gasp.

Cecotto also made several appearances in Team Bigazzi's McLaren F1 GTR, including a couple of wins in Brazil in 1996, sharing the car with Nelson Piquet. After racing in European Touring Cars for BMW in 2000, Johnny moved to the German V8Star series with outstanding success, being crowned champion in both 2001 and 2002. Thereafter, he scaled down his racing activities, making a single appearance in the 2003 ALMS Series in the Rafanelli Ferrari. Since then, Cecotto has spent time guiding the career path of his son, Johnny Cecotto Jnr, who had risen to the ranks of the GP2 series by 2011.

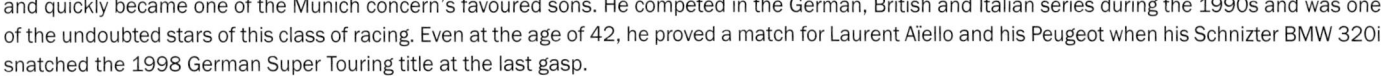

CECOTTO, Johnny (YV) b 25/1/1956, Caracas

1983 Championship position: 19th=   Wins: 0   Pole positions: 0   Fastest laps: 0   Points scored: 1

	Race	Circuit	No	Entrant	Tyres	Capacity/Car/Engine	Comment	Q Pos/Entries
13	BRAZILIAN GP	Rio	34	Theodore Racing Team	G	3.0 Theodore N183-Cosworth V8	3 laps behind	19/27
6	US GP WEST	Long Beach	34	Theodore Racing Team	G	3.0 Theodore N183-Cosworth V8	1 lap behind	17/28
11	FRENCH GP	Paul Ricard	34	Theodore Racing Team	G	3.0 Theodore N183-Cosworth V8	2 laps behind	17/29
ret	SAN MARINO GP	Imola	34	Theodore Racing Team	G	3.0 Theodore N183-Cosworth V8	accident damage	23/28
dnpq	MONACO GP	Monte Carlo	34	Theodore Racing Team	G	3.0 Theodore N183-Cosworth V8		26/28
10	BELGIAN GP	Spa	34	Theodore Racing Team	G	3.0 Theodore N183-Cosworth V8	1 lap behind	25/28
ret	US GP (DETROIT)	Detroit	34	Theodore Racing Team	G	3.0 Theodore N183-Cosworth V8	gear linkage	26/27
ret	CANADIAN GP	Montreal	34	Theodore Racing Team	G	3.0 Theodore N183-Cosworth V8	crown wheel and pinion	23/28
dnq	BRITISH GP	Silverstone	34	Theodore Racing Team	G	3.0 Theodore N183-Cosworth V8		27/29
11	GERMAN GP	Hockenheim	34	Theodore Racing Team	G	3.0 Theodore N183-Cosworth V8	1 lap behind	22/29
dnq	AUSTRIAN GP	Österreichring	34	Theodore Racing Team	G	3.0 Theodore N183-Cosworth V8		28/29
dnq	DUTCH GP	Zandvoort	34	Theodore Racing Team	G	3.0 Theodore N183-Cosworth V8		28/29
12	ITALIAN GP	Monza	34	Theodore Racing Team	G	3.0 Theodore N183-Cosworth V8	2 laps behind	26/29

1984 Championship position: Unplaced

ret	BRAZILIAN GP	Rio	20	Toleman Group Motorsport	P	1.5 t/c Toleman TG183B-Hart 4	turbo boost pressure	18/27
ret	SOUTH AFRICAN GP	Kyalami	20	Toleman Group Motorsport	P	1.5 t/c Toleman TG183B-Hart 4	tyre failure	19/27
ret	BELGIAN GP	Zolder	20	Toleman Group Motorsport	P	1.5 t/c Toleman TG183B-Hart 4	clutch	16/27
nc	SAN MARINO GP	Imola	20	Toleman Group Motorsport	P	1.5 t/c Toleman TG183B-Hart 4	pit stop/8 laps behind	19/28
ret	FRENCH GP	Dijon	20	Toleman Group Motorsport	M	1.5 t/c Toleman TG184-Hart 4	turbo	19/27
ret	MONACO GP	Monte Carlo	20	Toleman Group Motorsport	M	1.5 t/c Toleman TG184-Hart 4	spun off	18/27
9	CANADIAN GP	Montreal	20	Toleman Group Motorsport	M	1.5 t/c Toleman TG184-Hart 4	2 laps behind	20/26
ret	US GP (DETROIT)	Detroit	20	Toleman Group Motorsport	M	1.5 t/c Toleman TG184-Hart 4	clutch	17/27
ret	US GP (DALLAS)	Dallas	20	Toleman Group Motorsport	M	1.5 t/c Toleman TG184-Hart 4	hit wall	15/27
dnq	BRITISH GP	Brands Hatch	20	Toleman Group Motorsport	M	1.5 t/c Toleman TG184-Hart 4	crashed in practice – injured legs	- / -

GP Starts: 18   GP Wins: 0   Pole positions: 0   Fastest laps: 0   Points: 1

FRANÇOIS CEVERT

FRANÇOIS EVERT'S immense natural talent had been nurtured and developed over a four-year period in the Tyrrell team. He had been given what amounted to a personal master-class in the art of grand prix racing by Jackie Stewart and had learned so well that at the time of his shocking death at Watkins Glen in 1973, he was the finished article, ready to assume the mantle of a champion after his team leader's impending retirement.

Born in 1944 in occupied Paris, François' father was Charles Goldenberg, a successful jeweller who had escaped from Russia with his parents as a child. With the German occupation of the French capital, Goldenberg had joined the French resistance, and the three children assumed their mother's maiden name of Cevert to protect them from the attention of the Nazis.

François was introduced to the world of motorsport by his sister, Jacqueline, who was the girlfriend of the up-and-coming Jean-Pierre Beltoise, in whose footsteps he soon began to follow.

A Volant Shell award had seen François begin his racing career in 1967 at the wheel of his prize, an F3 Alpine. The season was something of a disaster, the old car proving very unreliable. Undismayed by this, he bought a Tecno for the following year and, after getting to grips with its inherent understeer, went on to take the French F3 championship. So impressed were the Italian manufacturers that they offered Cevert a place in their Formula 2 team for 1969. Despite his lack of experience, he took third place in the championship and a win in the Trophées de France meeting at Reims. He also made his grand prix debut in the car in the Formula 2 class of the German Grand Prix.

For 1970, François planned another season with Tecno as well as finally accepting an offer to drive for Matra in sports cars, which came via Beltoise, now his brother-in-law. But when Johnny Servoz-Gavin suddenly retired in mid-season, he took over the Tyrrell drive, largely on the recommendation of Stewart, who had been impressed with the Frenchman's performance in a Formula 2 race at Crystal Palace the previous year. Easing himself in sensibly with the March 701, the Frenchman scored a satisfying sixth place at Monza, but he really blossomed in 1971 with the superb Tyrrell, taking two excellent second places behind his leader at Paul Ricard and the Nürburgring, before posting his first (and only) grand prix win in the US Grand Prix.

The 1972 Formula 1 season was more difficult, perhaps not helped by Stewart's illness, and Cevert finished in the points on only three occasions. He also drove quite regularly in other formulas, dovetailing appearances in John Coombs' Elf-backed March in F2 with a full Can-Am programme (which saw a win at Donnybrooke) and a one-off drive at Le Mans, where he took a splendid second place for Matra with Howden Ganley.

Tyrrell were back at their best in 1973. Stewart, already intending to retire after one last season, used all his considerable gifts to take a third world championship, with François right behind him, the apprentice having matured to the point that he could be the faster man on occasion. Certainly it was felt that he could have taken victory in the German GP if he had so chosen, but in the event he had to be content with no fewer than five second-place finishes before that fateful day at Watkins Glen in October when, attempting to take pole position, he lost control of his car on a bumpy part of the track. The Tyrrell fishtailed out of control before flipping and crashing through the steel barriers with such ferocity that he stood no chance of survival.

France's most likely first world champion was gone, and Ken Tyrrell had lost the man who could perhaps have kept his team at the pinnacle in the post-Stewart era.

The dashing and handsome François had been widely seen as the prince in waiting: "The only thing I live for, hopefully, is racing."

"Its not a boring life for me, I've made my choice."

At breakfast on the morning of his death, he had been amused by a caption accompanying his photograph in a local newspaper, which described him as "intense and waiting". He smiled over his tea. "Aren't we all?" he asked.

CEVERT, François (F) b 25/2/1944, Paris – d 6/10/1973, Watkins Glen Circuit, New York State, USA

1969 Championship position: Unplaced

	Race	Circuit	No	Entrant	Tyres	Capacity/Car/Engine	Comment	Q Pos/Entries
ret	GERMAN GP (F2)	Nürburgring	28	Tecno Racing	D	1.6 Tecno F2/69-Cosworth 4 F2	gearbox	13/26

1970 Championship position: 22nd= Wins: 0 Pole positions: 0 Fastest laps: 0 Points scored: 1

	Race	Circuit	No	Entrant	Tyres	Capacity/Car/Engine	Comment	Q Pos/Entries
ret	DUTCH GP	Zandvoort	6	Tyrrell Racing Organisation	D	3.0 March 701-Cosworth V8	engine	15/24
11	FRENCH GP	Clermont Ferrand	2	Tyrrell Racing Organisation	D	3.0 March 701-Cosworth V8	1 lap behind	13/23
7	BRITISH GP	Brands Hatch	2	Tyrrell Racing Organisation	D	3.0 March 701-Cosworth V8	1 lap behind	15/25
7	GERMAN GP	Hockenheim	23	Tyrrell Racing Organisation	D	3.0 March 701-Cosworth V8	1 lap behind	14/25
ret	AUSTRIAN GP	Österreichring	2	Tyrrell Racing Organisation	D	3.0 March 701-Cosworth V8	engine	9/24
6	ITALIAN GP	Monza	20	Tyrrell Racing Organisation	D	3.0 March 701-Cosworth V8		=10/27
9	CANADIAN GP	St Jovite	2	Tyrrell Racing Organisation	D	3.0 March 701-Cosworth V8	pit stop – shock absorber/-5 laps	4/20
ret	US GP	Watkins Glen	2	Tyrrell Racing Organisation	D	3.0 March 701-Cosworth V8	lost wheel	17/27
ret	MEXICAN GP	Mexico City	2	Tyrrell Racing Organisation	D	3.0 March 701-Cosworth V8	engine	9/18

1971 Championship position: 3rd Wins: 1 Pole positions: 0 Fastest laps: 1 Points scored: 26

	Race	Circuit	No	Entrant	Tyres	Capacity/Car/Engine	Comment	Q Pos/Entries
ret	SOUTH AFRICAN GP	Kyalami	10	Elf Team Tyrrell	G	3.0 Tyrrell 002-Cosworth V8	accident	=8/25
7	SPANISH GP	Montjuich Park	12	Elf Team Tyrrell	G	3.0 Tyrrell 002-Cosworth V8	1 lap behind	12/22
ret	MONACO GP	Monte Carlo	12	Elf Team Tyrrell	G	3.0 Tyrrell 002-Cosworth V8	hit barrier/suspension – wheel	=15/23
ret	DUTCH GP	Zandvoort	6	Elf Team Tyrrell	G	3.0 Tyrrell 002-Cosworth V8	spun off/collision with Galli	12/24
2	FRENCH GP	Paul Ricard	12	Elf Team Tyrrell	G	3.0 Tyrrell 002-Cosworth V8		7/24
10	BRITISH GP	Silverstone	14	Elf Team Tyrrell	G	3.0 Tyrrell 002-Cosworth V8	pit stop – fuel pipe/3 laps behind	10/24
2	GERMAN GP	Nürburgring	3	Elf Team Tyrrell	G	3.0 Tyrrell 002-Cosworth V8	FL	5/23
ret	AUSTRIAN GP	Österreichring	12	Elf Team Tyrrell	G	3.0 Tyrrell 002-Cosworth V8	engine	3/22
3	ITALIAN GP	Monza	2	Elf Team Tyrrell	G	3.0 Tyrrell 002-Cosworth V8		5/24
6	CANADIAN GP	Mosport Park	12	Elf Team Tyrrell	G	3.0 Tyrrell 002-Cosworth V8	2 laps behind	3/27
1	US GP	Watkins Glen	9	Elf Team Tyrrell	G	3.0 Tyrrell 002-Cosworth V8		5/32

1972 Championship position: 6th= Wins: 0 Pole positions: 0 Fastest laps: 0 Points scored: 15

	Race	Circuit	No	Entrant	Tyres	Capacity/Car/Engine	Comment	Q Pos/Entries
ret	ARGENTINE GP	Buenos Aires	22	Elf Team Tyrrell	G	3.0 Tyrrell 002-Cosworth V8	gearbox	7/22
9	SOUTH AFRICAN GP	Kyalami	2	Elf Team Tyrrell	G	3.0 Tyrrell 002-Cosworth V8	pit stop – ignition/1 lap behind	=8/27
ret	SPANISH GP	Jarama	3	Elf Team Tyrrell	G	3.0 Tyrrell 002-Cosworth V8	ignition	12/26
18	MONACO GP	Monte Carlo	2	Elf Team Tyrrell	G	3.0 Tyrrell 002-Cosworth V8	electrics/10 laps behind	12/25
2	BELGIAN GP	Nivelles	8	Elf Team Tyrrell	G	3.0 Tyrrell 002-Cosworth V8		5/26
4	FRENCH GP	Clermont Ferrand	7	Elf Team Tyrrell	G	3.0 Tyrrell 002-Cosworth V8		=7/29
dns	"	"	7T/7	Elf Team Tyrrell	G	3.0 Tyrrell 005-Cosworth V8	practice only	– / –
ret	BRITISH GP	Brands Hatch	2	Elf Team Tyrrell	G	3.0 Tyrrell 002-Cosworth V8	spun off	=11/27
10	GERMAN GP	Nürburgring	7	Elf Team Tyrrell	G	3.0 Tyrrell 002-Cosworth V8	pit stop – tyre	5/27
dns	"	"	7T	Elf Team Tyrrell	G	3.0 Tyrrell 004-Cosworth V8	practice only	– / –
9	AUSTRIAN GP	Österreichring	2	Elf Team Tyrrell	G	3.0 Tyrrell 002-Cosworth V8	1 lap behind	20/26
ret	ITALIAN GP	Monza	2	Elf Team Tyrrell	G	3.0 Tyrrell 002-Cosworth V8	engine	14/27
dns	"	1T	Elf Team Tyrrell	G	3.0 Tyrrell 004-Cosworth V8	practice only	– / –
ret	CANADIAN GP	Mosport Park	2	Elf Team Tyrrell	G	3.0 Tyrrell 006-Cosworth V8	gearbox	=6/25
2	US GP	Watkins Glen	2	Elf Team Tyrrell	G	3.0 Tyrrell 006-Cosworth V8		4/32

François Cevert took his only grand prix victory in the 1971 US Grand Prix at Watkins Glen. The handsome young Frenchman would perish in a violent accident at the same track just three years later.

1973 Championship position: 4th		Wins: 0	Pole positions: 0	Fastest laps: 1	Points scored: 47			
2	ARGENTINE GP	Buenos Aires	8	Elf Team Tyrrell	G	3.0 Tyrrell 006-Cosworth V8		6/19
10	BRAZILIAN GP	Interlagos	4	Elf Team Tyrrell	G	3.0 Tyrrell 006-Cosworth V8	*pit stop – puncture/2 laps behind*	5/20
nc	SOUTH AFRICAN GP	Kyalami	4	Elf Team Tyrrell	G	3.0 Tyrrell 005-Cosworth V8	*3 stops – tyre & engine timing/-13 laps*	– / –
dns	" "	"	3	Elf Team Tyrrell	G	3.0 Tyrrell 006-Cosworth V8	*practice only – Stewart drove*	(9)/25
2	SPANISH GP	Montjuich Park	4	Elf Team Tyrrell	G	3.0 Tyrrell 006-Cosworth V8		3/22
2	BELGIAN GP	Zolder	6	Elf Team Tyrrell	G	3.0 Tyrrell 006-Cosworth V8	*FL*	4/23
4	MONACO GP	Monte Carlo	6	Elf Team Tyrrell	G	3.0 Tyrrell 006-Cosworth V8	*1 lap behind*	4/26
3	SWEDISH GP	Anderstorp	6	Elf Team Tyrrell	G	3.0 Tyrrell 006-Cosworth V8		2/22
dns	"	"	6T	Elf Team Tyrrell	G	3.0 Tyrrell 005-Cosworth V8	*practice only*	– / –
2	FRENCH GP	Paul Ricard	6	Elf Team Tyrrell	G	3.0 Tyrrell 006-Cosworth V8		4/25
5	BRITISH GP	Silverstone	6	Elf Team Tyrrell	G	3.0 Tyrrell 006-Cosworth V8		7/29
dns	"	"	43	Elf Team Tyrrell	G	3.0 Tyrrell 005-Cosworth V8	*practice only*	– / –
2	DUTCH GP	Zandvoort	6	Elf Team Tyrrell	G	3.0 Tyrrell 006-Cosworth V8		3/24
2	GERMAN GP	Nürburgring	6	Elf Team Tyrrell	G	3.0 Tyrrell 006-Cosworth V8		3/23
ret	AUSTRIAN GP	Österreichring	6	Elf Team Tyrrell	G	3.0 Tyrrell 006-Cosworth V8	*collision with Merzario*	10/25
dns	"	"	6T	Elf Team Tyrrell	G	3.0 Tyrrell 005-Cosworth V8	*practice only*	– / –
5	ITALIAN GP	Monza	6	Elf Team Tyrrell	G	3.0 Tyrrell 006-Cosworth V8		11/25
dns	"	"	6T	Elf Team Tyrrell	G	3.0 Tyrrell 005-Cosworth V8	*practice only*	– / –
ret	CANADIAN GP	Mosport Park	6	Elf Team Tyrrell	G	3.0 Tyrrell 006-Cosworth V8	*collision with Scheckter*	6/26
dns	US GP	Watkins Glen	6	Elf Team Tyrrell	G	3.0 Tyrrell 006-Cosworth V8	*fatal practice accident*	(4)/28

GP Starts: 47   GP Wins: 1   Pole positions: 0   Fastest laps: 2   Points: 89

EUGÈNE CHABOUD

WITH his friend Jean Trémoulet, Eugène Chaboud began racing late in 1936 with a Delahaye. The pair competed together until 1938 when, after winning the Le Mans 24-hour race, they went their separate ways.

After the Second World War, Chaboud soon returned to racing, being involved with Paul Vallée's Ecurie France team as sporting director and lead driver with his Delahaye 135S. In 1947, the team acquired a 1939 Talbot monoplace with which he lost no time in winning races at Marseilles and Perpignan. Then the drive was given to Louis Chiron, so Chaboud and Charles Pozzi left in disgust and set up their own team.

Eugène emerged as French champion, and for 1948 they created Ecurie Leutitia, with Chaboud still racing his Delahaye. He took sixth place in the 1949 French GP and was very unlucky at Le Mans when the car caught fire while leading the race by some nine miles; eventually, he had to abandon it.

Chaboud's chance to race in more competitive machinery than the Delahaye came in 1950, when he was invited to drive a Lago-Talbot in place of the injured Eugène Martin. Sharing the car with Philippe Étancelin, he finished fifth in the French Grand Prix.

In the Le Mans 24-hours of 1952, Chaboud lay sixth until, after the 22-hour mark, he crashed the Talbot. While lying under the overturned car waiting to be extricated, he had leisure to decide that this was a good time to call it a day...

JAY CHAMBERLAIN

AN SCCA sports car racer, Jay Chamberlain competed almost exclusively in Lotus cars, for which he was an early US distributor in Burbank, California.

Chamberlain travelled to Europe in 1957 and finished ninth at Le Mans (with Herbert Mackay-Fraser), winning the 1100cc class. He took the event very seriously and spent many hours of preparation, including ensuring that all the Dunlop tyres matched, which resulted in a major improvement in handling. A fortnight later, he took second in the 1500cc Lotus in a sports car race at Rouen, behind Ron Flockhart's similar car, before the teams moved on to Reims. He crashed his Lotus in practice for the 12-hour race, receiving serious injuries that required him to be sent to a Paris hospital. The dreadful weekend for Lotus would continue, as his Le Mans partner, Mackay-Fraser, perished after crashing in the F2 support race.

The American recovered in time to return to Le Mans in 1958, but he crashed at Mulsanne, thankfully this time without harm. After racing a Formula Junior Lotus back in the States, Jay tried his hand at a Formula 1 season in Europe with a Lotus 18, but his only result of any note was a fifth in the minor Lavant Cup (for four-cylinder cars only) at Goodwood. He also ventured to Chimay and took a fourth place in the GP des Frontières in a Formula Junior Cooper.

CHABOUD, Eugène (F) b 12/4/1907, Lyon – d 28/12/1983, Montfermeil

1950 Championship position: 15th=   Wins: 0   Pole positions: 0   Fastest laps: 0   Points scored: 1

	Race	Circuit	No	Entrant	Tyres	Capacity/Car/Engine	Comment	Q Pos/Entries
ret	BELGIAN GP	Spa	20	Ecurie Leutitia	D	4.5 Talbot-Lago T26C 6	engine	11/14
dns	FRENCH GP	Reims	24	Ecurie Leutitia	D	4.5 Talbot-Lago T26C 6		(10)/20
5*	"	"	16	Philippe Étancelin	D	4.5 Talbot-Lago T26C-DA 6	*took over Étancelin's car/-5 laps	– / –

1951 Championship position: Unplaced

	Race	Circuit	No	Entrant	Tyres	Capacity/Car/Engine	Comment	Q Pos/Entries
8	FRENCH GP	Reims	44	Eugène Chaboud	D	4.5 Talbot-Lago T26C-GS 6	8 laps behind	14/23

GP Starts: 3   GP Wins: 0   Pole positions: 0   Fastest laps: 0   Points: 1

CHAMBERLAIN, Jay (USA) b 29/12/1925 Hollywood, California – d 1/8/2001, Tuscon, Arizona

1962 Championship position: Unplaced

	Race	Circuit	No	Entrant	Tyres	Capacity/Car/Engine	Comment	Q Pos/Entries
15	BRITISH GP	Aintree	46	Ecurie Excelsior	D	1.5 Lotus 18-Climax 4	11 laps behind	20/21
dnq	GERMAN GP	Nürburgring	30	Ecurie Excelsior	D	1.5 Lotus 18-Climax 4		29/30
dnq	ITALIAN GP	Monza	26	Ecurie Excelsior	D	1.5 Lotus 18-Climax 4		29/30

GP Starts: 1   GP Wins: 0   Pole positions: 0   Fastest laps: 0   Points: 0

KARUN CHANDHOK

A CHARMING and eloquent man, Karun Chandhok is a perfect ambassador to represent his native India in Formula 1, but sadly he has not been able to pin down a full-time ride where he could prove he was more than a journeyman racer with good connections.

Early success in his homeland and then winning the F2000 Formula Asia title in 2001 sent him to Britain, where he spent three seasons in Formula 3, the first two in the national class. Then he tried his hand at the Formula Renault 3.5 Series and also represented India in the A1GP series. His career only gained momentum, however, when he convincingly won the 2006 V6 Asia by Renault championship. A more confident Chandhok then moved into the GP2 series where, with three different teams, he managed to take two wins in his three seasons.

Despite his connections with Vijay Mallya, Karun was disappointed not to be able to gain the vacant seat at Force India when Giancarlo Fisichella left for Ferrari towards the end of 2009, but he was finally able to find his way on to the Formula 1 grid with the fledgling Hispania team for 2010. Given the circumstances, he did a terrific job in making the finish in eight of his ten races, before being stood down largely for financial considerations. He had done enough, however, to earn the third-driver role at Team Lotus for 2011, where he gained some Friday track time and an unexpected start in the German GP when Jarno Trulli stepped aside, having experienced trouble with the car's power steering.

With F1 looking out of reach for Chandhok, he opted to race sports protoypes in the FIA Endurance Championship in 2012.

CHANDHOK, Karun (IND) b 19/1/1984, Madras

2010 Championship position: Unplaced

	Race	Circuit	No	Entrant	Tyres	Capacity/Car/Engine	Comment	Q Pos/Entries
ret	BAHRAIN GP	Sakhir Circuit	20	HTR F1 Team	B	2.4 HRT F110-Cosworth V8	accident on lap 1	24/24
14	AUSTRALIAN GP	Melbourne	20	HTR F1 Team	B	2.4 HRT F110-Cosworth V8	5 laps behind	24/24
15	MALAYSIAN GP	Sepang	20	HTR F1 Team	B	2.4 HRT F110-Cosworth V8	5 laps behind	22/24
17	CHINESE GP	Shanghai Circuit	20	HTR F1 Team	B	2.4 HRT F110-Cosworth V8	started from pitlane/-4 laps	24/24
ret	SPANISH GP	Barcelona	20	HTR F1 Team	B	2.4 HRT F110-Cosworth V8	collision – accident damage	23/24
14/ret	MONACO GP	Monte Carlo	20	HTR F1 Team	B	2.4 HRT F110-Cosworth V8	hit by Trulli/8 laps behind	23/24
ret	TURKISH GP	Istanbul Park	20	HTR F1 Team	B	2.4 HRT F110-Cosworth V8	fuel pump	24/24
18	CANADIAN GP	Montreal	20	HTR F1 Team	B	2.4 HRT F110-Cosworth V8	5 laps behind	24/24
18	EUROPEAN GP	Valencia	20	HTR F1 Team	B	2.4 HRT F110-Cosworth V8	2 laps behind	23/24
19	BRITISH GP	Silverstone	20	HTR F1 Team	B	2.4 HRT F110-Cosworth V8	2 laps behind	23/24

2011 Championship position: Unplaced

	Race	Circuit	No	Entrant	Tyres	Capacity/Car/Engine	Comment	Q Pos/Entries
app	AUSTRALIAN GP	Melbourne	21	Team Lotus	P	2.4 Lotus T128-Renault V8	3rd driver in practice 1 only – no time	– / –
app	TURKISH GP	Istanbul Park	20	Team Lotus	P	2.4 Lotus T128-Renault V8	ran as 3rd driver in practice 1 only	– / –
app	EUROPEAN GP	Valencia	21	Team Lotus	P	2.4 Lotus T128-Renault V8	3rd driver in practice 1 only – no time	– / –
app	BRITISH GP	Silverstone	20	Team Lotus	P	2.4 Lotus T128-Renault V8	ran as 3rd driver in practice 1 only	– / –
20	GERMAN GP	Hockenheim	20	Team Lotus	P	2.4 Lotus T128-Renault V8	4 laps behind	– / –
app	BELGIAN GP	Spa	20	Team Lotus	P	2.4 Lotus T128-Renault V8	ran as 3rd driver in practice 1 only	– / –
app	ITALIAN GP	Monza	21	Team Lotus	P	2.4 Lotus T128-Renault V8	ran as 3rd driver in practice 1 only	– / –
app	JAPANESE GP	Suzuka	20	Team Lotus	P	2.4 Lotus T128-Renault V8	ran as 3rd driver in practice 1 only	– / –
app	KOREAN GP	Yeongam	21	Team Lotus	P	2.4 Lotus T128-Renault V8	ran as 3rd driver in practice 1 only	– / –
app	INDIAN GP	Buddh Circuit	21	Team Lotus	P	2.4 Lotus T128-Renault V8	ran as 3rd driver in practice 1 only	– / –

GP Starts: 11   GP Wins: 0   Pole positions: 0   Fastest laps: 0   Points: 0

DAVE CHARLTON

AFTER club racing with an Austin Healey, Dave Charlton moved into South Africa's major league in 1962, racing under the intriguingly titled Ecurie Tomahawk banner. Driving a four-cylinder Lotus 20, he fared reasonably well on the local scene, but the car was not even good enough to qualify for practice in the 1965 Grand Prix. The purchase of a Brabham BT11 brought him to the forefront in South Africa's national series and helped ensure that he would be on the grid for the country's feature race as well. Having built his reputation with Scuderia Scribante, he was invited to England in early 1968 to test a works Cooper; also he took in the BOAC 500 sports car race in Sid Taylor's Lola T70. Unfortunately, a huge moment coming out of Paddock Hill bend caused him to hit the bank at Druids!

In 1970, Dave purchased the ex-Jo Bonnier Lotus 49C, which he used to devastating effect, cleaning up with seven wins to put an end to the championship run of John Love in the F1/FA series. This led to a deal to drive a works Brabham in the following year's grand prix, where he qualified well ahead of Graham Hill. Although his race ended with an engine failure, his impressive showing helped him to secure a lucrative long-term sponsorship from Lucky Strike.

Meanwhile, as a valuable Lotus customer, Charlton ventured to Europe for a planned two-race stint with a third works car. Unfortunately, he made the briefest of appearances, after team-mate Dave Walker shunted his car at Zandvoort. Then, at Silverstone, his engine suffered from a broken oil line on the opening lap.

His team's cigarette sponsorship allowed Charlton to purchase a Lotus 72 (after his 49 was severely damaged in the 1971 Natal Winter Trophy), and he raced the new car with great success at home, scoring nine victories in winning the 1972 series by a country mile, to the chagrin of his great rival, John Love.

During the South African winter of that year, Charlton arranged to ship the car to the Lotus factory so that it could be brought up to date, and this seemed a good opportunity to try his luck with it in Europe. In the end, his three-race sortie was not a success. The upgrades had removed the previous reliability the car had enjoyed, while Charlton himself was suffering from an inner-ear infection, which caused spells of dizziness and double vision – not ideal, as his three races were held at undulating tracks that included the Charade and Nürburgring circuits.

Charlton blotted his copybook by spinning out of the 1973 Grand Prix and causing a multiple shunt, but success would continue unabated when the Lotus was replaced by a McLaren M23. He comfortably won the 1974 series, but was extremely lucky to prevail over his new young challenger, Ian Scheckter, the following season – his consistency paid off, six second places and one win being enough. The 1976 season would see the beginning of the end of Charlton's domination. The championship was now run to Formula Atlantic rules, and his Modus did not inspire quite the same awe among his competitors. By mid-1978, he had lost his long-time sponsorship deal and eventually forsook single-seaters for saloons, which he raced with great gusto into the early 1980s.

CHARLTON, Dave (ZA) b 27/10/1936, Brotton, nr Redcar, Yorkshire, England

1965 Championship position: Unplaced

	Race	Circuit	No	Entrant	Tyres	Capacity/Car/Engine	Comment	Q Pos/Entries
dnpq	SOUTH AFRICAN GP	East London	32	Ecurie Tomahawk	D	1.5 Lotus 20-Ford 4	dnq for official practice	– / –

1967 Championship position: Unplaced

nc	SOUTH AFRICAN GP	Kyalami	19	Scuderia Scribante	–	2.7 Brabham BT11-Climax 4	17 laps behind	=7/18

1968 Championship position: Unplaced

ret	SOUTH AFRICAN GP	Kyalami	22	Scuderia Scribante	F	3.0 Brabham BT11-Repco V8	crown wheel and pinion	=14/23

1970 Championship position: Unplaced

12/ret	SOUTH AFRICAN GP	Kyalami	25	Scuderia Scribante	F	3.0 Lotus 49C-Cosworth V8	puncture/7 laps behind	13/24

1971 Championship position: Unplaced

ret	SOUTH AFRICAN GP	Kyalami	15	Motor Racing Developments	G	3.0 Brabham BT33-Cosworth V8	valve spring	12/25
dns	DUTCH GP	Zandvoort	12	Gold Leaf Team Lotus	F	3.0 Lotus 72D-Cosworth V8	Walker crashed car during practice	– / –
ret	BRITISH GP	Silverstone	2	Gold Leaf Team Lotus	F	3.0 Lotus 72D-Cosworth V8	engine - loose oil pipe	13/24

1972 Championship position: Unplaced

ret	SOUTH AFRICAN GP	Kyalami	26	Scuderia Scribante-Lucky Strike	F	3.0 Lotus 72D-Cosworth V8	fuel pressure - seized fuel pump	17/27
dnq	FRENCH GP	Clermont Ferrand	29	Scuderia Scribante-Lucky Strike	F	3.0 Lotus 72D-Cosworth V8		29/29
ret	BRITISH GP	Brands Hatch	29	Scuderia Scribante-Lucky Strike	F	3.0 Lotus 72D-Cosworth V8	gearbox	24/27
ret	GERMAN GP	Nürburgring	29	Scuderia Scribante-Lucky Strike	F	3.0 Lotus 72D-Cosworth V8	driver unwell	26/27

1973 Championship position: Unplaced

ret	SOUTH AFRICAN GP	Kyalami	25	Scuderia Scribante-Lucky Strike	F	3.0 Lotus 72D-Cosworth V8	spun - caused multiple accident	13/25

1974 Championship position: Unplaced

19	SOUTH AFRICAN GP	Kyalami	23	Scuderia Scribante-Lucky Strike	G	3.0 McLaren M23-Cosworth V8	pit stop - collision-Robarts/-7 laps	20/27

1975 Championship position: Unplaced

14	SOUTH AFRICAN GP	Kyalami	31	Lucky Strike Racing	G	3.0 McLaren M23-Cosworth V8	2 laps behind	20/28

GP Starts: 11   GP Wins: 0   Pole positions: 0   Fastest laps: 0   Points: 0

EDDIE CHEEVER

EDDIE CHEEVER has enjoyed such a long innings in motor racing that it is perhaps easy to forget the startling impact he made on Formula 3 in 1975, when barely 18 years old, or the fact that two years later he had raced successfully for the Project Four team in Formula 2 (taking a superb win at Rouen in 1977) and the BMW Junior touring car team with their 320i in the German national series.

Cheever had his first stab at grands prix in 1978 when, after failing to qualify the hapless Theodore for the first two races, he switched to the Hesketh team, which at least enabled him to make the grid, but had little else to recommend it. Then it was back to Formula 2 for the rest of the year and a series of morale-sapping incidents that undermined his reputation, despite second-place finishes at Rouen and Enna.

Now no longer quite the hot property of just 12 months earlier, Eddie threw in his lot with Osella for another season of Formula 2 in 1979, and enjoyed a happy year with the little Italian outfit, taking three wins (Silverstone, Pau and Zandvoort). When the team took the bold decision to enter grand prix racing the following year, naturally Cheever went with them. To say it was a character building season would be an understatement, and he certainly found out about life at the back of the grid. There was a little success to savour, however, for he joined the Lancia sports car team, winning a round of the World Championship of Makes at Mugello with Riccardo Patrese, and taking second places at Brands Hatch and Watkins Glen with Michele Alboreto.

A move to Tyrrell in 1981 found Cheever's career moving in the right direction, the American picking up points on no fewer than five occasions

before being tempted to the Ligier team for 1982, where, when he managed to finish, it was usually in the points, including a second place at Detroit. Eddie was chosen to partner Alain Prost at Renault in 1983, a season that would be his big opportunity to make the jump into the very front rank of driver talent. Although there were flashes of brilliance, he could not sustain them, and while he performed more than respectably, especially in qualifying, his performances were always judged against Prost's – a no-win situation. In the event, a switch to the Benetton Alfa team meant two seasons of disappointment and mechanical unreliability, but never did he ease his forceful driving style or pay much attention to the subtle art of fuel economy. If the turbo engine lasted, all well and good; if not, then it was going out in a big way – and it usually did.

Out in the cold in 1986, save for a race for Lola at Detroit in place of the indisposed Patrick Tambay, Eddie drove the TWR Jaguar in endurance racing, winning at Silverstone and finishing well elsewhere, but the lure of Formula 1 was still great and he joined Arrows for three seasons, during which his incredible enthusiasm sustained him through the frustrations of usually being no more than a midfield runner. There were occasional gems, such as his drives into third place at Monza in 1988 and Phoenix in 1989, where he hounded Patrese to the finish. But the down side was his increasing irritation with the team, which manifested itself on the track, particularly at Spa, where he was reprimanded for obstructive driving tactics.

Seeing no future in hanging on in Formula 1, Cheever joined the Indy Car trail in 1990, where in truth his form was something of a disappointment considering the abundant skill he possessed. A chance to build a solid platform for success with Chip Ganassi's team came and went, despite a second place at Phoenix and a fourth at Indianapolis in 1992. Subsequently, he teamed up with A.J. Foyt in a combustible partnership that came close to a win at Nazareth in 1995, but, predictably perhaps, failed to last the season.

Then the ever-uncompromising Eddie set his sights on the IRL with a win in the Indy 500 as his ultimate goal. After finishing 11th with John Menard's car in 1996, he decided to form his own team in 1997 and had the immediate bonus of a lucky win in the season opener at Walt Disney World. Mission was accomplished in 1998 when, starting from an unpromising 17th on the grid, he sped to a superbly judged Indy 500 win. Driving beautifully, he led 76 of the 200 laps and even survived a collision with a back-marker.

Cheever became a mainstay the IRL, winning the 1999 opener at Walt Disney World and taking seventh place overall. The following year was his best, with third place overall and a win at Pikes Peak Raceway. In 1991, he dropped back to seventh overall and took what would be his final IRL win in Kansas.

Despite backing from Red Bull, Cheever's team were no longer a force, as their Infiniti engine was overpowered by Chevrolet in an all-oval race schedule. He posted fifth places in the Indianapolis 500 and at Chicagoland, but with little else achieved he announced his retirement from driving.

Cheever returned to competition in 2005 in the Grand Prix Masters series, before a full-time commitment the following year with his own team in the Grand Am sports car series and a partial return to the IRL. At 48, he was no longer a force. Indeed, his return was most notable for unsavoury on-track incidents, at Watkins Glen in 2006, when he was accused of forcing both Marco Andretti and Danica Patrick off the track. Lack of finance led to him winding up his IRL team after competing in just seven races.

Cheever ran an Indy Pro Series team for a couple of seasons, with his nephew Richard Antinucci taking a couple of wins in 2007. Since then, he has concentrated on sports cars in the Rolex Grand Am series, acquiring the rights to the FABCAR chassis and marketing this as the Coyote-Cheever Prototype.

CHEEVER, Eddie (USA) b 10/1/1958, Phoenix, Arizona

1978 Championship position: Unplaced

	Race	Circuit	No	Entrant	Tyres	Capacity/Car/Engine	Comment	Q Pos/Entries
dnq	ARGENTINE GP	Buenos Aires	32	Theodore Racing	G	3.0 Theodore TR1-Cosworth V8		26/27
dnq	BRAZILIAN GP	Rio	32	Theodore Racing	G	3.0 Theodore TR1-Cosworth V8		26/28
ret	SOUTH AFRICAN GP	Kyalami	24	Olympus Cameras/Hesketh Racing	G	3.0 Hesketh 308E-Cosworth V8	engine – oil line	25/30

1980 Championship position: Unplaced

	Race	Circuit	No	Entrant	Tyres	Capacity/Car/Engine	Comment	Q Pos/Entries
dnq	ARGENTINE GP	Buenos Aires	31	Osella Squadra Corse	G	3.0 Osella FA1-Cosworth V8		28/28
dnq	BRAZILIAN GP	Interlagos	31	Osella Squarda Corse	G	3.0 Osella FA1-Cosworth V8		28/28
ret	SOUTH AFRICAN GP	Kyalami	31	Osella Squadra Corse	G	3.0 Osella FA1-Cosworth V8	accident	23/28
ret	US GP WEST	Long Beach	31	Osella Squadra Corse	G	3.0 Osella FA1-Cosworth V8	driveshaft	19/27
dnq	BELGIAN GP	Zolder	31	Osella Squadra Corse	G	3.0 Osella FA1-Cosworth V8		27/27
dnq	MONACO GP	Monte Carlo	31	Osella Squadra Corse	G	3.0 Osella FA1-Cosworth V8		22/27
ret	FRENCH GP	Paul Ricard	31	Osella Squadra Corse	G	3.0 Osella FA1-Cosworth V8	engine	21/27
ret	BRITISH GP	Brands Hatch	31	Osella Squadra Corse	G	3.0 Osella FA1-Cosworth V8	rear suspension	20/27
ret	GERMAN GP	Hockenheim	31	Osella Squadra Corse	G	3.0 Osella FA1-Cosworth V8	gearbox	18/26
ret	AUSTRIAN GP	Österreichring	31	Osella Squadra Corse	G	3.0 Osella FA1-Cosworth V8	wheel bearing	19/25
ret	DUTCH GP	Zandvoort	31	Osella Squadra Corse	G	3.0 Osella FA1-Cosworth V8	engine	19/28
12	ITALIAN GP	Imola	31	Osella Squadra Corse	G	3.0 Osella FA1-Cosworth V8	3 laps behind	17/28
ret	CANADIAN GP	Montreal	31	Osella Squadra Corse	G	3.0 Osella FA1-Cosworth V8	fuel pressure	14/28
ret	US GP EAST	Watkins Glen	31	Osella Squadra Corse	G	3.0 Osella FA1-Cosworth V8	suspension	16/27

1981 Championship position: 11th=   Wins: 0   Pole positions: 0   Fastest laps: 0   Points scored: 10

	Race	Circuit	No	Entrant	Tyres	Capacity/Car/Engine	Comment	Q Pos/Entries
5	US GP WEST	Long Beach	3	Tyrrell Racing	M	3.0 Tyrrell 010-Cosworth V8		8/29
nc	BRAZILIAN GP	Rio	3	Tyrrell Racing	M	3.0 Tyrrell 010-Cosworth V8	pit stops – collision damage/-13 laps	14/30
ret	ARGENTINE GP	Buenos Aires	3	Tyrrell Racing	M	3.0 Tyrrell 010-Cosworth V8	clutch	13/29
ret	SAN MARINO GP	Imola	3	Tyrrell Racing	M	3.0 Tyrrell 010-Cosworth V8	collision with Giacomelli	19/30
6	BELGIAN GP	Zolder	3	Tyrrell Racing	M	3.0 Tyrrell 010-Cosworth V8		8/31
5	MONACO GP	Monte Carlo	3	Tyrrell Racing	M	3.0 Tyrrell 010-Cosworth V8	2 laps behind	15/31
nc	SPANISH GP	Jarama	3	Tyrrell Racing	M	3.0 Tyrrell 010-Cosworth V8	long pit stop/19 laps behind	20/30
13	FRENCH GP	Dijon	3	Tyrrell Racing	M	3.0 Tyrrell 010-Cosworth V8	3 laps behind	19/29
4	BRITISH GP	Silverstone	3	Tyrrell Racing	M	3.0 Tyrrell 010-Cosworth V8	1 lap behind	23/30
5	GERMAN GP	Hockenheim	3	Tyrrell Racing	A	3.0 Tyrrell 011-Cosworth V8		18/30
dnq	AUSTRIAN GP	Österreichring	3	Tyrrell Racing	G	3.0 Tyrrell 011-Cosworth V8		25/28
dnq	"	"	3	Tyrrell Racing	G	3.0 Tyrrell 010-Cosworth V8		-/-
ret	DUTCH GP	Zandvoort	3	Tyrrell Racing	G	3.0 Tyrrell 011-Cosworth V8	accident – suspension failure	22/30
ret	ITALIAN GP	Monza	3	Tyrrell Racing	G	3.0 Tyrrell 011-Cosworth V8	spun off	17/30
12/ret	CANADIAN GP	Montreal	3	Tyrrell Racing	G	3.0 Tyrrell 011-Cosworth V8	engine/7 laps behind	14/30
ret	CAESARS PALACE GP	Las Vegas	3	Tyrrell Racing	G	3.0 Tyrrell 011-Cosworth V8	engine	19/30

1982 Championship position: 12th   Wins: 0   Pole positions: 0   Fastest laps: 0   Points scored: 15

	Race	Circuit	No	Entrant	Tyres	Capacity/Car/Engine	Comment	Q Pos/Entries
ret	SOUTH AFRICAN GP	Kyalami	25	Equipe Talbot Gitanes	M	3.0 Talbot Ligier JS17-Matra V12	misfire	17/30
ret	BRAZILIAN GP	Rio	25	Equipe Talbot Gitanes	M	3.0 Talbot Ligier JS17-Matra V12	water leak	26/31
ret	US GP WEST	Long Beach	25	Equipe Talbot Gitanes	M	3.0 Talbot Ligier JS17B-Matra V12	gearbox	13/31
3*	BELGIAN GP	Zolder	25	Equipe Talbot Gitanes	M	3.0 Talbot Ligier JS17B-Matra V12	*3rd place car disqualified/-1 lap	16/32
ret	MONACO GP	Monte Carlo	25	Equipe Talbot Gitanes	M	3.0 Talbot Ligier JS19-Matra V12	engine	16/31
2	US GP (DETROIT)	Detroit	25	Equipe Talbot Gitanes	M	3.0 Talbot Ligier JS17B-Matra V12	aggregate of two parts	9/28
10/ret	CANADIAN GP	Montreal	25	Equipe Talbot Gitanes	M	3.0 Talbot Ligier JS17B-Matra V12	out of fuel	12/29
dnq	DUTCH GP	Zandvoort	25	Equipe Talbot Gitanes	M	3.0 Talbot Ligier JS19-Matra V12		29/31
ret	BRITISH GP	Brands Hatch	25	Equipe Talbot Gitanes	M	3.0 Talbot Ligier JS19-Matra V12	engine	24/30
16	FRENCH GP	Paul Ricard	25	Equipe Talbot Gitanes	M	3.0 Talbot Ligier JS19-Matra V12	3 pit stops – tyres-skirts/-5 laps	19/30
ret	GERMAN GP	Hockenheim	25	Equipe Talbot Gitanes	M	3.0 Talbot Ligier JS19-Matra V12	handling	13/30
ret	AUSTRIAN GP	Österreichring	25	Equipe Talbot Gitanes	M	3.0 Talbot Ligier JS19-Matra V12	engine	22/29

Long tall Cheever in the Talbot-Ligier taking second place in the 1982 US Grand Prix at Detroit. The race was stopped due to an accident, but the American drove in his usual forceful style to his best ever finish.

nc	SWISS GP	Dijon	25	Equipe Talbot Gitanes	M	3.0 Talbot Ligier JS19-Matra V12	2 pit stops – tyres/10 laps behind	16/29
6	ITALIAN GP	Monza	25	Equipe Talbot Gitanes	M	3.0 Talbot Ligier JS19-Matra V12	1 lap behind	14/30
3	CAESARS PALACE GP	Las Vegas	25	Equipe Talbot Gitanes	M	3.0 Talbot Ligier JS19-Matra V12		4/30

1983 Championship position: 6th=   Wins: 0   Pole positions: 0   Fastest laps: 0   Points scored: 22

ret	BRAZILIAN GP	Rio	16	Equipe Renault Elf	M	1.5 t/c Renault RE30C V6	turbo	8/27
13/ret	US GP WEST	Long Beach	16	Equipe Renault Elf	M	1.5 t/c Renault RE30C V6	gearbox/8 laps behind	15/28
3	FRENCH GP	Paul Ricard	16	Equipe Renault Elf	M	1.5 t/c Renault RE40 V6		2/29
ret	SAN MARINO GP	Imola	16	Equipe Renault Elf	M	1.5 t/c Renault RE40 V6	turbo	6/28
ret	MONACO GP	Monte Carlo	16	Equipe Renault Elf	M	1.5 t/c Renault RE40 V6	engine cut out	3/28
3	BELGIAN GP	Spa	16	Equipe Renault Elf	M	1.5 t/c Renault RE40 V6		8/28
ret	US GP (DETROIT)	Detroit	16	Equipe Renault Elf	M	1.5 t/c Renault RE40 V6	distributor	7/27
2	CANADIAN GP	Montreal	16	Equipe Renault Elf	M	1.5 t/c Renault RE40 V6		6/28
ret	BRITISH GP	Silverstone	16	Equipe Renault Elf	M	1.5 t/c Renault RE40 V6	engine – head gasket	7/29
ret	GERMAN GP	Hockenheim	16	Equipe Renault Elf	M	1.5 t/c Renault RE40 V6	fuel injection pump	6/29
4	AUSTRIAN GP	Österreichring	16	Equipe Renault Elf	M	1.5 t/c Renault RE40 V6		8/29
ret	DUTCH GP	Zandvoort	16	Equipe Renault Elf	M	1.5 t/c Renault RE40 V6	electrics	11/29
3	ITALIAN GP	Monza	16	Equipe Renault Elf	M	1.5 t/c Renault RE40 V6		7/29
10	EUROPEAN GP	Brands Hatch	16	Equipe Renault Elf	M	1.5 t/c Renault RE40 V6	2 pit stops – tyres-visor/-1 lap	7/29
6	SOUTH AFRICAN GP	Kyalami	16	Equipe Renault Elf	M	1.5 t/c Renault RE40 V6	1 lap behind	14/26

1984 Championship position: 16th=   Wins: 0   Pole positions: 0   Fastest laps: 0   Points scored: 3

4	BRAZILIAN GP	Rio	23	Benetton Team Alfa Romeo	G	1.5 t/c Alfa Romeo 184T V8	1 lap behind	12/27
ret	SOUTH AFRICAN GP	Kyalami	23	Benetton Team Alfa Romeo	G	1.5 t/c Alfa Romeo 184T V8	radiator	16/27
ret	BELGIAN GP	Zolder	23	Benetton Team Alfa Romeo	G	1.5 t/c Alfa Romeo 184T V8	engine	11/27
7*/ret	SAN MARINO GP	Imola	23	Benetton Team Alfa Romeo	G	1.5 t/c Alfa Romeo 184T V8	*5th car dsq/out of fuel/-2 laps	8/28
ret	FRENCH GP	Dijon	23	Benetton Team Alfa Romeo	G	1.5 t/c Alfa Romeo 184T V8	engine	17/27
dnq	MONACO GP	Monte Carlo	23	Benetton Team Alfa Romeo	G	1.5 t/c Alfa Romeo 184T V8		23/27
11*/ret	CANADIAN GP	Montreal	23	Benetton Team Alfa Romeo	G	1.5 t/c Alfa Romeo 184T V8	*10th car dsq/out of fuel/-7 laps	11/26
ret	US GP (DETROIT)	Detroit	23	Benetton Team Alfa Romeo	G	1.5 t/c Alfa Romeo 184T V8	engine	8/27
ret	US GP (DALLAS)	Dallas	23	Benetton Team Alfa Romeo	G	1.5 t/c Alfa Romeo 184T V8	hit wall	14/27
ret	BRITISH GP	Brands Hatch	23	Benetton Team Alfa Romeo	G	1.5 t/c Alfa Romeo 184T V8	accident damage	18/27
ret	GERMAN GP	Hockenheim	23	Benetton Team Alfa Romeo	G	1.5 t/c Alfa Romeo 184T V8	engine	18/27
ret	AUSTRIAN GP	Österreichring	23	Benetton Team Alfa Romeo	G	1.5 t/c Alfa Romeo 184T V8	engine	16/28
13*/ret	DUTCH GP	Zandvoort	23	Benetton Team Alfa Romeo	G	1.5 t/c Alfa Romeo 184T V8	*8th/9th dsq/out of fuel/-6 laps	17/27
9*/ret	ITALIAN GP	Monza	23	Benetton Team Alfa Romeo	G	1.5 t/c Alfa Romeo 184T V8	out of fuel/6 laps behind	10/27
ret	EUROPEAN GP	Nürburgring	23	Benetton Team Alfa Romeo	G	1.5 t/c Alfa Romeo 184T V8	fuel pump	13/26
17	PORTUGUESE GP	Estoril	23	Benetton Team Alfa Romeo	G	1.5 t/c Alfa Romeo 184T V8	pit stop/6 laps behind	14/27

1985 Championship position: Unplaced

ret	BRAZILIAN GP	Rio	23	Benetton Team Alfa Romeo	G	1.5 t/c Alfa Romeo 185T V8	engine	18/25
ret	PORTUGUESE GP	Estoril	23	Benetton Team Alfa Romeo	G	1.5 t/c Alfa Romeo 185T V8	started from pit lane/engine	14/26
ret	SAN MARINO GP	Imola	23	Benetton Team Alfa Romeo	G	1.5 t/c Alfa Romeo 185T V8	engine	12/26
ret	MONACO GP	Monte Carlo	23	Benetton Team Alfa Romeo	G	1.5 t/c Alfa Romeo 185T V8	alternator	4/26
17	CANADIAN GP	Montreal	23	Benetton Team Alfa Romeo	G	1.5 t/c Alfa Romeo 185T V8	pit stop – electrics/6 laps behind	11/25
9	US GP (DETROIT)	Detroit	23	Benetton Team Alfa Romeo	G	1.5 t/c Alfa Romeo 185T V8	pit stop – puncture/2 laps behind	7/25
10	FRENCH GP	Paul Ricard	23	Benetton Team Alfa Romeo	G	1.5 t/c Alfa Romeo 185T V8	1 lap behind	18/26
ret	BRITISH GP	Silverstone	23	Benetton Team Alfa Romeo	G	1.5 t/c Alfa Romeo 185T V8	turbo	22/26
ret	GERMAN GP	Nürburgring	23	Benetton Team Alfa Romeo	G	1.5 t/c Alfa Romeo 184T V8	turbo	18/27
ret	AUSTRIAN GP	Österreichring	23	Benetton Team Alfa Romeo	G	1.5 t/c Alfa Romeo 184T V8	turbo	20/27
ret	DUTCH GP	Zandvoort	23	Benetton Team Alfa Romeo	G	1.5 t/c Alfa Romeo 184T V8	turbo	20/27
ret	ITALIAN GP	Monza	23	Benetton Team Alfa Romeo	G	1.5 t/c Alfa Romeo 184T V8	engine	17/26
ret	BELGIAN GP	Spa	23	Benetton Team Alfa Romeo	G	1.5 t/c Alfa Romeo 184T V8	gearbox	19/24
11	EUROPEAN GP	Brands Hatch	23	Benetton Team Alfa Romeo	G	1.5 t/c Alfa Romeo 184T V8	2 laps behind	18/27
ret	SOUTH AFRICAN GP	Kyalami	23	Benetton Team Alfa Romeo	G	1.5 t/c Alfa Romeo 184T V8	collision with Ghinzani & Patrese	14/21
ret	AUSTRALIAN GP	Adelaide	23	Benetton Team Alfa Romeo	G	1.5 t/c Alfa Romeo 184T V8	engine	13/25

1986 Championship position: Unplaced

ret	US GP (DETROIT)	Detroit	16	Team Haas (USA) Ltd	G	1.5 t/c Lola THL2-Cosworth V6	drive pegs	10/26

1987 Championship position: 10th   Wins: 0   Pole positions: 0   Fastest laps: 0   Points scored: 8

ret	BRAZILIAN GP	Rio	18	USF&G Arrows Megatron	G	1.5 t/c Arrows A10-Megatron 4	engine	14/23
ret	SAN MARINO GP	Imola	18	USF&G Arrows Megatron	G	1.5 t/c Arrows A10-Megatron 4	engine	10/27
4	BELGIAN GP	Spa	18	USF&G Arrows Megatron	G	1.5 t/c Arrows A10-Megatron 4	1 lap behind	11/26
ret	MONACO GP	Monte Carlo	18	USF&G Arrows Megatron	G	1.5 t/c Arrows A10-Megatron 4	head gasket	6/26
6/ret	US GP (DETROIT)	Detroit	18	USF&G Arrows Megatron	G	1.5 t/c Arrows A10-Megatron 4	out of fuel/3 laps behind	6/26
ret	FRENCH GP	Paul Ricard	18	USF&G Arrows Megatron	G	1.5 t/c Arrows A10-Megatron 4	knocked off ignition switch	14/26
ret	BRITISH GP	Silverstone	18	USF&G Arrows Megatron	G	1.5 t/c Arrows A10-Megatron 4	engine	14/26
ret	GERMAN GP	Hockenheim	18	USF&G Arrows Megatron	G	1.5 t/c Arrows A10-Megatron 4	throttle cable	15/26
8	HUNGARIAN GP	Hungaroring	18	USF&G Arrows Megatron	G	1.5 t/c Arrows A10-Megatron 4	hit Warwick – pit stops/-2 laps	11/26
ret	AUSTRIAN GP	Österreichring	18	USF&G Arrows Megatron	G	1.5 t/c Arrows A10-Megatron 4	puncture	12/26
ret	ITALIAN GP	Monza	18	USF&G Arrows Megatron	G	1.5 t/c Arrows A10-Megatron 4	driveshaft	13/28
6	PORTUGUESE GP	Estoril	18	USF&G Arrows Megatron	G	1.5 t/c Arrows A10-Megatron 4	2 laps behind	11/27
8/ret	SPANISH GP	Jerez	18	USF&G Arrows Megatron	G	1.5 t/c Arrows A10-Megatron 4	out of fuel	13/28
4	MEXICAN GP	Mexico City	18	USF&G Arrows Megatron	G	1.5 t/c Arrows A10-Megatron 4		12/27
9	JAPANESE GP	Suzuka	18	USF&G Arrows Megatron	G	1.5 t/c Arrows A10-Megatron 4	1 lap behind	13/27
ret	AUSTRALIAN GP	Adelaide	18	USF&G Arrows Megatron	G	1.5 t/c Arrows A10-Megatron 4	engine	11/27

1988 Championship position: 12th   Wins: 0   Pole positions: 0   Fastest laps: 0   Points scored: 6

8	BRAZILIAN GP	Rio	18	USF&G Arrows Megatron	G	1.5 t/c Arrows A10B-Megatron 4	1 lap behind	15/31
7	SAN MARINO GP	Imola	18	USF&G Arrows Megatron	G	1.5 t/c Arrows A10B-Megatron 4	1 lap behind	7/31
ret	MONACO GP	Monte Carlo	18	USF&G Arrows Megatron	G	1.5 t/c Arrows A10B-Megatron 4	electrics	9/30
6	MEXICAN GP	Mexico City	18	USF&G Arrows Megatron	G	1.5 t/c Arrows A10B-Megatron 4	1 lap behind	7/30
ret	CANADIAN GP	Montreal	18	USF&G Arrows Megatron	G	1.5 t/c Arrows A10B-Megatron 4	throttle return spring	8/31

Cheever had a three-year spell at Arrows, which was largely spent in midfield anonymity, before heading off to race in Indy cars and an eventual triumph in the 1998 Indianapolis 500.

ret	US GP (DETROIT)	Detroit	18	USF&G Arrows Megatron	G	1.5 t/c Arrows A10B-Megatron 4	engine		15/31
11	FRENCH GP	Paul Ricard	18	USF&G Arrows Megatron	G	1.5 t/c Arrows A10B-Megatron 4	handling/fuel problems/-2 laps		13/31
7	BRITISH GP	Silverstone	18	USF&G Arrows Megatron	G	1.5 t/c Arrows A10B-Megatron 4	1 lap behind		13/31
10	GERMAN GP	Hockenheim	18	USF&G Arrows Megatron	G	1.5 t/c Arrows A10B-Megatron 4	engine problems/1 lap behind		15/31
ret	HUNGARIAN GP	Hungaroring	18	USF&G Arrows Megatron	G	1.5 t/c Arrows A10B-Megatron 4	brakes		14/31
6*	BELGIAN GP	Spa	18	USF&G Arrows Megatron	G	1.5 t/c Arrows A10B-Megatron 4	*3rd & 4th cars dsq/1 lap behind		11/31
3	ITALIAN GP	Monza	18	USF&G Arrows Megatron	G	1.5 t/c Arrows A10B-Megatron 4			5/31
ret	PORTUGUESE GP	Estoril	18	USF&G Arrows Megatron	G	1.5 t/c Arrows A10B-Megatron 4	turbo		18/31
ret	SPANISH GP	Jerez	18	USF&G Arrows Megatron	G	1.5 t/c Arrows A10B-Megatron 4	handling		25/31
ret	JAPANESE GP	Suzuka	18	USF&G Arrows Megatron	G	1.5 t/c Arrows A10B-Megatron 4	turbo		15/31
ret	AUSTRALIAN GP	Adelaide	18	USF&G Arrows Megatron	G	1.5 t/c Arrows A10B-Megatron 4	engine		18/31

1989 Championship position: 11th=   Wins: 0   Pole positions: 0   Fastest laps: 0   Points scored: 6

ret	BRAZILIAN GP	Rio	10	USF&G Arrows	G	3.5 Arrows A11-Cosworth V8	hit by Schneider	24/38
9	SAN MARINO GP	Imola	10	USF&G Arrows	G	3.5 Arrows A11-Cosworth V8	broken exhaust/2 laps behind	21/39
7	MONACO GP	Monte Carlo	10	USF&G Arrows	G	3.5 Arrows A11-Cosworth V8	spun – collision – Arnoux/-2 laps	20/38
7	MEXICAN GP	Mexico City	10	USF&G Arrows	G	3.5 Arrows A11-Cosworth V8	1 lap behind	24/39
3	US GP (PHOENIX)	Phoenix	10	USF&G Arrows	G	3.5 Arrows A11-Cosworth V8	brakes fading at finish	17/39
ret	CANADIAN GP	Montreal	10	USF&G Arrows	G	3.5 Arrows A11-Cosworth V8	engine – electrics	16/39
7	FRENCH GP	Paul Ricard	10	USF&G Arrows	G	3.5 Arrows A11-Cosworth V8	1 lap behind	25/39
dnq	BRITISH GP	Silverstone	10	USF&G Arrows	G	3.5 Arrows A11-Cosworth V8		28/39
12/ret	GERMAN GP	Hockenheim	10	USF&G Arrows	G	3.5 Arrows A11-Cosworth V8	fuel pick-up/5 laps behind	25/39
5	HUNGARIAN GP	Hungaroring	10	USF&G Arrows	G	3.5 Arrows A11-Cosworth V8	lost 4th place on last lap	16/39
ret	BELGIAN GP	Spa	10	USF&G Arrows	G	3.5 Arrows A11-Cosworth V8	lost wheel/warned for baulking	24/39
dnq	ITALIAN GP	Monza	10	USF&G Arrows	G	3.5 Arrows A11-Cosworth V8		27/39
ret	PORTUGUESE GP	Estoril	10	USF&G Arrows	G	3.5 Arrows A11-Cosworth V8	engine cut out – crashed	26/39
ret	SPANISH GP	Jerez	10	USF&G Arrows	G	3.5 Arrows A11-Cosworth V8	engine	23/38
8*	JAPANESE GP	Suzuka	10	USF&G Arrows	G	3.5 Arrows A11-Cosworth V8	*1st place car dsq/1 lap behind	24/39
ret	AUSTRALIAN GP	Adelaide	10	USF&G Arrows	G	3.5 Arrows A11-Cosworth V8	spun off in rain	22/39

GP Starts: 132   GP Wins: 0   Pole positions: 0   Fastest laps: 0   Points: 70

CHIESA, Andrea (CH) b 6/5/1964, Milan

1992 Championship position: Unplaced

	Race	Circuit	No	Entrant	Tyres	Capacity/Car/Engine	Comment	Q Pos/Entries
dnq	SOUTH AFRICAN GP	Kyalami	14	Fondmetal	G	3.5 Fondmetal GR01-Ford HB V8		28/30
ret	MEXICAN GP	Mexico City	14	Fondmetal	G	3.5 Fondmetal GR01-Ford HB V8	spun off	23/30
dnq	BRAZILIAN GP	Interlagos	14	Fondmetal	G	3.5 Fondmetal GR01-Ford HB V8		27/31
ret	SPANISH GP	Barcelona	14	Fondmetal	G	3.5 Fondmetal GR01-Ford HB V8	spun off	20/32
dnq	SAN MARINO GP	Imola	14	Fondmetal	G	3.5 Fondmetal GR01-Ford HB V8		28/32
dnq	MONACO GP	Monte Carlo	14	Fondmetal	G	3.5 Fondmetal GR01-Ford HB V8		29/32
dnq	CANADIAN GP	Montreal	14	Fondmetal	G	3.5 Fondmetal GR01-Ford HB V8		29/32
ret	FRENCH GP	Magny Cours	14	Fondmetal	G	3.5 Fondmetal GR02-Ford HB V8	collision with Gugelmin on lap 1	26/30
dnq	BRITISH GP	Silverstone	14	Fondmetal	G	3.5 Fondmetal GR01-Ford HB V8		29/32
dnq	GERMAN GP	Hockenheim	14	Fondmetal	G	3.5 Fondmetal GR02-Ford HB V8		29/32

GP Starts: 3   GP Wins: 0   Pole positions: 0   Fastest laps: 0   Points: 0

ANDREA CHIESA

A SWISS national born in Milan, Andrea Chiesa spent five years in karts before making a solid start in Italian F3 in 1986. Despite being hampered by problems with his VW engine, he managed a couple of third places and a pole position in the season's finale, which caught the eye. For 1987, he switched team to Euroracing, thus gaining the ubiquitous Alfa power in his Dallara. He surged out of the blocks with three wins in the first four races, but then his season tailed off and Enrico Bertaggia pipped him to the title by five points.

Stepping up to F3000, Chiesa struggled in 1988, notching just a single point with the Cobra Motorsports Lola, but things improved the following year after a switch to Roni Motorsport, Running a Reynard-Ford, he won at Enna and finished second at Vallelunga to claim sixth in the final points standings.

Chiesa's third season in the formula, with Paul Stewart Racing, was much the same, and taking three second places and two sixths earned him seventh in the final table. Another change of team to Apotomax in 1991 was an utter disaster: he (and team-mate Paul Belmondo) failed to score even a point with the competitive Reynard. The Swiss driver was replaced by Frenchman Emmanuel Collard towards the end of the season.

Such are the vagaries of motor racing, however, that when the Formula 1 team line-ups were confirmed for 1992, Andrea was confirmed at Fondmetal. He was out of his depth, though, and his record of three starts (two spins, one collision) and seven DNQs tells the sorry tale. For Chiesa, the F1 dream was over.

Chiesa briefly reappeared in 1993, racing for the Euromotorsports team in the opening round of the Indy Car series at Surfers Paradise, Australia. Qualifying 19th out of 26 starters, he managed only two laps before an electrical failure sidelined his car. Pressure to return to the family business precluded further competition, but after three years away from the sport he briefly returned to the track in a Riley & Scott with Alex Caffi at Laguna Seca in 1996. The partnership was successfully renewed in 1998, when the pair scored a couple of third places in the ISRS series at the Paul Ricard and Le Mans (Bugatti) rounds.

In 2001, Chiesa made occasional appearances in sports and GT events, before he teamed up with ex-F1 driver Loris Kessel in his Ferrari 360 Modena at Spa the following year, when the pair won their class. This led to a fruitful partnership, the wealthy Kessel running the Ferrari in the Italian GT series. The Swiss duo won the championship in both 2003 and 2004, before switching to a Ferrari 575 in which they placed second and third overall in the next two seasons.

In 2007, Chiesa appeared at Le Mans in a GT2 Spyker C8 with Italian co-drivers Andrea Bellichi and Alex Caffi. The following year, he returned in the same car, but this time with an all-Swiss driver line-up, posting retirements on both occasions.

Still enjoying the cut and thrust of competition, Andrea then entered the Superstar series in 2009 with a Maserati Quattroporte. The Swiss team's car was overweight and in need of development, but he plugged away throughout the 2010 season. Just as things were looking up and the car was becoming more competitive, he was shocked to find that his services were no longer required mid-way through the 2011 season.

ETTORE CHIMERI

E TTORE CHIMERI was one of the local drivers who bolstered the grids for the two-race Temporada series when top-flight motorsport returned briefly to the Argentine in 1960. He failed to finish the championship race, but took the outdated Maserati 250F to fourth place in the Formula Libre Buenos Aires GP, admittedly, an event of huge attrition.

Tragically, two weeks later, Chimeri was killed in practice for a sports car race in Cuba.

CHIMERI, Ettore (I) b 4/6/1921, Lodi, nr Milan – d 27/2/1960, Cuba

1960 Championship position: Unplaced

	Race	Circuit	No	Entrant	Tyres	Capacity/Car/Engine	Comment	Q Pos/Entries
ret	ARGENTINE GP	Buenos Aires	44	Ettore Chimeri	D	2.5 Maserati 250F 6	electrics/driver exhaustion	21/22

GP Starts: 1   GP Wins: 0   Pole positions: 0   Fastest laps: 0   Points: 0

LOUIS CHIRON

THE bulk of Louis Chiron's long motor racing story falls outside the scope of this book, but it is worthwhile outlining his pre-world championship exploits, which began in the mid-1920s with a Bugatti, the make that would be synonymous with the first part of his career. The 1928 season saw him victorious in the Rome, Marne, Spanish and Italian GPs, with victories in the German and Spanish GPs following in 1929. He also took a Delage to compete at Indianapolis, finishing a creditable seventh after a long tyre stop. More success came in 1930, when he added the European and Lyons GPs to his tally, and in 1931, still with the Bugatti, he took a brilliant win in the Monaco GP and shared a French GP triumph with Achille Varzi.

Chiron was tempted away to Scuderia Ferrari for the 1933 season to race their Alfa Romeos, and he remained with them until 1936, when the might of Mercedes and Auto Union had become virtually irresistible. He cut down his racing almost to the point of retirement in the immediate pre-war years, although he did find time to win the 1937 French GP in a sports Talbot.

As soon as was practicable after the war, Chiron was out in his Talbot once more. Outright success eluded him in 1946, but he won the 1947 French GP at Montlhéry, a victory he would repeat at Reims two years later. In 1950 – the first season of the newly created world championship – Chiron campaigned a 4CLT Maserati without success, except for a fine third place in his native Monte Carlo. After just one grand prix the following season, he abandoned the Maserati in favour of the trusty old Lago-Talbot, but the car was generally unreliable. The 1952 season started with near disaster when he sustained serious burns after his Maserati-Platé caught fire at Syracuse. He did not compete for the rest of the season, but returned in 1953 at the wheel of the latest F2 OSCA, which, though attractive, failed to live up to his expectations.

At the start of the 1954 season, Chiron was 54 years old, but he still had not had enough of winning, and he finally triumphed in the Monte Carlo Rally in a Lancia. Invited to handle a works Lancia in the 1955 Monaco GP, he obliged with sixth place. When he finally retired, Prince Rainier asked him to run the Principality's two great events, which he did up until the 1979 Monaco Grand Prix, just a month before his death

CHIRON, Louis (MC) b 3/8/1899, Monte Carlo – d 22/6/1979, Monte Carlo

1950 Championship position: 9th= Wins: 0 Pole positions: 0 Fastest laps: 0 Points scored: 4

	Race	Circuit	No	Entrant	Tyres	Capacity/Car/Engine	Comment	Q Pos/Entries
ret	BRITISH GP	Silverstone	19	Officine Alfieri Maserati	P	1.5 s/c Maserati 4CLT/48 4	oil leak/clutch	11/21
3	MONACO GP	Monte Carlo	48	Officine Alfieri Maserati	P	1.5 s/c Maserati 4CLT/48 4	2 laps behind	8/21
9	SWISS GP	Bremgarten	26	Officine Alfieri Maserati	P	1.5 s/c Maserati 4CLT/48 4	3 laps behind	16/18
ret	FRENCH GP	Reims	30	Officine Alfieri Maserati	P	1.5 s/c Maserati 4CLT/48 4	engine	14/20
ret	ITALIAN GP	Monza	6	Officine Alfieri Msaerati	P	1.5 s/c Maserati 4CLT/48 4	oil pressure	19/27

1951 Championship position: Unplaced

7	SWISS GP	Bremgarten	30	Enrico Platé	P	1.5 s/c Maserati 4CLT/48 4	2 laps behind	19/21
ret	BELGIAN GP	Spa	18	Ecurie Rosier	D	4.5 Lago-Talbot T26C 6	engine	9/13
6	FRENCH GP	Reims	42	Ecurie Rosier	D	4.5 Lago-Talbot T26C 6	6 laps behind	8/23
ret	BRITISH GP	Silverstone	23	Ecurie Rosier	D	4.5 Lago-Talbot T26C 6	brakes	13/20
ret	GERMAN GP	Nürburgring	85	Ecurie Rosier	D	4.5 Lago-Talbot T26C 6	ignition/engine	13/23
ret	ITALIAN GP	Monza	20	Ecurie Rosier	D	4.5 Lago-Talbot T26C 6	ignition	17/22
ret	SPANISH GP	Pedralbes	30	Ecurie Rosier	D	4.5 Lago-Talbot T26C 6	engine	12/20

1953 Championship position: Unplaced

nc	FRENCH GP	Reims	32	Louis Chiron	P	2.0 OSCA 20 6	17 laps behind	25/25
dns	BRITISH GP	Silverstone	27	Louis Chiron	P	2.0 OSCA 20 6		– /29
dns	SWISS GP	Bremgarten	12	Louis Chiron	P	2.0 OSCA 20 6		– /23
10	ITALIAN GP	Monza	32	Louis Chiron	P	2.0 OSCA 20 6	8 laps behind	25/30

1955 Championship position: Unplaced

6	MONACO GP	Monte Carlo	32	Scuderia Lancia	P	2.5 Lancia D50 V8	5 laps behind	19/22

1956 Championship position: Unplaced

dns	MONACO GP	Monte Carlo	34	Scuderia Centro Sud	P	2.5 Maserati 250F 6	two blown engines in practice	– /19

1958 Championship position: Unplaced

dnq	MONACO GP	Monte Carlo	56	André Testut	P	2.5 Maserati 250F 6	practiced Testut's car	– / –

GP Starts: 15 GP Wins: 0 Pole positions: 0 Fastest laps: 0 Points: 4

JOHNNY CLAES

A BELGIAN born in Fulham, London, whose mother was Scottish, Johnny Claes' first passion was jazz, but he became involved in motor racing after a chance visit to the 1947 French Grand Prix, where his bilingualism allowed him to act as an interpreter to the English drivers.

Johnny's father was wealthy, so when he tried his hand at racing in 1948, a Talbot was duly ordered for him, which saw much service in both 1949 and 1950. However, his first real success came at the wheel of an HWM in the 1950 GP des Frontières at Chimay, a race he would win again the following season, this time in a Simca-Gordini.

With his Talbot effectively redundant following the adoption of Formula 2 regulations for world championship grands prix, Claes secured drives with the Gordini, HWM and Connaught teams during the 1952 and 1953 seasons. Although he found the competition tough at this level, he tasted real success in the 1953 Liège–Rome–Liège Rally, which he won despite having to drive the car single-handed for 52 hours after his co-driver was taken ill.

By 1954, Johnny was a sick man and he raced little, although a visit to Le Mans with a Porsche saw him finish 12th overall (with Pierre Stasser) and take victory in the 1500cc class.

He was more active in 1955, the highlight of his season being third place at Le Mans in the Ecurie Belgique Jaguar with Jacques Swaters. His last competitive event was the Liège–Rome–Liège Rally of that year, in which he took third place, partnered by Lucien Bianchi. After that his health deteriorated rapidly and, laid low by tuberculosis, he died in February, 1956, aged just 39.

CLAES, Johnny (B) b 11/8/1916, Fulham, London, England – d 3/2/1956, Brussels

1950 Championship position: Unplaced

	Race	Circuit	No	Entrant	Tyres	Capacity/Car/Engine	Comment	Q Pos/Entries
11	BRITISH GP	Silverstone	18	Ecurie Belge	D	4.5 Talbot-Lago T26C 6	6 laps behind	21/21
7	MONACO GP	Monte Carlo	6	Ecurie Belge	D	4.5 Talbot-Lago T26C 6	6 laps behind	19/21
10	SWISS GP	Bremgarten	4	Ecurie Belge	D	4.5 Talbot-Lago T26C 6	3 laps behind	14/18
8	BELGIAN GP	Spa	24	Ecurie Belge	D	4.5 Talbot-Lago T26C 6	3 laps behind	14/14
ret	FRENCH GP	Reims	42	Ecurie Belge	D	4.5 Talbot-Lago T26C 6	overheating	15/20
ret	ITALIAN GP	Monza	2	Ecurie Belge	D	4.5 Talbot-Lago T26C 6	overheating	22/27

1951 Championship position: Unplaced

	Race	Circuit	No	Entrant	Tyres	Capacity/Car/Engine	Comment	Q Pos/Entries
13	SWISS GP	Bremgarten	2	Ecurie Belge	D	4.5 Talbot-Lago T26C-DA 6	7 laps behind	18/21
7	BELGIAN GP	Spa	16	Ecurie Belge	D	4.5 Talbot-Lago T26C-DA 6	3 laps behind	11/13
ret	FRENCH GP	Reims	28	Ecurie Belge	D	4.5 Talbot-Lago T26C-DA 6	crashed into a house by circuit	12/23
13	BRITISH GP	Silverstone	25	Ecurie Belge	D	4.5 Talbot-Lago T26C-DA 6	10 laps behind	14/20
11	GERMAN GP	Nürburgring	94	Ecurie Belge	D	4.5 Talbot-Lago T26C-DA 6	3 laps behind	18/23
ret	ITALIAN GP	Monza	26	Ecurie Belge	D	4.5 Talbot-Lago T26C-DA 6	oil pump	21/22
ret	SPANISH GP	Pedralbes	36	Ecurie Belge	D	4.5 Talbot-Lago T26C-DA 6	hit straw bales	15/20

1952 Championship position: Unplaced

	Race	Circuit	No	Entrant	Tyres	Capacity/Car/Engine	Comment	Q Pos/Entries
8	BELGIAN GP	Spa	18	Equipe Gordini	E	2.0 Gordini Type 16S 6 sports	Formula 2 engine/3 laps behind	19/22
ret	FRENCH GP	Rouen	32	Ecurie Belge	E	1.5 Gordini Type 15 4	engine	19/20
14	BRITISH GP	Silverstone	27	Ecurie Belge	E	1.5 Gordini Type 15 4	6 laps behind	23/32
nc	GERMAN GP	Nürburgring	113	HW Motors Ltd	D	2.0 HWM-Alta 4	rear axle bearing/3 laps behind	32/32
dnq	ITALIAN GP	Monza	66	Vickomtesse de Walckiers	E	1.5 Gordini Type 15 4	no practice time set	– /35

1953 Championship position: Unplaced

	Race	Circuit	No	Entrant	Tyres	Capacity/Car/Engine	Comment	Q Pos/Entries
nc	DUTCH GP	Zandvoort	30	Ecurie Belge	E	2.0 Connaught A-Lea Francis 4	38 laps behind	17/20
ret	BELGIAN GP	Spa	6	Officine Alfieri Maserati	P	2.0 Maserati A6GCM 6	Fangio took over and then crashed	10/22
nc	FRENCH GP	Reims	48	Ecurie Belge	E	2.0 Connaught A-Lea Francis 4	7 laps behind	21/25
ret	GERMAN GP	Nürburgring	12	Ecurie Belge	E	2.0 Connaught A-Lea Francis 4		25/35
ret	ITALIAN GP	Monza	26	Ecurie Belge	E	2.0 Connaught A-Lea Francis 4	loose fuel line	30/30

1955 Championship position: Unplaced

	Race	Circuit	No	Entrant	Tyres	Capacity/Car/Engine	Comment	Q Pos/Entries
dns	BELGIAN GP	Spa	38	Stirling Moss Ltd	D	2.5 Maserati 250F 6	engine trouble in practice	14/14
nc	DUTCH GP	Zandvoort	30	Equipe Nationale Belge	E	2.5 Ferrari 500/625 4	22 laps behind	16/16

GP Starts: 23   GP Wins: 0   Pole positions: 0   Fastest laps: 0   Points: 0

JIM CLARK

IT really was a different era, the mid-1960s. There was no hype, the grand prix world was just a small close-knit community of rivals who were still friends, and the 'mega-buck' world of sponsorship was only just looming around the corner. Jim Clark's tragic death in a relatively meaningless Formula 2 race at Hockenheim on 7th April, 1968, was a savage blow to everyone connected with the sport, which from that day seemed to change: suddenly it was more of a business.

That Jimmy was not part of the new commercial order perversely seemed somehow fitting, yet in reality he was the supreme modern professional racing driver of his day, becoming a tax exile to maximise his earnings, and employing a manager to run his farming affairs back home in Scotland.

It was this well-off agricultural environment that provided the background to Clark's early motor racing activities – just minor rallies and trials to start with, before he graduated to the Porsche with which he began to make his name in 1958. Despite strong parental opposition, young Jimmy was soon racing for the Border Reivers in their Jaguar D-Type, a little Lotus Elite and the rather more potent Lister Jaguar with which he took 12 wins in the 1959 season. He agreed to drive for Aston Martin's grand prix team in 1960, but the project was delayed and he was released to Lotus for Formula 2 and Junior racing. However, once Lotus had him under contract, Colin Chapman lost no time in promoting him to the grand prix team, although the priority was the Junior championship, in which he tied for the title with Trevor Taylor. He was also committed to the Reivers sports car team, sharing the third-placed Aston Martin DBR 1 with Roy Salvadori in the Le Mans 24-hours, a race he disliked so much that he refused to participate in it after the Lotus 23 failed to pass scrutineering in 1962.

The 1961 season saw the introduction of the new 1.5-litre formula, and Clark could concentrate fully on the championship grands prix and the proliferation of lesser meetings that were organised. He took his first F1 win at Pau, but the year saw little luck come the Scotsman's way, culminating in the tragic collision with Wolfgang von Trips' Ferrari at Monza in September, from which he was fortunate indeed to emerge shocked, but unscathed. The end-of-season sunshine races in South Africa provided instant and welcome rehabilitation, however, with Jimmy winning the non-championship Rand, Natal and South African GPs.

For 1962, Chapman built the magnificent monocoque Lotus 25. Propelled by the Climax V8 engine and driven by Jimmy, it simply became the standard setter for the next three years. Much is made of the heartbreaking failure at East London, which cost Clark the championship, but that is harsh indeed on Graham Hill, who suffered equal bad luck earlier in the season and fully deserved the crown. There were no hiccoughs in 1963, though, as Jimmy scorched to the title, winning no fewer than seven championship grands prix and non-title races at Pau, Imola, Silverstone, Karlskoga and Oulton Park. Lotus also made their first assault on USAC racing, with Clark shaking Indianapolis to its roots with the funny little rear-engined car and taking second place on its first appearance. To prove this was no fluke, later in the season he won the Milwaukee 200. The revolution had truly begun.

Jimmy was still indisputably the man to beat in 1964, but unreliability, particularly with the new Lotus 33, saw the title pass to Surtees at the very last gasp in Mexico. Clark had thrilled the fans as never before, however, particularly those in Britain who were also lucky enough to watch him three-wheeling the Lotus Ford Cortina with such abandon.

Having seen the championship lost, Clark and Chapman were in no mood to face a repeat of their misfortunes in 1965, and after a highly successful winter Tasman series, which yielded five wins, their world championship rivals were subjected to the full onslaught of the car's performance and Jimmy's brilliance. Leaving aside Monaco (which he skipped to win the Indy 500), he won the first six grands prix of the season to put the outcome of the championship beyond doubt by August.

The new 3-litre formula for once found Chapman without a ready answer, Team Lotus having to make do with 2-litre Climax engines until the BRM H16s became available. This put Clark in the unusual position of an underdog, which made for a fascinating year, illuminated by superb drives at Zandvoort, where he used all his powers to pilot a sick car into third place, and at Watkins Glen, where he took the BRM H16 engine to its only championship victory. But, untypically, there were rare moments when he let his frustrations show, such as when he slid off in the wet at the Nürburgring.

The following year saw the advent of the Lotus 49-Cosworth V8, and Clark gave us the full repertoire of his bounteous gifts. That Denny Hulme won the championship seemed almost unimportant (yes, it really was different in those days!), for all eyes were on Clark. Moments that live fresh in the memory to this day for those lucky enough to have experienced them include a crushing win on the car's debut at Zandvoort; one of grand prix racing's greatest ever drives at Monza, where he made up almost a whole lap on the opposition only to run short of fuel on the last lap, having regained the lead; and his skill in bringing the car home at Watkins Glen with the rear suspension broken and the wheel angled drunkenly as he crossed the finish line.

The 1968 season began in typical Clark fashion, with an unruffled win in the South African Grand Prix to take his tally of world championship grand prix victories to 25, overhauling the legendary Juan Fangio's then record total. Little did the world suspect that he would never compete in a grand prix again. For after another enjoyable trip down-under, during which he won four Tasman races from seven starts, and a Formula 2 race at Barcelona, came Hockenheim...

Well over 40 years have passed since Clark's death, but he stands as one of the truly great drivers of any era. On the track, only Ayrton Senna and Michael Schumacher in modern times could compare, for both these drivers set the benchmark for their peers with performances that were often truly extraordinary. It is a shame that, while the brilliance of their performances has been captured for posterity, such were the times that the magnificence of Jimmy's career went largely unrecorded on moving film in any great detail. Indeed, interviews are also exceedingly rare, and thus those too young to have seen him race sadly will have to make do with very much second best by way of the written word.

CLARK, Jim (GB) b 4/3/1936, Kilmany, Fifeshire, Scotland – d 7/4/1968, Hockenheim Circuit, Germany

1960 Championship position: 8th=   Wins: 0   Pole positions: 0   Fastest laps: 0   Points scored: 8

	Race	Circuit	No	Entrant	Tyres	Capacity/Car/Engine	Comment	Q Pos/Entries
ret	DUTCH GP	Zandvoort	6	Team Lotus	D	2.5 Lotus 18-Climax 4	transmission	11/21
5	BELGIAN GP	Spa	18	Team Lotus	D	2.5 Lotus 18-Climax 4	2 laps behind	10/18
5	FRENCH GP	Reims	24	Team Lotus	D	2.5 Lotus 18-Climax 4	1 lap behind	10/23
16	BRITISH GP	Silverstone	8	Team Lotus	D	2.5 Lotus 18-Climax 4	pit stop – suspension/-9 laps	8/25
3	PORTUGUESE GP	Oporto	14	Team Lotus	D	2.5 Lotus 18-Climax 4		8/16
16	US GP	Riverside	12	Team Lotus	D	2.5 Lotus 18-Climax 4	hit Surtees – pit stop/-14 laps	5/23

1961 Championship position: 7th=   Wins: 0   Pole positions: 0   Fastest laps: 1   Points scored: 11

	Race	Circuit	No	Entrant	Tyres	Capacity/Car/Engine	Comment	Q Pos/Entries
10	MONACO GP	Monte Carlo	28	Team Lotus	D	1.5 Lotus 21-Climax 4	2 pit stops – plugs/11 laps behind	3/21
3	DUTCH GP	Zandvoort	15	Team Lotus	D	1.5 Lotus 21-Climax 4	FL	11/17
12	BELGIAN GP	Spa	34	Team Lotus	D	1.5 Lotus 21-Climax 4	2 pit stops – gear change/-6 laps	16/25
3	FRENCH GP	Reims	8	Team Lotus	D	1.5 Lotus 21-Climax 4		5/26
ret	BRITISH GP	Aintree	18	Team Lotus	D	1.5 Lotus 21-Climax 4	oil leak	8/30
4	GERMAN GP	Nürburgring	14	Team Lotus	D	1.5 Lotus 21-Climax 4		8/27
ret	ITALIAN GP	Monza	36	Team Lotus	D	1.5 Lotus 21-Climax 4	collision with von Trips	7/33
7	US GP	Watkins Glen	14	Team Lotus	D	1.5 Lotus 21-Climax 4	pit stop – clutch/14 laps behind	=5/19

1962 Championship position: 2nd   Wins: 3   Pole positions: 6   Fastest laps: 5   Points scored: 30

	Race	Circuit	No	Entrant	Tyres	Capacity/Car/Engine	Comment	Q Pos/Entries
9	DUTCH GP	Zandvoort	4	Team Lotus	D	1.5 Lotus 25-Climax V8	pit stop – clutch/10 laps behind	3/20
dns	"	"	4	Team Lotus	D	1.5 Lotus 24-Climax V8	practice only	- / -
ret	MONACO GP	Monte Carlo	18	Team Lotus	D	1.5 Lotus 25-Climax V8	clutch/FL	1/21
dns	"	" "	18	Team Lotus	D	1.5 Lotus 24-Climax V8	practice only	- / -
1	BELGIAN GP	Spa	16	Team Lotus	D	1.5 Lotus 25-Climax V8	FL	12/20
dns	"	"	16	Team Lotus	D	1.5 Lotus 24-Climax V8	practice only	- / -
ret	FRENCH GP	Rouen	12	Team Lotus	D	1.5 Lotus 25-Climax V8	suspension	1/17
dns	"	"	12	Team Lotus	D	1.5 Lotus 24-Climax V8	practice only	- / -
1	BRITISH GP	Aintree	20	Team Lotus	D	1.5 Lotus 25-Climax V8	FL	1/21
dns	"	"	20	Team Lotus	D	1.5 Lotus 24-Climax V8	practice only	- / -
4	GERMAN GP	Nürburgring	5	Team Lotus	D	1.5 Lotus 25-Climax V8	stalled on grid – last away	3/30
ret	ITALIAN GP	Monza	20	Team Lotus	D	1.5 Lotus 25-Climax V8	transmission	1/30
1	US GP	Watkins Glen	8	Team Lotus	D	1.5 Lotus 25-Climax V8	FL	1/20
ret	SOUTH AFRICAN GP	East London	1	Team Lotus	D	1.5 Lotus 25-Climax V8	oil leak/FL	1/17

1963 WORLD CHAMPION   Wins: 7   Pole positions: 7   Fastest laps: 6   Points scored: 73

	Race	Circuit	No	Entrant	Tyres	Capacity/Car/Engine	Comment	Q Pos/Entries
8/ret	MONACO GP	Monte Carlo	9	Team Lotus	D	1.5 Lotus 25-Climax V8	gear selection/22 laps behind	1/17
1	BELGIAN GP	Spa	1	Team Lotus	D	1.5 Lotus 25-Climax V8	FL	8/20
1	DUTCH GP	Zandvoort	6	Team Lotus	D	1.5 Lotus 25-Climax V8	FL	1/19
1	FRENCH GP	Reims	18	Team Lotus	D	1.5 Lotus 25-Climax V8	FL	1/21
dns	"	"	22	Team Lotus	D	1.5 Lotus 24-Climax V8	practice only	- / -
1	BRITISH GP	Silverstone	4	Team Lotus	D	1.5 Lotus 25-Climax V8		1/23
2	GERMAN GP	Nürburgring	3	Team Lotus	D	1.5 Lotus 25-Climax V8	engine on 7 cylinders	1/26
1	ITALIAN GP	Monza	8	Team Lotus	D	1.5 Lotus 25-Climax V8	FL	3/28
3	US GP	Watkins Glen	8	Team Lotus	D	1.5 Lotus 25-Climax V8	left on the grid – battery/FL/-1 lap	2/21
1	MEXICAN GP	Mexico City	8	Team Lotus	D	1.5 Lotus 25-Climax V8	FL	1/21
1	SOUTH AFRICAN GP	East London	1	Team Lotus	D	1.5 Lotus 25-Climax V8		1/21

1964 Championship position: 3rd   Wins: 3   Pole positions: 5   Fastest laps: 4   Points scored: 32

	Race	Circuit	No	Entrant	Tyres	Capacity/Car/Engine	Comment	Q Pos/Entries
4/ret	MONACO GP	Monte Carlo	12	Team Lotus	D	1.5 Lotus 25-Climax V8	engine/4 laps behind	1/20
1	DUTCH GP	Zandvoort	18	Team Lotus	D	1.5 Lotus 25-Climax V8	FL	2/18
1	BELGIAN GP	Spa	23	Team Lotus	D	1.5 Lotus 25-Climax V8		=6/20
dns	"	"	2	Team Lotus	D	1.5 Lotus 33-Climax V8	practice only	- / -
ret	FRENCH GP	Rouen	2	Team Lotus	D	1.5 Lotus 25-Climax V8	engine	1/17
dns	"	"	2	Team Lotus	D	1.5 Lotus 33-Climax V8	practice only	- / -
1	BRITISH GP	Brands Hatch	1	Team Lotus	D	1.5 Lotus 25-Climax V8	FL	1/25
dns	"	" "	1	Team Lotus	D	1.5 Lotus 33-Climax V8	practice only	- / -
ret	GERMAN GP	Nürburgring	1	Team Lotus	D	1.5 Lotus 33-Climax V8	engine	2/24
ret	AUSTRIAN GP	Zeltweg	1	Team Lotus	D	1.5 Lotus 33-Climax V8	driveshaft	3/20
ret	ITALIAN GP	Monza	8	Team Lotus	D	1.5 Lotus 25-Climax V8	engine	4/25
dns	"	"	8	Team Lotus	D	1.5 Lotus 33-Climax V8	practice only	- / -
ret	US GP	Watkins Glen	1	Team Lotus	D	1.5 Lotus 25-Climax V8	fuel injection/Spence took car	1/19
7/ret	"	" "	2	Team Lotus	D	1.5 Lotus 33-Climax V8	fuel starvation/Spence's car/FL	- / -
5/ret	MEXICAN GP	Mexico City	1	Team Lotus	D	1.5 Lotus 33-Climax V8	engine – oil leak/FL/1 lap behind	1/19
dns	"	"	1	Team Lotus	D	1.5 Lotus 25-Climax V8	practice only	- / -

1965 WORLD CHAMPION   Wins: 6   Pole positions: 6   Fastest laps: 6   Points scored: 54

	Race	Circuit	No	Entrant	Tyres	Capacity/Car/Engine	Comment	Q Pos/Entries
1	SOUTH AFRICAN GP	East London	5	Team Lotus	D	1.5 Lotus 33-Climax V8	FL	1/25
1	BELGIAN GP	Spa	17	Team Lotus	D	1.5 Lotus 33-Climax V8	FL	2/21
dns	"	"	17	Team Lotus	D	1.5 Lotus 25-Climax V8	practice only	- / -
1	FRENCH GP	Clermont Ferrand	6	Team Lotus	D	1.5 Lotus 25-Climax V8	FL	1/17
dns	"	" "	6	Team Lotus	D	1.5 Lotus 33-Climax V8	practice only	- / -
1	BRITISH GP	Silverstone	5	Team Lotus	D	1.5 Lotus 33-Climax V8		1/23
dns	"	"	77	Team Lotus	D	1.5 Lotus 25-Climax V8	practice only	- / -
1	DUTCH GP	Zandvoort	6	Team Lotus	D	1.5 Lotus 33-Climax V8	FL	=2/17
1	GERMAN GP	Nürburgring	1	Team Lotus	D	1.5 Lotus 33-Climax V8	FL	1/22
10/ret	ITALIAN GP	Monza	24	Team Lotus	D	1.5 Lotus 33-Climax V8	fuel pump/FL/12 laps behind	1/23
dns	"	"	28	Team Lotus	D	1.5 Lotus 25-Climax V8	practice only	- / -
ret	US GP	Watkins Glen	5	Team Lotus	D	1.5 Lotus 25-Climax V8	engine	2/18
dns	"	" "	6	Team Lotus	D	1.5 Lotus 25-Climax V8	practice only	- / -
ret	MEXICAN GP	Mexico City	5	Team Lotus	D	1.5 Lotus 33-Climax V8	engine	1/18

1966 Championship position: 6th   Wins: 0   Pole positions: 2   Fastest laps: 0   Points scored: 16

ret	MONACO GP	Monte Carlo	4	Team Lotus	F	2.0 Lotus 33-Climax V8	*suspension*	1/16
ret	BELGIAN GP	Spa	10	Team Lotus	F	2.1 Lotus 33-Climax V8	*engine*	10/18
dns	FRENCH GP	Reims	2	Team Lotus	F	2.0 Lotus 33-Climax V8	*hit in face by a bird in practice*	– / –
4	BRITISH GP	Brands Hatch	1	Team Lotus	F	2.0 Lotus 33-Climax V8	*pit stop – brakes/1 lap behind*	5/20
3	DUTCH GP	Zandvoort	6	Team Lotus	F	2.0 Lotus 33-Climax V8	*2 pit stops – water/2 laps behind*	=2/18
dns	"	"	8	Team Lotus	F	2.0 Lotus 33-BRM V8	*practice only*	– / –
ret	GERMAN GP	Nürburgring	1	Team Lotus	F	2.0 Lotus 33-Climax V8	*slid off road*	1/30
ret	ITALIAN GP	Monza	(20) 22	Team Lotus	F	3.0 Lotus 43-BRM H16	*gearbox (ran no. 20 in practice)*	3/22
1	US GP	Watkins Glen	1	Team Lotus	F	3.0 Lotus 43-BRM H16		2/19
dns	"	" "	1/2	Team Lotus	F	2.0 Lotus 33-Climax V8	*practice only*	– / –
ret	MEXICAN GP	Mexico City	1	Team Lotus	F	3.0 Lotus 43-BRM H16	*gearbox*	2/19

1967 Championship position: 3rd   Wins: 4   Pole positions: 6   Fastest laps: 5   Points scored: 41

ret	SOUTH AFRICAN GP	Kyalami	7	Team Lotus	F	3.0 Lotus 43-BRM H16	*engine*	3/18
ret	MONACO GP	Monte Carlo	12	Team Lotus	F	2.0 Lotus 33-Climax V8	*shock absorber/FL*	=4/18
1	DUTCH GP	Zandvoort	5	Team Lotus	F	3.0 Lotus 49-Cosworth V8	*FL*	8/17
6	BELGIAN GP	Spa	21	Team Lotus	F	3.0 Lotus 49-Cosworth V8	*pit stop – plugs/1 lap behind*	1/18
ret	FRENCH GP	Le Mans	6	Team Lotus	F	3.0 Lotus 49-Cosworth V8	*crown wheel and pinion*	4/15
1	BRITISH GP	Silverstone	5	Team Lotus	F	3.0 Lotus 49-Cosworth V8		1/21
ret	GERMAN GP	Nürburgring	3	Team Lotus	F	3.0 Lotus 49-Cosworth V8	*suspension*	1/25
ret	CANADIAN GP	Mosport Park	3	Team Lotus	F	3.0 Lotus 49-Cosworth V8	*wet ignition/FL*	1/19
3	ITALIAN GP	Monza	20	Team Lotus	F	3.0 Lotus 49-Cosworth V8	*out of fuel last lap when 1st/FL*	1/18
1	US GP	Watkins Glen	5	Team Lotus	F	3.0 Lotus 49-Cosworth V8	*despite rear suspension failure*	2/18
1	MEXICAN GP	Mexico City	5	Team Lotus	F	3.0 Lotus 49-Cosworth V8	*FL*	1/19

1968 Championship position: 11th   Wins: 1   Pole positions: 1   Fastest laps: 1   Points scored: 9

1	SOUTH AFRICAN GP	Kyalami	4	Team Lotus	F	3.0 Lotus 49-Cosworth V8	*FL*	1/23

GP Starts: 72   GP Wins: 25   Pole positions: 33   Fastest laps: 28   Points: 274

Jim Clark's 25th and final grand prix win came at Kyalami in 1968. It was also the last race for Lotus in their classic green and yellow livery.

PETER COLLINS' death at the Nürburgring in August, 1958, just two weeks after his wonderful performance at the British Grand Prix at Silverstone, left the racing world shocked. For although indisputably he was one of the fastest men around, he was also regarded as being one of the safest. Handsome and congenial, the young Collins graduated from the 500cc school, driving Coopers and then the JBS-Norton in 1951, both on the circuits and in hill-climbs, winning his class with BTD at Prescott and Shelsley Walsh.

With Formula 2 effectively becoming the premier racing class in 1952, John Heath of HWM signed the promising Collins to partner Stirling Moss and Lance Macklin in a three-car team that roamed the Continent over the next two seasons. Peter proved to be extremely quick, but the cars were fragile, and decent finishes were few and far between, although he managed a second place at Les Sables d'Olonne in 1952 and a third at the Eifelrennen the following year.

Collins' potential had been spotted by Aston Martin, who took him into their sports car squad with immediate results. Sharing a DB3 with Pat Griffiths, he won the 1952 BARC Goodwood nine-hours and the 1953 Tourist Trophy, and he achieved many other good results (including second places at Le Mans in 1955 with Paul Frère and in 1956 with Moss) in what would be a very happy association with the team.

In 1954, Peter was recruited by Tony Vandervell to drive his Ferrari 'Thinwall Special', with which he delighted British crowds in the popular Libre events of the day, winning at Snetterton and Goodwood. He was also one of the first to handle the new Vanwall Special, but at this stage it was still very much in its infancy. Having found him a constant thorn in their flesh in Libre racing, BRM signed him for a full season in 1955, but in the event their programme was behind schedule and mainly he raced the Owen team's Maserati 250F until the P25 was ready. Late in the year, he ran the new car in the Gold Cup at Oulton Park, where it proved staggeringly quick before he retired it, erroneously as it turned out, due to a lack of oil pressure.

Peter accepted the opportunity to join Ferrari in 1956 alongside the great Juan Fangio with glee, and 'the Maestro' would have a big influence on his racing. From then on, he began to take a much more serious attitude to his craft, though thankfully he never lost his fun-loving, light-hearted spirit off the track. For a new boy at the Scuderia, he settled in very quickly. After handing his machine to Fangio at Monaco, he took grand prix wins in Belgium and France, and then shared second place at Silverstone. Although he drew a blank at the Nürburgring, come the Italian GP at Monza he still had an outside chance of the championship. When Fangio was forced to retire his car early in the race, Peter was asked to hand over his car to the Argentinian at a pit stop, and he did so without hesitation, even though it meant the end of his own title bid. His actions were particularly appreciated by Enzo Ferrari, who had a special affection for the loyal Englishman from that moment on. However, the 1957 season was not one of the Scuderia's better ones, and Peter scored Formula 1 wins only in the relatively minor Syracuse and Naples grands prix, and third places in France and Germany, where Fangio put on such an unforgettable display.

The following season began promisingly for Collins with sports car victories in the Buenos Aires 1000km and the Sebring 12-hours, driving with Phil Hill. He had already raced the new Ferrari Dino 246 at the tail end of the previous year, finishing fourth in the Modena GP, and a win in the International Trophy race at Silverstone boded well for a Ferrari revival. Arriving at the Nürburgring for the German Grand Prix, Peter lay third in the championship standings, behind Mike Hawthorn and Moss, but in the race, with Tony Brooks leading in the Vanwall and Peter in hot pursuit, it seems he made a simple, but costly error of judgement, clipping a bank, which somersaulted the car at over 100mph over a hedge and into a field. The luckless Collins was hurled from his machine, suffering severe head injuries from which he died soon after in hospital in Bonn, without regaining consciousness.

Peter Collins put on a flawless display to win the 1958 British Grand Prix at Silverstone in the Ferrari 246 Dino V6. Two weeks later, he was killed in the German Grand Prix.

COLLINS, Peter (GB) b 6/11/1931, Kidderminster, Worcestershire – d 3/8/1958, Bonn, Germany

1952 Championship position: Unplaced

	Race	Circuit	No	Entrant	Tyres	Capacity/Car/Engine	Comment	Q Pos/Entries
ret	SWISS GP	Bremgarten	18	HW Motors Ltd	D	2.0 HWM-Alta 4	broken halfshaft – spun off	6/21
ret	BELGIAN GP	Spa	26	HW Motors Ltd	D	2.0 HWM-Alta 4	driveshaft	11/22
6	FRENCH GP	Rouen	22	HW Motors Ltd	D	2.0 HWM-Alta 4	7 laps behind	7/20
ret	BRITISH GP	Silverstone	29	HW Motors Ltd	D	2.0 HWM-Alta 4	ignition/crankshaft	14/32
dnq	GERMAN GP	Nürburgring	111	HW Motors Ltd	D	2.0 HWM-Alta 4	crankshaft – insufficient practice	-/32
dnq	ITALIAN GP	Monza	54	HW Motors Ltd	D	2.0 HWM-Alta 4		28/35

1953 Championship position: Unplaced

	Race	Circuit	No	Entrant	Tyres	Capacity/Car/Engine	Comment	Q Pos/Entries
8	DUTCH GP	Zandvoort	36	HW Motors Ltd	D	2.0 HWM-Alta 4	6 laps behind	16/20
ret	BELGIAN GP	Spa	26	HW Motors Ltd	D	2.0 HWM-Alta 4	clutch	16/22
13	FRENCH GP	Reims	28	HW Motors Ltd	D	2.0 HWM-Alta 4	8 laps behind	17/25
ret	BRITISH GP	Silverstone	2	HW Motors Ltd	D	2.0 HWM-Alta 4	spun off	23/29

1954 Championship position: Unplaced

	Race	Circuit	No	Entrant	Tyres	Capacity/Car/Engine	Comment	Q Pos/Entries
ret	BRITISH GP	Silverstone	20	G A Vandervell	P	2.3 Vanwall 4	cylinder head gasket	11/31
7	ITALIAN GP	Monza	10	G A Vandervell	P	2.4 Vanwall 4	5 laps behind	16/21
dns	SPANISH GP	Pedralbes	42	G A Vandervell	P	2.4 Vanwall 4	practice accident	– / –

1955 Championship position: Unplaced

	Race	Circuit	No	Entrant	Tyres	Capacity/Car/Engine	Comment	Q Pos/Entries
ret	BRITISH GP	Aintree	42	Owen Racing Organisation	D	2.5 Maserati 250F 6	clutch	24/25
ret	ITALIAN GP	Monza	32	Officine Alfieri Maserati	P	2.5 Maserati 250F 6	rear suspension	11/22

1956 Championship position: 3rd   Wins: 2   Pole positions: 0   Fastest laps: 0   Points scored: 25

	Race	Circuit	No	Entrant	Tyres	Capacity/Car/Engine	Comment	Q Pos/Entries
ret	ARGENTINE GP	Buenos Aires	36	Scuderia Ferrari	E	2.5 Ferrari 555 V8	collision with Piotti	9/15
2*	MONACO GP	Monte Carlo	26	Scuderia Ferrari	E	2.5 Lancia-Ferrari D50 V8	*Fangio took over	9/19
1	BELGIAN GP	Spa	8	Scuderia Ferrari	E	2.5 Lancia-Ferrari D50 V8		3/16
1	FRENCH GP	Reims	14	Scuderia Ferrari	E	2.5 Lancia-Ferrari D50 V8		3/20
ret	BRITISH GP	Silverstone	2	Scuderia Ferrari	E	2.5 Lancia-Ferrari D50 V8	oil pressure	4/28
2*	"	"	4	Scuderia Ferrari	E	2.5 Lancia-Ferrari D50 V8	*took de Portago's car/1 lap behind	– / –
ret	GERMAN GP	Nürburgring	2	Scuderia Ferrari	E	2.5 Lancia-Ferrari D50 V8	split fuel pipe	2/21
ret*	"	"	5	Scuderia Ferrari	E	2.5 Lancia-Ferrari D50 V8	*took de Portago's car/accident	– / –
2*	ITALIAN GP	Monza	26	Scuderia Ferrari	E	2.5 Lancia-Ferrari D50 V8	*Fangio took over car	7/26

1957 Championship position: 7th=   Wins: 0   Pole positions: 0   Fastest laps: 0   Points scored: 8

	Race	Circuit	No	Entrant	Tyres	Capacity/Car/Engine	Comment	Q Pos/Entries
ret	ARGENTINE GP	Buenos Aires	10	Scuderia Ferrari	E	2.5 Lancia-Ferrari D50 V8	clutch	5/16
6*	"	" "	18	Scuderia Ferrari	E	2.5 Lancia-Ferrari D50A V8	*Perdisa & von Trips co-drove/-2 laps	– / –
ret	MONACO GP	Monte Carlo	26	Scuderia Ferrari	E	2.5 Lancia-Ferrari 801 V8	accident with Moss & Hawthorn	2/21
dns	"	"	26	Scuderia Ferrari	E	2.5 Lancia-Ferrari D50A V8	practice only	– / –
3	FRENCH GP	Rouen	12	Scuderia Ferrari	E	2.5 Lancia-Ferrari 801 V8		5/15
ret	BRITISH GP	Aintree	12	Scuderia Ferrari	E	2.5 Lancia-Ferrari 801 V8	water leak/took Trintignant's car	8/19
4*	"	"	16	Scuderia Ferrari	E	2.5 Lancia-Ferrari 801 V8	*drove 4 laps – no points awarded	– / –
3	GERMAN GP	Nürburgring	7	Scuderia Ferrari	E	2.5 Lancia-Ferrari 801 V8		4/24
ret	ITALIAN GP	Monza	30	Scuderia Ferrari	E	2.5 Lancia-Ferrari 801 V8	engine	7/19

1958 Championship position: 5th=   Wins: 1   Pole positions: 0   Fastest laps: 0   Points scored: 14

	Race	Circuit	No	Entrant	Tyres	Capacity/Car/Engine	Comment	Q Pos/Entries
ret	ARGENTINE GP	Buenos Aires	18	Scuderia Ferrari	E	2.4 Ferrari Dino 246 V6	rear axle on grid	3/10
3	MONACO GP	Monte Carlo	36	Scuderia Ferrari	E	2.4 Ferrari Dino 246 V6		9/28
ret	DUTCH GP	Zandvoort	4	Scuderia Ferrari	E	2.4 Ferrari Dino 246 V6	gearbox seized – spun off	10/17
ret	BELGIAN GP	Spa	14	Scuderia Ferrari	E	2.4 Ferrari Dino 246 V6	engine – overheating	4/20
5	FRENCH GP	Reims	42	Scuderia Ferrari	E	2.4 Ferrari Dino 246 V6	out of fuel last lap	4/21
1	BRITISH GP	Silverstone	1	Scuderia Ferrari	E	2.4 Ferrari Dino 246 V6		6/21
ret	GERMAN GP	Nürburgring	2	Scuderia Ferrari	E	2.4 Ferrari Dino 246 V6	fatal accident	4/26

GP Starts: 32   GP Wins: 3   Pole positions: 0   Fastest laps: 0   Points: 47

BERNARD COLLOMB

A FORMER motorcycle racer from Nice, Bernard Collomb acquired a Cooper-Climax Formula 2 car that he raced briefly in 1960, embarking on a more ambitious programme of F1 races the following year. Fourth at Vienna and sixth at Naples were his best results in the car, which was replaced in mid-season by a new Cooper T53 with no discernible improvement in his results. Unfortunately, this car was burnt out in practice for the 1962 Brussels GP, but Bernard reappeared in mid-1962 with another Cooper, achieving fifth place in the Mediterranean GP at Enna.

Then Collomb bought himself a Lotus 24-Climax V8 for 1963, but he was ill-equipped to drive it to its full potential. It was given occasional unsuccessful outings in 1964, before being destroyed by fire on the way back to France from the 1965 Syracuse GP, where he had finished seventh. A Lotus 35 F2 car was then purchased, which again saw little action after he crashed it in the 1966 Barcelona F2 race. By the 1968 season, he had wisely given up thoughts of success in single-seaters and could be found racing the little Alpine GT car.

COLLOMB, Bernard (F) b 7/10/1930, Annecy – d 19/9/2011, La Colle-sur-Loup

1961	Championship position: Unplaced							
	Race	Circuit	No	Entrant	Tyres	Capacity/Car/Engine	Comment	Q Pos/Entries
ret	FRENCH GP	Reims	52	Bernard Collomb	D	1.5 Cooper T53-Climax 4	valve	21/26
ret	GERMAN GP	Nürburgring	38	Bernard Collomb	D	1.5 Cooper T53-Climax 4	engine	26/27
1962	Championship position: Unplaced							
ret	GERMAN GP	Nürburgring	31	Bernard Collomb	D	1.5 Cooper T53-Climax 4	gearbox	22/30
1963	Championship position: Unplaced							
dnq	MONACO GP	Monte Carlo	24	Bernard Collomb	D	1.5 Lotus 24-Climax V8		17/17
10	GERMAN GP	Nürburgring	28	Bernard Collomb	D	1.5 Lotus 24-Climax V8	5 laps behind	21/26
1964	Championship position: Unplaced							
dnq	MONACO GP	Monte Carlo	3	Bernard Collomb	D	1.5 Lotus 24-Climax V8		20/20

GP Starts: 4   GP Wins: 0   Pole positions: 0   Fastest laps: 0   Points: 0

ÉRIK COMAS

WITH Jean Alesi and Éric Bernard, Érik Comas is one of a trio of French drivers whose careers were closely intertwined as they made inexorable progress into Formula 1 along the French motor racing conveyor-belt, but ultimately only Alesi stayed the course.

A French karting champion in 1983, Comas was soon sampling cars, racing a Renault 5 previously driven by Alesi, with which he won the Volant Elf at Paul Ricard, then moving up to Formule Renault as number two to Bernard in 1985. Scoring consistently, he finished second on points to his team-mate, but only fourth overall after his lowest scores had been discounted, but he made no mistake a year later.

This led to a seat in the Winfield team in the national Formula 3 series in 1987, but Comas found himself as number two to Bernard once more and was somewhat overshadowed, although he did finish sixth in the final placings. For 1988, he was chosen to lead the ORECA team, normally an absolute guarantee of success in French F3. He delivered, but only just, pipping Éric Cheli to the title after a fraught season spent developing the

team's Dallara. However, the job was done and once again he followed Bernard on the upward path, joining him in the DAMS F3000 team for the 1989 season. After a slow start, Comas soon shone and by the season's end, it was his turn to outshine his team-mate. Two wins at Le Mans and another at Dijon brought him level with Alesi at the top of the points standings, but Jean was champion by virtue of an extra win. Érik finished the job in 1990; still with DAMS, but now number-one driver, he won four of the 11 rounds to clinch the title, and now he was ready for Formula 1.

On paper, a two-year contract with Ligier alongside the experienced Thierry Boutsen seemed to be ideal. The first season with the Lamborghini-engined car would allow Érik a chance to learn the ropes, and the second, 1992, with Renault power, would put him in the front rank. Best-laid plans do not always work out, however, and with the team already split into factions, any potential assets it held had been dissipated, while his working relationship with Boutsen was such that they were barely on speaking terms.

For the 1993 and 1994 seasons, he found refuge in the Larrousse team, making the best of a car run on very meagre resources. His sixth place at Monza in '93 was a fine achievement, but with the shortage of top seats in Formula 1 and a whole new generation of chargers knocking on the door, Comas had missed his big chance to make it to the very top. Personally he felt that Elf, who do so much for French drivers in the junior formulas, should have insisted that at least one of his compatriots be given an opportunity in a front-running team.

Subsequently. Érik found employment (and immediate success) driving in the All-Japan GT Championship in a Toyota Supra in 1996, which led to an offer by Nissan to race their Skyline GT model alongside Aguri Suzuki in 1997. He rapidly became a key member of the NISMO team and was crowned All-Japan GT champion in 1998 and 1999. He was also involved with the TWR-run Nissan prototype challenge, finishing sixth at Le Mans in 1998 with the R390 and winning the Fuji 1000km (with Satoshi Motoyama and Yukio Kagayama) in 1999 with the R391.

Comas became a mainstay in the All-Japan GT Championship, campaigning the NISMO-Nissan since 2000 (with the exception of 2003, when he raced for TOMS Toyota). In 2005, he returned to Europe to race for Pescarolo Sport, taking the prototype to second place at Le Mans and sharing the driving duties with Jean-Christophe Boullion and Rob Collard.

In 2000, Érik founded CRM (Comas Race Management), which provided television coverage of Super GT racing in Japan to European viewers. The following year, he expanded into the field of driver management, and in 2007 his company handled the careers of Stéphane Sarrazin, Loic Duval, André Couto and Ronnie Quintarelli.

After retiring from competition in 2006, Érik founded Comas Historic Racing, which allows customers to compete in historic rallies, and he also became involved in the world of electric cars, winning this special category in the Monte Carlo Alternative Energy Rally in both 2010 and 2011.

COMAS, Érik (F) b 28/9/1963, Romans, nr Valence

1991 Championship position: Unplaced

	Race	Circuit	No	Entrant	Tyres	Capacity/Car/Engine	Comment	Q Pos/Entries
dnq	US GP (PHOENIX)	Phoenix	26	Ligier Gitanes	G	3.5 Ligier JS35-Lamborghini V12		27/34
ret	BRAZILIAN GP	Interlagos	26	Ligier Gitanes	G	3.5 Ligier JS35-Lamborghini V12	spun off	23/34
10	SAN MARINO GP	Imola	26	Ligier Gitanes	G	3.5 Ligier JS35-Lamborghini V12	4 laps behind	19/34
10	MONACO GP	Monte Carlo	26	Ligier Gitanes	G	3.5 Ligier JS35-Lamborghini V12	2 laps behind	23/34
8	CANADIAN GP	Montreal	26	Ligier Gitanes	G	3.5 Ligier JS35-Lamborghini V12	1 lap behind	26/34
dnq	MEXICAN GP	Mexico City	26	Ligier Gitanes	G	3.5 Ligier JS35-Lamborghini V12		27/34
11	FRENCH GP	Magny Cours	26	Ligier Gitanes	G	3.5 Ligier JS35B-Lamborghini V12	2 laps behind	14/34
dnq	BRITISH GP	Silverstone	26	Ligier Gitanes	G	3.5 Ligier JS35B-Lamborghini V12		27/34
ret	GERMAN GP	Hockenheim	26	Ligier Gitanes	G	3.5 Ligier JS35B-Lamborghini V12	engine – oil pressure	26/34
10	HUNGARIAN GP	Hungaroring	26	Ligier Gitanes	G	3.5 Ligier JS35B-Lamborghini V12	2 laps behind	25/34
ret	BELGIAN GP	Spa	26	Ligier Gitanes	G	3.5 Ligier JS35B-Lamborghini V12	engine	26/34
11	ITALIAN GP	Monza	26	Ligier Gitanes	G	3.5 Ligier JS35B-Lamborghini V12	1 lap behind	22/34
11	PORTUGUESE GP	Estoril	26	Ligier Gitanes	G	3.5 Ligier JS35B-Lamborghini V12	1 lap behind	23/34
ret	SPANISH GP	Barcelona	26	Ligier Gitanes	G	3.5 Ligier JS35B-Lamborghini V12	electrics	25/33
ret	JAPANESE GP	Suzuka	26	Ligier Gitanes	G	3.5 Ligier JS35B-Lamborghini V12	alternator	20/31
18	AUSTRALIAN GP	Adelaide	26	Ligier Gitanes	G	3.5 Ligier JS35B-Lamborghini V12	rain-shortened race/1 lap behind	22/32

1992 Championship position: 11th   Wins: 0   Pole positions: 0   Fastest laps: 0   Points scored: 4

	Race	Circuit	No	Entrant	Tyres	Capacity/Car/Engine	Comment	Q Pos/Entries
7	SOUTH AFRICAN GP	Kyalami	26	Ligier Gitanes Blondes	G	3.5 Ligier JS37-Renault V10	lack of downforce/2 laps behind	13/30
9	MEXICAN GP	Mexico City	26	Ligier Gitanes Blondes	G	3.5 Ligier JS37-Renault V10	2 laps behind	26/30
ret	BRAZILIAN GP	Interlagos	26	Ligier Gitanes Blondes	G	3.5 Ligier JS37-Renault V10	engine	15/31
ret	SPANISH GP	Barcelona	26	Ligier Gitanes Blondes	G	3.5 Ligier JS37-Renault V10	spun off	10/32
9	SAN MARINO GP	Imola	26	Ligier Gitanes Blondes	G	3.5 Ligier JS37-Renault V10	2 laps behind	13/32
10	MONACO GP	Monte Carlo	26	Ligier Gitanes Blondes	G	3.5 Ligier JS37-Renault V10	2 laps behind	23/32
6	CANADIAN GP	Montreal	26	Ligier Gitanes Blondes	G	3.5 Ligier JS37-Renault V10	1 lap behind	22/32
5	FRENCH GP	Magny Cours	26	Ligier Gitanes Blondes	G	3.5 Ligier JS37-Renault V10	1 lap behind	10/30
8	BRITISH GP	Silverstone	26	Ligier Gitanes Blondes	G	3.5 Ligier JS37-Renault V10	1 lap behind	10/32
6	GERMAN GP	Hockenheim	26	Ligier Gitanes Blondes	G	3.5 Ligier JS37-Renault V10		7/32
ret	HUNGARIAN GP	Hungaroring	26	Ligier Gitanes Blondes	G	3.5 Ligier JS37-Renault V10	collision with Boutsen lap 1	11/31
dns	BELGIAN GP	Spa	26	Ligier Gitanes Blondes	G	3.5 Ligier JS37-Renault V10	accident in untimed practice	– /31
ret	ITALIAN GP	Monza	26	Ligier Gitanes Blondes	G	3.5 Ligier JS37-Renault V10	spun off	15/28
ret	PORTUGUESE GP	Estoril	26	Ligier Gitanes Blondes	G	3.5 Ligier JS37-Renault V10	over-revved engine	14/26
ret	JAPANESE GP	Suzuka	26	Ligier Gitanes Blondes	G	3.5 Ligier JS37-Renault V10	engine – oil pressure	8/26
ret	AUSTRALIAN GP	Adelaide	26	Ligier Gitanes Blondes	G	3.5 Ligier JS37-Renault V10	over-revved engine	9/26

1993 Championship position: 20th=   Wins: 0   Pole positions: 0   Fastest laps: 0   Points scored: 1

	Race	Circuit	No	Entrant	Tyres	Capacity/Car/Engine	Comment	Q Pos/Entries
ret	SOUTH AFRICAN GP	Kyalami	20	Larrousse F1	G	3.5 Larrousse LH93-Lamborghini V12	engine	19/26
10	BRAZILIAN GP	Interlagos	20	Larrousse F1	G	3.5 Larrousse LH93-Lamborghini V12	stop & go penalty/2 laps behind	17/26
9	EUROPEAN GP	Donington	20	Larrousse F1	G	3.5 Larrousse LH93-Lamborghini V12	4 laps behind	17/26
ret	SAN MARINO GP	Imola	20	Larrousse F1	G	3.5 Larrousse LH93-Lamborghini V12	no oil pressure	17/26
9	SPANISH GP	Barcelona	20	Larrousse F1	G	3.5 Larrousse LH93-Lamborghini V12	2 laps behind	14/26
ret	MONACO GP	Monte Carlo	20	Larrousse F1	G	3.5 Larrousse LH93-Lamborghini V12	collision with Brundle	10/26
8	CANADIAN GP	Montreal	20	Larrousse F1	G	3.5 Larrousse LH93-Lamborghini V12	1 lap behind	13/26
16/ret	FRENCH GP	Magny Cours	20	Larrousse F1	G	3.5 Larrousse LH93-Lamborghini V12	gearbox/6 laps behind	9/26
ret	BRITISH GP	Silverstone	20	Larrousse F1	G	3.5 Larrousse LH93-Lamborghini V12	driveshaft at start	17/26
ret	GERMAN GP	Hockenheim	20	Larrousse F1	G	3.5 Larrousse LH93-Lamborghini V12	clutch at start	16/26
ret	HUNGARIAN GP	Hungaroring	20	Larrousse F1	G	3.5 Larrousse LH93-Lamborghini V12	oil leak	18/26
ret	BELGIAN GP	Spa	20	Larrousse F1	G	3.5 Larrousse LH93-Lamborghini V12	fuel pump/oil pressure	19/25
6	ITALIAN GP	Monza	20	Larrousse F1	G	3.5 Larrousse LH93-Lamborghini V12	2 laps behind	20/26
11	PORTUGUESE GP	Estoril	20	Larrousse F1	G	3.5 Larrousse LH93-Lamborghini V12	3 laps behind	22/26
ret	JAPANESE GP	Suzuka	20	Larrousse F1	G	3.5 Larrousse LH93-Lamborghini V12	engine	21/24
12	AUSTRALIAN GP	Adelaide	20	Larrousse F1	G	3.5 Larrousse LH93-Lamborghini V12	3 laps behind	21/24

1994 Championship position: 23rd   Wins: 0   Pole positions: 0   Fastest laps: 0   Points scored: 2

	Race	Circuit	No	Entrant	Tyres	Capacity/Car/Engine	Comment	Q Pos/Entries
9	BRAZILIAN GP	Interlagos	20	Tourtel Larrousse F1	G	3.5 Larrousse LH94-Ford HB V8	3 laps behind	13/28
6	PACIFIC GP	T.I. Circuit	20	Tourtel Larrousse F1	G	3.5 Larrousse LH94-Ford HB V8	collision – pit stop/2 laps behind	16/28
ret	SAN MARINO GP	Imola	20	Tourtel Larrousse F1	G	3.5 Larrousse LH94-Ford HB V8	did not take part in restart	18/28
10	MONACO GP	Monte Carlo	20	Tourtel Larrousse F1	G	3.5 Larrousse LH94-Ford HB V8	lost clutch/3 laps behind	13/24
ret	SPANISH GP	Barcelona	20	Tourtel Larrousse F1	G	3.5 Larrousse LH94-Ford HB V8	water leak	16/27
ret	CANADIAN GP	Montreal	20	Tourtel Larrousse F1	G	3.5 Larrousse LH94-Ford HB V8	clutch	21/27
ret	FRENCH GP	Magny Cours	20	Tourtel Larrousse F1	G	3.5 Larrousse LH94-Ford HB V8	engine	20/28
ret	BRITISH GP	Silverstone	20	Tourtel Larrousse F1	G	3.5 Larrousse LH94-Ford HB V8	engine	22/28
6	GERMAN GP	Hockenheim	20	Tourtel Larrousse F1	G	3.5 Larrousse LH94-Ford HB V8		22/28
8	HUNGARIAN GP	Hungaroring	20	Tourtel Larrousse F1	G	3.5 Larrousse LH94-Ford HB V8	2 laps behind	21/28
ret	BELGIAN GP	Spa	20	Tourtel Larrousse F1	G	3.5 Larrousse LH94-Ford HB V8	engine	22/28
8	ITALIAN GP	Monza	20	Tourtel Larrousse F1	G	3.5 Larrousse LH94-Ford HB V8	1 lap behind	24/28
ret	PORTUGUESE GP	Estoril	20	Tourtel Larrousse F1	G	3.5 Larrousse LH94-Ford HB V8	accident	22/28
ret	EUROPEAN GP	Jerez	20	Tourtel Larrousse F1	G	3.5 Larrousse LH94-Ford HB V8	electrics	23/28
9	JAPANESE GP	Suzuka	20	Tourtel Larrousse F1	G	3.5 Larrousse LH94-Ford HB V8	1 lap behind	22/28

GP Starts: 59   GP Wins: 0   Pole positions: 0   Fastest laps: 0   Points: 7

COMOTTI, Gianfranco (I) b 24/7/1906, Brescia – d 10/5/1963, Bergamo

1950 Championship position: Unplaced

	Race	Circuit	No	Entrant	Tyres	Capacity/Car/Engine	Comment	Q Pos/Entries
ret	ITALIAN GP	Monza	62	Scuderia Milano	P	1.5 s/c Maserati Milano-Speluzzi 4	engine	26/27

1952 Championship position: Unplaced

12	FRENCH GP	Rouen	38	Scuderia Marzotto	P	2.0 Ferrari 166 V12	14 laps behind	18/20

GP Starts: 2   GP Wins: 0   Pole positions: 0   Fastest laps: 0   Points: 0

GIANFRANCO COMOTTI

THE best days of Gianfranco Comotti's career were before the Second World War, when he raced an Alfa Romeo and a Lago-Talbot with some success. He won the 1933 Naples GP in the former and came close to winning the 1937 French GP at Reims in the latter. After leading for a while, he finally had to settle for second place, behind Louis Chiron. After hostilities had ceased, Comotti made a return to competition, moving to France to join the Ecurie France team and race their Lago-Talbots. Although these trusty machines were certainly not the fleetest, they were reliable, and he took one into fourth place in the 1948 French GP, some nine miles adrift of the winner. He also finished seventh in the Italian GP in Turin.

Back in Italy, Comotti linked up with the Ruggeri brothers to race their latest Maserati-based Milano car in 1950, but due to a lack of funds these machines were never properly developed and he left to join Scuderia Marzotto. In 1951, he finished second at Grenzlandring in a Ferrari 166 F2, and the following year he raced even more regularly for the team, third in the Naples GP and sixth at Syracuse being his best finishes. Franco also made a one-off Maserati appearance for the Escuderia Bandeirantes at AVUS, before bringing his career, which had lasted for more than two decades, to a close. Subsequently, he worked on the Continent with oil and petroleum giant BP.

GEORGE CONSTANTINE

A VERY successful driver in SCCA events, Constantine drove his production Jaguar XK120 in East Coast races in the early 1950s. Then he progressed to more powerful machinery, winning the 1956 Watkins Glen GP in a Jaguar D-Type. The 1959 season was his best, and he scored many wins in an Aston Martin DBR2, including the Nassau Trophy, to earn the USSC Driver of the Year award with Walt Hansgen.

It was not surprising, therefore, that Constantine was one of the local attractions in the inaugural US Grand Prix at Sebring in a rented Cooper.

Constantine's career continued into the early 1960s, the veteran driving a Kelso-Lister Chevy (known as a 'Kelischev') with verve in both East and West Coast events

Switching to a Ferrari, Constantine was sixth (and class winner) in a 246S (with Jim Hall), and in the John Bunch-owned Ferrari 250TR he won that year's Watkins Glen Grand Prix. In the same machine, he was fifth (and class winner) in the 1962 Daytona Continental three-hour race with Gaston Audrey. After dropping out of the Sebring 12-hour race a month later, he called time on his career.

JOHN CORDTS

JOHN CORDTS was born in Germany, but grew up in Sweden, before moving to Canada with his wife and first child. He enjoyed some success in the mid-1960s racing sports cars in Canada. He took a fifth place in the 1966 Player's 200 at Mosport, and once he got his hands on a McLaren M2B, results in the USRRC championship improved. A couple of outings in Can-Am in 1968 encouraged him to become a regular in this series between 1969 and 1974, driving a succession of Chevrolet-powered McLarens.

Cordts' best result by far was a second place in the Road America round at Elkhart Lake in 1974, but by then the once vibrant series had lost much of its credibility. He also took part in numerous Trans-Am events with a Pontiac Firebird.

After retiring to Western Canada, Cordt became well known for his beautiful wood carvings; recently he wrote his autobiography, entitled *Blood, Sweat and Turnips*.

CONSTANTINE, George (USA) b 22/2/1918, Southbridge, Massachusetts – d 7/1/1968, Massachusets

1959	Championship position: Unplaced							
	Race	Circuit	No	Entrant	Tyres	Capacity/Car/Engine	Comment	Q Pos/Entries
ret	US GP	Sebring	16	Mike Taylor	D	2.5 Cooper T45-Climax 4	head gasket	15/19

GP Starts: 1 GP Wins: 0 Pole positions: 0 Fastest laps: 0 Points: 0

CORDTS, John (CDN) b 23/7/1935, Hamburg, Germany

1969	Championship position: Unplaced							
	Race	Circuit	No	Entrant	Tyres	Capacity/Car/Engine	Comment	Q Pos/Entries
ret	CANADIAN GP	Mosport Park	26	Paul Seitz	D	2.7 Brabham BT23B-Climax 4	oil leak	19/20

GP Starts: 1 GP Wins: 0 Pole positions: 0 Fastest laps: 0 Points: 0

DAVID COULTHARD

DESPITE being a 13-time winner and the scorer of more than 500 championship points, sadly David Coulthard was never a world champion. The equable Scot must look back on his long and very successful Formula 1 career perhaps just a little wistfully. Is he a case of what might have been?

With great parental encouragement, Coulthard was driving karts by the age of eight and was such a natural that it was inevitable that he would go racing seriously. His breakthrough came in 1989, with his move into Junior Formula Ford 1600. He dominated both championships, then joined Paul Stewart Racing in 1990 to contest the British Vauxhall Lotus Challenge and GM Lotus Euroseries. He might have won the former, but a broken leg sustained in an accident at Spa stymied the young Scot's chances, and he ended up a disappointed fourth overall. Staying with PSR in 1991, he moved up to F3 and waged a season-long battle, before just losing out to Rubens Barrichello. There was, however, the satisfaction of winning the prestigious European Marlboro Masters of F3 race at Zandvoort, and he followed this up with a stunning drive to win the end-of-season race at Macau – proof indeed that David was a true star in the making.

Coulthard took the step up to F3000 for 1992, and for a while struggled to find his feet, but by the end of the year he was on the podium and looking a good bet for honours in 1993, when he switched to the Pacific team. A first win was duly delivered at Enna, but his season tailed off somewhat thereafter. By then, he had had a number of outings as a test driver for the Williams-Renault team, and he quickly impressed with his positive feedback. He was appointed the team's official test driver for 1994 and was contemplating a third year in F3000 when the dreadful news of Ayrton Senna's death came from Imola. As a result, David stepped into the grand prix arena and, in the inevitable turmoil that followed, displayed remarkable maturity for one so inexperienced.

Relaxed and easy off track, David showed tremendous poise behind the wheel. Always aware of the need for him to back Damon Hill's title bid, he was the perfect team-mate and, given his performances, must have been disappointed to have to surrender his seat to Nigel Mansell for the last three races of the year. The uncertainty regarding his immediate future was clearly unsettling, and he hedged his bets by signing a contract with McLaren for 1995. In the event, a tribunal confirmed that he would remain at Williams, but his early-season form was decidedly patchy. He was constantly troubled by tonsillitis, and it was only after his tonsils were removed that his real ability became apparent. He would have won the British Grand Prix but for a stop-go penalty incurred through no fault of his own, but his dream of a grand prix win was finally realised with a truly dominant performance at Estoril. On the debit side, though, he tended to make a number of elementary mistakes that cost him dear, culminating in the embarrassment of sliding into the wall on the pit-lane entry in Adelaide.

David eventually moved to McLaren for 1996, but experienced a difficult first season with the team. Uncomfortable with the handling of the car, he was often a tad slower than team-mate Mika Häkkinen and, apart from being unlucky not to win in Monaco, generally delivered less than he promised. The 1997 season began with a win in Australia, which signified that McLaren were back after three lean years, and it was generally a more convincing campaign for the Scot. He was evenly matched with Häkkinen and, having scored another victory at Monza, stepped aside to allow his team-mate to win the season's finale at Jerez.

Coulthard did the same in the 1998 Australian Grand Prix, following a pre-race agreement, but in some ways it proved to be his undoing. Häkkinen upped his game as the season progressed to mount his successful championship bid and David, with just a single win at Imola, was left to play the subordinate role in the team. This pattern continued in 1999, Coulthard rarely making the absolute most of his equipment. On his day,

he had the legs of everybody – no one could catch him at Spa, Magny-Cours or Sepang – but only the first of these races earned him the win he deserved. McLaren kept both drivers for 2000 and, as previously, the Scot harboured hopes that this would be his year. Despite never qualifying outside the top four, however, ultimately he was beaten by both his team-mate and the eventual champion, Michael Schumacher, following a run of relatively poor finishes late in the year.

The 2001 campaign brought similar optimistic claims from the Coulthard camp. The Scot, charged with much of the pre-season testing of the new MP4-16, remained confident that he could take the championship fight to Schumacher and Ferrari. Having recorded wins in Brazil and Austria, he appeared to be in a strong championship position, but things began to unravel at Monaco where, after he had taken a superb pole position, his car failed to start on the grid. Left to begin his race from the back of the field, he was bottled up for much of the time behind Enrique Bernoldi's Arrows, which destroyed his chances of at least rescuing a podium finish. Out of the top two until Belgium – while Schumacher took four wins – David was forced to fight it out with Rubens Barrichello for the runner-up slot and his best ever finish in the title race.

McLaren freshened their line-up for 2002, when Coulthard had to face up to the challenge of Kimi Räikkönen, whose pace he struggled to match in qualifying. He had the upper hand in the races, however, and took the team's only win of the year with a superb drive at Monaco, which helped erase the painful memories of the previous year.

The following season started on a high with a magnificent victory in Australia, but he began to struggle thereafter, seemingly unable to come to terms with the new single-lap qualifying format. Too often he was left in recovery mode from mid-grid positions, which restricted his chances of victory, and he could only take seventh in the championship, some 40 points adrift of the championship chasing Räikkönen. DC's ninth and final season with McLaren, in 2004, wasn't a happy one, as it began with the MP4-19 being off the pace. Things improved when the updated car arrived in mid-season, but in a year littered with collisions there were no wins and, worse still, no podiums.

Although Coulthard's future at the highest level looked uncertain, eventually he secured a drive with new team Red Bull Racing to remain on the grid in 2005. Having signed a one-year deal, he made a storming debut in Melbourne to take fourth place, and his subsequent feisty performances in one of the less fancied machines had garnered another five finishes in the points by mid-season. DC's efforts were rewarded with a new contract for an additional year, and with Red Bull signing a deal to run Ferrari engines things looked quite positive. Apart from a superb third place at his home circuit of Monaco, however, the car and engine package largely underperformed, leaving the Scot marking time and looking towards 2007, when the first Adrian Newey designed car, with Renault engine, came on stream. It was a season of rapid expansion, and the car's ongoing development throughout the season masked numerous reliability issues that saw him finish a slightly disappointed tenth in the standings.

The 2008 season should have brought more reward for both Coulthard and his team, but he only had the satisfaction of taking the team's sole podium, in Canada. However, ten collisions and/or accidents in the 18 races told their own story. His final outing, in Brazil, ended on the first lap when he was the innocent victim of a collision at the first turn. Even so, having played a key role in persuading Adrian Newey to leave McLaren to join Red Bull, David's long lasting contribution to the rise of the team cannot be underestimated.

Working as a Red Bull ambassador, Coulthard also successfully took up a commentator's role on TV with the BBC, while in 2010 he decided to race again in the DTM series, joining Mücke Motorsport to race an older-spec C-class Mercedes.

COULTHARD, David (GB) b 27/3/71, Twynholm, Kirkcudbright, Scotland

1994 Championship position: 8th   Wins: 0   Pole positions: 0   Fastest laps: 2   Points scored: 14

	Race	Circuit	No	Entrant	Tyres	Capacity/Car/Engine	Comment	Q Pos/Entries
ret	SPANISH GP	Barcelona	2	Rothmans Williams Renault	G	3.5 Williams FW16-Renault V10	electrics	9/27
5	CANADIAN GP	Montreal	2	Rothmans Williams Renault	G	3.5 Williams FW16-Renault V10	1 lap behind	5/27
5*	BRITISH GP	Silverstone	2	Rothmans Williams Renault	G	3.5 Williams FW16-Renault V10	*2nd place car disqualified/-1 lap	7/28
ret	GERMAN GP	Hockenheim	2	Rothmans Williams Renault	G	3.5 Williams FW16B-Renault V10	electrics/FL	6/28
ret	HUNGARIAN GP	Hungaroring	2	Rothmans Williams Renault	G	3.5 Williams FW16B-Renault V10	spun off	3/28
4*	BELGIAN GP	Spa	2	Rothmans Williams Renault	G	3.5 Williams FW16B-Renault V10	*1st place car disqualified	7/28
6/ret	ITALIAN GP	Monza	2	Rothmans Williams Renault	G	3.5 Williams FW16B-Renault V10	out of fuel when 2nd/1 lap behind	5/28
2	PORTUGUESE GP	Estoril	2	Rothmans Williams Renault	G	3.5 Williams FW16B-Renault V10	FL	3/28

1995 Championship position: 3rd   Wins: 1   Pole positions: 5   Fastest laps: 2   Points scored: 49

	Race	Circuit	No	Entrant	Tyres	Capacity/Car/Engine	Comment	Q Pos/Entries
2	BRAZILIAN GP	Interlagos	6	Rothmans Williams Renault	G	3.0 Williams FW17-Renault V10		3/26
ret	ARGENTINE GP	Buenos Aires	6	Rothmans Williams Renault	G	3.0 Williams FW17-Renault V10	clutch	1/26
4	SAN MARINO GP	Imola	6	Rothmans Williams Renault	G	3.0 Williams FW17-Renault V10		3/26
ret	SPANISH GP	Barcelona	6	Rothmans Williams Renault	G	3.0 Williams FW17-Renault V10	gearbox	4/26
ret	MONACO GP	Monte Carlo	6	Rothmans Williams Renault	G	3.0 Williams FW17-Renault V10	gearbox	3/26
ret	CANADIAN GP	Montreal	6	Rothmans Williams Renault	G	3.0 Williams FW17-Renault V10	spun off on lap 1	3/24
3	FRENCH GP	Magny Cours	6	Rothmans Williams Renault	G	3.0 Williams FW17-Renault V10		3/24
3	BRITISH GP	Silverstone	6	Rothmans Williams Renault	G	3.0 Williams FW17-Renault V10	stop & go pen for speeding in pits	3/24
2	GERMAN GP	Hockenheim	6	Rothmans Williams Renault	G	3.0 Williams FW17-Renault V10		3/24
2	HUNGARIAN GP	Hungaroring	6	Rothmans Williams Renault	G	3.0 Williams FW17-Renault V10		2/24
ret	BELGIAN GP	Spa	6	Rothmans Williams Renault	G	3.0 Williams FW17-Renault V10	gearbox/FL	5/24
ret	ITALIAN GP	Monza	6	Rothmans Williams Renault	G	3.0 Williams FW17-Renault V10	wheel-bearing	1/24
1	PORTUGUESE GP	Estoril	6	Rothmans Williams Renault	G	3.0 Williams FW17-Renault V10	FL	1/24
3	EUROPEAN GP	Nürburgring	6	Rothmans Williams Renault	G	3.0 Williams FW17B-Renault V10		1/24
2	PACIFIC GP	T.I. Circuit	6	Rothmans Williams Renault	G	3.0 Williams FW17B-Renault V10		1/24
ret	JAPANESE GP	Suzuka	6	Rothmans Williams Renault	G	3.0 Williams FW17B-Renault V10	spun off	6/24
ret	AUSTRALIAN GP	Adelaide	6	Rothmans Williams Renault	G	3.0 Williams FW17B-Renault V10	hit barrier on pitlane entry	2/24

1996 Championship position: 7th   Wins: 0   Pole positions: 0   Fastest laps: 0   Points scored: 18

	Race	Circuit	No	Entrant	Tyres	Capacity/Car/Engine	Comment	Q Pos/Entries
ret	AUSTRALIAN GP	Melbourne	8	Marlboro McLaren Mercedes	G	3.0 McLaren MP4/11-Mercedes V10	started from pits/stuck throttle	13/22
ret	BRAZILIAN GP	Interlagos	8	Marlboro McLaren Mercedes	G	3.0 McLaren MP4/11-Mercedes V10	spun off	14/22
7	ARGENTINE GP	Buenos Aires	8	Marlboro McLaren Mercedes	G	3.0 McLaren MP4/11-Mercedes V10		9/22
3	EUROPEAN GP	Nürburgring	8	Marlboro McLaren Mercedes	G	3.0 McLaren MP4/11-Mercedes V10		6/22
ret	SAN MARINO GP	Imola	8	Marlboro McLaren Mercedes	G	3.0 McLaren MP4/11-Mercedes V10	led early race/hydraulic failure	4/22
2	MONACO GP	Monte Carlo	8	Marlboro McLaren Mercedes	G	3.0 McLaren MP4/11-Mercedes V10		5/22
ret	SPANISH GP	Barcelona	8	Marlboro McLaren Mercedes	G	3.0 McLaren MP4/11-Mercedes V10	collision with Lamy at start	14/22
4	CANADIAN GP	Montreal	8	Marlboro McLaren Mercedes	G	3.0 McLaren MP4/11-Mercedes V10		10/22
6	FRENCH GP	Magny Cours	8	Marlboro McLaren Mercedes	G	3.0 McLaren MP4/11-Mercedes V10	1 lap behind	7/22
5	BRITISH GP	Silverstone	8	Marlboro McLaren Mercedes	G	3.0 McLaren MP4/11-Mercedes V10		9/22
5	GERMAN GP	Hockenheim	8	Marlboro McLaren Mercedes	G	3.0 McLaren MP4/11-Mercedes V10		7/20
ret	HUNGARIAN GP	Hungaroring	8	Marlboro McLaren Mercedes	G	3.0 McLaren MP4/11-Mercedes V10	engine	9/20
ret	BELGIAN GP	Spa	8	Marlboro McLaren Mercedes	G	3.0 McLaren MP4/11-Mercedes V10	spun off	4/20
ret	ITALIAN GP	Monza	8	Marlboro McLaren Mercedes	G	3.0 McLaren MP4/11-Mercedes V10	suspension damage – spun off	5/20
13	PORTUGUESE GP	Estoril	8	Marlboro McLaren Mercedes	G	3.0 McLaren MP4/11-Mercedes V10	collision with Häkkinen/-2 laps	8/20
8	JAPANESE GP	Suzuka	8	Marlboro McLaren Mercedes	G	3.0 McLaren MP4/11-Mercedes V10	collision with Diniz	8/20

1997 Championship position: 3rd=   Wins: 2   Pole positions: 0   Fastest laps: 1   Points scored: 36

	Race	Circuit	No	Entrant	Tyres	Capacity/Car/Engine	Comment	Q Pos/Entries
1	AUSTRALIAN GP	Melbourne	10	West McLaren Mercedes	G	3.0 McLaren MP4/12-Mercedes V10		4/24
10	BRAZILIAN GP	Interlagos	10	West McLaren Mercedes	G	3.0 McLaren MP4/12-Mercedes V10	1 lap behind	12/22
ret	ARGENTINE GP	Buenos Aires	10	West McLaren Mercedes	G	3.0 McLaren MP4/12-Mercedes V10	collision with Ralf Schumacher	10/22
ret	SAN MARINO GP	Imola	10	West McLaren Mercedes	G	3.0 McLaren MP4/12-Mercedes V10	engine	10/22
ret	MONACO GP	Monte Carlo	10	West McLaren Mercedes	G	3.0 McLaren MP4/12-Mercedes V10	spun off on lap 1	6/22
6	SPANISH GP	Barcelona	10	West McLaren Mercedes	G	3.0 McLaren MP4/12-Mercedes V10	tyre problems	3/22
7	CANADIAN GP	Montreal	10	West McLaren Mercedes	G	3.0 McLaren MP4/12-Mercedes V10	led race – gear problems at stop/FL	5/22
7/ret	FRENCH GP	Magny Cours	10	West McLaren Mercedes	G	3.0 McLaren MP4/12-Mercedes V10	rammed off by Alesi/1 lap behind	9/22
4	BRITISH GP	Silverstone	10	West McLaren Mercedes	G	3.0 McLaren MP4/12-Mercedes V10		6/22
ret	GERMAN GP	Hockenheim	10	West McLaren Mercedes	G	3.0 McLaren MP4/12-Mercedes V10	transmission	8/22
ret	HUNGARIAN GP	Hungaroring	10	West McLaren Mercedes	G	3.0 McLaren MP4/12-Mercedes V10	alternator	8/22
ret	BELGIAN GP	Spa	10	West McLaren Mercedes	G	3.0 McLaren MP4/12-Mercedes V10	spun off in wet on slick tyres	10/22
1	ITALIAN GP	Monza	10	West McLaren Mercedes	G	3.0 McLaren MP4/12-Mercedes V10		6/22
2	AUSTRIAN GP	A1-Ring	10	West McLaren Mercedes	G	3.0 McLaren MP4/12-Mercedes V10		10/22
ret	LUXEMBOURG GP	Nürburgring	10	West McLaren Mercedes	G	3.0 McLaren MP4/12-Mercedes V10	engine	6/22
10*/ret	JAPANESE GP	Suzuka	10	West McLaren Mercedes	G	3.0 McLaren MP4/12-Mercedes V10	*5th car disqualified/engine/-1 lap	6/22
2	EUROPEAN GP	Jerez	10	West McLaren Mercedes	G	3.0 McLaren MP4/12-Mercedes V10	allowed Häkkinen past to win	11/22

1998 Championship position: 3rd   Wins: 1   Pole positions: 3   Fastest laps: 3   Points scored: 56

	Race	Circuit	No	Entrant	Tyres	Capacity/Car/Engine	Comment	Q Pos/Entries
2	AUSTRALIAN GP	Melbourne	7	West McLaren Mercedes	B	3.0 McLaren MP4/13-Mercedes V10	allowed Häkkinen past to win	2/22
2	BRAZILIAN GP	Interlagos	7	West McLaren Mercedes	B	3.0 McLaren MP4/13-Mercedes V10		2/22
6	ARGENTINE GP	Buenos Aires	7	West McLaren Mercedes	B	3.0 McLaren MP4/13-Mercedes V10	collision with M Schumacher	1/22
1	SAN MARINO GP	Imola	7	West McLaren Mercedes	B	3.0 McLaren MP4/13-Mercedes V10		1/22
2	SPANISH GP	Barcelona	7	West McLaren Mercedes	B	3.0 McLaren MP4/13-Mercedes V10		2/22
ret	MONACO GP	Monte Carlo	7	West McLaren Mercedes	B	3.0 McLaren MP4/13-Mercedes V10	engine	2/22
ret	CANADIAN GP	Montreal	7	West McLaren Mercedes	B	3.0 McLaren MP4/13-Mercedes V10	throttle mechanism	1/22
6	FRENCH GP	Magny Cours	7	West McLaren Mercedes	B	3.0 McLaren MP4/13-Mercedes V10	refuelling problems/FL/-1 lap	3/22
ret	BRITISH GP	Silverstone	7	West McLaren Mercedes	B	3.0 McLaren MP4/13-Mercedes V10	spun off	4/22
2	AUSTRIAN GP	A1-Ring	7	West McLaren Mercedes	B	3.0 McLaren MP4/13-Mercedes V10	hit by Salo on lap 1/FL	14/22
2	GERMAN GP	Hockenheim	7	West McLaren Mercedes	B	3.0 McLaren MP4/13-Mercedes V10	FL	2/22
2	HUNGARIAN GP	Hungaroring	7	West McLaren Mercedes	B	3.0 McLaren MP4/13-Mercedes V10		2/22
7	BELGIAN GP	Spa	7	West McLaren Mercedes	B	3.0 McLaren MP4/13-Mercedes V10	hit by M Schumacher/-5 laps	2/22

ret	ITALIAN GP	Monza	7	West McLaren Mercedes	B	3.0 McLaren MP4/13-Mercedes V10	engine	4/22
3	LUXEMBOURG GP	Nürburgring	7	West McLaren Mercedes	B	3.0 McLaren MP4/13-Mercedes V10		5/22
3	JAPANESE GP	Suzuka	7	West McLaren Mercedes	B	3.0 McLaren MP4/13-Mercedes V10		3/22

1999 Championship position: 4th   Wins: 2   Pole positions: 0   Fastest laps: 3   Points scored: 48

ret	AUSTRALIAN GP	Melbourne	2	West McLaren Mercedes	B	3.0 McLaren MP4/14-Mercedes V10	hydraulics	2/22
ret	BRAZILIAN GP	Interlagos	2	West McLaren Mercedes	B	3.0 McLaren MP4/14-Mercedes V10	gearbox	2/22
2	SAN MARINO GP	Imola	2	West McLaren Mercedes	B	3.0 McLaren MP4/14-Mercedes V10		2/22
ret	MONACO GP	Monte Carlo	2	West McLaren Mercedes	B	3.0 McLaren MP4/14-Mercedes V10	oil leak	3/22
2	SPANISH GP	Barcelona	2	West McLaren Mercedes	B	3.0 McLaren MP4/14-Mercedes V10		3/22
7	CANADIAN GP	Montreal	2	West McLaren Mercedes	B	3.0 McLaren MP4/14-Mercedes V10	stop & go penalty	4/22
ret	FRENCH GP	Magny Cours	2	West McLaren Mercedes	B	3.0 McLaren MP4/14-Mercedes V10	led early in the race/FL	4/22
1	BRITISH GP	Silverstone	2	West McLaren Mercedes	B	3.0 McLaren MP4/14-Mercedes V10		3/22
2	AUSTRIAN GP	A1-Ring	2	West McLaren Mercedes	B	3.0 McLaren MP4/14-Mercedes V10	collision with Häkkinen at start	2/22
5	GERMAN GP	Hockenheim	2	West McLaren Mercedes	B	3.0 McLaren MP4/14-Mercedes V10	collision – Irvine new nose wing/FL	3/22
2	HUNGARIAN GP	Hungaroring	2	West McLaren Mercedes	B	3.0 McLaren MP4/14-Mercedes V10	FL	3/22
1	BELGIAN GP	Spa	2	West McLaren Mercedes	B	3.0 McLaren MP4/14-Mercedes V10	nudged Häkkinen at first corner	2/22
5	ITALIAN GP	Monza	2	West McLaren Mercedes	B	3.0 McLaren MP4/14-Mercedes V10		3/22
ret	EUROPEAN GP	Nürburgring	2	West McLaren Mercedes	B	3.0 McLaren MP4/14-Mercedes V10	spun off when in lead	2/22
ret	MALAYSIAN GP	Sepang	2	West McLaren Mercedes	B	3.0 McLaren MP4/14-Mercedes V10	fuel pressure	3/22
ret	JAPANESE GP	Suzuka	2	West McLaren Mercedes	B	3.0 McLaren MP4/14-Mercedes V10	gearbox	3/22

2000 Championship position: 3rd   Wins: 3   Pole positions: 2   Fastest laps: 3   Points scored: 73

ret	AUSTRALIAN GP	Melbourne	2	West McLaren Mercedes	B	3.0 McLaren MP4/15-Mercedes V10	engine	2/22
2/dsq*	BRAZILIAN GP	Interlagos	2	West McLaren Mercedes	B	3.0 McLaren MP4/15-Mercedes V10	*front wing setting too low after race	2/22
3	SAN MARINO GP	Imola	2	West McLaren Mercedes	B	3.0 McLaren MP4/15-Mercedes V10		3/22
1	BRITISH GP	Silverstone	2	West McLaren Mercedes	B	3.0 McLaren MP4/15-Mercedes V10		4/22
2	SPANISH GP	Barcelona	2	West McLaren Mercedes	B	3.0 McLaren MP4/15-Mercedes V10		4/22
3	EUROPEAN GP	Nürburgring	2	West McLaren Mercedes	B	3.0 McLaren MP4/15-Mercedes V10	hampered by dry set-up on wet track	1/22
1	MONACO GP	Monte Carlo	2	West McLaren Mercedes	B	3.0 McLaren MP4/15-Mercedes V10		3/22
7	CANADIAN GP	Montreal	2	West McLaren Mercedes	B	3.0 McLaren MP4/15-Mercedes V10	grid infringement/stop & go penalty	2/22
1	FRENCH GP	Magny Cours	2	West McLaren Mercedes	B	3.0 McLaren MP4/15-Mercedes V10	FL	2/22
2	AUSTRIAN GP	A1-Ring	2	West McLaren Mercedes	B	3.0 McLaren MP4/15-Mercedes V10	FL	2/22
3	GERMAN GP	Hockenheim	2	West McLaren Mercedes	B	3.0 McLaren MP4/15-Mercedes V10		1/22
3	HUNGARIAN GP	Hungaroring	2	West McLaren Mercedes	B	3.0 McLaren MP4/15-Mercedes V10		2/22
4	BELGIAN GP	Spa	2	West McLaren Mercedes	B	3.0 McLaren MP4/15-Mercedes V10		5/22
ret	ITALIAN GP	Monza	2	West McLaren Mercedes	B	3.0 McLaren MP4/15-Mercedes V10	multiple accident on lap 1	5/22
5	U S GP	Indianapolis	2	West McLaren Mercedes	B	3.0 McLaren MP4/15-Mercedes V10	jumped start – stop & go penalty/FL	2/22
3	JAPANESE GP	Suzuka	2	West McLaren Mercedes	B	3.0 McLaren MP4/15-Mercedes V10		3/22
2	MALAYSIAN GP	Sepang	2	West McLaren Mercedes	B	3.0 McLaren MP4/15-Mercedes V10		3/22

2001 Championship position: 2nd   Wins: 2   Pole positions: 2   Fastest laps: 3   Points scored: 65

2	AUSTRALIAN GP	Melbourne	4	West McLaren Mercedes	B	3.0 McLaren MP4/16-Mercedes V10		6/22
3	MALAYSIAN GP	Sepang	4	West McLaren Mercedes	B	3.0 McLaren MP4/16-Mercedes V10		8/22
1	BRAZILIAN GP	Interlagos	4	West McLaren Mercedes	B	3.0 McLaren MP4/16-Mercedes V10		5/22
2	SAN MARINO GP	Imola	4	West McLaren Mercedes	B	3.0 McLaren MP4/16-Mercedes V10	hampered by tyre problems	1/22
5	SPANISH GP	Barcelona	4	West McLaren Mercedes	B	3.0 McLaren MP4/16-Mercedes V10	stalled/started from back of grid	3/22
1	AUSTRIAN GP	A1-Ring	4	West McLaren Mercedes	B	3.0 McLaren MP4/16-Mercedes V10	FL	7/22
5	MONACO GP	Monte Carlo	4	West McLaren Mercedes	B	3.0 McLaren MP4/16-Mercedes V10	stalled/started at back of grid/FL	1/22
ret	CANADIAN GP	Montreal	4	West McLaren Mercedes	B	3.0 McLaren MP4/16-Mercedes V10	engine	3/22
3	EUROPEAN GP	Nürburgring	4	West McLaren Mercedes	B	3.0 McLaren MP4/16-Mercedes V10		5/22
4	FRENCH GP	Magny Cours	4	West McLaren Mercedes	B	3.0 McLaren MP4/16-Mercedes V10	pitlane stop & go penalty/FL	3/22
ret	BRITISH GP	Silverstone	4	West McLaren Mercedes	B	3.0 McLaren MP4/16-Mercedes V10	collision damage – later spun off	3/22
ret	GERMAN GP	Hockenheim	4	West McLaren Mercedes	B	3.0 McLaren MP4/16-Mercedes V10	engine	5/22
3	HUNGARIAN GP	Hungaroring	4	West McLaren Mercedes	B	3.0 McLaren MP4/16-Mercedes V10	slow second fuel stop	2/22
2	BELGIAN GP	Spa	4	West McLaren Mercedes	B	3.0 McLaren MP4/16-Mercedes V10		9/22
ret	ITALIAN GP	Monza	4	West McLaren Mercedes	B	3.0 McLaren MP4/16-Mercedes V10	engine	6/22
3	U S GP	Indianapolis	4	West McLaren Mercedes	B	3.0 McLaren MP4/16-Mercedes V10		7/22
3	JAPANESE GP	Suzuka	4	West McLaren Mercedes	B	3.0 McLaren MP4/16-Mercedes V10	Häkkinen gave up third place	7/22

Back in business. Coulthard's win in the opening race of the 1997 season at Melbourne put McLaren back on the victory trail after the team had gone without a win for three seasons. It was also the first victory in what would prove to be a hugely successful alliance with engine partner Mercedes-Benz.

Monaco maestro. One of David's finest victories came in the 2002 Monaco Grand Prix, where he drove a masterful race to beat Michael Schumacher.

2002 Championship position: 5th   Wins: 1   Pole positions: 0   Fastest laps: 1   Points scored: 41

ret	AUSTRALIAN GP	Melbourne	3	West McLaren Mercedes	M	3.0 McLaren MP4/17-Mercedes V10	gearbox	4/22
ret	MALAYSIAN GP	Sepang	3	West McLaren Mercedes	M	3.0 McLaren MP4/17-Mercedes V10	engine	6/22
3	BRAZILIAN GP	Interlagos	3	West McLaren Mercedes	M	3.0 McLaren MP4/17-Mercedes V10		4/22
6	SAN MARINO GP	Imola	3	West McLaren Mercedes	M	3.0 McLaren MP4/17-Mercedes V10	lack of grip/1 lap behind	6/22
3	SPANISH GP	Barcelona	3	West McLaren Mercedes	M	3.0 McLaren MP4/17-Mercedes V10		7/21
6	AUSTRIAN GP	A1-Ring	3	West McLaren Mercedes	M	3.0 McLaren MP4/17-Mercedes V10		8/22
1	MONACO GP	Monte Carlo	3	West McLaren Mercedes	M	3.0 McLaren MP4/17-Mercedes V10	led entire race	2/22
2	CANADIAN GP	Montreal	3	West McLaren Mercedes	M	3.0 McLaren MP4/17-Mercedes V10		8/22
ret	EUROPEAN GP	Nürburgring	3	West McLaren Mercedes	M	3.0 McLaren MP4/17-Mercedes V10	hit by Montoya	5/22
10	BRITISH GP	Silverstone	3	West McLaren Mercedes	M	3.0 McLaren MP4/17-Mercedes V10	2 laps behind	6/22
3	FRANCE GP	Magny Cours	3	West McLaren Mercedes	M	3.0 McLaren MP4/17-Mercedes V10	drive through penalty/FL	6/21
5	GERMAN GP	Hockenheim	3	West McLaren Mercedes	M	3.0 McLaren MP4/17-Mercedes V10	1 lap behind	9/22
5	HUNGARIAN GP	Hungaroring	3	West McLaren Mercedes	M	3.0 McLaren MP4/17-Mercedes V10		10/20
4	BELGIAN GP	Spa	3	West McLaren Mercedes	M	3.0 McLaren MP4/17-Mercedes V10		6/20
7	ITALIAN GP	Monza	3	West McLaren Mercedes	M	3.0 McLaren MP4/17-Mercedes V10		7/20
3	U S GP	Indianapolis	3	West McLaren Mercedes	M	3.0 McLaren MP4/17-Mercedes V10		3/20
ret	JAPANESE GP	Suzuka	3	West McLaren Mercedes	M	3.0 McLaren MP4/17-Mercedes V10	throttle control	3/20

2003 Championship position: 7th   Wins: 1   Pole positions: 0   Fastest laps: 0   Points scored: 51

1	AUSTRALIAN GP	Melbourne	5	West McLaren Mercedes	M	3.0 McLaren MP4/17D-Mercedes V10	helped by good team strategy	11/20
ret	MALAYSIAN GP	Sepang	5	West McLaren Mercedes	M	3.0 McLaren MP4/17D-Mercedes V10	broken electrical connection	4/20
4	BRAZILIAN GP	Interlagos	5	West McLaren Mercedes	M	3.0 McLaren MP4/17D-Mercedes V10		2/20
5	SAN MARINO GP	Imola	5	West McLaren Mercedes	M	3.0 McLaren MP4/17D-Mercedes V10		12/20
ret	SPANISH GP	Barcelona	5	West McLaren Mercedes	M	3.0 McLaren MP4/17D-Mercedes V10	collision with Button	8/20
5	AUSTRIAN GP	A1-Ring	5	West McLaren Mercedes	M	3.0 McLaren MP4/17D-Mercedes V10		14/20
7	MONACO GP	Monte Carlo	5	West McLaren Mercedes	M	3.0 McLaren MP4/17D-Mercedes V10		6/19
ret	CANADIAN GP	Montreal	5	West McLaren Mercedes	M	3.0 McLaren MP4/17D-Mercedes V10	gearbox	11/20
15/ret	EUROPEAN GP	Nürburgring	5	West McLaren Mercedes	M	3.0 McLaren MP4/17D-Mercedes V10	spun off avoiding Alonso/-4 laps	9/20
5	FRANCE GP	Magny Cours	5	West McLaren Mercedes	M	3.0 McLaren MP4/17D-Mercedes V10	delayed at final pitstop	5/20
5	BRITISH GP	Silverstone	5	West McLaren Mercedes	M	3.0 McLaren MP4/17D-Mercedes V10	lost carbon-fibre cockpit surround	12/20
2	GERMAN GP	Hockenheim	5	West McLaren Mercedes	M	3.0 McLaren MP4/17D-Mercedes V10		10/20
5	HUNGARIAN GP	Hungaroring	5	West McLaren Mercedes	M	3.0 McLaren MP4/17D-Mercedes V10		9/20
ret	ITALIAN GP	Monza	5	West McLaren Mercedes	M	3.0 McLaren MP4/17D-Mercedes V10	fuel pressure	8/20
ret	U S GP	Indianapolis	5	West McLaren Mercedes	M	3.0 McLaren MP4/17D-Mercedes V10	gearbox	8/20
3	JAPANESE GP	Suzuka	5	West McLaren Mercedes	M	3.0 McLaren MP4/17D-Mercedes V10		7/20

2004 Championship position: 9th=   Wins: 0   Pole positions: 0   Fastest laps: 0   Points scored: 23

8	AUSTRALIAN GP	Melbourne	5	West McLaren Mercedes	M	3.0 McLaren MP19-Mercedes V10	1 lap behind	12/20
6	MALAYSIAN GP	Sepang	5	West McLaren Mercedes	M	3.0 McLaren MP19-Mercedes V10		9/20
ret	BAHRAIN GP	Sakhir Circuit	5	West McLaren Mercedes	M	3.0 McLaren MP19-Mercedes V10	hydraulics	10/20
12	SAN MARINO GP	Imola	5	West McLaren Mercedes	M	3.0 McLaren MP19-Mercedes V10	collision with Alonso/1 lap behind	11/20
10	SPANISH GP	Barcelona	5	West McLaren Mercedes	M	3.0 McLaren MP19-Mercedes V10	delayed at pitstops	10/20
ret	MONACO GP	Monte Carlo	5	West McLaren Mercedes	M	3.0 McLaren MP19-Mercedes V10	accident damage – hit by Fisichella	8/20
ret	EUROPEAN GP	Nürburgring	5	West McLaren Mercedes	M	3.0 McLaren MP19-Mercedes V10	*no time set/engine	*20/20
6*	CANADIAN GP	Montreal	5	West McLaren Mercedes	M	3.0 McLaren MP19-Mercedes V10	*2nd/5th/8th cars dsq/-1 lap	9/20
7	U S GP	Indianapolis	5	West McLaren Mercedes	M	3.0 McLaren MP19-Mercedes V10	minor body damage/1 lap behind	12/20
6	FRENCH GP	Magny Cours	5	West McLaren Mercedes	M	3.0 McLaren MP19B-Mercedes V10		3/20
7	BRITISH GP	Silverstone	5	West McLaren Mercedes	M	3.0 McLaren MP19B-Mercedes V10		6/20
4	GERMAN GP	Hockenheim	5	West McLaren Mercedes	M	3.0 McLaren MP19B-Mercedes V10	collision and debris damage	4/20
9	HUNGARIAN GP	Hungaroring	5	West McLaren Mercedes	M	3.0 McLaren MP19B-Mercedes V10	wrong tyre choice/1 lap behind	12/20
7	BELGIAN GP	Spa	5	West McLaren Mercedes	M	3.0 McLaren MP19B-Mercedes V10	tyre and collision damage	4/20
6	ITALIAN GP	Monza	5	West McLaren Mercedes	M	3.0 McLaren MP19B-Mercedes V10	started from pitlane	10/20
9	CHINESE GP	Shanghai	5	West McLaren Mercedes	M	3.0 McLaren MP19B-Mercedes V10	collision – R Schum'er – wheel change	9/20

ret	JAPANESE GP	Suzuka	5	West McLaren Mercedes	M	3.0 McLaren MP19B-Mercedes V10	collision – R Schumacher	8/20
11	BRAZILIAN GP	Interlagos	5	West McLaren Mercedes	M	3.0 McLaren MP19B-Mercedes V10	1 lap behind	13/20

2005 Championship position: 12th   Wins: 0   Pole positions: 0   Fastest laps: 0   Points scored: 24

4	AUSTRALIAN GP	Melbourne	14	Red Bull Racing	M	3.0 Red Bull RB1-Cosworth V10	very competitive drive	5/20
6	MALAYSIAN GP	Sepang	14	Red Bull Racing	M	3.0 Red Bull RB1-Cosworth V10	highest ever British points scorer	8/20
8	BAHRAIN GP	Sakhir Circuit	14	Red Bull Racing	M	3.0 Red Bull RB1-Cosworth V10	1 lap behind	14/20
11*	SAN MARINO GP	Imola	14	Red Bull Racing	M	3.0 Red Bull RB1-Cosworth V10	*3rd & 5th cars dsq/-1 lap	14/20
8	SPANISH GP	Barcelona	14	Red Bull Racing	M	3.0 Red Bull RB1-Cosworth V10	1 lap behind	9/18
ret	MONACO GP	Monte Carlo	14	Red Bull Racing	M	3.0 Red Bull RB1-Cosworth V10	hit by M Schumacher	7/18
4	EUROPEAN GP	Nürburgring	14	Red Bull Racing	M	3.0 Red Bull RB1-Cosworth V10	drive-through penalty	12/20
7	CANADIAN GP	Montreal	14	Red Bull Racing	M	3.0 Red Bull RB1-Cosworth V10	oversteer/1 lap behind	12/20
dns*	U S GP	Indianapolis	14	Red Bull Racing	M	3.0 Red Bull RB1-Cosworth V10	*withdrawn after parade lap	16/20
10	FRENCH GP	Magny Cours	14	Red Bull Racing	M	3.0 Red Bull RB1-Cosworth V10	1 lap behind	15/20
13	BRITISH GP	Silverstone	14	Red Bull Racing	M	3.0 Red Bull RB1-Cosworth V10	1 lap behind	13/20
7	GERMAN GP	Hockenheim	14	Red Bull Racing	M	3.0 Red Bull RB1-Cosworth V10		11/20
ret	HUNGARIAN GP	Hungaroring	14	Red Bull Racing	M	3.0 Red Bull RB1-Cosworth V10	hit Alonso's lost front wing on track	13/20
7	TURKISH GP	Istanbul	14	Red Bull Racing	M	3.0 Red Bull RB1-Cosworth V10		12/20
15	ITALIAN GP	Monza	14	Red Bull Racing	M	3.0 Red Bull RB1-Cosworth V10	pit stop – collision damage/-1 lap	11/20
ret	BELGIAN GP	Spa	14	Red Bull Racing	M	3.0 Red Bull RB1-Cosworth V10	engine	12/20
ret	BRAZILIAN GP	Interlagos	14	Red Bull Racing	M	3.0 Red Bull RB1-Cosworth V10	suspension – hit Pizzonia on lap 1	16/20
6	JAPANESE GP	Suzuka	14	Red Bull Racing	M	3.0 Red Bull RB1-Cosworth V10		6/20
9	CHINESE GP	Shanghai	14	Red Bull Racing	M	3.0 Red Bull RB1-Cosworth V10		7/20

2006 Championship position: 13th   Wins: 0   Pole positions: 0   Fastest laps: 0   Points scored: 14

10	BAHRAIN GP	Sakhir Circuit	14	Red Bull Racing	M	2.4 Red Bull RB2-Ferrari V8	flat-spotted tyre – severe vibration	13/22
ret	MALAYSIAN GP	Sepang	14	Red Bull Racing	M	2.4 Red Bull RB2-Ferrari V8	hydraulics	11/22
8*	AUSTRALIAN GP	Melbourne	14	Red Bull Racing	M	2.4 Red Bull RB2-Ferrari V8	*gained point after S Speed penalty	12/22
ret	SAN MARINO GP	Imola	14	Red Bull Racing	M	2.4 Red Bull RB2-Ferrari V8	driveshaft	14/22
ret	EUROPEAN GP	Nürburgring	14	Red Bull Racing	M	2.4 Red Bull RB2-Ferrari V8	collision damage	14/22
14	SPANISH GP	Barcelona	14	Red Bull Racing	M	2.4 Red Bull RB2-Ferrari V8	*no time set/poor brakes/-1 lap	*22/22
3	MONACO GP	Monte Carlo	14	Red Bull Racing	M	2.4 Red Bull RB2-Ferrari V8	first podium for Red Bull	9/22
12	BRITISH GP	Silverstone	14	Red Bull Racing	M	2.4 Red Bull RB2-Ferrari V8	understeer/1 lap behind	11/22
8	CANADIAN GP	Montreal	14	Red Bull Racing	M	2.4 Red Bull RB2-Ferrari V8	1 lap behind	16/22
7	U S GP	Indianapolis	14	Red Bull Racing	M	2.4 Red Bull RB2-Ferrari V8	1 lap behind	17/22
9	FRENCH GP	Magny Cours	14	Red Bull Racing	M	2.4 Red Bull RB2-Ferrari V8	1 lap behind	10/22
11	GERMAN GP	Hockenheim	14	Red Bull Racing	M	2.4 Red Bull RB2-Ferrari V8	collision – R Schumacher/-1 lap	10/22
5	HUNGARIAN GP	Hungaroring	14	Red Bull Racing	M	2.4 Red Bull RB2-Ferrari V8	1 lap behind	13/22
ret/15	TURKISH GP	Istanbul	14	Red Bull Racing	M	2.4 Red Bull RB2-Ferrari V8	gearbox/3 laps behind	17/22
12	ITALIAN GP	Monza	14	Red Bull Racing	M	2.4 Red Bull RB2-Ferrari V8	1 lap behind	14/22
9	CHINESE GP	Shanghai	14	Red Bull Racing	M	2.4 Red Bull RB2-Ferrari V8	collision-Massa/plus half-spin later	12/22
ret	JAPANESE GP	Suzuka	14	Red Bull Racing	M	2.4 Red Bull RB2-Ferrari V8	gearbox	17/22
ret	BRAZILIAN GP	Interlagos	14	Red Bull Racing	M	2.4 Red Bull RB2-Ferrari V8	gearbox	19/22

2007 Championship position: 10th   Wins: 0   Pole positions: 0   Fastest laps: 0   Points scored: 14

ret	AUSTRALIAN GP	Melbourne	14	Red Bull Racing	B	2.4 Red Bull RB3-Renault V8	accident – drove into and over Wurz	19/22
ret	MALAYSIAN GP	Sepang	14	Red Bull Racing	B	2.4 Red Bull RB3-Renault V8	faulty brake pedal	13/22
ret	BAHRAIN GP	Sakhir Circuit	14	Red Bull Racing	B	2.4 Red Bull RB3-Renault V8	driveshaft	21/22
5	SPANISH GP	Barcelona	14	Red Bull Racing	B	2.4 Red Bull RB3-Renault V8	good drive without third gear	9/22
14	MONACO GP	Monte Carlo	14	Red Bull Racing	B	2.4 Red Bull RB3-Renault V8	collision Liuzzi – wing damage/-2 laps	11/22
ret	CANADIAN GP	Montreal	14	Red Bull Racing	B	2.4 Red Bull RB3-Renault V8	gearbox	14/22
ret	U S GP	Indianapolis	14	Red Bull Racing	B	2.4 Red Bull RB3-Renault V8	lap 1 collision damage – oil cooler	11/22
13	FRENCH GP	Magny Cours	14	Red Bull Racing	B	2.4 Red Bull RB3-Renault V8	1 lap behind	16/22
11	BRITISH GP	Silverstone	14	Red Bull Racing	B	2.4 Red Bull RB3-Renault V8	1 lap behind	12/22
5	EUROPEAN GP	Nürburgring	14	Red Bull Racing	B	2.4 Red Bull RB3-Renault V8		20/22
11	HUNGARIAN GP	Hungaroring	14	Red Bull Racing	B	2.4 Red Bull RB3-Renault V8	inconsistent handling/-1 lap	11/22
10	TURKISH GP	Istanbul	14	Red Bull Racing	B	2.4 Red Bull RB3-Renault V8	inconsistent handling	13/22
ret	ITALIAN GP	Monza	14	Red Bull Racing	B	2.4 Red Bull RB3-Renault V8	front wing failure – lap 1 accident	20/22
ret	BELGIAN GP	Spa	14	Red Bull Racing	B	2.4 Red Bull RB3-Renault V8	hydraulics	13/22
4	JAPANESE GP	Suzuka	14	Red Bull Racing-	B	2.4 Red Bull RB3-Renault V8		13/22
8	CHINESE GP	Shanghai	14	Red Bull Racing-	B	2.4 Red Bull RB3-Renault V8		59/22
9	BRAZILIAN GP	Interlagos	14	Red Bull Racing-	B	2.4 Red Bull RB3-Renault V8	1 lap behind	9/22

2008 Championship position: 16th   Wins: 0   Pole positions: 0   Fastest laps: 0   Points scored: 8

ret	AUSTRALIAN GP	Melbourne	9	Red Bull Racing-	B	2.4 Red Bull RB4-Renault V8	hit by Massa – accident damage	8/22
9	MALAYSIAN GP	Sepang	9	Red Bull Racing-	B	2.4 Red Bull RB4-Renault V8	graining on tyres in first stint	12/22
18	BAHRAIN GP	Sakhir Circuit	9	Red Bull Racing-	B	2.4 Red Bull RB4-Renault V8	collision – Button/1 lap behind	17/22
12	SPANISH GP	Barcelona	9	Red Bull Racing-	B	2.4 Red Bull RB4-Renault V8	hit by Glock – puncture/-1 lap	17/22
9	TURKISH GP	Istanbul	9	Red Bull Racing-	B	2.4 Red Bull RB4-Renault V8		10/20
ret	MONACO GP	Monte Carlo	9	Red Bull Racing-	B	2.4 Red Bull RB4-Renault V8	crashed in rain	10/20
3	CANADIAN GP	Montreal	9	Red Bull Racing-	B	2.4 Red Bull RB4-Renault V8	lucky with strategy	13/20
9	FRENCH GP	Magny Cours	9	Red Bull Racing-	B	2.4 Red Bull RB4-Renault V8		9/20
ret	BRITISH GP	Silverstone	9	Red Bull Racing-	B	2.4 Red Bull RB4-Renault V8	collision – Vettel on lap 1	11/20
13	GERMAN GP	Hockenheim	9	Red Bull Racing-	B	2.4 Red Bull RB4-Renault V8	collision with Barrichello	10/20
11	HUNGARIAN GP	Hungaroring	9	Red Bull Racing-	B	2.4 Red Bull RB4-Renault V8		13/20
17	EUROPEAN GP	Valencia	9	Red Bull Racing-	B	2.4 Red Bull RB4-Renault V8	spun – damaged bargeboard/-1 lap	17/20
11	BELGIAN GP	Spa	9	Red Bull Racing-	B	2.4 Red Bull RB4-Renault V8	1 lap behind	14/20
16	ITALIAN GP	Monza	9	Red Bull Racing-	B	2.4 Red Bull RB4-Renault V8	collision – new front wing/-1 lap	13/20
7	SINGAPORE GP	Singapore Circuit	9	Red Bull Racing-	B	2.4 Red Bull RB4-Renault V8		14/20
ret	JAPANESE GP	Suzuka	9	Red Bull Racing-	B	2.4 Red Bull RB4-Renault V8	crashed – hit by Nakajima on lap 1	11/20
10	CHINESE GP	Shanghai	9	Red Bull Racing-	B	2.4 Red Bull RB4-Renault V8	one-stop strategy	16/20
ret	BRAZILIAN GP	Interlagos	9	Red Bull Racing-	B	2.4 Red Bull RB4-Renault V8	collision damage on lap 1	14/20

GP Starts: 246   GP Wins: 13   Pole positions: 12   Fastest laps: 18   Points: 535

PIERS COURAGE

PIERS COURAGE was the eldest son of the chairman of the Courage brewery group, but any thought that such a connection was an asset to his motor racing aspirations was a mistake. While his initial racing experience was gained by regularly gyrating the Lotus Seven funded by his father, after that he was on his own as far as finance was concerned.

Courage teamed up with old pal Jonathan Williams in 1964, and the pair terrorised the circuits of Europe, initially with a Lotus 22. Although they went under the grandiose Anglo-Swiss Racing Team banner, in reality Courage and Williams lived the sort of hand-to-mouth existence that most privateers had to endure, but third place at Reims and second at Zandvoort in a Brabham encouraged Piers to contest a full F3 season in 1965.

Charles Lucas entered a pair of Brabhams for Piers and Frank Williams, and it proved to be a very successful campaign for Courage, with four wins in major events at Silverstone, Goodwood, Caserta and Reims. This led to an invitation to race the Lotus 41 F3 car for 1966, and although it was inferior to the rival Brabhams, he still managed a string of wins, earning a ride in Ron Harris' works Formula 2 Lotus in the German Grand Prix, where he blotted his copybook by crashing out.

BRM signed both Courage and Chris Irwin for 1967, the idea being to run them under the Tim Parnell banner, grooming them for a drive in the works team in the future. It all went sour very quickly for Piers, however, all his good work being repeatedly undone by silly spins. After the Monaco Grand Prix, Parnell stuck with Irwin, and Piers had to content himself with a season of Formula 2 in John Coombs' McLaren. His speed was not in doubt and some excellent drives netted him fourth place in the non-graded drivers' championship, but – and it was a big but – the disturbing tendency to crash remained, with major shunts at Pau, Enna and Brands Hatch. Coombs advised him to quit, but he was determined to continue.

Early in 1968, Piers bought the McLaren from Coombs and took it down-under to contest the Tasman series. Pitted against the Lotuses of Jim Clark and Graham Hill, Chris Amon's Ferrari and McLaren's BRM in the seven-race series, he was second, fourth, fifth, third, third and fifth before the final round at Longford. In pouring rain, he simply out-drove the opposition – Clark included – to win the race, but more importantly finally established his credibility.

Turning down an offer to replace the late Jim Clark at Lotus, was a brave one, but Piers felt he needed a season of solid finishes under his belt without the immediate pressure that driving one of Chapman's cars would bring. Instead he kept his word to race with Tim Parnell in the second-string BRM squad. In a season of tragedy, the death of Mike Spence opened up a seat in the works team, but Dickie Attwood was given the nod, so Piers remained in situ, scoring a splendid fourth at Monza. He also teamed up with his old pal, Frank Williams in Formula 2, and so successful was their partnership that it was decided to enter F1 with a Brabham in 1969.

Aside from a shunt at the Nürburgring, things could hardly have gone better, Courage driving superbly for the fledgling outfit to take second places at Monaco and Watkins Glen. He was also still racing in Formula 2, scoring a win at Enna and five third places, while an invitation to join the Matra team for Le Mans saw him take fourth place with Jean-Pierre Beltoise.

For 1970, Williams took the brave and possibly foolhardy step of running the newly constructed de Tomaso-Ford in place of the proven Brabham. The early part of the season was inconclusive, with only a third place in the non-championship International Trophy to show for their efforts. Meanwhile, Piers busied himself in a hectic schedule of endurance events for Alfa Romeo, highlighted by a win with Andrea de Adamich in the Buenos Aires 1000km.

By the time of the Dutch GP at Zandvoort, in June, progress seemed to have been made with the de Tomaso, which was placed ninth on the grid, but in the race tragedy struck when Courage slid wide, ran up a bank and crashed. The red car rolled over and burst into a huge ball of flames, and the unfortunate Piers stood no chance of surviving the inferno. However, it seems that he was already dead, having been struck on the helmet by a front wheel that had detached itself on the initial impact.

COURAGE, Piers (GB) b 27/5/1942, Colchester, Essex – d 21/6/1970, Zandvoort Circuit, Netherlands

	Race	Circuit	No	Entrant	Tyres	Capacity/Car/Engine	Comment	Q Pos/Entries
	1966 Championship position: Unplaced							
ret	GERMAN GP (F2)	Nürburgring	32	Ron Harris-Team Lotus	D	1.0 Lotus 44-Cosworth 4	crashed	24/30
	1967 Championship position: Unplaced							
ret	SOUTH AFRICAN GP	Kyalami	16	Reg Parnell Racing Ltd	D	2.0 Lotus 25-BRM V8	engine – oil pipe	18/18
ret	MONACO GP	Monte Carlo	6	Reg Parnell Racing Ltd	D	2.1 BRM P261 V8	spun off and then stalled	=12/18
dns	BRITISH GP	Silverstone	16	Reg Parnell Racing Ltd	D	2.1 BRM P261 V8	Irwin drove car in race	(16)/21
	1968 Championship position: 19th= Wins: 0 Pole positions: 0 Fastest laps: 0 Points scored: 4							
ret	SPANISH GP	Jarama	5	Reg Parnell Racing Ltd	D	3.0 BRM P126 V12	fuel metering unit	11/14
ret	MONACO GP	Monte Carlo	16	Reg Parnell Racing Ltd	D	3.0 BRM P126 V12	rear sub-frame fracture	11/18
ret	BELGIAN GP	Spa	14	Reg Parnell Racing Ltd	D	3.0 BRM P126 V12	engine	7/18
ret	DUTCH GP	Zandvoort	20	Reg Parnell Racing Ltd	D	3.0 BRM P126 V12	accident	14/19
6	FRENCH GP	Rouen	36	Reg Parnell Racing Ltd	D	3.0 BRM P126 V12	pit stop – tyres/3 laps behind	15/18
8	BRITISH GP	Brands Hatch	20	Reg Parnell Racing Ltd	D	3.0 BRM P126 V12	pit stops – misfire/8 laps behind	16/20
8	GERMAN GP	Nürburgring	22	Reg Parnell Racing Ltd	D	3.0 BRM P126 V12		8/20
4	ITALIAN GP	Monza	27	Reg Parnell Racing Ltd	D	3.0 BRM P126 V12	1 lap behind	18/24
ret	CANADIAN GP	St Jovite	24	Reg Parnell Racing Ltd	D	3.0 BRM P126 V12	transmission	15/22
7/ret	US GP	Watkins Glen	22	Reg Parnell Racing Ltd	D	3.0 BRM P126 V12	broken suspension bolt/-10 laps	14/21
ret	MEXICAN GP	Mexico City	22	Reg Parnell Racing Ltd	D	3.0 BRM P126 V12	overheating	19/21
	1969 Championship position: 8th Wins: 0 Pole positions: 0 Fastest laps: 0 Points scored: 16							
ret	SPANISH GP	Montjuich Park	11	Frank Williams Racing Cars	D	3.0 Brabham BT26A-Cosworth V8	engine – valve spring	11/14
2	MONACO GP	Monte Carlo	16	Frank Williams Racing Cars	D	3.0 Brabham BT26A-Cosworth V8		=8/16
ret	DUTCH GP	Zandvoort	16	Frank Williams Racing Cars	D	3.0 Brabham BT26A-Cosworth V8	clutch	9/15
ret	FRENCH GP	Clermont Ferrand	9	Frank Williams Racing Cars	D	3.0 Brabham BT26A-Cosworth V8	nose-cone mounting	11/13
5	BRITISH GP	Silverstone	16	Frank Williams Racing Cars	D	3.0 Brabham BT26A-Cosworth V8	1 lap behind	10/17
ret	GERMAN GP	Nürburgring	17	Frank Williams Racing Cars	D	3.0 Brabham BT26A-Cosworth V8	accident	7/26
5	ITALIAN GP	Monza	32	Frank Williams Racing Cars	D	3.0 Brabham BT26A-Cosworth V8	low fuel pressure	4/15
ret	CANADIAN GP	Mosport Park	21	Frank Williams Racing Cars	D	3.0 Brabham BT26A-Cosworth V8	fuel leak	10/20
2	US GP	Watkins Glen	18	Frank Williams Racing Cars	D	3.0 Brabham BT26A-Cosworth V8		9/18
10	MEXICAN GP	Mexico City	18	Frank Williams Racing Cars	D	3.0 Brabham BT26A-Cosworth V8	spin – pit stop/4 laps behind	9/17

1970 Championship position: Unplaced

ret	SOUTH AFRICAN GP	Kyalami	22	Frank Williams Racing Cars	D	3.0 de Tomaso 505-Cosworth V8	*suspension*	20/24
dns	SPANISH GP	Jarama	12	Frank Williams Racing Cars	D	3.0 de Tomaso 505-Cosworth V8	*accident in practice*	(8)/22
nc	MONACO GP	Monte Carlo	24	Frank Williams Racing Cars	D	3.0 de Tomaso 505-Cosworth V8	*pit stop – steering box/-22 laps*	9/21
ret	BELGIAN GP	Spa	7	Frank Williams Racing Cars	D	3.0 de Tomaso 505-Cosworth V8	*low oil pressure*	12/18
ret	DUTCH GP	Zandvoort	4	Frank Williams Racing Cars	D	3.0 de Tomaso 505-Cosworth V8	*fatal accident*	9/24

GP Starts: 28   GP Wins: 0   Pole positions: 0   Fastest laps: 0   Points: 20

Piers Courage leads Jack Brabham on his way to a fine second place in the 1969 US Grand Prix at Watkins Glen. His partnership with Frank Williams that year was a productive one, but a switch to the de Tomaso chassis in 1970 would bring disaster at Zandvoort.

CHRIS CRAFT

CHRIS CRAFT began racing in a Ford Anglia in 1962 and soon built a reputation as one of Britain's foremost saloon car drivers, particularly with the Team Broadspeed Escort (1968–70). After F3 with a Tecno, he moved into sports cars, driving a Chevron in 1968, then teaming up with Alain de Cadenet to race his Porsche 908 and McLaren M8C. It was this association that led to his brief and rather unhappy flirtation with Formula 1.

The foray would be a mere punctuation mark in a massive volume, however, for Chris continued to race sports and F5000 machines in the early 1970s, then returned successfully to saloons (1976–79) with a Ford Capri. His career, which ran into hundreds of races, stretched into the 1980s with the Dome sports car project.

Under the banner of The Light Car Company, Craft oversaw the production and marketing of Gordon Murray's open-wheeled Rocket roadster, a fun machine that evoked the spirit of an earlier age.

CRAFT, Chris (GB) b 17/11/1939, Porthleven, nr Helston, Cornwall

1971 Championship position: Unplaced

	Race	Circuit	No	Entrant	Tyres	Capacity/Car/Engine	Comment	Q Pos/Entries
dns	CANADIAN GP	Mosport Park	26	Ecurie Evergreen	G	3.0 Brabham BT33-Cosworth V8	*engine*	(25)/27
ret	US GP	Watkins Glen	24	Ecurie Evergreen	G	3.0 Brabham BT33-Cosworth V8	*chunking tyres/suspension*	30/32

GP Starts: 1   GP Wins: 0   Pole positions: 0   Fastest laps: 0   Points: 0

CRAWFORD, Jim (GB) b 13/2/1948, Dunfermline, Fifeshire, Scotland – d 6/8/2002 Terre Verde, Florida, USA

1975 Championship position: Unplaced

	Race	Circuit	No	Entrant	Tyres	Capacity/Car/Engine	Comment	Q Pos/Entries
ret	BRITISH GP	Silverstone	6	John Player Team Lotus	G	3.0 Lotus 72F-Cosworth V8	*spun off in rain*	25/28
13	ITALIAN GP	Monza	6	John Player Team Lotus	G	3.0 Lotus 72F-Cosworth V8	*6 laps behind*	25/28

GP Starts: 2   GP Wins: 0   Pole positions: 0   Fastest laps: 0   Points: 0

JIM CRAWFORD

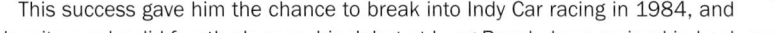

JIM CRAWFORD began his racing career as a mechanic working in Formula Atlantic, who proved to be quicker in the car than his young charge, and this led to an offer from Derek Bennett to drive a works Chevron late in 1973. He built his own car for 1974, just losing the Formula Atlantic title to John Nicholson. However, his performances earned him a testing contract with Lotus and a couple of grand prix outings in 1975, when he was again runner-up in the Atlantic series.

An expected Formula 2 drive in 1976 did not materialise and Crawford's career stalled. He spent 1978 in Formula 3 and '79 back in Atlantic, before finding a ride in the Aurora AFX F1/F2 series in 1980, winning the F2 class in a Chevron. After putting together a full season in Formula 2 in 1981 in an ex-works Toleman without much success, he dropped down to the rather weak five-race British Formula 1 series and had little trouble scoring wins in rounds 2, 3 and 4, to take the title in an AMCO Racing Ensign. This allowed him to skip the final round and try his luck in the USA.

It was a wise move, which revived and extended his career. Driving an F1 Ensign N180B, he joined the Can-Am series mid-way through the 1992 season and immediately made his mark, taking fifth in the standings. This encouraged a return the following season when, with a much revised machine, now renamed RKN180-Ford, he waged a no-holds-barred battle with Jacques Villeneuve Snr, just losing out by a mere three points in the title chase. He was back for more in 1984, this time in a modified March chassis. Despite three wins, once again he was runner-up.

This success gave him the chance to break into Indy Car racing in 1984, and despite a splendid fourth place on his debut at Long Beach, he remained in back-marker teams and failed to find a full-time ride.

Driving a March Buick, Crawford was a pace-setter in qualifying for the 1987 Indianapolis 500, but disaster struck when he was making an attempt on pole position. Losing control of his car in turn 1, he speared his car head-first into the wall, receiving serious foot and ankle injuries that put him out of action for the rest of the year.

Jim limped back to the Brickyard in 1988 and, after qualifying 18th, scorched through the field to lead the race at half-distance, before slipping down to a sixth-place finish. He was out again the following year looking for a win. After qualifying a fine fourth, despite a crash, he dropped out of the race on lap 135. It would be a downhill slide from then on, as he largely confined himself to racing only at the Speedway in the month of May. He finished 15th in 1990, but posted retirements in 1991 and 1992. On his last race appearance in '93, he made it to the finish in 24th place, but was running eight laps down.

After two more unsuccessful attempts to make the field in 1994 and 1995, Crawford settled with his family in St Petersburg, Florida, working as a fishing boat captain. He died in 2002 of liver failure.

ANTONIO CREUS

ANTONIO CREUS had a thirst for speed on two wheels and four, and was always curious about whatever type of machine he raced, wishing to improve every aspect of his driving along the way.

A native of Madrid, he was one of a large group of amateur enthusiasts who enjoyed the cut and thrust of competition, mainly for fun. To this end, he imported a succession of Pegasus sports cars, which he used on the road as well as for racing.

Obviously this compromise meant that they were at a serious disadvantage when pitted against pure racing machinery, so Creus upped the stakes with a Ferrari 750 Monza, which he used in 1957/58. The car was fast, but fragile and no results were achieved.

Creus got his first taste of F1 at the 1958 Syracuse Grand Prix in a Maserati, but he crashed out and did not return to single-seater action until the beginning of the 1960 season, when he made his one and only start in the Argentine Grand Prix. In a race of extreme heat, he was forced to retire after being affected by exhaust fumes. He failed to finish the Formula Libre Buenos Aires City Grand Prix and, in truth, he disliked the whole F1 experience, feeling that the cars were far too dangerous for his sense of self-preservation. He happily retired from driving, and spent a number of years working on engines and preparing cars while taking part in local races and rallies in less potent machines.

CREUS, Antonio Rodolfo Antonio Creus (E) b 24/10/1924, Madrid – d 19/2/1966, Madrid

1960	Championship position: Unplaced								
	Race	Circuit	No	Entrant	Tyres	Capacity/Car/Engine		Comment	Q Pos/Entries
ret	ARGENTINE GP	Buenos Aires	12	Antonio Creus	D	2.5 Maserati 250F 6		electrics/sunstroke	22/22
	GP Starts: 1	GP Wins: 0	Pole positions: 0	Fastest laps: 0	Points: 0				

TONY CROOK

ALTHOUGH he competed in only a couple of world championship grands prix, between 1946 and 1955 Tony Crook was one of Britain's most active racers, mainly on home soil, in single-seaters and sports categories. He actually won the first post-war circuit race at Gransden Lodge in Raymond Mays' 328 Fraser Nash BMW, and raced this and a 2.9-litre Alfa Romeo with huge success in the late 1940s.

In 1950, Tony began racing the Bristol-engined cars for the first time, and with his Frazer Nash he racked up countless wins and places over the next three years. He finished second to Mike Hawthorn in the 1951 Goodwood racing season, and his mercurial presence enlivened many a national meeting. A highlight in this period was a fine third place with the Frazer Nash in the 1952 sports car-only Monaco GP.

In 1953, Crook purchased a pukka single-seater Cooper-Bristol MkII, and he enjoyed many spirited battles with his friend and rival, Roy Salvadori. He also had a MkI Cooper modified to compete in sports events and raced both cars in tandem. For 1954, Tony had the MkII car rebuilt as an all-purpose 1 1/2-seater and took great delight in seeing off the challenges of Salvadori in his Maserati and Archie Scott-Brown in his Lister Bristol. He went on to compete in more than 400 races, sprints and hill-climbs, setting countless lap records and BTDs. His last race was the Goodwood 12-hours in which, during the night, he had the misfortune to spin on oil and be rammed by Stirling Moss. Tony was hospitalised for two weeks and during that time decided to retire.

Then he acquired Bristol Cars Limited, remaining resolutely at the helm of this idiosyncratic bespoke luxury car business until 2001, when he sold his interest. However, he remained on board until retirement in 2007, aged 87. Sadly, the business went into administration in 2011.

GEOFFREY CROSSLEY

AFTER starting racing with a pre-war Riley, Geoffrey Crossley ambitiously ordered the second Alta (GP2) from Geoffrey Taylor and upon delivery took it to compete in the 1949 Belgian Grand Prix at Spa. This may have seemed a bold step, but he was under the guidance of his friend, Johnny Claes, and wisely took things easy to finish seventh.

Crossley made occasional appearances with the car over the next couple of years, picking up sixth place in the Jersey Road Race in 1950. It seems he was unhappy with the costs of operating and maintaining this machine, however, and dropped out of the racing scene to attend to the day-to-day running of his Saxendale Motors business near Nottingham.

He made a brief reappearance in 1955, when his homemade Berkshire Special appeared at the Goodwood Easter meeting. The car performed so poorly that it was immediately withdrawn and never raced again.

CROOK, Anthony (GB) b 16/2/1920, Manchester

1952 Championship position: Unplaced

	Race	Circuit	No	Entrant	Tyres	Capacity/Car/Engine	Comment	Q Pos/Entries
nc	BRITISH GP	Silverstone	23	T A D Crook	D	2.0 Frazer Nash 421-Bristol 6	10 laps behind	25/32

1953 Championship position: Unplaced

	Race	Circuit	No	Entrant	Tyres	Capacity/Car/Engine	Comment	Q Pos/Entries
ret	BRITISH GP	Silverstone	22	T A D Crook	D	2.0 Cooper T20-Bristol 6	fuel feed on start line	25/29

GP Starts: 2   GP Wins: 0   Pole positions: 0   Fastest laps: 0   Points: 0

CROSSLEY, Geoffrey (GB) b 11/5/1921, Baslow, nr Bakewell, Derbyshire – d 7/1/2002, Headington, Oxfordshire

1950 Championship position: Unplaced

	Race	Circuit	No	Entrant	Tyres	Capacity/Car/Engine	Comment	Q Pos/Entries
ret	BRITISH GP	Silverstone	24	Geoffrey Crossley	D	1.5 s/c Alta GP 4	transmission	17/21
9	BELGIAN GP	Spa	26	Geoffrey Crossley	D	1.5 s/c Alta GP 4	5 laps behind	12/14

GP Starts: 2   GP Wins: 0   Pole positions: 0   Fastest laps: 0   Points: 0

JÉRÔME d'AMBRÔSIO

BORN in Belgium, but of Italian descent, Jérôme d'Ambrôsio began racing karts in 1995 and spent seven years in the category, before working his way methodically through junior Formula Renault single-seater categories until 2006. The following year, he graduated to the F3000 Euroseries and, despite missing the first eight races, scored well after his debut to finish fifth overall. Then he moved to the International Masters series for 2007 and won five of the 16 races to take the title in convincing fashion.

Naturally enough, d'Ambrôsio had his eye on the GP2 series and he joined the DAMS team, taking two second-place finishes in his debut season. In the winter GP2 Asia Series, he finished runner-up to team-mate Kamui Kobayashi. The Belgian remained with the team for 2010 and gained a big boost to his career with a win in the Sprint race at Monaco. Although other good results were hard to come by, a second place at Monza helped him to 12th overall in the standings.

Having already signed with Gravity Management, d'Ambrôsio was nominated as Lotus Renault's reserve driver, but didn't figure in the car, so he was given the role of third driver with Marussia Virgin for four races in preparation for a full-time drive in 2011. Given the largely thankless task of making an impression with the MVR-02, he did a pretty decent job. Certainly he was not outclassed by his vastly experienced team-mate, Timo Glock, and he brought the car home to a finish in all bar three races. For 2012, d'Ambrôsio joined the Lotus Renault team to act as reserve driver, while another driver from the Gravity stable, Charles Pic, began his F1 apprenticeship with the Banbury-based team.

d'AMBROISIO, Jérôme (B) b 27/12/1985, Etterbeek, Belgium

	2010			Championship position: Unplaced				
app	SINGAPORE GP	Marina Bay Circuit	25	Marussia Virgin Racing	P	2.4 Virgin MVR-01-Cosworth V8	ran as 3rd driver in practice 1 only	– / –
app	JAPANESE GP	Suzuka	25	Marussia Virgin Racing	P	2.4 Virgin MVR-01-Cosworth V8	ran as 3rd driver in practice 1 only	– / –
app	KOREAN GP	Yeongam	25	Marussia Virgin Racing	P	2.4 Virgin MVR-01-Cosworth V8	ran as 3rd driver in practice 1 only	– / –
app	BRAZILIAN GP	Interlagos	25	Marussia Virgin Racing	P	2.4 Virgin MVR-02-Cosworth V8	ran as 3rd driver in practice 1 only	– / –
	2011			Championship position: Unplaced				
14*	AUSTRALIAN GP	Melbourne	25	Marussia Virgin Racing	P	2.4 Virgin MVR-02-Cosworth V8	*16th but 7 & 8th cars dsq/-4 laps	22/24
ret	MALAYSIAN GP	Sepang	25	Marussia Virgin Racing	P	2.4 Virgin MVR-02-Cosworth V8	hit kerb/lost electrics	22/24
20	CHINESE GP	Shanghai Circuit	25	Marussia Virgin Racing	P	2.4 Virgin MVR-02-Cosworth V8	2 laps behind	21/24
20	TURKISH GP	Istanbul Park	25	Marussia Virgin Racing	P	2.4 Virgin MVR-02-Cosworth V8	2 laps behind	20/24
20	SPANISH GP	Barcelona	25	Marussia Virgin Racing	P	2.4 Virgin MVR-02-Cosworth V8	2 laps behind	23/24
15	MONACO GP	Monte Carlo	25	Marussia Virgin Racing	P	2.4 Virgin MVR-02-Cosworth V8	3 laps behind	22/24
14	CANADIAN GP	Montreal	25	Marussia Virgin Racing	P	2.4 Virgin MVR-02-Cosworth V8	1 lap behind	24/24
22	EUROPEAN GP	Valencia	25	Marussia Virgin Racing	P	2.4 Virgin MVR-02-Cosworth V8	2 laps behind	23/24
17	BRITISH GP	Silverstone	25	Marussia Virgin Racing	P	2.4 Virgin MVR-02-Cosworth V8	2 laps behind	22/24
18	GERMAN GP	Hockenheim	25	Marussia Virgin Racing	P	2.4 Virgin MVR-02-Cosworth V8	3 laps behind	22/24
19	HUNGARIAN GP	Hungaroring	25	Marussia Virgin Racing	P	2.4 Virgin MVR-02-Cosworth V8	5 laps behind	24/24
17	BELGIAN GP	Spa	25	Marussia Virgin Racing	P	2.4 Virgin MVR-02-Cosworth V8	1 lap behind	21/24
ret	ITALIAN GP	Monza	25	Marussia Virgin Racing	P	2.4 Virgin MVR-02-Cosworth V8	gearbox	22/24
18	SINGAPORE GP	Marina Bay Circuit	25	Marussia Virgin Racing	P	2.4 Virgin MVR-02-Cosworth V8	2 laps behind	22/24
21	JAPANESE GP	Suzuka	25	Marussia Virgin Racing	P	2.4 Virgin MVR-02-Cosworth V8	2 laps behind	20/24
20	KOREAN GP	Yeongam	25	Marussia Virgin Racing	P	2.4 Virgin MVR-02-Cosworth V8	1 lap behind	22/24
16	INDIAN GP	Buddh Circuit	25	Marussia Virgin Racing	P	2.4 Virgin MVR-02-Cosworth V8	3 laps behind	23/24
ret	ABU DHABI GP	Yas Marina Circuit	25	Marussia Virgin Racing	P	2.4 Virgin MVR-02-Cosworth V8	brakes	22/24
19	BRAZILIAN GP	Interlagos	25	Marussia Virgin Racing	P	2.4 Virgin MVR-02-Cosworth V8	3 laps behind	23/24

GP Starts: 19   GP Wins: 0   Pole positions: 0   Fastest laps: 0   Points: 0

FRITZ d'OREY

FRITZ D'OREY'S parents were from Portugal, but his grandfather was German, which probably accounts for his forename. The family were wealthy Packard car importers, and the young Fritz was soon behind the wheel of a Porsche Spyder. In 1958, he acquired an ex-Chico Landi F1 Ferrari and raced it extensively in Brazil, Uruguay and Argentina; his successes led to an invitation to race in Europe.

Having safely negotiated the French Grand Prix, Fritz crashed and wrote off the Maserati at Aintree, which cut short his F1 plans for the season, but later he drove the TecMec at Sebring, although he was glad to retire the machine, which he felt was too dangerous. Wins in Formula Junior at the GP de Messina and in sports cars in the Austrian GP with a Ferrari Testa Rossa led to the 22-year-old d'Orey signing a contract with Ferrari to race their sports cars in 1960.

Describing himself as "a child and very crazy", Fritz escaped a huge crash at Monza when trying to keep pace with Phil Hill, before suffering a much more serious accident at Le Mans, where he slammed his Ferrari into a tree. Having sustained serious head injuries, he spent eight months in hospital before making a full recovery, but he never raced again.

d'OREY, Fritz (BR) b 25/3/1938 São Paulo

1959 Championship position: Unplaced

	Race	Circuit	No	Entrant	Tyres	Capacity/Car/Engine	Comment	Q Pos/Entries
nc	FRENCH GP	Reims	38	Scuderia Centro Sud	D	2.5 Maserati 250F 6	10 laps behind	18/22
ret	BRITISH GP	Aintree	40	Scuderia Centro Sud	D	2.5 Maserati 250F 6	out of brakes – crashed	20/30
ret	US GP	Sebring	15	Camoradi USA	D	2.5 Tec Mec Maserati 250F 6	oil leak	17/19

GP Starts: 3   GP Wins: 0   Pole positions: 0   Fastest laps: 0   Points: 0

CRISTIANO da MATTA

A LTHOUGH highly rated when he joined the list of Brazilians to have made it to Formula 1, Cristiano da Matta never really settled in the grand prix arena and, rather hastily perhaps, Toyota's management decided he was not the man for them.

The son of a multiple Brazilian touring car champion, da Matta began his career in karts, producing a string of local, regional and national titles. Success followed in Formula Ford: he won the Brazilian championship in 1993, before stepping up to the Brazilian Formula 3 series the following year. Despite running against more seasoned campaigners, he clinched the title in his first season and immediately switched his attention to Europe in search of a path to F1.

He travelled to Britain in 1995 to contest the British F3 series with West Surrey Racing, but he failed to hit it off with team boss Dick Bennetts and the season was less successful than perhaps it should have been. A move to F3000 the following year was equally frustrating. He displayed flashes of speed, but could only finish eighth overall in his Pacific-run Lola.

Cristiano decided that perhaps his future lay elsewhere, so he joined the Indy Lights series with top team Brian Stewart Racing. In his debut season, he placed third overall and claimed Rookie of the Year honours. Looking to make the jump to Champ Cars, he needed to show his potential in his second year in the category, and despite a mid-season slump, he got the job done with Tasman racing, clinching the title with two races to spare.

Having impressed many people in the top category, da Matta made his Champ Car debut in 1999, driving for Arciero-Wells. Unfazed by the step up, he scored what was the highest finish to date for a Toyota-powered car, when he came home fourth on the Nazareth oval. His season was punctuated by accidents and mechanical failures, however, and he scored points in only four of the 20 races. In his sophomore year, he stayed put and drove for the renamed PPI Motorsports squad, taking his first victory at Chicago and placing tenth in the championship standings. That performance alerted the crack Newman-Haas team to his possibilities and, in 2001, he was hired to partner Christian Fittipaldi. Despite being regarded as the junior partner in the line-up, the Brazilian took his Toyota-powered Lola to three victories and a total of five podium finishes as he finished fifth in the championship. This proved to be the launch pad for his successful title bid with Newman-Haas in 2002, and this time he dominated the series with seven poles, seven victories and a total of 11 podium finishes to take the title at a canter. With the CART championship in his grasp, da Matta attracted the attention of F1, notably the Toyota brand that had powered him to Champ Car success.

At the time, Toyota had its own F1 team with a big budget and, having discarded drivers Allan McNish and Mika Salo after just one season, looked to da Matta to light up the F1 season in the manner of Juan Pablo Montoya. Unfortunately, Toyota wasn't able to run near the front of the grid. An accident at the first race in Australia aside, da Matta made a solid – if unspectacular – start to his F1 career. Highlights of the season included a stint as race leader during the British GP at Silverstone and a superb third on the grid in Japan, and his ten points outscored his experienced team-mate, Olivier Panis.

The following season things did not go so well, however, as the Toyota was still unreliable – and slow. Cristiano was effectively made the scapegoat as the team sought to turn its fortunes around, and in mid-season he was replaced by reserve driver Ricardo Zonta.

His F1 adventure over, Cristiano returned to Champ Cars and found a seat at the ambitious PKV Racing outfit. After a slow start, he picked up a rather fortuitous win at Portland, but (apart from a pole at Cleveland) he generally struggled to make an impression on the series he had once dominated. For 2006, at first he had trouble finding a ride, but eventually secured a berth with Dale Coyne Racing, where he put in some spirited performances.

When RuSPORT made their surprising mid-season decision to release A.J. Allmendinger, Cristiano was offered the drive. The Brazilian was soon up to speed and posted a fine second place at San José, before disaster struck. While testing at Elkhart Lake, his car struck a deer crossing the track and his helmet took much of the impact. Initially, there were fears for his life, but despite very serious head injuries, he survived to begin the long road to recovery.

It was two years before Cristiano made a tentative return to the track, sharing a Riley sports car with Jimmy Vasser at Laguna Seca early in 2008. He spent the rest of the year looking for a ride, but no offers to race were forthcoming and he went to work in his design business in Brazil. There was a brief flirtation with IVECO about the possibility of truck racing, but a real return to action came in 2011, when he shared a Jaguar RSR with old friend and adversary Bruno Junqueira in the GT class of the ALMS.

da MATTA, Cristiano (BR) b 19/9/1973, Belo Horizonte

2003 Championship position: 13th   Wins: 0   Pole positions: 0   Fastest laps: 0   Points scored: 10

	Race	Circuit	No	Entrant	Tyres	Capacity/Car/Engine	Comment	Q Pos/Entries
ret	AUSTRALIAN GP	Melbourne	21	Pansonic Toyota Racing	M	3.0 Toyota TF103-V10	spun off	16/20
11	MALAYSIAN GP	Sepang	21	Pansonic Toyota Racing	M	3.0 Toyota TF103-V10	1 lap behind	11/20
10	BRAZILIAN GP	Interlagos	21	Pansonic Toyota Racing	M	3.0 Toyota TF103-V10	1 lap behind	18/20
12	SAN MARINO GP	Imola	21	Pansonic Toyota Racing	M	3.0 Toyota TF103-V10	1 lap behind	13/20
6	SPANISH GP	Barcelona	21	Pansonic Toyota Racing	M	3.0 Toyota TF103-V10	1 lap behind	13/20
10	AUSTRIAN GP	A1-Ring	21	Pansonic Toyota Racing	M	3.0 Toyota TF103-V10	1 lap behind	11/20
9	MONACO GP	Monte Carlo	21	Pansonic Toyota Racing	M	3.0 Toyota TF103-V10	1 lap behind	10/19
11/ret	CANADIAN GP	Montreal	21	Pansonic Toyota Racing	M	3.0 Toyota TF103-V10	suspension/6 laps behind	9/20
ret	EUROPEAN GP	Nürburgring	21	Pansonic Toyota Racing	M	3.0 Toyota TF103-V10	engine	10/20
11	FRENCH GP	Magny Cours	21	Pansonic Toyota Racing	M	3.0 Toyota TF103-V10	1 lap behind	13/20
7	BRITISH GP	Silverstone	21	Pansonic Toyota Racing	M	3.0 Toyota TF103-V10	briefly led race	6/20
6	GERMAN GP	Hockenheim	21	Pansonic Toyota Racing	M	3.0 Toyota TF103-V10	1 lap behind	9/20
11	HUNGARIAN GP	Hungaroring	21	Pansonic Toyota Racing	M	3.0 Toyota TF103-V10	2 laps behind	15/20
ret	ITALIAN GP	Monza	21	Pansonic Toyota Racing	M	3.0 Toyota TF103-V10	puncture – spun off	12/20
9	UNITED STATES GP	Indianapolis	21	Pansonic Toyota Racing	M	3.0 Toyota TF103-V10	2 laps behind	9/20
7	JAPANESE GP	Suzuka	21	Pansonic Toyota Racing	M	3.0 Toyota TF103-V10		3/20

2004 Championship position: 16th=   Wins: 0   Pole positions: 0   Fastest laps: 0   Points scored: 3

	Race	Circuit	No	Entrant	Tyres	Capacity/Car/Engine	Comment	Q Pos/Entries
12	AUSTRALIAN GP	Melbourne	16	Pansonic Toyota Racing	M	3.0 Toyota TF104-V10	stalled at 2nd pit stop	13/20
9	MALAYSIAN GP	Sepang	16	Pansonic Toyota Racing	M	3.0 Toyota TF104-V10	1 lap behind	10/20
10	BAHRAIN GP	Bahrain Circuit	16	Pansonic Toyota Racing	M	3.0 Toyota TF104-V10	1 lap behind	9/20
ret	SAN MARINO GP	Imola	16	Pansonic Toyota Racing	M	3.0 Toyota TF104-V10	disabled traction control/spun off	10/20
13	SPANISH GP	Barcelona	16	Pansonic Toyota Racing	M	3.0 Toyota TF104-V10		11/20
6	MONACO GP	Monte Carlo	16	Pansonic Toyota Racing	M	3.0 Toyota TF104-V10	drive-through penalty/-1 lap	15/20
ret	EUROPEAN GP	Nürburgring	16	Pansonic Toyota Racing	M	3.0 Toyota TF104-V10	hit by Ralf Schumacher on lap 1	11/20
dsq*	CANADIAN GP	Montreal	16	Pansonic Toyota Racing	M	3.0 Toyota TF104-V10	8th/*brake duct infringement	12/20
ret	U S GP	Indianapolis	16	Pansonic Toyota Racing	M	3.0 Toyota TF104-V10	gearbox	11/20
14	FRENCH GP	Magny Cours	16	Pansonic Toyota Racing	M	3.0 Toyota TF104-V10	1 lap behind	11/20
13	BRITISH GP	Silverstone	16	Pansonic Toyota Racing	M	3.0 Toyota TF104-V10	1 lap behind	13/20
ret	GERMAN GP	Hockenheim	16	Pansonic Toyota Racing	M	3.0 Toyota TF104-V10	puncture – spun off	15/20

GP Starts: 28   GP Wins: 0   Pole positions: 0   Fastest laps: 0   Points: 13

NANO da SILVA RAMOS

HOLDING dual French and Brazilian nationality, Nano da Silva Ramos took part in his first races in Rio with an MG, but he wasn't really interested in the sport until he returned to France and purchased an Aston Martin DB2, with which he won the Rallye de Sable in 1953. He belonged to a group of racing enthusiasts that included Harry Schell and Ed Nelson. He also ignited a passion for racing in Alfonso de Portago, with whom he would become great friends.

After making his debut at Le Mans the following year, Ramos raced with the Gordini team in 1955 and 1956, driving their grand prix and sports cars, and suffering the usual mixture of speed and unreliability associated with that marque. In single-seaters, he finished fifth in the 1956 International Trophy and did well to claim points at Monaco, but achieved little else, while in sports car racing he scored a win for the team at Montlhéry against very poor opposition.

Équipe Gordini were on their last legs early in 1957, but Ramos took sixth place at Pau in the stream-liner before their demise. With the violent deaths of his friends, Alfonso de Potago and Edmund Nelson, in the Mille Miglia, he was persuaded to retire from competition by his wife, who was pregnant at the time. But he couldn't stay away for long and was back in 1958 with a 250GT Ferrari, winning at Spa. He returned in an Alan Brown Cooper the following year to finish second. In 1959, Nano raced briefly for Scuderia Centro Sud, claiming a very distant fourth in their outdated Maserati 250F in the Aintree 200, before sharing a works Ferrari with Cliff Allison at Le Mans. He raced just once more, with a Porsche in a sports car event, the Rio Grand Prix in 1960. Finally he gave way to the entreaties of his long-suffering wife who, sick with worry that he might be killed, had been begging him to retire.

da SILVA RAMOS, 'Nano' Hernano (F/BR) b 7/12/1925, Paris

1955 Championship position: Unplaced

	Race	Circuit	No	Entrant	Tyres	Capacity/Car/Engine	Comment	Q Pos/Entries
8	DUTCH GP	Zandvoort	22	Equipe Gordini	E	2.5 Gordini Type 16 6	8 laps behind	14/16
ret	BRITISH GP	Aintree	24	Equipe Gordini	E	2.5 Gordini Type 16 6	engine	18/25
ret	ITALIAN GP	Monza	22	Equipe Gordini	E	2.5 Gordini Type 16 6	fuel pump	18/22
dns	"	"	24	Equipe Gordini	E	2.5 Gordini Type 32 8	practice only	– / –

1956 Championship position: 15th=   Wins: 0   Pole positions: 0   Fastest laps: 0   Points scored: 2

	Race	Circuit	No	Entrant	Tyres	Capacity/Car/Engine	Comment	Q Pos/Entries
5	MONACO GP	Monte Carlo	6	Equipe Gordini	E	2.5 Gordini Type 16 6	7 laps behind	14/19
8	FRENCH GP	Reims	32	Equipe Gordini	E	2.5 Gordini Type 32 8	4 laps behind	14/20
ret	BRITISH GP	Silverstone	14	Equipe Gordini	E	2.5 Gordini Type 32 8	rear axle	26/28
ret	ITALIAN GP	Monza	8	Equipe Gordini	E	2.5 Gordini Type 32 8	engine	21/26

GP Starts: 7   GP Wins: 0   Pole positions: 0   Fastest laps: 0   Points: 2

DAIGH, Chuck (USA) b 29/11/1923, Long Beach, California – d 29/04/2008, Newport Beach, California

	1960 Championship position: Unplaced								
	Race	Circuit	No	Entrant	Tyres	Capacity/Car/Engine	Comment		Q Pos/Entries
dnq	MONACO GP	Monte Carlo	46	Reventlow Automobiles Inc	(G) D	2.4 Scarab 4	tried Goodyear tyres in practice		21/24
dns	DUTCH GP	Zandvoort	22	Reventlow Automobiles Inc	D	2.4 Scarab 4	dispute over start money		(19)/21
ret	BELGIAN GP	Spa	30	Reventlow Automobiles Inc	D	2.4 Scarab 4	engine		18/18
dns	FRENCH GP	Reims	26	Reventlow Automobiles Inc	D	2.4 Scarab 4	engine failure in practice		(23)/23
ret	BRITISH GP	Silverstone	3	Cooper Car Co	D	2.5 Cooper T51-Climax 4	engine – overheating		19/25
10	US GP	Riverside	23	Reventlow Automobiles Inc	D	2.4 Scarab 4	3 laps behind		18/23

GP Starts: 3   GP Wins: 0   Pole positions: 0   Fastest laps: 0   Points: 0

CHUCK DAIGH

CHUCK DAIGH appears in this book mainly because of his involvement in the ambitious, but unsuccessful, Scarab project in 1960, but his contribution to US motor sport as a driver, mechanic, engine guru and more was immense.

The son of a Los Angeles garage owner, Chuck and his brother, Harold, were brought up in the hot rod culture of the inter-war years, before becoming embroiled in the Second World War. On enlisting, given his mechanical background, he applied to serve in the Army's motor corps, but instead found himself a paratrooper seeing front-line action in Italy and Normandy as the Axis forces were defeated.

Post-war, the brothers soon caused a stir with their track roadster, Chuck starting to make a name for himself as a very able pilot. His first proper sports car race came in 1953 with a Frazer Nash, which was followed by a Jaguar special. His first victory was at the wheel of a Kurtis-Lincoln, and then he drove for Troutman-Barnes in a modified Kurtis-Mercury with great success in 1955/56.

Chuck had been hired by Ford to work on their USAC driving programme, overseeing the success of Johnny Mantz in 1956. Also he was part of the Ford team that broke speed and endurance records on the Bonneville Salt Flats. In 1957, he took a Ford to the paved ovals at Indianapolis and Milwaukee, and broke the stock car track records of both. Surprisingly, he was fired by Ford, but lost no time in joining rivals Chevrolet. It was a short-lived post, however, for the manufacturer pulled out of racing when safety concerns were raised about stock cars.

When Lance Reventlow decided to build the powerful Chevrolet-engined Scarab sports car, Chuck was brought on board and soon became responsible for the engine, suspension and brakes as the potent machine took shape. This Mk1 car proved to be very successful, with Daigh winning the Governor's Cup (beating Walt Hansgen's Lister) and the Nassau Trophy, and famously defeating Phil Hill's Ferrari at Riverside.

Buoyed by Chuck's success, Reventlow commissioned a front-engined F1 car, but by the time it appeared in 1960, it had been rendered almost obsolete by the rear-engined Cooper and Lotus cars. Chuck struggled manfully against the odds, but the car was withdrawn after just three races, reappearing only on home soil at season's end. Daigh meanwhile had the chance to try a proper F1 car at the British GP, where he drove a third works Cooper. Amazingly, the Scarab raced again, being wheeled out for the Inter-Continental Formula in 1961. Chuck finished seventh in the International Trophy race, but after he crashed in practice for the British Empire Trophy – suffering a cracked pelvis – the car was seen no more.

Fortunately, Daigh was seen again, racing one of Jim Hall's early Chaparrals at Sebring in 1962, and he tasted victory at Mosport in 1963, when he won the Player's 200 sports car race in a Lotus 19.

Chuck also enjoyed himself immensely competing in offshore powerboat racing. Later in life, he began building a Bonneville streamliner in his Costa Mesa garage. Sadly, he died in 2008 after a short illness, before he could see the project through. Chuck Daigh was a modest man of many talents who would be remembered fondly by all who knew him.

DALMAS, Yannick (F) b 28/7/1961, Le Beausset, nr Toulon

	1987 Championship position: Unplaced								
	Race	Circuit	No	Entrant	Tyres	Capacity/Car/Engine	Comment		Q Pos/Entries
9	MEXICAN GP	Mexico City	29	Larrousse Calmels	G	3.5 Lola LC87-Cosworth V8	4th non-turbo/4 laps behind		23/27
14/ret*	JAPANESE GP	Suzuka	29	Larrousse Calmels	G	3.5 Lola LC87-Cosworth V8	electrics/*3rd non-turbo/-4 laps		23/27
5*	AUSTRALIAN GP	Adelaide	29	Larrousse Calmels	G	3.5 Lola LC87-Cosworth V8	*2nd non-turbo – no points scored		21/27
	1988 Championship position: Unplaced								
ret	BRAZILIAN GP	Rio	29	Larrousse Calmels	G	3.5 Lola LC88-Cosworth V8	engine cut out		17/31
12	SAN MARINO GP	Imola	29	Larrousse Calmels	G	3.5 Lola LC88-Cosworth V8	broken front wing/2 laps behind		19/31
7	MONACO GP	Monte Carlo	29	Larrousse Calmels	G	3.5 Lola LC88-Cosworth V8	spin/1 lap behind		21/30
9	MEXICAN GP	Mexico City	29	Larrousse Calmels	G	3.5 Lola LC88-Cosworth V8	3 laps behind		22/30
dnq	CANADIAN GP	Montreal	29	Larrousse Calmels	G	3.5 Lola LC88-Cosworth V8			29/31
7	US GP (DETROIT)	Detroit	29	Larrousse Calmels	G	3.5 Lola LC88-Cosworth V8	2 laps behind		25/31
13	FRENCH GP	Paul Ricard	29	Larrousse Calmels	G	3.5 Lola LC88-Cosworth V8	pit stop – loose seat belts/-2 laps		19/31
13	BRITISH GP	Silverstone	29	Larrousse Calmels	G	3.5 Lola LC88-Cosworth V8	2 laps behind		23/31
ret	GERMAN GP	Hockenheim	29	Larrousse Calmels	G	3.5 Lola LC88-Cosworth V8	clutch		21/31
9	HUNGARIAN GP	Hungaroring	29	Larrousse Calmels	G	3.5 Lola LC88-Cosworth V8	collision – Sala/misfire/-3 laps		17/31
ret	BELGIAN GP	Spa	29	Larrousse Calmels	G	3.5 Lola LC88-Cosworth V8	engine		23/31
ret	ITALIAN GP	Monza	29	Larrousse Calmels	G	3.5 Lola LC88-Cosworth V8	spun – holed oil tank		25/31

YANNICK DALMAS

FRENCH F3 in the mid-1980s must have been bewildering. Potential world champions were two a penny as the conveyor-belt churned out hot-shots one after another: brothers Alain and Michel Ferté, Olivier Grouillard, Pierre-Henri Raphanel, Jean Alesi, Éric Bernard, Michel Trollé, Érik Comas – and Yannick Dalmas.

The reigning French Formule Renault champion, Yannick took the number-two seat to Raphanel in the all-conquering ORECA F3 team for 1985 and duly finished second in the championship. The next year it was his turn to lead the team, and he won six of the 11 races, impressing all watchers with his flair and speed.

Yannick moved up to F3000 for 1987, but his machinery did not always work as well as one would have expected. However, when things were right he flew. The Frenchman also literally cheated death when he escaped shaken, but largely unhurt after a 170mph meeting with the guardrail that left him in the remains of his Onyx-March in the middle of the track. Amazingly, every car that followed avoided the wreck and any further carnage. After missing the next round at Spa, he recovered in fine style to inherit a last-gasp victory (when leader Roberto Moreno ran out of fuel) at Pau on his return, and then took the win in the season's finale at Jarama to register a slightly disappointing fifth place in the championship. But for Dalmas, it mattered little. He had already been given his grand prix chance by Larrousse in Mexico, and a fifth place (no points scored, being a non-regular driver) in Australia at season's end made his place in the F1 team for 1988 a formality.

The year was a personal disaster. Early-season shunts blunted Yannick's confidence. Then what appeared to be an ear problem that sidelined him towards the end of the season turned out to be a life-threatening bout of Legionnaires' disease.

He returned to the Larrousse équipe for 1989, but a string of non-qualifications led to his leaving the team in mid-season in favour of Michele Alboreto. Taking a seat at AGS merely hastened his depressing slide and, while he did manage to qualify the car on occasion in 1990, it must have been a great relief when Peugeot offered him the chance to re-establish his career with a place in their sports car team. Paired with Keke Rosberg, he won two races (Magny-Cours and Mexico City), and in 1992 he shared the World Sports Car Drivers' title with Derek Warwick after winning at Le Mans, Silverstone and Fuji, also finishing second at Monza and Donington.

With Peugeot competing only at Le Mans in 1993 (where Yannick finished second with Thierry Boutsen and Teo Fabi), he drove a Peugeot 405 in the French Supertourisme series, continuing in 1994 to take fourth in the final standings. Undoubtedly the highlight of his year was a second Le Mans win (with Mauro Baldi and Hurley Haywood for Porsche), for his subsequent brief grand prix reappearance for Larrousse passed almost unnoticed.

Although Yannick scored a third Le Mans win in 1995 with a McLaren F1 GTR, he concentrated on his drive in the DTM/ITC series with the Opel Joest team. His two seasons in this category brought little reward, however, the frustrated driver dissatisfied with his equipment.

The 1997 season started with a win in a Ferrari 333SP at Sebring, and then Dalmas was delighted to sign for Porsche to race their 911 GT1 prototype. He quickly became the cornerstone of the team's efforts, his serious and professional approach being much admired by all his co-drivers. He formed a particularly strong pairing with Allan McNish in 1998, when the Porsche was bettered only by the works Mercedes CLKs. The company's withdrawal from competition in 1999 left him without a regular drive, but he was quickly snapped up by BMW Motorsport, enabling him to notch up a fourth Le Mans win with Pierluigi Martini and Jo Winkelhock in the BMW V12 LMR.

Subsequently, he made two unsuccessful sorties at the La Sarthe track with Oreca, before taking seventh place (in his 12th and final appearance) in 2002, sharing an Audi R8 with Seiji Ara and Hiroki Katoh.

ret	PORTUGUESE GP	Estoril	29	Larrousse Calmels	G	3.5 Lola LC88-Cosworth V8	alternator belt	15/31
11	SPANISH GP	Jerez	29	Larrousse Calmels	G	3.5 Lola LC88-Cosworth V8	1 lap behind	16/31
	1989 Championship position: Unplaced							
dnq	BRAZILIAN GP	Rio	29	Larrousse Calmels	G	3.5 Lola LC88B-Lamborghini V12		27/38
ret/dns	SAN MARINO GP	Imola	29	Equipe Larrousse	G	3.5 Lola LC89-Lamborghini V12	engine on dummy grid	(26)/39
dnq	MONACO GP	Monte Carlo	29	Equipe Larrousse	G	3.5 Lola LC89-Lamborghini V12		28/39
dnq	MEXICAN GP	Mexico City	29	Equipe Larrousse	G	3.5 Lola LC89-Lamborghini V12		29/39
dnq	US GP (PHOENIX)	Phoenix	29	Equipe Larrousse	G	3.5 Lola LC89-Lamborghini V12		30/39
dnq	CANADIAN GP	Montreal	29	Equipe Larrousse	G	3.5 Lola LC89-Lamborghini V12		28/39
dnpq	BRITISH GP	Silverstone	41	Automobiles Gonfaronaise Sportive	G	3.5 AGS JH23B-Cosworth V8		35/39
dnpq	GERMAN GP	Hockenheim	41	Automobiles Gonfaronaise Sportive	G	3.5 AGS JH23B-Cosworth V8		31/39
dnpq	"	"	41	Automobiles Gonfaronaise Sportive	G	3.5 AGS JH24-Cosworth V8		–/–
dnpq	HUNGARIAN GP	Hungaroring	41	Automobiles Gonfaronaise Sportive	G	3.5 AGS JH23B-Cosworth V8		33/39
dnpq	BELGIAN GP	Spa	41	Automobiles Gonfaronaise Sportive	G	3.5 AGS JH24-Cosworth V8		37/39
dnpq	ITALIAN GP	Monza	41	Automobiles Gonfaronaise Sportive	G	3.5 AGS JH24-Cosworth V8		37/39
excl	PORTUGUESE GP	Estoril	41	Automobiles Gonfaronaise Sportive	G	3.5 AGS JH24-Cosworth V8	practised on wrong tyres	38/38
dnpq	SPANISH GP	Jerez	41	Automobiles Gonfaronaise Sportive	G	3.5 AGS JH24-Cosworth V8		35/39
dnpq	JAPANESE GP	Suzuka	41	Automobiles Gonfaronaise Sportive	G	3.5 AGS JH24-Cosworth V8		38/39
dnpq	AUSTRALIAN GP	Adelaide	41	Automobiles Gonfaronaise Sportive	G	3.5 AGS JH24-Cosworth V8		37/39

1990 Championship position: Unplaced

dnpq	US GP (PHOENIX)	Phoenix	18	Automobiles Gonfaronaise Sportive	G	3.5 AGS JH24-Cosworth V8			32/35
ret	BRAZILIAN GP	Interlagos	18	Automobiles Gonfaronaise Sportive	G	3.5 AGS JH24-Cosworth V8	*front suspension*		26/35
dnpq	MONACO GP	Monte Carlo	18	Automobiles Gonfaranaise Sportive	G	3.5 AGS JH25-Cosworth V8			32/35
dnpq	CANADIAN GP	Montreal	18	Automobiles Gonfaronaise Sportive	G	3.5 AGS JH25-Cosworth V8			32/35
dnpq	MEXICAN GP	Mexico City	18	Automobiles Gonfaronaise Sportive	G	3.5 AGS JH25-Cosworth V8			31/35
17	FRENCH GP	Paul Ricard	18	Automobiles Gonfaronaise Sportive	G	3.5 AGS JH25-Cosworth V8	*5 laps behind*		26/35
dnpq	BRITISH GP	Silverstone	18	Automobiles Gonfaronaise Sportive	G	3.5 AGS JH25-Cosworth V8			32/35
dnq	GERMAN GP	Hockenheim	18	Automobiles Gonfaronaise Sportive	G	3.5 AGS JH25-Cosworth V8			29/35
dnq	HUNGARIAN GP	Hungaroring	18	Automobiles Gonfaronaise Sportive	G	3.5 AGS JH25-Cosworth V8			27/35
dnq	BELGIAN GP	Spa	18	Automobiles Gonfaronaise Sportive	G	3.5 AGS JH25-Cosworth V8			29/33
nc	ITALIAN GP	Monza	18	Automobiles Gonfaronaise Sportive	G	3.5 AGS JH25-Cosworth V8	*pit stops/8 laps behind*		24/33
ret	PORTUGUESE GP	Estoril	18	Automobiles Gonfaronaise Sportive	G	3.5 AGS JH25-Cosworth V8	*driveshaft*		25/33
9	SPANISH GP	Jerez	18	Automobiles Gonfaronaise Sportive	G	3.5 AGS JH25-Cosworth V8	*1 lap behind*		24/33
dnq	JAPANESE GP	Suzuka	18	Automobiles Gonfaronaise Sportive	G	3.5 AGS JH25-Cosworth V8			29/30
dnq	AUSTRALIAN GP	Adelaide	18	Automobiles Gonfaronaise Sportive	G	3.5 AGS JH25-Cosworth V8			28/30

1994 Championship position: Unplaced

ret	ITALIAN GP	Monza	19	Tourtel Larrousse F1	G	3.5 Larrousse LH94-Ford HB V8	*accident*	23/28
14	PORTUGUESE GP	Estoril	19	Tourtel Larrousse F1	G	3.5 Larrousse LH94-Ford HB V8	*2 laps behind*	23/28

GP Starts: 23 (24)   GP Wins: 0   Pole positions: 0   Fastest laps: 0   Points: 2

DEREK DALY

QUICK, but accident-prone may be an unfair judgement of Derek Daly, but the likeable Irishman certainly had to endure more than his fair share of incidents during his grand prix career.

Early experience in the harum-scarum world of stock cars led Derek into Formula Ford in his native Ireland. To finance his efforts, he went to Australia to work in the tin mines with his friend and fellow aspiring racer, David Kennedy. He earned enough to finance his season, winning the 1975 national championship. Then it was across the Irish Sea to try his luck in Formula Ford for 1976. It was a tough year for Daly, who was living out of a converted coach and perpetually strapped for cash, but all was made worthwhile when he won the Formula Ford Festival at the end of the season.

Derek stepped up to Formula 3 for 1977 and, driving a Chevron, won the BP championship ahead of Nelson Piquet, while a one-off drive saw him finish fifth on his Formula 2 debut at Estoril. So impressive was this performance that he was given the seat for 1978, and offers also came in for Formula 1. He did a deal with Hesketh and made a sensational debut in the rain at the International Trophy race, leading all the big names until he spun off. Reality soon dawned, however, as he failed to qualify for the first three races and quit in disgust. Luckily, Ensign needed a replacement for Jacky Ickx, and Daly was back, scoring his first point in Canada. He was persuaded to stay on for 1979, but the revamped car was outclassed, and after Monaco he returned to his successful ICI Formula 2 ride. This left him available to step into the Tyrrell team, initially in place of the indisposed Jean-Pierre Jarier. A superb drive at Watkins Glen ended in him spinning out, but Tyrrell had seen enough to offer him a drive for 1980. Again, it was a story of hit and miss, the season yielding a pair of fourth places and a couple of huge shunts.

For 1981, Daly was forced to take a step backwards. The RAM March was not competitive and the atmosphere in the team was tense, but he never gave up. Then Theodore threw him a lifeline, which put him back on the grid in 1982, and with Carlos Reutemann's sudden decision to retire, he found himself catapulted into the Williams team. It was a difficult season, however; he supported Rosberg with some classy drives, but was dumped at the end of the year.

Then Daly took the decision to turn his back on F1 and try his luck in Indy cars. After a handful of rides in '83 and some promising performances early in 1984, his career was nearly ended by a huge crash at Michigan, which badly smashed both his legs. After a long and painful recovery, he made a tentative comeback to Indy cars late in 1986, and then raced in endurance events for Jaguar and in IMSA for Nissan before announcing his retirement in 1992.

Derek has since slipped effortlessly into the role of TV commentator on grand prix and Indy car racing on Speedvision. Also, he is a very busy professional speaker, who addresses some of the largest businesses in the USA. His Derek Daly Academy is linked to the Skip Barber Racing Schools, and he has published a best-selling book on the motivational aspects of racing called Race To Win.

Daly's son, Conor, having won the Star Mazda championship in 2010, is currently striving to break into the top echelons of the sport, having raced in both Indy Lights and GP3 in 2011.

DALY, Derek (IRL) b 11/3/1953, Dundrum, Dublin

1978 Championship position: 19th=   Wins: 0   Pole positions: 0   Fastest laps: 0   Points scored: 1

	Race	Circuit	No	Entrant	Tyres	Capacity/Car/Engine	Comment	Q Pos/Entries
dnpq	US GP WEST	Long Beach	24	Olympus Cameras with Hesketh	G	3.0 Hesketh 308E-Cosworth V8		30/30
dnpq	MONACO GP	Monte Carlo	24	Olympus Cameras with Hesketh	G	3.0 Hesketh 308E-Cosworth V8		26/30
dnq	BELGIAN GP	Zolder	24	Olympus Cameras with Hesketh	G	3.0 Hesketh 308E-Cosworth V8		26/30
dnq	FRENCH GP	Paul Ricard	22	Team Tissot Ensign	G	3.0 Ensign N177-Cosworth V8		28/29
ret	BRITISH GP	Brands Hatch	22	Team Tissot Ensign	G	3.0 Ensign N177-Cosworth V8	lost wheel – crashed	15/30
dsq	AUSTRIAN GP	Österreichring	22	Team Tissot Ensign	G	3.0 Ensign N177-Cosworth V8	outside assistance after spin	19/31
ret	DUTCH GP	Zandvoort	22	Team Tissot Ensign	G	3.0 Ensign N177-Cosworth V8	driveshaft	16/33
10	ITALIAN GP	Monza	22	Team Tissot Ensign	G	3.0 Ensign N177-Cosworth V8		18/32
8	US GP EAST	Watkins Glen	22	Team Tissot Ensign	G	3.0 Ensign N177-Cosworth V8	1 lap behind	19/27
6	CANADIAN GP	Montreal	22	Team Tissot Ensign	G	3.0 Ensign N177-Cosworth V8		15/28

1979 Championship position: Unplaced

	Race	Circuit	No	Entrant	Tyres	Capacity/Car/Engine	Comment	Q Pos/Entries
11	ARGENTINE GP	Buenos Aires	22	Team Ensign	G	3.0 Ensign N177-Cosworth V8	2 laps behind	24/26
13	BRAZILIAN GP	Interlagos	22	Team Ensign	G	3.0 Ensign N177-Cosworth V8	1 lap behind	23/26
dnq	SOUTH AFRICAN GP	Kyalami	22	Team Ensign	G	3.0 Ensign N179-Cosworth V8		26/26
ret	US GP WEST	Long Beach	22	Team Ensign	G	3.0 Ensign N179-Cosworth V8	collision with Rebaque	26/26
dnq	SPANISH GP	Jarama	22	Team Ensign	G	3.0 Ensign N177-Cosworth V8		25/27
dnq	BELGIAN GP	Zolder	22	Team Ensign	G	3.0 Ensign N177-Cosworth V8		27/28
dnq	MONACO GP	Monte Carlo	22	Team Ensign	G	3.0 Ensign N179-Cosworth V8		24/25
8	AUSTRIAN GP	Österreichring	4	Candy Tyrrell Team	G	3.0 Tyrrell 009-Cosworth V8	1 lap behind	11/26
ret	CANADIAN GP	Montreal	33	Candy Tyrrell Team	G	3.0 Tyrrell 009-Cosworth V8	engine	24/29
ret	US GP EAST	Watkins Glen	33	Candy Tyrrell Team	G	3.0 Tyrrell 009-Cosworth V8	spun off	15/30

1980 Championship position: 10th=   Wins: 0   Pole positions: 0   Fastest laps: 0   Points scored: 6

	Race	Circuit	No	Entrant	Tyres	Capacity/Car/Engine	Comment	Q Pos/Entries
4	ARGENTINE GP	Buenos Aires	4	Candy Tyrrell Team	G	3.0 Tyrrell 009-Cosworth V8		22/28
14	BRAZILIAN GP	Interlagos	4	Candy Tyrrell Team	G	3.0 Tyrrell 009-Cosworth V8	2 laps behind	24/28
ret	SOUTH AFRICAN GP	Kyalami	4	Candy Tyrrell Team	G	3.0 Tyrrell 010-Cosworth V8	puncture	16/28
8	US GP WEST	Long Beach	4	Candy Tyrrell Team	G	3.0 Tyrrell 010-Cosworth V8	1 lap behind	14/27
9	BELGIAN GP	Zolder	4	Candy Tyrrell Team	G	3.0 Tyrrell 010-Cosworth V8	2 laps behind	11/27
ret	MONACO GP	Monte Carlo	4	Candy Tyrrell Team	G	3.0 Tyrrell 010-Cosworth V8	multiple accident on lap 1	12/27
11	FRENCH GP	Paul Ricard	4	Candy Tyrrell Team	G	3.0 Tyrrell 010-Cosworth V8	2 laps behind	20/27
4	BRITISH GP	Brands Hatch	4	Candy Tyrrell Team	G	3.0 Tyrrell 010-Cosworth V8	1 lap behind	10/27
10	GERMAN GP	Hockenheim	4	Candy Tyrrell Team	G	3.0 Tyrrell 010-Cosworth V8	1 lap behind	22/26
ret	AUSTRIAN GP	Österreichring	4	Candy Tyrrell Team	G	3.0 Tyrrell 010-Cosworth V8	sheared brake disc – crashed	10/25
ret	DUTCH GP	Zandvoort	4	Candy Tyrrell Team	G	3.0 Tyrrell 010-Cosworth V8	broken disc brake – big crash	23/28
ret	ITALIAN GP	Imola	4	Candy Tyrrell Team	G	3.0 Tyrrell 010-Cosworth V8	spun off	22/28
ret/dns	CANADIAN GP	Montreal	4	Candy Tyrrell Team	G	3.0 Tyrrell 010-Cosworth V8	startline crash – did not restart	20/28
ret	US GP EAST	Watkins Glen	4	Candy Tyrrell Team	G	3.0 Tyrrell 010-Cosworth V8	hit by de Cesaris	21/27

1981 Championship position: Unplaced

	Race	Circuit	No	Entrant	Tyres	Capacity/Car/Engine	Comment	Q Pos/Entries
dnq	US GP WEST	Long Beach	17	March Grand Prix Team	M	3.0 March 811-Cosworth V8		26/29
dnq	BRAZILIAN GP	Rio	17	March Grand Prix Team	M	3.0 March 811-Cosworth V8		30/30
dnq	ARGENTINE GP	Buenos Aires	17	March Grand Prix Team	M	3.0 March 811-Cosworth V8		27/29
dnq	SAN MARINO GP	Imola	18	March Grand Prix Team	M	3.0 March 811-Cosworth V8		26/30
dnq	BELGIAN GP	Zolder	18	March Grand Prix Team	M	3.0 March 811-Cosworth V8	practice times disallowed	-/31
dnpq	MONACO GP	Monte Carlo	18	March Grand Prix Team	M	3.0 March 811-Cosworth V8		28/31
16	SPANISH GP	Jarama	17	March Grand Prix Team	M	3.0 March 811-Cosworth V8	5 laps behind	22/30
ret	FRENCH GP	Dijon	17	March Grand Prix Team	A	3.0 March 811-Cosworth V8	engine	20/29
7	BRITISH GP	Silverstone	17	March Grand Prix Team	A	3.0 March 811-Cosworth V8	2 laps behind	17/30
ret	GERMAN GP	Hockenheim	17	March Grand Prix Team	A	3.0 March 811-Cosworth V8	steering tie rod	21/30
11	AUSTRIAN GP	Österreichring	17	March Grand Prix Team	A	3.0 March 811-Cosworth V8	6 laps behind	19/28
ret	DUTCH GP	Zandvoort	17	March Grand Prix Team	A	3.0 March 811-Cosworth V8	suspension	19/30
ret	ITALIAN GP	Monza	17	March Grand Prix Team	A	3.0 March 811-Cosworth V8	gearbox	19/30
8	CANADIAN GP	Montreal	17	March Grand Prix Team	A	3.0 March 811-Cosworth V8	2 laps behind	20/30
dnq	CAESARS PALACE GP	Las Vegas	17	March Grand Prix Team	A	3.0 March 811-Cosworth V8		27/30

1982 Championship position: 13th   Wins: 0   Pole positions: 0   Fastest laps: 0   Points scored: 8

	Race	Circuit	No	Entrant	Tyres	Capacity/Car/Engine	Comment	Q Pos/Entries
14	SOUTH AFRICAN GP	Kyalami	33	Theodore Racing Team	A	3.0 Theodore TY01-Cosworth V8	clutch/brake problems/-4 laps	24/30
ret	BRAZILIAN GP	Rio	33	Theodore Racing Team	A	3.0 Theodore TY02-Cosworth V8	puncture – spun off	20/31
ret	US GP WEST	Long Beach	33	Theodore Racing Team	A	3.0 Theodore TY02-Cosworth V8	ran off track – stalled car	22/31
ret	BELGIAN GP	Zolder	5	TAG Williams Team	G	3.0 Williams FW08-Cosworth V8	ran off road	15/32
6/ret	MONACO GP	Monte Carlo	5	TAG Williams Team	G	3.0 Williams FW08-Cosworth V8	gearbox – accident/2 laps behind	8/31
5	US GP (DETROIT)	Detroit	5	TAG Williams Team	G	3.0 Williams FW08-Cosworth V8		12/28
7/ret	CANADIAN GP	Montreal	5	TAG Williams Team	G	3.0 Williams FW08-Cosworth V8	out of fuel/2 laps behind	13/29
5	DUTCH GP	Zandvoort	5	TAG Williams Team	G	3.0 Williams FW08-Cosworth V8	1 lap behind	12/31
5	BRITISH GP	Brands Hatch	5	TAG Williams Team	G	3.0 Williams FW08-Cosworth V8		10/30
7	FRENCH GP	Paul Ricard	5	TAG Williams Team	G	3.0 Williams FW08-Cosworth V8	1 lap behind	11/30
ret	GERMAN GP	Hockenheim	5	TAG Williams Team	G	3.0 Williams FW08-Cosworth V8	engine	20/30
ret	AUSTRIAN GP	Österreichring	5	TAG Williams Team	G	3.0 Williams FW08-Cosworth V8	hit by de Cesaris	9/29
9	SWISS GP	Dijon	5	TAG Williams Team	G	3.0 Williams FW08-Cosworth V8	1 lap behind	7/29
ret	ITALIAN GP	Monza	5	TAG Williams Team	G	3.0 Williams FW08-Cosworth V8	hit by Guerrero – suspension damage	13/30
6	CAESARS PALACE GP	Las Vegas	5	TAG Williams Team	G	3.0 Williams FW08-Cosworth V8	1 lap behind	14/30

GP Starts: 48 (49)   GP Wins: 0   Pole positions: 0   Fastest laps: 0   Points: 15

CHRISTIAN DANNER

THE son of Professor Maximilian Danner, an engineer who founded the Allianz (AZT) automotive research department in 1971, which was the first institute of its kind, pioneering crash testing and safety research, Christian became involved in motorsport at about the same time by racing (and regularly crashing) a Renault 5 in Germany. He soon came to the attention of Manfred Cassani, who was looking for a young driver to promote.

Danner was given a BMW M1 to race in the German G4 championship and a couple of ProCar GP support races, and he did so well in these that BMW signed him on a three-year contract to race in the works March F2 team. With no single-seater experience, he struggled in 1981 – his first season – and he was usually overshadowed by the team's lead drivers, Thierry Boutsen, Corrado Fabi, Johnny Cecotto and Beppe Gabbiani, but by the end of 1983 he was not far off the pace, as witnessed by his pole position at the Nürburgring.

Unfortunately for Christian, BMW then pulled the plug on their F2 programme, and at first he was left without a drive for 1984, eventually joining the Bob Sparshott team. That season was dominated by the Ralt-Hondas, but Danner was up there with the rest, and with a minimal budget he tackled the inaugural F3000 season in 1985 with the same team. This would be his breakthrough year. Not the quickest driver, but certainly the most consistent, he became the formula's first champion. This brought him a grand prix opportunity at Zakspeed, and then a contract with Osella for 1986, which was bought out in mid-season when Arrows needed a replacement for the badly injured Marc Surer.

Christian rejoined Zakspeed in 1987 and, paired with Martin Brundle, performed quite well given the equipment available. He was on the sidelines in 1988, but could have had the dubious privilege of a EuroBrun drive from mid-season had he not been too tall to fit into the car. The following season saw his final shot at F1, driving the Rial for the autocratic Günther Schmid. He scored a distant fourth at Phoenix, but finally quit as the team slid into oblivion.

Christian spent the next few years as a real globetrotter, competing in Japanese F3000, Indy cars and the GTCC, driving a BMW in 1991. Landing a works-backed Alfa in the DTM/ITC run by Schübel, he put in some very strong performances, and was rewarded with outright wins in 1995 at Helsinki and Norisring.

Christian was a co-owner with Andreas Leberle of the Project Indy CART team, which always competed on very limited resources. He managed to drive in a couple of Indy car races himself in 1995, the first of which, in Miami, brought the team a remarkable seventh place, despite his having to resort to an elderly '93 Lola. It is a testament to his racing abilities that, in 1997, even two years away from CART proved to be no barrier. At short notice, he hopped into the Payton/Coyne Lola at Detroit and picked up the team's first point of the year with a solid 12th-place finish.

Lack of finance downed Project Indy's plans, so Christian's racing activities were centred on the German Super Touring series with an Alfa Romeo. In 2005/06, he took part in the short-lived Grand Prix Masters series, taking second behind Nigel Mansell at Losail, and third at Silverstone, sharing the podium with Eddie Cheever and Eric van der Poele.

In recent years, Christian has run a sponsorship consultancy business, worked as a TV commentator for RTL on German TV and contributed features to various motorsport publications. He is currently a safety ambassador for Allianz, helping to raise awareness of road safety issues. He is also in demand as a motivational speaker to business management groups.

DANNER, Christian (D) b 4/4/1958, Munich

1985 Championship position: Unplaced

	Race	Circuit	No	Entrant	Tyres	Capacity/Car/Engine	Comment	Q Pos/Entries
ret	BELGIAN GP	Spa	30	West Zakspeed Racing	G	1.5 t/c Zakspeed 841 4	gearbox	22/24
ret	EUROPEAN GP	Brands Hatch	30	West Zakspeed Racing	G	1.5 t/c Zakspeed 841 4	engine	25/27

1986 Championship position: 18th=   Wins: 0   Pole positions: 0   Fastest laps: 0   Points scored: 1

	Race	Circuit	No	Entrant	Tyres	Capacity/Car/Engine	Comment	Q Pos/Entries
ret	BRAZILIAN GP	Rio	22	Osella Squadra Corse	P	1.5 t/c Osella FA1F-Alfa Romeo V8	engine	24/25
ret	SPANISH GP	Jerez	22	Osella Squadra Corse	P	1.5 t/c Osella FA1F-Alfa Romeo V8	engine	23/25
ret	SAN MARINO GP	Imola	22	Osella Squadra Corse	P	1.5 t/c Osella FA1F-Alfa Romeo V8	electrics	25/26
dnq	MONACO GP	Monte Carlo	22	Osella Squadra Corse	P	1.5 t/c Osella FA1F-Alfa Romeo V8		24/26
ret	BELGIAN GP	Spa	22	Osella Squadra Corse	P	1.5 t/c Osella FA1F-Alfa Romeo V8	started from pit lane/engine	25/25
ret	CANADIAN GP	Montreal	22	Osella Squadra Corse	P	1.5 t/c Osella FA1F-Alfa Romeo V8	turbo	25/25
dnp	"	"	17	Barclay Arrows BMW	G	1.5 t/c Arrows A8-BMW 4	contractual problems	– / –
ret	US GP (DETROIT)	Detroit	17	Barclay Arrows BMW	G	1.5 t/c Arrows A8-BMW 4	electrics – fuel metering unit	19/26
11	FRENCH GP	Paul Ricard	17	Barclay Arrows BMW	G	1.5 t/c Arrows A8-BMW 4	stalled on grid/4 laps behind	18/26
ret/dns	BRITISH GP	Brands Hatch	17	Barclay Arrows BMW	G	1.5 t/c Arrows A8-BMW 4	accident at first start/did not restart	23/26
ret	GERMAN GP	Hockenheim	17	Barclay Arrows BMW	G	1.5 t/c Arrows A8-BMW 4	turbo	17/26
ret	HUNGARIAN GP	Hungaroring	17	Barclay Arrows BMW	G	1.5 t/c Arrows A9-BMW 4	rear suspension	21/26
dns	"	"	17	Barclay Arrows BMW	G	1.5 t/c Arrows A8-BMW 4	practice only	– / –
6	AUSTRIAN GP	Österreichring	17	Barclay Arrows BMW	G	1.5 t/c Arrows A8-BMW 4	3 laps behind	22/26
8	ITALIAN GP	Monza	17	Barclay Arrows BMW	G	1.5 t/c Arrows A8-BMW 4	2 laps behind	16/27
11	PORTUGUESE GP	Estoril	17	Barclay Arrows BMW	G	1.5 t/c Arrows A8-BMW 4	3 laps behind	22/27

			No	Entrant	Tyres	Capacity/Car/Engine	Comment	Q Pos/Entries
9	MEXICAN GP	Mexico City	17	Barclay Arrows BMW	G	1.5 t/c Arrows A8-BMW 4	*2 laps behind*	20/26
ret	AUSTRALIAN GP	Adelaide	17	Barclay Arrows BMW	G	1.5 t/c Arrows A8-BMW 4	*engine*	24/26

1987 Championship position: Unplaced

			No	Entrant	Tyres	Capacity/Car/Engine	Comment	Q Pos/Entries
9	BRAZILIAN GP	Rio	10	West Zakspeed Racing	G	1.5 t/c Zakspeed 861 4	*3 laps behind*	17/23
7	SAN MARINO GP	Imola	10	West Zakspeed Racing	G	1.5 t/c Zakspeed 861 4	*2 laps behind*	19/27
ret	BELGIAN GP	Spa	10	West Zakspeed Racing	G	1.5 t/c Zakspeed 871 4	*brakes – spun off*	20/26
excl*	MONACO GP	Monte Carlo	10	West Zakspeed Racing	G	1.5 t/c Zakspeed 871 4	**practice incident with Alboreto*	– /26
8	US GP (DETROIT)	Detroit	10	West Zakspeed Racing	G	1.5 t/c Zakspeed 871 4	*3 laps behind*	16/26
ret	FRENCH GP	Paul Ricard	10	West Zakspeed Racing	G	1.5 t/c Zakspeed 871 4	*engine*	19/26
ret	BRITISH GP	Silverstone	10	West Zakspeed Racing	G	1.5 t/c Zakspeed 871 4	*gearbox*	18/26
ret	GERMAN GP	Hockenheim	10	West Zakspeed Racing	G	1.5 t/c Zakspeed 871 4	*driveshaft*	20/26
ret	HUNGARIAN GP	Hungaroring	10	West Zakspeed Racing	G	1.5 t/c Zakspeed 871 4	*engine cut out*	23/26
9	AUSTRIAN GP	Österreichring	10	West Zakspeed Racing	G	1.5 t/c Zakspeed 871 4	*started from pit lane/3 laps behind*	20/26
9	ITALIAN GP	Monza	10	West Zakspeed Racing	G	1.5 t/c Zakspeed 871 4	*2 laps behind*	16/28
ret/dns	PORTUGUESE GP	Estoril	10	West Zakspeed Racing	G	1.5 t/c Zakspeed 871 4	*accident in first start*	16/27
ret	SPANISH GP	Jerez	10	West Zakspeed Racing	G	1.5 t/c Zakspeed 871 4	*gearbox*	22/28
ret	MEXICAN GP	Mexico City	10	West Zakspeed Racing	G	1.5 t/c Zakspeed 871 4	*hit Johansson*	17/27
ret	JAPANESE GP	Suzuka	10	West Zakspeed Racing	G	1.5 t/c Zakspeed 871 4	*accident*	17/27
7*	AUSTRALIAN GP	Adelaide	10	West Zakspeed Racing	G	1.5 t/c Zakspeed 871 4	**2nd place car dsq/3 laps behind*	24/27

1989 Championship position: 21st=   Wins: 0   Pole positions: 0   Fastest laps: 0   Points scored: 3

			No	Entrant	Tyres	Capacity/Car/Engine	Comment	Q Pos/Entries
14/ret	BRAZILIAN GP	Rio	38	Rial Racing	G	3.5 Rial ARC2-Cosworth V8	*gearbox/5 laps behind*	17/38
dnq	SAN MARINO GP	Imola	38	Rial Racing	G	3.5 Rial ARC2-Cosworth V8		29/38
dnq	MONACO GP	Monte Carlo	38	Rial Racing	G	3.5 Rial ARC2-Cosworth V8		27/38
12	MEXICAN GP	Mexico City	38	Rial Racing	G	3.5 Rial ARC2-Cosworth V8	*2 laps behind*	23/39
4	US GP (PHOENIX)	Phoenix	38	Rial Racing	G	3.5 Rial ARC2-Cosworth V8	*1 lap behind*	26/39
8	CANADIAN GP	Montreal	38	Rial Racing	G	3.5 Rial ARC2-Cosworth V8	*3 laps behind*	23/39
dnq	FRENCH GP	Paul Ricard	38	Rial Racing	G	3.5 Rial ARC2-Cosworth V8		29/39
dnq	BRITISH GP	Silverstone	38	Rial Racing	G	3.5 Rial ARC2-Cosworth V8		30/39
dnq	GERMAN GP	Hockenheim	38	Rial Racing	G	3.5 Rial ARC2-Cosworth V8		29/39
dnq	HUNGARIAN GP	Hungaroring	38	Rial Racing	G	3.5 Rial ARC2-Cosworth V8		29/39
dnq	BELGIAN GP	Spa	38	Rial Racing	G	3.5 Rial ARC2-Cosworth V8		29/39
dnq	ITALIAN GP	Monza	38	Rial Racing	G	3.5 Rial ARC2-Cosworth V8		28/39
dnq	PORTUGUESE GP	Estoril	38	Rial Racing	G	3.5 Rial ARC2-Cosworth V8		31/39

GP Starts: 34 (36)   GP Wins: 0   Pole positions: 0   Fastest laps: 0   Points: 4

JORGE DAPONTE

AN amateur Argentinian driver, Jorge Daponte bought a Maserati 4CLT with the help of his uncles, both former drivers, and drove it to ninth in the Perón Grand Prix at the Costanera Norte circuit. A week later, at the same track in the Eva Perón Grand Prix, he was the final healthy runner left at the finish and took fourth place behind Froilán Gonzáles, Karl Kling and Hermann Lang.

In 1952, Daponte was on hand at the opening of the Autódromo Municipal where, in front of an estimated crowd of 550,000 for the Perón Grand Prix, again he took fourth place. Two weeks later, he competed in Piriápolis, Uruguay, where he finished eighth with his Maserati.

In 1953, Jorge took part in the Sebring 12-hours, sharing a Maserati with Fritz Koster, but their car was disqualified for making a wrong manoeuvre during a pit stop. In May of that year, he ran some laps at the Indianapolis 500, but failed to qualify.

After his return home, Daponte began to race in the Fuerza Libre, held on dirt tracks dotted around the country, and he soon became a leading competitor with his Chevrolet-engined special. By the end of the year, he was second to champion Alfredo Pián and ahead of Jesus Ricardo Iglesias.

Daponte entered his home grand prix with an old Maserati in 1954, but was forced out with transmission trouble. He retained the car for the Buenos Aires City GP a fortnight later, but was involved in a freak accident when it skidded on a patch of oil, striking and killing team owner Enrico Platé, who was standing away from the pits. Later in the year, Jorge ventured to Europe to drive his 1953 Maserati. In a couple of non-championship races, he was fourth at Rouen and fifth at Pescara, but in both events he was the last healthy runner. For the Italian GP at Monza, he was some ten seconds off the pace in practice and circulated steadily in the race, but was ten laps behind at the finish. After his frustrating European excursion, he went to the USA, where he took part in some oval dirt-track racing and ended the year as a participant in the famous Carrera Panamericana. In 1955, he competed again in the Argentine national Fuerza Libre championship, and although he took part in some other competitions, he soon withdrew from racing.

In March, 1963, in his native Buenos Aires, Daponte was found dead, having committed suicide by shooting himself in the head.

DAPONTE, Jorge (RA)   b 5/6/1923, Buenos Aires – d 9/3/1963, Buenos Aires

1954 Championship position: Unplaced

	Race	Circuit	No	Entrant	Tyres	Capacity/Car/Engine	Comment	Q Pos/Entries
ret	ARGENTINE GP	Buenos Aires	34	Jorge Daponte	P	2.5 Maserati A6GCM/250F 6	*transmission*	18/18
nc	ITALIAN GP	Monza	8	Jorge Daponte	P	2.5 Maserati A6GCM/250F 6	*10 laps behind*	19/21

GP Starts: 2   GP Wins: 0   Pole positions: 0   Fastest laps: 0   Points: 0

ANTHONY DAVIDSON

A CONTEMPORARY of Jenson Button in his karting days, Anthony Davidson proved to be such an assiduous test driver for Honda that he found himself largely restricted to this valuable role, which harmed his long-term grand prix prospects.

He spent a long time in karting, winning numerous titles, before a switch to Formula Ford in 1999 that yielded immediate dividends, which he built on the following year with the Formula Ford Festival title and the runner-up spot in the British championship. His performances netted the McLaren/Autosport Young Driver Award.

Gaining a seat with Carlin Motorsport, partnered by Takuma Sato, Davidson made a good fist of challenging for the Formula 3 title in his debut year, but despite winning six races, he had to give best to his Japanese team-mate. He also added wins in the prestigious Pau Grand Prix, the Elf Masters and the European Cup for good measure, but ended his year in hospital, having crashed heavily in practice for the Macau GP.

Davidson elected not to chase a race seat in F3000 for 2002, preferring instead to concentrate on his burgeoning test role with BAR. His pace began to get him noticed elsewhere, however, and when Alex Yoong was 'rested' by Minardi for two races, he got the call to replace him. Sadly, he failed to shine and retired from both events after spinning out.

He remained in the testing role at BAR the following year, despite also being named as official reserve at Jaguar Racing, and rekindled his racing ambitions by contesting the Sebring and Le Mans sports car events with the Prodrive Veloqx team, taking second in class at the former.

While Davidson remained the third driver at BAR, rule changes for 2004 meant that he got the chance to display his potential to a bigger audience in Friday practice. Williams were impressed and were reported to be chasing in his services, but in the end being tied to a long-term contract proved to be a stumbling block and he remained at Brackley. In 2005, another rare race opportunity came his way after a feverish Sato became indisposed in Malaysia, but his Honda retired with engine failure on lap three. Passed over for a race seat, it was back to testing for 2006, once again supporting Button and the newly recruited Rubens Barrichello.

Davidson's loyalty was finally rewarded when Honda placed him in the Super Aguri team alongside Sato for 2007. It was of course a season of low expectations as the team tried desperately to make progress. He qualified superbly on occasion given the equipment, but fared less well in the races, failing to break into the top ten finishers. Despite persistent rumours of an imminent demise, the team made it on to the grid for the 2008 opener in Melbourne, but with Honda finally withdrawing their support, the financially beleaguered team soon closed its doors.

With any further F1 opportunities seemingly out of reach, Davidson looked to sports car racing in 2009, driving an Aston Martin LMP1 at Le Mans and then accepting a GT outing for Nissan in the Spa 24-hours. This led to him finding a place in the Peugeot team to race their 908 Hdi FAP for 2010. His debut at Sebring saw a commanding win (with Alex Wurz and Marc Gené), and he also took a victory at Silverstone (with Nicolas Minassian).

The following year brought a win at Spa (with Wurz and Gené once more), but a month later the trio could do no better than fourth in their bid to take victory at La Sarthe. With the French giant suddenly pulling the plug on their programme at the end of the year, Davidson lost no time in securing a seat in the Toyota sports car squad with their Le Mans TS030 hybrid challenger.

Having already successfully worked for the BBC in a commentating role, Davidson joined Sky Sports as a member of the team for their wall-to-wall coverage of the 2012 grand prix season.

DAVIDSON, Anthony (GB) b 18/4/1979, Hemel Hempstead, Hertfordshire

	Race	Circuit	No	Entrant	Tyres	Capacity/Car/Engine	Comment	Q Pos/Entries
	2002 Championship position: Unplaced							
ret	HUNGARIAN GP	Hungaroring	22	KL Minardi Asiatech	M	3.0 Minardi PS02-Asiatech V10	*spun off*	20/20
ret	BELGIAN GP	Spa	22	KL Minardi Asiatech	M	3.0 Minardi PS02-Asiatech V10	*spun off*	20/20
	2004 Championship position: Unplaced							
app	AUSTRALIAN GP	Melbourne	35	Lucky Strike BAR Honda	M	3.0 BAR 006-Honda V10	*ran as 3rd driver in practice only*	– /–
app	MALAYSIAN GP	Sepang	35	Lucky Strike BAR Honda	M	3.0 BAR 006-Honda V10	*ran as 3rd driver in practice only*	– /–
app	BAHRAIN GP	Sakhir Circuit	35	Lucky Strike BAR Honda	M	3.0 BAR 006-Honda V10	*ran as 3rd driver in practice only*	– /–
app	SAN MARINO GP	Imola	35	Lucky Strike BAR Honda	M	3.0 BAR 006-Honda V10	*ran as 3rd driver in practice only*	– /–
app	SPANISH GP	Barcelona	35	Lucky Strike BAR Honda	M	3.0 BAR 006-Honda V10	*ran as 3rd driver in practice only*	– /–
app	MONACO GP	Monte Carlo	35	Lucky Strike BAR Honda	M	3.0 BAR 006-Honda V10	*ran as 3rd driver in practice only*	– /–
app	EUROPEAN GP	Nürburgring	35	Lucky Strike BAR Honda	M	3.0 BAR 006-Honda V10	*ran as 3rd driver in practice only*	– /–
app	CANADIAN GP	Montreal	35	Lucky Strike BAR Honda	M	3.0 BAR 006-Honda V10	*ran as 3rd driver in practice only*	– /–
app	US GP	Indianapolis	35	Lucky Strike BAR Honda	M	3.0 BAR 006-Honda V10	*ran as 3rd driver in practice only*	– /–
app	FRENCH GP	Magny Cours	35	Lucky Strike BAR Honda	M	3.0 BAR 006-Honda V10	*ran as 3rd driver in practice only*	– /–
app	BRITISH GP	Silverstone	35	Lucky Strike BAR Honda	M	3.0 BAR 006-Honda V10	*ran as 3rd driver in practice only*	– /–
app	GERMAN GP	Hockenheim	35	Lucky Strike BAR Honda	M	3.0 BAR 006-Honda V10	*ran as 3rd driver in practice only*	– /–
app	HUNGARIAN GP	Hungaroring	35	Lucky Strike BAR Honda	M	3.0 BAR 006-Honda V10	*ran as 3rd driver in practice only*	– /–
app	BELGIAN GP	Spa	35	Lucky Strike BAR Honda	M	3.0 BAR 006-Honda V10	*ran as 3rd driver in practice only*	– /–
app	ITALIAN GP	Monza	35	Lucky Strike BAR Honda	M	3.0 BAR 006-Honda V10	*ran as 3rd driver in practice only*	– /–
app	CHINESE GP	Shanghai	35	Lucky Strike BAR Honda	M	3.0 BAR 006-Honda V10	*ran as 3rd driver in practice only*	– /–
app	JAPANESE GP	Suzuka	35	Lucky Strike BAR Honda	M	3.0 BAR 006-Honda V10	*ran as 3rd driver in practice only*	– /–
app	BRAZILIAN GP	Interlagos	35	Lucky Strike BAR Honda	M	3.0 BAR 006-Honda V10	*ran as 3rd driver in practice only*	– /–

2005 Championship position: Unplaced

ret	MALAYSIAN GP	Sepang	4	BAR Lucky Strike Honda	M	3.0 BAR 007-Honda V10	engine – oil leak	15/20

2006 Championship position: Unplaced

app	BAHRAIN GP	Sakhir Circuit	36	Lucky Strike Honda Racing F1 Team	M	2.4 Honda RA106-V8	ran as 3rd driver in practice only	– /–
app	MALAYSIAN GP	Sepang	36	Lucky Strike Honda Racing F1 Team	M	2.4 Honda RA106-V8	ran as 3rd driver in practice only	– /–
app	AUSTRALIAN GP	Melbourne	36	Lucky Strike Honda Racing F1 Team	M	2.4 Honda RA106-V8	ran as 3rd driver in practice only	– /–
app	SAN MARINO GP	Imola	36	Lucky Strike Honda Racing F1 Team	M	2.4 Honda RA106-V8	ran as 3rd driver in practice only	– /–
app	EUROPEAN GP	Nürburgring	36	Lucky Strike Honda Racing F1 Team	M	2.4 Honda RA106-V8	ran as 3rd driver in practice only	– /–
app	SPANISH GP	Barcelona	36	Lucky Strike Honda Racing F1 Team	M	2.4 Honda RA106-V8	ran as 3rd driver in practice only	– /–
app	MONACO GP	Monte Carlo	36	Lucky Strike Honda Racing F1 Team	M	2.4 Honda RA106-V8	ran as 3rd driver in practice only	– /–
app	BRITISH GP	Silverstone	36	Lucky Strike Honda Racing F1 Team	M	2.4 Honda RA106-V8	ran as 3rd driver in practice only	– /–
app	CANADIAN GP	Montreal	36	Lucky Strike Honda Racing F1 Team	M	2.4 Honda RA106-V8	ran as 3rd driver in practice only	– /–
app	US GP	Indianapolis	36	Lucky Strike Honda Racing F1 Team	M	2.4 Honda RA106-V8	ran as 3rd driver in practice only	– /–
app	FRENCH GP	Magny Cours	36	Lucky Strike Honda Racing F1 Team	M	2.4 Honda RA106-V8	ran as 3rd driver in practice only	– /–
app	GERMAN GP	Hockenheim	36	Lucky Strike Honda Racing F1 Team	M	2.4 Honda RA106-V8	ran as 3rd driver in practice only	– /–
app	HUNGARIAN GP	Hungaroring	36	Lucky Strike Honda Racing F1 Team	M	2.4 Honda RA106-V8	ran as 3rd driver in practice only	– /–
app	TURKISH GP	Istanbul	36	Lucky Strike Honda Racing F1 Team	M	2.4 Honda RA106-V8	ran as 3rd driver in practice only	– /–
app	ITALIAN GP	Monza	36	Lucky Strike Honda Racing F1 Team	M	2.4 Honda RA106-V8	ran as 3rd driver in practice only	– /–
app	CHINESE GP	Shanghai	36	Lucky Strike Honda Racing F1 Team	M	2.4 Honda RA106-V8	ran as 3rd driver in practice only	– /–
app	JAPANESE GP	Suzuka	36	Lucky Strike Honda Racing F1 Team	M	2.4 Honda RA106-V8	ran as 3rd driver in practice only	– /–
app	BRAZILIAN GP	Interlagos	36	Lucky Strike Honda Racing F1 Team	M	2.4 Honda RA106-V8	ran as 3rd driver in practice only	– /–

2007 Championship position: Unplaced

16	AUSTRALIAN GP	Melbourne	23	Super Aguri Racing	B	2.4 Super Aguri SA07-Honda V8	collision with Albers/2 laps behind	11/22
16	MALAYSIAN GP	Sepang	23	Super Aguri Racing	B	2.4 Super Aguri SA07-Honda V8	anti-stall pit stop delay/-1 lap	18/22
16/ret	BAHRAIN GP	Bahrain	23	Super Aguri Racing	B	2.4 Super Aguri SA07-Honda V8	engine/6 laps behind	13/22
11	SPANISH GP	Barcelona	23	Super Aguri Racing	B	2.4 Super Aguri SA07-Honda V8	1 lap behind	15/22
18	MONACO GP	Monte Carlo	23	Super Aguri Racing	B	2.4 Super Aguri SA07-Honda V8	collision/drive-thru penalty/-2 laps	17/22
11	CANADIAN GP	Montreal	23	Super Aguri Racing	B	2.4 Super Aguri SA07-Honda V8	one stop strategy/tyre graining	17/22
11	US GP	Indianapolis	23	Super Aguri Racing	B	2.4 Super Aguri SA07-Honda V8	1 lap behind	16/22
ret	FRENCH GP	Magny Cours	23	Super Aguri Racing	B	2.4 Super Aguri SA07-Honda V8	accident damage	20/22
ret	BRITISH GP	Silverstone	23	Super Aguri Racing	B	2.4 Super Aguri SA07-Honda V8	mechanical	19/22
12	EUROPEAN GP	Nürburgring	23	Super Aguri Racing	B	2.4 Super Aguri SA07-Honda V8	1 lap behind	15/22
ret	HUNGARIAN GP	Hungaroring	23	Super Aguri Racing	B	2.4 Super Aguri SA07-Honda V8	accident	15/22
14	TURKISH GP	Istanbul	23	Super Aguri Racing	B	2.4 Super Aguri SA07-Honda V8	1 lap behind	11/22
14	ITALIAN GP	Monza	23	Super Aguri Racing	B	2.4 Super Aguri SA07-Honda V8	early collision – Vettel/1 lap behind	14/22
16	BELGIAN GP	Spa	23	Super Aguri Racing	B	2.4 Super Aguri SA07-Honda V8	started from pitlane/1 lap behind	17/22
ret	JAPANESE GP	Suzuka	23	Super Aguri Racing	B	2.4 Super Aguri SA07-Honda V8	throttle sensor	19/22
ret	CHINESE GP	Shanghai	23	Super Aguri Racing	B	2.4 Super Aguri SA07-Honda V8	brakes – accident	15/22
14	BRAZILIAN GP	Interlagos	23	Super Aguri Racing	B	2.4 Super Aguri SA07-Honda V8	hit by Sutil/3 laps behind	20/22

2008 Championship position: Unplaced

ret	AUSTRALIAN GP	Melbourne	19	Super Aguri Racing	B	2.4 Super Aguri SA08A-Honda V8	multiple colllison on lap 1	22/22
15	MALAYSIAN GP	Sepang	19	Super Aguri Racing	B	2.4 Super Aguri SA08A-Honda V8	1 lap behind	22/22
16	BAHRAIN GP	Bahrain	19	Super Aguri Racing	B	2.4 Super Aguri SA08A-Honda V8	1 lap behind	21/22
ret	SPANISH GP	Barcelona	19	Super Aguri Racing	B	2.4 Super Aguri SA08A-Honda V8	holed radiator	21/22

GP Starts: 24   GP Wins: 0   Pole positions: 0   Fastest laps: 0   Points: 0

COLIN DAVIS

SON of the legendary S.C.H. 'Sammy' Davis, Colin began his career in 1954 with a Cooper Norton, using Formula 3 as a good learning vehicle before switching to sports cars to pursue his intended aim of racing in long-distance events. Unusually for an Englishman, with so much racing available in his homeland, he soon made Italy the centre of his activities, driving for de Tomaso, for Scuderia Centro Sud in grands prix and sports car races, and, from 1960, for Scuderia Serenissima.

Colin was also a leading runner in Formula Junior, winning at Albi in 1959 and at Pau in 1960. He was the winner of the second Monza Lottery Grand Prix in 1960 in a Fiat Osca. His greatest success still lay ahead, though; he would win the 1964 Targa Florio in a works Porsche 904 GT with Emilio Pucci. This led to other races for the Stuttgart team: he finished second in the 1965 Targa with Gerhard Mitter and fourth at Le Mans in 1966 with Jo Siffert.

After retiring, he moved to South Africa, where he still resides today.

DAVIS, Colin (GB) b 29/7/1932, Marylebone, London

1959 Championship position: Unplaced

	Race	Circuit	No	Entrant	Tyres	Capacity/Car/Engine	Comment	Q Pos/Entries
ret	FRENCH GP	Reims	20	Scuderia Centro Sud	D	2.5 Cooper T51-Maserati 4	oil pipe	17/22
11	ITALIAN GP	Monza	40	Scuderia Centro Sud	D	2.5 Cooper T51-Maserati 4	4 laps behind	18/21

GP Starts: 2   GP Wins: 0   Pole positions: 0   Fastest laps: 0   Points: 0

ANDREA de ADAMICH

WITH success in the 1965 Italian F3 championship and the 1966 European touring car series in an Alfa Romeo Giulia GTA behind him, Andrea de Adamich was given a works debut for Ferrari in the non-championship F1 Spanish GP at Jarama late in 1967 – finishing ninth after a puncture – but his grand prix career as a Ferrari driver faltered at the first hurdle with an accident at Kyalami in 1968, and came undone shortly afterwards when a crash in practice for the Race of Champions at Brands Hatch inflicted neck injuries that sidelined him for much of the season. Despite a victorious comeback with the works Ferrari Dino T166, which saw him win two races and the championship in the South American Formula 2 Temporada series, the Italian's big chance had gone.

Undaunted, Andrea busied himself in the newly inaugurated F5000/FA series for Team Surtees on both sides of the Atlantic, before returning to F1 in 1970, initially with backing from Alfa Romeo, racing their engine in a variety of 'third' works cars. A switch to Ford power made possible occasional good placings, but leg injuries sustained in the multiple accident caused by Jody Scheckter in the 1973 British Grand Prix brought his Formula 1 career to a premature end.

In parallel to his activities in grand prix racing, de Adamich was a works driver for Alfa Romeo in their successful T33 sports cars from 1970 to 1974, winning the Brands Hatch 1000km and the Watkins Glen six-hours in 1971. When his hectic racing schedule allowed, he also competed in Can-Am, touring cars and hill-climbs. After his retirement in 1974, he returned to the grand prix scene as a respected motorsport journalist and TV commentator.

de ADAMICH, Andrea (I) b 3/10/1941, Trieste

1968 Championship position: Unplaced

	Race	Circuit	No	Entrant	Tyres	Capacity/Car/Engine	Comment	Q Pos/Entries
ret	SOUTH AFRICAN GP	Kyalami	10	Scuderia Ferrari SpA SEFAC	F	3.0 Ferrari 312/67 V12	spun off on oil – crashed heavily	7/23

1970 Championship position: Unplaced

	Race	Circuit	No	Entrant	Tyres	Capacity/Car/Engine	Comment	Q Pos/Entries
dnq	SPANISH GP	Jarama	20	Bruce McLaren Motor Racing	G	3.0 McLaren M7D-Alfa Romeo V8	*not seeded	*13/22
dnq	MONACO GP	Monte Carlo	10	Bruce McLaren Motor Racing	G	3.0 McLaren M7D-Alfa Romeo V8		18/21
dnq	DUTCH GP	Zandvoort	21	Bruce McLaren Motor Racing	G	3.0 McLaren M14D-Alfa Romeo V8	*not seeded	*19/24
nc	FRENCH GP	Clermont Ferrand	16	Bruce McLaren Motor Racing	G	3.0 McLaren M7D-Alfa Romeo V8	pit stops – water pipe/-9 laps	15/23
dns	BRITISH GP	Brands Hatch	11	Bruce McLaren Motor Racing	G	3.0 McLaren M7D-Alfa Romeo V8	leaking fuel tank	(19)/25
dnq	GERMAN GP	Hockenheim	20	Bruce McLaren Motor Racing	G	3.0 McLaren M14D-Alfa Romeo V8		22/25
12	AUSTRIAN GP	Österreichring	22	Bruce McLaren Motor Racing	G	3.0 McLaren M14D-Alfa Romeo V8	engine off song/3 laps behind	14/24
8	ITALIAN GP	Monza	34	Bruce McLaren Motor Racing	G	3.0 McLaren M14D-Alfa Romeo V8	pit stop – tyres/fuel/7 laps behind	13/27
ret	CANADIAN GP	St Jovite	8	Bruce McLaren Motor Racing	G	3.0 McLaren M14D-Alfa Romeo V8	engine	=11/20
dnq	US GP	Watkins Glen	10	Bruce McLaren Motor Racing	G	3.0 McLaren M14D-Alfa Romeo V8		27/27

1971 Championship position: Unplaced

	Race	Circuit	No	Entrant	Tyres	Capacity/Car/Engine	Comment	Q Pos/Entries
13	SOUTH AFRICAN GP	Kyalami	8	STP-March	F	3.0 March 711-Alfa Romeo V8	4 laps behind	22/25
ret	SPANISH GP	Montjuich Park	17	STP-March	F	3.0 March 711-Alfa Romeo V8	transmission	18/22
ret	FRENCH GP	Paul Ricard	19	STP-March	F	3.0 March 711-Alfa Romeo V8	engine	21/24
nc	BRITISH GP	Silverstone	19	STP-March	F	3.0 March 711-Alfa Romeo V8	pit stops – electrics/12 laps behind	24/24
ret	GERMAN GP	Nürburgring	16	STP-March	F	3.0 March 711-Alfa Romeo V8	fuel injection	20/23
ret	ITALIAN GP	Monza	23	STP-March	F	3.0 March 711-Alfa Romeo V8	engine	20/24
11	US GP	Watkins Glen	27	STP-March	F	3.0 March 711-Alfa Romeo V8	2 laps behind	28/32

1972 Championship position: 16th=   Wins: 0   Pole positions: 0   Fastest laps: 0   Points scored: 3

	Race	Circuit	No	Entrant	Tyres	Capacity/Car/Engine	Comment	Q Pos/Entries
ret	ARGENTINE GP	Buenos Aires	20	Ceramica Pagnossin Team Surtees	F	3.0 Surtees TS9B-Cosworth V8	fuel line	14/22
nc	SOUTH AFRICAN GP	Kyalami	18	Ceramica Pagnossin Team Surtees	F	3.0 Surtees TS9B-Cosworth V8	pit stop-brakes/10 laps behind	=20/27
4	SPANISH GP	Jarama	26	Ceramica Pagnossin Team Surtees	F	3.0 Surtees TS9B-Cosworth V8	1 lap behind	13/26
7	MONACO GP	Monte Carlo	12	Ceramica Pagnossin Team Surtees	F	3.0 Surtees TS9B-Cosworth V8	3 laps behind	=18/25
ret	BELGIAN GP	Nivelles	36	Ceramica Pagnossin Team Surtees	F	3.0 Surtees TS9B-Cosworth V8	engine	10/26
14	FRENCH GP	Clermont Ferrand	28	Ceramica Pagnossin Team Surtees	F	3.0 Surtees TS9B-Cosworth V8	pit stop – puncture/1 lap behind	13/29
ret	BRITISH GP	Brands Hatch	23	Ceramica Pagnossin Team Surtees	F	3.0 Surtees TS9B-Cosworth V8	spun off	=20/27
13	GERMAN GP	Nürburgring	16	Ceramica Pagnossin Team Surtees	F	3.0 Surtees TS9B-Cosworth V8	pit stop – handling/1 lap behind	20/27
14	AUSTRIAN GP	Österreichring	11	Ceramica Pagnossin Team Surtees	F	3.0 Surtees TS9B-Cosworth V8	pit stops – engine/3 laps behind	13/26
ret	ITALIAN GP	Monza	9	Ceramica Pagnossin Team Surtees	F	3.0 Surtees TS9B-Cosworth V8	brake calliper	21/27
ret	CANADIAN GP	Mosport Park	23	Ceramica Pagnossin Team Surtees	F	3.0 Surtees TS9B-Cosworth V8	gearbox	15/25
ret	US GP	Watkins Glen	25	Ceramica Pagnossin Team Surtees	F	3.0 Surtees TS9B-Cosworth V8	collision with Ganley	19/32

1973 Championship position: 15th=   Wins: 0   Pole positions: 0   Fastest laps: 0   Points scored: 3

	Race	Circuit	No	Entrant	Tyres	Capacity/Car/Engine	Comment	Q Pos/Entries
8	SOUTH AFRICAN GP	Kyalami	12	Ceramica Pagnossin Team Surtees	F	3.0 Surtees TS9B-Cosworth V8	2 laps behind	20/25
ret	SPANISH GP	Montjuich Park	21	Ceramica Pagnossin MRD	G	3.0 Brabham BT37-Cosworth V8	hub failure – accident	17/22
4	BELGIAN GP	Zolder	9	Ceramica Pagnossin MRD	G	3.0 Brabham BT37-Cosworth V8	1 lap behind	18/23
7	MONACO GP	Monte Carlo	9	Ceramica Pagnossin MRD	G	3.0 Brabham BT37-Cosworth V8	3 laps behind	26/26
ret	FRENCH GP	Paul Ricard	9	Ceramica Pagnossin MRD	G	3.0 Brabham BT37-Cosworth V8	driveshaft	13/25
ret/dns	BRITISH GP	Silverstone	9	Ceramica Pagnossin MRD	G	3.0 Brabham BT42-Cosworth V8	accident at first start/broken leg	20/29

GP Starts: 29 (30)   GP Wins: 0   Pole positions: 0   Fastest laps: 0   Points: 6

ELIO de ANGELIS

FROM a wealthy background, Elio de Angelis had the reputation of being a cocky rich kid when he stepped from karting into Italian F3 at the beginning of 1977. Winning his third ever F3 race, he snatched the championship at the very last gasp from Piercarlo Ghinzani, and took an impressive seventh in the European series. After a controversial win in the 1978 Monaco F3 race, he moved up to Formula 2, but endured a fairly barren year and, since he was not slow to show his feelings, was seen as something of a spoilt prima donna.

It may have been a considerable gamble, but at the age of just 20, the inexperienced de Angelis joined a Shadow team that was in steep decline. With the exuberance of youth and not a little skill, the young Roman extracted the very best from a poor car, and his performances were not lost on Colin Chapman, who signed him for 1980. He made a great start for Lotus, taking a brilliant second place in Brazil, and – one or two silly incidents apart – soon settled down to become a most consistent points finisher over the next couple of seasons, the highlight of which was a hair's-breadth win over Keke Rosberg in the 1982 Austrian GP.

The following year was a transitional period for the team as they strug-gled to gain reliability from their Renault turbo-engined car, and results were thin on the ground. It was the reverse in 1984, though, as a string of excellent placings saw Elio leading the world championship by mid-season, but in the end he had to settle for third place in the points table behind Niki Lauda and Alain Prost.

De Angelis had spent four seasons vying somewhat inconclusively for number-one status with Nigel Mansell, but the arrival of Ayrton Senna in 1985 soon put the Roman in the shade, a lucky win at Imola following Prost's disqualification notwithstanding.

Accepting the situation would not change in his favour, Elio joined Brabham in 1986 to race their radical, but complex 'lowline' BT55. He managed just one finish, however, and that after losing a wheel, before a routine testing session at Paul Ricard in mid-May ended in catastrophe when the Brabham was thought to have suffered a component failure, crashing heavily at 180mph. His injuries were so severe that he stood no chance of survival, dying in hospital a few hours later. The entire motor racing world mourned the loss of a popular driver who had long since earned the respect of his peers.

ANGELIS, Elio de (I) b 26/3/1958, Rome – d 15/5/1986, Marseille, France

1979 Championship position: 15th= Wins: 0 Pole positions: 0 Fastest laps: 0 Points scored: 3

	Race	Circuit	No	Entrant	Tyres	Capacity/Car/Engine	Comment	Q Pos/Entries
7	ARGENTINE GP	Buenos Aires	18	Interscope Shadow Racing Team	G	3.0 Shadow DN9-Cosworth V8	1 lap behind	16/26
12	BRAZILIAN GP	Interlagos	18	Interscope Shadow Racing Team	G	3.0 Shadow DN9-Cosworth V8	1 lap behind	20/26
ret	SOUTH AFRICAN GP	Kyalami	18	Interscope Shadow Racing Team	G	3.0 Shadow DN9-Cosworth V8	spun off	=14/26
7	US GP WEST	Long Beach	18	Interscope Shadow Racing Team	G	3.0 Shadow DN9-Cosworth V8	2 laps behind	21/26
ret	SPANISH GP	Jarama	18	Interscope Shadow Racing Team	G	3.0 Shadow DN9-Cosworth V8	engine	22/27
ret	BELGIAN GP	Zolder	18	Interscope Shadow Racing Team	G	3.0 Shadow DN9-Cosworth V8	hit Giacomelli	24/28
dnq	MONACO GP	Monte Carlo	18	Interscope Shadow Racing Team	G	3.0 Shadow DN9-Cosworth V8		21/25
dnq/16	FRENCH GP	Dijon	18	Interscope Shadow Racing Team	G	3.0 Shadow DN9-Cosworth V8	started as 1st reserve/-5 laps	25/27
12*	BRITISH GP	Silverstone	18	Interscope Shadow Racing Team	G	3.0 Shadow DN9-Cosworth V8	*1min penalty – jump start/-3 laps	12/26
11	GERMAN GP	Hockenheim	18	Interscope Shadow Racing Team	G	3.0 Shadow DN9-Cosworth V8	2 laps behind	21/26
ret	AUSTRIAN GP	Österreichring	18	Interscope Shadow Racing Team	G	3.0 Shadow DN9-Cosworth V8	engine	22/26
ret	DUTCH GP	Zandvoort	18	Interscope Shadow Racing Team	G	3.0 Shadow DN9-Cosworth V8	driveshaft	22/26
ret	ITALIAN GP	Monza	18	Interscope Shadow Racing Team	G	3.0 Shadow DN9-Cosworth V8	distributor rotor arm	24/28
ret	CANADIAN GP	Montreal	18	Interscope Shadow Racing Team	G	3.0 Shadow DN9-Cosworth V8	broken rotor arm	23/29
4	US GP EAST	Long Beach	18	Interscope Shadow Racing Team	G	3.0 Shadow DN9-Cosworth V8		20/30

1980 Championship position: 7th Wins: 0 Pole positions: 0 Fastest laps: 0 Points scored: 13

	Race	Circuit	No	Entrant	Tyres	Capacity/Car/Engine	Comment	Q Pos/Entries
ret	ARGENTINE GP	Buenos Aires	12	Team Essex Lotus	G	3.0 Lotus 81-Cosworth V8	suspension	5/28
2	BRAZILIAN GP	Interlagos	12	Team Essex Lotus	G	3.0 Lotus 81-Cosworth V8		7/28
ret	SOUTH AFRICAN GP	Kyalami	12	Team Essex Lotus	G	3.0 Lotus 81-Cosworth V8	spun off	14/28
ret	US GP WEST	Long Beach	12	Team Essex Lotus	G	3.0 Lotus 81-Cosworth V8	multiple accident – broken foot	20/27
10/ret	BELGIAN GP	Zolder	12	Team Essex Lotus	G	3.0 Lotus 81-Cosworth V8	spun off/3 laps behind	8/27
9/ret	MONACO GP	Monte Carlo	12	Team Essex Lotus	G	3.0 Lotus 81-Cosworth V8	spun off into wall/8 laps behind	14/27
ret	FRENCH GP	Paul Ricard	12	Team Essex Lotus	G	3.0 Lotus 81-Cosworth V8	clutch	14/27
ret	BRITISH GP	Brands Hatch	12	Team Essex Lotus	G	3.0 Lotus 81-Cosworth V8	rear suspension	14/27
16/ret	GERMAN GP	Hockenheim	12	Team Essex Lotus	G	3.0 Lotus 81-Cosworth V8	wheel bearing/2 laps behind	11/26
6	AUSTRIAN GP	Österreichring	12	Team Essex Lotus	G	3.0 Lotus 81-Cosworth V8		9/25
ret	DUTCH GP	Zandvoort	12	Team Essex Lotus	G	3.0 Lotus 81-Cosworth V8	collision with Pironi	11/28
4	ITALIAN GP	Imola	12	Team Essex Lotus	G	3.0 Lotus 81-Cosworth V8	1 lap behind	18/28
10	CANADIAN GP	Montreal	12	Team Essex Lotus	G	3.0 Lotus 81-Cosworth V8	damaged skirt/2 laps behind	17/28
4	US GP EAST	Watkins Glen	12	Team Essex Lotus	G	3.0 Lotus 81-Cosworth V8		4/27

1981 Championship position: 8th Wins: 0 Pole positions: 0 Fastest laps: 0 Points scored: 14

	Race	Circuit	No	Entrant	Tyres	Capacity/Car/Engine	Comment	Q Pos/Entries
ret	US GP WEST	Long Beach	11	Team Essex Lotus	M	3.0 Lotus 81-Cosworth V8	hit wall	13/29
dns	"	"	11T	Team Essex Lotus	M	3.0 Lotus 88-Cosworth V8	car banned by scrutineers	-/-
5	BRAZILIAN GP	Rio	11	Team Essex Lotus	M	3.0 Lotus 81-Cosworth V8		10/30
6	ARGENTINE GP	Buenos Aires	11	Team Essex Lotus	M	3.0 Lotus 81-Cosworth V8	1 lap behind	10/29
5	BELGIAN GP	Zolder	11	Team Essex Lotus	M	3.0 Lotus 81-Cosworth V8		14/31
ret	MONACO GP	Monte Carlo	11	Team Essex Lotus	M	3.0 Lotus 87-Cosworth V8	engine	6/31
5	SPANISH GP	Jarama	11	John Player Team Lotus	M	3.0 Lotus 87-Cosworth V8		10/30
6	FRENCH GP	Dijon	11	John Player Team Lotus	M	3.0 Lotus 87-Cosworth V8	1 lap behind	8/29
ret	BRITISH GP	Silverstone	11	John Player Team Lotus	G	3.0 Lotus 87-Cosworth V8	retired after being black-flagged	22/30
dns	"		11	John Player Team Lotus	G	3.0 Lotus 88B-Cosworth V8	practice only	-/-
7	GERMAN GP	Hockenheim	11	John Player Team Lotus	G	3.0 Lotus 87-Cosworth V8	1 lap behind	14/30
7	AUSTRIAN GP	Österreichring	11	John Player Team Lotus	G	3.0 Lotus 87-Cosworth V8	1 lap behind	9/28
5	DUTCH GP	Zandvoort	11	John Player Team Lotus	G	3.0 Lotus 87-Cosworth V8	1 lap behind	9/30
4	ITALIAN GP	Monza	11	John Player Team Lotus	G	3.0 Lotus 87-Cosworth V8		11/30
6	CANADIAN GP	Montreal	11	John Player Team Lotus	G	3.0 Lotus 87-Cosworth V8	1 lap behind	7/30
ret	CAESARS PALACE GP	Las Vegas	11	John Player Team Lotus	G	3.0 Lotus 87-Cosworth V8	water leak	15/30

1982 Championship position: 9th Wins: 1 Pole positions: 0 Fastest laps: 0 Points scored: 23

	Race	Circuit	No	Entrant	Tyres	Capacity/Car/Engine	Comment	Q Pos/Entries
8	SOUTH AFRICAN GP	Kyalami	11	John Player Team Lotus	G	3.0 Lotus 87B-Cosworth V8	1 lap behind	15/30
ret	BRAZILIAN GP	Rio	11	John Player Team Lotus	G	3.0 Lotus 91-Cosworth V8	hit by Baldi	11/31
5*	US GP WEST	Long Beach	11	John Player Team Lotus	G	3.0 Lotus 91-Cosworth V8	*3rd place car dsq/1 lap behind	16/31
4*	BELGIAN GP	Zolder	11	John Player Team Lotus	G	3.0 Lotus 91-Cosworth V8	*3rd place car dsq/2 laps behind	13/32
5	MONACO GP	Monte Carlo	11	John Player Team Lotus	G	3.0 Lotus 91-Cosworth V8	1 lap behind	15/31
ret	US GP (DETROIT)	Detroit	11	John Player Team Lotus	G	3.0 Lotus 91-Cosworth V8	gearbox	8/28
4	CANADIAN GP	Montreal	11	John Player Team Lotus	G	3.0 Lotus 91-Cosworth V8	1 lap behind	10/29
ret	DUTCH GP	Zandvoort	11	John Player Team Lotus	G	3.0 Lotus 91-Cosworth V8	handling	15/31
4	BRITISH GP	Brands Hatch	11	John Player Team Lotus	G	3.0 Lotus 91-Cosworth V8		7/30
ret	FRENCH GP	Paul Ricard	11	John Player Team Lotus	G	3.0 Lotus 91-Cosworth V8	fuel pressure	13/30
ret	GERMAN GP	Hockenheim	11	John Player Team Lotus	G	3.0 Lotus 91-Cosworth V8	transmission	14/30
1	AUSTRIAN GP	Österreichring	11	John Player Team Lotus	G	3.0 Lotus 91-Cosworth V8	won by 0.050s from Rosberg	7/29
6	SWISS GP	Dijon	11	John Player Team Lotus	G	3.0 Lotus 91-Cosworth V8	1 lap behind	15/29
ret	ITALIAN GP	Monza	11	John Player Team Lotus	G	3.0 Lotus 91-Cosworth V8	handling/sticking throttle	17/30
ret	CAESARS PALACE GP	Las Vegas	11	John Player Team Lotus	G	3.0 Lotus 91-Cosworth V8	engine	20/30

1983 Championship position: 17th= Wins: 0 Pole positions: 1 Fastest laps: 0 Points scored: 2

	Race	Circuit	No	Entrant	Tyres	Capacity/Car/Engine	Comment	Q Pos/Entries
dsq*	BRAZILIAN GP	Rio	11	John Player Team Lotus	P	3.0 Lotus 91-Cosworth V8	*disqualified – did not practise this car	-/-
dns	"	"	11	John Player Team Lotus	P	1.5 t/c Lotus 93T-Renault V6	turbo on warm-up lap – changed cars	13/27
ret	US GP WEST	Long Beach	11	John Player Team Lotus	P	1.5 t/c Lotus 93T-Renault V6	tyres	5/28
ret	FRENCH GP	Paul Ricard	11	John Player Team Lotus	P	1.5 t/c Lotus 93T-Renault V6	electrics	5/29
ret	SAN MARINO GP	Imola	11	John Player Team Lotus	P	1.5 t/c Lotus 93T-Renault V6	poor handling/driver gave up	9/28
ret	MONACO GP	Monte Carlo	11	John Player Team Lotus	P	1.5 t/c Lotus 93T-Renault V6	driveshaft	19/28
9	BELGIAN GP	Spa	11	John Player Team Lotus	P	1.5 t/c Lotus 93T-Renault V6	1 lap behind	13/28
ret	US GP (DETROIT)	Detroit	11	John Player Team Lotus	P	1.5 t/c Lotus 93T-Renault V6	transmission	4/27
ret	CANADIAN GP	Montreal	11	John Player Team Lotus	P	1.5 t/c Lotus 93T-Renault V6	throttle linkage	11/28
ret	BRITISH GP	Silverstone	11	John Player Team Lotus	P	1.5 t/c Lotus 94T-Renault V6	engine – turbo fire	4/29
ret	GERMAN GP	Hockenheim	11	John Player Team Lotus	P	1.5 t/c Lotus 94T-Renault V6	overheating	11/29

ret	AUSTRIAN GP	Österreichring	11	John Player Team Lotus	P	1.5 t/c Lotus 94T-Renault V6	spun – hit Giacomelli	– / –
dns	"	"	11	John Player Team Lotus	P	1.5 t/c Lotus 93T-Renault V6	practice only – qualifying car	12/29
ret	DUTCH GP	Zandvoort	11	John Player Team Lotus	P	1.5 t/c Lotus 94T-Renault V6	fuel metering unit	3/29
5	ITALIAN GP	Monza	11	John Player Team Lotus	P	1.5 t/c Lotus 94T-Renault V6		8/29
ret	EUROPEAN GP	Brands Hatch	11	John Player Team Lotus	P	1.5 t/c Lotus 94T-Renault V6	engine	1/29
ret	SOUTH AFRICAN GP	Kyalami	11	John Player Team Lotus	P	1.5 t/c Lotus 94T-Renault V6	engine – misfire	11/26

1984 Championship position: 3rd   Wins: 0   Pole positions: 1   Fastest laps: 0   Points scored: 34

3	BRAZILIAN GP	Rio	11	John Player Team Lotus	G	1.5 t/c Lotus 95T-Renault V6		1/27
7	SOUTH AFRICAN GP	Kyalami	11	John Player Team Lotus	G	1.5 t/c Lotus 95T-Renault V6	pit stop – throttle cable/4 laps behind	7/27
5	BELGIAN GP	Zolder	11	John Player Team Lotus	G	1.5 t/c Lotus 95T-Renault V6	1 lap behind	5/27
3/ret	SAN MARINO GP	Imola	11	John Player Team Lotus	G	1.5 t/c Lotus 95T-Renault V6	out of fuel/1 lap behind	11/28
5	FRENCH GP	Dijon	11	John Player Team Lotus	G	1.5 t/c Lotus 95T-Renault V6		2/27
5*	MONACO GP	Monte Carlo	11	John Player Team Lotus	G	1.5 t/c Lotus 95T-Renault V6	*3rd place car dsq/half points	11/27
4	CANADIAN GP	Montreal	11	John Player Team Lotus	G	1.5 t/c Lotus 95T-Renault V6	1 lap behind	3/26
2*	US GP (DETROIT)	Detroit	11	John Player Team Lotus	G	1.5 t/c Lotus 95T-Renault V6	*2nd place car disqualified	5/27
3	US GP (DALLAS)	Dallas	11	John Player Team Lotus	G	1.5 t/c Lotus 95T-Renault V6	1 lap behind	2/27
4	BRITISH GP	Brands Hatch	11	John Player Team Lotus	G	1.5 t/c Lotus 95T-Renault V6	1 lap behind	4/27
ret	GERMAN GP	Hockenheim	11	John Player Team Lotus	G	1.5 t/c Lotus 95T-Renault V6	turbo	2/27
ret	AUSTRIAN GP	Österreichring	11	John Player Team Lotus	G	1.5 t/c Lotus 95T-Renault V6	engine	3/28
4	DUTCH GP	Zandvoort	11	John Player Team Lotus	G	1.5 t/c Lotus 95T-Renault V6	1 lap behind	3/27
ret	ITALIAN GP	Monza	11	John Player Team Lotus	G	1.5 t/c Lotus 95T-Renault V6	gearbox	3/27
ret	EUROPEAN GP	Nürburgring	11	John Player Team Lotus	G	1.5 t/c Lotus 95T-Renault V6	turbo	23/26
5	PORTUGUESE GP	Estoril	11	John Player Team Lotus	G	1.5 t/c Lotus 95T-Renault V6		5/27

1985 Championship position: 5th   Wins: 1   Pole positions: 1   Fastest laps: 0   Points scored: 33

3	BRAZILIAN GP	Rio	11	John Player Special Team Lotus	G	1.5 t/c Lotus 97T-Renault V6	1 lap behind	3/25
4	PORTUGUESE GP	Estoril	11	John Player Special Team Lotus	G	1.5 t/c Lotus 97T-Renault V6	1 lap behind	4/26
1*	SAN MARINO GP	Imola	11	John Player Special Team Lotus	G	1.5 t/c Lotus 97T-Renault V6	*1st place car disqualified	3/26
3	MONACO GP	Monte Carlo	11	John Player Special Team Lotus	G	1.5 t/c Lotus 97T-Renault V6		9/26
5	CANADIAN GP	Montreal	11	John Player Special Team Lotus	G	1.5 t/c Lotus 97T-Renault V6		1/25
5	US GP (DETROIT)	Detroit	11	John Player Special Team Lotus	G	1.5 t/c Lotus 97T-Renault V6		8/25
5	FRENCH GP	Paul Ricard	11	John Player Special Team Lotus	G	1.5 t/c Lotus 97T-Renault V6		7/26
nc	BRITISH GP	Silverstone	11	John Player Special Team Lotus	G	1.5 t/c Lotus 97T-Renault V6	pit stop – engine/28 laps behind	8/26
ret	GERMAN GP	Hockenheim	11	John Player Special Team Lotus	G	1.5 t/c Lotus 97T-Renault V6	engine	7/27
5	AUSTRIAN GP	Österreichring	11	John Player Special Team Lotus	G	1.5 t/c Lotus 97T-Renault V6		7/27
5	DUTCH GP	Zandvoort	11	John Player Special Team Lotus	G	1.5 t/c Lotus 97T-Renault V6	1 lap behind	11/27
6	ITALIAN GP	Monza	11	John Player Special Team Lotus	G	1.5 t/c Lotus 97T-Renault V6	1 lap behind	6/26
ret	BELGIAN GP	Spa	11	John Player Special Team Lotus	G	1.5 t/c Lotus 97T-Renault V6	turbo	9/24
5	EUROPEAN GP	Brands Hatch	11	John Player Special Team Lotus	G	1.5 t/c Lotus 97T-Renault V6	1 lap behind	9/27
ret	SOUTH AFRICAN GP	Kyalami	11	John Player Special Team Lotus	G	1.5 t/c Lotus 97T-Renault V6	engine	6/21
dsq*	AUSTRALIAN GP	Adelaide	11	John Player Special Team Lotus	G	1.5 t/c Lotus 97T-Renault V6	*excluded – changed grid position	10/25

1986 Championship position: Unplaced

8	BRAZILIAN GP	Rio	8	Motor Racing Developments	P	1.5 t/c Brabham BT55-BMW 4	lost wheel/3 laps behind	14/25
ret	SPANISH GP	Jerez	8	Motor Racing Developments	P	1.5 t/c Brabham BT55-BMW 4	gearbox	15/25
ret	SAN MARINO GP	Imola	8	Motor Racing Developments	P	1.5 t/c Brabham BT55-BMW 4	engine	19/26
ret	MONACO GP	Monte Carlo	8	Motor Racing Developments	P	1.5 t/c Brabham BT55-BMW 4	engine intercooler	20/26

GP Starts: 108   GP Wins: 2   Pole positions: 3   Fastest laps: 0   Points: 122

Austrian Grand Prix, 1982. With arm aloft, Elio de Angelis in his JPS Lotus beats Keke Rosberg and his Williams across the line by just 0.005 second, taking his only grand prix win.

CAREL de BEAUFORT

THE last truly amateur driver to compete in grand prix racing on a regular basis, Carel de Beaufort metamorphosed from the roly-poly dilettante of his early racing career into a much more serious and competent performer – without losing his perennially sunny disposition – to earn the respect of his fellow competitors.

De Beaufort began his racing career with production Porsche Spyders in 1956 and was soon itching to pit himself against the stars of the day, racing his Porsche RSK sports car in the Formula 2 category of the 1957 German Grand Prix. He had to content himself with occasional grand prix outings until the 1961 season, however, when he acquired the ex-Stirling Moss Rob Walker Porsche 718.

This car, with its four-cylinder engine, saw extensive service over the next four seasons, the broad-shouldered count – invariably driving in stockinged feet – battling nobly against more powerful fuel-injected cars. His orange machine was entered in non-championship races the length and breadth of Europe, enjoying its greatest successes in 1963, with second places in the Syracuse and Rome grands prix, and third in the Austrian Grand Prix at Zeltweg.

De Beaufort plugged away into the 1964 season with the veteran Porsche, but in practice for the German Grand Prix he crashed heavily at the Bergwerk corner. His car may have hit a patch of oil, causing it to spin off the track and down an embankment. The unlucky driver was hurled from his machine into a tree, sustaining multiple injuries from which there was to no recovery. Despite the best effort of a specialist neurological unit, he died the following day in hospital in Düsseldorf.

de BEAUFORT, Count Carel Godin Count Carel Pieter Antoni Jan Hubertus Godin de Beaufort (NL) b 10/4/1934, Maarsbergen – d 2/8/1964, Cologne

1957 Championship position: Unplaced

	Race	Circuit	No	Entrant	Tyres	Capacity/Car/Engine	Comment	Q Pos/Entries
14	GERMAN GP (F2)	Nürburgring	27	Ecurie Maarsbergen	D	1.5 Porsche 550RS F4 sports car	3rd in F2 class/2 laps behind	20/24

1958 Championship position: Unplaced

	Race	Circuit	No	Entrant	Tyres	Capacity/Car/Engine	Comment	Q Pos/Entries
11	DUTCH GP	Zandvoort	18	Ecurie Maarsbergen	D	1.5 Porsche RSK F4 sports car	6 laps behind	17/17
ret	GERMAN GP (F2)	Nürburgring	18	Ecurie Maarsbergen	D	1.5 Porsche RSK F4 sports car	mechanical	18/26

1959 Championship position: Unplaced

	Race	Circuit	No	Entrant	Tyres	Capacity/Car/Engine	Comment	Q Pos/Entries
10	DUTCH GP	Zandvoort	15	Ecurie Maarsbergen	D	1.5 Porsche RSK F4 sports car	7 laps behind	14/25
9*	FRENCH GP	Reims	42	Scuderia Ugolini	D	2.5 Maserati 250F 6	*8th place car disqualified/-10 laps	20/22

1960 Championship position: Unplaced

	Race	Circuit	No	Entrant	Tyres	Capacity/Car/Engine	Comment	Q Pos/Entries
8	DUTCH GP	Zandvoort	20	Ecurie Maarsbergen	D	1.5 Cooper T51-Climax 4 F2	6 laps behind	18/21

1961 Championship position: Unplaced

	Race	Circuit	No	Entrant	Tyres	Capacity/Car/Engine	Comment	Q Pos/Entries
14	DUTCH GP	Zandvoort	8	Ecurie Maarsbergen	D	1.5 Porsche 718 F4	3 laps behind	17/17
11	BELGIAN GP	Spa	22	Ecurie Maarsbergen	D	1.5 Porsche 718 F4	2 laps behind	14/25
ret	FRENCH GP	Reims	14	Ecurie Maarsbergen	D	1.5 Porsche 718 F4	engine – overheating	17/26
16	BRITISH GP	Aintree	56	Ecurie Maarsbergen	D	1.5 Porsche 718 F4	6 laps behind	=18/30
14	GERMAN GP	Nürburgring	31	Ecurie Maarsbergen	D	1.5 Porsche 718 F4	1 lap behind	17/27
7	ITALIAN GP	Monza	74	Ecurie Maarsbergen	D	1.5 Porsche 718 F4	2 laps behind	15/33

1962 Championship position: 16th= Wins: 0 Pole positions: 0 Fastest laps: 0 Points scored: 2

	Race	Circuit	No	Entrant	Tyres	Capacity/Car/Engine	Comment	Q Pos/Entries
6	DUTCH GP	Zandvoort	14	Ecurie Maarsbergen	D	1.5 Porsche 718 F4	4 laps behind	14/20
dnq	MONACO GP	Monte Carlo	44	Ecurie Maarsbergen	D	1.5 Porsche 718 F4		20/21
7	BELGIAN GP	Spa	7	Ecurie Maarsbergen	D	1.5 Porsche 718 F4	2 laps behind	13/20
6	FRENCH GP	Rouen	38	Ecurie Maarsbergen	D	1.5 Porsche 718 F4	3 laps behind	17/17
14	BRITISH GP	Aintree	54	Ecurie Maarsbergen	D	1.5 Porsche 718 F4	6 laps behind	17/21
13	GERMAN GP	Nürburgring	18	Ecurie Maarsbergen	D	1.5 Porsche 718 F4		8/30
10	ITALIAN GP	Monza	32	Ecurie Maarsbergen	D	1.5 Porsche 718 F4	5 laps behind	20/30
ret	US GP	Watkins Glen	12	Ecurie Maarsbergen	D	1.5 Porsche 718 F4	hit guard rail	14/20
11/ret	SOUTH AFRICAN GP	East London	15	Ecurie Maarsbergen	D	1.5 Porsche 718 F4	fuel pump/12 laps behind	16/17

1963 Championship position: 14th= Wins: 0 Pole positions: 0 Fastest laps: 0 Points scored: 2

	Race	Circuit	No	Entrant	Tyres	Capacity/Car/Engine	Comment	Q Pos/Entries
6	BELGIAN GP	Spa	29	Ecurie Maarsbergen	D	1.5 Porsche 718 F4	2 laps behind	18/20
9	DUTCH GP	Zandvoort	32	Ecurie Maarsbergen	D	1.5 Porsche 718 F4	5 laps behind	19/19
10	BRITISH GP	Silverstone	23	Ecurie Maarsbergen	D	1.5 Porsche 718 F4	6 laps behind	21/23
ret	GERMAN GP	Nürburgring	17	Ecurie Maarsbergen	D	1.5 Porsche 718 F4	lost wheel	17/26
dnq	ITALIAN GP	Monza	28	Ecurie Maarsbergen	D	1.5 Porsche 718 F4		24/28
6	US GP	Watkins Glen	12	Ecurie Maarsbergen	D	1.5 Porsche 718 F4	11 laps behind	19/21
10	MEXICAN GP	Mexico City	12	Ecurie Maarsbergen	D	1.5 Porsche 718 F4	7 laps behind	18/21
10	SOUTH AFRICAN GP	East London	14	Ecurie Maarsbergen	D	1.5 Porsche 718 F4	6 laps behind	20/21

1964 Championship position: Unplaced

	Race	Circuit	No	Entrant	Tyres	Capacity/Car/Engine	Comment	Q Pos/Entries
ret	DUTCH GP	Zandvoort	28	Ecurie Maarsbergen	D	1.5 Porsche 718 F4	valve	17/18
dns	GERMAN GP	Nürburgring	29	Ecurie Maarsbergen	D	1.5 Porsche 718 F4	fatal practice accident	(23)/24

GP Starts: 28 GP Wins: 0 Pole positions: 0 Fastest laps: 0 Points: 4

ANDREA de CESARIS

ANDREA DE CESARIS spent more than a decade trying to live down the reputation of being a wild and erratic performer, who was only competing in the top echelon by virtue of his powerful sponsorship connections. As is usually the case, there was more than a grain of truth in the sniping, although by the early 1990s, the enfant terrible had matured into a very professional performer.

A former world karting champion, 18-year-old Andrea was campaigning a Ralt run by Tiga's Tim Schenken in the 1978 British F3 championship. He continued in the formula the following year with Team Tiga's March, and although he won six rounds of the Vandervell series, the silly mistakes that would become a feature of his Formula 1 career were already apparent, spoiling his championship chances. He finished second to Italian Chico Serra at the season's end.

Joining Ron Dennis' Project Four outfit for the 1980 season, de Cesaris enjoyed a successful debut in the New Zealand Pacific series, winning

both races at Pukekohe, before racing a March 802 in Formula 2. He was paired with Serra, who soon gained the upper hand and number-one treatment in the team. Andrea's vast potential was there to be seen, however, and once a problematical tyre situation was eradicated he looked a real prospect, winning the final race at Misano and a well-earned promotion to the McLaren team, newly acquired (with continued Marlboro backing) by Dennis for 1981.

The season began badly when Andrea crashed into Alain Prost on the first lap at Long Beach, and roller-coastered downhill as the number of accidents mounted alarmingly. In most cases, it would have been "Goodbye and thank you very much", but luckily he was welcomed back by Alfa Romeo, for whom he had made his grand prix debut at the end of 1980. Although there were still many moments of desperation, in his two seasons with the team, he produced with some excellent performances, including a great drive at Spa in 1983, when he comfortably led

the first half of the race before trouble hit.

With the Alfa operation siphoned off to Pavanello's Euroracing in 1984, Andrea was found a place in the Ligier team, where all the bad traits and indiscipline that had been largely eradicated the previous year soon returned. He was extremely lucky to emerge unharmed from a huge barrel-rolling crash in Austria in 1985, and after one more race Ligier replaced him with Philippe Streiff.

Nothing if not a survivor, de Cesaris was back once more in 1986, this time leading the Minardi team, but it was an uncomfortable year in which he was overshadowed by team-mate Alessandro Nannini, despite first call on equipment. Team hopping was an art at which he would become well practised. Fetching up at Brabham in 1987, he proved the talent was still there with excellent performances at Spa, Estoril, Jerez and Mexico, but so were the equally lacklustre displays. It was the same sweet-and-sour cocktail at Rial in 1988, with an impressive drive at Detroit, where he showed remarkable restraint to finish fourth. Then he had a two-year tenure at Dallara, where the 'Jekyll and Hyde' character was even more in evidence, with 'Mr Hyde' playing the dominant role.

Just when it seemed that the game was up and de Cesaris' chequered grand prix career could go no further, he was a shock choice for Jordan for 1991. If the new team was a revelation then so was he, driving better than ever and coming very close to a second place at Spa before his engine failed at the death. Although not retained, his performances took him to Tyrrell for 1992, where his racecraft and new-found maturity helped bring the team much-needed points on four occasions. Sadly, 1993 found Tyrrell in deep trouble, struggling with a new Yamaha engine, and there was little sign of the de Cesaris we had seen in the previous two years.

After 14 seasons and close on 200 starts, Andrea began the 1994 season without a drive, but with Jordan's Eddie Irvine suspended, he was soon back in business, albeit for just two races. At Monaco, he drove sensibly to take fourth place, which must have helped his cause no end, since Sauber were searching for a replacement for the injured Karl Wendlinger. Apart from a sixth place in France, however, it was hardly an auspicious grand prix swansong, for there would be no more F1 comebacks.

After more than a decade away from the track, Andrea was tempted back behind the wheel to compete in the Grand Prix Masters race at Kyalami in November, 2005. The Italian impressed with his competitive spirit and nearly claimed a podium, just losing out to his former Brabham team-mate, Riccardo Patrese. He was back for more in 2006, but without much luck in the two races held.

de CESARIS, Andrea (I) b 31/5/1959, Rome

1980 Championship position: Unplaced

	Race	Circuit	No	Entrant	Tyres	Capacity/Car/Engine	Comment	Q Pos/Entries
ret	CANADIAN GP	Montreal	22	Marlboro Team Alfa Romeo	G	3.0 Alfa Romeo 179 V12	engine	8/28
ret	US GP EAST	Watkins Glen	22	Marlboro Team Alfa Romeo	G	3.0 Alfa Romeo 179 V12	collision with Daly	10/27

1981 Championship position: 18th= Wins: 0 Pole positions: 0 Fastest laps: 0 Points scored: 1

	Race	Circuit	No	Entrant	Tyres	Capacity/Car/Engine	Comment	Q Pos/Entries
ret	US GP WEST	Long Beach	8	McLaren International	M	3.0 McLaren M29F-Cosworth V8	hit Prost	22/29
ret	BRAZILIAN GP	Rio	8	McLaren International	M	3.0 McLaren M29F-Cosworth V8	electrics	20/30
11	ARGENTINE GP	Buenos Aires	8	McLaren International	M	3.0 McLaren M29F-Cosworth V8	2 laps behind	18/29
6	SAN MARINO GP	Imola	8	McLaren International	M	3.0 McLaren M29F-Cosworth V8		14/30
ret	BELGIAN GP	Zolder	8	McLaren International	M	3.0 McLaren M29F-Cosworth V8	gearbox	23/31
ret	MONACO GP	Monte Carlo	8	McLaren International	M	3.0 McLaren MP4-Cosworth V8	collision with Prost	11/31
ret	SPANISH GP	Jarama	8	McLaren International	M	3.0 McLaren MP4-Cosworth V8	accident	14/30
11	FRENCH GP	Dijon	8	McLaren International	M	3.0 McLaren MP4-Cosworth V8	2 laps behind	5/29
ret	BRITISH GP	Silverstone	8	McLaren International	M	3.0 McLaren MP4-Cosworth V8	accident with Villeneuve	6/30
ret	GERMAN GP	Hockenheim	8	McLaren International	M	3.0 McLaren MP4-Cosworth V8	spun off	10/30
8	AUSTRIAN GP	Österreichring	8	McLaren International	M	3.0 McLaren MP4-Cosworth V8	1 lap behind	18/28
dns	DUTCH GP	Zandvoort	8	McLaren International	M	3.0 McLaren MP4-Cosworth V8	withdrawn after practice accidents	(13)/30
7/ret	ITALIAN GP	Monza	8	McLaren International	M	3.0 McLaren MP4-Cosworth V8	puncture – accident	16/30
ret	CANADIAN GP	Montreal	8	McLaren International	M	3.0 McLaren MP4-Cosworth V8	spun off	13/30
12	CAESARS PALACE GP	Las Vegas	8	McLaren International	M	3.0 McLaren MP4-Cosworth V8	pit stops – tyres – handling/-6 laps	14/30

1982 Championship position: 17th= Wins: 0 Pole positions: 1 Fastest laps: 0 Points scored: 5

	Race	Circuit	No	Entrant	Tyres	Capacity/Car/Engine	Comment	Q Pos/Entries
13	SOUTH AFRICAN GP	Kyalami	22	Marlboro Team Alfa Romeo	M	3.0 Alfa Romeo 179D V12	4 laps behind	16/30
ret	BRAZILIAN GP	Rio	22	Marlboro Team Alfa Romeo	M	3.0 Alfa Romeo 182 V12	loose undertray	10/31
ret	US GP WEST	Long Beach	22	Marlboro Team Alfa Romeo	M	3.0 Alfa Romeo 182 V12	hit wall when 2nd	1/31
ret	SAN MARINO GP	Imola	22	Marlboro Team Alfa Romeo	M	3.0 Alfa Romeo 182 V12	fuel pump	7/14
ret	BELGIAN GP	Zolder	22	Marlboro Team Alfa Romeo	M	3.0 Alfa Romeo 182 V12	gear linkage	7/32
3/ret	MONACO GP	Monte Carlo	22	Marlboro Team Alfa Romeo	M	3.0 Alfa Romeo 182 V12	out of fuel on last lap	7/31
ret	US GP (DETROIT)	Detroit	22	Marlboro Team Alfa Romeo	M	3.0 Alfa Romeo 182 V12	transmission	2/28
6/ret	CANADIAN GP	Montreal	22	Marlboro Team Alfa Romeo	M	3.0 Alfa Romeo 182 V12	out of fuel when 3rd/2 laps behind	9/29
ret	DUTCH GP	Zandvoort	22	Marlboro Team Alfa Romeo	M	3.0 Alfa Romeo 182 V12	electrics	9/31
ret	BRITISH GP	Brands Hatch	22	Marlboro Team Alfa Romeo	M	3.0 Alfa Romeo 182 V12	electrics	11/30
ret	FRENCH GP	Paul Ricard	22	Marlboro Team Alfa Romeo	M	3.0 Alfa Romeo 182 V12	puncture – accident	7/30
ret	GERMAN GP	Hockenheim	22	Marlboro Team Alfa Romeo	M	3.0 Alfa Romeo 182 V12	collision – broken oil radiator	9/30
ret	AUSTRIAN GP	Österreichring	22	Marlboro Team Alfa Romeo	M	3.0 Alfa Romeo 182 V12	collision at start – Giacomelli & Daly	11/29
10	SWISS GP	Dijon	22	Marlboro Team Alfa Romeo	M	3.0 Alfa Romeo 182 V12	2 laps behind	5/29
10	ITALIAN GP	Monza	22	Marlboro Team Alfa Romeo	M	3.0 Alfa Romeo 182 V12	pit stop – ignition/2 laps behind	9/30
dns	"	"	22	Marlboro Team Alfa Romeo	M	1.5 t/c Alfa Romeo 182T V8	practice only	- / -
9	CAESARS PALACE GP	Las Vegas	22	Marlboro Team Alfa Romeo	M	3.0 Alfa Romeo 182 V12	3 laps behind	18/30

1983 Championship position: 8th Wins: 0 Pole positions: 0 Fastest laps: 1 Points scored: 15

	Race	Circuit	No	Entrant	Tyres	Capacity/Car/Engine	Comment	Q Pos/Entries
excl*	BRAZILIAN GP	Rio	22	Marlboro Team Alfa Romeo	M	1.5 t/c Alfa Romeo 183T V8	*missed weight check – excluded	- / -
ret	US GP WEST	Long Beach	22	Marlboro Team Alfa Romeo	M	1.5 t/c Alfa Romeo 183T V8	gearbox	19/28
12	FRENCH GP	Paul Ricard	22	Marlboro Team Alfa Romeo	M	1.5 t/c Alfa Romeo 183T V8	pit stop – fuel-tyres/4 laps behind	7/29
ret	SAN MARINO GP	Imola	22	Marlboro Team Alfa Romeo	M	1.5 t/c Alfa Romeo 183T V8	distributor	8/28
ret	MONACO GP	Monte Carlo	22	Marlboro Team Alfa Romeo	M	1.5 t/c Alfa Romeo 183T V8	gearbox	7/28
ret	BELGIAN GP	Spa	22	Marlboro Team Alfa Romeo	M	1.5 t/c Alfa Romeo 183T V8	engine when 2nd/led race/FL	3/28
ret	US GP (DETROIT)	Detroit	22	Marlboro Team Alfa Romeo	M	1.5 t/c Alfa Romeo 183T V8	turbo	8/27
ret	CANADIAN GP	Montreal	22	Marlboro Team Alfa Romeo	M	1.5 t/c Alfa Romeo 183T V8	engine	8/28
8	BRITISH GP	Silverstone	22	Marlboro Team Alfa Romeo	M	1.5 t/c Alfa Romeo 183T V8	1 lap behind	9/29
2	GERMAN GP	Hockenheim	22	Marlboro Team Alfa Romeo	M	1.5 t/c Alfa Romeo 183T V8		3/29
ret	AUSTRIAN GP	Österreichring	22	Marlboro Team Alfa Romeo	M	1.5 t/c Alfa Romeo 183T V8	out of fuel	11/29
ret	DUTCH GP	Zandvoort	22	Marlboro Team Alfa Romeo	M	1.5 t/c Alfa Romeo 183T V8	engine	8/29
ret	ITALIAN GP	Monza	22	Marlboro Team Alfa Romeo	M	1.5 t/c Alfa Romeo 183T V8	spun off	6/29
4	EUROPEAN GP	Brands Hatch	22	Marlboro Team Alfa Romeo	M	1.5 t/c Alfa Romeo 183T V8		14/29
2	SOUTH AFRICAN GP	Kyalami	22	Marlboro Team Alfa Romeo	M	1.5 t/c Alfa Romeo 183T V8		9/26

1984 Championship position: 16th= Wins: 0 Pole positions: 0 Fastest laps: 0 Points scored: 3

	Race	Circuit	No	Entrant	Tyres	Capacity/Car/Engine	Comment	Q Pos/Entries
ret	BRAZILIAN GP	Rio	26	Ligier Loto	M	1.5 t/c Ligier JS23-Renault V6	started spare car from pits/gearbox	14/27
5	SOUTH AFRICAN GP	Kyalami	26	Ligier Loto	M	1.5 t/c Ligier JS23-Renault V6	2 laps behind	14/27
ret	BELGIAN GP	Zolder	26	Ligier Loto	M	1.5 t/c Ligier JS23-Renault V6	spun off	13/27
6*/ret	SAN MARINO GP	Imola	26	Ligier Loto	M	1.5 t/c Ligier JS23-Renault V6	*5th place car dsq/out of fuel	12/28
10	FRENCH GP	Dijon	26	Ligier Loto	M	1.5 t/c Ligier JS23-Renault V6	started as 1st reserve/-2 laps	27/27
ret	MONACO GP	Monte Carlo	26	Ligier Loto	M	1.5 t/c Ligier JS23-Renault V6	accident damage	7/27
ret	CANADIAN GP	Montreal	26	Ligier Loto	M	1.5 t/c Ligier JS23-Renault V6	brakes	10/26
ret	US GP (DETROIT)	Detroit	26	Ligier Loto	M	1.5 t/c Ligier JS23-Renault V6	overheating	12/27
ret	US GP (DALLAS)	Dallas	26	Ligier Loto	M	1.5 t/c Ligier JS23-Renault V6	hit wall	16/27
10	BRITISH GP	Brands Hatch	26	Ligier Loto	M	1.5 t/c Ligier JS23-Renault V6	3 laps behind	19/27
7	GERMAN GP	Hockenheim	26	Ligier Loto	M	1.5 t/c Ligier JS23-Renault V6	1 lap behind	11/27
ret	AUSTRIAN GP	Österreichring	26	Ligier Loto	M	1.5 t/c Ligier JS23-Renault V6	fuel injection	18/28
ret	DUTCH GP	Zandvoort	26	Ligier Loto	M	1.5 t/c Ligier JS23-Renault V6	engine	14/27
ret	ITALIAN GP	Monza	26	Ligier Loto	M	1.5 t/c Ligier JS23-Renault V6	engine	16/27
7	EUROPEAN GP	Nürburgring	26	Ligier Loto	M	1.5 t/c Ligier JS23-Renault V6	2 laps behind	17/26
12	PORTUGUESE GP	Estoril	26	Ligier Loto	M	1.5 t/c Ligier JS23-Renault V6	1 lap behind	20/27

1985 Championship position: 17th Wins: 0 Pole positions: 0 Fastest laps: 0 Points scored: 3

	Race	Circuit	No	Entrant	Tyres	Capacity/Car/Engine	Comment	Q Pos/Entries
ret	BRAZILIAN GP	Rio	25	Equipe Ligier	P	1.5 t/c Ligier JS25-Renault V6	hit Arnoux	13/25
ret	PORTUGUESE GP	Estoril	25	Equipe Ligier	P	1.5 t/c Ligier JS25-Renault V6	tyres/handling	8/26
ret	SAN MARINO GP	Imola	25	Equipe Ligier	P	1.5 t/c Ligier JS25-Renault V6	spun off	13/26

4	MONACO GP	Monte Carlo	25	Equipe Ligier	P	1.5 t/c Ligier JS25-Renault V6	1 lap behind	8/26
14	CANADIAN GP	Montreal	25	Equipe Ligier Gitanes	P	1.5 t/c Ligier JS25-Renault V6	spin – hit Winkelhock – pit stop/-3 laps	15/25
10	US GP (DETROIT)	Detroit	25	Equipe Ligier Gitanes	P	1.5 t/c Ligier JS25-Renault V6	2 laps behind	17/25
ret	FRENCH GP	Paul Ricard	25	Equipe Ligier Gitanes	P	1.5 t/c Ligier JS25-Renault V6	driveshaft	13/26
ret	BRITISH GP	Silverstone	25	Equipe Ligier Gitanes	P	1.5 t/c Ligier JS25-Renault V6	clutch	7/26
ret	GERMAN GP	Nürburgring	25	Equipe Ligier Gitanes	P	1.5 t/c Ligier JS25-Renault V6	collision – broken steering arm	14/27
ret	AUSTRIAN GP	Österreichring	25	Equipe Ligier Gitanes	P	1.5 t/c Ligier JS25-Renault V6	accident – rolled car	18/27
ret	DUTCH GP	Zandvoort	25	Equipe Ligier Gitanes	P	1.5 t/c Ligier JS25-Renault V6	turbo	18/27

1986 Championship position: Unplaced

ret	BRAZILIAN GP	Rio	23	Minardi Team	P	1.5 t/c Minardi M185B-MM V6	turbo	22/25
ret	SPANISH GP	Jerez	23	Minardi Team	P	1.5 t/c Minardi M185B-MM V6	differential	24/25
ret	SAN MARINO GP	Imola	23	Minardi Team	P	1.5 t/c Minardi M185B-MM V6	engine	23/26
dnq	MONACO GP	Monte Carlo	23	Minardi Team	P	1.5 t/c Minardi M185B-MM V6		25/26
ret	BELGIAN GP	Spa	23	Minardi Team	P	1.5 t/c Minardi M185B-MM V6	out of fuel	19/25
ret	CANADIAN GP	Montreal	23	Minardi Team	P	1.5 t/c Minardi M185B-MM V6	gearbox	21/25
ret	US GP (DETROIT)	Detroit	23	Minardi Team	P	1.5 t/c Minardi M185B-MM V6	gearbox	23/26
ret	FRENCH GP	Paul Ricard	23	Minardi Team	P	1.5 t/c Minardi M185B-MM V6	turbo	23/26
ret	BRITISH GP	Brands Hatch	23	Minardi Team	P	1.5 t/c Minardi M185B-MM V6	electrics	21/26
ret	GERMAN GP	Hockenheim	23	Minardi Team	P	1.5 t/c Minardi M185B-MM V6	gearbox	23/26
ret	HUNGARIAN GP	Hungaroring	23	Minardi Team	P	1.5 t/c Minardi M186-MM V6	engine	20/26
ret	AUSTRIAN GP	Österreichring	23	Minardi Team	P	1.5 t/c Minardi M186-MM V6	clutch	23/26
dns	"	"	23	Minardi Team	P	1.5 t/c Minardi M185B-MM V6	practice only	– / –
ret	ITALIAN GP	Monza	23	Minardi Team	P	1.5 t/c Minardi M186-MM V6	engine	21/27
ret	PORTUGUESE GP	Estoril	23	Minardi Team	P	1.5 t/c Minardi M186-MM V6	spun off	16/27
8	MEXICAN GP	Mexico City	23	Minardi Team	P	1.5 t/c Minardi M186-MM V6	2 laps behind	22/26
ret	AUSTRALIAN GP	Adelaide	23	Minardi Team	P	1.5 t/c Minardi M186-MM V6	fire extinguisher set off	11/26

1987 Championship position: 14th= | Wins: 0 | Pole positions: 0 | Fastest laps: 0 | Points scored: 4

ret	BRAZILIAN GP	Rio	8	Motor Racing Developments Ltd	G	1.5 t/c Brabham BT56-BMW 4	gearbox	13/23
ret	SAN MARINO GP	Imola	8	Motor Racing Developments Ltd	G	1.5 t/c Brabham BT56-BMW 4	spun off	15/27
3/ret	BELGIAN GP	Spa	8	Motor Racing Developments Ltd	G	1.5 t/c Brabham BT56-BMW 4	out of fuel/1 lap behind	13/26
ret	MONACO GP	Monte Carlo	8	Motor Racing Developments Ltd	G	1.5 t/c Brabham BT56-BMW 4	suspension	21/26
ret	US GP (DETROIT)	Detroit	8	Motor Racing Developments Ltd	G	1.5 t/c Brabham BT56-BMW 4	gearbox	17/26
ret	FRENCH GP	Paul Ricard	8	Motor Racing Developments Ltd	G	1.5 t/c Brabham BT56-BMW 4	turbo	11/26
ret	BRITISH GP	Silverstone	8	Motor Racing Developments Ltd	G	1.5 t/c Brabham BT56-BMW 4	broken fuel line – fire	9/26
ret	GERMAN GP	Hockenheim	8	Motor Racing Developments Ltd	G	1.5 t/c Brabham BT56-BMW 4	engine	7/26
ret	HUNGARIAN GP	Hungaroring	8	Motor Racing Developments Ltd	G	1.5 t/c Brabham BT56-BMW 4	gearbox	13/26
ret	AUSTRIAN GP	Österreichring	8	Motor Racing Developments Ltd	G	1.5 t/c Brabham BT56-BMW 4	turbo	10/26
ret	ITALIAN GP	Monza	8	Motor Racing Developments Ltd	G	1.5 t/c Brabham BT56-BMW 4	suspension	10/28
ret	PORTUGUESE GP	Estoril	8	Motor Racing Developments Ltd	G	1.5 t/c Brabham BT56-BMW 4	engine	13/27
ret	SPANISH GP	Jerez	8	Motor Racing Developments Ltd	G	1.5 t/c Brabham BT56-BMW 4	gearbox	10/28
ret	MEXICAN GP	Mexico City	8	Motor Racing Developments Ltd	G	1.5 t/c Brabham BT56-BMW 4	incident with Senna	10/27
ret	JAPANESE GP	Suzuka	8	Motor Racing Developments Ltd	G	1.5 t/c Brabham BT56-BMW 4	turbo	11/27
8*/ret	AUSTRALIAN GP	Adelaide	8	Motor Racing Developments Ltd	G	1.5 t/c Brabham BT56-BMW 4	*2nd car dsq/spun off/-4 laps	10/27

1988 Championship position: 15th | Wins: 0 | Pole positions: 0 | Fastest laps: 0 | Points scored: 3

ret	BRAZILIAN GP	Rio	22	Rial Racing	G	3.5 Rial ARC1-Cosworth V8	engine	14/31
ret	SAN MARINO GP	Imola	22	Rial Racing	G	3.5 Rial ARC1-Cosworth V8	started from pits/suspension	16/31
ret	MONACO GP	Monte Carlo	22	Rial Racing	G	3.5 Rial ARC1-Cosworth V8	oil pressure	19/30
ret	MEXICAN GP	Mexico City	22	Rial Racing	G	3.5 Rial ARC1-Cosworth V8	gearbox	12/30
9/ret	CANADIAN GP	Montreal	22	Rial Racing	G	3.5 Rial ARC1-Cosworth V8	out of fuel/3 laps behind	12/31
4	US GP (DETROIT)	Detroit	22	Rial Racing	G	3.5 Rial ARC1-Cosworth V8	1 lap behind	12/31
10	FRENCH GP	Paul Ricard	22	Rial Racing	G	3.5 Rial ARC1-Cosworth V8	wheel stuck at pit stop/-2 laps	12/31
ret	BRITISH GP	Silverstone	22	Rial Racing	G	3.5 Rial ARC1-Cosworth V8	clutch	14/31
13	GERMAN GP	Hockenheim	22	Rial Racing	G	3.5 Rial ARC1-Cosworth V8	pit stop - tyres/2 spins/-2 laps	14/31
ret	HUNGARIAN GP	Hungaroring	22	Rial Racing	G	3.5 Rial ARC1-Cosworth V8	driveshaft – c.v. joint	18/31
ret	BELGIAN GP	Spa	22	Rial Racing	G	3.5 Rial ARC1-Cosworth V8	accident with Arnoux	19/31
ret	ITALIAN GP	Monza	22	Rial Racing	G	3.5 Rial ARC1-Cosworth V8	collision with Martini – suspension	18/31
ret	PORTUGUESE GP	Estoril	22	Rial Racing	G	3.5 Rial ARC1-Cosworth V8	driveshaft	12/31
ret	SPANISH GP	Jerez	22	Rial Racing	G	3.5 Rial ARC1-Cosworth V8	engine	23/31
ret	JAPANESE GP	Suzuka	22	Rial Racing	G	3.5 Rial ARC1-Cosworth V8	overheating	14/31
8/ret	AUSTRALIAN GP	Adelaide	22	Rial Racing	G	3.5 Rial ARC1-Cosworth V8	out of fuel/5 laps behind	15/31

1989 Championship position: 16th | Wins: 0 | Pole positions: 0 | Fastest laps: 0 | Points scored: 4

13/ret	BRAZILIAN GP	Rio	22	Scuderia Italia	P	3.5 Dallara 189-Cosworth V8	engine/4 laps behind	15/38
10	SAN MARINO GP	Imola	22	Scuderia Italia	P	3.5 Dallara 189-Cosworth V8	spin/2 laps behind	16/39
13	MONACO GP	Monte Carlo	22	Scuderia Italia	P	3.5 Dallara 189-Cosworth V8	collision - Piquet-pit stop/-4 laps	10/38
ret	MEXICAN GP	Mexico City	22	Scuderia Italia	P	3.5 Dallara 189-Cosworth V8	fuel pump	12/39
ret	US GP (PHOENIX)	Phoenix	22	Scuderia Italia	P	3.5 Dallara 189-Cosworth V8	fuel pump/5 laps behind	13/39
3	CANADIAN GP	Montreal	22	Scuderia Italia	P	3.5 Dallara 189-Cosworth V8		9/39
dnq	FRENCH GP	Paul Ricard	22	Scuderia Italia	P	3.5 Dallara 189-Cosworth V8		27/39
ret	BRITISH GP	Silverstone	22	Scuderia Italia	P	3.5 Dallara 189-Cosworth V8	gearbox	25/39
7	GERMAN GP	Hockenheim	22	Scuderia Italia	P	3.5 Dallara 189-Cosworth V8	1 lap behind	21/39
ret	HUNGARIAN GP	Hungaroring	22	Scuderia Italia	P	3.5 Dallara 189-Cosworth V8	clutch	18/39
11	BELGIAN GP	Spa	22	Scuderia Italia	P	3.5 Dallara 189-Cosworth V8	3 spins/1 lap behind	18/39
ret	ITALIAN GP	Monza	22	Scuderia Italia	P	3.5 Dallara 189-Cosworth V8	engine - electrics	17/39
ret	PORTUGUESE GP	Estoril	22	Scuderia Italia	P	3.5 Dallara 189-Cosworth V8	engine	19/39
7	SPANISH GP	Jerez	22	Scuderia Italia	P	3.5 Dallara 189-Cosworth V8	pit stop - tyres/1 lap behind	15/38
10	JAPANESE GP	Suzuka	22	Scuderia Italia	P	3.5 Dallara 189-Cosworth V8	collision with Pirro-pit stop/-2 laps	16/39
ret	AUSTRALIAN GP	Adelaide	22	Scuderia Italia	P	3.5 Dallara 189-Cosworth V8	spun off in rain	9/39

1990 Championship position: Unplaced

ret	US GP (PHOENIX)	Phoenix	22	Scuderia Italia	P	3.5 BMS Dallara 190-Cosworth V8	engine	3/35
ret	BRAZILIAN GP	Interlagos	22	Scuderia Italia	P	3.5 BMS Dallara 190-Cosworth V8	collision with Alesi	9/35
ret	SAN MARINO GP	Imola	22	Scuderia Italia	P	3.5 BMS Dallara 190-Cosworth V8	wheel hub	18/34
ret	MONACO GP	Monte Carlo	22	Scuderia Italia	P	3.5 BMS Dallara 190-Cosworth V8	throttle linkage	12/35
ret	CANADIAN GP	Montreal	22	Scuderia Italia	P	3.5 BMS Dallara 190-Cosworth V8	transmission	25/35
13	MEXICAN GP	Mexico City	22	Scuderia Italia	P	3.5 BMS Dallara 190-Cosworth V8	1 lap behind	15/35
15/dsq*	FRENCH GP	Paul Ricard	22	Scuderia Italia	P	3.5 BMS Dallara 190-Cosworth V8	*car underweight/2 laps behind	21/35
ret	BRITISH GP	Silverstone	22	Scuderia Italia	P	3.5 BMS Dallara 190-Cosworth V8	gearbox	23/35
dnq	GERMAN GP	Hockenheim	22	Scuderia Italia	P	3.5 BMS Dallara 190-Cosworth V8		30/35
ret	HUNGARIAN GP	Hungaroring	22	Scuderia Italia	P	3.5 BMS Dallara 190-Cosworth V8	engine – oil leak	10/35
ret	BELGIAN GP	Spa	22	Scuderia Italia	P	3.5 BMS Dallara 190-Cosworth V8	engine	20/33
10	ITALIAN GP	Monza	22	Scuderia Italia	P	3.5 BMS Dallara 190-Cosworth V8	pit stop – tyres/2 laps behind	25/33
ret	PORTUGUESE GP	Estoril	22	Scuderia Italia	P	3.5 BMS Dallara 190-Cosworth V8	sticking throttle	18/33
ret	SPANISH GP	Jerez	22	Scuderia Italia	P	3.5 BMS Dallara 190-Cosworth V8	engine – dropped valve	17/33
ret	JAPANESE GP	Suzuka	22	Scuderia Italia	P	3.5 BMS Dallara 190-Cosworth V8	spun off	26/30
ret	AUSTRALIAN GP	Adelaide	22	Scuderia Italia	P	3.5 BMS Dallara 190-Cosworth V8	electrics	15/30

1991 Championship position: 9th Wins: 0 Pole positions: 0 Fastest laps: 0 Points scored: 9

dnpq	US GP (PHOENIX)	Phoenix	33	Team 7UP Jordan	G	3.5 Jordan 191-Ford HB V8		31/34
ret	BRAZILIAN GP	Interlagos	33	Team 7UP Jordan	G	3.5 Jordan 191-Ford HB V8	engine cut out – spun off	13/34
ret	SAN MARINO GP	Imola	33	Team 7UP Jordan	G	3.5 Jordan 191-Ford HB V8	gear linkage	11/34
ret	MONACO GP	Monte Carlo	33	Team 7UP Jordan	G	3.5 Jordan 191-Ford HB V8	throttle cable	10/34
4	CANADIAN GP	Montreal	33	Team 7UP Jordan	G	3.5 Jordan 191-Ford HB V8		11/34
4/ret	MEXICAN GP	Mexico City	33	Team 7UP Jordan	G	3.5 Jordan 191-Ford HB V8	throttle potentiometer/1 lap behind	11/34
6	FRENCH GP	Magny Cours	33	Team 7UP Jordan	G	3.5 Jordan 191-Ford HB V8	1 lap behind	13/34
ret	BRITISH GP	Silverstone	33	Team 7UP Jordan	G	3.5 Jordan 191-Ford HB V8	accident – suspension failure	13/34
5	GERMAN GP	Hockenheim	33	Team 7UP Jordan	G	3.5 Jordan 191-Ford HB V8		7/34
7	HUNGARIAN GP	Hungaroring	33	Team 7UP Jordan	G	3.5 Jordan 191-Ford HB V8	1 lap behind	17/34
13/ret	BELGIAN GP	Spa	33	Team 7UP Jordan	G	3.5 Jordan 191-Ford HB V8	engine – overheating when 2nd	11/34
7	ITALIAN GP	Monza	33	Team 7UP Jordan	G	3.5 Jordan 191-Ford HB V8		14/34
8	PORTUGUESE GP	Estoril	33	Team 7UP Jordan	G	3.5 Jordan 191-Ford HB V8	1 lap behind	14/34
ret	SPANISH GP	Barcelona	33	Team 7UP Jordan	G	3.5 Jordan 191-Ford HB V8	electrics	17/33
ret	JAPANESE GP	Suzuka	33	Team 7UP Jordan	G	3.5 Jordan 191-Ford HB V8	spun off	11/31
8	AUSTRALIAN GP	Adelaide	33	Team 7UP Jordan	G	3.5 Jordan 191-Ford HB V8	rain-shortened race	12/32

1992 Championship position: 9th Wins: 0 Pole positions: 0 Fastest laps: 0 Points scored: 8

ret	SOUTH AFRICAN GP	Kyalami	4	Tyrrell Racing Organisation	G	3.5 Tyrrell 020B-Ilmor V10	engine	10/30
5	MEXICAN GP	Mexico City	4	Tyrrell Racing Organisation	G	3.5 Tyrrell 020B-Ilmor V10	1 lap behind	11/30
ret	BRAZILIAN GP	Interlagos	4	Tyrrell Racing Organisation	G	3.5 Tyrrell 020B-Ilmor V10	electrics	13/31
ret	SPANISH GP	Barcelona	4	Tyrrell Racing Organisation	G	3.5 Tyrrell 020B-Ilmor V10	oil pressure	11/32
14/ret	SAN MARINO GP	Imola	4	Tyrrell Racing Organisation	G	3.5 Tyrrell 020B-Ilmor V10	fuel pressure/5 laps behind	14/32
ret	MONACO GP	Monte Carlo	4	Tyrrell Racing Organisation	G	3.5 Tyrrell 020B-Ilmor V10	gearbox	10/32
5	CANADIAN GP	Montreal	4	Tyrrell Racing Organisation	G	3.5 Tyrrell 020B-Ilmor V10	1 lap behind	14/32
ret	FRENCH GP	Magny Cours	4	Tyrrell Racing Organisation	G	3.5 Tyrrell 020B-Ilmor V10	spun off	19/30
ret	BRITISH GP	Silverstone	4	Tyrrell Racing Organisation	G	3.5 Tyrrell 020B-Ilmor V10	suspension – spun off	18/32
ret	GERMAN GP	Hockenheim	4	Tyrrell Racing Organisation	G	3.5 Tyrrell 020B-Ilmor V10	engine	20/32
8	HUNGARIAN GP	Hungaroring	4	Tyrrell Racing Organisation	G	3.5 Tyrrell 020B-Ilmor V10	2 laps behind	19/31
8	BELGIAN GP	Spa	4	Tyrrell Racing Organisation	G	3.5 Tyrrell 020B-Ilmor V10	1 lap behind	13/30
6	ITALIAN GP	Monza	4	Tyrrell Racing Organisation	G	3.5 Tyrrell 020B-Ilmor V10	1 lap behind	21/28
9	PORTUGUESE GP	Estoril	4	Tyrrell Racing Organisation	G	3.5 Tyrrell 020B-Ilmor V10	2 laps behind	12/26
4	JAPANESE GP	Suzuka	4	Tyrrell Racing Organisation	G	3.5 Tyrrell 020B-Ilmor V10	1 lap behind	9/26
ret	AUSTRALIAN GP	Adelaide	4	Tyrrell Racing Organisation	G	3.5 Tyrrell 020B-Ilmor V10	fuel pressure – fire	7/26

1993 Championship position: Unplaced

ret	SOUTH AFRICAN GP	Kyalami	4	Tyrrell Racing Organisation	G	3.5 Tyrrell 020C-Yamaha V10	transmission on grid at start	23/26
ret	BRAZILIAN GP	Interlagos	4	Tyrrell Racing Organisation	G	3.5 Tyrrell 020C-Yamaha V10	engine – electrics	23/26
ret	EUROPEAN GP	Donington	4	Tyrrell Racing Organisation	G	3.5 Tyrrell 020C-Yamaha V10	gearbox	25/26
ret	SAN MARINO GP	Imola	4	Tyrrell Racing Organisation	G	3.5 Tyrrell 020C-Yamaha V10	gearbox	18/26
dsq	SPANISH GP	Barcelona	4	Tyrrell Racing Organisation	G	3.5 Tyrrell 020C-Yamaha V10	black-flagged for push start	24/26
10	MONACO GP	Monte Carlo	4	Tyrrell Racing Organisation	G	3.5 Tyrrell 020C-Yamaha V10	2 laps behind	19/26
ret	CANADIAN GP	Montreal	4	Tyrrell Racing Organisation	G	3.5 Tyrrell 020C-Yamaha V10	active suspension problems/spun off	19/26
15	FRENCH GP	Magny Cours	4	Tyrrell Racing Organisation	G	3.5 Tyrrell 020C-Yamaha V10	4 laps behind	25/26
ret	BRITISH GP	Silverstone	4	Tyrrell Racing Organisation	G	3.5 Tyrrell 021-Yamaha V10	pit stops after collision/steering	21/26
ret	GERMAN GP	Hockenheim	4	Tyrrell Racing Organisation	G	3.5 Tyrrell 021-Yamaha V10	gearbox	19/26
11	HUNGARIAN GP	Hungaroring	4	Tyrrell Racing Organisation	G	3.5 Tyrrell 021-Yamaha V10	pit stop – transmission/-5 laps-	22/26
ret	BELGIAN GP	Spa	4	Tyrrell Racing Organisation	G	3.5 Tyrrell 021-Yamaha V10	engine	17/25
ret	ITALIAN GP	Monza	4	Tyrrell Racing Organisation	G	3.5 Tyrrell 021-Yamaha V10	oil pressure	18/26
12	PORTUGUESE GP	Estoril	4	Tyrrell Racing Organisation	G	3.5 Tyrrell 021-Yamaha V10	spin/water leak/3 laps behind	17/26
ret	JAPANESE GP	Suzuka	4	Tyrrell Racing Organisation	G	3.5 Tyrrell 021-Yamaha V10	collision with Gounon – puncture	18/24
13	AUSTRALIAN GP	Adelaide	4	Tyrrell Racing Organisation	G	3.5 Tyrrell 021-Yamaha V10	4 laps behind	15/24

1994 Championship position: 18th= Wins: 0 Pole positions: 0 Fastest laps: 0 Points scored: 4

ret	SAN MARINO GP	Imola	15	Sasol Jordan	G	3.5 Jordan 194-Hart V10	driver fatigue – spun off	21/28
4	MONACO GP	Monte Carlo	15	Sasol Jordan	G	3.5 Jordan 194-Hart V10	1 lap behind	14/24
ret	CANADIAN GP	Montreal	29	Sauber AG	G	3.5 Sauber C13-Mercedes Benz V10	engine	14/27
6	FRENCH GP	Magny Cours	29	Sauber AG	G	3.5 Sauber C13-Mercedes Benz V10	2 laps behind	11/28
ret	BRITISH GP	Silverstone	29	Sauber AG	G	3.5 Sauber C13-Mercedes Benz V10	engine	18/28
ret	GERMAN GP	Hockenheim	29	Sauber AG	G	3.5 Sauber C13-Mercedes Benz V10	multiple accident at start	18/28
ret	HUNGARIAN GP	Hungaroring	29	Sauber AG	G	3.5 Sauber C13-Mercedes Benz V10	collision with Morbidelli	17/28
ret	BELGIAN GP	Spa	29	Sauber AG	G	3.5 Sauber C13-Mercedes Benz V10	sticking throttle	15/28
ret	ITALIAN GP	Monza	29	Sauber AG	G	3.5 Sauber C13-Mercedes Benz V10	engine	8/28
ret	PORTUGUESE GP	Estoril	29	Sauber AG	G	3.5 Sauber C13-Mercedes Benz V10	spun off	17/28
ret	EUROPEAN GP	Jerez	29	Sauber AG	G	3.5 Sauber C13-Mercedes Benz V10	accelerator	18/28

GP Starts: 208   GP Wins: 0   Pole positions: 1   Fastest laps: 1   Points: 59

de FILIPPIS, Maria-Teresa (I) b 11/11/1926

1958 Championship position: Unplaced

	Race	Circuit	No	Entrant	Tyres	Capacity/Car/Engine	Comment	Q Pos/Entries
dnq	MONACO GP	Monte Carlo	44	Maria-Teresa de Filippis	P	2.5 Maserati 250F 6		=22/28
10	BELGIAN GP	Spa	26	Maria-Teresa de Filippis	P	2.5 Maserati 250F 6	2 laps behind	19/20
ret	PORTUGUESE GP	Oporto	30	Scuderia Centro Sud	P	2.5 Maserati 250F 6	mechanical	15/15
ret	ITALIAN GP	Monza	42	Maria-Teresa de Filippis	P	2.5 Maserati 250F 6	engine	21/21

1959 Championship position: Unplaced

	Race	Circuit	No	Entrant	Tyres	Capacity/Car/Engine	Comment	Q Pos/Entries
dnq	MONACO GP	Monte Carlo	4	Dr Ing F Porsche KG	D	1.5 Behra-Porsche F4 F2		21/24

GP Starts: 3   GP Wins: 0   Pole positions: 0   Fastest laps: 0   Points: 0

MARIA-TERESA de FILIPPIS

MARIA-TERESA DE FILIPPIS made a little bit of grand prix history when she became the first woman to start a world championship grand prix, having competed successfully for a number of years in Italian national sports car racing, first with a little OSCA and then, from 1955, with a more powerful Maserati.

With the help, initially, of Luigi Musso, she broke into Formula 1 in 1958, scoring a fifth place at Syracuse in a rather thin field, before tackling four grands prix in her Maserati 250F. Maria-Teresa was then taken under the wing of Jean Behra for 1959, but after his death at AVUS, she immediately retired from racing to start a family.

After many years away, she renewed his association with the sport through her involvement in the Société des Anciens Pilotes and the Maserati Club, in which she served as president.

EMMANUEL de GRAFFENRIED

ALTHOUGH his racing activities began well before the Second World War in his native Switzerland, with both a 3-litre Alfa Romeo and a Type 6C Maserati, it was the immediate post-war years that saw 'Toulo' – as he was popularly known – at his zenith.

In 1946, he formed Team Autosport with former Mercedes driver Christian Kautz, the pair acquiring a new four-cylinder Maserati that de Graffenried drove to fifth place in the Prix de Geneva. He finished third in the car at Lausanne the following year, then drove splendidly to finish second to Farina in Geneva, and third in the Monaco GP behind Farina and Chiron in 1948, before his season was overshadowed by the death of Kautz in the Grand Prix de l'Europe at Bremgarten.

'Toulo' enjoyed his greatest triumph in 1949, winning the British Grand Prix in his latest San Remo-type 4CLT/48 Maserati, backing this up with second places in the Pau, Zandvoort and Swedish GPs, and the Jersey Road Race in St Helier, as well as many other placings. He continued to race the car into the 1950 season, but by then it was a little long in the tooth. However, his performances were such that Alfa Romeo invited him to race for their team in the Grand Prix des Nations at Geneva, where he performed creditably to finish second to Juan Fangio, but only two seconds ahead of Piero Taruffi after more than two hours' racing on the demanding street circuit.

Although de Graffenried was forced to continue racing his faithful Maserati in 1951, Alfa invited him to join their all-conquering team for three grands prix that year, and again he acquitted himself more than respectably. With the new Formula 2 rules in force for 1952, he drove Enrico Platé's Maseratis without achieving much success in the championship races, but picked up third places at Cadours and Aix-les-Bains.

Things were very different in 1953, however. Now at the wheel of the latest Maserati A6GCM model, he enjoyed some memorable races, winning the Syracuse GP, the Eifelrennen F2 race and the Lavant Cup at Goodwood. Installing a 2.5-litre engine in the car, he raced it briefly in 1954, as well as competing in a Maserati sports car, which he took to South

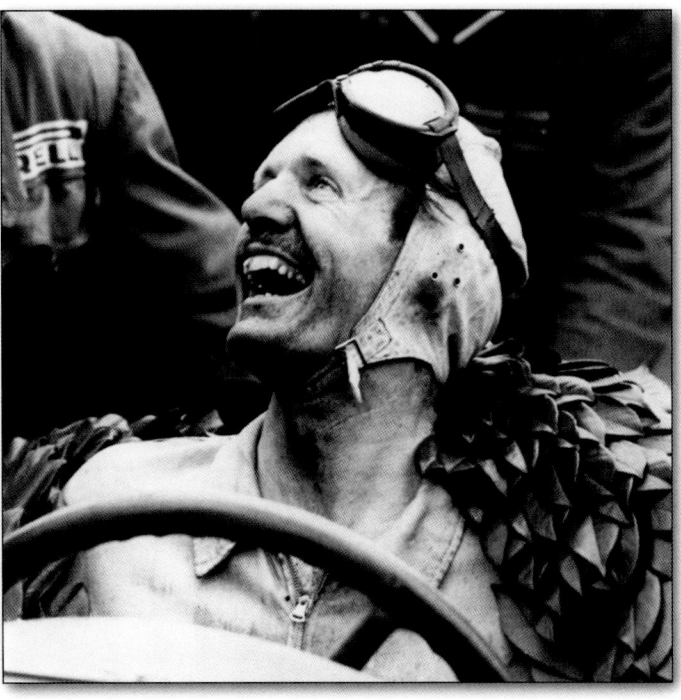

America early in the season, winning the Circuit of Gavea race at Rio and the São Paulo GP. He raced little after this, having a few sports car outings in Ferraris and Maseratis before making a final grand prix appearance at Monza in 1956.

De Graffenried built up a successful car dealership in Lausanne, which at first sold Alfa Romeo's, and later Rolls Royces and Ferraris. 'Toulo' was not lost to the grand prix world, however, for he was closely involved with the sport and was seen regularly at the circuits over the next three decades. His death in 2007, at the age of 92, marked the last link with the era of the pre-war drivers.

de GRAFFENRIED, Baron Emmanuel (CH) b 18/5/1914, Paris, France – d 22/1/2007, Lonay, Switzerland

1950 Championship position: Unplaced

	Race	Circuit	No	Entrant	Tyres	Capacity/Car/Engine	Comment	Q Pos/Entries
ret	BRITISH GP	Silverstone	20	Emmanuel de Graffenried	P	1.5 s/c Maserati 4CLT/48 4	engine	8/21
ret	MONACO GP	Monte Carlo	52	Emmanuel de Graffenried	P	1.5 s/c Maserati 4CLT/48 4	multiple accident	12/21
6	SWISS GP	Bremgarten	32	Emmanuel de Graffenried	P	1.5 s/c Maserati 4CLT/48 4	2 laps behind	11/18
6	ITALIAN GP	Monza	38	Emmanuel de Graffenried	P	1.5 s/c Maserati 4CLT/48 4	8 laps behind	17/27

1951 Championship position: 12th=   Wins: 0   Pole positions: 0   Fastest laps: 0   Points scored: 2

	Race	Circuit	No	Entrant	Tyres	Capacity/Car/Engine	Comment	Q Pos/Entries
5	SWISS GP	Bremgarten	26	Alfa Romeo SpA	P	1.5 s/c Alfa Romeo 159 8	2 laps behind	5/21
ret	FRENCH GP	Reims	18	Enrico Platé	P	1.5 s/c Maserati 4CLT/48 4	transmission	16/23
ret	GERMAN GP	Nürburgring	79	Enrico Platé	P	1.5 s/c Maserati 4CLT/48 4	engine	16/23
ret	ITALIAN GP	Monza	36	Alfa Romeo SpA	P	1.5 s/c Alfa Romeo 159 8	supercharger drive	9/22
6	SPANISH GP	Pedralbes	26	Alfa Romeo SpA	P	1.5 s/c Alfa Romeo 159 8	4 laps behind	6/20

1952 Championship position: Unplaced

	Race	Circuit	No	Entrant	Tyres	Capacity/Car/Engine	Comment	Q Pos/Entries
6	SWISS GP	Bremgarten	38	Enrico Platé	P	2.0 Maserati 4CLT/Platé 4	4 laps behind	8/21
ret*	FRENCH GP	Rouen	16	Enrico Platé	P	2.0 Maserati 4CLT/Platé 4	*Schell took over/brakes	11/20
19	BRITISH GP	Silverstone	32	Enrico Platé	P	2.0 Maserati 4CLT/Platé 4	no practice time set/9 laps behind	– /32
dnq	ITALIAN GP	Monza	60	Enrico Platé	P	2.0 Maserati 4CLT/Platé 4	engine	27/35

1953 Championship position: 7th   Wins: 0   Pole positions: 0   Fastest laps: 0   Points scored: 7

	Race	Circuit	No	Entrant	Tyres	Capacity/Car/Engine	Comment	Q Pos/Entries
5	DUTCH GP	Zandvoort	18	Emmanuel de Graffenried	P	2.0 Maserati A6GCM 6	2 laps behind	7/20
4	BELGIAN GP	Spa	30	Emmanuel de Graffenried	P	2.0 Maserati A6GCM 6	1 lap behind	9/22
7	FRENCH GP	Reims	46	Emmanuel de Graffenried	P	2.0 Maserati A6GCM 6	2 laps behind	9/25
ret	BRITISH GP	Silverstone	31	Emmanuel de Graffenried	P	2.0 Maserati A6GCM 6	clutch	26/29
5	GERMAN GP	Nürburgring	17	Emmanuel de Graffenried	P	2.0 Maserati A6GCM 6	1 lap behind	11/35
ret	SWISS GP	Bremgarten	42	Emmanuel de Graffenried	P	2.0 Maserati A6GCM 6	transmission	8/23
ret	ITALIAN GP	Monza	58	Emmanuel de Graffenried	P	2.0 Maserati A6GCM 6	engine	9/30

1954 Championship position: Unplaced

	Race	Circuit	No	Entrant	Tyres	Capacity/Car/Engine	Comment	Q Pos/Entries
8	ARGENTINE GP	Buenos Aires	30	Emmanuel de Graffenried	P	2.5 Maserati A6GCM/250F 6	4 laps behind	13/18
ret*	BELGIAN GP	Spa	50	Emmanuel de Graffenried	P	2.5 Maserati A6GCM/250F 6	*camera car only – not 'racing'	– / –
ret*	SPANISH GP	Pedralbes	22	Emmanuel de Graffenried	P	2.5 Maserati A6GCM/250F 6	*Volonterio also drove car/engine	21/22

1956 Championship position: Unplaced

	Race	Circuit	No	Entrant	Tyres	Capacity/Car/Engine	Comment	Q Pos/Entries
7	ITALIAN GP	Monza	14	Scuderia Centro Sud	P	2.5 Maserati 250F 6	4 laps behind	19/26

GP Starts: 22   GP Wins: 0   Pole positions: 0   Fastest laps: 0   Points: 9

PIET (PETER) de KLERK

PETER DE KLERK got his first foothold in motor racing as a mechanic. Indeed he worked his passage from Durban to London to learn about racing cars and spent a short spell working for Colin Chapman. On his return to his homeland, he found employment with Syd van der Vyver, who also gave him his first chance to race. Moving to Johannesburg, he helped Doug Serrurier and Ernest Pieterse to build the Alfa special in 1960, but it was 1962 before the eager de Klerk managed to get behind the wheel.

De Klerk quickly began to gain good results with the car and subsequently was entrusted with a Brabham-Climax, with which he was able to challenge more strongly local maestro John Love. He always seemed to be 'bridesmaid', however, finishing second on numerous occasions, before temporarily abandoning single-seaters at the end of 1965, when Mike de Udy offered him the chance to race abroad in his Porsche Carrera 6 sports cars. He took a fine sixth place in a works Porsche at Le Mans in 1966, then resumed his South African career in late 1968 with Love's old Brabham BT20. In 1970, he joined Love at Team Gunston, racing a Brabham BT26 and winning the Republic Trophy race at Kyalami. In 1971, he switched to the rival Scribante, but naturally perhaps played a subordinate role to team boss Dave Charlton until he called time on single-seaters at the end of 1972. His last hurrah as a driver was a win in the Chevron B19 at the Natal Easter Trophy sports car race.

de KLERK, Peter (ZA) b 16/3/1935, Pilgrim's Rest, Transvaal

1963 Championship position: Unplaced

	Race	Circuit	No	Entrant	Tyres	Capacity/Car/Engine	Comment	Q Pos/Entries
ret	SOUTH AFRICAN GP	East London	18	Otelle Nucci	D	1.5 Alfa Special 4	gearbox	16/21

1965 Championship position: Unplaced

	Race	Circuit	No	Entrant	Tyres	Capacity/Car/Engine	Comment	Q Pos/Entries
10	SOUTH AFRICAN GP	East London	20	Otelle Nucci	D	1.5 Alfa Special 4	6 laps behind	17/25

1969 Championship position: Unplaced

	Race	Circuit	No	Entrant	Tyres	Capacity/Car/Engine	Comment	Q Pos/Entries
nc	SOUTH AFRICAN GP	Kyalami	19	Jack Holme	D	3.0 Brabham BT20-Repco V8	pit stop – clutch/13 laps behind	17/18

1970 Championship position: Unplaced

	Race	Circuit	No	Entrant	Tyres	Capacity/Car/Engine	Comment	Q Pos/Entries
11	SOUTH AFRICAN GP	Kyalami	24	Team Gunston	F	3.0 Brabham BT26A-Cosworth V8	pit stop/5 laps behind	21/24

GP Starts: 4   GP Wins: 0   Pole positions: 0   Fastest laps: 0   Points: 0

PEDRO de la ROSA

IT was the end of a long and winding road for Pedro de la Rosa when he finally found his way on to the grand prix grid in 1999. After racing karts from an early age, the Spaniard became the national Fiat Uno champion in 1989 and took the Formula Ford title the following year, before moving to Formula Renault in Britain. This championship was duly added to the list in 1992, and when he graduated to Formula 3 in 1993, his upward career curve seemed untroubled. However, a satisfactory sixth place in that learning year was followed by a nightmare season, when, saddled with an uncompetitive Renault engine, he could only watch as Jan Magnussen blitzed the rest of the field. Fortunately, a late-season engine change proved there was nothing wrong with the driver, who by then had decided to further his career in Japanese Formula 3.

Driving for TOM's, de la Rosa trounced the opposition with eight pole positions and eight wins from the nine rounds of the series, ensuring a move up to Formula Nippon for 1996. In his first year at this level, he was always quick, but was let down by his lack of experience, which denied him better finishes. He was a good learner, though, and the following season he took his Nova Engineering Lola to the championship title with six wins from the ten rounds. As if his cup were not already overflowing, he also clinched the All-Japan GT championship in a Toyota Supra.

Seeing no purpose in racing in the European F3000 series, Pedro secured backing from Repsol and negotiated a place for himself as the Jordan test driver for 1998, impressing all concerned with his technical feedback. His ability to make a healthy contribution to the Arrows sponsorship budget no doubt was a huge factor in Tom Walkinshaw's decision to sign the Spaniard the following season, but he soon proved his worth by scoring a priceless point for the team on his grand prix debut in Melbourne.

Thereafter, lack of development saw Arrows treading water, but Pedro was held in high esteem by the team, and he was retained at Arrows for 2000. The new A21 had been flying in testing, but despite phenomenal straight-line speed in certain races, it flattered to deceive on more than one occasion. A couple of sixth places left him languishing in 15th place overall at the end of the year, but it was a surprise when he was dropped in favour of Enrique Bernoldi.

Then Pedro opted to join Jaguar, where initially he acted as a test driver, but he soon found himself in the race seat after Luciano Burti was dropped, The recalcitrant Jaguar R2 was not the best car to have, however, and he managed just three points in 13 races, but it was enough to see him retained for 2002. His second year with Jaguar was another difficult one, the team's R3 chassis being a disaster, and no points were scored.

De la Rosa appeared set for the F1 wilderness for 2003, until McLaren-Mercedes swooped to sign him as a test driver on the back of two successful 'development' outings at Jerez and Barcelona. Thus the Spaniard became McLaren's fourth driver, testing alongside Alex Wurz and race drivers David Coulthard and Kimi Räikkönen.

Pedro remained a vital part of Ron Dennis' squad in 2004, performing the same role and, for 2005, getting a fresh chance to impress the pit lane as he took on a share of the third driver role, running in the Friday morning practice sessions. Indeed, when Juan Pablo Montoya was sidelined by a 'tennis injury', he stepped up to the plate in Bahrain, taking a solid fifth

place for the team.

With Alex Wurz moving to Williams, the Spaniard became the de-facto third driver for 2006, and following the shock mid-season departure of Juan Pablo Montoya, he found himself with a chance to show his talent in a competitive car. In his eight starts, Pedro was placed in the points on five occasions, and he came tantalisingly close to winning the Hungarian Grand Prix, only losing out to Jenson Button. However, his performances were not deemed strong enough to gain him a race seat in 2007.

Thus the unassuming de la Rosa returned to his duties as the team's test driver, until he was tempted back into race action for the 2010 season by Sauber, who were restructuring following the pull-out of BMW. His performances were respectable, but before the season was out Nick Heidfeld had been drafted in to replace him.

So it was back to McLaren and more development work at Woking, save for a last-minute call-up in Montreal in 2011, to stand in for the indisposed Sergio Pérez at Sauber.

It seemed that this might have been his final race in F1, but at the end of the season Pedro was announced as the lead driver for HRT. With a change of ownership, the tiny Spanish team were undergoing a major restructuring, and with his vast knowledge, he was seen as a valuable asset in the team's efforts to progress from the back of the grid.

de la ROSA, Pedro (ESP) b 24/2/1971, Barcelona

	1999 Championship position: 17th=		Wins: 0	Pole positions: 0	Fastest laps: 0	Points scored: 1		
	Race	Circuit	No	Entrant	Tyres	Capacity/Car/Engine	Comment	Q Pos/Entries
6	AUSTRALIAN GP	Melbourne	14	Arrows	B	3.0 Arrows A20 V10	*scored a point in first Grand Prix*	18/22
ret	BRAZILIAN GP	Interlagos	14	Arrows	B	3.0 Arrows A20 V10	*hydraulics*	18/22
ret	SAN MARINO GP	Imola	14	Arrows	B	3.0 Arrows A20 V10	*collision with Wurz*	17/22
ret	MONACO GP	Monte Carlo	14	Arrows	B	3.0 Arrows A20 V10	*gearbox*	21/22
11	SPANISH GP	Barcelona	14	Arrows	B	3.0 Arrows A20 V10	*2 laps behind*	19/22
ret	CANADIAN GP	Montreal	14	Arrows	B	3.0 Arrows A20 V10	*transmission*	20/22
11	FRENCH GP	Magny Cours	14	Arrows	B	3.0 Arrows A20 V10	*1 lap behind*	21/22

ret	BRITISH GP	Silverstone	14	Arrows	B	3.0 Arrows A20 V10	gearbox at restart	20/22
ret	AUSTRIAN GP	A1-Ring	14	Arrows	B	3.0 Arrows A20 V10	spun off	21/22
ret	GERMAN GP	Hockenheim	14	Arrows	B	3.0 Arrows A20 V10	brakes – spun off	20/22
15	HUNGARIAN GP	Hungaroring	14	Arrows	B	3.0 Arrows A20 V10	2 laps behind	20/22
ret	BELGIAN GP	Spa	14	Arrows	B	3.0 Arrows A20 V10	transmission	22/22
ret	ITALIAN GP	Monza	14	Arrows	B	3.0 Arrows A20 V10	accident damage	21/22
ret	EUROPEAN GP	Nürburgring	14	Arrows	B	3.0 Arrows A20 V10	gearbox	22/22
ret	MALAYSIAN GP	Sepang	14	Arrows	B	3.0 Arrows A20 V10	engine	20/22
13	JAPANESE GP	Suzuka	14	Arrows	B	3.0 Arrows A20 V10	2 laps behind	21/22

2000 Championship position: 15= Wins: 0 Pole positions: 0 Fastest laps: 0 Points scored: 2

ret	AUSTRALIAN GP	Melbourne	18	Arrows Supertec	B	3.0 Arrows A21-Supertec V10	broken track rod – accident	12/22
8	BRAZILIAN GP	Interlagos	18	Arrows Supertec	B	3.0 Arrows A21-Supertec V10	1 lap behind	16/22
ret	SAN MARINO GP	Imola	18	Arrows Supertec	B	3.0 Arrows A21-Supertec V10	gearbox-spun off	13/22
ret	BRITISH GP	Silverstone	18	Arrows Supertec	B	3.0 Arrows A21-Supertec V10	electrics	19/22
ret	SPANISH GP	Barcelona	18	Arrows Supertec	B	3.0 Arrows A21-Supertec V10	*time disallowed/collision with Alesi	*9/22
6	EUROPEAN GP	Nürburgring	18	Arrows Supertec	B	3.0 Arrows A21-Supertec V10	1 lap behind	12/22
dns	MONACO GP	Monte Carlo	18	Arrows Supertec	B	3.0 Arrows A21-Supertec V10	collision in first start with Button	16/22
ret	CANADIAN GP	Montreal	18	Arrows Supertec	B	3.0 Arrows A21-Supertec V10	collision with Diniz	9/22
ret	FRENCH GP	Magny Cours	18	Arrows Supertec	B	3.0 Arrows A21-Supertec V10	gearbox	13/22
ret	AUSTRIAN GP	A1-Ring	18	Arrows Supertec	B	3.0 Arrows A21-Supertec V10	gearbox	12/22
6	GERMAN GP	Hockenheim	18	Arrows Supertec	B	3.0 Arrows A21-Supertec V10		5/22
16	HUNGARIAN GP	Hungaroring	18	Arrows Supertec	B	3.0 Arrows A21-Supertec V10	hit by Villeneuve/4 laps behind	15/22
16	BELGIAN GP	Spa	18	Arrows Supertec	B	3.0 Arrows A21-Supertec V10	2 laps behind	16/22
ret	ITALIAN GP	Monza	18	Arrows Supertec	B	3.0 Arrows A21-Supertec V10	multiple accident on lap 1	10/22
ret	U S GP	Indianapolis	18	Arrows Supertec	B	3.0 Arrows A21-Supertec V10	gearbox	18/22
12	JAPANESE GP	Suzuka	18	Arrows Supertec	B	3.0 Arrows A21-Supertec V10	1 lap behind	13/22
ret	MALAYSIAN GP	Sepang	18	Arrows Supertec	B	3.0 Arrows A21-Supertec V10	collision – Heidfeld/Diniz on lap 1	14/22

2001 Championship position: 16th Wins: 0 Pole positions: 0 Fastest laps: 0 Points scored: 3

ret	SPANISH GP	Barcelona	19	Jaguar Racing	M	3.0 Jaguar R2-Cosworth V10	collision with Frentzen	20/22
ret	AUSTRIAN GP	A1-Ring	19	Jaguar Racing	M	3.0 Jaguar R2-Cosworth V10	transmission	14/22
ret	MONACO GP	Monte Carlo	19	Jaguar Racing	M	3.0 Jaguar R2-Cosworth V10	hydraulics	14/22
6	CANADIAN GP	Montreal	19	Jaguar Racing	M	3.0 Jaguar R2-Cosworth V10	1 lap behind	14/22
8	EUROPEAN GP	Nürburgring	19	Jaguar Racing	M	3.0 Jaguar R2-Cosworth V10	1 lap behind	16/22
14	FRENCH GP	Magny Cours	19	Jaguar Racing	M	3.0 Jaguar R2-Cosworth V10	2 laps behind	14/22
12	BRITISH GP	Silverstone	19	Jaguar Racing	M	3.0 Jaguar R2-Cosworth V10	2 laps behind	13/22
ret	GERMAN GP	Hockenheim	19	Jaguar Racing	M	3.0 Jaguar R2-Cosworth V10	ran into back of Heidfeld at start	9/22
11	HUNGARIAN GP	Hungaroring	19	Jaguar Racing	M	3.0 Jaguar R2-Cosworth V10	2 laps behind	13/22
ret	BELGIAN GP	Spa	19	Jaguar Racing	M	3.0 Jaguar R2-Cosworth V10	accident damage	10/22
5	ITALIAN GP	Monza	19	Jaguar Racing	M	3.0 Jaguar R2-Cosworth V10	good team strategy	10/22
12	U S GP	Indianapolis	19	Jaguar Racing	M	3.0 Jaguar R2-Cosworth V10	1 lap behind	16/22
ret	JAPANESE GP	Suzuka	19	Jaguar Racing	M	3.0 Jaguar R2-Cosworth V10	oil leak	16/22

2002 Championship position: Unplaced

8	AUSTRALIAN GP	Melbourne	17	Jaguar Racing	M	3.0 Jaguar R3-Cosworth V10	electrical problem/5 laps behind	20/22
10	MALAYSIAN GP	Sepang	17	Jaguar Racing	M	3.0 Jaguar R3-Cosworth V10	2 laps behind	17/22
8	BRAZILIAN GP	Interlagos	17	Jaguar Racing	M	3.0 Jaguar R3-Cosworth V10	1 lap behind	11/22
ret	SAN MARINO GP	Imola	17	Jaguar Racing	M	3.0 Jaguar R3-Cosworth V10	driveshaft	21/22
ret	SPANISH GP	Barcelona	17	Jaguar Racing	M	3.0 Jaguar R3-Cosworth V10	spun off	16/21
ret	AUSTRIAN GP	A1-Ring	17	Jaguar Racing	M	3.0 Jaguar R3-Cosworth V10	throttle on lap 1	19/22
10	MONACO GP	Monte Carlo	17	Jaguar Racing	M	3.0 Jaguar R3-Cosworth V10	2 laps behind	20/22
ret	CANADIAN GP	Montreal	17	Jaguar Racing	M	3.0 Jaguar R3-Cosworth V10	gearbox	16/22
11	EUROPEAN GP	Nürburgring	17	Jaguar Racing	M	3.0 Jaguar R3-Cosworth V10	1 lap behind	16/22
11	BRITISH GP	Silverstone	17	Jaguar Racing	M	3.0 Jaguar R3-Cosworth V10	2 laps behind	21/22
9	FRANCE GP	Magny Cours	17	Jaguar Racing	M	3.0 Jaguar R3-Cosworth V10	2 laps behind	15/21
ret	GERMAN GP	Hockenheim	17	Jaguar Racing	M	3.0 Jaguar R3-Cosworth V10	transmission on lap1	20/22
13	HUNGARIAN GP	Hungaroring	17	Jaguar Racing	M	3.0 Jaguar R3-Cosworth V10	2 laps behind	15/20
ret	BELGIAN GP	Spa	17	Jaguar Racing	M	3.0 Jaguar R3-Cosworth V10	suspension	11/20
ret	ITALIAN GP	Monza	17	Jaguar Racing	M	3.0 Jaguar R3-Cosworth V10	chopped by Massa/accident damage	8/20
ret	UNITED STATES GP	Indianapolis	17	Jaguar Racing	M	3.0 Jaguar R3-Cosworth V10	transmission	17/20
ret	JAPANESE GP	Suzuka	17	Jaguar Racing	M	3.0 Jaguar R3-Cosworth V10	transmission	17/20

2005 Championship position: 19th= Wins: 0 Pole positions: 0 Fastest laps: 1 Points scored: 4

app	AUSTRALIAN GP	Melbourne	35	West McLaren Mercedes	M	3.0 McLaren MP4/20-Cosworth V10	ran as 3rd driver in practice only	-/-
app	MALAYSIAN GP	Sepang	35	West McLaren Mercedes	M	3.0 McLaren MP4/20-Cosworth V10	ran as 3rd driver in practice only	-/-
5	BAHRAIN GP	Bahrain	10	West McLaren Mercedes	M	3.0 McLaren MP4/20-Cosworth V10	FL	8/20
app	SAN MARINO GP	Imola	35	West McLaren Mercedes	M	3.0 McLaren MP4/20-Cosworth V10	ran as 3rd driver in practice only	-/-
app	SPANISH GP	Barcelona	35	West McLaren Mercedes	M	3.0 McLaren MP4/20-Cosworth V10	ran as 3rd driver in practice only	-/-
app	CANADIAN GP	Montreal	35	West McLaren Mercedes	M	3.0 McLaren MP4/20-Cosworth V10	ran as 3rd driver in practice only	-/-
app	US GP	Indianapolis	35	West McLaren Mercedes	M	3.0 McLaren MP4/20-Cosworth V10	ran as 3rd driver in practice only	-/-
app	FRENCH GP	Magny Cours	35	West McLaren Mercedes	M	3.0 McLaren MP4/20-Cosworth V10	ran as 3rd driver in practice only	-/-
app	BRITISH GP	Silverstone	35	West McLaren Mercedes	M	3.0 McLaren MP4/20-Cosworth V10	ran as 3rd driver in practice only	-/-
app	TURKISH GP	Istanbul	35	West McLaren Mercedes	M	3.0 McLaren MP4/20-Cosworth V10	ran as 3rd driver in practice only	-/-
app	ITALIAN GP	Monza	35	West McLaren Mercedes	M	3.0 McLaren MP4/20-Cosworth V10	ran as 3rd driver in practice only	-/-
app	JAPANESE GP	Suzuka	35	West McLaren Mercedes	M	3.0 McLaren MP4/20-Cosworth V10	ran as 3rd driver in practice only	-/-
app	CHINESE GP	Shanghai Circuit	35	West McLaren Mercedes	M	3.0 McLaren MP4/20-Cosworth V10	ran as 3rd driver in practice only	-/-

2006 Championship position: 11th= Wins: 0 Pole positions: 0 Fastest laps: 0 Points scored: 19

7	FRENCH GP	Magny Cours	4	McLaren Mercedes	M	2.4 McLaren MP4/21-Mercedes V8		8/22
ret	GERMAN GP	Hockenheim	4	McLaren Mercedes	M	2.4 McLaren MP4/21-Mercedes V8	fuel pump	9/22
2	HUNGARIAN GP	Hungaroring	4	McLaren Mercedes	M	2.4 McLaren MP4/21-Mercedes V8	first podium	5/22
5	TURKISH GP	Istanbul	4	McLaren Mercedes	M	2.4 McLaren MP4/21-Mercedes V8	1st corner delay	12/22

ret	ITALIAN GP	Monza	4	McLaren Mercedes	M	2.4 McLaren MP4/21-Mercedes V8	engine	7/22
5	CHINESE GP	Shanghai	4	McLaren Mercedes	M	2.4 McLaren MP4/21-Mercedes V8		7/22
11	JAPANESE GP	Suzuka	4	McLaren Mercedes	M	2.4 McLaren MP4/21-Mercedes V8	1 lap behind	13/22
8	BRAZILIAN GP	Interlagos	4	McLaren Mercedes	M	2.4 McLaren MP4/21-Mercedes V8	one-stop strategy	12/22

2010 Championship position: 17th Wins: 0 Pole positions: 0 Fastest laps: 0 Points scored: 6

ret	BAHRAIN GP	Sakhir Circuit	22	BMW Sauber F1 Team	B	2.4 Sauber C29-Ferrari V8	hydraulics	14/24
12	AUSTRALIAN GP	Melbourne	22	BMW Sauber F1 Team	B	2.4 Sauber C29-Ferrari V8		12/24
dns	MALAYSIAN GP	Sepang	22	BMW Sauber F1 Team	B	2.4 Sauber C29-Ferrari V8	engine failure before start	12/24
ret	CHINESE GP	Shanghai Circuit	22	BMW Sauber F1 Team	B	2.4 Sauber C29-Ferrari V8	engine	17/24
ret	SPANISH GP	Barcelona	22	BMW Sauber F1 Team	B	2.4 Sauber C29-Ferrari V8	accident damage after collision	12/24
ret	MONACO GP	Monte Carlo	22	BMW Sauber F1 Team	B	2.4 Sauber C29-Ferrari V8	hydraulics	15/24
11	TURKISH GP	Istanbul Park	22	BMW Sauber F1 Team	B	2.4 Sauber C29-Ferrari V8		13/24
ret	CANADIAN GP	Montreal	22	BMW Sauber F1 Team	B	2.4 Sauber C29-Ferrari V8	engine	17/24
11*	EUROPEAN GP	Valencia	22	BMW Sauber F1 Team	B	2.4 Sauber C29-Ferrari V8	* 5 second post-race penalty	16/24
12	BRITISH GP	Silverstone	22	BMW Sauber F1 Team	B	2.4 Sauber C29-Ferrari V8	hit by Sutil – rear wing damage	11/24
17	GERMAN GP	Hockenheim	22	BMW Sauber F1 Team	B	2.4 Sauber C29-Ferrari V8	collision – pit stop – new nose/-2 laps	15/24
7	HUNGARIAN GP	Hungaroring	22	BMW Sauber F1 Team	B	2.4 Sauber C29-Ferrari V8	1 lap behind	9/24
11	BELGIAN GP	Spa	22	BMW Sauber F1 Team	B	2.4 Sauber C29-Ferrari V8	engine change – started from back	22/24
14	ITALIAN GP	Monza	22	BMW Sauber F1 Team	B	2.4 Sauber C29-Ferrari V8	1 lap behind	17/24

2011 Championship position: Unplaced

12	CANADIAN GP	Montreal	17	Sauber F1 Team	P	2.4 Sauber C30-Ferrari V8	stood in for the unfit Pérez	17/24

GP Starts: 86   GP Wins: 0   Pole positions: 0   Fastest laps: 1   Points: 35

ALFONSO de PORTAGO

ONE of the most colourful characters ever to have been seen in motor racing, Alfonso 'Fon' de Portago was a fantastic all-round sportsman. A Spanish nobleman, he was three times French amateur champion jockey, and he appeared twice at Aintree – where he never raced cars – in the Grand National steeplechase; he was an international-class swimmer; and in addition he formed the Spanish bobsleigh team to take part in the 1956 Winter Olympics.

'Fon' took up motor racing in 1954, briefly sharing Harry Schell's big 4.5-litre Ferrari on its way to second place in the Buenos Aires 1000km, but usually he handled less potent machinery to begin with, his Maserati 2-litre winning a race at Metz.

In 1955, de Portago joined Scuderia Ferrari, and while his F1 outings were restricted to non-championship races, his sports car programme saw him take second in the Venezuelan GP and win the Governor's Cup at Nassau. He was included in Ferrari's large grand prix squad during 1956, sharing the second-place car in the British GP with Peter Collins, while in sports cars the highlight of his season was a win in the Tour de France in his Ferrari GT.

The 1957 season started well with a shared fifth place in the Argentine GP and success in sports car events, de Portago taking a win at Montlhéry, and third places in both the Buenos Aires 1000km and the Cuban GP, the latter after a brilliant drive when time was lost at a long pit stop. He was unhappy about taking part in the Mille Miglia, which he considered unnecessarily dangerous, but he competed nevertheless, only for disaster to strike less than 120km before the finish. It is thought that a tyre burst, hurling the Ferrari of de Portago and his long-time friend and co-driver, Ed Nelson, into the crowd. Ten unfortunate spectators were killed, along with the car's occupants, and the famous road race was banned forthwith by the Italian government.

de PORTAGO, Alfonso (E) b 11/10/1928, London, England – d 12/5/1957, Mille Miglia, between Goito and Guidizzolo, Italy

1956 Championship position: 12th= Wins: 0 Pole positions: 0 Fastest laps: 0 Points scored: 3

	Race	Circuit	No	Entrant	Tyres	Capacity/Car/Engine	Comment	Q Pos/Entries
ret	FRENCH GP	Reims	16	Scuderia Ferrari	E	2.5 Lancia-Ferrari D50 V8	gearbox	9/20
2*	BRITISH GP	Silverstone	4	Scuderia Ferrari	E	2.5 Lancia-Ferrari D50 V8	*Collins took over car/1 lap behind	12/28
10*	"	"	3	Scuderia Ferrari	E	2.5 Lancia-Ferrari D50 V8	*took Castellotti's car/9 laps behind	– / –
ret*	GERMAN GP	Nürburgring	5	Scuderia Ferrari	E	2.5 Lancia-Ferrari D50 V8	*Collins took over and crashed	10/21
ret	ITALIAN GP	Monza	30	Scuderia Ferrari	E	2.5 Lancia-Ferrari D50 V8	puncture	9/26

1957 Championship position: 16th= Wins: 0 Pole positions: 0 Fastest laps: 0 Points scored: 1

5*	ARGENTINE GP	Buenos Aires	20	Scuderia Ferrari	E	2.5 Lancia-Ferrari D50A V8	*took over González's car/-2 laps	– /16

GP Starts: 5   GP Wins: 0   Pole positions: 0   Fastest laps: 0   Points: 4

MAX de TERRA

ANOTHER Swiss 'gentleman racer' who competed in the late 1940s and early 1950s, Max de Terra was usually seen in minor events and hill-climbs. He made up the numbers at a handful of major races in his native country and drove at a sedate pace throughout.

Having raced a Cisitalia D46 in the 1950 Prix de Berne, finishing tenth (and last), he arranged to drive Alfred Dattner's Simca in the 1952 Swiss GP. The following year, he appeared at the wheel of an old Ferrari 166 entered by Rudi Fischer's Espadon team, plodding around to finish eighth, some 14 laps in arrears.

ALESSANDRO de TOMASO

A USEFUL sports car driver in his native Argentina, first with a Maserati T200S and then the little OSCA, Alessandro de Tomaso made his grand prix debut in an old Ferrari in his home event in 1957, before travelling to Europe to drive the small-capacity OSCA, winning the Index of Performance at Le Mans in 1958. After racing his Cooper-OSCA hybrid at Sebring in 1959, he retired from racing.

Alessandro had married American heiress Isabelle Haskell (a notable sports car racer in her own right), and the newly-weds set up de Tomaso Automobili, basing themselves in Modena to build prototypes and racing cars. In 1960, he helped to develop the ISIS-Fiat Formula Junior car, which was based on a Cooper model, and subsequently went on to build Formula 1 cars on two occasions. In 1962, he over-ambitiously built a sleek flat-four-engined car that proved to be hopelessly slow in the hands of Nasif Estéfano and, in the 1970 GianPaulo Dallara, penned a car that was campaigned by the privateer Williams team. Tragically, just when progress was being made, Piers Courage crashed fatally in the Dutch Grand Prix. The project struggled on with rapidly waning enthusiasm from all sides, and the partnership folded at the end of the season.

He was more successful in his road car business, however, producing numerous exotic luxury cars, of which the Pantera supercar is perhaps the most famous.

De Tomaso also bought many Italian concerns that had fallen on hard times, such as the Benelli and Moto Guzzi motorcycle firms. His most notable acquisition was Maserati, which had gone bankrupt in 1975. With the help of the Italian government, he revived the marque, which eventually was sold to FIAT in 1993.

That was the year that Alessandro suffered a stroke that confined him to a wheelchair until his death a decade later.

---

de TERRA, Max (CH) b 6/10/1918, Zürich – d 29/12/1982, Zolikon, Zürich

	1952	Championship position: Unplaced						
	Race	Circuit	No	Entrant	Tyres	Capacity/Car/Engine	Comment	Q Pos/Entries
ret	SWISS GP	Bremgarten	50	Alfred Daettner	E	1.5 Simca Gordini Type 11 4	magneto	21/21
	1953	Championship position: Unplaced						
nc	SWISS GP	Bremgarten	40	Ecurie Espadon	P	2.0 Ferrari 166C V12	14 laps behind	19/23

GP Starts: 2 GP Wins: 0 Pole positions: 0 Fastest laps: 0 Points: 0

de TOMASO, Alessandro (RA) b 10/7/1928, Buenos Aires – d 21/5/2003, Modena, Italy

	1957	Championship position: Unplaced						
	Race	Circuit	No	Entrant	Tyres	Capacity/Car/Engine	Comment	Q Pos/Entries
9	ARGENTINE GP	Buenos Aires	26	Scuderia Centro Sud	P	2.5 Ferrari 500/625 4	9 laps behind	12/16
	1959	Championship position: Unplaced						
ret	US GP	Sebring	14	Automobili OSCA	D	2.0 Cooper T43-OSCA 4	brakes	14/19

GP Starts: 2 GP Wins: 0 Pole positions: 0 Fastest laps: 0 Points: 0

de TORNACO, Baron Charles (B) b 7/6/1927, Brussels – d 18/9/1953, Modena Autodrome, Italy

	1952	Championship position: Unplaced						
	Race	Circuit	No	Entrant	Tyres	Capacity/Car/Engine	Comment	Q Pos/Entries
7	BELGIAN GP	Spa	34	Ecurie Francorchamps	E	2.0 Ferrari 500 4	3 laps behind	13/22
ret	DUTCH GP	Zandvoort	24	Ecurie Francorchamps	E	2.0 Ferrari 500 4	engine	17/18
dnq	ITALIAN GP	Monza	70	Ecurie Francorchamps	E	2.0 Ferrari 500 4		25/35
	1953	Championship position: Unplaced						
dns	BELGIAN GP	Spa	44	Ecurie Francorchamps	E	2.0 Ferrari 500 4	practice only	– /22

GP Starts: 2 GP Wins: 0 Pole positions: 0 Fastest laps: 0 Points: 0

CHARLES de TORNACO

THE wealthy son of 1920s racer Baron de Tornaco, the young Charles, encouraged by long-time friend Jacques Swaters, took part in the 1949 Spa 24-hours with a BMW, and then drove a Veritas in the 1950 event, before helping found Ecurie Belgique.

In truth, Charles was not a talented driver, but his enthusiasm was such that when the team re-grouped as Ecurie Francorchamps in 1952, he remained, racing their Ferrari T500, although his best result that year was a fourth place at Chimay in an HWM.

De Tornaco raced less regularly in 1953, but in practice for the Modena GP, he rolled the Ferrari, fracturing his skull and breaking his neck. Scandalously, no proper medical assistance was present, and he died on the way to hospital in an ordinary car.

EMILIO de VILLOTA

THE young Emilio de Villota began racing in 1967. He competed successfully in the Renault TS Cup series in 1970, and then with a SEAT 1430 the following year, before graduating from university and taking up employment with the Banco Ibérico, where eventually he found himself in the commercial department. Emilio developed his racing activities by sharing a Ford Capri RS2600 with the late Jorge de Bagration. They took second place in the Jarama four-hours with former F1 driver Mário Araújo Cabral.

In 1976, de Villota took part in the British Shellsport F5000 Championship, driving the Ex-John F1 Lyncar, and despite his inexperience held his own against the likes of David Purley, Derek Bell, Guy Edwards, Mike Wilds and Alan Jones.

With the backing of both Iberian Airways and Banco Ibérico, Emilio gave up his day job and set about the enormous task of tackling grand prix racing. He had a budget 100,000 pesetas (the equivalent of around 16 million euros in 1977), when he bought a McLaren M23 chassis, equipped with a Ford Cosworth V8 engine and Goodyear tires. "The chassis cost us 12,000 pesetas [two million euros]; each engine, 9000 pesetas [1.5 million euros]. We bought three engines for the entire year; each weekend we used only two sets of tires." Villota's team had three fully-paid members and four helpers, and perhaps inevitably found themselves out of their depth. Having failed in his attempt at his personal Everest, de Villota did have the satisfaction of taking three race wins from just six starts in the Group 8 series.

With the loss of his Banco Ibérico sponsorship, the Spaniard settled for a return to Britain and the newly introduced Aurora F1 AFX series, where he thought he could shine in a competitive car. In truth, his 1978 season was something of a let-down, after trivial faults blighted his car when well placed, leaving him in third place overall, a long way behind Tony Trimmer. However, de Villota became a staunch supporter of the championship during its short life. Acquiring the ex-Nilsson Lotus 78 helped him to take a run of four wins and a second place in just five starts, but reliability issues saw the title slip from his grasp, and he ended up in third place overall once again. He finally clinched the title in 1980 with his RAM Racing Williams FW07, snaring five victories in beating team-mate Elisio Salazar to the title. Less happy was his appearance in the 1980 Spanish GP (later stripped of its championship status), where he was embroiled with Jacques Laffite's Ligier and Carlos Reutemann's Williams in their dice for the lead.

After the AFX series folded, de Villota turned to sports cars with sparring partner Edwards, his Banco Occidental/Ultramar Team Lola T600 winning the Enna six-hours and the Flying Tigers 1000 at Brands Hatch. He also tried to compete with his Williams in the 1981 Spanish Grand Prix, but despite being invited to the event, he fell victim to infighting between rival factions within the governing bodies of Spanish motorsport. During the practice sessions, he found that his entry had been withdrawn at the behest of FISA.

There was more sports car racing in 1982, this time teamed with the likes of David Hobbs, Desiré Wilson and Alain de Cadanet, among others, in the Grid Plaza Racing Cosworth, before he was back to Formula 1 for a completely fruitless five-race spell in the hopeless works March, run by his old colleagues at RAM. In 1983, de Villota completed just a couple of races in Formula 2: with a Gresham Racing March to take ninth at Silverstone, and a home appearance at Jarama with a works Minardi. He was more concerned, however, with the foundation of his Escuela Pilotos Emilio de Villota at the Jarama circuit. This highly successful racing school took up much of his time, but he continued to race sporadically, most successfully in 1986, paired with Fermin Velez. The Spaniards took fifth place in the Silverstone 1000km, fourth at the Le Mans 24-hours and third at the Nürburgring 1000km.

De Villota's son, Emilio Jnr, and daughter, Maria, have both taken up competition in recent seasons, while Emilio runs a team in the Spanish Formula 3 championship and two cars in the Superleague Series. Maria had signed to work with F1 team Marussia Virgin in 2012.

de VILLOTA, Emilio (E) b 26/7/1946, Madrid

	Race	Circuit	No	Entrant	Tyres	Capacity/Car/Engine	Comment	Q Pos/Entries
	1976 Championship position: Unplaced							
dnq	SPANISH GP	Jarama	33	RAM Racing	G	3.0 Brabham BT44B-Cosworth V8		28/30
	1977 Championship position: Unplaced							
13	SPANISH GP	Jarama	36	Iberia Airlines	G	3.0 McLaren M23-Cosworth V8	5 laps behind	23/31
dnq	BELGIAN GP	Zolder	36	Iberia Airlines	G	3.0 McLaren M23-Cosworth V8		28/32
dnq	SWEDISH GP	Anderstorp	36	Iberia Airlines	G	3.0 McLaren M23-Cosworth V8		26/31

	Race	Circuit	No	Entrant	Tyres	Capacity/Car/Engine	Comment	Q Pos/Entries
dnq	BRITISH GP	Silverstone	36	Iberia Airlines	G	3.0 McLaren M23-Cosworth V8		30/36
dnq	GERMAN GP	Hockenheim	36	Iberia Airlines	G	3.0 McLaren M23-Cosworth V8		26/30
17/ret	AUSTRIAN GP	Österreichring	36	Iberia Airlines	G	3.0 McLaren M23-Cosworth V8	collision with course car/-4 laps	26/30
dnq	ITALIAN GP	Monza	36	Iberia Airlines	G	3.0 McLaren M23-Cosworth V8		29/34
	1978 Championship position: Unplaced							
dnq	SPANISH GP	Jarama	28	Centro Aseguredor F1	G	3.0 McLaren M23-Cosworth V8		27/28
	1981 Championship position: Unplaced							
dns	SPANISH GP	Jarama	37	Equipe Banco Occidental	M	3.0 Williams FW07-Cosworth V8	in breach of Concorde Agreement	- / -
	1982 Championship position: Unplaced							
dnpq	BELGIAN GP	Zolder	19	LBT Team March	A	3.0 March 821-Cosworth V8		32/32
dnpq	MONACO GP	Monte Carlo	19	LBT Team March	A	3.0 March 821-Cosworth V8		31/31
dnq	US GP (DETROIT)	Detroit	19	LBT Team March	A	3.0 March 821-Cosworth V8		27/28
dnq	CANADIAN GP	Montreal	19	LBT Team March	A	3.0 March 821-Cosworth V8		28/29
dnpq	DUTCH GP	Zandvoort	19	LBT Team March	A	3.0 March 821-Cosworth V8		31/31

GP Starts: 2 GP Wins: 0 Pole positions: 0 Fastest laps: 0 Points: 0

JEAN-DENIS DELÉTRAZ

WITH the cost of competing in Formula 1 escalating out of sight in the mid-1990s, the more impoverished teams towards the back of the grid increasingly looked to drivers who could bring a healthy sponsorship to make ends meet. Thus began the worrying trend of pilots of modest pedigree making up the numbers. Certainly Jean-Denis Delétraz's qualifications to compete at the highest level looked questionable, especially given his lack of recent top-flight competition, when he turned up to drive for Larrousse in Adelaide in 1994.

The wealthy Swiss driver had made a promising start to his career in French FF1600 in 1985, but achieved little in two seasons of Formula 3 thereafter. His F3000 credentials were bolstered by a couple of third places for the GDBA team in 1988, but otherwise his record was unimpressive. Given Pacific's desperate financial state at the end of 1995, they could have been excused for taking any lifeline thrown when he bought his rides, but the deal merely delayed the team's inevitable demise.

Delétraz has since continued his racing activities quite competitively in sports cars, campaigning a McLaren F1 GTR, the factory Lotus GT and a Ferrari 333SP in partnership with Fabien Giroix. Since 2000, he has been a mainstay of the FIA GT Series, handling such powerful machinery as Ferrari, Lister and Lamborghini with no little skill. He was LMP675 class winner at Le Mans in both 2002 and 2003. In 2006, he raced an Aston Martin DBR9 in the FIA GT Championship.

DELÉTRAZ, Jean-Denis (CH) b 1/10/1963, Geneva

	Race	Circuit	No	Entrant	Tyres	Capacity/Car/Engine	Comment	Q Pos/Entries
	1994 Championship position: Unplaced							
ret	AUSTRALIAN GP	Adelaide	20	Tourtel Larrousse	G	3.5 Larrousse LH94-Ford HB V8	gearbox	25/26
	1995 Championship position: Unplaced							
ret	PORTUGUESE GP	Estoril	16	Pacific Grand Prix Ltd	G	3.0 Pacific PR02-Ford ED V8	driver suffering cramp	24/24
nc	EUROPEAN GP	Nürburgring	16	Pacific Grand Prix Ltd	G	3.0 Pacific PR02-Ford ED V8	7 laps behind	24/24

GP Starts: 3 GP Wins: 0 Pole positions: 0 Fastest laps: 0 Points: 0

DEPAILLER, Patrick (F) b 9/8/1944, Clermont-Ferrand – d 1/8/1980, Hockenheim, Germany

	Race	Circuit	No	Entrant	Tyres	Capacity/Car/Engine	Comment	Q Pos/Entries
	1972 Championship position: Unplaced							
nc	FRENCH GP	Clermont Ferrand	8	Elf Team Tyrrell	G	3.0 Tyrrell 004-Cosworth V8	pit stops - suspension/-5 laps	=17/29
7	US GP	Watkins Glen	3	Elf Team Tyrrell	G	3.0 Tyrrell 004-Cosworth V8	1 lap behind	11/32
	1974 Championship position: 9th Wins: 0 Pole positions: 1 Fastest laps: 1 Points scored: 14							
6	ARGENTINE GP	Buenos Aires	4	Elf Team Tyrrell	G	3.0 Tyrrell 005-Cosworth V8		15/26
8	BRAZILIAN GP	Interlagos	4	Elf Team Tyrrell	G	3.0 Tyrrell 005-Cosworth V8	1 lap behind	16/25
4	SOUTH AFRICAN GP	Kyalami	4	Elf Team Tyrrell	G	3.0 Tyrrell 005-Cosworth V8		15/27
8	SPANISH GP	Jarama	4	Elf Team Tyrrell	G	3.0 Tyrrell 006-Cosworth V8	3 laps behind	=17/28
ret	BELGIAN GP	Nivelles	4	Elf Team Tyrrell	G	3.0 Tyrrell 007-Cosworth V8	brake strap	11/32
9	MONACO GP	Monte Carlo	4	Elf Team Tyrrell	G	3.0 Tyrrell 006-Cosworth V8	started from back of grid/-4 laps	- / -
dns	"	" "	4	Elf Team Tyrrell	G	3.0 Tyrrell 007-Cosworth V8	practised in this car	=4/28
2	SWEDISH GP	Anderstorp	4	Elf Team Tyrrell	G	3.0 Tyrrell 007-Cosworth V8	FL	1/28
6	DUTCH GP	Zandvoort	4	Elf Team Tyrrell	G	3.0 Tyrrell 007-Cosworth V8		8/27
8	FRENCH GP	Dijon	4	Elf Team Tyrrell	G	3.0 Tyrrell 006-Cosworth V8	1 lap behind	- / -
dns	" "	"	4	Elf Team Tyrrell	G	3.0 Tyrrell 007-Cosworth V8	accident in practice	9/30
ret	BRITISH GP	Brands Hatch	4	Elf Team Tyrrell	G	3.0 Tyrrell 007-Cosworth V8	engine	10/34
ret	GERMAN GP	Nürburgring	4	Elf Team Tyrrell	G	3.0 Tyrrell 007-Cosworth V8	hit guard rail	5/32
ret	AUSTRIAN GP	Österreichring	4	Elf Team Tyrrell	G	3.0 Tyrrell 007-Cosworth V8	collision with Ickx	14/31
11	ITALIAN GP	Monza	4	Elf Team Tyrrell	G	3.0 Tyrrell 007-Cosworth V8	2 laps behind	=9/31
5	CANADIAN GP	Mosport Park	4	Elf Team Tyrrell	G	3.0 Tyrrell 007-Cosworth V8		7/30

PATRICK DEPAILLER

THE archetypal wiry little Frenchman, a cigarette perpetually hanging from the corner of his mouth, Patrick Depailler was something of a free spirit – a throwback to an earlier age, who lived for the moment and raced accordingly.

Schooled in the French F3 championship, Patrick spent three seasons between 1967 and 1969 driving a works Alpine-Renault, but also had occasional races in the Alpine sports-prototype, taking a third place in the Monza 1000km of 1968. A switch to Formula 2 with the Elf-Pygmée team for 1970 proved something of a disaster, the final straw being a practice crash at the Salzburgring, from which he was lucky to escape with slight burns. Luckily he still had the faith of Elf, who backed him again the following year, but this time in a Tecno. Apart from a sixth place at Pau, however, little went right for Depailler at this level, but he was more than happy to race the works Alpine-Renault once more, becoming the 1971 French F3 champion.

By 1972, he was already 28 years of age and had left it quite late in motor racing terms if he were going to make the leap up into the big time. After winning the Monaco F3 race, it was third time lucky in his attempt to crack Formula 2; he took second places in the races at Pau, Enna and Albi. His performances in the Elf/John Coombs March 722 put him in the frame for a couple of rides with his old chum, Ken Tyrrell. It was more of the same in 1973, when once again a win in F2 just seemed to elude him; this time around, poor Patrick had to settle for no fewer than four second places, and even worse was to follow. A motorcycle accident left him with a broken leg and he was forced to miss the two drives in North America that Tyrrell had lined up for him.

Fortunately his leg was quick to mend, and he was in the Tyrrell team full time in 1974 with Jody Scheckter as his team-mate. In a highly competitive year, he brought the Tyrrell home in the points on six occasions and took a pole in Sweden, the first time a Frenchman had achieved this feat in a world championship race, while in Formula 2 he finally broke his long dry spell, winning four rounds, at Pau, Mugello, Hockenheim and Vallelunga.

Patrick stuck with Tyrrell to become Formula 1 racing's 'nearly-man' over the next three seasons, taking seven second places in grands prix (and another in the 1975 non-title Swiss GP), before an emotional triumph at Monaco in 1978.

Lured to Ligier for the 1979 season, when the team were at their zenith, he won the Spanish GP and lay equal third in the championship when a mid-season hang-gliding accident sidelined him with serious leg injuries.

Having struggled back to fitness, Patrick joined Alfa Romeo in 1980, shrugging aside the frustrations of developing the unreliable car. He was beginning to make real progress when, in a solitary test session at Hockenheim, something went wrong with the car, probably broken suspension, depositing the helpless driver into the Armco at massive speed. He stood no chance of survival.

Depailler had lived life to the full, and even in darker moments, as he fought the pain of his injuries, it would not be long before a broad smile would emerge, crinkling his face with laughter lines. And that is a fitting way to remember him.

6	US GP	Watkins Glen	4	Elf Team Tyrrell	G	3.0 Tyrrell 007-Cosworth V8		13/30

1975 Championship position: 9th   Wins: 0   Pole positions: 0   Fastest laps: 1   Points scored: 12

5	ARGENTINE GP	Buenos Aires	4	Elf Team Tyrrell	G	3.0 Tyrrell 007-Cosworth V8		8/23
ret	BRAZILIAN GP	Interlagos	4	Elf Team Tyrrell	G	3.0 Tyrrell 007-Cosworth V8	front suspension – crashed	9/23
3	SOUTH AFRICAN GP	Kyalami	4	Elf Team Tyrrell	G	3.0 Tyrrell 007-Cosworth V8		5/28
ret	SPANISH GP	Montjuich Park	4	Elf Team Tyrrell	G	3.0 Tyrrell 007-Cosworth V8	multiple accident – lost wheel	7/26
5	MONACO GP	Monte Carlo	4	Elf Team Tyrrell	G	3.0 Tyrrell 007-Cosworth V8	FL	12/26
4	BELGIAN GP	Zolder	4	Elf Team Tyrrell	G	3.0 Tyrrell 007-Cosworth V8		12/24
12	SWEDISH GP	Anderstorp	4	Elf Team Tyrrell	G	3.0 Tyrrell 007-Cosworth V8	2 laps behind	2/26
9	DUTCH GP	Zandvoort	4	Elf Team Tyrrell	G	3.0 Tyrrell 007-Cosworth V8	2 laps behind	13/25
6	FRENCH GP	Paul Ricard	4	Elf Team Tyrrell	G	3.0 Tyrrell 007-Cosworth V8		13/26
9/ret	BRITISH GP	Silverstone	4	Elf Team Tyrrell	G	3.0 Tyrrell 007-Cosworth V8	spun off in rain/2 laps behind	17/28
9	GERMAN GP	Nürburgring	4	Elf Team Tyrrell	G	3.0 Tyrrell 007-Cosworth V8	pit stop – suspension/1 lap behind	4/26
11	AUSTRIAN GP	Österreichring	4	Elf Team Tyrrell	G	3.0 Tyrrell 007-Cosworth V8	1 lap behind	7/30
7	ITALIAN GP	Monza	4	Elf Team Tyrrell	G	3.0 Tyrrell 007-Cosworth V8	1 lap behind	12/28
ret	US GP	Watkins Glen	4	Elf Team Tyrrell	G	3.0 Tyrrell 007-Cosworth V8	collision with Pace	8/24

1976 Championship position: 4   Wins: 0   Pole positions: 0   Fastest laps: 1   Points scored: 39

2	BRAZILIAN GP	Interlagos	4	Elf Team Tyrrell	G	3.0 Tyrrell 007-Cosworth V8		9/22
9	SOUTH AFRICAN GP	Kyalami	4	Elf Team Tyrrell	G	3.0 Tyrrell 007-Cosworth V8	1 lap behind	6/25
3	US GP WEST	Long Beach	4	Elf Team Tyrrell	G	3.0 Tyrrell 007-Cosworth V8		2/27
ret	SPANISH GP	Jarama	4	Elf Team Tyrrell	G	3.0 Tyrrell P34-Cosworth V8	brake failure – crashed	3/30
ret	BELGIAN GP	Zolder	4	Elf Team Tyrrell	G	3.0 Tyrrell P34-Cosworth V8	engine	4/29
3	MONACO GP	Monte Carlo	4	Elf Team Tyrrell	G	3.0 Tyrrell P34-Cosworth V8		4/25
2	SWEDISH GP	Anderstorp	4	Elf Team Tyrrell	G	3.0 Tyrrell P34-Cosworth V8		4/27
2	FRENCH GP	Paul Ricard	4	Elf Team Tyrrell	G	3.0 Tyrrell P34-Cosworth V8		3/30
ret	BRITISH GP	Brands Hatch	4	Elf Team Tyrrell	G	3.0 Tyrrell P34-Cosworth V8	engine	5/30
ret	GERMAN GP	Nürburgring	4	Elf Team Tyrrell	G	3.0 Tyrrell P34-Cosworth V8	collision with Regazzoni	3/28
ret	AUSTRIAN GP	Österreichring	4	Elf Team Tyrrell	G	3.0 Tyrrell P34-Cosworth V8	suspension	13/25
7	DUTCH GP	Zandvoort	4	Elf Team Tyrrell	G	3.0 Tyrrell P34-Cosworth V8		14/27
6	ITALIAN GP	Monza	4	Elf Team Tyrrell	G	3.0 Tyrrell P34-Cosworth V8		4/29
2	CANADIAN GP	Mosport Park	4	Elf Team Tyrrell	G	3.0 Tyrrell P34-Cosworth V8	FL	4/27
ret	US GP EAST	Watkins Glen	4	Elf Team Tyrrell	G	3.0 Tyrrell P34-Cosworth V8	detached fuel line	7/27
2	JAPANESE GP	Mount Fuji	4	Elf Team Tyrrell	G	3.0 Tyrrell P34-Cosworth V8	1 lap behind	13/27

1977 Championship position: 8th=   Wins: 0   Pole positions: 0   Fastest laps: 0   Points scored: 20

ret	ARGENTINE GP	Buenos Aires	4	Elf Team Tyrrell	G	3.0 Tyrrell P34-Cosworth V8	engine – overheating	3/21
ret	BRAZILIAN GP	Interlagos	4	Elf Team Tyrrell	G	3.0 Tyrrell P34-Cosworth V8	spun off	6/22
3	SOUTH AFRICAN GP	Kyalami	4	Elf Team Tyrrell	G	3.0 Tyrrell P34-Cosworth V8		4/23
4	US GP WEST	Long Beach	4	Elf Team Tyrrell	G	3.0 Tyrrell P34-Cosworth V8		12/22
ret	SPANISH GP	Jarama	4	Elf Team Tyrrell	G	3.0 Tyrrell P34-Cosworth V8	engine	10/31
ret	MONACO GP	Monte Carlo	4	Elf Team Tyrrell	G	3.0 Tyrrell P34-Cosworth V8	brakes/gearbox	8/26
dns	"	" "	4	Elf Team Tyrrell	G	3.0 Tyrrell 007-Cosworth V8	practice only	– / –
8	BELGIAN GP	Zolder	4	Elf Team Tyrrell	G	3.0 Tyrrell P34-Cosworth V8	1 lap behind	5/32
4	SWEDISH GP	Anderstorp	4	Elf Team Tyrrell	G	3.0 Tyrrell P34-Cosworth V8		6/31
ret	FRENCH GP	Dijon	4	Elf Team Tyrrell	G	3.0 Tyrrell P34-Cosworth V8	collision with Stuck	12/30
ret	BRITISH GP	Silverstone	4	Elf Team Tyrrell	G	3.0 Tyrrell P34-Cosworth V8	brake failure – crashed	18/36
ret	GERMAN GP	Hockenheim	4	Elf Team Tyrrell	G	3.0 Tyrrell P34-Cosworth V8	engine	15/30
13	AUSTRIAN GP	Österreichring	4	Elf Team Tyrrell	G	3.0 Tyrrell P34-Cosworth V8	1 lap behind	10/30
ret	DUTCH GP	Zandvoort	4	Elf Team Tyrrell	G	3.0 Tyrrell P34-Cosworth V8	engine	11/34
ret	ITALIAN GP	Monza	4	Elf Team Tyrrell	G	3.0 Tyrrell P34-Cosworth V8	engine	13/34
14	US GP EAST	Watkins Glen	4	Elf Team Tyrrell	G	3.0 Tyrrell P34-Cosworth V8	3 laps behind	8/27
2	CANADIAN GP	Mosport Park	4	Elf Team Tyrrell	G	3.0 Tyrrell P34-Cosworth V8		6/27
3	JAPANESE GP	Mount Fuji	4	Elf Team Tyrrell	G	3.0 Tyrrell P34-Cosworth V8		15/23

1978 Championship position: 5th   Wins: 1   Pole positions: 0   Fastest laps: 0   Points scored: 34

3	ARGENTINE GP	Buenos Aires	4	Elf Team Tyrrell	G	3.0 Tyrrell 008-Cosworth V8		10/26
ret	BRAZILIAN GP	Rio	4	Elf Team Tyrrell	G	3.0 Tyrrell 008-Cosworth V8	damaged brake cylinder	11/28
2	SOUTH AFRICAN GP	Kyalami	4	Elf Team Tyrrell	G	3.0 Tyrrell 008-Cosworth V8	lost lead on last lap – fuel pick up	11/30
3	US GP WEST	Long Beach	4	Elf Team Tyrrell	G	3.0 Tyrrell 008-Cosworth V8		12/30
1	MONACO GP	Monte Carlo	4	Elf Team Tyrrell	G	3.0 Tyrrell 008-Cosworth V8		5/30
ret	BELGIAN GP	Zolder	4	Elf Team Tyrrell	G	3.0 Tyrrell 008-Cosworth V8	gearbox	13/30
ret	SPANISH GP	Jarama	4	Elf Team Tyrrell	G	3.0 Tyrrell 008-Cosworth V8	engine	12/29
ret	SWEDISH GP	Anderstorp	4	Elf Team Tyrrell	G	3.0 Tyrrell 008-Cosworth V8	suspension – broken upright	12/27
ret	FRENCH GP	Paul Ricard	4	Elf Team Tyrrell	G	3.0 Tyrrell 008-Cosworth V8	engine	13/29
4	BRITISH GP	Brands Hatch	4	Elf Team Tyrrell	G	3.0 Tyrrell 008-Cosworth V8		10/30
ret	GERMAN GP	Hockenheim	4	Elf Team Tyrrell	G	3.0 Tyrrell 008-Cosworth V8	accident with Tambay at start	13/30
2	AUSTRIAN GP	Österreichring	4	Elf Team Tyrrell	G	3.0 Tyrrell 008-Cosworth V8		13/31
ret	DUTCH GP	Zandvoort	4	Elf Team Tyrrell	G	3.0 Tyrrell 008-Cosworth V8	engine	12/33
11	ITALIAN GP	Monza	4	Elf Team Tyrrell	G	3.0 Tyrrell 008-Cosworth V8		16/32
ret	US GP EAST	Watkins Glen	4	Elf Team Tyrrell	G	3.0 Tyrrell 008-Cosworth V8	loose hub	12/27
5	CANADIAN GP	Montreal	4	Elf Team Tyrrell	G	3.0 Tyrrell 008-Cosworth V8		13/28

1979 Championship position: 6th=   Wins: 0   Pole positions: 0   Fastest laps: 1   Points scored: 22

4	ARGENTINE GP	Buenos Aires	25	Gitanes Ligier	G	3.0 Ligier JS11-Cosworth V8	pit stop – misfire	2/26
2	BRAZILIAN GP	Interlagos	25	Gitanes Ligier	G	3.0 Ligier JS11-Cosworth V8		2/26
ret	SOUTH AFRICAN GP	Kyalami	25	Gitanes Ligier	G	3.0 Ligier JS11-Cosworth V8	spun off	5/26
5	US GP WEST	Long Beach	25	Gitanes Ligier	G	3.0 Ligier JS11-Cosworth V8	lost 4th gear	4/26
1	SPANISH GP	Jarama	25	Gitanes Ligier	G	3.0 Ligier JS11-Cosworth V8		2/27
ret	BELGIAN GP	Zolder	25	Gitanes Ligier	G	3.0 Ligier JS11-Cosworth V8	hit barrier	2/28
5/ret	MONACO GP	Monte Carlo	25	Gitanes Ligier	G	3.0 Ligier JS11-Cosworth V8	engine/FL/2 laps behind	3/25

1980 Championship position: Unplaced

	Race	Circuit	No	Entrant	Tyres	Capacity/Car/Engine	Comment	Q Pos/Entries
ret	ARGENTINE GP	Buenos Aires	22	Marlboro Team Alfa Romeo	G	3.0 Alfa Romeo 179 V12	engine	23/28
ret	BRAZILIAN GP	Interlagos	22	Marlboro Team Alfa Romeo	G	3.0 Alfa Romeo 179 V12	electrics	21/28
nc	SOUTH AFRICAN GP	Kyalami	22	Marlboro Team Alfa Romeo	G	3.0 Alfa Romeo 179 V12	pitstops – engine/25 laps behind	7/28
ret	US GP WEST	Long Beach	22	Marlboro Team Alfa Romeo	G	3.0 Alfa Romeo 179 V12	suspension	3/27
ret	BELGIAN GP	Zolder	22	Marlboro Team Alfa Romeo	G	3.0 Alfa Romeo 179 V12	exhaust	10/27
ret	MONACO GP	Monte Carlo	22	Marlboro Team Alfa Romeo	G	3.0 Alfa Romeo 179 V12	engine	7/27
ret	FRENCH GP	Paul Ricard	22	Marlboro Team Alfa Romeo	G	3.0 Alfa Romeo 179 V12	handling	10/27
ret	BRITISH GP	Brands Hatch	22	Marlboro Team Alfa Romeo	G	3.0 Alfa Romeo 179 V12	engine	8/27

GP Starts: 95   GP Wins: 2   Pole positions: 1   Fastest laps: 4   Points: 141

LUCAS DI GRASSI

I SUPPOSE when Lucas di Grassi finally made it into Formula 1 in 2010, he had scaled his own personal Everest. All that toil to reach the summit, a brief sojourn to take in the landscape, and then back down again to climb lesser summits in the future.

Another 'Paulinista' following in the tracks of his heroes, Ayrton Senna and Rubens Barrichello, di Grassi took the karting route and junior single-seaters, before contesting the F3 Sudamericana championship in 2002. Despite a nasty crash that curtailed his season, he still finished runner-up and was deemed ready for the move to Europe to compete in the British Formula 3 series.

Di Grassi's first year with Hitech produced a couple of wins that convinced Manor Motorsport of his potential. For the 2005 season, he moved to the F3 Euroseries in a strong field that contained not only Lewis Hamilton and Adrian Sutil, but also a young Sebastian Vettel. It was pretty well Lewis all the way, but Lucas was one of the three drivers to pick up the scraps with wins at Oschersleben and the prestigious end-of-season non-championship Macau race.

The Brazilian moved up to GP2 for 2006 with Durango and delivered a few points-scoring finishes in a low-key season. Moving to ART Grand Prix meant having to raise his game, and he put in a determined championship challenge, which included a win in Istanbul to finish runner-up to the much more experienced Timo Glock. In 2008, he took up a role as test driver for Renault, but soon was back in GP2 action with Campos. Despite his late start to the season, with three wins, di Grassi had a shot at the title, but a collision at Spa with championship rival Giorgio Pantano effectively ended his title hopes.

With no further options, Lucas was back for more GP2 in 2009. While he was a consistent finisher, he could do no better than third in the championship, behind runaway champion Nico Hülkenberg.

With Manor Motorsport moving into Formula 1 in 2010, di Grassi was chosen to partner Glock in what would be a chastening experience for the rechristened Virgin Racing team. The Brazilian was left to do no more than make up the numbers, battling with fellow strugglers HRT and trying to avoid the wooden spoon for last place among the constructors.

It's a sad fact that the conveyor belt from the junior classes is overloaded with drivers who have little chance of a permanent stay in F1. Thus di Grassi took on the role of chief tyre tester for Pirelli in 2011. It looked as though he would be joining Peugeot for their sports car programme in 2012, but with their sudden withdrawal, it seems his competition future may now lie in Indy cars.

di GRASSI, Lucas (BR) b 11/8/1984, São Paulo

	Race	Circuit	No	Entrant	Tyres	Capacity/Car/Engine	Comment	Q Pos/Entries
	2010 Championship position: Unplaced							
ret	BAHRAIN GP	Sakhir Circuit	25	Virgin Racing	B	2.4 Virgin VR-01-Cosworth V8	hydraulics	22/24
ret	AUSTRALIAN GP	Melbourne	25	Virgin Racing	B	2.4 Virgin VR-01-Cosworth V8	hydraulics	22/24
14	MALAYSIAN GP	Sepang	25	Virgin Racing	B	2.4 Virgin VR-01-Cosworth V8	3 laps behind	24/24
ret	CHINESE GP	Shanghai Circuit	25	Virgin Racing	B	2.4 Virgin VR-01-Cosworth V8	clutch	22/24
ret	SPANISH GP	Barcelona	25	Virgin Racing	B	2.4 Virgin VR-01-Cosworth V8	3 laps behind	22/24
ret	MONACO GP	Monte Carlo	25	Virgin Racing	B	2.4 Virgin VR-01-Cosworth V8	loose rear wheel	21/24
19	TURKISH GP	Istanbul Park	25	Virgin Racing	B	2.4 Virgin VR-01-Cosworth V8	3 laps behind	23/24
19	CANADIAN GP	Montreal	25	Virgin Racing	B	2.4 Virgin VR-01-Cosworth V8	5 laps behind	23/24
17	EUROPEAN GP	Valencia	25	Virgin Racing	B	2.4 Virgin VR-01-Cosworth V8	1 lap behind	21/24
ret	BRITISH GP	Silverstone	25	Virgin Racing	B	2.4 Virgin VR-01-Cosworth V8	hydraulics	22/24
ret	GERMAN GP	Hockenheim	25	Virgin Racing	B	2.4 Virgin VR-01-Cosworth V8	suspension failure – spun off	24/24
18	HUNGARIAN GP	Hungaroring	25	Virgin Racing	B	2.4 Virgin VR-01-Cosworth V8	4 laps behind	22/24
17	BELGIAN GP	Spa	25	Virgin Racing	B	2.4 Virgin VR-01-Cosworth V8	1 lap behind	23/24
20/ret	ITALIAN GP	Monza	25	Virgin Racing	B	2.4 Virgin VR-01-Cosworth V8	suspension/3 laps behind	22/24
15	SINGAPORE GP	Marina Bay Circuit	25	Virgin Racing	B	2.4 Virgin VR-01-Cosworth V8	2 laps behind	20/24
dns	JAPANESE GP	Suzuka	25	Virgin Racing	B	2.4 Virgin VR-01-Cosworth V8	crashed on formation lap	21/24
ret	KOREAN GP	Yeongam	25	Virgin Racing	B	2.4 Virgin VR-01-Cosworth V8	spun off	22/24
nc	BRAZILIAN GP	Interlagos	25	Virgin Racing	B	2.4 Virgin VR-01-Cosworth V8	long stop – suspension repairs/-9 laps	22/24
18	ABU DHABI GP	Yas Marina Circuit	25	Virgin Racing	B	2.4 Virgin VR-01-Cosworth V8	2 laps behind	22/24

GP Starts: 18   GP Wins: 0   Pole positions: 0   Fastest laps: 0   Points: 0

PAUL DI RESTA

THE cousin of racers Dario and Marino Franchitti, it was perhaps natural that the young Paul di Resta would choose to pursue a motorsport career. Certainly their experiences and network of contacts have helped him in his measured path to the summit of the sport.

Di Resta began karting at the age of eight, and he raced them until he was old enough to be eligible to race cars. His debut came in the 2002 Formula Renault Winter Series, which led to a full season the following year. Having learned the circuits, he followed in Lewis Hamilton's footsteps by joining the Manor Motorsport squad for 2004, where he took four wins and third place in the series. Still with Manor, the Scot graduated to the F3 Euroseries for the 2005 season, alongside Lucas di Grassi. It was a year when there was a great depth of talent, led by runaway winner Hamilton, not to mention Adrian Sutil and a fellow rookie by the name of Sebastian Vettel. Paul took a while to find his feet, but with his meticulous approach, he scored points in eight rounds to finish a creditable 12th overall.

Once again, di Resta tracked Hamilton's career path by taking his vacated seat in the top-running ASM Team alongside Vettel. The pair proceeded to slug it out in a head-to-head battle for the Euroseries crown. Neither driver could build up a meaningful advantage as they traded wins (5–4 to di Resta) throughout a season's racing, which was only decided in the Scot's favour on Vettel's home turf of Hockenheim.

Paul's career then stood at a crossroads, and with Mercedes keen to nurture his talents, he moved to the DTM series to run in an '05-spec C-class car run by Persson Motorsports. He soon made people take notice by recording two second places, going on to claim a very impressive fifth place overall, ahead of top talent such as Bernd Schneider, Mika Häkkinen and Gary Paffett. His reward was a top car for 2008, but his failure to score in the opening round counted against him in a cut-and-thrust battle with Audi's Timo Scheider, who pipped him to the title by four points. The following year, he slipped to third with only a single win, before finally cracking it in 2010, winning his inter-team battle with Bruno Spengler and Paffett as the HWA squad took a 1-2-3 in the championship battle.

By then, Paul had already been placed in the Force India F1 team as reserve driver, gaining valuable experience with the knowledge that he had a race seat for the 2011 season. His debut season was as the man himself, quietly impressive. There were ups and downs to be sure, but he pretty well matched up to his team-mate, Adrian Sutil, to the extent that the German was released in favour of Nico Hülkenberg.

The pairing of the two young drivers for 2012 is intriguing, as both appear to be real contenders for a seat with a top team in the future. If either fails to measure up to the other, however, then their dreams of being a future world champion might well start to fade.

DI RESTA, Paul (GB) b 16/4/1986, Livingston

	Race	Circuit	No	Entrant	Tyres	Capacity/Car/Engine	Comment	Q Pos/Entries
	2010 Championship position: Unplaced							
app	AUSTRALIAN GP	Melbourne	14	Force India F1 Team	B	2.4 Force India VJM03-Mercedes V8	ran as 3rd driver in practice 1 only	– / –
app	MALAYSIAN GP	Sepang	15	Force India F1 Team	P	2.4 Force India VJM03-Mercedes V8	ran as 3rd driver in practice 1 only	– / –
app	CHINESE GP	Shanghai Circuit	15	Force India F1 Team	P	2.4 Force India VJM03-Mercedes V8	ran as 3rd driver in practice 1 only	– / –
app	SPANISH GP	Barcelona	14	Force India F1 Team	P	2.4 Force India VJM03-Mercedes V8	ran as 3rd driver in practice 1 only	– / –
app	EUROPEAN GP	Valencia	14	Force India F1 Team	P	2.4 Force India VJM03-Mercedes V8	ran as 3rd driver in practice 1 only	– / –
app	BRITISH GP	Silverstone	15	Force India F1 Team	P	2.4 Force India VJM03-Mercedes V8	ran as 3rd driver in practice 1 only	– / –
app	HUNGARIAN GP	Hungaroring	15	Force India F1 Team	P	2.4 Force India VJM03-Mercedes V8	ran as 3rd driver in practice 1 only	– / –
app	ITALIAN GP	Monza	14	Force India F1 Team	P	2.4 Force India VJM03-Mercedes V8	ran as 3rd driver in practice 1 only	– / –
	2011 Championship position: 13th Wins: 0 Pole positions: 0 Fastest laps: 0 Points scored: 27							
10	AUSTRALIAN GP	Melbourne	15	Force India F1 Team	P	2.4 Force India VJM04-Mercedes V8	12th but 7 & 8th cars dsq/-1 lap	14/24
10	MALAYSIAN GP	Sepang	15	Force India F1 Team	P	2.4 Force India VJM04-Mercedes V8	2 laps behind	14/24
11	CHINESE GP	Shanghai Circuit	15	Force India F1 Team	P	2.4 Force India VJM04-Mercedes V8		8/24
ret	TURKISH GP	Istanbul Park	15	Force India F1 Team	P	2.4 Force India VJM04-Mercedes V8	loose wheel after pit stop	13/24
12	SPANISH GP	Barcelona	15	Force India F1 Team	P	2.4 Force India VJM04-Mercedes V8	1 lap behind	16/24
12	MONACO GP	Monte Carlo	15	Force India F1 Team	P	2.4 Force India VJM04-Mercedes V8	2 laps behind	14/24
18/ret	CANADIAN GP	Montreal	15	Force India F1 Team	P	2.4 Force India VJM04-Mercedes V8	drive-through pen/puncture/-3 laps	11/24
14	EUROPEAN GP	Valencia	15	Force India F1 Team	P	2.4 Force India VJM04-Mercedes V8	1 lap behind	12/24
10	BRITISH GP	Silverstone	15	Force India F1 Team	P	2.4 Force India VJM04-Mercedes V8	collision with Buemi/1 lap behind	18/24
11	GERMAN GP	Hockenheim	15	Force India F1 Team	P	2.4 Force India VJM04-Mercedes V8	hit by Heidfeld/1 lap behind	12/24
7	HUNGARIAN GP	Hungaroring	15	Force India F1 Team	P	2.4 Force India VJM04-Mercedes V8	1 lap behind	11/24
11	BELGIAN GP	Spa	15	Force India F1 Team	P	2.4 Force India VJM04-Mercedes V8		18/24
8	ITALIAN GP	Monza	15	Force India F1 Team	P	2.4 Force India VJM04-Mercedes V8	1 lap behind	11/24
6	SINGAPORE GP	Marina Bay Circuit	15	Force India F1 Team	P	2.4 Force India VJM04-Mercedes V8		10/24
12	JAPANESE GP	Suzuka	15	Force India F1 Team	P	2.4 Force India VJM04-Mercedes V8		12/24
10	KOREAN GP	Yeongam	15	Sahara Force India F1 Team	P	2.4 Force India VJM04-Mercedes V8		9/24
13	INDIAN GP	Buddh Circuit	15	Sahara Force India F1 Team	P	2.4 Force India VJM04-Mercedes V8	3-stop race/1 lap behind	13/24
9	ABU DHABI GP	Yas Marina Circuit	15	Sahara Force India F1 Team	P	2.4 Force India VJM04-Mercedes V8		10/24
8	BRAZILIAN GP	São Paulo	15	Sahara Force India F1 Team	P	2.4 Force India VJM04-Mercedes V8	1 lap behind	11/24

GP Starts: 19   GP Wins: 0   Pole positions: 0   Fastest laps: 0   Points: 27

PEDRO DINIZ

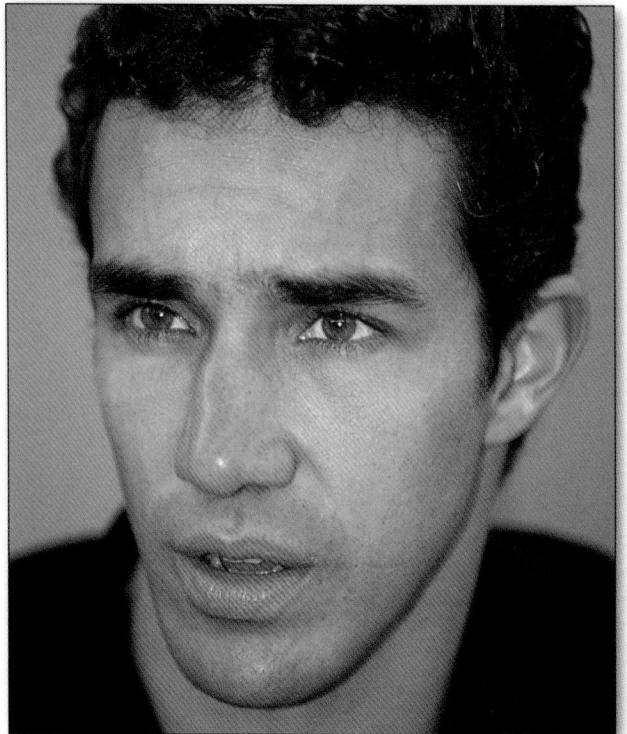

PEDRO DINIZ'S father was a racer in his day; he also headed the CBD distribution company, one of Brazil's largest, and the Pao de Acucar supermarket chain. In the past, Diniz Sr had been able to generate money by offering preferential product placement in his stores, so young Pedro was well funded to take a stab at racing. He completed a year in the Sud-Am F3 series, before heading to Europe in 1991, where he secured a seat in the crack West Surrey Racing team. A season spent alongside the very quick Rubens Barrichello and Jordi Gené highlighted his shortcomings, and a move to Edenbridge Racing in 1992 showed he still had much to learn.

For 1993, Diniz jumped up to compete in F3000 with Forti Corse, but he was out of his depth. Staying on for 1994, he conjured up one fourth-place finish at Estoril, but the Brazilian's performances, while showing some promise, failed to convince.

Thus eyebrows were raised when Diniz's name appeared on the 1995 F1 entry list, paired with fellow countryman Roberto Moreno at Forti. In the event, his performance was neat and tidy, and he proved evenly matched with his experienced colleague. The car was clearly uncompetitive, however, and with a massive personal sponsorship budget, he lost no time in obtaining a drive for 1996 at Ligier, where his goal was to secure a championship point, which he achieved on two occasions.

For 1997, Diniz (accompanied by his wad of cash) was tempted away by Tom Walkinshaw to join his newly reconstructed Arrows team as number two to Damon Hill. Again, he silenced the doubters with a number of more-than-respectable performances. He even managed to out-qualify and out-race the reigning world champion at Spa, of all places, and took a career-best fifth place in the Luxembourg Grand Prix. For 1998, the Brazilian was paired with Mika Salo and again had his moments, interestingly scoring points at the two classic circuits of Monaco and Spa.

It was patently obvious to Diniz that to climb further up the grid, he needed a better car than Arrows had thus far provided, so he was on the move once more. Brushing aside threats of litigation for breach of contract, he prepared to test himself against Jean Alesi at Sauber. Amazingly, he outscored his team leader by three points to two, which proved nothing more than, on this occasion, that modest consistency paid more dividends than blinkered audacity.

After drawing a blank in 2000, Diniz stepped out of the cockpit, and his family took a share in the Prost team for 2001. It proved to be a salutary and expensive exercise for the wealthy Brazilians, who brought Parmalat sponsorship, which paid for the leasing of the team's Ferrari engines. Before the season ended, however, Diniz and Prost had fallen out, and his interest had waned as the team headed in a tailspin towards an eventual crash.

Pedro returned to Brazil and became the prime mover behind the introduction of the 2-litre Brazilian Formula Renault Championship, which ran until 2006. Subsequently, he has been involved with a variety of business ventures with a number of companies.

DINIZ, Pedro Paulo (BR) b 22/5/1970, São Paulo

	Race	Circuit	No	Entrant	Tyres	Capacity/Car/Engine	Comment	Q Pos/Entries
	1995 Championship position: Unplaced							
10	BRAZILIAN GP	Interlagos	21	Parmalat Forti Ford	G	3.0 Forti FG01-Ford ED V8	7 laps behind	25/26
nc	ARGENTINE GP	Buenos Aires	21	Parmalat Forti Ford	G	3.0 Forti FG01-Ford ED V8	9 laps behind	25/26
nc	SAN MARINO GP	Imola	21	Parmalat Forti Ford	G	3.0 Forti FG01-Ford ED V8	7 laps behind	26/26
ret	SPANISH GP	Barcelona	21	Parmalat Forti Ford	G	3.0 Forti FG01-Ford ED V8	gearbox	26/26
10	MONACO GP	Monte Carlo	21	Parmalat Forti Ford	G	3.0 Forti FG01-Ford ED V8	6 laps behind	22/26
ret	CANADIAN GP	Montreal	21	Parmalat Forti Ford	G	3.0 Forti FG01-Ford ED V8	gearbox	24/24
ret	FRENCH GP	Magny Cours	21	Parmalat Forti Ford	G	3.0 Forti FG01-Ford ED V8	collision with Martini on lap 1	23/24
ret	BRITISH GP	Silverstone	21	Parmalat Forti Ford	G	3.0 Forti FG01-Ford ED V8	gearbox	20/24
ret	GERMAN GP	Hockenheim	21	Parmalat Forti Ford	G	3.0 Forti FG01-Ford ED V8	started from pit lane/brakes	21/24
ret	HUNGARIAN GP	Hungaroring	21	Parmalat Forti Ford	G	3.0 Forti FG01-Ford ED V8	engine	23/24
13	BELGIAN GP	Spa	21	Parmalat Forti Ford	G	3.0 Forti FG01-Ford ED V8	2 laps behind	24/24
9	ITALIAN GP	Monza	21	Parmalat Forti Ford	G	3.0 Forti FG01-Ford ED V8	3 laps behind	23/24
16	PORTUGUESE GP	Estoril	21	Parmalat Forti Ford	G	3.0 Forti FG01-Ford ED V8	5 laps behind	22/24
13	EUROPEAN GP	Nürburgring	21	Parmalat Forti Ford	G	3.0 Forti FG01-Ford ED V8	5 laps behind	22/24
17	PACIFIC GP	T.I. Circuit	21	Parmalat Forti Ford	G	3.0 Forti FG01-Ford ED V8	6 laps behind	21/24
ret	JAPANESE GP	Suzuka	21	Parmalat Forti Ford	G	3.0 Forti FG01-Ford ED V8	spun off	21/24
7	AUSTRALIAN GP	Adelaide	21	Parmalat Forti Ford	G	3.0 Forti FG01-Ford ED V8	4 laps behind	21/24
	1996 Championship position: 15th Wins: 0 Pole positions: 0 Fastest laps: 0 Points scored: 2							
10	AUSTRALIAN GP	Melbourne	10	Ligier Gauloises-Blondes	G	3.0 Ligier JS43-Mugen Honda V10	collision with Brundle/2 laps behind	20/22
8	BRAZILIAN GP	Interlagos	10	Ligier Gauloises-Blondes	G	3.0 Ligier JS43-Mugen Honda V10	*practice time disallowed/-2 laps	-*/22
ret	ARGENTINE GP	Buenos Aires	10	Ligier Gauloises-Blondes	G	3.0 Ligier JS43-Mugen Honda V10	car caught fire after refuelling	18/22
10	EUROPEAN GP	Nürburgring	10	Ligier Gauloises-Blondes	G	3.0 Ligier JS43-Mugen Honda V10	1 lap behind	17/22
7	SAN MARINO GP	Imola	10	Ligier Gauloises-Blondes	G	3.0 Ligier JS43-Mugen Honda V10	1 lap behind	17/22
ret	MONACO GP	Monte Carlo	10	Ligier Gauloises-Blondes	G	3.0 Ligier JS43-Mugen Honda V10	transmission	17/22
6	SPANISH GP	Barcelona	10	Ligier Gauloises-Blondes	G	3.0 Ligier JS43-Mugen Honda V10	spin/2 laps behind	17/22
ret	CANADIAN GP	Montreal	10	Ligier Gauloises-Blondes	G	3.0 Ligier JS43-Mugen Honda V10	engine	18/22

ret	FRENCH GP	Magny Cours	10	Ligier Gauloises-Blondes	G	3.0 Ligier JS43-Mugen Honda V10	*engine*	12/22
ret	BRITISH GP	Silverstone	10	Ligier Gauloises-Blondes	G	3.0 Ligier JS43-Mugen Honda V10	*engine*	18/22
ret	GERMAN GP	Hockenheim	10	Ligier Gauloises-Blondes	G	3.0 Ligier JS43-Mugen Honda V10	*engine*	11/20
ret	HUNGARIAN GP	Hungaroring	10	Ligier Gauloises-Blondes	G	3.0 Ligier JS43-Mugen Honda V10	*collision with Salo on lap 1*	15/20
ret	BELGIAN GP	Spa	10	Ligier Gauloises-Blondes	G	3.0 Ligier JS43-Mugen Honda V10	*engine*	15/20
6	ITALIAN GP	Monza	10	Ligier Gauloises-Blondes	G	3.0 Ligier JS43-Mugen Honda V10	*1 lap behind*	14/20
ret	PORTUGUESE GP	Estoril	10	Ligier Gauloises-Blondes	G	3.0 Ligier JS43-Mugen Honda V10	*spun off*	18/20
ret	JAPANESE GP	Suzuka	10	Ligier Gauloises-Blondes	G	3.0 Ligier JS43-Mugen Honda V10	*spun off*	16/20

1997 Championship position: 16th= Wins: 0 Pole positions: 0 Fastest laps: 0 Points scored: 2

10	AUSTRALIAN GP	Melbourne	2	Danka Arrows Yamaha	B	3.0 Arrows A18-Yamaha V10	*4 laps behind*	22/24
ret	BRAZILIAN GP	Interlagos	2	Danka Arrows Yamaha	B	3.0 Arrows A18-Yamaha V10	*spun off*	16/22
ret	ARGENTINE GP	Buenos Aires	2	Danka Arrows Yamaha	B	3.0 Arrows A18-Yamaha V10	*engine*	22/22
ret	SAN MARINO GP	Imola	2	Danka Arrows Yamaha	B	3.0 Arrows A18-Yamaha V10	*hydraulics*	17/22
ret	MONACO GP	Monte Carlo	2	Danka Arrows Yamaha	B	3.0 Arrows A18-Yamaha V10	*spun off on lap 1*	16/22
ret	SPANISH GP	Barcelona	2	Danka Arrows Yamaha	B	3.0 Arrows A18-Yamaha V10	*engine*	21/22
8	CANADIAN GP	Montreal	2	Danka Arrows Yamaha	B	3.0 Arrows A18-Yamaha V10	*1 lap behind*	16/22
ret	FRENCH GP	Magny Cours	2	Danka Arrows Yamaha	B	3.0 Arrows A18-Yamaha V10	*spun off*	16/22
ret	BRITISH GP	Silverstone	2	Danka Arrows Yamaha	B	3.0 Arrows A18-Yamaha V10	*engine*	17/22
ret	GERMAN GP	Hockenheim	2	Danka Arrows Yamaha	B	3.0 Arrows A18-Yamaha V10	*collision with Herbert*	16/22
ret	HUNGARIAN GP	Hungaroring	2	Danka Arrows Yamaha	B	3.0 Arrows A18-Yamaha V10	*alternator*	19/22
7*	BELGIAN GP	Spa	2	Danka Arrows Yamaha	B	3.0 Arrows A18-Yamaha V10	**5th place car disqualified*	8/22
ret	ITALIAN GP	Monza	2	Danka Arrows Yamaha	B	3.0 Arrows A18-Yamaha V10	*broken suspension – spun off*	17/22
13/ret	AUSTRIAN GP	A1-Ring	2	Danka Arrows Yamaha	B	3.0 Arrows A18-Yamaha V10	*shock absorber/4 laps behind*	17/22
5	LUXEMBOURG GP	Nürburgring	2	Danka Arrows Yamaha	B	3.0 Arrows A18-Yamaha V10		15/22
12	JAPANESE GP	Suzuka	2	Danka Arrows Yamaha	B	3.0 Arrows A18-Yamaha V10	*1 lap behind*	16/22
ret	EUROPEAN GP	Jerez	2	Danka Arrows Yamaha	B	3.0 Arrows A18-Yamaha V10	*spun off*	13/22

1998 Championship position: 13= Wins: 0 Pole positions: 0 Fastest laps: 0 Points scored: 3

ret	AUSTRALIAN GP	Melbourne	16	Danka Zepter Arrows	B	3.0 Arrows A19-V10	*gearbox*	20/22
ret	BRAZILIAN GP	Interlagos	16	Danka Zepter Arrows	B	3.0 Arrows A19-V10	*transmission*	22/22
ret	ARGENTINE GP	Buenos Aires	16	Danka Zepter Arrows	B	3.0 Arrows A19-V10	*gearbox*	18/22
ret	SAN MARINO GP	Imola	16	Danka Zepter Arrows	B	3.0 Arrows A19-V10	*engine*	18/22
ret	SPANISH GP	Barcelona	16	Danka Zepter Arrows	B	3.0 Arrows A19-V10	*engine*	15/22
6	MONACO GP	Monte Carlo	16	Danka Zepter Arrows	B	3.0 Arrows A19-V10	*1 lap behind*	12/22
9	CANADIAN GP	Montreal	16	Danka Zepter Arrows	B	3.0 Arrows A19-V10	*1 lap behind*	19/22
14	FRENCH GP	Magny Cours	16	Danka Zepter Arrows	B	3.0 Arrows A19-V10	*2 laps behind*	17/22
ret	BRITISH GP	Silverstone	16	Danka Zepter Arrows	B	3.0 Arrows A19-V10	*spun off*	13/22
ret	AUSTRIAN GP	A1-Ring	16	Danka Zepter Arrows	B	3.0 Arrows A19-V10	*collision damage*	13/22
ret	GERMAN GP	Hockenheim	16	Danka Zepter Arrows	B	3.0 Arrows A19-V10	*throttle*	18/22
11	HUNGARIAN GP	Hungaroring	16	Danka Zepter Arrows	B	3.0 Arrows A19-V10	*3 laps behind*	12/22
5	BELGIAN GP	Spa	16	Danka Zepter Arrows	B	3.0 Arrows A19-V10		16/22
ret	ITALIAN GP	Monza	16	Danka Zepter Arrows	B	3.0 Arrows A19-V10	*spun off*	20/22
ret	LUXEMBOURG GP	Nürburgring	16	Danka Zepter Arrows	B	3.0 Arrows A19-V10	*hydraulics*	17/22
ret	JAPANESE GP	Suzuka	16	Danka Zepter Arrows	B	3.0 Arrows A19-V10	*spun off*	18/22

1999 Championship position: 13th= Wins: 0 Pole positions: 0 Fastest laps: 0 Points scored: 3

ret	AUSTRALIAN GP	Melbourne	12	Red Bull Sauber Petronas	B	3.0 Sauber C18-Petronas V10	*transmission*	14/22
ret	BRAZILIAN GP	Interlagos	12	Red Bull Sauber Petronas	B	3.0 Sauber C18-Petronas V10	*spun off*	15/22
ret	SAN MARINO GP	Imola	12	Red Bull Sauber Petronas	B	3.0 Sauber C18-Petronas V10	*spun off*	15/22
ret	MONACO GP	Monte Carlo	12	Red Bull Sauber Petronas	B	3.0 Sauber C18-Petronas V10	*brakes – crashed*	15/22
ret	SPANISH GP	Barcelona	12	Red Bull Sauber Petronas	B	3.0 Sauber C18-Petronas V10	*gearbox*	12/22
6	CANADIAN GP	Montreal	12	Red Bull Sauber Petronas	B	3.0 Sauber C18-Petronas V10		18/22
ret	FRENCH GP	Magny Cours	12	Red Bull Sauber Petronas	B	3.0 Sauber C18-Petronas V10	*transmission*	11/22
6	BRITISH GP	Silverstone	12	Red Bull Sauber Petronas	B	3.0 Sauber C18-Petronas V10		12/22
6	AUSTRIAN GP	A1-Ring	12	Red Bull Sauber Petronas	B	3.0 Sauber C18-Petronas V10		16/22
ret	GERMAN GP	Hockenheim	12	Red Bull Sauber Petronas	B	3.0 Sauber C18-Petronas V10	*hit by Villeneuve on lap 1*	16/22
ret	HUNGARIAN GP	Hungaroring	12	Red Bull Sauber Petronas	B	3.0 Sauber C18-Petronas V10	*spun off*	12/22
ret	BELGIAN GP	Spa	12	Red Bull Sauber Petronas	B	3.0 Sauber C18-Petronas V10	*spun off*	18/22
ret	ITALIAN GP	Monza	12	Red Bull Sauber Petronas	B	3.0 Sauber C18-Petronas V10	*spun off*	16/22
ret	EUROPEAN GP	Nürburgring	12	Red Bull Sauber Petronas	B	3.0 Sauber C18-Petronas V10	*collision with Wurz – rolled car*	13/22
ret	MALAYSIAN GP	Sepang	12	Red Bull Sauber Petronas	B	3.0 Sauber C18-Petronas V10	*spun off*	17/22
11	JAPANESE GP	Suzuka	12	Red Bull Sauber Petronas	B	3.0 Sauber C18-Petronas V10	*1 lap behind*	17/22

2000 Championship position: Unplaced

ret	AUSTRALIAN GP	Melbourne	16	Red Bull Sauber Petronas	B	3.0 Sauber C19-Petronas V10	*transmission*	19/22
dns	BRAZILIAN GP	Interlagos	16	Red Bull Sauber Petronas	B	3.0 Sauber C19-Petronas V10	*cars withdrawn after wing failures*	(20)/22
8	SAN MARINO GP	Imola	16	Red Bull Sauber Petronas	B	3.0 Sauber C19-Petronas V10	*1 lap behind*	10/22
11	BRITISH GP	Silverstone	16	Red Bull Sauber Petronas	B	3.0 Sauber C19-Petronas V10	*1 lap behind*	13/22
ret	SPANISH GP	Barcelona	16	Red Bull Sauber Petronas	B	3.0 Sauber C19-Petronas V10	*spun off on lap 1*	16/22
7	EUROPEAN GP	Nürburgring	16	Red Bull Sauber Petronas	B	3.0 Sauber C19-Petronas V10	*2 laps behind*	16/22
ret	MONACO GP	Monte Carlo	16	Red Bull Sauber Petronas	B	3.0 Sauber C19-Petronas V10	*hit barrier – wheel damage*	19/22
10	CANADIAN GP	Montreal	16	Red Bull Sauber Petronas	B	3.0 Sauber C19-Petronas V10		19/22
11	FRANCE GP	Magny Cours	16	Red Bull Sauber Petronas	B	3.0 Sauber C19-Petronas V10	*1 lap behind*	15/22
9	AUSTRIAN GP	A1-Ring	16	Red Bull Sauber Petronas	B	3.0 Sauber C19-Petronas V10	*1 lap behind*	11/22
ret	GERMAN GP	Hockenheim	16	Red Bull Sauber Petronas	B	3.0 Sauber C19-Petronas V10	*collision with Alesi*	19/22
ret	HUNGARIAN GP	Hungaroring	16	Red Bull Sauber Petronas	B	3.0 Sauber C19-Petronas V10	*engine*	13/22
11	BELGIAN GP	Spa	16	Red Bull Sauber Petronas	B	3.0 Sauber C19-Petronas V10		15/22
8	ITALIAN GP	Monza	16	Red Bull Sauber Petronas	B	3.0 Sauber C19-Petronas V10	*1 lap behind*	16/22
8	U S GP	Indianapolis	16	Red Bull Sauber Petronas	B	3.0 Sauber C19-Petronas V10	*1 lap behind*	9/22
11	JAPANESE GP	Suzuka	16	Red Bull Sauber Petronas	B	3.0 Sauber C19-Petronas V10	*1 lap behind*	20/22
ret	MALAYSIAN GP	Sepang	16	Red Bull Sauber Petronas	B	3.0 Sauber C19-Petronas V10	*accident – de la Rosa and Heidfeld*	20/22

GP Starts: 98   GP Wins: 0   Pole positions: 0   Fastest laps: 0   Points: 10

DOLHEM, José (F) b 26/4/1944, Paris – d 16/4/1988, nr St Etienne

1974 Championship position: Unplaced

	Race	Circuit	No	Entrant	Tyres	Capacity/Car/Engine	Comment	Q Pos/Entries
dnq	FRENCH GP	Dijon	18	Bang & Olufsen Team Surtees	F	3.0 Surtees TS16-Cosworth V8		27/30
dnq	ITALIAN GP	Monza	19	Team Surtees	F	3.0 Surtees TS16-Cosworth V8		26/31
ret	US GP	Watkins Glen	18	Team Surtees	F	3.0 Surtees TS16-Cosworth V8	*withdrawn after Koinigg's accident*	26/30

GP Starts: 1   GP Wins: 0   Pole positions: 0   Fastest laps: 0   Points: 0

JOSÉ DOLHEM

ALTHOUGH he had dabbled in racing in 1964 at the wheel of a Lotus Seven, it was not until José Dolhem had completed his university studies in engineering and economics in 1969 that he returned to the sport, having won the prized Volant Shell award.

Dolhem was regarded as something of a playboy racer in his early days. Certainly his 1972 Formula 2 season with a March was undistinguished, and in his only race in the same category the following year, the Rouen GP, where he drove for Team Surtees, he crashed on the warm-up lap for the final after finishing third in his qualifying heat.

No doubt bringing much-needed finance, José raced for Surtees in both grands prix and Formula 2 in 1974, but then his career was interrupted by a neck injury sustained while skiing early in 1975. He continued to race in F2 on and off – at first with Fred Opert's Chevron in 1976, and later with Kauhsen and AGS cars – but success didn't come until 1979. The half-brother of the late Didier Pironi, Dolhem lost his life in a private plane crash in April, 1988.

MARTIN DONNELLY

A graduate of FF2000, Martin Donnelly made an immediate impact on the Marlboro Formula 3 series in his first season in 1986, winning four races and finishing third overall in the rankings. A favourite for the title the following year, he had a disastrous early-season run that ruined his chances. Only when he switched to the Cellnet Intersport team did things improve and he returned to the winner's circle.

Donnelly remained in F3 for a third year in 1988, but in mid-season he jumped ship, much to Intersport's chagrin, to join Eddie Jordan's Q8 F3000 team. In just four races, the Ulsterman took two wins and two second places. Things seemed set fair for a championship challenge in 1989, but after a win at Vallelunga had been wiped out, he lost the initiative to new team-mate Jean Alesi, despite a victory at Brands Hatch.

Meanwhile Donnelly had made an eye-catching GP debut for Arrows, and he signed to drive for Lotus in 1990. Although the car was not one of the best, he impressed nevertheless, until disaster struck in practice for the Spanish GP. He was very fortunate to survive when his car disintegrated after impact with the barriers, being tossed on to the track still strapped to the seat and the remnants of the car; only first-class medical help at trackside saved his life. Happily, he recovered to race again on occasion, and successfully run his own team in the junior formulas.

DONNELLY, Martin (GB) b 26/3/1964, Belfast, Northern Ireland

1989 Championship position: Unplaced

	Race	Circuit	No	Entrant	Tyres	Capacity/Car/Engine	Comment	Q Pos/Entries
12	FRENCH GP	Paul Ricard	9	USF&G Arrows Team	G	3.5 Arrows A11-Cosworth V8	*started from pit lane/3 laps behind*	14/39

1990 Championship position: Unplaced

	Race	Circuit	No	Entrant	Tyres	Capacity/Car/Engine	Comment	Q Pos/Entries
dns	US GP (PHOENIX)	Phoenix	12	Camel Team Lotus	G	3.5 Lotus 102-Lamborghini V12	*ignition failure on dummy grid*	(19)/35
ret	BRAZILIAN GP	Interlagos	12	Camel Team Lotus	G	3.5 Lotus 102-Lamborghini V12	*leg cramps – spun off*	14/35
8	SAN MARINO GP	Imola	12	Camel Team Lotus	G	3.5 Lotus 102-Lamborghini V12	*1 lap behind*	12/34
ret	MONACO GP	Monte Carlo	12	Camel Team Lotus	G	3.5 Lotus 102-Lamborghini V12	*gearbox*	11/35
ret	CANADIAN GP	Montreal	12	Camel Team Lotus	G	3.5 Lotus 102-Lamborghini V12	*engine*	12/35
8	MEXICAN GP	Mexico City	12	Camel Team Lotus	G	3.5 Lotus 102-Lamborghini V12	*tyre problems*	12/35
12	FRENCH GP	Paul Ricard	12	Camel Team Lotus	G	3.5 Lotus 102-Lamborghini V12	*handling problems/1 lap behind*	17/35
ret	BRITISH GP	Silverstone	12	Camel Team Lotus	G	3.5 Lotus 102-Lamborghini V12	*engine*	14/35
ret	GERMAN GP	Hockenheim	12	Camel Team Lotus	G	3.5 Lotus 102-Lamborghini V12	*clutch*	20/35
7	HUNGARIAN GP	Hungaroring	12	Camel Team Lotus	G	3.5 Lotus 102-Lamborghini V12	*1 lap behind*	18/35
12	BELGIAN GP	Spa	12	Camel Team Lotus	G	3.5 Lotus 102-Lamborghini V12	*understeer/exhaust/1 lap behind*	22/23
ret	ITALIAN GP	Monza	12	Camel Team Lotus	G	3.5 Lotus 102-Lamborghini V12	*engine*	11/33
ret	PORTUGUESE GP	Estoril	12	Camel Team Lotus	G	3.5 Lotus 102-Lamborghini V12	*alternator*	15/33
dns	SPANISH GP	Jerez	12	Camel Team Lotus	G	3.5 Lotus 102-Lamborghini V12	*severely injured in practice accident*	(23)/33

GP Starts: 13   GP Wins: 0   Pole positions: 0   Fastest laps: 0   Points: 0

MARK DONOHUE

A GRADUATE engineer, Mark Donohue merely dabbled in racing at first, but he was good enough to take a class of the SCCA production sports car championship in 1961 in an Elva Courier. Then he raced a Formula Junior Elva and a TVR, before taking a championship double in 1965 with a Lotus 23 in SCCA class C and a Mustang in class B. By this time, he had been taken under the wing of Walt Hansgen, who was leading the works Ford MkII sports car challenge in 1966. The pair shared second place at Sebring that year, Donohue's first major placing, but his mentor was tragically killed while testing at the Le Mans in April. Then Mark renewed an old association with Roger Penske, taking his Group 7 Lola-Chevrolet to victory at Mosport in Can-Am, before winning the 1967 and 1968 US Road Racing Championships.

Penske also entered Donohue in the Trans-Am championship in 1968, and he won ten of the 13 events to lift the title easily, repeating the trick the following year with six wins from 12 starts. The 1969 season also saw Penske's first appearance at the Indy 500 as an entrant, Donohue qualifying fourth and finishing seventh to earn the Rookie of the Year title. He finished second in the race in 1970, driving a Lola-Ford, and later on that season raced in Formula A, winning two of the three rounds he entered. Penske expanded his racing activities in 1971, and Mark faced a hectic schedule of Trans-Am (taking his third title), USAC (winning the Pocono 500 and the Michigan 200 in a McLaren) and sports car events, sharing a blue Ferrari 512M with David Hobbs. However, his performance of the year was undoubtedly his grand prix debut at Mosport, where he took a superb third place in Penske's McLaren M19A.

Grand prix racing was just a diversion at this stage, for in 1972 Mark continued to race in USAC, duly winning the Indianapolis 500 in a Penske McLaren, and returned to Can-Am, where his title chances were ruined by a testing accident that sidelined him for a couple of months. He was back in 1973, however, and made no mistake this time around, taking six race victories and the championship in a Porsche 917. He announced his retirement at the end of the year, but was tempted back behind the wheel late in 1974 to apply his superb development expertise to the Penske grand prix challenger.

Mark was persuaded to race the car in 1975, but it was a disappointment to all concerned, and Penske replaced it in mid-season with an 'off-the-shelf' March. He was practising in the car for the Austrian GP when a tyre is thought to have deflated, sending the March into catch fencing and over the Armco barrier. One marshal was killed and another seriously injured. At first, though dazed, Mark was sitting up and talking. He seemed to have escaped relatively unharmed, but it soon became apparent that all was not well and he lapsed into unconsciousness. Despite undergoing brain surgery, he died three days later in Graz hospital.

DONOHUE, Mark (USA) b 18/3/1937, Summit, New Jersey – d 19/8/1975, Graz, Austria

	1971 Championship position: 16th=	Wins: 0		Pole positions: 0	Fastest laps: 0		Points scored: 4		
	Race	Circuit	No	Entrant	Tyres	Capacity/Car/Engine	Comment		Q Pos/Entries
3	CANADIAN GP	Mosport Park	10	Penske-White Racing	G	3.0 McLaren M19A-Cosworth V8			=7/27
dns	US GP	Watkins Glen	31	Penske-White Racing	G	3.0 McLaren M19A-Cosworth V8	practised – but raced USAC event		(19)/32
	1974 Championship position: Unplaced								
12	CANADIAN GP	Mosport Park	66	Penske Cars	G	3.0 Penske PC1-Cosworth V8	2 laps behind		24/30
ret	US GP	Watkins Glen	66	Penske Cars	G	3.0 Penske PC1-Cosworth V8	rear suspension bracket		14/30
	1975 Championship position: 15th	Wins: 0		Pole positions: 0	Fastest laps: 0		Points scored: 4		
7	ARGENTINE GP	Buenos Aires	28	Penske Cars	G	3.0 Penske PC1-Cosworth V8	1 lap behind		16/23
ret	BRAZILIAN GP	Interlagos	28	Penske Cars	G	3.0 Penske PC1-Cosworth V8	handling		15/23
8	SOUTH AFRICAN GP	Kyalami	28	Penske Cars	G	3.0 Penske PC1-Cosworth V8	1 lap behind		18/28
ret	SPANISH GP	Montjuich Park	28	Penske Cars	G	3.0 Penske PC1-Cosworth V8	spun off on Scheckter's oil		17/26
ret	MONACO GP	Monte Carlo	28	Penske Cars	G	3.0 Penske PC1-Cosworth V8	hit guard rail		16/26
11	BELGIAN GP	Zolder	28	Penske Cars	G	3.0 Penske PC1-Cosworth V8	handling problems/3 laps behind		21/24
5	SWEDISH GP	Anderstorp	28	Penske Cars	G	3.0 Penske PC1-Cosworth V8			16/26
8	DUTCH GP	Zandvoort	28	Penske Cars	G	3.0 Penske PC1-Cosworth V8	1 lap behind		18/25
ret	FRENCH GP	Paul Ricard	28	Penske Cars	G	3.0 Penske PC1-Cosworth V8	driveshaft		18/26
5/ret	BRITISH GP	Silverstone	28	Penske Cars	G	3.0 March 751-Cosworth V8	spun off in rainstorm/1 lap behind		15/28
ret	GERMAN GP	Nürburgring	28	Penske Cars	G	3.0 March 751-Cosworth V8	puncture		19/26
dns	AUSTRIAN GP	Österreichring	28	Penske Cars	G	3.0 March 751-Cosworth V8	fatal accident in practice		(21)/30
	GP Starts: 14	GP Wins: 0		Pole positions: 0	Fastest laps: 0		Points: 8		

ROBERT DOORNBOS

WHILE most of his peers in their teens were learning their trade in karts, merely dreaming of making it to Formula 1, Robert Doornbos was happily hitting tennis balls at national level in his native Holland. However, after accepting an invitation to attend the 1998 Belgian Grand Prix as a guest of Williams, he was immediately smitten by motor racing, and henceforth his sporting ambitions were channelled away from the tennis court and on to the race track.

Finishing as runner-up in the 1999 Opel Lotus UK Winter Series showed an undoubted aptitude for motor sport, and the following season Doornbos competed in Belgian Formula Ford, finishing second overall. Then he opted to move up to the scholarship class of British F3, where he notched two wins. The young Dutchman also had his fair share of incidents, however, and ended up fifth in the final points standings.

Instead of graduating to the senior F3 class in Britain, Doornbos returned to the Continent to take a place with Team Ghinzani in the German F3 series. Although an outright win proved elusive, he did manage a couple of second-place finishes, eventually taking 11th overall. Remaining with the team, this time in the Formula 3 Euro Series, he opened the fol-

lowing season with a fine second place, behind Ryan Briscoe at Hockenheim, but thereafter he only found occasional podiums. Without doubt, his most pleasing result was a second on aggregate in the Korean Super Prix at the end of the year.

Motor racing is all about being in the right team at the right time, and Doornbos shrewdly accepted the role of number-two driver to Vitantonio Liuzzi in the Arden International squad to contest the 2004 International F3000 Championship. In a tightly-knit outfit, the Dutchman, although overshadowed by his more experienced Italian team-mate, was extremely competitive and took third place in the championship, the highlight of which was a win in the wet at Spa after gambling on a late set-up change just before the race.

Already eyeing an opportunity to break into Formula 1, Doornbos seized the chance to replace Giorgio Pantano at Jordan for the final three races of the year, where he took on the role of Friday tester with relish.

Electing not to compete in the newly introduced GP2 series that replaced F3000 in 2005, initially he retained his reserve-driver role at Jordan, before the opportunity came to race for Minardi after Patrick Friesacher ran out of cash. He joined compatriot Christijan Albers at the German Grand Prix at Hockenheim in July, the duo becoming the first all-Dutch pairing to race together for a grand prix team.

For 2006, Robert secured the third-driver role at Red Bull and with it the chance to measure his progress against a proven yardstick in the shape of the experienced David Coulthard. When second driver Christian Klien's performances failed to match the team's expectations, Doornbos was promoted for the final three races of the season. The Dutchman performed respectfully enough, but the seat was already earmarked for Mark Webber in 2007.

Itching to get back to racing action, Doornbos looked to the Champ Car series, where he secured a seat with the Minardi Team USA, performing very well indeed by scoring wins at Mont Tremblant and San Jose, on his way to take third overall and Rookie of the Year honours. Sadly, the series was on its last legs and was merged with the IRL at the start of 2008, leaving him to jump to another series, the Superleague, where he successfully represented AC Milan, scoring two wins in the 12-round championship.

In 2009, Doornbos headed to the States again to race in the IRL for Newman Haas Lanigan, before a late-season switch to HVM Racing. Unfortunately, no results of any note where obtained. He did record a victory in the A1GP series, however, while briefly representing the Netherlands in Portimão.

In 2010, it was back to Superleague action, this time representing the Brazilian club Corinthians with a team based in Belgium. In the main, he ran in the mid-field, scraping a single podium at Zolder. He reappeared in 2011 in Superleague Formula, a series where countries were represented rather than clubs. This time, he briefly represented the Japan team, before the series came to an abrupt end, along with, for the time being at least, Doornbos' career.

DOORNBOS, Robert (NL) b 23/9/1981, Rotterdam

	Race	Circuit	No	Entrant	Tyres	Capacity/Car/Engine	Comment	Q Pos/Entries
	2004 Championship position: Unplaced							
app	CHINESE GP	Shanghai Circuit	39	Jordan Toyota	B	3.0 Jordan EJ14-Cosworth V10	*ran as 3rd driver in practice only*	– /–
app	JAPANESE GP	Suzuka	39	Jordan Toyota	B	3.0 Jordan EJ14-Cosworth V10	*ran as 3rd driver in practice only*	– /–
app	BRAZILIAN GP	Interlagos	39	Jordan Toyota	B	3.0 Jordan EJ14-Cosworth V10	*ran as 3rd driver in practice only*	– /–
	2005 Championship position: Unplaced							
app	AUSTRALIAN GP	Melbourne	39	Jordan Toyota	B	3.0 Jordan EJ15-Toyota V10	*ran as 3rd driver in practice only*	– /–
app	MALAYSIAN GP	Sepang	39	Jordan Toyota	B	3.0 Jordan EJ15-Toyota V10	*ran as 3rd driver in practice only*	– /–
app	BAHRAIN GP	Sakhir Circuit	39	Jordan Toyota	B	3.0 Jordan EJ15-Toyota V10	*ran as 3rd driver in practice only*	– /–
app	SAN MARINO GP	Imola	39	Jordan Toyota	B	3.0 Jordan EJ15-Toyota V10	*ran as 3rd driver in practice only*	– /–
app	SPANISH GP	Barcelona	39	Jordan Toyota	B	3.0 Jordan EJ15-Toyota V10	*ran as 3rd driver in practice only*	– /–
app	MONACO GP	Monte Carlo	39	Jordan Toyota	B	3.0 Jordan EJ15-Toyota V10	*ran as 3rd driver in practice only*	– /–
app	U S GP	Indianapolis	39	Jordan Toyota	B	3.0 Jordan EJ15-Toyota V10	*ran as 3rd driver in practice only*	– /–
app	FRENCH GP	Magny Cours	39	Jordan Toyota	B	3.0 Jordan EJ15-Toyota V10	*ran as 3rd driver in practice only*	– /–

	Race	Circuit	No	Entrant	Tyres	Capacity/Car/Engine	Comment	Q Pos/Entries
app	BRITISH GP	Silverstone	39	Jordan Toyota	B	3.0 Jordan EJ15-Toyota V10	ran as 3rd driver in practice only	- /-
18	GERMAN GP	Hockenheim	20	Minardi Cosworth	B	3.0 Minardi PS05-Cosworth V10	4 laps behind	17/20
ret	HUNGARIAN GP	Hungaroring	20	Minardi Cosworth	B	3.0 Minardi PS05-Cosworth V10	hydraulics	19/20
13	TURKISH GP	Istanbul	20	Minardi Cosworth	B	3.0 Minardi PS05-Cosworth V10	*no practice time/3 laps behind	*20/20
18	ITALIAN GP	Monza	20	Minardi Cosworth	B	3.0 Minardi PS05-Cosworth V10	2 laps behind	18/20
13	BELGIAN GP	Spa	20	Minardi Cosworth	B	3.0 Minardi PS05-Cosworth V10	3 laps behind	17/20
ret	BRAZILIAN GP	Interlagos	20	Minardi Cosworth	B	3.0 Minardi PS05-Cosworth V10	*no practice time/oil pipe	*20/20
14	JAPANESE GP	Suzuka	20	Minardi Cosworth	B	3.0 Minardi PS05-Cosworth V10	2 laps behind	15/20
14	CHINESE GP	Shanghai	20	Minardi Cosworth	B	3.0 Minardi PS05-Cosworth V10	1 lap behind	20/20
	2006 Championship position: Unplaced							
app	BAHRAIN GP	Sakhir Circuit	37	Red Bull Racing	M	3.0 Red Bull RB2-Ferrari V8	ran as 3rd driver in practice only	- /-
app	MALAYSIAN GP	Sepang	37	Red Bull Racing	M	3.0 Red Bull RB2-Ferrari V8	ran as 3rd driver in practice only	- /-
app	AUSTRALIAN GP	Melbourne	37	Red Bull Racing	M	3.0 Red Bull RB2-Ferrari V8	ran as 3rd driver in practice only	- /-
app	SAN MARINO GP	Imola	37	Red Bull Racing	M	3.0 Red Bull RB2-Ferrari V8	ran as 3rd driver in practice only	- /-
app	EUROPEAN GP	Nürburgring	37	Red Bull Racing	M	3.0 Red Bull RB2-Ferrari V8	ran as 3rd driver in practice only	- /-
app	SPANISH GP	Barcelona	37	Red Bull Racing	M	3.0 Red Bull RB2-Ferrari V8	ran as 3rd driver in practice only	- /-
app	MONACO GP	Monte Carlo	37	Red Bull Racing	M	3.0 Red Bull RB2-Ferrari V8	ran as 3rd driver in practice only	- /-
app	BRITISH GP	Silverstone	37	Red Bull Racing	M	3.0 Red Bull RB2-Ferrari V8	ran as 3rd driver in practice only	- /-
app	CANADA	Montreal	37	Red Bull Racing	M	3.0 Red Bull RB2-Ferrari V8	ran as 3rd driver in practice only	- /-
app	U S GP	Indianapolis	37	Red Bull Racing	M	3.0 Red Bull RB2-Ferrari V8	ran as 3rd driver in practice only	- /-
app	FRENCH GP	Magny Cours	37	Red Bull Racing	M	3.0 Red Bull RB2-Ferrari V8	ran as 3rd driver in practice only	- /-
app	GERMAN GP	Hockenheim	37	Red Bull Racing	M	3.0 Red Bull RB2-Ferrari V8	ran as 3rd driver in practice only	- /-
app	HUNGARIAN GP	Hungaroring	37	Red Bull Racing	M	3.0 Red Bull RB2-Ferrari V8	ran as 3rd driver in practice only	- /-
app	TURKISH GP	Istanbul	37	Red Bull Racing	M	3.0 Red Bull RB2-Ferrari V8	ran as 3rd driver in practice only	- /-
app	ITALIAN GP	Monza	37	Red Bull Racing	M	3.0 Red Bull RB2-Ferrari V8	ran as 3rd driver in practice only	- /-
12	CHINESE GP	Shanghai	15	Red Bull Racing	M	3.0 Red Bull RB2-Ferrari V8	1 lap behind	10/20
13	JAPANESE GP	Suzuka	15	Red Bull Racing	M	3.0 Red Bull RB2-Ferrari V8	1 lap behind	18/20
12	BRAZILIAN GP	Interlagos	15	Red Bull Racing	M	3.0 Red Bull RB2-Ferrari V8	*engine penalty/1 lap behind	*15/20

GP Starts: 11   GP Wins: 0   Pole positions: 0   Fastest laps: 0   Points: 0

DOWNING, Ken (GB) b 5/12/1917, Chesterton, Staffordshire – d 3/7/2004, Monte Carlo

1952 Championship position: Unplaced

	Race	Circuit	No	Entrant	Tyres	Capacity/Car/Engine	Comment	Q Pos/Entries
9	BRITISH GP	Silverstone	4	Connaught Engineering	D	2.0 Connaught A-Lea Francis 4	3 laps behind	5/32
ret	DUTCH GP	Zandvoort	22	Kenneth Downing	D	2.0 Connaught A-Lea Francis 4	oil pressure	13/18

GP Starts: 2   GP Wins: 0   Pole positions: 0   Fastest laps: 0   Points: 0

DRAKE, Bob Robert Elden Drake (USA) b 14/12/1919, San Francisco, California – d 18/4/1990 Woodland Hills, California

1960 Championship position: Unplaced

	Race	Circuit	No	Entrant	Tyres	Capacity/Car/Engine	Comment	Q Pos/Entries
13	US GP	Riverside	20	Joe Lubin	D	2.5 Maserati 250F 6	7 laps behind	22/23

GP Starts: 1   GP Wins: 0   Pole positions: 0   Fastest laps: 0   Points: 0

KEN DOWNING

A DIRECTOR of numerous companies, Ken Downing was a supporter of the Connaught marque who also raced briefly in the early 1950s. He scored 17 wins in club events with his sports Connaught in 1951, before racing the A-Type model in 1953. Apart from a couple of grand prix appearances, he was seen little in major races, but did finish second in the GP of Chimay, being caught at the last gasp by Paul Frère's HWM in a thrilling finish.

After briefly racing an Aston Martin DB3S in 1953, Downing retired from the track, later emigrating to South Africa in 1955.

BOB DRAKE

L OS ANGELES restaurateur Bob Drake was an SCCA racer who began competing around California in 1953 with an MG TD. The following season, he scored a win at Palm Springs in Tony Parravano's Ferrari 375, but was seen most often in either a Triumph TR2 or Porsche 356 throughout the 1955 season.

Drake ramped up his appearances in 1956 by competing in very tasty variety of machinery, including a Ferrari 166, a Mercedes 300SL and an Aston Martin DB3, enjoying some success. He continued to race enthusiastically in 1957, with Joe Lubin's Cooper added to his portfolio of rides.

Over the next couple of years, Drake raced only sporadically, but still notched up wins in his Cooper. For 1960, he raced Lubin's newly acquired Maserati Tipo 61 and Max Balchowsky's Ol' Yaller MkII with great success. Thus he was a big local draw when the US Grand Prix was held for the only time at Riverside. His sole grand prix showing was most notable for being the last appearance at world championship level for the wonderful, but aged, Maserati 250F, one of Formula 1 racing's greatest creations. Drake qualified some 11 seconds slower than pole-position man Stirling Moss, but kept himself out of the way of the leaders to record a steady finish.

In 1961, Drake's last full season, he was back to winning ways in SCCA sports cars with Ol' Yaller, then in MkIII guise. The following year, he made just one appearance, sharing the victorious Ferrari 250GTB with Ken Miles in the Riverside six-hours.

DRIVER, 'Paddy' Ernest Gould Driver (ZA) b 19/5/1934, Johannesburg

1963 Championship position: Unplaced

	Race	Circuit	No	Entrant	Tyres	Capacity/Car/Engine	Comment	Q Pos/Entries
dns	SOUTH AFRICAN GP	East London	15	Selby Auto Spares	D	1.5 Lotus 24-BRM V8	*practice accident*	(22)/22

1974 Championship position: Unplaced

	Race	Circuit	No	Entrant	Tyres	Capacity/Car/Engine	Comment	Q Pos/Entries
ret	SOUTH AFRICAN GP	Kyalami	30	Team Gunston	G	3.0 Lotus 72E-Cosworth V8	*clutch slip*	26/27

GP Starts: 1   GP Wins: 0   Pole positions: 0   Fastest laps: 0   Points: 0

DROGO, Piero (I) b 8/8/1926, Vignale, Monteferrato – d 28/4/1973, Bologna

1960 Championship position: Unplaced

	Race	Circuit	No	Entrant	Tyres	Capacity/Car/Engine	Comment	Q Pos/Entries
8	ITALIAN GP	Monza	12	Scuderia Colonia	D	1.5 Cooper T43-Climax 4 F2	*5 laps behind*	15/16

GP Starts: 1   GP Wins: 0   Pole positions: 0   Fastest laps: 0   Points: 0

PADDY DRIVER

PADDY DRIVER made just one grand prix start, which may mislead the casual observer to believe that he was another racing journeyman who just made up the numbers. In fact, he enjoyed a remarkable 40-year racing career, during which he raced with and against some of the great competitors on both two and four wheels. Throughout his remarkable long career, he was seen as both a formidable and scrupulously fair opponent, whose sense of fun and joie de vivre was infectious.

Driver was a top-notch motorcycle rider, having made his name originally on Nortons, before moving to the embryonic Suzuki team and then the advanced, but impoverished and luckless EMC. If fate had been kinder to him, he might have had a world title on two wheels, but nonetheless he was one of those brave souls who competed on the 'Continental Circus'.

In 1963, Paddy flirted briefly with Formula Junior car racing in Europe, helped by Tony Marsh. At the end of the year, driving a rented Lotus 24, he finished seventh on aggregate in the Rand Grand Prix at Kyalami, but an end-over-end shunt in practice for the South African GP a fortnight later, when a steering arm broke, destroyed the car. Miraculously, Paddy emerged shaken, but unscathed (and £2,000 lighter!).

Paddy returned to motorcycle competition with his privateer AJS/Matchless, on which he finished third in the 1965 500cc World Championship, behind the works-backed MV Agustas of Mike Hailwood and Giacomo Agostini.

In 1969, after a couple of years spent developing his property business, Paddy's career on four wheels really began to take off, when he purchased an F5000 Lola. From then on, he enjoyed success in this category, winning the title in 1971 and '73. Early in 1974, at 39 years old, he was a surprise choice to replace the legendary John Love at Team Gunston, driving their Lotus 72s. It wasn't a happy time for him, though, and he finished third in the series, behind Dave Charlton and team-mate Ian Scheckter.

Driver was nothing if not versatile. He regularly raced in the Kylami nine-hours, paired with his great pal Mike Hailwood among many others. With Eddie Keizan, he also won the 1972 Roof of Africa Rally in a Toyota Landcruiser. Once the South African single-seater series went over to Formula Atlantic, Paddy switched to saloon cars with a Mazda, in which he continued racing with his customary verve into the 1980s.

PIERO DROGO

PIERO DROGO raced extensively on the South American continent in sports cars and saloons. He took seventh in the 1956 Venezuelan GP at Caracas, and in 1957 won his class with a Ferrari Testa Rossa in the Buenos Aires 1000km. Fourth place overall in the same event a year later encouraged him to head for Europe to try his luck, but his first visit to Le Mans ended in disappointment when the car was eliminated in an accident.

Having based himself in Italy, Drogo ran out of money in 1959, but to keep body and soul together found employment as a mechanic for Stanguellini. His opportunity to race in a grand prix came when he was invited to help fill the grid for the 1960 Italian event, which had been boycotted by the British teams. Subsequently he formed Carrozzeria Sportscars in the early 1960s, which created a number of rebodied Ferraris known as 'breadvans', because of their squared-off backs, as well as the bodies for the lovely P-type Ferrari's.

Drogo lost his life in a road accident in 1972, when his car ploughed into the back of an unlit truck that had broken down in a tunnel.

JOHNNY DUMFRIES

LOOKING at his record, it is clear that Johnny Dumfries did little wrong and plenty right, yet his career petered out while those of many drivers with less ability have endured.

More formally known as the Earl of Dumfries, Johnny was determined to make it in his own right as a racing driver, and he showed some promise and not a little speed when taken under the wing of Dave Morgan to race in Formula 3 in 1983. He landed a plum drive in the BP-backed Dave Price Racing team for 1984, and the season exceeded his wildest expectations: he won the Marlboro F3 championship at home and nearly repeated the feat in the European series, achieving a magnificent total of 15 wins. His stock was justifiably high, and for 1985 he joined Onyx for a season in F3000, but a bright start soon faded, and by mid-season he was out of work.

Luckily for Johnny, help was at hand in the form of Ayrton Senna, who declined to accept Derek Warwick as his new team-mate at Lotus, as he was entitled to do under the terms of his contract. This gave Dumfries his big chance, but while he let no one down, he was naturally very much the number two to Senna in all things. He did, however, score three points and handled himself pretty well. Politics of one sort had helped him into the team, and unfortunately the revolving door took him straight back out when an engine deal with Honda meant that Satoru Nakajima would be Senna's partner in 1987. Johnny did some testing for Benetton in 1989 and 1990, and then went into endurance racing, with drives in both Porsches and Toyotas, but the unquestioned highlight was his win at Le Mans (with Jan Lammers and Andy Wallace) in 1988 in the TWR Jaguar.

After one last appearance at Le Mans in a Cougar C26S-Porsche, Dumfries slipped quietly from the racing scene and resumed life as the Earl of Dumfries. He succeeded his father in 1993 as the 7th Marquis of Bute, although he prefers to be known more simply as John Bute.

DUMFRIES, Johnny (GB) b 26/4/1958, Rothesay, Isle of Bute, Scotland

1986 Championship position: 13th=   Wins: 0   Pole positions: 0   Fastest laps: 0   Points scored: 3

	Race	Circuit	No	Entrant	Tyres	Capacity/Car/Engine	Comment	Q Pos/Entries
9	BRAZILIAN GP	Rio	11	John Player Special Team Lotus	G	1.5 t/c Lotus 98T-Renault V6	2 pit stops – misfire/3 laps behind	11/25
ret	SPANISH GP	Jerez	11	John Player Special Team Lotus	G	1.5 t/c Lotus 98T-Renault V6	gearbox	10/25
ret	SAN MARINO GP	Imola	11	John Player Special Team Lotus	G	1.5 t/c Lotus 98T-Renault V6	wheel bearing	17/26
dnq	MONACO GP	Monte Carlo	11	John Player Special Team Lotus	G	1.5 t/c Lotus 98T-Renault V6		22/26
ret	BELGIAN GP	Spa	11	John Player Special Team Lotus	G	1.5 t/c Lotus 98T-Renault V6	spun off – holed radiator	13/25
ret	CANADIAN GP	Montreal	11	John Player Special Team Lotus	G	1.5 t/c Lotus 98T-Renault V6	accident with Johansson	16/25
7	US GP (DETROIT)	Detroit	11	John Player Special Team Lotus	G	1.5 t/c Lotus 98T-Renault V6	2 laps behind	14/26
ret	FRENCH GP	Paul Ricard	11	John Player Special Team Lotus	G	1.5 t/c Lotus 98T-Renault V6	engine	12/26
7	BRITISH GP	Brands Hatch	11	John Player Special Team Lotus	G	1.5 t/c Lotus 98T-Renault V6	3 laps behind	10/26
ret	GERMAN GP	Hockenheim	11	John Player Special Team Lotus	G	1.5 t/c Lotus 98T-Renault V6	holed water radiator	12/26
5	HUNGARIAN GP	Hungaroring	11	John Player Special Team Lotus	G	1.5 t/c Lotus 98T-Renault V6	2 laps behind	8/26
ret	AUSTRIAN GP	Österreichring	11	John Player Special Team Lotus	G	1.5 t/c Lotus 98T-Renault V6	engine	15/26
ret	ITALIAN GP	Monza	11	John Player Special Team Lotus	G	1.5 t/c Lotus 98T-Renault V6	gearbox	17/27
9	PORTUGUESE GP	Estoril	11	John Player Special Team Lotus	G	1.5 t/c Lotus 98T-Renault V6	2 laps behind	15/27
ret	MEXICAN GP	Mexico City	11	John Player Special Team Lotus	G	1.5 t/c Lotus 98T-Renault V6	electrics	17/26
6	AUSTRALIAN GP	Adelaide	11	John Player Special Team Lotus	G	1.5 t/c Lotus 98T-Renault V6	2 laps behind	14/26

GP Starts: 15   GP Wins: 0   Pole positions: 0   Fastest laps: 0   Points: 3

EATON, George (CDN) b 12/11/1945, Toronto, Ontario

1969 Championship position: Unplaced

	Race	Circuit	No	Entrant	Tyres	Capacity/Car/Engine	Comment	Q Pos/Entries
ret	US GP	Watkins Glen	22	Owen Racing Organisation	D	3.0 BRM P138 V12	engine	18/18
ret	MEXICAN GP	Mexico City	22	Owen Racing Organisation	D	3.0 BRM P138 V12	gearbox	17/17

1970 Championship position: Unplaced

ret	SOUTH AFRICAN GP	Kyalami	21	Owen Racing Organisation	F	3.0 BRM P139 V12	engine	23/24
dnq	SPANISH GP	Jarama	21	Owen Racing Organisation	F	3.0 BRM P153 V12		22/22
dnq	MONACO GP	Monte Carlo	15	Yardley Team BRM	F	3.0 BRM P153 V12		21/21
ret	DUTCH GP	Zandvoort	3	Yardley Team BRM	F	3.0 BRM P153 V12	loose oil tank	18/24
12	FRENCH GP	Clermont Ferrand	4	Yardley Team BRM	F	3.0 BRM P153 V12	pit stop – plug lead/2 laps behind	19/23
ret	BRITISH GP	Brands Hatch	24	Yardley Team BRM	F	3.0 BRM P153 V12	oil pressure	=16/25
11	AUSTRIAN GP	Österreichring	18	Yardley Team BRM	F	3.0 BRM P153 V12	2 laps behind	23/24
ret	ITALIAN GP	Monza	12	Yardley Team BRM	F	3.0 BRM P153 V12	overheating	23/27
10	CANADIAN GP	St Jovite	16	Yardley Team BRM	F	3.0 BRM P153 V12	pit stop/5 laps behind	=8/20
ret	US GP	Watkins Glen	21	Yardley Team BRM	F	3.0 BRM P153 V12	engine	14/27

1971 Championship position: Unplaced

15	CANADIAN GP	Mosport Park	28	Yardley Team BRM	F	3.0 BRM P160 V12	collision with Peterson/-5 laps	21/27

GP Starts: 11   GP Wins: 0   Pole positions: 0   Fastest laps: 0   Points: 0

GEORGE EATON

THE affluent scion of the T. Eaton Company Limited, the famous Canadian department store and office empire, George Eaton obviously had the wherewithal to go racing, graduating to a McLaren M1C via a fearsome Cobra. After a few races late in 1967, Eaton ran the car in Can-Am the following season, his best finish being a very impressive third at Laguna Seca in the wet.

Having ordered a new McLaren M12 for Can-Am and a McLaren M10 for Formula A, he was a front-runner in both series, which brought an invitation to race the works BRM in the final two grands prix of 1969. This contact led to a deal for Eaton to drive for BRM in F1 for the full season in 1970, as well as racing their P54 prototype in Can-Am. All in all, though, it proved to be a great disappointment for both parties, leaving George somewhat disillusioned.

Eaton raced for BRM once more in 1971, and also handled Ferrari sports cars at Sebring, Le Mans and Watkins Glen. But with success proving elusive, he gradually lost interest, and after taking part in the 1972 Daytona six-hour race, he left the scene to pursue other interests. Subsequently he took over the running of the family firm, but was unable to halt the steep decline in the fortunes of this once powerful institution. He stepped down in 1997 and the company filed for bankruptcy two years later. Its assets were bought by rival chain Sears.

GUY EDWARDS

ALTHOUGH not a front-rank driver, Guy Edwards, an intelligent and personable individual, had a talent for securing funding from sponsorship sources previously unconnected with motorsport, and with this backing he was able to rise from 2-litre sports cars via F5000 into Formula 1. Guy's first taste of grands prix ended bitterly when he lost his drive after a wrist injury had sidelined him from the Embassy Hill team. Then he arranged substantial sponsorship to drive for Hesketh in 1976, but the team was in decline, and results were poor, while one last stab in the hopeless Stanley-BRM is best forgotten.

Perhaps realising his limitations, Edwards settled for a satisfying few seasons competing at national level and occasionally beyond, mainly racing grand prix machinery in the popular Aurora F1 series, before retiring from driving to become a successful sponsorship consultant, a role that has made him a millionaire.

In the austere financial climate of the early 1990s, Edwards was employed by Team Lotus in 1992 to find a major sponsor for the once great marque. He managed to bring Castrol on board, but further substantial backing could not be found and their relationship ended somewhat acrimoniously in 1994.

Subsequently Guy moved out of motor racing to sell sponsorship opportunities in the world of commerce. His son, Sean, has been bitten by the racing bug and is a top competitor in the Porsche Supercup.

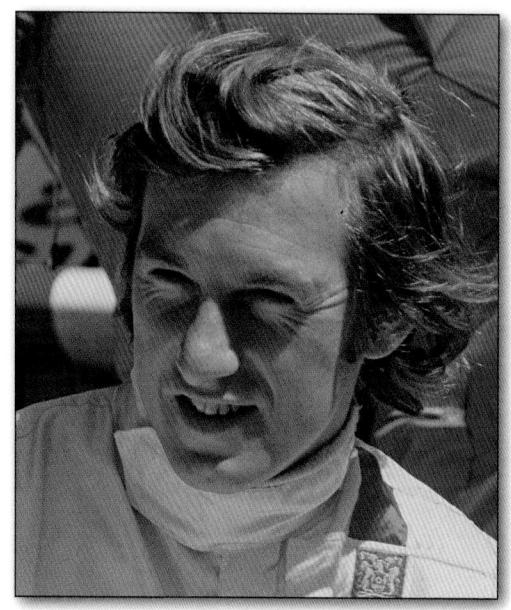

EDWARDS, Guy (GB) b 30/12/1942, Macclesfield, Cheshire

	Race	Circuit	No	Entrant	Tyres	Capacity/Car/Engine	Comment	Q Pos/Entries
	1974 Championship position: Unplaced							
11	ARGENTINE GP	Buenos Aires	27	Embassy Racing with Graham Hill	F	3.0 Lola T370-Cosworth V8	2 laps behind	25/26
ret	BRAZILIAN GP	Interlagos	27	Embassy Racing with Graham Hill	F	3.0 Lola T370-Cosworth V8	engine	25/25
dnq	SPANISH GP	Jarama	27	Embassy Racing with Graham Hill	F	3.0 Lola T370-Cosworth V8		27/28
12	BELGIAN GP	Nivelles	27	Embassy Racing with Graham Hill	F	3.0 Lola T370-Cosworth V8	3 laps behind	21/32
8	MONACO GP	Monte Carlo	27	Embassy Racing with Graham Hill	F	3.0 Lola T370-Cosworth V8	2 laps behind	26/28
7	SWEDISH GP	Anderstorp	27	Embassy Racing with Graham Hill	F	3.0 Lola T370-Cosworth V8	1 lap behind	18/28
ret	DUTCH GP	Zandvoort	27	Embassy Racing with Graham Hill	F	3.0 Lola T370-Cosworth V8	fuel system	14/27
15	FRENCH GP	Dijon	27	Embassy Racing with Graham Hill	F	3.0 Lola T370-Cosworth V8	3 laps behind	20/30
dns	BRITISH GP	Brands Hatch	27	Embassy Racing with Graham Hill	F	3.0 Lola T370-Cosworth V8	injury from previous race	– / –
dnq	GERMAN GP	Nürburgring	27	Embassy Racing with Graham Hill	F	3.0 Lola T370-Cosworth V8		29/32
	1976 Championship position: Unplaced							
dnq	BELGIAN GP	Zolder	25	Penthouse Rizla Racing with Hesketh	G	3.0 Hesketh 308D-Cosworth V8		29/29
17	FRENCH GP	Paul Ricard	25	Penthouse Rizla Racing with Hesketh	G	3.0 Hesketh 308D-Cosworth V8	1 lap behind	25/30
ret	BRITISH GP	Brands Hatch	25	Penthouse Rizla Racing with Hesketh	G	3.0 Hesketh 308D-Cosworth V8	accident	25/30
15	GERMAN GP	Nürburgring	25	Penthouse Rizla Racing with Hesketh	G	3.0 Hesketh 308D-Cosworth V8	1 lap behind	25/28
dns	ITALIAN GP	Monza	25	Penthouse Rizla Racing with Hesketh	G	3.0 Hesketh 308D-Cosworth V8	withdrew – allowed Watson to race	(23)/29
20	CANADIAN GP	Mosport Park	25	Penthouse Rizla Racing with Hesketh	G	3.0 Hesketh 308D-Cosworth V8	5 laps behind	24/27
	1977 Championship position: Unplaced							
dnpq	BRITISH GP	Silverstone	35	Rotary Watches-Stanley BRM	G	3.0 Stanley BRM P207 V12		33/36

GP Starts: 11   GP Wins: 0   Pole positions: 0   Fastest laps: 0   Points: 0

VIC ELFORD

VIC ELFORD was something of a star performer in every type of racing to which he turned his hand, and it is a great shame he was not seen in a competitive grand prix car earlier in his career, which was largely spent rallying, sprinkled with whatever circuit racing his limited finances would allow.

Elford was a Ford works driver from 1964 until he switched to Porsche, going on to win the Group 3 title in 1967 and the Monte Carlo Rally in 1968. By then, he had become an established member of the Porsche sports car team and produced some dazzling performances, winning the Daytona 24-hours (after doing the lion's share of the driving), the Targa Florio – a truly epic performance – and the Nürburgring 1000km. Cooper, searching for a driver, offered him a seat for the French GP, where he duly finished fourth first time out in the rain. He completed the season with them, but then the team folded.

For 1969, Elford continued with Porsche in sports car racing (taking time out to finish 11th in the Daytona 500 in a Dodge!) and drove for privateer Colin Crabbe in F1. Things looked promising until he was involved in Mario Andretti's accident at the German GP, his McLaren hitting debris from the American's car. He crashed badly and was lucky to escape with nothing worse than a broken arm and collarbone.

The crash effectively spelt the end of Elford's grand prix career, but he was soon back in the Porsche and driving as well as ever, winning the 1970 Nürburgring 1000km with Kurt Ahrens Jr. He drove for BRM in the German GP of 1971, but was not really given a fair crack of the whip.

He raced on, driving for Porsche and Alfa Romeo in endurance events, handling Chaparrals, McLarens and Shadows in Can-Am, and a Chevron in F2, and even won a Trans-Am race in a Camaro at Watkins Glen before finally retiring in 1974. Then he was responsible for overseeing the start-up and running of the French Inaltera project, which raced at Le Mans in both 1976 and '77.

Elford was also briefly team manager of the ATS F1 team in the second half of the 1977 season, before moving to the United States, where he was responsible for running the Renault Cup in the IMSA Champion Spark Plug Championship.

He has since resumed his successful association with the Porsche marque. The creation of the Porsche Owners Driving School allowed Vic to offer his considerable expertise to those lucky enough to be able to purchase the fabulous Stuttgart sports machines.

ELFORD, Vic (GB) b 10/6/1935, Peckham, London

1968 Championship position: 17th= Wins: 0 Pole positions: 0 Fastest laps: 0 Points scored: 5

	Race	Circuit	No	Entrant	Tyres	Capacity/Car/Engine	Comment	Q Pos/Entries
4	FRENCH GP	Rouen	30	Cooper Car Co	F	3.0 Cooper T86B-BRM V12	pit stop – tyres/2 laps behind	18/18
ret	BRITISH GP	Brands Hatch	15	Cooper Car Co	F	3.0 Cooper T86B-BRM V12	engine	17/20
ret	GERMAN GP	Nürburgring	20	Cooper Car Co	F	3.0 Cooper T86B-BRM V12	accident	5/20
ret	ITALIAN GP	Monza	23	Cooper Car Co	F	3.0 Cooper T86B-BRM V12	lost brakes – spun off	22/24
5	CANADIAN GP	St Jovite	21	Cooper Car Co	F	3.0 Cooper T86B-BRM V12	4 laps behind	17/22
ret	US GP	Watkins Glen	18	Cooper Car Co	F	3.0 Cooper T86B-BRM V12	engine – camshaft	17/21
8	MEXICAN GP	Mexico City	18	Cooper Car Co	F	3.0 Cooper T86B-BRM V12	2 laps behind	17/21

1969 Championship position: 13th= Wins: 0 Pole positions: 0 Fastest laps: 0 Points scored: 3

	Race	Circuit	No	Entrant	Tyres	Capacity/Car/Engine	Comment	Q Pos/Entries
7	MONACO GP	Monte Carlo	12	Colin Crabbe-Antique Automobiles	G	3.0 Cooper T86B-Maserati V12	6 laps behind	16/16
10	DUTCH GP	Zandvoort	18	Colin Crabbe-Antique Automobiles	G	3.0 McLaren M7A-Cosworth V8	6 laps behind	15/15
5	FRENCH GP	Clermont Ferrand	10	Colin Crabbe-Antique Automobiles	G	3.0 McLaren M7A-Cosworth V8	1 lap behind	10/13
6	BRITISH GP	Silverstone	19	Colin Crabbe-Antique Automobiles	G	3.0 McLaren M7A-Cosworth V8	2 laps behind	11/17
ret	GERMAN GP	Nürburgring	12	Colin Crabbe-Antique Automobiles	G	3.0 McLaren M7A-Cosworth V8	hit debris from Andretti's crash	6/25

1971 Championship position: Unplaced

	Race	Circuit	No	Entrant	Tyres	Capacity/Car/Engine	Comment	Q Pos/Entries
11/ret	GERMAN GP	Nürburgring	22	Yardley Team BRM	F	3.0 BRM P160 V12	pit stop – coil/1 lap behind	18/23

GP Starts: 13 GP Wins: 0 Pole positions: 0 Fastest laps: 0 Points: 8

EMERY, Paul (GB) b 12/11/1916, Chiswick, London – d 3/2/1992, Epsom, Surrey

1956 Championship position: Unplaced

	Race	Circuit	No	Entrant	Tyres	Capacity/Car/Engine	Comment	Q Pos/Entries
ret	BRITISH GP	Silverstone	32	Emeryson Cars	D	2.5 Emeryson-Alta 4	ignition	23/28

1958 Championship position: Unplaced

dnq	MONACO GP	Monte Carlo	14	B C Ecclestone	A	2.5 Connaught B-Alta 4		22/28

GP Starts: 1 GP Wins: 0 Pole positions: 0 Fastest laps: 0 Points: 0

PAUL EMERY

PAUL EMERY was one of those characters in life who was always chasing success, rarely found it, but had a hell of a good time along the way.

Emery and his father were indefatigable builders of specials, based on whatever components were available at the time. Given the name Emeryson, these machines were always technically interesting in some respect, but the finance essential for their development was always lacking.

Paul, a 500cc racer of some note who also raced a Lotus sports car in 1955, developed an Emeryson-Alta, in which in 1956 he finished second, to Stirling Moss no less, at Crystal Palace before racing it in the British Grand Prix.

Then he worked on the Connaughts owned by Bernie Ecclestone, before going on to build the Emeryson F1 cars for ENB and Scirocco-Powell. Eventually, he abandoned his Formula 1 ambitions, however, jumping from project to project, most of which remained unrealised, until finally finding a niche building and driving oval-track midget racers.

TOMAS ENGE

ALWAYS seen as a quick driver throughout his long and varied career, Tomas Enge, a Czech, has competed in a myriad of categories, including a very brief spell at the top of the ladder when he raced for Prost in 2001.

Tomas had motorsport in his blood courtesy of his father, Bretislav, who had raced touring cars in the 1970s. He began his racing career in karts, before eventually graduating to Formula Ford, where he ran alongside another rising star, Nick Heidfeld. The pair proved to be the class of the 1995 field, taking first and third overall, with Enge following in Heidfeld's footsteps as series champion the following year.

Despite a largely unrewarding spell in F3, Enge had graduated to F3000 by 1999, and some feisty performances and a podium at Magny-Cours led to the offer of an F1 test role with Jordan for 2000. A win at Hockenheim was the high point of a largely mediocre F3000 campaign, but there was an upturn the following year when he joined Nordic Racing, moving from mid-grid to front-runner almost overnight.

Despite Enge winning twice – at Barcelona and the Nürburgring – it was team-mate Justin Wilson who took the 2001 F3000 title, but third place in the series did not deter his admirers in F1 and, when Luciano Burti was injured in a shunt during the Belgian Grand Prix, former world champion Alain Prost called on Enge. Sadly, the Prost-Acer, gave him little chance to shine and, with the cash-strapped operation going under that winter, his chances of an extended stay in F1 evaporated.

Enge's F3000 performances stood him in good stead, however, and leading team Arden International decided to run the man from Liberec for 2002. With plenty of experience under his belt, he proved to be a real force in the series, winning four races and appearing on course for the title. However, after failing a routine drugs test following the Hungaroring race, his crown was handed to season-long rival Sébastien Bourdais.

At the same time, Enge was beginning to build a reputation as a promising sports car racer, and he decided to follow this route full-time in 2003, the highlight being a win in the GTS class at Le Mans in a Ferrari. He remained eager to continue his single-seater career, however, and in an effort to return to F1, decided to have one last crack at F3000. Unfortunately, it did not quite work out, and he struggled to string together the sort of results that his ability deserved, eventually finishing fourth overall. He also tried oval racing for the first time, entering two Indy Racing League events with Patrick Racing once his F3000 commitments had been met.

This foray gave Tomas the opportunity to pursue his IRL career with Panther Racing in 2005. Running the ageing Chevrolet engine against the massed ranks of Honda and Toyota powered cars gave him little chance to succeed in his 14 starts that year, but he did post a best finish of fifth at Sonoma.

When the A1 GP series became a reality at the tail end of 2005, Enge was naturally the first choice for a place in the Czech Republic car, and after a couple of podiums and a number of strong finishes, he finally gave his country a victory in the feature race at Shanghai in April, 2006. He continued to compete in the series until early 2008.

Having joined the Peterson ALMS team for 2007, things started badly for Tomas when he crashed heavily at an ALMS race at St Petersburg, suffering a broken elbow and cracked ribs, but he bounced back to take a class win at Salt Lake City, before an on-track clash with Mika Salo at Mid-Ohio led to his immediate dismissal from the team. His talents were soon in demand elsewhere, however, and he began his association with the works Aston Martin team, as well as racing for the Modena team, finishing second in the LMGT1 category. He also competed in the Czech touring car championship, taking eight wins on his way to the title.

In 2009, Tomas finished fourth at Le Mans (with Jan Charouz and Stefan Mücke) in the works Aston Martin LMP1, before joining the Young Driver AMR team to contest the newly inaugurated FIA GT1 World Championship for 2010. He took the Aston Martin DBR9 to an outright win at the Nürburgring (with Darren Turner), and fourth in the series overall. In 2011, he was paired with Alex Mueller, placing fourth overall once again, with four podium finishes.

ENGE, Tomáš (CZ) b 19/1/1976, Liberec

2001 Championship position: Unplaced

	Race	Circuit	No	Entrant	Tyres	Capacity/Car/Engine	Comment	Q Pos/Entries
12	ITALIAN GP	Monza	23	Prost Acer	M	3.0 Prost AP04-Acer V10	1 lap behind	20/22
14	UNITED STATES GP	Indianapolis	23	Prost Acer	M	3.0 Prost AP04-Acer V10	1 lap behind	21/22
ret	JAPANESE GP	Suzuka	23	Prost Acer	M	3.0 Prost AP04-Acer V10	wheel bearing	19/22

GP Starts: 3   GP Wins: 0   Pole positions: 0   Fastest laps: 0   Points: 0

ENGLAND, Paul (AUS) b 28/3/1929, Melbourne, Victoria

1957 Championship position: Unplaced

	Race	Circuit	No	Entrant	Tyres	Capacity/Car/Engine	Comment	Q Pos/Entries
ret	GERMAN GP (F2)	Nürburgring	26	Ridgeway Managements	D	1.5 Cooper T41-Climax 4	distributor	23/24

GP Starts: 1   GP Wins: 0   Pole positions: 0   Fastest laps: 0   Points: 0

PAUL ENGLAND

PAUL ENGLAND was originally a young engineer working for the Repco concern in Melbourne in the mid-1950s when he was involved in a number of performance-related projects.

He constructed his own sports car, the AUSCA, with a fibreglass body based on a Maserati A6GCS sports car, which used a Holden engine. Following a big crash at Phillip Island, which virtually wrecked the machine, Paul decided to travel to England, following in the footsteps of Jack Brabham. Naturally he headed to the Cooper workshops in Surbiton and took the opportunity of racing in the Formula 2 class of the German Grand Prix.

Upon his return to Australia, he set up his own highly specialised engineering business, concentrating on engine development, most notably with the Coventry Climax FPF 2.5- and 2.7-litre engines.

Paul carried on competing in hill-climbs with his 4WD, VW-powered twin-engined AUSCA, and was crowned Australian champion in 1970, 1973 and 1974.

Although Paul has since retired, his son and eldest daughter continue to run Paul England Performance Engineering, with a workshop in Essendon, Victoria, providing crankshaft grinding and precision dynamic balancing services to the performance automotive industry.

HARALD ERTL

HARALD ERTL was a journalist/racer who competed in Formula Vee, Super Vee and Formula 3 in Germany between 1969 and 1970. He made the move into touring cars in 1971 with an Alfa Romeo, before entering the European touring car series, the undoubted highlight being victory in the 1973 Tourist Trophy with Derek Bell in a BMW.

With finance from Warsteiner Breweries, Ertl broke into Formula 1 briefly in 1975, driving for Hesketh, and did a solid job. This encouraged him to undertake a full season the following year, but the car was not competitive and he was no James Hunt. However, he did come close to scoring a point at Brands Hatch.

Ertl attempted to compete in five more races the following year, but the updated 308E was well past its best. He had to wait until mid-1978 to get another chance on the F1 stage, when Sachs hooked up with Ensign. He was never quite able to make the points – although he was desperately unlucky to lose sixth place at Hockenheim when his engine failed. After failing to pre-qualify for the Italian Grand Prix, he switched teams to another poor car, the ATS, in a desperate attempt to make the grid. He failed.

During this period, Ertl was also dipping in and out of Formula 2, but was rarely more than a mid-field runner. In 1980, he made one more grand prix attempt, at Hockenheim for ATS, but again failed to qualify. By then, however, he was established as a leading light in the German G5 championship in BMW and Ford Capri turbos. He did not race in 1981, but planned a return to action in the Renault Turbo Cup for 1982.

A charming and popular figure around the circuits, Harald was killed in a light aeroplane crash in April, 1982. His brother-in-law, who was piloting the plane, which suffered an engine failure, was also killed. His wife and son, who were also on board, survived, although both were seriously injured.

ERTL, Harald (A) b 31/8/1948, Zell am See – d 7/4/1982, nr Glessen, Germany

1975 Championship position: Unplaced

	Race	Circuit	No	Entrant	Tyres	Capacity/Car/Engine	Comment	Q Pos/Entries
8	GERMAN GP	Nürburgring	25	Warsteiner Brewery	G	3.0 Hesketh 308B-Cosworth V8		23/26
ret	AUSTRIAN GP	Österreichring	32	Warsteiner Brewery	G	3.0 Hesketh 308B-Cosworth V8	electrics	27/30
9	ITALIAN GP	Monza	34	Warsteiner Brewery	G	3.0 Hesketh 308B-Cosworth V8	1 lap behind	17/28

1976 Championship position: Unplaced

	Race	Circuit	No	Entrant	Tyres	Capacity/Car/Engine	Comment	Q Pos/Entries
15	SOUTH AFRICAN GP	Kyalami	24	Hesketh Racing	G	3.0 Hesketh 308D-Cosworth V8	4 laps behind	24/25
dnq	US GP WEST	Long Beach	24	Hesketh Racing	G	3.0 Hesketh 308D-Cosworth V8		26/27
dnq	SPANISH GP	Jarama	24	Hesketh Racing	G	3.0 Hesketh 308D-Cosworth V8		29/30
ret	BELGIAN GP	Zolder	24	Hesketh Racing	G	3.0 Hesketh 308D-Cosworth V8	engine	24/29
dnq	MONACO GP	Monte Carlo	24	Hesketh Racing	G	3.0 Hesketh 308D-Cosworth V8		24/25
ret	SWEDISH GP	Anderstorp	24	Hesketh Racing	G	3.0 Hesketh 308D-Cosworth V8	spun off – could not restart	23/27
dnq/ret	FRENCH GP	Paul Ricard	24	Hesketh Racing	G	3.0 Hesketh 308D-Cosworth V8	started illegally/driveshaft	29/30
7*	BRITISH GP	Brands Hatch	24	Hesketh Racing	G	3.0 Hesketh 308D-Cosworth V8	*1st place car disqualified/-3 laps	24/30
ret/dns	GERMAN GP	Nürburgring	24	Hesketh Racing	G	3.0 Hesketh 308D-Cosworth V8	crashed at 1st start – did not restart	22/28
8	AUSTRIAN GP	Österreichring	24	Hesketh Racing	G	3.0 Hesketh 308D-Cosworth V8	1 lap behind	20/25
ret	DUTCH GP	Zandvoort	24	Hesketh Racing	G	3.0 Hesketh 308D-Cosworth V8	spun off – could not restart	24/27
16/ret	ITALIAN GP	Monza	24	Hesketh Racing	G	3.0 Hesketh 308D-Cosworth V8	driveshaft/3 laps behind	19/29
dns	CANADIAN GP	Mosport Park	24	Hesketh Racing	G	3.0 Hesketh 308D-Cosworth V8	practice accident with Amon	(23)/27
13	US GP EAST	Watkins Glen	24	Hesketh Racing	G	3.0 Hesketh 308D-Cosworth V8	hit Merzario – pit stop/-5 laps	21/27
8	JAPANESE GP	Mount Fuji	24	Hesketh Racing	G	3.0 Hesketh 308D-Cosworth V8	1 lap behind	22/27

1977 Championship position: Unplaced

	Race	Circuit	No	Entrant	Tyres	Capacity/Car/Engine	Comment	Q Pos/Entries
ret	SPANISH GP	Jarama	25	Hesketh Racing	G	3.0 Hesketh 308E-Cosworth V8	radiator	18/31
dnq	MONACO GP	Monte Carlo	25	Hesketh Racing	G	3.0 Hesketh 308E-Cosworth V8		23/26
9	BELGIAN GP	Zolder	25	Hesketh Racing	G	3.0 Hesketh 308E-Cosworth V8	1 lap behind	25/32
16	SWEDISH GP	Anderstorp	25	Hesketh Racing	G	3.0 Hesketh 308E-Cosworth V8	4 laps behind	23/31
dnq	FRENCH GP	Dijon	25	Hesketh Racing	G	3.0 Hesketh 308E-Cosworth V8		25/30

1978 Championship position: Unplaced

	Race	Circuit	No	Entrant	Tyres	Capacity/Car/Engine	Comment	Q Pos/Entries
11/ret	GERMAN GP	Hockenheim	23	Sachs Racing	G	3.0 Ensign N177-Cosworth V8	engine/4 laps behind	23/30
ret	AUSTRIAN GP	Österreichring	23	Sachs Racing	G	3.0 Ensign N177-Cosworth V8	collision with Patrese at restart	24/31
dnpq	DUTCH GP	Zandvoort	23	Sachs Racing	G	3.0 Ensign N177-Cosworth V8		31/33
dnpq	ITALIAN GP	Monza	23	Sachs Racing	G	3.0 Ensign N177-Cosworth V8		29/32
dnq	"	"	10	ATS Engineering	G	3.0 ATS HS1-Cosworth V8		26/32

1980 Championship position: Unplaced

	Race	Circuit	No	Entrant	Tyres	Capacity/Car/Engine	Comment	Q Pos/Entries
dnq	GERMAN GP	Hockenheim	10	Team ATS	G	3.0 ATS D4-Cosworth V8		26/26

GP Starts: 18 (19) GP Wins: 0 Pole positions: 0 Fastest laps: 0 Points: 0

ESTÉFANO, Nasif (RA) b 18/11/1932, Concepción, Tucumán – d 21/10/1973 Aimogasta, nr Conceptión-Tucamán

1960 Championship position: Unplaced

	Race	Circuit	No	Entrant	Tyres	Capacity/Car/Engine	Comment	Q Pos/Entries
14	ARGENTINE GP	Buenos Aires	10	Nasif Estéfano/Scuderia Centro Sud	D	2.5 Maserati 250F 6	10 laps behind	20/22

1962 Championship position: Unplaced

	Race	Circuit	No	Entrant	Tyres	Capacity/Car/Engine	Comment	Q Pos/Entries
dnq	ITALIAN GP	Monza	34	Scuderia de Tomaso	D	1.5 de Tomaso 801 F8		30/30

GP Starts: 1 GP Wins: 0 Pole positions: 0 Fastest laps: 0 Points: 0

ESTÉFANO, Nasif

ONE of five children of Lebanese immigrant stock, Nasif Estéfano grew up in Argentina and became hooked on speed shortly after leaving school. He and his brothers soon began racing locally, and Nasif recorded his first win in 1955. Then he ventured into national competitions, but it was not until 1959 that he made his breakthrough, at a 500-mile race at Rafaelo, where he qualified fourth and caught the eye and admiration of Juan Fangio. This led to his participation in the 1960 Argentine Grand Prix, where he was rented a somewhat tired, old Maserati 250F; nonetheless, he left a favourable impression.

In 1961, Nasif sold virtually everything he had to raise $7,000, which he paid to Alessandro de Tomaso to race his F1 car in 1962. In the event, the machine did not appear until Monza, where it was unprepared and hopelessly off the pace. When he tried to race this hopeless machine the following season, it lasted one lap in the Rome GP before the clutch failed. Having lost his money and feeling cheated, the talented driver lost no time back at home in claiming his national F1 championship in 1964, driving a Chevrolet special. Back in Europe, he shared a Porsche 904GTS with compatriot Andrea Vianini in the Reims 12-hour race, taking a brilliant fifth place overall and GT-class victory.

On his return to South America, Estéfano quickly asserted his skills to become 1965 and 1966 GT champion in an Alfa. He was regarded as perhaps the cream of local talent when the visiting teams from Europe contested the F3 Temporada series in 1966. Subsequently he concentrated on racing sports touring cars and the 'Turismo Carretera' long-distance events. It was in one of these that he lost his life in October, 1973. In an unexplained accident, he lost control of his Ford on a long fast bend and was thrown from the car as it rolled to destruction. It is thought a brake pedal may have sheared.

PHILIPPE ÉTANCELIN

EASILY recognisable by his trademark reversed cap, 'Phi Phi', as Philippe Étancelin was known to his friends, began racing in 1927, scoring a big win at Reims with his Bugatti in his first season. In 1929, he won at Reims once more, and claimed further victories at Antibes, Comminges and La Baule, while success continued into 1930 with wins at Pau and in the Algerian GP.

Late in 1931, Étancelin took the decision to order an Alfa Romeo, which he ran relatively successfully until rule changes for 1934 forced him to switch to a Maserati. He often finished second or third with this car over the next few seasons, outright successes mainly eluding him, although he did win at Pau in 1936, and had previously shared the 1934 Le Mans winning car with Chinetti.

After the Second World War, Étancelin took an Alfa Romeo to the first race in Paris, but it would be 1948 before he could compete regularly, after taking delivery of a Lago-Talbot. The car was raced to good effect in 1949, 'Phi Phi' winning the Paris GP and finishing second at Marseilles, Monza and Brno. In 1950 – the first season of the world championship – Étancelin picked up a couple of fifth places, racing his now elderly Talbot on through the 1951 season and into the following year in the few F1 and Libre events for which it was still eligible.

By 1953, this hard trier had virtually retired from racing after finishing third with Pierre Levegh (racing pseudonym of Pierre Bouillin) in the Casablanca three-hours, but the Rouen GP of that year was a non-championship event, so the organisers, invited Formula 1 cars to compete as well in the hope of bolstering the grid. 'Phi Phi' was a local man and could not resist the temptation to dust off his trusty Talbot to take up the challenge to the works Ferraris. To the immense delight of a partisan crowd, he brought the car home in third place, thus finishing a wonderful career in splendid fashion.

ÉTANCELIN, Philippe (F) b 28/12/1896, Rouen – d 13/10/1981, Neuilly sur Seine, nr Paris

1950 Championship position: 10th= Wins: 0 Pole positions: 0 Fastest laps: 0 Points scored: 3

	Race	Circuit	No	Entrant	Tyres	Capacity/Car/Engine	Comment	Q Pos/Entries
8	BRITISH GP	Silverstone	16	Philippe Étancelin	D	4.5 Talbot-Lago T26C 6	5 laps behind	14/21
ret	MONACO GP	Monte Carlo	14	Philippe Étancelin	D	4.5 Talbot-Lago T26C 6	oil pipe	4/21
ret	SWISS GP	Bremgarten	42	Philippe Étancelin	D	4.5 Talbot-Lago T26C 6	gearbox	6/18
ret	BELGIAN GP	Spa	16	Automobiles Talbot-Darracq	D	4.5 Talbot-Lago T26C-DA 6	overheating	6/14
5*	FRENCH GP	Reims	16	Philippe Étancelin	D	4.5 Talbot-Lago T26C-DA 6	*Chaboud took over/5 laps behind	4/20
5	ITALIAN GP	Monza	24	Philippe Étancelin	D	4.5 Talbot-Lago T26C 6	5 laps behind	16/27

1951 Championship position: Unplaced

	Race	Circuit	No	Entrant	Tyres	Capacity/Car/Engine	Comment	Q Pos/Entries
10	SWISS GP	Bremgarten	4	Philippe Étancelin	D	4.5 Talbot-Lago T26C-DA 6	3 laps behind	12/21
ret	BELGIAN GP	Spa	20	Philippe Étancelin	D	4.5 Talbot-Lago T26C-DA 6	transmission	10/13
ret	FRENCH GP	Reims	38	Philippe Étancelin	D	4.5 Talbot-Lago T26C-DA 6	engine	10/23
ret	GERMAN GP	Nürburgring	86	Philippe Étancelin	D	4.5 Talbot-Lago T26C-DA 6	gearbox	21/23
8	SPANISH GP	Pedralbes	34	Philippe Étancelin	D	4.5 Talbot-Lago T26C-DA 6	7 laps behind	13/20

1952 Championship position: Unplaced

	Race	Circuit	No	Entrant	Tyres	Capacity/Car/Engine	Comment	Q Pos/Entries
8	FRENCH GP	Rouen	28	Escuderia Bandeirantes	P	2.0 Maserati A6GCM 6	7 laps behind	16/20

GP Starts: 12 GP Wins: 0 Pole positions: 0 Fastest laps: 0 Points: 3

EVANS, Bob (GB) b 11/6/1947, Waddington, Lincolnshire

1975 Championship position: Unplaced

	Race	Circuit	No	Entrant	Tyres	Capacity/Car/Engine	Comment	Q Pos/Entries
15	SOUTH AFRICAN GP	Kyalami	14	Stanley BRM	G	3.0 BRM P201 V12	2 laps behind	24/28
ret	SPANISH GP	Montjuich Park	14	Stanley BRM	G	3.0 BRM P201 V12	fuel metering unit	23/26
dnq	MONACO GP	Monte Carlo	14	Stanley BRM	G	3.0 BRM P201 V12		22/26
9	BELGIAN GP	Zolder	14	Stanley BRM	G	3.0 BRM P201 V12	2 laps behind	20/24
13	SWEDISH GP	Anderstorp	14	Stanley BRM	G	3.0 BRM P201 V12	2 laps behind	23/26
ret	DUTCH GP	Zandvoort	14	Stanley BRM	G	3.0 BRM P201 V12	gearbox	20/25
17	FRENCH GP	Paul Ricard	14	Stanley BRM	G	3.0 BRM P201 V12	2 laps behind	25/26
ret	AUSTRIAN GP	Österreichring	14	Stanley BRM	G	3.0 BRM P201 V12	engine	25/30
ret	ITALIAN GP	Monza	14	Stanley BRM	G	3.0 BRM P201 V12	engine –electrics	20/28

1976 Championship position: Unplaced

	Race	Circuit	No	Entrant	Tyres	Capacity/Car/Engine	Comment	Q Pos/Entries
10	SOUTH AFRICAN GP	Kyalami	5	John Player Team Lotus	G	3.0 JPS Lotus 77-Cosworth V8	1 lap behind	23/25
dnq	US GP WEST	Long Beach	5	John Player Team Lotus	G	3.0 JPS Lotus 77-Cosworth V8		24/27
ret	BRITISH GP	Brands Hatch	32	RAM Racing	G	3.0 Brabham BT44B-Cosworth V8	gearbox	22/30

GP Starts: 10 GP Wins: 0 Pole positions: 0 Fastest laps: 0 Points: 0

BOB EVANS

BOB EVANS was one of many British drivers of the period who, having worked tremendously hard to reach Formula 1, had neither the machinery nor the opportunity to show what they could really do. He had begun his racing career in a Sprite, before moving into Formula Ford and then F3 in 1971, but only after he had recovered from a broken neck sustained in a crash while testing at Castle Combe.

It was F5000 that provided Bob with his big breakthrough. With a solid season in a Trojan under his belt, he was supplied a Lola T332 for 1974 by long-time supporter Alan McKechnie, and he duly swept to the Rothmans championship, picking up the first-place Grovewood Award in the process.

This led to an offer to drive for BRM in 1975. The car was well past its best, and it was to Evans' credit that he plugged away so valiantly in the face of adversity. Things looked better for 1976, when Colin Chapman, impressed with his performances, gave him a testing contract – and three races, the best of which was the Race of Champions, when sadly the car ran out fuel and fourth place was lost.

Apart from a RAM drive in the British GP later that year, and a one-off outing to 11th place in the Hexagon Penske in the 1977 Race of Champions, that was that for Evans, who returned to the relative obscurity of the Aurora championship in a Surtees TS19 in 1978.

CORRADO FABI

HAVING started his racing career at the age of 12, raced a Formula 3 car before he was 18 and become a convincing European Formula 2 champion by the age of 21, Corrado Fabi was clearly a young man in a hurry – but where was he headed? Towards a brief Formula 1 career and racing oblivion, as it turned out, for today who remembers Teo's younger brother, who promised so much three decades ago?

So swift was his rise to prominence (1979 – half a season in Italian F3; 1980 – third in the European F3 championship; 1981 – third in the European Formula 2 championship; 1982 – European Formula 2 champion) that it seemed certain he was a potential world champion.

Then it was into grands prix, and a cold shower of reality, with the back-of-the-grid Osella team in 1983. Struggling to qualify must have been a culture shock for the easy-going Corrado, and after three races in a competitive car, standing in for Teo at Brabham in 1984, no more was seen of the younger Fabi in Formula 1. At the end of that season, he appeared briefly in CART for the Forsythe team (again following his brother), making four appearances, which included a sixth place at Phoenix.

With the death of his father, Corrado committed himself to family business interests, but for a brief and unsuccessful return to the track in 1987 with Genoa Racing in F3000.

FABI, Corrado (I) b 12/4/1961, Milan

1983 Championship position: Unplaced

	Race	Circuit	No	Entrant	Tyres	Capacity/Car/Engine	Comment	Q Pos/Entries
ret	BRAZILIAN GP	Rio	31	Osella Squadra Corse	M	3.0 Osella FA1D-Cosworth V8	engine	24/27
dnq	US GP WEST	Long Beach	31	Osella Squadra Corse	M	3.0 Osella FA1D-Cosworth V8		27/28
ret	FRENCH GP	Paul Ricard	31	Osella Squadra Corse	M	3.0 Osella FA1D-Cosworth V8	engine	23/29
ret	SAN MARINO GP	Imola	31	Osella Squadra Corse	M	3.0 Osella FA1D-Cosworth V8	spun off	26/28
dnq	MONACO GP	Monte Carlo	31	Osella Squadra Corse	M	3.0 Osella FA1D-Cosworth V8		24/28
ret	BELGIAN GP	Spa	31	Osella Squadra Corse	M	3.0 Osella FA1D-Cosworth V8	rear suspension	24/28
dnq	US GP (DETROIT)	Detroit	31	Osella Squadra Corse	M	3.0 Osella FA1D-Cosworth V8		27/27
ret	CANADIAN GP	Montreal	31	Osella Squadra Corse	M	3.0 Osella FA1D-Cosworth V8	engine	25/28
dnq	BRITISH GP	Silverstone	31	Osella Squadra Corse	M	3.0 Osella FA1E-Alfa Romeo V12		28/29
dnq	GERMAN GP	Hockenheim	31	Osella Squadra Corse	M	3.0 Osella FA1E-Alfa Romeo V12		28/29
10	AUSTRIAN GP	Österreichring	31	Osella Squadra Corse	M	3.0 Osella FA1E-Alfa Romeo V12	3 laps behind	26/29
11/ret	DUTCH GP	Zandvoort	31	Osella Squadra Corse	M	3.0 Osella FA1E-Alfa Romeo V12	engine	25/29
ret	ITALIAN GP	Monza	31	Osella Squadra Corse	M	3.0 Osella FA1E-Alfa Romeo V12	oil union	25/29
dnq	EUROPEAN GP	Brands Hatch	31	Osella Squadra Corse	M	3.0 Osella FA1E-Alfa Romeo V12		28/29
ret	SOUTH AFRICAN GP	Kyalami	31	Osella Squadra Corse	M	3.0 Osella FA1E-Alfa Romeo V12	engine	25/26

1984 Championship position: Unplaced

	Race	Circuit	No	Entrant	Tyres	Capacity/Car/Engine	Comment	Q Pos/Entries
ret	MONACO GP	Monte Carlo	2	MRD International	M	1.5 t/c Brabham BT53-BMW 4	water in electrics/spun off	15/27
ret	CANADIAN GP	Montreal	2	MRD International	M	1.5 t/c Brabham BT53-BMW 4	lost turbo boost	16/26
7	US GP (DALLAS)	Dallas	2	MRD International	M	1.5 t/c Brabham BT53-BMW 4	3 laps behind	11/27

GP Starts: 12   GP Wins: 0   Pole positions: 0   Fastest laps: 0   Points: 0

TEO FABI

TEO FABI was fortunate enough to have a foot in both the Formula 1 and Indy car camps. Sadly for the Italian, however, he was unable to make the most of either opportunity.

The European karting champion of 1975, Teo began his rise to prominence with fourth place in the 1978 European F3 championship, followed by a trip down-under to win the New Zealand Formula Pacific series. This set up a season in Formula 2 for 1979 with a semi-works March, but Fabi took a while to find his feet and finished a disappointed tenth in the final standings.

With the backing of Robin Herd, who rated him very highly, Teo led the works March Formula 2 effort in 1980. The season was dominated by the Toleman pair of Brian Henton and Derek Warwick, but Fabi was third, and seemed certain to join the March F1 team for 1981 until the drive went to Derek Daly at the eleventh hour. Instead, he opted for a season in Can-Am with the Paul Newman team's March 817 and won four races, but the more consistent Geoff Brabham took the title.

In 1982, the Toleman team gave Teo a grand prix opportunity that he would soon regret taking. The year was a disaster and his stock in Europe was low, but help was at hand and, with Herd's backing, he got himself a ride in Indy cars for 1983. He immediately made a name for himself when he put the Forsythe March on pole for the Indy 500 – only his second outing for the team – and led the race for 23 laps until an engine failure put him out at just before quarter-distance. However, he was the undisputed Rookie of the Year and went on to score four wins that season (at Pocono, Mid-Ohio, Laguna Seca and Phoenix) to finish runner-up to the ultra-consistent Al Unser Snr, who ironically only posted a single win.

Teo then took on a punishing schedule for 1984, accepting an offer to continue in Indy cars while racing in F1 for Brabham whenever commitments allowed; in the end, he gave up the Indy ride to concentrate full time on F1. Rejoining Toleman for 1985, he earned pole position at the Nürburgring, which indicated the car's potential, but reliability was elusive. After the takeover by Benetton, he stayed on, and the 1986 BMW-powered car proved very fast, Teo taking two pole positions, but its reliability was poor and he was generally overshadowed by his outstanding team-mate, Gerhard Berger. In 1987, Thierry Boutsen lined up alongside Fabi, and the two drivers proved to be very evenly matched in a season that yielded just a single podium for the little Italian. When Benetton decided that Alessandro Nannini would partner Boutsen in 1988, Teo realised that his chances of finding a top seat in F1 were slim and opted for a return to Indy cars in 1988, with the ambitious Porsche project. This was fraught with many problems over its three-year life, but it yielded a single win, in 1989 at Mid-Ohio. That season was his most successful with the project, and he reached fourth place in the standings.

Teo then turned successfully to endurance racing with TWR Jaguar, winning the 1991 drivers' championship, mainly by dint of his consistent finishes. He had to be content with a place in the Toyota team at Le Mans the following year, but set up yet another return to Indy cars for 1993, although his tenure with the Pennzoil Hall/VDS team would prove largely undistinguished. However, he did score a fine second place at Le Mans for Peugeot, sharing the 905 prototype with Boutsen and Yannick Dalmas In a 1-2-3 finish for the French concern.

The 1995 season saw a real return to form, however, as Teo joined forces once more with Jerry Forsythe and Robin Herd. Often a frontrunner, the little Italian was distinctly unlucky not to pick up a win, but his performances were not deemed sufficient for him to retain his seat and he was passed over in favour of Indy Lights sensation Greg Moore.

Teo made a brief return to CART action in 1996, substituting for the injured Mark Blundell with PacWest. His races at Long Beach and Nazareth were as low-key as the Italian himself, who then slipped quietly away from the racing scene to join the family talc business.

FABI, Teo (I) b 9/3/1955, Milan

1982 Championship position: Unplaced

	Race	Circuit	No	Entrant	Tyres	Capacity/Car/Engine	Comment	Q Pos/Entries
dnq	SOUTH AFRICAN GP	Kyalami	36	Candy Toleman Motorsport	P	1.5 t/c Toleman TG181B-Hart 4	no time recorded	– / –
dnq	BRAZILIAN GP	Rio	36	Candy Toleman Motorsport	P	1.5 t/c Toleman TG181B-Hart 4		27/31
dnq	US GP WEST	Long Beach	36	Candy Toleman Motorsport	P	1.5 t/c Toleman TG181C-Hart 4		27/31
nc	SAN MARINO GP	Imola	36	Toleman Group Motorsport	P	1.5 t/c Toleman TG181C-Hart 4	pit stop/8 laps behind	10/14
ret	BELGIAN GP	Zolder	36	Toleman Group Motorsport	P	1.5 t/c Toleman TG181C-Hart 4	brakes	23/32
dnpq	MONACO GP	Monte Carlo	36	Toleman Group Motorsport	P	1.5 t/c Toleman TG181C-Hart 4		27/31
dnq	DUTCH GP	Zandvoort	36	Toleman Group Motorsport	P	1.5 t/c Toleman TG181C-Hart 4		28/31
ret	BRITISH GP	Brands Hatch	36	Toleman Group Motorsport	P	1.5 t/c Toleman TG181C-Hart 4	startline accident	15/30
ret	FRENCH GP	Paul Ricard	36	Toleman Group Motorsport	P	1.5 t/c Toleman TG181C-Hart 4	oil pump drive	21/30
dnq	GERMAN GP	Hockenheim	36	Toleman Group Motorsport	P	1.5 t/c Toleman TG181C-Hart 4	no time recorded	– / –
ret	AUSTRIAN GP	Österreichring	36	Toleman Group Motorsport	P	1.5 t/c Toleman TG181C-Hart 4	driveshaft	17/29
ret	SWISS GP	Dijon	36	Toleman Group Motorsport	P	1.5 t/c Toleman TG181C-Hart 4	misfire	23/29
ret	ITALIAN GP	Monza	36	Toleman Group Motorsport	P	1.5 t/c Toleman TG181C-Hart 4	engine cut out	22/30
dnq	CAESARS PALACE GP	Las Vegas	36	Toleman Group Motorsport	P	1.5 t/c Toleman TG181C-Hart 4		28/30

1984 Championship position: 12th   Wins: 0   Pole positions: 0   Fastest laps: 0   Points scored: 9

	Race	Circuit	No	Entrant	Tyres	Capacity/Car/Engine	Comment	Q Pos/Entries
ret	BRAZILIAN GP	Rio	2	MRD International	M	1.5 t/c Brabham BT53-BMW 4	turbo	16/27
ret	SOUTH AFRICAN GP	Kyalami	2	MRD International	M	1.5 t/c Brabham BT53-BMW 4	turbo compressor	6/27
ret	BELGIAN GP	Zolder	2	MRD International	M	1.5 t/c Brabham BT53-BMW 4	spun off	18/27
ret	SAN MARINO GP	Imola	2	MRD International	M	1.5 t/c Brabham BT53-BMW 4	turbo	9/28
9	FRENCH GP	Dijon	2	MRD International	M	1.5 t/c Brabham BT53-BMW 4	1 lap behind	18/27
3*	US GP (DETROIT)	Detroit	2	MRD International	M	1.5 t/c Brabham BT53-BMW 4	*2nd place car disqualified	23/27
ret	BRITISH GP	Brands Hatch	2	MRD International	M	1.5 t/c Brabham BT53-BMW 4	electrics	14/27
ret	GERMAN GP	Hockenheim	2	MRD International	M	1.5 t/c Brabham BT53-BMW 4	lost turbo boost	8/27
4	AUSTRIAN GP	Österreichring	2	MRD International	M	1.5 t/c Brabham BT53-BMW 4		7/28
5	DUTCH GP	Zandvoort	2	MRD International	M	1.5 t/c Brabham BT53-BMW 4	1 lap behind	10/27
ret	ITALIAN GP	Monza	2	MRD International	M	1.5 t/c Brabham BT53-BMW 4	engine/broken oil line	5/27
ret	EUROPEAN GP	Nürburgring	2	MRD International	M	1.5 t/c Brabham BT53-BMW 4	gearbox	10/26

1985 Championship position: Unplaced   Wins: 0   Pole positions: 1   Fastest laps: 0   Points scored: 0

	Race	Circuit	No	Entrant	Tyres	Capacity/Car/Engine	Comment	Q Pos/Entries
ret	MONACO GP	Monte Carlo	19	Toleman Group Motorsport	P	1.5 t/c Toleman TG185-Hart 4	turbo	20/26
ret	CANADIAN GP	Montreal	19	Toleman Group Motorsport	P	1.5 t/c Toleman TG185-Hart 4	started from pit lane/turbo	18/25
ret	US GP (DETROIT)	Detroit	19	Toleman Group Motorsport	P	1.5 t/c Toleman TG185-Hart 4	clutch	13/25
14/ret	FRENCH GP	Paul Ricard	19	Toleman Group Motorsport	P	1.5 t/c Toleman TG185-Hart 4	fuel pressure/4 laps behind	19/26
ret	BRITISH GP	Silverstone	19	Toleman Group Motorsport	P	1.5 t/c Toleman TG185-Hart 4	crown wheel and pinion	9/26
ret	GERMAN GP	Nürburgring	19	Toleman Group Motorsport	P	1.5 t/c Toleman TG185-Hart 4	clutch	1/27
ret	AUSTRIAN GP	Österreichring	19	Toleman Group Motorsport	P	1.5 t/c Toleman TG185-Hart 4	electrics	6/27
ret	DUTCH GP	Zandvoort	19	Toleman Group Motorsport	P	1.5 t/c Toleman TG185-Hart 4	wheel bearing	5/27
12	ITALIAN GP	Monza	19	Toleman Group Motorsport	P	1.5 t/c Toleman TG185-Hart 4	2 pit stops – handling/4 laps behind	15/26
ret	BELGIAN GP	Spa	19	Toleman Group Motorsport	P	1.5 t/c Toleman TG185-Hart 4	throttle linkage	11/24
ret	EUROPEAN GP	Brands Hatch	19	Toleman Group Motorsport	P	1.5 t/c Toleman TG185-Hart 4	engine	20/27
ret	SOUTH AFRICAN GP	Kyalami	19	Toleman Group Motorsport	P	1.5 t/c Toleman TG185-Hart 4	engine	7/21
ret	AUSTRALIAN GP	Adelaide	19	Toleman Group Motorsport	P	1.5 t/c Toleman TG185-Hart 4	engine	24/25

1986 Championship position: 15th   Wins: 0   Pole positions: 2   Fastest laps: 1   Points scored: 2

	Race	Circuit	No	Entrant	Tyres	Capacity/Car/Engine	Comment	Q Pos/Entries
10	BRAZILIAN GP	Rio	19	Benetton Formula Ltd	P	1.5 t/c Benetton B186-BMW 4	pit stop – electrics/5 laps behind	12/25
5	SPANISH GP	Jerez	19	Benetton Formula Ltd	P	1.5 t/c Benetton B186-BMW 4	hit Laffite – pit stop/1 lap behind	9/25
ret	SAN MARINO GP	Imola	19	Benetton Formula Ltd	P	1.5 t/c Benetton B186-BMW 4	engine	10/26
ret	MONACO GP	Monte Carlo	19	Benetton Formula Ltd	P	1.5 t/c Benetton B186-BMW 4	brakes	16/26
7	BELGIAN GP	Spa	19	Benetton Formula Ltd	P	1.5 t/c Benetton B186-BMW 4	collision with Tambay/1 lap behind	6/25
ret	CANADIAN GP	Montreal	19	Benetton Formula Ltd	P	1.5 t/c Benetton B186-BMW 4	battery	15/25
ret	US GP (DETROIT)	Detroit	19	Benetton Formula Ltd	P	1.5 t/c Benetton B186-BMW 4	gearbox	17/26
ret	FRENCH GP	Paul Ricard	19	Benetton Formula Ltd	P	1.5 t/c Benetton B186-BMW 4	engine misfire	9/26
ret	BRITISH GP	Brands Hatch	19	Benetton Formula Ltd	P	1.5 t/c Benetton B186-BMW 4	fuel system	7/26
ret	GERMAN GP	Hockenheim	19	Benetton Formula Ltd	P	1.5 t/c Benetton B186-BMW 4	accident at start	9/26
ret	HUNGARIAN GP	Hungaroring	19	Benetton Formula Ltd	P	1.5 t/c Benetton B186-BMW 4	transmission – spun off	13/26
ret	AUSTRIAN GP	Österreichring	19	Benetton Formula Ltd	P	1.5 t/c Benetton B186-BMW 4	engine	1/26
ret	ITALIAN GP	Monza	19	Benetton Formula Ltd	P	1.5 t/c Benetton B186-BMW 4	started from back/puncture/FL	1/27
8	PORTUGUESE GP	Estoril	19	Benetton Formula Ltd	P	1.5 t/c Benetton B186-BMW 4	2 laps behind	5/27
ret	MEXICAN GP	Mexico City	19	Benetton Formula Ltd	P	1.5 t/c Benetton B186-BMW 4	engine	9/26
10	AUSTRALIAN GP	Adelaide	19	Benetton Formula Ltd	P	1.5 t/c Benetton B186-BMW 4	2 pit stops – tyres/5 laps behind	13/26

1987 Championship position: 9th   Wins: 0   Pole positions: 0   Fastest laps: 1   Points scored: 12

	Race	Circuit	No	Entrant	Tyres	Capacity/Car/Engine	Comment	Q Pos/Entries
ret	BRAZILIAN GP	Rio	19	Benetton Formula Ltd	G	1.5 t/c Benetton B187-Cosworth V6	turbo	4/23
ret	SAN MARINO GP	Imola	19	Benetton Formula Ltd	G	1.5 t/c Benetton B187-Cosworth V6	turbo/FL	5/27
ret	BELGIAN GP	Spa	19	Benetton Formula Ltd	G	1.5 t/c Benetton B187-Cosworth V6	engine – oil pump drive belt	9/26
8	MONACO GP	Monte Carlo	19	Benetton Formula Ltd	G	1.5 t/c Benetton B187-Cosworth V6	2 laps behind	12/26
ret	US GP (DETROIT)	Detroit	19	Benetton Formula Ltd	G	1.5 t/c Benetton B187-Cosworth V6	accident with Cheever	8/26
5/ret	FRENCH GP	Paul Ricard	19	Benetton Formula Ltd	G	1.5 t/c Benetton B187-Cosworth V6	driveshaft/3 laps behind	7/26
6	BRITISH GP	Silverstone	19	Benetton Formula Ltd	G	1.5 t/c Benetton B187-Cosworth V6	2 laps behind	6/26
ret	GERMAN GP	Hockenheim	19	Benetton Formula Ltd	G	1.5 t/c Benetton B187-Cosworth V6	engine	9/26
ret	HUNGARIAN GP	Hungaroring	19	Benetton Formula Ltd	G	1.5 t/c Benetton B187-Cosworth V6	gearbox	12/26
3	AUSTRIAN GP	Österreichring	19	Benetton Formula Ltd	G	1.5 t/c Benetton B187-Cosworth V6	1 lap behind	5/26
7	ITALIAN GP	Monza	19	Benetton Formula Ltd	G	1.5 t/c Benetton B187-Cosworth V6	1 lap behind	7/28
4/ret	PORTUGUESE GP	Estoril	19	Benetton Formula Ltd	G	1.5 t/c Benetton B187-Cosworth V6	out of fuel/1 lap behind	10/27
ret	SPANISH GP	Jerez	19	Benetton Formula Ltd	G	1.5 t/c Benetton B187-Cosworth V6	engine	6/28
5	MEXICAN GP	Mexico City	19	Benetton Formula Ltd	G	1.5 t/c Benetton B187-Cosworth V6	2 laps behind	6/27
ret	JAPANESE GP	Suzuka	19	Benetton Formula Ltd	G	1.5 t/c Benetton B187-Cosworth V6	engine	6/27
ret	AUSTRALIAN GP	Adelaide	19	Benetton Formula Ltd	G	1.5 t/c Benetton B187-Cosworth V6	brakes	9/27

GP Starts: 64   GP Wins: 0   Pole positions: 3   Fastest laps: 2   Points: 23

FABRE, Pascal (F) b 9/1/1960, Lyon

1987 Championship position: Unplaced

	Race	Circuit	No	Entrant	Tyres	Capacity/Car/Engine	Comment	Q Pos/Entries
12*	BRAZILIAN GP	Rio	14	Team El Charro AGS	G	3.5 AGS JH22-Cosworth V8	*3rd non-turbo/6 laps behind	22/23
13*	SAN MARINO GP	Imola	14	Team El Charro AGS	G	3.5 AGS JH22-Cosworth V8	*3rd non-turbo/6 laps behind	26/27
10/ret	BELGIAN GP	Spa	14	Team El Charro AGS	G	3.5 AGS JH22-Cosworth V8	*3rd non-turbo/electrics/-5 laps	25/26
13*	MONACO GP	Monte Carlo	14	Team El Charro AGS	G	3.5 AGS JH22-Cosworth V8	*3rd non-turbo/7 laps behind	24/26
12*	US GP (DETROIT)	Detroit	14	Team El Charro AGS	G	3.5 AGS JH22-Cosworth V8	*3rd non-turbo/5 laps behind	26/26
9*	FRENCH GP	Paul Ricard	14	Team El Charro AGS	G	3.5 AGS JH22-Cosworth V8	*3rd non-turbo/6 laps behind	26/26
9*	BRITISH GP	Silverstone	14	Team El Charro AGS	G	3.5 AGS JH22-Cosworth V8	*2nd non-turbo/6 laps behind	26/26
ret	GERMAN GP	Hockenheim	14	Team El Charro AGS	G	3.5 AGS JH22-Cosworth V8	engine	25/26
13*	HUNGARIAN GP	Hungaroring	14	Team El Charro AGS	G	3.5 AGS JH22-Cosworth V8	*4th non-turbo/5 laps behind	26/26
nc	AUSTRIAN GP	Österreichring	14	Team El Charro AGS	G	3.5 AGS JH22-Cosworth V8	started from pit lane/7 laps behind	26/26
dnq	ITALIAN GP	Monza	14	Team El Charro AGS	G	3.5 AGS JH22-Cosworth V8		28/28
dnq	PORTUGUESE GP	Estoril	14	Team El Charro AGS	G	3.5 AGS JH22-Cosworth V8		27/27
ret	SPANISH GP	Jerez	14	Team El Charro AGS	G	3.5 AGS JH22-Cosworth V8	clutch	25/26
dnq	MEXICAN GP	Mexico City	14	Team El Charro AGS	G	3.5 AGS JH22-Cosworth V8		27/27

GP Starts: 11   GP Wins: 0   Pole positions: 0   Fastest laps: 0   Points: 0

PASCAL FABRE

ALTHOUGH he seemed quite promising in his first season of Formula 2 in 1982, when paired with the very quick Philippe Streiff in the little AGS team, Pascal Fabre was forced to drop back into European F3 the following year. Despite a bright start, lack of finance forced his Martini off the grid before the season was out. Back in F2 in 1984, he surprised many with his speed in a March-BMW, winning at Hockenheim in mid-season, only to depart abruptly from his team due to financial differences.

Fabre's plans for a Formula 3000 drive in 1985 fell through, and he had to settle for a single race at the end of the year before arranging a full season with a minimal budget in 1986. A winning start at Silverstone, followed by a second at Vallelunga, gave him an early-season lead that he was unable to maintain, slumping down to seventh in the championship table.

Prompted no doubt by Fabre's past links with the team, AGS chose him to drive their F1 challenger in 1987. The car was slow, but he flogged away, usually bringing it to the finish, until he was replaced by the talented Roberto Moreno, who lost little time in scoring the team's first championship point.

Fabre moved on to sports cars, most notably with the Courage-Porsche project between 1989 and 1994, and then opted for the GT classes, racing a McLaren GT and a Ferrari 333SP. His most notable result was fifth place at Le Mans in 2001 in a Reynard, shared with Marc Gené and Jean-Denis Délétraz.

LUIGI FAGIOLI

KNOWN affectionately as the 'old Abruzzi robber', Luigi Fagioli was one of Italy's greatest drivers and a true individualist, who often found himself at odds with those in authority. His career started in 1926, but he really shot to fame upon joining the Maserati team in 1930. Over the next three seasons, he won occasionally, but often was out of luck, which prompted him to join Ferrari's Alfa Romeo team in the second half of the 1933 season. Soon he had won the GPs of Pescara, Comminges, Marseilles and Italy, which brought an invitation to drive for Mercedes-Benz as number-two driver in 1934.

In his first race, the Eifelrennen, irked at being told to stay behind the sister entry of Manfred von Brauchitsch, Fagioli showed his displeasure by parking his car out on the circuit and returning to the pits on foot. It was not the last time he found himself in conflict with the team, but that did not stop him from winning the Italian and Spanish GPs that year, and those at Monaco, AVUS and Barcelona the following season. He continued with the team for 1936, before moving to their great rivals, Auto Union, but he was forced to miss much of the season through illness, although he was fifth at Tripoli.

In fact, Fagioli did not return to the grand prix arena until 1950, with the all-conquering Alfa Romeo team. His experience stood him in good stead, and some cold and calculating performances brought him third place in the world championship. He was retained for 1951, but at the French GP he was hauled from the car at a pit stop as he recovered from an early spin to allow Juan Fangio to take over and complete the race, the Argentinian going on to win. This was the last straw for the proud Fagioli, and he never raced a grand prix car again.

Turning to his own OSCA, Fagioli won his class in the Mille Miglia, a feat that he repeated in 1952 at the wheel of a Lancia Aurelia tourer. More remarkable was the fact that he was third overall, ahead of many pure sports racers. That year, the Monaco GP was held for sports cars only, and during practice he lost control of his car in the tunnel and broadsided out into a stone balustrade. Thrown out, he was taken to hospital unconscious, with a broken arm and leg. Four days later, he regained consciousness and seemed to be out of danger, but three weeks after the crash, he suffered a relapse – with a complete failure of the nervous system – and died, aged 54.

FAGIOLI, Luigi (I) b 9/6/1898, Osimo, nr Ancona – d 20/6/1952, Monte Carlo, Monaco

1950 Championship position: 3rd   Wins: 0   Pole positions: 0   Fastest laps: 0   Points scored: 28

	Race	Circuit	No	Entrant	Tyres	Capacity/Car/Engine	Comment	Q Pos/Entries
2	BRITISH GP	Silverstone	3	Alfa Romeo SpA	P	1.5 s/c Alfa Romeo 158 8		2/21
ret	MONACO GP	Monte Carlo	36	Alfa Romeo SpA	P	1.5 s/c Alfa Romeo 158 8	multiple accident on lap 1	5/21
2	SWISS GP	Bremgarten	12	Alfa Romeo SpA	P	1.5 s/c Alfa Romeo 158 8		3/18
2	BELGIAN GP	Spa	12	Alfa Romeo SpA	P	1.5 s/c Alfa Romeo 158 8		3/14
2	FRENCH GP	Reims	4	Alfa Romao SpA	P	1.5 s/c Alfa Romeo 158 8		3/20
3	ITALIAN GP	Monza	36	Alfa Romeo SpA	P	1.5 s/c Alfa Romeo 158 8		5/27

1951 Championship position: 9th   Wins: 1 (shared)   Pole positions: 0   Fastest laps: 0   Points scored: 4

	Race	Circuit	No	Entrant	Tyres	Capacity/Car/Engine	Comment	Q Pos/Entries
1*	FRENCH GP	Reims	8	Alfa Romeo SpA	P	1.5 s/c Alfa Romeo 159 8	*Fangio took over car	7/23
11*	"	"	4	Alfa Romeo SpA	P	1.5 s/c Alfa Romeo 159 8	*took Fangio's car/22 laps behind	- / -

GP Starts: 7   GP Wins: 1*(shared)   Pole positions: 0   Fastest laps: 0   Points: 32

JACK FAIRMAN

AN engineer, Jack Fairman began competing in 1934 with a 12/50 Alvis in trials, soon moving on to hill-climbs and events at Brooklands. These remained his staple diet until the Second World War intervened, during which he saw service in the Tank Corps.

Jack's career moved on to a wider stage in the late 1940s, when he raced at Le Mans and Spa for the first time. Strong as an ox, and an extremely safe and reliable driver, he was ideally suited to long-distance sports car racing, in which he raced with distinction for Bristol, Jaguar, Ecurie Ecosse and Aston Martin during the 1950s. His greatest successes came in 1959 when, driving the Aston, he won the Nürburgring 1000km (with Stirling Moss at his brilliant best) and the Tourist Trophy at Goodwood (with Moss and Carroll Shelby).

With his engineering background, Fairman was also in great demand as a test driver and was instrumental in developing the Connaught GP car, being rewarded with points finishes in each of his two grand prix appearances in 1956.

Jack seemed to thrive on picking up irregular rides here and there, and raced a bewildering succession of machines in different categories (including, on occasion, works cars from Cooper and BRM, and the Rob Walker 4WD Ferguson) during an extremely long career that lasted into the early 1960s. His final Formula 1 race was in 1963 at the City of Imola GP, where he took over one of de Beaufort's Ecurie Maarsbergen Porsches at short notice, finishing a distant seventh.

FAIRMAN, Jack (GB) b 15/3/1913, Smallfield, nr Horley, Surrey – d 7/2/2002, Rugby, Warwickshire

1953 Championship position: Unplaced

	Race	Circuit	No	Entrant	Tyres	Capacity/Car/Engine	Comment	Q Pos/Entries
ret	BRITISH GP	Silverstone	4	John Heath	D	2.0 HWM-Alta 4	clutch	27/29
nc	ITALIAN GP	Monza	20	Connaught Engineering	D	2.0 Connaught A-Lea Francis 4	19 laps behind	22/30

1955 Championship position: Unplaced

	Race	Circuit	No	Entrant	Tyres	Capacity/Car/Engine	Comment	Q Pos/Entries
dns	BRITISH GP	Aintree	34	Connaught Engineering	D	2.5 Connaught B-Alta 4	engine problems	(21)/25

1956 Championship position: 8th   Wins: 0   Pole positions: 0   Fastest laps: 0   Points scored: 5

	Race	Circuit	No	Entrant	Tyres	Capacity/Car/Engine	Comment	Q Pos/Entries
4	BRITISH GP	Silverstone	21	Connaught Engineering	P	2.5 Connaught B-Alta 4	3 laps behind	21/28
5	ITALIAN GP	Monza	6	Connaught Engineering	P/A	2.5 Connaught B-Alta 4	3 laps behind	16/26

1957 Championship position: Unplaced

	Race	Circuit	No	Entrant	Tyres	Capacity/Car/Engine	Comment	Q Pos/Entries
ret	BRITISH GP	Aintree	24	Owen Racing Organisation	D	2.5 BRM P25 4	engine	16/19

1958 Championship position: Unplaced

	Race	Circuit	No	Entrant	Tyres	Capacity/Car/Engine	Comment	Q Pos/Entries
ret	BRITISH GP	Silverstone	14	B C Ecclestone	D	2.5 Connaught B-Alta 4	ignition	19/21
8	MOROCCAN GP	Casablanca	32	Cooper Car Co	D	2.0 Cooper T45-Climax 4	3 laps behind	11/25

1959 Championship position: Unplaced

	Race	Circuit	No	Entrant	Tyres	Capacity/Car/Engine	Comment	Q Pos/Entries
ret	BRITISH GP	Aintree	38	High Efficiency Motors	D	2.2 Cooper T45-Climax 4	gearbox	15/30
ret	ITALIAN GP	Monza	22	High Efficiency Motors	D	2.5 Cooper T45-Maserati 4	engine	20/21

1960 Championship position: Unplaced

	Race	Circuit	No	Entrant	Tyres	Capacity/Car/Engine	Comment	Q Pos/Entries
ret	BRITISH GP	Silverstone	23	C T Atkins	D	2.5 Cooper T51-Climax 4	fuel pump	15/25

1961 Championship position: Unplaced

	Race	Circuit	No	Entrant	Tyres	Capacity/Car/Engine	Comment	Q Pos/Entries
dsq*	BRITISH GP	Aintree	26	R R C Walker Racing Team	D	1.5 Ferguson P99-Climax 4	Moss took car/*earlier push start	20/30
ret	ITALIAN GP	Monza	30	Fred Tuck	D	1.5 Cooper T45-Climax 4	engine	26/33

GP Starts: 12   GP Wins: 0   Pole positions: 0   Fastest laps: 0   Points: 5

JUAN MANUEL FANGIO

JUAN MANUEL FANGIO will always be 'the Maestro' and justifiably so. For all his phenomenal achievements in grand prix racing – five world championships and 24 wins from just 51 starts – it was as much the way he conducted himself outside the cockpit that created an aura that exists to this day.

Fangio's origins were humble. The son of an Italian immigrant family, he grew up in Argentina in a motoring environment, working in a garage from the age of 11 to supplement the family income. He saved everything he could towards the purchase of a Model T Ford, which he raced secretly before switching to a Ford V8 special and the real beginnings of his competition career. Supported by the people of his home town, Balcarce, he acquired a Chevrolet and won the 1940 Gran Premio del Norte, a 5,900-mile road race, scoring his first major success. Throughout the next seven years, he raced in these marathons with a Chevrolet, often competing with 'Los Gálvez' for top honours.

When Achille Varzi, Luigi Villoresi, Giuseppe Farina and Jean-Pierre Wimille were invited to appear in Libre events in 1948, Fangio was among their local opposition, and he performed so well that he was sponsored for a brief trip to Europe in 1948, driving a Simca-Gordini at Reims before returning home with a Maserati 4CLT.

For 1949, Fangio was back in Europe and, at the age of 38, enjoyed a staggering debut season, winning his first race at San Remo, and following it up with wins at Perpignan, Marseilles, Pau, Albi and Monza. This led to an invitation to join the Alfa Romeo team in 1950, and eventually he finished second in the world championship to Farina, despite winning three of the six races. He also won at Pescara, Geneva and San Remo in the Alfa, and at Pau and Angoulême in a Maserati. After handling the pre-war Mercedes in the early-season Libre events back in Argentina, he took the first of his five titles in 1951, before Alfa withdrew from competition.

In 1952, the newly crowned champion started the year in imperious form on his home continent, winning six Libre events in Argentina, Brazil and Uruguay, before returning to Europe to drive for Maserati. However, Fangio crashed at the Monza GP and was lucky to escape with his life, suffering concussion and a broken vertebra in his neck when he was thrown from the car. He convalesced in Balcarce for the rest of the season, and had leisure to ponder the thin dividing line between glory and disaster, but it did not prevent him from undertaking an even bigger racing schedule in 1953. He drove Maserati's A6GCM to victory in the Italian and Modena GPs, and also took the opportunity to return to his roots by winning the Carrera Panamericana road race in a works Lancia.

Fangio's stature was unrivalled, and Mercedes-Benz made it their top priority to sign him when they re-entered racing in 1954. While the cars were being prepared, he continued to drive for Maserati, winning the first two races of the season before scoring another four wins in the silver machine. The combination of Fangio's sublime talent and German technology was overwhelming, and if the car lasted he generally won. Such was his mastery that it is thought he allowed team-mates Karl Kling and Stirling Moss to take victories at AVUS and Aintree respectively, although he never admitted it. Despite being a relatively old man in grand prix terms by that stage, he had all the resources necessary to maintain his dominant position, his seemingly inexhaustible talents being equal to the demands of any situation. If there was a corner that needed to be taken flat out, then Fangio would do it; his physical strength and stamina allowed him to cope with broiling heat or pouring rain; and his powers of concentration enabled him to annihilate the opposition when his car ran well, or nurse a sick machine to the chequered flag when lesser mortals would have given up.

The Argentinian also had the acumen to choose the best machinery available and then make the best possible use of it. Even an uncomfortable year at Scuderia Ferrari in 1956, where he could have been undermined by the young Italian pretenders, did not prevent him from taking a fourth world championship, but he moved back to Maserati for 1957 and, with the 250F in the final stages of its useful development, took his fifth and perhaps finest championship win, highlighted by one of grand prix racing's greatest ever performances at the Nürburgring, where he overhauled Mike Hawthorn and Peter Collins to win a sensational German GP, having gambled that a pit stop for fresh tyres would pay off rather than running non-stop as did the Ferraris. His personal standards were such that at each track he set out to better his previous performances there. He was the world champion and it was expected, but at the Italian GP even he could not defeat Moss, by then nearly his equal as a driver. With the advantage of driving one of the emerging Vanwalls, Moss repeated the win at Pescara, and the writing was on the wall for Fangio. Having no wish to return to Ferrari, and with Maserati winding down their operation, his thoughts were perhaps turning to retirement, but in the event he carried on into 1958 as an independent, selecting his races. After a fourth place in the Argentine GP, he took his final win in the Libre Buenos Aires GP. Then he was tempted to Indianapolis to take part in the famous 500 and, despite being given a car that was far from new, duly passed his qualification tests, but he was unhappy with the machine. Perhaps fortuitously, he was forced to return home to deal with an urgent matter relating to his garage business and thus missed the race, which was marred by tragedy after a multiple crash on the first lap.

For Fangio, there was just one more grand prix, and it was perhaps one of his best. Coming home fourth, he could have been lapped right at the finish by the winner, Hawthorn, who chose to spare him this indignity. However, the spectators were unaware that he had raced without the benefit of a clutch from early on. With the engine turning at 8,000rpm, 'the Maestro' had relied on his ears to judge when to change gear throughout the race in a remarkable display that demonstrated his legendary empathy with his machinery. He went home to Balcarce and never returned as a driver, deciding that the time was right for him to stop. Of course his presence graced the circuits on many further occasions, and he held a magnetic attraction for young and old alike, who recognised that they were rubbing shoulders not only with a legendary racing driver, but also with a man of great sincerity and generosity of heart to whom the sport owes a great debt.

Fangio and Moss demonstrate the might of their Mercedes as they cruise to an easy 1-2 victory in the 1955 Dutch Grand Prix at Zandvoort. The team would pull out of motor racing following the Le Mans disaster later that year.

FANGIO, Juan Manuel (RA) b 24/6/1911, Balcarce, Buenos Aires – d 17/7/1995, Balcarce, Buenos Aires

1950 Championship position: 2nd   Wins: 3   Pole positions: 4   Fastest laps: 3   Points scored: 27

	Race	Circuit	No	Entrant	Tyres	Capacity/Car/Engine	Comment	Q Pos/Entries
ret	BRITISH GP	Silverstone	1	Alfa Romeo SpA	P	1.5 s/c Alfa Romeo 158 8	oil pipe	3/21
1	MONACO GP	Monte Carlo	34	Alfa Romeo SpA	P	1.5 s/c Alfa Romeo 158 8	FL	1/21
ret	SWISS GP	Bremgarten	14	Alfa Romeo SpA	P	1.5 s/c Alfa Romeo 158 8	valve	1/18
1	BELGIAN GP	Spa	10	Alfa Romeo SpA	P	1.5 s/c Alfa Romeo 158 8		2/14
1	FRENCH GP	Reims	6	Alfa Romeo SpA	P	1.5 s/c Alfa Romeo 158 8	FL	1/20
ret	ITALIAN GP	Monza	18	Alfa Romeo SpA	P	1.5 s/c Alfa Romeo 158 8	gearbox/FL	1/27
ret	"	"	60	Alfa Romeo SpA	P	1.5 s/c Alfa Romeo 158 8	took over Taruffi's Car	- / -

1951 WORLD CHAMPION   Wins: 3 (1 shared)   Pole positions: 4   Fastest laps: 5   Points scored: 37

	Race	Circuit	No	Entrant	Tyres	Capacity/Car/Engine	Comment	Q Pos/Entries
1	SWISS GP	Bremgarten	24	Alfa Romeo SpA	P	1.5 s/c Alfa Romeo 159 8	FL	1/21
9	BELGIAN GP	Spa	2	Alfa Romeo SpA	P	1.5 s/c Alfa Romeo 159 8	jammed rear wheel in pits/FL	1/13
11*	FRENCH GP	Reims	4	Alfa Romeo SpA	P	1.5 s/c Alfa Romeo 159 8	*Fagioli took over	1/23
1*	"	"	8	Alfa Romeo SpA	P	1.5 s/c Alfa Romeo 159 8	*took over Fagioli's car/FL	- / -
2	BRITISH GP	Silverstone	2	Alfa Romeo SpA	P	1.5 s/c Alfa Romeo 159 8		2/20
2	GERMAN GP	Nürburgring	75	Alfa Romeo SpA	P	1.5 s/c Alfa Romeo 159 8	FL	3/23
ret	ITALIAN GP	Monza	38	Alfa Romeo SpA	P	1.5 s/c Alfa Romeo 159 8	engine	1/22
1	SPANISH GP	Pedralbes	22	Alfa Romeo SpA	P	1.5 s/c Alfa Romeo 159 8	FL	2/20

1953 Championship position: 2nd   Wins: 1   Pole positions: 2   Fastest laps: 2 (1 shared)   Points scored: 29

	Race	Circuit	No	Entrant	Tyres	Capacity/Car/Engine	Comment	Q Pos/Entries
ret	ARGENTINE GP	Buenos Aires	2	Officine Alfieri Maserati	P	2.0 Maserati A6GCM 6	universal joint	2/16
ret	DUTCH GP	Zandvoort	12	Officine Alfieri Maserati	P	2.0 Maserati A6GCM 6	rear axle	2/20
ret	BELGIAN GP	Spa	4	Officine Alfieri Maserati	P	2.0 Maserati A6GCM 6	engine	1/22
ret	"	"	6	Officine Alfieri Maserati	P	2.0 Maserati A6GCM 6	took Claes' car/steering failed - crashed	- / -
2	FRENCH GP	Reims	18	Officine Alfieri Maserati	P	2.0 Maserati A6GCM 6	FL (shared)	4/25
2	BRITISH GP	Silverstone	23	Officine Alfieri Maserati	P	2.0 Maserati A6GCM 6		4/29
2	GERMAN GP	Nürburgring	5	Officine Alfieri Maserati	P	2.0 Maserati A6GCM 6		2/35
4*	SWISS GP	Bremgarten	32	Officine Alfieri Maserati	P	2.0 Maserati A6GCM 6	*Bonetto took over/1 lap behind	1/23
ret	"	"	30	Officine Alfieri Maserati	P	2.0 Maserati A6GCM 6	*took Bonetto's car	- / -
1	ITALIAN GP	Monza	50	Officine Alfieri Maserati	P	2.0 Maserati A6GCM 6	FL	2/30

1954 WORLD CHAMPION   Wins: 6   Pole positions: 5   Fastest laps: 3 (1 shared)   Points scored: 57.14

	Race	Circuit	No	Entrant	Tyres	Capacity/Car/Engine	Comment	Q Pos/Entries
1	ARGENTINE GP	Buenos Aires	2	Officine Alfieri Maserati	P	2.5 Maserati 250F 6		3/18
1	BELGIAN GP	Spa	26	Officine Alfieri Maserati	P	2.5 Maserati 250F 6	FL	1/15
1	FRENCH GP	Reims	18	Daimler Benz AG	C	2.5 Mercedes-Benz W196 str 8		1/22
4	BRITISH GP	Silverstone	1	Daimler Benz AG	C	2.5 Mercedes-Benz W196 str 8	FL (shared)/1 lap behind	1/31
1	GERMAN GP	Nürburgring	18	Daimler Benz AG	C	2.5 Mercedes-Benz W196 8		1/23
1	SWISS GP	Bremgarten	4	Daimler Benz AG	C	2.5 Mercedes-Benz W196 8	FL	2/15
1	ITALIAN GP	Monza	16	Daimler Benz AG	C	2.5 Mercedes-Benz W196 str 8		1/21
3	SPANISH GP	Pedralbes	2	Daimler Benz AG	C	2.5 Mercedes-Benz W196 8	1 lap behind	2/22

1955 WORLD CHAMPION   Wins: 4   Pole positions: 3   Fastest laps: 3   Points scored: 41

	Race	Circuit	No	Entrant	Tyres	Capacity/Car/Engine	Comment	Q Pos/Entries
1	ARGENTINE GP	Buenos Aires	2	Daimler Benz AG	C	2.5 Mercedes-Benz W196 8	FL	2/22
ret	MONACO GP	Monte Carlo	2	Daimler Benz AG	C	2.5 Mercedes-Benz W196 8	rear axle/FL	1/22
1	BELGIAN GP	Spa	10	Daimler Benz AG	C	2.5 Mercedes-Benz W196 8	FL	2/14
1	DUTCH GP	Zandvoort	8	Daimler Benz AG	C	2.5 Mercedes-Benz W196 8		1/16
2	BRITISH GP	Aintree	10	Daimler Benz AG	C	2.5 Mercedes-Benz W196 8		2/25
1	ITALIAN GP	Monza	18	Daimler Benz AG	C	2.5 Mercedes-Benz W196 str 8		1/22

1956 WORLD CHAMPION   Wins: 2 (1 shared)   Pole positions: 6   Fastest laps: 4   Points scored: 33

	Race	Circuit	No	Entrant	Tyres	Capacity/Car/Engine	Comment	Q Pos/Entries
ret	ARGENTINE GP	Buenos Aires	30	Scuderia Ferrari	E	2.5 Lancia-Ferrari D50 V8	fuel pump	1/15
1*	"	"	34	Scuderia Ferrari	E	2.5 Lancia-Ferrari D50 V8	*took over Musso's car/FL	- / -
4*	MONACO GP	Monte Carlo	20	Scuderia Ferrari	E	2.5 Lancia-Ferrari D50 V8	*Castellotti took over car/-6 laps	1/19
2*	"	"	26	Scuderia Ferrari	E	2.5 Lancia-Ferrari D50 V8	*took over Collins' car/FL no points	- / -

ret	BELGIAN GP	Spa	2	Scuderia Ferrari	E	2.5 Lancia-Ferrari D50 V8	transmission	1/16
4	FRENCH GP	Reims	10	Scuderia Ferrari	E	2.5 Lancia-Ferrari D50 V8	pit stop – split fuel pipe/FL	1/20
1	BRITISH GP	Silverstone	1	Scuderia Ferrari	E	2.5 Lancia-Ferrari D50 V8		2/28
1	GERMAN GP	Nürburgring	1	Scuderia Ferrari	E	2.5 Lancia-Ferrari D50 V8	FL	1/21
8*	ITALIAN GP	Monza	22	Scuderia Ferrari	E	2.5 Lancia-Ferrari D50 V8	*Castellotti took over car/-4 laps	1/26
2*	"	"	26	Scuderia Ferrari	E	2.5 Lancia-Ferrari D50 V8	*took over Collins' car	– / –

1957 WORLD CHAMPION Wins: 4 Pole positions: 4 Fastest laps: 2 Points scored: 46

1	ARGENTINE GP	Buenos Aires	2	Officine Alfieri Maserati	P	2.5 Maserati 250F 6		2/16
1	MONACO GP	Monte Carlo	32	Officine Alfieri Maserati	P	2.5 Maserati 250F 6	FL	1/21
dns	"	"	32	Officine Alfieri Maserati	P	2.5 Maserati 250F V12	practice only	– / –
1	FRENCH GP	Rouen	2	Officine Alfieri Maserati	P	2.5 Maserati 250F 6		1/15
ret	BRITISH GP	Aintree	2	Officine Alfieri Maserati	P	2.5 Maserati 250F 6	engine	4/19
1	GERMAN GP	Nürburgring	1	Officine Alfieri Maserati	P	2.5 Maserati 250F 6	FL	1/24
2	PESCARA GP	Pescara	2	Officine Alfieri Maserati	P	2.5 Maserati 250F 6		1/16
dns	"	"	2	Officine Alfieri Maserati	P	2.5 Maserati 250F V12	practice only	– / –
2	ITALIAN GP	Monza	2	Officine Alfieri Maserati	P	2.5 Maserati 250F 6		4/19
dns	"	"	2	Officine Alfieri Maserati	P	2.5 Maserati 250F V12	practice only	– / –

1958 Championship position: 14th Wins: 0 Pole positions: 1 Fastest laps: 1 Points scored: 7

4	ARGENTINE GP	Buenos Aires	2	Scuderia Sud Americana	P	2.5 Maserati 250F 6	FL	1/10
4	FRENCH GP	Reims	34	Juan Manuel Fangio	P	2.5 Maserati 250F 6	lost clutch	8/21

GP Starts: 51   GP Wins: 24   Pole positions: 29   Fastest laps: 23   Points: 277.14

Fangio's finest year came in 1957, at the wheel of a Maserati, when he saw off the stern challenge of the British Vanwall cars. Pictured above in splendid sunshine, he negotiates the hairpin on his way to victory in the French GP at Rouen-les-Essarts.

By general consensus, the 1957 German Grand Prix was Fangio's greatest race. After a scintillating drive, the maestro celebrates his stunning triumph with his defeated Ferrari rivals Peter Collins and Mike Hawthorn. It would be the Argentinian's 24th and final world championship victory.

GIUSEPPE FARINA

VERY much his own man, a private person, Giuseppe 'Nino' Farina did not make any great attempts to mix and guarded his private life jealously. He even played down his achievement in becoming world champion in 1950, refusing to become involved in the razzmatazz that followed.

By the time Farina won the title, he was one of the most senior campaigners still regularly active, having made his competition debut in the Aosta-St

Bernard hill-climb as far back as 1932. It was a chastening experience, for he crashed and ended up in hospital, but this would be only the first of many accidents sustained in a long career by this tough, aristocratic Italian who seemed totally indestructible.

After driving a Maserati with little success, Farina's first break came when he raced an Alfa Romeo under the tutelage of the great Tazio Nuvolari. At that time, the red cars were outclassed by the mighty German machines and the young Farina often ran out of road in his desperate attempts to keep pace. He did win the Naples GP in 1937, however, and was Italian champion in the years 1937–39, with further successes in the Alfa Romeo 158 at the Antwerp GP, Coppa Ciano and Prix de Berne. He also gave a fantastic display at the 1939 Swiss GP with the underpowered Alfa, leading many faster cars before giving way. Having won the Tripoli GP, Farina was probably reaching his peak when the Second World War suspended all racing activity, but in 1946 he returned to immediate effect, winning the GP des Nations at Geneva. Enzo Ferrari had great regard for his ability; he excelled on fast courses with his imperious, upright, arms-at-length driving style.

In 1948, Farina drove an independent Maserati, winning at Monaco, Geneva and Mar del Plata, and he continued with the car into the following season, when he won the Lausanne GP and finished second in the International Trophy, but he also drove for Ferrari, winning the Rosario GP in a Tipo 166.

When Alfa Romeo returned to action in 1950, Farina joined Juan Fangio and Luigi Fagioli in the classic 158s and, keeping a cool head and showing tremendous courage, took the first ever world championship for drivers. In 1951, he remained with Alfa and won the Belgian GP, but was outshone by Fangio; he would find the same problem when he joined Ferrari the following year. With Alberto Ascari sweeping all before him, 'Nino' was left in his wake, picking up wins only in the minor GPs at Naples and Monza. He was none too happy to play second fiddle, but generally was unable to match the searing pace set by his team-mate, although he did take a brilliant win in the German GP after losing a wheel. When Ascari moved to Lancia for 1954, Farina sniffed another title chance after a bright start to the season, which included a win in the Syracuse GP, but after crashing in the Mille Miglia, he recovered only to be involved in a very nasty incident at Monza, where his car caught fire, leaving him with badly burned legs.

Farina bravely returned in 1955, needing morphine to complete the Argentine GP, in which he shared two cars. He also took points at Monaco and Spa. His injuries caused him to announce his retirement at the end of the season, but he was soon back in a half-hearted attempt to qualify at Indianapolis, before yet another accident in practice at the Monza Supercortemaggiore race, which left him with a broken collarbone. Having recovered once more, he returned to Indy, but after his car was crashed with fatal results by a young American, Keith Andrews, he lost interest and retired for good.

It was ironic that after surviving so many racing accidents, Farina should lose his life in a road accident in 1966, when crashed his Lotus Cortina en-route to the French Grand Prix.

FARINA, Giuseppe (I) b 30/10/1906, Turin – d 30/6/1966, Aiguebelle, nr Chambéry, France

1950 WORLD CHAMPION Wins: 3   Pole positions: 2   Fastest laps: 4   Points scored: 30

	Race	Car	No	Entrant	Tyres	Capacity/Car/Engine	Comment	Q Pos/Entries
1	BRITISH GP	Silverstone	2	Alfa Romeo SpA	P	1.5 s/c Alfa Romeo 158 8	FL	1/21
ret	MONACO GP	Monte Carlo	32	Alfa Romeo SpA	P	1.5 s/c Alfa Romeo 158 8	multiple accident on lap 1	2/21
1	SWISS GP	Bremgarten	16	Alfa Romeo SpA	P	1.5 s/c Alfa Romeo 158 8	FL	2/18
4	BELGIAN GP	Spa	8	Alfa Romeo SpA	P	1.5 s/c Alfa Romeo 158 8	long pit stop/FL	1/14
ret	FRENCH GP	Reims	2	Alfa Romeo SpA	P	1.5 s/c Alfa Romeo 158 8	fuel pump	2/20
1	ITALIAN GP	Monza	10	Alfa Romeo SpA	P	1.5 s/c Alfa Romeo 158 8		3/27

1951 Championship position: 4th   Wins: 1   Pole positions: 0   Fastest laps: 1   Points scored: 22

	Race	Car	No	Entrant	Tyres	Capacity/Car/Engine	Comment	Q Pos/Entries
3	SWISS GP	Bremgarten	22	Alfa Romeo SpA	P	1.5 s/c Alfa Romeo 159 8		2/21
1	BELGIAN GP	Spa	4	Alfa Romeo SpA	P	1.5 s/c Alfa Romeo 159 8		2/13
5	FRENCH GP	Reims	2	Alfa Romeo SpA	P	1.5 s/c Alfa Romeo 159 8	4 laps behind	2/23
ret	BRITISH GP	Silverstone	1	Alfa Romeo SpA	P	1.5 s/c Alfa Romeo 159 8	slipping clutch/FL	3/20
ret	GERMAN GP	Nürburgring	76	Alfa Romeo SpA	P	1.5 s/c Alfa Romeo 159 8	engine – overheating	4/23
ret	ITALIAN GP	Monza	34	Alfa Romeo SpA	P	1.5 s/c Alfa Romeo 159 8	engine	2/22
3*	"	"	40	Alfa Romeo SpA	P	1.5 s/c Alfa Romeo 159 8	*took Bonetto's car/FL/1 lap behind	– / –
3	SPANISH GP	Pedralbes	20	Alfa Romeo SpA	P	1.5 s/c Alfa Romeo 159 8		4/20

1952 Championship position: 2nd   Wins: 0   Pole positions: 2   Fastest laps: 0   Points scored: 27

	Race	Car	No	Entrant	Tyres	Capacity/Car/Engine	Comment	Q Pos/Entries
ret	SWISS GP	Bremgarten	28	Scuderia Ferrari	P	2.0 Ferrari 500 4	magneto	1/21
ret	"	"	32	Scuderia Ferrari	P	2.0 Ferrari 500 4	took over Simon's car/magneto	– / –
2	BELGIAN GP	Spa	2	Scuderia Ferrari	P	2.0 Ferrari 500 4		2/22
2	FRENCH GP	Rouen	10	Scuderia Ferrari	P	2.0 Ferrari 500 4	1 lap behind	2/20
6	BRITISH GP	Silverstone	16	Scuderia Ferrari	P	2.0 Ferrari 500 4	pit stop – plugs/3 laps behind	1/32
2	GERMAN GP	Nürburgring	102	Scuderia Ferrari	E	2.0 Ferrari 500 4		2/32
2	DUTCH GP	Zandvoort	4	Scuderia Ferrari	P	2.0 Ferrari 500 4		2/18
4	ITALIAN GP	Monza	10	Scuderia Ferrari	P	2.0 Ferrari 500 4		3/35

1953 Championship position: 3rd   Wins: 1   Pole positions: 0   Fastest laps: 0   Points scored: 32

	Race	Car	No	Entrant	Tyres	Capacity/Car/Engine	Comment	Q Pos/Entries
ret	ARGENTINE GP	Buenos Aires	12	Scuderia Ferrari	P	2.0 Ferrari 500 4	boy killed running into car's path	4/16
2	DUTCH GP	Zandvoort	6	Scuderia Ferrari	P	2.0 Ferrari 500 4		3/20
ret	BELGIAN GP	Spa	12	Scuderia Ferrari	P	2.0 Ferrari 500 4	engine	4/22
5	FRENCH GP	Reims	14	Scuderia Ferrari	P	2.0 Ferrari 500 4		6/25
3	BRITISH GP	Silverstone	6	Scuderia Ferrari	P	2.0 Ferrari 500 4	2 laps behind	5/29
1	GERMAN GP	Nürburgring	2	Scuderia Ferrari	P	2.0 Ferrari 500 4		3/35
2	SWISS GP	Bremgarten	24	Scuderia Ferrari	P	2.0 Ferrari 500 4		3/23
2	ITALIAN GP	Monza	6	Scuderia Ferrari	P	2.0 Ferrari 500 4		3/30

1954 Championship position: 7th=   Wins: 0   Pole positions: 1   Fastest laps: 0   Points scored: 6

	Race	Car	No	Entrant	Tyres	Capacity/Car/Engine	Comment	Q Pos/Entries
2	ARGENTINE GP	Buenos Aires	10	Scuderia Ferrari	P	2.5 Ferrari 625 4		1/18
ret	BELGIAN GP	Spa	4	Scuderia Ferrari	P	2.5 Ferrari 553 4	ignition	3/15
dns	"	"	4	Scuderia Ferrari	P	2.5 Ferrari 625 4	practice only	– / –

1955 Championship position: 5th   Wins: 0   Pole positions: 0   Fastest laps: 0   Points scored: 10.33

	Race	Car	No	Entrant	Tyres	Capacity/Car/Engine	Comment	Q Pos/Entries
3	ARGENTINE GP	Buenos Aires	10	Scuderia Ferrari	E	2.5 Ferrari 625/555 4	Maglioli/Trintignant also drove/-2 laps	5/22
2	"	" "	12	Scuderia Ferrari	E	2.5 Ferrari 625/555 4	Gonzalez's car/Trintignant also drove	– / –
4	MONACO GP	Monte Carlo	42	Scuderia Ferrari	E	2.5 Ferrari 625 4	1 lap behind	14/22
3	BELGIAN GP	Spa	2	Scuderia Ferrari	E	2.5 Ferrari 555 4		4/14
dns	ITALIAN GP	Monza	2	Scuderia Ferrari	E	2.5 Lancia D50 V8	withdrawn – tyre trouble in practice	5/22

GP Starts: 33   GP Wins: 5   Pole positions: 5   Fastest laps: 5   Points: 127.33

The first ever world champion. Italian veteran Giuseppe Farina, in classic straight-arm pose, driving the all-conquering Alfa Romeo 158 to victory in the 1950 British Grand Prix at Silverstone.

category produced fourth overall in the British series with Paul Stewart Racing, and remaining with PSR, Firman graduated to Formula Three for 1995, and again surprised many by finishing second overall to fellow Briton Oliver Gavin. Despite his supposed rookie status, however, Firman also managed to beat off a strong field to win the prestigious Marlboro Masters at Zandvoort.

He remained in Formula 3 the following year, to claim the title of the British domestic series, beating drivers such as Juan Pablo Montoya, and controversially took a win at the end of year Macau Grand Prix after causing the race to be halted. Such success should have led to offers from F3000 teams, but lacking the necessary finance, he opted to try his luck in Japan, where he contested both the F3000 equivalent Formula Nippon series and the national GT championship.

The Japanese adventure went on to last for fully six seasons, with Firman driving for such as TMS, Nova and Nakajima in his time in F Nippon and SARD Toyota in sportscars. Always a threat for race wins in the single-seater series, he eventually won the title on the back of four individual victories with ex-F1 driver Satoru Nakajima's team in 2002, and added runners-up honours in the GT championship for good measure.

Firman finally made the breakthrough into the top flight with a place at Jordan for 2003, but the F1 dream turned into something of a nightmare for Firman, however, as the Jordan-Ford EJ13 proved to be a less than competitive proposition. A solitary eighth place finish put him onto the scoreboard, but a practice accident at the Hungaroring saw him sit out two races with concussion and inner ear problems before returning, to compete in two more races.

Dropped in favour of more moneyed rivals ahead of the 2004 campaign, Ralf was left to scrabble around for drives outside of Formula 1, eventually, Firman again returned to the Far East, landing a deal to race for Honda in the renamed Japanese Super GT series. Sharing the NSX with Daisuke Ito, the pair came close to taking the 2005 Championship, but a slip from Ito in the final round cost them dear and a non-points scoring finish meant they lost out to Yuchi Tachikawa and Tora Takagi at the last gasp.

Firman also returned to open wheel action, representing Ireland in the A1GP series where he was a consistent front-runner without gaining the results that his performances had often merited.

He therefore returned to his spiritual racing home and a regular diet of Super GT racing. In 2007 Ralf, again paired with Ito, finally took the title in the Super GT GT500 class with NSX, and In 2009 Firman (with Takuya Izawa) notched up two wins on their way to the runner's up slot.

Despite a 2010 win in the prestigious Pokka GT race at Suzuka (with Yuji Ide and Takashi Kobayashi), little else was achieved, and Firman became less active. In 2011 Ralph was seen in Europe once more, racing a Ferrari F458 Italia at the 6 Hours of Imola.

RALPH FIRMAN

BEING born into a motor racing family (his father Ralph senior founded Van Diemen) put Ralph Firman Jr in line for a career in the sport from an early age but, typical of so many British hopefuls, his route to the top came via Karting and the Junior Formula.

His progress was steady rather than sensational, but both Junior and Senior Kart titles were gained before a switch Formula Vauxhall Junior series in 1993 to learn his craft. It was immediately clear that Firman knew what to do, as he took nine wins and ten poles during the year, landing him the prestigious McLaren Autosport Young Driver Award, and prompting a move up to Formula Vauxhall for 1994. His first year in a slicks-and-wings

---

FIRMAN, Ralf (GB) b 20/5/1975, Norwich, Norfolk

2003 Championship position: 19th= Wins: 0 Pole positions: 0 Fastest laps: 0 Points scored: 1

	Race	Circuit	No	Entrant	Tyres	Capacity/Car/Engine	Comment	Q Pos/Entries
ret	AUSTRALIAN GP	Melbourne	12	Jordan Ford	B	3.0 Jordan EJ13-Ford Cosworth V10	crashed – possibly oil on track	17/20
10	MALAYSIAN GP	Sepang	12	Jordan Ford	B	3.0 Jordan EJ13-Ford Cosworth V10	low on fuel/1 lap behind	20/20
ret	BRAZILIAN GP	Interlagos	12	Jordan Ford	B	3.0 Jordan EJ13-Ford Cosworth V10	front suspension failure	16/20
ret	SAN MARINO GP	Imola	12	Jordan Ford	B	3.0 Jordan EJ13-Ford Cosworth V10	engine	19/20
8	SPANISH GP	Barcelona	12	Jordan Ford	B	3.0 Jordan EJ13-Ford Cosworth V10	first championship point	15/20
11	AUSTRIAN GP	A1-Ring	12	Jordan Ford	B	3.0 Jordan EJ13-Ford Cosworth V10	1 lap behind	16/20
12	MONACO GP	Monte Carlo	12	Jordan Ford	B	3.0 Jordan EJ13-Ford Cosworth V10	2 laps behind	16/19
ret	CANADIAN GP	Montreal	12	Jordan Ford	B	3.0 Jordan EJ13-Ford Cosworth V10	oil leak	19/20
11	EUROPEAN GP	Nürburgring	12	Jordan Ford	B	3.0 Jordan EJ13-Ford Cosworth V10	2 laps behind	14/20
15	FRANCE GP	Magny Cours	12	Jordan Ford	B	3.0 Jordan EJ13-Ford Cosworth V10	3 laps behind	18/20
13	BRITISH GP	Silverstone	12	Jordan Ford	B	3.0 Jordan EJ13-Ford Cosworth V10	1 lap behind	17/20
ret	GERMAN GP	Hockenheim	12	Jordan Ford	B	3.0 Jordan EJ13-Ford Cosworth V10	accident damage on lap 1	18/20
dns	HUNGARIAN GP	Hungaroring	12	Jordan Ford	B	3.0 Jordan EJ13-Ford Cosworth V10	Friday practice accident	–/–
ret	U S GP	Indianapolis	12	Jordan Ford	B	3.0 Jordan EJ13-Ford Cosworth V10	spun off	18/20
14	JAPANESE GP	Suzuka	12	Jordan Ford	B	3.0 Jordan EJ13-Ford Cosworth V10	2 laps behind	15/20

GP Starts: 14 GP Wins: 0 Pole positions: 0 Fastest laps: 0 Points: 1

RUDI FISCHER

A successful restaurateur and highly proficient amateur racer and hill-climb expert, Fischer enjoyed great success with his own single-seater Ferraris in the early fifties, run under the Ecurie Espadon (Team Swordfish) banner.

Encouraged by his form in a Simca in 1949, and a sixth place in the Prix de Berne, sharing an HWM with Moss, he acquired a V12 Ferrari for the 1951 season, which he drove to great effect, particularly in non-championship events, finishing second at Bordeaux, third at San Remo and Syracuse and fourth in the Dutch GP. That season he also won F2 events at AVUS, Aix-les-Bains and Angoulême and enjoyed success in hill-climbs.

For 1952 Rudi managed to buy one of the latest T500 Ferraris, and did justice to it by finishing second in the Swiss GP and third in the German GP at World Championship level, while victories at AVUS and in the Eifelrennen were the highlights of a productive programme of lesser races.

It was some surprise when this excellent and most underrated driver quit international racing at the end of the season, although he continued to make occasional appearances, mostly in hill-climbs, into the late fifties.

MIKE FISHER

FISHER raced a variety of machinery including a Lotus 18 and Porsche 906 and 910 sports cars, but was something of mystery when he entered the 1967 Canadian Grand Prix with the ex-Jim Clark Lotus 33 which had been bought that summer by Earl Chiles. In fact this car was the famous 'R11' with which the great Scotsman had utterly dominated the 1965 World Championship. The car was fitted with a 2-litre BRM unit for Fisher, who performed quite respectably both in Canada and in practice for the Mexican GP, where he was unfortunate not to start when a diaphragm 'worth five cents' on his fuel metering unit ruptured.

His racing career was then interrupted by the Vietnam war as Mike entered pilot training in 1968 and flew fighters (including the F-102, F-101, F-4 and F-15) until he was assigned to the Pentagon in 1994.

In 1997 Fisher briefly held the role of CART's executive vice-president of racing, but after only three races of the season quit his role by mutual consent.

FISCHER, Rudi (CH) b 19/5/1912, Stuttgart, Germany – d 30/12/1976, Lucerne

1951 Championship position: Unplaced

	Race	Circuit	No	Entrant	Tyres	Capacity/Car/Engine	Comment	Q Pos/Entries
11	SWISS GP	Bremgarten	38	Ecurie Espadon	P	2.5 Ferrari 212 V12	3 laps behind	10/21
6	GERMAN GP	Nürburgring	91	Ecurie Espadon	P	2.5 Ferrari 212 V12	1 lap behind	8/23
dns	ITALIAN GP	Monza	14	Ecurie Espadon	P	2.5 Ferrari 212 V12	practice crash	- / -

1952 Championship position: 4th= Wins: 0 Pole positions: 0 Fastest laps: 0 Points scored: 10

	Race	Circuit	No	Entrant	Tyres	Capacity/Car/Engine	Comment	Q Pos/Entries
2	SWISS GP	Bremgarten	42	Ecurie Espadon	P	2.0 Ferrari 500 4		5/21
11*	FRENCH GP	Rouen	36	Ecurie Espadon	P	2.0 Ferrari 212 V12	*Hirt took over/13 laps behind	17/20
dns	"	"	34	Ecurie Espadon	P	2.0 Ferrari 500 4	con-rod failure in practice	- / -
13	BRITISH GP	Silverstone	19	Ecurie Espadon	P	2.0 Ferrari 500 4	5 laps behind	15/32
3	GERMAN GP	Nürburgring	117	Ecurie Espadon	P	2.0 Ferrari 500 4		6/32
ret	ITALIAN GP	Monza	18	Ecurie Espadon	P	2.0 Ferrari 500 4	engine	14/35

GP Starts: 7 GP Wins: 0 Pole positions: 0 Fastest laps: 0 Points: 10

FISHER, Mike (US) b 13/3/1943, Hollywood, California

1967 Championship position: Unplaced

	Race	Circuit	No	Entrant	Tyres	Capacity/Car/Engine	Comment	Q Pos/Entries
11	CANADIAN GP	Mosport Park	6	Mike Fisher	F	2.0 Lotus 33-BRM V8	pit stops - electrics/-9 laps	18/19
ret/dns	MEXICAN GP	Mexico City	10	Mike Fisher	F	2.0 Lotus 33-BRM V8	fuel metering unit on grid	(18)/19

GP Starts: 1 (2) GP Wins: 0 Pole positions: 0 Fastest laps: 0 Points: 0

GIANCARLO FISICHELLA

A QUIET and easy-going Italian, Giancarlo Fisichella was surrounded by cars from an early age, when he played among the machines in his father's garage workshop. By the time he was ten, he was competing in the national Minikart series, and he soon progressed through the karting ranks, before moving up to Italian F3 in 1992. He spent two seasons learning his trade, before switching to the official RC Motorsport team. Then he simply scorched away from the opposition, winning ten of the 20 rounds of the series, and adding the prestigious one-off Monaco and Macau races to his impressive CV.

Obviously a talent to watch, Fisichella was snapped up by Minardi on a long-term contract and given the test-driver role for 1995, at the same time gaining experience and polishing his racecraft in the ITC with an Alfa Romeo 156. Another full season in the high-tech category was completed successfully in 1996, but of greater significance was his grand prix baptism with Minardi. Having joined Pedro Lamy in the Faenza squad, he immediately showed the speed to eclipse his team-mate, but the young lions blotted their copybooks by colliding on the opening lap at Monaco, when points were there for the taking. Fisichella was then obliged to make way for paying driver Giovanni Lavaggi, but his stock was high enough for him to be placed in the Jordan team for 1997, alongside Ralf Schumacher. It was 'Fisi' who looked the brighter prospect, however, which hastened the young Italian's transfer to Benetton after a contract wrangle between Jordan and Flavio Briatore was settled in court.

Fisichella undoubtedly brought a new sense of purpose to Benetton in 1998, and his two second places in Monaco and Montreal showed that here was a potential grand prix winner of the future. His second term presented a similar picture, when occasional outstanding performances, such as his second place in Canada, were mixed with lacklustre showings when he failed to impress. He was paired with Alexander Wurz for a third season, the new B200 appearing to be an improvement over its predecessor, and both drivers hoped to see more of the top six, only to be cruelly denied by a mid-season slump in form. 'Fisi' began the year well, inheriting second on David Coulthard's disqualification in Brazil, and then visiting the podium again in both Monaco and Canada. He ended the year being somewhat overshadowed by Wurz, but Benetton and Fisichella decided to stick with each other for 2001, when the Italian was partnered by Jenson Button, on loan from Williams for two years.

If that wasn't enough of an incentive to push harder that year, 'Fisi' also wanted to impress Renault bosses sufficiently to be considered as a potential employee for 2002. As things turned out, it wasn't to be, although the Italian comprehensively out-performed Button in the first two-thirds of the season and, despite scoring a podium finish against the odds in Belgium, he was already signing papers to take him back to Jordan for 2002. The Silverstone team provided a more settled environment, and armed with the latest Honda engine, Giancarlo was hopeful that he could score regular points and even grab the occasional podium.

It was far from an easy season, though, as the Jordan team struggled financially and Giancarlo was forced to settle for three fifth places – coming one after the other in Austria, Monaco and Canada – and one sixth place at the Hungarian GP. Other than that, it was a pretty dreary year, with eight retirements and little to smile about. He also missed the French GP following a heavy crash in practice prior to qualifying.

If 'Fisi' had hoped that 2003 would be a step forward and that the now Ford-powered Jordan would help him to more points finishes, he was sadly mistaken. More often than not, he struggled in the midfield rather than pushing for points, but an awful season had one good moment, when Fisichella found himself in the right place at the right time after Fernando Alonso decided to ignore yellow flags in Brazil and caused the race to be brought to a premature end. Initially, Kimi Räikkönen was declared the

winner, and a dejected Fisichella was awarded second place on the podium. In the week after the race, however, the stewards admitted that they had made an error and that, on count-back, the Italian had indeed been the leader. Fourteen days later, he got his hands on the winner's trophy, although he missed out on spraying the champagne from the top step.

The following season, Fisichella moved to Sauber in an attempt to restore his reputation as a front-line driver, and did enough to impress many up and down the pit lane. There may have been no major highs, but he was consistently there or thereabouts, thanks to some good driving and a solid car. His reward came in the form of nine points finishes, five in succession towards the end of the year and a best result of fourth in Canada. His form was enough to convince both Flavio Briatore and Frank Williams that they wanted him for 2005, the Italian eventually opting to return to Renault. His season started in the best possible way with a stunning victory in the Australian Grand Prix, but niggling problems dogged his title challenge, and he was soon overshadowed by team-mate Fernando Alonso, who steamed ahead to take the world championship. Nonetheless, on his day, 'Fisi' is still a contender for victory, although the closest he would come was a Suzuka, where he was sensationally defeated on the final lap by Räikkönen.

For 2006, Fisichella had the unenviable task of matching champion team-mate Alonso. Once again, however, his performances were typically uneven. An early-season flag-to-flag win in Malaysia was the undoubted highlight, and a number of classy performances – such as in Catalunya, Indianapolis, and Monza – helped him to an eventual fourth place in the championship. With the departure of Alonso to McLaren, he assumed the mantle of team leader with Renault and may have felt that he had a good shot at winning the world championship, but the team lost their way in the wind tunnel and struggled to adapt to their enforced change to Bridgestone tyres. The result was a less than competitive Renault R27 that struggled even to achieve a podium position. A reasonable early-season points haul ensured that Giancarlo would finish eighth in the 2007 table, but when it became clear that Renault would not be renewing his contract, the veteran appeared to be heading for enforced retirement.

Determined to prolong his grand prix career, the Italian tested impressively for the renamed and re-organised Force India Team. Well funded courtesy of billionaire owner Vijay Mallya, the team relied on Fisichella's vast experience to push forward in 2008. However, neither he nor team-mate Sutil managed to score a single point in that season, which turned into a long hard slog.

Changes over the winter included technical assistance from McLaren and a switch of engine suppliers from Ferrari to Mercedes, which put the team in a much more competitive position for 2009. Initially, better results were slow in coming, but by mid-season the VJM02 car suddenly sprang into life when Fisichella placed it on pole position for the Belgian Grand Prix. He may even have been able to take a fairy-tale first win for the team but for the intervention of the safety car, which allowed Räikkönen to pounce at the restart. Second place was almost as good as a win for Fisichella, who was immediately targeted to fill the gap at Ferrari left by the injured Felipe Massa. The Brazilian's stand-in, Luca Badoer, had already singularly failed to impress, and the Italian was chosen to step into the breach. Naturally, the offer of a place in the team for the balance of the year, plus a testing contract thereafter, was too good for an Italian driver to resist. Strangely, he just couldn't get to grips with the car and his first race at Monza was a huge let-down, as were his five subsequent appearances for the Prancing Horse.

Fisichella has since turned successfully to sports car racing. He was partnered by Gianmaria Bruni in a Ferrari 458 GTC, the experienced pair winning the 2011 Le Mans GTE class overall, helped by class wins at Spa and Silverstone.

FISICHELLA, Giancarlo (I) b 14/1/1973, Rome

1996 Championship position: Unplaced

	Race	Circuit	No	Entrant	Tyres	Capacity/Car/Engine	Comment	Q Pos/Entries
ret	AUSTRALIAN GP	Melbourne	21	Minardi Team	G	3.0 Minardi 195B-Ford EDM V8	clutch	16/22
13	EUROPEAN GP	Nürburgring	21	Minardi Team	G	3.0 Minardi 195B-Ford EDM V8	2 laps behind	18/22
ret	SAN MARINO GP	Imola	21	Minardi Team	G	3.0 Minardi 195B-Ford EDM V8	engine	19/22
ret	MONACO GP	Monte Carlo	21	Minardi Team	G	3.0 Minardi 195B-Ford EDM V8	collision with Lamy on lap 1	18/22
ret	SPANISH GP	Barcelona	21	Minardi Team	G	3.0 Minardi 195B-Ford EDM V8	collision damage at start	19/22
8	CANADIAN GP	Montreal	21	Minardi Team	G	3.0 Minardi 195B-Ford EDM V8	2 laps behind	16/22
ret	FRENCH GP	Magny Cours	21	Minardi Team	G	3.0 Minardi 195B-Ford EDM V8	fuel pressure	18/22
11	BRITISH GP	Silverstone	21	Minardi Team	G	3.0 Minardi 195B-Ford EDM V8	2 laps behind	19/22

1997 Championship position: 8th   Wins: 0   Pole positions: 0   Fastest laps: 1   Points scored: 20

	Race	Circuit	No	Entrant	Tyres	Capacity/Car/Engine	Comment	Q Pos/Entries
ret	AUSTRALIAN GP	Melbourne	12	B & H Total Jordan Peugeot	G	3.0 Jordan 197-Peugeot V10	spun off	14/24
8	BRAZILIAN GP	Interlagos	12	B & H Total Jordan Peugeot	G	3.0 Jordan 197-Peugeot V10		7/22
ret	ARGENTINE GP	Buenos Aires	12	B & H Total Jordan Peugeot	G	3.0 Jordan 197-Peugeot V10	collision with Ralf Schumacher	9/22
4	SAN MARINO GP	Imola	12	B & H Total Jordan Peugeot	G	3.0 Jordan 197-Peugeot V10		6/22
6	MONACO GP	Monte Carlo	12	B & H Total Jordan Peugeot	G	3.0 Jordan 197-Peugeot V10	1 lap behind	4/22
9	SPANISH GP	Barcelona	12	B & H Total Jordan Peugeot	G	3.0 Jordan 197-Peugeot V10	FL	8/22
3	CANADIAN GP	Montreal	12	B & H Total Jordan Peugeot	G	3.0 Jordan 197-Peugeot V10		6/22
9	FRENCH GP	Magny Cours	12	B & H Total Jordan Peugeot	G	3.0 Jordan 197-Peugeot V10	drove spare car/1 lap behind	11/22
7	BRITISH GP	Silverstone	12	B & H Total Jordan Peugeot	G	3.0 Jordan 197-Peugeot V10	1 lap behind	10/22
11	GERMAN GP	Hockenheim	12	B & H Total Jordan Peugeot	G	3.0 Jordan 197-Peugeot V10	puncture then oil cooler/-5 laps	2/22
ret	HUNGARIAN GP	Hungaroring	12	B & H Total Jordan Peugeot	G	3.0 Jordan 197-Peugeot V10	spun off	13/22
2	BELGIAN GP	Spa	12	B & H Total Jordan Peugeot	G	3.0 Jordan 197-Peugeot V10		4/22
4	ITALIAN GP	Monza	12	B & H Total Jordan Peugeot	G	3.0 Jordan 197-Peugeot V10		3/22
4	AUSTRIAN GP	A1-Ring	12	B & H Total Jordan Peugeot	G	3.0 Jordan 197-Peugeot V10		14/22
ret	LUXEMBOURG GP	Nürburgring	12	B & H Total Jordan Peugeot	G	3.0 Jordan 197-Peugeot V10	collision with Ralf Schumacher	4/22
7*	JAPANESE GP	Suzuka	12	B & H Total Jordan Peugeot	G	3.0 Jordan 197-Peugeot V10	*5th place car disqualified	9/22
11	EUROPEAN GP	Jerez	12	B & H Total Jordan Peugeot	G	3.0 Jordan 197-Peugeot V10		17/22

1998 Championship position: 9th   Wins: 0   Pole positions: 1   Fastest laps: 0   Points scored: 16

	Race	Circuit	No	Entrant	Tyres	Capacity/Car/Engine	Comment	Q Pos/Entries
ret	AUSTRALIAN GP	Melbourne	5	Mild Seven Benetton Playlife	B	3.0 Benetton B198-Playlife V10	broken rear wing support	7/22
6	BRAZILIAN GP	Interlagos	5	Mild Seven Benetton Playlife	B	3.0 Benetton B198-Playlife V10	1 lap behind	7/22
7	ARGENTINE GP	Buenos Aires	5	Mild Seven Benetton Playlife	B	3.0 Benetton B198-Playlife V10		10/22
ret	SAN MARINO GP	Imola	5	Mild Seven Benetton Playlife	B	3.0 Benetton B198-Playlife V10	spun off into wall	10/22
ret	SPANISH GP	Barcelona	5	Mild Seven Benetton Playlife	B	3.0 Benetton B198-Playlife V10	collision with Irvine	4/22
2	MONACO GP	Monte Carlo	5	Mild Seven Benetton Playlife	B	3.0 Benetton B198-Playlife V10		3/22
2	CANADIAN GP	Montreal	5	Mild Seven Benetton Playlife	B	3.0 Benetton B198-Playlife V10		4/22
9	FRENCH GP	Magny Cours	5	Mild Seven Benetton Playlife	B	3.0 Benetton B198-Playlife V10	1 lap behind	9/22
5	BRITISH GP	Silverstone	5	Mild Seven Benetton Playlife	B	3.0 Benetton B198-Playlife V10	1 lap behind	11/22
ret	AUSTRIAN GP	A1-Ring	5	Mild Seven Benetton Playlife	B	3.0 Benetton B198-Playlife V10	collision with Alesi	1/22
7	GERMAN GP	Hockenheim	5	Mild Seven Benetton Playlife	B	3.0 Benetton B198-Playlife V10		8/22
8	HUNGARIAN GP	Hungaroring	5	Mild Seven Benetton Playlife	B	3.0 Benetton B198-Playlife V10	1 lap behind	8/22
ret	BELGIAN GP	Spa	5	Mild Seven Benetton Playlife	B	3.0 Benetton B198-Playlife V10	ran into back of Nakano	7/22
8	ITALIAN GP	Monza	5	Mild Seven Benetton Playlife	B	3.0 Benetton B198-Playlife V10	1 lap behind	11/22
6	LUXEMBOURG GP	Nürburgring	5	Mild Seven Benetton Playlife	B	3.0 Benetton B198-Playlife V10		4/22
8	JAPANESE GP	Suzuka	5	Mild Seven Benetton Playlife	B	3.0 Benetton B198-Playlife V10		10/22

1999 Championship position: 9th   Wins: 0   Pole positions: 0   Fastest laps: 0   Points scored: 13

	Race	Circuit	No	Entrant	Tyres	Capacity/Car/Engine	Comment	Q Pos/Entries
4	AUSTRALIAN GP	Melbourne	9	Mild Seven Benetton Playlife	B	3.0 Benetton B199-Playlife V10	collision with Trulli - new nose cone	7/22
ret	BRAZILIAN GP	Interlagos	9	Mild Seven Benetton Playlife	B	3.0 Benetton B199-Playlife V10	clutch	5/22
5	SAN MARINO GP	Imola	9	Mild Seven Benetton Playlife	B	3.0 Benetton B199-Playlife V10	1 lap behind	16/22
5	MONACO GP	Monte Carlo	9	Mild Seven Benetton Playlife	B	3.0 Benetton B199-Playlife V10	1 lap behind	9/22
9	SPANISH GP	Barcelona	9	Mild Seven Benetton Playlife	B	3.0 Benetton B199-Playlife V10	lack of grip/1 lap behind	13/22
2	CANADIAN GP	Montreal	9	Mild Seven Benetton Playlife	B	3.0 Benetton B199-Playlife V10		7/22
ret	FRENCH GP	Magny Cours	9	Mild Seven Benetton Playlife	B	3.0 Benetton B199-Playlife V10	spun off	7/22
7	BRITISH GP	Silverstone	9	Mild Seven Benetton Playlife	B	3.0 Benetton B199-Playlife V10		17/22
12/ret	AUSTRIAN GP	A1-Ring	9	Mild Seven Benetton Playlife	B	3.0 Benetton B199-Playlife V10	engine/3 laps behind	12/22
ret	GERMAN GP	Hockenheim	9	Mild Seven Benetton Playlife	B	3.0 Benetton B199-Playlife V10	suspension failure after spin	10/22
ret	HUNGARIAN GP	Hungaroring	9	Mild Seven Benetton Playlife	B	3.0 Benetton B199-Playlife V10	fuel pressure	4/22
11	BELGIAN GP	Spa	9	Mild Seven Benetton Playlife	B	3.0 Benetton B199-Playlife V10	lack of grip	13/22
ret	ITALIAN GP	Monza	9	Mild Seven Benetton Playlife	B	3.0 Benetton B199-Playlife V10	nudged into spin	17/22
ret	EUROPEAN GP	Nürburgring	9	Mild Seven Benetton Playlife	B	3.0 Benetton B199-Playlife V10	spun off when leading	6/22
11	MALAYSIAN GP	Sepang	9	Mild Seven Benetton Playlife	B	3.0 Benetton B199-Playlife V10	collision damage/4 laps behind	11/22
14/ret	JAPANESE GP	Suzuka	9	Mild Seven Benetton Playlife	B	3.0 Benetton B199-Playlife V10	engine/5 laps behind	14/22

2000 Championship position: 6th   Wins: 0   Pole positions: 0   Fastest laps: 0   Points scored: 18

	Race	Circuit	No	Entrant	Tyres	Capacity/Car/Engine	Comment	Q Pos/Entries
5	AUSTRALIAN GP	Melbourne	11	Mild Seven Benetton Playlife	B	3.0 Benetton B200-Playlife V10		9/22
2*	BRAZILIAN GP	Interlagos	11	Mild Seven Benetton Playlife	B	3.0 Benetton B200-Playlife V10	*2nd place car disqualified	5/22
11	SAN MARINO GP	Imola	11	Mild Seven Benetton Playlife	B	3.0 Benetton B200-Playlife V10	1 lap behind	19/22
7	BRITISH GP	Silverstone	11	Mild Seven Benetton Playlife	B	3.0 Benetton B200-Playlife V10	1 lap behind	12/22
9	SPANISH GP	Barcelona	11	Mild Seven Benetton Playlife	B	3.0 Benetton B200-Playlife V10	1 lap behind	14/22
5	EUROPEAN GP	Nürburgring	11	Mild Seven Benetton Playlife	B	3.0 Benetton B200-Playlife V10	collision with Trulli/1 lap behind	7/22
3	MONACO GP	Monte Carlo	11	Mild Seven Benetton Playlife	B	3.0 Benetton B200-Playlife V10	despite puncture	8/22
3	CANADIAN GP	Montreal	11	Mild Seven Benetton Playlife	B	3.0 Benetton B200-Playlife V10	good race strategy	10/22
9	FRENCH GP	Magny Cours	11	Mild Seven Benetton Playlife	B	3.0 Benetton B200-Playlife V10	1 lap behind	14/22
ret	AUSTRIAN GP	A1-Ring	11	Mild Seven Benetton Playlife	B	3.0 Benetton B200-Playlife V10	punted off by Diniz on lap 1	8/22
ret	GERMAN GP	Hockenheim	11	Mild Seven Benetton Playlife	B	3.0 Benetton B200-Playlife V10	collision - M Schumacher on lap1	3/22
ret	HUNGARIAN GP	Hungaroring	11	Mild Seven Benetton Playlife	B	3.0 Benetton B200-Playlife V10	brakes	7/22
ret	BELGIAN GP	Spa	11	Mild Seven Benetton Playlife	B	3.0 Benetton B200-Playlife V10	electrics	11/22
11	ITALIAN GP	Monza	11	Mild Seven Benetton Playlife	B	3.0 Benetton B200-Playlife V10	clutch problems/1 lap behind	9/22

	Grand Prix	Circuit	No.	Team	Tyre	Car/Engine	Comments	Qual.
ret	UNITED STATES GP	Indianapolis	11	Mild Seven Benetton Playlife	B	3.0 Benetton B200-Playlife V10	*engine*	15/22
14	JAPANESE GP	Suzuka	11	Mild Seven Benetton Playlife	B	3.0 Benetton B200-Playlife V10	*1 lap behind*	12/22
9	MALAYSIAN GP	Sepang	11	Mild Seven Benetton Playlife	B	3.0 Benetton B200-Playlife V10	*1 lap behind*	13/22

2001 Championship position: 11th   Wins: 0   Pole positions: 0   Fastest laps: 0   Points scored: 8

	Grand Prix	Circuit	No.	Team	Tyre	Car/Engine	Comments	Qual.
13	AUSTRALIAN GP	Melbourne	7	Mild Seven Benetton Renault	M	3.0 Benetton B201-Renault V10	*broken exhaust/3 laps behind*	17/22
ret	MALAYSIAN GP	Sepang	7	Mild Seven Benetton Renault	M	3.0 Benetton B201-Renault V10	*fuel pressure*	16/22
6	BRAZILIAN GP	Interlagos	7	Mild Seven Benetton Renault	M	3.0 Benetton B201-Renault V10	*1 lap behind*	18/22
ret	SAN MARINO GP	Imola	7	Mild Seven Benetton Renault	M	3.0 Benetton B201-Renault V10	*misfire*	19/22
14	SPANISH GP	Barcelona	7	Mild Seven Benetton Renault	M	3.0 Benetton B201-Renault V10	*2 laps behind*	19/22
ret	AUSTRIAN GP	A1-Ring	7	Mild Seven Benetton Renault	M	3.0 Benetton B201-Renault V10	*engine*	19/22
ret	MONACO GP	Monte Carlo	7	Mild Seven Benetton Renault	M	3.0 Benetton B201-Renault V10	*accident – hit barrier*	10/22
ret	CANADIAN GP	Montreal	7	Mild Seven Benetton Renault	M	3.0 Benetton B201-Renault V10	*hit by Button – wheel damage*	18/22
11	EUROPEAN GP	Nürburgring	7	Mild Seven Benetton Renault	M	3.0 Benetton B201-Renault V10	*1 lap behind*	15/22
11	FRENCH GP	Magny Cours	7	Mild Seven Benetton Renault	M	3.0 Benetton B201-Renault V10	*collision – Verstappen/1 lap behind*	16/22
13	BRITISH GP	Silverstone	7	Mild Seven Benetton Renault	M	3.0 Benetton B201-Renault V10	*2 laps behind*	19/22
4	GERMAN GP	Hockenheim	7	Mild Seven Benetton Renault	M	3.0 Benetton B201-Renault V10		17/22
ret	HUNGARIAN GP	Hungaroring	7	Mild Seven Benetton Renault	M	3.0 Benetton B201-Renault V10	*engine*	15/22
3	BELGIAN GP	Spa	7	Mild Seven Benetton Renault	M	3.0 Benetton B201-Renault V10	*despite oil leak*	8/22
10	ITALIAN GP	Monza	7	Mild Seven Benetton Renault	M	3.0 Benetton B201-Renault V10	*1 lap behind*	14/22
8	UNITED STATES GP	Indianapolis	7	Mild Seven Benetton Renault	M	3.0 Benetton B201-Renault V10	*1 lap behind*	12/22
17/ret	JAPANESE GP	Suzuka	7	Mild Seven Benetton Renault	M	3.0 Benetton B201-Renault V10	*gearbox/6 laps behind*	6/22

2002 Championship position: 10th=   Wins: 0   Pole positions: 0   Fastest laps: 0   Points scored: 7

	Grand Prix	Circuit	No.	Team	Tyre	Car/Engine	Comments	Qual.
ret	AUSTRALIAN GP	Melbourne	9	DHL Jordan Honda	B	3.0 Jordan EJ12-Honda V10	*multiple accident at start*	8/22
13	MALAYSIAN GP	Sepang	9	DHL Jordan Honda	B	3.0 Jordan EJ12-Honda V10	*hit by Sato-rear wing change/-3 laps*	9/22
ret	BRAZILIAN GP	Interlagos	9	DHL Jordan Honda	B	3.0 Jordan EJ12-Honda V10	*engine*	14/22
ret	SAN MARINO GP	Imola	9	DHL Jordan Honda	B	3.0 Jordan EJ12-Honda V10	*hydraulic pressure*	15/22
ret	SPANISH GP	Barcelona	9	DHL Jordan Honda	B	3.0 Jordan EJ12-Honda V10	*hydraulics*	12/21
5	AUSTRIAN GP	A1-Ring	9	DHL Jordan Honda	B	3.0 Jordan EJ12-Honda V10		15/22
5	MONACO GP	Monte Carlo	9	DHL Jordan Honda	B	3.0 Jordan EJ12-Honda V10	*1 lap behind*	11/22
5	CANADIAN GP	Montreal	9	DHL Jordan Honda	B	3.0 Jordan EJ12-Honda V10	*good one-stop strategy*	6/22
ret	EUROPEAN GP	Nürburgring	9	DHL Jordan Honda	B	3.0 Jordan EJ12-Honda V10	*hit Sato – damage – later retired*	18/22
7	BRITISH GP	Silverstone	9	DHL Jordan Honda	B	3.0 Jordan EJ12-Honda V10	*1 lap behind*	17/22
dns	FRANCE GP	Magny Cours	9	DHL Jordan Honda	B	3.0 Jordan EJ12-Honda V10	*stood down after free practice crash*	– / –
ret	GERMAN GP	Hockenheim	9	DHL Jordan Honda	B	3.0 Jordan EJ12-Honda V10	*engine*	6/22
6	HUNGARIAN GP	Hungaroring	9	DHL Jordan Honda	B	3.0 Jordan EJ12-Honda V100		5/20
ret	BELGIAN GP	Spa	9	DHL Jordan Honda	B	3.0 Jordan EJ12-Honda V10	*engine*	14/20
8	ITALIAN GP	Monza	9	DHL Jordan Honda	B	3.0 Jordan EJ12-Honda V10		12/20
7	UNITED STATES GP	Indianapolis	9	DHL Jordan Honda	B	3.0 Jordan EJ12-Honda V10	*1 lap behind*	9/20
ret	JAPANESE GP	Suzuka	9	DHL Jordan Honda	B	3.0 Jordan EJ12-Honda V10	*engine*	8/20

2003 Championship position: 12   Wins: 1   Pole positions: 0   Fastest laps: 0   Points scored: 12

	Grand Prix	Circuit	No.	Team	Tyre	Car/Engine	Comments	Qual.
12/ret	AUSTRALIAN GP	Melbourne	11	Jordan Ford	B	3.0 Jordan EJ13-Ford Cosworth V10	*gearbox/6 laps behind*	13/20
ret	MALAYSIAN GP	Sepang	11	Jordan Ford	B	3.0 Jordan EJ13-Ford Cosworth V10	*left on grid at start*	14/20
1	BRAZILIAN GP	Interlagos	11	Jordan Ford	B	3.0 Jordan EJ13-Ford Cosworth V10	*race red-flagged – won on countback*	8/20
ret	SAN MARINO GP	Imola	11	Jordan Ford	B	3.0 Jordan EJ13-Ford Cosworth V10	*engine*	17/20
15/ret	SPANISH GP	Barcelona	11	Jordan Ford	B	3.0 Jordan EJ13-Ford Cosworth V10	*engine/5 laps behind*	17/20
ret	AUSTRIAN GP	A1-Ring	11	Jordan Ford	B	3.0 Jordan EJ13-Ford Cosworth V10	*fuel system*	9/20
10	MONACO GP	Monte Carlo	11	Jordan Ford	B	3.0 Jordan EJ13-Ford Cosworth V10	*1 lap behind*	12/19
ret	CANADIAN GP	Montreal	11	Jordan Ford	B	3.0 Jordan EJ13-Ford Cosworth V10	*gearbox*	16/20
12	EUROPEAN GP	Nürburgring	11	Jordan Ford	B	3.0 Jordan EJ13-Ford Cosworth V10	*2 laps behind*	13/20
ret	FRENCH GP	Magny Cours	11	Jordan Ford	B	3.0 Jordan EJ13-Ford Cosworth V10	*engine*	17/20
ret	BRITISH GP	Silverstone	11	Jordan Ford	B	3.0 Jordan EJ13-Ford Cosworth V10	*rear suspension failure*	15/20
13	GERMAN GP	Hockenheim	11	Jordan Ford	B	3.0 Jordan EJ13-Ford Cosworth V10	*7 laps behind*	12/20
ret	HUNGARIAN GP	Hungaroring	11	Jordan Ford	B	3.0 Jordan EJ13-Ford Cosworth V10	*engine*	13/20
10	ITALIAN GP	Monza	11	Jordan Ford	B	3.0 Jordan EJ13-Ford Cosworth V10	*1 lap behind*	13/20
7	U S GP	Indianapolis	11	Jordan Ford	B	3.0 Jordan EJ13-Ford Cosworth V10	*1 lap behind*	17/20
ret	JAPANESE GP	Suzuka	11	Jordan Ford	B	3.0 Jordan EJ13-Ford Cosworth V10	*spun off*	16/20

2004 Championship position: 11th   Wins: 0   Pole positions: 0   Fastest laps: 0   Points scored: 22

	Grand Prix	Circuit	No.	Team	Tyre	Car/Engine	Comments	Qual.
10	AUSTRALIAN GP	Melbourne	11	Sauber Petronas	B	3.0 Sauber C23-Petronas V10	*1 lap behind*	14/20
11	MALAYSIAN GP	Sepang	11	Sauber Petronas	B	3.0 Sauber C23-Petronas V10	*stalled at two pitstops/1 lap behind*	12/20
11	BAHRAIN GP	Sakhir Circuit	11	Sauber Petronas	B	3.0 Sauber C23-Petronas V10	*spin/gearbox problems/1 lap behind*	11/20
9	SAN MARINO GP	Imola	11	Sauber Petronas	B	3.0 Sauber C23-Petronas V10	**no time set/1 lap behind*	*18/20
7	SPANISH GP	Barcelona	11	Sauber Petronas	B	3.0 Sauber C23-Petronas V10		12/20
ret	MONACO GP	Monte Carlo	11	Sauber Petronas	B	3.0 Sauber C23-Petronas V10	*crashed into Coulthard*	10/20
6	EUROPEAN GP	Nürburgring	11	Sauber Petronas	B	3.0 Sauber C23-Petronas V100	**no time set*	*19/20
4*	CANADIAN GP	Montreal	11	Sauber Petronas	B	3.0 Sauber C23-Petronas V10	**2nd & 5th place cars dsq/-1 lap*	11/20
9/ret	U S GP	Indianapolis	11	Sauber Petronas	B	3.0 Sauber C23-Petronas V10	*hydraulic leak/5 laps behind*	14/20
12	FRENCH GP	Magny Cours	11	Sauber Petronas	B	3.0 Sauber C23-Petronas V10	*1 lap behind*	15/20
6	BRITISH GP	Silverstone	11	Sauber Petronas	B	3.0 Sauber C23-Petronas V10	**no time set*	*20/20
9	GERMAN GP	Hockenheim	11	Sauber Petronas	B	3.0 Sauber C23-Petronas V10	*wheel jammed at pitstop*	14/20
8	HUNGARIAN GP	Hungaroring	11	Sauber Petronas	B	3.0 Sauber C23-Petronas V10		8/20
5	BELGIAN GP	Spa	11	Sauber Petronas	B	3.0 Sauber C23-Petronas V10	*collision damage*	5/20
8	ITALIAN GP	Monza	11	Sauber Petronas	B	3.0 Sauber C23-Petronas V10		15/20
7	CHINESE GP	Shanghai	11	Sauber Petronas	B	3.0 Sauber C23-Petronas V10	*tyre-graining*	7/20
8	JAPANESE GP	Suzuka	11	Sauber Petronas	B	3.0 Sauber C23-Petronas V10		7/20
9	BRAZILIAN GP	Interlagos	11	Sauber Petronas	B	3.0 Sauber C23-Petronas V10		10/20

2005 Championship position: 5th   Wins: 1   Pole positions: 1   Fastest laps: 1   Points scored: 58

	Grand Prix	Circuit	No.	Team	Tyre	Car/Engine	Comments	Qual.
1	AUSTRALIAN GP	Melbourne	6	Mild Seven Renault F1 Team	M	3.0 Renault R25- V10		1/20
ret	MALAYSIAN GP	Sepang	6	Mild Seven Renault F1 Team	M	3.0 Renault R25- V10	*collision with Webber*	3/20
ret	BAHRAIN GP	Sakhir Circuit	6	Mild Seven Renault F1 Team	M	3.0 Renault R25- V10	*engine*	10/20
ret	SAN MARINO GP	Imola	6	Mild Seven Renault F1 Team	M	3.0 Renault R25- V10	*technical failure – spun off*	12/20
5	SPANISH GP	Barcelona	6	Mild Seven Renault F1 Team	M	3.0 Renault R25- V10	*pit stop – new nose/FL*	6/18

Fisichella leads the field on the opening lap of the 2006 Malaysian Grand Prix. The Italian scored a resounding victory for Renault, but his season was spent in the shadow of team-mate Fernando Alonso.

	GP	Circuit	No.	Team	Tyre	Engine	Notes	Laps
12	MONACO GP	Monte Carlo	6	Mild Seven Renault F1 Team	M	3.0 Renault R25- V10	excessive tyre wear/1 lap behind	4/18
6	EUROPEAN GP	Nürburgring	6	Mild Seven Renault F1 Team	M	3.0 Renault R25- V10	started from pitlane	9/20
ret	CANADIAN GP	Montreal	6	Mild Seven Renault F1 Team	M	3.0 Renault R25- V10	hydraulics	4/20
dns	U S GP	Indianapolis	6	Mild Seven Renault F1 Team	M	3.0 Renault R25- V10	withdrawn after parade lap	4/20
6	FRENCH GP	Magny Cours	6	Mild Seven Renault F1 Team	M	3.0 Renault R25- V10	fuel-rig delay/1 lap behind	6/20
4	BRITISH GP	Silverstone	6	Mild Seven Renault F1 Team	M	3.0 Renault R25- V10	stalled pit at second pitstop	7/20
4	GERMAN GP	Hockenheim	6	Mild Seven Renault F1 Team	M	3.0 Renault R25- V10		4/20
9	HUNGARIAN GP	Hungaroring	6	Mild Seven Renault F1 Team	M	3.0 Renault R25- V10	tyre and engine problems/-1 lap	9/20
4	TURKISH GP	Istanbul	6	Mild Seven Renault F1 Team	M	3.0 Renault R25- V10	fuel-rig delay	2/20
3	ITALIAN GP	Monza	6	Mild Seven Renault F1 Team	M	3.0 Renault R25- V10		9/20
ret	BELGIAN GP	Spa	6	Mild Seven Renault F1 Team	M	3.0 Renault R25- V10	*10-place grid penalty/accident	*3/20
5	BRAZILIAN GP	Interlagos	6	Mild Seven Renault F1 Team	M	3.0 Renault R25- V10	handling problems	3/20
2	JAPANESE GP	Suzuka	6	Mild Seven Renault F1 Team	M	3.0 Renault R25- V10	lost race to Räikkönen on last lap	3/20
4	CHINESE GP	Shanghai	6	Mild Seven Renault F1 Team	M	3.0 Renault R25- V10	drive thru penalty – blocked Räikkönen	2/20

2006 Championship position: 4th Wins: 1 Pole positions: 1 Fastest laps: 0 Points scored: 72

	GP	Circuit	No.	Team	Tyre	Engine	Notes	Laps
ret	BAHRAIN GP	Bahrain	2	Mild Seven Renault F1 Team-	M	2.4 Renault R26-V8	hydraulics	9/22
1	MALAYSIAN GP	Sepang	2	Mild Seven Renault F1 Team-	M	2.4 Renault R26-V8		1/22
5	AUSTRALIAN GP	Melbourne	2	Mild Seven Renault F1 Team-	M	2.4 Renault R26-V8	started from pits – great drive	00/22
8	SAN MARINO GP	Imola	2	Mild Seven Renault F1 Team-	M	2.4 Renault R26-V8	ran heavy fuel load on first stint	11/22
6	EUROPEAN GP	Nürburgring	2	Mild Seven Renault F1 Team-	M	2.4 Renault R26-V8		13/22
3	SPANISH GP	Barcelona	2	Mild Seven Renault F1 Team-	M	2.4 Renault R26-V8	handling problems	2/22
6	MONACO GP	Monte Carlo	2	Mild Seven Renault F1 Team-	M	2.4 Renault R26-V8	*blocking – dropped 4 grid places	*5/22
4	BRITISH GP	Silverstone	2	Mild Seven Renault F1 Team-	M	2.4 Renault R26-V8		5/22
4	CANADIAN GP	Montreal	2	Mild Seven Renault F1 Team-	M	2.4 Renault R26-V8	drive thru penalty for jumped start	2/22
3	U S GP	Indianapolis	2	Mild Seven Renault F1 Team-	M	2.4 Renault R26-V8	excellent drive	3/22
6	FRENCH GP	Magny Cours	2	Mild Seven Renault F1 Team-	M	2.4 Renault R26-V8	blistering tyres	7/22
6	GERMAN GP	Hockenheim	2	Mild Seven Renault F1 Team-	M	2.4 Renault R26-V8		5/22
ret	HUNGARIAN GP	Hungaroring	2	Mild Seven Renault F1 Team-	M	2.4 Renault R26-V8	accident – spun off in rain	8/22
6	TURKISH GP	Istanbul	2	Mild Seven Renault F1 Team-	M	2.4 Renault R26-V8	collision with Heidfeld on lap 1	4/22
4	ITALIAN GP	Monza	2	Mild Seven Renault F1 Team-	M	2.4 Renault R26-V8	one-stop fuel strategy	9/22
3	CHINESE GP	Shanghai	2	Mild Seven Renault F1 Team-	M	2.4 Renault R26-V8	slid off track to lose lead	2/22
3	JAPANESE GP	Suzuka	2	Mild Seven Renault F1 Team-	M	2.4 Renault R26-V8		6/22
6	BRAZILIAN GP	Interlagos	2	Mild Seven Renault F1 Team-	M	2.4 Renault R26-V8		6/22

2007 Championship position: 8th Wins: 0 Pole positions: 0 Fastest laps: 0 Points scored: 21

	GP	Circuit	No.	Team	Tyre	Engine	Notes	Laps
5	AUSTRALIAN GP	Melbourne	3	ING Renault F1 Team	B	2.4 Renault R27 V8	lack of grip	6/22
6	MALAYSIAN GP	Sepang	3	ING Renault F1 Team	B	2.4 Renault R27 V8		12/22
8	BAHRAIN GP	Bahrain	3	ING Renault F1 Team	B	2.4 Renault R27 V8		7/22
9	SPANISH GP	Barcelona	3	ING Renault F1 Team	B	2.4 Renault R27 V8	extra stop – fuel-rig problem/-1 lap	10/22
4	MONACO GP	Monte Carlo	3	ING Renault F1 Team	B	2.4 Renault R27 V8	1 lap behind	4/22
dsq*	CANADIAN GP	Montreal	3	ING Renault F1 Team	B	2.4 Renault R27 V8	*left pitlane against red light	9/22
9	U S GP	Indianapolis	3	ING Renault F1 Team	B	2.4 Renault R27 V8	one-stop strategy/1 lap behind	10/22
6	FRENCH GP	Magny Cours	3	ING Renault F1 Team	B	2.4 Renault R27 V8	understeer and tyre graining	5/22
8	BRITISH GP	Silverstone	3	ING Renault F1 Team	B	2.4 Renault R27 V8	1 lap behind	8/22
10	EUROPEAN GP	Nürburgring	3	ING Renault F1 Team	B	2.4 Renault R27 V8	1 lap behind	13/22
12	HUNGARIAN GP	Hungaroring	3	ING Renault F1 Team	B	2.4 Renault R27 V8	5-place grid pen – blocking/-1 lap	8/22
9	TURKISH GP	Istanbul	3	ING Renault F1 Team	B	2.4 Renault R27 V8	collision with Trulli	10/22
12	ITALIAN GP	Monza	3	ING Renault F1 Team	B	2.4 Renault R27 V8	1 lap behind	15/22
ret	BELGIAN GP	Spa	3	ING Renault F1 Team	B	2.4 Renault R27 V8	*started from pits/accident on lap 1	*11/22
5	JAPANESE GP	Suzuka	3	ING Renault F1 Team	B	2.4 Renault R27 V8		11/22
11	CHINESE GP	Shanghai	3	ING Renault F1 Team	B	2.4 Renault R27 V8		18/22
ret	BRAZILIAN GP	Interlagos	3	ING Renault F1 Team	B	2.4 Renault R27 V8	accident – collision with Nakajima	12/22

2008 Championship position: Unplaced

	GP	Circuit	No.	Team	Tyre	Engine	Notes	Laps
ret	AUSTRALIAN GP	Melbourne	21	Force India Formula One Team	B	2.4 Force India VJM-01-Ferrari V8	accident – hit by Glock on lap 1	17/22
12	MALAYSIAN GP	Sepang	21	Force India Formula One Team	B	2.4 Force India VJM-01-Ferrari V8	understeer in first stint/-1 lap	17/22
12	BAHRAIN GP	Bahrain	21	Force India Formula One Team	B	2.4 Force India VJM-01-Ferrari V8	1 lap behind	18/22
10	SPANISH GP	Barcelona	21	Force India Formula One Team	B	2.4 Force India VJM-01-Ferrari V8	1 lap behind	19/22
ret	TURKISH GP	Istanbul	21	Force India Formula One Team	B	2.4 Force India VJM-01-Ferrari V8	accident– collision with Nakajima	19/20

ret	MONACO GP	Monte Carlo	21	Force India Formula One Team	B	2.4 Force India VJM-01-Ferrari V8	gearbox		20/20
ret	CANADIAN GP	Montreal	21	Force India Formula One Team	B	2.4 Force India VJM-01-Ferrari V8	stalled at first stop – later spun off		18/20
18	FRENCH GP	Magny Cours	21	Force India Formula One Team	B	2.4 Force India VJM-01-Ferrari V8	1 lap behind		19/20
ret	BRITISH GP	Silverstone	21	Force India Formula One Team	B	2.4 Force India VJM-01-Ferrari V8	spun off		20/20
16*	GERMAN GP	Hockenheim	21	Force India Formula One Team	B	2.4 Force India VJM-01-Ferrari V8	25-sec pen – entered pits under s/car		20/20
15	HUNGARIAN GP	Hungaroring	21	Force India Formula One Team	B	2.4 Force India VJM-01-Ferrari V8	1 lap behind		19/20
14	EUROPEAN GP	Valencia	21	Force India Formula One Team	B	2.4 Force India VJM-01-Ferrari V8	1 lap behind		18/20
17	BELGIAN GP	Spa	21	Force India Formula One Team	B	2.4 Force India VJM-01-Ferrari V8	1 lap behind		20/20
ret	ITALIAN GP	Monza	21	Force India Formula One Team	B	2.4 Force India VJM-01-Ferrari V8	hit Coulthard – front wing failure		12/20
14	SINGAPORE GP	Singapore Circuit	21	Force India Formula One Team	B	2.4 Force India VJM-01-Ferrari V8	*no time set		*20/20
ret	JAPANESE GP	Suzuka	21	Force India Formula One Team	B	2.4 Force India VJM-01-Ferrari V8	gearbox		20/20
17	CHINESE GP	Shanghai	21	Force India Formula One Team	B	2.4 Force India VJM-01-Ferrari V8	1 lap behind		20/20
18	BRAZILIAN GP	Interlagos	21	Force India Formula One Team	B	2.4 Force India VJM-01-Ferrari V8	clutch problem/2 laps behind		19/20

2009 Championship position: 15th   Wins: 0   Pole positions: 1   Fastest laps: 0   Points scored: 8

11	AUSTRALIAN GP	Melbourne	21	Force India Formula One Team	B	2.4 Force India VJM-02-Mercedes V8			18/20
18/ret	MALAYSIAN GP	Sepang	21	Force India Formula One Team	B	2.4 Force India VJM-02-Mercedes V8	rain-shortened race/spun off/-2 laps		18/20
14	CHINESE GP	Shanghai	21	Force India Formula One Team	B	2.4 Force India VJM-02-Mercedes V8	1 lap behind		20/20
15	BAHRAIN GP	Bahrain	21	Force India Formula One Team	B	2.4 Force India VJM-02-Mercedes V8	1 lap behind		18/20
14	SPANISH GP	Barcelona	21	Force India Formula One Team	B	2.4 Force India VJM-02-Mercedes V8	1 lap behind		20/20
9	MONACO GP	Monte Carlo	21	Force India Formula One Team	B	2.4 Force India VJM-02-Mercedes V8			13/20
ret	TURKISH GP	Istanbul	21	Force India Formula One Team	B	2.4 Force India VJM-02-Mercedes V8	brakes		19/20
10	BRITISH GP	Silverstone	21	Force India Formula One Team	B	2.4 Force India VJM-02-Mercedes V8			16/20
11	GERMAN GP	Hockenheim	21	Force India Formula One Team	B	2.4 Force India VJM-02-Mercedes V8			18/20
14	HUNGARIAN GP	Hungaroring	21	Force India Formula One Team	B	2.4 Force India VJM-02-Mercedes V8	1 lap behind		17/20
12	EUROPEAN GP	Valencia	21	Force India Formula One Team	B	2.4 Force India VJM-02-Mercedes V8			17/20
2	BELGIAN GP	Spa	21	Force India Formula One Team	B	2.4 Force India VJM-02-Mercedes V8	Force India's 1st ever pole		1/20
9	ITALIAN GP	Monza	3	Scuderia Ferrari Marlboro	B	2.4 Ferrari F60 V8	replaced Badoer		14/20
13	SINGAPORE GP	Marina Bay Circuit	3	Scuderia Ferrari Marlboro	B	2.4 Ferrari F60 V8			18/20
12	JAPANESE GP	Suzuka	3	Scuderia Ferrari Marlboro	B	2.4 Ferrari F60 V8			16/20
10	BRAZILIAN GP	Interlagos	3	Scuderia Ferrari Marlboro	B	2.4 Ferrari F60 V8	*spun off in Q1		*20/20
16	ABU DHABI GP	Yas Marina Circuit	3	Scuderia Ferrari Marlboro	B	2.4 Ferrari F60 V8	1 lap behind		20/20

GP Starts: 229   GP Wins: 3   Pole positions: 4   Fastest laps: 2   Points: 275

JOHN FITCH

WITH just two grand prix races to his name, the uninitiated may think that John Fitch was just another insignificant run-of-the-mill driver – far from it.

Born into a wealthy family, and with a motoring background courtesy of his stepfather, Fitch served as a fighter pilot during the Second World War, and was held as a PoW after being shot down. In poor physical condition upon his release, he did not turn to motor racing until 1949, but soon became a major name in SCCA circles. In March 1951, on his first racing trip overseas, he won the Perón Grand Prix, a sports car race in Buenos Aires, driving an Allard-Cadillac. This victory brought him to the attention of millionaire racer and entrant Briggs Cunningham, who took him into his sports car team, which was attempting to win Le Mans and other long-distance events. John won the Sebring 12-hours, and finished third in the Cunningham at Le Mans in 1953, a season that also saw him have a go at single-seater racing with HWM in the Italian GP and finish fourth at Aix-les-Bains in a Cooper-Bristol; attempt to qualify for Indianapolis; and take part in the Monte Carlo and Alpine Rallies.

Having impressed Alfred Neubauer during a test in a 300SL Mercedes in 1952, Fitch finally got the call from the great man and found himself in the factory sports car team for 1955 and reserve driver (not used) at a couple of grands prix. Unfortunately this was the year of the Le Mans disaster, and Fitch's co-driver, 'Levegh' (Pierre Bouillin), was a central figure in the tragedy. John did have the satisfaction of sharing the winning Mercedes with Stirling Moss at Dundrod later in the year, however, before the Stuttgart team withdrew from racing.

Fitch then returned to the States, initially to help Chevrolet's sports car effort, which limited his racing somewhat, but nothing was allowed to get in the way of his annual pilgrimage to Sebring, which lasted until 1964. By then, he was fully involved in the management of the Lime Rock circuit, which was used for both racing and the testing of road cars.

FITCH, John (USA) b 4/8/1917, Indianapolis, Indiana

1953 Championship position: Unplaced

	Race	Circuit	No	Entrant	Tyres	Capacity/Car/Engine	Comment	Q Pos/Entries
ret	ITALIAN GP	Monza	18	HW Motors Ltd	D	2.0 HWM-Alta 4	engine	26/30

1955 Championship position: Unplaced

9	ITALIAN GP	Monza	40	Stirling Moss Ltd	D	2.5 Maserati 250F 6	4 laps behind	20/22

GP Starts: 2   GP Wins: 0   Pole positions: 0   Fastest laps: 0   Points: 0

CHRISTIAN FITTIPALDI

W ITH excellent backing from his Brazilian sponsors, and the guidance of his father, Wilson, himself a former grand prix driver, Christian Fittipaldi earned himself the right to become a Formula 1 driver on talent alone. Sadly, his grand prix career was spent driving mediocre machinery and he was unable to impress sufficiently to attract an offer from a front-line team, so he decided to pursue a career in CART.

With the Brazilian Formula 3 championship behind him, Christian travelled to Britain to race in the 1990 British F3 championship. Taking the number-two seat to Mika Häkkinen in the crack West Surrey Racing team, he finished fourth in the final standings, with just one win at Donington, but miles behind the Finns Häkkinen and Mika Salo in points. Moving up to F3000 for 1991 with Pacific Racing, young Christian was certainly fortunate to be in a Reynard chassis, but he held to his conviction that consistency would count and, when he had to, could show the pack a clean pair of heels, as he proved at Jerez and Nogaro. The championship was his, and thus he would soon become the third grand prix driver to emerge from this remarkable family.

Christian's first season with Minardi was interrupted when a practice crash at Magny-Cours inflicted back injuries that put him out for a spell, but after a shaky return he bounced back in Japan to score his first championship point. Continuing with the underfinanced Minardi team in 1993, he started well, but with the car less and less competitive as the season progressed, the Brazilian was stood down for the final two races to make room for the well-financed Jean-Marc Gounon.

Meanwhile Christian's sponsors and advisers were busy trying to arrange a switch to a bigger team for 1994. He moved another rung up the grand prix ladder with Footwork, but was disappointed not to have made it into a better-funded team with more chance of success. The season started brightly, however, and he was superb at Monaco with the neat Ford HB-engined car, qualifying sixth and running in fourth place, but things went downhill when the team became bogged down in trying to implement the post-Imola mid-season rule changes without the necessary resources.

Frustrated by his lack of progress and impatient for success, Christian abandoned his Formula 1 career to join the Indy car circuit in 1995. Naturally his first season with Derrick Walker was a period of learning, and the high point was undoubtedly lasting the distance to claim second place in the Indianapolis 500. For 1996, he obtained a seat alongside Michael Andretti at Newman-Haas, and at last he had the opportunity to shine, looking particularly impressive in the wet at Detroit and Portland. His prospects were bright for 1997, but only two races into the season he suffered a badly broken leg in an accident at Surfers Paradise and did extremely well upon his return to pick up his previous pace.

Despite fitting comfortably into the Newman-Haas camp, in Christian had thought a breakthrough was imminent, he would have been disappointed in 1998, when minor problems often blunted the team's challenge. However, he had shown in the past that patience is a virtue, and the 1999 season saw a much more complete driver. Not only did he win a CART race (at the 71st attempt, at Road America), but also he looked a possible PPG Cup champion, having finished among the top ten in each of the first seven races. Unfortunately he was involved in a nasty accident in testing at Gateway, suffering a subdural haematoma, which meant he was forced to sit on the sidelines for five races, which scuppered his title chances. Christian remained at Newman-Haas for three more seasons, scoring his second win at Fontana in 2000, but the steady driver was then completely overshadowed by the arrival of Brazilian compatriot Cristiano de Matta.

Christian then made an unimpressive switch to NASCAR with the once-illustrious Richard Petty Racing, with little by way of results, before tasting success again in the Rolex Grand Am series in 2004, driving a Doran-Pontiac to victory in the Daytona 24-hour race. Then he competed in the Brazilian Stock Car series against a number of ex-Formula 1 pilots before reappearing briefly on the International scene in 2006, taking over the Brazil A1GP entry from Nelson Piquet Jr without matching the youngster's impressive performances in the same car.

Success at Daytona put Christian in the frame for some appearances at Le Mans, where he raced in the GT class between 2006 and 2008. He signed to race full time in the 2008 ALMS Series for Andretti-Green, driving their Acura LMP2 Prototype alongside Bryan Herta. It was not a happy liaison, however, and despite a couple of sixth-place finishes, he was replaced after just four races. Then he switched back to the lesser Grand Am series with Eddie Cheever's team for the remainder of the 2008 season.

Next, Christian commuted to Brazil from his home in Key Biscayne, Florida, to compete in selected truck racing and stock car events, while in Grand Am, he finished third in the 2011 Daytona 24-hours in a Riley-Porsche, and posted a fifth in the Corvette Daytona Prototype in 2012. Looking to regain a more regular foothold in racing, he planned on joining the Italian Superstars series for a limited number of races initially. If it went well, he intended to make it a full season in 2013.

FITTIPALDI, Christian (BR) b 18/1/1971, São Paulo

1992 Championship position: 17th= Wins: 0 Pole positions: 0 Fastest laps: 0 Points scored: 1

	Race	Circuit	No	Entrant	Tyres	Capacity/Car/Engine	Comment	Q Pos/Entries
ret	SOUTH AFRICAN GP	Kyalami	23	Minardi Team	G	3.5 Minardi M191B-Lamborghini V12	electrics	20/30
ret	MEXICAN GP	Mexico City	23	Minardi Team	G	3.5 Minardi M191B-Lamborghini V12	spun off	17/30
ret	BRAZILIAN GP	Interlagos	23	Minardi Team	G	3.5 Minardi M191B-Lamborghini V12	gearbox	20/31
11	SPANISH GP	Barcelona	23	Minardi Team	G	3.5 Minardi M191B-Lamborghini V12	4 laps behind	22/32
ret	SAN MARINO GP	Imola	23	Minardi Team	G	3.5 Minardi M192-Lamborghini V12	transmission	25/32
8	MONACO GP	Monte Carlo	23	Minardi Team	G	3.5 Minardi M192-Lamborghini V12	1 lap behind	17/32
13/ret	CANADIAN GP	Montreal	23	Minardi Team	G	3.5 Minardi M192-Lamborghini V12	gearbox oil fire/4 laps behind	25/32
dnq	FRENCH GP	Magny Cours	23	Minardi Team	G	3.5 Minardi M192-Lamborghini V12	practice crash – injured back	28/30
dnq	BELGIAN GP	Spa	23	Minardi Team	G	3.5 Minardi M192-Lamborghini V12		27/30
dnq	ITALIAN GP	Monza	23	Minardi Team	G	3.5 Minardi M192-Lamborghini V12		27/28
12	PORTUGUESE GP	Estoril	23	Minardi Team	G	3.5 Minardi M192-Lamborghini V12	3 laps behind	26/26
6	JAPANESE GP	Suzuka	23	Minardi Team	G	3.5 Minardi M192-Lamborghini V12	1 lap behind	12/26
9	AUSTRALIAN GP	Adelaide	23	Minardi Team	G	3.5 Minardi M192-Lamborghini V12	2 laps behind	17/26

1993 Championship position: 13th= Wins: 0 Pole positions: 0 Fastest laps: 0 Points scored: 5

	Race	Circuit	No	Entrant	Tyres	Capacity/Car/Engine	Comment	Q Pos/Entries
4	SOUTH AFRICAN GP	Kyalami	23	Minardi Team	G	3.5 Minardi M193-Ford HB V8	1 lap behind	13/26
ret	BRAZILIAN GP	Interlagos	23	Minardi Team	G	3.5 Minardi M193-Ford HB V8	spun off in rainstorm	20/26
7	EUROPEAN GP	Donington	23	Minardi Team	G	3.5 Minardi M193-Ford HB V8	3 laps behind	16/26
ret	SAN MARINO GP	Imola	23	Minardi Team	G	3.5 Minardi M193-Ford HB V8	damaged steering	23/26
8	SPANISH GP	Barcelona	23	Minardi Team	G	3.5 Minardi M193-Ford HB V8	2 laps behind	20/26
5	MONACO GP	Monte Carlo	23	Minardi Team	G	3.5 Minardi M193-Ford HB V8	2 laps behind	17/26
9	CANADIAN GP	Montreal	23	Minardi Team	G	3.5 Minardi M193-Ford HB V8	gearbox trouble/2 laps behind	17/26
8	FRENCH GP	Magny Cours	23	Minardi Team	G	3.5 Minardi M193-Ford HB V8	ran without stop/1 lap behind	23/26
12/ret	BRITISH GP	Silverstone	23	Minardi Team	G	3.5 Minardi M193-Ford HB V8	gearbox/2 laps behind	19/26
11	GERMAN GP	Hockenheim	23	Minardi Team	G	3.5 Minardi M193-Ford HB V8	ran without stop/1 lap behind	20/26
ret	HUNGARIAN GP	Hungaroring	23	Minardi Team	G	3.5 Minardi M193-Ford HB V8	collision with Alesi – suspension	14/26
ret	BELGIAN GP	Spa	23	Minardi Team	G	3.5 Minardi M193-Ford HB V8	accident	22/25
8	ITALIAN GP	Monza	23	Minardi Team	G	3.5 Minardi M193-Ford HB V8	ran into Martini at finish/-2 laps	24/26
9	PORTUGUESE GP	Estoril	23	Minardi Team	G	3.5 Minardi M193-Ford HB V8	ran without stop/2 laps behind	24/26

1994 Championship position: 14th Wins: 0 Pole positions: 0 Fastest laps: 0 Points scored: 6

	Race	Circuit	No	Entrant	Tyres	Capacity/Car/Engine	Comment	Q Pos/Entries
ret	BRAZILIAN GP	Interlagos	9	Footwork Ford	G	3.5 Footwork FA15-Ford HB V8	gearbox	11/28
4	PACIFIC GP	T.I. Circuit	9	Footwork Ford	G	3.5 Footwork FA15-Ford HB V8	1 lap behind	9/28
13/ret	SAN MARINO GP	Imola	9	Footwork Ford	G	3.5 Footwork FA15-Ford HB V8	brakes/4 laps behind	16/28
ret	MONACO GP	Monte Carlo	9	Footwork Ford	G	3.5 Footwork FA15-Ford HB V8	gearbox	6/24
ret	SPANISH GP	Barcelona	9	Footwork Ford	G	3.5 Footwork FA15-Ford HB V8	engine	21/27
dsq*	CANADIAN GP	Montreal	9	Footwork Ford	G	3.5 Footwork FA15-Ford HB V8	6th on road – *car underweight	16/27
8	FRENCH GP	Magny Cours	9	Footwork Ford	G	3.5 Footwork FA15-Ford HB V8		18/28
9*	BRITISH GP	Silverstone	9	Footwork Ford	G	3.5 Footwork FA15-Ford HB V8	*2nd place car disqualified/-2 laps	20/28
4	GERMAN GP	Hockenheim	9	Footwork Ford	G	3.5 Footwork FA15-Ford HB V8		17/28
14/ret	HUNGARIAN GP	Hungaroring	9	Footwork Ford	G	3.5 Footwork FA15-Ford HB V8	8 laps behind/gearbox	16/28
ret	BELGIAN GP	Spa	9	Footwork Ford	G	3.5 Footwork FA15-Ford HB V8	engine	24/28
ret	ITALIAN GP	Monza	9	Footwork Ford	G	3.5 Footwork FA15-Ford HB V8	engine	19/28
8	PORTUGUESE GP	Estoril	9	Footwork Ford	G	3.5 Footwork FA15-Ford HB V8	1 lap behind	11/28
17	EUROPEAN GP	Jerez	9	Footwork Ford	G	3.5 Footwork FA15-Ford HB V8	long pit stop – nose cone/-3 laps	19/28
8	JAPANESE GP	Suzuka	9	Footwork Ford	G	3.5 Footwork FA15-Ford HB V8	1 lap behind	18/28
8	AUSTRALIAN GP	Adelaide	9	Footwork Ford	G	3.5 Footwork FA15-Ford HB V8	1 lap behind	19/28

GP Starts: 40 GP Wins: 0 Pole positions: 0 Fastest laps: 0 Points: 12

Christian Fittipaldi spent three years in F1, but having achieved just a couple of fourth places with Footwork in 1994, he opted for a more successful career in Indy cars.

EMERSON FITTIPALDI

CROWNED the youngest-ever world champion at 25 in 1972, Emerson Fittipaldi was one of the outstanding drivers of the 1970s, but a spectacularly ill-judged career move at the end of 1975 turned him into a grand prix racing also-ran, before he came back from retirement to forge a second magnificent career and conquer the world of Indy car racing.

Success in Brazil led Fittipaldi to turn his sights on Europe. The sale of his Formula Vee car financed a three-month trip to England in 1969, and he quickly made his mark in a Formula Ford Merlyn. Emerson's talent was obvious, and a move up to F3 in a Jim Russell Lotus 59 paid immediate dividends, the Brazilian winning a string of races, which gave him the confidence to move into Formula 2 with Mike Warner in 1970. Although an outright win eluded him, he finished virtually every race in the top six, and Colin Chapman soon had his signature on a Lotus F1 contract.

Fittipaldi was eased on to the grand prix scene with a Lotus 49C, but tragedy soon befell the team with the death of Jochen Rindt at Monza. Emerson was suddenly thrust into the spotlight upon the team's return at Watkins Glen, and he provided a great morale booster for Chapman by winning the race, albeit only after Pedro Rodriguez hit trouble late on. For 1971, he was given the number-one seat, but lost momentum after a mid-season road accident. Nevertheless he did remarkably well in his first full Formula 1 season and, with the Lotus 72 finely honed, he became the man to beat the following year. Victories in the Race of Champions and International Trophy provided the springboard for a mid-season burst of scintillating form that saw him claim the world championship.

Joined in the team by Ronnie Peterson for 1973, Emerson was quick straight out of the blocks with three wins in the first six grands prix, and a second title looked a formality, but then his year turned sour, particularly after a practice crash at Zandvoort left him with a niggling ankle injury. By the end of the season, he was somewhat overshadowed by Peterson and accepted a big-money offer from McLaren for 1974. It proved to be a wise decision, his smooth, unruffled driving and great tactical acumen bringing him his second world championship in an evenly contested season. The following year yielded just one grand prix win at Silverstone, Emerson keeping his head in a rainstorm while those all around were spinning out. In the end, though, Niki Lauda's Ferrari had the legs of his McLaren, and he had to settle for second place in the championship.

Then came the bombshell. Emerson would join the Copersucar-Fittipaldi team established by his brother, Wilson, for 1976 to drive the outfit's well-funded, but uncompetitive Brazilian-built challenger. From Olympian heights, he soon found himself in a valley of despair as the project struggled on, occasionally breaking into the top six, but achieving little else. A magnificent race at Rio in 1978, when he finished a brilliant second to Carlos Reutemann's Ferrari, and an excellent third place at Long Beach in 1980 were but isolated reminders of former glories. At the end of that season, he switched from driving to management duties, but the Fittipaldi team was finally forced to close its doors at the end of 1982.

Returning home to Brazil, Emerson concentrated on the family orange growing and automobile accessory businesses, not missing racing in the slightest. However, a few races in super karts for fun in 1983 led to an invitation to take part in an IMSA race at Miami early in 1984, and he enjoyed himself so much that he was soon tempted to accept an Indy car drive at Long Beach, finishing a remarkable fifth. The wheel-to-wheel racing ignited his lost passion for driving and soon he would get a big break, joining the Patrick Racing team to replace the severely injured Chip Ganassi. With Fittipaldi as the focal point, the team steadily grew in stature, ultimate success arriving in 1989, when he not only won the PPG Indy Car World Series title, but also took a famous last-gasp win in the Indy 500 after a coming-together with Al Unser Jnr on the penultimate lap.

'Emmo' joined Roger Penske's three-car team in 1990 and was one of the undoubted top guns in the Indy car championship. In 1993, he won the Indy 500 for the second time with a beautifully judged performance and finished second to Nigel Mansell in the points standings. Joined by Al Unser Jnr in an all-conquering three-car Penske squad for 1994, he proved that he still had plenty of racing mileage left. Despite recording only one win (at Phoenix), he was runner-up to the utterly dominant Unser in the PPG Cup ranking. His major disappointment came at Indianapolis, where he threw the car into the wall with the race all but won. After this season of plenty for Team Penske, 1995 came as a shock to the system, with Emmo and Unser struggling with the recalcitrant PC24. The nadir was the pair's failure to qualify at Indy, but there were some high spots, too, and Fittipaldi took a well-judged win at Nazareth.

Although the inevitable rumours of his retirement abounded, Fittipaldi had no intention of giving up competition, and he was back in 1996, running a Penske under the guidance of Carl Hogan. The Brazilian put in some spirited performances, but his season – and ultimately his career – came to an abrupt end when he crashed heavily in the Marlboro 500 at Michigan.

Suffering from a crushed vertebra in his neck, the 49-year-old spent five hours in surgery, being fortunate not to have sustained permanent injury. While recovering, Emmo still hankered after a return to action, but another accident – a light aircraft crash in his native Brazil – in 1997 left him with serious back injuries. Wisely all thoughts of racing again were abandoned, but he was still a regular on the CART scene, working with Penske to guide the career of the highly promising Brazilian Helio Castro-Neves.

After a period away from the track attending to a myriad of business interests, Emerson was tempted back to the Champ Car scene in 2003, when he formed Fittipaldi-Dingman Racing, which ran the promising Tiago Monteiro. Sadly the team was not particularly successful and folded after just one season.

Emerson was lured back into action again in 2005 in the Grand Prix Masters series, where he showed some of his more youthful competitors the way home with a feisty drive at Kyalami. In 2008, he was reunited with brother Wilson in action, driving a Porsche GT3 in the Brazilian GT3 series.

FITTIPALDI, Emerson (BR) b 12/12/1946, São Paulo

1970 Championship position: 10th   Wins: 1   Pole positions: 0   Fastest laps: 0   Points scored: 12

	Race	Circuit	No	Entrant	Tyres	Capacity/Car/Engine	Comment	Q Pos/Entries
8	BRITISH GP	Brands Hatch	28	Gold Leaf Team Lotus	F	3.0 Lotus 49C-Cosworth V8	2 laps behind	22/25
4	GERMAN GP	Hockenheim	17	Gold Leaf Team Lotus	F	3.0 Lotus 49C-Cosworth V8		13/25
15	AUSTRIAN GP	Österreichring	8	Gold Leaf Team Lotus	F	3.0 Lotus 49C-Cosworth V8	pit stop – fuel/5 laps behind	15/24
dns	ITALIAN GP	Monza	26	Gold Leaf Team Lotus	F	3.0 Lotus 72C-Cosworth V8	withdrawn after Rindt's fatal accident	25/27
1	US GP	Watkins Glen	24	Gold Leaf Team Lotus	F	3.0 Lotus 72C-Cosworth V8		3/27
ret	MEXICAN GP	Mexico City	24	Gold Leaf Team Lotus	F	3.0 Lotus 72C-Cosworth V8	engine	18/18

1971 Championship position: 6th   Wins: 0   Pole positions: 0   Fastest laps: 0   Points scored: 16

	Race	Circuit	No	Entrant	Tyres	Capacity/Car/Engine	Comment	Q Pos/Entries
ret	SOUTH AFRICAN GP	Kyalami	2	Gold Leaf Team Lotus	F	3.0 Lotus 72C-Cosworth V8	engine	=5/25
ret	SPANISH GP	Montjuich Park	2	Gold Leaf Team Lotus	F	3.0 Lotus 72C-Cosworth V8	rear suspension	14/22
5	MONACO GP	Monte Carlo	1	Gold Leaf Team Lotus	F	3.0 Lotus 72D-Cosworth V8	1 lap behind	17/23
3	FRENCH GP	Paul Ricard	1	Gold Leaf Team Lotus	F	3.0 Lotus 72D-Cosworth V8		17/24
3	BRITISH GP	Silverstone	1	Gold Leaf Team Lotus	F	3.0 Lotus 72D-Cosworth V8		3/24
ret	GERMAN GP	Nürburgring	8	Gold Leaf Team Lotus	F	3.0 Lotus 72D-Cosworth V8	oil leak	8/23
2	AUSTRIAN GP	Österreichring	2	Gold Leaf Team Lotus	F	3.0 Lotus 72D-Cosworth V8		5/22
8	ITALIAN GP	Monza	5	World Wide Racing	F	Turbine Lotus 56B-Pratt & Whitney	1 lap behind	18/24
7	CANADIAN GP	Mosport Park	2	Gold Leaf Team Lotus	F	3.0 Lotus 72D-Cosworth V8	2 laps behind	=4/27
nc	US GP	Watkins Glen	2	Gold Leaf Team Lotus	F	3.0 Lotus 72D-Cosworth V8	pit stops – throttle/10 laps behind	2/32

1972 WORLD CHAMPION   Wins: 5   Pole positions: 3   Fastest laps: 0   Points scored: 61

	Race	Circuit	No	Entrant	Tyres	Capacity/Car/Engine	Comment	Q Pos/Entries
ret	ARGENTINE GP	Buenos Aires	11	John Player Team Lotus	F	3.0 Lotus 72D-Cosworth V8	broken rear suspension	=5/22
2	SOUTH AFRICAN GP	Kyalami	8	John Player Team Lotus	F	3.0 Lotus 72D-Cosworth V8		=3/27
1	SPANISH GP	Jarama	5	John Player Team Lotus	F	3.0 Lotus 72D-Cosworth V8		3/26
3	MONACO GP	Monte Carlo	8	John Player Team Lotus	F	3.0 Lotus 72D-Cosworth V8	1 lap behind	1/25
1	BELGIAN GP	Nivelles	32	John Player Team Lotus	F	3.0 Lotus 72D-Cosworth V8		1/26
2	FRENCH GP	Clermont Ferrand	1	John Player Team Lotus	F	3.0 Lotus 72D-Cosworth V8		=7/29
1	BRITISH GP	Brands Hatch	8	John Player Team Lotus	F	3.0 Lotus 72D-Cosworth V8		2/27
ret	GERMAN GP	Nürburgring	2	John Player Team Lotus	F	3.0 Lotus 72D-Cosworth V8	gearbox casing – oil fire	3/27
1	AUSTRIAN GP	Österreichring	31	John Player Team Lotus	F	3.0 Lotus 72D-Cosworth V8		1/26
1	ITALIAN GP	Monza	6	World Wide Racing	F	3.0 Lotus 72D-Cosworth V8		6/27
11	CANADIAN GP	Mosport Park	5	John Player Team Lotus	F	3.0 Lotus 72D-Cosworth V8	pit stop – nose cone/gearbox/-2 laps	=4/25
ret	US GP	Watkins Glen	10	John Player Team Lotus	F	3.0 Lotus 72D-Cosworth V8	shock absorber	9/32

1973 Championship position: 2nd   Wins: 3   Pole positions: 1   Fastest laps: 5 (1 shared)   Points scored: 55

	Race	Circuit	No	Entrant	Tyres	Capacity/Car/Engine	Comment	Q Pos/Entries
1	ARGENTINE GP	Buenos Aires	2	John Player Team Lotus	G	3.0 Lotus 72D-Cosworth V8	FL	2/19
1	BRAZILIAN GP	Interlagos	1	John Player Team Lotus	G	3.0 Lotus 72D-Cosworth V8	FL (shared with Hulme)	2/20
3	SOUTH AFRICAN GP	Kyalami	1	John Player Team Lotus	G	3.0 Lotus 72D-Cosworth V8	FL	2/25
1	SPANISH GP	Montjuich Park	1	John Player Team Lotus	G	3.0 Lotus 72E-Cosworth V8		=7/22
3	BELGIAN GP	Zolder	1	John Player Team Lotus	G	3.0 Lotus 72E-Cosworth V8		9/23
2	MONACO GP	Monte Carlo	1	John Player Team Lotus	G	3.0 Lotus 72E-Cosworth V8	FL	5/26
12/ret	SWEDISH GP	Anderstorp	1	John Player Team Lotus	G	3.0 Lotus 72E-Cosworth V8	transmission/4 laps behind	4/22
ret	FRENCH GP	Paul Ricard	1	John Player Team Lotus	G	3.0 Lotus 72E-Cosworth V8	accident with Scheckter	3/25
ret	BRITISH GP	Silverstone	1	John Player Team Lotus	G	3.0 Lotus 72E-Cosworth V8	transmission – c.v. joint	=4/29
ret	DUTCH GP	Zandvoort	1	John Player Team Lotus	G	3.0 Lotus 72E-Cosworth V8	in pain after practice accident	16/24
6	GERMAN GP	Nürburgring	1	John Player Team Lotus	G	3.0 Lotus 72E-Cosworth V8		14/23
11/ret	AUSTRIAN GP	Österreichring	1	John Player Team Lotus	G	3.0 Lotus 72E-Cosworth V8	fuel pipe/6 laps behind	1/25
2	ITALIAN GP	Monza	1	John Player Team Lotus	G	3.0 Lotus 72E-Cosworth V8		4/25
2	CANADIAN GP	Mosport Park	1	John Player Team Lotus	G	3.0 Lotus 72E-Cosworth V8	FL	5/26
6	US GP	Watkins Glen	1	John Player Team Lotus	G	3.0 Lotus 72E-Cosworth V8		3/28

On his way to the championship for the first time, Emerson in the JPS Lotus leads the Ferrari of Jacky Ickx in the 1972 British Grand Prix at Brands Hatch. It was one of five victories delivered by the Brazilian in a hugely successful year.

Emerson Fittipaldi moved to McLaren in 1974 and took his second world championship at the wheel of the M23, after a close-fought battle with the Ferraris of Lauda and Reggazoni. Pictured left, he takes his first win for his new team in the Brazilian Grand Prix at Interlagos.

1974 WORLD CHAMPION Wins: 3   Pole positions: 2   Fastest laps: 0   Points scored: 55

10	ARGENTINE GP	Buenos Aires	5	Marlboro Team Texaco	G	3.0 McLaren M23-Cosworth V8	*knocked off ignition switch/-2 laps*	3/26
1	BRAZILIAN GP	Interlagos	5	Marlboro Team Texaco	G	3.0 McLaren M23-Cosworth V8		1/25
7	SOUTH AFRICAN GP	Kyalami	5	Marlboro Team Texaco	G	3.0 McLaren M23-Cosworth V8		5/27
3	SPANISH GP	Jarama	5	Marlboro Team Texaco	G	3.0 McLaren M23-Cosworth V8	*1 lap behind*	4/28
1	BELGIAN GP	Nivelles	5	Marlboro Team Texaco	G	3.0 McLaren M23-Cosworth V8		4/32
5	MONACO GP	Monte Carlo	5	Marlboro Team Texaco	G	3.0 McLaren M23-Cosworth V8	*1 lap behind*	=12/28
4	SWEDISH GP	Anderstorp	5	Marlboro Team Texaco	G	3.0 McLaren M23-Cosworth V8		9/28
3	DUTCH GP	Zandvoort	5	Marlboro Team Texaco	G	3.0 McLaren M23-Cosworth V8		3/27
ret	FRENCH GP	Dijon	5	Marlboro Team Texaco	G	3.0 McLaren M23-Cosworth V8	*engine*	5/30
2	BRITISH GP	Brands Hatch	5	Marlboro Team Texaco	G	3.0 McLaren M23-Cosworth V8		8/34
ret	GERMAN GP	Nürburgring	5	Marlboro Team Texaco	G	3.0 McLaren M23-Cosworth V8	*collision – Hulme – accident damage*	3/32
ret	AUSTRIAN GP	Österreichring	5	Marlboro Team Texaco	G	3.0 McLaren M23-Cosworth V8	*engine*	3/31
2	ITALIAN GP	Monza	5	Marlboro Team Texaco	G	3.0 McLaren M23-Cosworth V8		6/31
1	CANADIAN GP	Mosport Park	5	Marlboro Team Texaco	G	3.0 McLaren M23-Cosworth V8		1/30
4	US GP	Watkins Glen	5	Marlboro Team Texaco	G	3.0 McLaren M23-Cosworth V8		8/30

1975 Championship position: 2nd   Wins: 2   Pole positions: 0   Fastest laps: 1   Points scored: 45

1	ARGENTINE GP	Buenos Aires	1	Marlboro Team Texaco	G	3.0 McLaren M23-Cosworth V8		5/23
2	BRAZILIAN GP	Interlagos	1	Marlboro Team Texaco	G	3.0 McLaren M23-Cosworth V8		2/23
nc	SOUTH AFRICAN GP	Kyalami	1	Marlboro Team Texaco	G	3.0 McLaren M23-Cosworth V8	*pit stop – misfire/13 laps behind*	11/28
dns	SPANISH GP	Montjuich Park	1	Marlboro Team Texaco	G	3.0 McLaren M23-Cosworth V8	*protest at lack of track safety*	(26)/26
2	MONACO GP	Monte Carlo	1	Marlboro Team Texaco	G	3.0 McLaren M23-Cosworth V8		9/26
7	BELGIAN GP	Zolder	1	Marlboro Team Texaco	G	3.0 McLaren M23-Cosworth V8	*brake problems/1 lap behind*	8/24
8	SWEDISH GP	Anderstorp	1	Marlboro Team Texaco	G	3.0 McLaren M23-Cosworth V8	*handling problems/1 lap behind*	11/26
ret	DUTCH GP	Zandvoort	1	Marlboro Team Texaco	G	3.0 McLaren M23-Cosworth V8	*engine*	6/25
4	FRENCH GP	Paul Ricard	1	Marlboro Team Texaco	G	3.0 McLaren M23-Cosworth V8		10/26
1	BRITISH GP	Silverstone	1	Marlboro Team Texaco	G	3.0 McLaren M23-Cosworth V8		7/28
ret	GERMAN GP	Nürburgring	1	Marlboro Team Texaco	G	3.0 McLaren M23-Cosworth V8	*puncture – suspension damage*	=8/26
9	AUSTRIAN GP	Österreichring	1	Marlboro Team Texaco	G	3.0 McLaren M23-Cosworth V8	*1 lap behind*	3/30
2	ITALIAN GP	Monza	1	Marlboro Team Texaco	G	3.0 McLaren M23-Cosworth V8		3/28
2	US GP	Watkins Glen	1	Marlboro Team Texaco	G	3.0 McLaren M23-Cosworth V8	*FL*	2/24

1976 Championship position: 16th=   Wins: 0   Pole positions: 0   Fastest laps: 0   Points scored: 3

13	BRAZILIAN GP	Interlagos	30	Copersucar-Fittipaldi	G	3.0 Fittipaldi FD04-Cosworth V8	*misfire/3 laps behind*	5/22
17/ret	SOUTH AFRICAN GP	Kyalami	30	Copersucar-Fittipaldi	G	3.0 Fittipaldi FD04-Cosworth V8	*engine/4 laps behind*	21/25
6	US GP WEST	Long Beach	30	Copersucar-Fittipaldi	G	3.0 Fittipaldi FD04-Cosworth V8	*1 lap behind*	16/27
ret	SPANISH GP	Jarama	30	Copersucar-Fittipaldi	G	3.0 Fittipaldi FD04-Cosworth V8	*gear linkage*	19/30
dnq	BELGIAN GP	Zolder	30	Copersucar-Fittipaldi	G	3.0 Fittipaldi FD04-Cosworth V8		27/29
6	MONACO GP	Monte Carlo	30	Copersucar-Fittipaldi	G	3.0 Fittipaldi FD04-Cosworth V8	*1 lap behind*	7/25
ret	SWEDISH GP	Anderstorp	30	Copersucar-Fittipaldi	G	3.0 Fittipaldi FD04-Cosworth V8	*handling*	21/27
ret	FRENCH GP	Paul Ricard	30	Copersucar-Fittipaldi	G	3.0 Fittipaldi FD04-Cosworth V8	*engine – oil pressure*	21/30
6*	BRITISH GP	Brands Hatch	30	Copersucar-Fittipaldi	G	3.0 Fittipaldi FD04-Cosworth V8	**1st place car dsq/2 laps behind*	21/30
13	GERMAN GP	Nürburgring	30	Copersucar-Fittipaldi	G	3.0 Fittipaldi FD04-Cosworth V8		20/28
ret	AUSTRIAN GP	Österreichring	30	Copersucar-Fittipaldi	G	3.0 Fittipaldi FD04-Cosworth V8	*collision with Brambilla*	17/25
ret	DUTCH GP	Zandvoort	30	Copersucar-Fittipaldi	G	3.0 Fittipaldi FD04-Cosworth V8	*electrics*	17/27
15	ITALIAN GP	Monza	30	Copersucar-Fittipaldi	G	3.0 Fittipaldi FD04-Cosworth V8	*2 laps behind*	20/29
ret	CANADIAN GP	Mosport Park	30	Copersucar-Fittipaldi	G	3.0 Fittipaldi FD04-Cosworth V8	*exhaust and rear wing bracket*	17/27
9	US GP EAST	Watkins Glen	30	Copersucar-Fittipaldi	G	3.0 Fittipaldi FD04-Cosworth V8	*2 laps behind*	15/27
ret	JAPANESE GP	Mount Fuji	30	Copersucar-Fittipaldi	G	3.0 Fittipaldi FD04-Cosworth V8	*withdrew due to weather conditions*	23/27

1977 Championship position: 12th   Wins: 0   Pole positions: 0   Fastest laps: 0   Points scored: 11

4	ARGENTINE GP	Buenos Aires	28	Copersucar-Fittipaldi	G	3.0 Fittipaldi FD04-Cosworth V8		16/21
4	BRAZILIAN GP	Interlagos	28	Copersucar-Fittipaldi	G	3.0 Fittipaldi FD04-Cosworth V8	*1 lap behind*	16/22
10	SOUTH AFRICAN GP	Kyalami	28	Copersucar-Fittipaldi	G	3.0 Fittipaldi FD04-Cosworth V8		9/23
5	US GP WEST	Long Beach	28	Copersucar-Fittipaldi	G	3.0 Fittipaldi FD04-Cosworth V8		7/22
14	SPANISH GP	Jarama	28	Copersucar-Fittipaldi	G	3.0 Fittipaldi FD04-Cosworth V8	*vibration/overheating/5 laps behind*	19/31
ret	MONACO GP	Monte Carlo	28	Copersucar-Fittipaldi	G	3.0 Fittipaldi FD04-Cosworth V8	*engine*	18/26
ret	BELGIAN GP	Zolder	28	Copersucar-Fittipaldi	G	3.0 Fittipaldi F5-Cosworth V8	*water in electrics*	16/32

			No	Entrant	Tyres	Capacity/Car/Engine	Comment	Q Pos/Entries
18	SWEDISH GP	Anderstorp	28	Copersucar-Fittipaldi	G	3.0 Fittipaldi FD04-Cosworth V8	handling/6 laps behind	18/31
dns	"	"	28	Copersucar-Fittipaldi	G	3.0 Fittipaldi F5-Cosworth V8	accident in practice	- / -
11	FRENCH GP	Dijon	28	Copersucar-Fittipaldi	G	3.0 Fittipaldi F5-Cosworth V8	3 laps behind	22/30
ret	BRITISH GP	Silverstone	28	Copersucar-Fittipaldi	G	3.0 Fittipaldi F5-Cosworth V8	engine	22/36
dnq	GERMAN GP	Hockenheim	28	Copersucar-Fittipaldi	G	3.0 Fittipaldi F5-Cosworth V8		28/30
11	AUSTRIAN GP	Österreichring	28	Copersucar-Fittipaldi	G	3.0 Fittipaldi F5-Cosworth V8	1 lap behind	23/30
4	DUTCH GP	Zandvoort	28	Copersucar-Fittipaldi	G	3.0 Fittipaldi F5-Cosworth V8	1 lap behind	17/34
dnq	ITALIAN GP	Monza	28	Copersucar-Fittipaldi	G	3.0 Fittipaldi F5-Cosworth V8		26/34
13	US GP EAST	Watkins Glen	28	Copersucar-Fittipaldi	G	3.0 Fittipaldi F5-Cosworth V8	2 laps behind	18/27
ret	CANADIAN GP	Mosport Park	28	Copersucar-Fittipaldi	G	3.0 Fittipaldi F5-Cosworth V8	engine	19/27

1978 Championship position: 19th= Wins: 0 Pole positions: 0 Fastest laps: 0 Points scored: 17

			No	Entrant	Tyres	Capacity/Car/Engine	Comment	Q Pos/Entries
9	ARGENTINE GP	Buenos Aires	14	Fittipaldi Automotive	G	3.0 Fittipaldi F5A-Cosworth V8		17/27
2	BRAZILIAN GP	Rio	14	Fittipaldi Automotive	G	3.0 Fittipaldi F5A-Cosworth V8		7/28
ret	SOUTH AFRICAN GP	Kyalami	14	Fittipaldi Automotive	G	3.0 Fittipaldi F5A-Cosworth V8	driveshaft	16/30
8	US GP WEST	Long Beach	14	Fittipaldi Automotive	G	3.0 Fittipaldi F5A-Cosworth V8	1 lap behind	15/30
9	MONACO GP	Monte Carlo	14	Fittipaldi Automotive	G	3.0 Fittipaldi F5A-Cosworth V8	1 lap behind	20/30
ret	BELGIAN GP	Zolder	14	Fittipaldi Automotive	G	3.0 Fittipaldi F5A-Cosworth V8	collision with Ickx at start	15/30
ret	SPANISH GP	Jarama	14	Fittipaldi Automotive	G	3.0 Fittipaldi F5A-Cosworth V8	thottle linkage	15/29
6	SWEDISH GP	Anderstorp	14	Fittipaldi Automotive	G	3.0 Fittipaldi F5A-Cosworth V8	1 lap behind	13/27
ret	FRENCH GP	Paul Ricard	14	Fittipaldi Automotive	G	3.0 Fittipaldi F5A-Cosworth V8	rear suspension	15/29
ret	BRITISH GP	Brands Hatch	14	Fittipaldi Automotive	G	3.0 Fittipaldi F5A-Cosworth V8	engine	11/30
4	GERMAN GP	Hockenheim	14	Fittipaldi Automotive	G	3.0 Fittipaldi F5A-Cosworth V8		10/30
4	AUSTRIAN GP	Österreichring	14	Fittipaldi Automotive	G	3.0 Fittipaldi F5A-Cosworth V8	1 lap behind	6/31
5	DUTCH GP	Zandvoort	14	Fittipaldi Automotive	G	3.0 Fittipaldi F5A-Cosworth V8		10/33
8	ITALIAN GP	Monza	14	Fittipaldi Automotive	G	3.0 Fittipaldi F5A-Cosworth V8		13/32
5	US GP EAST	Watkins Glen	14	Fittipaldi Automotive	G	3.0 Fittipaldi F5A-Cosworth V8		13/27
ret	CANADIAN GP	Montreal	14	Fittipaldi Automotive	G	3.0 Fittipaldi F5A-Cosworth V8	collision with Stuck	6/28

1979 Championship position: 21st Wins: 0 Pole positions: 0 Fastest laps: 0 Points scored: 1

			No	Entrant	Tyres	Capacity/Car/Engine	Comment	Q Pos/Entries
6	ARGENTINE GP	Buenos Aires	14	Fittipaldi Automotive	G	3.0 Fittipaldi F5A-Cosworth V8	1 lap behind	11/26
11	BRAZILIAN GP	Interlagos	14	Fittipaldi Automotive	G	3.0 Fittipaldi F5A-Cosworth V8	1 lap behind	9/26
dns	"		14	Fittipaldi Automotive	G	3.0 Fittipaldi F6-Cosworth V8	practice only	- / -
13	SOUTH AFRICAN GP	Kyalami	14	Fittipaldi Automotive	G	3.0 Fittipaldi F6-Cosworth V8	4 laps behind	18/26
dns	" "	"	14	Fittipaldi Automotive	G	3.0 Fittipaldi F5A-Cosworth V8	practice only	- / -
ret	US GP WEST	Long Beach	14	Fittipaldi Automotive	G	3.0 Fittipaldi F5A-Cosworth V8	driveshaft	16/26
dns	" "	" "	14	Fittipaldi Automotive	G	3.0 Fittipaldi F6-Cosworth V8	practice only	- / -
11	SPANISH GP	Jarama	14	Fittipaldi Automotive	G	3.0 Fittipaldi F5A-Cosworth V8	1 lap behind	19/27
dns	"	"	14	Fittipaldi Automotive	G	3.0 Fittipaldi F6-Cosworth V8	practice only	- / -
9	BELGIAN GP	Zolder	14	Fittipaldi Automotive	G	3.0 Fittipaldi F5A-Cosworth V8	2 laps behind	23/28
ret	MONACO GP	Monte Carlo	14	Fittipaldi Automotive	G	3.0 Fittipaldi F5A-Cosworth V8	engine	17/25
ret	FRENCH GP	Paul Ricard	14	Fittipaldi Automotive	G	3.0 Fittipaldi F5A-Cosworth V8	engine - oil loss	18/27
ret	BRITISH GP	Silverstone	14	Fittipaldi Automotive	G	3.0 Fittipaldi F5A-Cosworth V8	engine	22/26
ret	GERMAN GP	Hockenheim	14	Fittipaldi Automotive	G	3.0 Fittipaldi F6A-Cosworth V8	electrics	22/26
ret	AUSTRIAN GP	Österreichring	14	Fittipaldi Automotive	G	3.0 Fittipaldi F6A-Cosworth V8	brakes	19/26
dns	"		14	Fittipaldi Automotive	G	3.0 Fittipaldi F5A-Cosworth V8	practice only	- / -
ret	DUTCH GP	Zandvoort	14	Fittipaldi Automotive	G	3.0 Fittipaldi F6A-Cosworth V8	electrics	21/26
dns	"	"	14	Fittipaldi Automotive	G	3.0 Fittipaldi F5A-Cosworth V8	practice only	- / -
8	ITALIAN GP	Monza	14	Fittipaldi Automotive	G	3.0 Fittipaldi F6A-Cosworth V8	1 lap behind	20/28
8	CANADIAN GP	Montreal	14	Fittipaldi Automotive	G	3.0 Fittipaldi F6A-Cosworth V8	wheel bearing problem/-5 laps	15/29
7	US GP EAST	Watkins Glen	14	Fittipaldi Automotive	G	3.0 Fittipaldi F6A-Cosworth V8	5 laps behind	23/30

1980 Championship position: 15th= Wins: 0 Pole positions: 0 Fastest laps: 0 Points scored: 5

			No	Entrant	Tyres	Capacity/Car/Engine	Comment	Q Pos/Entries
nc	ARGENTINE GP	Buenos Aires	20	Skol Fittipaldi Team	G	3.0 Fittipaldi F7-Cosworth V8	pit stops/16 laps behind	24/28
15	BRAZILIAN GP	Interlagos	20	Skol Fittipaldi Team	G	3.0 Fittipaldi F7-Cosworth V8	2 laps behind	19/28
8	SOUTH AFRICAN GP	Kyalami	20	Skol Fittipaldi Team	G	3.0 Fittipaldi F7-Cosworth V8	1 lap behind	18/28
3	US GP WEST	Long Beach	20	Skol Fittipaldi Team	G	3.0 Fittipaldi F7-Cosworth V8		24/27
ret	BELGIAN GP	Zolder	20	Skol Fittipaldi Team	G	3.0 Fittipaldi F7-Cosworth V8	electrics	24/27
6	MONACO GP	Monte Carlo	20	Skol Fittipaldi Team	G	3.0 Fittipaldi F7-Cosworth V8	2 laps behind	18/27
13/ret	FRENCH GP	Paul Ricard	20	Skol Fittipaldi Team	G	3.0 Fittipaldi F7-Cosworth V8	engine	24/27
12	BRITISH GP	Brands Hatch	20	Skol Fittipaldi Team	G	3.0 Fittipaldi F8-Cosworth V8	4 laps behind	22/27
ret	GERMAN GP	Hockenheim	20	Skol Fittipaldi Team	G	3.0 Fittipaldi F8-Cosworth V8	broken skirt	12/26
11	AUSTRIAN GP	Österreichring	20	Skol Fittipaldi Team	G	3.0 Fittipaldi F8-Cosworth V8	1 lap behind	23/25
ret	DUTCH GP	Zandvoort	20	Skol Fittipaldi Team	G	3.0 Fittipaldi F8-Cosworth V8	brakes	21/28
ret	ITALIAN GP	Imola	20	Skol Fittipaldi Team	G	3.0 Fittipaldi F8-Cosworth V8	hit guard rail	15/28
ret	CANADIAN GP	Montreal	20	Skol Fittipaldi Team	G	3.0 Fittipaldi F8-Cosworth V8	gearbox	16/28
ret	US GP EAST	Watkins Glen	20	Skol Fittipaldi Team	G	3.0 Fittipaldi F8-Cosworth V8	rear suspension	19/27

GP Starts: 144 GP Wins: 14 Pole positions: 6 Fastest laps: 6 Points: 281

FITTIPALDI, Wilson (BR) b 25/12/1943, São Paulo

1972 Championship position: Unplaced

	Race	Circuit	No	Entrant	Tyres	Capacity/Car/Engine	Comment	Q Pos/Entries
7	SPANISH GP	Jarama	22	Motor Racing Developments	G	3.0 Brabham BT33-Cosworth V8	2 laps behind	14/26
9	MONACO GP	Monte Carlo	21	Motor Racing Developments	G	3.0 Brabham BT33-Cosworth V8	3 laps behind	21/25
ret	BELGIAN GP	Nivelles	18	Motor Racing Developments	G	3.0 Brabham BT34-Cosworth V8	gearbox	18/26
8	FRENCH GP	Clermont Ferrand	19	Motor Racing Developments	G	3.0 Brabham BT34-Cosworth V8		16/29
12/ret	BRITISH GP	Brands Hatch	28	Motor Racing Developments	G	3.0 Brabham BT34-Cosworth V8	suspension/2 laps behind	22/27
7	GERMAN GP	Nürburgring	26	Motor Racing Developments	G	3.0 Brabham BT34-Cosworth V8		21/27
ret	AUSTRIAN GP	Österreichring	28	Motor Racing Developments	G	3.0 Brabham BT34-Cosworth V8	brake pipe	15/26
ret	ITALIAN GP	Monza	29	Motor Racing Developments	G	3.0 Brabham BT34-Cosworth V8	broken rear suspension	15/27

ret	CANADIAN GP	Mosport Park	9	Motor Racing Developments	G	3.0 Brabham BT34-Cosworth V8	*gearbox*	11/25
ret	US GP	Watkins Glen	30	Motor Racing Developments	G	3.0 Brabham BT34-Cosworth V8	*engine*	13/32

1973 Championship position: 15th= Wins: 0 Pole positions: 0 Fastest laps: 0 Points scored: 3

6	ARGENTINE GP	Buenos Aires	12	Motor Racing Developments	G	3.0 Brabham BT37-Cosworth V8	*1 lap behind*	12/19
ret	BRAZILIAN GP	Interlagos	18	Motor Racing Developments	G	3.0 Brabham BT37-Cosworth V8	*engine*	=11/20
ret	SOUTH AFRICAN GP	Kyalami	19	Motor Racing Developments	G	3.0 Brabham BT37-Cosworth V8	*gear selection*	17/25
10	SPANISH GP	Montjuich Park	17	Motor Racing Developments	G	3.0 Brabham BT42-Cosworth V8	*pit stop – throttle cable/-6 laps*	12/22
ret	BELGIAN GP	Zolder	11	Motor Racing Developments	G	3.0 Brabham BT42-Cosworth V8	*engine and brakes*	19/23
11/ret	MONACO GP	Monte Carlo	11	Motor Racing Developments	G	3.0 Brabham BT42-Cosworth V8	*split collector pot/7 laps behind*	9/26
ret	SWEDISH GP	Anderstorp	11	Motor Racing Developments	G	3.0 Brabham BT42-Cosworth V8	*accident on lap 1*	13/22
16/ret	FRENCH GP	Paul Ricard	11	Motor Racing Developments	G	3.0 Brabham BT42-Cosworth V8	*throttle linkage/4 laps behind*	19/25
ret	BRITISH GP	Silverstone	11	Motor Racing Developments	G	3.0 Brabham BT42-Cosworth V8	*oil pipe*	13/29
ret	DUTCH GP	Zandvoort	11	Motor Racing Developments	G	3.0 Brabham BT42-Cosworth V8	*spun off*	13/24
5	GERMAN GP	Nürburgring	11	Motor Racing Developments	G	3.0 Brabham BT42-Cosworth V8		13/23
ret	AUSTRIAN GP	Österreichring	11	Motor Racing Developments	G	3.0 Brabham BT42-Cosworth V8	*fuel metering unit*	16/25
ret	ITALIAN GP	Monza	11	Motor Racing Developments	G	3.0 Brabham BT42-Cosworth V8	*brakes*	16/25
11	CANADIAN GP	Mosport Park	11	Motor Racing Developments	G	3.0 Brabham BT42-Cosworth V8	*3 laps behind*	10/26
nc	US GP	Watkins Glen	11	Motor Racing Developments	G	3.0 Brabham BT42-Cosworth V8	*pit stops – various/7 laps behind*	26/28

1975 Championship position: Unplaced

ret	ARGENTINE GP	Buenos Aires	30	Copersucar-Fittipaldi	G	3.0 Copersucar FD01-Cosworth V8	*crashed*	23/23
13	BRAZILIAN GP	Interlagos	30	Copersucar-Fittipaldi	G	3.0 Copersucar FD02-Cosworth V8	*1 lap behind*	21/23
dnq	SOUTH AFRICAN GP	Kyalami	30	Copersucar-Fittipaldi	G	3.0 Copersucar FD02-Cosworth V8		27/28
ret	SPANISH GP	Montjuich Park	30	Copersucar-Fittipaldi	G	3.0 Copersucar FD02-Cosworth V8	*protest at lack of track safety*	21/26
dnq	MONACO GP	Monte Carlo	30	Copersucar-Fittipaldi	G	3.0 Copersucar FD02-Cosworth V8		26/26
12	BELGIAN GP	Zolder	30	Copersucar-Fittipaldi	G	3.0 Copersucar FD02-Cosworth V8	*3 laps behind*	24/24
17	SWEDISH GP	Anderstorp	30	Copersucar-Fittipaldi	G	3.0 Copersucar FD02-Cosworth V8	*pit stop/6 laps behind*	25/26
11	DUTCH GP	Zandvoort	30	Copersucar-Fittipaldi	G	3.0 Copersucar FD03-Cosworth V8	*4 laps behind*	24/25
dns	"	"	30T	Copersucar-Fittipaldi	G	3.0 Copersucar FD02-Cosworth V8	*practice only*	– / –
ret	FRENCH GP	Paul Ricard	30	Copersucar-Fittipaldi	G	3.0 Copersucar FD03-Cosworth V8	*engine*	23/26
19/ret	BRITISH GP	Silverstone	30	Copersucar-Fittipaldi	G	3.0 Copersucar FD03-Cosworth V8	*crashed in rain/6 laps behind*	24/28
ret	GERMAN GP	Nürburgring	30	Copersucar-Fittipaldi	G	3.0 Copersucar FD03-Cosworth V8	*engine*	22/26
dns	AUSTRIAN GP	Österreichring	30	Copersucar-Fittipaldi	G	3.0 Copersucar FD03-Cosworth V8	*practice accident – injured hand*	(20)/30
10	US GP	Watkins Glen	30	Copersucar-Fittipaldi	G	3.0 Copersucar FD03-Cosworth V8	*4 laps behind*	23/24

GP Starts: 35 GP Wins: 0 Pole positions: 0 Fastest laps: 0 Points: 3

WILSON FITTIPALDI

WILSON FITTIPALDI had to content himself with life as a racing driver for ever in the shadow of his brilliant younger brother, but that should not disguise the fact that he was a more than useful performer in his own right.

After a brief and dispiriting trip to Europe in 1966, Wilson returned to Brazil, where he raced saloons, sports cars and Formula Fords, as well as acting as engineer for Emerson's Super Vee efforts. He was back in Europe in 1970 to race in F3, and a good showing was enough to see him join his brother in Formula 2 in 1971, driving first a Lotus 69, then a March. Given his lack of experience, he fared well, taking fourth on his debut at Hockenheim, second at Vallelunga and third again at Hockenheim at season's end. A deal was struck with Bernie Ecclestone to race a Brabham in Formula 1 in 1972, as effectively the third driver to Carlos Reutemann and Graham Hill, but he did not enjoy the best of luck after a sixth place on his debut in the non-championship Brazilian GP. Things were better the following year, and his drive at Monaco was particularly impressive: he held third place in the BT42 when the fuel system failed. At least he scored some points in Argentina and Germany, however, and took an aggregate win in Formula 2 at Misano.

Wilson was now set on developing a grand prix car of his own, and much of 1974 was spent setting up the Copersucar-Fittipaldi team, which made its debut in 1975. The car was not a success, however, and he was a perpetual back-marker. At the end of the year came the shock announcement that Emerson would drive for the team in 1976, so the elder Fittipaldi happily retired to fill a management position in a project that was doomed to eventual failure.

A decade later, Wilson helped guide the racing career of his son, Christian, but he still found time to race himself occasionally. In the early 1990s, he drove Brazilian Stock cars. In 1994, he won the 23rd Brazilian 1000-mile race (Mil Milhas Brasileiras), sharing a Porsche 911 turbo. He also repeated the victory the following year. Aside from running his own stock car team, he returned to competition on occasion, including sharing a Porsche 997GT3 with brother Emerson in the Brazilian GT3 series in 2008.

FITZAU, Theo (D) b 10/2/1923 Köthen – d 18/3/1982 Gross-Gerau

1953 Championship position: Unplaced

	Race	Circuit	No	Entrant	Tyres	Capacity/Car/Engine	Comment	Q Pos/Entries
ret	GERMAN GP	Nürburgring	28	Helmut Niedermeyer	–	2.0 AFM 50-BMW 6		21/35

GP Starts: 1   GP Wins: 0   Pole positions: 0   Fastest laps: 0   Points: 0

FLINTERMAN, Jan (NL) b 2/10/1919 Den Haag – d 26/12/1992, Leiden

1952 Championship position: Unplaced

	Race	Circuit	No	Entrant	Tyres	Capacity/Car/Engine	Comment	Q Pos/Entries
ret	DUTCH GP	Zandvoort	20	Escuderia Bandeirantes	P	2.0 Maserati A6GCM 6	rear axle	15/18
9*	"	"	16	Escuderia Bandeirantes	P	2.0 Maserati A6GCM 6	*took Landi's car/7 laps behind	– / –

GP Starts: 1   GP Wins: 0   Pole positions: 0   Fastest laps: 0   Points: 0

THEO FITZAU

ORIGINALLY from Kothen, East Germany, Theodor 'Theo' Fitzau earned money to go racing by manufacturing soap. Most of his experience had been in an Eigenbau-BMW 328, and despite the small fields he was an enthusiastic competitor. He was second at Dessau in 1949, and fifth and final finisher at the Sachsenringrennen in 1950. The following season, he took third place at Halle behind Rudolf Krause and Ernst Klodwig in a DRS-Veritas BMW, and fourth at Leipzig.

In 1952, Fitzau dropped down to Formula 3 in the DDR championship, but the political climate in East Germany was adversely affecting both his soap business and his racing career. Thus, early in 1953, he defected to West Germany.

Fitzau's only world championship appearance was in Helmut Neidermayr's AFM in the 1953 German Grand Prix.

JAN FLINTERMAN

DESPITE being only 20 years of age at the outbreak of the Second World War, Jan Flinterman was already in the Dutch air force. He joined the RAF and flew Spitfires in Malta, then became a member of the famous 332 all-Dutch squadron, which was formed in 1943. He saw much active combat and was awarded the Distinguished Flying Cross. After the war, he flew RAF Meteor jets, before returning to Holland as a major in the Royal Dutch Air Force.

Flinterman began racing in 1950 with a Formula 3 Cooper-BSA, without much in the way of results. The first Dutch Grand Prix was staged in 1952, however, and the organisers wanted some local drivers to compete, so they arranged for him to drive one of the Bandeirante Maseratis, presumably in place of Eitel Cantoni. He broke a stub axle in this car early in the race, however, and then took over the sister car of Chico Landi, driving a spirited race to the finish and setting a lap time some five seconds better than he had managed in practice.

Later Flinterman became the MD of the Dutch airline Martinair Holland.

RON FLOCKHART

AFTER racing motorcycles, in 1948 Ron Flockhart switched to MG and JP-Vincent cars, before taking a serious step up with the purchase of an ERA D-Type in 1952. He enjoyed a fabulous 1953 season with the ex-Raymond Mays car, embarrassing many a newer machine in Formula Libre races. This brought him to the attention of BRM, who signed him up in 1954, initially to race in national Formula Libre events with the supercharged car. He also made his GP debut that season, taking over Bira's Maserati in the British GP before crashing.

In 1956, Ron was invited to race in sports cars for Ecurie Ecosse and won at Le Mans (with Ninian Sanderson) with their Jaguar E-Type, while he took full advantage of a last-minute opportunity to race for Connaught, finishing third in the Italian GP. The 1957 season saw him repeat his Le Mans success for Ecosse (this time with Ivor Bueb), but his luck with BRM was still out, an accident in the French GP leaving him with burns to an arm and legs. The following year was marred by further injury after a crash at Rouen in a sports car race, but he was back in action for 1959, winning the Lady Wigram Trophy in New Zealand and the minor Silver City Trophy at Snetterton for BRM. Easily his best effort that year was to finish sixth in the French GP when a stone smashed his goggles and he drove on gamely to the finish with the use of virtually only one eye and a badly cut face. After parting company with the Bourne concern, Flockhart raced for Alan Brown in Formula 2 in 1960, finishing second in the GP of Chimay, behind Jack Lewis, and fourth at Pau.

Ron also drove a single grand prix each for both Lotus and Cooper, but already his thoughts were turning towards his other passion, aviation. He had gained a pilot's licence in 1948, and now set about breaking flying records. He raced less frequently in 1961, and after taking part in three races in New Zealand and Australia with his Lotus 18 early in 1962, he was killed when his aeroplane broke up in turbulence while he was in Australia practising for a London-to-Sydney record attempt.

FLOCKHART, Ron (GB) b 16/6/1923, Edinburgh, Scotland – d 12/4/1962, Dandenong Ranges, nr Melbourne, Australia

1954 Championship position: Unplaced

	Race	Circuit	No	Entrant	Tyres	Capacity/Car/Engine	Comment	Q Pos/Entries
ret	BRITISH GP	Silverstone	6	Prince Bira	P	2.5 Maserati 250F 6	took over Bira's car/crashed	– /33
	1956	Championship position: 9th=		Wins: 0 Pole positions: 0 Fastest laps: 0 Points scored: 4				
ret	BRITISH GP	Silverstone	25	Owen Racing Organisation	D	2.5 BRM P25 4	engine	17/28
3	ITALIAN GP	Monza	4	Connaught Engineering	P/A	2.5 Connaught B-Alta 4	1 lap behind	24/26

1957 Championship position: Unplaced

| ret | MONACO GP | Monte Carlo | 6 | Owen Racing Organisation | D | 2.5 BRM P25 4 | timing gear | 11/21 |
| ret | FRENCH GP | Rouen | 26 | Owen Racing Organisation | D | 2.5 BRM P25 4 | accident – suffered burns | 11/15 |

1958 Championship position: Unplaced

| dnq | MONACO GP | Monte Carlo | 22 | R R C Walker Racing Team | D | 2.0 Cooper T43-Climax 4 | | 17/28 |
| ret | MOROCCAN GP | Casablanca | 20 | Owen Racing Organisation | D | 2.5 BRM P25 4 | camshaft | 15/25 |

1959 Championship position: Unplaced

ret	MONACO GP	Monte Carlo	20	Owen Racing Organisation	D	2.5 BRM P25 4	brake failure – spun off	10/24
6	FRENCH GP	Reims	44	Owen Racing Organisation	D	2.5 BRM P25 4		13/22
ret	BRITISH GP	Aintree	42	Owen Racing Organisation	D	2.5 BRM P25 4	spun off	11/30
7	PORTUGUESE GP	Oporto	8	Owen Racing Organisation	D	2.5 BRM P25 4	3 laps behind	11/16
13	ITALIAN GP	Monza	4	Owen Racing Organisation	D	2.5 BRM P25 4	5 laps behind	15/21

1960 Championship position: =19th   Wins: 0   Pole positions: 0   Fastest laps: 0   Points scored: 1

| 6 | FRENCH GP | Reims | 22 | Team Lotus | D | 2.5 Lotus 18-Climax 4 | 1 lap behind | 14/23 |
| ret | US GP | Riverside | 4 | Cooper Car Co | D | 2.5 Cooper T51-Climax 4 | transmission | 21/23 |

GP Starts: 13   GP Wins: 0   Pole positions: 0   Fastest laps: 0   Points: 5

FOITEK, Gregor (CH) b 27/3/1965, Zurich

1989 Championship position: Unplaced

	Race	Circuit	No	Entrant	Tyres	Capacity/Car/Engine	Comment	Q Pos/Entries
dnq	BRAZILIAN GP	Rio	33	EuroBrun Racing	P	3.5 EuroBrun ER188B-Judd V8		29/38
dnpq	SAN MARINO GP	Imola	33	EuroBrun Racing	P	3.5 EuroBrun ER188B-Judd V8		32/39
dnpq	MONACO GP	Monte Carlo	33	EuroBrun Racing	P	3.5 EuroBrun ER188B-Judd V8		35/38
dnpq	MEXICAN GP	Mexico City	33	EuroBrun Racing	P	3.5 EuroBrun ER188B-Judd V8		32/39
dnpq	US GP (PHOENIX)	Phoenix	33	EuroBrun Racing	P	3.5 EuroBrun ER188B-Judd V8		33/39
dnpq	CANADIAN GP	Montreal	33	EuroBrun Racing	P	3.5 EuroBrun ER188B-Judd V8		33/39
dnpq	FRENCH GP	Paul Ricard	33	EuroBrun Racing	P	3.5 EuroBrun ER188B-Judd V8		38/39
dnpq	BRITISH GP	Silverstone	33	EuroBrun Racing	P	3.5 EuroBrun ER188B-Judd V8		33/39
dnpq	GERMAN GP	Hockenheim	33	EuroBrun Racing	P	3.5 EuroBrun ER189-Judd V8		37/39
dnpq	"	"	33	EuroBrun Racing	P	3.5 EuroBrun ER188B-Judd V8		– / –
dnpq	HUNGARIAN GP	Hungaroring	33	EuroBrun Racing	P	3.5 EuroBrun ER189-Judd V8		37/39
dnpq	"	"	33	EuroBrun Racing	P	3.5 EuroBrun ER188B-Judd V8		– / –
dnpq	BELGIAN GP	Spa	33	EuroBrun Racing	P	3.5 EuroBrun ER188B-Judd V8		38/39
dnq	SPANISH GP	Jerez	38	Rial Racing	G	3.5 Rial ARC2-Cosworth V8	accident – rear wing collapsed	29/38

1990 Championship position: Unplaced

ret	US GP (PHOENIX)	Phoenix	7	Motor Racing Developments	P	3.5 Brabham BT58-Judd V8	collision with Grouillard	23/35
ret	BRAZILIAN GP	Interlagos	7	Motor Racing Developments	P	3.5 Brabham BT58-Judd V8	gear selection	22/35
ret	SAN MARINO GP	Imola	35	Moneytron Onyx	G	3.5 Onyx ORE 2-Cosworth V8	engine	24/34
7/ret	MONACO GP	Monte Carlo	35	Moneytron Onyx	G	3.5 Onyx ORE 2-Cosworth V8	collision – Bernard/6 laps behind	20/35
ret	CANADIAN GP	Montreal	35	Moneytron Onyx	G	3.5 Onyx ORE 2-Cosworth V8	over-revved engine	21/35
15	MEXICAN GP	Mexico City	35	Moneytron Onyx	G	3.5 Onyx ORE 2-Cosworth V8	brake problems/2 laps behind	23/35
dnq	FRENCH GP	Paul Ricard	35	Moneytron Onyx	G	3.5 Onyx ORE 2-Cosworth V8		29/35
dnq	BRITISH GP	Silverstone	35	Monteverdi Onyx Formula One	G	3.5 Onyx ORE 2-Cosworth V8		30/35
ret	GERMAN GP	Hockenheim	35	Monteverdi Onyx Formula One	G	3.5 Monteverdi ORE 2-Cosworth V8	spun off	26/35
dnq	HUNGARIAN GP	Hungaroring	35	Monteverdi Onyx Formula One	G	3.5 Monteverdi ORE 2-Cosworth V8		30/35

GP Starts: 7   GP Wins: 0   Pole positions: 0   Fastest laps: 0   Points: 0

GREGOR FOITEK

WINNING that curious anomaly, the Swiss F3 championship, in 1986 in a Dallara meant little; the wealthy Gregor Foitek's first season in F3000 the following year was a far more searching test. A poor start and a string of DNQs were overcome to some extent by switching teams to GA Motorsport in mid-season, although it was 1988 before he tasted success with a superb win at Vallelunga. But then came a worrying number of incidents, culminating in the Johnny Herbert crash at Brands Hatch, where Gregor's Lola was launched into a terrifying series of barrel rolls from which he was fortunate to escape with no more than a fractured wrist.

Moving into grands prix in 1989, Foitek spent a fruitless time trying in vain to qualify the EuroBrun, and he decided to quit while ahead when the rear wing fell off on his debut for Rial. He took his money to Brabham at the start of 1990 and at least made a couple starts, but then he moved to the Onyx team, which was on the way to oblivion after a Swiss gentleman by the name of Monteverdi took control. All in all, it was a sorry mess and before long Foitek had all but disappeared from view.

GEORGE FOLLMER

GEORGE FOLLMER was 39 when he first sampled life in Formula 1, thrown in at the deep end with the newly formed UOP Shadow team in 1973. At first, things went well, but as the season wore on he slipped further down the grid, and by the end of the year his grand prix tenure was over.

Although Follmer started racing in 1960, it was 1964/65 before he began competing seriously, becoming USRRC champion in the under-2-litre class with six wins in nine races in a Lotus-Porsche sports car. This led to an invitation to race a works Porsche 904 in the 1966 Sebring 12-hour race, in which he finished seventh with Peter Gregg, winning the under-2-litre class.

Still a part-time racer and full-time insurance broker, George financed his own Lola-Chevrolet for 1967 to race in USRRC events, but the car broke down repeatedly, and when Roger Penske offered him a Can-Am ride late in the season Follmer accepted, taking two third places and a sixth in his three races. The die was cast. Seeing how a serious team was run, George then embarked upon a professional racing career, competing successfully in USAC, Can-Am, Trans-Am and Formula A before his 1973 season with Shadow.

Following his sojourn in Formula 1, Follmer initially took a ride in NASCAR, but was soon tempted back into Can-Am by Shadow's Don Nichols. The next few seasons saw him on a regular diet of Can-Am, Trans-Am (winning the 1976 championship) and sports cars until his career was interrupted by a terrible practice crash at Laguna Seca in 1978, which left him with a broken leg and internal injuries. But despite still being in some pain from his leg injuries, he made a comeback in 1979 and continued racing into the early 1980s in Trans-Am with a Chevrolet Camaro.

FOLLMER, George (USA) b 27/1/1934, Phoenix, Arizona

1973 Championship position: 13th   Wins: 0   Pole positions: 0   Fastest laps: 0   Points scored: 5

	Race	Circuit	No	Entrant	Tyres	Capacity/Car/Engine	Comment	Q Pos/Entries
6	SOUTH AFRICAN GP	Kyalami	23	UOP Shadow Racing Team	G	3.0 Shadow DN1-Cosworth V8	2 laps behind	21/25
3	SPANISH GP	Montjuich Park	20	UOP Shadow Racing Team	G	3.0 Shadow DN1-Cosworth V8		=14/22
ret	BELGIAN GP	Zolder	16	UOP Shadow Racing Team	G	3.0 Shadow DN1-Cosworth V8	stuck throttle slides	11/23
dns	MONACO GP	Monte Carlo	16	UOP Shadow Racing Team	G	3.0 Shadow DN1-Cosworth V8	practice collision with Merzario	(20)/26
14	SWEDISH GP	Anderstorp	16	UOP Shadow Racing Team	G	3.0 Shadow DN1-Cosworth V8	6 laps behind	19/22
ret	FRENCH GP	Paul Ricard	16	UOP Shadow Racing Team	G	3.0 Shadow DN1-Cosworth V8	fuel-system – vapour lock	20/25
ret/dns	*BRITISH GP	Silverstone	16	UOP Shadow Racing Team	G	3.0 Shadow DN1-Cosworth V8	*accident at first start	=25/29
10	DUTCH GP	Zandvoort	16	UOP Shadow Racing Team	G	3.0 Shadow DN1-Cosworth V8	5 laps behind	22/24
ret	GERMAN GP	Nürburgring	16	UOP Shadow Racing Team	G	3.0 Shadow DN1-Cosworth V8	accident	22/23
ret	AUSTRIAN GP	Österreichring	16	UOP Shadow Racing Team	G	3.0 Shadow DN1-Cosworth V8	crown wheel and pinion	20/25
10	ITALIAN GP	Monza	16	UOP Shadow Racing Team	G	3.0 Shadow DN1-Cosworth V8	1 lap behind	21/25
17	CANADIAN GP	Mosport Park	16	UOP Shadow Racing Team	G	3.0 Shadow DN1-Cosworth V8	pit stop/7 laps behind	13/26
14	US GP	Watkins Glen	16	UOP Shadow Racing Team	G	3.0 Shadow DN1-Cosworth V8	2 laps behind	21/28

GP Starts: 11 (12)   GP Wins: 0   Pole positions: 0   Fastest laps: 0   Points: 5

FONTANA, Norberto (RA) b 20/1/1975, Arrecifes

1997 Championship position: Unplaced

	Race	Circuit	No	Entrant	Tyres	Capacity/Car/Engine	Comment	Q Pos/Entries
ret	FRENCH GP	Magny Cours	17	Red Bull Sauber Petronas	G	3.0 Sauber C16-Petronas V10	spun off	20/22
9	BRITISH GP	Silverstone	17	Red Bull Sauber Petronas	G	3.0 Sauber C16-Petronas V10	*times disallowed/1 lap behind	*14/22
9	GERMAN GP	Hockenheim	17	Red Bull Sauber Petronas	G	3.0 Sauber C16-Petronas V10	1 lap behind	18/22
14	EUROPEAN GP	Jerez	17	Red Bull Sauber Petronas	G	3.0 Sauber C16-Petronas V10	1 lap behind	18/22

GP Starts: 4   GP Wins: 0   Pole positions: 0   Fastest laps: 0   Points: 0

FORINI, Franco (CH) b 22/9/1958, Muralto, nr Locarno

1987 Championship position: Unplaced

	Race	Circuit	No	Entrant	Tyres	Capacity/Car/Engine	Comment	Q Pos/Entries
ret	ITALIAN GP	Monza	22	Osella Squadra Corse	G	1.5 t/c Osella FA1I-Alfa Romeo V8	turbo	26/28
ret	PORTUGUESE GP	Estoril	22	Osella Squadra Corse	G	1.5 t/c Osella FA1I-Alfa Romeo V8	rear wheel bearing	26/27
dnq	SPANISH GP	Jerez	22	Osella Squadra Corse	G	1.5 t/c Osella FA1I-Alfa Romeo V8		28/28

GP Starts: 2   GP Wins: 0   Pole positions: 0   Fastest laps: 0   Points: 0

FOTHERINGHAM-PARKER, Philip (GB) b 22/9/1907, Beckenham, Kent – d 15/10/1981, Beckley, nr Rye, East Sussex

1951 Championship position: Unplaced

	Race	Circuit	No	Entrant	Tyres	Capacity/Car/Engine	Comment	Q Pos/Entries
ret	BRITISH GP	Silverstone	17	Philip Fotheringham-Parker	D	1.5 s/c Maserati 4CL 4	oil pipe	16/20

GP Starts: 1   GP Wins: 0   Pole positions: 0   Fastest laps: 0   Points: 0

NORBERTO FONTANA

NORBERTO FONTANA was a highly impressive German F3 champion in 1995, with ten wins from 16 starts and the Marlboro Masters title to boot. The diminutive Argentinian defeated rivals such as Ralf Schumacher, Jarno Trulli and Alexander Wurz, but while these drivers went on to establish themselves as grand prix stars, Norberto was left to rue an unimpressive four-race stint at Sauber in 1997, deputising twice for the injured Gianni Morbidelli.

Norberto could well have grabbed a seat at Sauber at the beginning of 1996, had it not been for a neck injury sustained in an accident at the end-of-year F3 Macau GP in 1995. Instead, he had to be content with the test-driver role with the Swiss team and headed to Japan to compete in Formula Nippon.

During his three seasons in the Far East, Fontana, predictably, was a front-runner. He won four times, but the championship itself proved elusive and, with his ultimate goal a place on the Formula 1 grid, he opted to return to Europe in 1999 to contest the FIA F3000 series. It was not a move that brought much success, the well-funded Red Bull Sauber Junior Team star scoring a meagre four points to finish 13th in the final standings.

That left the Argentinian with no option but to look outside F1, and he opted to try his hand in the CART series with the Della Penna Team. He proved somewhat accident prone, however, and was replaced mid-way through the campaign after scoring just two points.

Thus Fontana returned to his homeland and soon found his feet in the premier TC2000 series, taking his first win in 2001. He scored his first championship win in 2002 in a Toyota, with whom he stayed until the end of 2009. Switching to Ford, he took the title again in 2010 in a Focus. By the end of the 2011 season, he had notched up 13 wins and four poles in this very competitive category. He also competed in the Tourismo Carretera, winning the series with a Dodge Polara in 2006. In addition, with the Dakar Rally relocated to South America, he took part in both the 2011 and 2012 events in his McRae buggy, but was forced to retire in both.

FRANCO FORINI

OF all the drivers to have raced a grand prix car in the 1980s, Franco Forini was probably one of the more surprising choices when Osella unfathomably decided to run a second car in the latter half of the 1987 season.

The Swiss driver had raced karts and touring cars before moving into Italian F3 in 1981. Forini also raced in European F3, before finally finding success in the 1983 Italian F3 series, taking a win and third place in the final standings. However all the class of '83 were a long way behind the champion, Ivan Capelli.

The following year, Forini was paired with Fabrizio Barbazza and, despite a couple of wins, he slipped to fifth overall. A switch to the Forti team and a competitive VW-powered carbon-fibre Dallara in 1985, however, saw him emerge as a worthy champion, ahead of Barbazza, Alessandro Caffi and Marco Apicella. He took six wins in the series and also finished second to British F3 champion Mauricio Gugelmin in the prestigious Monaco Formula 3 race.

Despite this success, Forini found it tough to get a regular seat in the Formula 3000 category in 1986. Apart from a solitary point – gained after a sixth place at Imola – a largely moribund F3000 season left him out of a drive of any kind until his chance at Osella. A wad of personal sponsorship money no doubt eased the way for him to take the drive, alongside his former F3 sparring partner, Caffi. It was a chastening time, however, as he was well off the pace of his younger and much more talented teammate in their hopelessly slow cars.

Forini went back to Formula 3 in both Germany and Italy over the next couple of seasons, but he couldn't repeat his earlier successes. After a sabbatical from competition, he re-appeared briefly in rallying, before finding success and enjoyment in numerous invitation karting events.

PHILIP FOTHERINGHAM-PARKER

A COMPANY director who raced intermittently in the immediate post-war years, Philip Fotheringham-Parker's greatest success was second place with a Maserati in the 1949 Wakefield Trophy race at the Curragh.

He raced the 4CLT in the 1951 British GP and also used it to win a very minor Formula 1 race at Winfield that year.

In 1953, he raced with Sydney Allard at Le Mans and took part in the 1954 Monte Carlo Rally in a Ford Zephyr.

HEINZ-HARALD FRENTZEN

FOR Heinz-Harald Frentzen, it was a long and sometimes frustrating road to the top, and even when he seemed to have climbed to the summit of Formula 1, with the chance of a lifetime at Williams in 1997, the likeable German had to prove himself all over again.

Frentzen raced karts from 1980 to 1985, taking a German junior championship, before three seasons in German FF2000, where he finished runner-up in 1987. This set up a move into the German Opel Lotus Challenge the following year, and not only did he take the title, but also he scored a couple of wins in the GM Lotus Euroseries.

It was in 1989 that motor-racing aficionados worldwide really started to take an interest in the trio of talented youngsters, Karl Wendlinger, Michael Schumacher and Frentzen, who were battling for the German F3 title. Eventually, the last two shared second place, just one point adrift of Wendlinger, but their performances were such that all three were earmarked to join the Mercedes-Benz Group C programme for 1990. In addition, Heinz-Harald found long-term backing from Camel to join Eddie Jordan in F3000.

It was now that Frentzen's career began to stall, however. Left in the third car at EJR and with no real experience, he struggled all year. With the troublesome Lola in 1991, things hardly improved, but worse would follow as Camel took its budget to Benetton with Schumacher for 1992, and Heinz-Harald was left high and dry without a drive of any sort.

Initially Frentzen agreed to race for March in 1993, but eventually backed away and plumped instead to go to Japan to compete in F3000 for Super Nova, in place of the indisposed Volker Weidler. The time he spent there did a great deal to build his confidence and, when the chance of a test for Sauber came in the autumn of 1993, he was equipped to make the most of it.

The first year in F1 saw Frentzen assume the team leadership after Wendlinger's accident and quickly become a top-six contender, despite the Sauber's obvious limitations. The quiet and unassuming man took another giant stride forward in 1995, working ceaselessly to push the Ford-engined car towards the front of the grid. In the second half of the season, he put in some superb drives to enhance his rising reputation. That he had come to be so highly regarded in just two seasons of Formula 1 in a car not good enough to challenge the leaders showed the reservoir of talent that he possessed.

Despite the introduction of the new Ford Zetec-R V10, however, the German's 1996 season was something of an anti-climax; he seemed less than fully committed when the Sauber C15 failed to come up to scratch. Williams, of course, had already made their move and controversially signed him to replace Damon Hill for the 1997 season. Life at Williams is never a bed of roses, and it would prove less than fertile ground for Frentzen, who failed to bloom in the harsh environment. A win at Imola and a string of podium finishes brought the runner-up position in the championship, behind team-mate Jacques Villeneuve, but there was a feeling that his contribution could, and should, have been much greater. Worse would follow for 1998, which turned into something of a nightmare for the mild-mannered Frentzen. The new narrow-track and grooved-tyre regulations found the Williams FW20 wanting, and he seemed resigned to his number-two status behind Villeneuve.

Frentzen was prematurely written off by many, but not by Eddie Jordan, who swiftly moved to bring the German on board for the 1999 season. A superb second place at the opening race in Australia provided him with an immediate and much-needed boost to his confidence and he simply never looked back. Team-mate Damon Hill was left floundering by his pace, and his smooth style and calmness under pressure brought two well-judged wins, which, together with a further ten top-six finishes, earned an impres-

sive third place in the championship table. More importantly, perhaps, he had regained his credibility as a top-rank driver.

For 2000, the German found himself partnered by rising Italian star Jarno Trulli in the wake of Hill's retirement. It was a disappointing season, with the radical looking EJ10 struggling to stay in touch with the likes of Williams and BAR, rather than challenging Ferrari and McLaren. Frentzen managed just two podiums after a reliability-plagued season.

The Frentzen/Trulli/Jordan axis remained together for much of 2001, but the year was disappointing for the German, since he was out-performed by his team-mate, especially in qualifying. By the time of the British Grand Prix, relations between the three-time GP winner and team boss Jordan were strained, and Frentzen, who had already missed the Canadian GP with concussion following a Monaco crash, was subsequently fired days before his home race. Four years later, Jordan revealed that the sacking was, in part, politically motivated by the fact that he needed to sign Takuma Sato to keep Honda power.

Frentzen was not out of work for very long, however, as Alain Prost moved swiftly to snap him up to replace the equally disaffected Jean Alesi. The result was a seat swap between the two veterans, the German sampling Ferrari power in the AP04 for the final five rounds. The French team was thrust into receivership towards the end of 2001, but Frentzen was determined to stay in F1 and subsequently secured an Arrows drive for 2002. The deal was for one year only, but then Arrows, like Prost the previous year, ran into financial difficulties and he left the outfit in August. He had signed to race for Sauber in 2003, again on a one-year contract, but made an early return to the Swiss team, replacing Felipe Massa for the 2002 US GP.

Frentzen's tenth season in F1 saw him come full circle with a full-time ride at Sauber, but the campaign was not the happy homecoming he had hoped for. Despite out-performing fellow Mönchengladbach native Nick Heidfeld, he managed just 13 points, based largely on third place in the penultimate race at Indianapolis to go with top-eight results in Australia and Brazil at the start of the year. That was not enough to convince Sauber to retain him for 2004, when he was replaced by returnee Felipe Massa.

With few realistic options for continuing his F1 career, Frentzen looked elsewhere for his racing. That search led him back home, to a seat in Opel's DTM squad for 2004. A moderate first season in an under-performing car nevertheless was deemed good enough for a second crack in 2005. Indeed, he finally notched a surprise podium place at Brno, but with Opel quitting the series at the end of the year, his future remained in limbo until, after protracted negotiations, he signed to drive the Abt Sportsline Audi.

For the first time in the DTM, Heinz-Harald had the chance to prove his competitiveness in a potentially winning machine, but Mercedes had the edge in 2006, and two trips to the podium were the best he could achieve, eventually placing seventh in the series. All had not been well behind the scenes, however, and he felt his established team-mates were being given preferential treatment. After the final race of the season, he let-rip about his unhappy lot in a TV interview, leaving Audi with little option but to dispense with his services.

Since then, Frentzen has raced sporadically, taking in the well-remunerated, but now defunct Speed Car series in 2008/09. He teamed up with Wendlinger and Andrea Piccini at Le Mans in 2008 to take a works Aston Martin DBR9 to fourth place in the GT1 class. He also introduced his own HHF hybrid concept car, based on the Gumpert Apollo, which competed in the 2008 Nürburgring 24-hour race.

In 2011, Frentzen was linked with the Indian-based i1 Super Series, a one-make sports car championship that was planned to run on circuits across Asia in 2013.

FRENTZEN, Heinz-Harald (D) b 18/5/1967, Mönchengladbach

1994 Championship position: 13th   Wins: 0   Pole positions: 0   Fastest laps: 0   Points scored: 7

	Race	Circuit	No	Entrant	Tyres	Capacity/Car/Engine	Comment	Q Pos/Entries
ret	BRAZILIAN GP	Interlagos	30	Sauber Mercedes	G	3.5 Sauber C13-Mercedes Benz V10	spun off	5/28
5	PACIFIC GP	T.I. Circuit	30	Sauber Mercedes	G	3.5 Sauber C13-Mercedes Benz V10	1 lap behind	11/28
7	SAN MARINO GP	Imola	30	Sauber Mercedes	G	3.5 Sauber C13-Mercedes Benz V10	1 lap behind	7/28
dns	MONACO GP	Monte Carlo	30	Sauber Mercedes	G	3.5 Sauber C13-Mercedes Benz V10	withdrawn after Wendlinger's crash	- / -
ret	SPANISH GP	Barcelona	30	Sauber Mercedes	G	3.5 Sauber C13-Mercedes Benz V10	gearbox	12/27
ret	CANADIAN GP	Montreal	30	Sauber Mercedes	G	3.5 Sauber C13-Mercedes Benz V10	spun off	10/27
4	FRENCH GP	Magny Cours	30	Sauber Mercedes	G	3.5 Sauber C13-Mercedes Benz V10		10/28
7*	BRITISH GP	Silverstone	30	Sauber Mercedes	G	3.5 Sauber C13-Mercedes Benz V10	*2nd place car disqualified/-1 lap	13/28
ret	GERMAN GP	Hockenheim	30	Sauber Mercedes	G	3.5 Sauber C13-Mercedes Benz V10	multiple accident at start	9/28
ret	HUNGARIAN GP	Hungaroring	30	Sauber Mercedes	G	3.5 Sauber C13-Mercedes Benz V10	gearbox	8/28
ret	BELGIAN GP	Spa	30	Sauber Mercedes	G	3.5 Sauber C13-Mercedes Benz V10	spun off	9/28
ret	ITALIAN GP	Monza	30	Sauber Mercedes	G	3.5 Sauber C13-Mercedes Benz V10	engine	11/28
ret	PORTUGUESE GP	Estoril	30	Sauber Mercedes	G	3.5 Sauber C13-Mercedes Benz V10	engine	9/28
6	EUROPEAN GP	Jerez	30	Sauber Mercedes	G	3.5 Sauber C13-Mercedes Benz V10	1 lap behind	4/28
6	JAPANESE GP	Suzuka	30	Sauber Mercedes	G	3.5 Sauber C13-Mercedes Benz V10		3/28
7	AUSTRALIAN GP	Adelaide	30	Sauber Mercedes	G	3.5 Sauber C13-Mercedes Benz V10	1 lap behind	10/28

1995 Championship position: 9th   Wins: 0   Pole positions: 0   Fastest laps: 0   Points scored: 15

	Race	Circuit	No	Entrant	Tyres	Capacity/Car/Engine	Comment	Q Pos/Entries
ret	BRAZILIAN GP	Interlagos	30	Red Bull Sauber Ford	G	3.0 Sauber C14-Ford Zetec-R V8	electrics	14/26
5	ARGENTINE GP	Buenos Aires	30	Red Bull Sauber Ford	G	3.0 Sauber C14-Ford Zetec-R V8	2 laps behind	9/26
6	SAN MARINO GP	Imola	30	Red Bull Sauber Ford	G	3.0 Sauber C14-Ford Zetec-R V8	1 lap behind	14/26
8	SPANISH GP	Barcelona	30	Red Bull Sauber Ford	G	3.0 Sauber C14-Ford Zetec-R V8	1 lap behind	12/26
6	MONACO GP	Monte Carlo	30	Red Bull Sauber Ford	G	3.0 Sauber C14-Ford Zetec-R V8	2 laps behind	14/26
ret	CANADIAN GP	Montreal	30	Red Bull Sauber Ford	G	3.0 Sauber C14-Ford Zetec-R V8	engine	12/24
10	FRENCH GP	Magny Cours	30	Red Bull Sauber Ford	G	3.0 Sauber C14-Ford Zetec-R V8	1 lap behind	12/24
6	BRITISH GP	Silverstone	30	Red Bull Sauber Ford	G	3.0 Sauber C14-Ford Zetec-R V8	1 lap behind	12/24
ret	GERMAN GP	Hockenheim	30	Red Bull Sauber Ford	G	3.0 Sauber C14-Ford Zetec-R V8	engine	11/24
5	HUNGARIAN GP	Hungaroring	30	Red Bull Sauber Ford	G	3.0 Sauber C14-Ford Zetec-R V8	1 lap behind	11/24
4	BELGIAN GP	Spa	30	Red Bull Sauber Ford	G	3.0 Sauber C14-Ford Zetec-R V8		10/24
3	ITALIAN GP	Monza	30	Red Bull Sauber Ford	G	3.0 Sauber C14-Ford Zetec-R V8		10/24
6	PORTUGUESE GP	Estoril	30	Red Bull Sauber Ford	G	3.0 Sauber C14-Ford Zetec-R V8	started from back/1 lap behind	5/24
ret	EUROPEAN GP	Nürburgring	30	Red Bull Sauber Ford	G	3.0 Sauber C14-Ford Zetec-R V8	collision with Diniz	8/24
7	PACIFIC GP	T.I. Circuit	30	Red Bull Sauber Ford	G	3.0 Sauber C14-Ford Zetec-R V8	1 lap behind	8/24
8	JAPANESE GP	Suzuka	30	Red Bull Sauber Ford	G	3.0 Sauber C14-Ford Zetec-R V8	1 lap behind	8/24
ret	AUSTRALIAN GP	Adelaide	30	Red Bull Sauber Ford	G	3.0 Sauber C14-Ford Zetec-R V8	gearbox	6/24

1996 Championship position: 12th   Wins: 0   Pole positions: 0   Fastest laps: 0   Points scored: 7

	Race	Circuit	No	Entrant	Tyres	Capacity/Car/Engine	Comment	Q Pos/Entries
8	AUSTRALIAN GP	Melbourne	15	Red Bull Sauber Ford	G	3.0 Sauber C15-Ford Zetec R V10	1 lap behind	9/22
ret	BRAZILIAN GP	Interlagos	15	Red Bull Sauber Ford	G	3.0 Sauber C15-Ford Zetec R V10	engine	14/22
ret	ARGENTINE GP	Buenos Aires	15	Red Bull Sauber Ford	G	3.0 Sauber C15-Ford Zetec R V10	spun off	11/22
ret	EUROPEAN GP	Nürburgring	15	Red Bull Sauber Ford	G	3.0 Sauber C15-Ford Zetec R V10	spun off – damaged front wing	10/22
ret	SAN MARINO GP	Imola	15	Red Bull Sauber Ford	G	3.0 Sauber C15-Ford Zetec R V10	brakes	10/22
4	MONACO GP	Monte Carlo	15	Red Bull Sauber Ford	G	3.0 Sauber C15-Ford Zetec R V10	collision/1 lap behind	9/22
4	SPANISH GP	Barcelona	15	Red Bull Sauber Ford	G	3.0 Sauber C15-Ford Zetec R V10	1 laps behind	11/22
ret	CANADIAN GP	Montreal	15	Red Bull Sauber Ford	G	3.0 Sauber C15-Ford Zetec R V10	gearbox	12/22
ret	FRENCH GP	Magny Cours	15	Red Bull Sauber Ford	G	3.0 Sauber C15-Ford Zetec R V10	throttle – spun off	13/22
8	BRITISH GP	Silverstone	15	Red Bull Sauber Ford	G	3.0 Sauber C15-Ford Zetec R V10	1 lap behind	11/22
8	GERMAN GP	Hockenheim	15	Red Bull Sauber Ford	G	3.0 Sauber C15-Ford Zetec R V10	1 lap behind	13/20
ret	HUNGARIAN GP	Hungaroring	15	Red Bull Sauber Ford	G	3.0 Sauber C15-Ford Zetec R V10	engine	10/20
ret	BELGIAN GP	Spa	15	Red Bull Sauber Ford	G	3.0 Sauber C15-Ford Zetec R V10	collision with Herbert & Panis	11/20
ret	ITALIAN GP	Monza	15	Red Bull Sauber Ford	G	3.0 Sauber C15-Ford Zetec R V10	spun off	13/20
7	PORTUGUESE GP	Estoril	15	Red Bull Sauber Ford	G	3.0 Sauber C15-Ford Zetec R V10	1 lap behind	11/20
6	JAPANESE GP	Suzuka	15	Red Bull Sauber Ford	G	3.0 Sauber C15-Ford Zetec R V10		7/20

1997 Championship position: 2nd   Wins: 1   Pole positions: 1   Fastest laps: 6   Points scored: 42

	Race	Circuit	No	Entrant	Tyres	Capacity/Car/Engine	Comment	Q Pos/Entries
8/ret	AUSTRALIAN GP	Melbourne	4	Rothmans Williams Renault	G	3.0 Williams FW19-Renault V10	brake disc failure – spun off/FL	2/24
9	BRAZILIAN GP	Interlagos	4	Rothmans Williams Renault	G	3.0 Williams FW19-Renault V10		8/22
ret	ARGENTINE GP	Buenos Aires	4	Rothmans Williams Renault	G	3.0 Williams FW19-Renault V10	clutch	2/22
1	SAN MARINO GP	Imola	4	Rothmans Williams Renault	G	3.0 Williams FW19-Renault V10	FL	2/22
ret	MONACO GP	Monte Carlo	4	Rothmans Williams Renault	G	3.0 Williams FW19-Renault V10	hit barriers	1/22
8	SPANISH GP	Barcelona	4	Rothmans Williams Renault	G	3.0 Williams FW19-Renault V10		2/22
4	CANADIAN GP	Montreal	4	Rothmans Williams Renault	G	3.0 Williams FW19-Renault V10		4/22
2	FRENCH GP	Magny Cours	4	Rothmans Williams Renault	G	3.0 Williams FW19-Renault V10		2/22
ret	BRITISH GP	Silverstone	4	Rothmans Williams Renault	G	3.0 Williams FW19-Renault V10	collision with Verstappen	2/22
ret	GERMAN GP	Hockenheim	4	Rothmans Williams Renault	G	3.0 Williams FW19-Renault V10	collision with Irvine	5/22
ret	HUNGARIAN GP	Hungaroring	4	Rothmans Williams Renault	G	3.0 Williams FW19-Renault V10	fuel valve/FL	6/22
3*	BELGIAN GP	Spa	4	Rothmans Williams Renault	G	3.0 Williams FW19-Renault V10	*5th place car disqualified	7/22
3	ITALIAN GP	Monza	4	Rothmans Williams Renault	G	3.0 Williams FW19-Renault V10		2/22
3	AUSTRIAN GP	A1-Ring	4	Rothmans Williams Renault	G	3.0 Williams FW19-Renault V10		4/22
3	LUXEMBOURG GP	Nürburgring	4	Rothmans Williams Renault	G	3.0 Williams FW19-Renault V10	FL	3/22
2	JAPANESE GP	Suzuka	4	Rothmans Williams Renault	G	3.0 Williams FW19-Renault V10	FL	6/22
6	EUROPEAN GP	Jerez	4	Rothmans Williams Renault	G	3.0 Williams FW19-Renault V10	FL	3/22

1998 Championship position: 7th=   Wins: 0   Pole positions: 0   Fastest laps: 0   Points scored: 17

	Race	Circuit	No	Entrant	Tyres	Capacity/Car/Engine	Comment	Q Pos/Entries
3	AUSTRALIAN GP	Melbourne	2	Winfield Williams	G	3.0 Williams FW20-Mechachrome V10	1 lap behind	6/22
5	BRAZILIAN GP	Interlagos	2	Winfield Williams	G	3.0 Williams FW20-Mechachrome V10	1 lap behind	3/22
9	ARGENTINE GP	Buenos Aires	2	Winfield Williams	G	3.0 Williams FW20-Mechachrome V10	1 lap behind	6/22
5	SAN MARINO GP	Imola	2	Winfield Williams	G	3.0 Williams FW20-Mechachrome V10		8/22
8	SPANISH GP	Barcelona	2	Winfield Williams	G	3.0 Williams FW20-Mechachrome V10	2 laps behind	13/22

ret	MONACO GP	Monte Carlo	2	Winfield Williams	G	3.0 Williams FW20-Mechachrome V10	*pushed off by Irvine*	5/22
ret	CANADIAN GP	Montreal	2	Winfield Williams	G	3.0 Williams FW20-Mechachrome V10	*pushed off by M Schumacher*	7/22
15/ret	FRENCH GP	Magny Cours	2	Winfield Williams	G	3.0 Williams FW20-Mechachrome V10	*collision – bent track rod/-3 laps*	8/22
ret	BRITISH GP	Silverstone	2	Winfield Williams	G	3.0 Williams FW20-Mechachrome V10	*spun off*	6/22
ret	AUSTRIAN GP	A1-Ring	2	Winfield Williams	G	3.0 Williams FW20-Mechachrome V10	*engine*	7/22
9	GERMAN GP	Hockenheim	2	Winfield Williams	G	3.0 Williams FW20-Mechachrome V10		10/22
5	HUNGARIAN GP	Hungaroring	2	Winfield Williams	G	3.0 Williams FW20-Mechachrome V10	*raced with intestinal bug*	7/22
4	BELGIAN GP	Spa	2	Winfield Williams	G	3.0 Williams FW20-Mechachrome V10		9/22
7	ITALIAN GP	Monza	2	Winfield Williams	G	3.0 Williams FW20-Mechachrome V10	*1 lap behind*	12/22
5	LUXEMBOURG GP	Nürburgring	2	Winfield Williams	G	3.0 Williams FW20-Mechachrome V10		7/22
5	JAPANESE GP	Suzuka	2	Winfield Williams	G	3.0 Williams FW20-Mechachrome V10		5/22

1999 Championship position: 3rd Wins: 2 Pole positions: 1 Fastest laps: 0 Points scored: 54

2	AUSTRALIAN GP	Melbourne	8	Benson & Hedges Jordan	B	3.0 Jordan 199-Mugen Honda V10		5/22
3/ret	BRAZILIAN GP	Interlagos	8	Benson & Hedges Jordan	B	3.0 Jordan 199-Mugen Honda V10	*stopped on last lap – low fuel*	8/22
ret	SAN MARINO GP	Imola	8	Benson & Hedges Jordan	B	3.0 Jordan 199-Mugen Honda V10	*slid off on Irvine's dropped oil*	7/22
4	MONACO GP	Monte Carlo	8	Benson & Hedges Jordan	B	3.0 Jordan 199-Mugen Honda V10		6/22
ret	SPANISH GP	Barcelona	8	Benson & Hedges Jordan	B	3.0 Jordan 199-Mugen Honda V10	*differential*	8/22
11/ret	CANADIAN GP	Montreal	8	Benson & Hedges Jordan	B	3.0 Jordan 199-Mugen Honda V10	*brake disc exploded – crashed*	6/22
1	FRENCH GP	Magny Cours	8	Benson & Hedges Jordan	B	3.0 Jordan 199-Mugen Honda V10		5/22
4	BRITISH GP	Silverstone	8	Benson & Hedges Jordan	B	3.0 Jordan 199-Mugen Honda V10		5/22
4	AUSTRIAN GP	A1-Ring	8	Benson & Hedges Jordan	B	3.0 Jordan 199-Mugen Honda V10		4/22
3	GERMAN GP	Hockenheim	8	Benson & Hedges Jordan	B	3.0 Jordan 199-Mugen Honda V10		2/22
4	HUNGARIAN GP	Hungaroring	8	Benson & Hedges Jordan	B	3.0 Jordan 199-Mugen Honda V10		5/22
3	BELGIAN GP	Spa	8	Benson & Hedges Jordan	B	3.0 Jordan 199-Mugen Honda V10		3/22
1	ITALIAN GP	Monza	8	Benson & Hedges Jordan	B	3.0 Jordan 199-Mugen Honda V10		2/22
ret	EUROPEAN GP	Nürburgring	8	Benson & Hedges Jordan	B	3.0 Jordan 199-Mugen Honda V10	*electrics when leading*	1/22
6	MALAYSIAN GP	Sepang	8	Benson & Hedges Jordan	B	3.0 Jordan 199-Mugen Honda V10	*fine drive from low grid position*	14/22
4	JAPANESE GP	Suzuka	8	Benson & Hedges Jordan	B	3.0 Jordan 199-Mugen Honda V10		4/22

2000 Championship position: 9th Wins: 0 Pole positions: 0 Fastest laps: 0 Points scored: 11

ret	AUSTRALIAN GP	Melbourne	5	Benson & Hedges Jordan	B	3.0 Jordan EJ10-Honda V10	*hydraulic leak – gearbox failure*	5/22
3*	BRAZILIAN GP	Interlagos	5	Benson & Hedges Jordan	B	3.0 Jordan EJ10-Honda V10	**2nd place car disqualified*	7/22
ret	SAN MARINO GP	Imola	5	Benson & Hedges Jordan	B	3.0 Jordan EJ10-Honda V10	*gearbox*	6/22
17/ret	BRITISH GP	Silverstone	5	Benson & Hedges Jordan	B	3.0 Jordan EJ10-Honda V10	*gearbox/transmission/6 laps behind*	2/22
6	SPANISH GP	Barcelona	5	Benson & Hedges Jordan	B	3.0 Jordan EJ10-Honda V10		8/22
ret	EUROPEAN GP	Nürburgring	5	Benson & Hedges Jordan	B	3.0 Jordan EJ10-Honda V10	*engine*	10/22
10/ret	MONACO GP	Monte Carlo	5	Benson & Hedges Jordan	B	3.0 Jordan EJ10-Honda V10	*crashed/8 laps behind*	4/22
ret	CANADIAN GP	Montreal	5	Benson & Hedges Jordan	B	3.0 Jordan EJ10-Honda V10	*brakes*	5/22
7	FRANCE GP	Magny Cours	5	Benson & Hedges Jordan	B	3.0 Jordan EJ10-Honda V10	*1 lap behind*	8/22
ret	AUSTRIAN GP	A1-Ring	5	Benson & Hedges Jordan	B	3.0 Jordan EJ10-Honda V10	*engine*	15/22
ret	GERMAN GP	Hockenheim	5	Benson & Hedges Jordan	B	3.0 Jordan EJ10-Honda V10	*low battery voltage*	17/22
6	HUNGARIAN GP	Hungaroring	5	Benson & Hedges Jordan	B	3.0 Jordan EJ10-Honda V10		6/22
6	BELGIAN GP	Spa	5	Benson & Hedges Jordan	B	3.0 Jordan EJ10-Honda V10		8/22
ret	ITALIAN GP	Monza	5	Benson & Hedges Jordan	B	3.0 Jordan EJ10-Honda V10	*multiple accident on lap 1*	8/22
3	UNITED STATES GP	Indianapolis	5	Benson & Hedges Jordan	B	3.0 Jordan EJ10-Honda V10		7/22
ret	JAPANESE GP	Suzuka	5	Benson & Hedges Jordan	B	3.0 Jordan EJ10-Honda V10	*hydraulics*	8/22
ret	MALAYSIAN GP	Sepang	5	Benson & Hedges Jordan	B	3.0 Jordan EJ10-Honda V10	*ran off track – electrics/hydraulics*	10/22

2001 Championship position: 12th= Wins: 0 Pole positions: 0 Fastest laps: 0 Points scored: 6

5	AUSTRALIAN GP	Melbourne	11	Benson & Hedges Jordan Honda	B	3.0 Jordan EJ11-Honda V10	*hit by Barrichello – great recovery*	4/22
4	MALAYSIAN GP	Sepang	11	Benson & Hedges Jordan Honda	B	3.0 Jordan EJ11-Honda V10	*despite clutch problem*	9/22
11/ret	BRAZILIAN GP	Interlagos	11	Benson & Hedges Jordan Honda	B	3.0 Jordan EJ11-Honda V10	*engine/8 laps behind*	8/22
6	SAN MARINO GP	Imola	11	Benson & Hedges Jordan Honda	B	3.0 Jordan EJ11-Honda V10	*1 lap behind*	9/22
ret	SPANISH GP	Barcelona	11	Benson & Hedges Jordan Honda	B	3.0 Jordan EJ11-Honda V10	*collision with de la Rosa*	8/22
ret	AUSTRIAN GP	A1-Ring	11	Benson & Hedges Jordan Honda	B	3.0 Jordan EJ11-Honda V10	*gearbox failure on grid*	11/22
dns	CANADIAN GP	Montreal	11	Benson & Hedges Jordan Honda	B	3.0 Jordan EJ11-Honda V10	*accident in Friday practice*	– / –
ret	MONACO GP	Monte Carlo	11	Benson & Hedges Jordan Honda	B	3.0 Jordan EJ11-Honda V10	*heavy crash exiting tunnel*	13/22
ret	EUROPEAN GP	Nürburgring	11	Benson & Hedges Jordan Honda	B	3.0 Jordan EJ11-Honda V10	*traction control failure – spun out*	8/22
8	FRENCH GP	Magny Cours	11	Benson & Hedges Jordan Honda	B	3.0 Jordan EJ11-Honda V10	*1 lap behind*	7/22
7	BRITISH GP	Silverstone	11	Benson & Hedges Jordan Honda	B	3.0 Jordan EJ11-Honda V10	*1 lap behind*	5/22
ret	HUNGARIAN GP	Hungaroring	22	Prost Acer	M	3.0 Prost AP04-Acer V10	*traction control failure – spun out*	16/22
9	BELGIAN GP	Spa	22	Prost Acer	M	3.0 Prost AP04-Acer V10	*1 lap behind*	4/22
ret	ITALIAN GP	Monza	22	Prost Acer	M	3.0 Prost AP04-Acer V10	*transmission*	12/22
10	UNITED STATES GP	Indianapolis	22	Prost Acer	M	3.0 Prost AP04-Acer V10	*1 lap behind*	15/22
12	JAPANESE GP	Suzuka	22	Prost Acer	M	3.0 Prost AP04-Acer V10	*1 lap behind*	15/22

2002 Championship position: 15th= Wins: 0 Pole positions: 0 Fastest laps: 0 Points scored: 2

dsq*	AUSTRALIAN GP	Melbourne	20	Orange Arrows	B	3.0 Arrows A23-Cosworth V10	*started from pits – *ignored red light*	15/22
11	MALAYSIAN GP	Sepang	20	Orange Arrows	B	3.0 Arrows A23-Cosworth V10	*2 laps behind*	11/22
ret	BRAZILIAN GP	Interlagos	20	Orange Arrows	B	3.0 Arrows A23-Cosworth V10	*rear track rod*	18/22
ret	SAN MARINO GP	Imola	20	Orange Arrows	B	3.0 Arrows A23-Cosworth V10	*fuel pressure*	13/22
6	SPANISH GP	Barcelona	20	Orange Arrows	B	3.0 Arrows A23-Cosworth V10		10/21
11	AUSTRIAN GP	A1-Ring	20	Orange Arrows	B	3.0 Arrows A23-Cosworth V10	*2 laps behind*	11/22
6	MONACO GP	Monte Carlo	20	Orange Arrows	B	3.0 Arrows A23-Cosworth V10	*1 lap behind*	12/22
13	CANADIAN GP	Montreal	20	Orange Arrows	B	3.0 Arrows A23-Cosworth V10	*1 lap behind*	19/22
13	EUROPEAN GP	Nürburgring	20	Orange Arrows	B	3.0 Arrows A23-Cosworth V10	*1 lap behind*	15/22
ret	BRITISH GP	Silverstone	20	Orange Arrows	B	3.0 Arrows A23-Cosworth V10	*engine*	16/22
dnq	FRENCH GP	Magny Cours	20	Orange Arrows	B	3.0 Arrows A23-Cosworth V10	*made only a token effort to qualify*	20/21
ret	GERMAN GP	Hockenheim	20	Orange Arrows	B	3.0 Arrows A23-Cosworth V10	*hydraulics*	15/20
13	UNITED STATES GP	Indianapolis	8	Sauber Petronas	B	3.0 Sauber C21-Petronas V10	*2 laps behind*	11/20

2003 Championship position: 11th   Wins: 0   Pole positions: 0   Fastest laps: 0   Points scored: 13

6	AUSTRALIAN GP	Melbourne	10	Sauber Petronas	B	3.0 Sauber C22-Petronas V10			4/20
9	MALAYSIAN GP	Sepang	10	Sauber Petronas	B	3.0 Sauber C22-Petronas V10	1 lap behind		13/20
5	BRAZILIAN GP	Interlagos	10	Sauber Petronas	B	3.0 Sauber C22-Petronas V10	race red flagged		14/20
11	SAN MARINO GP	Imola	10	Sauber Petronas	B	3.0 Sauber C22-Petronas V10	1 lap behind		14/20
ret	SPANISH GP	Barcelona	10	Sauber Petronas	B	3.0 Sauber C22-Petronas V10	suspension		10/20
dns*	AUSTRIAN GP	A1-Ring	10	Sauber Petronas	B	3.0 Sauber C22-Petronas V10	*clutch before first start		15/20
ret	MONACO GP	Monte Carlo	10	Sauber Petronas	B	3.0 Sauber C22-Petronas V10	crashed at swimming pool		15/19
ret	CANADIAN GP	Montreal	10	Sauber Petronas	B	3.0 Sauber C22-Petronas V10	electronics		10/20
9	EUROPEAN GP	Nürburgring	10	Sauber Petronas	B	3.0 Sauber C22-Petronas V10	1 lap behind		15/20
12	FRENCH GP	Magny Cours	10	Sauber Petronas	B	3.0 Sauber C22-Petronas V10	2 laps behind		16/20
12	BRITISH GP	Silverstone	10	Sauber Petronas	B	3.0 Sauber C22-Petronas V10			14/20
ret	GERMAN GP	Hockenheim	10	Sauber Petronas	B	3.0 Sauber C22-Petronas V10	accident		14/20
ret	HUNGARIAN GP	Hungaroring	10	Sauber Petronas	B	3.0 Sauber C22-Petronas V10	out of fuel		17/20
13/ret	ITALIAN GP	Monza	10	Sauber Petronas	B	3.0 Sauber C22-Petronas V10	transmission/2 laps behind		14/20
3	UNITED STATES GP	Indianapolis	10	Sauber Petronas	B	3.0 Sauber C22-Petronas V10			15/20
ret	JAPANESE GP	Suzuka	10	Sauber Petronas	B	3.0 Sauber C22-Petronas V10	engine		12/20

GP Starts: 156 (157)   GP Wins: 3   Pole positions: 2   Fastest laps: 6   Points: 174

PAUL FRÈRE

PAUL FRÈRE was a rarity in that he was not a full-time driver, preferring to maintain his profession as an international motoring journalist throughout a long and successful racing career.

Originally Frère was a champion rower in the immediate post-war years, before making his motor racing debut in the Spa 24-hours. He shared an MG with Jacques Swaters, the pair finishing fourth in class, but it was not until 1952 that he raced in earnest. After winning a big production car race in an Oldsmobile at Spa, he picked up a last-minute drive with HWM in the GP des Frontières at Chimay. Left on the grid at the start, he overhauled Ken Downing's Connaught right at the end of the race to score a surprise win. HWM's John Heath immediately offered him a drive in the forthcoming Belgian GP, and he delighted his entrant by bringing the car home in a splendid fifth place in the pouring rain.

Frère raced for HWM again in 1953; his luck was out this time in grands prix, but he did finish a brilliant second in the rain in the Eifelrennen. For 1954, he accepted a few rides with Gordini in Formula 1, and drove at Le Mans for the first time in a works Aston Martin DB3S sports car shared with Carroll Shelby.

The Sarthe classic became an important race in Frère's career. Second in the tragic 1955 race in an Aston (with Peter Collins), he was involved in a first-lap crash in a works Jaguar in 1956 and finished fourth in 1957 in the Equipe National Belge Jaguar entry. In 1958, he was in a works Porsche and took fourth (and second in class) with Eddie Barth. Back in the big-capacity class with a works Aston for 1959, he and Maurice Trintignant took second place (and second in class) behind the sister car of Roy Salvadori and Shelby. He won at last in 1960, sharing a works Ferrari 250 Testa Rossa with his great friend Olivier Gendebien. This partnership, incidentally, had been victorious in the Reims 12-hours of 1957.

Ferrari also gave Paul an opportunity to drive his Formula 1 cars, and he did not disappoint, taking fourth place in the 1955 Belgian GP and a quite magnificent second, behind Peter Collins, at Spa again in 1956. He made a brief return to single-seaters in 1960, his final season, winning the non-championship South African Grand Prix in an Equipe Nationale Belge Cooper. Then he showed his consistency and reliable driving skills on his return to Europe to take fifth places at Syracuse and Brussels, and sixth at Pau.

Following his retirement, Frère concentrated on his hugely successful journalistic career, as well as acting as an advisor to car manufacturers Honda, Mazda and particularly Porsche, with whom he had a very close working relationship. After his death in 2008, at the age of 92, a corner of the Spa-Francorchamps track was named in his honour.

FRÈRE, Paul (B)   b 30/1/1917, Sainte Adesse, Le Havre, France – d 23/3/2008, Saint-Paul-de-Vence, France

1952 Championship position: 11th=   Wins: 0   Pole positions: 0   Fastest laps: 0   Points scored: 2

	Race	Circuit	No	Entrant	Tyres	Capacity/Car/Engine	Comment	Q Pos/Entries
5	BELGIAN GP	Spa	28	HW Motors Ltd	D	2.0 HWM-Alta 4	2 laps behind	8/22
ret	GERMAN GP	Nürburgring	112	HW Motors Ltd	D	2.0 HWM-Alta 4	transmission	13/32
ret	DUTCH GP	Zandvoort	14	Ecurie Belge	E	1.5 Simca Gordini Type 15 4	clutch/gearbox	11/18
	1953 Championship position: Unplaced							
10	BELGIAN GP	Spa	24	HW Motors Ltd	D	2.0 HWM-Alta 4	6 laps behind	11/22
ret	SWISS GP	Bremgarten	14	HW Motors Ltd	D	2.0 HWM-Alta 4	engine	16/23

	1954 Championship position: Unplaced									
ret	BELGIAN GP	Spa	16	Equipe Gordini	E	2.0 Gordini Type 16 6		*engine*		10/15
ret	FRENCH GP	Reims	28	Equipe Gordini	E	2.0 Gordini Type 16 6		*rear axle*		19/22
ret	GERMAN GP	Nürburgring	10	Equipe Gordini	E	2.0 Gordini Type 16 6		*lost wheel*		6/23
	1955 Championship position: 11th		Wins: 0	Pole positions: 0	Fastest laps: 0	Points scored: 3				
8*	MONACO GP	Monte Carlo	48	Scuderia Ferrari	E	2.5 Ferrari 555 4		**took Taruffi's car/14 laps behind*		– /22
4	BELGIAN GP	Spa	6	Scuderia Ferrari	E	2.5 Ferrari 555 4				8/14
	1956 Championship position: 6th=		Wins: 0	Pole positions: 0	Fastest laps: 0	Points scored: 6				
2	BELGIAN GP	Spa	6	Scuderia Ferrari	E	2.5 Lancia-Ferrari D50 V8				8/16
	GP Starts: 11 GP Wins: 0 Pole positions: 0 Fastest laps: 0 Points: 11									

PATRICK FRIESACHER

THE young Patrick Friesacher raced motorcycles for five years before realising that his future lay on four wheels rather than two. Then his dogged determination saw him patiently climb the career ladder. He proved to be a strong contender in the Austrian national karting competition, twice placing third overall, before moving on to the international scene. This was despite suffering a serious accident that left him in hospital for six weeks and a wheelchair for seven after surgery was required to reconstruct his shin and heels.

Unfazed by the injuries, Friesacher returned to competition, having been selected as one of 26 young kart racers to try out for the famous La Filière racing school and its Formula Campus series. He proved instantly competitive, taking four poles and winning at Ledenon and on the streets of Pau to claim third overall in the points. This success led to the B class of the French F3 championship in 1999, where again he finished third overall after wins at Magny-Cours and Val de Vienne.

Then Friesacher moved closer to home to contest the 2000 German F3 series with Bertram Schafer Racing. Finding the series more competitive than in France, he finished sixth in the standings, managing to win races at the Sachsenring and Oschersleben, as well as take three poles and four other podiums.

Now in the Red Bull driver programme, Friesacher found himself propelled into the FIA F3000 championship, running with the new Red Bull Junior Team. Making steady, but not spectacular progress, he did just enough in his first two seasons to retain his backing and get a place in the Coloni team for 2003. A bright start was interrupted when he broke his arm in an accident in Spain, but he bounced back to take a maiden win at the Hungaroring. After losing his Red Bull backing, he moved to Super Nova for a fourth year in F3000, but it was not a happy sojourn. A mid-season return to Coloni brought an upturn in his fortunes and a repeat win in Hungary.

Signed by Minardi to pilot their special F1x2 two-seater cars at demonstration and sponsor events, Friesacher was not expected to feature in the Italian team's plans, until being offered a test in November, 2004. From there, he was understood to be in line for the permanent testing role, but when Nicolas Kiesa failed to come up with the finances necessary to secure a race seat, Patrick was signed up to partner Christijan Albers in an all-rookie team. The fledgling pair were pretty evenly matched for pace in 2005, with Patrick catching the eye at Monaco in particular. He also scored three world championship points as the sixth-placed finisher in the infamous six-car 'Bridgestone only' race at Indianapolis.

At the beginning of 2006, Friesacher replaced Mathias Lauda in the Team Austria car contesting the A1GP series round in Monterrey, Mexico. Given that he had not driven for more than half a season, he did well to score points in both the sprint and feature races.

In 2008, Friesacher signed with Risi Competizione to race their Ferrari 430 in the ALMS, making his debut in St Petersburg. Then he undertook testing of the A1GP's new chassis at Magny-Cours, where he had a nasty accident when the suspension failed. He was hospitalised him with three crushed vertebrae. Most recently, Friesacher has been demonstrating a Red Bull NASCAR 5.8-litre V8 Toyota Camry at events around Europe.

FRIESACHER, Patrick (A) b 26/9/1980, Wolfsburg

	2005 Championship position: 21st		Wins: 0	Pole positions: 0	Fastest laps: 0	Points scored: 3			
	Race	*Circuit*	*No*	*Entrant*	*Tyres*	*Capacity/Car/Engine*	*Comment*		*Q Pos/Entries*
17	AUSTRALIAN GP	Melbourne	20	European Minardi Cosworth	B	Minardi PS04B-3.0 Cosworth V10	*4 laps behind*		16/20
ret	MALAYSIAN GP	Sepang	20	European Minardi Cosworth	B	Minardi PS04B-3.0 Cosworth V10	*hit oil and spun off*		19/20
12	BAHRAIN GP	Bahrain	20	European Minardi Cosworth	B	Minardi PS04B-3.0 Cosworth V10	*3 laps behind*		20/20
ret	SAN MARINO GP	Imola	20	European Minardi Cosworth	B	Minardi PS05-3.0 Cosworth V10	*clutch*		19/20
ret	SPANISH GP	Barcelona	20	European Minardi Cosworth	B	Minardi PS05-3.0 Cosworth V10	*started from pitlane/spun off*		15/18
ret	MONACO GP	Monte Carlo	20	European Minardi Cosworth	B	Minardi PS05-3.0 Cosworth V10	*accident*		13/18
18	EUROPEAN GP	Nürburgring	20	European Minardi Cosworth	B	Minardi PS05-3.0 Cosworth V10	*oversteer/3 laps behind*		18/20
ret	CANADIAN GP	Montreal	20	European Minardi Cosworth	B	Minardi PS05-3.0 Cosworth V10	*hydraulics*		19/20
6	U S GP	Indianapolis	20	European Minardi Cosworth	B	Minardi PS05-3.0 Cosworth V10	*2 laps behind*		20/20
ret	FRENCH GP	Magny Cours	20	European Minardi Cosworth	B	Minardi PS05-3.0 Cosworth V10	*spun off – wrongly fitted tyre valve caps*		18/20
19	BRITISH GP	Silverstone	20	European Minardi Cosworth	B	Minardi PS05-3.0 Cosworth V10	*2 laps behind*		19/20
	GP Starts: 11 GP Wins: 0 Pole positions: 0 Fastest laps: 0 Points: 3								

FRY, Joe (GB) b 26/10/1915, Chipping Sodbury, Gloucestershire – d 29/7/1950, Blandford Camp, Dorset

1950 Championship position: Unplaced

	Race	Circuit	No	Entrant	Tyres	Capacity/Car/Engine	Comment	Q Pos/Entries
10*	BRITISH GP	Silverstone	10	Joe Fry	D	1.5 s/c Maserati 4CL 4	*Shawe-Taylor also drove car	20/21

GP Starts: 1   GP Wins: 0   Pole positions: 0   Fastest laps: 0   Points: 0

JOE FRY

A MAN of a quiet and retiring disposition, J.G. 'Joe' Fry was a sprint and hill-climb specialist who began developing a lightweight rear-engined special before the Second World War with his brother, David, and a small circle of devotees. Developments were resumed after the cessation of hostilities, and by 1949 he had broken Raymond Mays' record at Shelsley Walsh.

This sprint machine was one of the fastest in the country regardless of engine capacity. In its 1950 guise, the rear-engined 'Freikaiserwagen' was fitted with a potent twin-cylinder Blackburn air-cooled engine with two-stage supercharging, but in a minor meeting at Blandford Camp, in Dorset, Fry lost control of the machine on a fast bend and crashed with fatal results. Just a few weeks earlier, he had shared a Maserati with Brian Shawe-Taylor in the first ever world championship race, the 1950 British Grand Prix.

BEPPE GABBIANI

A FTER seven years in karting, Beppe Gabbiani, an Italian rich kid, decided to try his hand at F3 in 1977, immediately winning his first big race at Paul Ricard. Flushed with his success, he was soon in Formula 1, and by the end of the 1978 season he had had a couple of GP drives with Surtees in place of the injured Vittorio Brambilla.

Gabbiani's fortunes dipped in the first part of 1979, when he seemed to crash regularly in Formula 2, and a 'rent-a-drive' in a Shadow in a non-championship F1 race at Imola saw him fail to start after an embarrassing practice period. But to be fair, he was a quick driver, and he buckled down to rescue his season with second places in F2 at Mugello and Misano

His next season in F2 with Maurer brought little success after a late start, and for 1981 he joined Osella for a tilt at grands prix that found him out of his depth. The Italian's Formula 1 opportunities undoubtedly had come too soon, and he retrenched in 1982, returning to F2 with Maurer, where he faced a stern challenge from gifted team-mate Stefan Bellof. Given a real chance to demonstrate his class in 1983 with the top Onyx March team, Gabbiani started brilliantly, with four wins in the first five races, but the title eventually slipped from his grasp as the Ralt-Hondas of Jonathan Palmer and Mike Thackwell overwhelmed him.

After this disappointment, Gabbiani's front-line career dribbled away, a few further outings in Formula 2 and F3000 offering him little encouragement to continue. Then he turned to occasional outings in sports car racing, with Dome among others, but found much more enjoyment in the Touring and GT classes.

In the past two decades, Gabbiani has raced a huge variety of machinery, usually on an ad-hoc basis. In 2006, he shared a Creation Autosportif-Judd with Nicolas Minassian and Felipe Ortiz, and more recently he has successfully raced a BMW M3 with Pierro Necchi in the Italian Touring Car Endurance Championship. In 2011, Gabbiani could be found competing in the Lotus Cup.

GABBIANI, Beppe (I) b 2/1/1957, Piacenza

1978 Championship position: Unplaced

	Race	Circuit	No	Entrant	Tyres	Capacity/Car/Engine	Comment	Q Pos/Entries
dnq	US GP EAST	Watkins Glen	19	Team Surtees	G	3.0 Surtees TS20-Cosworth V8		27/27
dnq	CANADIAN GP	Montreal	19	Team Surtees	G	3.0 Surtees TS20-Cosworth V8		24/28

1981 Championship position: Unplaced

	Race	Circuit	No	Entrant	Tyres	Capacity/Car/Engine	Comment	Q Pos/Entries
ret	US GP WEST	Long Beach	32	Osella Squadra Corse	M	3.0 Osella FA1B-Cosworth V8	accident – broken suspension	24/29
dnq	BRAZILIAN GP	Rio	32	Osella Squadra Corse	M	3.0 Osella FA1B-Cosworth V8		27/30
dnq	ARGENTINE GP	Buenos Aires	32	Osella Squadra Corse	M	3.0 Osella FA1B-Cosworth V8		26/29
ret	SAN MARINO GP	Imola	32	Osella Squadra Corse	M	3.0 Osella FA1B-Cosworth V8	collision with Alboreto	20/30
ret	BELGIAN GP	Zolder	32	Osella Squadra Corse	M	3.0 Osella FA1B-Cosworth V8	engine	22/31
dnq	MONACO GP	Monte Carlo	31	Osella Squadra Corse	M	3.0 Osella FA1B-Cosworth V8		26/31
dnq	SPANISH GP	Jarama	31	Osella Squadra Corse	M	3.0 Osella FA1B-Cosworth V8		26/30
dnq	FRENCH GP	Dijon	31	Osella Squadra Corse	M	3.0 Osella FA1B-Cosworth V8		28/29
dnq	BRITISH GP	Silverstone	31	Osella Squadra Corse	M	3.0 Osella FA1B-Cosworth V8		30/30

dnq	GERMAN GP	Hockenheim	31	Osella Squadra Corse	M	3.0 Osella FA1B-Cosworth V8		27/30
dnq	AUSTRIAN GP	Österreichring	31	Osella Squadra Corse	M	3.0 Osella FA1B-Cosworth V8		28/28
dnq	DUTCH GP	Zandvoort	31	Osella Squadra Corse	M	3.0 Osella FA1B-Cosworth V8		29/30
dnq	ITALIAN GP	Monza	31	Osella Squadra Corse	M	3.0 Osella FA1B-Cosworth V8		26/30
dnq	CANADIAN GP	Montreal	31	Osella Squadra Corse	M	3.0 Osella FA1B-Cosworth V8		30/30
dnq	CAESARS PALACE GP	Las Vegas	31	Osella Squadra Corse	M	3.0 Osella FA1B-Cosworth V8		30/30

GP Starts: 3   GP Wins: 0   Pole positions: 0   Fastest laps: 0   Points: 0

BERTRAND GACHOT

A VERY confident and determined driver, Bertrand Gachot assiduously built his career to reach his goal of racing in a front-running Formula 1 team, only to throw it away with a moment of madness when an assault on a London taxi driver, after a traffic altercation, left him facing imprisonment.

Brilliantly successful in Formula Ford, winning the major British 1600 title in 1985 and the 2000 crown the following year after a torrid battle with Mark Blundell, Bertrand graduated to the British F3 championship with West Surrey Racing for 1987 and emerged as runner-up after another no-holds-barred battle, this time with Johnny Herbert.

A solid 1988 season in F3000 lacked only a win and Gachot finished fifth overall, quickly tying up a deal to race for the newly formed Onyx Grand Prix team in 1989. It was not a happy season though and, having been overshadowed by the experienced Stefan Johansson, he was replaced by JJ Lehto. After taking his sponsorship money to Rial for a couple more unproductive outings, he plunged into a disastrous 1990 season with the Coloni-Subaru. Then came the big break with Eddie Jordan's fledgling F1 team, whose new Gary Anderson-designed car was a revelation. Suddenly Gachot was really racing and showing his undoubted talent – until his shock incarceration. His drive with Jordan was lost, but undaunted he bounced back with the struggling Larrousse team. Bertrand's F1 career was on hold in 1993 – although he made a good Indy car debut at Toronto – while he finalised plans to lead Pacific's grand prix challenge in 1994.

Bertrand had worked ceaselessly to help find sponsorship for the team, and it must have been particularly hard for him to accept that the PR01 was a sub-standard car that had no prospect of improvement. Although the sparser grids in 1995 guaranteed that Pacific would at least be starting races, their second grand prix challenger proved no great step forward from the first, despite being a totally new design. As the team's financial situation worsened, Gachot stood down to allow pay-to-race drivers Giovanni Lavaggi and Jean-Denis Deletraz to provide a cash lifeline, but he did return for the last three races to see out the season. Given Pacific's previous track record of excellence in other formulas, there was plenty of sympathy for their plight, but there is no room for sentiment in F1, and the team followed Simtek into liquidation. For Keith Wiggins and Bertrand Gachot, a dream was over.

GACHOT, Bertrand (F) b 23/12/1962, Luxembourg

	Race	Circuit	No	Entrant	Tyres	Capacity/Car/Engine	Comment	Q Pos/Entries
1989	*Championship position: Unplaced*							
dnpq	BRAZILIAN GP	Rio	37	Moneytron Onyx	G	3.5 Onyx ORE 1-Cosworth V8		38/38
dnpq	SAN MARINO GP	Imola	37	Moneytron Onyx	G	3.5 Onyx ORE 1-Cosworth V8		31/39
dnpq	MONACO GP	Monte Carlo	37	Moneytron Onyx	G	3.5 Onyx ORE 1-Cosworth V8		34/38
dnpq	MEXICAN GP	Mexico City	37	Moneytron Onyx	G	3.5 Onyx ORE 1-Cosworth V8		31/39
dnpq	US GP (PHOENIX)	Phoenix	37	Moneytron Onyx	G	3.5 Onyx ORE 1-Cosworth V8		39/39
dnpq	CANADIAN GP	Montreal	37	Moneytron Onyx	G	3.5 Onyx ORE 1-Cosworth V8		32/39
13	FRENCH GP	Paul Ricard	37	Moneytron Onyx	G	3.5 Onyx ORE 1-Cosworth V8	*pit stop – overheating battery/-4 laps*	11/39
12	BRITISH GP	Silverstone	37	Moneytron Onyx	G	3.5 Onyx ORE 1-Cosworth V8	*raced spare car/2 laps behind*	21/39
dnq	GERMAN GP	Hockenheim	37	Moneytron Onyx	G	3.5 Onyx ORE 1-Cosworth V8		28/39
ret	HUNGARIAN GP	Hungaroring	37	Moneytron Onyx	G	3.5 Onyx ORE 1-Cosworth V8	*differential*	21/39
ret	BELGIAN GP	Spa	37	Moneytron Onyx	G	3.5 Onyx ORE 1-Cosworth V8	*wheel bearing – crashed*	23/39
ret	ITALIAN GP	Monza	37	Moneytron Onyx	G	3.5 Onyx ORE 1-Cosworth V8	*accident – holed radiator*	22/39
dnq	JAPANESE GP	Suzuka	39	Rial Racing	G	3.5 Rial ARC2-Cosworth V8		30/39
dnq	AUSTRALIAN GP	Adelaide	39	Rial Racing	G	3.5 Rial ARC2-Cosworth V8		29/39
1990	*Championship position: Unplaced*							
dnpq	US GP (PHOENIX)	Phoenix	31	Subaru Coloni Racing	G	3.5 Coloni FC189-Subaru F12	*no time set*	– /35
dnpq	BRAZILIAN GP	Interlagos	31	Subaru Coloni Racing	G	3.5 Coloni FC189-Subaru F12		33/35
dnpq	SAN MARINO GP	Imola	31	Subaru Coloni Racing	G	3.5 Coloni FC189-Subaru F12		31/34
dnpq	MONACO GP	Monte Carlo	31	Subaru Coloni Racing	G	3.5 Coloni FC189-Subaru F12		34/35
dnpq	CANADIAN GP	Montreal	31	Subaru Coloni Racing	G	3.5 Coloni FC189-Subaru F12		33/35
dnpq	MEXICAN GP	Mexico City	31	Subaru Coloni Racing	G	3.5 Coloni FC189-Subaru F12		33/35
dnpq	FRENCH GP	Paul Ricard	31	Subaru Coloni Racing	G	3.5 Coloni FC189-Subaru F12		34/35
dnpq	BRITISH GP	Silverstone	31	Subaru Coloni Racing	G	3.5 Coloni FC189-Subaru F12		34/35
dnpq	GERMAN GP	Hockenheim	31	Subaru Coloni Racing	G	3.5 Coloni FC189-Cosworth V8		33/35

	Race	Circuit	No	Entrant	Tyres	Capacity/Car/Engine	Comment	Q Pos/Entries
dnpq	HUNGARIAN GP	Hungaroring	31	Subaru Coloni Racing	G	3.5 Coloni FC189-Cosworth V8		32/35
dnq	BELGIAN GP	Spa	31	Subaru Coloni Racing	G	3.5 Coloni FC189-Cosworth V8		30/33
dnq	ITALIAN GP	Monza	31	Subaru Coloni Racing	G	3.5 Coloni FC189-Cosworth V8		30/33
dnq	PORTUGUESE GP	Estoril	31	Subaru Coloni Racing	G	3.5 Coloni FC189-Cosworth V8		30/33
dnq	SPANISH GP	Jerez	31	Subaru Coloni Racing	G	3.5 Coloni FC189-Cosworth V8		30/33
dnq	JAPANESE GP	Suzuka	31	Subaru Coloni Racing	G	3.5 Coloni FC189-Cosworth V8		30/30
dnq	AUSTRALIAN GP	Adelaide	31	Subaru Coloni Racing	G	3.5 Coloni FC189-Cosworth V8		30/30

1991 Championship position: 12= Wins: 0 Pole positions: 0 Fastest laps: 0 Points scored: 4

	Race	Circuit	No	Entrant	Tyres	Capacity/Car/Engine	Comment	Q Pos/Entries
10/ret	US GP (PHOENIX)	Phoenix	32	Team 7UP Jordan	G	3.5 Jordan 191-Ford HB V8	engine/6 laps behind	14/34
13/ret	BRAZILIAN GP	Interlagos	32	Team 7UP Jordan	G	3.5 Jordan 191-Ford HB V8	fuel pick-up/8 laps behind	10/34
ret	SAN MARINO GP	Imola	32	Team 7UP Jordan	G	3.5 Jordan 191-Ford HB V8	damage after earlier spin	12/34
8	MONACO GP	Monte Carlo	32	Team 7UP Jordan	G	3.5 Jordan 191-Ford HB V8	2 laps behind	24/34
5	CANADIAN GP	Montreal	32	Team 7UP Jordan	G	3.5 Jordan 191-Ford HB V8		14/34
ret	MEXICAN GP	Mexico City	32	Team 7UP Jordan	G	3.5 Jordan 191-Ford HB V8	spun off	20/34
ret	FRENCH GP	Magny Cours	32	Team 7UP Jordan	G	3.5 Jordan 191-Ford HB V8	spun off on first lap	19/34
6	BRITISH GP	Silverstone	32	Team 7UP Jordan	G	3.5 Jordan 191-Ford HB V8	1 lap behind	17/34
6	GERMAN GP	Hockenheim	32	Team 7UP Jordan	G	3.5 Jordan 191-Ford HB V8		11/34
9	HUNGARIAN GP	Hungaroring	32	Team 7UP Jordan	G	3.5 Jordan 191-Ford HB V8	spin/FL/1 lap behind	16/34
dnq	AUSTRALIAN GP	Adelaide	29	Larrousse F1	G	3.5 Lola L91-Cosworth V8		30/32

1992 Championship position: 17th= Wins: 0 Pole positions: 0 Fastest laps: 0 Points scored: 1

	Race	Circuit	No	Entrant	Tyres	Capacity/Car/Engine	Comment	Q Pos/Entries
ret	SOUTH AFRICAN GP	Kyalami	29	Central Park Venturi Larrousse	G	3.5 Venturi LC92-Lamborghini V12	suspension damage	22/30
11	MEXICAN GP	Mexico City	29	Central Park Venturi Larrousse	G	3.5 Venturi LC92-Lamborghini V12	engine misfire/3 laps behind	13/30
ret	BRAZILIAN GP	Interlagos	29	Central Park Venturi Larrousse	G	3.5 Venturi LC92-Lamborghini V12	rear suspension	18/31
ret	SPANISH GP	Barcelona	29	Central Park Venturi Larrousse	G	3.5 Venturi LC92-Lamborghini V12	engine	24/32
ret	SAN MARINO GP	Imola	29	Central Park Venturi Larrousse	G	3.5 Venturi LC92-Lamborghini V12	spun off	19/32
6	MONACO GP	Monte Carlo	29	Central Park Venturi Larrousse	G	3.5 Venturi LC92-Lamborghini V12	1 lap behind	15/32
dsq*	CANADIAN GP	Montreal	29	Central Park Venturi Larrousse	G	3.5 Venturi LC92-Lamborghini V12	shunted by Grouillard – *push start	19/32
ret	FRENCH GP	Magny Cours	29	Central Park Venturi Larrousse	G	3.5 Venturi LC92-Lamborghini V12	collision with Suzuki lap 1	13/30
ret	BRITISH GP	Silverstone	29	Central Park Venturi Larrousse	G	3.5 Venturi LC92-Lamborghini V12	rear wheel bearing	11/32
14	GERMAN GP	Hockenheim	29	Central Park Venturi Larrousse	G	3.5 Venturi LC92-Lamborghini V12	1 lap behind	25/32
ret	HUNGARIAN GP	Hungaroring	29	Central Park Venturi Larrousse	G	3.5 Venturi LC92-Lamborghini V12	collision with Suzuki	15/31
18/ret	BELGIAN GP	Spa	29	Central Park Venturi Larrousse	G	3.5 Venturi LC92-Lamborghini V12	spun off/4 laps behind	20/30
ret	ITALIAN GP	Monza	29	Central Park Venturi Larrousse	G	3.5 Venturi LC92-Lamborghini V12	engine	10/28
ret	PORTUGUESE GP	Estoril	29	Central Park Venturi Larrousse	G	3.5 Venturi LC92-Lamborghini V12	fuel pressure	13/26
ret	JAPANESE GP	Suzuka	29	Central Park Venturi Larrousse	G	3.5 Venturi LC92-Lamborghini V12	collision with Katayama	18/26
ret	AUSTRALIAN GP	Adelaide	29	Central Park Venturi Larrousse	G	3.5 Venturi LC92-Lamborghini V12	engine	21/26

1994 Championship position: Unplaced

	Race	Circuit	No	Entrant	Tyres	Capacity/Car/Engine	Comment	Q Pos/Entries
ret	BRAZILIAN GP	Interlagos	34	Pacific Grand Prix Ltd	G	3.5 Pacific PR01-Ilmor V10	hit by Beretta – spun off	25/28
dnq	PACIFIC GP	T.I. Circuit	34	Pacific Grand Prix Ltd	G	3.5 Pacific PR01-Ilmor V10		28/28
ret	SAN MARINO GP	Imola	34	Pacific Grand Prix Ltd	G	3.5 Pacific PR01-Ilmor V10	engine	25/28
ret	MONACO GP	Monte Carlo	34	Pacific Grand Prix Ltd	G	3.5 Pacific PR01-Ilmor V10	gearbox	23/24
ret	SPANISH GP	Barcelona	34	Pacific Grand Prix Ltd	G	3.5 Pacific PR01-Ilmor V10	wing damage	25/27
ret	CANADIAN GP	Montreal	34	Pacific Grand Prix Ltd	G	3.5 Pacific PR01-Ilmor V10	engine	26/27
dnq	FRENCH GP	Magny Cours	34	Pacific Grand Prix Ltd	G	3.5 Pacific PR01-Ilmor V10		27/28
dnq	BRITISH GP	Silverstone	34	Pacific Grand Prix Ltd	G	3.5 Pacific PR01-Ilmor V10		27/28
dnq	GERMAN GP	Hockenheim	34	Pacific Grand Prix Ltd	G	3.5 Pacific PR01-Ilmor V10		28/28
dnq	HUNGARIAN GP	Hungaroring	34	Pacific Grand Prix Ltd	G	3.5 Pacific PR01-Ilmor V10		27/28
dnq	BELGIAN GP	Spa	34	Pacific Grand Prix Ltd	G	3.5 Pacific PR01-Ilmor V10		27/28
dnq	ITALIAN GP	Monza	34	Pacific Grand Prix Ltd	G	3.5 Pacific PR01-Ilmor V10		27/28
dnq	PORTUGUESE GP	Estoril	34	Pacific Grand Prix Ltd	G	3.5 Pacific PR01-Ilmor V10		27/28
dnq	EUROPEAN GP	Jerez	34	Pacific Grand Prix Ltd	G	3.5 Pacific PR01-Ilmor V10		27/28
dnq	JAPANESE GP	Suzuka	34	Pacific Grand Prix Ltd	G	3.5 Pacific PR01-Ilmor V10		27/28
dnq	AUSTRALIAN GP	Adelaide	34	Pacific Grand Prix Ltd	G	3.5 Pacific PR01-Ilmor V10		28/28

1995 Championship position: Unplaced

	Race	Circuit	No	Entrant	Tyres	Capacity/Car/Engine	Comment	Q Pos/Entries
ret	BRAZILIAN GP	Interlagos	16	Pacific Grand Prix Ltd	G	3.0 Pacific PR02-Ford ED V8	gearbox	20/26
ret	ARGENTINE GP	Buenos Aires	16	Pacific Grand Prix Ltd	G	3.0 Pacific PR02-Ford ED V8	collision with Wendlinger	23/26
ret	SAN MARINO GP	Imola	16	Pacific Grand Prix Ltd	G	3.0 Pacific PR02-Ford ED V8	gearbox	22/26
ret	SPANISH GP	Barcelona	16	Pacific Grand Prix Ltd	G	3.0 Pacific PR02-Ford ED V8	fire	24/26
ret	MONACO GP	Monte Carlo	16	Pacific Grand Prix Ltd	G	3.0 Pacific PR02-Ford ED V8	gearbox	21/26
ret	CANADIAN GP	Montreal	16	Pacific Grand Prix Ltd	G	3.0 Pacific PR02-Ford ED V8	battery	20/24
ret	FRENCH GP	Magny Cours	16	Pacific Grand Prix Ltd	G	3.0 Pacific PR02-Ford ED V8	gearbox	22/24
12	BRITISH GP	Silverstone	16	Pacific Grand Prix Ltd	G	3.0 Pacific PR02-Ford ED V8	3 laps behind	21/24
ret	PACIFIC GP	T.I. Circuit	16	Pacific Grand Prix Ltd	G	3.0 Pacific PR02-Ford ED V8	hydraulics	24/24
ret	JAPANESE GP	Suzuka	16	Pacific Grand Prix Ltd	G	3.0 Pacific PR02-Ford ED V8	driveshaft bearing	23/24
8	AUSTRALIAN GP	Adelaide	16	Pacific Grand Prix Ltd	G	3.0 Pacific PR02-Ford ED V8	5 laps behind	23/24

GP Starts: 47 GP Wins: 0 Pole positions: 0 Fastest laps: 1 Points: 5

GAILLARD, Patrick (F) b 12/2/1952, Paris

1979 Championship position: Unplaced

	Race	Circuit	No	Entrant	Tyres	Capacity/Car/Engine	Comment	Q Pos/Entries
dnq	FRENCH GP	Dijon	22	Team Ensign	G	3.0 Ensign N179-Cosworth V8		26/27
13	BRITISH GP	Silverstone	22	Team Ensign	G	3.0 Ensign N179-Cosworth V8	3 laps behind	23/26
dnq	GERMAN GP	Hockenheim	22	Team Ensign	G	3.0 Ensign N179-Cosworth V8		25/26
ret	AUSTRIAN GP	Österreichring	22	Team Ensign	G	3.0 Ensign N179-Cosworth V8	front suspension	24/26
dnq	DUTCH GP	Zandvoort	22	Team Ensign	G	3.0 Ensign N179-Cosworth V8		25/26

GP Starts: 2 GP Wins: 0 Pole positions: 0 Fastest laps: 0 Points: 0

PATRICK GAILLARD

A GRADUATE of Formule Super Renault, Patrick Gaillard made his reputa-tion in Formula 3 with a Chevron, finishing third in the 1978 European championship in a works B43, and winning rounds at Imola and the Nürbur-gring. He moved into Formula 2 for the 1979 season, but soon stepped into the Ensign seat vacated by Derek Daly at the French Grand Prix. The car was extremely difficult to handle, however, and Patrick, though very brave, quali-fied only twice in five races, before he in turn was replaced by Marc Surer.

Gaillard made a brief return the following season to finish sixth in the infamous Spanish GP, which sadly for him, was subsequently downgraded from championship status. Then he picked up the odd Formula 2 ride and made sporadic sports car appearances before slipping from the limelight.

Thereafter, he became the chief instructor at the AGS driving school in the south of France.

NANNI GALLI

T he son of a wealthy textile merchant, Giovanni Galli began racing at the compara-tively late age of 24. He had anticipated that his family would be opposed to his early racing activities, so ran under the pseudonym 'Nanni', which stuck. He bought a Mini-Cooper with which he entered the 1965 Italian touring car championship and proceeded to take ten class wins in ten starts, before moving on to an Alfa Romeo GTA.

Galli began to forge a reputation in sports car racing in the factory Alfa Romeo T33 in 1967, although he had to wait until the following season for success, winning the Circuit of Mugello (with Lucien Bianchi and Nino Vaccarella), and finishing second in both the Targa Florio and the Imola 500km (both with Ignazio Giunti). He was a mainstay of the Autodelta sports car programme right through until 1972, with many top-six placings.

In tandem with his long-distance activities, Galli moved into single-seaters, initially with Tecno in Formula 2. Then he graduated to grand prix racing via an Alfa Romeo engine-supply deal, first at Monza in 1970 with McLaren and then with March in 1971. For 1972, he became involved in the well-funded, but unsuccessful Tecno F1 project, his best result being a third place in the poorly supported GP of the Italian Republic at Vallelunga. With Clay Regazzoni indisposed, he was invited to represent Ferrari in the French GP, but could finish no better than 13th.

For 1973, 'Nanni' joined Frank Williams to race his new Iso car, but after a handful of disappointing outings, he quit the team and announced his retirement, athough he would return briefly in 1974 at the wheel of a works Abarth sports car.

GALLI, Nanni (Giovanni) (I) b 2/10/1940, Bologna

	Race	Circuit	No	Entrant	Tyres	Capacity/Car/Engine	Comment	Q Pos/Entries
	1970 Championship position: Unplaced							
dnq	ITALIAN GP	Monza	36	Bruce McLaren Motor Racing	G	3.0 McLaren M7D-Alfa Romeo V8		27/27
	1971 Championship position: Unplaced							
dnq	MONACO GP	Monte Carlo	19	STP March	F	3.0 March 711-Alfa Romeo V8		21/23
ret	DUTCH GP	Zandvoort	18	STP March	F	3.0 March 711-Alfa Romeo V8	incident with Cevert – spun off	20/24
dns	FRENCH GP	Paul Ricard	33	STP March	F	3.0 March 711-Cosworth V8	Soler-Roig drove car in race	(20)/24
11	BRITISH GP	Silverstone	20	STP March	F	3.0 March 711-Cosworth V8	3 laps behind	21/24
12	GERMAN GP	Nürburgring	17	STP March	F	3.0 March 711-Alfa Romeo V8	broken engine mounting/-2 laps	21/23
12	AUSTRIAN GP	Österreichring	19	STP March	F	3.0 March 711-Alfa Romeo V8	pit stop/3 laps behind	15/22
ret	ITALIAN GP	Monza	22	STP March	F	3.0 March 711-Cosworth V8	electrics	19/24
16	CANADIAN GP	Mosport Park	18	STP March	F	3.0 March 711-Cosworth V8	7 laps behind	20/27
ret	US GP	Watkins Glen	26	STP March	F	3.0 March 711-Cosworth V8	steering and suspension	25/32
	1972 Championship position: Unplaced							
ret	BELGIAN GP	Nivelles	22	Martini Racing Team	F	3.0 Tecno PA123 F12	spun – hit by Regazzoni-suspension	24/26
13	FRENCH GP	Clermont Ferrand	30	Scuderia Ferrari SpA SEFAC	F	3.0 Ferrari 312B2 F12	1 lap behind	21/29
ret	BRITISH GP	Brands Hatch	30	Martini Racing Team	F	3.0 Tecno PA123 F12	spun off	=18/27
nc	AUSTRIAN GP	Österreichring	15	Martini Racing Team	F	3.0 Tecno PA123 F12	pit stops/9 laps behind	24/26
ret	ITALIAN GP	Monza	11	Martini Racing Team	F	3.0 Tecno PA123 F12	engine	23/27

1973 Championship position: Unplaced

	Race	Circuit	No	Entrant	Tyres	Capacity/Car/Engine	Comment	Q Pos/Entries
ret	ARGENTINE GP	Buenos Aires	36	Frank Williams Racing Cars	F	3.0 Iso Marlboro FX3B-Cosworth V8	*accessory belt to pumps*	16/19
9	BRAZILIAN GP	Interlagos	20	Frank Williams Racing Cars	F	3.0 Iso Marlboro FX3B-Cosworth V8	*2 laps behind*	18/20
11	SPANISH GP	Montjuich Park	24	Frank Williams Racing Cars	F	3.0 Iso Marlboro IR-Cosworth V8	*pitstop/6 laps behind*	20/22
ret	BELGIAN GP	Zolder	26	Frank Williams Racing Cars	F	3.0 Iso Marlboro IR-Cosworth V8	*engine*	17/23
ret	MONACO GP	Monte Carlo	26	Frank Williams Racing Cars	F	3.0 Iso Marlboro IR-Cosworth V8	*driveshaft*	22/26

GP Starts: 17　GP Wins: 0　Pole positions: 0　Fastest laps: 0　Points: 0

GÁLVEZ, Óscar Alfredo (RA)　b 17/8/1913, Buenos Aires – d 16/12/1989, Buenos Aires

1953 Championship position: 11th=　Wins: 0　Pole positions: 0　Fastest laps: 0　Points scored: 2

	Race	Circuit	No	Entrant	Tyres	Capacity/Car/Engine	Comment	Q Pos/Entries
5	ARGENTINE GP	Buenos Aires	8	Officine Alfieri Maserati	P	2.0 Maserati A6GCM 6	*1 lap behind*	9/16

GP Starts: 1　GP Wins: 0　Pole positions: 0　Fastest laps: 0　Points: 2

GAMBLE, Fred (USA)　b 17/3/1932, Pittsburgh, Pennsylvania

1960 Championship position: 0　Wins: 0　Pole positions: 0　Fastest laps: 0　Points scored: 0

	Race	Circuit	No	Entrant	Tyres	Capacity/Car/Engine	Comment	Q Pos/Entries
10	ITALIAN GP	Monza	28	Camoradi International	D	1.5 Behra-Porsche F4 F2	*9 laps behind*	14/16

GP Starts: 1　GP Wins: 0　Pole positions: 0　Fastest laps: 0　Points: 0

OSCAR ALFREDO GÁLVEZ

A GREAT talent hidden from Europe, Oscar Gálvez was the early rival and inspiration to Juan Fangio in their native Argentina, both before and after the Second World War. Oscar and his younger brother, Juan, set new standards of preparation and performance in the gruelling 'Turismo Carretara' road races that were so popular there, and they were usually seriously threatened only by 'the Maestro'. Such was the Galvez brothers' dominance in their Fords that between them they won every event, bar one, from 1949 to 1961. Oscar took five victories to his younger brother's nine.

Oscar was equally skilled at the art of circuit racing. Driving an Alfa Romeo, he won the Formula Libre Eva Perón Cup in 1949, beating Fangio, and was highly placed in the same event on a number of other occasions. It seems that the Gálvez brothers were opposed to the Perónist regime, however, and Oscar was 'overlooked' when the 'Argentine driver to Europe' scheme was instigated in 1949. The Invitation to drive a works Maserati in the 1953 race was his only grand prix; he finished fifth. It was a case of 'What if' for the world of grand prix racing.

In the absence of Fangio, 'Los Gálvez' continued to dominate South American road racing in their Fords through the 1950s and into the early 1960s, until disaster struck when Juan was killed in a crash early in 1963. Oscar raced on, but retired following a serious accident in 1964 to concentrate on managing the works-supported Ford team.

In tribute, the Buenos Aires circuit was renamed the Autódromo Oscar Gálvez in 1989, and in 2008 it was renamed once more as the Autódromo Juan y Oscar Gálvez to honour Argentina's greatest racing brothers.

FRED GAMBLE

A LTHOUGH never a serious F1 candidate – he never pretended to be – Fred Gamble, like all race fans, dreamed of one day driving in a grand prix. In his case, though, the dream came true. After gaining experience with Triumph and MGA cars in the USA, he stumbled across 'Lucky' Casner, a colourful personality and real wheeler-dealer. In 1960, they formed Scuderia Camoradi with the aim of tackling some of Europe's famous sports car races with a Maserati Birdcage and a Corvette. Fred was only allowed to race the latter car, and he drove within his limits to finish tenth at Le Mans.

By coincidence, the Camoradi base in Modena housed the ex-Behra Porsche F2 car and, knowing that the organisers of the Italian GP were anxious to fill the grid boycotted by the British teams, Fred contacted them and was amazed to be offered $1,000 starting money. In the race, he ran out of fuel out on the track and was forced to run half a mile back to his pit. Armed with a 5-gallon can, he refilled the car and eventually finished tenth and last! Gamble returned to the States at the end of the year and later worked on Shelby's Cobra project, before accepting an offer to join Goodyear in 1963. He was at the cutting edge of the tyre giant's move into grand prix racing and had the immense satisfaction of seeing two championships won in 1966 and 1967, before handing over the reins to Leo Mehl.

HOWDEN GANLEY

IT took a long time for Howden Ganley to realise his ambition of becoming a grand prix driver, which had been fired by a visit as a youngster in his native New Zealand to the grand prix at Ardmore in 1955. He sailed for England in 1961 with just £30 in his pocket and found employment as a mechanic preparing cars at a racing school. The urge to drive was satisfied occasionally over the next few years, but his engineering talent kept him well occupied (and paid), so his racing career was on hold.

It was 1967 before Howden embarked on a serious season of Formula 3 in his own new shiny Brabham, which had been financed by his engagement as crew chief for Skip Scott and Peter Revson in the 1966 Can-Am series. He plugged away in the formula for another two seasons, mixing it with the best, hoping for the big break that finally would come in 1970.

Given the opportunity to compete in F5000, Howden finished runner-up to Peter Gethin in the championship with a private McLaren M10B, and this success brought an offer to join the BRM team for 1971 as a junior driver. It was a mixed first season, but he scored some points at Monza and Watkins Glen, and in non-championship races finished second in the Oulton Park Gold Cup, fourth in the Jochen Rindt Memorial at Hockenheim and fifth in the Race of Champions. Continuing with BRM for 1972, he did not enjoy the best of seasons, again being restricted in the main from using the latest chassis. The high spot of his year came in a different arena, with second place at Le Mans, sharing a works Matra with François Cevert.

For 1973, Howden threw in his lot with Frank Williams and the Iso-FX3, which was a severe disappointment for all concerned, only a sixth place in Canada salvaging some pride. The season was redeemed a little by his inclusion in the Gulf/John Wyer sports car team, for whom his best result was second in the Spa 1000km in the Mirage with Vern Schuppan. At the beginning of 1974, Ganley raced for March in the first two grands prix, and took fifth in the GP Presidente Medici, a Brazilian non-championship race. Despite an offer to continue with March, unwisely in retrospect he opted to drive the mysterious F1 Maki. He was promised a deal that seemed too good to be true – and it was! The car suffered a suspension failure in practice for the German Grand Prix, and the unfortunate driver was left with serious foot and ankle injuries that effectively ended his grand prix career.

Howden then formed Tiga Cars with Tim Schenken and had plans to build an F1 car for Finnish hotshot Mikko Kozarowitzky, which fell through due to a lack of adequate finance. Over a 15-year period, however, Tiga were a successful presence, winning races in numerous classes from F2000 to Group C until the firm closed in 1989. Ganley, with his American wife Judy (herself a talented SCCA racer, who sadly passed away in 2007 after a long fight against cancer) then pursued numerous other business interests, splitting their time between the UK (where he acted as secretary to the BRDC) and their home in the USA.

GANLEY, Howden (NZ) b 24/12/1941, Hamilton

	1971 Championship position: 14th=		Wins: 0	Pole positions: 0		Fastest laps: 0	Points scored: 5		
	Race	Circuit	No	Entrant	Tyres	Capacity/Car/Engine	Comment	Q Pos/Entries
ret	SOUTH AFRICAN GP	Kyalami	27	Yardley BRM	F	3.0 BRM P153 V12	driver unwell	24/25
10	SPANISH GP	Montjuich Park	16	Yardley BRM	F	3.0 BRM P153 V12	4 laps behind	=16/22
dnq	MONACO GP	Monte Carlo	16	Yardley BRM	F	3.0 BRM P153 V12		19/23
7	DUTCH GP	Zandvoort	10	Yardley BRM	F	3.0 BRM P153 V12	4 laps behind	9/24
10	FRENCH GP	Paul Ricard	16	Yardley BRM	F	3.0 BRM P153 V12	1 lap behind	16/24
8	BRITISH GP	Silverstone	17	Yardley BRM	F	3.0 BRM P153 V12	pit stop – puncture/2 laps behind	11/24
ret	GERMAN GP	Nürburgring	23	Yardley BRM	F	3.0 BRM P153 V12	engine	14/23
ret	AUSTRIAN GP	Österreichring	15	Yardley BRM	F	3.0 BRM P160 V12	ignition	14/22
5	ITALIAN GP	Monza	19	Yardley BRM	F	3.0 BRM P160 V12		4/24
dns	CANADIAN GP	Mosport Park	16	Yardley BRM	F	3.0 BRM P160 V12	accident on warm-up lap	=(7)/27
4	US GP	Watkins Glen	16	Yardley BRM	F	3.0 BRM P160 V12		13/32
	1972 Championship position: 12=		Wins: 0	Pole positions: 0		Fastest laps: 0	Points scored: 4		
9	ARGENTINE GP	Buenos Aires	3	Marlboro BRM	F	3.0 BRM P160B V12	2 laps behind	13/22
nc	SOUTH AFRICAN GP	Kyalami	23	Marlboro BRM	F	3.0 BRM P160B V12	pit stop/9 laps behind	16/27
ret	SPANISH GP	Jarama	25	Marlboro BRM	F	3.0 BRM P160B V12	engine	20/26
ret	MONACO GP	Monte Carlo	19	Marlboro BRM	F	3.0 BRM P180 V12	collision – Hailwood – suspension	=18/25
8	BELGIAN GP	Nivelles	25	Marlboro BRM	F	3.0 BRM P160B V12	2 laps behind	15/26
dns	FRENCH GP	Clermont Ferrand	23	Marlboro BRM	F	3.0 BRM P160B V12	car driven by Beltoise	(22)/29
4	GERMAN GP	Nürburgring	17	Marlboro BRM	F	3.0 BRM P160C V12		18/27
6	AUSTRIAN GP	Österreichring	9	Marlboro BRM	F	3.0 BRM P160C V12		10/26
11	ITALIAN GP	Monza	22	Marlboro BRM	F	3.0 BRM P160C V12	pit stop/3 laps behind	17/27
10	CANADIAN GP	Mosport Park	15	Marlboro BRM	F	3.0 BRM P160C V12	2 laps behind	14/25
ret	US GP	Watkins Glen	16	Marlboro BRM	F	3.0 BRM P160C V12	engine	17/32

1973 Championship position: 19th=				Wins: 0	Pole positions: 0	Fastest laps: 0	Points scored: 1		
nc	ARGENTINE GP	Buenos Aires	38	Frank Williams Racing Cars	F	3.0 Iso Marlboro FX3B-Cosworth V8	pit stop/17 laps behind	19/19
7	BRAZILIAN GP	Interlagos	19	Frank Williams Racing Cars	F	3.0 Iso Marlboro FX3B-Cosworth V8	1 lap behind	16/20
10	SOUTH AFRICAN GP	Kyalami	21	Frank Williams Racing Cars	F	3.0 Iso Marlboro FX3B-Cosworth V8	pit stop – puncture/6 laps behind	19/25
ret	SPANISH GP	Montjuich Park	23	Frank Williams Racing Cars	F	3.0 Iso Marlboro IR-Cosworth V8	out of fuel	21/22
ret	BELGIAN GP	Zolder	25	Frank Williams Racing Cars	F	3.0 Iso Marlboro IR-Cosworth V8	throttle stuck/accident	21/23
ret	MONACO GP	Monte Carlo	25	Frank Williams Racing Cars	F	3.0 Iso Marlboro IR-Cosworth V8	driveshaft	10/26
11	SWEDISH GP	Anderstorp	25	Frank Willaims Racing Cars	F	3.0 Iso Marlboro IR-Cosworth V8	4 laps behind	11/22
14	FRENCH GP	Paul Ricard	25	Frank Williams Racing Cars	F	3.0 Iso Marlboro IR-Cosworth V8	3 laps behind	24/25
9	BRITISH GP	Silverstone	25	Frank Williams Racing Cars	F	3.0 Iso Marlboro IR-Cosworth V8	1 lap behind	18/29
9	DUTCH GP	Zandvoort	25	Frank Williams Racing Cars	F	3.0 Iso Marlboro IR-Cosworth V8	collision – Lauda – pit stop/-4 laps	15/24
dns	GERMAN GP	Nürburgring	25	Frank Williams Racing Cars	F	3.0 Iso Marlboro IR-Cosworth V8	practice accident	(19)/23
nc	AUSTRIAN GP	Österreichring	25	Frank Williams Racing Cars	F	3.0 Iso Marlboro IR-Cosworth V8	pit stop/10 laps behind	21/25
nc	ITALIAN GP	Monza	25	Frank Williams Racing Cars	F	3.0 Iso Marlboro IR-Cosworth V8	pit stops/11 laps behind	20/25
6	CANADIAN GP	Mosport Park	25	Frank Williams Racing Cars	F	3.0 Iso Marlboro IR-Cosworth V8	1 lap behind	22/26
12	US GP	Watkins Glen	25	Frank Williams Racing Cars	F	3.0 Iso Marlboro IR-Cosworth V8	pit stop/2 laps behind	20/28
1974 Championship position: Unplaced								
8/ret	ARGENTINE GP	Buenos Aires	10	March Engineering	G	3.0 March 741-Cosworth V8	out of fuel/1 lap behind	19/26
ret	BRAZILIAN GP	Interlagos	10	March Engineering	F	3.0 March 741-Cosworth V8	ignition	20/25
dnq	BRITISH GP	Brands Hatch	25	Maki Engineering	F	3.0 Maki F101-Cosworth V8		32/34
dnq	GERMAN GP	Nürburgring	25	Maki Engineering	F	3.0 Maki F101-Cosworth V8	injured in practice accident	32/32
GP Starts: 35	**GP Wins: 0**	**Pole positions: 0**		**Fastest laps: 0**	**Points: 10**			

FRANK GARDNER

ANOTHER driver whose brief grand prix career did no justice to his talent, Frank Gardner was one of the world's toughest, most determined and professional drivers, who was destined to enjoy an immensely long and successful career outside the sphere of Formula 1.

A typical Australian all-round sportsman, boxer, swimmer and motorcycle ace, Frank took up car racing in 1956/57, when he won 23 out of 24 races in a C-Type Jaguar to become NSW sports car champion. Inevitably he headed for England, where he found employment not as a driver, but as a mechanic for Aston Martin, Jim Russell and, in 1962, Jack Brabham's newly formed team, working on the Formula Junior cars. He drove the Brabham a few times that year, but turned down Jack's offer of a full-time ride for 1963 (taken instead by Denny Hulme), opting to join Ian Walker for a massively successful sports and Formula Junior programme.

This established Gardner as a serious proposition, and he moved to John Willment's team in 1964 to drive in Formula 2, also handling his stable of powerful sports and saloon cars. Ambitiously, the team moved into Formula 1 in 1965, but just were not up to it, although they did take an aggregate fourth place in the Race of Champions. Frank felt he had made a bit of a fool of himself and gave grand prix racing a wide berth, except for a couple of drives in 1968. He contested the Tasman series in a Brabham during this period, giving a good account of himself against the likes of Jim Clark, Graham Hill and Jackie Stewart, and did more Formula 2 in the MRP Lola and a works Brabham. He really established a niche in saloon cars, however, taking a string of championships from 1968 with Alan Mann's Escort and into the 1970s with both the Ford Mustang and Chevrolet Camaro. In fact, Gardner seemed to be racing virtually every weekend, as he was also contesting F5000 in the works Lola, taking the championship in both 1971 and '72, before suddenly quitting single-seaters after the Tasman series early in 1973 ("I drove like an old woman" was Frank's over-critical assessment after he won one round and took three second places). Gardner continued to thunder on in the Camaro until he returned to his homeland to race in the sports sedan championships, which he won in 1976 and '77. Truly he was a 'racing' driver in the very best sense of the word.

GARDNER, Frank (AUS) b 1/10/1930, Sydney, New South Wales – d 29/8/2009, Mermaid Waters, Queensland, New South Wales

	Race	Circuit	No	Entrant	Tyres	Capacity/Car/Engine	Comment	Q Pos/Entries
1964 Championship position: Unplaced								
ret	BRITISH GP	Brands Hatch	26	John Willment Automobiles	D	1.5 Brabham BT10-Ford 4	startline accident	19/25
1965 Championship position: Unplaced								
12	SOUTH AFRICAN GP	East London	16	John Willment Automobiles	D	1.5 Brabham BT11-BRM V8	pit stop/10 laps behind	15/25
ret	MONACO GP	Monte Carlo	11	John Willment Automobiles	D	1.5 Brabham BT11-BRM V8	engine mounting	=10/17
ret	BELGIAN GP	Spa	26	John Willment Automobiles	D	1.5 Brabham BT11-BRM V8	ignition	18/21
8	BRITISH GP	Silverstone	17	John Willment Automobiles	D	1.5 Brabham BT11-BRM V8	2 laps behind	13/23
11	DUTCH GP	Zandvoort	30	John Willment Automobiles	D	1.5 Brabham BT11-BRM V8	3 laps behind	=10/17
ret	GERMAN GP	Nürburgring	21	John Willment Automobiles	D	1.5 Brabham BT11-BRM V8	gearbox	18/22
ret	ITALIAN GP	Monza	46	John Willment Automobiles	D	1.5 Brabham BT11-BRM V8	engine	16/23
1968 Championship position: Unplaced								
dnq	ITALIAN GP	Monza	28	Bernard White Racing Ltd	G	3.0 BRM P261 V12		23/24
GP Starts: 8	**GP Wins: 0**	**Pole positions: 0**		**Fastest laps: 0**	**Points: 0**			

GARTNER, Jo (A) b 4/1/1954, Vienna – d 1/6/1986, Le Mans Circuit, France

1984 Championship position: Unplaced

	Race	Circuit	No	Entrant	Tyres	Capacity/Car/Engine	Comment	Q Pos/Entries
ret	SAN MARINO GP	Imola	30	Osella Squadra Corse	P	3.0 Osella FA1E-Alfa Romeo V12	engine	26/28
ret	BRITISH GP	Brands Hatch	30	Osella Squadra Corse	P	1.5 t/c Osella FA1F-Alfa Romeo V8	accident at start	27/27
ret	GERMAN GP	Nürburgring	30	Osella Squadra Corse	P	1.5 t/c Osella FA1F-Alfa Romeo V8	turbo	23/27
ret	AUSTRIAN GP	Österreichring	30	Osella Squadra Corse	P	1.5 t/c Osella FA1F-Alfa Romeo V8	engine	22/28
12*	DUTCH GP	Zandvoort	30	Osella Squadra Corse	P	1.5 t/c Osella FA1F-Alfa Romeo V8	*8th & 9th cars disqualified/-5 laps	23/27
5*	ITALIAN GP	Monza	30	Osella Squadra Corse	P	1.5 t/c Osella FA1F-Alfa Romeo V8	*not eligible for points/-2 laps	24/27
12/ret	EUROPEAN GP	Nürburgring	30	Osella Squadra Corse	P	1.5 t/c Osella FA1F-Alfa Romeo V8	fuel feed/7 laps behind	22/26
16/ret	PORTUGUESE GP	Estoril	30	Osella Squadra Corse	P	1.5 t/c Osella FA1F-Alfa Romeo V8	out of fuel/5 laps behind	24/27

GP Starts: 8   GP Wins: 0   Pole positions: 0   Fastest laps: 0   Points: 0

JO GARTNER

MUCH self-sacrifice and an iron determination to succeed against seemingly overwhelming odds kept Jo Gartner in motor racing when many drivers of lesser fibre would have fallen by the wayside.

From his early Formula 3 days (he was third in the 1978 European championship), Jo proved he had talent, but he was lacking finance and had to act as his own mechanic, running second-rate machinery for much of his Formula 2 career – although he did have his day, winning the Pau GP in 1983. Finding some backing, he got himself briefly into the Osella Grand Prix team in 1984, and even scored a fifth place for them at Monza, but against his expectations and much to his dismay, he was not retained for the following year.

Gartner then switched to sports car and IMSA racing, which he enjoyed, although he saw it as a means to get back into Formula 1. Sadly that was not to be, for he was killed instantly during the 1986 Le Mans 24-hours when his Porsche crashed on the Mulsanne Straight in the middle of the night.

TONY GAZE

AS an RAF pilot in the Second World War, Tony Gaze was a squadron leader flying Spitfires, which included sorties under the leadership of the famous Douglas Bader. He was shot down over France in 1943, but survived and, despite being injured, escaped captivity to return to England to resume his duties. By the end of hostilities, he had been credited with more than a dozen enemy kills and was awarded the DFC. His RAF base at Tangmere was close to the Duke of Richmond's Goodwood estate and, having driven around the perimeter track at RAF Westhampnett (on the estate), it was Gaze who suggested to Freddie March that it could be utilised for motor racing. Thus the Goodwood circuit was born in 1948.

Gaze was successful in hill-climbs in his native Australia in the immediate post-war years with a 1936 Alta, and he had married Kay Wakefield, (the widow of English racing driver Johnny Wakefield, who had been killed in the war). It was through her friends in racing circles that he was encouraged to return to the UK to try his hand. Initially he raced one of Geoffrey Taylor's Altas, before buying one of John Heath's HWMs to race briefly in grands prix during 1952, when Formula 2 cars were eligible for the world championship.

He soon turned his attention to sports car racing, an arena where he had more chance of success, and was lucky to survive a big crash in 1953 at Oporto, where he was thrown from his Aston Martin, which was wrecked. Over the next few seasons, Gaze raced a Maserati, HWM-Jaguar and Ferrari, both at home and abroad. He was also instrumental in encouraging Australian drivers, including Jack Brabham, to form 'The Kangaroo Stable', running their 3-litre sports cars in 1955. However, the Le Mans disaster saw many races cancelled and the short-lived team closed its doors.

Gaze was something of a pioneer with his regular racing trips down-under between 1954 and 1956, and he was a prime mover in the development of Australian motorsport, helping to bring European-style circuit racing to the continent. Thus he encouraged greater international competition in the years that followed, such as the Tasman series in the 1960s. After his retirement at the end of 1956, he took up gliding as a pastime and represented Australia in competition. Following the death of Kay, he subsequently married Diana Davidson, the widow of Australian great Lex Davidson, who had been killed in an accident in early 1965.

Although aged 91, Tony was well enough to join old adversary Sir Jack Brabham and others of the select band of Australian F1 drivers past and present at the Australian Grand Prix in Melbourne

GAZE, Tony (AUS) b 3/3/1920, Melbourne, Australia

1952 Championship position: Unplaced

	Race	Circuit	No	Entrant	Tyres	Capacity/Car/Engine	Comment	Q Pos/Entries
15	BELGIAN GP	Spa	42	Tony Gaze	D	2.0 HWM-Alta 4	6 laps behind	16/22
ret	BRITISH GP	Silverstone	28	Tony Gaze	D	2.0 HWM-Alta 4	cylinder head gasket	26/32
ret	GERMAN GP	Nürburgring	120	Tony Gaze	D	2.0 HWM-Alta 4	suspension	14/32
dnq	ITALIAN GP	Monza	56	Tony Gaze	D	2.0 HWM-Alta 4		30/35

GP Starts: 3   GP Wins: 0   Pole positions: 0   Fastest laps: 0   Points: 0

'GEKI' (Giacomo Russo)

RACING under the pseudonym 'Geki', Giacomo Russo was a talented driver from Milan who was a multiple Formula Junior champion in Italy during the early 1960s, graduating from the relatively primitive Stanguellini to a Lotus. He was always difficult to beat at Monza, and thus a local attraction come grand prix time each year; after hiring Rob Walker's car and failing to qualify in 1964, he was subsequently seen in a works Lotus.

After an abortive time with the Abarth F2 car in 1964, 'Geki' raced occasionally for the Alfa Romeo works team in sports cars and GTs during 1965/66, and was still competing successfully in Italian F3 with a Matra when he met his death at Caserta in 1967. Having been involved in a multiple pile-up, Swiss driver Fehr Beat jumped from his stricken car and ran back along the track to warn the leading bunch – which included 'Geki', who tragically was unable to avoid striking and killing his unfortunate rival. The Italian's Matra then ploughed into a concrete wall and he perished when the car burst into flames.

'GEKI' (RUSSO, Giacomo) (I) b 23/10/1937, Milan – d 18/6/1967, Caserta Circuit, nr Naples

1964 Championship position: Unplaced

	Race	Circuit	No	Entrant	Tyres	Capacity/Car/Engine	Comment	Q Pos/Entries
dnq	ITALIAN GP	Monza	36	R R C Walker Racing Team	D	1.5 Brabham BT11-BRM V8		23/25

1965 Championship position: Unplaced

ret	ITALIAN GP	Monza	28	Team Lotus	D	1.5 Lotus 25-Climax V8	gearbox oil seal	20/23

1966 Championship position: Unplaced

9	ITALIAN GP	Monza	(22) 20	Team Lotus	F	2.0 Lotus 33-Climax V8	5 laps behind/(no 22 in practice)	20/22

GP Starts: 2   GP Wins: 0   Pole positions: 0   Fastest laps: 0   Points: 0

GENDEBIEN, Olivier (B) b 12/1/1924, Brussels – d 2/10/1998, Tarascon, France

1956 Championship position: 15th=   Wins: 0   Pole positions: 0   Fastest laps: 0   Points scored: 2

	Race	Circuit	No	Entrant	Tyres	Capacity/Car/Engine	Comment	Q Pos/Entries
5	ARGENTINE GP	Buenos Aires	38	Scuderia Ferrari	E	2.5 Ferrari-Lancia 555/D50 V8	7 laps behind	10/15
ret	FRENCH GP	Reims	44	Scuderia Ferrari	E	2.5 Lancia-Ferrari D50 V8	clutch	11/20

1958 Championship position: Unplaced

6	BELGIAN GP	Spa	20	Scuderia Ferrari	E	2.4 Ferrari-Dino 246 V6	1 lap behind	6/20
ret	ITALIAN GP	Monza	20	Scuderia Ferrari	E	2.4 Ferrari-Dino 246 V6	suspension	5/21
ret	MOROCCAN GP	Casablanca	2	Scuderia Ferrari	E	2.4 Ferrari-Dino 246 V6	spun – hit by Picard	6/25

1959 Championship position: 11th   Wins: 0   Pole positions: 0   Fastest laps: 0   Points scored: 3

4	FRENCH GP	Reims	22	Scuderia Ferrari	D	2.4 Ferrari-Dino 246 V6		11/22
6	ITALIAN GP	Monza	38	Scuderia Ferrari	D	2.4 Ferrari-Dino 246 V6	1 lap behind	6/21

1960 Championship position: 6th   Wins: 0   Pole positions: 0   Fastest laps: 0   Points scored: 10

3	BELGIAN GP	Spa	34	Yeoman Credit Racing Team	D	2.5 Cooper T51-Climax 4	1 lap behind	5/18
2	FRENCH GP	Reims	44	Yeoman Credit Racing Team	D	2.5 Cooper T51-Climax 4		9/23
9	BRITISH GP	Silverstone	14	Yeoman Credit Racing Team	D	2.5 Cooper T51-Climax 4	3 laps behind	12/25
7	PORTUGUESE GP	Oporto	8	Yeoman Credit Racing Team	D	2.5 Cooper T51-Climax 4	stuck in top gear/9 laps behind	14/16
12	US GP	Riverside	7	Yeoman Credit Racing Team	D	2.5 Cooper T51-Climax 4	pit stop/6 laps behind	8/23

1961 Championship position: 13th=   Wins: 0   Pole positions: 0   Fastest laps: 0   Points scored: 3

dnq	MONACO GP	Monte Carlo	12	Equipe Nationale Belge	D	1.5 Emeryson-Maserati 4		20/21
4	BELGIAN GP	Spa	8	Scuderia Ferrari SpA SEFAC	D	1.5 Ferrari 156 V6		3/25
11*	US GP	Watkins Glen	21	UDT Laystall Racing Team	D	1.5 Lotus 18/21-Climax 4	*unwell – Gregory took over/-8 laps	15/19

GP Starts: 14   GP Wins: 0   Pole positions: 0   Fastest laps: 0   Points: 18

OLIVIER GENDEBIEN

A BELGIAN aristocrat, and former Second World War paratrooper, Olivier Gendebien spent some four years in forestry in the Congo, where he met rally driver Charles Fraikin, who was lamenting the lack of a co-driver with whom to compete back in Europe.

Gendebien then returned and raced a Veritas in the GP des Frontières at Chimay, finishing sixth, before joining Fraikin, initially to rally a Jaguar, the pair staying together until 1955. By the time they split, they had become known as 'the eternal bridesmaids' due to the number of times they had to be content with second place. Twice they just missed winning the Liège–Rome–Liège Rally but in 1955 it was third time lucky with a Mercedes 300SL. Without his partner, Olivier had great success, winning his class with a Plymouth in the Round Italy Rally, an Alfa Romeo (with Pierre Stasse) in the Tulip Rally and a Porsche in the Northern Roads Rally, all in 1954.

Such was the impression made that Gendebien was offered a contract to drive a works Ferrari in sports car events and selected grands prix. His first race for the team nearly ended in disaster, when in late 1955 he crashed heavily in practice for the Tourist Trophy at Dundrod, suffering concussion. He was fit for the start of 1956 and, with virtually no single-seater experience behind him, finished fifth on his grand prix debut at the Argentine GP, followed by sixth in the Mendoza GP. The season also saw a splendid run of results in sports car races, including second places at Buenos Aires and in the Super-cortemaggiore at Monza, and thirds in the Nürburgring 1000km, Targa Florio and Le Mans.

That would be the first of seven wonderful seasons that Gendebien spent in Ferrari's sports car team. Subsequently he won the Reims 12-hours in 1957 and '58, the Targa Florio in 1958, '61 and '62, Sebring in 1959, '60 and '61 and the Nürburgring 1000km in 1962, not forgetting his splendid achievement of four wins at Le Mans in 1958, '60, '61 and '62, after the last of which he retired.

Gendebien was no slouch in a grand prix car either. Although his outings were generally infrequent, whenever he raced a competitive machine, invariably he put it into the points, as a check on the accompanying statistics will show. However, it is as one of the greatest sports car drivers of any era that he will be best remembered.

GENÉ, Marc (ESP) b 29/3/1974, Sabadell

1999 Championship position: 17th=   Wins: 0   Pole positions: 0   Fastest laps: 0   Points scored: 1

	Race	Circuit	No	Entrant	Tyres	Capacity/Car/Engine	Comment	Q Pos/Entries
ret	AUSTRALIAN GP	Melbourne	21	Fondmetal Minardi Ford	B	3.0 Minardi M01-Ford Zetec R V10	collision with Trulli	22/22
9	BRAZILIAN GP	Interlagos	21	Fondmetal Minardi Ford	B	3.0 Minardi M01-Ford Zetec R V10	3 laps behind	20/22
9	SAN MARINO GP	Imola	21	Fondmetal Minardi Ford	B	3.0 Minardi M01-Ford Zetec R V10	3 laps behind	21/22
ret	MONACO GP	Monte Carlo	21	Fondmetal Minardi Ford	B	3.0 Minardi M01-Ford Zetec R V10	accident	22/22
ret	SPANISH GP	Barcelona	21	Fondmetal Minardi Ford	B	3.0 Minardi M01-Ford Zetec R V10	clutch on lap 1	21/22
8	CANADIAN GP	Montreal	21	Fondmetal Minardi Ford	B	3.0 Minardi M01-Ford Zetec R V10	1 lap behind	22/22
ret	FRENCH GP	Magny Cours	21	Fondmetal Minardi Ford	B	3.0 Minardi M01-Ford Zetec R V10	spun off in rain	19/22
15	BRITISH GP	Silverstone	21	Fondmetal Minardi Ford	B	3.0 Minardi M01-Ford Zetec R V10	2 laps behind	22/22
11	AUSTRIAN GP	A1-Ring	21	Fondmetal Minardi Ford	B	3.0 Minardi M01-Ford Zetec R V10	1 lap behind	22/22
9	GERMAN GP	Hockenheim	21	Fondmetal Minardi Ford	B	3.0 Minardi M01-Ford Zetec R V10	1 lap behind	15/22
17	HUNGARIAN GP	Hungaroring	21	Fondmetal Minardi Ford	B	3.0 Minardi M01-Ford Zetec R V10	3 laps behind	22/22
16	BELGIAN GP	Spa	21	Fondmetal Minardi Ford	B	3.0 Minardi M01-Ford Zetec R V10	1 lap behind	21/22
ret	ITALIAN GP	Monza	21	Fondmetal Minardi Ford	B	3.0 Minardi M01-Ford Zetec R V10	collision on lap 1	17/22
6	EUROPEAN GP	Nürburgring	21	Fondmetal Minardi Ford	B	3.0 Minardi M01-Ford Zetec R V10		20/22
9	MALAYSIAN GP	Sepang	21	Fondmetal Minardi Ford	B	3.0 Minardi M01-Ford Zetec R V10	1 lap behind	19/22
ret	JAPANESE GP	Suzuka	21	Fondmetal Minardi Ford	B	3.0 Minardi M01-Ford Zetec R V10	gearbox	20/22

2000 Championship position: Unplaced

	Race	Circuit	No	Entrant	Tyres	Capacity/Car/Engine	Comment	Q Pos/Entries
8	AUSTRALIAN GP	Melbourne	20	Telefonica Minardi Fondmetal	B	3.0 Minardi M02-Fondmetal Ford-Zetec V10	1 lap behind	18/22
ret	BRAZILIAN GP	Interlagos	20	Telefonica Minardi Fondmetal	B	3.0 Minardi M02-Fondmetal Ford-Zetec V10	engine	18/22
ret	SAN MARINO GP	Imola	20	Telefonica Minardi Fondmetal	B	3.0 Minardi M02-Fondmetal Ford-Zetec V10	spun off	21/22
14	BRITISH GP	Silverstone	20	Telefonica Minardi Fondmetal	B	3.0 Minardi M02-Fondmetal Ford-Zetec V10	1 lap behind	21/22
14	SPANISH GP	Barcelona	20	Telefonica Minardi Fondmetal	B	3.0 Minardi M02-Fondmetal Ford-Zetec V10	2 laps behind	21/22
ret	EUROPEAN GP	Nürburgring	20	Telefonica Minardi Fondmetal	B	3.0 Minardi M02-Fondmetal Ford-Zetec V10	throttle pedal	21/22
ret	MONACO GP	Monte Carlo	20	Telefonica Minardi Fondmetal	B	3.0 Minardi M02-Fondmetal Ford-Zetec V10	gearbox	21/22
16/ret	CANADIAN GP	Montreal	20	Telefonica Minardi Fondmetal	B	3.0 Minardi M02-Fondmetal Ford-Zetec V10	spun off	20/22
15	FRANCE GP	Magny Cours	20	Telefonica Minardi Fondmetal	B	3.0 Minardi M02-Fondmetal Ford-Zetec V10	2 laps behind	21/22

8	AUSTRIAN GP	A1-Ring	20	Telefonica Minardi Fondmetal	B	3.0 Minardi M02-Fondmetal Ford-Zetec V10	*1 lap behind*	20/22
ret	GERMAN GP	Hockenheim	20	Telefonica Minardi Fondmetal	B	3.0 Minardi M02-Fondmetal Ford-Zetec V10	*engine*	22/22
15	HUNGARIAN GP	Hungaroring	20	Telefonica Minardi Fondmetal	B	3.0 Minardi M02-Fondmetal Ford-Zetec V10	*3 laps behind*	21/22
14	BELGIAN GP	Spa	20	Telefonica Minardi Fondmetal	B	3.0 Minardi M02-Fondmetal Ford-Zetec V10	*1 lap behind*	21/22
9	ITALIAN GP	Monza	20	Telefonica Minardi Fondmetal	B	3.0 Minardi M02-Fondmetal Ford-Zetec V10	*1 lap behind*	21/22
12	UNITED STATES GP	Indianapolis	20	Telefonica Minardi Fondmetal	B	3.0 Minardi M02-Fondmetal Ford-Zetec V10	*1 lap behind*	22/22
ret	JAPANESE GP	Suzuka	20	Telefonica Minardi Fondmetal	B	3.0 Minardi M02-Fondmetal Ford-Zetec V10	*engine*	21/22
ret	MALAYSIAN GP	Sepang	20	Telefonica Minardi Fondmetal	B	3.0 Minardi M02-Fondmetal Ford-Zetec V10	*broken wheel spline*	21/22

2003 Championship position: 17th   Wins: 0   Pole positions: 0   Fastest laps: 0   Points scored: 4

5	ITALIAN GP	Monza	5	BMW WilliamsF1 Team	M	3.0 Williams FW25-BMW V10	*substitute for Ralf Schumacher*	5/20

2004 Championship position: Unplaced

10	FRENCH GP	Magny Cours	4	BMW WilliamsF1 Team	M	3.0 Williams FW26-BMW V10		8/20
12	BRITISH GP	Silverstone	4	BMW WilliamsF1 Team	M	3.0 Williams FW26-BMW V10	*handling problems*	12/20

GP Starts: 36   GP Wins: 0   Pole positions: 0   Fastest laps: 0   Points: 5

MARC GENÉ

ALTHOUGH the Spaniard had taken the Italian Superformula championship in 1994, Marc Gené's step up to British Formula 3 the following year proved somewhat disappointing when he struggled in the wake of his team-mate, Helio Castro-Neves. In mitigation, at this stage he was still studying at university, which naturally curtailed the amount of time he could devote to his racing.

Budget problems kept Marc out of action for much of 1996, but he managed to gain a place in the Pacific F3000 team at the start of 1997. Unfortunately, an accident in the second round at Pau left him with a cracked vertebra, which sidelined him for a month, and when he was fit to return his place in the team had gone. Although he was able to find another berth with Nordic for a couple of races, his season lay in tatters.

So it was back to his day job as an accountant in Spain and competition in the less-pressurised atmosphere of the Open Fortuna by Nissan single-seater series. Driving for Adrian Campos, Marc swept to a convincing championship win, chalking up six victories from 12 races. In truth, there wasn't a huge amount of competition for him to beat, but it gave his career a boost.

With Spanish communications giant Telefónica backing Minardi in 1999, Marc was suddenly a shock candidate for a place with the Faenza team, and immediately he impressed the Minardi hierarchy with his hard work and willingness to learn. Certainly he was not outclassed by his more experienced team-mate, Luca Badoer, and he had the great satisfaction of recording sixth place at the European Grand Prix. This single point pushed the little Italian team above the mega-rich British American Racing to ensure, for one season at least, that they were not bottom of the pile.

His promising debut season and links with Telefónica secured Gené's place in the team for 2000. Partnered by another rookie, Gaston Mazzacane, and powered by outdated Ford V10s, the Spaniard looked as though he would have his work cut out to reach the heights of '99, and so it proved as Minardi appeared to be on the brink of closure. Not wanting to wait too long and possibly be dragged down with the team, he opted to jump to Williams, where he acted as back-up to Ralf Schumacher and Juan Montoya for 2001. He continued to act as the team's official test driver in 2002 and for most of the 2003 season.

Gené found an outlet for his competitive side by returning to the Nissan World Series, where he ran with Adrian Campos Motorsport and instantly proved to be a winner. This meant that he was on the ball when he was given an unexpected opportunity to race for the Williams F1 team in the Italian GP, after Ralf Schumacher had been ruled out through injury. The Spaniard didn't let them down, finishing a career best fifth. He reverted to testing duties for the rest of the season – canning his Formula Nissan activities – and carried the role into 2004.

Following Ralf's crash at the US Grand Prix in June, Gené was drafted into the fold again, but this time he failed to do himself justice in either France or Britain, and subsequently was dropped in favour of fellow test driver Antonio Pizzonia. Apparently upset by his treatment, and the fact that he had been overlooked as a candidate to partner Mark Webber in the 2005 line-up, he decided it was time to move on and signed a deal to work alongside former Minardi team-mate Badoer at Ferrari.

With testing restrictions limiting Gené's role at Ferrari, the Italian team allowed the Spaniard to race the new factory Peugeot sports car in the LMES and at Le Mans in 2007. After a win in the Spa 1000km sports car race, he overcame a broken toe, sustained in practice for the 2008 Le Mans race, to take the 908 HDI prototype to second place in the race itself, behind rivals Audi.

The following year, Gené (with David Brabham and Alex Wurz) duly delivered the French concern their ultimate goal, a win in the prestigious Le Mans 24-hour race. He continued with the squad in 2010, scoring a season-opener win at Sebring and a fourth at Spa (both with Wurz and Anthony Davidson), but the trio went out of the Le Mans race with an engine failure. At the end of the season, his association with Ferrari came to an end and he was left with just his sports car commitments for 2011. Another win in the Spa 1000km proved to be his final victory for the team, as he and his cohorts could only finish fourth at Le Mans. A second place in the Petit Le Mans at Road Atlanta (with Nicolas Lapierre and Nicolas Minassian) would be the final chapter in his satisfying Peugeot story, for at the end of the season the team was disbanded.

BOB GERARD

BOB GERARD enjoyed an extremely long and active career in motor racing, from his early days as a trialist with a Riley in 1933 through to the early 1970s as an entrant.

At first, Bob was identified with the family Riley, but it was after the war that he really came into his own, with an ERA, winning the British Empire Trophy in 1947, '48 and '49, in addition to the 1949 Jersey Road Race. He also came close to winning that year's British Grand Prix, finishing second to Emmanuel de Graffenried.

As the 1950s dawned, the old ERA was placed sixth in a couple of grands prix, but it was only really suitable for national races, so Gerard had to wait until 1953, when he acquired a Cooper-Bristol, to prove his worth. He drove it doggedly, frequently putting more powerful cars to shame and regularly scoring respectable placings in minor Formula 2 and Libre events until 1956.

Gerard made his final GP appearance in 1957 at the wheel of the unsuccessful rear-engined Cooper-BG-Bristol, just missing the points. From 1959 to 1961, he happily drove a Turner in club events, before retiring from active service to enter a Cooper for John Taylor, mainly in non-championship races, later running Formula 2 cars for Alan Rollinson, Mike Beckwith and Peter Gethin among others.

GERINO GERINI

ITALIAN Gerino Gerini raced Ferrari sports cars in the mid-1950s, before switching to rivals Maserati.

The 1956 season started promisingly with a shared fourth place (with Chico Landi) in the Argentine GP, plus a third at Naples and a fifth at Syracuse, but then Gerini achieved nothing of note except a class win in the Maserati sports car at the Coppa Inter-Europa at Monza.

In fact, Gerini would not reappear in grands prix until 1958, when, apart from a distant sixth place at Caen, he struggled to make an impression in the by then elderly 250F. He briefly reappeared in sports cars in 1960, when his Ferrari crashed out of the Nürburgring 1000km.

GERARD, Bob (GB) b 19/1/1914, Leicester – d 26/1/1990, South Croxton, Leicester

	1950 Championship position: Unplaced								
	Race	Circuit	No	Entrant	Tyres	Capacity/Car/Engine		Comment	Q Pos/Entries
6	BRITISH GP	Silverstone	12	Bob Gerard	D	1.5 s/c ERA B/C-Type 6		3 laps behind	13/21
6	MONACO GP	Monte Carlo	26	Bob Gerard	D	1.5 s/c ERA A-Type 6		6 laps behind	16/21
	1951 Championship position: Unplaced								
11	BRITISH GP	Silverstone	8	Bob Gerard	D	1.5 s/c ERA B/C-Type 6		8 laps behind	10/20
	1953 Championship position: Unplaced								
11	FRENCH GP	Reims	38	Bob Gerard	D	2.0 Cooper T23-Bristol 6		5 laps behind	12/25
ret	BRITISH GP	Silverstone	17	Bob Gerard	D	2.0 Cooper T23-Bristol 6		front suspension	18/29
	1954 Championship position: Unplaced								
10	BRITISH GP	Silverstone	29	Bob Gerard	D	2.0 Cooper T23-Bristol 6		5 laps behind	18/31
	1956 Championship position: Unplaced								
11	BRITISH GP	Silverstone	26	Bob Gerard	D	2.2 Cooper T23-Bristol 6		13 laps behind	22/28
	1957 Championship position: Unplaced								
6	BRITISH GP	Aintree	38	Bob Gerard	D	2.2 Cooper BG43-Bristol 6		8 laps behind	18/19
	GP Starts: 8 GP Wins: 0 Pole positions: 0 Fastest laps: 0 Points: 0								

GERINI, Gerino (I) 10/8/1928, Rome

	1956 Championship position: 20= Wins: 0 Pole positions: 0 Fastest laps: 0 Points scored: 1.5								
	Race	Circuit	No	Entrant	Tyres	Capacity/Car/Engine		Comment	Q Pos/Entries
4*	ARGENTINE GP	Buenos Aires	10	Officine Alfieri Maserati	P	2.5 Maserati 250F 6		*shared with Landi/-6 laps	–/15
10	ITALIAN GP	Monza	42	Scuderia Guastalla	P	2.5 Maserati 250F 6		8 laps behind	17/26
	1958 Championship position: Unplaced								
dnq	MONACO GP	Monte Carlo	48	Scuderia Centro Sud	P	2.5 Maserati 250F 6			20/28
9	FRENCH GP	Reims	32	Scuderia Centro Sud	P	2.5 Maserati 250F 6		3 laps behind	15/21
ret	BRITISH GP	Silverstone	6	Scuderia Centro Sud	P	2.5 Maserati 250F 6		gearbox	18/21
ret	ITALIAN GP	Monza	40	Scuderia Centro Sud	P	2.5 Maserati 250F 6		mechanical	19/21
12*	MOROCCAN GP	Casablanca	28	Scuderia Centro Sud	P	2.5 Maserati 250F 6		*12th behind one F2 car/-5 laps	17/25
	GP Starts: 6 GP Wins: 0 Pole positions: 0 Fastest laps: 0 Points: 1.5								

PETER GETHIN

IT is perhaps unfair that Peter Gethin should be best remembered for his sensational grand prix win at Monza in 1971, when he took his BRM to a wonderful victory by the margin of one-hundredth of a second in a four-car dash to the line, for in fact he enjoyed a splendid career that spanned some 15 years and encompassed almost every category of the sport.

After an early start in a Lotus Seven in 1962, Peter soon became one of the country's top club sports car drivers in his Lotus 23. Then he moved into Formula 3 in 1965 with Charles Lucas, but his career really stood still until 1968, when he ran a full Formula 2 season with Frank Lythgoe, finishing strongly with a brilliant second at Albi and a third at Vallelunga after a Brabham had been acquired to replace a rather disappointing Chevron.

It was the introduction of F5000 in 1969 that really put Peter's career on the map. In a semi-works McLaren, he dominated the early part of the season with four straight wins and then defended his advantage grimly as his championship lead was whittled away. The final round ended in anti-climax with a collision, but the title went to Gethin, and he proved himself a more than worthy champion by retaining the crown convincingly the following year. By then, he was closely involved with the McLaren grand prix effort; having made a promising debut to finish sixth in the Race of Champions, he was brought into the team after the sad loss of Bruce McLaren in a testing accident at Goodwood; he also took over the vacant Can-Am drive, winning a round at Elkhart Lake.

Staying with McLaren for 1971, Peter continued to struggle to find form in grands prix, although he did finish second on aggregate in the International Trophy, and things came to a head in mid-season, when his strained relationship with team boss Teddy Mayer finally unravelled. Even so, it was something of a surprise to the F1 fraternity when he moved to BRM as a permanent replacement for Pedro Rodriguez, who had been killed at a sports car race at the Norisring.

Almost immediately, Gethin he took that dramatic victory in the Italian Grand Prix. "I deserved to win at Monza," he said. "Some people thought I was lucky, but in a sport like motor racing, you make your own good fortune to a very great degree. I thrashed the life out of that BRM V12 engine for much of the race to catch the leading bunch. And I was the one positioned in the right place at the right time as we came out of Parabolica for the final time and just managed to squeeze out Ronnie Peterson to take the win. François Cevert, who finished third, came over and complained that I pushed his Tyrrell wide on the last corner, but I told him I couldn't care less."

Then he repeated that triumph in the tragically shortened non-championship Victory Race at Brands Hatch, in which his team-mate, Jo Siffert, perished.

Hopes were high for 1972, but Peter endured a thin time of it with the BRM team, which was overstretched trying to run too many cars, An equally low-key season in Formula 2 with Chevron did bring an unexpected win in the Pau Grand Prix, which he regarded as his finest ever victory.

So, out of Formula 1, it was back to a season of F5000 action at home and abroad, which yielded a shock win in the Race of Champions. Gethin made a couple more unsuccessful grand prix appearances for BRM and Embassy Hill, but concentrated on F5000 with Chevron and VDS, and also raced in the newly revived Can-Am series, before retiring at the end of the 1977 season. He took the final race win of his career at Elkhart Lake in July, 1977 when, in the Team VDS Lola T333, he beat up-and-coming F1 star Gilles Villeneuve in his Wolf WD1.

Gethin later became involved with the March Formula 2 team, looking after the promising young Italian driver Beppe Gabbiani, and then had a brief spell with Toleman in Formula 1 in 1984, before setting up his own Formula 3000 team in 1986, running Adrian Campos, Dave Scott and Cathy Muller among others. It was not a success for all concerned, however, and Gethin pulled the plug to concentrate on running a racing drivers' school at Goodwood.

Later, Gethin served on the board of the BRDC between 2005 and 2008, but subsequently was diagnosed with a brain tumour, to which he succumbed in December, 2011. Many tributes flowed, most notably from his former teams, McLaren and Lola, which showed the high esteem in which this very popular man was still held.

GETHIN, Peter (GB) b 21/2/1940, Epsom, Surrey

1970 Championship position: 22nd=   Wins: 0   Pole positions: 0   Fastest laps: 0   Points scored: 1

	Race	Circuit	No	Entrant	Tyres	Capacity/Car/Engine	Comment	Q Pos/Entries
ret	DUTCH GP	Zandvoort	20	Bruce McLaren Motor Racing	G	3.0 McLaren M14A-Cosworth V8	spun off	11/24
ret	GERMAN GP	Hockenheim	24	Bruce McLaren Motor Racing	G	3.0 McLaren M14A-Cosworth V8	engine – throttle slides	17/25
10	AUSTRIAN GP	Österreichring	23	Bruce McLaren Motor Racing	G	3.0 McLaren M14A-Cosworth V8	1 lap behind	20/24
nc	ITALIAN GP	Monza	32	Bruce McLaren Motor Racing	G	3.0 McLaren M14A-Cosworth V8	pit stops - various/8 laps behind	18/27
6	CANADIAN GP	St Jovite	6	Bruce McLaren Motor Racing	G	3.0 McLaren M14A-Cosworth V8	2 laps behind	=11/20
14	US GP	Watkins Glen	9	Bruce McLaren Motor Racing	G	3.0 McLaren M14A-Cosworth V8	pit stop – tyres/8 laps behind	21/27
ret	MEXICAN GP	Mexico City	9	Bruce McLaren Motor Racing	G	3.0 McLaren M14A-Cosworth V8	engine	10/18

1971 Championship position: 9th   Wins: 1   Pole positions: 0   Fastest laps: 0   Points scored: 9

	Race	Circuit	No	Entrant	Tyres	Capacity/Car/Engine	Comment	Q Pos/Entries
ret	SOUTH AFRICAN GP	Kyalami	12	Bruce McLaren Motor Racing	G	3.0 McLaren M14A-Cosworth V8	loose fuel line	11/25
8	SPANISH GP	Montjuich Park	10	Bruce McLaren Motor Racing	G	3.0 McLaren M14A-Cosworth V8	2 laps behind	7/22
ret	MONACO GP	Monte Carlo	10	Bruce McLaren Motor Racing	G	3.0 McLaren M14A-Cosworth V8	hit chicane	14/23
nc	DUTCH GP	Zandvoort	28	Bruce McLaren Motor Racing	G	3.0 McLaren M19A-Cosworth V8	spin – pitstop/10 laps behind	23/24
9	FRENCH GP	Paul Ricard	10	Bruce McLaren Motor Racing	G	3.0 McLaren M19A-Cosworth V8	1 lap behind	19/24
ret	BRITISH GP	Silverstone	10	Bruce McLaren Motor Racing	G	3.0 McLaren M19A-Cosworth V8	oil pressure	14/24
ret	GERMAN GP	Nürburgring	20	Bruce McLaren Motor Racing	G	3.0 McLaren M19A-Cosworth V8	accident – damaged suspension	19/23
10	AUSTRIAN GP	Österreichring	23	Yardley BRM	F	3.0 BRM P160 V12	misfire/2 laps behind	16/22
1	ITALIAN GP	Monza	18	Yardley BRM	F	3.0 BRM P160 V12		11/24
14	CANADIAN GP	Mosport Park	15	Yardley BRM	F	3.0 BRM P160 V12	5 laps behind	=15/27
9	US GP	Watkins Glen	15	Yardley BRM	F	3.0 BRM P160 V12	broken valve spring/1 lap behind	23/32

1972 Championship position: 20   Wins: 0   Pole positions: 0   Fastest laps: 0   Points scored: 1

	Race	Circuit	No	Entrant	Tyres	Capacity/Car/Engine	Comment	Q Pos/Entries
ret	ARGENTINE GP	Buenos Aires	5	Marlboro BRM	F	3.0 BRM P160B V12	accident – broken fuel line	18/22
nc	SOUTH AFRICAN GP	Kyalami	11	Marlboro BRM	F	3.0 BRM P160B V12	pit stops/14 laps behind	=18/27
ret	SPANISH GP	Jarama	8	Marlboro BRM	F	3.0 BRM P180 V12	engine	21/26
ret/dsq	*MONACO GP	Monte Carlo	18	Marlboro BRM	F	3.0 BRM P160B V12	hit chicane/*reversed into pits	=5/25
ret	BELGIAN GP	Nivelles	24	Marlboro BRM	F	3.0 BRM P160B V12	fuel pump – engine misfire	17/26
dns	FRENCH GP	Clermont Ferrand	22	Marlboro BRM	F	3.0 BRM P160B V12	crashed in practice	(23)/29
ret	BRITISH GP	Brands Hatch	12	Marlboro BRM	F	3.0 BRM P160B V12	engine	16/27
13	AUSTRIAN GP	Österreichring	6	Marlboro BRM	F	3.0 BRM P160C V12	pit stops/3 laps behind	16/26
6	ITALIAN GP	Monza	23	Marlboro BRM	F	3.0 BRM P160C V12		12/27
ret	CANADIAN GP	Mosport Park	16	Marlboro BRM	F	3.0 BRM P160C V12	rear suspension mounting	=12/25
ret	US GP	Watkins Glen	14	Marlboro BRM	F	3.0 BRM P160C V12	engine	29/32

1973 Championship position: Unplaced

	Race	Circuit	No	Entrant	Tyres	Capacity/Car/Engine	Comment	Q Pos/Entries
ret	CANADIAN GP	Mosport Park	19	Marlboro BRM	F	3.0 BRM P160E V12	oil pump belt	25/26

1974 Championship position: Unplaced

	Race	Circuit	No	Entrant	Tyres	Capacity/Car/Engine	Comment	Q Pos/Entries
ret	BRITISH GP	Brands Hatch	27	Embassy Racing with Graham Hill	F	3.0 Lola T370-Cosworth V8	did not fit car properly/deflating tyre	=19/34

GP Starts: 30   GP Wins: 1   Pole positions: 0   Fastest laps: 0   Points: 11

Peter Gethin at Monza in 1971, driving
the BRM P160, in which he scored his
only world championship victory.

PIERCARLO GHINZANI

"BETTER to be at the back in Formula 1 than not to be in Formula 1 at all," said Piercarlo Ghinzani, and that's pretty well where he stayed in a grand prix career that spanned eight seasons, mostly at the tail-end of the grid.

It was all a long way from the start of Ghinzani's career when, after his 1970 debut in Italian Formula Ford, he began the slow climb up the motor racing ladder through Formula Italia to Formula 3 in 1973. His early days in Italian F3 were underfinanced, but he did finish second to Riccardo Patrese in 1976. Moving up to the European series in 1977, he did extremely well to take the title, his phlegmatic approach being vital in a team that was beset by upheaval. The next step into Formula 2 with a March was a big disappointment, which was a blow to his F1 aspirations.

However, salvation was nigh. In 1981, Ghinzani was called in by Osella after Giorgio Francia's credentials failed to satisfy FISA, and he qualified for the Belgian GP. This was the start of a long association with the little team, his best result being a much-needed fifth place at Dallas in 1984. He did take a brief sabbatical from them in mid-1985, when a second Toleman was entered, but returned to the fold for 1986. In grands prix, results were understandably hard to come by, but he had been successful in endurance events, winning the Fuji 1000km in a Porsche with Paulo Barilla.

In 1987, Ghinzani tried his luck in the Ligier team, which soured after an outburst from René Arnoux lost them their Alfa Romeo engine deal as the season dawned. Then it was on to an equally fruitless sojourn at Zakspeed, before a final season back at Osella. Ghinzani certainly had staying power: he started 74 grands prix, but more pointedly failed to qualify for another 31 – a real glutton for punishment.

In 1992, Piercarlo formed his own team, which has competed in a number of single-seater categories, including the Italian, German and Euro F3 series, as well as Italian F3000. He has also fielded Italy's car in the A1GP series.

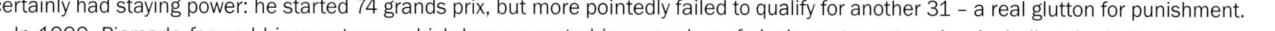

GHINZANI, Piercarlo (I) b 16/1/1952, Riviera d'Adda, Bergamo

1981 Championship position: Unplaced

	Race	Circuit	No	Entrant	Tyres	Capacity/Car/Engine	Comment	Q Pos/Entries
13	BELGIAN GP	Zolder	31	Osella Squadra Corse	M	3.0 Osella FA1B-Cosworth V8	spin – pit stop/4 laps behind	24/31
dnq	MONACO GP	Monte Carlo	32	Osella Squadra Corse	M	3.0 Osella FA1B-Cosworth V8		25/31

1983 Championship position: Unplaced

	Race	Circuit	No	Entrant	Tyres	Capacity/Car/Engine	Comment	Q Pos/Entries
dnq	BRAZILIAN GP	Rio	32	Osella Squadra Corse	M	3.0 Osella FA1D-Cosworth V8		27/27
dnq	US GP WEST	Long Beach	32	Osella Squadra Corse	M	3.0 Osella FA1D-Cosworth V8		28/28
dnq	FRENCH GP	Paul Ricard	32	Osella Squadra Corse	M	3.0 Osella FA1D-Cosworth V8		28/29
dnq	SAN MARINO GP	Imola	32	Osella Squadra Corse	M	3.0 Osella FA1E-Alfa Romeo V12		28/28
dnq	MONACO GP	Monte Carlo	32	Osella Squadra Corse	M	3.0 Osella FA1E-Alfa Romeo V12		27/28
dnq	BELGIAN GP	Spa	32	Osella Squadra Corse	M	3.0 Osella FA1E-Alfa Romeo V12		27/28
ret	US GP (DETROIT)	Detroit	32	Osella Squadra Corse	M	3.0 Osella FA1E-Alfa Romeo V12	overheating	24/27
dnq	CANADIAN GP	Montreal	32	Osella Squadra Corse	M	3.0 Osella FA1E-Alfa Romeo V12		28/28
ret	BRITISH GP	Silverstone	32	Osella Squadra Corse	M	3.0 Osella FA1E-Alfa Romeo V12	started from pits – fuel pressure	26/29
ret	GERMAN GP	Hockenheim	32	Osella Squadra Corse	M	3.0 Osella FA1E-Alfa Romeo V12	engine	26/29
11	AUSTRIAN GP	Österreichring	32	Osella Squadra Corse	M	3.0 Osella FA1E-Alfa Romeo V12	4 laps behind	25/29
dnq	DUTCH GP	Zandvoort	32	Osella Squadra Corse	M	3.0 Osella FA1E-Alfa Romeo V12		27/29
ret	ITALIAN GP	Monza	32	Osella Squadra Corse	M	3.0 Osella FA1E-Alfa Romeo V12	gearbox	23/29
nc	EUROPEAN GP	Brands Hatch	32	Osella Squadra Corse	M	3.0 Osella FA1E-Alfa Romeo V12	3 pit stops – throttle/13 laps behind	24/29
ret	SOUTH AFRICAN GP	Kyalami	32	Osella Squadra Corse	M	3.0 Osella FA1E-Alfa Romeo V12	engine	26/26

1984 Championship position: 19th Wins: 0 Pole positions: 0 Fastest laps: 0 Points scored: 2

	Race	Circuit	No	Entrant	Tyres	Capacity/Car/Engine	Comment	Q Pos/Entries
ret	BRAZILIAN GP	Rio	24	Osella Squadra Corse	P	1.5 t/c Osella FA1F-Alfa Romeo V8	gearbox	22/27
dns	SOUTH AFRICAN GP	Kyalami	24	Osella Squadra Corse	P	1.5 t/c Osella FA1F-Alfa Romeo V8	accident in a.m. warm up	27/27
ret	BELGIAN GP	Zolder	24	Osella Squadra Corse	P	1.5 t/c Osella FA1F-Alfa Romeo V8	transmission	20/27
dnq	SAN MARINO GP	Imola	24	Osella Squadra Corse	P	1.5 t/c Osella FA1F-Alfa Romeo V8		27/28
12*	FRENCH GP	Dijon	24	Osella Squadra Corse	P	1.5 t/c Osella FA1F-Alfa Romeo V8	*12th place car disqualified/-5 laps	26/27
7*	MONACO GP	Monte Carlo	24	Osella Squadra Corse	P	1.5 t/c Osella FA1F-Alfa Romeo V8	*3rd place car disqualified/-1 lap	19/27
ret	CANADIAN GP	Montreal	24	Osella Squadra Corse	P	1.5 t/c Osella FA1F-Alfa Romeo V8	gearbox	19/26
ret	US GP (DETROIT)	Detroit	24	Osella Squadra Corse	P	1.5 t/c Osella FA1F-Alfa Romeo V8	accident with Hesnault	26/27
5	US GP (DALLAS)	Dallas	24	Osella Squadra Corse	P	1.5 t/c Osella FA1F-Alfa Romeo V8	2 laps behind	18/27
9	BRITISH GP	Brands Hatch	24	Osella Squadra Corse	P	1.5 t/c Osella FA1F-Alfa Romeo V8	3 laps behind	21/27
ret	GERMAN GP	Hockenheim	24	Osella Squadra Corse	P	1.5 t/c Osella FA1F-Alfa Romeo V8	electrics	21/27
ret	AUSTRIAN GP	Österreichring	24	Osella Squadra Corse	P	1.5 t/c Osella FA1F-Alfa Romeo V8	gearbox	23/28
ret	DUTCH GP	Zandvoort	24	Osella Squadra Corse	P	1.5 t/c Osella FA1F-Alfa Romeo V8	fuel pump	21/27
7/ret	ITALIAN GP	Monza	24	Osella Squadra Corse	P	1.5 t/c Osella FA1F-Alfa Romeo V8	out of fuel/2 laps behind	22/27
ret	EUROPEAN GP	Nürburgring	24	Osella Squadra Corse	P	1.5 t/c Osella FA1F-Alfa Romeo V8	accident	20/27
ret	PORTUGUESE GP	Estoril	24	Osella Squadra Corse	P	1.5 t/c Osella FA1F-Alfa Romeo V8	engine	22/27

1985 Championship position: Unplaced

	Race	Circuit	No	Entrant	Tyres	Capacity/Car/Engine	Comment	Q Pos/Entries
12	BRAZILIAN GP	Rio	24	Osella Squadra Corse	P	1.5 t/c Osella FA1F-Alfa Romeo V8	4 laps behind	22/25
9	PORTUGUESE GP	Estoril	24	Osella Squadra Corse	P	1.5 t/c Osella FA1F-Alfa Romeo V8	6 laps behind	26/26
nc	SAN MARINO GP	Imola	24	Osella Squadra Corse	P	1.5 t/c Osella FA1G-Alfa Romeo V8	pit stop – gearbox/14 laps behind	22/26
dnq	MONACO GP	Monte Carlo	24	Osella Squadra Corse	P	1.5 t/c Osella FA1G-Alfa Romeo V8		21/26

ret	CANADIAN GP	Montreal	24	Osella Squadra Corse	P	1.5 t/c Osella FA1G-Alfa Romeo V8	engine	22/25
ret	US GP (DETROIT)	Detroit	24	Osella Squadra Corse	P	1.5 t/c Osella FA1G-Alfa Romeo V8	accident	22/25
15	FRENCH GP	Paul Ricard	24	Osella Squadra Corse	P	1.5 t/c Osella FA1G-Alfa Romeo V8	4 laps behind	24/26
ret	BRITISH GP	Silverstone	24	Osella Squadra Corse	P	1.5 t/c Osella FA1G-Alfa Romeo V8	accident damage on lap 1	25/26
ret/dns*	AUSTRIAN GP	Österreichring	20	Toleman Group Motorsport	P	1.5 t/c Toleman TG185-Hart 4	engine at first start/*did not restart	(19)/27
ret	DUTCH GP	Zandvoort	20	Toleman Group Motorsport	P	1.5 t/c Toleman TG185-Hart 4	engine	15/27
ret	ITALIAN GP	Monza	20	Toleman Group Motorsport	P	1.5 t/c Toleman TG185-Hart 4	stalled at start	21/26
ret	BELGIAN GP	Spa	20	Toleman Group Motorsport	P	1.5 t/c Toleman TG185-Hart 4	accident	16/24
ret	EUROPEAN GP	Brands Hatch	20	Toleman Group Motorsport	P	1.5 t/c Toleman TG185-Hart 4	engine	14/27
ret	SOUTH AFRICAN GP	Kyalami	20	Toleman Group Motorsport	P	1.5 t/c Toleman TG185-Hart 4	engine	13/21
ret	AUSTRALIAN GP	Adelaide	20	Toleman Group Motorsport	P	1.5 t/c Toleman TG185-Hart 4	clutch	21/25

1986 Championship position: Unplaced

ret	BRAZILIAN GP	Rio	21	Osella Squadra Corse	P	1.5 t/c Osella FA1G-Alfa Romeo V8	engine	23/25
ret	SPANISH GP	Jerez	21	Osella Squadra Corse	P	1.5 t/c Osella FA1G-Alfa Romeo V8	engine	21/25
ret	SAN MARINO GP	Imola	21	Osella Squadra Corse	P	1.5 t/c Osella FA1G-Alfa Romeo V8	out of fuel	26/25
dnq	MONACO GP	Monte Carlo	21	Osella Squadra Corse	P	1.5 t/c Osella FA1G-Alfa Romeo V8		21/26
ret	BELGIAN GP	Spa	21	Osella Squadra Corse	P	1.5 t/c Osella FA1G-Alfa Romeo V8	engine	24/25
ret	CANADIAN GP	Montreal	21	Osella Squadra Corse	P	1.5 t/c Osella FA1G-Alfa Romeo V8	gearbox	23/25
ret	US GP (DETROIT)	Detroit	21	Osella Squadra Corse	P	1.5 t/c Osella FA1G-Alfa Romeo V8	turbo	22/26
ret	FRENCH GP	Paul Ricard	21	Osella Squadra Corse	P	1.5 t/c Osella FA1H-Alfa Romeo V8	accident with Nannini	25/26
ret/dns*	BRITISH GP	Brands Hatch	21	Osella Squadra Corse	P	1.5 t/c Osella FA1G-Alfa Romeo V8	*accident in first start	24/26
ret	GERMAN GP	Hockenheim	21	Osella Squadra Corse	P	1.5 t/c Osella FA1G-Alfa Romeo V8	clutch	25/26
ret	HUNGARIAN GP	Hungaroring	21	Osella Squadra Corse	P	1.5 t/c Osella FA1G-Alfa Romeo V8	rear suspension	23/26
11	AUSTRIAN GP	Österreichring	21	Osella Squadra Corse	P	1.5 t/c Osella FA1G-Alfa Romeo V8	6 laps behind	25/26
ret	ITALIAN GP	Monza	21	Osella Squadra Corse	P	1.5 t/c Osella FA1G-Alfa Romeo V8	spun off – broken suspension	26/27
ret	PORTUGUESE GP	Estoril	21	Osella Squadra Corse	P	1.5 t/c Osella FA1G-Alfa Romeo V8	engine	24/27
ret	MEXICAN GP	Mexico City	21	Osella Squadra Corse	P	1.5 t/c Osella FA1G-Alfa Romeo V8	turbo	25/26
ret	AUSTRALIAN GP	Adelaide	21	Osella Squadra Corse	P	1.5 t/c Osella FA1G-Alfa Romeo V8	transmission	25/26

1987 Championship position: Unplaced

ret	SAN MARINO GP	Imola	26	Ligier Loto	G	1.5 t/c Ligier JS29B-Megatron 4	withdrawn – handling problems	20/27
7/ret	BELGIAN GP	Spa	26	Ligier Loto	G	1.5 t/c Ligier JS29B-Megatron 4	out of fuel/3 laps behind	17/26
12	MONACO GP	Monte Carlo	26	Ligier Loto	G	1.5 t/c Ligier JS29B-Megatron 4	4 laps behind	20/26
nc	US GP (DETROIT)	Detroit	26	Ligier Loto	G	1.5 t/c Ligier JS29B-Megatron 4	pit stop – clutch/12 laps behind	23/26
ret	FRENCH GP	Paul Ricard	26	Ligier Loto	G	1.5 t/c Ligier JS29C-Megatron 4	engine	17/26
excl*	BRITISH GP	Silverstone	26	Ligier Loto	G	1.5 t/c Ligier JS29C-Megatron 4	*disqualified in practice	19/26
ret	GERMAN GP	Hockenheim	26	Ligier Loto	G	1.5 t/c Ligier JS29C-Megatron 4	engine	17/26
12	HUNGARIAN GP	Hungaroring	26	Ligier Loto	G	1.5 t/c Ligier JS29C-Megatron 4	bad oversteer/3 laps behind	25/26
8	AUSTRIAN GP	Österreichring	26	Ligier Loto	G	1.5 t/c Ligier JS29C-Megatron 4	2 laps behind	18/26
8	ITALIAN GP	Monza	26	Ligier Loto	G	1.5 t/c Ligier JS29C-Megatron 4	2 laps behind	19/28
ret	PORTUGUESE GP	Estoril	26	Ligier Loto	G	1.5 t/c Ligier JS29C-Megatron 4	clutch	23/27
ret	SPANISH GP	Jerez	26	Ligier Loto	G	1.5 t/c Ligier JS29C-Megatron 4	ignition	23/28
ret	MEXICAN GP	Mexico City	26	Ligier Loto	G	1.5 t/c Ligier JS29C-Megatron 4	overheating	21/27
13/ret	JAPANESE GP	Suzuka	26	Ligier Loto	G	1.5 t/c Ligier JS29C-Megatron 4	out of fuel	25/27
ret	AUSTRALIAN GP	Adelaide	26	Ligier Loto	G	1.5 t/c Ligier JS29C-Megatron 4	engine	22/27

1988 Championship position: Unplaced

dnq	BRAZILIAN GP	Rio	9	West Zakspeed Racing	G	1.5 t/c Zakspeed 881 4		28/31
ret	SAN MARINO GP	Imola	9	West Zakspeed Racing	G	1.5 t/c Zakspeed 881 4	electrics	25/31
ret	MONACO GP	Monte Carlo	9	West Zakspeed Racing	G	1.5 t/c Zakspeed 881 4	gearbox	23/30
15	MEXICAN GP	Mexico City	9	West Zakspeed Racing	G	1.5 t/c Zakspeed 881 4	broken nose wing – pit stop/-6 laps	18/30
14/ret	CANADIAN GP	Montreal	9	West Zakspeed Racing	G	1.5 t/c Zakspeed 881 4	engine	22/31
dnq	US GP (DETROIT)	Detroit	9	West Zakspeed Racing	G	1.5 t/c Zakspeed 881 4		30/31
excl*	FRENCH GP	Paul Ricard	9	West Zakspeed Racing	G	1.5 t/c Zakspeed 881 4	*disqualified – missed weight check	(24)/31
dnq	BRITISH GP	Silverstone	9	West Zakspeed Racing	G	1.5 t/c Zakspeed 881 4		28/31
14	GERMAN GP	Hockenheim	9	West Zakspeed Racing	G	1.5 t/c Zakspeed 881 4	lost clutch/2 laps behind	23/31
dnq	HUNGARIAN GP	Hungaroring	9	West Zakspeed Racing	G	1.5 t/c Zakspeed 881 4		30/31
ret	BELGIAN GP	Spa	9	West Zakspeed Racing	G	1.5 t/c Zakspeed 881 4	engine – oil leak	24/31
ret	ITALIAN GP	Monza	9	West Zakspeed Racing	G	1.5 t/c Zakspeed 881 4	engine	16/31
dnq	PORTUGUESE GP	Estoril	9	West Zakspeed Racing	G	1.5 t/c Zakspeed 881 4		28/31
dnq	SPANISH GP	Jerez	9	West Zakspeed Racing	G	1.5 t/c Zakspeed 881 4		30/31
dnq	JAPANESE GP	Suzuka	9	West Zakspeed Racing	G	1.5 t/c Zakspeed 881 4		29/31
ret	AUSTRALIAN GP	Adelaide	9	West Zakspeed Racing	G	1.5 t/c Zakspeed 881 4	fuel pump	26/31

1989 Championship position: Unplaced

dnpq	BRAZILIAN GP	Rio	18	Osella Squadra Corse	P	3.5 Osella FA1M-Cosworth V8		32/38
dnpq	SAN MARINO GP	Imola	18	Osella Squadra Corse	P	3.5 Osella FA1M-Cosworth V8		33/39
dnpq	MONACO GP	Monte Carlo	18	Osella Squadra Corse	P	3.5 Osella FA1M-Cosworth V8		30/38
excl*	MEXICAN GP	Mexico City	18	Osella Squadra Corse	P	3.5 Osella FA1M-Cosworth V8	*disqualified for missing weight check	37/39
dnpq	US GP (PHOENIX)	Phoenix	18	Osella Squadra Corse	P	3.5 Osella FA1M-Cosworth V8		31/39
dnpq	CANADIAN GP	Montreal	18	Osella Squadra Corse	P	3.5 Osella FA1M-Cosworth V8		34/39
dnpq	FRENCH GP	Paul Ricard	18	Osella Squadra Corse	P	3.5 Osella FA1M-Cosworth V8		35/39
dnpq	BRITISH GP	Silverstone	18	Osella Squadra Corse	P	3.5 Osella FA1M-Cosworth V8		34/39
dnpq	GERMAN GP	Hockenheim	18	Osella Squadra Corse	P	3.5 Osella FA1M-Cosworth V8		34/39
ret	HUNGARIAN GP	Hungaroring	18	Osella Squadra Corse	P	3.5 Osella FA1M-Cosworth V8	electrics	22/39
dnpq	BELGIAN GP	Spa	18	Osella Squadra Corse	P	3.5 Osella FA1M-Cosworth V8		32/39
dnpq	ITALIAN GP	Monza	18	Osella Squadra Corse	P	3.5 Osella FA1M-Cosworth V8		33/39
dnpq	PORTUGUESE GP	Estoril	18	Osella Squadra Corse	P	3.5 Osella FA1M-Cosworth V8		33/39
ret	SPANISH GP	Jerez	18	Osella Squadra Corse	P	3.5 Osella FA1M-Cosworth V8	gearbox	25/38
dnpq	JAPANESE GP	Suzuka	18	Osella Squadra Corse	P	3.5 Osella FA1M-Cosworth V8		31/39
ret	AUSTRALIAN GP	Adelaide	18	Osella Squadra Corse	P	3.5 Osella FA1M-Cosworth V8	car hit by Piquet in rain	21/39

GP Starts: 74 (76)   GP Wins: 0   Pole positions: 0   Fastest laps: 0   Points: 2

BRUNO GIACOMELLI

BRUNO GIACOMELLI, who saw himself as "cool but enthusiastic", was undoubtedly a very talented performer who seemed to be well set for a successful grand prix career, but after he had been given some excellent early opportunities, his star waned and was eventually reduced to a distant flicker.

Giacomelli came through Formula Italia to contest the two 1976 British Formula 3 championships in a works-backed March-Toyota. He ran a close second to Rupert Keegan in a fiercely and bitterly contested BP Super Visco Championship, but did take the honours in the lesser Shellsport Series as well as scoring a prestigious win in the Monaco Formula 3 race.

Benefiting from the close attention of Robin Herd and the March factory, Giacomelli graduated to Formula 2 in 1977 and took three wins, but suffered through poor reliability. Enjoying substantial backing, he made his grand prix debut in 1978, driving a third works McLaren in selected races. His most notable contribution was to impede Niki Lauda's Brabham when being lapped, thus allowing Carlos Reutemann to snatch the lead and eventual victory in his Ferrari.

At this point, however, Giacomelli was still focusing on his Formula 2 campaign, in which he blitzed the opposition, winning eight of the 12 rounds in the works March-BMW to become the first Italian ever to win the title. His only serious title rival proved to be his team mate, Marc Surer, with a talented trio of Derek Daly, Eddie Cheever, and Keke Rosberg left trailing in their wake.

In 1979, Bruno joined the Alfa Romeo team for what would be very much a learning year, and his handful of appearances were inconclusive. He did make a strong impression at Monza in the new ground-effect car before overreaching himself and spinning off.

The gloves were off in 1980, and at first Giacomelli floundered, prone to silly errors that undid much good work. Then, after Patrick Depailler's death in a mid-season testing accident, he found himself leading the team and rose to the challenge magnificently. At the season's finale at Watkins Glen, he put in a magnificent effort to take pole and led the race with ease until an electrical problem robbed him of an odds-on maiden grand prix victory. This was probably the high-water mark in his career.

Perhaps Giacomelli lacked motivation, for while there were occasions during the next three seasons when his undoubted ability shone, all too often he seemed uninterested and at odds with his machinery, especially after he was eased out of the restructured Alfa squad and obliged to step down to the Candy Toleman Team, where was comprehensively outpaced by team-mate Derek Warwick.

Out of a grand prix drive from 1984, Giacomelli surfaced occasionally in Indy cars that year and in the following season, scoring a few reasonable finishes, with a best of fifth at Meadowlands for Patrick Racing in 1985. He also made appearances in sports car racing over the next few seasons to no great effect, so it was a considerable surprise when he was brought into the Life team in 1990 to replace the disenchanted Gary Brabham. The exercise was something of a joke, however, as Bruno rarely seemed to venture beyond the pit lane.

In 1995, Giacomelli was keeping his hand in by racing a Porsche in the Monza four-hour race, and after two seasons away from the tracks he garnered enough sponsorship in 1998 to contest the highly competitive Porsche Supercup series, where he performed more than respectably on occasion.

GIACOMELLI, Bruno (I) b 10/9/1952, Borgo Poncarale, Brescia

	1977 Championship position: Unplaced							
	Race	Circuit	No	Entrant	Tyres	Capacity/Car/Engine	Comment	Q Pos/Entries
ret	ITALIAN GP	Monza	14	Marlboro Team McLaren	G	3.0 McLaren M23-Cosworth V8	engine – spun off	15/34
	1978 Championship position: Unplaced							
8	BELGIAN GP	Zolder	33	Marlboro Team McLaren	G	3.0 McLaren M26-Cosworth V8	1 lap behind	21/30
ret	FRENCH GP	Paul Ricard	33	Marlboro Team McLaren	G	3.0 McLaren M26-Cosworth V8	engine	22/29
7	BRITISH GP	Brands Hatch	33	Marlboro Team McLaren	G	3.0 McLaren M26-Cosworth V8	1 lap behind	16/30
ret	DUTCH GP	Zandvoort	33	Marlboro Team McLaren	G	3.0 McLaren M26-Cosworth V8	spun off – stalled	19/33
14	ITALIAN GP	Monza	33	Marlboro Team McLaren	G	3.0 McLaren M26-Cosworth V8	1 lap behind	20/32
	1979 Championship position: Unplaced							
ret	BELGIAN GP	Zolder	35	Autodelta	G	3.0 Alfa Romeo 177 F12	hit by de Angelis	14/28
17	FRENCH GP	Dijon	35	Autodelta	G	3.0 Alfa Romeo 177 F12	pit stop/5 laps behind	17/27
ret	ITALIAN GP	Monza	35	Autodelta	G	3.0 Alfa Romeo 179 V12	spun off	18/28
dnp	CANADIAN GP	Montreal	35	Autodelta	G	3.0 Alfa Romeo 179 V12	had to pre qualify – entry withdrawn	– / –
ret	US GP EAST	Watkins Glen	35	Autodelta	G	3.0 Alfa Romeo 179 V12	spun avoiding Rosberg	18/30

1980 Championship position: 17th= Wins: 0 Pole positions: 1 Fastest laps: 0 Points scored: 4

5	ARGENTINE GP	Buenos Aires	23	Marlboro Team Alfa Romeo	G	3.0 Alfa Romeo 179 V12	1 lap behind	20/28
13	BRAZILIAN GP	Interlagos	23	Marlboro Team Alfa Romeo	G	3.0 Alfa Romeo 179 V12	1 lap behind	17/28
ret	SOUTH AFRICAN GP	Kyalami	23	Marlboro Team Alfa Romeo	G	3.0 Alfa Romeo 179 V12	engine	12/28
ret	US GP WEST	Long Beach	23	Marlboro Team Alfa Romeo	G	3.0 Alfa Romeo 179 V12	collison with Jones	6/27
ret	BELGIAN GP	Zolder	23	Marlboro Team Alfa Romeo	G	3.0 Alfa Romeo 179 V12	suspension	18/27
ret	MONACO GP	Monte Carlo	23	Marlboro Team Alfa Romeo	G	3.0 Alfa Romeo 179 V12	multiple accident	8/27
ret	FRENCH GP	Paul Ricard	23	Marlboro Team Alfa Romeo	G	3.0 Alfa Romeo 179 V12	handling	9/27
ret	BRITISH GP	Brands Hatch	23	Marlboro Team Alfa Romeo	G	3.0 Alfa Romeo 179 V12	spun off	6/27
5	GERMAN GP	Hockenheim	23	Marlboro Team Alfa Romeo	G	3.0 Alfa Romeo 179 V12		19/26
ret	AUSTRIAN GP	Österreichring	23	Marlboro Team Alfa Romeo	G	3.0 Alfa Romeo 179 V12	rear suspension	8/25
ret	DUTCH GP	Zandvoort	23	Marlboro Team Alfa Romeo	G	3.0 Alfa Romeo 179 V12	damaged skirt	8/28
ret	ITALIAN GP	Imola	23	Marlboro Team Alfa Romeo	G	3.0 Alfa Romeo 179 V12	puncture – spun off	4/28
ret	CANADIAN GP	Montreal	23	Marlboro Team Alfa Romeo	G	3.0 Alfa Romeo 179 V12	damaged skirt	4/28
ret	US GP EAST	Watkins Glen	23	Marlboro Team Alfa Romeo	G	3.0 Alfa Romeo 179 V12	electrics	1/27

1981 Championship position: 15th Wins: 0 Pole positions: 0 Fastest laps: 0 Points scored: 7

ret	US GP WEST	Long Beach	23	Marlboro Team Alfa Romeo	M	3.0 Alfa Romeo 179C V12	collision with Lammers	9/29
nc	BRAZILIAN GP	Rio	23	Marlboro Team Alfa Romeo	M	3.0 Alfa Romeo 179C V12	4 pit stops – electrics/-22 laps	6/30
10/ret	ARGENTINE GP	Buenos Aires	23	Marlboro Team Alfa Romeo	M	3.0 Alfa Romeo 179C V12	out of fuel/2 laps behind	22/29
ret	SAN MARINO GP	Imola	23	Marlboro Team Alfa Romeo	M	3.0 Alfa Romeo 179C V12	collision with Cheever	11/30
9	BELGIAN GP	Zolder	23	Marlboro Team Alfa Romeo	M	3.0 Alfa Romeo 179C V12		17/31
ret	MONACO GP	Monte Carlo	23	Marlboro Team Alfa Romeo	M	3.0 Alfa Romeo 179C V12	accident with Alboreto	18/31
10	SPANISH GP	Jarama	23	Marlboro Team Alfa Romeo	M	3.0 Alfa Romeo 179C V12		6/30
15	FRENCH GP	Dijon	23	Marlboro Team Alfa Romeo	M	3.0 Alfa Romeo 179C V12	3 laps behind	12/29
ret	BRITISH GP	Silverstone	23	Marlboro Team Alfa Romeo	M	3.0 Alfa Romeo 179D V12	gearbox	12/30
15	GERMAN GP	Hockenheim	23	Marlboro Team Alfa Romeo	M	3.0 Alfa Romeo 179D V12	2 laps behind	19/30
ret	AUSTRIAN GP	Österreichring	23	Marlboro Team Alfa Romeo	M	3.0 Alfa Romeo 179D V12	engine fire	16/28
ret	DUTCH GP	Zandvoort	23	Marlboro Team Alfa Romeo	M	3.0 Alfa Romeo 179C V12	suspension – crashed	14/30
8	ITALIAN GP	Monza	23	Marlboro Team Alfa Romeo	M	3.0 Alfa Romeo 179C V12	2 laps behind	10/30
4	CANADIAN GP	Montreal	23	Marlboro Team Alfa Romeo	M	3.0 Alfa Romeo 179C V12	1 lap behind	15/30
3	CAESARS PALACE GP	Las Vegas	23	Marlboro Team Alfa Romeo	M	3.0 Alfa Romeo 179C V12		8/30

1982 Championship position: 22= Wins: 0 Pole positions: 0 Fastest laps: 0 Points scored: 2

11	SOUTH AFRICAN GP	Kyalami	23	Marlboro Team Alfa Romeo	M	3.0 Alfa Romeo 179D V12	3 laps behind	19/30
ret	BRAZILIAN GP	Rio	23	Marlboro Team Alfa Romeo	M	3.0 Alfa Romeo 182 V12	engine	16/31
ret	US GP WEST	Long Beach	23	Marlboro Team Alfa Romeo	M	3.0 Alfa Romeo 182 V12	accident with Arnoux	5/31
ret	SAN MARINO GP	Imola	23	Marlboro Team Alfa Romeo	M	3.0 Alfa Romeo 182 V12	engine	6/14
ret	BELGIAN GP	Zolder	23	Marlboro Team Alfa Romeo	M	3.0 Alfa Romeo 182 V12	startline accident	17/32
ret	MONACO GP	Monte Carlo	23	Marlboro Team Alfa Romeo	M	3.0 Alfa Romeo 182 V12	transmission	3/31
ret	US GP (DETROIT)	Detroit	23	Marlboro Team Alfa Romeo	M	3.0 Alfa Romeo 182 V12	collision with Watson – hit barrier	6/28
ret	CANADIAN GP	Montreal	23	Marlboro Team Alfa Romeo	M	3.0 Alfa Romeo 182 V12	accident with Mansell	5/29
11	DUTCH GP	Zandvoort	23	Marlboro Team Alfa Romeo	M	3.0 Alfa Romeo 182 V12	2 laps behind	8/31
7	BRITISH GP	Brands Hatch	23	Marlboro Team Alfa Romeo	M	3.0 Alfa Romeo 182 V12	1 lap behind	14/30
9	FRENCH GP	Paul Ricard	23	Marlboro Team Alfa Romeo	M	3.0 Alfa Romeo 182 V12	1 lap behind	8/30
5	GERMAN GP	Hockenheim	23	Marlboro Team Alfa Romeo	M	3.0 Alfa Romeo 182 V12	1 lap behind	12/30
ret	AUSTRIAN GP	Österreichring	23	Marlboro Team Alfa Romeo	M	3.0 Alfa Romeo 182 V12	hit by de Cesaris	13/29
12	SWISS GP	Dijon	23	Marlboro Team Alfa Romeo	M	3.0 Alfa Romeo 182 V12	2 laps behind	9/29
ret	ITALIAN GP	Monza	23	Marlboro Team Alfa Romeo	M	3.0 Alfa Romeo 182 V12	broken side pod	8/30
10	CAESARS PALACE GP	Las Vegas	23	Marlboro Team Alfa Romeo	M	3.0 Alfa Romeo 182 V12	2 laps behind	16/30

1983 Championship position: 19th= Wins: 0 Pole positions: 0 Fastest laps: 0 Points scored: 1

ret	BRAZILIAN GP	Rio	36	Candy Toleman Motorsport	P	1.5 t/c Toleman TG183B-Hart 4	spun off	15/27
ret	US GP WEST	Long Beach	36	Candy Toleman Motorsport	P	1.5 t/c Toleman TG183B-Hart 4	battery – could not restart at pitstop	14/28
13/ret	FRENCH GP	Paul Ricard	36	Candy Toleman Motorsport	P	1.5 t/c Toleman TG183B-Hart 4	gearbox/5 laps behind	13/29
ret	SAN MARINO GP	Imola	36	Candy Toleman Motorsport	P	1.5 t/c Toleman TG183B-Hart 4	rear suspension	17/28
dnq	MONACO GP	Monte Carlo	36	Candy Toleman Motorsport	P	1.5 t/c Toleman TG183B-Hart 4		21/28
8	BELGIAN GP	Spa	36	Candy Toleman Motorsport	P	1.5 t/c Toleman TG183B-Hart 4		16/28
9	US GP (DETROIT)	Detroit	36	Candy Toleman Motorsport	P	1.5 t/c Toleman TG183B-Hart 4	1 lap behind	17/27
nc	CANADIAN GP	Montreal	36	Candy Toleman Motorsport	P	1.5 t/c Toleman TG183B-Hart 4	2 pit stops – engine/27 laps behind	10/28
ret	BRITISH GP	Silverstone	36	Candy Toleman Motorsport	P	1.5 t/c Toleman TG183B-Hart 4	turbo	12/29
ret	GERMAN GP	Hockenheim	36	Candy Toleman Motorsport	P	1.5 t/c Toleman TG183B-Hart 4	turbo	10/29
ret	AUSTRIAN GP	Österreichring	36	Candy Toleman Motorsport	P	1.5 t/c Toleman TG183B-Hart 4	accident damage	7/29
13	DUTCH GP	Zandvoort	36	Candy Toleman Motorsport	P	1.5 t/c Toleman TG183B-Hart 4	pit stop/4 laps behind	13/29
7	ITALIAN GP	Monza	36	Candy Toleman Motorsport	P	1.5 t/c Toleman TG183B-Hart 4		14/29
6	EUROPEAN GP	Brands Hatch	36	Candy Toleman Motorsport	P	1.5 t/c Toleman TG183B-Hart 4		12/29
ret	SOUTH AFRICAN GP	Kyalami	36	Candy Toleman Motorsport	P	1.5 t/c Toleman TG183B-Hart 4	turbo fire	16/26

1990 Championship position: Unplaced

dnpq	SAN MARINO GP	Imola	39	Life Racing Engines	P	3.5 Life L190 W12		33/34
dnpq	MONACO GP	Monte Carlo	39	Life Racing Engines	P	3.5 Life L190 W12		35/35
dnpq	CANADIAN GP	Montreal	39	Life Racing Engines	P	3.5 Life L190 W12		35/35
dnpq	MEXICAN GP	Mexico City	39	Life Racing Engines	P	3.5 Life L190 W12		35/35
dnpq	FRENCH GP	Paul Ricard	39	Life Racing Engines	P	3.5 Life L190 W12	no time recorded	– / –
dnpq	BRITISH GP	Silverstone	39	Life Racing Engines	P	3.5 Life L190 W12		35/35
dnpq	GERMAN GP	Hockenheim	39	Life Racing Engines	P	3.5 Life L190 W12		35/35
dnpq	HUNGARIAN GP	Hungaroring	39	Life Racing Engines	P	3.5 Life L190 W12		35/35
dnpq	BELGIAN GP	Spa	39	Life Racing Engines	P	3.5 Life L190 W12		33/33
dnpq	ITALIAN GP	Monza	39	Life Racing Engines	P	3.5 Life L190 W12		33/33
dnpq	PORTUGUESE GP	Estoril	39	Life Racing Engines	P	3.5 Life L190-Judd V8	no time recorded	– /33
dnpq	SPANISH GP	Jerez	39	Life Racing Engines	P	3.5 Life L190-Judd V8		33/33

GP Starts: 69   GP Wins: 0   Pole positions: 1   Fastest laps: 0   Points: 14

DICK GIBSON

A DIRECTOR of a motor company in Barnstaple, Dick Gibson bought Tony Crook's modified Cooper-Bristol to embark on competition, but soon switched to an A-Type Connaught, which he raced in 1955 and through 1956 with modest success. It was with the acquisition of a rear-engined Formula 2 Cooper, however, that he began to make a mark, sixth place in the International Coupe de Vitesse at Reims and seventh in the International Trophy at Silverstone being his best major placings in 1957.

Dick ran the Cooper again the following year, and after competing in New Zealand returned for the European season, before venturing to South Africa early in 1959. It was a worthwhile trip, for he won three (Natal, Cape Town and Pietermaritzburg) of the four races and claimed the RAC South African International Championship. Naturally he returned the following year, but after finishing seventh in the South African Grand Prix, he was involved in a nasty shunt at another meeting that left him hospitalised. The damaged car was shipped back to England and rebuilt, with Dick preferring to allow Keith Ballisat, George Pfaff and Vic Wilson to drive it under the Equipe Prideaux banner.

GIBSON, Dick (GB) b 16/4/1918, Bourne – d 17/12/2010, Cadíz, Spain

1957 Championship position: Unplaced

	Race	Circuit	No	Entrant	Tyres	Capacity/Car/Engine	Comment	Q Pos/Entries
ret	GERMAN GP (F2)	Nürburgring	29	R Gibson	D	1.5 Cooper T43-Climax 4 F2	steering	24/24

1958 Championship position: Unplaced

	Race	Circuit	No	Entrant	Tyres	Capacity/Car/Engine	Comment	Q Pos/Entries
ret	GERMAN GP (F2)	Nürburgring	19	R Gibson	D	1.5 Cooper T43-Climax 4 F2	mechanical	23/26

GP Starts: 2   GP Wins: 0   Pole positions: 0   Fastest laps: 0   Points: 0

GINTHER, Richie (USA) b 5/8/1930, Hollywood, California – d 20/9/1989, Touzac, nr Bordeaux, France

1960 Championship position: 8th=   Wins: 0   Pole positions: 0   Fastest laps: 0   Points scored: 8

	Race	Circuit	No	Entrant	Tyres	Capacity/Car/Engine	Comment	Q Pos/Entries
6	MONACO GP	Monte Carlo	34	Scuderia Ferrari	D	2.4 Ferrari-Dino 246MP V6	rear-engined prototype/-30 laps	9/24
6	DUTCH GP	Zandvoort	3	Scuderia Ferrari	D	2.4 Ferrari-Dino 246 V6	1 lap behind	12/21
dns	FRENCH GP	Reims	28	Reventlow Automobiles Inc	D	2.4 Scarab 4	engine problems	(20)/23
2	ITALIAN GP	Monza	18	Scuderia Ferrari	D	2.4 Ferrari-Dino 246 V6		2/16

1961 Championship position: 5   Wins: 0   Pole positions: 0   Fastest laps: 2 (1 shared)   Points scored: 16

	Race	Circuit	No	Entrant	Tyres	Capacity/Car/Engine	Comment	Q Pos/Entries
2	MONACO GP	Monte Carlo	36	Scuderia Ferrari SpA SEFAC	D	1.5 Ferrari 156 V6	FL (shared with Moss)	2/21
5	DUTCH GP	Zandvoort	2	Scuderia Ferrari SpA SEFAC	D	1.5 Ferrari 156 V6		3/17
3	BELGIAN GP	Spa	6	Scuderia Ferrari SpA SEFAC	D	1.5 Ferrari 156 V6	FL	5/25
15/ret	FRENCH GP	Reims	18	Scuderia Ferrari SpA SEFAC	D	1.5 Ferrari 156 V6	oil pressure/12 laps behind	3/26
3	BRITISH GP	Aintree	6	Scuderia Ferrari SpA SEFAC	D	1.5 Ferrari 156 V6		=1/30
8	GERMAN GP	Nürburgring	5	Scuderia Ferrari SpA SEFAC	D	1.5 Ferrari 156 V6		14/27
ret	ITALIAN GP	Monza	6	Scuderia Ferrari SpA SEFAC	D	1.5 Ferrari 156 V6	engine	4/33

1962 Championship position: 8th   Wins: 0   Pole positions: 0   Fastest laps: 0   Points scored: 10

	Race	Circuit	No	Entrant	Tyres	Capacity/Car/Engine	Comment	Q Pos/Entries
ret	DUTCH GP	Monza	18	Owen Racing Organisation	D	1.5 BRM P48/57 V8	pushed off by Trevor Taylor	7/20
ret	MONACO GP	Monte Carlo	8	Owen Racing Organisation	D	1.5 BRM P48/57 V8	stuck throttle – accident	=14/21
dns	" "	" "	8	Owen Racing Organisation	D	1.5 BRM P57 V8	practice only	– / –
ret	BELGIAN GP	Spa	2	Owen Racing Organisation	D	1.5 BRM P57 V8	gearbox	9/20
3	FRENCH GP	Rouen	10	Owen Racing Organisation	D	1.5 BRM P57 V8	car would not start on grid/-2 laps	10/17
13	BRITISH GP	Aintree	14	Owen Racing Organisation	D	1.5 BRM P57 V8	5 laps behind	=7/21
8	GERMAN GP	Nürburgring	12	Owen Racing Organisation	D	1.5 BRM P57 V8		7/30
2	ITALIAN GP	Monza	12	Owen Racing Organisation	D	1.5 BRM P57 V8		3/30
ret	US GP	Watkins Glen	5	Owen Racing Organisation	D	1.5 BRM P57 V8	engine/gearbox	2/20
7	SOUTH AFRICAN GP	East London	4	Owen Racing Organisation	D	1.5 BRM P57 V8	4 laps behind	=6/17

1963 Championship position: 2nd=   Wins: 0   Pole positions: 0   Fastest laps: 0   Points scored: 34

	Race	Circuit	No	Entrant	Tyres	Capacity/Car/Engine	Comment	Q Pos/Entries
2	MONACO GP	Monte Carlo	5	Owen Racing Organisation	D	1.5 BRM P57 V8		=3/17
4	BELGIAN GP	Spa	8	Owen Racing Organisation	D	1.5 BRM P57 V8	1 lap behind	9/20
5	DUTCH GP	Zandvoort	14	Owen Racing Organisation	D	1.5 BRM P57 V8	1 lap behind	=6/19
ret	FRENCH GP	Reims	4	Owen Racing Organisation	D	1.5 BRM P57 V8	holed radiator	12/21
4	BRITISH GP	Silverstone	2	Owen Racing Organisation	D	1.5 BRM P57 V8	1 lap behind	=7/23
3	GERMAN GP	Nürburgring	2	Owen Racing Organisation	D	1.5 BRM P57 V8		6/26
2	ITALIAN GP	Monza	10	Owen Racing Organisation	D	1.5 BRM P57 V8		4/28
2	US GP	Watkins Glen	2	Owen Racing Organisation	D	1.5 BRM P57 V8		4/21
3	MEXICAN GP	Mexico City	2	Owen Racing Organisation	D	1.5 BRM P57 V8		5/21
ret	SOUTH AFRICAN GP	East London	6	Owen Racing Organisation	D	1.5 BRM P57 V8	driveshaft	=7/21

RICHIE GINTHER

SMALL of stature and freckle-faced, Richie Ginther was always just outside the top echelon of grand prix talent, but on his day he was more than capable of delivering the goods. In many ways, he was the perfect number-two driver, being conscientious, reliable and an extremely fine tester, with a rare mechanical sympathy born of his early days as a skilled mechanic on both cars and aeroplanes during his national service.

Although Ginther had run an MG in 1951, it would be another two years before he really became involved in serious competition, when he shared Phil Hill's Ferrari in the Carrera Panamericana. The pair were lucky to emerge unscathed from a crash that wrote off the car, but they returned the following year to take second place behind Umberto Maglioli's works entry.

Richie then found employment with Ferrari importer Johnnie von Neumann, who gave him plenty of drives over the next few seasons, allowing him to make a big name for himself in West Coast racing. He came to the attention of Luigi Chinetti who, in turn, entered him in his Ferraris, Richie's programme including a visit to Le Mans in 1957.

Combining his job of running the car agency with a racing career was becoming something of a strain, but after Richie shared a Ferrari sports car with Wolfgang von Trips to take second place in the Buenos Aires 1000km, he was offered a four-race contract by the Scuderia. He quit his job and took the opportunity, moving to Italy with his wife. Although the sports car races yielded no success, his single-seater rides were a revelation. He was second in the Modena GP in the front-engined F2 car and made three grand prix starts, finishing an impressive sixth at Monaco

in the rear-engined prototype, and second at Monza in the boycotted Italian GP. Quickly realising his tremendous engineering expertise, Ferrari gave Richie the role of chief development driver in addition to his racing duties. In 1961, the team virtually swept the board with their 'sharknose' 156 V6 car, and Ginther really impressed with his spirited pursuit of Stirling Moss at Monaco. Surprisingly, he found himself surplus to requirements at the end of the year, but BRM were more than willing to take him into the fold.

Ginther made an ideal partner to Graham Hill, putting in much hard work as the Bourne team came good at last and won the world championship. The 1963 season was his most successful and consistent: he scored points in every grand prix, bar one, to finish equal second with his team-mate in the championship, behind runaway winner Jim Clark. Ginther stayed on for a third year in 1964, again proving his mechanical sympathy by finishing every grand prix.

It was all-change for 1965, when Ginther was hired to bring some much-needed experience to the still-fledgling Honda project. As the season wore on, the car became a real threat, until Richie had his greatest moment when he won the Mexican Grand Prix, the last race of the year. It must have been galling for all concerned that it marked the end of the 1.5-litre formula, for Honda would have been a very tough act to beat in 1966 under the old rules. As it was, they had to start again, and after filling in with a Cooper until the new car was finally made ready towards the end of the season, Ginther was fortunate to escape a huge accident in the Italian GP at Monza when a tyre failed.

For 1967, Honda went with John Surtees, and Richie joined up with Dan Gurney at Eagle. He lay second in the Race of Champions before retiring, but then surprisingly failed to qualify at Monaco. While practising for the Indianapolis 500, he suddenly decided that it was time to quit. He became involved in team management roles, for example running a Porsche 911 with Elliot Forbes-Robinson in 1971, before cutting his links with the sport and dropping out of the rat race to live in a camper in the desert.

He returned to the circuits in 1977, invited to the German GP at Hockenheim by Goodyear to present the winner, Niki Lauda, with a prize to mark the tyre company's 100th win, although many would not have recognised him with his moustache and long hair replacing the once familiar crew-cut.

It was a frail and sick Ginther who arrived at Donington in 1989 to attend BRM's 40th anniversary celebrations, and it was with much sadness, but little surprise, when the racing world learned of his death after a heart attack just days later while holidaying in France.

1964	Championship position: 4th=	Wins: 0	Pole positions: 0	Fastest laps: 0	Points scored: 23				
2	MONACO GP	Monte Carlo	7	Owen Racing Organisation	D	1.5 BRM P261 V8		1 lap behind	=8/20
11	DUTCH GP	Zandvoort	8	Owen Racing Organisation	D	1.5 BRM P261 V8		pit stop – fuel vaporisation/-16 laps	8/18
4	BELGIAN GP	Spa	2	Owen Racing Organisation	D	1.5 BRM P261 V8			8/20
5	FRENCH GP	Rouen	10	Owen Racing Organisation	D	1.5 BRM P261 V8			9/17
8	BRITISH GP	Brands Hatch	4	Owen Racing Organisation	D	1.5 BRM P261 V8		3 laps behind	14/25
7	GERMAN GP	Nürburgring	4	Owen Racing Organisation	D	1.5 BRM P261 V8		1 lap behind	11/24
2	AUSTRIAN GP	Zeltweg	4	Owen Racing Organisation	D	1.5 BRM P261 V8			=4/20
4	ITALIAN GP	Monza	20	Owen Racing Organisation	D	1.5 BRM P261 V8		1 lap behind	=9/25
4	US GP	Watkins Glen	4	Owen Racing Organisation	D	1.5 BRM P261 V8		3 laps behind	13/19
8	MEXICAN GP	Mexico City	4	Owen Racing Organisation	D	1.5 BRM P261 V8		1 lap behind	11/19

1965	Championship position: 7th=	Wins: 1	Pole positions: 0	Fastest laps: 0	Points scored: 11				
ret	MONACO GP	Monte Carlo	20	Honda R & D Co	G	1.5 Honda RA272 V12		driveshaft	17/17
6	BELGIAN GP	Spa	10	Honda R & D Co	G	1.5 Honda RA272 V12		1 lap behind	4/21
ret	FRENCH GP	Clermont Ferrand	26	Honda R & D Co	G	1.5 Honda RA272 V12		ignition	7/17
ret	BRITISH GP	Silverstone	11	Honda R & D Co	G	1.5 Honda RA272 V12		fuel injection	=3/23
6	DUTCH GP	Zandvoort	22	Honda R & D Co	G	1.5 Honda RA272 V12		led race/1 lap behind	=2/17
14/ret	ITALIAN GP	Monza	20	Honda R & D Co	G	1.5 Honda RA272 V12		ignition troubles/19 laps behind	17/23
7	US GP	Watkins Glen	11	Honda R & D Co	G	1.5 Honda RA272 V12		2 laps behind	3/18
1	MEXICAN GP	Mexico City (12)	11	Honda R & D Co	G	1.5 Honda RA272 V12			3/18

1966	Championship position: 11th	Wins: 0	Pole positions: 0	Fastest laps: 0	Points scored: 5				
ret	MONACO GP	Monte Carlo	9	Cooper Car Co	D	3.0 Cooper T81-Maserati V12		driveshaft	9/16
5	BELGIAN GP	Spa	18	Cooper Car Co	D	3.0 Cooper T81-Maserati V12		3 laps behind	8/18
ret	ITALIAN GP	Monza	18	Honda Racing Team	G	3.0 Honda RA273 V12		tyre threw tread – accident	7/22
nc	US GP	Watkins Glen	12	Honda Racing Team	G	3.0 Honda RA273 V12		pit stops – gearbox/27 laps behind	8/19
4	MEXICAN GP	Mexico City	12	Honda Racing Team	G	3.0 Honda RA273 V12		FL/1 lap behind	3/19

1967	Championship position: Unplaced								
dnq	MONACO GP	Monte Carlo	22	Anglo American Racers	G	3.0 Eagle T1G-Weslake V12			18/18

GP Starts: 52   GP Wins: 1   Pole positions: 0   Fastest laps: 3   Points: 107

**The Mexican Grand Prix was the final race of the
1.5-litre formula, and it was Ginther's only grand
prix victory. The American's Honda comfortably
outclassed the field.**

YVES GIRAUD-CABANTOUS

HAVING begun his long career in 1925, Yves Giraud-Cabantous had won his first race by 1927, the GP des Frontières at Chimay in a Salmson. Soon he began developing his own cars, and in 1930 he won the Bol d'Or 24-hour race in his own Caban. Later, he successfully raced a Bugatti and a Delahaye, in which he finished second at Le Mans.

After the Second World War, Yves joined the Ecurie France team, emerging victorious at Chimay, Montlhéry and San Remo in 1947, and winning the GP de Paris in 1948. He was also involved with the infamous CTA Arsenal project, before purchasing a Talbot that he raced extensively over the next five seasons.

In 1950, Yves joined the official Talbot team and, by finishing fourth in the British Grand Prix, became the first French driver to score world championship points. Financial difficulties led to the team being disbanded, but Giraud-Cabantous continued on his own with the Talbot, finishing third at Albi in 1952.Then he joined the HWM team for a number of races in 1952/53. His 'steady-as-she-goes' approach by this time was perhaps understandable, but he did bring the car home to the finish regularly.

In sports cars, Yves was second, sharing Louis Rosier's Talbot, in the Reims 12-hours of 1953, his last full season. He made occasional appearances over the next few years, in the little VP and Giaur sports cars, before retiring in 1957 to concentrate fully on his transport business.

GIRAUD-CABANTOUS, Yves (F) b 8/10/1904, Saint-Gaudens – d 30/3/1973, Paris

	1950	Championship position: 10th=		Wins: 0	Pole positions: 0	Fastest laps: 0	Points scored: 3		
	Race	Circuit	No	Entrant	Tyres	Capacity/Car/Engine		Comment	Q Pos/Entries
4	BRITISH GP	Silverstone	14	Automobiles Talbot-Darracq SA	D	4.5 Talbot-Lago T26C-DA 6		2 laps behind	6/21
ret	SWISS GP	Bremgarten	6	Automobiles Talbot-Darracq SA	D	4.5 Talbot-Lago T26C-DA 6		crashed	7/18
ret	BELGIAN GP	Spa	18	Automobiles Talbot-Darracq SA	D	4.5 Talbot-Lago T26C-DA 6		engine	9/14
8	FRENCH GP	Reims	18	Automobiles Talbot-Darracq SA	D	4.5 Talbot-Lago T26C-DA 6		12 laps behind	5/20
	1951		Championship position: 12=	Wins: 0	Pole positions: 0	Fastest laps: 0	Points scored: 2		
ret	SWISS GP	Bremgarten	6	Yves Giraud-Cabantous	D	4.5 Talbot-Lago T26C 6		ignition	15/21
5	BELGIAN GP	Spa	22	Yves Giraud-Cabantous	D	4.5 Talbot-Lago T26C 6		2 laps behind	8/13
7	FRENCH GP	Reims	46	Yves Giraud-Cabantous	D	4.5 Talbot-Lago T26C 6		6 laps behind	11/23
ret	GERMAN GP	Nürburgring	87	Yves Giraud-Cabantous	D	4.5 Talbot-Lago T26C 6		crashed	11/23
8	ITALIAN GP	Monza	24	Yves Giraud-Cabantous	D	4.5 Talbot-Lago T26C 6		8 laps behind	14/22
ret	SPANISH GP	Pedralbes	32	Yves Giraud-Cabantous	D	4.5 Talbot-Lago T26C 6		hit dog on track/overheating	14/20
	1952	Championship position: Unplaced							
10	FRENCH GP	Rouen	24	HW Motors Ltd	D	2.0 HWM-Alta 4		9 laps behind	10/20
	1953	Championship position: Unplaced							
14	FRENCH GP	Reims	30	HW Motors Ltd	D	2.0 HWM-Alta 4		10 laps behind	18/25
15	ITALIAN GP	Monza	16	HW Motors Ltd	D	2.0 HWM-Alta 4		13 laps behind	28/30

GP Starts: 13   GP Wins: 0   Pole positions: 0   Fastest laps: 0   Points: 5

IGNAZIO GIUNTI

FROM a well-to-do Rome family, Ignazio Giunti began racing in his teens, driving Alfas in hill-climbs and club events. He progressed to the works Alfa team in 1966, winning the touring car section of the European mountain-climb championship the following year. He was a regular member of the Autodelta sports car team in 1968, taking second in the Targa Florio and fourth (and a class win) at Le Mans with Nanni Galli, who was his regular partner through into 1969.

For 1970, Ignazio was signed by Ferrari for their successful sports car programme. He shared the winning 512S in the Sebring 12-hours, Targa Florio and Rand nine-hours, and took second place in the Monza 1000km and third in the Watkins Glen six-hours. Meanwhile he made a very impressive grand prix debut to finish fourth at Spa, earning three more drives.

Although Clay Regazzoni had laid claim to the number-two seat in F1, Giunti stayed with the team for 1971. In the season's first sports car race, the Buenos Aires 1000km, when unsighted by another car, he ploughed into the back of the Matra of Jean-Pierre Beltoise, which had run out of fuel and was being pushed along the track by its driver. The Ferrari somersaulted some 200 yards down the track, exploding into flames and leaving poor Giunti no chance of survival. Having sustained 70 per cent burns and multiple injuries, he died in hospital some two hours later.

GIUNTI, Ignazio (I) b 30/8/1941, Rome – d 10/1/1971, Buenos Aires, Argentina

1970	Championship position: 17th=		Wins: 0	Pole positions: 0	Fastest laps: 0	Points scored: 3		
	Race	Circuit	No	Entrant	Tyres	Capacity/Car/Engine	Comment	Q Pos/Entries
4	BELGIAN GP	Spa	28	Scuderia Ferrari SpA SEFAC	F	3.0 Ferrari 312B F12	pit stop – oil leak	8/18
14	FRENCH GP	Clermont Ferrand	11	Scuderia Ferrari SpA SEFAC	F	3.0 Ferrari 312B F12	pit stop – throttle/3 laps behind	11/23
7	AUSTRIAN GP	Österreichring	14	Scuderia Ferrari SpA SEFAC	F	3.0 Ferrari 312B F12	pit stop – wheel change/1 lap behind	5/24
ret	ITALIAN GP	Monza	6	Scuderia Ferrari SpA SEFAC	F	3.0 Ferrari 312B F12	overheating	5/27

GP Starts: 4   GP Wins: 0   Pole positions: 0   Fastest laps: 0   Points: 3

TIMO GLOCK

CARRIED in part by the wave of support for German drivers created by the success of the Schumacher brothers, Timo Glock enjoyed a rapid rise through the junior ranks, only to see his F1 ambitions stall just after he made the grade. Like any aspiring grand prix driver, he began his racing career in karts, although he didn't start until the age of 15, some seven or eight years after many of his counterparts. He proved capable enough, however, to consider a move into cars after only two seasons, despite not winning anything major.

With a fairly defined motorsport ladder in his homeland, Glock took his first steps in the Formula BMW Junior Cup, winning the 2000 title and setting himself up for the 'senior' championship the following year. With a season of experience – and confidence – under his belt, he duly clinched the ADAC title for Team Mamerow at the first time of asking, leaving him the option of Formula Renault or Formula 3 for 2002.

Having opted for the latter, Glock joined Opel Team KMS to contest the German championship and again adapted well, finishing third overall as best placed rookie driver. That introduction to F3 led to an invitation to contest the inaugural Euroseries in 2003, again with KMS. Up against a strong international field, including eventual winner Ryan Briscoe and runner-up Christian Klien, he finally broke through as an F3 driver, winning three races and finishing fifth overall.

While that performance in itself didn't cause a rush of interest from Formula 1 teams, access to German sponsorship was attractive and, with the support of Deutsche Post's Speed Academy, Glock signed up as official test and reserve driver for the Jordan team in 2004. While his deal restricted other racing activities, he didn't have to wait long to get back into the action, swapping his Friday practice role for the second race seat when sponsorship difficulties kept Giorgio Pantano out of the Canadian Grand Prix. Against the odds, and to Pantano's undoubted frustration, he managed to bring the otherwise poor EJ14 home in seventh place to earn a couple of points.

The German returned to testing duties from the next race, Pantano having ironed out his money problems, but he was called back into the fray when the lacklustre Italian was finally dropped ahead of the last three races of the year, in China, Japan and Brazil. No further points were forthcoming, however, and he hoped that his performances would stand him in good stead for the 2005 season, but that was not the case. Thwarted, he turned his attentions to the US-based Champ Car series where, after a series of promising tests, he picked up a seat at Rocketsports Racing. Timo certainly made his mark in his debut season, during which he experienced something of a wild ride in the Rocketsports machine. His commitment was total and, on occasion, led to on-track indiscretions that needed to be eliminated from his driving. Even so, his feisty performances won him the Rookie of The Year title and, although a victory just eluded him, he finished a creditable eighth in the final points standings.

Despite having built a strong reputation in Champ Car, Timo decided against a sophomore year, preferring to return to the unfinished business of Formula 1 via the supporting GP2 series in 2006. Although the year was largely dominated by Lewis Hamilton and Nelson Angelo Piquet, he did a great job in re-establishing his credentials, especially after a switch to iSports when he took a splendid racer's win at Hockenheim. A wrist injury hampered his chances of finishing higher than fourth in the final standings, but the following year he took the title on the back of five wins, sealing a place with Toyota as a replacement for Ralf Schumacher for 2008, despite the fact that he was still tied to BMW as a test driver. Once the matter was settled, he soon warmed to the task of trying to put the Japanese giants into the winner's circle; in taking second place in Hungary, behind his great friend, Heikki Kovalainen, he gave Toyota their best ever finish.

The 2009 season was Toyota's eighth since entering F1 and the pressure was on to produce the victory that was being demanded by the board of directors back in Japan. The TF109 challenger was equipped with a double diffuser à la Brawn and should have been a challenger, but once again it flattered to deceive. Timo started the season brightly, but soon became bogged down in mid-season. A tremendous second place in Singapore signalled the breakthrough, but a heavy crash in practice for the Japanese Grand Prix brought an early end to the German's season with a cracked vertebra. It was also the end of his Toyota career, as they finally pulled the plug on their F1 involvement.

Glock appeared to be lining up a drive for 2010 at Renault, alongside Robert Kubica, but eventually he took an offer from the Manor Motorsport team to head up their ambitious move into F1. The German has since spent his time struggling against the odds to move the car forwards from its position at the back of the grid. Despite rumours that he was looking for a seat elsewhere, he has signed a long-term deal with Marussia and seems happy to be in it for the long haul.

GLOCK, Timo (D) b 18/3/1982, Lindenfels

2004 Championship position: 19th   Wins: 0   Pole positions: 0   Fastest laps: 0   Points scored: 2

	Race	Circuit	No	Entrant	Tyres	Capacity/Car/Engine	Comment	Q Pos/Entries
app	AUSTRALIAN GP	Melbourne	39	Jordan Ford	B	3.0 Jordan EJ14-Cosworth V10	ran as 3rd driver in practice only	– /–
app	MALAYSIAN GP	Sepang	39	Jordan Ford	B	3.0 Jordan EJ14-Cosworth V10	ran as 3rd driver in practice only	– /–
app	BAHRAIN GP	Sakhir Circuit	39	Jordan Ford	B	3.0 Jordan EJ14-Cosworth V10	ran as 3rd driver in practice only	– /–
app	SAN MARINO GP	Imola	39	Jordan Ford	B	3.0 Jordan EJ14-Cosworth V10	ran as 3rd driver in practice only	– /–
app	SPANISH GP	Barcelona	39	Jordan Ford	B	3.0 Jordan EJ14-Cosworth V10	ran as 3rd driver in practice only	– /–
app	MONACO GP	Monte Carlo	39	Jordan Ford	B	3.0 Jordan EJ14-Cosworth V10	ran as 3rd driver in practice only	– /–
app	EUROPEAN GP	Nürburgring	39	Jordan Ford	B	3.0 Jordan EJ14-Cosworth V10	ran as 3rd driver in practice only	– /–
7*	CANADIAN GP	Montreal	19	Jordan Ford	B	3.0 Jordan EJ14-Cosworth V10	*2nd/5th/8th/10th cars dsq/-2 laps	16/20
app	U. S. GP	Indianapolis	39	Jordan Ford	B	3.0 Jordan EJ14-Cosworth V10	ran as 3rd driver in practice only	– /–
app	FRENCH GP	Magny Cours	39	Jordan Ford	B	3.0 Jordan EJ14-Cosworth V10	ran as 3rd driver in practice only	– /–
app	BRITISH GP	Silverstone	39	Jordan Ford	B	3.0 Jordan EJ14-Cosworth V10	ran as 3rd driver in practice only	– /–
app	GERMAN GP	Hockenheim	39	Jordan Ford	B	3.0 Jordan EJ14-Cosworth V10	ran as 3rd driver in practice only	– /–
app	HUNGARIAN GP	Hungaroring	39	Jordan Ford	B	3.0 Jordan EJ14-Cosworth V10	ran as 3rd driver in practice only	– /–
app	BELGIAN GP	Spa	39	Jordan Ford	B	3.0 Jordan EJ14-Cosworth V10	ran as 3rd driver in practice only	– /–
app	ITALIAN GP	Monza	39	Jordan Ford	B	3.0 Jordan EJ14-Cosworth V10	ran as 3rd driver in practice only	– /–
15	CHINESE GP	Shanghai Circuit	19	Jordan Ford	B	3.0 Jordan EJ14-Cosworth V10	tyre problems/two spins	17/20
15	JAPANESE GP	Suzuka	19	Jordan Ford	B	3.0 Jordan EJ14-Cosworth V10	2 laps behind	17/20
15	BRAZILIAN GP	São Paulo	19	Jordan Ford	B	3.0 Jordan EJ14-Cosworth V10	2 laps behind	18/20

2008 Championship position: 10th   Wins: 0   Pole positions: 0   Fastest laps: 0   Points scored: 25

	Race	Circuit	No	Entrant	Tyres	Capacity/Car/Engine	Comment	Q Pos/Entries
ret	AUSTRALIAN GP	Melbourne	12	Panasonic Toyota Racing	B	2.4 Toyota TF108-V8	accident	9/22
ret	MALAYSIAN GP	Sepang	12	Panasonic Toyota Racing	B	2.4 Toyota TF108-V8	accident	10/22
9	BAHRAIN GP	Sakhir Circuit	12	Panasonic Toyota Racing	B	2.4 Toyota TF108-V8		13/22
11	SPANISH GP	Barcelona	12	Panasonic Toyota Racing	B	2.4 Toyota TF108-V8	collision damage/1 lap behind	14/22
13	TURKISH GP	Istanbul	12	Panasonic Toyota Racing	B	2.4 Toyota TF108-V8		8/20
12	MONACO GP	Monte Carlo	12	Panasonic Toyota Racing	B	2.4 Toyota TF108-V8	collision damage/1 lap behind	8/20
4	CANADIAN GP	Montreal	12	Panasonic Toyota Racing	B	2.4 Toyota TF108-V8	one-stop strategy	11/20
11	FRENCH GP	Magny Cours	12	Panasonic Toyota Racing	B	2.4 Toyota TF108-V8	tyre graining and severe understeer	10/20
12	BRITISH GP	Silverstone	12	Panasonic Toyota Racing	B	2.4 Toyota TF108-V8	1 lap behind	12/20
ret	GERMAN GP	Hockenheim	12	Panasonic Toyota Racing	B	2.4 Toyota TF108-V8	rear suspension – big accident	11/20
2	HUNGARIAN GP	Hungaroring	12	Panasonic Toyota Racing	B	2.4 Toyota TF108-V8		5/20
7	EUROPEAN GP	Valencia	12	Panasonic Toyota Racing	B	2.4 Toyota TF108-V8	suffering with heavy cold	13/20
9	BELGIAN GP	Spa	12	Panasonic Toyota Racing	B	2.4 Toyota TF108-V8		13/20
11	ITALIAN GP	Monza	12	Panasonic Toyota Racing	B	2.4 Toyota TF108-V8	early spin	9/20
4	SINGAPORE GP	Marina Bay Circuit	12	Panasonic Toyota Racing	B	2.4 Toyota TF108-V8		8/20
ret	JAPANESE GP	Suzuka	12	Panasonic Toyota Racing	B	2.4 Toyota TF108-V8	rear suspension/broken seat mountings	8/20
7	CHINESE GP	Shanghai Circuit	12	Panasonic Toyota Racing	B	2.4 Toyota TF108-V8		13/20
6	BRAZILIAN GP	São Paulo	12	Panasonic Toyota Racing	B	2.4 Toyota TF108-V8		10/20

2009 Championship position: 10th   Wins: 0   Pole positions: 0   Fastest laps: 1   Points scored: 24

	Race	Circuit	No	Entrant	Tyres	Capacity/Car/Engine	Comment	Q Pos/Entries
4*	AUSTRALIAN GP	Melbourne	10	Panasonic Toyota Racing	B	2.4 Toyota TF109-V8	*4th place car dsq	6/20
3	MALAYSIAN GP	Sepang	10	Panasonic Toyota Racing	B	2.4 Toyota TF109-V8	rain-shortened race	5/20
7	CHINESE GP	Shanghai Circuit	10	Panasonic Toyota Racing	B	2.4 Toyota TF109-V8		14/20
7	BAHRAIN GP	Sakhir Circuit	10	Panasonic Toyota Racing	B	2.4 Toyota TF109-V8	trouble with medium tyres	2/20
10	SPANISH GP	Barcelona	10	Panasonic Toyota Racing	B	2.4 Toyota TF109-V8	1 lap behind	6/20
10	MONACO GP	Monte Carlo	10	Panasonic Toyota Racing	B	2.4 Toyota TF109-V8	started from pitlane/-1 lap	20/20
8	TURKISH GP	Istanbul	10	Panasonic Toyota Racing	B	2.4 Toyota TF109-V8		13/20
9	BRITISH GP	Silverstone	10	Panasonic Toyota Racing	B	2.4 Toyota TF109-V8		8/20
9	GERMAN GP	Nürburgring	10	Panasonic Toyota Racing	B	2.4 Toyota TF109-V8	one-stop strategy	19/20
6	HUNGARIAN GP	Hungaroring	10	Panasonic Toyota Racing	B	2.4 Toyota TF109-V8	excellent strategy	14/20
14	EUROPEAN GP	Valencia	10	Panasonic Toyota Racing	B	2.4 Toyota TF109-V8	collision – Buemi – damaged car/FL	13/20
10	BELGIAN GP	Spa	10	Panasonic Toyota Racing	B	2.4 Toyota TF109-V8		7/20
11	ITALIAN GP	Monza	10	Panasonic Toyota Racing	B	2.4 Toyota TF109-V8		16/20
2	SINGAPORE GP	Marina Bay Circuit	10	Panasonic Toyota Racing	B	2.4 Toyota TF109-V8		7/20
dns	JAPANESE GP	Suzuka	10	Panasonic Toyota Racing	B	2.4 Toyota TF109-V8	injured leg in practice crash	14/20

2010 Championship position: Unplaced

	Race	Circuit	No	Entrant	Tyres	Capacity/Car/Engine	Comment	Q Pos/Entries
ret	BAHRAIN GP	Sakhir Circuit	24	Virgin Racing	B	2.4 Virgin VR-01-Cosworth V8	gearbox	19/24
ret	AUSTRALIAN GP	Melbourne	24	Virgin Racing	B	2.4 Virgin VR-01-Cosworth V8	rear suspension	21/24
ret	MALAYSIAN GP	Sepang	24	Virgin Racing	B	2.4 Virgin VR-01-Cosworth V8	collision Trulli – accident damage	18/24
dns	CHINESE GP	Shanghai Circuit	24	Virgin Racing	B	2.4 Virgin VR-01-Cosworth V8	engine before start	22/24
18	SPANISH GP	Barcelona	24	Virgin Racing	B	2.4 Virgin VR-01-Cosworth V8	3 laps behind	21/24
ret	MONACO GP	Monte Carlo	24	Virgin Racing	B	2.4 Virgin VR-01-Cosworth V8	rear suspension	20/24
18	TURKISH GP	Istanbul Park	24	Virgin Racing	B	2.4 Virgin VR-01-Cosworth V8	3 laps behind	21/24
ret	CANADIAN GP	Montreal	24	Virgin Racing	B	2.4 Virgin VR-01-Cosworth V8	accident – steering	21/24
19*	EUROPEAN GP	Valencia	24	Virgin Racing	B	2.4 Virgin VR-01-Cosworth V8	*20-second post-race penalty/-2 laps	21/24
18	BRITISH GP	Silverstone	24	Virgin Racing	B	2.4 Virgin VR-01-Cosworth V8	2 laps behind	20/24
18	GERMAN GP	Hockenheim	24	Virgin Racing	B	2.4 Virgin VR-01-Cosworth V8	3 laps behind	20/24
16	HUNGARIAN GP	Hungaroring	24	Virgin Racing	B	2.4 Virgin VR-01-Cosworth V8	4 laps behind	19/24
18	BELGIAN GP	Spa	24	Virgin Racing	B	2.4 Virgin VR-01-Cosworth V8	1 lap behind	17/24
17	ITALIAN GP	Monza	25	Virgin Racing	B	2.4 Virgin VR-01-Cosworth V8	1 lap behind	22/24
ret	SINGAPORE GP	Marina Bay Circuit	25	Virgin Racing	B	2.4 Virgin VR-01-Cosworth V8	2 laps behind	20/24
dns	JAPANESE GP	Suzuka	25	Virgin Racing	B	2.4 Virgin VR-01-Cosworth V8	hydraulics	18/24
ret	KOREAN GP	Yeongam	25	Virgin Racing	B	2.4 Virgin VR-01-Cosworth V8	hit by Kovalainen – accident damage	20/24
20	BRAZILIAN GP	São Paulo	25	Virgin Racing	B	2.4 Virgin VR-01-Cosworth V8	2 laps behind	19/24
ret	ABU DHABI GP	Yas Marina Circuit	25	Virgin Racing	B	2.4 Virgin VR-01-Cosworth V8	gearbox	21/24

2011   Championship position: Unplaced

	Race	Circuit	No	Entrant	Tyres	Capacity/Car/Engine	Comment	Q Pos/Entries
nc	AUSTRALIAN GP	Melbourne	24	Marussia Virgin Racing	P	2.4 Virgin MVR-02-Cosworth V8	pit stop – repair to drive pegs/-9 laps	21/24

16	MALAYSIAN GP	Sepang	24	Marussia Virgin Racing	P	2.4 Virgin MVR-02-Cosworth V8	2 laps behind		21/24
21	CHINESE GP	Shanghai Circuit	24	Marussia Virgin Racing	P	2.4 Virgin MVR-02-Cosworth V8	2 laps behind		22/24
dns	TURKISH GP	Istanbul Park	24	Marussia Virgin Racing	P	2.4 Virgin MVR-02-Cosworth V8	gearbox		22/24
19	SPANISH GP	Barcelona	24	Marussia Virgin Racing	P	2.4 Virgin MVR-02-Cosworth V8	3 laps behind		20/24
ret	MONACO GP	Monte Carlo	24	Marussia Virgin Racing	P	2.4 Virgin MVR-02-Cosworth V8	rear suspension failure		21/24
15	CANADIAN GP	Montreal	24	Marussia Virgin Racing	P	2.4 Virgin MVR-02-Cosworth V8	1 lap behind		22/24
21	EUROPEAN GP	Valencia	24	Marussia Virgin Racing	P	2.4 Virgin MVR-02-Cosworth V8	2 laps behind		21/24
16	BRITISH GP	Silverstone	24	Marussia Virgin Racing	P	2.4 Virgin MVR-02-Cosworth V8	2 laps behind		20/24
17	GERMAN GP	Hockenheim	24	Marussia Virgin Racing	P	2.4 Virgin MVR-02-Cosworth V8	3 laps behind		20/24
17	HUNGARIAN GP	Hungaroring	24	Marussia Virgin Racing	P	2.4 Virgin MVR-02-Cosworth V8	4 laps behind		21/24
18	BELGIAN GP	Spa	24	Marussia Virgin Racing	P	2.4 Virgin MVR-02-Cosworth V8	drive – thru-hit di Resta/1 lap behind		20/24
15	ITALIAN GP	Monza	24	Marussia Virgin Racing	P	2.4 Virgin MVR-02-Cosworth V8	2 laps behind		21/24
ret	SINGAPORE GP	Marina Bay Circuit	24	Marussia Virgin Racing	P	2.4 Virgin MVR-02-Cosworth V8	spun off – suspension damage		21/24
20	JAPANESE GP	Suzuka	24	Marussia Virgin Racing	P	2.4 Virgin MVR-02-Cosworth V8	2 laps behind		21/24
18	KOREAN GP	Yeongam	24	Marussia Virgin Racing	P	2.4 Virgin MVR-02-Cosworth V8	1 lap behind		21/24
ret	INDIAN GP	Buddh Circuit	24	Marussia Virgin Racing	P	2.4 Virgin MVR-02-Cosworth V8	collsion damage – hit spinning car		24/24
19	ABU DHABI GP	Yas Marina Circuit	24	Marussia Virgin Racing	P	2.4 Virgin MVR-02-Cosworth V8	2 laps behind		20/24
ret	BRAZILIAN GP	São Paulo	24	Marussia Virgin Racing	P	2.4 Virgin MVR-02-Cosworth V8	lost rear wheel		24/24

GP Starts: 72   GP Wins: 0   Pole positions: 0   Fastest laps: 1   Points: 51

FRANCESCO GODIA SALES

ALSO known as Paco Godia, Francesco Godia Sales was a wealthy Spanish businessman who could afford to indulge his passion whenever he pleased. He made his grand prix debut in a Maserati 4CLT in the inaugural 1951 Spanish Grand Prix, although he only competed regularly between 1956 – when he became a member of the Maserati works team, on the understanding that his car could be taken if needed by a more senior driver – and 1958, when he entered the car himself after the factory's closure.

Not one to risk his neck unduly, Francesco gained placings in races of high attrition, as when he finished fourth in the German and Italian Grands Prix of 1956.

Perhaps the most fascinating feature of Francesco's long, but intermittent career – which spanned more than 20 years – was its variety: in 1949, he raced a vintage Delage to fourth place at Le Mans; on his second (and last) appearance at La Sarthe in 1958, he shared Jo Bonnier's Maserati 300S; and by the time his racing days were drawing to a close, in 1969, he was handling machines such as the Ford GT40 and Porsche 908 Spyder.

GODIA SALES, Francesco (E) b 21/3/1921, Barcelona – d 28/11/1990, Barcelona

1951 Championship position: Unplaced

	Race	Circuit	No	Entrant	Tyres	Capacity/Car/Engine	Comment	Q Pos/Entries
10	SPANISH GP	Pedralbes	44	Scuderia Milano	P	1.5 s/c Maserati 4CLT/48 4	10 laps behind	17/20

1954 Championship position: Unplaced

	Race	Circuit	No	Entrant	Tyres	Capacity/Car/Engine	Comment	Q Pos/Entries
6	SPANISH GP	Pedralbes	16	Officine Alfieri Maserati	P	2.5 Maserati 250F 6	4 laps behind	13/22

1956 Championship position: 6th=   Wins: 0   Pole positions: 0   Fastest laps: 0   Points scored: 6

ret	BELGIAN GP	Spa	36	Officine Alfieri Maserati	P	2.5 Maserati 250F 6	crashed	14/16
7	FRENCH GP	Reims	40	Officine Alfieri Maserati	P	2.5 Maserati 250F 6	4 laps behind	17/20
8	BRITISH GP	Silverstone	10	Officine Alfieri Maserati	P	2.5 Maserati 250F 6	7 laps behind	25/28
4	GERMAN GP	Nürburgring	20	Officine Alfieri Maserati	P	2.5 Maserati 250F 6	2 laps behind	16/21
4	ITALIAN GP	Monza	38	Officine Alfieri Maserati	P	2.5 Maserati 250F 6	1 lap behind	18/26

1957 Championship position: Unplaced

ret	GERMAN GP	Nürburgring	18	Francesco Godia-Sales	P	2.5 Maserati 250F 6	steering	21/24
ret	PESCARA GP	Pescara	10	Francesco Godia-Sales	P	2.5 Maserati 250F 6	engine	12/16
9	ITALIAN GP	Monza	10	Francesco Godia-Sales	P	2.5 Maserati 250F 6	6 laps behind	15/19

1958 Championship position: Unplaced

8	ARGENTINE GP	Buenos Aires	10	Francesco Godia-Sales	P	2.5 Maserati 250F 6	5 laps behind	9/10
dnq	MONACO GP	Monte Carlo	4	Francesco Godia-Sales	P	2.5 Maserati 250F 6		18/28
ret	BELGIAN GP	Spa	38	Francesco Godia-Sales	P	2.5 Maserati 250F 6	engine	18/20
ret	FRENCH GP	Reims	40	Francesco Godia-Sales	P	2.5 Maserati 250F 6	*Fangio set qualifying time/crashed	*11/21

GP Starts: 13   GP Wins: 0   Pole positions: 0   Fastest laps: 0   Points: 6

GOETHALS, Christian (B) b 4/8/1928, Heule, Kortrijk – d 26/2/2003, Kortrijk

1958 Championship position: Unplaced

	Race	Circuit	No	Entrant	Tyres	Capacity/Car/Engine	Comment	Q Pos/Entries
ret	GERMAN GP (F2)	Nürburgring	27	Ecurie Eperon d'Or	D	1.5 Cooper T43-Climax 4	fuel pump	24/26

GP Starts: 1   GP Wins: 0   Pole positions: 0   Fastest laps: 0   Points: 0

CHRISTIAN GOETHALS

AN amateur Belgian driver, Christian Goethals raced a Porsche Spyder in minor Continental events from the mid-1950s. With his brother, he took second place at Reims in 1956 in the up-to-1500cc sports car race and won the same class at Forez the following year.

Goethals acquired an F2 Cooper for 1958, but gained little success and soon returned to a Porsche RSK. In 1960, he finished fifth in the Buenos Aires 1000km and second in the GP de Spa, but after he crashed out of the Angola GP in Luanda later in the season, no more was seen of him and his Porsche on the circuits.

JOSÉ FROILAN GONZÁLEZ

THE press invariably tagged José Froilán González 'the Bull of the Pampas', and the name perfectly described the vast bulk of this unlikely-looking racing driver. However, he was called Pepe by his friends, who knew him as a kind-hearted, good-natured soul, despite his sometimes fearsome façade.

A surprisingly keen sportsman for one of his physique, González was a fair soccer player, swimmer and cyclist before he was old enough to begin a competition career racing motorcycles and then production cars. He caught the eye in 1949 at the wheel of a Maserati four-cylinder found for him by Juan Fangio and joined his compatriot in Europe in 1950, driving a Maserati without luck in the championship races, but taking a second place in the Albi GP.

González's breakthrough came in 1951, when he defeated the visiting Mercedes-Benz team in both the Libre races at Buenos Aires in a Ferrari 166, and he began his proper grand prix career as a works driver for Ferrari. His style, hunched over the wheel, hard on the throttle, sliding the car to the limits of the track – and beyond on many occasions – was far from pretty, but no one could argue with his speed, and he soon gained immortality by defeating the works Alfa Romeos in the 1951 British GP, becoming the first driver to win a world championship grand prix for the Scuderia.

José won the non-title Pescara GP before signing for Maserati for 1952, a season that saw him race in only one grand prix, although he also handled the brutish BRM V16, winning the Goodwood Trophy, and Vandervell's Thinwall Ferrari, in which he took the Richmond Trophy. He continued with Maserati as Fangio's teammate in 1953, but was in the shadow of his great friend and rival, before a crash in practice for a sports car race at Lisbon sidelined him for three months with a fractured vertebra.

Signed by Ferrari for 1954, González enjoyed his finest season, taking his 625 to another glorious win for the team over the, for once, hapless Mercedes, as well as claiming wins in the non-title International Trophy, and Bari and Bordeaux GPs. His year also saw four wins in sports cars, including Le Mans, where he shared the winning Ferrari with Maurice Trintignant, before a practice crash in the Tourist Trophy left him with an injured arm.

González returned home to Argentina and, apart from a visit to his beloved Silverstone to race the Vanwall in 1956, which ended with driveshaft failure at the start, mainly restricted his racing to home territory. His guest appearances in his home grands prix showed there was still considerable fire in his belly, and he duelled with Ascari's Lancia for the lead in 1955, before finishing second. After the 1957 race, however, he was content just to take part in his Chevrolet-engined Ferrari, turning his attention more to his motor business.

GONZÁLEZ, José Froilan (RA) b 5/10/1922, Arrecifes

1950 Championship position: Unplaced

	Race	Circuit	No	Entrant	Tyres	Capacity/Car/Engine	Comment	Q Pos/Entries
ret	MONACO GP	Monte Carlo	2	Scuderia Achille Varzi	P	1.5 s/c Maserati 4CLT/50 4	multiple accident/car on fire	3/21
ret	FRENCH GP	Reims	36	Scuderia Achille Varzi	P	1.5 s/c Maserati 4CLT/50 4	engine	8/20

1951 Championship position: 3rd   Wins: 1   Pole positions: 1   Fastest laps: 0   Points scored: 27

	Race	Circuit	No	Entrant	Tyres	Capacity/Car/Engine	Comment	Q Pos/Entries
ret	SWISS GP	Bremgarten	42	José Froilan González	D	4.5 Lago-Talbot T26-GS 6	oil pump	13/21
2*	FRENCH GP	Reims	14	Scuderia Ferrari	E	4.5 Ferrari 375 V12	*Ascari took over car	6/23
1	BRITISH GP	Silverstone	12	Scuderia Ferrari	P	4.5 Ferrari 375 V12		1/20
3	GERMAN GP	Nürburgring	74	Scuderia Ferrari	P	4.5 Ferrari 375 V12		2/23
2	ITALIAN GP	Monza	6	Scuderia Ferrari	P	4.5 Ferrari 375 V12		4/22
2	SPANISH GP	Pedralbes	6	Scuderia Ferrari	P	4.5 Ferrari 375 V12		3/20

1952 Championship position: 8th   Wins: 0   Pole positions: 0   Fastest laps: 1 (shared)   Points scored: 6.5

	Race	Circuit	No	Entrant	Tyres	Capacity/Car/Engine	Comment	Q Pos/Entries
2	ITALIAN GP	Monza	26	Officine Alfieri Maserati	P	2.0 Maserati A6GCM 6	FL (shared with Ascari)	5/35

1953 Championship position: 0   Wins: 0   Pole positions: 0   Fastest laps: 2 (1 shared)   Points scored: 14.5

	Race	Circuit	No	Entrant	Tyres	Capacity/Car/Engine	Comment	Q Pos/Entries
3	ARGENTINE GP	Buenos Aires	4	Officine Alfieri Maserati	P	2.0 Maserati A6GCM 6	1 lap behind	5/16
ret	DUTCH GP	Zandvoort	14	Officine Alfieri Maserati	P	2.0 Maserati A6GCM 6	rear axle	5/20
3*	"	"	16	Officine Alfieri Maserati	P	2.0 Maserati A6GCM 6	*took Bonetto's car/1 lap behind	– / –
ret	BELGIAN GP	Spa	2	Officine Alfieri Maserati	P	2.0 Maserati A6GCM 6	throttle/FL	3/22
3	FRENCH GP	Reims	20	Officine Alfieri Maserati	P	2.0 Maserati A6GCM 6		5/25
4	BRITISH GP	Silverstone	24	Officine Alfieri Maserati	P	2.0 Maserati A6GCM 6	FL (shared)/oil leak/2 laps behind	2/29

1954 Championship position: 2nd   Wins: 1   Pole positions: 1   Fastest laps: 3 (1 shared)   Points scored: 26.64

	Race	Circuit	No	Entrant	Tyres	Capacity/Car/Engine	Comment	Q Pos/Entries
3	ARGENTINE GP	Buenos Aires	12	Scuderia Ferrari	P	2.5 Ferrari 625 4	FL	2/18
ret	BELGIAN GP	Spa	6	Scuderia Ferrari	P	2.5 Ferrari 553/555 4	engine – oil pipe	2/15
4*	"	"	10	Scuderia Ferrari	P	2.5 Ferrari 625 4	*took Hawthorn's car/1 lap behind	– / –
ret	FRENCH GP	Reims	2	Scuderia Ferrari	P	2.5 Ferrari 553/555 4	engine	4/22
1	BRITISH GP	Silverstone	9	Scuderia Ferrari	P	2.5 Ferrari 625 4	FL (shared)	2/31
2*	GERMAN GP	Nürburgring	1	Scuderia Ferrari	P	2.5 Ferrari 625 4	*Hawthorn took over car	5/23
2	SWISS GP	Bremgarten	20	Scuderia Ferrari	P	2.5 Ferrari 625 4		1/16
ret	ITALIAN GP	Monza	32	Scuderia Ferrari	P	2.5 Ferrari 553 4	gearbox/FL	5/21
3*	"	"	38	Scuderia Ferrari	P	2.5 Ferrari 625 4	*shared Maglioli's car/2 laps behind	– / –

1955 Championship position: 12=   Wins: 0   Pole positions: 1   Fastest laps: 0   Points scored: 2

	Race	Circuit	No	Entrant	Tyres	Capacity/Car/Engine	Comment	Q Pos/Entries
2*	ARGENTINE GP	Buenos Aires	12	Scuderia Ferrari	E	2.5 Ferrari 625 4	*Farina/Trintignant also drove car	1/22

1956 Championship position: Unplaced

	Race	Circuit	No	Entrant	Tyres	Capacity/Car/Engine	Comment	Q Pos/Entries
ret	ARGENTINE GP	Buenos Aires	12	Officine Alfieri Maserati	P	2.5 Maserati 250F 6	valve	5/15
ret	BRITISH GP	Silverstone	18	Vandervell Products Ltd	P	2.5 Vanwall 4	driveshaft on grid	6/28

1957 Championship position: 14th=   Wins: 0   Pole positions: 0   Fastest laps: 0   Points scored: 1

	Race	Circuit	No	Entrant	Tyres	Capacity/Car/Engine	Comment	Q Pos/Entries
5*	ARGENTINE GP	Buenos Aires	20	Scuderia Ferrari	E	2.5 Lancia-Ferrari 801 V8	*shared with de Portago/-2 laps	10/16

1960 Championship position: Unplaced

	Race	Circuit	No	Entrant	Tyres	Capacity/Car/Engine	Comment	Q Pos/Entries
10	ARGENTINE GP	Buenos Aires	32	Scuderia Ferrari	D	2.4 Ferrari-Dino 246 V6	3 laps behind	11/22

GP Starts: 26   GP Wins: 2   Pole positions: 3   Fastest laps: 6   Points: 77.64

History in the making as González in his Ferrari T375 F1 defeats the Alfas to win the 1951 British Grand Prix at Silverstone. At the end of that season, Alfa Romeo withdrew and Ferrari became the team to beat in 1952.

OSCAR GONZÁLEZ

THE less-well-known González, Oscar, joined his Uruguayan compatriot, Alberto Uria, to share the latter's Maserati in the 1956 Argentine Grand Prix. After taking over the car, he circulated steadily around the circuit. By all accounts, he displayed impeccable track manners and did not interfere with the leaders as he was lapped with great regularity.

ALDO GORDINI

THE son of 'Le Sorcier', Aldo Gordini's name and Latin looks betrayed his Italian heritage, for father Amédée (born Amedeo) Gordini had settled in France after the First World War.

As the young Gordini grew up, not surprisingly, he became imbued with the racing activities of his father, who competed in the inter-war years and then began to build his own machines. However, the Second World War not only put paid to sporting competition once again, but also destroyed the Gordini factory.

So it was 1946 before Aldo went to work as a mechanic as Gordini reconstructed his team. The youngster had the urge to race and was allowed occasional outings, taking class honours in the Coupe du Salon at Montlhéry in both 1948 and 1949.

In 1950, Aldo drove the Type 11 car in selected Formula 2 races, taking second place at Cadours and fifth at Aix-les-Bains, and sharing fifth with Maurice Trintignant at Roubaix. The following year, which was his last as a racer, he drove in his only championship event at Reims, and once again took fifth place at Aix-les Bains.

HORACE GOULD

IN a period when fat Italians regularly occupied the cockpits of Formula 1 cars, to Horace Gould it seemed quite reasonable that a fat Bristolian should do the same. After all, he had spent a couple of seasons competing in a Cooper-Bristol – albeit usually in second-division races, with the notable exception of the 1954 British GP. So for 1955, he took himself off to Modena and bought a Maserati 250F, living a hand-to-mouth existence and scrounging parts from the factory to keep his machine on the grid.

Horace enjoyed a nomadic three seasons on the Continent, taking part in selected grands prix (his best result was fifth at Silverstone in 1956) and cannily entering his 'Maser' in non-championship races where starting money was good and the chances of decent placings were high. He finished third at Albi and fourth at Syracuse in 1955, second at Naples in 1956 and fourth, behind the three works Ferraris of Mike Hawthorn, Peter Collins and Luigi Musso, in the same race in 1957. Once the factory withdrew, it was really the end for Gould, who could no longer gain the assistance he needed to keep running the car. His last hurrah was a fourth place at Syracuse in 1958, although he was tempted back just one more time – to the boycotted 1960 Italian GP – where the old Maserati failed even to turn a wheel in practice due to crossed fuel lines. Horace, who later helped his son in his racing activities, died of a sudden heart attack in 1968.

GONZÁLEZ, Oscar (U) b 7/11/1923, Montevideo – d 24/2/1999, Montevideo

1956 Championship position: Unplaced								
	Race	Circuit	No	Entrant	Tyres	Capacity/Car/Engine	Comment	Q Pos/Entries
6*	ARGENTINE GP	Buenos Aires	16	Alberto Uria	–	2.5 Maserati A6GCM 6	*shared with Uria/10 laps behind	-/15
GP Starts: 1 GP Wins: 0 Pole positions: 0 Fastest laps: 0 Points: 0								

GORDINI, Aldo (F) b 20/5/1921, Bologna, Italy – d 28/1/1995, Paris

1951 Championship position: Unplaced								
	Race	Circuit	No	Entrant	Tyres	Capacity/Car/Engine	Comment	Q Pos/Entries
ret	FRENCH GP	Reims	36	Equipe Gordini	E	1.5 s/c Gordini Type 15 4	valve gear	17/23
GP Starts: 1 GP Wins: 0 Pole positions: 0 Fastest laps: 0 Points: 0								

GOULD, Horace (GB) b 20/9/1921, Southmead, Bristol – d 4/11/1968, Southmead, Bristol

1954 Championship position: Unplaced								
	Race	Circuit	No	Entrant	Tyres	Capacity/Car/Engine	Comment	Q Pos/Entries
nc	BRITISH GP	Silverstone	28	Goulds' Garage (Bristol)	D	2.0 Cooper T23-Bristol 6	pit stops/46 laps behind	20/31
1955 Championship position: Unplaced								
ret	DUTCH GP	Zandvoort	32	Goulds' Garage (Bristol)	D	2.5 Maserati 250F 6	crashed	15/16

ret	BRITISH GP	Aintree	48	Goulds' Garage (Bristol)	D	2.5 Maserati 250F 6	brakes	22/25
ret	ITALIAN GP	Monza	38	Officine Alfieri Maserati	D	2.5 Maserati 250F 6	suspension	21/22

1956 Championship position: 15th=   Wins: 0   Pole positions: 0   Fastest laps: 0   Points scored: 2

8	MONACO GP	Monte Carlo	18	Goulds' Garage (Bristol)	D	2.5 Maserati 250F 6	15 laps behind	18/19
ret	BELGIAN GP	Spa	26	Goulds' Garage (Bristol)	D	2.5 Maserati 250F 6	gearbox	15/16
5	BRITISH GP	Silverstone	31	Goulds' Garage (Bristol)	D	2.5 Maserati 250F 6	4 laps behind	14/28
ret	GERMAN GP	Nürburgring	19	Goulds' Garage (Bristol)	D	2.5 Maserati 250F 6	oil pressure	13/21

1957 Championship position: Unplaced

ret	MONACO GP	Monte Carlo	22	H H Gould	D	2.5 Maserati 250F 6	crashed	12/21
ret	FRENCH GP	Rouen	30	H H Gould	D	2.5 Maserati 250F 6	rear axle	14/15
dns	BRITISH GP	Aintree	30	H H Gould	D	2.5 Maserati 250F 6	injured in practice accident	(15)/19
ret	GERMAN GP	Nürburgring	19	H H Gould	D	2.5 Maserati 250F 6	rear axle	19/24
ret	PESCARA GP	Pescara	18	H H Gould	D	2.5 Maserati 250F 6	crashed	11/16
10	ITALIAN GP	Monza	14	H H Gould	D	2.5 Maserati 250F 6	9 laps behind	18/19

1958 Championship position: Unplaced

9	ARGENTINE GP	Buenos Aires	12	H H Gould	D	2.5 Maserati 250F 6	9 laps behind	10/10
dnq	MONACO GP	Monte Carlo	42	Scuderia Centro Sud	D	2.5 Maserati 250F 6	loan car	27/28
dns	DUTCH GP	Zandvoort	12	H H Gould	D	2.5 Maserati 250F 6	Gregory drove car in race	– / –

1960 Championship position: Unplaced

dns	ITALIAN GP	Monza	14	H H Gould	D	2.5 Maserati 250F 6	crossed fuel lines in ractice	– / –

GP Starts: 14   GP Wins: 0   Pole positions: 0   Fastest laps: 0   Points: 2

JEAN-MARC GOUNON

AFTER making an excellent debut to finish fourth overall in the 1988 French F3 championship, Jean-Marc Gounon convincingly took the title a year later in the ORECA Reynard. Then he became a stalwart of the F3000 scene from 1990 to 1992, making the best of things when he was in the right team, but perhaps the wrong chassis (a Ralt in 1991 and a Lola in 1992). He proved he was capable of being blindingly quick when circumstances allowed, and his wins at Pau and Vallelunga were just reward for his efforts.

At the end of 1993, at the relatively late age of 30, this amiable Frenchman finally realised his ambition of racing a Formula 1 car, having bought a ride for the year's last two races after waiting patiently for the opportunity, following the March team's collapse before the start of the season.

Although Gounon had hoped that his two drives for Minardi would lead to a full grand prix season in 1994, he was forced to bide his time by racing a BMW 318 in the French Supertourisme series, finishing a creditable fifth in the points standings. His chance to return to the grand prix stage came with Simtek, when he filled the seat tragically vacated by Roland Ratzenberger, and then by Andrea Montermini, who had crashed on his debut in Spain. Never able to do better than qualify on the last row of the grid, Jean-Marc nevertheless plugged away with great enthusiasm, his ninth place on his debut in France actually being the team's best result all year. However, when his sponsorship money eventually ran out, he was replaced by Mimmo Schiattarella.

Gounon then forged a rewarding career in sports car racing, excellent performances in 1996 with a Ferrari and the following season in a McLaren F1 GTR (second overall and a class winner at Le Mans) leading to a seat in the semi-works Persson Motorsport Mercedes CLK. In 1999, he raced a DAMS Lola and, paired with Éric Bernard or Christophe Tinseau, scored wins at Donington, Brno, the Nürburgring and Kyalami. Subsequently Gounon was active in the FIA GT championship through to the end of the 2007 season, the highlight of which was winning the Lamborghini GTR Super trophy in 2002.

GOUNON, Jean-Marc (F) b 1/1/1963, Aubenas

1993 Championship position: Unplaced

	Race	Circuit	No	Entrant	Tyres	Capacity/Car/Engine	Comment	Q Pos/Entries
ret	JAPANESE GP	Suzuka	23	Minardi Team	G	3.5 Minardi M193-Ford HB V8	collision – later called in by team	24/24
ret	AUSTRALIAN GP	Adelaide	23	Minardi Team	G	3.5 Minardi M193-Ford HB V8	spun off	22/24

1994 Championship position: Unplaced

9	FRENCH GP	Magny Cours	32	MTV Simtek Ford	G	3.5 Simtek S941-Ford HB V8	4 laps behind	26/28
16*	BRITISH GP	Silverstone	32	MTV Simtek Ford	G	3.5 Simtek S941-Ford HB V8	*2nd car disqualified/-3 laps	26/28
ret	GERMAN GP	Hockenheim	32	MTV Simtek Ford	G	3.5 Simtek S941-Ford HB V8	gearbox	26/28

	Race	Circuit	No	Entrant	Tyres	Capacity/Car/Engine	Comment	Q Pos/Entries
ret	HUNGARIAN GP	Hungaroroing	32	MTV Simtek Ford	G	3.5 Simtek S941-Ford HB V8	handling	26/28
11*	BELGIAN GP	Spa	32	MTV Simtek Ford	G	3.5 Simtek S941-Ford HB V8	*1st place car disqualified/-2 laps	25/28
ret	ITALIAN GP	Monza	32	MTV Simtek Ford	G	3.5 Simtek S941-Ford HB V8	transmission	25/28
15	PORTUGUESE GP	Estoril	32	MTV Simtek Ford	G	3.5 Simtek S941-Ford HB V8	4 laps behind	26/28

GP Starts: 9   GP Wins: 0   Pole positions: 0   Fastest laps: 0   Points: 0

GREENE, Keith (GB) b 5/1/1938, Leytonstone, London

1959 Championship position: Unplaced

	Race	Circuit	No	Entrant	Tyres	Capacity/Car/Engine	Comment	Q Pos/Entries
dnq	BRITISH GP	Aintree	54	Gilby Engineering Co Ltd	D	2.5 Cooper T45-Climax 4 F2		– /30

1960 Championship position: Unplaced

ret	BRITISH GP	Silverstone	22	Gilby Engineering Co Ltd	D	2.5 Cooper T45-Maserati 4	overheating	22/25

1961 Championship position: Unplaced

15	BRITISH GP	Aintree	54	Gilby Engineering Co Ltd	D	1.5 Gilby-Climax 4	6 laps behind	23/30

1962 Championship position: Unplaced

dns	BRITISH GP	Aintree	48	John Dalton	D	1.5 Lotus 18/21-Climax 4	practiced only - tried Shelly's car	– / –
ret	GERMAN GP	Nürburgring	27	Gilby Engineering Co Ltd	D	1.5 Gilby-BRM V8	front suspension	19/30
dnq	ITALIAN GP	Monza	56	Gilby Engineering Co Ltd	D	1.5 Gilby-BRM V8		23/30

GP Starts: 3   GP Wins: 0   Pole positions: 0   Fastest laps: 0   Points: 0

KEITH GREENE

GROWING up in the environment of his father Syd's Gilby Engineering concern, it was natural for young Keith Greene to want to try his hand. Entered by his father in handicaps and similar events soon after his 18th birthday, he soon got to grips with a Cooper-Climax sports car, replacing this with a Lotus XI for the 1958 season.

In 1959, Greene began his single-seater career, taking a splendid second place in the F2 Aintree 200. He continued with the Cooper until the 1961 season, when Gilby ambitiously built their own chassis for the 1.5-litre formula. It found no success at the very highest level, but did gain modest placings when fitted with a BRM V8 engine in 1962, Keith taking the car to third place in the Naples GP, behind the works Ferraris of Willy Mairesse and Lorenzo Bandini, and a trio of fourths at Brussels, Snetterton and Goodwood.

When the Formula 1 project was abandoned, Keith turned to sports and GT racing for the rest of the 1960s, before taking on management roles with a whole roster of teams through the 1970s and right into the 1990s.

GREGORY, Masten (USA) b 29/2/1932, Kansas City, Missouri – d 8/11/1985, Porto Ecole, nr Rome, Italy

1957 Championship position: 6th   Wins: 0   Pole positions: 0   Fastest laps: 0   Points scored: 10

	Race	Circuit	No	Entrant	Tyres	Capacity/Car/Engine	Comment	Q Pos/Entries
3	MONACO GP	Monte Carlo	2	Scuderia Centro Sud	P	2.5 Maserati 250F 6	2 laps behind	10/21
8	GERMAN GP	Nürburgring	16	Scuderia Centro Sud	P	2.5 Maserati 250F 6	1 lap behind	10/24
4	PESCARA GP	Pescara	14	Scuderia Centro Sud	P	2.5 Maserati 250F 6		7/16
4	ITALIAN GP	Monza	26	Scuderia Centro Sud	P	2.5 Maserati 250F 6	3 laps behind	11/19

1958 Championship position: Unplaced

ret	DUTCH GP	Zandvoort	12	H H Gould	D	2.5 Maserati 250F 6	fuel pump	14/17
ret	BELGIAN GP	Spa	30	Scuderia Centro Sud	D	2.5 Maserati 250F 6	engine	9/20
4*	ITALIAN GP	Monza	32	Temple Buell	D	2.5 Maserati 250F 6	Shelby co-drove car – no points allowed	11/21
6	MOROCCAN GP	Casablanca	22	Temple Buell	D	2.5 Maserati 250F 6	1 lap behind	13/25

1959 Championship position: 8th=   Wins: 0   Pole positions: 0   Fastest laps: 0   Points scored: 10

ret	MONACO GP	Monte Carlo	26	Cooper Car Co	D	2.5 Cooper T51-Climax 4	gearbox	11/24
3	DUTCH GP	Zandvoort	9	Cooper Car Co	D	2.5 Cooper T51-Climax 4		7/15
ret	FRENCH GP	Reims	10	Cooper Car Co	D	2.5 Cooper T51-Climax 4	exhaustion	7/22
7	BRITISH GP	Aintree	14	Cooper Car Co	D	2.5 Cooper T51-Climax 4	overheating/2 laps behind	5/30
ret	GERMAN GP	AVUS	3	Cooper Car Co	D	2.5 Cooper T51-Climax 4	engine in heat 1	5/16
2	PORTUGUESE GP	Monsanto	2	Cooper Car Co	D	2.5 Cooper T51-Climax 4	1 lap behind	3/16

1960 Championship position: Unplaced

12	ARGENTINE GP	Buenos Aires	2	Camoradi International	D	1.5 Behra-Porsche F4	4 laps behind	16/22
dnq	MONACO GP	Monte Carlo	40	Scuderia Centro Sud	D	2.5 Cooper T51-Maserati 4		20/24
dns	DUTCH GP	Zandvoort	19	Scuderia Centro Sud	D	2.5 Cooper T51-Maserati 4	starting money dispute	(16)/21
9	FRENCH GP	Reims	40	Scuderia Centro Sud	D	2.5 Cooper T51-Maserati 4	pit stop/13 laps behind	17/23
14	BRITISH GP	Silverstone	16	Scuderia Centro Sud	D	2.5 Cooper T51-Maserati 4	6 laps behind	14/25
ret	PORTUGUESE GP	Oporto	30	Scuderia Centro Sud	D	2.5 Cooper T51-Maserati 4	gearbox	11/16

1961 Championship position: Unplaced

dnq	MONACO GP	Monte Carlo	14	Camoradi International	D	1.5 Cooper T53-Climax 4			18/21
dnq	DUTCH GP	Zandvoort	17	Camoradi International	D	1.5 Cooper T53-Climax 4	'qualified' – but only on reserve list		(10)/17
10	BELGIAN GP	Spa	44	Camoradi International	D	1.5 Cooper T53-Climax 4	1 lap behind		12/25
12	FRENCH GP	Reims	36	Camoradi International	D	1.5 Cooper T53-Climax 4	pit stop/9 laps behind		16/26
11	BRITISH GP	Aintree	42	Camoradi International	D	1.5 Cooper T53-Climax 4	4 laps behind		16/30
ret	ITALIAN GP	Monza	22	UDT Laystall Racing Team	D	1.5 Lotus 18/21-Climax 4	rear suspension		=17/33
ret	US GP	Watkins Glen	22	UDT Laystall Racing Team	D	1.5 Lotus 18/21-Climax 4	gear selection		11/19
11*	"	" "	21	UDT Laystall Racing Team	D	1.5 Lotus 18/21-Climax 4	*took Gendebien's car/8 laps behind		– / –

1962 Championship position: 18th   Wins: 0   Pole positions: 0   Fastest laps: 0   Points scored: 1

ret	DUTCH GP	Zandvoort	10	UDT Laystall Racing Team	D	1.5 Lotus 18/21-Climax 4	driveshaft		16/20
dnq	MONACO GP	Monte Carlo	32	UDT Laystall Racing Team	D	1.5 Lotus 24-BRM V8	faster than 3 other starters		16/21
ret	BELGIAN GP	Spa	21	UDT Laystall Racing Team	D	1.5 Lotus 24-BRM V8	withdrawn after Ireland's accident		7/20
dns	"	"	20	UDT Laystall Racing Team	D	1.5 Lotus 24-Climax V8	practised in Ireland's car		– / –
ret	FRENCH GP	Rouen	34	UDT Laystall Racing Team	D	1.5 Lotus 24-Climax V8	ignition		7/17
7	BRITISH GP	Aintree	34	UDT Laystall Racing Team	D	1.5 Lotus 24-Climax V8	1 lap behind		14/21
12	ITALIAN GP	Monza	38	UDT Laystall Racing Team	D	1.5 Lotus 24-BRM V8	overheating & gearbox stops/-9 laps		6/30
6	US GP	Watkins Glen	16	UDT Laystall Racing Team	D	1.5 Lotus 24-BRM V8	1 lap behind		7/20

1963 Championship position: Unplaced

ret	FRENCH GP	Reims	48	Tim Parnell	D	1.5 Lotus 24-BRM V8	gearbox housing		19/21
11	BRITISH GP	Silverstone	21	Reg Parnell (Racing)	D	1.5 Lotus 24-BRM V8	7 laps behind		22/23
ret	ITALIAN GP	Monza	42	Tim Parnell	D	1.5 Lotus 24-BRM V8	engine		12/28
ret	US GP	Watkins Glen	17	Reg Parnell (Racing)	D	1.5 Lola Mk 4A-Climax V8	engine		=7/21
ret	MEXICAN GP	Mexico City	17	Reg Parnell (Racing)	D	1.5 Lola Mk 4A-Climax V8	radius arm bolt		14/21

1965 Championship position: Unplaced

ret	BELGIAN GP	Spa	29	Scuderia Centro Sud	D	1.5 BRM P57 V8	fuel pump		20/21
12	BRITISH GP	Silverstone	12	Scuderia Centro Sud	D	1.5 BRM P57 V8	pit stop/10 laps behind		19/23
8	GERMAN GP	Nürburgring	24	Scuderia Centro Sud	D	1.5 BRM P57 V8	1 lap behind		19/22
ret	ITALIAN GP	Monza	48	Scuderia Centro Sud	D	1.5 BRM P57 V8	gearbox		23/23

GP Starts: 38   GP Wins: 0   Pole positions: 0   Fastest laps: 0   Points: 21

MASTEN GREGORY

ALTHOUGH his father died when he was very young, Masten Gregory was born into a wealthy Kansas family and, much later, when his mother sold the family business, came into a great deal of money, some of which he immediately invested in some potent sports cars to further his fledgling racing career.

In the early days, he was 'hairy', but very fast, particularly when he received his Allard J2X and then the even more powerful C-Type Jaguar. His US exploits in this car led to an offer to drive in the 1954 Buenos Aires 1000km, and although his outing ended in retirement, the trip was still worthwhile, for he purchased the race-winning 4.5-litre Ferrari, which then he shipped to Europe.

In his first race, paired with the veteran Clemente Biondetti, Gregory finished fourth in the Reims 12-hours. The season turned out to be fruitful, with third place in the Portuguese GP, second in class at the Tourist Trophy and a win in the Nassau Trophy. More success followed over the next two seasons, before he took the plunge into grand prix racing with Scuderia Centro Sud in 1957. Having already shared the winning works Ferrari in the Argentine 1000km, he took a brilliant third place on his grand pPrix debut at Monaco, and later scored points at both Monza and Pescara. He stayed with the Maserati for 1958, but the car was past its best.

Next Masten negotiated a works drive with Cooper as number three to Jack Brabham and Bruce McLaren for 1959, and despite his position in the team, he gave some excellent performances, finishing third at Zandvoort and second at Monsanto, as well as producing a great drive at AVUS. However, after baling out of his Tojeiro-Jaguar in the Tourist Trophy at Goodwood when the steering failed, he sustained rib and shoulder injuries, which caused him to miss the season's remaining grands prix, and he found his services were not retained by Cooper for 1960. He was irked at this, to say the least, and returned to Scuderia Centro Sud to race their rather uncompetitive Maserati-engined Coopers, inevitably enjoying little success.

In 1961, Masten became involved with the American Camoradi outfit, running a Cooper in F1 and a Maserati in sports car racing. He won the Nürburgring 1000km in the 'Birdcage' Maserati with Lucky Casner, but in mid-season moved over to the UDT-Laystall team to race the more competitive Lotus 18. He continued with the team in 1962, partnered by Innes Ireland, and gained a victory in the minor Kanonloppet F1 race at Karlskoga in the Lotus, and a win in the Player's 200 at Mosport with a Lotus 19 sports car, but achieved little else.

The next few seasons saw Masten's grand prix career draw to a close with less and less competitive machinery, but there were compensations, including an unexpected triumph at Le Mans with Jochen Rindt in the NART Ferrari, which suddenly opened up a whole new career back in sports cars. Over the next five years (1966–71), he raced Ford GT40s, Ferrari P3s, Porsche 910s, Lola T70s and Alfa Romeo T33s among others before retiring after the 1972 Le Mans 24-hours. A chain-smoker, Masten died suddenly after a heart attack in 1985, aged just 53.

GEORGES GRIGNARD

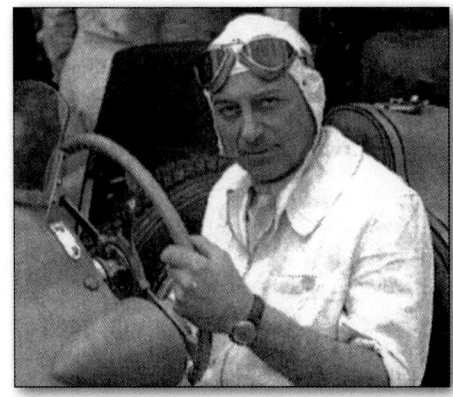

HAVING begun his career in rallying in the 1920s – he took part in the Monte Carlo Rallies of 1928 and '29 – George Grignard raced intermittently during the following decade while building up his garage business. After the Second World War, he reappeared in a Delahaye, which he raced for much of 1946. Then he joined the Ecurie Vallée team for 1947, but having disposed of the Delahaye, found himself virtually sidelined until late 1948, when he finally took delivery of a long-awaited Talbot. He soon became wedded to this beloved car and raced it extensively over the next few seasons, his best placings being third at Pau in 1949 and sixth at Rouen in 1953.

Not a particularly quick driver, Grignard nevertheless possessed mechanical sympathy and continued to compete, mainly in sports cars, until 1955, after which he retired to his garage business. He was still not finished with the Talbot marque, however, for in 1959 he took the opportunity to buy up all the liquidated stock, subsequently acting as a supplier to collectors around the world.

GRIGNARD, Georges (F) b 25/7/1905, Villeneuve-St-Georges – d 7/12/1977 Le Port Marly, Nr Verailles

	1951	Championship position: Unplaced							
	Race	Circuit	No	Entrant Tyres	Capacity/Car/Engine		Comment	Q Pos/Entries	
ret	SPANISH GP	Pedralbes	38	Georges Grignard		D	4.5 Lago-Talbot T26C-DA 6	overheating engine	16/20

GP Starts: 1   GP Wins: 0   Pole positions: 0   Fastest laps: 0   Points: 0

ROMAIN GROSJEAN

WILD and fast, Romain Grosjean has always possessed the sheer speed to take him to the very top of the sport, as a summary of his record will attest. The big question is can he temper his hallmark aggressive driving to avoid becoming a win-or-bust merchant?

After karting between 2000 and 2003, the Swiss national stepped into the shallow waters of the Formula Lista Swiss championship, immediately speeding to ten wins and the title, which led to a step up to the Formula Renault 2.0 French championship. There he took a win in his first year before returning in 2005 to dominate proceedings with ten wins and a second title on his CV.

The next move was to the F3 Euroseries, where the pattern repeated itself: consolidation and a win at the prestigious Pau meeting in year one, followed by the title in 2007 on the back of six victories.

By then, Romain was seen as a real prospect, and was snapped up by Renault to act as a reserve and test driver. Having joined ART Grand Prix for the 2008 GP2 Asia Series, he took another four wins, and convincingly beat Sébastien Buemi and Vitaly Petrov to claim his next championship, before taking on the FIA GP2 series proper. Rightly regarded as a title prospect, Grosjean's season took on a pattern that would become familiar over the next couple of years: brilliant and opportunistic overtaking with some dubious driving manoeuvres that endangered both himself and others. Nonetheless, he came fourth in his first year, helped by wins at Istanbul and Spa.

Grosjean's alliance with ART ultimately turned out to be an uneasy one, and he switched to champion team Barwa Addax for 2009 in an attempt to keep his championship-winning streak intact. Early wins at Barcelona and Monaco put him in a good position to chase the title by mid-season. When Nelson Piquet Junior's services were dispensed with, however, the chirpy Grosjean was thrown into the grand prix cauldron and thus abandoned his title ambitions. In his attempts to impress, though, he simply tried too hard, resulting in an error-strewn run of races where he seemed to be a magnet for trouble, not all of which was of his own making.

When Romain was dropped from the team for the 2010 season, it looked entirely possible that his big opportunity had come and gone, leaving the deflated driver to consider his future.

One thing Grosjean didn't lack was self-confidence, and he set about rebuilding his career by joining DAMS to contest the four-race GP2 Asia Series, which he promptly won, before successfully trying his hand at sports car racing with the Swiss Matech Competition team. In only four double-header races, he took two outright wins (with Thomas Mutsch) in the team's Ford GT1. Before long, though, he made a return to single-seaters, and the lifeline to his ultimate rehabilitation. He rejoined DAMS, at first in the lower-profile Auto GP series, where he wiped the floor with the opposition, and this success opened the door to the GP2 series once again. Two podiums showed he was still a serious contender, and it was no surprise that the team were keen to retain him to lead their attack in 2011. Clearly, the once headstrong youngster had matured into a more calculating performer, and he proceeded to dominate proceedings with five wins and a further five podiums, ensuring that his impressive run of championships remained intact.

Being a member of the Gravity Management Group of drivers pushed Grosjean to the forefront when Lotus-Renault made their decision on the second driver to partner Kimi Räikkönen in 2012. For the Swiss driver, it was a second chance well earned. Now he just needs to make the most of it.

GROSJEAN, Romain (F) b 17/4/1986, Geneva, Switzerland

2009 Championship position: Unplaced

	Race	Circuit	No	Entrant	Tyres	Capacity/Car/Engine	Comment	Q Pos/Entries
15	EUROPEAN GP	Valencia	8	ING Renault F1 Team	B	2.4 Renault R29-V8		14/20
ret	BELGIAN GP	Spa	8	ING Renault F1 Team	B	2.4 Renault R29-V8	collision with Button on lap 1	19/20
15	ITALIAN GP	Monza	8	ING Renault F1 Team	B	2.4 Renault R29-V8	accident damage/1 lap behind	12/20
ret	SINGAPORE GP	Marina Bay Circuit	8	Renault F1 Team	B	2.4 Renault R29-V8	brakes	18/20
16	JAPANESE GP	Suzuka	8	Renault F1 Team	B	2.4 Renault R29-V8	1 lap behind	18/20
13	BRAZILIAN GP	Interlagos	8	Renault F1 Team	B	2.4 Renault R29-V8	1 lap behind	13/20
18	ABU DHABI GP	Yas Marina Circuit	8	Renault F1 Team	B	2.4 Renault R29-V8	1 lap behind	19/20

2009 Championship position: Unplaced

	Race	Circuit	No	Entrant	Tyres	Capacity/Car/Engine	Comment	Q Pos/Entries
app	ABU DHABI GP	Yas Marina Circuit	9	Lotus Renault GP	P	2.4 Lotus T128-Renault V8	ran as 3rd driver in practice 1 only	– / –
app	BRAZILIAN GP	Interlagos	10	Lotus Renault GP	P	2.4 Lotus T128-Renault V8	ran as 3rd driver in practice 1 only	– / –

GP Starts: 7   GP Wins: 0   Pole positions: 0   Fastest laps: 0   Points: 0

OLIVIER GROUILLARD

EVEN from his earliest days in French Formula 3, Olivier Grouillard developed something of a reputation as a wild and uncompromising performer. After finishing fourth in the 1983 series, he graduated to the all-conquering Marlboro-backed ORECA team the following year and swept to the title, as was the established custom for the chosen incumbent. It was a close-run thing, however, Grouillard edging out his rival Frédéric Delavallade by just two points, 108 to 106.

Rustling up enough money for half a season in F3000 with ORECA in

1985, Grouillard made a good impression, coming close to a win at Enna. It was much the same the following year, when he was able to take part in only four races; he could have won at Mugello, but made a mistake and ended up in fourth place. Back with ORECA again in 1987, he showed speed, but was rather overshadowed by team-mate Yannick Dalmas, who was on a somewhat quicker path to Formula 1. But Olivier was nothing if not persistent, and for 1988 he got himself into the well-funded GDBA team, running works-backed Lolas. He finished runner-up to Roberto Moreno, winning two races and putting in some excellent performances.

At last Grouillard found himself in Formula 1 with Ligier, but after a bright start and a promising sixth place in the French Grand Prix, relations between the tempestuous youngster and his volcanic proprietor broke down and he was forced to seek alternative employment with Osella. The next two seasons were spent trying to qualify for races above all else, and the final straw with the Italian concern came when, against orders, he used his race car for pre-qualifying at the Portuguese Grand Prix. Apparently he was sent his dismissal notice by fax on the Monday after the race.

Grouillard lost no time in switching to another tail-ender team, AGS, for the briefest of flirtations at the end of the 1991 season, but with the team almost extinct, the future looked bleak. Once again, though, he dug himself out of a hole, finding the cash to join the underfinanced Tyrrell team. Freed from the perils of qualifying, he had a car that, at the very least, he could go racing with, but he was thoroughly outperformed by team-mate Andrea de Cesaris and succeeded only in attracting criticism for his bad track manners when being lapped.

For 1993, Grouillard took himself off to the States for a full season of Indy car racing, but while Nigel Mansell was heading for the championship with Newman Haas Racing, the Frenchman's tenure with Indy Regency Racing failed to create a worthwhile impression: he didn't make the field for the Indianapolis 500 and finished a lowly 28th in the final standings with a meagre four points from 11 starts.

Grouillard returned to Europe in 1994 and scratched around for a suitable ride. He competed at Le Mans in a Venturi 600LM and saw a huge upturn in his fortunes in GT racing. Having split with Giroix Racing in mid-1995 to join Dave Price, he finished the year with three straight wins at Silverstone, Nogaro and Zhuhai in China, sharing a Harrods-backed McLaren F1 GTR with Andy Wallace. The team stayed together for 1996, when more good top-six finishes were achieved, although there was only one outright win (at Silverstone).

In 1997, Grouillard took the opportunity to race a works Toyota Supra in the All-Japan GT championship, and partnered the Andrettis, father and son, in their unsuccessful attempt to win the Le Mans 24-hour race with the Courage C36-Porsche.

Driving the updated Courage C52 for La Filliere Pescarolo in 2000, Grouillard took fourth place at Le Mans and sixth at Silverstone with Sébastien Bourdais and Emmanuel Clérico.

GROUILLARD, Olivier (F) b 2/9/1958, Fenouillet, Toulouse

1989 Championship position: 26th=   Wins: 0   Pole positions: 0   Fastest laps: 0   Points scored: 1

	Race	Circuit	No	Entrant	Tyres	Capacity/Car/Engine	Comment	Q Pos/Entries
9	BRAZILIAN GP	Rio	26	Ligier Loto	G	3.5 Ligier JS33-Cosworth V8	oil leak/1 lap behind	22/38
dsq*	SAN MARINO GP	Imola	26	Ligier Loto	G	3.5 Ligier JS33-Cosworth V8	*car worked on between starts	10/39
ret	MONACO GP	Monte Carlo	26	Ligier Loto	G	3.5 Ligier JS33-Cosworth V8	gearbox	16/38
8	MEXICAN GP	Mexico City	26	Ligier Loto	G	3.5 Ligier JS33-Cosworth V8	lost clutch/1 lap behind	11/39
dnq	US GP (PHOENIX)	Phoenix	26	Ligier Loto	G	3.5 Ligier JS33-Cosworth V8		27/39
dnq	CANADIAN GP	Montreal	26	Ligier Loto	G	3.5 Ligier JS33-Cosworth V8		30/39
6	FRENCH GP	Paul Ricard	26	Ligier Loto	G	3.5 Ligier JS33-Cosworth V8	tyre & gearbox problems/1 lap behind	17/39
7	BRITISH GP	Silverstone	26	Ligier Loto	G	3.5 Ligier JS33-Cosworth V8	1 lap behind	24/39
ret	GERMAN GP	Hockenheim	26	Ligier Loto	G	3.5 Ligier JS33-Cosworth V8	input shaft	11/39
dnq	HUNGARIAN GP	Hungaroring	26	Ligier Loto	G	3.5 Ligier JS33-Cosworth V8		28/39
13	BELGIAN GP	Spa	26	Ligier Loto	G	3.5 Ligier JS33-Cosworth V8	1 lap behind	26/39
ret	ITALIAN GP	Monza	26	Ligier Loto	G	3.5 Ligier JS33-Cosworth V8	pit stop – gearbox/retired – exhaust	21/39
dnq	PORTUGUESE GP	Estoril	26	Ligier Loto	G	3.5 Ligier JS33-Cosworth V8		28/39
ret	SPANISH GP	Jerez	26	Ligier Loto	G	3.5 Ligier JS33-Cosworth V8	engine trumpet	24/38
ret	JAPANESE GP	Suzuka	26	Ligier Loto	G	3.5 Ligier JS33-Cosworth V8	engine	23/39
ret	AUSTRALIAN GP	Adelaide	26	Ligier Loto	G	3.5 Ligier JS33-Cosworth V8	hit wall in rain	24/39

1990 Championship position: Unplaced

	Race	Circuit	No	Entrant	Tyres	Capacity/Car/Engine	Comment	Q Pos/Entries
ret	US GP (PHOENIX)	Phoenix	14	Osella Squadra Corse	P	3.5 Osella FA1M-Cosworth V8	collision with Foitek	8/35
ret	BRAZILIAN GP	Interlagos	14	Osella Squadra Corse	P	3.5 Osella FA1M-Cosworth V8	collision with Alboreto	21/35
ret	SAN MARINO GP	Imola	14	Osella Squadra Corse	P	3.5 Osella FA1M-E-Cosworth V8	wheel bearing	23/34
dnq	MONACO GP	Monte Carlo	14	Osella Squadra Corse	P	3.5 Osella FA1M-E-Cosworth V8		28/35
13	CANADIAN GP	Montreal	14	Osella Squadra Corse	P	3.5 Osella FA1M-E-Cosworth V8	handling problems/5 laps behind	15/35
19	MEXICAN GP	Mexico City	14	Osella Squadra Corse	P	3.5 Osella FA1M-E-Cosworth V8	gear selection problems/-4 laps	20/35
dnpq	FRENCH GP	Paul Ricard	14	Osella Squadra Corse	P	3.5 Osella FA1M-E-Cosworth V8		31/35
dnq	BRITISH GP	Silverstone	14	Osella Squadra Corse	P	3.5 Osella FA1M-E-Cosworth V8		27/35
dnq	GERMAN GP	Hockenheim	14	Osella Squadra Corse	P	3.5 Osella FA1M-E-Cosworth V8		27/35
dnpq	HUNGARIAN GP	Hungaroring	14	Osella Squadra Corse	P	3.5 Osella FA1M-E-Cosworth V8		31/35
16	BELGIAN GP	Spa	14	Osella Squadra Corse	P	3.5 Osella FA1M-E-Cosworth V8	pit stop – tyres/2 laps behind	23/33
ret	ITALIAN GP	Monza	14	Osella Squadra Corse	P	3.5 Osella FA1M-E-Cosworth V8	wheel bearing	23/33
dnq	PORTUGUESE GP	Estoril	14	Osella Squadra Corse	P	3.5 Osella FA1M-E-Cosworth V8		27/33
ret	SPANISH GP	Jerez	14	Osella Squadra Corse	P	3.5 Osella FA1M-E-Cosworth V8	wheel bearing	21/33
dnq	JAPANESE GP	Suzuka	14	Osella Squadra Corse	P	3.5 Osella FA1M-E-Cosworth V8		27/30
13	AUSTRALIAN GP	Adelaide	14	Osella Squadra Corse	P	3.5 Osella FA1M-E-Cosworth V8	2 pit stops – tyres/handling/-7 laps	22/30

1991 Championship position: Unplaced

	Race	Circuit	No	Entrant	Tyres	Capacity/Car/Engine	Comment	Q Pos/Entries
dnpq	US GP (PHOENIX)	Phoenix	14	Fondmetal F1 SpA	G	3.5 Fomet FA1M-E-Cosworth V8		33/34
dnpq	BRAZILIAN GP	Interlagos	14	Fondmetal F1 SpA	G	3.5 Fomet FA1M-E-Cosworth V8		34/34
dnpq	SAN MARINO GP	Imola	14	Fondmetal F1 SpA	G	3.5 Fomet F1-Cosworth V8		32/34
dnpq	MONACO GP	Monte Carlo	14	Fondmetal F1 SpA	G	3.5 Fomet F1-Cosworth V8		34/34
dnpq	CANADIAN GP	Montreal	14	Fondmetal F1 SpA	G	3.5 Fomet F1-Cosworth V8		31/34
ret	MEXICAN GP	Mexico City	14	Fondmetal F1 SpA	G	3.5 Fomet F1-Cosworth V8	started from back/oil line	10/34
ret	FRENCH GP	Magny Cours	14	Fondmetal F1 SpA	G	3.5 Fomet F1-Cosworth V8	oil leak	21/34
dnpq	BRITISH GP	Silverstone	14	Fondmetal F1 SpA	G	3.5 Fomet F1-Cosworth V8		31/34
dnpq	GERMAN GP	Nürburgring	14	Fondmetal F1 SpA	G	3.5 Fomet F1-Cosworth V8		31/34
dnq	HUNGARIAN GP	Hungaroring	14	Fondmetal F1 SpA	G	3.5 Fomet F1-Cosworth V8		27/34
10	BELGIAN GP	Spa	14	Fondmetal F1 SpA	G	3.5 Fomet F1-Cosworth V8	1 lap behind	23/24
ret	ITALIAN GP	Monza	14	Fondmetal F1 SpA	G	3.5 Fomet F1-Cosworth V8	engine	26/34
dnpq	PORTUGUESE GP	Estoril	14	Fondmetal F1 SpA	G	3.5 Fomet F1-Cosworth V8		32/34
dnpq	SPANISH GP	Barcelona	17	Automobiles Gonfaronaise Sportive	G	3.5 AGS JH27-Cosworth V8		33/33

1992 Championship position: Unplaced

	Race	Circuit	No	Entrant	Tyres	Capacity/Car/Engine	Comment	Q Pos/Entries
ret	SOUTH AFRICAN GP	Kyalami	3	Tyrrell Racing Organisation	G	Tyrrell 020B-Ilmor V10	clutch	12/30
ret	MEXICAN GP	Mexico City	3	Tyrrell Racing Organisation	G	Tyrrell 020B-Ilmor V10	engine	16/30
ret	BRAZILIAN GP	Interlagos	3	Tyrrell Racing Organisation	G	Tyrrell 020B-Ilmor V10	engine	17/31
ret	SPANISH GP	Barcelona	3	Tyrrell Racing Organisation	G	Tyrrell 020B-Ilmor V10	spun off	15/32
8	SAN MARINO GP	Imola	3	Tyrrell Racing Organisation	G	Tyrrell 020B-Ilmor V10	2 laps behind	20/32
ret	MONACO GP	Monte Carlo	3	Tyrrell Racing Organisation	G	Tyrrell 020B-Ilmor V10	gearbox	24/32
12	CANADIAN GP	Montreal	3	Tyrrell Racing Organisation	G	Tyrrell 020B-Ilmor V10	2 laps behind	26/32
11	FRENCH GP	Magny Cours	3	Tyrrell Racing Organisation	G	Tyrrell 020B-Ilmor V10	3 laps behind	22/30
11	BRITISH GP	Kyalami	3	Tyrrell Racing Organisation	G	Tyrrell 020B-Ilmor V10	2 laps behind	20/32
ret	GERMAN GP	Hockenheim	3	Tyrrell Racing Organisation	G	Tyrrell 020B-Ilmor V10	overheating	14/32
ret	HUNGARIAN GP	Hungaroring	3	Tyrrell Racing Organisation	G	Tyrrell 020B-Ilmor V10	collision with Wendlinger	22/31
ret	BELGIAN GP	Spa	3	Tyrrell Racing Organisation	G	Tyrrell 020B-Ilmor V10	spun off lap 1	22/30
ret	ITALIAN GP	Monza	3	Tyrrell Racing Organisation	G	Tyrrell 020B-Ilmor V10	engine	18/28
ret	PORTUGUESE GP	Estoril	3	Tyrrell Racing Organisation	G	Tyrrell 020B-Ilmor V10	gearbox	15/26
ret	JAPANESE GP	Suzuka	3	Tyrrell Racing Organisation	G	Tyrrell 020B-Ilmor V10	spun off	21/26
ret	AUSTRALIAN GP	Adelaide	3	Tyrrell Racing Organisation	G	Tyrrell 020B-Ilmor V10	collision with Martini lap 1	13/26

GP Starts: 41   GP Wins: 0   Pole positions: 0   Fastest laps: 0   Points: 1

GUELFI, André (MA) b 6/5/1919, Mazagin (EL Jadida)

1958 Championship position: Unplaced

	Race	Circuit	No	Entrant	Tyres	Capacity/Car/Engine	Comment	Q Pos/Entries
15*	MOROCCAN GP (F2)	Casablanca (60)	48	André Guelfi	D	1.5 Cooper T45-Climax 4 F2	*4th in F2 class/5 laps behind	25/25

GP Starts: 1   GP Wins: 0   Pole positions: 0   Fastest laps: 0   Points: 0

ANDRÉ GUELFI

BORN in Morocco, but to a Corsican father, André Guelfi was a very useful performer, who mainly confined his racing activities to North Africa and France during a long competition career that stretched back to 1950, when he first raced a Delahaye. After driving a Jaguar, he came to prominence in 1953 racing a Gordini sports car, which he took to class and outright wins at Agadir. He shared a works car with Jean Behra in the 12-hour race at Casablanca that year, but it was retired with a broken shock absorber.

Joining the ever-changing roster of pilots at Gordini, Guelfi was given a single-seater appearance at Pescara in 1954, but his race ended on the first lap when the car caught fire. His true métier was in sports cars, however, and, with Jacky Pollet, he drove a works Gordini into sixth place at Le Mans, taking the 2000–3000cc class win. Although still racing mainly in Morocco – he was champion in 1955 – he continued to make regular sorties to France. In 1957, he finished a distant seventh in the Pau GP as the pale blue machines were reaching imminent extinction.

The new rear-engined Coopers were the way forward, and Guelfi made a good impression when he took second place in the Prix de Paris at Montlhéry in June 1958, only three seconds behind Henry Taylor in a similar car. With a Formula 2 class being added to bolster the field for the first (and only) Grand Prix of Morocco at season's end, he entered a car, but in truth was not as quick as could have been expected, although he stayed the distance to finish last.

Subsequently Guelfi raced on in Morocco through the 1960s, and as late as 1968 his name still appeared in the results when he took second place in a race in Rabat in a Porsche 911R.

Of far more interest than his modest racing exploits is Guelfi's remarkable life. In the 1930s, André worked on commission as a debt collector for a Swiss Bank, investing his sizeable earnings to make his first fortune in the sardine fishing and canning industry, which led to his famous soubriquet, 'Dédé de la Sardine'. After military service in Italy during the Second World War, he busied himself with his business and motor racing interests. In 1971, he moved to Paris and began dealing in property in a very big way. He married the niece of French President Georges Pompidou, which brought him close to the seat of government.

After moving to Lausanne in 1975, Guelfi became one a handful of powerful businessmen close to the powerful Spaniard Juan Antonio Samaranch, president of the International Olympic Committee. Moving in powerful political and financial circles, he was later employed as a 'Mr Fixit' and money mover for the then government owned oil giant Elf. Millions of francs were involved in bribery and corruption across Europe, and the scandal eventually brought down many involved, including German Chancellor Helmut Kohl. Despite his advanced years, Guelfi received a prison sentence and a hefty fine for his part in the murky dealings.

Once freed, Guelfi continued with his business affairs, claiming to have quit Switzerland for Malta following the revelation of details of his bank accounts to the French authorities during the Elf investigations.

MIGUEL ANGEL GUERRA

UNTIL the first-corner accident that eliminated Marco Apicella at Monza in 1993, the unfortunate Miguel Guerra had the unwanted tag of having just about the shortest grand prix career on record, for the Argentinian was barely a third of a lap into his debut, the 1981 San Marino Grand Prix, when he was pushed off the track and into a wall, sustaining a broken ankle and wrist in the process.

Guerra had three seasons in Formula 2 behind him: the first, in 1978, saw a few outings in a Chevron; the next, in a March, yielded his best finish (third place at Hockenheim); and then he endured a disappointing year with the troublesome Minardi.

Having recovered from his Imola crash, Guerra reappeared briefly in Formula 2 at the end of the 1981 season in the Adriatic GP at Misano, finishing a distant 13th. His racing career was far from over, however, and on his return to Argentina he became a front-runner in the Formula 2/3 CoDaSur series until 1987, when he made the switch to touring cars. He was crowned the Argentine TC2000 champion in 1989, driving a Renault Fuego, and was a regular competitor throughout the 1990s, before announcing his retirement in 2000. Subsequently he was president of the Top Race series, which runs V6-engined cars as an alternative the TC2000 category.

GUERRA, Miguel Angel (RA) b 31/8/1953, Buenos Aires

1981 Championship position: Unplaced

	Race	Circuit	No	Entrant	Tyres	Capacity/Car/Engine	Comment	Q Pos/Entries
dnq	US GP WEST	Long Beach	31	Osella Squadra Corse	M	3.0 Osella FA1B-Cosworth V8		27/29
dnq	BRAZILIAN GP	Rio	31	Osella Squadra Corse	M	3.0 Osella FA1B-Cosworth V8		28/30
dnq	ARGENTINE GP	Buenos Aires	31	Osella Squadra Corse	M	3.0 Osella FA1B-Cosworth V8		25/29
ret	SAN MARINO GP	Imola	31	Osella Squadra Corse	M	3.0 Osella FA1B-Cosworth V8	*spun – collision with Salazar – hit wall*	22/30

GP Starts: 1   GP Wins: 0   Pole positions: 0   Fastest laps: 0   Points: 0

ROBERTO GUERRERO

THE personable Roberto Guerrero, a Colombian, could have made a good career for himself in Formula 1 had he not chosen to move into Indy car racing at the end of 1983 when no suitable F1 drive was available, for, on his speedy passage to the top, he had already displayed genuine talent. Joint second in the British F3 series in the unfashionable Argo, and an immediate winner at Thruxton in his first Formula 2 season, Guerrero's fine performances caught the eye of Mo Nunn, who gave him the Ensign drive for 1982. He performed extremely well in difficult circumstances, as he did in his second season following the team's merger with Theodore.

So it was off to the States, and stardom: he finished second in the 1984 Indy 500 and won two races in 1987, at Phoenix and Mid-Ohio, before a crash while testing at Indy left him in a coma for 17 days. He made a full recovery, but his career never quite regained its earlier momentum, and he became bogged down in the largely disappointing Alfa Romeo Indy programme until he joined Kenny Bernstein's team in mid-1991. He took pole at Indy in 1992, but crashed on the warm-up lap and spent the rest of the campaign on the sidelines. Then he signed with Bernstein for a full season in 1993, but after a generally lacklustre year he lost his ride with three races remaining.

No longer capable of getting a full-time drive, Roberto, now a US citizen, joined forces with Pagan Racing in 1994 and did well to scrape into the Indy 500 as 33rd and final qualifier with a two-year-old Lola-Buick. Unfortunately he was posted as first retirement again when he spun into the wall. He remained with the little team for 1995, targeting the Brickyard once more (although he raced at Phoenix as a shakedown for the month of May), and this time things went much better. He finished a creditable 12th, having lost time under caution early on.

When the Indy Racing League was formed in 1996, it must have come as 'manna from heaven' to the likes of Guerrero. Not only did it give him a racing lifeline, but also it represented a tantalising opportunity to have his image engraved on the magnificent Borg Warner Trophy. Sadly that victory in the Indy 500 remained elusive. After a fifth place in 1996, he came agonisingly close in 1997 when, after a totally dominant performance, the race was snatched from his grasp by Al Unser Snr after clutch problems at a pit stop slowed him near the finish. Then he posted retirements in his final three appearances, his last two attempts at the Brickyard ending without qualifying in 2000 and 2001. Subsequently he switched to off-road competition in the Baja 1000, an endurance event held in Mexico's Baja California Peninsula.

GUERRERO, Roberto (COL/USA) b 16/11/1958, Medellin, Colombia

	1982 Championship position: Unplaced							
	Race	Circuit	No	Entrant	Tyres	Capacity/Car/Engine	Comment	Q Pos/Entries
dnp	SOUTH AFRICAN GP	Kyalami	14	Ensign Racing	A	3.0 Ensign N180B-Cosworth V8	withdrawn – injunction by Maurer	– / –
dnq	BRAZILIAN GP	Rio	14	Ensign Racing	A	3.0 Ensign N181-Cosworth V8		28/31
ret	US GP WEST	Long Beach	14	Ensign Racing	A	3.0 Ensign N181-Cosworth V8	hit wall	19/31
dnq	BELGIAN GP	Zolder	14	Ensign Racing	A	3.0 Ensign N181-Cosworth V8		29/32
dnq	MONACO GP	Monte Carlo	14	Ensign Racing	A	3.0 Ensign N181-Cosworth V8		26/31
ret	US GP (DETROIT)	Detroit	14	Ensign Racing	M	3.0 Ensign N181-Cosworth V8	accident with de Angelis	11/28
ret	CANADIAN GP	Montreal	14	Ensign Racing	M	3.0 Ensign N181-Cosworth V8	clutch	20/29
dnq	DUTCH GP	Zandvoort	14	Ensign Racing	M	3.0 Ensign N181-Cosworth V8		27/31
ret	BRITISH GP	Brands Hatch	14	Ensign Racing	M	3.0 Ensign N181-Cosworth V8	engine	19/30
dnq	FRENCH GP	Paul Ricard	14	Ensign Racing	M	3.0 Ensign N181-Cosworth V8		28/30
8	GERMAN GP	Hockenheim	14	Ensign Racing	M	3.0 Ensign N181-Cosworth V8	1 lap behind	22/30
ret	AUSTRIAN GP	Österreichring	14	Ensign Racing	M	3.0 Ensign N181-Cosworth V8	driveshaft	16/29
ret	SWISS GP	Dijon	14	Ensign Racing	M	3.0 Ensign N181-Cosworth V8	engine	19/29
nc	ITALIAN GP	Monza	14	Ensign Racing	M	3.0 Ensign N181-Cosworth V8	hit Daly – pit stops/12 laps behind	18/30
dns	CAESARS PALACE GP	Las Vegas	14	Ensign Racing	M	3.0 Ensign N181-Cosworth V8	engine in warm-up	(15)/30
	1983 Championship position: Unplaced							
nc	BRAZILIAN GP	Rio	33	Theodore Racing Team	G	3.0 Theodore N183-Cosworth V8	pit stop/10 laps behind	14/27
ret	US GP WEST	Long Beach	33	Theodore Racing Team	G	3.0 Theodore N183-Cosworth V8	gearbox	18/28
ret	FRENCH GP	Paul Ricard	33	Theodore Racing Team	G	3.0 Theodore N183-Cosworth V8	engine	22/29
ret	SAN MARINO GP	Imola	33	Theodore Racing Team	G	3.0 Theodore N183-Cosworth V8	incident with Sullivan	21/28
dnpq	MONACO GP	Monte Carlo	33	Theodore Racing Team	G	3.0 Theodore N183-Cosworth V8	no tyres	28/28
ret	BELGIAN GP	Spa	33	Theodore Racing Team	G	3.0 Theodore N183-Cosworth V8	engine	14/28
nc	US GP (DETROIT)	Detroit	33	Theodore Racing Team	G	3.0 Theodore N183-Cosworth V8	pit stop/22 laps behind	11/27
ret	CANADIAN GP	Montreal	33	Theodore Racing Team	G	3.0 Theodore N183-Cosworth V8	engine	21/28
16	BRITISH GP	Silverstone	33	Theodore Racing Team	G	3.0 Theodore N183-Cosworth V8	3 laps behind	21/29
ret	GERMAN GP	Hockenheim	33	Theodore Racing Team	G	3.0 Theodore N183-Cosworth V8	engine	24/29
ret	AUSTRIAN GP	Österreichring	33	Theodore Racing Team	G	3.0 Theodore N183-Cosworth V8	gearbox	21/29
12	DUTCH GP	Zandvoort	33	Theodore Racing Team	G	3.0 Theodore N183-Cosworth V8	incident with Jarier – pit stop/-4 laps	20/29
13	ITALIAN GP	Monza	33	Theodore Racing Team	G	3.0 Theodore N183-Cosworth V8	2 laps behind	21/29
12	EUROPEAN GP	Brands Hatch	33	Theodore Racing Team	G	3.0 Theodore N183-Cosworth V8	1 lap behind	21/29

GP Starts: 21   GP Wins: 0   Pole positions: 0   Fastest laps: 0   Points: 0

MAURICIO GUGELMIN

PRESENTABLE, articulate and displaying a mature approach to racing from his early days, Mauricio Gugelmin had a good deal of skill as well. He was born into a wealthy Brazilian family, his father being a timber merchant who collected antique cars, which no doubt captured the imagination of the youngster. He began his competition career with a succession of local karting titles, before claiming the national championship in 1980. A Formula Ford champion in 1981 in his native Brazil, he followed his friend and ex-karting rival Ayrton Senna to Europe, initially taking the same route to the top – FF1600 and FF2000, then Formula 3 with West Surrey Racing in 1985. Fast, safe and above all consistent, Mauricio took the title and rounded off the season, and his Formula 3 career, with a win in the prestigious Macau Grand Prix.

At the time, Gugelmin was sharing a house with Senna, and it was mooted that he might be given the second seat at Lotus in 1986, but it went instead to Johnny Dumfries, so the Brazilan moved into F3000 with West Surrey Racing for 1986, enduring a frustrating year fraught with problems. His fortunes improved the following season, however, when running a works Ralt-Honda with fellow Brazilian Roberto Moreno. He won the opening round at Silverstone, but a spate of mid-season non-finishes left him fourth in the points at season's end.

Mauricio then joined the Leyton House March team and was happy to remain with them for four seasons, during which he experienced the highs (third place in Brazil in 1989) and lows (a run of non-qualifications in 1990 when the car's sensitive chassis proved nearly impossible to set up) of Formula 1. In 1990, the team was sold and renamed Leyton House. By the end of 1991, the whole organisation was crumbling after 18 months of internal dissent and personnel changes, and Gugelmin, having failed to score a single point throughout the season, took his leave to join his old mentor, Ian Phillips, at Sasol Jordan. Although the year was a debacle for the team as they struggled with the underpowered Yamaha engine, Mauricio earned their respect by never giving less than his best.

Without a drive for 1993, Gugelmin made his Indy car debut for the enthusiastic Dick Simonin in the last three races of the season, and while he enjoyed little success he showed enough promise to decide that this was where his racing future lay.

Despite a minimal budget, Gugelmin joined Ganassi Racing in a team run quite separately from that of star driver Michael Andretti. The lack of a helping hand from an experienced team-mate and the absence of shared technical feedback (although there was some cross-fertilisation by mid-season) no doubt frustrated the Brazilian, who must have been pleased to out-qualify his illustrious peer on more than one occasion.

In 1995, Mauricio moved to the small, but promising PacWest Racing Group and really got moving with a career-best second place in the season-opener in Miami. Crucially this cemented his sponsorship for the year, allowing him to face the season with renewed confidence. At Indianapolis, he showed just how well he had adapted to oval racing by leading the most laps in the race, before handling problems caused him to fade to sixth at the finish. Thereafter, his form was patchy, but he bounced back at Laguna Seca with a strong third place.

The popular Gugelmin then became a fixture with Bruce McCaw's California-based team. Easily his best season Stateside was in 1997, when he posted his only CART victory to date at Vancouver and finished fourth in the championship.

Gugelmin raced on for another four seasons with PacWest, but never reached the top of the podium; a second place at Nazareth in 1999 was the closest he came to a victory. In 2001, his final season was traumatic. He suffered two massive crashes (at Texas and Chicago) and endured the loss of his young son, Guiliano, who suffered from cerebral palsy. The dreadful accident to Alex Zanardi at Lausitzring finally convinced the Brazilian that it was time to quit. Subsequently he returned to his native Brazil to run the family business with his brother and watch the progress of his surviving sons, who have taken to karting competition.

GUGELMIN, Mauricio (BR) b 20/4/1963, Joinville

1988 Championship position: 13th=		Wins: 0	Pole positions: 0	Fastest laps: 0	Points scored: 5		

	Race	Circuit	No	Entrant	Tyres	Capacity/Car/Engine	Comment	Q Pos/Entries
ret	BRAZILIAN GP	Rio	15	Leyton House March Racing Team	G	3.5 March 881-Judd V8	transmission on lap 1	13/31
15	SAN MARINO GP	Imola	15	Leyton House March Racing Team	G	3.5 March 881-Judd V8	fuel pick-up problems/2 laps behind	20/31
ret	MONACO GP	Monte Carlo	15	Leyton House March Racing Team	G	3.5 March 881-Judd V8	started from pits/electrics – engine	14/30
ret	MEXICAN GP	Mexico City	15	Leyton House March Racing Team	G	3.5 March 881-Judd V8	electrical short-circuit	16/30
ret	CANADIAN GP	Montreal	15	Leyton House March Racing Team	G	3.5 March 881-Judd V8	gearbox	18/31
ret	US GP (DETROIT)	Detroit	15	Leyton House March Racing Team	G	3.5 March 881-Judd V8	engine	13/31
8	FRENCH GP	Paul Ricard	15	Leyton House March Racing Team	G	3.5 March 881-Judd V8	lost clutch/1 lap behind	16/31

4	BRITISH GP	Silverstone	15	Leyton House March Racing Team	G	3.5 March 881-Judd V8		5/31
8	GERMAN GP	Hockenheim	15	Leyton House March Racing Team	G	3.5 March 881-Judd V8	1 lap behind	10/31
5	HUNGARIAN GP	Hungaroring	15	Leyton House March Racing Team	G	3.5 March 881-Judd V8	1 lap behind	8/31
ret	BELGIAN GP	Spa	15	Leyton House March Racing Team	G	3.5 March 881-Judd V8	clutch –spun off	13/31
8	ITALIAN GP	Monza	15	Leyton House March Racing Team	G	3.5 March 881-Judd V8	engine down on power	13/31
ret	PORTUGUESE GP	Estoril	15	Leyton House March Racing Team	G	3.5 March 881-Judd V8	engine	5/31
7	SPANISH GP	Jerez	15	Leyton House March Racing Team	G	3.5 March 881-Judd V8		11/31
10	JAPANESE GP	Suzuka	15	Leyton House March Racing Team	G	3.5 March 881-Judd V8	clutch problems/1 lap behind	13/31
ret	AUSTRALIAN GP	Adelaide	15	Leyton House March Racing Team	G	3.5 March 881-Judd V8	hit by Nakajima	19/31

1989 Championship position: 16th=   Wins: 0   Pole positions: 0   Fastest laps: 1   Points scored: 4

3	BRAZILIAN GP	Rio	15	Leyton House March Racing Team	G	3.5 March 881-Judd V8	2 pit stops – tyres	12/38
ret	SAN MARINO GP	Imola	15	Leyton House March Racing Team	G	3.5 March 881-Judd V8	clutch/puncture/retired – gearbox	19/39
ret	MONACO GP	Monte Carlo	15	Leyton House March Racing Team	G	3.5 March CG891-Judd V8	started from pitlane/engine	14/38
dnq	MEXICAN GP	Mexico City	15	Leyton House March Racing Team	G	3.5 March CG891-Judd V8		28/39
dsq	US GP (PHOENIX)	Phoenix	15	Leyton House March Racing Team	G	3.5 March CG891-Judd V8	topped up brake fluid in race	18/39
ret	CANADIAN GP	Montreal	15	Leyton House March Racing Team	G	3.5 March CG891-Judd V8	electrics	17/39
nc	FRENCH GP	Paul Ricard	15	Leyton House March Racing Team	G	3.5 March CG891-Judd V8	pit stop – misfire/FL	10/39
ret	BRITISH GP	Silverstone	15	Leyton House March Racing Team	G	3.5 March CG891-Judd V8	started from pitane/gearbox	6/39
ret	GERMAN GP	Hockenheim	15	Leyton House March Racing Team	G	3.5 March CG891-Judd V8	gearbox	14/39
ret	HUNGARIAN GP	Hungaroring	15	Leyton House March Racing Team	G	3.5 March CG891-Judd V8	electrics	13/39
7	BELGIAN GP	Spa	15	Leyton House March Racing Team	G	3.5 March CG891-Judd V8	1 lap behind	9/39
ret	ITALIAN GP	Monza	15	Leyton House March Racing Team	G	3.5 March CG891-Judd V8	throttle problems	25/39
10	PORTUGUESE GP	Estoril	15	Leyton House March Racing Team	G	3.5 March CG891-Judd V8	pit stop – tyres – stalled/-2 laps	14/39
ret	SPANISH GP	Jerez	15	Leyton House March Racing Team	G	3.5 March CG891-Judd V8	hit by Sala	26/38
7*	JAPANESE GP	Suzuka	15	Leyton House March Racing Team	G	3.5 March CG891-Judd V8	*1st place car disqualified/-1 lap	20/39
7	AUSTRALIAN GP	Adelaide	15	Leyton House March Racing Team	G	3.5 March CG891-Judd V8	4 laps behind	25/39

1990 Championship position: 18th   Wins: 0   Pole positions: 0   Fastest laps: 0   Points scored: 1

14	US GP (PHOENIX)	Phoenix	15	Leyton House March Racing Team	G	3.5 Leyton House CG901-Judd V8	pit stop – tyres/vibration/-6 laps	25/35
dns	"	"	15	Leyton House March Racing Team	G	3.5 March CG891-Judd V8	practice only	– / –
dnq	BRAZILIAN GP	Interlagos	15	Leyton House March Racing Team	G	3.5 Leyton House CG901-Judd V8		30/35
ret	SAN MARINO GP	Imola	15	Leyton House March Racing Team	G	3.5 Leyton House CG901-Judd V8	misfire – electrics	13/34
dnq	MONACO GP	Monte Carlo	15	Leyton House March Racing Team	G	3.5 Leyton House CG901-Judd V8		29/35
dnq	CANADIAN GP	Montreal	15	Leyton House March Racing Team	G	3.5 Leyton House CG901-Judd V8		28/35
dnq	MEXICAN GP	Mexico City	15	Leyton House March Racing Team	G	3.5 Leyton House CG901-Judd V8		29/25
ret	FRENCH GP	Paul Ricard	15	Leyton House March Racing Team	G	3.5 Leyton House CG901-Judd V8	engine when 4th	10/35
dns	BRITISH GP	Silverstone	15	Leyton House March Racing Team	G	3.5 Leyton House CG901-Judd V8	fuel pump on dummy grid	15/35
ret	GERMAN GP	Hockenheim	15	Leyton House March Racing Team	G	3.5 Leyton House CG901-Judd V8	engine	14/35
8	HUNGARIAN GP	Hungaroring	15	Leyton House March Racing Team	G	3.5 Leyton House CG901-Judd V8	brake problems – spin/1 lap behind	17/35
6	BELGIAN GP	Spa	15	Leyton House March Racing Team	G	3.5 Leyton House CG901-Judd V8	clutch problems	14/33
ret	ITALIAN GP	Monza	15	Leyton House March Racing Team	G	3.5 Leyton House CG901-Judd V8	engine	10/33
12	PORTUGUESE GP	Estoril	15	Leyton House March Racing Team	G	3.5 Leyton House CG901-Judd V8	driver unwell/2 laps behind	14/33
8	SPANISH GP	Jerez	15	Leyton House March Racing Team	G	3.5 Leyton House CG901-Judd V8	tyres & clutch problems/1 lap behind	12/33
ret	JAPANESE GP	Suzuka	15	Leyton House March Racing Team	G	3.5 Leyton House CG901-Judd V8	engine cut out	16/30
ret	AUSTRALIAN GP	Adelaide	15	Leyton House March Racing Team	G	3.5 Leyton House CG901-Judd V8	rear brakes	16/30

1991 Championship position: Unplaced

ret	US GP (PHOENIX)	Phoenix	15	Leyton House Racing	G	3.5 Leyton House CG911-Ilmor V10	gearbox	23/34
ret	BRAZILIAN GP	Interlagos	15	Leyton House Racing	G	3.5 Leyton House CG911-Ilmor V10	driver unwell – withdrew	8/34
12/ret	SAN MARINO	Imola	15	Leyton House Racing	G	3.5 Leyton House CG911-Ilmor V10	engine/6 laps behind	15/34
ret	MONACO GP	Monte Carlo	15	Leyton House Racing	G	3.5 Leyton House CG911-Ilmor V10	throttle cable	15/34
ret	CANADIAN GP	Montreal	15	Leyton House Racing	G	3.5 Leyton House CG911-Ilmor V10	engine	23/34
ret	MEXICAN GP	Mexico City	15	Leyton House Racing	G	3.5 Leyton House CG911-Ilmor V10	engine	21/34
7	FRENCH GP	Magny Cours	15	Leyton House Racing	G	3.5 Leyton House CG911-Ilmor V10	2 laps behind	9/34
ret	BRITISH GP	Silverstone	15	Leyton House Racing	G	3.5 Leyton House CG911-Ilmor V10	chassis vibration numbed leg	9/34
ret	GERMAN GP	Hockenheim	15	Leyton House Racing	G	3.5 Leyton House CG911-Ilmor V10	gearbox	16/34
11	HUNGARIAN GP	Hungaroring	15	Leyton House Racing	G	3.5 Leyton House CG911-Ilmor V10	2 laps behind	13/34
ret	BELGIAN GP	Spa	15	Leyton House Racing	G	3.5 Leyton House CG911-Ilmor V10		15/34
15	ITALIAN GP	Monza	15	Leyton House Racing	G	3.5 Leyton House CG911-Ilmor V10	no clutch/foot injury/4 laps behind	18/34
7	PORTUGUESE GP	Estoril	15	Leyton House Racing	G	3.5 Leyton House CG911-Ilmor V10	1 lap behind	7/34
7	SPANISH GP	Barcelona	15	Leyton House Racing	G	3.5 Leyton House CG911-Ilmor V10	1 lap behind	13/33
8	JAPANESE GP	Suzuka	15	Leyton House Racing	G	3.5 Leyton House CG911-Ilmor V10	1 lap behind	18/31
14/ret	AUSTRALIAN GP	Adelaide	15	Leyton House Racing	G	3.5 Leyton House CG911-Ilmor V10	crashed into pit lane entrance	14/32

1992 Championship position: Unplaced

11	SOUTH AFRICAN GP	Kyalami	33	Sasol Jordan Yamaha	G	3.5 Jordan 192-Yamaha V12	2 laps behind	23/30
ret	MEXICAN GP	Mexico City	33	Sasol Jordan Yamaha	G	3.5 Jordan 192-Yamaha V12	engine on lap 1	8/30
ret	BRAZILIAN GP	Interlagos	33	Sasol Jordan Yamaha	G	3.5 Jordan 192-Yamaha V12	gearbox	21/31
ret	SPANISH GP	Barcelona	33	Sasol Jordan Yamaha	G	3.5 Jordan 192-Yamaha V12	spun off	17/32
7	SAN MARINO GP	Imola	33	Sasol Jordan Yamaha	G	3.5 Jordan 192-Yamaha V12	2 laps behind	18/32
ret	MONACO GP	Monte Carlo	33	Sasol Jordan Yamaha	G	3.5 Jordan 192-Yamaha V12	transmission	13/32
ret	CANADIAN GP	Montreal	33	Sasol Jordan Yamaha	G	3.5 Jordan 192-Yamaha V12	transmission	24/32
ret	FRENCH GP	Magny Cours	33	Sasol Jordan Yamaha	G	3.5 Jordan 192-Yamaha V12	multiple collision on lap 1	24/30
ret	BRITISH GP	Silverstone	33	Sasol Jordan Yamaha	G	3.5 Jordan 192-Yamaha V12	engine	24/32
15	GERMAN GP	Nürburgring	33	Sasol Jordan Yamaha	G	3.5 Jordan 192-Yamaha V12	2 laps behind	23/32
10	HUNGARIAN GP	Hungaroring	33	Sasol Jordan Yamaha	G	3.5 Jordan 192-Yamaha V12	4 laps behind	21/31
14	BELGIAN GP	Spa	33	Sasol Jordan Yamaha	G	3.5 Jordan 192-Yamaha V12	2 laps behind	24/30
ret	ITALIAN GP	Monza	33	Sasol Jordan Yamaha	G	3.5 Jordan 192-Yamaha V12	transmission	26/28
ret	PORTUGUESE GP	Estoril	33	Sasol Jordan Yamaha	G	3.5 Jordan 192-Yamaha V12	electrics	20/26
ret	JAPANESE GP	Suzuka	33	Sasol Jordan Yamaha	G	3.5 Jordan 192-Yamaha V12	crashed	25/26
ret	AUSTRALIAN GP	Adelaide	33	Sasol Jordan Yamaha	G	3.5 Jordan 192-Yamaha V12	brake problem – crashed	20/26

GP Starts: 74   GP Wins: 0   Pole positions: 0   Fastest laps: 1   Points: 10

DAN GURNEY

SOME drivers seem to exude a natural warmth, and by their demeanour both on and off the track firmly entrench themselves in the hearts of motor racing fans around the globe. Dan Gurney certainly falls into that category. The universally popular American can look back over five decades on a staggering contribution to motorsport worldwide. Firstly as driver and then a constructor, he made significant marks in Formula 1, Indy car, sports car racing, NASCAR, Trans Am, Can-Am, F5000, IMSA and more. These many fine achievements merely underline his stature as one of the sport's least affected and most enthusiastic participants.

The son of an opera singer, Gurney revelled in the environment of his Riverside youth, taking little interest in his studies, but enjoying illicit drag racing at the local strips. After national service, he began his competition career in 1955 with a Triumph TR2, before building his reputation with a Porsche. By 1957, he was running a Ferrari entered by Frank Arciero, and was so successful that Luigi Chinetti arranged for him to race at Le Mans and Reims in 1958. In both races, his co-driver crashed the car, but Dan had shown sufficient promise to be offered a test with Ferrari later on that season.

Signing a contract with the wily Commendatore for the 1959 season, which bound him tightly, Gurney soon proved to be a major asset, particularly after the acrimonious departure of Jean Behra, scoring points in three of his four grands prix. The strictures of Maranello were such that he decided to join BRM for 1960, but it was an unhappy year, for the car was woefully unreliable – made even worse by a freak accident at Zandvoort where a small boy was killed when Dan's brakes failed and the car crashed into a prohibited area where the youngster was standing.

Joining Porsche for 1961, Gurney found that the four-cylinder car was reliable (he finished all but one of his 14 Formula 1 races), but not quite capable of winning. He stayed on for 1962 and gained some reward with the flat-eight car, winning his first grand prix at Rouen and then the non-title race at Solitude. This was the pinnacle of Porsche's achievements as a manufacturer in Formula 1, as they withdrew at season's end, leaving Dan to join Jack Brabham as the team's number-one driver for Formula 1, but free to continue his sports and USAC programme, which had begun so promisingly in 1962.

Having seen the promise exhibited by Jack Brabham's venture with his little rear-engined Cooper at the Indianapolis 500 in 1961, Gurney became the prime mover in getting both Ford and Lotus to the Speedway. That changed the face of racing forever, as the front-engined roadsters were soon consigned to the role of dinosaurs. Dan, though, was out of luck in his three appearances with the Lotus at the Brickyard, with a best finish of just seventh, while Jim Clark took his famous win in 1965.

Back in Europe with the Brabham team, again it was so near yet so far in grands prix, as Gurney repeatedly challenged Jim Clark, Graham Hill, John Surtees et al. Over the three seasons he was with 'Black Jack', he was almost invariably frustrated by sundry niggling problems that restricted him to 'just' two Formula 1 victories. It seems ironic that after his departure at the end of 1965, to build his own Eagle racers, the Brabham team, running Repco engines, should suddenly find the pace and reliability to take successive world championships with Brabham and Denny Hulme in 1966/67.

Meanwhile, with the new 3-litre formula introduced for 1966, Gurney's Anglo American Racers car looked superb in its dark blue livery, but it stood no chance of success until its punchless four-cylinder Climax engine was replaced by the complex, but potent Weslake V12 unit. By 1967, this was a truly competitive proposition, and Dan took victories in the non-championship Race of Champions at Brands Hatch and magnificently in the Belgian Grand Prix at Spa-Francorchamps, before the onslaught of

ubiquitous Ford-Cosworth V8 power eventually overwhelmed the project. However, June of that year was kind to Dan, who also shared a Ford GT40 with another American legend, A.J. Foyt, to win the Le Mans 24-hours. By then, Gurney was spending less of his time in Europe, extending his efforts into Can-Am and USAC racing, where he won the Rex Mays 100 at Riverside in 1967.

In 1968, Dan finished second in the Indianapolis 500 with his Eagle-Ford (Bobby Unser won in a customer Eagle-Offy) as well as winning races at Mosport and then Riverside once more.

Inevitably, Gurney's Formula 1 programme suffered in 1968 and he dropped the troublesome Eagle-Weslake in favour of running his own McLaren-Cosworth at the tail end of the season. Formula 1 seemed a thing of the past in 1969 as he developed his USAC programme, finishing second at Indy yet again, but winning at Donnybrooke. The following year, he won at Sears Point and was third at Indianapolis, before stepping into the breach at McLaren following Bruce's tragic death in a testing accident at Goodwood. After being away for more than a year, he never really had time to find his true pace in Formula 1, but he won two of the three Can-Am rounds he contested before problems over conflicting oil contracts precipitated his departure from the team. Realising that perhaps his best days were now behind him, he retired from racing, his place in the USAC team being filled by Bobby Unser, who would bring Eagle so much success in the 1970s. Happily Dan was not tempted to return full time, but he couldn't resist a one-off NASCAR outing in 1980 at his home track of Riverside, where he ran a superb third before gearbox trouble.

Gurney continued to enter his Eagles in USAC and had the satisfaction of winning Indy as a constructor once more, Gordon Johncock and Bobby Unser scoring victories in 1973 and 1975 respectively. Dan eventually withdrew from USAC single-seater racing, his team having recorded 22 wins and 33 pole positions between 1965 and 1986.

He ran ultra-successful programmes in IMSA from 1983, firstly with a GTU and then GTO Toyotas specially prepared by AAR. Between 1989 and 1993, the team entered the protoype Toyota GTP in the IMSA sports car championship with massive success. Juan Fangio II took the title in 1992 and 1993, and the team won the Sebring 12-hours in both of those years, with Andy Wallace partnering the Argentinian. The Eagle MkIII Toyota also took victory in the 1993 Daytona 24-hour race with P.J. Jones, Mark Dismore and Rocky Moran at the wheel.

Overall, this five-year programme yielded 23 pole positions and 26 wins, and encouraged the Japanese car giant to enter the world of Indy cars for the first time in 1996 with Gurney's team. However, the four-year alliance brought little but disappointment for Dan and his hard-working team at Santa Anna. The slow development of the Toyota powerplant, increasingly uncompetitive Goodyear tyres and the lack of a front-line driver were just some of the reasons why the Eagle failed to soar to the heights that the partners were expecting. Ironically, Toyota power would soon topple Honda and conquer the CART series, but their triumphs would be recorded elsewhere.

After dropping out of CART, AAR ran a car in the one-make Toyota Formula Atlantic series in 2000, with Dan's sons, Justin and Alex, running the team and driving respectively.

Having abandoned regular competition, Gurney and his AAR team looked for other markets in which to ply their expertise, building a limited-edition Alligator motorcycle, and successfully shifting to engineering projects contracted by the automotive, motorcycle and aviation industries. Most recently, AAR have been involved in building Highcroft Racing's Project 56. This radical DeltaWing car was intended to run at the Le Mans 24-hour race in 2012.

GURNEY, Dan (USA) b 13/4/1931, Port Jefferson, New York

1959 Championship position: 7th   Wins: 0   Pole positions: 0   Fastest laps: Points scored: 13

	Race	Circuit	No	Entrant	Tyres	Capacity/Car/Engine	Comment	Q Pos/Entries
ret	FRENCH GP	Reims	28	Scuderia Ferrari	D	2.4 Ferrari Dino 246 V6	*radiator*	12/22
2	GERMAN GP	AVUS	6	Scuderia Ferrari	D	2.4 Ferrari Dino 246 V6	*2nd heat 1/3rd heat 2*	3/16
3	PORTUGUESE GP	Monsanto	16	Scuderia Ferrari	D	2.4 Ferrari Dino 246 V6	*1 lap behind*	6/16
4	ITALIAN GP	Monza	36	Scuderia Ferrari	D	2.4 Ferrari Dino 246 V6		4/21

1960 Championship position: Unplaced

10/ret	MONACO GP	Monte Carlo	4	Owen Racing Organisation	D	2.5 BRM P48 4	*suspension/52 laps behind*	14/24
ret	DUTCH GP	Zandvoort	15	Owen Racing Organisation	D	2.5 BRM P48 4	*accident – brake failure*	6/21
ret	BELGIAN GP	Spa	8	Owen Racing Organisation	D	2.5 BRM P48 4	*engine*	12/21
ret	FRENCH GP	Reims	10	Owen Racing Organisation	D	2.5 BRM P48 4	*engine*	6/23
10	BRITISH GP	Silverstone	5	Owen Racing Organisation	D	2.5 BRM P48 4	*pit stop/3 laps behind*	6/25
ret	PORTUGUESE GP	Oporto	24	Owen Racing Organisation	D	2.5 BRM P48 4	*engine*	2/16
ret	US GP	Riverside	16	Owen Racing Organisation	D	2.5 BRM P48 4	*overheating*	3/23

1961 Championship position: 3rd=   Wins: 0   Pole positions: 0   Fastest laps: 0   Points scored: 21

5	MONACO GP	Monte Carlo	4	Porsche System Engineering	D	1.5 Porsche 718 F4	*2 laps behind*	11/21
10	DUTCH GP	Zandvoort	7	Porsche System Engineering	D	1.5 Porsche 787 F4	*1 lap behind*	6/17
6	BELGIAN GP	Spa	20	Porsche System Engineering	D	1.5 Porsche 718 F4		10/25
2	FRENCH GP	Reims	12	Porsche System Engineering	D	1.5 Porsche 718 F4		9/26
7	BRITISH GP	Aintree	10	Porsche System Engineering	D	1.5 Porsche 718 F4	*1 lap behind*	12/30
7	GERMAN GP	Nürburgring	9	Porsche System Engineering	D	1.5 Porsche 718 F4		7/27
2	ITALIAN GP	Monza	46	Porsche System Engineering	D	1.5 Porsche 718 F4		=12/33
dns	"	"	46	Porsche System Engineering	D	1.5 Porsche 787 F4	*practice only*	-/-
2	US GP	Watkins Glen	12	Porsche System Engineering	D	1.5 Porsche 718 F4		7/19

1962 Championship position: 5th   Wins: 1   Pole positions: 1   Fastest laps: 0   Points scored: 15

ret	DUTCH GP	Zandvoort	12	Porsche System Engineering	D	1.5 Porsche 804 F8	*gearbox*	8/20
ret	MONACO GP	Monte Carlo	4	Porsche System Engineering	D	1.5 Porsche 804 F8	*first corner accident*	=3/21
dns	BELGIAN GP	Spa	23	Autosport Team Wolfgang Seidel	D	1.5 Lotus 24-BRM V8	*car unraceworthy*	(20)/20
1	FRENCH GP	Rouen	30	Porsche System Engineering	D	1.5 Porsche 804 F8		6/17
9	BRITISH GP	Aintree	8	Porsche System Engineering	D	1.5 Porsche 804 F8	*2 laps behind*	6/21
3	GERMAN GP	Nürburgring	7	Porsche System Engineering	D	1.5 Porsche 804 F8		1/30
13/ret	ITALIAN GP	Monza	16	Porsche System Engineering	D	1.5 Porsche 804 F8	*engine/20 laps behind*	=6/30
5	US GP	Watkins Glen	10	Porsche System Engineering	D	1.5 Porsche 804 F8	*1 lap behind*	=4/20

1963 Championship position: 5th   Wins: 0   Pole positions: 0   Fastest laps: 1   Points scored: 19

ret	MONACO GP	Monte Carlo	4	Brabham Racing Organisation	D	1.5 Brabham BT7-Climax V8	*crown wheel and pinion*	6/17
3	BELGIAN GP	Spa	18	Brabham Racing Organisation	D	1.5 Brabham BT7-Climax V8	*1 lap behind*	2/20
2	DUTCH GP	Zandvoort	18	Brabham Racing Organisation	D	1.5 Brabham BT7-Climax V8	*1 lap behind*	14/19
5	FRENCH GP	Reims	8	Brabham Racing Organisation	D	1.5 Brabham BT7-Climax V8		3/21
ret	BRITISH GP	Silverstone	9	Brabham Racing Organisation	D	1.5 Brabham BT7-Climax V8	*engine*	2/23
ret	GERMAN GP	Nürburgring	10	Brabham Racing Organisation	D	1.5 Brabham BT7-Climax V8	*gearbox*	13/26
14/ret	ITALIAN GP	Monza	24	Brabham Racing Organisation	D	1.5 Brabham BT7-Climax V8	*fuel feed*	5/28
ret	US GP	Watkins Glen	6	Brabham Racing Organisation	D	1.5 Brabham BT7-Climax V8	*cracked chassis*	6/21
6	MEXICAN GP	Mexico City	6	Brabham Racing Organisation	D	1.5 Brabham BT7-Climax V8	*fuel starvation/3 laps behind*	4/21
2	SOUTH AFRICAN GP	East London	9	Brabham Racing Organisation	D	1.5 Brabham BT7-Climax V8	*FL*	3/21

1964 Championship position: 6th   Wins: 2   Pole positions: 2   Fastest laps: 2   Points scored: 19

ret	MONACO GP	Monte Carlo	6	Brabham Racing Organisation	D	1.5 Brabham BT7-Climax V8	*gearbox*	5/20
ret	DUTCH GP	Zandvoort	16	Brabham Racing Organisation	D	1.5 Brabham BT7-Climax V8	*steering wheel*	1/18
6/ret	BELGIAN GP	Spa	15	Brabham Racing Organisation	D	1.5 Brabham BT7-Climax V8	*out of fuel on last lap/FL*	1/20
1	FRENCH GP	Rouen	22	Brabham Racing Organisation	D	1.5 Brabham BT7-Climax V8		2/17
13	BRITISH GP	Brands Hatch	6	Brabham Racing Organisation	D	1.5 Brabham BT7-Climax V8	*pit stop – ignition/5 laps behind*	3/25
10	GERMAN GP	Nürburgring	5	Brabham Racing Organisation	D	1.5 Brabham BT7-Climax V8	*2 pit stops – overheating/1 lap behind*	3/24
ret	AUSTRIAN GP	Zeltweg	5	Brabham Racing Organisation	D	1.5 Brabham BT7-Climax V8	*front suspension/FL*	=4/20
10	ITALIAN GP	Monza	16	Brabham Racing Organisation	D	1.5 Brabham BT7-Climax V8	*pit stop – alternator/3 laps behind*	2/25
ret	US GP	Watkins Glen	6	Brabham Racing Organisation	D	1.5 Brabham BT7-Climax V8	*engine – oil pressure*	3/19
1	MEXICAN GP	Mexico City	6	Brabham Racing Organisation	D	1.5 Brabham BT7-Climax V8		2/19

1965 Championship position: 4th   Wins: 0   Pole positions: 0   Fastest laps: 1   Points scored: 25

ret	SOUTH AFRICAN GP	East London	8	Brabham Racing Organisation	G	1.5 Brabham BT11-Climax V8	*ignition*	9/25
10	BELGIAN GP	Spa	15	Brabham Racing Organisation	G	1.5 Brabham BT11-Climax V8	*pit stop – wet ignition/2 laps behind*	5/21
ret	FRENCH GP	Clermont Ferrand	14	Brabham Racing Organisation	G	1.5 Brabham BT11-Climax V8	*engine*	5/17
6	BRITISH GP	Silverstone	7	Brabham Racing Organisation	G	1.5 Brabham BT11-Climax V8	*drove Brabham's car/1 lap behind*	7/23
3	DUTCH GP	Zandvoort	16	Brabham Racing Organisation	G	1.5 Brabham BT11-Climax V8		5/17
3	GERMAN GP	Nürburgring	5	Brabham Racing Organisation	G	1.5 Brabham BT11-Climax V8		5/22
3	ITALIAN GP	Monza	12	Brabham Racing Organisation	G	1.5 Brabham BT11-Climax V8		9/23
2	US GP	Watkins Glen	8	Brabham Racing Organisation	G	1.5 Brabham BT11-Climax V8		8/18
2	MEXICAN GP	Mexico City	8	Brabham Racing Organisation	G	1.5 Brabham BT11-Climax V8	*FL*	2/18

1966 Championship position: 12th   Wins: 0   Pole positions: 0   Fastest laps: 0   Points scored: 4

nc	BELGIAN GP	Spa	27	Anglo American Racers	G	2.7 Eagle T1G-Climax 4	*pit stop – tyres/5 laps behind*	15/19
5	FRENCH GP	Reims	26	Anglo American Racers	G	2.7 Eagle T1G-Climax 4	*3 laps behind*	14/17
ret	BRITISH GP	Brands Hatch	16	Anglo American Racers	G	2.7 Eagle T1G-Climax 4	*engine*	3/20
ret	DUTCH GP	Zandvoort	10	Anglo American Racers	G	2.7 Eagle T1G-Climax 4	*engine – oil line*	4/18
7	GERMAN GP	Nürburgring	12	Anglo American Racers	G	2.7 Eagle T1G-Climax 4	*1 lap behind*	8/30
ret	ITALIAN GP	Monza	30	Anglo American Racers	G	3.0 Eagle T1G-Weslake V12	*oil temperature*	19/22
dns	"	"	34	Anglo American Racers	G	2.7 Eagle T1G-Climax 4	*practice only*	-/-
ret	US GP	Watkins Glen	15	Anglo American Racers	G	3.0 Eagle T1G-Weslake V12	*clutch slip*	14/19

			No	Entrant	Tyres	Capacity/Car/Engine	Comment	Q Pos/Entries
5	MEXICAN GP	Mexico City (16)	15	Anglo American Racers	G	2.7 Eagle T1G-Climax 4	1 lap behind/(also no 16 in practice)	9/19
dns	"	" "	15	Anglo American Racers	G	3.0 Eagle T1G-Weslake V12	practice only	– / –

1967 Championship position: 8th Wins: 1 Pole positions: 0 Fastest laps: 2 Points scored: 13

ret	SOUTH AFRICAN GP	Kyalami	9	Anglo American Racers	G	2.7 Eagle T1G-Climax 4	wishbone mounting	11/18
ret	MONACO GP	Monte Carlo	23	Anglo American Racers	G	3.0 Eagle T1G-Weslake V12	fuel pump drive	7/18
ret	DUTCH GP	Zandvoort	15	Anglo American Racers	G	3.0 Eagle T1G-Weslake V12	fuel injection	2/17
1	BELGIAN GP	Spa	36	Anglo American Racers	G	3.0 Eagle T1G-Weslake V12	FL	2/18
ret	FRENCH GP	Le Mans	9	Anglo American Racers	G	3.0 Eagle T1G-Weslake V12	fuel line	3/15
ret	BRITISH GP	Silverstone	9	Anglo American Racers	G	3.0 Eagle T1G-Weslake V12	clutch	5/21
ret	GERMAN GP	Nürburgring	9	Anglo American Racers	G	3.0 Eagle T1G-Weslake V12	driveshaft when leading/FL	5/25
3	CANADIAN GP	Mosport Park	10	Anglo American Racers	G	3.0 Eagle T1G-Weslake V12	1 lap behind	5/19
ret	ITALIAN GP	Monza	8	Anglo American Racers	G	3.0 Eagle T1G-Weslake V12	engine	5/18
ret	US GP	Watkins Glen	11	Anglo American Racers	G	3.0 Eagle T1G-Weslake V12	rear suspension	3/18
ret	MEXICAN GP	Mexico City	11	Anglo American Racers	G	3.0 Eagle T1G-Weslake V12	damaged radiator	3/19

1968 Championship position: 21st Wins: 0 Pole positions: 0 Fastest laps: 0 Points scored: 3

ret	SOUTH AFRICAN GP	Kyalami	6	Anglo American Racers	G	3.0 Eagle T1G-Weslake V12	oil leak/overheating	12/23
ret	MONACO GP	Monte Carlo	19	Anglo American Racers	G	3.0 Eagle T1G-Weslake V12	ignition	=17/18
ret	DUTCH GP	Zandvoort	18	Motor Racing Developments	G	3.0 Brabham BT24-Repco V8	sand in throttle slides	12/19
ret	BRITISH GP	Brands Hatch	24	Anglo American Racers	G	3.0 Eagle T1G-Weslake V12	fuel pump	=6/20
9	GERMAN GP	Nürburgring	14	Anglo American Racers	G	3.0 Eagle T1G-Weslake V12	pit stop – cut tyre	10/20
ret	ITALIAN GP	Monza	21	Anglo American Racers	G	3.0 Eagle T1G-Weslake V12	oil pressure	13/24
ret	CANADIAN GP	St Jovite	11	Anglo American Racers	G	3.0 McLaren M7A-Cosworth V8	overheating – oil pressure	=3/22
4	US GP	Watkins Glen	14	Anglo American Racers	G	3.0 McLaren M7A-Cosworth V8	1 lap behind	7/21
ret	MEXICAN GP	Mexico City	14	Anglo American Racers	G	3.0 McLaren M7A-Cosworth V8	rear suspension	5/21

1970 Championship position: 22nd = Wins: 0 Pole positions: 0 Fastest laps: 0 Points scored: 1

ret	DUTCH GP	Zandvoort	32	Bruce McLaren Motor Racing	G	3.0 McLaren M14A-Cosworth V8	timing gear	20/24
6	FRENCH GP	Clermont Ferrand	17	Bruce McLaren Motor Racing	G	3.0 McLaren M14A-Cosworth V8		17/23
ret	BRITISH GP	Brands Hatch	10	Bruce McLaren Motor Racing	G	3.0 McLaren M14A-Cosworth V8	engine – overheating	12/25

GP Starts: 86 GP Wins: 4 Pole positions: 3 Fastest laps: 6 Points: 133

HUBERT HAHNE

WITH only a very few exceptions, Hubert Hahne's racing career was spent in cars made or powered by BMW. He built his reputation in 1964–66, racing the works BMW 1800Ti touring cars in the European championship. Then a fine second place in the F2 class in the 1966 German GP in a Matra pointed him in the direction of single-seaters, and he became the non-graded works driver in the Lola-BMW for 1967 and a couple of races in 1968. That year, he returned to BMW tourers and also had the occasional Ford ride.

For 1969, Hubert was back with BMW's own F2 car, taking two second places at Hockenheim and a fourth in the Eifelrennen, although the season was marred by the death of Gerhard Mitter in practice for the German Grand Prix. He continued in Formula 2 with BMW in 1970, winning the Rhine Cup race at Hockenheim, but had little other success. Taking delivery of a March 701 for the German Grand Prix at Hockenheim, naturally he expected to do well at his favourite circuit, so there was much consternation when he failed to qualify the car. A disgruntled Hahne threatened legal action, contending that it had been delivered in an unraceworthy condition, but subsequently this was disproved by Ronnie Peterson in a test at Silverstone.

Following hard on the heels of Mitter's death, Hahne had survived a massive crash in practice for a Formula Two race in Enna, and apparently this began to sow the seeds of retirement in the driver's mind. After his unhappy experience with the F1 March, he called it a day. He set up a car dealership and with his many contacts has also worked as both a commentator and journalist.

HAHNE, Hubert (D) b 28/3/1935, Moers

1966 Championship position: Unplaced

	Race	Circuit	No	Entrant	Tyres	Capacity/Car/Engine	Comment	Q Pos/Entries
9*	GERMAN GP (F2)	Nürburgring	26	Tyrrell Racing Organisation	D	1.0 Matra MS5-BRM 4 F2	*2nd in F2 class/1 lap behind	28/30

1967 Championship position: Unplaced

ret	GERMAN GP	Nürburgring	17	Bayerische Motoren Werke	D	2.0 Lola T100-BMW 4 F2	front suspension	15/25

1968 Championship position: Unplaced

10	GERMAN GP	Nürburgring	18	Bayerische Motoren Werke	D	2.0 Lola T102-BMW 4 F2		18/20

1969 Championship position: Unplaced

dns	GERMAN GP (F2)	Nürburgring	23	Bayerische Motoren Werke	D	1.6 BMW 269-BMW 4 F2	withdrawn after Mitter's fatal accident	(17)/26

1970 Championship position: Unplaced

dnq	GERMAN GP	Hockenheim	26	Hubert Hahne	F	3.0 March 701-Cosworth V8		25/25

GP Starts: 3 GP Wins: 0 Pole positions: 0 Fastest laps: 0 Points: 0

MIKE HAILWOOD

DESPITE being the son of a brash millionaire, Mike Hailwood was totally without affectation and truly one of racing's 'nice guys'. He lived life to the full, but nevertheless was a dedicated sportsman who was undoubtedly one of motorcycle racing's greatest ever exponents – many consider him the greatest of them all – and a fine all-round racing driver who missed out on ultimate success, but still left a not inconsiderable mark on the four-wheeled sport.

By the age of 18, Hailwood was already a British motorcycle champion in four classes, winning his first world championship in 1961. During the next six seasons, he took a further eight world championships in the 500cc, 350cc and 250cc classes. His first taste of four-wheeled competition came in 1963 and, with a couple of Junior races satisfactorily completed, he briefly joined the Reg Parnell team in preparation for a full season the following year. He scored a world championship point at Monaco in 1964, but felt uncomfortable in the Formula 1 environment, perhaps frustrated at being an also-ran in one category and the top dog in the other. He did a few more races for Parnell in 1965, before concentrating almost exclusively on bikes once more, although he did enjoy some winter sunshine racing sports cars, winning the 1966 Dickie Dale three-hours in South Africa with David Hobbs in Bernard White's GT40.

Honda having pulled out of grand prix motorcycle racing at the end of 1967, the sport was heading for a period of essentially privateer participation, so Mike turned to cars once again from the beginning of 1969. The newly inaugurated F5000 series provided an ideal base to rebuild his career, and in tandem he began a successful sports car programme, mainly for John Wyer, finishing third at Le Mans in 1969. In 1971, he joined forces with John Surtees to race his F5000 car and benefited greatly from his guidance, taking second place in the series behind Frank Gardner. Late in the year, Surtees put Mike into his Formula 1 team for the Italian GP with startling results. In a great drive, he jousted for the lead in the four-car bunch that slipstreamed around the Monza circuit before finishing fourth.

Full of confidence, Hailwood lined up a massive programme with Surtees for 1972, undertaking the F2 Brazilian Torneio and F5000 Tasman series before the season proper had even started. A second place in the Race of Champions boded well for Formula 1, but his luck was definitely out. In South Africa, he put in an astounding drive to pressure Jackie Stewart, before his suspension broke, and at Monza he knew he had the opposition covered until the airbox blew off his Surtees. No one deserved a grand prix win more that year, but it was not to be. There was, however, the compensation of taking the European Formula 2 championship for Surtees with some excellent performances.

Unfortunately the progress made was not built upon in 1973, when unreliability beset the team to the extent that Mike failed to finish a single race in the points. In fact, his season was best remembered for a typical act of bravery, when he rescued Clay Regazzoni from his blazing car in South Africa to earn the George Medal. His only success came in endurance racing, where he shared the John Wyer Mirage with Derek Bell to win the Spa 1000km.

Frustrated at his lack of success with Surtees, Hailwood switched to McLaren in 1974, running a third works car in Yardley livery. Suddenly he was back in the frame, always running competitively until an accident at the German Grand Prix left him with such a badly broken leg that it spelled the end of his Grand Prix career.

Having announced his retirement in 1975, after a couple of years kicking his heels, 'Mike the Bike' was back. In a sensational return to the Isle of Man TT races in 1978, he won the Formula 1 event on a Ducati, and in 1979 he returned again to smash the lap record and take the Senior TT on a Suzuki. There were no more comebacks, however, for in 1981 Mike lost his life in a tragic road accident when his car ran into a lorry executing an illegal U-turn across a dual carriageway after he had nipped out for a fish and chip family supper. The entire world of racing, on both two wheels and four, were united in their grief at the loss of one of motorsport's most popular and genuine sons.

HAILWOOD, Mike (GB) b 2/4/1940, Great Milton Birmingham – d 23/3/1981, Birmingham

	1963 Championship position: Unplaced								
	Race	Circuit	No	Entrant	Tyres	Capacity/Car/Engine	Comment	Q Pos/Entries
8	BRITISH GP	Silverstone	20	Reg Parnell (Racing)	D	1.5 Lotus 24-Climax V8	4 laps behind	17/23
10	ITALIAN GP	Monza	40	Reg Parnell (Racing)	D	1.5 Lola Mk4-Climax V8	4 laps behind	18/28
	1964 Championship position: 19th= Wins: 0 Pole positions: 0 Fastest laps: 0 Points scored: 1							
6	MONACO GP	Monte Carlo	18	Reg Parnell (Racing)	D	1.5 Lotus 25-BRM V8	4 laps behind	15/20
12/ret	DUTCH GP	Zandvoort	12	Reg Parnell (Racing)	D	1.5 Lotus 25-BRM V8	crown wheel and pinion	14/18
8	FRENCH GP	Rouen	6	Reg Parnell (Racing)	D	1.5 Lotus 25-BRM V8	1 lap behind	13/17

ret	BRITISH GP	Brands Hatch	14	Reg Parnell (Racing)	D	1.5 Lotus 25-BRM V8	oil pipe	=12/25
ret	GERMAN GP	Nürburgring	15	Reg Parnell (Racing)	D	1.5 Lotus 25-BRM V8	engine	13/24
8	AUSTRIAN GP	Zeltweg	17	Reg Parnell (Racing)	D	1.5 Lotus 25-BRM V8	pit stop – suspension/-10 laps	=18/20
ret	ITALIAN GP	Monza	40	Reg Parnell (Racing)	D	1.5 Lotus 25-BRM V8	engine	=16/25
8/ret	US GP	Watkins Glen	14	Reg Parnell (Racing)	D	1.5 Lotus 25-BRM V8	oil pipe/9 laps behind	16/19
ret	MEXICAN GP	Mexico City	14	Reg Parnell (Racing)	D	1.5 Lotus 25-BRM V8	overheating	17/19

1965 Championship position: Unplaced

ret	MONACO GP	Monte Carlo	16	Reg Parnell (Racing)	D	1.5 Lotus 25-BRM V8	gearbox	=12/17

1971 Championship position: 18th=   Wins: 0   Pole positions: 0   Fastest laps: 0   Points scored: 3

4	ITALIAN GP	Monza	9	Team Surtees	F	3.0 Surtees TS9-Cosworth V8	0.18 sec behind winner Gethin	17/24
15/ret	US GP	Watkins Glen	20	Team Surtees	F	3.0 Surtees TS9-Cosworth V8	spun on oil – hit barrier	15/32

1972 Championship position: 8th   Wins: 0   Pole positions: 0   Fastest laps: 1   Points scored: 13

ret	SOUTH AFRICAN GP	Kyalami	17	Brooke Bond Oxo/Rob Walker/Team Surtees	F	3.0 Surtees TS9B-Cosworth V8	suspension when 2nd/FL	=3/27
ret	SPANISH GP	Jarama	15	Brooke Bond Oxo/Rob Walker/Team Surtees	F	3.0 Surtees TS9B-Cosworth V8	master switch solenoid	15/26
ret	MONACO GP	Monte Carlo	11	Brooke Bond Oxo/Rob Walker/Team Surtees	F	3.0 Surtees TS9B-Cosworth V8	hit by Ganley	11/25
4	BELGIAN GP	Nivelles	34	Brooke Bond Oxo/Rob Walker/Team Surtees	F	3.0 Surtees TS9B-Cosworth V8		8/26
6	FRENCH GP	Clermont Ferrand	26	Brooke Bond Oxo/Rob Walker/Team Surtees	F	3.0 Surtees TS9B-Cosworth V8		10/29
ret	BRITISH GP	Brands Hatch	21	Brooke Bond Oxo/Rob Walker/Team Surtees	F	3.0 Surtees TS9B-Cosworth V8	gearbox	7/27
ret	GERMAN GP	Nürburgring	14	Brooke Bond Oxo/Rob Walker/Team Surtees	F	3.0 Surtees TS9B-Cosworth V8	suspension	16/27
4	AUSTRIAN GP	Österreichring	25	Brooke Bond Oxo/Rob Walker/Team Surtees	F	3.0 Surtees TS9B-Cosworth V8		12/26
2	ITALIAN GP	Monza	10	Brooke Bond Oxo/Rob Walker/Team Surtees	F	3.0 Surtees TS9B-Cosworth V8		9/27
17/ret	US GP	Watkins Glen	23	Brooke Bond Oxo/Rob Walker/Team Surtees	F	3.0 Surtees TS9B-Cosworth V8	collision with Beuttler/-3 laps	14/32
dns	" " "	24T	Brooke Bond Oxo/Rob Walker/Team Surtees	F	3.0 Surtees TS14-Cosworth V8	practice only	- / -

1973 Championship position: Unplaced

ret	ARGENTINE GP	Buenos Aires	26	Brooke Bond Oxo/Rob Walker/Team Surtees	F	3.0 Surtees TS14A-Cosworth V8	driveshaft	10/19
ret	BRAZILIAN GP	Interlagos	5	Brooke Bond Oxo/Rob Walker/Team Surtees	F	3.0 Surtees TS14A-Cosworth V8	gearbox	14/20
ret	SOUTH AFRICAN GP	Kyalami	10	Brooke Bond Oxo/Rob Walker/Team Surtees	F	3.0 Surtees TS14A-Cosworth V8	accident/saved Regazzoni	12/25
ret	SPANISH GP	Montjuich Park	9	Brooke Bond Oxo/Rob Walker/Team Surtees	F	3.0 Surtees TS14A-Cosworth V8	started from pitlane/oil pipe	=9/22
ret	BELGIAN GP	Zolder	23	Brooke Bond Oxo/Rob Walker/Team Surtees	F	3.0 Surtees TS14A-Cosworth V8	spun off	13/23
8	MONACO GP	Monte Carlo	23	Brooke Bond Oxo/Rob Walker/Team Surtees	F	3.0 Surtees TS14A-Cosworth V8	pit stop – puncture/3 laps behind	=13/26
ret	SWEDISH GP	Anderstorp	23	Brooke Bond Oxo/Rob Walker/Team Surtees	F	3.0 Surtees TS14A-Cosworth V8	vibration caused by tyres	10/22
ret	FRENCH GP	Paul Ricard	23	Brooke Bond Oxo/Rob Walker/Team Surtees	F	3.0 Surtees TS14A-Cosworth V8	engine – oil leak	11/25
ret/dns*	BRITISH GP	Silverstone	23	Brooke Bond Oxo/Rob Walker/Team Surtees	F	3.0 Surtees TS14A-Cosworth V8	accident – 1st start/*did not restart	12/29
ret	DUTCH GP	Zandvoort	23	Brooke Bond Oxo/Rob Walker/Team Surtees	F	3.0 Surtees TS14A-Cosworth V8	electrics	24/24
14	GERMAN GP	Nürburgring	23	Brooke Bond Oxo/Rob Walker/Team Surtees	F	3.0 Surtees TS14A-Cosworth V8	1 lap behind	=17/23
10	AUSTRIAN GP	Österreichring	23	Brooke Bond Oxo/Rob Walker/Team Surtees	F	3.0 Surtees TS14A-Cosworth V8	pit stop – puncture/5 laps behind	15/25
7	ITALIAN GP	Monza	23	Brooke Bond Oxo/Rob Walker/Team Surtees	F	3.0 Surtees TS14A-Cosworth V8		8/25
9	CANADIAN GP	Mosport Park	23	Brooke Bond Oxo/Rob Walker/Team Surtees	F	3.0 Surtees TS14A-Cosworth V8	2 laps behind	12/26
ret	US GP	Watkins Glen	23	Brooke Bond Oxo/Rob Walker/Team Surtees	F	3.0 Surtees TS14A-Cosworth V8	broken suspension	7/28

1974 Championship position: 10=   Wins: 0   Pole positions: 0   Fastest laps: 0   Points scored: 12

4	ARGENTINE GP	Buenos Aires	33	Yardley Team McLaren	G	3.0 McLaren M23-Cosworth V8		9/26
5	BRAZILIAN GP	Interlagos	33	Yardley Team McLaren	G	3.0 McLaren M23-Cosworth V8	1 lap behind	7/25
3	SOUTH AFRICAN GP	Kyalami	33	Yardley Team McLaren	G	3.0 McLaren M23-Cosworth V8		=11/27
9	SPANISH GP	Jarama	33	Yardley Team McLaren	G	3.0 McLaren M23-Cosworth V8	3 laps behind	=17/28
7	BELGIAN GP	Nivelles	33	Yardley Team McLaren	G	3.0 McLaren M23-Cosworth V8	fuel starvation/1 lap behind	13/32
ret	MONACO GP	Monte Carlo	33	Yardley Team McLaren	G	3.0 McLaren M23-Cosworth V8	accident	=10/28
ret	SWEDISH GP	Anderstorp	33	Yardley Team McLaren	G	3.0 McLaren M23-Cosworth V8	fuel line	11/28
4	DUTCH GP	Zandvoort	33	Yardley Team McLaren	G	3.0 McLaren M23-Cosworth V8		4/27
7	FRENCH GP	Dijon	33	Yardley Team McLaren	G	3.0 McLaren M23-Cosworth V8	1 lap behind	6/30
ret	BRITISH GP	Brands Hatch	33	Yardley Team McLaren	G	3.0 McLaren M23-Cosworth V8	spun off – could not restart	=11/34
15/ret	GERMAN GP	Nürburgring	33	Yardley Team McLaren	G	3.0 McLaren M23-Cosworth V8	accident – leg injuries/-2 laps	12/32

GP Starts: 49 (50)   GP Wins: 0   Pole positions: 0   Fastest laps: 1   Points: 29

Hailwood finally established himself as a full-time Formula1 driver with Surtees in 1972. Pictured left, he hustles the TS14A around the rather bland Nivelles circuit in Belgium to an eventual fourth place. Note the rather hastily applied numbering on the side of the car!

MIKA HÄKKINEN

THIS Finnish driver has always seemed bound for great things. With the benefit of long-term sponsorship and the guiding hand of Keke Rosberg, Mika Häkkinen negotiated the slippery slope to the top in very short order, but still had the patience to bide his time when necessary. After sustaining very serious head injuries in practice for the Australian GP at the end of 1995, he came back with his appetite undiminished and eventually fulfilled his early promise by taking successive world championships with McLaren-Mercedes in 1998 and 1999.

A multiple karting champion in his native Finland, winner of three FF1600 titles in 1987 and GM Lotus Euroseries champion in 1988, Häkkinen had a pretty impressive CV to take into the 1989 Formula 3 season. Having opted to stay with the Dragon team that had served him so well in 1988, he found himself way off the pace, but he persevered and when he switched to the West Surrey Racing squad for the prestigious Cellnet F3 race at the end of the season, he promptly won it.

A deal was then concluded for 1990 and Mika never looked back, winning a total of 12 races at home and abroad. He took the British F3 championship and before the year was out had a Formula 1 seat with Lotus. In his first season in grand prix racing, the confident young Finn impressed everyone with his car control in a chassis that was never a match for the best, scoring points in only his third race. The following season, with a much better car, the team on the up and Ford HB engines, he firmly established himself in the top echelon, extracting the very maximum from the sleek Lotus 107.

Then came an unexpected opportunity that Häkkinen wisely grabbed. With Ayrton Senna prevaricating over his contract at McLaren, Ron Dennis lost little time in signing Mika as cover in case the Brazilian carried out his threat not to race. In the end, he contested the full season, and Mika was left sitting on the sidelines, waiting patiently for his opportunity, which finally came when Michael Andretti headed back home. In his first race, in Portugal, Mika out-qualified his master, and lay third until he ran wide and into a barrier. In his next race, in Japan, he was more circumspect, settling for a career-best third place in wildly fluctuating weather and track conditions.

For 1994, Häkkinen assumed the McLaren team leadership in the wake of Senna's departure for Williams. However, the optimism engendered by a new liaison with Peugeot soon evaporated and his year was spent in frustration, which sometimes turned into desperation, such was his desire to succeed. Ill-advised first-corner moves at Monaco and Hockenheim saw him eliminated, the latter indiscretion earning him a one-race ban. A much-heralded partnership with Mercedes Benz for 1995 brought promise of a new dawn for McLaren's sagging fortunes, but once more the team were never really on the pace, although Mika drove superbly in a handful of races, taking second places at Monza and Suzuka. His performance in Japan was all the more admirable, since he had undergone an appendectomy only ten days earlier, missing the previous weekend's Pacific GP.

Less than a fortnight after that sparkling performance came disaster in Adelaide: Mika was very close to losing his life and only prompt action saved him. The fun-loving Finn made a miraculously swift return, however, and after a shaky start soon proved he had lost none of the blinding speed he had always shown in the past. Indeed, the 1996 season was the one in which he established himself as a bona fide number-one driver; all that was missing was the breakthrough grand prix victory that he and team had been working so hard to achieve over the previous three years.

McLaren finally took the win in the opening race of the 1997 season at Melbourne, but unfortunately for the Finn it was David Coulthard's name that went into the record books. Undeterred, he continued to knock on the door, shrugging aside the heartbreak of a very late retirement when leading the British Grand Prix to bounce back with more determination than ever. He had to wait until the season's finale at Jerez, however, before taking the top step of the podium. Moreover, the victory was somewhat hollow because both Jacques Villeneuve and David Coulthard had allowed Häkkinen through to the chequered flag.

By 1998, however, his time had come. After Coulthard had stood by a pre-race agreement to allow the Finn to take first place in the Australian Grand Prix, Mika scorched away from his team-mate to begin a thrilling championship battle with Michael Schumacher. Wins in Brazil, Spain, Monaco, Austria and Germany were topped by perhaps his greatest triumph, at the Luxembourg Grand Prix, where he pulled out a top-drawer performance to defeat his Ferrari rival. His championship clincher in Japan was much easier after Schumacher stalled his car at the start.

Back-to-back titles are notoriously hard to achieve, and being the hot favourites for a repeat championship seemed to take its toll on McLaren and Häkkinen. Brilliant performances were interspersed with inexplicable lapses by both driver and team, who, it seemed, were going to lose the championship despite Schumacher's enforced absence after his Silverstone shunt. In the end, Mika's fluctuating title battle with Eddie Irvine and Ferrari was won with a truly dominant performance in Japan.

The Häkkinen-Coulthard axis remained in place at McLaren heading into 2000, the Finn chasing a third straight title, but while Michael Schumacher built up a comfortable cushion on which to mount his successful championship charge, Häkkinen appeared jaded. A mid-season rest worked wonders and he was back on form from Austria onwards, trouncing the field at the A1-Ring, and Hungary. He pulled off an amazing passing move at Spa to haul in Schumacher's points advantage, only to be pipped at the post at Suzuka's penultimate round.

Staying with McLaren for a ninth season in 2001, Häkkinen insisted that his motivation was higher than ever, but testing was blighted by engine failures on the latest Mercedes unit, and the season began with him being outshone by team-mate Coulthard. It quickly became clear that the Finn's heart wasn't entirely in it, especially after a win in Spain was lost when his clutch failed right at the finish. Then he announced a 12-month sabbatical and, with his mental burden lightened, ended the year with a win at Indianapolis, to add to another at Silverstone and fifth place in the drivers' points.

In 2002, Mika confirmed that he would not be returning to F1, his sabbatical turning into permanent retirement. 'The Flying Finn' had gone – from F1 at least. His retirement was interrupted by an outing on the Arctic Rally with Mitsubishi, and there were whispers that he was to accept a testing role in F1 – with anyone from Williams and BAR to McLaren. The speculation finally came to an end when he announced that he would indeed be returning to circuit racing – in the DTM for the 2005 season.

As part of the crack AMG Mercedes squad, Mika soon showed that he had lost little of his speed or motivation as he took a storming win at Spa in only his third race. Although the following season was less convincing, without a win and with only sixth place in the final standings, he remained a top-drawer attraction for the series.

At the end of the year, Häkkinen tested a 2006 McLaren MP4-21 for a full day at Barcelona, the suggestion being that he might make an F1 return. He was well off the pace set by McLaren's other drivers, however, and he had to accept that time had caught up with him as a grand prix driver.

Mika then committed himself to Mercedes and the DTM for a third successive year in 2007. His final season in this category yielded some bad luck, but brought a couple more wins before he signed off his second racing career. He now represents the Mercedes brand as one of their high-profile sporting ambassadors.

HÄKKINEN, Mika (SF) b 28/9/1968, Helsinki

1991 Championship position: 15th   Wins: 0   Pole positions: 0   Fastest laps: 0   Points scored: 2

	Race	Circuit	No	Entrant	Tyres	Capacity/Car/Engine	Comment	Q Pos/Entries
ret	US GP (PHOENIX)	Phoenix	11	Team Lotus	G	3.5 Lotus 102B-Judd V8	engine – oil union fire	13/34
9	BRAZILIAN GP	Interlagos	11	Team Lotus	G	3.5 Lotus 102B-Judd V8	3 laps behind	22/34
5	SAN MARINO GP	Imola	11	Team Lotus	G	3.5 Lotus 102B-Judd V8	3 laps behind	25/34
ret	MONACO GP	Monte Carlo	11	Team Lotus	G	3.5 Lotus 102B-Judd V8	oil leak – caught fire	26/34
ret	CANADIAN GP	Montreal	11	Team Lotus	G	3.5 Lotus 102B-Judd V8	spun off	24/34
9	MEXICAN GP	Mexico City	11	Team Lotus	G	3.5 Lotus 102B-Judd V8	2 laps behind	24/34
dnq	FRENCH GP	Magny Cours	11	Team Lotus	G	3.5 Lotus 102B-Judd V8		27/34
12	BRITISH GP	Silverstone	11	Team Lotus	G	3.5 Lotus 102B-Judd V8	2 laps behind	25/34
ret	GERMAN GP	Hockenheim	11	Team Lotus	G	3.5 Lotus 102B-Judd V8	engine	23/24
14	HUNGARIAN GP	Hungaroring	11	Team Lotus	G	3.5 Lotus 102B-Judd V8	3 laps behind	26/34
ret	BELGIAN GP	Spa	11	Team Lotus	G	3.5 Lotus 102B-Judd V8	engine	24/34
14	ITALIAN GP	Monza	11	Team Lotus	G	3.5 Lotus 102B-Judd V8	4 laps behind	25/34
14	PORTUGUESE GP	Estoril	11	Team Lotus	G	3.5 Lotus 102B-Judd V8	3 laps behind	26/34
ret	SPANISH GP	Barcelona	11	Team Lotus	G	3.5 Lotus 102B-Judd V8	spun off	21/33
ret	JAPANESE GP	Suzuka	11	Team Lotus	G	3.5 Lotus 102B-Judd V8	spun off	21/31
19	AUSTRALIAN GP	Adelaide	11	Team Lotus	G	3.5 Lotus 102B-Judd V8	race stopped at 14 laps/1 lap behind	25/32

1992 Championship position: 8   Wins: 0   Pole positions: 0   Fastest laps: 0   Points scored: 11

	Race	Circuit	No	Entrant	Tyres	Capacity/Car/Engine	Comment	Q Pos/Entries
9	SOUTH AFRICAN GP	Kyalami	11	Team Lotus	G	3.5 Lotus102D-Ford HB V8	2 laps behind	21/30
6	MEXICAN GP	Mexico City	11	Team Lotus	G	3.5 Lotus102D-Ford HB V8	1 lap behind	18/30
10	BRAZILIAN GP	Interlagos	11	Team Lotus	G	3.5 Lotus102D-Ford HB V8	4 laps behind	24/31
ret	SPANISH GP	Barcelona	11	Team Lotus	G	3.5 Lotus102D-Ford HB V8	spun off	21/32
dnq	SAN MARINO GP	Imola	11	Team Lotus	G	3.5 Lotus102D-Ford HB V8		27/32
ret	MONACO GP	Monte Carlo	11	Team Lotus	G	3.5 Lotus107-Ford HB V8	clutch	14/32
dns	"	" "	11	Team Lotus	G	3.5 Lotus102D-Ford HB V8	practice only	–/–
ret	CANADIAN GP	Montreal	11	Team Lotus	G	3.5 Lotus107-Ford HB V8	gearbox	10/32
4*	FRENCH GP	Magny Cours	11	Team Lotus	G	3.5 Lotus107-Ford HB V8	*aggregate of two parts/1 lap behind	11/30
6	BRITISH GP	Silverstone	11	Team Lotus	G	3.5 Lotus107-Ford HB V8		9/32
ret	GERMAN GP	Hockenheim	11	Team Lotus	G	3.5 Lotus107-Ford HB V8	engine	13/32
4	HUNGARIAN GP	Hungaroring	11	Team Lotus	G	3.5 Lotus107-Ford HB V8		16/31
6	BELGIAN GP	Spa	11	Team Lotus	G	3.5 Lotus107-Ford HB V8		8/30
ret	ITALIAN GP	Monza	11	Team Lotus	G	3.5 Lotus107-Ford HB V8	electrics	11/28
5	PORTUGUESE GP	Estoril	11	Team Lotus	G	3.5 Lotus107-Ford HB V8	1 lap behind	7/26
ret	JAPANESE GP	Suzuka	11	Team Lotus	G	3.5 Lotus107-Ford HB V8	engine	7/26
7	AUSTRALIAN GP	Adelaide	11	Team Lotus	G	3.5 Lotus107-Ford HB V8	1 lap behind	10/26

1993 Championship position: 15th=   Wins: 0   Pole positions: 0   Fastest laps: 0   Points scored: 4

	Race	Circuit	No	Entrant	Tyres	Capacity/Car/Engine	Comment	Q Pos/Entries
ret	PORTUGUESE GP	Estoril	7	Marlboro McLaren	G	3.5 McLaren MP4/8-Ford HB V8	accident – crashed into barrier	3/26
3	JAPANESE GP	Suzuka	7	Marlboro McLaren	G	3.5 McLaren MP4/8-Ford HB V8		3/24
ret	AUSTRALIAN GP	Adelaide	7	Marlboro McLaren	G	3.5 McLaren MP4/8-Ford HB V8	brakes	5/24

1994 Championship position: 4th   Wins: 0   Pole positions: 0   Fastest laps: 0   Points scored: 26

	Race	Circuit	No	Entrant	Tyres	Capacity/Car/Engine	Comment	Q Pos/Entries
ret	BRAZILIAN GP	Interlagos	7	Marlboro McLaren Peugeot	G	3.5 McLaren MP4/9-Peugeot V10	engine – electrics	8/28
ret	PACIFIC GP	T.I. Circuit	7	Marlboro McLaren Peugeot	G	3.5 McLaren MP4/9-Peugeot V10	hydraulics	4/28
3	SAN MARINO GP	Imola	7	Marlboro McLaren Peugeot	G	3.5 McLaren MP4/9-Peugeot V10		8/28
ret	MONACO GP	Monte Carlo	7	Marlboro McLaren Peugeot	G	3.5 McLaren MP4/9-Peugeot V10	first corner collision with Hill	2/24
ret	SPANISH GP	Barcelona	7	Marlboro McLaren Peugeot	G	3.5 McLaren MP4/9-Peugeot V10	engine	3/27
ret	CANADIAN GP	Montreal	7	Marlboro McLaren Peugeot	G	3.5 McLaren MP4/9-Peugeot V10	engine	7/27
ret	FRENCH GP	Magny Cours	7	Marlboro McLaren Peugeot	G	3.5 McLaren MP4/9-Peugeot V10	engine	9/28
3*	BRITISH GP	Silverstone	7	Marlboro McLaren Peugeot	G	3.5 McLaren MP4/9-Peugeot V10	*2nd place car disqualified	5/28
ret	GERMAN GP	Hockenheim	7	Marlboro McLaren Peugeot	G	3.5 McLaren MP4/9-Peugeot V10	instigated first corner accident	8/28
2*	BELGIAN GP	Spa	7	Marlboro McLaren Peugeot	G	3.5 McLaren MP4/9-Peugeot V10	*1st place car disqualified	8/28
3	ITALIAN GP	Monza	7	Marlboro McLaren Peugeot	G	3.5 McLaren MP4/9-Peugeot V10		7/28
3	PORTUGUESE GP	Estoril	7	Marlboro McLaren Peugeot	G	3.5 McLaren MP4/9-Peugeot V10		4/28
3	EUROPEAN GP	Jerez	7	Marlboro McLaren Peugeot	G	3.5 McLaren MP4/9-Peugeot V10		9/28
7	JAPANESE GP	Suzuka	7	Marlboro McLaren Peugeot	G	3.5 McLaren MP4/9-Peugeot V10		8/28
12/ret	AUSTRALIAN GP	Adelaide	7	Marlboro McLaren Peugeot	G	3.5 McLaren MP4/9-Peugeot V10	brakes – accident/5 laps behind	4/28

1995 Championship position: 7th   Wins: 0   Pole positions: 0   Fastest laps: 0   Points scored: 17

	Race	Circuit	No	Entrant	Tyres	Capacity/Car/Engine	Comment	Q Pos/Entries
4	BRAZILIAN GP	Interlagos	8	Marlboro McLaren Mercedes	G	3.0 McLaren MP4/10-Mercedes V10	1 lap behind	7/26
ret	ARGENTINE GP	Buenos Aires	8	Marlboro McLaren Mercedes	G	3.0 McLaren MP4/10-Mercedes V10	collision with Irvine on lap 1	5/26
5	SAN MARINO GP	Imola	8	Marlboro McLaren Mercedes	G	3.0 McLaren MP4/10-Mercedes V10	1 lap behind	6/26
ret	SPANISH GP	Barcelona	8	Marlboro McLaren Mercedes	G	3.0 McLaren MP4/10-Mercedes V10	fuel pressure	9/26
ret	MONACO GP	Monte Carlo	8	Marlboro McLaren Mercedes	G	3.0 McLaren MP4/10B-Mercedes V10	engine	6/26
ret	CANADIAN GP	Montreal	8	Marlboro McLaren Mercedes	G	3.0 McLaren MP4/10B-Mercedes V10	collision with Herbert on lap 1	7/24
7	FRENCH GP	Magny Cours	8	Marlboro McLaren Mercedes	G	3.0 McLaren MP4/10B-Mercedes V10	1 lap behind	8/24
ret	BRITISH GP	Silverstone	8	Marlboro McLaren Mercedes	G	3.0 McLaren MP4/10B-Mercedes V10	electrics	8/24
ret	GERMAN GP	Hockenheim	8	Marlboro McLaren Mercedes	G	3.0 McLaren MP4/10B-Mercedes V10	engine	7/24
ret	HUNGARIAN GP	Hungaroring	8	Marlboro McLaren Mercedes	G	3.0 McLaren MP4/10B-Mercedes V10	engine	5/24
ret	BELGIAN GP	Spa	8	Marlboro McLaren Mercedes	G	3.0 McLaren MP4/10B-Mercedes V10	spun off	3/24
2	ITALIAN GP	Monza	8	Marlboro McLaren Mercedes	G	3.0 McLaren MP4/10B-Mercedes V10		7/24
ret	PORTUGUESE GP	Estoril	8	Marlboro McLaren Mercedes	G	3.0 McLaren MP4/10B-Mercedes V10	engine	–/–
dns	"	"	8	Marlboro McLaren Mercedes	G	3.0 McLaren MP4/10C-Mercedes V10	set grid time in this car	13/24
8	EUROPEAN GP	Nürburgring	8	Marlboro McLaren Mercedes	G	3.0 McLaren MP4/10C-Mercedes V10	2 laps behind	9/24
2	JAPANESE GP	Suzuka	8	Marlboro McLaren Mercedes	G	3.0 McLaren MP4/10C-Mercedes V10		3/24
dns	AUSTRALIAN GP	Adelaide	8	Marlboro McLaren Mercedes	G	3.0 McLaren MP4/10B-Mercedes V10	accident in practice	(24)/24

1996 Championship position: 5th   Wins: 0   Pole positions: 0   Fastest laps: 0   Points scored: 31

	Race	Circuit	No	Entrant	Tyres	Capacity/Car/Engine	Comment	Q Pos/Entries
5	AUSTRALIAN GP	Melbourne	7	Marlboro McLaren Mercedes	G	3.0 McLaren MP4/11-Mercedes V10		5/22
4	BRAZILIAN GP	Interlagos	7	Marlboro McLaren Mercedes	G	3.0 McLaren MP4/11-Mercedes V10	spun off	7/22

ret	ARGENTINE GP	Buenos Aires	7	Marlboro McLaren Mercedes	G	3.0 McLaren MP4/11-Mercedes V10	*spun off*	8/22
8	EUROPEAN GP	Nürburgring	7	Marlboro McLaren Mercedes	G	3.0 McLaren MP4/11-Mercedes V10	*speeding in pits – stop & go penalty*	9/22
8	SAN MARINO GP	Imola	7	Marlboro McLaren Mercedes	G	3.0 McLaren MP4/11-Mercedes V10	*engine*	11/22
6/ret	MONACO GP	Monte Carlo	7	Marlboro McLaren Mercedes	G	3.0 McLaren MP4/11-Mercedes V10	*collision Salo & Irvine/5 laps behind*	8/22
5	SPANISH GP	Barcelona	7	Marlboro McLaren Mercedes	G	3.0 McLaren MP4/11-Mercedes V10	*1 lap behind*	10/22
5	CANADIAN GP	Montreal	7	Marlboro McLaren Mercedes	G	3.0 McLaren MP4/11-Mercedes V10	*spin/1 lap behind*	6/22
5	FRENCH GP	Magny Cours	7	Marlboro McLaren Mercedes	G	3.0 McLaren MP4/11-Mercedes V10	*lost 2nd and 3rd gears*	5/22
3	BRITISH GP	Silverstone	7	Marlboro McLaren Mercedes	G	3.0 McLaren MP4/11-Mercedes V10		4/22
ret	GERMAN GP	Hockenheim	7	Marlboro McLaren Mercedes	G	3.0 McLaren MP4/11-Mercedes V10	*gearbox*	4/20
4	HUNGARIAN GP	Hungaroring	7	Marlboro McLaren Mercedes	G	3.0 McLaren MP4/11-Mercedes V10	*1 lap behind*	7/20
3	BELGIAN GP	Spa	7	Marlboro McLaren Mercedes	G	3.0 McLaren MP4/11-Mercedes V10		6/20
3	ITALIAN GP	Monza	7	Marlboro McLaren Mercedes	G	3.0 McLaren MP4/11-Mercedes V10		4/20
ret	PORTUGUESE GP	Estoril	7	Marlboro McLaren Mercedes	G	3.0 McLaren MP4/11-Mercedes V10	*handling after collision damage*	7/20
3	JAPANESE GP	Suzuka	7	Marlboro McLaren Mercedes	G	3.0 McLaren MP4/11-Mercedes V10		5/20

1997 Championship position: 5th=   Wins: 1   Pole positions: 1   Fastest laps: 1   Points scored: 27

3	AUSTRALIAN GP	Melbourne	9	West McLaren Mercedes	G	3.0 McLaren MP4/12-Mercedes V10		6/24
4	BRAZILIAN GP	Interlagos	9	West McLaren Mercedes	G	3.0 McLaren MP4/12-Mercedes V10		4/22
5	ARGENTINE GP	Buenos Aires	9	West McLaren Mercedes	G	3.0 McLaren MP4/12-Mercedes V10		17/22
6	SAN MARINO GP	Imola	9	West McLaren Mercedes	G	3.0 McLaren MP4/12-Mercedes V10	*1 lap behind*	8/22
ret	MONACO GP	Monte Carlo	9	West McLaren Mercedes	G	3.0 McLaren MP4/12-Mercedes V10	*collision with Alesi*	8/22
7	SPANISH GP	Barcelona	9	West McLaren Mercedes	G	3.0 McLaren MP4/12-Mercedes V10		5/22
ret	CANADIAN GP	Montreal	9	West McLaren Mercedes	G	3.0 McLaren MP4/12-Mercedes V10	*lap 1 collision – lost rear wing*	9/22
ret	FRENCH GP	Magny Cours	9	West McLaren Mercedes	G	3.0 McLaren MP4/12-Mercedes V10	*engine*	10/22
ret	BRITISH GP	Silverstone	9	West McLaren Mercedes	G	3.0 McLaren MP4/12-Mercedes V10	*engine/led race*	3/22
3	GERMAN GP	Hockenheim	9	West McLaren Mercedes	G	3.0 McLaren MP4/12-Mercedes V10		3/22
ret	HUNGARIAN GP	Hungaroring	9	West McLaren Mercedes	G	3.0 McLaren MP4/12-Mercedes V10	*hydraulics*	4/22
dsq*	BELGIAN GP	Spa	9	West McLaren Mercedes	G	3.0 McLaren MP4/12-Mercedes V10	*3rd on road/*fuel irregularities*	5/22
9	ITALIAN GP	Monza	9	West McLaren Mercedes	G	3.0 McLaren MP4/12-Mercedes V10	*delayed by tyre problems/FL*	5/22
ret	AUSTRIAN GP	A1-Ring	9	West McLaren Mercedes	G	3.0 McLaren MP4/12-Mercedes V10	*engine*	2/22
ret	LUXEMBOURG GP	Nürburgring	9	West McLaren Mercedes	G	3.0 McLaren MP4/12-Mercedes V10	*engine*	1/22
4	JAPANESE GP	Suzuka	9	West McLaren Mercedes	G	3.0 McLaren MP4/12-Mercedes V10		4/22
1	EUROPEAN GP	Jerez	9	West McLaren Mercedes	G	3.0 McLaren MP4/12-Mercedes V10	*Coulthard gave up position*	5/22

1998 WORLD CHAMPION   Wins: 8   Pole positions: 9   Fastest laps: 6   Points scored: 100

1	AUSTRALIAN GP	Melbourne	8	West McLaren Mercedes	B	3.0 McLaren MP4/13-Mercedes V10	*Coulthard gave up leading position/FL*	1/22
1	BRAZILIAN GP	Interlagos	8	West McLaren Mercedes	B	3.0 McLaren MP4/13-Mercedes V10	*FL*	1/22
2	ARGENTINE GP	Buenos Aires	8	West McLaren Mercedes	B	3.0 McLaren MP4/13-Mercedes V10		3/22
ret	SAN MARINO GP	Imola	8	West McLaren Mercedes	B	3.0 McLaren MP4/13-Mercedes V10	*gearbox*	2/22
1	SPANISH GP	Barcelona	8	West McLaren Mercedes	B	3.0 McLaren MP4/13-Mercedes V10	*FL*	1/22
1	MONACO GP	Monte Carlo	8	West McLaren Mercedes	B	3.0 McLaren MP4/13-Mercedes V10	*FL*	1/22
ret	CANADIAN GP	Montreal	8	West McLaren Mercedes	B	3.0 McLaren MP4/13-Mercedes V10	*gearbox on lap 1*	2/22
3	FRENCH GP	Magny Cours	8	West McLaren Mercedes	B	3.0 McLaren MP4/13-Mercedes V10		1/22
2	BRITISH GP	Silverstone	8	West McLaren Mercedes	B	3.0 McLaren MP4/13-Mercedes V10	*survived mid-race spin in rain*	1/22
1	AUSTRIAN GP	A1-Ring	8	West McLaren Mercedes	B	3.0 McLaren MP4/13-Mercedes V10		3/22
1	GERMAN GP	Hockenheim	8	West McLaren Mercedes	B	3.0 McLaren MP4/13-Mercedes V10		1/22
6	HUNGARIAN GP	Hungaroring	8	West McLaren Mercedes	B	3.0 McLaren MP4/13-Mercedes V10	*handling problems/1 lap behind*	1/22
ret	BELGIAN GP	Spa	8	West McLaren Mercedes	B	3.0 McLaren MP4/13-Mercedes V10	*collision with Herbert*	1/22
4	ITALIAN GP	Monza	8	West McLaren Mercedes	B	3.0 McLaren MP4/13-Mercedes V10	*FL*	3/22
1	LUXEMBOURG GP	Nürburgring	8	West McLaren Mercedes	B	3.0 McLaren MP4/13-Mercedes V10	*FL*	3/22
1	JAPANESE GP	Suzuka	8	West McLaren Mercedes	B	3.0 McLaren MP4/13-Mercedes V10		2/22

Precision driving. Mika takes his McLaren as close to the barrier as possible in his round-the-houses win in the 1998 Monaco Grand Prix. The Finn took a further seven wins that season to claim the first of his two successive world championships.

1999 WORLD CHAMPION Wins: 5   Pole positions: 11   Fastest laps: 6   Points scored: 76

ret	AUSTRALIAN GP	Melbourne	1	West McLaren Mercedes	B	3.0 McLaren MP4/14-Mercedes V10	*throttle*	1/22
1	BRAZILIAN GP	Interlagos	1	West McLaren Mercedes	B	3.0 McLaren MP4/14-Mercedes V10	*FL*	1/22
ret	SAN MARINO GP	Imola	1	West McLaren Mercedes	B	3.0 McLaren MP4/14-Mercedes V10	*spun off when leading*	1/22
3	MONACO GP	Monte Carlo	1	West McLaren Mercedes	B	3.0 McLaren MP4/14-Mercedes V10	*FL*	1/22
1	SPANISH GP	Barcelona	1	West McLaren Mercedes	B	3.0 McLaren MP4/14-Mercedes V10		1/22
1	CANADIAN GP	Montreal	1	West McLaren Mercedes	B	3.0 McLaren MP4/14-Mercedes V10		2/22
2	FRENCH GP	Magny Cours	1	West McLaren Mercedes	B	3.0 McLaren MP4/14-Mercedes V10		14/22
ret	BRITISH GP	Silverstone	1	West McLaren Mercedes	B	3.0 McLaren MP4/14-Mercedes V10	*precautionary stop after lost wheel/FL*	1/22
3	AUSTRIAN GP	A1-Ring	1	West McLaren Mercedes	B	3.0 McLaren MP4/14-Mercedes V10	*recovered from lap 1 spin/FL*	1/22
ret	GERMAN GP	Hockenheim	1	West McLaren Mercedes	B	3.0 McLaren MP4/14-Mercedes V10	*tyre failure – crashed*	1/22
1	HUNGARIAN GP	Hungaroring	1	West McLaren Mercedes	B	3.0 McLaren MP4/14-Mercedes V10		1/22
2	BELGIAN GP	Spa	1	West McLaren Mercedes	B	3.0 McLaren MP4/14-Mercedes V10	*FL*	1/22
ret	ITALIAN GP	Monza	1	West McLaren Mercedes	B	3.0 McLaren MP4/14-Mercedes V10	*spun off when leading*	1/22
5	EUROPEAN GP	Nürburgring	1	West McLaren Mercedes	B	3.0 McLaren MP4/14-Mercedes V10	*delayed by wet-dry tyre changes/FL*	3/22
3	MALAYSIAN GP	Sepang	1	West McLaren Mercedes	B	3.0 McLaren MP4/14-Mercedes V10		4/22
1	JAPANESE GP	Suzuka	1	West McLaren Mercedes	B	3.0 McLaren MP4/14-Mercedes V10		2/22

2000 Championship position: 2nd   Wins: 4   Pole positions: 5   Fastest laps: 9   Points scored: 89

ret	AUSTRALIAN GP	Melbourne	1	West McLaren Mercedes	B	3.0 Mercedes MP4/15-Mercedes V10	*engine when in lead*	1/22
ret	BRAZILIAN GP	Interlagos	1	West McLaren Mercedes	B	3.0 Mercedes MP4/15-Mercedes V10	*engine– oil presure when in lead*	1/22
2	SAN MARINO GP	Imola	1	West McLaren Mercedes	B	3.0 Mercedes MP4/15-Mercedes V10	*FL*	1/22
2	BRITISH GP	Silverstone	1	West McLaren Mercedes	B	3.0 Mercedes MP4/15-Mercedes V10	*chassis problems/FL*	3/22
1	SPANISH GP	Barcelona	1	West McLaren Mercedes	B	3.0 Mercedes MP4/15-Mercedes V10	*FL*	2/22
2	EUROPEAN GP	Nürburgring	1	West McLaren Mercedes	B	3.0 Mercedes MP4/15-Mercedes V10		3/22
6	MONACO GP	Monte Carlo	1	West McLaren Mercedes	B	3.0 Mercedes MP4/15-Mercedes V10	*gearbox problems/1 lap behind/FL*	5/22
4	CANADIAN GP	Montreal	1	West McLaren Mercedes	B	3.0 Mercedes MP4/15-Mercedes V10	*FL*	4/22
2	FRENCH GP	Magny Cours	1	West McLaren Mercedes	B	3.0 Mercedes MP4/15-Mercedes V10		4/22
1	AUSTRIAN GP	A1-Ring	1	West McLaren Mercedes	B	3.0 Mercedes MP4/15-Mercedes V10		1/22
2	GERMAN GP	Hockenheim	1	West McLaren Mercedes	B	3.0 Mercedes MP4/15-Mercedes V10		4/22
1	HUNGARIAN GP	Hungaroring	1	West McLaren Mercedes	B	3.0 Mercedes MP4/15-Mercedes V10	*FL*	3/22
1	BELGIAN GP	Spa	1	West McLaren Mercedes	B	3.0 Mercedes MP4/15-Mercedes V10		1/22
2	ITALIAN GP	Monza	1	West McLaren Mercedes	B	3.0 Mercedes MP4/15-Mercedes V10	*FL*	3/22
ret	UNITED STATES GP	Indianapolis	1	West McLaren Mercedes	B	3.0 Mercedes MP4/15-Mercedes V10	*engine*	3/22
2	JAPANESE GP	Suzuka	1	West McLaren Mercedes	B	3.0 Mercedes MP4/15-Mercedes V10	*FL*	2/22
4	MALAYSIAN GP	Sepang	1	West McLaren Mercedes	B	3.0 Mercedes MP4/15-Mercedes V10	*FL*	2/22

Eventual winner Häkkinen speeds into an immediate lead at the start of the 1999 Hungarian Grand Prix. In close attendance are Irvine, Fisichella and Coulthard, with the yellow Jordans of Frentzen and Hill in pursuit.

2001 Championship position: 5th   Wins: 2   Pole positions: 0   Fastest laps: 3   Points scored: 37

	Race	Circuit	No	Entrant	Tyres	Capacity/Car/Engine	Comment	Q Pos/Entries
ret	AUSTRALIAN GP	Melbourne	3	West McLaren Mercedes	B	3.0 Mercedes MP4/16-Mercedes V10	broken suspension – accident	3/22
6	MALAYSIAN GP	Sepang	3	West McLaren Mercedes	B	3.0 Mercedes MP4/16-Mercedes V10	understeer/FL	4/22
ret	BRAZILIAN GP	Interlagos	3	West McLaren Mercedes	B	3.0 Mercedes MP4/16-Mercedes V10	stalled on grid	3/22
4	SAN MARINO GP	Imola	3	West McLaren Mercedes	B	3.0 Mercedes MP4/16-Mercedes V10		2/22
9/ret	SPANISH GP	Barcelona	3	West McLaren Mercedes	B	3.0 Mercedes MP4/16-Mercedes V10	leading on penultimate lap/clutch	2/22
ret	AUSTRIAN GP	A1-Ring	3	West McLaren Mercedes	B	3.0 Mercedes MP4/16-Mercedes V10	electronics	8/22
ret	MONACO GP	Monte Carlo	3	West McLaren Mercedes	B	3.0 Mercedes MP4/16-Mercedes V10	handling problem	3/22
3	CANADIAN GP	Montreal	3	West McLaren Mercedes	B	3.0 Mercedes MP4/16-Mercedes V10		8/22
6	EUROPEAN GP	Nürburgring	3	West McLaren Mercedes	B	3.0 Mercedes MP4/16-Mercedes V10	tyre balance problems	6/22
dns	FRANCE GP	Magny Cours	3	West McLaren Mercedes	B	3.0 Mercedes MP4/16-Mercedes V10	gearbox failure on dummy grid	4/22
1	BRITISH GP	Silverstone	3	West McLaren Mercedes	B	3.0 Mercedes MP4/16-Mercedes V10	FL	2/22
ret	GERMAN GP	Hockenheim	3	West McLaren Mercedes	B	3.0 Mercedes MP4/16-Mercedes V10	engine	3/22
5	HUNGARIAN GP	Hungaroring	3	West McLaren Mercedes	B	3.0 Mercedes MP4/16-Mercedes V10	FL	6/22
4	BELGIAN GP	Spa	3	West McLaren Mercedes	B	3.0 Mercedes MP4/16-Mercedes V10	handling problems	7/22
ret	ITALIAN GP	Monza	3	West McLaren Mercedes	B	3.0 Mercedes MP4/16-Mercedes V10	transmission	7/22
1	UNITED STATES GP	Indianapolis	3	West McLaren Mercedes	B	3.0 Mercedes MP4/16-Mercedes V10	*2nd place time disallowed	*4/22
4	JAPANESE GP	Suzuka	3	West McLaren Mercedes	B	3.0 Mercedes MP4/16-Mercedes V10		5/22

GP Starts: 161   GP Wins: 20   Pole positions: 26   Fastest laps: 25   Points: 420

BRUCE HALFORD

DESPITE possessing only limited experience, gained with a Cooper-Bristol, Bruce Halford ambitiously purchased the ex-Bira Maserati 250F in 1956. He also bought a passenger coach, stripped out most of the seats, put in a full-width access door at the rear and effectively built a transporter-cum-motorhome. He also undertook most of the driving duties as he trawled the Continent, living off starting and prize monies topped up by some trade sponsorship. Inevitably, perhaps, he tasted success only in minor F1 races, his best placing being third at the Caen Grand Prix in 1957. This result earned him an invitation to compete in the German Grand Prix, which would be followed by the appearances at Pescara and Monza to help extend his Continental adventure.

By 1958, the car was showing its age. Halford took another third at Caen before he switched to a Lister-Jaguar and a year of national sports car racing – which must certainly have sharpened his driving, for he was a much improved performer when he returned to single-seaters in 1959 with a new Lotus 16. However, his best result was a third in the Silver City Trophy race at Snetterton, guesting for the BRM team.

In 1960, Halford primarily handled a Cooper for the Yeoman Credit Team, mainly in non-championship events, with only moderate success. He made his last Formula 1 appearance at Goodwood in the 1961 Glover Trophy, taking an Emeryson to ninth place, and then he made a final trip to Le Mans, where he was lucky to escape serious injury after crashing the Ecurie Ecosse Cooper Monaco and being thrown out on to the track. Thereafter, he scaled down his racing activities to concentrate on the family hotel business in Torquay, while racing yachts with his brother, David, satisfied his sporting needs.

With the new-found popularity of historic racing in the late 1970s, Bruce returned to the circuits at the wheel of an immaculate Lotus 16 and enjoyed himself immensely in the friendly, but fiercely competitive atmosphere. Turning back the clock, he raced with great vigour through to the end of the 1981 season.

HALFORD, Bruce (GB) b 18/5/1931, Hampton-in-Arden, nr Birmingham, Warwickshire – d 2/12/2001, Churston Ferrers, Devon

1956 Championship position: Unplaced

	Race	Circuit	No	Entrant	Tyres	Capacity/Car/Engine	Comment	Q Pos/Entries
ret	BRITISH GP	Silverstone	29	Bruce Halford	D	2.5 Maserati 250F 6	engine	20/28
dsq*	GERMAN GP	Nürburgring	21	Bruce Halford	D	2.5 Maserati 250F 6	*push start after a spin	11/21
ret	ITALIAN GP	Monza	48	Bruce Halford	D	2.5 Maserati 250F 6	engine	22/26

1957 Championship position: Unplaced

	Race	Circuit	No	Entrant	Tyres	Capacity/Car/Engine	Comment	Q Pos/Entries
11	GERMAN GP	Nürburgring	15	Bruce Halford	D	2.5 Maserati 250F 6	1 lap behind	16/24
ret	PESCARA GP	Pescara	20	Bruce Halford	D	2.5 Maserati 250F 6	differential	14/16
ret	ITALIAN GP	Monza	16	Bruce Halford	D	2.5 Maserati 250F 6	engine	14/19

1959 Championship position: Unplaced

	Race	Circuit	No	Entrant	Tyres	Capacity/Car/Engine	Comment	Q Pos/Entries
ret	MONACO GP	Monte Carlo	44	John Fisher	D	1.5 Lotus 16-Climax 4	accident with Allison and von Trips	16/24

1960 Championship position: Unplaced

	Race	Circuit	No	Entrant	Tyres	Capacity/Car/Engine	Comment	Q Pos/Entries
dnq	MONACO GP	Monte Carlo	12	Fred Tuck Cars	D	2.5 Cooper T51-Climax 4		17/24
8/ret	FRENCH GP	Reims	48	Yeoman Credit Racing Team	D	2.5 Cooper T51-Climax 4	engine	16/23

GP Starts: 8   GP Wins: 0   Pole positions: 0   Fastest laps: 0   Points: 0

JIM HALL

IT is a pity that Jim Hall decided not to extend his season-long grand prix career and to return to the States, for undoubtedly he was a talented driver who could have gone much further in this sphere had he chosen to do so. As it was, Formula 1's loss was sports car racing's gain, for he set about building and racing a succession of just about the most exciting sports cars ever seen.

A multi-millionaire teenager after the death of his parents in an air crash, Hall soon became involved with racing and exotic cars, teaming up with Carroll Shelby to run a Texas Maserati dealership until he went into the oil business in 1958, continuing to race in SCCA events.

Hall made an impressive GP debut at Riverside in 1960, lying fifth until last-lap gremlins intervened. This encouraged him to race a Lotus in 1961 and '62 – without success, although he finished fourth in the non-championship 1962 Mexican GP. His 1963 season with BRP was quite encouraging: twice he finished in the points in GPs, he took fourth place in the Glover Trophy, and he recorded sixth in the Lombank Trophy and at Solitude.

With the Formula 1 bug out of his system, Hall set about completing the task he and Hap Sharp had first undertaken in 1962, namely building an advanced automatic-transmission sports car. Immersed in the Chaparral's innovative design, he continued to drive, regularly clocking up wins and placings, and in 1965 the car dominated USRRC sports car racing in North America. From 1966, he concentrated his driving activities on Can-Am, leaving the long-distance programme to Phil Hill, Jo Bonnier and Mike Spence until rule changes forced his Chaparral 2F out of competition.

However, in the 1968 Stardust GP at Las Vegas, Hall's Can-Am car ran into the back of a McLaren driven by Lothar Motschenbacher. The Chaparral flipped and was demolished, and he lay in hospital for nine weeks with multiple injuries. Apart from a couple of Trans-Am races in 1970, his racing career was over, but he continued to be involved with the sport throughout the 1970s, collaborating with Carl Haas in F5000 before making a successful move to Indy car racing with his own chassis. He pulled out at the end of the 1982 season and did not return until 1991. A fairy-tale first-time victory by John Andretti proved to be illusory, for the next three seasons saw the Pennzoil entry consistently underperforming.

In 1995, bolstered by the talents of Rookie of the Year Gil de Ferran, the team were back in business, taking a win in the season's finale at Laguna Seca. More success was anticipated in 1996, but despite another win in Cleveland, Jim, after much thought, decided the time was right to call it a day.

"It's been my life. It's been a lot of fun," he said. Certainly, the long, tall Texan took his leave having made an indelible mark on motor racing history.

Jim Hall contested the 1963 world championship in a less-than-competitive BRP Lotus 24-BRM, but he still managed to score points on two occasions. The tall American looks relaxed on his way to sixth place in the British Grand Prix at Silverstone.

HALL, Jim (USA) b 23/7/1935, Abilene, Texas

	Race	Circuit	No	Entrant	Tyres	Capacity/Car/Engine	Comment	Q Pos/Entries
1960 Championship position: Unplaced								
7	US GP	Riverside	24	Jim Hall	D	2.5 Lotus 18-Climax 4	2 laps behind	12/23
1961 Championship position: Unplaced								
ret	US GP	Watkins Glen	17	Jim Hall	D	1.5 Lotus 18-Climax 4	fuel leak	=18/19
1962 Championship position: Unplaced								
dns	US GP	Watkins Glen	25	Jim Hall	D	1.5 Lotus 21-Climax 4	engine – dropped valve	(18)/20
1963 Championship position: 12th Wins: 0 Pole positions: 0 Fastest laps: 0 Points scored: 3								
ret	MONACO GP	Monte Carlo	12	British Racing Partnership	D	1.5 Lotus 24-BRM V8	gearbox	13/17
ret	BELGIAN GP	Spa	5	British Racing Partnership	D	1.5 Lotus 24-BRM V8	accident in rain	=12/20
8	DUTCH GP	Zandvoort	42	British Racing Partnership	D	1.5 Lotus 24-BRM V8	3 laps behind	=17/19
11	FRENCH GP	Reims	34	British Racing Partnership	D	1.5 Lotus 24-BRM V8	pit stop/8 laps behind	18/21
6	BRITISH GP	Silverstone	12	British Racing Partnership	D	1.5 Lotus 24-BRM V8	2 laps behind	13/23
5	GERMAN GP	Nürburgring	20	British Racing Partnership	D	1.5 Lotus 24-BRM V8	1 lap behind	16/26
8	ITALIAN GP	Monza	30	British Racing Partnership	D	1.5 Lotus 24-BRM V8	2 laps behind	17/28
10/ret	US GP	Watkins Glen	16	British Racing Partnership	D	1.5 Lotus 24-BRM V8	gearbox	16/21
8	MEXICAN GP	Mexico City	16	British Racing Partnership	D	1.5 Lotus 24-BRM V8	5 laps behind	15/21
GP Starts: 11 GP Wins: 0 Pole positions: 0 Fastest laps: 0 Points: 3								

DUNCAN HAMILTON

A FORMER Fleet Air Arm pilot, Duncan Hamilton was a larger-than-life character who drove a pre-war Maserati 6C to fourth place in the inaugural 1948 Zandvoort Grand Prix in front of more than 100,000 fans.

It was 1951 before Hamilton really went racing seriously, however, after he managed to get hold of a Lago-Talbot, which he drove enthusiastically during that season. He made a couple of grand prix appearances, and took second place in the International Trophy and fifth in the non-championship Dutch GP. In addition, he recorded good placings in minor Libre events.

With Formula 2 becoming the premier category for 1952, Hamilton's car became redundant except for Libre events, so thereafter he had a handful of grand prix outings in John Heath's Formula 2 HWMs. His best placings were fourth in the 1952 Eifelrennen, and sixth in the Ulster Trophy at Dundrod and the Crystal Palace Trophy in '53.

However, Hamilton's greatest moments came in sports car racing. Having finished fourth in 1950 and then sixth in 1951 at Le Mans with a Nash-Healey, he and Tony Rolt finally won the race two years later in a works Jaguar D-Type. The pair were the first to break the 100mph average for the 24 hours with a speed of 108.85mph.

They returned the following season, this time in Duncan's own D-Type, and finished second after a thrilling chase of Froilán González's Ferrari in the wet. Hamilton scored further major wins in the Coupe de Paris at Montlhéry in 1954 and '56, and the 1956 Reims 12-hours with Ivor Bueb. It was this last race that lost him his seat in the Jaguar team, after he had ignored team orders to slow down and hold station behind the sister car of Paul Frère

Hamilton recorded numerous excellent placings elsewhere, however, including a third in the 1956 Swedish GP, where he shared a works Ferrari with Alfonso de Portago and Mike Hawthorn. After the death of a close friend in a road accident on the Guildford by-pass early in 1959, he retired from racing to concentrate on his successful garage business.

HAMILTON, Duncan (GB) b 30/4/1920, County Cork, Ireland – d 13/5/1994, Sherbourne, Dorset

	Race	Circuit	No	Entrant	Tyres	Capacity/Car/Engine	Comment	Q Pos/Entries
1951 Championship position: Unplaced								
12	BRITISH GP	Silverstone	18	Duncan Hamilton	D	4.5 Talbot-Lago T26C 6	9 laps behind	11/20
ret	GERMAN GP	Nürburgring	88	Duncan Hamilton	D	4.5 Talbot-Lago T26C 6	oil pressure	20/23
1952 Championship position: Unplaced								
ret	BRITISH GP	Silverstone	30	HW Motors Ltd	D	2.0 HWM-Alta 4	engine	11/32
7	DUTCH GP	Zandvoort	28	HW Motors Ltd	D	2.0 HWM-Alta 4	5 laps behind	10/18
1953 Championship position: Unplaced								
ret	BRITISH GP	Silverstone	3	HW Motors Ltd	D	2.0 HWM-Alta 4	clutch	17/29
GP Starts: 5 GP Wins: 0 Pole positions: 0 Fastest laps: 0 Points: 0								

GIVEN Lewis Hamilton's runaway successes in the sport's lower ranks, it was inevitable that one day he would strap himself into a McLaren-Mercedes to take part in his first grand prix, Once under the watchful eye of the meticulous Ron Dennis, his racing apprenticeship was carefully nurtured both on and off the track, to produce a young man inexorably bound for motor racing greatness.

Despite limited funds at the outset, but with massive encouragement from his father, Anthony, the youngster began racing when he was just eight. He quickly established himself at the head of the pack, becoming the British Cadet Kart champion in 1995, before embarking on an unprecedented trail of success, which culminated in him winning the 2000 world title. Having become the very best in karts, he made the decision to skip Formula Ford and head straight for the 2002 Formula Renault UK championship, which was justified when he took third overall. Although the temptation to move up to F3 was great, Hamilton opted to remain in Formula Renault in 2003, and it proved to be a wise move, with ten wins, eleven poles and nine fastest laps seeing him home.

Shrewdly, Hamilton was placed in the German-based F3 Euroseries for the 2004 season, where he was able to develop his career in a new environment. He had a solid debut year, taking one win and two thirds to end the season fifth in the standings, before dominating the inaugural Bahrain Super Prix and taking victory in race one at Macau.

In 2005, Hamilton left Manor to join the crack ASM team in the Euroseries. Backed by the existing series champions, the Briton blitzed the opposition, taking win after win to easily lift the title; 15 victories, 13 poles and 15 fastest laps underlined his dominance. His unstoppable rise was also illustrated in the blue-riband F3 events, where he seized the initiative to win the Marlboro Masters at Zandvoort, the Monaco GP support races and the Pau Grand Prix.

With all that achieved, Hamilton had only one more category to conquer before Formula 1, and while the GP2 Series would be a tough nut to crack, he took to it with aplomb. He was signed to ASM's sister team, ART Grand Prix, and was listed amid the pre-season favourites, despite his rookie status. Although a quiet opening round in Valencia yielded a maiden podium, he made short work of playing himself into the series, taking a double win in round three at the Nürburgring and going on to add three more victories – at Monaco and twice at Silverstone – before the season reached its mid-point. Although he failed to take another win, consistent podium finishes allowed him to get the job done, holding off a worthy challenge from Nelson Piquet Jr.

The conundrum for McLaren-Mercedes was what to do next with their embryonic grand prix star. Keep him in his testing role for further year, or perhaps place him with another Formula 1 team to gain experience, or give him the race seat alongside the newly arrived Fernando Alonso? Eventually, Ron Dennis decided that Hamilton's time had come, and a massively assured performance on his debut in Melbourne saw him take a stunning third place. Any doubters who thought that he would be a risk at this level were soon silenced as he tore into the season with four second-place finishes in a row, before taking glorious victories at Montreal and Indianapolis. Back in Europe, the winning run was halted, but two third places at Magny-Cours and Silverstone saw him record an astonishing nine consecutive podium finishes to comfortably sit atop the drivers' championship. His run was broken at the European Grand Prix, but he bounced right back to record another win in Hungary. That race saw the controversial practice spat that would unhinge the McLaren team and eventually bring about the departure of Fernando Alonso, but Hamilton seemed unfazed by the dispute.

The title seemed to be there for the taking following Hamilton's fourth win in the rain-hit Japanese Grand Prix, but the twists and turns of a dramatic season would bring yet more drama in the Chinese Grand Prix, where the youngster failed to negotiate the pit-lane entry and beached his car in the gravel. His desperate attempt to win the race, where just a solid haul of points would have been sufficient, had opened the door to his rivals in the title battle. The showdown in Brazil brought heartache for the Briton, when a mysterious glitch caused his car to slow, allowing Ferrari's Kimi Räikkönen to steal the championship at the death.

In 2008, Hamilton was determined to take the title at the second attempt and opened with a victory at Melbourne. However, he did not record another win until his brilliant wet-weather triumph in Monte Carlo. Things soured with his pit-lane faux pas in Montreal, where he crashed into Räikkönen, followed by a drive-through penalty, at Magny-Cours, which blunted his title ambitions. Typically, he responded with crushing victories in both Britain and Germany, but once again he was pegged back in his title quest. Spa provided the most contentious moment of the year, when Lewis was stripped of victory following what was deemed to be an illegal overtaking manoeuvre. He was back on form in China, taking a commanding victory, which gave him a seven-point advantage going into the final race of the season in Brazil. It was there that the gods smiled (or more accurately rained) on him when, in a thrilling finale, he snatched the championship by overtaking Timo Glock on the very last corner. Later he described it as the toughest race of his life, but after just 35 starts he had written himself into the record books as the sport's youngest ever world champion.

Lewis was then able to set his sights on his goal of being a multiple world champion and thus join the pantheon of all-time greats, but at the start of the 2009 season he found himself in uncharted waters, having to handle an uncompetitive car for the first time in his racing career. In addition, his reputation was sullied after he misled the stewards following the Australian Grand Prix. The fall-out from this tawdry affair seemed to affect the sensitive driver, and he was only able to recover his poise when McLaren brought the MP4-24 to a competitive pitch in the middle of the season, when he took a commanding victory in Hungary. Thereafter, he was always a factor and made up for a last-lap crash at Monza by winning the Singapore Grand Prix from pole position. It was a year when Brawn and Red Bull took the lion's share of the wins, however, and the former's Jenson Button took the title.

In 2010, McLaren with Hamilton, now joined by Button, were looking for a major improvement. Initially, it was the new world champion who stole the limelight, but Lewis struck back with a lucky win in Turkey and a convincing victory in Canada, where McLaren scored a 1-2 finish. Another victory at Spa put him into the title hunt, but accidents at Monza and Singapore left too much damage to repair and he was left to watch Sebastian Vettel take the title at Abu Dhabi, and with it his short-lived record as the youngest ever world champion.

Indeed, Vettel soon became Hamilton's nemesis, for in 2011 the German proved irresistible in his Red Bull. His position at McLaren also seemed less secure as Button's influence grew, and even a win in China could not stem his general disaffection, not only with his racing, but also his personal life. A rather clumsy approach to Red Bull was swiftly rebuffed and he cut a rather disconsolate figure as his season crumbled in a litany of collisions and errors that were not worthy of such a talent. Whatever his troubles, however, Lewis turned his season around with a dominant performance in Abu Dhabi to prove that he had not lost his winning touch.

Having reached the summit and conquered all before him in double-quick time, the mercurial Lewis Hamilton must play the long game, as no driver can expect to be in the best car every year. It is also inevitable perhaps, given his outrageous driving talent, that his frustrations will pour out when fortune does not smile on him. Surely more world titles are easily within his compass if he manages to put everything in place, both on and off the track.

HAMILTON, Lewis (GB) b 7/1/1985, Stevenage

2007 Championship position: 2nd   Wins: 4   Pole positions: 6   Fastest laps: 2   Points scored: 109

	Race	Circuit	No	Entrant	Tyres	Capacity/Car/Engine	Comment	Q Pos/Entries
3	AUSTRALIAN GP	Melbourne	2	Vodafone McLaren Mercedes	B	2.4 McLaren MP4/22-Mercedes V8		4/22
2	MALAYSIAN GP	Sepang	2	Vodafone McLaren Mercedes	B	2.4 McLaren MP4/22-Mercedes V8	FL	4/22
2	BAHRAIN GP	Sakhir Circuit	2	Vodafone McLaren Mercedes	B	2.4 McLaren MP4/22-Mercedes V8		2/22
2	SPANISH GP	Barcelona	2	Vodafone McLaren Mercedes	B	2.4 McLaren MP4/22-Mercedes V8		4/22
2	MONACO GP	Monte Carlo	2	Vodafone McLaren Mercedes	B	2.4 McLaren MP4/22-Mercedes V8		2/22
1	CANADIAN GP	Montreal	2	Vodafone McLaren Mercedes	B	2.4 McLaren MP4/22-Mercedes V8		1/22
1	U S GP	Indianapolis	2	Vodafone McLaren Mercedes	B	2.4 McLaren MP4/22-Mercedes V8		1/22
3	FRENCH GP	Magny Cours	2	Vodafone McLaren Mercedes	B	2.4 McLaren MP4/22-Mercedes V8		2/22
3	BRITISH GP	Silverstone	2	Vodafone McLaren Mercedes	B	2.4 McLaren MP4/22-Mercedes V8		1/22
9	EUROPEAN GP	Nürburgring	2	Vodafone McLaren Mercedes	B	2.4 McLaren MP4/22-Mercedes V8	spun – extracated from gravel/-1 lap	10/22
1	HUNGARIAN GP	Hungaroring	2	Vodafone McLaren Mercedes	B	2.4 McLaren MP4/22-Mercedes V8		1/22
5	TURKISH GP	Istanbul	2	Vodafone McLaren Mercedes	B	2.4 McLaren MP4/22-Mercedes V8	delayed by puncture	2/22
2	ITALIAN GP	Monza	2	Vodafone McLaren Mercedes	B	2.4 McLaren MP4/22-Mercedes V8		2/22
4	BELGIAN GP	Spa	2	Vodafone McLaren Mercedes	B	2.4 McLaren MP4/22-Mercedes V8		4/22
1	JAPANESE GP	Suzuka	2	Vodafone McLaren Mercedes	B	2.4 McLaren MP4/22-Mercedes V8	FL	1/22
ret	CHINESE GP	Shanghai Circuit	2	Vodafone McLaren Mercedes	B	2.4 McLaren MP4/22-Mercedes V8	spun off on pitlane entry	1/22
7	BRAZILIAN GP	Interlagos	2	Vodafone McLaren Mercedes	B	2.4 McLaren MP4/22-Mercedes V8	gearbox problems/1 lap behind	2/22

2008 WORLD CHAMPION   Wins: 5   Pole positions: 7   Fastest laps: 1   Points scored: 98

	Race	Circuit	No	Entrant	Tyres	Capacity/Car/Engine	Comment	Q Pos/Entries
1	AUSTRALIAN GP	Melbourne	22	Vodafone McLaren Mercedes	B	2.4 McLaren MP4/23-Mercedes V8		1/22
5	MALAYSIAN GP	Sepang	22	Vodafone McLaren Mercedes	B	2.4 McLaren MP4/23-Mercedes V8		4/22
13	BAHRAIN GP	Sakhir Circuit	22	Vodafone McLaren Mercedes	B	2.4 McLaren MP4/23-Mercedes V8	hit Alonso – accident damage/-1 lap	3/22
3	SPANISH GP	Barcelona	22	Vodafone McLaren Mercedes	B	2.4 McLaren MP4/23-Mercedes V8		5/22
2	TURKISH GP	Istanbul	22	Vodafone McLaren Mercedes	B	2.4 McLaren MP4/23-Mercedes V8	split Ferraris with great drive	3/20
1	MONACO GP	Monte Carlo	22	Vodafone McLaren Mercedes	B	2.4 McLaren MP4/23-Mercedes V8		3/20
ret	CANADIAN GP	Montreal	22	Vodafone McLaren Mercedes	B	2.4 McLaren MP4/23-Mercedes V8	ran into Räikkönen at pitlane exit	1/20
10	FRENCH GP	Magny Cours	22	Vodafone McLaren Mercedes	B	2.4 McLaren MP4/23-Mercedes V8	*grid penalty/drive-thru race penalty	*3/20
1	BRITISH GP	Silverstone	22	Vodafone McLaren Mercedes	B	2.4 McLaren MP4/23-Mercedes V8	great drive in conditions	4/20
1	GERMAN GP	Hockenheim	22	Vodafone McLaren Mercedes	B	2.4 McLaren MP4/23-Mercedes V8		1/20
5	HUNGARIAN GP	Hungaroring	22	Vodafone McLaren Mercedes	B	2.4 McLaren MP4/23-Mercedes V8	tyre failure – slid off – extra pit stop	1/20
2	EUROPEAN GP	Valencia	22	Vodafone McLaren Mercedes	B	2.4 McLaren MP4/23-Mercedes V8		2/20
3*	BELGIAN GP	Spa	22	Vodafone McLaren Mercedes	B	2.4 McLaren MP4/23-Mercedes V8	*1st but given 25-sec race penalty	1/20
7	ITALIAN GP	Monza	22	Vodafone McLaren Mercedes	B	2.4 McLaren MP4/23-Mercedes V8	extra pit stop – tyre gambles	15/20
3	SINGAPORE GP	Singapore Circuit	22	Vodafone McLaren Mercedes	B	2.4 McLaren MP4/23-Mercedes V8	lost time behind Coulthard	2/20
12	JAPANESE GP	Suzuka	22	Vodafone McLaren Mercedes	B	2.4 McLaren MP4/23-Mercedes V8	collision with Massa – drive thru pen	1/20
1	CHINESE GP	Shanghai Circuit	22	Vodafone McLaren Mercedes	B	2.4 McLaren MP4/23-Mercedes V8	FL	1/20
5	BRAZILIAN GP	Interlagos	22	Vodafone McLaren Mercedes	B	2.4 McLaren MP4/23-Mercedes V8	took 5th on last corner of last lap	4/20

2009 Championship position: 5th   Wins: 2   Pole positions: 4   Fastest laps: 0   Points scored: 49

	Race	Circuit	No	Entrant	Tyres	Capacity/Car/Engine	Comment	Q Pos/Entries
dsq*	AUSTRALIAN GP	Melbourne	1	Vodafone McLaren Mercedes	B	2.4 McLaren MP4/24-Mercedes V8	4th but mislead stewards post-race	15/20
7	MALAYSIAN GP	Sepang	1	Vodafone McLaren Mercedes	B	2.4 McLaren MP4/24-Mercedes V8	rain-shortened race	13/20
6	CHINESE GP	Shanghai Circuit	1	Vodafone McLaren Mercedes	B	2.4 McLaren MP4/24-Mercedes V8	tyre problems –two spins	9/20
4	BAHRAIN GP	Sakhir Circuit	1	Vodafone McLaren Mercedes	B	2.4 McLaren MP4/24-Mercedes V8		5/20
9	SPANISH GP	Barcelona	1	Vodafone McLaren Mercedes	B	2.4 McLaren MP4/24-Mercedes V8	handling – tyre problems/-1 lap	14/20
12	MONACO GP	Monte Carlo	1	Vodafone McLaren Mercedes	B	2.4 McLaren MP4/24-Mercedes V8	collision - Heidfeld/- 1 lap	16/20
13	TURKISH GP	Istanbul	1	Vodafone McLaren Mercedes	B	2.4 McLaren MP4/24-Mercedes V8		16/20
16	BRITISH GP	Silverstone	1	Vodafone McLaren Mercedes	B	2.4 McLaren MP4/24-Mercedes V8	1 lap behind	19/20
18	GERMAN GP	Nürburgring	1	Vodafone McLaren Mercedes	B	2.4 McLaren MP4/24-Mercedes V8	1 lap behind	5/20
1	HUNGARIAN GP	Hungaroring	1	Vodafone McLaren Mercedes	B	2.4 McLaren MP4/24-Mercedes V8	back on top with uprated car	4/20
2	EUROPEAN GP	Valencia	1	Vodafone McLaren Mercedes	B	2.4 McLaren MP4/24-Mercedes V8		1/20
ret	BELGIAN GP	Spa	1	Vodafone McLaren Mercedes	B	2.4 McLaren MP4/24-Mercedes V8	hit by Alguersuari on lap 1	12/20
12/ret	ITALIAN GP	Monza	1	Vodafone McLaren Mercedes	B	2.4 McLaren MP4/24-Mercedes V8	crashed on penultimate lap	1/20
1	SINGAPORE GP	Marina Bay Circuit	1	Vodafone McLaren Mercedes	B	2.4 McLaren MP4/24-Mercedes V8		1/20
3	JAPANESE GP	Suzuka	1	Vodafone McLaren Mercedes	B	2.4 McLaren MP4/24-Mercedes V8	gearbox and KERS problems	3/20
3	BRAZILIAN GP	Interlagos	1	Vodafone McLaren Mercedes	B	2.4 McLaren MP4/24-Mercedes V8		18/20
ret	ABU DHABI GP	Yas Island	1	Vodafone McLaren Mercedes	B	2.4 McLaren MP4/24-Mercedes V8	rear brakes	1/20

2010 Championship position: 4th   Wins: 3   Pole positions: 1   Fastest laps: 5   Points scored: 240

	Race	Circuit	No	Entrant	Tyres	Capacity/Car/Engine	Comment	Q Pos/Entries
3	BAHRAIN GP	Sakhir Circuit	2	Vodafone McLaren Mercedes	B	2.4 McLaren MP4/25-Mercedes V8		4/24
6	AUSTRALIAN GP	Melbourne	2	Vodafone McLaren Mercedes	B	2.4 McLaren MP4/25-Mercedes V8	minor collision/poor strategy	11/24
6	MALAYSIAN GP	Sepang	2	Vodafone McLaren Mercedes	B	2.4 McLaren MP4/25-Mercedes V8	lively battle with Petrov	20/24
2	CHINESE GP	Shanghai Circuit	2	Vodafone McLaren Mercedes	B	2.4 McLaren MP4/25-Mercedes V8	FL/four-stop strategy	6/24
14/ret	SPANISH GP	Barcelona	2	Vodafone McLaren Mercedes	B	2.4 McLaren MP4/25-Mercedes V8	wheel/tyre failure when 2nd/FL	3/24
5	MONACO GP	Monte Carlo	2	Vodafone McLaren Mercedes	B	2.4 McLaren MP4/25-Mercedes V8		5/24
1	TURKISH GP	Istanbul Park	2	Vodafone McLaren Mercedes	B	2.4 McLaren MP4/25-Mercedes V8		2/24
1	CANADIAN GP	Montreal	2	Vodafone McLaren Mercedes	B	2.4 McLaren MP4/25-Mercedes V8		1/24
2	EUROPEAN GP	Valencia	2	Vodafone McLaren Mercedes	B	2.4 McLaren MP4/25-Mercedes V8		3/24
2	BRITISH GP	Silverstone	2	Vodafone McLaren Mercedes	B	2.4 McLaren MP4/25-Mercedes V8		4/24
4	GERMAN GP	Hockenheim	2	Vodafone McLaren Mercedes	B	2.4 McLaren MP4/25-Mercedes V8		6/24
ret	HUNGARIAN GP	Hungaroring	2	Vodafone McLaren Mercedes	B	2.4 McLaren MP4/25-Mercedes V8	gearbox	5/24
1	BELGIAN GP	Spa	2	Vodafone McLaren Mercedes	B	2.4 McLaren MP4/25-Mercedes V8	FL	2/24
ret	ITALIAN GP	Monza	2	Vodafone McLaren Mercedes	B	2.4 McLaren MP4/25-Mercedes V8	ran into Massa – suspension	5/24
ret	SINGAPORE GP	Marina Bay Circuit	2	Vodafone McLaren Mercedes	B	2.4 McLaren MP4/25-Mercedes V8	hit Webber –damaged suspension	3/24
5	JAPANESE GP	Suzuka	2	Vodafone McLaren Mercedes	B	2.4 McLaren MP4/25-Mercedes V8	lost third gear	3/24
2	KOREAN GP	Yeongam	2	Vodafone McLaren Mercedes	B	2.4 McLaren MP4/25-Mercedes V8		4/24
4	BRAZILIAN GP	Interlagos	2	Vodafone McLaren Mercedes	B	2.4 McLaren MP4/25-Mercedes V8	FL	4/24
2	ABU DHABI GP	Yas Marina Circuit	2	Vodafone McLaren Mercedes	B	2.4 McLaren MP4/25-Mercedes V8	FL	2/24

2011 Championship position: 5th Wins: 3 Pole positions: 1 Fastest laps: 3 Points scored: 227

	Race	Circuit	No	Entrant	Tyre	Car/Engine	Comment	Q Pos/Entries
2	AUSTRALIAN GP	Melbourne	4	Vodafone McLaren Mercedes	P	2.4 McLaren MP4/26-Mercedes V8		2/24
8	MALAYSIAN GP	Sepang	4	Vodafone McLaren Mercedes	P	2.4 McLaren MP4/26-Mercedes V8	20-second penalty for blocking	2/24
1	CHINESE GP	Shanghai Circuit	4	Vodafone McLaren Mercedes	P	2.4 McLaren MP4/26-Mercedes V8		3/24
4	TURKISH GP	Istanbul Park	4	Vodafone McLaren Mercedes	P	2.4 McLaren MP4/26-Mercedes V8	four-pit stops – too much wing	4/24
3	SPANISH GP	Barcelona	4	Vodafone McLaren Mercedes	P	2.4 McLaren MP4/26-Mercedes V8	FL	3/24
6	MONACO GP	Monte Carlo	4	Vodafone McLaren Mercedes	P	2.4 McLaren MP4/26-Mercedes V8	20-sec penalty for causing an accident	9/24
ret	CANADIAN GP	Montreal	4	Vodafone McLaren Mercedes	P	2.4 McLaren MP4/26-Mercedes V8	damage after collison with Button	5/24
4	EUROPEAN GP	Valencia	4	Vodafone McLaren Mercedes	P	2.4 McLaren MP4/26-Mercedes V8		3/24
4	BRITISH GP	Silverstone	4	Vodafone McLaren Mercedes	P	2.4 McLaren MP4/26-Mercedes V8		10/24
1	GERMAN GP	Hockenheim	4	Vodafone McLaren Mercedes	P	2.4 McLaren MP4/26-Mercedes V8	FL	2/24
4	HUNGARIAN GP	Hungaroring	4	Vodafone McLaren Mercedes	P	2.4 McLaren MP4/26-Mercedes V8	drive-thru pen – forced di Resta off	2/24
ret	BELGIAN GP	Spa	4	Vodafone McLaren Mercedes	P	2.4 McLaren MP4/26-Mercedes V8	hit Kobayashi and ran into barriers	2/24
4	ITALIAN GP	Monza	4	Vodafone McLaren Mercedes	P	2.4 McLaren MP4/26-Mercedes V8	FL	2/24
5	SINGAPORE GP	Marina Bay Circuit	4	Vodafone McLaren Mercedes	P	2.4 McLaren MP4/26-Mercedes V8	collison with Massa – wing damage	4/24
5	JAPANESE GP	Suzuka	4	Vodafone McLaren Mercedes	P	2.4 McLaren MP4/26-Mercedes V8	collison with Massa	3/24
2	KOREAN GP	Yeongam	4	Vodafone McLaren Mercedes	P	2.4 McLaren MP4/26-Mercedes V8		2/24
7	INDIAN GP	Buddh Circuit	4	Vodafone McLaren Mercedes	P	2.4 McLaren MP4/26-Mercedes V8	collison with Massa – wing damage	2/24
1	ABU DHABI GP	Yas Marina Circuit	4	Vodafone McLaren Mercedes	P	2.4 McLaren MP4/26-Mercedes V8		2/24
ret	BRAZILIAN GP	Interlagos	4	Vodafone McLaren Mercedes	P	2.4 McLaren MP4/26-Mercedes V8	gearbox	4/24

GP Starts: 90 GP Wins: 17 Pole positions: 19 Fastest laps: 11 Points: 723

HAMPSHIRE, David (GB) b 29/12/1917, Mickleover, nr Derby – d 25/8/1990, Newton-Soleney, nr Burton-on-Trent, Derbyshire

1950 Championship position: Unplaced

	Race	Circuit	No	Entrant	Tyres	Capacity/Car/Engine	Comment	Q Pos/Entries
9	BRITISH GP	Silverstone	6	Scuderia Ambrosiana	D	1.5 s/c Maserati 4CLT/48 4	6 laps behind	16/21
ret	FRENCH GP	Reims	34	Scuderia Ambrosiana	D	1.5 s/c Maserati 4CLT/48 4	engine	18/20

GP Starts: 2 GP Wins: 0 Pole positions: 0 Fastest laps: 0 Points: 0

DAVID HAMPSHIRE

A COMPANY director who began racing a Maserati before the Second World War, David Hampshire enjoyed his principal successes between 1947 and 1949 driving an ERA. He finished second in the British Empire Trophy on the Isle of Man in 1948 and shared the car with bandleader Billy Cotton to take fourth place in the British GP in 1949.

The ERA was getting long in the tooth, however, so Hampshire was glad to take the opportunity to drive Reg Parnell's Scuderia Ambrosiana semi-works Maserati at a couple of grands prix.

Hampshire raced the car again in 1951, as well as wheeling out his venerable ERA for few minor outings. Also that year, he shared a works Aston Martin DB2 with Reg Parnell, the pair finishing seventh. He raced little thereafter, but reappeared in 1955 for a couple of outings in a Lister-Bristol, taking ninth (and a class win) with Peter Scott-Russell in the BARC nine-hour race at Goodwood.

WALT HANSGEN

O NE of the greatest American sports car drivers of the 1950s, Walt Hansgen was a seller, tuner and modifier of sports cars who was bitten by the racing bug in 1950. He built a mighty reputation with his own Jaguar XK120, before racing a D-Type for Briggs Cunningham from 1956. In 1958, he visited Britain to take delivery of a Lister-Jaguar, which he raced briefly before returning home to campaign the car with great success.

Walt made his grand prix debut at Watkins Glen in a Briggs Cunningham entered Cooper, but was involved in an accident when he was unable to avoid Olivier Gendebien's spinning car. His car vaulted the barriers, but he survived the heavy crash with light facial injuries.

At his first race at Indianapolis, in 1964, Walt drove superbly, finishing 12th, despite a long pit stop. This brought him to the attention of Lotus, who at the end of the year gave him a second world championship start at Watkins Glen. Driving the third works car, he took things steadily, climbing through the field to an eventual fifth-place finish.

But it was in sports cars that Hansgen really shone, taking victories in a wide variety of machines, including a Cooper-Monaco, before racing John Mecom's stable of cars, which boasted a Ferrari 250LM, a Lotus 19, a Scarab Chevrolet and a Lola T70. He began 1966 by sharing the Ford MkII with his protégé, Mark Donohue, taking third at Daytona and second at Sebring, but he crashed the car in the Le Mans 24-hours test weekend in April, 1966. Grievously injured, Walt was placed on life support in hospital, but there was no hope of recovery – he died a week later.

HANSGEN, Walt (USA) b 28/10/1919, Westfield, New Jersey – d 7/4/1966, Orléans, France

	1961 Championship position: Unplaced								
	Race	Circuit	No	Entrant	Tyres	Capacity/Car/Engine	Comment	Q Pos/Entries
ret	US GP	Watkins Glen	60	Momo Corporation	D	1.5 Cooper T53-Climax 4	accident	14/19
	1964 Championship position: 16th= Wins: 0 Pole positions: 0 Fastest laps: 0 Points scored: 2							
5	US GP	Watkins Glen	17	Team Lotus	D	1.5 Lotus 33-Climax V8	3 laps behind	17/19
	GP Starts: 2 GP Wins: 0 Pole positions: 0 Fastest laps: 0 Points: 2							

HARRIS, Mike (ZA) b 25/5/1939, Mulfulira, Zambia

	1962 Championship position: Unplaced								
	Race	Circuit	No	Entrant	Tyres	Capacity/Car/Engine	Comment	Q Pos/Entries
ret	SOUTH AFRICAN GP	East London	22	Mike Harris	D	1.5 Cooper T53-Alfa Romeo 4	big end bearings	14/17
	GP Starts: 1 GP Wins: 0 Pole positions: 0 Fastest laps: 0 Points: 0							

HARRISON, Cuth (GB) b 6/7/1906, Ecclesall, Sheffield – d 21/1/1981, Sheffield

	1950 Championship position: Unplaced								
	Race	Circuit	No	Entrant	Tyres	Capacity/Car/Engine	Comment	Q Pos/Entries
7	BRITISH GP	Silverstone	11	Cuth Harrison	D	1.5 s/c ERA B Type 6	3 laps behind	15/21
ret	MONACO GP	Monte Carlo	24	Cuth Harrison	D	1.5 s/c ERA B Type 6	multiple accident	14/21
ret	ITALIAN GP	Monza	32	Cuth Harrison	D	1.5 s/c ERA B Type 6	engine	21/27
	GP Starts: 3 GP Wins: 0 Pole positions: 0 Fastest laps: 0 Points: 0							

MIKE HARRIS

WITH third place in the 1962 Rhodesian Grand Prix and that country's championship to his name, Mike Harris entered the series of races staged around the end-of-year South African Grand Prix with an ex-Reg Parnell Cooper fitted with an Alfa engine.

Unfortunately, Mike's luck was out and he retired from all three events. A puncture ended his Natal Grand Prix, and he also failed to finish his qualifying heat of the Rand Grand Prix, thus missing the final.

The championship race at East London appears to have been Harris' last major single-seater outing, for he did not race at national level thereafter.

CUTH HARRISON

AN extremely enthusiastic amateur driver, T.C. 'Cuth' Harrison raced an ERA C-Type – mainly in national events, where his duels with Bob Gerard were lively indeed, but also occasionally on the Continent, finishing sixth in the 1949 Italian Grand Prix.

The 1950 season, his last with the car, brought no success in grands prix, but he did finish second in the British Empire Trophy in the Isle of Man, before concentrating on his thriving garage business in Sheffield and returning to trials with an 1172cc Harford, with which he was the 1952 RAC champion.

Harrison's name is still widely seen today, particularly in the north of England, due to a successful Ford car dealership he began developing in the 1950s.

BRIAN HART

FOR 25 years, Brian Hart designed and built racing engines for Formula 2 and then Formula 1, with the Toleman, RAM, Jordan, Footwork and Arrows teams among his customers. Long before that, however, he enjoyed a more than worthy career as a driver.

Between 1958 and 1963, Hart scored numerous wins in Formula Junior and sports car events with Lotus and Terrier chassis, taking third place in the Grovewood Awards for 1963.

Moving up to F2, Brian gained an almost immediate victory in the Pergusa GP, driving a Ron Harris entered Lotus, and although he stepped back into F3 in 1966, he would become an F2 mainstay, mostly racing for Bob Gerard, for whom he won the 1969 Rhine Cup race at Hockenheim after a great drive.

As his flourishing engine business grew, Hart inevitably found less time to go racing and eventually he retired at the end of the 1971 season.

HART, Brian (GB) b 7/9/1936, Enfield, Middlesex

1967 Championship position: Unplaced

	Race	Circuit	No	Entrant	Tyres	Capacity/Car/Engine	Comment	Q Pos/Entries
12*	GERMAN GP (F2)	Nürburgring	25	Ron Harris	F	1.6 Protos-Cosworth 4 F2	*4th in F2 class/3 laps behind	24/25

GP Starts: 1 GP Wins: 0 Pole positions: 0 Fastest laps: 0 Points: 0

HASEMI, Masahiro (J) b 13/11/1945, Tokyo

1976 Championship position: Unplaced

	Race	Circuit	No	Entrant	Tyres	Capacity/Car/Engine	Comment	Q Pos/Entries
11	JAPANESE GP	Mount Fuji	51	Kojima Engineering	D	3.0 Kojima KE007-Cosworth V8	pit stop – tyres/7 laps behind	10/27

GP Starts: 1 GP Wins: 0 Pole positions: 0 Fastest laps: 0 Points: 0

HAWKINS, Paul (AUS) b 12/10/1937, Melbourne, Victoria – d 26/5/1969, Oulton Park, Cheshire, England

1965 Championship position: Unplaced

	Race	Circuit	No	Entrant	Tyres	Capacity/Car/Engine	Comment	Q Pos/Entries
9	SOUTH AFRICAN GP	East London	18	John Willment Automobiles	D	1.5 Brabham BT10-Ford 4 F2	4 laps behind	16/25
10/ret	MONACO GP	Monte Carlo	10	DW Racing Enterprises	D	1.5 Lotus 33-Climax V8	crashed into harbour/-21 laps	=14/17
ret	GERMAN GP	Nürburgring	22	DW Racing Enterprises	D	1.5 Lotus 33-Climax V8	oil pipe	20/22

GP Starts: 3 GP Wins: 0 Pole positions: 0 Fastest laps: 0 Points: 0

MASAHIRO HASEMI

A FORMER motocross rider, Masahiro Hasemi turned to cars with a Nissan Bluebird and rightly earned a reputation as one of Japan's finest drivers, having been a champion in Formula 2 (1980) and Group C sports cars (1990 with Anders Olofsson). He was also the Japanese Touring Car champion in 1989, 1991 and 1992 with a Nissan Skyline.

In Formula 1, Hasemi caused a stir with the locally built Kojima on his only grand prix appearance in 1976. Benefiting from special Dunlop wet-weather tyres, he set fastest lap in the pouring rain, before they – and his challenge – faded.

Hasemi was often seen outside Japan as a member of the Nissan sports-prototype team, competing regularly at Le Mans, but he enjoyed his greatest international success when he won the 1992 Daytona 24-hours with compatriots Kazuyoshi Hoshino and Toshio Suzuki.

Although he finally retired from competition at the end of 2000, Masahiro continued to run his Hasemi Sport Team in the All-Japan Super GT Championship, in both the GT500 and GT300 classes, as well as a team contesting the Japanese F3 series.

PAUL HAWKINS

P AUL 'HAWKEYE' HAWKINS was another of those tough Aussies who travelled to Britain in the early 1960s with no money, but plenty of determination to further their racing careers and the willingness to graft ceaselessly to achieve their goal. He found employment in the Healey factory in 1960, with an opportunity to race their Sprites. This led to two happy seasons with Ian Walker's sports car and Formula Junior teams, before he was tempted to join John Willment in 1964 to race all sorts of cars, taking an aggregate second place in the Rand GP and winning the Rhodesian GP in an F2 Brabham, the same car that he used to make his world championship debut in South Africa in 1965.

Back in Europe, Paul had an unproductive time in Dickie Stoop's Lotus 33, which he crashed spectacularly into the harbour at Monaco, but he won the F2 Eifelrennen in an Alexis. Apart from a few F1 races with Tim Parnell early in 1966, he turned his attention to sports cars, which offered him a better opportunity to show his talent. Racing his own Ford GT40, he achieved numerous excellent wins and countless placings during 1967 and '68, his trips to South Africa proving particularly fruitful. He was also in demand by the top sports car teams of the period as a freelance, winning the 1967 Targa Florio for Porsche (with Rolf Stommelen), and the 1967 Paris 1000km (with Jacky Ickx) and the 1968 Monza 1000km (with David Hobbs) for John Wyer.

With his Lola T70 run by the factory, 'Hawkeye' embarked on a season of sports car racing in 1969, and it was a sad loss to the sport when this no-nonsense character died after crashing into a tree during the Tourist Trophy race at Oulton Park.

BLOND and debonair, Mike Hawthorn was in the vanguard of the new wave of English talent that came to the fore in grand prix racing in the early 1950s, and to him fell the signal honour of becoming Great Britain's first ever world champion driver.

Mike's rise was meteoric, winning a championship grand prix barely two years after his circuit racing debut in a Riley in 1951. During that first full season, he won the Leinster Trophy and the Ulster Handicap, as well as the Brooklands Memorial Trophy for his consistent successes throughout the year at Goodwood. For 1952, he took delivery of one of the new Cooper-Bristols, which had been purchased for him by a family friend, Bob Chase, the team being run by his father, Leslie. The season started well with F2 and Libre wins at the Goodwood Easter meeting, before he headed for the Continent and fourth place on his grand prix debut at Spa. Certainly the car was quite useful, but Mike coaxed far more from it than anyone else with his uninhibited driving.

A minor meeting at Boreham saw a fantastic display of Mike's ability. In pouring rain, he left the great Luigi Villoresi floundering in his 4.5-litre Ferrari until the track dried and the little Cooper was overhauled. The Italian went back to Italy to report to Ferrari that he had unearthed a new British star. Arriving at Modena for the late-season grand prix, Mike was invited to drive for the Scuderia in 1953, and had plenty of time to consider the offer, as he crashed the Cooper in practice and found himself hospitalised. He duly joined Ferrari's star-studded line-up and wisely took things easy to begin with, watching and learning from his more experienced team-mates.

It would be a magnificent first season for the Englishman abroad, and he finished every championship grand prix bar one in the points, the highlight being a glorious victory, over Juan Fangio no less, in the French GP at Reims after a wheel-to-wheel battle to the flag. Beyond the world championship, Hawthorn won the International Trophy and the Ulster Trophy at Dundrod, while in sports cars he took the Spa 24-hours with Giuseppe Farina, his achievements earning him a BRDC Gold Star.

The 1954 season began badly when Mike crashed at Syracuse, receiv-

ing serious burns to his arms and legs, and then there was a furore over his exemption from national service due to a kidney ailment, followed by the death of his father in a road accident. He decided that it would be impossible to run the family garage business if he stayed at Maranello, so after signing off with a win at Pedralbes, he moved to Vanwall for 1955, but the new car needed further development and he was seriously unimpressed with the disarray of Vanderwell's organisation. Even in victory, Mike was followed by controversy, for when he won the Le Mans 24-hours for Jaguar with Ivor Bueb, he found the finger of blame pointed towards him as the unwitting instigator of the tragedy that killed more than 80 people. Some semblance of order was restored with an end-of-season return to Ferrari by way of the Lancia team, which they had just taken over, and a splendid drive for Jaguar in the Tourist Trophy.

Mike's desire to honour his contract with the sports car team for 1956 meant that he had to join BRM for Formula 1, and the cars' unreliability restricted him to just a handful of outings. He decided that for success, he had to drive for an Italian team, and he was welcomed back to Ferrari to drive alongside his great mate, Peter Collins. The atmosphere, so strained in 1956, was completely different upon Mike's return and soon he was back to his consistent best. The magnificent Fangio bestrode the 1957 season in his Maserati, but when the Argentinian retired early in 1958, the title was there to be taken. Ironically, the threat to Ferrari came from Vanwall, who had been so shambolic during Mike's brief tenure as a driver. He paced himself brilliantly, taking risks when necessary, but making sure that he finished at all costs. The death of Collins in the German GP hit him very hard and, with Luigi Musso and Stuart Lewis-Evans also having lost their lives that year, Hawthorn, newly crowned as world champion, announced his retirement.

Mike was planning both marriage and an expansion of his garage business when, on a rainy January morning in 1959, he lost control of his potent Jaguar near Guildford and was killed instantly when it wrapped itself around a tree.

HAWTHORN, Mike (GB) b 10/4/1929, Mexborough, Yorkshire – d 22/1/1959, Guildford-by-pass, Surrey

1952 Championship position: 4th=   Wins: 0   Pole positions: 0   Fastest laps: 0   Points scored: 10

	Race	Circuit	No	Entrant	Tyres	Capacity/Car/Engine	Comment	Q Pos/Entries
4	BELGIAN GP	Spa	8	L D Hawthorn	D	2.0 Cooper T20-Bristol 6	2 pit stops – fuel leak/1 lap behind	6/22
ret	FRENCH GP	Rouen	42	A H M Bryde	D	2.0 Cooper T20-Bristol 6	ignition	15/20
3	BRITISH GP	Silverstone	9	L D Hawthorn	D	2.0 Cooper T20-Bristol 6	2 laps behind	7/32
4	DUTCH GP	Zandvoort	32	L D Hawthorn	D	2.0 Cooper T20-Bristol 6	2 laps behind	3/18
nc	ITALIAN GP	Monza	42	L D Hawthorn	D	2.0 Cooper T20-Bristol 6	long pit stop – magneto/-38 laps	12/35

1953 Championship position: 4   Wins: 1   Pole positions: 0   Fastest laps: 0   Points scored: 27

	Race	Circuit	No	Entrant	Tyres	Capacity/Car/Engine	Comment	Q Pos/Entries
4	ARGENTINE GP	Buenos Aires	16	Scuderia Ferrari	P	2.0 Ferrari 500 4	1 lap behind	6/16
4	DUTCH GP	Zandvoort	8	Scuderia Ferrari	P	2.0 Ferrari 500 4	1 lap behind	6/20
6	BELGIAN GP	Spa	14	Scuderia Ferrari	P	2.0 Ferrari 500 4	1 lap behind	7/22
1	FRENCH GP	Reims	16	Scuderia Ferrari	P	2.0 Ferrari 500 4		7/25
5	BRITISH GP	Silverstone	8	Scuderia Ferrari	P	2.0 Ferrari 500 4	spin – pit stop/3 laps behind	3/29
3	GERMAN GP	Nürburgring	3	Scuderia Ferrari	P	2.0 Ferrari 500 4		4/35
3	SWISS GP	Bremgarten	26	Scuderia Ferrari	P	2.0 Ferrari 500 4		7/23
4	ITALIAN GP	Monza	8	Scuderia Ferrari	P	2.0 Ferrari 500 4	1 lap behind	6/30

1954 Championship position: 3   Wins: 1   Pole positions: 0   Fastest laps: 1 (shared)   Points scored: 24.64

	Race	Circuit	No	Entrant	Tyres	Capacity/Car/Engine	Comment	Q Pos/Entries
dsq	ARGENTINE GP	Buenos Aires	14	Scuderia Ferrari	P	2.5 Ferrari 625 4	push start after spin	4/18
4*	BELGIAN GP	Spa	10	Scuderia Ferrari	P	2.5 Ferrari 625 4	exhaust fumes/*Gonzalez took over	5/15
ret	FRENCH GP	Reims	6	Scuderia Ferrari	P	2.5 Ferrari 553 4	engine	8/22
2	BRITISH GP	Silverstone	11	Scuderia Ferrari	P	2.5 Ferrari 625 4	FL (shared)	3/31
ret	GERMAN GP	Nürburgring	3	Scuderia Ferrari	P	2.5 Ferrari 625 4	rear axle	2/23
2*	"	"	1	Scuderia Ferrari	P	2.5 Ferrari 625 4	*took over Gonzalez's car	- / -
ret	SWISS GP	Bremgarten	22	Scuderia Ferrari	P	2.5 Ferrari 625 4	fuel pump	6/16
2	ITALIAN GP	Monza	40	Scuderia Ferrari	P	2.5 Ferrari 625 4	1 lap behind	7/21
1	SPANISH GP	Pedralbes	38	Scuderia Ferrari	P	2.5 Ferrari 553 4		3/22

1955 Championship position: Unplaced

	Race	Circuit	No	Entrant	Tyres	Capacity/Car/Engine	Comment	Q Pos/Entries
ret	MONACO GP	Monte Carlo	18	Vandervell Products Ltd	P	2.5 Vanwall 4	throttle linkage	12/22
ret	BELGIAN GP	Spa	40	Vandervell Products Ltd	P	2.5 Vanwall 4	gearbox	9/14
7	DUTCH GP	Zandvoort	2	Scuderia Ferrari	E	2.5 Ferrari 555 4	pit stop/3 laps behind	5/16
dns	"	"	2	Scuderia Ferrari	E	2.5 Ferrari 625 4	practice only	- / -

	Race	Circuit	No	Team		Car/Engine	Notes	Grid
6*	BRITISH GP	Aintree	16	Scuderia Ferrari	E	2.5 Ferrari 625 4	*unwell – Castellotti took car/-3 laps	12/25
ret	ITALIAN GP	Monza	6	Scuderia Ferrari	E	2.5 Ferrari 555 4	gearbox mounting	14/22
dns	"	"	T	Scuderia Ferrari	E	2.5 Lancia D50 V8	practice only – did not fit in car	- / -

1956 Championship position: 9th=   Wins: 0   Pole positions: 0   Fastest laps: 0   Points scored: 4

	Race	Circuit	No	Team		Car/Engine	Notes	Grid
3	ARGENTINE GP	Buenos Aires	14	Owen Racing Organisation	D	2.5 Maserati 250F 6	2 laps behind	8/15
dns	MONACO GP	Monte Carlo	10	Owen Racing Organisation	D	2.5 BRM P25 4	engine problems in practice	10/19
dns	BELGIAN GP	Spa	38	Officine Alfieri Maserati	P	2.5 Maserati 250F 6	ill-feeling at Mike driving works car	(13)/16
10*	FRENCH GP	Reims	24	Vandervell Products Ltd	P	2.5 Vanwall 4	*Schell took over car/5 laps behind	6/20
ret	BRITISH GP	Silverstone	23	Owen Racing Organisation	D	2.5 BRM P25 4	oil leak – universal joint	3/28

1957 Championship position: 4th   Wins: 0   Pole positions: 0   Fastest laps: 0   Points scored: 13

	Race	Circuit	No	Team		Car/Engine	Notes	Grid
ret	ARGENTINE GP	Buenos Aires	16	Scuderia Ferrari	E	2.5 Lancia-Ferrari D50A V8	clutch	7/16
ret	MONACO GP	Monte Carlo	28	Scuderia Ferrari	E	2.5 Lancia-Ferrari D50A V8	accident with Moss and Collins	5/21
7/ret	"	"	24	Scuderia Ferrari	E	2.5 Lancia-Ferrari 801 V8	shared with von Trips/engine/-5 laps	- / -
4	FRENCH GP	Rouen	14	Scuderia Ferrari	E	2.5 Lancia-Ferrari 801 V8	1 lap behind	7/15
3	BRITISH GP	Aintree	10	Scuderia Ferrari	E	2.5 Lancia-Ferrari 801 V8		5/19
2	GERMAN GP	Nürburgring	8	Scuderia Ferrari	E	2.5 Lancia-Ferrari 801 V8		2/24
6	ITALIAN GP	Monza	34	Scuderia Ferrari	E	2.5 Lancia-Ferrari 801 V8	pit stop – oil pipe/4 laps behind	10/19

1958 WORLD CHAMPION   Wins: 1   Pole positions: 3   Fastest laps: 5   Points scored: 49

	Race	Circuit	No	Team		Car/Engine	Notes	Grid
3	ARGENTINE GP	Buenos Aires	20	Scuderia Ferrari	E	2.4 Ferrari Dino 246 V6		2/10
ret	MONACO GP	Monte Carlo	38	Scuderia Ferrari	E	2.4 Ferrari Dino 246 V6	fuel pump/FL	6/28
5	DUTCH GP	Zandvoort	5	Scuderia Ferrari	E	2.4 Ferrari Dino 246 V6	1 lap behind	6/17
2	BELGIAN GP	Spa	16	Scuderia Ferrari	E	2.4 Ferrari Dino 246 V6	FL	1/20
1	FRENCH GP	Reims	4	Scuderia Ferrari	E	2.4 Ferrari Dino 246 V6	FL	1/21
2	BRITISH GP	Silverstone	2	Scuderia Ferrari	E	2.4 Ferrari Dino 246 V6	FL	4/21
ret	GERMAN GP	Nürburgring	3	Scuderia Ferrari	E	2.4 Ferrari Dino 246 V6	clutch	1/26
2	PORTUGUESE GP	Oporto	22	Scuderia Ferrari	E	2.4 Ferrari Dino 246 V6	FL	2/15
2	ITALIAN GP	Monza	14	Scuderia Ferrari	E	2.4 Ferrari Dino 246 V6		3/21
2	MOROCCAN GP	Casablanca	6	Scuderia Ferrari	E	2.4 Ferrari Dino 246 V6		1/25

GP Starts: 45   GP Wins: 3   Pole positions: 4   Fastest laps: 6 (1 shared)   Points: 127.64

Mike Hawthorn negotiates the fast and dangerous Reims-Geaux circuit in his Ferrari Dino 246. His utterly dominant victory in the 1958 French Grand Prix was the Englishman's only win in his championship winning season.

BOY HAYJE

A FORMER saloon car racer and Dutch Formula Ford champion, and a protégé of Toine Hezemans, Boy Hayje raced the ex-James Hunt March 731 in F5000 in 1975 without realising much by way of results. Thus he switched to Formula 3 in 1976, a year that saw him make a promising GP debut at Zandvoort. With backing from his loyal sponsors, he secured a seat in the RAM March team for 1977, a move that proved disastrous for all concerned, the Dutchman departing abruptly following his non-qualification at his home grand prix. Then he took his backing to Fred Opert in Formula 2 for 1978, achieving just a couple of seventh-places finishes.

Thereafter, Hayje perhaps found his true level, and success came his way at last, racing in the European Renault 5 Turbo championship. In 1983, he also ventured to the USA and competed in some IMSA races, taking third and the GTU class win at Riverside in a BMW 320i with Roberto Moreno, and a win outright at Laguna Seca. The latter earned him a few drives with Dan Gurney's AAR Toyota Celicas and an appearance in BMW M1 Procar at Portland. The following year, he returned for more action, driving a LolaT616-Mazda prototype on both sides of the Atlantic.

Hayje retired to run a family owned 4x4 garage in Belgium.

WILLI HEEKS

A SKILLED pilot who drove the BMW-engined Formula 2 AFM cars with great verve, Willi Heeks scored wins in 1950 in the Maipokalrennen at Hockenheim and at Dessau. The following year saw him carry the challenge to the Veritas marque once more, but his best placing was third at the Nürburgring in the Eifelrennen.

Competition in Germany at the time was vibrant and there were plenty of excellent drivers like Heeks who were rarely seen racing outside their own country. By 1953, the AFM was no longer competitive and Willi joined the ranks of the Veritas runners, although most of his major races ended in retirement. He did cause something of a stir in the German Grand Prix when his car led the Ferrari of Louis Rosier before eventually breaking down.

Subsequently, Heeks drove a Mercedes 220S with Erwin Bauer in a number of races during 1956, including the Nürburgring 1000km.

HAYJE, 'Boy' Johan (NL) b 3/5/1949, Amsterdam

	1976 Championship position: Unplaced							
	Race	Circuit	No	Entrant	Tyres	Capacity/Car/Engine	Comment	Q Pos/Entries
ret	DUTCH GP	Zandvoort	39	F & S Properties	G	3.0 Penske PC3-Cosworth V8	driveshaft	21/27
	1977 Championship position: Unplaced							
ret	SOUTH AFRICAN GP	Kyalami	33	RAM Racing/F & S Properties	G	3.0 March 761-Cosworth V8	gearbox	21/23
dnq	SPANISH GP	Jarama	33	RAM Racing/F & S Properties	G	3.0 March 761-Cosworth V8		28/31
dnq	MONACO GP	Monte Carlo	33	RAM Racing/F & S Properties	G	3.0 March 761-Cosworth V8		22/26
nc	BELGIAN GP	Zolder	33	RAM Racing/F & S Properties	G	3.0 March 761-Cosworth V8	7 laps behind	27/32
dnq	SWEDISH GP	Anderstorp	33	RAM Racing/F & S Properties	G	3.0 March 761-Cosworth V8		28/31
dnq	DUTCH GP	Zandvoort	33	RAM Racing/F & S Properties	G	3.0 March 761-Cosworth V8		31/34

GP Starts: 3   GP Wins: 0   Pole positions: 0   Fastest laps: 0   Points:

HEEKS, Willi (D) b 13/2/1922, Moorlage, nr Detmold – d 13/8/1996, Bocholt

	1952 Championship position: Unplaced							
	Race	Circuit	No	Entrant	Tyres	Capacity/Car/Engine	Comment	Q Pos/Entries
ret	GERMAN GP	Nürburgring	123	Willi Heeks	–	2.0 AFM-BMW 6	engine	9/32
	1953 Championship position: Unplaced							
ret	GERMAN GP	Nürburgring	23	Willi Heeks	–	2.0 Veritas Meteor 6	transmission	18/35

GP Starts: 2   GP Wins: 0   Pole positions: 0   Fastest laps: 0   Points: 0

NICK HEIDFELD

A TOP talent who drew admiration from many of his Formula 1 peers, Nick Heidfeld somehow failed to bridge the small gap that separates the elite from the best of the rest. When Lotus-Renault dropped him from their line-up mid-way through the 2011 season, it seemed as though the German's time in Formula 1 was finally over. He ended up with the unwanted statistic of having made the most grand prix starts (183) without recording a victory. It is not that he wasn't close, as attested by his eight second places, also a record for a non-winning driver.

Like so many others, Heidfeld began in karting, competing in various classes and championships before making his car racing debut in the 1994 German FFord series. Eight victories in nine starts gained the attention of the German media as he set about winning the 1600cc class, which laid the foundation for a move to higher things. The following year saw him finish as runner-up in the overall standings, with a maiden championship title in the concurrent German Zetec series. In 1996, he entered the German F3 championship, making an immediate impact by claiming third overall, behind future F1 rival Jarno Trulli. The following year, he made sure that the title was his, although a close look at his competition that year shows it was hardly a vintage crop. Nevertheless, the icing on the cake was when he took the Monaco Formula 3 race to add to his growing reputation.

F3000 was the logical progression for 1998, and Nick impressed again by fighting for the title with eventual champion Juan Pablo Montoya, the pair sharing seven wins from the 12-race season. Heidfeld stayed in the formula for a second season, and this time he had little opposition as he romped to the title, seizing the trophy well before the end of the year. Given his involvement with the McLaren-backed West Competition squad, and his F1 testing duties, many expected that he would be promoted into the Woking operation's grand prix team. Although that move didn't materialise, such was the impact he had made on the F1 paddock that he lined up alongside veteran Jean Alesi in former world champion Alain Prost's team. It was a long, hard season for the German, who had been used to success. Luckily, the pressure on him was not so great and, despite not scoring a point, his reputation remained intact. He made a welcome switch to Sauber for 2001.

The German was on the pace from the very first race and, surprisingly, the Swiss team did not suffer a fade away in mid-season; both Heidfeld and rookie team-mate Kimi Räikkönen were able to ruffle the feathers of the established midfield teams. Between them, the youngest duo on the grid racked up 21 points, good enough for fourth in the constructors' championship, while Heidfeld got the better of Räikkönen by a small margin in the drivers' standings, taking eighth overall with 12 points, including a first podium finish in Brazil. It was the Finn, however, who was chosen by McLaren to replace the retiring Mika Häkkinen, despite Heidfeld's links with the team during his junior career.

The "oversight", as Heidfeld referred to the decision, must have been a crushing blow to his morale, but he plugged away in midfield anonymity, putting in some good performances to pick up the scraps. His third successive season with Sauber, on the whole, was another largely disappointing campaign. The main highlight was a fifth place at the United States GP. Along with eighth places in Malaysia and at the Nürburgring, that was as good as it got, indicating the German's only points-scoring positions.

The following year brought a change of scene for Heidfeld, since he had been dropped by Sauber to make way for Giancarlo Fisichella. He grabbed a Formula 1 lifeline at Jordan, a deal only confirmed at the end of January. The team was on the wane, however, and the gritty Heidfeld had to make the most of a difficult season, the EJ14 not being particularly competitive. His efforts, though, were noted by most in the pit lane and, despite his best results coming in the early part of the season, with seventh at Monaco and eighth in Canada, his reputation was largely restored. De-

nied the chance to move to Williams as a replacement for the injured Ralf Schumacher mid-season, he finally got his chance to move to Grove after winning a shoot-out with test driver Antonio Pizzonia.

Partnering Mark Webber in 2005 (his first season in a really top-flight operation), Heidfeld rose to the challenge magnificently. After recording second place in a gruelling Monaco Grand Prix, he took pole position at the Nürburgring, backing up his speed with another second-place finish in the race. After being largely under-valued by the Formula 1 fraternity, suddenly he became BMW's favoured son, and his future prospects brightened even more when the news came that Williams and their engine partner were to go their separate ways for 2006. Although his season was ended prematurely, after a heavy crash during testing at Monza, he had already signed a long-term deal to join the new BMW-Sauber team as their number-one driver.

Having certainly earned his big chance with a major manufacturer, Heidfeld faced a transitional year with the newly assembled team. First, he gained the upper hand over the experienced Jacques Villeneuve, only to face a stiffer challenge from the sensational Robert Kubica. A podium place in Hungary and a further nine points-scoring finishes underlined his unobtrusively efficient driving skills, but the spectacular mid-season arrival of the Polish driver and the advancement of highly-favoured third driver Sebastian Vettel changed the landscape somewhat.

With the very competitive BMW Sauber F1.07, Nick was up to the challenge, however, and during 2007 he was consistently the leading pursuer of the dominant Ferrari-McLaren axis. Fourteen points-scoring finishes (all but one of them in the top six) were a testament to his immaculate driving, which maximised the car's potential; the highlight of his season was a second-place finish in the Canadian Grand Prix. He started 2008 in fine style with yet another second place in the Australian Grand Prix, but just couldn't find that elusive victory, having to settle for the second place on the podium on another three occasions that year. Once again, he was ultra-consistent, scoring points in 11 of the 18 races, to finish in sixth place at the end of another year when he had been so near, yet so far.

BMW's smooth progress towards the pinnacle in F1 came off the rails in 2009, when they were one of the biggest victims of the double-diffuser saga. While Brawn swept away to an unassailable championship lead, the team from Hinwil failed to react until far too late in the season and, after picking up a second place in the rainstorms of Malaysia, Heidfeld was forced to make do and mend until an upgraded car arrived late in the year. Thirteenth in the final points standing was bad enough, but worse was to come when BMW followed Toyota out of the sport due to the economic crisis, which left Nick out of work.

Heidfeld was soon taken on by Mercedes to act as their test driver, but before taking the wheel, he accepted the role of tyre tester for Pirelli, ahead of the Italian company entering the sport. This turned out to be another short-term appointment, as Peter Sauber called on him to replace the out-of-favour Pedro de la Rosa for the final five races of the year. Not figuring in Sauber's plans for 2011, however, Nick seemed to be off the F1 grid again, but Robert Kubica's terrible pre-season accident in a rally car opened up a seat at Lotus-Renault following the German's successful test. His third place at Sepang promised much for the season, but thereafter he largely disappointed with his performances, especially in comparison to his less-experienced team-mate, Vitaly Petrov. He was axed following the Hungarian Grand Prix and replaced by Bruno Senna. Statistics do not tell the whole story, but the final points tally for the three drivers made interesting reading: Petrov 18 starts, 37 points; Heidfeld 11 starts, 34 points; Senna 8 starts, 2 points...

Heidfeld's grand prix career seems finally to have come to an end with his move into sports car racing to compete in the FIA Endurance Championship with Rebellion Racing for 2012.

HEIDFELD, Nick (D) b 10/5/1977, Mönchengladbach

2000 Championship position: Unplaced

	Race	Circuit	No	Entrant	Tyres	Capacity/Car/Engine	Comment	Q Pos/Entries
9	AUSTRALIAN GP	Melbourne	15	Gauloises Prost Renault	B	3.0 Prost AP03-Peugeot V10	*2 laps behind*	15/22
ret	BRAZILIAN GP	Interlagos	14	Gauloises Prost Renault	B	3.0 Prost AP03-Peugeot V10	*engine*	19/22
ret	SAN MARINO GP	Imola	14	Gauloises Prost Renault	B	3.0 Prost AP03-Peugeot V10	*hydraulics*	22/22
ret	BRITISH GP	Silverstone	14	Gauloises Prost Renault	B	3.0 Prost AP03-Peugeot V10	*engine*	17/22
16	SPANISH GP	Barcelona	14	Gauloises Prost Renault	B	3.0 Prost AP03-Peugeot V10	*3 laps behind*	20/22
excl*	EUROPEAN GP	Nürburgring	14	Gauloises Prost Renault	B	3.0 Prost AP03-Peugeot V10	**excluded – car underweight*	*13/22
8	MONACO GP	Monte Carlo	14	Gauloises Prost Renault	B	3.0 Prost AP03-Peugeot V10	*1 lap behind*	18/22
ret	CANADIAN GP	Montreal	14	Gauloises Prost Renault	B	3.0 Prost AP03-Peugeot V10	*engine fire*	21/22
12	FRENCH GP	Magny Cours	14	Gauloises Prost Renault	B	3.0 Prost AP03-Peugeot V10	*1 lap behind*	16/22
ret	AUSTRIAN GP	A1-Ring	14	Gauloises Prost Renault	B	3.0 Prost AP03-Peugeot V10	*collision with Alesi*	13/22
12/ret	GERMAN GP	Hockenheim	14	Gauloises Prost Renault	B	3.0 Prost AP03-Peugeot V10	*alternator/5 laps behind*	13/22
ret	HUNGARIAN GP	Hungaroring	14	Gauloises Prost Renault	B	3.0 Prost AP03-Peugeot V10	*battery voltage*	19/22
ret	BELGIAN GP	Spa	14	Gauloises Prost Renault	B	3.0 Prost AP03-Peugeot V10	*engine*	14/22
ret	ITALIAN GP	Monza	14	Gauloises Prost Renault	B	3.0 Prost AP03-Peugeot V10	*spun off*	20/22
9	UNITED STATES GP	Indianapolis	14	Gauloises Prost Renault	B	3.0 Prost AP03-Peugeot V10	*1 lap behind*	16/22
ret	JAPANESE GP	Suzuka	14	Gauloises Prost Renault	B	3.0 Prost AP03-Peugeot V10	*broken rear suspension*	16/22
ret	MALAYSIAN GP	Sepang	14	Gauloises Prost Renault	B	3.0 Prost AP03-Peugeot V10	*lap 1 collision - Diniz & de la Rosa*	19/22

2001 Championship position: 7th= Wins: 0 Pole positions: 0 Fastest laps: 0 Points scored: 12

	Race	Circuit	No	Entrant	Tyres	Capacity/Car/Engine	Comment	Q Pos/Entries
4	AUSTRALIAN GP	Melbourne	16	Red Bull Sauber Petronas	B	3.0 Sauber C20-Petronas V10		10/22
ret	MALAYSIAN GP	Sepang	16	Red Bull Sauber Petronas	B	3.0 Sauber C20-Petronas V10	*spun off*	11/22
3	BRAZILIAN GP	Interlagos	16	Red Bull Sauber Petronas	B	3.0 Sauber C20-Petronas V10	*1 lap behind*	9/22
7	SAN MARINO GP	Imola	16	Red Bull Sauber Petronas	B	3.0 Sauber C20-Petronas V10	*1 lap behind*	12/22
6	SPANISH GP	Barcelona	16	Red Bull Sauber Petronas	B	3.0 Sauber C20-Petronas V10		10/22
9	AUSTRIAN GP	A1-Ring	16	Red Bull Sauber Petronas	B	3.0 Sauber C20-Petronas V10	*2 laps behind*	6/22
ret	MONACO GP	Monte Carlo	16	Red Bull Sauber Petronas	B	3.0 Sauber C20-Petronas V10	*hit barrier on lap 1*	16/22
ret	CANADIAN GP	Montreal	16	Red Bull Sauber Petronas	B	3.0 Sauber C20-Petronas V10	*collision with Irvine*	11/22
ret	EUROPEAN GP	Nürburgring	16	Red Bull Sauber Petronas	B	3.0 Sauber C20-Petronas V10	*driveshaft failure*	10/22
6	FRENCH GP	Magny Cours	16	Red Bull Sauber Petronas	B	3.0 Sauber C20-Petronas V10	*1 lap behind*	9/22
6	BRITISH GP	Silverstone	16	Red Bull Sauber Petronas	B	3.0 Sauber C20-Petronas V10	*1 lap behind*	9/22
ret	GERMAN GP	Hockenheim	16	Red Bull Sauber Petronas	B	3.0 Sauber C20-Petronas V10	*rear-ended by de la Rosa*	7/22
6	HUNGARIAN GP	Hungaroring	16	Red Bull Sauber Petronas	B	3.0 Sauber C20-Petronas V10	*1 lap behind*	7/22
ret	BELGIAN GP	Spa	16	Red Bull Sauber Petronas	B	3.0 Sauber C20-Petronas V10	*accident at second start*	14/22
11	ITALIAN GP	Monza	16	Red Bull Sauber Petronas	B	3.0 Sauber C20-Petronas V10	*1 lap behind*	8/22
6	UNITED STATES GP	Indianapolis	16	Red Bull Sauber Petronas	B	3.0 Sauber C20-Petronas V10		6/22
9	JAPANESE GP	Suzuka	16	Red Bull Sauber Petronas	B	3.0 Sauber C20-Petronas V10	*1 lap behind*	10/22

2002 Championship position: 10= Wins: 0 Pole positions: 0 Fastest laps: 0 Points scored: 7

	Race	Circuit	No	Entrant	Tyres	Capacity/Car/Engine	Comment	Q Pos/Entries
ret	AUSTRALIAN GP	Melbourne	7	Sauber Petronas	B	3.0 Sauber C21-Petronas V10	*multiple accident on lap 1*	10/22
5	MALAYSIAN GP	Sepang	7	Sauber Petronas	B	3.0 Sauber C21-Petronas V10	*1 lap behind*	7/22
ret	BRAZILIAN GP	Interlagos	7	Sauber Petronas	B	3.0 Sauber C21-Petronas V10	*loose front brake disc*	9/22
10	SAN MARINO GP	Imola	7	Sauber Petronas	B	3.0 Sauber C21-Petronas V10	*poor pitstop – drive thru penalty/-1 lap*	7/22
4	SPANISH GP	Barcelona	7	Sauber Petronas	B	3.0 Sauber C21-Petronas V10		8/21
ret	AUSTRIAN GP	A1-Ring	7	Sauber Petronas	B	3.0 Sauber C21-Petronas V10	*lost control – big collision with Sato*	5/22
8	MONACO GP	Monte Carlo	7	Sauber Petronas	B	3.0 Sauber C21-Petronas V10	*2 laps behind*	17/22
12	CANADIAN GP	Montreal	7	Sauber Petronas	B	3.0 Sauber C21-Petronas V10	*2 drive-through penalties/1 lap behind*	7/22
7	EUROPEAN GP	Nürburgring	7	Sauber Petronas	B	3.0 Sauber C21-Petronas V10	*1 lap behind*	9/22
6	BRITISH GP	Silverstone	7	Sauber Petronas	B	3.0 Sauber C21-Petronas V10	*1 lap behind*	10/22
7	FRENCH GP	Magny Cours	7	Sauber Petronas	B	3.0 Sauber C21-Petronas V10	*traction control problems/1 lap behind*	10/21
6	GERMAN GP	Hockenheim	7	Sauber Petronas	B	3.0 Sauber C21-Petronas V10	*allowed into 6th by Massa*	10/22
9	HUNGARIAN GP	Hungaroring	7	Sauber Petronas	B	3.0 Sauber C21-Petronas V10	*1 lap behind*	8/20
10	BELGIAN GP	Spa	7	Sauber Petronas	B	3.0 Sauber C21-Petronas V10	*1 lap behind*	18/20
10	ITALIAN GP	Monza	7	Sauber Petronas	B	3.0 Sauber C21-Petronas V10		15/20
9	UNITED STATES GP	Indianapolis	7	Sauber Petronas	B	3.0 Sauber C21-Petronas V10	*1 lap behind*	10/20
7	JAPANESE GP	Suzuka	7	Sauber Petronas	B	3.0 Sauber C21-Petronas V10	*1 lap behind*	12/20

2003 Championship position: 14th= Wins: 0 Pole positions: 0 Fastest laps: 0 Points scored: 6

	Race	Circuit	No	Entrant	Tyres	Capacity/Car/Engine	Comment	Q Pos/Entries
ret	AUSTRALIAN GP	Melbourne	9	Sauber Petronas	B	3.0 Sauber C22-Petronas V10	*broken suspension*	7/20
8	MALAYSIAN GP	Sepang	9	Sauber Petronas	B	3.0 Sauber C22-Petronas V10	*gearchange problems/1 lap behind*	6/20
ret	BRAZILIAN GP	Interlagos	9	Sauber Petronas	B	3.0 Sauber C22-Petronas V10	*engine*	12/20
10	SAN MARINO GP	Imola	9	Sauber Petronas	B	3.0 Sauber C22-Petronas V10	*1 lap behind*	11/20
10	SPANISH GP	Barcelona	9	Sauber Petronas	B	3.0 Sauber C22-Petronas V10	*2 laps behind*	14/20
ret	AUSTRIAN GP	A1-Ring	9	Sauber Petronas	B	3.0 Sauber C22-Petronas V10	*engine*	4/20
11	MONACO GP	Monte Carlo	9	Sauber Petronas	B	3.0 Sauber C22-Petronas V10	*2 laps behind*	14/19
ret	CANADIAN GP	Montreal	9	Sauber Petronas	B	3.0 Sauber C22-Petronas V10	*engine*	12/20
8	EUROPEAN GP	Nürburgring	9	Sauber Petronas	B	3.0 Sauber C22-Petronas V10	**no time set/1 lap behind*	*20/20
13	FRANCE GP	Magny Cours	9	Sauber Petronas	B	3.0 Sauber C22-Petronas V10	*2 laps behind*	15/20
17	BRITISH GP	Silverstone	9	Sauber Petronas	B	3.0 Sauber C22-Petronas V10	*2 laps behind*	16/20
10	GERMAN GP	Hockenheim	9	Sauber Petronas	B	3.0 Sauber C22-Petronas V10	*2 laps behind*	15/20
9	HUNGARIAN GP	Hungaroring	9	Sauber Petronas	B	3.0 Sauber C22-Petronas V10	*1 lap behind*	11/20
9	ITALIAN GP	Monza	9	Sauber Petronas	B	3.0 Sauber C22-Petronas V10	*1 lap behind*	16/20
5	UNITED STATES GP	Indianapolis	9	Sauber Petronas	B	3.0 Sauber C22-Petronas V10		13/20
9	JAPANESE GP	Suzuka	9	Sauber Petronas	B	3.0 Sauber C22-Petronas V10		11/20

2004 Championship position: 16= Wins: 0 Pole positions: 0 Fastest laps: 0 Points scored: 3

	Race	Circuit	No	Entrant	Tyres	Capacity/Car/Engine	Comment	Q Pos/Entries
ret	AUSTRALIAN GP	Melbourne	18	Jordan Ford	B	3.0 Jordan EJ14-Cosworth V10	*faulty clutch – collision in pits*	15/20
ret	MALAYSIAN GP	Sepang	18	Jordan Ford	B	3.0 Jordan EJ14-Cosworth V10	*gearbox failure*	15/20
15	BAHRAIN GP	Bahrain Circuit	18	Jordan Ford	B	3.0 Jordan EJ14-Cosworth V10	*brake problems/1 lap behind*	15/20
ret	SAN MARINO GP	Imola	18	Jordan Ford	B	3.0 Jordan EJ14-Cosworth V10	*transmission*	16/20
ret	SPANISH GP	Barcelona	18	Jordan Ford	B	3.0 Jordan EJ14-Cosworth V10	*hydraulics – gearbox failure*	15/20

7	MONACO GP	Monte Carlo	18	Jordan Ford	B	3.0 Jordan EJ14-Cosworth V10	*2 laps behind*	17/20	
10	EUROPEAN GP	Nürburgring	18	Jordan Ford	B	3.0 Jordan EJ14-Cosworth V10	*1 lap behind*	13/20	
8*	CANADIAN GP	Montreal	18	Jordan Ford	B	3.0 Jordan EJ14-Cosworth V10	*2nd/5th/8th/10th cars dsq/-2 laps*	15/20	
ret	U S GP	Indianapolis	18	Jordan Ford	B	3.0 Jordan EJ14-Cosworth V10	*engine*	16/20	
16	FRENCH GP	Magny Cours	18	Jordan Ford	B	3.0 Jordan EJ14-Cosworth V10	*2 laps behind*	17/20	
15	BRITISH GP	Silverstone	18	Jordan Ford	B	3.0 Jordan EJ14-Cosworth V10	*1 lap behind*	17/20	
ret	GERMAN GP	Hockenheim	18	Jordan Ford	B	3.0 Jordan EJ14-Cosworth V10	*handling*	18/20	
12	HUNGARIAN GP	Hungaroring	18	Jordan Ford	B	3.0 Jordan EJ14-Cosworth V10	*2 laps behind*	16/20	
11	BELGIAN GP	Spa	18	Jordan Ford	B	3.0 Jordan EJ14-Cosworth V10	*engine cut-out problems/4 laps behind*	16/20	
14	ITALIAN GP	Monza	18	Jordan Ford	B	3.0 Jordan EJ14-Cosworth V10	*1 lap behind*	17/20	
13	CHINESE GP	Shanghai	18	Jordan Ford	B	3.0 Jordan EJ14-Cosworth V10	*1 lap behind*	14/20	
13	JAPANESE GP	Suzuka	18	Jordan Ford	B	3.0 Jordan EJ14-Cosworth V10	*1 lap behind*	16/20	
ret	BRAZILIAN GP	Interlagos	18	Jordan Ford	B	3.0 Jordan EJ14-Cosworth V10	*clutch*	17/20	

2005 Championship position: 11th   Wins: 0   Pole positions: 1   Fastest laps: 0   Points scored: 28

ret	AUSTRALIAN GP	Melbourne	6	BMW WilliamsF1 Team	M	3.0 Williams FW27-BMW V10	*collision with M Schumacher*	7/20
3	MALAYSIAN GP	Sepang	6	BMW WilliamsF1 Team	M	3.0 Williams FW27-BMW V10		10/20
ret	BAHRAIN GP	Bahrain	6	BMW WilliamsF1 Team	M	3.0 Williams FW27-BMW V10	*engine*	4/20
6*	SAN MARINO GP	Imola	6	BMW WilliamsF1 Team	M	3.0 Williams FW27-BMW V10	*3rd & 5th place cars disqualified*	8/20
10	SPANISH GP	Barcelona	6	BMW WilliamsF1 Team	M	3.0 Williams FW27-BMW V10	*1 lap behind*	17/18
2	MONACO GP	Monte Carlo	6	BMW WilliamsF1 Team	M	3.0 Williams FW27-BMW V10		6/18
2	EUROPEAN GP	Nürburgring	6	BMW WilliamsF1 Team	M	3.0 Williams FW27-BMW V10		1/20
ret	CANADIAN GP	Montreal	6	BMW WilliamsF1 Team	M	3.0 Williams FW27-BMW V10	*engine*	13/20
dns*	U S GP	Indianapolis	6	BMW WilliamsF1 Team	M	3.0 Williams FW27-BMW V10	*withdrawn after parade lap*	15/20
14	FRENCH GP	Magny Cours	6	BMW WilliamsF1 Team	M	3.0 Williams FW27-BMW V10	*6 pitstops-handling/4 laps behind*	14/20
12	BRITISH GP	Silverstone	6	BMW WilliamsF1 Team	M	3.0 Williams FW27-BMW V10	*poor aerodynamics/1 lap behind*	14/20
11	GERMAN GP	Hockenheim	6	BMW WilliamsF1 Team	M	3.0 Williams FW27-BMW V10	*handling inbalance/1 lap behind*	7/20
6	HUNGARIAN GP	Hungaroring	6	BMW WilliamsF1 Team	M	3.0 Williams FW27-BMW V10	*two-stop strategy/reduced engine revs*	12/20
ret	TURKISH GP	Istanbul	6	BMW WilliamsF1 Team	M	3.0 Williams FW27-BMW V10	*tyre failure against undertray*	6/20

2006 Championship position: 9th   Wins: 0   Pole positions: 0   Fastest laps: 0   Points scored: 23

12	BAHRAIN GP	Bahrain	16	BMW Sauber F1 Team	M	2.4 BMW Sauber F1.06-BMW V8	*1 lap behind*	10/22
ret	MALAYSIAN GP	Sepang	16	BMW Sauber F1 Team	M	2.4 BMW Sauber F1.06-BMW V8	*engine*	15/22
4	AUSTRALIAN GP	Melbourne	16	BMW Sauber F1 Team	M	2.4 BMW Sauber F1.06-BMW V8		8/22
13	SAN MARINO GP	Imola	16	BMW Sauber F1 Team	M	2.4 BMW Sauber F1.06-BMW V8	*1 lap behind*	15/22
10	EUROPEAN GP	Nürburgring	16	BMW Sauber F1 Team	M	2.4 BMW Sauber F1.06-BMW V8	*1 lap behind*	15/22
8	SPANISH GP	Barcelona	16	BMW Sauber F1 Team	M	2.4 BMW Sauber F1.06-BMW V8	*1 lap behind*	10/22
7	MONACO GP	Monte Carlo	16	BMW Sauber F1 Team	M	2.4 BMW Sauber F1.06-BMW V8	*1 lap behind*	16/22
7	BRITISH GP	Silverstone	16	BMW Sauber F1 Team	M	2.4 BMW Sauber F1.06-BMW V8	*gearchange problems*	9/22
7	CANADIAN GP	Montreal	16	BMW Sauber F1 Team	M	2.4 BMW Sauber F1.06-BMW V8	*1 lap behind*	13/22
ret	U S GP	Indianapolis	16	BMW Sauber F1 Team	M	2.4 BMW Sauber F1.06-BMW V8	*multiple accident on lap 1*	10/22
8	FRENCH GP	Magny Cours	16	BMW Sauber F1 Team	M	2.4 BMW Sauber F1.06-V8	*1 lap behind*	12/22
ret	GERMAN GP	Hockenheim	16	BMW Sauber F1 Team	M	2.4 BMW Sauber F1.06-V8	*collision damage – hit by Villeneuve*	16/22
3	HUNGARIAN GP	Hungaroring	16	BMW Sauber F1 Team	M	2.4 BMW Sauber F1.06-V8	*hit by M Schumacher – steering damage*	11/22
14	TURKISH GP	Istanbul	16	BMW Sauber F1 Team	M	2.4 BMW Sauber F1.06-V8	*lap 1 collision with Fisichella/-2 laps*	6/22
8	ITALIAN GP	Monza	16	BMW Sauber F1 Team	M	2.4 BMW Sauber F1.06-V8		3/22
7	CHINESE GP	Shanghai	16	BMW Sauber F1 Team	M	2.4 BMW Sauber F1.06-V8	*hit by Sato and later Barrichello*	8/22
8	JAPANESE GP	Suzuka	16	BMW Sauber F1 Team	M	2.4 BMW Sauber F1.06-V8	*tyre graining*	9/22
17/ret	BRAZILIAN GP	Interlagos	16	BMW Sauber F1 Team	M	2.4 BMW Sauber F1.06-V8	*collision Liuzzi – later suspension failure*	8/22

2007 Championship position: 00   Wins: 0   Pole positions: 0   Fastest laps: 0   Points scored: 00

4	AUSTRALIAN GP	Melbourne	9	BMW Sauber F1 Team	B	2.4 BMW Sauber F1.07-V8		3/22
4	MALAYSIAN GP	Sepang	9	BMW Sauber F1 Team	B	2.4 BMW Sauber F1.07-V8		5/22
4	BAHRAIN GP	Bahrain	9	BMW Sauber F1 Team	B	2.4 BMW Sauber F1.07-V8		5/22
ret	SPANISH GP	Barcelona	9	BMW Sauber F1 Team	B	2.4 BMW Sauber F1.07-V8	*gearbox*	7/22
6	MONACO GP	Monte Carlo	9	BMW Sauber F1 Team	B	2.4 BMW Sauber F1.07-V8	*strategy thwarted by safety car/-1 lap*	7/22
2	CANADIAN GP	Montreal	9	BMW Sauber F1 Team	B	2.4 BMW Sauber F1.07-V8		3/22
ret	U S GP	Indianapolis	9	BMW Sauber F1 Team	B	2.4 BMW Sauber F1.07-V8	*hydraulic leak*	5/22
5	FRENCH GP	Magny Cours	9	BMW Sauber F1 Team	B	2.4 BMW Sauber F1.07-V8		7/22
6	BRITISH GP	Silverstone	9	BMW Sauber F1 Team	B	2.4 BMW Sauber F1.07-V8		9/22
6	GERMAN GP	Nürburgring	9	BMW Sauber F1 Team	B	2.4 BMW Sauber F1.07-V8	*minor collision with Kubica*	4/22
3	HUNGARIAN GP	Hungaroring	9	BMW Sauber F1 Team	B	2.4 BMW Sauber F1.07-V8		3/22
4	TURKISH GP	Istanbul	9	BMW Sauber F1 Team	B	2.4 BMW Sauber F1.07-V8		6/22
4	ITALIAN GP	Monza	9	BMW Sauber F1 Team	B	2.4 BMW Sauber F1.07-V8		4/22
5	BELGIAN GP	Spa	9	BMW Sauber F1 Team	B	2.4 BMW Sauber F1.07-V8	*ran wide at start - good recovery drive to 5th*	7/22
14/ret	JAPANESE GP	Suzuka	9	BMW Sauber F1 Team	B	2.4 BMW Sauber F1.07-V8	*accident damage/engine/2 laps behind*	5/22
7	CHINESE GP	Shanghai	9	BMW Sauber F1 Team	B	2.4 BMW Sauber F1.07-V8	*hampered by tyre changes during race*	8/22
6	BRAZILIAN GP	Interlagos	9	BMW Sauber F1 Team	B	2.4 BMW Sauber F1.07-V8		6/22

2008 Championship position: 6th   Wins: 0   Pole positions: 0   Fastest laps: 2   Points scored: 60

2	AUSTRALIAN GP	Melbourne	3	BMW Sauber F1 Team	B	2.4 BMW Sauber F1.08-V8		5/22
6	MALAYSIAN GP	Sepang	3	BMW Sauber F1 Team	B	2.4 BMW Sauber F1.08-V8	*FL*	7/22
4	BAHRAIN GP	Bahrain	3	BMW Sauber F1 Team	B	2.4 BMW Sauber F1.08-V8		6/22
9	SPANISH GP	Barcelona	3	BMW Sauber F1 Team	B	2.4 BMW Sauber F1.08-V8	*drive-thru penalty – pitted under safety car*	9/22
5	TURKISH GP	Istanbul	3	BMW Sauber F1 Team	B	2.4 BMW Sauber F1.08-V8		9/22
14	MONACO GP	Monte Carlo	3	BMW Sauber F1 Team	B	2.4 BMW Sauber F1.08-V8	*collision – hit by Alonso/4 laps behind*	13/20
2	CANADIAN GP	Montreal	3	BMW Sauber F1 Team	B	2.4 BMW Sauber F1.08-V8	*finished second to team mate Kubica*	13/22
13	FRENCH GP	Magny Cours	3	BMW Sauber F1 Team	B	2.4 BMW Sauber F1.08-V8	*handling*	8/22
2	BRITISH GP	Silverstone	3	BMW Sauber F1 Team	B	2.4 BMW Sauber F1.08-V8	*drove superbly to preserve tyres*	5/22
4	GERMAN GP	Hockenheim	3	BMW Sauber F1 Team	B	2.4 BMW Sauber F1.08-V8	*FL*	12/22
10	HUNGARIAN GP	Hungaroring	3	BMW Sauber F1 Team	B	2.4 BMW Sauber F1.08-V8		16/22
9	EUROPEAN GP	Valencia	3	BMW Sauber F1 Team	B	2.4 BMW Sauber F1.08-V8	*in trouble with soft tyres*	8/22
2*	BELGIAN GP	Spa	3	BMW Sauber F1 Team	B	2.4 BMW Sauber F1.08-V8	*3rd - but 1st place car penalised 25 sec*	5/22
5	ITALIAN GP	Monza	3	BMW Sauber F1 Team	B	2.4 BMW Sauber F1.08-V8		10/22

6	SINGAPORE GP	Singapore Circuit	3	BMW Sauber F1 Team	B	2.4 BMW Sauber F1.08-V8		6/22
9	JAPANESE GP	Suzuka	3	BMW Sauber F1 Team	B	2.4 BMW Sauber F1.08-V8	*ran one-stop race*	16/22
5	CHINESE GP	Shanghai	3	BMW Sauber F1 Team	B	2.4 BMW Sauber F1.08-V8	*grid penalty for impeding*	7/22
10	BRAZILIAN GP	Interlagos	3	BMW Sauber F1 Team	B	2.4 BMW Sauber F1.08-V8	*1 lap behind*	8/22

2009 Championship position: 13th Wins: 0 Pole positions: 0 Fastest laps: 0 Points scored: 19

10	AUSTRALIAN GP	Melbourne	6	BMW Sauber F1 Team	B	2.4 BMW Sauber F1.09-V8		11/20
2	MALAYSIAN GP	Sepang	6	BMW Sauber F1 Team	B	2.4 BMW Sauber F1.09-V8	*rain-shortened race*	11/20
12	CHINESE GP	Shanghai	6	BMW Sauber F1 Team	B	2.4 BMW Sauber F1.09-V8		11/20
19	BAHRAIN GP	Bahrain	6	BMW Sauber F1 Team	B	2.4 BMW Sauber F1.09-V8	*dreadful handling/1 lap behind*	14/20
7	SPANISH GP	Barcelona	7	BMW Sauber F1 Team	B	2.4 BMW Sauber F1.09-V8	*good drive in difficult handling car*	13/20
11	MONACO GP	Monte Carlo	7	BMW Sauber F1 Team	B	2.4 BMW Sauber F1.09-V8	*1 lap behind*	17/20
11	TURKISH GP	Istanbul	7	BMW Sauber F1 Team	B	2.4 BMW Sauber F1.09-V8		11/20
15	BRITISH GP	Silverstone	7	BMW Sauber F1 Team	B	2.4 BMW Sauber F1.09-V8	*1 lap behind*	15/20
10	GERMAN GP	Nürburgring	7	BMW Sauber F1 Team	B	2.4 BMW Sauber F1.09-V8	*lost time at pit stop*	11/20
11	HUNGARIAN GP	Hungaroring	7	BMW Sauber F1 Team	B	2.4 BMW Sauber F1.09-V8		16/20
11	EUROPEAN GP	Valencia	7	BMW Sauber F1 Team	B	2.4 BMW Sauber F1.09-V8		11/20
5	BELGIAN GP	Spa	7	BMW Sauber F1 Team	B	2.4 BMW Sauber F1.09-V8	*made wrong tyre choice for first stint*	3/20
7	ITALIAN GP	Monza	7	BMW Sauber F1 Team	B	2.4 BMW Sauber F1.09-V8	*good drive from fifteenth on the grid*	15/20
ret	SINGAPORE GP	Singapore Circuit	7	BMW Sauber F1 Team	B	2.4 BMW Sauber F1.09-V8	*taken out by Sutil*	8/20
6	JAPANESE GP	Suzuka	7	BMW Sauber F1 Team	B	2.4 BMW Sauber F1.09-V8	*delayed by wheel change at pit stop*	6/20
ret	BRAZILIAN GP	Interlagos	7	BMW Sauber F1 Team	B	2.4 BMW Sauber F1.09-V8	*out of fuel*	19/20
5	ABU DHABI GP	Yas Marina Circuit	7	BMW Sauber F1 Team	B	2.4 BMW Sauber F1.09-V8	*good battle with Barrichello*	8/20

2010 Championship position: 18 Wins: 0 Pole positions: 0 Fastest laps: 0 Points scored: 6

ret	SINGAPORE GP	Marina Bay Circuit	22	BMW Sauber F1 Team	B	2.4 BMW Sauber F1.10-V8	*accident – collision with Schumacher*	15/24
8	JAPANESE GP	Suzuka	22	BMW Sauber F1 Team	B	2.4 BMW Sauber F1.10-V8		11/24
9	KOREAN GP	Yeongam	22	BMW Sauber F1 Team	B	2.4 BMW Sauber F1.10-V8		13/24
17	BRAZILIAN GP	Interlagos	22	BMW Sauber F1 Team	B	2.4 BMW Sauber F1.10-V8	*drive thru pen – ignored blue flags/-1 lap*	16/24
11	ABU DHABI GP	Yas Marina Circuit	22	BMW Sauber F1 Team	B	2.4 BMW Sauber F1.10-V8		4/24

2011 Championship position: 11th Wins: 0 Pole positions: 0 Fastest laps: 0 Points scored: 34

12*	AUSTRALIAN GP	Melbourne	9	Lotus Renault GP	P	2.4 Lotus Renault R31-V8	*debris damage/*14th - 7 & 8th cars dsq/-1 lap*	18/24
3	MALAYSIAN GP	Sepang	9	Lotus Renault GP	P	2.4 Lotus Renault R31-V8		6/24
12	CHINESE GP	Shanghai	9	Lotus Renault GP	P	2.4 Lotus Renault R31-V8		16/24
7	TURKISH GP	Istanbul	9	Lotus Renault GP	P	2.4 Lotus Renault R31-V8		9/24
8	SPANISH GP	Barcelona	9	Lotus Renault GP	P	2.4 Lotus Renault R31-V8	*1 lap behind/*no time set*	*24/24
8	MONACO GP	Monte Carlo	9	Lotus Renault GP	P	2.4 Lotus Renault R31-V8		16/24
ret	CANADIAN GP	Montreal	9	Lotus Renault GP	P	2.4 Lotus Renault R31-V8	*ran into Kobayashi – lost front wing*	9/24
10	EUROPEAN GP	Valencia	9	Lotus Renault GP	P	2.4 Lotus Renault R31-V8		9/24
8	BRITISH GP	Silverstone	9	Lotus Renault GP	P	2.4 Lotus Renault R31-V8		16/24
ret	GERMAN GP	Hockenheim	9	Lotus Renault GP	P	2.4 Lotus Renault R31-V8	*collision with Buemi*	11/24
ret	HUNGARIAN GP	Hungaroring	9	Lotus Renault GP	P	2.4 Lotus Renault R31-V8	*exhaust system/car on fire*	14/24

GP Starts: 183 GP Wins: 0 Pole positions: 1 Fastest laps: 2 Points: 259

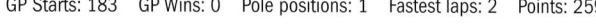

THEO HELFRICH

A MANAGER in the motor trade in Mannheim, the balding Theo Helfrich enjoyed considerable success in the early 1950s and was one of Germany's best 'lesser-known' pilots. Driving a Veritas, he won at Hockenheim in 1950, and over the next year or so scored some excellent placings with the car, bringing an invitation from Mercedes-Benz to race one of their three 300SLs at Le Mans. Paired with Helmut Niedermayr, he took a fine second place, behind the Fritz Riess/Hermann Lang car.

In 1953, Helfrich raced a single-seater Veritas and won the German Formula 2 championship, as well as helping to develop the little Borgward sports car. He and Günther Bechem took the potent little machine into third place overall and easily won the 750–1500cc class. Although he handled Hans Klenk's car in place of its injured owner in the 1954 German Grand Prix, the rule changes that had swept away Formula 2 in favour of the new 2.5-litre F1 rendered it obsolete. Thus he purchased an F3 Cooper and proceeded to win in hill-climbs and minor races, taking seven victories in ten outings that year. Perhaps his most notable performance, though, was second to Stirling Moss in that year's Eifelrennen. Purchasing a 1500cc Porsche Spyder, Helfrich raced on for a couple more years, taking fifth place at Rouen in 1956.

HELFRICH, Theo (D) b 13/5/1913, Frankfurt-am-Main – d 29/4/1978, Ludwigshafen

1952 Championship position: Unplaced

	Race	Circuit	No	Entrant	Tyres	Capacity/Car/Engine	Comment	Q Pos/Entries
ret	GERMAN GP	Nürburgring	122	Theo Helfrich	–	2.0 Veritas RS 6		18/32

1953 Championship position: Unplaced

12	GERMAN GP	Nürburgring	24	Theo Helfrich	–	2.0 Veritas RS 6	*2 laps behind*	28/35

1954 Championship position: Unplaced

ret	GERMAN GP	Nürburgring	22	Hans Klenk	–	2.0 Klenk Meteor-BMW 6	*engine*	21/23

GP Starts: 3 GP Wins: 0 Pole positions: 0 Fastest laps: 0 Points: 0

BRIAN HENTON

CAREER setbacks that would have made a less determined character throw in the towel only seemed to encourage the tough, no-nonsense Brian Henton to get stuck in once more and prove his critics wrong. With three seasons of Formula Vee and Super Vee racing behind him, he took the plunge into F3, initially with his own GRD, before a move into the works March F3 team for 1974 really put him on the map. Easily winning the Lombard and Forward Trust championships, he graduated to Formula 2, and a brief and salutary stint with Lotus. This was followed by an abortive 1976 season, after a planned drive with Tom Wheatcroft foundered after just one race, leaving him to start all over again.

Henton's patriotic private British Formula One March got him back on the F1 grid, but he soon ran out of funds, so it was back to Formula 2 for 1978, when he enjoyed some success in his own car, and 1979, when he finished a close second to Marc Surer in the championship, winning at Mugello and Misano. With BP and Toleman behind him, he made no mistake the following year, taking the title and establishing himself as a serious F1 proposition once more.

Brian had certainly earned his move back into grands prix with Toleman, but the season was another major disappointment, the underdeveloped car being beset by turbo problems. He could have sunk without trace, but he managed to find a seat for 1982, first with Arrows, deputising for the injured Marc Surer, and then at Tyrrell in place of Slim Borgudd. He did a solid job, nearly making the points, and was credited with fastest lap at Brands Hatch, but it was not enough for Tyrrell to retain him. A one-off drive into fourth place for Theodore in the 1983 Race of Champions rounded off a very good career, which eventually failed to meet his expectations, but not for want of trying.

HENTON, Brian (GB) b 19/9/1946, Derby

1975 Championship position: Unplaced

	Race	Circuit	No	Entrant	Tyres	Capacity/Car/Engine	Comment	Q Pos/Entries
16/ret	BRITISH GP	Silverstone	15	John Player Team Lotus	G	3.0 JPS Lotus 72E-Cosworth V8	crashed in rainstorm/3 laps behind	21/28
dns	AUSTRIAN GP	Österreichring	6	John Player Team Lotus	G	3.0 JPS Lotus 72F-Cosworth V8	accident in practice	(23)/30
nc	US GP	Watkins Glen	6	John Player Team Lotus	G	3.0 JPS Lotus 72F-Cosworth V8	pit stop/10 laps behind	19/24

1977 Championship position: Unplaced

10	US GP WEST	Long Beach	10	Team Rothmans International	G	3.0 March 761B-Cosworth V8	3 laps behind	18/22
dnq	SPANISH GP	Jarama	38	British Formula One Racing Team	G	3.0 March 761B-Cosworth V8		29/31
dnq	BRITISH GP	Silverstone	38	British Formula One Racing Team	G	3.0 March 761B-Cosworth V8		29/36
dnq	AUSTRIAN GP	Österreichring	38	British Formula One Racing Team	G	3.0 March 761B-Cosworth V8		27/30
dsq	DUTCH GP	Zandvoort	38	HB Bewaking Alarm Systems	G	3.0 Boro/Ensign N175-Cosworth V8	push start after spin	23/34
dnq	ITALIAN GP	Monza	38	HB Bewaking Alarm Systems	G	3.0 Boro/Ensign N175-Cosworth V8		28/34

1978 Championship position: Unplaced

dns	AUSTRIAN GP	Österreichring	18	Team Surtees	G	3.0 Surtees TS20-Cosworth V8	tried Keegan's car in practice	– / –

1981 Championship position: Unplaced

dnq	SAN MARINO GP	Imola	35	Candy Toleman Motorsport	M	1.5 t/c Toleman TG181-Hart 4		30/30
dnq	BELGIAN GP	Zolder	35	Candy Toleman Motorsport	P	1.5 t/c Toleman TG181-Hart 4		30/31
dnpq	MONACO GP	Monte Carlo	35	Candy Toleman Motorsport	P	1.5 t/c Toleman TG181-Hart 4		30/31
dnq	SPANISH GP	Jarama	35	Candy Toleman Motorsport	P	1.5 t/c Toleman TG181-Hart 4		28/30
dnq	FRENCH GP	Dijon	35	Candy Toleman Motorsport	P	1.5 t/c Toleman TG181-Hart 4		26/29
dnq	BRITISH GP	Silverstone	35	Candy Toleman Motorsport	P	1.5 t/c Toleman TG181-Hart 4		26/30
dnq	GERMAN GP	Hockenheim	35	Candy Toleman Motorsport	P	1.5 t/c Toleman TG181-Hart 4		26/30
dnq	AUSTRIAN GP	Österreichring	35	Candy Toleman Motorsport	P	1.5 t/c Toleman TG181-Hart 4		27/28
dnq	DUTCH GP	Zandvoort	35	Candy Toleman Motorsport	P	1.5 t/c Toleman TG181-Hart 4		26/30
10	ITALIAN GP	Monza	35	Candy Toleman Motorsport	P	1.5 t/c Toleman TG181-Hart 4	3 laps behind	23/30
dnq	CANADIAN GP	Montreal	35	Candy Toleman Motorsport	P	1.5 t/c Toleman TG181-Hart 4		27/30
dnq	CAESARS PALACE GP	Las Vegas	35	Candy Toleman Motorsport	P	1.5 t/c Toleman TG181-Hart 4		29/30

1982 Championship position: Unplaced   Fastest laps: 1

dnq	SOUTH AFRICAN GP	Kyalami	29	Arrows Racing Team	P	3.0 Arrows A4-Cosworth V8		29/30
dnq	BRAZILIAN GP	Rio	29	Arrows Racing Team	P	3.0 Arrows A4-Cosworth V8		29/31
ret	US GP WEST	Long Beach	29	Arrows Racing Team	P	3.0 Arrows A4-Cosworth V8	accident	20/31
ret	SAN MARINO GP	Imola	4	Team Tyrrell	G	3.0 Tyrrell 011-Cosworth V8	clutch	11/14
ret	BELGIAN GP	Zolder	4	Team Tyrrell	G	3.0 Tyrrell 011-Cosworth V8	engine	22/32
8	MONACO GP	Monte Carlo	4	Team Tyrrell	G	3.0 Tyrrell 011-Cosworth V8	pit stop – puncture/4 laps behind	17/31
9	US GP (DETROIT)	Detroit	4	Team Tyrrell	G	3.0 Tyrrell 011-Cosworth V8	pit stop/2 laps behind	20/28
nc	CANADIAN GP	Montreal	4	Team Tyrrell	G	3.0 Tyrrell 011-Cosworth V8	hit barrier – pitstop/11 laps behind	26/29
ret	DUTCH GP	Zandvoort	4	Team Tyrrell	G	3.0 Tyrrell 011-Cosworth V8	throttle linkage	20/31
8	BRITISH GP	Brands Hatch	4	Team Tyrrell	G	3.0 Tyrrell 011-Cosworth V8	pit stop – tyres/FL/1 lap behind	17/30
10	FRENCH GP	Paul Ricard	4	Team Tyrrell	G	3.0 Tyrrell 011-Cosworth V8	1 lap behind	23/30
7	GERMAN GP	Hockenheim	4	Team Tyrrell	G	3.0 Tyrrell 011-Cosworth V8	1 lap behind	18/30
ret	AUSTRIAN GP	Österreichring	4	Team Tyrrell	G	3.0 Tyrrell 011-Cosworth V8	engine	19/29
11	SWISS GP	Dijon	4	Team Tyrrell	G	3.0 Tyrrell 011-Cosworth V8	2 laps behind	18/29
ret	ITALIAN GP	Monza	4	Team Tyrrell	G	3.0 Tyrrell 011-Cosworth V8	collision with Daly – spun off	20/30
8	CAESARS PALACE GP	Las Vegas	4	Team Tyrrell	G	3.0 Tyrrell 011-Cosworth V8	1 lap behind	19/30

GP Starts: 19   GP Wins: 0   Pole positions: 0   Fastest laps: 1   Points: 0

PERHAPS Britain's most talented young prospect of the 1980s, Johnny Herbert built a successful career for himself in the world of grand prix racing. Indeed, 1999 saw him take an unlikely, but well-deserved win in the European Grand Prix to add to his emotional and hugely popular victories at Silverstone and Monza in 1995. Yet one wonders if the horrific crash at Brands Hatch in 1988, which interrupted his meteoric rise, somehow robbed his career of an impetus that might have seen him become a true contender for the world championship.

Having started racing karts at the age of ten, Herbert worked his way through the classes, taking numerous championships on the way, before graduating to FF1600 and winning the prestigious Brands Hatch Formula Ford Festival in 1985. His path then crossed that of Eddie Jordan, who took him into Formula 3 in 1987. He duly won the title and with it a Benetton test, which led to an option to drive for the team in 1989, so it was a season of F3000 next. That started brilliantly with a win at Jerez, followed by a number of highly competitive drives before that fateful leg shattering Brands accident.

During his recovery, Johnny had the goal of reaching the grid in Brazil to make his debut for Benetton, and after months of painful rehabilitation, he not only drove in Rio, but also took the car into fourth place. As the year progressed, however, it became clear that he was still handicapped by his injuries, and he was summarily replaced by the less-talented Emanuele Pirro. For the immediate future, he had to step down to Japanese F3000, take the occasional F1 ride and wait for another chance (an unexpected victory at Le Mans with Mazda in 1991 provided a highlight).

Luckily, Johnny's old mentor at Benetton, Peter Collins, had moved and was busy reviving the fortunes of Lotus; Herbert was very much the man he wanted for the job. Taken back into the team full time early in 1991, he repeatedly showed that he had the talent to win, but unfortunately the car did not. Locked into a contract at Lotus, he was left trapped and frustrated as the team struggled on against overwhelming odds during the 1994 season. He lost heart and, despite a morale-boosting fourth place on the grid at Monza, his relationship with team boss and father figure Collins soured to the point that a split was inevitable.

Both parties must have been relieved when Flavio Briatore bought out his contract in September that year, for not only did Collins receive some much-needed finance to stagger on at Lotus, but also Johnny was given a contract that would see him through to the end of 1995. Initially, he was placed at Ligier, but after a fine performance at Jerez, he was whisked into the Benetton team in the hope that he might assist Michaels Schumacher's title bid.

As already mentioned, 1995 was the year when Johnny found tangible success; indeed, apart from his two wins, his consistency brought him within a whisker of taking third place in the world championship. Unfortunately, his status at Benetton was very much that of the number two to Schumacher, and his gripes to the press after a disappointing showing in the Belgian Grand Prix could not have helped his cause.

Not retained at season's end, Herbert found a ride at Sauber and, after a somewhat frosty start when his experience was under-utilised in testing, he gradually won the team's confidence, especially after team-mate Heinz-Harald Frentzen seemed to lose his motivation. Third place at Monaco was the best result in a year littered with retirements, but despite Sauber's loss of the Ford engine deal to Stewart, Herbert had done enough to earn a new contract with the Swiss constructor. He became the team's mainstay and was charged with the task of developing the new Sauber C16 with its Petronas (née Ferrari) engine largely on his own.

The car was a capable points scorer, but never a likely winner, and the ever-optimistic Herbert made the best of his situation. Things changed for the worse in 1998, however, with the arrival of Jean Alesi. Simply, the two drivers failed to gel, and Johnny appeared to be worn down as much by the Frenchman's histrionics as by his edge in speed on the track.

Herbert was considered a touch fortunate to secure a two-year deal with Stewart Grand Prix beginning in 1999, but after a quiet first half to the season, he picked up the pace and duly supplied the team's aforementioned maiden grand prix win. Another superb drive in Malaysia gave a further boost to his confidence as he prepared to welcome Eddie Irvine on board as his new team-mate in the restructured Jaguar team for 2000. The new car was difficult and unpredictable to drive, but despite this Herbert gave his best and was probably relieved to be told that his services would not be required in 2001. His last race ended in a 150mph shunt when the suspension failed; he was lucky to escape unhurt.

Thereafter, Johnny busied himself largely in sports car racing, initially as a front-runner in the ALMS with Champion Racing in an Audi R8, taking six outright wins between 2001 and 2004. He also finished second at Le Mans on three consecutive occasions between 2002 and 2004.

Herbert continued to enjoy his racing and was the champion of the 2008 Speedcar series. He also had a brief spell in the British Touring Car Championship in 2009 with a Honda Civic.

HERBERT, Johnny (GB) b 25/6/1964, Brentwood, Essex

1989 Championship position: 14th=   Wins: 0   Pole positions: 0   Fastest laps: 0   Points scored: 5

	Race	Circuit	No	Entrant	Tyres	Capacity/Car/Engine	Comment	Q Pos/Entries
4	BRAZILIAN GP	Rio	20	Benetton Formula	G	3.5 Benetton B188-Cosworth V8		10/38
11	SAN MARINO GP	Imola	20	Benetton Formula	G	3.5 Benetton B188-Cosworth V8	*spin/2 laps behind*	23/39
14	MONACO GP	Monte Carlo	20	Benetton Formula	G	3.5 Benetton B188-Cosworth V8	*hit Arnoux/pit stop – new wing/-4 laps*	24/38
15	MEXICAN GP	Mexico City	20	Benetton Formula	G	3.5 Benetton B188-Cosworth V8	*pit stops – gearbox – tyres/-3 laps*	18/39
5	US GP (PHOENIX)	Phoenix	20	Benetton Formula	G	3.5 Benetton B188-Cosworth V8	*lost 4th gear/1 lap behind*	25/39
dnq	CANADIAN GP	Montreal	20	Benetton Formula	G	3.5 Benetton B188-Cosworth V8		29/39
ret	BELGIAN GP	Spa	4	Tyrrell Racing Organisation	G	3.5 Tyrrell 018-Cosworth V8	*spun off and hit barrier*	16/39
dnq	PORTUGUESE GP	Estoril	4	Tyrrell Racing Organisation	G	3.5 Tyrrell 018-Cosworth V8		27/39

1990 Championship position: Unplaced

	Race	Circuit	No	Entrant	Tyres	Capacity/Car/Engine	Comment	Q Pos/Entries
ret	JAPANESE GP	Suzuka	12	Camel Team Lotus	G	3.5 Lotus 102-Lamborghini V12	*engine*	15/30
ret	AUSTRALIAN GP	Adelaide	12	Camel Team Lotus	G	3.5 Lotus 102-Lamborghini V12	*clutch*	18/30

1991 Championship position: Unplaced

	Race	Circuit	No	Entrant	Tyres	Capacity/Car/Engine	Comment	Q Pos/Entries
dnq	CANADIAN GP	Montreal	12	Team Lotus	G	3.5 Lotus 102B-Judd V8		30/34
10	MEXICAN GP	Mexico City	12	Team Lotus	G	3.5 Lotus 102B-Judd V8	*2 laps behind*	25/34
10	FRENCH GP	Magny Cours	12	Team Lotus	G	3.5 Lotus 102B-Judd V8	*left at start – gears/2 laps behind*	20/34
14/ret	BRITISH GP	Silverstone	12	Team Lotus	G	3.5 Lotus 102B-Judd V8	*engine/4 laps behind*	24/34
7	BELGIAN GP	Spa	12	Team Lotus	G	3.5 Lotus 102B-Judd V8		21/34
ret	PORTUGUESE GP	Estoril	12	Team Lotus	G	3.5 Lotus 102B-Judd V8	*engine/gearbox*	22/34
ret	JAPANESE GP	Suzuka	12	Team Lotus	G	3.5 Lotus 102B-Judd V8	*engine cut out*	23/31

11	AUSTRALIAN GP	Adelaide	12	Team Lotus	G	3.5 Lotus 102B-Judd V8	*race stopped at 14 laps*	21/32

1992 Championship position: 14th= Wins: 0 Pole positions: 0 Fastest laps: 0 Points scored: 2

6	SOUTH AFRICAN GP	Kyalami	12	Team Lotus	G	3.5 Lotus 102D-Ford HB V8	*1 lap behind*	11/30
7	MEXICAN GP	Mexico City	12	Team Lotus	G	3.5 Lotus 102D-Ford HB V8	*1 lap behind*	12/30
ret	BRAZILIAN GP	Interlagos	12	Team Lotus	G	3.5 Lotus 102D-Ford HB V8	*taken off by Boutsen and Comas*	26/31
ret	SPANISH GP	Barcelona	12	Team Lotus	G	3.5 Lotus 102D-Ford HB V8	*spun off*	26/32
ret	SAN MARINO GP	Imola	12	Team Lotus	G	3.5 Lotus 107-Ford HB V8	*gearbox*	26/32
ret	MONACO GP	Monte Carlo	12	Team Lotus	G	3.5 Lotus 107-Ford HB V8	*handling – slid into barriers*	9/32
ret	CANADIAN GP	Montreal	12	Team Lotus	G	3.5 Lotus 107-Ford HB V8	*clutch*	6/32
6*	FRENCH GP	Magny Cours	12	Team Lotus	G	3.5 Lotus 107-Ford HB V8	**aggregate of two parts/1 lap behind*	12/30
ret	BRITISH GP	Silverstone	12	Team Lotus	G	3.5 Lotus 107-Ford HB V8	*gearbox*	7/32
ret	GERMAN GP	Hockenheim	12	Team Lotus	G	3.5 Lotus 107-Ford HB V8	*engine cut out*	11/32
ret	HUNGARIAN GP	Hungaroring	12	Team Lotus	G	3.5 Lotus 107-Ford HB V8	*spun avoiding Comas/Boutsen*	13/31
13/ret	BELGIAN GP	Spa	12	Team Lotus	G	3.5 Lotus 107-Ford HB V8	*engine/2 laps behind*	10/30
ret	ITALIAN GP	Monza	12	Team Lotus	G	3.5 Lotus 107-Ford HB V8	*engine*	13/28
ret	PORTUGUESE GP	Estoril	12	Team Lotus	G	3.5 Lotus 107-Ford HB V8	*collision – bent steering arm*	9/26
ret	JAPANESE GP	Suzuka	12	Team Lotus	G	3.5 Lotus 107-Ford HB V8	*gearbox*	6/26
13	AUSTRALIAN GP	Adelaide	12	Team Lotus	G	3.5 Lotus 107-Ford HB V8	*pit stop – nose & track rod/-4 laps*	12/26

1993 Championship position: 9th Wins: 0 Pole positions: 0 Fastest laps: 0 Points scored: 11

ret	SOUTH AFRICAN GP	Kyalami	12	Team Lotus	G	3.5 Lotus 107B-Ford HB V8	*fuel pressure*	17/26
4	BRAZILIAN GP	Interlagos	12	Team Lotus	G	3.5 Lotus 107B-Ford HB V8		12/26
4	EUROPEAN GP	Donington	12	Team Lotus	G	3.5 Lotus 107B-Ford HB V8	*1 lap behind*	11/26
8/ret	SAN MARINO GP	Imola	12	Team Lotus	G	3.5 Lotus 107B-Ford HB V8	*engine*	12/26
ret	SPANISH GP	Barcelona	12	Team Lotus	G	3.5 Lotus 107B-Ford HB V8	*started from back/active failure*	10/26
ret	MONACO GP	Monte Carlo	12	Team Lotus	G	3.5 Lotus 107B-Ford HB V8	*gearbox failed – crashed*	14/26
10	CANADIAN GP	Montreal	12	Team Lotus	G	3.5 Lotus 107B-Ford HB V8	*lack of grip/2 laps behind*	20/26
ret	FRENCH GP	Magny Cours	12	Team Lotus	G	3.5 Lotus 107B-Ford HB V8	*spun off*	19/26
4	BRITISH GP	Silverstone	12	Team Lotus	G	3.5 Lotus 107B-Ford HB V8		7/26
10	GERMAN GP	Hockenheim	12	Team Lotus	G	3.5 Lotus 107B-Ford HB V8	*actuator problem/1 lap behind*	13/26
ret	HUNGARIAN GP	Hungaroring	12	Team Lotus	G	3.5 Lotus 107B-Ford HB V8	*spun and stalled*	20/26
5	BELGIAN GP	Spa	12	Team Lotus	G	3.5 Lotus 107B-Ford HB V8	*1 lap behind*	10/25
ret	ITALIAN GP	Monza	12	Team Lotus	G	3.5 Lotus 107B-Ford HB V8	*crashed at Parabolica*	7/26
ret	PORTUGUESE GP	Estoril	12	Team Lotus	G	3.5 Lotus 107B-Ford HB V8	*crashed*	14/26
11	JAPANESE GP	Suzuka	12	Team Lotus	G	3.5 Lotus 107B-Ford HB V8	*2 laps behind*	19/24
ret	AUSTRALIAN GP	Adelaide	12	Team Lotus	G	3.5 Lotus 107B-Ford HB V8	*hydraulics*	20/24

1994 Championship position: Unplaced

7	BRAZILIAN GP	Interlagos	12	Team Lotus	G	3.5 Lotus 107C-Mugen Honda V10	*2 laps behind*	21/28
7	PACIFIC GP	T.I. Circuit	12	Team Lotus	G	3.5 Lotus 107C-Mugen Honda V10	*3 laps behind*	23/28
10	SAN MARINO GP	Imola	12	Team Lotus	G	3.5 Lotus 107C-Mugen Honda V10	*2 laps behind*	20/28
ret	MONACO GP	Monte Carlo	12	Team Lotus	G	3.5 Lotus 107C-Mugen Honda V10	*gearbox*	16/24
ret	SPANISH GP	Barcelona	12	Team Lotus	G	3.5 Lotus 109-Mugen Honda V10	*spun off*	22/27
8	CANADIAN GP	Montreal	12	Team Lotus	G	3.5 Lotus 109-Mugen Honda V10	*1 lap behind*	17/27
7	FRENCH GP	Magny Cours	12	Team Lotus	G	3.5 Lotus 109-Mugen Honda V10	*2 laps behind*	19/28
11*	BRITISH GP	Silverstone	12	Team Lotus	G	3.5 Lotus 109-Mugen Honda V10	**2nd place car disqualified/-2 laps*	21/28
ret	GERMAN GP	Hockenheim	12	Team Lotus	G	3.5 Lotus 109-Mugen Honda V10	*collision with Brundle on lap 1*	15/28
ret	HUNGARIAN GP	Hungaroring	12	Team Lotus	G	3.5 Lotus 109-Mugen Honda V10	*electrics*	24/28
12*	BELGIAN GP	Spa	12	Team Lotus	G	3.5 Lotus 109-Mugen Honda V10	**1st place car disqualified/-3 laps*	20/28
ret	ITALIAN GP	Monza	12	Team Lotus	G	3.5 Lotus 109-Mugen Honda V10	*engine*	4/28
11	PORTUGUESE GP	Estoril	12	Team Lotus	G	3.5 Lotus 109-Mugen Honda V10	*1 lap behind*	20/28
8	EUROPEAN GP	Jerez	25	Ligier Gitanes Blondes	G	3.5 Ligier JS39B-Renault V10	*1 lap behind*	7/28
ret	JAPANESE GP	Suzuka	6	Mild Seven Benetton Ford	G	3.5 Benetton B194-Ford Zetec-R V8	*accident*	5/28
ret	AUSTRALIAN GP	Adelaide	6	Mild Seven Benetton Ford	G	3.5 Benetton B194-Ford Zetec-R V8	*gearbox*	7/28

1995 Championship position: 4th Wins: 2 Pole positions: 0 Fastest laps: 0 Points scored: 45

ret	BRAZILIAN GP	Interlagos	2	Mild Seven Benetton Renault	G	3.0 Benetton B195-Renault V10	*collision with Suzuki*	4/26
4	ARGENTINE GP	Buenos Aires	2	Mild Seven Benetton Renault	G	3.0 Benetton B195-Renault V10	*1 lap behind*	11/26
7	SAN MARINO GP	Imola	2	Mild Seven Benetton Renault	G	3.0 Benetton B195-Renault V10	*2 laps behind*	8/26
2	SPANISH GP	Barcelona	2	Mild Seven Benetton Renault	G	3.0 Benetton B195-Renault V10		7/26
4	MONACO GP	Monte Carlo	2	Mild Seven Benetton Renault	G	3.0 Benetton B195-Renault V10		7/26
ret	CANADIAN GP	Montreal	2	Mild Seven Benetton Renault	G	3.0 Benetton B195-Renault V10	*collision with Häkkinen*	6/24
ret	FRENCH GP	Magny Cours	2	Mild Seven Benetton Renault	G	3.0 Benetton B195-Renault V10	*collision with Alesi*	10/24
1	BRITISH GP	Silverstone	2	Mild Seven Benetton Renault	G	3.0 Benetton B195-Renault V10		5/24
4	GERMAN GP	Hockenheim	2	Mild Seven Benetton Renault	G	3.0 Benetton B195-Renault V10		9/24
4	HUNGARIAN GP	Hungaroring	2	Mild Seven Benetton Renault	G	3.0 Benetton B195-Renault V10	*1 lap behind*	9/24
7	BELGIAN GP	Spa	2	Mild Seven Benetton Renault	G	3.0 Benetton B195-Renault V10		4/24
1	ITALIAN GP	Monza	2	Mild Seven Benetton Renault	G	3.0 Benetton B195-Renault V10		8/24
7	PORTUGUESE GP	Estoril	2	Mild Seven Benetton Renault	G	3.0 Benetton B195-Renault V10	*1 lap behind*	6/24
5	EUROPEAN GP	Nürburgring	2	Mild Seven Benetton Renault	G	3.0 Benetton B195-Renault V10	*1 lap behind*	7/24
6	PACIFIC GP	T.I. Circuit	2	Mild Seven Benetton Renault	G	3.0 Benetton B195-Renault V10	*1 lap behind*	7/24
3	JAPANESE GP	Suzuka	2	Mild Seven Benetton Renault	G	3.0 Benetton B195-Renault V10		9/24
ret	AUSTRALIAN GP	Adelaide	2	Mild Seven Benetton Renault	G	3.0 Benetton B195-Renault V10	*driveshaft*	8/24

1996 Championship position: 14th Wins: 0 Pole positions: 0 Fastest laps: 0 Points scored: 4

ret/dns*	AUSTRALIAN GP	Melbourne	14	Red Bull Sauber Ford	G	3.0 Sauber C15-Ford Zetec R V10	**car damaged in first start*	14/22
ret	BRAZILIAN GP	Interlagos	14	Red Bull Sauber Ford	G	3.0 Sauber C15-Ford Zetec R V10	*engine*	12/22
9	ARGENTINE GP	Buenos Aires	14	Red Bull Sauber Ford	G	3.0 Sauber C15-Ford Zetec R V10	*1 lap behind*	17/22
7	EUROPEAN GP	Nürburgring	14	Red Bull Sauber Ford	G	3.0 Sauber C15-Ford Zetec R V10		12/22
ret	SAN MARINO GP	Imola	14	Red Bull Sauber Ford	G	3.0 Sauber C15-Ford Zetec R V10	*engine*	15/22
3	MONACO GP	Monte Carlo	14	Red Bull Sauber Ford	G	3.0 Sauber C15-Ford Zetec R V10		13/22
ret	SPANISH GP	Barcelona	14	Red Bull Sauber Ford	G	3.0 Sauber C15-Ford Zetec R V10	*spun off*	9/22
7	CANADIAN GP	Montreal	14	Red Bull Sauber Ford	G	3.0 Sauber C15-Ford Zetec R V10	*1 lap behind*	15/22

dsq*/11	FRENCH GP	Magny Cours	14	Red Bull Sauber Ford	G	3.0 Sauber C15-Ford Zetec R V10	*front deflector dimensions	17/22
ret	BRITISH GP	Silverstone	14	Red Bull Sauber Ford	G	3.0 Sauber C15-Ford Zetec R V10	1 lap behind	13/22
ret	GERMAN GP	Hockenheim	14	Red Bull Sauber Ford	G	3.0 Sauber C15-Ford Zetec R V10	gearbox sensor	14/20
ret	HUNGARIAN GP	Hungaroring	14	Red Bull Sauber Ford	G	3.0 Sauber C15-Ford Zetec R V10	engine	8/20
ret	BELGIAN GP	Spa	14	Red Bull Sauber Ford	G	3.0 Sauber C15-Ford Zetec R V10	collision with Frentzen & Panis	12/20
9/ret	ITALIAN GP	Monza	14	Red Bull Sauber Ford	G	3.0 Sauber C15-Ford Zetec R V10	engine/2 laps behind	12/20
8	PORTUGUESE GP	Estoril	14	Red Bull Sauber Ford	G	3.0 Sauber C15-Ford Zetec R V10	1 lap behind	12/20
10	JAPANESE GP	Suzuka	14	Red Bull Sauber Ford	G	3.0 Sauber C15-Ford Zetec R V10		13/20

1997 Championship position: 10th   Wins: 0   Pole positions: 0   Fastest laps: 0   Points scored: 15

ret	AUSTRALIAN GP	Melbourne	16	Red Bull Sauber Petronas	G	3.0 Sauber C16-Petronas V10	collision at first corner	7/24
7	BRAZILIAN GP	Interlagos	16	Red Bull Sauber Petronas	G	3.0 Sauber C16-Petronas V10		13/22
4	ARGENTINE GP	Buenos Aires	16	Red Bull Sauber Petronas	G	3.0 Sauber C16-Petronas V10		8/22
ret	SAN MARINO GP	Imola	16	Red Bull Sauber Petronas	G	3.0 Sauber C16-Petronas V10	electrics	7/22
ret	MONACO GP	Monte Carlo	16	Red Bull Sauber Petronas	G	3.0 Sauber C16-Petronas V10	crashed into barrier	7/22
5	SPANISH GP	Barcelona	16	Red Bull Sauber Petronas	G	3.0 Sauber C16-Petronas V10		10/22
5	CANADIAN GP	Montreal	16	Red Bull Sauber Petronas	G	3.0 Sauber C16-Petronas V10		13/22
8	FRENCH GP	Magny Cours	16	Red Bull Sauber Petronas	G	3.0 Sauber C16-Petronas V10	1 lap behind	14/22
ret	BRITISH GP	Silverstone	16	Red Bull Sauber Petronas	G	3.0 Sauber C16-Petronas V10	transmission	9/22
ret	GERMAN GP	Hockenheim	16	Red Bull Sauber Petronas	G	3.0 Sauber C16-Petronas V10	collision with Diniz	14/22
3	HUNGARIAN GP	Hungaroring	16	Red Bull Sauber Petronas	G	3.0 Sauber C16-Petronas V10		10/22
4*	BELGIAN GP	Spa	16	Red Bull Sauber Petronas	G	3.0 Sauber C16-Petronas V10	*3rd place car disqualified	11/22
ret	ITALIAN GP	Monza	16	Red Bull Sauber Petronas	G	3.0 Sauber C16-Petronas V10	hit by Ralf Schumacher	12/22
8	AUSTRIAN GP	A1-Ring	16	Red Bull Sauber Petronas	G	3.0 Sauber C16-Petronas V10		12/22
7	LUXEMBOURG GP	Nürburgring	16	Red Bull Sauber Petronas	G	3.0 Sauber C16-Petronas V10		16/22
6*	JAPANESE GP	Suzuka	16	Red Bull Sauber Petronas	G	3.0 Sauber C16-Petronas V10	*5th place car disqualified	8/22
8	EUROPEAN GP	Jerez	16	Red Bull Sauber Petronas	G	3.0 Sauber C16-Petronas V10		14/22

1998 Championship position: 15th=   Wins: 0   Pole positions: 0   Fastest laps: 0   Points scored: 1

6	AUSTRALIAN GP	Melbourne	15	Red Bull Sauber Petronas	G	3.0 Sauber C17-Petronas V10	1 lap behind	6/22
11/ret	BRAZILIAN GP	Interlagos	15	Red Bull Sauber Petronas	G	3.0 Sauber C17-Petronas V10	neck strain/5 laps behind	14/22
ret	ARGENTINE GP	Buenos Aires	15	Red Bull Sauber Petronas	G	3.0 Sauber C17-Petronas V10	collision with Hill – puncture	12/22
ret	SAN MARINO GP	Imola	15	Red Bull Sauber Petronas	G	3.0 Sauber C17-Petronas V10	puncture	11/22
7	SPANISH GP	Barcelona	15	Red Bull Sauber Petronas	G	3.0 Sauber C17-Petronas V10	1 lap behind	7/22
7	MONACO GP	Monte Carlo	15	Red Bull Sauber Petronas	G	3.0 Sauber C17-Petronas V10	1 lap behind	9/22
ret	CANADIAN GP	Montreal	15	Red Bull Sauber Petronas	G	3.0 Sauber C17-Petronas V100	spun off	12/22
8	FRENCH GP	Magny Cours	15	Red Bull Sauber Petronas	G	3.0 Sauber C17-Petronas V10	1 lap behind	13/22
ret	BRITISH GP	Silverstone	15	Red Bull Sauber Petronas	G	3.0 Sauber C17-Petronas V10	spun off	9/22
8	AUSTRIAN GP	A1-Ring	15	Red Bull Sauber Petronas	G	3.0 Sauber C17-Petronas V10	1 lap behind	18/22
ret	GERMAN GP	Hockenheim	15	Red Bull Sauber Petronas	G	3.0 Sauber C17-Petronas V10	gearbox	12/22
10	HUNGARIAN GP	Hungaroring	15	Red Bull Sauber Petronas	G	3.0 Sauber C17-Petronas V10	1 lap behind	15/22
ret	BELGIAN GP	Spa	15	Red Bull Sauber Petronas	G	3.0 Sauber C17-Petronas V10	collision with Häkkinen on lap 1	12/22
ret	ITALIAN GP	Monza	15	Red Bull Sauber Petronas	G	3.0 Sauber C17-Petronas V10	spun off	15/22
ret	LUXEMBOURG GP	Nürburgring	15	Red Bull Sauber Petronas	G	3.0 Sauber C17-Petronas V10	engine	13/22
10	JAPANESE GP	Suzuka	15	Red Bull Sauber Petronas	G	3.0 Sauber C17-Petronas V10	1 lap behind	11/22

1999 Championship position: 8   Wins: 1   Pole positions: 0   Fastest laps: 0   Points scored: 15

ret/dns*	AUSTRALIAN GP	Melbourne	17	Stewart Ford	B	3.0 Stewart SF3 Ford CR1 V10	*oil leak on parade lap	(13)/22
ret	BRAZILIAN GP	Interlagos	17	Stewart Ford	B	3.0 Stewart SF3 Ford CR1 V10	hydraulics	10/22
10/ret	SAN MARINO GP	Imola	17	Stewart Ford	B	3.0 Stewart SF3 Ford CR1 V10	engine/4 laps behind	12/22
ret	MONACO GP	Monte Carlo	17	Stewart Ford	B	3.0 Stewart SF3 Ford CR1 V10	suspension failure	13/22
ret	SPANISH GP	Barcelona	17	Stewart Ford	B	3.0 Stewart SF3 Ford CR1 V10	transmission	14/22
5	CANADIAN GP	Montreal	17	Stewart Ford	B	3.0 Stewart SF3 Ford CR1 V10		10/22
ret	FRENCH GP	Magny Cours	17	Stewart Ford	B	3.0 Stewart SF3 Ford CR1 V10	gearbox	9/22
12	BRITISH GP	Silverstone	17	Stewart Ford	B	3.0 Stewart SF3 Ford CR1 V10		11/22
14	AUSTRIAN GP	A1-Ring	17	Stewart Ford	B	3.0 Stewart SF3 Ford CR1 V10	collision damage – new wing/-4 laps	6/22
11/ret	GERMAN GP	Hockenheim	17	Stewart Ford	B	3.0 Stewart SF3 Ford CR1 V10	gearbox/5 laps behind	17/22
11	HUNGARIAN GP	Hungaroring	17	Stewart Ford	B	3.0 Stewart SF3 Ford CR1 V10	1 lap behind	10/22
ret	BELGIAN GP	Spa	17	Stewart Ford	B	3.0 Stewart SF3 Ford CR1 V10	wheel bearing/brakes	10/22
ret	ITALIAN GP	Monza	17	Stewart Ford	B	3.0 Stewart SF3 Ford CR1 V10	clutch	15/22
1	EUROPEAN GP	Nürburgring	17	Stewart Ford	B	3.0 Stewart SF3 Ford CR1 V10		14/22
4	MALAYSIAN GP	Sepang	17	Stewart Ford	B	3.0 Stewart SF3 Ford CR1 V10		5/22
7	JAPANESE GP	Suzuka	17	Stewart Ford	B	3.0 Stewart SF3 Ford CR1 V10	1 lap behind	8/22

2000 Championship position: Unplaced

ret	AUSTRALIAN GP	Melbourne	8	Jaguar Racing	B	3.0 Jaguar R1-Cosworth V10	clutch	20/22
ret	BRAZILIAN GP	Interlagos	8	Jaguar Racing	B	3.0 Jaguar R1-Cosworth V10	gearbox	17/22
10	SAN MARINO GP	Imola	8	Jaguar Racing	B	3.0 Jaguar R1-Cosworth V10	1 lap behind	17/22
12	BRITISH GP	Silverstone	8	Jaguar Racing	B	3.0 Jaguar R1-Cosworth V10	stalled at 2nd pit stop/1 lap behind	14/22
13	SPANISH GP	Barcelona	8	Jaguar Racing	B	3.0 Jaguar R1-Cosworth V10	1 lap behind	15/22
11/ret	EUROPEAN GP	Nürburgring	8	Jaguar Racing	B	3.0 Jaguar R1-Cosworth V10	pushed off by Wurz/6 laps behind	17/22
9	MONACO GP	Monte Carlo	8	Jaguar Racing	B	3.0 Jaguar R1-Cosworth V10	2 laps behind	11/22
ret	CANADIAN GP	Montreal	8	Jaguar Racing	B	3.0 Jaguar R1-Cosworth V10	gearbox	11/22
ret	FRENCH GP	Magny Cours	8	Jaguar Racing	B	3.0 Jaguar R1-Cosworth V10	clutch	11/22
7	AUSTRIAN GP	A1-Ring	8	Jaguar Racing	B	3.0 Jaguar R1-Cosworth V10	1 lap behind	16/22
ret	GERMAN GP	Hockenheim	8	Jaguar Racing	B	3.0 Jaguar R1-Cosworth V10	gearbox	8/22
ret	HUNGARIAN GP	Hungaroring	8	Jaguar Racing	B	3.0 Jaguar R1-Cosworth V10	gearshift	17/22
8	BELGIAN GP	Spa	8	Jaguar Racing	B	3.0 Jaguar R1-Cosworth V10		9/22
ret	ITALIAN GP	Monza	8	Jaguar Racing	B	3.0 Jaguar R1-Cosworth V10	hit by de la Rosa	18/22
11	UNITED STATES GP	Indianapolis	8	Jaguar Racing	B	3.0 Jaguar R1-Cosworth V10	nose damage delay/1 lap behind	19/22
7	JAPANESE GP	Suzuka	8	Jaguar Racing	B	3.0 Jaguar R1-Cosworth V10	1 lap behind	10/22
ret	MALAYSIAN GP	Sepang	8	Jaguar Racing	B	3.0 Jaguar R1-Cosworth V10	rear suspension failure – big shunt	12/22

GP Starts: 161 (162)   GP Wins: 3   Pole positions: 0   Fastest laps: 0   Points: 98

HANS HERRMANN

YOUNG Hans Herrmann displayed considerable promise both in a Veritas (ninth in the German GP and fourth at the AVUSrennen) and a Porsche sports car in 1953, which earned him a golden opportunity to drive for Mercedes-Benz on their return to grand prix and sports car racing in 1954. Although naturally somewhat overshadowed by his more experienced peers, he scored good championship finishes at Bremgarten and Monza, and took third behind Karl Kling and Juan Fangio in what amounted to a Mercedes demonstration race against meagre opposition at AVUS. He still drove for Porsche in sports cars, and won the support race at AVUS and another at the Nürburgring. Better still, he took sixth in the Mille Miglia, again winning the up-to-1500cc class, before venturing to Mexico to compete in the Carrera Panamericana. In another superb drive, he drove his Porsche 550 Spyder to third overall and naturally won his class.

Prospects were promising indeed for the young German in 1955, but after sharing fourth place with Stirling Moss and Kling in the searing heat of Argentina, a practice accident for the next grand prix, at Monte Carlo, put Hans in hospital with cracked vertebrae and broken ribs.

With Mercedes' withdrawal from racing after the Le Mans tragedy, Herrmann, now fully recovered, joined Porsche for 1956 and, with Wolfgang von Trips, took sixth (and a class win) at Sebring. Sharing a Ferrari with Olivier Gendebien, he was third in the Targa Florio that year, but then became a mainstay of the Porsche team. He was third at Le Mans with Jean Behra in 1958 and fourth in the Nürburgring 1000km the following year with Umberto Maglioli. Sadly his subsequent grand prix appearances were generally restricted to less-than-competitive machinery, and he caused a stir only with his spectacular crash in the 1959 German GP at AVUS, where he was thrown from his BRM, fortunately without serious injury.

Hans enjoyed some excellent drives in Formula 2 for Porsche in 1960, taking second at Solitude, fourth at Modena and fifth in the non-championship German Grand Prix. He found real success throughout the decade in sports cars, however, winning the Sebring 12-hours (1960 and 1968), the Daytona 24-hours (1968), the Targa Florio (1960) and the Paris 1000km (1968). He was involved in the incredible finish at Le Mans in 1969, when his Porsche was pipped by Jacky Ickx's Ford, but he made amends a year later to bow out on a high note, retiring from racing after winning the Sarthe classic in a Porsche 917 with Richard Attwood.

FRANÇOIS HESNAULT

SUCCESSIVE seasons in the French Formula 3 championship saw François Hesnault take the runner-up slot in 1983, only a couple of points shy of Michel Ferté. Both drivers had scored five wins apiece.

Hesnault also took a fine second place at Magny-Cours in his only appearance in the European series that season, but it still came as a bit of a surprise when he was drafted into the Ligier team in 1984. The Frenchman acquitted himself respectably enough, however, sometimes proving more than a match for his team-mate, Andrea de Cesaris, particularly at Dijon, where he was forced to stand down to allow the Italian into the race.

A move to Brabham in 1985 proved a big let-down, with a shaken Hesnault leaving the team after just four races, having been lucky to escape injury in a massive testing accident at Paul Ricard. He did reappear later in the season, however, at the wheel of a Renault that acted as a camera car in the German Grand Prix.

HANS HEYER

WITH a natty Tyrolean hat as his trademark, Hans Heyer was a popular figure in 1970s touring car racing. He was European touring car champion in 1974, driving a Ford Escort RS2000, and among his wins that year was the prestigious round at the Nürburgring, where, after 38 laps and 531.18 miles of racing, he and Klaus Ludwig defeated the 3-litre Capri of Niki Lauda, Toine Hezemans and Dieter Glemser.

In subsequent seasons, Heyer raced a Porsche 934 turbo, taking second at Imola in 1976; produced another superb drive to claim third place and a class win at the Nürburgring in 1977 in an RS 1800 Escort; and then drove a Mercedes 450SLC to third places at Monza and the Salzburgring the following year.

Heyer's appearance in this section of the book is made under rather false pretences, for he failed to qualify the ATS-entered Penske for the 1977 German Grand Prix and was placed as third reserve. Somehow he managed to get on to the grid for his only grand prix start. Subsequently he was disqualified, but his race had already ended with a gear linkage failure.

HERRMANN, Hans (D) b 23/2/1928, Stuttgart

	1953 Championship position: Unplaced							
	Race	Circuit	No	Entrant	Tyres	Capacity/Car/Engine	Comment	Q Pos/Entries
9	GERMAN GP	Nürburgring	32	Hans Herrmann	–	2.0 Veritas Meteor 6	1 lap behind	14/35

	1954 Championship position: 6th	Wins: 0	Pole positions: 0	Fastest laps: 1	Points scored: 8			
ret	FRENCH GP	Reims	22	Daimler Benz AG	C	2.5 Mercedes Benz W196 8 str	engine/FL	7/22
ret	GERMAN GP	Nürburgring	20	Daimler Benz AG	C	2.5 Mercedes Benz W196 8 str	fuel pipe	4/23
3	SWISS GP	Bremgarten	6	Daimler Benz AG	C	2.5 Mercedes Benz W196 8	1 lap behind	7/16
4	ITALIAN GP	Monza	12	Daimler Benz AG	C	2.5 Mercedes Benz W196 8	pit stop – plugs/3 laps behind	8/21
ret	SPANISH GP	Pedralbes	6	Daimler Benz AG	C	2.5 Mercedes Benz W196 8	fuel injection pump	9/22

	1955 Championship position: 17th=	Wins: 0	Pole positions: 0	Fastest laps: 0	Points scored: 1			
4*	ARGENTINE GP	Buenos Aires	8	Daimler Benz AG	C	2.5 Mercedes Benz W196 8	*Moss & Kling co-drove/2 laps behind	10/22
dns	MONACO GP	Monte Carlo	4	Daimler Benz AG	C	2.5 Mercedes Benz W196 8	accident – internal injuries	– / –

	1957 Championship position: Unplaced							
dnq	MONACO GP	Monte Carlo	40	Officine Alfieri Maserati	P	2.5 Maserati 250F 6		18/21
ret	GERMAN GP	Nürburgring	17	Scuderia Centro Sud	P	2.5 Maserati 250F 6	broken chassis	11/24

	1958 Championship position: Unplaced							
ret	GERMAN GP	Nürburgring	17	Scuderia Centro Sud	P	2.5 Maserati 250F 6	engine	20/26
ret	ITALIAN GP	Monza	24	Jo Bonnier	P	2.5 Maserati 250F 6	engine	18/21
9	MOROCCAN GP	Casablanca	24	Jo Bonnier	P	2.5 Maserati 250F 6	3 laps behind	18/25

	1959 Championship position: Unplaced							
ret	BRITISH GP	Aintree	24	Scuderia Centro Sud	D	2.5 Cooper T51-Maserati 4	clutch	19/30
ret	GERMAN GP	AVUS	11	British Racing Partnership	D	2.5 BRM P25 4	8th heat 1/crashed heat 2	11/16

	1960 Championship position: 19th=	Wins: 0	Pole positions: 0	Fastest laps: 0	Points scored: 1			
6	ITALIAN GP	Monza	26	Porsche System Engineering	D	1.5 Porsche 718 F4	F2 car/3 laps behind	10/16

	1961 Championship position: Unplaced							
9	MONACO GP	Monte Carlo	6	Porsche System Engineering	D	1.5 Porsche 718 F4	pit stop/9 laps behind	12/21
15	DUTCH GP	Zandvoort	9	Ecurie Maarsbergen	D	1.5 Porsche 718 F4	3 laps behind	13/17
13	GERMAN GP	Nürburgring	11	Porsche System Engineering	D	1.5 Porsche 718 F4	1 lap behind	11/27

	1966 Championship position: Unplaced							
11*	GERMAN GP (F2)	Nürburgring	28	Roy Winkelmann Racing	–	1.0 Brabham BT18-Cosworth 4 F2	*4th in F2 class/1 lap behind	23/30

	1969 Championship position: Unplaced							
dns	GERMAN GP (F2)	Nürburgring	21	Roy Winkelmann Racing	F	1.6 Lotus 59B-Cosworth 4	withdrawn after Mitter's fatal accident	(26)/26

GP Starts: 18   GP Wins: 0   Pole positions: 0   Fastest laps: 1   Points: 10

HESNAULT, François (F) b 30/12/1956, Neuilly-sur-Seine, nr Paris

	1984 Championship position: Unplaced							
	Race	Circuit	No	Entrant	Tyres	Capacity/Car/Engine	Comment	Q Pos/Entries
ret	BRAZILIAN GP	Rio	25	Ligier Loto	M	1.5 t/c Ligier JS23-Renault V6	overheating	20/27
10	SOUTH AFRICAN GP	Kyalami	25	Ligier Loto	M	1.5 t/c Ligier JS23-Renault V6	hit by Brundle/4 laps behind	17/27
ret	BELGIAN GP	Zolder	25	Ligier Loto	M	1.5 t/c Ligier JS23-Renault V6	radiator	23/27
ret	SAN MARINO GP	Imola	25	Ligier Loto	M	1.5 t/c Ligier JS23-Renault V6	hit by Laffite	17/28
dns	FRENCH GP	Dijon	25	Ligier Loto	M	1.5 t/c Ligier JS23-Renault V6	withdrawn to allow de Cesaris to race	(15)/27
ret	MONACO GP	Monte Carlo	25	Ligier Loto	M	1.5 t/c Ligier JS23-Renault V6	water in the electrics	17/27
ret	CANADIAN GP	Montreal	25	Ligier Loto	M	1.5 t/c Ligier JS23-Renault V6	turbo	13/26
ret	US GP (DETROIT)	Detroit	25	Ligier Loto	M	1.5 t/c Ligier JS23-Renault V6	accident with Ghinzani	18/27
ret	US GP (DALLAS)	Dallas	25	Ligier Loto	M	1.5 t/c Ligier JS23-Renault V6	hit wall on lap 1	19/27
ret	BRITISH GP	Brands Hatch	25	Ligier Loto	M	1.5 t/c Ligier JS23-Renault V6	electrics	20/27
8	GERMAN GP	Hockenheim	25	Ligier Loto	M	1.5 t/c Ligier JS23-Renault V6	1 lap behind	17/27
8	AUSTRIAN GP	Österreichring	25	Ligier Loto	M	1.5 t/c Ligier JS23-Renault V6	2 laps behind	21/28
7	DUTCH GP	Zandvoort	25	Ligier Loto	M	1.5 t/c Ligier JS23-Renault V6	2 laps behind	20/27
ret	ITALIAN GP	Monza	25	Ligier Loto	M	1.5 t/c Ligier JS23-Renault V6	spun off	18/27
10	EUROPEAN GP	Nürburgring	25	Ligier Loto	M	1.5 t/c Ligier JS23-Renault V6	3 laps behind	19/26
ret	PORTUGUESE GP	Estoril	25	Ligier Loto	M	1.5 t/c Ligier JS23-Renault V6	electrics	21/27

	1985 Championship position: Unplaced							
ret	BRAZILIAN GP	Rio	8	Motor Racing Developments	P	1.5 t/c Brabham BT54-BMW 4	accident	17/25
ret	PORTUGUESE GP	Estoril	8	Motor Racing Developments	P	1.5 t/c Brabham BT54-BMW 4	electrics	19/26
ret	SAN MARINO GP	Imola	8	Motor Racing Developments	P	1.5 t/c Brabham BT54-BMW 4	engine	20/26
dnq	MONACO GP	Monte Carlo	8	Motor Racing Developments	P	1.5 t/c Brabham BT54-BMW 4		25/26
ret	GERMAN GP	Nürburgring	14	Equipe Renault Elf	G	1.5 t/c Renault RE60 V6	clutch	23/27

GP Starts: 19   GP Wins: 0   Pole positions: 0   Fastest laps: 0   Points: 0

HEYER, Hans (D) b 16/3/1943, Mönchengladbach

	1977 Championship position: Unplaced							
	Race	Circuit	No	Entrant	Tyres	Capacity/Car/Engine	Comment	Q Pos/Entries
dnq/ret	GERMAN GP	Hockenheim	35	ATS Racing Team	G	3.0 Penske PC4-Cosworth V8	dnq – but started illegally/gear linkage	27/30

GP Starts: 1   GP Wins: 0   Pole positions: 0   Fastest laps: 0   Points: 0

DAMON HILL

EARNING his success the hard way, just like his father Graham, Damon Hill had to work his way to the top with plenty of determination, but little in the way of the financial help, which is such a crucial element in modern-day racing. Sadly, of course, his illustrious father had not been able to offer him the benefit of his experience, but it is to Damon's great credit that, once he had decided on a career in motor sport, he progressed entirely on his own merits. There can have been no one in the F1 paddock who begrudged him his success when, in 1996, he emulated his father in winning the world championship.

In fact, at first Damon was more interested in bikes than cars and made his competition debut on two wheels, which led him into a job as a motorcycle courier while he worked on his fledgling career. After a brief taste of Formula Ford at the end of 1983, he was drawn into the world of motor racing and, with the help of Brands Hatch supremo John Webb in the form of free tuition and a little promotion, he went racing seriously in 1985, enjoying a very competitive year of Formula Ford. His elevation to Formula 3 for 1986 with Murray Taylor Racing may have been a little premature, but he finished ninth in the championship and then proved himself in the formula during a two-year spell at Intersport, winning splendidly at Zandvoort and Spa in 1987, and taking two more victories in 1988, including the prestigious grand prix support race at Silverstone.

Damon then moved up to F3000 for 1989 and gave a good account of himself in the troubled Footwork, before switching to Middlebridge the following year, when luck was not on his side in terms of results. More importantly, though, he established himself as a genuine racer, capable of beating anyone in the field. A third year of F3000 in 1991 should have brought some real success at last, but his Lola was no match for the Reynards and his first win remained elusive. There was, however, the consolation of a Williams testing contract, and the following year his work for the team helped ensure that the damage to his reputation arising from a calamitous half-season with Brabham, when he managed to qualify only twice, was merely superficial. So impressed was Patrick Head with his contribution that he became Damon's strongest advocate when the chance arose of a grand prix drive with the team in 1993.

The way Damon handled his first year in a top team was exemplary in every respect. Unfazed by a couple of early gaffes at Kyalami and Imola, he pushed team leader Alain Prost harder and harder as the season wore on, while remaining acutely aware of the delicate political situation within the team. The fact that he won three grands prix was a bonus, his drive at Spa, where he withstood severe pressure from Schumacher, demonstrating that he had the stuff of which real winners are made. In 1994, he faced his biggest test with the arrival of Ayrton Senna. Tragically, within three races, he was faced with the task of rebuilding shattered morale at Williams in the way his father had done at Lotus in 1968. In Damon's case, he still had comparatively little experience, but rose to the challenge magnificently. Nigel Mansell's return in France prompted Hill to raise his game and push back the veteran's claim to a full-time seat alongside him. Then at Silverstone came a win in the British Grand Prix, a triumph made so special because it is a race his father never won.

In a season of drama and controversy, Damon took advantage of Schumacher's disqualifications and enforced absence through suspension to close the gap sufficiently to enable him still to win the championship. A superb drive in the wet at Suzuka was worthy of the German at his best, so it was all to play for in Adelaide. The manner in which the title was decided, when Schumacher bounced back off the wall into Hill's path, was unsatisfactory to say the least, and his critics thought Hill should have avoided the situation. In any event, the title was lost, but Damon's exemplary reaction in the aftermath spoke volumes about him as a person.

The slate was wiped clean for 1995 and, with the latest Williams FW17 in formidable form, Damon set out on the championship trail with renewed vigour. A potential victory in Brazil was lost with suspension failure, but two consecutive wins seemed to indicate that the Englishman was on course for the title. Unfortunately, Schumacher and Benetton had other ideas, and he soon found himself on the ropes as the German ruthlessly exploited every weakness in the Williams' armour. It was not until Hungary that the tide was stemmed, but, just as in boxing, winning occasional rounds does not win the fight. Despite Damon's dominant performance in the final race at Adelaide, this world championship bout went to Schumacher on points by a comfortable margin.

When you have a multi-million-dollar contract and you drive for one of the world's leading grand prix teams, then expectations are naturally high, as Damon had found during the two seasons he had been leading the Williams challenge. For such a polite and genuinely decent individual, it must have been hurtful to have been thrown more brickbats than bouquets by a despicable element of the press, who lay waiting to pounce on any error with glee. It goes with the territory, they would say, but the treatment meted out to him at times during this period was disgraceful.

Undoubtedly the 1996 season was Damon's best ever chance of taking the championship. With the advantage of his major rivals bedding down in new teams, and a rookie partner in Jacques Villeneuve, he could have had no excuses for failing. In the event, of course, mission was accomplished, the popular Englishman winning eight of the 16 races to pip his team-mate to the crown. The only shadow over his season was the decision by Frank Williams to dispense with his services in favour of Heinz-Harald Frentzen, leaving him with no chance to secure a top ride in 1997.

So, after protracted negotiations with Jordan, Damon threw in his lot with Tom Walkinshaw at Arrows, amid much brave talk of winning races. In the event, he very nearly did, a superb drive in Hungary bringing second place after the car hit trouble on the penultimate lap. Otherwise it was a different story as the unfancied team struggled to make an impact, with Damon and his ambitious employer failing to see eye to eye. He joined up with Eddie Jordan for 1998, tempted by a healthy retainer and the prospect of Mugen Honda-powered cars. At first it seemed like a huge mistake for all concerned, as he struggled to make any impact in a poorly developed car, and it wasn't until the air was cleared in mid-season that things moved in the right direction. Fourth places at Hockenheim and the Hungaroring preceded the now-famous wet-race win at Spa with which Damon was finally able to realise Eddie Jordan's dreams of a grand prix victory for his team.

Grand prix racing has little room for sentiment, however, as Damon soon found out in 1999, when he was overshadowed by his new team-mate, Heinz-Harald Frentzen. So unhappy was he with his performances in the new generation of Formula 1 car that he contemplated immediate retirement after a miserable showing in the French Grand Prix. As it transpired, he continued in somewhat tentative fashion until the season's end. Physically, he emerged unscathed, but his racer's reputation received a bit of a bruising.

Damon then developed his business interests, which included car dealerships, and in 2006 he became the president of the BRDC. His discretion and quiet diplomacy were at the forefront of long and sometimes difficult negotiations that eventually led to the Silverstone track being awarded the rights to hold the British Grand Prix for a 17-year period.

HILL, Damon (GB) b 17/9/1960, Hampstead, London

1992 Championship position: Unplaced

	Race	Circuit	No	Entrant	Tyres	Capacity/Car/Engine	Comment	Q Pos/Entries
dnq	SPANISH GP	Barcelona	8	Motor Racing Developments Ltd	G	3.5 Brabham BT60B-Judd V10		30/32
dnq	SAN MARINO GP	Imola	8	Motor Racing Developments Ltd	G	3.5 Brabham BT60B-Judd V10		29/32
dnq	MONACO GP	Monte Carlo	8	Motor Racing Developments Ltd	G	3.5 Brabham BT60B-Judd V10		28/32
dnq	CANADIAN GP	Montreal	8	Motor Racing Developments Ltd	G	3.5 Brabham BT60B-Judd V10		30/32
dnq	FRENCH GP	Magny Cours	8	Motor Racing Developments Ltd	G	3.5 Brabham BT60B-Judd V10		30/30
16	BRITISH GP	Silverstone	8	Motor Racing Developments Ltd	G	3.5 Brabham BT60B-Judd V10	4 laps behind	26/32
dnq	GERMAN GP	Hockenheim	8	Motor Racing Developments Ltd	G	3.5 Brabham BT60B-Judd V10		30/32
11	HUNGARIAN GP	Hungaroring	8	Motor Racing Developments Ltd	G	3.5 Brabham BT60B-Judd V10	4 laps behind	25/31

1993 Championship position: 3rd Wins: 3 Pole positions: 2 Fastest laps: 4 Points scored: 69

	Race	Circuit	No	Entrant	Tyres	Capacity/Car/Engine	Comment	Q Pos/Entries
ret	SOUTH AFRICAN GP	Kyalami	0	Canon Williams Team	G	3.5 Williams FW15C-Renault V10	accident with Zanardi	4/26
2	BRAZILIAN GP	Interlagos	0	Canon Williams Team	G	3.5 Williams FW15C-Renault V10		2/26
2	EUROPEAN GP	Donington	0	Canon Williams Team	G	3.5 Williams FW15C-Renault V10		2/26
ret	SAN MARINO GP	Imola	0	Canon Williams Team	G	3.5 Williams FW15C-Renault V10	spun off	2/26
ret	SPANISH GP	Barcelona	0	Canon Williams Team	G	3.5 Williams FW15C-Renault V10	engine	2/26
2	MONACO GP	Monte Carlo	0	Canon Williams Team	G	3.5 Williams FW15C-Renault V10	despite collision with Berger	4/26
3	CANADIAN GP	Montreal	0	Canon Williams Team	G	3.5 Williams FW15C-Renault V10		2/26
2	FRENCH GP	Magny Cours	0	Canon Williams Team	G	3.5 Williams FW15C-Renault V10		1/26
ret	BRITISH GP	Silverstone	0	Canon Williams Team	G	3.5 Williams FW15C-Renault V10	engine/FL	2/26
15/ret	GERMAN GP	Hockenheim	0	Canon Williams Team	G	3.5 Williams FW15C-Renault V10	blown tyre when leading/2 laps behind	2/26
1	HUNGARIAN GP	Hungaroring	0	Canon Williams Team	G	3.5 Williams FW15C-Renault V10		2/26
1	BELGIAN GP	Spa	0	Canon Williams Team	G	3.5 Williams FW15C-Renault V10		2/25
1	ITALIAN GP	Monza	0	Canon Williams Team	G	3.5 Williams FW15C-Renault V10	FL	2/26
3	PORTUGUESE GP	Estoril	0	Canon Williams Team	G	3.5 Williams FW15C-Renault V10	started from back of grid/FL	1/26
4	JAPANESE GP	Suzuka	0	Canon Williams Team	G	3.5 Williams FW15C-Renault V10	pit stop – puncture	6/24
3	AUSTRALIAN GP	Adelaide	0	Canon Williams Team	G	3.5 Williams FW15C-Renault V10	FL	3/24

1994 Championship position: 2nd Wins: 6 Pole positions: 2 Fastest laps: 6 Points scored: 91

	Race	Circuit	No	Entrant	Tyres	Capacity/Car/Engine	Comment	Q Pos/Entries
2	BRAZILIAN GP	Interlagos	0	Rothmans Williams Renault	G	3.5 Williams FW16-Renault V10	1 lap behind	4/28
ret	PACIFIC GP	T.I. Circuit	0	Rothmans Williams Renault	G	3.5 Williams FW16-Renault V10	transmission	3/28
6	SAN MARINO GP	Imola	0	Rothmans Williams Renault	G	3.5 Williams FW16-Renault V10	pit stop – collision damage/FL	4/28
ret	MONACO GP	Monte Carlo	0	Rothmans Williams Renault	G	3.5 Williams FW16-Renault V10	first corner collision with Häkkinen	4/24
1	SPANISH GP	Barcelona	0	Rothmans Williams Renault	G	3.5 Williams FW16-Renault V10		2/27
2	CANADIAN GP	Montreal	0	Rothmans Williams Renault	G	3.5 Williams FW16-Renault V10		4/27
2	FRENCH GP	Magny Cours	0	Rothmans Williams Renault	G	3.5 Williams FW16-Renault V10	FL	1/28
1	BRITISH GP	Silverstone	0	Rothmans Williams Renault	G	3.5 Williams FW16-Renault V10	FL	1/28
8	GERMAN GP	Hockenheim	0	Rothmans Williams Renault	G	3.5 Williams FW16B-Renault V10	collision with Katayama/1 lap behind	3/28
2	HUNGARIAN GP	Hungaroring	0	Rothmans Williams Renault	G	3.5 Williams FW16B-Renault V10		2/28
1*	BELGIAN GP	Spa	0	Rothmans Williams Renault	G	3.5 Williams FW16B-Renault V10	*1st place car disqualified/FL	3/28
1	ITALIAN GP	Monza	0	Rothmans Williams Renault	G	3.5 Williams FW16B-Renault V10	FL	3/28
1	PORTUGUESE GP	Estoril	0	Rothmans Williams Renault	G	3.5 Williams FW16B-Renault V10		2/28
2	EUROPEAN GP	Jerez	0	Rothmans Williams Renault	G	3.5 Williams FW16B-Renault V10		2/28
1	JAPANESE GP	Suzuka	0	Rothmans Williams Renault	G	3.5 Williams FW16B-Renault V10	FL	2/28
ret	AUSTRALIAN GP	Adelaide	0	Rothmans Williams Renault	G	3.5 Williams FW16B-Renault V10	collision with M. Schumacher	3/28

1995 Championship position: 2nd Wins: 4 Pole positions: 7 Fastest laps: 4 Points scored: 69

	Race	Circuit	No	Entrant	Tyres	Capacity/Car/Engine	Comment	Q Pos/Entries
ret	BRAZILIAN GP	Interlagos	5	Rothmans Williams Renault	G	3.0 Williams FW17-Renault V10	suspension	1/26
1	ARGENTINE GP	Buenos Aires	5	Rothmans Williams Renault	G	3.0 Williams FW17-Renault V10		2/26
1	SAN MARINO GP	Imola	5	Rothmans Williams Renault	G	3.0 Williams FW17-Renault V10		4/26
4	SPANISH GP	Barcelona	5	Rothmans Williams Renault	G	3.0 Williams FW17-Renault V10	FL	5/26
2	MONACO GP	Monte Carlo	5	Rothmans Williams Renault	G	3.0 Williams FW17-Renault V10		1/26
ret	CANADIAN GP	Montreal	5	Rothmans Williams Renault	G	3.0 Williams FW17-Renault V10	gearbox	2/24
2	FRENCH GP	Magny Cours	5	Rothmans Williams Renault	G	3.0 Williams FW17-Renault V10		1/24
ret	BRITISH GP	Silverstone	5	Rothmans Williams Renault	G	3.0 Williams FW17-Renault V10	collision with M. Schumacher/FL	1/24
ret	GERMAN GP	Hockenheim	5	Rothmans Williams Renault	G	3.0 Williams FW17-Renault V10	spun off	1/24
1	HUNGARIAN GP	Hungaroring	5	Rothmans Williams Renault	G	3.0 Williams FW17-Renault V10	FL	1/24
2	BELGIAN GP	Spa	5	Rothmans Williams Renault	G	3.0 Williams FW17-Renault V10	stop & go penalty for speeding in pits	8/24
ret	ITALIAN GP	Monza	5	Rothmans Williams Renault	G	3.0 Williams FW17-Renault V10	ran into back of M. Schumacher	4/24
3	PORTUGUESE GP	Estoril	5	Rothmans Williams Renault	G	3.0 Williams FW17-Renault V10		2/24
ret	EUROPEAN GP	Nürburgring	5	Rothmans Williams Renault	G	3.0 Williams FW17B-Renault V10	collision with Alesi/later spun off	2/24
3	PACIFIC GP	T.I. Circuit	5	Rothmans Williams Renault	G	3.0 Williams FW17B-Renault V10		2/24
ret	JAPANESE GP	Suzuka	5	Rothmans Williams Renault	G	3.0 Williams FW17B-Renault V10	stop & go penalty/later spun off	4/24
1	AUSTRALIAN GP	Adelaide	5	Rothmans Williams Renault	G	3.0 Williams FW17B-Renault V10	FL	1/24

1996 WORLD CHAMPION Wins: 8 Pole positions: 9 Fastest laps: 5 Points scored: 97

	Race	Circuit	No	Entrant	Tyres	Capacity/Car/Engine	Comment	Q Pos/Entries
1	AUSTRALIAN GP	Melbourne	5	Rothmans Williams Renault	G	3.0 Williams FW18-Renault V10		2/22
1	BRAZILIAN GP	Interlagos	5	Rothmans Williams Renault	G	3.0 Williams FW18-Renault V10	FL	1/22
1	ARGENTINE GP	Buenos Aires	5	Rothmans Williams Renault	G	3.0 Williams FW18-Renault V10		1/22
4	EUROPEAN GP	Nürburgring	5	Rothmans Williams Renault	G	3.0 Williams FW18-Renault V10	poor start/slow pit stop/FL	1/22
1	SAN MARINO GP	Imola	5	Rothmans Williams Renault	G	3.0 Williams FW18-Renault V10	FL	2/22
ret	MONACO GP	Monte Carlo	5	Rothmans Williams Renault	G	3.0 Williams FW18-Renault V10	engine/led race	2/22
ret	SPANISH GP	Barcelona	5	Rothmans Williams Renault	G	3.0 Williams FW18-Renault V10	spun off	1/22
1	CANADIAN GP	Montreal	5	Rothmans Williams Renault	G	3.0 Williams FW18-Renault V10		1/22
1	FRENCH GP	Magny Cours	5	Rothmans Williams Renault	G	3.0 Williams FW18-Renault V10		2/22
ret	BRITISH GP	Silverstone	5	Rothmans Williams Renault	G	3.0 Williams FW18-Renault V10	wheel bearing failure – spun off	1/22
1	GERMAN GP	Hockenheim	5	Rothmans Williams Renault	G	3.0 Williams FW18-Renault V10	FL	1/20
2	HUNGARIAN GP	Hungaroring	5	Rothmans Williams Renault	G	3.0 Williams FW18-Renault V10	FL	2/20
5	BELGIAN GP	Spa	5	Rothmans Williams Renault	G	3.0 Williams FW18-Renault V10	long pit stop	2/20

Damon Hill takes his Williams FW18-Renault to victory in the 1996 German Grand Prix at Hockenheim. The Englishman deservedly took the title that year, ahead of rookie team-mate Jacques Villeneuve.

ret	ITALIAN GP	Monza	5	Rothmans Williams Renault	G	3.0 Williams FW18-Renault V10	clipped tyre stack – spun off	1/20
2	PORTUGUESE GP	Estoril	5	Rothmans Williams Renault	G	3.0 Williams FW18-Renault V10		1/20
1	JAPANESE GP	Suzuka	5	Rothmans Williams Renault	G	3.0 Williams FW18-Renault V10		2/20

1997 Championship position: 12th   Wins: 0   Pole positions: 0   Fastest laps: 0   Points scored: 7

ret/dns*	AUSTRALIAN GP	Melbourne	1	Danka Arrows Yamaha	B	3.0 Arrows A18-Yamaha V10	*throttle sensor on parade lap	20/24
17/ret	BRAZILIAN GP	Interlagos	1	Danka Arrows Yamaha	B	3.0 Arrows A18-Yamaha V10	engine fire	9/22
ret	ARGENTINE GP	Buenos Aires	1	Danka Arrows Yamaha	B	3.0 Arrows A18-Yamaha V10	engine	13/22
ret	SAN MARINO GP	Imola	1	Danka Arrows Yamaha	B	3.0 Arrows A18-Yamaha V10	ran into back of Nakano	15/22
ret	MONACO GP	Monte Carlo	1	Danka Arrows Yamaha	B	3.0 Arrows A18-Yamaha V10	collision with Irvine	13/22
ret	SPANISH GP	Barcelona	1	Danka Arrows Yamaha	B	3.0 Arrows A18-Yamaha V10	engine	15/22
9	CANADIAN GP	Montreal	1	Danka Arrows Yamaha	B	3.0 Arrows A18-Yamaha V10	1 lap behind	15/22
12	FRENCH GP	Magny Cours	1	Danka Arrows Yamaha	B	3.0 Arrows A18-Yamaha V10	3 laps behind	17/22
6	BRITISH GP	Silverstone	1	Danka Arrows Yamaha	B	3.0 Arrows A18-Yamaha V10		12/22
8	GERMAN GP	Hockenheim	1	Danka Arrows Yamaha	B	3.0 Arrows A18-Yamaha V10	1 lap behind	13/22
2	HUNGARIAN GP	Hungaroring	1	Danka Arrows Yamaha	B	3.0 Arrows A18-Yamaha V10	led race until hydraulic problem	3/22
13*/ret	BELGIAN GP	Spa	1	Danka Arrows Yamaha	B	3.0 Arrows A18-Yamaha V10	wheel nut/*3rd place car disqualified	9/22
ret	ITALIAN GP	Monza	1	Danka Arrows Yamaha	B	3.0 Arrows A18-Yamaha V10	engine	14/22
7	AUSTRIAN GP	A1-Ring	1	Danka Arrows Yamaha	B	3.0 Arrows A18-Yamaha V10		7/22
8	LUXEMBOURG GP	Nürburgring	1	Danka Arrows Yamaha	B	3.0 Arrows A18-Yamaha V10		13/22
11*	JAPANESE GP	Suzuka	1	Danka Arrows Yamaha	B	3.0 Arrows A18-Yamaha V10	*5th place car disqualified/-1 lap	17/22
ret	EUROPEAN GP	Jerez	1	Danka Arrows Yamaha	B	3.0 Arrows A18-Yamaha V10	hydraulics	4/22

1998 Championship position: 6   Wins: 1   Pole positions: 0   Fastest laps: 0   Points scored: 20

8	AUSTRALIAN GP	Melbourne	9	B & H Jordan Mugen Honda	G	3.0 Jordan 198-Mugen Honda V10	1 lap behind	10/22
dsq*	BRAZILIAN GP	Interlagos	9	B & H Jordan Mugen Honda	G	3.0 Jordan 198-Mugen Honda V10	*car underweight/10th on road	11/22
8	ARGENTINE GP	Buenos Aires	9	B & H Jordan Mugen Honda	G	3.0 Jordan 198-Mugen Honda V10	1 lap behind	9/22
10/ret	SAN MARINO GP	Imola	9	B & H Jordan Mugen Honda	G	3.0 Jordan 198-Mugen Honda V10	engine/5 laps behind	7/22
ret	SPANISH GP	Barcelona	9	B & H Jordan Mugen Honda	G	3.0 Jordan 198-Mugen Honda V10	engine	8/22
8	MONACO GP	Monte Carlo	9	B & H Jordan Mugen Honda	G	3.0 Jordan 198-Mugen Honda V10	2 laps behind	15/22
ret	CANADIAN GP	Montreal	9	B & H Jordan Mugen Honda	G	3.0 Jordan 198-Mugen Honda V10	electrics	10/22
ret	FRENCH GP	Magny Cours	9	B & H Jordan Mugen Honda	G	3.0 Jordan 198-Mugen Honda V10	hydraulics	7/22
ret	BRITISH GP	Silverstone	9	B & H Jordan Mugen Honda	G	3.0 Jordan 198-Mugen Honda V10	spun off	7/22
7	AUSTRIAN GP	A1-Ring	9	B & H Jordan Mugen Honda	G	3.0 Jordan 198-Mugen Honda V10		15/22
4	GERMAN GP	Hockenheim	9	B & H Jordan Mugen Honda	G	3.0 Jordan 198-Mugen Honda V10		5/22
4	HUNGARIAN GP	Hungaroring	9	B & H Jordan Mugen Honda	G	3.0 Jordan 198-Mugen Honda V10		4/22
1	BELGIAN GP	Spa	9	B & H Jordan Mugen Honda	G	3.0 Jordan 198-Mugen Honda V10	first win for Jordan team	3/22
6	ITALIAN GP	Monza	9	B & H Jordan Mugen Honda	G	3.0 Jordan 198-Mugen Honda V10		14/22
9	LUXEMBOURG GP	Nürburgring	9	B & H Jordan Mugen Honda	G	3.0 Jordan 198-Mugen Honda V10	1 lap behind	10/22
4	JAPANESE GP	Suzuka	9	B & H Jordan Mugen Honda	G	3.0 Jordan 198-Mugen Honda V10		8/22

1999 Championship position: 11=-   Wins: 0   Pole positions: 0   Fastest laps: 0   Points scored: 7

ret	AUSTRALIAN GP	Melbourne	7	Benson & Hedges Jordan	B	3.0 Jordan 199-Mugen Honda V10	lap 1 collision with Trulli spun off	9/22
ret	BRAZILIAN GP	Interlagos	7	Benson & Hedges Jordan	B	3.0 Jordan 199-Mugen Honda V10	collision with Wurz	7/22
4	SAN MARINO GP	Imola	7	Benson & Hedges Jordan	B	3.0 Jordan 199-Mugen Honda V10	1 lap behind	8/22
ret	MONACO GP	Monte Carlo	7	Benson & Hedges Jordan	B	3.0 Jordan 199-Mugen Honda V10	collision with Ralf Schumacher	17/22
7	SPANISH GP	Barcelona	7	Benson & Hedges Jordan	B	3.0 Jordan 199-Mugen Honda V10	1 lap behind	11/22
ret	CANADIAN GP	Montreal	7	Benson & Hedges Jordan	B	3.0 Jordan 199-Mugen Honda V10	crashed	14/22
ret	FRENCH GP	Magny Cours	7	Benson & Hedges Jordan	B	3.0 Jordan 199-Mugen Honda V10	engine	18/22
5	BRITISH GP	Silverstone	7	Benson & Hedges Jordan	B	3.0 Jordan 199-Mugen Honda V10		6/22
8	AUSTRIAN GP	A1-Ring	7	Benson & Hedges Jordan	B	3.0 Jordan 199-Mugen Honda V10	1 lap behind	11/22
ret	GERMAN GP	Hockenheim	7	Benson & Hedges Jordan	B	3.0 Jordan 199-Mugen Honda V10	unhappy with brakes	8/22
6	HUNGARIAN GP	Hungaroring	7	Benson & Hedges Jordan	B	3.0 Jordan 199-Mugen Honda V10		6/22
6	BELGIAN GP	Spa	7	Benson & Hedges Jordan	B	3.0 Jordan 199-Mugen Honda V10		4/22
10	ITALIAN GP	Monza	7	Benson & Hedges Jordan	B	3.0 Jordan 199-Mugen Honda V10	lost time in pit stop	9/22
ret	EUROPEAN GP	Nürburgring	7	Benson & Hedges Jordan	B	3.0 Jordan 199-Mugen Honda V10	electrics	7/22
ret	MALAYSIAN GP	Sepang	7	Benson & Hedges Jordan	B	3.0 Jordan 199-Mugen Honda V10	collision with Fisichella	9/22
ret	JAPANESE GP	Suzuka	7	Benson & Hedges Jordan	B	3.0 Jordan 199-Mugen Honda V10	driver retired car	12/22

GP Starts: 115 (116)   GP Wins: 22   Pole positions: 20   Fastest laps: 19   Points: 360

GRAHAM HILL

GRAHAM HILL captured the public's imagination like no other racing driver of the period. Ordinary people, particularly those who had only a passing interest in the sport, took to this suave, but somehow homely character, who could charm and amuse in a way that, say, the reserved Jim Clark, opinionated John Surtees or rather earnest Jackie Stewart could not. This may have been due, in part, to the fact that he had started his career from nothing and shown unbelievable single-mindedness and much courage, not to mention an appetite for hard work, to reach the very top of his profession.

Hill's early days were spent scrounging drives in return for his services as a mechanic, before he began racing regularly in 1956 in Lotus and Cooper sports cars. In fact, he was working as a mechanic for Colin Chapman, who didn't consider him that seriously as a driver until he had proved himself elsewhere. When Lotus entered grand prix racing in 1958, Graham was back as a driver, making his debut at Monaco, where a wheel fell off. His two seasons with the fragile Lotus 16 were largely unsuccessful, the cars suffering all sorts of failures.

For 1960, Hill joined BRM, who had won a grand prix and theoretically were better placed to further his career. He missed the chance of his first grand prix win at Silverstone that year when, after taking the lead from Jack Brabham, a slight error brought a heavy penalty when he spun into retirement. If outright victory was still elusive, then at least now he was finishing races. He was also consolidating his position as a fine all-rounder by driving for Porsche in Formula 2 and sports cars, taking third and a class win in the Buenos Aires 1000km with Jo Bonnier. After another barren year in 1961, when the British four-cylinder cars were outclassed by Ferrari, it was win or bust for the BRM team, which faced the threat of closure if success was not achieved in 1962. Armed with the new V8-engined car, Graham responded brilliantly by winning the Dutch GP and then, after losing seemingly certain triumphs in both the Monaco and French GPs, he took the BRM to three more victories to claim a thoroughly deserved first world championship.

The next three seasons saw some magnificent racing, Hill battling it out for supremacy with Clark, Surtees, Dan Gurney et al, and coming very close to a second title in Mexico City in 1964, where an accidental collision with Lorenzo Bandini cost him his chance. However, the championship seemed to be of less importance in those days, each race carrying more weight in its own right. Memorably he took a hat trick of wins in both the Monaco and US GPs, but there were many great drives that brought only podium finishes, such was the level of competition.

Graham was certainly one of the most active drivers of the period, and every weekend he seemed to be flying somewhere to race, handling a bewildering array of machinery, from Seattle to Kyalami, or Karlskoga to Pukekohe. Driving Ferrari sports and GT cars for Maranello Concessionaires, he won the 1963 and 1964 Tourist Trophy races, and the 1964 Reims 12-hours and Paris 1000km, as well as taking second place at Le Mans the same year – all co-driving with Bonnier. He was unable to add to his tally of grand prix wins during the first year of the 3-litre formula in 1966, but he scored a contentious victory after a confused finish at the Indianapolis 500.

It was a great surprise when Hill moved camps in 1967, joining Jim Clark at Lotus, to race the new Ford-Cosworth-engined Lotus 49. Its potential was enormous, and Graham was back in the hunt, but he had to endure a string of disappointments as his car fell prey to niggling maladies. Everything changed on 7th April, 1968, however, when the team was devastated by the death of Jim Clark at Hockenheim. Graham helped restore morale by immediately winning the next two races in Spain and Monaco, and as the season wore on he resisted the challenges of Stewart and Denny Hulme to take his second championship. Joined by Jochen Rindt in 1969, he won his fifth Monaco GP, but soon was overshadowed by the Austrian, and the season ended in near-disaster when he was thrown from his Lotus at Watkins Glen after a tyre deflated, suffering badly broken legs.

Then aged 40, many believed it was time for Graham to retire, but he was no quitter and sheer bloody-mindedness saw him back in the cockpit of Rob Walker's Lotus at Kyalami, despite still being almost unable to walk. Surprisingly he managed some points finishes early on and drove superbly in the Race of Champions to take fourth place, despite gearbox trouble, but with Walker's Lotus 72 late in arriving, the season petered out. Moving to Brabham for 1971, he won the International Trophy in the new 'lobster-claw' BT34, but had a thin time of it elsewhere. In Formula 2, he led the smart Rondel team, winning a thrilling race at Thruxton from Ronnie Peterson to show there was life in the old dog yet, but in truth a slow decline had already set in. His second season at Brabham was thoroughly lacklustre, and the year was illuminated only by his victory in the Le Mans 24-hours for Matra with Henri Pescarolo. Thus he enjoyed the unique achievement of winning the world championship, the Indy 500 and the Sarthe classic.

With no prospect of a decent works drive in grands prix, Hill took the logical step of setting up his own team, showing some spirit with the difficult-to-handle Shadow in 1973, but getting nowhere fast in the reliable, but heavy Lola the following year. In 1975, he took the decision to build his own car, but after failing to qualify at Monaco he remained out of the cockpit until he announced his retirement at the British Grand Prix. By then, he had taken on Tony Brise and felt he had in his charge a future world champion.

However, returning from a test session with the team's latest car at Paul Ricard in late November, 1975, Hill, piloting his own plane, clipped the tree tops in dense fog over Arkley golf course while approaching Elstree airfield and crashed. Not only did one of motor racing's great figures perish, but so too did poor Brise and four other team members.

HILL, Graham (GB) b 15/2/1929, Hampstead, London – d 29/11/1975, Arkley, nr Barnet, Hertfordshire

1958 Championship position: Unplaced

	Race	Circuit	No	Entrant	Tyres	Capacity/Car/Engine	Comment	Q Pos/Entries
ret	MONACO GP	Monte Carlo	26	Team Lotus	D	2.0 Lotus 12-Climax 4	broken half shaft – lost wheel	15/28
ret	DUTCH GP	Zandvoort	16	Team Lotus	D	2.0 Lotus 12-Climax 4	overheating	13/17
ret	BELGIAN GP	Spa	42	Team Lotus	D	2.0 Lotus 12-Climax 4	engine	15/20
ret	FRENCH GP	Reims	24	Team Lotus	D	2.0 Lotus 16-Climax 4	overheating	19/21
ret	BRITISH GP	Silverstone	16	Team Lotus	D	2.0 Lotus 16-Climax 4	overheating – oil pressure	14/21
ret	GERMAN GP (F2)	Nürburgring	25	Team Lotus	D	1.5 Lotus 16-Climax 4	oil pipe	25/26
ret	PORTUGUESE GP	Oporto	20	Team Lotus	D	2.2 Lotus 16-Climax 4	spun off	12/15
6	ITALIAN GP	Monza	38	Team Lotus	D	2.2 Lotus 16-Climax 4	pit stop – misfire/8 laps behind	12/21
16	MOROCCAN GP	Casablanca	36	Team Lotus	D	2.0 Lotus 16-Climax 4	behind four F2 cars/7 laps behind	12/25

1959 Championship position: Unplaced

	Race	Circuit	No	Entrant	Tyres	Capacity/Car/Engine	Comment	Q Pos/Entries
ret	MONACO GP	Monte Carlo	40	Team Lotus	D	2.5 Lotus 16-Climax 4	fire	14/24
7	DUTCH GP	Zandvoort	14	Team Lotus	D	2.5 Lotus 16-Climax 4	pit stop – smoke in car/2 laps behind	5/15
ret	FRENCH GP	Reims	32	Team Lotus	D	2.5 Lotus 16-Climax 4	radiator	14/22
9	BRITISH GP	Aintree	28	Team Lotus	D	2.5 Lotus 16-Climax 4	spin/5 laps behind	9/30
ret	GERMAN GP	AVUS	16	Team Lotus	D	2.5 Lotus 16-Climax 4	gearbox in heat 1	10/16
ret	PORTUGUESE GP	Monsanto	11	Team Lotus	D	2.5 Lotus 16-Climax 4	split fuel tank – spun – hit by Phil Hill	15/16
ret	ITALIAN GP	Monza	18	Team Lotus	D	2.5 Lotus 16-Climax 4	clutch	10/21

1960 Championship position: 13th= Wins: 0 Pole positions: 0 Fastest laps: 1 Points scored: 4

	Race	Circuit	No	Entrant	Tyres	Capacity/Car/Engine	Comment	Q Pos/Entries
ret	ARGENTINE GP	Buenos Aires	42	Owen Racing Organisation	D	2.5 BRM P25 4	overheating	3/22
7/ret	MONACO GP	Monte Carlo	6	Owen Racing Organisation	D	2.5 BRM P48 4	spun off	6/24
3	DUTCH GP	Zandvoort	16	Owen Racing Organisation	D	2.5 BRM P48 4		5/21
ret	BELGIAN GP	Spa	10	Owen Racing Organisation	D	2.5 BRM P48 4	engine	=6/18
ret	FRENCH GP	Reims	12	Owen Racing Organisation	D	2.5 BRM P48 4	stalled on grid – hit by Trintignant	3/23
ret	BRITISH GP	Silverstone	4	Owen Racing Organisation	D	2.5 BRM P48 4	spun off when leading/FL	2/25
ret	PORTUGUESE GP	Oporto	22	Owen Racing Organisation	D	2.5 BRM P48 4	gearbox	5/16
ret	US GP	Riverside	17	Owen Racing Organisation	D	2.5 BRM P48 4	gearbox	11/23

1961 Championship position: 13th= Wins: 0 Pole positions: 0 Fastest laps: 0 Points scored: 3

	Race	Circuit	No	Entrant	Tyres	Capacity/Car/Engine	Comment	Q Pos/Entries
ret	MONACO GP	Monte Carlo	18	Owen Racing Organisation	D	1.5 BRM P48/57-Climax 4	fuel pump	4/21
8	DUTCH GP	Zandvoort	4	Owen Racing Organisation	D	1.5 BRM P48/57-Climax 4		5/17
ret	BELGIAN GP	Spa	36	Owen Racing Organisation	D	1.5 BRM P48/57-Climax 4	oil leak	6/25
6	FRENCH GP	Reims	22	Owen Racing Organisation	D	1.5 BRM P48/57-Climax 4		6/26
ret	BRITISH GP	Aintree	20	Owen Racing Organisation	D	1.5 BRM P48/57-Climax 4	engine	11/30
ret	GERMAN GP	Nürburgring	17	Owen Racing Organisation	D	1.5 BRM P48/57-Climax 4	accident	6/27
ret	ITALIAN GP	Monza	24	Owen Racing Organisation	D	1.5 BRM P48/57-Climax 4	engine	5/33
dns	"	"	24	Owen Racing Organisation	D	1.5 BRM P57 V8	practice only	– / –
5	US GP	Watkins Glen	4	Owen Racing Organisation	D	1.5 BRM P48/57-Climax 4	1 lap behind	2/19

1962 WORLD CHAMPION Wins: 4 Pole positions: 1 Fastest laps: 3 Points scored: 52

	Race	Circuit	No	Entrant	Tyres	Capacity/Car/Engine	Comment	Q Pos/Entries
1	DUTCH GP	Zandvoort	17	Owen Racing Organisation	D	1.5 BRM P57 V8		2/20
6/ret	MONACO GP	Monte Carlo	10	Owen Racing Organisation	D	1.5 BRM P57 V8	engine/8 laps behind	2/21
2	BELGIAN GP	Spa	1	Owen Racing Organisation	D	1.5 BRM P57 V8		1/20

The 1962 world championship title was decided in far-off East London, where Graham Hill won the South African GP after Jim Clark's Lotus retired. Close scrutiny of the season shows that the BRM driver fully deserved his crown, after suffering retirements himself in both the Monaco and French grands prix when comfortably in command of both races.

Mr Monaco. In one of his finest drives, Graham Hill completed a hat trick of wins in the Monaco Grand Prix between 1963 and 1965 in his BRM. By then, the Belle Époque architecture in the Mediterranean tax haven had begun to be replaced by luxury high-rise apartment blocks. Note the cast-iron lamp-post base with just a sandbag placed in front, offering little protection for a driver in a collision.

					D			
9	FRENCH GP	Rouen	8	Owen Racing Organisation	D	1.5 BRM P57 V8	*pit stop – fuel injection/FL/-10 laps*	2/17
4	BRITISH GP	Aintree	12	Owen Racing Organisation	D	1.5 BRM P57 V8		=4/21
1	GERMAN GP	Nürburgring	11	Owen Racing Organisation	D	1.5 BRM P57 V8	*FL*	2/30
1	ITALIAN GP	Monza	14	Owen Racing Organisation	D	1.5 BRM P57 V8	*FL*	2/30
2	US GP	Watkins Glen	4	Owen Racing Organisation	D	1.5 BRM P57 V8		3/20
1	SOUTH AFRICAN GP	East London	3	Owen Racing Organisation	D	1.5 BRM P57 V8		2/17

1963 Championship position: 2nd=   Wins: 2   Pole positions: 2   Fastest laps: 0   Points scored: 29

					D			
1	MONACO GP	Monte Carlo	6	Owen Racing Organisation	D	1.5 BRM P57 V8		2/17
ret	BELGIAN GP	Spa	7	Owen Racing Organisation	D	1.5 BRM P57 V8	*gearbox*	1/20
ret	DUTCH GP	Zandvoort	12	Owen Racing Organisation	D	1.5 BRM P57 V8	*overheating*	2/19
dns	"	"	12	Owen Racing Organisation	D	1.5 BRM P61 V8	*practice only*	- / -
dsq/3*	FRENCH GP	Reims	2	Owen Racing Organisation	D	1.5 BRM P61 V8	**disqualified for a push start*	2/21
dns	"	"	2	Owen Racing Organisation	D	1.5 BRM P57 V8	*practice only*	- / -
3	BRITISH GP	Silverstone	1	Owen Racing Organisation	D	1.5 BRM P57 V8	*ran low on fuel on last lap when 2nd*	3/23
ret	GERMAN GP	Nürburgring	1	Owen Racing Organisation	D	1.5 BRM P57 V8	*gearbox*	4/26
dns	"	"	1	Owen Racing Organisation	D	1.5 BRM P61 V8	*practice only*	- / -
ret	ITALIAN GP	Monza	12	Owen Racing Organisation	D	1.5 BRM P61 V8	*clutch*	2/28
dns	"	"	12	Owen Racing Organisation	D	1.5 BRM P57 V8	*practice only*	- / -
1	US GP	Watkins Glen	1	Owen Racing Organisation	D	1.5 BRM P57 V8		1/21
4	MEXICAN GP	Mexico City	1	Owen Racing Organisation	D	1.5 BRM P57 V8	*1 lap behind*	3/21
3	SOUTH AFRICAN GP	East London	5	Owen Racing Organisation	D	1.5 BRM P57 V8	*1 lap behind*	6/21

1964 Championship position: 2nd   Wins: 2   Pole positions: 1   Fastest laps: 1   Points scored: 41

					D			
1	MONACO GP	Monte Carlo	8	Owen Racing Organisation	D	1.5 BRM P261 V8	*FL*	=3/20
4	DUTCH GP	Zandvoort	6	Owen Racing Organisation	D	1.5 BRM P261 V8	*1 lap behind*	3/18
5/ret	BELGIAN GP	Spa	1	Owen Racing Organisation	D	1.5 BRM P261 V8	*out of fuel last lap*	2/20
2	FRENCH GP	Rouen	8	Owen Racing Organisation	D	1.5 BRM P261 V8		6/17
2	BRITISH GP	Brands Hatch	3	Owen Racing Organisation	D	1.5 BRM P261 V8		2/25
2	GERMAN GP	Nürburgring	3	Owen Racing Organisation	D	1.5 BRM P261 V8		5/24
ret	AUSTRIAN GP	Zeltweg	3	Owen Racing Organisation	D	1.5 BRM P261 V8	*distributor drive*	1/20
ret	ITALIAN GP	Monza	18	Owen Racing Organisation	D	1.5 BRM P261 V8	*clutch on startline*	3/25
1	US GP	Watkins Glen	3	Owen Racing Organisation	D	1.5 BRM P261 V8		4/19
11	MEXICAN GP	Mexico City	3	Owen Racing Organisation	D	1.5 BRM P261 V8	*hit by Bandini when 2nd/2 laps behind*	6/19

1965 Championship position: 2nd   Wins: 2   Pole positions: 4   Fastest laps: 3   Points scored: 47

					D			
3	SOUTH AFRICAN GP	East London	3	Owen Racing Organisation	D	1.5 BRM P261 V8		5/25
1	MONACO GP	Monte Carlo	3	Owen Racing Organisation	D	1.5 BRM P261 V8	*FL*	1/17
5	BELGIAN GP	Spa	7	Owen Racing Organisation	D	1.5 BRM P261 V8	*1 lap behind*	1/21
5	FRENCH GP	Clermont Ferrand	10	Owen Racing Organisation	D	1.5 BRM P261 V8	*1 lap behind*	13/17
2	BRITISH GP	Silverstone	3	Owen Racing Organisation	D	1.5 BRM P261 V8	*FL*	2/23
4	DUTCH GP	Zandvoort	10	Owen Racing Organisation	D	1.5 BRM P261 V8		1/17
2	GERMAN GP	Nürburgring	9	Owen Racing Organisation	D	1.5 BRM P261 V8		3/22
2	ITALIAN GP	Monza	30	Owen Racing Organisation	D	1.5 BRM P261 V8		4/23

	GP	Circuit	No	Team		Engine	Notes	Grid/Fin
1	US GP	Watkins Glen	3	Owen Racing Organisation	D	1.5 BRM P261 V8	*FL*	1/18
ret	MEXICAN GP	Mexico City	3	Owen Racing Organisation	D	1.5 BRM P261 V8	*engine*	5/18

1966 Championship position: 5th   Wins: 0   Pole positions: 0   Fastest laps: 0   Points scored: 17

	GP	Circuit	No	Team		Engine	Notes	Grid/Fin
3	MONACO GP	Monte Carlo	11	Owen Racing Organisation	D	2.0 BRM P261 V8	*1 lap behind*	4/16
dns	"	" "	11T	Owen Racing Organisation	G	3.0 BRM P83 H16	*practice only*	- / -
ret	BELGIAN GP	Spa	14	Owen Racing Organisation	D	2.0 BRM P261 V8	*spun off in rainstorm*	9/18
ret	FRENCH GP	Reims	16	Owen Racing Organisation	D	2.0 BRM P261 V8	*engine*	8/17
dns	"	"	T2	Owen Racing Organisation	G	3.0 BRM P83 H16	*practice only*	- / -
3	BRITISH GP	Brands Hatch	3	Owen Racing Organisation	G	2.0 BRM P261 V8	*1 lap behind*	4/20
2	DUTCH GP	Zandvoort	12	Owen Racing Organisation	G	2.0 BRM P261 V8	*1 lap behind*	7/18
4	GERMAN GP	Nürburgring	5	Owen Racing Organisation	G	2.0 BRM P261 V8		10/30
ret	ITALIAN GP	Monza	26	Owen Racing Organisation	G	3.0 BRM P83 H16	*engine – camshaft*	11/22
dns	"	"	26	Owen Racing Organisation	G	2.0 BRM P261 V8	*practice only*	- / -
ret	US GP	Watkins Glen	3	Owen Racing Organisation	G	3.0 BRM P83 H16	*crown wheel and pinion*	5/19
ret	MEXICAN GP	Mexico City	3	Owen Racing Organisation	G	3.0 BRM P83 H16	*engine*	7/19

1967 Championship position: 6th=   Wins: 0   Pole positions: 3   Fastest laps: 2   Points scored: 15

	GP	Circuit	No	Team		Engine	Notes	Grid/Fin
ret	SOUTH AFRICAN GP	Kyalami	8	Team Lotus	F	3.0 Lotus 43-BRM H16	*hit kerb*	15/18
2	MONACO GP	Monte Carlo	14	Team Lotus	F	2.1 Lotus 33-BRM V8	*1 lap behind*	8/18
ret	DUTCH GP	Zandvoort	6	Team Lotus	F	3.0 Lotus 49-Cosworth V8	*timing gears*	1/17
ret	BELGIAN GP	Spa	22	Team Lotus	F	3.0 Lotus 49-Cosworth V8	*gearbox*	3/18
ret	FRENCH GP	Le Mans	7	Team Lotus	F	3.0 Lotus 49-Cosworth V8	*gearbox/FL*	1/15
ret	BRITISH GP	Silverstone	6	Team Lotus	F	3.0 Lotus 49-Cosworth V8	*engine*	2/21
ret	GERMAN GP	Nürburgring	4	Team Lotus	F	3.0 Lotus 49-Cosworth V8	*rear suspension mounting*	14/25
4	CANADIAN GP	Mosport Park	4	Team Lotus	F	3.0 Lotus 49-Cosworth V8	*2 laps behind*	2/19
ret	ITALIAN GP	Monza	22	Team Lotus	F	3.0 Lotus 49-Cosworth V8	*engine*	8/18
2	US GP	Watkins Glen	6	Team Lotus	F	3.0 Lotus 49-Cosworth V8	*gearbox problems/FL*	1/18
ret	MEXICAN GP	Mexico City	6	Team Lotus	F	3.0 Lotus 49-Cosworth V8	*driveshaft – universal joint*	4/19

1968 WORLD CHAMPION   Wins: 3   Pole positions: 2   Fastest laps: 0   Points scored: 48

	GP	Circuit	No	Team		Engine	Notes	Grid/Fin
2	SOUTH AFRICAN GP	Kyalami	5	Team Lotus	F	3.0 Lotus 49-Cosworth V8		2/23
1	SPANISH GP	Jarama	10	Gold Leaf Team Lotus	F	3.0 Lotus 49-Cosworth V8		6/14
1	MONACO GP	Monte Carlo	9	Gold Leaf Team Lotus	F	3.0 Lotus 49B-Cosworth V8		1/18
ret	BELGIAN GP	Spa	1	Gold Leaf Team Lotus	F	3.0 Lotus 49B-Cosworth V8	*driveshaft – universal joint*	14/18
9/ret	DUTCH GP	Zandvoort	3	Gold Leaf Team Lotus	F	3.0 Lotus 49B-Cosworth V8	*spun off/9 laps behind*	3/19
ret	FRENCH GP	Rouen	12	Gold Leaf Team Lotus	F	3.0 Lotus 49B-Cosworth V8	*driveshaft*	9/18
ret	BRITISH GP	Brands Hatch	8	Gold Leaf Team Lotus	F	3.0 Lotus 49B-Cosworth V8	*driveshaft – universal joint*	1/20
2	GERMAN GP	Nürburgring	3	Gold Leaf Team Lotus	F	3.0 Lotus 49B-Cosworth V8		4/20
ret	ITALIAN GP	Monza	16	Gold Leaf Team Lotus	F	3.0 Lotus 49B-Cosworth V8	*lost wheel*	5/24
4	CANADIAN GP	St Jovite	3	Gold Leaf Team Lotus	F	3.0 Lotus 49B-Cosworth V8	*pit stop – vibration/4 laps behind*	5/22
2	US GP	Watkins Glen	10	Gold Leaf Team Lotus	F	3.0 Lotus 49B-Cosworth V8		3/21
1	MEXICAN GP	Mexico City	10	Gold Leaf Team Lotus	F	3.0 Lotus 49B-Cosworth V8		3/21

1969 Championship position: 7th   Wins: 1   Pole positions: 0   Fastest laps: 0   Points scored: 19

	GP	Circuit	No	Team		Engine	Notes	Grid/Fin
2	SOUTH AFRICAN GP	Kyalami	1	Gold Leaf Team Lotus	F	3.0 Lotus 49B-Cosworth V8		=7/18
ret	SPANISH GP	Montjuich Park	1	Gold Leaf Team Lotus	F	3.0 Lotus 49B-Cosworth V8	*accident – rear wing collapsed*	3/14
1	MONACO GP	Monte Carlo	1	Gold Leaf Team Lotus	F	3.0 Lotus 49B-Cosworth V8		4/16
7	DUTCH GP	Zandvoort	1	Gold Leaf Team Lotus	F	3.0 Lotus 49B-Cosworth V8	*pit stop – handling/2 laps behind*	3/15
dns	"	"	1T	Gold Leaf Team Lotus	F	3.0 Lotus 63-Cosworth V8	*practice only*	- / -
6	FRENCH GP	Clermont Ferrand	1	Gold Leaf Team Lotus	F	3.0 Lotus 49B-Cosworth V8	*1 lap behind*	8/13
7	BRITISH GP	Silverstone	1	Gold Leaf Team Lotus	F	3.0 Lotus 49B-Cosworth V8	*pit stop – fuel/2 laps behind*	12/17
dns	"	"	1T	Gold Leaf Team Lotus	F	3.0 Lotus 63-Cosworth V8	*practice only*	- / -
dns	"	"	9	Motor Racing Developments	G	3.0 Brabham BT26A-Cosworth V8	*waiting for his Lotus to arrive*	- / -
4	GERMAN GP	Nürburgring	1	Gold Leaf Team Lotus	F	3.0 Lotus 49B-Cosworth V8		9/26

'Gives you wings' had a very different meaning in 1968, when Graham Hill clinched his second world championship with a victory at the wheel of his Lotus 49B in Mexico City. These hideous appendages were quite rightly banned early in the following season, after both Hill and his team-mate, Rindt, suffered structural failures that could have brought much more serious consequences.

9/ret	ITALIAN GP	Monza	2	Gold Leaf Team Lotus	F	3.0 Lotus 49B-Cosworth V8	*driveshaft/5 laps behind*	9/15
ret	CANADIAN GP	Mosport Park	1	Gold Leaf Team Lotus	F	3.0 Lotus 49B-Cosworth V8	*engine*	7/20
ret	US GP	Watkins Glen	1	Gold Leaf Team Lotus	F	3.0 Lotus 49B-Cosworth V8	*puncture – thrown out – broken legs*	4/18

1970 Championship position: 13th   Wins: 0   Pole positions: 0   Fastest laps: 0   Points scored: 7

6	SOUTH AFRICAN GP	Kyalami	11	Rob Walker Racing Team	F	3.0 Lotus 49C-Cosworth V8	*1 lap behind*	19/24
4	SPANISH GP	Jarama	6	Rob Walker Racing Team	F	3.0 Lotus 49C-Cosworth V8	*1 lap behind*	18/22
5	MONACO GP	Monte Carlo	1	Brooke Bond Oxo Racing/Rob Walker	F	3.0 Lotus 49C-Cosworth V8	*raced borrowed works car/-1 lap*	12/21
ret	BELGIAN GP	Spa	23	Brooke Bond Oxo Racing/Rob Walker	F	3.0 Lotus 49C-Cosworth V8	*engine*	16/18
nc	DUTCH GP	Zandvoort	15	Brooke Bond Oxo Racing/Rob Walker	F	3.0 Lotus 49C-Cosworth V8	*pit stop – handling/9 laps behind*	21/24
10	FRENCH GP	Clermont Ferrand	8	Brooke Bond Oxo Racing/Rob Walker	F	3.0 Lotus 49C-Cosworth V8	*1 lap behind*	20/23
6	BRITISH GP	Brands Hatch	14	Brooke Bond Oxo Racing/Rob Walker	F	3.0 Lotus 49C-Cosworth V8	*1 lap behind*	23/25
ret	GERMAN GP	Hockenheim	9	Brooke Bond Oxo Racing/Rob Walker	F	3.0 Lotus 49C-Cosworth V8	*engine*	21/25
dns	ITALIAN GP	Monza	28	Brooke Bond Oxo Racing/Rob Walker	F	3.0 Lotus 72C-Cosworth V8	*withdrawn after Rindt's fatal accident*	(16)/27
nc	CANADIAN GP	St Jovite	9	Brooke Bond Oxo Racing/Rob Walker	F	3.0 Lotus 72C-Cosworth V8	*pit stop – gearbox/13 laps behind*	20/20
ret	US GP	Watkins Glen	14	Brooke Bond Oxo Racing/Rob Walker	F	3.0 Lotus 72C-Cosworth V8	*clutch*	10/27
ret	MEXICAN GP	Mexico City	14	Brooke Bond Oxo Racing/Rob Walker	F	3.0 Lotus 72C-Cosworth V8	*overheating*	8/18

1971 Championship position: 21st   Wins: 0   Pole positions: 0   Fastest laps: 0   Points scored: 2

9	SOUTH AFRICAN GP	Kyalami	14	Motor Racing Developments	G	3.0 Brabham BT33-Cosworth V8	*pit stop – rear wing/2 laps behind*	19/25
ret	SPANISH GP	Montjuich Park	7	Motor Racing Developments	G	3.0 Brabham BT34-Cosworth V8	*steering*	15/22
ret	MONACO GP	Monte Carlo	7	Motor Racing Developments	G	3.0 Brabham BT34-Cosworth V8	*hit wall at Tabac*	=9/23
10	DUTCH GP	Zandvoort	24	Motor Racing Developments	G	3.0 Brabham BT34-Cosworth V8	*5 laps behind*	16/24
ret	FRENCH GP	Paul Ricard	7	Motor Racing Developments	G	3.0 Brabham BT34-Cosworth V8	*oil pressure*	4/24
ret	BRITISH GP	Silverstone	7	Motor Racing Developments	G	3.0 Brabham BT34-Cosworth V8	*hit by Oliver on grid*	16/24
9	GERMAN GP	Nürburgring	24	Motor Racing Developments	G	3.0 Brabham BT34-Cosworth V8	*left on grid*	13/23
5	AUSTRIAN GP	Österreichring	7	Motor Racing Developments	G	3.0 Brabham BT34-Cosworth V8		8/22
11/ret	ITALIAN GP	Monza	10	Motor Racing Developments	G	3.0 Brabham BT34-Cosworth V8	*gearbox/7 laps behind*	14/24
ret	CANADIAN GP	Mosport Park	37	Motor Racing Developments	G	3.0 Brabham BT34-Cosworth V8	*spun off*	=15/27
7	US GP	Watkins Glen	22	Motor Racing Developments	G	3.0 Brabham BT34-Cosworth V8	*1 lap behind*	20/32

1972 Championship position: 12th   Wins: 0   Pole positions: 0   Fastest laps: 0   Points scored: 4

ret	ARGENTINE GP	Buenos Aires	1	Motor Racing Developments	G	3.0 Brabham BT33-Cosworth V8	*fuel pump/tyre problems*	=16/22
6	SOUTH AFRICAN GP	Kyalami	19	Motor Racing Developments	G	3.0 Brabham BT33-Cosworth V8	*1 lap behind*	14/27
10	SPANISH GP	Jarama	18	Motor Racing Developments	G	3.0 Brabham BT37-Cosworth V8	*spin/4 laps behind*	23/26
12	MONACO GP	Monte Carlo	20	Motor Racing Developments	G	3.0 Brabham BT37-Cosworth V8	*4 laps behind*	=18/25
ret	BELGIAN GP	Nivelles	17	Motor Racing Developments	G	3.0 Brabham BT37-Cosworth V8	*rear upright*	16/26
10	FRENCH GP	Clermont Ferrand	18	Motor Racing Developments	G	3.0 Brabham BT37-Cosworth V8	*hit by Beltoise*	24/29
ret	BRITISH GP	Brands Hatch	26	Motor Racing Developments	G	3.0 Brabham BT37-Cosworth V8	*spun off*	=20/27
6	GERMAN GP	Nürburgring	11	Motor Racing Developments	G	3.0 Brabham BT37-Cosworth V8		15/27
ret	AUSTRIAN GP	Österreichring	16	Motor Racing Developments	G	3.0 Brabham BT37-Cosworth V8	*fuel metering unit*	14/26
5	ITALIAN GP	Monza	28	Motor Racing Developments	G	3.0 Brabham BT37-Cosworth V8	*brake problems*	13/27
8	CANADIAN GP	Mosport Park	7	Motor Racing Developments	G	3.0 Brabham BT37-Cosworth V8	*1 lap behind*	17/25
11	US GP	Watkins Glen	28	Motor Racing Developments	G	3.0 Brabham BT37-Cosworth V8	*spin/2 laps behind*	28/32

1973 Championship position: Unplaced

ret	SPANISH GP	Montjuich Park	25	Embassy Racing	G	3.0 Shadow DN1-Cosworth V8	*brakes*	22/22
9	BELGIAN GP	Zolder	12	Embassy Racing	G	3.0 Shadow DN1-Cosworth V8	*pit stop – plug lead/5 laps behind*	23/23
ret	MONACO GP	Monte Carlo	12	Embassy Racing	G	3.0 Shadow DN1-Cosworth V8	*rear suspension*	25/26
ret	SWEDISH GP	Anderstorp	12	Embassy Racing	G	3.0 Shadow DN1-Cosworth V8	*ignition*	18/22
10	FRENCH GP	Paul Ricard	12	Embassy Racing	G	3.0 Shadow DN1-Cosworth V8	*1 lap behind*	16/25
ret	BRITISH GP	Silverstone	12	Embassy Racing	G	3.0 Shadow DN1-Cosworth V8	*steering rack/front subframe*	27/29
nc	DUTCH GP	Zandvoort	12	Embassy Racing	G	3.0 Shadow DN1-Cosworth V8	*4 pit stops – water/16 laps behind*	17/24
13	GERMAN GP	Nürburgring	12	Embassy Racing	G	3.0 Shadow DN1-Cosworth V8		20/23
ret	AUSTRIAN GP	Österreichring	12	Embassy Racing	G	3.0 Shadow DN1-Cosworth V8	*rear suspension mounting*	22/25
14	ITALIAN GP	Monza	12	Embassy Racing	G	3.0 Shadow DN1-Cosworth V8	*1 lap behind*	22/25
16	CANADIAN GP	Mosport Park	12	Embassy Racing	G	3.0 Shadow DN1-Cosworth V8	*4 pit stops – various/7 laps behind*	17/26
13	US GP	Watkins Glen	12	Embassy Racing	G	3.0 Shadow DN1-Cosworth V8	*pit stop – puncture/2 laps behind*	19/28

1974 Championship position: 18th   Wins: 0   Pole positions: 0   Fastest laps: 0   Points scored: 1

ret	ARGENTINE GP	Buenos Aires	26	Embassy Racing with Graham Hill	F	3.0 Lola T370-Cosworth V8	*engine*	=17/26
11	BRAZILIAN GP	Interlagos	26	Embassy Racing with Graham Hill	F	3.0 Lola T370-Cosworth V8	*1 lap behind*	21/25
12	SOUTH AFRICAN GP	Kyalami	26	Embassy Racing with Graham Hill	F	3.0 Lola T370-Cosworth V8	*1 lap behind*	18/27
ret	SPANISH GP	Jarama	26	Embassy Racing with Graham Hill	F	3.0 Lola T370-Cosworth V8	*engine*	20/28
8	BELGIAN GP	Nivelles	26	Embassy Racing with Graham Hill	F	3.0 Lola T370-Cosworth V8	*2 laps behind*	29/32
7	MONACO GP	Monte Carlo	26	Embassy Racing with Graham Hill	F	3.0 Lola T370-Cosworth V8	*2 laps behind*	=21/28
6	SWEDISH GP	Anderstorp	26	Embassy Racing with Graham Hill	F	3.0 Lola T370-Cosworth V8	*1 lap behind*	15/28
ret	DUTCH GP	Zandvoort	26	Embassy Racing with Graham Hill	F	3.0 Lola T370-Cosworth V8	*loose clutch housing bolts*	19/27
13	FRENCH GP	Dijon	26	Embassy Racing with Graham Hill	F	3.0 Lola T370-Cosworth V8	*2 laps behind*	21/30
13	BRITISH GP	Brands Hatch	26	Embassy Racing with Graham Hill	F	3.0 Lola T370-Cosworth V8	*2 pit stops – punctures/-6 laps*	22/34
9	GERMAN GP	Nürburgring	26	Embassy Racing with Graham Hill	F	3.0 Lola T370-Cosworth V8		19/32
12	AUSTRIAN GP	Österreichring	26	Embassy Racing with Graham Hill	F	3.0 Lola T370-Cosworth V8	*pit stop – tyres/6 laps behind*	21/31
8	ITALIAN GP	Monza	26	Embassy Racing with Graham Hill	F	3.0 Lola T370-Cosworth V8	*1 lap behind*	21/31
14	CANADIAN GP	Mosport Park	26	Embassy Racing with Graham Hill	F	3.0 Lola T370-Cosworth V8	*3 laps behind*	20/30
8	US GP	Watkins Glen	26	Embassy Racing with Graham Hill	F	3.0 Lola T370-Cosworth V8	*1 lap behind*	24/30

1975 Championship position: Unplaced

10	ARGENTINE GP	Buenos Aires	22	Embassy Racing with Graham Hill	G	3.0 Lola T370-Cosworth V8	*1 lap behind*	21/23
12	BRAZILIAN GP	Interlagos	22	Embassy Racing with Graham Hill	G	3.0 Lola T370-Cosworth V8	*1 lap behind*	20/23
dns	SOUTH AFRICAN GP	Kyalami	22	Embassy Racing with Graham Hill	G	3.0 Lola T370-Cosworth V8	*practice accident – car damaged*	(28)/28
dnq	MONACO GP	Monte Carlo	23	Embassy Racing with Graham Hill	G	3.0 Hill GH1-Cosworth V8		21/26
dnq	"	" "	23T	Embassy Racing with Graham Hill	G	3.0 Lola T370-Cosworth V8		- / -

GP Starts: 176   GP Wins: 14   Pole positions: 13   Fastest laps: 10   Points: 289

P HIL Hill will always be remembered as the man who became America's first world champion when he took the 1961 crown, driving a Ferrari in a tragic finale at Monza. Yet that season, he won only two grands prix, and they were his only victories in small-capacity racing cars. In a long career, he was overwhelmingly more effective and successful in big, powerful sports machines.

After business studies on the West Coast, Phil decided he preferred working on cars to the office life, and by 1950 he was racing an MG TC, which was duly replaced by a succession of machines, all of which were hard-earned by the sweat of his brow. In 1952, he got a big break with a drive in Alan Guiberson's Ferrari, taking sixth place in the Carrera Panamericana, but the following year he fared badly and briefly considered retirement. He was persuaded to continue, however, and second place in the 1954 Carrera was a marvellous morale booster. Then his career took off in a big way Stateside: he won the 1955 SCCA championship, and after he had finished second in the 1956 Buenos Aires 1000km, he was given a contract to drive sports cars for the Scuderia. He won the Swedish GP and the Messina five-hours that season in works cars, and added more good results the following year, including a win in the Venezuelan GP at Caracas with Peter Collins.

By 1958, Phil was itching to get his hands on a grand prix car, but Ferrari seemed unwilling to give him the opportunity he craved, save for a little practice at the Libre Buenos Aires GP. Enzo felt he was best suited to sports cars, and Hill proved as much when he won at Buenos Aires and Sebring, and then put in a brilliant drive in the wet to win Le Mans with Olivier Gendebien. By then, however, his need to race in Formula 1 bordered on the obsessional, so he hired Jo Bonnier's Maserati to give himself a debut at the French GP. Perhaps Ferrari took the hint, because come the German GP Hill was handed the team's F2 car, and then at Monza he was entrusted with the real thing – a Ferrari 246 – taking third and fastest lap. By backing off at the finish of the Moroccan GP to allow Mike Hawthorn to move into second place and thus take the championship, Phil did his standing no harm and he became a full-time grand prix team member thereafter. He spent 1959 learning the art of grand prix driving, sometimes proving a little ragged in his approach and indulging in some hairy moments, but taking fourth place in the championship nevertheless. By 1960, the big front-engined cars were almost on the point of obsoles-

cence, but Hill gave the dinosaurs one last hurrah by winning the rather hollow Italian GP held on Monza's banked circuit, which was boycotted by the British teams.

The following season would be his finest. In addition to winning the Sebring 12-hours and Le Mans for the second time with Gendebien, he took the little 'shark-nose' Ferrari to victory at Spa and Monza to be crowned as world champion in the saddest of circumstances following the terrible death of his team-mate and championship rival, Wolfgang von Trips. Things progress quickly in Formula 1, however, and in 1962 Ferrari were totally eclipsed, leaving him with a few placings, but no hope of defending his title. He was still regarded as one of the finest exponents of sports car racing, though, and confirmed it by winning Le Mans for the third time with Gendebien, as well as the Nürburgring 1000km.

Such was the disharmony at Maranello that year that Phil joined what was effectively a breakaway group to race the ATS in 1963. To say it was a disastrous move would be an understatement, and it effectively destroyed his grand prix career. Initially left without a drive, he was called into the Cooper team following the tragic loss of Tim Mayer at Longford, but it was an unhappy liaison, his confidence hitting rock bottom at Zeltweg, where he wrote off two cars. This resulted in the ignominy of being dropped for Monza, but he was reinstated for the final two races.

Save for a drive in Gurney's Eagle at Monza in 1966, Phil's grand prix career was over, but he still had something left. He had been a key member of the Ford works sports car effort in 1964/65, but a move to Jim Hall's Chaparral team gave the twilight of his career a final glow. In 1966, he won the Nürburgring 1000km with Bonnier and a Can-Am round at Laguna Seca. In his final season, he took a memorable victory at Brands Hatch, sharing the Chaparral 2F with Mike Spence.

After this last win, Phil drifted into contented retirement, building a business restoring vintage cars and keeping in touch with the sport as a TV commentator. He was a regular participant in historic events and oversaw the racing career of his son, Derek, in the junior formulas on both sides of the Atlantic.

Sadly, Phil contracted Parkinson's disease, an illness he bore with his typical quiet dignity. He still continued to attend as many historic events as possible, the Monterey Historic Automobile Races in August, 2008, being his last public appearance. He passed away in hospital shortly afterwards.

HILL, Phil (USA) b 20/4/1927, Miami, Florida – d 28/8/2008, Salinas, California

	1958 Championship position: 10	Wins: 0	Pole positions: 0		Fastest laps: 1	Points scored: 9				
	Race	Circuit	No	Entrant	Tyres	Capacity/Car/Engine		Comment		Q Pos/Entries
7	FRENCH GP	Reims	36	Joakim Bonnier	P	2.5 Maserati 250F 6		1 lap behind		13/21
9*	GERMAN GP (F2)	Nürburgring	23	Scuderia Ferrari	E	1.5 Ferrari Dino 156 V6 F2		*5th in F2 class		13/26
3	ITALIAN GP	Monza	18	Scuderia Ferrari	E	2.4 Ferrari Dino 246 V6		FL		7/21
3	MOROCCAN GP	Casablanca	4	Scuderia Ferrari	E	2.4 Ferrari Dino 246 V6				5/25
	1959 Championship position: 4th	Wins: 0	Pole positions: 0		Fastest laps: 1	Points scored: 20				
4	MONACO GP	Monte Carlo	48	Scuderia Ferrari	D	2.4 Ferrari Dino 246 V6		3 spins – pit stop – wheels/-3 laps		5/24
6	DUTCH GP	Zandvoort	3	Scuderia Ferrari	D	2.4 Ferrari Dino 246 V6		2 laps behind		12/15
2	FRENCH GP	Reims	26	Scuderia Ferrari	D	2.4 Ferrari Dino 246 V6				3/22
3	GERMAN GP	AVUS	5	Scuderia Ferrari	D	2.4 Ferrari Dino 246 V6		3rd heat 1/2nd heat 2		6/16
ret	PORTUGUESE GP	Monsanto	15	Scuderia Ferrari	D	2.4 Ferrari Dino 246 V6		hit a spinning Graham Hill		7/16
2	ITALIAN GP	Monza	32	Scuderia Ferrari	D	2.4 Ferrari Dino 246 V6		FL		5/21
ret	US GP	Sebring	5	Scuderia Ferrari	D	2.4 Ferrari Dino 246 V6		clutch		8/19
	1960 Championship position: 5th	Wins: 1	Pole positions: 1		Fastest laps: 2 (1 shared)	Points scored: 16				
8	ARGENTINE GP	Buenos Aires	26	Scuderia Ferrari	D	2.4 Ferrari Dino 246 V6		3 laps behind		6/22
3	MONACO GP	Monte Carlo	36	Scuderia Ferrari	D	2.4 Ferrari Dino 246 V6				10/24
ret	DUTCH GP	Zandvoort	1	Scuderia Ferrari	D	2.4 Ferrari Dino 246 V6		engine		13/21
4	BELGIAN GP	Spa	24	Scuderia Ferrari	D	2.4 Ferrari Dino 246 V6		pit stop – fuel leak/FL (shared)/-1 lap		4/18
12/ret	FRENCH GP	Reims	2	Scuderia Ferrari	D	2.4 Ferrari Dino 246 V6		transmission		2/23
7	BRITISH GP	Silverstone	10	Scuderia Ferrari	D	2.4 Ferrari Dino 246 V6		2 laps behind		10/25
ret	PORTUGUESE GP	Oporto	26	Scuderia Ferrari	D	2.4 Ferrari Dino 246 V6		hit straw bales		10/16
1	ITALIAN GP	Monza	20	Scuderia Ferrari	D	2.4 Ferrari Dino 246 V6		FL		1/16
6	US GP	Riverside	9	Yeoman Credit Racing Team	D	2.5 Cooper T51-Climax 4		1 lap behind		13/23

Phil Hill enters the famous 'Karussel' in his Ferrrari during practice for the 1961 German Grand Prix. He was on his way to setting the first ever sub-nine-minute lap of the daunting 22.810km Nordschliefe mountain circuit. Wet weather on race day stymied the American's chances of a win, but third place kept him on course in his successful championship quest.

	Race	Circuit	No	Entrant	Tyres	Capacity/Car/Engine	Comment	Q Pos/Entries
1961 WORLD CHAMPION Wins: 2 Pole positions: 5 Fastest laps: 2 Points scored: 38								
3	MONACO GP	Monte Carlo	38	Scuderia Ferrari SpA SEFAC	D	1.5 Ferrari 156 V6		5/21
2	DUTCH GP	Zandvoort	1	Scuderia Ferrari SpA SEFAC	D	1.5 Ferrari 156 V6		1/17
1	BELGIAN GP	Spa	4	Scuderia Ferrari SpA SEFAC	D	1.5 Ferrari 156 V6		1/25
9	FRENCH GP	Reims	16	Scuderia Ferrari SpA SEFAC	D	1.5 Ferrari 156 V6	spin/FL/2 laps behind	1/26
2	BRITISH GP	Aintree	2	Scuderia Ferrari SpA SEFAC	D	1.5 Ferrari 156 V6		1/30
3	GERMAN GP	Nürburgring	4	Scuderia Ferrari SpA SEFAC	D	1.5 Ferrari 156 V6	FL	1/26
1	ITALIAN GP	Monza	2	Scuderia Ferrari SpA SEFAC	D	1.5 Ferrari 156 V6		3/33
1962 Championship position: 6th Wins: 0 Pole positions: 0 Fastest laps: 0 Points scored: 14								
3	DUTCH GP	Zandvoort	1	Scuderia Ferrari SpA SEFAC	D	1.5 Ferrari 156 V6		9/20
2	MONACO GP	Monte Carlo	36	Scuderia Ferrari SpA SEFAC	D	1.5 Ferrari 156 V6		9/21
3	BELGIAN GP	Spa	9	Scuderia Ferrari SpA SEFAC	D	1.5 Ferrari 156 V6		4/20
ret	BRITISH GP	Aintree	2	Scuderia Ferrari SpA SEFAC	D	1.5 Ferrari 156 V6	ignition	=11/21
ret	GERMAN GP	Nürburgring	1	Scuderia Ferrari SpA SEFAC	D	1.5 Ferrari 156 V6	shock absorbers	12/30
11	ITALIAN GP	Monza	10	Scuderia Ferrari SpA SEFAC	D	1.5 Ferrari 156 V6	pit stop – tyres/5 laps behind	15/30
dns	US GP	Watkins Glen	11	Porsche System Engineering	D	1.5 Porsche 804 F8	practiced only, as Bonnier was unwell	– / –
1963 Championship position: Unplaced								
ret	BELGIAN GP	Spa	26	Automobili Tourisimo Sport	D	1.5 ATS 100 V8	gearbox	17/20
ret	DUTCH GP	Zandvoort	24	Automobili Tourisimo Sport	D	1.5 ATS 100 V8	rear hub	13/19
nc	FRENCH GP	Reims	42	Ecurie Filipinetti	D	1.5 Lotus 24-BRM V8	pit stops – fuel pump/19 laps behind	13/21
11	ITALIAN GP	Monza	16	Automobili Tourisimo Sport	D	1.5 ATS 100 V8	pit stops – various/7 laps behind	14/28
ret	US GP	Watkins Glen	25	Automobili Tourisimo Sport	D	1.5 ATS 100 V8	oil pump	15/21
ret	MEXICAN GP	Mexico City	25	Automobili Tourisimo Sport	D	1.5 ATS 100 V8	rear suspension	17/21
1964 Championship position: 19th= Wins: 0 Pole positions: 0 Fastest laps: 0 Points scored: 1								
9/ret	MONACO GP	Monte Carlo	9	Cooper Car Co	D	1.5 Cooper T73-Climax V8	rear suspension	=8/20
8	DUTCH GP	Zandvoort	22	Cooper Car Co	D	1.5 Cooper T73-Climax V8	4 laps behind	9/18
ret	BELGIAN GP	Spa	21	Cooper Car Co	D	1.5 Cooper T73-Climax V8	engine	15/20
7	FRENCH GP	Rouen	14	Cooper Car Co	D	1.5 Cooper T73-Climax V8	1 lap behind	10/17
6	BRITISH GP	Brands Hatch	10	Cooper Car Co	D	1.5 Cooper T73-Climax V8	2 laps behind	15/25
ret	GERMAN GP	Nürburgring	10	Cooper Car Co	D	1.5 Cooper T73-Climax V8	engine	8/24
ret	AUSTRIAN GP	Zeltweg	10	Cooper Car Co	D	1.5 Cooper T66-Climax V8	accident – car written off	20/20
dns	"	"	10	Cooper Car Co	D	1.5 Cooper T73-Climax V8	accident in practice	– / –
ret	US GP	Watkins Glen	10	Cooper Car Co	D	1.5 Cooper T73-Climax V8	ignition	19/19
9/ret	MEXICAN GP	Mexico City	10	Cooper Car Co	D	1.5 Cooper T73-Climax V8	engine/2 laps behind	15/19
1966 Championship position: Unplaced								
dns	MONACO GP	Monte Carlo	20	Phil Hill/20th Century Fox	F	1.5 Lotus 33-Climax V8	camera car only – not competing	– / –
dns	BELGIAN GP	Spa	28	Phil Hill/20th Century Fox	F	4.7 McLaren-Ford V8	camera car only – not competing	– / –
dnq	ITALIAN GP	Monza	34	Anglo American Racers	G	2.7 Eagle T1G-Climax 4		21/22

GP Starts: 48 GP Wins: 3 Pole positions: 6 Fastest laps: 6 Points: 98

HIRT, Peter (CH) b 30/3/1910, Zurich – d 26/6/1992, Küsnacht, Zurich

	Race	Circuit	No	Entrant	Tyres	Capacity/Car/Engine	Comment	Q Pos/Entries
1951 Championship position: Unplaced								
ret	SWISS GP	Bremgarten	52	Peter Hirt	–	2.0 Veritas Meteor 6	fuel pump on lap 1	16/21
1952 Championship position: Unplaced								
7	SWISS GP	Bremgarten	44	Ecurie Espadon	P	2.0 Ferrari 212 V12	6 laps behind	19/21
11*	FRENCH GP	Rouen	36	Ecurie Espadon	P	2.0 Ferrari 212 V12	*took over Fischer's car/13 laps behind	– / –
ret	BRITISH GP	Silverstone	20	Ecurie Espadon	P	2.0 Ferrari 212 V12	brakes	24/32
1953 Championship position: Unplaced								
ret	SWISS GP	Bremgarten	38	Ecurie Espadon	P	2.0 Ferrari 500 4	water pump	17/23

GP Starts: 5 GP Wins: 0 Pole positions: 0 Fastest laps: 0 Points: 0

PETER HIRT

ALONG with Max de Terra, Peter Hirt was a gentleman Swiss driver who occasionally took part in major races and never remotely troubled the leaders.

Hirt purchased one of Loof's Veritas-Meteors with fellow countryman Paul Glauser and ran it during the 1950 and 1951 seasons, but it proved very unreliable in his hands, regularly posting early retirements.

He was glad to join forces with Rudi Fischer in 1952, when the Swiss pair ran Formula 2 Ferraris under the Ecurie Espadon (swordfish) banner. He drove the old T212 car with no great success, however, and after having a bash in the team's T500 at Bremgarten late in 1953, he was seen no more on the circuits at major level.

DAVID HOBBS

WITH only the occasional foray into grand prix racing, David Hobbs forged a very satisfying career for himself over three decades, starting in the early 1960s with Lotus and Jaguar sports cars, before graduating to Formula Junior, Formula 2 and then 'big-banger' sports cars with the Lola T70 in 1965.

Hobbs' first Formula 1 break came with Bernard White's BRM, in which he finished third in the 1966 Syracuse GP. He also made a couple of grand prix appearances the following year in the outdated car. This led to a contract with Team Surtees in 1967, largely racing the troublesome Lola-Aston Martin sports car. He had hoped for a full-time Formula 1 ride with his boss at Honda, but the slow development of the Japanese machines eventually precluded all but a single single grand prix appearance at Monza in 1968, shortly before the whole project was closed down.

Happily, Hobbs had already established himself in the top league of sports car racing that year with the John Wyer team by winning the Monza 1000km (with Paul Hawkins) in a Ford GT40. At the end of the year, he shared the winning Mirage-Ford with Jacky Ickx in the Rand nine-hours at Kyalami.

The advent of F5000/Formula A in 1969 provided a profitable furrow for David to plough over the next few seasons, firstly with Surtees in 1969 and 1970, and then by racing full time in the USA. Driving Carl Hogan's Lola in the States, he won the 1971 L&M Championship after taking five wins in the eight-round series. He also signed with Penske to race their Ferrari 512M alongside Mark Donohue. This brought about another grand prix drive at Watkins Glen, when Donohue was eventually committed to a USAC race at Trenton. The pair shared the McLaren during practice, the car being largely set up in favour of the American. In the race, Hobbs took the car to a steady tenth place. That year, he made the first of his four starts in the Indianapolis 500, fifth place in a McLaren in the 1974 race being his best finish. Later that season, he returned briefly to Formula 1, drafted in by McLaren for a couple of grands prix following Mike Hailwood's accident in the German Grand Prix.

The sheer variety of cars that Hobbs drove throughout a career that encompassed Formula 1, Formula 2, Endurance, Can-Am, F5000, Touring cars, IMSA and even a couple of NASCAR appearances is simply bewildering. In the 1990s, he still raced occasionally, before concentrating on his role as a TV commentator in America, which he performed with all the characteristic professionalism one would expect from this seasoned racer. He also owns a car dealership in Milwaukee, Wisconsin, where he now resides.

HOBBS, David (GB) b 9/6/1939, Leamington Spa, Warwickshire

	Race	Circuit	No	Entrant	Tyres	Capacity/Car/Engine	Comment	Q Pos/Entries
	1967 Championship position: Unplaced							
8	BRITISH GP	Silverstone	20	Bernard White Racing	G	2.0 BRM P261 V8	*3 laps behind*	14/21
10*	GERMAN GP (F2)	Nürburgring	27	Lola Cars Ltd	F	1.6 Lola T100-BMW 4 F2	*3rd in F2 class/2 laps behind*	20/25
9	CANADIAN GP	Mosport Park	12	Bernard White Racing	G	2.0 BRM P261 V8	*5 laps behind*	12/19
	1968 Championship position: Unplaced							
ret	ITALIAN GP	Monza	15	Honda Racing	F	3.0 Honda RA301 V12	*engine*	15/24
	1971 Championship position: Unplaced							
10	US GP	Watkins Glen	31	Penske White Racing	G	3.0 McLaren M19A-Cosworth V8	*stood in for Donohue/1 lap behind*	24/32
	1974 Championship position: Unplaced							
7	AUSTRIAN GP	Österreichring	33	Yardley Team McLaren	G	3.0 McLaren M23-Cosworth V8	*1 lap behind*	17/31
9	ITALIAN GP	Monza	33	Yardley Team McLaren	G	3.0 McLaren M23-Cosworth V8	*1 lap behind*	23/31

GP Starts: 7 GP Wins: 0 Pole positions: 0 Fastest laps: 0 Points: 0

HOFFMANN, Ingo (BR) b 18/2/1953, São Paulo

1976 Championship position: Unplaced

	Race	Circuit	No	Entrant	Tyres	Capacity/Car/Engine	Comment	Q Pos/Entries
11	BRAZILIAN GP	Interlagos	31	Copersucar-Fittipaldi	G	3.0 Copersucar FD03-Cosworth V8	1 lap behind	20/22
dnq	US GP WEST	Long Beach	31	Copersucar-Fittipaldi	G	3.0 Copersucar FD04-Cosworth V8		22/27
dnq	SPANISH GP	Jarama	31	Copersucar-Fittipaldi	G	3.0 Copersucar FD04-Cosworth V8		30/30
dnq	FRENCH GP	Paul Ricard	31	Copersucar-Fittipaldi	G	3.0 Copersucar FD04-Cosworth V8		28/30

1977 Championship position: Unplaced

	Race	Circuit	No	Entrant	Tyres	Capacity/Car/Engine	Comment	Q Pos/Entries
ret	ARGENTINE GP	Buenos Aires	29	Copersucar-Fittipaldi	G	3.0 Copersucar FD04-Cosworth V8	engine	19/21
7	BRAZILIAN GP	Interlagos	29	Copersucar-Fittipaldi	G	3.0 Copersucar FD04-Cosworth V8	2 laps behind	19/22

GP Starts: 3   GP Wins: 0   Pole positions: 0   Fastest laps: 0   Points: 0

HOSHINO, Kazuyoshi (J) b 1/7/1947, Shizuoka Prefecture

1976 Championship position: Unplaced

	Race	Circuit	No	Entrant	Tyres	Capacity/Car/Engine	Comment	Q Pos/Entries
ret	JAPANESE GP	Mount Fuji	52	Heros Racing	B	3.0 Tyrrell 007-Cosworth V8	used up tyres – no more available	21/27

1977 Championship position: Unplaced

	Race	Circuit	No	Entrant	Tyres	Capacity/Car/Engine	Comment	Q Pos/Entries
11	JAPANESE GP	Mount Fuji	52	Heros Racing	B	3.0 Kojima KE009-Cosworth V8	2 laps behind	11/23

GP Starts: 2   GP Wins: 0   Pole positions: 0   Fastest laps: 0   Points: 0

INGO HOFFMANN

A TALENTED driver, Ingo Hoffmann's potential as a Formula 1 racer was laid waste by a disastrous spell in the Fittipaldi brothers' Copersucar team. That lost opportunity for worldwide fame has since been forgotten, however, for Ingo became Brazil's greatest ever stock car driver, breaking all records in the process.

A top Super Vee and saloon car driver in his native country, Ingo travelled to Britain in 1975 with the support of Wilson Fittipaldi and contested the F3 series in a March. A handful of F5000 appearances were also arranged so that he could become acclimatised to big-engined single-seaters, before his planned move into Formula 1 with Fittipaldi.

With the team beset by all sorts of problems, inevitably Hoffmann's difficulties were very much secondary to those of the team leader, and he was only given four outings in 1976. Even worse followed. After just two races of the 1977 season, the second car was withdrawn, leaving Ingo to concentrate on a programme of Formula 2 for Project Four with a Ralt. Although outright success eluded him in this class, he proved to be a very quick and tough competitor, producing some great performances, particularly in 1978, his last season in Europe, in the Project Four March. It is a shame that a second grand prix chance did not go the Brazilian's way.

On his return home in 1979, Ingo became a participant in the newly formed Brazilian Stock Car Championship, and his first title came the following year. He went on to amass an incredible 12 titles, three of which were shared with Antonio Giombelli. At the end of 2008, the now legendary Hoffmann took honourable retirement after 30 consecutive seasons in the class.

KAZUYOSHI HOSHINO

H IS remarkable performance in the rain-sodden 1976 Japanese GP with a private Tyrrell on Bridgestone tyres confirmed Kazuyoshi Hoshino as one of Japan's leading drivers. Indeed, many believe he is Japan's greatest ever racer

Kazuyoshi was a works Nissan driver as far back as 1969, and since then he swept the board in many forms of domestic racing, being a four-times Formula 2/F3000 champion, as well as a multiple grand champion. The 1993 season saw the veteran snatch the Japanese F3000 title for the third time, at the wheel of a Lola, from the grasp of a clutch of young and hungry European drivers. Typically, he continued to be ultra-competitive in Formula Nippon right up to the end of 1996, his final year in single-seaters.

Hoshino was also a regular member of the Nissan sports car team, winning the Daytona 24-hours in 1992 with compatriots Masahiro Hasemi and Toshio Suzuki. He also finished third at Le Mans in 1998 in the Nissan R390, with Aguri Suzuki and Masahiro Kageyama.

In 1994, Kazuyoshi took the All-Japan touring car title outright, having previously shared the crown with Toshio Suzuki in 1990. Then he concentrated on racing a Nissan in the Japanese GT and Touring Car championships. Suffering from persistent back problems, however, he finally called it a day in 2002 to concentrate on running his own Formula Nippon team.

NICO HÜLKENBERG

WITH a CV as impressive as Nico Hülkenberg's, one would have expected him to have been given a place in a top Formula 1 team, but thus far the very talented German has been restricted to showing flashes of brilliance, highlighted by his opportunistic pole position for Williams on a damp track for the 2010 Brazilian Grand Prix. Hülkenberg's junior career was truly stellar. In karting, he won junior and senior titles in both Germany and Italy, and on moving to cars in 2005 he immediately dominated in Formula BMW, winning nine of the 20 races to edge out Sébastien Buemi. Then he stepped up to the German F3 series and took a win in his rookie season, but his career profile was raised immensely when he tore up the 2006/07 season in the A1GP series. Representing his country, he took the title virtually single-handedly with nine wins from just 20 starts.

Not surprisingly, Nico was hot property and joined the ASM team for 2007, when he finished a solid third, behind team-mate Romain Grosjean. The following year was all about 'The Hulk' as he won seven of the season's feature races to take a crushing Euroseries championship victory and his inevitable promotion to GP2. Being given a seat in the ART team was a huge plus, but he proved just how rapidly he had progressed, by dominating the series in his rookie year, recording five wins on the way to the title.

Starting his Formula 1 career at Williams with the vastly experienced Rubens Barrichello was a perfect way for young Nico to learn the ropes. Scoring a point in only his third race helped ease the pressure, and although there were a few indifferent races, his performances in qualifying, where he made Q3 on seven occasions, showed he had the speed. Despite his impressive debut year, however, he lost his place to Pastor Maldonado, but soon joined Force India as their third driver for 2011. The German's rapid rise was brought to a temporary halt, but his employment as partner to Paul di Resta in 2012 promises to be very interesting indeed as both talented drivers battle for supremacy.

HÜLKENBERG, Nico (D) b 19/8/1987, Emmerich

2010 Championship position: 14   Wins: 0   Pole positions: 1   Fastest laps: 0   Points scored: 22

	Race	Circuit	No	Entrant	Tyres	Capacity/Car/Engine	Comment	Q Pos/Entries
14	BAHRAIN GP	Sakhir Circuit	10	AT&T Williams	B	2.4 Williams FW32 Cosworth V8	spin- extra pit stop/1 lap behind	13/24
ret	AUSTRALIAN GP	Melbourne	10	AT&T Williams	B	2.4 Williams FW32 Cosworth V8	multiple collision on lap 1	8/24
10	MALAYSIAN GP	Sepang	10	AT&T Williams	B	2.4 Williams FW32 Cosworth V8	extra stop – faulty steering wheel	5/24
15	CHINESE GP	Shanghai Circuit	10	AT&T Williams	B	2.4 Williams FW32 Cosworth V8	1 lap behind	16/24
16	SPANISH GP	Barcelona	10	AT&T Williams	B	2.4 Williams FW32 Cosworth V8	damaged floor/2 laps behind	13/24
ret	MONACO GP	Monte Carlo	10	AT&T Williams	B	2.4 Williams FW32 Cosworth V8	lost front wing – accident on lap 1	11/24
17	TURKISH GP	Istanbul Park	10	AT&T Williams	B	2.4 Williams FW32 Cosworth V8	collision Buemi– puncture/-1 lap	15/24
13	CANADIAN GP	Montreal	10	AT&T Williams	B	2.4 Williams FW32 Cosworth V8	1 lap behind	12/24
ret	EUROPEAN GP	Valencia	10	AT&T Williams	B	2.4 Williams FW32 Cosworth V8	overheating exhaust/tyre damage	8/24
10	BRITISH GP	Silverstone	10	AT&T Williams	B	2.4 Williams FW32 Cosworth V8		13/24
13	GERMAN GP	Hockenheim	10	AT&T Williams	B	2.4 Williams FW32 Cosworth V8	left out on supersofts too long/-1 lap	10/24
6	HUNGARIAN GP	Hungaroring	10	AT&T Williams	B	2.4 Williams FW32 Cosworth V8		10/24
14	BELGIAN GP	Spa	10	AT&T Williams	B	2.4 Williams FW32 Cosworth V8	electrical problems/1 lap behind	8/24
7	ITALIAN GP	Monza	10	AT&T Williams	B	2.4 Williams FW32 Cosworth V8	good battle with Webber	8/24
10	SINGAPORE GP	Yas Marina Circuit	10	AT&T Williams	B	2.4 Williams FW32 Cosworth V8	20-sec penalty for missing chicane	12/24
ret	JAPANESE GP	Suzuka	10	AT&T Williams	B	2.4 Williams FW32 Cosworth V8	suspension/hit by Petrov on lap 1	9/24
10	KOREAN GP	Yeongam	10	AT&T Williams	B	2.4 Williams FW32 Cosworth V8	late stop for slow puncture	11/24
8	BRAZILIAN GP	Interlagos	10	AT&T Williams	B	2.4 Williams FW32 Cosworth V8	vibration problems/1 lap behind	1/24
16	ABU DHABI GP	Yas Marina Circuit	10	AT&T Williams	B	2.4 Williams FW32 Cosworth V8		15/24

2011 Championship position: Unplaced

	Race	Circuit	No	Entrant	Tyres	Capacity/Car/Engine	Comment	Q Pos/Entries
app	AUSTRALIAN GP	Melbourne	15	Force India F1 Team	P	2.4 Force India VJM04-Mercedes V8	ran as 3rd driver in practice 1 only	– / –
app	MALAYSIAN GP	Sepang	15	Force India F1 Team	P	2.4 Force India VJM04-Mercedes V8	ran as 3rd driver in practice 1 only	– / –
app	CHINESE GP	Shanghai Circuit	14	Force India F1 Team	P	2.4 Force India VJM04-Mercedes V8	ran as 3rd driver in practice 1 only	– / –
app	TURKISH GP	Istanbul Park	14	Force India F1 Team	P	2.4 Force India VJM04-Mercedes V8	ran as 3rd driver in practice 1 only	– / –
app	SPANISH GP	Barcelona	15	Force India F1 Team	P	2.4 Force India VJM04-Mercedes V8	ran as 3rd driver in practice 1 only	– / –
app	CANADIAN GP	Montreal	14	Force India F1 Team	P	2.4 Force India VJM04-Mercedes V8	ran as 3rd driver in practice 1 only	– / –
app	EUROPEAN GP	Valencia	15	Force India F1 Team	P	2.4 Force India VJM04-Mercedes V8	ran as 3rd driver in practice 1 only	– / –
app	BRITISH GP	Silverstone	14	Force India F1 Team	P	2.4 Force India VJM04-Mercedes V8	ran as 3rd driver in practice 1 only	– / –
app	GERMAN GP	Hockenheim	15	Force India F1 Team	P	2.4 Force India VJM04-Mercedes V8	ran as 3rd driver in practice 1 only	– / –
app	HUNGARIAN GP	Hungaroring	14	Force India F1 Team	P	2.4 Force India VJM04-Mercedes V8	ran as 3rd driver in practice 1 only	– / –
app	BELGIAN GP	Spa	14	Force India F1 Team	P	2.4 Force India VJM04-Mercedes V8	ran as 3rd driver in practice 2 only	– / –
app	ITALIAN GP	Monza	15	Force India F1 Team	P	2.4 Force India VJM04-Mercedes V8	ran as 3rd driver in practice 1 only	– / –
app	JAPANESE GP	Suzuka	14	Force India F1 Team	P	2.4 Force India VJM04-Mercedes V8	ran as 3rd driver in practice 1 only	– / –
app	BRAZILIAN GP	Interlagos	14	Sahara Force India F1 Team	P	2.4 Force India VJM04-Mercedes V8	ran as 3rd driver in practice 1 only	– / –

GP Starts: 19   GP Wins: 0   Pole positions: 0   Fastest laps: 1   Points: 22

IF there can be such a thing as an unfashionable world champion, then Denny Hulme was just that. Self-effacing to the point of anonymity in his public persona, he eschewed the glamorous trappings that grand prix racing had to offer, but in fact he was no shrinking violet and his inner determination was second to none, born of many years working as a humble mechanic.

After making an impact on the local scene, Hulme travelled to Europe in 1960 with George Lawton on the 'New Zealand Driver to Europe' scheme, racing a Cooper in Formula 2 and Formula Junior around the Continent. Unfortunately poor Lawton was killed at Roskilde Ring, but Hulme carried on before returning home to contest his local series early in 1961. He was soon back in Europe, however, carving out a reputation for himself in Ken Tyrrell's Cooper and the works Brabham, having replaced the retired Gavin Youl.

While still working as a mechanic at Brabham, Hulme took over the leadership of the Junior team in 1963, winning seven of the 14 races he entered. Although top-flight chances were limited, Jack was shrewd enough to realise the young New Zealander's potential and took him down to the 1964 Tasman series, where he won at Levin and finished second in the New Zealand GP. Supporting his boss in the Formula 2 championship that year, Denny won two races, at Clermont Ferrand and Zolder, with plenty of other good placings besides. In 1965, Brabham had the problem of running himself, Dan Gurney and Hulme, so he shuffled the pack to ensure that Hulme was well prepared for the 3-litre formula; Denny backed 'Black Jack' superbly in 1966 as his mentor enjoyed an Indian summer and took the championship. As well as having another successful Formula 2 season, he also raced sports cars, taking second place at Le Mans with Ken Miles in a Ford GT40, and winning the Tourist Trophy and Martini International in Sid Taylor's Lola.

In 1967, it was Hulme's turn to take the spotlight. His wins in the Monaco and German GPs were the outstanding performances, but he scored points in all but two races to edge out his boss and claim the drivers' crown for himself. Typically thinking ahead, Denny had already decided to join forces with fellow 'Kiwi' Bruce McLaren in 1968, and he started the year in the team's new bright orange livery. An early-season win in the International Trophy and then third to Bruce in the Race of Champions indicated things were on the right track, and sure enough Hulme's consistent approach put him in with an outside chance of the title after wins at Monza and Mont Tremblant. In the end, though, his efforts fell short, but as a team McLaren had established themselves as a front-line outfit in both Formula 1 and Can-Am, which proved a lucrative sideline for both driver and constructor. Hulme took the Can-Am title that year, but this success could have been a double-edged sword, for the 1969 grand prix season only provided Denny with an end-of-season win in Mexico.

The following season should have been a real breakthrough year for the team, but instead it was one of catastrophe as McLaren was killed in a testing accident and Hulme was involved in a practice crash at Indy, which left him with nasty burns to hands and feet. That the team recovered so well from Bruce's loss was a great credit to Denny, who hid his own devastation and gave the team a new sense of purpose by winning the Can-Am championship for the second time. From then on, the tough New Zealander's approach became more circumspect. If he could sniff the scent of victory, he would really get stuck in, as we saw at Kyalami in 1972 and in Sweden in 1973, but generally he drove within his limits. He was always a factor, even in his final season in 1974, when he pounced to claim a win in Argentina after a patient race. But after he had been on the scene of Peter Revson's fatal accident at Kyalami, he was generally content to let younger lions risk their necks before unobtrusively easing himself into a retirement of sorts.

Although Formula 1 was in the past, the lure of competition was too strong for Hulme, and from 1978 he raced touring cars and trucks as and when the fancy took him, with all the grit and determination he had showed in his heyday. He was competing in the Bathurst 1000km in October, 1992, when suddenly he swiped the Armco barrier, before veering his BMW M3 across the track onto the grass alongside the opposite barrier. For a while nothing happened, and when marshals arrived they found that Denny was dead, still strapped into the car, having apparently suffered a heart attack at the early age of 56.

HULME, Denny (Clive Denis) (NZ) b 18/6/1936, Nelson – d 4/10/1992, Bathurst Circuit, NSW, Australia

1965 Championship position: 11th   Wins: 0   Pole positions: 0   Fastest laps: 0   Points scored: 5

	Race	Circuit	No	Entrant	Tyres	Capacity/Car/Engine	Comment	Q Pos/Entries
8	MONACO GP	Monte Carlo	2	Brabham Racing Organisation	G	1.5 Brabham BT7-Climax V8	pit stop/8 laps behind	8/17
4	FRENCH GP	Clermont Ferrand	16	Brabham Racing Organisation	G	1.5 Brabham BT11-Climax V8		6/17
ret	BRITISH GP	Silverstone	14	Brabham Racing Organisation	G	1.5 Brabham BT7-Climax V8	alternator belt	=9/23
5	DUTCH GP	Zandvoort	14	Brabham Racing Organisation	G	1.5 Brabham BT11-Climax V8	1 lap behind	7/17
ret	GERMAN GP	Nürburgring	6	Brabham Racing Organisation	G	1.5 Brabham BT7-Climax V8	fuel leak	13/22
ret	ITALIAN GP	Monza	14	Brabham Racing Organisation	G	1.5 Brabham BT11-Climax V8	suspension	12/23

1966 Championship position: 4th   Wins: 0   Pole positions: 0   Fastest laps: 1   Points scored: 18

	Race	Circuit	No	Entrant	Tyres	Capacity/Car/Engine	Comment	Q Pos/Entries
ret	MONACO GP	Monte Carlo	8	Brabham Racing Organisation	G	2.5 Brabham BT22-Climax 4	driveshaft	6/16
ret	BELGIAN GP	Spa	4	Brabham Racing Organisation	G	2.5 Brabham BT22-Climax 4	collision with Siffert	13/18
3	FRENCH GP	Reims	14	Brabham Racing Organisation	G	3.0 Brabham BT20-Repco V8	fuel pick up problem/2 laps behind	9/17
dns	"	"	12	Brabham Racing Organisation	G	3.0 Brabham BT19-Repco V8	practice only	– / –
2	BRITISH GP	Brands Hatch	6	Brabham Racing Organisation	G	3.0 Brabham BT20-Repco V8		2/20
ret	DUTCH GP	Zandvoort	18	Brabham Racing Organisation	G	3.0 Brabham BT20-Repco V8	ignition/FL	=2/18
ret	GERMAN GP	Nürburgring	4	Brabham Racing Organisation	G	3.0 Brabham BT20-Repco V8	ignition	16/30
3	ITALIAN GP	Monza	12	Brabham Racing Organisation	G	3.0 Brabham BT20-Repco V8		10/22
ret	US GP	Watkins Glen	6	Brabham Racing Organisation	G	3.0 Brabham BT20-Repco V8	oil pressure	7/19
3	MEXICAN GP	Mexico City	6	Brabham Racing Organisation	G	3.0 Brabham BT20-Repco V8	1 lap behind	6/19

1967 WORLD CHAMPION   Wins: 2   Pole positions: 0   Fastest laps: 2   Points scored: 51

	Race	Circuit	No	Entrant	Tyres	Capacity/Car/Engine	Comment	Q Pos/Entries
4	SOUTH AFRICAN GP	Kyalami	2	Brabham Racing Organisation	G	3.0 Brabham BT20-Repco V8	2 pit stops – brakes/FL/2 laps behind	2/18
1	MONACO GP	Monte Carlo	9	Brabham Racing Organisation	G	3.0 Brabham BT20-Repco V8		=4/18
3	DUTCH GP	Zandvoort	2	Brabham Racing Organisation	G	3.0 Brabham BT20-Repco V8		=6/17
ret	BELGIAN GP	Spa	26	Brabham Racing Organisation	G	3.0 Brabham BT19-Repco V8	engine	14/18
2	FRENCH GP	Le Mans	4	Brabham Racing Organisation	G	3.0 Brabham BT24-Repco V8		6/15
2	BRITISH GP	Silverstone	2	Brabham Racing Organisation	G	3.0 Brabham BT24-Repco V8	FL	4/21
1	GERMAN GP	Nürburgring	2	Brabham Racing Organisation	G	3.0 Brabham BT24-Repco V8		2/25
2	CANADIAN GP	Mosport Park	2	Brabham Racing Organisation	G	3.0 Brabham BT24-Repco V8		3/19
ret	ITALIAN GP	Monza	18	Brabham Racing Organisation	G	3.0 Brabham BT24-Repco V8	overheating engine	6/18

Mr Consistency. Denny Hulme was crowned the 1967 world champion after posting eight points-scoring finishes from 11 races. The undoubted highlights were high-profile wins at Monte Carlo and the Nürburgring *(right)* with his Brabham BT24-Repco.

3	US GP	Watkins Glen	2	Brabham Racing Organisation	G	3.0 Brabham BT24-Repco V8	1 lap behind	6/18
3	MEXICAN GP	Mexico City	2	Brabham Racing Organisation	G	3.0 Brabham BT24-Repco V8	1 lap behind	6/19

1968 Championship position: 3rd   Wins: 2   Pole positions: 0   Fastest laps: 0   Points scored: 33

5	SOUTH AFRICAN GP	Kyalami	1	Bruce McLaren Motor Racing	G	3.0 McLaren M5A-BRM V12	2 laps behind	9/23
2	SPANISH GP	Jarama	1	Bruce McLaren Motor Racing	G	3.0 McLaren M7A-Cosworth V8		3/14
5	MONACO GP	Monte Carlo	12	Bruce McLaren Motor Racing	G	3.0 McLaren M7A-Cosworth V8	long pit stop – driveshaft/-7 laps	=9/18
ret	BELGIAN GP	Spa	6	Bruce McLaren Motor Racing	G	3.0 McLaren M7A-Cosworth V8	driveshaft	5/18
ret	DUTCH GP	Zandvoort	1	Bruce McLaren Motor Racing	G	3.0 McLaren M7A-Cosworth V8	damp ignition	7/19
5	FRENCH GP	Rouen	8	Bruce McLaren Motor Racing	G	3.0 McLaren M7A-Cosworth V8	2 laps behind	4/18
4	BRITISH GP	Brands Hatch	1	Bruce McLaren Motor Racing	G	3.0 McLaren M7A-Cosworth V8	1 lap behind	=10/20
7	GERMAN GP	Nürburgring	1	Bruce McLaren Motor Racing	G	3.0 McLaren M7A-Cosworth V8		11/20
1	ITALIAN GP	Monza	1	Bruce McLaren Motor Racing	G	3.0 McLaren M7A-Cosworth V8		7/24
1	CANADIAN GP	St Jovite	1	Bruce McLaren Motor Racing	G	3.0 McLaren M7A-Cosworth V8		=6/22
ret	US GP	Watkins Glen	1	Bruce McLaren Motor Racing	G	3.0 McLaren M7A-Cosworth V8	spun off	5/21
ret	MEXICAN GP	Mexico City	1	Bruce McLaren Motor Racing	G	3.0 McLaren M7A-Cosworth V8	suspension collapsed – crashed	4/21

1969 Championship position: 6th   Wins: 1   Pole positions: 0   Fastest laps: 0   Points scored: 20

3	SOUTH AFRICAN GP	Kyalami	5	Bruce McLaren Motor Racing	G	3.0 McLaren M7A-Cosworth V8		3/18
4	SPANISH GP	Montjuich Park	5	Bruce McLaren Motor Racing	G	3.0 McLaren M7A-Cosworth V8		8/14
6	MONACO GP	Monte Carlo	3	Bruce McLaren Motor Racing	G	3.0 McLaren M7A-Cosworth V8	pit stop – handling/3 laps behind	12/16
4	DUTCH GP	Zandvoort	7	Bruce McLaren Motor Racing	G	3.0 McLaren M7A-Cosworth V8	unwell/2 laps behind	7/15
8	FRENCH GP	Clermont Ferrand	4	Bruce McLaren Motor Racing	G	3.0 McLaren M7A-Cosworth V8	brake problems/3 laps behind	2/13
ret	BRITISH GP	Silverstone	5	Bruce McLaren Motor Racing	G	3.0 McLaren M7A-Cosworth V8	engine	3/17
ret	GERMAN GP	Nürburgring	9	Bruce McLaren Motor Racing	G	3.0 McLaren M7A-Cosworth V8	transmission	5/26
7	ITALIAN GP	Monza	16	Bruce McLaren Motor Racing	G	3.0 McLaren M7A-Cosworth V8	brake problems/2 laps behind	2/15
ret	CANADIAN GP	Mosport Park	5	Bruce McLaren Motor Racing	G	3.0 McLaren M7A-Cosworth V8	distributor	=5/20
ret	US GP	Watkins Glen	5	Bruce McLaren Motor Racing	G	3.0 McLaren M7A-Cosworth V8	gear selection	2/18
1	MEXICAN GP	Mexico City	5	Bruce McLaren Motor Racing	G	3.0 McLaren M7A-Cosworth V8		4/17

1970 Championship position: 4th   Wins: 0   Pole positions: 0   Fastest laps: 0   Points scored: 27

2	SOUTH AFRICAN GP	Kyalami	6	Bruce McLaren Motor Racing	G	3.0 McLaren M14A-Cosworth V8		6/24
ret	SPANISH GP	Jarama	5	Bruce McLaren Motor Racing	G	3.0 McLaren M14A-Cosworth V8	rotor arm shaft	2/22
4	MONACO GP	Monte Carlo	11	Bruce McLaren Motor Racing	G	3.0 McLaren M14A-Cosworth V8		3/21
4	FRENCH GP	Clermont Ferrand	19	Bruce McLaren Motor Racing	G	3.0 McLaren M14D-Cosworth V8		7/23
3	BRITISH GP	Brands Hatch	9	Bruce McLaren Motor Racing	G	3.0 McLaren M14D-Cosworth V8		=4/25
3	GERMAN GP	Hockenheim	4	Bruce McLaren Motor Racing	G	3.0 McLaren M14A-Cosworth V8		16/25
ret	AUSTRIAN GP	Österreichring	21	Bruce McLaren Motor Racing	G	3.0 McLaren M14A-Cosworth V8	engine	=11/24
4	ITALIAN GP	Monza	30	Bruce McLaren Motor Racing	G	3.0 McLaren M14A-Cosworth V8		9/27
ret	CANADIAN GP	St Jovite	5	Bruce McLaren Motor Racing	G	3.0 McLaren M14A-Cosworth V8	flywheel	15/20
7	US GP	Watkins Glen	8	Bruce McLaren Motor Racing	G	3.0 McLaren M14A-Cosworth V8	2 laps behind	11/27
3	MEXICAN GP	Mexico City	8	Bruce McLaren Motor Racing	G	3.0 McLaren M14A-Cosworth V8		14/18

1971 Championship position: 9   Wins: 0   Pole positions: 0   Fastest laps: 1   Points scored: 9

6	SOUTH AFRICAN GP	Kyalami	11	Bruce McLaren Motor Racing	G	3.0 McLaren M19A-Cosworth V8	suspension problems/1 lap behind	=5/25
5	SPANISH GP	Montjuich Park	9	Bruce McLaren Motor Racing	G	3.0 McLaren M19A-Cosworth V8		9/22
4	MONACO GP	Monte Carlo	9	Bruce McLaren Motor Racing	G	3.0 McLaren M19A-Cosworth V8		6/23
12	DUTCH GP	Zandvoort	26	Bruce McLaren Motor Racing	G	3.0 McLaren M19A-Cosworth V8	7 laps behind	14/24
ret	FRENCH GP	Paul Ricard	9	Bruce McLaren Motor Racing	G	3.0 McLaren M19A-Cosworth V8	ignition	11/24
ret	BRITISH GP	Silverstone	9	Bruce McLaren Motor Racing	G	3.0 McLaren M19A-Cosworth V8	engine	8/24
ret	GERMAN GP	Nürburgring	18	Bruce McLaren Motor Racing	G	3.0 McLaren M19A-Cosworth V8	fuel leak	6/23
ret	AUSTRIAN GP	Österreichring	9	Bruce McLaren Motor Racing	G	3.0 McLaren M19A-Cosworth V8	engine	9/22
4	CANADIAN GP	Mosport Park	9	Bruce McLaren Motor Racing	G	3.0 McLaren M19A-Cosworth V8	FL/1 lap behind	10/27
ret	US GP	Watkins Glen	7	Bruce McLaren Motor Racing	G	3.0 McLaren M19A-Cosworth V8	spun off on oil	3/32

1972 Championship position: 3rd   Wins: 1   Pole positions: 0   Fastest laps: 1   Points scored: 39

Pos	GP	Circuit	No	Team	Tyre	Car	Notes	Grid
2	ARGENTINE GP	Buenos Aires	17	Yardley Team McLaren	G	3.0 McLaren M19A-Cosworth V8		4/22
1	SOUTH AFRICAN GP	Kyalami	12	Yardley Team McLaren	G	3.0 McLaren M19A-Cosworth V8		=3/27
ret	SPANISH GP	Jarama	11	Yardley Team McLaren	G	3.0 McLaren M19C-Cosworth V8	gearbox	2/26
dns	"	"	11	Yardley Team McLaren	G	3.0 McLaren M19C-Cosworth V8	practice only	-/-
15	MONACO GP	Monte Carlo	14	Yardley Team McLaren	G	3.0 McLaren M19C-Cosworth V8	hit guard rail/6 laps behind	7/25
dns	"	" "	14T	Yardley Team McLaren	G	3.0 McLaren M19A-Cosworth V8	practice only	-/-
3	BELGIAN GP	Nivelles	9	Yardley Team McLaren	G	3.0 McLaren M19A-Cosworth V8		3/26
dns	"	"	9T	Yardley Team McLaren	G	3.0 McLaren M19A-Cosworth V8	practice only - not timed	-/-
7	FRENCH GP	Clermont Ferrand	2	Yardley Team McLaren	G	3.0 McLaren M19C-Cosworth V8	pit stop - puncture	2/29
dns	"	" "	2T	Yardley Team McLaren	G	3.0 McLaren M19A-Cosworth V8	practice only	-/-
5	BRITISH GP	Brands Hatch	18	Yardley Team McLaren	G	3.0 McLaren M19C-Cosworth V8	1 lap behind	=11/27
ret	GERMAN GP	Nürburgring	3	Yardley Team McLaren	G	3.0 McLaren M19C-Cosworth V8	engine	10/27
2	AUSTRIAN GP	Österreichring	12	Yardley Team McLaren	G	3.0 McLaren M19C-Cosworth V8	FL	7/26
dns	"	"	12T	Yardley Team McLaren	G	3.0 McLaren M19A-Cosworth V8	practice only	-/-
3	ITALIAN GP	Monza	14	Yardley Team McLaren	G	3.0 McLaren M19C-Cosworth V8		5/27
dns	"	"	14T	Yardley Team McLaren	G	3.0 McLaren M19A-Cosworth V8	practice only	-/-
3	CANADIAN GP	Mosport Park	18	Yardley Team McLaren	G	3.0 McLaren M19C-Cosworth V8		2/25
dns	"	"	18T	Yardley Team McLaren	G	3.0 McLaren M19A-Cosworth V8	practice only	-/-
3	US GP	Watkins Glen	19	Yardley Team McLaren	G	3.0 McLaren M19C-Cosworth V8		3/22

1973 Championship position: 6th   Wins: 1   Pole positions: 1   Fastest laps: 3 (1 shared)   Points scored: 26

Pos	GP	Circuit	No	Team	Tyre	Car	Notes	Grid
5	ARGENTINE GP	Buenos Aires	14	Yardley Team McLaren	G	3.0 McLaren M19C-Cosworth V8	1 lap behind	8/19
3	BRAZILIAN GP	Interlagos	7	Yardley Team McLaren	G	3.0 McLaren M19C-Cosworth V8	FL (shared with Fittipaldi)	5/20
5	SOUTH AFRICAN GP	Kyalami	5	Yardley Team McLaren	G	3.0 McLaren M23-Cosworth V8	pit stop - puncture/2 laps behind	1/25
6	SPANISH GP	Montjuich Park	5	Yardley Team McLaren	G	3.0 McLaren M23-Cosworth V8	pit stop - wheel/1 lap behind	2/22
7	BELGIAN GP	Zolder	7	Yardley Team McLaren	G	3.0 McLaren M23-Cosworth V8	spin - pit stop/3 laps behind	2/23
6	MONACO GP	Monte Carlo	7	Yardley Team McLaren	G	3.0 McLaren M23-Cosworth V8	pit stop - gear linkage/2 laps behind	3/26
1	SWEDISH GP	Anderstorp	7	Yardley Team McLaren	G	3.0 McLaren M23-Cosworth V8	FL	6/22
8	FRENCH GP	Paul Ricard	7	Yardley Team McLaren	G	3.0 McLaren M23-Cosworth V8	pit stop - tyre/FL	6/25
3	BRITISH GP	Silverstone	7	Yardley Team McLaren	G	3.0 McLaren M23-Cosworth V8		=2/29
ret	DUTCH GP	Zandvoort	7	Yardley Team McLaren	G	3.0 McLaren M23-Cosworth V8	engine	4/24
12	GERMAN GP	Nürburgring	7	Yardley Team McLaren	G	3.0 McLaren M23-Cosworth V8	pit stop - exhaust	8/23
8	AUSTRIAN GP	Österreichring	7	Yardley Team McLaren	G	3.0 McLaren M23-Cosworth V8	3 pit stops - plugs/1 lap behind	3/25
15	ITALIAN GP	Monza	7	Yardley Team McLaren	G	3.0 McLaren M23-Cosworth V8	spin - pit stop/2 laps behind	3/25
13	CANADIAN GP	Mosport Park	7	Yardley Team McLaren	G	3.0 McLaren M23-Cosworth V8	pit stop - puncture/5 laps behind	7/26
4	US GP	Watkins Glen	7	Yardley Team McLaren	G	3.0 McLaren M23-Cosworth V8		9/28

1974 Championship position: 7th   Wins: 1   Pole positions: 0   Fastest laps: 1   Points scored: 20

Pos	GP	Circuit	No	Team	Tyre	Car	Notes	Grid
1	ARGENTINE GP	Buenos Aires	6	Marlboro Team Texaco	G	3.0 McLaren M23-Cosworth V8		10/26
12	BRAZILIAN GP	Interlagos	6	Marlboro Team Texaco	G	3.0 McLaren M23-Cosworth V8	pit stop - front tyres/1 lap behind	11/25
9	SOUTH AFRICAN GP	Kyalami	6	Marlboro Team Texaco	G	3.0 McLaren M23-Cosworth V8	1 lap behind	9/27
6	SPANISH GP	Jarama	56	Marlboro Team Texaco	G	3.0 McLaren M23-Cosworth V8	pit stop - suspension/2 laps behind	8/28
6	BELGIAN GP	Nivelles	6	Marlboro Team Texaco	G	3.0 McLaren M23-Cosworth V8	FL	12/32
ret	MONACO GP	Monte Carlo	6	Marlboro Team Texaco	G	3.0 McLaren M23-Cosworth V8	collision with Beltoise	=12/28
ret	SWEDISH GP	Anderstorp	6	Marlboro Team Texaco	G	3.0 McLaren M23-Cosworth V8	suspension	12/28
ret	DUTCH GP	Zandvoort	6	Marlboro Team Texaco	G	3.0 McLaren M23-Cosworth V8	ignition	9/27
6	FRENCH GP	Dijon	6	Marlboro Team Texaco	G	3.0 McLaren M23-Cosworth V8		11/30
7	BRITISH GP	Brands Hatch	6	Marlboro Team Texaco	G	3.0 McLaren M23-Cosworth V8	1 lap behind	=19/34
ret	GERMAN GP	Nürburgring	6	Marlboro Team Texaco	G	3.0 McLaren M23-Cosworth V8	accident on starting grid	7/32
dsq*	"	"	5T	Marlboro Team Texaco	G	3.0 McLaren M23-Cosworth V8	*restarted illegally from pits in spare car	-/-
2	AUSTRIAN GP	Österreichring	6	Marlboro Team Texaco	G	3.0 McLaren M23-Cosworth V8		10/31
6	ITALIAN GP	Monza	6	Marlboro Team Texaco	G	3.0 McLaren M23-Cosworth V8	1 lap behind	19/31
6	CANADIAN GP	Mosport Park	6	Marlboro Team Texaco	G	3.0 McLaren M23-Cosworth V8	1 lap behind	14/30
ret	US GP	Watkins Glen	6	Marlboro Team Texaco	G	3.0 McLaren M23-Cosworth V8	engine	17/30

GP Starts: 112   GP Wins: 8   Pole positions: 1   Fastest laps: 9 (1 shared)   Points: 248

Hulme's final season opened with his eighth and final grand prix win in the 1974 Argentine Grand Prix, before 'The Bear' slipped quietly away from the scene, having made a tremendous contribution to both the Brabham and McLaren marques.

SOME drivers are cut out for the big stage, and undoubtedly James Hunt was a prime example. Here was a man who, having been quick, but not at all convincing in his early career, took to grand prix racing like the proverbial duck to water, confounding his critics, who had given him the unkind, but not entirely inappropriate nickname of 'Hunt the Shunt'.

Despite being the son of a Surrey stockbroker, James had to finance his early racing career largely from his own pocket, stacking the shelves in his local Sainsbury's supermarket to be able to race his Mini, before moving into Formula Ford in 1968 with an Alexis and then a Merlyn Mk11A in 1969. Mid-way through the season, he moved up to F3 with a Brabham BT21B, but found the competition hot, gaining success only in Libre events at Brands Hatch.

It was during the 1970 season, when James was equipped with a Lotus 59, that people began to sit up and take notice, and not only because of his wins at Rouen and Zolder, for late in the season he was involved in a last-corner collision with Dave Morgan, which saw the irate James exact pugilistic retribution on the spot. His penchant for attracting controversy followed him into the 1971 season, which was littered with accidents and mechanical gremlins, but once again he proved beyond doubt that when trouble stayed away he was a serious contender. March certainly thought so, as they signed him for their STP-backed works car in 1972, but the team fell apart and James joined forces with Lord Hesketh's Dastle F3 team. Almost immediately, Hesketh took the plunge into Formula 2 and Hunt placed the team's car on the front row at the Salzburgring in his first race. After a really good drive, he was forced to pull out with engine trouble, but crucially he had proved to himself that he was good enough. In the next race, he gave a superb display at Oulton Park to finish third. Now there was no stopping the upward momentum of 'young Master James'.

Third place in the 1973 Race of Champions with a hired Surtees convinced Lord Hesketh that Hunt had the talent for the big time, and James proved that his faith was not misplaced, putting in some sensational performances once the team had acquired a March 731. His drives at Zandvoort and Watkins Glen, where he dogged the Lotus of Ronnie Peterson, stood out. The Hesketh bandwagon was really gathering pace by then, and in 1974 the team launched their own car, which proved an immediate success. Hunt won the International Trophy before embarking on an up-and-down grand prix season, which was marred by trivial mechanical failures and some misjudgements on the part of the driver. However, it included some race-performance gems, such as in Austria, where he drove from 18th after a pit stop to third at the finish. His reputation was such that Dan Gurney invited him to the States to drive his Eagle in US F5000 for three races, his best result being a second at the Monterey GP. He also sampled sports cars, taking fourth at the Nürburgring 750km with Vern Schuppan and Derek Bell in John Wyer's Gulf-Ford.

That Hunt was a top-drawer racer was finally confirmed in 1975, when he drove the Hesketh to a magnificent win in the Dutch GP, defeating Niki Lauda's Ferrari. To prove it was no fluke, he took three second places that year before the financial burden of running the team independently became too great for its aristocratic patron. Briefly, James looked to be without a drive for 1976, but with Emerson Fittipaldi's sudden defection to his family's Copersucar-backed project, he found himself alongside Jochen Mass at McLaren. It was a season of high drama, controversy and courage, which saw James and great pal Lauda fight it out for the championship in a fashion that captured the imagination of the world and surely was instrumental in increasing the sport's popularity in subsequent years.

James soon asserted his number-one status in the team by claiming pole in Brazil, and then winning the Race of Champions and International Trophy. His first grand prix win for McLaren was contentious. He was reinstated after a post-race disqualification in Spain, but a victory in France kept him in touch, and then came the famous British GP at Brands. Having been taken out by Clay Regazzoni in a first-corner mêlée, he won the restarted race, but then was disqualified. His championship chances seemed over, but after Lauda's fiery accident at the Nürburgring, he had an outside chance. By the time the Austrian had bravely returned to the cockpit, Hunt had made inroads into his points lead, and once on a roll he proved difficult to resist, with two brilliant wins in Canada and the USA. The showdown in Japan was hyped more intensely than anything ever seen before, and while his rival withdrew, he stayed out on a flooded track to take third place and the coveted championship.

By then, James was a public figure way beyond the confines of the sport, and perhaps this began to affect his racing. In 1977, he still put in some superb performances to win at Silverstone, Watkins Glen and Fuji, but his refusal to appear on the rostrum at the final race showed the more petulant side of his nature. By that time, the ground-effect Lotus was in the ascendancy and McLaren were slow to follow this route, which left Hunt struggling in 1978, although it has to be said that the driver's apparent lack of motivation certainly didn't help matters. Feeling a move would be beneficial for all concerned, he switched to Walter Wolf for one final season in 1979, but the car proved difficult to handle and he seemed generally disinclined to give his all when there was little chance of outright success. Abruptly, and with no regrets, he quit the cockpit after the Monaco GP.

However, another career soon opened up for the extremely articulate and self-opinionated Hunt. He joined Murray Walker in the BBC's commentary booth to form a wonderful partnership, enlivening many a dreary race with his astute and pithy comments. By the early 1990s, despite well-publicised money worries, his roller-coaster personal life had at last become settled, and it was a great shock when he died in 1993 after a massive heart attack at the age of 45.

HUNT, James (GB) b 29/8/1947, Belmont, nr Sutton, Surrey – d 15/6/1993, Wimbledon, London

	1973 Championship position: 8th		Wins: 0	Pole positions: 0	Fastest laps: 2	Points scored: 14			
	Race	Circuit	No	Entrant	Tyres	Capacity/Car/Engine	Comment		Q Pos/Entries
9/ret	MONACO GP	Monte Carlo	27	Hesketh Racing	F	3.0 March 731-Cosworth V8	engine/5 laps behind		18/26
6	FRENCH GP	Paul Ricard	27	Hesketh Racing	F	3.0 March 731-Cosworth V8			14/25
4	BRITISH GP	Silverstone	27	Hesketh Racing	F	3.0 March 731-Cosworth V8	FL		11/29
3	DUTCH GP	Zandvoort	27	Hesketh Racing	F	3.0 March 731-Cosworth V8			7/24
ret	AUSTRIAN GP	Österreichring	27	Hesketh Racing	F	3.0 March 731-Cosworth V8	fuel metering unit		9/25
dns	ITALIAN GP	Monza	27	Hesketh Racing	F	3.0 March 731-Cosworth V8	car damaged in practice		(25)/25
7	CANADIAN GP	Mosport Park	27	Hesketh Racing	F	3.0 March 731-Cosworth V8	pit stop – tyres/2 laps behind		15/26
2	US GP	Watkins Glen	27	Hesketh Racing	F	3.0 March 731-Cosworth V8	FL		5/28
	1974 Championship position: 8th		Wins: 0	Pole positions: 0	Fastest laps: 0	Points scored: 15			
ret	ARGENTINE GP	Buenos Aires	24	Hesketh Racing	F	3.0 March 731-Cosworth V8	overheating		5/26
9	BRAZILIAN GP	Interlagos	24	Hesketh Racing	F	3.0 March 731-Cosworth V8	1 lap behind		18/25
ret	SOUTH AFRICAN GP	Kyalami	24	Hesketh Racing	F	3.0 Hesketh 308-Cosworth V8	c.v. joint		14/27
10	SPANISH GP	Jarama	24	Hesketh Racing	F	3.0 Hesketh 308-Cosworth V8	pit stop – tyres/brakes/3 laps behind		11/28
ret	BELGIAN GP	Nivelles	24	Hesketh Racing	F	3.0 Hesketh 308-Cosworth V8	rear suspension		9/32

A touch of opposite lock from 'Master James' as he wrestles with his McLaren M23 during the 1976 Dutch Grand Prix. That season's compulsive championship battle with Niki Lauda sparked a massive interest in the sport that mushroomed with the ensuing worldwide television coverage.

ret	MONACO GP	Monte Carlo	24	Hesketh Racing	F	3.0 Hesketh 308-Cosworth V8	driveshaft	=7/28
3	SWEDISH GP	Anderstorp	24	Hesketh Racing	F	3.0 Hesketh 308-Cosworth V8		6/27
ret	DUTCH GP	Zandvoort	24	Hesketh Racing	F	3.0 Hesketh 308-Cosworth V8	collision with Pryce	6/27
ret	FRENCH GP	Dijon	24	Hesketh Racing	F	3.0 Hesketh 308-Cosworth V8	collision with Pryce	10/30
ret	BRITISH GP	Brands Hatch	24	Hesketh Racing	F	3.0 Hesketh 308-Cosworth V8	rear suspension – accident	=5/34
ret	GERMAN GP	Nürburgring	24	Hesketh Racing	F	3.0 Hesketh 308-Cosworth V8	transmission	13/32
3	AUSTRIAN GP	Österreichring	24	Hesketh Racing	F	3.0 Hesketh 308-Cosworth V8	pit stop – tyre	7/31
ret	ITALIAN GP	Monza	24	Hesketh Racing	F	3.0 Hesketh 308-Cosworth V8	engine	8/31
4	CANADIAN GP	Mosport Park	24	Hesketh Racing	F	3.0 Hesketh 308-Cosworth V8		8/30
3	US GP	Watkins Glen	24	Hesketh Racing	F	3.0 Hesketh 308-Cosworth V8	fuel problems	2/30
1975	Championship position: 4th	Wins: 1	Pole positions: 0	Fastest laps: 1	Points scored: 33			
2	ARGENTINE GP	Buenos Aires	24	Hesketh Racing	G	3.0 Hesketh 308B-Cosworth V8	FL	6/23
6	BRAZILIAN GP	Interlagos	24	Hesketh Racing	G	3.0 Hesketh 308B-Cosworth V8		7/23
ret	SOUTH AFRICAN GP	Kyalami	24	Hesketh Racing	G	3.0 Hesketh 308B-Cosworth V8	fuel metering unit	12/28
ret	SPANISH GP	Montjuich Park	24	Hesketh Racing	G	3.0 Hesketh 308B-Cosworth V8	spun off	3/26
ret	MONACO GP	Monte Carlo	24	Hesketh Racing	G	3.0 Hesketh 308B-Cosworth V8	hit guard rail	11/26
ret	BELGIAN GP	Zolder	24	Hesketh Racing	G	3.0 Hesketh 308B-Cosworth V8	gear linkage	11/24
ret	SWEDISH GP	Anderstorp	24	Hesketh Racing	G	3.0 Hesketh 308B-Cosworth V8	brake pipe leakage	13/26
1	DUTCH GP	Zandvoort	24	Hesketh Racing	G	3.0 Hesketh 308B-Cosworth V8	pit stop – tyres	3/25
2	FRENCH GP	Paul Ricard	24	Hesketh Racing	G	3.0 Hesketh 308B-Cosworth V8		3/26
4/ret	BRITISH GP	Silverstone	24	Hesketh Racing	G	3.0 Hesketh 308B-Cosworth V8	spun off in rainstorm/1 lap behind	9/28
ret	GERMAN GP	Nürburgring	24	Hesketh Racing	G	3.0 Hesketh 308B-Cosworth V8	rear hub	=8/26
2*	AUSTRIAN GP	Österreichring	24	Hesketh Racing	G	3.0 Hesketh 308B-Cosworth V8	*rain shortened race – half points	2/30
5	ITALIAN GP	Monza	24	Hesketh Racing	G	3.0 Hesketh 308C-Cosworth V8		8/28
4	US GP	Watkins Glen	24	Hesketh Racing	G	3.0 Hesketh 308C-Cosworth V8		15/24
dns	"	" "	24	Hesketh Racing	G	3.0 Hesketh 308B-Cosworth V8	practice only	- / -
1976 WORLD CHAMPION		Wins: 5	Pole positions: 8	Fastest laps: 2	Points scored: 69			
ret	BRAZILIAN GP	Interlagos	11	Marlboro Team McLaren	G	3.0 McLaren M23-Cosworth V8	stuck throttle – crashed	1/22
2	SOUTH AFRICAN GP	Kyalami	11	Marlboro Team McLaren	G	3.0 McLaren M23-Cosworth V8		1/25
ret	US GP WEST	Long Beach	11	Marlboro Team McLaren	G	3.0 McLaren M23-Cosworth V8	collision with Depailler	3/27
1	SPANISH GP	Jarama	11	Marlboro Team McLaren	G	3.0 McLaren M23-Cosworth V8	disqualified but later reinstated	1/30
ret	BELGIAN GP	Zolder	11	Marlboro Team McLaren	G	3.0 McLaren M23-Cosworth V8	transmission	3/29
ret	MONACO GP	Monte Carlo	11	Marlboro Team McLaren	G	3.0 McLaren M23-Cosworth V8	engine	14/25
5	SWEDISH GP	Anderstorp	11	Marlboro Team McLaren	G	3.0 McLaren M23-Cosworth V8		8/27
1	FRENCH GP	Paul Ricard	11	Marlboro Team McLaren	G	3.0 McLaren M23-Cosworth V8		1/30
dsq*	BRITISH GP	Brands Hatch	11	Marlboro Team McLaren	G	3.0 McLaren M23-Cosworth V8	*used spare car in restart/1st on road	2/30
1	GERMAN GP	Nürburgring	11	Marlboro Team McLaren	G	3.0 McLaren M23-Cosworth V8	race restarted	1/28
4	AUSTRIAN GP	Österreichring	11	Marlboro Team McLaren	G	3.0 McLaren M23-Cosworth V8	FL	1/25
1	DUTCH GP	Zandvoort	11	Marlboro Team McLaren	G	3.0 McLaren M23-Cosworth V8		2/27
ret	ITALIAN GP	Monza	11	Marlboro Team McLaren	G	3.0 McLaren M23-Cosworth V8	ran off circuit – stuck in sand	27/29
1	CANADIAN GP	Mosport Park	11	Marlboro Team McLaren	G	3.0 McLaren M23-Cosworth V8		1/27
1	US GP EAST	Watkins Glen	11	Marlboro Team McLaren	G	3.0 McLaren M23-Cosworth V8	FL	1/27
3	JAPANESE GP	Mount Fuji	11	Marlboro Team McLaren	G	3.0 McLaren M23-Cosworth V8	pit stop – tyre/1 lap behind	2/27
1977	Championship position: 5th	Wins: 3	Pole positions: 6	Fastest laps: 3	Points scored: 40			
ret	ARGENTINE GP	Buenos Aires	1	Marlboro Team McLaren	G	3.0 McLaren M23-Cosworth V8	suspension mounting/FL	1/21
2	BRAZILIAN GP	Interlagos	1	Marlboro Team McLaren	G	3.0 McLaren M23-Cosworth V8	FL	1/22
4	SOUTH AFRICAN GP	Kyalami	1	Marlboro Team McLaren	G	3.0 McLaren M23-Cosworth V8		1/23
7	US GP WEST	Long Beach	1	Marlboro Team McLaren	G	3.0 McLaren M23-Cosworth V8	hit Watson – pit stop/1 lap behind	8/22
ret	SPANISH GP	Jarama	1	Marlboro Team McLaren	G	3.0 McLaren M26-Cosworth V8	engine	7/31
ret	MONACO GP	Monte Carlo	1	Marlboro Team McLaren	G	3.0 McLaren M23-Cosworth V8	engine	7/26

			No	Entrant	Tyres	Capacity/Car/Engine	Comment	Q Pos/Entries
7	BELGIAN GP	Zolder	1	Marlboro Team McLaren	G	3.0 McLaren M26-Cosworth V8	1 lap behind	– / –
dns	"	"	1	Marlboro Team McLaren	G	3.0 McLaren M23-Cosworth V8	set grid time in this car	9/32
12	SWEDISH GP	Anderstorp	1	Marlboro Team McLaren	G	3.0 McLaren M26-Cosworth V8	1 lap behind	3/31
3	FRENCH GP	Dijon	1	Marlboro Team McLaren	G	3.0 McLaren M26-Cosworth V8		2/30
1	BRITISH GP	Silverstone	1	Marlboro Team McLaren	G	3.0 McLaren M26-Cosworth V8	FL	1/36
ret	GERMAN GP	Hockenheim	1	Marlboro Team McLaren	G	3.0 McLaren M26-Cosworth V8	fuel pump	4/30
ret	AUSTRIAN GP	Österreichring	1	Marlboro Team McLaren	G	3.0 McLaren M26-Cosworth V8	engine	2/30
ret	DUTCH GP	Zandvoort	1	Marlboro Team McLaren	G	3.0 McLaren M26-Cosworth V8	collision with Andretti	3/34
ret	ITALIAN GP	Monza	1	Marlboro Team McLaren	G	3.0 McLaren M26-Cosworth V8	spun off	1/34
1	US GP EAST	Watkins Glen	1	Marlboro Team McLaren	G	3.0 McLaren M26-Cosworth V8		1/27
ret	CANADIAN GP	Mosport Park	1	Marlboro Team McLaren	G	3.0 McLaren M26-Cosworth V8	hit Mass	2/27
1	JAPANESE GP	Mount Fuji	1	Marlboro Team McLaren	G	3.0 McLaren M26-Cosworth V8		2/23

1978 Championship position: 13   Wins: 0   Pole positions: 0   Fastest laps: 0   Points scored: 8

			No	Entrant	Tyres	Capacity/Car/Engine	Comment	Q Pos/Entries
4	ARGENTINE GP	Buenos Aires	7	Marlboro Team McLaren	G	3.0 McLaren M26-Cosworth V8		6/27
ret	BRAZILIAN GP	Rio	7	Marlboro Team McLaren	G	3.0 McLaren M26-Cosworth V8	spun off	2/28
ret	SOUTH AFRICAN GP	Kyalami	7	Marlboro Team McLaren	G	3.0 McLaren M26-Cosworth V8	engine	3/30
ret	US GP WEST	Long Beach	7	Marlboro Team McLaren	G	3.0 McLaren M26-Cosworth V8	spun off – damaged suspension	7/30
ret	MONACO GP	Monte Carlo	7	Marlboro Team McLaren	G	3.0 McLaren M26-Cosworth V8	anti-roll bar	6/30
ret	BELGIAN GP	Zolder	7	Marlboro Team McLaren	G	3.0 McLaren M26-Cosworth V8	startline collision with Patrese	6/30
6	SPANISH GP	Jarama	7	Marlboro Team McLaren	G	3.0 McLaren M26-Cosworth V8	pit stop – tyres/1 lap behind	4/29
8	SWEDISH GP	Anderstorp	7	Marlboro Team McLaren	G	3.0 McLaren M26-Cosworth V8	1 lap behind	14/27
3	FRENCH GP	Paul Ricard	7	Marlboro Team McLaren	G	3.0 McLaren M26-Cosworth V8	driver unwell	4/29
ret	BRITISH GP	Brands Hatch	7	Marlboro Team McLaren	G	3.0 McLaren M26-Cosworth V8	spun off	14/30
dns	"	"	7	Marlboro Team McLaren	G	3.0 McLaren M26E-Cosworth V8	practice only	– / –
dsq	GERMAN GP	Hockenheim	7	Marlboro Team McLaren	G	3.0 McLaren M26-Cosworth V8	took short cut to pits	8/30
ret	AUSTRIAN GP	Österreichring	7	Marlboro Team McLaren	G	3.0 McLaren M26-Cosworth V8	collision with Daly	8/31
10	DUTCH GP	Zandvoort	7	Marlboro Team McLaren	G	3.0 McLaren M26-Cosworth V8	handling problems/1 lap behind	7/33
ret	ITALIAN GP	Monza	7	Marlboro Team McLaren	G	3.0 McLaren M26-Cosworth V8	distributor	10/32
7	US GP EAST	Watkins Glen	7	Marlboro Team McLaren	G	3.0 McLaren M26-Cosworth V8	1 lap behind	6/27
ret	CANADIAN GP	Montreal	7	Marlboro Team McLaren	G	3.0 McLaren M26-Cosworth V8	spun off	19/28

1979 Championship position: Unplaced

			No	Entrant	Tyres	Capacity/Car/Engine	Comment	Q Pos/Entries
ret	ARGENTINE GP	Buenos Aires	20	Olympus Cameras Wolf Racing	G	3.0 Wolf WR7-Cosworth V8	electrics	18/26
ret	BRAZILIAN GP	Interlagos	20	Olympus Cameras Wolf Racing	G	3.0 Wolf WR7-Cosworth V8	loose steering rack	10/26
8	SOUTH AFRICAN GP	Kyalami	20	Olympus Cameras Wolf Racing	G	3.0 Wolf WR7-Cosworth V8	1 lap behind	13/26
ret	US GP WEST	Long Beach	20	Olympus Cameras Wolf Racing	G	3.0 Wolf WR8-Cosworth V8	driveshaft	8/26
ret	SPANISH GP	Jarama	20	Olympus Cameras Wolf Racing	G	3.0 Wolf WR8-Cosworth V8	brakes	15/27
dns	"	"	20	Olympus Cameras Wolf Racing	G	3.0 Wolf WR8-Cosworth V8	practice only	– / –
ret	BELGIAN GP	Zolder	20	Olympus Cameras Wolf Racing	G	3.0 Wolf WR8-Cosworth V8	spun off	9/28
dns	"	"	20	Olympus Cameras Wolf Racing	G	3.0 Wolf WR7-Cosworth V8	practice only	– / –
ret	MONACO GP	Monte Carlo	20	Olympus Cameras Wolf Racing	G	3.0 Wolf WR7-Cosworth V8	c.v. joint	10/25

GP Starts: 92   GP Wins: 10   Pole positions: 14   Fastest laps: 8   Points: 179

HUTCHISON, Gus (USA) b 26/4/1937, Atlanta, Georgia

1970 Championship position: Unplaced

	Race	Circuit	No	Entrant	Tyres	Capacity/Car/Engine	Comment	Q Pos/Entries
ret	US GP	Watkins Glen	31	Champlin Racing/Gus Hutchison	G	3.0 Brabham BT26A-Cosworth V8	loose supplementary fuel tank	22/27

GP Starts: 1   GP Wins: 0   Pole positions: 0   Fastest laps: 0   Points: 0

GUS HUTCHISON

AN amateur racer from Dallas, Gus Hutchison, who had gained a degree in chemistry, began racing in 1956 in the SCCA. It was 1964, however, when he began to make an impact in the divisional championships of the Formula Junior category; the following year, he was divisional champion in the modified class F, before moving to Formula B in 1966.

The acquisition of brand-new Lotus 41C-BRM put Hutchison at the forefront of his category. He was the US Formula B Continental champion in 1967, having won four of the five races. He also swept the board in his yellow Lotus in the Southwest division, winning each of the first seven races he entered.

Hutchison did not race at all in the next two seasons, but in late in 1969, he bought the ex-Jacky Ickx Brabham BT26 to race in the 1970 season of the Formula A SCCA Continental series. He won with the car at Sears Point and Dallas, before switching to a Lola T190-Chevrolet V8

Gus took the Brabham to Watkins Glen for that year's United States Grand Prix, but sadly his only grand prix appearance ended early on with a fuel leak.

Although busy with his engine business, HRE (Hutchison Racing Engines), Gus was still a regular competitor in the L & M F5000 series through to the end of 1974, with both a Lola T300 and then a March 73A/B chassis. He scored some good top-ten finishes, but he was always at a big disadvantage against more potent machinery and very professional drivers, who inevitably kept him low on the results sheets.

IN Jacky Ickx, grand prix racing had a prodigy with the brio of Jochen Rindt and the controlled circumspection of Jackie Stewart, absolutely brilliant in the wet and endowed with such natural driving gifts that surely the world championship should have been a formality. In the end, though, that was not to be, as his mercurial powers became diluted in a succession of less-competitive cars.

The son of a famous motor racing journalist, Jacky was three times Belgium's motorcycle trials champion before he moved to cars, quickly becoming the man to beat in his Lotus Cortina and taking his national saloon car championship in 1965. Although only 21, he was pitched straight into a season of Formula 2 in 1966, under the guidance of Ken Tyrrell, who could see his vast potential. It was at the following year's German GP that the young Jacky caused a sensation by qualifying the little Matra third fastest in practice, and though he had to start with the other Formula 2 cars at the back of the grid, he soon carved his way through the field to fourth place before his suspension broke. Now a hot property, he was a guest driver for Cooper at Monza, where he scored his first championship point, before signing for Ferrari in 1968.

Jacky's first great win was not long in coming: he demonstrated sublime control in the wet to win at Rouen, and his consistent placings left him with an outside chance of taking the championship, until a practice crash in Canada scuppered his hopes. By then, he was already regarded as one of the world's very best sports car drivers: racing for John Wyer, he had won the Spa 1000km twice, in addition to scoring victories at Brands Hatch, Watkins Glen and Kyalami. So anxious were Gulf to keep their prize asset that they arranged for him to join Brabham for 1969. In the light of Ferrari's plight that year, it was a smart move, Ickx reaching the heights of his considerable brilliance by defeating Jackie Stewart in the German GP. Another win followed in Canada, but he had to be content with the runner-up spot in the championship that year. Meanwhile, the wisdom of Gulf's decision was demonstrated when Jacky took a sensational last-gasp victory at Le Mans over Hans Herrmann's Porsche.

In 1970, Jacky rejoined Ferrari to race in both Formula 1 and sports car events, but once again he was the 'nearly man', just failing to overhaul the late Jochen Rindt's points total after winning three grands prix. Apart from a non-title win in the Rindt Memorial race at Hockenheim, and yet another masterful display in the wet at Zandvoort, the following grand prix season was not as competitive as he would have hoped, while in 1972 Ferrari were still a potent force, but not consistent enough. Predictably he took another superb win at the Nürburgring, as well as chalking up brilliant victories in the team's sports cars, races at Daytona, Sebring, Brands Hatch, the Österreichring and Watkins Glen all surrendering to the Belgian that year.

Ferrari having fallen into one of their periodical troughs in 1973, Ickx's patience had run out by mid-season and he quit the team, freelancing for McLaren and Williams before joining Ronnie Peterson at Lotus for 1974. Apart from a memorable win in the Race of Champions, however, it was a disastrous move, the bewildered Belgian switching back and forth between the almost undriveable new Lotus 76 and the by then venerable 72E. Things became even worse in 1975, and he and Lotus parted company in mid-season. By then, his Formula 1 career was in the balance, and a move to the Wolf-Williams team at the beginning of 1976 tipped him into the also-ran category. A brief spell at Ensign, ironically replacing Chris Amon, showed that the spark was still there, but a nasty crash at Watkins Glen convinced him that his highly successful sports car career was a better bet.

Jacky completed a remarkable hat trick of Le Mans wins between 1975 and 1977, and won a string of rounds of the World Championship of Makes in the Martini Porsche, partnered by Jochen Mass. In 1979, he was back in the grand prix world, replacing the injured Patrick Depailler at Ligier, but sadly it was not a successful return, the finesse of his driving style not suiting the ground-effect cars of the time. Racing in Can-Am for Jim Hall, he took the 1979 title, before concentrating almost exclusively on endurance racing in the 1980s. After taking a fifth Le Mans win in 1981, he became a key member of the Rothmans Porsche team the following season and won the drivers' world championship, scoring a record sixth win at Le Mans in addition to victories at Spa, Fuji and Brands Hatch.

In 1983, Ickx drove a Mercedes 280G to victory in the Paris-Dakar, an event he would revisit with his daugher, Vanina, in 2000.

Jacky continued to race successfully through to the end of the 1985 season, which was clouded by an accident at Spa that caused the death of Stefan Bellof. He took honourable retirement, hailed not only as one of the all-time greats of sports car racing, but also, by those who remembered his halcyon days, as one of grand prix racing's most brilliant talents.

Total control. Jacky Ickx takes his first grand prix in the pouring rain at Rouen in 1968 for Ferrari, after correctly gambling on running wet-weather tyres from the start.

ICKX, Jacky (B) b 1/1/1945, Ixelles, Brussels

1966 Championship position: Unplaced

	Race	Circuit	No	Entrant	Tyres	Capacity/Car/Engine	Comment	Q Pos/Entries
ret	GERMAN GP (F2)	Nürburgring	27	Ken Tyrrell Racing	D	1.0 Matra MS5-Cosworth 4 F2	*transmission (F2 car)*	17/30

1967 Championship position: 19th= Wins: 0 Pole positions: 0 Fastest laps: 0 Points scored: 1

	Race	Circuit	No	Entrant	Tyres	Capacity/Car/Engine	Comment	Q Pos/Entries
ret	GERMAN GP (F2)	Nürburgring	29	Ken Tyrrell Racing	D	1.6 Matra MS7-Cosworth 4 F2	*suspension (FL in F2 class)*	3/25
6	ITALIAN GP	Monza	32	Cooper Car Co	F	3.0 Cooper T81B-Maserati V12	*puncture on last lap/2 laps behind*	15/18
ret	US GP	Watkins Glen	21	Cooper Car Co	F	3.0 Cooper T86-Maserati V12	*overheating*	16/18

1968 Championship position: 4th Wins: 1 Pole positions: 1 Fastest laps: 0 Points scored: 27

	Race	Circuit	No	Entrant	Tyres	Capacity/Car/Engine	Comment	Q Pos/Entries
ret	SOUTH AFRICAN GP	Kyalami	9	Scuderia Ferrari SpA SEFAC	F	3.0 Ferrari 312/67 V12	*oil tank/driver exhausted*	=10/23
ret	SPANISH GP	Jarama	21	Scuderia Ferrari SpA SEFAC	F	3.0 Ferrari 312/67/68 V12	*ignition*	8/14
3	BELGIAN GP	Spa	23	Scuderia Ferrari SpA SEFAC	F	3.0 Ferrari 312/67/68 V12		3/18
4	DUTCH GP	Zandvoort	10	Scuderia Ferrari SpA SEFAC	F	3.0 Ferrari 312/68 V12	*2 laps behind*	6/19
1	FRENCH GP	Rouen	26	Scuderia Ferrari SpA SEFAC	F	3.0 Ferrari 312/68 V12		3/18
3	BRITISH GP	Brands Hatch	6	Scuderia Ferrari SpA SEFAC	F	3.0 Ferrari 312/68 V12	*1 lap behind*	12/20
4	GERMAN GP	Nürburgring	9	Scuderia Ferrari SpA SEFAC	F	3.0 Ferrari 312/68 V12	*pitstops – visor problem*	1/20
3	ITALIAN GP	Monza	8	Scuderia Ferrari SpA SEFAC	F	3.0 Ferrari 312/68 V12		4/24
dns	CANADIAN GP	St Jovite	10	Scuderia Ferrari SpA SEFAC	F	3.0 Ferrari 312/68 V12	*practice accident – broken leg*	(=13)/22
ret	MEXICAN GP	Mexico City	7	Scuderia Ferrari SpA SEFAC	F	3.0 Ferrari 312/68 V12	*ignition*	15/21

1969 Championship position: 2nd Wins: 2 Pole positions: 2 Fastest laps: 3 (1 shared) Points scored: 37

	Race	Circuit	No	Entrant	Tyres	Capacity/Car/Engine	Comment	Q Pos/Entries
ret	SOUTH AFRICAN GP	Kyalami	15	Motor Racing Developments	G	3.0 Brabham BT26A-Cosworth V8	*starter solenoid after pit stop*	14/18
6/ret	SPANISH GP	Montjuich Park	4	Motor Racing Developments	G	3.0 Brabham BT26A-Cosworth V8	*rear suspension/7 laps behind*	7/14
ret	MONACO GP	Monte Carlo	6	Motor Racing Developments	G	3.0 Brabham BT26A-Cosworth V8	*rear suspension*	7/16
5	DUTCH GP	Zandvoort	12	Motor Racing Developments	G	3.0 Brabham BT26A-Cosworth V8		5/15
3	FRENCH GP	Clermont Ferrand	11	Motor Racing Developments	G	3.0 Brabham BT26A-Cosworth V8		4/13
2	BRITISH GP	Silverstone	7	Motor Racing Developments	G	3.0 Brabham BT26A-Cosworth V8	*low on fuel last lap/1 lap behind*	4/17
1	GERMAN GP	Nürburgring	6	Motor Racing Developments	G	3.0 Brabham BT26A-Cosworth V8	*FL*	1/26
10/ret	ITALIAN GP	Monza	26	Motor Racing Developments	G	3.0 Brabham BT26A-Cosworth V8	*oil pressure/6 laps behind*	15/15
1	CANADIAN GP	Mosport Park	11	Motor Racing Developments	G	3.0 Brabham BT26A-Cosworth V8	*FL (shared with Brabham)*	1/20
ret	US GP	Watkins Glen	7	Motor Racing Developments	G	3.0 Brabham BT26A-Cosworth V8	*engine*	8/18
2	MEXICAN GP	Mexico City	7	Motor Racing Developments	G	3.0 Brabham BT26A-Cosworth V8	*FL*	2/17

1970 Championship position: 2nd Wins: 3 Pole positions: 4 Fastest laps: 4 (1 shared) Points scored: 40

	Race	Circuit	No	Entrant	Tyres	Capacity/Car/Engine	Comment	Q Pos/Entries
ret	SOUTH AFRICAN GP	Kyalami	17	Scuderia Ferrari SpA SEFAC	F	3.0 Ferrari 312B F12	*engine*	5/24
ret	SPANISH GP	Jarama	2	Scuderia Ferrari SpA SEFAC	F	3.0 Ferrari 312B F12	*collision with Oliver – suffered burns*	7/22
ret	MONACO GP	Monte Carlo	26	Scuderia Ferrari SpA SEFAC	F	3.0 Ferrari 312B F12	*driveshaft*	5/21
8	BELGIAN GP	Spa	27	Scuderia Ferrari SpA SEFAC	F	3.0 Ferrari 312B F12	*pit stop – fuel leak/2 laps behind*	4/18
3	DUTCH GP	Zandvoort	25	Scuderia Ferrari SpA SEFAC	F	3.0 Ferrari 312B F12	*pit stop – puncture/FL/1 lap behind*	3/24
ret	FRENCH GP	Clermont Ferrand	10	Scuderia Ferrari SpA SEFAC	F	3.0 Ferrari 312B F12	*engine*	1/23
ret	BRITISH GP	Brands Hatch	3	Scuderia Ferrari SpA SEFAC	F	3.0 Ferrari 312B F12	*differential*	3/25
2	GERMAN GP	Hockenheim	10	Scuderia Ferrari SpA SEFAC	F	3.0 Ferrari 312B F12	*FL*	1/25
1	AUSTRIAN GP	Österreichring	12	Scuderia Ferrari SpA SEFAC	F	3.0 Ferrari 312B F12	*FL (shared with Regazzoni)*	3/24
ret	ITALIAN GP	Monza	2	Scuderia Ferrari SpA SEFAC	F	3.0 Ferrari 312B F12	*clutch*	1/27
1	CANADIAN GP	St Jovite	18	Scuderia Ferrari SpA SEFAC	F	3.0 Ferrari 312B F12		2/20
4	US GP	Watkins Glen	3	Scuderia Ferrari SpA SEFAC	F	3.0 Ferrari 312B F12	*pit stop – fuel leak/FL/1 lap behnd*	1/27
1	MEXICAN GP	Mexico City	3	Scuderia Ferrari SpA SEFAC	F	3.0 Ferrari 312B F12	*FL*	3/18

Ickx leads team-mate Regazzoni in their beautiful Ferrari 312Bs as they head for a 1-2 finish in the 1970 Austrian Grand Prix. The Belgian was second to the late Jochen Rindt in that year's championship chase, and sadly he never came close to challenging for the title again.

1971 Championship position: 4th=   Wins: 1   Pole positions: 2   Fastest laps: 3   Points scored: 19

Result	Grand Prix	Circuit	No	Team	Tyre	Car	Notes	Grid
8	SOUTH AFRICAN GP	Kyalami	4	Scuderia Ferrari SpA SEFAC	F	3.0 Ferrari 312B F12	1 lap behind	=8/25
2	SPANISH GP	Montjuich Park	4	Scuderia Ferrari SpA SEFAC	F	3.0 Ferrari 312B F12	FL	1/22
3	MONACO GP	Monte Carlo	4	Scuderia Ferrari SpA SEFAC	F	3.0 Ferrari 312B2 F12		2/23
1	DUTCH GP	Zandvoort	2	Scuderia Ferrari SpA SEFAC	F	3.0 Ferrari 312B2 F12	wet race/FL	1/24
ret	FRENCH GP	Paul Ricard	4	Scuderia Ferrari SpA SEFAC	F	3.0 Ferrari 312B2 F12	engine	3/24
ret	BRITISH GP	Silverstone	4	Scuderia Ferrari SpA SEFAC	F	3.0 Ferrari 312B2 F12	engine	6/24
ret	GERMAN GP	Nürburgring	4	Scuderia Ferrari SpA SEFAC	F	3.0 Ferrari 312B2 F12	spun off	2/23
ret	AUSTRIAN GP	Österreichring	4	Scuderia Ferrari SpA SEFAC	F	3.0 Ferrari 312B2 F12	electrics – plug leads	6/22
ret	ITALIAN GP	Monza	3	Scuderia Ferrari SpA SEFAC	F	3.0 Ferrari 312B F12	engine damper	2/24
dns	"	"	3	Scuderia Ferrari SpA SEFAC	F	3.0 Ferrari 312B2 F12	practice only	– / –
8	CANADIAN GP	Mosport Park	4	Scuderia Ferrari SpA SEFAC	F	3.0 Ferrari 312B2 F12	2 laps behind	=11/27
ret	US GP	Watkins Glen	32	Scuderia Ferrari SpA SEFAC	F	3.0 Ferrari 312B F12	alternator fell off/FL	8/32
dns	"	"	4	Scuderia Ferrari SpA SEFAC	F	3.0 Ferrari 312B2 F12	practice only	– / –

1972 Championship position: 4th   Wins: 1   Pole positions: 4   Fastest laps: 3   Points scored: 27

Result	Grand Prix	Circuit	No	Team	Tyre	Car	Notes	Grid
3	ARGENTINE GP	Buenos Aires	8	Scuderia Ferrari SpA SEFAC	F	3.0 Ferrari 312B2 F12		8/22
8	SOUTH AFRICAN GP	Kyalami	5	Scuderia Ferrari SpA SEFAC	F	3.0 Ferrari 312B2 F12	1 lap behind	7/27
2	SPANISH GP	Jarama	4	Scuderia Ferrari SpA SEFAC	F	3.0 Ferrari 312B2 F12	FL	1/26
2	MONACO GP	Monte Carlo	6	Scuderia Ferrari SpA SEFAC	F	3.0 Ferrari 312B2 F12		2/25
ret	BELGIAN GP	Nivelles	29	Scuderia Ferrari SpA SEFAC	F	3.0 Ferrari 312B2 F12	fuel injection	4/26
11	FRENCH GP	Clermont Ferrand	3	Scuderia Ferrari SpA SEFAC	F	3.0 Ferrari 312B2 F12	1 lap behind	4/29
ret	BRITISH GP	Brands Hatch	5	Scuderia Ferrari SpA SEFAC	F	3.0 Ferrari 312B2 F12	oil pressure/led race	1/27
1	GERMAN GP	Nürburgring	4	Scuderia Ferrari SpA SEFAC	F	3.0 Ferrari 312B2 F12	FL	1/27
ret	AUSTRIAN GP	Österreichring	18	Scuderia Ferrari SpA SEFAC	F	3.0 Ferrari 312B2 F12	fuel pressure	9/26
ret	ITALIAN GP	Monza	4	Scuderia Ferrari SpA SEFAC	F	3.0 Ferrari 312B2 F12	electrics/FL	1/27
12	CANADIAN GP	Mosport Park	10	Scuderia Ferrari SpA SEFAC	F	3.0 Ferrari 312B2 F12	pit stop – puncture/3 laps behind	8/25
5	US GP	Watkins Glen	7	Scuderia Ferrari SpA SEFAC	F	3.0 Ferrari 312B2 F12		12/32

1973 Championship position: 9th   Wins: 0   Pole positions: 0   Fastest laps: 0   Points scored: 12

Result	Grand Prix	Circuit	No	Team	Tyre	Car	Notes	Grid
4	ARGENTINE GP	Buenos Aires	18	Scuderia Ferrari SpA SEFAC	G	3.0 Ferrari 312B2 F12		3/19
5	BRAZILIAN GP	Interlagos	9	Scuderia Ferrari SpA SEFAC	G	3.0 Ferrari 312B2 F12	pit stop – puncture/1 lap behind	3/20
ret	SOUTH AFRICAN GP	Kyalami	8	Scuderia Ferrari SpA SEFAC	G	3.0 Ferrari 312B2 F12	accident with Regazzoni & Hailwood	11/25
12	SPANISH GP	Montjuich Park	7	Scuderia Ferrari SpA SEFAC	G	3.0 Ferrari 312B3 F12	pit stop – brakes/6 laps behind	6/22
ret	BELGIAN GP	Zolder	3	Scuderia Ferrari SpA SEFAC	G	3.0 Ferrari 312B3 F12	oil pump	3/23
ret	MONACO GP	Monte Carlo	3	Scuderia Ferrari SpA SEFAC	G	3.0 Ferrari 312B3 F12	driveshaft	7/26
6	SWEDISH GP	Anderstorp	3	Scuderia Ferrari SpA SEFAC	G	3.0 Ferrari 312B3 F12	1 lap behind	8/22
5	FRENCH GP	Paul Ricard	3	Scuderia Ferrari SpA SEFAC	G	3.0 Ferrari 312B3 F12		12/25G
8	BRITISH GP	Silverstone	3	Scuderia Ferrari SpA SEFAC	G	3.0 Ferrari 312B3 F12		19/29
3	GERMAN GP	Nürburgring	30	Yardley Team McLaren	G	3.0 McLaren M23-Cosworth V8		4/23
8	ITALIAN GP	Monza	3	Scuderia Ferrari SpA SEFAC	G	3.0 Ferrari 312B3 F12	clipped chicane/1 lap behind	14/25
7	US GP	Watkins Glen	26	Frank Williams Racing Cars	F	3.0 Iso Marlboro IR-Cosworth V8	1 lap behind	24/28

1974 Championship position: 10th   Wins: 0   Pole positions: 0   Fastest laps: 0   Points scored: 12

Result	Grand Prix	Circuit	No	Team	Tyre	Car	Notes	Grid
ret	ARGENTINE GP	Buenos Aires	2	John Player Team Lotus	G	3.0 Lotus 72E-Cosworth V8	transmission	7/26
3	BRAZILIAN GP	Interlagos	2	John Player Team Lotus	G	3.0 Lotus 72E-Cosworth V8	1 lap behind	5/25
ret	SOUTH AFRICAN GP	Kyalami	2	John Player Team Lotus	G	3.0 Lotus 76-Cosworth V8	brake balance/hit by Peterson	10/27
ret	SPANISH GP	Jarama	2	John Player Team Lotus	G	3.0 Lotus 76-Cosworth V8	leaking brake fluid	5/28
ret	BELGIAN GP	Nivelles	2	John Player Team Lotus	G	3.0 Lotus 76-Cosworth V8	brakes	16/32
ret	MONACO GP	Monte Carlo	2	John Player Team Lotus	G	3.0 Lotus 72E-Cosworth V8	gearbox	19/28
dns	"	"	2T	John Player Team Lotus	G	3.0 Lotus 76-Cosworth V8	practice only	– / –
ret	SWEDISH GP	Anderstorp	2	John Player Team Lotus	G	3.0 Lotus 72E-Cosworth V8	oil pressure	7/28
11	DUTCH GP	Zandvoort	2	John Player Team Lotus	G	3.0 Lotus 72E-Cosworth V8	pit stop – loose wheel/4 laps behind	18/27
dns	"	"	2T	John Player Team Lotus	G	3.0 Lotus 76-Cosworth V8	practice only	– / –
5	FRENCH GP	Dijon	2	John Player Team Lotus	G	3.0 Lotus 72E-Cosworth V8		13/30
3	BRITISH GP	Brands Hatch	2	John Player Team Lotus	G	3.0 Lotus 72E-Cosworth V8		=11/34
5	GERMAN GP	Nürburgring	2	John Player Team Lotus	G	3.0 Lotus 72E-Cosworth V8		9/32
ret	AUSTRIAN GP	Österreichring	2	John Player Team Lotus	G	3.0 Lotus 76-Cosworth V8	collision with Depailler	– / –
dns	"	"	2T	John Player Team Lotus	G	3.0 Lotus 72E-Cosworth V8	used to set grid time	22/31
ret	ITALIAN GP	Monza	2	John Player Team Lotus	G	3.0 Lotus 76-Cosworth V8	throttle linkage	16/31
13	CANADIAN GP	Mosport Park	2	John Player Team Lotus	G	3.0 Lotus 72E-Cosworth V8	2 laps behind	21/30
dns	"	"	2T	John Player Team Lotus	G	3.0 Lotus 76-Cosworth V8	practice only	– / –
ret	US GP	Watkins Glen	2	John Player Team Lotus	G	3.0 Lotus 72E-Cosworth V8	hit guard rail	16/30

1975 Championship position: 16th   Wins: 0   Pole positions: 0   Fastest laps: 0   Points scored: 3

Result	Grand Prix	Circuit	No	Team	Tyre	Car	Notes	Grid
8	ARGENTINE GP	Buenos Aires	6	John Player Team Lotus	G	3.0 Lotus 72E-Cosworth V8	1 lap behind	18/23
9	BRAZILIAN GP	Interlagos	6	John Player Team Lotus	G	3.0 Lotus 72E-Cosworth V8		12/23
12	SOUTH AFRICAN GP	Kyalami	6	John Player Team Lotus	G	3.0 Lotus 72E-Cosworth V8	2 laps behind	21/28
2*	SPANISH GP	Montjuich Park	6	John Player Team Lotus	G	3.0 Lotus 72E-Cosworth V8	*shortened race – half points only	16/26
8	MONACO GP	Monte Carlo	6	John Player Team Lotus	G	3.0 Lotus 72E-Cosworth V8	1 lap behind	14/26
ret	BELGIAN GP	Zolder	6	John Player Team Lotus	G	3.0 Lotus 72E-Cosworth V8	front brake shaft	16/24
15	SWEDISH GP	Anderstorp	6	John Player Team Lotus	G	3.0 Lotus 72E-Cosworth V8	3 laps behind	18/26
ret	DUTCH GP	Zandvoort	6	John Player Team Lotus	G	3.0 Lotus 72E-Cosworth V8	engine	21/25
ret	FRENCH GP	Paul Ricard	6	John Player Team Lotus	G	3.0 Lotus 72F-Cosworth V8	brake shaft	19/26

1976 Championship position: Unplaced

Result	Grand Prix	Circuit	No	Team	Tyre	Car	Notes	Grid
8	BRAZILIAN GP	Interlagos	20	Frank Williams Racing Cars	G	3.0 Wolf Williams FW05-Cosworth V8	1 lap behind	19/22
16	SOUTH AFRICAN GP	Kyalami	20	Frank Williams Racing Cars	G	3.0 Wolf Williams FW05-Cosworth V8	pit stop/5 laps behind	19/25
dnq	US GP WEST	Long Beach	20	Frank Williams Racing Cars	G	3.0 Wolf Williams FW05-Cosworth V8		25/27
7	SPANISH GP	Jarama	20	Walter Wolf Racing	G	3.0 Wolf Williams FW05-Cosworth V8	1 lap behind	21/30
dnq	BELGIAN GP	Zolder	20	Walter Wolf Racing	G	3.0 Wolf Williams FW05-Cosworth V8		28/29
dnq	MONACO GP	Monte Carlo	20	Walter Wolf Racing	G	3.0 Wolf Williams FW05-Cosworth V8		21/25
10	FRENCH GP	Paul Ricard	20	Walter Wolf Racing	G	3.0 Wolf Williams FW05-Cosworth V8	1 lap behind	19/30

dnq	BRITISH GP	Silverstone	20	Walter Wolf Racing	G	3.0 Wolf Williams FW05-Cosworth V8			27/30
ret	DUTCH GP	Zandvoort	22	Team Ensign	G	3.0 Ensign N176-Cosworth V8	electrics		11/27
10	ITALIAN GP	Monza	22	Team Ensign	G	3.0 Ensign N176-Cosworth V8			10/29
13	CANADIAN GP	Mosport Park	22	Team Ensign	G	3.0 Ensign N176-Cosworth V8	1 lap behind		16/27
ret	US GP EAST	Watkins Glen	22	Team Ensign	G	3.0 Ensign N176-Cosworth V8	accident – broken ankle and burns		19/27

1977 Championship position: Unplaced

10	MONACO GP	Monte Carlo	22	Team Tissot Ensign with Castrol	G	3.0 Ensign N177-Cosworth V8	1 lap behind		17/26

1978 Championship position: Unplaced

ret	MONACO GP	Monte Carlo	22	Team Tissot Ensign	G	3.0 Ensign N177-Cosworth V8	brakes		16/30
12	BELGIAN GP	Zolder	22	Team Tissot Ensign	G	3.0 Ensign N177-Cosworth V8	multiple accident – pit stop/-6 laps		22/30
ret	SPANISH GP	Jarama	22	Team Tissot Ensign	G	3.0 Ensign N177-Cosworth V8	engine		21/29
dnq	SWEDISH GP	Anderstorp	22	Team Tissot Ensign	G	3.0 Ensign N177-Cosworth V8			27/27

1979 Championship position: 15th=   Wins: 0   Pole positions: 0   Fastest laps: 0   Points scored: 3

ret	FRENCH GP	Dijon	25	Ligier Gitanes	G	3.0 Ligier JS11-Cosworth V8	engine		14/27
6	BRITISH GP	Silverstone	25	Ligier Gitanes	G	3.0 Ligier JS11-Cosworth V8	1 lap behind		=16/26
ret	GERMAN GP	Hockenheim	25	Ligier Gitanes	G	3.0 Ligier JS11-Cosworth V8	burst tyre		14/26
ret	AUSTRIAN GP	Österreichring	25	Ligier Gitanes	G	3.0 Ligier JS11-Cosworth V8	engine		21/26
5	DUTCH GP	Zandvoort	25	Ligier Gitanes	G	3.0 Ligier JS11-Cosworth V8	1 lap behind		20/26
ret	ITALIAN GP	Monza	25	Ligier Gitanes	G	3.0 Ligier JS11-Cosworth V8	engine		11/28
ret	CANADIAN GP	Montreal	25	Ligier Gitanes	G	3.0 Ligier JS11-Cosworth V8	gearbox		16/29
ret	US GP EAST	Watkins Glen	25	Ligier Gitanes	G	3.0 Ligier JS11-Cosworth V8	spun off		24/30

GP Starts: 116   GP Wins: 8   Pole positions: 13   Fastest laps: 14   Points: 181

YUJI IDE

STEPPING into Fomula 1 is a daunting experience for any driver, but few will have entered the red-hot crucible with the odds stacked quite so high against him as against 31-year-old Japanese driver Yuji Ide, who joined Super Aguri for the 2006 season. A poor command of English, a hastily assembled team, an aged interim chassis, virtually no testing and no experience of grand prix circuits (save Suzuka) put him at the bottom of a very steep learning curve.

After his involvement in an accident with Christijan Albers on the opening lap at Imola, the FIA revoked his Super Licence, causing the hapless Ide to be demoted to test-driver status; he quickly headed back to Japan. Yet perhaps Ide should not be blamed for grasping the opportunity to take part in Formula 1 when it was offered to him, for he had spent the previous 15 years climbing the motorsport ladder.

After four years successfully competing in karts, Yuji moved into the Japanese F3 series in 1994, his best season being 2000, when he finished runner-up. He ventured to Europe in 2002 to compete in the French F3 championship with a Dallara-Renault, managing a single win in heat two at Croix-en-Ternois and eventually claiming seventh place in the overall standings.

For 2003, Ide returned home and finally graduated to the very competitive Formula Nippon series, where he quickly became a front-runner. After placing seventh in his debut year, he moved up to third in the final standings the following season.

In 2005, Yuji improved again to take the runner-up spot, proving to be the closest challenger to the champion, Satoshi Motoyama, by scoring two wins in the eight-race series. This success paved the way to his brief and bruising F1 experience.

Ide quickly picked up the threads of his career in both Formula Nippon and the Super GT Series in Japan, but he rarely figured much above the midfield runners.

IDE, Yuji (J) b 21/01/1975, Saitima

2006 Championship position: Unplaced

	Race	Circuit	No	Entrant	Tyres	Capacity/Car/Engine	Comment	Q Pos/Entries
ret	BAHRAIN GP	Bahrain	23	Super Aguri Racing	B	2.4 Super Aguri SA05-Honda V8	engine	21/22
ret	MALAYSIAN GP	Sepang	23	Super Aguri Racing	B	2.4 Super Aguri SA05-Honda V8	engine	22/22
13	AUSTRALIAN GP	Melbourne	23	Super Aguri Racing	B	2.4 Super Aguri SA05-Honda V8	1 lap behind	22/22
ret	SAN MARINO GP	Imola	23	Super Aguri Racing	B	2.4 Super Aguri SA05-Honda V8	accident with Albers – rear suspension	22/22

GP Starts: 4   GP Wins: 0   Pole positions: 0   Fastest laps: 0   Points: 0

IGLESIAS, Jésus Ricardo (RA) b 22/2/1922, Pergamino, nr Buenos Aires – d Pergamino, nr Buenos Aires 11/7/2005

1955 Championship position: Unplaced

	Race	Circuit	No	Entrant	Tyres	Capacity/Car/Engine	Comment	Q Pos/Entries
ret	ARGENTINE GP	Buenos Aires	42	Equipe Gordini	E	2.5 Gordini Type 16 6	transmission/exhaustion	17/22

GP Starts: 1   GP Wins: 0   Pole positions: 0   Fastest laps: 0   Points: 0

JÉSUS IGLESIAS

AN Argentinian driver, Jésus Iglesias was very fast indeed in his Chevrolet special and was invited to handle one of the works Gordinis in the 1955 Argentine GP. Even though he was more used to the conditions than most of the visiting drivers, it seems he succumbed to the broiling heat, although he did last some 38 of the 96 laps.

Iglesias appears to have driven a Maserati into 16th place in the well-supported Buenos Aires City GP, a Libre event held a couple of weeks after his outing in the French car. Thereafter, it was back to his Chevrolet special, in which he earned some glory by taking second place in the 500-mile race at Rafaelo in 1956. Two years later, he achieved fame of a kind by contriving to collide with Stirling Moss on the opening lap of the Buenos Aires Libre GP. The first heat of the race was started in wet conditions and he powered from the back of the grid, braking far too late for the first corner. He ran at unabated speed into Moss' Cooper, sending the little machine some three to four feet into the air before it shot off the circuit towards a crowd of photographers. Both cars were hors de combat. Fortunately no one was hurt, although if the unpleasant incident had had more serious results, Iglesias may have gained worldwide notoriety.

TAKI INOUE

PRESS handouts from Formula 1 teams tell you little you really want to know about a driver. You know the sort of thing: residence, hobbies, favourite music, favourite singers, favourite food, etc. How about Monte Carlo, shopping, jazz and rock, Eric Clapton and globefish? Well, that's a lot more interesting than Taki Inoue's racing exploits, which date back to 1985 and the Fuji Freshman championship. He travelled to England to compete in FF1600 in 1987, before returning home to tackle Japanese F3 until 1993, the sum total of his achievements being a few fourth places.

A move into Japanese F3000 with a top team, Super Nova, still brought little by way of results, but that didn't prevent Inoue from gaining a Super Licence to race for Simtek in the Japanese Grand Prix. Result? He spun into the pit wall along the straight.

Far from that being the end of Inoue's grand prix CV, he found the necessary funding to buy a seat at Footwork for the whole 1995 season; Jackie Oliver must have needed the money. "His learning curve has been steep, but his performance very flat," Oliver was quoted as saying in Autocourse. Indeed, it was two bizarre incidents in which he was involved (happily without serious injury) that left the most impression: the first when his Footwork was overturned by the course car in Monaco while being towed back to the pits, the second in Hungary, where he was knocked flying by a rescue vehicle attending the scene after his car had broken down.

Back to the press handout – Learned profession: racing driver. Mmm…

INOUE, Taki (J) b 5/9/1963, Kobe

	Race	Circuit	No	Entrant	Tyres	Capacity/Car/Engine	Comment	Q Pos/Entries
	1994 Championship position: Unplaced							
ret	JAPANESE GP	Suzuka	32	MTV Simtek Ford	G	3.5 Simtek S941-Ford HB V8	crashed into pit wall in rain	26/28
	1995 Championship position: 0		Wins: 0	Pole positions: 0	Fastest laps: 0	Points scored: 0		
ret	BRAZILIAN GP	Interlagos	10	Footwork Hart	G	3.0 Footwork FA16-Hart V8	fire	21/26
ret	ARGENTINE GP	Buenos Aires	10	Footwork Hart	G	3.0 Footwork FA16-Hart V8	spun off	26/26
ret	SAN MARINO GP	Imola	10	Footwork Hart	G	3.0 Footwork FA16-Hart V8	spun off	19/26
ret	SPANISH GP	Barcelona	10	Footwork Hart	G	3.0 Footwork FA16-Hart V8	engine – fire	18/26
ret	MONACO GP	Monte Carlo	10	Footwork Hart	G	3.0 Footwork FA16-Hart V8	gearbox	26/26
9	CANADIAN GP	Montreal	10	Footwork Hart	G	3.0 Footwork FA16-Hart V8	2 laps behind	22/24
ret	FRENCH GP	Magny Cours	10	Footwork Hart	G	3.0 Footwork FA16-Hart V8	collision with Katayama on lap 1	18/24
ret	BRITISH GP	Silverstone	10	Footwork Hart	G	3.0 Footwork FA16-Hart V8	spun off	19/24
ret	GERMAN GP	Hockenheim	10	Footwork Hart	G	3.0 Footwork FA16-Hart V8	gearbox	19/24
ret	HUNGARIAN GP	Hungaroring	10	Footwork Hart	G	3.0 Footwork FA16-Hart V8	engine	18/24
12	BELGIAN GP	Spa	10	Footwork Hart	G	3.0 Footwork FA16-Hart V8	1 lap behind	18/24
8	ITALIAN GP	Monza	10	Footwork Hart	G	3.0 Footwork FA16-Hart V8	1 lap behind	20/24
15	PORTUGUESE GP	Estoril	10	Footwork Hart	G	3.0 Footwork FA16-Hart V8	3 laps behind	19/24
dns	EUROPEAN GP	Nürburgring	10	Footwork Hart	G	3.0 Footwork FA16-Hart V8	electrics before start	(21)/24
ret	PACIFIC GP	T.I. Circuit	10	Footwork Hart	G	3.0 Footwork FA16-Hart V8	engine	20/24
12	JAPANESE GP	Suzuka	10	Footwork Hart	G	3.0 Footwork FA16-Hart V8	2 laps behind	19/24
ret	AUSTRALIAN GP	Adelaide	10	Footwork Hart	G	3.0 Footwork FA16-Hart V8	accident	19/24

GP Starts: 17 (18)   GP Wins: 0   Pole positions: 0   Fastest laps: 0   Points: 0

INNES IRELAND

IT was all-change: the front-engined cars were out, as was the casual racing attire and devil-may-care attitude, but Innes Ireland carried the spirit of a fast disappearing age into the 1960s, and in career terms it cost him dear.

The son of a veterinary surgeon, Innes showed no inclination to follow the same path and instead took up an engineering apprenticeship. After dabbling in racing between 1952 and 1955, a period that saw him complete his national service as a paratrooper, he really put his career into gear with a Lotus XI in 1956. He began to build his reputation in 1957 and 1958,

racing both his own car and the Ecurie Ecosse Jaguar D-Type.

A class win in the Lotus at the Reims 12-hours impressed Colin Chapman sufficiently for him to sign Innes for the 1959 season, and he took a fourth place in the International Trophy before making an impressive grand prix debut at Zandvoort. The cars were very unreliable, however, and little else was achieved until the 1960 season, when the new rear-engined Lotus 18 proved sensationally quick. On its debut in Argentina, Ireland led comfortably until the gear linkage broke, and then at home he stormed to

victory in the Glover Trophy at Goodwood, ahead of Stirling Moss, and the International Trophy, putting Jack Brabham in his place. Although a grand prix victory would not be his that season, he enjoyed a fabulous year, for in addition to the wins mentioned, he took the Lombank Trophy and recorded some excellent placings, as well as Formula 2 wins at both Goodwood and Oulton Park.

The 1961 season started badly for Innes with a heavy crash at Monaco when he selected the wrong gear, but despite a fractured kneecap he was soon back in his stride, producing a splendid performance to win the Solitude GP, followed by a win in the Flugplatzrennen at Zeltweg. His great moment arrived at the end of the season, when he won the US GP after a textbook drive. Then, much to his chagrin, he was released from his contract by Chapman, who had decided that he wanted youngsters Jim Clark and Trevor Taylor to race for him in 1962. That effectively was the end of Innes' front-line career.

Joining the UDT-Laystall team, Innes found success in sports cars, winning the Tourist Trophy in a 250 GTO, but he endured a largely frustrating time in single-seaters. He won the Crystal Palace Trophy in 1962, and the following season (the team having been renamed BRP) he enjoyed a respectable early-season run in non-championship events with both a Lotus 24 and the team's own BRP chassis, winning the Glover Trophy, and finishing third at Snetterton, second at Aintree, fourth at Silverstone and third at Solitude, before an accident at Seattle in a sports car race left him with a dislocated hip.

In 1964, Innes plugged away with the disappointing BRP, claiming a victory in the Daily Mirror Trophy at Snetterton, but the team closed its doors at the end of the year, leaving him to find a berth in the Parnell Racing team for 1965. His off-track popularity was as high as ever, but sadly by then he was less than reliable as a driver. Appearing late for a practice session in Mexico led to him being dismissed on the spot, but Tim Parnell must have forgiven him, as he raced for the team again in the 1966 South African GP.

Innes then found employment racing sports cars, sharing a Ford GT40 with Chris Amon to take fifth place in the Spa 1000km. He drew down the curtain on his single-seater career late in 1966, when he joined Bernard White's suitably 'happy-go-lucky' équipe and took fourth place in the Gold Cup at Oulton Park, before his last two grand prix appearances in the USA and Mexico. His hell-raising lifestyle had not fitted in with the new professionalism of the age, but this unique character, who could both charm and outrage in short order, continued to be happily associated with the sport in both journalistic and organisational capacities on and off until his death from cancer in 1993.

IRELAND, Innes (GB) b 12/6/1930, Mytholroyd, nr Todmorden, Yorkshire – d 22/10/1993, Reading, Berkshire

1959 Championship position: 10th=   Wins: 0   Pole positions: 0   Fastest laps: 0   Points scored: 5

	Race	Circuit	No	Entrant	Tyres	Capacity/Car/Engine	Comment	Q Pos/Entries
4	DUTCH GP	Zandvoort	12	Team Lotus	D	2.5 Lotus 16-Climax 4	1 lap behind	9/15
ret	FRENCH GP	Reims	34	Team Lotus	D	2.5 Lotus 16-Climax 4	front hub bearing	15/22
dnp	BRITISH GP	Aintree	30	Team Lotus	D	2.5 Lotus 16-Climax 4	driver unwell – car raced by Stacey	– / –
ret	GERMAN GP	AVUS	15	Team Lotus	D	2.5 Lotus 16-Climax 4	gear selection/cwp – heat 1	13/16
ret	PORTUGUESE GP	Monsanto	12	Team Lotus	D	2.5 Lotus 16-Climax 4	gearbox	16/16
ret	ITALIAN GP	Monza	20	Team Lotus	D	2.5 Lotus 16-Climax 4	brakes	14/21
5	US GP	Sebring	10	Team Lotus	D	2.5 Lotus 16-Climax 4	3 laps behind	9/19

1960 Championship position: 4th   Wins: 0   Pole positions: 0   Fastest laps: 1 (shared)   Points scored: 18

	Race	Circuit	No	Entrant	Tyres	Capacity/Car/Engine	Comment	Q Pos/Entries
6	ARGENTINE GP	Buenos Aires	20	Team Lotus	D	2.5 Lotus 18-Climax 4	gear linkage – spin/1 lap behind	2/22
9	MONACO GP	Monte Carlo	22	Team Lotus	D	2.5 Lotus 18-Climax 4	long pit stop – engine/44 laps behind	7/24
2	DUTCH GP	Zandvoort	4	Team Lotus	D	2.5 Lotus 18-Climax 4		3/21
ret	BELGIAN GP	Spa	14	Team Lotus	D	2.5 Lotus 18-Climax 4	spun off/FL (shared)	8/18
7	FRENCH GP	Reims	20	Team Lotus	D	2.5 Lotus 18-Climax 4	pit stop – suspension/7 laps behind	4/23
3	BRITISH GP	Silverstone	7	Team Lotus	D	2.5 Lotus 18-Climax 4		5/25
6	PORTUGUESE GP	Oporto	16	Team Lotus	D	2.5 Lotus 18-Climax 4	pit stop – fuel feed problems/-7 laps	7/16
2	US GP	Riverside	10	Team Lotus	D	2.5 Lotus 18-Climax 4		7/23

1961 Championship position: 6th   Wins: 1   Pole positions: 0   Fastest laps: 0   Points scored: 12

	Race	Circuit	No	Entrant	Tyres	Capacity/Car/Engine	Comment	Q Pos/Entries
dns	MONACO GP	Monte Carlo	30	Team Lotus	D	1.5 Lotus 21-Climax 4	accident in practice	(10)/21
ret	BELGIAN GP	Spa	32	Team Lotus	D	1.5 Lotus 21-Climax 4	engine	18/25
4	FRENCH GP	Reims	6	Team Lotus	D	1.5 Lotus 21-Climax 4		10/26
10	BRITISH GP	Aintree	16	Team Lotus	D	1.5 Lotus 21-Climax 4	despite spin/3 laps behind	7/30
ret	GERMAN GP	Nürburgring	15	Team Lotus	D	1.5 Lotus 21-Climax 4	fire	16/27
ret	ITALIAN GP	Monza	38	Team Lotus	D	1.5 Lotus 18/21-Climax 4	chassis frame	– / –
dns	"	"	38	Team Lotus	D	1.5 Lotus 21-Climax 4	practice only/car used by Moss for race	9/33
1	US GP	Watkins Glen	15	Team Lotus	D	1.5 Lotus 21-Climax 4		8/19

1962 Championship position: 16   Wins: 0   Pole positions: 0   Fastest laps: 0   Points scored: 3

	Race	Circuit	No	Entrant	Tyres	Capacity/Car/Engine	Comment	Q Pos/Entries
ret	DUTCH GP	Zandvoort	9	UDT Laystall Racing Team	D	1.5 Lotus 24-Climax V8	locked brake – overturned	6/20
ret	MONACO GP	Monte Carlo	34	UDT Laystall Racing Team	D	1.5 Lotus 24-Climax V8	fuel pump	8/21
dns	"	" "	34	UDT Laystall Racing Team	D	1.5 Lotus 18-Climax V8	practice only	– / –
ret	BELGIAN GP	Spa	20	UDT Laystall Racing Team	D	1.5 Lotus 24-Climax V8	rear suspension	=5/20
dns	"	"	21	UDT Laystall Racing Team	D	1.5 Lotus 24-BRM V8	practice only – drove Gregory's car	– / –
ret	FRENCH GP	Rouen	36	UDT Laystall Racing Team	D	1.5 Lotus 24-Climax V8	puncture	8/17
16	BRITISH GP	Aintree	32	UDT Laystall Racing Team	D	1.5 Lotus 24-Climax V8	gear selection on grid/14 laps behind	3/21
ret	ITALIAN GP	Monza	40	UDT Laystall Racing Team	D	1.5 Lotus 24-Climax V8	front suspension	=4/30
8	US GP	Watkins Glen	15	UDT Laystall Racing Team	D	1.5 Lotus 24-Climax V8	pit stop/4 laps behind	16/20
5	SOUTH AFRICAN GP	East London	11	UDT Laystall Racing Team	D	1.5 Lotus 24-Climax V8	1 lap behind	4/17

1963 Championship position: 9th=   Wins: 0   Pole positions: 0   Fastest laps: 0   Points scored: 6

	Race	Circuit	No	Entrant	Tyres	Capacity/Car/Engine	Comment	Q Pos/Entries
ret	MONACO GP	Monte Carlo	14	British Racing Partnership	D	1.5 Lotus 24-BRM V8	accident – wrong gear selection	5/17
ret	BELGIAN GP	Spa	4	British Racing Partnership	D	1.5 BRP Mk1-BRM V8	gear selection	7/20
dns	"	"	4	British Racing Partnership	D	1.5 Lotus 24-BRM V8	practice only	– / –
4	DUTCH GP	Zandvoort	30	British Racing Partnership	D	1.5 BRP Mk1-BRM V8	1 lap behind	=6/19
dns	"	"	30	British Racing Partnership	D	1.5 Lotus 24-BRM V8	practice only	– / –
9	FRENCH GP	Reims	32	British Racing Partnership	D	1.5 BRP Mk1-BRM V8	pit stop – gearbox/4 laps behind	3/21
dsq*	BRITISH GP	Silverstone	11	British Racing Partnership	D	1.5 BRP Mk1-BRM V8	ignition at pit stop led to*push start	=10/23
dns	"	"	11	British Racing Partnership	D	1.5 Lotus 24-BRM V8	practice only	– / –
ret	GERMAN GP	Nürburgring	14	British Racing Partnership	D	1.5 Lotus 24-BRM V8	collision with Bandini	11/26
dns	"	"	14	British Racing Partnership	D	1.5 BRP Mk1-BRM V8	accident in practice	– / –
4/ret	ITALIAN GP	Monza	32	British Racing Partnership	D	1.5 BRP Mk1-BRM V8	engine	10/28

1964 Championship position: 12th   Wins: 0   Pole positions: 0   Fastest laps: 0   Points scored: 4

	Race	Circuit	No	Entrant	Tyres	Capacity/Car/Engine	Comment	Q Pos/Entries
dns	MONACO GP	Monte Carlo	14	British Racing Partnership	D	1.5 Lotus 24-BRM V8	practice accident	(17)/20
10	BELGIAN GP	Spa	3	British Racing Partnership	D	1.5 BRP Mk1-BRM V8	pit stop/4 laps behind	16/20
ret	FRENCH GP	Rouen	16	British Racing Partnership	D	1.5 BRP Mk1-BRM V8	accident	11/17
10	BRITISH GP	Brands Hatch	11	British Racing Partnership	D	1.5 BRP Mk2-BRM V8	engine problems/3 laps behind	10/25
5	AUSTRIAN GP	Zeltweg	14	British Racing Partnership	D	1.5 BRP Mk2-BRM V8	pit stop – engine/3 laps behind	11/20
5	ITALIAN GP	Monza	46	British Racing Partnership	D	1.5 BRP Mk2-BRM V8	fuel feed problems/1 lap behind	=12/25
ret	US GP	Watkins Glen	11	British Racing Partnership	D	1.5 BRP Mk2-BRM V8	gear lever	10/19
12	MEXICAN GP	Mexico City	11	British Racing Partnership	D	1.5 BRP Mk2-BRM V8	pit stop/4 laps behind	16/19

1965 Championship position: Unplaced

	Race	Circuit	No	Entrant	Tyres	Capacity/Car/Engine	Comment	Q Pos/Entries
13	BELGIAN GP	Spa	22	Reg Parnell (Racing)	D	1.5 Lotus 25-BRM V8	pit stop/5 laps behind	16/21
ret	FRENCH GP	Clermont Ferrand	22	Reg Parnell (Racing)	D	1.5 Lotus 25-BRM V8	gearbox	17/17
ret	BRITISH GP	Silverstone	23	Reg Parnell (Racing)	D	1.5 Lotus 25-BRM V8	engine	15/23
10	DUTCH GP	Zandvoort	38	Reg Parnell (Racing)	D	1.5 Lotus 25-BRM V8	2 laps behind	13/17
9	ITALIAN GP	Monza	38	Reg Parnell (Racing)	D	1.5 Lotus 25-BRM V8	2 laps behind	18/23
ret	US GP	Watkins Glen	22	Reg Parnell (Racing)	D	1.5 Lotus 25-BRM V8	unwell with influenza	18/18
dns	MEXICAN GP	Mexico City	22	Reg Parnell (Racing)	D	1.5 Lotus 25-BRM V8	late for practice – dropped by team	(13)/18

1966 Championship position: Unplaced

	Race	Circuit	No	Entrant	Tyres	Capacity/Car/Engine	Comment	Q Pos/Entries
ret	US GP	Watkins Glen	10	Bernard White Racing	D	2.0 BRM P261 V8	flat battery	17/19
ret	MEXICAN GP	Mexico City	10	Bernard White Racing	D	2.0 BRM P261 V8	gearbox	17/19

GP Starts: 50   GP Wins: 1   Pole positions: 0   Fastest laps: 1 (shared)   Points: 47

A BOLD, but ultimately unsuccessful attempt by Eddie Irvine to wrest the drivers' championship from Mika Häkkinen not only saved the 1999 season from McLaren domination, but also gave the Ulsterman the platform to demonstrate the talents that for so long had been subjugated to the needs of Michael Schumacher.

Many onlookers were surprised at his emergence, but Eddie's early career had promised a great deal, from his beginnings in the British and Irish FF1600 series. Driving a works Van Diemen, he won both the RAC British and Esso FF1600 championships in 1987, amassing 14 victories, and to crown his year he also took the Brands Hatch Formula Ford Festival in convincing style. Moving up to Formula 3 in 1988, he found winning a tougher proposition; he managed eight top-three placings, but just could not break the dominance of JJ Lehto and Gary Brabham.

Eddie's graduation to F3000 the following season with Pacific found the team struggling, but Irvine got stuck in and never gave up. His reward was a move to Eddie Jordan's team in 1990, and he rapidly developed into a front-runner, winning at Hockenheim and finishing third in the championship. Subsequently opting to continue his career in the Japanese F3000 series, he finished sixth in the final table in 1991 and 1992, and was very unfortunate to lose the 1993 championship to Kazuyoshi Hoshino after scoring more points than the veteran. Highly thought of by Toyota, he drove for the company in Japan in 1992 and also at Le Mans in 1993, when he was fourth and set fastest lap, and 1994, when he came second and was class winner with Mauro Martini and Jeff Krosnoff.

Eddie was given his F1 chance by Jordan at Suzuka in 1993, and rarely can a grand prix debut have caused so much controversy. As he battled with Damon Hill for sixth place, revelling in the tricky conditions, first he obstructed and then had the temerity to repass the race leader, Ayrton Senna, who was attempting to lap him; in the closing stages, he punted Derek Warwick off to claim his first championship point; and then he suffered a physical and verbal assault from the irate Brazilian after the race. It certainly moved the self-assured Ulsterman to centre stage, if only for a weekend.

Signed for a full season of grand prix racing with Jordan in 1994, Irvine was soon embroiled in further controversy. He was blamed for a four-car pile-up in Brazil and received a harsh one-race ban. Quite reasonably, he appealed, but was sent away with his punishment increased threefold! A less resilient character than the Ulsterman might have suffered a loss of confidence, but he bounced back all the stronger, a late-season drive to fourth place at Jerez being the best of a number of fine displays.

In 1995, Irvine matured even further to outshine team-mate Rubens Barrichello more often than not. His performances in qualifying were particularly impressive, but it still came as a mild shock when it was announced that he would be joining Michael Schumacher at Ferrari in 1996.

This proved to be the chance of a lifetime for Irvine, who was astute enough to accept his subordinate role to the German, on the sound basis that a spell at Maranello could only improve his standing as a driver. His first season brought little in terms of worthwhile finishes, nor was he given sufficient testing to enable him to back his team leader as effectively as he would have wished, but he carved a comfortable and profitable niche for himself, wearing an air of casual indifference or open defiance depending upon his mood.

The 1998 season saw an even more confident Eddie raise his game, and he not only became a reliably consistent points scorer, but also had the look of a genuine contender for victory should the opportunity arise. However, few people anticipated that the opening race of 1999 at Melbourne would bring that first grand prix win, and that then he would be sucked into the vortex of a thrilling championship battle with the McLarens of Mika Häkkinen and David Coulthard. Picking up Ferrari's challenge after Schumacher's unfortunate Silverstone accident, he realistically assessed his situation and took the fight to the McLaren pair with great tenacity, and he was predictably consummate in waging a war of mind games.

Despite help from Mika Salo and a returning Schumacher, in the end Eddie came up just short and had to give best to Häkkinen in Japan. By way of consolation, there was a multi-million-pound move to Jaguar for 2000, and the chance to emerge from Schumacher's shadow and prove he had what it took to be a team leader.

In the event, Eddie's three-year tenure was one of frustration and underachievement. He gave of his best under trying circumstances as managements were hired and fired by parent company Ford in an attempt to find a quick fix. His first season was hobbled by reliability problems with the Cosworth engine and aerodynamic shortcomings with the R1 chassis, resulting in a meagre four points for a season's toil.

Things needed to look up in 2001, and they did – just – with Irvine managing to post a fine podium finish at Monaco to paper over the cracks. The Irishman didn't see eye to eye with team boss Bobby Rahal, who was replaced by Niki Lauda, so a third season began with the team still in a state of flux. Once again, the R3 chassis was not competitive from the outset, and even mid-season upgrades failed to deal with its inherent lack of stiffness. His fourth place in the season-opener in Melbourne was largely due to the first-lap multiple collision that eliminated eight contenders. He drove impeccably to third place at Monza, but the season only yielded eight points. Given that his massive retainer had yielded so little return over the three years, it was no real surprise that Jaguar's hierarchy decided not to renew his contract.

There was a possibility that Irvine would renew his links with Jordan for 2003, but in the end the Ulsterman opted for retirement. He had already amassed a considerable personal fortune through property investment, and he continued to dabble in various media and sporting activities, the most notable of which is Eddie Irvine Sports, a leisure and sporting complex near his native Bangor, County Down, in Northern Ireland.

IRVINE, Eddie (GB) b 10/11/1965, Conlig, Co Down, Northern Ireland

	1993 Championship position: 20th=		Wins: 0	Pole positions: 0		Fastest laps: 0	Points scored: 1			
	Race	Circuit	No	Entrant	Tyres	Capacity/Car/Engine		Comment		Q Pos/Entries
6	JAPANESE GP	Suzuka	15	Team Sasol Jordan	G	3.5 Jordan 193-Hart V10				8/24
ret	AUSTRALIAN GP	Adelaide	15	Team Sasol Jordan	G	3.5 Jordan 193-Hart V10		suspension damage after spin		19/24
	1994 Championship position: 14th=		Wins: 0	Pole positions: 0		Fastest laps: 0	Points scored: 6			
ret	BRAZILIAN GP	Interlagos	15	Sasol Jordan	G	3.5 Jordan 194-Hart V10		hit Verstappen – multiple crash		16/28
6	SPANISH GP	Barcelona	15	Sasol Jordan	G	3.5 Jordan 194-Hart V10		1 lap behind		13/27
ret	CANADIAN GP	Montreal	15	Sasol Jordan	G	3.5 Jordan 194-Hart V10		spun off		8/27
ret	FRENCH GP	Magny Cours	15	Sasol Jordan	G	3.5 Jordan 194-Hart V10		gearbox		6/28
ret/dns	BRITISH GP	Silverstone	15	Sasol Jordan	G	3.5 Jordan 194-Hart V10		engine failure on parade lap		12/28
ret	GERMAN GP	Hockenheim	15	Sasol Jordan	G	3.5 Jordan 194-Hart V10		multiple accident at start		10/28
ret	HUNGARIAN GP	Hungaroring	15	Sasol Jordan	G	3.5 Jordan 194-Hart V10		collision – Barrichello & Katayama		7/28
13*/ret	BELGIAN GP	Spa	15	Sasol Jordan	G	3.5 Jordan 194-Hart V10		*1st placed car dsq/alternator/-4 laps		4/28
ret	ITALIAN GP	Monza	15	Sasol Jordan	G	3.5 Jordan 194-Hart V10		engine		9/28

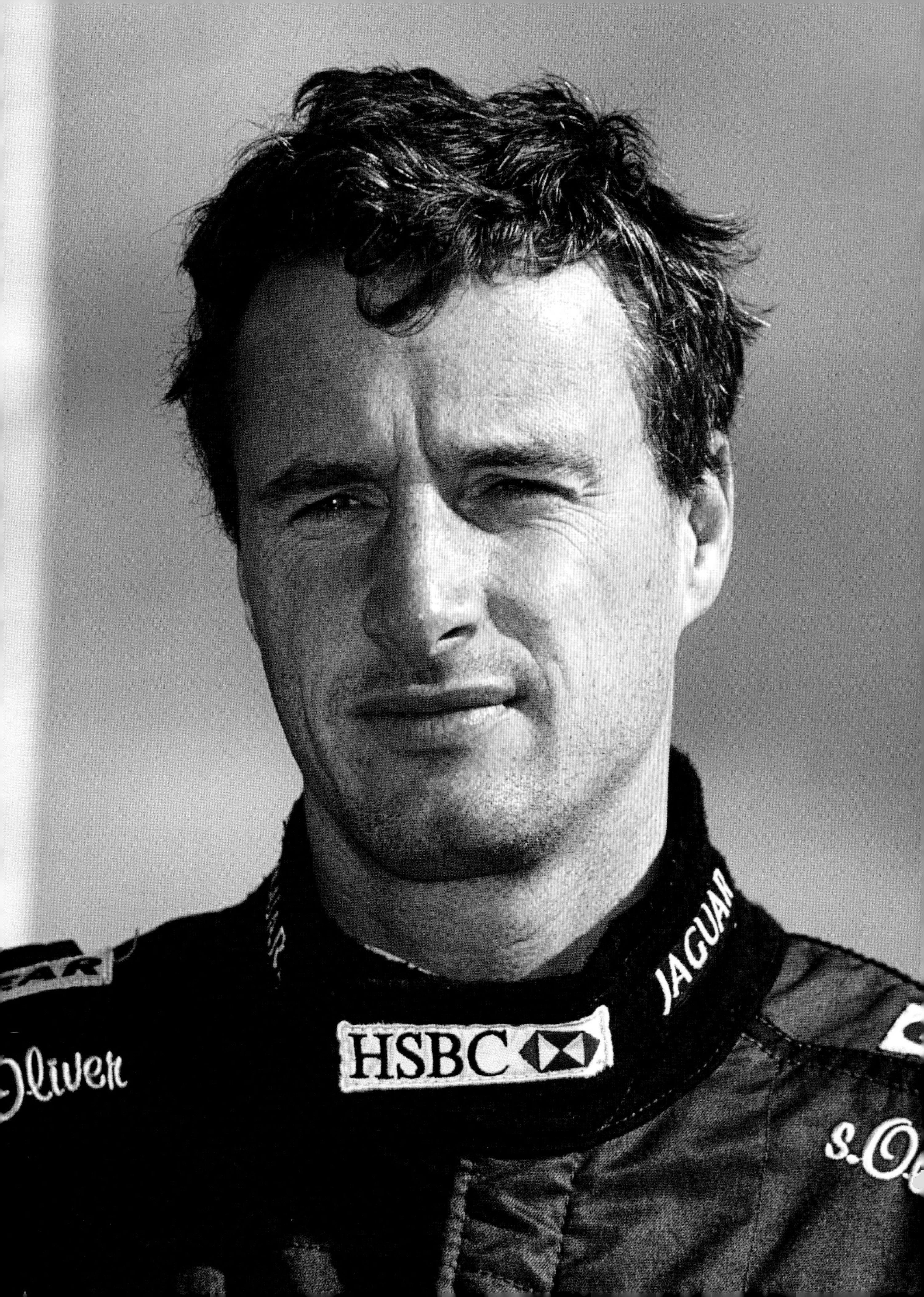
HSBC
JAGUAR
Oliver

7	PORTUGUESE GP	Estoril	15	Sasol Jordan	G	3.5 Jordan 194-Hart V10	*1 lap behind*	13/28
4	EUROPEAN GP	Jerez	15	Sasol Jordan	G	3.5 Jordan 194-Hart V10		10/28
5	JAPANESE GP	Suzuka	15	Sasol Jordan	G	3.5 Jordan 194-Hart V10		6/28
ret	AUSTRALIAN GP	Adelaide	15	Sasol Jordan	G	3.5 Jordan 194-Hart V10	*spun off*	6/28

1995 Championship position: 12th Wins: 0 Pole positions: 0 Fastest laps: 0 Points scored: 10

ret	ARGENTINE GP	Buenos Aires	15	Total Jordan Peugeot	G	3.0 Jordan 195-Peugeot V10	*gearbox*	8/26
ret	BRAZILIAN GP	Interlagos	15	Total Jordan Peugeot	G	3.0 Jordan 195-Peugeot V10	*engine*	4/26
8	SAN MARINO GP	Imola	15	Total Jordan Peugeot	G	3.0 Jordan 195-Peugeot V10	*2 laps behind*	7/26
5	SPANISH GP	Barcelona	15	Total Jordan Peugeot	G	3.0 Jordan 195-Peugeot V10	*1 lap behind*	6/26
ret	MONACO GP	Monte Carlo	15	Total Jordan Peugeot	G	3.0 Jordan 195-Peugeot V10	*broken wheel rim*	9/26
3	CANADIAN GP	Montreal	15	Total Jordan Peugeot	G	3.0 Jordan 195-Peugeot V10		8/24
9	FRENCH GP	Magny Cours	15	Total Jordan Peugeot	G	3.0 Jordan 195-Peugeot V10	*1 lap behind*	11/24
ret	BRITISH GP	Silverstone	15	Total Jordan Peugeot	G	3.0 Jordan 195-Peugeot V10	*electrics*	7/24
9	GERMAN GP	Hockenheim	15	Total Jordan Peugeot	G	3.0 Jordan 195-Peugeot V10	*engine*	6/24
13/ret	HUNGARIAN GP	Hungaroring	15	Total Jordan Peugeot	G	3.0 Jordan 195-Peugeot V10	*clutch/7 laps behind*	7/24
ret	BELGIAN GP	Spa	15	Total Jordan Peugeot	G	3.0 Jordan 195-Peugeot V10	*car caught fire in refuelling*	7/24
ret	ITALIAN GP	Monza	15	Total Jordan Peugeot	G	3.0 Jordan 195-Peugeot V10	*engine*	12/24
10	PORTUGUESE GP	Estoril	15	Total Jordan Peugeot	G	3.0 Jordan 195-Peugeot V10	*1 lap behind*	10/24
6	EUROPEAN GP	Nürburgring	15	Total Jordan Peugeot	G	3.0 Jordan 195-Peugeot V10	*1 lap behind*	5/24
11	PACIFIC GP	T.I. Circuit	15	Total Jordan Peugeot	G	3.0 Jordan 195-Peugeot V10	*2 laps behind*	6/24
4	JAPANESE GP	Suzuka	15	Total Jordan Peugeot	G	3.0 Jordan 195-Peugeot V10		7/24
ret	AUSTRALIAN GP	Adelaide	15	Total Jordan Peugeot	G	3.0 Jordan 195-Peugeot V10	*engine*	9/24

1996 Championship position: 10 Wins: 0 Pole positions: 0 Fastest laps: 0 Points scored: 11

3	AUSTRALIAN GP	Melbourne	2	Scuderia Ferrari	G	3.0 Ferrari F310-V10		3/22
7	BRAZILIAN GP	Interlagos	2	Scuderia Ferrari	G	3.0 Ferrari F310-V10	*misfire/handling/1 lap behind*	10/22
5	ARGENTINE GP	Buenos Aires	2	Scuderia Ferrari	G	3.0 Ferrari F310-V10		10/22
ret	EUROPEAN GP	Nürburgring	2	Scuderia Ferrari	G	3.0 Ferrari F310-V10	*collision with Panis*	7/22
4	SAN MARINO GP	Imola	2	Scuderia Ferrari	G	3.0 Ferrari F310-V10		6/22
7/ret	MONACO GP	Monte Carlo	2	Scuderia Ferrari	G	3.0 Ferrari F310-V10	*collision with Salo & Häkkinen/-7 laps*	7/22
ret	SPANISH GP	Barcelona	2	Scuderia Ferrari	G	3.0 Ferrari F310-V10	*spun off on lap 1*	6/22
ret	CANADIAN GP	Montreal	2	Scuderia Ferrari	G	3.0 Ferrari F310-V10	*spun – broken suspension*	5/22
ret	FRENCH GP	Magny Cours	2	Scuderia Ferrari	G	3.0 Ferrari F310-V10	*gearbox*	10/22
ret	BRITISH GP	Silverstone	2	Scuderia Ferrari	G	3.0 Ferrari F310-V10	*gearbox bearing*	10/22
ret	GERMAN GP	Hockenheim	2	Scuderia Ferrari	G	3.0 Ferrari F310-V10	*gearbox*	8/20
ret	HUNGARIAN GP	Hungaroring	2	Scuderia Ferrari	G	3.0 Ferrari F310-V10	*gearbox*	4/20
ret	BELGIAN GP	Spa	2	Scuderia Ferrari	G	3.0 Ferrari F310-V10	*gearbox*	9/20
ret	ITALIAN GP	Monza	2	Scuderia Ferrari	G	3.0 Ferrari F310-V10	*hit tyre stack – damaged suspension*	7/20
5	PORTUGUESE GP	Estoril	2	Scuderia Ferrari	G	3.0 Ferrari F310-V10	*hit by Berger on last lap*	6/20
ret	JAPANESE GP	Suzuka	2	Scuderia Ferrari	G	3.0 Ferrari F310-V10	*collision with Berger*	6/20

1997 Championship position: 7th Wins: 0 Pole positions: 0 Fastest laps: 0 Points scored: 24

ret	AUSTRALIAN GP	Melbourne	6	Scuderia Ferrari Marlboro	G	3.0 Ferrari F310B-V10	*first corner collision*	5/24
16	BRAZILIAN GP	Interlagos	6	Scuderia Ferrari Marlboro	G	3.0 Ferrari F310B-V10	*ill-fitting belts in spare car/-2 laps*	14/22
2	ARGENTINE GP	Buenos Aires	6	Scuderia Ferrari Marlboro	G	3.0 Ferrari F310B-V10		7/22
3	SAN MARINO GP	Imola	6	Scuderia Ferrari Marlboro	G	3.0 Ferrari F310B-V10		9/22
3	MONACO GP	Monte Carlo	6	Scuderia Ferrari Marlboro	G	3.0 Ferrari F310B-V10		13/22
12	SPANISH GP	Barcelona	6	Scuderia Ferrari Marlboro	G	3.0 Ferrari F310B-V10	*stop & go penalty – blocking/-1 lap*	11/22
ret	CANADIAN GP	Montreal	6	Scuderia Ferrari Marlboro	G	3.0 Ferrari F310B-V10	*spun off on lap 1*	12/22
3	FRENCH GP	Magny Cours	6	Scuderia Ferrari Marlboro	G	3.0 Ferrari F310B-V10		5/22
ret	BRITISH GP	Silverstone	6	Scuderia Ferrari Marlboro	G	3.0 Ferrari F310B-V10	*driveshaft*	7/22
ret	GERMAN GP	Hockenheim	6	Scuderia Ferrari Marlboro	G	3.0 Ferrari F310B-V10	*collision with Frentzen*	10/22
9/ret	HUNGARIAN GP	Hungaroring	6	Scuderia Ferrari Marlboro	G	3.0 Ferrari F310B-V10	*collision with Nakano/1 lap behind*	5/22
10*/ret	BELGIAN GP	Spa	6	Scuderia Ferrari Marlboro	G	3.0 Ferrari F310B-V10	*3rd car dsq/collision with Diniz/-1 lap*	17/22
8	ITALIAN GP	Monza	6	Scuderia Ferrari Marlboro	G	3.0 Ferrari F310B-V10		10/22
ret	AUSTRIAN GP	A1-Ring	6	Scuderia Ferrari Marlboro	G	3.0 Ferrari F310B-V10	*hit Alesi – collision damage*	8/22
ret	LUXEMBOURG GP	Nürburgring	6	Scuderia Ferrari Marlboro	G	3.0 Ferrari F310B-V10	*engine*	14/22
3	JAPANESE GP	Suzuka	6	Scuderia Ferrari Marlboro	G	3.0 Ferrari F310B-V10		3/22
5	EUROPEAN GP	Jerez	6	Scuderia Ferrari Marlboro	G	3.0 Ferrari F310B-V10		7/22

1998 Championship position: 4th Wins: 0 Pole positions: 0 Fastest laps: 0 Points scored: 48

4	AUSTRALIAN GP	Melbourne	4	Scuderia Ferrari Marlboro	G	3.0 Ferrari F300-V10	*1 lap behind*	8/22
8	BRAZILIAN GP	Interlagos	4	Scuderia Ferrari Marlboro	G	3.0 Ferrari F300-V10	*1 lap behind*	6/22
3	ARGENTINE GP	Buenos Aires	4	Scuderia Ferrari Marlboro	G	3.0 Ferrari F300-V10		4/22
3	SAN MARINO GP	Imola	4	Scuderia Ferrari Marlboro	G	3.0 Ferrari F300-V10		6/22
ret	SPANISH GP	Barcelona	4	Scuderia Ferrari Marlboro	G	3.0 Ferrari F300-V10	*collision with Fisichella*	10/22
3	MONACO GP	Monte Carlo	4	Scuderia Ferrari Marlboro	G	3.0 Ferrari F300-V10		7/22
3	CANADIAN GP	Montreal	4	Scuderia Ferrari Marlboro	G	3.0 Ferrari F300-V10		8/22
2	FRENCH GP	Magny Cours	4	Scuderia Ferrari Marlboro	G	3.0 Ferrari F300-V10		4/22
3	BRITISH GP	Silverstone	4	Scuderia Ferrari Marlboro	G	3.0 Ferrari F300-V10		5/22
4	AUSTRIAN GP	A1-Ring	4	Scuderia Ferrari Marlboro	G	3.0 Ferrari F300-V10		8/22
8	GERMAN GP	Hockenheim	4	Scuderia Ferrari Marlboro	G	3.0 Ferrari F300-V10		6/22
ret	HUNGARIAN GP	Hungaroring	4	Scuderia Ferrari Marlboro	G	3.0 Ferrari F300-V10	*gearbox*	5/22
ret	BELGIAN GP	Spa	4	Scuderia Ferrari Marlboro	G	3.0 Ferrari F300-V10	*spun off*	5/22
2	ITALIAN GP	Monza	4	Scuderia Ferrari Marlboro	G	3.0 Ferrari F300-V10		5/22
4	LUXEMBOURG GP	Nürburgring	4	Scuderia Ferrari Marlboro	G	3.0 Ferrari F300-V10		2/22
2	JAPANESE GP	Suzuka	4	Scuderia Ferrari Marlboro	G	3.0 Ferrari F300-V10		4/22

1999 Championship position: 2nd Wins: 4 Pole positions: 0 Fastest laps: 1 Points scored: 74

1	AUSTRALIAN GP	Melbourne	4	Scuderia Ferrari Marlboro	B	3.0 Ferrari F399-V10		6/22
5	BRAZILIAN GP	Interlagos	4	Scuderia Ferrari Marlboro	B	3.0 Ferrari F399-V10	*pit stop – air resevoir/1 lap behind*	6/22
ret	SAN MARINO GP	Imola	4	Scuderia Ferrari Marlboro	B	3.0 Ferrari F399-V10	*engine*	4/22
2	MONACO GP	Monte Carlo	4	Scuderia Ferrari Marlboro	B	3.0 Ferrari F399-V10		4/22

4	SPANISH GP	Barcelona	4	Scuderia Ferrari Marlboro	B	3.0 Ferrari F399-V10		2/22
3	CANADIAN GP	Montreal	4	Scuderia Ferrari Marlboro	B	3.0 Ferrari F399-V10	*FL*	3/22
6	FRENCH GP	Magny Cours	4	Scuderia Ferrari Marlboro	B	3.0 Ferrari F399-V10		17/22
2	BRITISH GP	Silverstone	4	Scuderia Ferrari Marlboro	B	3.0 Ferrari F399-V10		4/22
1	AUSTRIAN GP	A1-Ring	4	Scuderia Ferrari Marlboro	B	3.0 Ferrari F399-V10		3/22
1	GERMAN GP	Hockenheim	4	Scuderia Ferrari Marlboro	B	3.0 Ferrari F399-V10	*team mate Salo gave up lead*	5/22
3	HUNGARIAN GP	Hungaroring	4	Scuderia Ferrari Marlboro	B	3.0 Ferrari F399-V10		2/22
4	BELGIAN GP	Spa	4	Scuderia Ferrari Marlboro	B	3.0 Ferrari F399-V10	*wrong set-up on car*	6/22
6	ITALIAN GP	Monza	4	Scuderia Ferrari Marlboro	B	3.0 Ferrari F399-V10		8/22
7	EUROPEAN GP	Nürburgring	4	Scuderia Ferrari Marlboro	B	3.0 Ferrari F399-V10		9/22
1	MALAYSIAN GP	Sepang	4	Scuderia Ferrari Marlboro	B	3.0 Ferrari F399-V10		2/22
3	JAPANESE GP	Suzuka	4	Scuderia Ferrari Marlboro	B	3.0 Ferrari F399-V10		5/22

2000 Championship position: 13th   Wins: 0   Pole positions: 0   Fastest laps: 0   Points scored: 4

ret	AUSTRALIAN GP	Melbourne	7	Jaguar Racing	B	3.0 Jaguar R1-Cosworth V10	*spun off to avoid de la Rosa's debris*	7/22
ret	BRAZILIAN GP	Interlagos	7	Jaguar Racing	B	3.0 Jaguar R1-Cosworth V10	*spun off*	6/22
7	SAN MARINO GP	Imola	7	Jaguar Racing	B	3.0 Jaguar R1-Cosworth V10	*1 lap behind*	7/22
13	BRITISH GP	Silverstone	7	Jaguar Racing	B	3.0 Jaguar R1-Cosworth V10	*stalled at 2nd pitstop/1 lap behind*	9/22
11	SPANISH GP	Barcelona	7	Jaguar Racing	B	3.0 Jaguar R1-Cosworth V10	*1 lap behind*	10/22
ret	EUROPEAN GP	Nürburgring	7	Jaguar Racing	B	3.0 Jaguar R1-Cosworth V10	*hit by Ralf Schumacher – lost wing*	8/22
4	MONACO GP	Monte Carlo	7	Jaguar Racing	B	3.0 Jaguar R1-Cosworth V10	*despite heavy steering*	10/22
13	CANADIAN GP	Montreal	7	Jaguar Racing	B	3.0 Jaguar R1-Cosworth V10	*clutch – started from pitlane/-3 laps*	16/22
13	FRENCH GP	Magny Cours	7	Jaguar Racing	B	3.0 Jaguar R1-Cosworth V10	*extra pit stops for fuel/2 laps behind*	6/22
dns	AUSTRIANGP	A1-Ring	7	Jaguar Racing	B	3.0 Jaguar R1-Cosworth V10	*unwell – withdrew after Friday practice*	- / -
10	GERMAN GP	Hockenheim	7	Jaguar Racing	B	3.0 Jaguar R1-Cosworth V10	*grip problems*	10/22
8	HUNGARIAN GP	Hungaroring	7	Jaguar Racing	B	3.0 Jaguar R1-Cosworth V10	*fuel pressure problem/1 lap behind*	10/22
10	BELGIAN GP	Spa	7	Jaguar Racing	B	3.0 Jaguar R1-Cosworth V10	*tyre balance problems on wets*	12/22
ret	ITALIAN GP	Monza	7	Jaguar Racing	B	3.0 Jaguar R1-Cosworth V10	*multiple accident on lap 1*	14/22
7	UNITED STATES GP	Indianapolis	7	Jaguar Racing	B	3.0 Jaguar R1-Cosworth V10		17/22
8	JAPANESE GP	Suzuka	7	Jaguar Racing	B	3.0 Jaguar R1-Cosworth V10	*delay at pitstop/1 lap behind*	7/22
6	MALAYSIAN GP	Sepang	7	Jaguar Racing	B	3.0 Jaguar R1-Cosworth V10		7/22

2001 Championship position: 12th=   Wins: 0   Pole positions: 0   Fastest laps: 0   Points scored: 6

11	AUSTRALIAN GP	Melbourne	18	Jaguar Racing	M	3.0 Jaguar R2-Cosworth V10	*engine misfire/extra fuel/1 lap behind*	12/22
ret	MALAYSIAN GP	Sepang	18	Jaguar Racing	M	3.0 Jaguar R2-Cosworth V10	*hit by Verstappen – water leak*	12/22
ret	BRAZILIAN GP	Interlagos	18	Jaguar Racing	M	3.0 Jaguar R2-Cosworth V10	*spun off*	13/22
ret	SAN MARINO GP	Imola	18	Jaguar Racing	M	3.0 Jaguar R2-Cosworth V10	*engine*	13/22
ret	SPANISH GP	Barcelona	18	Jaguar Racing	M	3.0 Jaguar R2-Cosworth V10	*engine*	13/22
7	AUSTRIAN GP	A1-Ring	18	Jaguar Racing	M	3.0 Jaguar R2-Cosworth V10	*1 lap behind*	13/22
3	MONACO GP	Monte Carlo	18	Jaguar Racing	M	3.0 Jaguar R2-Cosworth V10		6/22
ret	CANADIAN GP	Montreal	18	Jaguar Racing	M	3.0 Jaguar R2-Cosworth V10	*collision with Heidfeld*	15/22
7	EUROPEAN GP	Nürburgring	18	Jaguar Racing	M	3.0 Jaguar R2-Cosworth V10		12/22
ret	FRENCH GP	Magny Cours	18	Jaguar Racing	M	3.0 Jaguar R2-Cosworth V10	*engine*	12/22
9	BRITISH GP	Silverstone	18	Jaguar Racing	M	3.0 Jaguar R2-Cosworth V10	*1 lap behind*	15/22
ret	GERMAN GP	Hockenheim	18	Jaguar Racing	M	3.0 Jaguar R2-Cosworth V10	*fuel blockage*	11/22
ret	HUNGARIAN GP	Hungaroring	18	Jaguar Racing	M	3.0 Jaguar R2-Cosworth V10	*spun off on opening lap*	14/22
ret/dns*	BELGIAN GP	Spa	18	Jaguar Racing	M	3.0 Jaguar R2-Cosworth V10	**accident with Burti in 1st start*	17/22

Eddie Irvine had a shot at the 1999 world championship after Michael Schumacher was sidelined by his accident at Silverstone. The Ferrari driver won the German Grand Prix *(left)*, but ultimately failed in his title bid.

	Race	Circuit	No	Entrant	Tyres	Capacity/Car/Engine	Comment	Q Pos/Entries
ret	ITALIAN GP	Monza	18	Jaguar Racing	M	3.0 Jaguar R2-Cosworth V10	engine – oil leak/misfire	13/22
5	UNITED STATES GP	Indianapolis	18	Jaguar Racing	M	3.0 Jaguar R2-Cosworth V10		14/22
ret	JAPANESE GP	Suzuka	18	Jaguar Racing	M	3.0 Jaguar R2-Cosworth V10	fuel rig failure – no fuel available	13/22

2002 Championship position: 9th Wins: 0 Pole positions: 0 Fastest laps: 0 Points scored: 8

	Race	Circuit	No	Entrant	Tyres	Capacity/Car/Engine	Comment	Q Pos/Entries
4	AUSTRALIAN GP	Melbourne	16	Jaguar Racing	M	3.0 Jaguar R3-Cosworth V10	1 lap behind	19/22
ret	MALAYSIAN GP	Sepang	16	Jaguar Racing	M	3.0 Jaguar R3-Cosworth V10	hydraulics – clutch failure	20/22
7	BRAZILIAN GP	Interlagos	16	Jaguar Racing	M	3.0 Jaguar R3-Cosworth V10	1 lap behind	13/22
ret	SAN MARINO GP	Imola	16	Jaguar Racing	M	3.0 Jaguar R3-Cosworth V10	driveshaft	18/22
ret	SPANISH GP	Barcelona	16	Jaguar Racing	M	3.0 Jaguar R3-Cosworth V10	*all times disallowed/hydraulics	*–/–
ret	AUSTRIAN GP	A1-Ring	16	Jaguar Racing	M	3.0 Jaguar R3-Cosworth V10	hydraulics	20/22
9	MONACO GP	Monte Carlo	16	Jaguar Racing	M	3.0 Jaguar R3-Cosworth V10	2 laps behind	21/22
ret	CANADIAN GP	Montreal	16	Jaguar Racing	M	3.0 Jaguar R3-Cosworth V10	engine	14/22
ret	EUROPEAN GP	Nürburgring	16	Jaguar Racing	M	3.0 Jaguar R3-Cosworth V10	hydraulics	17/22
ret	BRITISH GP	Silverstone	16	Jaguar Racing	M	3.0 Jaguar R3-Cosworth V10	spun off	19/22
ret	FRENCH GP	Magny Cours	16	Jaguar Racing	M	3.0 Jaguar R3-Cosworth V10	rear wing failed – spun off	9/21
ret	GERMAN GP	Hockenheim	16	Jaguar Racing	M	3.0 Jaguar R3-Cosworth V10	brake fluid leak	16/22
ret	HUNGARIAN GP	Hungaroring	16	Jaguar Racing	M	3.0 Jaguar R3-Cosworth V10	engine misfire	16/20
6	BELGIAN GP	Spa	16	Jaguar Racing	M	3.0 Jaguar R3-Cosworth V10		8/20
3	ITALIAN GP	Monza	16	Jaguar Racing	M	3.0 Jaguar R3-Cosworth V10	excellent drive	5/20
10	UNITED STATES GP	Indianapolis	16	Jaguar Racing	M	3.0 Jaguar R3-Cosworth V10	1 lap behind	13/20
9	JAPANESE GP	Suzuka	16	Jaguar Racing	M	3.0 Jaguar R3-Cosworth V10	lacking grip/1 lap behind	14/20

GP Starts: 146 (147) GP Wins: 4 Pole positions: 0 Fastest laps: 1 Points: 191

CHRIS IRWIN

AN outstanding prospect, Chris Irwin made an immediate impression in his first full Formula 3 season in 1964, taking third in the Grovewood Awards. Further success in F3 with the Chequered Flag Merlyn earned him a works Formula 2 drive for that marque in 1965. Then he gained a works drive for Brabham in 1966, concentrating on F3, but occasionally racing in F2, where he scored a fine third place in the Albi GP. Given an old four-cylinder-engined Brabham, he finished seventh on his GP debut at Brands Hatch, impressing Tim Parnell, who signed him along with Piers Courage to share the semi-works BRM for 1967.

In fact, Courage made a tardy start to the season. After scoring a fourth at Sandown Park and a third at Longford in the Tasman series, however, followed by sixth place in the Race of Champions and fourth at Syracuse in Parnell's old Lotus 25-BRM, Irwin took his chance with some solid and sensible drives in both the 2-litre car and the heavy, unreliable H16, which he took to fifth in the French GP.

Chris had also joined up with John Surtees to race the works Lola in Formula 2, brilliantly winning the 1968 Eifelrennen race at the Nürburgring and finishing third at Zolder. His performance in the F2 race brought a return to the 'Ring in Alan Mann's Ford PL3 sports car in place of poor Mike Spence, who had opted to drive at Indianapolis.

Irwin's promising career ended in a catastrophic practice crash. It is thought that he may have hit a hare on track and dislodged the bodywork. After cresting the Flugplatz, the airborne car flipped over into the trees, ripping off the roof. The luckless driver received very serious head injuries, which left him in a coma for over a week, although eventually he made a recovery, but he never raced again.

IRWIN, Chris (GB) b 27/6/1942, Wandsworth, London

1966 Championship position: Unplaced

	Race	Circuit	No	Entrant	Tyres	Capacity/Car/Engine	Comment	Q Pos/Entries
7	BRITISH GP	Brands Hatch	7	Brabham Racing Organisation	G	2.7 Brabham BT11-Climax 4	2 laps behind	12/20

1967 Championship position: 16th= Wins: 0 Pole positions: 0 Fastest laps: 0 Points scored: 2

	Race	Circuit	No	Entrant	Tyres	Capacity/Car/Engine	Comment	Q Pos/Entries
7	DUTCH GP	Zandvoort	18	Reg Parnell Motor Racing	F	2.0 Lotus 25-BRM V8	2 laps behind	13/17
ret	BELGIAN GP	Spa	17	Reg Parnell Motor Racing	D	2.0 BRM P261 V8	engine	15/18
5/ret	FRENCH GP	Le Mans	15	Reg Parnell Motor Racing	G	3.0 BRM P83 H16	engine/4 laps behind	9/15
dns	"	" "	15	Reg Parnell Motor Racing	D/G	2.0 BRM P261 V8	practice only/Stewart in race	–/–
7	BRITISH GP	Silverstone	15	Reg Parnell Motor Racing	D	2.0 BRM P261 V8	3 laps behind	13/21
dns	"	"	15	Reg Parnell Motor Racing	G	3.0 BRM P83 H16	practice only/Stewart drove in race	–/–
7*	GERMAN GP	Nürburgring	18	Reg Parnell Motor Racing	G	3.0 BRM P83 H16	pit stop – gearbox/*9th on road/-2 laps	19/25
ret	CANADIAN GP	Mosport Park	17	Reg Parnell Motor Racing	G	3.0 BRM P83 H16	spun off	11/19
ret	ITALIAN GP	Monza	38	Reg Parnell Motor Racing	G	3.0 BRM P83 H16	injection pump drive	16/18
ret	US GP	Watkins Glen	17	Reg Parnell Motor Racing	G	3.0 BRM P83 H16	engine	14/18
ret	MEXICAN GP	Mexico City	17	Reg Parnell Motor Racing	G	3.0 BRM P83 H16	low oil pressure	15/19

GP Starts: 10 GP Wins: 1 Pole positions: 0 Fastest laps: 0 Points: 2

JEAN-PIERRE JABOUILLE

SUCCESS was a long time coming for popular French-man Jean-Pierre Jabouille who, while never one to take the eye, certainly knew how to make the best use of the machinery at his disposal.

With no previous experience, Jean-Pierre competed in the R8 Renault Gordini series in 1966 and won a few races, earning an invitation to drive in French F3 in a team with the more seasoned Philippe Vidal. The F3 scene was very competitive, but Jabouille made his mark in 1968, when he ran and maintained his own car, keeping out of trouble and earning enough prize money from one race to make it to the next. That year, the series was dominated by François Cevert, but Jean-Pierre won five races to finish runner-up and gain an end-of-year Formula 2 ride with Matra at Hockenheim.

Alpine offered him a contract for 1969 as number two to Patrick Depailler, and he stayed with the team as a test and development driver over the next few seasons, his rather fragmented racing programme doing little to further his ambitions. There were outings for Pygmée in F2 in 1970 and for Elf-Tecno the following season, when he finished second at Pau. He also tried his hand at sports cars, taking a splendid second place in the Paris 1000km in a Ferrari 512S. The Frenchman's career seemed to be stuck in something of a rut in 1972, when he received decidedly 'second best' treatment in the Elf/John Coombs team and made his feelings known. When he was given a March 722, things improved and he took second place at Mantorp Park. His lot was much the same in 1973, when a lot of his time was given over to the development of the Alpine A440 sports car, but he was loaned to Matra for Le Mans, sharing the third-placed car with Jean-Pierre Jaussaud.

In 1974, Jabouille made a couple of unsuccessful attempts to qualify for a grand prix with Williams and Surtees, so he concentrated on the same mix as the year before, only this time with more success. In Formula 2, he won his first race at Hockenheim and, racing the

Alpine, he finished runner-up in the European 2-litre series. Seconded to Matra for Le Mans again, he finished third once more, this time with François Migault. Determined to improve upon his somewhat patchy record of success in Formula 2, he took the brave step of constructing his own chassis for 1975, with the support of Elf. He lost out to great chum Pierre Laffite in the championship, but thanks to his connections with Elf, he at least had the consolation of a decent grand prix opportunity, qualifying the Tyrrell for the French GP. It was a popular triumph when he finally clinched the Formula 2 title in 1976 with three wins; no one begrudged the Parisian his hard-earned triumph.

Having achieved his goal, Jabouille undertook the development work on the F1 Renault turbo project, accepting the early disappointments with equanimity as failure heaped upon failure over the first two seasons, until the glorious moment for France and Renault when the car finally came good – fittingly at Dijon – in 1979. Although overshadowed by the sparkling René Arnoux in 1980, Jean-Pierre took a shrewd and well-judged win at the Öster-reichring, before a crash in Montreal after a suspension failure left him with badly broken legs. Having already agreed to join Ligier for 1981, he made it back into the cockpit for the start of the season, but it soon became painfully obvious that he was far from fit and, with his leg injuries slow to heal, he decided to retire in mid-season.

Missing the thrill of competition, Jean-Pierre soon returned to the circuits, racing in the French Supertourisme series. His vast engineering and devel-opment experience later made a valuable contribution to Peugeot's successful sports car racing programme, and in 1993 he shared the third-placed car at Le Mans, before succeeding Jean Todt at the head of the French company's motorsport division as they prepared to enter grand prix racing as engine supplier to McLaren in 1994. It proved to be a torrid baptism for Peugeot, the newcomers perhaps having underestimated the level of technol-ogy required to compete at the highest level. Certainly, partnering McLaren, who were in a trough after so many seasons of greatness, made the task even harder, and Eddie Jordan was delighted to step in and embrace the French giant, but after another troubled and inconclusive year in 1995, it was Jabouille's head that rolled when victory seemed no nearer.

In 1997, Jean-Pierre formed his own very successful sports car team, initially running a Porsche 911 GT1 for Mauro Baldi and Emmanuel Collard, and then a Ferrari 333SP, with which Baldi and Laurent Redon took an outright win at Spa in 1999 in the International Sports Racing Series. In 2002, Jabouille joined Phillipe Alliot's GT team as a technical director. Now retired, he still attends historic meetings and tends to his classic car collection.

Jabouille's great day. The thoughtful Frenchman gave Renault their first win of the modern grand prix era when he took their turbo challenger to victory at Dijon in 1979.

JABOUILLE, Jean-Pierre (F) b 1/10/1942, Paris

1974 Championship position: Unplaced

	Race	Circuit	No	Entrant	Tyres	Capacity/Car/Engine	Comment	Q Pos/Entries
dnq	FRENCH GP	Dijon	21	Frank Williams Racing Cars	F	3.0 Iso Marlboro FW01-Cosworth V8		25/30
dnq	AUSTRIAN GP	Österreichring	19	Team Surtees	F	3.0 Surtees TS16-Cosworth V8		30/31

1975 Championship position: Unplaced

	Race	Circuit	No	Entrant	Tyres	Capacity/Car/Engine	Comment	Q Pos/Entries
12	FRENCH GP	Paul Ricard	15	Elf Team Tyrrell	G	3.0 Tyrrell 007-Cosworth V8		21/26

1977 Championship position: Unplaced

	Race	Circuit	No	Entrant	Tyres	Capacity/Car/Engine	Comment	Q Pos/Entries
ret	BRITISH GP	Silverstone	15	Equipe Renault Elf	M	1.5 t/c Renault RS01 V6	turbo	21/36
ret	DUTCH GP	Zandvoort	15	Equipe Renault Elf	M	1.5 t/c Renault RS01 V6	rear suspension	10/34
ret	ITALIAN GP	Monza	15	Equipe Renault Elf	M	1.5 t/c Renault RS01 V6	engine	20/34
ret	US GP EAST	Watkins Glen	15	Equipe Renault Elf	M	1.5 t/c Renault RS01 V6	alternator	14/27
dnq	CANADIAN GP	Mosport Park	15	Equipe Renault Elf	M	1.5 t/c Renault RS01 V6		27/27

1978 Championship position: 17th   Wins: 0   Pole positions: 0   Fastest laps: 0   Points scored: 3

	Race	Circuit	No	Entrant	Tyres	Capacity/Car/Engine	Comment	Q Pos/Entries
ret	SOUTH AFRICAN GP	Kyalami	15	Equipe Renault Elf	M	1.5 t/c Renault RS01 V6	engine – misfire	6/30
ret	US GP WEST	Long Beach	15	Equipe Renault Elf	M	1.5 t/c Renault RS01 V6	turbo	13/30
10	MONACO GP	Monte Carlo	15	Equipe Renault Elf	M	1.5 t/c Renault RS01 V6	brake problem/4 laps behind	12/30
nc	BELGIAN GP	Zolder	15	Equipe Renault Elf	M	1.5 t/c Renault RS01 V6	3 pit stops – brakes/14 laps behind	10/30
13	SPANISH GP	Jarama	15	Equipe Renault Elf	M	1.5 t/c Renault RS01 V6	4 laps behind	11/29
ret	SWEDISH GP	Anderstorp	15	Equipe Renault Elf	M	1.5 t/c Renault RS01 V6	engine	10/27
ret	FRENCH GP	Paul Ricard	15	Equipe Renault Elf	M	1.5 t/c Renault RS01 V6	engine	11/29

	Race	Circuit	No	Entrant	Tyres	Capacity/Car/Engine	Comment	Q Pos/Entries
ret	BRITISH GP	Brands Hatch	15	Equipe Renault Elf	M	1.5 t/c Renault RS01 V6	engine	12/30
ret	GERMAN GP	Hockenheim	15	Equipe Renault Elf	M	1.5 t/c Renault RS01 V6	engine	9/30
ret	AUSTRIAN GP	Österreichring	15	Equipe Renault Elf	M	1.5 t/c Renault RS01 V6	gearbox	3/31
ret	DUTCH GP	Zandvoort	15	Equipe Renault Elf	M	1.5 t/c Renault RS01 V6	engine	9/33
ret	ITALIAN GP	Monza	15	Equipe Renault Elf	M	1.5 t/c Renault RS01 V6	engine	3/32
4	US GP EAST	Watkins Glen	15	Equipe Renault Elf	M	1.5 t/c Renault RS01 V6		9/27
12	CANADIAN GP	Montreal	15	Equipe Renault Elf	M	1.5 t/c Renault RS01 V6	pit stop/5 laps behind	22/28

1979 Championship position: 13th Wins: 1 Pole positions: 4 Fastest laps: 0 Points scored: 9

	Race	Circuit	No	Entrant	Tyres	Capacity/Car/Engine	Comment	Q Pos/Entries
ret	ARGENTINE GP	Buenos Aires	15	Equipe Renault Elf	M	1.5 t/c Renault RS01 V6	engine	12/26
10	BRAZILIAN GP	Interlagos	15	Equipe Renault Elf	M	1.5 t/c Renault RS01 V6	stalled on grid/1 lap behind	7/26
ret	SOUTH AFRICAN GP	Kyalami	15	Equipe Renault Elf	M	1.5 t/c Renault RS01 V6	engine	1/26
dns	US GP WEST	Long Beach	15	Equipe Renault Elf	M	1.5 t/c Renault RS01 V6	practice accident – injured arm	(20)/26
ret	SPANISH GP	Jarama	15	Equipe Renault Elf	M	1.5 t/c Renault RS10 V6	turbo	9/27
ret	BELGIAN GP	Zolder	15	Equipe Renault Elf	M	1.5 t/c Renault RS10 V6	turbo	17/28
8	MONACO GP	Monte Carlo	15	Equipe Renault Elf	M	1.5 t/c Renault RS10 V6	pit stops – engine/8 laps behind	20/25
1	FRENCH GP	Dijon	15	Equipe Renault Elf	M	1.5 t/c Renault RS10 V6		1/27
ret	BRITISH GP	Silverstone	15	Equipe Renault Elf	M	1.5 t/c Renault RS10 V6	engine	2/26
ret	GERMAN GP	Hockenheim	15	Equipe Renault Elf	M	1.5 t/c Renault RS10 V6	spun off	1/26
ret	AUSTRIAN GP	Österreichring	15	Equipe Renault Elf	M	1.5 t/c Renault RS10 V6	clutch/gearbox	3/26
ret	DUTCH GP	Zandvoort	15	Equipe Renault Elf	M	1.5 t/c Renault RS10 V6	clutch	4/26
14/ret	ITALIAN GP	Monza	15	Equipe Renault Elf	M	1.5 t/c Renault RS10 V6	engine	1/28
ret	CANADIAN GP	Montreal	15	Equipe Renault Elf	M	1.5 t/c Renault RS10 V6	brakes	7/29
ret	US GP EAST	Watkins Glen	15	Equipe Renault Elf	M	1.5 t/c Renault RS10 V6	camshaft belt	8/30

1980 Championship position: 8th Wins: 1 Pole positions: 2 Fastest laps: 0 Points scored: 9

	Race	Circuit	No	Entrant	Tyres	Capacity/Car/Engine	Comment	Q Pos/Entries
ret	ARGENTINE GP	Buenos Aires	15	Equipe Renault Elf	M	1.5 t/c Renault RE20 V6	gearbox	9/28
ret	BRAZILIAN GP	Interlagos	15	Equipe Renault Elf	M	1.5 t/c Renault RE20 V6	turbo	1/28
ret	SOUTH AFRICAN GP	Kyalami	15	Equipe Renault Elf	M	1.5 t/c Renault RE20 V6	puncture	1/28
10	US GP WEST	Long Beach	15	Equipe Renault Elf	M	1.5 t/c Renault RE20 V6	pit stop – brakes/9 laps behind	11/27
ret	BELGIAN GP	Zolder	15	Equipe Renault Elf	M	1.5 t/c Renault RE20 V6	clutch	=5/27
ret	MONACO GP	Monte Carlo	15	Equipe Renault Elf	M	1.5 t/c Renault RE20 V6	gearbox	16/27
ret	FRENCH GP	Paul Ricard	15	Equipe Renault Elf	M	1.5 t/c Renault RE20 V6	transmission	6/27
ret	BRITISH GP	Brands Hatch	15	Equipe Renault Elf	M	1.5 t/c Renault RE20 V6	engine	13/27
ret	GERMAN GP	Hockenheim	15	Equipe Renault Elf	M	1.5 t/c Renault RE20 V6	engine	2/26
1	AUSTRIAN GP	Österreichring	15	Equipe Renault Elf	M	1.5 t/c Renault RE20 V6		2/25
ret	DUTCH GP	Zandvoort	15	Equipe Renault Elf	M	1.5 t/c Renault RE20 V6	handling/differential	2/28
ret	ITALIAN GP	Imola	15	Equipe Renault Elf	M	1.5 t/c Renault RE20 V6	gearbox	2/28
ret	CANADIAN GP	Montreal	15	Equipe Renault Elf	M	1.5 t/c Renault RE20 V6	suspension failure – accident	13/28

1981 Championship position: Unplaced

	Race	Circuit	No	Entrant	Tyres	Capacity/Car/Engine	Comment	Q Pos/Entries
dns	BRAZILIAN GP	Rio	25	Equipe Talbot Gitanes	M	3.0 Talbot Ligier JS17-Matra V12	withdrawn in practice/Jarier drove	(26)/30
dnq	ARGENTINE GP	Buenos Aires	25	Equipe Talbot Gitanes	M	3.0 Talbot Ligier JS17-Matra V12		28/29
nc	SAN MARINO GP	Imola	25	Equipe Talbot Gitanes	M	3.0 Talbot Ligier JS17-Matra V12	pit stops – engine/15 laps behind	18/30
ret	BELGIAN GP	Zolder	25	Equipe Talbot Gitanes	M	3.0 Talbot Ligier JS17-Matra V12	transmission	16/31
dnq	MONACO GP	Monte Carlo	25	Equipe Talbot Gitanes	M	3.0 Talbot Ligier JS17-Matra V12		22/31
ret	SPANISH GP	Jarama	25	Equipe Talbot Gitanes	M	3.0 Talbot Ligier JS17-Matra V12	brakes	19/30

GP Starts: 49 GP Wins: 2 Pole positions: 6 Fastest laps: 0 Points: 21

JOHN JAMES

AN engineer by profession, John James had his first race in a Lea Francis at Brooklands immediately before the Second World War, and when competition resumed he competed in hill-climbs and sprints with a Monza-type 2.3 Alfa Romeo. For the 1948 season, he acquired a 4.9-litre Type 54 Bugatti for similar competition, before reverting to a Sunbeam that had been in storage throughout the war and had been completely rebuilt. It was this car that gained him a fourth place in the 1949 Wakefield Trophy at the Curragh in Eire.

In 1951, John purchased a Maserati 4CLT from Reg Parnell and, apart from his appearance in the British Grand Prix, he piloted it to eighth places in both the Woodcote Cup and the Daily Graphic Trophy races at Goodwood. With the change in regulations in 1952 rendering the 4CLT suitable only for Formula Libre events, he used it mainly for fun in sprints until his retirement from the sport the following year.

JAMES, John (GB) b 10/5/1914, Packwood, nr Hockley Heath, Warwickshire – d 27/1/2002, Slierna, Malta

	Race	Circuit	No	Entrant	Tyres	Capacity/Car/Engine	Comment	Q Pos/Entries
	1951 Championship position: Unplaced							
ret	BRITISH GP	Silverstone	16	John James	D	1.5 s/c Maserati 4CLT/48 4	radiator	17/20

GP Starts: 1 GP Wins: 0 Pole positions: 0 Fastest laps: 0 Points: 0

JEAN-PIERRE JARIER

ALTHOUGH this Frenchman had a few fleeting moments in grand prix racing when nobody could touch him, ultimately the inconsistent Jean-Pierre Jarier flattered to deceive and the once bright promise soon faded.

After impressing in saloons and Formula France, Jean-Pierre graduated to the highly competitive French F3 series, finishing third in the championship in 1970 with a Tecno, before making an assault on the European Formula 2 championship in 1971. He took the Shell Arnold team's March to a couple of third-place finishes at Albi and Vallelunga, and had his first taste of grand prix racing when the team hired the ex-Hubert Hahne March 701 for the Italian GP, bringing the car home in a steady 12th place.

Unfortunately, Jarier's career took a step backwards the following year when the Shell Arnold team ran out of funds just after he had taken third place at Monza in the Lottery GP. The wealthy José Dolhem took over the ride, so it was back to the harum-scarum world of Formula 3, but then came his big break. Signed to lead the March Formula 2 team, he also found himself promoted to Formula 1 after Chris Amon was sensationally dismissed before the start of the 1973 season. Not surprisingly, he was a little overwhelmed in grands prix, but nevertheless was unlucky not to have scored the occasional point, but in Formula 2 it was a different story, as he stormed to the European championship with eight victories in 13 rounds.

Now in demand, Jarier signed for Shadow in 1974 as number two to Peter Revson, but the American was soon tragically killed at Kyalami, leav-ing the burden of leading the team on the young Frenchman's shoulders. He responded with much courage, taking third place in the International Trophy and then the Monaco GP. He was also a key member of the Matra sports car team that year, sharing the winning car at Spa with Jacky Ickx, and at the Nürburgring, Watkins Glen, Paul Ricard and Brands Hatch with Jean-Pierre Beltoise.

The following season started sensationally for Jarier. On pole in Argentina, he was unlucky to strip his clutch. Then, when leading in Brazil by the proverbial country mile, a metering unit failed. This dominance did not last, however, his season disintegrating in a series of spins and crashes while team-mate Tom Pryce was busy asserting himself.

Jarier gathered his resources for 1976. In the Brazilian GP, he lay a splendid second and was closing on the leader, Niki Lauda, when unluckily he crashed out on James Hunt's oil. Things were never the same after that, the moody Frenchman becoming increasingly disenchanted with life at Shadow, who dropped him at the end of the season.

Although Jarier hoped for a drive at Ligier in 1977, in the event he found himself in the ATS team, running the Penske. A sixth place on his debut boded well, but the car was never really more than a midfield runner and he failed to score any further points. Towards the end of the season, he spent a brief period back at Shadow and then had a one-off outing with Ligier. Meanwhile, Alfa Romeo, aware of his superb sports car displays with Matra, had invited him to drive their T33 cars at Dijon and Paul Ricard; he won both races with Arturo Merzario. He also raced a Mirage-Renault at Le Mans that year, taking second place with Vern Schuppan.

Jarier was back with ATS in 1978, but achieved little, quitting the team in mid-season. His whole career was suddenly revived at the end of the year, however, when he took over the Lotus seat left vacant by the death of Ronnie Peterson. At Watkins Glen, he set fastest lap and was in third place until he ran out of fuel near the end, and then in Montreal 'Jumper' put the Lotus on pole and fairly streaked away from the field until a small leak in a brake pipe ended his dominance. Ken Tyrrell, looking for a replacement for the Ligier-bound Patrick Depailler, gave Jarier the opportunity to build on his swiftly restored credibility. His two seasons with the team yielded ten points-scoring finishes, but the cars were not world beaters, nor did the Frenchman seem totally involved once he realised there was nothing to aim for.

Early in 1981, Jarier deputised for the still injury-troubled Jean-Pierre Jabouille at Ligier, before taking the only drive available at Osella. He stayed on for 1982, but apart from a splendid fourth place for the little team at Imola, he lost interest badly as the year wore on. He was in the last-chance saloon the following season; he had finally secured a place in the Ligier line-up, but unfortunately the car was not quite the competitive proposition he had dreamed of racing in previous years. On the one occasion a victory was possible, he made a hash of things, running into the back of Keke Rosberg at Long Beach when well placed.

After a decade as a grand prix driver, Jarier was forced to face the fact that he was no longer in demand, so he quietly slipped out of single-seater racing, contenting himself in the French Supertourisme series for many years. In the early 1990s, 'Jumper' – now somewhat plumper – acquitted himself nobly in the Global GT series: driving a Porsche 911SR, he won rounds at Paul Ricard and Suzuka (with Bob Wollek and Jesús Pareja) in 1994, and in 1995 he took second place in a Porsche GTZ at both Jerez and Paul Ricard.

Despite his 'advancing' years, Jarier still had few peers in his class of GT racing. He was French GT champion for the first time in 1998 and, again driving one of his beloved Porsche 911s, he repeated the feat in 1999. In 2000, he switched to a Chrysler Viper GTS-R with which he raced competitively through to the end of 2002 in the FIA GT Championship. After just a handful of races in France the following year, however, he retired after more than three decades of competition.

JARIER, Jean-Pierre (F) b 10/7/1946, Charenton, nr Paris

1971 Championship position: Unplaced

	Race	Circuit	No	Entrant	Tyres	Capacity/Car/Engine	Comment	Q Pos/Entries
12	ITALIAN GP	Monza	26	Shell Arnold	G	3.0 March 701-Cosworth V8	*pit stops – brakes/8 laps behind*	24/24

1973 Championship position: Unplaced

	Race	Circuit	No	Entrant	Tyres	Capacity/Car/Engine	Comment	Q Pos/Entries
ret	ARGENTINE GP	Buenos Aires	24	STP March Racing Team	G	3.0 March 721G-Cosworth V8	*gear linkage*	17/19
ret	BRAZILIAN GP	Interlagos	11	STP March Racing Team	G	3.0 March 721G-Cosworth V8	*gearbox*	15/20
nc	SOUTH AFRICAN GP	Kyalami	14	STP March Racing Team	G	3.0 March 721G-Cosworth V8	*13 laps behind*	18/25
ret	BELGIAN GP	Zolder	14	STP March Racing Team	G	3.0 March 731-Cosworth V8	*accident*	16/23
ret	MONACO GP	Monte Carlo	14	STP March Racing Team	G	3.0 March 731-Cosworth V8	*gearbox*	=13/26
ret	SWEDISH GP	Anderstorp	14	STP March Racing Team	G	3.0 March 731-Cosworth V8	*throttle cable*	20/22
ret	FRENCH GP	Paul Ricard	14	STP March Racing Team	G	3.0 March 731-Cosworth V8	*driveshaft*	7/25
ret	AUSTRIAN GP	Österreichring	14	March Racing Team	G	3.0 March 731-Cosworth V8	*engine*	12/25
nc	CANADIAN GP	Mosport Park	18	March Racing Team	G	3.0 March 731-Cosworth V8	*spun off/gearbox/9 laps behind*	23/26
11/ret	US GP	Watkins Glen	18	March Racing Team	G	3.0 March 731-Cosworth V8	*accident/2 laps behind*	18/28

1974 Championship position: 14th   Wins: 0   Pole positions: 0   Fastest laps: 0   Points scored: 6

	Race	Circuit	No	Entrant	Tyres	Capacity/Car/Engine	Comment	Q Pos/Entries
ret	ARGENTINE GP	Buenos Aires	17	UOP Shadow Racing Team	G	3.0 Shadow DN1-Cosworth V8	*collision with Revson*	16/26
ret	BRAZILIAN GP	Interlagos	17	UOP Shadow Racing Team	G	3.0 Shadow DN1-Cosworth V8	*brakes*	19/25
nc	SPANISH GP	Jarama	17	UOP Shadow Racing Team	G	3.0 Shadow DN3-Cosworth V8	*hit by Merzario – pit stop/-11 laps*	13/28
13	BELGIAN GP	Nivelles	17	UOP Shadow Racing Team	G	3.0 Shadow DN3-Cosworth V8	*3 laps behind*	17/32
3	MONACO GP	Monte Carlo	17	UOP Shadow Racing Team	G	3.0 Shadow DN3-Cosworth V8		6/28
5	SWEDISH GP	Anderstorp	17	UOP Shadow Racing Team	G	3.0 Shadow DN3-Cosworth V8		8/28
ret	DUTCH GP	Zandvoort	17	UOP Shadow Racing Team	G	3.0 Shadow DN3-Cosworth V8	*clutch*	7/27
12	FRENCH GP	Dijon	17	UOP Shadow Racing Team	G	3.0 Shadow DN3-Cosworth V8	*1 lap behind*	12/30
ret	BRITISH GP	Brands Hatch	17	UOP Shadow Racing Team	G	3.0 Shadow DN3-Cosworth V8	*suspension*	=15/34
8	GERMAN GP	Nürburgring	17	UOP Shadow Racing Team	G	3.0 Shadow DN3-Cosworth V8		18/32
8	AUSTRIAN GP	Österreichring	17	UOP Shadow Racing Team	G	3.0 Shadow DN3-Cosworth V8	*fuel problems – pit stop/-2 laps*	24/31
ret	ITALIAN GP	Monza	17	UOP Shadow Racing Team	G	3.0 Shadow DN3-Cosworth V8	*engine*	=9/31
ret	CANADIAN GP	Mosport Park	17	UOP Shadow Racing Team	G	3.0 Shadow DN3-Cosworth V8	*driveshaft*	5/30
10	US GP	Watkins Glen	17	UOP Shadow Racing Team	G	3.0 Shadow DN3-Cosworth V8	*2 laps behind*	10/30

1975 Championship position: 18th   Wins: 0   Pole positions: 2   Fastest laps: 1   Points scored: 1.5

	Race	Circuit	No	Entrant	Tyres	Capacity/Car/Engine	Comment	Q Pos/Entries
ret/dns*	ARGENTINE GP	Buenos Aires	17	UOP Shadow Racing Team	G	3.0 Shadow DN5-Cosworth V8	*crown wheel and pinion in warm-up	(1)/23
ret	BRAZILIAN GP	Interlagos	17	UOP Shadow Racing Team	G	3.0 Shadow DN5-Cosworth V8	*fuel metering unit/FL*	1/23
ret	SOUTH AFRICAN GP	Kyalami	17	UOP Shadow Racing Team	G	3.0 Shadow DN5-Cosworth V8	*engine*	13/28
4	SPANISH GP	Montjuich Park	17	UOP Shadow Racing Team	G	3.0 Shadow DN5-Cosworth V8	*shortened race – half points/-1 lap*	10/26
ret	MONACO GP	Monte Carlo	17	UOP Shadow Racing Team	G	3.0 Shadow DN5-Cosworth V8	*spun – hit barrier on lap 1*	3/26
ret	BELGIAN GP	Zolder	17	UOP Shadow Racing Team	G	3.0 Shadow DN5-Cosworth V8	*spun off*	10/24
ret	SWEDISH GP	Anderstorp	17	UOP Shadow Racing Team	G	3.0 Shadow DN5-Cosworth V8	*engine*	3/26
ret	DUTCH GP	Zandvoort	17	UOP Shadow Racing Team	G	3.0 Shadow DN5-Cosworth V8	*puncture – spun off*	10/25
8	FRENCH GP	Paul Ricard	17	UOP Shadow Racing Team	G	3.0 Shadow DN5-Cosworth V8		4/26
14/ret	BRITISH GP	Silverstone	17	UOP Shadow Racing Team	G	3.0 Shadow DN5-Cosworth V8	*spun off/3 laps behind*	11/28
ret	GERMAN GP	Nürburgring	17	UOP Shadow Racing Team	G	3.0 Shadow DN5-Cosworth V8	*puncture*	12/26
ret	AUSTRIAN GP	Österreichring	17	UOP Shadow Racing Team	G	3.0 Shadow DN7-Matra V12	*fuel injection*	14/30
ret	ITALIAN GP	Monza	17	UOP Shadow Racing Team	G	3.0 Shadow DN7-Matra V12	*fuel pump*	13/28
ret	US GP	Watkins Glen	17	UOP Shadow Racing Team	G	3.0 Shadow DN5-Cosworth V8	*wheel bearing*	4/24
dns	"	" "	17	UOP Shadow Racing Team	G	3.0 Shadow DN7-Matra V12	*practice only*	– / –

1976 Championship position: Unplaced

	Race	Circuit	No	Entrant	Tyres	Capacity/Car/Engine	Comment	Q Pos/Entries
ret	BRAZILIAN GP	Interlagos	17	Shadow Racing Team	G	3.0 Shadow DN5-Cosworth V8	*spun off on Hunt's oil/FL*	3/22
ret	SOUTH AFRICAN GP	Kyalami	17	Shadow Racing Team	G	3.0 Shadow DN5-Cosworth V8	*radiator/engine*	15/25
7	US GP WEST	Long Beach	17	Shadow Racing Team	G	3.0 Shadow DN5-Cosworth V8	*1 lap behind*	7/27
ret	SPANISH GP	Jarama	17	Shadow Racing Team	G	3.0 Shadow DN5-Cosworth V8	*electrics*	15/30
9	BELGIAN GP	Zolder	17	Shadow Racing Team	G	3.0 Shadow DN5-Cosworth V8	*1 lap behind*	14/29
8	MONACO GP	Monte Carlo	17	Shadow Racing Team	G	3.0 Shadow DN5-Cosworth V8	*2 laps behind*	10/25
12	SWEDISH GP	Anderstorp	17	Shadow Racing Team	G	3.0 Shadow DN5-Cosworth V8	*1 lap behind*	14/27
12	FRENCH GP	Paul Ricard	17	Shadow Racing Team	G	3.0 Shadow DN5-Cosworth V8	*1 lap behind*	15/30
9	BRITISH GP	Brands Hatch	17	Shadow Racing Team	G	3.0 Shadow DN5-Cosworth V8	*pit stop/6 laps behind*	23/30
11	GERMAN GP	Nürburgring	17	Shadow Racing with Tabatip	G	3.0 Shadow DN5-Cosworth V8		23/28
ret	AUSTRIAN GP	Österreichring	17	Shadow Racing with Tabatip	G	3.0 Shadow DN5-Cosworth V8	*fuel pump*	18/25
10	DUTCH GP	Zandvoort	17	Shadow Racing Team	G	3.0 Shadow DN5-Cosworth V8	*1 lap behind*	20/27
19	ITALIAN GP	Monza	17	Shadow Racing Team	G	3.0 Shadow DN5-Cosworth V8	*pit stop/5 laps behind*	17/29
18	CANADIAN GP	Mosport Park	17	Shadow Racing Team	G	3.0 Shadow DN5-Cosworth V8	*3 laps behind*	18/27
10	US GP EAST	Watkins Glen	17	Shadow Racing Team	G	3.0 Shadow DN5-Cosworth V8	*2 laps behind*	16/27
10	JAPANESE GP	Mount Fuji	17	Shadow Racing Team	G	3.0 Shadow DN5-Cosworth V8	*4 laps behind*	15/27

1977 Championship position: 19th   Wins: 0   Pole positions: 0   Fastest laps: 0   Points scored: 1

	Race	Circuit	No	Entrant	Tyres	Capacity/Car/Engine	Comment	Q Pos/Entries
6	US GP WEST	Long Beach	34	ATS Racing Team	G	3.0 Penske PC4-Cosworth V8	*1 lap behind*	9/22
dnq	SPANISH GP	Jarama	34	ATS Racing Team	G	3.0 Penske PC4-Cosworth V8	*driver unwell*	26/31
11	MONACO GP	Monte Carlo	34	ATS Racing Team	G	3.0 Penske PC4-Cosworth V8	*pit stop/2 laps behind*	12/26
11	BELGIAN GP	Zolder	34	ATS Racing Team	G	3.0 Penske PC4-Cosworth V8	*2 laps behind*	26/32
8	SWEDISH GP	Anderstorp	34	ATS Racing Team	G	3.0 Penske PC4-Cosworth V8		17/31
ret	FRENCH GP	Dijon	34	ATS Racing Team	G	3.0 Penske PC4-Cosworth V8	*gearbox problem – spun off*	19/30
9	BRITISH GP	Silverstone	34	ATS Racing Team	G	3.0 Penske PC4-Cosworth V8	*1 lap behind*	20/36
ret	GERMAN GP	Hockenheim	34	ATS Racing Team	G	3.0 Penske PC4-Cosworth V8	*damage from startline accident*	12/30
14	AUSTRIAN GP	Österreichring	34	ATS Racing Team	G	3.0 Penske PC4-Cosworth V8	*pit stop/2 laps behind*	18/30
ret	DUTCH GP	Zandvoort	34	ATS Racing Team	G	3.0 Penske PC4-Cosworth V8	*engine*	21/34
ret	ITALIAN GP	Monza	34	ATS Racing Team	G	3.0 Penske PC4-Cosworth V8	*engine*	18/34
9	US GP EAST	Watkins Glen	16	Shadow Racing Team	G	3.0 Shadow DN8-Cosworth V8	*1 lap behind*	16/27

Jarier competed in well over a hundred grands prix without scoring a victory. His most productive years were spent with Tyrrell, where he managed to gain a couple of podiums in the 009 car in 1979. However, he was out of luck at Monaco *(left)*, where he was forced to retire with broken suspension.

ret	JAPANESE GP	Mount Fuji	27	Ligier Gitanes	G	3.0 Ligier JS7-Matra V12	*engine*	17/23

1978 Championship position: Unplaced   Pole positions: 1   Fastest laps: 1

12	ARGENTINE GP	Buenos Aires	10	ATS Racing Team	G	3.0 ATS HS1-Cosworth V8	*1 lap behind*	11/26
dns	BRAZILIAN GP	Rio	10	ATS Racing Team	G	3.0 ATS HS1-Cosworth V8	*car driven by Mass*	(16)/28
8	SOUTH AFRICAN GP	Kyalami	10	ATS Racing Team	G	3.0 ATS HS1-Cosworth V8	*1 lap behind*	17/30
11	US GP WEST	Long Beach	10	ATS Racing Team	G	3.0 ATS HS1-Cosworth V8	*pit stop – hit Brambilla/5 laps behind*	19/30
dnq	MONACO GP	Monte Carlo	10	ATS Racing Team	G	3.0 ATS HS1-Cosworth V8		23/30
dnq	GERMAN GP	Hockenheim	10	ATS Racing Team	G	3.0 ATS HS1-Cosworth V8		26/30
15/ret	US GP EAST	Watkins Glen	55	John Player Team Lotus	G	3.0 JPS Lotus 79-Cosworth V8	*out of fuel/FL/4 laps behind*	8/27
ret	CANADIAN GP	Montreal	55	John Player Team Lotus	G	3.0 JPS Lotus 79-Cosworth V8	*oil leak*	1/28

1979 Championship position: 10=   Wins: 0   Pole positions: 0   Fastest laps: 0   Points scored: 14

ret	ARGENTINE GP	Buenos Aires	4	Team Tyrrell	G	3.0 Tyrrell 009-Cosworth V8	*engine*	4/26
ret/dns*	BRAZILIAN GP	Interlagos	4	Team Tyrrell	G	3.0 Tyrrell 009-Cosworth V8	**electrics on parade lap*	(15)/26
3	SOUTH AFRICAN GP	Kyalami	4	Team Tyrrell	G	3.0 Tyrrell 009-Cosworth V8		9/26
6	US GP WEST	Long Beach	4	Team Tyrrell	G	3.0 Tyrrell 009-Cosworth V8	*pit stop – tyres/1 lap behind*	7/26
5	SPANISH GP	Jarama	4	Team Tyrrell	G	3.0 Tyrrell 009-Cosworth V8		12/27
11	BELGIAN GP	Zolder	4	Candy Team Tyrrell	G	3.0 Tyrrell 009-Cosworth V8	*pit stops – skirts/3 laps behind*	11/28
ret	MONACO GP	Monte Carlo	4	Candy Team Tyrrell	G	3.0 Tyrrell 009-Cosworth V8	*broken rear upright*	6/25
5	FRENCH GP	Dijon	4	Candy Team Tyrrell	G	3.0 Tyrrell 009-Cosworth V8		10/27
3	BRITISH GP	Silverstone	4	Candy Team Tyrrell	G	3.0 Tyrrell 009-Cosworth V8	*1 lap behind*	=16/26
ret	DUTCH GP	Zandvoort	4	Candy Team Tyrrell	G	3.0 Tyrrell 009-Cosworth V8	*jammed throttle – spun off*	16/26
6	ITALIAN GP	Monza	4	Candy Team Tyrrell	G	3.0 Tyrrell 009-Cosworth V8		16/28
ret	CANADIAN GP	Montreal	4	Candy Team Tyrrell	G	3.0 Tyrrell 009-Cosworth V8	*engine*	13/29
ret	US GP EAST	Watkins Glen	4	Candy Team Tyrrell	G	3.0 Tyrrell 009-Cosworth V8	*collision with Daly – spun off*	11/30

1980 Championship position: 10=   Wins: 0   Pole positions: 0   Fastest laps: 0   Points scored: 6

ret	ARGENTINE GP	Buenos Aires	3	Candy Team Tyrrell	G	3.0 Tyrrell 009-Cosworth V8	*accident damage*	18/28
12	BRAZILIAN GP	Interlagos	3	Candy Team Tyrrell	G	3.0 Tyrrell 009-Cosworth V8	*1 lap behind*	22/28
7	SOUTH AFRICAN GP	Kyalami	3	Candy Team Tyrrell	G	3.0 Tyrrell 010-Cosworth V8	*1 lap behind*	13/28
ret	US GP WEST	Long Beach	3	Candy Team Tyrrell	G	3.0 Tyrrell 010-Cosworth V8	*multiple collision*	12/27
5	BELGIAN GP	Zolder	3	Candy Team Tyrrell	G	3.0 Tyrrell 010-Cosworth V8	*1 lap behind*	9/27
ret	MONACO GP	Monte Carlo	3	Candy Team Tyrrell	G	3.0 Tyrrell 010-Cosworth V8	*multiple collision lap 1*	9/27
14	FRENCH GP	Paul Ricard	3	Candy Team Tyrrell	G	3.0 Tyrrell 010-Cosworth V8	*2 pit stops – side pod/4 laps behind*	16/27
5	BRITISH GP	Brands Hatch	3	Candy Team Tyrrell	G	3.0 Tyrrell 010-Cosworth V8	*1 lap behind*	11/27
15	GERMAN GP	Hockenheim	3	Candy Team Tyrrell	G	3.0 Tyrrell 010-Cosworth V8	*1 lap behind*	23/26
ret	AUSTRIAN GP	Österreichring	3	Candy Team Tyrrell	G	3.0 Tyrrell 010-Cosworth V8	*engine*	13/25
5	DUTCH GP	Zandvoort	3	Candy Team Tyrrell	G	3.0 Tyrrell 010-Cosworth V8		17/28
ret	ITALIAN GP	Imola	3	Candy Team Tyrrell	G	3.0 Tyrrell 010-Cosworth V8	*brakes*	12/28
7	CANADIAN GP	Montreal	3	Candy Team Tyrrell	G	3.0 Tyrrell 010-Cosworth V8	*1 lap behind*	15/28
nc	US GP EAST	Watkins Glen	3	Candy Team Tyrrell	G	3.0 Tyrrell 010-Cosworth V8	*pit stops/19 laps behind*	22/27

1981 Championship position: Unplaced

ret	US GP WEST	Long Beach	25	Equipe Talbot Gitanes	M	3.0 Talbot Ligier JS17-Matra V12	*fuel pump*	10/29
7	BRAZILIAN GP	Rio	25	Equipe Talbot Gitanes	M	3.0 Talbot Ligier JS17-Matra V12		23/30
8	BRITISH GP	Silverstone	32	Osella Squadra Corse	M	3.0 Osella FA1B-Cosworth V8	*pit stop/3 laps behind*	20/30
8	GERMAN GP	Hockenheim	32	Osella Squadra Corse	M	3.0 Osella FA1B-Cosworth V8	*1 lap behind*	17/30
10	AUSTRIAN GP	Österreichring	32	Osella Squadra Corse	M	3.0 Osella FA1B-Cosworth V8	*2 laps behind*	14/28
ret	DUTCH GP	Zandvoort	32	Osella Squadra Corse	M	3.0 Osella FA1B-Cosworth V8	*gearbox*	18/30
9	ITALIAN GP	Monza	32	Osella Squadra Corse	M	3.0 Osella FA1C-Cosworth V8	*2 laps behind*	18/30
ret	CANADIAN GP	Montreal	32	Osella Squadra Corse	M	3.0 Osella FA1C-Cosworth V8	*collision with Rebaque*	23/30
ret	CAESARS PALACE GP	Las Vegas	32	Osella Squadra Corse	M	3.0 Osella FA1C-Cosworth V8	*transmission*	21/30

1982 Championship position: 20th   Wins: 0   Pole positions: 0   Fastest laps: 0   Points scored: 3

ret	SOUTH AFRICAN GP	Kyalami	31	Osella Squadra Corse	P	3.0 Osella FA1C-Cosworth V8	spun avoiding Mansell – lap 1	26/30
9*	BRAZILIAN GP	Rio	31	Osella Squadra Corse	P	3.0 Osella FA1C-Cosworth V8	*1st & 2nd place dsq/3 laps behind	23/31
ret	US GP WEST	Long Beach	31	Osella Squadra Corse	P	3.0 Osella FA1C-Cosworth V8	engine	10/31
4	SAN MARINO GP	Imola	31	Osella Squadra Corse	P	3.0 Osella FA1C-Cosworth V8	1 lap behind	9/14
ret	BELGIAN GP	Zolder	31	Osella Squadra Corse	P	3.0 Osella FA1C-Cosworth V8	broken rear wing	18/32
dnq	MONACO GP	Monte Carlo	31	Osella Squadra Corse	P	3.0 Osella FA1C-Cosworth V8		25/31
ret	US GP (DETROIT)	Detroit	31	Osella Squadra Corse	P	3.0 Osella FA1C-Cosworth V8	electrics	22/28
dns*	CANADIAN GP	Montreal	31	Osella Squadra Corse	P	3.0 Osella FA1C-Cosworth V8	*withdrawn after Paletti's accident	(18)/29
14	DUTCH GP	Zandvoort	31	Osella Squadra Corse	P	3.0 Osella FA1C-Cosworth V8	pit stop/3 laps behind	23/31
ret	BRITISH GP	Brands Hatch	31	Osella Squadra Corse	P	3.0 Osella FA1C-Cosworth V8	accident with Serra	18/30
ret	FRENCH GP	Paul Ricard	31	Osella Squadra Corse	P	3.0 Osella FA1C-Cosworth V8	driveshaft	17/30
ret	GERMAN GP	Hockenheim	31	Osella Squadra Corse	P	3.0 Osella FA1D-Cosworth V8	steering	21/30
dnq	AUSTRIAN GP	Österreichring	31	Osella Squadra Corse	P	3.0 Osella FA1D-Cosworth V8		28/29
ret	SWISS GP	Dijon	31	Osella Squadra Corse	P	3.0 Osella FA1D-Cosworth V8	engine	17/29
ret	ITALIAN GP	Monza	31	Osella Squadra Corse	P	3.0 Osella FA1D-Cosworth V8	lost rear wheel – accident	15/30
dnq	CAESARS PALACE GP	Las Vegas	31	Osella Squadra Corse	P	3.0 Osella FA1D-Cosworth V8	accident in practice	27/30

1983 Championship position: Unplaced

ret	BRAZILIAN GP	Rio	25	Equipe Ligier Gitanes	M	3.0 Ligier JS21-Cosworth V8	rear suspension	12/27
ret	US GP WEST	Long Beach	25	Equipe Ligier Gitanes	M	3.0 Ligier JS21-Cosworth V8	accident with Rosberg	10/28
9	FRENCH GP	Paul Ricard	25	Equipe Ligier Gitanes	M	3.0 Ligier JS21-Cosworth V8	1 lap behind	20/29
ret	SAN MARINO GP	Imola	25	Equipe Ligier Gitanes	M	3.0 Ligier JS21-Cosworth V8	holed radiator	19/28
ret	MONACO GP	Monte Carlo	25	Equipe Ligier Gitanes	M	3.0 Ligier JS21-Cosworth V8	hydraulic suspension pump	9/28
ret	BELGIAN GP	Spa	25	Equipe Ligier Gitanes	M	3.0 Ligier JS21-Cosworth V8	accident with Watson	21/28
ret	US GP (DETROIT)	Detroit	25	Equipe Ligier Gitanes	M	3.0 Ligier JS21-Cosworth V8	seized wheel nut	19/27
ret	CANADIAN GP	Montreal	25	Equipe Ligier Gitanes	M	3.0 Ligier JS21-Cosworth V8	gearbox	16/28
10	BRITISH GP	Silverstone	25	Equipe Ligier Gitanes	M	3.0 Ligier JS21-Cosworth V8	pit stop – tyres/2 laps behind	25/29
8	GERMAN GP	Hockenheim	25	Equipe Ligier Gitanes	M	3.0 Ligier JS21-Cosworth V8	pit stop – tyres/1 lap behind	19/29
7	AUSTRIAN GP	Österreichring	25	Equipe Ligier Gitanes	M	3.0 Ligier JS21-Cosworth V8	pit stop – tyres/2 laps behind	20/29
ret	DUTCH GP	Zandvoort	25	Equipe Ligier Gitanes	M	3.0 Ligier JS21-Cosworth V8	suspension	22/29
9	ITALIAN GP	Monza	25	Equipe Ligier Gitanes	M	3.0 Ligier JS21-Cosworth V8	1 lap behind	19/29
ret/dns*	EUROPEAN GP	Brands Hatch	25	Equipe Ligier Gitanes	M	3.0 Ligier JS21-Cosworth V8	*transmission failure on grid	(22)/29
10	SOUTH AFRICAN GP	Kyalami	25	Equipe Ligier Gitanes	M	3.0 Ligier JS21-Cosworth V8	4 laps behind	21/26

GP Starts: 132 (135)   GP Wins: 0   Pole positions: 3   Fastest laps: 3   Points: 31.5

MAX JEAN

RACE entry listings show this driver as Jean Max – apparently an error that was perpetuated. Max Jean spent much of his early career involved in the Formula Ford and F3 GRAC projects. He really shot to prominence nationally in 1968 by taking the Formula Ford Championship with 11 wins from 17 starts in a series that featured Jean-Pierre Jarier and Gérard Larrousse.

This success saw the GRAC team build their own F3 car for 1969, but decent results were few and far between, and Jean parted company with his long-time employer. With Motul backing, he ran a works-assisted Tecno in 1970 and immediately put himself at the sharp end of the races held in France. Despite second-place finishes at Nogaro and Magny-Cours, his performances were deemed a trifle disappointing given the competitiveness of his car. He also competed in a couple of Formula 2 races with a works Tecno, taking a creditable seventh place at Paul Ricard.

Retaining Motul backing for 1971, Jean raced briefly in Formula 2 for Williams, retiring at Pau and crashing out at Rouen. With that year's French Grand Prix being held at the Paul Ricard circuit, the local boy was given a chance to participate in a March 701, but gearbox problems left him well adrift at the finish. Opportunities started to dry up after this, save for a couple of Formula 2 races for Rondel at Pau and Albi early in 1972.

Returning to the well-funded French Formula 3 championship for 1973 proved to be a big disappointment for Jean, who rarely showed the form expected of him, despite being in a cracking ORECA Martini chassis. With Motul cutting back their sponsorship in the wake of the global oil crisis, Jean drifted into retirement. Subsequently, he built a successful transport business that now is run by his sons.

JEAN, Max ("Jean Max") (F) b 27/7/1943, Marseille

1971 Championship position: Unplaced

	Race	Circuit	No	Entrant	Tyres	Capacity/Car/Engine	Comment	Q Pos/Entries
nc	FRENCH GP	Paul Ricard	28	Frank Williams Racing Cars	G	3.0 March 701-Cosworth V8	pit stops/9 laps behind	23/24

GP Starts: 1   GP Wins: 0   Pole positions: 0   Fastest laps: 0   Points: 0

STEFAN JOHANSSON

BRIGHT, bubbly and immensely likeable, Stefan Johansson had gathered together all the credentials required to take him to the top in grand prix racing. Somehow, though, it never quite happened for him, despite golden opportunities with two front-running teams.

Stefan's father had raced Mini-Coopers, and the youngster was soon competing in karts, before moving up the Swedish racing ladder in various third-hand single-seaters, which he frequently had to drive above and beyond their limit to gain a modicum of success. He first hit the headlines in 1976 when still a complete novice by managing to shunt current Formula 3 big-shot Riccardo Patrese out of a European championship round. His F3 progress stuttered on over the next few seasons, raising eyebrows by his wild and sometimes not so wonderful driving, but eventually he began to make some solid progress until forced to return home when his money ran out.

It was in 1979 that things started to fall into place for Johansson. After a poor start to his British F3 championship campaign with a Chevron, a switch to a March chassis seemed to work wonders and he was on the pace thereafter. Then came a quite unexpected opportunity with the Shadow team at the beginning of 1980. In retrospect, he shouldn't have taken up the offer, for inevitably his reputation suffered when he failed to qualify in Argentina and Brazil, but at least he was able to return to a seat in the top Project Four F3 team, going on to win the Vandervell championship after a great tussle with Kenneth Acheson. Understandably on a high, he moved into Formula 2 with a Toleman and finished fourth in the final

standings, gaining victories at Hockenheim and Mantorp Park. Joining the Spirit-Honda team for 1982, he looked a good bet for championship honours, but it wasn't his year – bad luck seemed to dog his heels throughout the season.

Stefan moved into Formula 1 with Spirit and Honda in 1983, and by general consensus the Swede did a fine job with a far from sorted machine, but he found himself out of work when Honda abandoned the project to move to Williams. He decided to drive anything and everything in 1984, travelling the globe to race in an effort to prove his worth, and it worked. Tyrrell called him in to replace the injured Martin Brundle, before political problems forced the team's withdrawal, and then Toleman gave him an opportunity and were sufficiently impressed to make plans to run him in 1985. In the event, the team were unable to obtain tyres, which in truth worked in Stefan's favour, for he was available to take over from René Arnoux at Ferrari just one race into the 1985 season. This was his main chance, and he grabbed it with some gutsy race performances, bringing the car home regularly to earn a contract for 1986.

Johansson's second season was fraught with endless technical problems, but the ever-smiling Swede plugged away and was lucky enough to be given a second top-line chance with McLaren in 1987. Again some of his races were excellent, but too often he qualified poorly, leaving much to do to retrieve the situation once the racing started. The decision to bring Ayrton Senna in to partner Alain Prost for 1988 saw Johansson seeking employment elsewhere, and he could hardly have found a worse berth than Ligier. The season was a write-off and things looked little better in 1989 with the new Onyx outfit, but to his credit he helped to establish the team's credibility with a terrific third place in Portugal. Just to show there is no such thing as loyalty in grand prix racing, poor Johansson was dumped just two races into the 1990 season in favour of the well-financed Gregor Foitek.

Desperate to stay in Formula 1, Stefan signed to drive for AGS in 1991, but when the team changed hands he found himself redundant once more, and a few outings for Footwork, in place of the injured Alex Caffi, did him no favours, as the team were in the midst of a crisis with the ill-fated Porsche engine that was not of their own making.

For 1992, Johansson found a niche in Indy car racing with Tony Bettenhausen's small team. Over the next four seasons, he was generally a midfield runner, but the acquisition of an up-to-date Reynard for 1996 at last gave him a realistic chance of success. In the event, it was a largely disappointing year for the Swede, and at the end of it he was so disillusioned that he didn't even bother to look for another ride. He soon found enjoyment in his racing again, however, when he won the 1997 Sebring 12-hours in Team Scandia's Ferrari 333SP, and things became even better when he shared Joest Racing's Le Mans-winning Porsche WSC95 with Michele Alboreto and Tom Kristensen. He continued to race in selected sports car events, most notably in 2002, when he shared a Champion Racing Audi R8 with Johnny Herbert.

In 1997, Johansson set up an Indy Lights team, and one of his graduates was future IRL champion Scott Dixon, who's career Stefan subsequently went on to manage.

Stefan took the brave step of fielding a Champ Car team in 2003, and although under-funded, they did take a fortuitous win with Ryan Hunter-Reay. Sadly the team folded after just one year, and Johansson eventually returned to sports car action in 2005 with Ganassi's Grand Am Team.

In 2007, Johansson raced in the ALMS with Highcroft Racing, sharing the Acura ARX-01A with David Brabham to take fifth overall in the final standings. While continuing to make occasional appearances, such as the Speedcar series, he now devotes much of his time to his burgeoning business interests, most notably marketing his Stefan Johansson Växjö watches, which he designs personally. Given his interest in art and design, he is planning to expand the brand into other areas of the luxury goods market.

JOHANSSON, Stefan (S) b 8/9/1956, Växjö

1980 Championship position: Unplaced

	Race	Circuit	No	Entrant	Tyres	Capacity/Car/Engine	Comment	Q Pos/Entries
dnq	ARGENTINE GP	Buenos Aires	17	Shadow Cars	G	3.0 Shadow DN11-Cosworth V8		26/28
dnq	BRAZILIAN GP	Interlagos	17	Shadow Cars	G	3.0 Shadow DN11-Cosworth V8		27/28

1983 Championship position: Unplaced

	Race	Circuit	No	Entrant	Tyres	Capacity/Car/Engine	Comment	Q Pos/Entries
ret	BRITISH GP	Silverstone	40	Spirit Racing	G	1.5 t/c Spirit 201-Honda V6	fuel pump belt	14/29
ret	GERMAN GP	Hockenheim	40	Spirit Racing	G	1.5 t/c Spirit 201C-Honda V6	engine	13/29
12	AUSTRIAN GP	Österreichring	40	Spirit Racing	G	1.5 t/c Spirit 201C-Honda V6	2 pit stops – hit by Alboreto/-5 laps	16/29
7	DUTCH GP	Zandvoort	40	Spirit Racing	G	1.5 t/c Spirit 201C-Honda V6	pit stop – tyres/2 laps behind	16/29
ret	ITALIAN GP	Monza	40	Spirit Racing	G	1.5 t/c Spirit 201-Honda V6	distributor	17/29
14	EUROPEAN GP	Brands Hatch	40	Spirit Racing	G	1.5 t/c Spirit 201-Honda V6	pit stop – tyres/2 laps behind	19/29

1984 Championship position: 16th= Wins: 0 Pole positions: 0 Fastest laps: 0 Points scored: 3

	Race	Circuit	No	Entrant	Tyres	Capacity/Car/Engine	Comment	Q Pos/Entries
ret/dsq*	BRITISH GP	Brands Hatch	3	Tyrrell Racing Organisation	G	3.0 Tyrrell 012-Cosworth V8	accident damage/*after Dutch GP	25/27
9/dsq*	GERMAN GP	Hockenheim	3	Tyrrell Racing Organisation	G	3.0 Tyrrell 012-Cosworth V8	9th on road/*after Dutch GP	26/27
dnq	AUSTRIAN GP	Österreichring	3	Tyrrell Racing Organisation	G	3.0 Tyrrell 012-Cosworth V8		27/27
8/dsq*	DUTCH GP	Zandvoort	3	Tyrrell Racing Organisation	G	3.0 Tyrrell 012-Cosworth V8	8th on road/*after Dutch GP	25/27
4	ITALIAN GP	Monza	19	Toleman Group Motorsport	M	1.5 t/c Toleman TG184-Hart 4	2 laps behind	17/27
ret	EUROPEAN GP	Nürburgring	20	Toleman Group Motorsport	M	1.5 t/c Toleman TG184-Hart 4	overheating	26/26
11	PORTUGESE GP	Estoril	20	Toleman Group Motorsport	M	1.5 t/c Toleman TG184-Hart 4	1 lap behind	10/27

1985 Championship position: 7th Wins: 0 Pole positions: 0 Fastest laps: 0 Points scored: 26

	Race	Circuit	No	Entrant	Tyres	Capacity/Car/Engine	Comment	Q Pos/Entries
7	BRAZILIAN GP	Rio	4	Tyrrell Racing Organisation	G	3.0 Tyrrell 012-Cosworth V8	pit stop – tyres/3 laps behind	23/25
8	PORTUGESE GP	Estoril	28	Scuderia Ferrari SpA SEFAC	G	1.5 t/c Ferrari 156/85 V6	pit stop – brakes/5 laps behind	11/26
6/ret	SAN MARINO GP	Imola	28	Scuderia Ferrari SpA SEFAC	G	1.5 t/c Ferrari 156/85 V6	out of fuel/3 laps behind	15/26
ret	MONACO GP	Monte Carlo	28	Scuderia Ferrari SpA SEFAC	G	1.5 t/c Ferrari 156/85 V6	accident damage	15/26
2	CANADIAN GP	Montreal	28	Scuderia Ferrari SpA SEFAC	G	1.5 t/c Ferrari 156/85 V6		4/25
2	US GP (DETROIT)	Detroit	28	Scuderia Ferrari SpA SEFAC	G	1.5 t/c Ferrari 156/85 V6		9/25
4	FRENCH GP	Paul Ricard	28	Scuderia Ferrari SpA SEFAC	G	1.5 t/c Ferrari 156/85 V6		16/26
ret	BRITISH GP	Silverstone	28	Scuderia Ferrari SpA SEFAC	G	1.5 t/c Ferrari 156/85 V6	hit spinning Tambay	11/26
9	GERMAN GP	Nürburgring	28	Scuderia Ferrari SpA SEFAC	G	1.5 t/c Ferrari 156/85 V6	pit stop – tyre-hit by Alboreto/-1 lap	2/27
4	AUSTRIAN GP	Österreichring	28	Scuderia Ferrari SpA SEFAC	G	1.5 t/c Ferrari 156/85 V6		12/27
ret	DUTCH GP	Zandvoort	28	Scuderia Ferrari SpA SEFAC	G	1.5 t/c Ferrari 156/85 V6	engine	17/27
5/ret	ITALIAN GP	Monza	28	Scuderia Ferrari SpA SEFAC	G	1.5 t/c Ferrari 156/85 V6	out of fuel/1 lap behind	10/26
ret	BELGIAN GP	Spa	28	Scuderia Ferrari SpA SEFAC	G	1.5 t/c Ferrari 156/85 V6	engine – spun off	5/24
ret	EUROPEAN GP	Brands Hatch	28	Scuderia Ferrari SpA SEFAC	G	1.5 t/c Ferrari 156/85 V6	electrics	13/27
4	SOUTH AFRICAN GP	Kyalami	28	Scuderia Ferrari SpA SEFAC	G	1.5 t/c Ferrari 156/85 V6	pit stop – tyres/1 lap behind	16/21
5	AUSTRALIAN GP	Adelaide	28	Scuderia Ferrari SpA SEFAC	G	1.5 t/c Ferrari 156/85 V6	pit stop – tyres/1 lap behind	15/25

1986 Championship position: 5th Wins: 0 Pole positions: 0 Fastest laps: 0 Points scored: 23

	Race	Circuit	No	Entrant	Tyres	Capacity/Car/Engine	Comment	Q Pos/Entries
ret	BRAZILIAN GP	Rio	28	Scuderia Ferrari SpA SEFAC	G	1.5 t/c Ferrari F1/86 V6	brakes – spun off	8/25
ret	SPANISH GP	Jerez	28	Scuderia Ferrari SpA SEFAC	G	1.5 t/c Ferrari F1/86 V6	brakes – accident	11/25
4	SAN MARINO GP	Imola	28	Scuderia Ferrari SpA SEFAC	G	1.5 t/c Ferrari F1/86 V6	pit stop – brakes/1 lap behind	7/26
10	MONACO GP	Monte Carlo	28	Scuderia Ferrari SpA SEFAC	G	1.5 t/c Ferrari F1/86 V6	handling problems/3 laps behind	15/26
3	BELGIAN GP	Spa	28	Scuderia Ferrari SpA SEFAC	G	1.5 t/c Ferrari F1/86 V6		11/25
ret	CANADIAN GP	Montreal	28	Scuderia Ferrari SpA SEFAC	G	1.5 t/c Ferrari F1/86 V6	accident with Dumfries	18/25
ret	US GP (DETROIT)	Detroit	28	Scuderia Ferrari SpA SEFAC	G	1.5 t/c Ferrari F1/86 V6	electrics	5/26
ret	FRENCH GP	Paul Ricard	28	Scuderia Ferrari SpA SEFAC	G	1.5 t/c Ferrari F1/86 V6	turbo	10/26
ret	BRITISH GP	Brands Hatch	28	Scuderia Ferrari SpA SEFAC	G	1.5 t/c Ferrari F1/86 V6	engine	18/26
11/ret	GERMAN GP	Hockenheim	28	Scuderia Ferrari SpA SEFAC	G	1.5 t/c Ferrari F1/86 V6	broken rear wing/3 laps behind	11/26
4	HUNGARIAN GP	Hungaroring	28	Scuderia Ferrari SpA SEFAC	G	1.5 t/c Ferrari F1/86 V6	2 pit stops – tyres/1 lap behind	7/26
3	AUSTRIAN GP	Österreichring	28	Scuderia Ferrari SpA SEFAC	G	1.5 t/c Ferrari F1/86 V6	2 pit stops – tyres/wing/2 laps behind	14/26
3	ITALIAN GP	Monza	28	Scuderia Ferrari SpA SEFAC	G	1.5 t/c Ferrari F1/86 V6		12/27
6	PORTUGESE GP	Estoril	28	Scuderia Ferrari SpA SEFAC	G	1.5 t/c Ferrari F1/86 V6	hit by Berger/1 lap behind	8/27
12/ret	MEXICAN GP	Mexico City	28	Scuderia Ferrari SpA SEFAC	G	1.5 t/c Ferrari F1/86 V6	turbo/4 laps behind	14/26
3	AUSTRALIAN GP	Adelaide	28	Scuderia Ferrari SpA SEFAC	G	1.5 t/c Ferrari F1/86 V6	1 lap behind	12/26

Johansson takes his Ferrari into second place in the 1985 Canadian Grand Prix. The popular Swedish driver never quite managed a grand prix victory, but did go on to enjoy a long and rewarding career in both Indy cars and sports prototypes.

1987 Championship position: 6th   Wins: 0   Pole positions: 0   Fastest laps: 0   Points scored: 30

	Race	Circuit	No	Entrant	Tyres	Capacity/Car/Engine	Comment	Q Pos/Entries
3	BRAZILIAN GP	Rio	2	Marlboro McLaren International	G	1.5 t/c McLaren MP4/3-TAG V6		10/23
4	SAN MARINO GP	Imola	2	Marlboro McLaren International	G	1.5 t/c McLaren MP4/3-TAG V6		9/27
2	BELGIAN GP	Spa	2	Marlboro McLaren International	G	1.5 t/c McLaren MP4/3-TAG V6		10/26
ret	MONACO GP	Monte Carlo	2	Marlboro McLaren International	G	1.5 t/c McLaren MP4/3-TAG V6	engine	7/26
7	US GP (DETROIT)	Detroit	2	Marlboro McLaren International	G	1.5 t/c McLaren MP4/3-TAG V6	pit stop – electrics/3 laps behind	11/26
8/ret	FRENCH GP	Paul Ricard	2	Marlboro McLaren International	G	1.5 t/c McLaren MP4/3-TAG V6	alternator belt/6 laps behind	9/26
ret	BRITISH GP	Silverstone	2	Marlboro McLaren International	G	1.5 t/c McLaren MP4/3-TAG V6	engine	10/26
2	GERMAN GP	Hockenheim	2	Marlboro McLaren International	G	1.5 t/c McLaren MP4/3-TAG V6	finished on 3 wheels	8/26
ret	HUNGARIAN GP	Hungaroring	2	Marlboro McLaren International	G	1.5 t/c McLaren MP4/3-TAG V6	transmission	8/26
7	AUSTRIAN GP	Österreichring	2	Marlboro McLaren International	G	1.5 t/c McLaren MP4/3-TAG V6	stop – puncture – loose wheel/-2 laps	14/26
6	ITALIAN GP	Monza	2	Marlboro McLaren International	G	1.5 t/c McLaren MP4/3-TAG V6		11/28
5	PORTUGUESE GP	Estoril	2	Marlboro McLaren International	G	1.5 t/c McLaren MP4/3-TAG V6	1 lap behind	8/27
3	SPANISH GP	Jerez	2	Marlboro McLaren International	G	1.5 t/c McLaren MP4/3-TAG V6		11/28
ret	MEXICAN GP	Mexico City	2	Marlboro McLaren International	G	1.5 t/c McLaren MP4/3-TAG V6	spun off	15/27
3	JAPANESE GP	Suzuka	2	Marlboro McLaren International	G	1.5 t/c McLaren MP4/3-TAG V6		10/27
ret	AUSTRALIAN GP	Adelaide	2	Marlboro McLaren International	G	1.5 t/c McLaren MP4/3-TAG V6	brakes	8/27

1988 Championship position: Unplaced

	Race	Circuit	No	Entrant	Tyres	Capacity/Car/Engine	Comment	Q Pos/Entries
9	BRAZILIAN GP	Rio	26	Ligier Loto	G	3.5 Ligier JS31-Judd V8	3 laps behind	21/31
dnq	SAN MARINO GP	Imola	26	Ligier Loto	G	3.5 Ligier JS31-Judd V8		28/31
ret	MONACO GP	Monte Carlo	26	Ligier Loto	G	3.5 Ligier JS31-Judd V8	electrics	26/30
10	MEXICAN GP	Mexico City	26	Ligier Loto	G	3.5 Ligier JS31-Judd V8	4 laps behind	24/30
ret	CANADIAN GP	Montreal	26	Ligier Loto	G	3.5 Ligier JS31-Judd V8	engine	25/31
ret	US GP (DETROIT)	Detroit	26	Ligier Loto	G	3.5 Ligier JS31-Judd V8	engine	18/31
dnq	FRENCH GP	Paul Ricard	26	Ligier Loto	G	3.5 Ligier JS31-Judd V8		30/31
dnq	BRITISH GP	Silverstone	26	Ligier Loto	G	3.5 Ligier JS31-Judd V8		29/31
dnq	GERMAN GP	Hockenheim	26	Ligier Loto	G	3.5 Ligier JS31-Judd V8		28/31
ret	HUNGARIAN GP	Hungaroring	26	Ligier Loto	G	3.5 Ligier JS31-Judd V8	stuck throttle	24/31
11*/ret	BELGIAN GP	Spa	26	Ligier Loto	G	3.5 Ligier JS31-Judd V8	cwp/*3rd & 4th cars dsq/-4 laps	20/31
dnq	ITALIAN GP	Monza	26	Ligier Loto	G	3.5 Ligier JS31-Judd V8		28/31
ret	PORTUGUESE GP	Estoril	26	Ligier Loto	G	3.5 Ligier JS31-Judd V8	engine	24/31
ret	SPANISH GP	Jerez	26	Ligier Loto	G	3.5 Ligier JS31-Judd V8	lost wheel	21/31
dnq	JAPANESE GP	Suzuka	26	Ligier Loto	G	3.5 Ligier JS31-Judd V8		27/31
9/ret	AUSTRALIAN GP	Adelaide	26	Ligier Loto	G	3.5 Ligier JS31-Judd V8	out of fuel/6 laps behind	22/31

1989 Championship position: 11th=   Wins: 0   Pole positions: 0   Fastest laps: 0   Points scored: 6

	Race	Circuit	No	Entrant	Tyres	Capacity/Car/Engine	Comment	Q Pos/Entries
dnpq	BRAZILIAN GP	Rio	36	Moneytron Onyx	G	3.5 Onyx ORE 1-Cosworth V8		37/38
dnpq	SAN MARINO GP	Imola	36	Moneytron Onyx	G	3.5 Onyx ORE 1-Cosworth V8		34/39
dnpq	MONACO GP	Monte Carlo	36	Moneytron Onyx	G	3.5 Onyx ORE 1-Cosworth V8		31/38
ret	MEXICAN GP	Mexico City	36	Moneytron Onyx	G	3.5 Onyx ORE 1-Cosworth V8	transmission	21/39
ret	US GP (PHOENIX)	Phoenix	36	Moneytron Onyx	G	3.5 Onyx ORE 1-Cosworth V8	puncture – suspension damage	19/39
dsq	CANADIAN GP	Montreal	36	Moneytron Onyx	G	3.5 Onyx ORE 1-Cosworth V8	trailing air gun/black flagged	18/39
5	FRENCH GP	Paul Ricard	36	Moneytron Onyx	G	3.5 Onyx ORE 1-Cosworth V8	throttle linkage problems/-1 lap	13/39
dnpq	BRITISH GP	Silverstone	36	Moneytron Onyx	G	3.5 Onyx ORE 1-Cosworth V8		31/39
ret	GERMAN GP	Hockenheim	36	Moneytron Onyx	G	3.5 Onyx ORE 1-Cosworth V8	rear wheel bearing	24/39
ret	HUNGARIAN GP	Hungaroring	36	Moneytron Onyx	G	3.5 Onyx ORE 1-Cosworth V8	gear selection	24/39
8	BELGIAN GP	Spa	36	Moneytron Onyx	G	3.5 Onyx ORE 1-Cosworth V8	1 lap behind	15/39
dnpq	ITALIAN GP	Monza	36	Moneytron Onyx	G	3.5 Onyx ORE 1-Cosworth V8		30/39
3	PORTUGUESE GP	Estoril	36	Moneytron Onyx	G	3.5 Onyx ORE 1-Cosworth V8		12/39
dnpq	SPANISH GP	Jerez	36	Moneytron Onyx	G	3.5 Onyx ORE 1-Cosworth V8		31/38
dnpq	JAPANESE GP	Suzuka	36	Moneytron Onyx	G	3.5 Onyx ORE 1-Cosworth V8		33/39
dnpq	AUSTRALIAN GP	Adelaide	36	Moneytron Onyx	G	3.5 Onyx ORE 1-Cosworth V8		31/39

1990 Championship position: Unplaced

	Race	Circuit	No	Entrant	Tyres	Capacity/Car/Engine	Comment	Q Pos/Entries
dnq	US GP (PHOENIX)	Phoenix	35	Moneytron Onyx Formula One	G	3.5 Onyx ORE 1-Cosworth V8		28/35
dnq	BRAZILIAN GP	Interlagos	35	Moneytron Onyx Formula One	G	3.5 Onyx ORE 1-Cosworth V8		27/35

1991 Championship position: Unplaced

	Race	Circuit	No	Entrant	Tyres	Capacity/Car/Engine	Comment	Q Pos/Entries
dnq	US GP (PHOENIX)	Phoenix	18	Automobiles Gonfaronaise Sportive	G	3.5 AGS JH25-Cosworth V8		29/34
dnq	BRAZILIAN GP	Interlagos	18	Automobiles Gonfaronaise Sportive	G	3.5 AGS JH25-Cosworth V8		28/34
ret	CANADIAN GP	Montreal	10	Footwork Grand Prix International	G	3.5 Footwork FA12-Porsche V12	engine	25/34
dnq	MEXICAN GP	Mexico City	10	Footwork Grand Prix International	G	3.5 Footwork FA12-Porsche V12		29/34
dnq	FRENCH GP	Magny Cours	10	Footwork Grand Prix International	G	3.5 Footwork FA12-Cosworth V8		30/34
dnq	BRITISH GP	Silverstone	10	Footwork Grand Prix International	G	3.5 Footwork FA12-Cosworth V8		28/34

GP Starts: 79   GP Wins: 0   Pole positions: 0   Fastest laps: 0   Points: 88

JOHNSON, Leslie (GB) b 22/3/1912 Walthamstow, London – d 8/6/1959, Withington, Gloucestershire

1950 Championship position: Unplaced

	Race	Circuit	No	Entrant	Tyres	Capacity/Car/Engine	Comment	Q Pos/Entries
ret	BRITISH GP	Silverstone	8	T A S O Mathieson	D	1.5 s/c ERA E type 6	supercharger	12/21

GP Starts: 1   GP Wins: 0   Pole positions: 0   Fastest laps: 0   Points: 0

JOHNSTONE, Bruce (ZA) b 30/1/1937, Durban

1962 Championship position: Unplaced

	Race	Circuit	No	Entrant	Tyres	Capacity/Car/Engine	Comment	Q Pos/Entries
9	SOUTH AFRICAN GP	East London	5	Owen Racing Organisation	D	1.5 BRM P48/57 V8	6 laps behind	17/17

GP Starts: 1   GP Wins: 0   Pole positions: 0   Fastest laps: 0   Points: 0

LESLIE JOHNSON

LESLIE JOHNSON was not born into a wealthy family; his father was a cabinetmaker with a small business, who died when Leslie was still in his teens. He took over the reigns to help support the family and soon began to make a success of the concern, which generated the funds to allow him to take up motorsport. He raced a Delage, a Talbot-Lago and an ERA E-Type with great gusto in the years immediately after the Second World War, and even became the chairman of the once illustrious ERA marque after taking control in late 1947.

Johnson took part in the 1950 British Grand Prix, the very first round of the world championship, at the wheel of an ERA, but his major driving successes were often achieved at the wheel of rival cars. In 1948, he won the Spa 24-hours sports car race in an Aston Martin, shared with St John Horsfall, and he was second at Spa again the following year, also in an Aston, this time with Charles Brackenbury.

In 1950, driving a Jaguar XK120, Johnson was third in the Tourist Trophy and fifth in the Mille Miglia; a year later, he came fourth in the Jaguar with Tony Rolt. Driving a Nash-Healey, he finished third at Le Mans with Tommy Wisdom in 1952, and also was fourth in class (despite shock absorber problems) in that year's Mille Miglia in the same machine. He collapsed with serious heart problems during the 1954 Monte Carlo Rally, which resulted in his enforced retirement from competition.

Johnson continued to run several businesses and was much loved by his employees, who it seems were exceptionally well cared for. Sadly in childhood he had suffered from illnesses that damaged his heart and kidneys, which eventually took their toll on this kindly man in 1959 at the early age of 46.

BRUCE JOHNSTONE

HAVING enhanced his reputation with a Volvo before entering single-seater competition, South African Bruce Johnstone really came to prominence nationally with a Cooper-Alfa in 1960, when he finished fourth in the Cape GP and then sixth in the Formula Libre South African Grand Prix, won by Paul Frère. Less than a year later, he finished runner-up to Syd van der Vyver in the 1961 South African championship and was invited to drive for the Yeoman Credit team, under the stewardship of Reg Parnell. It was not a happy partnership, however, as Johnstone crashed the car in the Natal GP and then in practice for the South African GP, rendering him a non-starter.

After travelling over to Europe in 1962, Bruce drove for Ian Walker, winning the up-to-1.5-litre class in the Nürburgring 1000km with Peter Ashdown in a Lotus 23 and taking fifth in the Vanwall Trophy at Snetterton with Walker's Formula Junior Lotus. Bruce also concluded a deal to drive a third works car for BRM in Europe and in South Africa at the end of that season. He did quite a bit of testing for the Bourne concern, but BRM would only give him one outing in the Gold Cup race at Oulton Park, where he finished fourth. Once back home, he was dismayed to find that he was given only a semi-works car for the Natal GP, which blew up in heat 2. Then he was forced to use carburettors rather than fuel injection in the same car to allow him to take part in his only world championship grand prix. After a pit stop to adjust the timing, he took the car to a ninth-place finish. In disgust, he abandoned the car in a nearby garage, leaving BRM to reclaim it at their own expense.

Undeniably, Johnstone was a talented and versatile driver, for he won the Rand nine-hours at Kyalami, sharing David Piper's Ferrari 250 GTO, but he was so upset at his treatment by BRM that year that he decided to retire from driving. A few years later, however, he returned to the sport as a key figure in gaining sponsorship for local drivers and events, such as the Springbok sports car series.

ALAN JONES, MBE

TOUGH and downright bloody-minded, Alan Jones might have been, but once he had established himself in the Williams team there were few to argue with the Australian's methods. Endowed with immense physical strength and bucket-loads of bravery, he became perhaps the 'ground-effect' era's most skilled practitioner, with a driving style that appeared brutal at times, but certainly produced results.

The son of Stan Jones, a famous 1950s Australian racer, young Alan left school to work in his father's Holden dealership. He raced a Mini and then an old Cooper before travelling to England in 1967, only to find that even a Formula Ford drive was out of his reach. Undaunted, he returned in 1970 with fellow racing aspirant Brian McGuire, and the Aussie pair set about running a couple of F3 Brabhams financed by buying and selling second-hand cars. Money was tight, Alan and wife Beverley living a hand-to-mouth existence to pay for the racing programme, but by 1973 he had a foot on the ladder to the top with a DART-entered GRD, with which he took second place in the John Player championship. Then came a setback when the team folded, leaving him with no drive for 1974, until one Harry Stiller came to the rescue. He ran the Australian in Formula Atlantic and, at the end of the year, Jones made a big impression in a one-off F5000 drive for John MacDonald.

Alan stepped up to Formula 1 in 1975 with Stiller's Hesketh, but the team managed only three grands prix before the owner packed his bags and went abroad for tax reasons, leaving the Australian high and dry. Then Graham Hill invited him to join the Embassy team in place of the injured Rolf Stommelen, and he took the car into fifth place at the Nürburgring before the German was fit to resume. Fortunately, John MacDonald found Jones a seat in his RAM F5000 car while he continued to look for a Formula 1 ride. After a sensational drive to second place in the 1976 Race of Champions at the wheel of a Surtees, he was placed under contract for the season, but relations soon became strained between team boss and driver, Jones being more interested in his US F5000 programme with Theodore, which brought wins at Mosport and Watkins Glen. He ended the F1 season with fourth place at Mount Fuji, but without the prospect of a grand prix ride after a complete breakdown of communications with Surtees.

Then, in 1977, tragedy worked in Alan's favour. When Tom Pryce was killed in South Africa, he took over the vacant seat at Shadow and seized the opportunity brilliantly, winning in Austria and scoring points finishes with some aggressive drives. Frank Williams, rebuilding his team in the wake of the Walter Wolf fiasco, saw Jones as just the sort of pragmatic charger he needed for 1978. At the wheel of Patrick Head's no-nonsense machine, the Aussie regularly put himself in among the leaders, often dogging the omnipotent Lotus 79s. Eleventh place in the championship was in no way a reflection of the team's competitiveness that year, but Alan had the satisfaction of also making his mark in Can-Am, taking the title in the Haas/Hall Lola T333.

The following season marked the true blossoming of Alan Jones the racing driver. The new ground-effect Williams FW07 proved that the imitator had leapfrogged the innovator, and in Alan's hands the car was simply stunning. A spate of retirements in the first half of the year torpedoed his title hopes, but four wins from five starts gave a fair indication of his late-season dominance. Nothing was left to chance in 1980, when he squeezed every ounce of potential from the car. He never once eased up, and certainly took no prisoners, winning the title with crushing dominance. There was no let-up in 1981 either as he headed towards self-imposed retirement; he still raced as if that first grand prix win had not yet been achieved, finishing on a high note with a lights-to-flag win at Caesar's Palace.

Perhaps the story should have ended there. But after racing Porsches back in Australia, and despite a broken leg sustained in a riding accident, Jones was tempted back in 1983. In his all-too-brief spell with Arrows, he took third in the Race of Champions and then raced at Long Beach, before pulling out when he was unable to agree a contract.

In mid-1985, Jones was called back into action for one race, substituting for the injured Mario Andretti in a CART race at Road America. Considering he had been out of the cockpit for more than a year, he was very happy to deliver the team a third-place finish in a rain-affected race. This set him up for his much awaited return to Formula 1 with Team Haas Lola later that season. Both technically and administratively, the project was something of a fiasco, leaving him to pick his way through the 1986 season with no more than occasional glimpses of his racing past. Wisely there were no further attempts to extend his grand prix career; instead he opted to tackle the thunderous Australian V8 Touring Car Series in tandem with his no-nonsense commentating role on Formula 1 for Channel Nine.

Jones spent more than a decade as both driver and team owner in the hairy-chested category with mixed results. After little success initially with a Ford Sierra, 1991 found him in a BMW M320 Evolution, taking fourth place in the series overall. He returned to Ford in 1993 and, in his best season, finished runner-up to team-mate Glen Seaton, running a pair of Falcons.

The next couple of years saw Alan slip down the rankings, but he remained a top-ten performer, and as the profile of this form of racing in Australia rose enormously, he found major sponsorship from Marlboro. He formed his own team in 1996, running Ford Falcons, but by mid-season he had lost his substantial backing and eventually sold his interest to return to driver duties with his previous employer, Tony Longhurst, for 1998. By then, however, his form had dipped and he made only occasional guest appearances in the big events, such as Bathurst, where he finished seventh in his final race, before quitting for good at the end of 2002.

Subsequently, Jones held a franchise for Australia in the A1GP series, which ran a number of drivers, including Will Power and Ryan Briscoe, as well as his adopted son, Christian Jones. He was also offered enough of a financial incentive to appear in the inaugural Grand Prix Masters race at Kyalami in 2005, but after setting times well off the pace, he wisely pulled out during practice, citing neck pains.

JONES, Alan (AUS) b 2/11/1946, Melbourne, Victoria

1975 Championship position: 17th   Wins: 0   Pole positions: 0   Fastest laps: 0   Points scored: 2

	Race	Circuit	No	Entrant	Tyres	Capacity/Car/Engine	Comment	Q Pos/Entries
ret	SPANISH GP	Montjuich Park	25	Custom Made Harry Stiller Racing	G	3.0 Hesketh 308B-Cosworth V8	*hit by Donohue*	20/26
ret	MONACO GP	Monte Carlo	26	Custom Made Harry Stiller Racing	G	3.0 Hesketh 308B-Cosworth V8	*lost wheel*	18/26
ret	BELGIAN GP	Zolder	26	Custom Made Harry Stiller Racing	G	3.0 Hesketh 308B-Cosworth V8	*hit by Laffite*	13/24
11	SWEDISH GP	Anderstorp	26	Custom Made Harry Stiller Racing	G	3.0 Hesketh 308B-Cosworth V8	*1 lap behind*	19/26
13	DUTCH GP	Zandvoort	22	Embassy Racing with Graham Hill	G	3.0 Hill GH1-Cosworth V8	*pit stop – tyres/5 laps behind*	17/25
16	FRENCH GP	Paul Ricard	22	Embassy Racing with Graham Hill	G	3.0 Hill GH1-Cosworth V8	*spin – pit stop/1 lap behind*	20/26
10	BRITISH GP	Silverstone	22	Embassy Racing with Graham Hill	G	3.0 Hill GH1-Cosworth V8	*2 pit stops – tyres/2 laps behind*	20/28
5	GERMAN GP	Nürburgring	22	Embassy Racing with Graham Hill	G	3.0 Hill GH1-Cosworth V8		21/26

1976 Championship position: 14th=   Wins: 0   Pole positions: 0   Fastest laps: 0   Points scored: 7

	Race	Circuit	No	Entrant	Tyres	Capacity/Car/Engine	Comment	Q Pos/Entries
nc	US GP WEST	Long Beach	19	Durex Team Surtees	G	3.0 Surtees TS19-Cosworth V8	*2 pit stops/10 laps behind*	19/27
9	SPANISH GP	Jarama	19	Durex Team Surtees	G	3.0 Surtees TS19-Cosworth V8	*1 lap behind*	20/30
5	BELGIAN GP	Zolder	19	Durex Team Surtees	G	3.0 Surtees TS19-Cosworth V8	*1 lap behind*	16/29
ret	MONACO GP	Monte Carlo	19	Durex Team Surtees	G	3.0 Surtees TS19-Cosworth V8	*collision with Reutemann*	19/25
13	SWEDISH GP	Anderstorp	19	Durex Team Surtees	G	3.0 Surtees TS19-Cosworth V8	*1 lap behind*	18/27
ret	FRENCH GP	Paul Ricard	19	Durex Team Surtees	G	3.0 Surtees TS19-Cosworth V8	*rear anti-roll bar*	18/30
5	BRITISH GP	Brands Hatch	19	Durex Team Surtees	G	3.0 Surtees TS19-Cosworth V8	*1 lap behind*	19/30
10	GERMAN GP	Nürburgring	19	Durex Team Surtees	G	3.0 Surtees TS19-Cosworth V8		14/28
ret	AUSTRIAN GP	Österreichring	19	Durex Team Surtees	G	3.0 Surtees TS19-Cosworth V8	*engine cut out – crashed*	15/25
8	DUTCH GP	Zandvoort	19	Durex Team Surtees	G	3.0 Surtees TS19-Cosworth V8	*1 lap behind*	16/27
12	ITALIAN GP	Monza	19	Durex Team Surtees	G	3.0 Surtees TS19-Cosworth V8	*pit stop – thought race stopped/-1 lap*	18/29
16	CANADIAN GP	Mosport Park	19	Durex Team Surtees	G	3.0 Surtees TS19-Cosworth V8	*pit stop/2 laps behind*	20/27
8	US GP EAST	Watkins Glen	19	Durex Team Surtees	G	3.0 Surtees TS19-Cosworth V8	*1 lap behind*	18/27
4	JAPANESE GP	Mount Fuji	19	Durex/Theodore Team Surtees	G	3.0 Surtees TS19-Cosworth V8	*1 lap behind*	20/27

1977 Championship position: 7th   Wins: 1   Pole positions: 0   Fastest laps: 0   Points scored: 22

	Race	Circuit	No	Entrant	Tyres	Capacity/Car/Engine	Comment	Q Pos/Entries
ret	US GP WEST	Long Beach	17	Shadow Racing Team	G	3.0 Shadow DN8-Cosworth V8	*gearbox*	14/22
ret	SPANISH GP	Jarama	17	Shadow Racing Team	G	3.0 Shadow DN8-Cosworth V8	*collision with Peterson*	14/31
6	MONACO GP	Monte Carlo	17	Shadow Racing Team	G	3.0 Shadow DN8-Cosworth V8		11/26
5	BELGIAN GP	Zolder	17	Shadow Racing Team	G	3.0 Shadow DN8-Cosworth V8		17/32
17	SWEDISH GP	Anderstorp	17	Shadow Racing Team	G	3.0 Shadow DN8-Cosworth V8	*2 pit stops – ignition/5 laps behind*	11/31
ret	FRENCH GP	Dijon	17	Shadow Racing Team	G	3.0 Shadow DN8-Cosworth V8	*driveshaft*	10/30
7	BRITISH GP	Silverstone	17	Shadow Racing Team	G	3.0 Shadow DN8-Cosworth V8	*1 lap behind*	12/36
ret	GERMAN GP	Hockenheim	17	Shadow Racing Team	G	3.0 Shadow DN8-Cosworth V8	*startline accident*	17/30
1	AUSTRIAN GP	Österreichring	17	Shadow Racing Team	G	3.0 Shadow DN8-Cosworth V8		14/30
ret	DUTCH GP	Zandvoort	17	Shadow Racing Team	G	3.0 Shadow DN8-Cosworth V8	*engine*	=13/34
3	ITALIAN GP	Monza	17	Shadow Racing Team	G	3.0 Shadow DN8-Cosworth V8		16/34
ret	US GP EAST	Watkins Glen	17	Shadow Racing Team	G	3.0 Shadow DN8-Cosworth V8	*accident with Peterson*	13/27
4	CANADIAN GP	Mosport Park	17	Shadow Racing Team	G	3.0 Shadow DN8-Cosworth V8		7/27
4	JAPANESE GP	Mount Fuji	17	Shadow Racing Team	G	3.0 Shadow DN8-Cosworth V8		12/23

1978 Championship position: 11th   Wins: 0   Pole positions: 0   Fastest laps: 2   Points scored: 11

	Race	Circuit	No	Entrant	Tyres	Capacity/Car/Engine	Comment	Q Pos/Entries
ret	ARGENTINE GP	Buenos Aires	27	Williams Grand Prix Engineering	G	3.0 Williams FW06-Cosworth V8	*fuel vapour lock*	14/27
11	BRAZILIAN GP	Rio	27	Williams Grand Prix Engineering	G	3.0 Williams FW06-Cosworth V8	*3 pit stops – tyres/5 laps behind*	8/28
4	SOUTH AFRICAN GP	Kyalami	27	Williams Grand Prix Engineering	G	3.0 Williams FW06-Cosworth V8		18/30
7	US GP WEST	Long Beach	27	Williams Grand Prix Engineering	G	3.0 Williams FW06-Cosworth V8	*broken front wings/FL/1 lap behind*	8/30
ret	MONACO GP	Monte Carlo	27	Williams Grand Prix Engineering	G	3.0 Williams FW06-Cosworth V8	*gearbox oil leak*	10/30
10	BELGIAN GP	Zolder	27	Williams Grand Prix Engineering	G	3.0 Williams FW06-Cosworth V8	*2 pit stops – tyres/-2 laps*	11/30
8	SPANISH GP	Jarama	27	Williams Grand Prix Engineering	G	3.0 Williams FW06-Cosworth V8	*1 lap behind*	18/29
ret	SWEDISH GP	Anderstorp	27	Williams Grand Prix Engineering	G	3.0 Williams FW06-Cosworth V8	*front wheel bearing seized*	9/27
5	FRENCH GP	Paul Ricard	27	Williams Grand Prix Engineering	G	3.0 Williams FW06-Cosworth V8		14/29
ret	BRITISH GP	Brands Hatch	27	Williams Grand Prix Engineering	G	3.0 Williams FW06-Cosworth V8	*driveshaft*	6/30
ret	GERMAN GP	Hockenheim	27	Williams Grand Prix Engineering	G	3.0 Williams FW06-Cosworth V8	*fuel vaporisation*	6/30
ret	AUSTRIAN GP	Österreichring	27	Williams Grand Prix Engineering	G	3.0 Williams FW06-Cosworth V8	*accident*	15/31
ret	DUTCH GP	Zandvoort	27	Williams Grand Prix Engineering	G	3.0 Williams FW06-Cosworth V8	*broken throttle cable*	11/33
13	ITALIAN GP	Monza	27	Williams Grand Prix Engineering	G	3.0 Williams FW06-Cosworth V8	*pit stop – tyre/1 lap behind*	6/32
2	US GP EAST	Watkins Glen	27	Williams Grand Prix Engineering	G	3.0 Williams FW06-Cosworth V8		3/27
9	CANADIAN GP	Montreal	27	Williams Grand Prix Engineering	G	3.0 Williams FW06-Cosworth V8	*handling problems/FL*	5/28

1979 Championship position: 3rd   Wins: 4   Pole positions: 3   Fastest laps: 1   Points scored: 43

	Race	Circuit	No	Entrant	Tyres	Capacity/Car/Engine	Comment	Q Pos/Entries
9	ARGENTINE GP	Buenos Aires	27	Albilad-Saudia Racing Team	G	3.0 Williams FW06-Cosworth V8	*pit stop – tyres/2 laps behind*	15/26
ret	BRAZILIAN GP	Interlagos	27	Albilad-Saudia Racing Team	G	3.0 Williams FW06-Cosworth V8	*fuel pressure*	13/26
ret	SOUTH AFRICAN GP	Kyalami	27	Albilad-Saudia Racing Team	G	3.0 Williams FW06-Cosworth V8	*rear suspension*	19/26
3	US GP WEST	Long Beach	27	Albilad-Saudia Racing Team	G	3.0 Williams FW06-Cosworth V8		10/26
ret	SPANISH GP	Jarama	27	Albilad-Saudia Racing Team	G	3.0 Williams FW07-Cosworth V8	*gear selection*	13/27
ret	BELGIAN GP	Zolder	27	Albilad-Saudia Racing Team	G	3.0 Williams FW07-Cosworth V8	*electrics*	4/28
ret	MONACO GP	Monte Carlo	27	Albilad-Saudia Racing Team	G	3.0 Williams FW07-Cosworth V8	*hit guard rail*	9/25
4	FRENCH GP	Dijon	27	Albilad-Saudia Racing Team	G	3.0 Williams FW07-Cosworth V8		7/27
ret	BRITISH GP	Silverstone	27	Albilad-Saudia Racing Team	G	3.0 Williams FW07-Cosworth V8	*water pump when leading race*	1/26
1	GERMAN GP	Hockenheim	27	Albilad-Saudia Racing Team	G	3.0 Williams FW07-Cosworth V8		2/26
1	AUSTRIAN GP	Österreichring	27	Albilad-Saudia Racing Team	G	3.0 Williams FW07-Cosworth V8		2/26
1	DUTCH GP	Zandvoort	27	Albilad-Saudia Racing Team	G	3.0 Williams FW07-Cosworth V8		2/26
9	ITALIAN GP	Monza	27	Albilad-Saudia Racing Team	G	3.0 Williams FW07-Cosworth V8	*pit stop – battery/1 lap behind*	4/28
1	CANADIAN GP	Montreal	27	Albilad-Saudia Racing Team	G	3.0 Williams FW07-Cosworth V8	*FL*	1/29
ret	US GP EAST	Watkins Glen	27	Albilad-Saudia Racing Team	G	3.0 Williams FW07-Cosworth V8	*lost rear wheel*	1/30

1980 WORLD CHAMPION   Wins: 5   Pole positions: 3   Fastest laps: 5   Points scored: 71

	Race	Circuit	No	Entrant	Tyres	Capacity/Car/Engine	Comment	Q Pos/Entries
1	ARGENTINE GP	Buenos Aires	27	Albilad-Williams Racing Team	G	3.0 Williams FW07-Cosworth V8	*FL*	1/28
3	BRAZILIAN GP	Interlagos	27	Albilad-Williams Racing Team	G	3.0 Williams FW07B-Cosworth V8		10/28

	Race	Circuit	No	Entrant	Tyres	Capacity/Car/Engine	Comment	Q Pos/Entries
ret	SOUTH AFRICAN GP	Kyalami	27	Albilad-Williams Racing Team	G	3.0 Williams FW07B-Cosworth V8	gearbox oiil cooler	8/28
ret	US GP WEST	Long Beach	27	Albilad-Williams Racing Team	G	3.0 Williams FW07B-Cosworth V8	collision with Giacomelli	5/27
2	BELGIAN GP	Zolder	27	Albilad-Williams Racing Team	G	3.0 Williams FW07B-Cosworth V8		1/27
ret	MONACO GP	Monte Carlo	27	Albilad-Williams Racing Team	G	3.0 Williams FW07B-Cosworth V8	differential	3/27
1	FRENCH GP	Paul Ricard	27	Albilad-Williams Racing Team	G	3.0 Williams FW07B-Cosworth V8	FL	4/27
1	BRITISH GP	Brands Hatch	27	Albilad-Williams Racing Team	G	3.0 Williams FW07B-Cosworth V8		3/27
3	GERMAN GP	Hockenheim	27	Albilad-Williams Racing Team	G	3.0 Williams FW07B-Cosworth V8	pit stop – puncture/FL	1/26
2	AUSTRIAN GP	Österreichring	27	Albilad-Williams Racing Team	G	3.0 Williams FW07B-Cosworth V8		3/25
11	DUTCH GP	Zandvoort	27	Albilad-Williams Racing Team	G	3.0 Williams FW07B-Cosworth V8	ran off road – pitstop/-3 laps	4/28
2	ITALIAN GP	Imola	27	Albilad-Williams Racing Team	G	3.0 Williams FW07B-Cosworth V8	FL	6/28
1	CANADIAN GP	Montreal	27	Albilad-Williams Racing Team	G	3.0 Williams FW07B-Cosworth V8		2/28
1	US GP EAST	Watkins Glen	27	Albilad-Williams Racing Team	G	3.0 Williams FW07B-Cosworth V8	FL	5/27

1981 Championship position: 3rd   Wins: 2   Pole positions: 0   Fastest laps: 5   Points scored: 46

1	US GP WEST	Long Beach	1	Albilad-Williams Racing Team	M	3.0 Williams FW07C-Cosworth V8	FL	2/29
2	BRAZILIAN GP	Rio	1	Albilad-Williams Racing Team	M	3.0 Williams FW07C-Cosworth V8		3/30
4	ARGENTINE GP	Buenos Aires	1	Albilad-Williams Racing Team	M	3.0 Williams FW07C-Cosworth V8	down on power engine	3/29
12	SAN MARINO GP	Imola	1	Albilad-Williams Racing Team	M	3.0 Williams FW07C-Cosworth V8	pit stop – front wing/-2 laps	8/30
ret	BELGIAN GP	Zolder	1	Albilad-Williams Racing Team	M	3.0 Williams FW07C-Cosworth V8	accident	6/31
2	MONACO GP	Monte Carlo	1	Albilad-Williams Racing Team	M	3.0 Williams FW07C-Cosworth V8	pit stop – fuel starvation/FL	7/31
7	SPANISH GP	Jarama	1	TAG Williams Team	M	3.0 Williams FW07C-Cosworth V8	went off when leading/FL	2/30
17	FRENCH GP	Dijon	1	TAG Williams Team	G	3.0 Williams FW07C-Cosworth V8	3 pit stops – steering/tyres/-4 laps	9/29
ret	BRITISH GP	Silverstone	1	TAG Williams Team	G	3.0 Williams FW07C-Cosworth V8	went off avoiding Villeneuve	7/30
11	GERMAN GP	Hockenheim	1	TAG Williams Team	G	3.0 Williams FW07C-Cosworth V8	pit stop – fuel starvation/-1 lap /FL	4/30
4	AUSTRIAN GP	Österreichring	1	TAG Williams Team	G	3.0 Williams FW07C-Cosworth V8		6/28
3	DUTCH GP	Zandvoort	1	TAG Williams Team	G	3.0 Williams FW07C-Cosworth V8	FL	4/30
2	ITALIAN GP	Monza	1	TAG Williams Team	G	3.0 Williams FW07C-Cosworth V8		5/30
ret	CANADIAN GP	Montreal	1	TAG Williams Team	G	3.0 Williams FW07C-Cosworth V8	handling	3/30
1	CAESARS PALACE GP	Las Vegas	1	TAG Williams Team	G	3.0 Wiliams FW07C-Cosworth V8		2/30

1983 Championship position: Unplaced

ret	US GP WEST	Long Beach	30	Arrows Racing Team	G	3.0 Arrows A6-Cosworth V8	driver discomfort	12/28

1985 Championship position: Unplaced

ret	ITALIAN GP	Monza	33	Team Haas (USA) Ltd	G	1.5 t/c Lola THL1-Hart 4	distributor	25/26
ret	EUROPEAN GP	Brands Hatch	33	Team Haas (USA) Ltd	G	1.5 t/c Lola THL1-Hart 4	holed water radiator	22/27
dns	SOUTH AFRICAN GP	Kyalami	33	Team Haas (USA) Ltd	G	1.5 t/c Lola THL1-Hart 4	driver unwell	(18)/21
ret	AUSTRALIAN GP	Adelaide	33	Team Haas (USA) Ltd	G	1.5 t/c Lola THL1-Hart 4	electrics	19/25

1986 Championship position: 12th   Wins: 0   Pole positions: 0   Fastest laps: 0   Points scored: 4

ret	BRAZILIAN GP	Rio	15	Team Haas (USA) Ltd	G	1.5 t/c Lola THL1-Hart 4	distributor rotor arm	19/25
ret	SPANISH GP	Jerez	15	Team Haas (USA) Ltd	G	1.5 t/c Lola THL1-Hart 4	accident with Palmer on lap 1	17/25
ret	SAN MARINO GP	Imola	15	Team Haas (USA) Ltd	G	1.5 t/c Lola THL2-Cosworth V6	radiator – overheating engine	21/26
ret	MONACO GP	Monte Carlo	15	Team Haas (USA) Ltd	G	1.5 t/c Lola THL2-Cosworth V6	incident with Streiff	18/26
11/ret	BELGIAN GP	Spa	15	Team Haas (USA) Ltd	G	1.5 t/c Lola THL2-Cosworth V6	out of fuel/3 laps behind	16/25
10	CANADIAN GP	Montreal	15	Team Haas (USA) Ltd	G	1.5 t/c Lola THL2-Cosworth V6	2 pit stops – tyres/-3 laps	13/25
ret	US GP (DETROIT)	Detroit	15	Team Haas (USA) Ltd	G	1.5 t/c Lola THL2-Cosworth V6	drive pegs	21/26
ret	FRENCH GP	Paul Ricard	15	Team Haas (USA) Ltd	G	1.5 t/c Lola THL2-Cosworth V6	accident	20/26
ret	BRITISH GP	Brands Hatch	15	Team Haas (USA) Ltd	G	1.5 t/c Lola THL2-Cosworth V6	throttle linkage	14/26
9	GERMAN GP	Hockenheim	15	Team Haas (USA) Ltd	G	1.5 t/c Lola THL2-Cosworth V6	started from back of grid/2 laps behind	19/26
ret	HUNGARIAN GP	Hungaroring	15	Team Haas (USA) Ltd	G	1.5 t/c Lola THL2-Cosworth V6	differential	10/26
4	AUSTRIAN GP	Österreichring	15	Team Haas (USA) Ltd	G	1.5 t/c Lola THL2-Cosworth V6	slipping clutch/2 laps behind	16/26
6	ITALIAN GP	Monza	15	Team Haas (USA) Ltd	G	1.5 t/c Lola THL2-Cosworth V6	2 pit stops – tyre balance-weight/-2 laps	18/27
ret	PORTUGESE GP	Estoril	15	Team Haas (USA) Ltd	G	1.5 t/c Lola THL2-Cosworth V6	brakes – spun off	17/27
ret	MEXICAN GP	Mexico City	15	Team Haas (USA) Ltd	G	1.5 t/c Lola THL2-Cosworth V6	gearbox/engine overheating	15/26
ret	AUSTRALIAN GP	Adelaide	15	Team Haas (USA) Ltd	G	1.5 t/c Lola THL2-Cosworth V6	engine	15/26

GP Starts: 116   GP Wins: 12   Pole positions: 6   Fastest laps: 13   Points: 206

OSWALD KARCH

IN the early 1950s, Oswald Karch raced on both sides of the East/West German border and, in common with many other competitors at the time, he drove a BMW-Eigenbau. After the 1950 season, however, this was replaced with the almost equally ubiquitous Veritas RS two-seater sports.

Apart from appearing in the German Grand Prix in 1953, Karch enjoyed quite a successful national racing season in 1954 with the elderly sports car. He also took the machine to Morocco to race in the Casablanca 12-hour race, where he took sixth place in the hotly contested 751–2000cc class, sharing the driving duties with Willy Sturzebecker.

KARCH, Oswald (D) b 6/3/1917, Ludwigshafen – d 28/01/2009, Mannheim

1953 Championship position: Unplaced

	Race	Circuit	No	Entrant	Tyres	Capacity/Car/Engine	Comment	Q Pos/Entries
ret	GERMAN GP	Nürburgring	26	Oswald Karch	–	2.0 Veritas RS 6		34/35

GP Starts: 1   GP Wins: 0   Pole positions: 0   Fastest laps: 0   Points: 0

NARAIN KARTHIKEYAN

ON seeing his son's love for motorsport, Narain Karthikeyan's father, a former Indian rally champion and wealthy businessman, arranged for him to travel to Europe in 1992 to receive professional tuition at the Elf-Winfield school. Over the next couple of years, he learned the circuits and caught the eye by winning the 1994 Formula Ford winter series, before returning home to triumph eventually in the 1996 Formula Asia series. This success sent him back to the UK, where he spent a year in Formula Opel before a part-season with Carlin in the British F3 championship in 1998. He did well enough to gain a seat for 1999, and history was made when he became the first Indian to take pole and victory in the UK series, winning twice at Brands Hatch.

Narain continued to contest the British F3 series in 2000 with Paul Stewart, but no more wins were achieved. However, he did get to test a Formula 1 car with Jaguar. Having decided to find an alternative route to the top, he tried his hand at Formula Nippon in 2001, but he found little joy in this unfamiliar environment and opted to race in the newly formed Formula Nissan World Series between 2002 and 2004. His performances were mixed, but no doubt two race wins in his third season in the class helped him to a drive at Jordan for 2005, Collin Kolles having seen potential in both his driving and sponsorship links. There is little doubt that the Indian had the pace to step up, but sometimes his racecraft was lacking and he was overshadowed by the consistent speed of team-mate Tiago Monteiro for much of the time. It was a chance that the Indian felt he had to take, however, and he did score a fourth place at Indianapolis in the six-car Bridgestone runner's-only race.

Without a race drive for 2006, Narain secured a test driver's role at Williams to keep his F1 links alive, but he also raced in the A1GP in 2007 and 2008, winning at Zuhai in China and also the final race of the season at Brands Hatch.

In 2010, Narain tried his hand at the NASCAR Craftsman Truck Series, but achieved little in his nine starts; he also raced in the Superleague series representing PSV Eindhoven without much success.

Thus it was a major surprise when Karthikeyan returned to the F1 arena in 2011 with HRT, largely courtesy of sponsorship from the Tata Group. It was a season when the team was unable to afford to run anything more than a heavily updated car, which he raced with typical enthusiasm until he was stood down to make way for Daniel Ricciardo, whose drive had been paid for by Red Bull. Narain did get his seat back for the Indian Grand Prix, however, giving him the signal honor of competing in his home country's inaugural race, even if by then he was really just making up the numbers.

KARTHIKEYAN, Narain (I) b 14/1/1977, Madras

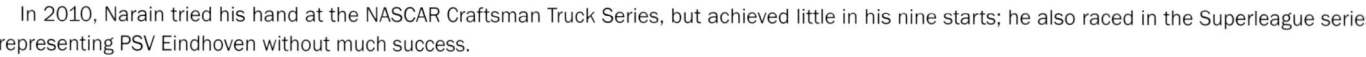

2005 Championship position: 16th   Wins: 0   Pole positions: 0   Fastest laps: 0   Points scored: 5

	Race	Circuit	No	Entrant	Tyres	Capacity/Car/Engine	Comment	Q Pos/Entries
15	AUSTRALIAN GP	Melbourne	19	Jordan Toyota	B	3.0 Jordan EJ15-Toyota V10	2 laps behind	12/20
11	MALAYSIAN GP	Sepang	18	Jordan Toyota	B	3.0 Jordan EJ15-Toyota V10	2 laps behind	17/20
ret	BAHRAIN GP	Bahrain	18	Jordan Toyota	B	3.0 Jordan EJ15-Toyota V10	electrics	18/20
12	SAN MARINO GP	Imola	18	Jordan Toyota	B	3.0 Jordan EJ15-Toyota V10	1 lap behind	17/20
13	SPANISH GP	Barcelona	18	Jordan Toyota	B	3.0 Jordan EJ15-Toyota V10	3 laps behind	13/18
ret	MONACO GP	Monte Carlo	18	Jordan Toyota	B	3.0 Jordan EJ15-Toyota V10	accident damage/hydraulics	16/18
16	EUROPEAN GP	Nürburgring	18	Jordan Toyota	B	3.0 Jordan EJ15-Toyota V10	1 lap behind	19/20
10	CANADIAN GP	Montreal	18	Jordan Toyota	B	3.0 Jordan EJ15-Toyota V10	electronics	17/20
4	U S GP	Indianapolis	18	Jordan Toyota	B	3.0 Jordan EJ15-Toyota V10	only six starters/1 lap behind	18/20
15	FRENCH GP	Magny Cours	18	Jordan Toyota	B	3.0 Jordan EJ15-Toyota V10	4 laps behind	17/20
ret	BRITISH GP	Silverstone	18	Jordan Toyota	B	3.0 Jordan EJ15-Toyota V10	electronics	17/20
16	GERMAN GP	Hockenheim	18	Jordan Toyota	B	3.0 Jordan EJ15-Toyota V10	3 laps behind	20/20
12	HUNGARIAN GP	Hungaroring	18	Jordan Toyota	B	3.0 Jordan EJ15-Toyota V10	3 laps behind	18/20
14	TURKISH GP	Hungaroring	18	Jordan Toyota	B	3.0 Jordan EJ15-Toyota V10	3 laps behind	19/20
20	ITALIAN GP	Monza	18	Jordan Toyota	B	3.0 Jordan EJ15-Toyota V10	3 laps behind	19/20
11	BELGIAN GP	Spa	18	Jordan Toyota	B	3.0 Jordan EJ15B-Toyota V10	1 lap behind	20/20
15	BRAZILIAN GP	Interlagos	18	Jordan Toyota	B	3.0 Jordan EJ15B-Toyota V10	3 laps behind	17/20
15	JAPANESE GP	Suzuka	18	Jordan Toyota	B	3.0 Jordan EJ15B-Toyota V10	extra pit stop – tyre/2 laps behind	11/20
ret	CHINESE GP	Shanghai	18	Jordan Toyota	B	3.0 Jordan EJ15B-Toyota V10	accident	15/20

2011 Championship position: Unplaced

	Race	Circuit	No	Entrant	Tyres	Capacity/Car/Engine	Comment	Q Pos/Entries
dnq	AUSTRALIAN GP	Melbourne	22	HRT F1 Team	P	2.4 HRT F111-Cosworth V8		24/24
ret	MALAYSIAN GP	Sepang	22	HRT F1 Team	P	2.4 HRT F111-Cosworth V8	overheating	24/24
23	CHINESE GP	Shanghai Circuit	22	HRT F1 Team	P	2.4 HRT F111-Cosworth V8	2 laps behind	24/24
21	TURKISH GP	Istanbul Park	22	HRT F1 Team	P	2.4 HRT F111-Cosworth V8	3 laps behind	23/24
21	SPANISH GP	Barcelona	22	HRT F1 Team	P	2.4 HRT F111-Cosworth V8	5 laps behind	22/24
ret	MONACO GP	Monte Carlo	22	HRT F1 Team	P	2.4 HRT F111-Cosworth V8	4 laps behind/*no time set	*23/24
17	CANADIAN GP	Montreal	22	HRT F1 Team	P	2.4 HRT F111-Cosworth V8	20-sec pen – missed corner/-1 lap	18/24
24	EUROPEAN GP	Valencia	22	HRT F1 Team	P	2.4 HRT F111-Cosworth V8	3 laps behind	24/24
app	GERMAN GP	Hockenheim	23	HRT F1 Team	P	2.4 HRT F111-Cosworth V8	drove in free practice 1 only	- / -
app	SINGAPORE GP	Marina Bay Circuit	22	HRT F1 Team	P	2.4 HRT F111-Cosworth V8	drove in free practice 1 only	- / -
app	JAPANESE GP	Suzuka	23	HRT F1 Team	P	2.4 HRT F111-Cosworth V8	drove in free practice 1 only	- / -
app	KOREAN GP	Yeongam	23	HRT F1 Team	P	2.4 HRT F111-Cosworth V8	drove in free practice 1 only	- / -
17	INDIAN GP	Buddh Circuit	22	HRT F1 Team	P	2.4 HRT F111-Cosworth V8	1 lap behind	22/24

GP Starts: 27   GP Wins: 0   Pole positions: 0   Fastest laps: 0   Points: 5

UKYO KATAYAMA

THE diminutive Japanese driver Ukyo Katayama first ventured to Europe some time before he entered grand prix racing with Larrousse in 1992, for he tried his hand at Formule Renault in France in 1986 and the French Formula 3 series in 1987, after winning junior 1600 single-seater championships at home: the Tsukuba class B title in 1983 and the Suzuka FFJ 1600 crown in 1984.

From 1988, Katayama concentrated on racing in his national F3000 series, finally becoming champion in 1991, although he did travel to Europe to drive the uncompetitive Footwork briefly at the beginning of 1989.

Given his F1 opportunity, Katayama was certainly committed. A possible first world championship point was lost in Canada when he buzzed the engine, but his lack of strength and stamina seemed to count against him. With the faith of sponsor Cabin intact, he moved to Tyrrell with Yamaha engines for 1993. Sadly the season was not a happy one, the promise of the new V10 being compromised by the shortcomings of the chassis, and poor Katayama was involved in a seemingly endless catalogue of spins in a desperate attempt to make up for its failings.

Just about everyone was writing off the little Japanese in terms of a grand prix career, but Ukyo blossomed in 1994. The new Tyrrell 022 was a much better chassis, and taking fifth place in the season's opening race at Interlagos would have done his confidence no harm. Despite the fact that he scored points on only two more occasions that year, his performances deserved more. He qualified fifth and ran in third at Hockenheim, before throttle trouble, and then put in two storming drives at Monza and Jerez, which went unrewarded.

Katayama's standing in the grand prix fraternity had risen immensely after his splendid season, so it must have been crushingly disappointing for him to be cast back into the role of also-ran once more in 1995, when Tyrrell failed to make the progress they expected. It must also be said that the arrival of Mika Salo certainly placed him under pressure.

Ukyo stayed with the team for a fourth season in 1996, largely, it is thought, because of the substantial backing of Mild Seven. His form was more competitive, but health problems eventually blunted his motivation, especially after a dispiriting run of retirements in mid-season. It was surprising, therefore, when he decided to continue in F1 with Minardi in 1997, but given the need to adapt to the different language and culture, he performed respectably. Tellingly, though, he was outshone by his novice team-mate, Jarno Trulli, and he came to the conclusion that it was time to step down and let a younger Japanese driver carry the hopes of his nation.

Ukyo still raced for Toyota, taking second place in both the Le Mans 24-hours and the Fuji 1000km in 1999 with their potent GT-One prototype. He contested the All-Japan GT series in both Nissan and Toyota machines, but since then has spent more of his time on his other passion, mountain climbing (he climbed Everest in 2002). He has also made several sorties to the Paris-Dakar Rally.

KATAYAMA, Ukyo (J) b 29/5/1963, Tokyo

1992 Championship position: Unplaced

	Race	Circuit	No	Entrant	Tyres	Capacity/Car/Engine	Comment	Q Pos/Entries
12	SOUTH AFRICAN GP	Kyalami	30	Central Park Venturi Larrousse	G	3.5 Venturi LC92-Lamborghini V12	4 laps behind	18/30
12	MEXICAN GP	Mexico City	30	Central Park Venturi Larrousse	G	3.5 Venturi LC92-Lamborghini V12	3 laps behind	24/30
9	BRAZILIAN GP	Interlagos	30	Central Park Venturi Larrousse	G	3.5 Venturi LC92-Lamborghini V12	3 laps behind	25/31
dnq	SPANISH GP	Barcelona	30	Central Park Venturi Larrousse	G	3.5 Venturi LC92-Lamborghini V12		27/32
ret	SAN MARINO GP	Imola	30	Central Park Venturi Larrousse	G	3.5 Venturi LC92-Lamborghini V12	spun off	17/32
dnpq	MONACO GP	Monte Carlo	30	Central Park Venturi Larrousse	G	3.5 Venturi LC92-Lamborghini V12		31/32
ret	CANADIAN GP	Montreal	30	Central Park Venturi Larrousse	G	3.5 Venturi LC92-Lamborghini V12	engine	11/32
ret	FRENCH GP	Magny Cours	30	Central Park Venturi Larrousse	G	3.5 Venturi LC92-Lamborghini V12	engine	18/30
ret	BRITISH GP	Silverstone	30	Central Park Venturi Larrousse	G	3.5 Venturi LC92-Lamborghini V12	gear linkage	16/32
ret	GERMAN GP	Hockenheim	30	Central Park Venturi Larrousse	G	3.5 Venturi LC92-Lamborghini V12	accident	16/32
ret	HUNGARIAN GP	Hungaroring	30	Central Park Venturi Larrousse	G	3.5 Venturi LC92-Lamborghini V12	engine	20/31
17	BELGIAN GP	Spa	30	Central Park Venturi Larrousse	G	3.5 Venturi LC92-Lamborghini V12	2 laps behind	26/30
9/ret	ITALIAN GP	Monza	30	Central Park Venturi Larrousse	G	3.5 Venturi LC92-Lamborghini V12	transmission – spun off/3 laps behind	23/28
ret	PORTUGUESE GP	Estoril	30	Central Park Venturi Larrousse	G	3.5 Venturi LC92-Lamborghini V12	spun off	25/26
11	JAPANESE GP	Suzuka	30	Central Park Venturi Larrousse	G	3.5 Venturi LC92-Lamborghini V12	1 lap behind	20/26
ret	AUSTRALIAN GP	Adelaide	30	Central Park Venturi Larrousse	G	3.5 Venturi LC92-Lamborghini V12	differential	26/26

1993 Championship position: Unplaced

	Race	Circuit	No	Entrant	Tyres	Capacity/Car/Engine	Comment	Q Pos/Entries
ret	SOUTH AFRICAN GP	Kyalami	3	Tyrrell Racing Organisation	G	3.5 Tyrrell 020C-Yamaha V10	transmission	21/26
ret	BRAZILIAN GP	Interlagos	3	Tyrrell Racing Organisation	G	3.5 Tyrrell 020C-Yamaha V10	crashed in rainstorm	22/26
ret	EUROPEAN GP	Donington	3	Tyrrell Racing Organisation	G	3.5 Tyrrell 020C-Yamaha V10	clutch failure	18/26
ret	SAN MARINO GP	Imola	3	Tyrrell Racing Organisation	G	3.5 Tyrrell 020C-Yamaha V10	engine – water leak	22/26
ret	SPANISH GP	Barcelona	3	Tyrrell Racing Organisation	G	3.5 Tyrrell 020C-Yamaha V10	spun off	23/26
ret	MONACO GP	Monte Carlo	3	Tyrrell Racing Organisation	G	3.5 Tyrrell 020C-Yamaha V10	oil leak	22/26
17	CANADIAN GP	Montreal	3	Tyrrell Racing Organisation	G	3.5 Tyrrell 020C-Yamaha V10	spin – pit stop/suspension/-5 laps	22/26
ret	FRENCH GP	Magny Cours	3	Tyrrell Racing Organisation	G	3.5 Tyrrell 020C-Yamaha V10	engine	21/26
13	BRITISH GP	Silverstone	3	Tyrrell Racing Organisation	G	3.5 Tyrrell 020C-Yamaha V10	4 laps behind	22/26
dns	"	"	3	Tyrrell Racing Organisation	G	3.5 Tyrrell 021-Yamaha V10	practice only	– / –

ret	GERMAN GP	Hockenheim	3	Tyrrell Racing Organisation	G	3.5 Tyrrell 021-Yamaha V10	spun off	21/26
10	HUNGARIAN GP	Hungaroring	3	Tyrrell Racing Organisation	G	3.5 Tyrrell 021-Yamaha V10	4 laps behind	23/26
15	BELGIAN GP	Spa	3	Tyrrell Racing Organisation	G	3.5 Tyrrell 021-Yamaha V10	4 laps behind	23/25
14	ITALIAN GP	Monza	3	Tyrrell Racing Organisation	G	3.5 Tyrrell 021-Yamaha V10	suspension/puncture/6 laps behind	17/26
dns	"	"	3	Tyrrell Racing Organisation	G	3.5 Tyrrell 020C-Yamaha V10	practice only	- / -
ret	PORTUGUESE GP	Estoril	3	Tyrrell Racing Organisation	G	3.5 Tyrrell 021-Yamaha V10	crashed	21/26
ret	JAPANESE GP	Suzuka	3	Tyrrell Racing Organisation	G	3.5 Tyrrell 021-Yamaha V10	engine	13/24
ret	AUSTRALIAN GP	Adelaide	3	Tyrrell Racing Organisation	G	3.5 Tyrrell 021-Yamaha V10	started from back of grid/crashed	18/24

1994 Championship position: 17th   Wins: 0   Pole positions: 0   Fastest laps: 0   Points scored: 5

5	BRAZILIAN GP	Interlagos	3	Tyrrell	G	3.5 Tyrrell 022-Yamaha V10	2 laps behind	10/28
ret	PACIFIC GP	T.I. Circuit	3	Tyrrell	G	3.5 Tyrrell 022-Yamaha V10	engine	14/28
5	SAN MARINO GP	Imola	3	Tyrrell	G	3.5 Tyrrell 022-Yamaha V10	1 lap behind	9/28
ret	MONACO GP	Monte Carlo	3	Tyrrell	G	3.5 Tyrrell 022-Yamaha V10	gearbox	11/24
ret	SPANISH GP	Barcelona	3	Tyrrell	G	3.5 Tyrrell 022-Yamaha V10	engine	10/27
ret	CANADIAN GP	Montreal	3	Tyrrell	G	3.5 Tyrrell 022-Yamaha V10	spun off	9/27
ret	FRENCH GP	Magny Cours	3	Tyrrell	G	3.5 Tyrrell 022-Yamaha V10	spun and stalled	14/28
6*	BRITISH GP	Silverstone	3	Tyrrell	G	3.5 Tyrrell 022-Yamaha V10	*2nd place car dsq/1 lap behind	8/28
ret	GERMAN GP	Hockenheim	3	Tyrrell	G	3.5 Tyrrell 022-Yamaha V10	sticking throttle	5/28
ret	HUNGARIAN GP	Hungaroring	3	Tyrrell	G	3.5 Tyrrell 022-Yamaha V10	collision with Barrichello & Irvine	5/28
ret	BELGIAN GP	Spa	3	Tyrrell	G	3.5 Tyrrell 022-Yamaha V10	engine	23/28
ret	ITALIAN GP	Monza	3	Tyrrell	G	3.5 Tyrrell 022-Yamaha V10	brake disc failure – accident	14/28
ret	PORTUGUESE GP	Estoril	3	Tyrrell	G	3.5 Tyrrell 022-Yamaha V10	started from pitlane/gearbox	6/28
7	EUROPEAN GP	Jerez	3	Tyrrell	G	3.5 Tyrrell 022-Yamaha V10	stalled at start/1 lap behind	13/28
ret	JAPANESE GP	Suzuka	3	Tyrrell	G	3.5 Tyrrell 022-Yamaha V10	spun off in rain	14/28
ret	AUSTRALIAN GP	Adelaide	3	Tyrrell	G	3.5 Tyrrell 022-Yamaha V10	spun off	15/28

1995 Championship position: Unplaced

ret	BRAZILIAN GP	Interlagos	3	Nokia Tyrrell Yamaha	G	3.0 Tyrrell 023-Yamaha V10	spun off	11/26
8	ARGENTINE GP	Buenos Aires	3	Nokia Tyrrell Yamaha	G	3.0 Tyrrell 023-Yamaha V10	3 laps behind	15/26
ret	SAN MARINO GP	Imola	3	Nokia Tyrrell Yamaha	G	3.0 Tyrrell 023-Yamaha V10	spun off	15/26
ret	SPANISH GP	Barcelona	3	Nokia Tyrrell Yamaha	G	3.0 Tyrrell 023-Yamaha V10	engine	17/26
ret	MONACO GP	Monte Carlo	3	Nokia Tyrrell Yamaha	G	3.0 Tyrrell 023-Yamaha V10	accident	15/26
ret	CANADIAN GP	Montreal	3	Nokia Tyrrell Yamaha	G	3.0 Tyrrell 023-Yamaha V10	engine	16/24
ret	FRENCH GP	Magny Cours	3	Nokia Tyrrell Yamaha	G	3.0 Tyrrell 023-Yamaha V10	collision with Inoue	19/24
ret	BRITISH GP	Silverstone	3	Nokia Tyrrell Yamaha	G	3.0 Tyrrell 023-Yamaha V10	fuel pressure	14/24
7	GERMAN GP	Hockenheim	3	Nokia Tyrrell Yamaha	G	3.0 Tyrrell 023-Yamaha V10	1 lap behind	17/24
ret	HUNGARIAN GP	Hungaroring	3	Nokia Tyrrell Yamaha	G	3.0 Tyrrell 023-Yamaha V10	accident	17/24
ret	BELGIAN GP	Spa	3	Nokia Tyrrell Yamaha	G	3.0 Tyrrell 023-Yamaha V10	spun off	15/24
nc	ITALIAN GP	Monza	3	Nokia Tyrrell Yamaha	G	3.0 Tyrrell 023-Yamaha V10	pit stop – sensor problem/-6 laps	17/24
ret/dns*	PORTUGUESE GP	Estoril	3	Nokia Tyrrell Yamaha	G	3.0 Tyrrell 023-Yamaha V10	*accident at first start	(16)/24
14	PACIFIC GP	T.I. Circuit	3	Nokia Tyrrell Yamaha	G	3.0 Tyrrell 023-Yamaha V10	3 laps behind	17/24
ret	JAPANESE GP	Suzuka	3	Nokia Tyrrell Yamaha	G	3.0 Tyrrell 023-Yamaha V10	spun off	14/24
ret	AUSTRALIAN GP	Adelaide	3	Nokia Tyrrell Yamaha	G	3.0 Tyrrell 023-Yamaha V10	engine	16/24

1996 Championship position: Unplaced

11	AUSTRALIAN GP	Melbourne	18	Tyrrell Yamaha	G	3.0 Tyrrell 024-Yamaha V10	3 laps behind	15/22
9	BRAZILIAN GP	Interlagos	18	Tyrrell Yamaha	G	3.0 Tyrrell 024-Yamaha V10	2 laps behind	16/22
ret	ARGENTINE GP	Buenos Aires	18	Tyrrell Yamaha	G	3.0 Tyrrell 024-Yamaha V10	tranmission	13/22
dsq*	EUROPEAN GP	Nürburgring	18	Tyrrell Yamaha	G	3.0 Tyrrell 024-Yamaha V10	*push start /12th on road	16/22
ret	SAN MARINO GP	Imola	18	Tyrrell Yamaha	G	3.0 Tyrrell 024-Yamaha V10	transmission	16/22
ret	MONACO GP	Monte Carlo	18	Tyrrell Yamaha	G	3.0 Tyrrell 024-Yamaha V10	stuck throttle - hit barrier	15/22
ret	SPANISH GP	Barcelona	18	Tyrrell Yamaha	G	3.0 Tyrrell 024-Yamaha V10	electrics	16/22
ret	CANADIAN GP	Montreal	18	Tyrrell Yamaha	G	3.0 Tyrrell 024-Yamaha V10	collision with Rosset	17/22
ret	FRENCH GP	Magny Cours	18	Tyrrell Yamaha	G	3.0 Tyrrell 024-Yamaha V10	engine	15/22
ret	BRITISH GP	Silverstone	18	Tyrrell Yamaha	G	3.0 Tyrrell 024-Yamaha V10	engine	12/22
ret	GERMAN GP	Hockenheim	18	Tyrrell Yamaha	G	3.0 Tyrrell 024-Yamaha V10	spun off	16/20
7	HUNGARIAN GP	Hungaroring	18	Tyrrell Yamaha	G	3.0 Tyrrell 024-Yamaha V10	3 laps behind	14/20
8	BELGIAN GP	Spa	18	Tyrrell Yamaha	G	3.0 Tyrrell 024-Yamaha V10		17/20
10	ITALIAN GP	Monza	18	Tyrrell Yamaha	G	3.0 Tyrrell 024-Yamaha V10	2 laps behind	16/20
12	PORTUGUESE GP	Estoril	18	Tyrrell Yamaha	G	3.0 Tyrrell 024-Yamaha V10	2 laps behind	14/20
ret	JAPANESE GP	Suzuka	18	Tyrrell Yamaha	G	3.0 Tyrrell 024-Yamaha V10	engine	14/20

1997 Championship position: Unplaced

ret	AUSTRALIAN GP	Melbourne	20	Minardi Team	B	3.0 Minardi M197-Hart V8	engine	15/24
18	BRAZILIAN GP	Interlagos	20	Minardi Team	B	3.0 Minardi M197-Hart V8	5 laps behind	18/22
ret	ARGENTINE GP	Buenos Aires	20	Minardi Team	B	3.0 Minardi M197-Hart V8	spun off	21/22
11	SAN MARINO GP	Imola	20	Minardi Team	B	3.0 Minardi M197-Hart V8	3 laps behind	22/22
10	MONACO GP	Monte Carlo	20	Minardi Team	B	3.0 Minardi M197-Hart V8	2 laps behind	20/22
ret	SPANISH GP	Barcelona	20	Minardi Team	B	3.0 Minardi M197-Hart V8	hydraulic pump	20/22
ret	CANADIAN GP	Montreal	20	Minardi Team	B	3.0 Minardi M197-Hart V8	stuck throttle – crashed	22/22
11	FRENCH GP	Magny Cours	20	Minardi Team	B	3.0 Minardi M197-Hart V8	2 laps behind	21/22
ret	BRITISH GP	Silverstone	20	Minardi Team	B	3.0 Minardi M197-Hart V8	spun into pit wall at start	19/22
ret	GERMAN GP	Hockenheim	20	Minardi Team	B	3.0 Minardi M197-Hart V8	out of fuel	22/22
10	HUNGARIAN GP	Hungaroring	20	Minardi Team	B	3.0 Minardi M197-Hart V8	1 lap behind	20/22
14*	BELGIAN GP	Spa	20	Minardi Team	B	3.0 Minardi M197-Hart V8	*3rd place car disqualified/-2 laps	20/22
ret	ITALIAN GP	Monza	20	Minardi Team	B	3.0 Minardi M197-Hart V8	puncture – hit barrier – retired in pits	21/22
11	AUSTRIAN GP	A1-Ring	20	Minardi Team	B	3.0 Minardi M197-Hart V8	2 laps behind	19/22
ret	LUXEMBOURG GP	Nürburgring	20	Minardi Team	B	3.0 Minardi M197-Hart V8	collision – suspension damage	22/22
ret	JAPANESE GP	Suzuka	20	Minardi Team	B	3.0 Minardi M197-Hart V8	engine	19/22
17	EUROPEAN GP	Jerez	20	Minardi Team	B	3.0 Minardi M197-Hart V8	1 lap behind	19/22

GP Starts: 94 (95)   GP Wins: 0   Pole positions: 0   Fastest laps: 0   Points: 5

RUPERT KEEGAN

THE much hyped Rupert Keegan did possess talent, but perhaps not quite as much as he and his father, Mike – backer and number-one fan – believed. Starting his career with a win first time out in a Ford Escort Mexico, he soon moved into Formula Ford, where he was quick, but erratic. A successful end to the 1974 season encouraged him to move into Formula 3 the following year with the ex-Henton March 743, but the season was punctuated by crashes, including a very nasty one at Thruxton.

Things changed dramatically in 1976, however, when a more consistent Rupert won nine rounds of the BP championship and the title to line up a seat in the Hesketh grand prix team for 1977. The car was awful, but Keegan emerged with great credit, qualifying for every race in which he was entered, only to jump out of the frying pan and into the fire by joining the ailing Surtees team in 1978.

Left with no alternatives, Rupert drove an Arrows in the 1979 Aurora F1 series, winning five rounds and the championship, but his return to the grand prix arena in 1980 with the RAM Williams brought little reward, and the same could be said of his final shot in the Rothmans March at the end of 1982. Then came a spell in endurance racing and a brief flirtation with Indy cars in 1985, when he took in three races, finishing in the points at Laguna Seca and Miami. In 1986, he failed to qualify for the Indianapolis 500, running a March-Buick.

Keegan quit racing to pursue a business career, but six years later he made just two starts in the Indy Lights series without success. In 1995, at the age of 40, he made a surprise reappearance back on the track, driving a Lister Storm at Le Mans.

KEEGAN, Rupert (GB) b 26/2/1955, Westcliff-on-Sea, Essex

1977 Championship position: Unplaced

	Race	Circuit	No	Entrant	Tyres	Capacity/Car/Engine	Comment	Q Pos/Entries
ret	SPANISH GP	Jarama	24	Penthouse Rizla Racing	G	3.0 Hesketh 308E-Cosworth V8	missed gearchange – accident	16/31
12	MONACO GP	Monte Carlo	24	Penthouse Rizla Racing	G	3.0 Hesketh 308E-Cosworth V8	broken anti-roll bar/3 laps behind	20/26
ret	BELGIAN GP	Zolder	24	Penthouse Rizla Racing	G	3.0 Hesketh 308E-Cosworth V8	spun off	19/32
13	SWEDISH GP	Anderstorp	24	Penthouse Rizla Racing	G	3.0 Hesketh 308E-Cosworth V8	handling problems/1 lap behind	24/31
10	FRENCH GP	Dijon	24	Penthouse Rizla Racing	G	3.0 Hesketh 308E-Cosworth V8	2 laps behind	14/30
ret	BRITISH GP	Silverstone	24	Penthouse Rizla Racing	G	3.0 Hesketh 308E-Cosworth V8	collision – Merzario – lost wheel	=13/36
ret	GERMAN GP	Hockenheim	24	Penthouse Rizla Racing	G	3.0 Hesketh 308E-Cosworth V8	accident – hit Ribeiro	23/30
7	AUSTRIAN GP	Österreichring	24	Penthouse Rizla Racing	G	3.0 Hesketh 308E-Cosworth V8	2 spins/1 lap behind	=20/30
ret	DUTCH GP	Zandvoort	24	Penthouse Rizla Racing	G	3.0 Hesketh 308E-Cosworth V8	accident	26/34
9	ITALIAN GP	Monza	24	Penthouse Rizla Racing	G	3.0 Hesketh 308E-Cosworth V8	pit stop/4 laps behind	23/34
8	US GP EAST	Watkins Glen	24	Penthouse Rizla Racing	G	3.0 Hesketh 308E-Cosworth V8	1 lap behind	20/27
ret	CANADIAN GP	Mosport Park	24	Penthouse Rizla Racing	G	3.0 Hesketh 308E-Cosworth V8	collision with Binder	25/27

1978 Championship position: Unplaced

	Race	Circuit	No	Entrant	Tyres	Capacity/Car/Engine	Comment	Q Pos/Entries
ret	ARGENTINE GP	Buenos Aires	18	Durex Team Surtees	G	3.0 Surtees TS19-Cosworth V8	overheating	19/27
ret	BRAZILIAN GP	Rio	18	Durex Team Surtees	G	3.0 Surtees TS19-Cosworth V8	accident	=24/28
ret	SOUTH AFRICAN GP	Kyalami	18	Durex Team Surtees	G	3.0 Surtees TS19-Cosworth V8	engine – oil line	23/30
dns	US GP WEST	Long Beach	18	Durex Team Surtees	G	3.0 Surtees TS19-Cosworth V8	practice accident	(22)/30
ret	MONACO GP	Monte Carlo	18	Durex Team Surtees	G	3.0 Surtees TS19-Cosworth V8	transmission	– / –
dns	"	"	18	Durex Team Surtees	G	3.0 Surtees TS20-Cosworth V8	practice only – set grid time	=18/30
dnq	BELGIAN GP	Zolder	18	Durex Team Surtees	G	3.0 Surtees TS20-Cosworth V8		25/30
11	SPANISH GP	Jarama	18	Durex Team Surtees	G	3.0 Surtees TS20-Cosworth V8	2 laps behind	23/29
dnq	SWEDISH GP	Anderstorp	18	Durex Team Surtees	G	3.0 Surtees TS20-Cosworth V8		25/27
ret	FRENCH GP	Paul Ricard	18	Durex Team Surtees	G	3.0 Surtees TS20-Cosworth V8	engine	23/29
dnq	BRITISH GP	Brands Hatch	18	Durex Team Surtees	G	3.0 Surtees TS20-Cosworth V8		28/30
dnq	"	" "	18	Durex Team Surtees	G	3.0 Surtees TS19-Cosworth V8		– / –
dnq	GERMAN GP	Hockenheim	18	Durex Team Surtees	G	3.0 Surtees TS20-Cosworth V8		27/30
dnq	AUSTRIAN GP	Österreichring	18	Durex Team Surtees	G	3.0 Surtees TS20-Cosworth V8		29/31
dns	DUTCH GP	Zandvoort	18	Durex Team Surtees	G	3.0 Surtees TS20-Cosworth V8	injured in pre-race warm-up	(25)/33

1980 Championship position: Unplaced

	Race	Circuit	No	Entrant	Tyres	Capacity/Car/Engine	Comment	Q Pos/Entries
11	BRITISH GP	Brands Hatch	50	RAM/Williams Grand Prix Engineering	G	3.0 Williams FW07-Cosworth V8	pit stop/3 laps behind	18/27
dnq	GERMAN GP	Hockenheim	50	RAM/Penthouse Rizla Racing	G	3.0 Williams FW07B-Cosworth V8		25/26
15	AUSTRIAN GP	Österreichring	50	RAM/Penthouse Rizla Racing	G	3.0 Williams FW07B-Cosworth V8	2 laps behind	20/25
dnq	DUTCH GP	Zandvoort	50	RAM/Penthouse Rizla Racing	G	3.0 Williams FW07B-Cosworth V8		25/28
11	ITALIAN GP	Imola	50	RAM/Penthouse Rizla Racing	G	3.0 Williams FW07B-Cosworth V8	2 laps behind	21/28
dnq	CANADIAN GP	Montreal	50	RAM/Penthouse Rizla Racing	G	3.0 Williams FW07B-Cosworth V8		27/28
9	US GP EAST	Watkins Glen	50	RAM/Penthouse Rizla Racing	G	3.0 Williams FW07B-Cosworth V8	2 laps behind	15/27

1982 Championship position: Unplaced

	Race	Circuit	No	Entrant	Tyres	Capacity/Car/Engine	Comment	Q Pos/Entries
dnq	GERMAN GP	Hockenheim	17	Rothmans March Grand Prix Team	A	3.0 March 821-Cosworth V8		29/30
ret	AUSTRIAN GP	Österreichring	17	Rothmans March Grand Prix Team	A	3.0 March 821-Cosworth V8	accident – bent steering arm	24/29
ret	SWISS GP	Dijon	17	Rothmans March Grand Prix Team	A	3.0 March 821-Cosworth V8	spun off	22/29
dnq	ITALIAN GP	Monza	17	Rothmans March Grand Prix Team	M	3.0 March 821-Cosworth V8		27/30
12	CAESARS PALACE GP	Las Vegas	17	Rothmans March Grand Prix Team	M	3.0 March 821-Cosworth V8	2 laps behind	25/30

GP Starts: 25   GP Wins: 0   Pole positions: 0   Fastest laps: 0   Points: 0

EDDIE KEIZAN

HAVING raced saloons in his native South Africa from the late 1960s, winning the championship twice, Eddie Keizan switched to a mixed diet of Formula Ford and sports car racing with a Lola T212 in 1971. It was the purchase of an F5000 Surtees in 1972, however, that put him on the map as Gold Star champion in that class.

Eddie then raced a Tyrrell 004 and an ex-Fittipaldi Lotus 72 in the domestic series, and naturally the local grands prix as well. He loved the Lotus, setting his fastest ever lap time at Kyalami with it, but it was unreliable and he endured a terrible run of mechanical failures.

At the end of 1975, it was decided that the South African championship was no longer able to sustain 'pukka' Formula 1 machinery for financial reasons, so henceforth the premier class would be for Formula Atlantic cars. These relatively underpowered machines held little appeal for Eddie, who moved into the South African touring car championship with his own team, running a BMW 535, and won the title twice more in 1977 and 1978.

Eddie crowned his career by scoring a great victory in the Wynn's 1000 at Kyalami in 1979, when he was forced to drive for most of the race after his co-driver, Helmut Kelleners, was taken ill, defeating such luminaries as John Watson, Jochen Mass, Marc Surer and Hans Stuck. When Ian Scheckter suffered a neck injury, Keizan was back in the BMW in the Wynn's in 1980, but this time an almost certain victory was lost when a driveshaft broke.

With his thriving business interests taking up more of his time, Eddie did not race again for ten years, but thereafter occasionally he donned his overalls to drive a BMW in South African endurance events.

JOE KELLY

ALTHOUGH born in South America, Joe Kelly was a larger-than-life motor dealer from Dublin, who had a tilt at grands prix with the last of Geoffrey Taylor's three GP Altas. This attractive machine never achieved any real success, but Kelly did manage to take a second place in the Wakefield Trophy handicap race, behind Duncan Hamilton's Maserati at the Curragh in 1950 and third place in the Ulster Trophy at Dundrod in 1952 against much better opposition.

With the introduction of rule changes favouring Formula 2, Kelly had his Alta extensively modified to take a Bristol engine. He raced this machine, renamed the IRA (Irish Racing Automobile), sporadically through 1952 and '53, but was far more interested in enjoying himself at the wheel of his Jaguar C-Type (particularly at the Curragh), which he raced in his inimitable hard-charging style through until 1955, when his career was brought to an end after a three-car accident at Oulton Park.

Kelly, who had sustained serious injuries and narrowly escaped the amputation of a badly damaged leg, then concentrated on his extensive business interests, which included the Ferrari dealership for Ireland and property development in the United Kingdom.

KEIZAN, Eddie (ZA) b 12/9/1944, Johannesburg

	Race	Circuit	No	Entrant	Tyres	Capacity/Car/Engine	Comment	Q Pos/Entries
	1973 Championship position: Unplaced							
nc	SOUTH AFRICAN GP	Kyalami	26	Blignaut-Lucky Strike Racing	F	3.0 Tyrrell 004-Cosworth V8	2 pit stops/12 laps behind	22/25
	1974 Championship position: Unplaced							
14	SOUTH AFRICAN GP	Kyalami	32	Blignaut-Embassy Racing SA	G	3.0 Tyrrell 004-Cosworth V8	2 laps behind	24/27
	1975 Championship position: Unplaced							
13	SOUTH AFRICAN GP	Kyalami	33	Team Gunston	G	3.0 Lotus 72E-Cosworth V8	2 laps behind	22/28
	GP Starts: 3 GP Wins: 0 Pole positions: 0 Fastest laps: 0 Points: 0							

KELLY, Joe (IRL) b 13/3/1913, Dublin – d 12/1993, Neston, Wirral, England

	Race	Circuit	No	Entrant	Tyres	Capacity/Car/Engine	Comment	Q Pos/Entries
	1950 Championship position: Unplaced							
nc	BRITISH GP	Silverstone	23	Joe Kelly	D	1.5 s/c Alta GP 4	pit stops/23 laps behind	19/21
	1951 Championship position: Unplaced							
nc	BRITISH GP	Silverstone	5	Joe Kelly	D	1.5 s/c Alta GP 4	pit stops/15 laps behind	18/20
	GP Starts: 2 GP Wins: 0 Pole positions: 0 Fastest laps: 0 Points: 0							

LORIS KESSEL

A SWISS garage owner and former Alfa saloon racer, Loris Kessel graduated from Formula 3 with no great record of success outside his native championship. A season of Formula 2 with a March in 1975 saw him briefly lead the opening race at Estoril and score a couple of fourth places at Hockenheim, but little else.

His undistinguished spell in the RAM F1 team in 1976 ended in legal acrimony, then followed a brief flirtation with the hopelessly slow Williams-based Apollon. Thereafter, he made occasional appearances in Formula 3 until 1981, when he returned to Formula 2, again without success. In 1993, however, after many years out of the spotlight, he raced in a Porsche 962C that finished seventh in the Le Mans 24-hours.

Kessel set up a luxury car dealership, concentrating on Ferraris and Maseratis, and this gave him the wherewithal to begin racing again. In 2000, he founded Loris Kessel Racing, but only really found time to return to the wheel on a regular basis in 2003, when he took part in the Italian GT series in a Ferrari 360 Modena with Andrea Chiesa. The Swiss pair enjoyed a successful partnership over the next few seasons, mainly running a Ferrari 575 Maranello GTC in both Italian GT and selected FIA GT races. His last season of competition was in 2008 when, in the GT Open at Valencia, he won his last podium alongside his son, Ronnie, who has since taken over the running of the family business following his father's death in 2010 after a long illness.

KESSEL, Loris (CH) b 1/4/1950, Lugano – d 15/5/2010, Montagnola

	Race	Circuit	No	Entrant	Tyres	Capacity/Car/Engine	Comment	Q Pos/Entries
1976 Championship position: Unplaced								
dnq	SPANISH GP	Jarama	32	RAM Racing	G	3.0 Brabham BT44B-Cosworth V8		26/30
12	BELGIAN GP	Zolder	32	RAM Racing	G	3.0 Brabham BT44B-Cosworth V8	pit stop/7 laps behind	23/29
ret	SWEDISH GP	Anderstorp	32	RAM Racing	G	3.0 Brabham BT44B-Cosworth V8	accident	26/27
dnq	FRENCH GP	Paul Ricard	32	RAM Racing	G	3.0 Brabham BT44B-Cosworth V8		30/30
nc	AUSTRIAN GP	Österreichring	32	RAM Racing	G	3.0 Brabham BT44B-Cosworth V8	pit stop – fuel union/10 laps behind	25/25
1977 Championship position: Unplaced								
dnq	ITALIAN GP	Monza	41	Jolly Club of Switzerland	G	3.0 Apollon-Williams FW03-Cosworth V8	crashed in practice	33/34

GP Starts: 3   GP Wins: 0   Pole positions: 0   Fastest laps: 0   Points: 0

NICOLAS KIESA

LIKE so many before him, Nicolas Kiesa began his motorsport career in karts and made an almost immediate impact, winning the national junior title in only his second season. The Dane continued in karts, winning more than 160 races, before switching to Formula Ford at the end of the 1997 season. Choosing to stay in this category eventually brought him the 1999 British title and a platform from which to step up to Formula 3.

Kiesa's two seasons in F3 yielded just a single win at Donington in 2000, and the following year he was forced to abandon the British series when his team folded, moving to German F3 in search of success. Despite his modest record, he managed to get a drive in F3000 for 2002 with PSM Racing. Initially the going was tough, but he did score points in the season's two closing races.

The high point of Kiesa's career came in 2003, when a switch of teams brought him an unexpected win at Monaco; a third in the next race perfectly positioned the Dane for a shot at Formula 1 with Minardi when Justin Wilson moved to Jaguar. Kiesa did what he could with the machinery and, although naturally slower than team-mate Jos Verstappen, he always brought the car to the finish.

When Minardi looked elsewhere for their drivers in 2004, Nicolas was left high and dry. Although forced to take a racing sabbatical, he stayed with the team on promotional duities, running their two-seater F1 car while working on an F1 return in 2005. This was finally achieved in mid-season when Robert Doornbos vacated his third-driver role at Jordan Grand Prix. His appearances were restricted to Friday practice only, and when the team was sold at the end of the year, he was not part of the new Midland regime's plans.

In 2006, Kiesa raced briefly in sports cars, with Aston Martin, when he took sixth overall (and third in the GT1 class) at Sebring. Then he drove a Lister to third place in the Le Mans Series in Istanbul. Later in the year, he had three races in the DTM, impressing in his 2004-spec Audi. Sadly a motocross accident prevented him from completing the year, and his chances of a ride in 2008 disappeared. Kiesa has since acted as a commentator on Danish TV, but has failed to find a permanent racing programme.

KIESA, Nicolas (DK) b 3/3/1978, Copenhagen

2003 Championship position: Unplaced

	Race	Circuit	No	Entrant	Tyres	Capacity/Car/Engine	Comment	Q Pos/Entries
12	GERMAN GP	Hockenheim	18	European Minardi Cosworth	B	3.0 Minardi PS03-Cosworth V10	5 laps behind	20/20
13	HUNGARIAN GP	Hungaroring	18	European Minardi Cosworth	B	3.0 Minardi PS03-Cosworth V10	4 laps behind	20/20
12	ITALIAN GP	Monza	18	European Minardi Cosworth	B	3.0 Minardi PS03-Cosworth V10	2 laps behind	19/20
11	UNITED STATES GP	Indianapolis	18	European Minardi Cosworth	B	3.0 Minardi PS03-Cosworth V10	4 laps behind	20/20
16	JAPANESE GP	Suzuka	18	European Minardi Cosworth	B	3.0 Minardi PS03-Cosworth V10	3 laps behind	18/20

2005 Championship position: Unplaced

	Race	Circuit	No	Entrant	Tyres	Capacity/Car/Engine	Comment	Q Pos/Entries
app	GERMAN GP	Hockenheim	39	Jordan Toyota	B	3.0 Jordan EJ15-Toyota V10	ran as 3rd driver in practice only	–/–
app	HUNGARIAN GP	Hungaroring	39	Jordan Toyota	B	3.0 Jordan EJ15-Toyota V10	ran as 3rd driver in practice only	–/–
app	TURKISH GP	Istanbul	39	Jordan Toyota	B	3.0 Jordan EJ15-Toyota V10	ran as 3rd driver in practice only	–/–
app	ITALIAN GP	Monza	39	Jordan Toyota	B	3.0 Jordan EJ15-Toyota V10	ran as 3rd driver in practice only	–/–
app	BELGIAN GP	Monza	39	Jordan Toyota	B	3.0 Jordan EJ15-Toyota V10	ran as 3rd driver in practice only	–/–
app	BRAZILIAN GP	Indianapolis	39	Jordan Toyota	B	3.0 Jordan EJ15B-Toyota V10	ran as 3rd driver in practice only	–/–
app	CHINESE GP	Suzuka	39	Jordan Toyota	B	3.0 Jordan EJ15B-Toyota V10	ran as 3rd driver in practice only	–/–

GP Starts: 5   GP Wins: 0   Pole positions: 0   Fastest laps: 0   Points: 0

KINNUNEN, Leo (Leo Juhani "Leska" Kinnunen) (SF) b 5/8/1943, Tampere

1974 Championship position: Unplaced

	Race	Circuit	No	Entrant	Tyres	Capacity/Car/Engine	Comment	Q Pos/Entries
dnq	BELGIAN GP	Nivelles	44	AAW Racing Team	F	3.0 Surtees TS16-Cosworth V8	gearbox failures	32/32
ret	SWEDISH GP	Anderstorp	23	AAW Racing Team	F	3.0 Surtees TS16-Cosworth V8	electrics – sparking plug	26/28
dnq	FRENCH GP	Dijon	23	AAW Racing Team	F	3.0 Surtees TS16-Cosworth V8		29/30
dnq	BRITISH GP	Brands Hatch	43	AAW Racing Team	F	3.0 Surtees TS16-Cosworth V8		34/34
dnq	AUSTRIAN GP	Österreichring	43	AAW Racing Team	F	3.0 Surtees TS16-Cosworth V8		27/31
dnq	ITALIAN GP	Monza	23	AAW Racing Team	F	3.0 Surtees TS16-Cosworth V8		31/31

GP Starts: 1   GP Wins: 0   Pole positions: 0   Fastest laps: 0   Points: 0

LEO KINNUNEN

LEO KINNUNEN raced successfully for a number of seasons in rallying, autocross and ice racing his native Finland, with Volvos and then Fiats. He also raced the exotic Lancia Stratos in 1974. In 1967, he finished a close second to Simon Lampinen in the Finnish Rally championship and also made his debut on circuits in F3 with an old Brabham. With better funding the following year, he successfully raced a Titan, beating visiting Swedes Ronnie Peterson and Reine Wisell at Ahvenisto.

Leo's career really gained momentum with the introduction of the Nordic Cup for sports cars in mid-1969. Handling a Porsche 908 with great aplomb, he scored wins at Anderstorp and Mantorp Park, and was invited to test a works Porsche 917. So impressive was his performance that he was immediately plucked from this relative obscurity to partner Pedro Rodriguez in the Gulf/Wyer sports car team for 1970, the pair winning at Daytona, Brands Hatch, Monza and Watkins Glen. There was friction, however, because the car was set up more to the Mexican's liking. There was talk of a grand prix drive at Lotus, but after his friend, Jochen Rindt, died at Monza, this came to nought.

Between 1971 and '73, Leo swept the board in Interserie racing with a Porsche 917 Spyder entered by AAW-Finland. The team folded at the beginnng of 1974, however, leaving Leo without a drive. He managed to scrape together enough to rent a Surtees, but working with the thinnest of resources, the team could only qualify for one race before folding.

After this debacle, Kinnunen returned successfully to sports car racing, competing in the Martini Porsche with Herbert Müller in 1975, and then Egon Evertz's private 934 turbo the following year.

HANS KLENK

AN ex-German air force pilot, Hans Klenk built specials in Stuttgart from 1950, but soon moved on to competing with the Veritas previously used by his friend, Karl Kling. In 1952, he was second at AVUS, behind Fischer's Ferrari, and at Grenzlandring. But the highlight of his competition career was undoubtedly joining Mercedes that year to take second in the Mille Miglia and then win the Carrera Panamericana with Kling in the 300SLR. Acting as navigator, he was very lucky to escape with minor facial cuts when the car's windsreen was hit by a vulture.

In 1953, Klenk was second to a Ferrari at AVUS once more, this time driven by Jacques Swaters, but a serious accident when testing a Mercedes brought his racing career to a premature end. In 1954, he built his own Klenk-Meteor, based on the Veritas, which was driven briefly by Theo Helfrich. Then he became the head of the racing department of Continental, the tyre manufacturer, and subsequently head of public relations.

KLENK, Hans (D) b 28/10/1919, Künzelsau – d 24/3/2009, Vellberg, Germany

1952 Championship position: Unplaced

	Race	Circuit	No	Entrant	Tyres	Capacity/Car/Engine	Comment	Q Pos/Entries
nc	GERMAN GP	Nürburgring	128	Hans Klenk	–	2.0 Veritas Meteor 6	4 laps behind	8/32

GP Starts: 1   GP Wins: 0   Pole positions: 0   Fastest laps: 0   Points: 0

CHRISTIAN KLIEN

AIDED by substantial support from Red Bull and no little talent, personable Christian Klien seemed to have the makings of a really front-rank grand prix driver and enjoyed a meteoric rise to the top. Sadly, once there, his progress stalled, and despite some good performances in difficult cars, he failed to convince at the top level, being cast aside for the never-ending conveyor belt of hopefuls on the roster of the energy drinks brand.

Born in the heart of Austria's alpine region, the young Klien found a perfect playground in the surrounding mountains, and it appeared that he had a future in ski racing – until his father took him to a local kart race. Immediately bitten by the motorsport bug, he was soon gaining experience and, gradually, winning trophies, including the Swiss junior title in 1996.

As soon as he was old enough, however, Klien moved into cars, starting with the 1999 Formula BMW Junior Cup in neighbouring Germany. He began in the best possible manner, winning his first ever car race at the Sachsenring, before adding a further four victories en route to fourth in the overall standings. Then two years were spent with Team Rosberg in the Formula BMW series, followed by Formula Renault in 2002, when he won four races and emerged the worthy champion. The following season, he joined the respected Mücke Motorsport team for the F3 Euroseries. Despite his inexperience, the likeable Austrian quickly proved to be one of the season's front-runners and, while Australian Ryan Briscoe took the title, he managed four race wins and five other podiums to end the season as runner-up. His biggest moment, however, came in the non-championship Marlboro Masters at Zandvoort where, against an elite international field, he controlled the race from the front and took the title.

Klien then received an unexpected chance to jump straight into Formula 1. His inclusion on the renowned Red Bull Junior Team programme had already marked him out as a prospective grand prix driver of the future, but brand owner Dietrich Mateschitz pushed for him to be included in the Jaguar Racing line-up for 2004, to partner Mark Webber. Initially he struggled to match the speed of his team-mate, and there were calls for him to be stood down in favour of more experienced alternatives, but he drove consistently and kept his head, raising his game as the year went on. Eventually he claimed his first F1 points for sixth place in Belgium.

For 2005, Jaguar was no more, but Red Bull took to the tracks as a fully-fledged team with the Austrian still on board as number two to the newly recruited David Coulthard. It was planned that he would share the seat in the number 15 car with F3000 champion Vitantonio Liuzzi, but in the event Christian took part in the majority of the races. He started brightly, scoring points in the first two races of the year, and then qualified seventh at Bahrain, where his car failed before the start. Subsequently, he handed his car to Liuzzi for a four-race spell, and upon his return struggled to gain his early-season sparkle, although a career-best fifth in the season's finale in China helped him cement his Red Bull place for 2006.

Klien's third season in Formula 1 yielded only a couple of single-point finishes before it became apparent that he would not be retained at the season's end. After refusing offers of support from Red Bull in other racing categories away from Formula 1, he was summarily replaced after the Italian Grand Prix, Robert Doornbos stepping up from the third-driver role. Still hoping to make a mark in grand prix racing, Christian joined the Honda team in 2007 as a test driver, supporting Jenson Button and Rubens Barrichello. When the possibility of a drive with Spyker arose, he was released from his contract, but in the end they opted to take Sakon Yamamoto's cash.

Christian lost no time in finding a place as a test driver with BMW Sauber in 2008 and 2009, and he resumed racing in sports cars with Peugeot, taking third place with the 908 HDi at Le Mans with F1 refugees Franck Montagny and Ricardo Zonta. In 2009, he returned to take sixth place with Nicolas Minassian and Pedro Lamy. When Pedro de la Rosa was chosen to partner Kamui Kobayashi at Sauber for the 2010 season, Klien's F1 prospects appeared to be finished, but newcomers Hispania took him on board. Initially, he was seen as an experienced hand to help Karun Chandhok and Bruno Senna, but ironically he eventually picked up a race seat at the expense of Yamamoto, who was 'indisposed' in Singapore.

In 2001, Klien was back in sports cars, this time with Aston Martin, failing to finish in the problematic AMR-One prototype at Le Mans, but picking up ninth at Silverstone in the older, faster and more reliable B09/60. Over the winter, he headed to Australia to appear as a guest driver in a Ford V8 at the Gold Coast 600 and then a Lotus Exige GT4 at the Bathurst 12-hours.

KLIEN, Christian (A) b 7/2/1983, Hohenems

2004 Championship position: 16th= Wins: 0 Pole positions: 0 Fastest laps: 0 Points scored: 3

	Race	Circuit	No	Entrant	Tyres	Capacity/Car/Engine	Comment	Q Pos/Entries
11	AUSTRALIAN GP	Melbourne	15	Jaguar Racing	M	3.0 Jaguar R5-Cosworth V10	*no time set/2 laps behind	*19/20
10	MALAYSIAN GP	Sepang	15	Jaguar Racing	M	3.0 Jaguar R5-Cosworth V10	delayed at pit stop/1 lap behind	13/20
14	BAHRAIN GP	Sakhir Circuit	15	Jaguar Racing	M	3.0 Jaguar R5-Cosworth V10	spin/1 lap behind	12/20
14	SAN MARINO GP	Imola	15	Jaguar Racing	M	3.0 Jaguar R5-Cosworth V10	poor handling/2 laps behind	14/20
ret	SPANISH GP	Barcelona	15	Jaguar Racing	M	3.0 Jaguar R5-Cosworth V10	throttle	16/20
ret	MONACO GP	Monte Carlo	15	Jaguar Racing	M	3.0 Jaguar R5-Cosworth V10	accident damage – hit barrier	14/20
12	EUROPEAN GP	Nürburgring	15	Jaguar Racing	M	3.0 Jaguar R5-Cosworth V10	1 lap behind	12/20
9*	CANADIAN GP	Montreal	15	Jaguar Racing	M	3.0 Jaguar R5-Cosworth V10	*2nd/5th/8th/10th cars dsq/-2 laps	10/20
ret	U S GP	Indianapolis	15	Jaguar Racing	M	3.0 Jaguar R5-Cosworth V10	ran into da Matta on lap 1	13/20
11	FRENCH GP	Magny Cours	15	Jaguar Racing	M	3.0 Jaguar R5-Cosworth V10	1 lap behind	13/20
14	BRITISH GP	Silverstone	15	Jaguar Racing	M	3.0 Jaguar R5-Cosworth V10	1 lap behind	14/20
10	GERMAN GP	Hockenheim	15	Jaguar Racing	M	3.0 Jaguar R5-Cosworth V10		12/20
13	HUNGARIAN GP	Hungaroring	15	Jaguar Racing	M	3.0 Jaguar R5-Cosworth V10	handling/2 laps behind	14/20
6	BELGIAN GP	Spa	15	Jaguar Racing	M	3.0 Jaguar R5-Cosworth V100		13/20
13	ITALIAN GP	Monza	15	Jaguar Racing	M	3.0 Jaguar R5-Cosworth V10	drive through penalty/1 lap behind	14/20
ret	CHINESE GP	Shanghai	15	Jaguar Racing	M	3.0 Jaguar R5-Cosworth V10	collison – damaged suspension	15/20
12	JAPANESE GP	Suzuka	15	Jaguar Racing	M	3.0 Jaguar R5-Cosworth V10	1 lap behind	14/20
14	BRAZILIAN GP	Interlagos	15	Jaguar Racing	M	3.0 Jaguar R5-Cosworth V10	2 laps behind	16/20

2005 Championship position: 14th= Wins: 0 Pole positions: 0 Fastest laps: 0 Points scored: 9

	Race	Circuit	No	Entrant	Tyres	Capacity/Car/Engine	Comment	Q Pos/Entries
7	AUSTRALIAN GP	Melbourne	15	Red Bull Racing	M	3.0 Red Bull RB1-Cosworth V10		6/20
8	MALAYSIAN GP	Sepang	15	Red Bull Racing	M	3.0 Red Bull RB1-Cosworth V10	lack of grip	7/20
dns*	BAHRAIN GP	Sakhir Circuit	15	Red Bull Racing	M	3.0 Red Bull RB1-Cosworth V10	*electrical failure on dummy grid	7/20
app	SAN MARINO GP	Imola	37	Red Bull Racing	M	3.0 Red Bull RB1-Cosworth V10	ran as 3rd driver in practice only	– / –
app	SPANISH GP	Barcelona	37	Red Bull Racing	M	3.0 Red Bull RB1-Cosworth V10	ran as 3rd driver in practice only	– / –
app	MONACO GP	Monte Carlo	37	Red Bull Racing	M	3.0 Red Bull RB1-Cosworth V10	ran as 3rd driver in practice only	– / –
app	EUROPEAN GP	Nürburgring	37	Red Bull Racing	M	3.0 Red Bull RB1-Cosworth V10	ran as 3rd driver in practice only	– / –
8	CANADIAN GP	Montreal	15	Red Bull Racing	M	3.0 Red Bull RB1-Cosworth V10	low grip and understeer/1 lap behind	16/20
dns*	U S GP	Indianapolis	15	Red Bull Racing	M	3.0 Red Bull RB1-Cosworth V10	*withdrawn after parade lap	14/20
ret	FRENCH GP	Magny Cours	15	Red Bull Racing	M	3.0 Red Bull RB1-Cosworth V10	engine – fuel pressure	16/20
14	BRITISH GP	Silverstone	15	Red Bull Racing	M	3.0 Red Bull RB1-Cosworth V10	tyre issues/1 lap behind	15/20
9	GERMAN GP	Hockenheim	15	Red Bull Racing	M	3.0 Red Bull RB1-Cosworth V10		10/20
ret	HUNGARIAN GP	Hungaroring	15	Red Bull Racing	M	3.0 Red Bull RB1-Cosworth V10	accident – hit by Villeneuve on lap 1	11/20
8	TURKISH GP	Hungaroring	15	Red Bull Racing	M	3.0 Red Bull RB1-Cosworth V10		10/20
13	ITALIAN GP	Monza	15	Red Bull Racing	M	3.0 Red Bull RB1-Cosworth V10	1 lap behind	13/20
9	BELGIAN GP	Spa	15	Red Bull Racing	M	3.0 Red Bull RB1-Cosworth V10	1 lap behind	16/20
9	BRAZILIAN GP	Interlagos	15	Red Bull Racing	M	3.0 Red Bull RB1-Cosworth V10	1 lap behind	6/20
9	JAPANESE GP	Suzuka	15	Red Bull Racing	M	3.0 Red Bull RB1-Cosworth V10		4/20
5	CHINESE GP	Shanghai	15	Red Bull Racing	M	3.0 Red Bull RB1-Cosworth V10		14/20

2006 Championship position: 18th Wins: 0 Pole positions: 0 Fastest laps: 0 Points scored: 2

	Race	Circuit	No	Entrant	Tyres	Capacity/Car/Engine	Comment	Q Pos/Entries
8	BAHRAIN GP	Sakhir Circuit	15	Red Bull Racing	M	2.4 Red Bull RB2-Ferrari V8		8/22
ret	MALAYSIAN GP	Sepang	15	Red Bull Racing	M	2.4 Red Bull RB2-Ferrari V8	hydraulics	9/22
ret	AUSTRALIAN GP	Melbourne	15	Red Bull Racing	M	2.4 Red Bull RB2-Ferrari V8	accident – brakes	14/22
ret	SAN MARINO GP	Imola	15	Red Bull Racing	M	2.4 Red Bull RB2-Ferrari V8	hydraulics	17/22
ret	EUROPEAN GP	Nürburgring	15	Red Bull Racing	M	2.4 Red Bull RB2-Ferrari V8	transmission	17/22
13	SPANISH GP	Barcelona	15	Red Bull Racing	M	2.4 Red Bull RB2-Ferrari V8	1 lap behind	15/22
ret	MONACO GP	Monte Carlo	15	Red Bull Racing	M	2.4 Red Bull RB2-Ferrari V8	transmission	12/22
14	BRITISH GP	Silverstone	15	Red Bull Racing	M	2.4 Red Bull RB2-Ferrari V8	1 lap behind	14/22
11	CANADIAN GP	Montreal	15	Red Bull Racing	M	2.4 Red Bull RB2-Ferrari V8	1 lap behind	12/22
ret	U S GP	Indianapolis	15	Red Bull Racing	M	2.4 Red Bull RB2-Ferrari V8	multiple accident on lap 1	16/22
12	FRENCH GP	Magny Cours	15	Red Bull Racing	M	2.4 Red Bull RB2-Ferrari V8	1 lap behind	13/22
8	GERMAN GP	Hockenheim	15	Red Bull Racing	M	2.4 Red Bull RB2-Ferrari V8		12/22
ret	HUNGARIAN GP	Hungaroring	15	Red Bull Racing	M	2.4 Red Bull RB2-Ferrari V8	accident	14/22
11	TURKISH GP	Istanbul	15	Red Bull Racing	M	2.4 Red Bull RB2-Ferrari V8	1 lap behind	11/22
11	ITALIAN GP	Monza	15	Red Bull Racing	M	2.4 Red Bull RB2-Ferrari V8	1 lap behind	16/22

2007 Championship position: Unplaced

	Race	Circuit	No	Entrant	Tyres	Capacity/Car/Engine	Comment	Q Pos/Entries
app	BRITISH GP	Silverstone	34	Honda Racing F1 Team	B	2.4 Honda RA107 V8	substitute for Button in 2nd practice only	– /–

2010 Championship position: Unplaced

	Race	Circuit	No	Entrant	Tyres	Capacity/Car/Engine	Comment	Q Pos/Entries
app	SPANISH GP	Barcelona	20	HRT F1 Team	B	2.4 HRT F1 10-Cosworth V8	ran as 3rd driver in practice 1 only	– /–
app	EUROPEAN GP	Valencia	20	HRT F1 Team	B	2.4 HRT F1 10-Cosworth V8	ran as 3rd driver in practice 1 only	– /–
ret	SINGAPORE GP	Marina Bay Circuit	20	HRT F1 Team	B	2.4 HRT F1 10-Cosworth V8	hydraulics	22/24
22	BRAZILIAN GP	Interlagos	20	HRT F1 Team	B	2.4 HRT F1 10-Cosworth V8	6 laps behind	23/24
20	ABU DHABI GP	Yas Marina Circuit	20	HRT F1 Team	B	2.4 HRT F1 10-Cosworth V8	2 laps behind	24/24

GP Starts: 49 GP Wins: 0 Pole positions: 0 Fastest laps: 0 Points: 14

KLING, Karl (D) b 16/9/1910, Glessen – d 18/3/2003, Gaienhofen

1954 Championship position: 5th Wins: 0 Pole positions: 0 Fastest laps: 1 Points scored: 12

	Race	Circuit	No	Entrant	Tyres	Capacity/Car/Engine	Comment	Q Pos/Entries
2	FRENCH GP	Reims	20	Daimler Benz AG	C	2.5 Mercedes-Benz W196 8 str		2/22
7	BRITISH GP	Silverstone	2	Daimler Benz AG	C	2.5 Mercedes-Benz W196 8	3 laps behind	6/31
4	GERMAN GP	Nürburgring	19	Daimler Benz AG	C	2.5 Mercedes-Benz W196 8	led race – suspension problems/FL	– /23
ret	SWISS GP	Bremgarten	8	Daimler Benz AG	C	2.5 Mercedes-Benz W196 8	injector pump drive	5/16
ret	ITALIAN GP	Monza	14	Daimler Benz AG	C	2.5 Mercedes-Benz W196 8 str	radius rod – crashed	4/21
5	SPANISH GP	Pedralbes	4	Daimler Benz AG	C	2.5 Mercedes-Benz W196 8	1 lap behind	12/22

	1955 Championship position: 11th	Wins: 0		Pole positions: 0		Fastest laps: 0	Points scored: 5			
ret	ARGENTINE GP	Buenos Aires	4	Daimler Benz AG	C	2.5 Mercedes-Benz W196 8		crashed	6/22
4*	"	"	8	Daimler Benz AG	C	2.5 Mercedes-Benz W196 8		*Moss & Herrmann co-drove/-2 laps	– / –
ret	BELGIAN GP	Spa	12	Daimler Benz AG	C	2.5 Mercedes-Benz W196 8		oil pipe	6/14
ret	DUTCH GP	Zandvoort	12	Daimler Benz AG	C	2.5 Mercedes-Benz W196 8		spun off	3/16
3	BRITISH GP	Aintree	14	Daimler Benz AG	C	2.5 Mercedes-Benz W196 8			4/25
ret	ITALIAN GP	Monza	20	Daimler Benz AG	C	2.5 Mercedes-Benz W196 8		gearbox	3/22

GP Starts: 11   GP Wins: 0   Pole positions: 0   Fastest laps: 1   Points: 17

KARL KLING

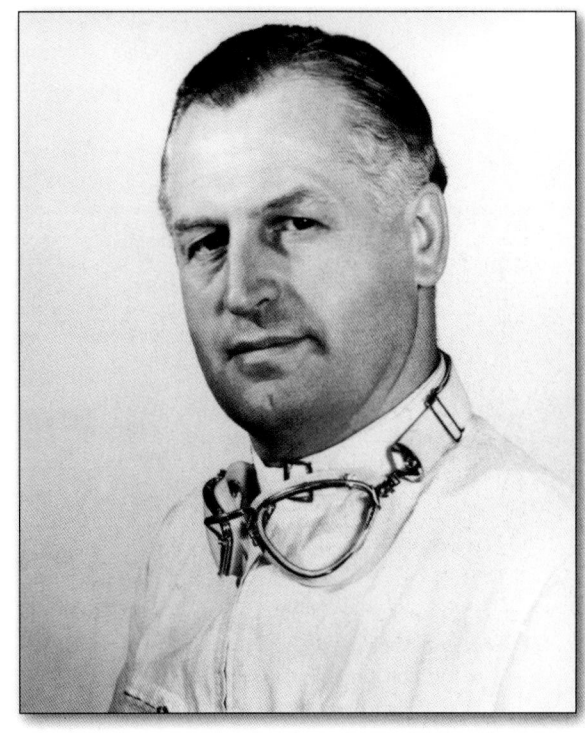

KARL KLING was very much the essence of Mercedes-Benz. He joined them in 1928 as a lowly reception clerk, but eventually rose to succeed the legendary Alfred Neubauer as head of the motorsport division in 1956.

He raced production cars in hill-climbs and trials as an amateur before the Second World War – during which he served as an aircraft mechanic in the Luftwaffe – but his racing career did not really start in earnest until 1947, when he scored a victory at Hockenheim with a BMW 328.

The next two seasons saw Kling crowned German sports car champion in the 2-litre class with the potent Veritas. In 1950, he raced the Veritas-Meteor in Formula 2, winning races at Grenzlandring and Solitude, and the Eifelrennen at the Nürburgring, which led to an invitation to help develop the pre-war Mercedes, which raced again at the start of 1951 in South America, taking second place in the Eva Perón Cup.

Leading the Mercedes 300SL sports car attack in 1952, Kling missed out at Le Mans, but made up for it elsewhere, winning the Carrera Panamericana and the Prix de Berne, and taking second in the Mille Miglia.

With Mercedes back in F1 in 1954, Kling was very much in the shadow of Juan Fangio. He finished just a tenth of a second behind 'the Maestro' after 61 laps of the Reims circuit, but was convinced he could have won the French Grand Prix that day had he not mistakenly thought the race was one lap shorter. He did win the non-championship Berlin GP at AVUS, although it was thought that the Argentinian had allowed him to take the victory.

Relegated in the pecking order in 1955 by the arrival of Stirling Moss, Karl did not enjoy much success in grands prix, but took third place at Aintree, behind the star duo, and shared the second-placed Mercedes sports car with Fangio in both the Tourist Trophy and the Targa Florio, before the team withdrew from competition at the end of the 1955 season following the Le Mans disaster.

Kling was the mastermind behind Mercedes-Benz's sucessful motorsport activities, such as the Gran Premio International Turismo in Argentina (between 1961 and 1964) and the Nürburgring six-hour races. In 1961, he ended his driving carer on a winning note, taking victory in the Algiers–Cape Town Rally at the wheel of a Mercedes 220SE.

ERNST KLODWIG

IF not quite the fastest of the drivers who competed in the East German national races, which ran from 1950 through to 1954, Ernst Klodwig was certainly one of the most consistent.

Klodwig was a regular top-three finisher – racing against the likes of Rudi Krause, Paul Geifzu and Edgar Barth – with his neat little 'Eigenbau' (self-built) BMW. The car was also often referred to as a 'Heck' (tail), on account of its rear-mounted engine, following the Auto Union philosophy.

In Klodwig's two German Grand Prix appearances in the West, the car made it to the chequered flag, but was so far off the pace that it was not officially classified as a finisher.

KLODWIG, Ernst (D) b 23/5/1903, Aschersleben – d 15/4/1973, Hamburg

	1952 Championship position: Unplaced							
	Race	Circuit	No	Entrant	Tyres	Capacity/Car/Engine	Comment	Q Pos/Entries
nc	GERMAN GP	Nürburgring	135	Ernst Klodwig	–	2.0 BMW-Heck Eigenbau 6	4 laps behind	29/32
	1953 Championship position: Unplaced							
nc	GERMAN GP	Nürburgring	37	Ernst Klodwig	–	2.0 BMW-Heck Eigenbau 6	3 laps behind	32/35

GP Starts: 2   GP Wins: 0   Pole positions: 0   Fastest laps: 0   Points: 0

KAMUI KOBAYASHI

BUT for an unfortunate crash that sidelined Timo Glock at Suzuki late in 2009, the Formula 1 career of Kamui Kobayashi might not have flourished at all. At the time, he was the reserve driver for Toyota, having just completed an undistinguished GP2 campaign with just a single podium to his name.

Given a brief window of opportunity to shine, the tigerish Japanese driver stunned everyone with his exuberant performances in Brazil and Abu Dhabi, putting himself at the front of the shop window of available driver talent.

Kamui had been a karting regular in Japan before moving to cars in 2004 and heading to Europe, initially in Formula Renault in both Italy and Germany. The following season saw the young hopeful make a real impact at this level by winning both the Italian and Eurocup championships, scoring six wins in both series.

Kobayashi then took the step up to the F3 Euroseries with the top ASM team, where naturally he found the level of competition pretty hot. His first year was spent learning the ropes while his stellar team-mates, Sebastian Vettel and Paul di Resta, battled for the title, but eighth overall was satisfactory enough. More would be expected in year two, and he did improve, including a win at Magny-Cours, to move up to fourth in the standings. Crucially, though, his new team-mates, Romain Grosjean and Nico Hülkenberg, shone more brightly and looked more convincing talents. Nevertheless, Toyota had taken him on to their driver strength, along with Kohei Hirate, in 2007 and they promoted him to the third-driver role for 2008, leaving him to gain experience in the GP2 Asia Series with DAMS, where he settled in well, taking a couple of wins on his way to sixth overall. His debut year in the main category started well with a win in the Barcelona Sprint race, but he couldn't repeat the success and struggled to score points thereafter, slipping down to finish a lowly 16th.

Crucially, Kamui soon erased the memories of that lacklustre season with another winter campaign in the GP2 Asia Series, where he took two wins to emerge as the champion by a comfortable margin. This success perhaps should have been the springboard to a sophomore GP2 championship challenge, but in the event he rarely figured at all, apart from a single podium at the Nürburgring.

Luckily, the aforementioned chance to shine for Toyota gave Kobayashi a career lifeline that he grabbed. Not everyone was enamoured by the Japanese driver's wild driving style, however; Jenson Button described him as "crazy".

With the shock withdrawal of Toyota, Kobayashi's F1 career could have been over almost immediately, but Sauber stepped in to give him the chance to prove the general consensus that he was the best talent to have emerged from Japan. His first year in the team was spent trying to coax the best from a car that was hardly the most competitive proposition, but his racecraft and trademark passing manoeuvres brought a decent haul of points.

In 2011, Kamui faced a new challenge in the form of team-mate Sergio Pérez. Both drivers were up against it as they fought to get an average car out of the midfield log jam, but Kobayashi emerged with more points. The distinct impression, however, is that the fearless Japanese driver needs access to more competitive machinery, otherwise his career may have reached its high point.

KOBAYASHI, Kamui (J) b 13/9/1986, Amagasaki, Hyogo

	2009 Championship position: 18th		Wins: 0	Pole positions: 0		Fastest laps: 0	Points scored: 3			
	Race	Circuit	No	Entrant	Tyres	Capacity/Car/Engine		Comment		Q Pos/Entries
app	JAPANESE GP	Suzuka	10	Panasonic Toyota Racing	B	2.4 Toyota TF109-V8		ran as 3rd driver in practice 1 only		- / -
9	BRAZILIAN GP	Interlagos	10	Panasonic Toyota Racing	B	2.4 Toyota TF109-V8		clashed with Nakajima		11/20
6	ABU DHABI GP	Yas Marina Circuit	10	Panasonic Toyota Racing	B	2.4 Toyota TF109-V8		ran good one-stop strategy		12/20
	2010 Championship position: 12th		Wins: 0	Pole positions: 0		Fastest laps: 0	Points scored: 32			
ret	BAHRAIN GP	Sakhir Circuit	23	BMW Sauber F1 Team	B	2.4 Sauber C29-Ferrari V8		hydraulics		16/24
ret	AUSTRALIAN GP	Melbourne	23	BMW Sauber F1 Team	B	2.4 Sauber C29-Ferrari V8		lost front wing - hit Rosberg on lap 1		16/24
ret	MALAYSIAN GP	Sepang	23	BMW Sauber F1 Team	B	2.4 Sauber C29-Ferrari V8		engine		9/24
ret	CHINESE GP	Shanghai Circuit	23	BMW Sauber F1 Team	B	2.4 Sauber C29-Ferrari V8		multiple collision on lap 1		15/24
12	SPANISH GP	Barcelona	23	BMW Sauber F1 Team	B	2.4 Sauber C29-Ferrari V8		1 lap behind		10/24
ret	MONACO GP	Monte Carlo	23	BMW Sauber F1 Team	B	2.4 Sauber C29-Ferrari V8		gearbox		16/24
10	TURKISH GP	Istanbul Park	23	BMW Sauber F1 Team	B	2.4 Sauber C29-Ferrari V8				10/24
ret	CANADIAN GP	Montreal	23	BMW Sauber F1 Team	B	2.4 Sauber C29-Ferrari V8		accident with Rosberg on lap 1		18/24
7	EUROPEAN GP	Valencia	23	BMW Sauber F1 Team	B	2.4 Sauber C29-Ferrari V8				18/24
6	BRITISH GP	Silverstone	23	BMW Sauber F1 Team	B	2.4 Sauber C29-Ferrari V8				12/24
11	GERMAN GP	Hockenheim	23	BMW Sauber F1 Team	B	2.4 Sauber C29-Ferrari V8		1 lap behind		12/24
9	HUNGARIAN GP	Hungaroring	23	BMW Sauber F1 Team	B	2.4 Sauber C29-Ferrari V8		1 lap behind		18/24
8	BELGIAN GP	Spa	23	BMW Sauber F1 Team	B	2.4 Sauber C29-Ferrari V8				19/24
ret	ITALIAN GP	Monza	23	BMW Sauber F1 Team	B	2.4 Sauber C29-Ferrari V8		gearbox		13/24
ret	SINGAPORE GP	Marina Bay Circuit	23	BMW Sauber F1 Team	B	2.4 Sauber C29-Ferrari V8		accident slid off on worn tyres		10/24
7	JAPANESE GP	Suzuka	23	BMW Sauber F1 Team	B	2.4 Sauber C29-Ferrari V8				14/24
8	KOREAN GP	Yeongam	23	BMW Sauber F1 Team	B	2.4 Sauber C29-Ferrari V8				12/24
10	BRAZILIAN GP	Interlagos	23	BMW Sauber F1 Team	B	2.4 Sauber C29-Ferrari V8		1 lap behind		12/24
14	ABU DHABI GP	Yas Marina Circuit	23	BMW Sauber F1 Team	B	2.4 Sauber C29-Ferrari V8				12/24

2011 Championship position: 12th	Wins: 0	Pole positions: 0	Fastest laps: 0	Points scored: 30				
dsq*	AUSTRALIAN GP	Melbourne	23	Sauber F1 Team	P	2.4 Sauber C30-Ferrari V8	8th *dsq – rear wing element illegal	9/24
7	MALAYSIAN GP	Sepang	23	Sauber F1 Team	P	2.4 Sauber C30-Ferrari V8		10/24
10	CHINESE GP	Shanghai Circuit	23	Sauber F1 Team	P	2.4 Sauber C30-Ferrari V8		13/24
10	TURKISH GP	Istanbul Park	23	Sauber F1 Team	P	2.4 Sauber C30-Ferrari V8	*no time set – started from back of grid	*24/24
10	SPANISH GP	Barcelona	23	Sauber F1 Team	P	2.4 Sauber C30-Ferrari V8	1st lap puncture/1 lap behind	10/24
5	MONACO GP	Monte Carlo	23	Sauber F1 Team	P	2.4 Sauber C30-Ferrari V8		13/24
7	CANADIAN GP	Montreal	23	Sauber F1 Team	P	2.4 Sauber C30-Ferrari V8	hit from behind behind by Heidfeld	13/24
16	EUROPEAN GP	Valencia	23	Sauber F1 Team	P	2.4 Sauber C30-Ferrari V8	1 lap behind	14/24
ret	BRITISH GP	Silverstone	23	Sauber F1 Team	P	2.4 Sauber C30-Ferrari V8	oil leak	8/24
9	GERMAN GP	Hockenheim	23	Sauber F1 Team	P	2.4 Sauber C30-Ferrari V8	1 lap behind	18/24
11	HUNGARIAN GP	Hungaroring	23	Sauber F1 Team	P	2.4 Sauber C30-Ferrari V8	1 lap behind	13/24
12	BELGIAN GP	Spa	23	Sauber F1 Team	P	2.4 Sauber C30-Ferrari V8	survived collision with Hamilton	12/24
ret	ITALIAN GP	Monza	23	Sauber F1 Team	P	2.4 Sauber C30-Ferrari V8	gearbox	17/24
14	SINGAPORE GP	Marina Bay Circuit	23	Sauber F1 Team	P	2.4 Sauber C30-Ferrari V8	2 laps behind	17/24
13	JAPANESE GP	Suzuka	23	Sauber F1 Team	P	2.4 Sauber C30-Ferrari V8		10/24
15	KOREAN GP	Yeongam	23	Sauber F1 Team	P	2.4 Sauber C30-Ferrari V8	1 lap behind	14/24
ret	INDIAN GP	Buddh Circuit	23	Sauber F1 Team	P	2.4 Sauber C30-Ferrari V8	hit by Glock on lap 1	18/24
10	ABU DHABI GP	Yas Marina Circuit	23	Sauber F1 Team	P	2.4 Sauber C30-Ferrari V8	1 lap behind	16/24
9	BRAZILIAN GP	Interlagos	23	Sauber F1 Team	P	2.4 Sauber C30-Ferrari V8	1 lap behind	16/24

GP Starts: 40   GP Wins: 0   Pole positions: 0   Fastest laps: 1   Points: 65

HELMUTH KOINIGG

ALTHOUGH Helmuth Koinigg came from a relatively affluent background, he found his lack of sufficient funds a great hindrance in his attempts to break into to the sport's higher echelons. His early sporting efforts had been directed towards gymnastics and ski-ing, before he gravitated towards motorsport.

Koinigg started with an old VW beetle in small events, but parental disapproval meant that funds were not forthcoming for him to progess further at this stage. Thus he left school and took a number of jobs to earn some money before attending university in Vienna.

It was 1969 when Koinigg got his real start in racing, after scraping together the funds to buy the ex-Niki Lauda Mini Cooper S. Four wins in his first five races soon attracted the attention of Helmut Marko, who invited him to become involved in his McNamara project in Formula Vee. Initially Koinigg was out of his depth, proving to be quick, but accident-prone. Marko and MacNamara were not discouraged, however, and he showed promise in some Formula Ford and F3 outings in 1970, along with his European Super Vee rides. In the event, the project ran out of funds in mid-season, but he soon picked up another ride with Bergmann in Formula Ford.

However, he was destined to spend the bulk of his short career trapped, albeit tre-mendously successfully, in Formula Vee and Super Vee, with only occasional outings in Formula Ford offering a glimpse of his natural talent on a wider stage.

Without the funds to race in Formula 2, in 1972 Koinning was forced to turn down the drive eventually taken by Lauda. Nonetheless, he buckled down to another diet of Super Vee, finishing a close second to Manfed Schurti in a two-horse battle. Staying with Berg-mann, he planned a dual assualt on Super Vee and a selected number of Formula 2 races with a modified March 722. In the event, he finally did the business in Super Vee, winning the Gold Cup, but the F2 plans were abandoned in favour of local hill-climb success.

Then Helmuth found himself in demand by the Ford Cologne team, and he made a big impression in both the Ford Capri and the Zakspeed Escort. His polished performances led to him to Martini Racing's G5 Porsche, before he raised the finance to hire a private Scuderia Finotto Brabham for the 1974 Austrian Grand Prix. Predictably, perhaps, he failed to qualify this poorly prepared and tired car, but he did well enough to interest John Surtees, who signed him up for the last two races of the year, with the prospect of a full-time drive in 1975. After a solid debut in Canada, in only his second race for the team, at Watkins Glen, the young Austrian suffered a suspension failure that pitched the car at speed through the catch fencing and into the Armco barrier. Unfortunately the car speared under the bottom section and he was decapitated. While the action continued without interruption, a tarpaulin was draped over the gruesome remains, which were dealt with after the race was run, Different times...

KOINIGG, Helmuth (A) b 3/11/1948, Vienna – d 6/10/1974, Watkins Glen Circuit, New York State, USA

	1974 Championship position: Unplaced							
	Race	Circuit	No	Entrant	Tyres	Capacity/Car/Engine	Comment	Q Pos/Entries
dnq	AUSTRIAN GP	Österreichring	32	Scuderia Finotto	G	3.0 Brabham BT42-Cosworth V8		31/31
10	CANADIAN GP	Mosport Park	19	Team Surtees	F	3.0 Surtees TS16-Cosworth V8	2 laps behind	22/30
ret	US GP	Watkins Glen	19	Team Surtees	F	3.0 Surtees TS16-Cosworth V8	fatal accident	23/30

GP Starts: 2   GP Wins: 0   Pole positions: 0   Fastest laps: 0   Points: 0

HEIKKI KOVALAINEN

DESPITE not having conquered the feeder championships that usually prove to be the passport to the top echelon, Heikki Kovalainen managed to find a way into Formula 1. Certainly, his karting credentials were as impressive as most, as he had won the Finnish Formula A championship in both 1999 and 2000. He also added the Scandinavian title and the Elf Masters at Bercy in the latter year to begin his association with Renault, opting for the French giant's UK-based series. Claiming an overall fourth place in his debut year and scoring two wins in the process earned him a place in the Renault Driver Development Programme, and his position helped him graduate to the British F3 championship for 2002 with Fortec Motorsport, the leading user of Renault's Sodomo engines. Although arguably the units were not as strong as the Mugen-Honda engines that dominated the British F3 field, Heikki got the most from his car to prove a consistent front-runner against a dominant Carlin Motorsport, taking five wins and three pole positions in a late-season surge to third in the championship.

Heikki continued his climb up the motorsport ladder when his next venture took him to the World Series by Nissan, where he defied his inexperience to

claim second in the standings, taking a win at the Lausitzring, even though generally outpaced by his title winning team-mate, Franck Montagny.

Nonetheless, Kovalainen had done enough to earn himself a test at both ends of the F1 scale, initially with Renault and then with Minardi. In the end, Renault decided to keep tabs on the Finn by signing him to be their second test driver after Montagny. This less-intensive role allowed him to continue racing and return to the World Series, this time with newcomers Pons Racing. With a year of experience under his belt, he was the dominant force in the championship throughout 2004, a mid-season flurry of strong results, including seven straight podiums and four wins, helping him well on the way to glory. Despite his triumph, however, the general lack of exposure for the World Series meant that he remained something of an unknown quantity to all but the most hardened of enthusiasts.

Renault retained Kovalainen as a test driver for a second season and helped him secure a drive with Arden in the GP2 series, where he promptly marked himself out as a championship contender by dominating during the first half of the year. In the end, Nico Rosberg got the better of him, but with both drivers scoring five wins apiece, they proved they were that year's outstanding talents.

When Renault learned that Fernando Alonso would be defecting to McLaren, they immediately promoted Kovalainen to the role of full-time test driver, and he spent the season being groomed to take over the Spaniard's racing role for 2007. Not short of confidence, he stated that he would be looking to win races in his first season, but the Finn was put on the back foot on his debut when he found that the R27 was not remotely a race winner. Under pressure after criticism from team principal Flavio Briatore for some tentative early-season performances, he finally got to grips with Formula 1 with top-six finishes in the North American races. From that point on, the Finn began to regularly overshadow team-mate Giancarlo Fischella, delivering a succession of points-scoring races that culminated in a brilliant second place behind Lewis Hamilton in the Japanese Grand Prix.

Kovalainen's career took a massive upturn when Alonso sought refuge back at Renault following his hasty departure from McLaren. It became clear that the Finn was not the preferred choice of partner for the double world champion, however, so unproven test driver Nelson Piquet Jr was chosen instead. Heikki was released to take up the offer of joining McLaren, and thus the chance of a lifetime dropped into his lap.

Not unnaturally, Heikki was somewhat eclipsed by the whirlwind surrounding Lewis Hamilton's successful championship quest. Things started to pick up, however, after he emerged unscathed from a high-speed crash when his McLaren suffered a wheel-rim failure in Spain. A well-taken pole position under tricky conditions at Silverstone only brought a somewhat disappointing fifth-place finish, but his maiden grand prix win in Hungary was just around the corner, even if it was achieved in slightly fortuitous circumstances following Felipe Massa's late retirement.

Unfortunately, the Finn's breakthrough victory was not really built upon during the remainder of the season. Even his second place behind Sebastian Vettel in the Italian Grand Prix was looked on as something of a missed opportunity. Indeed, his end-of-season form was something of a let-down. Surely much more was expected from him in 2009, but the McLaren MP4-24 initially proved to be uncompetitive and he endured a torrid start to the season. With only a fifth place garnered from the opening five races, Heikki's confidence seemed to suffer, and once the car was proved to be a winning machine by Hamilton, he was under pressure to deliver solid results. Having failed to make the podium, his tenure looked increasingly insecure. The end-of-season arrival of new world champion Jenson Button left him out work, but Tony Fernandes and his new Lotus team were more than happy to have him on board as they started their fledgling operation from the back of the grid.

Thus far, Heikki has driven his heart out without much prospect of reward. Indeed, the holy grail of tenth place and its valuable single championship point may have seemed as far out of reach as a grand prix victory. Nevertheless, he never complained and kept up a cheery presence as the team made slow progress towards the midfield. Maybe the easy-going Finn can no longer be considered as a candidate for a top seat elsewhere, but his immense value to his current employers is beyond doubt.

KOVALAINEN, Heikki (FIN) b 9/10/1981, Suomussalmi

2007 Championship position: 7th   Wins: 0   Pole positions: 0   Fastest laps: 0   Points scored: 30

	Race	Circuit	No	Entrant	Tyres	Capacity/Car/Engine	Comment	Q Pos/Entries
10	AUSTRALIAN GP	Melbourne	4	ING Renault F1 Team	B	2.4 Renault R27-V8	1 lap behind	13/22
8	MALAYSIAN GP	Sepang	4	ING Renault F1 Team	B	2.4 Renault R27-V8		11/22
9	BAHRAIN GP	Sakhir Circuit	4	ING Renault F1 Team	B	2.4 Renault R27-V8	heavy rear tyre wear	12/22
7	SPANISH GP	Barcelona	4	ING Renault F1 Team	B	2.4 Renault R27-V8	re-fuelling problem – extra stop	8/22
13/ret	MONACO GP	Monte Carlo	4	ING Renault F1 Team	B	2.4 Renault R27-V8	engine/2 laps behind	15/22
4	CANADIAN GP	Montreal	4	ING Renault F1 Team	B	2.4 Renault R27-V8		19/22
5	U S GP	Indianapolis	4	ING Renault F1 Team	B	2.4 Renault R27-V8		6/22
15	FRENCH GP	Magny Cours	4	ING Renault F1 Team	B	2.4 Renault R27-V8	hit by Trulli – puncture/1 lap behind	6/22
7	BRITISH GP	Silverstone	4	ING Renault F1 Team	B	2.4 Renault R27-V8	tyre problems/1 lap behind	7/22
8	EUROPEAN GP	Nürburgring	4	ING Renault F1 Team	B	2.4 Renault R27-V8	1 lap behind	7/22
8	HUNGARIAN GP	Hungaroring	4	ING Renault F1 Team	B	2.4 Renault R27-V8		12/22
6	TURKISH GP	Istanbul	4	ING Renault F1 Team	B	2.4 Renault R27-V8		7/22
7	ITALIAN GP	Monza	4	ING Renault F1 Team	B	2.4 Renault R27-V8		7/22
8	BELGIAN GP	Spa	4	ING Renault F1 Team	B	2.4 Renault R27-V8	ran wrong fuel-load strategy	10/22
2	JAPANESE GP	Suzuka	4	ING Renault F1 Team	B	2.4 Renault R27-V8		12/22
9	CHINESE GP	Shanghai Circuit	4	ING Renault F1 Team	B	2.4 Renault R27-V8		14/22
ret	BRAZILIAN GP	Interlagos	4	ING Renault F1 Team	B	2.4 Renault R27-V8	spun off –suspension – earlier damage	17/22

2008 Championship position: 7th   Wins: 1   Pole positions: 1   Fastest laps: 2   Points scored: 53

	Race	Circuit	No	Entrant	Tyres	Capacity/Car/Engine	Comment	Q Pos/Entries
5	AUSTRALIAN GP	Melbourne	23	Vodafone McLaren Mercedes	B	2.4 McLaren MP4/23-Mercedes V8	FL	3/22
3	MALAYSIAN GP	Sepang	23	Vodafone McLaren Mercedes	B	2.4 McLaren MP4/23-Mercedes V8	some tyre graining	3/22
5	BAHRAIN GP	Sakhir Circuit	23	Vodafone McLaren Mercedes	B	2.4 McLaren MP4/23-Mercedes V8	flat-spotted tyre/FL	5/22
ret	SPANISH GP	Barcelona	23	Vodafone McLaren Mercedes	B	2.4 McLaren MP4/23-Mercedes V8	big accident – wheel rim failure	6/22
12	TURKISH GP	Istanbul	23	Vodafone McLaren Mercedes	B	2.4 McLaren MP4/23-Mercedes V8	lap 1 collision – cut tyre/1 lap behind	2/20
8	MONACO GP	Monte Carlo	23	Vodafone McLaren Mercedes	B	2.4 McLaren MP4/23-Mercedes V8	*started from pits – gear selection	*4/20
9	CANADIAN GP	Montreal	23	Vodafone McLaren Mercedes	B	2.4 McLaren MP4/23-Mercedes V8	excessive tyre graining	7/20
4	FRENCH GP	Magny Cours	23	Vodafone McLaren Mercedes	B	2.4 McLaren MP4/23-Mercedes V8	grid penalty – blocking/collision with Trulli	6/20
5	BRITISH GP	Silverstone	23	Vodafone McLaren Mercedes	B	2.4 McLaren MP4/23-Mercedes V8	spun at Abbey/1 lap behind	1/20
5	GERMAN GP	Hockenheim	23	Vodafone McLaren Mercedes	B	2.4 McLaren MP4/23-Mercedes V8		3/20
1	HUNGARIAN GP	Hungaroring	23	Vodafone McLaren Mercedes	B	2.4 McLaren MP4/23-Mercedes V8		2/20
4	EUROPEAN GP	Valencia	23	Vodafone McLaren Mercedes	B	2.4 McLaren MP4/23-Mercedes V8		5/20
10/ret	BELGIAN GP	Spa	23	Vodafone McLaren Mercedes	B	2.4 McLaren MP4/23-Mercedes V8	gearbox/1 lap behind	3/20
2	ITALIAN GP	Monza	23	Vodafone McLaren Mercedes	B	2.4 McLaren MP4/23-Mercedes V8	glazed brake discs	2/20
10	SINGAPORE GP	Marina Bay Circuit	23	Vodafone McLaren Mercedes	B	2.4 McLaren MP4/23-Mercedes V8	brakes/trapped in traffic	5/20
ret	JAPANESE GP	Suzuka	23	Vodafone McLaren Mercedes	B	2.4 McLaren MP4/23-Mercedes V8	engine	3/20
ret	CHINESE GP	Shanghai Circuit	23	Vodafone McLaren Mercedes	B	2.4 McLaren MP4/23-Mercedes V8	hydraulic pressure	5/20
7	BRAZILIAN GP	Interlagos	23	Vodafone McLaren Mercedes	B	2.4 McLaren MP4/23-Mercedes V8		5/20

2009 Championship position: 12th   Wins: 0   Pole positions: 0   Fastest laps: 0   Points scored: 22

	Race	Circuit	No	Entrant	Tyres	Capacity/Car/Engine	Comment	Q Pos/Entries
ret	AUSTRALIAN GP	Melbourne	2	Vodafone McLaren Mercedes	B	2.4 McLaren MP4/24-Mercedes V8	lap 1 collision – suspension damage	14/20
ret	MALAYSIAN GP	Sepang	2	Vodafone McLaren Mercedes	B	2.4 McLaren MP4/24-Mercedes V8	spun off on lap 1	9/20
5	CHINESE GP	Shanghai Circuit	2	Vodafone McLaren Mercedes	B	2.4 McLaren MP4/24-Mercedes V8		12/20
12	BAHRAIN GP	Sakhir Circuit	2	Vodafone McLaren Mercedes	B	2.4 McLaren MP4/24-Mercedes V8	tyre problems – vibration	11/20
ret	SPANISH GP	Barcelona	2	Vodafone McLaren Mercedes	B	2.4 McLaren MP4/24-Mercedes V8	gearbox	18/20
ret	MONACO GP	Monte Carlo	2	Vodafone McLaren Mercedes	B	2.4 McLaren MP4/24-Mercedes V8	accident – hit kerb	7/20
14	TURKISH GP	Istanbul	2	Vodafone McLaren Mercedes	B	2.4 McLaren MP4/24-Mercedes V8	1 lap behind	14/20
ret	BRITISH GP	Silverstone	2	Vodafone McLaren Mercedes	B	2.4 McLaren MP4/24-Mercedes V8	accident damage – hit by Bourdais	13/20
8	GERMAN GP	Nürburgring	2	Vodafone McLaren Mercedes	B	2.4 McLaren MP4/24-Mercedes V8		6/20
5	HUNGARIAN GP	Hungaroring	2	Vodafone McLaren Mercedes	B	2.4 McLaren MP4/24-Mercedes V8		6/20
4	EUROPEAN GP	Valencia	2	Vodafone McLaren Mercedes	B	2.4 McLaren MP4/24-Mercedes V8	wrong tyres fitted at final pitstop	2/20
6	BELGIAN GP	Spa	2	Vodafone McLaren Mercedes	B	2.4 McLaren MP4/24-Mercedes V8	good one-stop strategy	15/20
6	ITALIAN GP	Monza	2	Vodafone McLaren Mercedes	B	2.4 McLaren MP4/24-Mercedes V8		4/20
7	SINGAPORE GP	Marina Bay Circuit	2	Vodafone McLaren Mercedes	B	2.4 McLaren MP4/24-Mercedes V8		10/20
11	JAPANESE GP	Suzuka	2	Vodafone McLaren Mercedes	B	2.4 McLaren MP4/24-Mercedes V8	collision with Sutil	9/20

Heikki's great day. The Finn scored his maiden grand prix win in the 2008 Hungarian Grand Prix after the late retirement of Ferrari's Felipe Massa.

	Race	Circuit	No	Entrant	Tyres	Capacity/Car/Engine	Comment	Q Pos/Entries
12*	BRAZILIAN GP	Interlagos	2	Vodafone McLaren Mercedes	B	2.4 McLaren MP4/24-Mercedes V8	*25-sec penalty – dragging fuel hose	17/20
11	ABU DHABI GP	Yas Island	2	Vodafone McLaren Mercedes	B	2.4 McLaren MP4/24-Mercedes V8		13/20

2010 Championship position: Unplaced

15	BAHRAIN GP	Sakhir Circuit	19	Lotus Racing	B	2.4 Lotus T127 Cosworth V8	2 laps behind	21/24
13	AUSTRALIAN GP	Melbourne	19	Lotus Racing	B	2.4 Lotus T127 Cosworth V8	2 laps behind	19/24
nc	MALAYSIAN GP	Sepang	19	Lotus Racing	B	2.4 Lotus T127 Cosworth V8	puncture/hydraulics/10 laps behind	15/24
14	CHINESE GP	Shanghai Circuit	19	Lotus Racing	B	2.4 Lotus T127 Cosworth V8	1 lap behind	21/24
dns*	SPANISH GP	Barcelona	19	Lotus Racing	B	2.4 Lotus T127 Cosworth V8	*gearbox software failure	20/24
ret	MONACO GP	Monte Carlo	19	Lotus Racing	B	2.4 Lotus T127 Cosworth V8	steering	18/24
ret	TURKISH GP	Istanbul Park	19	Lotus Racing	B	2.4 Lotus T127 Cosworth V8	hydraulics	20/24
16	CANADIAN GP	Montreal	19	Lotus Racing	B	2.4 Lotus T127 Cosworth V8	2 laps behind	19/24
ret	EUROPEAN GP	Valencia	19	Lotus Racing	B	2.4 Lotus T127 Cosworth V8	accident – big rear-end hit by Webber	20/24
17	BRITISH GP	Silverstone	19	Lotus Racing	B	2.4 Lotus T127 Cosworth V8	1 lap behind	19/24
ret	GERMAN GP	Hockenheim	19	Lotus Racing	B	2.4 Lotus T127 Cosworth V8	accident – collision with de la Rosa	24/24
14	HUNGARIAN GP	Hungaroring	19	Lotus Racing	B	2.4 Lotus T127 Cosworth V8	good race with Trulli/3 laps behind	20/24
16	BELGIAN GP	Spa	19	Lotus Racing	B	2.4 Lotus T127 Cosworth V8	1 lap behind	16/24
18	ITALIAN GP	Monza	19	Lotus Racing	B	2.4 Lotus T127 Cosworth V8	2 laps behind	19/24
ret/16	SINGAPORE GP	Marina Bay Circuit	19	Lotus Racing	B	2.4 Lotus T127 Cosworth V8	spun on own oil/fire/3 laps behind	19/24
12	JAPANESE GP	Suzuka	19	Lotus Racing	B	2.4 Lotus T127 Cosworth V8	1 lap behind	20/24
13	KOREAN GP	Yeongam	19	Lotus Racing	B	2.4 Lotus T127 Cosworth V8	1 lap behind	21/24
18	BRAZILIAN GP	Interlagos	19	Lotus Racing	B	2.4 Lotus T127 Cosworth V8	2 laps behind	21/24
17	ABU DHABI GP	Yas Marina Circuit	19	Lotus Racing	B	2.4 Lotus T127 Cosworth V8	1 lap behind	20/24

2011 Championship position: Unplaced

ret	AUSTRALIAN GP	Melbourne	20	Lotus Racing	P	2.4 Lotus T128 Renault V8	radiator leak	19/24
15	MALAYSIAN GP	Sepang	20	Lotus Racing	P	2.4 Lotus T128 Renault V8	1 lap behind	19/24
16	CHINESE GP	Shanghai Circuit	20	Lotus Racing	P	2.4 Lotus T128 Renault V8	1 lap behind	19/24
19	TURKISH GP	Istanbul Park	20	Lotus Racing	P	2.4 Lotus T128 Renault V8	2 laps behind	18/24
ret	SPANISH GP	Barcelona	20	Lotus Racing	P	2.4 Lotus T128 Renault V8	accident	15/24
14	MONACO GP	Monte Carlo	20	Lotus Racing	P	2.4 Lotus T128 Renault V8	2 laps behind	18/24
ret	CANADIAN GP	Montreal	20	Lotus Racing	P	2.4 Lotus T128 Renault V8	driveshaft	20/24
19	EUROPEAN GP	Valencia	20	Lotus Racing	P	2.4 Lotus T128 Renault V8	3 laps behind	18/24
ret	BRITISH GP	Silverstone	20	Lotus Racing	P	2.4 Lotus T128 Renault V8	electrics/gearbox	17/24
10	GERMAN GP	Hockenheim	20	Lotus Racing	P	2.4 Lotus T128 Renault V8	2 laps behind	19/24
ret	HUNGARIAN GP	Hungaroring	20	Lotus Racing	P	2.4 Lotus T128 Renault V8	water leak	19/24
15	BELGIAN GP	Spa	20	Lotus Racing	P	2.4 Lotus T128 Renault V8	1 lap behind	17/24
13	ITALIAN GP	Monza	20	Lotus Racing	P	2.4 Lotus T128 Renault V8	2 laps behind	20/24
16	SINGAPORE GP	Marina Bay Circuit	20	Lotus Racing	P	2.4 Lotus T128 Renault V8	2 laps behind	19/24
18	JAPANESE GP	Suzuka	20	Lotus Racing	P	2.4 Lotus T128 Renault V8		18/24
14	KOREAN GP	Yeongam	20	Lotus Racing	P	2.4 Lotus T128 Renault V8	1 lap behind	19/24
14	INDIAN GP	Buddh Circuit	20	Lotus Racing	P	2.4 Lotus T128 Renault V8	2 laps behind	19/24
17	ABU DHABI GP	Yas Marina Circuit	20	Lotus Racing	P	2.4 Lotus T128 Renault V8	1 lap behind	18/24
16	BRAZILIAN GP	Interlagos	20	Lotus Racing	P	2.4 Lotus T128 Renault V8	2 laps behind	19/24

GP Starts: 89 (90)   GP Wins: 1   Pole positions: 1   Fastest laps: 2   Points: 105

RUDI KRAUSE

Post-War Germany having been divided into two separate countries, the communist German Democratic Republic (DDR) in the East ran their own hotly-contested series between 1950 and '53, mainly on ad-hoc courses often created by closing sections of autobahn. Rudi Krause was a leading runner throughout, mainly in BMW-based specials. He took many top-three finishes and was well placed to win when faster drivers – such as Edgar Barth and his EMW – hit trouble.

Rudi ventured into the West and drove a Veritas sports at Avus in 1951, but he retired on the first lap. At this meeting, his great rival, Paul Greifzu, caused a stir by beating West Germany's finest with his BMW special. Sadly, the brilliant owner/driver lost his life in crash at Dessau the following year, but his widow had the car rebuilt and entrusted it to Rudi for the 1953 season.

Thus Rudi ventured westward once more to participate in the German Grand Prix. The car had a sports-type body with doors, and it seems that one of these came adrift and jammed a rear wheel. Krause was forced to stop and disentangle the offending item before rejoining the race to finish two laps adrift. He continued to race the car in the DDR and ran a final season of Formula 2 in 1954. However, the fields were thin and there was a distinct lack of interest, even among the competitors. Some events were cancelled, but he was left with enough points from the races completed to claim the championship crown. In the event, however, it was never awarded. He had to be content with the title of 'DDR-Bester' (best of the GDR). When the DDR championship ceased, he then turned to rallying with a BMW.

KRAUSE, Rudolf (D) b 30/3/1907, Oberrreichenbach – d 11/4/1987, Reichenbach

1952 Championship position: Unplaced

	Race	Circuit	No	Entrant	Tyres	Capacity/Car/Engine	Comment	Q Pos/Entries
ret	GERMAN GP	Nürburgring	136	Rudolf Krause	–	2.0 BMW-Reif 6	clutch	23/32

1953 Championship position: 0   Wins: 0   Pole positions: 0   Fastest laps: 0   Points scored: 0

14	GERMAN GP	Nürburgring	36	Dora Greifzu	–	2.0 BMW-Greifzu 6	2 laps behind	26/35

GP Starts: 2   GP Wins: 0   Pole positions: 0   Fastest laps: 0   Points: 0

ROBERT KUBICA

SOMETIMES a driver finds himself a seat in a Formula 1 car more because of his nationality and/or commercial viability than any outright talent. This was not the case with Robert Kubica, who had all the attributes of not only a front-line racer who just happened to be the first Polish driver to compete in grand prix racing, but also of a potential world champion and serial winner in the right car. Sadly, he may never be given the chance to take his massive natural talent to the highest level following his catastrophic rallying accident, which caused horrendous injuries and nearly claimed his life.

Robert began running around in a little off-road vehicle when just four years old and he spent time practising in a go-kart, under the tutelage of his father, long before he was able to take part in any official competition. He began his racing career in the Polish karting championship at the age of ten, winning six titles in three years before heading to Italy, where he soon showed his considerable talent, emerging as both the Italian and German champion, with the added bonus of prestigious wins at Monaco in both 1998 and 1999.

After taking fourth place overall in both the World and European karting championships the following season, Kubica finally graduated to Formula Renault in 2001, soon becoming a pacesetter in this discipline. Four wins helped him to finish runner-up in the 2002 Italian championship and he planned an assault on the Euroseries F3 championship the following year. Unfortunately, his Formula 3 debut was delayed after he sustained a badly broken arm as a passenger in a road accident, but upon his return in mid-season, he won at Norisring and finished a creditable 12th overall. In 2004, he was a front-runner again, but outright victory eluded him and he had to settle for seventh in the final standings.

A crucial decision to opt for World Series by Renault rather than GP2 in 2005 proved to be astute, as the Polish driver quickly took control of proceedings against more experienced campaigners. Four wins wrapped up the championship and guaranteed Kubica an end-of-season test at Barcelona in the F1 Renault. His lap times were so impressive that Mario Thiessen of BMW immediately signed him up as the BMW-Sauber team's test driver for 2006. After excelling in his duties as third driver in Friday testing throughout the first half of the season, he was unexpectedly pitched into action in place of the indisposed Jacques Villeneuve for the Hungarian Grand Prix. What a baptism it proved to be for the Pole, who out-qualified team-mate Nick Heidfeld in practice and then survived two spins in a rain-hit race to claim a plucky seventh place. Sadly, his BMW-Sauber was found to be underweight during post-race scrutineering and his points-scoring debut was wiped out. Nevertheless, he kept his seat at the expense of Villeneuve, and at the very next race, the Italian Grand Prix, he took a sensational third place. Although his subsequent results were less productive, a feisty performance in Japan proved him to be a true racer.

Initially, Kubica struggled somewhat in 2007, experiencing problems in adapting to the change to Bridgestone control tyres, but he soon started scoring points, before surviving a huge accident in the Canadian Grand Prix. Fortunately, his injuries were not serious, and after being rested from Indianapolis, he returned to score in eight of the ten remaining rounds, finishing the season in a highly satisfactory sixth place.

The 2008 season began with a stunning second place in Malaysia and a pole position in Bahrain. Then came an ultra-consistent run of top-six finishes, capped by Robert's (and BMW-Sauber's) first ever grand prix victory in Montreal. Thereafter, the team lost their edge slightly, but he kept them in with a fighting chance of taking the championship with some brilliant drives. These included a determined second place in Japan, where he resolutely held off Räikkönen's Ferrari. In the end, the BMW was not quite fast enough, but fourth overall was a fine achievement, and many pundits put him at the top of their own personal driver rankings.

If the Pole thought he might have been able to mount a championship challenge in 2009, he was in for a rude awakening. Without the double diffuser, the BMW-Sauber was off the pace and, in contrast to the previous season, Kubica had to wait seven races until he registered any points at all. It was not until Singapore that he had a competitive car, and despite a brilliant drive into second place in Brazil, it was all too little, too late as far as 2009 was concerned. More bad news followed when BMW pulled out of Formula 1, leaving him to find a home with Renault .

Starting afresh with a new team was no obstacle to Robert, who soon meshed with the long-standing team personnel to work on a car that had good driveability and was also reliable. Although it was not on a par with the Red Bulls or McLarens, he put in some excellent drives that brought another haul of points-scoring finishes, including eight in a row, starting with his second place in Melbourne. Once again, he demonstrated his outstanding talent in taking the car to podium positions at both Monaco and Spa, where a driver's skills are at a premium.

Sadly, Kubica's world crumbled around him when he crashed his Skoda Fabia during a national rally in Italy. In a freak accident, his car was pierced by a length of Armco barrier, which partially severed his right arm and left him with serious multiple fractures, requiring several lengthy operations throughout 2011. A further setback occurred at the beginning of 2012, when the luckless Pole reportedly slipped on ice at home and broke his right leg above the ankle, thus further delaying his recuperation ahead of a planned return to the cockpit.

KUBICA, Robert (POL) b 7/12/84, Krakow

2006 Championship position: 16th   Wins: 0   Pole positions: 0   Fastest laps: 0   Points scored: 6

	Race	Circuit	No	Entrant	Tyres	Capacity/Car/Engine	Comment	Q Pos/Entries
dsq*	HUNGARIAN GP	Hungaroring	17	BMW Sauber F1 Team	M	2.4 BMW Sauber F1.06-V8	*7th on road/*car underweight*	10/22
12	TURKISH GP	Istanbul	17	BMW Sauber F1 Team	M	2.4 BMW Sauber F1.06-V8	*excessive tyre graining/1 lap behind*	9/22
3	ITALIAN GP	Monza	17	BMW Sauber F1 Team	M	2.4 BMW Sauber F1.06-V8	*flat-spotted tyre*	6/22
12	CHINESE GP	Shanghai	17	BMW Sauber F1 Team	M	2.4 BMW Sauber F1.06-V8	*wrong gamble on tyre change/- 1 lap*	9/22
9	JAPANESE GP	Suzuka	17	BMW Sauber F1 Team	M	2.4 BMW Sauber F1.06-V8		12/22
9	BRAZILIAN GP	Interlagos	17	BMW Sauber F1 Team	M	2.4 BMW Sauber F1.06-V8		9/22

2007 Championship position: 6th   Wins: 0   Pole positions: 0   Fastest laps: 0   Points scored: 39

	Race	Circuit	No	Entrant	Tyres	Capacity/Car/Engine	Comment	Q Pos/Entries
ret	AUSTRALIAN GP	Melbourne	9	BMW Sauber F1 Team	B	2.4 BMW Sauber F1.07-V8	*gearbox*	5/22
18	MALAYSIAN GP	Sepang	9	BMW Sauber F1 Team	B	2.4 BMW Sauber F1.07-V8	*collision damage/brake problems/-1 lap*	7/22
6	BAHRAIN GP	Bahrain	9	BMW Sauber F1 Team	B	2.4 BMW Sauber F1.07-V8	*refuelling flap stuck open*	6/22
4	SPANISH GP	Barcelona	9	BMW Sauber F1 Team	B	2.4 BMW Sauber F1.07-V8		5/22
5	MONACO GP	Monte Carlo	9	BMW Sauber F1 Team	B	2.4 BMW Sauber F1.07-V8	*brake & traction control problems/-1 lap*	8/22
ret	CANADIAN GP	Montreal	9	BMW Sauber F1 Team	B	2.4 BMW Sauber F1.07-V8	*massive accident – shock and bruising*	8/22
4	FRENCH GP	Magny Cours	9	BMW Sauber F1 Team	B	2.4 BMW Sauber F1.07-V8		4/22
4	BRITISH GP	Silverstone	9	BMW Sauber F1 Team	B	2.4 BMW Sauber F1.07-V8	*held off Massa*	5/22
7	EUROPEAN GP	Nürburgring	9	BMW Sauber F1 Team	B	2.4 BMW Sauber F1.07-V8	*lap 1 collision with Heidfeld*	5/22
5	HUNGARIAN GP	Hungaroring	9	BMW Sauber F1 Team	B	2.4 BMW Sauber F1.07-V8		7/22
8	TURKISH GP	Istanbul	9	BMW Sauber F1 Team	B	2.4 BMW Sauber F1.07-V8	*lack of speed*	5/22
5	ITALIAN GP	Monza	9	BMW Sauber F1 Team	B	2.4 BMW Sauber F1.07-V8	*delayed at first pitstop*	6/22
9	BELGIAN GP	Spa	9	BMW Sauber F1 Team	B	2.4 BMW Sauber F1.07-V8		5/22
7	JAPANESE GP	Suzuka	9	BMW Sauber F1 Team	B	2.4 BMW Sauber F1.07-V8	*hit Hamilton – drive-through penalty*	10/22
ret	CHINESE GP	Shanghai	9	BMW Sauber F1 Team	B	2.4 BMW Sauber F1.07-V8	*hydraulics*	9/22
5	BRAZILIAN GP	Interlagos	9	BMW Sauber F1 Team	B	2.4 BMW Sauber F1.07-V8	*overheating engine*	7/22

2008 Championship position: 4th   Wins: 1   Pole positions: 1   Fastest laps: 0   Points scored: 75

	Race	Circuit	No	Entrant	Tyres	Capacity/Car/Engine	Comment	Q Pos/Entries
ret	AUSTRALIAN GP	Melbourne	4	BMW Sauber F1 Team	B	2.4 BMW Sauber F1.08-V8	*hit by Nakajima – accident damage*	2/22
2	MALAYSIAN GP	Sepang	4	BMW Sauber F1 Team	B	2.4 BMW Sauber F1.08-V8		6/22
3	BAHRAIN GP	Bahrain	4	BMW Sauber F1 Team	B	2.4 BMW Sauber F1.08-V8	*first pole position*	1/22
4	SPANISH GP	Barcelona	4	BMW Sauber F1 Team	B	2.4 BMW Sauber F1.08-V8		4/22
4	TURKISH GP	Istanbul	4	BMW Sauber F1 Team	B	2.4 BMW Sauber F1.08-V8		5/20
2	MONACO GP	Monte Carlo	4	BMW Sauber F1 Team	B	2.4 BMW Sauber F1.08-V8	*faultless drive in wet*	5/20
1	CANADIAN GP	Montreal	4	BMW Sauber F1 Team	B	2.4 BMW Sauber F1.08-V8		2/20
5	FRENCH GP	Magny Cours	4	BMW Sauber F1 Team	B	2.4 BMW Sauber F1.08-V8		7/20
ret	BRITISH GP	Silverstone	4	BMW Sauber F1 Team	B	2.4 BMW Sauber F1.08-V8	*spun off in wet conditions*	10/20
7	GERMAN GP	Hockenheim	4	BMW Sauber F1 Team	B	2.4 BMW Sauber F1.08-V8	*unable to heat tyres sufficiently*	7/20
8	HUNGARIAN GP	Hungaroring	4	BMW Sauber F1 Team	B	2.4 BMW Sauber F1.08-V8	*excessive oversteer*	4/20
3	EUROPEAN GP	Valencia	4	BMW Sauber F1 Team	B	2.4 BMW Sauber F1.08-V8		3/20
6	BELGIAN GP	Spa	4	BMW Sauber F1 Team	B	2.4 BMW Sauber F1.08-V8		8/20
3	ITALIAN GP	Monza	4	BMW Sauber F1 Team	B	2.4 BMW Sauber F1.08-V8		11/20
11	SINGAPORE GP	Marina Bay Circuit	4	BMW Sauber F1 Team	B	2.4 BMW Sauber F1.08-V8	*drive thru penalty - entered 'closed' pits*	4/20
2	JAPANESE GP	Suzuka	4	BMW Sauber F1 Team	B	2.4 BMW Sauber F1.08-V8	*held off Räikkönen*	6/20
6	CHINESE GP	Shanghai	4	BMW Sauber F1 Team	B	2.4 BMW Sauber F1.08-V8	*balance problems*	12/20
11	BRAZILIAN GP	Interlagos	4	BMW Sauber F1 Team	B	2.4 BMW Sauber F1.08-V8	*started wet race on dry tyres/-1 lap*	13/20

Kubica scored BMW's only grand prix win in the 2008 Canadian GP. Only a year earlier, he was lucky to have escaped serious injury in a monumental accident at the same circuit.

2009 Championship position: 14		Wins: 0	Pole positions: 0		Fastest laps: 0	Points scored: 17		
ret/14	AUSTRALIAN GP	Melbourne	5	BMW Sauber F1 Team	B	2.4 BMW Sauber F1.09-V8	accident –collision with Vettel	4/20
ret	MALAYSIAN GP	Sepang	5	BMW Sauber F1 Team	B	2.4 BMW Sauber F1.09-V8	engine –fire	8/20
13	CHINESE GP	Shanghai	5	BMW Sauber F1 Team	B	2.4 BMW Sauber F1.09-V8	ran into Trulli – continued after repairs	18/20
18	BAHRAIN GP	Bahrain	5	BMW Sauber F1 Team	B	2.4 BMW Sauber F1.09-V8	collision – Heidfeld nose damage/-1 lap	13/20
11	SPANISH GP	Barcelona	5	BMW Sauber F1 Team	B	2.4 BMW Sauber F1.09-V8	1 lap behind	10/20
ret	MONACO GP	Monte Carlo	5	BMW Sauber F1 Team	B	2.4 BMW Sauber F1.09-V8	brakes	18/20
7	TURKISH GP	Istanbul	5	BMW Sauber F1 Team	B	2.4 BMW Sauber F1.09-V8		10/20
13	BRITISH GP	Silverstone	5	BMW Sauber F1 Team	B	2.4 BMW Sauber F1.09-V8	1 lap behind	12/20
14	GERMAN GP	Nürburgring	5	BMW Sauber F1 Team	B	2.4 BMW Sauber F1.09-V8	tyre pressure problems	16/20
13	HUNGARIAN GP	Hungaroring	5	BMW Sauber F1 Team	B	2.4 BMW Sauber F1.09-V8		19/20
8	EUROPEAN GP	Valencia	5	BMW Sauber F1 Team	B	2.4 BMW Sauber F1.09-V8		10/20
4	BELGIAN GP	Spa	5	BMW Sauber F1 Team	B	2.4 BMW Sauber F1.09-V8	wrong order for tyre choice strategy	5/20
ret	ITALIAN GP	Monza	5	BMW Sauber F1 Team	B	2.4 BMW Sauber F1.09-V8	oil leak	13/20
8	SINGAPORE GP	Marina Bay Circuit	5	BMW Sauber F1 Team	B	2.4 BMW Sauber F1.09-V8	tyre degradation	9/20
9	JAPANESE GP	Suzuka	5	BMW Sauber F1 Team	B	2.4 BMW Sauber F1.09-V8		13/20
2	BRAZILIAN GP	Interlagos	5	BMW Sauber F1 Team	B	2.4 BMW Sauber F1.09-V8	great drive	8/20
10	ABU DHABI GP	Yas Marina Circuit	5	BMW Sauber F1 Team	B	2.4 BMW Sauber F1.09-V8		7/20
2010 Championship position: 8th		Wins: 0	Pole positions: 0		Fastest laps: 1	Points scored: 136		
11	BAHRAIN GP	Sakhir Circuit	11	Renault F1 Team	B	2.4 Renault R30-V8	hit by Sutil on lap 1	9/24
2	AUSTRALIAN GP	Melbourne	11	Renault F1 Team	B	2.4 Renault R30-V8		9/24
4	MALAYSIAN GP	Sepang	11	Renault F1 Team	B	2.4 Renault R30-V8		6/24
5	CHINESE GP	Shanghai Circuit	11	Renault F1 Team	B	2.4 Renault R30-V8		8/24
8	SPANISH GP	Barcelona	11	Renault F1 Team	B	2.4 Renault R30-V8		7/24
3	MONACO GP	Monte Carlo	11	Renault F1 Team	B	2.4 Renault R30-V8		2/24
6	TURKISH GP	Istanbul Park	11	Renault F1 Team	B	2.4 Renault R30-V8		7/24
7	CANADIAN GP	Montreal	11	Renault F1 Team	B	2.4 Renault R30-V8	reprimanded for dangerous manoeuvre/FL	8/24
5	EUROPEAN GP	Valencia	11	Renault F1 Team	B	2.4 Renault R30-V8		6/24
ret	BRITISH GP	Silverstone	11	Renault F1 Team	B	2.4 Renault R30-V8	driveshaft	6/24
7	GERMAN GP	Hockenheim	11	Renault F1 Team	B	2.4 Renault R30-V8	1 lap behind	7/24
ret	HUNGARIAN GP	Hungaroring	11	Renault F1 Team	B	2.4 Renault R30-V8	pit collision – Sutil – suspension	8/24
3	BELGIAN GP	Spa	11	Renault F1 Team	B	2.4 Renault R30-V8	lost time at pit stop	3/24
8	ITALIAN GP	Monza	11	Renault F1 Team	B	2.4 Renault R30-V8		9/24
7	SINGAPORE GP	Marina Bay Circuit	11	Renault F1 Team	B	2.4 Renault R30-V8	puncture – additional pit stop	8/24
ret	JAPANESE GP	Suzuka	11	Renault F1 Team	B	2.4 Renault R30-V8	lost unsecured rear wheel	4/24
5	KOREAN GP	Yeongam	11	Renault F1 Team	B	2.4 Renault R30-V8		8/24
9	BRAZILIAN GP	Interlagos	11	Renault F1 Team	B	2.4 Renault R30-V8	1 lap behind	7/24
5	ABU DHABI GP	Yas Marina Circuit	11	Renault F1 Team	B	2.4 Renault R30-V8	clutch problems at the start	11/24

GP Starts: 76   GP Wins: 1   Pole positions: 1   Fastest laps: 1   Points: 273

ROBERT LA CAZE

A LTHOUGH a French native, Robert La Caze lived in Morocco. He took his first victory at Marrakech circuit in 1951, and for several years therafter he was a leading figure on the motorsport scene in North Africa, where he raced and rallied various Simcas, Renaults, a Lancia and a Delahaye to great effect in the early part of the decade.

In 1954, Robert won the Moroccan International Rally in a Simca, and subsequently he raced a Mercedes 300SL. In 1956, he made an appearance at Le Mans in a works Gordini, shared with Hernando da Silva Ramos. The pair put on a feisty performance against the Ferraris before the clutch failed. They had the satisfaction, however, of setting the fastest race lap for their class.

Morocco having been given the honour of hosting a round of the Formula 1 World Championship in 1958, La Caze was invited to take part. Running a Formula 2 Cooper, he circulated steadily round the 7km track to take third in class, behind the works cars of Jack Brabham and Bruce McLaren.

Robert concentrated on his business interests thereafter, but when the Rally of Morocco was revived in 1967, the indomitable pilot was on hand to triumph with his Renault R8 Gordini.

After this success, La Caze returned the following year with an even more potent car, but he suffered a big accident early on and, having passed the age of 50, decided that retirement was probably a wise option. He continued to indulge his passion for speed, however, in aviation, boating and skiing.

La CAZE, Robert (MA) b 26/2/1917, Paris, France

1958 Championship position: Unplaced								
	Race	Circuit	No	Entrant	Tyres	Capacity/Car/Engine	Comment	Q Pos/Entries
14*	MOROCCAN GP	Casablanca	58	Robert la Caze	D	1.5 Cooper T45-Climax 4 F2	*3rd in F2 class/5 laps behind	23/25

GP Starts: 1   GP Wins: 0   Pole positions: 0   Fastest laps: 0   Points: 0

JACQUES LAFFITE

THE smiling countenance of Jacques Laffite brightened the grand prix scene for more than a decade, during which he was a consistent performer who really excelled only when his car was absolutely on the pace – but then he simply flew.

Laffite's introduction to the sport was as a mechanic to Jean-Pierre Jabouille during his 1968 Formula 3 season. Jacques resolved to race himself and started in Formula France, before getting a taste of Formula 3 in 1969, taking a third place at Magny-Cours behind Jean-Pierre Jaussaud and François Mazet. Lack of finance saw him return to Formula France, however, and it wasn't until the 1973 season that he made a big breakthrough. He won the French F3 championship in his Martini and came close to taking the British John Player title as well, his splendid season including big wins in the prestigious Monaco and Pau grands prix. His driving was a little wild at times, and his French F3 title rival, Michel Leclere, was generally considered a better prospect.

Buoyed by his succcess and with backing from BP France, Laffite moved into Formula 2 in 1974 with a March-BMW and soon established himself among the front-runners, finishing second at Pau and winning the next round at the Salzburgring.

Having tried a number of drivers during the first half of the season, Frank Williams decided to offer Jacques a ride for the the German Grand Prix and, although his race ended in a shunt, he impressed more than the previous incumbents and kept the seat for the rest of the year. Thus his Formula 2 challenge was set aside, although he still finished third overall, behind Patrick Depaillier and Hans Stuck, despite missing four rounds due to his F1 commitments.

The 1975 season was very busy for the Frenchman, who had to shuffle his F1 drives for Williams with a full season in Formula 2, racing a Martini-BMW. Laffite dominated proceedings, taking six wins and the European championship against a phalanx of talented, and better funded, Frenchmen: Michel Leclère, Patrick Tambay, Gérard Larrousse and Jean-Pierre Jabouuille. In grands prix, Frank's outfit were very much in the doldrums, but Laffite profited from others' misfortune to provide the team with a much-needed second place in Germany. He also tried his hand successfully at sports car racing, taking the Kauhsen/Autodelta Alfa T33 to victory at Dijon, Monza and the Nürburgring.

Laffite's performances were good enough to convince Guy Ligier that he should lead the new Ligier-Matra team for 1976, much to the chagarin of the originally nominated driver, Jean-Pierre Beltoise. Jacques quickly became a favourite son at Vichy, working hard to bring the car to a competitive pitch. A second place in Austria, and podiums at Zolder and Monza (where he took pole position) were enough to see him take a satisfactory seventh place in the championship standings. Despite his graded driver status (which meant he was ineligible to score points), Lafitte appeared in a couple of races with Fred Opert's Chevron, scoring second places at Pau and Nogaro.

Jacques' next two seasons with Ligier were a mixture of highs and lows. He scored his maiden win at Anderstorp in 1977 after a tremendous drive, albeit aided by big a slice of luck when leader Mario Andretti ran short of fuel. This was a historic moment, for it was the first time an all-Fench car had won a world championship grand prix.

It soon became clear that Cosworth power allied to ground-effects was a necessity for sustained success, so the following year saw the team treading water somewhat, as the ageing Matra powerplant was about to be pensioned off.

At the beginning of 1979, Jacques flashed to victory in the opening two grands prix, stunning the F1 fraternity, but such dominance could not be sustained, as development brought more questions than answers. Certainly the stimulus of new team-mate Patrick Depaillier kept him on his mettle, and after a mid-season hang-gliding accident sidelined his partner, the sharp edge went from his performances.

Laffite faced a new challenge in 1980, in the form of a new team-mate, Didier Pironi, who drove with tremendous verve; Jacques was overshadowed somewhat, but he plugged away and never gave less than 100 per cent. His reward came with a win at Hockenheim and a fourth place in the championship, just in front of his team-mate, who was heading out of the door to Ferrari.

Ligier made a return to Matra power in 1981 under the Talbot banner and, despite the new chassis/engine combination, the team enjoyed a remarkably consistent season. A strong mid-season run saw Laffite take two wins and make a late bid for the title, before finishing fourth, just behind Nelso Piquet, Carlos Reutemann and Alan Jones. The promise evaporated in 1982, however, and he managed only two points-scoring finishes all year. With Ligier reverting to Cosworth power for 1983, he decided to take up the tempting offer of partnering new world champion Keke Rosberg at Williams on a two-year contract.

Laffite's first campaign began soundly, but the Cosworth car became less and less competitive and he suffered the late-season embarrassment of non-qualification at Monza and Brands Hatch, and spinning off on the opening lap of the season's finale at Kyalami. Things failed to pick up in 1984, with a bouyant Rosberg extracting the very maximum from the car; the Frenchman's efforts often seemed pedestrian by comparison. In addition, a succession of engine failures can hardly have done much for the veteran's motivation.

Despite rumours of retirement, Jacques returned to Ligier, now with V6 Renault power, and rediscovered some of his old form, enough at least to ensure that his beaming smile appeared on the rostrum from time to time. The season ended on a high with a fine second place in Australia, and perhaps spurred by the arrival of René Arnoux, he produced some sparkling displays in 1986, even leading the Detroit race briefly. Then came a multiple shunt at the start at the British Grand Prix at Brands Hatch, which left the unlucky Jacques trapped in his car with both legs broken. His grand prix career was over.

Laffite returned to the circuits, however, enjoying the cut and thrust of the French touring car series over the ensuing seasons. In 1995, he was still a regular in the Supertourisme series, driving an Opel Vectra, and then for a while he raced mainly for fun in selected events.

He made a welcome return to the grand prix paddock, working for Ligier in a PR capacity, and then became the voice of Formula 1 in France, providing live commentary for the TF1 television broadcasts.

LAFFITE, Jacques (F) b 21/11/1943, Paris

1974 Championship position: Unplaced

	Race	Circuit	No	Entrant	Tyres	Capacity/Car/Engine	Comment	Q Pos/Entries
ret	GERMAN GP	Nürburgring	21	Frank Williams Racing Cars	F	3.0 Iso Marlboro FW02-Cosworth V8	accident – suspension damage	21/32
nc	AUSTRIAN GP	Österreichring	21	Frank Williams Racing Cars	F	3.0 Iso Marlboro FW02-Cosworth V8	wheel damage on grid/17 laps behind	12/31
ret	ITALIAN GP	Monza	21	Frank Williams Racing Cars	F	3.0 Iso Marlboro FW02-Cosworth V8	engine	17/31
15	CANADIAN GP	Mosport Park	21	Frank Williams Racing Cars	F	3.0 Iso Marlboro FW02-Cosworth V8	puncture/6 laps behind	18/30
ret	US GP	Watkins Glen	21	Frank Williams Racing Cars	F	3.0 Iso Marlboro FW02-Cosworth V8	rear wheel	11/30

1975 Championship position: 12th Wins: 0 Pole positions: 0 Fastest laps: 0 Points scored: 6

	Race	Circuit	No	Entrant	Tyres	Capacity/Car/Engine	Comment	Q Pos/Entries
ret	ARGENTINE GP	Buenos Aires	21	Frank Williams Racing Cars	G	3.0 Williams FW02-Cosworth V8	gearbox	17/23
11	BRAZILIAN GP	Interlagos	21	Frank Williams Racing Cars	G	3.0 Williams FW02-Cosworth V8	1 lap behind	19/23
nc	SOUTH AFRICAN GP	Kyalami	21	Frank Williams Racing Cars	G	3.0 Williams FW02-Cosworth V8	pit stop/9 laps behind	23/28
dnq	MONACO GP	Monte Carlo	21	Frank Williams Racing Cars	G	3.0 Williams FW04-Cosworth V8		19/26
ret	BELGIAN GP	Zolder	21	Frank Williams Racing Cars	G	3.0 Williams FW04-Cosworth V8	gearbox	17/24
ret	DUTCH GP	Zandvoort	21	Frank Williams Racing Cars	G	3.0 Williams FW04-Cosworth V8	engine	15/25
11	FRENCH GP	Paul Ricard	21	Frank Williams Racing Cars	G	3.0 Williams FW04-Cosworth V8		=15/26
ret	BRITISH GP	Silverstone	21	Frank Williams Racing Cars	G	3.0 Williams FW04-Cosworth V8	gearbox	19/28
2	GERMAN GP	Nürburgring	21	Frank Williams Racing Cars	G	3.0 Williams FW04-Cosworth V8		15/26
ret	AUSTRIAN GP	Österreichring	21	Frank Williams Racing Cars	G	3.0 Williams FW04-Cosworth V8	handling	12/30
ret	ITALIAN GP	Monza	21	Frank Williams Racing Cars	G	3.0 Williams FW04-Cosworth V8	gearbox	18/28
dns	US GP	Watkins Glen	21	Frank Williams Racing Cars	G	3.0 Williams FW04-Cosworth V8	visor cleaner fluid in eyes	(21)/24

1976 Championship position: 7th= Wins: 0 Pole positions: 1 Fastest laps: 0 Points scored: 20

	Race	Circuit	No	Entrant	Tyres	Capacity/Car/Engine	Comment	Q Pos/Entries
ret	BRAZILIAN GP	Interlagos	26	Ligier Gitanes	G	3.0 Ligier JS5-Matra V12	gear linkage	11/22
ret	SOUTH AFRICAN GP	Kyalami	26	Ligier Gitanes	G	3.0 Ligier JS5-Matra V12	engine	8/25
4	US GP WEST	Long Beach	26	Ligier Gitanes	G	3.0 Ligier JS5-Matra V12		12/27
12	SPANISH GP	Jarama	26	Ligier Gitanes	G	3.0 Ligier JS5-Matra V12	reinstated after disqualification/-3 laps	8/30
3	BELGIAN GP	Zolder	26	Ligier Gitanes	G	3.0 Ligier JS5-Matra V12		6/29
12/ret	MONACO GP	Monte Carlo	26	Ligier Gitanes	G	3.0 Ligier JS5-Matra V12	collision with Mass/3 laps behind	8/25
4	SWEDISH GP	Anderstorp	26	Ligier Gitanes	G	3.0 Ligier JS5-Matra V12		7/27
14	FRENCH GP	Paul Ricard	26	Ligier Gitanes	G	3.0 Ligier JS5-Matra V12	1 lap behind	13/30
ret/dsq*	BRITISH GP	Brands Hatch	26	Ligier Gitanes	G	3.0 Ligier JS5-Matra V12	suspension/*used spare car in restart	13/30
ret/dns*	GERMAN GP	Nürburgring	26	Ligier Gitanes	G	3.0 Ligier JS5-Matra V12	gearbox at 1st start/*did not restart	6/28
2	AUSTRIAN GP	Österreichring	26	Ligier Gitanes	G	3.0 Ligier JS5-Matra V12		5/25
ret	DUTCH GP	Zandvoort	26	Ligier Gitanes	G	3.0 Ligier JS5-Matra V12	oil pressure	10/27
3	ITALIAN GP	Monza	26	Ligier Gitanes	G	3.0 Ligier JS5-Matra V12		1/29
ret	CANADIAN GP	Mosport Park	26	Ligier Gitanes	G	3.0 Ligier JS5-Matra V12	oil pressure	9/27
ret	US GP EAST	Watkins Glen	26	Ligier Gitanes	G	3.0 Ligier JS5-Matra V12	burst tyre – suspension damage	12/27
7	JAPANESE GP	Mount Fuji	26	Ligier Gitanes	G	3.0 Ligier JS5-Matra V12	1 lap behind/FL	11/27

1977 Championship position: 10 Wins: 1 Pole positions: 0 Fastest laps: 1 Points scored: 18

	Race	Circuit	No	Entrant	Tyres	Capacity/Car/Engine	Comment	Q Pos/Entries
nc	ARGENTINE GP	Buenos Aires	26	Ligier Gitanes	G	3.0 Ligier JS7-Matra V12	3 pit stops – misfire/16 laps behind	15/21
ret	BRAZILIAN GP	Interlagos	26	Ligier Gitanes	G	3.0 Ligier JS7-Matra V12	accident	14/22
ret	SOUTH AFRICAN GP	Kyalami	26	Ligier Gitanes	G	3.0 Ligier JS7-Matra V12	accident – hit by Pryce's crashing car	12/23
9/ret	US GP WEST	Long Beach	26	Ligier Gitanes	G	3.0 Ligier JS7-Matra V12	electrics/2 laps behind	5/22
7	SPANISH GP	Jarama	26	Ligier Gitanes	G	3.0 Ligier JS7-Matra V12	pit stop – loose wheel/1 lap behind/FL	2/31
7	MONACO GP	Monte Carlo	26	Ligier Gitanes	G	3.0 Ligier JS7-Matra V12		16/26
ret	BELGIAN GP	Zolder	26	Ligier Gitanes	G	3.0 Ligier JS7-Matra V12	engine	10/32
1	SWEDISH GP	Anderstorp	26	Ligier Gitanes	G	3.0 Ligier JS7-Matra V12		8/31
8	FRENCH GP	Dijon	26	Ligier Gitanes	G	3.0 Ligier JS7-Matra V12	collision with Stuck – pitstop/-2 laps	5/30
6	BRITISH GP	Silverstone	26	Ligier Gitanes	G	3.0 Ligier JS7-Matra V12	1 lap behind	15/36
ret	GERMAN GP	Hockenheim	26	Ligier Gitanes	G	3.0 Ligier JS7-Matra V12	engine	6/30
ret	AUSTRIAN GP	Österreichring	26	Ligier Gitanes	G	3.0 Ligier JS7-Matra V12	oil leak onto tyres	6/30

Jacques and Ligier won the opening two races of the 1979 season in Argentina (left) and Brazil. Sadly for France, they were unable to conjure more victories.

2	DUTCH GP	Zandvoort	26	Ligier Gitanes	G	3.0 Ligier JS7-Matra V12		pit stop – overheating/2 laps behind	2/34
8	ITALIAN GP	Monza	26	Ligier Gitanes	G	3.0 Ligier JS7-Matra V12			8/34
7	US GP EAST	Watkins Glen	26	Ligier Gitanes	G	3.0 Ligier JS7-Matra V12		1 lap behind	10/27
ret	CANADIAN GP	Mosport Park	26	Ligier Gitanes	G	3.0 Ligier JS7-Matra V12		driveshaft	11/27
5/ret	JAPANESE GP	Mount Fuji	26	Ligier Gitanes	G	3.0 Ligier JS7-Matra V12		out of fuel/1 lap behind	5/23

1978 Championship position: 8th   Wins: 0   Pole positions: 0   Fastest laps: 0   Points scored: 19

16/ret	ARGENTINE GP	Buenos Aires	26	Ligier Gitanes	G	3.0 Ligier JS7-Matra V12	engine/2 laps behind	8/27
9	BRAZILIAN GP	Rio	26	Ligier Gitanes	G	3.0 Ligier JS7-Matra V12	pit stop – tyres/2 laps behind	14/28
5	SOUTH AFRICAN GP	Kyalami	26	Ligier Gitanes	G	3.0 Ligier JS7-Matra V12		13/30
dns	" "	" "	26	Ligier Gitanes	G	3.0 Ligier JS7-Matra V12	practice only	– / –
5	US GP WEST	Long Beach	26	Ligier Gitanes	G	3.0 Ligier JS7-Matra V12		– / –
dns	" "	" "	26	Ligier Gitanes	G	3.0 Ligier JS7/9-Matra V12	practice only – set grid time	14/30
ret	MONACO GP	Monte Carlo	26	Ligier Gitanes	G	3.0 Ligier JS9-Matra V12	gearbox	15/30
dns	" "	" "	26	Ligier Gitanes	G	3.0 Ligier JS7-Matra V12	practice only	– / –
5/ret	BELGIAN GP	Zolder	26	Ligier Gitanes	G	3.0 Ligier JS7-Matra V12	hit by Reutemann/1 lap behind	14/30
3	SPANISH GP	Jarama	26	Ligier Gitanes	G	3.0 Ligier JS9-Matra V12		=9/29
dns	" "	" "	26	Ligier Gitanes	G	3.0 Ligier JS7/9-Matra V12	practice only	– / –
7	SWEDISH GP	Anderstorp	26	Ligier Gitanes	G	3.0 Ligier JS9-Matra V12	1 lap behind	11/27
dns	"	"	26	Ligier Gitanes	G	3.0 Ligier JS7/9-Matra V12	practice only	– / –
7	FRENCH GP	Paul Ricard	26	Ligier Gitanes	G	3.0 Ligier JS9-Matra V12		10/29
10	BRITISH GP	Brands Hatch	26	Ligier Gitanes	G	3.0 Ligier JS9-Matra V12	2 pit stops – tyres/3 laps behind	7/30
3	GERMAN GP	Hockenheim	26	Ligier Gitanes	G	3.0 Ligier JS9-Matra V12		7/30
5	AUSTRIAN GP	Österreichring	26	Ligier Gitanes	G	3.0 Ligier JS9-Matra V12	1 lap behind	5/31
8	DUTCH GP	Zandvoort	26	Ligier Gitanes	G	3.0 Ligier JS9-Matra V12	1 lap behind	6/33
4	ITALIAN GP	Monza	26	Ligier Gitanes	G	3.0 Ligier JS9-Matra V12		8/32
11	US GP EAST	Watkins Glen	26	Ligier Gitanes	G	3.0 Ligier JS9-Matra V12	pit stop – tyre/1 lap behind	10/27
ret	CANADIAN GP	Montreal	26	Ligier Gitanes	G	3.0 Ligier JS9-Matra V12	transmission	10/28

1979 Championship position: 4th   Wins: 2   Pole positions: 4   Fastest laps: 2   Points scored: 36

1	ARGENTINE GP	Buenos Aires	26	Ligier Gitanes	G	3.0 Ligier JS11-Cosworth V8	FL	1/26
1	BRAZILIAN GP	Rio	26	Ligier Gitanes	G	3.0 Ligier JS11-Cosworth V8	FL	1/26
ret	SOUTH AFRICAN GP	Kyalami	26	Ligier Gitanes	G	3.0 Ligier JS11-Cosworth V8	puncture – spun off	6/26
ret	US GP WEST	Long Beach	26	Ligier Gitanes	G	3.0 Ligier JS11-Cosworth V8	started from pit lane/brakes	5/26
ret	SPANISH GP	Jarama	26	Ligier Gitanes	G	3.0 Ligier JS11-Cosworth V8	engine	1/27
2	BELGIAN GP	Zolder	26	Ligier Gitanes	G	3.0 Ligier JS11-Cosworth V8		1/28
ret	MONACO GP	Monte Carlo	26	Ligier Gitanes	G	3.0 Ligier JS11-Cosworth V8	gearbox	5/25
8	FRENCH GP	Dijon	26	Ligier Gitanes	G	3.0 Ligier JS11-Cosworth V8	1 lap behind	8/27
ret	BRITISH GP	Silverstone	26	Ligier Gitanes	G	3.0 Ligier JS11-Cosworth V8	engine – plugs	10/26
3	GERMAN GP	Hockenheim	26	Ligier Gitanes	G	3.0 Ligier JS11-Cosworth V8		3/26
3	AUSTRIAN GP	Österreichring	26	Ligier Gitanes	G	3.0 Ligier JS11-Cosworth V8		8/26
3	DUTCH GP	Zandvoort	26	Ligier Gitanes	G	3.0 Ligier JS11-Cosworth V8		7/26
ret	ITALIAN GP	Monza	26	Ligier Gitanes	G	3.0 Ligier JS11-Cosworth V8	engine	7/28
ret	CANADIAN GP	Montreal	26	Ligier Gitanes	G	3.0 Ligier JS11-Cosworth V8	engine	5/29
ret	US GP EAST	Watkins Glen	26	Ligier Gitanes	G	3.0 Ligier JS11-Cosworth V8	spun off	4/30

1980 Championship position: 4th   Wins: 1   Pole positions: 1   Fastest laps: 1   Points scored: 34

ret	ARGENTINE GP	Buenos Aires	26	Equipe Ligier Gitanes	G	3.0 Ligier JS11/15-Cosworth V8	engine	2/28
ret	BRAZILIAN GP	Interlagos	26	Equipe Ligier Gitanes	G	3.0 Ligier JS11/15-Cosworth V8	electrics	5/28
2	SOUTH AFRICAN GP	Kyalami	26	Equipe Ligier Gitanes	G	3.0 Ligier JS11/15-Cosworth V8		4/28
ret	US GP WEST	Long Beach	26	Equipe Ligier Gitanes	G	3.0 Ligier JS11/15-Cosworth V8	puncture – suspension	13/27
11	BELGIAN GP	Zolder	26	Equipe Ligier Gitanes	G	3.0 Ligier JS11/15-Cosworth V8	pit stop – engine/4 laps behind/FL	3/27
2	MONACO GP	Monte Carlo	26	Equipe Ligier Gitanes	G	3.0 Ligier JS11/15-Cosworth V8		5/27
3	FRENCH GP	Paul Ricard	26	Equipe Ligier Gitanes	G	3.0 Ligier JS11/15-Cosworth V8		1/27
ret	BRITISH GP	Brands Hatch	26	Equipe Ligier Gitanes	G	3.0 Ligier JS11/15-Cosworth V8	wheel/tyre failure – crashed	2/27
1	GERMAN GP	Hockenheim	26	Equipe Ligier Gitanes	G	3.0 Ligier JS11/15-Cosworth V8		5/26
4	AUSTRIAN GP	Österreichring	26	Equipe Ligier Gitanes	G	3.0 Ligier JS11/15-Cosworth V8		5/25
3	DUTCH GP	Zandvoort	26	Equipe Ligier Gitanes	G	3.0 Ligier JS11/15-Cosworth V8		6/28
9	ITALIAN GP	Imola	26	Equipe Ligier Gitanes	G	3.0 Ligier JS11/15-Cosworth V8	1 lap behind	20/28
8/ret	CANADIAN GP	Montreal	26	Equipe Ligier Gitanes	G	3.0 Ligier JS11/15-Cosworth V8	out of fuel/2 laps behind	9/28
5	US GP EAST	Watkins Glen	26	Equipe Ligier Gitanes	G	3.0 Ligier JS11/15-Cosworth V8	1 lap behind	12/27

1981 Championship position: 4th   Wins: 2   Pole positions: 1   Fastest laps: 1   Points scored: 44

ret	US GP WEST	Long Beach	26	Equipe Talbot Gitanes	M	3.0 Talbot Ligier JS17-Matra V12	collision with Cheever	12/29
6	BRAZILIAN GP	Rio	26	Equipe Talbot Gitanes	M	3.0 Talbot Ligier JS17-Matra V12		16/30
ret	ARGENTINE GP	Buenos Aires	26	Equipe Talbot Gitanes	M	3.0 Talbot Ligier JS17-Matra V12	vibration/handling	21/29
ret	SAN MARINO GP	Imola	26	Equipe Talbot Gitanes	M	3.0 Talbot Ligier JS17-Matra V12	accident with Arnoux	10/30
2	BELGIAN GP	Zolder	26	Equipe Talbot Gitanes	M	3.0 Talbot Ligier JS17-Matra V12		9/31
3	MONACO GP	Monte Carlo	26	Equipe Talbot Gitanes	M	3.0 Talbot Ligier JS17-Matra V12		8/31
2	SPANISH GP	Jarama	26	Equipe Talbot Gitanes	M	3.0 Talbot Ligier JS17-Matra V12		1/30
ret	FRENCH GP	Dijon	26	Equipe Talbot Gitanes	M	3.0 Talbot Ligier JS17-Matra V12	front suspension	6/29
3	BRITISH GP	Silverstone	26	Equipe Talbot Gitanes	M	3.0 Talbot Ligier JS17-Matra V12	1 lap behind	14/30
3	GERMAN GP	Hockenheim	26	Equipe Talbot Gitanes	M	3.0 Talbot Ligier JS17-Matra V12		7/30
1	AUSTRIAN GP	Österreichring	26	Equipe Talbot Gitanes	M	3.0 Talbot Ligier JS17-Matra V12	FL	4/28
ret	DUTCH GP	Zandvoort	26	Equipe Talbot Gitanes	M	3.0 Talbot Ligier JS17-Matra V12	collision with Reutemann	6/30
ret	ITALIAN GP	Monza	26	Equipe Talbot Gitanes	M	3.0 Talbot Ligier JS17-Matra V12	puncture	4/30
1	CANADIAN GP	Montreal	26	Equipe Talbot Gitanes	M	3.0 Talbot Ligier JS17-Matra V12		10/30
6	CAESARS PALACE GP	Las Vegas	26	Equipe Talbot Gitanes	M	3.0 Talbot Ligier JS17-Matra V12	pit stop-tyres	12/30

1982 Championship position: 17th=   Wins: 0   Pole positions: 0   Fastest laps: 0   Points scored: 5

ret	SOUTH AFRICAN GP	Kyalami	26	Equipe Talbot Gitanes	M	3.0 Talbot Ligier JS17-Matra V12	fuel vaporisation – misfire	11/30
ret	BRAZILIAN GP	Rio	26	Equipe Talbot Gitanes	M	3.0 Talbot Ligier JS17-Matra V12	handling/misfire	24/31
ret	US GP WEST	Long Beach	26	Equipe Talbot Gitanes	M	3.0 Talbot Ligier JS17B-Matra V12	ran off track and stalled	15/31

The last podium for the V12 Matra engine as Laffite, driving the Talbot-Ligier, takes third place in the 1982 Austrian Grand Prix.

9	BELGIAN GP	Zolder	26	Equipe Talbot Gitanes	M	3.0 Talbot Ligier JS17B-Matra V12	pit stop – tyres/4 laps behind	19/32
ret	MONACO GP	Monte Carlo	26	Equipe Talbot Gitanes	M	3.0 Talbot Ligier JS19-Matra V12	handling	18/31
6	US GP (DETROIT)	Detroit	26	Equipe Talbot Gitanes	M	3.0 Talbot Ligier JS17B-Matra V12	1 lap behind	13/28
ret	CANADIAN GP	Montreal	26	Equipe Talbot Gitanes	M	3.0 Talbot Ligier JS17B-Matra V12	handling	19/29
ret	DUTCH GP	Zandvoort	26	Equipe Talbot Gitanes	M	3.0 Talbot Ligier JS19-Matra V12	handling	21/31
ret	BRITISH GP	Brands Hatch	26	Equipe Talbot Gitanes	M	3.0 Talbot Ligier JS19-Matra V12	gearbox	20/30
14	FRENCH GP	Paul Ricard	26	Equipe Talbot Gitanes	M	3.0 Talbot Ligier JS19-Matra V12	3 pit stops – handling – tyres/-3 laps	16/30
ret	GERMAN GP	Hockenheim	26	Equipe Talbot Gitanes	M	3.0 Talbot Ligier JS19-Matra V12	handling	16/30
3	AUSTRIAN GP	Österreichring	26	Equipe Talbot Gitanes	M	3.0 Talbot Ligier JS19-Matra V12	1 lap behind	14/29
ret	SWISS GP	Dijon	26	Equipe Talbot Gitanes	M	3.0 Talbot Ligier JS19-Matra V12	skirts/handling	13/29
ret	ITALIAN GP	Monza	26	Equipe Talbot Gitanes	M	3.0 Talbot Ligier JS19-Matra V12	gearbox	21/29
ret	CAESARS PALACE GP	Las Vegas	26	Equipe Talbot Gitanes	M	3.0 Talbot Ligier JS19-Matra V12	ignition	11/30

1983 Championship position: 11th   Wins: 0   Pole positions: 0   Fastest laps: 0   Points scored: 11

4	BRAZILIAN GP	Rio	2	TAG Williams Team	G	3.0 Williams FW08C-Cosworth V8		18/27
4	US GP WEST	Long Beach	2	TAG Williams Team	G	3.0 Williams FW08C-Cosworth V8	1 lap behind	4/28
6	FRENCH GP	Paul Ricard	2	TAG Williams Team	G	3.0 Williams FW08C-Cosworth V8	pit stop – fuel/1 lap behind	19/29
7	SAN MARINO GP	Imola	2	TAG Williams Team	G	3.0 Williams FW08C-Cosworth V8	pit stop – fuel/1 lap behind	16/28
ret	MONACO GP	Monte Carlo	2	TAG Williams Team	G	3.0 Williams FW08C-Cosworth V8	gearbox	8/28
6	BELGIAN GP	Spa	2	TAG Williams Team	G	3.0 Williams FW08C-Cosworth V8		11/28
5	US GP (DETROIT)	Detroit	2	TAG Williams Team	G	3.0 Williams FW08C-Cosworth V8		20/27
ret	CANADIAN GP	Montreal	2	TAG Williams Team	G	3.0 Williams FW08C-Cosworth V8	gearbox	13/28
12	BRITISH GP	Silverstone	2	TAG Williams Team	G	3.0 Williams FW08C-Cosworth V8	pit stop – fuel/2 laps behind	20/29
6	GERMAN GP	Hockenheim	2	TAG Williams Team	G	3.0 Williams FW08C-Cosworth V8	1 lap behind	15/29
ret	AUSTRIAN GP	Österreichring	2	TAG Williams Team	G	3.0 Williams FW08C-Cosworth V8	collision with Ghinzani and Surer	24/29
ret	DUTCH GP	Zandvoort	2	TAG Williams Team	G	3.0 Williams FW08C-Cosworth V8	tyres	17/29
dnq	ITALIAN GP	Monza	2	TAG Williams Team	G	3.0 Williams FW08C-Cosworth V8		28/29
dnq	EUROPEAN GP	Brands Hatch	2	TAG Williams Team	G	3.0 Williams FW08C-Cosworth V8		29/29
ret	SOUTH AFRICAN GP	Kyalami	2	TAG Williams Team	G	1.5 t/c Williams FW09-Honda V6	spun off on lap 1	10/26

1984 Championship position: 14th=   Wins: 0   Pole positions: 0   Fastest laps: 0   Points scored: 5

ret	BRAZILIAN GP	Rio	5	Williams Grand Prix Engineering	G	1.5 t/c Williams FW09-Honda V6	electrics	13/27
ret	SOUTH AFRICAN GP	Kyalami	5	Williams Grand Prix Engineering	G	1.5 t/c Williams FW09-Honda V6	c.v. joint	11/27
ret	BELGIAN GP	Zolder	5	Williams Grand Prix Engineering	G	1.5 t/c Williams FW09-Honda V6	electrics	15/27
ret	SAN MARINO GP	Imola	5	Williams Grand Prix Engineering	G	1.5 t/c Williams FW09-Honda V6	engine	15/28
8	FRENCH GP	Dijon	5	Williams Grand Prix Engineering	G	1.5 t/c Williams FW09-Honda V6	1 lap behind	12/27
8*	MONACO GP	Monte Carlo	5	Williams Grand Prix Engineering	G	1.5 t/c Williams FW09-Honda V6	*3rd place car dsq/1 lap behind	16/27
ret	CANADIAN GP	Montreal	5	Williams Grand Prix Engineering	G	1.5 t/c Williams FW09-Honda V6	lost turbo boost	17/26
5*	US GP (DETROIT)	Detroit	5	Williams Grand Prix Engineering	G	1.5 t/c Williams FW09-Honda V6	*2nd place car dsq/1 lap behind	19/27
4	US GP (DALLAS)	Dallas	5	Williams Grand Prix Engineering	G	1.5 t/c Williams FW09-Honda V6	2 laps behind	24/27
ret	BRITISH GP	Brands Hatch	5	Williams Grand Prix Engineering	G	1.5 t/c Williams FW09B-Honda V6	water pump	16/27
ret	GERMAN GP	Hockenheim	5	Williams Grand Prix Engineering	G	1.5 t/c Williams FW09B-Honda V6	engine	12/27
ret	AUSTRIAN GP	Österreichring	5	Williams Grand Prix Engineering	G	1.5 t/c Williams FW09B-Honda V6	engine	11/28
ret	DUTCH GP	Zandvoort	5	Williams Grand Prix Engineering	G	1.5 t/c Williams FW09B-Honda V6	engine	8/27
ret	ITALIAN GP	Monza	5	Williams Grand Prix Engineering	G	1.5 t/c Williams FW09B-Honda V6	turbo	13/27
ret	EUROPEAN GP	Nürburgring	5	Williams Grand Prix Engineering	G	1.5 t/c Williams FW09B-Honda V6	engine	14/26
14	PORTUGUESE GP	Estoril	5	Williams Grand Prix Engineering	G	1.5 t/c Williams FW09B-Honda V6	2 pit stops – bodywork/3 laps behind	15/27

1985 Championship position: 9   Wins: 0   Pole positions: 0   Fastest laps: 1   Points scored: 16

6	BRAZILIAN GP	Rio	26	Equipe Ligier	P	1.5 t/c Ligier JS25-Renault V6	hit de Cesaris – pit stop/2 laps behind	15/25
ret	PORTUGUESE GP	Estoril	26	Equipe Ligier	P	1.5 t/c Ligier JS25-Renault V6	tyres/handling	18/26
ret	SAN MARINO GP	Imola	26	Equipe Ligier	P	1.5 t/c Ligier JS25-Renault V6	turbo	16/26
6	MONACO GP	Monte Carlo	26	Equipe Ligier	P	1.5 t/c Ligier JS25-Renault V6	spin/1 lap behind	16/26
8	CANADIAN GP	Montreal	26	Equipe Ligier Gitanes	P	1.5 t/c Ligier JS25-Renault V6	1 minute penalty – jumped start/-1 lap	19/25
12	US GP (DETROIT)	Detroit	26	Equipe Ligier Gitanes	P	1.5 t/c Ligier JS25-Renault V6	pit stop/5 laps behind	16/25
ret	FRENCH GP	Paul Ricard	26	Equipe Ligier Gitanes	P	1.5 t/c Ligier JS25-Renault V6	turbo	15/26

3	BRITISH GP	Silverstone	26	Equipe Ligier Gitanes	P	1.5 t/c Ligier JS25-Renault V6	*1 lap behind*	16/26
3	GERMAN GP	Nürburgring	26	Equipe Ligier Gitanes	P	1.5 t/c Ligier JS25-Renault V6		13/27
ret	AUSTRIAN GP	Österreichring	26	Equipe Ligier Gitanes	P	1.5 t/c Ligier JS25-Renault V6	*lost wheel – crashed*	15/27
ret	DUTCH GP	Zandvoort	26	Equipe Ligier Gitanes	P	1.5 t/c Ligier JS25-Renault V6	*electrics*	13/27
ret	ITALIAN GP	Monza	26	Equipe Ligier Gitanes	P	1.5 t/c Ligier JS25-Renault V6	*engine*	20/26
11/ret	BELGIAN GP	Spa	26	Equipe Ligier Gitanes	P	1.5 t/c Ligier JS25-Renault V6	*hit barrier/5 laps behind*	17/24
ret	EUROPEAN GP	Brands Hatch	26	Equipe Ligier Gitanes	P	1.5 t/c Ligier JS25-Renault V6	*engine/FL*	10/27
2	AUSTRALIAN GP	Adelaide	26	Equipe Ligier Gitanes	P	1.5 t/c Ligier JS25-Renault V6		20/25

1986 Championship position: 8   Wins: 0   Pole positions: 0   Fastest laps: 0   Points scored: 14

3	BRAZILIAN GP	Rio	26	Equipe Ligier	P	1.5 t/c Ligier JS27-Renault V6		5/25
ret	SPANISH GP	Jerez	26	Equipe Ligier	P	1.5 t/c Ligier JS27-Renault V6	*driveshaft*	8/25
ret	SAN MARINO GP	Imola	26	Equipe Ligier	P	1.5 t/c Ligier JS27-Renault V6	*transmission*	14/26
6	MONACO GP	Monte Carlo	26	Equipe Ligier	P	1.5 t/c Ligier JS27-Renault V6	*started from back/1 lap behind*	7/26
5	BELGIAN GP	Spa	26	Equipe Ligier	P	1.5 t/c Ligier JS27-Renault V6		17/25
7	CANADIAN GP	Montreal	26	Equipe Ligier	P	1.5 t/c Ligier JS27-Renault V6	*1 lap behind*	8/25
2	US GP (DETROIT)	Detroit	26	Equipe Ligier	P	1.5 t/c Ligier JS27-Renault V6		6/26
6	FRENCH GP	Paul Ricard	26	Equipe Ligier	P	1.5 t/c Ligier JS27-Renault V6	*2 pit stops – tyres/1 lap behind*	11/26
ret/dns	BRITISH GP	Brands Hatch	26	Equipe Ligier	P	1.5 t/c Ligier JS27-Renault V6	*accident – 1st start/did not restart*	19/26

GP Starts: 174 (176)   GP Wins: 6   Pole positions: 7   Fastest laps: 7   Points: 228

FRANCK LAGORCE

THIS quiet Frenchman is yet another in the ever lengthening queue of grand prix aspirants to have graduated with honours from F3000, only to find no outlet for their talent, for Franck Lagorce had shown in the junior formulas that he was a fine prospect. After six seasons of karting, his car racing career was given a flying start in 1987 with second place in the Volant Ekron and the opportunity to move into FF1600. In 1990, he stepped into Formule Renault and finished second in the championship, before two seasons in French Formula 3 with a Dallara-Opel, which culminated in his being crowned champion in 1992.

Joining DAMS to tackle F3000 in 1993, Lagorce was number two to Olivier Panis, and although the latter took the crown, Franck's role was not entirely subordinate, for he won the final two rounds at Magny-Cours and Nogaro to take equal fourth in the series with Gil de Ferran. He switched to the rival Apomatox team in 1994, scoring another two fine wins (at Silverstone and Hockenheim), but in truth he let the championship slip through his fingers after looking a good bet throughout the year. He finished just two points shy of Jean-Cristophe Boullion.

Already the official reserve and test driver with Ligier, Franck was given a tantalising glimpse of grand prix racing with a couple of end-of-season drives, but he spent 1995 consigned to his testing role.

In 1996, Franck returned to racing to win the Renault Spyder series, and he joined Henri Pescarolo and Rob Collard in the Courage at Le Mans in 1996, taking seventh place. Deciding that he would rather be in a factory-backed sports car than struggling with a back-of-the-grid Formula 1 team, he abandoned his efforts to find a place on the grand prix stage and opted to partner Éric Bernard in the DAMS-run Panoz for 1997. Then he joined Nissan for their 1998 Le Mans programme, taking the 390 to a fifth place with John Neilsen and Michael Krumm. No doubt these performances helped him secure a seat in the Mercedes works team for the 1999 Le Mans 24-hours. Hopes of a win were dashed, however, when the prototype was withdrawn on safety grounds, following team-mate Peter Dumbreck's airborne flip into the woods during the race.

Between 2000 and 2001, Franck continued to race sports cars for Team Cadillac and Panoz, before joining Pescarolo Sport to help their Le Mans project. His best results were elsewhere, however, with a fourth place at Estoril and a third at Dijon (with Stéphane Sarrazin) in 2002. The following season, he won at a round of the GT Championship Nogaro (with Soheil Ayari) and took second place in both the Spa 1000km (with Sarrazin) and the 1000km of Le Mans, held on the Bugatti circuit (with Sarrazin and Sébastien Bourdais).

From 2004, Franck acted as a commentator on Eurosport France for the GP2 Series and the Le Mans 24-hours. He also returned to his first love, karting, helping in the development of young talent. He has raced infrequently, apart from a single appearance at Spa in the Le Mans Series in 2009, but he has been heavily involved with the Andros Trophy, joining ORECA's star-studded line-up to race their Skoda Fabias.

LAGORCE, Franck (F) b 1/9/1968, L'Hay-Les-Roses, nr Paris

1994 Championship position: Unplaced

	Race	Circuit	No	Entrant	Tyres	Capacity/Car/Engine	Comment	Q Pos/Entries
ret	JAPANESE GP	Suzuka	25	Ligier Gitanes Blondes	G	3.5 Ligier JS39B-Renault V10	*touched by Martini – spun off*	20/28
11	AUSTRALIAN GP	Adelaide	25	Ligier Gitanes Blondes	G	3.5 Ligier JS39B-Renault V10	*2 laps behind*	20/28

GP Starts: 2   GP Wins: 0   Pole positions: 0   Fastest laps: 0   Points: 0

JAN LAMMERS

IN a career stretching back more than 35 years, Jan Lammers has tried his hand at most forms of racing, achieving his earliest success as the Dutch Group 1 saloon car champion. Progressing through the single-seater formulas, the pint-sized Dutchman took the 1978 European F3 championship by the narrowest of margins with a Ralt, tied on points with Anders Olofsson, but declared the winner on the basis of his best 12 scores. His performenaces that year drew universal praise, not only for his aggressive, but scrupulously clean driving manners, but also his personable manner off track.

Lammers' impressive championship win earned him his big chance with the restructured Shadow team, alongside fellow European F3 competitor Elio de Angelis, for 1979. This meant there was no need for him to compete in Formula 2, whereas perhaps a season's experience at that next level might have been beneficial in the long term.

The Shadow cars, without the benefit of ground-effects, were well off the pace, but while de Angelis showed he was a talent to be nurtured, Lammers looked a little out of his depth. Out of the frying pan, he moved to the ATS team for 1980. After failing to qualify in the two opening races, he startled the Formula 1 fraternity at Long Beach by qualifying his car fourth on the grid, but sadly his race ended on lap one with a driveshaft failure.

With the team contracting to a single entry, Lammers was released to join Ensign, who were seeking a permanent replacement for the injured Clay Regazzoni. The car was certainly not as good as the ATS, and the Dutchman struggled to make the grid for most of the year.

In 1981, Lammers returned to ATS, but his tenure was short after two DNQs in four races; his services were dispensed with by team owner Gunther Schmidt. This left him out of a drive until he was given the chance to join Theodore early in the 1982 season, after Williams bought out the contract of Derek Daly. Lammers' cause was not helped by a practice accident at Long Beach, where he understeered into a wall and broke a thumb, which caused him to miss the Canadian GP. On his return, he did well to qualify for his home race at Zandvoort, but failure to make the races at Silverstone and Paul Ricard sealed his fate, and Tommy Byrne was the next hopeful to take his chance.

After his grand prix career seemed to have fizzled out, Jan enjoyed a productive spell in the Richard Lloyd Porsche sports car team, before having a crack at Indy car racing, driving for Forsythe in 1985. He took part in five races and scored a heartening fifth place at Laguna Seca. He was back for more CART action at the beginning of 1986, but his failure to qualify the Machinists Union car at Indianapolis outweighed three top-ten finishes from just five starts, ending his Indy car dreams.

Jan would soon enjoy his greatest successes, however, in the TWR Jaguar team, partnering John Watson to three wins (Jarama, Monza and Mount Fuji) in 1987, and then winning the Le Mans 24-hours in 1988 with Johnny Dumfries and Andy Wallace. He also won the Daytona 24-hour race for Jaguar twice (1988 and '90). After racing in Japanese F3000 in 1991, where he finished 11th in the standings with the Dome-Mugen-Honda, Lammers joined the Toyota sports car team for Le Mans in 1992, finishing eighth.

After a record gap of more than 11 years, Lammers made an unexpected return to Formula 1 at the end of the year with March, contesting the two closing races of the year. Plans for a full grand prix season in 1993 came to nought, however, when the financially bereft Bicester team was finally forced to close its doors, leaving him to take in a limited programme of European F3000, where he certainly proved he could take the heat with the up-and-coming talent. Sadly the team folded befor the season ended

Jan was a somewhat surprising choice to race the TWR Volvo estate alongside Rickard Rydell in the 1994 BTCC, and although excellent progress was made in the car's debut year, he still hankered after a single-seater career. The Dutchman kicked off 1995 with a win in the F3000/F2 invitation race at Kyalami, and then took second place in the Sebring 12-hours in a Ferrari with Derek Bell and Wallace, before he lined up with Vortex for a projected full season in F3000. Unfortunately, he rarely rose above the midfield positions and quit in frustration after just three races.

From 1996, Lammers concentrated on sports car and GT racing, initially competing with the factory Lotus team and then with the Konrad Motorsports Lola. In 2001, he launched his own Racing For Holland Team, which successfully ran a Dome S101-Judd in the FIA GT championship through until 2007. He returned to single-seater action in 2005 as the team owner of the Dutch A1GP franchise. A strong driver line-up helped to bring some success during the three years the series ran, when Jos Verstappen, Jeroen Bleekemolen and Robert Doornbos all tasted victory.

For Jan, even in in his mid-50s, the thirst for competition still burned bright, and he found his thrills by tackling the Dakar Rally (relocated to South America) between 2010 and 2012 with his massive GINAF truck.

LAMMERS, Jan (NL) b 2/6/1956, Zandvoort

	1979 Championship position: Unplaced								
	Race	Circuit	No	Entrant	Tyres	Capacity/Car/Engine	Comment	Q Pos/Entries
ret	ARGENTINE GP	Buenos Aires	17	Samson Shadow Racing Team	G	3.0 Shadow DN9-Cosworth V8	transmission	21/26
14	BRAZILIAN GP	Interlagos	17	Samson Shadow Racing Team	G	3.0 Shadow DN9-Cosworth V8	1 lap behind	21/26
ret	SOUTH AFRICAN GP	Kyalami	17	Samson Shadow Racing Team	G	3.0 Shadow DN9-Cosworth V8	collision with Rebaque	21/26
ret	US GP WEST	Long Beach	17	Samson Shadow Racing Team	G	3.0 Shadow DN9-Cosworth V8	collision with Pironi – bent suspension	14/26
12	SPANISH GP	Jarama	17	Samson Shadow Racing Team	G	3.0 Shadow DN9-Cosworth V8	2 laps behind	24/27

10	BELGIAN GP	Zolder	17	Samson Shadow Racing Team	G	3.0 Shadow DN9-Cosworth V8	*2 laps behind*	21/28
dnq	MONACO GP	Monte Carlo	17	Samson Shadow Racing Team	G	3.0 Shadow DN9-Cosworth V8		23/25
18	FRENCH GP	Dijon	17	Samson Shadow Racing Team	G	3.0 Shadow DN9-Cosworth V8	*pit stop/7 laps behind*	21/27
11	BRITISH GP	Silverstone	17	Samson Shadow Racing Team	G	3.0 Shadow DN9-Cosworth V8	*3 laps behind*	21/26
10	GERMAN GP	Hockenheim	17	Samson Shadow Racing Team	G	3.0 Shadow DN9-Cosworth V8	*1 lap behind*	20/26
ret	AUSTRIAN GP	Österreichring	17	Samson Shadow Racing Team	G	3.0 Shadow DN9-Cosworth V8	*accident*	23/26
ret	DUTCH GP	Zandvoort	17	Samson Shadow Racing Team	G	3.0 Shadow DN9-Cosworth V8	*gearbox*	23/26
dnq	ITALIAN GP	Monza	17	Samson Shadow Racing Team	G	3.0 Shadow DN9-Cosworth V8		25/28
9	CANADIAN GP	Montreal	17	Samson Shadow Racing Team	G	3.0 Shadow DN9-Cosworth V8	*5 laps behind*	21/29
dnq	US GP EAST	Watkins Glen	17	Samson Shadow Racing Team	G	3.0 Shadow DN9-Cosworth V8		27/30

1980 Championship position: Unplaced

dnq	ARGENTINE GP	Buenos Aires	10	Team ATS	G	3.0 ATS D3-Cosworth V8		27/28
dnq	BRAZILIAN GP	Interlagos	10	Team ATS	G	3.0 ATS D3-Cosworth V8		25/28
dnq	SOUTH AFRICAN GP	Kyalami	9	Team ATS	G	3.0 ATS D3-Cosworth V8	*replaced injured Surer*	28/28
ret	US GP WEST	Long Beach	9	Team ATS	G	3.0 ATS D4-Cosworth V8	*driveshaft on lap 1*	4/27
12/ret	BELGIAN GP	Zolder	9	Team ATS	G	3.0 ATS D4-Cosworth V8	*engine/8 laps behind*	15/27
nc	MONACO GP	Monte Carlo	9	Team ATS	G	3.0 ATS D4-Cosworth V8	*hit Patrese – pitstop/12 laps behind*	13/27
dnq	FRENCH GP	Paul Ricard	14	Unipart Racing Team	G	3.0 Ensign N180-Cosworth V8		26/27
dnq	BRITISH GP	Brands Hatch	14	Unipart Racing Team	G	3.0 Ensign N180-Cosworth V8		25/27
14	GERMAN GP	Hockenheim	14	Unipart Racing Team	G	3.0 Ensign N180-Cosworth V8	*1 lap behind*	24/26
dnq	AUSTRIAN GP	Österreichring	14	Unipart Racing Team	G	3.0 Ensign N180-Cosworth V8		25/25
dnq	DUTCH GP	Zandvoort	14	Unipart Racing Team	G	3.0 Ensign N180-Cosworth V8		26/28
dnq	ITALIAN GP	Imola	14	Unipart Racing Team	G	3.0 Ensign N180-Cosworth V8		27/28
12	CANADIAN GP	Montreal	14	Unipart Racing Team	G	3.0 Ensign N180-Cosworth V8	*4 laps behind*	19/28
dnq/ret	US GP EAST	Watkins Glen	14	Unipart Racing Team	G	3.0 Ensign N180-Cosworth V8	*1st reserve/steering mounting*	25/27

1981 Championship position: Unplaced

ret	US GP WEST	Long Beach	9	Team ATS	M	3.0 ATS D4-Cosworth V8	*collision with Giacomelli*	21/29
dnq	BRAZILIAN GP	Rio	9	Team ATS	M	3.0 ATS D4-Cosworth V8		25/30
12	ARGENTINE GP	Buenos Aires	9	Team ATS	M	3.0 ATS D4-Cosworth V8	*pit stop/2 laps behind*	23/29
dnq	SAN MARINO GP	Imola	9	Team ATS	M	3.0 ATS D4-Cosworth V8		27/30

1982 Championship position: Unplaced

dnq	BELGIAN GP	Zolder	33	Theodore Racing Team	A	3.0 Theodore TY02-Cosworth V8		30/32
dnq	MONACO GP	Monte Carlo	33	Theodore Racing Team	G	3.0 Theodore TY02-Cosworth V8		22/31
dns	US GP (DETROIT)	Detroit	33	Theodore Racing Team	G	3.0 Theodore TY02-Cosworth V8	*injured in unofficial practice*	– / –
ret	DUTCH GP	Zandvoort	33	Theodore Racing Team	G	3.0 Theodore TY02-Cosworth V8	*engine*	26/31
dnq	BRITISH GP	Brands Hatch	33	Theodore Racing Team	G	3.0 Theodore TY02-Cosworth V8		28/30
dnq	FRENCH GP	Paul Ricard	33	Theodore Racing Team	G	3.0 Theodore TY02-Cosworth V8		27/30

1992 Championship position: Unplaced

ret	JAPANESE GP	Suzuka	16	March F1	G	3.5 March CG911-Ilmor V10	*clutch*	23/26
12	AUSTRALIAN GP	Adelaide	16	March F1	G	3.5 March CG911-Ilmor V10	*3 laps behind*	25/26

GP Starts: 23 GP Wins: 0 Pole positions: 0 Fastest laps: 0 Points: 0

LAMY, Pedro (P) b 20/3/1972, Aldeia Galega

1993 Championship position: Unplaced

	Race	Circuit	No	Entrant	Tyres	Capacity/Car/Engine	Comment	Q Pos/Entries
11/ret	ITALIAN GP	Monza	11	Team Lotus	G	3.5 Lotus 107B-Ford HB V8	*engine/4 laps behind*	26/26
ret	PORTUGUESE GP	Estoril	11	Team Lotus	G	3.5 Lotus 107B-Ford HB V8	*accident*	18/26
13/ret	JAPANESE GP	Suzuka	11	Team Lotus	G	3.5 Lotus 107B-Ford HB V8	*accident*	20/24
ret	AUSTRALIAN GP	Adelaide	11	Team Lotus	G	3.5 Lotus 107B-Ford HB V8	*collision with Katayama on lap 1*	23/24

1994 Championship position: Unplaced

10	BRAZILIAN GP	Interlagos	11	Team Lotus	G	3.5 Lotus 107C-Mugen Honda V10	*3 laps behind*	24/28
8	PACIFIC GP	T.I. Circuit	11	Team Lotus	G	3.5 Lotus 107C-Mugen Honda V10	*4 laps behind*	24/28
ret	SAN MARINO GP	Imola	11	Team Lotus	G	3.5 Lotus 107C-Mugen Honda V10	*hit Lehto at first start*	22/28
11	MONACO GP	Monte Carlo	11	Team Lotus	G	3.5 Lotus 107C-Mugen Honda V10	*5 laps behind*	19/24

1995 Championship position: 17th= Wins: 0 Pole positions: 0 Fastest laps: 0 Points scored: 1

9	HUNGARIAN GP	Hungaroring	23	Minardi Scuderia Italia	G	3.0 Minardi M195-Ford EDM V8	*3 laps behind*	15/24
10	BELGIAN GP	Spa	23	Minardi Scuderia Italia	G	3.0 Minardi M195-Ford EDM V8		17/24
ret	ITALIAN GP	Monza	23	Minardi Scuderia Italia	G	3.0 Minardi M195-Ford EDM V8	*differential on lap 1*	19/24
ret	PORTUGUESE GP	Estoril	23	Minardi Scuderia Italia	G	3.0 Minardi M195-Ford EDM V8	*gearbox*	17/24
9	EUROPEAN GP	Nürburgring	23	Minardi Scuderia Italia	G	3.0 Minardi M195-Ford EDM V8	*3 laps behind*	16/24
13	PACIFIC GP	T.I. Circuit	23	Minardi Scuderia Italia	G	3.0 Minardi M195-Ford EDM V8	*3 laps behind*	14/24
11	JAPANESE GP	Suzuka	23	Minardi Scuderia Italia	G	3.0 Minardi M195-Ford EDM V8	*2 laps behind*	17/24
6	AUSTRALIAN GP	Adelaide	23	Minardi Scuderia Italia	G	3.0 Minardi M195-Ford EDM V8	*3 laps behind*	17/24

1996 Championship position: Unplaced

ret	AUSTRALIAN GP	Melbourne	20	Minardi Team	G	3.0 Minardi 195B-Ford EDM V8	*seat belts*	17/22
10	BRAZILIAN GP	Interlagos	20	Minardi Team	G	3.0 Minardi 195B-Ford EDM V8	*3 laps behind*	18/22
ret	ARGENTINE GP	Buenos Aires	20	Minardi Team	G	3.0 Minardi 195B-Ford EDM V8	*differential*	19/22
12	EUROPEAN GP	Nürburgring	20	Minardi Team	G	3.0 Minardi 195B-Ford EDM V8	*2 laps behind*	19/22
9	SAN MARINO GP	Imola	20	Minardi Team	G	3.0 Minardi 195B-Ford EDM V8	*2 laps behind*	18/22
ret	MONACO GP	Monte Carlo	20	Minardi Team	G	3.0 Minardi 195B-Ford EDM V8	*collision with Fisichella*	19/22
ret	SPANISH GP	Barcelona	20	Minardi Team	G	3.0 Minardi 195B-Ford EDM V8	*collision damage at start*	18/22
ret	CANADIAN GP	Montreal	20	Minardi Team	G	3.0 Minardi 195B-Ford EDM V8	*hit by Brundle*	19/22
12	FRENCH GP	Magny Cours	20	Minardi Team	G	3.0 Minardi 195B-Ford EDM V8	*3 laps behind*	19/22
ret	BRITISH GP	Silverstone	20	Minardi Team	G	3.0 Minardi 195B-Ford EDM V8	*hydraulic pressure*	20/22
12	GERMAN GP	Hockenheim	20	Minardi Team	G	3.0 Minardi 195B-Ford EDM V8	*2 laps behind*	18/20
ret	HUNGARIAN GP	Hungaroring	20	Minardi Team	G	3.0 Minardi 195B-Ford EDM V8	*suspension*	19/20

10	BELGIAN GP	Spa	20	Minardi Team	G	3.0 Minardi 195B-Ford EDM V8	1 lap behind	19/20
ret	ITALIAN GP	Monza	20	Minardi Team	G	3.0 Minardi 195B-Ford EDM V8	engine	18/20
16	PORTUGUESE GP	Estoril	20	Minardi Team	G	3.0 Minardi 195B-Ford EDM V8	5 laps behind	19/20
12	JAPANESE GP	Suzuka	20	Minardi Team	G	3.0 Minardi 195B-Ford EDM V8	2 laps behind	18/20

GP Starts: 32   GP Wins: 0   Pole positions: 0   Fastest laps: 0   Points: 1

PEDRO LAMY

A FORMER motocrosser and karting champion, Pedro Lamy won the Portuguese FF1600 title in 1989 and quickly graduated to the GM Lotus Euroseries. Blindingly fast in pre-season testing, he suffered a shock when the racing began, as he struggled to qualify, but a switch of teams soon helped restore his confidence and he ended the season strongly by winning the final round of the German series, thus ensuring a move to replace champion Rubens Barrichello in the Draco Racing team for 1991. He was straight out of the traps with a succession of wins, building up such a healthy points cushion that he could even afford to have a couple of shunts at Spa and Imola on his way to the championship.

With sound backing and shrewd management, Pedro opted for a season of German Formula 3 for 1992, and this was the year when he really came to prominence. Having totally dominated proceedings in his WTS Reynard-Opel, he won 11 races in the 26-round series and underlined his mastery when he also won the big Marlboro Masters Zandvoort meeting.

A year in F3000 furthered Pedro's reputation as a very quick driver – albeit sometimes erratic, and some of his track manners were dubious to say the least. He won one race, at Pau, and remained in contention for the title until the final round, when a collision cost him his chance. By then, he had been called into the Lotus line-up at Monza, to replace the unfit Alex Zanardi. He had a tough baptism, but with the backing of Portuguese sponsors, secured a full-time ride with the team for 1994.

Pedro's season suffered a setback at Imola, where he was fortunate to escape unscathed when his Lotus ran into the back of JJ Lehto's stalled Benetton, and soon was shattered when he was involved in a massive testing accident at Silverstone. His car ended up over the barriers; he suffered fractured and dislocated knees, and a broken wrist, but it could have been much worse. Happily, he made an amazingly swift recovery and soon was back in the paddock looking to get back into competition at the earliest opportunity.

In the event, Pedro had to wait until the middle of 1995, when Minardi finally decided to dispense with the services of Pierluigi Martini, but he was quickly back in the groove, matching the performances of team-mate Luca Badoer. Sixth place at the season's finale in Adelaide brought the softly-spoken Lamy his first world championship point, and a seat with the team in 1996.

With the demise of Simtek, Pacific and Forti, Minardi were once again consigned to the back of the field, and Lamy's main challenge came from his team-mates, Giancarlo Fisichella, Tarso Marques and later Giovanni Lavaggi. Fisichella in particular proved a stern test, and when the pair took each other out on the first lap at Monaco, Giancarlo Minardi not unnaturally castigated his young chargers. Unfortunately Pedro was out of the grand prix frame for 1997, but he successfully chased a GT ride with Porsche, taking fifth at Le Mans.

Pedro joined Olivier Beretta to race the works Chrysler Viper in 1998, and the pair stormed to the GT2 title, scoring eight wins in their class. Still ambitious, though, he was keen to move up to prototypes and, after winning a place in the works Mercedes squad for Le Mans, alongside Bernd Schneider and Franck Lagorce, the Portuguese driver sampled life in the American Le Mans Series with a BMW V12 LM.

After two seasons (2000/01) without much success in the DTM, racing Keke Rosberg's Mercedes, Pedro opted for action in the German V8 Star series, emerging as champion in 2003. More victories came the following year, when he won the GTS Le Mans Endurance Series driving the Larbre-Ferrari.

After he won the opening FIA GT round at Monza, Lamy's talents were utilised as a member of the Pro-drive Aston Martin team, where he shared the winning car in round three of the 2005 FIA GT Championship at Silverstone. Reverting to the trusty Ferrari 550 Maranello, he certainly lit up the tracks with some stirring performances. The Portuguese driver also tasted success at the wheel of a BMW M3, winning the Nürburgring 24-hour race twice over the classic 15.769-mile circuit.

In 2006, Lamy was part of the Aston Martin squad that contested the GT1 class of the American Le Mans Series; in 2007, he moved back into the prototype class with Peugeot as part of the French car giant's attack on the LMS series, taking three wins with co-driver Stéphane Sarrazin in the 908 Hdi. In the Le Mans 24-hours, Sébastien Bourdais was added, the trio posting a second-place finish, behind the winning Audi. Lamy and Sarrazzin took two more LMS wins for Peugeot in 2008, but could only finish fourth in the rankings.

In 2010, Pedro won the Nürburgring 24-hours for the fifth time, driving for BMW Motorsport, and now he is tied with Marcel Tiemann for the record number of wins at this famous race. Back in protoypes, with the Peugeot 908, he recorded wins at Spa in the LMS and in the Petit LeMans at Road Atlanta. In 2011, he had to settle for second place at Le Mans again (with Simon Pagenaud and Bourdais) when the Peugeot drivers had to cede victory once more to Audi. With the French concern's withdrawal from racing, Lamy planned to extend his long racing career In the World Endurance Championship with a Chevrolet Corvette.

CHICO LANDI

PERHAPS the first great Brazilian driver, Chico Landi raced mainly at home and therefore his immense talent was not really appreciated on the international stage. Racing from as early as 1934, he built a fine record with his Alfa Romeo, including winning the Rio de Janeiro GP in 1941, 1947 and 1948. He was well nigh unbeatable on home soil during and after the Second World War, driving his monoposto Alfa and Maserati, or in big Buicks, Cadillacs and Mercurys (running on Syngas due to fuel rationing). He was already 40 years old when he became the first Brazilian ace to try his luck in Europe, and he won the minor Bari GP in a Ferrari T166 in 1948. However, his subsequent appearances at world championship level were rarely in the most competitive of machines.

In the early 1950s, Landi was often the finest of the home racers on South American soil, giving best only to the likes of Juan Fangio and Froilán González. In 1952, he made a number of appearances in Europe in the Bandeirantes Maserati and a Ferrari T375, in which he recorded second places in the Formula Libre races at Albi and Boreham. He took the car back to Brazil and raced it successfully, before switching to sports cars with a Ferrari 250 and a Maserati 300S.

From the mid-1950s, Landi carried on winning races in both a Porsche and a Ferrari-Corvette. He targeted the Mil Mahas Brasil, finally winning the event in 1960 in a modified 2-litre Alfa Romeo. He continued to race this machine until 1964, when he acquired a Porsche Carrera 2. Chico was still winning races as late as 1969, and when he finally called it quits in 1973, at the age of 66, his career record over nearly 40 years was extraordinary. From 178 starts, he had recorded 53 victories, giving a win rate approaching 30 per cent.

LANDI, 'Chico' (Francisco Sacco) (BR) b 14/7/1907, São Paulo – d 7/6/1989, São Paulo

1951 Championship position: Unplaced

	Race	Circuit	No	Entrant	Tyres	Capacity/Car/Engine	Comment	Q Pos/Entries
ret	ITALIAN GP	Monza	12	Francisco Landi	P	4.5 Ferrari 375 V12	transmission on lap 1	16/22

1952 Championship position: Unplaced

	Race	Circuit	No	Entrant	Tyres	Capacity/Car/Engine	Comment	Q Pos/Entries
9*	DUTCH GP	Zandvoort	16	Escuderia Bandeirantes	P	2.0 Maserati A6GCM 6	*Flinterman took over car/-7 laps	16/18
8	ITALIAN GP	Monza	48	Escuderia Bandeirantes	P	2.0 Maserati A6GCM 6	4 laps behind	18/35

1953 Championship position: Unplaced

	Race	Circuit	No	Entrant	Tyres	Capacity/Car/Engine	Comment	Q Pos/Entries
ret	SWISS GP	Bremgarten	4	Escuderia Bandeirantes	P	2.0 Maserati A6GCM 6	gearbox	20/23
ret	ITALIAN GP	Monza	42	Scuderia Milano	P	2.0 Maserati A6GCM 6	engine – piston	21/30

1956 Championship position: 20th=   Wins: 0   Pole positions: 0   Fastest laps: 0   Points scored: 1.5

	Race	Circuit	No	Entrant	Tyres	Capacity/Car/Engine	Comment	Q Pos/Entries
4*	ARGENTINE GP	Buenos Aires	10	Officine Alfieri Maserati	P	2.5 Maserati 250F 6	*Gerini took over car/6 laps behind	11/15

GP Starts: 6   GP Wins: 0   Pole positions: 0   Fastest laps: 0   Points: 1.5

LANG, Hermann (D) b 6/4/1909, Bad Cannstatt, nr Stuttgart – d 19/10/1987, Bad Cannstatt, nr Stuttgart

1953 Championship position: 11th=   Wins: 0   Pole positions: 0   Fastest laps: 0   Points scored: 2

	Race	Circuit	No	Entrant	Tyres	Capacity/Car/Engine	Comment	Q Pos/Entries
5	SWISS GP	Bremgarten	34	Officine Alfieri Maserati	P	2.0 Maserati A6GCM 6	stood in for González/3 laps behind	11/23

1954 Championship position: Unplaced

	Race	Circuit	No	Entrant	Tyres	Capacity/Car/Engine	Comment	Q Pos/Entries
ret	GERMAN GP	Nürburgring	21	Daimler Benz AG	C	2.5 Mercedes-Benz W196 8	spun off	11/23

GP Starts: 2   GP Wins: 0   Pole positions: 0   Fastest laps: 0   Points: 2

HERMANN LANG

ONE of the true stars of pre-war racing, Hermann Lang had been a motorcycling champion in 1930 and 1931 before he joined Mercedes in 1933, initially working in the experimental department and then, in 1934, as Luigi Fagioli's mechanic. Given his chance to race the following season, young Lang immediately tamed the fearsome silver beasts and became a full team member in 1937, celebrating with wins at Tripoli and AVUS. He added six more major victories to his tally before the Second World War interrupted his career, when he was undoubtedly at his peak.

When peace returned, Hermann was back in action immediately. He rejoined the Mercedes team for their South American trip in February, 1951, finishing second in the Perón Cup and third in the Eva Perón Cup. Then he raced the team's 300SL cars in 1952, winning the Le Mans 24-hours (with Fritz Riess) and the Nürburgring sports car race, and scoring second places in the Prix de Berne and the Carrera Panamericana.

In 1953, Lang made a surprise return to grands prix, replacing the injured Froilán González in the Maserati team at Spa and taking fifth place. In truth, he was past his prime at this level, but when Mercedes returned to GP racing in 1954, he was invited to drive in the German Grand Prix. His race ended in disappointment, however, when he spun off while challenging team-mate Karl Kling for second place. He retired from competition immediately after this race, but for many years continued to demonstrate the famous cars that had brought him so much success early in his racing days.

NICOLA LARINI

THE talented Nicola Larini is yet another example of a driver who, having achieved success in the junior formulas, reached Formula 1, only to endure the frustration of making up the numbers at the back of the grid. However, the little Italian at least had the satisfaction of an opportunity to show his prowess at Ferrari when, standing in for the indisposed Jean Alesi, he took a splendid second place in the tragic San Marino Grand Prix at Imola in 1994.

Larini's first win in a racing car came in a Fiat Abarth in 1984; later that season he switched to Italian F3, qualifying fourth fastest for his first race. Driving a Martini-Alfa Romeo the following year, he won two races and finished sixth in the championship. He was taken under the wing of Enzo Coloni and upstaged his team leader, Marco Apicella, to win a very high-quality 1986 Italian Formula 3 championship in a Dallara, racing against the likes of Alex Caffi and Stefano Modena. He had a brief taste of F3000 with Coloni at Enna and again the following year with the rival Forti Corse

team, where he failed to qualify for both of his races.

Coloni then gave him his grand prix debut in the team's new bright yellow FC187 at the end of 1987, before he joined Osella for a couple of character-building seasons, when he never gave less than 100 per cent. Particularly noteworthy were his drives at Imola and Montreal in 1989, a season when he was among a whole gaggle of hopefuls who had to endure pre-qualifying.

After an unhappy season with Ligier in 1990, when he could look forward to starting every race in an otherwise mediocre machine, Nicola threw in his lot with the ambitious, but ill-starred Modena team. Once again he had to endure the qualifying lottery and only managed to qualify for four races before the team foundered. Having been given a testing contract by Ferrari to develop their active suspension system, he re-established his reputation as a class driver by winning the 1992 Italian touring car championship for Alfa Romeo. At the end of the year, he was given a couple of outings by Ferrari, after they had dispensed with the services of the disillusioned Ivan Capelli. Sadly technical problems prevented him from making a bid for the points.

Nicola's stock rose even higher in 1993, when he moved with Alfa Romeo into the high-profile DTM German series, regularly destroying the opposition with some brilliant drives to take the title.

Early in 1994, Larini received another chance to make a mark in Formula 1, deputising for the injured Jean Alesi at both the Pacific Grand Prix, where he was caught up in a first-corner accident, and San Marino Grand Prix, where he rose to the occasion magnificently to take a career-best second place, behind Michael Schumacher. Sadly his achievement was largely forgotten in the aftermath of the deaths of Roland Ratzenberger and Ayrton Senna.

Back in the DTM, Nicola found himself evenly matched with team-mate Alessandro Nannini, the pair finishing the 1994 season just a point apart, With Mercedes dominant, Larini finished third overall, with four wins to Nannini's three. The following year saw the Mercedes juggernaut steamroller the opposition, but Larini was easily the best of the rest in sixth place overall. In 1996, with the series renamed the International Touring Car series, Larini was somewhat overshadowed by Nannini this time around, but at least he managed to post wins at Mugello and São Paulo. Although he was placed 11th overall, he remained not only a popular and formidable competitor, but also one of the category's star attractions.

Larini's continuing role as Ferrari test driver led to a grand prix return in 1997, when he was found a seat at Sauber. But, after he had scored a point in his first race, his dream opportunity turned into a nightmare and he was dropped amid some unsavoury mud-slinging by both sides.

Relieved to be out of a team in which he claimed the ambience had been terrible, Nicola continued to race for Alfa Romeo in European Super Touring and the national Italian Superturismo championships. Seeking a greater challenge, he joined Chevrolet in 2005 to compete in the World Touring Car Championship. He competed for five seasons in the category, making more than 100 race starts, with a fifth place overall in 2007 being his highest ranking. In his final season before retirement, he finally scored a long-awaited and much deserved victory in Morocco.

LARINI, Nicola (I) b 19/3/1964, Lido di Camaiore

		1987 Championship position: Unplaced							
	Race	Circuit	No	Entrant	Tyres	Capacity/Car/Engine	Comment		Q Pos/Entries
dnq	ITALIAN GP	Monza	32	Enzo Coloni Racing Car System	G	3.5 Coloni FC187-Cosworth V8			27/28
ret	SPANISH GP	Jerez	32	Enzo Coloni Racing Car System	G	3.5 Coloni FC187-Cosworth V8	suspension		26/28
		1988 Championship position: Unplaced							
dnq	BRAZILIAN GP	Rio	21	Osella Squadra Corse	G	1.5 t/c Osella FA1I-Alfa Romeo V8			29/31
excl*	SAN MARINO GP	Imola	21	Osella Squadra Corse	G	1.5 t/c Osella FA1L-Alfa Romeo V8	*failed to pass scrutineering		- /31
9	MONACO GP	Monte Carlo	21	Osella Squadra Corse	G	1.5 t/c Osella FA1L-Alfa Romeo V8	3 laps behind		25/30
dnq	MEXICAN GP	Mexico City	21	Osella Squadra Corse	G	1.5 t/c Osella FA1L-Alfa Romeo V8			28/30
dnq	CANADIAN GP	Montreal	21	Osella Squadra Corse	G	1.5 t/c Osella FA1L-Alfa Romeo V8			28/31

ret	US GP (DETROIT)	Detroit	21	Osella Squadra Corse	G	1.5 t/c Osella FA1L-Alfa Romeo V8	engine	27/31
ret	FRENCH GP	Paul Ricard	21	Osella Squadra Corse	G	1.5 t/c Osella FA1L-Alfa Romeo V8	driveshaft	25/31
19/ret	BRITISH GP	Silverstone	21	Osella Squadra Corse	G	1.5 t/c Osella FA1L-Alfa Romeo V8	out of fuel/5 laps behind	26/31
ret	GERMAN GP	Hockenheim	21	Osella Squadra Corse	G	1.5 t/c Osella FA1L-Alfa Romeo V8	started from pit lane/turbo pipe	18/31
dnpq	HUNGARIAN GP	Hungaroring	21	Osella Squadra Corse	G	1.5 t/c Osella FA1L-Alfa Romeo V8		31/31
ret	BELGIAN GP	Spa	21	Osella Squadra Corse	G	1.5 t/c Osella FA1L-Alfa Romeo V8	electrics	26/31
ret	ITALIAN GP	Monza	21	Osella Squadra Corse	G	1.5 t/c Osella FA1L-Alfa Romeo V8	engine	17/31
12	PORTUGUESE GP	Estoril	21	Osella Squadra Corse	G	1.5 t/c Osella FA1L-Alfa Romeo V8	pit stop – steering/fuel/7 laps behind	25/31
ret	SPANISH GP	Jerez	21	Osella Squadra Corse	G	1.5 t/c Osella FA1L-Alfa Romeo V8	suspension	14/31
ret	JAPANESE GP	Suzuka	21	Osella Squadra Corse	G	1.5 t/c Osella FA1L-Alfa Romeo V8	lost wheel	24/31
dnpq	AUSTRALIAN GP	Adelaide	21	Osella Squadra Corse	G	1.5 t/c Osella FA1L-Alfa Romeo V8		31/31

1989 Championship position: Unplaced

dsq	BRAZILIAN GP	Rio	17	Osella Squadra Corse	P	3.5 Osella FA1M-Cosworth V8	started from wrong grid position	19/38
12/ret	SAN MARINO GP	Imola	17	Osella Squadra Corse	P	3.5 Osella FA1M-Cosworth V8	broken hub – crashed/6 laps behind	14/39
dnpq	MONACO GP	Monte Carlo	17	Osella Squadra Corse	P	3.5 Osella FA1M-Cosworth V8		32/38
dnpq	MEXICAN GP	Mexico City	17	Osella Squadra Corse	P	3.5 Osella FA1M-Cosworth V8		33/39
dnpq	US GP (PHOENIX)	Phoenix	17	Osella Squadra Corse	P	3.5 Osella FA1M-Cosworth V8		34/39
ret	CANADIAN GP	Montreal	17	Osella Squadra Corse	P	3.5 Osella FA1M-Cosworth V8	electrics	15/39
dnpq	FRENCH GP	Paul Ricard	17	Osella Squadra Corse	P	3.5 Osella FA1M-Cosworth V8		31/39
ret	BRITISH GP	Silverstone	17	Osella Squadra Corse	P	3.5 Osella FA1M-Cosworth V8	started from pitlane/handling	17/39
dnpq	GERMAN GP	Hockenheim	17	Osella Squadra Corse	P	3.5 Osella FA1M-Cosworth V8		32/39
dnpq	HUNGARIAN GP	Hungaroring	17	Osella Squadra Corse	P	3.5 Osella FA1M-Cosworth V8		31/39
dnpq	BELGIAN GP	Spa	17	Osella Squadra Corse	P	3.5 Osella FA1M-Cosworth V8		31/39
ret	ITALIAN GP	Monza	17	Osella Squadra Corse	P	3.5 Osella FA1M-Cosworth V8	gearbox	24/39
excl*	PORTUGUESE GP	Estoril	17	Osella Squadra Corse	P	3.5 Osella FA1M-Cosworth V8	*excluded – missed weight check	35/39
ret	SPANISH GP	Jerez	17	Osella Squadra Corse	P	3.5 Osella FA1M-Cosworth V8	suspension – crashed	11/38
ret	JAPANESE GP	Suzuka	17	Osella Squadra Corse	P	3.5 Osella FA1M-Cosworth V8	brakes	10/39
ret/dns*	AUSTRALIAN GP	Adelaide	17	Osella Squadra Corse	P	3.5 Osella FA1M-Cosworth V8	*electrics on the grid at 2nd start	11/39

1990 Championship position: Unplaced

ret	US GP (PHOENIX)	Phoenix	25	Ligier Gitanes	G	3.5 Ligier JS33B-Cosworth V8	stuck throttle	13/35
11	BRAZILIAN GP	Interlagos	25	Ligier Gitanes	G	3.5 Ligier JS33B-Cosworth V8	pit stop – tyres/3 laps behind	20/35
10	SAN MARINO GP	Imola	25	Ligier Gitanes	G	3.5 Ligier JS33B-Cosworth V8	gearbox problems/2 laps behind	21/34
ret	MONACO GP	Monte Carlo	25	Ligier Gitanes	G	3.5 Ligier JS33B-Cosworth V8	gearbox/differential	17/35
ret	CANADIAN GP	Montreal	25	Ligier Gitanes	G	3.5 Ligier JS33B-Cosworth V8	hit by Boutsen	20/35
16	MEXICAN GP	Mexico City	25	Ligier Gitanes	G	3.5 Ligier JS33B-Cosworth V8	2 laps behind	24/35
14	FRENCH GP	Paul Ricard	25	Ligier Gitanes	G	3.5 Ligier JS33B-Cosworth V8	brake problems/2 laps behind	19/35
10	BRITISH GP	Silverstone	25	Ligier Gitanes	G	3.5 Ligier JS33B-Cosworth V8	2 laps behind	21/35
10	GERMAN GP	Hockenheim	25	Ligier Gitanes	G	3.5 Ligier JS33B-Cosworth V8	2 pit stops – tyres/2 laps behind	22/35
11	HUNGARIAN GP	Hungaroring	25	Ligier Gitanes	G	3.5 Ligier JS33B-Cosworth V8	1 lap behind	25/35
14	BELGIAN GP	Spa	25	Ligier Gitanes	G	3.5 Ligier JS33B-Cosworth V8	2 pit stops – handling – tyres/-2 laps	21/33
11	ITALIAN GP	Monza	25	Ligier Gitanes	G	3.5 Ligier JS33B-Cosworth V8	2 laps behind	26/33
10	PORTUGUESE GP	Estoril	25	Ligier Gitanes	G	3.5 Ligier JS33B-Cosworth V8	pit stop – tyres/2 laps behind	23/33
7	SPANISH GP	Jerez	25	Ligier Gitanes	G	3.5 Ligier JS33B-Cosworth V8	1 lap behind	20/33
7	JAPANESE GP	Suzuka	25	Ligier Gitanes	G	3.5 Ligier JS33B-Cosworth V8	pit stop – tyres/1 lap behind	18/30
10	AUSTRALIAN GP	Adelaide	25	Ligier Gitanes	G	3.5 Ligier JS33B-Cosworth V8	2 laps behind	12/30

1991 Championship position: Unplaced

7	US GP (PHOENIX)	Phoenix	34	Modena Team SpA	G	3.5 Lambo 291-Lamborghini V12	3 laps behind	17/34
dnpq	BRAZILIAN GP	Interlagos	34	Modena Team SpA	G	3.5 Lambo 291-Lamborghini V12		32/34
dnpq	SAN MARINO GP	Imola	34	Modena Team SpA	G	3.5 Lambo 291-Lamborghini V12		33/34
dnpq	MONACO GP	Monte Carlo	34	Modena Team SpA	G	3.5 Lambo 291-Lamborghini V12		31/34
dnpq	CANADIAN GP	Montreal	34	Modena Team SpA	G	3.5 Lambo 291-Lamborghini V12		32/34
excl*	MEXICAN GP	Mexico City	34	Modena Team SpA	G	3.5 Lambo 291-Lamborghini V12	*rear wing height infringement	31/34
dnpq	FRENCH GP	Paul Ricard	34	Modena Team SpA	G	3.5 Lambo 291-Lamborghini V12		32/34
dnpq	BRITISH GP	Silverstone	34	Modena Team SpA	G	3.5 Lambo 291-Lamborghini V12		32/34
ret	GERMAN GP	Hockenheim	34	Modena Team SpA	G	3.5 Lambo 291-Lamborghini V12	spun avoiding Blundell on lap 1	24/34
16	HUNGARIAN GP	Hungaroring	34	Modena Team SpA	G	3.5 Lambo 291-Lamborghini V12	3 laps behind	24/34
dnq	BELGIAN GP	Spa	34	Modena Team SpA	G	3.5 Lambo 291-Lamborghini V12		28/34
16	ITALIAN GP	Monza	34	Modena Team SpA	G	3.5 Lambo 291-Lamborghini V12	5 laps behind	23/34
dnq	PORTUGUESE GP	Estoril	34	Modena Team SpA	G	3.5 Lambo 291-Lamborghini V12		29/34
dnq	SPANISH GP	Barcelona	34	Modena Team SpA	G	3.5 Lambo 291-Lamborghini V12		28/33
dnq	JAPANESE GP	Suzuka	34	Modena Team SpA	G	3.5 Lambo 291-Lamborghini V12		28/31
ret	AUSTRALIAN GP	Adelaide	34	Modena Team SpA	G	3.5 Lambo 291-Lamborghini V12	collision with Alesi	19/32

1992 Championship position: Unplaced

12	JAPANESE GP	Suzuka	28	Scuderia Ferrari SpA	G	3.5 Fiat Ferrari F9200 V12	left at start/active car/1 lap behind	11/26
11	AUSTRALIAN GP	Adelaide	28	Scuderia Ferrari SpA	G	3.5 Fiat Ferrari F9200 V12	again left at start – clutch/-2 laps	19/26

1994 Championship position: 14th= Wins: 0 Pole positions: 0 Fastest laps: 0 Points scored: 6

ret	PACIFIC GP	T.I. Circuit	27	Scuderia Ferrari	G	3.5 Fiat Ferrari 412T1 V12	ran off track and into Senna – lap 1	7/28
2	SAN MARINO GP	Imola	27	Scuderia Ferrari	G	3.5 Fiat Ferrari 412T1 V12		6/28

1997 Championship position: 19th Wins: 0 Pole positions: 0 Fastest laps: 0 Points scored: 1

6	AUSTRALIAN GP	Melbourne	17	Red Bull Sauber Petronas	G	3.0 Sauber C16-Petronas V10		13/24
11	BRAZILIAN GP	Interlagos	17	Red Bull Sauber Petronas	G	3.0 Sauber C16-Petronas V10	1 lap behind	19/22
ret	ARGENTINE GP	Buenos Aires	17	Red Bull Sauber Petronas	G	3.0 Sauber C16-Petronas V10	spun off	14/22
7	SAN MARINO GP	Imola	17	Red Bull Sauber Petronas	G	3.0 Sauber C16-Petronas V10	1 lap behind	12/22
ret	MONACO GP	Monte Carlo	17	Red Bull Sauber Petronas	G	3.0 Sauber C16-Petronas V10	accident	11/22

GP Starts: 48 (49) GP Wins: 0 Pole positions: 0 Fastest laps: 0 Points: 7

OSCAR LARRAURI

DESPITE having raced in Argentinian F3 from 1979, Oscar 'Poppy' Larrauri found the going tough when he made the move to Europe, until he secured the top drive in the Pavanello Euroracing F3 team for 1982. Then he showed his mettle, winning seven races and the European championship. Unfortunately his aspirations were soon blunted by an unhappy Formula 2 liaison with Minardi that left him out in the cold as far as single-seaters were concerned. However, he began a long and rewarding association with Walter Brun, racing the Swiss entrant's Group C Porsche sports cars through to the early 1990s, the high spot being a win at Jerez in 1986.

Brun's over-ambitious move into Formula 1 was a different story, however, and 'Poppy' was left struggling to qualify uncompetitive machinery. Subsequently he embarked on a busy racing career based in Italy, where he drove a Jolly Club Ferrari 348 in the GT Supercar championship in 1993 and '94. At the end of that season, he took a Ferrari F40 to victory in the final round of the All-Japan GT championship; success continued in 1995, when he shared the victorious Porsche 962 K8 at the Daytona 24-hours. The bulk of the year was spent contesting the Italian Superturismo series in a Jolly Club Alfa T155

In 1996, Larrauri returned to race for the first time in a decade in his native Argentina, and he took consecutive Super Touring titles in 1997 and '98 with a BMW 320i, before retiring from competition to pursue a political career and run his cold-storage business. He did not lose all links with motorsport however, as he became involved with the launch of Miguel Angel Guerra's Top Race V6 series.

LARRAURI, Oscar (RA) b 19/8/1954, Buenos Aires

1988 Championship position: Unplaced

	Race	Circuit	No	Entrant	Tyres	Capacity/Car/Engine	Comment	Q Pos/Entries
ret/dns	BRAZILIAN GP	Rio	32	EuroBrun Racing	G	3.5 EuroBrun ER188-Cosworth V8	electrics on parade lap	(26)/31
dnq	SAN MARINO GP	Imola	32	EuroBrun Racing	G	3.5 EuroBrun ER188-Cosworth V8		27/31
ret	MONACO GP	Monte Carlo	32	EuroBrun Racing	G	3.5 EuroBrun ER188-Cosworth V8	accident	18/31
13	MEXICAN GP	Mexico City	32	EuroBrun Racing	G	3.5 EuroBrun ER188-Cosworth V8	handling/battery problems/-4 laps	26/30
ret	CANADIAN GP	Montreal	32	EuroBrun Racing	G	3.5 EuroBrun ER188-Cosworth V8	accident	24/31
ret	US GP (DETROIT)	Detroit	32	EuroBrun Racing	G	3.5 EuroBrun ER188-Cosworth V8	gearbox	24/31
ret	FRENCH GP	Paul Ricard	32	EuroBrun Racing	G	3.5 EuroBrun ER188-Cosworth V8	clutch	27/31
dnq	BRITISH GP	Silverstone	32	EuroBrun Racing	G	3.5 EuroBrun ER188-Cosworth V8		27/31
16	GERMAN GP	Hockenheim	32	EuroBrun Racing	G	3.5 EuroBrun ER188-Cosworth V8	2 laps behind	26/31
dnq	HUNGARIAN GP	Hungaroring	32	EuroBrun Racing	G	3.5 EuroBrun ER188-Cosworth V8		27/31
dnpq	BELGIAN GP	Spa	32	EuroBrun Racing	G	3.5 EuroBrun ER188-Cosworth V8		31/31
dnpq	ITALIAN GP	Monza	32	EuroBrun Racing	G	3.5 EuroBrun ER188-Cosworth V8		31/31
dnpq	PORTUGUESE GP	Estoril	32	EuroBrun Racing	G	3.5 EuroBrun ER188-Cosworth V8		31/31
dnq	SPANISH GP	Jerez	32	EuroBrun Racing	G	3.5 EuroBrun ER188-Cosworth V8		28/31
dnq	JAPANESE GP	Suzuka	32	EuroBrun Racing	G	3.5 EuroBrun ER188-Cosworth V8		28/31
ret	AUSTRALIAN GP	Adelaide	32	EuroBrun Racing	G	3.5 EuroBrun ER188-Cosworth V8	half shaft – spun off	25/31

1989 Championship position: Unplaced

	Race	Circuit	No	Entrant	Tyres	Capacity/Car/Engine	Comment	Q Pos/Entries
dnpq	ITALIAN GP	Monza	33	EuroBrun Racing	P	3.5 EuroBrun ER189-Judd V8		36/39
dnpq	"	"	33	EuroBrun Racing	P	3.5 EuroBrun ER188B-Judd V8		- / -
dnpq	PORTUGUESE GP	Estoril	33	EuroBrun Racing	P	3.5 EuroBrun ER189-Judd V8		34/39
dnpq	"	"	33	EuroBrun Racing	P	3.5 EuroBrun ER188B-Judd V8		- / -
dnpq	SPANISH GP	Jerez	33	EuroBrun Racing	P	3.5 EuroBrun ER189-Judd V8		37/38
dnpq	"	"	33	EuroBrun Racing	P	3.5 EuroBrun ER188B-Judd V8		- / -
dnpq	JAPANESE GP	Suzuka	33	EuroBrun Racing	P	3.5 EuroBrun ER189-Judd V8		35/39
dnpq	AUSTRALIAN GP	Adelaide	33	EuroBrun Racing	P	3.5 EuroBrun ER189-Judd V8		35/39

GP Starts: 7 (8)   GP Wins: 0   Pole positions: 0   Fastest laps: 0   Points: 0

LARRETA, Alberto Rodriguez (Alberto Jorge RODRIGUEZ LARRETA) (RA) b 14/1/1934, Buenos Aires – d 11/3/1977, Buenos Aires

1960 Championship position: Unplaced

	Race	Circuit	No	Entrant	Tyres	Capacity/Car/Engine	Comment	Q Pos/Entries
9	ARGENTINE GP	Buenos Aires	46	Team Lotus	D	2.5 Lotus 16-Climax 4	ran in 3rd works car/3 laps behind	15/22

GP Starts: 1   GP Wins: 0   Pole positions: 0   Fastest laps: 0   Points: 0

LARROUSSE, Gérard (F) b 23/5/1940, Lyon

1974 Championship position: Unplaced

	Race	Circuit	No	Entrant	Tyres	Capacity/Car/Engine	Comment	Q Pos/Entries
ret	BELGIAN GP	Nivelles	43	Scuderia Finotto	G	3.0 Brabham BT42-Cosworth V8	chunking tyres	28/32
dnq	FRENCH GP	Dijon	43	Scuderia Finotto	G	3.0 Brabham BT42-Cosworth V8		30/30

GP Starts: 1   GP Wins: 0   Pole positions: 0   Fastest laps: 0   Points: 0

ALBERTO-JORGE 'LARRY' RODRÍGUEZ LARRETA

AN amateur driver, Alberto-Jorge Rodríguez Larreta came from a wealthy family with a motorsport heritage (his father, Alberto, triumphed in the Marseilles GP in 1924). He made his racing debut at the age of 19 in 1953, driving a Cisitalia 1.100, and it did not take him long to record his first victory. At 21, he participated in the 1955 500 miles of Rafaela, driving a 1953 Ferrari 250MM and winning the bronze medal in the sports championship. In his early racing days, he used the name Jorge, to distinguish himself from his father, but his friends called him 'Larry', a pseudonym that he often used himself. Throughout his career, he raced in all manner of disciplines, such as sports, race, rally and Turismo Carretera (the most popular touring car racing series in Argentina). Competing in this huge variety of machines also changed his style of driving, which became less spectacular, but remained very effective.

In 1960, the ACA (Automóvil Club Argentino) arranged for Larreta to drive a third works Lotus in the Argentine Grand Prix. He had hoped that this would lead to more F1 opportunities, but sadly no further chances came his way, as his country dropped off the world championship calendar thereafter.

Despite having to take over the family estate, Larreta continued to race in 'tin tops', going on to complete a very successful career. In 1969, he drove a Torino 380W coupé in the Marathon de la Route at the Nürburgring. Despite completing the most laps during the 84-hour event, his team was penalised and relegated to a still impressive fourth overall and a class win. That year was one of his best, for he won eight races in the Torino from a total of 15. Having retired from the sport in 1971, he remained close to racing circles until his untimely death from a heart attack some six years later.

GÉRARD LARROUSSE

AFTER a distinguished career in rallying between 1961 and 1965 with Simca and Renault Gordini cars, Gérard Larrouse switched to the German BMW and NSU marques in 1966 to take second place in the French Rally Championship. The following year, he reverted successfully to the Renault marque, undertaking both rally and circuit competition with an Alpine A110. He shared the car at the Le Mans 24-hours with a young Patrick Depailler, but was forced into retirement.

The following year, Larrousse again split his racing activities between rallies and circuits, taking a sixth in the Paris 1000km at Montlhéry and a ninth in the Nürburgring 1000km with the Alpine A220, again with Depailler.

Then the versatile Gérard became an official works driver for Porsche, racing in both rallies and long-distance events. He made an immediate impact in both disciplines, taking rally wins in the Tour de France and the Tour de Corse. He shared the second-place Porsche 908 with Hans Herrmann, which finished second at Le Mans in 1969, and took class wins in the 911GT at Sebring, Spa, Magny-Cours and Monza.

Larrousse built a fine reputation in prototype racing, taking the Nürburgring 1000km and the Spa 1000km in 1970 with the Porsche 908. In 1971, driving for Martini racing, he shared the winning Porsche 917 in the Sebring 12-hours and the Nürburgring 1000km with Vic Elford, and the victorious Matra 650 in the Tour de France with Johnny Rives. In addition, he drove Jo Siffert's Chevron B19 in the European 2-litre championship. In 1972, he raced for ill-fated Ecurie Bonnier in the Swede's 2-litre Lola T282, and for Ford with Jochen Mass in the European Touring Car championship.

Gérard then enjoyed two fabulously successful years with Matra in 1973 and 1974, during which, partnered by Henri Pescarolo, he won the Le Mans 24-hours twice, and added further victories at Vallelunga, Dijon, the Österreichring, Watkins Glen, Imola and Kyalami. In 1974, he was also the European 2-litre champion in an Alpine A441-Renault.

That was the year Larrousse briefly sampled the ambience of Formula 1, but he had a miserable time with the poorly prepared 'rent-a-drive' Finotto Brabham, scraping on to the grid at Nivelles, but failing to qualify for his home race at Dijon.

In 1975, Larrousse joined forces with Jean-Pierre Jabouille to undertake a season of Formula 2 with their space-frame Elf A367-BMW. He won the Jim Clark Trophy at Hockenheim on aggregate first time out, and took second places at Enna and Silverstone to finish a very creditable fourth in the series, behind Jacques Laffite, Michel Leclère and Patrick Tambay. In addition, they ran a limited sports car programme for Renault with the A441, winning at Mugello with Jabouille and taking third at Watkins Glen with Jean-Pierre Jarier. At the end of that season, Gérard was appointed competitions manager at Renault, overseeing the development of their 1977 Formula 1 turbo car. Later he moved to Ligier, before establishing his own team, which competed on minimal budgets and was supported by a murky collection of sponsors from 1987 through to 1994, when the financial climate forced Larrousse to close its doors, after a possible merger with French F3000 champions and grand prix aspirants DAMS came to nought.

SOME try to buck the system, but usually fail, while others play the game and manipulate it to their own ends. Niki Lauda managed to do both, the adroitness of his off-track political and business manoeuvrings being matched by that of his driving and racecraft, which saw him win three world titles.

After a couple of seasons in which he struggled to make an impression in Formula Vee, Formula 3 and sports cars, with a Porsche 908, Lauda took a bank loan to finance a season of Formula 2 in a semi-works March and a one-off drive in his home grand prix in 1971.

Although Niki's results were hardly inspiring, there were fleeting glimpses of his talent. Already the quiet self-confidence was there, as was the inner determination to overcome every setback, and he effectively mortgaged himself to the hilt to buy a seat in the works March team alongside Ronnie Peterson for 1972. To say the F1 season was disastrous is almost an understatement; the dreadful 721X proved absolutely hopeless. Fortunately, the Formula 2 March 722 was competitive, at least allowing Niki to compete with his peers. His win in the spring John Player F2 race at Oulton Park was one indication of his potential, his ability to closely match Ronnie Peterson's testing times another. Even so, March discarded him right at the end of the year, and he virtually saved his career by joining BRM for 1973 in a pay-as-you-race deal, which he knew would be difficult to honour.

When Lauda managed to overshadow his team-mates in the early races, took his first championship points at Zolder and held third place in the Monaco GP, he was able to put his contract problems behind him, but only by locking himself into a three-year deal. There were a few successful touring car races for BMW, which proved quite lucrative, but most important was the fact that on the recommendation of Clay Regazzoni, he had been targeted by Ferrari for 1974. Contract or not, there was no way Louis Stanley was going to stop Niki from heading for Maranello, and the young Austrian wriggled his way out of the deal. Displaying typical pragmatism, he set about his new task at Ferrari with a huge programme of testing and constant development, which paid immediate dividends. After a very poor season in 1973, Ferrari were back, and Niki's second place in the season's opener set the tone. His first win (at Jarama) soon followed, as did a succession of pole positions to make him the season's pace setter. There was another win (at Zandvoort) and three more second places, but an end-of-season dip in form and a rash of retirements cost him his title chance.

For a driver in his first year with a front-line team, Niki had performed admirably, but privately he was convinced that in 1975 the title would be his, and once the transverse-gearbox car was introduced there was no stopping him. Nine pole positions and five grand prix wins (complemented by victory in the International Trophy) saw the Austrian sweep to his first championship, and 1976 showed every sign of going the same way, with five wins, two second places and a third in the season's first nine races. This included a brave race at Jarama, where he drove with broken ribs, and of course the controversial British Grand Prix, where his rival, James Hunt, was disqualified.

Then came the German Grand Prix and the fiery crash at the Nürburgring, which so nearly took Niki's life. Although badly burned around the head, he returned (having missed the Austrian and Dutch races) to defend his title just weeks later at Monza, whee he claimed an emotional fourth place. The fact that ultimately he failed to retain his crown was largely irrelevant in the grand scheme of things, despite the dreadful treatment the Italian press meted out to him after his decision to pull out of the Japanese Grand Prix. Even at Maranello there were doubters who thought he had lost his 'bottle', however, and Carlos Reutemann was brought into the team, much to Lauda's annoyance.

Inwardly, Niki must have relished the challenge, and with a perfect blend of aggression and circumspection he all but humiliated his new team-mate the following season to prove to the hierarchy that he was still the boss. A second title was duly won with a succession of measured performances, where he maximised every opportunity to score points. Then, having proved his point, and with a characteristic lack of sentiment, he announced that he was moving to Bernie Ecclestone's Brabham team. After he collected the three points he needed to confirm his second title at Watkins Glen, the disenchanted driver opted out of appearing in the season's last two races in Canada and Japan.

Niki's two years with Brabham brought only limited success; the Alfa engine was unreliable and unsuited to the new ground-effects technology that Lotus had so brilliantly created. An avenue for success was briefly opened when he won the Swedish Grand Prix in the notorious fan car, but this was swiftly banned, officially on the grounds of safety.

Lauda did win the Italian GP in 1978, but only after Mario Andretti and Gilles Villeneuve had both been penalised for jumping the start. The following season was demoralising, as his car suffered a succession of mishaps that left him with a meagre four points to show for his effort. A win in the meaningless non-title Dino Ferrari Trophy at Imola came just before fly-away races at the end of the year. At Montreal, he tried the new Cosworth-engined BT49 in free practice and made the shock decision to retire there and then.

Niki stayed away for two years, during which he built up his airline business, before being tempted back in 1982. Perhaps it was his ego, the money, or maybe just the challenge of proving the inevitable doubters wrong. One thing was for sure: once he had demonstrated to himself that the speed was still there, he wasn't going to mess around. There was a job to be done in developing John Barnard's innovative McLaren MP4 and Niki was just the man to do it. The Austrian took only three races to post a win (at Long Beach), followed by another victory at Brands Hatch. True, there were occasional lapses and lacklustre performances in the Cosworth car, but once his attention turned to the TAG turbo-powered machine at the end of 1983, he was fully focused. He needed to be for 1984, when he was joined by Alain Prost.

Using all his experience, the wily Lauda hung on to the Frenchman's tail, and despite only taking five wins to Prost's seven, the veteran only needed a second place at the season's final race in Estoril to claim his third world championship by the narrowest of margins after a fabulous year for McLaren. His final season perhaps went according to expectation, as the still hungry Prost forced the pace, while Niki was happy to adopt a more tactical approach. Unfortunately his year was blighted by unreliability, and finishes were few and far between. At Zandvoort, however, we saw Lauda the racer one last time as he kept his McLaren in front of Prost's sister-car in a Formula 3-style battle to the finish. This time, Niki stayed retired, but in 1992 he was invited to act as a consultant to Ferrari as they attempted to recapture the glory days, but most of the 1990s were spent running his airline, Lauda Air, from which eventually he was ousted following a takeover by his rivals, Austrian Air.

Niki made a shock return to Formula 1 in 2001 at Jaguar Racing, eventually succeeding Bobby Rahal as team principal. It was a turbulent period for the under-achieving outfit and, predictably perhaps, Lauda's head rolled in another reshuffle at the end of the 2002 season.

Typically, Lauda bounced back, setting up another airline business, Niki, in association with Air Berlin, running flights out of Austria. In 2009, at the age of 60, he became a father once again when his 30-year-old second wife, Birgit, delivered twins. She had already donated one of her kidneys to her husband, who had previously received a similar transplant from his brother. Lauda has long been an F1 paddock regular with his work as a commentator for Austrian and German TV.

LAUDA, Niki (A) b 22/2/1949, Vienna

1971 Championship position: Unplaced

	Race	Circuit	No	Entrant	Tyres	Capacity/Car/Engine	Comment	Q Pos/Entries
ret	AUSTRIAN GP	Österreichring	26	STP March Racing Team	F	3.0 March 711-Cosworth V8	handling	21/22

1972 Championship position: Unplaced

	Race	Circuit	No	Entrant	Tyres	Capacity/Car/Engine	Comment	Q Pos/Entries
11	ARGENTINE GP	Buenos Aires	15	STP March Racing Team	G	3.0 March 721-Cosworth V8	2 laps behind	22/22
7	SOUTH AFRICAN GP	Kyalami	4	STP March Racing Team	G	3.0 March 721-Cosworth V8	1 lap behind	=20/27
ret	SPANISH GP	Jarama	24	STP March Racing Team	G	3.0 March 721X-Cosworth V8	sticking throttle	25/26
16	MONACO GP	Monte Carlo	4	STP March Racing Team	G	3.0 March 721X-Cosworth V8	pit stop – wheel/fuel leak/-6 laps	=22/25
12	BELGIAN GP	Nivelles	12	STP March Racing Team	G	3.0 March 721X-Cosworth V8	handling problems/3 laps behind	25/26
dns	"	"	14	Clarke-Mordaunt-Guthrie Racing	G	3.0 March 721G-Cosworth V8	practice only	- / -
ret	FRENCH GP	Clermont Ferrand	14	STP March Racing Team	G	3.0 March 721G-Cosworth V8	loose driveshaft	25/29
9	BRITISH GP	Brands Hatch	4	STP March Racing Team	G	3.0 March 721G-Cosworth V8	3 laps behind	=18/27
ret	GERMAN GP	Nürburgring	23	STP March Racing Team	G	3.0 March 721G-Cosworth V8	split oil tank	24/27
10	AUSTRIAN GP	Österreichring	4	STP March Racing Team	G	3.0 March 721G-Cosworth V8	1 lap behind	22/26
13	ITALIAN GP	Monza	18	STP March Racing Team	G	3.0 March 721G-Cosworth V8	pit stop – throttle slides/5 laps behind	20/27
dsq	CANADIAN GP	Mosport Park	26	STP March Racing Team	G	3.0 March 721G-Cosworth V8	outside assistance on track	=19/25
nc	US GP	Watkins Glen	5	STP March Racing Team	G	3.0 March 721G-Cosworth V8	pit stop – fuel pressure/10 laps behind	26/32

1973 Championship position: 17th Wins: 0 Pole positions: 0 Fastest laps: 0 Points scored: 2

	Race	Circuit	No	Entrant	Tyres	Capacity/Car/Engine	Comment	Q Pos/Entries
ret	ARGENTINE GP	Buenos Aires	34	Marlboro BRM	F	3.0 BRM P160C V12	oil pressure	13/19
8	BRAZILIAN GP	Interlagos	16	Marlboro BRM	F	3.0 BRM P160C V12	stopped – electrics/2 laps behind	13/20
ret	SOUTH AFRICAN GP	Kyalami	17	Marlboro BRM	F	3.0 BRM P160D V12	engine	10/25
ret	SPANISH GP	Montjuich Park	16	Marlboro BRM	F	3.0 BRM P160E V12	tyres	11/22
5	BELGIAN GP	Zolder	21	Marlboro BRM	F	3.0 BRM P160E V12	pit stop – fuel/1 lap behind	14/23
ret	MONACO GP	Monte Carlo	21	Marlboro BRM	F	3.0 BRM P160E V12	gearbox	6/26
13	SWEDISH GP	Anderstorp	21	Marlboro BRM	F	3.0 BRM P160E V12	pit stop – engine/5 laps behind	15/22
9	FRENCH GP	Paul Ricard	21	Marlboro BRM	F	3.0 BRM P160E V12		17/25
12	BRITISH GP	Silverstone	21	Marlboro BRM	F	3.0 BRM P160E V12	pit stop – tyres/4 laps behind	=8/29
ret	DUTCH GP	Zandvoort	21	Marlboro BRM	F	3.0 BRM P160E V12	tyres/fuel pump	11/24
ret	GERMAN GP	Nürburgring	21	Marlboro BRM	F	3.0 BRM P160E V12	crashed – fractured wrist	5/23
dns	AUSTRIAN GP	Österreichring	21	Marlboro BRM	F	3.0 BRM P160E V12	still in pain from German GP injury	(25)/25
ret	ITALIAN GP	Monza	21	Marlboro BRM	F	3.0 BRM P160E V12	tyre failure – accident	15/25
ret	CANADIAN GP	Mosport Park	21	Marlboro BRM	F	3.0 BRM P160E V12	transmission	8/26
ret	US GP	Watkins Glen	21	Marlboro BRM	F	3.0 BRM P160E V12	fuel pump	22/28

1974 Championship position: 4th Wins: 2 Pole positions: 9 Fastest laps: 3 Points scored: 38

	Race	Circuit	No	Entrant	Tyres	Capacity/Car/Engine	Comment	Q Pos/Entries
2	ARGENTINE GP	Buenos Aires	12	Scuderia Ferrari SpA SEFAC	G	3.0 Ferrari 312B3 F12		8/26
ret	BRAZILIAN GP	Interlagos	12	Scuderia Ferrari SpA SEFAC	G	3.0 Ferrari 312B3 F12	broken wing stay	3/25
16/ret	SOUTH AFRICAN GP	Kyalami	12	Scuderia Ferrari SpA SEFAC	G	3.0 Ferrari 312B3 F12	ignition/4 laps behind	1/27
1	SPANISH GP	Jarama	12	Scuderia Ferrari SpA SEFAC	G	3.0 Ferrari 312B3 F12	FL	1/28
2	BELGIAN GP	Nivelles	12	Scuderia Ferrari SpA SEFAC	G	3.0 Ferrari 312B3 F12		3/32
ret	MONACO GP	Monte Carlo	12	Scuderia Ferrari SpA SEFAC	G	3.0 Ferrari 312B3 F12	ignition	1/28
ret	SWEDISH GP	Anderstorp	12	Scuderia Ferrari SpA SEFAC	G	3.0 Ferrari 312B3 F12	transmission	3/28
1	DUTCH GP	Zandvoort	12	Scuderia Ferrari SpA SEFAC	G	3.0 Ferrari 312B3 F12		1/27
2	FRENCH GP	Dijon	12	Scuderia Ferrari SpA SEFAC	G	3.0 Ferrari 312B3 F12		1/30
5	BRITISH GP	Brands Hatch	12	Scuderia Ferrari SpA SEFAC	G	3.0 Ferrari 312B3 F12	trapped in blocked pits/1 lap behind/FL	=1/34
ret	GERMAN GP	Nürburgring	12	Scuderia Ferrari SpA SEFAC	G	3.0 Ferrari 312B3 F12	hit Scheckter	1/32
ret	AUSTRIAN GP	Österreichring	12	Scuderia Ferrari SpA SEFAC	G	3.0 Ferrari 312B3 F12	engine	1/31
ret	ITALIAN GP	Monza	12	Scuderia Ferrari SpA SEFAC	G	3.0 Ferrari 312B3 F12	engine	1/31
ret	CANADIAN GP	Mosport Park	12	Scuderia Ferrari SpA SEFAC	G	3.0 Ferrari 312B3 F12	hit barrier when leading/FL	2/30
ret	US GP	Watkins Glen	12	Scuderia Ferrari SpA SEFAC	G	3.0 Ferrari 312B3 F12	front suspension	5/30

1975 WORLD CHAMPION Wins: 5 Pole positions: 9 Fastest laps: 2 Points scored: 64.5

	Race	Circuit	No	Entrant	Tyres	Capacity/Car/Engine	Comment	Q Pos/Entries
6	ARGENTINE GP	Buenos Aires	12	Scuderia Ferrari SpA SEFAC	G	3.0 Ferrari 312B3 F12		4/23
5	BRAZILIAN GP	Interlagos	12	Scuderia Ferrari SpA SEFAC	G	3.0 Ferrari 312B3 F12		4/23
5	SOUTH AFRICAN GP	Kyalami	12	Scuderia Ferrari SpA SEFAC	G	3.0 Ferrari 312T F12		4/28
dns	"	"	12	Scuderia Ferrari SpA SEFAC	G	3.0 Ferrari 312B3 F12	practice only	- / -
ret	SPANISH GP	Montjuich Park	12	Scuderia Ferrari SpA SEFAC	G	3.0 Ferrari 312T F12	hit by Andretti	1/26
1	MONACO GP	Monte Carlo	12	Scuderia Ferrari SpA SEFAC	G	3.0 Ferrari 312T F12		1/26
1	BELGIAN GP	Zolder	12	Scuderia Ferrari SpA SEFAC	G	3.0 Ferrari 312T F12		1/24
1	SWEDISH GP	Anderstorp	12	Scuderia Ferrari SpA SEFAC	G	3.0 Ferrari 312T F12	FL	5/26
2	DUTCH GP	Zandvoort	12	Scuderia Ferrari SpA SEFAC	G	3.0 Ferrari 312T F12	FL	1/25
1	FRENCH GP	Paul Ricard	12	Scuderia Ferrari SpA SEFAC	G	3.0 Ferrari 312T F12		1/26
8	BRITISH GP	Silverstone	12	Scuderia Ferrari SpA SEFAC	G	3.0 Ferrari 312T F12	2 laps behind	3/28
3	GERMAN GP	Nürburgring	12	Scuderia Ferrari SpA SEFAC	G	3.0 Ferrari 312T F12	pit stops – tyre problems	1/26
6*	AUSTRIAN GP	Österreichring	12	Scuderia Ferrari SpA SEFAC	G	3.0 Ferrari 312T F12	*rain shortened race – half points	1/30
3	ITALIAN GP	Monza	12	Scuderia Ferrari SpA SEFAC	G	3.0 Ferrari 312T F12		1/28
1	US GP	Watkins Glen	12	Scuderia Ferrari SpA SEFAC	G	3.0 Ferrari 312T F12		1/24

1976 Championship position: 2nd Wins: 4 Pole positions: 3 Fastest laps: 4 Points scored: 68

	Race	Circuit	No	Entrant	Tyres	Capacity/Car/Engine	Comment	Q Pos/Entries
1	BRAZILIAN GP	Interlagos	1	Scuderia Ferrari SpA SEFAC	G	3.0 Ferrari 312T F12		2/22
1	SOUTH AFRICAN GP	Kyalami	1	Scuderia Ferrari SpA SEFAC	G	3.0 Ferrari 312T F12	FL	2/25
2	US GP WEST	Long Beach	1	Scuderia Ferrari SpA SEFAC	G	3.0 Ferrari 312T F12		4/27
2	SPANISH GP	Jarama	1	Scuderia Ferrari SpA SEFAC	G	3.0 Ferrari 312T2 F12		2/30
1	BELGIAN GP	Zolder	1	Scuderia Ferrari SpA SEFAC	G	3.0 Ferrari 312T2 F12	FL	1/29
dns	"	"	1	Scuderia Ferrari SpA SEFAC	G	3.0 Ferrari 312T F12	practice only	- / -
1	MONACO GP	Monte Carlo	1	Scuderia Ferrari SpA SEFAC	G	3.0 Ferrari 312T2 F12		1/25
3	SWEDISH GP	Anderstorp	1	Scuderia Ferrari SpA SEFAC	G	3.0 Ferrari 312T2 F12		5/27
ret	FRENCH GP	Paul Ricard	1	Scuderia Ferrari SpA SEFAC	G	3.0 Ferrari 312T2 F12	engine/FL	2/30
1*	BRITISH GP	Brands Hatch	1	Scuderia Ferrari SpA SEFAC	G	3.0 Ferrari 312T2 F12	*1st place car disqualified/FL	1/30

ret/dns*	GERMAN GP	Nürburgring	1	Scuderia Ferrari SpA SEFAC	G	3.0 Ferrari 312T2 F12	*accident at first start – badly burnt	2/28
4	ITALIAN GP	Monza	1	Scuderia Ferrari SpA SEFAC	G	3.0 Ferrari 312T2 F12		5/29
8	CANADIAN GP	Mosport Park	1	Scuderia Ferrari SpA SEFAC	G	3.0 Ferrari 312T2 F12		6/27
3	US GP EAST	Watkins Glen	1	Scuderia Ferrari SpA SEFAC	G	3.0 Ferrari 312T2 F12		5/27
ret	JAPANESE GP	Mount Fuji	1	Scuderia Ferrari SpA SEFAC	G	3.0 Ferrari 312T2 F12	withdrew due to weather conditions	3/27

1977 WORLD CHAMPION Wins: 3 Pole positions: 2 Fastest laps: 3 Points scored: 72

ret	ARGENTINE GP	Buenos Aires	11	Scuderia Ferrari SpA SEFAC	G	3.0 Ferrari 312T2 F12	fuel metering unit	4/21
3	BRAZILIAN GP	Interlagos	11	Scuderia Ferrari SpA SEFAC	G	3.0 Ferrari 312T2 F12		13/22
1	SOUTH AFRICAN GP	Kyalami	11	Scuderia Ferrari SpA SEFAC	G	3.0 Ferrari 312T2 F12		3/23
2	US GP WEST	Long Beach	11	Scuderia Ferrari SpA SEFAC	G	3.0 Ferrari 312T2 F12	FL	1/22
dns	SPANISH GP	Jarama	11	Scuderia Ferrari SpA SEFAC	G	3.0 Ferrari 312T2 F12	broken rib in Sunday a.m. warm-up	(3)/31
2	MONACO GP	Monte Carlo	11	Scuderia Ferrari SpA SEFAC	G	3.0 Ferrari 312T2 F12		6/26
2	BELGIAN GP	Zolder	11	Scuderia Ferrari SpA SEFAC	G	3.0 Ferrari 312T2 F12		11/32
ret	SWEDISH GP	Anderstorp	11	Scuderia Ferrari SpA SEFAC	G	3.0 Ferrari 312T2 F12	handling	15/31
5	FRENCH GP	Dijon	11	Scuderia Ferrari SpA SEFAC	G	3.0 Ferrari 312T2 F12		9/30
2	BRITISH GP	Silverstone	11	Scuderia Ferrari SpA SEFAC	G	3.0 Ferrari 312T2 F12		3/36
1	GERMAN GP	Hockenheim	11	Scuderia Ferrari SpA SEFAC	G	3.0 Ferrari 312T2 F12	FL	3/30
2	AUSTRIAN GP	Österreichring	11	Scuderia Ferrari SpA SEFAC	G	3.0 Ferrari 312T2 F12		1/30
1	DUTCH GP	Zandvoort	11	Scuderia Ferrari SpA SEFAC	G	3.0 Ferrari 312T2 F12	FL	4/34
2	ITALIAN GP	Monza	11	Scuderia Ferrari SpA SEFAC	G	3.0 Ferrari 312T2 F12		5/34
4	US GP EAST	Watkins Glen	11	Scuderia Ferrari SpA SEFAC	G	3.0 Ferrari 312T2 F12		7/27

1978 Championship position: 4th Wins: 2 Pole positions: 1 Fastest laps: 4 Points scored: 44

2	ARGENTINE GP	Buenos Aires	1	Parmalat Racing Team	G	3.0 Brabham BT45C-Alfa Romeo F12		5/27
3	BRAZILIAN GP	Rio	1	Parmalat Racing Team	G	3.0 Brabham BT45C-Alfa Romeo F12		10/28
ret	SOUTH AFRICAN GP	Kyalami	1	Parmalat Racing Team	G	3.0 Brabham BT46-Alfa Romeo F12	engine	1/30
ret	US GP WEST	Long Beach	1	Parmalat Racing Team	G	3.0 Brabham BT46-Alfa Romeo F12	ignition	3/30
2	MONACO GP	Monte Carlo	1	Parmalat Racing Team	G	3.0 Brabham BT46-Alfa Romeo F12	FL	3/30
ret	BELGIAN GP	Zolder	1	Parmalat Racing Team	G	3.0 Brabham BT46-Alfa Romeo F12	hit by Scheckter at start	3/30
ret	SPANISH GP	Jarama	1	Parmalat Racing Team	G	3.0 Brabham BT46-Alfa Romeo F12	engine	6/29
1	SWEDISH GP	Anderstorp	1	Parmalat Racing Team	G	3.0 Brabham BT46B-Alfa Romeo F12	only win for fan car/FL	3/27
ret	FRENCH GP	Paul Ricard	1	Parmalat Racing Team	G	3.0 Brabham BT46-Alfa Romeo F12	engine	3/29
2	BRITISH GP	Brands Hatch	1	Parmalat Racing Team	G	3.0 Brabham BT46-Alfa Romeo F12	FL	4/30
ret	GERMAN GP	Hockenheim	1	Parmalat Racing Team	G	3.0 Brabham BT46-Alfa Romeo F12	engine	3/30
dns	"	"	1	Parmalat Racing Team	G	3.0 Brabham BT46C-Alfa Romeo F12	practice only	- / -
ret	AUSTRIAN GP	Österreichring	1	Parmalat Racing Team	G	3.0 Brabham BT46-Alfa Romeo F12	crashed	12/31
3	DUTCH GP	Zandvoort	1	Parmalat Racing Team	G	3.0 Brabham BT46-Alfa Romeo F12	FL	3/33
1*	ITALIAN GP	Monza	1	Parmalat Racing Team	G	3.0 Brabham BT46-Alfa Romeo F12	*1st & 2nd cars penalised 1 minute	4/32
ret	US GP EAST	Watkins Glen	1	Parmalat Racing Team	G	3.0 Brabham BT46-Alfa Romeo F12	engine	5/27
ret	CANADIAN GP	Montreal	1	Parmalat Racing Team	G	3.0 Brabham BT46-Alfa Romeo F12	brakes – accident	7/28

Niki Lauda, in his Ferrari 312T2, battles with Mario Andretti during the 1977 Dutch Grand Prix at Zandvoort.

Niki Lauda took his third world championship in 1984, beating team-mate Alain Prost by a mere half-point. One of his five wins came in the French Grand Prix, held at the Dijon track.

	1979 Championship position: 14th		Wins: 0	Pole positions: 0		Fastest laps: 0	Points scored: 4		
ret	ARGENTINE GP	Buenos Aires	5	Parmalat Racing Team	G	3.0 Brabham BT48-Alfa Romeo V12	fuel pressure		– / –
dns	"	" "	5	Parmalat Racing Team	G	3.0 Brabham BT46-Alfa Romeo F12	practice only – set grid time		23/26
ret	BRAZILIAN GP	Interlagos	5	Parmalat Racing Team	G	3.0 Brabham BT48-Alfa Romeo V12	gear linkage		12/26
6	SOUTH AFRICAN GP	Kyalami	5	Parmalat Racing Team	G	3.0 Brabham BT48-Alfa Romeo V12	pit stop – tyres/1 lap behind		4/26
ret	US GP WEST	Long Beach	5	Parmalat Racing Team	G	3.0 Brabham BT48-Alfa Romeo V12	collision with Tambay		11/26
ret	SPANISH GP	Jarama	5	Parmalat Racing Team	G	3.0 Brabham BT48-Alfa Romeo V12	water leak		6/27
ret	BELGIAN GP	Zolder	5	Parmalat Racing Team	G	3.0 Brabham BT48-Alfa Romeo V12	engine		13/28
ret	MONACO GP	Monte Carlo	5	Parmalat Racing Team	G	3.0 Brabham BT48-Alfa Romeo V12	accident with Pironi		4/25
ret	FRENCH GP	Dijon	5	Parmalat Racing Team	G	3.0 Brabham BT48-Alfa Romeo V12	spun off – could not restart		6/27
ret	BRITISH GP	Silverstone	5	Parmalat Racing Team	G	3.0 Brabham BT48-Alfa Romeo V12	brakes		6/26
ret	GERMAN GP	Hockenheim	5	Parmalat Racing Team	G	3.0 Brabham BT48-Alfa Romeo V12	engine		7/26
ret	AUSTRIAN GP	Österreichring	5	Parmalat Racing Team	G	3.0 Brabham BT48-Alfa Romeo V12	oil leak		4/26
ret	DUTCH GP	Zandvoort	5	Parmalat Racing Team	G	3.0 Brabham BT48-Alfa Romeo V12	withdrew – wrist injury		9/26
4	ITALIAN GP	Monza	5	Parmalat Racing Team	G	3.0 Brabham BT48-Alfa Romeo V12			9/28
dnp	CANADIAN GP	Montreal	5	Parmalat Racing Team	G	3.0 Brabham BT49-Cosworth V8	quit after Friday a.m. practice		– / –
	1982 Championship position: 5th		Wins: 2	Pole positions: 0		Fastest laps: 1	Points scored: 30		
4	SOUTH AFRICAN GP	Kyalami	8	Marlboro McLaren International	M	3.0 McLaren MP4-Cosworth V8			13/30
ret	BRAZILIAN GP	Rio	8	Marlboro McLaren International	M	3.0 McLaren MP4B-Cosworth V8	hit by Reutemann		5/31
1	US GP WEST	Long Beach	8	Marlboro McLaren International	M	3.0 McLaren MP4B-Cosworth V8	FL		2/31
dsq*	BELGIAN GP	Zolder	8	Marlboro McLaren International	M	3.0 McLaren MP4B-Cosworth V8	3rd on road/*car underweight		4/32
ret	MONACO GP	Monte Carlo	8	Marlboro McLaren International	M	3.0 McLaren MP4B-Cosworth V8	engine		12/31
ret	US GP (DETROIT)	Detroit	8	Marlboro McLaren International	M	3.0 McLaren MP4B-Cosworth V8	hit Rosberg		10/28
ret	CANADIAN GP	Montreal	8	Marlboro McLaren International	M	3.0 McLaren MP4B-Cosworth V8	clutch		11/29
4	DUTCH GP	Zandvoort	8	Marlboro McLaren International	M	3.0 McLaren MP4B-Cosworth V8			5/31
1	BRITISH GP	Brands Hatch	8	Marlboro McLaren International	M	3.0 McLaren MP4B-Cosworth V8			5/30
8	FRENCH GP	Paul Ricard	8	Marlboro McLaren International	M	3.0 McLaren MP4B-Cosworth V8	pit stop – tyres/1 lap behind		9/30
dns	GERMAN GP	Hockenheim	8	Marlboro McLaren International	M	3.0 McLaren MP4B-Cosworth V8	hurt wrist in practice		(8)/30
5	AUSTRIAN GP	Österreichring	8	Marlboro McLaren International	M	3.0 McLaren MP4B-Cosworth V8	1 lap behind		10/29
3	SWISS GP	Dijon	8	Marlboro McLaren International	M	3.0 McLaren MP4B-Cosworth V8			4/29
ret	ITALIAN GP	Monza	8	Marlboro McLaren International	M	3.0 McLaren MP4B-Cosworth V8	handling/brakes		10/30
ret	CAESARS PALACE GP	Las Vegas	8	Marlboro McLaren International	M	3.0 McLaren MP4B-Cosworth V8	engine		13/30
	1983 Championship position: 10th		Wins: 0	Pole positions: 0		Fastest laps: 1	Points scored: 12		
3	BRAZILIAN GP	Rio	8	Marlboro McLaren International	M	3.0 McLaren MP4/1C-Cosworth V8			9/27
2	US GP WEST	Long Beach	8	Marlboro McLaren International	M	3.0 McLaren MP4/1C-Cosworth V8	FL		23/28
ret	FRENCH GP	Paul Ricard	8	Marlboro McLaren International	M	3.0 McLaren MP4/1C-Cosworth V8	wheel bearing		12/29
ret	SAN MARINO GP	Imola	8	Marlboro McLaren International	M	3.0 McLaren MP4/1C-Cosworth V8	hit barrier		18/28
dnq	MONACO GP	Monte Carlo	8	Marlboro McLaren International	M	3.0 McLaren MP4/1C-Cosworth V8			22/28

	Race	Circuit	No	Entrant	Tyres	Capacity/Car/Engine	Comment	Q Pos/Entries
ret	BELGIAN GP	Spa	8	Marlboro McLaren International	M	3.0 McLaren MP4/1C-Cosworth V8	engine	15/28
ret	US GP (DETROIT)	Detroit	8	Marlboro McLaren International	M	3.0 McLaren MP4/1C-Cosworth V8	shock absorber	18/27
ret	CANADIAN GP	Montreal	8	Marlboro McLaren International	M	3.0 McLaren MP4/1C-Cosworth V8	spun off – could not restart	19/28
6	BRITISH GP	Silverstone	8	Marlboro McLaren International	M	3.0 McLaren MP4/1C-Cosworth V8	pit stop – tyres/1 lap behind	15/29
dsq*	GERMAN GP	Hockenheim	8	Marlboro McLaren International	M	3.0 McLaren MP4/1C-Cosworth V8	5th on road/*reversed into pits	18/29
6	AUSTRIAN GP	Österreichring	8	Marlboro McLaren International	M	3.0 McLaren MP4/1C-Cosworth V8	pit stop – tyres/2 laps behind	14/29
ret	DUTCH GP	Zandvoort	8	Marlboro McLaren International	M	1.5 t/c McLaren MP4/1E-TAG V6	brakes	19/29
ret	ITALIAN GP	Monza	8	Marlboro McLaren International	M	1.5 t/c McLaren MP4/1E-TAG V6	electrics	13/29
ret	EUROPEAN GP	Brands Hatch	8	Marlboro McLaren International	M	1.5 t/c McLaren MP4/1E-TAG V6	engine	13/29
11/ret	SOUTH AFRICAN GP	Kyalami	8	Marlboro McLaren International	M	1.5 t/c McLaren MP4/1E-TAG V6	electrics/6 laps behind	12/26

1984 WORLD CHAMPION   Wins: 5   Pole positions: 0   Fastest laps: 5   Points scored: 72

	Race	Circuit	No	Entrant	Tyres	Capacity/Car/Engine	Comment	Q Pos/Entries
ret	BRAZILIAN GP	Rio	8	Marlboro McLaren International	M	1.5 t/c McLaren MP4/2-TAG V6	electrics	6/27
1	SOUTH AFRICAN GP	Kyalami	8	Marlboro McLaren International	M	1.5 t/c McLaren MP4/2-TAG V6		8/27
ret	BELGIAN GP	Zolder	8	Marlboro McLaren International	M	1.5 t/c McLaren MP4/2-TAG V6	water pump	14/27
ret	SAN MARINO GP	Imola	8	Marlboro McLaren International	M	1.5 t/c McLaren MP4/2-TAG V6	engine	5/28
1	FRENCH GP	Dijon	8	Marlboro McLaren International	M	1.5 t/c McLaren MP4/2-TAG V6		9/27
ret	MONACO GP	Monte Carlo	8	Marlboro McLaren International	M	1.5 t/c McLaren MP4/2-TAG V6	spun off	8/27
2	CANADIAN GP	Montreal	8	Marlboro McLaren International	M	1.5 t/c McLaren MP4/2-TAG V6		8/26
ret	US GP (DETROIT)	Detroit	8	Marlboro McLaren International	M	1.5 t/c McLaren MP4/2-TAG V6	electrics	10/27
9/ret	US GP (DALLAS)	Dallas	8	Marlboro McLaren International	M	1.5 t/c McLaren MP4/2-TAG V6	hit wall/FL/7 laps behind	5/27
1	BRITISH GP	Brands Hatch	8	Marlboro McLaren International	M	1.5 t/c McLaren MP4/2-TAG V6	FL	3/27
2	GERMAN GP	Hockenheim	8	Marlboro McLaren International	M	1.5 t/c McLaren MP4/2-TAG V6		7/27
1	AUSTRIAN GP	Österreichring	8	Marlboro McLaren International	M	1.5 t/c McLaren MP4/2-TAG V6	FL	4/28
2	DUTCH GP	Zandvoort	8	Marlboro McLaren International	M	1.5 t/c McLaren MP4/2-TAG V6		6/27
1	ITALIAN GP	Monza	8	Marlboro McLaren International	M	1.5 t/c McLaren MP4/2-TAG V6	FL	4/27
4	EUROPEAN GP	Nürburgring	8	Marlboro McLaren International	M	1.5 t/c McLaren MP4/2-TAG V6		15/26
2	PORTUGESE GP	Estoril	8	Marlboro McLaren International	M	1.5 t/c McLaren MP4/2-TAG V6	FL	11/27

1985   Championship position: 10th   Wins: 1   Pole positions: 0   Fastest laps: 1   Points scored: 14

	Race	Circuit	No	Entrant	Tyres	Capacity/Car/Engine	Comment	Q Pos/Entries
ret	BRAZILIAN GP	Rio	1	Marlboro McLaren International	G	1.5 t/c McLaren MP4/2B-TAG V6	fuel metering unit	9/25
ret	PORTUGESE GP	Estoril	1	Marlboro McLaren International	G	1.5 t/c McLaren MP4/2B-TAG V6	engine	7/26
4	SAN MARINO GP	Imola	1	Marlboro McLaren International	G	1.5 t/c McLaren MP4/2B-TAG V6	gearbox problems/1 lap behind	8/26
ret	MONACO GP	Monte Carlo	1	Marlboro McLaren International	G	1.5 t/c McLaren MP4/2B-TAG V6	spun off – could not restart	14/26
ret	CANADIAN GP	Montreal	1	Marlboro McLaren International	G	1.5 t/c McLaren MP4/2B-TAG V6	engine	17/25
ret	US GP (DETROIT)	Detroit	1	Marlboro McLaren International	G	1.5 t/c McLaren MP4/2B-TAG V6	brakes	12/25
ret	FRENCH GP	Paul Ricard	1	Marlboro McLaren International	G	1.5 t/c McLaren MP4/2B-TAG V6	gearbox	6/26
ret	BRITISH GP	Silverstone	1	Marlboro McLaren International	G	1.5 t/c McLaren MP4/2B-TAG V6	electrics	10/26
5	GERMAN GP	Nürburgring	1	Marlboro McLaren International	G	1.5 t/c McLaren MP4/2B-TAG V6	pit stop – loose wheel/FL	12/27
ret	AUSTRIAN GP	Österreichring	1	Marlboro McLaren International	G	1.5 t/c McLaren MP4/2B-TAG V6	engine	3/27
1	DUTCH GP	Zandvoort	1	Marlboro McLaren International	G	1.5 t/c McLaren MP4/2B-TAG V6		10/27
ret	ITALIAN GP	Monza	1	Marlboro McLaren International	G	1.5 t/c McLaren MP4/2B-TAG V6	transmission	16/26
dns	BELGIAN GP	Spa	1	Marlboro McLaren International	G	1.5 t/c McLaren MP4/2B-TAG V6	injured wrist in practice accident	– / –
ret	SOUTH AFRICAN GP	Kyalami	1	Marlboro McLaren International	G	1.5 t/c McLaren MP4/2B-TAG V6	turbo	8/21
ret	AUSTRALIAN GP	Adelaide	1	Marlboro McLaren International	G	1.5 t/c McLaren MP4/2B-TAG V6	brake problem – hit wall	16/25

GP Starts: 170 (171)   GP Wins: 25   Pole positions: 24   Fastest laps: 24   Points: 420.5

ROGER LAURENT

A MEMBER of the famed Ecurie Belgique, Roger Laurent raced the team's Veritas RS, before making occasional appearances in their newly acquired Lago-Talbot in 1951, taking seventh place at Albi. The following year, he ventured to Helsinki to win an F1 race against entirely local opposition, without an F1 car among them!

Subsequently renamed Ecurie Francorchamps, the team ran a Ferrari T500 in 1952, but with Charles de Tornaco behind the wheel at Spa, Laurent hired an HWM for the grand prix. It was his turn to try the T500 in the German GP, and he finished a solid sixth. He coaxed a few other decent placings from the yellow-painted machine, most notably second at Chimay in 1953 and fourth at Syracuse in 1954.

Laurent also enjoyed quite a successful time in the team's sports car programme, particularly when the Jaguar XK120 was replaced by a C-Type in 1954. He was third in the Dutch GP for sports machines and, with Jacques Swaters, third at Reims and then fourth at Le Mans. A crash in practice for a race at Bari in 1955 left him with a broken leg, but he returned when fit.

Roger's final racing season was in 1956, when once again he took fourth place at Le Mans in a Jaguar D-Type, shared with Freddy Rouselle.

LAURENT, Roger (B)   b 21/2/1913, Liège – d 6/2/1977, Uccle

1952   Championship position: Unplaced

	Race	Circuit	No	Entrant	Tyres	Capacity/Car/Engine	Comment	Q Pos/Entries
12	BELGIAN GP	Spa	30	HW Motors Ltd	D	2.0 HWM-Alta 4	4 laps behind	20/22
6	GERMAN GP	Nürburgring	119	Ecurie Francorchamps	E	2.0 Ferrari 500 4	2 laps behind	17/32

GP Starts: 2   GP Wins: 0   Pole positions: 0   Fastest laps: 0   Points: 0

GIOVANNI LAVAGGI

AN Italian of noble ancestry, Giovanni Lavaggi is a former consultant engineer with a degree in mechanical engineering from Milan University. He began competing in local rallies, but then got his kicks skiing and hang-gliding, until a broken leg ended this sometimes dangerous pastime. Despite parental discouragement, he returned to motorsport on the tracks, rather than gravel, and quickly found a niche, successfully handling a Kremer Porsche 962 sports car in 1989. With Formula 1 his long-term aim, however, he cut down on his business commitments to spend a preparatory year in F3000. His 1992 season with Crypton was disappointing to say the least: he failed to qualify for eight of ten races.

Undaunted by the collapse of the March F1 team, for whom he had hoped to drive, the personable and friendly Lavaggi enjoyed a year in Interserie, where he emerged as the champion, and had a brief tilt at Indy car racing in 1994, before raising enough finance to buy his four-race stint at Pacific in 1995. He briefly returned to the grand prix stage once more the following season with cash-strapped Minardi, where, to his credit, he was not that far off the pace of team-mate Pedro Lamy. Results, inevitably perhaps, may not have been achieved, but Lavaggi enjoyed every moment of his spell in Formula 1, jauntily filling the paddock with his own sense of film-star fun and glamour!

In reality, Lavaggi had found his true level in sports car racing, his victory in the 1995 Daytona 24-hour race, in which he shared a Kremer Porsche, being the undoubted highlight of his career. When his flourishing business interests allowed, he was an enthusiastic owner-driver in the World Sportscar Championship, initially with a Ferrari. In 2001, he scored an unlikely win in the Monza 1000km with a Ferrari 333SP, after being beached in the gravel. In 2006, he also became the constructor of his own machine, the Lavaggi LS1, but little was achieved with this protoype.

CHRIS LAWRENCE

A CLUB driver from the late 1950s in MGs and particularly Morgans, with which he clocked up some modest triumphs, Chris Lawrence ran a London engine tuning business and became involved in the ill-fated Deep-Sanderson sports car project of 1963/64.

With the introduction of the 3-litre formula in 1966, Chris raced a shoestring Cooper T73-Ferrari special, which he took to fifth place in the Gold Cup race at Oulton Park, before his two grand prix appearances. In 1967, he finished eighth (and last) in the Race of Champions, after which the cars were destroyed by fire at Silverstone. Then he worked in France, designing a luxury Grand Tourer called the Monica. Sadly this project foundered in the oil crisis of the early 1970s, which had an adverse effect on his business.

Chris spent the next 15 years in America, mainly fettling classic cars, before returning to Britain in 1992 to work briefly for Marcos. Then he approached Charles Morgan and persuaded him to agree to the production of a completely new car, the futuristic Aero 8, which could be used on both road and track. He had the immense satisfaction of seeing his creation race to the finish at Le Mans in 2004. The Aero is a fine legacy of Chris, who died from cancer in 2011. It ensured that the Malvern-based Morgan Motor Company had a machine that was more relevant to 21st-century motoring to market alongside its ever-popular classic models.

LAVAGGI, Giovanni (I) b 18/2/1958, Sicily

1995 Championship position: Unplaced

	Race	Circuit	No	Entrant	Tyres	Capacity/Car/Engine	Comment	Q Pos/Entries
ret	GERMAN GP	Hockenheim	16	Pacific Grand Prix Ltd	G	3.0 Pacific PR02-Ford ED V8	gearbox	24/24
ret	HUNGARIAN GP	Hungaroring	16	Pacific Grand Prix Ltd	G	3.0 Pacific PR02-Ford ED V8	spun off	24/24
ret	BELGIAN GP	Spa	16	Pacific Grand Prix Ltd	G	3.0 Pacific PR02-Ford ED V8	gearbox	23/24
ret	ITALIAN GP	Monza	16	Pacific Grand Prix Ltd	G	3.0 Pacific PR02-Ford ED V8	spun off	24/24

1996 Championship position: Unplaced

	Race	Circuit	No	Entrant	Tyres	Capacity/Car/Engine	Comment	Q Pos/Entries
dnq	GERMAN GP	Hockenheim	21	Minardi Team	G	3.0 Minardi 195B-Ford EDM V8	not within 107% of pole time	20/20
10/ret	HUNGARIAN GP	Hungaroring	21	Minardi Team	G	3.0 Minardi 195B-Ford EDM V8	spun off/8 laps behind	20/20
dnq	BELGIAN GP	Spa	21	Minardi Team	G	3.0 Minardi 195B-Ford EDM V8	not within 107% of pole time	20/20
ret	ITALIAN GP	Monza	21	Minardi Team	G	3.0 Minardi 195B-Ford EDM V8	engine	20/20
15	PORTUGUESE GP	Estoril	21	Minardi Team	G	3.0 Minardi 195B-Ford EDM V8	5 laps behind	20/20
dnq	JAPANESE GP	Suzuka	21	Minardi Team	G	3.0 Minardi 195B-Ford EDM V8	not within 107% of pole time	20/20

GP Starts: 7   GP Wins: 0   Pole positions: 0   Fastest laps: 0   Points: 0

LAWRENCE, Chris (GB) b 27/7/1933, Ealing, London – d 13/8/2011, Burghill, Herefordshire

1966 Championship position: Unplaced

	Race	Circuit	No	Entrant	Tyres	Capacity/Car/Engine	Comment	Q Pos/Entries
11	BRITISH GP	Brands Hatch	24	J A Pearce Engineering Ltd	D	2.9 Cooper T73-Ferrari V12	7 laps behind	19/20
ret	GERMAN GP	Nürburgring	20	J A Pearce Engineering Ltd	D	2.9 Cooper T73-Ferrari V12	front suspension	27/30

GP Starts: 2   GP Wins: 0   Pole positions: 0   Fastest laps: 0   Points: 0

MICHEL LECLÈRE

A RELATIVELY late starter at 22, Michel Leclère began racing in the Renault 8A Challenge series, before embarking on a single-seater career in 1970 in Alpine Formula France. Steady progress followed as he tidied up his hitherto rough-and-ready driving style to take championship honours the following season. This gained him promotion to the French F3 championship and a seat in the works Alpine-Renault. He won first time out and put in some stellar performances, such as his wins at Rouen and at Thruxton, to take the title after holding off a strong challenge from Jacques Coulon's Martini. Frustratingly, he was forced to remain in situ for 1973, when he was unable to beat Jacques Laffite's Martini. Elf finally moved him up to their F2 works outfit for 1974, when he did a solid job in a learning season, taking good placings, but no wins.

Victories would come, however, in the following season, when Michel was placed in the Elf March Team. After a difficult period of adjustment, he won races at Rouen, Zolder and Silverstone, to take second in the final standings, earning an F1 debut with Tyrrell and a grand prix contract with Wolf-Williams for 1976.

In the event, the car was awful and the team despondent, and poor Leclère was jettisoned in mid-season, along with the once great Jacky Ickx, who was no faster in the recalcitrant machine. The Frenchman returned to familiar F2 territory with the Elf-Renault to take fourth in the championship. Sadly his career never really recovered after a disastrous F2 season with Kauhsen in 1977, which destroyed any chance of a Formula 1 comeback. Thereafter, he scratched about with only occasional sports car and single-seater outings before quitting for good.

Subsequently, he used his experience to offer his services as a high-performance driving instructor. Recently he has been involved with the Renault H&C Classic Team, demonstrating some of their stable of historic Formula 1 cars at events around Europe.

NEVILLE LEDERLE

R IGHTLY regarded as one of his country's outstanding prospects, Neville Lederle made an immediate impression on South African racing with his Lotus 18 late in 1961. This promise was confirmed the following year, when he finished sixth in the South African GP, to score a point in what would be his only grand prix start. This achievement proved to be a double-edged sword, however, for he was classed as a graded driver and therefore was not eligible to score points in Formula Junior or national races outside South Africa.

Neville stayed at home in 1963, dominating his domestic series with a string of wins in his Lotus 21, until a practice accident at the Rand nine-hours sports car race left him sidelined with a broken leg. He missed that year's grand prix and also the 1964 Springbok series, after his injury proved very slow to heal. This, coupled with increasing business commitments, prompted his retirement, although he did bring the old Lotus out for the end-of-season Rand Grand Prix and the South African Grand Prix in January 1965, when, as fastest non-qualifier, he just failed to make the grid.

LECLÈRE, Michel (F) b 18/3/1946, Mantes la Jolie, nr Paris

	1975 Championship position: Unplaced							
	Race	Circuit	No	Entrant	Tyres	Capacity/Car/Engine	Comment	Q Pos/Entries
ret	US GP	Watkins Glen	15	Elf Team Tyrrell	G	3.0 Tyrrell 007-Cosworth V8	engine	20/24
	1976 Championship position: Unplaced							
13	SOUTH AFRICAN GP	Kyalami	21	Frank Williams Racing Cars	G	3.0 Williams FW05-Cosworth V8	2 laps behind	22/25
dnq	US GP WEST	Long Beach	21	Frank Williams Racing Cars	G	3.0 Williams FW05-Cosworth V8		21/27
10	SPANISH GP	Jarama	21	Walter Wolf Racing	G	3.0 Williams FW05-Cosworth V8	2 laps behind	23/30
11	BELGIAN GP	Zolder	21	Walter Wolf Racing	G	3.0 Williams FW05-Cosworth V8	2 laps behind	25/29
11	MONACO GP	Monte Carlo	21	Walter Wolf Racing	G	3.0 Williams FW05-Cosworth V8	2 laps behind	18/25
ret	SWEDISH GP	Anderstorp	21	Walter Wolf Racing	G	3.0 Williams FW05-Cosworth V8	engine	25/27
13	FRENCH GP	Paul Ricard	21	Walter Wolf Racing	G	3.0 Williams FW05-Cosworth V8	1 lap behind	22/30

GP Starts: 7   GP Wins: 0   Pole positions: 0   Fastest laps: 0   Points: 0

LEDERLE, Neville (ZA) b 25/9/1938, Theunisssen, Winburg, Orange Free State

	1962 Championship position: 18th= Wins: 0 Pole positions: 0 Fastest laps: 0 Points scored: 1							
	Race	Circuit	No	Entrant	Tyres	Capacity/Car/Engine	Comment	Q Pos/Entries
6	SOUTH AFRICAN GP	East London	20	Neville Lederle	D	1.5 Lotus 21-Climax 4	4 laps behind	10/17
	1965 Championship position: Unplaced							
dnq	SOUTH AFRICAN GP	East London	23	Scuderia Scribante	D	1.5 Lotus 21-Climax 4		=21/25

GP Starts: 1   GP Wins: 0   Pole positions: 0   Fastest laps: 0   Points: 1

LEES, Geoff (GB) b 1/5/1951, Atherstone, Warwickshire

	Race	Circuit	No	Entrant	Tyres	Capacity/Car/Engine	Comment	Q Pos/Entries
	1978 Championship position: Unplaced							
dnq	BRITISH GP	Brands Hatch	23	Mario Deliotti Racing	G	3.0 Ensign N175-Cosworth V8		29/30
	1979 Championship position: Unplaced							
7	GERMAN GP	Hockenheim	4	Candy Tyrrell Team	G	3.0 Tyrrell 009-Cosworth V8	*1 lap behind*	16/26
	1980 Championship position: Unplaced							
13/ret	SOUTH AFRICAN GP	Kyalami	17	Shadow Cars	G	3.0 Shadow DN11-Cosworth V8	*suspension failure/8 laps behind*	25/28
dnq	US GP WEST	Long Beach	17	Shadow Cars	G	3.0 Shadow DN11-Cosworth V8	*unwell – withdrawn after 1st practice*	26/27
dnq	BELGIAN GP	Zolder	17	Shadow Cars	G	3.0 Shadow DN12-Cosworth V8		25/27
dnq	MONACO GP	Monte Carlo	17	Shadow Cars	G	3.0 Shadow DN12-Cosworth V8		23/27
dnq	FRENCH GP	Paul Ricard	17	Shadow Cars	G	3.0 Shadow DN12-Cosworth V8		25/27
ret	DUTCH GP	Zandvoort	41	Unipart Racing Team	G	3.0 Ensign N180-Cosworth V8	*accident with Brambilla*	24/28
dnq	ITALIAN GP	Imola	41	Unipart Racing Team	G	3.0 Ensign N180-Cosworth V8		28/28
dnq	US GP EAST	Watkins Glen	51	RAM/Theodore/Rainbow Jeans Racing	G	3.0 Williams FW07B-Cosworth V8	*no time recorded*	– /27
	1982 Championship position: Unplaced							
ret/dns*	CANADIAN GP	Montreal	33	Theodore Racing Team	G	3.0 Theodore TY02-Cosworth V8	*accident at 1st start/*did not restart*	25/29
12	FRENCH GP	Paul Ricard	12	John Player Team Lotus	G	3.0 Lotus 91-Cosworth V8	*pit stop – puncture/2 laps behind*	24/30

GP Starts: 4 (5)   GP Wins: 0   Pole positions: 0   Fastest laps: 0   Points: 0

GEOFF LEES

APROFESSIONAL racing driver in the truest sense of the word, Geoff Lees never really had the Formula 1 opportunities that his talent demanded, but nevertheless he enjoyed continued success in virtually every other type of racing he tried. A Formula Ford champion in the mid-1970s, he soon moved into F3 with a works Chevron, then tackled the Aurora F1 series and Can-Am, and won the Macau GP twice, while taking the occasional grand prix chances that came his way.

In 1981, Geoff won the European Formula 2 championship with the Ralt-Honda, but even this did not bring him the big chance he had hoped for, and eventually he turned his back on Europe. For many years, he lived in Japan, where he married a local girl and carved out a fine career, winning the F2 title in 1983 and the Grand Champion series on four occasions. His vast experience was also put to great effect as leader of the TOM'S Toyota sports car team. In 1992, driving a Toyota TS010 with Hitoshi Ogawa, he won at Monza, ahead of the works Peugeot, and was fifth-placed and highest non-Peugeot points scorer that season.

Between 1995 and mid-1997, Geoff led the Lister Storm line-up, mainly partnering Tiff Needell, but continued lack of success blunted his enthusiasm and he found a more rewarding berth with the GTC team, racing their McLaren F1 GTRs.

In 1998, his great experience was still in demand by Toyota for their Le Mans challenge. The race brought heartbreak, however, for Lees and co-drivers Thierry Boutsen and Ralf Kelleners, after a possible first victory at the Sarthe circuit was lost when their car failed just 80 minutes from the finish while leading. His final appearance at Le Mans came in Thomas Bscher's BMW 12LM, but the car was sidelined by an accident.

After a sabbatical to pursue business interests, Lees returned to full-time racing in the All-Japan GT series with his own team in 2002, finally retiring at the end of 2005.

ARTHUR LEGAT

IF ever a driver was identified with just one circuit, then it must be dear old Arthur Legat, who first saw competition at the Chimay track in Belgium when it opened in 1926, for he was still in action there some 30 years later! This fast and very dangerous 6.754-mile temporary road course close to the French border hosted the annual Grand Prix des Fontières, and was a magnet for semi-professional and amateur racers who came to test their skills. In his younger days, Legat won the race twice with his Bugatti T37A, in 1931 and 1932; he actually appeared there 25 times in total.

Having bought a Veritas-Meteor for the 1951 season, Legat then wheeled out the machine almost unchanged for occasional outings during the next few seasons, venturing to Spa for the Belgian Grand Prix in 1952 and 1953, when the German machine conformed to the then current Formula 2 regulations.

LEGAT, Arthur (B) b 1/11/1898, Haine-Saint-Paul – d 23/2/1960, Haine-Saint-Pierre

1952	Championship position: Unplaced							
	Race	Circuit	No	Entrant	Tyres	Capacity/Car/Engine	Comment	Q Pos/Entries
nc	BELGIAN GP	Spa	38	Arthur Legat	E	2.0 Veritas Meteor 6	5 laps behind	21/22
1953	Championship position: Unplaced							
ret	BELGIAN GP	Spa	36	Arthur Legat	E	2.0 Veritas Meteor 6	transmission	19/22

GP Starts: 2   GP Wins: 0   Pole positions: 0   Fastest laps: 0   Points: 0

JJ LEHTO

INVOLVED in motorsport since taking up karting at the age of six, JJ Lehto built up a tremendous record in the junior formulas, winning the Scandinavian FF1600 championship in 1986, before travelling to England in 1987 to claim the titles in both the British and European FF2000 series. His career carefully nurtured and guided by Keke Rosberg, he moved into Formula 3 in 1988 with the Pacific Racing team that had brought his FF2000 success. After a devastatingly successful start to the season, he cruised to yet another championship, with a total of eight wins and only a late-season charge from Gary Brabham by way of serious competition.

Lehto and Pacific found things tougher when they moved up to F3000, however, the Finn enjoying only modest success (and being somewhat overshadowed by team-mate Eddie Irvine) before replacing the out-of-favour Bertrand Gachot at Onyx late in 1989. This proved to be his salvation, for a sparkling qualifying performance in the Spanish Grand Prix effectively cemented his place in the team. The following season was wasted, however, after the once promising little team fell into the hands of Peter Monteverdi and quickly folded after the Hungarian GP.

Then Lehto signed a two-year deal with Scuderia Italia. The first season, with Judd engines, was generally encouraging, the team making progress,

and JJ scored his first podium finish at Imola, but the switch to Ferrari engines in 1992 proved dispiriting and his once sky-high reputation was beginning to be questioned. Certainly his career had not yet produced the success that had been widely expected. Still highly thought of, however, he joined the Sauber team for 1993. Early-season promise evaporated when internal politics divided the team into two camps, but perhaps tellingly team-mate Karl Wendlinger appeared to be the better long-term prospect.

Given his F1 record, JJ was seen as fortunate to gain a chance at Benetton in 1994, and it seemed certain to be his best ever opportunity to make the breakthrough to the front rank. Unfortunately, it all went horribly wrong when a testing crash left him with fractured neck vertebrae; his confidence never fully recovered. Inconsistent qualifying performances led to him being replaced by Jos Verstappen, and when he did make a return, due to Michael Schumacher's enforced absence, he was slower than his less-experienced team-mate. Perhaps it might have been different if he had joined a front-line team much earlier in his career, or maybe he just wasn't all he was cracked up to be in the first place...

In 1995, Lehto took up the challenge of the DTM/ITC with Opel, but without doubt the season's high spot was his win at Le Mans with Yannick Dalmas and Masanori Sekiya in a McLaren F1 GTR. Indeed, sports car racing brought a welcome upturn in his fortunes. In 1997, driving a Schnitzer-run McLaren F1 GTR, the Finn won four rounds outright (at Hockenheim, Helsinki, Spa and Mugello) and was easily the best of the drivers challenging the might of the silver Mercedes.

Shrewd management brought Lehto a chance to take a crack at CART in 1998, when he joined veteran team owner Carl Hogan to race a Reynard-Mercedes. Surprisingly, perhaps, he shone on the ovals, but struggled somewhat on the road courses. All seemed set fair for a continuation of this partnership, however, until he was unceremoniously dumped just before the start of the 1999 season. Poor Lehto's career seemed to lie in tatters, but sports cars proved to be his salvation once again. A win in the Sebring 12-hours for BMW led to a contract to race Schnitzer's BMW V12 LM in the American Le Mans Series, where he formed a strong partnership once more with Steve Soper, winning at Sears Point, Laguna Seca and Las Vegas.

After racing for Cadillac in the ALMS and a one-off appearance for Opel in the DTM, JJ found a berth with the Champion Audi squad for the 2003 season, and he enjoyed a tremendously successful period. Paired with Marco Werner, he won the 2004 ALMS title and in 2005, with Tom Kristensen on board, the pair took victory in the Le Mans 24-hour race, as well as claiming the top step of the podium at Sebring, Atlanta and Lime Rock in the American Le Mans Series.

Appearances at Daytona in 2007 and Sepang in the Speedcars Malaysian GP support race drew a line under JJ's competition career, but the Finn continued to fulfill his long-term TV commentator's role.

JJ's personal life took a tragic turn in June, 2010, when he was injured in a speedboat accident that cost the life of his passenger. Subsequently he was sentenced to two years and four months in prison after it was discovered that the boat had been travelling at nearly 80km/h in an area where the speed limit was 5km/h, and that Lehto had been drunk at the time. He was jailed in December, 2011, but immediately lodged an appeal against his sentence.

LEHTO JJ (Jyrki Jarvilehto) (SF) b 31/1/1966, Espoo

1989 Championship position: Unplaced

	Race	Circuit	No	Entrant		Tyres	Capacity/Car/Engine	Comment	Q Pos/Entries
dnpq	PORTUGUESE GP	Estoril	37	Moneytron Onyx		G	3.5 Onyx ORE 1-Cosworth V8		32/39
ret	SPANISH GP	Jerez	37	Moneytron Onyx		G	3.5 Onyx ORE 1-Cosworth V8	gearbox	17/38
dnpq	JAPANESE GP	Suzuka	37	Moneytron Onyx		G	3.5 Onyx ORE 1-Cosworth V8		36/39
ret	AUSTRALIAN GP	Adelaide	37	Moneytron Onyx		G	3.5 Onyx ORE 1-Cosworth V8	engine – electrics	17/39

1990 Championship position: Unplaced

	Race	Circuit	No	Entrant	Tyres	Capacity/Car/Engine	Comment	Q Pos/Entries
dnq	US GP (PHOENIX)	Phoenix	36	Moneytron Onyx Formula One	G	3.5 Onyx ORE 1-Cosworth V8	no time recorded	– /35
dnq	BRAZILIAN GP	Interlagos	36	Moneytron Onyx Formula One	G	3.5 Onyx ORE 1-Cosworth V8		28/35
12	SAN MARINO GP	Imola	36	Moneytron Onyx Formula One	G	3.5 Onyx ORE 1B-Cosworth V8	engine problems/2 laps behind	26/34
ret	MONACO GP	Monte Carlo	36	Moneytron Onyx Formula One	G	3.5 Onyx ORE 1B-Cosworth V8	gearbox	26/35
ret	CANADIAN GP	Montreal	36	Moneytron Onyx Formula One	G	3.5 Onyx ORE 1B-Cosworth V8	engine	22/35
ret	MEXICAN GP	Mexico City	36	Moneytron Onyx Formula One	G	3.5 Onyx ORE 1B-Cosworth V8	engine	27/35
dnq	FRENCH GP	Paul Ricard	36	Moneytron Onyx Formula One	G	3.5 Onyx ORE 1B-Cosworth V8		30/35
dnq	BRITISH GP	Silverstone	36	Monteverdi Onyx Formula One	G	3.5 Onyx ORE 1B-Cosworth V8		29/35
nc	GERMAN GP	Hockenheim	36	Monteverdi Onyx Formula One	G	3.5 Monteverdi ORE 1B-Cosworth V8	misfire/bodywork/6 laps behind	25/35
dnq	HUNGARIAN GP	Hungaroring	36	Monteverdi Onyx Formula One	G	3.5 Monteverdi ORE 1B-Cosworth V8		29/35

1991 Championship position: 12th=   Wins: 0   Pole positions: 0   Fastest laps: 0   Points scored: 4

	Race	Circuit	No	Entrant	Tyres	Capacity/Car/Engine	Comment	Q Pos/Entries
ret	US GP (PHOENIX)	Phoenix	22	Scuderia Italia SpA	P	3.5 BMS Dallara 191-Judd V10	clutch	10/34
ret	BRAZILIAN GP	Interlagos	22	Scuderia Italia SpA	P	3.5 BMS Dallara 191-Judd V10	alternator	19/34
3	SAN MARINO GP	Imola	22	Scuderia Italia SpA	P	3.5 BMS Dallara 191-Judd V10	1 lap behind	16/34
11	MONACO GP	Monte Carlo	22	Scuderia Italia SpA	P	3.5 BMS Dallara 191-Judd V10	3 laps behind	13/34
ret	CANADIAN GP	Montreal	22	Scuderia Italia SpA	P	3.5 BMS Dallara 191-Judd V10	engine	17/34
ret	MEXICAN GP	Mexico City	22	Scuderia Italia SpA	P	3.5 BMS Dallara 191-Judd V10	engine	16/34
ret	FRENCH GP	Magny Cours	22	Scuderia Italia SpA	P	3.5 BMS Dallara 191-Judd V10	puncture	26/34
13	BRITISH GP	Silverstone	22	Scuderia Italia SpA	P	3.5 BMS Dallara 191-Judd V10	3 laps behind	11/34
ret	GERMAN GP	Hockenheim	22	Scuderia Italia SpA	P	3.5 BMS Dallara 191-Judd V10	engine	20/34
ret	HUNGARIAN GP	Hungaroring	22	Scuderia Italia SpA	P	3.5 BMS Dallara 191-Judd V10	engine	12/34
ret	BELGIAN GP	Spa	22	Scuderia Italia SpA	P	3.5 BMS Dallara 191-Judd V10	engine	14/34
ret	ITALIAN GP	Monza	22	Scuderia Italia SpA	P	3.5 BMS Dallara 191-Judd V10	puncture – suspension	20/24
ret	PORTUGUESE GP	Estoril	22	Scuderia Italia SpA	P	3.5 BMS Dallara 191-Judd V10	gear linkage	18/34
8	SPANISH GP	Barcelona	22	Scuderia Italia SpA	P	3.5 BMS Dallara 191-Judd V10	1 lap behind	15/33
ret	JAPANESE GP	Suzuka	22	Scuderia Italia SpA	P	3.5 BMS Dallara 191-Judd V10	spun avoiding de Cesaris	12/31
12*	AUSTRALIAN GP	Phoenix	22	Scuderia Italia SpA	P	3.5 BMS Dallara 191-Judd V10	*rain shortened race	11/32

1992 Championship position: Unplaced

	Race	Circuit	No	Entrant	Tyres	Capacity/Car/Engine	Comment	Q Pos/Entries
ret	SOUTH AFRICAN GP	Kyalami	21	Scuderia Italia SpA	G	3.5 BMS Dallara 192-Ferrari V12	final drive	24/30
8	MEXICAN GP	Mexico City	21	Scuderia Italia SpA	G	3.5 BMS Dallara 192-Ferrari V12	1 lap behind	7/30
8	BRAZILIAN GP	Interlagos	21	Scuderia Italia SpA	G	3.5 BMS Dallara 192-Ferrari V12	2 laps behind	16/31
ret	SPANISH GP	Barcelona	21	Scuderia Italia SpA	G	3.5 BMS Dallara 192-Ferrari V12	spun off	12/32
11/ret	SAN MARINO GP	Imola	21	Scuderia Italia SpA	G	3.5 BMS Dallara 192-Ferrari V12	engine cut out/3 laps behind	16/32
9	MONACO GP	Monte Carlo	21	Scuderia Italia SpA	G	3.5 BMS Dallara 192-Ferrari V12	2 laps behind	20/32
9	CANADIAN GP	Montreal	21	Scuderia Italia SpA	G	3.5 BMS Dallara 192-Ferrari V12	1 lap behind	23/32
9*	FRENCH GP	Magny Cours	21	Scuderia Italia SpA	G	3.5 BMS Dallara 192-Ferrari V12	*aggregate of 2 parts/2 laps behind	17/30
13	BRITISH GP	Silverstone	21	Scuderia Italia SpA	G	3.5 BMS Dallara 192-Ferrari V12	2 laps behind	19/32
10	GERMAN GP	Hockenheim	21	Scuderia Italia SpA	G	3.5 BMS Dallara 192-Ferrari V12	1 lap behind	21/32
dnq	HUNGARIAN GP	Hungaroring	21	Scuderia Italia SpA	G	3.5 BMS Dallara 192-Ferrari V12		28/31
7	BELGIAN GP	Spa	21	Scuderia Italia SpA	G	3.5 BMS Dallara 192-Ferrari V12	1 lap behind	16/30
11/ret	ITALIAN GP	Monza	21	Scuderia Italia SpA	G	3.5 BMS Dallara 192-Ferrari V12	electrics – engine/6 laps behind	14/28
ret	PORTUGUESE GP	Estoril	21	Scuderia Italia SpA	G	3.5 BMS Dallara 192-Ferrari V12	accident damage	19/26
9	JAPANESE GP	Suzuka	21	Scuderia Italia SpA	G	3.5 BMS Dallara 192-Ferrari V12	1 lap behind	22/26
ret	AUSTRALIAN GP	Phoenix	21	Scuderia Italia SpA	G	3.5 BMS Dallara 192-Ferrari V12	gearbox	24/26

1993 Championship position: 13th=   Wins: 0   Pole positions: 0   Fastest laps: 0   Points scored: 5

	Race	Circuit	No	Entrant	Tyres	Capacity/Car/Engine	Comment	Q Pos/Entries
5	SOUTH AFRICAN GP	Kyalami	30	Sauber	G	3.5 Sauber C12-Ilmor V10	2 laps behind	6/26
ret	BRAZILIAN GP	Interlagos	30	Sauber	G	3.5 Sauber C12-Ilmor V10	electrics	7/26
ret	EUROPEAN GP	Donington	30	Sauber	G	3.5 Sauber C12-Ilmor V10	started spare car from pit lane/handling	7/26
4/ret	SAN MARINO GP	Imola	30	Sauber	G	3.5 Sauber C12-Ilmor V10	engine/2 laps behind	16/26
ret	SPANISH GP	Barcelona	30	Sauber	G	3.5 Sauber C12-Ilmor V10	engine	9/26
ret	MONACO GP	Monte Carlo	30	Sauber	G	3.5 Sauber C12-Ilmor V10	collision with Wendlinger	11/26
7	CANADIAN GP	Montreal	30	Sauber	G	3.5 Sauber C12-Ilmor V10	lost 2nd & 3rd gears/1 lap behind	11/26
ret	FRENCH GP	Magny Cours	30	Sauber	G	3.5 Sauber C12-Ilmor V10	gearbox	18/26
8	BRITISH GP	Silverstone	30	Sauber	G	3.5 Sauber C12-Ilmor V10	1 lap behind	16/26
ret	GERMAN GP	Hockenheim	30	Sauber	G	3.5 Sauber C12-Ilmor V10	stuck throttle – spun out	18/26
ret	HUNGARIAN GP	Hungaroring	30	Sauber	G	3.5 Sauber C12-Ilmor V10	engine	15/26
9	BELGIAN GP	Spa	30	Sauber	G	3.5 Sauber C12-Ilmor V10	understeer/1 lap behind	9/25
ret	ITALIAN GP	Monza	30	Sauber	G	3.5 Sauber C12-Ilmor V10	started from back of grid/lap 1 accident	13/26
7	PORTUGUESE GP	Estoril	30	Sauber	G	3.5 Sauber C12-Ilmor V10	stop & go penalty/2 laps behind	12/26
8	JAPANESE GP	Suzuka	30	Sauber	G	3.5 Sauber C12-Ilmor V10	collision – Brundle/1 lap behind	11/24
ret	AUSTRALIAN GP	Phoenix	30	Sauber	G	3.5 Sauber C12-Ilmor V10	stuck throttle – accident	12/24

1994 Championship position: 24th=   Wins: 0   Pole positions: 0   Fastest laps: 0   Points scored: 1

	Race	Circuit	No	Entrant	Tyres	Capacity/Car/Engine	Comment	Q Pos/Entries
ret	SAN MARINO GP	Imola	6	Mild Seven Benetton Ford	G	3.5 Benetton B194-Ford Zetec-R V8	stalled on grid – hit by Lamy	5/28
7	MONACO GP	Monte Carlo	6	Mild Seven Benetton Ford	G	3.5 Benetton B194-Ford Zetec-R V8	1 lap behind	17/24
ret	SPANISH GP	Barcelona	6	Mild Seven Benetton Ford	G	3.5 Benetton B194-Ford Zetec-R V8	engine	4/27
6	CANADIAN GP	Montreal	6	Mild Seven Benetton Ford	G	3.5 Benetton B194-Ford Zetec-R V8	1 lap behind	20/27
9	ITALIAN GP	Monza	5	Mild Seven Benetton Ford	G	3.5 Benetton B194-Ford Zetec-R V8	1 lap behind	20/28
ret	PORTUGUESE GP	Estoril	5	Mild Seven Benetton Ford	G	3.5 Benetton B194-Ford Zetec-R V8	spun off	14/28
ret	JAPANESE GP	Suzuka	29	Sauber Mercedes	G	3.5 Sauber C13-Mercedes Benz V10	engine on lap 1	15/28
10	AUSTRALIAN GP	Adelaide	29	Sauber Mercedes	G	3.5 Sauber C13-Mercedes Benz V10	2 laps behind	17/28

GP Starts: 62   GP Wins: 0   Pole positions: 0   Fastest laps: 0   Points: 10

LAMBERTO LEONI

A FORMULA Italia champion, Lamberto Leoni proved to be a quick driver in Italian Formula 3, but without gaining the necessary solid results. Moving up to Formula 2 in 1977, he unexpectedly won the Adriatic Grand Prix on aggregate in his Ferrari-engined Chevron, after a dismal start to the season in a Ralt. After failing to qualify his 'rent-a-drive' works Surtees at Monza in 1977, he joined Ensign for the following year, but only made the grid once in four outings and swiftly departed the team. From then on, Leoni's career stuttered on with occasional outings in Formula 2, seemingly with the aim of keeping his licence intact, but then he tackled F3000 more seriously and enjoyed some success, before being sidelined after a massive shunt at the Österreichring in 1986.

Having formed his own FIRST F3000 team, Lamberto returned more determined than ever in 1987, enjoying a consistent final season to finish in eighth place, tied with his up-and-coming driver, Gabriele Tarquini.

Leoni retired from driving to concentrate on management duties, initially guiding the fortunes of Pierluigi Martini and Marco Apicella. The team performed respectably enough, gaining some decent finishes, but had to wait until 1989 for Fabrizio Giovarnari to post their first victory.

At the same time, Leoni tried, over-ambitiously, to get into Formula 1 with the shambolic Life F1 project, which seriously undermined his F3000 operation. Eventually he lost the services of star driver Apicella, and his team slipped from being contenders to also-rans.

The FIRST team finally collapsed early in 1991, after a legal wrangle with former driver Giovanni Bonnano. Leoni then switched successfully to powerboat racing for a while, before reappearing as an entrant in F3000 Italia in 1999, running Thomas Biagi.

LES LESTON

A STAR of the exciting 500cc Formula 3 racing of the early 1950s, Les Leston scored an early British victory on the Continent in 1952, winning the Luxembourg GP. A runner-up in 1952 and '53, he finally claimed the crown in 1954 at the wheel of a works Cooper, before concentrating on sports car racing, enjoying a successful 1955 season in Peter Bell's Connaught.

In the main, Les raced John Willment's Cooper sports in 1956, but handled a Connaught in the Italian GP and took third place in the Richmond Trophy with the same car. In 1957, he raced a Formula 2 Cooper in national events, drove for BRM in the British GP and took sixth place in the Nürburgring 1000km for Aston Martin. However, after escaping with a shaking from a massive crash at Caen in 1958, when his F2 Lotus seized, he concentrated on his expanding racewear business. He did not desert the circuits, though, having great fun in the early 1960s in his red Lotus Elite with the famous 'DAD 10' plate.

LEONI, Lamberto (I) b 24/5/1953, Argenta, Ferrara

	1977 Championship position: Unplaced							
	Race	Circuit	No	Entrant	Tyres	Capacity/Car/Engine	Comment	Q Pos/Entries
dnq	ITALIAN GP	Monza	18	Team Surtees	G	3.0 Surtees TS19-Cosworth V8		27/34
	1978 Championship position: Unplaced							
ret	ARGENTINE GP	Buenos Aires	23	Team Tissot Ensign	G	3.0 Ensign N177-Cosworth V8	engine	22/27
ret/dns*	BRAZILIAN GP	Rio	23	Team Tissot Ensign	G	3.0 Ensign N177-Cosworth V8	*driveshaft on parade lap	(17)/28
dnq	SOUTH AFRICAN GP	Kyalami	22	Team Tissot Ensign	G	3.0 Ensign N177-Cosworth V8		29/30
dnq	US GP WEST	Long Beach	22	Team Tissot Ensign	G	3.0 Ensign N177-Cosworth V8		26/30

GP Starts: 1 (2)   GP Wins: 0   Pole positions: 0   Fastest laps: 0   Points: 0

LESTON, Les (GB) b 16/12/1920, Nottingham

	1956 Championship position: Unplaced							
	Race	Circuit	No	Entrant	Tyres	Capacity/Car/Engine	Comment	Q Pos/Entries
ret	ITALIAN GP	Monza	2	Connaught Engineering	P/A	2.5 Connaught-Alta B Type 4	torsion bar	20/26
	1957 Championship position: Unplaced							
dnq	MONACO GP	Monte Carlo	16	Cooper Car Co	D	1.5 Cooper T43-Climax 4		21/21
ret	BRITISH GP	Aintree	26	Owen Racing Organisation	D	2.5 BRM P25 4	engine	12/19

GP Starts: 2   GP Wins: 0   Pole positions: 0   Fastest laps: 0   Points: 0

'LEVEGH' (Bouillin, Pierre) (F) b 22/12/1905, Paris – d 11/6/1955, Le Mans Circuit

	1950 Championship position: Unplaced							
	Race	Circuit	No	Entrant	Tyres	Capacity/Car/Engine	Comment	Q Pos/Entries
7	BELGIAN GP	Spa	22	'Pierre Levegh'	D	4.5 Lago-Talbot T26C 6	2 laps behind	10/14
ret	FRENCH GP	Reims	22	'Pierre Levegh'	D	4.5 Lago-Talbot T26C 6	engine	9/20
ret	ITALIAN GP	Monza	56	'Pierre Levegh'	D	4.5 Lago-Talbot T26C 6		20/27
	1951 Championship position: Unplaced							
8	BELGIAN GP	Spa	26	'Pierre Levegh'	D	4.5 Lago-Talbot T26C 6	4 laps behind	13/13
9	GERMAN GP	Nürburgring	90	'Pierre Levegh'	D	4.5 Lago-Talbot T26C 6	2 laps behind	19/23
ret	ITALIAN GP	Monza	22	'Pierre Levegh'	D	4.5 Lago-Talbot T26C 6	engine	20/22

GP Starts: 6   GP Wins: 0   Pole positions: 0   Fastest laps: 0   Points: 0

'LEVEGH'

ULTIMATELY a tragic figure, 'Levegh' (real name Pierre Bouillin) competed under the name of his uncle, a racer in the early part of the 20th century. From before the Second World War, he was obsessed with the Le Mans 24-hour race, waiting patiently for an opportunity to take part in this classic and finally achieving his ambition as relief driver in the Talbot team in 1938. After the war, he raced a Delage, taking second at Pau in 1947, before acquiring a Talbot in 1949, which he raced in grands prix in 1950 and '51.

'Levegh' finished fourth at Le Mans in a works Talbot in 1951, but was dissatisfied with the car's performance and resolved to return the following year in his own car, which he prepared himself at huge expense. His investment was very nearly rewarded after he drove the car single-handedly for more than 22 hours, only to lose a massive lead when he missed a gearchange and damaged the engine.

His dream of victory seemed over, but in 1955 Alfred Neubauer, remembering his exploits, offered 'Levegh' a drive in the works Mercedes. By some strange premonition, the Frenchman had voiced his unease at the narrowness of the straight in front of the pits, and it was his misfortune to be involved in a collision at this point that catapulted his car into the crowd, killing him and 80 others in the worst disaster in motor racing history.

JACK LEWIS

NOW an almost forgotten figure in motor racing, Jack Lewis showed plenty of natural talent, but perhaps not the necessary resilience to overcome the setbacks that are a part of any sport.

In 1958, Lewis purchased the ex-Bueb F3 Cooper and won three races in his first season, which encouraged him to move into Formula 2 in 1959 with a Cooper. Despite setting the fastest practice time for the Pau GP (ahead of Jack Brabham and Maurice Trintignant) and taking third in the Aintree 200, he was frustrated by organisers' general reluctance to accept his entry, and returned to the tracks in 1960 well prepared to prove himself a serious competitor. He did just that, winning the Autocar F2 British Championship, as well as races at Chimay and Montlhéry.

For 1961, Lewis set out on the grand prix trail with a Cooper, setting 12th-fastest practice time on his debut at Spa and fighting off Tony Brooks' late challenge to take fourth place in the Italian GP. Given 'grade A' driver status, he then bought a BRM 48/57 for 1962, which he took to third in the Pau Grand Prix, but he failed to qualify at Monaco and was so dissatisfied with the car that it was returned to the factory.

Back in his Cooper, Lewis seemed to lose heart, feeling his reputation had suffered after the BRM episode, and it was a despondent Welshman who slipped into retirement at the age of just 27.

LEWIS, Jack (GB) b 1/11/1936, Stroud, Gloucestershire

1961 Championship position: 13th= Wins: 0 Pole positions: 0 Fastest laps: 0 Points scored: 3

	Race	Circuit	No	Entrant	Tyres	Capacity/Car/Engine	Comment	Q Pos/Entries
9	BELGIAN GP	Spa	40	H & L Motors	D	1.5 Cooper T53-Climax 4	1 lap behind	13/25
ret	FRENCH GP	Reims	44	H & L Motors	D	1.5 Cooper T53-Climax 4	overheating	18/26
ret	BRITISH GP	Aintree	46	H & L Motors	D	1.5 Cooper T53-Climax 4	steering	=14/30
9	GERMAN GP	Nürburgring	28	H & L Motors	D	1.5 Cooper T53-Climax 4		18/27
4	ITALIAN GP	Monza	60	H & L Motors	D	1.5 Cooper T53-Climax 4		16/33

1962 Championship position: Unplaced

	Race	Circuit	No	Entrant	Tyres	Capacity/Car/Engine	Comment	Q Pos/Entries
8	DUTCH GP	Zandvoort	21	Ecurie Galloise	D	1.5 Cooper T53-Climax 4	pit stop/10 laps behind	19/20
dnq*	MONACO GP	Monte Carlo	24	Ecurie Galloise	D	1.5 BRM P48/57 V8	*faster than 3 guaranteed starters	=14/21
ret	FRENCH GP	Rouen	42	Ecurie Galloise	D	1.5 Cooper T53-Climax 4	brakes – hit Graham Hill	16/17
10	BRITISH GP	Aintree	42	Ecurie Galloise	D	1.5 Cooper T53-Climax 4	3 laps behind	15/21
ret	GERMAN GP	Nürburgring	20	Ecurie Galloise	D	1.5 Cooper T53-Climax 4	front shock absorber	21/30

GP Starts: 9 GP Wins: 0 Pole positions: 0 Fastest laps: 0 Points: 3

STUART LEWIS-EVANS

WITH his father 'Pop' a noted Formula 3 racer in his own right, it was no surprise when Stuart Lewis-Evans followed in his footsteps. In 1951, he began racing with a Cooper MkIV in the Junior championship. He soon became one of the formula's leading exponents, taking an important win at the Silverstone International meeting in 1952. He spent five seasons in this cut-and-thrust environment before Connaught gave him a chance to race at the end of 1956 at one of his happy hunting grounds, Brands Hatch. The newcomer drove a blinding race into second and cemented a place for himself on the team for 1957

Encouraging early-season performances, including a victory in the Richmond Trophy at Goodwood and running second at the Naples GP before retirement, were followed by a fourth place in his first grand prix start at Monaco. Shortly after, the team disbanded, leaving Lewis-Evans high and dry.

Fortunately, a vacancy arose at the next grand prix where, with Stirling Moss and Tony Brooks indisposed, Stuart was co-opted into the Vanwall team for the rest of 1957. Some of his drives were brilliant: at Reims for example, where he qualified alongside Juan Fangio on the front row and led the race, before problems dropped him to third; and in Morocco, where he was second, behind Jean Behra's works Maserati. In world championship races, he displayed a rare blend of speed and finesse, but had only a fifth to show for his efforts at Pescara.

Although a slight, frail figure, Lewis-Evans embarked on a daunting racing programme in 1958, beginning with a couple of races in a Connaught in New Zealand. The cars had been bought by one Bernie Ecclestone, who would become Stuart's personal manager. Back in Europe, he competed very successfully in Formula 2 with a Cooper for BRP, and in sports cars for Aston Martin, sharing the third-placed DBR with Carroll Shelby in the Tourist Trophy at Goodwwod.

Driving for Vanwall in grands prix, Lewis-Evans played a crucial part in gaining the constructors' championship for the team, backing Moss and Brooks, but, in what should have been a glorious finale to the year in Morocco, his car crashed in flames after its transmission had locked. The poor driver was extricated from the wreckage suffering from terrible burns and, despite being flown back to England for expert attention, he succumbed to his injuries in the specialist burns unit at East Grinstead some six days later.

LEWIS-EVANS, Stuart (GB) b 20/4/1930, Luton, Bedfordshire – d 25/10/1958, East Grinstead, Sussex

1957 Championship position: 10th= Wins: 0 Pole positions: 0 Fastest laps: 0 Points scored: 5

	Race	Circuit	No	Entrant	Tyres	Capacity/Car/Engine	Comment	Q Pos/Entries
4	MONACO GP	Monte Carlo	10	Connaught Engineering	D	2.5 Connaught-Alta B Type 4	3 laps behind	13/21
ret	FRENCH GP	Rouen	18	Vandervell Products Ltd	P	2.5 Vanwall 4	steering	10/15
7	BRITISH GP	Aintree	22	Vandervell Products Ltd	P	2.5 Vanwall 4	pit stop – throttle/8 laps behind	6/19
ret	GERMAN GP	Nürburgring	12	Vandervell Products Ltd	P	2.5 Vanwall 4	gearbox	9/24
5	PESCARA GP	Pescara	30	Vandervell Products Ltd	P	2.5 Vanwall 4	pit stop – tyres/1 lap behind	8/16
ret	ITALIAN GP	Monza	20	Vandervell Products Ltd	P	2.5 Vanwall 4	cracked cylinder head	1/19

1958 Championship position: 9th= Wins: 0 Pole positions: 0 Fastest laps: 0 Points scored: 11

	Race	Circuit	No	Entrant	Tyres	Capacity/Car/Engine	Comment	Q Pos/Entries
ret	MONACO GP	Monte Carlo	32	Vandervell Products Ltd	D	2.5 Vanwall 4	overheating	7/28
ret	DUTCH GP	Zandvoort	3	Vandervell Products Ltd	D	2.5 Vanwall 4	engine	1/17
3	BELGIAN GP	Spa	6	Vandervell Products Ltd	D	2.5 Vanwall 4		11/20
ret*	FRENCH GP	Reims	12	Vandervell Products Ltd	D	2.5 Vanwall 4	engine/*Brooks took over car	10/21
4	BRITISH GP	Silverstone	9	Vandervell Products Ltd	D	2.5 Vanwall 4		7/21
3	PORTUGESE GP	Oporto	6	Vandervell Products Ltd	D	2.5 Vanwall 4	1 lap behind	3/15
ret	ITALIAN GP	Monza	30	Vandervell Products Ltd	D	2.5 Vanwall 4	overheating	4/21
ret	MOROCCAN GP	Casablanca	12	Vandervell Products Ltd	D	2.5 Vanwall 4	engine – crashed – suffered fatal burns	3/25

GP Starts: 14 GP Wins: 0 Pole positions: 2 Fastest laps: 0 Points: 16

LIGIER, Guy (F) b 12/7/1930, Vichy

	Race	Circuit	No	Entrant	Tyres	Capacity/Car/Engine	Comment	Q Pos/Entries
1966 Championship position: Unplaced								
nc	MONACO GP	Monte Carlo	21	Guy Ligier	D	3.0 Cooper T81-Maserati V12	*pit stop/25 laps behind*	15/16
nc	BELGIAN GP	Spa	22	Guy Ligier	D	3.0 Cooper T81-Maserati V12	*4 laps behind*	12/18
nc	FRENCH GP	Reims	42	Guy Ligier	D	3.0 Cooper T81-Maserati V12	*6 laps behind*	11/17
10	BRITISH GP	Brands Hatch	19	Guy Ligier	D	3.0 Cooper T81-Maserati V12	*5 laps behind*	17/20
9	DUTCH GP	Zandvoort	36	Guy Ligier	D	3.0 Cooper T81-Maserati V12	*6 laps behind*	17/18
dns	GERMAN GP	Nürburgring	18	Guy Ligier	D	3.0 Cooper T81-Maserati V12	*practice accident – broken knee*	–./30
1967 Championship position: 19th= Wins: 0 Pole positions: 0 Fastest laps: 0 Points scored: 1								
10	BELGIAN GP	Spa	32	Guy Ligier	F	3.0 Cooper T81-Maserati V12	*3 laps behind*	18/18
nc	FRENCH GP	Le Mans	16	Guy Ligier	F	3.0 Cooper T81-Maserati V12	*pit stop/12 laps behind*	15/15
10	BRITISH GP	Silverstone	18	Guy Ligier	F	3.0 Brabham BT20-Repco V8	*4 laps behind*	21/21
6	GERMAN GP	Nürburgring	15	Guy Ligier	F	3.0 Brabham BT20-Repco V8	*8th behind F2 cars/1 lap behind*	25/25
ret	ITALIAN GP	Monza	12	Guy Ligier	F	3.0 Brabham BT20-Repco V8	*engine*	18/18
ret	US GP	Watkins Glen	19	Guy Ligier	F	3.0 Brabham BT20-Repco V8	*camshaft*	17/18
11	MEXICAN GP	Mexico City	19	Guy Ligier	F	3.0 Brabham BT20-Repco V8	*4 laps behind*	19/19

GP Starts: 12   GP Wins: 0   Pole positions: 2   Fastest laps: 0   Points: 1

GUY LIGIER

THE uncompromising Guy Ligier came late on to the motor racing scene, after a distinguished rugby career. A close friend and business partner of Jo Schlesser, he began racing in 1963 with a Porsche Carrera, then moved into endurance racing with a Porsche 904GT. He competed in Formula 2 in 1964, gaining some minor success in a Brabham BT10, with fifth in the Pergusa GP, and sixth places at both Albi and Montlhéry. In 1965, he raced a Ford GT, winning the sports and GT race at Albi, but achieving little of note elsewhere.

Taking delivery of a Cooper-Maserati, Ligier joined the grand prix circus in 1966, but his season ended early when he sustained a smashed kneecap after crashing in practice for the German GP. Undaunted, he returned in 1967, eventually replacing the Cooper with a more competitive Brabham and scoring his only championship point at the Nürburgring. He did record a major success in sports cars that year, however, winning the Reims 12-hours in a Ford GT40 with Jo Schlesser.

In 1968, Guy returned to Formula 2, but he quit in mid-season, disillusioned after Schlesser's death at Rouen. He returned the following year with the ex-Alan Mann Escort, however, before building a prototype sports car that he debuted successfully in 1970. The sports car programme eventually led to a Formula 1 machine being built for 1976 and, although the Ligier team often failed to make the most of their resources, particularly as they had substantial support from the Mitterand government, the blue cars were a constant presence on the grid until the end of 1996. By then, though, Ligier had sold most of his shareholding (in 1992/93). In 1997, he finally disposed of his remaining 18 per cent interest in the team to Flavio Briatore for what amounted to a knock-down price. When subsequently the Italian sold the team on for a handsome profit, the unhappy founder was left contemplating recourse to the courts in an attempt to gain fairer compensation.

Away from the tracks, Ligier made a fortune in the fertiliser business, before returning to automobiles, this time with micro cars. In 2004, he acquired a majority shareholding in race car builder Automobiles Martini, which went on produce an open sports protoype, the Ligier JS49 CN.

ROBERTO LIPPI

A HIGHLY rated Italian driver, Roberto Lippi began racing sports cars in the mid-1950s. In 1955, he shared a Maserati with Giorgio Scarlatti to take eighth place in the Targa Florio, and he was Italian 750cc sports champion in 1957. He came to real prominence nationally with the introduction of Formula Junior in 1958, driving the Stanguellini-Fiat. He won the inaugural event of this series and subsequently went on to take the championship. He remained a leading runner in this class over the next couple of seasons, but was less successful in 1960, when he switched to a de Sanctis.

Lippi's Formula 1 experiences were less happy: plugging away in the uncompetitive de Tomaso-OSCA 4, his best results were scored at his favourite home track of Vallelunga in 1961 (fifth) and 1963 (fourth). He briefly returned to Formula Junior in 1963, racing a Cooper-Ford with his customary verve against much younger competitors.

LIPPI, Roberto (I) b 17/10/1926, Rome

	1961 Championship position: Unplaced							
	Race	Circuit	No	Entrant	Tyres	Capacity/Car/Engine	Comment	Q Pos/Entries
ret	ITALIAN GP	Monza	52	Scuderia Settecolli	D	1.5 de Tomaso F1-OSCA 4	engine	32/33
	1962 Championship position: Unplaced							
dnq	ITALIAN GP	Monza	50	Scuderia Settecolli	D	1.5 de Tomaso F1-OSCA 4		28/30
	1963 Championship position: Unplaced							
dnq	ITALIAN GP	Monza	44	Scuderia Settecolli	D	1.5 de Tomaso F1-Ferrari V6		28/28

GP Starts: 1   GP Wins: 0   Pole positions: 0   Fastest laps: 0   Points: 0

VITANTONIO LIUZZI

A KARTING win over world champion Michael Schumacher in 2001 brought Vitantonio Liuzzi to the racing world's full attention and, having gained success in Formula Renault 2000 in Germany and Italian F3, he was signed up by Red Bull, who helped fast-track him to the top flight.

Liuzzi was handed a seat in F3000 with Red Bull's junior team, which was run by Coloni Motorsport. His first year in the series produced a second place at the Nürburgring plus five fourth-place finishes that belied his rookie status, leaving him fourth overall, just behind close rival Giorgio Pantano. This promise earned him an opportunity to join Christian Horner's Arden International for 2004, a move that cemented his burgeoning reputation, as he romped to the title on the back of a record-equalling seven race wins to clinch the GP2 title in convincing manner.

Although Liuzzi appeared to be heading for Sauber, he was edged out by former world champion Jacques Villeneuve, but then fate took a helpful hand in the Italian's career. With Jaguar Racing ailing badly and owners Ford about to pull the plug, Red Bull staged a last-ditch buy-out, fulfilling Dietrich Mateschitz's dream of owning his own F1 team. The experienced David Coulthard was hired to provide some knowledge and guidance, while Jaguar incumbent Christian Klien was under contract and still in place. With both youngsters backed by Red Bull, it was decided that they would share the second seat, Klien driving three races before Liuzzi finally made his F1 debut on home soil at Imola. Scoring the final point on offer was certainly a promising start, but he only retained the seat for a further three races before Klien took over for the rest of the season.

For 2006, Vitantonio was given his chance of a full-time ride in the newly formed Toro Rosso team, alongside American Scott Speed. With very restricted testing and a lack of in-house development, not much was expected from the team, except perhaps beating the other minnows. In the event, Liuzzi highlighted the season for the team with a well-earned eighth place at Indianapolis and with it the precious point to put the team into ninth place in the constructors' standings.

Hopes for an improvement in 2007 were buoyed by the acquisition of Ferrari engines from the parent Red Bull team, but it was a fractious year when both drivers fell out of favour with the team bosses. Liuzzi's uncertain position was not helped by the stunning form of Sebastian Vettel, who had replaced Speed by mid-season. However, inclement weather conditions at the Chinese Grand Prix gave the Toro Rosso team the opportunity to grab points that were going begging, and 'Tonio' took a career-best sixth, two places behind Vettel. It was too late to save the Italian's place, though, as the decision had been made to hire Champ Car star Sébastien Bourdais, which left him frantically searching for another foothold in Formula 1.

The Italian found a role as test driver for the emerging Force India Team in 2008, and he patiently bided his time until the opportunity for a race seat arose. Meanwhile, he kept his hand in by taking three wins and making some decent money in the Middle East Speedcar series, and then representing Italy in four rounds of the A1GP series during the early part of 2009. His chance to get back into F1 finally came when Ferrari came calling for Giancarlo Fisichella. Force India had just hit a sweet spot with their car, and 'Toni' was fortunate to be handed the drive for Monza. After a fine qualifying effort, he was holding fourth place when he was forced to retire. Sadly, the car never quite lived up to the promise of that day and he dropped back into midfield obscurity.

Nonetheless, Liuzzi was handed a full-time seat for the 2010 season. The VJM03 was a solid midfield runner and capable of points-scoring finishes, which he and team-mate Adrian Sutil delivered with regularity, but the Italian struggled to make much of an impression on his German partner. Despite having a valid contract, he lost his drive when the promising Paul di Resta became the preferred choice at Force India for 2011.

Liuzzi was linked with Lotus-Renault as a replacement for the injured Robert Kubica, but eventually he fetched up at the Hispania Racing Team to extend his stay in Formula 1. Naturally enough, he could do very little to show his worth in the back-marker team. His most high-profile moment came at Monza, where he lost control on the opening lap of the Italian Grand Prix, wiping out not only his HRT, but also the cars of the innocent Vitaly Petrov and Nico Rosberg.

With the Spanish team being reorganized, and despite being under contract, Liuzzi was muscled aside once more when the sponsorship-rich Narain Karthikeyan returned with his finance. While finding a way back into F1 was still a burning ambition, 'Tonio' opted to compete in the Italian Superstars series with a Mercedes in 2012.

LIUZZI, Vitantonio (I) b 6/8/1980, Milan

2005 Championship position: 23=   Wins: 0   Pole positions: 0   Fastest laps: 0   Points scored: 1

	Race	Circuit	No	Entrant	Tyres	Capacity/Car/Engine	Comment	Q Pos/Entries
app	AUSTRALIAN GP	Melbourne	37	Red Bull Racing	M	3.0 Red Bull RB1-Cosworth V8	ran as 3rd driver in practice only	- /-
app	MALAYSIAN GP	Sepang	37	Red Bull Racing	M	3.0 Red Bull RB1-Cosworth V8	ran as 3rd driver in practice only	- /-
app	BAHRAIN GP	Sakhir Circuit	37	Red Bull Racing	M	3.0 Red Bull RB1-Cosworth V8	ran as 3rd driver in practice only	- /-
8	SAN MARINO GP	Imola	15	Red Bull Racing	M	3.0 Red Bull RB1-Cosworth V8		16/20
ret	SPANISH GP	Barcelona	15	Red Bull Racing	M	3.0 Red Bull RB1-Cosworth V8	spun off – engine cut out	11/18
ret	MONACO GP	Monte Carlo	15	Red Bull Racing	M	3.0 Red Bull RB1-Cosworth V8	accident – suspension damage	12/18
9	EUROPEAN GP	Nürburgring	15	Red Bull Racing	M	3.0 Red Bull RB1-Cosworth V8		14/20
app	FRENCH GP	Magny Cours	37	Red Bull Racing	M	3.0 Red Bull RB1-Cosworth V8	ran as 3rd driver in practice only	- /-
app	BRITISH GP	Silverstone	37	Red Bull Racing	M	3.0 Red Bull RB1-Cosworth V8	ran as 3rd driver in practice only	- /-
app	GERMAN GP	Hockenheim	37	Red Bull Racing	M	3.0 Red Bull RB1-Cosworth V8	ran as 3rd driver in practice only	- /-
app	HUNGARIAN GP	Hungaroring	37	Red Bull Racing	M	3.0 Red Bull RB1-Cosworth V8	ran as 3rd driver in practice only	- /-
aap	TURKISH GP	Istanbul	37	Red Bull Racing	M	3.0 Red Bull RB1-Cosworth V8	ran as 3rd driver in practice only	- /-
app	ITALIAN GP	Monza	37	Red Bull Racing	M	3.0 Red Bull RB1-Cosworth V8	ran as 3rd driver in practice only	- /-
app	BELGIAN GP	Spa	37	Red Bull Racing	M	3.0 Red Bull RB1-Cosworth V8	ran as 3rd driver in practice only	- /-
app	JAPANESE GP	Suzuka	37	Red Bull Racing	M	3.0 Red Bull RB1-Cosworth V8	ran as 3rd driver in practice only	- /-
app	CHINESE GP	Shanghai	37	Red Bull Racing	M	3.0 Red Bull RB1-Cosworth V8	ran as 3rd driver in practice only	- /-

2006 Championship position: 00   Wins: 0   Pole positions: 0   Fastest laps: 0   Points scored: 1

	Race	Circuit	No	Entrant	Tyres	Capacity/Car/Engine	Comment	Q Pos/Entries
11	BAHRAIN GP	Sakhir Circuit	20	Scuderia Toro Rosso	B	3.0 Toro Rosso STR01-Cosworth V8		15/22
11	MALAYSIAN GP	Sepang	20	Scuderia Toro Rosso	B	3.0 Toro Rosso STR01-Cosworth V8	1 lap behind	18/22
ret	AUSTRALIAN GP	Melbourne	20	Scuderia Toro Rosso	B	3.0 Toro Rosso STR01-Cosworth V8	accident	13/22
14	SAN MARINO GP	Imola	20	Scuderia Toro Rosso	B	3.0 Toro Rosso STR01-Cosworth V8	1 lap behind	16/22
ret	EUROPEAN GP	Nürburgring	20	Scuderia Toro Rosso	B	3.0 Toro Rosso STR01-Cosworth V8	accident – multiple collision on lap 1	16/22
15/ret	SPANISH GP	Barcelona	20	Scuderia Toro Rosso	B	3.0 Toro Rosso STR01-Cosworth V8	hydraulics/3 laps behind	16/22
10	MONACO GP	Monte Carlo	20	Scuderia Toro Rosso	B	3.0 Toro Rosso STR01-Cosworth V8	1 lap behind	13/22
13	BRITISH GP	Silverstone	20	Scuderia Toro Rosso	B	3.0 Toro Rosso STR01-Cosworth V8	1 lap behind	13/22
13	CANADIAN GP	Montreal	20	Scuderia Toro Rosso	B	3.0 Toro Rosso STR01-Cosworth V8	2 laps behind	15/22
8	U S GP	Indianapolis	20	Scuderia Toro Rosso	B	3.0 Toro Rosso STR01-Cosworth V8	1 lap behind/first point for Toro Rosso	21/22
13	FRENCH GP	Magny Cours	20	Scuderia Toro Rosso	B	3.0 Toro Rosso STR01-Cosworth V8	started from back of grid/1 lap behind	17/22
10	GERMAN GP	Hockenheim	20	Scuderia Toro Rosso	B	3.0 Toro Rosso STR01-Cosworth V8	1 lap behind	17/22
ret	HUNGARIAN GP	Hungaroring	20	Scuderia Toro Rosso	B	3.0 Toro Rosso STR01-Cosworth V8	accident – rear ended by Räikkönen	17/22
ret	TURKISH GP	Istanbul	20	Scuderia Toro Rosso	B	3.0 Toro Rosso STR01-Cosworth V8	differential failure – spun off	19/22
14	ITALIAN GP	Monza	20	Scuderia Toro Rosso	B	3.0 Toro Rosso STR01-Cosworth V8	1 lap behind	17/22
10	CHINESE GP	Shanghai	20	Scuderia Toro Rosso	B	3.0 Toro Rosso STR01-Cosworth V8	1 lap behind	14/22
14	JAPANESE GP	Suzuka	20	Scuderia Toro Rosso	B	3.0 Toro Rosso STR01-Cosworth V8	1 lap behind	15/22
13	BRAZILIAN GP	Interlagos	20	Scuderia Toro Rosso	B	3.0 Toro Rosso STR01-Cosworth V8	1 lap behind	16/22

2007 Championship position: 18   Wins: 0   Pole positions: 0   Fastest laps: 0   Points scored: 3

	Race	Circuit	No	Entrant	Tyres	Capacity/Car/Engine	Comment	Q Pos/Entries
14	AUSTRALIAN GP	Melbourne	18	Scuderia Toro Rosso	B	2.4 Toro Rosso STR02-Ferrari V8	1 lap behind	20/22
17	MALAYSIAN GP	Sepang	18	Scuderia Toro Rosso	B	2.4 Toro Rosso STR02-Ferrari V8	1 lap behind	16/22
ret	BAHRAIN GP	Bahrain	18	Scuderia Toro Rosso	B	2.4 Toro Rosso STR02-Ferrari V8	hydraulics	18/22
ret	SPANISH GP	Barcelona	18	Scuderia Toro Rosso	B	2.4 Toro Rosso STR02-Ferrari V8	hydraulics	16/22
ret	MONACO GP	Monte Carlo	18	Scuderia Toro Rosso	B	2.4 Toro Rosso STR02-Ferrari V8	accident – lap 1 collision – Couthard	13/22
ret	CANADIAN GP	Montreal	18	Scuderia Toro Rosso	B	2.4 Toro Rosso STR02-Ferrari V8	accident – suspension failure	12/22
17/ret	U S GP	Indianapolis	18	Scuderia Toro Rosso	B	2.4 Toro Rosso STR02-Ferrari V8	water pressure/5 laps behind	19/22
ret	FRENCH GP	Magny Cours	18	Scuderia Toro Rosso	B	2.4 Toro Rosso STR02-Ferrari V8	accident- hit by Davidson on lap 1	17/22
16/ret	BRITISH GP	Silverstone	18	Scuderia Toro Rosso	B	2.4 Toro Rosso STR02-Ferrari V8	gearbox	16/22
ret	EUROPEAN GP	Nürburgring	18	Scuderia Toro Rosso	B	2.4 Toro Rosso STR02-Ferrari V8	accident – crashed out in heavy rain	19/22
ret	HUNGARIAN GP	Hungaroring	18	Scuderia Toro Rosso	B	2.4 Toro Rosso STR02-Ferrari V8	electronics	16/22
15	TURKISH GP	Istanbul	18	Scuderia Toro Rosso	B	2.4 Toro Rosso STR02-Ferrari V8	gearshift problems/1 lap behind	17/22
17	ITALIAN GP	Monza	18	Scuderia Toro Rosso	B	2.4 Toro Rosso STR02-Ferrari V8	tired engine/1 lap behind	19/22
12	BELGIAN GP	Spa	18	Scuderia Toro Rosso	B	2.4 Toro Rosso STR02-Ferrari V8	1 lap behind	15/22
9*	JAPANESE GP	Suzuka	18	Scuderia Toro Rosso	B	2.4 Toro Rosso STR02-Ferrari V8	*8th – but given 25-sec penalty	15/22
6	CHINESE GP	Shanghai	18	Scuderia Toro Rosso	B	2.4 Toro Rosso STR02-Ferrari V8	survived collision with R Schumacher	11/22
13	BRAZILIAN GP	Interlagos	18	Scuderia Toro Rosso	B	2.4 Toro Rosso STR02-Ferrari V8	extra stop – collision damage/-2 laps	14/22

2009 Championship position: Unplaced

	Race	Circuit	No	Entrant	Tyres	Capacity/Car/Engine	Comment	Q Pos/Entries
ret	ITALIAN GP	Monza	21	Force India F1 Team	B	2.4 Force India VJM02-Mercedes V8	driveshaft	7/20
14	SINGAPORE GP	Marina Bay Circuit	21	Force India F1 Team	B	2.4 Force India VJM02-Mercedes V8		20/20
14	JAPANESE GP	Suzuka	21	Force India F1 Team	B	2.4 Force India VJM02-Mercedes V8		19/20
11	BRAZILIAN GP	Interlagos	21	Force India F1 Team	B	2.4 Force India VJM02-Mercedes V8		15/22
15	ABU DHABI GP	Yas Marina Circuit	21	Force India F1 Team	B	2.4 Force India VJM02-Mercedes V8		17/22

2010 Championship position: 12th   Wins: 0   Pole positions: 0   Fastest laps: 0   Points scored: 32

	Race	Circuit	No	Entrant	Tyres	Capacity/Car/Engine	Comment	Q Pos/Entries
9	BAHRAIN GP	Sakhir Circuit	15	Force India F1 Team	B	2.4 Force India VJM03-Mercedes V8		12/24
7	AUSTRALIAN GP	Melbourne	15	Force India F1 Team	B	2.4 Force India VJM03-Mercedes V8		13/24
ret	MALAYSIAN GP	Sepang	15	Force India F1 Team	B	2.4 Force India VJM03-Mercedes V8	throttle	10/24
ret	CHINESE GP	Shanghai Circuit	15	Force India F1 Team	B	2.4 Force India VJM03-Mercedes V8	caused multiple accident on lap 1	18/24
15/ret	SPANISH GP	Barcelona	15	Force India F1 Team	B	2.4 Force India VJM03-Mercedes V8	engine//2 laps behind	10/24
9*	MONACO GP	Monte Carlo	15	Force India F1 Team	B	2.4 Force India VJM03-Mercedes V8	*10th – but 6th place car demoted	10/24
13	TURKISH GP	Istanbul Park	15	Force India F1 Team	B	2.4 Force India VJM03-Mercedes V8	1 lap behind	18/24
9	CANADIAN GP	Montreal	15	Force India F1 Team	B	2.4 Force India VJM03-Mercedes V8	1 lap behind	6/24
16*	EUROPEAN GP	Valencia	15	Force India F1 Team	B	2.4 Force India VJM03-Mercedes V8	*5-sec pen – speeding behind safety car	14/24
11	BRITISH GP	Silverstone	15	Force India F1 Team	B	2.4 Force India VJM03-Mercedes V8		15/24
16	GERMAN GP	Hockenheim	15	Force India F1 Team	B	2.4 Force India VJM03-Mercedes V8	ran off track – extra pitstop/-2 laps	12/24
13	HUNGARIAN GP	Hungaroring	15	Force India F1 Team	B	2.4 Force India VJM03-Mercedes V8	1 lap behind	16/24
10	BELGIAN GP	Spa	15	Force India F1 Team	B	2.4 Force India VJM03-Mercedes V8		14/24
12	ITALIAN GP	Monza	15	Force India F1 Team	B	2.4 Force India VJM03-Mercedes V8		20/24
ret	SINGAPORE GP	Marina Bay Circuit	15	Force India F1 Team	B	2.4 Force India VJM03-Mercedes V8	hit by Heidfeld – broken suspension	17/24
ret	JAPANESE GP	Suzuka	15	Force India F1 Team	B	2.4 Force India VJM03-Mercedes V8	accident - hit by Massa on lap 1	17/24

6	KOREAN GP	Yeongam	15	Force India F1 Team	B	2.4 Force India VJM03-Mercedes V8			18/24
ret	BRAZILIAN GP	Interlagos	15	Force India F1 Team	B	2.4 Force India VJM03-Mercedes V8	accident - rear suspension failure		17/24
ret	ABU DHABI GP	Yas Marina Circuit	15	Force India F1 Team	B	2.4 Force India VJM03-Mercedes V8	accident - hit stationary Schumacher		16/24

2011 Championship position: Unplaced

dnq	AUSTRALIAN GP	Melbourne	23	HRT F1 Team	P	2.4 HRT F111-Cosworth V8		23/24
ret	MALAYSIAN GP	Sepang	23	HRT F1 Team	P	2.4 HRT F111-Cosworth V8	precautionary – damaged rear wing	23/24
22	CHINESE GP	Shanghai Circuit	23	HRT F1 Team	P	2.4 HRT F111-Cosworth V8	jump start – drive thu penalty/-2 laps	23/24
22	TURKISH GP	Istanbul Park	23	HRT F1 Team	P	2.4 HRT F111-Cosworth V8	4 laps behind	21/24
ret	SPANISH GP	Barcelona	23	HRT F1 Team	P	2.4 HRT F111-Cosworth V8	gearbox	21/24
16	MONACO GP	Monte Carlo	23	HRT F1 Team	P	2.4 HRT F111-Cosworth V8	3 laps behind/*no time set	*24/24
13	CANADIAN GP	Montreal	23	HRT F1 Team	P	2.4 HRT F111-Cosworth V8	1 lap behind	21/24
23	EUROPEAN GP	Valencia	23	HRT F1 Team	P	2.4 HRT F111-Cosworth V8	3 laps behind	22/24
18	BRITISH GP	Silverstone	23	HRT F1 Team	P	2.4 HRT F111-Cosworth V8	2 laps behind	23/24
ret	GERMAN GP	Hockenheim	23	HRT F1 Team	P	2.4 HRT F111-Cosworth V8	electrics	23/24
20	HUNGARIAN GP	Hungaroring	23	HRT F1 Team	P	2.4 HRT F111-Cosworth V8	5 laps behind	22/24
19	BELGIAN GP	Spa	23	HRT F1 Team	P	2.4 HRT F111-Cosworth V8	1 lap behind	22/24
ret	ITALIAN GP	Monza	23	HRT F1 Team	P	2.4 HRT F111-Cosworth V8	caused multiple accident on lap 1	24/24
20	SINGAPORE GP	Marina Bay Circuit	23	HRT F1 Team	P	2.4 HRT F111-Cosworth V8	5 laps behind	24/24
23	JAPANESE GP	Suzuka	23	HRT F1 Team	P	2.4 HRT F111-Cosworth V8	3 laps behind/*no time set	*24/24
21	KOREAN GP	Yeongam	23	HRT F1 Team	P	2.4 HRT F111-Cosworth V8	3 laps behind	23/24
20	ABU DHABI GP	Yas Marina Circuit	23	HRT F1 Team	P	2.4 HRT F111-Cosworth V8	2 laps behind	23/24
ret	BRAZILIAN GP	Interlagos	23	HRT F1 Team	P	2.4 HRT F111-Cosworth V8	alternator	21/24

GP Starts: 80   GP Wins: 0   Pole positions: 0   Fastest laps: 0   Points: 26

LELLA LOMBARDI

IN 1975, Lella Lombardi became the first and thus far only woman to finish in the top six in a grand prix (albeit one that had been shortened and only counted for half points). Having always harboured an ambition to go racing, she drove in Formula Monza and Formula 3 with Lotus and Brabham cars, before winning the Italian Ford Mexico championship in 1973.

In 1974, Lella was signed to race the Shellsport-Luxembourg Lola T330 in F5000 and silenced her critics by finishing fourth in the final standings. Despite failing to make the the grid for the grand prix at Brands Hatch, she found backing from Lavazza to embark on an F1 season with March in 1975, the result in Spain being the obvious high point. Although she did extremely well to finish seventh in the German Grand Prix, she was denied a start for Williams at Watkins Glen when the ignition failed on her car on the warm-up lap. Her hopes of continuing with March in 1976 were dashed when she lost her backing after the first race of the season, and she was pushed out of the team by Ronnie Peterson's hasty switch from Lotus. Lella's brief flirtation with the always troubled RAM team was predictably fruitless.

Although squeezed out of Formula 1, Lella continued her racing career, mainly in sports cars, through into the early 1980s. She enjoyed some excellent results in the Osella prototype with Giorgio Francia, the pair winning the Ignazio Giunti Trophy at Vallelunga in 1979, and the Ore di Mugello in 1981, a year that also saw them finish second in the Monza 1000km.

It was with great sadness that the motor racing world learned of Lella's tragically early death, at the age of 50, from cancer in March, 1992.

LOMBARDI, Lella (I) b 26/3/1943, Frugarolo, nr Alessandria – d 3/3/1992, Milan

1974 Championship position: Unplaced

	Race	Circuit	No	Entrant	Tyres	Capacity/Car/Engine	Comment	Q Pos/Entries
dnq	BRITISH GP	Brands Hatch	208	Allied Polymer Group	G	3.0 Brabham BT42-Cosworth V8		=28/34

1975 Championship position: 21st   Wins: 0   Pole positions: 0   Fastest laps: 0   Points scored: 0.5

ret	SOUTH AFRICAN GP	Kyalami	10	March Engineering	G	3.0 March 741-Cosworth V8	engine	26/28
6*	SPANISH GP	Montjuich Park	10	Lavazza March	G	3.0 March 751-Cosworth V8	*half points – shortened race/-2 laps	24/26
dnq	MONACO GO	Monte Carlo	10	Lavazza March	G	3.0 March 751-Cosworth V8		25/26
ret	BELGIAN GP	Zolder	10	Lavazza March	G	3.0 March 751-Cosworth V8	engine – oil leak	23/24
ret	SWEDISH GP	Anderstorp	10	Lavazza March	G	3.0 March 751-Cosworth V8	fuel metering unit	24/26
14	DUTCH GP	Zandvoort	10	Lavazza March	G	3.0 March 751-Cosworth V8	pit stop - tyres/5 laps behind	23/25
18	FRENCH GP	Paul Ricard	10	Lavazza March	G	3.0 March 751-Cosworth V8	pit stop – handling/4 laps behind	26/26
ret	BRITISH GP	Silverstone	29	Lavazza March	G	3.0 March 751-Cosworth V8	ignition	22/28
7	GERMAN GP	Nürburgring	29	Lavazza March	G	3.0 March 751-Cosworth V8		25/26
17	AUSTRIAN GP	Österreichring	29	Lavazza March	G	3.0 March 751-Cosworth V8	3 laps behind	22/30
ret	ITALIAN GP	Monza	29	Lavazza March	G	3.0 March 751-Cosworth V8	brake failure – crashed	24/28
dns	US GP	Watkins Glen	20	Frank Williams Racing Cars	G	3.0 Williams FW04-Cosworth V8	ignition failure on warm up lap	(24)/24

1976 Championship position: Unplaced

14	BRAZILIAN GP	Interlagos	10	Lavazza March	G	3.0 March 761-Cosworth V8	pit stop – engine/4 laps behind	22/22
dnq	BRITISH GP	Brands Hatch	33	RAM Racing with Lavazza	G	3.0 Brabham BT44B-Cosworth V8		30/30
dnq	GERMAN GP	Nürburgring	33	RAM Racing with Lavazza	G	3.0 Brabham BT44B-Cosworth V8	legal wrangle – car impounded	27/28
12	AUSTRIAN GP	Österreichring	33	RAM Racing with Lavazza	G	3.0 Brabham BT44B-Cosworth V8	4 laps behind	24/25

GP Starts: 12   GP Wins: 0   Pole positions: 0   Fastest laps: 0   Points: 0.5

ERNST LOOF

A GERMAN motorcycle champion eight times between 1930 and 1938, Ernst Loof worked for BMW, building the sports car that von Hanstein used to win the Brescia 1000-miles before the Second World War.

However, it is as designer and engineer of the splendid Veritas machines of the late 1940s and early 1950s that Loof is best remembered. He seldom took the wheel, but did appear in the 1953 German Grand Prix, the marque's last season in top-flight competition. Sadly, by then, the venture had gone into bankruptcy.

Thereafter, Loof returned to work for BMW in 1954, but by then he had begun to develop cancer. Suffering from a brain tumour, he died after a long illness in 1956.

HENRI LOUVEAU

A LTHOUGH not a driver of the first rank, Henri Louveau was a more than useful performer, whose best days were in the immediate post-war years. In 1946, he drove a Maserati 4CL, winning at Lille, where he shared with Raymond Sommer, and gaining second places at Forez, Perpignan and Albi. The following year, he was second at Lyon and third at Pau with the 'Maser'. He also raced a recently purchased Delage with success, taking second at Perpignan once more, third at Marseilles, fifth in the Jersey Road Race and sixth in the Italian GP.

The Delage was put to good use over the next three seasons, with seconds at Montlhéry and Chimay in 1948, third at Pescara in 1949 and fourth at Rouen in 1950. But the most thrilling of Henri's races in the car must have been the 1949 Le Mans 24-hours, when he was second, having driven at grand prix pace over the last couple of hours and just failed to overhaul the sick car of Luigi Chinetti, which was touring to the finish.

Having handled Louis Rosier's Talbot in the 1950 Italian GP, Henri planned to race the car regularly in the 1951 season, which began with a series of non-championship events. He started with fourth at Syracuse, crashed at Pau (where he was lucky to escape without injury after the car flipped), then took eighth at San Remo, sixth at Bordeaux, eleventh in the rain-halted International Trophy and fourth in the Paris GP at Montlhéry. A week later came the championship race at the fearsome Bremgarten road circuit in Berne. With the track made even more treacherous by wet conditions, Henri's Talbot skidded off the road, struck a barrier and overturned in a repeat of his Pau crash. This time, he was not so fortunate, suffering concussion and a fractured leg, which prompted his retirement from racing.

LOOF, Ernst (D) b 4/7/1907, Neindorf – d 3/3/1956, Bonn

	1953 Championship position: Unplaced							
	Race	Circuit	No	Entrant	Tyres	Capacity/Car/Engine	Comment	Q Pos/Entries
ret	GERMAN GP	Nürburgring	30	Ernst Loof	–	2.0 Veritas Meteor 6	fuel pump	31/35
	GP Starts: 1 GP Wins: 0 Pole positions: 0 Fastest laps: 0 Points: 0							

LOUVEAU, Henri (F) b 25/1/1910, Suresnes – d 7/1/1991, Orléans

	1950 Championship position: Unplaced							
	Race	Circuit	No	Entrant	Tyres	Capacity/Car/Engine	Comment	Q Pos/Entries
ret	ITALIAN GP	Monza	64	Ecurie Louis Rosier	D	4.5 Lago-Talbot T26C-GS 6		14/27
	1951 Championship position: Unplaced							
ret	SWISS GP	Bremgarten	10	Ecurie Louis Rosier	D	4.5 Lago-Talbot T26C 6	hit telegraph pole – suffered broken leg 11/21	
	GP Starts: 2 GP Wins: 0 Pole positions: 0 Fastest laps: 0 Points: 0							

LOVE, John (RSR) b 7/12/1924, Bulawayo – d 25/4/2005, Bulawayo

	1962 Championship position: Unplaced							
	Race	Circuit	No	Entrant	Tyres	Capacity/Car/Engine	Comment	Q Pos/Entries
8	SOUTH AFRICAN GP	East London	18	John Love	D	1.5 Cooper T55-Climax 4	4 laps behind	12/17
	1963 Championship position: Unplaced							
9	SOUTH AFRICAN GP	East London	19	John Love	D	1.5 Cooper T55-Climax 4	5 laps behind	13/21
	1964 Championship position: Unplaced							
dnq	ITALIAN GP	Monza	24	Cooper Car Co	D	1.5 Cooper T73-Climax V8	engine seized in practice	24/25
	1965 Championship position: Unplaced							
ret	SOUTH AFRICAN GP	East London	17	John Love	D	1.5 Cooper T55-Climax 4	driveshaft	18/25

1967 Championship position: 11th=		Wins: 0	Pole positions: 0	Fastest laps: 0	Points scored: 6			
2	SOUTH AFRICAN GP Kyalami	17	John Love	F	2.7 Cooper T79-Climax 4		*pit stop – fuel pick up when in lead*	5/18
1968 Championship position: Unplaced								
9	SOUTH AFRICAN GP Kyalami	17	Team Gunston	F	3.0 Brabham BT20-Repco V8		*5 laps behind*	17/23
1969 Championship position: Unplaced								
ret	SOUTH AFRICAN GP Kyalami	16	Team Gunston	D	3.0 Lotus 49-Cosworth V8		*ignition*	11/18
1970 Championship position: Unplaced								
8	SOUTH AFRICAN GP Kyalami	23	Team Gunston	D	3.0 Lotus 49-Cosworth V8		*2 laps behind*	22/24
1971 Championship position: Unplaced								
ret	SOUTH AFRICAN GP Kyalami	24	Team Peco/Gunston	F	3.0 March 701-Cosworth V8		*differential*	21/25
1972 Championship position: Unplaced								
16/ret	SOUTH AFRICAN GP Kyalami	27	Team Gunston	F	3.0 Surtees TS9-Cosworth V8		*puncture – spun off/6 laps behind*	26/27

GP Starts: 9   GP Wins: 0   Pole positions: 0   Fastest laps: 0   Points: 6

JOHN LOVE

ONE the great figures in South African motorsport, John Love was from Rhodesia (now Zimbabwe) and he began racing motorcyles immediately upon his return from war service in Italy and the Middle East. After starting with a Cooper-JAP in 1954, he began to take racing seriously, and the purchase of the championship winning Jennings-Riley special for the 1958 season allowed him to pit his talents against the cream of the local crop. In 1959, together with another local hopeful, Jimmy Shield, he ventured to Europe, where he purchased a D-Type Jaguar that he raced briefly before shipping it back to race in South African events.

Still ambitious to succeed in Europe, Love arranged to race a Formula Junior Lola that he prepared and maintained himself. A fine drive at Albi caught the eye of Ken Tyrrell, while a subsequent second place and the fastest lap at the Nürburgring led to a successful test that saw him enter the Tyrrell fold. Despite blotting is copybook with a crash at Pescara, the

Rhodesian went back to South Africa with the exciting prospect of a really competitive Formula Junior ride to look forward to in 1961. Meanwhile, he wasted little time in impressing everyone at home with a superb win in the the Rand nine-hours in a Porsche Spyder and some outstanding performances in a T51 Cooper-Maserati, which included a win at Killarney.

Love was partnered by Tony Maggs, and the 'Tyrrell twins' were pretty evenly matched, both taking regular wins in the two seasons they drove together. Love gained five victories in 1961 and a further four the following season, before a very nasty crash at Albi in September, 1962, left him with a badly damaged elbow. Ironically, his accident was triggered by his team-mate's spin. Only a week earlier, he had clinched the British Saloon Car Championship after his seventh win of the year in Mini Cooper-Austin.

Unfortunately, Love's injury scuppered a test for a possible Cooper drive in 1963 and, not wishing to continue in Formula Junior, he returned to South Africa with a T55 'Slimline' Cooper to compete in the domestic championship. Another chance in Formula 1 came at short notice when Cooper offered John the chance to race the second works car at Monza. Sadly it failed him early on in practice, leaving him unable to qualify...

The first of Love's six South African championships came in 1964, and his tally was only halted by a determined rival, Dave Charlton, with whom he had some ding-dong battles over the years. Success generally eluded him in the home world championship grands prix, though, with the notable exception of the 1967 event, when only a late pit stop for fuel prevented him from taking what would have been an incredible fairy-tale victory. In fact, he had fitted extra fuel tanks to his light Tasman car to complete the full grand prix distance, but unfortunately one of the Bendix fuel pumps failed, necessitating the late stop that cost him the lead. However, his second-place finish, behind Rodriguez, was still an amazing achievement.

To stave off the ever-growing threat to his national crown, Love first acquired a Brabham BT20-Repco V8 and then, in 1969, a Lotus 49 complete with Cosworth engine. His vice-like grip on proceedings was finally broken in 1970, when he had a troubled time after switching to a March 701, enduring endless mechanical and reliability problems. Dave Charlton took the championship to begin his own era of dominance in South Africa. Love, with his Surtees TS9 or his Brabham BT33, just could not match the pace of his deadly rival in his beautifully prepared Lotus 72C.

In 1973, Team Gunston were running John and his team-mate, Ian Scheckter, in Formula 2 Chevrons, which plainly could not compete with Charlton's F1 car. Left to battle for the subsidiary honours, the old hand was outpaced by the young charger, and when the team returned to F1-spec machines for 1974, Love was dropped in favour of Paddy Driver. This brought an end to a long and illustrious career, which did have a sentimental last hurrah late in 1979, when Team Gunston invited him back to compete in a couple of Formula Atlantic races. After retiring from competition, he was involved in a car dealership in Bulawayo. He died of cancer in April 2005, aged 80.

PETE LOVELY

ONE of the most enduring figures of the amateur US motorsport scene, Pete Lovely began racing specials on dirt tracks in the Pacific North West area in the late 1940s. Subsequently, he graduated to a Jaguar XK120 and built a couple of very competitive Porsche derivatives in 1954.

The following season, Pete fitted a Porsche engine and VW transaxle into a Cooper Mk8 chassis, racing the special (known affectionately as the Lovely 'Pooper') very successfully. He won the 1955 SCCA F-Modified Championship for under-1500cc cars, often having been involved in some stirring battles with Ken Miles.

Pete and Jack McAfee caused a stir in the 1956 Sebring 12-hours when their privately entered Porsche 550 Spyder gave the similar works entry, driven by Wolfgang von Trips and Hans Herrman, a run for its money, finishing just one place behind in seventh overall. Lovely would return even more successfully in 1960, taking third place overall in Jack Nethercott's Ferrari 250 Testa Rossa.

In November 1957, Lovely became the first man to win a race at the newly opened Laguna Seca Raceway, when he took his Ferrari to the chequered flag. In 1958, he travelled to Europe to visit the Lotus factory with a view to purchasing a sports car. After a successful test, he agreed to race a Lotus XV model at Le Mans, but his race ended when co-driver Jay Chamberlain crashed the machine. A couple of weeks later, however, success was achieved when he shared a Lotus with Innes Ireland to easily take a class win at the Reims 12-hour race.

For the 1959 season, Lovely arranged to join Lotus, partnering Graham Hill, but the American had a short tenure in the number-two seat. Hampered by low oil pressure, he was not classified in the International Trophy Race at Silverstone, after an extremely promising practice, and more disappointment followed. His chances of a hoped-for grand prix debut at Monaco were effectively dashed when the team's transporter broke down, leaving the unfortunate rookie just one practice session in which to try to qualify an unsorted car.

Disenchanted, Lovely returned to America, but he did appear in the following year's grand prix at Riverside, driving a Formula 2 Cooper with a Ferrari sports car engine. Not surprisingly, it was not competitive, but he brought it home in 11th place, six laps down. With Formula Junior burgeoning in the USA, he equipped himself with a Lotus 18 to win races at Las Vegas and Nassau in 1961, and the following year he found more success in a Lotus 22 at Daytona and Seattle. He also campaigned a Lotus 23 sports car, finishing fifth in the first heat of the 1962 Pacific North West Grand Prix, and later he ran a Lotus Cortina at West Coast meetings. From then on, his racing largely took a back seat while he built a highly successful Volkswagen dealership in Seattle, Washington State. Eventually, the urge to be involved in grand prix racing again took hold, and he boldly purchased a Lotus 49 to race in the final three races of the 1969 season, which were all held on the American continent. By then well past 40 years of age, he sensibly drove well within his limits and was encouraged to venture to Europe early in the 1970 season.

After shunting his car into the Brands Hatch Armco in the Race of Champions, Lovely trailed his 49B home 13th on aggregate in the International Trophy at Silverstone. Undaunted, the ever-enthusiastic American reappeared in mid-season at Zandvoort, where gearbox trouble left him two seconds away from qualification. It was the same story at Clermont-Ferrand, where he was out of his depth on the mountain circuit, but he was on the grid at Brands Hatch, sharing the back row with two other Lotus 49s driven by Graham Hill and grand prix debutant Emerson Fittipaldi. Eventually, he struggled to the finish, with a borrowed rain tyre on one corner, too far behind to be officially classified. Lovely's last tilt at Formula 1 that season came in the US Grand Prix, where he just failed to make the cut.

With the 49B outdated and the cost of a new Formula 1 car prohibitive, Lovely came up with the novel idea of purchasing a Lotus 69 F2 car and grafting the whole of the Cosworth rear-end package on to the chassis. This concept was somewhat more successful when taken up by Mike Beuttler and, in turn, the March works team in 1972. However, Chris Craft's late withdrawal saw Pete promoted from first reserve to contest a rain-sodden Canadian Grand Prix; he was also allowed to start at Watkins Glen, but a flat battery and excessive vibration in the race left him out of the classified finishers once more.

For a couple of years (1979 and 1980), Lovely turned team entrant in the Can-Am series and ran Gary Cove in the 2-litre class, first with a Chevron and then a Ralt. Despite his advancing years, he remained a leading light on the US historic racing scene. He continued to race contemporary machinery from his racing days, including his incredibly valuable Lotus 49. This was beautifully restored by Pete Lovely Racing, based in his home town of Tacoma, Washington, a company dedicated to maintaining and restoring vintage racers to the highest standards.

LOVELY, Pete (USA) b 11/4/1926, Livingston, Montana – d 15/5/2011, Takoma, Washington

	1959	Championship position: Unplaced							
	Race	Circuit	No	Entrant	Tyres	Capacity/Car/Engine	Comment		Q Pos/Entries
dnq	MONACO GP	Monte Carlo	42	Team Lotus	D	2.5 Lotus 16-Climax 4			22/24
	1960	Championship position: Unplaced							
11	US GP	Riverside	25	Fred Armbruster	D	2.4 Cooper T45-Ferrari 4	6 laps behind		20/23

1969 Championship position: 0	Wins: 0	Pole positions: 0	Fastest laps: 0	Points scored: 0					
7	CANADIAN GP	Mosport Park	25	Pete Lovely Volkswagen Inc	F	3.0 Lotus 49B-Cosworth V8	9 laps behind	16/20
ret	US GP	Watkins Glen	21	Pete Lovely Volkswagen Inc	F	3.0 Lotus 49B-Cosworth V8	driveshaft	16/18
9	MEXICAN GP	Mexico City	21	Pete Lovely Volkswagen Inc	F	3.0 Lotus 49B-Cosworth V8	3 laps behind	16/17
1970 Championship position: Unplaced								
dnq	DUTCH GP	Zandvoort	31	Pete Lovely Volkswagen Inc	F	3.0 Lotus 49B-Cosworth V8		23/24
dnq	FRENCH GP	Clermont Ferrand	25	Pete Lovely Volkswagen Inc	F	3.0 Lotus 49B-Cosworth V8		22/23
nc	BRITISH GP	Brands Hatch	29	Pete Lovely Volkswagen Inc	F	3.0 Lotus 49B-Cosworth V8	pit stop – tyres/11 laps behind	24/25
dnq	US GP	Watkins Glen	28	Pete Lovely Volkswagen Inc	F	3.0 Lotus 49B-Cosworth V8		26/27
1971 Championship position: Unplaced								
nc	CANADIAN GP	Mosport Park	35	Pete Lovely Volkswagen Inc	F	3.0 Lotus 69-Cosworth V8	pit stop – fuel/9 laps behind	26/27
nc	US GP	Watkins Glen	30	Pete Lovely Volkswagen Inc	F	3.0 Lotus 69-Cosworth V8	pit stop – fuel/10 laps behind	32/32

GP Starts: 7   GP Wins: 0   Pole positions: 0   Fastest laps: 0   Points: 0

ROGER LOYER

FROM a modest background – his father was a taxi driver – as a youngster, Roger Loyer was always in contact with cars. Indeed, he began his working life as a chauffer and mechanic, before taking up motorcycle racing in 1928. He enjoyed great success with a Velocette before trying his hand at cars in 1938. The Second World War took away a huge chunk of his competition career, but after a few one-off drives, he co-founded a team to drive the little Cisitalia D46 between 1947 and 1949. Then he joined Equipe Gordini in 1950 to race their Formula 2 Simca Gordini, the best result coming in the minor Circuit of Médoc race near Bordeaux. Over the next few seasons, he appeared mainly in sports cars for the Gordini concern, winning the Coupe du Salon at Montlhéry, and at Agen in 1953.

Roger's one opportunity at grand prix level came at the beginning of 1954 in the Argentine Grand Prix, and he also drove the same Gordini Type 16 in the Buenos Aires City Libre GP a couple of weeks later. He was forced to retire his car, but took over Élie Bayol's machine to finish a distant tenth.

Loyer made a couple of sports car appeances for Gordini in 1956 and then apparently retired, but in 1960 he made a surprise return in the new Formula Junior. Although well past 50 years of age, he took an Elva-DKW to a win in the Coupe d l'USA at Montlhery, but achieved little else of note.

JEAN LUCAS

TURNING to racing after beginning his career in rallies, Jean Lucas recorded his best results behind the wheel of sports cars, winning at Spa in 1949 and Montlhéry the following year in Luigi Chinetti's Ferrari. In 1953, he joined Gordini as team manager and occasional driver, although he could still be seen racing his own Ferrari under the Los Amigos banner in popular North African events, such as those held at Agadir and Marrakesh. It was only when urgent business matters called Robert Manzon away from the Monza circuit that he stood in to make his solitary world championship appearance.

In 1956, Lucas took an old Ferrari 625 to fifth place in the Caen GP, and in 1957 he finished second in the F2 Coupe de Vitesse at Reims in Alan Brown's Cooper. He also took third place in his Los Amigos Jaguar D-Type at Le Mans that year, but when driving John du Puy's Maserati 250F in the end-of-season Moroccan GP, he overturned the car and was badly injured.

Realising that he would not be able to race again to his fullest abilities, Lucas threw himself into administrative roles within the sport, as well as co-founding the magazine Sport-Auto with Gérard Crombac in 1962; he moved on to other publishing projects when his interest in motorsport waned.

LOYER, Roger (F) b 5/8/1907, Paris – d 24/3/1988, Boulogne, Billancourt

1954 Championship position: Unplaced								
	Race	Circuit	No	Entrant	Tyres	Capacity/Car/Engine	Comment	Q Pos/Entries
ret	ARGENTINE GP	Buenos Aires	22	Equipe Gordini	E	2.5 Gordini Type 16 6	lack of oil	16/18

GP Starts: 1   GP Wins: 0   Pole positions: 0   Fastest laps: 0   Points: 0

LUCAS, Jean (F) b 25/4/1917, Le Mans – d 27/9/2003, Saint-Martin-de Ré

1955 Championship position: Unplaced								
	Race	Circuit	No	Entrant	Tyres	Capacity/Car/Engine	Comment	Q Pos/Entries
ret	ITALIAN GP	Monza	24	Equipe Gordini	E	2.5 Gordini Type 32 8	subbed for Manzon/engine	22/22
dns	"	"	22	Equipe Gordini	E	2.5 Gordini Type 16 6	practice only	– / –

GP Starts: 1   GP Wins: 0   Pole positions: 0   Fastest laps: 0   Points: 0

BRETT LUNGER

AN heir to the DuPont family, Brett Lunger began racing in 1965 with a Corvette, later graduating to Can-Am with a Caldwell-Chevrolet in 1968, but by his own admission he did not really know how to race properly; he did it for fun more than anything else.

Lunger dropped out of Princeton University and volunteered to fight in Vietnam with the Marines during 1969 and 1970, serving with distinction in an elite front-line reconnaissance squadron.

His racing career having been on hold, Lunger returned to the track in 1971, when he took part in the L & M F5000 series, racing an ex-Penske Lola T192 and finishing third in the championship. No doubt encouraged that he could progress his career more quickly, he travelled to Europe to race in Formula 2 with a works supported March 722 and soon found the level of competition hot, adopting a steady approach to his learning curve. He found more success back in the States, winning two races in Carl Hogan's LolaT300 to share third place overall in the series with Brian Redman.

It was something of a repeat diet the folowing year, Brett running a works supported Chevron in Formula 2 on occasion, but he seemed far more interested in the Rothmans F5000 series in the UK (where he took wins at Snetterton and Mallory) and the L & M Series back home

Lunger largely stayed in the USA for his F5000 action in 1974, signing up with Dan Gurney's ambitious Jorgensen Eagle. Initially the car was overweight and not able to match the Lola opposition, but the American plugged away to finish the year with a good deal of credit, if only fifth place in the standings, to show for his efforts.

Finally, come 1975, he was given a taste of grand prix racing with Hesketh, contesting three races in a second car alongside James Hunt.

During the next three seasons, the personable American, armed with a sizeable budget, slogged on without any real signs of making a breakthrough, even though he had some decent cars at his disposal, including McLaren M23 and M26 machines run by B & S Fabrications.

Perhaps Lunger's most notable contribution to Formula 1 was his bravery in the aftermath of Niki Lauda's fiery accident in the 1976 German Grand Prix. As the Austrian struggled to get free on his own, Lunger jumped on top of the Ferrari, grabbed the Austrian by his shoulders and, with the help of Arturo Merzario, who unbuckled the seatbelts, dragged the driver out of the car to safety.

Statistically, Lunger's best ever result of fourth place was achieved at the 1978 Daily Express International Trophy race, but this event was affected by rain and he finished just behind Tony Trimmer, both some three laps down on the winner, Keke Rosberg. Eventually, after a financial falling-out between driver and team towards the end of the season, Brett took his cash to Mo Nunn and made the grid in the US Grand Prix with a one-off ride for Ensign. It was his last grand prix appearance, after which he briefly drove in sports car events.

In 1979, Lunger joined George Follmer and Derek Bell in a Porsche 935/79 to take third place at the Riverside six-hour race, while later in the year he crossed to Watkins Glen to share a similar car with Elliott Forbes-Robinson and Randolph Townsend, which came home fourth.

After retiring from motor racing, Lunger remained a very competitive individual, and even in his 50s he was racing in marathons and cycling events. In 2003, he and his wife, Caroline, both licensed pilots, joined the Angel Flight Network. They give their time and pay all out-of-pocket-expenses to fly sick patients to hospital when they cannot fund the costs of transport themselves.

LUNGER, Brett (USA) b 14/11/1945, Wilmington, Delaware

	1975 Championship position: Unplaced							
	Race	Circuit	No	Entrant	Tyres	Capacity/Car/Engine	Comment	Q Pos/Entries
13	AUSTRIAN GP	Österreichring	25	Hesketh Racing	G	3.0 Hesketh 308B-Cosworth V8	1 lap behind	17/30
10	ITALIAN GP	Monza	25	Hesketh Racing	G	3.0 Hesketh 308B-Cosworth V8	2 laps behind	21/28
ret	US GP	Watkins Glen	25	Hesketh Racing	G	3.0 Hesketh 308B-Cosworth V8	missed gearchange – crashed	18/24
	1976 Championship position: Unplaced							
11	SOUTH AFRICAN GP	Kyalami	18	Team Surtees	G	3.0 Surtees TS19-Cosworth V8	1 lap behind	20/25
dnq	US GP WEST	Long Beach	18	Team Surtees	G	3.0 Surtees TS19-Cosworth V8		27/27
dnq	SPANISH GP	Jarama	18	Team Surtees	G	3.0 Surtees TS19-Cosworth V8		25/30

	Race	Circuit	No	Entrant	Tyres	Capacity/Car/Engine	Comment	Q Pos/Entries
ret	BELGIAN GP	Zolder	18	Team Surtees	G	3.0 Surtees TS19-Cosworth V8	electrics	26/29
15	SWEDISH GP	Anderstorp	18	Team Surtees	G	3.0 Surtees TS19-Cosworth V8	2 laps behind	24/24
16	FRENCH GP	Paul Ricard	18	Team Surtees	G	3.0 Surtees TS19-Cosworth V8	1 lap behind	23/30
ret	BRITISH GP	Brands Hatch	18	Team Surtees	G	3.0 Surtees TS19-Cosworth V8	gearbox	18/30
ret/dns*	GERMAN GP	Nürburgring	18	Team Surtees	G	3.0 Surtees TS19-Cosworth V8	in Lauda's crash/*did not restart	24/28
10/ret	AUSTRIAN GP	Österreichring	18	Team Surtees	G	3.0 Surtees TS19-Cosworth V8	brake failure – crashed/3 laps behind	16/25
14	ITALIAN GP	Monza	18	Team Surtees	G	3.0 Surtees TS19-Cosworth V8	stopped – thought race halted/-2 laps	25/29
15	CANADIAN GP	Mosport Park	18	Team Surtees	G	3.0 Surtees TS19-Cosworth V8	2 laps behind	22/27
11	US GP EAST	Watkins Glen	18	Team Surtees	G	3.0 Surtees TS19-Cosworth V8	2 laps behind	24/27
1977 Championship position: Unplaced								
14	SOUTH AFRICAN GP	Kyalami	30	Chesterfield Racing	G	3.0 March 761-Cosworth V8	2 laps behind	23/23
ret	US GP WEST	Long Beach	30	Chesterfield Racing	G	3.0 March 761-Cosworth V8	collision with Reutemann	21/22
10	SPANISH GP	Jarama	30	Chesterfield Racing	G	3.0 March 761-Cosworth V8	3 laps behind	25/31
dns	BELGIAN GP	Zolder	30	Chesterfield Racing	G	3.0 McLaren M23-Cosworth V8	car unready after engine change	(22)/32
11	SWEDISH GP	Anderstorp	30	Chesterfield Racing	G	3.0 McLaren M23-Cosworth V8	1 lap behind	22/31
dnq	FRENCH GP	Dijon	30	Chesterfield Racing	G	3.0 McLaren M23-Cosworth V8		25/30
13	BRITISH GP	Silverstone	30	Chesterfield Racing	G	3.0 McLaren M23-Cosworth V8	pit stop/4 laps behind	19/36
ret	GERMAN GP	Hockenheim	30	Chesterfield Racing	G	3.0 McLaren M23-Cosworth V8	damage from startline accident	21/30
10	AUSTRIAN GP	Österreichring	30	Chesterfield Racing	G	3.0 McLaren M23-Cosworth V8	1 lap behind	17/30
9	DUTCH GP	Zandvoort	30	Chesterfield Racing	G	3.0 McLaren M23-Cosworth V8	2 laps behind	20/34
ret	ITALIAN GP	Monza	30	Chesterfield Racing	G	3.0 McLaren M23-Cosworth V8	engine	22/34
10	US GP EAST	Watkins Glen	30	Chesterfield Racing	G	3.0 McLaren M23-Cosworth V8	2 laps behind	17/27
11/ret	CANADIAN GP	Mosport Park	30	Chesterfield Racing	G	3.0 McLaren M23-Cosworth V8	engine/4 laps behind	20/27
1978 Championship position: Unplaced								
13	ARGENTINE GP	Buenos Aires	30	Liggett Group/B & S Fabrications	G	3.0 McLaren M23-Cosworth V8	1 lap behind	24/27
ret	BRAZILIAN GP	Rio	30	Liggett Group/B & S Fabrications	G	3.0 McLaren M23-Cosworth V8	overheating	13/28
11	SOUTH AFRICAN GP	Kyalami	30	Liggett Group/B & S Fabrications	G	3.0 McLaren M23-Cosworth V8	2 laps behind	20/30
dnq	US GP WEST	Long Beach	30	Liggett Group/B & S Fabrications	G	3.0 McLaren M23-Cosworth V8		25/30
dnpq	MONACO GP	Monte Carlo	30	Liggett Group/B & S Fabrications	G	3.0 McLaren M26-Cosworth V8		29/30
7	BELGIAN GP	Zolder	30	Liggett Group/B & S Fabrications	G	3.0 McLaren M26-Cosworth V8	1 lap behind	24/30
dnq	SPANISH GP	Jarama	30	Liggett Group/B & S Fabrications	G	3.0 McLaren M26-Cosworth V8		26/29
dnq	"	"	30	Liggett Group/B & S Fabrications	G	3.0 McLaren M23-Cosworth V8		- / -
dnq	SWEDISH GP	Anderstorp	30	Liggett Group/B & S Fabrications	G	3.0 McLaren M26-Cosworth V8		26/27
dnq	"	"	30	Liggett Group/B & S Fabrications	G	3.0 McLaren M23-Cosworth V8		- / -
ret	FRENCH GP	Paul Ricard	30	Liggett Group/B & S Fabrications	G	3.0 McLaren M26-Cosworth V8	engine	24/29
dns	"	"	30	Liggett Group/B & S Fabrications	G	3.0 McLaren M23-Cosworth V8	practice only	- / -
8	BRITISH GP	Brands Hatch	30	Liggett Group/B & S Fabrications	G	3.0 McLaren M26-Cosworth V8	1 lap behind	24/30
dnpq	GERMAN GP	Hockenheim	30	Liggett Group/B & S Fabrications	G	3.0 McLaren M26-Cosworth V8		=29/30
8	AUSTRIAN GP	Österreichring	30	Liggett Group/B & S Fabrications	G	3.0 McLaren M26-Cosworth V8	pit stop – tyres/2 laps behind	17/31
ret	DUTCH GP	Zandvoort	30	Liggett Group/B & S Fabrications	G	3.0 McLaren M26-Cosworth V8	engine	21/33
ret/dns*	ITALIAN GP	Monza	30	Liggett Group/B & S Fabrications	G	3.0 McLaren M26-Cosworth V8	startline accident/*did not restart	21/32
13	US G P EAST	Watkins Glen	23	Team Tissot Ensign	G	3.0 Ensign N177-Cosworth V8	broken gear lever/1 lap behind	24/27

GP Starts: 32 (34) GP Wins: 0 Pole positions: 0 Fastest laps: 0 Points: 0

MIKE MacDOWEL

A KEEN amateur racer, Mike MacDowel made a name for himself in the 1172cc Lotus sports car in 1955 with ten wins and five second places. This success earned him a place in the Cooper works team for 1956 with their latest sports model.

MacDowel's only grand prix appearance came in 1957 at Reims (a track he disliked because the edges of the flat, fast bends were hard to see) when his car was taken over in mid-race by Jack Brabham. Later in the year, however, he finished second in the Prix de Paris at Montlhéry.

After a lengthy period away from racing, MacDowel returned to action on the hill-climb scene in 1968, winning the RAC championships in 1973 and '74 in his potent 5-litre Repco-engined Brabham BT36X. Although past the age of 60, looking extremely fit and trim, he was still competing in hill-climbs in the early 1990s, and afterwards he enjoyed his appearances at the hugely popular historic racing festivals.

MacDOWEL, Mike (GB) b 13/9/1932, Great Yarmouth, Norfolk

	Race	Circuit	No	Entrant	Tyres	Capacity/Car/Engine	Comment	Q Pos/Entries
1957 Championship position: Unplaced								
7*	FRENCH GP	Rouen	24	Cooper Car Co	D	1.5 Cooper T43-Climax 4	*Brabham took over car/-9 laps	15/15

GP Starts: 1 GP Wins: 0 Pole positions: 0 Fastest laps: 0 Points: 0

MACKAY-FRASER, Herbert (USA) b 23/6/1927, Pernambuco,(now Recife) Brazil – d 14/7/1957, Reims-Gueux Circuit, France

1957 Championship position: Unplaced

	Race	Circuit	No	Entrant	Tyres	Capacity/Car/Engine	Comment	Q Pos/Entries
ret	FRENCH GP	Rouen	28	Owen Racing Organisation	D	2.5 BRM P25 4	transmission	12/15

GP Starts: 1   GP Wins: 0   Pole positions: 0   Fastest laps: 0   Points: 0

HERBERT MACKAY-FRASER

BORN in Brazil, to American parents who owned a coffee plantation, Herbert Mackay-Fraser tried his hand at ranching in Wyoming before moving to California. There he began racing an XK120 Jaguar, and his career took off. After returning to Brazil, he settled in Rio de Janeiro and began competing in national events with a Ferrari 750 Monza. It was always his ambition to race in Europe, however, and in June, 1955, he shipped his Ferrari across the Atlantic to compete under the Kangaroo Stable banner.

Basing himself in London, he soon became integrated in the British motor racing scene, driving for Colin Chapman's fledgling sports car team at home, and taking in a number of races on the Continent in his own Ferrari and with his great friend, Jo Bonnier, in the latter's Maserati during 1956. He really made a name for himself in the Reims 12-hour race, however, which he led superbly in Ivor Bueb's Lotus until engine troubles intervened.

In 1957, eager to continue his successful association with Lotus, 'Mack' was chosen to partner Cliff Allison in the team. At Spa, he put in a brilliant drive to claim a class win and seventh place overall with the 2-litre Lotus, ahead of some much more potent machinery.

On 7th July, Herbert made an impressive debut for BRM in the French Grand Prix at Rouen, which augured well for the future, but sadly a week later he was dead. 'Mack' had been assigned the streamliner 1500cc Lotus F2 car in the Coupe de Vitesse at the ultra-fast triangular road circuit at Reims. While slipstreaming the faster cars of Roy Salvadori and Maurice Trintignant, he lost control of the Lotus on the fast Gueux curve just after the pits. His car ran into a low roadside ditch and somersaulted into a field. The luckless American was thrown out, sustaining fatal injuries to which he succumbed on the way to hospital. Perhaps due to his Scottish ancestry, he was buried in the nearby local Cemetiere de l'Ouest, which contains Commonwealth war graves, 'as a soldier fallen in battle far from home'. His funeral on 23rd July, 1957, was attended by members of the Automobile Club of Champagne.

LANCE MACKLIN

A POLISHED and extremely stylish driver, Lance Macklin spent the bulk of his career racing for John Heath's under-financed HWM team, and his grand prix career suffered through the cars' lack of reliability.

Early experience with an Invicta and then a Maserati led to Macklin joining HWM for 1950, when he immediately made his mark with a second place at Naples, and thirds at Mettet and Périgueux. The minor Continental races provided a happy hunting ground for the team at this time, with good starting and prize money on offer. Macklin continued to pick up many good places over the next few seasons, highlighted by a superb win in the 1952 International Trophy at Silverstone.

Lance also raced occasionally for Aston Martin, finishing third at Le Mans in 1951, but four years later he became involved in the catastrophic accident at the Sarthe circuit that claimed so many lives, when the Mercedes driven by 'Levegh' was launched off the back of his Healey and wreckage flew into the crowd. By some miracle, Macklin survived unhurt. He continued to race that year, but after a narrow escape in the Tourist Trophy at Dundrod, where he crashed to avoid a multiple accident in which two drivers were killed and another seriously injured, he decided to call it a day.

The ramifications of the Le Mans affair rumbled on, Lance initially taking most of the blame. Subsequently, however, it was shown that Mike Hawthorn's late decision to dive into the pits had caused Macklin to swerve in avoidance, which triggered the terrible chain of events that followed. Later he worked in a sales capacity for exclusive car dealerships in both Paris and London.

MACKLIN, Lance (GB) b 2/9/1919, Kensington, London – d 29/8/2002, Tenterden, Kent

1952 Championship position: Unplaced

	Race	Circuit	No	Entrant	Tyres	Capacity/Car/Engine	Comment	Q Pos/Entries
ret	SWISS GP	Bremgarten	20	HW Motors Ltd	D	2.0 HWM-Alta 4	*withdrawn – suspension problems*	12/21
11	BELGIAN GP	Spa	24	HW Motors Ltd	D	2.0 HWM-Alta 4	*4 laps behind*	14/22
9	FRENCH GP	Rouen	20	HW Motors Ltd	D	2.0 HWM-Alta 4	*7 laps behind*	14/20
15	BRITISH GP	Silverstone	31	HW Motors Ltd	D	2.0 HWM-Alta 4	*6 laps behind*	29/32
8	DUTCH GP	Zandvoort	26	HW Motors Ltd	D	2.0 HWM-Alta 4	*6 laps behind*	9/18
dnq	ITALIAN GP	Monza	52	HW Motors Ltd	D	2.0 HWM-Alta 4		32/35

1953 Championship position: Unplaced

	Race	Circuit	No	Entrant	Tyres	Capacity/Car/Engine	Comment	Q Pos/Entries
ret	DUTCH GP	Zandvoort	38	HW Motors Ltd	D	2.0 HWM-Alta 4	*throttle*	15/20
ret	BELGIAN GP	Spa	22	HW Motors Ltd	D	2.0 HWM-Alta 4	*engine*	17/22
ret	FRENCH GP	Reims	26	HW Motors Ltd	D	2.0 HWM-Alta 4	*clutch*	16/25
ret	BRITISH GP	Silverstone	1	HW Motors Ltd	D	2.0 HWM-Alta 4	*clutch housing*	12/29
ret	SWISS GP	Bremgarten	16	HW Motors Ltd	D	2.0 HWM-Alta 4	*engine – valve*	15/23
ret	ITALIAN GP	Monza	14	HW Motors Ltd	D	2.0 HWM-Alta 4	*engine*	27/30

1954 Championship position: Unplaced

	Race	Circuit	No	Entrant	Tyres	Capacity/Car/Engine	Comment	Q Pos/Entries
ret	FRENCH GP	Reims	32	HW Motors Ltd	D	2.0 HWM-Alta 4	*engine*	15/22

1955 Championship position: Unplaced

	Race	Circuit	No	Entrant	Tyres	Capacity/Car/Engine	Comment	Q Pos/Entries
dnq	MONACO GP	Monte Carlo	22	Stirling Moss Ltd	D	2.5 Maserati 250F 6		21/22
8	BRITISH GP	Aintree	46	Stirling Moss Ltd	D	2.5 Maserati 250F 6	*11 laps behind*	16/25

GP Starts: 13   GP Wins: 0   Pole positions: 0   Fastest laps: 0   Points: 0

DAMIEN MAGEE

AN Ulsterman who showed potential in the junior formulas from his early days, Damien Magee always seemed to be scratching around for a decent ride. With no substantial backing to speak of, he was forced to drive any sort of car he could get his hands on. Never less than 100 per cent committed, no sooner would poor Magee get a car going well than it seemed to be sold from under him.

After leaving school, Magee went straight into the motor trade in Belfast and soon found himself in a Lotus XI, winning three races on his first outing. Suitably encouraged, he managed to raise enough backing to move up to Formula Ford, winning the Scottish Formula Ford title in 1970. Commuting across from Ireland and preparing the car himself, he tackled the British Formula Ford season in 1972 and was reasonably successful, moving up to Formula 3 with a works Palliser the following year.

Despite a chronic lack of finance, the Ulsterman continued into 1973, taking some fine placings, before a huge shunt at Thruxton saw the car written off and its driver very lucky indeed to escape injury. Fortunately, an Irish car wheeler-dealer, Tony 'Monkey' Brown, came to the rescue and provided Magee with a Brabham, with which he recorded a third place in the Monaco Formula 3 Monaco GP race. Sadly this would be the end of his season, as the car was sold by its owner.

For the 1975 season, Magee agreed to race a works Palliser in FF2000, but soon split after a disagreement. So it was back to F5000 with a very second-hand Trojan, in which his sheer commitment caught the eye. Indeed, Bernie Ecclestone was instrumental in his only grand prix start, which came at very short notice when he replaced Arturo Merzario in Sweden for Williams. Despite missing the first practice, Magee did a sound job, nursing a difficult handling car to the finish.

After an enjoyable trip to Canada to race Alan McCall's Tui on a shoestring budget in the Atlantic series, Magee finished off the year in F5000, before finally landing a deal with Hexagon to race a full season in the Shellsport F5000 series the following year. Always a strong contender, he won a round at Oulton Park in the team's March 751, and consistent finishes put him into a clear second place in the championship, behind David Purley, despite leaving the team before the season was out after shunting the Penske at Oulton Park.

In Formula 1, Magee drove an elderly RAM BT42B with verve in the Silverstone International Trophy, before suffering an engine failure. Later in the season, he tried unsuccessfully to qualify the RAM-Brabham BT44B at Paul Ricard. The Irishman was out of a drive once more when the 1977 season opened, and he had to wait until August before taking over a Lola previously driven by Keith Holland. In truth, the car's engine was rather tired, but he salvaged a second place at Snetterton as the series itself stumbled into oblivion.

MAGEE, Damien (GB) b 17/11/1945, Belfast, Northern Ireland

1975 Championship position: Unplaced

	Race	Circuit	No	Entrant	Tyres	Capacity/Car/Engine	Comment	Q Pos/Entries
14	SWEDISH GP	Anderstorp	20	Frank Williams Racing Cars	G	3.0 Williams FW03-Cosworth V8	*2 laps behind*	22/26

1976 Championship position: Unplaced

	Race	Circuit	No	Entrant	Tyres	Capacity/Car/Engine	Comment	Q Pos/Entries
dnq	FRENCH GP	Paul Ricard	33	RAM Racing	G	3.0 Brabham BT44B-Cosworth V8		27/30

GP Starts: 1   GP Wins: 0   Pole positions: 0   Fastest laps: 0   Points: 0

TONY MAGGS

WITH only a handful of races in an Austin-Healey in South Africa behind him, Tony Maggs travelled to England in 1959 to gain experience, and his talent was quickly recognised. Initially he raced a Lotus XI-Climax, winning his second race at Goodwood and soon progressing to a Formula 2 Cooper. At the end of the year, he bought a Tojeiro-Jaguar, which he shipped back to South Africa to race over the winter months. Allthough the machine proved troublesome, he did win a race in the Transvaal

Maggs returned to England in 1960 to race a variety of machines, finishing third in the Vanwall Trophy in a Cooper and doing well in the Formula Junior Gemini. To underscore his versatility, he had his first taste of front-line sports cars by sharing an Aston Martin DB4GT with Jim Clark in the Paris 1000km. His handful of outings in the F2 car earned him his big break when Ken Tyrrell signed him for a season of Formula Junior in 1961 with his Cooper-BMC, alongside Rhodesian John Love.

The two drivers, who soon became known as the 'Tyrrell Twins', began cutting a swathe through Europe, despite being at a power disadvantage to Ford-engined machines raced by the Lotus pair of Peter Arundell and Trevor Taylor. While the Lotus prevailed at home, on the Continent Tony won six races and shared the European Formula Junior title with Jo Siffert, who was running on a different schedule, given the bewildering number of events taking place at the time. Maggs also made a steady start in grand prix racing with Louise Bryden-Brown's Lotus 18, impressing the Cooper F1 team. With Jack Brabham leaving to form his own team, Tony and John Love were the two candidates for the seat. There was little to choose between them, but since Tony was 13 years younger, he was eventually signed as number two to Bruce McLaren.

Tony was always at his best on fast flowing circuits, and with a reliable car the always consistent South African scored some fine placings over the next two seasons, second-place finishes in the French Grand Prix at Rouen and Reims in successive years being the highlights for a Cooper team that was slowly losing its competitive edge.

The 1963 season was a busy one for Maggs, who drove the Bowmaker Lola in the Tasman Series and helped develop the new Lola GT. He shared a Porsche with Jo Bonnier at Le Mans, and at the end of the year scored a fine win in the Rand nine-hour race, sharing David Piper's Ferrari GTO.

Tony was not retained by Cooper for 1964, so he joined the Italian Centro Sud team to race their elderly BRM P57 cars. According to Maggs, "The team management was shambolic and the cars were poorly prepared." Things got off to a bad start at Zandvoort, where he was lucky to escape serious injury after rolling his car into a ditch; at the next race, at Spa, the team's transporter broke down on the way to the circuit. When it did arrive, he was a non-starter with an engine problem; there was no spare for the race. It was something of a miracle that he actually went on to score points on two occasions, albeit only after faster cars failed to make the finish. With no real F1 prospects in sight, he undertook a programme of Formula 2 in an MRP Lola and sports cars in David Piper's Ferrari GTO, the pair repeating their Rand nine-hours triumph at Kyalami.

After handling Parnell's Lotus in the 1965 South African GP, Maggs raced abroad for the last time. He took second place in the Rome GP, fourth at both Oulton Park and Pau in MRP's F2 Lola, and third place in the Sebring 12-hours with David Piper in his Ferrari 250 LM.

Tony had planned to race the Surtees Lola in Formula 2, but when he crashed his Brabham in a national race at Pietermaritzburg, a small boy standing in a prohibited area was hit and killed. Distraught, Maggs immediately retired from racing.

This unfortunate incident obviously left its mark on Tony, who took the boy's death very hard, and he distanced himself from the motor racing scene thereafter to concentrate on the family's farming interests. In 1967, he was very lucky to escape with his life when he was involved in a light aircraft crash. He escaped unhurt, but then suffered serious burns while attempting to help the other passengers escape.

In his later years, Tony was able to make occasional visits to races and catch up with many old friends, and happily recount tales of a different life as a buccanering racer from a different age.

MAGGS, Tony (ZA) b 9/2/1937, Pretoria – d 2/6/2009, Caledon, South Africa

	1961 Championship position: Unplaced								
	Race	Circuit	No	Entrant	Tyres	Capacity/Car/Engine	Comment		Q Pos/Entries
13	BRITISH GP	Aintree	50	Louise Bryden-Brown	D	1.5 Lotus 18-Climax 4	6 laps behind		24/30
11	GERMAN GP	Nürburgring	33	Louise Bryden-Brown	D	1.5 Lotus 18-Climax 4	1 lap behind		22/27

	1962 Championship position: 7th	Wins: 0	Pole positions: 0	Fastest laps: 0	Points scored: 13				
5	DUTCH GP	Zandvoort	7	Cooper Car Co	D	1.5 Cooper T55-Climax 4	2 laps behind		15/20
ret	MONACO GP	Monte Carlo	16	Cooper Car Co	D	1.5 Cooper T55-Climax 4	gearbox		19/21
ret	BELGIAN GP	Spa	26	Cooper Car Co	D	1.5 Cooper T60-Climax V8	gearbox		10/20
2	FRENCH GP	Rouen	24	Cooper Car Co	D	1.5 Cooper T60-Cliamx V8	1 lap behind		11/17
6	BRITISH GP	Aintree	18	Cooper Car Co	D	1.5 Cooper T60-Climax V8	1 lap behind		13/21
9	GERMAN GP	Nürburgring	10	Cooper Car Co	D	1.5 Cooper T55-Climax 4			23/30
dns	"	"	10	Cooper Car Co	D	1.5 Cooper T60-Climax V8	accident in practice		- / -

	Race	Circuit	No	Entrant	Tyres	Capacity/Car/Engine	Comment	Q Pos/Entries
7	ITALIAN GP	Monza	30	Cooper Car Co	D	1.5 Cooper T60-Climax V8	*1 lap behind*	12/30
7	US GP	Watkins Glen	22	Cooper Car Co	D	1.5 Cooper T60-Climax V8	*3 laps behind*	10/20
3	SOUTH AFRCAN GP	East London	9	Cooper Car Co	D	1.5 Cooper T60-Climax V8		=6/17
	1963 Championship position: 8th		Wins: 0	Pole positions: 0		Fastest laps: 0	Points scored: 9	
5	MONACO GP	Monte Carlo	8	Cooper Car Co	D	1.5 Cooper T66-Climax V8	*2 laps behind*	10/17
7/ret	BELGIAN GP	Spa	15	Cooper Car Co	D	1.5 Cooper T66-Climax V8	*accident in rain/5 laps behind*	4/20
ret	DUTCH GP	Zandvoort	22	Cooper Car Co	D	1.5 Cooper T66-Climax V8	*overheating*	9/19
2	FRENCH GP	Reims	12	Cooper Car Co	D	1.5 Cooper T66-Climax V8		8/21
9	BRITISH GP	Silverstone	7	Cooper Car Co	D	1.5 Cooper T66-Climax V8	*4 laps behind*	=7/23
ret	GERMAN GP	Nürburgring	6	Cooper Car Co	D	1.5 Cooper T66-Climax V8	*camshaft*	10/26
6	ITALIAN GP	Monza	20	Cooper Car Co	D	1.5 Cooper T66-Climax V8	*2 laps behind*	13/28
ret	US GP	Watkins Glen	4	Cooper Car Co	D	1.5 Cooper T66-Climax V8	*ignition*	9/21
ret	MEXICAN GP	Mexico City	4	Cooper Car Co	D	1.5 Cooper T66-Climax V8	*engine*	13/21
7	SOUTH AFRICAN GP	East London	11	Cooper Car Co	D	1.5 Cooper T66-Climax V8	*3 laps behind*	10/21
	1964 Championship position: 12th		Wins: 0	Pole positions: 0		Fastest laps: 0	Points scored: 4	
dns	DUTCH GP	Zandvoort	30	Scuderia Centro Sud	D	1.5 BRM P57 V8	*accident in practice*	(15)/18
dns	BELGIAN GP	Spa	7	Scuderia Centro Sud	D	1.5 BRM P57 V8	*engine failure in practice*	(18)/20
ret	BRITISH GP	Brands Hatch	17	Scuderia Centro Sud	D	1.5 BRM P57 V8	*gearbox*	23/25
6	GERMAN GP	Nürburgring	26	Scuderia Centro Sud	D	1.5 BRM P57 V8	*1 lap behind*	16/24
4	AUSTRIAN GP	Zeltweg	19	Scuderia Centro Sud	D	1.5 BRM P57 V8	*3 laps behind*	=18/20
	1965 Championship position: Unplaced							
11	SOUTH AFRICAN GP	East London	15	Reg Parnell (Racing)	D	1.5 Lotus 25-BRM V8	*overheating - 2 pit stops/8 laps behind*	13/25

GP Starts: 25   GP Wins: 0   Pole positions: 0   Fastest laps: 0   Points: 26

UMBERTO MAGLIOLI

A MOST accomplished sports car driver for nearly two decades, the pipe smoking Umberto Maglioli found his grand prix opportunities severely limited, given his position as a junior Ferrari driver. He had made his reputation as national production car champion in 1952 with Lancia, then had won the 1953 Targa Florio and the Carrera Panamericana in 1954 in the marque's cars. Despite success at Maranello in hill-climbs and sports car races, which included victories in the Pescara 12-hours, Buenos Aires 1000km and Circuit of Mugello, Umberto joined Maserati for 1956, again racing only occasionally in grands prix, but he also began the start of a long and fruitful association with Porsche by winning the Targa Florio with Wolfgang von Trips.

A practice crash at Salzburg in 1957 sidelined Maglioli with leg injuries, but he bounced back in 1959, winning the Sebring 12-hours with Hans Herrmann. Little success came his way in the early 1960s, but a return to the Ferrari sports car team in 1963 saw him take third places at Le Mans and in the Nürburgring 1000km, followed by another win at Sebring in 1964.

Throughout the rest of the decade, Maglioli continued to race a variety of potent machines, including a Ford GT40 and the works Porsche 907. In the latter, paired with Vic Elford, he won the Targa Florio in 1968, his last major victory.

MAGLIOLI, Umberto (I) b 5/6/1928, Bioglio, Vercelli – d 7/2/1999, Monza

	Race	Circuit	No	Entrant	Tyres	Capacity/Car/Engine	Comment	Q Pos/Entries
	1953 Championship position: Unplaced							
8	ITALIAN GP	Monza	10	Scuderia Ferrari	P	2.0 Ferrari 553 4	*5 laps behind*	11/30
	1954 Championship position: 15th=		Wins: 0	Pole positions: 0		Fastest laps: 0	Points scored: 2	
9	ARGENTINE GP	Buenos Aires	16	Scuderia Ferrari	P	2.5 Ferrari 625 4	*5 laps behind*	12/18
7	SWISS GP	Bremgarten	24	Scuderia Ferrari	P	2.5 Ferrari 553 4	*5 laps behind*	11/16
3*	ITALIAN GP	Monza	38	Scuderia Ferrari	P	2.5 Ferrari 625 4	**Gonzalez took over/2 laps behind*	13/21
	1955 Championship position: 16th=		Wins: 0	Pole positions: 0		Fastest laps: 0	Points scored: 1.33	
3*	ARGENTINE GP	Buenos Aires	10	Scuderia Ferrari	E	2.5 Ferrari 625 4	**shared with Farina/Trintignant/-2 laps*	(22)/22
6	ITALIAN GP	Monza	12	Scuderia Ferrari	E	2.5 Ferrari 555 4	*1 lap behind*	12/22
	1956 Championship position: Unplaced							
ret	BRITISH GP	Silverstone	12	Scuderia Guastalla	P	2.5 Maserati 250F 6	*gearbox*	24/28
ret	GERMAN GP	Nürburgring	8	Officine Alfieri Maserati	P	2.5 Maserati 250F 6	*steering*	7/21
ret*	ITALIAN GP	Monza	46	Officine Alfieri Maserati	P	2.5 Maserati 250F 6	**Behra took over/steering*	13/26
	1957 Championship position: Unplaced							
ret	GERMAN GP (F2)	Nürburgring	20	Dr Ing F Porsche KG	–	1.5 Porsche 550RS F4	*engine*	15/24

GP Starts: 10   GP Wins: 0   Pole positions: 0   Fastest laps: 0   Points: 3.33

JAN MAGNUSSEN

WHEN 5ft 5in Dane Jan Magnussen decimated the opposition to win the British Formula 3 championship with Paul Stewart Racing in 1994, taking an amazing 14 wins from 18 starts, comparisons with the late Ayrton Senna were perhaps inevitable. Certainly Jackie Stewart regarded him as a potential world champion of the future. Sadly, thus far, that dazzling promise has remained unfulfilled, and Magnussen's name soon disappeared from the Formula 1 team managers' shortlists.

A hugely successful karting career, which culminated in the senior world crown in 1990, set Magnussen on the path to the top in motorsport. Without any sponsorship to speak of, he drove in FF1600 in 1992 and not only took that title, but also capped it with a stunning display to win the prestigious end-of-year Formula Ford Festival at Brands Hatch. A year in the Vauxhall Euroseries had its ups and downs, but still his innate talent shone through, and two late-season F3 drives with PSR cemented his place for 1994, leading to the aforementioned success.

Signed by McLaren as a test driver, Jan also joined Mercedes for their DTM/ITC programme, which represented a great opportunity for the young Dane to work with a major manufacturer. Initially, he hankered for single-seater action, but after his season was interrupted by a broken leg, sustained in a bizarre paddock accident when he fell off his scooter, he returned more fully focused, eventually taking a win at Estoril and second place to Bernd Schneider in the ten-round ITC series, and eighth in the parallel DTM.

At the end of the season, Jan gave an assured performance on his debut at the Pacific Grand Prix, but with no suitable F1 seat available he was obliged to continue in the Mercedes ITC team in 1996. A chance of single-seater action came in the form of a few Indy car outings, initially with Penske, replacing the injured Paul Tracy, and then with Hogan, filling in for Emerson Fittipaldi. The heavy Penske chassis did him no favours, but given his lack of testing, Jan did a solid enough job.

When Paul and Jackie Stewart made the transition to Formula 1 for 1997, Jan was given the second seat alongside Rubens Barrichello, but it proved to be a traumatic debut season for the Dane, who failed to match the pace of his more experienced team-mate. Fortunately, as the year wore on, he seemed to be getting to grips with the task and he was kept on for 1998 in the hope that he could make the big breakthrough. In the event, his confidence seemed to be eroded by the team's criticism of his perceived lack of performance and, after scoring his first ever championship point in Montreal, he was summarily dropped in favour of Jos Verstappen.

Looking to reinvigorate his flagging career, Magnussen opted to race sports cars and shone immediately with Panoz Racing's sports roadster in the American Le Mans Series. He had another crack at CART in 1999 with a seven-race stint for Pat Patrick, but only one top-ten finish told its own story – Jan's single-seater dreams were over.

Back in sports cars in 2000 with Panoz, Jan and co-driver David Brabham took their front-engined challenger into battle with the might of both Audi and BMW, and won the Nürburgring 1000km outright. The following year, the pair picked up another two wins at Portland and Mid-Ohio, and in 2002 they slayed the mighty Audis twice more, at Road America and Washington, DC.

For 2003, Magnussen switched to a Ferrari 550 Maranello in the GTS class of the ALMS, as well as taking time to commute across the Atlantic to win the Danish touring car championship, which he would win again in 2009.

In 2004, Jan began an amazing sequence of successes at the Le Mans 24-hour race. Driving a Chevrolet Corvette, and partnered by Olivier Beretta and Oliver Gavin, he took the GT1 class for thee years in row. After second places in the same class in 2007/08, he took a fourth GT1 win the following year with Johnny O'Connell and Ron Fellows.

In 2007, Jan returned to full-time ALMS participation with Corvette and took three class wins; he was the GT1 champion (with O'Connell) the following year, racking up another eight class victories. In 2009, he scored Corvette's first GT2 victory at Mosport after a thrilling race and continued as a mainstay of the Corvette Racing programme, bringing the Chevrolet marque's success. In 2011, he became the only driver to have taken a race class win in each of the 13 years of the ALMS. He was also voted the series' most popular driver on three occasions.

Meanwhile, Jan has been watching the fast moving career of his oldest son, Kevin, who has already made a big impact as runner-up in the 2011 British Formula 3 series. The 19-year-old has been employed by McLaren as a test and development driver, which can only help his future Formula 1 ambitions.

MAGNUSSEN, Jan (DK) b 4/7/1973, Roskilde

1995 Championship position: Unplaced

	Race	Circuit	No	Entrant	Tyres	Capacity/Car/Engine	Comment	Q Pos/Entries
10	PACIFIC GP	T.I. Circuit	8	Marlboro McLaren Mercedes	G	3.0 McLaren MP4/10B-Mercedes V10	*2 laps behind*	12/24

1997 Championship position: Unplaced

	Race	Circuit	No	Entrant	Tyres	Capacity/Car/Engine	Comment	Q Pos/Entries
ret	AUSTRALIAN GP	Melbourne	23	Stewart Ford	B	3.0 Stewart SF1-Ford Zetec-R V10	*suspension*	19/24
ret/dns*	BRAZILIAN GP	Interlagos	23	Stewart Ford	B	3.0 Stewart SF1-Ford Zetec-R V10	**accident at first start*	20/22
10/ret	ARGENTINE GP	Buenos Aires	23	Stewart Ford	B	3.0 Stewart SF1-Ford Zetec-R V10	*engine/6 laps behind*	15/22
ret	SAN MARINO GP	Imola	23	Stewart Ford	B	3.0 Stewart SF1-Ford Zetec-R V10	*spun off*	16/22
7	MONACO GP	Monte Carlo	23	Stewart Ford	B	3.0 Stewart SF1-Ford Zetec-R V10	*1 lap behind*	19/22
13	SPANISH GP	Barcelona	23	Stewart Ford	B	3.0 Stewart SF1-Ford Zetec-R V10	*1 lap behind*	22/22
ret	CANADIAN GP	Montreal	23	Stewart Ford	B	3.0 Stewart SF1-Ford Zetec-R V10	*accident on lap 1*	21/22
ret	FRENCH GP	Magny Cours	23	Stewart Ford	B	3.0 Stewart SF1-Ford Zetec-R V10	*brakes*	15/22
ret	BRITISH GP	Silverstone	23	Stewart Ford	B	3.0 Stewart SF1-Ford Zetec-R V10	*engine*	15/22
ret	GERMAN GP	Hockenheim	23	Stewart Ford	B	3.0 Stewart SF1-Ford Zetec-R V10	*engine*	12/22
ret	HUNGARIAN GP	Hungaroring	23	Stewart Ford	B	3.0 Stewart SF1-Ford Zetec-R V10	*collision damage*	17/22
12	BELGIAN GP	Spa	23	Stewart Ford	B	3.0 Stewart SF1-Ford Zetec-R V10	*1 lap behind*	18/22
ret	ITALIAN GP	Monza	23	Stewart Ford	B	3.0 Stewart SF1-Ford Zetec-R V10	*transmission*	13/22
ret	AUSTRIAN GP	A1-Ring	23	Stewart Ford	B	3.0 Stewart SF1-Ford Zetec-R V10	*engine*	6/22
ret	LUXEMBOURG GP	Nürburgring	23	Stewart Ford	B	3.0 Stewart SF1-Ford Zetec-R V10	*driveshaft*	12/22
ret	JAPANESE GP	Suzuka	23	Stewart Ford	B	3.0 Stewart SF1-Ford Zetec-R V10	*spun off*	14/22
9	EUROPEAN GP	Jerez	23	Stewart Ford	B	3.0 Stewart SF1-Ford Zetec-R V10		11/22

1998 Championship position: 15th= Wins: 0 Pole positions: 0 Fastest laps: 0 Points scored: 1

	Race	Circuit	No	Entrant	Tyres	Capacity/Car/Engine	Comment	Q Pos/Entries
ret	AUSTRALIAN GP	Melbourne	19	Stewart Ford	B	3.0 Stewart SF2-Ford Zetec R V10	*collision with Ralf Schumacher*	18/22
10	BRAZILIAN GP	Interlagos	19	Stewart Ford	B	3.0 Stewart SF2-Ford Zetec R V10	*2 laps behind*	16/22
ret	ARGENTINE GP	Buenos Aires	19	Stewart Ford	B	3.0 Stewart SF2-Ford Zetec R V10	*transmission*	22/22
ret	SAN MARINO GP	Imola	19	Stewart Ford	B	3.0 Stewart SF2-Ford Zetec R V10	*gearbox*	20/22
12	SPANISH GP	Barcelona	19	Stewart Ford	B	3.0 Stewart SF2-Ford Zetec R V10	*2 laps behind*	20/22
ret	MONACO GP	Monte Carlo	19	Stewart Ford	B	3.0 Stewart SF2-Ford Zetec R V10	*suspension failure*	17/22
6	CANADIAN GP	Montreal	19	Stewart Ford	B	3.0 Stewart SF2-Ford Zetec R V10		20/22

GP Starts: 24 (25) GP Wins: 0 Pole positions: 0 Fastest laps: 0 Points: 1

GUY MAIRESSE

A TOUGH and independent character with a big heart, Guy Mairesse built a long-distance haulage business from modest beginnings as a lorry driver before the Second World War. He became interested in racing after Paul Vallée invited him to the 1946 Coupe du Salon, purely as a spectator. After winning the 1947 Lyons-Charbonnières Rally, he bought a Delahaye from Vallée for 1948, which he took to victory at Chimay.

Joining his great friend's Ecurie France team for 1949, to race the Lago-Talbot, Mairesse took fourth at Pau and fifth at Albi; in 1950, teamed with Pierre Meyrat, he finished second at Le Mans in a Talbot 'monoplace'. On the Vallée team's demise, he bought the Le Mans car and a Talbot T26C, prepared by Giraud Cabantous, which he raced in only a couple of grands prix in 1951, due to his increasing business commitments.

At the start of 1952, Mairesse sold his cars, but still appeared occasionally in machines provided by others, and it was while practising for the Coupe de Paris at Montlhéry in 1954 that he lost his life, swerving to avoid a slower car and crashing into a concrete wall.

MAIRESSE, Guy (F) b 10/8/1910, La Capelle, l'Aisne – d 24/4/1954, Montlhéry Circuit, nr Paris

1950 Championship position: 0 Wins: 0 Pole positions: 0 Fastest laps: 0 Points scored: 0

	Race	Circuit	No	Entrant	Tyres	Capacity/Car/Engine	Comment	Q Pos/Entries
ret	ITALIAN GP	Monza	40	Guy Mairesse	D	4.5 Lago-Talbot T26C 6		11/27

1951 Championship position: 0 Wins: 0 Pole positions: 0 Fastest laps: 0 Points scored: 0

	Race	Circuit	No	Entrant	Tyres	Capacity/Car/Engine	Comment	Q Pos/Entries
nc	SWISS GP	Bremgarten	40	Guy Mairesse	D	4.5 Lago-Talbot T26C 6	*11 laps behind*	21/21
9	FRENCH GP	Reims	48	Guy Mairesse	D	4.5 Lago-Talbot T26C 6	*11 laps behind*	19/23

GP Starts: 3 GP Wins: 0 Pole positions: 0 Fastest laps: 0 Points: 0

MAIRESSE, Willy (B) b 1/10/1928 Momignies – d 9/9/1969 Ostend

1960 Championship position: 13th= Wins: 0 Pole positions: 0 Fastest laps: 0 Points scored: 4

	Race	Circuit	No	Entrant	Tyres	Capacity/Car/Engine	Comment	Q Pos/Entries
ret	BELGIAN GP	Spa	22	Scuderia Ferrari	D	2.4 Ferrari Dino 246 V6	*transmission*	13/18
ret	FRENCH GP	Reims	6	Scuderia Ferrari	D	2.4 Ferrari Dino 246 V6	*transmission*	11/23
3	ITALIAN GP	Monza	16	Scuderia Ferrari	D	2.4 Ferrari Dino 246 V6	*gearbox problems/1 lap behind*	3/16

1961 Championship position: Unplaced

	Race	Circuit	No	Entrant	Tyres	Capacity/Car/Engine	Comment	Q Pos/Entries
ret	BELGIAN GP	Spa	10	Equipe Nationale Belge	D	1.5 Lotus 18-Climax 4	*hired Tony Marsh's car/ignition*	– /25
dns	"	"	10	Equipe Nationale Belge	D	1.5 Emeryson 1003-Maserati 4	*car too slow*	– / –

ret	FRENCH GP	Reims	48	Team Lotus	D	1.5 Lotus 21-Climax 4	*hired 3rd works car/fuel system*	20/26
ret	GERMAN GP	Nürburgring	6	Scuderia Ferrari SpA SEFAC	D	1.5 Ferrari 156 V6	*crashed*	13/27

1962 Championship position: 14th=   Wins: 0   Pole positions: 0   Fastest laps: 0   Points scored: 3

7/ret	MONACO GP	Monte Carlo	40	Scuderia Ferrari SpA SEFAC	D	1.5 Ferrari 156 V6	*oil pressure/10 laps behind*	=3/21
ret	BELGIAN GP	Spa	10	Scuderia Ferrari SpA SEFAC	D	1.5 Ferrari 156 V6	*huge accident with Trevor Taylor*	=5/20
4	ITALIAN GP	Monza	8	Scuderia Ferrari SpA SEFAC	D	1.5 Ferrari 156 V6		10/30

1963 Championship position: Unplaced

ret	MONACO GP	Monte Carlo	20	Scuderia Ferrari SpA SEFAC	D	1.5 Ferrari 156 V6	*transmission*	7/17
ret	BELGIAN GP	Spa	10	Scuderia Ferrari SpA SEFAC	D	1.5 Ferrari 156 V6	*engine*	3/20
ret	GERMAN GP	Nürburgring	8	Scuderia Ferrari SpA SEFAC	D	1.5 Ferrari 156 V6	*crashed*	7/26

1965 Championship position: Unplaced

dns	BELGIAN GP	Spa	28	Scuderia Centro Sud	D	1.5 BRM P57 V8	*Gregory's car – did only 1 practice lap*	21/21

GP Starts: 12   GP Wins: 0   Pole positions: 0   Fastest laps: 0   Points: 7

WILLY MAIRESSE

A DRIVER who raced with a grim determination and who frequently came unstuck, Willy Mairesse suffered a whole series of lurid accidents that burned and battered his small frame, but never dented his fearless approach.

Mairesse sprang to prominence in 1956, when he took his second-hand Mercedes 300SL to victory in the Liège–Rome–Liège Rally, beating the favourite, Olivier Gendebien, in the process, which sparked a bitter rivalry between the two Belgians. In 1957, Willy over-reached himself, wrecking a series of expensive cars, and he was lucky that Ferrari importer Jacques Swaters rescued him from probable obscurity by furnishing him with a Ferrari Berlinetta for 1958, which he took to second place in the Reims 12-hours.

Willy clashed with Gendebien once more in the 1959 Tour de France, defeating his rival on a number of timed stages, but missing out on overall victory. Ferrari took an interest in the little man, however, and offered him a drive in the 1960 Targa Florio. He finished fourth and was immediately taken into the works team for both F1 and sports cars.

Handling the outdated front-engined Ferrari Dino 246, Mairesse languished in midfield obscurity at Spa and Reims, before transmission failures ended his runs. He soon scored his best ever grand prix result, however, with a third place behind Phil Hill and Richie Ginther in a Ferrari 1-2-3 in the Italian Grand Prix at Monza. This clean sweep was somwhat hollow, though, as the race had been boycotted by all of the British teams.

Late in the year, he scored the first of two successive Tour de France victories in a Ferrari 250GT, but only after Gendebien, of all people, and his co-driver Lucien Bianchi had helped to manhandle Mairesse's car from a ditch. This gutsy display from Willy made him Ferrari's blue-eyed boy and he was retained to race in the sports car team for 1961. He also took GT wins in the Auvergne Trophy at Clermont-Ferrand and the Spa Grand Prix. In addition, he scored a fine place at Le Mans with Michael Parkes, and another second in the Paris 1000km at Montlhéry with Lucien Bianchi.

Initially out of the frame for a Formula 1 ride, Mairesse threw in his lot with Equipe Nationale Belge, driving their Emerysons to tenth (and last) place in the Brussels Grand Prix and an even more distant 11th at Syracuse. When the ENB machine proved unraceworthy at Spa, they hastily hired Tony Marsh's Lotus so that the Belgian could compete. At Reims, he turned up with no drive, but no doubt a wad of cash persuaded Colin Chapman to allow him to take the wheel of the team's spare car. In the race itself, he pulled into the pits with fuel vaporisation problems. He was given another Ferrari F1 chance at the Nürburgring, where he crashed out, but another win in the Tour de France may have kept him employed in 1962, when he accepted the role of test driver vacated by Richie Ginther, who had decided to move to BRM.

The season started promisingly enough, with wins in the Brussels and Naples GPs, before more success with a tremendous victory in the Targa Florio (with Gendebien and Ricardo Rodriguez). At the Belgian Grand Prix, though, Mairesse was involved in a lurid high-speed accident after colliding with Trevor Taylor, receiving burns that kept him out of action until a comeback at Monza, which netted fourth place.

Mairesse survived the Ferrari clear-out to partner John Surtees in 1963, but his erratic performances culminated in a needless accident at the German Grand Prix, where he wrote off the car and put himself out of racing for the remainder of the season. Although his Ferrari works career was finally at an end, he was still a more than useful sports car driver and rejoined Equipe Nationale Belge, winning the 1964 Angola GP in their Ferrari GTO and the Spa 500km in 1965. His last major win came the following year, when he shared a Filipinetti Porsche Carrera with Herbert Müller to win the Targa Florio once more. His accident-prone career finally came to an end at the 1968 Le Mans 24-hours, when a door flew open on his Ford GT40, causing him to crash heavily. He suffered severe head injuries that left him unconscious for two weeks. He never fully recovered, and after a year spent in poor health, and with no prospect of a return to racing, he committed suicide in an Ostend hotel room.

PASTOR MALDONADO

WITHOUT the benefit of Venezuelan oil money, it is more than likely that Pastor Maldonado would struggle to find a place on the Formula 1 grid, despite his more than decent record in the junior single-seater categories. Perhaps his somewhat chequered early career, which involved no little controversy and quite a few changes of team, marked him down as a midfielder at best. It took his GP2 championship winning campaign of 2010 to convince the doubters that he was worthy of a place in F1, having made slow, but sure progress since his debut year in the class in 2007.

The young Maldonado found his early sporting thrills on a BMX bike, before being captivated by go-karts after a visit to his local Maracay track. Once he had tasted the thrill of mini karts, the obsession took hold, and he competed in the class both at home and abroad, until he felt he was ready to progress to cars at the start of the 2002 season.

Maldonado chose Formula Renault and, after a satisfactory introduction, proved to be the class of the field in Italy in 2004, taking eight wins and six pole positions on his cruise to the title. This success brought a first taste of grand prix machinery with an acceptable test in the Minardi, which drew praise from Paul Stoddart. It was too early to make the jump, however, and he chose to compete in the World Series by Renault for 2005. His foray into the class came to an abrupt halt at Monaco, though, when he picked up a four-race ban after failing to obey yellow flags and seriously injuring a marshal. Thus he transferred to the Italian F3000 championship to compete in four events, taking a win in his final appearance at Magione. Remaining in the World Series for the 2006 season, the Venezuelan was a front-runner and took two wins to finish third overall in the standings; he would have won had he not been stripped of a victory at Misano for a technical infringement. After losing his appeal, the deduction of those 15 points proved crucial to his title quest.

For 2007, Maldonado graduated to the GP2 series and soon made his mark with an impressive win in Monaco, but he looked ragged elsewhere. Unfortunately, his season was cut short when he broke his collarbone while training on his mountain bike. Having joined Piquet Sports for 2008, initially he struggled to find his form, but a strong finish to the year was highlighted by a Sprint race win at Spa, which pushed him up to fifth in the standings and a place in the top ART Grand Prix team for 2009, paired with the brilliant young Nico Hülkenberg. It was a salutary year for the personable Maldonado who, despite managing a couple of high-profile wins at Monaco and Silverstone, was comprehensively outpaced by his young German team-mate, who stormed to the title while Pastor could do no better than sixth.

A return to the familiar surroundings of the Rappax squad (formerly Piquet Sports) proved to be the right move for Maldonado, who really was looking at win or bust in his fourth successive year in the class. However, six wins in mid-season gave him enough of an advantage over his younger opponents, the most notable of whom was Sergio Pérez.

It was somewhat ironic that Maldonado finally found himself in Formula 1 at Williams, as replacement for none other than Hülkenberg. It was a tough baptism for the Venezuelan rookie, who had bought into the worst season in the once great team's history. He impressed doubters with his never-say-die approach, however, and was very unfortunate to lose a points finish at Monaco, where he was punted out by an errant Lewis Hamilton. Despite the lack of results – he had to wait until Spa to register his first and only point of the year – generally he looked more convincing than his experienced team-mate, Rubens Barrichello, shading the Brazilian 10–9 in qualifying. With the team undergoing a radical overhaul for 2012, Maldonado's healthy budget ensured that he would remain on board, no doubt hoping that the new package and Renault power would give him the chance to make a real mark on Formula 1 at long last.

MALDONADO, Pastor (YV) b 9/3/1985, Maracay

2011 Championship position: 19th   Wins: 0   Pole positions: 0   Fastest laps: 0   Points scored: 1

	Race	Circuit	No	Entrant	Tyres	Capacity/Car/Engine	Comment	Q Pos/Entries
ret	AUSTRALIAN GP	Melbourne	11	AT&T Williams	P	2.4 Williams FW33-Cosworth V8	transmission	15/24
ret	MALAYSIAN GP	Sepang	11	AT&T Williams	P	2.4 Williams FW33-Cosworth V8	coil	18/24
18	CHINESE GP	Shanghai Circuit	11	AT&T Williams	P	2.4 Williams FW33-Cosworth V8	1 lap behind	17/24
17	TURKISH GP	Istanbul Park	11	AT&T Williams	P	2.4 Williams FW33-Cosworth V8	poor balance/1 lap behind	14/24
15	SPANISH GP	Barcelona	11	AT&T Williams	P	2.4 Williams FW33-Cosworth V8	1 lap behind	9/24
ret	MONACO GP	Monte Carlo	11	AT&T Williams	P	2.4 Williams FW33-Cosworth V8	accident – hit by Hamilton	8/24
ret	CANADIAN GP	Montreal	11	AT&T Williams	P	2.4 Williams FW33-Cosworth V8	spun off	12/24
18	EUROPEAN GP	Valencia	11	AT&T Williams	P	2.4 Williams FW33-Cosworth V8	puncture/1 lap behind	13/24
14	BRITISH GP	Silverstone	11	AT&T Williams	P	2.4 Williams FW33-Cosworth V8	1 lap behind	7/24
14	GERMAN GP	Hockenheim	11	AT&T Williams	P	2.4 Williams FW33-Cosworth V8	tyre wear/1 lap behind	13/24
16	HUNGARIAN GP	Hungaroring	11	AT&T Williams	P	2.4 Williams FW33-Cosworth V8	2 laps behind	17/24
10	BELGIAN GP	Spa	11	AT&T Williams	P	2.4 Williams FW33-Cosworth V8		16/24
11	ITALIAN GP	Monza	11	AT&T Williams	P	2.4 Williams FW33-Cosworth V8	1 lap behind	13/24
11	SINGAPORE GP	Marina Bay Circuit	11	AT&T Williams	P	2.4 Williams FW33-Cosworth V8	1 lap behind	13/24
14	JAPANESE GP	Suzuka	11	AT&T Williams	P	2.4 Williams FW33-Cosworth V8		14/24
ret	KOREAN GP	Yeongam	11	AT&T Williams	P	2.4 Williams FW33-Cosworth V8	engine	16/24
ret	INDIAN GP	Buddh Circuit	11	AT&T Williams	P	2.4 Williams FW33-Cosworth V8	gearbox	14/24
14	ABU DHABI GP	Yas Marina Circuit	11	AT&T Williams	P	2.4 Williams FW33-Cosworth V8	30-sec pen – ignored flags-1 lap	17/24
14	BRAZILIAN GP	Interlagos	11	AT&T Williams	P	2.4 Williams FW33-Cosworth V8	accident	18/24

GP Starts: 19   GP Wins: 0   Pole positions: 0   Fastest laps: 0   Points: 1

NIGEL MANSELL, OBE, CBE

If you look at it objectively, there were two Nigel Mansells. One belonged to sections of the motor racing press, who saw him as the whingeing, ungracious 'chip-on-the-shoulder' Brit, who courted success and disaster in equal measure, but actually was a brilliant racing driver, good for endless column inches and therefore a lucrative source of income. The second Mansell belonged to the 'man in the street', who didn't give a damn about the scribblings of the journalists, but was content merely to revel in the many scintillating displays served up by one of the bravest, and most committed and entertaining drivers of his age, a man who still retained the common touch even if he was a superstar. In truth, of course, he was a mixture of all these things; it really just depends on your perspective. I prefer to concentrate on the latter persona, for his remarkable deeds in a racing car are of primary concern in a book of this nature.

Mansell's story is well chronicled, but his dogged refusal to give up when the early part of his career seemed to be leading nowhere marked him down as a potential champion, even if his results in Formula 3 at the time indicated otherwise. The man most responsible for helping his career over that crucial first hurdle was none other than Colin Chapman, who knew a good 'un' when he saw one and placed him in the Lotus team as a test driver. When given his grand prix debut in Austria, Mansell endured acute discomfort from petrol that leaked into his cockpit to tough it out until the engine failed. This was just the stuff that Lotus needed as they slipped from their pedestal in the early 1980s.

Certainly there were still rough edges, and Mansell made plenty of mistakes, but there were virtues, too. He absolutely gave his all, in contrast to team-mate Elio de Angelis, who could lose heart when his car was not performing. When Chapman died of a sudden heart attack in December, 1982, it was a crushing blow for Nigel, not least because he had lost his greatest believer. His level of competitiveness was raised, however, when the team received their new Renault turbo-powered, Gérard Ducarouge-designed car mid-way through the following season, as he demonstrated in the European GP at Brands Hatch, but he endured a generally unhappy time in 1984. A probable win in the rain at Monaco was thrown away when he slithered into the Armco, and there were many at that stage who doubted that he would ever win a grand prix.

Mansell's move to Williams in 1985 changed everything. After quickly coming to terms with Keke Rosberg, he broke his duck at last and continued his new-found form into the 1986 season, putting new team-mate Nelson Piquet in the shade with a series of brilliant drives to take five grand prix wins. The championship seemed to be there for the taking, but a gaffe in the penultimate round in Mexico, where he failed to put the car into gear on the grid, cost him dear. Under pressure at the final race in Adelaide, poor Nigel had the race covered and the championship within his grasp until a tyre failure sent him crashing out. Undaunted, he bounced back in 1987, this time clocking up six wins in the Williams-Honda, but a practice crash at Suzuka handed the title to team-mate Piquet. Then the Williams team lost their Honda engines to McLaren, and Nigel was forced to spend a year in purgatory with the Judd-powered car, although in the rain at Silverstone he drove quite brilliantly into second place.

Accepting a massive offer from Maranello, Mansell entered Ferrari folklore with a first-time-out win in Brazil and carried the fight to McLaren with captivating brio. His victory in Hungary, after a stunning bit of opportunism in traffic, was the highlight of a brilliant season, which was soured some-

what when a skirmish with Ayrton Senna in Portugal led to his suspension from the Spanish GP a week later. Greater disenchantment followed in 1990, when Alain Prost joined the Ferrari payroll. The little Frenchman hi-jacked the team's attentions with four early-season wins, prompting Mansell to announce his retirement. An offer from Williams to return to Didcot in 1991 was enough to persuade him to continue, however, and it was a decision he would not regret. Although driving as well as ever, his slow start to the season eventually counted against him, for despite a mid-season burst of five wins, punctuated by a heartbreaking pit-stop fiasco in Portugal, he was unable to overhaul Senna in the race for the title.

In 1992, Nigel finally got the job done. With what was undeniably the best car, he fairly scorched away with the championship, taking five straight wins at the start of the season. Apart from an ill-judged clash with Senna in Canada, he hardly put a foot wrong and thoroughly earned his world championship. Sadly, his relationship with Williams had deteriorated to the point that an agreement could not be reached for him to continue in 1993 and, with both parties seemingly unable (or unwilling) to compromise, he headed off to the States and a new life in Indy car racing with Newman-Haas Lola.

Proving all the doubters wrong, Nigel not only won the PPG Cup at his first attempt, but – a crash at Phoenix apart – also made light of the black art of racing on ovals to such effect that he was almost omnipotent. He was very unlucky to miss out on a first-time win in the Indy 500 at the last gasp, when a full-course yellow saw him outfumbled by the wily Emerson Fittipaldi. Perhaps more importantly, however, he had found a new environment in which he felt appreciated, and this showed in his contented demeanour. Sadly, it did not last. Penske wheeled out a new car in 1994, which left everyone else trailing in its wake, and Nigel's motivation, such a crucial part of his success, appeared to be less than total. The chance to return to grand prix racing in the wake of Senna's death proved irresistible, but despite an end-of-season win at Adelaide, Williams decided to stick with Damon Hill and David Coulthard for 1995.

With hindsight, , a fully charged Mansell might have been a better choice to challenge Michael Schumacher's dominance. Instead, a multi-million-dollar marriage of convenience was forged with Marlboro McLaren Mercedes, which ended in farce when first he couldn't fit properly in the car and then gave up when the expensively redesigned machine failed to meet his expectations. It was a rather sad epitaph to his grand prix career.

Mansell then made a handful of over-hyped touring car appearances for Ford in the BTCC during 1998, which gave his legions of loyal fans a few last glimpses of track action – until 1995/96, when he signed up for the Grand Prix Masters. Typically, he was the most impressive of the over-45-year-old F1 veterans, taking two wins from three races held.

The temptation to compete alongside his two sons, Greg and Leo, was enough to tempt Nigel back into action in 2010, when he set up the Beachdean Mansell Motorsport team. His sons, already racing an LMP1 Ginetta-Zytek, were joined at Le Mans by their father. Sadly, their race ended early, when a puncture caused Nigel to crash out, very heavily, happily without serious injury.

Already an Officer of the Order of the British Empire (OBE), Mansell was appointed a Commander of the Order (CBE) in the 2012 New Year Honours for services to children and young people, following his work as president of UK Youth.

MANSELL, Nigel (GB) b 8/8/1953, Baughton, Upton on Severn, Worcestershire

1980 Championship position: Unplaced

	Race	Circuit	No	Entrant	Tyres	Capacity/Car/Engine	Comment	Q Pos/Entries
ret	AUSTRIAN GP	Österreichring	43	Team Essex Lotus	G	3.0 Lotus 81B-Cosworth V8	engine	24/25
ret	DUTCH GP	Zandvoort	43	Team Essex Lotus	G	3.0 Lotus 81B-Cosworth V8	brake failure – spun off	16/28
dnq	ITALIAN GP	Imola	43	Team Essex Lotus	G	3.0 Lotus 81B-Cosworth V8		25/28

1981 Championship position: 14th= Wins: 0 Pole positions: 0 Fastest laps: 0 Points scored: 8

	Race	Circuit	No	Entrant	Tyres	Capacity/Car/Engine	Comment	Q Pos/Entries
ret	US GP WEST	Long Beach	12	Team Essex Lotus	M	3.0 Lotus 81-Cosworth V8	hit wall	7/29
11	BRAZILIAN GP	Rio	12	Team Essex Lotus	M	3.0 Lotus 81-Cosworth V8	1 lap behind	13/30
ret	ARGENTINE GP	Buenos Aires	12	Team Essex Lotus	M	3.0 Lotus 81-Cosworth V8	engine	15/31
3	BELGIAN GP	Zolder	12	Team Essex Lotus	M	3.0 Lotus 81-Cosworth V8		10/31
ret	MONACO GP	Monte Carlo	12	Team Essex Lotus	M	3.0 Lotus 87-Cosworth V8	rear suspension	3/31
6	SPANISH GP	Jarama	12	John Player Team Lotus	M	3.0 Lotus 87-Cosworth V8		11/30
7	FRENCH GP	Dijon	12	John Player Team Lotus	M	3.0 Lotus 87-Cosworth V8	1 lap behind	13/29
dnq	BRITISH GP	Silverstone	12	John Player Team Lotus	G	3.0 Lotus 87-Cosworth V8		27/30
dns	"	"	12	John Player Team Lotus	G	3.0 Lotus 88B-Cosworth V8	car disqualified during practice	– / –
ret	GERMAN GP	Hockenheim	12	John Player Team Lotus	G	3.0 Lotus 87-Cosworth V8	fuel leak	15/30
ret	AUSTRIAN GP	Österreichring	12	John Player Team Lotus	G	3.0 Lotus 87-Cosworth V8	engine	11/28
ret	DUTCH GP	Zandvoort	12	John Player Team Lotus	G	3.0 Lotus 87-Cosworth V8	electrics	17/30
ret	ITALIAN GP	Monza	12	John Player Team Lotus	G	3.0 Lotus 87-Cosworth V8	handling	12/30
ret	CANADIAN GP	Montreal	12	John Player Team Lotus	G	3.0 Lotus 87-Cosworth V8	accident with Prost	5/30
4	CAESARS PALACE GP	Las Vegas	12	John Player Team Lotus	G	3.0 Lotus 87-Cosworth V8		9/30

1982 Championship position: 14th= Wins: 0 Pole positions: 0 Fastest laps: 0 Points scored: 7

	Race	Circuit	No	Entrant	Tyres	Capacity/Car/Engine	Comment	Q Pos/Entries
ret	SOUTH AFRICAN GP	Kyalami	12	John Player Team Lotus	G	3.0 Lotus 87B-Cosworth V8	electrics	18/30
3*	BRAZILIAN GP	Rio	12	John Player Team Lotus	G	3.0 Lotus 91-Cosworth V8	*1st and 2nd place cars disqualified	14/31
7	US GP WEST	Long Beach	12	John Player Team Lotus	G	3.0 Lotus 91-Cosworth V8	2 laps behind	17/31
ret	BELGIAN GP	Zolder	12	John Player Team Lotus	G	3.0 Lotus 91-Cosworth V8	clutch	9/32
4	MONACO GP	Monte Carlo	12	John Player Team Lotus	G	3.0 Lotus 91-Cosworth V8	1 lap behind	11/31
ret	US GP (DETROIT)	Detroit	12	John Player Team Lotus	G	3.0 Lotus 91-Cosworth V8	engine	7/28
ret	CANADIAN GP	Montreal	12	John Player Team Lotus	G	3.0 Lotus 91-Cosworth V8	accident with Giacomelli	14/29
ret	BRITISH GP	Brands Hatch	12	John Player Team Lotus	G	3.0 Lotus 91-Cosworth V8	handling & driver discomfort	23/30
9	GERMAN GP	Hockenheim	12	John Player Team Lotus	G	3.0 Lotus 91-Cosworth V8	pit stop – in pain/2 laps behind	19/30
ret	AUSTRIAN GP	Österreichring	12	John Player Team Lotus	G	3.0 Lotus 91-Cosworth V8	engine	12/29
8	SWISS GP	Dijon	12	John Player Team Lotus	G	3.0 Lotus 91-Cosworth V8	1 lap behind	26/29
7	ITALIAN GP	Monza	12	John Player Team Lotus	G	3.0 Lotus 91-Cosworth V8	1 lap behind	23/30
ret	CAESARS PALACE GP	Las Vegas	12	John Player Team Lotus	G	3.0 Lotus 91-Cosworth V8	accident with Baldi	21/30

1983 Championship position: 0 Wins: 0 Pole positions: 0 Fastest laps: 1 Points scored: 0

	Race	Circuit	No	Entrant	Tyres	Capacity/Car/Engine	Comment	Q Pos/Entries
12	BRAZILIAN GP	Rio	12	John Player Team Lotus	P	3.0 Lotus 92-Cosworth V8	pit stop – tyres/2 laps behind	22/27
12	US GP WEST	Long Beach	12	John Player Team Lotus	P	3.0 Lotus 92-Cosworth V8	3 pitstops – tyres/handling/-3 laps	13/28
ret	FRENCH GP	Paul Ricard	12	John Player Team Lotus	P	3.0 Lotus 92-Cosworth V8	handling/driver discomfort	18/29
12/ret	SAN MARINO GP	Imola	12	John Player Team Lotus	P	3.0 Lotus 92-Cosworth V8	broken rear wing – spun/-4 laps	15/28
ret	MONACO GP	Monte Carlo	12	John Player Team Lotus	P	3.0 Lotus 92-Cosworth V8	accident with Alboreto	14/28
ret	BELGIAN GP	Spa	12	John Player Team Lotus	P	3.0 Lotus 92-Cosworth V8	gearbox	19/28
6	US GP (DETROIT)	Detroit	12	John Player Team Lotus	P	3.0 Lotus 92-Cosworth V8	1 lap behind	14/27
ret	CANADIAN GP	Montreal	12	John Player Team Lotus	P	3.0 Lotus 92-Cosworth V8	handling/tyres	18/28
4	BRITISH GP	Silverstone	12	John Player Team Lotus	P	1.5 t/c Lotus 94T-Renault V6	pit stop – fuel	– / –
dns	"	"	12	John Player Team Lotus	P	1.5 t/c Lotus 93T-Renault V6	practice only/set grid time	18/29
ret	GERMAN GP	Hockenheim	12	John Player Team Lotus	P	1.5 t/c Lotus 94T-Renault V6	engine	– / –
dns	"	"	12	John Player Team Lotus	P	1.5 t/c Lotus 93T-Renault V6	practice only/set grid time	17/29
5	AUSTRIAN GP	Österreichring	12	John Player Team Lotus	P	1.5 t/c Lotus 94T-Renault V6	pit stop – fuel/1 lap behind	3/29
ret	DUTCH GP	Zandvoort	12	John Player Team Lotus	P	1.5 t/c Lotus 94T-Renault V6	spun off	5/29
8	ITALIAN GP	Monza	12	John Player Team Lotus	P	1.5 t/c Lotus 94T-Renault V6		11/29
3	EUROPEAN GP	Brands Hatch	12	John Player Team Lotus	P	1.5 t/c Lotus 94T-Renault V6	FL	3/29
nc	SOUTH AFRICAN GP	Kyalami	12	John Player Team Lotus	P	1.5 t/c Lotus 94T-Renault V6	pit stops – gear linkage/tyres/-9 laps	7/26

1984 Championship position: 9th Wins: 0 Pole positions: 1 Fastest laps: 0 Points scored: 13

	Race	Circuit	No	Entrant	Tyres	Capacity/Car/Engine	Comment	Q Pos/Entries
ret	BRAZILIAN GP	Rio	12	John Player Team Lotus	G	1.5 t/c Lotus 95T-Renault V6	slid off track	5/27
ret	SOUTH AFRICAN GP	Kyalami	12	John Player Team Lotus	G	1.5 t/c Lotus 95T-Renault V6	turbo inlet duct	3/27
ret	BELGIAN GP	Zolder	12	John Player Team Lotus	G	1.5 t/c Lotus 95T-Renault V6	clutch	10/27
ret	SAN MARINO GP	Imola	12	John Player Team Lotus	G	1.5 t/c Lotus 95T-Renault V6	brake failure – crashed	18/28
3	FRENCH GP	Dijon	12	John Player Team Lotus	G	1.5 t/c Lotus 95T-Renault V6		6/27
ret	MONACO GP	Monte Carlo	12	John Player Team Lotus	G	1.5 t/c Lotus 95T-Renault V6	hit barrier when leading	2/27
6	CANADIAN GP	Montreal	12	John Player Team Lotus	G	1.5 t/c Lotus 95T-Renault V6	gearbox problems/2 laps behind	7/26
ret	US GP (DETROIT)	Detroit	12	John Player Team Lotus	G	1.5 t/c Lotus 95T-Renault V6	gearbox	3/27
6/ret	US GP (DALLAS)	Dallas	12	John Player Team Lotus	G	1.5 t/c Lotus 95T-Renault V6	gearbox/3 laps behind	1/27
ret	BRITISH GP	Brands Hatch	12	John Player Team Lotus	G	1.5 t/c Lotus 95T-Renault V6	gearbox	8/27
4	GERMAN GP	Hockenheim	12	John Player Team Lotus	G	1.5 t/c Lotus 95T-Renault V6		16/27
ret	AUSTRIAN GP	Österreichring	12	John Player Team Lotus	G	1.5 t/c Lotus 95T-Renault V6	engine	8/28
3	DUTCH GP	Zandvoort	12	John Player Team Lotus	G	1.5 t/c Lotus 95T-Renault V6		12/27
ret	ITALIAN GP	Monza	12	John Player Team Lotus	G	1.5 t/c Lotus 95T-Renault V6	spun off	7/27
ret	EUROPEAN GP	Nürburgring	12	John Player Team Lotus	G	1.5 t/c Lotus 95T-Renault V6	engine	8/26
ret	PORTUGUESE GP	Estoril	12	John Player Team Lotus	G	1.5 t/c Lotus 95T-Renault V6	lost brake fluid – spun off	6/27

1985 Championship position: 6th Wins: 2 Pole positions: 1 Fastest laps: 1 Points scored: 31

	Race	Circuit	No	Entrant	Tyres	Capacity/Car/Engine	Comment	Q Pos/Entries
ret	BRAZILIAN GP	Rio	5	Canon Williams Honda Team	G	1.5 t/c Williams FW10-Honda V6	broken exhaust/accident damage	5/25
5	PORTUGUESE GP	Estoril	5	Canon Williams Honda Team	G	1.5 t/c Williams FW10-Honda V6	started from pitlane/2 laps behind	9/26
5	SAN MARINO GP	Imola	5	Canon Williams Honda Team	G	1.5 t/c Williams FW10-Honda V6	gearbox problems/2 laps behind	7/26
7	MONACO GP	Monte Carlo	5	Canon Williams Honda Team	G	1.5 t/c Williams FW10-Honda V6	brake problems/1 lap behind	2/26
6	CANADIAN GP	Montreal	5	Canon Williams Honda Team	G	1.5 t/c Williams FW10-Honda V6		16/25

ret	US GP (DETROIT)	Detroit	5	Canon Williams Honda Team	G	1.5 t/c Williams FW10-Honda V6	brake problems – crashed	2/25
dns	FRENCH GP	Paul Ricard	5	Canon Williams Honda Team	G	1.5 t/c Williams FW10-Honda V6	accident in practice	(8)/26
ret	BRITISH GP	Silverstone	5	Canon Williams Honda Team	G	1.5 t/c Williams FW10-Honda V6	clutch	5/26
6	GERMAN GP	Nürburgring	5	Canon Williams Honda Team	G	1.5 t/c Williams FW10-Honda V6		10/27
ret	AUSTRIAN GP	Österreichring	5	Canon Williams Honda Team	G	1.5 t/c Williams FW10-Honda V6	engine	2/27
6	DUTCH GP	Zandvoort	5	Canon Williams Honda Team	G	1.5 t/c Williams FW10-Honda V6	pit stop – tyres/1 lap behind	7/27
11/ret	ITALIAN GP	Monza	5	Canon Williams Honda Team	G	1.5 t/c Williams FW10-Honda V6	engine/FL/4 laps behind	3/26
2	BELGIAN GP	Spa	5	Canon Williams Honda Team	G	1.5 t/c Williams FW10-Honda V6		7/24
1	EUROPEAN GP	Brands Hatch	5	Canon Williams Honda Team	G	1.5 t/c Williams FW10-Honda V6		3/27
1	SOUTH AFRICAN GP	Kyalami	5	Canon Williams Honda Team	G	1.5 t/c Williams FW10-Honda V6		1/21
ret	AUSTRALIAN GP	Adelaide	5	Canon Williams Honda Team	G	1.5 t/c Williams FW10-Honda V6	transmission	2/25

1986 Championship position: 2nd Wins: 5 Pole positions: 2 Fastest laps: 4 Points scored: 72

ret	BRAZILIAN GP	Rio	5	Canon Williams Honda Team	G	1.5 t/c Williams FW11-Honda V6	accident with Senna on lap 1	3/25
2	SPANISH GP	Jerez	5	Canon Williams Honda Team	G	1.5 t/c Williams FW11-Honda V6	FL	3/25
ret	SAN MARINO	Imola	5	Canon Williams Honda Team	G	1.5 t/c Williams FW11-Honda V6	engine	3/26
4	MONACO GP	Monte Carlo	5	Canon Williams Honda Team	G	1.5 t/c Williams FW11-Honda V6		2/26
1	BELGIAN GP	Spa	5	Canon Williams Honda Team	G	1.5 t/c Williams FW11-Honda V6		5/25
1	CANADIAN GP	Montreal	5	Canon Williams Honda Team	G	1.5 t/c Williams FW11-Honda V6		1/25
5	US GP (DETROIT)	Detroit	5	Canon Williams Honda Team	G	1.5 t/c Williams FW11-Honda V6	pit stop – tyres/1 lap behind	2/26
1	FRENCH GP	Paul Ricard	5	Canon Williams Honda Team	G	1.5 t/c Williams FW11-Honda V6	FL	2/26
1	BRITISH GP	Brands Hatch	5	Canon Williams Honda Team	G	1.5 t/c Williams FW11-Honda V6	FL	2/26
3	GERMAN GP	Hockenheim	5	Canon Williams Honda Team	G	1.5 t/c Williams FW11-Honda V6		6/26
3	HUNGARIAN GP	Hungaroring	5	Canon Williams Honda Team	G	1.5 t/c Williams FW11-Honda V6	pit stop – tyres/handling/-1 lap	4/26
ret	AUSTRIAN GP	Österreichring	5	Canon Williams Honda Team	G	1.5 t/c Williams FW11-Honda V6	driveshaft – c.v. joint	6/26
2	ITALIAN GP	Monza	5	Canon Williams Honda Team	G	1.5 t/c Williams FW11-Honda V6		3/27
1	PORTUGUESE GP	Estoril	5	Canon Williams Honda Team	G	1.5 t/c Williams FW11-Honda V6	FL	2/27
5	MEXICAN GP	Mexico City	5	Canon Williams Honda Team	G	1.5 t/c Williams FW11-Honda V6	last away/pitstop – tyres/1 lap behind	3/26
ret	AUSTRALIAN GP	Adelaide	5	Canon Williams Honda Team	G	1.5 t/c Williams FW11-Honda V6	tyre failure – crashed	1/26

1987 Championship position: 2nd Wins: 6 Pole positions: 8 Fastest laps: 3 Points scored: 61

6	BRAZILIAN GP	Rio	5	Canon Williams Honda Team	G	1.5 t/c Williams FW11B-Honda V6	pit stop – paper in radiator/-1 lap	1/23
1	SAN MARINO GP	Imola	5	Canon Williams Honda Team	G	1.5 t/c Williams FW11B-Honda V6		2/27
ret	BELGIAN GP	Spa	5	Canon Williams Honda Team	G	1.5 t/c Williams FW11B-Honda V6	collision with Senna – accident damage	1/26
ret	MONACO GP	Monte Carlo	5	Canon Williams Honda Team	G	1.5 t/c Williams FW11B-Honda V6	wastegate pipe	1/26
5	US GP (DETROIT)	Detroit	5	Canon Williams Honda Team	G	1.5 t/c Williams FW11B-Honda V6	pit stop – tyres-wheel stuck/-1 lap	1/26
1	FRENCH GP	Paul Ricard	5	Canon Williams Honda Team	G	1.5 t/c Williams FW11B-Honda V6		1/26
1	BRITISH GP	Silverstone	5	Canon Williams Honda Team	G	1.5 t/c Williams FW11B-Honda V6	FL	2/26
ret	GERMAN GP	Hockenheim	5	Canon Williams Honda Team	G	1.5 t/c Williams FW11B-Honda V6	engine/FL	1/26
14/ret	HUNGARIAN GP	Hungaroring	5	Canon Williams Honda Team	G	1.5 t/c Williams FW11B-Honda V6	lost wheel nut/6 laps behind	1/26
1	AUSTRIAN GP	Österreichring	5	Canon Williams Honda Team	G	1.5 t/c Williams FW11B-Honda V6	FL	2/26
3	ITALIAN GP	Monza	5	Canon Williams Honda Team	G	1.5 t/c Williams FW11B-Honda V6		2/28
ret	PORTUGUESE GP	Estoril	5	Canon Williams Honda Team	G	1.5 t/c Williams FW11B-Honda V6	electrics	2/27
1	SPANISH GP	Jerez	5	Canon Williams Honda Team	G	1.5 t/c Williams FW11B-Honda V6		2/28
1	MEXICAN GP	Mexico City	5	Canon Williams Honda Team	G	1.5 t/c Williams FW11B-Honda V6		1/27
dns	JAPANESE GP	Suzuka	5	Canon Williams Honda Team	G	1.5 t/c Williams FW11B-Honda V6	practice accident – injured back	(7)/27

Hail the hero. Mansell takes the plaudits after his victory in the 1986 British Grand Prix while a deflated Nelson Piquet ponders his teammate's astonishing speed.

'Il Leone'. Mansell spent two years with Ferrari and immediately won the hearts of the 'tifosi' with his typically committed performances. One of the highlights was a sensational victory in the 1989 Hungarian Grand Prix after taking his car from a lowly 12th place on the grid.

	1988 Championship position: 9th		Wins: 0	Pole positions: 0		Fastest laps: 1	Points scored: 12		
ret	BRAZILIAN GP	Rio	5	Canon Williams Team	G	3.5 Williams FW12-Judd V8		overheating/electrics	2/31
ret	SAN MARINO GP	Imola	5	Canon Williams Team	G	3.5 Williams FW12-Judd V8		engine/electrics	11/31
ret	MONACO GP	Monte Carlo	5	Canon Williams Team	G	3.5 Williams FW12-Judd V8		accident with Alboreto	5/30
ret	MEXICAN GP	Mexico City	5	Canon Williams Team	G	3.5 Williams FW12-Judd V8		engine	14/30
ret	CANADIAN GP	Montreal	5	Canon Williams Team	G	3.5 Williams FW12-Judd V8		engine	9/31
ret	US GP (DETROIT)	Detroit	5	Canon Williams Team	G	3.5 Williams FW12-Judd V8		electrics	6/31
ret	FRENCH GP	Paul Ricard	5	Canon Williams Team	G	3.5 Williams FW12-Judd V8		suspension	9/31
2	BRITISH GP	Silverstone	5	Canon Williams Team	G	3.5 Williams FW12-Judd V8		FL	11/31
ret	GERMAN GP	Hockenheim	5	Canon Williams Team	G	3.5 Williams FW12-Judd V8		spun off	11/31
ret	HUNGARIAN GP	Hungaroring	5	Canon Williams Team	G	3.5 Williams FW12-Judd V8		driver exhaustion	2/31
ret	PORTUGUESE GP	Estoril	5	Canon Williams Team	G	3.5 Williams FW12-Judd V8		spun off	6/31
2	SPANISH GP	Jerez	5	Canon Williams Team	G	3.5 Williams FW12-Judd V8			3/31
ret	JAPANESE GP	Suzuka	5	Canon Williams Team	G	3.5 Williams FW12-Judd V8		spun off – hit Piquet	8/31
ret	AUSTRALIAN GP	Adelaide	5	Canon Williams Team	G	3.5 Williams FW12-Judd V8		brakes – spun off	3/31
	1989 Championship position: 4th		Wins: 2	Pole positions: 0		Fastest laps: 3	Points scored: 38		
1	BRAZILIAN GP	Rio	27	Scuderia Ferrari SpA SEFAC	G	3.5 Ferrari 640 V12			6/38
ret	SAN MARINO GP	Imola	27	Scuderia Ferrari SpA SEFAC	G	3.5 Ferrari 640 V12		gearbox	3/39
ret	MONACO GP	Monte Carlo	27	Scuderia Ferrari SpA SEFAC	G	3.5 Ferrari 640 V12		gear selection	5/38
ret	MEXICAN GP	Mexico City	27	Scuderia Ferrari SpA SEFAC	G	3.5 Ferrari 640 V12		gearbox/FL	3/39
ret	US GP (PHOENIX)	Phoenix	27	Scuderia Ferrari SpA SEFAC	G	3.5 Ferrari 640 V12		alternator	4/39
dsq*	CANADIAN GP	Montreal	27	Scuderia Ferrari SpA SEFAC	G	3.5 Ferrari 640 V12		*started from pits before start	5/39
2	FRENCH GP	Paul Ricard	27	Scuderia Ferrari SpA SEFAC	G	3.5 Ferrari 640 V12		started from pit lane	3/39
2	BRITISH GP	Silverstone	27	Scuderia Ferrari SpA SEFAC	G	3.5 Ferrari 640 V12		FL	3/39
3	GERMAN GP	Hockenheim	27	Scuderia Ferrari SpA SEFAC	G	3.5 Ferrari 640 V12			3/39
1	HUNGARIAN GP	Hungaroring	27	Scuderia Ferrari SpA SEFAC	G	3.5 Ferrari 640 V12		FL	12/39
3	BELGIAN GP	Spa	27	Scuderia Ferrari SpA SEFAC	G	3.5 Ferrari 640 V12			6/39
ret	ITALIAN GP	Monza	27	Scuderia Ferrari SpA SEFAC	G	3.5 Ferrari 640 V12		gearbox	3/39
dsq*/ret	PORTUGUESE GP	Estoril	27	Scuderia Ferrari SpA SEFAC	G	3.5 Ferrari 640 V12		*reversed in pits/collision – Senna	3/39
ret	JAPANESE GP	Suzuka	27	Scuderia Ferrari SpA SEFAC	G	3.5 Ferrari 640 V12		engine	4/39
ret	AUSTRALIAN GP	Adelaide	27	Scuderia Ferrari SpA SEFAC	G	3.5 Ferrari 640 V12		spun off in rain	7/39
	1990 Championship position: 5th		Wins: 1	Pole positions: 3		Fastest laps: 3	Points scored: 37		
ret	US GP (PHOENIX)	Phoenix	2	Scuderia Ferrari SpA SEFAC	G	3.5 Ferrari 641 V12		spun off – gearbox/clutch	17/35
4	BRAZILIAN GP	Interlagos	2	Scuderia Ferrari SpA SEFAC	G	3.5 Ferrari 641 V12		pit stop – tyres-anti-roll bar	5/35
ret	SAN MARINO GP	Imola	2	Scuderia Ferrari SpA SEFAC	G	3.5 Ferrari 641/2 V12		engine	5/34
ret	MONACO GP	Monte Carlo	2	Scuderia Ferrari SpA SEFAC	G	3.5 Ferrari 641/2 V12		battery/electrics	7/35
3	CANADIAN GP	Montreal	2	Scuderia Ferrari SpA SEFAC	G	3.5 Ferrari 641/2 V12			7/35
2	MEXICAN GP	Mexico City	2	Scuderia Ferrari SpA SEFAC	G	3.5 Ferrari 641/2 V12			4/35
18/ret	FRENCH GP	Paul Ricard	2	Scuderia Ferrari SpA SEFAC	G	3.5 Ferrari 641/2 V12		engine/FL/8 laps behind	1/35
ret	BRITISH GP	Silverstone	2	Scuderia Ferrari SpA SEFAC	G	3.5 Ferrari 641/2 V12		gearbox/FL	1/35
ret	GERMAN GP	Hockenheim	2	Scuderia Ferrari SpA SEFAC	G	3.5 Ferrari 641/2 V12		undertray damage	4/35
17/ret	HUNGARIAN GP	Hungaroring	2	Scuderia Ferrari SpA SEFAC	G	3.5 Ferrari 641/2 V12		collision with Berger/6 laps behind	5/35
ret	BELGIAN GP	Spa	2	Scuderia Ferrari SpA SEFAC	G	3.5 Ferrari 641/2 V12		handling problems	5/33

4	ITALIAN GP	Monza	2	Scuderia Ferrari SpA SEFAC	G	3.5 Ferrari 641/2 V12	throttle problems	4/33
1	PORTUGUESE GP	Estoril	2	Scuderia Ferrari SpA SEFAC	G	3.5 Ferrari 641/2 V12		1/33
2	SPANISH GP	Jerez	2	Scuderia Ferrari SpA SEFAC	G	3.5 Ferrari 641/2 V12		3/33
ret	JAPANESE GP	Suzuka	2	Scuderia Ferrari SpA SEFAC	G	3.5 Ferrari 641/2 V12	driveshaft	3/30
2	AUSTRALIAN GP	Adelaide	2	Scuderia Ferrari SpA SEFAC	G	3.5 Ferrari 641/2 V12	FL	3/30

1991 Championship position: 2nd   Wins: 5   Pole positions: 2   Fastest laps: 6   Points scored: 72

ret	US GP	Phoenix	5	Canon Williams Team	G	3.5 Williams FW14-Renault V10	gearbox	4/34
ret	BRAZILIAN GP	Interlagos	5	Canon Williams Team	G	3.5 Williams FW14-Renault V10	gearbox/FL	3/34
ret	SAN MARINO GP	Imola	5	Canon Williams Team	G	3.5 Williams FW14-Renault V10	collision with Brundle	4/34
2	MONACO GP	Monte Carlo	5	Canon Williams Team	G	3.5 Williams FW14-Renault V10		5/34
6/ret	CANADIAN GP	Montreal	5	Canon Williams Team	G	3.5 Williams FW14-Renault V10	leading – engine cut out on last lap/FL	2/34
2	MEXICAN GP	Mexico City	5	Canon Williams Team	G	3.5 Williams FW14-Renault V10	FL	2/34
1	FRENCH GP	Magny Cours	5	Canon Williams Team	G	3.5 Williams FW14-Renault V10	FL	4/34
1	BRITISH GP	Silverstone	5	Canon Williams Team	G	3.5 Williams FW14-Renault V10	FL	1/34
1	GERMAN GP	Hockenheim	5	Canon Williams Team	G	3.5 Williams FW14-Renault V10		1/34
2	HUNGARIAN GP	Hungaroring	5	Canon Williams Team	G	3.5 Williams FW14-Renault V10		3/34
ret	BELGIAN GP	Spa	5	Canon Williams Team	G	3.5 Williams FW14-Renault V10	voltage regulator	3/34
1	ITALIAN GP	Monza	5	Canon Williams Team	G	3.5 Williams FW14-Renault V10		2/34
dsq*	PORTUGUESE GP	Estoril	5	Canon Williams Team	G	3.5 Williams FW14-Renault V10	*wheel change in pitlane/FL	4/34
1	SPANISH GP	Barcelona	5	Canon Williams Team	G	3.5 Williams FW14-Renault V10		2/33
ret	JAPANESE GP	Suzuka	5	Canon Williams Team	G	3.5 Williams FW14-Renault V10	spun off	3/31
2*	AUSTRALIAN GP	Adelaide	5	Canon Williams Team	G	3.5 Williams FW14-Renault V10	race stopped at 14 laps/*half points	3/32

1992 WORLD CHAMPION   Wins: 9   Pole positions: 14   Fastest laps: 8   Points scored: 108

1	SOUTH AFRICAN GP	Kyalami	5	Canon Williams Team	G	3.5 Williams FW14B-Renault V10	FL	1/30
1	MEXICAN GP	Mexico City	5	Canon Williams Team	G	3.5 Williams FW14B-Renault V10		1/30
1	BRAZILIAN GP	Interlagos	5	Canon Williams Team	G	3.5 Williams FW14B-Renault V10		1/31
1	SPANISH GP	Barcelona	5	Canon Williams Team	G	3.5 Williams FW14B-Renault V10	FL	1/32
1	SAN MARINO GP	Imola	5	Canon Williams Team	G	3.5 Williams FW14B-Renault V10		1/32
2	MONACO GP	Monte Carlo	5	Canon Williams Team	G	3.5 Williams FW14B-Renault V10	pit stop for tyres when leading/FL	1/32
ret	CANADIAN GP	Montreal	5	Canon Williams Team	G	3.5 Williams FW14B-Renault V10	spun off trying to pass Senna	3/32
1	FRENCH GP	Magny Cours	5	Canon Williams Team	G	3.5 Williams FW14B-Renault V10	aggregate of 2 parts/FL	1/30
1	BRITISH GP	Silverstone	5	Canon Williams Team	G	3.5 Williams FW14B-Renault V10	FL	1/32
1	GERMAN GP	Hockenheim	5	Canon Williams Team	G	3.5 Williams FW14B-Renault V10		1/32
2	HUNGARIAN GP	Hungaroring	5	Canon Williams Team	G	3.5 Williams FW14B-Renault V10	FL	2/31
2	BELGIAN GP	Spa	5	Canon Williams Team	G	3.5 Williams FW14B-Renault V10		1/30
ret	ITALIAN GP	Monza	5	Canon Williams Team	G	3.5 Williams FW14B-Renault V10	hydraulics/gearbox/FL	1/28
1	PORTUGUESE GP	Estoril	5	Canon Williams Team	G	3.5 Williams FW14B-Renault V10		1/26
ret	JAPANESE GP	Suzuka	5	Canon Williams Team	G	3.5 Williams FW14B-Renault V10	engine/FL	1/26
ret	AUSTRALIAN GP	Adelaide	5	Canon Williams Team	G	3.5 Williams FW14B-Renault V10	hit by Senna	1/26

1994 Championship position: 9th   Wins: 1   Pole positions: 1   Fastest laps: 0   Points scored: 13

ret	FRENCH GP	Magny Cours	2	Rothmans Williams Renault	G	3.5 Williams FW16-Renault V10	transmission	2/28
ret	EUROPEAN GP	Jerez	2	Rothmans Williams Renault	G	3.5 Williams FW16B-Renault V10	spun off	3/28
4	JAPANESE GP	Suzuka	2	Rothmans Williams Renault	G	3.5 Williams FW16B-Renault V10		4/28
1	AUSTRALIAN GP	Adelaide	2	Rothmans Williams Renault	G	3.5 Williams FW16B-Renault V10		1/28

1995 Championship position: Unplaced

10	SAN MARINO GP	Imola	7	Marlboro McLaren Mercedes	G	3.0 McLaren MP4/10B-Mercedes V10	2 laps behind	9/26
ret	SPANISH GP	Barcelona	7	Marlboro McLaren Mercedes	G	3.0 McLaren MP4/10B-Mercedes V10	poor handling – driver retired car	10/26

GP Starts: 187   GP Wins: 31   Pole positions: 32   Fastest laps: 30   Points: 482

Job done. Nigel Mansell returned to Williams and finally nailed that elusive world championship in 1992. Pictured left, he takes his 'Red 5' to victory in the Portuguese Grand Prix at Estoril.

SERGIO MANTOVANI

A YOUNG Italian businessman, Sergio Mantovani made a good impression in both sports and touring cars in 1952, finishing sixth in the Bari GP (second in class) in a Ferrari, and second in the GT class of the Pescara 12-hours in a Lancia Aurelia.

Mantovani's success prompted him to buy a Maserati, and he was soon assimilated into the works team, sharing a 2-litre sports car with Juan Fangio to take third in the 1953 Targa Florio, and winning the Circuit of Caserta. This led to a drive in that year's Italian GP, although he had to hand his car over to Luigi Musso in the race.

In 1954, Mantovani became a good, solid team member who could be relied upon to look after the car and bring it home, taking fifth places in the German and Swiss grands prix, and thirds in both the Syracuse and Rome non-championship events.

Retained in the squad for 1955, Sergio was involved in a practice crash at the Valentino GP in Turin, sustaining serious leg injuries that resulted in the amputation of one limb above the knee.

Although Mantovani's racing career was over, he became a member of the Italian Sporting Commission and thus retained his links with the sport.

MANTOVANI, Sergio (I) b 22/5/1929, Cusano Milanino, nr Milan – d 23/2/2001 Milan

1953 Championship position: Unplaced

	Race	Circuit	No	Entrant	Tyres	Capacity/Car/Engine	Comment	Q Pos/Entries
7*	ITALIAN GP	Monza	56	Officine Alfieri Maserati	P	2.0 Maserati A6GCM 6	*Musso took over/4 laps behind	12/30

1954 Championship position: 12th= Wins: 0 Pole positions: 0 Fastest laps: 0 Points scored: 4

	Race	Circuit	No	Entrant	Tyres	Capacity/Car/Engine	Comment	Q Pos/Entries
7	BELGIAN GP	Spa	30	Officine Alfieri Maserati	P	2.5 Maserati 250F 6	2 laps behind	11/15
dns	FRENCH GP	Reims	40	Officine Alfieri Maserati	P	2.5 Maserati 250F 6	practice only	– /22
5	GERMAN GP	Nürburgring	7	Officine Alfieri Maserati	P	2.5 Maserati 250F 6		15/23
5	SWISS GP	Bremgarten	28	Officine Alfieri Maserati	P	2.5 Maserati 250F 6	2 laps behind	9/16
9	ITALIAN GP	Monza	18	Officine Alfieri Maserati	P	2.5 Maserati 250F 6	pit stop/6 laps behind	9/21
ret	SPANISH GP	Pedralbes	12	Officine Alfieri Maserati	P	2.5 Maserati 250F 6	brake problems – crashed	10/22

1955 Championship position: Unplaced

	Race	Circuit	No	Entrant	Tyres	Capacity/Car/Engine	Comment	Q Pos/Entries
ret	ARGENTINE GP	Buenos Aires	20	Officine Alfieri Maserati	P	2.5 Maserati 250F 6	*Musso/Behra co-drove/fuel feed	19/22
7*	"	" "	22	Officine Alfieri Maserati	P	2.5 Maserati 250F 6	*Musso/Schell co-drove/-13 laps	– / –

GP Starts: 7 GP Wins: 0 Pole positions: 0 Fastest laps: 0 Points: 4

MANZON, Robert (F) b 12/4/1917, Marseille

1950 Championship position: 10th= Wins: 0 Pole positions: 0 Fastest laps: 0 Points scored: 3

	Race	Circuit	No	Entrant	Tyres	Capacity/Car/Engine	Comment	Q Pos/Entries
ret	MONACO GP	Monte Carlo	10	Equipe Simca Gordini	E	1.5 s/c Simca-Gordini Type 15 4	multiple accident	11/21
4	FRENCH GP	Reims	44	Equipe Simca Gordini	E	1.5 s/c Simca-Gordini Type 15 4	3 laps behind	13/20
ret	ITALIAN GP	Monza	44	Equipe Simca Gordini	E	1.5 s/c Simca-Gordini Type 15 4	transmission	10/27

1951 Championship position: Unplaced

	Race	Circuit	No	Entrant	Tyres	Capacity/Car/Engine	Comment	Q Pos/Entries
ret	FRENCH GP	Reims	30	Equipe Simca Gordini	E	1.5 s/c Simca-Gordini Type 15 4	engine	23/23
7	GERMAN GP	Nürburgring	82	Equipe Simca Gordini	E	1.5 s/c Simca-Gordini Type 15 4	1 lap behind	9/23
ret	ITALIAN GP	Monza	46	Equipe Simca Gordini	E	1.5 s/c Simca-Gordini Type 15 4	radiator	13/22
9	SPANISH GP	Pedralbes	14	Equipe Simca Gordini	E	1.5 s/c Simca-Gordini Type 15 4	7 laps behind	9/20

1952 Championship position: 6th Wins: 0 Pole positions: 0 Fastest laps: 0 Points scored: 9

	Race	Circuit	No	Entrant	Tyres	Capacity/Car/Engine	Comment	Q Pos/Entries
ret	SWISS GP	Bremgarten	8	Equipe Gordini	E	2.0 Gordini Type 16 6	cooling damper	3/21
3	BELGIAN GP	Spa	14	Equipe Gordini	E	2.0 Gordini Type 16 6		4/22
4	FRENCH GP	Rouen	2	Equipe Gordini	E	2.0 Gordini Type 16 6	3 laps behind	5/20
ret	BRITISH GP	Silverstone	24	Equipe Gordini	E	2.0 Gordini Type 16 6	transmission	4/32
ret	GERMAN GP	Nürburgring	107	Equipe Gordini	E	2.0 Gordini Type 16 6	lost wheel	4/32
5	DUTCH GP	Zandvoort	10	Equipe Gordini	E	2.0 Gordini Type 16 6	3 laps behind	8/18
14	ITALIAN GP	Monza	2	Equipe Gordini	E	2.0 Gordini Type 16 6	9 laps behind	7/35

1953 Championship position: Unplaced

	Race	Circuit	No	Entrant	Tyres	Capacity/Car/Engine	Comment	Q Pos/Entries
ret	ARGENTINE GP	Buenos Aires	26	Equipe Gordini	E	2.0 Gordini Type 16 6	lost wheel	8/16

1954 Championship position: 12th= Wins: 0 Pole positions: 0 Fastest laps: 0 Points scored: 4

3	FRENCH GP	Reims	34	Equipe Rosier	P	2.5 Ferrari 625 4	*1 lap behind*	12/22
ret	BRITISH GP	Silverstone	14	Equipe Rosier	P	2.5 Ferrari 625 4	*cracked cylinder block*	15/31
9	GERMAN GP	Nürburgring	24	Equipe Rosier	P	2.5 Ferrari 625 4	*2 laps behind*	12/23
dns	SWISS GP	Bremgarten	24	Scuderia Ferrari	P	2.5 Ferrari 553 4	*practice accident*	– / –
ret	ITALIAN GP	Monza	6	Equipe Rosier	P	2.5 Ferrari 625 4	*engine*	15/21
ret	SPANISH GP	Pedralbes	20	Equipe Rosier	P	2.5 Ferrari 625 4	*engine*	17/22

1955 Championship position: Unplaced

ret	MONACO GP	Monte Carlo	8	Equipe Gordini	E	2.5 Gordini Type 16 6	*gearbox*	13/22
dns	"	" "	8	Equipe Gordini	E	2.5 Gordini Type 32 8	*practice only*	– / –
ret	DUTCH GP	Zandvoort	20	Equipe Gordini	E	2.5 Gordini Type 16 6	*transmission*	11/16
ret	BRITISH GP	Aintree	22	Equipe Gordini	E	2.5 Gordini Type 16 6	*transmission*	11/25

1956 Championship position: Unplaced

ret	MONACO GP	Monte Carlo	2	Equipe Gordini	E	2.5 Gordini Type 16 6	*brakes – crashed*	12/19
dns	"	" "	2	Equipe Gordini	E	2.5 Gordini Type 32 8	*practice only*	– / –
9	FRENCH GP	Reims	30	Equipe Gordini	E	2.5 Gordini Type 32 8	*5 laps behind*	15/20
9	BRITISH GP	Silverstone	15	Equipe Gordini	E	2.5 Gordini Type 32 8	*7 laps behind*	18/28
ret	GERMAN GP	Nürburgring	10	Equipe Gordini	E	2.5 Gordini Type 32 8	*suspension*	15/21
ret	ITALIAN GP	Monza	10	Equipe Gordini	E	2.5 Gordini Type 32 8	*gearbox*	23/26

GP Starts: 28   GP Wins: 0   Pole positions: 0   Fastest laps: 0   Points: 16

ROBERT MANZON

RACING his own 1100cc Cisitalia in 1947, Robert Manzon took wins at Angoulême and Comminges, and chased the Simca Gordinis impressively enough in other events to persuade Amédée 'Le Sorcier' Gordini to sign him mid-way through the 1948 season. In his first race, at the Circuit des Ramparts in Angoulême (a circuit on which he always shone), he led the final lap and set fastest lap before retirement.

Manzon became a mainstay of the team, and in 1949 he was second to Maurice Trintignant at Angoulême and runner-up to Sommer at Lausanne. He also won the Bol d'Or at Montlhéry in a production Simca sports car with a special 1000cc engine. The cars were gaining a reputation for unreliabilty, however, because their engines were so highly stressed, but when they lasted, good results often followed. In 1950, Manzon took fourth place in the world championship French GP at Reims, while in the Formula 2 category he won the GP of Perigueux and the Circuit of Mettet in Belgium, and was second at Roubaix and third in the Swiss GP at Bremgarten. The following season, he triumphed only once, at Mettet again, but took second places at Les Sables d'Olonne, Rouen and Cadours.

Gordini introduced the new six-cylinder car for 1952, and this brought a much-needed boost in competitiveness. Robert put the extra performance to good use with some fine placings in the championship grands prix, including an excellent third at Spa, behind the works Ferraris. His best non-title race finish was a second place shared with Bira at Marseilles, while in Gordini sports cars he won the Coupe du Salon at Montlhéry. One of his best ever performances came at the beginning of 1953 in the Argentine GP, where he lay second after a great drive before the car shed a wheel. He took fifth in the subsequent Libre race at Buenos Aires, but on his return to France he quit the team, racing a Lancia sports car for the remainder of the year, before joining Louis Rosier's équipe in 1954. His best result was undoubtedly a third place behind two Mercedes-Benz cars making their stunning debut at Reims, although he did take a second at Bordeaux behind Froilán González's works Ferrari.

In 1955, Manzon was back in his spiritual home with 'Le Sorcier', but unhappily he gained no real success, just a fifth place at Bordeaux. The following year saw heartbreak at Monaco, where he lay third until a gearbox failure just three laps from the finish. He did take a couple of wins – at the Naples GP, where he inherited the lead after the works Ferraris failed, and in the Pescara sports car race where, in the team's 2-litre sports car, he defeated Piero Taruffi's Ferrari after an outstanding drive. Then the much-underrated Manzon decided to retire for both family and business reasons at the end of the season.

MARIMÓN, Onofre (RA) b 19/12/1923, Cordoba – d 31/7/1954, Nürburgring, Germany

	1951 Championship position: Unplaced							
	Race	Circuit	No	Entrant	Tyres	Capacity/Car/Engine	Comment	Q Pos/Entries
ret	FRENCH GP	Reims	50	Scuderia Milano	P	1.5 s/c Maserati 4CLT/Milano 4	engine	15/23
	1953 Championship position: 9th= Wins: 0 Pole positions: 0 Fastest laps: 0 Points scored: 4							
3	BELGIAN GP	Spa	28	Officine Alfieri Maserati	P	2.0 Maserati A6GCM 6	1 lap behind	6/22
9	FRENCH GP	Reims	22	Officine Alfieri Maserati	P	2.0 Maserati A6GCM 6	5 laps behind	8/25
ret	BRITISH GP	Silverstone	26	Officine Alfieri Maserati	P	2.0 Maserati A6GCM 6	engine	7/29
ret	GERMAN GP	Nürburgring	8	Officine Alfieri Maserati	P	2.0 Maserati A6GCM 6	suspension	8/35
ret	SWISS GP	Bremgarten	36	Officine Alfieri Maserati	P	2.0 Maserati A6GCM 6	oil pipe	5/23
ret	ITALIAN GP	Monza	54	Officine Alfieri Maserati	P	2.0 Maserati A6GCM 6	hit Ascari's spinning car	4/30
	1954 Championship position: 10th= Wins: 0 Pole positions: 0 Fastest laps: 1 (shared) Points scored: 4.14							
ret	ARGENTINE GP	Buenos Aires	4	Officine Alfieri Maserati	P	2.5 Maserati 250F 6	spun off	6/18
ret	BELGIAN GP	Spa	28	Officine Alfieri Maserati	P	2.5 Maserati 250F 6	engine	4/15
ret	FRENCH GP	Reims	12	Officine Alfieri Maserati	P	2.5 Maserati 250F 6	gearbox	5/22
3	BRITISH GP	Silverstone	33	Officine Alfieri Maserati	P	2.5 Maserati 250F 6	1 lap behind/FL (shared)	28/31
dns	GERMAN GP	Nürburgring	6	Officine Alfieri Maserati	P	2.5 Maserati 250F 6	fatal accident in practice	(8)/23

GP Starts: 11   GP Wins: 0   Pole positions: 0   Fastest laps: 1   Points: 8.14

ONOFRE MARIMÓN

A PROTÉGÉ of Juan Fangio, who had frequently raced against his cigar-chewing father, Domingo, in the long-distance South American road races, Onofre Marimón first made his mark in 1949 in a Chevrolet special prepared by Fangio's younger bother, Ruben. He finished second to Froilán González at Cordoba and continued to progress rapidly the following year, taking second behind Juan Gálvez in the Tour of Cordoba, and winning the races at Mar del Plata, La Cumbre and elsewhere in his Meccanica Nacional special.

The urge to race in Europe was overwhelming, and Marimón made a brief visit in 1951, sharing a Talbot with González at Le Mans until they were forced to retire the car with a holed radiator. The following week, he made his grand prix debut, racing for back-marker Scuderia Milano in the French Grand Prix. It was a short-lived experience, the car retiring after just three laps.

Nicknamed 'Pinnocchio', Marimón returned for a full season in 1953 as a member of the works Maserati team, under the guidance of his mentors, Fangio and González. He made an immediate impression with a classified third place in the Belgian Grand Prix, behind the dominant Ferraris of Alberto Ascari and Luigi Villoresi, and a second to Fangio in the non-championship Modena Grand Prix, a race boycotted by Ferrari.

In 1954, with Fangio having been lured to Mercedes and González to Ferrari, Onofre found himself as effective Maserati team leader, and he did well in the early-season races, winning the Rome GP at Castel Fusano and finishing third at Pau. In championship races, he tried hard to emulate his peers, but in practice for the German Grand Prix, perhaps through missing a gear, he locked a wheel and failed to negotiate a corner. His Maserati plunged through a hedge and somersaulted down a slope, leaving him trapped in the upturned machine. His injuries were so severe that he had no chance of survival, and he was given the last rights by a priest.

MARKO, Helmut (A) b 27/4/1943, Graz

	1971 Championship position: Unplaced							
	Race	Circuit	No	Entrant	Tyres	Capacity/Car/Engine	Comment	Q Pos/Entries
dns	GERMAN GP	Nürburgring	27	Ecurie Bonnier	G	3.0 McLaren M7C-Cosworth V8	practice only – only did 1 lap	– / –
11	AUSTRIAN GP	Österreichring	16	Yardley-BRM	F	3.0 BRM P153 V12	2 laps behind	17/22
ret	ITALIAN GP	Monza	21	Yardley-BRM	F	3.0 BRM P153 V12	engine	12/24
dns	"	"	20T	Yardley-BRM	F	3.0 BRM P160 V12	practice only	– / –
12	CANADIAN GP	Mosport Park	31	Yardley-BRM	F	3.0 BRM P153 V12	pit stop-fuel/4 laps behind	19/27
13	US GP	Watkins Glen	17	Yardley-BRM	F	3.0 BRM P160 V12	pit stop-fuel/2 laps behind	17/32
	1972 Championship position: Unplaced							
10	ARGENTINE GP	Buenos Aires	7	Austria-Marlboro BRM	F	3.0 BRM P153 V12	2 laps behind	19/22
14	SOUTH AFRICAN GP	Kyalami	24	Austria-Marlboro BRM	F	3.0 BRM P153 V12	3 laps behind	23/27
8	MONACO GP	Monte Carlo	26	Austria-Marlboro BRM	F	3.0 BRM P153B V12	3 laps behind	17/25
10	BELGIAN GP	Nivelles	27	Austria-Marlboro BRM	F	3.0 BRM P153B V12	2 laps behind	23/26
ret	FRENCH GP	Clermont Ferrand	25	Austria-Marlboro BRM	F	3.0 BRM P160B V12	stone pierced visor/serious eye injury	6/29

GP Starts: 9   GP Wins: 0   Pole positions: 0   Fastest laps: 0   Points: 0

DR HELMUT MARKO

LIKE many Austrian drivers, Helmut Marko, whose racing career had been delayed while he gained a doctorate in law, cut his teeth on Super Vee racers. In 1969, he drove the works McNamara in Formula 3, but he had already tried his hand in sports cars, on which he concentrated the following year.

Driving Martini Racing's Porsche, Marko soon established himself, finishing third at Le Mans in 1970 and then going on to win the classic race with Gijs van Lennep a year later.

Luck generally deserted Helmut in other major events, but he handled a little Lola T212 sports car, entered by Karl von Wendt, to devastating effect in 1971, winning the Auvergne Trophy, the Cape three-hours and three rounds of the European 2-litre championship. By then, he had made a solid start to his grand prix career, his initial hire-drive agreement with BRM proving so satisfactory that soon he became a full team member.

For the 1972 season, Marko had a BRM contract for Formula 1 and a seat in the Alfa Romeo sports car team, for whom he scored second places in both the Targa Florio and the Österreichring 1000km, and thirds at the Daytona 24-hour race and the Nürburgring 1000km. His F1 season started well with fourth place in the non-championship Brazilian Grand Prix, but in the French Grand Prix at Clermont-Ferrand, a freak accident saw a stone thrown up by another car shatter his visor and embed itself in his eye. He was able to bring the car safely to a halt, but the sight of the eye could not be saved, and a potentially fine grand prix career was lost.

Subsequently, Marko stayed within the sport, initially working for Renault Austria. He also guided the fledgling career of the ill-fated Helmuth Koinigg. Later he formed a successful F3 team, which showcased the talent of a young Gerhard Berger and later Karl Wendlinger. Marko then set up a Formula 3000 team, taking Jörg Müller to the title in 1996. Less happy was his association with Juan Pablo Montoya the following year, despite the Colombian taking three wins. In 1999, Marko's close association with Dieter Mateschitz led to his F3000 squad running under the Red Bull banner, initially with Enrique Bernoldi, followed by Ricardo Mauricio and Patrick Friesacher, none of whom was particularly successful.

Marko disbanded the team to take on the role of supervising the Red Bull driver development programme. He oversaw the progress of Christian Klien and Toni Liuzzi at Red Bull, and was instrumental in the recruitment of Sebastian Vettel from BMW. Now a powerful figure in Red Bull Racing, the Austrian wields huge influence over drivers' careers. Jaime Alguersuari and Sébastien Buemi, for example, found themselves discarded at Toro Rosso after not being deemed future championship material.

MARQUES, Tarso Tarso Marques Anibal Santanna (BR) b 19/1/1976, Curitiba

1996 Championship position: Unplaced

	Race	Circuit	No	Entrant	Tyres	Capacity/Car/Engine	Comment	Q Pos/Entries
ret	BRAZILIAN GP	Interlagos	21	Minardi Team	G	3.0 Minardi 195B-Ford EDM V8	*practice time disallowed/spun off	*– /22
ret	ARGENTINE GP	Buenos Aires	21	Minardi Team	G	3.0 Minardi 195B-Ford EDM V8	collision with Brundle	14/22

1997 Championship position: Unplaced

	Race	Circuit	No	Entrant	Tyres	Capacity/Car/Engine	Comment	Q Pos/Entries
ret	FRENCH GP	Magny Cours	21	Minardi Team	B	3.0 Minardi M197-Hart V8	engine	22/22
10	BRITISH GP	Silverstone	21	Minardi Team	B	3.0 Minardi M197-Hart V8	1 lap behind	21/22
ret	GERMAN GP	Hockenheim	21	Minardi Team	B	3.0 Minardi M197-Hart V8	transmission	21/22
12	HUNGARIAN GP	Hungaroring	21	Minardi Team	B	3.0 Minardi M197-Hart V8	2 laps behind	22/22
ret	BELGIAN GP	Spa	21	Minardi Team	B	3.0 Minardi M197-Hart V8	spun off	22/22
14	ITALIAN GP	Monza	21	Minardi Team	B	3.0 Minardi M197-Hart V8	2 laps behind	22/22
exc*	AUSTRIAN GP	A1-Ring	21	Minardi Team	B	3.0 Minardi M197-Hart V8	*excluded – car underweight	–*/22
ret	LUXEMBOURG GP	Nürburgring	21	Minardi Team	B	3.0 Minardi M197-Hart V8	engine	22/22
ret	JAPANESE GP	Suzuka	21	Minardi Team	B	3.0 Minardi M197-Hart V8	gearbox	20/22
15	EUROPEAN GP	Jerez	21	Minardi Team	B	3.0 Minardi M197-Hart V8	1 lap behind	20/22

2001 Championship position: Unplaced

	Race	Circuit	No	Entrant	Tyres	Capacity/Car/Engine	Comment	Q Pos/Entries
ret	AUSTRALIAN GP	Melbourne	20	European Minardi F1	M	3.0 Minardi PS01-European V10	*outside 107% time/electrical	*22/22
14	MALAYSIAN GP	Sepang	20	European Minardi F1	M	3.0 Minardi PS01-European V10	4 laps behind	21/22
9	BRAZILIAN GP	Interlagos	20	European Minardi F1	M	3.0 Minardi PS01-European V10	3 laps behind	22/22
ret	SAN MARINO GP	Imola	20	European Minardi F1	M	3.0 Minardi PS01-European V10	engine	22/22
16	SPANISH GP	Barcelona	20	European Minardi F1	M	3.0 Minardi PS01-European V10	3 laps behind	22/22
ret	AUSTRIAN GP	A1-Ring	20	European Minardi F1	M	3.0 Minardi PS01-European V10	gearbox	22/22
ret	MONACO GP	Monte Carlo	20	European Minardi F1	M	3.0 Minardi PS01-European V10	transmission	22/22
9	CANADIAN GP	Montreal	20	European Minardi F1	M	3.0 Minardi PS01-European V10	3 laps behind	22/22
ret	EUROPEAN GP	Nürburgring	20	European Minardi F1	M	3.0 Minardi PS01-European V10	gearbox	22/22
15	FRENCH GP	Magny Cours	20	European Minardi F1	M	3.0 Minardi PS01-European V10	3 laps behind	22/22
dnq	BRITISH GP	Silverstone	20	European Minardi F1	M	3.0 Minardi PS01-European V10	outside 107% time	22/22
ret	GERMAN GP	Hockenheim	20	European Minardi F1	M	3.0 Minardi PS01-European V10	engine	22/22
ret	HUNGARIAN GP	Hungaroring	20	European Minardi F1	M	3.0 Minardi PS01-European V10	engine	22/22
13	BELGIAN GP	Spa	20	European Minardi F1	M	3.0 Minardi PS01-European V10	*outside 107% time/3 laps behind	*22/22

GP Starts: 24   GP Wins: 0   Pole positions: 0   Fastest laps: 0   Points: 0

TARSO MARQUES

THE son of renowned Brazilian motorsport figure Pablo de Tarso, Tarso Marques was able to rely on family backing to propel him rapidly along the path towards Formula 1, but he did not have the staying power to remain in the top flight for any length of time. As ever, he started out in karting, and proved to have the ability to progress by winning both regional and national titles. Moving into cars at the age 16, he tore through the Formula Chevrolet and F3 series at home, becoming the youngest ever race winner in the category.

In 1994, aged just 18, Marques travelled to Europe and ambitiously tackled the F3000 series with Vortex, eventually scoring points at Magny-Cours. The following season saw him run for DAMS and take a win at Estoril, on his way to fifth overall, but in truth, the opposition that year were hardly the cream of the crop

Marques had done enough to get a foot in the door at Minardi and was given a start in the two South American races, making a splash in the Brazilian Grand Prix by passing no fewer than 11 cars in his opening lap at a rain-soaked Interlagos before spinning out. Having stepped down to test-driver duties, he was forced to wait until halfway through the following season before being given another chance, when Jarno Trulli left for Prost. Unable to better tenth place, however, he was released at the end of the year and, with no offers of a drive, spent 1998 tyre testing for Bridgestone.

The Brazilian then looked at the American Champ Car series, and in 1999 he was offered the chance to replace injured veteran Al Unser Jr at Team Penske for three races. Unfortunately, that year was a fallow one for the squad, being saddled with a less than competitive tyre, engine and chassis combination. Marques joined forces with Payton-Coyne the following year, but running with the largely unproven Swift chassis made for a difficult campaign, and he managed just 11 points and 25th in the season's standings.

Despite having been dropped by Minardi at the end of 1997, Marques managed to engineer a return to Formula 1 for the 2001 season. As before, the Italian team was a back-marker in the top flight and always on the look-out for sponsorship to stay afloat. Tarso managed most of the season, largely in the shadow of Fernando Alonso, and best finishes of ninth in Brazil and Canada could not prevent his seat from going to wealthy Malaysian Alex Yoong for the final three races of the year.

For the next two seasons, little was heard from the Brazilian. He finally returned to Champ Cars in 2004, reunited with former boss Dale Coyne for two races at the start of the season, before being replaced by Gastón Mazzacane. Then he returned to the team for the Mexico City finale after the Argentinian stepped down to concentrate on finding the budget for 2005. Marques then returned to Brazil, initially to compete in the Renault Megane and Clio series, but stood in for Christian Fittipaldi at Team Land Avallone in the stock car series. Taking a first ever win for his new team landed the Brazilian a full-time seat for 2008 in the well-funded Sky Team, racing a Peugeot 307 alongside Luciano Burti.

Having failed a drug test taken after the final race of the 2009 season, Marques was eventually suspended from racing for two years for having taken anabolic steroids, Since his enforced retirement, he has been concentrating on running his business, creating custom motorbikes and hot rods back in his home town of Curitiba.

LESLIE MARR

A FLIGHT lieutenant in the Royal Air Force specialising in radar, Leslie Marr took up painting while in Palestine during the Second World War and continued his studies as a member of the artists' collective known as the Borough Group, which was founded in 1946 in the Borough area of London. After this circle of abstract expressionists disbanded in 1951, he decided to try his hand at motorsport.

At first, Marr mainly raced his Connaught in national events during 1952/53, before trying his hand against tougher opposition in 1954, when he gained his greatest success in Libre events, placing third in the Glover Trophy and third in the Formula 2 class in the Aintree 200. By 1955, Marr had taken delivery of a B-Type model, but after the British Grand Prix he raced it infrequently until early 1956, when he drove splendidly to finish fourth in the New Zealand GP, after starting from the back of the grid without benefit of practice. Then he took third place in the Lady Wigram Trophy at Christchurch.

Subsequently, Marr developed a promising career as a documentary film maker, but soon rediscovered his first passion, painting. Over the past half-century, he has become a well-regarded artist who exhibits his works extensively.

MARR, Leslie (GB) b 14/8/1922, Durham

	Race	Circuit	No	Entrant	Tyres	Capacity/Car/Engine	Comment	Q Pos/Entries
	1954 Championship position: Unplaced							
13	BRITISH GP	Silverstone	23	Leslie Marr	D	2.0 Connaught-Lea Francis A Type 4	*8 laps behind*	22/31
	1955 Championship position: Unplaced							
ret	BRITISH GP	Aintree	38	Leslie Marr	D	2.5 Connaught-Alta B Type 4 str	*brake pipe – spun off*	19/25
	GP Starts: 2 GP Wins: 0 Pole positions: 0 Fastest laps: 0 Points: 0							

TONY MARSH

HILL-CLIMBS, trials, sprints, rallies – in fact, almost every type of four-wheeled competition was sampled by Tony Marsh in the early 1950s, when, at the wheel of the ex-Peter Collins Cooper, he won his first three RAC hill-climb championships.

In 1957, Marsh bought a Formula 2 Cooper, which he used to dominate Libre events at home and also raced on the Continent, making his debut in the German Grand Prix, where he took fourth in the F2 class. Over the next three seasons, he sensibly raced the Cooper in events where success was a realistic proposition, his best result being a win in the 1960 Lewis-Evans Trophy at Brands Hatch.

For 1961, Tony obtained a Lotus 18, which he drove in grands prix and even hill-climbs, winning five of the six events he entered, but despite a third on aggregate in the Brussels GP, he soon set it aside in favour of a BRM. Then, in 1962, a planned season with a works-tended BRM ended in legal action, as he felt the machine was unraceworthy.

From then on, Marsh concentrated fully on the hill-climb scene, eventually replacing the BRM with a fearsome 4.3-litre Marsh-Oldsmobile special, with which he took another three titles in succession (1965–67) to add to those won in the 1950s. Then he took a sabbatical from racing to look after his business interests and indulge in other sporting pastimes, such as ski-bob racing, aviation, windsurfing and shooting, but he returned to speed trials and hill-climbs on and off until just a year before his death, aged 77, in 2009.

EUGÈNE MARTIN

POSSESSING a broad engineering background, Eugène Martin began racing a BMW/Frazer-Nash in the late 1940s and soon modified it extensively, subsequently winning races at Angoulême and the GP of Lyons in 1947.

The latter victory put Martin in demand, and he briefly tried the CTA Arsenal before racing the Jicey during 1948/49. Having been invited to join Talbot for 1950, he crashed in only his second race for the team at Berne and was seriously injured, prompting his temporary retirement. He reappeared occasionally, however, having acquired the Jicey, and drove a works Gordini at the 1954 Pau GP, which would be his final race and unfortunately ended in a crash.

Then he concentrated on his new role as technical director of the Salmson company, whose machines would bear a marked resemblance to the Martin cars Eugène had briefly marketed in 1952/53.

MARSH, Tony (GB) b 20/7/1931, Stourbridge, Worcestershire – d 7/5/2009, Petersfield, Hampshire

	1957 Championship position: Unplaced								
	Race	Circuit	No	Entrant	Tyres	Capacity/Car/Engine	Comment	Q Pos/Entries
15*	GERMAN GP (F2)	Nürburgring	25	Ridgeway Managements	D	1.5 Cooper T43-Climax 4 F2	*4th in F2 class/5 laps behind	22/24
	1958 Championship position: Unplaced							
8*	GERMAN GP (F2)	Nürburgring	30	Tony Marsh	D	1.5 Cooper T45-Climax 4 F2	*4th in F2 class	17/26
	1961 Championship position: Unplaced							
dns	BELGIAN GP	Spa	42	Tony Marsh	D	1.5 Lotus 18-Climax 4	no starting money offered	(20)/25
ret	BRITISH GP	Aintree	48	Tony Marsh	D	1.5 Lotus 18-Climax 4	ignition	27/30
15	GERMAN GP	Nürburgring	37	Tony Marsh	D	1.5 Lotus 18-Climax 4	2 laps behind	20/27
	GP Starts: 4 GP Wins: 0 Pole positions: 0 Fastest laps: 0 Points: 0							

MARTIN, Eugène (F) b 24/3/1915, Suresnes, - d 12/10/2006 Aytré

	1950 Championship position: Unplaced							
	Race	Circuit	No	Entrant	Tyres	Capacity/Car/Engine	Comment	Q Pos/Entries
ret	BRITISH GP	Silverstone	17	Automobiles Talbot-Darracq SA	D	4.5 Lago-Talbot T26C-DA 6	engine – oil pressure	7/21
ret	SWISS GP	Bremgarten	8	Automobiles Talbot-Darracq SA	D	4.5 Lago-Talbot T26C-DA 6	crashed – injured	9/18
	GP Starts: 2 GP Wins: 0 Pole positions: 0 Fastest laps: 0 Points: 0							

PIERLUIGI MARTINI

LITTLE Pierluigi Martini had the resilience to shrug off a disastrous debut year in grand prix racing and sensibly return to shallower waters until he was truly ready to plunge back into the deep end. Then he became a well-respected member of the grand prix community, albeit with only a tantalising hint of joining the elite band of winners.

The nephew of 1970s Italian racer Giancarlo Martini, Pierluigi spent a couple of years hidden in Italian F3, driving the ubiquitous Dallara before emerging as something of a surprise European F3 champion in 1983. At the wheel of a Pavesi Ralt, he put together a late-season run to snatch the title at the very last from under the nose of John Nielsen, but a second place on his Formula 2 debut in a Minardi that season may have given him ideas above his station. After he had tested a Brabham, but failed to land a drive, 1984 saw a hapless attempt to qualify a works Toleman at the Italian GP at Monza, while his lack of experience was merely amplified during the 1985 season. The task of leading the single-ton Minardi challenge was beyond him and he dropped back to F3000 for the 1986 season with the Pavesi team.

It proved to be a good decision for, freed from the pressure of Formula 1, Martini soon found his feet to put in a determined bid for the championship, winning rounds at Imola and Mugello, and taking second places in Enna and Birmingham. Any hopes of a title win were dashed, however, when he was disqualified in the final round at Jarama after some illegal tinkering with the car between the two parts of the interrupted race. The team lost their way the following year, constantly switching Ralt chassis, and Pierluigi largely wasted his time. A move to the FIRST team in 1988 bounced him back to the front, despite being hampered by a difficult March chassis, and a victory at Enna kept his interest in the series alive, even though he had made a surprise return to grand prix racing with Minardi.

Scoring the team's first-ever championship point on his comeback in Detroit, the Italian soon found himself the spearhead of the little Faenza outfit's upward progress. In 1989, he hauled them from the brink of the pre-qualification abyss to a brief, but brilliant moment at Estoril where, for one glorious lap, a Minardi led a grand prix. At the last race of the year in Adelaide, he qualified third on the grid, but had to settle for a distant sixth place on unsuitable Pirelli race tyres. The following season proved relatively uneventful while Minardi waited with eager anticipation for the Ferrari power that they hoped would place them among the front-runners.

Sadly for Martini, the partnership was hardly a distinguished one, and at the end of the year he moved to Scuderia Italia along with the V12 engines. It was akin to being transferred from one First Division football team to another when the player was eyeing a move to the Premiership. Enduring a year of endless frustrations, he found himself without a drive when the team concluded a deal to race Lolas in 1993. He wasn't to know how lucky he was to miss out on that débâcle. He bided his time, before keeping his grand prix career alive with a mid-season return to the homely confines of Minardi. After all this time, it was difficult to imagine him breaking out of the ranks of the also-ran teams – no matter how much he may have deserved the chance previously, and so it proved. For the most part, he ran in midfield anonymity until the middle of the 1995 season, when his drive was taken by up-and-coming Portuguese driver Pedro Lamy.

Although Martini's grand prix sojourn had come to an end, he accepted the opportunity of racing Scuderia Italia's Porsche 911 GT1 in 1997 and took a win in Joest's Porsche WSC95 at Donington with Stefan Johansson. The pinnacle of the Italian's career finally arrived in 1999, when he partnered Yannick Dalmas and Jo Winkelhock to victory at Le Mans, driving a works BMW V12 LMR.

Martini has since made occasional returns to the circuits in the Grand Prix Masters in 2005/06 and then the Italian Superstars series in 2009.

MARTINI, Pierluigi (I) b 23/4/1961, Lugo di Romagna, nr Ravenna

1984 Championship position: Unplaced

	Race	Circuit	No	Entrant	Tyres	Capacity/Car/Engine	Comment	Q Pos/Entries
dnq	ITALIAN GP	Monza	20	Toleman Group Motorsport	M	1.5 t/c Toleman TG184-Hart 4		27/27

1985 Championship position: Unplaced

	Race	Circuit	No	Entrant	Tyres	Capacity/Car/Engine	Comment	Q Pos/Entries
ret	BRAZILIAN GP	Rio	29	Minardi Team	P	3.0 Minardi M185-Cosworth V8	engine	25/25
ret	PORTUGUESE GP	Estoril	29	Minardi Team	P	3.0 Minardi M185-Cosworth V8	started from pitlane/spun off	25/26
ret	SAN MARINO GP	Imola	29	Minardi Team	P	1.5 t/c Minardi M185-MM V6	turbo	19/26
dnq	MONACO GP	Monte Carlo	29	Minardi Team	P	1.5 t/c Minardi M185-MM V6	no time set – knee injury in practice	– /26
ret	CANADIAN GP	Montreal	29	Minardi Team	P	1.5 t/c Minardi M185-MM V6	accident	25/25
ret	US GP (DETROIT)	Detroit	29	Minardi Team	P	1.5 t/c Minardi M185-MM V6	engine	25/25
ret	FRENCH GP	Paul Ricard	29	Minardi Team	P	1.5 t/c Minardi M185-MM V6	accident with Berger	25/26
ret	BRITISH GP	Silverstone	29	Minardi Team	P	1.5 t/c Minardi M185-MM V6	transmission	23/26
11/ret	GERMAN GP	Nürburgring	29	Minardi Team	P	1.5 t/c Minardi M185-MM V6	engine/5 laps behind	27/27
ret	AUSTRIAN GP	Österreichring	29	Minardi Team	P	1.5 t/c Minardi M185-MM V6	suspension	26/27
ret	DUTCH GP	Zandvoort	29	Minardi Team	P	1.5 t/c Minardi M185-MM V6	accident	24/27
ret	ITALIAN GP	Monza	29	Minardi Team	P	1.5 t/c Minardi M185-MM V6	fuel pump	23/26
12	BELGIAN GP	Spa	29	Minardi Team	P	1.5 t/c Minardi M185-MM V6	5 laps behind	24/24
ret	EUROPEAN GP	Brands Hatch	29	Minardi Team	P	1.5 t/c Minardi M185-MM V6	accident	26/27
ret	SOUTH AFRICAN GP	Kyalami	29	Minardi Team	P	1.5 t/c Minardi M185-MM V6	radiator	19/21
8	AUSTRALIAN GP	Adelaide	29	Minardi Team	P	1.5 t/c Minardi M185-MM V6	4 laps behind	23/25

1988 Championship position: 16th= — Wins: 0 — Pole positions: 0 — Fastest laps: 0 — Points scored: 1

	Race	Circuit	No	Entrant	Tyres	Capacity/Car/Engine	Comment	Q Pos/Entries
6	US GP (DETROIT)	Detroit	23	Lois Minardi Team	G	3.5 Minardi M188-Cosworth V8	1 lap behind	16/31
15	FRENCH GP	Paul Ricard	23	Lois Minardi Team	G	3.5 Minardi M188-Cosworth V8	3 laps behind	22/31
15	BRITISH GP	Silverstone	23	Lois Minardi Team	G	3.5 Minardi M188-Cosworth V8	2 laps behind	19/31
dnq	GERMAN GP	Hockenheim	23	Lois Minardi Team	G	3.5 Minardi M188-Cosworth V8		30/31
ret	HUNGARIAN GP	Hungaroring	23	Lois Minardi Team	G	3.5 Minardi M188-Cosworth V8	collision with Piquet	16/31
dnq	BELGIAN GP	Spa	23	Lois Minardi Team	G	3.5 Minardi M188-Cosworth V8		28/31
ret	ITALIAN GP	Monza	23	Lois Minardi Team	G	3.5 Minardi M188-Cosworth V8	engine	14/31
ret	PORTUGUESE GP	Estoril	23	Lois Minardi Team	G	3.5 Minardi M188-Cosworth V8	engine	14/31
ret	SPANISH GP	Jerez	23	Lois Minardi Team	G	3.5 Minardi M188-Cosworth V8	gearbox	20/31
13	JAPANESE GP	Suzuka	23	Lois Minardi Team	G	3.5 Minardi M188-Cosworth V8	2 laps behind	17/31
7	AUSTRALIAN GP	Adelaide	23	Lois Minardi Team	G	3.5 Minardi M188-Cosworth V8	2 laps behind	14/31

1989 Championship position: 14th= — Wins: 0 — Pole positions: 0 — Fastest laps: 0 — Points scored: 5

	Race	Circuit	No	Entrant	Tyres	Capacity/Car/Engine	Comment	Q Pos/Entries
ret	BRAZILIAN GP	Rio	23	Minardi Team SpA	P	3.5 Minardi M188B-Cosworth V8	engine mounting	16/38
ret	SAN MARINO GP	Imola	23	Minardi Team SpA	P	3.5 Minardi M188B-Cosworth V8	gearbox	11/39
ret	MONACO GP	Monte Carlo	23	Minardi Team SpA	P	3.5 Minardi M188B-Cosworth V8	clutch	11/38
ret	MEXICAN GP	Mexico City	23	Minardi Team SpA	P	3.5 Minardi M189-Cosworth V8	engine	22/39
ret	US GP (PHOENIX)	Phoenix	23	Minardi Team SpA	P	3.5 Minardi M189-Cosworth V8	engine	15/39
ret	CANADIAN GP	Montreal	23	Minardi Team SpA	P	3.5 Minardi M189-Cosworth V8	collision with Modena	11/39
ret	FRENCH GP	Paul Ricard	23	Minardi Team SpA	P	3.5 Minardi M189-Cosworth V8	overheating	23/39
5	BRITISH GP	Silverstone	23	Minardi Team SpA	P	3.5 Minardi M189-Cosworth V8	pit stop – paper in radiator/-1 lap	11/39
9	GERMAN GP	Hockenheim	23	Minardi Team SpA	P	3.5 Minardi M189-Cosworth V8	chassis problems/1 lap behind	13/39
ret	HUNGARIAN GP	Hungaroring	23	Minardi Team SpA	P	3.5 Minardi M189-Cosworth V8	wheel bearing	10/39
9	BELGIAN GP	Spa	23	Minardi Team SpA	P	3.5 Minardi M189-Cosworth V8	pit stop – tyres/1 lap behind	14/39
7	ITALIAN GP	Monza	23	Minardi Team SpA	P	3.5 Minardi M189-Cosworth V8	1 lap behind	15/39
5	PORTUGUESE GP	Estoril	23	Minardi Team SpA	P	3.5 Minardi M189-Cosworth V8	led race for one lap/1 lap behind	5/39
ret	SPANISH GP	Jerez	23	Minardi Team SpA	P	3.5 Minardi M189-Cosworth V8	spun off	4/38
6	AUSTRALIAN GP	Adelaide	23	Minardi Team SpA	P	3.5 Minardi M189-Cosworth V8	3 laps behind	3/39

1990 Championship position: Unplaced

	Race	Circuit	No	Entrant	Tyres	Capacity/Car/Engine	Comment	Q Pos/Entries
7	US GP (PHOENIX)	Phoenix	23	SCM Minardi Team	P	3.5 Minardi M189-Cosworth V8	pit stop – tyres/1 lap behind	2/35
9	BRAZILIAN GP	Interlagos	23	SCM Minardi Team	P	3.5 Minardi M189-Cosworth V8	pit stop – tyres/brakes/2 laps behind	8/35
dns	SAN MARINO GP	Imola	23	SCM Minardi Team	P	3.5 Minardi M190-Cosworth V8	accident in practice	(10)/34
ret	MONACO GP	Monte Carlo	23	SCM Minardi Team	P	3.5 Minardi M190-Cosworth V8	electrics	8/35
ret	CANADIAN GP	Montreal	23	SCM Minardi Team	P	3.5 Minardi M190-Cosworth V8	hit by Suzuki	16/35
12	MEXICAN GP	Mexico City	23	SCM Minardi Team	P	3.5 Minardi M190-Cosworth V8	engine down on power/1 lap behind	7/35
ret	FRENCH GP	Paul Ricard	23	SCM Minardi Team	P	3.5 Minardi M190-Cosworth V8	electrics	23/35
ret	BRITISH GP	Silverstone	23	SCM Minardi Team	P	3.5 Minardi M190-Cosworth V8	alternator	18/35
ret	GERMAN GP	Hockenheim	23	SCM Minardi Team	P	3.5 Minardi M190-Cosworth V8	engine	15/35
ret	HUNGARIAN GP	Hungaroring	23	SCM Minardi Team	P	3.5 Minardi M190-Cosworth V8	collision with Alesi	14/35
15	BELGIAN GP	Spa	23	SCM Minardi Team	P	3.5 Minardi M190-Cosworth V8	understeer/2 laps behind	16/33
ret	ITALIAN GP	Monza	23	SCM Minardi Team	P	3.5 Minardi M190-Cosworth V8	suspension	15/33
11	PORTUGUESE GP	Estoril	23	SCM Minardi Team	P	3.5 Minardi M190-Cosworth V8	2 laps behind	16/33
ret	SPANISH GP	Jerez	23	SCM Minardi Team	P	3.5 Minardi M190-Cosworth V8	loose wheel	11/33
8	JAPANESE GP	Suzuka	23	SCM Minardi Team	P	3.5 Minardi M190-Cosworth V8	1 lap behind	11/30
9	AUSTRALIAN GP	Adelaide	23	SCM Minardi Team	P	3.5 Minardi M190-Cosworth V8	2 laps behind	10/30

1991 Championship position: 11th — Wins: 0 — Pole positions: 0 — Fastest laps: 0 — Points scored: 6

	Race	Circuit	No	Entrant	Tyres	Capacity/Car/Engine	Comment	Q Pos/Entries
9/ret	US GP (PHOENIX)	Phoenix	23	SCM Minardi Team	G	3.5 Minardi M191-Ferrari V12	engine	15/34
ret	BRAZILIAN GP	Interlagos	23	SCM Minardi Team	G	3.5 Minardi M191-Ferrari V12	spun off	20/34
4	SAN MARINO GP	Imola	23	SCM Minardi Team	G	3.5 Minardi M191-Ferrari V12	2 laps behind	9/34
12	MONACO GP	Monte Carlo	23	SCM Minardi Team	G	3.5 Minardi M191-Ferrari V12	stop & go penalty/6 laps behind	14/34
7	CANADIAN GP	Montreal	23	SCM Minardi Team	G	3.5 Minardi M191-Ferrari V12	started from pitlane/1 lap behind	18/34
ret	MEXICAN GP	Mexico City	23	SCM Minardi Team	G	3.5 Minardi M191-Ferrari V12	spun off on Berger's dropped oil	15/34
9	FRENCH GP	Magny Cours	23	SCM Minardi Team	G	3.5 Minardi M191-Ferrari V12	2 laps behind	12/34
9	BRITISH GP	Silverstone	23	SCM Minardi Team	G	3.5 Minardi M191-Ferrari V12	1 lap behind	23/34
ret	GERMAN GP	Hockenheim	23	SCM Minardi Team	G	3.5 Minardi M191-Ferrari V12	spun off on own oil	10/34
ret	HUNGARIAN GP	Hungaroring	23	SCM Minardi Team	G	3.5 Minardi M191-Ferrari V12	engine	18/34
12	BELGIAN GP	Spa	23	SCM Minardi Team	G	3.5 Minardi M191-Ferrari V12	2 laps behind	9/34

ret	ITALIAN GP	Monza	23	SCM Minardi Team	G	3.5 Minardi M191-Ferrari V12	spun off – brakes	10/34
4	PORTUGUESE GP	Estoril	23	SCM Minardi Team	G	3.5 Minardi M191-Ferrari V12		8/34
13	SPANISH GP	Barcelona	23	SCM Minardi Team	G	3.5 Minardi M191-Ferrari V12	2 laps behind	19/33
ret	JAPANESE GP	Suzuka	23	SCM Minardi Team	G	3.5 Minardi M191-Ferrari V12	clutch	7/31
ret	AUSTRALIAN GP	Adelaide	23	SCM Minardi Team	G	3.5 Minardi M191-Ferrari V12	spun off in heavy rain	10/32

1992 Championship position: 14th=   Wins: 0   Pole positions: 0   Fastest laps: 0   Points scored: 2

ret	SOUTH AFRICAN GP	Kyalami	22	Scuderia Italia SpA	G	3.5 BMS Dallara 192-Ferrari V12	clutch	25/30
ret	MEXICAN GP	Mexico City	22	Scuderia Italia SpA	G	3.5 BMS Dallara 192-Ferrari V12	handling	9/30
ret	BRAZILIAN GP	Interlagos	22	Scuderia Italia SpA	G	3.5 BMS Dallara 192-Ferrari V12	clutch	8/31
6	SPANISH GP	Barcelona	22	Scuderia Italia SpA	G	3.5 BMS Dallara 192-Ferrari V12	2 laps behind	13/32
6	SAN MARINO GP	Imola	22	Scuderia Italia SpA	G	3.5 BMS Dallara 192-Ferrari V12	1 lap behind	15/32
ret	MONACO GP	Monte Carlo	22	Scuderia Italia SpA	G	3.5 BMS Dallara 192-Ferrari V12	accident lap 1	18/32
8	CANADIAN GP	Montreal	22	Scuderia Italia SpA	G	3.5 BMS Dallara 192-Ferrari V12	1 lap behind	15/32
10	FRENCH GP	Magny Cours	22	Scuderia Italia SpA	G	3.5 BMS Dallara 192-Ferrari V12	aggregate of two parts/2 laps behind	25/30
15	BRITISH GP	Silverstone	22	Scuderia Italia SpA	G	3.5 BMS Dallara 192-Ferrari V12	3 laps behind	22/32
11	GERMAN GP	Hockenheim	22	Scuderia Italia SpA	G	3.5 BMS Dallara 192-Ferrari V12	1 lap behind	18/32
ret	HUNGARIAN GP	Hungaroring	22	Scuderia Italia SpA	G	3.5 BMS Dallara 192-Ferrari V12	gearbox	26/31
ret	BELGIAN GP	Spa	22	Scuderia Italia SpA	G	3.5 BMS Dallara 192-Ferrari V12	spun off on lap 1	19/30
8	ITALIAN GP	Monza	22	Scuderia Italia SpA	G	3.5 BMS Dallara 192-Ferrari V12	1 lap behind	22/28
ret	PORTUGUESE GP	Estoril	22	Scuderia Italia SpA	G	3.5 BMS Dallara 192-Ferrari V12	puncture from Patrese's debris	21/26
10	JAPANESE GP	Suzuka	22	Scuderia Italia SpA	G	3.5 BMS Dallara 192-Ferrari V12	1 lap behind	19/26
ret	AUSTRALIAN GP	Adelaide	22	Scuderia Italia SpA	G	3.5 BMS Dallara 192-Ferrari V12	collision with Grouillard on lap 1	14/26

1993 Championship position: Unplaced

ret	BRITISH GP	Silverstone	24	Minardi Team	G	3.5 Minardi M193-Ford HB V8	cramp in arm	20/26
14	GERMAN GP	Hockenheim	24	Minardi Team	G	3.5 Minardi M193-Ford HB V8	1 lap behind	22/26
ret	HUNGARIAN GP	Hungaroring	24	Minardi Team	G	3.5 Minardi M193-Ford HB V8	spun off	7/26
ret	BELGIAN GP	Spa	24	Minardi Team	G	3.5 Minardi M193-Ford HB V8	spun off	21/25
7	ITALIAN GP	Monza	24	Minardi Team	G	3.5 Minardi M193-Ford HB V8	hit by C Fittipaldi at finish/-2 laps	22/26
8	PORTUGUESE GP	Estoril	24	Minardi Team	G	3.5 Minardi M193-Ford HB V8	2 laps behind	19/26
10	JAPANESE GP	Suzuka	24	Minardi Team	G	3.5 Minardi M193-Ford HB V8	2 laps behind	22/24
ret	AUSTRALIAN GP	Adelaide	24	Minardi Team	G	3.5 Minardi M193-Ford HB V8	gearbox	16/24

1994 Championship position: 18th=   Wins: 0   Pole positions: 0   Fastest laps: 0   Points scored: 4

8	BRAZILIAN GP	Interlagos	23	Minardi Scuderia Italia	G	3.5 Minardi M193B-Ford HB V8	2 laps behind	15/28
ret	PACIFIC GP	T.I. Circuit	23	Minardi Scuderia Italia	G	3.5 Minardi M193B-Ford HB V8	electrics	17/28
ret	SAN MARINO GP	Imola	23	Minardi Scuderia Italia	G	3.5 Minardi M193B-Ford HB V8	spun off	14/28
ret	MONACO GP	Monte Carlo	23	Minardi Scuderia Italia	G	3.5 Minardi M193B-Ford HB V8	collision with Morbidelli on lap 1	9/24
5	SPANISH GP	Barcelona	23	Minardi Scuderia Italia	G	3.5 Minardi M193B-Ford HB V8	1 lap behind	18/27
9	CANADIAN GP	Montreal	23	Minardi Scuderia Italia	G	3.5 Minardi M194-Ford HB V8	1 lap behind	15/27
5	FRENCH GP	Magny Cours	23	Minardi Scuderia Italia	G	3.5 Minardi M194-Ford HB V8	2 laps behind	16/28
10*	BRITISH GP	Silverstone	23	Minardi Scuderia Italia	G	3.5 Minardi M194-Ford HB V8	*2nd place car disqualified/-2 laps	14/28
ret	GERMAN GP	Hockenheim	23	Minardi Scuderia Italia	G	3.5 Minardi M194-Ford HB V8	multiple accident on lap 1	20/28
ret	HUNGARIAN GP	Hungaroring	23	Minardi Scuderia Italia	G	3.5 Minardi M194-Ford HB V8	spun off	15/28
8*	BELGIAN GP	Spa	23	Minardi Scuderia Italia	G	3.5 Minardi M194-Ford HB V8	*1st place car disqualified/-1 lap	10/28
ret	ITALIAN GP	Monza	23	Minardi Scuderia Italia	G	3.5 Minardi M194-Ford HB V8	spun off	18/28
12	PORTUGUESE GP	Estoril	23	Minardi Scuderia Italia	G	3.5 Minardi M194-Ford HB V8	2 laps behind	18/28
15	EUROPEAN GP	Jerez	23	Minardi Scuderia Italia	G	3.5 Minardi M194-Ford HB V8	2 laps behind	17/28
ret	JAPANESE GP	Suzuka	23	Minardi Scuderia Italia	G	3.5 Minardi M194-Ford HB V8	touched Lagorce – spun off	16/28
9	AUSTRALIAN GP	Adelaide	23	Minardi Scuderia Italia	G	3.5 Minardi M194-Ford HB V8	2 laps behind	18/28

1995 Championship position: Unplaced

ret/dns*	BRAZILIAN GP	Interlagos	23	Minardi Scuderia Italia	G	3.0 Minardi M195-Ford EDM V8	*gearbox on parade lap	(17)/26
ret	ARGENTINE GP	Buenos Aires	23	Minardi Scuderia Italia	G	3.0 Minardi M195-Ford EDM V8	spun off	16/26
12	SAN MARINO GP	Imola	23	Minardi Scuderia Italia	G	3.0 Minardi M195-Ford EDM V8	4 laps behind	18/26
14	SPANISH GP	Barcelona	23	Minardi Scuderia Italia	G	3.0 Minardi M195-Ford EDM V8	3 laps behind	19/26
7	MONACO GP	Monte Carlo	23	Minardi Scuderia Italia	G	3.0 Minardi M195-Ford EDM V8	2 laps behind	18/26
ret	CANADIAN GP	Montreal	23	Minardi Scuderia Italia	G	3.0 Minardi M195-Ford EDM V8	throttle	17/24
ret	FRENCH GP	Magny Cours	23	Minardi Scuderia Italia	G	3.0 Minardi M195-Ford EDM V8	gearbox	20/24
7	BRITISH GP	Silverstone	23	Minardi Scuderia Italia	G	3.0 Minardi M195-Ford EDM V8	1 lap behind	15/24
ret	GERMAN GP	Hockenheim	23	Minardi Scuderia Italia	G	3.0 Minardi M195-Ford EDM V8	engine	20/24

GP Starts: 118 (119)   GP Wins: 0   Pole positions: 0   Fastest laps: 0   Points: 18

Pierluigi Martini never had a truly front-running car to show his talent, but the neat little 1989 Minardi M189-Cosworth thrust him into the limelight on a number of occasions.

JOCHEN MASS

PERHAPS lacking the killer instinct that separates winners from the rest, Jochen Mass nevertheless was a very talented racing driver who appeared to be destined for the very top on the evidence of his early career. This began in 1970 with an Alfa saloon, before he joined Ford Germany to race their Capri. He really shot to prominence in 1972 by winning the European touring car championship for drivers after major wins at Spa, Zandvoort, Silverstone and Jarama. In addition to a planned F3 programme, he also made his Formula 2 debut in the works March, scoring a superb win in the Eifelrennen.

Retaining his Ford touring car links, Mass signed for the Surtees Formula 2 team in 1973, winning the rounds at Kinnekulle and Hockenheim. He finished a solid second in the championship standings and also earned his grand prix debut at Silverstone. Unfortunately, his car was wiped out in the Jody Scheckter-instigated multiple shunt, but he was soon back in action, taking seventh place in the German GP.

Promoted to the Surtees F1 team full time in 1974, Jochen enjoyed a useful start to the year with a fourth place in the Medici GP in Brasilia and then second in the International Trophy race. Once the grand prix season proper got under way, however, things soon began to go wrong, a succession of technical maladies afflicting the team. Things reached boiling point when a superb drive in the German GP was ended by engine failure, prompting him to follow Carlos Pace's example and quit in frustration. Picking up the vacant Yardley McLaren seat for the final two races of the season, Mass was offered a full works ride in place of the retired Denny Hulme for 1975 and emerged as an excellent number two to Fittipaldi, winning the shortened Spanish GP in Barcelona, and impressing mightily at both Paul Ricard and Watkins Glen.

The German's subordinate role in the team continued during the next two seasons as James Hunt breezed in to highlight the gulf that exists between champions and contenders. Jochen had his moments, though, and was distinctly unlucky not to win the 1976 German GP, his gamble to run on slicks looking likely to pay off until Niki Lauda's accident halted proceedings. He could be relied upon to provide the team with plenty of top-six finishes, however, and was happy to deliver. In 1977, a couple of Formula 2 races for March brought him victories at Hockenheim and the Nürburgring, and he began his long and tremendously successful sports car partnership with Jacky Ickx, winning three rounds of the World Championship of Makes in the Martini Racing Porsche.

Making the break from an increasingly downtrodden existence at McLaren, Mass joined the ATS team as number-one driver in 1978, but the season was desperately disappointing and ended prematurely when he suffered a broken knee and thigh in a testing accident at Silverstone. It was to his credit that he made a strong comeback in 1979 with Arrows. Despite being in an outclassed car, he put in some spirited drives, none more stirring than at Monaco, where he lay third until brake problems intervened. Continuing with the team for another season, he proved a consistent performer yet again. Ironically, his best placing was second in the Spanish GP, which subsequently was denied championship status, but he produced another excellent display at Monaco. Out of a drive for 1981, he concentrated on sports car and G5 racing, before an unhappy return to the grand prix arena with the RAM team in 1982.

Disillusioned after this final year of F1, Mass turned to sports car racing full time. With Rothmans Porsche, he took eight wins between 1982 and 1985, before briefly switching to IMSA, and after racing a Brun Porsche in 1987, he joined Sauber, which eventually became the full works Mercedes-Benz team. He remained a very capable driver and his huge experience made him the ideal tutor to the German company's young lions, Michael Schumacher, Karl Wendlinger and Heinz-Harald Frentzen. Jochen scored three wins in 1988 and added five more in 1989, including a long-awaited and much-deserved victory at Le Mans. In 1990, he won another two rounds, but there were no successes the following year, when the programme was running down as Sauber looked towards Formula 1. In 1992, he moved into a team management role in the German touring car championship, but continued to enjoy his racing, mainly in GT cars.

Jochen was also a TV commentator and regular in the grand prix paddock, but more recently he has represented the Mercedes-Benz marque, enthusiastically demonstrating their priceless classic machines at historic festivals around the globe.

MASS, Jochen (D) b 30/9/1946, Dorfen, nr Munich

1973 Championship position: Unplaced

	Race	Circuit	No	Entrant	Tyres	Capacity/Car/Engine	Comment	Q Pos/Entries
ret/dns	BRITISH GP	Silverstone	31	Team Surtees	F	3.0 Surtees TS14A-Cosworth V8	*multiple accident at 1st start*	=14/29
7	GERMAN GP	Nürburgring	31	Team Surtees	F	3.0 Surtees TS14A-Cosworth V8		15/23
ret	US GP	Watkins Glen	30	Team Surtees	F	3.0 Surtees TS14A-Cosworth V8	*engine*	17/28

1974 Championship position: Unplaced

	Race	Circuit	No	Entrant	Tyres	Capacity/Car/Engine	Comment	Q Pos/Entries
ret	ARGENTINE GP	Buenos Aires	19	Team Surtees	F	3.0 Surtees TS16-Cosworth V8	*engine*	=17/26
17	BRAZILIAN GP	Interlagos	19	Team Surtees	F	3.0 Surtees TS16-Cosworth V8	*pit stop/2 laps behind*	10/25
ret	SOUTH AFRICAN GP	Kyalami	19	Team Surtees	F	3.0 Surtees TS16-Cosworth V8	*withdrawn after accident*	17/27
ret	SPANISH GP	Jarama	19	Bang & Olufsen Team Surtees	F	3.0 Surtees TS16-Cosworth V8	*gearbox*	19/28
ret	BELGIAN GP	Nivelles	19	Bang & Olufsen Team Surtees	F	3.0 Surtees TS16-Cosworth V8	*broken right rear upright*	26/32
dns	MONACO GP	Monte Carlo	19	Bang & Olufsen Team Surtees	F	3.0 Surtees TS16-Cosworth V8	*lack of suspension parts*	(=16)/28
ret	SWEDISH GP	Anderstorp	19	Bang & Olufsen Team Surtees	F	3.0 Surtees TS16-Cosworth V8	*suspension*	22/30
ret	DUTCH GP	Zandvoort	19	Bang & Olufsen Team Surtees	F	3.0 Surtees TS16-Cosworth V8	*c.v. joint*	20/27
ret	FRENCH GP	Dijon	19	Bang & Olufsen Team Surtees	F	3.0 Surtees TS16-Cosworth V8	*clutch*	18/30
14	BRITISH GP	Brands Hatch	19	Bang & Olufsen Team Surtees	F	3.0 Surtees TS16-Cosworth V8	*pit stop – puncture/7 laps behind*	=15/34
ret	GERMAN GP	Nürburgring	19	Bang & Olufsen Team Surtees	F	3.0 Surtees TS16-Cosworth V8	*engine*	10/32
16	CANADIAN GP	Mosport Park	33	Yardley Team McLaren	G	3.0 McLaren M23-Cosworth V8	*pit stop after spin/8 laps behind*	12/30
7	US GP	Watkins Glen	33	Yardley Team McLaren	G	3.0 McLaren M23-Cosworth V8		20/30

1975 Championship position: 7th   Wins: 1   Pole positions: 0   Fastest laps: 1   Points scored: 20

	Race	Circuit	No	Entrant	Tyres	Capacity/Car/Engine	Comment	Q Pos/Entries
14	ARGENTINE GP	Buenos Aires	2	Marlboro Team Texaco	G	3.0 McLaren M23-Cosworth V8	*hit Scheckter – pit stop/3 laps behind*	13/23
3	BRAZILIAN GP	Interlagos	2	Marlboro Team Texaco	G	3.0 McLaren M23-Cosworth V8		10/23
6	SOUTH AFRICAN GP	Kyalami	2	Marlboro Team Texaco	G	3.0 McLaren M23-Cosworth V8		16/28
1*	SPANISH GP	Montjuich Park	2	Marlboro Team Texaco	G	3.0 McLaren M23-Cosworth V8	*race stopped/*half points awarded*	11/26
6	MONACO GP	Monte Carlo	2	Marlboro Team Texaco	G	3.0 McLaren M23-Cosworth V8		15/26
ret	BELGIAN GP	Zolder	2	Marlboro Team Texaco	G	3.0 McLaren M23-Cosworth V8	*collision with Watson*	15/24
ret	SWEDISH GP	Anderstorp	2	Marlboro Team Texaco	G	3.0 McLaren M23-Cosworth V8	*water leak*	14/26
ret	DUTCH GP	Zandvoort	2	Marlboro Team Texaco	G	3.0 McLaren M23-Cosworth V8	*engine cut out – crashed*	8/25
3	FRENCH GP	Paul Ricard	2	Marlboro Team Texaco	G	3.0 McLaren M23-Cosworth V8	*FL*	7/26
7/ret	BRITISH GP	Silverstone	2	Marlboro Team Texaco	G	3.0 McLaren M23-Cosworth V8	*accident in rainstorm/1 lap behind*	10/28
ret	GERMAN GP	Nürburgring	2	Marlboro Team Texaco	G	3.0 McLaren M23-Cosworth V8	*tyre failure – crashed on lap 1*	6/26
4*	AUSTRIAN GP	Österreichring	2	Marlboro Team Texaco	G	3.0 McLaren M23-Cosworth V8	*rain shortened race – half points awarded*	9/30
ret	ITALIAN GP	Monza	2	Marlboro Team Texaco	G	3.0 McLaren M23-Cosworth V8	*damaged suspension*	5/28
3	US GP	Watkins Glen	2	Marlboro Team Texaco	G	3.0 McLaren M23-Cosworth V8		9/24

1976 Championship position: 9th   Wins: 0   Pole positions: 0   Fastest laps: 1   Points scored: 19

	Race	Circuit	No	Entrant	Tyres	Capacity/Car/Engine	Comment	Q Pos/Entries
6	BRAZILIAN GP	Interlagos	12	Marlboro Team McLaren	G	3.0 McLaren M23-Cosworth V8		6/22
3	SOUTH AFRICAN GP	Kyalami	12	Marlboro Team McLaren	G	3.0 McLaren M23-Cosworth V8		4/25
5	US GP WEST	Long Beach	12	Marlboro Team McLaren	G	3.0 McLaren M23-Cosworth V8		14/27
ret	SPANISH GP	Jarama	12	Marlboro Team McLaren	G	3.0 McLaren M23-Cosworth V8	*engine/FL*	4/30
6	BELGIAN GP	Zolder	12	Marlboro Team McLaren	G	3.0 McLaren M23-Cosworth V8	*1 lap behind*	18/29
5	MONACO GP	Monte Carlo	12	Marlboro Team McLaren	G	3.0 McLaren M23-Cosworth V8	*1 lap behind*	11/25
11	SWEDISH GP	Anderstorp	12	Marlboro Team McLaren	G	3.0 McLaren M23-Cosworth V8	*1 lap behind*	13/27
15	FRENCH GP	Paul Ricard	12	Marlboro Team McLaren	G	3.0 McLaren M23-Cosworth V8	*hit by Reutemann – pit stop/1 lap behind*	14/30
ret	BRITISH GP	Brands Hatch	12	Marlboro Team McLaren	G	3.0 McLaren M23-Cosworth V8	*clutch*	12/30
3	GERMAN GP	Nürburgring	12	Marlboro Team McLaren	G	3.0 McLaren M23-Cosworth V8		9/28
7	AUSTRIAN GP	Österreichring	12	Marlboro Team McLaren	G	3.0 McLaren M23-Cosworth V8		12/25
9	DUTCH GP	Zandvoort	12	Marlboro Team McLaren	G	3.0 McLaren M26-Cosworth V8	*1 lap behind*	15/27
dns	"	"	12	Marlboro Team McLaren	G	3.0 McLaren M23-Cosworth V8	*practice only*	- / -
ret	ITALIAN GP	Monza	12	Marlboro Team McLaren	G	3.0 McLaren M23-Cosworth V8	*ignition*	- / -
dns	"	"	12	Marlboro Team McLaren	G	3.0 McLaren M26-Cosworth V8	*practice only – set grid time*	28/29
5	CANADIAN GP	Mosport Park	12	Marlboro Team McLaren	G	3.0 McLaren M23-Cosworth V8		11/27

Jochen's only grand prix victory came in the 1975 Spanish Grand Prix at the Montjuich street circuit. The race was halted after just 29 laps, following an accident in which Rolf Stommelen's car crashed into the crowd, killing five spectators.

4	US GP EAST	Watkins Glen	12	Marlboro Team McLaren	G	3.0 McLaren M23-Cosworth V8		17/27
ret	JAPANESE GP	Mount Fuji	12	Marlboro Team McLaren	G	3.0 McLaren M23-Cosworth V8	*slid off track*	12/27

1977 Championship position: 6 Wins: 0 Pole positions: 0 Fastest laps: 0 Points scored: 25

ret	ARGENTINE GP	Buenos Aires	2	Marlboro Team McLaren	G	3.0 McLaren M23-Cosworth V8	*engine cut out – spun off*	5/21
ret	BRAZILIAN GP	Interlagos	2	Marlboro Team McLaren	G	3.0 McLaren M23-Cosworth V8	*spun off*	4/22
5	SOUTH AFRICAN GP	Kyalami	2	Marlboro Team McLaren	G	3.0 McLaren M23-Cosworth V8		13/23
ret	US GP WEST	Long Beach	2	Marlboro Team McLaren	G	3.0 McLaren M23-Cosworth V8	*rear end vibration*	15/22
4	SPANISH GP	Jarama	2	Marlboro Team McLaren	G	3.0 McLaren M23-Cosworth V8		9/31
4	MONACO GP	Monte Carlo	2	Marlboro Team McLaren	G	3.0 McLaren M23-Cosworth V8		9/26
ret	BELGIAN GP	Zolder	2	Marlboro Team McLaren	G	3.0 McLaren M23-Cosworth V8	*spun off*	6/32
2	SWEDISH GP	Anderstorp	2	Marlboro Team McLaren	G	3.0 McLaren M23-Cosworth V8		9/31
9	FRENCH GP	Dijon	2	Marlboro Team McLaren	G	3.0 McLaren M23-Cosworth V8	*hit Reutemann – pitstop/-2 laps*	7/30
4	BRITISH GP	Silverstone	2	Marlboro Team McLaren	G	3.0 McLaren M26-Cosworth V8		11/36
dns	"	"	2	Marlboro Team McLaren	G	3.0 McLaren M23-Cosworth V8	*practice only*	– / –
ret	GERMAN GP	Hockenheim	2	Marlboro Team McLaren	G	3.0 McLaren M26-Cosworth V8	*gearbox*	13/30
dns	"	"	2	Marlboro Team McLaren	G	3.0 McLaren M26-Cosworth V8	*practice only*	– / –
6	AUSTRIAN GP	Österreichring	2	Marlboro Team McLaren	G	3.0 McLaren M26-Cosworth V8	*pit stop/1 lap behind*	9/30
ret	DUTCH GP	Zandvoort	2	Marlboro Team McLaren	G	3.0 McLaren M26-Cosworth V8	*hit by Jones*	=13/34
4	ITALIAN GP	Monza	2	Marlboro Team McLaren	G	3.0 McLaren M26-Cosworth V8		9/34
ret	US GP EAST	Watkins Glen	2	Marlboro Team McLaren	G	3.0 McLaren M26-Cosworth V8	*fuel pump belt*	15/27
3	CANADIAN GP	Mosport Park	2	Marlboro Team McLaren	G	3.0 McLaren M26-Cosworth V8	*despite being hit by Hunt*	5/27
ret	JAPANESE GP	Mount Fuji	2	Marlboro Team McLaren	G	3.0 McLaren M26-Cosworth V8	*engine*	=8/23

1978 Championship position: Unplaced

11	ARGENTINE GP	Buenos Aires	9	ATS Racing Team	G	3.0 ATS HS1-Cosworth V8		13/27
7	BRAZILIAN GP	Rio	9	ATS Racing Team	G	3.0 ATS HS1-Cosworth V8	*1 lap behind*	20/28
ret	SOUTH AFRICAN GP	Kyalami	9	ATS Racing Team	G	3.0 ATS HS1-Cosworth V8	*engine*	15/30
ret	US GP WEST	Long Beach	9	ATS Racing Team	G	3.0 ATS HS1-Cosworth V8	*brake master cylinder*	16/30
dnq	MONACO GP	Monte Carlo	9	ATS Racing Team	G	3.0 ATS HS1-Cosworth V8		21/30
11	BELGIAN GP	Zolder	9	ATS Racing Team	G	3.0 ATS HS1-Cosworth V8	*pit stop – tyres/2 laps behind*	16/30
9	SPANISH GP	Jarama	9	ATS Racing Team	G	3.0 ATS HS1-Cosworth V8	*pit stop – tyres/1 lap behind*	17/29
13	SWEDISH GP	Anderstorp	9	ATS Racing Team	G	3.0 ATS HS1-Cosworth V8	*2 laps behind*	19/27
13	FRENCH GP	Paul Ricard	9	ATS Racing Team	G	3.0 ATS HS1-Cosworth V8	*1 lap behind*	25/29
nc	BRITISH GP	Brands Hatch	9	ATS Racing Team	G	3.0 ATS HS1-Cosworth V8	*pit stop/10 laps behind*	26/30
ret	GERMAN GP	Hockenheim	9	ATS Racing Team	G	3.0 ATS HS1-Cosworth V8	*suspension breakage*	22/30
dnq	AUSTRIAN GP	Österreichring	9	ATS Racing Team	G	3.0 ATS HS1-Cosworth V8		28/31
dnq	DUTCH GP	Zandvoort	9	ATS Racing Team	G	3.0 ATS HS1-Cosworth V8		30/33

1979 Championship position: 15th Wins: 0 Pole positions: 0 Fastest laps: 0 Points scored: 3

8	ARGENTINE GP	Buenos Aires	30	Warsteiner Arrows Racing Team	G	3.0 Arrows A1B-Cosworth V8	*2 laps behind*	14/26
7	BRAZILIAN GP	Interlagos	30	Warsteiner Arrows Racing Team	G	3.0 Arrows A1B-Cosworth V8	*1 lap behind*	19/26
12	SOUTH AFRICAN GP	Kyalami	30	Warsteiner Arrows Racing Team	G	3.0 Arrows A1B-Cosworth V8	*pit stop – tyre/4 laps behind*	20/26
9	US GP WEST	Long Beach	30	Warsteiner Arrows Racing Team	G	3.0 Arrows A1B-Cosworth V8	*2 laps behind*	13/26
8	SPANISH GP	Jarama	30	Warsteiner Arrows Racing Team	G	3.0 Arrows A1B-Cosworth V8		17/27
ret	BELGIAN GP	Zolder	30	Warsteiner Arrows Racing Team	G	3.0 Arrows A1B-Cosworth V8	*spun off – could not restart*	22/28
6	MONACO GP	Monte Carlo	30	Warsteiner Arrows Racing Team	G	3.0 Arrows A1B-Cosworth V8	*pit stop – brake cooler/7 laps behind*	8/25
15	FRENCH GP	Dijon	30	Warsteiner Arrows Racing Team	G	3.0 Arrows A2-Cosworth V8	*handling/5 laps behind*	22/27
ret	BRITISH GP	Silverstone	30	Warsteiner Arrows Racing Team	G	3.0 Arrows A2-Cosworth V8	*gearbox*	20/26
6	GERMAN GP	Hockenheim	30	Warsteiner Arrows Racing Team	G	3.0 Arrows A2-Cosworth V8	*1 lap behind*	18/26
ret	AUSTRIAN GP	Österreichring	30	Warsteiner Arrows Racing Team	G	3.0 Arrows A2-Cosworth V8	*engine*	20/26
6	DUTCH GP	Zandvoort	30	Warsteiner Arrows Racing Team	G	3.0 Arrows A2-Cosworth V8	*2 laps behind*	18/26
ret	ITALIAN GP	Monza	30	Warsteiner Arrows Racing Team	G	3.0 Arrows A2-Cosworth V8	*suspension*	21/28
dnq	CANADIAN GP	Montreal	30	Warsteiner Arrows Racing Team	G	3.0 Arrows A2-Cosworth V8		25/29
dnq	US GP EAST	Watkins Glen	30	Warsteiner Arrows Racing Team	G	3.0 Arrows A2-Cosworth V8		26/30

1980 Championship position: 17th Wins: 0 Pole positions: 0 Fastest laps: 0 Points scored: 4

ret	ARGENTINE GP	Buenos Aires	30	Warsteiner Arrows Racing Team	G	3.0 Arrows A3-Cosworth V8	*gearbox*	14/28
10	BRAZILIAN GP	Interlagos	30	Warsteiner Arrows Racing Team	G	3.0 Arrows A3-Cosworth V8	*1 lap behind*	16/28
6	SOUTH AFRICAN GP	Kyalami	30	Warsteiner Arrows Racing Team	G	3.0 Arrows A3-Cosworth V8	*1 lap behind*	=19/23
7	US GP WEST	Long Beach	30	Warsteiner Arrows Racing Team	G	3.0 Arrows A3-Cosworth V8	*pit stop – hit by Zunino/1 lap behind*	17/27
ret	BELGIAN GP	Zolder	30	Warsteiner Arrows Racing Team	G	3.0 Arrows A3-Cosworth V8	*spun off*	13/27
4	MONACO GP	Monte Carlo	30	Warsteiner Arrows Racing Team	G	3.0 Arrows A3-Cosworth V8	*1 lap behind*	15/27
10	FRENCH GP	Paul Ricard	30	Warsteiner Arrows Racing Team	G	3.0 Arrows A3-Cosworth V8	*1 lap behind*	15/27
13	BRITISH GP	Brands Hatch	30	Warsteiner Arrows Racing Team	G	3.0 Arrows A3-Cosworth V8	*pit stop – steering wheel/7 laps behind*	24/27
8	GERMAN GP	Hockenheim	30	Warsteiner Arrows Racing Team	G	3.0 Arrows A3-Cosworth V8		17/26
dnq	AUSTRIAN GP	Österreichring	30	Warsteiner Arrows Racing Team	G	3.0 Arrows A3-Cosworth V8	*practice crash – no time set*	– / –
11	CANADIAN GP	Montreal	30	Warsteiner Arrows Racing Team	G	3.0 Arrows A3-Cosworth V8	*3 laps behind*	21/28
ret	US GP EAST	Watkins Glen	30	Warsteiner Arrows Racing Team	G	3.0 Arrows A3-Cosworth V8	*driveshaft*	24/27

1982 Championship position: Unplaced

12	SOUTH AFRICAN GP	Kyalami	17	March Grand Prix Team	P	3.0 March 821-Cosworth V8	*3 laps behind*	22/30
8*	BRAZILIAN GP	Rio	17	Rothmans March Grand Prix Team	P	3.0 March 821-Cosworth V8	*pit stop/*1st & 2nd cars dsq/-2 laps*	22/31
8	US GP WEST	Long Beach	17	Rothmans March Grand Prix Team	P	3.0 March 821-Cosworth V8	*2 laps behind*	21/31
ret	BELGIAN GP	Zolder	17	Rothmans March Grand Prix Team	P	3.0 March 821-Cosworth V8	*engine*	27/32
dnq	MONACO GP	Monte Carlo	17	Rothmans March Grand Prix Team	A	3.0 March 821-Cosworth V8		23/31
7	US GP (DETROIT)	Detroit	17	Rothmans March Grand Prix Team	A	3.0 March 821-Cosworth V8	*1 lap behind*	18/28
11	CANADIAN GP	Montreal	17	Rothmans March Grand Prix Team	A	3.0 March 821-Cosworth V8	*pit stop/4 laps behind*	22/29
ret	DUTCH GP	Zandvoort	17	Rothmans March Grand Prix Team	A	3.0 March 821-Cosworth V8	*engine*	24/31
10	BRITISH GP	Brands Hatch	17	Rothmans March Grand Prix Team	A	3.0 March 821-Cosworth V8	*pit stop/3 laps behind*	25/30
10	FRENCH GP	Paul Ricard	17	Rothmans March Grand Prix Team	A	3.0 March 821-Cosworth V8	*accident with Baldi*	26/30
dns	GERMAN GP	Hockenheim	17	Rothmans March Grand Prix Team	A	3.0 March 821-Cosworth V8	*discomfort – injured ribs – Keegan drove*	– / –

GP Starts: 104 (105)   GP Wins: 1   Pole positions: 0   Fastest laps: 2   Points: 71

FELIPE MASSA

A WORLD champion for fewer than ten seconds. Can any racing driver have had the sport's ultimate prize within his grasp and then had it snatched away in such a fashion? That was Felipe Massa's unkind fate in the 2008 season's dying moments on a rain-soaked Interlagos track as the gods smiled on Lewis Hamilton. Given the pressure that the Brazilian must have been under, his performance in front of his home crowd was masterly. Pole position and a mistake-free drive to victory under the treacherous conditions was everything that could have been asked of him and more. The fact that it was not quite enough must have been devastating for him, but in defeat he showed the qualities of a true champion, both on and off the track.

Like those countrymen who had preceded him, Massa began his racing career in the competitive Brazilian karting scene. Having made his debut at the age of nine, he finished fourth in the São Paulo junior series, before gaining similar results as he worked his way through the various age groups. In all, he remained in karts until the age of 17, when he made the switch to single-seaters in the equally competitive Formula Chevrolet category in 1998. A fifth-place finish in the Brazilian equivalent of the successful Formula Opel championship was his initial reward, before a return the following season saw him clinch the title.

Having gone almost as high as possible on the South American single-seater ladder, Massa decided to head for Europe for the 2000 season. Opting for a relatively low-key entrance, he contested the Italian and European Formula Renault series, before making the unusual jump into F3000 for 2001. That move proved to be valuable, however, as he dominated the secondary Euro F3000 category with the Draco Racing team, clinching the title with one round remaining.

Felipe's performances attracted the attention of noted talent scout Peter Sauber and, despite misgivings from other parties, he was duly signed for the 2002 season. It was a wild debut year in Formula 1 for the 20-year-old Brazilian, who took part in his first race at the Australian Grand Prix and bounced back from retirement in Melbourne to score his first F1 points second time out at engine supplier Petronas' home race in Malaysia. Points finishes continued to come throughout the season, but more often than not they were interspersed with accidents as his exciting driving style frequently got the better of him. He was also dropped for the United States GP as the result of having earned a ten-place grid penalty at Monza.

The young Brazilian had often overreached himself and failed to ally his prodigious speed with the disciplines of a grand prix car's characteristics. Fortunately, he was allowed to step out for a season, before returning to rebuild a Formula 1 career that has seen him blossom into not only a grand prix winner, but also a true championship contender.

Peter Sauber decided not to renew Massa's race contract for the following year, but accepted Ferrari's offer to take him on as a test driver in the hope that he would develop on the test track during 2003. The Brazilian duly returned to the Sauber fold for 2004, signing a two-year deal to partner the experienced Giancarlo Fisichella. Felipe showed that he had lost little of his raw pace, but some of the rough edges had definitely been knocked off during his time at Maranello, and the Sauber team was able to challenge for points at just about every race. He recorded best finishes of fourth in Belgium and fifth in Monaco on his way to 12th overall, while the Sauber team eventually slipped back to sixth in the constructors' stakes.

Felipe remained at Hinwil for a third season. Partnered by 1997 world champion Jacques Villeneuve, the Brazilian soon asserted his authority as the Canadian struggled to find his form. Indeed, Massa proved to be a very consistent performer, out-qualifying his team-mate 13–6 and generally making the most of the car's performance deficit in comparison to the bigger teams. With Nicolas Todt as his manager, eyebrows were raised when he was chosen to take the place of Rubens Barrichello alongside Michael Schumacher at Ferrari for 2006.

This would be the acid test for Massa, a chance finally to determine whether he was a top-drawer performer who could win races from the front. Having overcome a tardy start to the year, when he trashed two chassis in Melbourne, he rapidly grew in confidence and often matched the great Schumacher for pace. Indeed, his pole position in Turkey proved to be crucial in that it enabled him to take a maiden win in Istanbul, after pitting ahead of his team-mate under caution. His season ended on an unbelievable high when he took pole position and then scored a commanding win in front of his countrymen at Interlagos. Scoring third place in the championship with two wins and three pole positions, and amassing 90 points was more than enough proof that his place in the team was justified.

In 2007, Felipe was teamed with Kimi Räikkönen, the number-one slot at Ferrari seemingly up for grabs. He rose to the challenge of taking on the Finn, managing to eclipse him on a number of occasions, and claiming wins in Spain and Bahrain. A further win in Turkey put the Brazilian into a four-way championship battle, but retirement in the following race at Monza effectively blunted his title ambitions. From then on, he was prepared to back Räikkönen's successful championship bid, emphasising the value of having a potential race-winning driver who is also very much a team player...

The 2008 season began with Massa very much on the back foot, following disappointing performances in the first two races, and rumours were circulating that his place on the team potentially was at risk. The Brazilian immediately bounced back to win at a canter in Bahrain, however, and after further victories in Istanbul and Magny-Cours, he found himself at the top of the championship table. Thereafter, he became embroiled in the see-saw title battle with Lewis Hamilton that ebbed back and forth until that dramatic finale in Brazil.

Massa had to start all over again in 2009, and given the fact that Ferrari were on the back foot following the Brawn team's onslaught, he acquitted himself well, squeezing everything he could from the F60 while they started to play catch-up and using its KERS to help make up for a lack of downforce. His first podium came nine races into the season at the Nürburgring, which told its own story. The next race would not only shape his season, but also possibly the rest of his career. Under sunny August skies at the Hungaroring, Felipe was engaged in the usual qualifying routine, having reached Q3, when he was hit on the helmet by an 800-gram coil spring, which had come adrift from Rubens Barrichello's Brawn. Knocked unconscious, the Brazilian speared his Ferrari into the tyre wall, and a dreadful silence descended upon the track. The world of Formula 1 held its collective breath until the good news came that, while he had sustained a fractured skull, his injuries were not life threatening and his physical recovery would be complete. His season was over, so he concentrated on getting fit for 2010.

Despite a strong start to the year, Massa seemed to take a while to regain his racing edge. Perhaps the defining moment of his season (and maybe his future career) came at the German Grand Prix at Hockenheim where, in complete control of the race, he was given team orders to move aside and allow Fernando Alonso to take the victory.

Never more was Massa's position in the team laid bare, and he really never seemed to recover from the realisation that his status had been clearly defined as the number-two driver. This position was reinforced in 2011, when he never really featured as a truly competitive proposition. He could only manage a personal best of fifth on five occasions, and he trailed team-mate Alonso by a massive 139 points at the end of the year. Although possessing a contract with Ferrari for 2012, the Brazilian's tenure seems to be permanently under threat. Since his is one of the most coveted seats on the grid, there will be no shortage of eager candidates should he continue to under-achieve.

MASSA, Felipe (BR) b 25/4/1981, São Paulo

2002 Championship position: 12th=   Wins: 0   Pole positions: 0   Fastest laps: 0   Points scored: 4

	Race	Circuit	No	Entrant	Tyres	Capacity/Car/Engine	Comment	Q Pos/Entries
ret	AUSTRALIAN GP	Melbourne	8	Sauber Petronas	B	3.0 Sauber C21-Petronas V10	multiple accident at start	9/22
6	MALAYSIAN GP	Sepang	8	Sauber Petronas	B	3.0 Sauber C21-Petronas V10	1 lap behind	14/22
ret	BRAZILIAN GP	Interlagos	8	Sauber Petronas	B	3.0 Sauber C21-Petronas V10	spun out by Webber	12/22
8	SAN MARINO GP	Imola	8	Sauber Petronas	B	3.0 Sauber C21-Petronas V10	1 lap behind	11/22
5	SPANISH GP	Barcelona	8	Sauber Petronas	B	3.0 Sauber C21-Petronas V10		11/21
ret	AUSTRIAN GP	A1-Ring	8	Sauber Petronas	B	3.0 Sauber C21-Petronas V10	rear suspension damage	7/22
ret	MONACO GP	Monte Carlo	8	Sauber Petronas	B	3.0 Sauber C21-Petronas V10	collison – de la Rosa/later crashed	13/22
9	CANADIAN GP	Montreal	8	Sauber Petronas	B	3.0 Sauber C21-Petronas V10	1 lap behind	12/22
6	EUROPEAN GP	Nürburgring	8	Sauber Petronas	B	3.0 Sauber C21-Petronas V10	1 lap behind	11/22
9	BRITISH GP	Silverstone	8	Sauber Petronas	B	3.0 Sauber C21-Petronas V10	1 lap behind	11/22
ret	FRENCH GP	Magny Cours	8	Sauber Petronas	B	3.0 Sauber C21-Petronas V10	transmission	12/21
7	GERMAN GP	Hockenheim	8	Sauber Petronas	B	3.0 Sauber C21-Petronas V10	1 lap behind	14/22
7	HUNGARIAN GP	Hungaroring	8	Sauber Petronas	B	3.0 Sauber C21-Petronas V10		7/22
ret	BELGIAN GP	Spa	8	Sauber Petronas	B	3.0 Sauber C21-Petronas V10	engine	17/22
ret	ITALIAN GP	Monza	8	Sauber Petronas	B	3.0 Sauber C21-Petronas V10	collision with de la Rosa – suspension	14/22
ret	JAPANESE GP	Suzuka	8	Sauber Petronas	B	3.0 Sauber C21-Petronas V10	lost downforce – spun off	15/22

2004 Championship position: 12th   Wins: 0   Pole positions: 0   Fastest laps: 0   Points scored: 12

	Race	Circuit	No	Entrant	Tyres	Capacity/Car/Engine	Comment	Q Pos/Entries
ret	AUSTRALIAN GP	Melbourne	12	Sauber Petronas	B	3.0 Sauber C23-Petronas V10	engine seized – spun off	11/20
8	MALAYSIAN GP	Sepang	12	Sauber Petronas	B	3.0 Sauber C23-Petronas V10	clutch problems/1 lap behind	11/20
12	BAHRAIN GP	Sakhir Circuit	12	Sauber Petronas	B	3.0 Sauber C23-Petronas V10	tyre problems/1 lap behind	13/20
10	SAN MARINO GP	Imola	12	Sauber Petronas	B	3.0 Sauber C23-Petronas V10	1 lap behind	12/20
9	SPANISH GP	Barcelona	12	Sauber Petronas	B	3.0 Sauber C23-Petronas V10		17/20
5	MONACO GP	Monte Carlo	12	Sauber Petronas	B	3.0 Sauber C23-Petronas V10	1 lap behind	16/20
9	EUROPEAN GP	Nürburgring	12	Sauber Petronas	B	3.0 Sauber C23-Petronas V10	collision damage/1 lap behind	16/20
ret	CANADIAN GP	Montreal	12	Sauber Petronas	B	3.0 Sauber C23-Petronas V10	*no time set/suspension – accident	*19/20
ret	U S GP	Indianapolis	12	Sauber Petronas	B	3.0 Sauber C23-Petronas V10	hit by Klien on lap 1	15/20
13	FRANCE GP	Magny Cours	12	Sauber Petronas	B	3.0 Sauber C23-Petronas V10	1 lap behind	16/20
9	BRITISH GP	Silverstone	12	Sauber Petronas	B	3.0 Sauber C23-Petronas V10		10/20
18	GERMAN GP	Hockenheim	12	Sauber Petronas	B	3.0 Sauber C23-Petronas V10	1 lap behind	16/20
ret	HUNGARIAN GP	Hungaroring	12	Sauber Petronas	B	3.0 Sauber C23-Petronas V10	*no practice time set/brakes	*20/20
4	BELGIAN GP	Spa	12	Sauber Petronas	B	3.0 Sauber C23-Petronas V10	rear wing change	8/20
12	ITALIAN GP	Monza	12	Sauber Petronas	B	3.0 Sauber C23-Petronas V10	hit Heidfeld – wing change/-1 lap	16/20
8	CHINESE GP	Shanghai Circuit	12	Sauber Petronas	B	3.0 Sauber C23-Petronas V10		4/20
9	JAPANESE GP	Suzuka	12	Sauber Petronas	B	3.0 Sauber C23-Petronas V10	*no practice time set	*19/20
8	BRAZILIAN GP	Interlagos	12	Sauber Petronas	B	3.0 Sauber C23-Petronas V10	briefly led race	4/20

2005 Championship position: 13th   Wins: 0   Pole positions: 0   Fastest laps: 0   Points scored: 11

	Race	Circuit	No	Entrant	Tyres	Capacity/Car/Engine	Comment	Q Pos/Entries
10	AUSTRALIAN GP	Melbourne	12	Sauber Petronas	M	Sauber C24-3.0-Petronas V10	*no practice time set – heavy rain	*20/20
10	MALAYSIAN GP	Sepang	12	Sauber Petronas	M	Sauber C24-3.0-Petronas V10	handling problems/1 lap behind	14/20
7	BAHRAIN GP	Sakhir Circuit	12	Sauber Petronas	M	Sauber C24-3.0-Petronas V10	1 lap behind	12/20
10	SAN MARINO GP	Imola	12	Sauber Petronas	M	Sauber C24-3.0-Petronas V10	*3rd & 5th cars dsq/1 lap behind	18/20
11/ret	SPANISH GP	Barcelona	12	Sauber Petronas	M	Sauber C24-3.0-Petronas V10	broken wheel rim/3 laps behind	10/18
9	MONACO GP	Monte Carlo	12	Sauber Petronas	M	Sauber C24-3.0-Petronas V10	collision with Villeneuve/1 lap behind	11/18
14	EUROPEAN GP	Nürburgring	12	Sauber Petronas	M	Sauber C24-3.0-Petronas V10	tyre change/1 lap behind	11/20
4	CANADIAN GP	Montreal	12	Sauber Petronas	M	Sauber C24-3.0-Petronas V10	excellent drive	11/20
ret/dns*	U S GP	Indianapolis	12	Sauber Petronas	M	Sauber C24-3.0-Petronas V10	*withdrawn after parade lap	10/20
ret	FRENCH GP	Magny Cours	12	Sauber Petronas	M	Sauber C24-3.0-Petronas V10	hydraulics	9/20
10	BRITISH GP	Silverstone	12	Sauber Petronas	M	Sauber C24-3.0-Petronas V10	anti-stall failed at start/1 lap behind	16/20
8	GERMAN GP	Hockenheim	12	Sauber Petronas	M	Sauber C24-3.0-Petronas V10		13/20
14	HUNGARIAN GP	Hungaroring	12	Sauber Petronas	M	Sauber C24-3.0-Petronas V10	replaced coils/fire/7 laps behind	14/20
ret	TURKISH GP	Hungaroring	12	Sauber Petronas	M	Sauber C24-3.0-Petronas V10	engine	8/20
9	ITALIAN GP	Monza	12	Sauber Petronas	M	Sauber C24-3.0-Petronas V10	oversteer	15/20
10	BELGIAN GP	Spa	12	Sauber Petronas	M	Sauber C24-3.0-Petronas V10	1 lap behind	8/20
11	BRAZILIAN GP	Interlagos	12	Sauber Petronas	M	Sauber C24-3.0-Petronas V10	poor traction/1 lap behind	9/20
10	JAPANESE GP	Suzuka	12	Sauber Petronas	M	Sauber C24-3.0-Petronas V10		10/20
6	CHINESE GP	Shanghai Circuit	12	Sauber Petronas	M	Sauber C24-3.0-Petronas V10	flat-spotted tyre	11/20

2006 Championship position: 3rd   Wins: 2   Pole positions: 3   Fastest laps: 2   Points scored: 80

	Race	Circuit	No	Entrant	Tyres	Capacity/Car/Engine	Comment	Q Pos/Entries
9	BAHRAIN GP	Sakhir Circuit	6	Scuderia Ferrari Marlboro	B	2.4 Ferrari 248F1-V8	tyre change delay at pitstop	4/22
5	MALAYSIAN GP	Sepang	6	Scuderia Ferrari Marlboro	B	2.4 Ferrari 248F1-V8	one-stop strategy	16/22
ret	AUSTRALIAN GP	Melbourne	6	Scuderia Ferrari Marlboro	B	2.4 Ferrari 248F1-V8	accident – crashed at first corner	16/22
4	SAN MARINO GP	Imola	6	Scuderia Ferrari Marlboro	B	2.4 Ferrari 248F1-V8		4/22
3	EUROPEAN GP	Nürburgring	6	Scuderia Ferrari Marlboro	B	2.4 Ferrari 248F1-V8		3/22
4	SPANISH GP	Barcelona	6	Scuderia Ferrari Marlboro	B	2.4 Ferrari 248F1-V8	FL	4/22
9	MONACO GP	Monte Carlo	6	Scuderia Ferrari Marlboro	B	2.4 Ferrari 248F1-V8	*no time set/1 lap behind	*22/22
5	BRITISH GP	Silverstone	6	Scuderia Ferrari Marlboro	B	2.4 Ferrari 248F1-V8		4/22
5	CANADIAN GP	Montreal	6	Scuderia Ferrari Marlboro	B	2.4 Ferrari 248F1-V8		10/22
2	U S GP	Indianapolis	6	Scuderia Ferrari Marlboro	B	2.4 Ferrari 248F1-V8		2/22
3	FRENCH GP	Magny Cours	6	Scuderia Ferrari Marlboro	B	2.4 Ferrari 248F1-V8		2/22
2	GERMAN GP	Hockenheim	6	Scuderia Ferrari Marlboro	B	2.4 Ferrari 248F1-V8		3/22
7	HUNGARIAN GP	Hungaroring	6	Scuderia Ferrari Marlboro	B	2.4 Ferrari 248F1-V8	1 lap behind	2/22
1	TURKISH GP	Istanbul	6	Scuderia Ferrari Marlboro	B	2.4 Ferrari 248F1-V8	FL	1/22
9	ITALIAN GP	Monza	6	Scuderia Ferrari Marlboro	B	2.4 Ferrari 248F1-V8	flat-spotted tyre	4/22
ret	CHINESE GP	Shanghai Circuit	6	Scuderia Ferrari Marlboro	B	2.4 Ferrari 248F1-V8	collision Coulthard – supsension damage	13/22
2	JAPANESE GP	Suzuka	6	Scuderia Ferrari Marlboro	B	2.4 Ferrari 248F1-V8		1/22
1	BRAZILIAN GP	Interlagos	6	Scuderia Ferrari Marlboro	B	2.4 Ferrari 248F1-V8		1/22

Champion performance. Felipe Massa dominated the 2008 Brazilian Grand Prix, but his brilliant victory was not enough to deny Lewis Hamilton, who snatched the title in a dramatic finish.

	2007 Championship position: 4th	Wins: 3	Pole positions: 6	Fastest laps: 6		Points scored: 94			
6	AUSTRALIAN GP	Melbourne	5	Scuderia Ferrari Marlboro	B	2.4 Ferrari F2007-V8			16/22
5	MALAYSIAN GP	Sepang	5	Scuderia Ferrari Marlboro	B	2.4 Ferrari F2007-V8	ran off track trying to pass Hamilton		1/22
1	BAHRAIN GP	Sakhir Circuit	5	Scuderia Ferrari Marlboro	B	2.4 Ferrari F2007-V8	FL		1/22
1	SPANISH GP	Barcelona	5	Scuderia Ferrari Marlboro	B	2.4 Ferrari F2007-V8	FL		1/22
3	MONACO GP	Monte Carlo	5	Scuderia Ferrari Marlboro	B	2.4 Ferrari F2007-V8			3/22
dsq*	CANADIAN GP	Montreal	5	Scuderia Ferrari Marlboro	B	2.4 Ferrari F2007-V8	*left pit exit against red light		5/22
3	U S GP	Indianapolis	5	Scuderia Ferrari Marlboro	B	2.4 Ferrari F2007-V8			3/22
2	FRENCH GP	Magny Cours	5	Scuderia Ferrari Marlboro	B	2.4 Ferrari F2007-V8	FL		1/22
5	BRITISH GP	Silverstone	5	Scuderia Ferrari Marlboro	B	2.4 Ferrari F2007-V8	*started from pitlane		*4/22
2	EUROPEAN GP	Nürburgring	5	Scuderia Ferrari Marlboro	B	2.4 Ferrari F2007-V8	FL		3/22
13	HUNGARIAN GP	Hungaroring	5	Scuderia Ferrari Marlboro	B	2.4 Ferrari F2007-V8	1 lap behind		14/22
1	TURKISH GP	Istanbul	5	Scuderia Ferrari Marlboro	B	2.4 Ferrari F2007-V8			1/22
ret	ITALIAN GP	Monza	5	Scuderia Ferrari Marlboro	B	2.4 Ferrari F2007-V8	damper in rear suspension		3/22
2	BELGIAN GP	Spa	5	Scuderia Ferrari Marlboro	B	2.4 Ferrari F2007-V8	FL		2/22
6	JAPANESE GP	Suzuka	5	Scuderia Ferrari Marlboro	B	2.4 Ferrari F2007-V8	early race tyre problems		4/22
3	CHINESE GP	Shanghai	5	Scuderia Ferrari Marlboro	B	2.4 Ferrari F2007-V8	FL		3/22
2	BRAZILIAN GP	Interlagos	5	Scuderia Ferrari Marlboro	B	2.4 Ferrari F2007-V8			1/22
	2008 Championship position: 2nd	Wins: 6	Pole positions: 6	Fastest laps: 3		Points scored: 97			
ret	AUSTRALIAN GP	Melbourne	2	Scuderia Ferrari Marlboro	B	2.4 Ferrari F2008-V8	engine		4/22
ret	MALAYSIAN GP	Sepang	2	Scuderia Ferrari Marlboro	B	2.4 Ferrari F2008-V8	spun off		1/22
1	BAHRAIN GP	Sakhir Circuit	2	Scuderia Ferrari Marlboro	B	2.4 Ferrari F2008-V8			2/22
2	SPANISH GP	Barcelona	2	Scuderia Ferrari Marlboro	B	2.4 Ferrari F2008-V8			3/22
1	TURKISH GP	Istanbul	2	Scuderia Ferrari Marlboro	B	2.4 Ferrari F2008-V8			1/20
3	MONACO GP	Monte Carlo	2	Scuderia Ferrari Marlboro	B	2.4 Ferrari F2008-V8	ran off track and lost time		1/20
5	CANADIAN GP	Montreal	2	Scuderia Ferrari Marlboro	B	2.4 Ferrari F2008-V8	fuel-rig malfunction caused extra pitstop		6/20
1	FRENCH GP	Magny Cours	2	Scuderia Ferrari Marlboro	B	2.4 Ferrari F2008-V8			2/20
13	BRITISH GP	Silverstone	2	Scuderia Ferrari Marlboro	B	2.4 Ferrari F2008-V8	spin/2 laps behind		9/20
3	GERMAN GP	Hockenheim	2	Scuderia Ferrari Marlboro	B	2.4 Ferrari F2008-V8	balance and brake problems		2/20
17/ret	HUNGARIAN GP	Hungaroring	2	Scuderia Ferrari Marlboro	B	2.4 Ferrari F2008-V8	engine failure when leading race		3/20
1	EUROPEAN GP	Valencia	2	Scuderia Ferrari Marlboro	B	2.4 Ferrari F2008-V8	FL		1/20
1*	BELGIAN GP	Spa	2	Scuderia Ferrari Marlboro	B	2.4 Ferrari F2008-V8	*1st place car demoted to 3rd place		2/20
6	ITALIAN GP	Monza	2	Scuderia Ferrari Marlboro	B	2.4 Ferrari F2008-V8			6/20

13	SINGAPORE GP	Marina Bay Circuit	2	Scuderia Ferrari Marlboro	B	2.4 Ferrari F2008-V8	*left pit with refuelling hose attached*	1/20
7	JAPANESE GP	Suzuka	2	Scuderia Ferrari Marlboro	B	2.4 Ferrari F2008-V8	*hit Hamilton – drive through penalty/FL*	5/20
2	CHINESE GP	Shanghai	2	Scuderia Ferrari Marlboro	B	2.4 Ferrari F2008-V8		3/20
1	BRAZILIAN GP	Interlagos	2	Scuderia Ferrari Marlboro	B	2.4 Ferrari F2008-V8	*FL/lost championship on final lap*	1/20

2009 Championship position: 11th   Wins: 0   Pole positions: 0   Fastest laps: 1   Points scored: 22

ret	AUSTRALIAN GP	Melbourne	4	Scuderia Ferrari Marlboro	B	2.4 Ferrari F2009-V8	*front suspension*	7/20
9	MALAYSIAN GP	Sepang	4	Scuderia Ferrari Marlboro	B	2.4 Ferrari F2009-V8	*rain-shortened race*	16/20
ret	CHINESE GP	Shanghai Circuit	4	Scuderia Ferrari Marlboro	B	2.4 Ferrari F2009-V8	*electrics*	13/20
14	BAHRAIN GP	Sakhir Circuit	4	Scuderia Ferrari Marlboro	B	2.4 Ferrari F2009-V8	*multiple collision on lap 1/1 lap behind*	8/20
6	SPANISH GP	Barcelona	4	Scuderia Ferrari Marlboro	B	2.4 Ferrari F2009-V8		4/20
4	MONACO GP	Monte Carlo	4	Scuderia Ferrari Marlboro	B	2.4 Ferrari F2009-V8	*FL*	5/20
6	TURKISH GP	Istanbul	4	Scuderia Ferrari Marlboro	B	2.4 Ferrari F2009-V8	*short on downforce*	7/20
4	BRITISH GP	Silverstone	4	Scuderia Ferrari Marlboro	B	2.4 Ferrari F2009-V8		11/20
3	GERMAN GP	Hockenheim	4	Scuderia Ferrari Marlboro	B	2.4 Ferrari F2009-V8		8/20
dns	HUNGARIAN GP	Hungaroring	4	Scuderia Ferrari Marlboro	B	2.4 Ferrari F2009-V8	*seriously injured in qualifying*	(10)/20

2010 Championship position: 6th   Wins: 0   Pole positions: 0   Fastest laps: 0   Points scored: 144

2	BAHRAIN GP	Sakhir Circuit	7	Scuderia Ferrari Marlboro	B	2.4 Ferrari F10 V8		2/24
3	AUSTRALIAN GP	Melbourne	7	Scuderia Ferrari Marlboro	B	2.4 Ferrari F10 V8		5/24
7	MALAYSIAN GP	Sepang	7	Scuderia Ferrari Marlboro	B	2.4 Ferrari F10 V8		21/24
9	CHINESE GP	Shanghai Circuit	7	Scuderia Ferrari Marlboro	B	2.4 Ferrari F10 V8		7/24
6	SPANISH GP	Barcelona	7	Scuderia Ferrari Marlboro	B	2.4 Ferrari F10 V8	*collision – Chandhok – damaged front wing*	9/24
4	MONACO GP	Monte Carlo	7	Scuderia Ferrari Marlboro	B	2.4 Ferrari F10 V8		4/24
7	TURKISH GP	Istanbul Park	7	Scuderia Ferrari Marlboro	B	2.4 Ferrari F10 V8		8/24
15	CANADIAN GP	Montreal	7	Scuderia Ferrari Marlboro	B	2.4 Ferrari F10 V8	*20-sec pen – speeding in pitlane/-1 lap*	7/24
11	EUROPEAN GP	Valencia	7	Scuderia Ferrari Marlboro	B	2.4 Ferrari F10 V8		5/24
15	BRITISH GP	Silverstone	7	Scuderia Ferrari Marlboro	B	2.4 Ferrari F10 V8	*extra pit stop after spin*	7/24
2	GERMAN GP	Hockenheim	7	Scuderia Ferrari Marlboro	B	2.4 Ferrari F10 V8	*allow*	3/24
4	HUNGARIAN GP	Hungaroring	7	Scuderia Ferrari Marlboro	B	2.4 Ferrari F10 V8		4/24
4	BELGIAN GP	Spa	7	Scuderia Ferrari Marlboro	B	2.4 Ferrari F10 V8		6/24
3	ITALIAN GP	Monza	7	Scuderia Ferrari Marlboro	B	2.4 Ferrari F10 V8		3/24
8	SINGAPORE GP	Marina Bay Circuit	7	Scuderia Ferrari Marlboro	B	2.4 Ferrari F10 V8	*no time set/early stop ran long stint	*24/24
ret	JAPANESE GP	Suzuka	7	Scuderia Ferrari Marlboro	B	2.4 Ferrari F10 V8	*accident – ran into Liuzzi on lap 1*	12/24
3	KOREAN GP	Yeongam	7	Scuderia Ferrari Marlboro	B	2.4 Ferrari F10 V8	*two-part race*	6/24
15	BRAZILIAN GP	Interlagos	7	Scuderia Ferrari Marlboro	B	2.4 Ferrari F10 V8	*extra pit stop – loose wheel nut/-1 lap*	9/24
10	ABU DHABI GP	Yas Marina Circuit	7	Scuderia Ferrari Marlboro	B	2.4 Ferrari F10 V8		6/24

2011 Championship position: 6th   Wins: 0   Pole positions: 0   Fastest laps: 2   Points scored: 118

7	AUSTRALIAN GP	Melbourne	5	Scuderia Ferrari Marlboro	P	2.4 Ferrari F150th Italia V8	*9th on road – but 7 & 8th cars dsq/FL*	8/24
5	MALAYSIAN GP	Sepang	5	Scuderia Ferrari Marlboro	P	2.4 Ferrari F150th Italia V8		7/24
6	CHINESE GP	Shanghai Circuit	5	Scuderia Ferrari Marlboro	P	2.4 Ferrari F150th Italia V8		6/24
11	TURKISH GP	Istanbul Park	5	Scuderia Ferrari Marlboro	P	2.4 Ferrari F150th Italia V8	*delayed at pit stops*	10/24
ret	SPANISH GP	Barcelona	5	Scuderia Ferrari Marlboro	P	2.4 Ferrari F150th Italia V8	*gearbox*	8/24
ret	MONACO GP	Monte Carlo	5	Scuderia Ferrari Marlboro	P	2.4 Ferrari F150th Italia V8	*accident after collision*	6/24
6	CANADIAN GP	Montreal	5	Scuderia Ferrari Marlboro	P	2.4 Ferrari F150th Italia V8		3/24
5	EUROPEAN GP	Valencia	5	Scuderia Ferrari Marlboro	P	2.4 Ferrari F150th Italia V8		5/24
5	BRITISH GP	Silverstone	5	Scuderia Ferrari Marlboro	P	2.4 Ferrari F150th Italia V8		4/24
5	GERMAN GP	Hockenheim	5	Scuderia Ferrari Marlboro	P	2.4 Ferrari F150th Italia V8		5/24
6	HUNGARIAN GP	Hungaroring	5	Scuderia Ferrari Marlboro	P	2.4 Ferrari F150th Italia V8	*FL*	4/24
8	BELGIAN GP	Spa	5	Scuderia Ferrari Marlboro	P	2.4 Ferrari F150th Italia V8	*puncture*	6/24
6	ITALIAN GP	Monza	5	Scuderia Ferrari Marlboro	P	2.4 Ferrari F150th Italia V8	*hit by Webber – spin*	6/24
9	SINGAPORE GP	Marina Bay Circuit	5	Scuderia Ferrari Marlboro	P	2.4 Ferrari F150th Italia V8	*hit by Hamilton – puncture*	6/24
7	JAPANESE GP	Suzuka	5	Scuderia Ferrari Marlboro	P	2.4 Ferrari F150th Italia V8	*hit by Hamilton – minor collision damage*	4/24
6	KOREAN GP	Yeongam	5	Scuderia Ferrari Marlboro	P	2.4 Ferrari F150th Italia V8		5/24
ret	INDIAN GP	Buddh Circuit	5	Scuderia Ferrari Marlboro	P	2.4 Ferrari F150th Italia V8	*hit by kerb – damaged front suspension*	6/24
5	ABU DHABI GP	Yas Marina Circuit	5	Scuderia Ferrari Marlboro	P	2.4 Ferrari F150th Italia V8		6/24
5	BRAZILIAN GP	Interlagos	5	Scuderia Ferrari Marlboro	P	2.4 Ferrari F150th Italia V8		7/24

GP Starts: 152   GP Wins: 11   Pole positions: 15   Fastest laps: 14   Points: 582

MAX, Jean (see JEAN, Max)

MAY, Michael (CH) b 18/8/1934, Stuttgart, Germany

1961 Championship position: Unplaced

	Race	Circuit	No	Entrant	Tyres	Capacity/Car/Engine	Comment	Q Pos/Entries
ret	MONACO GP	Monte Carlo	8	Scuderia Colonia	D	1.5 Lotus 18-Climax 4	*oil pipe*	14/21
11	FRENCH GP	Reims	46	Scuderia Colonia	D	1.5 Lotus 18-Climax 4	*4 laps behind*	22/26
dns	GERMAN GP	Nürburgring	25	Scuderia Colonia	D	1.5 Lotus 18-Climax 4	*accident in practice*	27/27

GP Starts: 2   GP Wins: 0   Pole positions: 0   Fastest laps: 0   Points: 0

MAYER, Timmy (USA) b 22/2/1938, Dalton, Pennsylvania – d 28/2/1964, Longford Circuit, Tasmania, Australia

1962 Championship position: Unplaced

	Race	Circuit	No	Entrant	Tyres	Capacity/Car/Engine	Comment	Q Pos/Entries
ret	US GP	Watkins Glen	23	Cooper Car Co	D	1.5 Cooper T53-Climax 4	*ignition*	12/20

GP Starts: 1   GP Wins: 0   Pole positions: 0   Fastest laps: 0   Points: 0

MICHAEL MAY

PRINCIPALLY an engineer, Michael May first caused something of stir when he and his brother, Pierre, turned up at the Nürburgring 1000km race in 1956. Their otherwise standard Porsche 550 Spyder sported a huge rear aerofoil that was way ahead of its time. Some excellent practice times brought a swift protest from Porsche boss Hüschke von Hanstein, which saw the device banned forthwith on the grounds of safety. It would be nearly a decade before Jim Hall and Chaparral utilised the idea to stunning effect.

With the introduction of Formula Junior in 1959, May instantly became one the new category's leading stars, winning the prestigious Monaco race with his Stanguellini. His talent for racing on street circuits was reinforced by a second place at Pau a fortnight later, but after comfortably winning his heat at Albi, the Swiss driver was very lucky indeed to escape unharmed after rolling his car in the final. A second place in the Eifelrennen emphasised his natural talent, but the arrival of the rear-engined Lotus 18s in 1960, and a clutch of very fast British drivers led by Jim Clark, Peter Arundell and Trevor Taylor, pushed May and his fellow Continentals into the margins. The best he could manage at Monaco this time around was a dispirited tenth, lapped by the winner, Clark.

For 1961, May was given a chance to race Wolfgang Seidel's Scuderia Colonia Lotus 18 and he showed some promise, particularly at Monaco. A big practice crash at the Nürburgring, however, persuaded him to retire from the sport to pursue his original vocation, working on fuel injection development with Porsche, for whom he was also a test driver, and then Ferrari.

TIM MAYER

WHILE studying English Literature at Yale in 1959, Tim Mayer began racing an Austin-Healey, finishing fourth overall in the Production Class D after a series of wins. This encouraged him to moved up to Formula Junior for 1960, having purchased a Lotus 18, with which he scored some fine placings before writing off the car at Louisville. He managed to combine his racing activities with national service and raced a Cooper Monaco purchased from Roger Penske, as well as his Formula Junior T56.

It was during the 1962 season that Mayer began to be seen as a real prospect, after recording a number of big wins with his Cooper Formula Junior and taking the SCCA championship in the process. This brought him his only grand prix appearance at Watkins Glen, in an outdated four-cylinder Cooper T53 as the third 'works' car.

Following his discharge from the Army, Tim headed to Europe in mid-1963 to race his Cooper Monaco and secured a seat in Ken Tyrrell's Formula Junior team. Despite his unfamiliarity with the circuits, he scored a number of top-six finishes and, along with his brother, Teddy, arranged to join Bruce McLaren and Cooper to contest the Tasman series in Australia and New Zealand at the beginning of 1964.

Charles Cooper was concerned about Mayer's lack of perceived status 'down under', so Bruce, greatly aided by Eoin Young and sharing the costs with the Mayers, went it alone, effectively setting up the famous McLaren marque in the process. Pitted against the works Brabhams of 'Black Jack' and Denny Hulme, Mayer and his mentor soon had their lightweight Coopers up to speed. Timmy took third place in the New Zealand Grand Prix and then shadowed Bruce home to finish second at Teretonga Park.

The team then journeyed across to Australia, where fuel starvation robbed Mayer of a second place at Sandown Park. He did manage to finish third at Warwick Farm, however, before retiring with engine failure at Lakeside. The series' final race was held at the challenging Longford road circuit in Teretonga. Bruce had already taken the Tasman Championship and Timmy had more than proved himself ready to take up the number-two seat at Cooper for the forthcoming world championship season.

Tragically it was not to be, for when having a real go for the fastest lap in practice, Mayer lost control of his car over a tricky hump at over 130mph. The car became airborne and crashed into a tree, hurling the luckless driver from the wreckage; he died from a broken neck. Doubtless Timmy would have been an integral part of the exciting McLaren team that Bruce and Teddy Mayer would soon develop into grand prix giants.

FRANÇOIS MAZET

IN 1968, François Mazet made a good impact on his debut in the French F3 series, and his promise was fulfilled the following year when he took his nimble Shell-backed Tecno to his country's championship. Defeating rivals such Jean-Pierre Jabouille, Jean-Pierre Jaussaud and Patrick Depailler made him appear to be a potentially top-drawer talent, but his move into Formula 2 in 1970 proved to be a huge disappointment. Despite gaining a drive in a works-assisted Brabham, the Frenchman could only muster two points (from a fifth-place finish at Pau) throughout a troubled year.

Effectively, Mazet was written off as serious talent. His friendship with Jo Siffert led to him driving a Formula 2 Chevron B18C when the F1 ace was committed elsewhere. A fourth place in the non-championship Pau GP was the best result he could muster, but nonetheless 'Seppi' arranged for Mazet to handle his March 701 at Paul Ricard. Qualifying dead last, the Parisian kept out of trouble, but ended up five laps down at the finish.

Aside from single-seaters that year, Mazet also contested a handful of races for Ford Germany in the European Touring Car Championship.

In 1972, Mazet teamed up with Jean Todt to contest the Tour de France in a Ford GT70 rally car. Unfortunately, the potent 3-litre machine went out after an accident and his competition career came to close. Later he was heavily involved with the Essex Petroleum sponsorship of Lotus in the early 1980s, but today is better known for his famous lemon growing business near Menton on the Côte d'Azur.

GASTON MAZZACANE

ARGENTINA has not been well represented in Formula 1 since the days of Carlos Reutemann and, given the opportunities he was afforded, Gaston Mazzacane was not about to add anything significant to the country's illustrious F1 history. After taking his first steps in karting, the young driver proved quite adept at the discipline, winning both regional and national titles in his homeland, before finally making the step up to cars in 1992, initially with a Datsun 280ZX

Having proved that he was no slouch yet again, Gaston returned to open-wheel competition in the hotly contested South American F3 series. Against expectation for a rookie, he managed to record five race wins and attracted attention from Europe, which he realised was where he needed to make his name to progress up the racing ladder.

Despite effectively being a step back down the ladder, Mazzacane appeared initially in the Italian Formula 2000 series, running with proven winners RC Motorsport. Again, he impressed, taking the title at his first attempt, before signing a deal to move up to the national F3 championship with BVM Racing for 1995. He had already enjoyed a couple of

outings in one of RC's F3 machines in 1994, but the BVM team proved no match and Mazzacane slumped to an unrepresentative 17th in the standings.

Disillusioned at the thought of having to spend another year in F3, but buoyed by a brief taste of F3000 with Autosport Racing in 1994, the Argentinian decided to throw in his lot with the higher series for 1996, but the story remained the same. Several low-key appearances and one DNQ punctuated both the 1996 and '97 campaigns, and a switch of teams to the respected Astromega camp did little to reverse his fortunes, with a grand total of two points to show for his efforts. Again disillusioned, Mazzacane quit F3000 to concentrate on finding an F1 drive for 1999 and landed the Minardi test role on the back of sponsorship from Argentina. He split the season with a sports prototype campaign in the International Sportscar Racing Series, which at least yielded a return to the top step of the podium.

Although he did not set the world alight in testing, Mazzacane's F1 role morphed into a full race seat the following season, as part-owner Telefónica pressed for a South American driver to partner Marc Gené. A best finish of eighth at an attrition-strewn European GP punctuated a series of lowly results and retirements; backing or not, Mazzacane was cast off by F1's weakest team, only to resurface at Prost the following year.

Backed by Argentinian TV company PSN, Gaston was an attractive proposition for the cash-strapped French team, but he lasted just four races and two 12th-place finishes before again being released. Despite professing to have secured a drive with the still-born Phoenix team that was supposed to have risen from the ashes of Arrows in 2002, and then being linked to rides in both the IRL and FIA F3000 for 2003, he appeared to have vanished from the international racing radar until he resurfaced at Dale Coyne's Champ Car team in 2004. He contested a competent part-season in place of Tarso Marques before surprisingly stepping down again for the final two races.

Mazaccane reappeared on the international scene at the beginning of 2007, when he took part in the Rolex 24-hours. Unfortunately, the Argentinian was involved in the race's biggest accident when he lost control of his Porsche. Taken to hospital for observation, happily, he was soon released with no lasting injuries. He returned to competition in both touring cars and truck racing, and it was in the latter category that he had another lucky escape from injury in 2009, when he wrote off his Mercedes at Guaporé.

MAZET, François (F) b 26/2/1943, Paris

1971 Championship position: Unplaced

	Race	Circuit	No	Entrant	Tyres	Capacity/Car/Engine	Comment	Q Pos/Entries
13	FRENCH GP	Paul Ricard	34	Jo Siffert Automobiles	F	3.0 March 701-Cosworth V8	5 laps behind	24/24

GP Starts: 1   GP Wins: 0   Pole positions: 0   Fastest laps: 0   Points: 0

MAZZACANE, Gaston (ARG) b 8/5/1975, La Plata

2000 Championship position: Unplaced

	Race	Circuit	No	Entrant	Tyres	Capacity/Car/Engine	Comment	Q Pos/Entries
ret	AUSTRALIAN GP	Melbourne	21	Telefonica Minardi Fondmetal	B	3.0 Minardi M02-Fondmetal Ford-Zetec R V10	gearbox	22/22
10	BRAZILIAN GP	Interlagos	21	Telefonica Minardi Fondmetal	B	3.0 Minardi M02-Fondmetal Ford-Zetec R V10	2 laps behind	21/22
13	SAN MARINO GP	Imola	21	Telefonica Minardi Fondmetal	B	3.0 Minardi M02-Fondmetal Ford-Zetec R V10	2 laps behind	20/22
15	BRITISH GP	Silverstone	21	Telefonica Minardi Fondmetal	B	3.0 Minardi M02-Fondmetal Ford-Zetec R V10	1 lap behind	22/22
15	SPANISH GP	Barcelona	21	Telefonica Minardi Fondmetal	B	3.0 Minardi M02-Fondmetal Ford-Zetec R V10	2 laps behind	22/22
8	EUROPEAN GP	Nürburgring	21	Telefonica Minardi Fondmetal	B	3.0 Minardi M02-Fondmetal Ford-Zetec R V10	2 laps behind	22/22
ret	MONACO GP	Monte Carlo	21	Telefonica Minardi Fondmetal	B	3.0 Minardi M02-Fondmetal Ford-Zetec R V10	crashed at St Dévote	22/22
12	CANADIAN GP	Montreal	21	Telefonica Minardi Fondmetal	B	3.0 Minardi M02-Fondmetal Ford-Zetec R V10	1 lap behind	22/22
ret	FRANCE GP	Magny Cours	21	Telefonica Minardi Fondmetal	B	3.0 Minardi M02-Fondmetal Ford-Zetec R V10	spun off	22/22
12	AUSTRIAN GP	A1-Ring	21	Telefonica Minardi Fondmetal	B	3.0 Minardi M02-Fondmetal Ford-Zetec R V10	3 laps behind	22/22
11	GERMAN GP	Hockenheim	21	Telefonica Minardi Fondmetal	B	3.0 Minardi M02-Fondmetal Ford-Zetec R V10		21/22
ret	HUNGARIAN GP	Hungaroring	21	Telefonica Minardi Fondmetal	B	3.0 Minardi M02-Fondmetal Ford-Zetec R V10	engine	22/22
17	BELGIAN GP	Spa	21	Telefonica Minardi Fondmetal	B	3.0 Minardi M02-Fondmetal Ford-Zetec R V10	2 laps behind	22/22
10	ITALIAN GP	Monza	21	Telefonica Minardi Fondmetal	B	3.0 Minardi M02-Fondmetal Ford-Zetec R V10	1 lap behind	22/22
ret	UNITED STATES GP	Indianapolis	21	Telefonica Minardi Fondmetal	B	3.0 Minardi M02-Fondmetal Ford-Zetec R V10	engine	21/22
15	JAPANESE GP	Suzuka	21	Telefonica Minardi Fondmetal	B	3.0 Minardi M02-Fondmetal Ford-Zetec R V10	2 laps behind	22/22
13/ret	MALAYSIAN GP	Sepang	21	Telefonica Minardi Fondmetal	B	3.0 Minardi M02-Fondmetal Ford-Zetec R V10	6 laps behind	22/22

2001 Championship position: Unplaced

	Race	Circuit	No	Entrant	Tyres	Capacity/Car/Engine	Comment	Q Pos/Entries
ret	AUSTRALIAN GP	Melbourne	23	Prost Acer	M	3.0 Prost AP04-Acer V10	brakes	20/22
12	MALAYSIAN GP	Sepang	23	Prost Acer	M	3.0 Prost AP04-Acer V10	2 laps behind	20/22
ret	BRAZILIAN GP	Interlagos	23	Prost Acer	M	3.0 Prost AP04-Acer V10	clutch	21/22
ret	SAN MARINO GP	Imola	23	Prost Acer	M	3.0 Prost AP04-Acer V10	engine	20/22

GP Starts: 21   GP Wins: 0   Pole positions: 0   Fastest laps: 0   Points: 0

KENNETH McALPINE

THE wealthy Kenneth McAlpine, a member of the famous civil engineering family, was trained as a pilot by the US Navy and later became a flight instructor towards the end of the Second World War. After the hostilities had ceased, he soon found his thrills as a hill-climber and speed-triallist. He also became a major benefactor of the Connaught team, having originally entrusted the race preparation of his Maserati 8CM to Rodney Clarke's Continental Cars Ltd. McAlpine was enthused into supplying the capital to build the Connaught L3 sports car, which was soon followed by their beautifully presented Formula 2 A-Type car, which raced in selected grands prix between 1952 and 1955.

Despite being fully involved in the company's construction projects, McAlpine crammed in as many racing appearances as his busy workload would allow. Faced with the punishing tax regime of the time, Kenneth cleverly bankrolled his racing activities through his part-ownership of Connaught, much of the team's expenditure apparently being a tax-deductible business expense.

Although McAlpine competed in a total of seven grand prix races, his best results were achieved in the less rarefied atmosphere of Libre events, where he took third place in the 1954 Glover Trophy. He enjoyed some success with the team's sports car during this period and finished second in the British Empire Trophy in 1955, his final racing season, before concentrating fully on his business interests, which included McAlpine Helicopters. In 1971, he also oversaw the creation and development of the famous Lamberhurst Vineyard, which subsequently he sold in 1994. He was awarded the OBE for both his contribution to business and his charitable work.

McALPINE, Ken (GB) b 21/9/1920, Chobham, Surrey

1952 Championship position: Unplaced

	Race	Circuit	No	Entrant	Tyres	Capacity/Car/Engine	Comment	Q Pos/Entries
16	BRITISH GP	Silverstone	3	Connaught Engineering	D	2.0 Connaught-Lea Francis A Type 4	6 laps behind	17/32
ret	ITALIAN GP	Monza	28	Connaught Engineering	D	2.0 Connaught-Lea Francis A Type 4	rear suspension	22/35

1953 Championship position: Unplaced

	Race	Circuit	No	Entrant	Tyres	Capacity/Car/Engine	Comment	Q Pos/Entries
ret	DUTCH GP	Zandvoort	28	Connaught Engineering	D	2.0 Connaught-Lea Francis A Type 4	engine	14/20
ret	BRITISH GP	Silverstone	11	Connaught Engineering	D	2.0 Connaught-Lea Francis A Type 4	split hose on startline	13/29
13	GERMAN GP	Nürburgring	16	Connaught Engineering	D	2.0 Connaught-Lea Francis A Type 4	2 laps behind	16/35
nc	ITALIAN GP	Monza	24	Connaught Engineering	D	2.0 Connaught-Lea Francis A Type 4	pit stops/24 laps behind	18/30

1955 Championship position: Unplaced

	Race	Circuit	No	Entrant	Tyres	Capacity/Car/Engine	Comment	Q Pos/Entries
ret	BRITISH GP	Aintree	32	Connaught Engineering	D	2.5 Connaught-Alta B Type 4 str	oil pressure	17/25

GP Starts: 7   GP Wins: 0   Pole positions: 0   Fastest laps: 0   Points: 0

BRUCE McLAREN

OF all the many motor racing fatalities of the era, the death of Bruce McLaren was perhaps the most shocking. By general consensus the safest driver in the sport, his fatal accident while testing his Can-Am McLaren at Goodwood in 1970 was greeted with utter disbelief, despite the high driver death toll at the time.

Having arrived in Europe in March, 1958, virtually unknown, but with the endorsement of Jack Brabham and on a scholarship from the New Zealand Grand Prix Association, McLaren began his career in sensational fashion. In Formula 2 with a works Cooper, he took a class win and fifth overall in the German Grand Prix and, showing a maturity beyond his years, mixed it with seasoned competitors on unfamiliar tracks to such good effect that he finished runner-up in the Autocar F2 championship. Promoted to the F1 works team with Brabham in 1959, Bruce was completely unfazed in the top flight and at the end of the season became the youngest ever grand prix winner (at 22) when he won the US GP at Sebring.

The 1960 season opened with another triumph, this time in Argentina, but for the rest of the year Bruce was content to understudy Brabham as he headed towards a second successive title. There is no doubt that he learned much from his mentor, who moved on at the end of 1961 to build his own cars. Unfortunately, Cooper's fortunes began to decline, although McLaren picked up a fortunate win at Monaco and also won the non-title Reims GP. During this period, he was happy to spend the winter months back home, competing in the Tasman series, which provided him with a number of wins. In 1964, he was forced to enter his own cars 'down under', and thus Bruce McLaren Motor Racing was born.

That year also saw a great ambition fulfilled when he won the New Zealand GP at his eighth attempt. Tragedy struck, however, with the death of Tim Mayer, whom Bruce had taken under his wing; the young American's elder brother, Teddy, stayed on to become a pillar of the new team, which slowly took shape over the next two seasons. Initially the programme centred on the Cooper Zerex Special sports car, later developments of which would lead towards the team's successful Can-Am cars, which formed the basis of McLaren's emergence as a constructor. Meanwhile, Bruce plugged away faithfully at Cooper to the end of the 1965 season, but his various freelance activities, which included racing for Ford in endurance events, had grown to such an extent that a break was inevitable.

Bruce introduced the white Formula 1 McLaren in 1966, but his season was hampered by the lack of a suitable engine and the demands of a sports car programme with the McLaren Elva Oldsmobile, which by then was really taking off in North America. However, the highlight of the year was winning the Le Mans 24-hours for Ford with Chris Amon.

The pace of expansion continued in 1967, when McLaren was totally involved in F1, now with BRM power. However, this was still an interim unit. Indeed, Bruce was glad to race Dan Gurney's second Eagle for a spell after Richie Ginther's sudden retirement rather than use his own machine. A Formula 2 version of the car appeared for the first time, which Bruce drove when sports car and F1 commitments permitted. In addition, he shared the victorious Ford MkII with Mario Andretti at the Sebring 12-hours, and also won rounds of the growing Can-Am series at Monterey and Riverside on his way to the title.

Clearly the task of heading the team, and developing and driving the cars was becoming too much for Bruce to handle on his own, and he tempted Denny Hulme from Brabham for 1968 to take some of the weight off his shoulders. It was a move that showed his wisdom, for he was quite prepared to play second fiddle to the new world champion, although when the mood took him McLaren the racer, for so long closeted, was allowed to re-emerge, as at Brands Hatch, where he unleashed a stunning performance to win the Race of Champions in the bright tangerine M7A. Onlookers that day must have wondered just what reservoirs of talent remained untapped. Shortly afterwards, he took his final grand prix win at Spa, but it was Hulme who led the team's title challenge for the rest of the season. However, the ever-consistent Bruce enjoyed the uper hand in 1969, finishing third in the championship, behind Jackie Stewart and Jacky Ickx. He also took the Can-Am title for the second time, dominating the series with six outright victories and three second places.

Although there were hints of impending retirement, Bruce carried on racing into 1970, when plans were afoot to tackle Indianapolis after the success of the Can-Am cars. In due course, a McLaren would win the Indy 500, but sadly the team's founder and inspiration was not around to witness the success. He perished on a sunny June afternoon when a piece of bodywork flew from the car, sending it out of control. Poor Bruce was killed instantly when the car careered into a disused marshals' post.

Mention the name McLaren today and most people will immediately think of the wonderful sleek silver and red cars that have established so many records. But Ron Dennis, of all people, can surely testify that all those lucky enough either to have met the remarkable New Zealander or seen him in action will never forget the man with the silver helmet in the tangerine car who began it all nearly five decades ago.

McLAREN

McLAREN, Bruce (NZ) b 30/8/1937, Auckland – d 2/6/1970, Goodwood Circuit, Sussex, England

1958 Championship position: Unplaced

	Race	Circuit	No	Entrant	Tyres	Capacity/Car/Engine	Comment	Q Pos/Entries
5*	GERMAN GP (F2)	Nürburgring	20	Cooper Car Co	D	1.5 Cooper T45-Climax 4 F2	*1st in F2 class/no points awarded	15/26
13*	MOROCCAN GP (F2)	Casablanca	52	Cooper Car Co	D	1.5 Cooper T45-Climax 4	*2nd in F2 class	21/25

1959 Championship position: 6th   Wins: 1   Pole positions: 0   Fastest laps: 1 (shared)   Points scored: 16.5

	Race	Circuit	No	Entrant	Tyres	Capacity/Car/Engine	Comment	Q Pos/Entries
5*	MONACO GP	Monte Carlo	22	Cooper Car Co	D	2.2 Cooper T51-Climax 4	*4 laps behind	13/24
5	FRENCH GP	Reims	12	Cooper Car Co	D	2.2 Cooper T51-Climax 4		10/22
3	BRITISH GP	Aintree	16	Cooper Car Co	D	2.5 Cooper T51-Climax 4	FL (shared with Moss)	6/30
ret	GERMAN GP	AVUS	2	Cooper Car Co	D	2.5 Cooper T51-Climax 4	4th in heat 1/clutch – heat 2	9/16
ret	PORTUGUESE GP	Monsanto	3	Cooper Car Co	D	2.5 Cooper T51-Climax 4	clutch	8/16
ret	ITALIAN GP	Monza	8	Cooper Car Co	D	2.5 Cooper T51-Climax 4	engine	9/21
1	US GP	Sebring	9	Cooper Car Co	D	2.5 Cooper T51-Climax 4		10/19

1960 Champßionship position: 2nd   Wins: 1   Pole positions: 0   Fastest laps: 1   Points scored: 37

	Race	Circuit	No	Entrant	Tyres	Capacity/Car/Engine	Comment	Q Pos/Entries
1	ARGENTINE GP	Buenos Aires	16	Cooper Car Co	D	2.5 Cooper T51-Climax 4		12/22
2	MONACO GP	Monte Carlo	10	Cooper Car Co	D	2.5 Cooper T53-Climax 4	FL	11/24
ret	DUTCH GP	Zandvoort	12	Cooper Car Co	D	2.5 Cooper T53-Climax 4	driveshaft	9/21
2	BELGIAN GP	Spa	4	Cooper Car Co	D	2.5 Cooper T53-Climax 4		14/18
3	FRENCH GP	Reims	18	Cooper Car Co	D	2.5 Cooper T53-Climax 4		7/23
4	BRITISH GP	Silverstone	2	Cooper Car Co	D	2.5 Cooper T53-Climax 4	1 lap behind	3/25
2	PORTUGUESE GP	Oporto	4	Cooper Car Co	D	2.5 Cooper T53-Climax 4		6/16
3	US GP	Riverside	3	Cooper Car Co	D	2.5 Cooper T53-Climax 4		10/23

1961 Championship position: 7th=   Wins: 0   Pole positions: 0   Fastest laps: 0   Points scored: 11

	Race	Circuit	No	Entrant	Tyres	Capacity/Car/Engine	Comment	Q Pos/Entries
6	MONACO GP	Monte Carlo	26	Cooper Car Co	D	1.5 Cooper T55-Climax 4	5 laps behind	7/21
12	DUTCH GP	Zandvoort	11	Cooper Car Co	D	1.5 Cooper T55-Climax 4	2 laps behind	14/17
ret	BELGIAN GP	Spa	30	Cooper Car Co	D	1.5 Cooper T55-Climax 4	ignition	15/25
5	FRENCH GP	Reims	4	Cooper Car Co	D	1.5 Cooper T55-Climax 4		8/26
8	BRITISH GP	Aintree	14	Cooper Car Co	D	1.5 Cooper T55-Climax 4	1 lap behind	=14/30
6	GERMAN GP	Nürburgring	2	Cooper Car Co	D	1.5 Cooper T55-Climax 4		12/27
3	ITALIAN GP	Monza	12	Cooper Car Co	D	1.5 Cooper T55-Climax 4		14/33
4	US GP	Watkins Glen	2	Cooper Car Co	D	1.5 Cooper T55-Climax 4		=3/19

1962 Championship position: 3rd   Wins: 1   Pole positions: 0   Fastest laps: 1   Points scored: 32

	Race	Circuit	No	Entrant	Tyres	Capacity/Car/Engine	Comment	Q Pos/Entries
ret	DUTCH GP	Zandvoort	6	Cooper Car Co	D	1.5 Cooper T60-Climax V8	gearbox/FL	5/20
1	MONACO GP	Monte Carlo	14	Cooper Car Co	D	1.5 Cooper T60-Climax V8		=3/21
ret	BELGIAN GP	Spa	25	Cooper Car Co	D	1.5 Cooper T60-Climax V8	oil pressure	2/20
4	FRENCH GP	Rouen	22	Cooper Car Co	D	1.5 Cooper T60-Climax V8	pit stop/3 laps behind	3/17
3	BRITISH GP	Aintree	16	Cooper Car Co	D	1.5 Cooper T60-Climax V8		=4/21
5	GERMAN GP	Nürburgring	9	Cooper Car Co	D	1.5 Cooper T60-Climax V8		5/30
3	ITALIAN GP	Monza	28	Cooper Car Co	D	1.5 Cooper T60-Climax V8		=4/30
3	US GP	Watkins Glen	21	Cooper Car Co	D	1.5 Cooper T60-Climax V8	1 lap behind	6/20
2	SOUTH AFRICAN GP	East London	8	Cooper Car Co	D	1.5 Cooper T60-Climax V8		=6/17

1963 Championship position: 6th   Wins: 0   Pole positions: 0   Fastest laps: 0   Points scored: 17

	Race	Circuit	No	Entrant	Tyres	Capacity/Car/Engine	Comment	Q Pos/Entries
3	MONACO GP	Monte Carlo	7	Cooper Car Co	D	1.5 Cooper T66-Climax V8		8/17
2	BELGIAN GP	Spa	14	Cooper Car Co	D	1.5 Cooper T66-Climax V8		5/20
ret	DUTCH GP	Zandvoort	20	Cooper Car Co	D	1.5 Cooper T66-Climax V8	gearbox	3/19
12/ret	FRENCH GP	Reims	10	Cooper Car Co	D	1.5 Cooper T66-Climax V8	ignition/11 laps behind	6/21
ret	BRITISH GP	Silverstone	6	Cooper Car Co	D	1.5 Cooper T66-Climax V8	engine	6/23
ret	GERMAN GP	Nürburgring	5	Cooper Car Co	D	1.5 Cooper T66-Climax V8	car failure – crashed	5/26
3	ITALIAN GP	Monza	18	Cooper Car Co	D	1.5 Cooper T66-Climax V8	1 lap behind	8/28
11/ret	US GP	Watkins Glen	3	Cooper Car Co	D	1.5 Cooper T66-Climax V8	fuel pump/36 laps behind	11/21
ret	MEXICAN GP	Mexico City	3	Cooper Car Co	D	1.5 Cooper T66-Climax V8	engine	6/21
4	SOUTH AFRICAN GP	East London	10	Cooper Car Co	D	1.5 Cooper T66-Climax V8	1 lap behind	9/21

1964 Championship position: 7th   Wins: 0   Pole positions: 0   Fastest laps: 0   Points scored: 13

	Race	Circuit	No	Entrant	Tyres	Capacity/Car/Engine	Comment	Q Pos/Entries
ret	MONACO GP	Monte Carlo	10	Cooper Car Co	D	1.5 Cooper T66-Climax V8	oil leak – main bearing	10/20
dns	" " "	10	Cooper Car Co	D	1.5 Cooper T73-Climax V8	practice only	– / –
7	DUTCH GP	Zandvoort	24	Cooper Car Co	D	1.5 Cooper T73-Climax V8	2 laps behind	5/18
2	BELGIAN GP	Spa	20	Cooper Car Co	D	1.5 Cooper T73-Climax V8		=6/20
6	FRENCH GP	Rouen	12	Cooper Car Co	D	1.5 Cooper T73-Climax V8	1 lap behind	7/17
ret	BRITISH GP	Brands Hatch	9	Cooper Car Co	D	1.5 Cooper T73-Climax V8	gearbox	6/25
ret	GERMAN GP	Nürburgring	9	Cooper Car Co	D	1.5 Cooper T73-Climax V8	engine	7/24
ret	AUSTRIAN GP	Zeltweg	9	Cooper Car Co	D	1.5 Cooper T73-Climax V8	engine	9/20
2	ITALIAN GP	Monza	26	Cooper Car Co	D	1.5 Cooper T73-Climax V8		5/25
ret	US GP	Watkins Glen	9	Cooper Car Co	D	1.5 Cooper T73-Climax V8	engine	5/19
7	MEXICAN GP	Mexico City	9	Cooper Car Co	D	1.5 Cooper T73-Climax V8	1 lap behind	10/19

1965 Championship position: 8th=   Wins: 0   Pole positions: 0   Fastest laps: 0   Points scored: 10

	Race	Circuit	No	Entrant	Tyres	Capacity/Car/Engine	Comment	Q Pos/Entries
5	SOUTH AFRICAN GP	East London	9	Cooper Car Co	D	1.5 Cooper T77-Climax V8	1 lap behind	8/25
5	MONACO GP	Monte Carlo	7	Cooper Car Co	D	1.5 Cooper T77-Climax V8	2 laps behind	7/17
3	BELGIAN GP	Spa	4	Cooper Car Co	D	1.5 Cooper T77-Climax V8	1 lap behind	9/21
ret	FRENCH GP	Clermont Ferrand	18	Cooper Car Co	D	1.5 Cooper T77-Climax V8	steering	9/17
10	BRITISH GP	Silverstone	9	Cooper Car Co	D	1.5 Cooper T77-Climax V8	3 laps behind	11/23
ret	DUTCH GP	Zandvoort	18	Cooper Car Co	D	1.5 Cooper T77-Climax V8	transmission	9/17
ret	GERMAN GP	Nürburgring	11	Cooper Car Co	D	1.5 Cooper T77-Climax V8	gear selection	10/22
5	ITALIAN GP	Monza	16	Cooper Car Co	D	1.5 Cooper T77-Climax V8	1 lap behind	11/23
ret	US GP	Watkins Glen	9	Cooper Car Co	D	1.5 Cooper T77-Climax V8	no oil pressure	9/18

	Race	Circuit		Entrant		Car/Engine	Notes	
ret	MEXICAN GP	Mexico City	9	Cooper Car Co	D	1.5 Cooper T77-Climax V8	*gear selection*	15/18

1966 Championship position: 14th= | Wins: 0 | Pole positions: 0 | Fastest laps: 0 | Points scored: 3

ret	MONACO GP	Monte Carlo	2	Bruce McLaren Motor Racing	F	3.0 McLaren M2B-Ford V8	*oil leak*	=10/16
dns	BELGIAN GP	Spa	24	Bruce McLaren Motor Racing	F	3.0 McLaren M2B-Serenissima V8	*bearings in practice*	(16)/19
6	BRITISH GP	Brands Hatch	14	Bruce McLaren Motor Racing	F	3.0 McLaren M2B-Serenissima V8	*2 laps behind*	13/20
dns	DUTCH GP	Zandvoort	20	Bruce McLaren Motor Racing	F	3.0 McLaren M2B-Serenissima V8	*engine in practice*	(14)/18
5	US GP	Watkins Glen	17	Bruce McLaren Motor Racing	F	3.0 McLaren M2B-Ford V8	*3 laps behind*	11/19
ret	MEXICAN GP	Mexico City	17	Bruce McLaren Motor Racing	F	3.0 McLaren M2B-Ford V8	*engine*	15/19

1967 Championship position: 14th | Wins: 0 | Pole positions: 0 | Fastest laps: 0 | Points scored: 3

4	MONACO GP	Monte Carlo	16	Bruce McLaren Motor Racing	G	2.1 McLaren M4B-BRM V8	*pit stop – battery/3 laps behind*	=9/18
ret	DUTCH GP	Zandvoort	17	Bruce McLaren Motor Racing	G	2.1 McLaren M4B-BRM V8	*spun off*	14/17
ret	FRENCH GP	Le Mans	8	Anglo American Racers	G	3.0 Eagle T1G-Weslake V12	*ignition drive*	5/15
ret	BRITISH GP	Silverstone	10	Anglo American Racers	G	3.0 Eagle T1G-Weslake V12	*engine*	10/21
ret	GERMAN GP	Nürburgring	10	Anglo American Racers	G	3.0 Eagle T1G-Weslake V12	*oil pipe leak*	6/25
7	CANADIAN GP	Mosport Park	19	Bruce McLaren Motor Racing	G	3.0 McLaren M5A-BRM V12	*pit stop – battery/4 laps behind*	6/19
ret	ITALIAN GP	Monza	4	Bruce McLaren Motor Racing	G	3.0 McLaren M5A-BRM V12	*engine*	3/18
ret	US GP	Watkins Glen	14	Bruce McLaren Motor Racing	G	3.0 McLaren M5A-BRM V12	*water pipe*	9/18
ret	MEXICAN GP	Mexico City	14	Bruce McLaren Motor Racing	G	3.0 McLaren M5A-BRM V12	*oil pressure*	8/19

1968 Championship position: 5th | Wins: 1 | Pole positions: 0 | Fastest laps: 0 | Points scored: 22

ret	SPANISH GP	Jarama	2	Bruce McLaren Motor Racing	G	3.0 McLaren M7A-Cosworth V8	*oil loss*	=4/14
ret	MONACO GP	Monte Carlo	14	Bruce McLaren Motor Racing	G	3.0 McLaren M7A-Cosworth V8	*spun off*	7/10
1	BELGIAN GP	Spa	5	Bruce McLaren Motor Racing	G	3.0 McLaren M7A-Cosworth V8		6/18
ret	DUTCH GP	Zandvoort	2	Bruce McLaren Motor Racing	G	3.0 McLaren M7A-Cosworth V8	*crashed*	8/19
8	FRENCH GP	Rouen	10	Bruce McLaren Motor Racing	G	3.0 McLaren M7A-Cosworth V8	*pit stop – tyres/4 laps behind*	6/18
7	BRITISH GP	Brands Hatch	2	Bruce McLaren Motor Racing	G	3.0 McLaren M7A-Cosworth V8	*3 laps behind*	=10/20
13	GERMAN GP	Nürburgring	2	Bruce McLaren Motor Racing	G	3.0 McLaren M7A-Cosworth V8	*1 lap behind*	16/20
ret	ITALIAN GP	Monza	2	Bruce McLaren Motor Racing	G	3.0 McLaren M7A-Cosworth V8	*oil loss*	2/24
2	CANADIAN GP	St Jovite	2	Bruce McLaren Motor Racing	G	3.0 McLaren M7A-Cosworth V8	*1 lap behind*	8/22
6	US GP	Watkins Glen	2	Bruce McLaren Motor Racing	G	3.0 McLaren M7A-Cosworth V8	*pit stop – fuel/5 laps behind*	10/21
2	MEXICAN GP	Mexico City	2	Bruce McLaren Motor Racing	G	3.0 McLaren M7A-Cosworth V8		9/21

1969 Championship position: 3rd | Wins: 0 | Pole positions: 0 | Fastest laps: 0 | Points scored: 26

5	SOUTH AFRICAN GP	Kyalami	6	Bruce McLaren Motor Racing	G	3.0 McLaren M7A-Cosworth V8	*1 lap behind*	=7/18
2	SPANISH GP	Montjuich Park	6	Bruce McLaren Motor Racing	G	3.0 McLaren M7C-Cosworth V8	*2 laps behind*	13/14
5	MONACO GP	Monte Carlo	4	Bruce McLaren Motor Racing	G	3.0 McLaren M7C-Cosworth V8	*1 lap behind*	11/16
ret	DUTCH GP	Zandvoort	6	Bruce McLaren Motor Racing	G	3.0 McLaren M7C-Cosworth V8	*front stub axle*	6/15
4	FRENCH GP	Clermont Ferrand	5	Bruce McLaren Motor Racing	G	3.0 McLaren M7C-Cosworth V8	*1 lap behind*	7/13
3	BRITISH GP	Silverstone	6	Bruce McLaren Motor Racing	G	3.0 McLaren M7C-Cosworth V8	*1 lap behind*	=7/17
3	GERMAN GP	Nürburgring	10	Bruce McLaren Motor Racing	G	3.0 McLaren M7C-Cosworth V8		8/24
4	ITALIAN GP	Monza	18	Bruce McLaren Motor Racing	G	3.0 McLaren M7C-Cosworth V8		5/15
5	CANADIAN GP	Mosport Park	4	Bruce McLaren Motor Racing	G	3.0 McLaren M7C-Cosworth V8	*3 laps behind*	=8/20
ret/dns*	US GP	Watkins Glen	6	Bruce McLaren Motor Racing	G	3.0 McLaren M7C-Cosworth V8	**engine on parade lap*	(6)/18
ret	MEXICAN GP	Mexico City	6	Bruce McLaren Motor Racing	G	3.0 McLaren M7C-Cosworth V8	*fuel system*	7/17

1970 Championship position: 14th | Wins: 0 | Pole positions: 0 | Fastest laps: 0 | Points scored: 6

ret	SOUTH AFRICAN GP	Kyalami	5	Bruce McLaren Motor Racing	G	3.0 McLaren M14A-Cosworth V8	*engine*	10/24
2	SPANISH GP	Jarama	11	Bruce McLaren Motor Racing	G	3.0 McLaren M14A-Cosworth V8	*1 lap behind*	12/22
ret	MONACO GP	Monte Carlo	12	Bruce McLaren Motor Racing	G	3.0 McLaren M14A-Cosworth V8	*hit chicane – suspension damage*	10/21

GP Starts: 100 (101) GP Wins: 4 Pole positions: 0 Fastest laps: 3 Points: 196.5

Bruce McLaren had the immense satisfaction of scoring his own team's maiden grand prix victory in the 1968 Belgian Grand Prix. Although it had been a lucky win, after six years without a victory, the Kiwi savoured his success.

ALLAN McNISH

HAVING attempted to gain a place in Formula 1 by acting as a hardworking and uncomplaining test driver on and off for 13 years, Allan McNish only ever enjoyed one full season of grand prix racing with Toyota, by which time the talented Scot had established himself in sports car racing with Audi. He would go on to become one of the modern-day greats in the category.

McNish began racing in karts when he was 11 years old and quickly proved his ability – aided by his diminutive stature – by landing Scottish and British titles over a six-year period. After success in Formula Ford, he was teamed with Mika Häkkinen to contest both the British Formula Vauxhall and European Formula Opel championships. The pair proved to be the drivers to beat in 1988, taking race wins in both categories and sealing the two titles between them, McNish winning the British crown and finishing as runner-up in Europe. Both graduated to F3 with Marlboro the following year, when Allan joined the top West Surrey Racing squad, where he immediately became a front-runner and ended up battling for the title with Australia's David Brabham, only losing out at the final round.

McNish secured a test-driver role at McLaren for 1990 and also a top seat in F3000 at DAMS, for whom he scored two wins in his debut year, looking well set for an eventual rise to the top tier. Things didn't go as planned for the Scot, however, and he failed to build on his early promise, being released by McLaren to find a home with Benetton as a test driver in the hope of gaining an F1 seat alongside Michael Schumacher. As it transpired, that call never came, and he pursued his on-off F3000 career until the end of 1995. After failing to break into Indy cars, he decided to take up an offer to race for Porsche in North America in 1997, and three wins in the GT class earned him a works drive at Le Mans the following year, when he triumphed in the 911 GT1. For 2000, he made the switch to the Audi marque, where he took six wins and claimed the ALMS title in fine style.

No doubt Allan's longstanding reputation as a test driver helped persuade Toyota to take him on board with the promise of a seat for the 2002 season alongside Mika Salo. After much anticipation, his year in F1 was something of an anticlimax. A possible championship point in Malaysia was lost after a delayed pit stop cost him time, and by the end of the year both he and Salo were out. So it was back to test-driver duties once more, this time with Renault in 2003, but with Fernando Alonso and Jarno Trulli firmly ensconsed, there was no likelihood of an F1 drive.

McNish soon made a welcome return to Audi, where he immediately won the Sebring 12-hour race, followed by ELMS wins at Silverstone and in the Nürburgring 1000km. In 2006 and 2007, paired with Rinaldo Capello, he won two more ALMS titles, chalking up ten outright wins in the LMP1 Audi. In 2008, he claimed a second win at Le Mans (with Capello and Tom Kristensen) and continued to be one of the leading contenders for victory as the German marque battled head to head with Peugeot.

In the 2011 Le Mans 24-hour race, McNish was extremely lucky to escape without injury after his Audi touched a slower car and cart-wheeled to destruction against the tyre barriers. The Scot bounced back, however, to take his fourth win at Sebring with the Audi R18 in 2012.

McNISH, Allan (GB) b 29/12/1969, Dumfries, Scotland

	Race	Circuit	No	Entrant	Tyres	Car/Engine	Comment	Q Pos/Entries
	2002 Championship position: Unplaced							
ret	AUSTRALIAN GP	Melbourne	25	Panasonic Toyota Racing	M	3.0 Toyota TF102-V10	multiple accident at start	16/22
7	MALAYSIAN GP	Sepang	25	Panasonic Toyota Racing	M	3.0 Toyota TF102-V10	bungled tyre stop/1 lap behind	19/22
ret	BRAZILIAN GP	Interlagos	25	Panasonic Toyota Racing	M	3.0 Toyota TF102-V10	spun off	16/22
ret	SAN MARINO GP	Imola	25	Panasonic Toyota Racing	M	3.0 Toyota TF102-V10	transmission failure on grid	17/22
8	SPANISH GP	Barcelona	25	Panasonic Toyota Racing	M	3.0 Toyota TF102-V10	1 lap behind	19/22
9	AUSTRIAN GP	A1-Ring	25	Panasonic Toyota Racing	M	3.0 Toyota TF102-V10		14/22
ret	MONACO GP	Monte Carlo	25	Panasonic Toyota Racing	M	3.0 Toyota TF102-V10	clipped kerb and spun into barrier	10/22
ret	CANADIAN GP	Montreal	25	Panasonic Toyota Racing	M	3.0 Toyota TF102-V10	collision de la Rosa – later spun off	20/22
14	EUROPEAN GP	Nürburgring	25	Panasonic Toyota Racing	M	3.0 Toyota TF102-V10	painful shoulder/1 lap behind	13/22
ret	BRITISH GP	Silverstone	25	Panasonic Toyota Racing	M	3.0 Toyota TF102-V10	clutch failure on line at start	15/22
11/ret	FRENCH GP	Magny Cours	25	Panasonic Toyota Racing	M	3.0 Toyota TF102-V10	engine/7 laps behind	17/22
ret	GERMAN GP	Hockenheim	25	Panasonic Toyota Racing	M	3.0 Toyota TF102-V10	engine	17/22
14	HUNGARIAN GP	Hungaroring	25	Panasonic Toyota Racing	M	3.0 Toyota TF102-V10	2 laps behind	18/20
9	BELGIAN GP	Spa	25	Panasonic Toyota Racing	M	3.0 Toyota TF102-V10	1 lap behind	13/20
ret	ITALIAN GP	Monza	25	Panasonic Toyota Racing	M	3.0 Toyota TF102-V10	damaged rear suspension	13/20
15	UNITED STATES GP	Indianapolis	25	Panasonic Toyota Racing	M	3.0 Toyota TF102-V10	2 laps behind	16/20
dns	JAPANESE GP	Suzuka	25	Panasonic Toyota Racing	M	3.0 Toyota TF102-V10	heavy practice accident	(18)/20
	2003 Championship position: Unplaced							
app	AUSTRALIAN GP	Melbourne	34	Mild Seven Renault F1 Team	B	3.0 Renault R23-V10	ran as 3rd driver in private testing	– / –
app	MALAYSIAN GP	Sepang	34	Mild Seven Renault F1 Team	B	3.0 Renault R23-V10	ran as 3rd driver in private testing	– / –
app	BRAZILIAN GP	Interlagos	34	Mild Seven Renault F1 Team	B	3.0 Renault R23-V10	ran as 3rd driver in private testing	– / –
app	SAN MARINO GP	Imola	34	Mild Seven Renault F1 Team	B	3.0 Renault R23-V10	ran as 3rd driver in private testing	– / –
app	SPANISH GP	Barcelona	34	Mild Seven Renault F1 Team	B	3.0 Renault R23-V10	ran as 3rd driver in private testing	– / –
app	AUSTRIAN GP	A1-Ring	34	Mild Seven Renault F1 Team	B	3.0 Renault R23-V10	ran as 3rd driver in private testing	– / –
app	MONACO GP	Monte Carlo	34	Mild Seven Renault F1 Team	B	3.0 Renault R23-V10	ran as 3rd driver in private testing	– / –
app	CANADIAN GP	Montreal	34	Mild Seven Renault F1 Team	B	3.0 Renault R23-V10	ran as 3rd driver in private testing	– / –
app	EUROPEAN GP	Nürburgring	34	Mild Seven Renault F1 Team	B	3.0 Renault R23-V10	ran as 3rd driver in private testing	– / –
app	BRITISH GP	Silverstone	34	Mild Seven Renault F1 Team	B	3.0 Renault R23-V10	ran as 3rd driver in private testing	– / –
	GP Starts: 16 GP Wins: 0 Pole positions: 0 Fastest laps: 0 Points: 0							

GRAHAM McRAE

ANOTHER Kiwi driver-constructor who followed in the eminent footsteps of the late Bruce McLaren, Graham McRae was a tough and forthright competitor who found much success outside the rarified world of Formula 1.

From an engineering background, McRae began his racing activities with homebuilt specials, followed by an MG and a Jaguar, paid for by his mechanical skills. At the end of 1967, he bought a Brabham BT6 Formula Junior car that gradually he developed into his first self-built McRae chassis. This car took him to the national formula championship, and with it the prize of a trip to Europe for 1969.

McRae campaigned a well-worn Brabham BT23C with mixed results in a number of European Formula 2 championship races, taking a fourth place on aggregate at Zolder. In the less competitive national Formula Libre events, however, he notched wins at Silverstone and Brands Hatch. With his money all gone, he headed home to New Zealand and managed to obtain a drive in a McLaren M10A, with which he raced very successfully in the winter months, taking victories at Invercargill and Surfers Paradise.

Fifth place in the Tasman series and another Gold Star championship with his own McRae brought about a swift return to Britain, this time with a McLaren M10B to challenge for honours in the Guards F5000 championship. He talked up his chances big time, which soon earned him the nickname 'Cassius'. Like the famous boxer,

McRae proved to be a very tough competitor, matching the likes of Peter Gethin and Frank Gardner, and despite enduring several high-speed shunts, he finally took a win at the season's finale at Brands Hatch.

The car was shipped 'down under' for the 1971 Tasman Series, where McRae emerged as the worthy champion, having taken a trio wins in the process. Later in the year, he was back in Europe with the M10B and carried on his winning ways, taking three victories before a very nasty accident at Hockenhiem left him with burns to his hands. He was soon back in business, however, building his own F5000 car under the Leda Cars banner and sponsored by STP. The Leda GM1 won the New Zealander a second successive Tasman title, before he took on a punishing schedule of races in championships on both sides of the Atlantic.

To his credit, McRae lived up to his words. He was the man to beat in the Rothmans Series before heading Stateside, to clinch the L & M title against a strong field. Then he returned to Europe, where he found backing to help buy the Leda concern. He finished third in the UK series, but could well have beaten Gijs van Lennep and Brian Redman had he not been competing on two fronts. Success continued when he took a third consecutive Tasman title at the beginning of 1973, before embarking on yet another two-pronged attack on F5000. It was a frustrating season, however, that yielded little save for a single victory at Mallory Park.

Even so, that year, McRae did take part in the two biggest events of his career. His STP backing brought him a drive in the Indianapolis 500. The event, marred by rain and postponements, was a tragic one, but despite his retirement, he was accorded the honour of top rookie. His only grand prix appearance came a few weeks later, but it was less than a happy experience, for his race lasted less than one lap after the throttle slides of his Williams jammed. The forthright driver was quick to voice his displeasure at the poor preparation of his car.

McRae then surprised many by suddenly selling off the manufacturing side of his business to Roger Penske, before concentrating his efforts on piloting his beautifully prepared McRae GM2. A bid for a fourth consecutive Tasman Championship foundered in 1974 and he endured little luck thereafter as F5000 declined as a category. In retirement, he went into business in Auckland building replica Porches, before ill health curtailed his activities.

McRAE, Graham (NZ) b 5/3/1940, Wellington

	Race	Circuit	No	Entrant	Tyres	Capacity/Car/Engine	Comment	Q Pos/Entries
1973	Championship position: Unplaced							
ret	BRITISH GP	Silverstone	26	Frank Williams Racing Cars	F	3.0 Iso Marlboro IR-Cosworth V8	*sticking throttle on lap 1*	28/29
	GP Starts: 1	GP Wins: 0	Pole positions: 0	Fastest laps: 0	Points: 0			

CARLOS MENDITÉGUY

A FINE all-round sportsman and top-ranked polo player in the early 1940s, Carlos Menditéguy was also a scratch golfer who began his racing successes in 1950, when he won at Mar del Plata in a Ferrari sports car. However, it was in the 1951 Perón Cup races that his performances in an old Alfa Romeo took the eye. There were two big events held early in the following year, and 'Charly' took sixth in his Maserati in the opening race, in front of an estimated 550,000 fans. For the second race a week later, he was lent a Ferrari and showed his ability by finishing second only to Juan Fangio.

From then on, Carlos was a regular local attraction when the big European teams visited for the grands prix and the accompanying Buenos Aires Libre races.

In 1953, Menditéguy found a place on the Gordini team for the very first world championship race to be held in Argentina, but he was forced to retire by a gearbox failure. He would not even make the start a year later, after the engine in the Marimón 2-litre Maserati blew up during practice.

In 1955, Menditéguy was a guest driver in the Maserati works team, but he was still out of luck, collecting Pablo Birger on lap two. In a race held in scorching heat, the Argentinian was then employed as a relief driver in the number 26 machine before it cried enough. However, he did record a sixth place in the Buenos Aires City Grand Prix. Later in the season, he was invited to take part in the Italian Grand Prix, where he drove sensibly to take fifth place, after good battle with Umberto Magioli's Ferrari.

In the 1956 Argentine GP, Menditéguy led the race until, missing a gear, he broke a half-shaft and slid the Maserati into a fence. Another fine drive in the Mendoza GP yielded only fourth place, after low oil pressure had blunted his challenge, but he did share the winning Maserati sports car with Stirling Moss in the Buenos Aires 1000km.

A very fine third place in the 1957 Argentine Grand Prix persuaded Maserati to give him an opportunity to race in Europe, but he had an unhappy sojourn, feeling that his car was the least well prepared, while the team opined that he was too hard on the machinery. In mid-season, he returned to Argentina in disgust.

In 1958, Carlos took a seventh in the Argentine GP, a race in which he suffered several spectacular spins and made a pit stop for refreshment! He actually missed the start of the Buenos Aires City GP, his place on the grid being taken by Paco Godia. When Carlos finally arrived, he soon took over the Maserati and went on to record third place on aggregate. In 1960, in the last Argentine Grand Prix for more than a decade, he showed his talent had not deserted him by piloting a Centro Sud Cooper into fourth place.

Apart from his single-seater adventures, Menditéguy was a frequent competitor in the Turismo Carretera, the fearsome long-distance road races held on the open roads of Argentina. Although he was always a strong factor, often taking stage wins, he never achieved his ambition of winning the event outright. In the Turismo Carretera Gran Premio of 1963, when just 16km from the finish, his car broke down. He handed his co-driver, 'Negro' Linares, his lighter, and told him to pour a little petrol on the car and burn it.

Carlos then became a successful horse trainer, before the onset of diabetes and Parkinson's disease. He died in 1973 from a heart attack following an operation. He was buried in La Recoleta Cemetery in Buenos Aires, where his casket can be seen through a glass window on the north side of the family vault.

MENDITÉGUY, Carlos (RA) b 10/8/1915, Buenos Aires – d 28/4/1973 Buenos Aires

	Race	Circuit	No	Entrant	Tyres	Capacity/Car/Engine	Comment	Q Pos/Entries
	1953 Championship position: Unplaced							
ret	ARGENTINE GP	Buenos Aires	32	Equipe Gordini	E	2.0 Gordini Type 16 6	gearbox	10/16
	1954 Championship position: Unplaced							
dns	ARGENTINE GP	Buenos Aires	36	Onofre Marimón	P	2.0 Maserati A6GCM/250F 6	engine in practice	(9)/18
	1955 Championship position: 12=	Wins: 0	Pole positions: 0	Fastest laps: 0	Points scored: 2			
ret	ARGENTINE GP	Buenos Aires	24	Officine Alfieri Maserati	P	2.5 Maserati 250F 6	crashed	13/22
ret	" "	26	Officine Alfieri Maserati	P	2.5 Maserati 250F 6	Bucci/Schell co-drove/fuel feed	– / –
5	ITALIAN GP	Monza	34	Officine Alfieri Maserati	P	2.5 Maserati 250F 6	1 lap behind	16/22
	1956 Championship position: Unplaced							
ret	ARGENTINE GP	Buenos Aires	6	Officine Alfieri Maserati	P	2.5 Maserati 250F 6	half-shaft/led race	6/15
	1957 Championship position: 12th=	Wins: 0	Pole positions: 0	Fastest laps: 0	Points scored: 4			
3	ARGENTINE GP	Buenos Aires	8	Officine Alfieri Maserati	P	2.5 Maserati 250F 6	1 lap behind	8/16
ret	MONACO GP	Monte Carlo	36	Officine Alfieri Maserati	P	2.5 Maserati 250F 6	crashed at chicane	7/21
ret	FRENCH GP	Rouen	8	Officine Alfieri Maserati	P	2.5 Maserati 250F 6	engine	9/15
ret	BRITISH GP	Aintree	8	Officine Alfieri Maserati	P	2.5 Maserati 250F 6	transmission	11/19
	1958 Championship position: Unplaced							
7	ARGENTINE GP	Buenos Aires	6	Scuderia Sud Americana	P	2.5 Maserati 250F 6	4 laps behind	6/10
	1960 Championship position: 16th=	Wins: 0	Pole positions: 0	Fastest laps: 0	Points scored: 3			
4	ARGENTINE GP	Buenos Aires	6	Scuderia Centro Sud	D	2.5 Cooper T51-Maserati 4		12/22
	GP Starts: 10 Pole positions: 0 Fastest laps: 0 Points: 9							

ARTURO MERZARIO

KNOWN as 'Little Art', Arturo Merzario made his name in the late 1960s with works Fiat Abarths in both GT and European mountain-climb events. If one race in particular advanced his career prospects, then it was the Mugello GP in 1969, which he won after a superb drive in the Abarth 2-litre, beating the likes of Nino Vaccarella and Andrea de Adamich. This brought an invitation to join the Ferrari sports car team for 1970, which was the start of a three-year association with the Scuderia.

Merzario's best season was probably 1972, when he made a sparkling grand prix debut at Brands Hatch, winning the Spa 1000km with Brian Redman, the Targa Florio with Sandro Munari and the Rand nine-hours with Clay Regazzoni in the 312P. In addition, racing for Abarth, he was crowned European 2-litre champion. The following season saw Ferrari in something of a trough, but Merzario knuckled down to a hit-and-miss season of Formula 1 while

team leader Jacky Ickx just gave up. His feisty spirit appealed to Frank Williams, who signed him for 1974. The season began with a third place in the Medici GP at Brasilia, but once the serious business began, success was elusive. The pair ploughed on into the 1975 season, but Merzario's fortunes in Formula 1 could hardly have been worse. By mid-season, he had quit Williams to concentrate on his commitments with the Alfa sports car team, taking their T33 to wins at Dijon, Monza, Enna and the Nürburgring. After a brief liaison with Copersucar at Monza, Arturo lined up a works March drive for 1976, but the strain of running a four-car team showed and, unhappy with his lot, the Italian grabbed the chance to join Wolf-Williams in mid-season following the sudden departure of Ickx.

With no other options open to him, Merzario entered his own March in 1977, before the money ran out due to a lack of results. He had a good one-off drive for Shadow in Austria, but this was overlooked due to Alan Jones' splendid win in the sister car. While his grand prix career had been heading for the rocks for some time, Arturo managed to salvage his reputation somewhat by continuing his sports car success with Alfa Romeo, and in 1977 he won championship rounds at Dijon, Enna, Estoril and Paul Ricard in Autodelta's last fling. The following year, he took the brave and ultimately completely foolhardy step of fielding his own F1 chassis. Two versions of this appalling device were built during the next two seasons, but the cars rarely looked capable of qualifying. Very much the poorer, but seemingly no wiser, the little Italian persisted with his folly in 1980, making an equally fruitless attempt to mix it with the constructors in Formula 2 with his Merzario M1-BMW, which was just as embarrassing as his grand prix 'contender'.

Arturo returned to the tracks once more in the 1990s, winning the inaugural Maserati Bi-turbo Cup race at Imola in 1995 and, after driving in the Porsche Supercup, the jaunty Italian continued to be a spirited competitor in various sports car races at both national and international level. He also became a regular fixture on the historic circuit, driving some of the machines from his halcyon days.

MERZARIO, Arturo (I) b 11/3/1943, Civenna, Como

	1972 Championship position: 20th		Wins: 0	Pole positions: 0		Fastest laps: 0	Points scored: 1		
	Race	Circuit	No	Entrant	Tyres	Capacity/Car/Engine	Comment		Q Pos/Entries
6	BRITISH GP	Brands Hatch	6	Scuderia Ferrari SpA SEFAC	F	3.0 Ferrari 312B2 F12	pit stop – tyre/1 lap behind		=8/27
12	GERMAN GP	Nürburgring	19	Scuderia Ferrari SpA SEFAC	F	3.0 Ferrari 312B2 F12	pit stop – oil pressure/1 lap behind		22/27
	1973 Championship position: 12th		Wins: 0	Pole positions: 0		Fastest laps: 0	Points scored: 6		
9	ARGENTINE GP	Buenos Aires	20	Scuderia Ferrari SpA SEFAC	G	3.0 Ferrari 312B2 F12	gearbox problems/4 laps behind		14/19
4	BRAZILIAN GP	Interlagos	10	Scuderia Ferrari SpA SEFAC	G	3.0 Ferrari 312B2 F12	1 lap behind		17/20
4	SOUTH AFRICAN GP	Kyalami	9	Scuderia Ferrari SpA SEFAC	G	3.0 Ferrari 312B2 F12	1 lap behind		15/25
ret	MONACO GP	Monte Carlo	4	Scuderia Ferrari SpA SEFAC	G	3.0 Ferrari 312B3 F12	oil pressure		16/26
7	FRENCH GP	Paul Ricard	4	Scuderia Ferrari SpA SEFAC	G	3.0 Ferrari 312B3 F12			10/25
7	AUSTRIAN GP	Österreichring	4	Scuderia Ferrari SpA SEFAC	G	3.0 Ferrari 312B3 F12	1 lap behind		6/25
ret	ITALIAN GP	Monza	4	Scuderia Ferrari SpA SEFAC	G	3.0 Ferrari 312B3 F12	hit chicane – suspension damage		7/25
15	CANADIAN GP	Mosport Park	4	Scuderia Ferrari SpA SEFAC	G	3.0 Ferrari 312B3 F12	pit stops – lost nose cone/-5 laps		20/26
16	US GP	Watkins Glen	4	Scuderia Ferrari SpA SEFAC	G	3.0 Ferrari 312B3 F12	pit stop – rear wing/4 laps behind		12/28
	1974 Championship position: 17th		Wins: 0	Pole positions: 0		Fastest laps: 0	Points scored: 4		
ret	ARGENTINE GP	Buenos Aires	20	Frank Williams Racing Cars	G	3.0 Iso Marlboro FW01-Cosworth V8	engine		13/26
ret	BRAZILIAN GP	Interlagos	20	Frank Williams Racing Cars	G	3.0 Iso Marlboro FW01-Cosworth V8	dirt in throttle slides		9/25
6	SOUTH AFRICAN GP	Kyalami	20	Frank Williams Racing Cars	G	3.0 Iso Marlboro FW02-Cosworth V8			3/27
ret	SPANISH GP	Jarama	20	Frank Williams Racing Cars	G	3.0 Iso Marlboro FW03-Cosworth V8	hit and vaulted barrier		7/28
ret	BELGIAN GP	Nivelles	20	Frank Williams Racing Cars	G	3.0 Iso Marlboro FW03-Cosworth V8	driveshaft		6/32

ret	MONACO GP	Monte Carlo	20	Frank Williams Racing Cars	G	3.0 Iso Marlboro FW03-Cosworth V8	*multiple accident*	14/28
dns	"	"	20T	Frank Williams Racing Cars	G	3.0 Iso Marlboro FW03-Cosworth V8	*practice only*	- / -
dns	SWEDISH GP	Anderstorp	20	Frank Williams Racing Cars	G	3.0 Iso Marlboro FW03-Cosworth V8	*unwell*	28/28
ret	DUTCH GP	Zandvoort	20	Frank Williams Racing Cars	G	3.0 Iso Marlboro FW03-Cosworth V8	*gearbox*	21/27
9	FRENCH GP	Dijon	20	Frank Williams Racing Cars	G	3.0 Iso Marlboro FW03-Cosworth V8	*1 lap behind*	15/30
ret	BRITISH GP	Brands Hatch	20	Frank Williams Racing Cars	G	3.0 Iso Marlboro FW03-Cosworth V8	*engine*	=15/34
dns	"	"	20	Frank Williams Racing Cars	G	3.0 Iso Marlboro FW03-Cosworth V8	*practice only*	- / -
ret	GERMAN GP	Nürburgring	20	Frank Williams Racing Cars	G	3.0 Iso Marlboro FW03-Cosworth V8	*throttle linkage*	16/32
ret	AUSTRIAN GP	Österreichring	20	Frank Williams Racing Cars	G	3.0 Iso Marlboro FW03-Cosworth V8	*fuel pressure*	9/31
4	ITALIAN GP	Monza	20	Frank Williams Racing Cars	G	3.0 Iso Marlboro FW03-Cosworth V8		15/31
ret	CANADIAN GP	Mosport Park	20	Frank Williams Racing Cars	G	3.0 Iso Marlboro FW03-Cosworth V8	*handling*	19/30
ret	US GP	Watkins Glen	20	Frank Williams Racing Cars	G	3.0 Iso Marlboro FW03-Cosworth V8	*extinguisher – electrical short*	15/30

1975 Championship position: Unplaced

nc	ARGENTINE GP	Buenos Aires	20	Frank Williams Racing Cars	G	3.0 Williams FW03-Cosworth V8	*2 stops – fuel metering unit/-9 laps*	20/23
ret	BRAZILIAN GP	Interlagos	20	Frank Williams Racing Cars	G	3.0 Williams FW03-Cosworth V8	*fuel metering unit*	11/23
ret	SOUTH AFRICAN GP	Kyalami	20	Frank Williams Racing Cars	G	3.0 Williams FW03-Cosworth V8	*engine*	15/28
ret	SPANISH GP	Montjuich Park	20	Frank Williams Racing Cars	G	3.0 Williams FW04-Cosworth V8	*withdrew in protest on circuit safety*	(25)/26
dnq	MONACO GP	Monte Carlo	20	Frank Williams Racing Cars	G	3.0 Williams FW03-Cosworth V8		20/26
ret	BELGIAN GP	Zolder	20	Frank Williams Racing Cars	G	3.0 Williams FW03-Cosworth V8	*clutch*	19/24
11	ITALIAN GP	Monza	30	Copersucar-Fittipaldi	G	3.0 Fittipaldi FD03-Cosworth V8	*4 laps behind*	26/28

1976 Championship position: Unplaced

dnq	US GP WEST	Long Beach	35	Ovoro Team March	G	3.0 March 761-Cosworth V8		23/27
ret	SPANISH GP	Jarama	35	Ovoro Team March	G	3.0 March 761-Cosworth V8	*gear linkage*	18/30
ret	BELGIAN GP	Zolder	35	Ovoro Team March	G	3.0 March 761-Cosworth V8	*engine*	21/29
dnq	MONACO GP	Monte Carlo	35	Ovoro Team March	G	3.0 March 761-Cosworth V8	*accident in practice*	25/25
14/ret	SWEDISH GP	Anderstorp	35	Ovoro Team March	G	3.0 March 761-Cosworth V8	*engine/2 laps behind*	19/27
9	FRENCH GP	Paul Ricard	35	Ovoro Team March	G	3.0 March 761-Cosworth V8		20/30
ret	BRITISH GP	Brands Hatch	35	Ovoro Team March	G	3.0 March 761-Cosworth V8	*engine*	9/30
ret	GERMAN GP	Nürburgring	20	Walter Wolf Racing	G	3.0 Williams FW05-Cosworth V8	*brakes*	21/28
ret	AUSTRIAN GP	Österreichring	20	Walter Wolf Racing	G	3.0 Williams FW05-Cosworth V8	*spun off*	21/25
ret	DUTCH GP	Zandvoort	20	Walter Wolf Racing	G	3.0 Williams FW05-Cosworth V8	*spun off*	23/27
dns	ITALIAN GP	Monza	20	Walter Wolf Racing	G	3.0 Williams FW05-Cosworth V8	*withdrawn after practice*	(24)/29
ret	CANADIAN GP	Mosport Park	20	Walter Wolf Racing	G	3.0 Williams FW05-Cosworth V8	*spun off*	25/27
ret	US GP EAST	Watkins Glen	20	Walter Wolf Racing	G	3.0 Williams FW05-Cosworth V8	*spun – hit by Ertl*	25/27
ret	JAPANESE GP	Mount Fuji	20	Walter Wolf Racing	G	3.0 Williams FW05-Cosworth V8	*gearbox*	19/27

1977 Championship position: Unplaced

ret	SPANISH GP	Jarama	37	Team Merzario	G	3.0 March 761B-Cosworth V8	*suspension*	21/31
dnq	MONACO GP	Monte Carlo	37	Team Merzario	G	3.0 March 761B-Cosworth V8		21/26
14	BELGIAN GP	Zolder	37	Team Merzario	G	3.0 March 761B-Cosworth V8	*pit stop-tyres-fuel pump/-5 laps*	14/32
ret	FRENCH GP	Dijon	37	Team Merzario	G	3.0 March 761B-Cosworth V8	*gearbox*	18/30
ret	BRITISH GP	Silverstone	37	Team Merzario	G	3.0 March 761B-Cosworth V8	*driveshaft*	17/36
dnq	GERMAN GP	Hockenheim	37	Team Merzario	G	3.0 March 761B-Cosworth V8		29/30
ret	AUSTRIAN GP	Österreichring	16	Shadow Racing Team	G	3.0 Shadow DN8-Cosworth V8	*gear linkage*	=20/31
dnq	DUTCH GP	Zandvoort	37	Team Merzario	G	3.0 March 761B-Cosworth V8		28/34

1978 Championship position: Unplaced

ret	ARGENTINE GP	Buenos Aires	37	Team Merzario	G	3.0 Merzario A1-Cosworth V8	*differential*	20/27
dnq	BRAZILIAN GP	Rio	37	Team Merzario	G	3.0 Merzario A1-Cosworth V8		=24/28
ret	SOUTH AFRICAN GP	Kyalami	37	Team Merzario	G	3.0 Merzario A1-Cosworth V8	*radius rod mounting*	26/30
ret	US GP WEST	Long Beach	37	Team Merzario	G	3.0 Merzario A1-Cosworth V8	*gearbox*	21/30
dnpq	MONACO GP	Monte Carlo	37	Team Merzario	G	3.0 Merzario A1-Cosworth V8		30/30
dnpq	BELGIAN GP	Zolder	37	Team Merzario	G	3.0 Merzario A1-Cosworth V8		30/30
dnq	SPANISH GP	Jarama	37	Team Merzario	G	3.0 Merzario A1-Cosworth V8		25/29
nc	SWEDISH GP	Anderstorp	37	Team Merzario	G	3.0 Merzario A1-Cosworth V8	*pit stop/8 laps behind*	22/27
dnq	FRENCH GP	Paul Ricard	37	Team Merzario	G	3.0 Merzario A1-Cosworth V8		27/29
ret	BRITISH GP	Brands Hatch	37	Team Merzario	G	3.0 Merzario A1-Cosworth V8	*fuel pump*	23/30
dnq	GERMAN GP	Hockenheim	37	Team Merzario	G	3.0 Merzario A1-Cosworth V8		28/30
dnq	AUSTRIAN GP	Österreichring	37	Team Merzario	G	3.0 Merzario A1-Cosworth V8		27/31
ret	DUTCH GP	Zandvoort	37	Team Merzario	G	3.0 Merzario A1-Cosworth V8	*engine*	27/33
ret	ITALIAN GP	Monza	37	Team Merzario	G	3.0 Merzario A1-Cosworth V8	*engine*	22/32
ret	US GP EAST	Watkins Glen	37	Team Merzario	G	3.0 Merzario A1-Cosworth V8	*gearbox oil leak*	26/27
dnq	CANADIAN GP	Montreal	37	Team Merzario	G	3.0 Merzario A1-Cosworth V8		25/28

1979 Championship position: Unplaced

ret/dns	ARGENTINE GP	Buenos Aires	24	Team Merzario	G	3.0 Merzario A1B-Cosworth V8	*accident in first start*	22/26
dnq	BRAZILIAN GP	Rio	24	Team Merzario	G	3.0 Merzario A1B-Cosworth V8		26/26
dnq	SOUTH AFRICAN GP	Kyalami	24	Team Merzario	G	3.0 Merzario A1B-Cosworth V8		25/26
ret	US GP WEST	Long Beach	24	Team Merzario	G	3.0 Merzario A1B-Cosworth V8	*engine*	24/26
dns	"	"	24	Team Merzario	G	3.0 Merzario A2-Cosworth V8	*practice only*	- / -
dnq	SPANISH GP	Jarama	24	Team Merzario	G	3.0 Merzario A2-Cosworth V8		26/27
dnq	BELGIAN GP	Zolder	24	Team Merzario	G	3.0 Merzario A2-Cosworth V8		26/28
dnq	FRENCH GP	Dijon	24	Team Merzario	G	3.0 Merzario A2-Cosworth V8		27/27
dnq	BRITISH GP	Silverstone	24	Team Merzario	G	3.0 Merzario A2-Cosworth V8		26/26
dnq	GERMAN GP	Hockenheim	24	Team Merzario	G	3.0 Merzario A2-Cosworth V8		26/26
dnq	AUSTRIAN GP	Österreichring	24	Team Merzario	G	3.0 Merzario A2-Cosworth V8		26/26
dnq	DUTCH GP	Zandvoort	24	Team Merzario	G	3.0 Merzario A2-Cosworth V8		26/26
dnq	ITALIAN GP	Monza	24	Team Merzario	G	3.0 Merzario A2-Cosworth V8		27/28
dnq	CANADIAN GP	Montreal	24	Team Merzario	G	3.0 Merzario A2-Cosworth V8		29/29
dnq	US GP EAST	Watkins Glen	24	Team Merzario	G	3.0 Merzario A2-Cosworth V8		30/30

GP Starts: 56 (57)   GP Wins: 0   Pole positions: 0   Fastest laps: 0   Points: 11

ROBERTO MIÈRES

A NATURAL athlete, Roberto Mières excelled at rowing, yachting and rugby until a broken leg ended his interest in the oval-ball game. After reaching championship class at tennis, he turned to motorsport with an MG. This was soon replaced by a Mercedes SSK, with which he won an important race at Rosario. Racing the ex-Achille Varzi Bugatti, he won the Argentine sports car championship and, as a result, was invited to accompany Juan Fangio and Froilán González on a short trip to Europe, during which he took a Ferrari to fourth in the Geneva GP of 1950.

Returning home, Mières waited for an opportunity to race abroad once more, which finally came in 1953, when Gordini invited him to replace the injured Jean Behra. Little came his way in terms of results, but he drove brilliantly to finish fourth in the F1 Albi GP with the F2 car. In 1954, he ordered a Maserati 250F, but he started the season with the interim A6GCM/250 and scored a superb second place in the Buenos Aires City GP. He was frustrated by the non-appearance of his new car for most of the year, but made the best of it, taking third at Pau and fourth in the International Trophy at Silverstone. When the 250F eventually arrived, Mières immediately took fourth places in the Swiss and Spanish GPs, so impressing the factory that he was taken on for 1955.

Ably supporting team leader Behra, Mières enjoyed a consistent season, doing particularly well in non-championship races; he took second in the Turin GP, and third at both Pau and Bordeaux. Political upheaval at home prompted him to retire from grands prix at the end of 1955 to tend to his business interests, and he returned to his earlier passion of yachting.

However, Roberto was tempted back behind the wheel. He finished fourth In the 1957 Buenos Aires 1000km in the Ecurie Ecosse Jaguar D-Type, while in 1958 he raced a Centro Sud Maserati 250F in the Buenos Aires City GP, and shared a works Porsche with Edgar Barth and Fritz d'Orey in the 1000km, claiming a class win and fifth place overall.

Subsequently, Mières raced occasionally in the USA, and took part in single-seater and saloon car events at home until 1962/63, when he decided to concentrate on his considerable competition yachting skills. He later moved to Uruguay where, for more than thirty years, he owned and ran a farm in Punta del Este.

MIÈRES, Roberto (RA) b 3/12/1924, Mar del Plata – d 26/1/2012, Uruguay

	Race	Circuit	No	Entrant	Tyres	Capacity/Car/Engine	Comment	Q Pos/Entries
1953 Championship position: Unplaced								
ret	DUTCH GP	Zandvoort	22	Equipe Gordini	E	2.0 Gordini Type 16 6	transmission	19/20
ret	FRENCH GP	Reims	8	Equipe Gordini	E	2.0 Gordini Type 16 6	rear axle	24/25
6	ITALIAN GP	Monza	40	Equipe Gordini	E	2.0 Gordini Type 16 6	3 laps behind	16/30
1954 Championship position: 7th= Wins: 0 Pole positions: 0 Fastest laps: 0 Points scored: 6								
ret	ARGENTINE GP	Buenos Aires	32	Roberto Mières	P	2.5 Maserati A6GCM/250F 6	engine	8/18
ret	BELGIAN GP	Spa	24	Roberto Mières	P	2.5 Maserati A6GCM/250F 6	fire	12/15
ret	FRENCH GP	Reims	16	Roberto Mières	P	2.5 Maserati A6GCM/250F 6	engine	11/22
6	BRITISH GP	Silverstone	4	Roberto Mières	P	2.5 Maserati A6GCM/250F 6	3 laps behind	31/31
ret	GERMAN GP	Nürburgring	8	Roberto Mières	P	2.5 Maserati 250F 6	fuel tank leak	17/23
4	SWISS GP	Bremgarten	30	Officine Alfieri Maserati	P	2.5 Maserati 250F 6	2 laps behind	12/16
ret	ITALIAN GP	Monza	24	Officine Alfieri Maserati	P	2.5 Maserati 250F 6	suspension	10/21
4	SPANISH GP	Pedralbes	10	Officine Alfieri Maserati	P	2.5 Maserati 250F 6	1 lap behind	11/22
1955 Championship position: 7th Wins: 0 Pole positions: 0 Fastest laps: 1 Points scored: 7								
5	ARGENTINE GP	Buenos Aires	18	Officine Alfieri Maserati	P	2.5 Maserati 250F 6	5 laps behind	16/22
ret	MONACO GP	Monte Carlo	36	Officine Alfieri Maserati	P	2.5 Maserati 250F 6	rear axle	6/22
5*	BELGIAN GP	Spa	24	Officine Alfieri Maserati	P	2.5 Maserati 250F 6	*Behra took over car/1 lap behind	11/14
4	DUTCH GP	Zandvoort	16	Officine Alfieri Maserati	P	2.5 Maserati 250F 6	FL/1 lap behind	7/16
ret	BRITISH GP	Aintree	6	Officine Alfieri Maserati	P	2.5 Maserati 250F 6	engine	6/25
7	ITALIAN GP	Monza	28	Officine Alfieri Maserati	P	2.5 Maserati 250F 6	2 laps behind	7/22
GP Starts: 17 GP Wins: 0 Pole positions: 0 Fastest laps: 1 Points: 13								

FRANÇOIS MIGAULT

A FORMER Volant Shell winner, François Migault appeared to have a promising future when he shone in Formula 3 during the 1970 and '71 seasons with a Tecno. His first Formula 2 races brought fourth place at Albi and fifth at Rouen, and then he made his first attempt at grands prix with the enthusiastic, but naïve Connew project in 1972.

François marked time somewhat in 1973 with the F2 Pygmée, before joining compatriots Jean-Pierre Beltoise and Henri Pescarolo in the Motul-backed BRM team for 1974. Despite making do with the worst of machinery, as befitted the third driver, he did well to qualify the car for most of the races, his best result being a fifth place in the International Trophy. Subsequently, he scraped a handful of rides in 1975 with Hill and Williams, but nothing of note was achieved before an equally moribund year in Formula 2 with the works Osella in 1976.

Already experienced in sports cars, François had shared a Matra with Jean-Pierre Jabouille to take third place at Le Mans in 1974, and went one better in 1976, finishing second in the Mirage GR8.

In the 1990s, François was active in the USA, racing a Kudzu-Buick in IMSA, and then he became a racing instructor. He was still a regular at his local Sarthe circuit, continuing to race there until 2004, although outright success eluded him in the end. Migault died on 29th January, 2012, after a long battle with cancer.

MIGAULT, François (F) b 4/12/1944, Le Mans – d 29/1/2012 Parigné-L'Evêque

1972 Championship position: Unplaced

	Race	Circuit	No	Entrant	Tyres	Capacity/Car/Engine	Comment	Q Pos/Entries
dns	BRITISH GP	Brands Hatch	34	Darnvall Connew Racing Team	F	3.0 Connew PC1-Cosworth V8	suspension in practice	(27)/27
ret	AUSTRIAN GP	Österreichring	29	Darnvall Connew Racing Team	F	3.0 Connew PC1-Cosworth V8	rear wishbone mounting point	26/26

1974 Championship position: Unplaced

	Race	Circuit	No	Entrant	Tyres	Capacity/Car/Engine	Comment	Q Pos/Entries
ret	ARGENTINE GP	Buenos Aires	37	Team BRM	F	3.0 BRM P160E V12	water leak	24/26
16	BRAZILIAN GP	Interlagos	37	Team BRM	F	3.0 BRM P160E V12	2 laps behind	23/25
15	SOUTH AFRICAN GP	Kyalami	37	Team BRM	F	3.0 BRM P160E V12	3 laps behind	25/27
ret	SPANISH GP	Jarama	37	Team BRM	F	3.0 BRM P160E V12	engine	23/28
16	BELGIAN GP	Nivelles	37	Team BRM	F	3.0 BRM P160E V12	3 laps behind	25/32
ret	MONACO GP	Monte Carlo	37	Team BRM	F	3.0 BRM P160E V12	brake failure – crashed	=21/28
ret	DUTCH GP	Zandvoort	37	Team BRM	F	3.0 BRM P201 V12	gear linkage	– / –
dns	"	"	37	Team BRM	F	3.0 BRM P160E V12	practice only – Pescarolo drove in race	25/27
14	FRENCH GP	Dijon	37	Team BRM	F	3.0 BRM P160E V12	2 laps behind	22/30
nc	BRITISH GP	Brands Hatch	37	Team BRM	F	3.0 BRM P160E V12	2 pit stops – rear wing/13 laps behind	14/34
dnq	GERMAN GP	Nürburgring	37	Team BRM	F	3.0 BRM P160E V12		27/32
ret	ITALIAN GP	Monza	37	Team BRM	F	3.0 BRM P201 V12	gearbox	24/31

1975 Championship position: Unplaced

	Race	Circuit	No	Entrant	Tyres	Capacity/Car/Engine	Comment	Q Pos/Entries
nc	SPANISH GP	Montjuich Park	23	Embassy Racing with Graham Hill	G	3.0 Hill GH1-Cosworth V8	hit Peterson – pit stop/11 laps behind	22/26
ret	BELGIAN GP	Zolder	22	Embassy Racing with Graham Hill	G	3.0 Hill GH1-Cosworth V8	rear suspension sub-frame	22/24
dns	FRENCH GP	Paul Ricard	20	Frank Williams Racing Cars	G	3.0 Williams FW03-Cosworth V8	engine in practice	(24)/26

GP Starts: 13   GP Wins: 0   Pole positions: 0   Fastest laps: 0   Points: 0

JOHN MILES

THE son of the late thespian Sir Bernard Miles, John chose not to follow his father into the theatre, but pursued a racing career instead, gaining numerous victories at club level in his Diva-Ford in 1964. Under the wing of Willment, he continued his winning ways in 1965 and received a third-place Grovewood Award.

Having scored nine consecutive wins with the Willment Lotus Elan at the start of 1966, John soon became involved with the works team, racing the GT Europa and F3 Lotus 41 in 1967 and 1968 with tremendous success. A planned season with Lotus in Formula 2 in 1969 never took off, but he did finish third in the Rome GP and fifth at Hockhenheim from three starts, before Colin Chapman entrusted him with the task of developing the Lotus 63 4WD car in five grands prix.

John's reward was a place alongside Jochen Rindt in the Lotus team for the 1970 season, which started well with a fifth place in the Lotus 49C in South Africa, but gradually declined as his apprehension over the fragility of the new Lotus 72 steadily grew. After Rindt's fatal crash at Monza, Miles was summarily replaced by Reine Wisell, and that was the end of his grand prix career. He did make a brief appearance for BRM in the non-championship Jochen Rindt Memorial race at Hockenheim the following season, while racing for the DART sports car team, but he soon retired from racing to concentrate on his new occupation as a motoring journalist, road-testing cars, before returning to Lotus Cars in an engineering capacity.

MILES, John (GB) b 14/6/1943, Islington, London

1969 Championship position: Unplaced

	Race	Circuit	No	Entrant	Tyres	Capacity/Car/Engine	Comment	Q Pos/Entries
ret	FRENCH GP	Clermont Ferrand	14	Gold Leaf Team Lotus	F	3.0 Lotus 63-Cosworth V8	fuel pump belt	12/13
10	BRITISH GP	Silverstone	9	Gold Leaf Team Lotus	F	3.0 Lotus 63-Cosworth V8	pit stop – gearbox/9 laps behind	14/17
ret	ITALIAN GP	Monza	6	Gold Leaf Team Lotus	F	3.0 Lotus 63-Cosworth V8	engine	14/15
ret	CANADIAN GP	Mosport Park	3	Gold Leaf Team Lotus	F	3.0 Lotus 63-Cosworth V8	gearbox	11/20
ret	MEXICAN GP	Mexico City	9	Gold Leaf Team Lotus	F	3.0 Lotus 63-Cosworth V8	fuel pump	11/17

1970 Championship position: 19th=   Wins: 0   Pole positions: 0   Fastest laps: 0   Points scored: 2

	Race	Circuit	No	Entrant	Tyres	Capacity/Car/Engine	Comment	Q Pos/Entries
5	SOUTH AFRICAN GP	Kyalami	10	Gold Leaf Team Lotus	F	3.0 Lotus 49C-Cosworth V8	1 lap behind	14/24
dnq	SPANISH GP	Jarama	19	Gold Leaf Team Lotus	F	3.0 Lotus 72-Cosworth V8	not seeded	15/22
dnq	"	" "	19	Gold Leaf Team Lotus	F	3.0 Lotus 49C-Cosworth V8		– / –
dnq	MONACO GP	Monte Carlo	2	Gold Leaf Team Lotus	F	3.0 Lotus 49C-Cosworth V8	practice only	19/21
dnq	"	" "	2T	Gold Leaf Team Lotus	F	3.0 Lotus 72-Cosworth V8		– / –
ret	BELGIAN GP	Spa	21	Gold Leaf Team Lotus	F	3.0 Lotus 72B-Cosworth V8	gear selection/tyres	13/18
dns	"	"	21	Gold Leaf Team Lotus	F	3.0 Lotus 49C-Cosworth V8	practice only – Rindt drove in race	– / –
7	DUTCH GP	Zandvoort	12	Gold Leaf Team Lotus	F	3.0 Lotus 72B-Cosworth V8	2 laps behind	8/24
8	FRENCH GP	Clermont Ferrand	7	Gold Leaf Team Lotus	F	3.0 Lotus 72B-Cosworth V8		18/23
ret	BRITISH GP	Brands Hatch	6	Gold Leaf Team Lotus	F	3.0 Lotus 72C-Cosworth V8	engine	7/25
ret	GERMAN GP	Hockenheim	16	Gold Leaf Team Lotus	F	3.0 Lotus 72C-Cosworth V8	engine	10/25
ret	AUSTRIAN GP	Österreichring	7	Gold Leaf Team Lotus	F	3.0 Lotus 72C-Cosworth V8	front brake-shaft	10/24
dns	ITALIAN GP	Monza	24	Gold Leaf Team Lotus	F	3.0 Lotus 72C-Cosworth V8	withdrawn after Rindt's fatal accident	(19)/27

GP Starts: 12   GP Wins: 0   Pole positions: 0   Fastest laps: 0   Points: 2

MILHOUX, André (B) 9/12/1928, Bressoux, Liege

1956 Championship position: Unplaced

	Race	Circuit	No	Entrant	Tyres	Capacity/Car/Engine	Comment	Q Pos/Entries
ret	GERMAN GP	Nürburgring	11	Equipe Gordini	E	2.5 Gordini Type 32 8	engine – misfire	21/21

GP Starts: 1   GP Wins: 0   Pole positions: 0   Fastest laps: 0   Points: 0

ANDRÉ MILHOUX

A USEFUL sports and production car driver, André Milhoux took part in the 1956 German Grand Prix as a substitute for André Pilette, who had injured himself in practice. It was his only single-seater appearance of note.

Milhoux had successfully handled huge Plymouths and Fords in Belgian events, and had partnered compatriot Paul Frère to win the 2-litre touring car class in the 1953 Mille Miglia, driving a Chrysler – highly unsuitable, one would think, for this event.

Subsequently, André moved into pukka sports machines. He finished fifth overall with Wolfgang Seidel in the 1955 Le Mans 24-hours (taking second place in the 1100–1500cc class), and fourth in the Paris 1000km in 1956, sharing an Equipe National Belge Ferrari with Pilette. He crashed heavily in practice for the 1958 Spa GP driving one of the team's yellow Ferraris and was lucky to escape unhurt, so he quit while he was ahead.

GERHARD MITTER

A N outstanding driver, Gerhard Mitter was an infrequent grand prix competitor who surely deserved more opportunities at the highest level, as he demonstrated with his fourth place in Carel de Beaufort's old Porsche in the 1963 German GP. As it was, he had to be content with just the annual outing at the Nürburgring, mainly in the Formula 2 class.

Gerhard was a top Formula Junior driver in the early 1960s with his DKW-engined Lotus before joining Porsche in 1964. He would become a mainstay of the German company's endurance racing programme, winning the Austrian GP in 1966 and the Targa Florio in 1969, and gaining many other fine placings. Also, he was European mountain-climb champion three times between 1966 and 1968.

In 1969, Mitter became involved in the development of the Dornier-built BMW F2 contender, but he crashed fatally during practice for that year's German GP, it is thought because a wheel came off the car.

MITTER, Gerhard (D) b 30/8/1935, Schönlinde – d 1/8/1969, Nürburgring Circuit

1963 Championship position: 12th   Wins: 0   Pole positions: 0   Fastest laps: 0   Points scored: 3

	Race	Circuit	No	Entrant	Tyres	Capacity/Car/Engine	Comment	Q Pos/Entries
ret	DUTCH GP	Zandvoort	34	Ecurie Maarsbergen	D	1.5 Porsche 718 F4	clutch	16/19
4	GERMAN GP	Nürburgring	26	Ecurie Maarsbergen	D	1.5 Porsche 718 F4		15/25
	1964 Championship position: Unplaced							
9	GERMAN GP	Nürburgring	23	Team Lotus	D	1.5 Lotus 25-Climax V8	1 lap behind	19/24
	1965 Championship position: Unplaced							
ret	GERMAN GP	Nürburgring	3	Team Lotus	D	1.5 Lotus 25-Climax V8	water hose	12/22
	1966 Championship position: Unplaced							
dns	GERMAN GP	Nürburgring	30	Ron Harris Team Lotus	D	1.0 Lotus 44-Cosworth 4 F2	not fully fit after a crash at Spa	(11)/30
	1967 Championship position: Unplaced							
ret	GERMAN GP (F2)	Nürburgring	20	Gerhard Mitter	D	1.6 Brabham BT23-Cosworth 4 F2	engine	23/25
	1969 Championship position: Unplaced							
dns	GERMAN GP (F2)	Nürburgring	24	Bayerische Motoren Werke	D	BMW 269-4 F2	car lost wheel – fatal accident	(25)/25

GP Starts: 5   GP Wins: 0   Pole positions: 0   Fastest laps: 0   Points: 3

STEFANO MODENA

HAVING served notice in karting that he was a man to watch, when Stefano Modena finally got into Formula 3 he soon became a front-runner, taking fourth place in the Italian championship in 1986. Also, he impressed the F1 fraternity with a superb second place in the Monaco Grand Prix support race and earned the title of 'European Champion' after victory in the one-off meeting at Imola.

After obtaining substantial backing, Modena moved straight into F3000 with the Onyx team and took the championship at the first attempt, winning three races (at Vallelunga, Birmingham and Imola), but it was the way he went about the whole business that marked him as a special talent. Much was expected of the tousle-haired Italian when he entered grand prix racing, but after an end-of-season ride with Brabham, he was forced to endure a discouraging learning year in 1988 with the uncompetitive EuroBrun, before being given a chance to really show what he could do with Brabham in 1989.

Modena finished in third place at Monaco, but the team lacked the financial resources to progress, so then he marked time until 1991, when he moved to a Tyrrell team newly equipped with Honda power. Things started well with yet another superb display at Monaco, which ended with a broken engine when he was running second, behind Ayrton Senna. Then he took second place in the next race in Canada, but as the season wore on he seemed to lose heart too easily.

It was a surprise when Modena was signed to drive the Jordan-Yamaha in 1992, but the team endured a troubled season, and the enigmatic Italian was temperamentally unsuited to the situation. He scored a point in the last race of the year, but was consigned to the wilderness for 1993, racing a BMW in the Italian touring car championship.

All was not lost for Modena, however, since his excellent form in the Alfa Romeo T155 during the early part of 1994 gained the Superturismo driver a passport to the higher-profile DTM late in the season. He made a sensational debut at AVUS, qualifying third, winning both heats and thoroughly eclipsing the established Alfa aces. Naturally, in light of his drives in the series' final three rounds, he was signed to race for a full DTM/ITC season with hopes high for even greater success. In reality, in 1995, Alfa became lost in a mire of technical problems and, in common with his colleagues, he had to pick up the scraps left by Mercedes and Opel.

Modena, who had harboured hopes of gaining a ride in CART, then became a mainstay of the German Super Touring championship. The 1997 season with the ageing Alfa 155 was a disaster, and the arrival of the 156 model the following year rarely allowed him to finish in the top ten, but 1999 saw an upturn in the Italian's fortunes as the 156 at last became a competitive proposition. He had a season in the DTM with Opel before deciding to retire from competition. He has also acted as a tester for Bridgestone on occasion, at their track near his home in Rome.

MODENA, Stefano (I) b 12/5/1963, Modena

1987 Championship position: Unplaced

	Race	Circuit	No	Entrant	Tyres	Capacity/Car/Engine	Comment	Q Pos/Entries
ret	AUSTRALIAN GP	Adelaide	7	Motor Racing Developments	G	1.5 t/c Brabham BT56-BMW 4	driver exhaustion	15/27

1988 Championship position: Unplaced

	Race	Circuit	No	Entrant	Tyres	Capacity/Car/Engine	Comment	Q Pos/Entries
ret	BRAZILIAN GP	Rio	33	EuroBrun Racing	G	3.5 EuroBrun ER188-Cosworth V8	engine cut out – fuel pump	24/31
nc	SAN MARINO GP	Imola	33	EuroBrun Racing	G	3.5 EuroBrun ER188-Cosworth V8	gearbox trouble/8 laps behind	26/31
excl*	MONACO GP	Monte Carlo	33	EuroBrun Racing	G	3.5 EuroBrun ER188-Cosworth V8	*missed weight check	– /30
excl*	MEXICAN GP	Mexico City	33	EuroBrun Racing	G	3.5 EuroBrun ER188-Cosworth V8	*rear wing height infringement	– /30
12	CANADIAN GP	Montreal	33	EuroBrun Racing	G	3.5 EuroBrun ER188-Cosworth V8	3 laps behind	15/31
ret	US GP (DETROIT)	Detroit	33	EuroBrun Racing	G	3.5 EuroBrun ER188-Cosworth V8	spun off	19/31
14	FRENCH GP	Paul Ricard	33	EuroBrun Racing	G	3.5 EuroBrun ER188-Cosworth V8	3 laps behind	20/31
12	BRITISH GP	Silverstone	33	EuroBrun Racing	G	3.5 EuroBrun ER188-Cosworth V8	1 lap behind	20/31
ret	GERMAN GP	Hockenheim	33	EuroBrun Racing	G	3.5 EuroBrun ER188-Cosworth V8	engine	25/31
11	HUNGARIAN GP	Hungaroring	33	EuroBrun Racing	G	3.5 EuroBrun ER188-Cosworth V8	4 laps behind	26/31
dnq	BELGIAN GP	Spa	33	EuroBrun Racing	G	3.5 EuroBrun ER188-Cosworth V8		29/31
dnq	ITALIAN GP	Monza	33	EuroBrun Racing	G	3.5 EuroBrun ER188-Cosworth V8		30/31
dnq	PORTUGUESE GP	Estoril	33	EuroBrun Racing	G	3.5 EuroBrun ER188-Cosworth V8		29/31
13	SPANISH GP	Jerez	33	EuroBrun Racing	G	3.5 EuroBrun ER188-Cosworth V8	2 laps behind	26/31
dnq	JAPANESE GP	Suzuka	33	EuroBrun Racing	G	3.5 EuroBrun ER188-Cosworth V8		30/31
ret	AUSTRALIAN GP	Adelaide	33	EuroBrun Racing	G	3.5 EuroBrun ER188-Cosworth V8	driveshaft	20/31

1989 Championship position: 16th= Wins: 0 Pole positions: 0 Fastest laps: 0 Points scored: 4

	Race	Circuit	No	Entrant	Tyres	Capacity/Car/Engine	Comment	Q Pos/Entries
ret	BRAZILIAN GP	Rio	8	Motor Racing Developments	P	3.5 Brabham BT58-Judd V8	driveshaft – c.v.joint	14/38
ret	SAN MARINO GP	Imola	8	Motor Racing Developments	P	3.5 Brabham BT58-Judd V8	spun into barrier	17/39
3	MONACO GP	Monte Carlo	8	Motor Racing Developments	P	3.5 Brabham BT58-Judd V8	1 lap behind	8/38
10	MEXICAN GP	Mexico City	8	Motor Racing Developments	P	3.5 Brabham BT58-Judd V8	1 lap behind	9/39
ret	US GP (PHOENIX)	Phoenix	8	Motor Racing Developments	P	3.5 Brabham BT58-Judd V8	brakes	7/39
ret	CANADIAN GP	Montreal	8	Motor Racing Developments	P	3.5 Brabham BT58-Judd V8	collision with Martini	7/39
ret	FRENCH GP	Paul Ricard	8	Motor Racing Developments	P	3.5 Brabham BT58-Judd V8	engine	22/39
ret	BRITISH GP	Silverstone	8	Motor Racing Developments	P	3.5 Brabham BT58-Judd V8	engine	14/39
ret	GERMAN GP	Hockenheim	8	Motor Racing Developments	P	3.5 Brabham BT58-Judd V8	engine	16/39
11	HUNGARIAN GP	Hungaroring	8	Motor Racing Developments	P	3.5 Brabham BT58-Judd V8	damaged nose cone/1 lap behind	8/39
ret	BELGIAN GP	Spa	8	Motor Racing Developments	P	3.5 Brabham BT58-Judd V8	started from pit lane/handling	8/39
excl*	ITALIAN GP	Monza	8	Motor Racing Developments	P	3.5 Brabham BT58-Judd V8	*missed weight check	–/39
14	PORTUGUESE GP	Estoril	8	Motor Racing Developments	P	3.5 Brabham BT58-Judd V8	shock absorber/misfire/2 laps behind	11/39
ret	SPANISH GP	Jerez	8	Motor Racing Developments	P	3.5 Brabham BT58-Judd V8	engine cut out – electrics	12/38
ret	JAPANESE GP	Suzuka	8	Motor Racing Developments	P	3.5 Brabham BT58-Judd V8	alternator	9/39
8	AUSTRALIAN GP	Adelaide	8	Motor Racing Developments	P	3.5 Brabham BT58-Judd V8	6 laps behind	8/39

1990 Championship position: 16th= Wins: 0 Pole positions: 0 Fastest laps: 0 Points scored: 2

	Race	Circuit	No	Entrant	Tyres	Capacity/Car/Engine	Comment	Q Pos/Entries
5	US GP (PHOENIX)	Phoenix	8	Motor Racing Developments	P	3.5 Brabham BT58-Judd V8	went up escape road	10/35
ret	BRAZILIAN GP	Interlagos	8	Motor Racing Developments	P	3.5 Brabham BT58-Judd V8	spun off	12/35
ret	SAN MARINO GP	Imola	8	Motor Racing Developments	P	3.5 Brabham BT58-Judd V8	brakes	15/34
ret	MONACO GP	Monte Carlo	8	Motor Racing Developments	P	3.5 Brabham BT59-Judd V8	transmission	14/35
7	CANADIAN GP	Montreal	8	Motor Racing Developments	P	3.5 Brabham BT59-Judd V8	2 laps behind	10/35
11	MEXICAN GP	Mexico City	8	Motor Racing Developments	P	3.5 Brabham BT59-Judd V8	1 lap behind	10/35
13	FRENCH GP	Paul Ricard	8	Motor Racing Developments	P	3.5 Brabham BT59-Judd V8	2 laps behind	20/35
9	BRITISH GP	Silverstone	8	Motor Racing Developments	P	3.5 Brabham BT59-Judd V8	spin – pit stop/2 laps behind	20/35
ret	GERMAN GP	Hockenheim	8	Motor Racing Developments	P	3.5 Brabham BT59-Judd V8	clutch on startline	17/35
ret	HUNGARIAN GP	Hungaroring	8	Motor Racing Developments	P	3.5 Brabham BT59-Judd V8	engine	20/35
17/ret	BELGIAN GP	Spa	8	Motor Racing Developments	P	3.5 Brabham BT59-Judd V8	engine/5 laps behind	13/33
ret	ITALIAN GP	Monza	8	Motor Racing Developments	P	3.5 Brabham BT59-Judd V8	engine	17/33
ret	PORTUGUESE GP	Estoril	8	Motor Racing Developments	P	3.5 Brabham BT59-Judd V8	gearbox	24/33
ret	SPANISH GP	Jerez	8	Motor Racing Developments	P	3.5 Brabham BT59-Judd V8	collision with Tarquini	25/33
ret	JAPANESE GP	Suzuka	8	Motor Racing Developments	P	3.5 Brabham BT59-Judd V8	spun off	22/30
12	AUSTRALIAN GP	Adelaide	8	Motor Racing Developments	P	3.5 Brabham BT59-Judd V8	pit stop – tyres/4 laps behind	17/30

1991 Championship position: 8th Wins: 0 Pole positions: 0 Fastest laps: 0 Points scored: 10

	Race	Circuit	No	Entrant	Tyres	Capacity/Car/Engine	Comment	Q Pos/Entries
4	US GP (PHOENIX)	Phoenix	4	Braun Tyrrell Honda	P	3.5 Tyrrell 020-Honda V10		11/34
ret	BRAZILIAN GP	Interlagos	4	Braun Tyrrell Honda	P	3.5 Tyrrell 020-Honda V10	gearshift	9/34
ret	SAN MARINO GP	Imola	4	Braun Tyrrell Honda	P	3.5 Tyrrell 020-Honda V10	transmission	6/34
ret	MONACO GP	Monte Carlo	4	Braun Tyrrell Honda	P	3.5 Tyrrell 020-Honda V10	lay 2nd for 42 laps/engine	2/34
2	CANADIAN GP	Montreal	4	Braun Tyrrell Honda	P	3.5 Tyrrell 020-Honda V10		9/34
11	MEXICAN GP	Mexico City	4	Braun Tyrrell Honda	P	3.5 Tyrrell 020-Honda V10	3 tyre stops/2 laps behind	8/34
ret	FRENCH GP	Magny Cours	4	Braun Tyrrell Honda	P	3.5 Tyrrell 020-Honda V10	gearbox	11/34
7	BRITISH GP	Silverstone	4	Braun Tyrrell Honda	P	3.5 Tyrrell 020-Honda V10	1 lap behind	10/34
13	GERMAN GP	Hockenheim	4	Braun Tyrrell Honda	P	3.5 Tyrrell 020-Honda V10	3 tyre stops/4 laps behind	14/34
12	HUNGARIAN GP	Hungaroring	4	Braun Tyrrell Honda	P	3.5 Tyrrell 020-Honda V10	2 laps behind	8/34
ret	BELGIAN GP	Spa	4	Braun Tyrrell Honda	P	3.5 Tyrrell 020-Honda V10	oil leak/fire	10/34
ret	ITALIAN GP	Monza	4	Braun Tyrrell Honda	P	3.5 Tyrrell 020-Honda V10	engine	13/34
ret	PORTUGUESE GP	Estoril	4	Braun Tyrrell Honda	P	3.5 Tyrrell 020-Honda V10	engine	12/34
16	SPANISH GP	Jerez	4	Braun Tyrrell Honda	P	3.5 Tyrrell 020-Honda V10	3 laps behind	14/33
6	JAPANESE GP	Suzuka	4	Braun Tyrrell Honda	P	3.5 Tyrrell 020-Honda V10	1 lap behind	14/31
10	AUSTRALIAN GP	Adelaide	4	Braun Tyrrell Honda	P	3.5 Tyrrell 020-Honda V10	race stopped at 14 laps	9/32

1992 Championship position: 17th= Wins: 0 Pole positions: 0 Fastest laps: 0 Points scored: 1

	Race	Circuit	No	Entrant	Tyres	Capacity/Car/Engine	Comment	Q Pos/Entries
dnq	SOUTH AFRICAN GP	Kyalami	32	Sasol Jordan Yamaha	G	3.5 Jordan 192-Yamaha V12		29/30
ret	MEXICAN GP	Mexico City	32	Sasol Jordan Yamaha	G	3.5 Jordan 192-Yamaha V12	started from pitlane/gearbox	15/30
ret	BRAZILIAN GP	Interlagos	32	Sasol Jordan Yamaha	G	3.5 Jordan 192-Yamaha V12	gearbox	12/31
dnq	SPANISH GP	Barcelona	32	Sasol Jordan Yamaha	G	3.5 Jordan 192-Yamaha V12		29/32

ret	SAN MARINO GP	Imola	32	Sasol Jordan Yamaha	G	3.5 Jordan 192-Yamaha V12	*started from pitlane/gearbox*	23/32
ret	MONACO GP	Monte Carlo	32	Sasol Jordan Yamaha	G	3.5 Jordan 192-Yamaha V12	*crashed at Casino square*	21/32
ret	CANADIAN GP	Montreal	32	Sasol Jordan Yamaha	G	3.5 Jordan 192-Yamaha V12	*started from back of grid/transmission*	17/32
ret	FRENCH GP	Magny Cours	32	Sasol Jordan Yamaha	G	3.5 Jordan 192-Yamaha V12	*engine*	20/30
ret	BRITISH GP	Silverstone	32	Sasol Jordan Yamaha	G	3.5 Jordan 192-Yamaha V12	*engine*	23/32
dnq	GERMAN GP	Hockenheim	32	Sasol Jordan Yamaha	G	3.5 Jordan 192-Yamaha V12		27/32
ret	HUNGARIAN GP	Hungaroring	32	Sasol Jordan Yamaha	G	3.5 Jordan 192-Yamaha V12	*hit by Grouillard*	24/31
15	BELGIAN GP	Spa	32	Sasol Jordan Yamaha	G	3.5 Jordan 192-Yamaha V12	*2 laps behind*	17/30
dnq	ITALIAN GP	Monza	32	Sasol Jordan Yamaha	G	3.5 Jordan 192-Yamaha V12		28/28
13	PORTUGUESE GP	Estoril	32	Sasol Jordan Yamaha	G	3.5 Jordan 192-Yamaha V12	*3 laps behind*	24/26
7	JAPANESE GP	Suzuka	32	Sasol Jordan Yamaha	G	3.5 Jordan 192-Yamaha V12	*1 lap behind*	17/26
6	AUSTRALIAN GP	Adelaide	32	Sasol Jordan Yamaha	G	3.5 Jordan 192-Yamaha V12	*1 lap behind*	15/26

GP Starts: 70   GP Wins: 0   Pole positions: 0   Fastest laps: 0   Points: 17

FRANCK MONTAGNY

AT the beginning of 2006, Franck Montagny's career seemed to have stalled completely. Having been discarded by Renault after two years as their reserve driver, the amiable Frenchman had tried unsuccessfully to break into Champ Cars and had been left without the prospect of a regular drive. However, when the Super Aguri Racing project became a reality, his testing abilities brought him a swift return to Formula 1. Then he suddenly found himself promoted to a race seat after the struggling Yuchi Ide was stood down.

For Montagny, it was the reward for a decade's hard work and his dogged refusal to quit even when a horrendous crash in Formula Renault in 1986 had left him with broken vertebrae and seriously injured legs. Only skilled work by the surgeons saved his promising racing career, which so far had seen him gain Rookie of the Year honours in French Formule Renault in 1995. After graduating to French Formula 3, more race wins continued to come his way, and in 1998 he chalked up a run of eight successive victories in a bitter championship battle that eventually went the way of the Belgian David Saelens by a mere three points.

Montagny then secured a seat with the DAMS team for F3000 in 1999 and showed flashes of promise in his rookie season to finish tenth in the final points standings. Obviously, hopes were high for his second season in the formula, but only five points were mustered and the Frenchman was forced to take a step back in 2001. He opted to compete in the Spanish Formula Nissan Series, which proved to be a wise move, for he eclipsed the previous series records set by Fernando Alonso on his way to the title, ahead of Tomas Scheckter. Now back on an upward curve, Franck was promoted to the Telefónica World Series by Nissan. He did not disappoint, taking three victories on his way to third place in the championship, behind the much more experienced champion Ricardo Zonta. Building upon this platform in 2003, he scorched his way to nine victories and the title he richly deserved, which gave him his big break into Formula 1 as test driver in the Renault team.

Along with his single-seater rides, Franck began a serious sports car career with DAMS and then Team Oreca. Successive Le Mans appearances brought improving finishes between 2002 and 2006, when he took the Pescarolo-Judd to a fine second place with Eric Hélary and Sébastien Loeb.

In F1, for 2004, Franck was involved in the development of the R24, and he must have been disappointed when overlooked after the unemployed Jacques Villeneuve was drafted into the team to replace Jarno Trulli at the tail end of the season. He continued to pound around the test tracks in 2005 as he helped fine-tune the championship winning R25, and he also made a brief appearance for Jordan-Toyota at the European GP as their Friday-only driver. His season ended in uncertainty, as he was released from Renault, who had placed their faith in Heikki Kovalainen.

Happily for Montagny, as one door closed, another opened, courtesy of Ide's aforementioned demotion. Franck appeared in a race seat at the European Grand Prix. He did a good enough job for the team in the SA05 car, but eventually was replaced for the balance of the season by Sakon Yamamoto, who was entrusted with the pukka 2006 machine from the German Grand Prix onwards.

With Super Aguri signing experienced Honda tester Anthony Davidson to race for them in 2007, Montagny was quickly snapped up by Toyota as their main development driver, where he remained for the season. Meanwhile, he took to the tracks in the A1GP series and then grabbed a potential showcase for his talents in Champ Car. On his debut for the Forsythe Petit team at Long Beach, the Frenchman scored an excellent second place, only to find the series amalgamated with the IRL and his team ceasing operations. He found more racing action at Andretti Green in the ALMS LM2 class, impressing mightily and finishing his part-season on a high, with a third overall and a class win at Laguna Seca with Tony Kanaan.

Montagny's performances put him in demand in the sports car category and he was signed up by Peugeot to join a strong driver line-up in their Le Mans assault. It was a case of 'so near' for Franck who, in four attempts between 2008 and 2011, finished third twice and second once in the 908 HDi protoype. However, there was the compensation of important victories elsewhere, such as a hat trick of wins in the Petit Le Mans between 2009 and 2011. Following the sudden withdrawal from competition of the French team, Toyota quickly recruited Montagny to contest the new World Endurance Championship with their new Le Mans prototype.

MONTAGNY Franck (F) b 5/5/1978, Feurs

2003 Championship position: Unplaced

	Race	Circuit	No	Entrant	Tyres	Capacity/Car/Engine	Comment	Q Pos/Entries
app	FRENCH GP	Magny Cours	34	Mild Seven Renault F1 Team	M	3.0 Renault R23-V10	ran as 3rd driver in practice only	– / –

2005 Championship position: Unplaced

app	EUROPEAN GP	Nürburgring	39	Jordan Toyota	B	3.0 Jordan EJ15-Toyota V10	ran as 3rd driver in practice only	– / –

2006 Championship position: Unplaced

ret	EUROPEAN GP	Nürburgring	23	Super Aguri F1 Team	B	2.4 Super Aguri SA05-Honda V8	hydraulics	22/22
ret	SPANISH GP	Barcelona	23	Super Aguri F1 Team	B	2.4 Super Aguri SA05-Honda V8	driveshaft	21/22
16	MONACO GP	Monte Carlo	23	Super Aguri F1 Team	B	2.4 Super Aguri SA06-Honda V8	3 laps behind	21/22
18	BRITISH GP	Silverstone	23	Super Aguri F1 Team	B	2.4 Super Aguri SA06-Honda V8	3 laps behind	21/22
ret	CANADIAN GP	Montreal	23	Super Aguri F1 Team	B	2.4 Super Aguri SA06-Honda V8	engine	22/22
ret	U S GP	Indianapolis	23	Super Aguri F1 Team	B	2.4 Super Aguri SA06-Honda V8	multiple accident on lap 1	22/22
16	FRENCH GP	Magny Cours	23	Super Aguri F1 Team	B	2.4 Super Aguri SA06-Honda V8	3 laps behind	21/22
app	TURKISH GP	Istanbul	41	Super Aguri F1 Team	B	2.4 Super Aguri SA05-Honda V8	ran as 3rd driver in practice only	– / –
app	ITALIAN GP	Monza	41	Super Aguri F1 Team	B	2.4 Super Aguri SA05-Honda V8	ran as 3rd driver in practice only	– / –
app	JAPANESE GP	Suzuka	41	Super Aguri F1 Team	B	2.4 Super Aguri SA05-Honda V8	ran as 3rd driver in practice only	– / –
app	CHINESE GP	Shanghai Circuit	41	Super Aguri F1 Team	B	2.4 Super Aguri SA05-Honda V8	ran as 3rd driver in practice only	– / –
app	BRAZILIAN GP	Interlagos	41	Super Aguri F1 Team	B	2.4 Super Aguri SA05-Honda V8	ran as 3rd driver in practice only	– / –

GP Starts: 7   GP Wins: 0   Pole positions: 0   Fastest laps: 0   Points: 0

TIAGO MONTEIRO

DESPITE a relatively late introduction to motorsport, Tiago Monteiro proved to have talent when, at 21, he started racing in the French Porsche Carrera Cup in 1997. This encouraged him to jump straight to French Formula 3 the following season. He took rookie honours in 1998, before good progress the next year produced a sixth place overall and a first win at Albi. The Portuguese driver had two more attempts at winning the elusive title, but he was runner-up in both 2000 and 2001, taking four wins in each season.

Having finally taken the plunge to move up the racing ladder, Monteiro landed a plum seat at Super Nova for the 2002 FIA F3000 series, but then largely squandered the opportunity by overdriving. He finished a somewhat lowly 12th place in the series with just five top-ten finishes to his credit.

Disillusioned by then in F3000 and unable to find a vacancy in Formula 1, Monteiro turned his attention to America, finding a place in the Champ Car series with the new Fittipaldi-Dingman operation. Pole position in the Mexico City finale was the highlight of a season otherwise littered with mechanical problems, but he had restored much of his reputation as a racer. With the team not entering the 2004 campaign and the desire to pursue an F1 drive still burning, he returned to Europe, joining Carlin Motorsport for the Nissan World Series. A string of strong performances, including five wins, saw him mount the greatest threat to eventual champion Heikki Kovalainen, as well as earning rookie honours.

Monteiro's F1 ambitions were also back on track, as Minardi had offered him the role of test driver for the season. While not running with the team at grand prix meetings, the Portuguese driver did make sporadic outings during the season and also was involved with the team's F1x2 project. Those performances, plus his relationship with Formula Nissan team boss Trevor Carlin, eventually stood him in good stead. Following a takeover at Jordan, Carlin was installed as team boss by new owner Alex Shnaider, and Monteiro got the call to partner former World Series rival Narain Karthikeyan in an all-rookie line-up for 2005.

Despite his inexperience, Tiago soon adapted to his new surroundings. Indeed. his calm and cerebral approach immediately produced an impressive run of 16 consecutive finishes. The highlights were a podium place in the six-car United States Grand Prix, following the Michelin tyre fiasco, and a gritty eighth place on merit at Spa in the wet. Deservedly, he was retained in the team when it was rebranded as Midland for 2007, and he was pretty evenly matched with his new team-mate, Christijan Albers. Indeed, the pair locked wheels more than once on the track, causing expensive damage to their machines and dismay to the tightly-budgeted team.

No points were garnered by the likeable Portuguese driver during the campaign, although he came mighty close in Hungary, after finishing ninth, and in the end-of-season takeover by the Dutch Spyker, Monteiro found himself surplus to requirements.

Tiago accepted an invitation to test a WTCC Seat León at Valencia and quickly adapted to the world of front-wheel-drive super-touring cars. He became a fixture in the series from 2007. Thus far, he has recorded four victories, despite the withdrawal of works support at the end of 2009, and despite the disadvantage of a non-factory car, he remains a competitive force. Fifth place overall in 2010 and sixth in 2011 were good rewards for his efforts.

MONTEIRO, Tiago (P) b 24/7/1976, Massarelos, Porto

2005 Championship position: 16th   Wins: 0   Pole positions: 0   Fastest laps: 0   Points scored: 7

	Race	Circuit	No	Entrant	Tyres	Capacity/Car/Engine	Comment	Q Pos/Entries
16	AUSTRALIAN GP	Melbourne	18	Jordan Toyota	B	3.0 Jordan EJ15-Toyota V10	2 laps behind	14/20
12	MALAYSIAN GP	Sepang	18	Jordan Toyota	B	3.0 Jordan EJ15-Toyota V10	spun on oil/3 laps behind	18/20
10	BAHRAIN GP	Sakhir Circuit	18	Jordan Toyota	B	3.0 Jordan EJ15-Toyota V10	2 laps behind	17/20
13*	SAN MARINO GP	Imola	18	Jordan Toyota	B	3.0 Jordan EJ15-Toyota V10	*3rd & 5th cars disqualified/-2 laps	17/20
12	SPANISH GP	Barcelona	18	Jordan Toyota	B	3.0 Jordan EJ15-Toyota V10	3 laps behind	18/18
13	MONACO GP	Monte Carlo	18	Jordan Toyota	B	3.0 Jordan EJ15-Toyota V10	3 laps behind	15/18
15	EUROPEAN GP	Nürburgring	18	Jordan Toyota	B	3.0 Jordan EJ15-Toyota V10	drive-through penalty/1 lap behind	17/20
10	CANADIAN GP	Montreal	18	Jordan Toyota	B	3.0 Jordan EJ15-Toyota V10	3 laps behind	18/20
3	U S GP	Indianapolis	18	Jordan Toyota	B	3.0 Jordan EJ15-Toyota V10	1 lap behind	17/20
13	FRENCH GP	Magny Cours	18	Jordan Toyota	B	3.0 Jordan EJ15-Toyota V10	3 laps behind	19/20
17	BRITISH GP	Silverstone	18	Jordan Toyota	B	3.0 Jordan EJ15-Toyota V10	*no time set/2 laps behind	*20/20
17	GERMAN GP	Hockenheim	18	Jordan Toyota	B	3.0 Jordan EJ15-Toyota V10	collision – Villeneuve/3 laps behind	18/20
13	HUNGARIAN GP	Hungaroring	18	Jordan Toyota	B	3.0 Jordan EJ15-Toyota V10	*no time set/4 laps behind	*20/20
15	TURKISH GP	Hungaroring	18	Jordan Toyota	B	3.0 Jordan EJ15-Toyota V10	3 laps behind	15/20
17	ITALIAN GP	Monza	18	Jordan Toyota	B	3.0 Jordan EJ15B-Toyota V10	lap 1 bodywork damage/-2 laps	17/20
8	BELGIAN GP	Spa	18	Jordan Toyota	B	3.0 Jordan EJ15B-Toyota V10	1 lap behind	19/20
ret	BRAZILIAN GP	Interlagos	18	Jordan Toyota	B	3.0 Jordan EJ15B-Toyota V10	engine	13/20
13	JAPANESE GP	Suzuka	18	Jordan Toyota	B	3.0 Jordan EJ15B-Toyota V10	*no time set/1 lap behind	*20/20
11	CHINESE GP	Shanghai	18	Jordan Toyota	B	3.0 Jordan EJ15B-Toyota V10		19/20

2006 Championship position: Unplaced

	Race	Circuit	No	Entrant	Tyres	Capacity/Car/Engine	Comment	Q Pos/Entries
17	BAHRAIN GP	Sakhir Circuit	18	MF1 Team	B	2.4 Midland M16-Toyota V8	started from pitlane/2 laps behind	19/22
13	MALAYSIAN GP	Sepang	18	MF1 Team	B	2.4 Midland M16-Toyota V8	2 laps behind	20/22
ret	AUSTRALIAN GP	Melbourne	18	MF1 Team	B	2.4 Midland M16-Toyota V8	hydraulics	20/22
16	SAN MARINO GP	Imola	18	MF1 Team	B	2.4 Midland M16-Toyota V8	2 laps behind	19/22
12	EUROPEAN GP	Nürburgring	18	MF1 Team	B	2.4 Midland M16-Toyota V8	1 lap behind	20/22
16	SPANISH GP	Barcelona	18	MF1 Team	B	2.4 Midland M16-Toyota V8	3 laps behind	18/22
15	MONACO GP	Monte Carlo	18	MF1 Team	B	2.4 Midland M16-Toyota V8	2 laps behind	18/22
16	BRITISH GP	Silverstone	18	MF1 Team	B	2.4 Midland M16-Toyota V8	2 laps behind	16/22
14	CANADIAN GP	Montreal	18	MF1 Team	B	2.4 Midland M16-Toyota V8	4 laps behind	19/22
ret	U S GP	Indianapolis	18	MF1 Team	B	2.4 Midland M16-Toyota V8	hit by Sato- accident damage	15/22
ret	FRENCH GP	Magny Cours	18	MF1 Team	B	2.4 Midland M16-Toyota V8	differential – spin	20/22
14/dsq*	GERMAN GP	Hockenheim	18	MF1 Team	B	2.4 Midland M16-Toyota V8	14th on road *dsq – illegal rear wing	20/22
9	HUNGARIAN GP	Hungaroring	18	MF1 Team	B	2.4 Midland M16-Toyota V8	3 laps behind	16/22
ret	TURKISH GP	Istanbul	18	MF1 Team	B	2.4 Midland M16-Toyota V8	multiple collision on lap 1	20/22
ret	ITALIAN GP	Monza	18	Spyker MF1 Team	B	2.4 Spyker M16-Toyota V8	brakes	20/22
ret	CHINESE GP	Shanghai Circuit	18	Spyker MF1 Team	B	2.4 Spyker M16-Toyota V8	spun off	20/22
16	JAPANESE GP	Suzuka Shanghai	18	Spyker MF1 Team	B	2.4 Spyker M16-Toyota V8	2 laps behind	21/22
15	BRAZILIAN GP	Interlagos	18	Spyker MF1 Team	B	2.4 Spyker M16-Toyota V8	*no time set/2 laps behind	*22/22

GP Starts: 37   GP Wins: 0   Pole positions: 0   Fastest laps: 0   Points: 7

MONTERMINI, Andrea (I) b 30/5/1964, Sassuolo

1994 Championship position: Unplaced

	Race	Circuit	No	Entrant	Tyres	Capacity/Car/Engine	Comment	Q Pos/Entries
dnq	SPANISH GP	Barcelona	32	MTV Simtek Ford	G	3.5 Simtek S941-Ford HB V8	injured in practice accident	27/27

1995 Championship position: Unplaced

	Race	Circuit	No	Entrant	Tyres	Capacity/Car/Engine	Comment	Q Pos/Entries
9	BRAZILIAN GP	Interlagos	17	Pacific Grand Prix Ltd	G	3.0 Pacific PR02-Ford ED V8	6 laps behind	22/26
ret	ARGENTINE GP	Buenos Aires	17	Pacific Grand Prix Ltd	G	3.0 Pacific PR02-Ford ED V8	suspension damage	22/26
ret	SAN MARINO GP	Imola	17	Pacific Grand Prix Ltd	G	3.0 Pacific PR02-Ford ED V8	gearbox	24/26
ret/dns	SPANISH GP	Barcelona	17	Pacific Grand Prix Ltd	G	3.0 Pacific PR02-Ford ED V8	gearbox on parade lap	(23)/26
dsq*	MONACO GP	Monte Carlo	17	Pacific Grand Prix Ltd	G	3.0 Pacific PR02-Ford ED V8	jump start – *ignored black flag	25/26
ret	CANADIAN GP	Montreal	17	Pacific Grand Prix Ltd	G	3.0 Pacific PR02-Ford ED V8	gearbox	21/24
nc	FRENCH GP	Magny Cours	17	Pacific Grand Prix Ltd	G	3.0 Pacific PR02-Ford ED V8	10 laps behind	21/24
ret	BRITISH GP	Silverstone	17	Pacific Grand Prix Ltd	G	3.0 Pacific PR02-Ford ED V8	spun off	24/24
8	GERMAN GP	Hockenheim	17	Pacific Grand Prix Ltd	G	3.0 Pacific PR02-Ford ED V8	3 laps behind	23/24
12	HUNGARIAN GP	Hungaroring	17	Pacific Grand Prix Ltd	G	3.0 Pacific PR02-Ford ED V8	4 laps behind	22/24
ret	BELGIAN GP	Spa	17	Pacific Grand Prix Ltd	G	3.0 Pacific PR02-Ford ED V8	fuel pressure	21/24
ret/dns	ITALIAN GP	Monza	17	Pacific Grand Prix Ltd	G	3.0 Pacific PR02-Ford ED V8	accident at first start	(21)/24
ret	PORTUGUESE GP	Estoril	17	Pacific Grand Prix Ltd	G	3.0 Pacific PR02-Ford ED V8	gearbox	21/24
ret	EUROPEAN GP	Nürburgring	17	Pacific Grand Prix Ltd	G	3.0 Pacific PR02-Ford ED V8	out of fuel	20/24
ret	PACIFIC GP	T.I. Circuit	17	Pacific Grand Prix Ltd	G	3.0 Pacific PR02-Ford ED V8	gearbox	23/24
ret	JAPANESE GP	Suzuka	17	Pacific Grand Prix Ltd	G	3.0 Pacific PR02-Ford ED V8	spun off	20/24
ret	AUSTRALIAN GP	Adelaide	17	Pacific Grand Prix Ltd	G	3.0 Pacific PR02-Ford ED V8	gearbox	22/24

1996 Championship position: Unplaced

	Race	Circuit	No	Entrant	Tyres	Capacity/Car/Engine	Comment	Q Pos/Entries
dnq	AUSTRALIAN GP	Melbourne	23	Forti Grand Prix	G	3.0 Forti FG01 95B-Ford Zetec R V8	not within 107% of pole time	22/22
ret	BRAZILIAN GP	Interlagos	23	Forti Grand Prix	G	3.0 Forti FG01 95B-Ford Zetec R V8	4 laps behind	20/22
10	ARGENTINE GP	Buenos Aires	23	Forti Grand Prix	G	3.0 Forti FG01 95B-Ford Zetec R V8	3 laps behind	22/22
dnq	EUROPEAN GP	Nürburgring	23	Forti Grand Prix	G	3.0 Forti FG01 95B-Ford Zetec R V8	not within 107% of pole time	21/22
dnq	SAN MARINO GP	Imola	23	Forti Grand Prix	G	3.0 Forti FG0-Ford Zetec R V8	not within 107% of pole time	22/22
dns	MONACO GP	Monte Carlo	23	Forti Grand Prix	G	3.0 Forti FG03-Ford Zetec R V8	accident in warm up	22/22
dnq	SPANISH GP	Barcelona	23	Forti Grand Prix	G	3.0 Forti FG03-Ford Zetec R V8		22/22
ret	CANADIAN GP	Montreal	23	Forti Grand Prix	G	3.0 Forti FG03-Ford Zetec R V8	loose ballast	22/22
ret	FRENCH GP	Magny Cours	23	Forti Grand Prix	G	3.0 Forti FG03-Ford Zetec R V8	electrics	22/22
dnq	BRITISH GP	Silverstone	23	Forti Grand Prix	G	3.0 Forti FG03-Ford Zetec R V8		21/22
dnp	GERMAN GP	Hockenheim	23	Forti Grand Prix	G	3.0 Forti FG01 95B-Ford Zetec R V8	cars did not practice	- / -

GP Starts: 19 (21)   GP Wins: 0   Pole positions: 0   Fastest laps: 0   Points: 0

ANDREA MONTERMINI

WHEN Andrea Montermini crashed his Simtek heavily during practice for the 1994 Spanish GP and was taken to hospital with relatively minor ankle and foot injuries, a number of observers thought that it might be the last grand prix racing would see of the little Italian, rather cruelly commenting that he was not good enough to take part at this exalted level. Of course he did return, albeit only with back-of-the-grid strugglers Pacific and Forti, and succeeded in winning the respect of the Formula 1 paddock, his racer's appetite remaining undimmed despite overwhelming odds.

A closer look at Andrea's racing history reveals a good deal of success during the early stages of his long career, which began in 1987 in Italian Formula Alfa Boxer. Fourth place in the 1988 Italian F3 standings was supplemented by a splendid second place in the Monaco F3 race the following year. Montermini then spent three seasons in European F3000 between 1990 and 1992. His first year with Madgwick was promising, the second, in a difficult-to-tame Ralt, perhaps less so. However, the Italian's final season in the formula, though beset by financial problems that saw him swap teams from the defunct Il Barone Rampante to Forti Corse, brought him second place in the championship with three wins (at Pau, Spa and Albacete) to his credit.

In 1993, Andrea caused a stir in Indy car circles when he arrived in Detroit to drive a year-old Lola for the Euromotorsports team. Sixth place in practice was impressive, and fourth at the finish an outstanding achievement.

Following the collapse of Forti in mid-1996, Montermini largely pursued his career in sports cars, initially impressing with Gianpiero Moretti's Ferrari in 1997. Wins in the Professional Racing Series at Lime Rock, Pikes Peak Raceway and Sebring led to a Nissan works drive at Le Mans in 1998, when, teamed with Jan Lammers and Érik Comas, he took sixth place, a feat that he repeated a year later at the wheel of a Courage-Nissan in company with fellow countrymen Alex Caffi and Domenico Schiattarella.

The diminutive Italian joined Dan Gurney's underperforming CART team for a four-race spell towards the end of 1999, scoring a couple of points on his debut in Vancouver, but he failed to find a full-time drive in that very competitive category.

Since 2001, Andrea has raced in sports and GT cars, and he has been a regular in the Porsche Supercup. He was fifth overall in the 2006 Italian GT Championship with a Saleen 57-R.

In 2008, Montermini won the International GT open series in a Ferrari F430, and in 2010 he was the Italian Gran Turismo GT2 champion, again behind the wheel of a Ferrari F430 GT2, entered by Villorba Corse. Along with his racing schedule Andrea also acts as a race driving instructor at the International Circuit of Misano Adriatico.

ROBIN MONTGOMERIE-CHARRINGTON

POPULARLY known as 'Monty', Robin Montgomerie-Charrington was an enthusiastic amateur who raced an 1100cc JAP-engined Cooper. In truth, however, he was no match for the leading exponents, such as Eric Brandon and Alan Brown, who could be relied upon to extract the maximum potential from these extremely rapid little rear-engined machines.

Another of Robin's F3 competitors was Bill Aston, who set about building his Formula 2 contender, the Aston-Butterworth, for the 1952 season. 'Monty' became involved and duly purchased one of these machines, which was finished in a pale blue livery. This was the national racing colour of the United States, and apparently it reflected the financial input of an American benefactor.

Montgomerie-Charrington fared no better than Aston during the machines' short racing history, his only result of note being third place in the Grand Prix des Frontières at Chimay, despite coasting to a halt when out of fuel on the last lap. Before the 1952 season was out, 'Monty' had abandoned his racing activities and emigrated to the USA.

MONTGOMERIE-CHARRINGTON, Robin (GB) b 22/6/1915, Mayfair, London – d 3/4/2007 Moreton-in-Marsh

	Race	Circuit	No	Entrant	Tyres	Capacity/Car/Engine	Comment	Q Pos/Entries
	1952 Championship position: Unplaced							
ret	BELGIAN GP	Spa	40	Robin Montgomerie-Charrington	D	2.0 Aston Butterworth F4	misfire	15/22
	GP Starts: 1 GP Wins: 0 Pole positions: 0 Fastest laps: 0 Points: 0							

JUAN PABLO MONTOYA

HAVING achieved so much in his career and given his immense talent, it seems churlish to think that, with his sudden defection to NASCAR in 2006, Juan Pablo Montoya left the grand prix arena with a sense of failure. When the Colombian made his belated entrance in 2001, having made his mark on the Champ Car scene prior to joining Williams, he was seen as the man most likely to topple the omnipotent Michael Schumacher at Ferrari. His early enthusiasm and zest were gradually worn down, however, until he became so disillusioned with the whole environment of Formula 1 that he felt it was not worth pursuing the world championship, which had been his goal since he had started racing karts at the tender age of five.

As he grew older, Montoya progressed to higher kart classes, eventually contesting the 1990 and 1991 world championships. Then he went to the USA to the Skip Barber school to compete successfully in the Saab Pro Series. In 1995, he journeyed to Europe to race in the Formula Vauxhall series with Paul Stewart Racing. Four wins, four poles and two lap records finally netted him third overall and set him up for a crack at the prestigious British F3 championship.

Ever keen to reach the top, Montoya spent just one year in F3, notching two wins, one pole position and five fastest laps, before moving on again, this time to the International F3000 series. Running with Marko RSM, the Colombian made a strong start, taking three wins in his rookie season and just losing out to Ricardo Zonta. Then he jumped ship to join the crack Super Nova outfit for 1998. This was just the environment he needed, and he duly took the title on the back of four wins and seven pole positions to see off the challenge of Nick Heidfeld. His title campaign was supplemented by test-driving duties for the Williams GP squad, but a hoped-for elevation to F1 in 1999 was not forthcoming and, eager for action, he was happy to take the offer of a drive in the CART series when Williams mooted an exchange deal for Alex Zanardi.

The young Colombian took up where Zanardi had left off, going on to dominate his rookie season. Consecutive wins in Long Beach, Nazareth and Rio de Janeiro provided an early-season hat trick, and a further four wins – accompanied by seven pole positions – were enough to seal his double success. It was also Ganassi's fourth straight title, and it marked out Montoya as a special talent. He stayed for a second season in Champ Cars and was a hot favourite for back-to-back titles, but he had to turn the all-new Lola-Toyota combination into a winner to do so. In the end, the task defeated him, leaving him a lowly ninth in the series. However, he did have the considerable kudos of notching a rookie win in the Indianapolis 500 with Ganassi's Target machine. Leading 167 of the 200 laps, he became the first Colombian winner of the 'Blue Riband' event, and the first rookie to win since Graham Hill in 1966.

Frank Williams decided to take up his option on Montoya for 2001, and he was being tipped as a potential race winner before the year got under way in anger. There was little love lost between Juan and his established team-mate, Ralf Schumacher, and it was interesting to watch who got the upper hand on and off the track. Williams, despite their results, suffered a poor year in terms of reliability, and Montoya seemed to bear the brunt of it. Great drives were interspersed with unreliability, until victory number one finally arrived at Monza, and he went on to end the year strongly with an inspired second place in Japan.

In 2002, it was the German who scored the team's only win of the year, but Juan showed his searing pace in taking five consecutive poles and third place in the drivers' championship, one place ahead of his team-mate. The 2003 season saw Montoya really come to the fore, joining a three-way battle for the title with Kimi Räikkönen and Michael Schumacher. He made it tough for himself, however: at the opening grand prix of the season, the Colombian threw away the chance of victory when he spun while leading, and then he picked up just seven more points in the next five races. Victory in Monte Carlo saw his season pick up, starting a run of eight consecutive podium finishes, including a stunning win at Hockenheim. Going into the final two races of the season, he was back in with a shot at his first F1 title, but it all fell apart at the US Grand Prix, where an incident with Rubens Barrichello earned him a drive-through penalty.

Before the 2004 season even started, Montoya had decided he would leave Williams in 2005, opting to sign a deal with Team McLaren-Mercedes. The year was a big disappointment, as the Williams-BMW FW26 wasn't as competitive as hoped, and he had to wait until the final race in Brazil to take his only win of the year.

Montoya's McLaren career did not really start off as expected. Having been sidelined for two races by an injured shoulder – reportedly from playing tennis – on his return, he found that his car was plagued by technical failures, but the Colombian did not help his cause by making avoidable driver errors. Mid-season, however, things began to click for Montoya, who won the British Grand Prix in commanding style and then added wins at Monza and Interlagos, although there were still avoidable errors, which left him only fourth in the overall standings.

Montoya and team-mate Kimi Räikkönen began the 2006 season in the knowledge that Fernando Alonso was already guaranteed one of the seats in the team for 2007, and it seemed to affect the Colombian more than the Finn. Things began badly after a wretched race in Melbourne, which ended in him damaging the car after running over a kerb. Two further disastrous races followed. In Canada, he clipped a wall and broke his suspension, and at Indianapolis he ran into the back of his team-mate on the opening lap, eliminating them both. Disenchanted with his position at McLaren, and with Formula 1 in general, he made a mid-season announcement that he had reached an agreement to join his former employer, Chip Ganassi, in NASCAR for 2007.

Just as rapidly, McLaren-Mercedes removed the Colombian from his race seat, and he was contractually forced to sit out much of the rest of the year before being allowed to make his Nextel Cup debut at Homestead. It was a fiery affair. Juan Pablo's car was pitched into a wall, which ruptured a fuel cell, causing the car to be engulfed in flames and halting the race. Fortunately, he emerged unscathed from his luridly liveried number 07 Dodge Avenger.

The following year started brightly for the Colombian, who shared driving duties in the Ganassi team's Riley-Lexus with Scott Pruett and Salvador Duran. They won the Rolex Daytona 24-hours before Juan Pablo hit the gruelling NASCAR trail. By mid-season, he had taken his first Sprint Cup win, at Infineon Raceway, although this was only one of two road courses on the schedule. In addition, he added a second-tier Nationwide win in Mexico City. He would have to wait another 113 races to record his next victory – at Watkins Glen in 2010 – but a victory on an oval proved elusive. In 2009, Juan Pablo came very close to taking a win in the Allstate 400 at Indianapolis, but he had to surrender a commanding lead after picking up a drive-through penalty for speeding in the pit lane. That year was his most convincing in the series to date. With a best finish of second place at Pocono, he became the first foreign-born driver to qualify for the Chase for the Sprint Cup title, eventually taking eighth in the overall standings.

Meanwhile, the Colombian's brilliant road-course skills were put to good use by Ganassi, Montoya claiming a second successive Rolex 24-hours win in 2008, before being edged out of a personal hat trick of victories the following year, when he lost out to David Donohue's Porsche by the margin of just 0.167 second in a thrilling finish after 24 hours of racing.

Now aged 36, Montoya seems settled in the harum-scarum oval environment, but for fans of Formula 1 and circuit racing in general, there is the undeniable feeling that his sublime talent could have been better utilised over the past five seasons than in simply driving stock cars around in circles...

MONTOYA Juan Pablo, (COL) b 20/9/1975, Bogotá

2001 Championship position: 6th   Wins: 1   Pole positions: 3   Fastest laps: 3   Points scored: 31

	Race	Circuit	No	Entrant	Tyres	Capacity/Car/Engine	Comment	Q Pos/Entries
ret	AUSTRALIAN GP	Melbourne	6	BMW WilliamsF1 Team	M	3.0 Williams FW23-BMW V10	engine	11/22
ret	MALAYSIAN GP	Sepang	6	BMW WilliamsF1 Team	M	3.0 Williams FW23-BMW V10	started spare car from pitlane/spun off	6/22
ret	BRAZILIAN GP	Interlagos	6	BMW WilliamsF1 Team	M	3.0 Williams FW23-BMW V10	led race – punted off by Verstappen	4/22
ret	SAN MARINO GP	Imola	6	BMW WilliamsF1 Team	M	3.0 Williams FW23-BMW V10	clutch	7/22
2	SPANISH GP	Barcelona	6	BMW WilliamsF1 Team	M	3.0 Williams FW23-BMW V10		12/22
ret	AUSTRIAN GP	A1-Ring	6	BMW WilliamsF1 Team	M	3.0 Williams FW23-BMW V10	hydraulics	2/22
ret	MONACO GP	Monte Carlo	6	BMW WilliamsF1 Team	M	3.0 Williams FW23-BMW V10	glanced barrier – crashed out	7/22
ret	CANADIAN GP	Montreal	6	BMW WilliamsF1 Team	M	3.0 Williams FW23-BMW V10	clipped kerb – hit barrier	10/22
2	EUROPEAN GP	Nürburgring	6	BMW WilliamsF1 Team	M	3.0 Williams FW23-BMW V10	FL	3/22
ret	FRENCH GP	Magny Cours	6	BMW WilliamsF1 Team	M	3.0 Williams FW23-BMW V10	engine	6/22
4	BRITISH GP	Silverstone	6	BMW WilliamsF1 Team	M	3.0 Williams FW23-BMW V10		8/22
ret	GERMAN GP	Hockenheim	6	BMW WilliamsF1 Team	M	3.0 Williams FW23-BMW V10	fuel-rig delay/engine overheated/FL	1/22
8	HUNGARIAN GP	Hungaroring	6	BMW WilliamsF1 Team	M	3.0 Williams FW23-BMW V10	1 lap behind	8/22
ret	BELGIAN GP	Spa	6	BMW WilliamsF1 Team	M	3.0 Williams FW23-BMW V10	started first race from back/engine	1/22
1	ITALIAN GP	Monza	6	BMW WilliamsF1 Team	M	3.0 Williams FW23-BMW V10		1/22
ret	UNITED STATES GP	Indianapolis	6	BMW WilliamsF1 Team	M	3.0 Williams FW23-BMW V10	hydraulic failure/FL	3/22
2	JAPANESE GP	Suzuka	6	BMW WilliamsF1 Team	M	3.0 Williams FW23-BMW V10		2/22

2002 Championship position: 3rd   Wins: 0   Pole positions: 7   Fastest laps: 3   Points scored: 50

	Race	Circuit	No	Entrant	Tyres	Capacity/Car/Engine	Comment	Q Pos/Entries
2	AUSTRALIAN GP	Melbourne	6	BMW WilliamsF1 Team	M	3.0 Williams FW24-BMW V10		6/22
2	MALAYSIAN GP	Sepang	6	BMW WilliamsF1 Team	M	3.0 Williams FW24-BMW V10	collision – M Schumacher. – drive-thru pen/FL	2/22
5	BRAZILIAN GP	Interlagos	6	BMW WilliamsF1 Team	M	3.0 Williams FW24-BMW V10	collision – M.Schumacher – pit stop/FL	1/22
4	SAN MARINO GP	Imola	6	BMW WilliamsF1 Team	M	3.0 Williams FW24-BMW V10		4/22
2	SPANISH GP	Barcelona	6	BMW WilliamsF1 Team	M	3.0 Williams FW24-BMW V10		4/21
3	AUSTRIAN GP	A1-Ring	6	BMW WilliamsF1 Team	M	3.0 Williams FW24-BMW V10		4/22
ret	MONACO GP	Monte Carlo	6	BMW WilliamsF1 Team	M	3.0 Williams FW24-BMW V10	engine	1/22
ret	CANADIAN GP	Montreal	6	BMW WilliamsF1 Team	M	3.0 Williams FW24-BMW V10	engine/FL	1/22
ret	EUROPEAN GP	Nürburgring	6	BMW WilliamsF1 Team	M	3.0 Williams FW24-BMW V10	spun – collided with Coulthard	1/22
3	BRITISH GP	Silverstone	6	BMW WilliamsF1 Team	M	3.0 Williams FW24-BMW V10		1/22
4	FRENCH GP	Magny Cours	6	BMW WilliamsF1 Team	M	3.0 Williams FW24-BMW V10	balance problems	1/21
2	GERMAN GP	Hockenheim	6	BMW WilliamsF1 Team	M	3.0 Williams FW24-BMW V10		4/22
11	HUNGARIAN GP	Hungaroring	6	BMW WilliamsF1 Team	M	3.0 Williams FW24-BMW V10	spun – damaged car on kerb/-1 lap	4/20
3	BELGIAN GP	Spa	6	BMW WilliamsF1 Team	M	3.0 Williams FW24-BMW V10		5/20
ret	ITALIAN GP	Monza	6	BMW WilliamsF1 Team	M	3.0 Williams FW24-BMW V10	front suspension	1/20
4	U S GP	Indianapolis	6	BMW WilliamsF1 Team	M	3.0 Williams FW24-BMW V10	wrongly-timed pit stop	4/20
4	JAPANESE GP	Suzuka	6	BMW WilliamsF1 Team	M	3.0 Williams FW24-BMW V10	handling problems	6/20

2003 Championship position: 3rd   Wins: 2   Pole positions: 1   Fastest laps: 3   Points scored: 82

	Race	Circuit	No	Entrant	Tyres	Capacity/Car/Engine	Comment	Q Pos/Entries
2	AUSTRALIAN GP	Melbourne	3	BMW WilliamsF1 Team	M	3.0 Williams FW25-BMW V10	spun away lead to Coulthard	3/20
12	MALAYSIAN GP	Sepang	3	BMW WilliamsF1 Team	M	3.0 Williams FW25-BMW V10	hit by Pizzonia – new rear wing/3 laps behind	8/20
ret	BRAZILIAN GP	Interlagos	3	BMW WilliamsF1 Team	M	3.0 Williams FW25-BMW V10	slid off greasy track	9/20
7	SAN MARINO GP	Imola	3	BMW WilliamsF1 Team	M	3.0 Williams FW25-BMW V10	refuelling glitch – extra pitstop	4/20
4	SPANISH GP	Barcelona	3	BMW WilliamsF1 Team	M	3.0 Williams FW25-BMW V10		9/20
ret	AUSTRIAN GP	A1-Ring	3	BMW WilliamsF1 Team	M	3.0 Williams FW25-BMW V10	engine – water pressure	3/20
1	MONACO GP	Monte Carlo	3	BMW WilliamsF1 Team	M	3.0 Williams FW25-BMW V10	won despite overheating engine	3/19
3	CANADIAN GP	Montreal	3	BMW WilliamsF1 Team	M	3.0 Williams FW25-BMW V10	electronic & gearchange problems	2/20
2	EUROPEAN GP	Nürburgring	3	BMW WilliamsF1 Team	M	3.0 Williams FW25-BMW V10	collision with Michael Schumacher	4/20
2	FRANCE GP	Magny Cours	3	BMW WilliamsF1 Team	M	3.0 Williams FW25-BMW V10	upset at team's pit strategies/FL	2/20
2	BRITISH GP	Silverstone	3	BMW WilliamsF1 Team	M	3.0 Williams FW25-BMW V10		7/20
1	GERMAN GP	Hockenheim	3	BMW WilliamsF1 Team	M	3.0 Williams FW25-BMW V10	FL	1/20
3	HUNGARIAN GP	Hungaroring	3	BMW WilliamsF1 Team	M	3.0 Williams FW25-BMW V10	spin/FL	4/20
2	ITALIAN GP	Monza	3	BMW WilliamsF1 Team	M	3.0 Williams FW25-BMW V10	frustrated lapping cars	2/20
6	U S GP	Indianapolis	3	BMW WilliamsF1 Team	M	3.0 Williams FW25-BMW V10	hit Barrichello – drive-through penalty/-1 lap	4/20
ret	JAPANESE GP	Suzuka	3	BMW WilliamsF1 Team	M	3.0 Williams FW25-BMW V10	hydraulics	2/20

2004 Championship position: 5th   Wins: 1   Pole positions: 0   Fastest laps: 1   Points scored: 58

	Race	Circuit	No	Entrant	Tyres	Capacity/Car/Engine	Comment	Q Pos/Entries
5	AUSTRALIAN GP	Melbourne	3	BMW WilliamsF1 Team	M	3.0 Williams FW26-BMW V10	delayed at 3rd pitstop	3/20
2	MALAYSIAN GP	Sepang	3	BMW WilliamsF1 Team	M	3.0 Williams FW26-BMW V10	FL	4/20
13	BAHRAIN GP	Sakhir Circuit	3	BMW WilliamsF1 Team	M	3.0 Williams FW26-BMW V10	jammed in 4th gear/1 lap behind	3/20
3	SAN MARINO GP	Imola	3	BMW WilliamsF1 Team	M	3.0 Williams FW26-BMW V10		3/20
ret	SPANISH GP	Barcelona	3	BMW WilliamsF1 Team	M	3.0 Williams FW26-BMW V10	brakes	2/20
4	MONACO GP	Monte Carlo	3	BMW WilliamsF1 Team	M	3.0 Williams FW26-BMW V10	1 lap behind	9/20
8	EUROPEAN GP	Nürburgring	3	BMW WilliamsF1 Team	M	3.0 Williams FW26-BMW V10	collision – Ralf Schumacher/1 lap behind	8/20
dsq*	CANADIAN GP	Montreal	3	BMW WilliamsF1 Team	M	3.0 Williams FW26-BMW V10	5th on road/*brake-duct infringement	4/20
dsq*	U S GP	Indianapolis	3	BMW WilliamsF1 Team	M	3.0 Williams FW26-BMW V10	*switched to spare car too late	5/20
8	FRANCE GP	Magny Cours	3	BMW WilliamsF1 Team	M	3.0 Williams FW26-BMW V10	bruised neck from practice/spin	6/20
5	BRITISH GP	Silverstone	3	BMW WilliamsF1 Team	M	3.0 Williams FW26-BMW V10		7/20
5	GERMAN GP	Hockenheim	3	BMW WilliamsF1 Team	M	3.0 Williams FW26-BMW V10	tyre blistering	7/20
4	HUNGARIAN GP	Hungaroring	3	BMW WilliamsF1 Team	M	3.0 Williams FW26-BMW V10		7/20
ret	BELGIAN GP	Spa	3	BMW WilliamsF1 Team	M	3.0 Williams FW26-BMW V10	tyre failure – suspension damage	11/20
5	ITALIAN GP	Monza	3	BMW WilliamsF1 Team	M	3.0 Williams FW26-BMW V10		2/20
5	CHINESE GP	Shanghai	3	BMW WilliamsF1 Team	M	3.0 Williams FW26-BMW V10		10/20
7	JAPANESE GP	Suzuka	3	BMW WilliamsF1 Team	M	3.0 Williams FW26-BMW V10		13/20
1	BRAZILIAN GP	Interlagos	3	BMW WilliamsF1 Team	M	3.0 Williams FW26-BMW V10	FL	2/20

2005 Championship position: 4th   Wins: 3   Pole positions: 2   Fastest laps: 1   Points scored: 60

	Race	Circuit	No	Entrant	Tyres	Capacity/Car/Engine	Comment	Q Pos/Entries
6	AUSTRALIAN GP	Melbourne	10	West McLaren Mercedes	M	McLaren MP4/20-3.0 Mercedes V10	untidy race	9/20
4	MALAYSIAN GP	Sepang	10	West McLaren Mercedes	M	McLaren MP4/20-3.0 Mercedes V10	flat-spotted tyre	11/20
7	SPANISH GP	Barcelona	10	West McLaren Mercedes	M	McLaren MP4/20-3.0 Mercedes V10	spin/extra fuel stop/1 lap behind	7/18
5	MONACO GP	Monte Carlo	10	West McLaren Mercedes	M	McLaren MP4/20-3.0 Mercedes V10	practice incident – sent back of grid	17/18

7	EUROPEAN GP	Nürburgring	10	West McLaren Mercedes	M	McLaren MP4/20-3.0 Mercedes V10	hit by Webber – collision damage	5/20
dsq*	CANADIAN GP	Montreal	10	West McLaren Mercedes	M	McLaren MP4/20-3.0 Mercedes V10	*black-flagged – exiting pits against red light	5/20
ret/dns*	U S GP	Indianapolis	10	West McLaren Mercedes	M	McLaren MP4/20-3.0 Mercedes V10	*withdrawn after parade lap	11/20
ret	FRENCH GP	Magny Cours	10	West McLaren Mercedes	M	McLaren MP4/20-3.0 Mercedes V10	hydraulics	8/20
1	BRITISH GP	Silverstone	10	West McLaren Mercedes	M	McLaren MP4/20-3.0 Mercedes V10		4/20
2	GERMAN GP	Hockenheim	10	West McLaren Mercedes	M	McLaren MP4/20-3.0 Mercedes V10	*no time set/great drive from back of field	*19/20
ret	HUNGARIAN GP	Hungaroring	10	West McLaren Mercedes	M	McLaren MP4/20-3.0 Mercedes V10	driveshaft	2/20
3	TURKISH GP	Hungaroring	10	West McLaren Mercedes	M	McLaren MP4/20-3.0 Mercedes V10	collision with Monteiro – spin – handling/FL	4/20
1	ITALIAN GP	Monza	10	West McLaren Mercedes	M	McLaren MP4/20-3.0 Mercedes V10	*given pole – Raikkonen engine penalty	*(2) 1/20
ret	BELGIAN GP	Spa	10	West McLaren Mercedes	M	McLaren MP4/20-3.0 Mercedes V10	collision with Pizzonia	1/20
1	BRAZILIAN GP	Interlagos	10	West McLaren Mercedes	M	McLaren MP4/20-3.0 Mercedes V10		2/20
ret	JAPANESE GP	Suzuka	10	West McLaren Mercedes	M	McLaren MP4/20-3.0 Mercedes V10	*no time set/accident on lap 1	*18/20
ret	CHINESE GP	Shanghai	10	West McLaren Mercedes	M	McLaren MP4/20-3.0 Mercedes V10	engine	5/20

2006 Championship position: 8th   Wins: 0   Pole positions: 0   Fastest laps: 0   Points scored: 26

4	BAHRAIN GP	Sakhir Circuit	4	McLaren Mercedes	M	2.4 McLaren MP4/21-Mercedes V8	set-up problems	5/22
4	MALAYSIAN GP	Sepang	4	McLaren Mercedes	M	2.4 McLaren MP4/21-Mercedes V8	understeer	6/22
ret	AUSTRALIAN GP	Melbourne	4	McLaren Mercedes	M	2.4 McLaren MP4/21-Mercedes V8	hit kerb – electrics switched off engine	5/22
3	SAN MARINO GP	Imola	4	McLaren Mercedes	M	2.4 McLaren MP4/21-Mercedes V8		7/22
ret	EUROPEAN GP	Nürburgring	4	McLaren Mercedes	M	2.4 McLaren MP4/21-Mercedes V8	engine	9/22
ret	SPANISH GP	Barcelona	4	McLaren Mercedes	M	2.4 McLaren MP4/21-Mercedes V8	spun off	12/22
2	MONACO GP	Monte Carlo	4	McLaren Mercedes	M	2.4 McLaren MP4/21-Mercedes V8		6/22
6	BRITISH GP	Silverstone	4	McLaren Mercedes	M	2.4 McLaren MP4/21-Mercedes V8		8/22
ret	CANADIAN GP	Montreal	4	McLaren Mercedes	M	2.4 McLaren MP4/21-Mercedes V8	collision Rosberg/later hit wall	7/22
ret	U S GP	Indianapolis	4	McLaren Mercedes	M	2.4 McLaren MP4/21-Mercedes V8	collision with Räikkönen	11/22

GP Starts: 94   GP Wins: 7   Pole positions: 13   Fastest laps: 12   Points: 307

GIANNI MORBIDELLI

FROM a racing background (his family produced world championship winning motorcycles), Gianni Morbidelli raced karts from 1981 to 1986, before moving into Italian F3. Although certainly he was quick, he was prone to accidents, which spoiled his 1988 season, but the following year he deservedly claimed the crown with his Forti Corse Dallara, earning a testing contract with Ferrari.

The 1990 season saw Morbidelli make a brief unscheduled grand prix debut for Dallara in place of the indisposed Emanuele Pirro, before he concentrated on his planned F3000 campaign with Forti, which got off to a slow start. Once he got to grips with the Lola, he scored a fine win at Enna and, with the lacklustre Paolo Barilla out of favour at Minardi, he finished the season back in Formula 1 with the luxury of a contract in his pocket for a full season with the Faenza team (and Ferrari power) in 1991. The campaign failed to live up to expectations, but Gianni impressed enough for Ferrari to draft him in to replace the departed Alain Prost in Australia, where he finished sixth in the rain-shortened race to earn a half-point.

Morbidelli returned to Minardi in 1992, but the season was spent in the mire once more as they struggled to develop their Lamborghini-powered car. Without the necessary sponsorship to retain his place, he was jettisoned and left to race in the Italian touring car championship with an Alfa Romeo. Luckily, Jack Oliver had faith in his abilities and drafted him into his Footwork team to renew his grand prix career in 1994. With customer Cosworth power, they were never going to be in the hunt for major honours, but Gianni scored three priceless points to help keep his seat as paying drivers hovered in the hope that Oliver would take their money. So highly did Oliver think of Morbidelli that he retained his services in 1995 as team leader, no doubt assisted by the arrival of Taki Inoue, who brought the team much-needed finance. Sixth place in Canada was a bonus, but within another race Morbidelli was forced on to the sidelines as Max Papis bought his way in. Fortunately for Oliver, he was able to recall Gianni for the final three races, and he was rewarded with a really well-earned podium finish at Adelaide, despite facing the reality of having to look elsewhere for a drive.

Morbidelli's reinstatement to the grand prix ranks with Sauber in 1997 came after Nicola Larini's bust-up with the team. He would find that the number-two seat in the Swiss outfit was no easy berth. Any chance of making an impression was stymied when he broke his arm badly in a testing accident, which forced him out for three races, and the season ended with another injury after a practice crash in Japan.

Looking for a fresh challenge in 1998, Gianni turned to touring cars, driving for Volvo in the BTCC. By his own admission, he found it difficult to adapt to front-wheel drive, but he was not the first ex-grand prix driver to fail to adjust to the demands of this specialised form of racing. However, he found the rear-wheel-drive BMWs far more to his liking in the European Touring Car Championship, which he contested between 2000 and 2002. Since then, Morbidelli has been a very highly regarded competitor in touring and GT cars.

In 2006, Gianni raced an Alfa Romeo T156 in the World Touring Car Championship, before reverting to the Italian Superstars Championship in 2007. Racing an Audi RS4, he took the first two successive championship victories in the class, while the 2009 title came in an M3 BMW. He also showed that he could race the big 6-litre stock cars in the Speedcar Series, winning the 2008/09 title ahead of Johnny Herbert and Toni Liuzzi.

In 2011, Morbidelli returned to Audi to race the RS4 in the Superstar Series, while preparing the new RS5 for an all-out assault on the title against strong opposition in 2012.

MORBIDELLI, Gianni (I) b 13/1/1968, Pesaro, nr Rimini

1990 Championship position: Unplaced

	Race	Circuit	No	Entrant	Tyres	Capacity/Car/Engine	Comment	Q Pos/Entries
dnq	US GP (PHOENIX)	Phoenix	21	Scuderia Italia	P	3.5 BMS Dallara F190-Cosworth V8		29/35
14	BRAZILIAN GP	Interlagos	21	Scuderia Italia	P	3.5 BMS Dallara F190-Cosworth V8	pit stop – jammed throttle/7 laps behind	16/35
ret	JAPANESE GP	Suzuka	24	SCM Minardi Team	P	3.5 Minardi M190-Cosworth V8	spun off	20/30
ret	AUSTRALIAN GP	Adelaide	24	SCM Minardi Team	P	3.5 Minardi M190-Cosworth V8	gearbox	20/30

1991 Championship position: 24th Wins: 0 Pole positions: 0 Fastest laps: 0 Points scored: 0.5

	Race	Circuit	No	Entrant	Tyres	Capacity/Car/Engine	Comment	Q Pos/Entries
ret	US GP (PHOENIX)	Phoenix	24	SCM Minardi Team	G	3.5 Minardi M191-Ferrari V12	gearbox	26/34
8	BRAZILIAN GP	Interlagos	24	SCM Minardi Team	G	3.5 Minardi M191-Ferrari V12	2 laps behind	21/34
ret	SAN MARINO GP	Imola	24	SCM Minardi Team	G	3.5 Minardi M191-Ferrari V12	gearbox	8/34
ret	MONACO GP	Monte Carlo	24	SCM Minardi Team	G	3.5 Minardi M191-Ferrari V12	gearbox	17/34
ret	CANADIAN GP	Montreal	24	SCM Minardi Team	G	3.5 Minardi M191-Ferrari V12	spun off	15/34
7	MEXICAN GP	Mexico City	24	SCM Minardi Team	G	3.5 Minardi M191-Ferrari V12	1 lap behind	23/34
ret	FRENCH GP	Magny Cours	24	SCM Minardi Team	G	3.5 Minardi M191-Ferrari V12	spun off	10/34
11	BRITISH GP	Silverstone	24	SCM Minardi Team	G	3.5 Minardi M191-Ferrari V12	2 laps behind	20/34
ret	GERMAN GP	Hockenheim	24	SCM Minardi Team	G	3.5 Minardi M191-Ferrari V12	differential	19/34
13	HUNGARIAN GP	Hungaroring	24	SCM Minardi Team	G	3.5 Minardi M191-Ferrari V12	2 laps behind	23/34
ret	BELGIAN GP	Spa	24	SCM Minardi Team	G	3.5 Minardi M191-Ferrari V12	clutch	19/34
9	ITALIAN GP	Monza	24	SCM Minardi Team	G	3.5 Minardi M191-Ferrari V12	1 lap behind	17/34
9	PORTUGUESE GP	Estoril	24	SCM Minardi Team	G	3.5 Minardi M191-Ferrari V12	1 lap behind	13/34
14/ret	SPANISH GP	Barcelona	24	SCM Minardi Team	G	3.5 Minardi M191-Ferrari V12	spun off	16/33
ret	JAPANESE GP	Suzuka	24	SCM Minardi Team	G	3.5 Minardi M191-Ferrari V12	wheel bearing	8/31
6*	AUSTRALIAN GP	Adelaide	27	Scuderia Ferrari SpA	G	3.5 Ferrari 643 V12	shortened race/*half points only	8/32

1992 Championship position: Unplaced

	Race	Circuit	No	Entrant	Tyres	Capacity/Car/Engine	Comment	Q Pos/Entries
ret	SOUTH AFRICAN GP	Kyalami	24	Minardi Team	G	3.5 Minardi M191B-Lamborghini V12	engine	19/30
ret	MEXICAN GP	Mexico City	24	Minardi Team	G	3.5 Minardi M191B-Lamborghini V12	spun off	21/30
7	BRAZILIAN GP	Interlagos	24	Minardi Team	G	3.5 Minardi M191B-Lamborghini V12	2 laps behind	23/31
ret	SPANISH GP	Barcelona	24	Minardi Team	G	3.5 Minardi M191B-Lamborghini V12	handling	25/32
ret	SAN MARINO GP	Imola	24	Minardi Team	G	3.5 Minardi M192-Lamborghini V12	transmission	21/32
ret	MONACO GP	Monte Carlo	24	Minardi Team	G	3.5 Minardi M192-Lamborghini V12	flat battery	12/32
11	CANADIAN GP	Montreal	24	Minardi Team	G	3.5 Minardi M192-Lamborghini V12	2 laps behind	13/32
8	FRENCH GP	Magny Cours	24	Minardi Team	G	3.5 Minardi M192-Lamborghini V12	aggregate of two parts/1 lap behind	16/30
17/ret	BRITISH GP	Silverstone	24	Minardi Team	G	3.5 Minardi M192-Lamborghini V12	engine/6 laps behind	25/32
12	GERMAN GP	Hockenheim	24	Minardi Team	G	3.5 Minardi M192-Lamborghini V12	1 lap behind	26/32
dnq	HUNGARIAN GP	Hungaroring	24	Minardi Team	G	3.5 Minardi M192-Lamborghini V12		27/31
16	BELGIAN GP	Spa	24	Minardi Team	G	3.5 Minardi M192-Lamborghini V12	2 laps behind	23/30
ret	ITALIAN GP	Monza	24	Minardi Team	G	3.5 Minardi M192-Lamborghini V12	engine	12/28
14	PORTUGUESE GP	Estoril	24	Minardi Team	G	3.5 Minardi M192-Lamborghini V12	3 laps behind	18/26
14	JAPANESE GP	Suzuka	24	Minardi Team	G	3.5 Minardi M192-Lamborghini V12	2 laps behind	14/26
10	AUSTRALIAN GP	Adelaide	24	Minardi Team	G	3.5 Minardi M192-Lamborghini V12	2 laps behind	16/26

1994 Championship position: 22 Wins: 0 Pole positions: 0 Fastest laps: 0 Points scored: 3

	Race	Circuit	No	Entrant	Tyres	Capacity/Car/Engine	Comment	Q Pos/Entries
ret	BRAZILIAN GP	Interlagos	10	Footwork Ford	G	3.5 Footwork FA15-Ford HB V8	gearbox	6/28
ret	PACIFIC GP	T.I. Circuit	10	Footwork Ford	G	3.5 Footwork FA15-Ford HB V8	engine	13/28
ret	SAN MARINO GP	Imola	10	Footwork Ford	G	3.5 Footwork FA15-Ford HB V8	engine	11/28
ret	MONACO GP	Monte Carlo	10	Footwork Ford	G	3.5 Footwork FA15-Ford HB V8	collision with Martini on lap 1	7/24
ret	SPANISH GP	Barcelona	10	Footwork Ford	G	3.5 Footwork FA15-Ford HB V8	fuel filter	15/27
ret	CANADIAN GP	Montreal	10	Footwork Ford	G	3.5 Footwork FA15-Ford HB V8	engine	11/27
ret	FRENCH GP	Magny Cours	10	Footwork Ford	G	3.5 Footwork FA15-Ford HB V8	collision with Panis	22/28
ret	BRITISH GP	Silverstone	10	Footwork Ford	G	3.5 Footwork FA15-Ford HB V8	split fuel pipe	16/28
5	GERMAN GP	Hockenheim	10	Footwork Ford	G	3.5 Footwork FA15-Ford HB V8		16/28
ret	HUNGARIAN GP	Hungaroring	10	Footwork Ford	G	3.5 Footwork FA15-Ford HB V8	collision with de Cesaris	19/28
6*	BELGIAN GP	Spa	10	Footwork Ford	G	3.5 Footwork FA15-Ford HB V8	1 lap behind	14/28
ret	ITALIAN GP	Monza	10	Footwork Ford	G	3.5 Footwork FA15-Ford HB V8	collision with Zanardi	17/28
9	PORTUGUESE GP	Estoril	10	Footwork Ford	G	3.5 Footwork FA15-Ford HB V8	1 lap behind	16/28
11	EUROPEAN GP	Jerez	10	Footwork Ford	G	3.5 Footwork FA15-Ford HB V8	1 lap behind	8/28
ret	JAPANESE GP	Suzuka	10	Footwork Ford	G	3.5 Footwork FA15-Ford HB V8	crashed in rainstorm	12/28
ret	AUSTRALIAN GP	Adelaide	10	Footwork Ford	G	3.5 Footwork FA15-Ford HB V8	oil leak	21/28

1995 Championship position: 14th= Wins: 0 Pole positions: 0 Fastest laps: 0 Points scored: 5

	Race	Circuit	No	Entrant	Tyres	Capacity/Car/Engine	Comment	Q Pos/Entries
ret	BRAZILIAN GP	Interlagos	9	Footwork Hart	G	3.0 Footwork FA16-Hart V8	fuel pump	13/26
ret	ARGENTINE GP	Buenos Aires	9	Footwork Hart	G	3.0 Footwork FA16-Hart V8	electrics	12/26
13	SAN MARINO GP	Imola	9	Footwork Hart	G	3.0 Footwork FA16-Hart V8	4 laps behind	11/26
11	SPANISH GP	Barcelona	9	Footwork Hart	G	3.0 Footwork FA16-Hart V8	2 laps behind	14/26
9	MONACO GP	Monte Carlo	9	Footwork Hart	G	3.0 Footwork FA16-Hart V8	4 laps behind	13/26
6	CANADIAN GP	Montreal	9	Footwork Hart	G	3.0 Footwork FA16-Hart V8	1 lap behind	13/24
14	FRENCH GP	Magny Cours	9	Footwork Hart	G	3.0 Footwork FA16-Hart V8	3 laps behind	16/24
ret	PACIFIC GP	T.I. Circuit	9	Footwork Hart	G	3.0 Footwork FA16-Hart V8	engine	19/24
ret	JAPANESE GP	Suzuka	9	Footwork Hart	G	3.0 Footwork FA16-Hart V8	spun off	15/24
3	AUSTRALIAN GP	Adelaide	9	Footwork Hart	G	3.0 Footwork FA16-Hart V8	2 laps behind	13/24

1997 Championship position: Unplaced

	Race	Circuit	No	Entrant	Tyres	Capacity/Car/Engine	Comment	Q Pos/Entries
14	SPANISH GP	Barcelona	17	Red Bull Sauber Petronas	G	3.0 Sauber C16-Petronas V10	2 laps behind	13/22
10	CANADIAN GP	Montreal	17	Red Bull Sauber Petronas	G	3.0 Sauber C16-Petronas V10	1 lap behind	18/22
ret	HUNGARIAN GP	Hungaroring	17	Red Bull Sauber Petronas	G	3.0 Sauber C16-Petronas V10	engine	15/22
9*	BELGIAN GP	Spa	17	Red Bull Sauber Petronas	G	3.0 Sauber C16-Petronas V10	*3rd place car dsq	13/22
12	ITALIAN GP	Monza	17	Red Bull Sauber Petronas	G	3.0 Sauber C16-Petronas V10	1 lap behind	18/22
9	AUSTRIAN GP	A1-Ring	17	Red Bull Sauber Petronas	G	3.0 Sauber C16-Petronas V10		13/22
9	LUXEMBOURG GP	Nürburgring	17	Red Bull Sauber Petronas	G	3.0 Sauber C16-Petronas V10	1 lap behind	19/22
dns	JAPANESE GP	Suzuka	17	Red Bull Sauber Petronas	G	3.0 Sauber C16-Petronas V10	practice accident – hurt wrist	(18)/22

GP Starts: 67   GP Wins: 0   Pole positions: 0   Fastest laps: 0   Points: 8.5

ROBERTO MORENO

A CHILDHOOD friend and karting companion of Nelson Piquet, Roberto Moreno travelled to Europe in 1979; he soon made a big impact in a Royale, and then in 1980 he won 15 races and the British FF1600 championship. A testing contract with Lotus gave him the funds to sustain a Formula 3 career, while a win in the Australian GP with a Ralt (beating Piquet and Alan Jones) at the end of 1981 raised his profile greatly. He started 1982 in Formula Atlantic in the USA, before his disastrous grand prix outing for Lotus at Zandvoort, where he failed to qualify, which greatly handicapped his career for a number of years. In 1984, he finished second to team-mate Mike Thackwell in the F2 championship, but a chance of an F1 return with Toleman foundered when the team failed to gain a tyre deal. This led Roberto to try his hand at Indy car racing with Rick Galles and, while results were disappointing, the little Brazilian certainly impressed.

Returning to Europe in 1987, Moreno was back with Ralt in F3000, but his luck was out. Despite leading round after round, his car always seemed to hit trouble and he managed to win only one race, at Enna. Fortune did smile with a return to grands prix with the little AGS team, in which amazingly he scored a point in the Australian Grand Prix. Lack of funding forced him to stay in F3000 for 1988, but once again he showed his talent by clinching the championship, winning four of the 11 rounds.

Roberto took up a drive with back-markers Coloni and then joined EuroBrun, only for the team to fold. Dramatically, he was given the Benetton seat in place of the injured Alessandro Nannini, and a sensational debut in Japan saw him finish second to team-mate Piquet and gain a well-earned contract for 1991. His big season was something of an anti-climax, however, and when Michael Schumacher was snatched from Jordan, he was turfed out, ironically after his best race of the year at Spa. A disconsolate Roberto saw out the season being shuffled around by Jordan and Minardi. He was back at square one in 1992, this time with the hapless Andrea Moda outfit. He showed unbelievable qualities to brilliantly qualify the car at Monaco, but when the team was finally thrown out of the championship, he was left with no option but to find a ride in touring cars. It was quite a surprise when it was announced that he would partner Pedro Diniz in the new Forti Corse F1 team in 1995, but the all-Brazilian driver pairing were forced to spend most of their races looking in their mirrors as the leaders lapped them with monotonous regularity.

In 1996, after a ten-year absence, Roberto returned to Indy car racing with the underfinanced Payton-Coyne Racing. His professionalism brought its reward with a superb third place in the U.S. 500 at Michigan, the team's best ever finish. Initially without a ride for 1997, he was soon in action as a replacement for the injured Christian Fittipaldi at Newman-Haas. The fact that he outqualified team-mate Michael Andretti three times in six races raised a few eyebrows. The following season began with two races for Project Indy before he quit, and it seemed that his only future lay in the IRL. Indeed, he started 1999 in that category, before another call into CART action as a substitute for Mark Blundell at PacWest, followed by a further stand-in role at Newman-Haas. Roberto's efforts were recognised at last when 'Supersub' finally was given the full-time ride he deserved with Patrick Racing for 2000. He did not let his team down, and at the age of 41, he made a worthy challenge for the title. The highlight of Moreno's year was his dominant victory from pole position at Cleveland. He remained with Patrick for 2001, but his season was less happy, and despite a win in Vancouver, he was out of a ride for the 2002 season.

Another comeback was conjured by the never-say-die Moreno, who found himself in the Herdez team in 2003. His wealth of experience was of huge benefit to the team and he played a full part in their success, which included a 1-2 finish at Surfers Paradise. Despite announcing his retirement, he was soon back behind the wheel, testing the Panoz chassis in 2006. Moreover, his racing career was not quite over. While acting as a driver coach to Ed Carpenter for 2006, he stood in for the indisposed youngster at an IRL race at St Petersburg. In 2007, he stood in for Alex Figge in Champ Car at Houston, taking 12th place, and then he was a late replacement at Indianapolis for the injured Stéphan Gregoire – amazingly, he qualified the old Panoz. It was only his third start in the 500, his first having been some 21 years earlier! In 2008, Moreno's front-line career came to a close with a race in the last ever Champ Car event at Long Beach, before the series was merged with the IRL.

MORENO, Roberto 'Pupo' (BR) b 11/2/1959, Rio de Janeiro

	Race	Circuit	No	Entrant	Tyres	Capacity/Car/Engine	Comment	Q Pos/Entries
	1982 Championship position: Unplaced							
dnq	DUTCH GP	Zandvoort	12	John Player Team Lotus	G	3.0 Lotus 91-Cosworth V8		30/31
	1987 Championship position: 19th= Wins: 0 Pole positions: 0 Fastest laps: 0 Points scored: 1							
ret	JAPANESE GP	Suzuka	14	Team El Charro AGS	G	3.5 AGS JH22-Cosworth V8	engine – fuel injection	27/27
6*	AUSTRALIAN GP	Adelaide	14	Team El Charro AGS	G	3.5 AGS JH22-Cosworth V8	*3rd non-turbo/3 laps behind	25/27
	1989 Championship position: Unplaced							
dnq	BRAZILIAN GP	Rio	31	Coloni SpA	P	3.5 Coloni FC188B-Cosworth V8		30/38
dnq	SAN MARINO GP	Imola	31	Coloni SpA	P	3.5 Coloni FC188B-Cosworth V8		30/39
ret	MONACO GP	Monte Carlo	31	Coloni SpA	P	3.5 Coloni FC188B-Cosworth V8	gearbox	25/38
dnq	MEXICAN GP	Mexico City	31	Coloni SpA	P	3.5 Coloni FC188B-Cosworth V8		30/39
dnq	US GP (PHOENIX)	Phoenix	31	Coloni SpA	P	3.5 Coloni FC188B-Cosworth V8		28/39
ret	CANADIAN GP	Montreal	31	Coloni SpA	P	3.5 Coloni FC189-Cosworth V8	transmission	26/39
dns	"	"	31	Coloni SpA	P	3.5 Coloni FC188B-Cosworth V8	practice only	– / –
dnq	FRENCH GP	Paul Ricard	31	Coloni SpA	P	3.5 Coloni FC189-Cosworth V8		30/39
ret	BRITISH GP	Silverstone	31	Coloni SpA	P	3.5 Coloni FC189-Cosworth V8	gearbox	23/39

dnpq	GERMAN GP	Hockenheim	31	Coloni SpA	P	3.5 Coloni FC189-Cosworth V8		35/39
dnpq	HUNGARIAN GP	Hungaroring	31	Coloni SpA	P	3.5 Coloni FC189-Cosworth V8		36/39
dnpq	BELGIAN GP	Spa	31	Coloni SpA	P	3.5 Coloni FC189-Cosworth V8		33/39
dnpq	ITALIAN GP	Monza	31	Coloni SpA	P	3.5 Coloni FC189-Cosworth V8		32/39
ret	PORTUGUESE GP	Estoril	31	Coloni SpA	P	3.5 Coloni FC189-Cosworth V8	*electrics*	15/39
dnpq	SPANISH GP	Jerez	31	Coloni SpA	P	3.5 Coloni FC189-Cosworth V8		32/38
dnpq	JAPANESE GP	Suzuka	31	Coloni SpA	P	3.5 Coloni FC189-Cosworth V8		32/39
dnpq	AUSTRALIAN GP	Adelaide	31	Coloni SpA	P	3.5 Coloni FC189-Cosworth V8		34/39

1990 Championship position: 10th   Wins: 0   Pole positions: 0   Fastest laps: 0   Points scored: 6

13	US GP (PHOENIX)	Phoenix	33	EuroBrun Racing	P	3.5 EuroBrun ER189-Judd V8	*pit stop – flat battery/5 laps behind*	16/35
dnpq	BRAZILIAN GP	Interlagos	33	EuroBrun Racing	P	3.5 EuroBrun ER189-Judd V8		32/35
ret	SAN MARINO GP	Imola	33	EuroBrun Racing	P	3.5 EuroBrun ER189-Judd V8	*sticking throttle on lap 1*	25/34
dnq	MONACO GP	Monte Carlo	33	EuroBrun Racing	P	3.5 EuroBrun ER189-Judd V8		30/35
dnq	CANADIAN GP	Montreal	33	EuroBrun Racing	P	3.5 EuroBrun ER189-Judd V8		27/35
excl	MEXICAN GP	Mexico City	33	EuroBrun Racing	P	3.5 EuroBrun ER189B-Judd V8	*push start after practice spin*	26/35
dnpq	FRENCH GP	Paul Ricard	33	EuroBrun Racing	P	3.5 EuroBrun ER189B-Judd V8		32/35
dnpq	BRITISH GP	Silverstone	33	EuroBrun Racing	P	3.5 EuroBrun ER189B-Judd V8		31/35
dnpq	GERMAN GP	Hockenheim	33	EuroBrun Racing	P	3.5 EuroBrun ER189B-Judd V8		32/35
dnpq	HUNGARIAN GP	Hungaroring	33	EuroBrun Racing	P	3.5 EuroBrun ER189B-Judd V8		33/35
dnpq	BELGIAN GP	Spa	33	EuroBrun Racing	P	3.5 EuroBrun ER189B-Judd V8		31/33
dnpq	ITALIAN GP	Monza	33	EuroBrun Racing	P	3.5 EuroBrun ER189B-Judd V8		31/33
dnpq	PORTUGUESE GP	Estoril	33	EuroBrun Racing	P	3.5 EuroBrun ER189B-Judd V8		31/33
dnpq	SPANISH GP	Jerez	33	EuroBrun Racing	P	3.5 EuroBrun ER189B-Judd V8		31/33
2	JAPANESE GP	Suzuka	19	Benetton Formula	G	3.5 Benetton B190-Ford HB V8		9/30
7	AUSTRALIAN GP	Adelaide	19	Benetton Formula	G	3.5 Benetton B190-Ford HB V8	*pit stop – tyres/1 lap behind*	8/30

1991 Championship position: 10th   Wins: 0   Pole positions: 0   Fastest laps: 1   Points scored: 8

ret	US GP (PHOENIX)	Phoenix	19	Camel Benetton Ford	G	3.5 Benetton B190B-Ford HB V8	*hit Patrese's spun car*	8/34
7	BRAZILIAN GP	Interlagos	19	Camel Benetton Ford	G	3.5 Benetton B190B-Ford HB V8	*1 lap behind*	14/34
13/ret	SAN MARINO GP	Imola	19	Camel Benetton Ford	G	3.5 Benetton B190B-Ford HB V8	*gearbox/engine/7 laps behind*	13/34
4	MONACO GP	Monte Carlo	19	Camel Benetton Ford	G	3.5 Benetton B190B-Ford HB V8	*1 lap behind*	8/34
ret	CANADIAN GP	Montreal	19	Camel Benetton Ford	G	3.5 Benetton B190B-Ford HB V8	*spun off – suspension damage*	5/34
5	MEXICAN GP	Mexico City	19	Camel Benetton Ford	G	3.5 Benetton B190B-Ford HB V8	*1 lap behind*	9/34
ret	FRENCH GP	Magny Cours	19	Camel Benetton Ford	G	3.5 Benetton B190B-Ford HB V8	*driver unwell*	8/34
ret	BRITISH GP	Silverstone	19	Camel Benetton Ford	G	3.5 Benetton B190B-Ford HB V8	*gearbox*	7/34
8	GERMAN GP	Hockenheim	19	Camel Benetton Ford	G	3.5 Benetton B190B-Ford HB V8	*1 lap behind*	9/34
8	HUNGARIAN GP	Hungaroring	19	Camel Benetton Ford	G	3.5 Benetton B190B-Ford HB V8	*1 lap behind*	15/34
4	BELGIAN GP	Spa	19	Camel Benetton Ford	G	3.5 Benetton B190B-Ford HB V8	*FL*	8/34
ret	ITALIAN GP	Monza	32	Team 7UP Jordan	G	3.5 Jordan 191-Ford HB V8	*spun off – brakes*	9/34
10	PORTUGUESE GP	Estoril	32	Team 7UP Jordan	G	3.5 Jordan 191-Ford HB V8	*1 lap behind*	16/34
16	AUSTRALIAN GP	Adelaide	24	Minardi Team	G	3.5 Minardi M191-Ferrari V12	*rain shortened race/1 lap behind*	18/32

1992 Championship position: Unplaced

dnpq	BRAZILIAN GP	Interlagos	34	Andrea Moda Formula	G	3.5 Moda S921-Judd V10		31/31
dnpq	SPANISH GP	Barcelona	34	Andrea Moda Formula	G	3.5 Moda S921-Judd V10		31/32
dnpq	SAN MARINO GP	Imola	34	Andrea Moda Formula	G	3.5 Moda S921-Judd V10		31/32
ret	MONACO GP	Monte Carlo	34	Andrea Moda Formula	G	3.5 Moda S921-Judd V10	*engine*	26/32
dnpq	CANADIAN GP	Montreal	34	Andrea Moda Formula	G	3.5 Moda S921-Judd V10		31/32
dnp	FRENCH GP	Magny Cours	34	Andrea Moda Formula	G	3.5 Moda S921-Judd V10	*team failed to arrive*	- / -
dnpq	BRITISH GP	Silverstone	34	Andrea Moda Formula	G	3.5 Moda S921-Judd V10		31/32
dnpq	GERMAN GP	Hockenheim	34	Andrea Moda Formula	G	3.5 Moda S921-Judd V10		31/32
dnq	HUNGARIAN GP	Hungaroring	34	Andrea Moda Formula	G	3.5 Moda S921-Judd V10		30/31
dnq	BELGIAN GP	Spa	34	Andrea Moda Formula	G	3.5 Moda S921-Judd V10		28/30
excl	ITALIAN GP	Monza	34	Andrea Moda Formula	G	3.5 Moda S921-Judd V10	*team excluded*	- / -

1995 Championship position: Unplaced

ret	BRAZILIAN GP	Interlagos	22	Parmalat Forti Ford	G	3.0 Forti FG01-Ford ED V8	*spun off*	23/26
nc	ARGENTINE GP	Buenos Aires	22	Parmalat Forti Ford	G	3.0 Forti FG01-Ford ED V8	*9 laps behind*	24/26
nc	SAN MARINO GP	Imola	22	Parmalat Forti Ford	G	3.0 Forti FG01-Ford ED V8	*7 laps behind*	25/26
ret	SPANISH GP	Barcelona	22	Parmalat Forti Ford	G	3.0 Forti FG01-Ford ED V8	*water pump*	25/26
ret	MONACO GP	Monte Carlo	22	Parmalat Forti Ford	G	3.0 Forti FG01-Ford ED V8	*brake pipe*	24/26
ret	CANADIAN GP	Montreal	22	Parmalat Forti Ford	G	3.0 Forti FG01-Ford ED V8	*blocked fuel line*	23/24
16	FRENCH GP	Magny Cours	22	Parmalat Forti Ford	G	3.0 Forti FG01-Ford ED V8	*6 laps behind*	24/24
ret	BRITISH GP	Silverstone	22	Parmalat Forti Ford	G	3.0 Forti FG01-Ford ED V8	*hydraulic pressure*	22/24
ret	GERMAN GP	Hockenheim	22	Parmalat Forti Ford	G	3.0 Forti FG01-Ford ED V8	*driveshaft*	22/24
ret	HUNGARIAN GP	Hungaroring	22	Parmalat Forti Ford	G	3.0 Forti FG01-Ford ED V8	*gearshift failure*	21/24
14	BELGIAN GP	Spa	22	Parmalat Forti Ford	G	3.0 Forti FG01-Ford ED V8	*2 laps behind*	22/24
ret/dns	ITALIAN GP	Monza	22	Parmalat Forti Ford	G	3.0 Forti FG01-Ford ED V8	*accident at first start*	(22)/24
17	PORTUGUESE GP	Estoril	22	Parmalat Forti Ford	G	3.0 Forti FG01-Ford ED V8	*7 laps behind*	23/24
ret	EUROPEAN GP	Nürburgring	22	Parmalat Forti Ford	G	3.0 Forti FG01-Ford ED V8	*driveshaft*	23/24
16	PACIFIC GP	T.I. Circuit	22	Parmalat Forti Ford	G	3.0 Forti FG01-Ford ED V8	*5 laps behind*	22/24
ret	JAPANESE GP	Suzuka	22	Parmalat Forti Ford	G	3.0 Forti FG01-Ford ED V8	*gearbox on lap 1*	22/24
ret	AUSTRALIAN GP	Adelaide	22	Parmalat Forti Ford	G	3.0 Forti FG01-Ford ED V8	*accident*	20/24

GP Starts: 41 (42)   GP Wins: 0   Pole positions: 0   Fastest laps: 1   Points: 15

MORGAN, Dave (GB) b 7/8/1944, Shepton Mallet, Somerset

1975 Championship position: Unplaced

	Race	Circuit	No	Entrant	Tyres	Capacity/Car/Engine	Comment	Q Pos/Entries
18/ret	BRITISH GP	Silverstone	19	National Organs-Team Surtees	G	3.0 Surtees TS16-Cosworth V8	*crashed in rainstorm/6 laps behind*	23/28

GP Starts: 1   GP Wins: 0   Pole positions: 0   Fastest laps: 0   Points: 0

DAVE MORGAN

HAVING begun racing in 1965 with a Mini Cooper, Dave Morgan progressed to Formula 3 in 1970 with a March 703, and a highly competitive season ended in a controversial accident with James Hunt at Crystal Palace. Morgan was suspended for 12 months for 'dangerous driving', but subsequently he was allowed to continue his racing activities in 1971 in Formula Atlantic. Moving up to Formula 2, he took his private Brabham BT35 to a surprise, but well-deserved win at Mallory Park, and later in the year came a brilliant drive at Salzburgring, where he won the first heat and finished third in heat 2.

After two seasons in the formula and a few more decent placings, Morgan successfully returned to Formula Atlantic in 1974. Then, with the support of his sponsors, he organised his one grand prix drive with a Surtees in 1975. Unfortunately, he was one of the many victims who crashed in the rainstorm that eventually halted proceedings. After a couple of outings sharing John Lepp's March sports car, he retired from the circuits. He did return in 1980 and 1981, however, racing a Colt Lancer in the RAC Tricentrol British Saloon Car Championship.

In the early 1990s, he acted as Eric van de Poele's engineer in F3000 and Formula 1, before heading to Mexico to work in the thriving junior single-seater series, later moving over to CART. On his return to Europe, he worked in the Renault World Series with Robert Kubica before moving to South Africa.

SILVIO MOSER

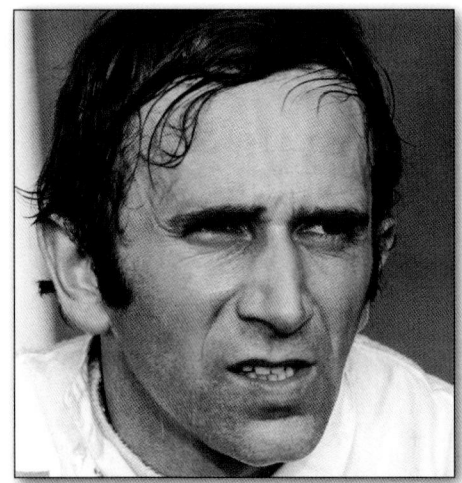

AFTER racing Alfas in the early 1960s, pleasant little Swiss driver Silvio Moser switched to junior single-seaters in 1964 with huge success, both in European F3 and in the Temporada series, winning all four rounds in his Formula Junior Lotus.

Moser moved into Formula 2 with his own team, but continued to race in F3, where he was more competitive, winning races at Syracuse, La Chatre and Rosario. Then he switched to Formula 1 full time, initially with an elderly Cooper-ATS, then with the ex-Ligier Brabham, scoring a fifth place at Zandvoort in 1968 and a sixth at Watkins Glen in 1969.

Silvio embarked on a disastrous 1970 season with the hopeless Bellasi-Ford, which scuppered his immediate grand prix expectations. Returning to Formula 2, he drove a Brabham in 1971 and '72, taking second at the Monza Lottery GP, but he had a thin time of it with a Surtees in 1973. He was planning to race a March in Formula 2 in 1974, as well as to make a return to grands prix with a Bretscher Brabham, but he crashed a Lola sports car heavily in the Monza 1000km, sustaining serious internal and head injuries. Despite several operations, poor Moser died in hospital the following month without regaining consciousness.

MOSER, Silvio (CH) b 24/4/1941, Zurich – d 26/5/1974, Locarno

	Race	Circuit	No	Entrant	Tyres	Capacity/Car/Engine	Comment	Q Pos/Entries
	1966 Championship position: Unplaced							
dns	GERMAN GP (F2)	Nürburgring	35	Silvio Moser	D	1.0 Brabham BT16-Cosworth 4 F2	engine in practice	(29)/30
	1967 Championship position: Unplaced							
ret	BRITISH GP	Silverstone	22	Charles Vögele	D	2.7 Cooper T77-ATS V8	engine – no oil pressure	20/21
	1968 Championship position: 23rd Wins: 0 Pole positions: 0 Fastest laps: 0 Points scored: 2							
dnq	MONACO GP	Monte Carlo	21	Charles Vögele	G	3.0 Brabham BT20-Repco V8		16/18
5	DUTCH GP	Zandvoort	22	Charles Vögele	G	3.0 Brabham BT20-Repco V8	3 laps behind	17/19
nc	BRITISH GP	Brands Hatch	19	Charles Vögele	G	3.0 Brabham BT20-Repco V8	pit stops – gearbox/28 laps behind	19/20
dnp	GERMAN GP	Nürburgring	23	Charles Vögele	G	3.0 Brabham BT20-Repco V8	oil pump failed – seized bearings	– / –
dnq	ITALIAN GP	Monza	12	Charles Vögele	G	3.0 Brabham BT20-Repco V8		24/24
	1969 Championship position: 16th= Wins: 0 Pole positions: 0 Fastest laps: 0 Points scored: 1							
ret	MONACO GP	Monte Carlo	17	Silvio Moser Racing Team	G	3.0 Brabham BT24-Cosworth V8	driveshaft	=14/16
ret	DUTCH GP	Zandvoort	17	Silvio Moser Racing Team	G	3.0 Brabham BT24-Cosworth V8	steering/electrics	14/15
7	FRENCH GP	Clermont Ferrand	12	Silvio Moser Racing Team	G	3.0 Brabham BT24-Cosworth V8	2 laps behind	13/13
ret	ITALIAN GP	Monza	36	Silvio Moser Racing Team	G	3.0 Brabham BT24-Cosworth V8	fuel leak	13/15
ret	CANADIAN GP	Mosport Park	20	Silvio Moser Racing Team	G	3.0 Brabham BT24-Cosworth V8	put off road by Pease	20/20
6	US GP	Watkins Glen	19	Silvio Moser Racing Team	G	3.0 Brabham BT24-Cosworth V8	pit stop/10 laps behind	17/18
11/ret	MEXICAN GP	Mexico City	19	Silvio Moser Racing Team	G	3.0 Brabham BT24-Cosworth V8	fuel leak/5 laps behind	13/17
	1970 Championship position: Unplaced							
dnq	DUTCH GP	Zandvoort	29	Silvio Moser Racing Team	G	3.0 Bellasi-Cosworth V8		24/24
dnq	FRENCH GP	Clermont Ferrand	24	Silvio Moser Racing Team	G	3.0 Bellasi-Cosworth V8		21/23
dnq	GERMAN GP	Nürburgring	27	Silvio Moser Racing Team	G	3.0 Bellasi-Cosworth V8		24/25
ret	AUSTRIAN GP	Österreichring	24	Silvio Moser Racing Team	G	3.0 Bellasi-Cosworth V8	radiator	24/24
dnq	ITALIAN GP	Monza	56	Silvio Moser Racing Team	G	3.0 Bellasi-Cosworth V8		26/27
	1971 Championship position: Unplaced							
ret	ITALIAN GP	Monza	27	Jolly Club Switzerland	G	3.0 Bellasi-Cosworth V8	shock absorber	22/24
	GP Starts: 12 GP Wins: 0 Pole positions: 0 Fastest laps: 0 Points: 3							

SIR STIRLING MOSS, OBE

THE long career and many brilliant deeds of Stirling Moss far outstrip the space available to describe them here, and his successes are also far too numerous to list. Thus a broad brush must be used to give an impression of this patriotic and ultra-professional driver, who had a clear idea of his own worth. Without vanity, he quite soundly reasoned that the world championship, which the British public was so desperate for him to win, was utterly meaningless as a measure of a driver's abilities. Painstaking and thorough in his approach, in his prime his mastery of the skills of his profession was absolute. Capable of driving just about any machine with equal excellence, he never gave less than 100 per cent and, no matter what the situation, he simply never gave up.

Stirling's career began in 1947 with a BMW 328, but he soon started scrapping it out in the rough and tumble of 500cc racing with a Cooper-JAP. In 1950, he scored his first major success, winning the Tourist Trophy in a Jaguar XK120, and during the next three seasons he drove a variety of cars – HWM, Formula 3 Kieft, Frazer-Nash and Jaguar – sampling success in all of them. Only the ERA G-Type was a complete failure, and by 1953 Stirling's talents were coveted by Ferrari.

Actually, Moss had his eyes fixed on a seat with Mercedes-Benz, but Alfred Neubauer was not yet convinced that the youngster was ready. So for the 1954 season, he bought a Maserati 250F and promptly took third place at Spa. Later in the year, he accepted the offer of a works car and duly led the Mercedes of Juan Fangio at Monza until the oil tank split. Seeing his massive talent, the German team lost no time in signing him up for the 1955 season alongside the 'Maestro'.

In world championship grands prix, Stirling watched and learned much from his august partner, scoring a famous victory in the British Grand Prix in the July sunshine at Aintree. He also won the Mille Miglia and the Targa Florio in the silver sports cars. Unfortunately, the Le Mans disaster prompted Mercedes' withdrawal from the sport, and while Fangio decamped to Ferrari, Stirling joined Maserati as their number-one driver for 1956.

Despite brilliant wins at Monaco and Monza, retirements elsewhere cost Stirling dear, and the championship (with the help of Peter Collins) went the way of the fortunate Argentine on this occasion. It was a very productive year overall, however, with no fewer than 16 race wins in the 250F, the Maserati 300TS and the Vanwall among others.

Stirling's patriotism was rewarded at last when Vanwall offered him a machine worthy of his talents in 1957, and in the British Grand Prix he fulfilled a long-held ambition by giving a green car victory in a world championship grand prix after taking over Tony Brooks' sister entry. There were further wins at Pescara and Monza, and hopes were high for the championship in 1958. He started the season with a quite brilliant win against the odds in Rob Walker's little Cooper, before resuming the fight in Vandervell's machines. Once again the unreliability of the car torpedoed his personal title chances. He scored four victories to rival Mike Hawthorn's one, but the Ferrari driver's consistent finishes held sway. There was some consolation for Tony Vandervell, however, since with Brooks and Stuart Lewis-Evans backing up Moss, the team took the constructors' title before withdrawing from grand prix racing at the season's end.

By then, Moss had ceased to worry unduly about the championship. Certainly Ferrari would have given anything to sign him, but he preferred the comfortable ambience of Walker's little team, with Rob himself offering discreet guidance and Alf Francis fettling the cars. Stirling perhaps hindered his chances by switching about a bit too often, surmising that the BRP BRM would be better suited to Reims and Aintree, although he won in Portugal and Italy in the Walker Cooper.

In 1960, Stirling had the choice of a Cooper and the new Lotus 18, which he used to win the Monaco Grand Prix – and give the marque its first ever victory – before disaster struck in practice for the Belgian Grand Prix, when his Lotus shed a wheel, leaving him suffering from serious back injuries. Characteristically, he set himself impossible targets for his comeback and returned in time to take another predictable win at the end of the year at Riverside.

In 1961, we saw the true genius of Moss in two grands prix at Monaco and particularly the Nürburgring, where he defeated the shark-nose Ferrari 156 V6 cars of Phil Hill and Wolfgang von Trips. Inevitably, these victories were just outcrops of a seam of success that ran through the season, into the winter months at Nassau, and then across the world early in 1962 in Australia and New Zealand. On his return to Britain, Moss drove the pale green UDT-entered Lotus to seventh in the Lombank Trophy, before heading down to Goodwood for the Easter Monday meeting and the final race of his top-line career.

Why Stirling crashed is still not clear, but his car was wrecked and he was hospitalised with serious head injuries. His recuperation was slow this time. Almost a year later, he tried a car in a private test, but his fears were realised. The sharp edge of his reflexes had gone, and wisely he decided not to race again, thus leaving intact memories of a driver who always competed at the peak of his powers. Then he launched himself into myriad business ventures, many of which kept him in touch with the sport. In the late 1970s, he was tempted back to the track, mainly for fun, in historic cars and saloons.

With the millennium approaching and having just celebrated his 70th birthday, Stirling (who had received an OBE in 1959) was given a knighthood in the 2000 New Year Honours. It was a fitting confirmation of the high esteem in which this truly great driver was held. In 2006, he was awarded the FIA gold medal in recognition of his outstanding contribution to motorsport.

Stirling survived a three-storey plunge down a lift shaft at home in March, 2010, but he broke both ankles and four bones in his feet. He recovered, however, to get back behind the wheel again. At Le Mans in 2011, he announced that he was giving up track action, but despite being an octogenerian, Sir Stirling shows little sign of slowing down, and remains a much loved and vibrant presence in motorsport.

MOSS, Stirling (GB) b 17/9/1929, West Kensington, London

1951 Championship position: Unplaced

	Race	Circuit	No	Entrant	Tyres	Capacity/Car/Engine	Comment	Q Pos/Entries
8	SWISS GP	Bremgarten	14	HW Motors Ltd	D	2.0 HWM-Alta 4	2 laps behind	14/21

1952 Championship position: Unplaced

	Race	Circuit	No	Entrant	Tyres	Capacity/Car/Engine	Comment	Q Pos/Entries
ret	SWISS GP	Bremgarten	46	HW Motors Ltd	D	2.0 HWM-Alta 4	withdrawn – hub failure on team-mate's car	9/21
ret	BELGIAN GP	Spa	32	ERA Ltd	D	2.0 ERA G Type-Bristol 6	engine	10/22
ret	BRITISH GP	Silverstone	12	ERA Ltd	D	2.0 ERA G Type-Bristol 6	engine	16/32
ret	DUTCH GP	Zandvoort	36	ERA Ltd	D	2.0 ERA G Type-Bristol 6	*no practice time set/engine	*- /18
ret	ITALIAN GP	Monza	32	Connaught Engineering	D	2.0 Connaught-Lea Francis A Type 4	engine – push rod	9/35

1953 Championship position: Unplaced

	Race	Circuit	No	Entrant	Tyres	Capacity/Car/Engine	Comment	Q Pos/Entries
9	DUTCH GP	Zandvoort	34	Connaught Engineering	D	2.0 Connaught-Lea Francis A Type 4	7 laps behind	9/20
ret	FRENCH GP	Reims	36	Cooper Car Co	D	2.0 Cooper Alta Special-4	clutch	13/25
6	GERMAN GP	Nürburgring	19	Cooper Car Co	D	2.0 Cooper Alta Special T2-4	1 lap behind	12/35
13	ITALIAN GP	Monza	28	Cooper Car Co	D	2.0 Cooper Alta Special T23-4	pit stop – fuel leak/10 laps behind	10/30

1954 Championship position: 10th=   Wins: 0   Pole positions: 0   Fastest laps: 1 (shared)   Points scored: 4.14

	Race	Circuit	No	Entrant	Tyres	Capacity/Car/Engine	Comment	Q Pos/Entries
3	BELGIAN GP	Spa	22	Equipe Moss	P	2.5 Maserati 250F 6	1 lap behind	9/15
ret	BRITISH GP	Silverstone	7	A E Moss	P	2.5 Maserati 250F 6	gearbox/FL (shared)	4/31
ret	GERMAN GP	Nürburgring	16	A E Moss	P	2.5 Maserati 250F 6	engine	3/23
ret	SWISS GP	Bremgarten	32	Officine Alfieri Maserati	P	2.5 Maserati 250F 6	oil pressure	3/16
nc	ITALIAN GP	Monza	28	Officine Alfieri Maserati	P	2.5 Maserati 250F 6	split oil tank/9 laps behind	3/21
ret	SPANISH GP	Pedralbes	8	Officine Alfieri Maserati	P	2.5 Maserati 250F 6	oil pump	6/22

1955 Championship position: 2nd   Wins: 1   Pole positions: 1   Fastest laps: 2   Points scored: 23

	Race	Circuit	No	Entrant	Tyres	Capacity/Car/Engine	Comment	Q Pos/Entries
ret	ARGENTINE GP	Buenos Aires	6	Daimler Benz AG	C	2.5 Mercedes-Benz W196 8	fuel system vapour lock	8/22
4*	"	"	8	Daimler Benz AG	C	2.5 Mercedes-Benz W196 8	*Herrmann/Kling also drove car	- / -
9/ret	MONACO GP	Monte Carlo	6	Daimler Benz AG	C	2.5 Mercedes-Benz W196 8	engine/19 laps behind	3/22
2	BELGIAN GP	Spa	14	Daimler Benz AG	C	2.5 Mercedes-Benz W196 8		3/14
2	DUTCH GP	Zandvoort	10	Daimler Benz AG	C	2.5 Mercedes-Benz W196 8		2/16
1	BRITISH GP	Aintree	12	Daimler Benz AG	C	2.5 Mercedes-Benz W196 8	FL	1/25
ret	ITALIAN GP	Monza	16	Daimler Benz AG	C	2.5 Mercedes-Benz W196 8 str	engine/FL	2/22

1956 Championship position: 2nd   Wins: 2   Pole positions: 1   Fastest laps: 3   Points scored: 28

	Race	Circuit	No	Entrant	Tyres	Capacity/Car/Engine	Comment	Q Pos/Entries
ret	ARGENTINE GP	Buenos Aires	2	Officine Alfieri Maserati	P	2.5 Maserati 250F 6	engine	7/15
1	MONACO GP	Monte Carlo	28	Officine Alfieri Maserati	P	2.5 Maserati 250F 6		2/19
ret	BELGIAN GP	Spa	30	Officine Alfieri Maserati	P	2.5 Maserati 250F 6	lost wheel	2/16
3*	"	"	34	Officine Alfieri Maserati	P	2.5 Maserati 250F 6	*took over Perdisa's car/FL	- / -
ret	FRENCH GP	Reims	2	Officine Alfieri Maserati	P	2.5 Maserati 250F 6	gear lever	8/20
5*	"	"	6	Officine Alfieri Maserati	P	2.5 Maserati 250F 6	*took Perdisa's car/2 laps behind	- / -
ret	BRITISH GP	Silverstone	7	Officine Alfieri Maserati	P	2.5 Maserati 250F 6	gearbox/FL	1/28
2	GERMAN GP	Nürburgring	7	Officine Alfieri Maserati	P	2.5 Maserati 250F 6		4/21
1	ITALIAN GP	Monza	36	Officine Alfieri Maserati	P	2.5 Maserati 250F 6	FL	6/26

1957 Championship position: 2nd   Wins: 3 (1 shared)   Pole positions: 2   Fastest laps: 3   Points scored: 25

	Race	Circuit	No	Entrant	Tyres	Capacity/Car/Engine	Comment	Q Pos/Entries
8	ARGENTINE GP	Buenos Aires	4	Officine Alfieri Maserati	P	2.5 Maserati 250F 6	pit stop – throttle/7 laps behind/FL	1/16
ret	MONACO GP	Monte Carlo	18	Vandervell Products Ltd	P	2.5 Vanwall 4	hit chicane	3/21
ret	BRITISH GP	Aintree	18	Vandervell Products Ltd	P	2.5 Vanwall 4	Brooks took over car/engine	1/19
1*	"	"	20	Vandervell Products Ltd	P	2.5 Vanwall 4	*took over from Brooks/FL	- / -
5	GERMAN GP	Nürburgring	10	Vandervell Products Ltd	P	2.5 Vanwall 4	suspension problems	7/24
1	PESCARA GP	Pescara	26	Vandervell Products Ltd	P	2.5 Vanwall 4	FL	2/16
1	ITALIAN GP	Monza	18	Vandervell Products Ltd	P	2.5 Vanwall 4		2/19

Moss guides the 'Silver Arrow' to his first ever grand prix win in the 1955 British Grand Prix at Aintree. Note the patriotic Union Jack sticker on the car's fuel tank.

Driving a Vanwall, Moss won the 1957 Pescara Grand Prix at a canter. After nearly three hours of racing around the 25.575km road circuit, the brilliant young driver finished over two minutes ahead of his nearest challenger, Fangio.

1958 Championship position: 2nd   Wins: 4   Pole positions: 3   Fastest laps: 3   Points scored: 41

1	ARGENTINE GP	Buenos Aires	14	R R C Walker Racing Team	C	1.9 Cooper T43-Climax 4	tyres worn out at finish	7/10
ret	MONACO GP	Monte Carlo	28	Vandervell Products Ltd	D	2.5 Vanwall 4	engine	8/28
1	DUTCH GP	Zandvoort	1	Vandervell Products Ltd	D	2.5 Vanwall 4	FL	2/17
ret	BELGIAN GP	Spa	2	Vandervell Products Ltd	D	2.5 Vanwall 4	dropped valve	3/20
2	FRENCH GP	Reims	8	Vandervell Products Ltd	D	2.5 Vanwall 4		6/21
ret	BRITISH GP	Silverstone	7	Vandervell Products Ltd	D	2.5 Vanwall 4	engine	1/21
ret	GERMAN GP	Nürburgring	7	Vandervell Products Ltd	D	2.5 Vanwall 4	magneto/FL	3/26
1	PORTUGUESE GP	Oporto	2	Vandervell Products Ltd	D	2.5 Vanwall 4		1/15
ret	ITALIAN GP	Monza	26	Vandervell Products Ltd	D	2.5 Vanwall 4	gearbox	1/21
1	MOROCCAN GP	Casablanca	8	Vandervell Products Ltd	D	2.5 Vanwall 4	FL	2/25

1959 Championship position: 3rd   Wins: 2   Pole positions: 4   Fastest laps: 4 (1 shared)   Points scored: 25.5

ret	MONACO GP	Monte Carlo	30	R R C Walker Racing Team	D	2.5 Cooper T51-Climax 4	transmission	1/24
dns	"	" "	30	R R C Walker Racing Team	D	2.5 Cooper T51-BRM 4	practice only	-/-
ret	DUTCH GP	Zandvoort	11	R R C Walker Racing Team	D	2.5 Cooper T51-Climax 4	gearbox/FL	3/15
dns	"	"	15	Ecurie Maarsbergen	D	1.5 Porsche-RSK F4 sports	practice only	-/-
dsq	FRENCH GP	Reims	2	British Racing Partnership	D	2.5 BRM P25 4	outside assistance after spin/FL	4/22
2	BRITISH GP	Aintree	6	British Racing Partnership	D	2.5 BRM P25 4	FL (shared with McLaren)	7/30
ret	GERMAN GP	AVUS	7	R R C Walker Racing Team	D	2.5 Cooper T51-Climax 4	transmission (in heat 1)	2/16
1	PORTUGUESE GP	Monsanto	4	R R C Walker Racing Team	D	2.5 Cooper T51-Climax 4	FL	1/16
1	ITALIAN GP	Monza	14	R R C Walker Racing Team	D	2.5 Cooper T51-Climax 4		1/21
ret	US GP	Sebring	7	R R C Walker Racing Team	D	2.5 Cooper T51-Climax 4	transmission	1/19

1960 Championship position: 3rd   Wins: 2   Pole positions: 4   Fastest laps: 2   Points scored: 19

ret	ARGENTINE GP	Buenos Aires	36	R R C Walker Racing Team	D	2.5 Cooper T51-Climax 4	suspension/FL	1/22
3*	"	" "	38	R R C Walker Racing Team	D	2.5 Cooper T51-Climax 4	*took over from Trintignant/no points	-/-
dns	"	" "	36	R R C Walker Racing Team	D	2.5 Cooper T43-Climax 4	practice only	-/-
1	MONACO GP	Monte Carlo	28	R R C Walker Racing Team	D	2.5 Lotus 18-Climax 4		1/24
dns	"	" "	T	Reventlow Automobiles Inc	G/D	2.5 Scarab 4	practice only	-/-
4	DUTCH GP	Zandvoort	7	R R C Walker Racing Team	D	2.5 Lotus 18-Climax 4	pit stop when leading/FL	1/21
dns	BELGIAN GP	Spa	12	R R C Walker Racing Team	D	2.5 Lotus 18-Cliamx 4	seriously injured in practice accident	(3)/18
dsq	PORTUGUESE GP	Oporto	12	R R C Walker Racing Team	D	2.5 Lotus 18-Climax 4	pushed car against traffic flow	4/16
dns	"	" "	12	R R C Walker Racing Team	D	2.5 Cooper T51-Climax 4	practice only	-/-
1	US GP	Riverside	5	R R C Walker Racing Team	D	2.5 Lotus 18-Climax 4		1/23

1961 Championship position: 3rd   Wins: 2   Pole positions: 1   Fastest laps: 1 (shared)   Points scored: 21

1	MONACO GP	Monte Carlo	20	R R C Walker Racing Team	D	1.5 Cooper T53-Climax 4	FL (shared with Ginther)	1/21
dns	"	" "	20	R R C Walker Racing Team	D	1.5 Cooper T53-Climax 4	practice only	-/-
4	DUTCH GP	Zandvoort	14	R R C Walker Racing Team	D	1.5 Lotus 18-Climax 4		4/17
dns	"	"	14	R R C Walker Racing Team	D	1.5 Cooper T53-Climax 4	practice only	-/-
8	BELGIAN GP	Spa	14	R R C Walker Racing Team	D	1.5 Lotus 18/21-Climax 4		8/25
ret	FRENCH GP	Reims	26	R R C Walker Racing Team	D	1.5 Lotus 18/21-Climax 4	brake pipe	4/26
dns	"	"	26	UDT-Laystall Racing Team	D	1.5 Lotus 18-Climax 4	practice only	-/-
ret	BRITISH GP	Aintree	28	R R C Walker Racing Team	D	1.5 Lotus 18/21-Climax 4	brake pipe	5/30
dsq*	"	"	26	R R C Walker Racing Team	D	1.5 Ferguson P99-Climax 4	took Fairman's car/*push start	-/-
1	GERMAN GP	Nürburgring	7	R R C Walker Racing Team	D	1.5 Lotus 18/21-Climax 4		3/27
ret	ITALIAN GP	Monza	28	R R C Walker Racing Team	D	1.5 Lotus 21-Climax 4	drove Ireland's car/wheel bearing	
dns	"	" "	28	R R C Walker Racing Team	D	1.5 Lotus 18/21-Climax 4	practice only/set grid time in this car	11/33
dns	"	" "	28	R R C Walker Racing Team	D	1.5 Lotus 18/21-Climax V8	practice only	-/-
ret	US GP	Watkins Glen	7	R R C Walker Racing Team	D	1.5 Lotus 18/21-Climax 4	engine	=3/19
dns	"	" "	7	R R C Walker Racing Team	D	1.5 Lotus 18/21-Climax V8	practice only	-/-

GP Starts: 66   GP Wins: 16 (1 shared)   Pole positions: 16   Fastest laps: 19   Points: 186.64

MUNARON, Gino (I) b 2/4/1928, Turin – d 22/11/2009, Valenza Po, Alessandria, Italy

1960 Championship position: Unplaced

	Race	Circuit	No	Entrant	Tyres	Capacity/Car/Engine	Comment	Q Pos/Entries
13	ARGENTINE GP	Buenos Aires	14	Gino Munaron	D	2.5 Maserati 250F 6	*8 laps behind*	19/22
dnq	MONACO GP	Monte Carlo	30	Scuderia Eugenio Castellotti	D	2.5 Cooper T51-Ferrari 4	*shared car with Scarlatti*	– / –
ret	FRENCH GP	Reims	30	Scuderia Eugenio Castellotti	D	2.5 Cooper T51-Ferrari 4	*transmission*	19/23
15	BRITISH GP	Silverstone	21	Scuderia Eugenio Castellotti	D	2.5 Cooper T51-Ferrari 4	*7 laps behind*	– /25
ret	ITALIAN GP	Monza	4	Scuderia Eugenio Castellotti	D	2.5 Cooper T51-Ferrari 4	*oil pipe*	8/16

GP Starts: 4   GP Wins: 0   Pole positions: 0   Fastest laps: 0   Points: 0

GINO MUNARON

ALTHOUGH not of the top echelon, Gino Munaron was a very professional driver who raced a whole roster of sports and touring cars throughout the decade from 1955 to 1965. Apart from handling his own machines, he was an occasional works driver for Ferrari, Maserati and Osca during the 1950s, and among his best placings were first at Hyeres in 1955 (Ferrari), third at Pescara and fourth at Bari in 1956 (Maserati), third in the Reims 12-hours in 1957 (single-handed, Ferrari 250GT), third in the Venezuelan GP at Caracas (Ferrari) and third once more in the Auvergne Trophy at Clermont-Ferrand in 1959 (Osca).

In 1960, Munaron drove an elderly Maserati 250F in the Argentine GP, and on his return to Europe he linked up with the Scuderia Castellotti, racing their Cooper-Ferrari without success in a handful of races. The following year, he entered a Cooper T43-Alfa for the Syracuse Grand Prix, but failed to qualify, reappearing in the Castellotti Cooper in a couple of Inter-Continental races (for 2.5-litre machines) held in Britain later that season. Although his single-seater career petered out, Gino would race GT cars for a few seasons to come. He drove the works Alfa Romeo Giulia TI in 1964, scoring a fifth place (with Andrea de Adamich) in the Spa 24-hours and second in the Coppa Inter Europa four–hours at Monza.

DAVID MURRAY

A CHARTERED accountant by profession, David Murray also ran a motor business and was involved in the wine trade in Edinburgh. After some competition in an MG, he joined up with the wealthy David Hampshire to race his ERA at a number of Continental events during the 1949 season. These included the French Grand Prix at Reims, where he retired with piston trouble, and the Italian Grand Prix, where he escaped unhurt after crashing at the Monza circuit. His most notable success was victory in an International race in Copenhagen.

For the 1950 season, David ended up with a Maserati 4CLT/48, which was more than capable of tackling the newly inaugurated world championship. Under the grandiose banner of Reg Parnell's Scuderia Ambrosiana, he and Hampshire took in selected events, David recording a sixth place in the non-championship Dutch Grand Prix. It was the same diet of high-profile races mixed with more modest Libre events and hill-climbs the following year, when Murray was very lucky to escape injury after he crashed the Maserati heavily in practice for the German Grand Prix. Undaunted, the Scotsman pressed on, having already agreed the purchase of the ex-Peter Whitehead Ferrari 125/166 F2 car. He raced this at Pescara, finishing eighth, and non-started at Bari.

By then, however, David (now past 40) was under pressure from his wife to stop racing, but he soon found an outlet for his enthusiasm by helping a group of enthusiastic young talents to race their Jaguar XK120s under the Ecurie Ecosse banner. The team also acquired a Cooper-Bristol for the 1952 season, and David could not resist the temptation of racing it at the British Grand Prix, before settling down to mastermind the team's fortunes from the pit counter.

Throughout the 1950s, the Edinburgh team successfully raced their potent Jaguars at home and abroad, culminating in the dark blue cars' wonderful triumphs at Le Mans in 1956 and 1957. Ecosse continued racing into the 1960s on a much more modest level, but financially all was not well for Murray and his various business enterprises. In 1968, he faced bankruptcy for unpaid income tax and fled to the Canary Islands, where he lived in impoverished circumstances until his death in 1975, from a heart attack following a car crash.

MURRAY, David (GB) b 28/12/1909, Edinburgh, Scotland – d 5/4/1973, Las Palmas, Canary Islands, Spain

	1950 Championship position: Unplaced							
	Race	Circuit	No	Entrant	Tyres	Capacity/Car/Engine	Comment	Q Pos/Entries
ret	BRITISH GP	Silverstone	5	Scuderia Ambrosiana	D	1.5 s/c Maserati 4CLT/48 4	engine	18/21
dns	FRENCH GP	Reims	34	Scuderia Ambrosiana	D	1.5 s/c Maserati 4CLT/48 4	car raced by Hampshire	19/20
ret	ITALIAN GP	Monza	50	Scuderia Ambrosiana	D	1.5 s/c Maserati 4CLT/48 4	gearbox/engine – valves	24/27
	1951 Championship position: Unplaced							
ret	BRITISH GP	Silverstone	15	Scuderia Ambrosiana	D	1.5 s/c Maserati 4CLT/48 4	engine – valve springs	15/20
dns	GERMAN GP	Nürburgring	89	Scuderia Ambrosiana	D	1.5 s/c Maserati 4CLT/48 4	accident in practice	(23)/23
	1952 Championship position: Unplaced							
ret	BRITISH GP	Silverstone	7	Ecurie Ecosse	D	2.0 Cooper T20-Bristol 6	engine – spark plugs	22/32

GP Starts: 4   GP Wins: 0   Pole positions: 0   Fastest laps: 0   Points: 0

LUIGI MUSSO

BORN of a wealthy family, Luigi Musso was one of five brothers, two of whom, Luciano and Giuseppe, he followed into the sport with initially some unexciting performances. In a Patriarca-Giannini Fiat 750, he entered the 1950 Targa Florio, but blotted his copybook by crashing into a statue of Garibaldi! His brothers, meanwhile, shared tenth place in their Ferrari.

Slowly Luigi gained experience, and for 1952 he acquired a Giaur-Giannini with which he began to establish a reputation as a rising star. Once he got hold of one of the latest Maserati sports cars for 1953, he proved almost unbeatable as he sped to the Italian 2-litre sports car championship. So impressed were Maserati that he and Sergio Mantovani shared a car at that year's Italian Grand Prix, both drivers being given 38 laps each.

Musso was signed up by the Alfieri brothers to race the works sports for 1954, when again he was sports car champion of Italy, winning the Circuit of Senigallia, and taking second in the Targa Florio (behind Piero Taruffi's Lancia) and third in the Mille Miglia. In single-seaters, he only came into the team after the death of Onofre Marimón, inheriting a lucky win in the Pescara Grand Prix, but taking a fine second place behind Mike Hawthorn's Ferrari in the Spanish Grand Prix at season's end.

For 1955, Musso undertook another busy schedule of racing, scoring points only at Zandvoort, but taking second places in non-championship races at Syracuse, Bordeaux and Naples. Driving the Maserati T300S in sports car events, his only win came at the Monza Supercortemaggiore race with Jean Behra, just days after the death of Alberto Ascari.

In 1956, Luigi was invited to join the Scuderia Ferrari, and the association began on a high note when he shared the winning car with Juan Fangio in the Argentine Grand Prix, following this with a second place in the Syracuse Grand Prix. Unfortunately, a crash in the Nürburgring 1000km left him temporarily sidelined with a broken arm, although he made a contentious comeback at the Italian Grand Prix, first refusing to hand his car to the waiting Fangio at a pit stop. He proceeded to take the lead at Monza and looked set for his first singleton victory, only for his steering to fail after a tyre threw a tread.

Despite friction with English drivers Mike Hawthorn and Peter Collins, Musso stayed on for 1957, after Fangio departed for the less political atmosphere at Maserati. Once more he was something of a 'nearly' man, as outright success seemed continually to elude him in world championship races. He was a runner-up in both France and Britain, as well as in the non-title Syracuse and Modena grands prix, although he did take a victory at last at non-championship Reims in the GP de Marne. This sequence continued into 1958, when a succession of yet more second places (Argentine Grand Prix, Buenos Aires City Libre race, Buenos Aires 1000km, Sebring 12-hours and Monaco Grand Prix) was only broken when he lapped a weak field to take victory in the Syracuse Grand Prix and then a fine sports car win with Olivier Gendebien in the Targa Florio.

Musso headed the world championship table after the Monte Carlo race, but failed to score any points at Zandvoort and then crashed his Ferrari at Spa after a tyre failure. This put him out of action for Le Mans, but he arrived at Reims for the French GP, determined to make up for lost ground. Rumour has it that he was doubly motivated to take a win, as by then he was in considerable debt due to his heavy gambling losses. Early in the race, he was chasing team-mate Hawthorn for the lead when he ran wide on the long Gueux curve at 150mph. The car careered into a ditch and flipped into a wheat field, Musso being flung from the car and suffering serious injuries. The last of an ill-fated generation of Italian grand prix drivers, he succumbed in hospital later that evening.

MUSSO, Luigi (I) b 28/7/1924, Rome – d 6/7/1958, Reims Circuit, France

1953 Championship position: Unplaced

	Race	Circuit	No	Entrant	Tyres	Capacity/Car/Engine	Comment	Q Pos/Entries
7*	ITALIAN GP	Monza	56	Officine Alfieri Maserati	P	2.0 Maserati A6GCM 6	*took over Mantovani's car/4 laps behind – /30	

1954 Championship position: 7th= Wins: 0 Pole positions: 0 Fastest laps: 0 Points scored: 6

	Race	Circuit	No	Entrant	Tyres	Capacity/Car/Engine	Comment	Q Pos/Entries
dns	ARGENTINE GP	Buenos Aires	6	Officine Alfieri Maserati	P	2.5 Maserati A6GCM/250F 6	engine in practice	7/18
ret	ITALIAN GP	Monza	20	Officine Alfieri Maserati	P	2.5 Maserati 250F 6	transmission	14/21
2	SPANISH GP	Pedralbes	14	Officine Alfieri Maserati	P	2.5 Maserati 250F 6		7/22

1955 Championship position: 8th= Wins: 0 Pole positions: 0 Fastest laps: 0 Points scored: 6

	Race	Circuit	No	Entrant	Tyres	Capacity/Car/Engine	Comment	Q Pos/Entries
7*	ARGENTINE GP	Buenos Aires	22	Officine Alfieri Maserati	P	2.5 Maserati 250F 6	*Mantovani/Schell co-drove/-13 laps	18/22
ret	"	"	20	Officine Alfieri Maserati	P	2.5 Maserati 250F 6	fuel feed/Behra/Mantovani co-drove	– / –
ret	MONACO GP	Monte Carlo	38	Officine Alfieri Maserati	P	2.5 Maserati 250F 6	transmission	8/22
7	BELGIAN GP	Spa	22	Officine Alfieri Maserati	P	2.5 Maserati 250F 6	2 laps behind	7/14
3	DUTCH GP	Zandvoort	18	Officine Alfieri Maserati	P	2.5 Maserati 250F 6		4/16
5	BRITISH GP	Silverstone	4	Officine Alfieri Maserati	P	2.5 Maserati 250F 6	1 lap behind	9/25
ret	ITALIAN GP	Monza	30	Officine Alfieri Maserati	P	2.5 Maserati 250F 6	gearbox	10/22

1956 Championship position: 9th= Wins: 0 Pole positions: 0 Fastest laps: 0 Points scored: 4

	Race	Circuit	No	Entrant	Tyres	Capacity/Car/Engine	Comment	Q Pos/Entries
1*	ARGENTINE GP	Buenos Aires	34	Scuderia Ferrari	E	2.5 Lancia-Ferrari D50 V8	*Fangio took over car	3/15
ret	"	"	30	Scuderia Ferrari	E	2.5 Lancia-Ferrari D50 V8	switched to Fangio's car/fuel pump	– / –
ret	MONACO GP	Monte Carlo	24	Scuderia Ferrari	E	2.5 Lancia-Ferrari D50 V8	crashed avoiding Fangio	8/19
ret*	GERMAN GP	Nurburging	4	Scuderia Ferrari	E	2.5 Lancia-Ferrari D50 V8	*Castellotti took car – crashed	5/21
ret	ITALIAN GP	Monza	28	Scuderia Ferrari	E	2.5 Lancia-Ferrari D50 V8	accident – steering arm	3/26

1957 Championship position: 3rd Wins: 0 Pole positions: 0 Fastest laps: 1 Points scored: 16

	Race	Circuit	No	Entrant	Tyres	Capacity/Car/Engine	Comment	Q Pos/Entries
ret	ARGENTINE GP	Buenos Aires	12	Scuderia Ferrari	E	2.5 Lancia-Ferrari D50A V8	clutch	6/16
2	FRENCH GP	Rouen	10	Scuderia Ferrari	E	2.5 Lancia-Ferrari 801 V8	FL	3/15
2	BRITISH GP	Aintree	14	Scuderia Ferrari	E	2.5 Lancia-Ferrari 801 V8		10/19
4	GERMAN GP	Nürburgring	6	Scuderia Ferrari	E	2.5 Lancia-Ferrari 801 V8		8/24
ret	PESCARA GP	Pescara	34	Scuderia Ferrari	E	2.5 Lancia-Ferrari 801 V8	split oil tank – seized engine	3/16
8	ITALIAN GP	Monza	32	Scuderia Ferrari	E	2.5 Lancia-Ferrari 801 V8	5 laps behind	9/19

1958 Championship position: 7th= Wins: 0 Pole positions: 0 Fastest laps: 0 Points scored: 12

	Race	Circuit	No	Entrant	Tyres	Capacity/Car/Engine	Comment	Q Pos/Entries
2	ARGENTINE GP	Buenos Aires	16	Scuderia Ferrari	E	2.4 Ferrari Dino 246 V6		5/10
2	MONACO GP	Monte Carlo	34	Scuderia Ferrari	E	2.4 Ferrari Dino 246 V6		10/28
7	DUTCH GP	Zandvoort	6	Scuderia Ferrari	E	2.4 Ferrari Dino 246 V6	pit stop/2 laps behind	12/17
ret	BELGIAN GP	Spa	18	Scuderia Ferrari	E	2.4 Ferrari Dino 246 V6	tyre – crashed at Stavelot	2/20
ret	FRENCH GP	Reims	2	Scuderia Ferrari	E	2.4 Ferrari Dino 246 V6	fatal accident	2/21

GP Starts: 24   GP Wins: 1(shared)   Pole positions: 0   Fastest laps: 1   Points: 44

'NACKE, Bernhard' (D) see BECHEM, Karl-Günther

1952 Championship position: Unplaced

	Race	Circuit	No	Entrant	Tyres	Capacity/Car/Engine	Comment	Q Pos/Entries
ret	GERMAN GP	Nürburgring	130	'Bernhard Nacke'	–	2.0 BMW-Eigenbau 6	sparking plugs	30/32

GP Starts: 1   GP Wins: 0   Pole positions: 0   Fastest laps: 0   Points: 0

NAKAJIMA, Kazuki (J) b 11/1/1985, Okazaki City

2007 Championship position: Unplaced

	Race	Circuit	No	Entrant	Tyres	Capacity/Car/Engine	Comment	Q Pos/Entries
app	AUSTRALIAN GP	Melbourne	8	AT&T Williams	B	2.4 Williams FW29-Toyota V8	ran as 3rd driver in practice 1 only	– /–
app	MALAYSIAN GP	Sepang	8	AT&T Williams	B	2.4 Williams FW29-Toyota V8	ran as 3rd driver in practice 1 only	– /–
app	CANADIAN GP	Montreal	8	AT&T Williams	B	2.4 Williams FW29-Toyota V8	ran as 3rd driver in practice 1 only	– /–
app	US GP	Indianapolis	8	AT&T Williams	B	2.4 Williams FW29-Toyota V8	ran as 3rd driver in practice 1 only	– /–
app	CHINESE GP	Shanghai	8	AT&T Williams	B	2.4 Williams FW29-Toyota V8	ran as 3rd driver in practice 1 only	– /–
10	BRAZILIAN GP	Interlagos	17	AT&T Williams	B	2.4 Williams FW29-Toyota V8	hit mechanic at pit stop/1 lap behind	19/22

2008 Championship position: 15th Wins: 0 Pole positions: 0 Fastest laps: 0 Points scored: 9

	Race	Circuit	No	Entrant	Tyres	Capacity/Car/Engine	Comment	Q Pos/Entries
6	AUSTRALIAN GP	Melbourne	8	AT&T Williams	B	2.4 Williams FW30-Toyota V8	caused collision/stop - new nose/-1 lap	14/22
17	MALAYSIAN GP	Sepang	8	AT&T Williams	B	2.4 Williams FW30-Toyota V8	started from back/puncture/-2 laps	18/22
14	BAHRAIN GP	Bahrain	8	AT&T Williams	B	2.4 Williams FW30-Toyota V8	spun on oil/1 lap behind	16/22
7	SPANISH GP	Barcelona	8	AT&T Williams	B	2.4 Williams FW30-Toyota V8		12/22
ret	TURKISH GP	Istanbul	8	AT&T Williams	B	2.4 Williams FW30-Toyota V8	collision damage with Fisichella	16/20
7	MONACO GP	Monte Carlo	8	AT&T Williams	B	2.4 Williams FW30-Toyota V8		14/20
ret	CANADIAN GP	Montreal	8	AT&T Williams	B	2.4 Williams FW30-Toyota V8	collision with Button - accident damage	12/20
15	FRENCH GP	Magny Cours	8	AT&T Williams	B	2.4 Williams FW30-Toyota V8	1 lap behind	16/20
8	BRITISH GP	Silverstone	8	AT&T Williams	B	2.4 Williams FW30-Toyota V8	1 lap behind	15/20
14	GERMAN GP	Hockenheim	8	AT&T Williams	B	2.4 Williams FW30-Toyota V8		16/20
13	HUNGARIAN GP	Hungaroring	8	AT&T Williams	B	2.4 Williams FW30-Toyota V8	one-stop strategy/1 lap behind	17/20
15	EUROPEAN GP	Valencia	8	AT&T Williams	B	2.4 Williams FW30-Toyota V8	1 lap behind	11/20
14	BELGIAN GP	Spa	8	AT&T Williams	B	2.4 Williams FW30-Toyota V8	1 lap behind	19/20
12	ITALIAN GP	Monza	8	AT&T Williams	B	2.4 Williams FW30-Toyota V8		18/20
8	SINGAPORE GP	Singapore Circuit	8	AT&T Williams	B	2.4 Williams FW30-Toyota V8		10/20
15	JAPANESE GP	Suzuka	8	AT&T Williams	B	2.4 Williams FW30-Toyota V8	1 lap behind	14/20
12	CHINESE GP	Shanghai	8	AT&T Williams	B	2.4 Williams FW30-Toyota V8		17/20
17	BRAZILIAN GP	Interlagos	8	AT&T Williams	B	2.4 Williams FW30-Toyota V8	2 laps behind	16/20

2009 Championship position: Unplaced

ret	AUSTRALIAN GP	Melbourne	17	AT&T Williams	B	2.4 Williams FW31-Toyota V8	accident – hit wall	13/20
12	MALAYSIAN GP	Sepang	17	AT&T Williams	B	2.4 Williams FW31-Toyota V8	rain-shortened race	12/20
ret	CHINESE GP	Shanghai	17	AT&T Williams	B	2.4 Williams FW31-Toyota V8	transmission	15/20
ret	BAHRAIN GP	Bahrain	17	AT&T Williams	B	2.4 Williams FW31-Toyota V8	engine – oil pressure	12/20
13	SPANISH GP	Barcelona	17	AT&T Williams	B	2.4 Williams FW31-Toyota V8	1 lap behind	11/20
15/ret	MONACO GP	Monte Carlo	17	AT&T Williams	B	2.4 Williams FW31-Toyota V8	accident/2 laps behind	10/20
12	TURKISH GP	Istanbul	17	AT&T Williams	B	2.4 Williams FW31-Toyota V8	wheel jammed – lost time in pit stop	12/20
11	BRITISH GP	Silverstone	17	AT&T Williams	B	2.4 Williams FW31-Toyota V8		5/20
12	GERMAN GP	Nürburgring	17	AT&T Williams	B	2.4 Williams FW31-Toyota V8	nudged wide by Trulli on lap 1	13/20
9	HUNGARIAN GP	Hungaroring	17	AT&T Williams	B	2.4 Williams FW31-Toyota V8		9/20
18/ret	EUROPEAN GP	Valencia	17	AT&T Williams	B	2.4 Williams FW31-Toyota V8	puncture caused gearbox damage/-3 laps	17/20
13	BELGIAN GP	Spa	17	AT&T Williams	B	2.4 Williams FW31-Toyota V8		18/20
10	ITALIAN GP	Monza	17	AT&T Williams	B	2.4 Williams FW31-Toyota V8		17/20
9	SINGAPORE GP	Singapore Circuit	17	AT&T Williams	B	2.4 Williams FW31-Toyota V8		11/20
15	JAPANESE GP	Suzuka	17	AT&T Williams	B	2.4 Williams FW31-Toyota V8		17/20
ret	BRAZILIAN GP	Interlagos	17	AT&T Williams	B	2.4 Williams FW31-Toyota V8	muscled off track by Kobayashi	11/20
13	ABU DHABI GP	Yas Island	17	AT&T Williams	B	2.4 Williams FW31-Toyota V8		14/20

GP Starts: 36   GP Wins: 0   Pole positions: 0   Fastest laps: 0   Points: 9

KAZUKI NAKAJIMA

BEING the son of Satoru Nakajima, a former Nippon champion and grand prix stalwart with more than 70 GP starts, it is no surprise that Kazuki took up the sport. Interestingly, though, he made his own way to the top and not via patronage from his father's team or long-standing Honda connections. In fact, his elevation to a full-time Formula 1 ride came courtesy of a long-term commitment by car giant Toyota, and briefly (until the arrival of Kamui Kobayashi) he supplanted Takuma Sato in his nation's conciousness as the leading Japanese driver.

The young Nakajima started his career in karts and eventually he became the Suzuka Formula ICA champion in 1999. This success earned him a place in the Toyota Young Drivers Program and soon he started competing in the various junior single-seater classes. In 2003, he won the Formula Toyota championship, which took him into the very competitive Japanese F3 series. In a very satisfactory debut season, he won two races and finished a creditable fifth. The following year, again he won two races on his way to the runner-up slot with his Dallara-Toyota.

For the 2006 season, Kazuki ventured to Europe to compete in the F3 Euro Series, partnered in the Manor Mortorsport team by fellow countryman Kohei Hirate. He was generally overshadowed by his team-mate, eventually finishing a creditable seventh in the overall standings. There was mild surprise after the largely unproven Nakajima landed a position with Williams-Toyota as a test driver in 2007, when he also continued to develop his skills in the GP2 series.

Joining the well-fancied DAMS team, the Japanese charger soon proved that he had the outright pace to be a championship contender, but his campaign was punctuated by a number of accidents that prevented him from chalking up a victory. There were a number of podium visits, with a best finish of second in the feature race at the Hungaroring, but he could only manage to finish fifth in the overall series standings.

A bonus for Nakajima was an early chance to impress, when Williams handed him a grand prix debut in the season's finale in Brazil. He certainly didn't go unnoticed, impressively posting the fifth fastest lap around the challenging Interlagos circuit. He did blot his copybook somewhat, however, when he skittled three of his mechanics in a misjudged pit stop. Happily, no serious injuries were sustained, and Nakajima took his car into a steady tenth place at the finish.

Confirmed as the partner to Nico Rosberg in the AT&T Williams team for 2008, Kazuki started his season well with a sixth-place finish (and his first three championship points, following the disqualification of Rubens Barrichello) in Australia. He continued to pick up points here and there, despite the FW30 becoming less competitive as the season progressed. Impressively, he posted just two retirements, and his seventh place in the wet (which might have been fifth but for a pit stop glitch) at Monaco was the model of disciplined driving. Concentrating on bringing the car home safely to the finish paid dividends for Nakajima, who showed great resilience in race situations. Indeed, his main weakness was in qualifying, where he made the Q3 session only once.

Nakajima's sophomore season brought no points, although he did come close on a couple of occasions, and his performance level was closer to team-mate Rosberg than in his debut year. With the team losing their Toyota engine deal and opting for Cosworth power for 2010, it was all change on the driver front at Grove as the experienced Barrichello and GP2 champion Nico Hülkenberg were brought in, pushing Kazuki out in the cold.

Nakajima was linked to the Stefan Grand Prix consortium, who had hoped to buy the assets of the recently disbanded Toyota F1 team, but with no super licence granted the project was abandoned.

In 2011, Kazuki returned to Formula Nippon with TOMS Team Toyota, finishing second in the standings to team-mate André Lotterer. He was chosen to race the new Toyota Le Mans challenger in 2012, pencilled in to drive the hybrid LMP1 car with Alex Wurz and Nicolas Lapierre.

SATORU NAKAJIMA

FROM a farming family near Okazaki, the young Satoru Nakajima gained some driving experience within the confines of his parents' land. As soon as he gained his driver's licence, he went racing, winning a novice series at Suzuka. His rise to prominence began in 1977, when he finished a strong third in the All Japan Formula 2000 championship, and he repeated the feat a year later in Formula 2, winning his first race in a Nova-BMW. Moving from Heroes Racing to Tetsu Isukawa for 1979 was a backward step initially, but once Satoru got to grips with his March 792, he became a force again.

In 1980, Nakajima took two wins in the six-race series to finish third once more, but his big breakthrough was not far away. Armed with a March chassis and Honda power he scorched to his first title in 1981 by a massive margin over reigning champion Kazuyoshi Hoshino. He claimed a second consecutive crown the following year, his best score of four wins from six starts providing a maximum possible of 80 points. Satoru then split from Isukawa to run a privateer March, and despite a win in the first race of the 1983 season, he could only take fourth place overall, behind champion Geoff Lees.

The Japanese driver moved teams once more, back to Heroes Racing, and reclaimed his crown after holding off a determined challenge from title rival Stefan Johansson at a thrilling finale at Suzuka. The following year, he won the title at a canter, racking up five wins in the eight-race series, and he made it three in a row in 1986 (the final year of Formula 2's existence), despite only taking a singleton victory.

Not surprisingly, the five-time champion was chosen by Honda to represent them on the grand prix stage, and they put him into the Lotus team alongside the brilliant Ayrton Senna. Inevitably, the Japanese driver appeared in an unfavourable light compared to the dazzling Brazilian during his first season, and his number-two status continued when Nelson Piquet took over as team leader in 1988/89. Satoru quietly got on with the job, however, despite the fortunes of the Hethel outfit being in decline. His last race for the team was in the wet at Adelaide in 1989, and he astonished everyone when he made a mockery of the conditions to finish fourth and take fastest lap.

With help from long-time sponsors Honda and Epson, Satoru moved to Tyrrell in 1990, gaining the odd point with the nimble Cosworth-powered car. Then he endured a disappointing final year in F1, despite having Honda V10 power. It was with some relief that he retired from the sport, his head held high and no longer having to carry the burden of his fanatical countrymen's expectations. Having pulled out of Formula 1 at the end of 1992, Honda subsequently developed their own chassis for a possible return. Nakajima tested it in 1993 and 1994, but eventually the project was dropped in favour of the engine giant's US racing plans.

A huge name in Japan after his grand prix exploits, Nakajima earned millions from endorsements and advertising, and founded his own Formula Nippon team in 1989. Four times this has provided the series champion (Tom Coronel in 1999, Toranosuke Takagi in 2000, Ralph Firman in 2002 and Loïc Duval in 2009). In addition, André Lotterer, who finished second in the 2004 championship, actually tied on points with eventual champion Richard Lyons.

With excellent financial backing from long-time sponsor Epson, Nakajima Racing is also a regular competitor in the Super GT series. They ran the venerable Honda NSX until the car was finally replaced in 2010 by the HSV-010.

Satoru's elder son, Kazuki, having successfully competed in the 2006 German Formula 3 championship, was taken on as a test driver by Williams-Toyota and, after a year in the GP2 series with the DAMS team, was included in the Formula 1 team for 2008 and 2009. His younger son, Daisuke, hoping to follow in his elder sibling's footsteps, drove for the Nakajima Racing team in Formula Nippon in 2011.

NAKAJIMA, Satoru (J) b 23/2/1953, Okazaki City

	1987 Championship position: 11th	Wins: 0	Pole positions: 0		Fastest laps: 0	Points scored: 7		
	Race	Circuit	No	Entrant	Tyres	Capacity/Car/Engine	Comment	Q Pos/Entries
7	BRAZILIAN GP	Rio	11	Camel Team Lotus Honda	G	1.5 t/c Lotus 99T-Honda V6	*pit stop – tyres/2 laps behind*	12/23
6	SAN MARINO GP	Imola	11	Camel Team Lotus Honda	G	1.5 t/c Lotus 99T-Honda V6	*pit stop – tyres/2 laps behind*	13/27
5	BELGIAN GP	Spa	11	Camel Team Lotus Honda	G	1.5 t/c Lotus 99T-Honda V6	*pit stop – tyres/1 lap behind*	15/26
10	MONACO GP	Monte Carlo	11	Camel Team Lotus Honda	G	1.5 t/c Lotus 99T-Honda V6	*hit by Alliot/Capelli – pit stop/-3 laps*	17/26
ret	US GP (DETROIT)	Detroit	11	Camel Team Lotus Honda	G	1.5 t/c Lotus 99T-Honda V6	*accident with Campos*	24/26
nc	FRENCH GP	Paul Ricard	11	Camel Team Lotus Honda	G	1.5 t/c Lotus 99T-Honda V6	*pit stops – tyre-wheel problems/-9 laps*	16/26

Pos	GP	Circuit	No	Team	T	Car	Notes	Q
4	BRITISH GP	Silverstone	11	Camel Team Lotus Honda	G	1.5 t/c Lotus 99T-Honda V6	*pit stop – tyres/2 laps behind*	12/26
ret	GERMAN GP	Hockenheim	11	Camel Team Lotus Honda	G	1.5 t/c Lotus 99T-Honda V6	*turbo*	14/26
ret	HUNGARIAN GP	Hungaroring	11	Camel Team Lotus Honda	G	1.5 t/c Lotus 99T-Honda V6	*driveshaft*	17/26
13	AUSTRIAN GP	Österreichring	11	Camel Team Lotus Honda	G	1.5 t/c Lotus 99T-Honda V6	*pit stop – puncture/-3 laps*	13/26
11	ITALIAN GP	Monza	11	Camel Team Lotus Honda	G	1.5 t/c Lotus 99T-Honda V6	*spin/pit stop – tyres/3 laps behind*	14/28
8	PORTUGUESE GP	Estoril	11	Camel Team Lotus Honda	G	1.5 t/c Lotus 99T-Honda V6	*pit stop – tyres/2 laps behind*	15/27
9	SPANISH GP	Jerez	11	Camel Team Lotus Honda	G	1.5 t/c Lotus 99T-Honda V6	*pit stop – tyres/2 laps behind*	18/28
ret	MEXICAN GP	Mexico City	11	Camel Team Lotus Honda	G	1.5 t/c Lotus 99T-Honda V6	*hit Warwick*	16/27
6	JAPANESE GP	Suzuka	11	Camel Team Lotus Honda	G	1.5 t/c Lotus 99T-Honda V6		12/27
ret	AUSTRALIAN GP	Adelaide	11	Camel Team Lotus Honda	G	1.5 t/c Lotus 99T-Honda V6	*hydraulic leak*	14/27

1988 Championship position: 16th   Wins: 0   Pole positions: 0   Fastest laps: 0   Points scored: 1

Pos	GP	Circuit	No	Team	T	Car	Notes	Q
6	BRAZILIAN GP	Rio	2	Camel Team Lotus Honda	G	1.5 t/c Lotus 100T-Honda V6	*pit stop – tyres/1 lap behind*	10/31
8	SAN MARINO GP	Imola	2	Camel Team Lotus Honda	G	1.5 t/c Lotus 100T-Honda V6	*1 lap behind*	12/31
dnq	MONACO GP	Monte Carlo	2	Camel Team Lotus Honda	G	1.5 t/c Lotus 100T-Honda V6		27/30
ret	MEXICAN GP	Mexico City	2	Camel Team Lotus Honda	G	1.5 t/c Lotus 100T-Honda V6	*turbo*	6/30
11	CANADIAN GP	Montreal	2	Camel Team Lotus Honda	G	1.5 t/c Lotus 100T-Honda V6	*pit stop – tyres/3 laps behind*	13/31
dnq	US GP (DETROIT)	Detroit	2	Camel Team Lotus Honda	G	1.5 t/c Lotus 100T-Honda V6		28/31
7	FRENCH GP	Paul Ricard	2	Camel Team Lotus Honda	G	1.5 t/c Lotus 100T-Honda V6	*pit stop – tyres/handling/1 lap behind*	8/31
10	BRITISH GP	Silverstone	2	Camel Team Lotus Honda	G	1.5 t/c Lotus 100T-Honda V6	*lost 5th gear/1 lap behind*	10/31
9	GERMAN GP	Hockenheim	2	Camel Team Lotus Honda	G	1.5 t/c Lotus 100T-Honda V6	*1 lap behind*	8/31
7	HUNGARIAN GP	Hungaroring	2	Camel Team Lotus Honda	G	1.5 t/c Lotus 100T-Honda V6	*hit by Streiff/3 laps behind*	19/31
ret	BELGIAN GP	Spa	2	Camel Team Lotus Honda	G	1.5 t/c Lotus 100T-Honda V6	*engine*	8/31
ret	ITALIAN GP	Monza	2	Camel Team Lotus Honda	G	1.5 t/c Lotus 100T-Honda V6	*engine*	12/31
ret	PORTUGUESE GP	Estoril	2	Camel Team Lotus Honda	G	1.5 t/c Lotus 100T-Honda V6	*accident damage*	16/31
ret	SPANISH GP	Jerez	2	Camel Team Lotus Honda	G	1.5 t/c Lotus 100T-Honda V6	*spun off*	15/31
7	JAPANESE GP	Suzuka	2	Camel Team Lotus Honda	G	1.5 t/c Lotus 100T-Honda V6	*1 lap behind*	6/31
ret	AUSTRALIAN GP	Adelaide	2	Camel Team Lotus Honda	G	1.5 t/c Lotus 100T-Honda V6	*hit Gugelmin*	13/31

1989 Championship position: 21   Wins: 0   Pole positions: 0   Fastest laps: 1   Points scored: 3

Pos	GP	Circuit	No	Team	T	Car	Notes	Q
8	BRAZILIAN GP	Rio	12	Camel Team Lotus	G	3.5 Lotus 101-Judd V8	*2 pit stops – tyres/clutch/1 lap behind*	21/38
nc	SAN MARINO GP	Imola	12	Camel Team Lotus	G	3.5 Lotus 101-Judd V8	*pit stop – electrics/12 laps behind*	24/39
dnq	MONACO GP	Monte Carlo	12	Camel Team Lotus	G	3.5 Lotus 101-Judd V8		29/38
ret	MEXICAN GP	Mexico City	12	Camel Team Lotus	G	3.5 Lotus 101-Judd V8	*gearbox – spun off*	15/39
ret	US GP (PHOENIX)	Phoenix	12	Camel Team Lotus	G	3.5 Lotus 101-Judd V8	*throttle cable bracket*	23/39
dnq	CANADIAN GP	Montreal	12	Camel Team Lotus	G	3.5 Lotus 101-Judd V8		27/39
ret	FRENCH GP	Paul Ricard	12	Camel Team Lotus	G	3.5 Lotus 101-Judd V8	*electrics – engine cut out*	19/39
8	BRITISH GP	Silverstone	12	Camel Team Lotus	G	3.5 Lotus 101-Judd V8	*1 lap behind*	16/39
ret	GERMAN GP	Hockenheim	12	Camel Team Lotus	G	3.5 Lotus 101-Judd V8	*spun off*	18/39
ret	HUNGARIAN GP	Hungaroring	12	Camel Team Lotus	G	3.5 Lotus 101-Judd V8	*collision with Warwick*	20/39
dnq	BELGIAN GP	Spa	12	Camel Team Lotus	G	3.5 Lotus 101-Judd V8		27/39
10	ITALIAN GP	Monza	12	Camel Team Lotus	G	3.5 Lotus 101-Judd V8	*2 pit stops – tyres/2 laps behind*	19/39
7	PORTUGUESE GP	Estoril	12	Camel Team Lotus	G	3.5 Lotus 101-Judd V8	*1 lap behind*	25/39
ret	SPANISH GP	Jerez	12	Camel Team Lotus	G	3.5 Lotus 101-Judd V8	*hit by Capelli – spun off*	18/38
ret	JAPANESE GP	Suzuka	12	Camel Team Lotus	G	3.5 Lotus 101-Judd V8	*engine*	12/39
4	AUSTRALIAN GP	Adelaide	12	Camel Team Lotus	G	3.5 Lotus 101-Judd V8	*FL in the rain*	23/39

1990 Championship position: 14th   Wins: 0   Pole positions: 0   Fastest laps: 0   Points scored: 3

Pos	GP	Circuit	No	Team	T	Car	Notes	Q
6	US GP (PHOENIX)	Phoenix	3	Tyrrell Racing Organisation	P	3.5 Tyrrell 018-Cosworth V8	*1 lap behind*	11/35
8	BRAZILIAN GP	Interlagos	3	Tyrrell Racing Organisation	P	3.5 Tyrrell 018-Cosworth V8	*collision with Senna/1 lap behind*	19/35
ret	SAN MARINO GP	Imola	3	Tyrrell Racing Organisation	P	3.5 Tyrrell 019-Cosworth V8	*hit Capelli on lap 1*	20/34
ret	MONACO GP	Monte Carlo	3	Tyrrell Racing Organisation	P	3.5 Tyrrell 019-Cosworth V8	*suspension*	21/35
11	CANADIAN GP	Montreal	3	Tyrrell Racing Organisation	P	3.5 Tyrrell 019-Cosworth V8	*3 laps behind*	13/35
ret	MEXICAN GP	Mexico City	3	Tyrrell Racing Organisation	P	3.5 Tyrrell 019-Cosworth V8	*collision with Suzuki*	9/35
ret	FRENCH GP	Paul Ricard	3	Tyrrell Racing Organisation	P	3.5 Tyrrell 019-Cosworth V8	*transmission*	15/35
ret	BRITISH GP	Silverstone	3	Tyrrell Racing Organisation	P	3.5 Tyrrell 019-Cosworth V8	*electrics*	12/35
ret	GERMAN GP	Hockenheim	3	Tyrrell Racing Organisation	P	3.5 Tyrrell 019-Cosworth V8	*engine*	13/35
ret	HUNGARIAN GP	Hungaroring	3	Tyrrell Racing Organisation	P	3.5 Tyrrell 019-Cosworth V8	*spun off*	15/35
ret	BELGIAN GP	Spa	3	Tyrrell Racing Organisation	P	3.5 Tyrrell 019-Cosworth V8	*misfire*	10/33
6	ITALIAN GP	Monza	3	Tyrrell Racing Organisation	P	3.5 Tyrrell 019-Cosworth V8	*1 lap behind*	14/33
dns	PORTUGUESE GP	Estoril	3	Tyrrell Racing Organisation	P	3.5 Tyrrell 019-Cosworth V8	*withdrawn – driver unwell*	(20)/33
ret	SPANISH GP	Jerez	3	Tyrrell Racing Organisation	P	3.5 Tyrrell 019-Cosworth V8	*spun off*	14/33
6	JAPANESE GP	Suzuka	3	Tyrrell Racing Organisation	P	3.5 Tyrrell 019-Cosworth V8		14/30
ret	AUSTRALIAN GP	Adelaide	3	Tyrrell Racing Organisation	P	3.5 Tyrrell 019-Cosworth V8	*spun off*	13/30

1991 Championship position: 15th   Wins: 0   Pole positions: 0   Fastest laps: 0   Points scored: 2

Pos	GP	Circuit	No	Team	T	Car	Notes	Q
5	US GP (PHOENIX)	Phoenix	3	Braun Tyrrell Honda	P	3.5 Tyrrell 020-Honda V10	*1 lap behind*	16/34
ret	BRAZILIAN GP	Interlagos	3	Braun Tyrrell Honda	P	3.5 Tyrrell 020-Honda V10	*spun off*	16/34
ret	SAN MARINO GP	Imola	3	Braun Tyrrell Honda	P	3.5 Tyrrell 020-Honda V10	*transmission*	10/34
ret	MONACO GP	Monte Carlo	3	Braun Tyrrell Honda	P	3.5 Tyrrell 020-Honda V10	*spun and stalled*	11/34
10	CANADIAN GP	Montreal	3	Braun Tyrrell Honda	P	3.5 Tyrrell 020-Honda V10	*2 laps behind*	12/34
12	MEXICAN GP	Mexico City	3	Braun Tyrrell Honda	P	3.5 Tyrrell 020-Honda V10	*3 laps behind*	13/34
ret	FRENCH GP	Magny Cours	3	Braun Tyrrell Honda	P	3.5 Tyrrell 020-Honda V10	*spun off*	18/34
8	BRITISH GP	Silverstone	3	Braun Tyrrell Honda	P	3.5 Tyrrell 020-Honda V10	*1 lap behind*	15/34
ret	GERMAN GP	Hockenheim	3	Braun Tyrrell Honda	P	3.5 Tyrrell 020-Honda V10	*gearbox*	13/34
15	HUNGARIAN GP	Hungaroring	3	Braun Tyrrell Honda	P	3.5 Tyrrell 020-Honda V10	*3 laps behind*	14/34
ret	BELGIAN GP	Spa	3	Braun Tyrrell Honda	P	3.5 Tyrrell 020-Honda V10	*slid off at Les Combes*	22/34
ret	ITALIAN GP	Monza	3	Braun Tyrrell Honda	P	3.5 Tyrrell 020-Honda V10	*sticking throttle*	15/34
13	PORTUGUESE GP	Estoril	3	Braun Tyrrell Honda	P	3.5 Tyrrell 020-Honda V10	*3 laps behind*	21/34
17	SPANISH GP	Barcelona	3	Braun Tyrrell Honda	P	3.5 Tyrrell 020-Honda V10	*3 laps behind*	18/33
ret	JAPANESE GP	Suzuka	3	Braun Tyrrell Honda	P	3.5 Tyrrell 020-Honda V10	*suspension*	15/31
ret	AUSTRALIAN GP	Adelaide	3	Braun Tyrrell Honda	P	3.5 Tyrrell 020-Honda V10	*collision with Boutsen*	24/32

GP Starts: 74   GP Wins: 0   Pole positions: 0   Fastest laps: 1   Points: 16

SHINJI NAKANO

SHINJI NAKANO began racing karts at the age of 13 in 1984 and spent a successful five years in the discipline until switching to Japanese Formula 3 in 1989. Then he took the brave decision to try the Formula Opel Lotus Euroseries for two seasons in 1990/91, but endured a thin time of it and returned to Japan for 1992 to race for Satoru Nakajima in both F3000 and Formula 3.

This over-ambitious schedule proved to be Shinji's undoing, and he decided to concentrate solely on Formula 3 in 1993 in a bid to restart his now flagging career. Helped greatly by Mugen Honda boss Hirotoshita Honda, he moved back up to the All-Japan F3000 championship the following year and gradually worked his way to the front end of the grid, finishing sixth overall in the ten-round 1996 championship placings.

Shinji's connections were crucial in his placement in the Prost team for 1997, where at first he was all at sea. Certainly Alain Prost gave little time to his number-two driver and pushed hard to drop him from the team, but in the end Mr Honda stood firm and his protégé was safe. Having accepted the situation, Prost spent some time helping Shinji to come to terms with Formula 1, with the result that his performances improved no end in the second half of the season.

For 1998, Nakano was found a seat at Minardi, where he did a tidy job under difficult circumstances, but not unnaturally nothing in the way of startling results was achieved. A few days' testing for the Jordan team was the only action that he could find in 1999, but he struck a deal to race in CART in 2000. Driving a Honda-powered car for Walker Racing, he started confidently in his new environment, but a heavy shunt in testing at Milwaukee dented his confidence. In addition, he was at a disadvantage by being in a single-car team, so he switched to Fernandez Racing, where he had an experienced crew and a proven team-mate against whom he could measure his performances.

Nakano's two seasons yielded some modest results (fourth at Toronto in 2002 being the best), and the enigmatic Japanese driver switched camps to the Indy Racing League for 2003. In fact, he competed in only two events, finishing 11th at Motegi and then a solid 14th in the Indianapolis 500 for Beck Motorsports. Then he returned to Japan to a more palatable diet of sports and GT racing. In 2004, he raced a Team Kunimitsu Honda NSX, before linking up with Courage to race their prototype. In 2007, he finished second in both 1000km races at Sugo and Okayama in the Team Mugen Courage C70. Although racing infrequently, he took a win in 2009 at Okayama in a Pescarolo shared with the experienced Christophe Tinseau. Since 2005, Nakano has also competed in the Le Mans 24-hour race on five occasions. His best finish came in 2011, when he took 14th (and fifth in LMP2 class) with a privately entered Pescarolo-Judd.

NAKANO, Shinji (J) b 1/4/1971, Oksaka

	1997	Championship position: 16th=		Wins: 0	Pole positions: 0		Fastest laps: 0	Points scored: 2		
	Race	Circuit	No	Entrant		Tyres	Capacity/Car/Engine		Comment	Q Pos/Entries
7	AUSTRALIAN GP	Melbourne	15	Prost Gauloise Blondes		B	3.0 Prost JS45-Mugen Honda V10		1 lap behind	16/24
14	BRAZILIAN GP	Interlagos	15	Prost Gauloise Blondes		B	3.0 Prost JS45-Mugen Honda V10		1 lap behind	15/22
ret	ARGENTINE GP	Buenos Aires	15	Prost Gauloise Blondes		B	3.0 Prost JS45-Mugen Honda V10		engine	20/22
ret	SAN MARINO GP	Imola	15	Prost Gauloise Blondes		B	3.0 Prost JS45-Mugen Honda V10		shunted off by Hill	18/22
ret	MONACO GP	Monte Carlo	15	Prost Gauloise Blondes		B	3.0 Prost JS45-Mugen Honda V10		spun off	21/22
ret	SPANISH GP	Barcelona	15	Prost Gauloise Blondes		B	3.0 Prost JS45-Mugen Honda V10		gearbox	16/22
6	CANADIAN GP	Montreal	15	Prost Gauloise Blondes		B	3.0 Prost JS45-Mugen Honda V10			19/22
ret	FRENCH GP	Magny Cours	15	Prost Gauloise Blondes		B	3.0 Prost JS45-Mugen Honda V10		spun off	12/22
11/ret	BRITISH GP	Silverstone	15	Prost Gauloise Blondes		B	3.0 Prost JS45-Mugen Honda V10		engine	15/22
7	GERMAN GP	Hockenheim	15	Prost Gauloise Blondes		B	3.0 Prost JS45-Mugen Honda V10			17/22
6	HUNGARIAN GP	Hungaroring	15	Prost Gauloise Blondes		B	3.0 Prost JS45-Mugen Honda V10			16/22
ret	BELGIAN GP	Spa	15	Prost Gauloise Blondes		B	3.0 Prost JS45-Mugen Honda V10		spun off	16/22
11	ITALIAN GP	Monza	15	Prost Gauloise Blondes		B	3.0 Prost JS45-Mugen Honda V10			15/22
ret	AUSTRIAN GP	A-1 Ring	15	Prost Gauloise Blondes		B	3.0 Prost JS45-Mugen Honda V10		engine	16/22
ret	LUXEMBOURG GP	Nürburgring	15	Prost Gauloise Blondes		B	3.0 Prost JS45-Mugen Honda V10		engine	17/22
ret	JAPANESE GP	Suzuka	15	Prost Gauloise Blondes		B	3.0 Prost JS45-Mugen Honda V10		wheel bearing	15/22
10	EUROPEAN GP	Jerez	15	Prost Gauloise Blondes		B	3.0 Prost JS45-Mugen Honda V10			15/22
	1998	Championship position: Unplaced								
ret	AUSTRALIAN GP	Melbourne	22	Fondmetal Minardi Ford		B	3.0 Minardi M198-Ford Zetec r V10		driveshaft	22/22
ret	BRAZILIAN GP	Interlagos	22	Fondmetal Minardi Ford		B	3.0 Minardi M198-Ford Zetec r V10		spun off	18/22
13	ARGENTINE GP	Buenos Aires	22	Fondmetal Minardi Ford		B	3.0 Minardi M198-Ford Zetec r V10		3 laps behind	19/22
ret	SAN MARINO GP	Imola	22	Fondmetal Minardi Ford		B	3.0 Minardi M198-Ford Zetec r V10		engine	21/22
14	SPANISH GP	Barcelona	22	Fondmetal Minardi Ford		B	3.0 Minardi M198-Ford Zetec r V10		2 laps behind	20/22
9	MONACO GP	Monte Carlo	22	Fondmetal Minardi Ford		B	3.0 Minardi M198-Ford Zetec r V10		2 laps behind	19/22
7	CANADIAN GP	Montreal	22	Fondmetal Minardi Ford		B	3.0 Minardi M198-Ford Zetec r V10		1 lap behind	18/22
17/ret	FRENCH GP	Magny Cours	22	Fondmetal Minardi Ford		B	3.0 Minardi M198-Ford Zetec r V10		engine/6 laps behind	21/22
8	BRITISH GP	Silverstone	22	Fondmetal Minardi Ford		B	3.0 Minardi M198-Ford Zetec r V10		2 laps behind	21/22
11	AUSTRIAN GP	A-1 Ring	22	Fondmetal Minardi Ford		B	3.0 Minardi M198-Ford Zetec r V10		1 lap behind	21/22
ret	GERMAN GP	Hockenheim	22	Fondmetal Minardi Ford		B	3.0 Minardi M198-Ford Zetec r V10		gearbox	20/22

15	HUNGARIAN GP	Hungaroring	22	Fondmetal Minardi Ford	B	3.0 Minardi M198-Ford Zetec r V10	*3 laps behind*	19/22
8	BELGIAN GP	Spa	22	Fondmetal Minardi Ford	B	3.0 Minardi M198-Ford Zetec r V10	*5 laps behind*	21/22
ret	ITALIAN GP	Monza	22	Fondmetal Minardi Ford	B	3.0 Minardi M198-Ford Zetec r V10	*engine*	21/22
15	LUXEMBOURG GP	Nürburgring	22	Fondmetal Minardi Ford	B	3.0 Minardi M198-Ford Zetec r V10	*2 laps behind*	20/22
ret	JAPANESE GP	Suzuka	22	Fondmetal Minardi Ford	B	3.0 Minardi M198-Ford Zetec r V10	*throttle*	20/22

GP Starts: 33   GP Wins: 0   Pole positions: 0   Fastest laps: 0   Points: 2

ALESSANDRO NANNINI

THE beaming countenance and charming manner of Alessandro Nannini were among the more pleasing aspects of life in the Formula 1 paddock in the late 1980s. Certainly it was grand prix racing's loss when his career was wrecked so devastatingly by a helicopter accident in which his right arm was severed. Surgeons were able to re-attach the limb, but controlling an F1 car was beyond him. The popular Italian's misfortune seemed all the more cruel, since his grand prix prospects had been at their zenith.

Sandro began his racing activities off road with a Lancia Stratos, before turning to circuit racing in 1981 in Formula Italia. Then he took a big jump into Formula 2 with Minardi in 1982, replacing the team's previous star, Michele Alboreto, who had moved into F1 with Tyrrell. Nannini soon proved

himself a worthy successor, and by the end of the season he had taken a second place at Misano. In 1983, Minardi produced a promising, but initially unworkable new car, and he had to resort to the old chassis to take another second place, this time at the Nürburgring. By 1984, still loyal to the team, his F2 career was really treading water, but everyone had seen his talent, and Lancia signed him to drive for their sports car team between 1984 and 1986.

Having dispensed with the services of Pierluigi Martini, Minardi entered two cars in 1986, Sandro being very much the number two (in theory at least) to the experienced Andrea de Cesaris. He spent two seasons with the little team, which in truth had little hope of success. However, he made his mark and, unlike a number of other grand prix talents, managed to escape to a front-line team before too many seasons at the back of the field could dull his edge. Chosen to partner Thierry Boutsen at Benetton, he proved more than a match for the Belgian, making the rostrum on two occasions. He was thrust into the position of team leader in 1989 and took some time to adjust to the situation, but once the new Ford engine arrived his season began to take off. He won the Japanese GP on a technical 'knockout' after Ayrton Senna was excluded following his tête-à-tête with Alain Prost, and then took a fine second to Boutsen's Williams in the rain-soaked Australian GP.

In 1990, Sandro was joined by the experienced and cunning Nelson Piquet, who immediately established a rapport with John Barnard in developing the B190. Having been somewhat overshadowed, Nannini suddenly found his form again at Hockenheim, where he led until finally giving best to Senna. The battle with the Brazilian was rejoined in Hungary, where Ayrton crassly elbowed the Benetton out of second place, ending Sandro's chances of a win. Certainly the Italian's star was in the ascendant, and reportedly there was a Ferrari contract being bandied about, if not for 1991, then certainly for some time in the future.

It all proved academic after the helicopter accident, but Nannini fought back bravely, to the admiration and great pleasure of the motor racing world. In 1992, he raced an Alfa Romeo successfully in the Italian touring car championship, before proving that he was not in the Alfa team on sentiment alone with some fine displays in the 1993 German series, backing team-mate Nicola Larini superbly as they defeated the Mercedes on home territory.

After a blindingly good start to 1994, the problems of developing the second-evolution Alfa Romeo told on Nannini, whose performances became somewhat erratic, but he bounced back to form in 1996, winning seven rounds of the marathon 26-race ITC series to finish third in the championship. With the collapse of the ITC, he moved into the FIA GT series for 1997 with a works Mercedes CLK-GTR, but it was a mixed year in which only four second-place finishes were achieved. Sandro then retired from competition to build Gruppo Nannini, which includes a chain of up-market coffee shops and patisseries. He is also heavily involved in local politics in Tuscany and is a potential candidate to run for mayor of his home town of Siena.

NANNINI, Alessandro (I) b 7/7/1959, Siena

1986 Championship position: Unplaced

	Race	Circuit	No	Entrant	Tyres	Capacity/Car/Engine	Comment	Q Pos/Entries
ret	BRAZILIAN GP	Rio	24	Minardi Team	P	1.5 t/c Minardi M185B-MM V6	clutch	25/25
ret/dns*	SPANISH GP	Jerez	24	Minardi Team	P	1.5 t/c Minardi M185B-MM V6	*differential on parade lap	(25)/25
ret	SAN MARINO GP	Imola	24	Minardi Team	P	1.5 t/c Minardi M185B-MM V6	collision – suspension damage	18/26
dnq	MONACO GP	Monte Carlo	24	Minardi Team	P	1.5 t/c Minardi M185B-MM V6		26/26
ret	BELGIAN GP	Spa	24	Minardi Team	P	1.5 t/c Minardi M185B-MM V6	gearbox	22/25
ret	CANADIAN GP	Montreal	24	Minardi Team	P	1.5 t/c Minardi M185B-MM V6	turbo	20/25
ret	US GP (DETROIT)	Detroit	24	Minardi Team	P	1.5 t/c Minardi M185B-MM V6	turbo	24/26
ret	FRENCH GP	Paul Ricard	24	Minardi Team	P	1.5 t/c Minardi M185B-MM V6	accident with Ghinzani	19/26
ret	BRITISH GP	Brands Hatch	24	Minardi Team	P	1.5 t/c Minardi M185B-MM V6	started from pits/driveshaft	20/26
ret	GERMAN GP	Hockenheim	24	Minardi Team	P	1.5 t/c Minardi M185B-MM V6	overheating	22/26
ret	HUNGARIAN GP	Hungaroring	24	Minardi Team	P	1.5 t/c Minardi M185B-MM V6	engine	17/26
ret	AUSTRIAN GP	Österreichring	24	Minardi Team	P	1.5 t/c Minardi M185B-MM V6	suspension – spun off	19/26
dns	"	"	24	Minardi Team	P	1.5 t/c Minardi M186-MM V6	practice only	– / –
ret	ITALIAN GP	Monza	24	Minardi Team	P	1.5 t/c Minardi M185B-MM V6	electrics	19/27
ret	PORTUGUESE GP	Estoril	24	Minardi Team	P	1.5 t/c Minardi M185B-MM V6	gearbox	18/27
14	MEXICAN GP	Mexico City	24	Minardi Team	P	1.5 t/c Minardi M185B-MM V6	pit stop – tyres/4 laps behind	24/26
ret	AUSTRALIAN GP	Adelaide	24	Minardi Team	P	1.5 t/c Minardi M185B-MM V6	crashed into barrier	18/26

1987 Championship position: Unplaced

	Race	Circuit	No	Entrant	Tyres	Capacity/Car/Engine	Comment	Q Pos/Entries
ret	BRAZILIAN GP	Rio	24	Minardi Team	G	1.5 t/c Minardi M/187-MM V6	suspension	15/23
ret	SAN MARINO GP	Imola	24	Minardi Team	G	1.5 t/c Minardi M/187-MM V6	turbo	17/27
ret	BELGIAN GP	Spa	24	Minardi Team	G	1.5 t/c Minardi M/187-MM V6	turbo	14/26
ret	MONACO GP	Monte Carlo	24	Minardi Team	G	1.5 t/c Minardi M/187-MM V6	electrics	13/26
ret	US GP (DETROIT)	Detroit	24	Minardi Team	G	1.5 t/c Minardi M/187-MM V6	gearbox	18/26
ret	FRENCH GP	Paul Ricard	24	Minardi Team	G	1.5 t/c Minardi M/187-MM V6	turbo	15/26
ret	BRITISH GP	Silverstone	24	Minardi Team	G	1.5 t/c Minardi M/187-MM V6	engine	15/26
ret	GERMAN GP	Hockenheim	24	Minardi Team	G	1.5 t/c Minardi M/187-MM V6	engine	16/26
11	HUNGARIAN GP	Hungaroring	24	Minardi Team	G	1.5 t/c Minardi M/187-MM V6	3 laps behind	20/26
ret	AUSTRIAN GP	Österreichring	24	Minardi Team	G	1.5 t/c Minardi M/187-MM V6	engine	15/26
16/ret	ITALIAN GP	Monza	24	Minardi Team	G	1.5 t/c Minardi M/187-MM V6	out of fuel/5 laps behind	18/28
11/ret	PORTUGUESE GP	Estoril	24	Minardi Team	G	1.5 t/c Minardi M/187-MM V6	out of fuel/4 laps behind	14/27
ret	SPANISH GP	Jerez	24	Minardi Team	G	1.5 t/c Minardi M/187-MM V6	turbo	21/28
ret	MEXICAN GP	Mexico City	24	Minardi Team	G	1.5 t/c Minardi M/187-MM V6	turbo	14/27
ret	JAPANESE GP	Suzuka	24	Minardi Team	G	1.5 t/c Minardi M/187-MM V6	engine	15/27
ret	AUSTRALIAN GP	Adelaide	24	Minardi Team	G	1.5 t/c Minardi M/187-MM V6	hit wall	13/27

1988 Championship position: 9th   Wins: 0   Pole positions: 0   Fastest laps: 1   Points scored: 12

	Race	Circuit	No	Entrant	Tyres	Capacity/Car/Engine	Comment	Q Pos/Entries
ret	BRAZILIAN GP	Rio	19	Benetton Formula	G	3.5 Benetton B188-Cosworth V8	overheating	12/31
6	SAN MARINO GP	Imola	19	Benetton Formula	G	3.5 Benetton B188-Cosworth V8	1 lap behind	4/31
ret	MONACO GP	Monte Carlo	19	Benetton Formula	G	3.5 Benetton B188-Cosworth V8	gearbox	6/30
7	MEXICAN GP	Mexico City	19	Benetton Formula	G	3.5 Benetton B188-Cosworth V8	2 laps behind	8/30
ret	CANADIAN GP	Montreal	19	Benetton Formula	G	3.5 Benetton B188-Cosworth V8	ignition/water leak	5/31
ret	US GP (DETROIT)	Detroit	19	Benetton Formula	G	3.5 Benetton B188-Cosworth V8	front suspension damage	7/31
6	FRENCH GP	Paul Ricard	19	Benetton Formula	G	3.5 Benetton B188-Cosworth V8	1 lap behind	6/31
3	BRITISH GP	Silverstone	19	Benetton Formula	G	3.5 Benetton B188-Cosworth V8	two spins	8/31

Nannini scored his only grand prix victory in the 1989 Japanese Grand Prix at Suzuka. His Benetton was declared the winner after Senna was disqualified for receiving a push-start in his McLaren.

18	GERMAN GP	Hockenheim	19	Benetton Formula	G	3.5 Benetton B188-Cosworth V8	*pit stop – throttle cable/4 laps behind/FL*	6/31
ret	HUNGARIAN GP	Hungaroring	19	Benetton Formula	G	3.5 Benetton B188-Cosworth V8	*water pipe leak*	5/31
dsq*	BELGIAN GP	Spa	19	Benetton Formula	G	3.5 Benetton B188-Cosworth V8	*4th on road/*illegal fuel*	7/31
9	ITALIAN GP	Monza	19	Benetton Formula	G	3.5 Benetton B188-Cosworth V8	*started from pitlane/1 lap behind*	9/31
ret	PORTUGUESE GP	Estoril	19	Benetton Formula	G	3.5 Benetton B188-Cosworth V8	*exhausted due to chassis vibration*	9/31
3	SPANISH GP	Jerez	19	Benetton Formula	G	3.5 Benetton B188-Cosworth V8		5/31
5	JAPANESE GP	Suzuka	19	Benetton Formula	G	3.5 Benetton B188-Cosworth V8		12/31
ret	AUSTRALIAN GP	Adelaide	19	Benetton Formula	G	3.5 Benetton B188-Cosworth V8	*spun off – could not restart*	8/31

	1989 Championship position: 6th		Wins: 1	Pole positions: 0	Fastest laps: 0	Points scored: 32		
6	BRAZILIAN GP	Rio	19	Benetton Formula	G	3.5 Benetton B188-Cosworth V8	*2 pit stops – tyres/broken wing stay*	11/38
3	SAN MARINO GP	Imola	19	Benetton Formula	G	3.5 Benetton B188-Cosworth V8	*vibration/1 lap behind*	7/39
8	MONACO GP	Monte Carlo	19	Benetton Formula	G	3.5 Benetton B188-Cosworth V8	*brakes – clipped barrier/3 laps behind*	15/38
4	MEXICAN GP	Mexico City	19	Benetton Formula	G	3.5 Benetton B188-Cosworth V8		13/39
ret	US GP (PHOENIX)	Phoenix	19	Benetton Formula	G	3.5 Benetton B188-Cosworth V8	*driver exhausted*	3/39
dsq*	CANADIAN GP	Montreal	19	Benetton Formula	G	3.5 Benetton B188-Cosworth V8	**started from pits before green light*	13/39
ret	FRENCH GP	Paul Ricard	19	Benetton Formula	G	3.5 Benetton B189-Ford V8	*suspension*	4/39
3	BRITISH GP	Silverstone	19	Benetton Formula	G	3.5 Benetton B189-Ford V8	*broken exhaust*	9/39
ret	GERMAN GP	Hockenheim	19	Benetton Formula	G	3.5 Benetton B189-Ford V8	*ignition*	7/39
ret	HUNGARIAN GP	Hungaroring	19	Benetton Formula	G	3.5 Benetton B189-Ford V8	*gearbox*	7/39
5	BELGIAN GP	Spa	19	Benetton Formula	G	3.5 Benetton B189-Ford V8		7/39
ret	ITALIAN GP	Monza	19	Benetton Formula	G	3.5 Benetton B189-Ford V8	*brakes*	8/39
4	PORTUGUESE GP	Estoril	19	Benetton Formula	G	3.5 Benetton B189-Ford V8		13/39
ret	SPANISH GP	Jerez	19	Benetton Formula	G	3.5 Benetton B189-Ford V8	*spun off*	14/38
1*	JAPANESE GP	Suzuka	19	Benetton Formula	G	3.5 Benetton B189-Ford V8	**1st place car disqualified*	6/39
2	AUSTRALIAN GP	Adelaide	19	Benetton Formula	G	3.5 Benetton B189-Ford V8	*broken exhaust*	4/39

	1990	Championship position: 8th	Wins: 0	Pole positions: 0	Fastest laps: 1	Points scored: 21		
11	US GP (PHOENIX)	Phoenix	19	Benetton Formula	G	3.5 Benetton B189B-Ford V8	*2 pit stops – accident damage/-2 laps*	22/35
10/ret	BRAZILIAN GP	Interlagos	19	Benetton Formula	G	3.5 Benetton B189B-Ford V8	*collision with de Cesaris/3 laps behind*	15/35
3	SAN MARINO GP	Imola	19	Benetton Formula	G	3.5 Benetton B190-Ford V8	*FL*	9/34
ret	MONACO GP	Monte Carlo	19	Benetton Formula	G	3.5 Benetton B190-Ford V8	*oil pressure*	16/35
ret	CANADIAN GP	Montreal	19	Benetton Formula	G	3.5 Benetton B190-Ford V8	*spun off*	4/35
4	MEXICAN GP	Mexico City	19	Benetton Formula	G	3.5 Benetton B190-Ford V8		14/35
16*/ret	FRENCH GP	Paul Ricard	19	Benetton Formula	G	3.5 Benetton B190-Ford V8	**15th placed car dsq/engine/-5 laps*	5/35
ret	BRITISH GP	Silverstone	19	Benetton Formula	G	3.5 Benetton B190-Ford V8	*hit Patrese – spun and stalled*	13/35
2	GERMAN GP	Hockenheim	19	Benetton Formula	G	3.5 Benetton B190-Ford V8	*led race*	9/35
ret	HUNGARIAN GP	Hungaroring	19	Benetton Formula	G	3.5 Benetton B190-Ford V8	*collision with Senna*	7/35
4	BELGIAN GP	Spa	19	Benetton Formula	G	3.5 Benetton B190-Ford V8		6/33
8	ITALIAN GP	Monza	19	Benetton Formula	G	3.5 Benetton B190-Ford V8	*long pit stop – tyres/1 lap behind*	8/33
6	PORTUGUESE GP	Estoril	19	Benetton Formula	G	3.5 Benetton B190-Ford V8		9/33
3	SPANISH GP	Jerez	19	Benetton Formula	G	3.5 Benetton B190-Ford V8		9/33

GP Starts: 76 (77)   GP Wins: 1   Pole positions: 0   Fastest laps: 2   Points: 65

EMANUELE NASPETTI

DRIVING for the top-notch Forti team, Emanuele Naspetti won a titanic struggle with Mauro Martini to clinch the 1988 Italian F3 championship in only his second year of racing cars, having been competing in karts between 1980 and '86.

After drawing a blank in his first season of F3000, Naspetti was taken under the wing of Eddie Jordan in 1990, but again he disappointed, scoring but a single point. It was a different story in 1991, however, when the Italian came out of his shell. After switching from a Lola to a Reynard chassis, he strung together a run of four consecutive victories at Enna, Hockenheim, Brands Hatch and Spa, raising doubts about the legality of his Heini Mader-tended Cosworth engines. In the end, his title chances fizzled out, but he stayed in the formula with Forti for a fourth year in 1992, winning the opening race at Pau. Then he jumped at the chance of joining the Formula 1 March team, replacing Paul Belmondo in mid-season. Proving surprisingly quick to adapt to his new surroundings, he clung tenaciously to team-mate Karl Wendlinger for most of his debut race at Spa.

Emanuele spent much of 1993 frustrated at the lack of a Formula 1 drive, but he did make a one-off appearance for Jordan in Portugal as a reward for his efforts as a test driver during the year.

After that, he carved out a niche for himself in the Italian Superturismo series with a BMW 320i. Only a controversial stop-and-go penalty in the final round cost him the chance of the title in 1996, but he made amends the following year by dominating the championship. Subsequently, he hankered after a return to single-seaters and visited the States to investigate the possibility of a ride in CART, but nothing materialised and he continued to race in Italy, where his BMW had to play second fiddle to Fabrizio Giovanardi's Alfa Romeo.

In 2001, Naspetti switched his racing activities to the sports and GT championships, and raced a Rafanelli-Ferrari and later a Panoz in the American Le Mans Series, before returning to touring cars with BMW in 2006.

NASPETTI, Emanuele (I) b 24/2/1968, Ancona

1992 Championship position: Unplaced

	Race	Circuit	No	Entrant	Tyres	Capacity/Car/Engine	Comment	Q Pos/Entries
12	BELGIAN GP	Spa	17	March F1	G	3.5 March CG911-Ilmor V10	1 lap behind	21/30
ret	ITALIAN GP	Monza	17	March F1	G	3.5 March CG911-Ilmor V10	collision – Wendlinger-spun off	24/28
11	PORTUGUESE GP	Estoril	17	March F1	G	3.5 March CG911-Ilmor V10	3 laps behind	23/26
13	JAPANESE GP	Suzuka	17	March F1	G	3.5 March CG911-Ilmor V10	2 laps behind	26/26
ret	AUSTRALIAN GP	Adelaide	17	March F1	G	3.5 March CG911-Ilmor V10	gearbox	23/26

1993 Championship position: Unplaced

	Race	Circuit	No	Entrant	Tyres	Capacity/Car/Engine	Comment	Q Pos/Entries
ret	PORTUGUESE GP	Estoril	15	Sasol Jordan	G	3.5 Jordan 193-Hart V10	engine – fire	23/26

GP Starts: 6   GP Wins: 0   Pole positions: 0   Fastest laps: 0   Points: 0

NATILI, Massimo (I) b 28/7/1935, Ronciglione, Viterbo

1961 Championship position: Unplaced

	Race	Circuit	No	Entrant	Tyres	Capacity/Car/Engine	Comment	Q Pos/Entries
ret	BRITISH GP	Aintree	62	Scuderia Centro Sud	D	1.5 Cooper T51-Maserati 4	gearbox	28/30
dnq	ITALIAN GP	Monza	58	Scuderia Centro Sud	D	1.5 Cooper T51-Maserati 4	practised – but entry taken by Pirocchi	– / –

GP Starts: 1   GP Wins: 0   Pole positions: 0   Fastest laps: 0   Points: 0

MASSIMO NATILI

AFTER racing a Fiat 500 and Giaur 750 sports, and very little Formula Junior experience, Massimo Natili was one of a number of promising drivers tested by Scuderia Centro Sud. He was given a handful of F1 outings in 1961 (at Syracuse, Posillipo, Aintree and Monza), none of which brought him any success.

In 1962, he finished third overall to champion 'Geki' (Giacomo Russo) in his de Sanctis, but he was lucky to survive a crash in a Monza FJ race, when a spectator pulled him from his blazing car with burns to face and legs, He reappeared briefly for Centro Sud in the F1 Rome Grand Prix in 1963, retiring in the first heat.

In Formula 3, Natili took a sixth place in the 1964 Rome GP with a Joly Club Brabham-Giannini. He continued to race competitively in Italian Formula 3 with a Brabham and was the 1965 1-litre national sports car champion with a Lotus 23. In 1966, he shared a Bizzarini Ferrari 553 GT Strada at Le Mans with Sam Posey, but the car was disqualified for infringing safety regulations in the pits.

After retiring from racing, Natili established a car dealership, BMW Natili, near Viterbo, in the Lazio region of Italy.

BRIAN NAYLOR

A SUCCESSFUL motor dealer from Stockport and former merchant navy chief radio officer, who had been awarded the American Silver star for gallantry during the Second World War, Brian Naylor began racing quite late, when past the age of 30, in 1954 with a 500cc Cooper-Norton and then a Cooper-MG, but soon he switched to a Lotus chassis.

In 1955, Naylor began to experiment by mating a Maserati 105S engine to a Lotus XI chassis. This combination proved troublesome at first, but after much hard work, he used it to clock up more than a dozen victories over the length and breadth of Britain.

Naylor continued to race the sports car successfully in 1957, but also bought a Formula 2 Cooper, which he raced in selected events, including grands prix, over the next two years. He was never content to drive standard fare, and after the success of the Maserati-engined Lotus, he developed his own JBW-Maserati sports car. Then, less successfully, he replaced one Italian unit for another when a 3-litre Ferrari powerplant was introduced.

The Maserati engine was earmarked for yet another JBW creation, this time a Cooper-based single-seater, which Naylor ran with some success in minor Formula Libre events. He always drove within his limits, but invariably the rear-engined machine was outclassed in the selected Formula 1 and Inter-Continental races in which it competed.

Ill health brought about Naylor's retirement at the end of the 1961 season.

NAYLOR, Brian (GB) b 24/3/1923, Salford, Manchester – d 8/8/1989, Marbella, Spain

	1957 Championship position: Unplaced							
	Race	Circuit	No	Entrant	Tyres	Capacity/Car/Engine	Comment	Q Pos/Entries
13*	GERMAN GP (F2)	Nürburgring	28	J B Naylor	D	1.5 Cooper T43-Climax 4 F2	*2nd in F2 class/2 laps behind	17/24
	1958 Championship position: Unplaced							
ret	GERMAN GP (F2)	Nürburgring	29	J B Naylor	D	1.5 Cooper T45-Climax 4 F2	fuel pump	21/26
	1959 Championship position: Unplaced							
ret	BRITISH GP	Aintree	36	J B Naylor	D	2.5 JBW-Maserati 4	transmission	14/30
	1960 Championship position: Unplaced							
dnq	MONACO GP	Monte Carlo	20	J B Naylor	D	2.5 JBW-Maserati 4		19/24
13	BRITISH GP	Silverstone	25	J B Naylor	D	2.5 JBW-Maserati 4	pit stop/5 laps behind	18/25
ret	ITALIAN GP	Monza	6	J B Naylor	D	2.5 JBW-Maserati 4	gearbox	7/16
ret	US GP	Riverside	21	J B Naylor	D	2.5 JBW-Maserati 4	engine	17/23
	1961 Championship position: Unplaced							
ret	ITALIAN GP	Monza	14	J B Naylor	D	1.5 JBW-Climax 4	engine	31/33

GP Starts: 7   GP Wins: 0   Pole positions: 0   Fastest laps: 0   Points: 0

NEEDELL, Tiff (GB) b 29/10/1951, Havant, Hampshire

	1980 Championship position: Unplaced							
	Race	Circuit	No	Entrant	Tyres	Capacity/Car/Engine	Comment	Q Pos/Entries
ret	BELGIAN GP	Zolder	14	Unipart Racing Team	G	3.0 Ensign N180-Cosworth V8	engine	23/27
dnq	MONACO GP	Monte Carlo	14	Unipart Racing Team	G	3.0 Ensign N180-Cosworth V8		26/27

GP Starts: 1   GP Wins: 0   Pole positions: 0   Fastest laps: 0   Points: 0

TIFF NEEDELL

TIFF NEEDELL spent the formative years of his racing career in Formula Ford, benefiting from a Lotus 69 that he had won in a competition run by Autosport magazine. Perenially underfunded compared to his rivals, he began to make progress in 1974 when he drove the semi-works Eldon; the following year brought the Hampshire man some real success at last. A mid-season switch to a Crossle chassis brought him 12 wins, the FF1600 Townsend Thorenson championship and a commendation in the Grovewood Awards.

Having switched to the FF2000 class for 1976, Needell finished as runner-up, but surprisingly, perhaps, landed the premier Grovewood Award ahead of Rupert Keegan and Derek Warwick. This gave him the chance to join the Unipart-backed March Formula 3 team. His two-year stint in Formula 3 was largely spent in frustration, driving excellently, but pitting his underpowered Triumph-engined machine against much more powerful Toyota propelled cars. Despite a promising one-off drive for Toleman in Formula 2, he was left with only the prospect of a shared drive in the Aurora AFX F1 series for Chevron in 1979. In mid-season, he was refused an F1 super licence after Ensign had approached him about racing in that year's British Grand Prix. In 1980, however, in the aftermath of Clay Regazzoni's accident at Long Beach, he did get an F1 opportunity at last.

Tiff did extremely well to qualify the car for the Belgian Grand Prix, but his failure to make the cut at Monaco resulted in the drive going to Jan Lammers, much to his chagrin. Then he headed to Japan to compete in Formula 2 races, before foresaking single-seaters completely and concentrating on myriad Group C sports cars. Ultimately most of these projects ended in failure, but he did finish third at Le Mans in 1990, sharing a Porsche 962 with Anthony Reid and David Sears.

In 1993, Tiff appeared occasionally in the BTTC with a third works Nissan, which was run mainly for development purposes, and in mid-1994 he took over the troublesome Nissan vacated by Eric van der Poele, but could do little to alter the car's uncompetitive state. Then it was back to sports car racing over the next few seasons with the potent front-engined Lister-Storm.

By the time Tiff retired from competition, he had long since been more active in his successful career as a TV presenter, occasional racing commentator and magazine journalist. He has also been very successful doing voice-overs and as an after-dinner speaker.

PATRICK NÈVE

A ONE-TIME pupil at the Jim Russell driving school, Patrick Nève later worked as an instructor to finance his own racing activities, but he gained enough success in the school's Merlyn to set himself up for a successful year in 1974, winning the STP Formula Ford championship in a Lola T340.

Having moved up to Formula 3 in 1975, Patrick drove well enough in the Safir to gain a test with Brabham and a drive with the RAM team in 1976. After a couple of non-championship races, he was bundled out of the car by Emilio de Villota's banknotes in Spain, but raced in Belgium before departing for a one-off drive with Ensign.

The following year could have seen Patrick make his breakthrough. He led a Formula 2 race at Silverstone until suspension problems dropped him to third place, but then spent an unhappy grand prix season with the post-Wolf Frank Williams team, running a March. The relationship ended in acrimony after the Canadian Grand Prix and his career never really recovered.

After an abortive attempt to make the grid in Belgium in 1978, Nève's planned season of Formula 2 with Kauhsen fell through when the German's sponsors pulled out, leaving the Belgian to race the unsuccessful Pilbeam. Thereafter, he appeared only occasionally in BMW Procars and touring cars. In the 1990s, he entered cars in races under the Patrick Nève Racing banner while also running a sports promotion agency in Brussels.

NÈVE, Patrick (B) b 13/10/1949, Liège

1976 Championship position: Unplaced

	Race	Circuit	No	Entrant	Tyres	Capacity/Car/Engine	Comment	Q Pos/Entries
ret	BELGIAN GP	Zolder	33	Tissot RAM Racing	G	3.0 Brabham BT44B-Cosworth V8	driveshaft c.v. joint	19/29
18	FRENCH GP	Paul Ricard	22	Team Ensign	G	3.0 Ensign N176-Cosworth V8	1 lap behind	26/30

1977 Championship position: Unplaced

	Race	Circuit	No	Entrant	Tyres	Capacity/Car/Engine	Comment	Q Pos/Entries
12	SPANISH GP	Jarama	27	Williams Grand Prix Engineering	G	3.0 March 761-Cosworth V8	pit stop/4 laps behind	22/31
10	BELGIAN GP	Zolder	27	Williams Grand Prix Engineering	G	3.0 March 761-Cosworth V8	pit stop – tyres/2 laps behind	24/32
15	SWEDISH GP	Anderstorp	27	Williams Grand Prix Engineering	G	3.0 March 761-Cosworth V8	3 laps behind	20/31
dnq	FRENCH GP	Dijon	27	Williams Grand Prix Engineering	G	3.0 March 761-Cosworth V8		24/30
10	BRITISH GP	Silverstone	27	Williams Grand Prix Engineering	G	3.0 March 761-Cosworth V8	2 laps behind	26/36
dnq	GERMAN GP	Hockenheim	27	Williams Grand Prix Engineering	G	3.0 March 761-Cosworth V8		25/30
9	AUSTRIAN GP	Österreichring	27	Williams Grand Prix Engineering	G	3.0 March 761-Cosworth V8	1 lap behind	22/30
dnq	DUTCH GP	Zandvoort	27	Williams Grand Prix Engineering	G	3.0 March 761-Cosworth V8		27/34
7	ITALIAN GP	Monza	27	Williams Grand Prix Engineering	G	3.0 March 761-Cosworth V8	2 laps behind	24/34
18	US GP EAST	Watkins Glen	27	Williams Grand Prix Engineering	G	3.0 March 761-Cosworth V8	4 laps behind	24/27
ret	CANADIAN GP	Mosport Park	27	Williams Grand Prix Engineering	G	3.0 March 761-Cosworth V8	oil pressure	21/27

1978 Championship position: Unplaced

	Race	Circuit	No	Entrant	Tyres	Capacity/Car/Engine	Comment	Q Pos/Entries
dnpq	BELGIAN GP	Zolder	–	Patrick Neve	G	3.0 March 781S-Cosworth V8	dnq for official practice sessions	– / –

GP Starts: 10 GP Wins: 0 Pole positions: 0 Fastest laps: 0 Points: 0

NICHOLSON, John (NZ) b 6/10/1941, Auckland

1974 Championship position: Unplaced

	Race	Circuit	No	Entrant	Tyres	Capacity/Car/Engine	Comment	Q Pos/Entries
dnq	BRITISH GP	Brands Hatch	29	Pinch (Plant) Ltd	F	3.0 Lyncar 006-Cosworth V8		31/34

1975 Championship position: Unplaced

	Race	Circuit	No	Entrant	Tyres	Capacity/Car/Engine	Comment	Q Pos/Entries
17/ret	BRITISH GP	Silverstone	32	Pinch (Plant) Ltd	G	3.0 Lyncar 006-Cosworth V8	crashed in rainstorm/5 laps behind	26/28

GP Starts: 1 GP Wins: 0 Pole positions: 0 Fastest laps: 0 Points: 0

NIEDERMAYR, Helmut (D) b 29/11/1915, Munich – d 3/4/1985, Cristiansted, Virgin Is, US

1952 Championship position: Unplaced

	Race	Circuit	No	Entrant	Tyres	Capacity/Car/Engine	Comment	Q Pos/Entries
nc	GERMAN GP	Nürburgring	124	Helmut Niedermayr	–	2.0 AFM-BMW 6	3 laps behind	22/32

GP Starts: 1 GP Wins: 0 Pole positions: 0 Fastest laps: 0 Points: 0

NIEMANN, Brausch (ZA) b 7/1/1939, Durban

1963 Championship position: Unplaced

	Race	Circuit	No	Entrant	Tyres	Capacity/Car/Engine	Comment	Q Pos/Entries
14	SOUTH AFRICAN GP	East London	21	Ted Lanfear	D	1.5 Lotus 22-Ford 4	19 laps behind	15/21

1965 Championship position: Unplaced

	Race	Circuit	No	Entrant	Tyres	Capacity/Car/Engine	Comment	Q Pos/Entries
dnq	SOUTH AFRICAN GP	East London	27	Ted Lanfear	D	1.5 Lotus 22-Ford 4		24/25

GP Starts: 1 GP Wins: 0 Pole positions: 0 Fastest laps: 0 Points: 0

JOHN NICHOLSON

HAVING already tasted success in his native New Zealand with a Lotus-Ford and then Brabham BT18, John Nicholson made his way to England and, with experience of rebuilding engines in his native land, walked straight into a job at McLaren in 1969, working on their Can-Am engines. His driving talents were also put to use, as he was assigned testing duties with the team; no doubt this gave him the taste for more action. When his urge to compete resurfaced, he quickly became a leading figure in Formula Atlantic, initially in 1971 with a March 702-Vegatune and then with his own Lyncar-Piper, in which he finished third overall in the 1972 series. After he had added his own BDA powerplant, there was no stopping him, and the Kiwi claimed the Atlantic title in both 1973 and '74.

By the start of 1973, Nicholson had established his own thriving engine business, servicing and preparing Cosworths for McLaren and Hill among others, which prevented him from undertaking a major racing programme abroad, but he did dip into Formula 1 with the Lyncar (a typical F1 kit car of the time) in British events, his best result being sixth at the 1974 Race of Champions.

Plans to purchase a McLaren M23 and have a real go fell through, much to Nicholson's dismay, but he did race on, making a few appearances in Alan McCall's Tui in the UK and Canada in 1975.

For 1976, Nicholson bought a March 752, in which he struggled to qualify in the European Formula 2 championship, but he was more effective in the Shellsport F5000 series. Then he took in the Peter Stuyvesant New Zealand series early in 1977 with a Modus, before concentrating on his business commitments and indulging his passion for speed with a new-found interest in powerboat racing.

HELMUT NIEDERMAYR

ONE of a number of enthusiastic racers who ran homebuilt specials, Helmut Niedermayr raced his own AFM 50-BMW and Veritas machines. Within a couple of months in the summer of 1952, he surely experienced the high and low points of his career. At the end of June, he shared the second-place Mercedes-Benz 300SL with Theo Helfrich at the Le Mans 24-hour race, and at the beginning of August he lost control of his Veritas-Meteor and crashed into the crowd at the Grenzlandring circuit, killing at least 13 spectators and injuring many others.

Understandably, Niedermayr made the decision to retire, but he did enter his elderly AFM for Theo Fitzau to race in the 1953 German Grand Prix

Eventually, Helmut returned to the track, appearing briefly in Hans Klenk's special in the 1954 Berlin Grand Prix at AVUS. Having struggled with steering problems on the Klenk-Meteor, he was not classified at the finish. Thereafter, he made occasional appearances, driving a Porsche, in rallies and sports car events.

BRAUSCH NIEMANN

BRAUSCH NIEMANN achieved amazing feats in a wide-wheeled Lotus Seven, seemingly held together with lashings of masking tape and known as either the 'coffin on cotton reels' or 'masked marvel'. Even so, it often put to shame far more potent machinery in South Africa's vibrant national racing scene in the early 1960s.

This led to Niemann's chance to race Ted Lanfer's Formula Junior Lotus 22, in which he took numerous top-six places between 1963 and 1965. After driving Lotus 23 and 30 sports cars (with Neville Lederle and David Prophet), and then a Lotus Ford Cortina, he turned to racing enduro motorcycles, winning the South African championship in 1979.

After running a Kawasaki dealership in South Africa, Niemann subsequently moved to Wales and set up a specialist exhaust company.

GUNNAR NILSSON

A CHEERY and gregarious Swede, Gunnar Nilsson was always his own man, and the courage and dignity he showed after being diagnosed with terminal cancer said as much about him as his all-too-brief motor racing career.

Having made a late start in the sport, Gunnar had his first full season of racing in Formula Super Vee in 1973, learning a great deal in a short time from the experienced Freddy Kottulinsky, who was instrumental in his early development. He also tried his hand at Formula 2 at Norisring and, given his novice status, did remarkably well to finish a lucky fourth on aggregate with a GRD. In 1974, he raced in the German Polifac F3 championship in a private March and impressed sufficiently to bargain his way into the works team, contesting the British series alongside Alex Ribeiro in 1975. Things could hardly have started better, as he won the first race at Thruxton to set up his year, which ended with him taking the BP championship. An end-of-season switch to Formula Atlantic merely underlined his talent, as he won the last five rounds in succession in a Chevron B29.

Although tied to March and BMW for 1976, Nilsson got together with Ronnie Peterson to contrive a swap deal that saw Gunnar join the Lotus team at a time when it was at a low ebb. It was a gamble, but it soon paid off, as he ended up on the rostrum in his third race. The arrival of Mario Andretti only strengthened the team's hand as they sought to recapture past glories, and Gunnar benefited greatly from the American driver's guidance. Ken Tyrrell, no less, predicted that here was a future world champion – praise indeed.

Happy to stay with Lotus for another year in 1977, Nilsson maintained his upward momentum during the first half of the season, culminating in his only grand prix win in the wet at Zolder, where memorably he moved through the field before picking off the leader, Niki Lauda, with clinical precision. The second half of the year saw a sudden downturn in his fortunes, however, as inconsistency set in. Of course no one knew it, but the cancer he had developed was already well advanced.

With Peterson returning to the Lotus fold for 1978, Gunnar signed for the newly formed Arrows team, but in the event he was never well enough to drive the car. By the following autumn, he was fighting to live just long enough to see his Gunnar Nilsson Cancer Treatment Campaign successfully launched. He passed away that October.

NILSSON, Gunnar (S) b 20/11/1948, Helsingborg – d 20/10/1978, Hammersmith, London

1976 Championship position: 10th   Wins: 0   Pole positions: 0   Fastest laps: 0   Points scored: 11

	Race	Circuit	No	Entrant	Tyres	Capacity/Car/Engine	Comment	Q Pos/Entries
ret	SOUTH AFRICAN GP	Kyalami	6	John Player Team Lotus	G	3.0 Lotus 77-Cosworth V8	clutch	25/25
ret	US GP WEST	Long Beach	6	John Player Team Lotus	G	3.0 Lotus 77-Cosworth V8	suspension – crashed	20/27
3	SPANISH GP	Jarama	6	John Player Team Lotus	G	3.0 Lotus 77-Cosworth V8		7/30
ret	BELGIAN GP	Zolder	6	John Player Team Lotus	G	3.0 Lotus 77-Cosworth V8	crashed	22/29
ret	MONACO GP	Monte Carlo	6	John Player Team Lotus	G	3.0 Lotus 77-Cosworth V8	engine	16/25
ret	SWEDISH GP	Anderstorp	6	John Player Team Lotus	G	3.0 Lotus 77-Cosworth V8	spun into barrier	6/27
ret	FRENCH GP	Paul Ricard	6	John Player Team Lotus	G	3.0 Lotus 77-Cosworth V8	transmission	12/30
ret	BRITISH GP	Brands Hatch	6	John Player Team Lotus	G	3.0 Lotus 77-Cosworth V8	engine	14/30
5	GERMAN GP	Nürburgring	6	John Player Team Lotus	G	3.0 Lotus 77-Cosworth V8		16/28
3	AUSTRIAN GP	Österreichring	6	John Player Team Lotus	G	3.0 Lotus 77-Cosworth V8		4/25
ret	DUTCH GP	Zandvoort	6	John Player Team Lotus	G	3.0 Lotus 77-Cosworth V8	crashed on oil	13/27
13	ITALIAN GP	Monza	6	John Player Team Lotus	G	3.0 Lotus 77-Cosworth V8	pit stop – broken nose cone/-1 lap	12/29
12	CANADIAN GP	Mosport Park	6	John Player Team Lotus	G	3.0 Lotus 77-Cosworth V8	last away at start/1 lap behind	15/27
ret	US GP EAST	Watkins Glen	6	John Player Team Lotus	G	3.0 Lotus 77-Cosworth V8	engine	20/27
6	JAPANESE GP	Mount Fuji	6	John Player Team Lotus	G	3.0 Lotus 77-Cosworth V8	1 lap behind	16/27

1977 Championship position: 8th   Wins: 1   Pole positions: 0   Fastest laps: 1   Points scored: 20

	Race	Circuit	No	Entrant	Tyres	Capacity/Car/Engine	Comment	Q Pos/Entries
dns	ARGENTINE GP	Buenos Aires	6	John Player Team Lotus	G	3.0 Lotus 78-Cosworth V8	Andretti drove car	(10)/21
5	BRAZILIAN GP	Interlagos	6	John Player Team Lotus	G	3.0 Lotus 78-Cosworth V8	2 pitstops – tyres/-1 lap	10/22
12	SOUTH AFRICAN GP	Kyalami	6	John Player Team Lotus	G	3.0 Lotus 78-Cosworth V8	pit stop – tyres – new nose/-1 lap	10/23
8	US GP WEST	Long Beach	6	John Player Team Lotus	G	3.0 Lotus 78-Cosworth V8	1 lap behind	16/22
5	SPANISH GP	Jarama	6	John Player Team Lotus	G	3.0 Lotus 78-Cosworth V8		12/31
ret	MONACO GP	Monte Carlo	6	John Player Team Lotus	G	3.0 Lotus 78-Cosworth V8	gearbox	13/26
1	BELGIAN GP	Zolder	6	John Player Team Lotus	G	3.0 Lotus 78-Cosworth V8	FL	3/32
19/ret	SWEDISH GP	Anderstorp	6	John Player Team Lotus	G	3.0 Lotus 78-Cosworth V8	wheel bearing/8 laps behind	7/31
4	FRENCH GP	Dijon	6	John Player Team Lotus	G	3.0 Lotus 78-Cosworth V8		3/30
3	BRITISH GP	Silverstone	6	John Player Team Lotus	G	3.0 Lotus 78-Cosworth V8		5/36
ret	GERMAN GP	Hockenheim	6	John Player Team Lotus	G	3.0 Lotus 78-Cosworth V8	engine	9/30
ret	AUSTRIAN GP	Österreichring	6	John Player Team Lotus	G	3.0 Lotus 78-Cosworth V8	engine	16/30
ret	DUTCH GP	Zandvoort	6	John Player Team Lotus	G	3.0 Lotus 78-Cosworth V8	hit Reutemann	5/34
ret	ITALIAN GP	Monza	6	John Player Team Lotus	G	3.0 Lotus 78-Cosworth V8	broken front upright	19/34
ret	US GP EAST	Watkins Glen	6	John Player Team Lotus	G	3.0 Lotus 78-Cosworth V8	hit by Peterson	12/27
ret	CANADIAN GP	Mosport Park	6	John Player Team Lotus	G	3.0 Lotus 78-Cosworth V8	throttle stuck – crashed	4/27
ret	JAPANESE GP	Mount Fuji	6	John Player Team Lotus	G	3.0 Lotus 78-Cosworth V8	gearbox	14/23

GP Starts: 31   GP Wins: 1   Pole positions: 0   Fastest laps: 1   Points: 31

HIDEKI NODA

THE inscrutable Japanese are famed for their polite and formal manner, but the self-deprecating Hideki Noda goes against the stereotype. Perhaps it is because much of his racing career has been in Europe that he has developed a Western sense of humour. He travelled from Japan to contest the 1989 Vauxhall and GM Lotus series, and then F3 with a Ralt. The high point in this class came in 1991, when he won at Silverstone.

Three years in F3000 brought steady, but hardly spectacular progress, although Hideki took a third at Enna in 1994. "People think I'm useless," said the ever-smiling Noda as eyebrows were raised when he found a seat at Larrousse at the end of 1994. However, he did a neat and tidy job in a poor car – a lot better than most people expected. Plans to join Simtek for a series of races in 1995 came to nought when the team folded, and to add insult to injury, it appears that they had taken his deposit...

Hideki then switched to the Indy Lights series, where he was quick, but erratic. The highlight of his two years in the States came at Portland in 1997, when he became the first Japanese driver to win a CART-sanctioned event.

In 1998, Noda returned to Japan to race successfully in both Formula Nippon and the All-Japan GT championship, driving the Hoshino team's Ralt in the former and a Toyota Supra with co-driver Wayne Gardner in the latter. For the 2003 season, Noda launched his own Formula Nippon squad, Team Mohn, but three seasons in the category yielded little in the way of results and more in the way of outlandish hairstyles. Hideki was briefly seen behind the wheel of Japan's A1GP challenger, scoring some points before opting out after the franchise ran into funding problems

RODNEY NUCKEY

AFTER showing a great deal of skill in his own F3 Cooper-Norton during the 1952 season, his record including wins at Falkenberg and Skarpnack in Sweden, Rodney Nuckey was sufficiently encouraged to purchase a Formula 2 Cooper-Bristol, which he put to good use in 1953, taking a third place in the Syracuse Grand Prix, fourth in the London Trophy at Crystal Palace and fifth in the Eifelrennen. In 1954, he raced mainly in Formula Libre events and in the F3 Cooper. He toured Europe, taking wins in Vaxjo, Sweden, and Bressiure and Montauban. After marrying his first Scandinavian wife in 1955, he stopped racing, eventually moving to Australia and then to the Philippines, where he subsequently remarried and started a family.

ROBERT O'BRIEN

RUMOURS abounded that Robert O'Brien was actually a CIA operative, and considerable mystery surrounds him, but he was definitely a sports car racer who took fourth place in the 1952 Sebring 12-hour race in a Ferrari. Then he toured Europe in a Cadillac, pulling a Frazer-Nash racer around on a trailer. He hired Johnny Claes' Simca-Gordini T15 for the Belgian Grand Prix, qualified for the last spot on the grid and finished in 14th place, six laps down on race winner Alberto Ascari. After he left racing, O'Brien concentrated on his business ventures, which included involvement in car dealerships and spares retailing, in both his home state of New Jersey and in New York.

NODA, Hideki (J) b 7/3/1969, Osaka

	1994	Championship position: Unplaced						
	Race	Circuit	No	Entrant	Tyres	Capacity/Car/Engine	Comment	Q Pos/Entries
ret	EUROPEAN GP	Jerez	19	Tourtel Larrousse F1	G	3.5 Larrousse LH94-Ford HB V8	gearbox	24/28
ret	JAPANESE GP	Suzuka	19	Tourtel Larrousse F1	G	3.5 Larrousse LH94-Ford HB V8	started from pits/fuel injection	23/28
ret	AUSTRALIAN GP	Adelaide	19	Tourtel Larrousse F1	G	3.5 Larrousse LH94-Ford HB V8	oil leak	23/28

GP Starts: 3   GP Wins: 0   Pole positions: 0   Fastest laps: 0   Points: 0

NUCKEY, Rodney (GB) b 26/6/1929, Wood Green, London – d 29/6/2000, Manilla, Philippines

	1953	Championship position: Unplaced						
	Race	Circuit	No	Entrant	Tyres	Capacity/Car/Engine	Comment	Q Pos/Entries
11	GERMAN GP	Nürburgring	40	Rodney Nuckey	D	2.0 Cooper T23-Bristol 6	2 laps behind	20/35
	1954	Championship position: Unplaced						
dns	BRITISH GP	Silverstone	30	Ecurie Richmond	D	2.0 Cooper T23-Bristol 6	Brandon drove car	– / –

GP Starts: 1   GP Wins: 0   Pole positions: 0   Fastest laps: 0   Points: 0

O'BRIEN, Robert (USA) b 11/4/1908, Lyndhurst, New Jersey – d 10/2/1987, Hackensack, New Jersey

	1952	Championship position: Unplaced						
	Race	Circuit	No	Entrant	Tyres	Capacity/Car/Engine	Comment	Q Pos/Entries
nc	BELGIAN GP	Spa	44	Robert O'Brien	E	1.5 Simca-Gordini Type 15 4	6 laps behind	22/22

GP Starts: 1   GP Wins: 0   Pole positions: 0   Fastest laps: 0   Points: 0

JACKIE OLIVER

IT'S hard to believe that the still youthful looking Jackie Oliver has been involved in motorsport for over 50 years, having started with a Mini way back in 1961. He really came to prominence, however, driving a Lotus Elan, with which he embarrassed many a more powerful GT car in 1965, before moving into single-seaters the following year, when he showed much promise, but achieved little success in Formula 3.

Jackie's breakthrough year was 1967, when he drove the Lotus Components F2 car, doing himself a power of good in the eyes of Colin Chapman by taking fifth overall and the F2 class win in the German GP. With the death of Jim Clark at Hockenheim, Oliver was promoted into the Lotus team as number two to Graham Hill, but he had something of a torrid baptism, crashing in both the Monaco and French GPs before redeeming himself with a splendid performance at Brands Hatch, where he led the British GP until engine failure.

Seen as nothing more than a stopgap by Chapman, who had set his heart on having Jochen Rindt in the team, Oliver bowed out with a fine third place in Mexico to take up a two-year contract with BRM.

The following season was a miserable one for BRM, but Oliver salvaged his year by racing for John Wyer's Gulf team. Paired with Jacky Ickx, he won at Sebring and then they scored a famous victory at Le Mans, Jackie's contribution to which is often overlooked. The second year of his BRM deal brought scarcely more joy than the first, even though he had the excellent P153 to drive. Apart from a fifth place in Austria and a third in the Gold Cup at Oulton Park, the catalogue of retirements made depressing reading. Jackie's sharp, young, Essex personality didn't sit well with Louis Stanley, who preferred drivers typical of a different era, so a parting of the ways was probably inevitable. The season was not completely lost, however, for he ventured into Can-Am with the Autocast project and took three second places. Meanwhile, he returned to sports cars with Wyer, winning the Daytona 24-hours and Monza 1000km, but was released when he was invited to race Don Nichols' Shadow in Can-Am. Keen to keep his Formula 1 career afloat, Oliver arranged some drives in a third McLaren, and his versatility was proven when he stood in for Mark Donohue in Penske's Trans-Am Javelin to take third place at Riverside.

With the 1972 British GP being held at Brands Hatch (one of Jackie's favourite circuits), he drove for BRM, but he spent most of the season testing Shadow's latest Can-Am car. He got on well with Don Nichols, and when Shadow entered grand prix racing the following year, Oliver had one of the drives. It was a perplexing season, the DN1 chassis proving difficult to sort, but in a wet race in Canada he took third place – although many insist that in fact he won, as the lap charts were thrown into confusion by the use of a pace car.

Oliver concentrated on Can-Am alone in 1974, and it paid off handsomely when he won the series at the fourth attempt in Nichols' machines. Although increasingly involved in the management side of things, Oliver contested the 1975 and 1976 US F5000 series, before a Formula 1 swansong as a driver in 1977. He took the Shadow DN8 into fifth place at the Race of Champions, and later in the year he raced in his final grand prix in Sweden, finishing ninth.

Along with Alan Rees and Tony Southgate, Oliver quit Shadow at the end of the year and unveiled the 1978 Arrows Formula 1 car, which subsequently was the subject of legal action by Nichols over design copyright. Jackie then spent the next decade keeping Arrows on the F1 grid, but in 1990 he sold out to the Japanese Footwork concern, whose name the team took. He remained at the helm as a director, however, and regained control of the team at the end of 1993, when the parent company hit financial difficulties in Japan. The Arrows name was back.

In 1996, Oliver sold a major portion of the team to Tom Walkinshaw and was content to take a back-seat role as the new incumbent set about trying to end Arrows' winless streak. At the start of 1999, Jackie finally disposed of his remaining interest in the team that he had founded, walking away an exceedingly wealthy man after the reportedly massive buy-out.

In the past decade, as a board member of the BRDC, Jackie has been instrumental in the planning and execution of the improvement work on the much-revamped Silverstone circuit. After Lord March offered an invitation to try out a Porsche at Goodwood, he has been tempted back into on-track action, racing classic saloons for fun at historic festivals.

OLIVER, Jackie Keith Jack Oliver (GB) b 14/8/1942, Chadwell Heath, nr Romford, Essex

	Race	Circuit	No	Entrant	Tyres	Capacity/Car/Engine	Comment	Q Pos/Entries
	1967 Championship position: Unplaced							
5*	GERMAN GP (F2)	Nürburgring	24	Lotus Components Ltd	F	1.6 Lotus 48-Cosworth 4 F2	*1st in F2 class/no points scored	16/25
	1968 Championship position: 13th=		Wins: 0	Pole positions: 0	Fastest laps: 1	Points scored: 6		
ret	MONACO GP	Monte Carlo	10	Gold Leaf Team Lotus	F	3.0 Lotus 49-Cosworth V8	collision with McLaren	13/18
5/ret	BELGIAN GP	Spa	2	Gold Leaf Team Lotus	F	3.0 Lotus 49B-Cosworth V8	driveshaft/2 laps behind	15/18
nc	DUTCH GP	Zandvoort	4	Gold Leaf Team Lotus	F	3.0 Lotus 49B-Cosworth V8	pit stops – water in electrics/-10 laps	10/19
dns	FRENCH GP	Rouen	14	Gold Leaf Team Lotus	F	3.0 Lotus 49B-Cosworth V8	car destroyed in practice accident	(11)/18
ret	BRITISH GP	Brands Hatch	9	Gold Leaf Team Lotus	F	3.0 Lotus 49B-Cosworth V8	transmission	2/20
11	GERMAN GP	Nürburgring	21	Gold Leaf Team Lotus	F	3.0 Lotus 49B-Cosworth V8	1 lap behind	13/20

ret	ITALIAN GP	Monza	19	Gold Leaf Team Lotus	F	3.0 Lotus 49B-Cosworth V8	transmission/FL (disputed)	12/24
ret	CANADIAN GP	St Jovite	4	Gold Leaf Team Lotus	F	3.0 Lotus 49B-Cosworth V8	transmission	9/22
dns	US GP	Watkins Glen	11	Gold Leaf Team Lotus	F	3.0 Lotus 49B-Cosworth V8	accident in practice	(16)/21
3	MEXICAN GP	Mexico City	11	Gold Leaf Team Lotus	F	3.0 Lotus 49B-Cosworth V8		14/21

1969 Championship position: 16th=   Wins: 0   Pole positions: 0   Fastest laps: 0   Points scored: 1

7	SOUTH AFRICAN GP	Kyalami	11	Owen Racing Organisation	D	3.0 BRM P133 V12	pit stop/3 laps behind	15/18
ret	SPANISH GP	Montjuich Park	12	Owen Racing Organisation	D	3.0 BRM P133 V12	burst oil pipe	10/14
ret	MONACO GP	Monte Carlo	15	Owen Racing Organisation	D	3.0 BRM P133 V12	hit Attwood – damaged front wishbone	13/16
ret	DUTCH GP	Zandvoort	15	Owen Racing Organisation	D	3.0 BRM P133 V12	gear selection	13/15
ret	BRITISH GP	Silverstone	15	Owen Racing Organisation	D	3.0 BRM P133 V12	transmission	13/17
ret	GERMAN GP	Nürburgring	15	Owen Racing Organisation	D	3.0 BRM P138 V12	damaged sump	16/26
ret	ITALIAN GP	Monza	12	Owen Racing Organisation	D	3.0 BRM P139 V12	oil pressure	11/15
dns	"	"	12	Owen Racing Organisation	D	3.0 BRM P138 V12	practice only	– / –
ret	CANADIAN GP	Mosport Park	15	Owen Racing Organisation	D	3.0 BRM P139 V12	engine	12/20
ret	US GP	Watkins Glen	15	Owen Racing Organisation	D	3.0 BRM P139 V12	engine	14/18
6	MEXICAN GP	Mexico City	15	Owen Racing Organisation	D	3.0 BRM P139 V12	2 laps behind	12/17

1970 Championship position: 19th=   Wins: 0   Pole positions: 0   Fastest laps: 0   Points scored: 2

ret	SOUTH AFRICAN GP	Kyalami	19	Owen Racing Organisation	D	3.0 BRM P153 V12	gear selection	12/24
ret	SPANISH GP	Jarama	15	Yardley Team BRM	D	3.0 BRM P153 V12	broken stub axle – hit Ickx – fire	11/22
ret	MONACO GP	Monte Carlo	16	Yardley Team BRM	D	3.0 BRM P153 V12	engine – throttle cable	17/21
ret	BELGIAN GP	Spa	2	Yardley Team BRM	D	3.0 BRM P153 V12	engine	14/18
ret	DUTCH GP	Zandvoort	2	Yardley Team BRM	D	3.0 BRM P153 V12	engine	5/24
ret	FRENCH GP	Clermont Ferrand	5	Yardley Team BRM	D	3.0 BRM P153 V12	engine	12/23
ret	BRITISH GP	Brands Hatch	23	Yardley Team BRM	D	3.0 BRM P153 V12	engine	=4/25
ret	GERMAN GP	Hockenheim	18	Yardley Team BRM	D	3.0 BRM P153 V12	engine	18/25
5	AUSTRIAN GP	Österreichring	16	Yardley Team BRM	D	3.0 BRM P153 V12	1 lap behind	13/24
ret	ITALIAN GP	Monza	8	Yardley Team BRM	D	3.0 BRM P153 V12	engine	6/27
nc	CANADIAN GP	St Jovite	15	Yardley Team BRM	D	3.0 BRM P153 V12	long pit stop – broken wishbone/-38 laps	10/20
ret	US GP	Watkins Glen	20	Yardley Team BRM	D	3.0 BRM P153 V12	engine	7/27
7	MEXICAN GP	Mexico City	20	Yardley Team BRM	D	3.0 BRM P153 V12	1 lap behind	13/18

1971 Championship position: Unplaced

ret	BRITISH GP	Silverstone	11	Bruce McLaren Motor Racing	G	3.0 McLaren M14A-Cosworth V8	hit Hill at start – broke radius rod	22/24
9	AUSTRIAN GP	Österreichring	10	Bruce McLaren Motor Racing	G	3.0 McLaren M19A-Cosworth V8	1 lap behind	22/22
7	ITALIAN GP	Monza	14	Bruce McLaren Motor Racing	G	3.0 McLaren M14A-Cosworth V8		13/24

1972 Championship position: Unplaced

ret	BRITISH GP	Brands Hatch	14	Marlboro BRM	F	3.0 BRM P160B V12	rear radius rod	=14/27

1973 Championship position: 14th   Wins: 0   Pole positions: 0   Fastest laps: 0   Points scored: 4

ret	SOUTH AFRICAN GP	Kyalami	22	UOP Shadow Racing Team	G	3.0 Shadow DN1-Cosworth V8	engine	14/25
ret	SPANISH GP	Montjuich Park	19	UOP Shadow Racing Team	G	3.0 Shadow DN1-Cosworth V8	oil leak	13/22
ret	BELGIAN GP	Zolder	17	UOP Shadow Racing Team	G	3.0 Shadow DN1-Cosworth V8	accident	22/23
10	MONACO GP	Monte Carlo	17	UOP Shadow Racing Team	G	3.0 Shadow DN1-Cosworth V8	6 laps behind	23/26
ret	SWEDISH GP	Anderstorp	17	UOP Shadow Racing Team	G	3.0 Shadow DN1-Cosworth V8	transmission	17/22
ret	FRENCH GP	Paul Ricard	17	UOP Shadow Racing Team	G	3.0 Shadow DN1-Cosworth V8	clutch	21/25
ret/dns	BRITISH GP	Silverstone	17	UOP Shadow Racing Team	G	3.0 Shadow DN1-Cosworth V8	hit Lauda in first start	=25/29
ret	DUTCH GP	Zandvoort	17	UOP Shadow Racing Team	G	3.0 Shadow DN1-Cosworth V8	stuck throttle – hit barrier	10/24
8	GERMAN GP	Nürburgring	17	UOP Shadow Racing Team	G	3.0 Shadow DN1-Cosworth V8		=17/23
ret	AUSTRIAN GP	Österreichring	17	UOP Shadow Racing Team	G	3.0 Shadow DN1-Cosworth V8	fuel leak	18/25
11	ITALIAN GP	Monza	17	UOP Shadow Racing Team	G	3.0 Shadow DN1-Cosworth V8	1 lap behind	19/25
3	CANADIAN GP	Mosport Park	17	UOP Shadow Racing Team	G	3.0 Shadow DN1-Cosworth V8		14/26
15	US GP	Watkins Glen	17	UOP Shadow Racing Team	G	3.0 Shadow DN1-Cosworth V8	pit stop – loose wheels/4 laps behind	23/28

1977 Championship position: Unplaced

9	SWEDISH GP	Anderstorp	16	Shadow Racing Team	G	3.0 Shadow DN8-Cosworth V8		16/31

GP Starts: 49 (50)   GP Wins: 0   Pole positions: 0   Fastest laps: 1   Points: 13

Oliver convincingly led the 1968 British Grand Prix at Brands Hatch in his Lotus 49B, before transmission failure sent him into retirement at half-distance.

DANNY ONGAIS

BORN in Hawaii, Danny Ongais first found fame as a drag racer with the Vel's Parnelli team, before trying his hand in SCCA national racing in 1974. Then he tackled US F5000 with Interscope Racing's Lola in 1975 and 1976, and although a win eluded him, he was a regular contender. The following season, Interscope ran him in USAC racing – where he shone, taking a win at Michigan – and in IMSA, where he won two rounds in a Porsche 935 turbo. He made his grand prix debut at the end-of-year North American rounds in the team's Penske.

Danny's struggles in F1 in 1978 – he scraped on to the grid for the first two grands prix in the works Ensign, then floundered with the embarrassing Interscope Shadow – were in sharp contrast to his rapidly blossoming career in USAC, where he took five wins in the Parnelli VPJ6.

Although Danny enjoyed further success for Interscope in IMSA sports car events, winning the 1979 Daytona 24-hours in a Porsche and taking third place the following year, this was the high point of his Indy car career, as he would suffer appalling leg injuries in a crash at Indianapolis in 1981. Happily, he recovered to make a return to the track, but although he raced on until 1987, he was never quite the same force again.

It came as a huge surprise when Danny came out of retirement in 1996 after Scott Brayton was killed in practice for the Indy 500. The veteran brought the Menard Lola home in a splendid seventh place, however, which encouraged him to race in the event the following May.

Unfortunately, it was not a happy return, for he crashed heavily when the engine in his car blew during his first lap of qualifying, resulting in an overnight stay in hospital. He was inducted into the Motorsports Hall of Fame of America in 2000, in the drag racing category.

ARTHUR OWEN

A DIRECTOR of a jewellery business in St Helier, Jersey, Arthur Owen not unnaturally gained his early competition experience on the Bouley Bay hill-climb in the early 1950s with a Skinner special. By the middle of the decade, he and his friend, Bill Knight, had acquired a potent Cooper sports car and set about breaking speed records at Montlhéry and Monza.

Although he was only an occasional circuit racer, Owen was invited to take part in the 1960 Italian Grand Prix, which was boycotted by the major English teams because the organisers had insisted on including the banked part of the circuit. Then he turned his attention to the hills, unleashing his 2.2-litre Type 53 Cooper 'Lowline' on the opposition. After coming close to winning the British hill-climb championship in 1961, he made no mistake the following year.

In 1963 and '64, Owen raced a Lotus 23 sports car. He was one of a select group of drivers invited to compete in the inaugural race held at the Suzuka circuit.

ONGAIS, Danny (USA) b 21/5/1942, Honolulu, Hawaii

	Race	Circuit	No	Entrant	Tyres	Capacity/Car/Engine	Comment	Q Pos/Entries
	1977 Championship position: Unplaced							
ret	US GP EAST	Watkins Glen	14	Interscope Racing	G	3.0 Penske PC4-Cosworth V8	*spun off*	26/27
7	CANADIAN GP	Mosport Park	14	Interscope Racing	G	3.0 Penske PC4-Cosworth V8	*2 laps behind*	22/27
	1978 Championship position: Uuplaced							
ret	ARGENTINE GP	Buenos Aires	22	Team Tissot Ensign	G	3.0 Ensign N177-Cosworth V8	*rotor arm*	21/27
ret	BRAZILIAN GP	Rio	22	Team Tissot Ensign	G	3.0 Ensign N177-Cosworth V8	*brake disc mounting bolt*	23/28
dnpq	US GP WEST	Long Beach	39	Interscope Racing	G	3.0 Shadow DN9-Cosworth V8		29/30
dnpq	DUTCH GP	Zandvoort	39	Interscope Racing	G	3.0 Shadow DN9-Cosworth V8		32/33
	GP Starts: 4　GP Wins: 0　Pole positions: 0　Fastest laps: 0　Points: 0							

OWEN, Arthur (GB) b 23/3/1915, Forest Gate, London – d 13/4/2002, Vilamoura, Portugal

	Race	Circuit	No	Entrant	Tyres	Capacity/Car/Engine	Comment	Q Pos/Entries
	1960 Championship position: Unplaced							
ret	ITALIAN GP	Monza	8	Arthur Owen	D	2.2 Cooper T45-Climax 4	*locked brakes – suspension damage*	11/16
	GP Starts: 1　GP Wins: 0　Pole positions: 0　Fastest laps: 0　Points: 0							

CARLOS PACE

ALONG-TIME friend and rival of the Fittipaldi brothers – fellow Paulistas – Carlos Pace raced for most of the 1960s in Brazil, beginning in karts where his opponents included Wilson Fittipaldi. Driving a variety of machines from Renault Gordinis to Formula Vee cars and a potent Alfa Romeo T33/2, he took the Brazilian national championship three years in a row between 1967 and 1969.

Together with Wilson Fittipaldi, Carlos arrived in Europe in 1970 to contest a very competitive Formula 3 series with a Lotus 59 entered by Jim Russell. Despite his lack of knowledge of the British circuits, he was soon very much one of the front-runners, and by the end of the year he had collected the Forward Trust championship.

After spending his winter at home, where he endured a disappointing Torneio series with an F3 Lotus 59, Carlos returned with a healthy dose of sponsorship, which was eagerly accepted by Frank Williams, who provided a March for the Formula 2 season. Pace managed to win a non-championship round on aggregate at Imola, although the entry for this race wasn't one of the best. In the 11-race series, poor reliability was largely responsible for him failing to score a point.

Williams was keen to run Pace in his second F1 car in 1972, and the pair went 50/50 on a deal. While the unfortunate number-one driver, Henri Pescarolo, had a dreadful time, Carlos made good progress in the old March, taking valuable championship points in two of his first four races.

Broadening his horizons, Carlos raced briefly in Formula 2 with Pygmée, and then joined Ferrari's sports car team to take second place (with Helmut Marko) in the Österreichring 1000km, which brought an invitation from Gulf to race their Mirage at Watkins Glen, where he took third place with Derek Bell. Late in the 1972 season, he dropped a bombshell on Williams by announcing his intention to join Surtees in 1973, and by the end-of-year John Player Challenge Race at Brands Hatch, he was already installed in one of 'Big John's' cars, taking a very promising second place in the Surtees TS9B.

In 1973, he raced regularly for Surtees in Formula 1 and was a revelation. The highlights were his two points-scoring performances in Germany and Austria, but too many mechanical problems left him lowly placed in the final championship table. In tandem with F1, he drove for Ferrari in sports car events and, teamed with Arturo Merzario, took a string of top-six placings, including second at both the Le Mans 24-hours and the Nürburgring 1000km.

Despite the poor reliability of the Surtees, Carlos was persuaded to stay with the team for 1974. He took a fourth place in his home grand prix and then a ninth in the non-championship Grand Prix de Presidente Medici in Brasilia, before a succession of niggling problems blighted his prospects. Suddenly, in mid-season, he quit in frustration, stating, "I would prefer not to drive in another grand prix this year rather than drive a Surtees." A divorce settlement was reached and Carlos tried (and failed) to qualify a poorly prepared Hexagon BT42 at Dijon, while Bernie Ecclestone set about taking him into the Brabham team at the expense of Rikki von Opel.

Alongside Carlos Reutemann, he soon proved to be every bit as competitive as his Argentinian team-mate. A great drive in Austria was halted by a broken fuel line when victory seemed possible, and he posted fastest race laps at Monza and Watkins Glen, where a second-place finish served due notice of his intentions for the 1975 season.

The highlight of Pace's career came at Interlagos, his first grand prix win being recorded in front of his ecstatic home fans, but luck rarely went his way throughout the rest of the year. He drove some extremely hard races, made some mistakes and generally was more convincing than Reutemann. His competitiveness was severely blunted in 1976, however, when Brabham ran Alfa Romeo engines, but he got stuck in and never gave up in his efforts to develop the car. It was a question of 'if only' for much of the season; he could have achieved much more than his best of two fourth-place finishes. By the end of the year, he was enthusiastic about his prospects for 1977, especially as now he was leading the team, following Reutemann's move to Ferrari.

Second place in the season opening Argentine Grand Prix vindicated Pace's optimism, but a chance to record another home win in Brazil was lost after a mistake ended in a collision. Just prior to the start of the European season came the terrible news of his death in a light plane crash in Brazil. He was married with two young children. In 1985, the Interlagos track was renamed Autodrómo José Carlos Pace in his honour.

PACE, Carlos (BR) b 6/10/1944, São Paulo – d 18/3/1977, nr São Paulo

1972 Championship position: 16th=   Wins: 0   Pole positions: 0   Fastest laps: 0   Points scored: 3

	Race	Circuit	No	Entrant	Tyres	Capacity/Car/Engine	Comment	Q Pos/Entries
17	SOUTH AFRICAN GP	Kyalami	22	Team Williams-Motul	G	3.0 March 711-Cosworth V8	*delayed start – fuel pump/6 laps behind*	24/27
6	SPANISH GP	Jarama	29	Team Williams-Motul	G	3.0 March 711-Cosworth V8	*1 lap behind*	16/26
17	MONACO GP	Monte Carlo	23	Team Williams-Motul	G	3.0 March 711-Cosworth V8	*pit stop – electrics/8 laps behind*	24/25
5	BELGIAN GP	Nivelles	16	Team Williams-Motul	G	3.0 March 711-Cosworth V8	*1 lap behind*	11/26
ret	FRENCH GP	Clermont Ferrand	17	Team Williams-Motul	G	3.0 March 711-Cosworth V8	*engine*	11/29
ret	BRITISH GP	Brands Hatch	25	Team Williams-Motul	G	3.0 March 711-Cosworth V8	*collision with Reutemann/differential*	13/27
nc	GERMAN GP	Nürburgring	21	Team Williams-Motul	G	3.0 March 711-Cosworth V8	*long pit stop – handling/3 laps behind*	11/27
nc	AUSTRIAN GP	Österreichring	23	Team Williams-Motul	G	3.0 March 711-Cosworth V8	*pit stop – fuel leak/8 laps behind*	=17/26
ret	ITALIAN GP	Monza	26	Team Williams-Motul	G	3.0 March 711-Cosworth V8	*hit by Regazzoni at chicane*	18/27
9/ret	CANADIAN GP	Mosport Park	29	Team Williams-Motul	G	3.0 March 711-Cosworth V8	*fuel pressure/2 laps behind*	18/25
ret	US GP	Watkins Glen	27	Team Williams-Motul	G	3.0 March 711-Cosworth V8	*fuel injection*	15/32

1973 Championship position: 11th   Wins: 0   Pole positions: 0   Fastest laps: 2   Points scored: 7

	Race	Circuit	No	Entrant	Tyres	Capacity/Car/Engine	Comment	Q Pos/Entries
ret	ARGENTINE GP	Buenos Aires	28	Brooke Bond Oxo-Team Surtees	F	3.0 Surtees TS14A-Cosworth V8	*suspension*	15/19
ret	BRAZILIAN GP	Interlagos	6	Brooke Bond Oxo-Team Surtees	F	3.0 Surtees TS14A-Cosworth V8	*suspension*	6/20
ret	SOUTH AFRICAN GP	Kyalami	11	Brooke Bond Oxo-Team Surtees	F	3.0 Surtees TS14A-Cosworth V8	*burst tyre – crashed*	9/25
ret	SPANISH GP	Montjuich Park	10	Brooke Bond Oxo-Team Surtees	F	3.0 Surtees TS14A-Cosworth V8	*driveshaft*	16/22
8	BELGIAN GP	Zolder	24	Brooke Bond Oxo-Team Surtees	F	3.0 Surtees TS14A-Cosworth V8	*pitstop – rear wing/4 laps behind*	=7/23
ret	MONACO GP	Monte Carlo	24	Brooke Bond Oxo-Team Surtees	F	3.0 Surtees TS14A-Cosworth V8	*driveshaft*	17/26
10	SWEDISH GP	Anderstorp	24	Brooke Bond Oxo-Team Surtees	F	3.0 Surtees TS14A-Cosworth V8	*pit stop – tyres – vibration/3 laps behind*	16/22
13	FRENCH GP	Paul Ricard	24	Brooke Bond Oxo-Team Surtees	F	3.0 Surtees TS14A-Cosworth V8	*pit stop – tyres/3 laps behind*	18/25
ret/dns	BRITISH GP	Silverstone	24	Brooke Bond Oxo-Team Surtees	F	3.0 Surtees TS14A-Cosworth V8	*multiple accident in first start*	=14/29
7	DUTCH GP	Zandvoort	24	Brooke Bond Oxo-Team Surtess	F	3.0 Surtees TS14A-Cosworth V8	*pit stop – tyres/engine/3 laps behind*	8/24
4	GERMAN GP	Nürburgring	24	Brooke Bond Oxo-Team Surtees	F	3.0 Surtees TS14A-Cosworth V8	*FL*	=11/23
3	AUSTRIAN GP	Österreichring	24	Brooke Bond Oxo-Team Surtees	F	3.0 Surtees TS14A-Cosworth V8	*FL*	8/25
ret	ITALIAN GP	Monza	24	Brooke Bond Oxo-Team Surtees	F	3.0 Surtees TS14A-Cosworth V8	*tyre failure*	5/25
ret	CANADIAN GP	Mosport Park	24	Brooke Bond Oxo-Team Surtees	F	3.0 Surtees TS14A-Cosworth V8	*broken wheel*	19/26
ret	US GP	Watkins Glen	24	Brooke Bond Oxo-Team Surtees	F	3.0 Surtees TS14A-Cosworth V8	*broken suspension*	10/28

1974 Championship position: 12th   Wins: 0   Pole positions: 0   Fastest laps: 2   Points scored: 11

	Race	Circuit	No	Entrant	Tyres	Capacity/Car/Engine	Comment	Q Pos/Entries
ret	ARGENTINE GP	Buenos Aires	18	Team Surtees	F	3.0 Surtees TS16-Cosworth V8	*engine*	11/26
4	BRAZILIAN GP	Interlagos	18	Team Surtees	F	3.0 Surtees TS16-Cosworth V8	*1 lap behind*	12/25
11	SOUTH AFRICAN GP	Kyalami	18	Bang & Olufsen Team Surtees	F	3.0 Surtees TS16-Cosworth V8	*1 lap behind*	2/27
13	SPANISH GP	Jarama	18	Bang & Olufsen Team Surtees	F	3.0 Surtees TS16-Cosworth V8	*2 pit stops – tyres/6 laps behind*	15/28
ret	BELGIAN GP	Nivelles	18	Bang & Olufsen Team Surtees	F	3.0 Surtees TS16-Cosworth V8	*tyre vibration*	8/32
ret	MONACO GP	Monte Carlo	18	Bang & Olufsen Team Surtees	F	3.0 Surtees TS16-Cosworth V8	*multiple accident*	18/28
ret	SWEDISH GP	Anderstorp	18	Bang & Olufsen Team Surtees	F	3.0 Surtees TS16-Cosworth V8	*poor handling – withdrawn*	24/28
dnq	FRENCH GP	Dijon	34	Hexagon Racing with John Goldie	F	3.0 Brabham BT42-Cosworth V8		24/30
9	BRITISH GP	Brands Hatch	8	Motor Racing Developments	G	3.0 Brabham BT44-Cosworth V8	*1 lap behind*	=19/34
12	GERMAN GP	Nürburgring	8	Motor Racing Developments	G	3.0 Brabham BT44-Cosworth V8	*pitstop – handling*	17/32
ret	AUSTRIAN GP	Österreichring	8	Motor Racing Developmants	G	3.0 Brabham BT44-Cosworth V8	*fuel line*	4/31
5	ITALIAN GP	Monza	8	Motor Racing Developments	G	3.0 Brabham BT44-Cosworth V8	*pit stop – tyre/1 lap behind/FL*	3/31
8	CANADIAN GP	Mosport Park	8	Motor Racing Developments	G	3.0 Brabham BT44-Cosworth V8	*pit stop – tyre/1 lap behind*	9/30
2	US GP	Watkins Glen	8	Motor Racing Developments	G	3.0 Brabham BT44-Cosworth V8	*FL*	4/30

1975 Championship position: 6th   Wins: 1   Pole positions: 1   Fastest laps: 1   Points scored: 24

	Race	Circuit	No	Entrant	Tyres	Capacity/Car/Engine	Comment	Q Pos/Entries
ret	ARGENTINE GP	Buenos Aires	8	Martini Racing	G	3.0 Brabham BT44B-Cosworth V8	*engine*	2/23
1	BRAZILIAN GP	Interlagos	8	Martini Racing	G	3.0 Brabham BT44B-Cosworth V8		6/23
4	SOUTH AFRICAN GP	Kyalami	8	Martini Racing	G	3.0 Brabham BT44B-Cosworth V8	*FL*	1/28

A dream win on home soil for Carlos Pace as he takes his Brabham to victory in the 1975 Brazilian Grand Prix. Tragically, his life would be cut short a year later in a light aircraft accident.

ret	SPANISH GP	Montjuich Park	8	Martini Racing	G	3.0 Brabham BT44B-Cosworth V8	accident avoiding Stommelen	14/26
3	MONACO GP	Monte Carlo	8	Martini Racing	G	3.0 Brabham BT44B-Cosworth V8		8/26
8	BELGIAN GP	Zolder	8	Martini Racing	G	3.0 Brabham BT44B-Cosworth V8	1 lap behind	2/24
ret	SWEDISH GP	Anderstorp	8	Martini Racing	G	3.0 Brabham BT44B-Cosworth V8	spun off	6/26
5	DUTCH GP	Zandvoort	8	Martini Racing	G	3.0 Brabham BT44B-Cosworth V8	pit stop – tyres/1 lap behind	9/25
ret	FRENCH GP	Paul Ricard	8	Martini Racing	G	3.0 Brabham BT44B-Cosworth V8	driveshaft	=5/26
2/ret	BRITISH GP	Silverstone	8	Martini Racing	G	3.0 Brabham BT44B-Cosworth V8	spun off in rainstorm/1 lap behind	2/28
ret	GERMAN GP	Nürburgring	8	Martini Racing	G	3.0 Brabham BT44B-Cosworth V8	rear upright	2/26
ret	AUSTRIAN GP	Österreichring	8	Martini Racing	G	3.0 Brabham BT44B-Cosworth V8	engine	6/30
ret	ITALIAN GP	Monza	8	Martini Racing	G	3.0 Brabham BT44B-Cosworth V8	throttle linkage	10/28
ret	US GP	Watkins Glen	8	Martini Racing	G	3.0 Brabham BT44B-Cosworth V8	collision with Depailler	16/24

1976 Championship position: 14th= Wins: 0 Pole positions: 0 Fastest laps: 0 Points scored: 7

10	BRAZILIAN GP	Interlagos	8	Martini Racing	G	3.0 Brabham BT45-Alfa Romeo F12	1 lap behind	10/22
ret	SOUTH AFRICAN GP	Kyalami	8	Martini Racing	G	3.0 Brabham BT45-Alfa Romeo F12	engine	14/25
9	US GP WEST	Long Beach	8	Martini Racing	G	3.0 Brabham BT45-Alfa Romeo F12	pit stop – handling/3 laps behind	13/27
6	SPANISH GP	Jarama	8	Martini Racing	G	3.0 Brabham BT45-Alfa Romeo F12	1 lap behind	11/30
ret	BELGIAN GP	Zolder	8	Martini Racing	G	3.0 Brabham BT45-Alfa Romeo F12	electrics	9/29
9	MONACO GP	Monte Carlo	8	Martini Racing	G	3.0 Brabham BT45-Alfa Romeo F12	2 laps behind	13/25
8	SWEDISH GP	Anderstorp	8	Martini Racing	G	3.0 Brabham BT45-Alfa Romeo F12		10/27
4	FRENCH GP	Paul Ricard	8	Martini Racing	G	3.0 Brabham BT45-Alfa Romeo F12		5/30
8	BRITISH GP	Brands Hatch	8	Martini Racing	G	3.0 Brabham BT45-Alfa Romeo F12	pit stops – tyres/3 laps behind	16/30
4	GERMAN GP	Nürburgring	8	Martini Racing	G	3.0 Brabham BT45-Alfa Romeo F12		7/28
ret	AUSTRIAN GP	Österreichring	8	Martini Racing	G	3.0 Brabham BT45-Alfa Romeo F12	brake failure – hit barrier	8/25
ret	DUTCH GP	Zandvoort	8	Martini Racing	G	3.0 Brabham BT45-Alfa Romeo F12	oil leak	9/27
ret	ITALIAN GP	Monza	8	Martini Racing	G	3.0 Brabham BT45-Alfa Romeo F12	engine	3/29
7	CANADIAN GP	Mosport Park	8	Martini Racing	G	3.0 Brabham BT45-Alfa Romeo F12		10/27
ret	US GP EAST	Watkins Glen	8	Martini Racing	G	3.0 Brabham BT45-Alfa Romeo F12	collision with Mass	10/27
ret	JAPANESE GP	Mount Fuji	8	Martini Racing	G	3.0 Brabham BT45-Alfa Romeo F12	withdrew due to weather conditions	6/27

1977 Championship position: 15th= Wins: 0 Pole positions: 0 Fastest laps: 0 Points scored: 6

2	ARGENTINE GP	Buenos Aires	8	Martini Racing	G	3.0 Brabham BT45-Alfa Romeo F12		6/21
ret	BRAZILIAN GP	Interlagos	8	Martini Racing	G	3.0 Brabham BT45-Alfa Romeo F12	accident damage	5/22
13	SOUTH AFRICAN GP	Kyalami	8	Martini Racing	G	3.0 Brabham BT45B-Alfa Romeo F12	pit stops – tyres/2 laps behind	2/23
dns	" "	"	8	Martini Racing	G	3.0 Brabham BT45-Alfa Romeo F12	practice only	– / –

GP Starts: 71 (72) GP Wins: 1 Pole positions: 1 Fastest laps: 5 Points: 58

PAGANI, Nello (I) b 11/10/1911, Milan – d 19/10/2003, Miazzina

1950 Championship position: Unplaced

	Race	Circuit	No	Entrant	Tyres	Capacity/Car/Engine	Comment	Q Pos/Entries
7	SWISS GP	Bremgarten	2	Scuderia Achille Varzi	P	1.5 s/c Maserati 4CLT/48 4	3 laps behind	15/18

GP Starts: 1 GP Wins: 0 Pole positions: 0 Fastest laps: 0 Points: 0

NELLO PAGANI

AN aristocratic Italian, Nello Pagani first and foremost was a motorcycle racer, who won the inaugural 125cc World Championship in 1949 on a Mondial and finished second in the 500cc class on an MV Agusta.

Pagani was a talented car racer, too, as witnessed by his wins at Pau in 1947 and 1948 in a Maserati, although his appearances on four wheels were necessarily limited.

In 1950, Pagani drove a Maserati to seventh in his only grand prix appearance, at Bremgarten, and took a fourth at the Modena GP in a Simca-Gordini. Although he appeared occasionally thereafter, taking second in class in the Mille Miglia with an OSCA in 1952, he was more involved with the bike world, later managing the legendary MV Agusta team.

PALETTI, Riccardo (I) b 15/6/1958, Milan – d 13/6/1982, Montreal, Canada

1982 Championship position: Unplaced

	Race	Circuit	No	Entrant	Tyres	Capacity/Car/Engine	Comment	Q Pos/Entries
dnq	SOUTH AFRICAN GP	Kyalami	32	Osella Squadra Corse	P	3.0 Osella FA1C-Cosworth V8		28/30
dnpq	BRAZILIAN GP	Rio	32	Osella Squadra Corse	P	3.0 Osella FA1C-Cosworth V8		31/31
dnq	US GP WEST	Long Beach	32	Osella Squadra Corse	P	3.0 Osella FA1C-Cosworth V8		28/31
ret	SAN MARINO GP	Imola	32	Osella Squadra Corse	P	3.0 Osella FA1C-Cosworth V8	suspension	13/14
dnpq	BELGIAN GP	Zolder	32	Osella Sqaudra Corse	P	3.0 Osella FA1C-Cosworth V8		31/32
dnpq	MONACO GP	Monte Carlo	32	Osella Squadra Corse	P	3.0 Osella FA1C-Cosworth V8		28/31
dns	US GP (DETROIT)	Detroit	32	Osella Squadra Corse	P	3.0 Osella FA1C-Cosworth V8	crashed in a.m. warm-up	(23)/28
ret/dns	CANADIAN GP	Montreal	32	Osella Squadra Corse	P	3.0 Osella FA1C-Cosworth V8	fatal accident at first start	23/26

GP Starts: 1 (2) GP Wins: 0 Pole positions: 0 Fastest laps: 0 Points: 0

RICCARDO PALETTI

HAVING begun racing at 19 in Italian SuperFord, Riccardo Paletti soon graduated to Italian Formula 3 and then, after just 15 races in that series, made the big jump into Formula 2 – albeit briefly – at the end of 1979.

Back for more at the end of 1980, Paletti drove sensibly within his limits and, with the benefit of winter testing, he joined the Onyx team full time for 1981. The year started well with his March taking a second place at Silverstone to Mike Thackwell and a third at Thruxton. Then his season tailed off disappointingly, however, in a mixture of accidents and engine failures, apart from a sixth place in the Rome GP at Vallelunga.

With the help of generous sponsorship (reportedly more than $1m) courtesy of his father, an importer of Pioneer hi-fi equipment, Paletti was installed in the tiny Osella team for 1982. Thirty years later, the young Italian probably would have been refused a super licence. In the event, he was left slightly in fear of jumping into F1 with so little experience.

Undoubtedly Paletti faced a steep learning curve. In the eight races he entered, he failed to get on the grid for six of them and was well off the pace of his experienced team-mate, Jean-Pierre Jarier. Sadly he never had the chance to progress, for in Montreal his Osella accelerated away from its place at the tail of the grid and hurtled into the back of Didier Pironi's stalled Ferrari at over 100mph with devastating consequences.

It was a gruesome accident, the car catching fire briefly, while poor Paletti was trapped in the mangled wreck for more than 25 minutes. He suffered massive internal injuries and was pronounced dead in hospital shortly afterwards.

TORSTEN PALM

AFTER a little rallying in a Volvo, Torsten Palm entered a strong Scandinavian Formula 3 series with a Brabham BT21B in 1969, making a very good impression indeed. He did well enough to be included in the Swedish team (with Ronnie Peterson and Freddy Kottulinsky) that won that year's European Challenge at Karlskoga. Then he joined up with Picko Troberg for the 1970 season, and five wins helped him to take the Swedish title. In addition, he helped his country retain the European Challenge, this time at Thruxton. For 1971, he ventured to Brazil for the F3 Torneio series, before returning home to sew up another Swedish title with relative ease. When he stepped up to compete in a couple of European races, however, things did not go so well and he struggled to compete with the big names in his newly-acquired Brabham BT35.

Without the required financial backing to compete at the top level, Palm found himself trapped in Swedish Formula 3, narrowly losing his title to Conny Andersson in 1972 and slipping further down the pecking order the following year. He did find enough, however, to take in three European races with a Surtees, and his spectacular driving brought mixed results, but included a fine third place at Karlskoga. A one-off drive for Team Pierre Robert at Salzburgring, as a substitute for the graded Reine Wisell, ended in retirement, but it brought the Swede some more outings in 1974, when he managed to cause quite a stir at Karlskoga by qualifying the old GRD in fourth place.

In 1975, Palm grabbed the chance to participate at the top level. With backing from Polar Caravans, he took over the 'rent-a-drive' works Hesketh for the Monaco and Swedish grands prix. He did not disgrace himself at Anderstorp, driving steadily until running out of fuel just before the finish. That race really marked the end of his career. Still lacking the backing to put together a racing programme, the Swede preferred to put his efforts behind the promising Eje Elgh, who enjoyed a long and successful career outside Formula 1. In the 1990s, Torsten returned to his early roots, occasionally competing in rallies, but by then much of his time was absorbed by running his car dealership.ß

PALM, Torsten (S) b 23/7/1947, Kristinehamn

	1975 Championship position: Unplaced							
	Race	Circuit	No	Entrant	Tyres	Capacity/Car/Engine	Comment	Q Pos/Entries
dnq	MONACO GP	Monte Carlo	25	Polar Caravans	G	3.0 Hesketh 308B-Cosworth V8		24/26
10/ret	SWEDISH GP	Anderstorp	32	Polar Caravans	G	3.0 Hesketh 308B-Cosworth V8	out of fuel/2 laps behind	21/26
	GP Starts: 1 GP Wins: 0 Pole positions: 0 Fastest laps: 0 Points: 0							

JONATHAN PALMER

A BRILLIANT early career for Jonathan Palmer failed to deliver the fully competitive grand prix car his efforts had so obviously merited, so another talent was never truly tested at the highest level.

Palmer's racing career took a back seat while he qualified as a doctor, but early races with a Van Diemen in 1979 and 1980 earned him a drive with Dick Bennett's crack Formula 3 team for 1981. In a superb year, he took seven pole positions and eight wins, and set ten fastest laps to win the Marlboro F3 championship by a large margin from his rivals. A move into Formula 2 with the Ralt team brought him back down to earth with a jolt, as they struggled to find a competitive set-up. It was a different story in 1983 when, with the full attention of Honda, Jonathan and team-mate Mike Thackwell dominated proceedings. Palmer won six of the 12 rounds (five of them in a row at the end of the season) with a display of brilliant driving backed by much planning and hard work behind the scenes.

After a drive for Williams in the 1983 European GP, Palmer found himself with the RAM team and then the ambitious, but overstretched Zakspeed outfit, struggling even to gain sight of a top-six finish. Luckily he kept his competitive edge sharpened in sports cars. Driving a Richard Lloyd Porsche, he won at Brands Hatch in 1984 with Jan Lammers, and finished second at Le Mans in 1985. In 1987, he won the Norisring race with Mauro Baldi in Brun's Porsche.

By then, Palmer was at the start of a three-year association with Tyrrell. For the first two years, spent struggling with a Cosworth against the turbo brigade, all he could do was pick up the crumbs, but some excellent drives brought hard-earned points for the team, and Jonathan won the Jim Clark Trophy for top non-turbo driver in 1987. A competitive new chassis allowed him to take a splendid fifth at Imola in 1989, but his form sagged after the arrival of Jean Alesi, who stole the show. The season's finale saw him despondent after failing to qualify; his grand prix career was over.

In 1990, he acted as a test driver for McLaren-Honda and returned to competition in sports cars with a Porsche 962, but after the sudden death of James Hunt, the personable and ever talkative Palmer moved into a commentator's role for BBC TV.

Jonathan then set up his own ultra-professional junior single-seater series, Formula Palmer Audi. At a realistic cost, the identically prepared cars offered up-and-coming young drivers the chance to show their skills as they sought to make their way in the sport. It ran between 1998 and 2010, and gave a number of budding talents the chance to begin their professional careers. Palmer managed the first FPA winner, Justin Wilson, and helped the Sheffield man to achieve his goal of reaching Formula 1 before embarking on a successful Indy car career.

Palmer also set up an impressive track-day facility at Bedford Autodrome, spanning some 384 acres. This impressive facility safely caters for motorsport enthusiasts seeking thrills in an array of fast cars. In 2004, Palmer was a member of a consortium that took control of Cadwell Park, Oulton Park, Snetterton and Brands Hatch. Since then, running MotorSport Vision, he has invested much of his time in reviving the fortunes of these famous British tracks.

The Palmer name may yet reappear at grand prix level, his eldest son, Jolyon, having competed in Formula 2 and moved up to GP2 in 2011. His brother, Will, is also making his way in the sport further down the ladder.

PALMER, Jonathan (GB) b 7/11/1956, Lewisham, London

1983 Championship position: Unplaced

	Race	Circuit	No	Entrant	Tyres	Capacity/Car/Engine	Comment	Q Pos/Entries
13	EUROPEAN GP	Brands Hatch	42	TAG Williams Team	G	3.0 Williams FW08C-Cosworth V8	pit stop – tyres/2 laps behind	25/29

1984 Championship position: Unplaced

	Race	Circuit	No	Entrant	Tyres	Capacity/Car/Engine	Comment	Q Pos/Entries
8*	BRAZILIAN GP	Rio	10	Skoal Bandit Formula 1 Team	P	1.5 t/c RAM 01-Hart 4	*5th place car disqualified/-3 laps	27/27
ret	SOUTH AFRICAN GP	Kyalami	10	Skoal Bandit Formula 1 Team	P	1.5 t/c RAM 01-Hart 4	gearbox/electrics	21/27
10*	BELGIAN GP	Zolder	10	Skoal Bandit Formula 1 Team	P	1.5 t/c RAM 02-Hart 4	*5th car disqualified/pit stop/-6 laps	26/27
9*	SAN MARINO GP	Imola	10	Skoal Bandit Formula 1 Team	P	1.5 t/c RAM 02-Hart 4	*5th place car disqualified/-3 laps	25/28
13*	FRENCH GP	Dijon	10	Skoal Bandit Formula 1 Team	P	1.5 t/c RAM 02-Hart 4	*12th place car disqualified/-7 laps	22/27
dnq	MONACO GP	Monte Carlo	10	Skoal Bandit Formula 1 Team	P	1.5 t/c RAM 02-Hart 4		25/27
ret	US GP (DETROIT)	Detroit	10	Skoal Bandit Formula 1 Team	P	1.5 t/c RAM 02-Hart 4	tyre failure – accident	24/27
ret	US GP (DALLAS)	Dallas	10	Skoal Bandit Formula 1 Team	P	1.5 t/c RAM 02-Hart 4	electrics	25/27
ret	BRITISH GP	Brands Hatch	10	Skoal Bandit Formula 1 Team	P	1.5 t/c RAM 02-Hart 4	steering failure – accident	23/27
ret	GERMAN GP	Hockenheim	10	Skoal Bandit Formula 1 Team	P	1.5 t/c RAM 02-Hart 4	turbo	25/27
9	AUSTRIAN GP	Österreichring	10	Skoal Bandit Formula 1 Team	P	1.5 t/c RAM 02-Hart 4	2 laps behind	24/28
9*	DUTCH GP	Zandvoort	10	Skoal Bandit Formula 1 Team	P	1.5 t/c RAM 02-Hart 4	*8th & 9th cars disqualified/-4 laps	22/27
ret	ITALIAN GP	Monza	10	Skoal Bandit Formula 1 Team	P	1.5 t/c RAM 02-Hart 4	oil pressure	26/27
ret	EUROPEAN GP	Nürburgring	10	Skoal Bandit Formula 1 Team	P	1.5 t/c RAM 02-Hart 4	turbo	21/26

	GP	Circuit	No	Team	Tyre	Engine	Comment	Grid
ret	PORTUGUESE GP	Estoril	10	Skoal Bandit Formula 1 Team	P	1.5 t/c RAM 02-Hart 4	*gearbox*	26/27

1985 Championship position: Unplaced

	GP	Circuit	No	Team	Tyre	Engine	Comment	Grid
ret	PORTUGUESE GP	Estoril	30	West Zakspeed Racing	G	1.5 t/c Zakspeed 841 4	*suspension damage*	23/26
ret/dns	SAN MARINO GP	Imola	30	West Zakspeed Racing	G	1.5 t/c Zakspeed 841 4	*engine misfire on parade lap*	(17)/26
11	MONACO GP	Monte Carlo	30	West Zakspeed Racing	G	1.5 t/c Zakspeed 841 4	*spin/4 laps behind*	19/26
ret	FRENCH GP	Paul Ricard	30	West Zakspeed Racing	G	1.5 t/c Zakspeed 841 4	*engine*	22/26
ret	BRITISH GP	Silverstone	30	West Zakspeed Racing	G	1.5 t/c Zakspeed 841 4	*engine*	24/26
ret	GERMAN GP	Nürburgring	30	West Zakspeed Racing	G	1.5 t/c Zakspeed 841 4	*alternator belt*	24/27
ret	AUSTRIAN GP	Österreichring	30	West Zakspeed Racing	G	1.5 t/c Zakspeed 841 4	*engine*	25/27
ret	DUTCH GP	Zandvoort	30	West Zakspeed Racing	G	1.5 t/c Zakspeed 841 4	*engine – oil pressure*	23/27

1986 Championship position: Unplaced

	GP	Circuit	No	Team	Tyre	Engine	Comment	Grid
ret	BRAZILIAN GP	Rio	14	West Zakspeed Racing	G	1.5 t/c Zakspeed 861 4	*cracked airbox*	21/25
ret	SPANISH GP	Jerez	14	West Zakspeed Racing	G	1.5 t/c Zakspeed 861 4	*accident with Jones*	16/25
ret	SAN MARINO GP	Imola	14	West Zakspeed Racing	G	1.5 t/c Zakspeed 861 4	*started from pit lane/brakes*	20/26
12	MONACO GP	Monte Carlo	14	West Zakspeed Racing	G	1.5 t/c Zakspeed 861 4	*pit stop/4 laps behind*	19/26
nc	BELGIAN GP	Spa	14	West Zakspeed Racing	G	1.5 t/c Zakspeed 861 4	*pit stops – alternator belt/-6 laps*	20/25
ret	CANADIAN GP	Montreal	14	West Zakspeed Racing	G	1.5 t/c Zakspeed 861 4	*started from pitlane/engine*	22/25
8	US GP (DETROIT)	Detroit	14	West Zakspeed Racing	G	1.5 t/c Zakspeed 861 4	*2 laps behind*	20/26
ret	FRENCH GP	Paul Ricard	14	West Zakspeed Racing	G	1.5 t/c Zakspeed 861 4	*engine*	22/26
9	BRITISH GP	Brands Hatch	14	West Zakspeed Racing	G	1.5 t/c Zakspeed 861 4	*pit stop/6 laps behind*	22/26
ret	GERMAN GP	Hockenheim	14	West Zakspeed Racing	G	1.5 t/c Zakspeed 861 4	*engine*	16/26
10	HUNGARIAN GP	Hungaroring	14	West Zakspeed Racing	G	1.5 t/c Zakspeed 861 4	*pit stop – brakes/6 laps behind*	24/26
ret	AUSTRIAN GP	Österreichring	14	West Zakspeed Racing	G	1.5 t/c Zakspeed 861 4	*engine*	21/26
ret	ITALIAN GP	Monza	14	West Zakspeed Racing	G	1.5 t/c Zakspeed 861 4	*engine*	22/27
12	PORTUGUESE GP	Estoril	14	West Zakspeed Racing	G	1.5 t/c Zakspeed 861 4	*3 laps behind*	20/27
10/ret	MEXICAN GP	Mexico City	14	West Zakspeed Racing	G	1.5 t/c Zakspeed 861 4	*out of fuel/3 laps behind*	18/26
9/ret	AUSTRALIAN GP	Adelaide	14	West Zakspeed Racing	G	1.5 t/c Zakspeed 861 4	*trailing bodywork/5 laps behind*	21/26

1987 Championship position: 11th (winner non-turbo Jim Clark Cup) Wins: 0 Pole positions: 0 Fastest laps: 0 Points scored: 7

	GP	Circuit	No	Team	Tyre	Engine	Comment	Grid
10*	BRAZILIAN GP	Rio	3	Data General Team Tyrrell	G	3.5 Tyrrell-DG016-Cosworth V8	*1st non-turbo/3 laps behind*	18/23
ret	SAN MARINO GP	Imola	3	Data General Team Tyrrell	G	3.5 Tyrrell-DG016-Cosworth V8	*clutch*	25/27
ret/dns*	BELGIAN GP	Spa	3	Data General Team Tyrrell	G	3.5 Tyrrell-DG016-Cosworth V8	*accident with Streiff/*did not restart*	24/26
5*	MONACO GP	Monte Carlo	3	Data General Team Tyrrell	G	3.5 Tyrrell-DG016-Cosworth V8	*1st non-turbo/2 laps behind*	15/26
11*	US GP (DETROIT)	Detroit	3	Data General Team Tyrrell	G	3.5 Tyrrell-DG016-Cosworth V8	*1st non-turbo/3 laps behind*	13/26
7*	FRENCH GP	Paul Ricard	3	Data General Team Tyrrell	G	3.5 Tyrrell-DG016-Cosworth V8	*2nd non-turbo/4 laps behind*	24/26
8*	BRITISH GP	Silverstone	3	Data General Team Tyrrell	G	3.5 Tyrrell-DG016-Cosworth V8	*1st non-turbo/5 laps behind*	24/26
5*	GERMAN GP	Hockenheim	3	Data General Team Tyrrell	G	3.5 Tyrrell-DG016-Cosworth V8	*2nd non-turbo/1 lap behind*	23/26
7*	HUNGARIAN GP	Hungaroring	3	Data General Team Tyrrell	G	3.5 Tyrrell-DG016-Cosworth V8	*1st non-turbo/2 laps behind*	16/26
14*	AUSTRIAN GP	Österreichring	3	Data General Team Tyrrell	G	3.5 Tyrrell-DG016-Cosworth V8	*3rd non-turbo/5 laps behind*	24/26
14*	ITALIAN GP	Monza	3	Data General Team Tyrrell	G	3.5 Tyrrell-DG016-Cosworth V8	*3rd non-turbo/3 laps behind*	22/28
10*	PORTUGUESE GP	Estoril	3	Data General Team Tyrrell	G	3.5 Tyrrell-DG016-Cosworth V8	*2nd non-turbo/3 laps behind*	24/27
ret	SPANISH GP	Jerez	3	Data General Team Tyrrell	G	3.5 Tyrrell-DG016-Cosworth V8	*hit by Arnoux*	16/28
7*	MEXICAN GP	Mexico City	3	Data General Team Tyrrell	G	3.5 Tyrrell-DG016-Cosworth V8	*2nd non-turbo/3 laps behind*	22/27
8*	JAPANESE GP	Suzuka	3	Data General Team Tyrrell	G	3.5 Tyrrell-DG016-Cosworth V8	*1st non-turbo/1 lap behind*	20/27
4*	AUSTRALIAN GP	Adelaide	3	Data General Team Tyrrell	G	3.5 Tyrrell-DG016-Cosworth V8	*1st non-turbo/2 laps behind*	19/27

1988 Championship position: 13th Wins: 0 Pole positions: 0 Fastest laps: 0 Points scored: 5

	GP	Circuit	No	Team	Tyre	Engine	Comment	Grid
ret	BRAZILIAN GP	Rio	3	Tyrrell Racing Organisation	G	3.5 Tyrrell 017-Cosworth V8	*transmission*	22/31
14	SAN MARINO GP	Imola	3	Tyrrell Racing Organisation	G	3.5 Tyrrell 017-Cosworth V8	*engine problem/2 laps behind*	23/31
5	MONACO GP	Monte Carlo	3	Tyrrrel Racing Organisation	G	3.5 Tyrrell 017-Cosworth V8	*1 lap behind*	10/30
dnq	MEXICAN GP	Mexico City	3	Tyrrel Racing Organisation	G	3.5 Tyrrell 017-Cosworth V8		27/30
6	CANADIAN GP	Montreal	3	Tyrrell Racing Organisation	G	3.5 Tyrrell 017-Cosworth V8	*cockpit problems/2 laps behind*	19/31
5	US GP (DETROIT)	Detroit	3	Tyrrell Racing Organisation	G	3.5 Tyrrell 017-Cosworth V8	*1 lap behind*	17/31
ret	FRENCH GP	Paul Ricard	3	Tyrrell Racing Organisation	G	3.5 Tyrrell 017-Cosworth V8	*engine*	23/31
ret	BRITISH GP	Silverstone	3	Tyrrell Racing Organisation	G	3.5 Tyrrell 017-Cosworth V8	*transmission*	17/31
11	GERMAN GP	Hockenheim	3	Tyrrell Racing Organisation	G	3.5 Tyrrell 017-Cosworth V8	*1 lap behind*	24/31
ret	HUNGARIAN GP	Hungaroring	3	Tyrrell Racing Organisation	G	3.5 Tyrrell 017-Cosworth V8	*engine cut out*	21/31
12*/ret	BELGIAN GP	Spa	3	Tyrrell Racing Organisation	G	3.5 Tyrrell 017-Cosworth V8	*throttle/*3rd & 4th cars dsq/-4 laps*	21/31
dnq	ITALIAN GP	Monza	3	Tyrrell Racing Organisation	G	3.5 Tyrrell 017-Cosworth V8		27/31
ret	PORTUGUESE GP	Estoril	3	Tyrrell Racing Organisation	G	3.5 Tyrrell 017-Cosworth V8	*overheating*	22/31
ret	SPANISH GP	Jerez	3	Tyrrell Racing Organisation	G	3.5 Tyrrell 017-Cosworth V8	*accident – water radiator*	22/31
12	JAPANESE GP	Suzuka	3	Tyrrell Racing Organisation	G	3.5 Tyrrell 017-Cosworth V8	*1 lap behind*	16/31
ret	AUSTRALIAN GP	Adelaide	3	Tyrrell Racing Organisation	G	3.5 Tyrrell 017-Cosworth V8	*transmission*	17/31

1989 Championship position: 23rd= Wins: 0 Pole positions: 0 Fastest laps: 1 Points scored: 2

	GP	Circuit	No	Team	Tyre	Engine	Comment	Grid
7	BRAZILIAN GP	Rio	3	Tyrrell Racing Organisation	G	3.5 Tyrrell 017B-Cosworth V8	*1 lap behind*	18/38
6*	SAN MARINO GP	Imola	3	Tyrrell Racing Organisation	G	3.5 Tyrrell 018-Cosworth V8	*spin/1 lap behind*	–/–
dns	" " "	3	Tyrrell Racing Organisation	G	3.5 Tyrrell 017B-Cosworth V8	*practice only – set grid time*	25/39
9	MONACO GP	Monte Carlo	3	Tyrrell Racing Organisation	G	3.5 Tyrrell 018-Cosworth V8	*3 laps behind*	23/38
ret	MEXICAN GP	Mexico City	3	Tyrrell Racing Organisation	G	3.5 Tyrrell 018-Cosworth V8	*throttle linkage*	14/39
9/ret	US GP (PHOENIX)	Phoenix	3	Tyrrell Racing Organisation	G	3.5 Tyrrell 018-Cosworth V8	*fuel shortage/6 laps behind*	21/39
ret	CANADIAN GP	Montreal	3	Tyrrell Racing Organisation	G	3.5 Tyrrell 018-Cosworth V8	*hit wall/FL*	14/39
10	FRENCH GP	Paul Ricard	3	Tyrrell Racing Organisation	G	3.5 Tyrrell 018-Cosworth V8	*5 pit stops – hit by Arnoux/2 laps behind*	9/39
ret	BRITISH GP	Silverstone	3	Tyrrell Racing Organisation	G	3.5 Tyrrell 018-Cosworth V8	*spun off*	18/39
ret	GERMAN GP	Hockenheim	3	Tyrrell Racing Organisation	G	3.5 Tyrrell 018-Cosworth V8	*throttle cable*	19/39
13	HUNGARIAN GP	Hungaroring	3	Tyrrell Racing Organisation	G	3.5 Tyrrell 018-Cosworth V8	*pit stop – broken injector/4 laps behind*	19/39
14	BELGIAN GP	Spa	3	Tyrrell Racing Organisation	G	3.5 Tyrrell 018-Cosworth V8	*misfire/2 laps behind*	21/39
ret	ITALIAN GP	Monza	3	Tyrrell Racing Organisation	G	3.5 Tyrrell 018-Cosworth V8	*started from back of grid/engine*	14/39
6	PORTUGUESE GP	Estoril	3	Tyrrell Racing Organisation	G	3.5 Tyrrell 018-Cosworth V8	*1 lap behind*	18/39
10	SPANISH GP	Jerez	3	Tyrrell Racing Organisation	G	3.5 Tyrrell 018-Cosworth V8	*misfire/2 laps behind*	13/38
ret	JAPANESE GP	Suzuka	3	Tyrrell Racing Organisation	G	3.5 Tyrrell 018-Cosworth V8	*fuel leak*	26/39
dnq	AUSTRALIAN GP	Adelaide	3	Tyrrell Racing Organisation	G	3.5 Tyrrell 018-Cosworth V8		27/39

GP Starts: 82 (84)   GP Wins: 0   Pole positions: 0   Fastest laps: 1   Points: 14

OLIVIER PANIS

FOLLOWING the traditional karting, Pilote Elf and Formule Renault junior route, the quiet and impeccably mannered Olivier Panis emerged as a champion in 1989 to earn a move into French F3. His first year, in a Dallara, brought fourth place in the championship, while in the second, despite taking five wins and six poles in a Ralt, he was narrowly beaten to the title by Christophe Bouchut. Then he took the well-trodden path to F3000 with the Apomatox team. It was a tough year, as he struggled with the Lola chassis, but he still impressed enough to land the plum drive with DAMS for 1993. True to its reputation, this amazingly hard-fought series yet again saw the points spread evenly among the leading contenders, but it was Panis who finished at the head of the table, in front of fellow grand prix aspirants Pedro Lamy, David Coulthard, Gil de Ferran and Olivier Beretta.

Over the next two years, with the backing and confidence of Elf, Panis quietly established himself as a grand prix regular, shunting other rivals such as Érik Comas, Eric Bernard and Beretta, and even younger chargers like Franck Lagorce and Jean-Christophe Boullion into touch.

Given his chance at Ligier, Olivier made a remarkably assured start to his Formula 1 career, highlighted by his second place in a German Grand Prix that was decimated by accidents. Paired with the experienced Martin Brundle and Aguri Suzuki in 1995, he handled the politics of being a Frenchman in an increasingly cosmopolitan team with aplomb, and his second place in the end-of-season race at Adelaide no doubt helped him survive the winter reshuffles. He was undisputed team leader in 1996, paired with the wealthy, but inexperienced Pedro Diniz as the financially pressured outfit faced up to life as one of grand prix racing's poorer relations. Despite the Ligier JS43 suffering from traction problems, Panis got

the best out of the car wherever he could and was a shock winner of the rain-hit Monaco Grand Prix. Revelling in the slippery conditions, he drove quite superbly on the day and resisted the challenge of David Coulthard's McLaren for much of the latter part of the race.

Ligier having been taken over by Alain Prost prior to the start of the 1997 season, Panis became the newly renamed Prost team's spearhead, and he kicked off the season in fine style, scoring the revamped organisation's – and Bridgestone's – first ever points with a fifth place in Australia. Third in Brazil and second in Spain saw the Frenchman driving at the top of his form, until disaster struck when he crashed violently in the Canadian Grand Prix in Montreal. Both of his legs were badly broken and he spent several months recuperating. Happily, he was fit enough to return before the end of the season, but it was very much a case of 'what might have been'.

The promise of 1997 gave way to gloom in 1998, when the first true Prost challenger was compromised by seemingly incurable handling problems. Things did not improve much in 1999 and, when Olivier's relationship with Alain Prost reached rock bottom by mid-year, it became clear that his tenure with the team was over. Having put himself under the management of Keke Rosberg, however, the Frenchman soon found alternative employment, signing a testing contract for McLaren-Mercedes.

Sitting out the 2000 campaign proved to be a wise move, as Panis regularly topped the testing times, both in the winter and throughout the regular season, meaning that he was seen seriously as a candidate by other F1 teams. In the end, it was British American Racing that moved first and signed the Frenchman, who replaced the lacklustre Ricardo Zonta. Panis looked an early threat for points, but could do no better than the occasional top-six finish and a share of 14th place in the championship.

Going into the 2002 campaign, Olivier endured another string of retirements, and BAR had to wait until Silverstone to score its first points, Jacques Villeneuve coming home fourth and Panis fifth. Together with a sixth place at Monza, however, that was it in terms of points for the Frenchman, four more retirements bringing his total to 12 in 17 events, ten of which were due to mechanical failures beyond his control.

Olivier then made a move to Toyota, where his bad luck continued. Although he qualified in the top six on four occasions, he never really got the chance to build on those performances on race day, ending the season with just six points and 15th in the title race. The following year was not much better, and he ended the season once again with only six points. Despite having elected to retire from active racing, he remained at Toyota to act as third driver along with Ricardo Zonta, and he signed a two-year deal to work on development for the Cologne-based team before finally taking his leave at the end of 2006.

In 2007, Panis took on an advisory role with DAMS to work with their A1GP drivers, before making a return to action in 2008, when he joined the Oreca Courage squad to race their Le Mans challenger. He found success in 2009, winning the Silverstone 1000km and, after the squad acquired a Peugeot 908, he notched up a further victory at Portimao in 2010 and a notable triumph in the 2011 Sebring 12-hour race. In 2011, he took fifth place at Le Mans, but announced that he would not enter again, following the huge accident that befell Audi drivers Allan McNish and Mike Rockenfeller.

In 2009, Olivier competed in the French GT championship, sharing a Corvette with Eric Debard to win the championship. The pair continued to race together, switching to a Mercedes SL63 for 2011. Not content with restricting himself to action in the traditional racing season, since 2005, Panis has been a convert to the Andros Trophy ice racing series, driving a Skoda in 2012 with great success.

As a member of Lagardere Unlimited, Panis has also been employed as technical advisor to young French hopeful Charles Pic, who graduated to Formula 1 with Marussia for 2012.

PANIS, Olivier (F) b 2/9/1966, Lyon

1994 Championship position: 11th Wins: 0 Pole positions: 0 Fastest laps: 0 Points scored: 9

	Race	Circuit	No	Entrant	Tyres	Capacity/Car/Engine	Comment	Q Pos/Entries
11	BRAZILIAN GP	Interlagos	26	Ligier Gitanes Blondes	G	3.5 Ligier JS39B-Renault V10	3 laps behind	19/28
9	PACIFIC GP	T.I. Circuit	26	Ligier Gitanes Blondes	G	3.5 Ligier JS39B-Renault V10	5 laps behind	22/28
11	SAN MARINO GP	Imola	26	Ligier Gitanes Blondes	G	3.5 Ligier JS39B-Renault V10	2 laps behind	19/28
9	MONACO GP	Monte Carlo	26	Ligier Gitanes Blondes	G	3.5 Ligier JS39B-Renault V10	2 laps behind	20/24
7	SPANISH GP	Barcelona	26	Ligier Gitanes Blondes	G	3.5 Ligier JS39B-Renault V10	2 laps behind	19/27
12	CANADIAN GP	Montreal	26	Ligier Gitanes Blondes	G	3.5 Ligier JS39B-Renault V10	2 laps behind	19/27
ret	FRENCH GP	Magny Cours	26	Ligier Gitanes Blondes	G	3.5 Ligier JS39B-Renault V10	collision with Morbidelli	13/28
12*	BRITISH GP	Silverstone	26	Ligier Gitanes Blondes	G	3.5 Ligier JS39B-Renault V10	*2nd place car dsq/2 laps behind	15/28
2	GERMAN GP	Hockenheim	26	Ligier Gitanes Blondes	G	3.5 Ligier JS39B-Renault V10		12/28
6	HUNGARIAN GP	Hungaroring	26	Ligier Gitanes Blondes	G	3.5 Ligier JS39B-Renault V10	1 lap behind	9/28
7*	BELGIAN GP	Spa	26	Ligier Gitanes Blondes	G	3.5 Ligier JS39B-Renault V10	*1st place car disqualified/1 lap behind	17/28
10	ITALIAN GP	Monza	26	Ligier Gitanes Blondes	G	3.5 Ligier JS39B-Renault V10	2 laps behind	6/28
9/dsq*	PORTUGUESE GP	Estoril	26	Ligier Gitanes Blondes	G	3.5 Ligier JS39B-Renault V10	*disqualified – excessive skid block wear	15/28
9	EUROPEAN GP	Jerez	26	Ligier Gitanes Blondes	G	3.5 Ligier JS39B-Renault V10	1 lap behind	11/28
11	JAPANESE GP	Suzuka	26	Ligier Gitanes Blondes	G	3.5 Ligier JS39B-Renault V10	1 lap behind	19/28
5	AUSTRALIAN GP	Adelaide	26	Ligier Gitanes Blondes	G	3.5 Ligier JS39B-Renault V10	1 lap behind	12/28

1995 Championship position: 8th Wins: 0 Pole positions: 0 Fastest laps: 0 Points scored: 16

	Race	Circuit	No	Entrant	Tyres	Capacity/Car/Engine	Comment	Q Pos/Entries
ret	BRAZILIAN GP	Interlagos	26	Ligier Gitanes Blondes	G	3.0 Ligier JS41-Mugen Honda V10	spun off on lap 1	10/26
7	ARGENTINE GP	Buenos Aires	26	Ligier Gitanes Blondes	G	3.0 Ligier JS41-Mugen Honda V10	2 laps behind	18/26
9	SAN MARINO GP	Imola	26	Ligier Gitanes Blondes	G	3.0 Ligier JS41-Mugen Honda V10	2 laps behind	12/26
6	SPANISH GP	Barcelona	26	Ligier Gitanes Blondes	G	3.0 Ligier JS41-Mugen Honda V10	1 lap behind	15/26
ret	MONACO GP	Monte Carlo	26	Ligier Gitanes Blondes	G	3.0 Ligier JS41-Mugen Honda V10	accident	12/26
4	CANADIAN GP	Montreal	26	Ligier Gitanes Blondes	G	3.0 Ligier JS41-Mugen Honda V10		11/24
8	FRENCH GP	Magny Cours	26	Ligier Gitanes Blondes	G	3.0 Ligier JS41-Mugen Honda V10	1 lap behind	6/24
4	BRITISH GP	Silverstone	26	Ligier Gitanes Blondes	G	3.0 Ligier JS41-Mugen Honda V10		13/24
ret	GERMAN GP	Hockenheim	26	Ligier Gitanes Blondes	G	3.0 Ligier JS41-Mugen Honda V10	engine	12/24
6	HUNGARIAN GP	Hungaroring	26	Ligier Gitanes Blondes	G	3.0 Ligier JS41-Mugen Honda V10	1 lap behind	10/24
9	BELGIAN GP	Spa	26	Ligier Gitanes Blondes	G	3.0 Ligier JS41-Mugen Honda V10		9/24
ret	ITALIAN GP	Monza	26	Ligier Gitanes Blondes	G	3.0 Ligier JS41-Mugen Honda V10	spun off	13/24
ret	PORTUGUESE GP	Estoril	26	Ligier Gitanes Blondes	G	3.0 Ligier JS41-Mugen Honda V10	spun off	11/24
ret	EUROPEAN GP	Nürburgring	26	Ligier Gitanes Blondes	G	3.0 Ligier JS41-Mugen Honda V10	spun off	14/24
8	PACIFIC GP	T.I. Circuit	26	Ligier Gitanes Blondes	G	3.0 Ligier JS41-Mugen Honda V10	2 laps behind	9/24
5	JAPANESE GP	Suzuka	26	Ligier Gitanes Blondes	G	3.0 Ligier JS41-Mugen Honda V10	1 lap behind	11/24
2	AUSTRALIAN GP	Adelaide	26	Ligier Gitanes Blondes	G	3.0 Ligier JS41-Mugen Honda V10	2 laps behind	12/24

1996 Championship position: 9th Wins: 1 Pole positions: 0 Fastest laps: 0 Points scored: 13

	Race	Circuit	No	Entrant	Tyres	Capacity/Car/Engine	Comment	Q Pos/Entries
7	AUSTRALIAN GP	Melbourne	9	Ligier Gauloises-Blondes	G	3.0 Ligier JS43-Mugen Honda V10	1 lap behind	11/22
6	BRAZILIAN GP	Interlagos	9	Ligier Gauloises-Blondes	G	3.0 Ligier JS43-Mugen Honda V10	1 lap behind	15/22
8	ARGENTINE GP	Buenos Aires	9	Ligier Gauloises-Blondes	G	3.0 Ligier JS43-Mugen Honda V10		12/22
ret	EUROPEAN GP	Nürburgring	9	Ligier Gauloises-Blondes	G	3.0 Ligier JS43-Mugen Honda V10	collision with Irvine	15/22
ret	SAN MARINO GP	Imola	9	Ligier Gauloises-Blondes	G	3.0 Ligier JS43-Mugen Honda V10	gearbox	13/22
1	MONACO GP	Monte Carlo	9	Ligier Gauloises-Blondes	G	3.0 Ligier JS43-Mugen Honda V10		14/22
ret	SPANISH GP	Barcelona	9	Ligier Gauloises-Blondes	G	3.0 Ligier JS43-Mugen Honda V10	spun off	8/22
ret	CANADIAN GP	Montreal	9	Ligier Gauloises-Blondes	G	3.0 Ligier JS43-Mugen Honda V10	alternator	11/22
7	FRENCH GP	Magny Cours	9	Ligier Gauloises-Blondes	G	3.0 Ligier JS43-Mugen Honda V10	1 lap behind	9/22
ret	BRITISH GP	Silverstone	9	Ligier Gauloises-Blondes	G	3.0 Ligier JS43-Mugen Honda V10	handling	16/22
7	GERMAN GP	Hockenheim	9	Ligier Gauloises-Blondes	G	3.0 Ligier JS43-Mugen Honda V10		12/20
5	HUNGARIAN GP	Hungaroring	9	Ligier Gauloises-Blondes	G	3.0 Ligier JS43-Mugen Honda V10	1 lap behind	11/20
ret	BELGIAN GP	Spa	9	Ligier Gauloises-Blondes	G	3.0 Ligier JS43-Mugen Honda V10	collision with Frentzen & Herbert	12/20
ret	ITALIAN GP	Monza	9	Ligier Gauloises-Blondes	G	3.0 Ligier JS43-Mugen Honda V10	spun off	11/20
10	PORTUGUESE GP	Estoril	9	Ligier Gauloises-Blondes	G	3.0 Ligier JS43-Mugen Honda V10	1 lap behind	15/20
7	JAPANESE GP	Suzuka	9	Ligier Gauloises-Blondes	G	3.0 Ligier JS43-Mugen Honda V10		12/20

1997 Championship position: 9th Wins: 0 Pole positions: 0 Fastest laps: 0 Points scored: 16

	Race	Circuit	No	Entrant	Tyres	Capacity/Car/Engine	Comment	Q Pos/Entries
5	AUSTRALIAN GP	Melbourne	14	Prost Gauloise Blondes	B	3.0 Prost JS45-Mugen Honda V10		9/24
3	BRAZILIAN GP	Interlagos	14	Prost Gauloise Blondes	B	3.0 Prost JS45-Mugen Honda V10		5/22
ret	ARGENTINE GP	Buenos Aires	14	Prost Gauloise Blondes	B	3.0 Prost JS45-Mugen Honda V10	hydraulic leak	3/22
8	SAN MARINO GP	Imola	14	Prost Gauloise Blondes	B	3.0 Prost JS45-Mugen Honda V10	failed damper/1 lap behind	4/22
4	MONACO GP	Monte Carlo	14	Prost Gauloise Blondes	B	3.0 Prost JS45-Mugen Honda V10		12/22
2	SPANISH GP	Barcelona	14	Prost Gauloise Blondes	B	3.0 Prost JS45-Mugen Honda V10		12/22
11/ret	CANADIAN GP	Montreal	14	Prost Gauloise Blondes	B	3.0 Prost JS45-Mugen Honda V10	accident/broken legs/3 laps behind	10/22
6	LUXEMBOURG GP	Nürburgring	14	Prost Gauloise Blondes	B	3.0 Prost JS45-Mugen Honda V10		11/22
ret	JAPANESE GP	Suzuka	14	Prost Gauloise Blondes	B	3.0 Prost JS45-Mugen Honda V10	engine	10/22
7	EUROPEAN GP	Jerez	14	Prost Gauloise Blondes	B	3.0 Prost JS45-Mugen Honda V10		9/22

1998 Championship position: Unplaced

	Race	Circuit	No	Entrant	Tyres	Capacity/Car/Engine	Comment	Q Pos/Entries
9	AUSTRALIAN GP	Melbourne	11	Gauloises Prost Peugeot	B	3.0 Prost AP01-Peugeot V10	1 lap behind	21/22
ret	BRAZILIAN GP	Interlagos	11	Gauloises Prost Peugeot	B	3.0 Prost AP01-Peugeot V10	engine	9/22
15/ret	ARGENTINE GP	Buenos Aires	11	Gauloises Prost Peugeot	B	3.0 Prost AP01-Peugeot V10	engine/7 laps behind	15/22
11/ret	SAN MARINO GP	Imola	11	Gauloises Prost Peugeot	B	3.0 Prost AP01-Peugeot V10	engine/6 laps behind	13/22
16/ret	SPANISH GP	Barcelona	11	Gauloises Prost Peugeot	B	3.0 Prost AP01-Peugeot V10	engine/5 laps behind	12/22
ret	MONACO GP	Monte Carlo	11	Gauloises Prost Peugeot	B	3.0 Prost AP01-Peugeot V10	suspension	18/22
ret	CANADIAN GP	Montreal	11	Gauloises Prost Peugeot	B	3.0 Prost AP01-Peugeot V10	engine	15/22
11	FRENCH GP	Magny Cours	11	Gauloises Prost Peugeot	B	3.0 Prost AP01-Peugeot V10	2 laps behind	16/22
ret	BRITISH GP	Silverstone	11	Gauloises Prost Peugeot	B	3.0 Prost AP01-Peugeot V10	spun off	16/22
ret	AUSTRIAN GP	A-1 Ring	11	Gauloises Prost Peugeot	B	3.0 Prost AP01-Peugeot V10	clutch	10/22
15	GERMAN GP	Hockenheim	11	Gauloises Prost Peugeot	B	3.0 Prost AP01-Peugeot V10	1 lap behind	16/22
12	HUNGARIAN GP	Hungaroring	11	Gauloises Prost Peugeot	B	3.0 Prost AP01-Peugeot V10	3 laps behind	20/22
ret/dns*	BELGIAN GP	Spa	11	Gauloises Prost Peugeot	B	3.0 Prost AP01-Peugeot V10	*accident at first start	15/22

ret	ITALIAN GP	Monza	11	Gauloises Prost Peugeot	B	3.0 Prost AP01-Peugeot V10	*rear vibration*	9/22
12	LUXEMBOURG GP	Nürburgring	11	Gauloises Prost Peugeot	B	3.0 Prost AP01-Peugeot V10	*2 laps behind*	15/22
11	JAPANESE GP	Suzuka	11	Gauloises Prost Peugeot	B	3.0 Prost AP01-Peugeot V10	*1 lap behind*	13/22

1999 Championship position: 15th=   Wins: 0   Pole positions: 0   Fastest laps: 0   Points scored: 2

ret	AUSTRALIAN GP	Melbourne	18	Gauloises Prost Peugeot	B	3.0 Prost AP02-Peugeot V10	*stuck wheel nut*	20/22
6	BRAZILIAN GP	Interlagos	18	Gauloises Prost Peugeot	B	3.0 Prost AP02-Peugeot V10	*1 lap behind*	12/22
ret	SAN MARINO GP	Imola	18	Gauloises Prost Peugeot	B	3.0 Prost AP02-Peugeot V10	*throttle*	11/22
ret	MONACO GP	Monte Carlo	18	Gauloises Prost Peugeot	B	3.0 Prost AP02-Peugeot V10	*engine*	18/22
ret	SPANISH GP	Barcelona	18	Gauloises Prost Peugeot	B	3.0 Prost AP02-Peugeot V10	*gearbox hydraulics*	15/22
9	CANADIAN GP	Montreal	18	Gauloises Prost Peugeot	B	3.0 Prost AP02-Peugeot V10	*1 lap behind*	15/22
8	FRENCH GP	Magny Cours	18	Gauloises Prost Peugeot	B	3.0 Prost AP02-Peugeot V10		3/22
13	BRITISH GP	Silverstone	18	Gauloises Prost Peugeot	B	3.0 Prost AP02-Peugeot V10		15/22
10	AUSTRIAN GP	A-1 Ring	18	Gauloises Prost Peugeot	B	3.0 Prost AP02-Peugeot V10	*1 lap behind*	18/22
6	GERMAN GP	Hockenheim	18	Gauloises Prost Peugeot	B	3.0 Prost AP02-Peugeot V10		7/22
10	HUNGARIAN GP	Hungaroring	18	Gauloises Prost Peugeot	B	3.0 Prost AP02-Peugeot V10	*1 lap behind*	14/22
13	BELGIAN GP	Spa	18	Gauloises Prost Peugeot	B	3.0 Prost AP02-Peugeot V10		17/22
11	ITALIAN GP	Monza	18	Gauloises Prost Peugeot	B	3.0 Prost AP02-Peugeot V10	*1 lap behind*	10/22
9	EUROPEAN GP	Nürburgring	18	Gauloises Prost Peugeot	B	3.0 Prost AP02-Peugeot V10	*1 lap behind*	5/22
ret	MALAYSIAN GP	Sepang	18	Gauloises Prost Peugeot	B	3.0 Prost AP02-Peugeot V10	*engine*	12/22
ret	JAPANESE GP	Suzuka	18	Gauloises Prost Peugeot	B	3.0 Prost AP02-Peugeot V10	*gearbox*	6/22

2001 Championship position: 14th=   Wins: 0   Pole positions: 0   Fastest laps: 0   Points scored: 5

7*	AUSTRALIAN GP	Melbourne	9	Lucky Strike BAR Honda	B	3.0 BAR 03-Honda V10	**4th – but 25-sec pen passed yellow flag*	9/22
ret	MALAYSIAN GP	Sepang	9	Lucky Strike BAR Honda	B	3.0 BAR 03-Honda V10	*oil tank on fire*	10/22
4	BRAZILIAN GP	Interlagos	9	Lucky Strike BAR Honda	B	3.0 BAR 03-Honda V10	*delayed at second pitstop/1 lap behind*	11/22
8	SAN MARINO GP	Imola	9	Lucky Strike BAR Honda	B	3.0 BAR 03-Honda V10	*1 lap behind*	8/22
7	SPANISH GP	Barcelona	9	Lucky Strike BAR Honda	B	3.0 BAR 03-Honda V10		11/22
5	AUSTRIAN GP	A1-Ring	9	Lucky Strike BAR Honda	B	3.0 BAR 03-Honda V10		10/22
ret	MONACO GP	Monte Carlo	9	Lucky Strike BAR Honda	B	3.0 BAR 03-Honda V10	*steering*	12/22
ret	CANADIAN GP	Montreal	9	Lucky Strike BAR Honda	B	3.0 BAR 03-Honda V10	*brakes*	6/22
ret	EUROPEAN GP	Nürburgring	9	Lucky Strike BAR Honda	B	3.0 BAR 03-Honda V10	*electrical fault in gearbox – spun off*	13/22
9	FRENCH GP	Magny Cours	9	Lucky Strike BAR Honda	B	3.0 BAR 03-Honda V10	*1 lap behind*	11/22
ret	BRITISH GP	Silverstone	9	Lucky Strike BAR Honda	B	3.0 BAR 03-Honda V10	*pushed off by Villeneuve on lap 1*	11/22
7	GERMAN GP	Hockenheim	9	Lucky Strike BAR Honda	B	3.0 BAR 03-Honda V10	*incident with Trulli*	13/22
ret	HUNGARIAN GP	Hungaroring	9	Lucky Strike BAR Honda	B	3.0 BAR 03-Honda V10	*hydraulics*	11/22
11	BELGIAN GP	Spa	9	Lucky Strike BAR Honda	B	3.0 BAR 03-Honda V10	*stop & go penalty – pit exit/-1 lap*	11/22
9	ITALIAN GP	Monza	9	Lucky Strike BAR Honda	B	3.0 BAR 03-Honda V10	*1 lap behind*	17/22
11	UNITED STATES GP	Indianapolis	9	Lucky Strike BAR Honda	B	3.0 BAR 03-Honda V10	*1 lap behind*	13/22
13	JAPANESE GP	Suzuka	9	Lucky Strike BAR Honda	B	3.0 BAR 03-Honda V10	*2 laps behind*	17/22

2002 Championship position: 14th   Wins: 0   Pole positions: 0   Fastest laps: 0   Points scored: 3

ret	AUSTRALIAN GP	Melbourne	12	Lucky Strike BAR Honda	B	3.0 BAR 004-Honda V10	*multiple accident on lap 1*	12/22
ret	MALAYSIAN GP	Sepang	12	Lucky Strike BAR Honda	B	3.0 BAR 004-Honda V10	*clutch bearing*	18/22
ret	BRAZILIAN GP	Interlagos	12	Lucky Strike BAR Honda	B	3.0 BAR 004-Honda V10	*transmission*	17/22
ret	SAN MARINO GP	Imola	12	Lucky Strike BAR Honda	B	3.0 BAR 004-Honda V10	*throttle – engine*	12/22
ret	SPANISH GP	Barcelona	12	Lucky Strike BAR Honda	B	3.0 BAR 004-Honda V10	*broken exhaust*	13/21
ret	AUSTRIAN GP	A1-Ring	12	Lucky Strike BAR Honda	B	3.0 BAR 004-Honda V10	*seized engine – spun off*	9/22
ret	MONACO GP	Monte Carlo	12	Lucky Strike BAR Honda	B	3.0 BAR 004-Honda V10	*punted off by Button*	18/22
8	CANADIAN GP	Montreal	12	Lucky Strike BAR Honda	B	3.0 BAR 004-Honda V10	*1 lap behind*	11/22
9	EUROPEAN GP	Nürburgring	12	Lucky Strike BAR Honda	B	3.0 BAR 004-Honda V10	*1 lap behind*	12/22
5	BRITISH GP	Silverstone	12	Lucky Strike BAR Honda	B	3.0 BAR 004-Honda V10	*1 lap behind*	13/22
ret	FRENCH GP	Magny Cours	12	Lucky Strike BAR Honda	B	3.0 BAR 004-Honda V10	*collision with Sato/later retired-vibration*	11/21
ret	GERMAN GP	Hockenheim	12	Lucky Strike BAR Honda	B	3.0 BAR 004-Honda V10	*seized engine – spun off*	7/22
12	HUNGARIAN GP	Hungaroring	12	Lucky Strike BAR Honda	B	3.0 BAR 004-Honda V10	*low oil pressure/1 lap behind*	12/22
12/ret	BELGIAN GP	Spa	12	Lucky Strike BAR Honda	B	3.0 BAR 004-Honda V10	*engine/5 laps behind*	15/20
6	ITALIAN GP	Monza	12	Lucky Strike BAR Honda	B	3.0 BAR 004-Honda V10	*good pit strategy*	16/20
12	UNITED STATES GP	Indianapolis	12	Lucky Strike BAR Honda	B	3.0 BAR 004-Honda V10	*1 lap behind*	12/20
ret	JAPANESE GP	Suzuka	12	Lucky Strike BAR Honda	B	3.0 BAR 004-Honda V10	*throttle control*	16/20

2003 Championship position: 14th=   Wins: 0   Pole positions: 0   Fastest laps: 0   Points scored: 6

ret	AUSTRALIAN GP	Melbourne	20	Panasonic Toyota Racing	M	3.0 Toyota TF103-V10	*fuel system*	5/20
ret	MALAYSIAN GP	Sepang	20	Panasonic Toyota Racing	M	3.0 Toyota TF103-V10	*fuel pick-up*	10/20
ret	BRAZILIAN GP	Interlagos	20	Panasonic Toyota Racing	M	3.0 Toyota TF103-V10	*hit by Firman's out of control car*	15/20
9	SAN MARINO GP	Imola	20	Panasonic Toyota Racing	M	3.0 Toyota TF103-V10	*1 lap behind*	10/20
ret	SPANISH GP	Barcelona	20	Panasonic Toyota Racing	M	3.0 Toyota TF103-V10	*gearbox*	6/20
ret	AUSTRIAN GP	A1-Ring	20	Panasonic Toyota Racing	M	3.0 Toyota TF103-V10	*hit debris – suspension damage*	11/20
13	MONACO GP	Monte Carlo	20	Panasonic Toyota Racing	M	3.0 Toyota TF103-V10	*no grip/4 laps behind*	17/19
8	CANADIAN GP	Montreal	20	Panasonic Toyota Racing	M	3.0 Toyota TF103-V10	*1 lap behind*	7/20
ret	EUROPEAN GP	Nürburgring	20	Panasonic Toyota Racing	M	3.0 Toyota TF103-V10	*brake problems/spun off*	7/20
8	FRENCH GP	Magny Cours	20	Panasonic Toyota Racing	M	3.0 Toyota TF103-V10	*1 lap behind*	10/20
11	BRITISH GP	Silverstone	20	Panasonic Toyota Racing	M	3.0 Toyota TF103-V10		13/20
5	GERMAN GP	Hockenheim	20	Panasonic Toyota Racing	M	3.0 Toyota TF103-V10	*1 lap behind*	7/20
ret	HUNGARIAN GP	Hungaroring	20	Panasonic Toyota Racing	M	3.0 Toyota TF103-V10	*gearbox*	10/20
ret	ITALIAN GP	Monza	20	Panasonic Toyota Racing	M	3.0 Toyota TF103-V10	*brakes*	9/20
ret	UNITED STATES GP	Indianapolis	20	Panasonic Toyota Racing	M	3.0 Toyota TF103-V10	*spun off*	3/20
10	JAPANESE GP	Suzuka	20	Panasonic Toyota Racing	M	3.0 Toyota TF103-V10		4/20

2004 Championship position: 14th=   Wins: 0   Pole positions: 0   Fastest laps: 0   Points scored: 6

13	AUSTRALIAN GP	Melbourne	17	Panasonic Toyota Racing	M	3.0 Toyota TF104-V10	**no time set/2 laps behind*	*18/20
12	MALAYSIAN GP	Sepang	17	Panasonic Toyota Racing	M	3.0 Toyota TF104-V10	*spin/drive-through penalty/-1 lap*	14/20
9	BAHRAIN GP	Bahrain Circuit	17	Panasonic Toyota Racing	M	3.0 Toyota TF104-V10	*1 lap behind*	8/20
11	SAN MARINO GP	Imola	17	Panasonic Toyota Racing	M	3.0 Toyota TF104-V10	*1 lap behind*	13/20
ret	SPANISH GP	Barcelona	17	Panasonic Toyota Racing	M	3.0 Toyota TF104-V10	*hydraulics*	7/20

8	MONACO GP	Monte Carlo	17	Pansonic Toyota Racing	M	3.0 Toyota TF104-V10	started from pitlane/3 laps behind	13/20
11	EUROPEAN GP	Nürburgring	17	Pansonic Toyota Racing	M	3.0 Toyota TF104-V10	tyre problems/1 lap behind	10/20
dsq*	CANADIAN GP	Montreal	17	Pansonic Toyota Racing	M	3.0 Toyota TF104-V10	10th/*brake duct infringement	13/20
5	U S GP	Indianapolis	17	Pansonic Toyota Racing	M	3.0 Toyota TF104-V10		8/20
15	FRENCH GP	Magny Cours	17	Pansonic Toyota Racing	M	3.0 Toyota TF104-V10	2 laps behind	14/20
ret	BRITISH GP	Silverstone	17	Pansonic Toyota Racing	M	3.0 Toyota TF104-V10	fire extinguisher discharged	17/20
14	GERMAN GP	Hockenheim	17	Pansonic Toyota Racing	M	3.0 Toyota TF104-V10	started from pitlane/1 lap behind	9/20
11	HUNGARIAN GP	Hungaroring	17	Pansonic Toyota Racing	M	3.0 Toyota TF104-V10	1 lap behind	13/20
8	BELGIAN GP	Spa	17	Pansonic Toyota Racing	M	3.0 Toyota TF104-V10	collision damage	9/20
ret	ITALIAN GP	Monza	17	Pansonic Toyota Racing	M	3.0 Toyota TF104-V10	hit Pizzonia – spun off	13/20
14	CHINESE GP	Shanghai	17	Pansonic Toyota Racing	M	3.0 Toyota TF104-V10	1 lap behind	8/20
14	JAPANESE GP	Suzuka	16	Pansonic Toyota Racing	M	3.0 Toyota TF104-V10	2 laps behind	10/20

2005 Championship position: Unplaced

| app | FRENCH GP | Magny Cours | 38 | Pansonic Toyota Racing | M | 3.0 Toyota TF105-V10 | ran as 3rd driver in practice 1 only | - /- |

GP Starts: 158   GP Wins: 1   Pole positions: 0   Fastest laps: 0   Points: 76

GIORGIO PANTANO

A FRONT-RUNNER throughout his career, Giorgio Pantano had undoubted ability, but somehow failed to convince a succession of team bosses that he deserved a place in Formula 1, when perhaps lesser talents were given more opportunities.

The Italian was seen as the unofficial king of karting, taking a whole raft of titles, which made him a hot property once he had gorged himself on trophies at this level. Buoyed by pace in the Formula Palmer Audi series, Pantano began his ascent of the racing ladder proper in the German Formula 3 championship. He got off to a flying start by winning on his debut and, after adding three further victories and seven podiums, took the 2000 title in his first season.

Despite testing for Benetton, Pantano opted for a year in F3000 with Astromega in 2001. It wasn't a good year for either driver or team, but he elevated himself to ninth in the final standings with a victory in the final round at Monza. With this experience, he was tipped as one of the favourites to win the 2002 title. Eventually, he landed a seat at Coloni Motorsport and even gave the Italian team its first F3000 victory, in Barcelona, but despite adding further wins at Hockenheim and Spa, he had to settle for second place in the final standings.

After more F1 tests with both Williams and Minardi, it was back to F3000. After a last-gasp deal with the midfield Durango team, the Italian produced impressive performances again, taking the team to two victories en route to an eventual third overall, behind eventual champion Bjorn Wirdheim.

Pantano seemed all set to drive for Jaguar in 2004, but at the last minute Christian Klien took the seat courtesy of a huge chunk of Red Bull cash. Instead, Giorgio managed to secure a place at Jordan, alongside Nick Heidfeld. The jump up to F1 was a big one and he struggled to make an impact. Wrangles over sponsorship payments caused unrest, and he was stood down for the Canadian Grand Prix, where his replacement, Timo Glock, picked up a couple of points. Pantano returned to the fray next time out, but continued retirements – some of his own making – prevented him from improving on the 13th places he had achieved at Sepang and the Nürburgring. After Monza, he opted not to complete the season, deciding that he was wasting his family's dwindling sponsorship funds.

Giorgio attempted to reboot his career by joining the brand-new GP2 Series, eventually signing a late deal with Super Nova. However, the switch did not provide him with the career boost he had envisaged. Early-season performances were mostly lacklustre, but by mid-season he had managed to put together a number of top-three finishes, and eventually he placed sixth overall in the final rankings.

Already the Italian was eyeing other career opportunities, this time in the United States, where he picked up a couple of road-course rides with Ganassi Racing. Even a fourth place at Watkins Glen brought no offers of a full-time ride anywhere in 2006, however, and he was forced on to the sidelines until a mid-season return to GP2 with Giancarlo Fisichella's team got his career moving again. Three wins, including a double-header at Monza, showed he was still a talent, but there was still no interest from within the F1 paddock. So it was back to GP2, this time with Campos GP, and another decent campaign that brought another two wins and third in the championship, behind Timo Glock. While the German succeeded in finding his way back into F1 on the back of his GP2 return, Giorgio was not so fortunate. In 2008, he joined Racing Engineering and, having built an early-season advantage, managed to keep his head to claim the title against strong opposition. It must have been galling for the Italian to watch all six drivers below him in the final points table be given F1 opportunities.

As the GP2 champion, Pantano was no longer allowed to compete in the series, so he found himself effectively in racing limbo and was forced to drop down to the Super League series in 2009. Then he chose to mix it in the new Auto GP series (which was Euro F3000 rebranded), but failed to make much of an impression against a clutch of hungry young hopefuls and older hands whom he had comfortably seen off in his halcyon GP2 days.

In 2011, Pantano had one last throw of the dice, heading to America once more to try to get a foothold in Indy car racing. His three-race spell as a substitute for the injured Justin Wilson failed to bring the results he had hoped for, leaving him with few options for the future.

So, was Pantano just unlucky, or never good enough for a long-term career in Formula 1? Perhaps the answer is a bit of both...

PANTANO, Giorgio (I) b 4/2/1979, Padua

2004 Championship position: Unplaced

	Race	Circuit	No	Entrant		Tyres	Capacity/Car/Engine	Comment	Q Pos/Entries
14	AUSTRALIAN GP	Melbourne	19	Jordan Ford		B	3.0 Jordan EJ14-Cosworth V10	5 laps behind	16/20
13	MALAYSIAN GP	Sepang	19	Jordan Ford		B	3.0 Jordan EJ14-Cosworth V10	2 laps behind	18/20
16	BAHRAIN GP	Bahrain Circuit	19	Jordan Ford		B	3.0 Jordan EJ14-Cosworth V10	brakes & differential/1 lap behind	16/20
ret	SAN MARINO GP	Imola	19	Jordan Ford		B	3.0 Jordan EJ14-Cosworth V10	hydraulics	15/20
ret	SPANISH GP	Barcelona	19	Jordan Ford		B	3.0 Jordan EJ14-Cosworth V10	hydraulics	19/20
ret	MONACO GP	Monte Carlo	19	Jordan Ford		B	3.0 Jordan EJ14-Cosworth V10	hydraulics	18/20
13	EUROPEAN GP	Nürburgring	19	Jordan Ford		B	3.0 Jordan EJ14-Cosworth V10	2 laps behind	15/20
ret	U S GP	Indianapolis	19	Jordan Ford		B	3.0 Jordan EJ14-Cosworth V10	collision damage on lap 1	17/20
17	FRENCH GP	Magny Cours	19	Jordan Ford		B	3.0 Jordan EJ14-Cosworth V10	3 laps behind	18/20
ret	BRITISH GP	Silverstone	19	Jordan Ford		B	3.0 Jordan EJ14-Cosworth V10	spun off	15/20
15	GERMAN GP	Hockenheim	19	Jordan Ford		B	3.0 Jordan EJ14-Cosworth V10	puncture/3 laps behind	17/20
ret	HUNGARIAN GP	Hungaroring	19	Jordan Ford		B	3.0 Jordan EJ14-Cosworth V10	gearbox	17/20
ret	BELGIAN GP	Spa	19	Jordan Ford		B	3.0 Jordan EJ14-Cosworth V10	hit by Bruni on lap 1	19/20
ret	ITALIAN GP	Monza	19	Jordan Ford		B	3.0 Jordan EJ14-Cosworth V10	spun off	18/20

GP Starts: 14   GP Wins: 0   Pole positions: 0   Fastest laps: 0   Points: 0

MAX PAPIS

AFTER starting in karting, Max Papis spent three years racing in Italian Formula 3, culminating in sixth place overall in 1992. He stepped up to F3000 the following year with the Vortex team and enjoyed a solid first season. Then he switched to Mythos for another crack in the next season, and jaws soon dropped when the Italian proved utterly dominant at Barcelona with a performance he could not repeat throughout the year. Taken under the wing of former Lotus boss Peter Collins, who had given him an F1 test in 1994, Papis proved that he had more to offer than many would have supposed once he got behind the wheel of a Footwork in 1995, and he certainly relished his chance to briefly join the grand prix ranks. Only the late challenge of Jean-Christophe Boullion, who pipped him for sixth place, denied Papis a championship point at Monza.

The Italian raced Gianpiero Moretti's Ferrari 333SP sports car in America in 1996, and his impressive performances caught the eye of the Arciero-Wells team, who gave him his CART chance after the tragic death of Jeff Krosnoff. For much of 1997 and 1998, Max was handicapped by the lack of horsepower from the Toyota engine, but he comfortably eclipsed team-mates Hiro Matsushita and Robbie Gordon. The big breakthrough came for Papis when Bobby Rahal put him into one of his cars for 1999. Only cruel luck robbed him of a deserved victory on the last lap of the US 500, but throughout the season he had consistently shown that his day would surely come. And so it did in 2000, at the season-opener at Homestead, where the Italian scored a close win from Roberto Moreno. The rest of the season was something of a let-down, however, only a second-place finish at Detroit being noteworthy. The Italian picked up another two wins the following season (in the wet at Portland and at Laguna Seca), but unfortunately he blotted his copybook in tangling with team-mate Kenny Bräck on more than one occasion. Despite a second-place finish in the finale at Fontana, to finish sixth in the final points standings, Rahal dispensed with his services.

Max started 2002 on a high note, sharing the winning Dallara Judd in the Daytona 24-hour race, but was left without much in the way of a ride thereafter. He threw in his lot with the fledgling Sigma Autosport team and, despite the lack of resources, he managed the extraordinary feat of gaining podium placings in Long Beach and Milwaukee, before the team folded in mid-season. This allowed him to fill in for both Penske and Cheever in the IRL during the rest of that season. Max also returned briefly to Champ Car duties in 2003 for a seven-race mid-season stint with PK Racing, but then turned his attentions to the American Le Mans Series, racing a Chip Ganassi entered Riley-Lexus (he and Scott Pruett were 2004 champions), a works backed Chevrolet Corvette at Le Mans and latterly a Krohn Riley-Pontiac. He also put in an appearance for Italy in the A1GP race at Laguna Seca in March, 2006, finishing seventh in the feature race. Since 2006, Papis has concentrated largely on trying to forge a career in NASCAR, contesting 35 premier Sprint Cup races (2008–10) and a few Nationwide events, before settling into regular rides in the third-tier Camping World Truck Cup series.

PAPIS, Max (Massimiliano) (I) b 3/10/1969, Como

1995 Championship position: Unplaced

	Race	Circuit	No	Entrant		Tyres	Capacity/Car/Engine	Comment	Q Pos/Entries
ret	BRITISH GP	Silverstone	9	Footwork Hart		G	3.0 Footwork FA16-Hart V8	accident – slid off track	17/24
ret	GERMAN GP	Hockenheim	9	Footwork Hart		G	3.0 Footwork FA16-Hart V8	transmission on startline	15/24
ret	HUNGARIAN GP	Hungaroring	9	Footwork Hart		G	3.0 Footwork FA16-Hart V8	brakes	20/24
ret	BELGIAN GP	Spa	9	Footwork Hart		G	3.0 Footwork FA16-Hart V8	spun off	20/24
7	ITALIAN GP	Monza	9	Footwork Hart		G	3.0 Footwork FA16-Hart V8	1 lap behind	15/24
ret/dns	PORTUGUESE GP	Estoril	9	Footwork Hart		G	3.0 Footwork FA16-Hart V8	gearbox at first start	(20)/24
12	EUROPEAN GP	Nürburgring	9	Footwork Hart		G	3.0 Footwork FA16-Hart V8	3 laps behind	17/24

GP Starts: 6 (7)   GP Wins: 0   Pole positions: 0   Fastest laps: 0   Points: 0

MICHAEL PARKES

BORN into a motoring family (his father was the chairman of Alvis cars), Mike Parkes first took to the circuits with an MG TD while working as an engineer with the Rootes group, but soon graduated to a Frazer Nash.

Mike started to race seriously in 1957 with a Lotus, which earned him an invitation from Colin Chapman to act as reserve driver for the works team at Le Mans. Then he became involved with David Fry's Formula 2 project, which was intended for Stuart Lewis-Evans. Apart from the occasional Libre success in minor events during 1958/59, the car was not really competitive and Mike failed to qualify it for the F2 class of the British GP at Aintree.

A few outings in Sir Gawaine Baillie's Lotus Elite during 1960 showed Mike's potential, but brought little by way of results. His breakthrough came in 1961, however, when he raced for Tommy Sopwith's Equipe Endeavour in GT and Formula Junior events, and also handled Maranello Concessionaires' Ferrari GT, winning races regularly in all classes. Undoubtedly the high point of his season was the Le Mans 24-hours, in which he shared a Ferrari 3-litre Testa Rossa with Willy Mairesse to take a superb second place.

Although Mike began 1962 with a rare Formula 1 outing at Mallory Park, taking fourth place in the 1000 Guineas race in a Bowmaker Cooper, his immediate future remained in the sports and GT category. His superb form of the previous year was repeated with much the same machinery, his tally including a hat trick of wins in one day at Brands Hatch. Another fine outing brought second place in the Nürburgring 1000km in the works Ferrari, and it was no surprise when he joined the Scuderia for the 1963 season as development engineer and reserve driver.

Over the next three seasons, Mike became one the world's leading sports car drivers, winning the Sebring 12-hours and Spa 500km in 1964 – a season cut short by a testing accident – and the Monza 1000km in 1965. After John Surtees' sudden departure from the team, he was elevated to grand prix status and, with a special long chassis to accommodate his 6ft 4in frame, he took second place on his debut in the French GP and repeated the feat at Monza. His success in sports cars continued: he won the Monza and Spa 1000km in 1966, and finished second at Daytona, Monza and Le Mans in 1967, a season that started with much promise when he dead-heated with Ludovico Scarfiotti to share a win at Syracuse and then demolished the opposition in the International Trophy at Silverstone. Disaster struck in the Belgian GP, however, where he crashed his Ferrari and suffered serious leg injuries.

Mike continued in a management role at Ferrari while he recovered from the accident, and made a tentative return in the Paris 1000km in 1969, returning to the track in 1970 and 1971 for NART and Scuderia Filipinetti. Although he could not repeat his previous triumphs, he produced some useful performances, including a superb drive to fifth place in the 1972 Targa Florio with Peter Westbury in the little Lola T212. Then he was involved in the Fiat 128 touring car programme before moving to Lancia to help develop the Stratos. Tragically, he was killed in a road accident in 1977, when his car was involved in a collision with a lorry.

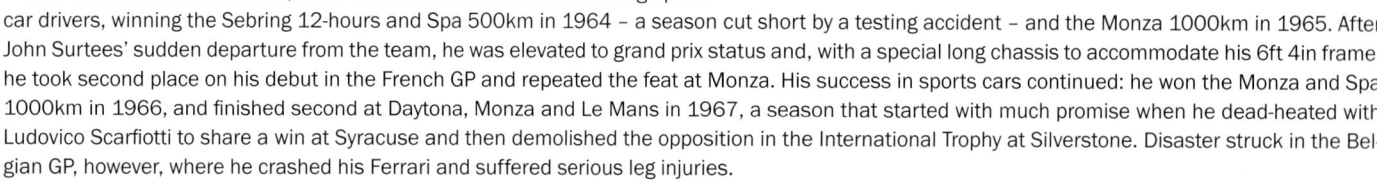

PARKES, Michael (GB) b 24/9/1931, Richmond, Surrey – d 28/8/1977, nr Turin, Italy

	1959 Championship position: Unplaced								
	Race	Circuit	No	Entrant	Tyres	Capacity/Car/Engine	Comment		Q Pos/Entries
dnq	BRITISH GP (F2)	Aintree	60	David Fry	D	1.5 Fry-Climax 4 F2			– /30
	1966 Championship position: 8th=	Wins: 0	Pole positions: 1	Fastest laps: 0	Points scored: 12				
2	FRENCH GP	Reims	22	Scuderia Ferrari SpA SEFAC	F	3.0 Ferrari 312/66-V12			3/17
ret	DUTCH GP	Zandvoort	4	Scuderia Ferrari SpA SEFAC	F	3.0 Ferrari 312/66-V12	spun off		5/18
ret	GERMAN GP	Nürburgring	10	Scuderia Ferrari SpA SEFAC	D	3.0 Ferrari 312/66-V12	engine failure – crashed		7/30
2	ITALIAN GP	Monza	4	Scuderia Ferrari SpA SEFAC	F	3.0 Ferrari 312/66-V12			1/22
	1967 Championship position: 16th=	Wins: 0	Pole positions: 0	Fastest laps: 0	Points scored: 2				
5	DUTCH GP	Zandvoort	4	Scuderia Ferrari SpA SEFAC	F	3.0 Ferrari 312/66-V12	1 lap behind		10/17
ret	BELGIAN GP	Spa	3	Scuderia Ferrari SpA SEFAC	F	3.0 Ferrari 312/66-V12	went off on oil – suffered broken legs		8/18
	GP Starts: 6	GP Wins: 0	Pole positions: 1	Fastest laps: 0	Points: 14				

PARNELL, Reg (GB) b 2/7/1911, Derby – d 7/1/1964, Derby

	1950 Championship position: 7th=	Wins: 0	Pole positions: 0	Fastest laps: 0	Points scored: 4				
	Race	Circuit	No	Entrant	Tyres	Capacity/Car/Engine	Comment		Q Pos/Entries
3	BRITISH GP	Silverstone	4	Alfa Romeo SpA	P	1.5 s/c Alfa Romeo 158 8	guest driver for Alfa Romeo		4/21
ret	FRENCH GP	Reims	32	Scuderia Ambrosiana	D	1.5 s/c Maserati 4CLT/48 4	engine		12/20
	1951 Championship position: 8th	Wins: 0	Pole positions: 0	Fastest laps: 0	Points scored: 5				
4	FRENCH GP	Reims	26	G A Vandervell	P	4.5 Ferrari T375/Thinwall Spl V12	4 laps behind		9/23
5	BRITISH GP	Silverstone	6	BRM Ltd	D	1.5 s/c BRM P15 V16	5 laps behind		20/20
dns	ITALIAN GP	Monza	30	BRM Ltd	D	1.5 s/c BRM P15 V16	engine in practice		(8)/22

1952 Championship position: Unplaced								
7	BRITISH GP	Silverstone	8	A H M Bryde	D	2.0 Cooper T20-Bristol 6	*3 laps behind*	6/32
1954 Championship position: Unplaced								
ret	BRITISH GP	Silverstone	12	Scuderia Ambrosiana	A	2.5 Ferrari 500/625 4	*water jacket*	14/31

GP Starts: 6   GP Wins: 0   Pole positions: 0   Fastest laps: 0   Points: 9

REG PARNELL

SOMETHING of a wayward performer in his youth (his licence was withdrawn from 1937 to 1939 following a serious accident at Silverstone), Reg Parnell matured to become one of Britain's most seasoned professionals and later a respected elder statesman, guiding the fortunes of a new generation of grand prix talent.

The Derbyshire pig farmer began racing in 1935 with an MG Magnette and found success immediately before the Second World War with a 4.7-litre Bugatti. The war years robbed Reg of a large part of what should have been the prime of his career, but he did not idle his time away, purchasing a vast array of temporarily redundant racing machinery in readiness for peace.

Racing a Maserati and an E-Type ERA bought from Peter Whitehead, Reg soon began tackling Continental races with great gusto, but eventually the Maserati 4CLT/48 brought more success, particularly at Goodwood, where he seemed to be able to win at will.

Such was the respect he commanded that Reg was invited to drive a works Alfa Romeo in the very first world championship race at Silverstone in 1950, finishing an excellent third.

In 1951, Reg drove Tony Vandervell's 'Thinwall Special' Ferrari to points finishes in two grands prix, and won the International Trophy at Silverstone when the race was abandoned after a rainstorm. Less happy was his association with BRM and their problematic V16 car, which defeated even his efforts.

Reg found the ready-made Ferrari T500 – no longer a grand prix challenger due to the change in formula – just the ticket for national events and chalked up many successes during the 1954 season. Later he drove Rob Walker's Connaught on occasion, as well as a Ferrari Super Squalo, which he used to win the 1957 New Zealand GP and the South Island race at Dunedin, before retiring to take up the full-time team manager's job at Aston Martin, having been a key member of the team since the early 1950s.

When David Brown pulled out of racing, Reg was immediately in demand, and he spent 1961 and 1962 overseeing the Yeoman Credit and Bowmaker Lola teams, before setting up his own Reg Parnell Racing team. This was still in its infancy when, at the age of 52, the sturdy Parnell died unexpectedly of peritonitis after a routine appendix operation in January, 1964.

TIM PARNELL

BIG, bluff and affable, Tim Parnell never managed to match the success of his father, Reg, on the circuits, but he had an enjoyable career in minor Formula 1 and F2 races in the late 1950s and early 1960s. Suitably encouraged by a sound Formula Junior season in 1960, he purchased a Lotus 18 in 1961, which he hauled to the far corners of the Continent in search of limited success.

Illness curtailed his 1962 campaign, but he returned in 1963, only for the sudden death of his father the following January to thrust him into the role of running the Parnell team. He remained a team manager for the rest of the decade, latterly with the BRM works team. He also ran his own outfit, working with drivers such as Mike Spence (1966) and Pedro Rodriguez (1969).

PARNELL, Tim (GB) b 25/6/1932, Derby

	Race	Circuit	No	Entrant	Tyres	Capacity/Car/Engine	Comment	Q Pos/Entries
1959 Championship position: Unplaced								
dnq	BRITISH GP (F2)	Aintree	66	R H H Parnell	D	1.5 Cooper T45-Climax 4		– /30
1961 Championship position: Unplaced								
ret	BRITISH GP	Aintree	38	Tim Parnell	D	1.5 Lotus 18-Climax 4	*clutch*	29/30
10	ITALIAN GP	Monza	16	Tim Parnell	D	1.5 Lotus 18-Climax 4	*3 laps behind*	27/33
1963 Championship position: Unplaced								
dnq	GERMAN GP	Nürburgring	30	Tim Parnell	D	1.5 Lotus 18/21-Climax 4		25/26

GP Starts: 2   GP Wins: 0   Pole positions: 0   Fastest laps: 0   Points: 0

AT the end of the 1993 season, the curtain finally fell on Riccardo Patrese's Formula 1 career, during which he had competed in a staggering total of 256 world championship grands prix. During the 17 seasons that he had spent racing at the highest level, he had matured from a wild and cocksure enfant terrible into a contented and charming elder statesman, happy still to be part of the scene that had changed so much during his marathon innings.

A former karting whizz-kid who took the world title in 1974, Patrese moved into cars the following year in Formula Italia. He finished as runner-up to Bruno Giacomelli and then embarked on a full season of Formula 3 in 1976. The ensuing fierce battle with Conny Andersson for the European championship went all the way to a bitter final round, before the title fell to the Italian. Riccardo then enjoyed a successful year in Formula 2 with a Chevron, but before long he had been propelled into the Shadow team to replace Renzo Zorzi.

While his off-track demeanour ruffled a few feathers, there was certainly no doubting Patrese's talent behind the wheel. He was part of the new breakaway Arrows team at the start of 1978, and he was sensationally quick, leading comfortably in South Africa until an engine failure robbed him of a deserved victory. Unfortunately, his driving still had some rough edges, and in the emotional aftermath of Ronnie Peterson's accident at Monza, he was targeted for blame. The treatment he received would have broken a lesser man, but he simply got on with the job, although in retrospect, staying loyal to Arrows could have been his biggest mistake. From 1979 through to 1981, he struggled to find sustained success with cars that showed occasional, but unfulfilled promise, and secretly he must have regretted turning down the tempting opportunities he had been offered in 1978.

A move to Brabham put Riccardo in a truly competitive environment, but a lucky win at Monaco was the highlight of an inconclusive year, disfigured by a rash of mistakes. It was a similar story in 1983, when he tossed away victory at Imola early in the season, but signed off from the Brabham team with a perfect display at Kyalami to show what might have been. Certainly he had time to ponder his wasted chances over the next few years as he became caught in a depressing downward spiral, struggling with the Benetton sponsored Alfa for two seasons, before returning to a Brabham

team that was beginning its terminal decline. At least, he had been able to savour the taste of success in his role as a works driver for Lancia Martini, with wins at Silverstone and the Nürburgring in 1982, Kyalami in 1984 and Spa a year later.

When Patrese was picked for the second Williams drive, most observers felt that he was extremely lucky to have been given such an opportunity, but he failed to pull up any trees with the Judd-engined car in 1988. In the following season, with Nigel Mansell off to Ferrari and Renault power at his disposal, however, a rejuvenated Riccardo appeared. Relaxed and confident, he forged an excellent working relationship with Patrick Head and was largely responsible for the development work that put the Didcot team back at the top of the pile. Certainly he was unlucky not to have won at least two races that year, but he put that to rights in 1990 with an emotional win at Imola, helping to erase his painful memories of 1983.

Even the return of Mansell in 1991 – which he took with great equanimity – failed to blunt his spirit, and he gave as good as he got, particularly in the first half of the season. Victories in Mexico and Portugal set the seal on what probably was his best ever year. Statistically, the following season, when he was runner-up to Mansell in the world championship, was more successful, but his performances were less convincing. He was very fortunate to escape unharmed after a horrifying coming-together with Helmut Berger at Estoril, but showed his steel by bouncing back with a win at Suzuka.

Having accepted a lucrative contract with Benetton for 1993, Riccardo found it difficult to rediscover his recent sparkling form. A depressing early-season run had been arrested by mid-summer, but by then the Benetton management had decided to dispense with the services of grand prix racing's most experienced campaigner.

Subsequently, Riccardo took a well-paid drive in the German Super Touring series with Ford, but the Mondeo was never more than a midfield runner. Apart from a one-off return to Le Mans with Nissan in 1997, he eased himself into comfortable and well-deserved retirement, although (like former team-mate Nigel Mansell) he was tempted back into the cockpit to compete in the Kyalami Grand Prix Masters at the end of 2005, taking a highly impressive third place.

Riccardo Patrese leads Alain Prost, Didier Pironi and Andrea de Cesaris in the early stages of the 1982 Monaco Grand Prix. The Italian eventually scored his maiden win in a chaotic rain-affected finish.

PATRESE, Riccardo (I) b 17/4/1954, Padua

1977 Championship position: 19th= Wins: 0 Pole positions: 0 Fastest laps: 0 Points scored: 1

	Race	Circuit	No	Entrant	Tyres	Capacity/Car/Engine	Comment	Q Pos/Entries
9	MONACO GP	Monte Carlo	16	Shadow Racing Team	G	3.0 Shadow DN8-Cosworth V8	1 lap behind	15/26
ret	BELGIAN GP	Zolder	16	Shadow Racing Team	G	3.0 Shadow DN8-Cosworth V8	crashed	15/32
ret	FRENCH GP	Dijon	16	Shadow Racing Team	G	3.0 Shadow DN8-Cosworth V8	clutch/engine	15/30
ret	BRITISH GP	Silverstone	16	Shadow Racing Team	G	3.0 Shadow DN8-Cosworth V8	fuel pressure	25/36
10/ret	GERMAN GP	Hockenheim	16	Shadow Racing Team	G	3.0 Shadow DN8-Cosworth V8	lost wheel/5 laps behind	16/30
13	DUTCH GP	Zandvoort	16	Shadow Racing Team	G	3.0 Shadow DN8-Cosworth V8	pit stop/8 laps behind	16/34
ret	ITALIAN GP	Monza	16	Shadow Racing Team	G	3.0 Shadow DN8-Cosworth V8	spun off on oil	=6/34
10/ret	CANADIAN GP	Mosport Park	16	Shadow Racing Team	G	3.0 Shadow DN8-Cosworth V8	spun off/4 laps behind	8/27
6	JAPANESE GP	Mount Fuji	16	Shadow Racing Team	G	3.0 Shadow DN8-Cosworth V8	1 lap behind	13/23

1978 Championship position: 11th= Wins: 0 Pole positions: 0 Fastest laps: 0 Points scored: 11

	Race	Circuit	No	Entrant	Tyres	Capacity/Car/Engine	Comment	Q Pos/Entries
10	BRAZILIAN GP	Rio	36	Arrows Racing Team	G	3.0 Arrows FA1-Cosworth V8	2 pit stops – fuel/4 laps behind	18/28
ret	SOUTH AFRICAN GP	Kyalami	35	Arrows Racing Team	G	3.0 Arrows FA1-Cosworth V8	engine/led race	7/30
6	US GP WEST	Long Beach	35	Arrows Racing Team	G	3.0 Arrows FA1-Cosworth V8	pit stop – tyre/1 lap behind	9/30
6	MONACO GP	Monte Carlo	35	Arrows Racing Team	G	3.0 Arrows FA1-Cosworth V8		14/30
ret	BELGIUM GP	Zolder	35	Arrows Racing Team	G	3.0 Arrows FA1-Cosworth V8	rear suspension	8/30
ret	SPANISH GP	Jarama	35	Arrows Racing Team	G	3.0 Arrows FA1-Cosworth V8	engine	8/29
2	SWEDISH GP	Anderstorp	35	Arrows Racing Team	G	3.0 Arrows FA1-Cosworth V8		5/27
8	FRENCH GP	Paul Ricard	35	Arrows Racing Team	G	3.0 Arrows FA1-Cosworth V8		12/29
ret	BRITISH GP	Brands Hatch	35	Arrows Racing Team	G	3.0 Arrows FA1-Cosworth V8	rear suspension after puncture	5/30
9	GERMAN GP	Hockenheim	35	Arrows Racing Team	G	3.0 Arrows FA1-Cosworth V8	1 lap behind	14/30
ret	AUSTRIAN GP	Österreichring	35	Arrows Racing Team	G	3.0 Arrows A1-Cosworth V8	collision with Ertl at restart	16/31
ret	DUTCH GP	Zandvoort	35	Arrows Racing Team	G	3.0 Arrows A1-Cosworth V8	collision with Pironi	13/33
ret	ITALIAN GP	Monza	35	Arrows Racing Team	G	3.0 Arrows A1-Cosworth V8	engine	12/32
4	CANADIAN GP	Montreal	35	Arrows Racing Team	G	3.0 Arrows A1-Cosworth V8		12/28

1979 Championship position: 19th= Wins: 0 Pole positions: 0 Fastest laps: 0 Points scored: 2

	Race	Circuit	No	Entrant	Tyres	Capacity/Car/Engine	Comment	Q Pos/Entries
dns	ARGENTINE GP	Buenos Aires	29	Warsteiner Arrows Racing Team	G	3.0 Arrows A1B-Cosworth V8	accident in a.m. warm-up	(13)/26
9	BRAZILIAN GP	Interlagos	29	Warsteiner Arrows Racing Team	G	3.0 Arrows A1B-Cosworth V8	1 lap behind	16/26
11	SOUTH AFRICAN GP	Kyalami	29	Warsteiner Arrows Racing Team	G	3.0 Arrows A1B-Cosworth V8	3 laps behind	16/26
ret	US GP WEST	Long Beach	29	Warsteiner Arrows Racing Team	G	3.0 Arrows A1B-Cosworth V8	brakes	9/26
10	SPANISH GP	Jarama	29	Warsteiner Arrows Racing Team	G	3.0 Arrows A1B-Cosworth V8	1 lap behind	16/27
5	BELGIUM GP	Zolder	29	Warsteiner Arrows Racing Team	G	3.0 Arrows A1B-Cosworth V8		16/28
ret	MONACO GP	Monte Carlo	29	Warsteiner Arrows Racing Team	G	3.0 Arrows A1B-Cosworth V8	suspension	15/25
14	FRENCH GP	Dijon	29	Warsteiner Arrows Racing Team	G	3.0 Arrows A2-Cosworth V8	3 laps behind	19/27
ret	BRITISH GP	Silverstone	29	Warsteiner Arrows Racing Team	G	3.0 Arrows A2-Cosworth V8	gearbox	19/26
dns	"	"	29	Warsteiner Arrows Racing Team	G	3.0 Arrows A1B-Cosworth V8	practice only	- / -
ret	GERMAN GP	Hockenheim	29	Warsteiner Arrows Racing Team	G	3.0 Arrows A2-Cosworth V8	puncture	19/26
ret	AUSTRIAN GP	Österreichring	29	Warsteiner Arrows Racing Team	G	3.0 Arrows A2-Cosworth V8	rear suspension	13/26
ret	DUTCH GP	Zandvoort	29	Warsteiner Arrows Racing Team	G	3.0 Arrows A2-Cosworth V8	brake failure – spun off	19/26
13	ITALIAN GP	Monza	29	Warsteiner Arrows Racing Team	G	3.0 Arrows A2-Cosworth V8	pit stop/3 laps behind	17/28
ret	CANADIAN GP	Montreal	29	Warsteiner Arrows Racing Team	G	3.0 Arrows A1B-Cosworth V8	spun off – could not restart	14/29
dns	"	"	29	Warsteiner Arrows Racing Team	G	3.0 Arrows A2-Cosworth V8	practice only	- / -
ret	US GP EAST	Watkins Glen	29	Warsteiner Arrows Racing Team	G	3.0 Arrows A2-Cosworth V8	rear suspension	19/30

1980 Championship position: 9th Wins: 0 Pole positions: 0 Fastest laps: 1 Points scored: 7

	Race	Circuit	No	Entrant	Tyres	Capacity/Car/Engine	Comment	Q Pos/Entries
ret	ARGENTINE GP	Buenos Aires	29	Warsteiner Arrows Racing Team	G	3.0 Arrows A3-Cosworth V8	engine	7/28
6	BRAZILIAN GP	Interlagos	29	Warsteiner Arrows Racing Team	G	3.0 Arrows A3-Cosworth V8	1 lap behind	14/28
ret	SOUTH AFRICAN GP	Kyalami	29	Warsteiner Arrows Racing Team	G	3.0 Arrows A3-Cosworth V8	locked brakes – accident	11/28
2	US GP WEST	Long Beach	29	Warsteiner Arrows Racing Team	G	3.0 Arrows A3-Cosworth V8		8/27
ret	BELGIUM GP	Zolder	29	Warsteiner Arrows Racing Team	G	3.0 Arrows A3-Cosworth V8	spun off	16/27
8	MONACO GP	Monte Carlo	29	Warsteiner Arrows Racing Team	G	3.0 Arrows A3-Cosworth V8	hit by Arnoux – pit stop/-3 laps/FL	11/27
9	FRENCH GP	Paul Ricard	29	Warsteiner Arrows Racing Team	G	3.0 Arrows A3-Cosworth V8	1 lap behind	18/27
9	BRITISH GP	Brands Hatch	29	Warsteiner Arrows Racing Team	G	3.0 Arrows A3-Cosworth V8	3 laps behind	21/27
9	GERMAN GP	Hockenheim	29	Warsteiner Arrows Racing Team	G	3.0 Arrows A3-Cosworth V8	1 lap behind	10/26
14	AUSTRIAN GP	Österreichring	29	Warsteiner Arrows Racing Team	G	3.0 Arrows A3-Cosworth V8	1 lap behind	18/25
ret	DUTCH GP	Zandvoort	29	Warsteiner Arrows Racing Team	G	3.0 Arrows A3-Cosworth V8	engine	14/28
ret	ITALIAN GP	Imola	29	Warsteiner Arrows Racing Team	G	3.0 Arrows A3-Cosworth V8	engine	7/28
ret	CANADIAN GP	Montreal	29	Warsteiner Arrows Racing Team	G	3.0 Arrows A3-Cosworth V8	collision with Prost	11/28
ret	US GP EAST	Watkins Glen	29	Warsteiner Arrows Racing Team	G	3.0 Arrows A3-Cosworth V8	spun off	20/27

1981 Championship position: 11th= Wins: 0 Pole positions: 0 Fastest laps: 0 Points scored: 10

	Race	Circuit	No	Entrant	Tyres	Capacity/Car/Engine	Comment	Q Pos/Entries
ret	US GP WEST	Long Beach	29	Arrows Racing Team	M	3.0 Arrows A3-Cosworth V8	fuel filter/led race	1/29
3	BRAZILIAN GP	Rio	29	Arrows Racing Team	M	3.0 Arrows A3-Cosworth V8		4/30
7	ARGENTINE GP	Buenos Aires	29	Arrows Racing Team	M	3.0 Arrows A3-Cosworth V8	1 lap behind	9/29
2	SAN MARINO GP	Imola	29	Arrows Racing Team	M	3.0 Arrows A3-Cosworth V8		9/30
ret/*dns	BELGIUM GP	Zolder	29	Arrows Racing Team	M	3.0 Arrows A3-Cosworth V8	hit by Stohr at start/*did not restart	4/31
ret	MONACO GP	Monte Carlo	29	Arrows Racing Team	M	3.0 Arrows A3-Cosworth V8	gearbox	5/31
ret	SPANISH GP	Jarama	29	Arrows Racing Team	M	3.0 Arrows A3-Cosworth V8	engine	12/30
14	FRENCH GP	Dijon	29	Arrows Racing Team	M	3.0 Arrows A3-Cosworth V8	3 laps behind	18/29
10/ret	BRITISH GP	Silverstone	29	Arrows Racing Team	P	3.0 Arrows A3-Cosworth V8	engine/4 laps behind	10/30
ret	GERMAN GP	Hockenheim	29	Arrows Racing Team	P	3.0 Arrows A3-Cosworth V8	engine	13/30
ret	AUSTRIAN GP	Österreichring	29	Arrows Racing Team	P	3.0 Arrows A3-Cosworth V8	engine	10/28
ret	DUTCH GP	Zandvoort	29	Arrows Racing Team	P	3.0 Arrows A3-Cosworth V8	suspension	10/30
ret	ITALIAN GP	Monza	29	Arrows Racing Team	P	3.0 Arrows A1-Cosworth V8	gearbox	20/30
ret	CANADIAN GP	Montreal	29	Arrows Racing Team	P	3.0 Arrows A3-Cosworth V8	spun off	18/30
11	CAESARS PALACE GP	Las Vegas	29	Arrows Racing Team	P	3.0 Arrows A3-Cosworth V8	2 pit stops/4 laps behind	11/30

1982 Championship position: 10th Wins: 1 Pole positions: 0 Fastest laps: 2 Points scored: 21

	Race	Circuit	No	Entrant	Tyres	Capacity/Car/Engine	Comment	Q Pos/Entries
ret	SOUTH AFRICAN GP	Kyalami	2	Parmalat Racing Team	G	1.5 t/c Brabham BT50-BMW 4	turbo bearing	4/30

ret	BRAZILIAN GP	Rio	2	Parmalat Racing Team	G	3.0 Brabham BT49D-Cosworth V8	driver fatigue	9/31
3*	US GP WEST	Long Beach	2	Parmalat Racing Team	G	3.0 Brabham BT49C-Cosworth V8	*3rd place car disqualified	18/31
dns	" "	" "	2	Parmalat Racing Team	G	3.0 Brabham BT49C-Cosworth V8	practice only – accident damage	– / –
ret	BELGIUM GP	Zolder	2	Parmalat Racing Team	G	1.5 t/c Brabham BT50-BMW 4	spun off	11/32
1	MONACO GP	Monte Carlo	2	Parmalat Racing Team	G	3.0 Brabham BT49D-Cosworth V8	FL	2/31
ret	US GP (DETROIT)	Detroit	2	Parmalat Racing Team	G	3.0 Brabham BT49D-Cosworth V8	hit barrier	14/28
2	CANADIAN GP	Montreal	2	Parmalat Racing Team	G	3.0 Brabham BT49D-Cosworth V8		8/29
15	DUTCH GP	Zandvoort	2	Parmalat Racing Team	G	1.5 t/c Brabham BT50-BMW 4	pit stop – gear linkage/3 laps behind	10/31
ret	BRITISH GP	Brands Hatch	2	Parmalat Racing Team	G	1.5 t/c Brabham BT50-BMW 4	stalled at start – hit by Arnoux	2/30
ret	FRENCH GP	Paul Ricard	2	Parmalat Racing Team	G	1.5 t/c Brabham BT50-BMW 4	engine/FL	4/30
ret	GERMAN GP	Hockenheim	2	Parmalat Racing Team	G	1.5 t/c Brabham BT50-BMW 4	engine	6/30
ret	AUSTRIAN GP	Österreichring	2	Parmalat Racing Team	G	1.5 t/c Brabham BT50-BMW 4	engine	2/29
5	SWISS GP	Dijon	2	Parmalat Racing Team	G	1.5 t/c Brabham BT50-BMW 4	1 lap behind	3/29
ret	ITALIAN GP	Monza	2	Parmalat Racing Team	G	1.5 t/c Brabham BT50-BMW 4	clutch	4/30
ret	CAESARS PALACE GP	Las Vegas	2	Parmalat Racing Team	G	1.5 t/c Brabham BT50-BMW 4	clutch	5/30

1983 Championship position: 9th=   Wins: 1   Pole positions: 1   Fastest laps: 1   Points scored: 13

ret	BRAZILIAN GP	Rio	6	Fila Sport	M	1.5 t/c Brabham BT52-BMW 4	exhaust	7/27
10/ret	US GP WEST	Long Beach	6	Fila Sport	M	1.5 t/c Brabham BT52-BMW 4	distributor/3 laps behind	11/28
ret	FRENCH GP	Paul Ricard	6	Fila Sport	M	1.5 t/c Brabham BT52-BMW 4	overheating	3/29
ret	SAN MARINO GP	Imola	6	Fila Sport	M	1.5 t/c Brabham BT52-BMW 4	spun off when leading/FL	5/28
ret	MONACO GP	Monte Carlo	6	Fila Sport	M	1.5 t/c Brabham BT52-BMW 4	electrics	17/28
ret	BELGIUM GP	Spa	6	Fila Sport	M	1.5 t/c Brabham BT52-BMW 4	engine	6/28
ret	US GP (DETROIT)	Detroit	6	Fila Sport	M	1.5 t/c Brabham BT52-BMW 4	brakes	15/27
ret	CANADIAN GP	Montreal	6	Fila Sport	M	1.5 t/c Brabham BT52-BMW 4	gearbox	5/28
ret	BRITISH GP	Silverstone	6	Fila Sport	M	1.5 t/c Brabham BT52B-BMW 4	turbo	5/29
3	GERMAN GP	Hockenheim	6	Fila Sport	M	1.5 t/c Brabham BT52B-BMW 4		8/29
ret	AUSTRIAN GP	Österreichring	6	Fila Sport	M	1.5 t/c Brabham BT52B-BMW 4	overheating	6/29
9	DUTCH GP	Zandvoort	6	Fila Sport	M	1.5 t/c Brabham BT52B-BMW 4	pit stop – fuel/2 laps behind	6/29
ret	ITALIAN GP	Monza	6	Fila Sport	M	1.5 t/c Brabham BT52B-BMW 4	electrics/engine	1/29
7	EUROPEAN GP	Brands Hatch	6	Fila Sport	M	1.5 t/c Brabham BT52B-BMW 4		2/29
1	SOUTH AFRICAN GP	Kyalami	6	Fila Sport	M	1.5 t/c Brabham BT52B-BMW 4		3/26

1984 Championship position: 13th   Wins: 0   Pole positions: 0   Fastest laps: 0   Points scored: 8

ret	BRAZILIAN GP	Rio	22	Benetton Team Alfa Romeo	G	1.5 t/c Alfa Romeo 184T V8	gearbox	11/27
4	SOUTH AFRICAN GP	Kyalami	22	Benetton Team Alfa Romeo	G	1.5 t/c Alfa Romeo 184T V8	2 laps behind	18/27
ret	BELGIUM GP	Zolder	22	Benetton Team Alfa Romeo	G	1.5 t/c Alfa Romeo 184T V8	ignition	7/27
ret	SAN MARINO GP	Imola	22	Benetton Team Alfa Romeo	G	1.5 t/c Alfa Romeo 184T V8	electrics	10/28
ret	FRENCH GP	Dijon	22	Benetton Team Alfa Romeo	G	1.5 t/c Alfa Romeo 184T V8	engine	16/27
ret	MONACO GP	Monte Carlo	22	Benetton Team Alfa Romeo	G	1.5 t/c Alfa Romeo 184T V8	steering	14/27
ret	CANADIAN GP	Montreal	22	Benetton Team Alfa Romeo	G	1.5 t/c Alfa Romeo 184T V8	crashed	14/26
ret	US GP (DETROIT)	Detroit	22	Benetton Team Alfa Romeo	G	1.5 t/c Alfa Romeo 184T V8	spun off – suspension damage	25/27
ret	US GP (DALLAS)	Dallas	22	Benetton Team Alfa Romeo	G	1.5 t/c Alfa Romeo 184T V8	hit wall	21/27
12*/ret	BRITISH GP	Brands Hatch	22	Benetton Team Alfa Romeo	G	1.5 t/c Alfa Romeo 184T V8	out of fuel/*11th car disqualified/-5 laps	17/27
ret	GERMAN GP	Hockenheim	22	Benetton Team Alfa Romeo	G	1.5 t/c Alfa Romeo 184T V8	fuel metering unit	20/27
10/ret	AUSTRIAN GP	Österreichring	22	Benetton Team Alfa Romeo	G	1.5 t/c Alfa Romeo 184T V8	out of fuel/3 laps behind	13/28
ret	DUTCH GP	Zandvoort	22	Benetton Team Alfa Romeo	G	1.5 t/c Alfa Romeo 184T V8	engine	18/27
3	ITALIAN GP	Monza	22	Benetton Team Alfa Romeo	G	1.5 t/c Alfa Romeo 184T V8	1 lap behind	9/27
6	EUROPEAN GP	Nürburgring	22	Benetton Team Alfa Romeo	G	1.5 t/c Alfa Romeo 184T V8	1 lap behind	9/26
8	PORTUGUESE GP	Estoril	22	Benetton Team Alfa Romeo	G	1.5 t/c Alfa Romeo 184T V8	1 lap behind	12/27

1985 Championship position: Unplaced

ret	BRAZILIAN GP	Rio	22	Benetton Team Alfa Romeo	G	1.5 t/c Alfa Romeo 185T V8	puncture	14/25
ret	PORTUGUESE GP	Estoril	22	Benetton Team Alfa Romeo	G	1.5 t/c Alfa Romeo 185T V8	spun off	13/26
ret	SAN MARINO GP	Imola	22	Benetton Team Alfa Romeo	G	1.5 t/c Alfa Romeo 185T V8	engine	18/26
ret	MONACO GP	Monte Carlo	22	Benetton Team Alfa Romeo	G	1.5 t/c Alfa Romeo 185T V8	accident with Piquet	12/26
10	CANADIAN GP	Montreal	22	Benetton Team Alfa Romeo	G	1.5 t/c Alfa Romeo 185T V8	2 laps behind	13/25
ret	US GP (DETROIT)	Detroit	22	Benetton Team Alfa Romeo	G	1.5 t/c Alfa Romeo 185T V8	electrics	14/25
11	FRENCH GP	Paul Ricard	22	Benetton Team Alfa Romeo	G	1.5 t/c Alfa Romeo 185T V8	1 lap behind	17/26
9	BRITISH GP	Silverstone	22	Benetton Team Alfa Romeo	G	1.5 t/c Alfa Romeo 185T V8	3 laps behind	14/26
ret	GERMAN GP	Nürburgring	22	Benetton Team Alfa Romeo	G	1.5 t/c Alfa Romeo 184T V8	gearbox	9/27
ret	AUSTRIAN GP	Österreichring	22	Benetton Team Alfa Romeo	G	1.5 t/c Alfa Romeo 184T V8	engine	10/27
ret	DUTCH GP	Zandvoort	22	Benetton Team Alfa Romeo	G	1.5 t/c Alfa Romeo 184T V8	turbo	19/27
ret	ITALIAN GP	Monza	22	Benetton Team Alfa Romeo	G	1.5 t/c Alfa Romeo 184T V8	exhaust	13/26
ret	BELGIUM GP	Spa	22	Benetton Team Alfa Romeo	G	1.5 t/c Alfa Romeo 184T V8	engine	15/24
9	EUROPEAN GP	Brands Hatch	22	Benetton Team Alfa Romeo	G	1.5 t/c Alfa Romeo 184T V8	2 laps behind	11/27
ret	SOUTH AFRICAN GP	Kyalami	22	Benetton Team Alfa Romeo	G	1.5 t/c Alfa Romeo 184T V8	hit by Cheever on lap 1	12/21
ret	AUSTRALIAN GP	Adelaide	22	Benetton Team Alfa Romeo	G	1.5 t/c Alfa Romeo 184T V8	exhaust	14/25

1986 Championship position: 15th=   Wins: 0   Pole positions: 0   Fastest laps: 0   Points scored: 2

ret	BRAZILIAN GP	Rio	7	Motor Racing Developments Ltd	P	1.5 t/c Brabham BT55-BMW 4	split water pipe	10/25
ret	SPANISH GP	Jerez	7	Motor Racing Developments Ltd	P	1.5 t/c Brabham BT55-BMW 4	gearbox	14/25
6/ret	SAN MARINO GP	Imola	7	Motor Racing Developments Ltd	P	1.5 t/c Brabham BT55-BMW 4	out of fuel/2 laps behind	16/26
ret	MONACO GP	Monte Carlo	7	Motor Racing Developments Ltd	P	1.5 t/c Brabham BT55-BMW 4	fuel pump	6/26
8	BELGIUM GP	Spa	7	Motor Racing Developments Ltd	P	1.5 t/c Brabham BT55-BMW 4	started from pit lane/1 lap behind	15/25
ret	CANADIAN GP	Montreal	7	Motor Racing Developments Ltd	P	1.5 t/c Brabham BT55-BMW 4	turbo	9/25
6	US GP (DETROIT)	Detroit	7	Motor Racing Developments Ltd	P	1.5 t/c Brabham BT55-BMW 4	1 lap behind	8/26
7	FRENCH GP	Paul Ricard	7	Motor Racing Developments Ltd	P	1.5 t/c Brabham BT55-BMW 4	2 laps behind	16/26
ret	BRITISH GP	Brands Hatch	7	Motor Racing Developments Ltd	P	1.5 t/c Brabham BT54-BMW 4	engine	15/26
ret	GERMAN GP	Hockenheim	7	Motor Racing Developments Ltd	P	1.5 t/c Brabham BT55-BMW 4	turbo	7/26
ret	HUNGARIAN GP	Hungaroring	7	Motor Racing Developments Ltd	P	1.5 t/c Brabham BT55-BMW 4	spun off	14/26
ret	AUSTRIAN GP	Österreichring	7	Motor Racing Developments Ltd	P	1.5 t/c Brabham BT55-BMW 4	engine	4/26
ret	ITALIAN GP	Monza	7	Motor Racing Developments Ltd	P	1.5 t/c Brabham BT55-BMW 4	accident with Tambay	10/27
ret	PORTUGUESE GP	Estoril	7	Motor Racing Developments Ltd	P	1.5 t/c Brabham BT55-BMW 4	engine	9/27

Result	Race	Circuit	No.	Entrant	Tyre	Car/Engine	Notes	Grid
13/ret	MEXICAN GP	Mexico City	7	Motor Racing Developments Ltd	P	1.5 t/c Brabham BT55-BMW 4	spun off/4 laps behind	5/26
ret	AUSTRALIAN GP	Adelaide	7	Motor Racing Developments Ltd	P	1.5 t/c Brabham BT55-BMW 4	engine – electrics	19/26

1987 Championship position: 13th   Wins: 0   Pole positions: 0   Fastest laps: 0   Points scored: 6

Result	Race	Circuit	No.	Entrant	Tyre	Car/Engine	Notes	Grid
ret	BRAZILIAN GP	Rio	7	Motor Racing Developments Ltd	G	1.5 t/c Brabham BT56-BMW 4	loose battery	11/23
9	SAN MARINO GP	Imola	7	Motor Racing Developments Ltd	G	1.5 t/c Brabham BT56-BMW 4	2 laps behind	8/27
ret	BELGIUM GP	Spa	7	Motor Racing Developments Ltd	G	1.5 t/c Brabham BT56-BMW 4	clutch	8/26
ret	MONACO GP	Monte Carlo	7	Motor Racing Developments Ltd	G	1.5 t/c Brabham BT56-BMW 4	electrics	10/26
9	US GP (DETROIT)	Detroit	7	Motor Racing Developments Ltd	G	1.5 t/c Brabham BT56-BMW 4	spun – hit Palmer/3 laps behind	9/26
ret	FRENCH GP	Paul Ricard	7	Motor Racing Developments Ltd	G	1.5 t/c Brabham BT56-BMW 4	transmission	12/26
ret	BRITISH GP	Silverstone	7	Motor Racing Developments Ltd	G	1.5 t/c Brabham BT56-BMW 4	fuel metering unit	11/26
ret	GERMAN GP	Hockenheim	7	Motor Racing Developments Ltd	G	1.5 t/c Brabham BT56-BMW 4	turbo	11/26
5	HUNGARIAN GP	Hungaroring	7	Motor Racing Developments Ltd	G	1.5 t/c Brabham BT56-BMW 4	1 lap behind	10/26
ret	AUSTRIAN GP	Österreichring	7	Motor Racing Developments Ltd	G	1.5 t/c Brabham BT56-BMW 4	engine	8/26
ret	ITALIAN GP	Monza	7	Motor Racing Developments Ltd	G	1.5 t/c Brabham BT56-BMW 4	engine	9/28
ret	PORTUGUESE GP	Estoril	7	Motor Racing Developments Ltd	G	1.5 t/c Brabham BT56-BMW 4	engine	7/27
13	SPANISH GP	Jerez	7	Motor Racing Developments Ltd	G	1.5 t/c Brabham BT56-BMW 4	4 laps behind	9/28
3	MEXICAN GP	Mexico City	7	Motor Racing Developments Ltd	G	1.5 t/c Brabham BT56-BMW 4		8/27
11/ret	JAPANESE GP	Suzuka	7	Motor Racing Developments Ltd	G	1.5 t/c Brabham BT56-BMW 4	engine/2 laps behind	9/27
9/ret	AUSTRALIAN GP	Adelaide	5	Canon Williams Team		1.5 t/c Williams FW11B-Honda V6	engine/6 laps behind	7/27

1988 Championship position: 11th   Wins: 0   Pole positions: 0   Fastest laps: 0   Points scored: 8

Result	Race	Circuit	No.	Entrant	Tyre	Car/Engine	Notes	Grid
ret	BRAZILIAN GP	Rio	6	Canon Williams Team	G	3.5 Williams FW12-Judd V8	overheating	8/31
13	SAN MARINO GP	Imola	6	Canon Williams Team	G	3.5 Williams FW12-Judd V8	precautionary stop – handling/-2 laps	6/31
6	MONACO GP	Monte Carlo	6	Canon Williams Team	G	3.5 Williams FW12-Judd V8	1 lap behind	8/30
ret	MEXICAN GP	Mexico City	6	Canon Williams Team	G	3.5 Williams FW12-Judd V8	engine	17/30
ret	CANADIAN GP	Montreal	6	Canon Williams Team	G	3.5 Williams FW12-Judd V8	engine	11/31
ret	US GP (DETROIT)	Detroit	6	Canon Williams Team	G	3.5 Williams FW12-Judd V8	electrics	10/31
ret	FRENCH GP	Paul Ricard	6	Canon Williams Team	G	3.5 Williams FW12-Judd V8	brakes	15/31
8	BRITISH GP	Silverstone	6	Canon Williams Team	G	3.5 Williams FW12-Judd V8	1 lap behind	15/31
ret	GERMAN GP	Hockenheim	6	Canon Williams Team	G	3.5 Williams FW12-Judd V8	slid off	13/31
6	HUNGARIAN GP	Hungaroring	6	Canon Williams Team	G	3.5 Williams FW12-Judd V8	1 lap behind	6/31
ret	BELGIUM GP	Spa	6	Canon Williams Team	G	3.5 Williams FW12-Judd V8	engine	5/31
7	ITALIAN GP	Monza	6	Canon Williams Team	G	3.5 Williams FW12-Judd V8		10/31
ret	PORTUGUESE GP	Estoril	6	Canon Williams Team	G	3.5 Williams FW12-Judd V8	radiator	11/31
5	SPANISH GP	Jerez	6	Canon Williams Team	G	3.5 Williams FW12-Judd V8	fined $10,000 – practice incident	7/31
6	JAPANESE GP	Suzuka	6	Canon Williams Team	G	3.5 Williams FW12-Judd V8		11/31
4	AUSTRALIAN GP	Adelaide	6	Canon Williams Team	G	3.5 Williams FW12-Judd V8		6/31

1989 Championship position: 3rd   Wins: 0   Pole positions: 1   Fastest laps: 1   Points scored: 40

Result	Race	Circuit	No.	Entrant	Tyre	Car/Engine	Notes	Grid
ret	BRAZILIAN GP	Rio	6	Canon Williams Team	G	3.5 Williams FW12C-Renault V10	engine/led race/FL	2/38
ret	SAN MARINO GP	Imola	6	Canon Williams Team	G	3.5 Williams FW12C-Renault V10	engine	4/39
15	MONACO GP	Monte Carlo	6	Canon Williams Team	G	3.5 Williams FW12C-Renault V10	pit stop – wing end/4 laps behind	7/38
2	MEXICAN GP	Mexico City	6	Canon Williams Team	G	3.5 Williams FW12C-Renault V10		5/39
2	US GP (PHOENIX)	Phoenix	6	Canon Williams Team	G	3.5 Williams FW12C-Renault V10		14/39
2	CANADIAN GP	Montreal	6	Canon Williams Team	G	3.5 Williams FW12C-Renault V10	pit stop – tyres/led race	3/39
3	FRENCH GP	Paul Ricard	6	Canon Williams Team	G	3.5 Williams FW12C-Renault V10	spin	8/39
ret	BRITISH GP	Silverstone	6	Canon Williams Team	G	3.5 Williams FW12C-Renault V10	stone burst radiator – crashed	5/39
4	GERMAN GP	Hockenheim	6	Canon Williams Team	G	3.5 Williams FW12C-Renault V10	pitstop – tyres/vibration/gearbox/-1 lap	5/39
ret	HUNGARIAN GP	Hungaroring	6	Canon Williams Team	G	3.5 Williams FW12C-Renault V10	engine/led race	1/39
ret	BELGIAN GP	Spa	6	Canon Williams Team	G	3.5 Williams FW12C-Renault V10	collision with Alboreto	5/39
4	ITALIAN GP	Monza	6	Canon Williams Team	G	3.5 Williams FW12C-Renault V10	handling problems	5/39
ret	PORTUGUESE GP	Estoril	6	Canon Williams Team	G	3.5 Williams FW13-Renault V10	overheating	6/39
dns	"	"	6	Canon Williams Team	G	3.5 Williams FW12C-Renault V10	practice only	-/-
5	SPANISH GP	Jerez	6	Canon Williams Team	G	3.5 Williams FW12C-Renault V10		6/38
dns	"	"	6	Canon Williams Team	G	3.5 Williams FW13-Renault V10	practice only	-/-
2*	JAPANESE GP	Suzuka	6	Canon Williams Team	G	3.5 Williams FW13-Renault V10	*1st place car disqualified	5/39
3	AUSTRALIAN GP	Adelaide	6	Canon Williams Team	G	3.5 Williams FW13-Renault V10		6/39

1990 Championship position: 7th   Wins: 1   Pole positions: 0   Fastest laps: 4   Points scored: 23

Result	Race	Circuit	No.	Entrant	Tyre	Car/Engine	Notes	Grid
9	US GP (PHOENIX)	Phoenix	6	Canon Williams Renault	G	3.5 Williams FW13B-Renault V10	hit Grouillard – pit stop/1 lap behind	12/35
13/ret	BRAZILIAN GP	Interlagos	6	Canon Williams Renault	G	3.5 Williams FW13B-Renault V10	oil cooler/6 laps behind	4/35
1	SAN MARINO GP	Imola	6	Canon Williams Renault	G	3.5 Williams FW13B-Renault V10		3/34
ret	MONACO GP	Monte Carlo	6	Canon Williams Renault	G	3.5 Williams FW13B-Renault V10	electrics – engine	4/35
ret	CANADIAN GP	Montreal	6	Canon Williams Renault	G	3.5 Williams FW13B-Renault V10	brakes	9/35
9	MEXICAN GP	Mexico City	6	Canon Williams Renault	G	3.5 Williams FW13B-Renault V10	spin – pit stop – tyres	2/35
6	FRENCH GP	Paul Ricard	6	Canon Williams Renault	G	3.5 Williams FW13B-Renault V10	pit stop – tyres/misfire	6/35
ret	BRITISH GP	Silverstone	6	Canon Williams Renault	G	3.5 Williams FW13B-Renault V10	collision damage – undertray	7/35
5	GERMAN GP	Hockenheim	6	Canon Williams Renault	G	3.5 Williams FW13B-Renault V10	pit stop – tyres	5/35
4	HUNGARIAN GP	Hungaroring	6	Canon Williams Renault	G	3.5 Williams FW13B-Renault V10	pit stop – tyres/FL	2/35
ret	BELGIAN GP	Spa	6	Canon Williams Renault	G	3.5 Williams FW13B-Renault V10	gearbox	7/33
5	ITALIAN GP	Monza	6	Canon Williams Renault	G	3.5 Williams FW13B-Renault V10	pit stop – tyres	7/33
7	PORTUGUESE GP	Estoril	6	Canon Williams Renault	G	3.5 Williams FW13B-Renault V10	long pit stop – tyres/FL/1 lap behind	5/33
5	SPANISH GP	Jerez	6	Canon Williams Renault	G	3.5 Williams FW13B-Renault V10	2 pit stops – tyres/FL	6/33
4	JAPANESE GP	Suzuka	6	Canon Williams Renault	G	3.5 Williams FW13B-Renault V10	pit stop – tyres/FL	8/30
6	AUSTRALIAN GP	Adelaide	6	Canon Williams Renault	G	3.5 Williams FW13B-Renault V10	spin – pit stop – tyres/1 lap behind	6/30

1991 Championship position: 3rd   Wins: 2   Pole positions: 4   Fastest laps: 3   Points scored: 53

Result	Race	Circuit	No.	Entrant	Tyre	Car/Engine	Notes	Grid
ret	US GP (PHOENIX)	Phoenix	6	Canon Williams Team	G	3.5 Williams FW14-Renault V10	gearbox/spun	3/34
2	BRAZILIAN GP	Interlagos	6	Canon Williams Team	G	3.5 Williams FW14-Renault V10		2/34
ret	SAN MARINO GP	Imola	6	Canon Williams Team	G	3.5 Williams FW14-Renault V10	electrics/engine	2/34
ret	MONACO GP	Monte Carlo	6	Canon Williams Team	G	3.5 Williams FW14-Renault V10	hit Modena's oil – crashed	3/34
3	CANADIAN GP	Montreal	6	Canon Williams Team	G	3.5 Williams FW14-Renault V10		1/34
1	MEXICAN GP	Mexico City	6	Canon Williams Team	G	3.5 Williams FW14-Renault V10		1/34

5	FRENCH GP	Magny Cours	6	Canon Williams Team	G	3.5 Williams FW14-Renault V10	*1 lap behind*	1/34
ret	BRITISH GP	Silverstone	6	Canon Williams Team	G	3.5 Williams FW14-Renault V10	*collision with Berger on lap 1*	3/34
2	GERMAN GP	Hockenheim	6	Canon Williams Team	G	3.5 Williams FW14-Renault V10	*FL*	4/34
3	HUNGARIAN GP	Hungaroring	6	Canon Williams Team	G	3.5 Williams FW14-Renault V10		2/34
5	BELGIAN GP	Spa	6	Canon Williams Team	G	3.5 Williams FW14-Renault V10		17/34
ret	ITALIAN GP	Monza	6	Canon Williams Team	G	3.5 Williams FW14-Renault V10	*clutch*	4/34
1	PORTUGUESE GP	Estoril	6	Canon Williams Team	G	3.5 Williams FW14-Renault V10		1/34
3	SPANISH GP	Barcelona	6	Canon Williams Team	G	3.5 Williams FW14-Renault V10	*FL*	4/33
3	JAPANESE GP	Suzuka	6	Canon Williams Team	G	3.5 Williams FW14-Renault V10		5/31
5	AUSTRALIAN GP	Adelaide	6	Canon Williams Team	G	3.5 Williams FW14-Renault V10	*rain shortened race stopped at 14 laps*	4/32

1992 Championship position: 2nd Wins: 1 Pole positions: 0 Fastest laps: 2 Points scored: 56

2	SOUTH AFRICAN GP	Kyalami	6	Canon Williams Team	G	3.5 Williams FW14B-Renault V10		4/30
2	MEXICAN GP	Mexico City	6	Canon Williams Team	G	3.5 Williams FW14B-Renault V10		2/30
2	BRAZILIAN GP	Interlagos	6	Canon Williams Team	G	3.5 Williams FW14B-Renault V10	*FL*	2/31
ret	SPANISH GP	Barcelona	6	Canon Williams Team	G	3.5 Williams FW14B-Renault V10	*spun off*	4/32
2	SAN MARINO GP	Imola	6	Canon Williams Team	G	3.5 Williams FW14B-Renault V10	*FL*	2/32
3	MONACO GP	Monte Carlo	6	Canon Williams Team	G	3.5 Williams FW14B-Renault V10		2/32
ret	CANADIAN GP	Montreal	6	Canon Williams Team	G	3.5 Williams FW14B-Renault V10	*gearbox*	2/32
2*	FRENCH GP	Magny Cours	6	Canon Williams Team	G	3.5 Williams FW14B-Renault V10	**aggregate of two parts*	2/30
2	BRITISH GP	Silverstone	6	Canon Williams Team	G	3.5 Williams FW14B-Renault V10		2/32
8/ret	GERMAN GP	Hockenheim	6	Canon Williams Team	G	3.5 Williams FW14B-Renault V10	*spun off and stalled/FL/1 lap behind*	2/32
ret	HUNGARIAN GP	Hungaroring	6	Canon Williams Team	G	3.5 Williams FW14B-Renault V10	*engine*	1/31
3	BELGIAN GP	Spa	6	Canon Williams Team	G	3.5 Williams FW14B-Renault V10		4/30
5	ITALIAN GP	Monza	6	Canon Williams Team	G	3.5 Williams FW14B-Renault V10	*led until car stuck in 4th gear*	4/28
ret	PORTUGUESE GP	Estoril	6	Canon Williams Team	G	3.5 Williams FW14B-Renault V10	*crashed after hitting Berger*	2/26
1	JAPANESE GP	Suzuka	6	Canon Williams Team	G	3.5 Williams FW14B-Renault V10		2/24
ret	AUSTRALIAN GP	Adelaide	6	Canon Williams Team	G	3.5 Williams FW14B-Renault V10	*fuel pressure*	3/26

1993 Championship position: 5th Wins: 0 Pole positions: 0 Fastest laps: 0 Points scored: 20

ret	SOUTH AFRICAN GP	Kyalami	6	Camel Benetton Ford	G	3.5 Benetton B192B-Ford HB V8	*spun off*	7/26
ret	BRAZILIAN GP	Interlagos	6	Camel Benetton Ford	G	3.5 Benetton B192B-Ford HB V8	*active suspension*	6/26
5	EUROPEAN GP	Donington	6	Camel Benetton Ford	G	3.5 Benetton B193B-Ford HB V8	*2 laps behind*	10/26
ret	SAN MARINO GP	Imola	6	Camel Benetton Ford	G	3.5 Benetton B193B-Ford HB V8	*spun off and stalled on lap 1*	11/26
4	SPANISH GP	Barcelona	6	Camel Benetton Ford	G	3.5 Benetton B193B-Ford HB V8	*1 lap behind*	5/26
ret	MONACO GP	Monte Carlo	6	Camel Benetton Ford	G	3.5 Benetton B193B-Ford HB V8	*engine*	6/26
ret	CANADIAN GP	Montreal	6	Camel Benetton Ford	G	3.5 Benetton B193B-Ford HB V8	*driver cramp*	4/26
10	FRENCH GP	Magny Cours	6	Camel Benetton Ford	G	3.5 Benetton B193B-Ford HB V8	*pit stop – collision – C Fittipaldi/-2 laps*	12/26
3	BRITISH GP	Silverstone	6	Camel Benetton Ford	G	3.5 Benetton B193B-Ford HB V8		5/26
5	GERMAN GP	Hockenheim	6	Camel Benetton Ford	G	3.5 Benetton B193B-Ford HB V8		7/26
2	HUNGARIAN GP	Hungaroring	6	Camel Benetton Ford	G	3.5 Benetton B193B-Ford HB V8		5/26
6	BELGIAN GP	Spa	6	Camel Benetton Ford	G	3.5 Benetton B193B-Ford HB V8	*1 lap behind*	8/25
5	ITALIAN GP	Monza	6	Camel Benetton Ford	G	3.5 Benetton B193B-Ford HB V8	*active suspension/1 lap behind*	10/26
16/ret	PORTUGUESE GP	Estoril	6	Camel Benetton Ford	G	3.5 Benetton B193B-Ford HB V8	*hit Warwick – spun off/8 laps behind*	7/26
ret	JAPANESE GP	Suzuka	6	Camel Benetton Ford	G	3.5 Benetton B193B-Ford HB V8	*oil on tyres – crashed*	10/27
8/ret	AUSTRALIAN GP	Adelaide	6	Camel Benetton Ford	G	3.5 Benetton B193B-Ford HB V8	*engine/2 laps behind*	9/24

GP Starts: 255 (256)   GP Wins: 6   Pole positions: 8   Fastest laps: 13   Points: 281

The popular Patrese enjoyed a five-year spell with Williams, but only won four races between 1988 and 1992. Pictured left, the veteran Italian takes the FW14 to victory in the 1991 Mexican Grand Prix.

AL PEASE

BORN in England, Al Pease joined the army at the age of 17 and soon found himself stationed in India, before switching to the RAF for wartime service in Rhodesia and Egypt. After the hostilities had ended, he found employment as an illustrator in the USA, before finally settling in Canada, where he succeeded in developing his career in the graphic arts. Indeed, Pease ran his own commercial art company, which worked for some major clients for more than 25 years. Gainfully employed, Pease began racing a Riley for fun in the early 1950s, before moving on to MGs. He made quite a mark with a potent supercharged MGB, before buying a pure racing machine, a Lotus 23, with which he finished eighth in the 1963 Canadian Grand Prix for sports cars. His business connections with BMC led him to a successful racing campaign with a Mini during the 1964 season, and by 1967 he had acquired a Lotus 47 sports car, which was sponsored by Castrol Canada.

Then the oil giant purchased an uncompetitive Eagle-Climax and asked Pease to run it in the inaugural 1967 Canadian Grand Prix at Mosport. At the start of rain-sodden race, the car refused to fire up, and the race was six laps old before he was on his way. Later he spun and stalled. Unable to restart the engine, he hotfooted it back to the pits and returned to his car to fit a new battery. He struggled on, crossing the line some 43 laps down on the winner! He returned for the big race again the following year, but engine problems precluded a start this time round.

For 1969, Pease tried his hand at the Formula A Series with a Lola T140, taking third place in the opener at Mosport, but achieving little else of note. He returned to the same track for the grand prix once more with the venerable Eagle. Despite qualifying respectably, he proved to be nothing but a dangerous mobile chicane in the race, and after a number of close calls with the fast boys, he was rightly black-flagged for being too slow.

Subsequently, Pease raced a Brabham BT23B-Climax in the 1970 season, winning the last ever race at Harewood Acres, before his business responsibilities forced an end to his racing activities. Later he acted as the secretary of the Canadian Race Drivers Association and then was drawn into the Canadian vintage racing scene in the 1980s, rebuilding and restoring a number of machines, a hobby that he took into his retirement in Tennessee, USA.

PEASE, Al (CDN) b 15/10/1921, Darlington, GB

	Race	Circuit	No	Entrant		Tyres	Capacity/Car/Engine	Comment	Q Pos/Entries
	1967 Championship position: Unplaced								
nc	CANADIAN GP	Mosport Park	11	Castrol Oils Ltd		G	2.7 Eagle T1G-Climax 4	*43 laps behind*	16/19
	1968 Championship position: Unplaced								
dns	CANADIAN GP	St Jovite	25	Castrol Oils Ltd		G	2.7 Eagle T1G-Climax 4	*engine failure in practice*	(17)/20
	1969 Championship position: Unplaced								
dsq*	CANADIAN GP	Mosport Park	69	John Maryon		F	2.7 Eagle T1G-Climax 4	**black flagged – too slow*	17/20
	GP Starts: 2 GP Wins: 0 Pole positions: 0 Fastest laps: 0 Points: 0								

PENSKE, Roger (USA) b 20/2/1937, Shaker Heights, Ohio

	Race	Circuit	No	Entrant		Tyres	Capacity/Car/Engine	Comment	Q Pos/Entries
	1961 Championship position: Unplaced								
8	US GP	Watkins Glen	6	John M Wyatt III		D	1.5 Cooper T53-Climax 4	*4 laps behind*	16/19
	1962 Championship position: Unplaced								
9	US GP	Watkins Glen	14	Dupont Team Zerex		D	1.5 Lotus 24-Climax V8	*4 laps behind*	13/20
	GP Starts: 2 GP Wins: 0 Pole positions: 0 Fastest laps: 0 Points: 0								

PERDISA, Cesare (I) b 21/10/1932, Bologna – d 10/5/1998, Bologna

	Race	Circuit	No	Entrant		Tyres	Capacity/Car/Engine	Comment	Q Pos/Entries
	1955 Championship position: 12th= Wins: 0 Pole positions: 0 Fastest laps: 0 Points scored: 2								
ret*	MONACO GP	Monte Carlo	40	Officine Alfieri Maserati		P	2.5 Maserati 250F 6	**Behra took over and spun off*	11/22
3*	"	" "	34	Officine Alfieri Maserati		P	2.5 Maserati 250F 6	**took over Behra's car/1 lap behind*	- / -
8	BELGIAN GP	Spa	26	Officine Alfieri Maserati		P	2.5 Maserati 250F 6	*3 laps behind*	13/14
	1956 Championship position: 12th= Wins: 0 Pole positions: 0 Fastest laps: 0 Points scored: 3								
7	MONACO GP	Monte Carlo	32	Officine Alfieri Maserati		P	2.5 Maserati 250F 6	*pit stops/14 laps behind*	7/19
3*	BELGIAN GP	Spa	34	Officine Alfieri Maserati		P	2.5 Maserati 250F 6	**Moss took over*	9/16
5*	FRENCH GP	Reims	6	Officine Alfieri Maserati		P	2.5 Maserati 250F 6	**Moss took over/2 laps behind*	13/20
7	BRITISH GP	Silverstone	9	Officine Alfieri Maserati		P	2.5 Maserati 250F 6	*6 laps behind*	15/28
dns	GERMAN GP	Nürburgring	8	Officine Alfieri Maserati		P	2.5 Maserati 250F 6	*injured – Maglioli drove car*	(6)/21
	1957 Championship position: Unplaced								
6*	ARGENTINE GP	Buenos Aires	18	Scuderia Ferrari		E	2.5 Lancia-Ferrari D50 V8	**Collins/von Trips co-drove/-2 laps*	11/16
	GP Starts: 7 GP Wins: 0 Pole positions: 0 Fastest laps: 0 Points: 5								

ROGER PENSKE

ROGER PENSKE the racing driver has long since disappeared into the mists of time, to be replaced by the imposing figure who has built a vast business empire and progressively developed a small racing team, with Mark Donohue as first driver, into one of the premier powers in US racing, winning a record number of Indianapolis 500 victories (15 up to and including the 2011 event).

However, Penske was a very good driver indeed. Racing a Porsche RSK, he won the SCCA 'F' category championship in 1960, before acquiring a Cooper-Monaco, which he modified and later renamed the Zerex Special. Between 1961 and 1963, he gained many successes with this car and performed equally well in others sports cars, such as John Mecom's Ferrari GTO.

Penske's F1 drives in the United States Grand Prix of 1961 and 1962 offered him little but the chance to rub shoulders with the stars of the day, although he did bring his cars home to the finish. In 1964, he raced in future rival Jim Hall's Chaparral team, winning races at Monterey and Nassau, and taking second place in the Riverside Grand Prix. At the end of the season, he retired from driving to start his entrepreneurial business career, which now encompasses many facets of the automobile industry worldwide.

Penske himself is reputed to have a net worth of well over $1 billion, but despite his myriad business responsibilities, the 75-year-old remains a committed racer at heart, never happier than when directing operations from the pit wall.

Apart from his long-standing successes in Indy car racing, Penske has been victorious in many other forms of racing. His team competed in Formula 1 (with John Watson winning the 1976 Austrian Grand Prix), sports protoypes (in the ALMS with Porsche, taking the LMP2 honours three times between 2006 and 2008) and NASCAR (where his team finally clinched a victory in the 2008 Daytona 500 with Ryan Newman).

CESARE PERDISA

FROM a wealthy publishing background, Cesare Perdisa first made his mark on the racing scene in 1954 with some excellent drives in his Maserati T200S sports car, finishing fourth at the Imola Grand Prix, fifth in the Portuguese GP and third at Syracuse. Proving that this was no flash in the pan, in the 1955 season he took wins at the Imola Shell GP and the Bari GP, and second place at the Monza Supercortemaggiore in works machines; at his first grand prix, at Monaco, Jean Behra took over his car to share a third-place finish.

After missing the early-season Argentine races due to appendicitis, Perdisa was back in harness by Monaco, but again his points finishes were due in part to the efforts of another driver, this time Stirling Moss. He was injured in a practice crash at the German Grand Prix and did not race for the Maserati team again.

Lining up for rivals Ferrari in Argentina at the start of 1957, he took a shared sixth place in the grand prix, seventh in the Buenos Aires City Grand Prix, and a win in the 1000km sports car race with co-drivers Masten Gregory, Eugenio Castellotti and Luigi Musso. On returning to Europe, however, his closest friend, Castellotti, was killed testing at Modena and Cesare lost all heart for racing, announcing that he would not race for some time. His place in the Ferrari for the Mille Miglia was taken by the ill-fated Alphonse de Portago. Perhaps due to pressure from his family, Cesare suddenly announced his retirement from racing and transferred his sporting interests to equestrianism, while working in the family business. His name is still remembered with the Cesare Perdisa Trophy, which is awarded to the winner of the Bologna-Raticosa Pass, a 6km run that celebrates the original 42km uphill mountain climb that he contested so fiercely in 1954, when he lost out to Castellotti by just five seconds.

SERGIO PÉREZ

THE Mexican nation had to wait 30 years to see one of its countrymen grace the grand prix stage, in the shape of journeyman racer Héctor Rebaque, who failed to cause even a ripple of excitement with his performances. Fast forward to 27th March, 2011, and the 21-year-old Sergio Pérez stunned onlookers by completing the 58 laps of the Australian Grand Prix at Melbourne by taking just a single pit stop on his way to seventh place in his Sauber-Ferrari. The debut performance from the Mexican rookie was worthy of the Rodriguez brothers, and it was such a shame that a technical error by the team caused him to be disqualified from the results. Perhaps most importantly, 'Checo' had made an immediate impression on the F1 fraternity; his top-line career had received the perfect kick-start. He was up and running.

Sergio began karting at the age of seven, and a year later he was the youngest driver to win the Junior category, before going on to become the champion in 1998. He continued to record successes in the karting classes at home and, occasionally, in the USA. At the tender age of 14, he graduated to cars in the Midwestern League in the National Formula Skip Barber series, becoming the youngest driver to achieve a podium; he was also awarded Rookie of the Year honours.

Pérez then moved to Europe in 2005 to compete in Formula BMW Germany, where he shone despite his tender years. Choosing to consolidate in the following year, the young Mexican joined the Mücke Motorsport team and recorded two podiums on his way to sixth in the standings.

Aged just 17, Sergio joined the British F3 series in 2007 to compete in the National class, which he took with 14 triumphs from just 21 starts. Inevitable promotion to the F3 Championship class in 2008 saw him take an early win at Croft and then a double-header victory at Monza. His early-season lead was eventually whittled away, however, and despite a further

win at Brands Hatch, he had to settle for fourth place in the standings. At the end of the year, he moved up to the GP2 Asia Series, taking wins in both Bahrain and Qatar for Campos, which put the youngster much in demand. Eventually, he secured a place in the Arden team for the GP2 series, where he scored a couple of podiums at Valencia in what was generally seen as a learning year.

A return to the Barwa Addax team (formerly Campos) in 2010 saw the Mexican really blossom, taking five wins, including a victory in the Monaco Grand Prix meeting. He was runner-up only to the much more experienced Pastor Maldonado. In October, 2010, with substantial backing from his homeland in the form of Telmex, Pérez was confirmed at Sauber; he had secured his place in Formula 1 before the age of 21.

Sergio's amazing debut performance in Melbourne perhaps raised expectations too high, for he achieved little in the next three races, before receiving a severe setback when he crashed very heavily in practice for the Monaco Grand Prix. After he lost control of his Sauber on the way out of the tunnel, the car suffered a massive side impact at the chicane, and he was lucky to escape with just heavy concussion, which ruled him out of the race. The after-effects of this crash ruled him out of the next race in Montreal, but the youngster soon returned to form with a then career-best seventh place at Silverstone. Sauber immediately confirmed his place on the team for 2012, and the Mexican lost no time in extending his future options by joining Ferrari's driver academy, which earned him a September test day – alongside Jules Bianchi – in a 2009 Ferrari.

With Felipe Massa's place on the Ferrari team looking ever less secure, Pérez appears to be a likely candidate to partner Fernando Alonso in the future, provided of course that he continues to impress with the Sauber team and its Ferrari engines.

PÉREZ, Sergio (MEX) b 26/12/1990, Guadalajara, Jalisco

2011 Championship position: 16th   Wins: 0   Pole positions: 0   Fastest laps: 0   Points scored: 14

	Race	Circuit	No	Entrant	Tyres	Capacity/Car/Engine	Comment	Q Pos/Entries
dsq*	AUSTRALIAN GP	Melbourne	23	Sauber F1 Team	P	2.4 Sauber C30-Ferrari V8	7th *dsq – rear wing element illegal	13/24
ret	MALAYSIAN GP	Sepang	23	Sauber F1 Team	P	2.4 Sauber C30-Ferrari V8	hit debris/extinguisher killed electrics	16/24
17	CHINESE GP	Shanghai Circuit	23	Sauber F1 Team	P	2.4 Sauber C30-Ferrari V8	1 lap behind	12/24
14	TURKISH GP	Istanbul Park	23	Sauber F1 Team	P	2.4 Sauber C30-Ferrari V8	1 lap behind	15/24
9	SPANISH GP	Barcelona	23	Sauber F1 Team	P	2.4 Sauber C30-Ferrari V8	1 lap behind	12/24
dns*	MONACO GP	Monte Carlo	23	Sauber F1 Team	P	2.4 Sauber C30-Ferrari V8	*injured in qualifying accident	10/24
dns	CANADIAN GP	Montreal	23	Sauber F1 Team	P	2.4 Sauber C30-Ferrari V8	driver unwell - withdrew after practice 1	– / –
11	EUROPEAN GP	Valencia	23	Sauber F1 Team	P	2.4 Sauber C30-Ferrari V8	1 lap behind	16/24
7	BRITISH GP	Silverstone	23	Sauber F1 Team	P	2.4 Sauber C30-Ferrari V8		12/24
11	GERMAN GP	Hockenheim	23	Sauber F1 Team	P	2.4 Sauber C30-Ferrari V8	1 lap behind	15/24
15	HUNGARIAN GP	Hungaroring	23	Sauber F1 Team	P	2.4 Sauber C30-Ferrari V8	2 laps behind	10/24
ret	BELGIAN GP	Spa	23	Sauber F1 Team	P	2.4 Sauber C30-Ferrari V8	collision – Buemi – drive thru/rear axle	9/24
ret	ITALIAN GP	Monza	23	Sauber F1 Team	P	2.4 Sauber C30-Ferrari V8	gearbox	15/24
10	SINGAPORE GP	Marina Bay Circuit	23	Sauber F1 Team	P	2.4 Sauber C30-Ferrari V8	1 lap behind	11/24
8	JAPANESE GP	Suzuka	23	Sauber F1 Team	P	2.4 Sauber C30-Ferrari V8		17/24
16	KOREAN GP	Yeongam	23	Sauber F1 Team	P	2.4 Sauber C30-Ferrari V8	excessive tyre wear/1 lap behind	17/24
10	INDIAN GP	Buddh Circuit	23	Sauber F1 Team	P	2.4 Sauber C30-Ferrari V8	1 lap behind	17/24
11	ABU DHABI GP	Yas Marina Circuit	23	Sauber F1 Team	P	2.4 Sauber C30-Ferrari V8	1 lap behind	11/24
13	BRAZILIAN GP	Interlagos	23	Sauber F1 Team	P	2.4 Sauber C30-Ferrari V8	1 lap behind	17/24

GP Starts: 17   GP Wins: 0   Pole positions: 0   Fastest laps: 0   Points: 14

Pérez made a big impact on his Grand Prix debut, running his Sauber-Ferrari to an truly impressive seventh place finish in the 2011 Australian GP. Sadly for the young Mexican, a technical infringement by the team, saw him disqualified from the results.

PERKINS, Larry (AUS) b 18/3/1950, Murrayville, Victoria

1974 Championship position: Unplaced

	Race	Circuit	No	Entrant	Tyres	Capacity/Car/Engine	Comment	Q Pos/Entries
dnq	GERMAN GP	Nürburgring	30	Dalton-Amon International	F	3.0 Amon AF101-Cosworth V8	practice crash – hit barrier	30/32

1976 Championship position: Unplaced

13	SPANISH GP	Jarama	37	HB Bewaking Alarm Systems	G	3.0 Boro Ensign N175-Cosworth V8	pit stop/3 laps behind	24/30
8	BELGIAN GP	Zolder	37	HB Bewaking Alarm Systems	G	3.0 Boro Ensign N175-Cosworth V8	1 lap behind	20/29
dnq	MONACO GP	Monte Carlo	37	HB Bewaking Alarm Systems	G	3.0 Boro Ensign N175-Cosworth V8		23/25
ret	SWEDISH GP	Anderstorp	37	HB Bewaking Alarm Systems	G	3.0 Boro Ensign N175-Cosworth V8	engine	22/27
ret	DUTCH GP	Zandvoort	27	HB Bewaking Alarm Systems	G	3.0 Boro Ensign N175-Cosworth V8	spun off	19/27
ret	ITALIAN GP	Monza	40	HB Bewaking Alarm Systems	G	3.0 Boro Ensign N175-Cosworth V8	engine	13/29
17	CANADIAN GP	Mosport Park	7	Martini Racing	G	3.0 Brabham BT45-Alfa Romeo F12	spin/2 laps behind	19/27
ret	US GP EAST	Watkins Glen	7	Martini Racing	G	3.0 Brabham BT45-Alfa Romeo F12	front suspension	13/27
ret	JAPANESE GP	Mount Fuji	7	Martini Racing	G	3.0 Brabham BT45-Alfa Romeo F12	withdrawn due to weather conditions	17/27

1977 Championship position: Unplaced

ret	BRAZILIAN GP	Interlagos	14	Rotary Watches Stanley BRM	G	3.0 BRM P207 V12	engine – lost water	22/22
15	SOUTH AFRICAN GP	Kyalami	14	Rotary Watches Stanley BRM	G	3.0 BRM P201B/204 V12	engine on 10 cylinders/5 laps behind	22/23
12	BELGIAN GP	Zolder	18	Team Surtees	G	3.0 Surtees TS19-Cosworth V8	2 pit stops – tyres/3 laps behind	23/32
dnq	SWEDISH GP	Anderstorp	18	Team Surtees	G	3.0 Surtees TS19-Cosworth V8		27/31
dnq	FRENCH GP	Dijon	18	Team Surtees	G	3.0 Surtees TS19-Cosworth V8		27/30

GP Starts: 11   GP Wins: 0   Pole positions: 0   Fastest laps: 0   Points: 0

LARRY PERKINS

A FFECTIONATELY known as the 'Cowangie Kid', because he came from the tiny village of that name in Victoria, Larry Perkins began an early love affair with all things automotive, inspired by his father, who was a racer in the 1950s. He came to Britain on the heels of Tim Schenken, with just as big a reputation, having blazed a winning trail through Formula Vee, Formula Ford and Australian F2 in three successive seasons between 1970 and 1972

Once in Europe, Perkins finished fifth in the 1972 Formula Ford Festival, before taking a shot at Formula 3 in 1973, his season improving after he switched to a works Brabham. In 1974, he was involved in the ill-fated Amon F1 project and an unhappy attempt to qualify at the Nürburgring, before re-establishing his career after dropping back into Formula 3 in 1975 with the works Ralt. On a limited budget compared to main rivals Gunnar Nilsson, Alex Ribeiro and Conny Andersson, he picked up wins and with them the European Cup.

Perkins landed a deal to drive the Boro (née Ensign) for the first part of 1976 and put in some determined performances before his big chance came with Brabham, replacing the Ferrari-bound Carlos Reutemann for the final three races of the season. To be frank, Larry failed to make the most of his chance and was definitely ruled out of contention for a full-time ride in 1977 when John Watson became available.

Next, Perkins signed a contract to race the truly awful Stanley-BRM in 1977, but after just two races he gratefully jumped from the sinking ship. Subsequently, he appeared briefly and unsuccessfully with Surtees, an inevitable parting of the ways occurring at the French Grand Prix, where the Australian was replaced by Patrick Tambay for the final practice session.

After returning to Australia, Larry – now something of a big fish in a small pond – was soon back to winning form in Formula Pacific, and he regained some pride by winning the 1979 Australian F5000 series, before concentrating on a long, hugely successful and rewarding career in touring car racing.

Larry won the famous Bathurst race six times – three times with Peter Brock (1982, '83 and '84), once with Gregg Hansford (1993) and twice with Russell Ingall (1995 and 1997). He scored a number of other notable victories in the category, but somehow never managed to clinch the V8 Supercar Championship before his retirement from driving at the end of 2003. A much respected engineer and engine builder, he continued to oversee his Team Perkins entries in V8 Supercar, until withdrawal of manufacturer support prompted him to close the operation at the end of 2008. His franchises were taken over by Kelly Racing, who fielded Larry's son, Jack, running the number 11 made so famous by his father and his team over the years.

XAVIER PERROT

A SWISS garage owner, Xavier Perrot began competing in the early 1960s in strictly national racing events and hill-climbs with such machines as an Abarth-Simca and then a Lotus 23.

In 1968, Perrot purchased an ex-Winkelmann Racing Brabham to race in Formula 2, but found himself out of his depth. Not easily discouraged, he returned for more in 1969, and by mid-season he was looking more of a serious proposition, taking sixth in the F2 class in the German GP and fourth in the Rhine Cup at Hockenheim.

In 1970, Perrot equipped himself with the latest March 702 and gained a somewhat lucky win in the Preis von Deutschland at the Nürburgring, after Derek Bell ran into trouble on the last lap. This was the best result of the underrated Swiss driver's career. He continued in Formula 2 in 1971 and into early 1972, gaining some useful results; he actually drove Jo Siffert's March 701 in the Jochen Rindt Memorial Trophy F1 race at Hockenheim to finish 11th. Finding his F2 car ideally suited to hill-climbs, he returned to this form of the sport, winning the European Hill Climb Championship in 1972.

PERROT, Xavier (CH) b 1/2/1932, Zurich – d 8/12/2008, Zurich

	1969 Championship position: Unplaced							
	Race	Circuit	No	Entrant	Tyres	Capacity/Car/Engine	Comment	Q Pos/Entries
10*	GERMAN GP (F2)	Nürburgring	30	Squadra Tartaruga	F	1.6 Brabham BT23C-Cosworth 4 F2		24/26
	GP Starts: 1 GP Wins: 0 Pole positions: 0 Fastest laps: 0 Points: 0							

HENRI PESCAROLO

H AVING begun his lengthy involvement with the sport in a minor way during 1965, when he raced a Lotus Seven, Henri Pescarolo was offered the third place in the Matra Formula 3 team for the following year. It proved to be something of a false start to his F3 career, as his car was not ready until mid-season. It was a different story in 1967, however, when he became the man to beat, winning the European championship. His victories that year included the important events at Barcelona, Monaco, Rouen and Zandvoort, so his promotion to the Formula 2 team in 1968 was a formality. Supporting Jean-Pierre Beltoise, he put in some excellent drives, taking second places at Barcelona, Hockenheim, Zandvoort and Hockenheim again, before finishing the year with his first win at Albi. Highly regarded by Matra, he was given a run in the second V12 car in the end-of-season grands prix.

Pescarolo's career then received a major setback when, while testing the Matra sports car at Le Mans, he crashed on the Mulsanne Straight and suffered serious burns, which laid him low until mid-season. He did well to return at the German GP, where he took the F2 Matra into fifth place overall and won the small-capacity class; the season ended on a bright note when he shared the MS630 sports car with Beltoise to win the Paris 1000km at Montlhéry. With Matra committed to their own grand prix project once more, Beltoise returned from his year with Tyrrell and Pescarolo joined him in the V12s. Henri put in some solid performances that year, a third place at Monaco being his best finish. He was also a member of the sports car squad, taking victory in the Buenos Aires 1000km with Beltoise.

Pescarolo was surplus to requirements at Matra in 1971 and took some backing from Motul to Williams, which enabled the team to go racing in both F1 and F2. Henri started the season with the old March 701 and picked up a second place on aggregate in the non-title Argentine GP, but Frank Williams soon became over-extended both financially and logistically, which showed in the team's preparation and lack of competitiveness as the year wore on. Meanwhile, Pescarolo pursued a parallel programme in sports cars with Alfa Romeo, winning the BOAC 1000km with Andrea de Adamich.

Despite all the problems, Henri was back in the Williams fold in 1972. It turned out to be a miserable season for all concerned, as his March 721 was involved in a succession of crashes that required extensive and expensive rebuilds. To cap it all, the prototype Politoys was written off in the midst of all this on its Brands Hatch debut. Fortunately, Pescarolo escaped the carnage largely unhurt and was buoyed up by his Le Mans win with Graham Hill in the Matra. Racing for the smart Rondel squad in Formula 2, he also won at Enna that year, and took another victory at Thruxton in 1973 after bringing Motul sponsorship to the team. With only the occasional grand prix ride that season, he returned to Matra for a hugely successful programme of sports car racing, winning at Vallelunga, Dijon, Le Mans (for the second time), the Österreichring and Watkins Glen.

With Motul backing once more, Pescarolo made a full-time return to grand prix racing with BRM in 1974, but the team had lost their way, and his only decent finish came in the International Trophy, where he was fourth. His partnership with Gérard Larrousse at Matra was still a potent one, however: he completed a hat trick of Le Mans victories, and scored other wins at Monza and the Österreichring. By then, of course, he was widely recognised as one of sports car racing's best talents, and in 1975 he returned to Alfa Romeo, winning rounds at Spa, the Österreichring and Watkins Glen, all with Derek Bell.

Henri made a last attempt to find success in Formula 1 with a privately entered Surtees in 1976, but neither he nor the car was remotely competitive. From then on, he concentrated on his sports car career, taking a fourth win at Le Mans in 1984 and raising his tally of world championship victories to 21 by the end of 1986.

In 1991, Pescarolo shared the winning Porsche at the Daytona 24-hour race, and subsequently he continued his career Stateside in IMSA, before focusing his efforts on Le Mans with the Courage C36.

More recently, Henri has looked after Elf's La Filière young driver scheme, which has helped so many French drivers to the top echelons of the sport. In 1999, he entered his own Courage C36-Porsche to register a remarkable 33rd Le Mans 24-hours start and finished in ninth place.

In 2000, Pescarolo began concentrating on management duties, founding Pescarolo Sport with the long-term aim of winning the Le Mans 24-hour race with a French team. Having tried in vain to win the big prize with the Courage-Peugeot combination, he opted for an all-new Pescarolo-Judd in 2004, and the new car finished fourth, behind a trio of all-powerful Audis.

Pescarolo came tantalisingly close to achieving his ambition in 2005, when his car (piloted by the French trio of Érik Comas, Eric Hélary and Jean-Christophe Boullion) was placed second, splitting the Audis. Victory was achieved in the Le Mans Endurance Series, however, where Pescarolo Sport took both the manufacturers' and drivers' crowns with wins at Monza and Istanbul.

While Henri has long since retired from circuit competition, he fulfills his insatiable appetite for speed by undertaking gruelling rally raids, such as the famous Dakar event, and various aeronautic challenges involving planes and helicopters.

PESCAROLO, Henri (F) b 25/9/1942, Paris

1968 Championship position: Unplaced

	Race	Circuit	No	Entrant	Tyres	Capacity/Car/Engine	Comment	Q Pos/Entries
ret	CANADIAN GP	St Jovite	19	Matra Sports	D	3.0 Matra MS11 V12	oil pressure	=20/22
dns	US GP	Watkins Glen	21T	Matra Sports	D	3.0 Matra MS11 V12	engine trouble in practice	(21)/21
9	MEXICAN GP	Mexico City	9	Matra Sports	D	3.0 Matra MS11 V12	3 laps behind	20/21

1969 Championship position: Unplaced

	Race	Circuit	No	Entrant	Tyres	Capacity/Car/Engine	Comment	Q Pos/Entries
5*	GERMAN GP (F2)	Nürburgring	26	Matra Sports	D	1.6 Matra MS7-Cosworth 4	*1st in F2 class/no points scored	14/26

1970 Championship position: 12th Wins: 0 Pole positions: 0 Fastest laps: 0 Points scored: 8

	Race	Circuit	No	Entrant	Tyres	Capacity/Car/Engine	Comment	Q Pos/Entries
7	SOUTH AFRICAN GP	Kyalami	4	Equipe Matra Elf	G	3.0 Matra-Simca MS120 V12	2 laps behind	18/24
ret	SPANISH GP	Jarama	22	Equipe Matra Elf	G	3.0 Matra-Simca MS120 V12	engine – con rod	10/22
3	MONACO GP	Monte Carlo	9	Equipe Matra Elf	G	3.0 Matra-Simca MS120 V12		7/21
6/ret	BELGIAN GP	Spa	26	Equipe Matra Elf	G	3.0 Matra-Simca MS120 V12	out of fuel/1 lap behind	17/18
8	DUTCH GP	Zandvoort	24	Equipe Matra Elf	G	3.0 Matra-Simca MS120 V12	2 laps behind	13/24
5	FRENCH GP	Clermont Ferrand	20	Equipe Matra Elf	G	3.0 Matra-Simca MS120 V12		8/23
ret	BRITISH GP	Brands Hatch	8	Equipe Matra Elf	G	3.0 Matra-Simca MS120 V12	spun off	13/25
6	GERMAN GP	Hockenheim	14	Equipe Matra Elf	G	3.0 Matra-Simca MS120 V12	pit stop – gearbox/1 lap behind	5/25
14	AUSTRIAN GP	Österreichring	20	Equipe Matra Elf	G	3.0 Matra-Simca MS120 V12	pit stop – wheel change/4 laps behind	12/24
ret	ITALIAN GP	Monza	42	Equipe Matra Elf	G	3.0 Matra-Simca MS120 V12	engine – valve spring	17/27
7	CANADIAN GP	St Jovite	24	Equipe Matra Elf	G	3.0 Matra-Simca MS120 V12	tyres worn out/3 laps behind	=8/20
8	US GP	Watkins Glen	7	Equipe Matra Elf	G	3.0 Matra-Simca MS120 V12	pit stops/3 laps behind	12/27
9	MEXICAN GP	Mexico City	7	Equipe Matra Elf	G	3.0 Matra-Simca MS120 V12	pit stop – gearbox/4 laps behind	11/18

1971 Championship position: 16th= Wins: 0 Pole positions: 0 Fastest laps: 1 Points scored: 4

	Race	Circuit	No	Entrant	Tyres	Capacity/Car/Engine	Comment	Q Pos/Entries
11	SOUTH AFRICAN GP	Kyalami	22	Frank Williams Racing Cars	G	3.0 March 701-Cosworth V8	2 laps behind	=16/25
ret	SPANISH GP	Montjuïch Park	27	Frank Williams Racing Cars	G	3.0 March 711-Cosworth V8	pit stop – rear wing-could not restart	11/22
8	MONACO GP	Monte Carlo	27	Frank Williams Racing Cars	G	3.0 March 711-Cosworth V8	pit stop – puncture/3 laps behind	13/23
13	DUTCH GP	Zandvoort	31	Frank Williams Racing Cars	G	3.0 March 711-Cosworth V8	spin – pitstop – nose cone/-8 laps	15/24
ret	FRENCH GP	Paul Ricard	27	Frank Williams Racing Cars	G	3.0 March 711-Cosworth V8	gearbox	18/24
4	BRITISH GP	Silverstone	26	Frank Williams Racing Cars	G	3.0 March 711-Cosworth V8	1 lap behind	17/24
ret	GERMAN GP	Nürburgring	14	Frank Williams Racing Cars	G	3.0 March 711-Cosworth V8	suspension	10/23
6	AUSTRIAN GP	Österreichring	25	Frank Williams Racing Cars	G	3.0 March 711-Cosworth V8		13/22
ret	ITALIAN GP	Monza	16	Frank Williams Racing Cars	G	3.0 March 711-Cosworth V8	suspension/FL	10/24
dns	CANADIAN GP	Mosport Park	27	Frank Williams Racing Cars	G	3.0 March 711-Cosworth V8	went off track in warm-up	(27)/27
ret	US GP	Watkins Glen	21	Frank Williams Racing Cars	G	3.0 March 711-Cosworth V8	engine	22/32

1972 Championship position: Unplaced

	Race	Circuit	No	Entrant	Tyres	Capacity/Car/Engine	Comment	Q Pos/Entries
8	ARGENTINE GP	Buenos Aires	23	Team Williams-Motul	G	3.0 March 721-Cosworth V8	2 laps behind	15/22
11	SOUTH AFRICAN GP	Kyalami	21	Team Williams-Motul	G	3.0 March 721-Cosworth V8	2 laps behind	22/27
11	SPANISH GP	Jarama	14	Team Williams-Motul	G	3.0 March 721-Cosworth V8	4 laps behind	19/26
ret	MONACO GP	Monte Carlo	22	Team Williams-Motul	G	3.0 March 721-Cosworth V8	aquaplaned – hit barrier	=8/25
nc	BELGIAN GP	Nivelles	15	Team Williams-Motul	G	3.0 March 721-Cosworth V8	pit stop – throttle problems/-26 laps	19/26
dns	FRENCH GP	Clermont Ferrand	16	Team Williams-Motul	G	3.0 March 721-Cosworth V8	crashed in practice	(12)/29
ret	BRITISH GP	Brands Hatch	24	Team Williams-Motul	G	3.0 Politoys FX3-Cosworth V8	steering failure – accident	26/27
ret	GERMAN GP	Nürburgring	20	Team Williams-Motul	G	3.0 March 721-Cosworth V8	crashed while 6th	9/27
dns	AUSTRIAN GP	Österreichring	22	Team Williams-Motul	G	3.0 March 721-Cosworth V8	accident in practice	(23)/26
dnq	ITALIAN GP	Monza	25	Team Williams-Motul	G	3.0 March 721-Cosworth V8	accident in practice	26/27
13	CANADIAN GP	Mosport Park	28	Team Williams-Motul	G	3.0 March 721-Cosworth V8	pit stop – handling/7 laps behind	21/25
14	US GP	Watkins Glen	26	Team Williams-Motul	G	3.0 March 721-Cosworth V8	2 laps behind	22/32

1973 Championship position: Unplaced

	Race	Circuit	No	Entrant	Tyres	Capacity/Car/Engine	Comment	Q Pos/Entries
8	SPANISH GP	Montjuïch Park	11	STP March Racing Team	G	3.0 March 731-Cosworth V8	2 laps behind	18/22
ret	FRENCH GP	Paul Ricard	26	Frank Williams Racing Cars	F	3.0 Iso Marlboro 1R-Cosworth V8	overheating	23/25
10	GERMAN GP	Nürburgring	26	Frank Williams Racing Cars	F	3.0 Iso Marlboro 1R-Cosworth V8		=11/23

1974 Championship position: Unplaced

	Race	Circuit	No	Entrant	Tyres	Capacity/Car/Engine	Comment	Q Pos/Entries
9	ARGENTINE GP	Buenos Aires	15	Motul Team BRM	F	3.0 BRM P160E V12	1 lap behind	21/26
14	BRAZILIAN GP	Interlagos	15	Motul Team BRM	F	3.0 BRM P160E V12	2 laps behind	22/25
18	SOUTH AFRICAN GP	Kyalami	15	Motul Team BRM	F	3.0 BRM P160E V12	2 pitstops – nose cone/6 laps behind	21/27
12	SPANISH GP	Jarama	15	Motul Team BRM	F	3.0 BRM P160E V12	pit stop/4 laps behind	21/28
ret	BELGIAN GP	Nivelles	15	Motul Team BRM	F	3.0 BRM P106E V12	spun off	15/32
ret	MONACO GP	Monte Carlo	15	Motul Team BRM	F	3.0 BRM P160E V12	gearbox	27/28
ret	SWEDISH GP	Anderstorp	15	Motul Team BRM	F	3.0 BRM P201 V12	fire on lap 1	19/28
ret	DUTCH GP	Zandvoort	15	Motul Team BRM	F	3.0 BRM P160E V12	handling	24/27
dns	"	"	15	Motul Team BRM	F	3.0 BRM P201 V12	practice only	– / –
ret	FRENCH GP	Dijon	15	Motul Team BRM	F	3.0 BRM P201 V12	clutch on startline	19/30
ret	BRITISH GP	Brands Hatch	15	Motul Team BRM	F	3.0 BRM P201 V12	engine	24/34
10	GERMAN GP	Nürburgring	15	Motul Team BRM	F	3.0 BRM P201 V12		24/32
ret	ITALIAN GP	Monza	15	Motul Team BRM	F	3.0 BRM P201 V12	engine	25/31

1976 Championship position: Unplaced

	Race	Circuit	No	Entrant	Tyres	Capacity/Car/Engine	Comment	Q Pos/Entries
dnq	MONACO GP	Monte Carlo	38	Team Norev Racing/BS Fabrications	G	3.0 Surtees TS19-Cosworth V8		22/25
ret	FRENCH GP	Paul Ricard	38	Team Norev Racing/BS Fabrications	G	3.0 Surtees TS19-Cosworth V8	rear hub	24/30
ret	BRITISH GP	Brands Hatch	38	Team Norev Racing/BS Fabrications	G	3.0 Surtees TS19-Cosworth V8	fuel pressure	26/30
dnq	GERMAN GP	Nürburgring	38	Team Norev Racing/BS Fabrications	G	3.0 Surtees TS19-Cosworth V8	fuel system problems	28/28
9	AUSTRIAN GP	Österreichring	38	Team Norev Racing/BS Fabrications	G	3.0 Surtees TS19-Cosworth V8	2 laps behind	22/25
11	DUTCH GP	Zandvoort	38	Team Norev Racing/BS Fabrications	G	3.0 Surtees TS19-Cosworth V8	1 lap behind	22/27
17	ITALIAN GP	Monza	38	Team Norev Racing/BS Fabrications	G	3.0 Surtees TS19-Cosworth V8	pit stop/3 laps behind	22/29
19	CANADIAN GP	Mosport Park	38	Team Norev Racing/BS Fabrications	G	3.0 Surtees TS19-Cosworth V8	3 laps behind	21/27
nc	US GP EAST	Watkins Glen	38	Team Norev Racing/BS Fabrications	G	3.0 Surtees TS19-Cosworth V8	hit chicane – pitstop/11 laps behind	26/27

GP Starts: 57   GP Wins: 0   Pole positions: 0   Fastest laps: 1   Points: 12

ALESSANDRO PESENTI-ROSSI

WITH only a few appearances in saloons and sports cars, Alessandro Pesenti-Rossi was regarded initially as an Italian national racer of little pedigree until 1974, when he did well in his GRD at home and undertook a couple of Formula 2 races with a Beta backed March, which brought decent finishes. In 1975, he really made his mark in Italian F3, where he was unlucky to miss out on a chance to take the title at the final race in Vallelunga. A rainstorm caused the race to be abandoned, leaving him one point shy of Luciano Pavesi in the title race. Meanwhile, he had managed to run in a few Formula 2 races in a Beta Tools backed March 742, running very competitively and consistently. His best placing was second on aggregate at Mugello, but the field was thin on talent, so his fourth at Vallelunga, behind Vittorio Brambilla, Jacques Laffite and Maurizio Flammini was perhaps more noteworthy.

After more promising performances in Formula 2 at the beginning of 1976, somewhat ambitiously perhaps, Sandro made his short-lived attempt to break into grand prix racing in mid-1976 with a privately entered Tyrrell 007. To be fair, at least he qualified for three of the four races in which he entered, and he brought the orange and white car to the finish, but in reality he was way off the pace. At the Nürburgring, he qualified 42 seconds slower than pole man James Hunt. He was far more respectable, however, at the Österreichring and Monza.

Sandro and his backers sensibly decided to invest their money more wisely the following year, when he returned to Formula 2 with a March 772, although three fourth places on home soil (at Vallelunga, Mugello and Misano) were the best he could muster. After he failed to qualify for the Preis von Württemberg at Hockenheim in a Chevron, at the start of 1978, no more was seen of the wiry Italian at this level.

JOSEF PETERS

A STALWART of both buoyant German domestic series of the early 1950s, Josef Peters drove a trusty two-seater Veritas. He made an assured debut at fearsomely fast Grenzlandring in 1950, taking fifth place. In 1951, he continued to obtain good results in the sports machine, and for 1952 he decided to run his Veritas Meteor to the new Formula 2 regulations.

Peters made regular trips into East Germany to take on the DDR's top drivers, but mostly he just seemed to make up the numbers. He finished third in the 1953 Formula 2 race at Grenzlandring – a meeting marred by the accident in which Helmut Niedermayr's car ran into the crowd with such devastating consequences.

The sports-bodied Veritas was put to good use in the 1953 Nürburgring 1000km, where Josef and Wolfgang Seidel took fifth place overall and won the 1500–2000cc class.

PESENTI-ROSSI, Alessandro (I) b 31/8/1942, Bergamo

1976 Championship position: Unplaced

	Race	Circuit	No	Entrant	Tyres	Capacity/Car/Engine	Comment	Q Pos/Entries
14	GERMAN GP	Nürburgring	40	Scuderia Gulf Rondini	G	3.0 Tyrrell 007-Cosworth V8	1 lap behind	26/28
11	AUSTRIAN GP	Österreichring	39	Scuderia Gulf Rondini	G	3.0 Tyrrell 007-Cosworth V8	3 laps behind	23/25
dnq	DUTCH GP	Zandvoort	40	Scuderia Gulf Rondini	G	3.0 Tyrrell 007-Cosworth V8		27/27
18	ITALIAN GP	Monza	37	Scuderia Gulf Rondini	G	3.0 Tyrrell 007-Cosworth V8	3 laps behind	21/29

GP Starts: 3   GP Wins: 0   Pole positions: 0   Fastest laps: 0   Points: 0

PETERS, Josef (D) b 16/9/1914, Düsseldorf – d 24/4/2001, Düsseldorf

1952 Championship position: Unplaced

	Race	Circuit	No	Entrant	Tyres	Capacity/Car/Engine	Comment	Q Pos/Entries
ret	GERMAN GP	Nürburgring	129	Josef Peters	–	2.0 Veritas RS 6-BMW 6 (sports car)		20/32

GP Starts: 1   GP Wins: 0   Pole positions: 0   Fastest laps: 0   Points: 0

RONNIE PETERSON

EVERYBODY loved Ronnie Peterson. Whatever your allegiances, the big blond Swede was the entertainer of the early 1970s, thrilling everyone with his astonishing car control. Just watching him drift a Lotus 72 through the old Woodcote Corner was worth the price of admission alone. With all that natural talent, surely he should have been a world champion; sadly, luck decreed otherwise.

Ronnie was Swedish karting champion between 1963 and 1966, and then switched to Formula 3, at first in a home-brewed special before acquiring a Tecno for 1968. This proved to be a wise move, as he took his national championship and on his sorties abroad showed talent to burn in recording wins at Hockenheim and a third place at Monaco. At this time, his big rival was compatriot Reine Wisell; he and Ronnie had many duels in the 1-litre F3 formula. Peterson won the prestigious Monaco race during a mega-successful 1969 season, in which he scored no fewer than 15 victories on his way to retaining his Swedish F3 title.

A couple of promising outings in Formula 2 showed that Peterson had something to offer at a higher level, and they brought the offer of a three-year contract with March from 1970. Initially, he was placed in a Colin Crabbe-entered F1 car, with which he gained some valuable experience in his first year, and he also ran a full season of Formula 2 guided by Malcolm Guthrie. The year yielded little by way of concrete results in either category, but he learned a huge amount, which was to put to good use the following year.

Promoted to the STP-March works team the following season, Ronnie quickly established himself as one of the grand prix racing world's leading talents, scoring four second places (Monaco, Silverstone, Monza and Mosport) to finish as runner-up in the world championship to Jackie Stewart. In Formula 2, he displayed Rindt-like qualities to take the European championship with four wins. Another two victories were recorded in non-championship events to emphasise his dominance over a very strong field of competitors.

Locked into the final year of his March deal, Peterson was lumbered with the very difficult 721X in 1972, and things improved only marginally when the hastily cobbled-together 721G was pressed into service.

Indeed there was a hint of desperation in Ronnie's driving on occasion, which drew doubts from some quarters as to whether he was championship material after all. His racing in Formula 2 was limited somewhat by a successful sports car programme for Ferrari; teamed with Tim Schenken, he won in both the Buenos Aires and the Nürburgring 1000km races and took four second places, at Daytona, Sebring, Brands Hatch and Watkins Glen.

Given joint number-one status with world champion Emerson Fittipaldi, Ronnie took the brave move of joining Lotus for 1973. Any doubts that had surfaced the previous season were swept away when the Swede proceeded to take nine pole positions and four grand prix wins. A poor start to the season (three retirements in the first four races) eventually counted against him, and third place in the championship certainly was not a true reflection of his efforts. So dominant was his form that Fittipaldi opted for McLaren for 1974, allowing Jacky Ickx to partner Peterson.

The season was desperately disappointing because of the difficulties experienced with the new Lotus 76, but the compensation for the Swede's army of admirers was the opportunity to savour his sublime driving talent a little longer at the wheel of the aged Lotus 72E. His wins at Monaco, Dijon and Monza were the stuff of true genius, but questions were being asked about his development abilities. His perceived lack of feedback meant that progress of the new Lotus challenger was not all it should have been. At Ferrari, Niki Lauda was proving that expertise in this area was becoming crucial to success.

Peterson was forced to soldier on in the old faithful 72E during 1975 while a new car was prepared, and he seriously considered defecting to the OUP Shadow team, but found extricating himself from his contract more difficult than he had imagined. Thus he was stuck with the old car, but could no longer compensate for its deficiencies. Not that it prevented him from driving in his usual 100 per cent manner, in contrast to team-mate Ickx, who just gave up the uneven battle and departed the team in mid-season.

Unfortunately, when the Type 77 was introduced at the opening race of 1976, it appeared to be another lemon, and then Ronnie contrived to collide with new team-mate Mario Andretti. This was the final straw, and he engineered a move out of Hethel and back to March for the rest of the season. In the underfinanced little team's car, he managed to score a brilliant win at Monza, but it really was a marriage of convenience, and the Swede was tempted away to join Tyrrell for 1977. However, the six-wheeler just was not suited to his style and he was regularly outpaced by team-mate Patrick Depailler. By the end of the year, his reputation had been seriously dented, but salvation was nigh. Colin Chapman took him back, albeit strictly as number two to Andretti, to race the superb Lotus 79.

Keeping his word, Peterson was content to play the support role in the team. Mario headed for his deserved championship win while Ronnie picked up the crumbs, in the shape of wins in South Africa and Austria. However, tragedy lay around the corner. At Monza, he became embroiled in a first-lap multiple crash, which left him suffering from severe leg injuries. Worse was to come, for in hospital complications set in. He slipped into a coma and within hours he was gone. The sense of disbelief was matched only by the grief felt throughout the motor racing world. For Lotus, what should have been a time of great joy became instead a period of hollow celebration.

More than 30 years have passed since Peterson's sad demise, but today there is a museum in his birthplace of Örebro, which no doubt will become a place of pilgrimage for those lucky enough to have seen him race, while younger visitors will have the opportunity to learn about Sweden's greatest racer.

PETERSON, Ronnie (S) b 14/2/1944, Orebro – d 11/9/1978, Milan, Italy

1970 Championship position: Unplaced

	Race	Circuit	No	Entrant	Tyres	Capacity/Car/Engine	Comment	Q Pos/Entries
7	MONACO GP	Monte Carlo	23	Antique Automobiles Racing Team	G	3.0 March 701-Cosworth V8	2 laps behind	13/21
nc	BELGIAN GP	Spa	14	Antique Automobiles Racing Team	G	3.0 March 701-Cosworth V8	spin – pit stop/8 laps behind	9/18
9	DUTCH GP	Zandvoort	22	Colin Crabbe Racing	G	3.0 March 701-Cosworth V8	2 laps behind	16/24
ret	FRENCH GP	Clermont Ferrand	18	Colin Crabbe Racing	G	3.0 March 701-Cosworth V8	transmission	9/23
9	BRITISH GP	Brands Hatch	27	Colin Crabbe Racing	G	3.0 March 701-Cosworth V8	pit stop – clutch/8 laps behind	14/25
ret	GERMAN GP	Hockenheim	22	Colin Crabbe Racing	G	3.0 March 701-Cosworth V8	engine	19/25
ret	ITALIAN GP	Monza	52	Colin Crabbe Racing	G	3.0 March 701-Cosworth V8	engine – camshaft	14/27
nc	CANADIAN GP	St Jovite	26	Colin Crabbe Racing	G	3.0 March 701-Cosworth V8	pit stops – fuel leak/25 laps behind	16/20
11	US GP	Watkins Glen	29	Colin Crabbe Racing	G	3.0 March 701-Cosworth V8	2 pit stops – tyres/4 laps behind	15/27

1971 Championship position: 2nd   Wins: 0   Pole positions: 0   Fastest laps: 0   Points scored: 33

	Race	Circuit	No	Entrant	Tyres	Capacity/Car/Engine	Comment	Q Pos/Entries
10	SOUTH AFRICAN GP	Kyalami	7	STP March Racing Team	F	3.0 March 711-Cosworth V8	pit stop – plug lead/2 laps behind	=13/25
ret	SPANISH GP	Montjuich Park	18	STP March Racing Team	F	3.0 March 711-Cosworth V8	ignition	13/22
2	MONACO GP	Monte Carlo	17	STP March Racing Team	F	3.0 March 711-Cosworth V8		8/23
4	DUTCH GP	Zandvoort	16	STP March Racing Team	F	3.0 March 711-Cosworth V8	2 laps behind	– / –
dns	"	"	16T	STP March Racing Team	F	3.0 March 711-Alfa Romeo V8	qualified in this car	13/24
ret	FRENCH GP	Paul Ricard	17	STP March Racing Team	F	3.0 March 711-Alfa Romeo V8	engine	12/24
2	BRITISH GP	Silverstone	18	STP March Racing Team	F	3.0 March 711-Cosworth V8		5/24
5	GERMAN GP	Nürburgring	15	STP March Racing Team	F	3.0 March 711-Cosworth V8	pit stop – radiator cover	7/23
8	AUSTRIAN GP	Österreichring	17	STP March Racing Team	F	3.0 March 711-Cosworth V8	handling problems/1 lap behind	11/22
2	ITALIAN GP	Monza	25	STP March Racing Team	F	3.0 March 711-Cosworth V8		6/24
2	CANADIAN GP	Mosport Park	17	STP March Racing Team	F	3.0 March 711-Cosworth V8		6/27
3	US GP	Watkins Glen	25	STP March Racing Team	F	3.0 March 711-Cosworth V8		12/32

1972 Championship position: 9th   Wins: 0   Pole positions: 0   Fastest laps: 0   Points scored: 12

	Race	Circuit	No	Entrant	Tyres	Capacity/Car/Engine	Comment	Q Pos/Entries
6	ARGENTINE GP	Buenos Aires	14	STP March Racing Team	G	3.0 March 721-Cosworth V8	spin/1 lap behind	10/22
5	SOUTH AFRICAN GP	Kyalami	3	STP March Racing Team	G	3.0 March 721-Cosworth V8	handling problems	=8/27
ret	SPANISH GP	Jarama	2	STP March Racing Team	G	3.0 March 721X-Cosworth V8	fuel leak/suspension/body damage	9/26
11	MONACO GP	Monte Carlo	3	STP March Racing Team	G	3.0 March 721X-Cosworth V8	hit Ickx – pit stop/4 laps behind	15/25
dns	"	" "	3T	STP March Racing Team	G	3.0 March 721-Cosworth V8	practice only	– / –
9	BELGIAN GP	Nivelles	11	STP March Racing Team	G	3.0 March 721X-Cosworth V8	2 laps behind	14/26
5	FRENCH GP	Clermont Ferrand	12	STP March Racing Team	G	3.0 March 721G-Cosworth V8	broken roll bar	9/29
7/ret	BRITISH GP	Brands Hatch	3	STP March Racing Team	G	3.0 March 721G-Cosworth V8	out of fuel – spun off/2 laps behind	=8/27
3	GERMAN GP	Nürburgring	10	STP March Racing Team	G	3.0 March 721G-Cosworth V8	spin	4/27
12	AUSTRIAN GP	Österreichring	5	STP March Racing Team	G	3.0 March 721G-Cosworth V8	pit stop – fuel/2 laps behind	11/26
9	ITALIAN GP	Monza	19	STP March Racing Team	G	3.0 March 721G-Cosworth V8	pit stop – handling/1 lap behind	24/27
dsq	CANADIAN GP	Mosport Park	25	STP March Racing Team	G	3.0 March 721G-Cosworth V8	push start after collision	3/25
4	US GP	Watkins Glen	4	STP March Racing Team	G	3.0 March 721G-Cosworth V8	accident in practice	27/32

1973 Championship position: 3rd   Wins: 4   Pole positions: 9   Fastest laps: 2   Points scored: 52

	Race	Circuit	No	Entrant	Tyres	Capacity/Car/Engine	Comment	Q Pos/Entries
ret	ARGENTINE GP	Buenos Aires	4	John Player Team Lotus	G	3.0 Lotus 72D-Cosworth V8	oil pressure	5/19
ret	BRAZILIAN GP	Interlagos	2	John Player Team Lotus	G	3.0 Lotus 72D-Cosworth V8	rear wheel	1/20
11	SOUTH AFRICAN GP	Kyalami	2	John Player Team Lotus	G	3.0 Lotus 72D-Cosworth V8	pit stop – throttle linkage/6 laps behind	4/25
ret	SPANISH GP	Montjuich Park	2	John Player Team Lotus	G	3.0 Lotus 72E-Cosworth V8	gearbox/FL	1/22
ret	BELGIAN GP	Zolder	2	John Player Team Lotus	G	3.0 Lotus 72E-Cosworth V8	spun off	1/23
3	MONACO GP	Monte Carlo	2	John Player Team Lotus	G	3.0 Lotus 72E-Cosworth V8	engine problems/1 lap behind	2/26
2	SWEDISH GP	Anderstorp	2	John Player Team Lotus	G	3.0 Lotus 72E-Cosworth V8	puncture on last lap when leading	1/22
1	FRENCH GP	Paul Ricard	2	John Player Team Lotus	G	3.0 Lotus 72E-Cosworth V8		5/25
2	BRITISH GP	Silverstone	2	John Player Team Lotus	G	3.0 Lotus 72E-Cosworth V8		1/29
11/ret	DUTCH GP	Zandvoort	2	John Player Team Lotus	G	3.0 Lotus 72E-Cosworth V8	gearbox/FL/6 laps behind	1/24
ret	GERMAN GP	Nürburgring	2	John Player Team Lotus	G	3.0 Lotus 72E-Cosworth V8	distributor	2/23
1	AUSTRIAN GP	Österreichring	2	John Player Team Lotus	G	3.0 Lotus 72E-Cosworth V8		2/25
1	ITALIAN GP	Monza	2	John Player Team Lotus	G	3.0 Lotus 72E-Cosworth V8		1/25
ret	CANADIAN GP	Mosport Park	2	John Player Team Lotus	G	3.0 Lotus 72E-Cosworth V8	puncture – spun off	1/26
1	US GP	Watkins Glen	2	John Player Team Lotus	G	3.0 Lotus 72E-Cosworth V8		1/28

Pure Peterson magic as the Swede takes his ageing Lotus 72E through Casino Square on his way to victory in the 1974 Monaco Grand Prix.

The 'ground-effect' 79 chassis gave Ronnie the platform to showcase his skills, but as the number-two driver at Lotus he was cast into a supporting role to Mario Andretti. A season of dazzling success for the Hethel team was made hollow by his death after an accident at Monza.

1974 Championship position: 5th — Wins: 3 — Pole positions: 1 — Fastest laps: 2 — Points scored: 35

13	ARGENTINE GP	Buenos Aires	1	John Player Team Lotus	G	3.0 Lotus 72E-Cosworth V8	*pit stop – battery – tyres/5 laps behind*	1/26
6	BRAZILIAN GP	Interlagos	1	John Player Team Lotus	G	3.0 Lotus 72E-Cosworth V8	*pit stop – tyre/1 lap behind*	4/25
ret	SOUTH AFRICAN GP	Kyalami	1	John Player Team Lotus	G	3.0 Lotus 76-Cosworth V8	*throttle – hit Ickx*	16/27
dns	"	"	1	John Player Team Lotus	G	3.0 Lotus 72E-Cosworth V8	*practice only*	– / –
ret	SPANISH GP	Jarama	1	John Player Team Lotus	G	3.0 Lotus 76-Cosworth V8	*engine*	2/28
ret	BELGIAN GP	Nivelles	1	John Player Team Lotus	G	3.0 Lotus 76-Cosworth V8	*fuel leak*	5/32
dns	"	"	1T	John Player Team Lotus	G	3.0 Lotus 72E-Cosworth V8	*practice only*	– / –
1	MONACO GP	Monte Carlo	1	John Player Team Lotus	G	3.0 Lotus 72E-Cosworth V8	FL	3/28
ret	SWEDISH GP	Anderstorp	1	John Player Team Lotus	G	3.0 Lotus 72E-Cosworth V8	*driveshaft*	5/28
dns	"	"	1T	John Player Team Lotus	G	3.0 Lotus 76-Cosworth V8	*practice only*	– / –
8	DUTCH GP	Zandvoort	1	John Player Team Lotus	G	3.0 Lotus 72E-Cosworth V8	*pit stop –tyres/FL/2 laps behind*	10/27
1	FRENCH GP	Dijon	1	John Player Team Lotus	G	3.0 Lotus 72E-Cosworth V8		2/30
dns	"	"	1T	John Player Team Lotus	G	3.0 Lotus 76-Cosworth V8	*practice only*	– / –
10	BRITISH GP	Brands Hatch	1	John Player Team Lotus	G	3.0 Lotus 72E-Cosworth V8	*pit stops – tyres/2 laps behind*	=1/34
4	GERMAN GP	Nürburgring	1	John Player Team Lotus	G	3.0 Lotus 76-Cosworth V8	*cobbled together race car*	– / –
dns	"	"	1	John Player Team Lotus	G	3.0 Lotus 72E-Cosworth V8	*crashed car in practice*	8/32
ret	AUSTRIAN GP	Österreichring	1	John Player Team Lotus	G	3.0 Lotus 72E-Cosworth V8	*driveshaft*	5/31
dns	"	"	1T	John Player Team Lotus	G	3.0 Lotus 76-Cosworth V8	*practice only*	– / –
1	ITALIAN GP	Monza	1	John Player Team Lotus	G	3.0 Lotus 72E-Cosworth V8		7/31
dns	"	"	1	John Player Team Lotus	G	3.0 Lotus 76-Cosworth V8	*practice only*	– / –
3	CANADIAN GP	Mosport Park	1	John Player Team Lotus	G	3.0 Lotus 72E-Cosworth V8		10/30
ret	US GP	Watkins Glen	1	John Player Team Lotus	G	3.0 Lotus 72E-Cosworth V8	*fuel line*	19/30

1975 Championship position: 12th= — Wins: 0 — Pole positions: 0 — Fastest laps: 0 — Points scored: 6

ret	ARGENTINE GP	Buenos Aires	5	John Player Team Lotus	G	3.0 Lotus 72E-Cosworth V8	*brakes/gearbox*	11/23
15	BRAZILIAN GP	Interlagos	5	John Player Team Lotus	G	3.0 Lotus 72E-Cosworth V8	*stalled on grid/2 laps behind*	16/23
10	SOUTH AFRICAN GP	Kyalami	5	John Player Team Lotus	G	3.0 Lotus 72E-Cosworth V8	*pitstop – tyres/1 lap behind*	8/28
ret	SPANISH GP	Montjuich Park	5	John Player Team Lotus	G	3.0 Lotus 72E-Cosworth V8	*collision with Migault*	12/26
4	MONACO GP	Monte Carlo	5	John Player Team Lotus	G	3.0 Lotus 72E-Cosworth V8		4/26
ret	BELGIAN GP	Zolder	5	John Player Team Lotus	G	3.0 Lotus 72E-Cosworth V8	*brake failure – crashed*	14/24
9	SWEDISH GP	Anderstorp	5	John Player Team Lotus	G	3.0 Lotus 72E-Cosworth V8	*1 lap behind*	9/26
15/ret	DUTCH GP	Zandvoort	5	John Player Team Lotus	G	3.0 Lotus 72E-Cosworth V8	*out of fuel/6 laps behind*	16/25
10	FRENCH GP	Paul Ricard	5	John Player Team Lotus	G	3.0 Lotus 72E-Cosworth V8		17/26
ret	BRITISH GP	Silverstone	5	John Player Team Lotus	G	3.0 Lotus 72E-Cosworth V8	*engine*	16/28
ret	GERMAN GP	Nürburgring	5	John Player Team Lotus	G	3.0 Lotus 72E-Cosworth V8	*clutch*	18/26
5*	AUSTRIAN GP	Österreichring	5	John Player Team Lotus	G	3.0 Lotus 72E-Cosworth V8	**rain-shortened race – half points*	13/30
ret	ITALIAN GP	Monza	5	John Player Team Lotus	G	3.0 Lotus 72E-Cosworth V8	*engine*	11/28
5	US GP	Watkins Glen	5	John Player Team Lotus	G	3.0 Lotus 72E-Cosworth V8		14/24

1976 Championship position: 11th= — Wins: 1 — Pole positions: 1 — Fastest laps: 1 — Points scored: 10

ret	BRAZILIAN GP	Interlagos	5	John Player Team Lotus	G	3.0 Lotus 77-Cosworth V8	*collision with Andretti*	18/22
ret	SOUTH AFRICAN GP	Kyalami	10	March Engineering	G	3.0 March 761-Cosworth V8	*accident with Depailler*	10/25
10	US GP WEST	Long Beach	10	Theodore Racing	G	3.0 March 761-Cosworth V8	*pit stop – boiling brake fluid/-3 laps*	6/27
ret	SPANISH GP	Jarama	10	March Engineering	G	3.0 March 761-Cosworth V8	*transmission*	16/30
ret	BELGIAN GP	Zolder	10	March Engineering	G	3.0 March 761-Cosworth V8	*spun avoiding Reutemann*	10/29
ret	MONACO GP	Monte Carlo	10	March Engineering	G	3.0 March 761-Cosworth V8	*spun off*	3/25
7	SWEDISH GP	Anderstorp	10	March Engineering	G	3.0 March 761-Cosworth V8		9/27
19/ret	FRENCH GP	Paul Ricard	10	March Engineering	G	3.0 March 761-Cosworth V8	*fuel metering unit/3 laps behind*	6/30
ret	BRITISH GP	Brands Hatch	10	March Engineering	G	3.0 March 761-Cosworth V8	*fuel pressure*	7/30
ret	GERMAN GP	Nürburgring	10	March Engineering	G	3.0 March 761-Cosworth V8	*accident – went off at Flugplatz*	11/28
6	AUSTRIAN GP	Österreichring	10	March Engineering	G	3.0 March 761-Cosworth V8		3/25
ret	DUTCH GP	Zandvoort	10	March Engineering	G	3.0 March 761-Cosworth V8	*oil pressure*	1/27
1	ITALIAN GP	Monza	10	March Engineering	G	3.0 March 761-Cosworth V8	FL	8/29
9	CANADIAN GP	Mosport Park	10	March Engineering	G	3.0 March 761-Cosworth V8	*1 lap behind*	2/27
ret	US GP EAST	Watkins Glen	10	March Engineering	G	3.0 March 761-Cosworth V8	*front suspension bulkhead*	3/27
ret	JAPANESE GP	Mount Fuji	10	March Engineering	G	3.0 March 761-Cosworth V8	*engine cut out*	9/27

1977 Championship position: 14th   Wins: 0   Pole positions: 0   Fastest laps: 1   Points scored: 7

			No	Entrant	Tyres	Capacity/Car/Engine	Comment	Q Pos/Entries
ret	ARGENTINE GP	Buenos Aires	3	Elf Team Tyrrell	G	3.0 Tyrrell P34-Cosworth V8	spun off	14/21
ret	BRAZILIAN GP	Interlagos	3	Elf Team Tyrrell	G	3.0 Tyrrell P34-Cosworth V8	accident avoiding Mass & Regazzoni	8/22
ret	SOUTH AFRICAN GP	Kyalami	3	Elf Team Tyrrell	G	3.0 Tyrrell P34-Cosworth V8	fuel pressure	7/23
ret	US GP WEST	Long Beach	3	Elf Team Tyrrell	G	3.0 Tyrrell P34-Cosworth V8	fuel line	10/22
8	SPANISH GP	Jarama	3	Elf Team Tyrrell	G	3.0 Tyrrell P34-Cosworth V8	1 lap behind	15/31
ret	MONACO GP	Monte Carlo	3	Elf Team Tyrrell	G	3.0 Tyrrell P34-Cosworth V8	brakes	4/26
3	BELGIAN GP	Zolder	3	Elf Team Tyrrell	G	3.0 Tyrrell P34-Cosworth V8		8/32
ret	SWEDISH GP	Anderstorp	3	Elf Team Tyrrell	G	3.0 Tyrrell P34-Cosworth V8	ignition	10/31
12	FRENCH GP	Dijon	3	Elf Team Tyrrell	G	3.0 Tyrrell P34-Cosworth V8	pit stop – tyres/3 laps behind	17/30
ret	BRITISH GP	Silverstone	3	Elf Team Tyrrell	G	3.0 Tyrrell P34-Cosworth V8	engine	10/36
9/ret	GERMAN GP	Hockenheim	3	Elf Team Tyrrell	G	3.0 Tyrrell P34-Cosworth V8	engine/5 laps behind	14/30
5	AUSTRIAN GP	Österreichring	3	Elf Team Tyrrell	G	3.0 Tyrrell P34-Cosworth V8		15/30
ret	DUTCH GP	Zandvoort	3	Elf Team Tyrrell	G	3.0 Tyrrell P34-Cosworth V8	ignition	7/34
6	ITALIAN GP	Monza	3	Elf Team Tyrrell	G	3.0 Tyrrell P34-Cosworth V8		12/34
16	US GP EAST	Watkins Glen	3	Elf Team Tyrrell	G	3.0 Tyrrell P34-Cosworth V8	pit stops – tyres/FL/3 laps behind	5/27
ret	CANADIAN GP	Mosport Park	3	Elf Team Tyrrell	G	3.0 Tyrrell P34-Cosworth V8	fuel leak	3/27
ret	JAPANESE GP	Mount Fuji	3	Elf Team Tyrrell	G	3.0 Tyrrell P34-Cosworth V8	hit by Villeneuve	18/23

1978 Championship position: 2nd   Wins: 2   Pole positions: 3   Fastest laps: 3   Points scored: 51

			No	Entrant	Tyres	Capacity/Car/Engine	Comment	Q Pos/Entries
5	ARGENTINE GP	Buenos Aires	6	John Player Team Lotus	G	3.0 Lotus 78-Cosworth V8		3/27
ret	BRAZILIAN GP	Rio	6	John Player Team Lotus	G	3.0 Lotus 78-Cosworth V8	collision with Villeneuve	1/28
1	SOUTH AFRICAN GP	Kyalami	6	John Player Team Lotus	G	3.0 Lotus 78-Cosworth V8	took lead on last lap	12/30
4	US GP WEST	Long Beach	6	John Player Team Lotus	G	3.0 Lotus 78-Cosworth V8	pit stop – tyres	6/30
ret	MONACO GP	Monte Carlo	6	John Player Team Lotus	G	3.0 Lotus 78-Cosworth V8	gearbox	7/30
2	BELGIAN GP	Zolder	6	John Player Team Lotus	G	3.0 Lotus 78-Cosworth V8	pit stop – tyre/FL	7/30
2	SPANISH GP	Jarama	6	John Player Team Lotus	G	3.0 Lotus 79-Cosworth V8		2/29
3	SWEDISH GP	Anderstorp	6	John Player Team Lotus	G	3.0 Lotus 79-Cosworth V8	held up by Patrese	4/27
2	FRENCH GP	Paul Ricard	6	John Player Team Lotus	G	3.0 Lotus 79-Cosworth V8		5/29
ret	BRITISH GP	Brands Hatch	6	John Player Team Lotus	G	3.0 Lotus 79-Cosworth V8	fuel pump	1/30
ret	GERMAN GP	Hockenheim	6	John Player Team Lotus	G	3.0 Lotus 79-Cosworth V8	gearbox/FL	2/30
1	AUSTRIAN GP	Österreichring	6	John Player Team Lotus	G	3.0 Lotus 79-Cosworth V8	FL	1/31
2	DUTCH GP	Zandvoort	6	John Player Team Lotus	G	3.0 Lotus 79-Cosworth V8		2/33
ret/dns*	ITALIAN GP	Monza	6	John Player Team Lotus	G	3.0 Lotus 78-Cosworth V8	*fatal accident at 1st start	– / –
dns	"	"	6	John Player Team Lotus	G	3.0 Lotus 79-Cosworth V8	car damaged in practice	(5)/32

GP Starts: 122 (123)   GP Wins: 10   Pole positions: 14   Fastest laps: 9   Points: 206

PETROV, Vitaly (RUS) b 8/9/1984, Vyborg, nr St Petersburg

2010 Championship position: 8th   Wins: 0   Pole positions: 0   Fastest laps: 1   Points scored: 136

	Race	Circuit	No	Entrant	Tyres	Capacity/Car/Engine	Comment	Q Pos/Entries
ret	BAHRAIN GP	Sakhir Circuit	12	Renault F1 Team	B	2.4 Renault R30-V8	front suspension mounting bolt	17/24
ret	AUSTRALIAN GP	Melbourne	12	Renault F1 Team	B	2.4 Renault R30-V8	spun off on slicks	18/24
ret	MALAYSIAN GP	Sepang	12	Renault F1 Team	B	2.4 Renault R30-V8	gearbox	11/24
7	CHINESE GP	Shanghai Circuit	12	Renault F1 Team	B	2.4 Renault R30-V8		14/24
11	SPANISH GP	Barcelona	12	Renault F1 Team	B	2.4 Renault R30-V8	1 lap behind	14/24
13/ret	MONACO GP	Monte Carlo	12	Renault F1 Team	B	2.4 Renault R30-V8	gearbox failure/5 laps behind	14/24
15	TURKISH GP	Istanbul Park	12	Renault F1 Team	B	2.4 Renault R30-V8	collision – Alonso – puncture/-1 lap/FL	9/24
17	CANADIAN GP	Montreal	12	Renault F1 Team	B	2.4 Renault R30-V8	2 drive-thru penalties/2 laps behind	14/24
14	EUROPEAN GP	Valencia	12	Renault F1 Team	B	2.4 Renault R30-V8		10/24
13	BRITISH GP	Silverstone	12	Renault F1 Team	B	2.4 Renault R30-V8	puncture –extra pit stop	16/24
10	GERMAN GP	Hockenheim	12	Renault F1 Team	B	2.4 Renault R30-V8	1 lap behind	13/24
5	HUNGARIAN GP	Hungaroring	12	Renault F1 Team	B	2.4 Renault R30-V8		7/24
9	BELGIAN GP	Spa	12	Renault F1 Team	B	2.4 Renault R30-V8	*no time set	*24/24
13	ITALIAN GP	Monza	12	Renault F1 Team	B	2.4 Renault R30-V8		15/24
11	SINGAPORE GP	Marina Bay Circuit	12	Renault F1 Team	B	2.4 Renault R30-V8	tangled with Hülkenberg	13/24
ret	JAPANESE GP	Suzuka	12	Renault F1 Team	B	2.4 Renault R30-V8	caused multiple collision on lap 1	13/24
ret	KOREAN GP	Yeongam	12	Renault F1 Team	B	2.4 Renault R30-V8	accident – hit pitlane barriers	15/24
16	BRAZILIAN GP	Interlagos	12	Renault F1 Team	B	2.4 Renault R30-V8	1 lap behind	10/24
6	ABU DHABI GP	Yas Marina Circuit	12	Renault F1 Team	B	2.4 Renault R30-V8	held Alonso at bay for the last 40 laps	10/24

2011   Championship position: 10th   Wins: 0   Pole positions: 0   Fastest laps: 0   Points scored: 37

			No	Entrant	Tyres	Capacity/Car/Engine	Comment	Q Pos/Entries
3	AUSTRALIAN GP	Melbourne	10	Renault F1 Team	P	2.4 Renault R31-V8		6/24
17/ret	MALAYSIAN GP	Sepang	10	Renault F1 Team	P	2.4 Renault R31-V8	hit kerb/broken steering column/-4 laps	13/24
9	CHINESE GP	Shanghai Circuit	10	Renault F1 Team	P	2.4 Renault R31-V8		10/24
9	TURKISH GP	Istanbul Park	10	Renault F1 Team	P	2.4 Renault R31-V8		7/24
11	SPANISH GP	Barcelona	10	Renault F1 Team	P	2.4 Renault R31-V8	1 lap behind	6/24
ret	MONACO GP	Monte Carlo	10	Renault F1 Team	P	2.4 Renault R31-V8	multiple collision – hit barriers	11/24
5	CANADIAN GP	Montreal	10	Renault F1 Team	P	2.4 Renault R31-V8		10/24
15	EUROPEAN GP	Valencia	10	Renault F1 Team	P	2.4 Renault R31-V8	1 lap behind	11/24
12	BRITISH GP	Silverstone	10	Renault F1 Team	P	2.4 Renault R31-V8		14/24
10	GERMAN GP	Hockenheim	10	Renault F1 Team	P	2.4 Renault R31-V8	1 lap behind	9/24
12	HUNGARIAN GP	Hungaroring	10	Renault F1 Team	P	2.4 Renault R31-V8	1 lap behind	12/24
9	BELGIAN GP	Spa	10	Renault F1 Team	P	2.4 Renault R31-V8	spin – brakes	10/24
ret	ITALIAN GP	Monza	10	Renault F1 Team	P	2.4 Renault R31-V8	multiple collision on lap 1	7/24
17	SINGAPORE GP	Marina Bay Circuit	10	Renault F1 Team	P	2.4 Renault R31-V8	2 laps behind	16/24
9	JAPANESE GP	Suzuka	10	Renault F1 Team	P	2.4 Renault R31-V8		9/24
7	KOREAN GP	Yeongam	10	Renault F1 Team	P	2.4 Renault R31-V8	hit Schumacher/damaged steering	8/24
11	INDIAN GP	Buddh Circuit	10	Renault F1 Team	P	2.4 Renault R31-V8	1 lap behind	11/24
13	ABU DHABI GP	Yas Marina Circuit	10	Renault F1 Team	P	2.4 Renault R31-V8	1 lap behind	12/24
10	BRAZILIAN GP	Interlagos	10	Renault F1 Team	P	2.4 Renault R31-V8	1 lap behind	15/24

GP Starts: 38   GP Wins: 0   Pole positions: 0   Fastest laps: 1   Points: 64

VITALY PETROV

THE first Russian driver to represent his country in Formula 1, Vitaly Petrov is also refreshingly different in that he was not a graduate of the karting classes. Instead, he chose to gain a degree in meteorology at the University of Moscow, and once his motorsport career launched into orbit, he became known at home as the 'Vyborg Rocket'.

Petrov's first taste of competition was in the Lada Cup during the 2001/02 season, when he proved to be utterly dominant.

Venturing abroad for the 2003 season, Petrov opted to work his way up the ladder via the various Formula Renault junior classes. Competing in both Italy and the UK, he scored a win in the 2.0-litre UK British Winter Series and was encouraged to return for selected appearances the following year.

Without further opportunities abroad, Vitaly stayed at home to join the newly introduced Lada Revolution challenge for small-capacity sports cars, becoming the 2005 champion with ten wins. He also took part in the single-seater F3-style Russian Formula 1600 championship, winning this short-lived series after taking five victories.

Ready to take his talents to Europe for 2006, Petrov opted for the Italian-based Euroseries F3000, taking four wins and third place overall, before graduating to the world-level GP2 series in mid-season. There he found the level of competition a whole lot tougher. Nonetheless, the following year he secured a seat with Campos, and his slow, but sure progress was developed alongside team-mate and series veteran Giorgio Pantano. He learnt well, and by the end of the year he had scored his first victory, at Valencia.

Another season in situ saw further progress up the GP2 ladder, but despite a further win at Valencia and a rise to seventh in the rankings, Petrov was hardly seen as a bona-fide grand prix candidate at this stage.

Once a driver reaches a fourth season in GP2, it's usually make or break time for their career ambitions, and the Russian had no excuses in 2009. Paired with the very fast, but flawed Romain Grosjean, initially he was a little overshadowed, but as the season wore on his consistency paid dividends, throwing him into the championship mix. Helped by Grosjean's elevation to the Renault F1 team, Vitaly became the de facto team leader and the only challenger to the runaway Nico Hülkenberg, until an engine failure at Spa blunted his chase and he was forced to settle for second place behind the German in the overall standings.

The door to Formula 1 was now ajar, and noises were made about the vast untapped Russian market and a network of potential sponsors; no doubt a reported sum of £13.5 million was attractive enough for the Renault team to take on the Russian alongside Robert Kubica. The newcomer took a while to acclimatise in a team that was in the midst of a huge re-organisation. A very fine fifth place in Hungary was the undoubted highlight, although his sixth place in the Abu Dhabi finale, where he held Fernando Alonso's Ferrari at bay, was probably just as praiseworthy.

For 2011, Petrov signed another contract for a further two years with the rebranded Lotus-Renault concern and was thrust into the team leadership following Kubica's pre-season rally accident. His drive to third place in Melbourne was a welcome and surprising boost for the team, and in the next few races his car was surprisingly competitive, allowing the Russian to garner a few points, before the lack of development and the leadership of Kubica began to tell.

Frustration had set in for the driver, who felt gagged by the terms of his contract, which prevented him from speaking about the situation – until in an interview with the Russian media he vented his spleen.

"I haven't criticised the team, despite losing out many times. How much have we lost in pit stops? How much have we lost with tactics? I can say that we have lost places in about ten races, if not more."

Petrov added that Renault's main issue had been the fact that they couldn't keep pace with the development of other teams, a series of parts

having been introduced that failed to work as planned; the team also ran into problems with the unique exhaust system fitted to the R31.

Not unnaturally, the team's hierarchy took a dim view of his outbursts and, despite his sponsorship links, decided that he was just not fast enough. They negotiated the return to F1 of Kimi Räikkönen and opted for the undoubtedly quick Romain Grosjean as his partner.

Thus Petrov found himself out of a drive. "I think it is quite clear," he said. "I have a contract. But I've said before that even the world champion Kimi Räikkönen was asked to leave F1 by Ferrari for a certain amount of money. This is a world where anything is possible, and it is hard to do anything if someone wants you to be removed."

Petrov and his management set about looking for another berth on the grid. With few options open to him, it seemed strange that a potential place at Williams was not seen as the best option.

Indeed, the Russian's statement seemed somewhat disingenuous. "Look at the queue of drivers at Williams. I believe there are 20 people eager to take the second place there. Thank God I'm not in it."

Instead, at the 11th hour, Petrov used his funding to turf Jarno Trulli from his seat at Caterham. It is hard to see where the driver can take his F1 career from this new baseline in the lower reaches of the grid. He may have stayed in the game, but in truth he appears only to be making up the numbers for the moment, and his main ambition must be to secure the team's first ever world championship point.

FRANÇOIS PICARD

HAVING begun racing in 1949 with a Renault 4CV, François Picard switched to a Porsche and used it to win the 1952 Circuit of Agadir. From 1953 on, he became a well-known Ferrari privateer, racing mainly in France and North Africa. He gained some good results partnering Charles Pozzi, the pair winning their class at both the Reims and Hyères 12-hour races in 1954.

Over the next two seasons, Picard ran a Ferrari 500 Monza, gaining numerous placings, including second at the 1955 Coupe de Paris, and third in the Agadir GP and Paris 1000km of 1956. He continued in sports cars until the Moroccan GP of 1958, when he drove in his first, and only, single-seater race in Rob Walker's Cooper. The unlucky Picard crashed into Olivier Gendebien's spinning car, sustaining serious injuries that left him incapacitated for six months. Happily, he recovered, but he never raced again.

ERNIE PIETERSE

A LEADING figure on the South African stage, Ernie Pieterse raced saloons and GTs, finishing third in an Alfa Giulietta GTI in the 1958 Rand nine-hours, before eventually joining the burgeoning single-seater series in the early 1960s.

Racing an Alfa-engined Heron Special in 1961, Pieterse scored his first single-seater victory at Kyalami; later that year, he won the Rhodesian GP at Belvedere. He continued with this car into 1962, but soon replaced it with an ex-works Lotus 21-Climax 4, becoming national champion after a thrilling season-long battle with Syd van der Vyver. Joining the Lawson Organisation should have brought even more success in 1963, but despite a whole clutch of top-three finishes through to the end of 1964, outright wins eluded him.

Pieterse slipped from competition at this level after failing to qualify for the South African GP on New Year's Day, 1965.

PICARD, François (F) b 26/4/1921, Villefranche-sur-Saone – d 29/4/1996, Nice

	1958 Championship position: 0 Wins: 0 Pole positions: 0 Fastest laps: 0 Points scored: 0							
	Race	Circuit	No	Entrant	Tyres	Capacity/Car/Engine	Comment	Q Pos/Entries
ret	MOROCCAN GP (F2) Casablanca		54	R R C Walker Racing Team	D	1.5 Cooper T43-Climax 4 F2	hit Gendebien's spinning car	24/25
	GP Starts: 1 GP Wins: 0 Pole positions: 0 Fastest laps: 0 Points: 0							

PIETERSE, Ernest (ZA) b 4/7/1938, Parow-Belleville

	1962 Championship position: Unplaced							
	Race	Circuit	No	Entrant	Tyres	Capacity/Car/Engine	Comment	Q Pos/Entries
10	SOUTH AFRICAN GP East London		14	Ernest Pieterse	D	1.5 Lotus 21-Climax 4	11 laps behind	=13/27
	1963 Championship position: Unplaced							
ret	SOUTH AFRICAN GP East London		7	Lawson Organisation	D	1.5 Lotus 21-Climax 4	engine	12/21
	1965 Championship position: Unplaced							
dnq	SOUTH AFRICAN GP East London		22	Lawson Organisation	D	1.5 Lotus 21-Climax 4		25/25
	GP Starts: 2 GP Wins: 0 Pole positions: 0 Fastest laps: 0 Points: 0							

PIETSCH, Paul (D) b 20/6/1911, Freiburg im Breisgau

	1950 Championship position: Unplaced							
	Race	Circuit	No	Entrant	Tyres	Capacity/Car/Engine	Comment	Q Pos/Entries
ret	ITALIAN GP	Monza	28	Paul Pietsch	P	1.5 s/c Maserati 4CLT/48	engine at start	27/27
	1951 Championship position: Unplaced							
ret	GERMAN GP	Nürburgring	78	Alfa Romeo SpA	P	1.5 s/c Alfa Romeo 159 8	spun off	7/23
	1952 Championship position: Unplaced							
ret	GERMAN GP	Nürburgring	127	Motor-Presse-Verlag	–	2.0 Veritas-Meteor 6	gearbox	7/32
	GP Starts: 3 GP Wins: 0 Pole positions: 0 Fastest laps: 0 Points: 0							

PAUL PIETSCH

A NOTABLE pre-war driver, Paul Pietsch enjoyed success aplenty in hill-climbs with a Bugatti and an Alfa Romeo 'Monza' during the 1930s. In 1935, he was invited to join the Auto Union team. He did not get many opportunities to race, but shared the third-place car in the 1935 Italian Grand Prix with Bernd Rosemeyer, before branching out on his own with a Maserati in 1937. He really made a name for himself when he led the 1939 German Grand Prix, until plug trouble dropped him to third.

After the Second World War, Pietsch concentrated on building up his thriving motoring publishing business, but still found time to race a Maserati and a Veritas, winning the Eifelrennen in the latter in 1951. He was given a guest drive in works Alfa Romeo for that year's German Grand Prix, but crashed heavily in the race when lying fifth, luckily escaping injury. After another serious accident with his Veritas at AVUS the following year, he decided to quit for good.

Pietsch's name is famous in Germany, since he founded one of the biggest car magazines in the country, *Auto Motor und Sport*. In June, 2011, his publishing house, Motor Presse, decided to celebrate his 100th birthday by arranging the Paul Pietsch Classic. This special event, covering over 400km through the Black Forest and the Rhine Valley, featured more than 100 priceless classic cars.

ANDRÉ PILETTE

A NDRÉ PILETTE'S father, who had finished fifth at Indianapolis in 1912 and taken third place in the French Grand Prix the same year, died when he was only three. Nevertheless, tales of his exploits set the youngster on course for a career in motorsport.

After gaining some experience in the late 1940s with his own machines, Pilette joined Ecurie Belgique, finally taking their Talbot to sixth place in the 1951 Belgian GP. Then, at the Dutch GP, he had the first of two huge accidents and was seriously injured (the second, at Albi in 1952, wrote off the Talbot).

Pilette reappeared in Johnny Claes' Connaught at the grand prix at Spa in 1953 and then aligned himself with Gordini for 1954. He competed in only three grands prix, but raced in a good number of non-title races, his best results being second places at Chimay and Cadours. Back with his countrymen to form Ecurie Nationale Belge in 1955, ironically he only found success in the Coupe de Paris in a Gordini. The 1956 season started well, but then he had another bad accident in practice for the German Grand Prix that sidelined him for nearly two years.

André finished fourth at Le Mans in 1959, with George Arents in a Ferrari 250GT, and then second in 1960, again in a Ferrari, with Ricardo Rodriguez.

In 1961, André reappeared in single-seaters with the ENB Emeryson-Climax, which proved a total flop. Being a glutton for punishment, however, he was back in 1963 with an old Lotus 18/21 Climax four-cylinder, before a final fling in the ex-Powell Scirocco in 1964. Subsequently, he opened a racing school at Zolder, at which he oversaw operations until the late 1980s.

PILETTE, André (B) b 6/10/1918, Paris, France – d 27/12/1993, Brussels

	1951 Championship position: Unplaced							
	Race	Circuit	No	Entrant	Tyres	Capacity/Car/Engine	Comment	Q Pos/Entries
6	BELGIAN GP	Spa	24	Ecurie Belgique	E	4.5 Lago-Talbot T26C 6	3 laps behind	12/13
	1953 Championship position: Unplaced							
nc	BELGIAN GP	Spa	40	Ecurie Belge	E	2.0 Connaught A Type-Lea Francis 4	7 laps behind	18/22
	1954 Championship position: 15th= Wins: 0 Pole positions: 0 Fastest laps: 0 Points scored: 2							
5	BELGIAN GP	Spa	18	Equipe Gordini	E	2.5 Gordini Type 16 6	1 lap behind	8/15
9	BRITISH GP	Silverstone	19	Equipe Gordini	E	2.5 Gordini Type 16 6	4 laps behind	12/31
ret	GERMAN GP	Nürburgring	12	Equipe Gordini	E	2.5 Gordini Type 16 6	suspension	20/23

1956 Championship position: Unplaced

	Race	Circuit	No	Entrant	Tyres	Capacity/Car/Engine	Comment	Q Pos/Entries
6*	MONACO GP	Monte Carlo	4	Equipe Gordini	E	2.5 Gordini Type 32 8	*took Bayol's car/12 laps behind	– /19
6	BELGIAN GP	Spa	20	Scuderia Ferrari	E	2.5 Lancia-Ferrari D50 V8	3 laps behind	16/16
11	FRENCH GP	Reims	34	Equipe Gordini	E	2.5 Gordini Type 16 6	6 laps behind	19/20
dns	GERMAN GP	Nürburgring	11	Equipe Gordini	E	2.5 Gordini Type 32 8	practice accident – cracked ribs	(18)/21

1961 Championship position: Unplaced

dnq	ITALIAN GP	Monza	68	André Pilette	D	1.5 Emeryson P-Climax 4		33/33

1963 Championship position: Unplaced

dnq	GERMAN GP	Nürburgring	29	Tim Parnell	D	1.5 Lotus 18/21-Climax 4		23/26
dnq	ITALIAN GP	Monza	46	André Pilette	D	1.5 Lotus 18/21-Climax 4		27/28

1964 Championship position: Unplaced

ret	BELGIAN GP	Spa	28	Equipe Scirocco Belge	D	1.5 Scirocco SP-Climax V8	engine	20/20
dnq	GERMAN GP	Nürburgring	28	Equipe Scirocco Belge	D	1.5 Scirocco SP-Climax V8		24/24

GP Starts: 9   GP Wins: 0   Pole positions: 0   Fastest laps: 0   Points: 2

TEDDY PILETTE

HAVING followed his father, André, into the sport, Teddy Pilette cleared his own path, setting out in Formula Junior in 1962, then having a spell with the Fiat-Abarth GT team.

In 1965, Teddy used a Fiat-Abarth saloon to win his class in the Belgian championship and then became involved in a long-term association with Count van der Straten's VDS team, first driving an Alfa Romeo T33 and then a Lola T70.

In 1971, Pilette began racing in F5000, which is where he enjoyed his greatest success, winning the European championship with a Chevron B28 in 1973 and repeating the feat with a Lola T400 in 1975, before heading for a season in the United States.

Undoubtedly a useful driver, Teddy finally emulated his father's achievement by starting a grand prix in 1974. However, the rented Brabham hardly helped his cause. Later he became another of the masochists who tried to qualify the lumbering Stanley-BRM for three races in 1977, even campaigning the dreadful car in the British Aurora AFX series the following year.

In the mid-1990s, Pilette returned briefly to the racing scene as a constructor with a Formula 3 car that carried his name. This ill-starred machine was hopelessly outclassed and soon consigned to history.

PILETTE, Teddy (B) b 26/7/1942, Brussels

1974 Championship position: Unplaced

	Race	Circuit	No	Entrant	Tyres	Capacity/Car/Engine	Comment	Q Pos/Entries
17	BELGIAN GP	Nivelles	34	Motor Racing Developments	G	3.0 Brabham BT42-Cosworth V8	pit stop – tyres/4 laps behind	27/32

1977 Championship position: Unplaced

dnq	GERMAN GP	Hockenheim	40	Stanley BRM	G	3.0 Stanley BRM P207 V12		30/30
dnq	DUTCH GP	Zandvoort	29	Stanley BRM	G	3.0 Stanley BRM P207 V12		33/34
dnq	ITALIAN GP	Monza	35	Stanley BRM	G	3.0 Stanley BRM P207 V12		31/34

GP Starts: 1   GP Wins: 0   Pole positions: 0   Fastest laps: 0   Points: 0

PIOTTI, Luigi (I), b 27/10/1913, Milan – d 19/4/1971, Godiasco

1955 Championship position: Unplaced

	Race	Circuit	No	Entrant	Tyres	Capacity/Car/Engine	Comment	Q Pos/Entries
dns	ITALIAN GP	Monza	46	Scuderia Volpini/Luigi Piotti	P	2.5 Arzani-Volpini 4	mechanical problems – no time set	– / –

1956 Championship position: Unplaced

ret	ARGENTINE GP	Buenos Aires	8	Officine Alfieri Maserati	P	2.5 Maserati 250F 6	collision with Collins	12/15
dns	GERMAN GP	Nürburgring	18	Luigi Piotti	P	2.5 Maserati 250F 6	car driven by Villoresi	– / –
6	ITALIAN GP	Monza	40	Luigi Piotti	P	2.5 Maserati 250F 6	3 laps behind	15/26

1957 Championship position: Unplaced

10	ARGENTINE GP	Buenos Aires	28	Luigi Piotti	P	2.5 Maserati 250F 6	10 laps behind	14/26
dnq	MONACO GP	Monte Carlo	42	Luigi Piotti	P	2.5 Maserati 250F 6		20/21
ret	PESCARA GP	Pescara	12	Luigi Piotti	P	2.5 Maserati 250F 6	engine	13/16
ret	ITALIAN GP	Monza	12	Luigi Piotti	P	2.5 Maserati 250F 6	engine	17/19

1958 Championship position: Unplaced

dnq	MONACO GP	Monte Carlos	54	Automobili OSCA	–	1.5 OSCA 4 sports car		26/28

GP Starts: 5   GP Wins: 0   Pole positions: 0   Fastest laps: 0   Points: 0

LUIGI PIOTTI

A BUSINESSMAN and part-time racer, Luigi Piotti achieved minor success in sports cars, including a class win in the 1952 Tour of Sicily in an OSCA, third place in a rather weak Targa Florio with a Lancia in 1954 and a win in the Hyères 12-hours the same year, sharing a Ferrari with Maurice Trintignant.

Piotti made his Formula 1 debut in 1955, taking seventh place in the Syracuse GP in a works Maserati 250F, before purchasing a car for the 1956 season, in which he proved hopelessly slow, especially in the Argentine Grand Prix where he continually baulked faster cars, eventually colliding with Peter Collins' Ferrari. Later in the season, he caused a furore at the Italian Grand Prix by using his car to push Stirling Moss' fuel-starved machine into the pits and thus give the Englishman a chance to win the race.

Luigi plodded on through the 1957 season with the Maserati, and after finding little success in an OSCA in 1958 wisely returned to a more sedate occupation.

DAVID PIPER

FROM farming stock, David Piper began his career by competing in sprints and hill-climbs, but soon hit the circuits in a little Lotus XI before buying a Lotus 16. By swapping engines, he was able to race this in both F1 and F2 in 1959/60, perhaps his best result in the car being a second place in the 1960 Lady Wigram Trophy in New Zealand.

In 1961, Piper joined Jo Siffert on the Continent for a season of Formula Junior racing, before returning home to drive the F1 Gilby in the Gold Cup. Although he entered a handful of national F1 races in 1962, he had become disillusioned with single-seaters and bought a Ferrari GTO, which gave his career a new lease of life. Between 1962 and 1970, he raced all over the world in his own Ferraris and later Porsches, winning races in places as far afield as South Africa, Angola, Sweden and Japan, but always proving a reliable driver and a consistent finisher.

In 1970, Piper crashed his Porsche 917 while working on the Steve McQueen film Le Mans; a tyre deflated and the car was all but destroyed. As a consequence, he had to have his right foot amputated. A hospital visit from none other than Second World War legless flying ace Douglas Bader made him realise that it could have been much worse, and he set about planning a racing return in spite of his disability.

Later on, Piper returned to race in historic events, and he has become the magical touchstone of these enjoyable festivals with his stable of racing thoroughbreds.

PIPER, David (GB) b 2/12/1930, Edgware, Middlesex

	Race	Circuit	No	Entrant	Tyres	Capacity/Car/Engine	Comment	Q Pos/Entries
	1959 Championship position: Unplaced							
ret	BRITISH GP	Aintree	64	Dorchester Service Station	D	1.5 Lotus 16-Climax 4 F2	engine – head gasket	22/30
	1960 Championship position: Unplaced							
dns	FRENCH GP	Reims	34	Robert Bodle Ltd	D	2.5 Lotus 16-Climax 4	engine in practice	(21)/23
12	BRITISH GP	Silverstone	26	Robert Bodle Ltd	D	2.5 Lotus 16-Climax 4	5 laps behind	24/25

GP Starts: 2   GP Wins: 0   Pole positions: 0   Fastest laps: 0   Points: 0

NELSON PIQUET

THREE world titles testify to the standing of Nelson Piquet, yet some might begrudge him his successes, feeling that they were not earned in the manner of a true champion. Of course, the Brazilian couldn't have cared less. Racing above all to please himself, he went about things in his own way, and that approach generally paid dividends. He was never happier than being in possession of some technical advantage to employ, and he felt no embarrassment at using that edge to beat his hapless rivals.

Having raced karts and Super Vee cars in Brazil, Nelson travelled to Europe in 1977 to tackle the European F3 series, winning two rounds after switching to a Ralt chassis. The following year, he concentrated on Formula 3 once more, this time in Britain. His initial object was to beat Brazilian rival Chico Serra, who was getting a good press back home, but eventually it was Derek Warwick who became his sternest challenger for the two championships on offer that year. They ended up taking one apiece, but by then Nelson was interesting Formula 1 teams.

Mo Nunn gave him a debut in his forgiving Ensign, before the heavy steering of the BS Fabrications McLaren posed more searching questions. However, his practice performance in the third Brabham-Alfa at Montreal prompted Bernie Ecclestone to offer him a contract for 1979.

A superb early-season drive in the Race of Champions took Nelson into second place, and although the grand prix season yielded little by way of hard results, his superb car control was always in evidence and he was clearly seen as a driver destined for the very top.

When Niki Lauda quit towards the end of the season, Brabham did not have far to look for a new team leader to handle the Cosworth-powered BT49 in 1980. Nelson took three grand prix wins (United States West, Dutch and Italian) and finished runner-up to the Williams of Alan Jones that year. There were mistakes that cost him dearly in the title race, but for a driver with so little experience probably it was to be expected. He did have the consolation of taking the honours in the BMW Procar Championship, edging out Alan Jones in the one-make series.

The Brazilian went all the way in 1981, claiming the first of his three world titles. Perhaps the Brabham BT49C was so good that, after a tense and closely fought season, Nelson typically did just enough to edge out Carlos Reutemann in the final race at Caesars Palace.

Realising that turbo power had become a necessity, Brabham spent the 1982 season bringing their new BMW-engined car to a competitive state – achieved when Nelson won in Montreal – and then trying to make it reliable. Eleventh place in the championship table told its story, a string of retirements having taken their toll.

The knowledge gained was incorporated into the design of Gordon Murray's flat-bottomed 1983 contender, which had been designed for the mid-race refuelling tactics the team had pioneered the previous year. At the wheel of the splendid little BT52, Piquet battled with Alain Prost for the title. In perhaps his finest year, the Brazilian adapted his tactics to suit every eventuality, blending raw speed and aggression with patience and intelligence, and whittling away the Frenchman's championship lead before taking the crown at the last gasp at Kyalami.

In 1984, the Brabham was no match for the McLarens of Lauda and Prost, and even Nelson was left to struggle in their wake. Digging deep, however, he conjured up nine pole positions, and back-to-back wins in Montreal and Detroit to salvage something from a disappointing year. The end of the superb Piquet-Brabham relationship came in 1985, after Nelson had been hamstrung by running uncompetitive Pirelli tyres, but there was one last win, at Paul Ricard, where the hard-compound Italian tyres held sway.

Unhappy to labour under such a disadvantage and ready to better his financial position, with what seemed perfect timing Piquet signed for Williams for 1986. The season should have been a walkover for the Didcot team, but the atmosphere soon became strained as Nigel Mansell refused to play second fiddle to Nelson and set about launching his own title bid. Williams refused to intervene by means of team orders, and the upshot was that Alain Prost stole the championship, leaving Nelson to fume over what he saw as Williams' indecisive handling of team tactics. Honda were not pleased either and would switch to McLaren at the end of the following season.

Piquet knew the score in 1987 and was determined to win the championship despite Mansell. With a good deal of fortune and some help from his luckless team-mate, he did just that. His third title may have been achieved more by stealth than by absolute speed, but the results justified the means in his book.

A two-year spell at Lotus was a complete disaster for all concerned. The massive retainer Nelson picked up from Camel was out of all proportion to his on-track return, and while his bank balance may never have been higher than it was at the end of 1989, never was his stock so low. His subsequent inclusion in the Benetton team for 1990 was greeted with huge surprise, but as the season wore on, the wisdom of the move became apparent.

Nelson struck up a good working relationship with John Barnard, and the pair took the Benetton B190 to a very competitive pitch, the Brazilian exploiting others' misfortune to win both the Japanese and Australian grands prix. Even his sternest critics were forced to admit that his drive in Adelaide was right out of the top drawer. He took one more very fortuitous (but highly satisfying) win, at Mansell's expense, in Canada the following year, before being swept away amid the personnel changes that engulfed the team that season.

With no suitable F1 offers on the table, Piquet decided to try his hand at the Indianapolis 500 in 1992. Unfortunately, a huge crash in practice left him with very badly crushed feet and legs, easily the most severe injuries he had suffered in his long career, and his rehabilitation was long and painful. He vowed never to return to the cockpit, but once fit he was back at the Brickyard in 1993, and by qualifying for the race he finished the job left uncompleted 12 months earlier.

Competing mainly for fun, Nelson renewed his links with BMW and raced a 320i tourer in long-distance events, both at home and in Europe, usually with Ingo Hoffmann and Johnny Cecotto. He also made a couple of visits to Le Mans with the Bigazzi McLaren F1 GTR, finishing eighth in 1996 with Cecotto and Danny Sullivan.

After F1, Nelson set about building a successful career in commerce in his native Brazil, including backing the development an anti-theft device for haulage trucks.

Nelson returned to the track in January 2006 and won the 50th edition of Mil Milhas Brasileiras (Brazilian 1000 miles) at the Interlagos racing track. He drove an Aston Martin DBR9 alongside his son, Nelsinho, and Christophe Bouchut and Hélio Castroneves. He also set up the Piquet Sports racing team, which helped the rising fortunes of Nelsinho through the junior classes to eventually win a seat in the Renault grand prix team for the 2008 season.

PIQUET, Nelson Nelson Piquet Souto Maior (BR) b 17/8/1952, Rio de Janeiro

1978 Championship position: Unplaced

	Race	Circuit	No	Entrant	Tyres	Capacity/Car/Engine	Comment	Q Pos/Entries
ret	GERMAN GP	Hockenheim	22	Team Tissot Ensign	G	3.0 Ensign N177-Cosworth V8	engine	21/30
ret	AUSTRIAN GP	Österreichring	29	BS Fabrications	G	3.0 McLaren M23-Cosworth V8	slid off in first part of two part race	20/31
ret	DUTCH GP	Zandvoort	29	BS Fabrications	G	3.0 McLaren M23-Cosworth V8	driveshaft	26/33
9	ITALIAN GP	Monza	29	BS Fabrications	G	3.0 McLaren M23-Cosworth V8		24/32
11	CANADIAN GP	Montreal	66	Parmalat Racing Team	G	3.0 Brabham BT46-Alfa Romeo F12	1 lap behind	14/28

1979 Championship position: 15th=   Wins: 0   Pole positions: 0   Fastest laps: 1   Points scored: 3

	Race	Circuit	No	Entrant	Tyres	Capacity/Car/Engine	Comment	Q Pos/Entries
ret/*dns	ARGENTINE GP	Buenos Aires	6	Parmalat Racing Team	G	3.0 Brabham BT46-Alfa Romeo F12	*accident at first start – hurt foot	20/26
ret	BRAZILIAN GP	Interlagos	6	Parmalat Racing Team	G	3.0 Brabham BT48-Alfa Romeo V12	hit Reutemann	22/26
7	SOUTH AFRICAN GP	Kyalami	6	Parmalat Racing Team	G	3.0 Brabham BT48-Alfa Romeo V12	1 lap behind	12/26
8	US GP WEST	Long Beach	6	Parmalat Racing Team	G	3.0 Brabham BT48-Alfa Romeo V12	pit stop – tyres/2 laps behind	12/26
ret	SPANISH GP	Jarama	6	Parmalat Racing Team	G	3.0 Brabham BT48-Alfa Romeo V12	fuel metering unit	7/27
ret	BELGIAN GP	Zolder	6	Parmalat Racing Team	G	3.0 Brabham BT48-Alfa Romeo V12	engine	3/28
7/ret	MONACO GP	Monte Carlo	6	Parmalat Racing Team	G	3.0 Brabham BT48-Alfa Romeo V12	driveshaft/8 laps behind	18/25
ret	FRENCH GP	Dijon	6	Parmalat Racing Team	G	3.0 Brabham BT48-Alfa Romeo V12	spun off	4/27
ret	BRITISH GP	Silverstone	6	Parmalat Racing Team	G	3.0 Brabham BT48-Alfa Romeo V12	spun off – could not restart	3/26
12/ret	GERMAN GP	Hockenheim	6	Parmalat Racing Team	G	3.0 Brabham BT48-Alfa Romeo V12	engine/3 laps behind	4/26
ret	AUSTRIAN GP	Österreichring	6	Parmalat Racing Team	G	3.0 Brabham BT48-Alfa Romeo V12	engine	7/26
4	DUTCH GP	Zandvoort	6	Parmalat Racing Team	G	3.0 Brabham BT48-Alfa Romeo V12	1 lap behind	11/26
ret	ITALIAN GP	Monza	6	Parmalat Racing Team	G	3.0 Brabham BT48-Alfa Romeo V12	collision with Regazzoni	8/28
ret	CANADIAN GP	Montreal	6	Parmalat Racing Team	G	3.0 Brabham BT49-Cosworth V8	gearbox	4/29
8/ret	US GP EAST	Watkins Glen	6	Parmalat Racing Team	G	3.0 Brabham BT49-Cosworth V8	driveshaft/FL/6 laps behind	2/30

1980 Championship position: 2nd   Wins: 3   Pole positions: 2   Fastest laps: 1   Points scored: 54

	Race	Circuit	No	Entrant	Tyres	Capacity/Car/Engine	Comment	Q Pos/Entries
2	ARGENTINE GP	Buenos Aires	5	Parmalat Racing Team	G	3.0 Brabham BT49-Cosworth V8		4/28
ret	BRAZILIAN GP	Interlagos	5	Parmalat Racing Team	G	3.0 Brabham BT49-Cosworth V8	suspension failure – accident	9/28
4	SOUTH AFRICAN GP	Kyalami	5	Parmalat Racing Team	G	3.0 Brabham BT49-Cosworth V8		3/28
1	US GP WEST	Long Beach	5	Parmalat Racing Team	G	3.0 Brabham BT49-Cosworth V8	FL	1/27
ret	BELGIAN GP	Zolder	5	Parmalat Racing Team	G	3.0 Brabham BT49-Cosworth V8	crashed into catch fencing	7/27
3	MONACO GP	Monte Carlo	5	Parmalat Racing Team	G	3.0 Brabham BT49-Cosworth V8		4/27
4	FRENCH GP	Paul Ricard	5	Parmalat Racing Team	G	3.0 Brabham BT49-Cosworth V8		8/27
2	BRITISH GP	Brands Hatch	5	Parmalat Racing Team	G	3.0 Brabham BT49-Cosworth V8		5/27
4	GERMAN GP	Hockenheim	5	Parmalat Racing Team	G	3.0 Brabham BT49-Cosworth V8		6/26
5	AUSTRIAN GP	Österreichring	5	Parmalat Racing Team	G	3.0 Brabham BT49-Cosworth V8		7/25
1	DUTCH GP	Zandvoort	5	Parmalat Racing Team	G	3.0 Brabham BT49-Cosworth V8		5/28
1	ITALIAN GP	Imola	5	Parmalat Racing Team	G	3.0 Brabham BT49-Cosworth V8		5/28
ret	CANADIAN GP	Montreal	5	Parmalat Racing Team	G	3.0 Brabham BT49-Cosworth V8	engine	1/28
ret	US GP EAST	Watkins Glen	5	Parmalat Racing Team	G	3.0 Brabham BT49-Cosworth V8	spun off – push started	2/27

1981 WORLD CHAMPION   Wins: 3   Pole positions: 4   Fastest laps: 1   Points scored: 50

	Race	Circuit	No	Entrant	Tyres	Capacity/Car/Engine	Comment	Q Pos/Entries
3	US GP WEST	Long Beach	5	Parmalat Racing Team	M	3.0 Brabham BT49C-Cosworth V8		4/29
12	BRAZILIAN GP	Rio	5	Parmalat Racing Team	M	3.0 Brabham BT49C-Cosworth V8	pit stop – tyres/2 laps behind	1/30
1	ARGENTINE GP	Buenos Aires	5	Parmalat Racing Team	M	3.0 Brabham BT49C-Cosworth V8	FL	1/29
1	SAN MARINO GP	Imola	5	Parmalat Racing Team	M	3.0 Brabham BT49C-Cosworth V8		5/30
ret	BELGIAN GP	Zolder	5	Parmalat Racing Team	M	3.0 Brabham BT49C-Cosworth V8	collision with Jones	2/31
ret	MONACO GP	Monte Carlo	5	Parmalat Racing Team	M	3.0 Brabham BT49C-Cosworth V8	spun off	1/31
ret	SPANISH GP	Jarama	5	Parmalat Racing Team	M	3.0 Brabham BT49C-Cosworth V8	collision with Andretti	9/30
3	FRENCH GP	Dijon	5	Parmalat Racing Team	M	3.0 Brabham BT49C-Cosworth V8		4/29
ret	BRITISH GP	Silverstone	5	Parmalat Racing Team	G	3.0 Brabham BT49C-Cosworth V8	tyre failure – accident	3/30
dns	"	"	5	Parmalat Racing Team	G	1.5 t/c Brabham BT50-BMW 4	practice only	– / –
1	GERMAN GP	Hockenheim	5	Parmalat Racing Team	G	3.0 Brabham BT49C-Cosworth V8		6/30
3	AUSTRIAN GP	Österreichring	5	Parmalat Racing Team	G	3.0 Brabham BT49C-Cosworth V8		7/28

Piquet took his maiden grand prix win in the 1980 United States West Grand Prix at Long Beach. The Brazilian would win 11 races for Brabham between 1979 and 1985.

Pos	Grand Prix	Circuit	No	Team	Tyre	Car/Engine	Notes	Grid
2	DUTCH GP	Zandvoort	5	Parmalat Racing Team	G	3.0 Brabham BT49C-Cosworth V8		3/30
6/ret	ITALIAN GP	Monza	5	Parmalat Racing Team	G	3.0 Brabham BT49C-Cosworth V8	engine failed on last lap/1 lap behind	6/30
5	CANADIAN GP	Montreal	5	Parmalat Racing Team	G	3.0 Brabham BT49C-Cosworth V8	1 lap behind	1/30
5	CAESARS PALACE GP	Las Vegas	5	Parmalat Racing Team	G	3.0 Brabham BT49C-Cosworth V8		4/30

1982 Championship position: 11th   Wins: 1   Pole positions: 1   Fastest laps: 3   Points scored: 20

Pos	Grand Prix	Circuit	No	Team	Tyre	Car/Engine	Notes	Grid
ret	SOUTH AFRICAN GP	Kyalami	1	Parmalat Racing Team	G	1.5 t/c Brabham BT50-BMW 4	spun off	2/30
dsq*	BRAZILIAN GP	Rio	1	Parmalat Racing Team	G	3.0 Brabham BT49D-Cosworth V8	1st on road/*water cooled brakes/FL	7/31
ret	US GP WEST	Long Beach	1	Parmalat Racing Team	G	3.0 Brabham BT49D-Cosworth V8	hit wall	6/31
5*	BELGIAN GP	Zolder	1	Parmalat Racing Team	G	1.5 t/c Brabham BT50-BMW 4	*3rd car disqualified/pitstop/-3 laps	10/32
ret	MONACO GP	Monte Carlo	1	Parmalat Racing Team	G	1.5 t/c Brabham BT50-BMW 4	gearbox	13/31
dnq	US GP (DETROIT)	Detroit	1	Parmalat Racing Team	G	1.5 t/c Brabham BT50-BMW 4		28/28
1	CANADIAN GP	Montreal	1	Parmalat Racing Team	G	1.5 t/c Brabham BT50-BMW 4		4/29
2	DUTCH GP	Zandvoort	1	Parmalat Racing Team	G	1.5 t/c Brabham BT50-BMW 4		3/31
ret	BRITISH GP	Brands Hatch	1	Parmalat Racing Team	G	1.5 t/c Brabham BT50-BMW 4	fuel metering unit	3/30
ret	FRENCH GP	Paul Ricard	1	Parmalat Racing Team	G	1.5 t/c Brabham BT50-BMW 4	engine	6/30
ret	GERMAN GP	Hockenheim	1	Parmalat Racing Team	G	1.5 t/c Brabham BT50-BMW 4	accident with Salazar/FL	4/30
ret	AUSTRIAN GP	Österreichring	1	Parmalat Racing Team	G	1.5 t/c Brabham BT50-BMW 4	engine/FL	1/29
4	SWISS GP	Dijon	1	Parmalat Racing Team	G	1.5 t/c Brabham BT50-BMW 4	pit stop – tyres/fuel/1 lap behind	6/29
ret	ITALIAN GP	Monza	1	Parmalat Racing Team	G	1.5 t/c Brabham BT50-BMW 4	clutch	2/30
ret	CAESARS PALACE GP	Las Vegas	1	Parmalat Racing Team	G	1.5 t/c Brabham BT50-BMW 4	spark plug electrode	12/30

1983 WORLD CHAMPION   Wins: 3   Pole positions: 1   Fastest laps: 4   Points scored: 59

Pos	Grand Prix	Circuit	No	Team	Tyre	Car/Engine	Notes	Grid
1	BRAZILIAN GP	Rio	5	Fila Sport	M	1.5 t/c Brabham BT52-BMW 4	FL	4/27
ret	US GP WEST	Long Beach	5	Fila Sport	M	1.5 t/c Brabham BT52-BMW 4	jammed throttle linkage	20/28
2	FRENCH GP	Paul Ricard	5	Fila Sport	M	1.5 t/c Brabham BT52-BMW 4	pit stop – fuel	6/29
ret	SAN MARINO GP	Imola	5	Fila Sport	M	1.5 t/c Brabham BT52-BMW 4	engine	2/28
2	MONACO GP	Monte Carlo	5	Fila Sport	M	1.5 t/c Brabham BT52-BMW 4	FL	6/28
4	BELGIAN GP	Spa	5	Fila Sport	M	1.5 t/c Brabham BT52-BMW 4		4/28
4	US GP (DETROIT)	Detroit	5	Fila Sport	M	1.5 t/c Brabham BT52-BMW 4		2/27
ret	CANADIAN GP	Montreal	5	Fila Sport	M	1.5 t/c Brabham BT52-BMW 4	throttle cable	3/28
2	BRITISH GP	Silverstone	5	Fila Sport	M	1.5 t/c Brabham BT52B-BMW 4		6/29
13/ret	GERMAN GP	Hockenheim	5	Fila Sport	M	1.5 t/c Brabham BT52B-BMW 4	fire – leaking fuel/3 laps behind	4/29
3	AUSTRIAN GP	Österreichring	5	Fila Sport	M	1.5 t/c Brabham BT52B-BMW 4		4/29
ret	DUTCH GP	Zandvoort	5	Fila Sport	M	1.5 t/c Brabham BT52B-BMW 4	accident with Prost	1/29
1	ITALIAN GP	Monza	5	Fila Sport	M	1.5 t/c Brabham BT52B-BMW 4	FL	4/29
1	EUROPEAN GP	Brands Hatch	5	Fila Sport	M	1.5 t/c Brabham BT52B-BMW 4		4/29
3	SOUTH AFRICAN GP	Kyalami	5	Fila Sport	M	1.5 t/c Brabham BT52B-BMW 4	FL	2/26

1984 Championship position: 5th   Wins: 2   Pole positions: 9   Fastest laps: 3 (1 shared)   Points scored: 29

Pos	Grand Prix	Circuit	No	Team	Tyre	Car/Engine	Notes	Grid
ret	BRAZILIAN GP	Rio	1	MRD International	M	1.5 t/c Brabham BT53-BMW 4	engine	7/27
ret	SOUTH AFRICAN GP	Kyalami	1	MRD International	M	1.5 t/c Brabham BT53-BMW 4	turbo	1/27
9*/ret	BELGIAN GP	Zolder	1	MRD International	M	1.5 t/c Brabham BT53-BMW 4	engine/*6th car disqualified/-4 laps	9/27
ret	SAN MARINO GP	Imola	1	MRD International	M	1.5 t/c Brabham BT53-BMW 4	turbo/FL	1/28
ret	FRENCH GP	Dijon	1	MRD International	M	1.5 t/c Brabham BT53-BMW 4	turbo	3/27
ret	MONACO GP	Monte Carlo	1	MRD International	M	1.5 t/c Brabham BT53-BMW 4	wet electrics	9/27
1	CANADIAN GP	Montreal	1	MRD International	M	1.5 t/c Brabham BT53-BMW 4	FL	1/26
1	US GP (DETROIT)	Detroit	1	MRD International	M	1.5 t/c Brabham BT53-BMW 4		1/27
ret	US GP (DALLAS)	Dallas	1	MRD International	M	1.5 t/c Brabham BT53-BMW 4	jammed throttle hit wall	12/27
7	BRITISH GP	Brands Hatch	1	MRD International	M	1.5 t/c Brabham BT53-BMW 4	lost turbo boost/1 lap behind	1/27
ret	GERMAN GP	Hockenheim	1	MRD International	M	1.5 t/c Brabham BT53-BMW 4	gearbox	5/27
2	AUSTRIAN GP	Österreichring	1	MRD International	M	1.5 t/c Brabham BT53-BMW 4		1/28
ret	DUTCH GP	Zandvoort	1	MRD International	M	3.0 Brabham BT53-BMW 4	oil pressure – loose oil union	2/27
ret	ITALIAN GP	Monza	1	MRD International	M	1.5 t/c Brabham BT53-BMW 4	engine	1/27
3	EUROPEAN GP	Nürburgring	1	MRD International	M	1.5 t/c Brabham BT53-BMW 4	FL (shared with Alboreto)	1/26
6	PORTUGUESE GP	Estoril	1	MRD International	M	1.5 t/c Brabham BT53-BMW 4	spin/1 lap behind	1/27

1985 Championship position: 8th   Wins: 1   Pole positions: 1   Fastest laps: 0   Points scored: 21

Pos	Grand Prix	Circuit	No	Team	Tyre	Car/Engine	Notes	Grid
ret	BRAZILIAN GP	Rio	7	Motor Racing Developments Ltd	P	1.5 t/c Brabham BT54-BMW 4	transmission	8/25
ret	PORTUGUESE GP	Estoril	7	Motor Racing Developments Ltd	P	1.5 t/c Brabham BT54-BMW 4	tyres/handling	10/26
8	SAN MARINO GP	Imola	7	Motor Racing Developments Ltd	P	1.5 t/c Brabham BT54-BMW 4	pit stop – tyres/out of fuel/-3 laps	9/26
ret	MONACO GP	Monte Carlo	7	Motor Racing Developments Ltd	P	1.5 t/c Brabham BT54-BMW 4	accident with Patrese	13/26
ret	CANADIAN GP	Montreal	7	Motor Racing Developments Ltd	P	1.5 t/c Brabham BT54-BMW 4	transmission	9/25
6	US GP (DETROIT)	Detroit	7	Motor Racing Developments Ltd	P	1.5 t/c Brabham BT54-BMW 4	1 lap behind	10/25
1	FRENCH GP	Paul Ricard	7	Motor Racing Developments Ltd	P	1.5 t/c Brabham BT54-BMW 4		5/26
4	BRITISH GP	Silverstone	7	Motor Racing Developmants Ltd	P	1.5 t/c Brabham BT54-BMW 4	1 lap behind	2/26
ret	GERMAN GP	Nürburgring	7	Motor Racing Developments Ltd	P	1.5 t/c Brabham BT54-BMW 4	turbo	6/27
ret	AUSTRIAN GP	Österreichring	7	Motor Racing Developments Ltd	P	1.5 t/c Brabham BT54-BMW 4	exhaust	5/27
8	DUTCH GP	Zandvoort	7	Motor Racing Developments Ltd	P	1.5 t/c Brabham BT54-BMW 4	stalled on grid/1 lap behind	1/27
2	ITALIAN GP	Monza	7	Motor Racing Developments Ltd	P	1.5 t/c Brabham BT54-BMW 4		4/26
5	BELGIAN GP	Spa	7	Motor Racing Developments Ltd	P	1.5 t/c Brabham BT54-BMW 4	1 lap behind	3/24
ret	EUROPEAN GP	Brands Hatch	7	Motor Racing Developments Ltd	P	1.5 t/c Brabham BT54-BMW 4	hit Rosberg's spinning car	2/27
ret	SOUTH AFRICAN GP	Kyalami	7	Motor Racing Developments Ltd	P	1.5 t/c Brabham BT54-BMW 4	engine	2/21
ret	AUSTRALIAN GP	Adelaide	7	Motor Racing Developments Ltd	P	1.5 t/c Brabham BT54-BMW 4	electrical fire	9/25

1986 Championship position: 3rd   Wins: 4   Pole positions: 2   Fastest laps: 7   Points scored: 69

Pos	Grand Prix	Circuit	No	Team	Tyre	Car/Engine	Notes	Grid
1	BRAZILIAN GP	Rio	6	Canon Williams Team	G	1.5 t/c Williams FW11-Honda V6	FL	2/25
ret	SPANISH GP	Jerez	6	Canon Williams Team	G	1.5 t/c Williams FW11-Honda V6	overheating	2/25
2	SAN MARINO GP	Imola	6	Canon Williams Team	G	1.5 t/c Williams FW11-Honda V6	FL	2/26
7	MONACO GP	Monte Carlo	6	Canon Williams Team	G	1.5 t/c Williams FW11-Honda V6	1 lap behind	11/26
ret	BELGIAN GP	Spa	6	Canon Williams Team	G	1.5 t/c Williams FW11-Honda V6	turbo boost control	1/25
3	CANADIAN GP	Montreal	6	Canon Williams Team	G	1.5 t/c Williams FW11-Honda V6	FL	3/25
ret	US GP (DETROIT)	Detroit	6	Canon Williams Team	G	1.5 t/c Williams FW11-Honda V6	hit wall/FL	3/26
3	FRENCH GP	Paul Ricard	6	Canon Williams Team	G	1.5 t/c Williams FW11-Honda V6		3/26

Piquet took his third world championship in 1987 at the wheel of the Williams FW11B-Honda after a season-long battle with team-mate Nigel Mansell. Never comfortable in the team, he switched to Lotus for 1988, taking the Honda engine deal with him, but it would prove to be an unsuccessful move for the Brazilian.

2	BRITISH GP	Brands Hatch	6	Canon Williams Team	G	1.5 t/c Williams FW11-Honda V6		1/26
1	GERMAN GP	Hockenheim	6	Canon Williams Team	G	1.5 t/c Williams FW11-Honda V6		5/26
1	HUNGARIAN GP	Hungaroring	6	Canon Williams Team	G	1.5 t/c Williams FW11-Honda V6	FL	2/26
ret	AUSTRIAN GP	Österreichring	6	Canon Williams Team	G	1.5 t/c Williams FW11-Honda V6	engine	7/26
1	ITALIAN GP	Monza	6	Canon Williams Team	G	1.5 t/c Williams FW11-Honda V6		6/27
3	PORTUGUESE GP	Estoril	6	Canon Williams Team	G	1.5 t/c Williams FW11-Honda V6		6/27
4	MEXICAN GP	Mexico City	6	Canon Williams Team	G	1.5 t/c Williams FW11-Honda V6	1 lap behind/FL	2/26
2	AUSTRALIAN GP	Adelaide	6	Canon Williams Team	G	1.5 t/c Williams FW11-Honda V6	precautionary tyre stop/FL	2/26

1987 WORLD CHAMPION Wins: 3 Pole positions: 4 Fastest laps: 4 Points scored: 76

2	BRAZILIAN GP	Rio	6	Canon Williams Team	G	1.5 t/c Williams FW11B-Honda V6	FL	2/23
dns	SAN MARINO GP	Imola	6	Canon Williams Team	G	1.5 t/c Williams FW11B-Honda V6	accident – not allowed to start	(3)/27
ret	BELGIAN GP	Spa	6	Canon Williams Team	G	1.5 t/c Williams FW11B-Honda V6	turbo sensor	2/26
2	MONACO GP	Monte Carlo	6	Canon Williams Team	G	1.5 t/c Williams FW11B-Honda V6		3/26
2	US GP (DETROIT)	Detroit	6	Canon Williams Team	G	1.5 t/c Williams FW11B-Honda V6		3/26
2	FRENCH GP	Paul Ricard	6	Canon Williams Team	G	1.5 t/c Williams FW11B-Honda V6	FL	4/26
2	BRITISH GP	Silverstone	6	Canon Williams Team	G	1.5 t/c Williams FW11B-Honda V6		1/26
1	GERMAN GP	Hockenheim	6	Canon Williams Team	G	1.5 t/c Williams FW11B-Honda V6		4/26
1	HUNGARIAN GP	Hungaroring	6	Canon Williams Team	G	1.5 t/c Williams FW11B-Honda V6	FL	3/26
2	AUSTRIAN GP	Österreichring	6	Canon Williams Team	G	1.5 t/c Williams FW11B-Honda V6		1/26
1	ITALIAN GP	Monza	6	Canon Williams Team	G	1.5 t/c Williams FW11B-Honda V6		1/28
3	PORTUGUESE GP	Estoril	6	Canon Williams Team	G	1.5 t/c Williams FW11B-Honda V6		4/27
4	SPANISH GP	Jerez	6	Canon Williams Team	G	1.5 t/c Williams FW11B-Honda V6		1/28
2	MEXICAN GP	Mexico City	6	Canon Williams Team	G	1.5 t/c Williams FW11B-Honda V6	FL	3/27
15/ret	JAPANESE GP	Suzuka	6	Canon Williams Team	G	1.5 t/c Williams FW11B-Honda V6	engine/5 laps behind	5/27
ret	AUSTRALIAN GP	Adelaide	6	Canon Williams Team	G	1.5 t/c Williams FW11B-Honda V6	brakes/gear linkage	3/27

1988 Championship position: 6th= Wins: 0 Pole positions: 0 Fastest laps: 0 Points scored: 22

3	BRAZILIAN GP	Rio	1	Camel Team Lotus Honda	G	1.5 t/c Lotus 100T-Honda V6		5/31
3	SAN MARINO GP	Imola	1	Camel Team Lotus Honda	G	1.5 t/c Lotus 100T-Honda V6		3/31
ret	MONACO GP	Monte Carlo	1	Camel Team Lotus Honda	G	1.5 t/c Lotus 100T-Honda V6	accident damage	11/30
ret	MEXICAN GP	Mexico City	1	Camel Team Lotus Honda	G	1.5 t/c Lotus 100T-Honda V6	engine	4/30
4	CANADIAN GP	Montreal	1	Camel Team Lotus Honda	G	1.5 t/c Lotus 100T-Honda V6	1 lap behind	6/31
ret	US GP (DETROIT)	Detroit	1	Camel Team Lotus Honda	G	1.5 t/c Lotus 100T-Honda V6	spun off	8/31
5	FRENCH GP	Paul Ricard	1	Camel Team Lotus Honda	G	1.5 t/c Lotus 100T-Honda V6	1 lap behind	7/31
5	BRITISH GP	Silverstone	1	Camel Team Lotus Honda	G	1.5 t/c Lotus 100T-Honda V6		7/31
ret	GERMAN GP	Hockenheim	1	Camel Team Lotus Honda	G	1.5 t/c Lotus 100T-Honda V6	dry tyres – wet race – spun off	5/31
8	HUNGARIAN GP	Hungaroring	1	Camel Team Lotus Honda	G	1.5 t/c Lotus 100T-Honda V6	hit Martini – pit stop/3 laps behind	13/31
4*	BELGIAN GP	Spa	1	Camel Team Lotus Honda	G	1.5 t/c Lotus 100T-Honda V6	*3rd & 4th place cars disqualified	9/31
ret	ITALIAN GP	Monza	1	Camel Team Lotus Honda	G	1.5 t/c Lotus 100T-Honda V6	clutch/spun off	7/31
ret	PORTUGUESE GP	Estoril	1	Camel Team Lotus Honda	G	1.5 t/c Lotus 100T-Honda V6	clutch	8/31
8	SPANISH GP	Jerez	1	Camel Team Lotus Honda	G	1.5 t/c Lotus 100T-Honda V6		9/31
ret	JAPANESE GP	Suzuka	1	Camel Team Lotus Honda	G	1.5 t/c Lotus 100T-Honda V6	driver unwell	5/31
3	AUSTRALIAN GP	Adelaide	1	Camel Team Lotus Honda	G	1.5 t/c Lotus 100T-Honda V6		5/31

1989 Championship position: 8th Wins: 0 Pole positions: 0 Fastest laps: 0 Points scored: 12

ret	BRAZILIAN GP	Rio	11	Camel Team Lotus	G	3.5 Lotus 101-Judd V8	fuel pump	9/38
ret	SAN MARINO GP	Imola	11	Camel Team Lotus	G	3.5 Lotus 101-Judd V8	engine	8/39
ret	MONACO GP	Monte Carlo	11	Camel Team Lotus	G	3.5 Lotus 101-Judd V8	collision with de Cesaris	19/38
11	MEXICAN GP	Mexico City	11	Camel Team Lotus	G	3.5 Lotus 101-Judd V8	understeer/1 lap behind	26/39
ret	US GP (PHOENIX)	Phoenix	11	Camel Team Lotus	G	3.5 Lotus 101-Judd V8	hit wall	22/39
4	CANADIAN GP	Montreal	11	Camel Team Lotus	G	3.5 Lotus 101-Judd V8	2 pit stops – tyres/low oil pressure	19/39
8	FRENCH GP	Paul Ricard	11	Camel Team Lotus	G	3.5 Lotus 101-Judd V8	2 pit stops – tyres/2 laps behind	20/39
4	BRITISH GP	Silverstone	11	Camel Team Lotus	G	3.5 Lotus 101-Judd V8		10/39
5	GERMAN GP	Hockenheim	11	Camel Team Lotus	G	3.5 Lotus 101-Judd V8	pit stop – tyres/1 lap behind	8/39

6	HUNGARIAN GP	Hungaroring	11	Camel Team Lotus	G	3.5 Lotus 101-Judd V8	pit stop – tyres	17/39
dnq	BELGIAN GP	Spa	11	Camel Team Lotus	G	3.5 Lotus 101-Judd V8		28/39
ret	ITALIAN GP	Monza	11	Camel Team Lotus	G	3.5 Lotus 101-Judd V8	spun avoiding Gachot	11/39
ret	PORTUGUESE GP	Estoril	11	Camel Team Lotus	G	3.5 Lotus 101-Judd V8	collision with Caffi	20/39
8	SPANISH GP	Jerez	11	Camel Team Lotus	G	3.5 Lotus 101-Judd V8	2 pit stops – tyres – puncture/-2 laps	7/38
4*	JAPANESE GP	Suzuka	11	Camel Team Lotus	G	3.5 Lotus 101-Judd V8	*1st place car disqualified	11/39
ret	AUSTRALIAN GP	Adelaide	11	Camel Team Lotus	G	3.5 Lotus 101-Judd V8	hit Ghinzani in rain	18/39

1990 Championship position: 3rd Wins: 2 Pole positions: 0 Fastest laps: 0 Points scored: 44

4	US GP (PHOENIX)	Phoenix	20	Benetton Formula	G	3.5 Benetton B189B-Ford HB V8	pit stop – tyres	6/35
6	BRAZILIAN GP	Interlagos	20	Benetton Formula	G	3.5 Benetton B189B-Ford HB V8	1 lap behind	13/35
5	SAN MARINO GP	Imola	20	Benetton Formula	G	3.5 Benetton B190-Ford HB V8	collision – Alesi/pit stop – tyres	8/34
dsq	MONACO GP	Monte Carlo	20	Benetton Formula	G	3.5 Benetton B190-Ford HB V8	spin – push start – black flagged	10/35
2	CANADIAN GP	Montreal	20	Benetton Formula	G	3.5 Benetton B190-Ford HB V8		5/35
6	MEXICAN GP	Mexico City	20	Benetton Formula	G	3.5 Benetton B190-Ford HB V8	pit stop – tyres	8/35
4	FRENCH GP	Paul Ricard	20	Benetton Formula	G	3.5 Benetton B190-Ford HB V8	pit stop – tyres	9/35
5	BRITISH GP	Silverstone	20	Benetton Formula	G	3.5 Benetton B190-Ford HB V8	started from back/lost bodywork	11/35
ret	GERMAN GP	Hockenheim	20	Benetton Formula	G	3.5 Benetton B190-Ford HB V8	engine	7/35
3	HUNGARIAN GP	Hungaroring	20	Benetton Formula	G	3.5 Benetton B190-Ford HB V8	electrical problems	9/35
5	BELGIAN GP	Spa	20	Benetton Formula	G	3.5 Benetton B190-Ford HB V8	understeer/no clutch	8/33
7	ITALIAN GP	Monza	20	Benetton Formula	G	3.5 Benetton B190-Ford HB V8	pit stop – puncture/1 lap behind	9/33
5	PORTUGUESE GP	Estoril	20	Benetton Formula	G	3.5 Benetton B190-Ford HB V8	pit stop – tyres	6/33
ret	SPANISH GP	Jerez	20	Benetton Formula	G	3.5 Benetton B190-Ford HB V8	electrics	8/33
1	JAPANESE GP	Suzuka	20	Benetton Formula	G	3.5 Benetton B190-Ford HB V8		6/30
1	AUSTRALIAN GP	Adelaide	20	Benetton Formula	G	3.5 Benetton B190-Ford HB V8		7/30

1991 Championship position: 6th Wins: 1 Pole positions: 0 Fastest laps: 0 Points scored: 26.5

3	US GP (PHOENIX)	Phoenix	20	Camel Benetton Ford	P	3.5 Benetton B190B-Ford HB V8		5/34
5	BRAZILIAN GP	Interlagos	20	Camel Benetton Ford	P	3.5 Benetton B190B-Ford HB V8		7/34
ret	SAN MARINO GP	Imola	20	Camel Benetton Ford	P	3.5 Benetton B191-Ford HB V8	spun off lap 1	14/34
ret	MONACO GP	Monte Carlo	20	Camel Benetton Ford	P	3.5 Benetton B191-Ford HB V8	hit by Berger – suspension damage	4/34
1	CANADIAN GP	Montreal	20	Camel Benetton Ford	P	3.5 Benetton B191-Ford HB V8		8/34
ret	MEXICAN GP	Mexico City	20	Camel Benetton Ford	P	3.5 Benetton B191-Ford HB V8	wheel bearing	6/34
8	FRENCH GP	Magny Cours	20	Camel Benetton Ford	P	3.5 Benetton B191-Ford HB V8	2 laps behind	7/34
5	BRITISH GP	Silverstone	20	Camel Benetton Ford	P	3.5 Benetton B191-Ford HB V8		8/34
ret	GERMAN GP	Hockenheim	20	Camel Benetton Ford	P	3.5 Benetton B191-Ford HB V8	engine	8/34
ret	HUNGARIAN GP	Hungaroring	20	Camel Benetton Ford	P	3.5 Benetton B191-Ford HB V8	gearbox	11/34
3	BELGIAN GP	Spa	20	Camel Benetton Ford	P	3.5 Benetton B191-Ford HB V8		6/34
6	ITALIAN GP	Monza	20	Camel Benetton Ford	P	3.5 Benetton B191-Ford HB V8		8/34
5	PORTUGUESE GP	Estoril	20	Camel Benetton Ford	P	3.5 Benetton B191-Ford HB V8		11/34
11	SPANISH GP	Barcelona	20	Camel Benetton Ford	P	3.5 Benetton B191-Ford HB V8	electrics/wet set-up/2 laps behind	10/33
7	JAPANESE GP	Suzuka	20	Camel Benetton Ford	P	3.5 Benetton B191-Ford HB V8	1 lap behind	10/30
4*	AUSTRALIAN GP	Adelaide	20	Camel Benetton Ford	P	3.5 Benetton B191-Ford HB V8	*rain shortened race – half points	5/32

GP Starts: 203 (204) GP Wins: 23 Pole positions: 24 Fastest laps: 23 Points: 485.5

PIQUET, Nelson Jr. Nelson Ângelo Tamsma Piquet Souto Maior (BR) b 25/7/1985, Heidelberg, Germany

2008 Championship position: 12th Wins: 0 Pole positions: 0 Fastest laps: 0 Points scored: 19

	Race	Circuit	No	Entrant	Tyres	Capacity/Car/Engine	Comment	Q Pos/Entries
ret	AUSTRALIAN GP	Melbourne	6	ING Renault F1 Team	B	2.4 Renault R28-V8	hit Glock damaged car – handling	21/22
11	MALAYSIAN GP	Sepang	6	ING Renault F1 Team	B	2.4 Renault R28-V8		13/22
ret	BAHRAIN GP	Sakhir Circuit	6	ING Renault F1 Team	B	2.4 Renault R28-V8	gearbox	14/22
ret	SPANISH GP	Barcelona	6	ING Renault F1 Team	B	2.4 Renault R28-V8	collision with Bourdais	10/22
15	TURKISH GP	Istanbul	6	ING Renault F1 Team	B	2.4 Renault R28-V8	1 lap behind	17/20
ret	MONACO GP	Monte Carlo	6	ING Renault F1 Team	B	2.4 Renault R28-V8	crashed at St Devote	17/20
ret	CANADIAN GP	Montreal	6	ING Renault F1 Team	B	2.4 Renault R28-V8	brakes	15/20
7	FRENCH GP	Magny Cours	6	ING Renault F1 Team	B	2.4 Renault R28-V8		11/20
ret	BRITISH GP	Silverstone	6	ING Renault F1 Team	B	2.4 Renault R28-V8	spun off	7/20
2	GERMAN GP	Hockenheim	6	ING Renault F1 Team	B	2.4 Renault R28-V8	helped by safety car and only one stop	17/20
6	HUNGARIAN GP	Hungaroring	6	ING Renault F1 Team	B	2.4 Renault R28-V8		10/20
11	EUROPEAN GP	Valencia	6	ING Renault F1 Team	B	2.4 Renault R28-V8	damaged front wing	15/20
ret	BELGIAN GP	Spa	6	ING Renault F1 Team	B	2.4 Renault R28-V8	accident – crashed out on damp track	12/20
10	ITALIAN GP	Monza	6	ING Renault F1 Team	B	2.4 Renault R28-V8		17/20
ret	SINGAPORE GP	Marina Bay Circuit	6	ING Renault F1 Team	B	2.4 Renault R28-V8	crashed car on team orders	16/20
4	JAPANESE GP	Suzuka	6	ING Renault F1 Team	B	2.4 Renault R28-V8		12/20
8	CHINESE GP	Shanghai	6	ING Renault F1 Team	B	2.4 Renault R28-V8		11/20
ret	BRAZILIAN GP	Interlagos	6	ING Renault F1 Team	B	2.4 Renault R28-V8	accident with Coulthard on lap 1	11/20

2009 Championship position: Unplaced

ret	AUSTRALIAN GP	Melbourne	8	ING Renault F1 Team	B	2.4 Renault R29-V8	spun off	17/20
13*	MALAYSIAN GP	Sepang	8	ING Renault F1 Team	B	2.4 Renault R29-V8	*rain-shortened race	17/20
16	CHINESE GP	Shanghai	8	ING Renault F1 Team	B	2.4 Renault R29-V8	2 laps behind	17/20
10	BAHRAIN GP	Sakhir Circuit	8	ING Renault F1 Team	B	2.4 Renault R29-V8		15/20
12	SPANISH GP	Barcelona	8	ING Renault F1 Team	B	2.4 Renault R29-V8	1 lap behind	12/20
ret	MONACO GP	Monte Carlo	8	ING Renault F1 Team	B	2.4 Renault R29-V8	shunted off by Buemi	12/20
16	TURKISH GP	Istanbul	8	ING Renault F1 Team	B	2.4 Renault R29-V8	1 lap behind	17/20
12	BRITISH GP	Silverstone	8	ING Renault F1 Team	B	2.4 Renault R29-V8	1 lap behind	14/20
13	GERMAN GP	Nürburgring	8	ING Renault F1 Team	B	2.4 Renault R29-V8		10/20
12	HUNGARIAN GP	Hungaroring	8	ING Renault F1 Team	B	2.4 Renault R29-V8		15/20

GP Starts: 28 GP Wins: 0 Pole positions: 0 Fastest laps: 0 Points: 19

NELSON PIQUET Jr

NELSON PIQUET JR had all the possible advantages to help him make a career as a racing driver in the junior classes: family wealth, an impeccable network of racing connections, first-class machinery and a good deal of talent, which shone through. Having attained his goal of reaching Formula 1, however, generally he failed to impress and, after being axed from his drive at Renault, he proceeded to lift the lid on a can of worms that essentially signed the death warrant of his future career in grand prix racing.

Born in Heidelberg, the young Piquet Jr spent his early years in Europe with his mother, his parents having separated soon after his birth. At the age of eight, however, he moved to Brazil to be with his father and soon began taking his first tentative steps in the karting world. By 2001, he was ready to move into the F3 Sudamerican series, and in his first season the rookie took a win and a pole in just seven starts, so he was well fancied as a contender in his sophomore year. Indeed, he was the dominant force, storming to the championship by taking 13 wins and 16 pole positions from his 17 starts.

Having travelled to Europe to build his burgeoning career, Piquet Jr chose to contest the BRDC British Formula 3 championship. The youngster soon got to grips with the competition and grew ever stronger as the season progressed, taking six wins and eight pole positions on his way to third place in the series. He further enhanced his reputation with a pole position and a second-place finish behind the F1-bound Christian Klien in the prestigious Marlboro Masters at Zandvoort. He was a firm favourite to take the title out-right in 2004, and the bookies were right: six wins and numerous podiums made him a worthy champion.

For 2005, Piquet Jr and his team moved up into the GP2 series, and for a while he looked out of his depth, but a win of the year at Spa settled his nerves and convinced the doubters that he had done enough to warrant another chance in the class. He was right on the pace the following year, and a win in the opening race in Valencia boded well, but soon he came up against the stunning talent of Lewis Hamilton, who quickly began to dominate the series. Indeed, it was to the Brazilian's credit that he carried the fight for the GP2 crown to the final round in Monza. In the end, Hamilton had enough of a points cushion to close out the championship, but Nelsinho had given him a good run for his money, the two youngsters being the series' outstanding talents. His performances were impressive enough to earn him a place as the test driver at Renault for 2007, before stepping up to a full-time ride alongside the returning Fernando Alonso.

Once the 2008 season opened, Piquet Jr endured a torrid spell of races when everything seemed to go against him. Indeed, it seemed that he might even be dropped in mid-season, but salvation came with his first points at Magny-Cours and a surprise second place at Hockenheim, where his one-stop strategy was aided by a safety car intervention. Late in the season, the youngster seemed to have blown his chances of retaining his seat when he crashed out of the Singapore Grand Prix. However, it transpired that he had been ordered to do this by team management in a successful ploy to help Fernando Alonso take victory. In return, he would retain his place in the team.

All this came out only after the crestfallen Piquet Jr had been released from his drive mid-way through the 2009 season, after he had failed to score a single point. Given immunity by the FIA in return for his testimony, the Brazilian settled old scores, but it left him to face a racing future in the relative wilderness. Having opted to try his hand in NASCAR in 2010, he made his debut in the second-tier Nationwide series and then became a strong contender in the Camping World Truck Series, taking his first victory at Bristol Speedway in March, 2012.

RENATO PIROCCHI

AFTER a promising start in small-capacity Stanguellini sports cars in the mid-1950s, Renato Pirocchi became one of the stars of the Italian Formula Junior series, then in its infancy. In 1959, he raced a Taraschi and began a friendly rivalry with Lorenzo Bandini, the pair enjoying a spectacular dice at Syracuse in particular. For the following year, Renato switched to a Stanguellini chassis, in common with most of his competitors, and ended a marvellous season as Italian champion, although probably his most important win was in the prestigious Havana GP in Cuba.

Pirocchi's brief flirtation with Formula 1 machinery in 1961 proved to be less successful. Driving a rather tired Cooper entered by the Pescara Racing Club, and on one occasion a Scuderia Centro Sud Cooper (as number two to his old sparring partner Bandini), he was at best a back-marker.

PIROCCHI, Renato (I) b 26/6/1933, Notaresco, Teramo – d 29/7/2002, Chieti, Pescara

	1961 Championship position: Unplaced								
	Race	Circuit	No	Entrant	Tyres	Capcity/Capacity/Car/Engine	Comment		Q Pos/Entries
12	ITALIAN GP	Monza	58	Pescara Racing Club	D	1.5 Cooper T51-Maserati 4	5 laps behind		29/33
	GP Starts: 1 GP Wins: 0 Pole positions: 0 Fastest laps: 0 Points: 0								

DIDIER PIRONI

DIDIER PIRONI'S ambition to become France's first-ever world champion driver was never realised. The crash at Hockenheim in 1982, which destroyed his career and almost cost him his legs, saw to that, leaving the cool and unemotional Frenchman to fight the greater battle of learning to walk again, while Alain Prost was enjoying his nation's plaudits in 1985.

Didier's interest in motor racing was awakened by a visit to a meeting with his cousin, José Dolhem, and as soon as he was old enough he attended the Winfield racing school, winning the prize of an Elf-sponsored Martini for 1973. It was a hard learning year for the young Frenchman who, rather than whingeing, clinically analysed all the ingredients that were lacking in his first season and set about putting them into place for his return in 1974. His attention to detail obviously paid dividends, for he became French Formule Renault champion at the wheel of a Martini Mk14.

Moving into Formule Super Renault in 1975 as number two to René Arnoux, Didier dutifully supported his team-mate, before taking over the number-one seat a year later. His dominance was almost total and he ran away with the championship, gaining promotion to the Elf Martini Formula 2 squad in 1977, again as number two to Arnoux. While he was finding his feet in this category, he gambled on dropping into Formula 3 for just one event, the Monaco race. His reasoning was sound, for a win there would be a valuable calling card in his future dealings. Naturally, mission was accomplished and he resumed his Formula 2 racing with the air of a man who knew his destiny. Raising his game, by the end of the year he had taken his first win at Estoril and earned a grand prix contract with Tyrrell for the 1978 season.

As one had come to expect of this coolest of customers, Didier's first tilt at the big time was accomplished with all the aplomb of a seasoned veteran. Finishing four of his first six races in the points perhaps raised expectations a little too high, as he ended the year with a few shunts. However, there was also the considerable kudos of a win at Le Mans in the Elf-backed Alpine-Renault to reinforce his burgeoning reputation. In fact, he was top of the turbo team's shopping list for 1979, but Tyrrell kept him to his contract. Thus he spent the year looking for an escape route, which he found in the shape of a move to Ligier for 1980.

Overshadowing the incumbent Jacques Laffite with some stunning drives, Pironi took his first grand prix win at Zolder and was unlucky not to have won the British GP at Brands Hatch after a brilliant drive through the field. With Jody Scheckter heading for retirement, another door opened for Pironi, who joined Gilles Villeneuve at Maranello for 1981. The new turbo cars were unrefined, but Gilles was at his brilliant best, leaving Pironi groping somewhat for the first time. Clearly a single fourth place was unacceptable to Ferrari, but it was doubly so to Pironi, who resolved not to be found wanting in 1982.

Four races into what would prove to be a bitter and tragic season came a flashpoint at Imola, where Pironi stole the win from Villeneuve on the last lap against team orders. All lines of communication between the two drivers were cut. Two weeks later, at Zolder, came the Canadian's horrendous fatal accident, making previous feuds irrelevant. Didier, now centre stage at Ferrari, unleashed a superb run of impressive performances that came to an end when, unsighted in pouring rain, he ran into Prost's Renault in practice for the German GP. It was the end of his season, and his total of 39 points left him tantalisingly within touching distance of the title before Keke Rosberg edged him out by a mere five points.

Although, almost miraculously, Pironi's feet and ankles were saved, he would never regain the feel and movement necessary to allow him to return to the cockpit. For thrills, he turned to the dangerous sport of powerboat racing, which became a lethal pastime when he crashed off the Isle of Wight in August, 1987.

PIRONI, Didier (F) b 26/3/1952, Villecresnes, nr Paris – d 23/8/1987, off the Isle of Wight, England

1978 Championship position: 15th   Wins: 0   Pole positions: 0   Fastest laps: 0   Points scored: 7

	Race	Circuit	No	Entrant	Tyres	Capacity/Car/Engine	Comment	Q Pos/Entries
14	ARGENTINE GP	Buenos Aires	3	Elf Team Tyrrell	G	3.0 Tyrrell 008-Cosworth V8	1 lap behind	23/27
6	BRAZILIAN GP	Rio	3	Elf Team Tyrrell	G	3.0 Tyrrell 008-Cosworth V8	1 lap behind	19/28
6	SOUTH AFRICAN GP	Kyalami	3	Elf Team Tyrrell	G	3.0 Tyrrell 008-Cosworth V8	1 lap behind	14/30
ret	US GP WEST	Long Beach	3	Elf Team Tyrrell	G	3.0 Tyrrell 008-Cosworth V8	gearbox	24/30
5	MONACO GP	Monte Carlo	3	Elf Team Tyrrell	G	3.0 Tyrrell 008-Cosworth V8		13/30
6	BELGIAN GP	Zolder	3	Elf Team Tyrrell	G	3.0 Tyrrell 008-Cosworth V8	1 lap behind	23/30
12	SPANISH GP	Jarama	3	Elf Team Tyrrell	G	3.0 Tyrrell 008-Cosworth V8	pit stop/distributor/4 laps behind	13/29
ret	SWEDISH GP	Anderstrop	3	Elf Team Tyrrell	G	3.0 Tyrrell 008-Cosworth V8	collision with Brambilla	17/27
10	FRENCH GP	Paul Ricard	3	Elf Team Tyrrell	G	3.0 Tyrrell 008-Cosworth V8		16/29
ret	BRITISH GP	Brands Hatch	3	Elf Team Tyrrell	G	3.0 Tyrrell 008-Cosworth V8	gearbox mounting bolts	19/30
5	GERMAN GP	Hockenheim	3	Elf Team Tyrrell	G	3.0 Tyrrell 008-Cosworth V8		16/30
ret	AUSTRIAN GP	Österreichring	3	Elf Team Tyrrell	G	3.0 Tyrrell 008-Cosworth V8	crashed	9/31
ret	DUTCH GP	Zandvoort	3	Elf Team Tyrrell	G	3.0 Tyrrell 008-Cosworth V8	accident with Patrese	17/33
ret/dns	ITALIAN GP	Monza	3	Elf Team Tyrrell	G	3.0 Tyrrell 008-Cosworth V8	accident at first start	(14)/32
10	US GP EAST	Watkins Glen	3	Elf Team Tyrrell	G	3.0 Tyrrell 008-Cosworth V8	1 lap behind	16/27
7	CANADIAN GP	Montreal	3	Elf Team Tyrrell	G	3.0 Tyrrell 008-Cosworth V8		18/28

1979 Championship position: 10th=   Wins: 0   Pole positions: 0   Fastest laps: 0   Points scored: 14

	Race	Circuit	No	Entrant	Tyres	Capacity/Car/Engine	Comment	Q Pos/Entries
ret/dns*	ARGENTINE GP	Buenos Aires	3	Team Tyrrell	G	3.0 Tyrrell 009-Cosworth V8	*accident at first start	(8)/26
4	BRAZILIAN GP	Interlagos	3	Team Tyrrell	G	3.0 Tyrrell 009-Cosworth V8		8/26
ret	SOUTH AFRICAN GP	Kyalami	3	Team Tyrrell	G	3.0 Tyrrell 009-Cosworth V8	throttle linkage	7/26
dsq*	US GP WEST	Long Beach	3	Team Tyrrell	G	3.0 Tyrrell 009-Cosworth V8	*push start after spin	17/26
6	SPANISH GP	Jarama	3	Team Tyrrell	G	3.0 Tyrrell 009-Cosworth V8		10/27
3	BELGIAN GP	Zolder	3	Candy Tyrrell Team	G	3.0 Tyrrell 009-Cosworth V8		12/28
ret	MONACO GP	Monte Carlo	3	Candy Tyrrell Team	G	3.0 Tyrrell 009-Cosworth V8	accident with Lauda	7/25
ret	FRENCH GP	Dijon	3	Candy Tyrrell Team	G	3.0 Tyrrell 009-Cosworth V8	suspension	11/27
10	BRITISH GP	Silverstone	3	Candy Tyrrell Team	G	3.0 Tyrrell 009-Cosworth V8	pit stop/2 laps behind	15/26
9	GERMAN GP	Hockenheim	3	Candy Tyrrell Team	G	3.0 Tyrrell 009-Cosworth V8	pit stop/1 lap behind	8/26
7	AUSTRIAN GP	Österreichring	3	Candy Tyrrell Team	G	3.0 Tyrrell 009-Cosworth V8	1 lap behind	10/26
ret	DUTCH GP	Zandvoort	3	Candy Tyrrell Team	G	3.0 Tyrrell 009-Cosworth V8	rear suspension	10/26
10	ITALIAN GP	Monza	3	Candy Tyrrell Team	G	3.0 Tyrrell 009-Cosworth V8	pit stop – hit by Watson/1 lap behind	12/28
5	CANADIAN GP	Montreal	3	Candy Tyrrell Team	G	3.0 Tyrrell 009-Cosworth V8	1 lap behind	6/29
3	US GP EAST	Watkins Glen	3	Candy Tyrrell Team	G	3.0 Tyrrell 009-Cosworth V8		10/30

1980 Championship position: 5th   Wins: 1   Pole positions: 2   Fastest laps: 2   Points scored: 32

	Race	Circuit	No	Entrant	Tyres	Capacity/Car/Engine	Comment	Q Pos/Entries
ret	ARGENTINE GP	Buenos Aires	25	Equipe Ligier Gitanes	G	3.0 Ligier JS11/15-Cosworth V8	engine	3/28
4	BRAZILIAN GP	Interlagos	25	Equipe Ligier Gitanes	G	3.0 Ligier JS11/15-Cosworth V8		2/28
3	SOUTH AFRICAN GP	Kyalami	25	Equipe Ligier Gitanes	G	3.0 Ligier JS11/15-Cosworth V8		5/28
6	US GP WEST	Long Beach	25	Equipe Ligier Gitanes	G	3.0 Ligier JS11/15-Cosworth V8	1 lap behind	9/27
1	BELGIAN GP	Zolder	25	Equipe Ligier Gitanes	G	3.0 Ligier JS11/15-Cosworth V8		2/27
ret	MONACO GP	Monte Carlo	25	Equipe Ligier Gitanes	G	3.0 Ligier JS11/15-Cosworth V8	gearbox/hit barrier when leading	1/27
2	FRENCH GP	Paul Ricard	25	Equipe Ligier Gitanes	G	3.0 Ligier JS11/15-Cosworth V8		=2/27
ret	BRITISH GP	Brands Hatch	25	Equipe Ligier Gitanes	G	3.0 Ligier JS11/15-Cosworth V8	rim/tyre failure/crashed/FL	1/27
ret	GERMAN GP	Hockenheim	25	Equipe Ligier Gitanes	G	3.0 Ligier JS11/15-Cosworth V8	driveshaft	7/26
ret	AUSTRIAN GP	Österreichring	25	Equipe Ligier Gitanes	G	3.0 Ligier JS11/15-Cosworth V8	handling	6/25
ret	DUTCH GP	Zandvoort	25	Equipe Ligier Gitanes	G	3.0 Ligier JS11/15-Cosworth V8	accident with de Angelis	15/28
6	ITALIAN GP	Imola	25	Equipe Ligier Gitanes	G	3.0 Ligier JS11/15-Cosworth V8	1 lap behind	13/28
3*	CANADIAN GP	Montreal	25	Equipe Ligier Gitanes	G	3.0 Ligier JS11/15-Cosworth V8	*1st – but 1 min pen jumped restart/FL	3/28
3	US GP EAST	Watkins Glen	25	Equipe Ligier Gitanes	G	3.0 Ligier JS11/15-Cosworth V8		7/27

1981 Championship position: 13th   Wins: 0   Pole positions: 0   Fastest laps: 1   Points scored: 9

	Race	Circuit	No	Entrant	Tyres	Capacity/Car/Engine	Comment	Q Pos/Entries
ret	US GP WEST	Long Beach	28	Scuderia Ferrari SpA SEFAC	M	1.5 t/c Ferrari 126CK V6	engine	11/29
ret	BRAZILIAN GP	Rio	28	Scuderia Ferrari SpA SEFAC	M	1.5 t/c Ferrari 126CK V6	collision with Prost	17/30
ret	ARGENTINE GP	Buenos Aires	28	Scuderia Ferrari SpA SEFAC	M	1.5 t/c Ferrari 126CK V6	engine	12/29
5	SAN MARINO GP	Imola	28	Scuderia Ferrari SpA SEFAC	M	1.5 t/c Ferrari 126CK V6		6/30
8	BELGIAN GP	Zolder	28	Scuderia Ferrari SpA SEFAC	M	1.5 t/c Ferrari 126CK V6	led race until brake problems	3/31
4	MONACO GP	Monte Carlo	28	Scuderia Ferrari SpA SEFAC	M	1.5 t/c Ferrari 126CK V6	1 lap behind	17/31
15	SPANISH GP	Jarama	28	Scuderia Ferrari SpA SEFAC	M	1.5 t/c Ferrari 126CK V6	pit stop/new nose/tyres/4 laps behind	13/30
5	FRENCH GP	Dijon	28	Scuderia Ferrari SpA SEFAC	M	1.5 t/c Ferrari 126CK V6	1 lap behind	14/29
ret	BRITISH GP	Silverstone	28	Scuderia Ferrari SpA SEFAC	M	1.5 t/c Ferrari 126CK V6	engine	4/30
ret	GERMAN GP	Hockenheim	28	Scuderia Ferrari SpA SEFAC	M	1.5 t/c Ferrari 126CK V6	engine	5/30
9	AUSTRIAN GP	Österreichring	28	Scuderia Ferrari SpA SEFAC	M	1.5 t/c Ferrari 126CK V6	1 lap behind	8/28
ret	DUTCH GP	Zandvoort	28	Scuderia Ferrari SpA SEFAC	M	1.5 t/c Ferrari 126CK V6	accident with Tambay	12/30
5	ITALIAN GP	Monza	28	Scuderia Ferrari SpA SEFAC	M	1.5 t/c Ferrari 126CK V6		8/30
ret	CANADIAN GP	Montreal	28	Scuderia Ferrari SpA SEFAC	M	1.5 t/c Ferrari 126CK V6	engine	12/30
9	CAESARS PALACE GP	Las Vegas	28	Scuderia Ferrari SpA SEFAC	M	1.5 t/c Ferrari 126CK V6	tyres/damage check/FL/2 laps behind	18/30

1982 Championship position: 2nd   Wins: 2   Pole positions: 2   Fastest laps: 2   Points scored: 39

	Race	Circuit	No	Entrant	Tyres	Capacity/Car/Engine	Comment	Q Pos/Entries
18	SOUTH AFRICAN GP	Kyalami	28	Scuderia Ferrari SpA SEFAC	G	1.5 t/c Ferrari 126C2 V6	pit stops/tyres/6 laps behind	6/30
6*	BRAZILIAN GP	Rio	28	Scuderia Ferrari SpA SEFAC	G	1.5 t/c Ferrari 126C2 V6	pit stop/tyres/*1st & 2nd cars dsq	8/31
ret	US GP WEST	Long Beach	28	Scuderia Ferrari SpA SEFAC	G	1.5 t/c Ferrari 126C2 V6	hit wall	9/31
1	SAN MARINO GP	Imola	28	Scuderia Ferrari SpA SEFAC	G	1.5 t/c Ferrari 126C2 V6	overtook Villeneuve on last lap/FL	4/14
dns	BELGIAN GP	Zolder	28	Scuderia Ferrari SpA SEFAC	G	1.5 t/c Ferrari 126C2 V6	withdrawn after Villeneuve's accident	(6)/32
2/ret	MONACO GP	Monte Carlo	28	Scuderia Ferrari SpA SEFAC	G	1.5 t/c Ferrari 126C2 V6	electrics/1 lap behind	5/31
3	US GP (DETROIT)	Detroit	28	Scuderia Ferrari SpA SEFAC	G	1.5 t/c Ferrari 126C2 V6		4/28
9	CANADIAN GP	Montreal	28	Scuderia Ferrari SpA SEFAC	G	1.5 t/c Ferrari 126C2 V6	pit stop/mechanical/FL/3 laps behind	1/29
1	DUTCH GP	Zandvoort	28	Scuderia Ferrari SpA SEFAC	G	1.5 t/c Ferrari 126C2 V6		4/31
2	BRITISH GP	Brands Hatch	28	Scuderia Ferrari SpA SEFAC	G	1.5 t/c Ferrari 126C2 V6		4/30
3	FRENCH GP	Paul Ricard	28	Scuderia Ferrari SpA SEFAC	G	1.5 t/c Ferrari 126C2 V6		3/30
dns	GERMAN GP	Hockenheim	28	Scuderia Ferrari SpA SEFAC	G	1.5 t/c Ferrari 126C2 V6	badly injured in practice accident	(1)/30

GP Starts: 68 (70)   GP Wins: 3   Pole positions: 4   Fastest laps: 5   Points: 101

EMANUELE PIRRO

EMANUELE PIRRO'S career has been a tale of ups and downs, as the unlucky Italian always seemed to fall short of ultimate success in most of the categories in which he raced. That was until he teamed up with Audi at the beginning of 1994 and took the Italian Superturismo championship by storm with his 80 Competition. Three successive titles represented a sweet success for the tall and lanky Roman, whose earlier exploits had promised so much.

Moving from karts to Formula Fiat, Pirro won the championship in 1980, before graduating to the European Formula 3 series, taking the runner-up slot behind Euroracing team-mate Oscar Larrauri in 1982. When the team went to F1 with Alfa Romeo in 1983, he had to find an F3 ride elsewhere, and after a bright start faded to third in the championship. Stepping up to Formula 2 for 1984 with Onyx, he established a good rapport with the team and stayed with them for F3000 in 1985, victories at Thruxton and Vallelunga earning him a Brabham F1 test that came to nought. So it was back to F3000 in 1986 and second place in the championship, behind Ivan Capelli. Despite closing the year with wins at Le Mans and Jarama, a mid-season slump had cost him the title chance.

Still seeking an F1 ride, Emanuele busied himself with some superb performances in BMW touring cars and took on the role of test driver for McLaren, before replacing Johnny Herbert at Benetton mid-way through 1989. His half-season was not productive enough, however, and he was dropped for 1990, when Nelson Piquet was signed up, leaving him to find a place in the Dallara squad for the next two seasons. With no worthwhile results to speak of and, crucially, precious few drives that caught the eye, he was passed over in favour of fresher talent in 1992 and switched to the Italian touring car championship with a Bigazzi BMW.

After being synonymous with the BMW marque on and off over the years, Pirro's switch to Audi was something of a surprise, but it paid off in a big way for both parties with his aforementioned hat trick of Superturismo titles. A switch to the German Super Touring championship brought another title in 1996, before the car was eventually handicapped by weight penalties and being made to run in two-wheel-drive configuration.

In 1999, Pirro and team-mate Frank Biela were drafted into the Audi Sport Team Joest sports car squad for Le Mans, where the touring car stars took third place with Didier Theys in the Audi R8R. This was the beginning of a tremendously successful new chapter in the driver's career. With co-drivers Tom Kristensen and Biela, he took a magnificent hat trick of wins at the Sarthe classic between 2000 and 2002. With Biela, he took the 2001 ALMS title, before works support was withdrawn for 2003. Along with Stefan Johansson and JJ Lehto, Pirro upheld the marque's honour by taking third place at Le Mans in the Champion Audi, and he repeated the result in both 2004 (with Marco Werner and Lehto) and 2005 (with Allan McNish and Biela). Having been regular competitors in the American Le Mans Series, Pirro and Biela wrapped up the championship in 2005 in the venerable Audi R8.

For 2006, Pirro, Biela and Marco Werner created history in the all-new Audi R10 TDI that became the first diesel-powered Le Mans 24-hour winner. The trio repeated their triumph the following year, taking Pirro's personal tally of victories to five. At the end of 2008, the popular Italian announced that he would be retiring from racing to take on an ambassadorial role with Audi, but the temptation to race proved too strong. In 2010, he joined the Drayson team to race their LMP1 Lola in selected events.

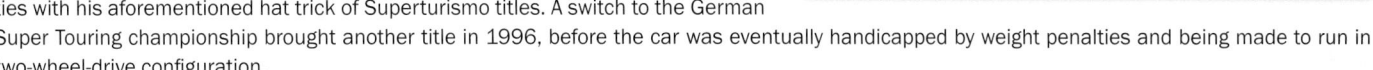

PIRRO Emanuele (I) b 12/1/1962, Rome

	Race	Circuit	No	Entrant	Tyres	Capacity/Car/Engine	Comment	Q Pos/Entries
1989	Championship position: 23rd=			Wins: 0	Pole positions: 0	Fastest laps: 0	Points scored: 2	
9	FRENCH GP	Paul Ricard	20	Benetton Formula Ltd	G	3.5 Benetton B188-Cosworth V8	2 laps behind	24/39
11	BRITISH GP	Silverstone	20	Benetton Formula Ltd	G	3.5 Benetton B188-Cosworth V8	2 laps behind	26/39
ret	GERMAN GP	Hockenheim	20	Benetton Formula Ltd	G	3.5 Benetton B189-Cosworth V8	accident	9/39
8	HUNGARIAN GP	Hungaroring	20	Benetton Formula Ltd	G	3.5 Benetton B189-Cosworth V8	1 lap behind	25/39
10	BELGIAN GP	Spa	20	Benetton Formula Ltd	G	3.5 Benetton B189-Cosworth V8	1 lap behind	13/39
ret	ITALIAN GP	Monza	20	Benetton Formula Ltd	G	3.5 Benetton B189-Cosworth V8	gearbox/clutch on lap 1	9/39
ret	PORTUGUESE GP	Estoril	20	Benetton Formula Ltd	G	3.5 Benetton B189-Cosworth V8	shock absorber	16/39
ret	SPANISH GP	Jerez	20	Benetton Formula Ltd	G	3.5 Benetton B189-Cosworth V8	leg cramp – spun off when 4th	10/38
ret	JAPANESE GP	Suzuka	20	Benetton Formula Ltd	G	3.5 Benetton B189-Cosworth V8	accident with de Cesaris	22/39
5	AUSTRALIAN GP	Adelaide	20	Benetton Formula Ltd	G	3.5 Benetton B189-Cosworth V8	2 laps behind	13/39
1990	Championship position: Unplaced							
ret	SAN MARINO GP	Imola	21	Scuderia Italia SpA	P	3.5 BMS Dallara 190-Cosworth V8	started from back of grid/engine	22/34
ret/dns*	MONACO GP	Monte Carlo	21	Scuderia Italia SpA	P	3.5 BMS Dallara 190-Cosworth V8	*stalled on dummy grid	(9)/35
ret	CANADIAN GP	Montreal	21	Scuderia Italia SpA	P	3.5 BMS Dallara 190-Cosworth V8	collided with Alboreto	19/35
ret	MEXICAN GP	Mexico City	21	Scuderia Italia SpA	P	3.5 BMS Dallara 190-Cosworth V8	engine	18/35
ret	FRENCH GP	Paul Ricard	21	Scuderia Italia SpA	P	3.5 BMS Dallara 190-Cosworth V8	brakes – spun off	24/35
11	BRITISH GP	Silverstone	21	Scuderia Italia SpA	P	3.5 BMS Dallara 190-Cosworth V8	2 laps behind	19/35
ret	GERMAN GP	Hockenheim	21	Scuderia Italia SpA	P	3.5 BMS Dallara 190-Cosworth V8	startline collision with Brabham	23/35
10	HUNGARIAN GP	Hungaroring	21	Scuderia Italia SpA	P	3.5 BMS Dallara 190-Cosworth V8	1 lap behind	13/35
ret	BELGIAN GP	Spa	21	Scuderia Italia SpA	P	3.5 BMS Dallara 190-Cosworth V8	cracked water pipe	17/33
ret	ITALIAN GP	Monza	21	Scuderia Italia SpA	P	3.5 BMS Dallara 190-Cosworth V8	gearbox – spun off	19/33

15	PORTUGUESE GP	Estoril	21	Scuderia Italia SpA	P	3.5 BMS Dallara 190-Cosworth V8	3 laps behind	13/33
ret	SPANISH GP	Jerez	21	Scuderia Italia SpA	P	3.5 BMS Dallara 190-Cosworth V8	throttle slides – spun off	16/33
ret	JAPANESE GP	Suzuka	21	Scuderia Italia SpA	P	3.5 BMS Dallara 190-Cosworth V8	alternator	19/30
ret	AUSTRALIAN GP	Adelaide	21	Scuderia Italia SpA	P	3.5 BMS Dallara 190-Cosworth V8	engine – electrics	21/30

1991 Championship position: 18th   Wins: 0   Pole positions: 0   Fastest laps: 0   Points scored: 1

ret	US GP (PHOENIX)	Phoenix	21	Scuderia Italia SpA	P	3.5 BMS Dallara 191-Judd V10	clutch	9/34
11	BRAZILIAN GP	Rio	21	Scuderia Italia SpA	P	3.5 BMS Dallara 191-Judd V10	3 laps behind	12/34
dnpq	SAN MARINO GP	Imola	21	Scuderia Italia SpA	P	3.5 BMS Dallara 191-Judd V10		31/34
6	MONACO GP	Monte Carlo	21	Scuderia Italia SpA	P	3.5 BMS Dallara 191-Judd V10	1 lap behind	12/34
9	CANADIAN GP	Montreal	21	Scuderia Italia SpA	P	3.5 BMS Dallara 191-Judd V10	1 lap behind	10/34
dnpq	MEXICAN GP	Mexico City	21	Scuderia Italia SpA	P	3.5 BMS Dallara 191-Judd V10		34/34
dnpq	FRENCH GP	Magny Cours	21	Scuderia Italia SpA	P	3.5 BMS Dallara 191-Judd V10		31/34
10	BRITISH GP	Silverstone	21	Scuderia Italia SpA	P	3.5 BMS Dallara 191-Judd V10	2 laps behind	18/34
10	GERMAN GP	Hockenheim	21	Scuderia Italia SpA	P	3.5 BMS Dallara 191-Judd V10	1 lap behind	18/34
ret	HUNGARIAN GP	Hungaroring	21	Scuderia Italia SpA	P	3.5 BMS Dallara 191-Judd V10	engine – oil pressure	7/34
8	BELGIAN GP	Spa	21	Scuderia Italia SpA	P	3.5 BMS Dallara 191-Judd V10	1 lap behind	25/34
10	ITALIAN GP	Monza	21	Scuderia Italia SpA	P	3.5 BMS Dallara 191-Judd V10	1 lap behind	16/34
ret	PORTUGUESE GP	Estoril	21	Scuderia Italia SpA	P	3.5 BMS Dallara 191-Judd V10	engine	17/34
15	SPANISH GP	Barcelona	21	Scuderia Italia SpA	P	3.5 BMS Dallara 191-Judd V10	3 laps behind	9/33
ret	JAPANESE GP	Suzuka	21	Scuderia Italia SpA	P	3.5 BMS Dallara 191-Judd V10	spun off avoiding de Cesaris	16/31
7*	AUSTRALIAN GP	Adelaide	21	Scuderia Italia SpA	P	3.5 BMS Dallara 191-Judd V10	*rain stopped race after 14 laps	13/32

GP Starts: 36 (37)   GP Wins: 0   Pole positions: 0   Fastest laps: 0   Points: 3

ANTÔNIO PIZZONIA

ANOTHER of the seemingly endless stream of Brazilians heading to Europe, chasing their Formula 1 dream, Antônio Pizzonia showed real talent, but ultimately failed to obtain a place on the grand prix stage, despite some impressive testing performances for the Williams team. He started racing karts at a young age, and despite living in the remote Manaus region of the Amazon, 'Jungle Boy', as he was affectionately nicknamed, was soon accumulating local and regional titles. At the age of 15, he had clinched the Brazilian national title and was being touted as a possible successor to such greats as Nelson Piquet and Ayrton Senna.

Antônio left Brazil to contest the 1996 US-based Barber Dodge series, where he finished second overall to set up a move to Britain to race in Formula Vauxhall Junior. He finished second overall in 1997, before taking the championship the following year. That success provided the platform for a move into Formula Renault, where he eased to the British title in his first season. He also finished as runner-up in the European series and, remaining with Manor the following season, took the next step up the ladder to British F3. Again, talent won out and the Brazilian clinched the title at his first attempt. F1 teams naturally showed an interest, and Williams offered him a deal for testing initially, but also guaranteed him support in F3000. In a competitive field, he managed one victory (at Hockenheim) en route to sixth in the final standings. The following year was slightly better. Remaining with Petrobras, he finished one place higher in the standings, but without a win in the campaign.

Jaguar Racing offered Pizzonia a full race contract for 2003 and, reluctantly released by Williams, he was signed up to partner rising star Mark Webber. The partnership, both with team and team-mate, never really gelled, and the Brazilian found himself made something of a scapegoat for poor performances. Despite a good drive at Silverstone, he was replaced by Justin Wilson and returned to Williams, where his testing abilities remained in high regard.

Pizzonia's move back to Grove was finally rewarded mid-way through 2004. With Ralf Schumacher injured and fellow test driver Marc Gené proving unconvincing, Antônio was finally given his chance. Three seventh places were punctuated by a tearful retirement at Spa, where a podium had looked possible, before Schumacher returned to action.

Antônio looked set for a full race seat in 2006, but was edged out by Nick Heidfeld after the pair went head-to-head in winter testing, leaving the Brazilian with another year of testing and reserve duties. He was given another opportunity to show his abilities, however, when Heidfeld was unavailable following a testing accident. His first race (at Monza) yielded a couple of points, but when GP2 champion Nico Rosberg and experienced tester Alex Wurz were both snapped up for 2006, he became surplus to requirements. Thus the Brazilian was forced to seek employment outside Formula 1, and he looked to the USA and the Champ Car series to put his career back on track. He managed to make four appearances for the Rocketsports Team, but no noteworthy results were forthcoming.

For 2007, Pizzonia decided that the best way to get back into Formula 1 was by way of the GP2 feeder series. Signing with Giancarlo Fisichella's FMS squad proved to be a disaster, however, as after scoring only a single point in five rounds, he was replaced by Adam Carroll.

Antônio retreated to Brazil, where he contested the competitive stock car series with a Peugeot 307 in 2008/09. He was more convincing in single-seaters, though, and represented Corinthians in the football-themed Superleague formula with a best result of second at Jerez.

Back in stock cars for the 2010 season, Pizzonia switched to a Chevrolet Astra, but could only manage a lowly 23rd in the final standings. In 2011, he briefly raced a Peugeot 408 in stock cars and a Ferrari 430 in the GT3 series.

PIZZONIA, Antônio Reginaldo Jr (BR) b 11/9/1980, Manaus

2003 Championship position: Unplaced

	Race	Circuit	No	Entrant	Tyres	Capacity/Car/Engine	Comment	Q Pos/Entries
13/ret	AUSTRALIAN GP	Melbourne	15	Jaguar Racing	M	3.0 Jaguar R4-Cosworth V10	suspension/6 laps behind	18/20
ret	MALAYSIAN GP	Sepang	15	Jaguar Racing	M	3.0 Jaguar R4-Cosworth V10	brake problem – spun off	15/20
ret	BRAZILIAN GP	Interlagos	15	Jaguar Racing	M	3.0 Jaguar R4-Cosworth V10	spun off on wet track	17/20
14	SAN MARINO GP	Imola	15	Jaguar Racing	M	3.0 Jaguar R4-Cosworth V10	2 laps behind	15/20
ret	SPANISH GP	Barcelona	15	Jaguar Racing	M	3.0 Jaguar R4-Cosworth V10	stalled on grid – hit by Räikkönen	16/20
9	AUSTRIAN GP	A1-Ring	15	Jaguar Racing	M	3.0 Jaguar R4-Cosworth V10	1 lap behind	8/20
ret	MONACO GP	Monte Carlo	15	Jaguar Racing	M	3.0 Jaguar R4-Cosworth V10	electrics	13/19
10/ret	CANADIAN GP	Montreal	15	Jaguar Racing	M	3.0 Jaguar R4-Cosworth V10	brakes/4 laps behind	13/20
10	EUROPEAN GP	Nürburgring	15	Jaguar Racing	M	3.0 Jaguar R4-Cosworth V10	1 lap behind	16/20
10	FRANCE GP	Magny Cours	15	Jaguar Racing	M	3.0 Jaguar R4-Cosworth V10	1 lap behind	11/20
ret	BRITISH GP	Silverstone	15	Jaguar Racing	M	3.0 Jaguar R4-Cosworth V10	engine	10/20

2004 Championship position: 14th=   Wins: 0   Pole positions: 0   Fastest laps: 0   Points scored: 6

	Race	Circuit	No	Entrant	Tyres	Capacity/Car/Engine	Comment	Q Pos/Entries
7	GERMAN GP	Hockenheim	4	BMW WIlliamsF1 Team	M	3.0 Williams FW26-BMW V10		10/20
7	HUNGARIAN GP	Hungaroring	4	BMW WIlliamsF1 Team	M	3.0 Williams FW26-BMW V10		6/20
ret	BELGIAN GP	Spa	4	BMW WIlliamsF1 Team	M	3.0 Williams FW26-BMW V10	gearbox failure when third	14/20
7	ITALIAN GP	Monza	4	BMW WIlliamsF1 Team	M	3.0 Williams FW26-BMW V10		8/20

2005 Championship position: 22nd   Wins: 0   Pole positions: 0   Fastest laps: 0   Points scored: 2

	Race	Circuit	No	Entrant	Tyres	Capacity/Car/Engine	Comment	Q Pos/Entries
7	ITALIAN GP	Monza	8	BMW WilliamsF1 Team	M	3.0 Williams FW27-BMW V10		16/20
15/ret	BELGIAN GP	Spa	8	BMW WilliamsF1 Team	M	3.0 Williams FW27-BMW V10	accident/5 laps behind	15/20
ret	BRAZILIAN GP	Interlagos	8	BMW WilliamsF1 Team	M	3.0 Williams FW27-BMW V10	accident	13/20
ret	JAPANESE GP	Suzuka	8	BMW WilliamsF1 Team	M	3.0 Williams FW27-BMW V10	accident	12/20
13	CHINESE GP	Shanghai	8	BMW WilliamsF1 Team	M	3.0 Williams FW27-BMW V10	1 lap behind	13/20

GP Starts: 20   GP Wins: 0   Pole positions: 0   Fastest laps: 0   Points: 8

POLLET, Jacques (F) b 28/7/1922, Roubaix – d 16/8/1997, Paris

1954 Championship position: Unplaced

	Race	Circuit	No	Entrant	Tyres	Capacity/Car/Engine	Comment	Q Pos/Entries
ret	FRENCH GP	Reims	26	Equipe Gordini	E	2.5 Gordini Type 16 6	engine	18/22
ret	SPANISH GP	Pedralbes	48	Equipe Gordini	E	2.5 Gordini Type 16 6	engine	16/22

1955 Championship position: Unplaced

	Race	Circuit	No	Entrant	Tyres	Capacity/Car/Engine	Comment	Q Pos/Entries
7	MONACO GP	Monte Carlo	10	Equipe Gordini	E	2.5 Gordini Type 16 6	9 laps behind	20/22
10	DUTCH GP	Zandvoort	24	Equipe Gordini	E	2.5 Gordini Type 16 6	10 laps behind	12/16
ret	ITALIAN GP	Monza	26	Equipe Gordini	E	2.5 Gordini Type 16 6	engine	19/22

GP Starts: 5   GP Wins: 0   Pole positions: 0   Fastest laps: 0   Points: 0

PON, Ben (NL) b 9/12/1936, Leiden

1962 Championship position: Unplaced

	Race	Circuit	No	Entrant	Tyres	Capacity/Car/Engine	Comment	Q Pos/Entries
ret	DUTCH GP	Zandvoort	15	Ecurie Maarsbergen	D	1.5 Porsche 787 F4	spun off	18/20

GP Starts: 1   GP Wins: 0   Pole positions: 0   Fastest laps: 0   Points: 0

JACQUES POLLET

AFTER breezing into the Gordini squad for a single race at Chimay in 1953, Jacques 'Jacky' Pollet was taken on as a trainee works driver the following season. In single-seaters, he took sixth in the Bordeaux GP and shared the third-placed car with Jean Behra at Caen. He led briefly at Chimay until a stone smashed his goggles, and he was moving back through the field when he crashed into the crowd, fatally injuring two spectators.

In sports machines, 'Jacky' won his class at Le Mans with André Guelfi and also won the Tour de France Rally with Hubert Gauthier. His association with the team continued in 1955, but apart from fourth at Albi, little was achieved. Thereafter, Pollet competed in a Mercedes 300S, finishing eighth overall (fourth in class) in the 1956 Mille Miglia.

BEN PON

A CLASS winner for Porsche at Le Mans in 1961, popular Dutchman Ben Pon's only grand prix appearance ended in embarrassment as, trying too hard early on, he spun out on oil in his works-loaned Porsche on lap three of the 1962 Dutch Grand Prix. It could easily have been tragic, for his car overturned and he was thrown out, only luckily escaping injury.

Over the next few seasons, Pon was at the forefront of the Porsche challenge in sports and GT events, usually under the Racing Team Holland banner, but occasionally as a member of the full works team. He won races in his 904GT at Limbourg, Solitude and Zandvoort, and was third and a class winner in the 1965 Spa 1000km in a 914GTS. At the end of that year, he retired from driving duties to run the Dutch Racing Team.

DENNIS POORE

A WEALTHY industrialist, Dennis Poore was British hill-climb champion in 1950 with his Alfa Romeo 3.8S. He briefly became a member of the Connaught Racing Syndicate in 1952, scoring a fine fourth place in the British Grand Prix, and at national level he won minor races at Charterhall and Boreham.

After severing his connections with the Send concern, Poore linked up with the Aston Martin sports car team for 1953, racing the DB3S at both Le Mans and Dundrod. His best result with the car came in 1955, when he won the Goodwood International nine-hours in a DB3S with Peter Walker.

Poore continued to race his old Alfa Romeo in numerous events during this period, winning the Dick Seaman Trophy race three times in a row between 1951 and 1953.

SAM POSEY

A VERSATILE American driver who loved the ambience of Formula 1 and wanted to make a real impact on the grand prix scene, Sam Posey never really had the chance to do so. He performed capably in Can-Am, Trans-Am and sports cars in the late 1960s, and finished fourth at Daytona and Le Mans in 1970, but his real success came in Formula A, where he challenged David Hobbs and Graham McRae for the championships of 1971 and 1972. After a brief tilt at USAC, during the course of which he finished fifth at both Indianapolis and Pocono with an Eagle-Offy in 1972, Sam raced the Norris Industries Talon in US F5000 in 1974 and briefly in 1976, until his sponsorship dried up. Thereafter, he focused his attentions on IMSA and was a Le Mans regular for many years. Racing a works 3.5-litre BMW CSL, he won the 1975 Sebring 12-hour race with Brian Redman, Hans Stuck and Allan Moffat.

When Sam decided to wind down his racing career, he took up a TV commentator's role. He covered not only motor racing, but also the Olympic Games and the Tour de France for ABC Television. Posey also writes, paints and is a model railway expert. Despite suffering from Parkinson's disease, he still has a slot on Speed Channel as part of a team of experts reviewing the Formula 1 races.

CHARLES POZZI

A SHREWD motor dealer who traded in luxury cars after the Second World War, Charles Pozzi was briefly associated with Paul Vallée's Ecurie France, before leaving together with Eugène Chaboud. The pair formed their own team, Ecurie Leutitia, usually fielding Delahayes, with one of which Pozzi won the 1949 Comminges GP at St Gaudens. In 1950, he shared Rosier's Talbot in the French GP, but for the most part he confined himself to sports cars, winning the Casablanca 12-hours in a Talbot in 1952.

During 1953/54, Pozzi raced François Picard's Ferrari, before business pressures forced his retirement, as he was by then the importer for both Chrysler and Rolls-Royce in France. He maintained his interest in the sport for many years and, having become the Ferrari importer, he entered Daytonas and 512Bs at Le Mans throughout the 1970s.

POORE, Dennis (GB) b 19/8/1916, West London – d 12/2/1987, Kensington, London

	1952 Championship position:10th=		Wins: 0	Pole positions: 0		Fastest laps: 0	Points scored: 3		
	Race	Circuit	No	Entrant	Tyres	Capacity/Car/Engine	Comment	Q Pos/Entries
4	BRITISH GP	Silverstone	6	Connaught Engineering	D	2.0 Connaught A Type-Lea Francis 4	2 laps behind	8/32
12	ITALIAN GP	Monza	30	Connaught Racing Syndicate	D	2.0 Connaught A Type-Lea Francis 4	6 laps behind	19/35
	GP Starts: 2	GP Wins: 0	Pole positions: 0	Fastest laps: 0	Points: 3			

POSEY, Sam (USA) b 26/5/1944, New York City, New York

	1971 Championship position: Unplaced							
	Race	Circuit	No	Entrant	Tyres	Capacity/Car/Engine	Comment	Q Pos/Entries
ret	US GP	Watkins Glen	19	Team Surtees	F	3.0 Surtees TS9-Cosworth V8	engine	18/32
	1972 Championship position: Unplaced							
12	US GP	Watkins Glen	34	Champcarr Inc	G	3.0 Surtees TS9B-Cosworth V8	2 laps behind	23/32
	GP Starts: 2	GP Wins: 0	Pole positions: 0	Fastest laps: 0	Points: 0			

POZZI, Charles (F) b 27/8/1909, Paris – d 28/2/2001, Paris

	1950 Championship position: Unplaced							
	Race	Circuit	No	Entrant	Tyres	Capacity/Car/Engine	Comment	Q Pos/Entries
6*	FRENCH GP	Reims	26	Charles Pozzi	D	4.5 Lago-Talbot T26C 6	*Rosier took over car/8 laps behind	16/20
	GP Starts: 1	GP Wins: 0	Pole positions: 0	Fastest laps: 0	Points: 0			

JACKIE PRETORIUS

A MEMBER of one of South Africa's most famous families, Jacob Pretorius was a descendent of one of the earliest Dutch settlers and was related to Marthinus Pretorius, the first president of South Africa and founder of the city of Pretoria.

Jackie began getting his kicks by performing hair-raising stunts in the aptly named Dunlop Hell Drivers Team, along with his pal Doug Serrurier, but a big crash left him with a broken pelvis. He headed for the relative safety of circuit racing and soon became a leading light on the thriving South African racing scene of the early 1960s. He handled the local Serrurier-built LDS-Climax in national events, but used a Lotus 21-Climax to finish ninth in the non-championship 1966 South African GP.

Between 1968 and 1970, he was very successful in Lola single-seaters and T70 sports cars entered by Serrurier, but his best season was when handling the Team Gunston Brabham BT26A in 1971, when he won championship races at Killarney and the Natal Roy Hesketh circuit. In 1972, he drove a Surtees TS5A in the championship, but couldn't quite win a race and had to be content with top-six placings.

At the 1973 South African Grand Prix, Jackie was called in by Williams to replace Nanni Galli, who had been injured in an earlier testing accident. Then he returned to action in the local series with his ex-Motul Brabham BT38. He quit racing at the end of that year to work for Wynn Oil, where he spent 34 years until his retirement.

In 2003, Jackie's wife, Shirley, was murdered during a burglary at his home and he was badly beaten. Tragically, in 2009, in another break-in at his home, he was viciously assaulted and died from his injuries in hospital some three weeks later.

DAVID PROPHET

N EVER a driver likely to make an impression above national level, Midlands motor trader David Prophet raced enthusiastically in some serious machinery for more than a decade. While competing in Formula Junior, he took his Brabham to South Africa late in the 1963 season and raced in the national grand prix. He also took sixth place on aggregate in the Rand GP and finished second in the Libre Rhodesian GP.

David raced in European F2 from 1964 to 1967 with little success, but found more joy in sports cars, particularly with the Lotus 30. In 1968/69, he raced his Ford GT40 and then a Lola T70, before becoming a regular competitor in Formula 5000 in 1970 with a McLaren 10B. He took this car to the non-championship 1971 Argentine GP to claim a lucrative fourth place on aggregate after more fancied runners had fallen by the wayside. He was killed in 1981 when the helicopter in which he was leaving the Silverstone circuit crashed just after take-off.

PRETORIUS, Jackie (ZA) b 22/11/1934, Potchefstroom, Transvaal – d 30/3/2009, Johannesburg

	1965 Championship position: Unplaced							
	Race	Circuit	No	Entrant	Tyres	Capacity/Car/Engine	Comment	Q Pos/Entries
dnpq	SOUTH AFRICAN GP	East London	29	Jackie Pretorius	D	1.5 LDS Mk1-Alfa Romeo 4	dnq for official practice	– / –
	1968 Championship position: Unplaced							
nc	SOUTH AFRICAN GP	Kyalami	23	Team Pretoria	F	2.7 Brabham BT11-Climax 4	10 laps behind	23/23
	1971 Championship position: Unplaced							
ret	SOUTH AFRICAN GP	Kyalami	25	Team Gunston	F	3.0 Brabham BT26A-Cosworth V8	engine	20/25
	1973 Championship position: Unplaced							
ret	SOUTH AFRICAN GP	Kyalami	20	Frank Williams Racing Cars	F	3.0 Iso Marlboro FX3B-Cosworth V8	overheating	24/25
	GP Starts: 3 GP Wins: 0 Pole positions: 0 Fastest laps: 0 Points: 0							

PROPHET, David (GB) b 9/10/1937, Hong Kong – d 29/3/1981, Silverstone, Northamptonshire

	1963 Championship position: Unplaced							
	Race	Circuit	No	Entrant	Tyres	Capacity/Car/Engine	Comment	Q Pos/Entries
ret	SOUTH AFRICAN GP	East London	22	David Prophet	D	1.5 Brabham BT6-Ford 4	oil pressure	14/21
	1965 Championship position: Unplaced							
14	SOUTH AFRICAN GP	East London	19	David Prophet Racing	D	1.5 Brabham BT10-Ford 4	14 laps behind	19/25
	GP Starts: 2 GP Wins: 0 Pole positions: 0 Fastest laps: 0 Points: 0							

ALAIN PROST

WHEN Alain Prost retired at the end of 1993, his record stood at four world championships, a total of 51 grand prix wins and nearly 800 points from 199 starts. Simple mathematics tell the story: an average of four points from every grand prix. Yet despite these staggering statistics, there are plenty of fans who wouldn't give the Frenchman the time of day. Perhaps only Jackie Stewart can divide opinion so sharply, and the issues were much clearer in his case, being centred on safety.

As the years roll by, however, Alain will rightly be lauded as one of the sport's absolute greats. Certainly a decade or two hence, there will be few, if any, followers of motor racing who will be able to understand the current dismissive attitude of an ill-informed minority towards his wonderful achievements.

Prost's racing career had been set on a stellar path from the start. After racing karts in the company of Eddie Cheever and Riccardo Patrese, he turned to cars in 1975, enrolling at the Winfield school. He won the traditional Pilote Elf prize of a car for the following season's Formule Renault series and certainly put it to good use, winning 12 of 13 races. Promotion to Formule Super Renault duly followed, and eight wins later that trophy went on the Prost mantelpiece as well. He moved into Formula 3 in 1978, but the Martini MK21B-Renault was not truly competitive until a close-season revamp saw it emerge as the Mk27. He proved virtually unbeatable with it, taking the European and French titles, and the all-important Monaco Formula 3 race. He was ready for Formula 1, and McLaren were the first takers.

In 1980, the team were not in great shape and were on the point of total transition, but Prost was unfazed and scored points in his first two grands prix. Even in that first season, the traits that later served him so well were there: the smooth driving style, the willingness to speak his mind honestly, and a genuine concern about the sport and its image.

The chance to join Renault for 1981 was too good to turn down, and Prost moved in to completely flummox partner René Arnoux. He scored three wins that year, displaying coolness under pressure and making very few mistakes. Fifth place in the final points did him an injustice.

It was more of the same in 1982, but only two more wins were added that year. There could have been many others if the Renault had not let Alain down so often. It was largely thanks to him that the RE30B reached such a competitive position, and he was just as formidable a force in 1983 with its successor. Apart from an error at Zandvoort, he hardly put a foot wrong, yet still the championship slipped through his fingers at the very last. Renault and the French press pointed the finger of blame at a bemused Prost, who took the only course of action possible and high-tailed it to McLaren, who knew better than to look a gift horse in the mouth.

While the Renault F1 effort slid into oblivion over the next two seasons, Alain was busy winning the small matter of 12 grands prix. In 1984, despite seven wins, he lost out to team-mate Niki Lauda by just half a point, but finally cracked it to become the first French world champion in 1985. All his hallmarks were on display in that first title-winning year. Meticulous in setting up his car and in race strategy, he raced hard when he needed to and weighed up the odds to maximise his return when his car was perhaps not the quickest. No wonder they called him 'The Professor'.

With Williams-Honda dominant in 1986, few gave Alain any hope of retaining his crown, but luck was on his side when Nigel Mansell and Nelson Piquet took vital points from each other in their internecine battle. Prost hung in, picking up every point possible and coaxed four wins from the McLaren-TAG to steal the title in Adelaide when both Williams faltered.

The following year, even Prost's powers were unable to halt the Williams steamroller, but he did overtake Jackie Stewart's long-standing total of grand prix wins in Portugal. Then, in 1988, Prost too had Honda power, but with the Japanese V6 came Ayrton Senna. That first season saw a McLaren carve-up, the pair winning all but one of the 16 races. Senna had the edge, taking eight wins to Prost's seven, and the little Frenchman appeared at times non-plussed by the Brazilian's sheer speed and had to settle for second-best for once. It should be noted that Alain actually totalled more points that year (105 to 94), but the scoring system required drivers to count only their 11 best scores from the 16-race season.

It was a different story in 1989; Alain raised his game and the battle was on, especially after a steady deterioration in the drivers' relationship. The title was settled in the Frenchman's favour when he subtly chopped the Brazilian at Suzuka. It was truly an awful way to decide a championship. Subsequently, tired of wrangles in a team that he had come to see as Senna's fiefdom, Prost headed off to Maranello

History repeated itself in 1990, except that Alain was now on the receiving end as Senna exacted his revenge by driving into the back of his Ferrari at the start. That wiped out a season's truly brilliant endeavour by Prost, who had moved into his new environment and immediately given the Italian team a real sense of purpose. Unfortunately, this was not maintained in 1991, when Maranello politics and intrigue reached new heights, and he became locked in bitter off-track arguments. When it finally arrived, the new 643 was disappointing, and by the season's end the Frenchman had been fired for his outspoken views.

Disillusioned, Prost took a year's sabbatical from the cockpit, despite massive pressure to join Ligier. This move left him plenty of time to weigh up his options, and by mid-1992 he had tied up a deal to race for Williams in 1993, expecting to partner Nigel Mansell. The Englishman chose to vacate his seat, however, leaving Prost in a very strong position to take his fourth world championship. He got the job done in his usual undramatic style, his season yielding 13 pole positions and another seven wins. With the prospect of Ayrton Senna joining the team in 1994, he concluded that he just didn't need the aggravation and announced that he was going to retire at the end of the season.

However, there were tempting opportunities to consider. He tested a McLaren-Peugeot early in 1994, but eventually confirmed his decision to retire. In the aftermath of Senna's death, he declared that he would not race again, but in 1995 he tested for McLaren once more, subsequently joining the team in a test and advisory capacity. With a new era already dawning in Formula 1, he took on a huge new challenge by buying the Ligier team, which was renamed Prost Grand Prix prior to the start of the 1997 season. He immediately set about a major overhaul of the under-performing French constructor, moving its base from Magny-Cours to the outskirts of Paris.

Like Jackie Stewart, Prost was an exacting taskmaster who expected, perhaps unrealistically, his drivers to match his own standards. In his five seasons as a team owner, he saw Olivier Panis (Spain, 1997) and Jarno Trulli (Europe, 1999) take his cars to second-place finishes. Otherwise there was little else to cheer, and by the start of the 2002 season bankruptcy had been declared, leaving debts of some US$30m; the blue of France disappeared from the grid.

Alain has successfully returned to competition in the Andros Trophy, claiming the championship in 2007 and 2008 with a Toyota Auris. In 2012, he made it a hat trick of titles behind the wheel of a Dacia Lodgy.

PROST, Alain (F) b 24/2/1955, Lorette, Saint-Chamond, nr St Etienne

1980 Championship position: 15th=   Wins: 0   Pole positions: 0   Fastest laps: 0   Points scored: 5

	Race	Circuit	No	Entrant	Tyres	Capacity/Car/Engine	Comment	Q Pos/Entries
6	ARGENTINE GP	Buenos Aires	8	Marlboro Team McLaren	G	3.0 McLaren M29-Cosworth V8	1 lap behind	12/28
5	BRAZILIAN GP	Interlagos	8	Marlboro Team McLaren	G	3.0 McLaren M29-Cosworth V8		13/28
dns	SOUTH AFRICAN GP	Kyalami	8	Marlboro Team McLaren	G	3.0 McLaren M29-Cosworth V8	practice accident – injured wrist	(22)/28
ret	BELGIAN GP	Zolder	8	Marlboro Team McLaren	G	3.0 McLaren M29-Cosworth V8	transmission	19/27
ret	MONACO GP	Monte Carlo	8	Marlboro Team McLaren	G	3.0 McLaren M29-Cosworth V8	multiple accident on first lap	10/27
ret	FRENCH GP	Paul Ricard	8	Marlboro Team McLaren	G	3.0 McLaren M29-Cosworth V8	transmission	7/27
6	BRITISH GP	Brands Hatch	8	Marlboro Team McLaren	G	3.0 McLaren M29-Cosworth V8	1 lap behind	7/27
11	GERMAN GP	Hockenheim	8	Marlboro Team McLaren	G	3.0 McLaren M29-Cosworth V8	pit stops/tyre/skirt problems	14/26
7	AUSTRIAN GP	Österreichring	8	Marlboro Team McLaren	G	3.0 McLaren M29-Cosworth V8		12/25
6	DUTCH GP	Zandvoort	8	Marlboro Team McLaren	G	3.0 McLaren M30-Cosworth V8		18/28
7	ITALIAN GP	Imola	8	Marlboro Team McLaren	G	3.0 McLaren M30-Cosworth V8	1 lap behind	24/28
ret	CANADIAN GP	Montreal	8	Marlboro Team McLaren	G	3.0 McLaren M30-Cosworth V8	suspension failure/accident	12/28
dns	US GP EAST	Watkins Glen	8	Marlboro Team McLaren	G	3.0 McLaren M30-Cosworth V8	injured in practice accident	(13)/27

1981 Championship position: 5th   Wins: 3   Pole positions: 2   Fastest laps: 1   Points scored: 43

	Race	Circuit	No	Entrant	Tyres	Capacity/Car/Engine	Comment	Q Pos/Entries
ret	US GP WEST	Long Beach	15	Equipe Renault Elf	M	1.5 t/c Renault RE22B V6	hit by de Cesaris	14/29
ret	BRAZILIAN GP	Rio	15	Equipe Renault Elf	M	1.5 t/c Renault RE22B V6	hit by Pironi	5/30
3	ARGENTINE GP	Buenos Aires	15	Equipe Renault Elf	M	1.5 t/c Renault RE22B V6		2/29
ret	SAN MARINO GP	Imola	15	Equipe Renault Elf	M	1.5 t/c Renault RE22B V6	gearbox	4/30
ret	BELGIAN GP	Zolder	15	Equipe Renault Elf	M	1.5 t/c Renault RE30 V6	clutch	12/31
ret	MONACO GP	Monte Carlo	15	Equipe Renault Elf	M	1.5 t/c Renault RE30 V6	engine	9/31
ret	SPANISH GP	Jarama	15	Equipe Renault Elf	M	1.5 t/c Renault RE30 V6	spun off	5/30
1*	FRENCH GP	Dijon	15	Equipe Renault Elf	M	1.5 t/c Renault RE30 V6	*aggregate of two parts/FL	3/29
ret	BRITISH GP	Silverstone	15	Equipe Renault Elf	M	1.5 t/c Renault RE30 V6	engine	2/30
2	GERMAN GP	Hockenheim	15	Equipe Renault Elf	M	1.5 t/c Renault RE30 V6		1/30
ret	AUSTRIAN GP	Österreichring	15	Equipe Renault Elf	M	1.5 t/c Renault RE30 V6	front suspension	2/28
1	DUTCH GP	Zandvoort	15	Equipe Renault Elf	M	1.5 t/c Renault RE30 V6		1/30
1	ITALIAN GP	Monza	15	Equipe Renault Elf	M	1.5 t/c Renault RE30 V6		3/30
ret	CANADIAN GP	Montreal	15	Equipe Renault Elf	M	1.5 t/c Renault RE30 V6	accident with Mansell	4/30
2	CAESARS PALACE GP	Las Vegas	15	Equipe Renault Elf	M	1.5 t/c Renault RE30 V6		5/30

1982 Championship position: 4th   Wins: 2   Pole positions: 5   Fastest laps: 4   Points scored: 34

	Race	Circuit	No	Entrant	Tyres	Capacity/Car/Engine	Comment	Q Pos/Entries
1	SOUTH AFRICAN GP	Kyalami	15	Equipe Renault Elf	M	1.5 t/c Renault RE30B V6	FL	5/30
1*	BRAZILIAN GP	Rio	15	Equipe Renault Elf	M	1.5 t/c Renault RE30B V6	*1st & 2nd place cars disqualified/FL	1/31
ret	US GP WEST	Long Beach	15	Equipe Renault Elf	M	1.5 t/c Renault RE30B V6	brake problems/hit wall	4/31
ret	SAN MARINO GP	Imola	15	Equipe Renault Elf	M	1.5 t/c Renault RE30B V6	engine	2/14
ret	BELGIAN GP	Zolder	15	Equipe Renault Elf	M	1.5 t/c Renault RE30B V6	spun off	1/32
7/ret	MONACO GP	Monte Carlo	15	Equipe Renault Elf	M	1.5 t/c Renault RE30B V6	spun off/3 laps behind	4/31
nc	US GP (DETROIT)	Detroit	15	Equipe Renault Elf	M	1.5 t/c Renault RE30B V6	pit stop/fuel pump/FL/8 laps behind	1/28
ret	CANADIAN GP	Montreal	15	Equipe Renault Elf	M	1.5 t/c Renault RE30B V6	engine	3/29
ret	DUTCH GP	Zandvoort	15	Equipe Renault Elf	M	1.5 t/c Renault RE30B V6	engine	2/31
6	BRITISH GP	Brands Hatch	15	Equipe Renault Elf	M	1.5 t/c Renault RE30B V6		8/30
2	FRENCH GP	Paul Ricard	15	Equipe Renault Elf	M	1.5 t/c Renault RE30B V6	Arnoux 'won' race against team orders	2/30
ret	GERMAN GP	Hockenheim	15	Equipe Renault Elf	M	1.5 t/c Renault RE30B V6	fuel injection	2/30
8/ret	AUSTRIAN GP	Österreichring	15	Equipe Renault Elf	M	1.5 t/c Renault RE30B V6	fuel injection/5 laps behind	3/29
2	SWISS GP	Dijon	15	Equipe Renault Elf	M	1.5 t/c Renault RE30B V6	FL	1/29
ret	ITALIAN GP	Monza	15	Equipe Renault Elf	M	1.5 t/c Renault RE30B V6	fuel injection	5/30
4	CAESARS PALACE GP	Las Vegas	15	Equipe Renault Elf	M	1.5 t/c Renault RE30B V6		1/30

Prost takes his Renault to victory in the 1983 French Grand Prix. Despite his four wins that year, ultimately the Frenchman lost out by just two points to Nelson Piquet in the championship battle.

Alain heads for victory in the 1985 Italian Grand Prix in his McLaren MP4/28. He ended the year with the distinction of becoming France's first ever world champion.

1983 Championship position: 2nd   Wins: 4   Pole positions: 3   Fastest laps: 3   Points scored: 57

7	BRAZILIAN GP	Rio	15	Equipe Renault Elf	M	1.5 t/c Renault RE30C V6	*1 lap behind*	2/27
11	US GP WEST	Long Beach	15	Equipe Renault Elf	M	1.5 t/c Renault RE40 V6	*pit stop/misfire/3 laps behind*	8/28
1	FRENCH GP	Paul Ricard	15	Equipe Renault Elf	M	1.5 t/c Renault RE40 V6	*FL*	1/29
2	SAN MARINO GP	Imola	15	Equipe Renault Elf	M	1.5 t/c Renault RE40 V6		4/28
3	MONACO GP	Monte Carlo	15	Equipe Renault Elf	M	1.5 t/c Renault RE40 V6		1/28
1	BELGIAN GP	Spa	15	Equipe Renault Elf	M	1.5 t/c Renault RE40 V6		1/28
8	US GP (DETROIT)	Detroit	15	Equipe Renault Elf	M	1.5 t/c Renault RE40 V6	*pit stop/fuel/1 lap behind*	13/27
5	CANADIAN GP	Montreal	15	Equipe Renault Elf	M	1.5 t/c Renault RE40 V6	*1 lap behind*	2/28
1	BRITISH GP	Silverstone	15	Equipe Renault Elf	M	1.5 t/c Renault RE40 V6	*FL*	3/29
4	GERMAN GP	Hockenheim	15	Equipe Renault Elf	M	1.5 t/c Renault RE40 V6		5/29
1	AUSTRIAN GP	Österreichring	15	Equipe Renault Elf	M	1.5 t/c Renault RE40 V6	*FL*	5/29
ret	DUTCH GP	Zandvoort	15	Equipe Renault Elf	M	1.5 t/c Renault RE40 V6	*collision with Piquet*	4/29
ret	ITALIAN GP	Monza	15	Equipe Renault Elf	M	1.5 t/c Renault RE40 V6	*turbo*	5/29
2	EUROPEAN GP	Brands Hatch	15	Equipe Renault Elf	M	1.5 t/c Renault RE40 V6		8/29
ret	SOUTH AFRICAN GP	Kyalami	15	Equipe Renault Elf	M	1.5 t/c Renault RE40 V6	*turbo*	5/26

1984 Championship position: 2nd   Wins: 7   Pole positions: 3   Fastest laps: 3   Points scored: 71.5

1	BRAZILIAN GP	Rio	7	Marlboro McLaren International	M	1.5 t/c McLaren MP4/2-TAG V6	*FL*	4/27
2	SOUTH AFRICAN GP	Kyalami	7	Marlboro McLaren International	M	1.5 t/c McLaren MP4/2-TAG V6	*started from pitlane*	5/27
ret	BELGIAN GP	Zolder	7	Marlboro McLaren International	M	1.5 t/c McLaren MP4/2-TAG V6	*distributor*	8/27
1	SAN MARINO GP	Imola	7	Marlboro McLaren International	M	1.5 t/c McLaren MP4/2-TAG V6		2/28
7	FRENCH GP	Dijon	7	Marlboro McLaren International	M	1.5 t/c McLaren MP4/2-TAG V6	*2 pit stops/loose wheel/FL*	5/27
1*	MONACO GP	Monte Carlo	7	Marlboro McLaren International	M	1.5 t/c McLaren MP4/2-TAG V6	**rain shortened race – half points*	1/27
3	CANADIAN GP	Montreal	7	Marlboro McLaren International	M	1.5 t/c McLaren MP4/2-TAG V6		2/26
4*	US GP (DETROIT)	Detroit	7	Marlboro McLaren International	M	1.5 t/c McLaren MP4/2-TAG V6	**2nd place car disqualified*	2/27
ret	US GP (DALLAS)	Dallas	7	Marlboro McLaren International	M	1.5 t/c McLaren MP4/2-TAG V6	*hit wall*	7/27
ret	BRITISH GP	Brands Hatch	7	Marlboro McLaren International	M	1.5 t/c McLaren MP4/2-TAG V6	*gearbox*	2/27
1	GERMAN GP	Hockenheim	7	Marlboro McLaren International	M	1.5 t/c McLaren MP4/2-TAG V6	*FL*	1/27
ret	AUSTRIAN GP	Österreichring	7	Marlboro McLaren International	M	1.5 t/c McLaren MP4/2-TAG V6	*spun off*	2/28
1	DUTCH GP	Zandvoort	7	Marlboro McLaren International	M	1.5 t/c McLaren MP4/2-TAG V6		1/27
ret	ITALIAN GP	Monza	7	Marlboro McLaren International	M	1.5 t/c McLaren MP4/2-TAG V6	*engine*	2/27
1	EUROPEAN GP	Nürburgring	7	Marlboro McLaren International	M	1.5 t/c McLaren MP4/2-TAG V6		2/26
1	PORTUGUESE GP	Estoril	7	Marlboro McLaren International	M	1.5 t/c McLaren MP4/2-TAG V6		2/27

1985 WORLD CHAMPION   Wins: 5   Pole positions: 2   Fastest laps: 5   Points scored: 76

1	BRAZILIAN GP	Rio	2	Marlboro McLaren International	G	1.5 t/c McLaren MP4/2B-TAG V6	*FL*	6/25
ret	PORTUGUESE GP	Estoril	2	Marlboro McLaren International	G	1.5 t/c McLaren MP4/2B-TAG V6	*spun off*	2/26
dsq*	SAN MARINO GP	Imola	2	Marlboro McLaren International	G	1.5 t/c McLaren MP4/2B-TAG V6	*1st on road/* dsq – car underweight*	6/26
1	MONACO GP	Monte Carlo	2	Marlboro McLaren International	G	1.5 t/c McLaren MP4/2B-TAG V6		5/26
3	CANADIAN GP	Montreal	2	Marlboro McLaren International	G	1.5 t/c McLaren MP4/2B-TAG V6		5/25
ret	US GP (DETROIT)	Detroit	2	Marlboro McLaren International	G	1.5 t/c McLaren MP4/2B-TAG V6	*brake failure/accident*	4/25
3	FRENCH GP	Paul Ricard	2	Marlboro McLaren International	G	1.5 t/c McLaren MP4/2B-TAG V6		4/26
1	BRITISH GP	Silverstone	2	Marlboro McLaren International	G	1.5 t/c McLaren MP4/2B-TAG V6	*FL*	3/26
2	GERMAN GP	Nürburgring	2	Marlboro McLaren International	G	1.5 t/c McLaren MP4/2B-TAG V6		3/27
1	AUSTRIAN GP	Österreichring	2	Marlboro McLaren International	G	1.5 t/c McLaren MP4/2B-TAG V6	*FL*	1/27
2	DUTCH GP	Zandvoort	2	Marlboro McLaren International	G	1.5 t/c McLaren MP4/2B-TAG V6	*FL*	3/27
1	ITALIAN GP	Monza	2	Marlboro McLaren International	G	1.5 t/c McLaren MP4/2B-TAG V6		5/26
3	BELGIAN GP	Spa	2	Marlboro McLaren International	G	1.5 t/c McLaren MP4/2B-TAG V6	*FL*	1/24
4	EUROPEAN GP	Brands Hatch	2	Marlboro McLaren International	G	1.5 t/c McLaren MP4/2B-TAG V6		6/27
3	SOUTH AFRICAN GP	Kyalami	2	Marlboro McLaren International	G	1.5 t/c McLaren MP4/2B-TAG V6		9/21
ret	AUSTRALIAN GP	Adelaide	2	Marlboro McLaren International	G	1.5 t/c McLaren MP4/2B-TAG V6	*engine*	4/25

1986 WORLD CHAMPION Wins: 4 Pole positions: 1 Fastest laps: 2 Points scored: 74

ret	BRAZILIAN GP	Rio	1	Marlboro McLaren International	G	1.5 t/c McLaren MP4/2C-TAG V6	engine	9/25
3	SPANISH GP	Jerez	1	Marlboro McLaren International	G	1.5 t/c McLaren MP4/2C-TAG V6		4/25
1	SAN MARINO GP	Imola	1	Marlboro McLaren International	G	1.5 t/c McLaren MP4/2C-TAG V6		4/26
1	MONACO GP	Monte Carlo	1	Marlboro McLaren International	G	1.5 t/c McLaren MP4/2C-TAG V6	FL	1/26
6	BELGIAN GP	Spa	1	Marlboro McLaren International	G	1.5 t/c McLaren MP4/2C-TAG V6	first lap collision and spin/FL	3/25
2	CANADIAN GP	Montreal	1	Marlboro McLaren International	G	1.5 t/c McLaren MP4/2C-TAG V6		4/25
3	US GP (DETROIT)	Detroit	1	Marlboro McLaren International	G	1.5 t/c McLaren MP4/2C-TAG V6		7/26
2	FRENCH GP	Paul Ricard	1	Marlboro McLaren International	G	1.5 t/c McLaren MP4/2C-TAG V6		5/26
3	BRITISH GP	Brands Hatch	1	Marlboro McLaren International	G	1.5 t/c McLaren MP4/2C-TAG V6		6/26
6/ret	GERMAN GP	Hockenheim	1	Marlboro McLaren International	G	1.5 t/c McLaren MP4/2C-TAG V6	out of fuel	2/26
ret	HUNGARIAN GP	Hungaroring	1	Marlboro McLaren International	G	1.5 t/c McLaren MP4/2C-TAG V6	accident with Arnoux	3/26
1	AUSTRIAN GP	Österreichring	1	Marlboro McLaren International	G	1.5 t/c McLaren MP4/2C-TAG V6		5/26
ret/dsq*	ITALIAN GP	Monza	1	Marlboro McLaren International	G	1.5 t/c McLaren MP4/2C-TAG V6	engine/*car change after green	2/27
2	PORTUGUESE GP	Estoril	1	Marlboro McLaren International	G	1.5 t/c McLaren MP4/2C-TAG V6		3/27
2	MEXICAN GP	Mexico City	1	Marlboro McLaren International	G	1.5 t/c McLaren MP4/2C-TAG V6		6/26
1	AUSTRALIAN GP	Adelaide	1	Marlboro McLaren International	G	1.5 t/c McLaren MP4/2C-TAG V6		4/26

1987 Championship position: 4th Wins: 3 Pole positions: 0 Fastest laps: 2 Points scored: 46

1	BRAZILIAN GP	Rio	1	Marlboro McLaren International	G	1.5 t/c McLaren MP4/3-TAG V6		5/23
ret	SAN MARINO GP	Imola	1	Marlboro McLaren International	G	1.5 t/c McLaren MP4/3-TAG V6	alternator	4/27
1	BELGIAN GP	Spa	1	Marlboro McLaren International	G	1.5 t/c McLaren MP4/3-TAG V6	FL	6/26
9/ret	MONACO GP	Monte Carlo	1	Marlboro McLaren International	G	1.5 t/c McLaren MP4/3-TAG V6	engine/3 laps behind	4/26
3	US GP (DETROIT)	Detroit	1	Marlboro McLaren International	G	1.5 t/c McLaren MP4/3-TAG V6		5/26
3	FRENCH GP	Paul Ricard	1	Marlboro McLaren International	G	1.5 t/c McLaren MP4/3-TAG V6		2/26
ret	BRITISH GP	Silverstone	1	Marlboro McLaren International	G	1.5 t/c McLaren MP4/3-TAG V6	clutch bearings/electrics	4/26
7/ret	GERMAN GP	Hockenheim	1	Marlboro McLaren International	G	1.5 t/c McLaren MP4/3-TAG V6	alternator belt/5 laps behind	3/26
3	HUNGARIAN GP	Hungaroring	1	Marlboro McLaren International	G	1.5 t/c McLaren MP4/3-TAG V6		4/26
6	AUSTRIAN GP	Österreichring	1	Marlboro McLaren International	G	1.5 t/c McLaren MP4/3-TAG V6	started from pit lane/2 laps behind	9/26
15	ITALIAN GP	Monza	1	Marlboro McLaren International	G	1.5 t/c McLaren MP4/3-TAG V6	pit stop – misfire/4 laps behind	5/28
1	PORTUGUESE GP	Estoril	1	Marlboro McLaren International	G	1.5 t/c McLaren MP4/3-TAG V6		3/27
2	SPANISH GP	Jerez	1	Marlboro McLaren International	G	1.5 t/c McLaren MP4/3-TAG V6		7/28
ret	MEXICAN GP	Mexico City	1	Marlboro McLaren International	G	1.5 t/c McLaren MP4/3-TAG V6	accident with Piquet	5/27
7	JAPANESE GP	Suzuka	1	Marlboro McLaren International	G	1.5 t/c McLaren MP4/3-TAG V6	pit stop – puncture/FL/1 lap behind	2/27
ret	AUSTRALIAN GP	Adelaide	1	Marlboro McLaren International	G	1.5 t/c McLaren MP4/3-TAG V6	brake problem – accident	2/27

1988 Championship position: 2nd Wins: 7 Pole positions: 2 Fastest laps: 7 Points scored: 95

1	BRAZILIAN GP	Rio	11	Honda Marlboro McLaren	G	1.5 t/c McLaren MP4/4-Honda V6		3/31
2	SAN MARINO GP	Imola	11	Honda Marlboro McLaren	G	1.5 t/c McLaren MP4/4-Honda V6	FL	2/31
1	MONACO GP	Monte Carlo	11	Honda Marlboro McLaren	G	1.5 t/c McLaren MP4/4-Honda V6		2/30
1	MEXICAN GP	Mexico City	11	Honda Marlboro McLaren	G	1.5 t/c McLaren MP4/4-Honda V6	FL	2/30
2	CANADIAN GP	Montreal	11	Honda Marlboro McLaren	G	1.5 t/c McLaren MP4/4-Honda V6		2/31
2	US GP (DETROIT)	Detroit	11	Honda Marlboro McLaren	G	1.5 t/c McLaren MP4/4-Honda V6	FL	4/31
1	FRENCH GP	Paul Ricard	11	Honda Marlboro McLaren	G	1.5 t/c McLaren MP4/4-Honda V6	FL	1/31
ret	BRITISH GP	Silverstone	11	Honda Marlboro McLaren	G	1.5 t/c McLaren MP4/4-Honda V6	handling in wet conditions	4/31
2	GERMAN GP	Hockenheim	11	Honda Marlboro McLaren	G	1.5 t/c McLaren MP4/4-Honda V6		2/31
2	HUNGARIAN GP	Hungaroring	11	Honda Marlboro McLaren	G	1.5 t/c McLaren MP4/4-Honda V6	FL	7/31
2	BELGIAN GP	Spa	11	Honda Marlboro McLaren	G	1.5 t/c McLaren MP4/4-Honda V6		2/31
ret	ITALIAN GP	Monza	11	Honda Marlboro McLaren	G	1.5 t/c McLaren MP4/4-Honda V6	engine	2/31
1	PORTUGUESE GP	Estoril	11	Honda Marlboro McLaren	G	1.5 t/c McLaren MP4/4-Honda V6		1/31
1	SPANISH GP	Jerez	11	Honda Marlboro McLaren	G	1.5 t/c McLaren MP4/4-Honda V6	FL	2/31
2	JAPANESE GP	Suzuka	11	Honda Marlboro McLaren	G	1.5 t/c McLaren MP4/4-Honda V6		2/31
1	AUSTRALIAN GP	Adelaide	11	Honda Marlboro McLaren	G	1.5 t/c McLaren MP4/4-Honda V6	FL	2/31

1989 WORLD CHAMPION Wins: 4 Pole positions: 2 Fastest laps: 5 Points scored: 81

2	BRAZILIAN GP	Rio	2	Honda Marlboro McLaren	G	3.5 McLaren MP4/5-Honda V10		5/38
2*	SAN MARINO GP	Imola	2	Honda Marlboro McLaren	G	3.5 McLaren MP4/5-Honda V10	*aggregate of two parts/FL	2/39
2	MONACO GP	Monte Carlo	2	Honda Marlboro McLaren	G	3.5 McLaren MP4/5-Honda V10	FL	2/38
5	MEXICAN GP	Mexico City	2	Honda Marlboro McLaren	G	3.5 McLaren MP4/5-Honda V10	wrong choice of tyre type	2/39
1	US GP (PHOENIX)	Phoenix	2	Honda Marlboro McLaren	G	3.5 McLaren MP4/5-Honda V10		2/39
ret	CANADIAN GP	Montreal	2	Honda Marlboro McLaren	G	3.5 McLaren MP4/5-Honda V10	suspension failure	1/39
1	FRENCH GP	Paul Ricard	2	Honda Marlboro McLaren	G	3.5 McLaren MP4/5-Honda V10		1/39
1	BRITISH GP	Silverstone	2	Honda Marlboro McLaren	G	3.5 McLaren MP4/5-Honda V10		2/39
2	GERMAN GP	Hockenheim	2	Honda Marlboro McLaren	G	3.5 McLaren MP4/5-Honda V10		2/39
4	HUNGARIAN GP	Hungaroring	2	Honda Marlboro McLaren	G	3.5 McLaren MP4/5-Honda V10	late pit stop – tyre	5/39
2	BELGIAN GP	Spa	2	Honda Marlboro McLaren	G	3.5 McLaren MP4/5-Honda V10	FL	2/39
1	ITALIAN GP	Monza	2	Honda Marlboro McLaren	G	3.5 McLaren MP4/5-Honda V10	FL	4/39
2	PORTUGUESE GP	Estoril	2	Honda Marlboro McLaren	G	3.5 McLaren MP4/5-Honda V10		4/39
3	SPANISH GP	Jerez	2	Honda Marlboro McLaren	G	3.5 McLaren MP4/5-Honda V10		3/38
ret	JAPANESE GP	Suzuka	2	Honda Marlboro McLaren	G	3.5 McLaren MP4/5-Honda V10	collision with Senna at chicane/FL	2/39
dns	AUSTRALIAN GP	Adelaide	2	Honda Marlboro McLaren	G	3.5 McLaren MP4/5-Honda V10	refused to start due to heavy rain	2/39

1990 Championship position: 2nd Wins: 5 Pole positions: 0 Fastest laps: 2 Points scored: 73

ret	US GP (PHOENIX)	Phoenix	1	Scuderia Ferrari SpA	G	3.5 Fiat Ferrari 641 V12	engine – oil leak	7/35
1	BRAZILIAN GP	Rio	1	Scuderia Ferrari SpA	G	3.5 Fiat Ferrari 641 V12		6/35
4	SAN MARINO GP	Imola	1	Scuderia Ferrari SpA	G	3.5 Fiat Ferrari 641 V12		6/34
ret	MONACO GP	Monte Carlo	1	Scuderia Ferrari SpA	G	3.5 Fiat Ferrari 641 V12	electrics	2/35
5	CANADIAN GP	Montreal	1	Scuderia Ferrari SpA	G	3.5 Fiat Ferrari 641 V12	worn brakes	3/35
1	MEXICAN GP	Mexico City	1	Scuderia Ferrari SpA	G	3.5 Fiat Ferrari 641 V12	FL	13/35
1	FRENCH GP	Paul Ricard	1	Scuderia Ferrari SpA	G	3.5 Fiat Ferrari 641 V12		4/35
1	BRITISH GP	Silverstone	1	Scuderia Ferrari SpA	G	3.5 Fiat Ferrari 641 V12		5/35
4	GERMAN GP	Hockenheim	1	Scuderia Ferrari SpA	G	3.5 Fiat Ferrari 641 V12		3/35
ret	HUNGARIAN GP	Hungaroring	1	Scuderia Ferrari SpA	G	3.5 Fiat Ferrari 641 V12	clutch seized – spun off	8/35

2	BELGIAN GP	Spa	1	Scuderia Ferrari SpA	G	3.5 Fiat Ferrari 641 V12	*FL*	3/33
2	ITALIAN GP	Monza	1	Scuderia Ferrari SpA	G	3.5 Fiat Ferrari 641 V12		2/33
3	PORTUGUESE GP	Estoril	1	Scuderia Ferrari SpA	G	3.5 Fiat Ferrari 641 V12		2/33
1	SPANISH GP	Jerez	1	Scuderia Ferrari SpA	G	3.5 Fiat Ferrari 641 V12		2/33
ret	JAPANESE GP	Suzuka	1	Scuderia Ferrari SpA	G	3.5 Fiat Ferrari 641 V12	*first corner crash with Senna*	2/30
3	AUSTRALIAN GP	Adelaide	1	Scuderia Ferrari SpA	G	3.5 Fiat Ferrari 641 V12		4/30

1991 Championship position: 5th   Wins: 0   Pole positions: 0   Fastest laps: 1   Points scored: 31

2	US GP (PHOENIX)	Phoenix	27	Scuderia Ferrari SpA	G	3.5 Fiat Ferrari 642 V12		2/34
4	BRAZILIAN GP	Interlagos	27	Scuderia Ferrari SpA	G	3.5 Fiat Ferrari 642 V12		6/34
ret/dns*	SAN MARINO GP	Imola	27	Scuderia Ferrari SpA	G	3.5 Fiat Ferrari 642 V12	**spun off on parade lap*	(3)/34
5	MONACO GP	Monte Carlo	27	Scuderia Ferrari SpA	G	3.5 Fiat Ferrari 642 V12	*late pit stop – tyres/FL/1 lap behind*	7/34
ret	CANADIAN GP	Montreal	27	Scuderia Ferrari SpA	G	3.5 Fiat Ferrari 642 V12	*gearbox*	4/34
ret	MEXICAN GP	Mexico City	27	Scuderia Ferrari SpA	G	3.5 Fiat Ferrari 642 V12	*alternator*	7/34
2	FRENCH GP	Magny Cours	27	Scuderia Ferrari SpA	G	3.5 Fiat Ferrari 643 V12		2/34
3	BRITISH GP	Silverstone	27	Scuderia Ferrari SpA	G	3.5 Fiat Ferrari 643 V12		5/34
ret	GERMAN GP	Hockenheim	27	Scuderia Ferrari SpA	G	3.5 Fiat Ferrari 643 V12	*spun off – unable to restart*	5/34
ret	HUNGARIAN GP	Hungaroring	27	Scuderia Ferrari SpA	G	3.5 Fiat Ferrari 643 V12	*engine*	4/34
ret	BELGIAN GP	Spa	27	Scuderia Ferrari SpA	G	3.5 Fiat Ferrari 643 V12	*engine*	2/34
3	ITALIAN GP	Monza	27	Scuderia Ferrari SpA	G	3.5 Fiat Ferrari 643 V12		5/34
ret	PORTUGUESE GP	Estoril	27	Scuderia Ferrari SpA	G	3.5 Fiat Ferrari 643 V12	*engine*	5/34
2	SPANISH GP	Barcelona	27	Scuderia Ferrari SpA	G	3.5 Fiat Ferrari 643 V12		6/33
4	JAPANESE GP	Suzuka	27	Scuderia Ferrari SpA	G	3.5 Fiat Ferrari 643 V12		4/31

1993 WORLD CHAMPION Championship position: 1st   Wins: 7   Pole positions: 13   Fastest laps: 6   Points scored: 99

1	SOUTH AFRICAN GP	Kyalami	2	Canon Williams Team	G	3.5 Williams FW15C-Renault V10	*FL*	1/26
ret	BRAZILIAN GP	Interlagos	2	Canon Williams Team	G	3.5 Williams FW15C-Renault V10	*spun off in rainstorm*	1/26
3	EUROPEAN GP	Donington	2	Canon Williams Team	G	3.5 Williams FW15C-Renault V10		1/26
1	SAN MARINO GP	Imola	2	Canon Williams Team	G	3.5 Williams FW15C-Renault V10	*FL*	1/26
1	SPANISH GP	Barcelona	2	Canon Williams Team	G	3.5 Williams FW15C-Renault V10		1/26
4	MONACO GP	Monte Carlo	2	Canon Williams Team	G	3.5 Williams FW15C-Renault V10	*jump start – stop & go penalty/FL*	1/26
1	CANADIAN GP	Montreal	2	Canon Williams Team	G	3.5 Williams FW15C-Renault V10		1/26
1	FRENCH GP	Magny Cours	2	Canon Williams Team	G	3.5 Williams FW15C-Renault V10		2/26
1	BRITISH GP	Silverstone	2	Canon Williams Team	G	3.5 Williams FW15C-Renault V10	*50th Grand Prix win*	1/26
1	GERMAN GP	Hockenheim	2	Canon Williams Team	G	3.5 Williams FW15C-Renault V10	*despite stop & go penalty*	1/26
12	HUNGARIAN GP	Hungaroring	2	Canon Williams Team	G	3.5 Williams FW15C-Renault V10	*started at back/pit stop – wing//FL/-7 laps*	1/26
3	BELGIAN GP	Spa	2	Canon Williams Team	G	3.5 Williams FW15C-Renault V10	*FL*	1/25
12/ret	ITALIAN GP	Monza	2	Canon Williams Team	G	3.5 Williams FW15C-Renault V10	*engine/5 laps behind*	1/26
2	PORTUGUESE GP	Estoril	2	Canon Williams Team	G	3.5 Williams FW15C-Renault V10		2/26
2	JAPANESE GP	Suzuka	2	Canon Williams Team	G	3.5 Williams FW15C-Renault V10	*FL*	1/24
2	AUSTRALIAN GP	Adelaide	2	Canon Williams Team	G	3.5 Williams FW15C-Renault V10		2/24

GP Starts: 199 (200)   GP Wins: 51   Pole positions: 33   Fastest laps: 41   Points: 798.5

After a year's sabbatical, Prost returned to action with Williams in 1993, claiming a fourth world title.

TOM PRYCE

TOM PRYCE'S death at Kyalami in 1977 robbed Britain of one of its great natural talents of the era. Had he survived, he surely would have gone on to achieve much greater things. The quiet and reserved Welshman had got into motor racing in 1970 via a competition in the Daily Express, in which he won a Lola T200 Formula Ford. He made a good start in the car before switching to the Formula Ford 100 series in 1971, where he dominated in his TAS Racing Royale. This success took him to the works Royale team to race in Formula Super Vee, before embarking on a Formula 3 season with the team in 1972. Unfortunately, this effort was hampered by a lack of finance, and Tom's season was interrupted by a broken leg sustained in a heat of the Monaco F3 race.

Royale ran Tom in Formula Atlantic in 1973, and he was enjoying a successful season when he was given an opportunity to drive the Motul Rondel F2 car in selected races. A second place at Norisring signified better things ahead, and sure enough in 1974 he joined the little Token team for the International Trophy and Belgian GP. When the team's entry for Monaco was refused due to the Welshman's lack of experience, he contested the F3 support race instead and, in an astonishing display of dominance, simply drove into the distance to win by the proverbial country mile.

With Shadow still looking for a suitable replacement for the late Peter Revson, Pryce was drafted into the team after Brian Redman had decided not to stay. In only his second race, at Dijon, he put the car on to the second row of the grid, which was enough for Don Nichols to decide he had found his man. The 1975 season started well with a win in the Race of Champions, but it was an up-and-down year, pole position for the British GP, and superb drives in both Germany and Austria being the highlights. The team received a major setback when UOP, their main sponsor, pulled out at the end of the year. The subsequent cash shortage certainly hindered both the team's and Tom's progress in 1976, the Welshman loyally staying on when plenty of others would have been seeking to better their lot elsewhere. The 1977 season began with new sponsors and a fresh enthusiasm, but a bizarre and horrendous accident at Kyalami cruelly cut him down. Thankfully, he was already dead as his car hurtled down the straight towards oblivion, having hit an errant marshal as he crossed the track carrying a fire extinguisher.

PRYCE, Tom (GB) b 11/6/1949, Ruthin, Denbighshire, North Wales – d 5/3/1977, Kyalami Circuit, South Africa

1974 Championship position: 18th= Wins: 0 Pole positions: 0 Fastest laps: 0 Points scored: 1

	Race	Circuit	No	Entrant	Tyres	Capacity/Car/Engine	Comment	Q Pos/Entries
ret	BELGIAN GP	Nivelles	42	Token Racing	F	3.0 Token RJ02-Cosworth V8	collision with Scheckter	20/32
ret	DUTCH GP	Zandvoort	16	UOP Shadow Racing Team	G	3.0 Shadow DN3-Cosworth V8	collision with Hunt	11/27
ret	FRENCH GP	Dijon	16	UOP Shadow Racing Team	G	3.0 Shadow DN3-Cosworth V8	collision with Hunt	3/30
8	BRITISH GP	Brands Hatch	16	UOP Shadow Racing Team	G	3.0 Shadow DN3-Cosworth V8	1 lap behind	=5/34
6	GERMAN GP	Nürburgring	16	UOP Shadow Racing Team	G	3.0 Shadow DN3-Cosworth V8		11/32
ret	AUSTRIAN GP	Österreichring	16	UOP Shadow Racing Team	G	3.0 Shadow DN3-Cosworth V8	spun off – could not restart	16/31
10	ITALIAN GP	Monza	16	UOP Shadow Racing Team	G	3.0 Shadow DN3-Cosworth V8	2 laps behind	22/31
ret	CANADIAN GP	Mosport Park	16	UOP Shadow Racing Team	G	3.0 Shadow DN3-Cosworth V8	engine	13/30
nc	US GP	Watkins Glen	16	UOP Shadow Racing Team	G	3.0 Shadow DN3-Cosworth V8	pit stops/nose cone/misfire/-12 laps	18/30

1975 Championship position: 10th Wins: 0 Pole positions: 1 Fastest laps: 0 Points scored: 8

	Race	Circuit	No	Entrant	Tyres	Capacity/Car/Engine	Comment	Q Pos/Entries
12/ret	ARGENTINE GP	Buenos Aires	16	UOP Shadow Racing Team	G	3.0 Shadow DN3B-Cosworth V8	transmission/2 laps behind	14/23
ret	BRAZILIAN GP	Interlagos	16	UOP Shadow Racing Team	G	3.0 Shadow DN3B-Cosworth V8	spun off	14/23
9	SOUTH AFRICAN GP	Kyalami	16	UOP Shadow Racing Team	G	3.0 Shadow DN5-Cosworth V8	1 lap behind	19/28
ret	SPANISH GP	Montjuich Park	16	UOP Shadow Racing Team	G	3.0 Shadow DN5-Cosworth V8	collision with Brise	8/26
ret	MONACO GP	Monte Carlo	16	UOP Shadow Racing Team	G	3.0 Shadow DN5-Cosworth V8	hit barrier – damaged rear wing	2/26
6	BELGIAN GP	Zolder	16	UOP Shadow Racing Team	G	3.0 Shadow DN5-Cosworth V8		5/24
ret	SWEDISH GP	Anderstorp	16	UOP Shadow Racing Team	G	3.0 Shadow DN5-Cosworth V8	spun off – could not restart	7/26
6	DUTCH GP	Zandvoort	16	UOP Shadow Racing Team	G	3.0 Shadow DN5-Cosworth V8	1 lap behind	12/25
ret	FRENCH GP	Paul Ricard	16	UOP Shadow Racing Team	G	3.0 Shadow DN5-Cosworth V8	transmission	=5/26
ret	BRITISH GP	Silverstone	16	UOP Shadow Racing Team	G	3.0 Shadow DN5-Cosworth V8	spun off	1/28
4	GERMAN GP	Nürburgring	16	UOP Shadow Racing Team	G	3.0 Shadow DN5-Cosworth V8		16/26
3*	AUSTRIAN GP	Österreichring	16	UOP Shadow Racing Team	G	3.0 Shadow DN5-Cosworth V8	*rain shortened race – half points	15/30
6	ITALIAN GP	Monza	16	UOP Shadow Racing Team	G	3.0 Shadow DN5-Cosworth V8		14/28
nc	US GP	Watkins Glen	16	UOP Shadow Racing Team	G	3.0 Shadow DN5-Cosworth V8	pit stops – misfire/7 laps behind	7/24

1976 Championship position: 11th= Wins: 0 Pole positions: 0 Fastest laps: 0 Points scored: 10

	Race	Circuit	No	Entrant	Tyres	Capacity/Car/Engine	Comment	Q Pos/Entries
3	BRAZILIAN GP	Interlagos	16	Shadow Racing Team	G	3.0 Shadow DN5-Cosworth V8		12/22
7	SOUTH AFRICAN GP	Kyalami	16	Shadow Racing Team	G	3.0 Shadow DN5-Cosworth V8	1 lap behind	7/25
ret	US GP WEST	Long Beach	16	Shadow Racing Team	G	3.0 Shadow DN5-Cosworth V8	driveshaft	5/27

8	SPANISH GP	Jarama	16	Shadow Racing Team	G	3.0 Shadow DN5-Cosworth V8	1 lap behind	22/30
10	BELGIAN GP	Zolder	16	Shadow Racing Team	G	3.0 Shadow DN5-Cosworth V8	2 laps behind	13/29
7	MONACO GP	Monte Carlo	16	Shadow Racing Team	G	3.0 Shadow DN5-Cosworth V8	1 lap behind	15/25
9	SWEDISH GP	Anderstorp	16	Shadow Racing Team	G	3.0 Shadow DN5-Cosworth V8	1 lap behind	12/27
8	FRENCH GP	Paul Ricard	16	Shadow Racing Team	G	3.0 Shadow DN5-Cosworth V8		16/30
4	BRITISH GP	Brands Hatch	16	Shadow Racing Team	G	3.0 Shadow DN5-Cosworth V8	1 lap behind	20/30
8	GERMAN GP	Nürburgring	16	Shadow Racing with Tabatip	G	3.0 Shadow DN5-Cosworth V8		18/28
ret	AUSTRIAN GP	Österreichring	16	Shadow Racing with Tabatip	G	3.0 Shadow DN5-Cosworth V8	brakes	6/25
4	DUTCH GP	Zandvoort	16	Shadow Racing Team	G	3.0 Shadow DN8-Cosworth V8		3/27
8	ITALIAN GP	Monza	16	Shadow Racing Team	G	3.0 Shadow DN8-Cosworth V8		15/29
11	CANADIAN GP	Mosport Park	16	Shadow Racing Team	G	3.0 Shadow DN8-Cosworth V8	1 lap behind	13/27
ret	US GP EAST	Watkins Glen	16	Shadow Racing Team	G	3.0 Shadow DN8-Cosworth V8	engine	9/27
ret	JAPANESE GP	Mount Fuji	16	Shadow Racing Team	G	3.0 Shadow DN8-Cosworth V8	engine – seized	14/27

1977 Championship position: 0   Wins: 0   Pole positions: 0   Fastest laps: 0   Points scored: 0

nc	ARGENTINE GP	Buenos Aires	16	Shadow Racing Team	G	3.0 Shadow DN8-Cosworth V8	pit stop – gear selection/8 laps behind	9/21
ret	BRAZILIAN GP	Interlagos	16	Shadow Racing Team	G	3.0 Shadow DN8-Cosworth V8	engine	12/22
ret	SOUTH AFRICAN GP	Kyalami	16	Shadow Racing Team	G	3.0 Shadow DN8-Cosworth V8	hit fire marshal – fatal accident	15/23

GP Starts: 42   GP Wins: 0   Pole positions: 1   Fastest laps: 0   Points: 19

DAVID PURLEY

SOME drivers leave behind memories far greater than the sum of their deeds, and David Purley was undoubtedly such a man: a model of personal courage, a great sportsman, and a fine racing driver as well. He began racing with a Cobra in 1968, then moved on to a Chevron GT, before taking a shot at Formula 3 in 1970 in his family-backed Lec Refrigeration Brabham. At this stage, he was a little wild and wayward, and he certainly relished the dangerous challenge presented by events such as the GP of Chimay, taking a hat trick of wins on this road circuit between 1970 and 1972.

By then, Purley had progressed to Formula 2, taking a splendid third place at Pau, but in 1973 he dropped down for a season of Formula Atlantic, during the course of which he hired a March to go grand prix racing for the first time. Although his results were unmemorable, his actions at the Dutch GP, where he single-handedly tried in vain to save poor Roger Williamson were certainly not. His bravery won him the George Medal and the admiration of the grand prix world.

In 1974, Purley teamed up with Peter Harper to race in Formula 2 once more and enjoyed a successful season, taking second places at the Salzburgring, Rouen and Enna, and in the end-of-year Macau GP. Then, back under his own Lec banner, he contested two seasons of F5000 with a Chevron, taking the Shellsport championship in 1976 with six victories.

Seeing Formula 1 as unfinished business, David commissioned his own Lec chassis to race in 1977, taking a sixth place in the Race of Champions and then briefly leading the wet Belgian GP during a round of pit stops. Disaster struck in practice for the British GP, however, when he crashed his car, sustaining horrendous multiple injuries that would have killed a man of lesser fortitude. Displaying incredible will to survive and then recover, he endured months of rehabilitation, subsequently racing his Porsche in club events in preparation for a serious return to the track in the Aurora series towards the end of 1979. He may have competed in only four rounds, but a fourth place at Snetterton was an amazing achievement.

Purley then restricted his racing to occasional club events, but his love for speed and danger remained unquenchable, and he took up aerobatics with a Pitts Special biplane. Fate caught up with him at last, however, in July, 1985, when his plane crashed into the sea off Bognor Regis. One of Britain's greatest characters had finally run out of luck.

PURLEY, David (GB) b 26/1/1945, Bognor Regis, Sussex – d 2/7/1985, off coast nr Bognor Regis, Sussex

1973 Championship position: Unplaced

	Race	Circuit	No	Entrant	Tyres	Capacity/Car/Engine	Comment	Q Pos/Entries
ret	MONACO GP	Monte Carlo	18	LEC Refrigeration Racing	F	3.0 March 731-Cosworth V8	oil tank	24/26
dns	BRITISH GP	Silverstone	18	LEC Refrigeration Racing	F	3.0 March 731-Cosworth V8	practice accident	(=16)/29
ret	DUTCH GP	Zandvoort	18	LEC Refrigeration Racing	F	3.0 March 731-Cosworth V8	stopped car to aid Williamson	21/24
15	GERMAN GP	Nürburgring	18	LEC Refrigeration Racing	F	3.0 March 731-Cosworth V8	1 lap behind	23/23
9	ITALIAN GP	Monza	29	LEC Refrigeration Racing	F	3.0 March 731-Cosworth V8	1 lap behind	24/25

1974 Championship position: Unplaced

dnq	BRITISH GP	Brands Hatch	42	Team Harper-Token Racing	F	3.0 Token RJ02-Cosworth V8		=25/34

1977 Championship position: Unplaced

dnq	SPANISH GP	Jarama	31	LEC Refrigeration Racing	G	3.0 LEC CRP1-Cosworth V8		30/31
13	BELGIAN GP	Zolder	31	LEC Refrigeration Racing	G	3.0 LEC CRP1-Cosworth V8	3 laps behind	20/32
14	SWEDISH GP	Anderstorp	31	LEC Refrigeration Racing	G	3.0 LEC CRP1-Cosworth V8	2 laps behind	19/31
ret	FRENCH GP	Dijon	31	LEC Refrigeration Racing	G	3.0 LEC CRP1-Cosworth V8	brake failure – accident	21/30
dnpq	BRITISH GP	Silverstone	31	LEC Refrigeration Racing	G	3.0 LEC CRP1-Cosworth V8	accident in pre-qualifying	31/36

GP Starts: 7   GP Wins: 0   Pole positions: 0   Fastest laps: 0   Points: 0

DIETER QUESTER

SINCE starting motor racing in 1965, after many years of competing in speedboats and on motorcycles, Dieter Quester has been identified with the BMW marque for the bulk of his long
career – not surprisingly, perhaps, since he had married Julianna, the daughter of Alexander von
Falkenhausen.

Dieter really came to prominence by winning the Austrian touring car championship in a BMW
1800 in 1966, and then his sideways driving style in the factory BMW took him to two consecutive
Division 3 European touring car titles in 1968/69. He was also part of BMW's largely under-devel-
oped Formula 2 programme, although he did manage a victory at Hockenheim at the end of 1970.
He switched to a March for a season of Formula 2 in 1971 and performed well, winning the Lottery
GP and scoring five second places. It was around this period, frustrated at being unable to get a
Formula 1 ride, that he seriously considered retirement, but he carried on and eventually drove a
rented Surtees in the 1974 Austrian GP.

Subsequently concentrating on saloons, Dieter was European G2 touring car champion in 1977
and a regular in the BMW Procar series of 1979/80. Throughout the 1990s, he was a more or less
permanent fixture in BMW touring cars in the European, German and Austrian championships, as
well as competing in a BMW M3 in the IMSA GT3 class in America through to 2003.

In 2000, Quester broke ranks and forsook his beloved BMW to race Porsche GTs backed by Red
Bull. In 2006, back with BMW, he won a 24-hour race at Dubai in a BMW M3 shared with Hans
Joachim-Stuck, Toto Wolff and Philipp Peter. He followed this with a victory in the Britcar 24-hours at Silverstone with a BMW Z4.

Although now past 70 years of age, but still looking trim and fit, Quester competes in historics and rallies in a beautiful BMW 507 convertible.

IAN RABY

A CAR dealer from Brighton, Ian Raby began racing in the early 1950s in Formula 3 with specials that
he christened 'Puddle Jumper', but he wasn't really competitive until he raced a Cooper in 1956.
After two years with Cooper and Elva sports cars, he returned to single-seaters in 1959/60 with both a
Cooper and a Hume-Climax, gaining success only in modest Formula Libre races.

In 1961/62, Raby raced mainly in Formula Junior, before buying the Gilby-BRM from Syd Greene
to race in Formula 1 in 1963. He gained a third place at Vallelunga in the Rome Grand Prix, but precious little else, and in 1964/65 he relied on a Brabham BT3-Climax, still doing no more than making
up the numbers.

With the new 3-litre formula in operation for 1966, Raby stepped down into F2 with a Brabham BT14-
Cosworth. He scored a good fourth place at the Eifelrennen, before a crash at Brands Hatch curtailed
his season. Despite his relatively old age, he undertook a full season of Formula 2 in 1967, gaining the
occasional top-six finish, before a serious crash at Zandvoort left him hospitalised with multiple injuries,
to which he succumbed some weeks later.

QUESTER, Dieter (A) b 30/5/1939, Vienna

	1969 Championship position: Unplaced							
	Race	Circuit	No	Entrant	Tyres	Capacity/Car/Engine	Comment	Q Pos/Entries
dns	GERMAN GP	Nürburgring	25	Bayerische Moteren Werke	D	1.6 BMW 269 4 F2	withdrawn after Mitter's accident	(21)/26
	1974 Championship position: Unplaced							
9	AUSTRIAN GP	Österreichring	30	Memphis International-Team Surtees	F	3.0 Surtees TS16-Cosworth V8	3 laps behind	23/31
	GP Starts: 1 GP Wins: 0 Pole positions: 0 Fastest laps: 0 Points: 0							

RABY, Ian (GB) b 22/9/1921, Woolwich, London – d 7/11/1967, Waterloo, London

	1963 Championship position: Unplaced							
	Race	Circuit	No	Entrant	Tyres	Capacity/Car/Engine	Comment	Q Pos/Entries
ret	BRITISH GP	Silverstone	26	Ian Raby (Racing)	D	1.5 Gilby-BRM V8	gearbox	19/23
dnq	GERMAN GP	Nürburgring	25	Ian Raby (Racing)	D	1.5 Gilby-BRM V8		24/26
dnq	ITALIAN GP	Monza	50	Ian Raby (Racing)	D	1.5 Gilby-BRM V8		22/28
	1964 Championship position: Unplaced							
ret	BRITISH GP	Brands Hatch	23	Ian Raby (Racing)	D	1.5 Brabham BT3-BRM V8	rear hub failure – accident	=16/25
dnq	ITALIAN GP	Monza	56	Ian Raby (Racing)	D	1.5 Brabham BT3-BRM V8		25/25
	1965 Championship position: Unplaced							
11	BRITISH GP	Silverstone	24	Ian Raby (Racing)	D	1.5 Brabham BT3-BRM V8	7 laps behind	20/23
dnq	GERMAN GP	Nürburgring	23	Ian Raby (Racing)	D	1.5 Brabham BT3-BRM V8		22/22
	GP Starts: 3 GP Wins: 0 Pole positions: 0 Fastest laps: 0 Points: 0							

BOBBY RAHAL

FROM the start, Bobby Rahal was refreshingly different from most American drivers, in that he wanted to go road racing and was prepared to travel to Europe to measure himself against the best talent around. After three years (1975–77) in Canadian Formula Atlantic, where he was somewhat overshadowed by the exploits of Gilles Villeneuve, he crossed the Atlantic for a selection of Formula 3 races with Walter Wolf Racing. He did well enough to be offered a drive with the team in the end-of-season United States and Canadian GPs, the latter in the old WR1 chassis, which had been dragged from a museum after he had pranged his WR5 in practice.

Determined to make the grade, Bobby returned to Europe in 1979 for a full Formula 2 season with a works Chevron, scoring some good finishes in a car that was not the most competitive in the series. That was the end of his dreams of Formula 1, however, for in 1980 he went Can-Am racing with Truesports, which was followed by a successful year in endurance events, where he won the Daytona 24-hours and took second place at Brands Hatch in a Porsche 935 turbo.

In 1982, Bobby moved into Indy cars, racing for Jim Trueman's Truesports once more. He won the Cleveland race and finished second in the PPG Cup to take Rookie of the Year honours.

Another race win followed in 1983 (Riverside) and a further two (Phoenix and Laguna Seca) the following year. Budweiser sponsorship for 1985 strengthened the team, and Rahal took another three wins to finish third in the series, behind father and son racers the Unsers. His standout year was 1986, when he won six races to take his first championship. His win in the Indianapolis 500 was especially emotional, as team owner Jim Trueman passed away just after the race. Despite switching to a Lola chassis for 1987, Rahal was still the man to beat, taking four wins on the way to a second consecutive title. The following year was less successful, due in part to the team running a Judd powerplant, but he managed a win in the 500-miler at Pocono.

Bobby decided it was time for a change, and for 1989 he moved to Kraco Racing and back to Cosworth power. A single win at Meadowlands and ninth in the standings were somewhat disappointing, and team owner Maurice Kranes merged his outfit with Rick Galles for the following season. The driver line-up of Bobby and Al Unser Jr was very strong, as Unser had taken the title in 1990, but Rahal was also a factor, with five second-place finishes, which included the Indianapolis 500.

In 1991, Rahal took a single win (at Meadowlands) and nine other top-three placings, but could only finish runner-up to Michael Andretti, before electing to join forces with Carl Hogan to form Rahal-Hogan Racing. Opting for the proven Lola-Chevrolet combination was a wise move, as Bobby won his third PPG CART title in 1992. He raced on to the end of the 1998 season, and although he failed to add to his 24 career wins, he remained a canny and robust racer who could never be discounted, given his still burning desire to succeed.

Having ended a fabulous driving career, Bobby continued to run his own highly professional outfit from the safer side of the pit wall. Indeed, his esteem was such that in 2001 Ford persuaded him to take over the running of the Jaguar F1 team, which was in need of a steady hand at the helm. Had it succeeded, his audacious attempt to persuade old friend Adrian Newey to join from McLaren probably would have turned the team's fortunes around, but the design genius opted to remain with the status quo, and a disappointed Rahal soon departed following another shake-up that saw him unceremoniously eased out by a new regime.

Having returned to the relative calm of racing in the USA, Rahal found himself at the centre of more controversy when, as a former CART stalwart, he decided to drop out of the Champ Car series and race in the rival Indy Racing League, in deference to his sponsors. This proved to be a shrewd move in 2004, when his young driver, Buddy Rice, won the Indianapolis 500 in commanding style. The following year's race may not have provided another win, but the achievement of his female driver, Danica Patrick, in finishing fourth caused a massive upsurge in media interest that far outweighed the performance. The 2006 season began tragically for Rahal and his team when newcomer Paul Dana was killed after an accident during practice for the season's opening race in Homestead. Rahal continued to compete fully in the IRL until 2008, but without the services of a truly front-line driver and a lack sufficient sponsorship, they scaled back their operation to compete in the Indianapolis 500 and other selected events.

In 2010, Bobby's son, Graham, drove for the team in the 500 and finished in 12th place. While out of open-wheel racing, his team has successfully run BMW M3s in the ALMS, taking many class wins and the overall GT class championships in both 2010 and 2011. The Rahal Letterman Lanigan team re-entered the IRL full time for 2012, with F1 refugee Takuma Sato as their lead driver.

RAHAL, Bobby (USA) b 10/1/1953, Medina, Ohio

1978 Championship position: Unplaced									
	Race	Circuit	No	Entrant	Tyres	Capacity/Car/Engine	Comment		Q Pos/Entries
12	US GP EAST	Watkins Glen	21	Walter Wolf Racing	G	3.0 Wolf WR5-Cosworth V8	*1 lap behind*		20/27
ret	CANADIAN GP	Montreal	21	Walter Wolf Racing	G	3.0 Wolf WR1-Cosworth V8	*fuel system*		20/28
dns	"	"	21	Walter Wolf Racing	G	3.0 Wolf WR5-Cosworth V8	*practice accident*		– / –

GP Starts: 2   GP Wins: 0   Pole positions: 0   Fastest laps: 0   Points: 0

W HEN Kimi Räikkönen clinched the world championship at the last gasp in 2007, even the least ardent of Ferrari fans would have conceded that he deserved his first title. After five seasons of taking the battle to the Prancing Horse with the fast, but often unreliable McLaren-Mercedes, it must have been a doubly satisfying triumph for the taciturn Finn, who prefers to let his performances do the talking.

A graduate of the World and European karting scene, the Finn had competed in just 23 events in single-seaters by the time Sauber gained his signature on an F1 contract, causing some concern among the establishment and governing body alike over his alleged inexperience. However, he was able to point to an extensive karting career as the foundation for his rapid escalation to the top flight.

When Räikkönen moved into cars, he had only a small budget to play with, so he dipped in and out of various junior championships until the end of 1999, when he scored four wins in the Formula Renault winter series. With Manor Motorsport in the same class for 2000, he proceeded to take seven wins, ten podiums, seven pole positions and six fastest laps from the ten-race series. Peter Sauber was first to offer him a maiden F1 test, if for no other reason than to prevent other teams from getting their hands on him!

With so few races under his belt, naturally there were serious concerns that Räikkönen could have been biting off more than he could chew, but the confident Finn quickly dispelled any doubts with his eye-catching testing performances, and Sauber moved quickly to secure his name on a contract. He set about proving his point in his 2001 F1 debut year, when a sixth place in Melbourne coupled with fourth places in Austria and Canada helped elevate him to a championship ranking of tenth – and attracted the attention of bigger teams. Before the end of the season, he had been chosen by McLaren to replace Mika Häkkinen for 2002.

Partnering the experienced David Coulthard, the Finn soon showed he had the upper hand in qualifying, and he also went well in the races, although reliability problems from Brazil onwards saw him notch up six successive retirements. Eventually, he ended the season with four podium finishes, one of which so nearly became his maiden win. He was robbed in France, however, when Allan McNish's Toyota engine dumped its oil on the track, causing him to run off line and allowing Michael Schumacher to snatch the win.

Räikkönen had a storming year in 2003, scoring his maiden F1 win in Malaysia and taking the battle for the title with Schumacher right down to the wire – the Finn lost out in the end by just two points. Ten podium finishes were a mark of his consistency and, with a little more luck, he might so easily have been the champion, despite running the ageing MP-17D after the replacement MP4-18 flopped in testing.

Kimi's third season with McLaren was bitterly disappointing, however, as the 2004 model MP4-19 was never up to the job of tackling Schumacher and Ferrari. In the early part of the season, both he and team-mate Coulthard struggled to achieve any creditable results prior to the introduction of the MP4-19B at Magny-Cours. The reworked car salvaged his year somewhat; following a second-place finish at the British GP, he went on to win in Belgium, beating Schumacher fair and square.

Räikkönen was hoping that McLaren would get it right for 2005, and the new MP4-20 proved to be an incredibly fast machine. Facing an uphill battle to regain ground lost to Fernando Alonso early in the season, Kimi hit back with wins in Spain, Monaco and Canada, which put him within striking distance of his young rival by mid-season, but he was always fighting a losing battle, as the Spaniard did more than enough to maintain his lead. The brilliant Finn scored four more wins in Hungary, Turkey, Belgium and Japan to cement second place in the drivers' table, 19 points behind Alonso and a massive 50 ahead of Michael Schumacher in third.

Naturally, Räikkönen started among the favourites for the championship chase in 2006, but it would be a somewhat patchy last shot at the title for McLaren. (It appears that he had already committed himself to Ferrari, although a formal announcement was only made at Monza.) On his day, the Finn was as quick as ever, taking three pole positions, but he was unable to translate any of them into a victory. Second place at Monza was a high point, while retirements at Monaco and the Hungaroring were the lows, especially when victories were more than possible.

With the retirement of Michael Schumacher, Kimi took his talents to Maranello, comfortable in the knowledge that they would embrace his laid-back manner. Much was expected from the Finn, who was reportedly on a $30m-a-year retainer. After storming to a maiden Ferrari win in the opening race of the season in Australia, he struggled somewhat as he adapted his style to the Bridgestone tyres after years of running on Michelins. Indeed, it was round eight in the championship before the title contender began to appear, Räikkönen taking back-to-back wins at Magny-Cours and Silverstone.

As the season began its second half, Räikkönen clung on to the McLaren pair of Lewis Hamilton and Alonso until the dominant win in the Belgian Grand Prix, which rekindled his seemingly faint title hopes. Third place in China seemed to be too little to maintain his title bid, but at last fate was kind to him. As Hamilton faltered, the Ferrari driver ended the season with two wins to take his tally for the season to six. In the final reckoning, he edged out the McLaren pair by a single point over the course of a tumultuous season.

Having reached the summit of motorsport achievement, like so many previous champions, Kimi found the successful defence of his title a step too far. His 2008 season began strongly enough, with two wins from the opening four races, but then things began to go wrong. A certain win was lost at Magny-Cours, where he suffered a broken exhaust, and his travails continued at Silverstone, where he did well to rescue fourth place in the wet conditions. From then on, however, his season began to unravel slowly, and after he crashed out of the Singapore Grand Prix, he was all but out of the championship chase and forced to play a supporting role to his team-mate, Felipe Massa.

Kimi's final year at Maranello turned out to be woefully inconsistent, and he had to wait until the sixth race of the season, at Monaco, to claim his first podium. He only seemed to assert himself in Hungary following team-mate Massa's qualifying accident. The high point of a rather flat year came at Spa, where he must have been grateful for KERS to see off the challenge of Giancarlo Fisichella's Force India. By then, however, the Ferrari hierarchy had begun moves to replace him with Alonso for 2010. With a reputedly massive pay-off, Räikkönen had looked toward a possible return to McLaren, but Jenson Button was seen as the ideal candidate to partner Hamilton.

With no viable F1 options open to him for 2010, Kimi decided to pursue his motorsport career in the World Rally Championship. Armed with Red Bull backing and a competitive seat in the Citroën C4, the Finn had a mixed year, scoring good results at the Jordan Rally and the Rally of Turkey, but failing to convince elsewhere. In 2001, he entered a works-run Citroën DS3 under the banner of his own ICE 1 Racing Team, but he only took part in six events before losing interest and decamping to the USA to have a brief look at NASCAR.

In the end, the 'Kimster' was tempted to return to the grand prix arena for 2012 with Lotus-Renault, who were prepared to meet the Finn's terms. Just how long the partnership will last will probably depend upon the team's ongoing progress. Given Räikkönen's determination to plough his own furrow, we can only wait to see if his fascinating comeback will last the course.

RÄIKKÖNEN, Kimi (SF) b 17/10/1979, Espoo

2001 Championship position: 10th   Wins: 0   Pole positions: 0   Fastest laps: 0   Points scored:9

	Race	Circuit	No	Entrant	Tyres	Capacity/Car/Engine	Comment	Q Pos/Entries
6	AUSTRALIAN GP	Melbourne	17	Red Bull Sauber Petronas	B	3.0 Sauber C20-Petronas V10		13/22
ret	MALAYSIAN GP	Sepang	17	Red Bull Sauber Petronas	B	3.0 Sauber C20-Petronas V10	clutch at start	14/22
ret	BRAZILIAN GP	Interlagos	17	Red Bull Sauber Petronas	B	3.0 Sauber C20-Petronas V10	spun off in rain	10/22
ret	SAN MARINO GP	Imola	17	Red Bull Sauber Petronas	B	3.0 Sauber C20-Petronas V10	loose steering wheel – crashed	10/22
8	SPANISH GP	Barcelona	17	Red Bull Sauber Petronas	B	3.0 Sauber C20-Petronas V10		9/22
4	AUSTRIAN GP	A1-Ring	17	Red Bull Sauber Petronas	B	3.0 Sauber C20-Petronas V10		9/22
10	MONACO GP	Monte Carlo	17	Red Bull Sauber Petronas	B	3.0 Sauber C20-Petronas V10	5 laps behind	15/22
4	CANADIAN GP	Montreal	17	Red Bull Sauber Petronas	B	3.0 Sauber C20-Petronas V10		7/22
10	EUROPEAN GP	Nürburgring	17	Red Bull Sauber Petronas	B	3.0 Sauber C20-Petronas V10	1 lap behind	9/22
7	FRENCH GP	Magny Cours	17	Red Bull Sauber Petronas	B	3.0 Sauber C20-Petronas V10	oversteer/1 lap behind	13/22
5	BRITISH GP	Silverstone	17	Red Bull Sauber Petronas	B	3.0 Sauber C20-Petronas V10	1 lap behind	7/22
ret	GERMAN GP	Hockenheim	17	Red Bull Sauber Petronas	B	3.0 Sauber C20-Petronas V10	driveshaft	8/22
7	HUNGARIAN GP	Hungaroring	17	Red Bull Sauber Petronas	B	3.0 Sauber C20-Petronas V10	1 lap behind	9/22
ret/dns*	BELGIAN GP	Spa	17	Red Bull Sauber Petronas	B	3.0 Sauber C20-Petronas V10	*transmission at first start	12/22
7	ITALIAN GP	Monza	17	Red Bull Sauber Petronas	B	3.0 Sauber C20-Petronas V10		9/22
ret	U S GP	Indianapolis	17	Red Bull Sauber Petronas	B	3.0 Sauber C20-Petronas V10	driveshaft	11/22
ret	JAPANESE GP	Suzuka	17	Red Bull Sauber Petronas	B	3.0 Sauber C20-Petronas V10	broken supension/spin – hit by Alesi	12/22

2002 Championship position: 6th   Wins: 0   Pole positions: 0   Fastest laps: 1   Points scored: 24

	Race	Circuit	No	Entrant	Tyres	Capacity/Car/Engine	Comment	Q Pos/Entries
3	AUSTRALIAN GP	Melbourne	4	West McLaren Mercedes	M	3.0 McLaren MP4/17-Mercedes V10	slid off avoiding Montoya/FL	5/22
ret	MALAYSIAN GP	Sepang	4	West McLaren Mercedes	M	3.0 McLaren MP4/17-Mercedes V10	engine – piston	5/22
12/ret	BRAZILIAN GP	Interlagos	4	West McLaren Mercedes	M	3.0 McLaren MP4/17-Mercedes V10	rear wheel hub failure/4 laps behind	5/22
ret	SAN MARINO GP	Imola	4	West McLaren Mercedes	M	3.0 McLaren MP4/17-Mercedes V10	exhaust – overheating suspension	5/22
ret	SPANISH GP	Barcelona	4	West McLaren Mercedes	M	3.0 McLaren MP4/17-Mercedes V10	rear wing failure	5/21
ret	AUSTRIAN GP	A1-Ring	4	West McLaren Mercedes	M	3.0 McLaren MP4/17-Mercedes V10	engine	6/22
ret	MONACO GP	Monte Carlo	4	West McLaren Mercedes	M	3.0 McLaren MP4/17-Mercedes V10	shunted by Barrichello – damaged car	6/22
4	CANADIAN GP	Montreal	4	West McLaren Mercedes	M	3.0 McLaren MP4/17-Mercedes V10	refuelling glitch – low on fuel	5/22
3	EUROPEAN GP	Nürburgring	4	West McLaren Mercedes	M	3.0 McLaren MP4/17-Mercedes V10		6/22
ret	BRITISH GP	Silverstone	4	West McLaren Mercedes	M	3.0 McLaren MP4/17-Mercedes V10	engine	5/22
2	FRENCH GP	Magny Cours	4	West McLaren Mercedes	M	3.0 McLaren MP4/17-Mercedes V10	hit oil patch to lose lead	4/21
ret	GERMAN GP	Hockenheim	4	West McLaren Mercedes	M	3.0 McLaren MP4/17-Mercedes V10	puncture – underbody damage – spun off	5/22
4	HUNGARIAN GP	Hungaroring	4	West McLaren Mercedes	M	3.0 McLaren MP4/17-Mercedes V10		11/20
ret	BELGIAN GP	Spa	4	West McLaren Mercedes	M	3.0 McLaren MP4/17-Mercedes V10	engine	2/20
ret	ITALIAN GP	Monza	4	West McLaren Mercedes	M	3.0 McLaren MP4/17-Mercedes V10	*best time disallowed/engine	*6/20
ret	U S GP	Indianapolis	4	West McLaren Mercedes	M	3.0 McLaren MP4/17-Mercedes V10	engine	6/20
3	JAPANESE GP	Suzuka	4	West McLaren Mercedes	M	3.0 McLaren MP4/17-Mercedes V10		4/20

2003 Championship position: 2nd   Wins: 1   Pole positions: 2   Fastest laps: 3   Points scored: 91

	Race	Circuit	No	Entrant	Tyres	Capacity/Car/Engine	Comment	Q Pos/Entries
3	AUSTRALIAN GP	Melbourne	6	West McLaren Mercedes	M	3.0 McLaren MP4/17D-Mercedes V10	started from pits/stop & go penalty/FL	15/20
1	MALAYSIAN GP	Sepang	6	West McLaren Mercedes	M	3.0 McLaren MP4/17D-Mercedes V10		7/20
2	BRAZILIAN GP	Interlagos	6	West McLaren Mercedes	M	3.0 McLaren MP4/17D-Mercedes V10	race stopped due to accident	4/20
2	SAN MARINO GP	Imola	6	West McLaren Mercedes	M	3.0 McLaren MP4/17D-Mercedes V10		6/20
ret	SPANISH GP	Barcelona	6	West McLaren Mercedes	M	3.0 McLaren MP4/17D-Mercedes V10	*no time/ran into back of Pizzonia	*20/20
2	AUSTRIAN GP	A1-Ring	6	West McLaren Mercedes	M	3.0 McLaren MP4/17D-Mercedes V10		2/20
2	MONACO GP	Monte Carlo	6	West McLaren Mercedes	M	3.0 McLaren MP4/17D-Mercedes V10	FL	2/19
6	CANADIAN GP	Montreal	6	West McLaren Mercedes	M	3.0 McLaren MP4/17D-Mercedes V10	*no time set	*20/20
ret	EUROPEAN GP	Nürburgring	6	West McLaren Mercedes	M	3.0 McLaren MP4/17D-Mercedes V10	engine when in lead/FL	1/20
4	FRANCE GP	Magny Cours	6	West McLaren Mercedes	M	3.0 McLaren MP4/17D-Mercedes V10		4/20
3	BRITISH GP	Silverstone	6	West McLaren Mercedes	M	3.0 McLaren MP4/17D-Mercedes V10		3/20
ret	GERMAN GP	Hockenheim	6	West McLaren Mercedes	M	3.0 McLaren MP4/17D-Mercedes V10	collision with Barrichello after start	5/20
2	HUNGARIAN GP	Hungaroring	6	West McLaren Mercedes	M	3.0 McLaren MP4/17D-Mercedes V10		7/20
4	ITALIAN GP	Monza	6	West McLaren Mercedes	M	3.0 McLaren MP4/17D-Mercedes V10		4/20
2	U S GP	Indianapolis	6	West McLaren Mercedes	M	3.0 McLaren MP4/17D-Mercedes V10	unlucky with weather conditions	1/20
2	JAPANESE GP	Suzuka	6	West McLaren Mercedes	M	3.0 McLaren MP4/17D-Mercedes V10		8/20

2004 Championship position: 7th   Wins: 1   Pole positions: 1   Fastest laps: 2   Points scored: 45

	Race	Circuit	No	Entrant	Tyres	Capacity/Car/Engine	Comment	Q Pos/Entries
ret	AUSTRALIAN GP	Melbourne	6	West McLaren Mercedes	M	3.0 McLaren MP4/19-Mercedes V10	engine	10/20
ret	MALAYSIAN GP	Sepang	6	West McLaren Mercedes	M	3.0 McLaren MP4/19-Mercedes V10	engine	5/20
ret	BAHRAIN GP	Sakhir Circuit	6	West McLaren Mercedes	M	3.0 McLaren MP4/19-Mercedes V10	*no time set/engine	*20/20
8	SAN MARINO GP	Imola	6	West McLaren Mercedes	M	3.0 McLaren MP4/19-Mercedes V10	*no time set/1 lap behind	*20/20
11	SPANISH GP	Barcelona	6	West McLaren Mercedes	M	3.0 McLaren MP4/19-Mercedes V10		13/20
ret	MONACO GP	Monte Carlo	6	West McLaren Mercedes	M	3.0 McLaren MP4/19-Mercedes V10	engine	5/20
ret	EUROPEAN GP	Nürburgring	6	West McLaren Mercedes	M	3.0 McLaren MP4/19-Mercedes V10	engine	4/20
5*	CANADIAN GP	Montreal	6	West McLaren Mercedes	M	3.0 McLaren MP4/19-Mercedes V10	*2nd/5th place cars disqualified/-1 lap	8/20
6	U S GP	Indianapolis	6	West McLaren Mercedes	M	3.0 McLaren MP4/19-Mercedes V10	engine problems/1 lap behind	7/20
7	FRENCH GP	Magny Cours	6	West McLaren Mercedes	M	3.0 McLaren MP4/19B-Mercedes V10		9/20
2	BRITISH GP	Silverstone	6	West McLaren Mercedes	M	3.0 McLaren MP4/19B-Mercedes V10		1/20
ret	GERMAN GP	Hockenheim	6	West McLaren Mercedes	M	3.0 McLaren MP4/19B-Mercedes V10	rear wing failure/FL	3/20
ret	HUNGARIAN GP	Hungaroring	6	West McLaren Mercedes	M	3.0 McLaren MP4/19B-Mercedes V10	fuel injection	10/20
1	BELGIAN GP	Spa	6	West McLaren Mercedes	M	3.0 McLaren MP4/19B-Mercedes V10	FL	10/20
ret	ITALIAN GP	Monza	6	West McLaren Mercedes	M	3.0 McLaren MP4/19B-Mercedes V10	engine – water leak	7/20
3	CHINESE GP	Shanghai	6	West McLaren Mercedes	M	3.0 McLaren MP4/19B-Mercedes V10		2/20
6	JAPANESE GP	Suzuka	6	West McLaren Mercedes	M	3.0 McLaren MP4/19B-Mercedes V10		12/20
2	BRAZILIAN GP	Interlagos	6	West McLaren Mercedes	M	3.0 McLaren MP4/19B-Mercedes V10		3/20

2005 Championship position: 2nd   Wins: 7   Pole positions: 6   Fastest laps: 9   Points scored: 112

	Race	Circuit	No	Entrant	Tyres	Capacity/Car/Engine	Comment	Q Pos/Entries
8	AUSTRALIAN GP	Melbourne	9	West McLaren Mercedes	M	3.0 McLaren MP4/20-Mercedes V10	stalled on grid – started from pitlane	10/20
9	MALAYSIAN GP	Sepang	9	West McLaren Mercedes	M	3.0 McLaren MP4/20-Mercedes V10	tyre failure/new tyre stop/FL	6/20
3	BAHRAIN GP	Sakhir Circuit	9	West McLaren Mercedes	M	3.0 McLaren MP4/20-Mercedes V10	strong drive through field	9/20

Kimi Räikkönen joined Ferrari in 2007, and benefited from the internecine rivalry between Alonso and Hamilton at McLaren. He snatched the title after having scored three wins in the final four races of the season.

ret	SAN MARINO GP	Imola	9	West McLaren Mercedes	M	3.0 McLaren MP4/20-Mercedes V10	driveshaft	1/20
1	SPANISH GP	Barcelona	9	West McLaren Mercedes	M	3.0 McLaren MP4/20-Mercedes V10		1/18
1	MONACO GP	Monte Carlo	9	West McLaren Mercedes	M	3.0 McLaren MP4/20-Mercedes V10		1/20
11/ret	EUROPEAN GP	Nürburgring	9	West McLaren Mercedes	M	3.0 McLaren MP4/20-Mercedes V10	suspension failure on last lap	2/20
1	CANADIAN GP	Montreal	9	West McLaren Mercedes	M	3.0 McLaren MP4/20-Mercedes V10	FL	7/20
ret/dns*	U S GP	Indianapolis	9	West McLaren Mercedes	M	3.0 McLaren MP4/20-Mercedes V10	*withdrawn after parade lap	2/20
2	FRENCH GP	Magny Cours	9	West McLaren Mercedes	M	3.0 McLaren MP4/20-Mercedes V10	*10-place penalty on grid/FL	*13/20
3	BRITISH GP	Silverstone	9	West McLaren Mercedes	M	3.0 McLaren MP4/20-Mercedes V10		2/20
ret	GERMAN GP	Hockenheim	9	West McLaren Mercedes	M	3.0 McLaren MP4/20-Mercedes V10	hydraulic leak/led race/FL	1/20
1	HUNGARIAN GP	Hungaroring	9	West McLaren Mercedes	M	3.0 McLaren MP4/20-Mercedes V10	FL	4/20
1	TURKISH GP	Hungaroring	9	West McLaren Mercedes	M	3.0 McLaren MP4/20-Mercedes V10		1/20
4	ITALIAN GP	Monza	9	West McLaren Mercedes	M	3.0 McLaren MP4/20-Mercedes V10	tyre problems/FL	1/20
1	BELGIAN GP	Spa	9	West McLaren Mercedes	M	3.0 McLaren MP4/20-Mercedes V10		2/20
2	BRAZILIAN GP	Interlagos	9	West McLaren Mercedes	M	3.0 McLaren MP4/20-Mercedes V10	FL	5/20
1	JAPANESE GP	Suzuka	9	West McLaren Mercedes	M	3.0 McLaren MP4/20-Mercedes V10	last lap win from Fisichella/FL	17/20
2	CHINESE GP	Shanghai	9	West McLaren Mercedes	M	3.0 McLaren MP4/20-Mercedes V10	FL	3/20

2006 Championship position: 5th   Wins: 0   Pole positions: 3   Fastest laps: 3   Points scored: 65

3	BAHRAIN GP	Sakhir Circuit	3	McLaren Mercedes	M	2.4 McLaren MP4/21-Mercedes V8	*no time set due to supension failure	*22/22
ret	MALAYSIAN GP	Sepang	3	McLaren Mercedes	M	2.4 McLaren MP4/21-Mercedes V8	hit by Klien – broken suspension	7/22
2	AUSTRALIAN GP	Melbourne	3	McLaren Mercedes	M	2.4 McLaren MP4/21-Mercedes V8	FL	4/22
5	SAN MARINO GP	Imola	3	McLaren Mercedes	M	2.4 McLaren MP4/21-Mercedes V8	handling problems	8/22
4	EUROPEAN GP	Nürburgring	3	McLaren Mercedes	M	2.4 McLaren MP4/21-Mercedes V8	wrong tyre choice	5/22
5	SPANISH GP	Barcelona	3	McLaren Mercedes	M	2.4 McLaren MP4/21-Mercedes V8	car lacked rear-end grip	9/22
ret	MONACO GP	Monte Carlo	3	McLaren Mercedes	M	2.4 McLaren MP4/21-Mercedes V8	engine failure	4/22
3	BRITISH GP	Silverstone	3	McLaren Mercedes	M	2.4 McLaren MP4/21-Mercedes V8		2/22
3	CANADIAN GP	Montreal	3	McLaren Mercedes	M	2.4 McLaren MP4/21-Mercedes V8	stalled at 2nd pit stop/FL	3/22
ret	U S GP	Indianapolis	3	McLaren Mercedes	M	2.4 McLaren MP4/21-Mercedes V8	multiple accident on lap 1	9/22
5	FRENCH GP	Magny Cours	3	McLaren Mercedes	M	2.4 McLaren MP4/21-Mercedes V8		6/22
3	GERMAN GP	Hockenheim	3	McLaren Mercedes	M	2.4 McLaren MP4/21-Mercedes V8		1/22
ret	HUNGARIAN GP	Hungaroring	3	McLaren Mercedes	M	2.4 McLaren MP4/21-Mercedes V8	ran into back of Liuzzi	1/22
ret	TURKISH GP	Istanbul	3	McLaren Mercedes	M	2.4 McLaren MP4/21-Mercedes V8	multiple collison on lap 1	8/22
2	ITALIAN GP	Monza	3	McLaren Mercedes	M	2.4 McLaren MP4/21-Mercedes V8	FL	1/22
ret	CHINESE GP	Shanghai	3	McLaren Mercedes	M	2.4 McLaren MP4/21-Mercedes V8	throttle	5/22
5	JAPANESE GP	Suzuka	3	McLaren Mercedes	M	2.4 McLaren MP4/21-Mercedes V8		11/22
5	BRAZILIAN GP	Interlagos	3	McLaren Mercedes	M	2.4 McLaren MP4/21-Mercedes V8		2/22

2007 WORLD CHAMPION   Wins: 6   Pole positions: 3   Fastest laps: 6   Points scored: 110

1	AUSTRALIAN GP	Melbourne	6	Scuderia Ferrari Marlboro	B	2.4 Ferrari F2007-V8	FL	1/22
3	MALAYSIAN GP	Sepang	6	Scuderia Ferrari Marlboro	B	2.4 Ferrari F2007-V8		3/22
3	BAHRAIN GP	Sakhir Circuit	6	Scuderia Ferrari Marlboro	B	2.4 Ferrari F2007-V8		3/22
ret	SPANISH GP	Barcelona	6	Scuderia Ferrari Marlboro	B	2.4 Ferrari F2007-V8	electrics	3/22
8	MONACO GP	Monte Carlo	6	Scuderia Ferrari Marlboro	B	2.4 Ferrari F2007-V8	accident in qualifying/1 lap behind	16/22
5	CANADIAN GP	Montreal	6	Scuderia Ferrari Marlboro	B	2.4 Ferrari F2007-V8		4/22
4	U S GP	Indianapolis	6	Scuderia Ferrari Marlboro	B	2.4 Ferrari F2007-V8	FL	4/22
1	FRENCH GP	Magny Cours	6	Scuderia Ferrari Marlboro	B	2.4 Ferrari F2007-V8		3/22
1	BRITISH GP	Silverstone	6	Scuderia Ferrari Marlboro	B	2.4 Ferrari F2007-V8	FL	2/22
ret	EUROPEAN GP	Nürburgring	6	Scuderia Ferrari Marlboro	B	2.4 Ferrari F2007-V8	hydraulics	1/22
2	HUNGARIAN GP	Hungaroring	6	Scuderia Ferrari Marlboro	B	2.4 Ferrari F2007-V8	close race with Hamilton/FL	4/22
2	TURKISH GP	Istanbul	6	Scuderia Ferrari Marlboro	B	2.4 Ferrari F2007-V8	FL	3/22

	Race	Circuit	No	Entrant	Tyres	Capacity/Car/Engine	Comment	Q Pos/Entries
3	ITALIAN GP	Monza	6	Scuderia Ferrari Marlboro	B	2.4 Ferrari F2007-V8		5/22
1	BELGIAN GP	Spa	6	Scuderia Ferrari Marlboro	B	2.4 Ferrari F2007-V8		1/22
3	JAPANESE GP	Suzuka	6	Scuderia Ferrari Marlboro	B	2.4 Ferrari F2007-V8	delayed by tyre mix up	3/22
1	CHINESE GP	Shanghai	6	Scuderia Ferrari Marlboro	B	2.4 Ferrari F2007-V8		2/22
1	BRAZILIAN GP	Interlagos	6	Scuderia Ferrari Marlboro	B	2.4 Ferrari F2007-V8	FL	3/22

2008 Championship position: 3rd   Wins: 2   Pole positions: 2   Fastest laps: 10   Points scored: 75

	Race	Circuit	No	Entrant	Tyres	Capacity/Car/Engine	Comment	Q Pos/Entries
8*/ret	AUSTRALIAN GP	Melbourne	1	Scuderia Ferrari Marlboro	B	2.4 Ferrari F2008-V8	*6th place car dsq/engine/-5 laps	16/22
1	MALAYSIAN GP	Sepang	1	Scuderia Ferrari Marlboro	B	2.4 Ferrari F2008-V8		2/22
2	BAHRAIN GP	Sakhir Circuit	1	Scuderia Ferrari Marlboro	B	2.4 Ferrari F2008-V8		4/22
1	SPANISH GP	Barcelona	1	Scuderia Ferrari Marlboro	B	2.4 Ferrari F2008-V8	FL	1/22
3	TURKISH GP	Istanbul	1	Scuderia Ferrari Marlboro	B	2.4 Ferrari F2008-V8	minor collision with Kovalainen/FL	4/20
9	MONACO GP	Monte Carlo	1	Scuderia Ferrari Marlboro	B	2.4 Ferrari F2008-V8	2 collisions/2 pit stops for new nose/FL	2/20
ret	CANADIAN GP	Montreal	1	Scuderia Ferrari Marlboro	B	2.4 Ferrari F2008-V8	rammed by Hamilton at pitlane exit/FL	3/20
2	FRENCH GP	Magny Cours	1	Scuderia Ferrari Marlboro	B	2.4 Ferrari F2008-V8	FL	1/20
4	BRITISH GP	Silverstone	1	Scuderia Ferrari Marlboro	B	2.4 Ferrari F2008-V8	struggled in late race wet conditions/FL	3/20
6	GERMAN GP	Hockenheim	1	Scuderia Ferrari Marlboro	B	2.4 Ferrari F2008-V8	brake and grip problems	6/20
3	HUNGARIAN GP	Hungaroring	1	Scuderia Ferrari Marlboro	B	2.4 Ferrari F2008-V8	suspension problem/FL	6/20
ret	EUROPEAN GP	Valencia	1	Scuderia Ferrari Marlboro	B	2.4 Ferrari F2008-V8	engine	4/20
18/ret	BELGIAN GP	Spa	1	Scuderia Ferrari Marlboro	B	2.4 Ferrari F2008-V8	accident – spun off/2 laps behind/FL	4/20
9	ITALIAN GP	Monza	1	Scuderia Ferrari Marlboro	B	2.4 Ferrari F2008-V8	low tyre temparatures/FL	14/20
15/ret	SINGAPORE GP	Marina Bay Circuit	1	Scuderia Ferrari Marlboro	B	2.4 Ferrari F2008-V8	accident – hit wall/4 laps behind/FL	3/20
3	JAPANESE GP	Suzuka	1	Scuderia Ferrari Marlboro	B	2.4 Ferrari F2008-V8		2/20
3	CHINESE GP	Shanghai	1	Scuderia Ferrari Marlboro	B	2.4 Ferrari F2008-V8		2/20
3	BRAZILIAN GP	Interlagos	1	Scuderia Ferrari Marlboro	B	2.4 Ferrari F2008-V8		3/20

2009 Championship position: 6th   Wins: 1   Pole positions: 0   Fastest laps: 0   Points scored: 48

	Race	Circuit	No	Entrant	Tyres	Capacity/Car/Engine	Comment	Q Pos/Entries
15/ret	AUSTRALIAN GP	Melbourne	3	Scuderia Ferrari Marlboro	B	2.4 Ferrari F2009-V8	spin-damage/differential failure	9/20
14	MALAYSIAN GP	Sepang	3	Scuderia Ferrari Marlboro	B	2.4 Ferrari F2009-V8	mistimed tyre change in wet	9/20
10	CHINESE GP	Shanghai	3	Scuderia Ferrari Marlboro	B	2.4 Ferrari F2009-V8	lack of grip	8/20
6	BAHRAIN GP	Sakhir Circuit	3	Scuderia Ferrari Marlboro	B	2.4 Ferrari F2009-V8		10/20
ret	SPANISH GP	Barcelona	3	Scuderia Ferrari Marlboro	B	2.4 Ferrari F2009-V8	hydraulics	16/20
3	MONACO GP	Monte Carlo	3	Scuderia Ferrari Marlboro	B	2.4 Ferrari F2009-V8		2/20
9	TURKISH GP	Istanbul	3	Scuderia Ferrari Marlboro	B	2.4 Ferrari F2009-V8		6/20
8	BRITISH GP	Silverstone	3	Scuderia Ferrari Marlboro	B	2.4 Ferrari F2009-V8		9/20
ret	GERMAN GP	Nürburgring	3	Scuderia Ferrari Marlboro	B	2.4 Ferrari F2009-V8	debris caused radiator damage	9/20
2	HUNGARIAN GP	Hungaroring	3	Scuderia Ferrari Marlboro	B	2.4 Ferrari F2009-V8		7/20
3	EUROPEAN GP	Valencia	3	Scuderia Ferrari Marlboro	B	2.4 Ferrari F2009-V8		6/20
1	BELGIAN GP	Spa	3	Scuderia Ferrari Marlboro	B	2.4 Ferrari F2009-V8		6/20
3	ITALIAN GP	Monza	3	Scuderia Ferrari Marlboro	B	2.4 Ferrari F2009-V8		3/20
10	SINGAPORE GP	Marina Bay Circuit	3	Scuderia Ferrari Marlboro	B	2.4 Ferrari F2009-V8	lack of grip	13/20
4	JAPANESE GP	Suzuka	3	Scuderia Ferrari Marlboro	B	2.4 Ferrari F2009-V8		8/20
6	BRAZILIAN GP	Interlagos	3	Scuderia Ferrari Marlboro	B	2.4 Ferrari F2009-V8		5/20
12	ABU DHABI GP	Yas Marina Circuit	3	Scuderia Ferrari Marlboro	B	2.4 Ferrari F2009-V8		11/20

GP Starts: 155 (157)   GP Wins: 18   Pole positions: 16   Fastest laps: 35   Points: 579

RAPHANEL, Pierre-Henri (F) b 27/5/1961, Algiers, Algeria

1988 Championship position: Unplaced

	Race	Circuit	No	Entrant	Tyres	Capacity/Car/Engine	Comment	Q Pos/Entries
dnq	AUSTRALIAN GP	Adelaide	29	Larrousse Calmels	G	3.5 Lola LC88-Cosworth V8		29/31

1989 Championship position: Unplaced

	Race	Circuit	No	Entrant	Tyres	Capacity/Car/Engine	Comment	Q Pos/Entries
dnpq	BRAZILIAN GP	Rio	32	Coloni SpA	P	3.5 Coloni FC188B-Cosworth V8		34/38
dnpq	SAN MARINO GP	Imola	32	Coloni SpA	P	3.5 Coloni FC188B-Cosworth V8		36/39
ret	MONACO GP	Monte Carlo	32	Coloni SpA	P	3.5 Coloni FC188B-Cosworth V8	gearbox	18/38
dnpq	MEXICAN GP	Mexico City	32	Coloni SpA	P	3.5 Coloni FC188B-Cosworth V8		39/39
dnpq	US GP (PHOENIX)	Phoenix	32	Coloni SpA	P	3.5 Coloni FC188B-Cosworth V8		32/39
dnpq	CANADIAN GP	Montreal	32	Coloni SpA	P	3.5 Coloni FC189-Cosworth V8		39/39
dnpq	FRENCH GP	Paul Ricard	32	Coloni SpA	P	3.5 Coloni FC189-Cosworth V8		36/39
dnpq	BRITISH GP	Silverstone	32	Coloni SpA	P	3.5 Coloni FC189-Cosworth V8		37/39
dnpq	GERMAN GP	Hockenheim	32	Coloni SpA	P	3.5 Coloni FC189-Cosworth V8		36/39
dnpq	HUNGARIAN GP	Hungaroring	32	Coloni SpA	P	3.5 Coloni FC189-Cosworth V8		39/39
dnq	BELGIAN GP	Spa	39	Rial Racing	G	3.5 Rial ARC2-Cosworth V8		30/39
dnq	ITALIAN GP	Monza	39	Rial Racing	G	3.5 Rial ARC2-Cosworth V8		29/39
dnq	PORTUGUESE GP	Estoril	39	Rial Racing	G	3.5 Rial ARC2-Cosworth V8		30/39
dnq	SPANISH GP	Jerez	39	Rial Racing	G	3.5 Rial ARC2-Cosworth V8		28/38
dnq	JAPANESE GP	Suzuka	38	Rial Racing	G	3.5 Rial ARC2-Cosworth V8		29/39
dnq	AUSTRALIAN GP	Adelaide	38	Rial Racing	G	3.5 Rial ARC2-Cosworth V8		29/39

GP Starts: 1   GP Wins: 0   Pole positions: 0   Fastest laps: 0   Points: 0

RATZENBERGER, Roland (A) b 4/7/1960, Salzburg – d 30/4/1994, Imola Circuit, Italy

1994 Championship position: Unplaced

	Race	Circuit	No	Entrant	Tyres	Capacity/Car/Engine	Comment	Q Pos/Entries
dnq	BRAZILIAN GP	Interlagos	32	MTV Simtek Ford	G	3.5 Simtek S941-Ford HB V8		27/28
11	PACIFIC GP	T.I. Circuit	32	MTV Simtek Ford	G	3.5 Simtek S941-Ford HB V8	5 laps behind	26/28
dns	SAN MARINO GP	Imola	32	MTV Simtek Ford	G	3.5 Simtek S941-Ford HB V8	fatal accident in practice	(26)/28

GP Starts: 1   GP Wins: 0   Pole positions: 0   Fastest laps: 0   Points: 0

PIERRE-HENRI RAPHANEL

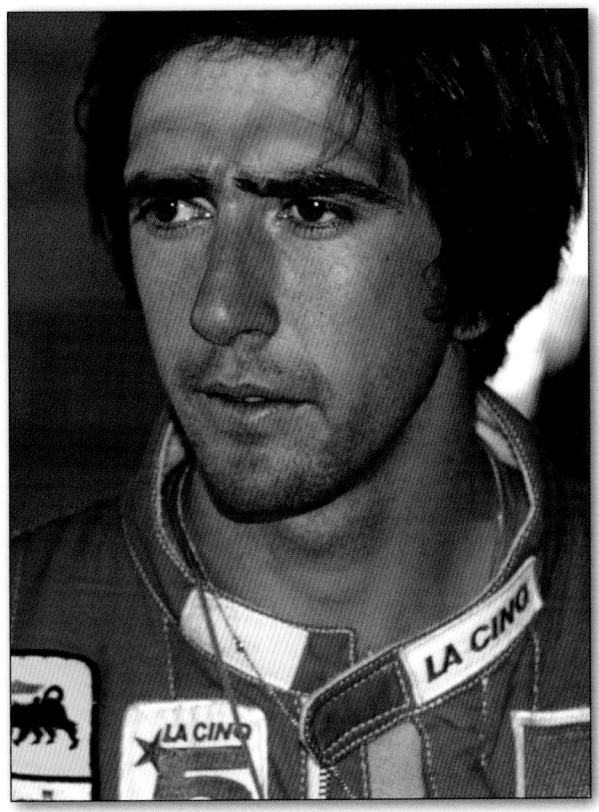

AFTER finishing third overall in the 1984 series, Pierre-Henri Raphanel was French Formula 3 champion in 1985, having successfully defended his early-season lead from ORECA team-mate Yannick Dalmas as the season wore on.

Promoted into the ORECA F3000 team for 1986, Raphanel soon found his feet and ended the season looking a good bet for honours in 1987. Somehow he failed to spark thereafter, however, enduring two lacklustre seasons. At the end of 1988, he stood in for former team-mate Dalmas at Larrousse, but gearbox problems stymied his chances of qualifying.

Having signed to race for Coloni in 1989, Raphanel found himself among the early risers attempting to pre-qualify, and he did extremely well to get on the grid at Monaco. A mid-season move to Rial merely meant that he could turn up a little later for practice, but he still found his Sundays free.

Subsequently, Pierre-Henri drove in Japanese Group C and touring cars, and figured in Toyota's Le Mans challenge, finishing second in 1992 (with Masanori Sekiya and Kenny Acheson). Then he enjoyed a successful career in sports cars, and after racing a Courage-Porsche at the Sarthe circuit with Pascal Fabre in 1994, he switched to GT racing with a McLaren F1 GTR between 1995 and 1997. The highlight of this period was another second-place finish at Le Mans in 1997 with car owner Lindsay Owen-Jones and David Brabham.

The following year, Raphanel took second at the Sarthe circuit again, in a McLaren GT1 partnered by Jean-Marc Gounon and Anders Olofsson. Elsewhere, he was an incredibly consistent top-six finisher.

In 1999, Pierre-Henri competed in the All-Japan touring car championship with a Toyota Supra with mixed results, so he returned to the FIA GT series in 2000 with a Panoz LMP roadster.

After 2006, Raphanel worked as the lead test driver and product specialist for Bugatti, and he is usually seen demonstrating the Veyron. In 2010, he set the production car speed record in the new Veyron Super Sport 16.4. The 1,200-horsepower (1,106 pound-feet of torque) monster propelled Raphanel to timed runs of 265.9 and 269.8mph on Volkswagen's Ehra-Lessien test track near Wolfsburg, averaging a maximum speed of 267.81mph.

ROLAND RATZENBERGER

WHEN Roland Ratzenberger was chosen, surprisingly, for the second seat at Simtek Grand Prix at the beginning of 1994, he had become something of a forgotten figure, having spent the previous four seasons making a very successful career for himself in Japan after his options in Europe had narrowed in 1989.

Victory in the Formula Ford Festival at Brands Hatch in 1986 had led to rides with BMW in the FIA world touring car championship, Formula 3 programmes in both Britain and Germany, and British F3000. Roland's record in all these disciplines was more than respectable, but it failed to open the doors to a higher echelon, so he headed east to continue his racing. He won in touring cars, F3000 and Group C with the SARD Toyota team, the latter category being a particular favourite.

Sadly, Roland's part on the grand prix stage was truly tragic, for the chance to show his undoubted talent was cruelly cut short when his Simtek crashed during practice for the San Marino Grand Prix at nearly 200mph, following a suspected front-wing failure caused by riding the kerbs too hard at Aqua Minerale on the previous lap. The subsequent lack of downforce meant that the Austrian was helpless, and he struck the wall on the approach to Villeneuve Curve. The impact sent the Simtek car spinning before finally coming to a halt several hundred yards down the hill in the middle of the track. It is thought that he died instantly from a broken neck.

HECTOR REBAQUE

AN ambitious young Mexican hot-shot, Hector Rebaque travelled to England in 1974 as a raw 18-year-old to try his hand at Formula Atlantic, as a protégé of Fred Opert in a Chevron. The following year, he moved into Formula 2 in Opert's Chevron, before returning across the pond to contest the Canadian Formula Atlantic series in 1975 and 1976.

Itching to get into grand prix racing, Hector joined the Hesketh team for a few outings in 1977, qualifying just once. Determined to succeed, he set up his own team the following season, fielding ex-works Lotus 78s, but he managed only one top-six finish, in Germany. For 1979, he had Lotus 79s at his disposal, but results remained discouraging, so he took the brave – if foolhardy – step of commissioning his own chassis, which only appeared for the last three grands prix of the year before the team folded.

In 1980, Hector kicked his heels until the opportunity arose to join Brabham in place of Ricardo Zunino. Now in a top-notch car, it was up to him to prove himself, and on occasion he showed a good turn of speed. In Argentina in 1981, for example, he had the BT49C in a comfortable second place until a rotor arm broke.

Rebaque briefly tried his hand at Indy car racing in 1982, luckily winning a race at Elkhart Lake when many of the leaders ran out of fuel. After a mid-season crash at Michigan, however, he developed a distinct aversion to ovals and retired at season's end, at the age of 29.

REBAQUE, Hector (MEX) b 5/2/1956, Mexico City

	Race	Circuit	No	Entrant	Tyres	Capacity/Car/Engine	Comment	Q Pos/Entries
1977	Championship position: Unplaced							
dnq	BELGIAN GP	Zolder	39	Hesketh Racing	G	3.0 Hesketh 308E-Cosworth V8		32/32
dnq	SWEDISH GP	Anderstorp	39	Hesketh Racing	G	3.0 Hesketh 308E-Cosworth V8		29/31
dnq	FRENCH GP	Dijon	39	Hesketh Racing	G	3.0 Hesketh 308E-Cosworth V8		28/30
ret	GERMAN GP	Hockenheim	25	Hesketh Racing	G	3.0 Hesketh 308E-Cosworth V8	battery	24/30
dnq	AUSTRIAN GP	Österreichring	25	Hesketh Racing	G	3.0 Hesketh 308E-Cosworth V8		29/30
dnq	DUTCH GP	Zandvoort	25	Hesketh Racing	G	3.0 Hesketh 308E-Cosworth V8		32/34
1978	Championship position: Unplaced							
dnq	ARGENTINE GP	Buenos Aires	25	Team Rebaque	G	3.0 Lotus 78-Cosworth V8		25/27
ret	BRAZILIAN GP	Rio	25	Team Rebaque	G	3.0 Lotus 78-Cosworth V8	driver fatigue	22/28
10	SOUTH AFRICAN GP	Kyalami	25	Team Rebaque	G	3.0 Lotus 78-Cosworth V8	1 lap behind	21/30
dnpq	US GP WEST	Long Beach	25	Team Rebaque	G	3.0 Lotus 78-Cosworth V8		28/30
dnpq	MONACO GP	Monte Carlo	25	Team Rebaque	G	3.0 Lotus 78-Cosworth V8		28/30
dnpq	BELGIAN GP	Zolder	25	Team Rebaque	G	3.0 Lotus 78-Cosworth V8		29/30
ret	SPANISH GP	Jarama	25	Team Rebaque	G	3.0 Lotus 78-Cosworth V8	exhaust system	20/29
12	SWEDISH GP	Anderstorp	25	Team Rebaque	G	3.0 Lotus 78-Cosworth V8	2 laps behind	21/27
dnq	FRENCH GP	Paul Ricard	25	Team Rebaque	G	3.0 Lotus 78-Cosworth V8		29/29
ret	BRITISH GP	Brands Hatch	25	Team Rebaque	G	3.0 Lotus 78-Cosworth V8	gearbox	21/30
6	GERMAN GP	Hockenheim	25	Team Rebaque	G	3.0 Lotus 78-Cosworth V8		18/30
ret	AUSTRIAN GP	Österreichring	25	Team Rebaque	G	3.0 Lotus 78-Cosworth V8	clutch	18/31
11	DUTCH GP	Zandvoort	25	Team Rebaque	G	3.0 Lotus 78-Cosworth V8	1 lap behind	20/33
dnq	ITALIAN GP	Monza	25	Team Rebaque	G	3.0 Lotus 78-Cosworth V8		25/32
ret	US GP EAST	Watkins Glen	25	Team Rebaque	G	3.0 Lotus 78-Cosworth V8	clutch	23/27
dnq	CANADIAN GP	Montreal	25	Team Rebaque	G	3.0 Lotus 78-Cosworth V8		26/28
1979	Championship position: Unplaced							
ret	ARGENTINE GP	Buenos Aires	31	Team Rebaque	G	3.0 Lotus 79-Cosworth V8	suspension	19/26
dnq	BRAZILIAN GP	Interlagos	31	Team Rebaque	G	3.0 Lotus 79-Cosworth V8		25/26
ret	SOUTH AFRICAN GP	Kyalami	31	Team Rebaque	G	3.0 Lotus 79-Cosworth V8	engine	23/26
ret	US GP WEST	Long Beach	31	Team Rebaque	G	3.0 Lotus 79-Cosworth V8	accident with Daly	25/26
ret	SPANISH GP	Jarama	31	Team Rebaque	G	3.0 Lotus 79-Cosworth V8	engine	23/27
ret	BELGIAN GP	Zolder	31	Team Rebaque	G	3.0 Lotus 79-Cosworth V8	driveshaft	15/28
12	FRENCH GP	Dijon	31	Team Rebaque	G	3.0 Lotus 79-Cosworth V8	2 laps behind	24/27
9	BRITISH GP	Silverstone	31	Team Rebaque	G	3.0 Lotus 79-Cosworth V8	2 laps behind	24/26
ret	GERMAN GP	Hockenheim	31	Team Rebaque	G	3.0 Lotus 79-Cosworth V8	handling	24/26
dnq	AUSTRIAN GP	Österreichring	31	Team Rebaque	G	3.0 Lotus 79-Cosworth V8		25/26
7	DUTCH GP	Zandvoort	31	Team Rebaque	G	3.0 Lotus 79-Cosworth V8	2 laps behind	24/26
dnq	ITALIAN GP	Monza	31	Team Rebaque	G	3.0 Rebaque HR100-Cosworth V8		28/28
ret	CANADIAN GP	Montreal	31	Team Rebaque	G	3.0 Rebaque HR100-Cosworth V8	engine mounting	22/29
dnq	US GP EAST	Watkins Glen	31	Team Rebaque	G	3.0 Rebaque HR100-Cosworth V8		28/30

1980 Championship position: Unplaced

7	BRITISH GP	Brands Hatch	6	Parmalat Racing Team	G	3.0 Brabham BT49-Cosworth V8	2 laps behind	17/27
ret	GERMAN GP	Hockenheim	6	Parmalat Racing Team	G	3.0 Brabham BT49-Cosworth V8	gearbox	15/26
10	AUSTRIAN GP	Österreichring	6	Parmalat Racing Team	G	3.0 Brabham BT49-Cosworth V8	1 lap behind	14/25
ret	DUTCH GP	Zandvoort	6	Parmalat Racing Team	G	3.0 Brabham BT49-Cosworth V8	gearbox	13/28
ret	ITALIAN GP	Imola	6	Parmalat Racing Team	G	3.0 Brabham BT49-Cosworth V8	broken rear suspension	9/28
6	CANADIAN GP	Montreal	6	Parmalat Racing Team	G	3.0 Brabham BT49-Cosworth V8	1 lap behind	10/28
ret	US GP EAST	Watkins Glen	6	Parmalat Racing Team	G	3.0 Brabham BT49-Cosworth V8	engine	8/27

1981 Championship position: Unplaced

ret	US GP WEST	Long Beach	6	Parmalat Racing Team	M	3.0 Brabham BT49C-Cosworth V8	accident	15/29
ret	BRAZILIAN GP	Rio	6	Parmalat Racing Team	M	3.0 Brabham BT49C-Cosworth V8	rear suspension damage	11/30
ret	ARGENTINE GP	Buenos Aires	6	Parmalat Racing Team	M	3.0 Brabham BT49C-Cosworth V8	distributor rotor arm	6/29
4	SAN MARINO GP	Imola	6	Parmalat Racing Team	M	3.0 Brabham BT49C-Cosworth V8		13/30
ret	BELGIAN GP	Zolder	6	Parmalat Racing Team	M	3.0 Brabham BT49C-Cosworth V8	accident	21/31
dnq	MONACO GP	Monte Carlo	6	Parmalat Racing Team	M	3.0 Brabham BT49C-Cosworth V8		23/31
ret	SPANISH GP	Jarama	6	Parmalat Racing Team	M	3.0 Brabham BT49C-Cosworth V8	gearbox	18/30
9	FRENCH GP	Dijon	6	Parmalat Racing Team	M	3.0 Brabham BT49C-Cosworth V8	2 laps behind	15/29
5	BRITISH GP	Silverstone	6	Parmalat Racing Team	G	3.0 Brabham BT49C-Cosworth V8	1 lap behind	13/30
4	GERMAN GP	Hockenheim	6	Parmalat Racing Team	G	3.0 Brabham BT49C-Cosworth V8		16/30
ret	AUSTRIAN GP	Österreichring	6	Parmalat Racing Team	G	3.0 Brabham BT49C-Cosworth V8	clutch	15/28
4	DUTCH GP	Zandvoort	6	Parmalat Racing Team	G	3.0 Brabham BT49C-Cosworth V8	1 lap behind	15/30
ret	ITALIAN GP	Monza	6	Parmalat Racing Team	G	3.0 Brabham BT49C-Cosworth V8	electrics	14/30
ret	CANADIAN GP	Montreal	6	Parmalat Racing Team	G	3.0 Brabham BT49C-Cosworth V8	spun off	6/30
ret	CAESARS PALACE GP	Las Vegas	6	Parmalat Racing Team	G	3.0 Brabham BT49C-Cosworth V8	spun off	16/30

GP Starts: 41   GP Wins: 0   Pole positions: 0   Fastest laps: 0   Points: 13

BRIAN REDMAN

THE 1959 season saw the start of Brian Redman's competition career, which began in the modest surroundings of Rufforth with a Morris 1000. Since those far-off days, the Lancastrian has probably raced on more of the world's circuits than most of his peers, but he is hardly a household name. It could have been so different, however, for undoubtedly he had the talent to become a grand prix winner, but his distaste of the high-pressure Formula 1 environment prompted him to turn his back on the grand prix paddock to enjoy an enormously successful and rewarding career in other forms of racing.

After early club-level outings with a Mini, Redman made a name for himself in 1965 with a Jaguar E-Type, before campaigning a Lola T70 in 1966. His career gradually gained momentum during 1967 in Formula 2 – with David Bridges' Lola – and sports car events; he won the Rand nine-hours in a Mirage with Jacky Ickx. In 1968, he had his first taste of grand prix racing with Cooper, which ended with a broken arm after a crash at Spa when his car's suspension failed. This came after a run of impressive performances, most notably victories in the BOAC 500 and Spa 1000km with Ickx in the GT40, and a brilliant drive in the Formula 2 Eifelrennen with the Ferrari Dino. The last brought an offer of a works drive, which he declined.

Redman then began a long period in sports car racing (1969–73) with Porsche and Ferrari, winning virtually all the major classics with the striking exception of Le Mans, which strangely eluded him. He made occasional returns to grand prix racing, usually as a replacement driver, but often without the benefit of testing and preparation. By this time, however, Brian had established himself as the man to beat in US F5000, winning three successive titles between 1974 and 1976 in the Haas/Hall Lola. After overcoming serious injuries received at the start of 1977, when his Can-Am Lola flipped, Brian was soon back, winning at Sebring in 1978 and taking the IMSA title in 1981.

Based in Jacksonville, Florida with a Porsche dealership, Redman subsequently graced a wide variety of classes, racing as competitively as ever and revelling in the less-pressured atmosphere of motorsport in North America. He also fronted the Redman-Bright F3000 team, which successfully ran Gonzalo Rodriguez before the Uruguayan driver's tragic death in a CART accident at Laguna Seca in 1999.

Even into his seventies, Brian still drives vintage race cars, organises and promotes historic motoring events, and provides individual and group driving instruction. In 2011, he was deservedly inducted into the International Motorsports Hall of Fame at Talladega.

REDMAN, Brian (GB) b 9/3/1937, Burnley, Lancashire

1968 Championship position: 19th=   Wins: 0   Pole positions: 0   Fastest laps: 0   Points scored: 4

	Race	Circuit	No	Entrant	Tyres	Capacity/Car/Engine	Comment	Q Pos/Entries
ret	SOUTH AFRICAN GP	Kyalami	14	Cooper Car Co	F	3.0 Cooper T81B-Maserati V12	overheating/oil leak	21/23
3	SPANISH GP	Jarama	14	Cooper Car Co	F	3.0 Cooper T86B-BRM V12	1 lap behind	13/14
ret	BELGIAN GP	Spa	16	Cooper Car Co	F	3.0 Cooper T86B-BRM V12	accident – broken suspension	10/18

1970 Championship position: Unplaced

	Race	Circuit	No	Entrant	Tyres	Capacity/Car/Engine	Comment	Q Pos/Entries
dnp	SOUTH AFRICAN GP	Kyalami	11	Rob Walker Racing Team	F	3.0 Lotus 49C-Cosworth V8	reserve driver on stand-by for Hill	– / –
dns	BRITISH GP	Brands Hatch	25	Frank Williams Racing Cars	D	3.0 de Tomaso 505-Cosworth V8	hub failure in practice	25/25
dnq	GERMAN GP	Hockenheim	25	Frank Williams Racing Cars	D	3.0 de Tomaso 505-Cosworth V8	unseeded car	20/25

1971 Championship position: Unplaced

	Race	Circuit	No	Entrant	Tyres	Capacity/Car/Engine	Comment	Q Pos/Entries
7	SOUTH AFRICAN GP	Kyalami	28	Team Surtees	F	3.0 Surtees TS7-Cosworth V8	1 lap behind	=16/25

1972 Championship position: 12th=   Wins: 0   Pole positions: 0   Fastest laps: 0   Points scored: 4

	Race	Circuit	No	Entrant	Tyres	Capacity/Car/Engine	Comment	Q Pos/Entries
5	MONACO GP	Monte Carlo	15	Yardley Team McLaren	G	3.0 McLaren M19A-Cosworth V8	pit stop – puncture/-3 laps	10/25
9	FRENCH GP	Clermont Ferrand	11	Yardley Team McLaren	G	3.0 McLaren M19A-Cosworth V8		15/29
5	GERMAN GP	Nürburgring	5	Yardley Team McLaren	G	3.0 McLaren M19A-Cosworth V8		19/27
ret	US GP	Watkins Glen	15	Marlboro BRM	F	3.0 BRM P180 V12	engine	24/32

1973 Championship position: Unplaced

	Race	Circuit	No	Entrant	Tyres	Capacity/Car/Engine	Comment	Q Pos/Entries
dsq	US GP	Watkins Glen	31	Shadow Racing Team	G	3.0 Shadow DN1-Cosworth V8	outside assistance – push start	13/28

1974 Championship position: Unplaced

	Race	Circuit	No	Entrant	Tyres	Capacity/Car/Engine	Comment	Q Pos/Entries
7	SPANISH GP	Jarama	16	UOP Shadow Racing Team	G	3.0 Shadow DN3-Cosworth V8	3 laps behind	22/28
18/ret	BELGIAN GP	Nivelles	16	UOP Shadow Racing Team	G	3.0 Shadow DN3-Cosworth V8	engine/5 laps behind	18/32
ret	MONACO GP	Monte Carlo	16	UOP Shadow Racing Team	G	3.0 Shadow DN3-Cosworth V8	multiple accident	=16/28

GP Starts: 12   GP Wins: 0   Pole positions: 0   Fastest laps: 0   Points: 8

ALAN REES

A VERY useful driver in Formula Junior, Alan Rees drove for the works Lotus team in 1962, taking three wins, before a crash in a Lotus 23 at the Nürburgring 1000km sports car race curtailed his season.

For 1963, Rees joined the Roy Winkelmann team, eventually becoming its mainstay as both driver and, later, team manager. Concentrating on Formula 2 between 1964 and 1968, he drove countless races in the team's Brabhams, often beating the stars of the day, such as Jochen Rindt, Jackie Stewart and Jim Clark. However, his grand prix opportunities were limited to a couple of races in the Winkelmann F2 car and a single outing in a rather tired works Cooper at the 1967 British Grand Prix.

By the end of 1968, Rees had decided that he was not going to progress any further as a drive, so he retired to the team manager's role, before becoming a founder member of March in 1969. Later he acted as team manager of Shadow (1973–76) and then Arrows, after his defection with Jackie Oliver. He remained in harness with Oliver through the sale and buy-back from Footwork, until finally the pair sold out to Tom Walkinshaw in 1996.

In 2010, Alan's son, Paul, sampled Formula 2 before turning to GT racing with a Ferrari.

REES, Alan (GB) b 12/1/1938, Langstone, nr Newport, Monmouthshire, Wales

1966 Championship position: Unplaced

	Race	Circuit	No	Entrant	Tyres	Capacity/Car/Engine	Comment	Q Pos/Entries
ret	GERMAN GP (F2)	Nürburgring	29	Roy Winkelmann Racing	–	1.0 Brabham BT18-Cosworth 4 F2	gearbox/engine	25/30

1967 Championship position: Unplaced

	Race	Circuit	No	Entrant	Tyres	Capacity/Car/Engine	Comment	Q Pos/Entries
9	BRITISH GP	Silverstone	14	Cooper Car Co	F	3.0 Cooper T81-Maserati V12	4 laps behind	15/21
7*	GERMAN GP (F2)	Nürburgring	22	Roy Winkelmann Racing	–	1.6 Brabham BT23-Cosworth 4 F2	*2nd in F2 class	17/25

GP Starts: 3   GP Wins: 0   Pole positions: 0   Fastest laps: 0   Points: 0

CLAY REGAZZONI

A DRIVER of the old school, Clay Regazzoni took no prisoners with his rough-and-ready approach to racing during his early days of Formula 3. And while he may have tempered his approach in the ensuing years, he was always liable to revert to type, leaving his competitors a little wary as they locked horns with the hard-racing Swiss.

After competing with a Healey Sprite, Clay joined forces with fellow countryman Silvio Moser to race F2 and F3 Brabhams in 1965/66, before switching to the Tecno marque. Regazzoni joined their works team in 1968 to compete in the European Formula 2 championship, where some of his driving tactics became a cause for concern. Things reached a low ebb in mid-season, when he was disqualified for overtaking at the site of an accident at Monza and then, in the next race at Zandvoort, was involved in Chris Lambert's fatal accident. The fall-out from this incident lasted for some considerable time, and although Regazzoni was absolved from blame, some mud would always stick.

The 1969 season brought an invitation from Ferrari to race their Formula 2 166 Dino, but little of note was achieved and Clay soon returned to the Tecno ranks. This proved a wise decision, for the team's F2 car really came good in 1970. Up to that point, he had been regarded as something of a Neanderthal, but wins at Hockenheim, Paul Ricard, Enna and Imola helped dispel this image, and he jumped into the Ferrari F1 team with no qualms at all. Fourth place on his debut was a great effort, but better was to come when, after a splendid second at the Österreichring, he took the ultimate prize for a Ferrari driver, a win in the Italian Grand Prix at Monza.

Clay's place was now secure, but over the next two seasons, apart from the Race of Champions in 1971, there were no more wins – some good performances to be sure, but too many incidents for the Scuderia's liking. Thus, at the end of 1972, he was released, but he soon found a seat with Marlboro-BRM.

Regazzoni took his change of circumstances with equanimity and started the season with a great drive in the Argentine GP, taking pole and leading the race for 30 laps, before troubles dropped him back. His year was largely spent in midfield anonymity, however, before a surprise recall to Ferrari, who were re-structuring after a terrible year; he would race alongside Niki Lauda. The 1974 season was probably the Swiss driver's finest. There were off-track excursions, but he was a remarkably consistent finisher and took a superb win at the Nür-burgring to get within touching distance of the world championship

Clay's value to Ferrari at this time was immense, proving to be the ideal foil for Lauda, quite capable of picking up the pieces if necessary, as in the non-title Swiss GP and then the Italian GP at Monza the following season. Unfor-tunately, there was still the occasional brainstorm, and his tactics at Watkins Glen, where he blatantly blocked Emerson Fittipaldi, were a disgrace. In 1976, we saw the same cocktail – a brilliant win at Long Beach and a crass first-cor-ner manoeuvre at Paddock Bend in the infamous British GP. Certainly his form began to tail off towards the end of that year, and his services were no longer required at Ferrari once the talents of Carlos Reutemann became available.

Joining the little Ensign squad for 1977 was akin to leaving The Ritz to dine at MacDonald's, but Regazzoni was happy just to be part of the scene. There were inevitable crashes of course, but a couple of fifth places near the end of the season kept Mo Nunn happy enough. Clay was tempted by the lure of Indianapolis that year and qualified in a Theodore McLaren, but was forced to retire the car in the race with a water leak.

Regazzoni's Swiss connections helped him into the Shadow team for 1978, but apart from a couple of fifth-place finishes, it was a pretty dismal year. It was difficult to see much future for him in Formula 1 by this stage, but Frank Williams took him on board. He reasoned that in good car, Clay had been almost as quick as Lauda, and his experience would be an asset in the team's newly expanded two-car operation. That hunch proved correct, as he won at Silverstone to score the Williams team's first ever grand prix victory, and a special place in their history. Sentiment didn't cloud Williams' judgement when it came to his 1980 line-up, however, and when Reutemann became available, Regazzoni was out...

Unperturbed, Clay counted his blessings and headed back to Ensign. The team had a healthier budget and a new car, but the season was only four races old when disaster struck. In the grand prix at Long Beach, his brake pedal snapped, leaving the red, white and blue machine to hurtle down the escape road into a concrete wall. Poor Regazzoni, trapped in the car for more than 25 minutes, sustained serious spinal damage in addition to a broken leg, which confined him to a wheelchair. Despite this crippling injury, however, he lost none of his enthusiasm for the sport, nor his zest for life.

After working regularly as a commentator for Swiss TV for more than a decade, Regazzoni started competing again in specially adapted saloon cars and karts. He started a driving school for handicapped people and was fully involved in developing the hand-control systems for their cars. It came as a huge shock to the motor racing fraternity worldwide when news of his death in a road crash filtered out from Italy just ten days before Christmas, 2006. His car had been involved in a head-on collision with a lorry on the autostrada near Palma. The cause of the accident was not clear, but he may have fallen asleep at the wheel of his Chrysler Voyager.

Strangely, Regazzoni was the third ex-Ferrari grand prix driver to perish in such a fashion. Both Giuseppe Farina and Michael Parkes had lost their lives after road traffic accidents.

REGAZZONI, 'Clay' (Gianclaudio) (CH) b 5/9/1939, Mendrisio, nr Lugano – d 15/12/2006, nr Parma

1970 Championship position: 3rd   Wins: 1   Pole positions: 1   Fastest laps: 3 (1 shared)   Points scored: 33

	Race	Circuit	No	Entrant	Tyres	Capacity/Car/Engine	Comment	Q Pos/Entries
4	DUTCH GP	Zandvoort	26	Scuderia Ferrari SpA SEFAC	F	3.0 Ferrari 312B F12	1 lap behind	6/24
4	BRITISH GP	Brands Hatch	4	Scuderia Ferrari SpA SEFAC	F	3.0 Ferrari 312B F12		6/25
ret	GERMAN GP	Hockenheim	15	Scuderia Ferrari SpA SEFAC	F	3.0 Ferrari 312B F12	gearbox problems – spun off	3/25
2	AUSTRIAN GP	Österreichring	27	Scuderia Ferrari SpA SEFAC	F	3.0 Ferrari 312B F12	FL (shared with Ickx)	2/24
1	ITALIAN GP	Monza	4	Scuderia Ferrari SpA SEFAC	F	3.0 Ferrari 312B F12	FL	3/27
2	CANADIAN GP	St Jovite	19	Scuderia Ferrari SpA SEFAC	F	3.0 Ferrari 312B F12	FL	3/20
13	US GP	Watkins Glen	4	Scuderia Ferrari SpA SEFAC	F	3.0 Ferrari 312B F12	pit stop – fuel pipe/7 laps behind	6/27
2	MEXICAN GP	Mexico City	4	Scuderia Ferrari SpA SEFAC	F	3.0 Ferrari 312B F12		1/18

1971 Championship position: 7th   Wins: 0   Pole positions: 1   Fastest laps: 0   Points scored: 13

	Race	Circuit	No	Entrant	Tyres	Capacity/Car/Engine	Comment	Q Pos/Entries
3	SOUTH AFRICAN GP	Kyalami	5	Scuderia Ferrari SpA SEFAC	F	3.0 Ferrari 312B F12		3/25
ret	SPANISH GP	Montjuich Park	5	Scuderia Ferrari SpA SEFAC	F	3.0 Ferrari 312B F12	engine	=2/25
dns	"	" "	5T	Scuderia Ferrari SpA SEFAC	F	3.0 Ferrari 312B2 F12	practice only	– / –
ret	MONACO GP	Monte Carlo	5	Scuderia Ferrari SpA SEFAC	F	3.0 Ferrari 312B2 F12	hit chicane – suspension	11/23
3	DUTCH GP	Zandvoort	3	Scuderia Ferrari SpA SEFAC	F	3.0 Ferrari 312B2 F12	late spin/1 lap behind	4/24
dns	"	"	3T	Scuderia Ferrari SpA SEFAC	F	3.0 Ferrari 312B2 F12	practice only	– / –
ret	FRENCH GP	Paul Ricard	5	Scuderia Ferrari SpA SEFAC	F	3.0 Ferrari 312B2 F12	spun off – damaged wheel	2/24
ret	BRITISH GP	Silverstone	5	Scuderia Ferrari SpA SEFAC	F	3.0 Ferrari 312B2 F12	engine	1/24
3	GERMAN GP	Nürburgring	6	Scuderia Ferrari SpA SEFAC	F	3.0 Ferrari 312B2 F12		4/23
dns	"	"	31	Scuderia Ferrari SpA SEFAC	F	3.0 Ferrari 312B F12	practice only	– / –
ret	AUSTRIAN GP	Österreichring	5	Scuderia Ferrari SpA SEFAC	F	3.0 Ferrari 312B2 F12	engine	4/22
ret	ITALIAN GP	Monza	4	Scuderia Ferrari SpA SEFAC	F	3.0 Ferrari 312B2 F12	engine damper	8/24
ret	CANADIAN GP	Mosport Park	5	Scuderia Ferrari SpA SEFAC	F	3.0 Ferrari 312B2 F12	electrical fire – accident	18/27
dns	"	" "	25T	Scuderia Ferrari SpA SEFAC	F	3.0 Ferrari 312B F12	practice only	– / –
6	US GP	Watkins Glen	5	Scuderia Ferrari SpA SEFAC	F	3.0 Ferrari 312B2 F12	spin	4/32

1972 Championship position: 6th=   Wins: 0   Pole positions: 0   Fastest laps: 0   Points scored: 15

	Race	Circuit	No	Entrant	Tyres	Capacity/Car/Engine	Comment	Q Pos/Entries
4	ARGENTINE GP	Buenos Aires	9	Scuderia Ferrari SpA SEFAC	F	3.0 Ferrari 312B2 F12		=5/22
12	SOUTH AFRICAN GP	Kyalami	6	Scuderia Ferrari SpA SEFAC	F	3.0 Ferrari 312B2 F12	pit stop – tyres/2 laps behind	2/27
3	SPANISH GP	Jarama	6	Scuderia Ferrari SpA SEFAC	F	3.0 Ferrari 312B2 F12	1 lap behind	8/26
ret	MONACO GP	Monte Carlo	7	Scuderia Ferrari SpA SEFAC	F	3.0 Ferrari 312B2 F12	hit barrier	3/25
ret	BELGIAN GP	Nivelles	30	Scuderia Ferrari SpA SEFAC	F	3.0 Ferrari 312B2 F12	hit Galli's spinning car	2/26
2	GERMAN GP	Nürburgring	9	Scuderia Ferrari SpA SEFAC	F	3.0 Ferrari 312B2 F12	hit Stewart on last lap	7/27
ret	AUSTRIAN GP	Österreichring	19	Scuderia Ferrari SpA SEFAC	F	3.0 Ferrari 312B2 F12	fuel pressure	2/26
ret	ITALIAN GP	Monza	5	Scuderia Ferrari SpA SEFAC	F	3.0 Ferrari 312B2 F12	hit Pace at chicane	4/27
5	CANADIAN GP	Mosport Park	11	Scuderia Ferrari SpA SEFAC	F	3.0 Ferrari 312B2 F12	handling problems	=6/25
8	US GP	Watkins Glen	8	Scuderia Ferrari SpA SEFAC	F	3.0 Ferrari 312B2 F12	exhaust fell off/1 lap behind	6/32

1973 Championship position: 17th=   Wins: 0   Pole positions: 1   Fastest laps: 0   Points scored: 2

	Race	Circuit	No	Entrant	Tyres	Capacity/Car/Engine	Comment	Q Pos/Entries
7	ARGENTINE GP	Buenos Aires	32	Marlboro BRM	F	3.0 BRM P160D V12	3 laps behind	1/19
6	BRAZILIAN GP	Interlagos	14	Marlboro BRM	F	3.0 BRM P160D V12	1 lap behind	4/20
ret	SOUTH AFRICAN GP	Kyalami	15	Marlboro BRM	F	3.0 BRM P160D V12	accident – rescued by Hailwood	5/25
9	SPANISH GP	Montjuich Park	14	Marlboro BRM	F	3.0 BRM P160E V12	pit stops – tyres/6 laps behind	=7/22
10/ret	BELGIAN GP	Zolder	19	Marlboro BRM	F	3.0 BRM P160E V12	spun off	12/23
ret	MONACO GP	Monte Carlo	19	Marlboro BRM	F	3.0 BRM P160E V12	boiling brake fluid	8/26
9	SWEDISH GP	Anderstorp	19	Marlboro BRM	F	3.0 BRM P160E V12	3 laps behind	12/22
12	FRENCH GP	Paul Ricard	19	Marlboro BRM	F	3.0 BRM P160E V12	1 lap behind	9/25
7	BRITISH GP	Silverstone	19	Marlboro BRM	F	3.0 BRM P160E V12		10/29
8	DUTCH GP	Zandvoort	19	Marlboro BRM	F	3.0 BRM P160E V12	2 pit stops – tyre – fuel/4 laps behind	12/24
ret	GERMAN GP	Nürburgring	19	Marlboro BRM	F	3.0 BRM P160E V12	engine	10/23
6	AUSTRIAN GP	Österreichring	19	Marlboro BRM	F	3.0 BRM P160E V12		14/25
ret	ITALIAN GP	Monza	19	Marlboro BRM	F	3.0 BRM P160E V12	coil	18/25
8	US GP	Watkins Glen	19	Marlboro BRM	F	3.0 BRM P160E V12	1 lap behind	16/28

1974 Championship position: 2nd   Wins: 1   Pole positions: 1   Fastest laps: 3   Points scored: 52

	Race	Circuit	No	Entrant	Tyres	Capacity/Car/Engine	Comment	Q Pos/Entries
3	ARGENTINE GP	Buenos Aires	11	Scuderia Ferrari SpA SEFAC	G	3.0 Ferrari 312B3 F12	FL	2/26
2	BRAZILIAN GP	Interlagos	11	Scuderia Ferrari SpA SEFAC	G	3.0 Ferrari 312B3 F12	FL	8/25
ret	SOUTH AFRICAN GP	Kyalami	11	Scuderia Ferrari SpA SEFAC	G	3.0 Ferrari 312B3 F12	oil pressure	6/27
2	SPANISH GP	Jarama	11	Scuderia Ferrari SpA SEFAC	G	3.0 Ferrari 312B3 F12		3/28
4	BELGIAN GP	Nivelles	11	Scuderia Ferrari SpA SEFAC	G	3.0 Ferrari 312B3 F12		1/32
4	MONACO GP	Monte Carlo	11	Scuderia Ferrari SpA SEFAC	G	3.0 Ferrari 312B3 F12		2/28
ret	SWEDISH GP	Anderstorp	11	Scuderia Ferrari SpA SEFAC	G	3.0 Ferrari 312B3 F12	transmission	4/28
2	DUTCH GP	Zandvoort	11	Scuderia Ferrari SpA SEFAC	G	3.0 Ferrari 312B3 F12		2/27
3	FRENCH GP	Dijon	11	Scuderia Ferrari SpA SEFAC	G	3.0 Ferrari 312B3 F12		4/30
4	BRITISH GP	Brands Hatch	11	Scuderia Ferrari SpA SEFAC	G	3.0 Ferrari 312B3 F12		=5/34
1	GERMAN GP	Nürburgring	11	Scuderia Ferrari SpA SEFAC	G	3.0 Ferrari 312B3 F12		2/32
5	AUSTRIAN GP	Österreichring	11	Scuderia Ferrari SpA SEFAC	G	3.0 Ferrari 312B3 F12	pit stop – tyre/FL	8/31
ret	ITALIAN GP	Monza	11	Scuderia Ferrari SpA SEFAC	G	3.0 Ferrari 312B3 F12	engine – oil seal	5/31
2	CANADIAN GP	Mosport Park	11	Scuderia Ferrari SpA SEFAC	G	3.0 Ferrari 312B3 F12		6/30
11	US GP	Watkins Glen	11	Scuderia Ferrari SpA SEFAC	G	3.0 Ferrari 312B3 F12	3 pit stops – handling/4 laps behind	9/30

1975 Championship position: 5th   Wins: 1   Pole positions: 0   Fastest laps: 4   Points scored: 25

	Race	Circuit	No	Entrant	Tyres	Capacity/Car/Engine	Comment	Q Pos/Entries
4	ARGENTINE GP	Buenos Aires	11	Scuderia Ferrari SpA SEFAC	G	3.0 Ferrari 312B3 F12		7/23
4	BRAZILIAN GP	Interlagos	11	Scuderia Ferrari SpA SEFAC	G	3.0 Ferrari 312B3 F12		5/23
16/ret	SOUTH AFRICAN GP	Kyalami	11	Scuderia Ferrari SpA SEFAC	G	3.0 Ferrari 312T F12	throttle linkage/7 laps behind	9/28
nc	SPANISH GP	Montjuich Park	11	Scuderia Ferrari SpA SEFAC	G	3.0 Ferrari 312T F12	pit stop – collision/4 laps behind	2/26
ret	MONACO GP	Monte Carlo	11	Scuderia Ferrari SpA SEFAC	G	3.0 Ferrari 312T F12	spun off – damaged suspension	6/26
5	BELGIAN GP	Zolder	11	Scuderia Ferrari SpA SEFAC	G	3.0 Ferrari 312T F12	pit stop – tyre/FL	4/24
3	SWEDISH GP	Anderstorp	11	Scuderia Ferrari SpA SEFAC	G	3.0 Ferrari 312T F12		12/26
3	DUTCH GP	Zandvoort	11	Scuderia Ferrari SpA SEFAC	G	3.0 Ferrari 312T F12		2/25

ret	FRENCH GP	Paul Ricard	11	Scuderia Ferrari SpA SEFAC	G	3.0 Ferrari 312T F12	*engine*	9/26
13	BRITISH GP	Silverstone	11	Scuderia Ferrari SpA SEFAC	G	3.0 Ferrari 312T F12	*pit stops – tyres/FL/2 laps behind*	4/28
ret	GERMAN GP	Nürburgring	11	Scuderia Ferrari SpA SEFAC	G	3.0 Ferrari 312T F12	*engine/FL*	5/26
7	AUSTRIAN GP	Österreichring	11	Scuderia Ferrari SpA SEFAC	G	3.0 Ferrari 312T F12		5/30
1	ITALIAN GP	Monza	11	Scuderia Ferrari SpA SEFAC	G	3.0 Ferrari 312T F12	*FL*	2/28
ret	US GP	Watkins Glen	11	Scuderia Ferrari SpA SEFAC	G	3.0 Ferrari 312T F12	*withdrawn in protest over reprimand*	11/24

1976 Championship position: 5th   Wins: 1   Pole positions: 1   Fastest laps: 3   Points scored: 31

7	BRAZILIAN GP	Interlagos	2	Scuderia Ferrari SpA SEFAC	G	3.0 Ferrari 312T F12	*pit stop/tyre*	4/22
ret	SOUTH AFRICAN GP	Kyalami	2	Scuderia Ferrari SpA SEFAC	G	3.0 Ferrari 312T F12	*engine*	9/25
1	US GP WEST	Long Beach	2	Scuderia Ferrari SpA SEFAC	G	3.0 Ferrari 312T F12	*FL*	1/27
11	SPANISH GP	Jarama	2	Scuderia Ferrari SpA SEFAC	G	3.0 Ferrari 312T2 F12	*pit stop – gear selection/3 laps behind*	5/30
2	BELGIAN GP	Zolder	2	Scuderia Ferrari SpA SEFAC	G	3.0 Ferrari 312T2 F12		2/29
14/ret	MONACO GP	Monte Carlo	2	Scuderia Ferrari SpA SEFAC	G	3.0 Ferrari 312T2 F12	*spun off/FL/5 laps behind*	2/25
6	SWEDISH GP	Anderstorp	2	Scuderia Ferrari SpA SEFAC	G	3.0 Ferrari 312T2 F12		11/27
ret	FRENCH GP	Paul Ricard	2	Scuderia Ferrari SpA SEFAC	G	3.0 Ferrari 312T2 F12	*engine – spun off*	4/30
ret/dsq*	BRITISH GP	Brands Hatch	2	Scuderia Ferrari SpA SEFAC	G	3.0 Ferrari 312T2 F12	*accident/*used T car in restart*	4/30
9	GERMAN GP	Nürburgring	2	Scuderia Ferrari SpA SEFAC	G	3.0 Ferrari 312T2 F12	*pit stop – nose cone*	5/28
2	DUTCH GP	Zandvoort	2	Scuderia Ferrari SpA SEFAC	G	3.0 Ferrari 312T2 F12	*FL*	5/27
2	ITALIAN GP	Monza	2	Scuderia Ferrari SpA SEFAC	G	3.0 Ferrari 312T2 F12		9/29
6	CANADIAN GP	Mosport Park	2	Scuderia Ferrari SpA SEFAC	G	3.0 Ferrari 312T2 F12	*1 lap behind*	12/27
7	US GP EAST	Watkins Glen	2	Scuderia Ferrari SpA SEFAC	G	3.0 Ferrari 312T2 F12	*1 lap behind*	14/27
5	JAPANESE GP	Mount Fuji	2	Scuderia Ferrari SpA SEFAC	G	3.0 Ferrari 312T2 F12	*pit stop – tyre*	7/27

1977 Championship position: 17th=   Wins: 0   Pole positions: 0   Fastest laps: 0   Points scored: 5

6	ARGENTINE GP	Buenos Aires	22	Team Tissot Ensign with Castrol	G	3.0 Ensign N177-Cosworth V8	*2 laps behind*	12/21
ret	BRAZILIAN GP	Interlagos	22	Team Tissot Ensign with Castrol	G	3.0 Ensign N177-Cosworth V8	*hit catch – fencing spun onto track*	9/22
9	SOUTH AFRICAN GP	Kyalami	22	Team Tissot Ensign with Castrol	G	3.0 Ensign N177-Cosworth V8		16/23
ret	US GP WEST	Long Beach	22	Team Tissot Ensign with Castrol	G	3.0 Ensign N177-Cosworth V8	*gearbox*	13/22
ret	SPANISH GP	Jarama	22	Team Tissot Ensign with Castrol	G	3.0 Ensign N177-Cosworth V8	*collision with Brambilla*	8/31
dnq	MONACO GP	Monte Carlo	22	Team Tissot Ensign with Castrol	G	3.0 Ensign N177-Cosworth V8		24/26
ret	BELGIAN GP	Zolder	22	Team Tissot Ensign with Castrol	G	3.0 Ensign N177-Cosworth V8	*engine*	13/32
7	SWEDISH GP	Anderstorp	22	Team Tissot Ensign with Castrol	G	3.0 Ensign N177-Cosworth V8		14/31
7	FRENCH GP	Dijon	22	Team Tissot Ensign with Castrol	G	3.0 Ensign N177-Cosworth V8	*1 lap behind*	16/30
dnq	BRITISH GP	Silverstone	22	Team Tissot Ensign with Castrol	G	3.0 Ensign N177-Cosworth V8		28/36
ret	GERMAN GP	Hockenheim	22	Team Tissot Ensign with Castrol	G	3.0 Ensign N177-Cosworth V8	*startline accident*	22/30
ret	AUSTRIAN GP	Österreichring	22	Team Tissot Ensign with Castrol	G	3.0 Ensign N177-Cosworth V8	*spun off*	11/30
ret	DUTCH GP	Zandvoort	22	Team Tissot Ensign with Castrol	G	3.0 Ensign N177-Cosworth V8	*throttle cable*	9/34
5	ITALIAN GP	Monza	22	Team Tissot Ensign with Castrol	G	3.0 Ensign N177-Cosworth V8		=6/34
5	US GP EAST	Watkins Glen	22	Team Tissot Ensign with Castrol	G	3.0 Ensign N177-Cosworth V8		19/27
ret	CANADIAN GP	Mosport Park	22	Team Tissot Ensign with Castrol	G	3.0 Ensign N177-Cosworth V8	*crashed on lap 1*	14/27
ret	JAPANESE GP	Mount Fuji	22	Team Tissot Ensign with Castrol	G	3.0 Ensign N177-Cosworth V8	*engine*	10/23

1978 Championship position: 16th=   Wins: 0   Pole positions: 0   Fastest laps: 0   Points scored: 4

15/ret	ARGENTINE GP	Buenos Aires	17	Shadow Racing Team	G	3.0 Shadow DN8-Cosworth V8	*pit stop – tyre/out of fuel/1 lap behind*	16/27
5	BRAZILIAN GP	Rio	17	Shadow Racing Team	G	3.0 Shadow DN8-Cosworth V8	*1 lap behind*	15/28
dnq	SOUTH AFRICAN GP	Kyalami	17	Shadow Racing Team	G	3.0 Shadow DN8-Cosworth V8		28/30
10	US GP WEST	Long Beach	17	Shadow Racing Team	G	3.0 Shadow DN8-Cosworth V8	*1 lap behind*	20/30
dnq	MONACO GP	Monte Carlo	17	Shadow Racing Team	G	3.0 Shadow DN9-Cosworth V8		22/30
ret	BELGIAN GP	Zolder	17	Shadow Racing Team	G	3.0 Shadow DN9-Cosworth V8	*differential*	18/30
15/ret	SPANISH GP	Jarama	17	Shadow Racing Team	G	3.0 Shadow DN9-Cosworth V8	*fuel union/8 laps behind*	22/29
5	SWEDISH GP	Anderstorp	17	Shadow Racing Team	G	3.0 Shadow DN9-Cosworth V8	*1 lap behind*	16/27
ret	FRENCH GP	Paul Ricard	17	Shadow Racing Team	G	3.0 Shadow DN9-Cosworth V8	*electrics*	17/29
ret	BRITISH GP	Brands Hatch	17	Shadow Racing Team	G	3.0 Shadow DN9-Cosworth V8	*gearbox*	17/30
dnq	GERMAN GP	Hockenheim	17	Shadow Racing Team	G	3.0 Shadow DN9-Cosworth V8		25/30
nc	AUSTRIAN GP	Österreichring	17	Shadow Racing Team	G	3.0 Shadow DN9-Cosworth V8	*pit stop – tyres/4 laps behind*	22/31
dnq	DUTCH GP	Zandvoort	17	Shadow Racing Team	G	3.0 Shadow DN9-Cosworth V8		28/33
nc	ITALIAN GP	Monza	17	Shadow Racing Team	G	3.0 Shadow DN9-Cosworth V8	*pit stops/7 laps behind*	15/32
14	US GP EAST	Watkins Glen	17	Shadow Racing Team	G	3.0 Shadow DN9-Cosworth V8	*pit stop – tyres/3 laps behind*	17/27
dnq	CANADIAN GP	Montreal	17	Shadow Racing Team	G	3.0 Shadow DN9-Cosworth V8		23/28

1979 Championship position: 5th   Wins: 1   Pole positions: 0   Fastest laps: 2   Points scored: 32

10	ARGENTINE GP	Buenos Aires	28	Albilad-Saudia Racing Team	G	3.0 Williams FW06-Cosworth V8	*pit stop – tyres/2 laps behind*	17/26
15	BRAZILIAN GP	Interlagos	28	Albilad-Saudia Racing Team	G	3.0 Williams FW06-Cosworth V8	*pit stop – damage check/2 laps behind*	17/26
9	SOUTH AFRICAN GP	Kyalami	28	Albilad-Saudia Racing Team	G	3.0 Williams FW06-Cosworth V8	*2 laps behind*	22/26
ret	US GP WEST	Long Beach	28	Albilad-Saudia Racing Team	G	3.0 Williams FW06-Cosworth V8	*engine*	15/26
ret	SPANISH GP	Jarama	28	Albilad-Saudia Racing Team	G	3.0 Williams FW07-Cosworth V8	*engine*	14/27
ret	BELGIAN GP	Zolder	28	Albilad-Saudia Racing Team	G	3.0 Williams FW07-Cosworth V8	*accident with J Scheckter & Villeneuve*	8/28
2	MONACO GP	Monte Carlo	28	Albilad-Saudia Racing Team	G	3.0 Williams FW07-Cosworth V8		16/25
6	FRENCH GP	Dijon	28	Albilad-Saudia Racing Team	G	3.0 Williams FW07-Cosworth V8		9/27
1	BRITISH GP	Silverstone	28	Albilad-Saudia Racing Team	G	3.0 Williams FW07-Cosworth V8	*FL*	4/26
2	GERMAN GP	Hockenheim	28	Albilad-Saudia Racing Team	G	3.0 Williams FW07-Cosworth V8		6/26
5	AUSTRIAN GP	Österreichring	28	Albilad-Saudia Racing Team	G	3.0 Williams FW07-Cosworth V8		6/26
ret	DUTCH GP	Zandvoort	28	Albilad-Saudia Racing Team	G	3.0 Williams FW07-Cosworth V8	*accident with Arnoux at start*	3/26
3	ITALIAN GP	Monza	28	Albilad-Saudia Racing Team	G	3.0 Williams FW07-Cosworth V8	*FL*	6/28
3	CANADIAN GP	Montreal	28	Albilad-Saudia Racing Team	G	3.0 Williams FW07-Cosworth V8		3/29
ret	US GP EAST	Watkins Glen	28	Albilad-Saudia Racing Team	G	3.0 Williams FW07-Cosworth V8	*collision with Piquet*	5/30

1980 Championship position: Unplaced

nc	ARGENTINE GP	Buenos Aires	14	Unipart Racing Team	G	3.0 Ensign N180-Cosworth V8	*3 pit stops – throttle/-9 laps*	15/28
ret	BRAZILIAN GP	Interlagos	14	Unipart Racing Team	G	3.0 Ensign N180-Cosworth V8	*handling*	12/28
9	SOUTH AFRICAN GP	Kyalami	14	Unipart Racing Team	G	3.0 Ensign N180-Cosworth V8	*1 lap behind*	=19/28
ret	US GP WEST	Long Beach	14	Unipart Racing Team	G	3.0 Ensign N180-Cosworth V8	*brake failure – accident*	23/27

GP Starts: 132   GP Wins: 5   Pole positions: 5   Fastest laps: 15   Points: 212

CARLOS REUTEMANN

RGENTINA'S most successful driver, apart from the great Juan Fangio, Carlos Reutemann was certainly the enigma of his times. Picturing some of his majestic grand prix wins, it seems impossible to believe that he was anything other than a world champion. Yet there were days when his performance was so lacklustre that you would cringe with embarrassment at his feeble showing. That was the contradiction of this deep-thinking perfectionist, who ultimately was unable to summon the consistency required to underpin any championship success.

Carlos was a cattle rancher's son from Santa Fe, Argentina, who began racing in 1965. Competing mainly in saloons, such as Ford Torinos, he soon became one of the country's top talents, gaining some valuable single-seater experience in the 1968 Temporada Formula 2 series. In 1970, he was chosen by the Automovil Club Argentino for a sponsored season in Europe racing a Brabham BT30. The year passed relatively uneventfully; he learned a great deal and produced the occasional top-six finish. After returning home, he served notice of his talent by taking an aggregate third place in the non-championship Argentine GP in an elderly McLaren M7C. Back in Europe for another season of Formula 2, he really came good in the latter stages of the year. Although he won only at Hockenheim, there were plenty of brilliant performances, and he finished runner-up to Ronnie Peterson in the final standings.

Having recently acquired the Brabham team, Bernie Ecclestone signed Carlos for 1972. The Argentinian made a sensational GP debut at Buenos Aires, putting the hitherto unloved Brabham BT34 on pole position before finishing seventh. Reutemann then won the non-title Brazilian GP at Interlagos to underline his vast promise, but his momentum was broken soon after his return to Europe, when a nasty crash at Thruxton in the F2 Rondel Brabham left him with a crushed ankle. This injury proved troublesome and slow to mend, which knocked his confidence for the rest of that year.

The 1973 season saw Carlos back in the groove, particularly once the new BT42 was introduced. There were flashes of brilliance and he soon became a regular top-six finisher. With the superb BT44 at his disposal at the start of 1974, he launched a ferocious opening onslaught, leading the first two grands prix before encountering problems and then winning the third, at Kyalami. Just as suddenly, however, his form vanished, before mysteriously reappearing when he won the Austrian GP with a stunning performance. There was another victory at Watkins Glen, which prompted thoughts that a world championship bid was on the cards for the following season, but once again he flattered to deceive. Winning the German GP was the high point, but he seemed unsettled by the competitive presence of new team-mate Carlos Pace. Things took a turn for the worse in 1976, when Brabham became involved in the Alfa engine project. The powerplant was woefully unreliable and Reutemann soon became fed up with the situation. He engineered his way out of his contract to join Ferrari, who were anxious to find a replacement for the recently injured Niki Lauda, but in the event he raced only at Monza before the Austrian made an amazing recovery and returned. Despite a win in the Brazilian GP at the beginning of 1977, he was completely overshadowed by Niki Lauda who, with total disdain, took great delight in heaping every possible humiliation upon the the somewhat bemused Argentinian.

Upon the two-fingered departure of 'the Rat' at the end of the year, Carlos was promoted to lead the Ferrari challenge in 1978. His form certainly improved, and he took four wins, including a brilliantly judged performance to outwit Lauda at Brands Hatch. Indeed, if his Michelin tyres had been more consistent he might have been able to mount a sustained championship challenge to Mario Andretti.

Despite this success, Carlos found himself unwanted by Ferrari, who had chosen Jody Scheckter, and he joined Lotus in 1979, which with hindsight was the worst possible move. Their title winning ground-effect car had peaked and was soon overtaken by Williams The new Lotus 80 was a technical nightmare, so Reutemann stuck resolutely with the 79; to be fair, he put in some brilliant early-season performances, which went largely unregarded. Results tailed off alarmingly in the second half of the season, and many thought that he was past his best.

Frank Williams still had faith in Carlos, however, and for 1980, without sentiment, Clay Regazzoni was dropped to make way for the Argentinian to be included in the team alongside Alan Jones. There were a few flashes of his brilliance, but it was a mystery that a driver of such experience should take such a long time to come to terms with his situation. A win at Monaco was achieved by caution more than outright speed, and he seemed content to let Jones force the pace as the highly motivated Australian charged towards his well-deserved world championship title.

The following season saw a far more aggressive Reutemann. He took the FOCA-only South African GP and then embarked on an early-season run of brilliant performances to gain a seemingly impregnable position. Then, from out of nowhere, came the slump. Whether the mid-season switch from Michelin back to Goodyear tyres was the cause, or other factors came into play, it is hard to say. In the event, the title went down to the line at Las Vegas, and Carlos set himself up for glory with an utterly brilliant lap to put the car on pole. Once the lights went green, however, he just seemed to fade away, his confidence apparently punctured by a mysterious handling problem encountered in the warm-up. A season's work appeared to be tossed away without so much as a whimper as Nelson Piquet snatched the title for Brabham by a point.

Reutemann was back leading the team in 1982, but perhaps the roll of the dice at Caesars Palace still weighed heavily on the mind of this introspective and complex man. Just two races into the season, he suddenly retired for reasons that have never really been explained. An enigma to the end.

Aside from Formula 1, Reutemann had been tempted to participate in the first Rally of Argentina in 1980, where he took third place in a Fiat. He repeated this performance in 1985 in a Peugeot, and these results made him the only driver to score championship points in both disciplines until Kimi Räikkönen managed to match his feat.

After suddenly deciding to quit grand prix racing, Reutemann pursued a lengthy career in politics, serving two terms as the governor of the Santa Fe province. Subsequently, he was elected to the national senate as a member of the Justicialist Party, but despite many calls from his supporters, so far he has declined to run for his country's presidency.

REUTEMANN, Carlos (RA) b 12/4/1942, Santa Fé

1972 Championship position: 16th Wins: 0 Pole positions: 1 Fastest laps: 0 Points scored: 3

	Race	Circuit	No	Entrant	Tyres	Capacity/Car/Engine	Comment	Q Pos/Entries
7	ARGENTINE GP	Buenos Aires	2	Motor Racing Developments	G	3.0 Brabham BT34-Cosworth V8	pit stop – loose air box/2 laps behind	1/22
ret	SOUTH AFRICAN GP	Kyalami	20	Motor Racing Developments	G	3.0 Brabham BT34-Cosworth V8	fuel line	15/27
13	BELGIAN GP	Nivelles	19	Motor Racing Developments	G	3.0 Brabham BT37-Cosworth V8	pit stops – clutch – gear lever/-4 laps	9/26
12	FRENCH GP	Clermont Ferrand	20	Motor Racing Developments	G	3.0 Brabham BT37-Cosworth V8	1 lap behind	=19/29
8	BRITISH GP	Brands Hatch	27	Motor Racing Developments	G	3.0 Brabham BT37-Cosworth V8	pit stop – wheels/3 laps behind	10/27
ret	GERMAN GP	Nürburgring	12	Motor Racing Developments	G	3.0 Brabham BT37-Cosworth V8	gearbox	6/27
ret	AUSTRIAN GP	Österreichring	17	Motor Racing Developments	G	3.0 Brabham BT37-Cosworth V8	fuel metering unit	5/26
ret	ITALIAN GP	Monza	30	Motor Racing Developments	G	3.0 Brabham BT37-Cosworth V8	hit chicane – suspension damage	11/27
4	CANADIAN GP	Mosport Park	8	Motor Racing Developments	G	3.0 Brabham BT37-Cosworth V8		9/25
ret	US GP	Watkins Glen	29	Motor Racing Developments	G	3.0 Brabham BT37-Cosworth V8	engine	5/32

1973 Championship position: 7th Wins: 0 Pole positions: 0 Fastest laps: 0 Points scored: 16

	Race	Circuit	No	Entrant	Tyres	Capacity/Car/Engine	Comment	Q Pos/Entries
ret	ARGENTINE GP	Buenos Aires	10	Motor Racing Developments	G	3.0 Brabham BT37-Cosworth V8	gearbox	9/19
11	BRAZILIAN GP	Interlagos	17	Motor Racing Developments	G	3.0 Brabham BT37-Cosworth V8	pit stop – fuel metering unit/-2 laps	7/20
7	SOUTH AFRICAN GP	Kyalami	18	Motor Racing Developments	G	3.0 Brabham BT37-Cosworth V8	pit stop – tyre/2 laps behind	8/25
ret	SPANISH GP	Montjuich Park	18	Motor Racing Developments	G	3.0 Brabham BT42-Cosworth V8	driveshaft	=14/22
ret	BELGIAN GP	Zolder	10	Motor Racing Developments	G	3.0 Brabham BT42-Cosworth V8	oil leak	=7/23
ret	MONACO GP	Monte Carlo	10	Motor Racing Developments	G	3.0 Brabham BT42-Cosworth V8	gearbox	19/26
4	SWEDISH GP	Anderstorp	10	Motor Racing Developments	G	3.0 Brabham BT42-Cosworth V8		5/22
3	FRENCH GP	Paul Ricard	10	Motor Racing Developments	G	3.0 Brabham BT42-Cosworth V8		8/25
6	BRITISH GP	Silverstone	10	Motor Racing Developments	G	3.0 Brabham BT42-Cosworth V8		=8/29
ret	DUTCH GP	Zandvoort	10	Motor Racing Developments	G	3.0 Brabham BT42-Cosworth V8	burst tyre	5/24
ret	GERMAN GP	Nürburgring	10	Motor Racing Developments	G	3.0 Brabham BT42-Cosworth V8	engine	10/23
4	AUSTRIAN GP	Österreichring	10	Motor Racing Developments	G	3.0 Brabham BT42-Cosworth V8		5/25
6	ITALIAN GP	Monza	10	Motor Racing Developments	G	3.0 Brabham BT42-Cosworth V8		10/25
8	CANADIAN GP	Mosport Park	10	Motor Racing Developments	G	3.0 Brabham BT42-Cosworth V8	pit stop – tyres/2 laps behind	4/26
3	US GP	Watkins Glen	10	Motor Racing Developments	G	3.0 Brabham BT42-Cosworth V8		2/28

1974 Championship position: 6th Wins: 3 Pole positions: 1 Fastest laps: 1 Points scored: 32

	Race	Circuit	No	Entrant	Tyres	Capacity/Car/Engine	Comment	Q Pos/Entries
7/ret	ARGENTINE GP	Buenos Aires	7	Motor Racing Developments	G	3.0 Brabham BT44-Cosworth V8	led race – out of fuel/1 lap behind	6/26
7	BRAZILIAN GP	Interlagos	7	Motor Racing Developments	G	3.0 Brabham BT44-Cosworth V8	led race – tyre problems/1 lap behind	2/25
1	SOUTH AFRICAN GP	Kyalami	7	Motor Racing Developments	G	3.0 Brabham BT44-Cosworth V8	FL	4/27
ret	SPANISH GP	Jarama	7	Motor Racing Developments	G	3.0 Brabham BT44-Cosworth V8	spun off	6/28
ret	BELGIAN GP	Nivelles	7	Motor Racing Developments	G	3.0 Brabham BT44-Cosworth V8	broken fuel line	24/32
ret	MONACO GP	Monte Carlo	7	Motor Racing Developments	G	3.0 Brabham BT44-Cosworth V8	hit Peterson	=7/28
ret	SWEDISH GP	Anderstorp	7	Motor Racing Developments	G	3.0 Brabham BT44-Cosworth V8	oil leak	10/28
12	DUTCH GP	Zandvoort	7	Motor Racing Developments	G	3.0 Brabham BT44-Cosworth V8	pit stop – tyres/4 laps behind	12/27
ret	FRENCH GP	Dijon	7	Motor Racing Developments	G	3.0 Brabham BT44-Cosworth V8	handling	8/30
6	BRITISH GP	Brands Hatch	7	Motor Racing Developments	G	3.0 Brabham BT44-Cosworth V8	spin/1 lap behind	4/34
3	GERMAN GP	Nürburgring	7	Motor Racing Developments	G	3.0 Brabham BT44-Cosworth V8		6/32
1	AUSTRIAN GP	Österreichring	7	Motor Racing Developments	G	3.0 Brabham BT44-Cosworth V8		2/31
ret	ITALIAN GP	Monza	7	Motor Racing Developments	G	3.0 Brabham BT44-Cosworth V8	gearbox bearing	2/31
9	CANADIAN GP	Mosport Park	7	Motor Racing Developments	G	3.0 Brabham BT44-Cosworth V8	pit stop – tyres/1 lap behind	4/30
1	US GP	Watkins Glen	7	Motor Racing Developments	G	3.0 Brabham BT44-Cosworth V8		1/30

1975 Championship position: 3rd Wins: 1 Pole positions: 0 Fastest laps: 0 Points scored: 37

	Race	Circuit	No	Entrant	Tyres	Capacity/Car/Engine	Comment	Q Pos/Entries
3	ARGENTINE GP	Buenos Aires	7	Martini Racing	G	3.0 Brabham BT44B-Cosworth V8	led race	3/23
8	BRAZILIAN GP	Interlagos	7	Martini Racing	G	3.0 Brabham BT44B-Cosworth V8	pit stop – tyre/led race	3/23
2	SOUTH AFRICAN GP	Kyalami	7	Martini Racing	G	3.0 Brabham BT44B-Cosworth V8		2/28
3*	SPANISH GP	Montjuich Park	7	Martini Racing	G	3.0 Brabham BT44B-Cosworth V8	race stopped/*half points/-1 lap	15/26
9	MONACO GP	Monte Carlo	7	Martini Racing	G	3.0 Brabham BT44B-Cosworth V8	wrong tyre choice/2 laps behind	10/26
3	BELGIAN GP	Zolder	7	Martini Racing	G	3.0 Brabham BT44B-Cosworth V8		6/24
2	SWEDISH GP	Anderstorp	7	Martini Racing	G	3.0 Brabham BT44B-Cosworth V8	led race	4/26
4	DUTCH GP	Zandvoort	7	Martini Racing	G	3.0 Brabham BT44B-Cosworth V8	pit stop – tyres/1 lap behind	5/25
14	FRENCH GP	Paul Ricard	7	Martini Racing	G	3.0 Brabham BT44B-Cosworth V8	pit stop – tyres/1 lap behind	11/26
ret	BRITISH GP	Silverstone	7	Martini Racing	G	3.0 Brabham BT44B-Cosworth V8	engine	8/28
1	GERMAN GP	Nürburgring	7	Martini Racing	G	3.0 Brabham BT44B-Cosworth V8		10/26
14	AUSTRIAN GP	Österreichring	7	Martini Racing	G	3.0 Brabham BT44B-Cosworth V8	1 lap behind	11/30
4	ITALIAN GP	Monza	7	Martini Racing	G	3.0 Brabham BT44B-Cosworth V8		7/28
ret	US GP	Watkins Glen	7	Martini Racing	G	3.0 Brabham BT44B-Cosworth V8	engine	3/24

1976 Championship position: 16th Wins: 0 Pole positions: 0 Fastest laps: 0 Points scored: 3

	Race	Circuit	No	Entrant	Tyres	Capacity/Car/Engine	Comment	Q Pos/Entries
12/ret	BRAZILIAN GP	Interlagos	7	Martini Racing	G	3.0 Brabham BT45-Alfa Romeo F12	out of fuel/3 laps behind	15/22
ret	SOUTH AFRICAN GP	Kyalami	7	Martini Racing	G	3.0 Brabham BT45-Alfa Romeo F12	engine	11/25
ret	US GP WEST	Long Beach	7	Martini Racing	G	3.0 Brabham BT45-Alfa Romeo F12	collision with Brambilla	10/27
4	SPANISH GP	Jarama	7	Martini Racing	G	3.0 Brabham BT45-Alfa Romeo F12	1 lap behind	12/30
ret	BELGIAN GP	Zolder	7	Martini Racing	G	3.0 Brabham BT45-Alfa Romeo F12	engine	12/29
ret	MONACO GP	Monte Carlo	7	Martini Racing	G	3.0 Brabham BT45-Alfa Romeo F12	collision with Jones	20/25
ret	SWEDISH GP	Anderstorp	7	Martini Racing	G	3.0 Brabham BT45-Alfa Romeo F12	engine	16/27
11	FRENCH GP	Paul Ricard	7	Martini Racing	G	3.0 Brabham BT45-Alfa Romeo F12	1 lap behind	10/30
ret	BRITISH GP	Brands Hatch	7	Martini Racing	G	3.0 Brabham BT45-Alfa Romeo F12	oil pressure	15/30
ret	GERMAN GP	Nürburgring	7	Martini Racing	G	3.0 Brabham BT45-Alfa Romeo F12	engine	10/28
ret	AUSTRIAN GP	Österreichring	7	Martini Racing	G	3.0 Brabham BT45-Alfa Romeo F12	clutch	14/25
ret	DUTCH GP	Zandvoort	7	Martini Racing	G	3.0 Brabham BT45-Alfa Romeo F12	clutch – fluid loss	12/27
9	ITALIAN GP	Monza	35	Scuderia Ferrari SpA SEFAC	G	3.0 Ferrari 312T2 F12		7/29

1977 Championship position: 4th Wins: 1 Pole positions: 0 Fastest laps: 0 Points scored: 42

	Race	Circuit	No	Entrant	Tyres	Capacity/Car/Engine	Comment	Q Pos/Entries
3	ARGENTINE GP	Buenos Aires	12	Scuderia Ferrari SpA SEFAC	G	3.0 Ferrari 312T2 F12		7/21
1	BRAZILIAN GP	Interlagos	12	Scuderia Ferrari SpA SEFAC	G	3.0 Ferrari 312T2 F12		2/22
8	SOUTH AFRICAN GP	Kyalami	12	Scuderia Ferrari SpA SEFAC	G	3.0 Ferrari 312T2 F12		8/23
ret	US GP WEST	Long Beach	12	Scuderia Ferrari SpA SEFAC	G	3.0 Ferrari 312T2 F12	collision with Lunger	4/22
2	SPANISH GP	Jarama	12	Scuderia Ferrari SpA SEFAC	G	3.0 Ferrari 312T2 F12		4/31

3	MONACO GP	Monte Carlo	12	Scuderia Ferrari SpA SEFAC	G	3.0 Ferrari 312T2 F12		3/26
ret	BELGIAN GP	Zolder	12	Scuderia Ferrari SpA SEFAC	G	3.0 Ferrari 312T2 F12	spun off	7/32
3	SWEDISH GP	Anderstorp	12	Scuderia Ferrari SpA SEFAC	G	3.0 Ferrari 312T2 F12		12/31
6	FRENCH GP	Dijon	12	Scuderia Ferrari SpA SEFAC	G	3.0 Ferrari 312T2 F12	1 lap behind	6/30
15	BRITISH GP	Silverstone	12	Scuderia Ferrari SpA SEFAC	G	3.0 Ferrari 312T2 F12	pit stop – brake problem/-6 laps	=13/36
4	GERMAN GP	Hockenheim	12	Scuderia Ferrari SpA SEFAC	G	3.0 Ferrari 312T2 F12		8/30
4	AUSTRIAN GP	Österreichring	12	Scuderia Ferrari SpA SEFAC	G	3.0 Ferrari 312T2 F12		5/30
6	DUTCH GP	Zandvoort	12	Scuderia Ferrari SpA SEFAC	G	3.0 Ferrari 312T2 F12	pit stop – wing damage/2 laps behind	6/34
ret	ITALIAN GP	Monza	12	Scuderia Ferrari SpA SEFAC	G	3.0 Ferrari 312T2 F12	spun off on oil	2/34
6	US GP EAST	Watkins Glen	12	Scuderia Ferrari SpA SEFAC	G	3.0 Ferrari 312T2 F12	1 lap behind	6/27
ret	CANADIAN GP	Mosport Park	12	Scuderia Ferrari SpA SEFAC	G	3.0 Ferrari 312T2 F12	fuel pressure	12/27
2	JAPANESE GP	Mount Fuji	12	Scuderia Ferrari SpA SEFAC	G	3.0 Ferrari 312T2 F12		7/23

1978 Championship position: 3rd Wins: 4 Pole positions: 2 Fastest laps: 2 Points scored: 48

7	ARGENTINE GP	Buenos Aires	11	Scuderia Ferrari SpA SEFAC	M	3.0 Ferrari 312T2 F12	pit stop – tyres	2/27
1	BRAZILIAN GP	Rio	11	Scuderia Ferrari SpA SEFAC	M	3.0 Ferrari 312T2 F12	FL	4/28
ret	SOUTH AFRICAN GP	Kyalami	11	Scuderia Ferrari SpA SEFAC	M	3.0 Ferrari 312T3 F12	spun off on oil	9/30
1	US GP WEST	Long Beach	11	Scuderia Ferrari SpA SEFAC	M	3.0 Ferrari 312T3 F12		1/30
8	MONACO GP	Monte Carlo	11	Scuderia Ferrari SpA SEFAC	M	3.0 Ferrari 312T3 F12	hit kerb – damaged tyres/1 lap behind	1/30
3	BELGIAN GP	Zolder	11	Scuderia Ferrari SpA SEFAC	M	3.0 Ferrari 312T3 F12		2/30
ret	SPANISH GP	Jarama	11	Scuderia Ferrari SpA SEFAC	M	3.0 Ferrari 312T3 F12	driveshaft – accident	3/29
10	SWEDISH GP	Anderstorp	11	Scuderia Ferrari SpA SEFAC	M	3.0 Ferrari 312T3 F12	pit stops – tyres/1 lap behind	8/27
18	FRENCH GP	Paul Ricard	11	Scuderia Ferrari SpA SEFAC	M	3.0 Ferrari 312T3 F12	pit stops – tyres/FL/5 laps behind	8/29
1	BRITISH GP	Brands Hatch	11	Scuderia Ferrari SpA SEFAC	M	3.0 Ferrari 312T3 F12		8/30
ret	GERMAN GP	Hockenheim	11	Scuderia Ferrari SpA SEFAC	M	3.0 Ferrari 312T3 F12	fuel vaporisation	12/30
dsq*	AUSTRIAN GP	Österreichring	11	Scuderia Ferrari SpA SEFAC	M	3.0 Ferrari 312T3 F12	*outside assistance after spin	4/31
7	DUTCH GP	Zandvoort	11	Scuderia Ferrari SpA SEFAC	M	3.0 Ferrari 312T3 F12		4/33
3	ITALIAN GP	Monza	11	Scuderia Ferrari SpA SEFAC	M	3.0 Ferrari 312T3 F12		11/32
1	US GP EAST	Watkins Glen	11	Scuderia Ferrari SpA SEFAC	M	3.0 Ferrari 312T3 F12		2/27
3	CANADIAN GP	Montreal	11	Scuderia Ferrari SpA SEFAC	M	3.0 Ferrari 312T3 F12		11/28

1979 Championship position: 6th= Wins: 0 Pole positions: 0 Fastest laps: 0 Points scored: 25

2	ARGENTINE GP	Buenos Aires	2	Martini Racing Team Lotus	G	3.0 Lotus 79-Cosworth V8		3/26
3	BRAZILIAN GP	Interlagos	2	Martini Racing Team Lotus	G	3.0 Lotus 79-Cosworth V8		3/26
5	SOUTH AFRICAN GP	Kyalami	2	Martini Racing Team Lotus	G	3.0 Lotus 79-Cosworth V8		11/26
ret	US GP WEST	Long Beach	2	Martini Racing Team Lotus	G	3.0 Lotus 79-Cosworth V8	started from pit lane/driveshaft	2/26
2	SPANISH GP	Jarama	2	Martini Racing Team Lotus	G	3.0 Lotus 79-Cosworth V8		8/27
4	BELGIAN GP	Zolder	2	Martini Racing Team Lotus	G	3.0 Lotus 79-Cosworth V8		10/28
3	MONACO GP	Monte Carlo	2	Martini Racing Team Lotus	G	3.0 Lotus 79-Cosworth V8		11/25
13/ret	FRENCH GP	Dijon	2	Martini Racing Team Lotus	G	3.0 Lotus 79-Cosworth V8	accident with Rosberg/3 laps behind	13/27
8	BRITISH GP	Silverstone	2	Martini Racing Team Lotus	G	3.0 Lotus 79-Cosworth V8	pit stop – tyre/2 laps behind	8/26
ret	GERMAN GP	Hockenheim	2	Martini Racing Team Lotus	G	3.0 Lotus 79-Cosworth V8	collision with Mass – spun off	13/26
ret	AUSTRIAN GP	Österreichring	2	Martini Racing Team Lotus	G	3.0 Lotus 79-Cosworth V8	handling	17/26
ret	DUTCH GP	Zandvoort	2	Martini Racing Team Lotus	G	3.0 Lotus 79-Cosworth V8	collision with Jarier	13/26
7	ITALIAN GP	Monza	2	Martini Racing Team Lotus	G	3.0 Lotus 79-Cosworth V8		13/28
ret	CANADIAN GP	Montreal	2	Martini Racing Team Lotus	G	3.0 Lotus 79-Cosworth V8	rear suspension	11/29
ret	US GP EAST	Watkins Glen	2	Martini Racing Team Lotus	G	3.0 Lotus 79-Cosworth V8	spun off	6/30

1980 Championship position: 3rd Wins: 1 Pole positions: 0 Fastest laps: 1 Points scored: 49

ret	ARGENTINE GP	Buenos Aires	28	Albilad-Williams Racing Team	G	3.0 Williams FW07B-Cosworth V8	engine	10/28
ret	BRAZILIAN GP	Interlagos	28	Albilad-Williams Racing Team	G	3.0 Williams FW07B-Cosworth V8	driveshaft	4/28
5	SOUTH AFRICAN GP	Kyalami	28	Albilad-Williams Racing Team	G	3.0 Williams FW07B-Cosworth V8	1 lap behind	6/28
ret	US GP WEST	Long Beach	28	Albilad-Williams Racing Team	G	3.0 Williams FW07B-Cosworth V8	driveshaft	7/27
3	BELGIAN GP	Zolder	28	Albilad-Williams Racing Team	G	3.0 Williams FW07B-Cosworth V8		4/27
1	MONACO GP	Monte Carlo	28	Albilad-Williams Racing Team	G	3.0 Williams FW07B-Cosworth V8	FL	2/27
6	FRENCH GP	Paul Ricard	28	Albilad-Williams Racing Team	G	3.0 Williams FW07B-Cosworth V8		5/27
3	BRITISH GP	Brands Hatch	28	Albilad-Williams Racing Team	G	3.0 Williams FW07B-Cosworth V8		4/27
2	GERMAN GP	Hockenheim	28	Albilad-Williams Racing Team	G	3.0 Williams FW07B-Cosworth V8		4/26
3	AUSTRIAN GP	Österreichring	28	Albilad-Williams Racing Team	G	3.0 Williams FW07B-Cosworth V8		4/25
4	DUTCH GP	Zandvoort	28	Albilad-Williams Racing Team	G	3.0 Williams FW07B-Cosworth V8		3/28
3	ITALIAN GP	Imola	28	Albilad-Williams Racing Team	G	3.0 Williams FW07B-Cosworth V8		3/28
2	CANADIAN GP	Montreal	28	Albilad-Williams Racing Team	G	3.0 Williams FW07B-Cosworth V8		5/28
2	US GP EAST	Watkins Glen	28	Albilad-Williams Racing Team	G	3.0 Williams FW07B-Cosworth V8		3/27

1981 Championship position: 2nd Wins: 2 Pole positions: 2 Fastest laps: 2 Points scored: 49

2	US GP WEST	Long Beach	2	Albilad-Williams Racing Team	M	3.0 Williams FW07C-Cosworth V8		3/29
1	BRAZILIAN GP	Rio	2	Albilad-Williams Racing Team	M	3.0 Williams FW07C-Cosworth V8		2/30
2	ARGENTINE GP	Buenos Aires	2	Albilad-Williams Racing Team	M	3.0 Williams FW07C-Cosworth V8		4/29
3	SAN MARINO GP	Imola	2	Albilad-Williams Racing Team	M	3.0 Williams FW07C-Cosworth V8		2/30
1	BELGIAN GP	Zolder	2	Albilad-Williams Racing Team	M	3.0 Williams FW07C-Cosworth V8	FL	1/31
ret	MONACO GP	Monte Carlo	2	Albilad-Williams Racing Team	M	3.0 Williams FW07C-Cosworth V8	gearbox	4/31
4	SPANISH GP	Jarama	2	TAG Williams Team	M	3.0 Williams FW07C-Cosworth V8		3/30
10	FRENCH GP	Dijon	2	TAG Williams Team	M	3.0 Williams FW07C-Cosworth V8	misfire/2 laps behind	7/29
2	BRITISH GP	Silverstone	2	TAG Williams Team	G	3.0 Williams FW07C-Cosworth V8		9/30
ret	GERMAN GP	Hockenheim	2	TAG Williams Team	G	3.0 Williams FW07C-Cosworth V8	engine	3/30
5	AUSTRIAN GP	Österreichring	2	TAG Williams Team	G	3.0 Williams FW07C-Cosworth V8		5/28
ret	DUTCH GP	Zandvoort	2	TAG Williams Team	G	3.0 Williams FW07C-Cosworth V8	accident with Laffite	5/30
3	ITALIAN GP	Monza	2	TAG Williams Team	G	3.0 Williams FW07C-Cosworth V8	FL	2/30
10	CANADIAN GP	Montreal	2	TAG Williams Team	G	3.0 Williams FW07C-Cosworth V8	wrong tyre choice in rain/3 laps behind	2/30
8	CAESARS PALACE GP	Las Vegas	2	TAG Williams Team	G	3.0 Williams FW07C-Cosworth V8	handling problems/1 lap behind	1/30

1982 Championship position: 15th= Wins: 0 Pole positions: 0 Fastest laps: 0 Points scored: 6

2	SOUTH AFRICAN GP	Kyalami	5	TAG Williams Team	G	3.0 Williams FW07C-Cosworth V8		8/30
ret	BRAZILIAN GP	Rio	5	TAG Williams Team	G	3.0 Williams FW07C-Cosworth V8	accident with Arnoux	6/31

GP Starts: 146 GP Wins: 12 Pole positions: 6 Fastest laps: 6 Points: 310

LANCE REVENTLOW

THE multi-millionaire son of Woolworth heiress Barbara Hutton, Lance Reventlow began competing in the mid-1950s with a Mercedes, before getting his hands on an 1100cc Cooper to race in the USA in 1956. The following year, he travelled to Europe to buy a Maserati sports car, which he crashed badly at Snetterton, escaping unharmed. He also raced an F2 Cooper briefly before returning home.

Reventlow then decided to build his own sports car, the Scarab, for 1958. It was a success and, with Chuck Daigh, he made ambitious plans for a front-engined grand prix car that the pair would drive, but when it finally appeared in 1960, the outdated design was hopelessly outclassed. So frustrated were the drivers that, by the British Grand Prix, the car had been temporarily abandoned in favour of a third works Cooper. Both practised in it, but Chuck was the faster and drove it in the race. They struggled on with the Scarab project in the hope of achieving some success in the 1961 Inter-Continental Formula, but when that folded, so did the team.

Reventlow returned to the States to race a new Scarab rear-engined sports car briefly, before losing interest in the sport completely. He was killed in 1972, when he was a passenger in a light aeroplane that crashed in bad weather over the Rocky Mountains.

REVENTLOW, Lance (USA) b 24/2/1936, London, England – d 24/7/1972, Colorado

1960 Championship position: Unplaced

	Race	Circuit	No	Entrant	Tyres	Capacity/Car/Engine	Comment	Q Pos/Entries
dnq	MONACO GP	Monte Carlo	48	Reventlow Automobiles Inc	G/D	2.4 Scarab 4		23/24
dns	DUTCH GP	Zandvoort	21	Reventlow Automobiles Inc	D	2.4 Scarab 4	dispute over starting money	21/21
ret	BELGIAN GP	Spa	28	Reventlow Automobiles Inc	D	2.4 Scarab 4	engine	16/18
dns	BRITISH GP	Silverstone	3	Cooper Car Co	D	2.5 Cooper T51-Climax 4	car driven by Daigh in race	(23)/25

GP Starts: 1   GP Wins: 0   Pole positions: 0   Fastest laps: 0   Points: 0

REVSON, Peter (USA) b 27/2/1939, New York City, New York – d 22/3/1974, Kyalami Circuit, South Africa

1964 Championship position: Unplaced

	Race	Circuit	No	Entrant	Tyres	Capacity/Car/Engine	Comment	Q Pos/Entries
dnq	MONACO GP	Monte Carlo	2	Revson Racing (America)	D	1.5 Lotus 24-BRM V8		19/20
dsq	BELGIAN GP	Spa	29	Reg Parnell (Racing)	D	1.5 Lotus 24-BRM V8	engine cut out – push start	10/20
dns	FRENCH GP	Rouen	36	Reg Parnell (Racing)	D	1.5 Lotus 25-BRM V8	car driven by Hailwood	– / –
ret	BRITISH GP	Brands Hatch	24	Revson Racing (America)	D	1.5 Lotus 24-BRM V8	gear selectors	=21/25
14	GERMAN GP	Nürburgring	27	Revson Racing (America)	D	1.5 Lotus 24-BRM V8	accident	18/24
13	ITALIAN GP	Monza	38	Revson Racing (America)	D	1.5 Lotus 24-BRM V8	6 laps behind	18/25

1971 Championship position: Unplaced

	Race	Circuit	No	Entrant	Tyres	Capacity/Car/Engine	Comment	Q Pos/Entries
ret	US GP	Watkins Glen	10	Elf Team Tyrrell	G	3.0 Tyrrell 001-Cosworth V8	clutch	21/32

1972 Championship position: 5th   Wins: 0   Pole positions: 1   Fastest laps: 0   Points scored: 23

	Race	Circuit	No	Entrant	Tyres	Capacity/Car/Engine	Comment	Q Pos/Entries
ret	ARGENTINE GP	Buenos Aires	18	Team Yardley McLaren	G	3.0 McLaren M19A-Cosworth V8	engine	3/22
3	SOUTH AFRICAN GP	Kyalami	14	Team Yardley McLaren	G	3.0 McLaren M19A-Cosworth V8		12/27
5	SPANISH GP	Jarama	20	Team Yardley McLaren	G	3.0 McLaren M19A-Cosworth V8	1 lap behind	11/26
7	BELGIAN GP	Nivelles	10	Team Yardley McLaren	G	3.0 McLaren M19A-Cosworth V8	2 laps behind	7/26
3	BRITISH GP	Brands Hatch	19	Team Yardley McLaren	G	3.0 McLaren M19A-Cosworth V8		3/27
3	AUSTRIAN GP	Österreichring	14	Team Yardley McLaren	G	3.0 McLaren M19C-Cosworth V8		4/26
dns	"	"	14T	Team Yardley McLaren	G	3.0 McLaren M19A-Cosworth V8	practice only	– / –
4	ITALIAN GP	Monza	15	Team Yardley McLaren	G	3.0 McLaren M19C-Cosworth V8		8/27
dns	"	"	14T	Team Yardley McLaren	G	3.0 McLaren M19A-Cosworth V8	practice only	– / –
2	CANADIAN GP	Mosport Park	19	Team Yardley McLaren	G	3.0 McLaren M19C-Cosworth V8		1/25
dns	"	" "	19T	Team Yardley McLaren	G	3.0 McLaren M19A-Cosworth V8	practice only	– / –
18/ret	US GP	Watkins Glen	20	Team Yardley McLaren	G	3.0 McLaren M19C-Cosworth V8	ignition/5 laps behind	2/32

1973 Championship position: 5th   Wins: 2   Pole positions: 0   Fastest laps: 0   Points scored: 38

	Race	Circuit	No	Entrant	Tyres	Capacity/Car/Engine	Comment	Q Pos/Entries
8	ARGENTINE GP	Buenos Aires	16	Yardley Team McLaren	G	3.0 McLaren M19C-Cosworth V8	tyre problems/4 laps behind	11/19
ret	BRAZILIAN GP	Interlagos	8	Yardley Team McLaren	G	3.0 McLaren M19C-Cosworth V8	gearbox	=11/20
2	SOUTH AFRICAN GP	Kyalami	6	Yardley Team McLaren	G	3.0 McLaren M19C-Cosworth V8		6/25
4	SPANISH GP	Montjuich Park	6	Yardley Team McLaren	G	3.0 McLaren M23-Cosworth V8	1 lap behind	5/22
ret	BELGIAN GP	Zolder	8	Yardley Team McLaren	G	3.0 McLaren M23-Cosworth V8	spun off	10/23
5	MONACO GP	Monte Carlo	8	Yardley Team McLaren	G	3.0 McLaren M23-Cosworth V8	2 laps behind	15/26
7	SWEDISH GP	Anderstorp	8	Yardley Team McLaren	G	3.0 McLaren M23-Cosworth V8	1 lap behind	7/22
1	BRITISH GP	Silverstone	8	Yardley Team McLaren	G	3.0 McLaren M23-Cosworth V8		=2/29
4	DUTCH GP	Zandvoort	8	Yardley Team McLaren	G	3.0 McLaren M23-Cosworth V8		6/24
9	GERMAN GP	Nürburgring	8	Yardley Team McLaren	G	3.0 McLaren M23-Cosworth V8		7/23
ret	AUSTRIAN GP	Österreichring	8	Yardley Team McLaren	G	3.0 McLaren M23-Cosworth V8	clutch	4/25
3	ITALIAN GP	Monza	8	Yardley Team McLaren	G	3.0 McLaren M23-Cosworth V8		2/25
1	CANADIAN GP	Mosport Park	8	Yardley Team McLaren	G	3.0 McLaren M23-Cosworth V8		2/26
5	US GP	Watkins Glen	8	Yardley Team McLaren	G	3.0 McLaren M23-Cosworth V8		8/28

1974 Championship position: Unplaced

	Race	Circuit	No	Entrant	Tyres	Capacity/Car/Engine	Comment	Q Pos/Entries
ret	ARGENTINE GP	Buenos Aires	16	UOP Shadow Racing Team	G	3.0 Shadow DN3-Cosworth V8	collision – Hailwood & Regazzoni	4/26
ret	BRAZILIAN GP	Interlagos	16	UOP Shadow Racing Team	G	3.0 Shadow DN3-Cosworth V8	overheating	6/25
dnp	SOUTH AFRICAN GP	Kyalami	16	UOP Shadow Racing Team	G	3.0 Shadow DN3-Cosworth V8	fatal crash in pre-race practice	– / –

GP Starts: 30   GP Wins: 2   Pole positions: 1   Fastest laps: 0   Points: 61

PETER REVSON

DESPITE his family being a part of the Revlon cosmetics empire, Peter Revson made his way in motor racing very much under his own steam. Initially, he was regarded rather unfairly as just another rich American playboy after his first unsuccessful attempts at grand prix racing. Eventually, however, he returned to fulfill his long-held ambition of winning a grand prix and, almost as importantly, to win the respect and admiration of his peers.

Peter's career started in Hawaii with a Morgan, which he shipped back to the States and raced there before trying his hand in a Formula Junior Taraschi. However, the lure of European racing, not to mention European culture, exerted a great pull on the young driver, who cashed in everything he could to finance his expedition in 1963. Leading the nomadic existence that was so typical of the time and often meant living out of the transporter, he raced a Formula Junior Cooper on the Continent and won the Copenhagen GP, but soon laid plans for a Formula 1 assault.

Reg Parnell's team had lost their sponsor and took Peter under their wing by way of a semi-works deal. His first tilt at Formula 1 in 1964 brought little cheer except a fourth place at Solitude, so he changed tack in 1965, joining the works Lotus F2 team run for the factory by Ron Harris. A win in the Eifelrennen was lost when he went off on the last lap, but he finished second. Dropping into F3, he also took the Monaco support race. Despite the season's progress, the gloss was wearing off Revson's European idyll and he headed back to the States to race a little Brabham BT8 sports car, winning his class at Seattle and Las Vegas.

For the 1966 season, Revson joined Skip Scott in a Ford GT40, and over the next three seasons he began to build his career in big sports cars in Can-Am and Trans-Am, before stepping back into single-seaters with a fine drive to fifth at Indianapolis in 1969. The following season, he took second at Sebring with actor Steve McQueen in a Porsche 908 and then raced the Carl Haas Lola in Can-Am. In 1971, he joined the McLaren team to contest the money spinning series, winning five rounds in the McLaren M8F; his performance in taking second place in the Indy 500 for McLaren raised his profile greatly. He was invited to drive for Tyrrell at Watkins Glen in a one-off grand prix return, before arranging a full season of both Formula 1 and Can-Am with McLaren in 1972. The team's F1 M19 wasn't quite a winner, but Peter did a superb job with three third-place finishes, followed by a second place in the Canadian Grand Prix. Despite having to miss some races due to clashing USAC commitments, the American finished an encouraging fifth overall in the championship.

Revson stayed with the team in 1973 and once behind the wheel of the new M23 proved a winner at last. His performance in the British Grand Prix was exemplary. On a damp track, he first grabbed the initiative and then controlled the later stages to score a beautifully judged victory. There was one more win to follow in the rain-soaked confusion of Mosport, but by then internal pressures were afflicting the team, and Peter in particular.

Emerson Fittipaldi was moving in for 1974 with massive support from Marlboro and Texaco, and Teddy Mayer was willing to run Revson only as a third entry in Yardley colours. Not surprisingly, the American decided to seek better treatment elsewhere, joining the up-and-coming Shadow team.

The season started with great promise as the new DN3 showed a fair turn of speed, but in pre-race testing for the South African Grand Prix at Kyalami, tragedy struck when a suspected suspension failure caused the car to crash into a guard rail. The Shadow was totally destroyed in the massive impact and Revson had no chance of survival.

JOHN RHODES

A FORMULA Junior regular in the early 1960s, John Rhodes raced the Midland Racing Partnership Cooper in 1961, victory in the minor Irish FJ championship providing the highlight of his season.

In 1962, Rhodes raced for Bob Gerard, taking 13th in the International Trophy in a Cooper and driving an Ausper-Ford in Formula Junior events. He signed to race for Ken Tyrrell in the formula the following year, but also began to drive the works Mini Coopers with which he became synonymous throughout the 1960s.

John's single-seater outings were confined to a few races with Bob Gerard's faithful old Cooper in 1965, the car proving to be very slow in his only grand prix appearance at Silverstone.

ALEX RIBEIRO

H AVING become the 1973 Brazilian Formula Ford champion with five wins from seven starts, Alex Ribeiro headed for Europe and an excellent first season in F3 with a works GRD, winning three rounds. His career continued its upward trend with a factory F3 March in 1975, which led to a full season for the team in Formula 2 in 1976. Although a win eluded him, with champion René Arnoux, he was usually the fastest man around.

Hiring a Hesketh, Alex made a steady F1 debut in the US GP, before taking on his only full grand prix season with a works March in 1977. It was a disastrous campaign, with drivers and manage-ment blaming each other for the cars' disappointing performances.

Back in Formula 2 in 1978 with his own 'Jesus Saves Racing' March 782, Alex initially dem-onstrated that he had lost none of his talent with a brilliant win at the Nürburgring, but gradually his season tailed off and the little team lost heart. In 1979, he reappeared with Fittipaldi at the non-championship Dino Ferrari GP, but retired early on. Later he was invited to drive for the team in the end-of-season North American races, but he failed to qualify the car on both occasions. Sub-sequently, Alex enjoyed a long career in touring cars, and occasionally Sud-Am single-seaters, back in his native Brazil.

RHODES, John (GB) b 18/8/1927, Wolverhampton, Staffordshire

	1965	Championship position: Unplaced							
	Race	Circuit	No	Entrant	Tyres	Capacity/Car/Engine	Comment	Q Pos/Entries
ret	BRITISH GP	Silverstone	20	Gerard Racing	D	1.5 Cooper T60-Climax V8	ignition	21/23
	GP Starts: 1	GP Wins: 0	Pole positions: 0	Fastest laps: 0	Points: 0			

RIBEIRO, Alex-Dias (BR) b 7/11/1948, Belo Horizonte

	1976	Championship position: Unplaced							
	Race	Circuit	No	Entrant	Tyres	Capacity/Car/Engine	Comment	Q Pos/Entries
12	US GP EAST	Watkins Glen	25	Hesketh Racing with Rizla/Penthouse	G	3.0 Hesketh 308D-Cosworth V8	2 laps behind	22/27
	1977	Championship position: Unplaced							
ret	ARGENTINE GP	Buenos Aires	9	Hollywood March Racing	G	3.0 March 761B-Cosworth V8	broken gear lever	20/21
ret	BRAZILIAN GP	Interlgos	9	Hollywood March Racing	G	3.0 March 761B-Cosworth V8	engine	21/22
ret	SOUTH AFRICAN GP	Kyalami	9	Hollywood March Racing	G	3.0 March 761B-Cosworth V8	engine	17/23
ret	US GP WEST	Long Beach	9	Hollywood March Racing	G	3.0 March 761B-Cosworth V8	gearbox oil leak	22/22
dnq	SPANISH GP	Jarama	9	Hollywood March Racing	G	3.0 March 761B-Cosworth V8		27/31
dnq	MONACO GP	Monte Carlo	9	Hollywood March Racing	G	3.0 March 761B-Cosworth V8	accident in practice	25/26
dnq	BELGIAN GP	Zolder	9	Hollywood March Racing	G	3.0 March 761B-Cosworth V8		30/32
dnq	SWEDISH GP	Anderstorp	9	Hollywood March Racing	G	3.0 March 761B-Cosworth V8		25/31
dnq	FRENCH GP	Dijon	9	Hollywood March Racing	G	3.0 March 761B-Cosworth V8		23/30
dnq	BRITISH GP	Silverstone	9	Hollywood March Racing	G	3.0 March 761B-Cosworth V8		27/36
8	GERMAN GP	Hockenheim	9	Hollywood March Racing	G	3.0 March 761B-Cosworth V8	1 lap behind	20/30
dnq	AUSTRIAN GP	Österreichring	9	Hollywood March Racing	G	3.0 March 761B-Cosworth V8	accident in practice	30/30
11	DUTCH GP	Zandvoort	9	Hollywood March Racing	G	3.0 March 761B-Cosworth V8	3 laps behind	24/34
dnq	ITALIAN GP	Monza	9	Hollywood March Racing	G	3.0 March 761B-Cosworth V8		25/34
15	US GP EAST	Watkins Glen	9	Hollywood March Racing	G	3.0 March 761B-Cosworth V8	3 laps behind	23/27
8	CANADIAN GP	Mosport Park	9	Hollywood March Racing	G	3.0 March 761B-Cosworth V8	2 laps behind	23/27
12	JAPANESE GP	Mount Fuji	9	Hollywood March Racing	G	3.0 March 761B-Cosworth V8	4 laps behind	23/23
	1979	Championship position: Unplaced							
dnq	CANADIAN GP	Montreal	19	Fittipaldi Automotive	G	3.0 Fittipaldi F6A-Cosworth V8		28/29
dnq	US GP EAST	Watkins Glen	19	Fittipaldi Automotive	G	3.0 Fittipaldi F6A-Cosworth V8		29/30
	GP Starts: 10	GP Wins: 0	Pole positions: 0	Fastest laps: 0	Points: 0			

DANIEL RICCIARDO

TOO few Australians have represented their country in Formula 1, so the addition of Daniel Ricciardo to the grid in 2011 was most welcome, especially as he has appeared to be such an outstanding prospect on his way to the top echelon since being taken into the Red Bull family.

Ricciardo raced karts in his native Western Australia from the age of nine until he graduated to Formula Ford in 2006. Winning the Formula BMW Asia Pacific Scholarship proved to be just the start of his heady rise after an outstanding performance in the world finals in Valencia.

After travelling to Europe to contest the Italian Formula Renault championship in 2007, by the following year, Ricciardo had wrapped up the Western European title and made a satisfactory debut in the F3 Euroseries. His big breakthrough came in 2009, however, when he gained a seat in the Carlin Motorsport team. He had the strongest car and he made the most of it, winning six races on his way to the title. Another step up to World Series by Renault for 2010 saw him the hot favourite for honours, and he certainly was the pacesetter, qualifying on the front row for all of the 17 races. That said, he did not have everything his own way in the races and was just pipped to the title by a mere two points.

By then, Red Bull had earmarked him as their next grand prix representative and, in 2011, they placed him at Toro Rosso as a reserve driver, before arranging for him to take over a seat at HRT to gain valuable race experience.

It was no surprise that he lined up for Toro Rosso in 2012, but the addition into the mix of the very talented Jean-Eric Vergne alongside him meant that his once expected serene transition to the Red Bull team was no longer a certainty.

FRITZ RIESS

HAVING shown much promise in Hermann Holbein's beautifully constructed HH single-seater in 1948, Fritz Riess switched to AFM and, in 1950, enjoyed some fine tussles with Toni Ulmen's Veritas-Meteor, winning the Eifelrennen and finishing second to Ulmen at Sachsenring. He continued with the team the following year, winning at the Riem airfield circuit and then taking second place, behind Paul Pietsch, in the Eifelrennen, before successfully joining the ranks of the Veritas runners in 1952 with his two-seater sports model.

Invited by Mercedes to join their team for Le Mans, Riess shared the winning 300SL with Hermann Lang and then finished third in the Prix de Berne at Bremgarten. He raced infrequently from 1953 onwards, but was still active in 1957, when he took a class win in the Nürburgring 1000km, again in a Mercedes-Benz 300SL.

RICCIARDO, Daniel (AUS) b 1/7/1989, Perth, Western Australia

2011 Championship position: Unplaced

	Race	Circuit	No	Entrant	Tyres	Capacity/Car/Engine	Comment	Q Pos/Entries
app	AUSTRALIAN GP	Melbourne	19	Scuderia Toro Rosso	P	2.4 Toro Rosso STR6-Ferrari V8	ran as 3rd driver in practice 1 only	– / –
app	MALAYSIAN GP	Sepang	18	Scuderia Toro Rosso	P	2.4 Toro Rosso STR6-Ferrari V8	ran as 3rd driver in practice 1 only	– / –
app	CHINESE GP	Shanghai Circuit	19	Scuderia Toro Rosso	P	2.4 Toro Rosso STR6-Ferrari V8	ran as 3rd driver in practice 1 only	– / –
app	TURKISH GP	Istanbul Park	19	Scuderia Toro Rosso	P	2.4 Toro Rosso STR6-Ferrari V8	ran as 3rd driver in practice 1 only	– / –
app	SPANISH GP	Barcelona	18	Scuderia Toro Rosso	P	2.4 Toro Rosso STR6-Ferrari V8	ran as 3rd driver in practice 1 only	– / –
app	MONACO GP	Monte Carlo	19	Scuderia Toro Rosso	P	2.4 Toro Rosso STR6-Ferrari V8	ran as 3rd driver in practice 1 only	– / –
app	CANADIAN GP	Montreal	18	Scuderia Toro Rosso	P	2.4 Toro Rosso STR6-Ferrari V8	ran as 3rd driver in practice 1 only	– / –
app	EUROPEAN GP	Valencia	18	Scuderia Toro Rosso	P	2.4 Toro Rosso STR6-Ferrari V8	ran as 3rd driver in practice 1 only	– / –
19	BRITISH GP	Silverstone	22	HRT F1 Team	P	2.4 HRT F111-Cosworth V8	3 laps behind	24/24
19	GERMAN GP	Hockenheim	22	HRT F1 Team	P	2.4 HRT F111-Cosworth V8	3 laps behind	24/24
18	HUNGARIAN GP	Hungaroring	22	HRT F1 Team	P	2.4 HRT F111-Cosworth V8	4 laps behind	23/24
ret	BELGIAN GP	Spa	22	HRT F1 Team	P	2.4 HRT F111-Cosworth V8	loose rear wheel	23/24
nc	ITALIAN GP	Monza	22	HRT F1 Team	P	2.4 HRT F111-Cosworth V8	long pit stop – water system/-14 laps	23/24
19	SINGAPORE GP	Marina Bay Circuit	22	HRT F1 Team	P	2.4 HRT F111-Cosworth V8	4 laps behind	23/24
22	JAPANESE GP	Suzuka	22	HRT F1 Team	P	2.4 HRT F111-Cosworth V8	2 laps behind/*no time set	*24/24
19	KOREAN GP	Yeongam	22	HRT F1 Team	P	2.4 HRT F111-Cosworth V8	1 lap behind/*no time set	*24/24
19	INDIAN GP	Buddh Circuit	23	HRT F1 Team	P	2.4 HRT F111-Cosworth V8	3 laps behind	21/24
ret	ABU DHABI GP	Yas Marina Circuit	22	HRT F1 Team	P	2.4 HRT F111-Cosworth V8	alternator	23/24
20	BRAZILIAN GP	Interlagos	22	HRT F1 Team	P	2.4 HRT F111-Cosworth V8	3 laps behind	21/24

GP Starts: 11   GP Wins: 0   Pole positions: 0   Fastest laps: 0   Points: 0

RIESS, Fritz (D) b 11/7/1922, Nuremburg – d 15/5/1991, Samedan, Switzerland

1952 Championship position: Unplaced

	Race	Circuit	No	Entrant	Tyres	Capacity/Car/Engine	Comment	Q Pos/Entries
7	GERMAN GP	Nürburgring	121	Fritz Riess	C	2.0 Veritas RS 6 (sports car)	2 laps behind	12/32

GP Starts: 1   GP Wins: 0   Pole positions: 0   Fastest laps: 0   Points: 0

JOCHEN RINDT

YOU really needed to see Jochen Rindt in action to appreciate his genius. The little skittering Formula 2 cars were thrown to the limits of their adhesion as he almost danced them to win after win. Then his phenomenal skill took the huge over-weight Cooper-Maserati into undreamt angles as the unwieldy beast was driven with such ferocity that, inevitably perhaps, finishes were few and far between.

Although Rindt had been around in Formula Junior and taken part in the non-championship 1963 Austrian Grand Prix, his potential remained largely hidden until he burst upon an unsuspecting British public at a big Formula 2 race at Crystal Palace in 1964. Sensationally, he defeated the established aces of the day in the formula that would become largely his personal domain in future years. With the Zeltweg race part of the championship calendar that year, he hired Rob Walker's Brabham. Although he retired in the race, he was keen to drive for Walker's équipe in 1965, but while Rob greatly admired the Austrian's talents he felt his career would be better nurtured at Cooper.

Rindt's first season with the team was spent learning the ropes under the tutelage of Bruce McLaren. The Cooper T77 was pretty uncompetitive, but he delivered a best result of fourth place at the Nürburgring. He could be found more regularly in Formula 2, where his ability shone and he took a win at Reims in the Winkelmann Brabham. The highlight of that year was at Le Mans, where he took a NART entered Ferrari 250LM to an unlikely victory with Masten Gregory, after outlasting the more fancied competitors.

Cooper's competitiveness was restored somewhat in 1966 when the new 3-litre formula was introduced. With McLaren leaving to pursue his dream of starting his own F1 team, Jochen emerged as a true front-runner, although he was pushed aside somewhat by the mid-season arrival of John Surtees, who had already enjoyed a long-standing relationship with team manager Roy Salvadori. By then, Rindt may have been regretting his decision to sign a three-year deal with Cooper, but promising finishes in the German, Italian and US grands prix proved to everyone that he was a winner in the making. Third place in the drivers' table was a satisfactory result for the season's work, but 1967 would start in the worst possible fashion when his new team-mate, Pedro Rodriguez, scored a lucky win at Kyalami. Soon it became obvious that he was trapped in a poor car, and he could only scrape two fourth-place finishes. In stark contrast, he spent his energies making up for it in Formula 2, taking Roy Winkelmann's Brabham to nine victories and four second places from 15 starts. It was a busy racing schedule for the Austrian, who also drove a works Porsche in selected sports car races and made his debut in the Indianapolis 500 after being very lucky to escape injury in a big practice crash.

Joining a Brabham team fresh from two world championships should have been the passport to well-deserved grand prix success, but it was not to be, despite Rindt enjoying a tremendous rapport with Jack Brabham. The latest Repco engine proved to be hopelessly unreliable and he was left with just a couple of third places at the end of the year. He also had a shot at Indianapolis in the team's BT25-Repco, but his race ended in retirement. His Formula 2 success continued unabated, however, with another six wins in Europe, but the lack of grand prix success led him to make the tough decision to abandon Brabham and accept a drive at Lotus alongside Graham Hill for 1969. Although he had equal status with the new world champion, it soon became clear during the Tasman series that he had the edge, winning races at Christchurch and Warwick Farm.

The European season started badly for Rindt, who crashed in the Spanish GP after his car's massive rear aerofoil collapsed, putting him into hospital. He was back to his best by the British Grand Prix, however, where he fought a glorious duel with Jackie Stewart's Matra before minor problems dropped him from contention. He could not be denied much longer, though, taking his long awaited maiden grand prix victory at Watkins Glen. Although Colin Chapman had supplied him with a car worthy of his talents, theirs was an uneasy alliance. Jochen would have liked to return to Brabham – a competitive force again – but in the end, lashings of money, the promise of total number-one status and a ground-breaking new car for 1970 held sway.

After starting the year in the old Lotus 49, taking second in the Race of Champions, Rindt gave the sensational looking Lotus 72 its debut in Spain. It still needed some development, however, and for Monaco he was back in the old car. It was there that he took perhaps his most famous victory, his incredible late-race charge forcing Jack Brabham into a final-corner error. The new 72 was finally considered fully raceworthy at Zandvoort, where he scored the first of four successive wins that put him within touching distance of the title. At Brands Hatch, he was very lucky, as Brabham ran out of fuel on the last lap, but at Hockenheim he and Jacky Ickx gave a wonderful display of high-speed artistry. Having previously agreed places on the circuit where overtaking manoeuvres were acceptable, both drivers fought a great battle within those parameters. At the finish, Chapman, who by then had grown much closer to Rindt than had seemed possible a year before, offered his congratulations. "A monkey could have won in your car today," was Jochen's retort. Following the loss of close friend Piers Courage, there were rumours of his retirement, but Rindt was tantalisingly close to claiming the world championship and the riches it would bring. Despite his apprehensions over the safety of Chapman's cars, he would compete for one more year in 1971 to reap the rewards of his efforts.

Then came Monza. Jochen was not sure that the 72 was the right car for the Italian Grand Prix, preferring the old 49. When the transporter arrived, however, the old cars were nowhere to be seen and the Austrian was left to sort out the 72 for practice.

After much debate, it was decided to run the car without its rear wing, which made it faster on the straights, but very nervous under braking. It was in this configuration that Jochen was running on his way down to the entrance to the Parabolica. Something broke on the car, which snapped left and veered at enormous speed into the barrier. The front of the Lotus was totally destroyed and poor Rindt, who was not wearing his crotch straps, submarined out of the front of the car. Having received massive chest and throat injuries, he was pronounced dead on arrival at hospital in Milan. A month later at Watkins Glen, the inexperienced Emerson Fittipaldi took the Lotus 72 to a surprise victory, thus ensuring that Rindt became the sport's first and to date, thankfully, only posthumous world champion.

RINDT, Jochen (A) b 18/4/1942, Mainz-am-Rhein, Germany – d 5/9/1970, Milan, Italy

1964 Championship position: Unplaced

	Race	Circuit	No	Entrant	Tyres	Capacity/Car/Engine	Comment	Q Pos/Entries
ret	AUSTRIAN GP	Zeltweg	12	Rob Walker Racing Team	D	1.5 Brabham BT11-BRM V8	steering	13/20

1965 Championship position: 13th   Wins: 0   Pole positions: 0   Fastest laps: 0   Points scored: 4

	Race	Circuit	No	Entrant	Tyres	Capacity/Car/Engine	Comment	Q Pos/Entries
ret	SOUTH AFRICAN GP	East London	10	Cooper Car Co	D	1.5 Cooper T73-Climax V8	electrics	10/25
dnq	MONACO GP	Monte Carlo	8	Cooper Car Co	D	1.5 Cooper T77-Climax V8		16/17
11	BELGIAN GP	Spa	5	Cooper Car Co	D	1.5 Cooper T77-Climax V8	3 laps behind	14/21
ret	FRENCH GP	Clermont Ferrand	20	Cooper Car Co	D	1.5 Cooper T77-Climax V8	collision with Amon	12/17
14/ret	BRITISH GP	Silverstone	10	Cooper Car Co	D	1.5 Cooper T77-Climax V8	engine	12/23
ret	DUTCH GP	Zandvoort	20	Cooper Car Co	D	1.5 Cooper T77-Climax V8	no oil pressure	14/17
4	GERMAN GP	Nürburgring	12	Cooper Car Co	D	1.5 Cooper T77-Climax V8		8/22
8	ITALIAN GP	Monza	18	Cooper Car Co	D	1.5 Cooper T77-Climax V8	2 laps behind	7/23
6	US GP	Watkins Glen	10	Cooper Car Co	D	1.5 Cooper T77-Climax V8	2 laps behind	=13/18
ret	MEXICAN GP	Mexico City	10	Cooper Car Co	D	1.5 Cooper T77-Climax V8	ignition	16/18

1966 Championship position: 3rd   Wins: 0   Pole positions: 0   Fastest laps: 0   Points scored: 24

	Race	Circuit	No	Entrant	Tyres	Capacity/Car/Engine	Comment	Q Pos/Entries
ret	MONACO GP	Monte Carlo	10	Cooper Car Co	D	3.0 Cooper T81-Maserati V12	engine	7/16
2	BELGIAN GP	Spa	19	Cooper Car Co	D	3.0 Cooper T81-Maserati V12		2/18
4	FRENCH GP	Reims	6	Cooper Car Co	D	3.0 Cooper T81-Maserati V12		5/17
5	BRITISH GP	Brands Hatch	11	Cooper Car Co	D	3.0 Cooper T81-Maserati V12	2 laps behind	7/20
ret	DUTCH GP	Zandvoort	26	Cooper Car Co	D	3.0 Cooper T81-Maserati V12	1 lap behind	6/18
3	GERMAN GP	Nürburgring	8	Cooper Car Co	D	3.0 Cooper T81-Maserati V12	crashed	9/30
4	ITALIAN GP	Monza	16	Cooper Car Co	F	3.0 Cooper T81-Maserati V12	flat tyre on last lap/1 lap behind	8/22
2	US GP	Watkins Glen	8	Cooper Car Co	F	3.0 Cooper T81-Maserati V12	1 lap behind	9/19
ret	MEXICAN GP	Mexico City	8	Cooper Car Co	F	3.0 Cooper T81-Maserati V12	lost wheel – suspension bolt	5/19

1967 Championship position: 11th=   Wins: 0   Pole positions: 0   Fastest laps: 0   Points scored: 6

	Race	Circuit	No	Entrant	Tyres	Capacity/Car/Engine	Comment	Q Pos/Entries
ret	SOUTH AFRICAN GP	Kyalami	3	Cooper Car Co	F	3.0 Cooper T81-Maserati V12	engine	=7/18
ret	MONACO GP	Monte Carlo	10	Cooper Car Co	F	3.0 Cooper T81-Maserati V12	gearbox	16/18
ret	DUTCH GP	Zandvoort	12	Cooper Car Co	F	3.0 Cooper T81B-Maserati V12	suspension	4/17
4	BELGIAN GP	Spa	29	Cooper Car Co	F	3.0 Cooper T81B-Maserati V12		=4/18
ret	FRENCH GP	Le Mans	12	Cooper Car Co	F	3.0 Cooper T81B-Maserati V12	engine	8/15
ret	BRITISH GP	Silverstone	11	Cooper Car Co	F	3.0 Cooper T86-Maserati V12	engine	8/21
dns	"	"	11	Cooper Car Co	F	3.0 Cooper T81B-Maserati V12	practice only	– / –
ret	GERMAN GP	Nürburgring	5	Cooper Car Co	F	3.0 Cooper T86-Maserati V12	engine – overheating	10/25
dns	"	"	5	Cooper Car Co	F	3.0 Cooper T81B-Maserati V12	practice only	– / –
ret	CANADIAN GP	Mosport Park	71	Cooper Car Co	F	3.0 Cooper T81-Maserati V12	ignition	8/19
dns	"	"	7	Cooper Car Co	F	3.0 Cooper T86-Maserati V12	engine in practice	– / –
4	ITALIAN GP	Monza	30	Cooper Car Co	F	3.0 Cooper T86-Maserati V12		11/18
ret	US GP	Watkins Glen	4	Cooper Car Co	F	3.0 Cooper T81B-Maserati V12	engine	8/19
dns	"	"	21	Cooper Car Co	F	3.0 Cooper T86-Maserati V12	Ickx drove car in race	– / –

1968 Championship position: 12th   Wins: 0   Pole positions: 2   Fastest laps: 0   Points scored: 8

	Race	Circuit	No	Entrant	Tyres	Capacity/Car/Engine	Comment	Q Pos/Entries
3	SOUTH AFRICAN GP	Kyalami	3	Brabham Racing Organisation	G	3.0 Brabham BT24-Repco V8		4/23
ret	SPANISH GP	Jarama	4	Brabham Racing Organisation	G	3.0 Brabham BT24-Repco V8	low oil pressure	=9/14
ret	MONACO GP	Monte Carlo	3	Brabham Racing Organisation	G	3.0 Brabham BT24-Repco V8	spun off	5/18
ret	BELGIAN GP	Spa	19	Brabham Racing Organisation	G	3.0 Brabham BT26-Repco V8	engine	17/18
ret	DUTCH GP	Zandvoort	6	Brabham Racing Organisation	G	3.0 Brabham BT26-Repco V8	damp ignition	2/19
ret	FRENCH GP	Rouen	2	Brabham Racing Organisation	G	3.0 Brabham BT26-Repco V8	fuel leak	1/18
ret	BRITISH GP	Brands Hatch	4	Brabham Racing Organisation	G	3.0 Brabham BT26-Repco V8	fuel system	5/20
dns	"	"	4	Brabham Racing Organisation	G	3.0 Brabham BT24-Repco V8	practice only	– / –
3	GERMAN GP	Nürburgring	5	Brabham Racing Organisation	G	3.0 Brabham BT26-Repco V8		3/20
ret	ITALIAN GP	Monza	11	Brabham Racing Organisation	G	3.0 Brabham BT26-Repco V8	engine	10/24
ret	CANADIAN GP	St Jovite	6	Brabham Racing Organisation	G	3.0 Brabham BT26-Repco V8	engine	1/22
ret	US GP	Watkins Glen	4	Brabham Racing Organisation	G	3.0 Brabham BT26-Repco V8	engine	6/21
ret	MEXICAN GP	Mexico City	4	Brabham Racing Organisation	G	3.0 Brabham BT26-Repco V8	ignition	10/21

1969 Championship position: 4th   Wins: 1   Pole positions: 5   Fastest laps: 2   Points scored: 22

	Race	Circuit	No	Entrant	Tyres	Capacity/Car/Engine	Comment	Q Pos/Entries
ret	SOUTH AFRICAN GP	Kyalami	2	Gold Leaf Team Lotus	F	3.0 Lotus 49B-Cosworth V8	fuel pump	2/18
ret	SPANISH GP	Montjuich Park	2	Gold Leaf Team Lotus	F	3.0 Lotus 49B-Cosworth V8	broken rear wing – accident//FL	1/14
ret	DUTCH GP	Zandvoort	2	Gold Leaf Team Lotus	F	3.0 Lotus 49B-Cosworth V8	driveshaft	1/15
ret	FRENCH GP	Clermont Ferrand	15	Gold Leaf Team Lotus	F	3.0 Lotus 49B-Cosworth V8	driver unwell – suffered double vision	3/13
4	BRITISH GP	Silverstone	2	Gold Leaf Team Lotus	F	3.0 Lotus 49B-Cosworth V8	pit stops – rear wing/fuel	1/17
ret	GERMAN GP	Nürburgring	2	Gold Leaf Team Lotus	F	3.0 Lotus 49B-Cosworth V8	ignition	3/26
2	ITALIAN GP	Monza	4	Gold Leaf Team Lotus	F	3.0 Lotus 49B-Cosworth V8		1/15
3	CANADIAN GP	Mosport Park	2	Gold Leaf Team Lotus	F	3.0 Lotus 49B-Cosworth V8		=2/20
dns	"	"	T	Gold Leaf Team Lotus	F	3.0 Lotus 63-Cosworth V8 4WD	practice only	– / –
1	US GP	Watkins Glen	2	Gold Leaf Team Lotus	F	3.0 Lotus 49B-Cosworth V8	FL	1/18
ret	MEXICAN GP	Mexico City	2	Gold Leaf Team Lotus	F	3.0 Lotus 49B-Cosworth V8	broken front suspension	6/17

1970 WORLD CHAMPION   Wins: 5   Pole positions: 3   Fastest laps: 1   Points scored: 45

	Race	Circuit	No	Entrant	Tyres	Capacity/Car/Engine	Comment	Q Pos/Entries
13/ret	SOUTH AFRICAN GP	Kyalami	9	Gold Leaf Team Lotus	F	3.0 Lotus 49C-Cosworth V8	engine/8 laps behind	4/24
ret	SPANISH GP	Jarama	3	Gold Leaf Team Lotus	F	3.0 Lotus 72-Cosworth V8	ignition	9/22
1	MONACO GP	Monte Carlo	3	Gold Leaf Team Lotus	F	3.0 Lotus 49C-Cosworth V8	FL	8/21
ret	BELGIAN GP	Spa	20	Gold Leaf Team Lotus	F	3.0 Lotus 49C-Cosworth V8	engine	2/18
dns	"	"	20	Gold Leaf Team Lotus	F	3.0 Lotus 72-Cosworth V8	practice only	– / –
1	DUTCH GP	Zandvoort	10	Gold Leaf Team Lotus	F	3.0 Lotus 72C-Cosworth V8		1/24
1	FRENCH GP	Clermont Ferrand	6	Gold Leaf Team Lotus	F	3.0 Lotus 72C-Cosworth V8		6/23
1	BRITISH GP	Brands Hatch	5	Gold Leaf Team Lotus	F	3.0 Lotus 72C-Cosworth V8		1/25
1	GERMAN GP	Hockenheim	2	Gold Leaf Team Lotus	F	3.0 Lotus 72C-Cosworth V8		2/25
ret	AUSTRIAN GP	Österreichring	6	Gold Leaf Team Lotus	F	3.0 Lotus 72C-Cosworth V8	engine	1/24
dns	ITALIAN GP	Monza	22	Gold Leaf Team Lotus	F	3.0 Lotus 72C-Cosworth V8	fatal accident in practice	(12)/27

GP Starts: 60   GP Wins: 6   Pole positions: 10   Fastest laps: 3   Points: 109

JOHN RISELEY-PRICHARD

ORIGINALLY just plain John Prichard, but he changed his name by deed poll in 1947, Risely-Prichard began his competition career modestly in 1952/53 at national level with a Riley. In 1954, however, he bought Rob Walker's Connaught, which he drove mainly in minor races, winning an obscure Formula 1 event at Davidstow, Cornwall, but also in that year's British Grand Prix.

John raced the Connaught for fun in Formula Libre events into the 1955 season, but when he let the young Tony Brooks take the wheel he soon realised his limitations as a driver. He shared a works Aston Martin with Brooks in that year's Le Mans 24-hour race, but in the wake of Levegh's terrible accident, his family is thought to have persuaded him to retire from the sport and concentrate on his profession as a Lloyd's insurance broker.

Riseley-Prichard was one of the original partners in the Ann Summers sex shop chain, before it was sold on. In his later years, he was caught up in a child pornography scandal, which resulted in his hurried departure to Thailand to escape justice.

He was reported to have died from AIDS in the remote village of Baan Kai Thuan, some hundred miles from Bankok, aged 69.

RICHARD ROBARTS

HAVING begun racing a Ginetta, Richard Robarts became a Formula Ford club racer in 1969 using Palliser and Elden chassis without making much of an impression.

Undaunted, Richard took the step up to Formula 3, initially with GRD, which was replaced in mid-season by a March 733. This gave him the impetus to challenge for victory on a regular basis, and a win in the final race of the year at Brands Hatch led to him sharing the Lombard North Central championship with Tony Brise. As luck would have it, Bernie Ecclestone was in attendance and liked what he saw. Negotiations were swiftly concluded and the young man from Essex took a giant step into Formula 1. He bought the second seat in the Brabham team for 1974, but when his backing fell through, he soon lost his place to the millionaire Rikki von Opel.

A hoped-for second chance with Williams in Sweden later that year failed to materialise when Tom Belso took over the car at the last minute, which left Robarts pretty much in the wilderness until he found the necessary sponsorship to go racing in Formula 2 in 1976 with a year-old March. Although he found the level of competition a bit too hot, he later enjoyed some success with occasional outings in the Shellsport G8 series.

RISELEY-PRICHARD, John (GB) b 17/1/1924, Hereford – d 8/7/1993 Baan Kai Thuan, Thailand

1954 Championship position: Unplaced

	Race	Circuit	No	Entrant	Tyres	Capacity/Car/Engine	Comment	Q Pos/Entries
ret	BRITISH GP	Silverstone	24	R R C Walker Racing Team	D	2.0 Connaught A Type-Lea Francis 4	spun off	21/31

GP Starts: 1   GP Wins: 0   Pole positions: 0   Fastest laps: 0   Points: 0

ROBARTS, Richard (GB) b 22/9/1944, Bicknacre, nr Chelmsford, Essex

1974 Championship position: Unplaced

	Race	Circuit	No	Entrant	Tyres	Capacity/Car/Engine	Comment	Q Pos/Entries
ret	ARGENTINE GP	Buenos Aires	8	Motor Racing Developments	G	3.0 Brabham BT44-Cosworth V8	gearbox	22/26
15	BRAZILIAN GP	Interlagos	8	Motor Racing Developments	G	3.0 Brabham BT44-Cosworth V8	2 laps behind	24/25
17	SOUTH AFRICAN GP	Kyalami	8	Motor Racing Developments	G	3.0 Brabham BT44-Cosworth V8	4 laps behind	23/27
dns	SWEDISH GP	Anderstorp	20	Frank Williams Racing Cars	G	3.0 Iso Marlboro FW02-Cosworth V8	car driven by Belsø	(25)/28

GP Starts: 3   GP Wins: 0   Pole positions: 0   Fastest laps: 0   Points: 0

PEDRO RODRIGUEZ

PEDRO RODRIGUEZ looked just great in a late-1960s grand prix car. His head seemed perpetually laid right back, and you could clearly see his eyes staring through the big aviator goggles as he went about his work. Aesthetics aside, that his talent went largely unregarded in Formula 1 is something of a mystery, and it was only right at the end of his life that his legend was forged.

Two years older than his brother, Ricardo, Pedro was racing bikes by the age of 12 and a Jaguar XK120 by the time he was 15. He was soon joined by his sibling, and the pair became notorious for their daring exploits in the late 1950s. Attracting the attention of Luigi Chinetti,

Pedro began racing his NART Ferraris, taking second place in the 1958 Nassau Trophy. The brothers eventually travelled to Europe and set about building a brilliant reputation in Chinetti's Ferraris, winning both the Nürburgring and Paris 1000km in 1961.

The death of Ricardo in Mexico at the end of 1962 was a devastating blow for Pedro, who nevertheless carried on racing, but was largely restricted to North America during 1963 and 1964. There were wins at Daytona in the GT class in 1963, and outright in 1964, sharing a GTO with Phil Hill. There were also end-of-year F1 drives for Lotus and Ferrari, but no offers of permanent grand prix employment came his

way, so the little Mexican stuck it out in sports car racing, taking such occasional single-seater opportunities as he was given.

For the 1967 South African GP, he was offered a works Cooper drive, but no deal beyond that single event. In a race of high attrition, he drove steadily to score a surprise win, a feat that eluded even Jochen Rindt during his spell with the team. Naturally, Rodriguez was taken on for the rest of the year, but the car was rapidly becoming uncompetitive, and he did well just to scrape the odd point thereafter. His season was also interrupted by injury when an accident at Enna in the F2 Protos left him sidelined with a broken foot.

Pedro joined BRM in 1968 and, after an unsuccessful Tasman series, started the season in fine form, taking a memorable second place in the Race of Champions when he sliced through the field after being left at the start. After a rather lucky second place behind MacLaren at Spa, the season slid into mediocrity as the team lost their way, and it was Pedro who paid the price, making way for John Surtees in 1969. As luck would have it, that would be a terrible year at Bourne, and he was fortunate to be out of the firing line, racing Tim Parnell's semi-works machine until he accepted an offer of a one-off drive in the equally disappointing Ferrari of that year.

Rodriguez had become much in demand as a sports car driver following his 1968 Le Mans victory with Lucien Bianchi in John Wyer's Ford GT40. He drove for both Ferrari and Matra the following year, before returning to Wyer in 1970. He was also back at BRM, and this time they had come up with a really good car in the P153. That year, Pedro left two races as a legacy to the portfolio of great motor racing performances. At Brands Hatch, driving the fearsome Gulf Porsche 917, he produced an unforgettable display in the rain to win the 1000km by a five-lap margin, and then in the Belgian GP at Spa he drove a masterful race, almost to the point of perfection, to beat Chris Amon's March.

He would score no more grand prix victories, only a win in the 1971 Rothmans Trophy at Oulton Park, but he continued to drive the Porsche with a fearlessness that was frightening. In 1971, he won the Daytona 24-hours, Monza 1000km and Spa 1000km with Jackie Oliver, and the Österreichring 1000km with Richard Attwood to confirm his position as sports car racing's leading exponent.

Pedro lived for racing and could not refuse the offer of a drive in an Interserie round at Norisring. Driving Herbert Müller's Ferrari 512M, he crashed heavily, it is thought because a tyre deflated. The car burst into flames, and when Pedro was finally released he was found to have succumbed to multiple injuries.

RODRIGUEZ, Pedro (MEX) b 18/1/1940, Mexico City – d 11/7/1971, Norisring Circuit, Germany

1963 Championship position: Unplaced

	Race	Circuit	No	Entrant	Tyres	Capacity/Car/Engine	Comment	Q Pos/Entries
ret	US GP	Watkins Glen	10	Team Lotus	D	1.5 Lotus 25-Climax V8	engine	=13/21
ret	MEXICAN GP	Mexico City	10	Team Lotus	D	1.5 Lotus 25-Climax V8	rear suspension	20/21

1964 Championship position: 19th= Wins: 0 Pole positions: 0 Fastest laps: 0 Points scored: 1

6	MEXICAN GP	Mexico City	18	North American Racing Team	D	1.5 Ferrari 156 V6	1 lap behind	9/19

1965 Championship position: 14th= Wins: 0 Pole positions: 0 Fastest laps: 0 Points scored: 2

5	US GP	Watkins Glen	14	North American Racing Team	D	1.5 Ferrari 1512 F12	1 lap behind	15/18
7	MEXICAN GP	Mexico City	14	North American Racing Team	D	1.5 Ferrari 1512 F12	3 laps behind	14/18

1966 Championship position: Unplaced

ret	FRENCH GP	Reims	2	Team Lotus	F	2.0 Lotus 33-Climax V8	engine – broken oil pipe	=12/27
ret	GERMAN GP (F2)	Nürburgring	31	Ron Harris-Team Lotus	D	1.0 Lotus 44-Cosworth 4 F2	engine	21/30
ret	US GP	Watkins Glen	11	Team Lotus	F	2.0 Lotus 33-BRM V8	starter motor after pitstop	10/19
ret	MEXICAN GP	Mexico City	11	Team Lotus	F	2.0 Lotus 33-Climax V8	gearbox	8/19

1967 Championship position: 6th= Wins: 1 Pole positions: 0 Fastest laps: 0 Points scored: 15

1	SOUTH AFRICAN GP	Kyalami	4	Cooper Car Co	F	3.0 Cooper T81-Maserati V12		4/18
5	MONACO GP	Monte Carlo	11	Cooper Car Co	F	3.0 Cooper T81-Maserati V12	4 laps behind	5/17
ret	DUTCH GP	Zandvoort	14	Cooper Car Co	F	3.0 Cooper T81-Maserati V12	gearbox	13/18
9/ret	BELGIAN GP	Spa	30	Cooper Car Co	F	3.0 Cooper T81-Maserati V12	engine/3 laps behind	13/18
6	FRENCH GP	Le Mans	14	Cooper Car Co	F	3.0 Cooper T81-Maserati V12	4 laps behind	13/15
5	BRITISH GP	Silverstone	12	Cooper Car Co	F	3.0 Cooper T81-Maserati V12	1 lap behind	9/21
8*	GERMAN GP	Nürburgring	6	Cooper Car Co	F	3.0 Cooper T81-Maserati V12	*11th behind 3 F2 cars/2 laps behind	11/25
dns	"	"	6	Cooper Car Co	F	3.0 Cooper T86-Maserati V12	practice only	– / –
6	MEXICAN GP	Mexico City	21	Cooper Car Co	F	3.0 Cooper T81B-Maserati V12	2 laps behind	13/19

1968 Championship position: 6th= Wins: 0 Pole positions: 0 Fastest laps: 1 Points scored: 18

ret	SOUTH AFRICAN GP	Kyalami	11	Owen Racing Organisation	G	3.0 BRM P126 V12	ignition/boiling fuel	=10/23
ret	SPANISH GP	Jarama	9	Owen Racing Organisation	G	3.0 BRM P133 V12	crashed	2/14
ret	MONACO GP	Monte Carlo	4	Owen Racing Organisation	G	3.0 BRM P133 V12	hit barrier	=9/18
2	BELGIAN GP	Spa	11	Owen Racing Organisation	G	3.0 BRM P133 V12		8/18
3	DUTCH GP	Zandvoort	15	Owen Racing Organisation	G	3.0 BRM P133 V12	1 lap behind	5/17
nc	FRENCH GP	Rouen	20	Owen Racing Organisation	G	3.0 BRM P133 V12	pit stops – gearbox/FL/7 laps behind	10/18
ret	BRITISH GP	Brands Hatch	10	Owen Racing Organisation	G	3.0 BRM P133 V12	timing chain	=13/20
dns	"	"	10	Owen Racing Organisation	G	3.0 BRM P126 V12	practice only	– / –
6	GERMAN GP	Nürburgring	10	Owen Racing Organisation	G	3.0 BRM P133 V12		14/20
ret	ITALIAN GP	Monza	26	Owen Racing Organisation	G	3.0 BRM P138 V12	engine	16/24
3	CANADIAN GP	St Jovite	16	Owen Racing Organisation	G	3.0 BRM P133 V12		12/22
ret	US GP	Watkins Glen	8	Owen Racing Organisation	G	3.0 BRM P133 V12	broken rear suspension	11/21
dns	"	"	8	Owen Racing Organisation	G	3.0 BRM P138 V12	practice only	– / –
4	MEXICAN GP	Mexico City	8	Owen Racing Organisation	G	3.0 BRM P133 V12	2 laps behind	12/21

1969 Championship position: 13th= Wins: 0 Pole positions: 0 Fastest laps: 0 Points scored: 3

ret	SOUTH AFRICAN GP	Kyalami	12	Reg Parnell (Racing) Ltd	D	3.0 BRM P126 V12	engine	16/18
ret	SPANISH GP	Montjuich Park	9	Reg Parnell (Racing) Ltd	D	3.0 BRM P126 V12	engine	14/14
ret	MONACO GP	Monte Carlo	10	Reg Parnell (Racing) Ltd	D	3.0 BRM P126 V12	engine	=14/16
ret	BRITISH GP	Silverstone	12	Scuderia Ferrari SpA SEFAC	F	3.0 Ferrari 312/68/69 V12	engine	=7/17
6	ITALIAN GP	Monza	10	Scuderia Ferrari SpA SEFAC	F	3.0 Ferrari 312/68/69 V12	2 laps behind	12/15
ret	CANADIAN GP	Mosport Park	6	North American Racing Team	F	3.0 Ferrari 312/68/69 V12	oil pressure	13/20
5	US GP	Watkins Glen	12	North American Racing Team	F	3.0 Ferrari 312/68/69 V12	7 laps behind	12/18
7	MEXICAN GP	Mexico City	12	North American Racing Team	F	3.0 Ferrari 312/68/69 V12	2 laps behind	15/17

1970 Championship position: 7th= Wins: 1 Pole positions: 0 Fastest laps: 0 Points scored: 23

9	SOUTH AFRICAN GP	Kyalami	20	Owen Racing Organisation	D	3.0 BRM P153 V12	pit stop – misfire/4 laps behind	16/24
ret	SPANISH GP	Jarama	10	Yardley Team BRM	D	3.0 BRM P153 V12	withdrawn after Oliver's crash	5/22
6	MONACO GP	Monte Carlo	17	Yardley Team BRM	D	3.0 BRM P153 V12	sticking throttle/2 laps behind	20/21
1	BELGIAN GP	Spa	1	Yardley Team BRM	D	3.0 BRM P153 V12		6/18
10	DUTCH GP	Zandvoort	1	Yardley Team BRM	D	3.0 BRM P153 V12	2 pit stops – loose nose cone/-3 laps	7/24
ret	FRENCH GP	Clermont Ferrand	3	Yardley Team BRM	D	3.0 BRM P153 V12	gearbox	10/23
ret	BRITISH GP	Brands Hatch	22	Yardley Team BRM	D	3.0 BRM P153 V12	spun off	=16/25
ret	GERMAN GP	Hockenheim	6	Yardley Team BRM	D	3.0 BRM P153 V12	ignition	8/25
4	AUSTRIAN GP	Österreichring	17	Yardley Team BRM	D	3.0 BRM P153 V12	1 lap behind	22/24
ret	ITALIAN GP	Monza	10	Yardley Team BRM	D	3.0 BRM P153 V12	engine	2/27
4	CANADIAN GP	St Jovite	14	Yardley Team BRM	D	3.0 BRM P153 V12	pit stop – fuel/1 lap behind	7/20
2	US GP	Watkins Glen	19	Yardley Team BRM	D	3.0 BRM P153 V12	pit stop when leading/fuel	4/27
6	MEXICAN GP	Mexico City	19	Yardley Team BRM	D	3.0 BRM P153 V12		7/18

1971 Championship position: 9= Wins: 0 Pole positions: 0 Fastest laps: 0 Points scored: 9

ret	SOUTH AFRICAN GP	Kyalami	16	Yardley-BRM	F	3.0 BRM P160 V12	overheating	10/25
dns	"	"	16T	Yardley-BRM	F	3.0 BRM P153 V12	practice only	– / –
4	SPANISH GP	Montjuich Park	14	Yardley-BRM	F	3.0 BRM P160 V12		4/22
9	MONACO GP	Monte Carlo	15	Yardley-BRM	F	3.0 BRM P160 V12	pit stop/wheel change/4 laps behind	5/23
dns	"	" "	15T	Yardley-BRM	F	3.0 BRM P153 V12	practice only	– / –
2	DUTCH GP	Zandvoort	8	Yardley-BRM	F	3.0 BRM P160 V12	led race	2/24
ret	FRENCH GP	Paul Ricard	15	Yardley-BRM	F	3.0 BRM P160 V12	coil	5/24

GP Starts: 55 GP Wins: 2 Pole positions: 0 Fastest laps: 1 Points: 71

RICARDO RODRIGUEZ

THE younger of the two racing Rodriguez brothers, Ricardo gave up bike racing at the age of 14, having won the Mexican championship, to race an Opel saloon. By 1957, he was already competing abroad, taking a class win in the Nassau Tourist Trophy with a Porsche Spyder.

The Rodriguez brothers travelled to Europe in 1960 with a NART Ferrari, although it was with André Pilette that Ricardo gained his best result, a second at Le Mans in a 250GT. Teamed with brother Pedro, he took third in the Sebring 12-hours and second in the Nürburgring 1000km.

Invited by the Scuderia to join their grand prix line-up for the Italian GP, Ricardo sensationally put the car on the front row of the grid alongside the ill-fated championship favourite, Wolfgang von Trips. Not surprisingly, he was signed by the team for a full season in 1962, but the car was far from the dominant machine of just a year earlier, and Ricardo, still a little wild and fearless, was employed selectively. In a bright start, the Mexican took second place at the Pau GP, before confirming his outstanding potential in a number of world championship rounds. In sports car racing, he was out of luck, except for a win in the Targa Florio, sharing a Ferrari 246 V6 with Olivier Gendebien and Willy Mairesse.

When Ferrari decided not to enter their cars for the non-championship Mexican GP, Ricardo arranged to race one of Rob Walker's Lotus-Climax V8s. Striving for pole position, the young charger came unstuck, crashing on the banking and dying from multiple injuries.

FRANCO ROL

A WEALTHY Italian aristocrat, Franco Rol was a gentleman racer who made more of a mark in sports cars than in single-seater competition. Equipped with a special short-chassis Alfa Romeo coupé, he tackled the classic road races in the late 1940s. In 1948, he led the Giro de Sicilia before retiring, but fared better the following season, finishing second in class. The same year he took a splendid third in the Mille Miglia.

In 1950, Rol joined up with Louis Chiron to race in the Platé Maseratis, which by then were well past their best, but he did manage a fifth place in the San Marino GP at Ospedaletti. His next chance to sample a monoposto came at the end of the following season at Monza with the newly built OSCA. It was hopelessly outclassed on its debut, but undaunted he reappeared with the car at the beginning of 1952 in the Valentino GP, where it expired with a blown gasket.

Franco was included in an expanded works Maserati driver line-up for the 1952 Italian GP, but his car failed on the 24th lap. His racing career was brought to an end after he suffered serious injuries while competing in the 1953 Tour of Sicily.

RODRIGUEZ, Ricardo (MEX) b 14/2/1942, Mexico City – d 1/11/1962, Mexico City

	1961 Championship position: Unplaced							
	Race	Circuit	No	Entrant	Tyres	Capacity/Car/Engine	Comment	Q Pos/Entries
ret	ITALIAN GP	Monza	8	Scuderia Ferrari SpA SEFAC	D	1.5 Ferrari 156 V6	fuel pump	2/33
	1962 Championship position: 12= Wins: 0 Pole positions: 0 Fastest laps: 0 Points scored: 4							
ret	DUTCH GP	Zandvoort	3	Scuderia Ferrari SpA SEFAC	D	1.5 Ferrari 156 V6	crashed	11/20
dns	MONACO GP	Monte Carlo	40T	Scuderia Ferrari SpA SEFAC	D	1.5 Ferrari 156 V6	practised in Mairesse's car	– / –
4	BELGIAN GP	Spa	12	Scuderia Ferrari SpA SEFAC	D	1.5 Ferrari 156 V6		=7/20
6	GERMAN GP	Nürburgring	3	Scuderia Ferrari SpA SEFAC	D	1.5 Ferrari 156 V6		10/30
14/ret	ITALIAN GP	Monza	4	Scuderia Ferrari SpA SEFAC	D	1.5 Ferrari 156 V6	pit stops – ignition/23 laps behind	11/30
	GP Starts: 5 GP Wins: 0 Pole positions: 0 Fastest laps: 0 Points: 4							

RODRÍGUEZ LARRETA, Alberto see LARRETA, Alberto RODRIGUEZ LARRETA

ROL, Franco (I) b 5/6/1908, Torino – d 18/6/1977, Rapallo

	1950 Championship position: Unplaced							
	Race	Circuit	NO	Entrant	Tyres	Capacity/Car/Engine	Comment	Q Pos/Entries
ret	MONACO GP	Monte Carlo	44	Officine Alfieri Maserati	P	1.5 s/c Maserati 4CLT/48 4	multiple accident	17/21
ret	FRENCH GP	Reims	28	Officine Alfieri Maserati	P	1.5 s/c Maserati 4CLT/48 4	engine	7/20
ret	ITALIAN GP	Monza	4	Officine Alfieri Maserati	P	1.5 s/c Maserati 4CLT/48 4		9/27
	1951 Championship position: Unplaced							
9	ITALIAN GP	Monza	44	OSCA Automobili	P	4.5 OSCA 4500G V12	13 laps behind	18/22
	1952 Championship position: Unplaced							
ret	ITALIAN GP	Monza	24	Officine Alfieri Maserati	P	2.0 Maserati A6GCM 6	engine	16/35
	GP Starts: 5 GP Wins: 0 Pole positions: 0 Fastest laps: 0 Points: 0							

TONY ROLT

EDUCATED at Eton and later the Royal Military Academy, Sandhurst, Anthony Peter Roylance Rolt was perhaps the brightest young talent of a generation of pre-war amateur drivers, winning the British Empire Trophy at Donington in an ERA as a 19-year-old before the outbreak of the Second World War. Having joined the army, he became an officer in the Rifle Brigade and was taken prisoner in May, 1940, after his platoon was outnumbered in a brave, but hopeless, attempt to defend Calais. Subsequently, he was awarded the Military Cross for his gallantry. He was sent to two PoW camps, from which he managed to escape, albeit briefly, before becoming a celebrated resident of Colditz Castle, where he was one of the instigators of an audacious escape plan that involved the building of a glider.

When peace returned, Rolt was soon back in action with an Alfa Romeo, a Delage and a Nash-Healey. Although he shared Peter Walker's ERA at the 1950 British GP, in the main he restricted himself to national racing, enjoying himself with Rob Walker's Delage in 1951 and, in his only HWM drive, taking second place in the 1952 International Trophy behind team-mate Lance Macklin.

Between 1953 and 1955, Rolt raced Walker's dark-blue Connaught with great success in national events, winning numerous Formula 2, Libre and handicap races. He also drove for the works Jaguar sports car team, paired with the extrovert Duncan Hamilton. This larger-than-life duo won the Le Mans 24-hour race in 1953, and took second places the following year at Le Mans and in the Reims 12-hours.

In 1955, Rolt retired from competition to concentrate on his motor manufacturing business, which converted ambulances and military vehicle to four-wheel drive. The company eventually became a leading supplier of design and engineering services to the motor industry.

BERTIL ROOS

HAVING grown up in an isolated part of Sweden, and with very little capital, no formal education and little knowledge of English, young Bertil Roos took the brave step of heading to North America to pursue his motorsport dream.

A graduate of the Opert driving school, where later he became an instructor, the self-confident Roos appeared to have a bright future after winning the 1973 US Super Vee title, and doing well in both European Formula 2 and Canadian Formula Atlantic.

Bertil's big opportunity came when Shadow invited him to drive their car in the 1974 Swedish Grand Prix, but it was an unhappy and brief alliance, the Swede failing to impress the team and subsequently being passed over in favour of Tom Pryce.

Thereafter, Roos returned to the States and, having founded his own racing school in 1975, continued to compete in Atlantic races and in Can-Am, where he was the 2-litre class champion in 1982 and 1983. The Bertil Roos Racing school continues to this day, but its founder ended his involvement after selling out in 1999 for a reported sum of US $500,000.

ROLT, Tony (GB) b 16/10/1918, Bordon, Hampshire – d 26/2/2008, Warwick, Warwickshire

	1950 Championship position: Unplaced							
	Race	Circuit	No	Entrant	Tyres	Capacity/Car/Engine	Comment	Q Pos/Entries
ret	BRITISH GP	Silverstone	9	Peter Walker	D	1.5 s/c ERA E Type 6	shared Peter Walker's car/gearbox	- / -
	1953 Championship position: Unplaced							
ret	BRITISH GP	Silverstone	14	R R C Walker Racing Team	D	2.0 Connaught A Type-Lea Francis 4	half shaft	10/29
	1955 Championship position: Unplaced							
ret*	BRITISH GP	Aintree	36	R R C Walker Racing Team	D	2.5 Connaught B Type-Alta 4	*car taken over by P Walker/throttle	15/25
	GP Starts: 3 GP Wins: 0 Pole positions: 0 Fastest laps: 0 Points: 0							

ROOS, Bertil (S) b 12/10/1943, Gothenburg

	1974 Championship position: Unplaced							
	Race	Circuit	No	Entrant	Tyres	Capacity/Car/Engine	Comment	Q Pos/Entries
ret	SWEDISH GP	Anderstorp	16	UOP Shadow Racing Team	G	3.0 Shadow DN3-Cosworth V8	transmission	23/28
	GP Starts: 1 GP Wins: 0 Pole positions: 0 Fastest laps: 0 Points: 0							

KEKE ROSBERG

THE buccaneering Keke Rosberg became a firm favourite in the mid-1980s after he had taken a surprise world championship win in a season clouded by tragedy. His subsequent exuberant performances, stabbing the turbo-powered Williams around the world's circuits with frightening commitment, did much to supply the entertainment factor that was often missing from the sport.

Born in Sweden of Finnish parentage, Keijo Rosberg was three times his country's karting champion before moving with equal success into the rough-and-tumble world of Formula Vee and Super Vee, taking the Castrol GTX title in the latter category in 1975. He found a seat in the Toj Formula 2 team in 1976, but apart from a fourth place at Rouen, this was not a successful alliance. By the end of the year, Keke had linked up with Fred Opert, who satisfied his insatiable appetite for racing in 1977 by running him first in New Zealand, where he took the Peter Stuyvesant title, and then in the European Formula 2 championship and the Labatt's Atlantic series in North America.

There was no let-up the following year, when Rosberg undertook a mind-numbing schedule that totalled some 40 races. His season's marathon stint for Opert included another visit to New Zealand to claim a second Stuyvesant title, a couple of Temporada races in Argentina and a six-race North American stint in the Labatts Formula Atlantic series, in which he claimed a win at Hamilton. In addition, he shoehorned in a part-season of Formula 2, which yielded an aggregate win at Donington and a second in the Eifelrennen.

As if this schedule was not enough, Keke moved into Formula 1 and scored a shock win in a rain-drenched International Trophy race for the new Theodore team. Although this result was something of a fluke, there was no doubting the Finn's stunning car control, and his name was noted as one to watch by Formula 1 team managers. In world championship races, of course, it was a different story, as he struggled to make an impression in two different teams and three different makes of car.

Initially resigned to a season out of Formula 1, Keke showed his talent by taking an emphatic win in a one-off F2 ride at Hockenheim in a Ron Dennis March, before heading to the States for the CitiCorp Can-Am series in 1979, where he was often quicker, but tellingly also more erratic than champion Jacky Ickx. An unexpected route back into grand prix racing opened after James Hunt's sudden retirement. Although his half-season in a difficult Wolf car failed to provide any satisfactory results, he was back in the frame to stay. When the Wolf team was amalgamated with Fittipaldi for 1980, Keke was part of the package, and on his maiden outing at Buenos Aires he scored his first championship points with a splendid third place. The team lacked the technical and financial resources to make a real impact, however, and Rosberg was forced to make up the numbers as the car became less and less competitive, until the end of 1981 when it closed its doors.

The cards suddenly began to fall for the Finn when he took over the Williams seat vacated by Alan Jones at the start of 1982. Within two races, the team's other star driver, Carlos Reutemann, had also walked away from grand prix racing, and suddenly Keke was leading the team. Showing incredible maturity for one not familiar with racing at the sharp end of the grid, he made the odd mistake, but maximised every potential points-scoring opportunity and took a splendidly thought-out win in the Swiss GP at Dijon. By the end of the year, he had overhauled the unfortunate Didier Pironi's points total and claimed a hard-fought world championship triumph. The following year saw Keke hampered by a lack of turbo power, but this didn't prevent him from taking a classic win on a damp track at Monaco, driving on slicks throughout. He took the Cosworth car into battle with great ferocity elsewhere, never admitting defeat when many others would have been content merely to cruise around.

When Keke finally got a turbo engine himself, he was frustrated by the poor handling of the Williams chassis, but nevertheless he scored perhaps the best win of his career in searing heat in Dallas in 1984, when most of his rivals failed to avoid a meeting with the concrete walls. His relationship with the Williams team (and in particular Patrick Head) was never completely harmonious and he wanted out at the end of the season. Forced to see out his contract, however, he got on with the job without further complaint, by then having decided he would only continue racing for another two years. Initially at least, he was unhappy with the arrival of Nigel Mansell for 1985, but he soon established a rapport with his new team-mate.

The season yielded a victory in Detroit and then, with a lucrative deal with McLaren waiting, he signed off from Williams with a sparkling win in Adelaide, before the start of the final short chapter of his grand prix career.

Having replaced the retired Niki Lauda, Keke was rather taken aback by his inability to come to terms with the talents of Alain Prost, and the partnership became something of disappointment for both sides, the Finn struggling to adapt the car to his particular style of driving.

Rosberg quit without regrets, but stayed closely involved with the sport, before making a return to the wheel in the World Sports Car Championship with Peugeot in 1991. With Yannick Dalmas, he took wins at both Magny-Cours and Mexico, before switching to the German touring car championship the following year to race a Mercedes. Apart from his role in guiding young Finnish talent (the careers of both Mika Häkkinen and JJ Lehto were under his shrewd stewardship), Keke formed his own DTM/ITC team, running works backed Opels led by the experienced Klaus Ludwig.

Following the collapse of this series, Rosberg concentrated his team's efforts on the German Super Touring series, together with Formula 3 and Formula BMW single-seater classes.

With the return of the DTM in 2000, Team Rosberg were back. Running year-old Mercedes with a mixture of up-and-coming drivers, the team found points hard to come by and pulled out at the end of 2004. After a year out, however, Rosberg switched camps and joined Audi for the 2006 season. Again the cars were always a year old, making outright success almost impossible. In 2011, he had his most successful season, with hard chargers Edoardo Mortara and Filipe Albuquerque both making their mark.

The junior single-seater classes provided the perfect environment for Keke's son, Nico, to begin to fulfill his serious motorsport ambitions. They provided the youngster with a championship winning car in Formula BMW in 2002, and two successful seasons in the F3 EuroSeries, before the youngster continued his steady climb towards Formula 1.

ROSBERG, Keke (Keijo) (SF) b 6/12/1948, Stockholm, Sweden

1978 Championship position: Unplaced

	Race	Circuit	No	Entrant	Tyres	Capacity/Car/Engine	Comment	Q Pos/Entries
ret	SOUTH AFRICAN GP	Kyalami	32	Theodore Racing Hong Kong	G	3.0 Theodore TR1-Cosworth V8	clutch/engine – fuel leak	24/30
dnpq	US GP WEST	Long Beach	32	Theodore Racing Hong Kong	G	3.0 Theodore TR1-Cosworth V8		27/30
dnpq	MONACO GP	Monte Carlo	32	Theodore Racing Hong Kong	G	3.0 Theodore TR1-Cosworth V8		25/30
dnq	BELGIAN GP	Zolder	32	Theodore Racing Hong Kong	G	3.0 Theodore TR1-Cosworth V8		27/30
dnpq	SPANISH GP	Jarama	32	Theodore Racing Hong Kong	G	3.0 Theodore TR1-Cosworth V8		29/29
15	SWEDISH GP	Anderstorp	10	ATS Racing Team	G	3.0 ATS HS1-Cosworth V8	pit stops – ignition/clutch/-7 laps	23/27
16	FRENCH GP	Paul Ricard	10	ATS Racing Team	G	3.0 ATS HS1-Cosworth V8	2 laps behind	26/29
ret	BRITISH GP	Brands Hatch	10	ATS Racing Team	G	3.0 ATS HS1-Cosworth V8	front suspension	22/30
10	GERMAN GP	Hockenheim	32	Theodore Racing Hong Kong	G	3.0 Wolf WR3-Cosworth V8	pit stop – nose cone/3 laps behind	19/30
nc	AUSTRIAN GP	Österreichring	32	Theodore Racing Hong Kong	G	3.0 Wolf WR3-Cosworth V8	pit stop – tyres/5 laps behind	25/31
ret	DUTCH GP	Zandvoort	32	Theodore Racing Hong Kong	G	3.0 Wolf WR4-Cosworth V8	stuck throttle – accident	24/33
dns	"	"	32	Theodore Racing Hong Kong	G	3.0 Wolf WR3-Cosworth V8	practice only	– / –
dnpq	ITALIAN GP	Monza	32	Theodore Racing Hong Kong	G	3.0 Wolf WR4-Cosworth V8		30/32
ret	US GP EAST	Watkins Glen	32	ATS Racing Team	G	3.0 ATS D1-Cosworth V8	gear linkage	15/27
nc	CANADIAN GP	Montreal	32	ATS Racing Team	G	3.0 ATS D1-Cosworth V8	pit stops/misfire/12 laps behind	21/28

1979 Championship position: Unplaced

	Race	Circuit	No	Entrant	Tyres	Capacity/Car/Engine	Comment	Q Pos/Entries
9	FRENCH GP	Dijon	20	Olympus Cameras Wolf Racing	G	3.0 Wolf WR8-Cosworth V8	gearbox problems/1 lap behind	16/27
ret	BRITISH GP	Silverstone	20	Olympus Cameras Wolf Racing	G	3.0 Wolf WR7-Cosworth V8	fuel system	14/26
dns	"	"	20	Olympus Cameras Wolf Racing	G	3.0 Wolf WR9-Cosworth V8	practice only	– / –
ret	GERMAN GP	Hockenheim	20	Olympus Cameras Wolf Racing	G	3.0 Wolf WR8-Cosworth V8	engine	17/26
dns	"	"	20	Olympus Cameras Wolf Racing	G	3.0 Wolf WR9-Cosworth V8	practice only	– / –
ret	AUSTRIAN GP	Österreichring	20	Olympus Cameras Wolf Racing	G	3.0 Wolf WR9-Cosworth V8	electrics	12/26
dns	"	"	20	Olympus Cameras Wolf Racing	G	3.0 Wolf WR8-Cosworth V8	practice only	– / –
ret	DUTCH GP	Zandvoort	20	Olympus Cameras Wolf Racing	G	3.0 Wolf WR9-Cosworth V8	engine	8/26
ret	ITALIAN GP	Monza	20	Olympus Cameras Wolf Racing	G	3.0 Wolf WR8-Cosworth V8	engine	23/28
dns	"	"	20	Olympus Cameras Wolf Racing	G	3.0 Wolf WR9-Cosworth V8	practice only	– / –
dnq	CANADIAN GP	Montreal	20	Olympus Cameras Wolf Racing	G	3.0 Wolf WR9-Cosworth V8		27/29
ret	US GP EAST	Watkins Glen	20	Olympus Cameras Wolf Racing	G	3.0 Wolf WR8/9-Cosworth V8	collision with Pironi	12/30

1980 Championship position: 10th= Wins: 0 Pole positions: 0 Fastest laps: 0 Points scored: 6

	Race	Circuit	No	Entrant	Tyres	Capacity/Car/Engine	Comment	Q Pos/Entries
3	ARGENTINE GP	Buenos Aires	21	Skol Fittipaldi Team	G	3.0 Fittipaldi F7-Cosworth V8		13/28
9	BRAZILIAN GP	Interlagos	21	Skol Fittipaldi Team	G	3.0 Fittipaldi F7-Cosworth V8	1 lap behind	15/28
ret	SOUTH AFRICAN GP	Kyalami	21	Skol Fittipaldi Team	G	3.0 Fittipaldi F7-Cosworth V8	brake failure – crashed	24/28
ret	US GP WEST	Long Beach	21	Skol Fittipaldi Team	G	3.0 Fittipaldi F7-Cosworth V8	overheating	22/27
7	BELGIAN GP	Zolder	21	Skol Fittipaldi Team	G	3.0 Fittipaldi F7-Cosworth V8	1 lap behind	21/27
dnq	MONACO GP	Monte Carlo	21	Skol Fittipaldi Team	G	3.0 Fittipaldi F7-Cosworth V8		24/27
ret	FRENCH GP	Paul Ricard	21	Skol Fittipaldi Team	G	3.0 Fittipaldi F7-Cosworth V8	crashed	23/27
dnq	BRITISH GP	Brands Hatch	21	Skol Fittipaldi Team	G	3.0 Fittipaldi F7-Cosworth V8		26/27
ret	GERMAN GP	Hockenheim	21	Skol Fittipaldi Team	G	3.0 Fittipaldi F8-Cosworth V8	wheel bearing	8/26
16	AUSTRIAN GP	Österreichring	21	Skol Fittipaldi Team	G	3.0 Fittipaldi F8-Cosworth V8	pit stop/2 laps behind	11/25
dnq	DUTCH GP	Zandvoort	21	Skol Fittipaldi Team	G	3.0 Fittipaldi F8-Cosworth V8		28/28
5	ITALIAN GP	Imola	21	Skol Fittipaldi Team	G	3.0 Fittipaldi F8-Cosworth V8	1 lap behind	11/28
9	CANADIAN GP	Montreal	21	Skol Fittipaldi Team	G	3.0 Fittipaldi F8-Cosworth V8	2 laps behind	6/28
10	US GP EAST	Watkins Glen	21	Skol Fittipaldi Team	G	3.0 Fittipaldi F8-Cosworth V8	2 laps behind	14/27

1981 Championship position: Unplaced

	Race	Circuit	No	Entrant	Tyres	Capacity/Car/Engine	Comment	Q Pos/Entries
ret	US GP WEST	Long Beach	20	Fittipaldi Automotive	M	3.0 Fittipaldi F8C-Cosworth V8	rotor arm	16/29
9	BRAZILIAN GP	Rio	20	Fittipaldi Automotive	M	3.0 Fittipaldi F8C-Cosworth V8	1 lap behind	12/30
ret	ARGENTINE GP	Buenos Aires	20	Fittipaldi Automotive	M	3.0 Fittipaldi F8C-Cosworth V8	fuel pump belt	8/29
ret	SAN MARINO GP	Imola	20	Fittipaldi Automotive	A	3.0 Fittipaldi F8C-Cosworth V8	engine	15/30
ret	BELGIAN GP	Zolder	20	Fittipaldi Automotive	A	3.0 Fittipaldi F8C-Cosworth V8	broken gear lever	11/31
dnq	MONACO GP	Monte Carlo	20	Fittipaldi Automotive	A/M	3.0 Fittipaldi F8C-Cosworth V8		21/31
12	SPANISH GP	Jarama	20	Fittipaldi Automotive	M	3.0 Fittipaldi F8C-Cosworth V8	2 laps behind	15/30
ret	FRENCH GP	Dijon	20	Fittipaldi Automotive	M	3.0 Fittipaldi F8C-Cosworth V8	broken rear cross beam	17/29
ret	BRITISH GP	Silverstone	20	Fittipaldi Automotive	M	3.0 Fittipaldi F8C-Cosworth V8	rear suspension	16/30
dnq	GERMAN GP	Hockenheim	20	Fittipaldi Automotive	M	3.0 Fittipaldi F8C-Cosworth V8		25/30
dnq	DUTCH GP	Zandvoort	20	Fittipaldi Automotive	P	3.0 Fittipaldi F8C-Cosworth V8		27/30
dnq	ITALIAN GP	Monza	20	Fittipaldi Automotive	P	3.0 Fittipaldi F8C-Cosworth V8		29/30
dnq	CANADIAN GP	Montreal	20	Fittipaldi Automotive	P	3.0 Fittipaldi F8C-Cosworth V8		25/30
10	CAESARS PALACE GP	Las Vegas	20	Fittipaldi Automotive	P	3.0 Fittipaldi F8C-Cosworth V8	2 laps behind	20/30

1982 WORLD CHAMPION Wins: 1 Pole positions: 1 Fastest laps: 0 Points scored: 44

	Race	Circuit	No	Entrant	Tyres	Capacity/Car/Engine	Comment	Q Pos/Entries
5	SOUTH AFRICAN GP	Kyalami	6	TAG Williams Team	G	3.0 Williams FW07C-Cosworth V8		7/30
dsq*	BRAZILIAN GP	Rio	6	TAG Williams Team	G	3.0 Williams FW07C-Cosworth V8	2nd on road/*illegal brakes	3/31
2	US GP WEST	Long Beach	6	TAG Williams Team	G	3.0 Williams FW07C-Cosworth V8		8/31
2	BELGIAN GP	Zolder	6	TAG Williams Team	G	3.0 Williams FW08-Cosworth V8		3/32
ret	MONACO GP	Monte Carlo	6	TAG Williams Team	G	3.0 Williams FW08-Cosworth V8	front suspension	6/31
4	US GP (DETROIT)	Detroit	6	TAG Williams Team	G	3.0 Williams FW08-Cosworth V8		3/28
ret	CANADIAN GP	Montreal	6	TAG Williams Team	G	3.0 Williams FW08-Cosworth V8	gearbox	7/29
3	DUTCH GP	Zandvoort	6	TAG Williams Team	G	3.0 Williams FW08-Cosworth V8		7/31
ret	BRITISH GP	Brands Hatch	6	TAG Williams Team	G	3.0 Williams FW08-Cosworth V8	fuel pressure	1/30
5	FRENCH GP	Paul Ricard	6	TAG Williams Team	G	3.0 Williams FW08-Cosworth V8		10/30
3	GERMAN GP	Hockenheim	6	TAG Williams Team	G	3.0 Williams FW08-Cosworth V8	1 lap behind	10/30

	Race	Circuit	No.	Team		Engine	Notes	Grid/Fin
2	AUSTRIAN GP	Österreichring	6	TAG Williams Team	G	3.0 Williams FW08-Cosworth V8		6/29
1	SWISS GP	Dijon	6	TAG Williams Team	G	3.0 Williams FW08-Cosworth V8		8/29
8	ITALIAN GP	Monza	6	TAG Williams Team	G	3.0 Williams FW08-Cosworth V8	*pit stop – lost rear wing/2 laps behind*	7/30
5	CAESARS PALACE GP	Las Vegas	6	TAG Williams Team	G	3.0 Williams FW08-Cosworth V8		6/30

1983 Championship position: 5th Wins: 1 Pole positions: 1 Fastest laps: 0 Points scored: 27

	Race	Circuit	No.	Team		Engine	Notes	Grid/Fin
dsq*	BRAZILIAN GP	Rio	1	TAG Williams Team	G	3.0 Williams FW08C-Cosworth V8	*push start at pit stop/2nd on road*	1/27
ret	US GP WEST	Long Beach	1	TAG Williams Team	G	3.0 Williams FW08C-Cosworth V8	*accident with Jarier*	3/28
5	FRENCH GP	Paul Ricard	1	TAG Williams Team	G	3.0 Williams FW08C-Cosworth V8	*1 lap behind*	16/29
4	SAN MARINO GP	Imola	1	TAG Williams Team	G	3.0 Williams FW08C-Cosworth V8	*1 lap behind*	11/28
1	MONACO GP	Monte Carlo	1	TAG Williams Team	G	3.0 Williams FW08C-Cosworth V8		5/28
5	BELGIAN GP	Spa	1	TAG Williams Team	G	3.0 Williams FW08C-Cosworth V8		9/28
2	US GP (DETROIT)	Detroit	1	TAG Williams Team	G	3.0 Williams FW08C-Cosworth V8		12/27
4	CANADIAN GP	Montreal	1	TAG Williams Team	G	3.0 Williams FW08C-Cosworth V8		9/28
11	BRITISH GP	Silverstone	1	TAG Williams Team	G	3.0 Williams FW08C-Cosworth V8	*pit stop – tyres/2 laps behind*	13/29
10	GERMAN GP	Hockenheim	1	TAG Williams Team	G	3.0 Williams FW08C-Cosworth V8	*pit stop – tyres/1 lap behind*	12/29
8	AUSTRIAN GP	Österreichring	1	TAG Williams Team	G	3.0 Williams FW08C-Cosworth V8	*pit stop – tyres/2 laps behind*	15/29
ret	DUTCH GP	Zandvoort	1	TAG Williams Team	G	3.0 Williams FW08C-Cosworth V8	*misfire*	23/29
11*	ITALIAN GP	Monza	1	TAG Williams Team	G	3.0 Williams FW08C-Cosworth V8	*9th on road – 1 min pen/-1 lap*	16/29
ret	EUROPEAN GP	Brands Hatch	1	TAG Williams Team	G	3.0 Williams FW08C-Cosworth V8	*engine*	16/29
5	SOUTH AFRICAN GP	Kyalami	1	TAG Williams Team	G	1.5 t/c Williams FW09-Honda V6	*pit stop – tyres/1 lap behind*	6/26

1984 Championship position: 8th Wins: 1 Pole positions: 0 Fastest laps: 0 Points scored: 20.5

	Race	Circuit	No.	Team		Engine	Notes	Grid/Fin
2	BRAZILIAN GP	Rio	6	Williams Grand Prix Engineering	G	1.5 t/c Williams FW09-Honda V6		9/27
ret	SOUTH AFRICAN GP	Kyalami	6	Williams Grand Prix Engineering	G	1.5 t/c Williams FW09-Honda V6	*loose wheel nut – lost wheel*	2/27
4/ret	BELGIAN GP	Zolder	6	Williams Grand Prix Engineering	G	1.5 t/c Williams FW09-Honda V6	*out of fuel/1 lap behind*	3/27
ret	SAN MARINO GP	Imola	6	Williams Grand Prix Engineering	G	1.5 t/c Williams FW09-Honda V6	*electrics*	3/28
6	FRENCH GP	Dijon	6	Williams Grand Prix Engineering	G	1.5 t/c Williams FW09-Honda V6	*1 lap behind*	4/27
4*	MONACO GP	Monte Carlo	6	Williams Grand Prix Engineering	G	1.5 t/c Williams FW09-Honda V6	*rain shortened race – half points*	10/27
ret	CANADIAN GP	Montreal	6	Williams Grand Prix Engineering	G	1.5 t/c Williams FW09-Honda V6	*fuel system*	15/26
ret	US GP (DETROIT)	Detroit	6	Williams Grand Prix Engineering	G	1.5 t/c Williams FW09-Honda V6	*exhaust/turbo*	21/27
1	US GP (DALLAS)	Dallas	6	Williams Grand Prix Engineering	G	1.5 t/c Williams FW09-Honda V6		8/27
ret	BRITISH GP	Brands Hatch	6	Williams Grand Prix Engineering	G	1.5 t/c Williams FW09B-Honda V6	*intercooler hose – engine*	5/27
ret	GERMAN GP	Hockenheim	6	Williams Grand Prix Engineering	G	1.5 t/c Williams FW09B-Honda V6	*electrics*	19/27
ret	AUSTRIAN GP	Österreichring	6	Williams Grand Prix Engineering	G	1.5 t/c Williams FW09B-Honda V6	*handling*	9/28
8*/ret	DUTCH GP	Zandvoort	6	Williams Grand Prix Engineering	G	1.5 t/c Williams FW09B-Honda V6	*8th & 9th cars dsq/out of fuel*	7/27
ret	ITALIAN GP	Monza	6	Williams Grand Prix Engineering	G	1.5 t/c Williams FW09B-Honda V6	*engine*	6/27
ret	EUROPEAN GP	Nürburgring	6	Williams Grand Prix Engineering	G	1.5 t/c Williams FW09B-Honda V6	*hit by Senna*	4/26
ret	PORTUGUESE GP	Estoril	6	Williams Grand Prix Engineering	G	1.5 t/c Williams FW09B-Honda V6	*engine*	4/27

1985 Championship position: 3rd Wins: 2 Pole positions: 2 Fastest laps: 3 Points scored: 40

	Race	Circuit	No.	Team		Engine	Notes	Grid/Fin
ret	BRAZILIAN GP	Rio	6	Canon Williams Team	G	1.5 t/c Williams FW10-Honda V6	*turbo*	2/25
ret	PORTUGUESE GP	Estoril	6	Canon Williams Team	G	1.5 t/c Williams FW10-Honda V6	*spun off*	3/26
ret	SAN MARINO GP	Imola	6	Canon Williams Team	G	1.5 t/c Williams FW10-Honda V6	*throttle linkage/brakes*	2/26
8	MONACO GP	Monte Carlo	6	Canon Williams Team	G	1.5 t/c Williams FW10-Honda V6	*2 laps behind*	7/26
4	CANADIAN GP	Montreal	6	Canon Williams Team	G	1.5 t/c Williams FW10-Honda V6		8/25
1	US GP (DETROIT)	Detroit	6	Canon Williams Team	G	1.5 t/c Williams FW10-Honda V6		5/25
2	FRENCH GP	Paul Ricard	6	Canon Williams Team	G	1.5 t/c Williams FW10-Honda V6	*FL*	1/26
ret	BRITISH GP	Silverstone	6	Canon Williams Team	G	1.5 t/c Williams FW10-Honda V6	*exhaust*	1/26
12/ret	GERMAN GP	Nürburgring	6	Canon Williams Team	G	1.5 t/c Williams FW10-Honda V6	*brake caliper/6 laps behind*	4/27
ret	AUSTRIAN GP	Österreichring	6	Canon Williams Team	G	1.5 t/c Williams FW10-Honda V6	*engine*	4/27
ret	DUTCH GP	Zandvoort	6	Canon Williams Team	G	1.5 t/c Williams FW10-Honda V6	*engine*	2/27
ret	ITALIAN GP	Monza	6	Canon Williams Team	G	1.5 t/c Williams FW10-Honda V6	*engine*	2/26
4	BELGIAN GP	Spa	6	Canon Williams Team	G	1.5 t/c Williams FW10-Honda V6		10/24
3	EUROPEAN GP	Brands Hatch	6	Canon Williams Team	G	1.5 t/c Williams FW10-Honda V6		4/27
2	SOUTH AFRICAN GP	Kyalami	6	Canon Williams Team	G	1.5 t/c Williams FW10-Honda V6	*FL*	3/21
1	AUSTRALIAN GP	Adelaide	6	Canon Williams Team	G	1.5 t/c Williams FW10-Honda V6	*FL*	3/25

1986 Championship position: 6th Wins: 0 Pole positions: 1 Fastest laps: 0 Points scored: 22

	Race	Circuit	No.	Team		Engine	Notes	Grid/Fin
ret	BRAZILIAN GP	Rio	2	Marlboro McLaren International	G	1.5 t/c McLaren MP4/2C-TAG V6	*engine*	7/25
4	SPANISH GP	Jerez	2	Marlboro McLaren International	G	1.5 t/c McLaren MP4/2C-TAG V6		5/25
5/ret	SAN MARINO GP	Imola	2	Marlboro McLaren International	G	1.5 t/c McLaren MP4/2C-TAG V6	*out of fuel/2 laps behind*	6/26
2	MONACO GP	Monte Carlo	2	Marlboro McLaren International	G	1.5 t/c McLaren MP4/2C-TAG V6		9/26
ret	BELGIAN GP	Spa	2	Marlboro McLaren International	G	1.5 t/c McLaren MP4/2C-TAG V6	*engine*	8/25
4	CANADIAN GP	Montreal	2	Marlboro McLaren International	G	1.5 t/c McLaren MP4/2C-TAG V6		6/25
ret	US GP (DETROIT)	Detroit	2	Marlboro McLaren International	G	1.5 t/c McLaren MP4/2C-TAG V6	*transmission*	9/26
4	FRENCH GP	Paul Ricard	2	Marlboro McLaren International	G	1.5 t/c McLaren MP4/2C-TAG V6		7/26
ret	BRITISH GP	Brands Hatch	2	Marlboro McLaren International	G	1.5 t/c McLaren MP4/2C-TAG V6	*gearbox*	5/26
5/ret	GERMAN GP	Hockenheim	2	Marlboro McLaren International	G	1.5 t/c McLaren MP4/2C-TAG V6	*out of fuel/1 lap behind*	1/26
ret	HUNGARIAN GP	Hungaroring	2	Marlboro McLaren International	G	1.5 t/c McLaren MP4/2C-TAG V6	*rear suspension*	5/26
9/ret	AUSTRIAN GP	Österreichring	2	Marlboro McLaren International	G	1.5 t/c McLaren MP4/2C-TAG V6	*electrics/5 laps behind*	3/26
4	ITALIAN GP	Monza	2	Marlboro McLaren International	G	1.5 t/c McLaren MP4/2C-TAG V6		8/27
ret	PORTUGUESE GP	Estoril	2	Marlboro McLaren International	G	1.5 t/c McLaren MP4/2C-TAG V6	*engine*	7/27
ret	MEXICAN GP	Mexico City	2	Marlboro McLaren International	G	1.5 t/c McLaren MP4/2C-TAG V6	*puncture*	11/26
ret	AUSTRALIAN GP	Adelaide	2	Marlboro McLaren International	G	1.5 t/c McLaren MP4/2C-TAG V6	*tyre failure when leading*	7/26

GP Starts: 114 GP Wins: 5 Pole positions: 5 Fastest laps: 3 Points: 159.5

NICO ROSBERG

HAVING been a karting champion in France when only 12 and then the youngest man ever to have driven a Formula 1 car (aged just 17 in December, 2002), Nico Rosberg's racing career has certainly been running in the fast lane. Of course, being the son of 1982 world champion Keke, who shrewdly guided his career, certainly opened doors for him, and he handled all the hurdles in the junior formulas with ever increasing assuredness. Living with his parents in Monaco, Nico was a very promising tennis player, but he opted to take up karting, as it dovetailed neatly with his education. The youngster spent five seasons in the discipline, before moving up to cars in 2002 to contest the BMW Formula series in Germany. The ease with which nine race wins and the title came was a surprise to the rookie, but it made for an easy and immediate graduation into the Formula 3 Euroseries with his father's Team Rosberg for 2003.

In a strong field, Nico drove an Opel-powered Dallara to a win at Le Mans and placed eighth overall in his debut year, finishing second to Christian Klien in the Rookie Cup. Much was expected for the following season, and a pair of wins in the opening round at Hockenheim seemed to signal a championship bid, but thereafter his challenge stuttered and, despite a win at the Nürburgring, the German passport holder, ended up a somewhat disappointed fourth in the standings.

In the 2005 season, Rosberg really came of age. Away from the familiar surroundings of his father's team, eventually he decided to join Formula 3 graduates ASM, renamed ART, for the newly introduced GP2 series. He immediately gelled with his new team, and after a hesitant start by all concerned, he finally delivered a win at Magny-Cours in July. This was fol-

lowed by another victory at Silverstone; suddenly he was looking like a championship contender. Thereafter, he continued to rack up points on a consistent basis, before taking both race wins at the Bahrain finale to edge out talented Finn Heikki Kovalainen, the pair of Formula 1 aspirants being well clear of the rest of the opposition.

Since Nico had already made a huge impression in his 2005 test role for Williams, it came as no surprise when he was chosen to partner Mark Webber in the team for 2006. Such was Frank Williams' belief in his young charge that he signed him to a long-term contract, confident that he had true world champion potential. Certainly he breezed on to the grand prix stage with a superb drive in Bahrain, taking seventh place after a pit stop to replace a nose cone. Qualifying third at Malaysia indicated that he was a top-draw driver in the making, but thereafter (apart from seventh place at the Nürburgring) his season slid downhill as the Williams-Cosworth became increasingly uncompetitive.

The team remained convinced of Rosberg's abilities, however, and hoped for better in 2007, when the latest challenger from Grove gained Toyota power. In his second season, we started to see the rough edges being rounded off and a much more assured performer emerging, particularly in the second half of the year with a string of well-judged drives into the points. His best race came in the season's finale at Interlagos, where he took his Williams into battle with the BMW Saubers and beat them to take a then career-best fourth place.

Indeed, as the 2008 season opened, Nico scored his first podium place in the Australian Grand Prix and the mood was buoyant, but the limitations of the Williams-Toyota were laid bare as other teams got into their stride. The German driver was left to struggle in midfield obscurity, scratching for occasional points. Aided by the safety car, he managed to pull off a splendid second place in the Renault manipulated Singapore Grand Prix, but by the end of the year he was languishing in 13th place in the overall standings.

Signing a contract extension to remain at Williams for 2009 showed admirable loyalty, and he drove with his usual calm and collected manner to score points in ten of the 17 races, more than doubling his 2008 tally. Even so, despite all the polish, it was as if something was lacking in the driver's make-up. Williams love a 'racer' above all else, and perhaps Rosberg lacked the outright aggression that separates the winners from those content merely to be members of the supporting cast. In the end, perhaps Sir Frank's decision to part company with Rosberg was simply a case of moving first, as the German had signed for the newly formed Mercedes F1 Team for 2010.

Being partnered with the legendary Michael Schumacher, fresh from a three-year retirement, was an extra challenge for Nico, who would be under huge scrutiny when compared to the seven-time champion. In the end, it was the youngster who held sway, with three podiums and a total of 15 points-scoring finishes from the season's 19 races. He ended the season in seventh place as the best of the rest, behind the elite trio of Red Bull, Ferrari and McLaren.

Rosberg continued to ply his trade in his usual manner throughout 2011, when his Mercedes was less capable of delivering results than in the previous year. He finished in seventh place once again, but this time around his final points tally was significantly reduced, and his superiority over team-mate Schumacher was not as marked.

The question now asked about Rosberg must be whether he will ever be a winner. If the mighty Mercedes can finally engineer a car that is fast enough, then he has the talent to deliver, but if not it seems that after six seasons, none of the major teams will be looking in his direction to refresh their driver line-ups. After clocking up more than 100 grands prix, he has started a long-term contract with the Stuttgart giant, which no doubt has given him the confidence that he can break that winless streak sooner rather than later.

ROSBERG, Nico (D) b 27/6/1985, Wiesbaden

2006 Championship position: 17th Wins: 0 Pole positions: 0 Fastest laps: 0 Points scored: 4

	Race	Circuit	No	Entrant	Tyres	Capacity/Car/Engine	Comment	Q Pos/Entries
7	BAHRAIN GP	Sakhir Circuit	10	WilliamsF1Team	B	2.4 Williams FW28-Cosworth V8	spin on lap 1/FL	12/22
ret	MALAYSIAN GP	Sepang	10	WilliamsF1Team	B	2.4 Williams FW28-Cosworth V8	engine – fire	3/22
ret	AUSTRALIAN GP	Melbourne	10	WilliamsF1Team	B	2.4 Williams FW28-Cosworth V8	taken out by Massa on lap 1	15/22
11	SAN MARINO GP	Imola	10	WilliamsF1Team	B	2.4 Williams FW28-Cosworth V8		13/22
7	EUROPEAN GP	Nürburgring	10	WilliamsF1Team	B	2.4 Williams FW28-Cosworth V8	started from back of grid	12/22
11	SPANISH GP	Barcelona	10	WilliamsF1Team	B	2.4 Williams FW28-Cosworth V8	1 lap behind	13/22
ret	MONACO GP	Monte Carlo	10	WilliamsF1Team	B	2.4 Williams FW28-Cosworth V8	exhaust	10/22
9	BRITISH GP	Silverstone	10	WilliamsF1Team	B	2.4 Williams FW28-Cosworth V8		12/22
ret	CANADIAN GP	Montreal	10	WilliamsF1Team	B	2.4 Williams FW28-Cosworth V8	collision with Montoya – hit wall	6/22
9	U S GP	Indianapolis	10	WilliamsF1Team	B	2.4 Williams FW28-Cosworth V8	1 lap behind	19/22
14	FRENCH GP	Magny Cours	10	WilliamsF1Team	B	2.4 Williams FW28-Cosworth V8	precautionary pit stop/2 laps behind	9/22
ret	GERMAN GP	Hockenheim	10	WilliamsF1Team	B	2.4 Williams FW28-Cosworth V8	accident	15/22
ret	HUNGARIAN GP	Hungaroring	10	WilliamsF1Team	B	2.4 Williams FW28-Cosworth V8	electrics	18/22
ret	TURKISH GP	Istanbul	10	WilliamsF1Team	B	2.4 Williams FW28-Cosworth V8	loss of water pressure	15/22
ret	ITALIAN GP	Monza	10	WilliamsF1Team	B	2.4 Williams FW28-Cosworth V8	hit kerbing – broken driveshaft	12/22
11	CHINESE GP	Shanghai	10	WilliamsF1Team	B	2.4 Williams FW28-Cosworth V8	1 lap behind	16/22
10	JAPANESE GP	Suzuka	10	WilliamsF1Team	B	2.4 Williams FW28-Cosworth V8	1 lap behind	10/22
ret	BRAZILIAN GP	Interlagos	10	WilliamsF1Team	B	2.4 Williams FW28-Cosworth V8	hit Webber/puncture/accident on lap 1	13/22

2007 Championship position: 9th Wins: 0 Pole positions: 0 Fastest laps: 0 Points scored: 20

	Race	Circuit	No	Entrant	Tyres	Capacity/Car/Engine	Comment	Q Pos/Entries
7	AUSTRALIAN GP	Melbourne	16	AT&T WilliamsF1Team	B	2.4 Williams FW29-Toyota V8	1 lap behind	12/22
ret	MALAYSIAN GP	Sepang	16	AT&T WilliamsF1Team	B	2.4 Williams FW29-Toyota V8	hydraulics	6/22
10	BAHRAIN GP	Sakhir Circuit	16	AT&T WilliamsF1Team	B	2.4 Williams FW29-Toyota V8		10/22
6	SPANISH GP	Barcelona	16	AT&T WilliamsF1Team	B	2.4 Williams FW29-Toyota V8		11/22
12	MONACO GP	Monte Carlo	16	AT&T WilliamsF1Team	B	2.4 Williams FW29-Toyota V8	1 lap behind	5/22
10	CANADIAN GP	Montreal	16	AT&T WilliamsF1Team	B	2.4 Williams FW29-Toyota V8	pitted under safety car –stop & go penalty	7/22
16/ret	U S GP	Indianapolis	16	AT&T WilliamsF1Team	B	2.4 Williams FW29-Toyota V8	oil leak –fire/5 laps behind	14/22
9	FRENCH GP	Magny Cours	16	AT&T WilliamsF1Team	B	2.4 Williams FW29-Toyota V8		9/22
12	BRITISH GP	Silverstone	16	AT&T WilliamsF1Team	B	2.4 Williams FW29-Toyota V8	1 lap behind	17/22
ret	EUROPEAN GP	Nürburgring	16	AT&T WilliamsF1Team	B	2.4 Williams FW29-Toyota V8	spun off	11/22
7	HUNGARIAN GP	Hungaroring	16	AT&T WilliamsF1Team	B	2.4 Williams FW29-Toyota V8	three-stop strategy	5/22
7	TURKISH GP	Istanbul	16	AT&T WilliamsF1Team	B	2.4 Williams FW29-Toyota V8		8/22
6	ITALIAN GP	Monza	16	AT&T WilliamsF1Team	B	2.4 Williams FW29-Toyota V8		8/22
6	BELGIAN GP	Spa	16	AT&T WilliamsF1Team	B	2.4 Williams FW29-Toyota V8		6/22
ret	JAPANESE GP	Fuji Speedway	16	AT&T WilliamsF1Team	B	2.4 Williams FW29-Toyota V8	electronics	6/22
16	CHINESE GP	Shanghai	16	AT&T WilliamsF1Team	B	2.4 Williams FW29-Toyota V8	collision – puncture/2 laps behind	16/22
4	BRAZILIAN GP	Interlagos	16	AT&T WilliamsF1Team	B	2.4 Williams FW29-Toyota V8		10/22

2008 Championship position: 13th Wins: 0 Pole positions: 0 Fastest laps: 0 Points scored: 17

	Race	Circuit	No	Entrant	Tyres	Capacity/Car/Engine	Comment	Q Pos/Entries
3	AUSTRALIAN GP	Melbourne	7	AT&T Williams	B	2.4 Williams FW30-Toyota V8		7/22
14	MALAYSIAN GP	Sepang	7	AT&T Williams	B	2.4 Williams FW30-Toyota V8	collision Glock – new front wing/-1 lap	16/22
8	BAHRAIN GP	Sakhir Circuit	7	AT&T Williams	B	2.4 Williams FW30-Toyota V8		8/22
ret	SPANISH GP	Barcelona	7	AT&T Williams	B	2.4 Williams FW30-Toyota V8	engine	15/22
8	TURKISH GP	Istanbul	7	AT&T Williams	B	2.4 Williams FW30-Toyota V8		11/20
ret	MONACO GP	Monte Carlo	7	AT&T Williams	B	2.4 Williams FW30-Toyota V8	accident – multiple collision	6/20
10	CANADIAN GP	Montreal	7	AT&T Williams	B	2.4 Williams FW30-Toyota V8	extra pit stop –new nose	5/20
16	FRENCH GP	Magny Cours	7	AT&T Williams	B	2.4 Williams FW30-Toyota V8	grid penalty from Canada/1 lap behind	15/20
9	BRITISH GP	Silverstone	7	AT&T Williams	B	2.4 Williams FW30-Toyota V8	started from pits/collision – Glock/-1 lap	18/20
10	GERMAN GP	Hockenheim	7	AT&T Williams	B	2.4 Williams FW30-Toyota V8		13/20
14	HUNGARIAN GP	Hungaroring	7	AT&T Williams	B	2.4 Williams FW30-Toyota V8	delayed pit stop –jammed fuel-rig/-1 lap	15/20
8	EUROPEAN GP	Valencia	7	AT&T Williams	B	2.4 Williams FW30-Toyota V8	suffering with heavy cold	9/20
12	BELGIAN GP	Spa	7	AT&T Williams	B	2.4 Williams FW30-Toyota V8	1 lap behind	15/20
14	ITALIAN GP	Monza	7	AT&T Williams	B	2.4 Williams FW30-Toyota V8	took wrong tyre strategy	5/20
2	SINGAPORE GP	Singapore Circuit	7	AT&T Williams	B	2.4 Williams FW30-Toyota V8		9/20
11	JAPANESE GP	Suzuka	7	AT&T Williams	B	2.4 Williams FW30-Toyota V8		15/20
15	CHINESE GP	Shanghai	7	AT&T Williams	B	2.4 Williams FW30-Toyota V8	wrong gearing/1 lap behind	15/20
12	BRAZILIAN GP	Interlagos	7	AT&T Williams	B	2.4 Williams FW30-Toyota V8	1 lap behind	18/20

2009 Championship position: 7th Wins: 0 Pole positions: 0 Fastest laps: 0 Points scored: 34.5

	Race	Circuit	No	Entrant	Tyres	Capacity/Car/Engine	Comment	Q Pos/Entries
6*	AUSTRALIAN GP	Melbourne	16	AT&T Williams	B	2.4 Williams FW31-Toyota V8	tyre problems/*4th place car dsq/FL	5/20
8	MALAYSIAN GP	Sepang	16	AT&T Williams	B	2.4 Williams FW31-Toyota V8	rain-shortened race – half points only	6/20
15	CHINESE GP	Shanghai	16	AT&T Williams	B	2.4 Williams FW31-Toyota V8	1 lap behind	7/20
9	BAHRAIN GP	Sakhir Circuit	16	AT&T Williams	B	2.4 Williams FW31-Toyota V8		9/20
8	SPANISH GP	Barcelona	16	AT&T Williams	B	2.4 Williams FW31-Toyota V8	inconsistent handling/1 lap behind	9/20
6	MONACO GP	Monte Carlo	16	AT&T Williams	B	2.4 Williams FW31-Toyota V8		6/20
5	TURKISH GP	Istanbul	16	AT&T Williams	B	2.4 Williams FW31-Toyota V8		9/20
5	BRITISH GP	Silverstone	16	AT&T Williams	B	2.4 Williams FW31-Toyota V8		7/20
4	GERMAN GP	Nürburgring	16	AT&T Williams	B	2.4 Williams FW31-Toyota V8	fuel system problem	15/20
4	HUNGARIAN GP	Hungaroring	16	AT&T Williams	B	2.4 Williams FW31-Toyota V8	slight delay at first pit stop	5/20
5	EUROPEAN GP	Valencia	16	AT&T Williams	B	2.4 Williams FW31-Toyota V8		7/20
8	BELGIAN GP	Spa	16	AT&T Williams	B	2.4 Williams FW31-Toyota V8	handling problems	10/20
16	ITALIAN GP	Monza	16	AT&T Williams	B	2.4 Williams FW31-Toyota V8	pit stop – debris/poor handling/-2 laps	18/20
11	SINGAPORE GP	Marina Bay Circuit	16	AT&T Williams	B	2.4 Williams FW31-Toyota V8	drive-thru penalty – over-rode pit exit line	3/20
5	JAPANESE GP	Suzuka	16	AT&T Williams	B	2.4 Williams FW31-Toyota V8		11/20
ret	BRAZILIAN GP	Interlagos	16	AT&T Williams	B	2.4 Williams FW31-Toyota V8	gearbox	7/20
9	ABU DHABI GP	Yas Marina Circuit	16	AT&T Williams	B	2.4 Williams FW31-Toyota V8		9/20

2010 Championship position: 7th Wins: 0 Pole positions: 0 Fastest laps: 0 Points scored: 142

	Race	Circuit	No	Entrant	Tyres	Capacity/Car/Engine	Comment	Q Pos/Entries
5	BAHRAIN GP	Sakhir Circuit	4	Mercedes GP Petronas F1 Team	B	2.4 Mercedes MGP W01-V8		5/24

5	AUSTRALIAN GP	Melbourne	4	Mercedes GP Petronas F1 Team B	2.4 Mercedes MGP W01-V8			6/24
3	MALAYSIAN GP	Sepang	4	Mercedes GP Petronas F1 Team B	2.4 Mercedes MGP W01-V8			2/24
3	CHINESE GP	Shanghai Circuit	4	Mercedes GP Petronas F1 Team B	2.4 Mercedes MGP W01-V8			4/24
13	SPANISH GP	Barcelona	4	Mercedes GP Petronas F1 Team B	2.4 Mercedes MGP W01-V8	jammed wheel-nut at pit stop/1 lap behind		8/24
7*	MONACO GP	Monte Carlo	4	Mercedes GP Petronas F1 Team B	2.4 Mercedes MGP W01-V8	*8th on road but 6th-placed car demoted		6/24
5	TURKISH GP	Istanbul Park	4	Mercedes GP Petronas F1 Team B	2.4 Mercedes MGP W01-V8			6/24
6	CANADIAN GP	Montreal	4	Mercedes GP Petronas F1 Team B	2.4 Mercedes MGP W01-V8			10/24
10	EUROPEAN GP	Valencia	4	Mercedes GP Petronas F1 Team B	2.4 Mercedes MGP W01-V8			12/24
3	BRITISH GP	Silverstone	4	Mercedes GP Petronas F1 Team B	2.4 Mercedes MGP W01-V8			5/24
8	GERMAN GP	Hockenheim	4	Mercedes GP Petronas F1 Team B	2.4 Mercedes MGP W01-V8	1 lap behind		9/24
ret	HUNGARIAN GP	Hungaroring	4	Mercedes GP Petronas F1 Team B	2.4 Mercedes MGP W01-V8	lost wheel in pitlane after pit stop		6/24
6	BELGIAN GP	Spa	4	Mercedes GP Petronas F1 Team B	2.4 Mercedes MGP W01-V8			12/24
5	ITALIAN GP	Monza	4	Mercedes GP Petronas F1 Team B	2.4 Mercedes MGP W01-V8			7/24
5	SINGAPORE GP	Marina Bay Circuit	4	Mercedes GP Petronas F1 Team B	2.4 Mercedes MGP W01-V8			7/24
17/ret	JAPANESE GP	Suzuka	4	Mercedes GP Petronas F1 Team B	2.4 Mercedes MGP W01-V8	accident – lost wheel/6 laps behind		7/24
ret	KOREAN GP	Yeongam	4	Mercedes GP Petronas F1 Team B	2.4 Mercedes MGP W01-V8	accident – hit by Webber's spinning car		5/24
6	BRAZILIAN GP	Interlagos	4	Mercedes GP Petronas F1 Team B	2.4 Mercedes MGP W01-V8			13/24
4	ABU DHABI GP	Yas Marina Circuit	4	Mercedes GP Petronas F1 Team B	2.4 Mercedes MGP W01-V8			9/24

2011 Championship position: 7th Wins: 0 Pole positions: 0 Fastest laps: 0 Points scored: 89

ret	AUSTRALIAN GP	Melbourne	8	Mercedes GP Petronas F1 Team P	2.4 Mercedes MGP W02-V8	hit by Barrichello – fractured water pipe		7/24
12	MALAYSIAN GP	Sepang	8	Mercedes GP Petronas F1 Team P	2.4 Mercedes MGP W02-V8	1 lap behind		9/24
5	CHINESE GP	Shanghai Circuit	8	Mercedes GP Petronas F1 Team P	2.4 Mercedes MGP W02-V8			4/24
5	TURKISH GP	Istanbul Park	8	Mercedes GP Petronas F1 Team P	2.4 Mercedes MGP W02-V8			3/24
7	SPANISH GP	Barcelona	8	Mercedes GP Petronas F1 Team P	2.4 Mercedes MGP W02-V8			7/24
11	MONACO GP	Monte Carlo	8	Mercedes GP Petronas F1 Team P	2.4 Mercedes MGP W02-V8	2 laps behind		7/24
11	CANADIAN GP	Montreal	8	Mercedes GP Petronas F1 Team P	2.4 Mercedes MGP W02-V8	hit Kobayashi – eventually lost front wing		6/24
7	EUROPEAN GP	Valencia	8	Mercedes GP Petronas F1 Team P	2.4 Mercedes MGP W02-V8			17/24
6	BRITISH GP	Silverstone	8	Mercedes GP Petronas F1 Team P	2.4 Mercedes MGP W02-V8			9/24
7	GERMAN GP	Hockenheim	8	Mercedes GP Petronas F1 Team P	2.4 Mercedes MGP W02-V8			6/24
9	HUNGARIAN GP	Hungaroring	8	Mercedes GP Petronas F1 Team P	2.4 Mercedes MGP W02-V8	1 lap behind		7/24
6	BELGIAN GP	Spa	8	Mercedes GP Petronas F1 Team P	2.4 Mercedes MGP W02-V8			5/24
ret	ITALIAN GP	Monza	8	Mercedes GP Petronas F1 Team P	2.4 Mercedes MGP W02-V8	multiple accident on lap 1		9/24
7	SINGAPORE GP	Marina Bay Circuit	8	Mercedes GP Petronas F1 Team P	2.4 Mercedes MGP W02-V8	1 lap behind		7/24
10	JAPANESE GP	Suzuka	8	Mercedes GP Petronas F1 Team P	2.4 Mercedes MGP W02-V8	*no time set		*23/24
8	KOREAN GP	Yeongam	8	Mercedes GP Petronas F1 Team P	2.4 Mercedes MGP W02-V8			7/24
6	INDIAN GP	Buddh Circuit	8	Mercedes GP Petronas F1 Team P	2.4 Mercedes MGP W02-V8	1 lap behind		7/24
6	ABU DHABI GP	Yas Marina Circuit	8	Mercedes GP Petronas F1 Team P	2.4 Mercedes MGP W02-V8			7/24
7	BRAZILIAN GP	Interlagos	8	Mercedes GP Petronas F1 Team P	2.4 Mercedes MGP W02-V8	1 lap behind		6/24

GP Starts: 108 GP Wins: 0 Pole positions: 0 Fastest laps: 2 Points: 306.5

ROSIER, Louis (F) b 5/11/1905, Chapdes-Beaufort, nr Clermont Ferrand – d 29/10/1956, Montlhéry, nr Paris

1950 Championship position: 4th Wins: 0 Pole positions: 0 Fastest laps: 0 Points scored: 13

	Race	Circuit	No	Entrant	Tyres	Capacity/Car/Engine	Comment	Q Pos/Entries
5	BRITISH GP	Silverstone	15	Ecurie Rosier	D	4.5 Lago-Talbot T26C 6	2 laps behind	9/21
ret	MONACO GP	Monte Carlo	16	Ecurie Rosier	D	4.5 Lago-Talbot T26C 6	multiple accident	10/21
3	SWISS GP	Bremgarten	10	Automobiles Talbot-Darracq SA	D	4.5 Lago-Talbot T26C-DA 6	1 lap behind	10/18
3	BELGIAN GP	Spa	14	Automobiles Talbot-Darracq SA	D	4.5 Lago-Talbot T26C-DA 6		=7/14
ret	FRENCH GP	Reims	20	Automobiles Talbot-Darracq SA	D	4.5 Lago-Talbot T26C-DA 6	overheating	6/20
6*	"	"	26	Charles Pozzi	D	4.5 Lago-Talbot T26C 6	*took over Pozzi's car/8 laps behind	– / –
4	ITALIAN GP	Monza	58		D	4.5 Lago-Talbot T26C 6	5 laps behind	13/27

1951 Championship position: 10= Wins: 0 Pole positions: 0 Fastest laps: 0 Points scored: 3

9	SWISS GP	Bremgarten	8	Ecurie Rosier	D	4.5 Lago-Talbot T26C-DA 6	3 laps behind	8/21
4	BELGIAN GP	Spa	14	Ecurie Rosier	D	4.5 Lago-Talbot T26C-DA 6	2 laps behind	7/13
ret	FRENCH GP	Reims	40	Ecurie Rosier	D	4.5 Lago-Talbot T26C-DA 6	transmisssion – rear axle	13/23
10	BRITISH GP	Silverstone	22	Ecurie Rosier	D	4.5 Lago-Talbot T26C-DA 6	7 laps behind	9/20
8	GERMAN GP	Nürburgring	84	Ecurie Rosier	D	4.5 Lago-Talbot T26C-DA 6	1 lap behind	15/23
7	ITALIAN GP	Monza	18	Ecurie Rosier	D	4.5 Lago-Talbot T26C-DA 6	7 laps behind	15/22
7	SPANISH GP	Pedrlbes	28	Ecurie Rosier	D	4.5 Lago-Talbot T26C-DA 6	6 laps behind	20/20

1952 Championship position: Unplaced

ret	SWISS GP	Bremgarten	12	Ecurie Rosier	D	2.0 Ferrari 500 4	crashed	20/21
ret	BELGIAN GP	Spa	22	Ecurie Rosier	D	2.0 Ferrari 500 4	transmission	17/22
ret	FRENCH GP	Rouen	14	Ecurie Rosier	D	2.0 Ferrari 500 4	engine	9/20
10	ITALIAN GP	Monza	62	Ecurie Rosier	D	2.0 Ferrari 500 4	5 laps behind	17/35

1953 Championship position: Unplaced

7	DUTCH GP	Zandvoort	10	Ecurie Rosier	D	2.0 Ferrari 500 4	4 laps behind	8/20
8	BELGIAN GP	Spa	32	Ecurie Rosier	D	2.0 Ferrari 500 4	3 laps behind	13/22
8	FRENCH GP	Reims	44	Ecurie Rosier	D	2.0 Ferrari 500 4	4 laps behind	10/25
10	BRITISH GP	Silverstone	9	Ecurie Rosier	D	2.0 Ferrari 500 4	12 laps behind	24/29
10	GERMAN GP	Nürburgring	20	Ecurie Rosier	D	2.0 Ferrari 500 4	1 lap behind	22/35
ret	SWISS GP	Bremgarten	10	Ecurie Rosier	D	2.0 Ferrari 500 4	spun off	14/23
nc	ITALIAN GP	Monza	64	Ecurie Rosier	D	2.0 Ferrari 500 4	15 laps behind	17/30

1954 Championship position: Unplaced

ret	ARGENTINE GP	Buenos Aires	24	Ecurie Rosier	D	2.5 Ferrari 500/625 4	spun off	14/18
ret	FRENCH GP	Reims	36	Ecurie Rosier	D	2.5 Ferrari 500/625 4	engine	13/22
ret	BRITISH GP	Silverstone	15	Ecurie Rosier	D	2.5 Ferrari 500/625 4	engine	30/31
8	GERMAN GP	Nürburgring	25	Ecurie Rosier	D	2.5 Ferrari 500/625 4	1 lap behind	18/23
8	ITALIAN GP	Monza	26	Officine Alfieri Maserati	P	2.5 Maserati 250F 6	6 laps behind	20/21

7	SPANISH GP	Pedralbes	26	Ecurie Rosier	P	2.5 Maserati 250F 6	*6 laps behind*	20/22
1955 Championship position: Unplaced								
ret	MONACO GP	Monte Carlo	14	Ecurie Rosier	P	2.5 Maserati 250F 6	*split oil tank*	17/22
9	BELGIAN GP	Spa	28	Ecurie Rosier	P	2.5 Maserati 250F 6	*3 laps behind*	12/14
9	DUTCH GP	Zandvoort	28	Ecurie Rosier	P	2.5 Maserati 250F 6	*8 laps behind*	13/16
1956 Championship position: 15th= Wins: 0 Pole positions: 0 Fastest laps: 0 Points scored: 2								
ret	MONACO GP	Monte Carlo	8	Ecurie Rosier	P	2.5 Maserati 250F 6	*engine*	15/19
8	BELGIAN GP	Spa	24	Ecurie Rosier	P	2.5 Maserati 250F 6	*3 laps behind*	10/16
6	FRENCH GP	Reims	36	Ecurie Rosier	P	2.5 Maserati 250F 6	*3 laps behind*	12/20
ret	BRITISH GP	Silverstone	27	Ecurie Rosier	P	2.5 Maserati 250F 6	*carburettor union*	27/28
5	GERMAN GP	Nürburgring	15	Ecurie Rosier	P	2.5 Maserati 250F 6	*3 laps behind*	14/21

GP Starts: 38   GP Wins: 0   Pole positions: 0   Fastest laps: 0   Points: 18

LOUIS ROSIER

A FORMER motorcycle racer and hill-climb specialist, Louis Rosier had just started to develop his racing career when the Second World War intervened, and it was 1947 before this garage owner from Clermont-Ferrand could compete on a wider stage.

Equipped with his self-prepared Talbot, Rosier won the 1947 Albi GP after more speedy opponents had dropped out, and this win set the tone for the rest of his career, for he usually raced well within his limits, placing great store on strategy and reliability as a route to success. In 1948, as a member of the Ecurie France team, he took delivery of a single-seater Lago-Talbot, winning the Grand Prix du Salon and finishing fourth at the Comminges, Pau and British GPs. The following season, with the Talbot probably at its peak relative to the opposition, he won the Belgian GP and, with a succession of steady finishes, was crowned champion of France, a title he held for four years.

Alfa Romeo ruled the roost in 1950, the year of the inaugural world championship, but the crafty Rosier was always well placed to pick up the pieces, and he took some good points-scoring finishes in championship grands prix, as well as winning the Albi and Dutch GPs. Adapting his Talbot to sports car specification, he also won that season's Le Mans 24-hour race with his son, Jean-Louis, although he was the pillar of the achievement, having driven for some 20 hours. By 1951, the Talbot was no longer a competitive proposition, but Louis still managed to coax the elderly car to the finish with astonishing consistency, winning the non-championship Dutch and Bordeaux GPs.

The 1952 season brought a change of regulations, and Rosier lost no time in getting his hands on a Ferrari T375 and a state-of-the-art Ferrari T500 F2 car. Naturally, the Italian machines were painted French blue, and he quickly put one of them to good use, winning the Albi GP in the big-engined model. For 1953, he continued with the same equipment, taking yet another win in the Albi GP and a victory in the Sables d'Olonne GP with the T500. His old Talbot was brought out for the Reims 12-hours, where he

took second place with Yves Giraud-Cabantous.

By then, Rosier was well past his best as a driver, but he pushed ahead undaunted the following season. After racing a Ferrari 625, he bought a Maserati 250F, which he continued to campaign in grands prix and non-championship events in a steady and reliable fashion, as well as handling his own Ferrari 3-litre sports car.

Ironically, he shared a Maserati T300S with Jean Behra to win the 1956 Paris 1000km, his last win, before returning to the Montlhéry circuit he knew so well in this Ferrari for the Coupe du Salon. In pouring rain, he overturned his car and suffered severe head injuries, from which he died three weeks later. He was posthumously awarded the French Order of the Nation.

RICARDO ROSSET

HAVING enjoyed a sound debut year in the 1993 British F3 championship, Ricardo Rosset's hopes were high for his second season in the class. In the end, however, he had to be content with a single win and numerous placings as Jan Magnussen swept all before him. The Brazilian moved up to F3000 in 1995, but few expected him to figure among the front-runners, especially as he was partnered in the Super Nova line-up by the highly experienced Vincenzo Sospiri. In the event, he proved almost the equal of his team leader in terms of speed and eventually took the runner-up slot behind the Italian.

Ricardo's performances brought a drive at Arrows in 1996, where initially he was well off the pace of team-mate Jos Verstappen, but he proved more impressive after a mid-season heart-to-heart with the team management.

Rosset then threw in his lot with Sospiri once more as Eric Broadley launched a brave, but ultimately foolhardy attempt to return Lola to the grand prix grids in 1997. After the débâcle of a debut in Australia, he was left with nothing but a testing contract at Tyrrell to fill his time and the budget to negotiate a seat in the team for 1998.

With Tyrrell effectively in its death throes, Ricardo struggled to make an impact, blaming a lack of technical support from the team, whom he claimed had ruined his career and destroyed his credibility.

The disillusioned Rosset spurned offers to race in the CART series and returned home to concentrate on the family clothing business, but he was tempted back to the track in 2008 to race a Ford GT in the Brazilian GT3 championship.

ROSSET, Ricardo (B) b São Paulo 27/7/1968

	Race	Circuit	No	Entrant	Tyres	Capacity/Car/Engine	Comment	Q Pos/Entries
1996 Championship position: Unplaced								
9	AUSTRALIAN GP	Melbourne	16	TWR Arrows	G	3.0 Footwork FA17-Hart V8	2 laps behind	18/22
ret	BRAZILIAN GP	Interlagos	16	TWR Arrows	G	3.0 Footwork FA17-Hart V8	spun into pit wall	19/22
ret	ARGENTINE GP	Buenos Aires	16	TWR Arrows	G	3.0 Footwork FA17-Hart V8	fuel pump	20/22
11	EUROPEAN GP	Nürburgring	16	TWR Arrows	G	3.0 Footwork FA17-Hart V8	2 laps behind	20/22
ret	SAN MARINO GP	Imola	16	TWR Arrows	G	3.0 Footwork FA17-Hart V8	out of fuel	20/22
ret	MONACO GP	Monte Carlo	16	TWR Arrows	G	3.0 Footwork FA17-Hart V8	spun off	20/22
ret	SPANISH GP	Barcelona	16	TWR Arrows	G	3.0 Footwork FA17-Hart V8	multiple collision on lap 1	20/22
ret	CANADIAN GP	Montreal	16	TWR Arrows	G	3.0 Footwork FA17-Hart V8	collision with Katayama	21/22
11	FRENCH GP	Magny Cours	16	TWR Arrows	G	3.0 Footwork FA17-Hart V8	3 laps behind	20/22
ret	BRITISH GP	Silverstone	16	TWR Arrows	G	3.0 Footwork FA17-Hart V8	*time disallowed/electrics	*17/22
11	GERMAN GP	Hockenheim	16	TWR Arrows	G	3.0 Footwork FA17-Hart V8	1 lap behind	19/20
8	HUNGARIAN GP	Hungaroring	16	TWR Arrows	G	3.0 Footwork FA17-Hart V8	3 laps behind	18/20
9	BELGIAN GP	Spa	16	TWR Arrows	G	3.0 Footwork FA17-Hart V8	1 lap behind	18/20
ret	ITALIAN GP	Monza	16	TWR Arrows	G	3.0 Footwork FA17-Hart V8	spun off	19/20
14	PORTUGUESE GP	Estoril	16	TWR Arrows	G	3.0 Footwork FA17-Hart V8	3 laps behind	17/20
13	JAPANESE GP	Suzuka	16	TWR Arrows	G	3.0 Footwork FA17-Hart V8	2 laps behind	19/20
1997 Championship position: Unplaced								
dnq	AUSTRALIAN GP	Melbourne	25	Mastercard Lola F1 Team	B	3.0 Lola T/97/30-Ford Zetec R V8	not within 107% of pole	24/24
dnp	BRAZILIAN GP	Interlagos	25	Mastercard Lola F1 Team	B	3.0 Lola T/97/30-Ford Zetec R V8	cars did not practice	- / -
1998 Championship position: Unplaced								
ret	AUSTRALIAN GP	Melbourne	20	Tyrrell Ford	G	3.0 Tyrrell 026-Ford Zetec R V10	gearbox	19/22
ret	BRAZILIAN GP	Interlagos	20	Tyrrell Ford	G	3.0 Tyrrell 026-Ford Zetec R V10	gearbox	21/22
14	ARGENTINE GP	Buenos Aires	20	Tyrrell Ford	G	3.0 Tyrrell 026-Ford Zetec R V10	4 laps behind	21/22
ret	SAN MARINO GP	Imola	20	Tyrrell Ford	G	3.0 Tyrrell 026-Ford Zetec R V10	engine	22/22
dnq	SPANISH GP	Barcelona	20	Tyrrell Ford	G	3.0 Tyrrell 026-Ford Zetec R V10		22/22
dnq	MONACO GP	Monte Carlo	20	Tyrrell Ford	G	3.0 Tyrrell 026-Ford Zetec R V10		22/22
8	CANADIAN GP	Montreal	20	Tyrrell Ford	G	3.0 Tyrrell 026-Ford Zetec R V10	1 lap behind	22/22
ret	FRENCH GP	Magny Cours	20	Tyrrell Ford	G	3.0 Tyrrell 026-Ford Zetec R V10	engine	18/22
ret	BRITISH GP	Silverstone	20	Tyrrell Ford	G	3.0 Tyrrell 026-Ford Zetec R V10	engine	22/22
12	AUSTRIAN GP	A1-Ring	20	Tyrrell Ford	G	3.0 Tyrrell 026-Ford Zetec R V10	2 laps behind	22/22
ret	GERMAN GP	Hockenheim	20	Tyrrell Ford	G	3.0 Tyrrell 026-Ford Zetec R V10	injured wrist in free practice	-/22
dnq	HUNGARIAN GP	Hungaroring	20	Tyrrell Ford	G	3.0 Tyrrell 026-Ford Zetec R V10		22/22
ret/dns	BELGIAN GP	Spa	20	Tyrrell Ford	G	3.0 Tyrrell 026-Ford Zetec R V10	accident at first start	20/22
12	ITALIAN GP	Monza	20	Tyrrell Ford	G	3.0 Tyrrell 026-Ford Zetec R V10	2 laps behind	18/22
ret	LUXEMBOURG GP	Nürburgring	20	Tyrrell Ford	G	3.0 Tyrrell 026-Ford Zetec R V10	engine	22/22
dnq	JAPANESE GP	Suzuka	20	Tyrrell Ford	G	3.0 Tyrrell 026-Ford Zetec R V10		22/22

GP Starts: 27 (28)　GP Wins: 0　Pole positions: 0　Fastest laps: 0　Points: 0

HUUB ROTHENGATTER

ATALL, genial Dutchman, Huub Rothengatter left school with few qualifications, but worked at a succession of jobs to pave the way to a grand prix career after a fairly unspectacular climb through the ranks.

Huub started in both German and European Formula 3 in his privately entered March, his first success coming in 1978 with a win at Hockenheim. Although the following season brought little reward in terms of points accrued, nonetheless he graduated to Formula 2 in 1979 with a Hart-powered Chevron B48. He was a little rough around the edges, however, and only garnered three points to finish 18th in the final standings.

The following season, equipped with a Toleman TG280, Huub improved immensely, scoring an excellent win at Zolder by beating Brian Henton, Siegfried Stohr and Derek Warwick fair and square.

At this point, Rothengatter harboured hopes of a Formula 1 ride, but in the event he missed the first half of 1981 completely, before making a brief return to Formula 2 with a March 812-BMW, his best result being a second place to Thiery Boutsen at the ultra-fast Enna circuit.

Huub was left kicking his heels on the sidelines until mid-way through the 1984 season, when surprisingly he was called into action with Spirit – now shorn of Honda power – to replace the disaffected Mauro Baldi. He did his best with uncompetitive machinery before Baldi's end-of-season return and went back to the sidelines before his next tilt at F1 windmills.

When Zakspeed inexplicitly decided to enter a second car early in 1986, Rothengatter readily accepted the poisoned chalice, being forced to scramble around at the back of the field. Basically he had been just making up the numbers, but he remained remarkably cheerful, clearly enjoying his bit part on the grand prix stage. However, his involvement with F1 did not end there. In the early 1990s, he helped fellow countryman Jos Verstappen to make it into grands prix and largely stay in the dog-eat-dog competition for rides between 1994 and 2003.

Rothengatter has since found a new and rewarding business career as the co-owner of EV-Box. Mainly based in Holland, they provide charging stations for electric vehicles, primarily for the corporate and the public sector.

ROTHENGATTER, 'Huub' Hubertus (NL) b 8/10/1954, Bussum, nr Hilversum

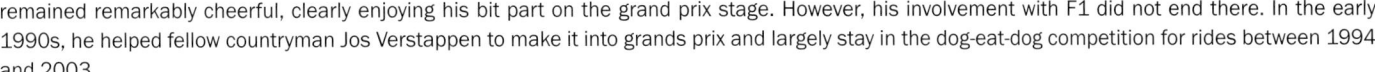

	1984 Championship position: Unplaced							
	Race	Circuit	No	Entrant	Tyres	Capacity/Car/Engine	Comment	Q Pos/Entries
nc	CANADIAN GP	Montreal	21	Spirit Racing	P	1.5 t/c Spirit 101-Hart 4	engine problems/14 laps behind	24/26
dnq	US GP (DETROIT)	Detroit	21	Spirit Racing	P	3.0 Spirit 101-Cosworth V8		27/27
ret	US GP (DALLAS)	Dallas	21	Spirit Racing	P	1.5 t/c Spirit 101-Hart 4	fuel leak in cockpit	23/27
nc	BRITISH GP	Brands Hatch	21	Spirit Racing	P	1.5 t/c Spirit 101-Hart 4	pit stop/nose cone/9 laps behind	22/27
9*	GERMAN GP	Hockenheim	21	Spirit Racing	P	1.5 t/c Spirit 101-Hart 4	*9th place car dsq/4 laps behind	24/27
nc	AUSTRIAN GP	Österreichring	21	Spirit Racing	P	1.5 t/c Spirit 101-Hart 4	pit stop – exhaust/28 laps behind	26/28
dnq*/ret	DUTCH GP	Zandvoort	21	Spirit Racing	P	1.5 t/c Spirit 101-Hart 4	allowed to start*/throttle cable	27/27
8	ITALIAN GP	Monza	21	Spirit Racing	P	1.5 t/c Spirit 101-Hart 4	3 laps behind	25/27
	1985 Championship position: Unplaced							
ret	GERMAN GP	Nürburgring	24	Osella Squadra Corse	P	1.5 t/c Osella FA1G-Alfa Romeo V8	gearbox	25/27
9	AUSTRIAN GP	Österreichring	24	Osella Squadra Corse	P	1.5 t/c Osella FA1G-Alfa Romeo V8	4 laps behind	24/27
nc	DUTCH GP	Zandvoort	24	Osella Squadra Corse	P	1.5 t/c Osella FA1G-Alfa Romeo V8	24 laps behind	26/27
ret	ITALIAN GP	Monza	24	Osella Squadra Corse	P	1.5 t/c Osella FA1G-Alfa Romeo V8	engine	22/26
nc	BELGIAN GP	Spa	24	Osella Squadra Corse	P	1.5 t/c Osella FA1G-Alfa Romeo V8	6 laps behind	23/24
dnq	EUROPEAN GP	Brands Hatch	24	Osella Squadra Corse	P	1.5 t/c Osella FA1G-Alfa Romeo V8		27/27
ret	SOUTH AFRICAN GP	Kyalami	24	Osella Squadra Corse	P	1.5 t/c Osella FA1G-Alfa Romeo V8	electrics	21/21
7	AUSTRALIAN GP	Adelaide	24	Osella Squadra Corse	P	1.5 t/c Osella FA1G-Alfa Romeo V8	4 laps behind	25/25
	1986 Championship position: Unplaced							
ret	SAN MARINO GP	Imola	29	West Zakspeed Racing	G	1.5 t/c Zakspeed 861 4	turbo	24/26
dnq	MONACO GP	Monte Carlo	29	West Zakspeed Racing	G	1.5 t/c Zakspeed 861 4		23/26
ret	BELGIAN GP	Spa	29	West Zakspeed Racing	G	1.5 t/c Zakspeed 861 4	alternator/battery	23/25
12	CANADIAN GP	Montreal	29	West Zakspeed Racing	G	1.5 t/c Zakspeed 861 4	6 laps behind	24/25
ret/dns*	US GP (DETROIT)	Detroit	29	West Zakspeed Racing	G	1.5 t/c Zakspeed 861 4	*electrics on parade lap	26/26
ret	FRENCH GP	Paul Ricard	29	West Zakspeed Racing	G	1.5 t/c Zakspeed 861 4	collision with Dumfries	24/26
ret	BRITISH GP	Brands Hatch	29	West Zakspeed Racing	G	1.5 t/c Zakspeed 861 4	engine	25/26
ret	GERMAN GP	Hockenheim	29	West Zakspeed Racing	G	1.5 t/c Zakspeed 861 4	gearbox	24/26
ret	HUNGARIAN GP	Hungaroring	29	West Zakspeed Racing	G	1.5 t/c Zakspeed 861 4	oil radiator	25/26
8	AUSTRIAN GP	Österreichring	29	West Zakspeed Racing	G	1.5 t/c Zakspeed 861 4	4 laps behind	24/26
ret	ITALIAN GP	Monza	29	West Zakspeed Racing	G	1.5 t/c Zakspeed 861 4	engine	24/27
ret	PORTUGUESE GP	Estoril	29	West Zakspeed Racing	G	1.5 t/c Zakspeed 861 4	transmission	26/27
dns	MEXICAN GP	Mexico City	29	West Zakspeed Racing	G	1.5 t/c Zakspeed 861 4	practice accident – no spare car	23/26
ret	AUSTRALIAN GP	Adelaide	29	West Zakspeed Racing	G	1.5 t/c Zakspeed 861 4	rear suspension	23/26

GP Starts: 25 (26)　GP Wins: 0　Pole positions: 0　Fastest laps: 0　Points: 0

LLOYD RUBY

AN Indianapolis 500 perennial, Lloyd Ruby began racing motorcycles on the Texas plains before moving on to midgets after the Second World War. Then he raced stock cars, but it was more than a decade before he joined the USAC trail, soon developing a reputation as a shrewd tactician who looked after his cars. He won seven championship races during a long career that ran from 1958 to 1977. He never succeeded in winning the 500, however – third place in 1964 was his best finish – although he came heartbreakingly close on a number of occasions. In 1969, he held the lead at the halfway mark when a routine pit stop went disastrously wrong. He was given the signal to go, but the fuel hose was still attached and a hole was ripped in the tank to destroy his best chance of a victory. Ironically, it was the Texan's misfortune that handed Mario Andretti his only 500 win.

In the early 1960s, Ruby also went sports car racing with a Lotus Monte Carlo, and became a local attraction at the 1961 US Grand Prix in a guest appearance in a Lotus 18. His mechanical sympathy prompted Ford to take him into their sports car team to develop their prototype, and he won the Daytona 24-hours in 1965 and 1966 with Ken Miles. This experienced pairing also took a win at Sebring in 1966, but injury in a light plane crash caused Lloyd to miss the Le Mans 24-hour race that year, and a very real chance of victory.

TROY RUTTMAN

WHILE Lloyd Ruby tried in vain to win the Indy 500 for more than two decades, Troy Ruttman was only 22 when he triumphed at the 'Brickyard' at only his fourth attempt in 1952, becoming the youngest driver to win the classic event. That could easily have been his last year in racing, however, for later he was seriously injured in a sprint car race at Cedar Rapids, Iowa, and didn't return to action until 1954. This accident had brought a halt to a sensational run of three AAA sprint car titles, Ruttman having won 16 races in just 51 starts. He returned to the Speedway in 1954 to finish fourth, but apart from leading briefly in 1960, he never was a factor in seven subsequent starts.

Thereafter, Ruttman raced less frequently, although he was invited to compete in the 1957 Two Worlds Trophy race at Monza, where he finished second. He returned for the race in 1958 and stayed on in Europe to briefly try his hand at grand prix racing with Scuderia Centro Sud. In conflict with the American racing authorities, allegedly over his love of gambling, he successfully took up stock car racing with Mercury, before suddenly announcing his retirement immediately after completing his final Indianapolis 500 in 1964, a race marred by the death of his friend, Eddie Sachs.

Ruttman suffered tragedy in his personal life with the death of his son, Troy Jr, who lost his life in a super modified sprint car accident in 1969. In his later years, his achievements were honoured when he was inducted into the National Sprint Car Hall of Fame. Following his death from lung cancer in 1997, Ruttman was similarly honoured by the Motor Sports Hall of Fame of America (2005), The National Midget Auto Racing Hall of Fame (2003) and the West Coast Stock Car Hall of Fame (2002).

RUBY, Lloyd (USA) Richard Lloyd Ruby b 12/1/1928, Wichita Falls, Texas – d 23/3/2009, Wichita Falls, Texas

1961 Championship position: Unplaced

	Race	Circuit	No	Entrant	Tyres	Capacity/Car/Engine	Comment	Q Pos/Entries
ret	US GP	Watkins Glen	26	J Frank Harrison	D	1.5 Lotus 18-Climax 4	magneto	=18/19

GP Starts: 1   GP Wins: 0   Pole positions: 0   Fastest laps: 0   Points: 0

RUSSO, Giacomo see 'Geki'

RUTTMAN, Troy (USA) b 11/3/1930, Mooreland, Oklahoma – d 19/5/1997, Lake Havasu City, Arizona

1958 Championship position: Unplaced

	Race	Circuit	No	Entrant	Tyres	Capacity/Car/Engine	Comment	Q Pos/Entries
10	FRENCH GP	Reims	30	Scuderia Centro Sud	P	2.5 Maserati 250F 6	5 laps behind	18/21
dns	GERMAN GP	Nürburgring	14	Scuderia Centro Sud	P	2.5 Maserati 250F 6	engine in practice	– /26

GP Starts: 1   GP Wins: 0   Pole positions: 0   Fastest laps: 0   Points: 0

RYAN, Peter (CDN) b 10/6/1940, Philadelphia, Pennsylvania USA, – d 2/7/1962, Paris, France

1961 Championship position: Unplaced

	Race	Circuit	No	Entrant	Tyres	Capacity/Car/Engine	Comment	Q Pos/Entries
9	US GP	Watkins Glen	16	J Wheeler Autosport	D	1.5 Lotus 18/21-Climax 4	4 laps behind	13/19

GP Starts: 1   GP Wins: 0   Pole positions: 0   Fastest laps: 0   Points: 0

SAID, 'Bob' (Boris) (USA) b 5/5/1932, New York City, New York – d 24/3/2002, Kirkland, Washington

1959 Championship position: Unplaced

	Race	Circuit	No	Entrant	Tyres	Capacity/Car/Engine	Comment	Q Pos/Entries
ret	US GP	Sebring	18	Connaught Cars-Paul Emery	D	2.5 Connaught C Type Alta 4	spun off on lap 1	13/19

GP Starts: 1   GP Wins: 0   Pole positions: 0   Fastest laps: 0   Points: 0

PETER RYAN

YOUNG Canadian Peter Ryan built a fine reputation during his tragically short career, initially at the wheel of a Porsche RS60 with which he won a thrilling Sundown GP at Harewood in 1961. That triumph was followed by victory in the Canadian GP at Mosport in a Lotus 23, Ryan beating a similar car handled by no less a driver than Stirling Moss.

In 1962, Peter came to Europe for a planned season of Formula Junior in a works Lotus, but in the event he was loaned to the Ian Walker stable. He immediately confirmed his promise by beating Peter Arundell in the works car at Mallory Park, but during a heat of the Coupe de Vitesse des Juniors at Reims, his Lotus was involved in a collision with the Gemini of Bill Moss. The young Canadian was thrown from his machine and died from internal injuries.

'BOB' SAID

AN amazing character, Boris 'Bob' Said was born in New York of Syrian-Russian parents, who interspersed his various sporting activities with an equally diverse business career, which saw him make and lose a fortune, before spectacularly restoring his finances once more.

Said holds the distinction of being the first American to win a post-war European race – at Rouen with an OSCA in 1953 – having already made his mark at home in a Jaguar and his Cisitalia sports car, with which he won the Seneca Cup at Watkins Glen. His seasons in Europe went pretty well; he won the Anerley Trophy in 1953 with the OSCA, then switched to a Ferrari 500 Mondial for 1954, taking second place the Trullo d'Oro at Castellana.

At the beginning of the 1955 season, Said had a lucky escape in the Sebring 12-hour race when his Ferrari collided with an ambulance on the way to the scene of another accident. He enjoyed his earlier Continental sojourns enough to venture back to Italy to take second place in the Bari Grand Prix.

In 1956, Said briefly dropped out of racing and moved to California, where he lost his $100,000 inheritance by dabbling in real estate. Undaunted, he moved to Montana, where he purchased a Thorium mine, which soon restored his finances and allowed him to return to the tracks in 1957, winning his class at Nassau with a Ferrari.

In February 1959, Said made his only start in NASCAR with a Chevrolet convertible in the inaugural Daytona 500 meeting. At the end of the season, he made it on to the grand prix stage in the inaugural US Grand Prix held at Sebring.

Having persuaded organiser Alec Ulmann to grant him an entry, Said eventually found a car in the shape of Paul Emery's ancient Connaught. The ever-enthusiastic Boris set off like a rocket from the start, passing a gaggle of cars before leaving his braking far too late for the first corner. He spun off and was unable to restart his engine: "I didn't even make single a corner!" That was also the last hurrah for Connaught in Formula 1.

Said continued to race in minor events until 1962 when, "dead broke", he borrowed $2,600 to venture into property speculation once more. This time, his dealings paid off and within two years he had made more than a million dollars.

After a return to Sebring one last time in 1966, when he took an AC Cobra to 15th place and second in class, Said took up a completely different sport and became a member of the US bobsleigh team, competing in both the 1968 and 1972 Winter Olympics.

Later he turned his talents to the world of film, acting as executive producer for an Emmy award-winning documentary, The Mystery of The Sphinx, hosted and narrated by Charlton Heston in 1993.

LUIS SALA

A TALENTED and charming Spanish driver, Luis Sala began racing in karts in 1976 and was Spain's Renault Cup champion in 1980. His career progressed to touring cars in an Alfa Sud, before he graduated to the Italian Formula 3 championship with the Pavesi team's Ralt-Alfa. He won a round of the series, but didn't pull up any trees. He was a different proposition, however, when he moved up to Formula 3000 with Pavesi the following season. Luis was well served by his team and, in his own quiet way, soon got to grips with the formula, winning two rounds at Enna and Birmingham. Backing up these victories with a consistent finishing record, he took fifth place in the points table.

This excellent first season earned Sala a place in the works Lola team for 1987, and again he won two races (at Donington and Le Mans), but was unable to stop Stefano Modena's title charge, having to settle for the runner-up slot, ahead of Roberto Moreno, Mauricio Gugelmin and Yannick Dalmas.

With Spanish backing, Sala joined former rival Adrian Campos at Minardi for 1988 and looked quite promising in the early races, but once his countryman had been replaced by Pierluigi Martini the picture changed. Suddenly Luis was very much second best within the team, particularly the following season when Minardi were quite capable of scoring points.

At the end of the year, Sala was out, but he went on to enjoy an excellent career with Nissan in Spanish touring cars, taking the championship in 1991 and 1993. He continued to race right up until 2008 when, after more than 380 races that yielded 46 victories, he retired from competition.

Sala combined his racing with commentating for TV, road car testing and race driver training, being a member of the programme for Young Pilots of the Circuit de Catalunya.

In 2001, Sala was employed by the HRT F1 team initially to act as a consultant, but then he was chosen to replace Colin Kolles as the team principal for the re-organised squad in the 2012 season.

SALA, Luis Perez (E) b 15/5/1959, Barcelona

1988 Championship position: Unplaced

	Race	Circuit	No	Entrant	Tyres	Capacity/Car/Engine	Comment	Q Pos/Entries
ret	BRAZILIAN GP	Rio	24	Lois Minardi Team	G	3.5 Minardi M188-Cosworth V8	rear wing mounting	20/31
11	SAN MARINO GP	Imola	24	Lois Minardi Team	G	3.5 Minardi M188-Cosworth V8	2 laps behind	18/31
ret	MONACO GP	Monte Carlo	24	Lois Minardi Team	G	3.5 Minardi M188-Cosworth V8	suspension	15/30
11	MEXICAN GP	Mexico City	24	Lois Minardi Team	G	3.5 Minardi M188-Cosworth V8	4 laps behind	25/30
13	CANADIAN GP	Montreal	24	Lois Minardi Team	G	3.5 Minardi M188-Cosworth V8	5 laps behind	21/31
ret	US GP (DETROIT)	Detroit	24	Lois Minardi Team	G	3.5 Minardi M188-Cosworth V8	gearbox	26/31
nc	FRENCH GP	Paul Ricard	24	Lois Minardi Team	G	3.5 Minardi M188-Cosworth V8	4 pit stops – electrics/10 laps behind	26/31
ret	BRITISH GP	Silverstone	24	Lois Minardi Team	G	3.5 Minardi M188-Cosworth V8	ran into back of Streiff	18/31
dnq	GERMAN GP	Hockenheim	24	Lois Minardi Team	G	3.5 Minardi M188-Cosworth V8		27/31
10	HUNGARIAN GP	Hungaroring	24	Lois Minardi Team	G	3.5 Minardi M188-Cosworth V8	4 laps behind	11/31
dnq	BELGIAN GP	Spa	24	Lois Minardi Team	G	3.5 Minardi M188-Cosworth V8		27/31
ret	ITALIAN GP	Monza	24	Lois Minardi Team	G	3.5 Minardi M188-Cosworth V8	gearbox	19/31
8	PORTUGUESE GP	Estoril	24	Lois Minardi Team	G	3.5 Minardi M188-Cosworth V8	2 laps behind	19/31
12	SPANISH GP	Jerez	24	Lois Minardi Team	G	3.5 Minardi M188-Cosworth V8	2 laps behind	24/31
15	JAPANESE GP	Suzuka	24	Lois Minardi Team	G	3.5 Minardi M188-Cosworth V8	2 laps behind	22/31
ret	AUSTRALIAN GP	Adelaide	24	Lois Minardi Team	G	3.5 Minardi M188-Cosworth V8	engine	21/31

1989 Championship position: 26th= Wins: 0 Pole positions: 0 Fastest laps: 0 Points scored: 1

	Race	Circuit	No	Entrant	Tyres	Capacity/Car/Engine	Comment	Q Pos/Entries
ret	BRAZILIAN GP	Rio	24	Lois Minardi Team	P	3.5 Minardi M188B-Cosworth V8	collision with Grouillard on lap 1	23/38
ret	SAN MARINO GP	Imola	24	Lois Minardi Team	P	3.5 Minardi M188B-Cosworth V8	spun off	15/39
ret	MONACO GP	Monte Carlo	24	Lois Minardi Team	P	3.5 Minardi M188B-Cosworth V8	engine/cockpit fire	26/38
dnq	MEXICAN GP	Mexico City	24	Lois Minardi Team	P	3.5 Minardi M189-Cosworth V8		27/39
ret	US GP (PHOENIX)	Phoenix	24	Lois Minardi Team	P	3.5 Minardi M189-Cosworth V8	overheating	20/39
ret	CANADIAN GP	Montreal	24	Lois Minardi Team	P	3.5 Minardi M189-Cosworth V8	started from pit lane/crashed	24/39
dnq	FRENCH GP	Paul Ricard	24	Lois Minardi Team	P	3.5 Minardi M189-Cosworth V8		28/39
6	BRITISH GP	Silverstone	24	Lois Minardi Team	P	3.5 Minardi M189-Cosworth V8	1 lap behind	15/39
dnq	GERMAN GP	Hockenheim	24	Lois Minardi Team	P	3.5 Minardi M189-Cosworth V8		27/39
ret	HUNGARIAN GP	Hungaroring	24	Lois Minardi Team	P	3.5 Minardi M189-Cosworth V8	accident with Modena	23/39
15	BELGIAN GP	Spa	24	Lois Minardi Team	P	3.5 Minardi M189-Cosworth V8	3 laps behind	25/39
8	ITALIAN GP	Monza	24	Lois Minardi Team	P	3.5 Minardi M189-Cosworth V8	2 laps behind	26/39
12	PORTUGUESE GP	Estoril	24	Lois Minardi Team	P	3.5 Minardi M189-Cosworth V8	2 laps behind	9/39
ret	SPANISH GP	Jerez	24	Lois Minardi Team	P	3.5 Minardi M189-Cosworth V8	collision with Gugelmin	21/38
ret	JAPANESE GP	Suzuka	24	Lois Minardi Team	P	3.5 Minardi M189-Cosworth V8	forced off by Nakajima on lap 1	14/39
dnq	AUSTRALIAN GP	Adelaide	24	Lois Minardi Team	P	3.5 Minardi M189-Cosworth V8		28/39

GP Starts: 26 GP Wins: 0 Pole positions: 0 Fastest laps: 0 Points: 1

ELISEO SALAZAR

THUS far the only Chilean driver to have represented his country in grand prix racing, Eliseo Salazar was a virtual unknown when he travelled to Britain in 1979 to contest the Vandervell Formula 3 championship, He made a good impression with some gritty performances, despite being saddled with the initially temperamental 'ground-effect' Ralt RT3 while his rivals ran more proven machinery. For 1980, the Chilean switched to the Aurora British F1 series with the RAM Racing Williams FW07 and won three races (including the once prestigious International Trophy), finishing second to his more experienced team-mate, Emilio de Villota, in the championship.

With much-needed financial backing available, Salazar joined the revamped March F1 team the following season. He soon became disillusioned, however, and took his cash to Ensign, where he put in some excellent performances, finishing in sixth place at Zandvoort, and impressing at Hockenheim and the Osterreichring.

For 1982, Eliseo joined the autocratic Gunther Schmid's ATS team, but apart from a flattering fifth place at Imola, where a large number of the FOCA teams staged a boycott, he was largely in the shadow of Manfred Winkelhock. However, his profile was raised massively, if perversely, when he was involved in a much-publicised incident at Hockenheim. After being involved in a collision with Nelson Piquet, while being lapped, subsequently the Chilean was assaulted by the irate Brazilian, who rained a flurry of blows on the bemused driver.

His options now limited if he wished to stay in Formula 1, Salazar went back to RAM for 1983. Perhaps predictably, however, things disintegrated rapidly, and after a string of non-qualifications he found himself out of a drive.

With the Chilean economic crisis restricting the supply of money, Salazar raced at home before a return to Europe in 1986 in F3000. His two seasons spent with four teams yielded virtually nothing, leaving him to look towards rebuilding his career in sports car racing.

A class win in the Fuji 1000km in a Spice SE88C kick-started his new career and took him into Tom Walkinshaw's Silk Cut Jaguar squad for Le Mans. In 1989, he took eighth place with the Ferté brothers, and in 1990 he had the heartbreak of missing out on being part of the winning driver team when he was stood down during the race and replaced by Martin Brundle after the Briton's car hit problems.

Suddenly the drives dried up and Salazar had to wait until the 1994 season to find a ride. Joining Giampiero Moretti's Momo-Ferrari team to race their 333SP produced a highly successful liaison that ended in a number of wins. This success helped the 40-year-old to find the backing to join Dick Simon's Indy car team for 1995. He did surprisingly well in this highly competitive series, appearing particularly comfortable on the ovals. Fourth place in the Indianapolis 500 was the year's high point, and then the veteran moved to the rival Indy Racing League.

Since then, Salazar's grit and determination have certainly been tested, the Chilean returning on three separate occasions from huge accidents that ended in broken limbs. He had one IRL victory to his credit, at Las Vegas in 1997, and a number of fine placings, including his highest finish of third for A.J. Foyt at Indianapolis in 2000. Despite a truncated season, he finished fourth in the standings; the following year, he was fifth. His third year with Foyt started well, but was marred by a big accident in practice for Indianapolis, which caused him to miss several races. He did briefly re-appear in single-seaters in the Grand Prix Masters in 2005/06, replacing Alan Jones without making any impression at all near the front of the field.

Having concentrated on the ALMS series, racing a Porsche 996 GT3 and a Ferrari 360 Modena in 2003, Salazar returned to Chile to take up rallying, in which he has competed regularly. Not content with winding down his career at this national level, he fulfilled another ambition by taking part in the Dakar Rally in 2008.

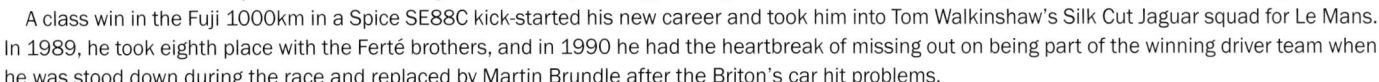

SALAZAR, Eliseo (RCH) b 14/11/1954, Santiago

1981 Championship position: 18th=   Wins: 0   Pole positions: 0   Fastest laps: 0   Points scored: 1

	Race	Circuit	No	Entrant	Tyres	Capacity/Car/Engine	Comment	Q Pos/Entries
dnq	US GP WEST	Long Beach	18	March Grand Prix Team	M	3.0 March 811-Cosworth V8		29/29
dnq	BRAZILIAN GP	Rio	18	March Grand Prix Team	M	3.0 March 811-Cosworth V8		29/30
dnq	ARGENTINE GP	Buenos Aires	18	March Grand Prix Team	M	3.0 March 811-Cosworth V8		29/29
ret	SAN MARINO GP	Imola	17	March Grand Prix Team	M	3.0 March 811-Cosworth V8	oil pressure	23/30
dnq	BELGIAN GP	Zolder	17	March Grand Prix Team	M	3.0 March 811-Cosworth V8		26/31
dnpq	MONACO GP	Monte Carlo	17	March Grand Prix Team	M	3.0 March 811-Cosworth V8		29/31
14	SPANISH GP	Jarama	14	Ensign Racing	M	3.0 Ensign N180B-Cosworth V8	3 laps behind	24/30
ret	FRENCH GP	Dijon	14	Ensign Racing	A	3.0 Ensign N180B-Cosworth V8	rear suspension	22/29
dnq	BRITISH GP	Silverstone	14	Ensign Racing	A	3.0 Ensign N180B-Cosworth V8		28/30

	Race	Circuit	No	Entrant	Tyres	Capacity/Car/Engine	Comment	Q Pos/Entries
nc	GERMAN GP	Hockenheim	14	Ensign Racing	A	3.0 Ensign N180B-Cosworth V8	pit stop – brakes/6 laps behind	23/30
ret	AUSTRIAN GP	Österreichring	14	Ensign Racing	A	3.0 Ensign N180B-Cosworth V8	engine	20/28
6	DUTCH GP	Zandvoort	14	Ensign Racing	A	3.0 Ensign N180B-Cosworth V8	2 laps behind	24/30
ret	ITALIAN GP	Monza	14	Ensign Racing	A	3.0 Ensign N180B-Cosworth V8	tyre failure	24/30
ret	CANADIAN GP	Montreal	14	Ensign Racing	A	3.0 Ensign N180B-Cosworth V8	spun off	24/30
nc	CAESARS PALACE GP	Las Vegas	14	Ensign Racing	A	3.0 Ensign N180B-Cosworth V8	brake problems/14 laps behind	24/30

1982 Championship position: 22nd=   Wins: 0   Pole positions: 0   Fastest laps: 0   Points scored: 2

9	SOUTH AFRICAN GP	Kyalami	10	Team ATS	A	3.0 ATS D5-Cosworth V8	2 laps behind	12/30
ret	BRAZILIAN GP	Rio	10	Team ATS	A	3.0 ATS D5-Cosworth V8	engine	18/31
ret	US GP WEST	Long Beach	10	Team ATS	A	3.0 ATS D5-Cosworth V8	hit wall	26/31
5	SAN MARINO GP	Imola	10	Team ATS	A	3.0 ATS D5-Cosworth V8	3 laps behind	14/14
ret	BELGIAN GP	Zolder	10	Team ATS	A	3.0 ATS D5-Cosworth V8	startline accident	20/32
ret	MONACO GP	Monte Carlo	10	Team ATS	M	3.0 ATS D5-Cosworth V8	fire extinguisher went off	20/31
ret	US GP (DETROIT)	Detroit	10	Team ATS	M	3.0 ATS D5-Cosworth V8	crashed	25/28
ret	CANADIAN GP	Montreal	10	Team ATS	M	3.0 ATS D5-Cosworth V8	transmission	24/29
13	DUTCH GP	Zandvoort	10	Team ATS	M	3.0 ATS D5-Cosworth V8	2 laps behind	25/31
dnq	BRITISH GP	Brands Hatch	10	Team ATS	M	3.0 ATS D5-Cosworth V8		29/30
ret	FRENCH GP	Paul Ricard	10	Team ATS	M	3.0 ATS D5-Cosworth V8	crashed	22/30
ret	GERMAN GP	Hockenheim	10	Team ATS	M	3.0 ATS D5-Cosworth V8	accident with Piquet	23/30
dnq	AUSTRIAN GP	Österreichring	10	Team ATS	M	3.0 ATS D5-Cosworth V8		29/29
14	SWISS GP	Dijon	10	Team ATS	M	3.0 ATS D5-Cosworth V8	3 laps behind	25/29
9	ITALIAN GP	Monza	10	Team ATS	M	3.0 ATS D5-Cosworth V8	2 laps behind	25/30
dnq	CAESARS PALACE GP	Las Vegas	10	Team ATS	M	3.0 ATS D5-Cosworth V8		29/30

1983 Championship position: Unplaced

14*	BRAZILIAN GP	Rio	17	RAM Automotive Team March	P	3.0 March RAM 01-Cosworth V8	*13th place car dsq/4 laps behind	26/27
ret	US GP WEST	Long Beach	17	RAM Automotive Team March	P	3.0 March RAM 01-Cosworth V8	gear linkage	25/28
dnq	FRENCH GP	Paul Ricard	17	RAM Automotive Team March	P	3.0 March RAM 01-Cosworth V8		27/29
dnq	SAN MARINO GP	Imola	17	RAM Automotive Team March	P	3.0 March RAM 01-Cosworth V8		27/28
dnq	MONACO GP	Monte Carlo	17	RAM Automotive Team March	P	3.0 March RAM 01-Cosworth V8		25/28
dnq	BELGIAN GP	Spa	17	RAM Automotive Team March	P	3.0 March RAM 01-Cosworth V8		28/28

GP Starts: 24   GP Wins: 0   Pole positions: 0   Fastest laps: 0   Points: 3

SALO, Mika (SF) b 25/9/1967, Helsinki

1994 Championship position: Unplaced

	Race	Circuit	No	Entrant	Tyres	Capacity/Car/Engine	Comment	Q Pos/Entries
10	JAPANESE GP	Suzuka	11	Team Lotus	G	3.5 Lotus 109-Mugen Honda V10	1 lap behind	25/28
ret	AUSTRALIAN GP	Adelaide	11	Team Lotus	G	3.5 Lotus 109-Mugen Honda V10	electrics	22/28

1995 Championship position: 14th=   Wins: 0   Pole positions: 0   Fastest laps: 0   Points scored: 5

7	BRAZILIAN GP	Interlagos	4	Nokia Tyrrell Yamaha	G	3.0 Tyrrell 023-Yamaha V10	2 laps behind	12/26
ret	ARGENTINE GP	Buenos Aires	4	Nokia Tyrrell Yamaha	G	3.0 Tyrrell 023-Yamaha V10	collision with Suzuki	7/26
ret	SAN MARINO GP	Imola	4	Nokia Tyrrell Yamaha	G	3.0 Tyrrell 023-Yamaha V10	engine	13/26
10	SPANISH GP	Barcelona	4	Nokia Tyrrell Yamaha	G	3.0 Tyrrell 023-Yamaha V10	1 lap behind	13/26
ret	MONACO GP	Monte Carlo	4	Nokia Tyrrell Yamaha	G	3.0 Tyrrell 023-Yamaha V10	started from pitlane/engine	17/26
7	CANADIAN GP	Montreal	4	Nokia Tyrrell Yamaha	G	3.0 Tyrrell 023-Yamaha V10	1 lap behind	15/24
15	FRENCH GP	Magny Cours	4	Nokia Tyrrell Yamaha	G	3.0 Tyrrell 023-Yamaha V10	3 laps behind	14/24
8	BRITISH GP	Silverstone	4	Nokia Tyrrell Yamaha	G	3.0 Tyrrell 023-Yamaha V10	1 lap behind	23/24
ret	GERMAN GP	Hockenheim	4	Nokia Tyrrell Yamaha	G	3.0 Tyrrell 023-Yamaha V10	clutch	13/24
ret	HUNGARIAN GP	Hungaroring	4	Nokia Tyrrell Yamaha	G	3.0 Tyrrell 023-Yamaha V10	throttle	16/24
8	BELGIAN GP	Spa	4	Nokia Tyrrell Yamaha	G	3.0 Tyrrell 023-Yamaha V10		11/24
5	ITALIAN GP	Monza	4	Nokia Tyrrell Yamaha	G	3.0 Tyrrell 023-Yamaha V10	1 lap behind	16/24
13	PORTUGUESE GP	Estoril	4	Nokia Tyrrell Yamaha	G	3.0 Tyrrell 023-Yamaha V10	2 laps behind	15/24
10	EUROPEAN GP	Nürburgring	4	Nokia Tyrrell Yamaha	G	3.0 Tyrrell 023-Yamaha V10	3 laps behind	15/24
12	PACIFIC GP	T.I. Circuit	4	Nokia Tyrrell Yamaha	G	3.0 Tyrrell 023-Yamaha V10	3 laps behind	18/24
6	JAPANESE GP	Suzuka	4	Nokia Tyrrell Yamaha	G	3.0 Tyrrell 023-Yamaha V10	1 lap behind	14/24
5	AUSTRALIAN GP	Adelaide	4	Nokia Tyrrell Yamaha	G	3.0 Tyrrell 023-Yamaha V10	3 laps behind	14/24

1996 Championship position: 13th   Wins: 0   Pole positions: 0   Fastest laps: 0   Points scored: 5

6	AUSTRALIAN GP	Melbourne	19	Tyrrell Yamaha	G	3.0 Tyrrell 024-Yamaha V10	3 laps behind	10/22
5	BRAZILIAN GP	Interlagos	19	Tyrrell Yamaha	G	3.0 Tyrrell 024-Yamaha V10	1 lap behind	11/22
ret	ARGENTINE GP	Buenos Aires	19	Tyrrell Yamaha	G	3.0 Tyrrell 024-Yamaha V10	throttle	16/22
dsq*	EUROPEAN GP	Nürburgring	19	Tyrrell Yamaha	G	3.0 Tyrrell 024-Yamaha V10	*10th but disqualified – car underweight	14/22
ret	SAN MARINO GP	Imola	19	Tyrrell Yamaha	G	3.0 Tyrrell 024-Yamaha V10	engine	8/22
5/ret	MONACO GP	Monte Carlo	19	Tyrrell Yamaha	G	3.0 Tyrrell 024-Yamaha V10	collison with Irvine & Häkikinen/-5 laps	11/22
dsq*	SPANISH GP	Barcelona	19	Tyrrell Yamaha	G	3.0 Tyrrell 024-Yamaha V10	*switched to spare car before start	12/22
ret	CANADIAN GP	Montreal	19	Tyrrell Yamaha	G	3.0 Tyrrell 024-Yamaha V10	engine	14/22
10	FRENCH GP	Magny Cours	19	Tyrrell Yamaha	G	3.0 Tyrrell 024-Yamaha V10	2 laps behind	14/22
7	BRITISH GP	Silverstone	19	Tyrrell Yamaha	G	3.0 Tyrrell 024-Yamaha V10	1 lap behind	14/22
9	GERMAN GP	Hockenheim	19	Tyrrell Yamaha	G	3.0 Tyrrell 024-Yamaha V10	1 laps behind	15/20
ret	HUNGARIAN GP	Hungaroring	19	Tyrrell Yamaha	G	3.0 Tyrrell 024-Yamaha V10	collision with Diniz	16/20
7	BELGIAN GP	Spa	19	Tyrrell Yamaha	G	3.0 Tyrrell 024-Yamaha V10		13/20
ret	ITALIAN GP	Monza	19	Tyrrell Yamaha	G	3.0 Tyrrell 024-Yamaha V10	engine	17/20
11	PORTUGUESE GP	Estoril	19	Tyrrell Yamaha	G	3.0 Tyrrell 024-Yamaha V10	1 lap behind	13/20
ret	JAPANESE GP	Suzuka	19	Tyrrell Yamaha	G	3.0 Tyrrell 024-Yamaha V10	engine	15/20

1997 Championship position: 16th=   Wins: 0   Pole positions: 0   Fastest laps: 0   Points scored: 2

ret	AUSTRALIAN GP	Melbourne	19	Tyrrell	G	3.0 Tyrrell 025-Ford ED4 V8	engine	18/24
13	BRAZILIAN GP	Interlagos	19	Tyrrell	G	3.0 Tyrrell 025-Ford ED4 V8	1 lap behind	22/22

MIKA SALO

MIKA SALO could easily have been the forgotten of the two Mikas following a hard-fought British Formula 3 championship in 1990, when the Finn from Helsinki pushed rival Mika Häkkinen all the way in the battle for the title. The champion was snapped up by Lotus, while, despite six wins to his credit, Salo was left without sufficient backing even to scrape up a ride in European F3000.

It must have been a choker for the uninhibited Salo, who had an almost unbroken list of successes in karts and FF1600 behind him in Scandinavia, but at least he had the lifeline of employment in Japan, testing and racing on behalf of Yokohama. Running on these tyres in the All-Japan F3000 championship failed to produce the most spectacular of results, but in his four-year stay in the Far East Mika built up a massive amount of experience. Thus he was ideally placed to step into a vacant seat at Lotus for the 1994 Japanese GP, where he seized his big chance to shine in a poor car, finishing tenth in the appalling race conditions without once making an error. From forgotten man, suddenly he was in demand and, when it became clear that Lotus had finally closed its doors, he joined Tyrrell for the 1995 season.

A sensational debut in Brazil could have yielded points but for Mika suffering cramp, and he spent the rest of the season overshadowing his team-mate, Ukyo Katayama. There were plenty of rough edges and his driving tactics were sometimes a little questionable, but he plugged on in a disappointing car to take three points-scoring finishes in the last six races. Undoubtedly the maturing Finn had the speed to go much further up the grand prix ladder, but after a bright start to the 1996 season, he found himself wondering if he could even finish a race, let alone challenge for a worthwhile result, given the fragility of the Yamaha engine.

Locked into a three-year deal with Tyrrell, Salo was joined in 1997 by the equally hungry Jos Verstappen. The young lions had customer Ford power, which increased reliability, but at the price of straight-line speed. When circumstances presented Mika with a chance to score points with the Tyrrell at Monaco, he drove a brilliant non-stop race to take fifth place and emphasise that his talent was largely being wasted.

It was something of a sideways move for Salo when he switched to Arrows for 1998 to replace Damon Hill. For the Finn, it was much the same situation as at Tyrrell – tidy, but none-too-quick machinery with questionable reliability. A fourth place was achieved at Monaco in the black car, but no other top-six finishes were forthcoming. With the team needing to take paying drivers for 1999, Salo found himself on the sidelines, but that meant he was free to take over from Ricardo Zonta at BAR for three races after the Brazilian sustained a foot injury. Then he was rapidly called back into action, this time with Ferrari, and he certainly made a lasting impression in the German Grand Prix, where he had total control of the race before moving aside to let team-mate Eddie Irvine take the ten points in his championship quest.

Mika's selflessness no doubt played a big part in him being offered a seat at Sauber for 2000, when he faced a reality check after his short substitute role for the Prancing Horse. Tenth in the championship was not enough to persuade him to stay on for 2001, however, despite overtures from the Swiss team to do so. Instead he signed with Toyota to spend a year testing for the Japanese car giant prior to their grand prix debut in 2002. Salo made a promising start, finishing sixth in the Australian GP, and scored another point in Brazil that brought high expectations. A poor run of results thereafter led the team management to heap the blame on the drivers, and both Salo and team-mate Allan McNish were paid off in short order.

Following Toyota's decision, Salo announced his retirement from F1 and turned his attention to other areas of the sport. In 2003, his single-seater career came to an end, despite having impressed in a handful of outings in America's then fading Champ Car World Series with former BAR employer Craig Pollock's PK Racing team.

Salo continued to compete instead in various sports cars. An attempt to win at Le Mans with Audi UK in 2003 failed when team-mate Frank Biela was forced to retire the R8 after running out of fuel. The Finn found a new niche in the GT class, helping to guide the GPC Giesse team to second in the 2004 Spa 24-hours while also developing the all-new Maserati MC12, a car he went on to debut, and win with, in the FIA GT Championship.

In mid-2006, Salo moved his family to Houston and joined the Risi Competizione team to compete in the GT2 class of the American Le Mans Series with a Ferrari 430GT. He was paired with Brazilian Jaime Melo, and the duo took the class win at Salt Lake City. Risi set their sights on winning the GT2 ALMS championship in 2007, and the pair took eight class wins on their way to the crown.

The following year was not so successful, with Porsche taking over, but Salo had the satisfaction of a GT2 class win at Le Mans, sharing the Risi Ferrari 430 with Gianmaria Bruni and Melo. A feat he repeated the following year, this time with Melo and Pierre Kaffer.

Subsequently, Salo flirted with the idea of racing in NASCAR, but got no further than a test. He returned to Europe and in 2011 resumed his commentator's role for Finnish TV.

8	ARGENTINE GP	Buenos Aires	19	Tyrrell	G	3.0 Tyrrell 025-Ford ED4 V8	*1 lap behind*	19/22
9	SAN MARINO GP	Imola	19	Tyrrell	G	3.0 Tyrrell 025-Ford ED4 V8	*2 laps behind*	19/22
5	MONACO GP	Monte Carlo	19	Tyrrell	G	3.0 Tyrrell 025-Ford ED4 V8	*ran without pit stop in rain*	14/22
ret	SPANISH GP	Barcelona	19	Tyrrell	G	3.0 Tyrrell 025-Ford ED4 V8	*puncture*	14/22
ret	CANADIAN GP	Montreal	19	Tyrrell	G	3.0 Tyrrell 025-Ford ED4 V8	*engine*	17/22
ret	FRENCH GP	Magny Cours	19	Tyrrell	G	3.0 Tyrrell 025-Ford ED4 V8	*engine*	19/22
ret	BRITISH GP	Silverstone	19	Tyrrell	G	3.0 Tyrrell 025-Ford ED4 V8	*engine*	18/22
ret	GERMAN GP	Hockenheim	19	Tyrrell	G	3.0 Tyrrell 025-Ford ED4 V8	*clutch*	19/22
13	HUNGARIAN GP	Hungaroring	19	Tyrrell	G	3.0 Tyrrell 025-Ford ED4 V8	*2 laps behind*	21/22
11*	BELGIAN GP	Spa	19	Tyrrell	G	3.0 Tyrrell 025-Ford ED4 V8	**3rd place car disqualified/-1 lap*	19/22
ret	ITALIAN GP	Monza	19	Tyrrell	G	3.0 Tyrrell 025-Ford ED4 V8	*engine*	19/22
ret	AUSTRIAN GP	A1-Ring	19	Tyrrell	G	3.0 Tyrrell 025-Ford ED4 V8	*transmission*	21/22
10	LUXEMBOURG GP	Nürburgring	19	Tyrrell	G	3.0 Tyrrell 025-Ford ED4 V8	*1 lap behind*	20/22
ret	JAPANESE GP	Suzuka	19	Tyrrell	G	3.0 Tyrrell 025-Ford ED4 V8	*engine*	22/22
12	EUROPEAN GP	Jerez	19	Tyrrell	G	3.0 Tyrrell 025-Ford ED4 V8	*1 lap behind*	21/22

1998 Championship position: 13=   Wins: 0   Pole positions: 0   Fastest laps: 0   Points scored: 3

ret	AUSTRALIAN GP	Melbourne	17	Danka Zepter Arrows	B	3.0 Arrows A19-V10	*electrics*	16/22
ret	BRAZILIAN GP	Interlagos	17	Danka Zepter Arrows	B	3.0 Arrows A19-V10	*engine*	20/22
ret	ARGENTINE GP	Buenos Aires	17	Danka Zepter Arrows	B	3.0 Arrows A19-V10	*gearbox*	17/22
9	SAN MARINO GP	Imola	17	Danka Zepter Arrows	B	3.0 Arrows A19-V10	*2 laps behind*	14/22
ret	SPANISH GP	Barcelona	17	Danka Zepter Arrows	B	3.0 Arrows A19-V10	*engine*	17/22
4	MONACO GP	Monte Carlo	17	Danka Zepter Arrows	B	3.0 Arrows A19-V10		8/22
ret	CANADIAN GP	Montreal	17	Danka Zepter Arrows	B	3.0 Arrows A19-V10	*crashed*	17/22
13	FRENCH GP	Magny Cours	17	Danka Zepter Arrows	B	3.0 Arrows A19-V10	*2 laps behind*	19/22
ret	BRITISH GP	Silverstone	17	Danka Zepter Arrows	B	3.0 Arrows A19-V10	*spun off*	14/22
ret	AUSTRIAN GP	A1-Ring	17	Danka Zepter Arrows	B	3.0 Arrows A19-V10	*collision damage*	6/22
14	GERMAN GP	Hockenheim	17	Danka Zepter Arrows	B	3.0 Arrows A19-V10	*1 lap behind*	17/22
ret	HUNGARIAN GP	Hungaroring	17	Danka Zepter Arrows	B	3.0 Arrows A19-V10	*hydraulic leak*	13/22
ret/dns	BELGIAN GP	Spa	17	Danka Zepter Arrows	B	3.0 Arrows A19-V10	*accident at first start*	18/22
ret	ITALIAN GP	Monza	17	Danka Zepter Arrows	B	3.0 Arrows A19-V10	*hydraulics*	16/22
14	LUXEMBOURG GP	Nürburgring	17	Danka Zepter Arrows	B	3.0 Arrows A19-V10	*2 laps behind*	16/22
ret	JAPANESE GP	Suzuka	17	Danka Zepter Arrows	B	3.0 Arrows A19-V10	*hydraulics*	15/22

1999 Championship position: 10th   Wins: 0   Pole positions: 0   Fastest laps: 0   Points scored: 10

7/ret	SAN MARINO GP	Imola	23	British American Racing	B	3.0 BAR 01-Supertec V10	*electrics/2 laps behind*	19/22
ret	MONACO GP	Monte Carlo	23	British American Racing	B	3.0 BAR 01-Supertec V10	*brakes*	12/22
8	SPANISH GP	Barcelona	23	British American Racing	B	3.0 BAR 01-Supertec V10	*1 lap behind*	16/22
9	AUSTRIAN GP	A1-Ring	3	Scuderia Marlboro Ferrari	B	3.0 Ferrari F399-V10	*1 lap behind*	7/22
2	GERMAN GP	Hockenheim	3	Scuderia Marlboro Ferrari	B	3.0 Ferrari F399-V10	*led race – allowed Irvine through to win*	4/22
12	HUNGARIAN GP	Hungaroring	3	Scuderia Marlboro Ferrari	B	3.0 Ferrari F399-V10	*2 laps behind*	18/22
7	BELGIAN GP	Spa	3	Scuderia Marlboro Ferrari	B	3.0 Ferrari F399-V10		9/22
3	ITALIAN GP	Monza	3	Scuderia Marlboro Ferrari	B	3.0 Ferrari F399-V10		6/22
ret	EUROPEAN GP	Nürburgring	3	Scuderia Marlboro Ferrari	B	3.0 Ferrari F399-V10	*brakes*	12/22

2000 Championship position: 10th=   Wins: 0   Pole positions: 0   Fastest laps: 0   Points scored: 6

dsq	AUSTRALIAN GP	Melbourne	17	Red Bull Sauber Petronas	B	3.0 Sauber C19-Petronas V10	*6th – but dsq for illegal front wing*	10/22
dns	BRAZILIAN GP	Interlagos	17	Red Bull Sauber Petronas	B	3.0 Sauber C19-Petronas V10	*cars withdrawn after wing failures*	22/22
6	SAN MARINO GP	Imola	17	Red Bull Sauber Petronas	B	3.0 Sauber C19-Petronas V10	*1 lap behind*	12/22
8	BRITISH GP	Silverstone	17	Red Bull Sauber Petronas	B	3.0 Sauber C19-Petronas V10	*understeer/1 lap behind*	18/22
7	SPANISH GP	Barcelona	17	Red Bull Sauber Petronas	B	3.0 Sauber C19-Petronas V10	*1 lap behind*	13/22
ret	EUROPEAN GP	Nürburgring	17	Red Bull Sauber Petronas	B	3.0 Sauber C19-Petronas V10	*driveshaft*	20/22
5	MONACO GP	Monte Carlo	17	Red Bull Sauber Petronas	B	3.0 Sauber C19-Petronas V10		13/22
ret	CANADIAN GP	Montreal	17	Red Bull Sauber Petronas	B	3.0 Sauber C19-Petronas V10	*engine*	15/22
10	FRENCH GP	Magny Cours	17	Red Bull Sauber Petronas	B	3.0 Sauber C19-Petronas V10	*1 lap behind*	12/22
6	AUSTRIAN GP	A1-Ring	17	Red Bull Sauber Petronas	B	3.0 Sauber C19-Petronas V10	*1 lap behind*	9/22
5	GERMAN GP	Hockenheim	17	Red Bull Sauber Petronas	B	3.0 Sauber C19-Petronas V10		15/22
10	HUNGARIAN GP	Hungaroring	17	Red Bull Sauber Petronas	B	3.0 Sauber C19-Petronas V10	*1 lap behind*	9/22
9	BELGIAN GP	Spa	17	Red Bull Sauber Petronas	B	3.0 Sauber C19-Petronas V10		18/22
7	ITALIAN GP	Monza	17	Red Bull Sauber Petronas	B	3.0 Sauber C19-Petronas V10		15/22
ret	UNITED STATES GP	Indianapolis	17	Red Bull Sauber Petronas	B	3.0 Sauber C19-Petronas V10	*spun off*	14/22
10	JAPANESE GP	Suzuka	17	Red Bull Sauber Petronas	B	3.0 Sauber C19-Petronas V10	*1 lap behind*	19/22
8	MALAYSIAN GP	Sepang	17	Red Bull Sauber Petronas	B	3.0 Sauber C19-Petronas V10	*1 lap behind*	17/22

2002 Championship position: 15th=   Wins: 0   Pole positions: 0   Fastest laps: 0   Points scored: 2

6	AUSTRALIAN GP	Melbourne	24	Panasonic Toyota Racing	M	3.0 Toyota TF102-V10	*2 laps behind*	14/22
12	MALAYSIAN GP	Sepang	24	Panasonic Toyota Racing	M	3.0 Toyota TF102-V10	*traction control problem/3 laps behind*	10/22
6	BRAZILIAN GP	Interlagos	24	Panasonic Toyota Racing	M	3.0 Toyota TF102-V10	*1 lap behind*	10/22
ret	SAN MARINO GP	Imola	24	Panasonic Toyota Racing	M	3.0 Toyota TF102-V10	*gearbox*	16/22
9	SPANISH GP	Barcelona	24	Panasonic Toyota Racing	M	3.0 Toyota TF102-V10	*puncture/1 lap behind*	17/22
8	AUSTRIAN GP	A1-Ring	24	Panasonic Toyota Racing	M	3.0 Toyota TF102-V10		10/22
ret	MONACO GP	Monte Carlo	24	Panasonic Toyota Racing	M	3.0 Toyota TF102-V10	*accident*	9/22
ret	CANADIAN GP	Montreal	24	Panasonic Toyota Racing	M	3.0 Toyota TF102-V10	*brakes*	18/22
ret	EUROPEAN GP	Nürburgring	24	Panasonic Toyota Racing	M	3.0 Toyota TF102-V10	*gearbox*	10/22
ret	BRITISH GP	Silverstone	24	Panasonic Toyota Racing	M	3.0 Toyota TF102-V10	*driveshaft*	8/22
ret	FRENCH GP	Magny Cours	24	Panasonic Toyota Racing	M	3.0 Toyota TF102-V10	*engine*	16/22
9	GERMAN GP	Hockenheim	24	Panasonic Toyota Racing	M	3.0 Toyota TF102-V10	*1 lap behind*	19/22
15	HUNGARIAN GP	Hungaroring	24	Panasonic Toyota Racing	M	3.0 Toyota TF102-V10	*penalty – pitlane infringement/-2 laps*	17/20
7	BELGIAN GP	Spa	24	Panasonic Toyota Racing	M	3.0 Toyota TF102-V10		9/22
11	ITALIAN GP	Monza	24	Panasonic Toyota Racing	M	3.0 Toyota TF102-V10	*drive-through penalty/1 lap behind*	10/20
14	UNITED STATES GP	Indianapolis	24	Panasonic Toyota Racing	M	3.0 Toyota TF102-V10	*2 laps behind*	19/20
8	JAPANESE GP	Suzuka	24	Panasonic Toyota Racing	M	3.0 Toyota TF102-V10	*1 lap behind*	13/20

GP Starts: 110   GP Wins: 0   Pole positions: 0   Fastest laps: 0   Points: 33

ROY SALVADORI

WHILE not possessing the talent of contemporaries Stirling Moss, Mike Hawthorn, Peter Collins and Tony Brooks, Roy Salvadori was a fine all-round driver, particularly in sports cars, who became a household name in Britain thanks to his many victories on home soil. Although born of Italian parents, Salvadori was very much a Londoner at heart, and he began racing for fun in 1946, before entering selected events the following year in an Alfa Romeo. Having decided to pursue a professional career, he sampled a variety of machines, including a Healey, a Jaguar and a Frazer Nash, on his way up the ladder.

In 1952, Roy campaigned a four-cylinder Ferrari in the British GP and a few other minor races, in addition to racing Tony Crook's Frazer Nash, but by then his sights were set on grand prix racing and he joined Connaught for the 1953 season. While he drew a blank in the world championship races, there were plenty of successful outings in national events. He was happy to compete in almost any type of machine and often took part in three or more races during a single race meeting.

Having joined Syd Greene to race his potent Maserati 250F, Salvadori again concentrated on events at home during 1954–56, but by then he was already a regular member of the Aston Martin sports car team, a role he would fulfill right to the end of their programme, which finished on such a high

note in 1959 when he shared the winning DBR1 at Le Mans with Carroll Shelby.

For 1957, Roy aligned himself with Cooper as they developed their rear-engined Formula 2 car in preparation for a full season of grands prix the following year. Fifth place in the British GP at Aintree put him among the championship points scorers for the first time, and in non-title races he took a second at Caen and a fourth at Reims. The 1958 season saw the Surbiton team's first sustained effort at the top level, and both Jack Brabham and Salvadori scored some excellent results. Roy's second place to Brooks in the German GP may have been distant, but it was a portent of even greater things to follow, but sadly he was not part of the great works Cooper triumph.

In 1959, Salvadori continued to drive Coopers in Formula 2, but for Tommy Atkins, his best result being a win in the London Trophy at Crystal Palace. Meanwhile, Aston Martin had ambitiously decided to embark on a grand prix programme of their own, and Roy would be one of the drivers. Crucially, however, they had adopted the traditional front-engined layout, which soon would be doomed to oblivion. Their cars were superbly crafted and beautifully turned out, but after Salvadori had scored a totally misleading second place in the International Trophy early in 1959, they proved to be a major disappointment. The engine just didn't possess enough power and, despite major modifications, the project was a hopeless failure, which drifted on into 1960, by which time the writing was well and truly on the wall.

The following season, Roy joined John Surtees in Reg Parnell's well-funded Yeoman Credit backed team racing Coopers. The Surbiton-built cars had had their day, however, as Colin Chapman had devoured every lesson they had offered and combined them with his own thinking to push his Lotus 18 and 21 models to the fore. Salvadori came as close as he ever would be to winning a grand prix at Watkins Glen that year; he was closing in on Innes Ireland's leading Lotus when his engine failed. The team had high hopes for 1962 with the new Lola chassis, but it was a desperately disappointing season for Salvadori, who was totally overshadowed by Surtees, almost being reduced to the role of hack driver. Wisely perhaps, he decided that grand prix success was beyond his reach, and he returned to sports and touring car racing with Tommy Atkins' Cooper Monaco, Shelby Cobra and Jaguar E-Type cars. Although his front-line career was behind him, there was no easing up in his driving style, for Roy had never taken any prisoners and he wasn't going to change his approach in the twilight of his career.

By the time he retired early in 1965, Salvadori had driven on most of the world's circuits. He knew the risks attendant on them, for he had seen many of his peers perish over his long career, and indeed had come perilously close to joining them on more than one occasion. He also knew his own worth, and the thought of racing without start money was anathema to him. After his driving days were over, he became the team manager at Cooper in 1966/67, before retiring to Monaco and an apartment overlooking the Monte Carlo circuit.

Until he was overtaken by ill health, Salvadori was a frequent visitor to historic festivals, and his apartment was always filled with old friends and colleagues at the end of May when the grand prix took over the principality.

SALVADORI, Roy (GB) b 12/5/1922, Dovercourt, Essex

1952 Championship position: Unplaced

	Race	Circuit	No	Entrant	Tyres	Capacity/Car/Engine	Comment	Q Pos/Entries
8	BRITISH GP	Silverstone	14	G Caprara	D	2.0 Ferrari 500 4	*3 laps behind*	19/32

1953 Championship position: Unplaced

	Race	Circuit	No	Entrant	Tyres	Capacity/Car/Engine	Comment	Q Pos/Entries
ret	DUTCH GP	Zandvoort	26	Connaught Engineering	D	2.0 Connaught A Type-Lea Francis 4	*engine*	11/20
ret	FRENCH GP	Reims	50	Connaught Engineering	D	2.0 Connaught A Type-Lea Francis 4	*ignition*	19/25
ret	BRITISH GP	Silverstone	12	Connaught Engineering	D	2.0 Connaught A Type-Lea Francis 4	*radius rod*	28/29
ret	GERMAN GP	Nürburgring	15	Connaught Engineering	D	2.0 Connaught A Type-Lea Francis 4	*engine*	13/35
ret	ITALIAN GP	Monza	22	Connaught Engineering	D	2.0 Connaught A Type-Lea Francis 4	*throttle cable*	14/30

1954 Championship position: Unplaced

	Race	Circuit	No	Entrant	Tyres	Capacity/Car/Engine	Comment	Q Pos/Entries
ret	FRENCH GP	Reims	44	Gilby Engineering Ltd	D	2.5 Maserati 250F 6	*driveshaft*	10/22
ret	BRITISH GP	Silverstone	5	Gilby Engineering Ltd	D	2.5 Maserati 250F 6	*gearbox*	7/31

1955 Championship position: Unplaced

	Race	Circuit	No	Entrant	Tyres	Capacity/Car/Engine	Comment	Q Pos/Entries
ret	BRITISH GP	Aintree	44	Gilby Engineering Ltd	D	2.5 Maserati 250F 6	*gearbox*	20/25

1956 Championship position: Unplaced

	Race	Circuit	No	Entrant	Tyres	Capacity/Car/Engine	Comment	Q Pos/Entries
ret	BRITISH GP	Silverstone	28	Gilby Engineering Ltd	D	2.5 Maserati 250F 6	*fuel starvation*	7/28
ret	GERMAN GP	Nürburgring	16	Gilby Engineering Ltd	D	2.5 Maserati 250F 6	*rear suspension*	9/21
nc	ITALIAN GP	Monza	44	Gilby Engineering Ltd	D	2.5 Maserati 250F 6	*9 laps behind*	14/26

1957 Championship position: 14th= Wins: 0 Pole positions: 0 Fastest laps: 0 Points scored: 2

	Race	Circuit	No	Entrant	Tyres	Capacity/Car/Engine	Comment	Q Pos/Entries
dnq	MONACO GP	Monte Carlo	8	Owen Racing Organisation	D	2.5 BRM P25 4		17/21
ret	FRENCH GP	Rouen	20	Vandervell Products Ltd	P	2.5 Vanwall 4	*engine*	6/15
5	BRITISH GP	Aintree	36	Cooper Car Co	D	2.0 Cooper T43-Climax 4	*5 laps behind*	14/19
ret	GERMAN GP (F2)	Nürburgring	23	Cooper Car Co	D	1.5 Cooper T43-Climax 4	*suspension*	14/24
ret	PESCARA GP	Pescara	22	Cooper Car Co	D	1.5 Cooper T43-Climax 4	*suspension*	15/16

1958 Championship position: 4th Wins: 0 Pole positions: 0 Fastest laps: 0 Points scored: 15

	Race	Circuit	No	Entrant	Tyres	Capacity/Car/Engine	Comment	Q Pos/Entries
ret	MONACO GP	Monte Carlo	18	Cooper Car Co	D	2.0 Cooper T45-Climax 4	*gearbox*	4/28
4	DUTCH GP	Zandvoort	7	Cooper Car Co	D	2.2 Cooper T45-Climax 4	*1 lap behind*	9/17
8	BELGIAN GP	Spa	24	Cooper Car Co	D	2.0 Cooper T45-Climax 4	*1 lap behind*	13/20
nc	FRENCH GP	Reims	20	Cooper Car Co	D	2.0 Cooper T45-Climax 4	*clutch slip/13 laps behind*	14/21
3	BRITISH GP	Silverstone	10	Cooper Car Co	D	2.2 Cooper T45-Climax 4		3/21
2	GERMAN GP	Nürburgring	10	Cooper Car Co	D	2.2 Cooper T45-Climax 4		6/26
9	PORTUGUESE GP	Oporto	16	Cooper Car Co	D	2.0 Cooper T45-Climax 4	*4 laps behind*	11/15
5	ITALIAN GP	Monza	6	Cooper Car Co	D	2.2 Cooper T45-Climax 4	*8 laps behind*	14/21
7	MOROCCAN GP	Casablanca	30	Cooper Car Co	D	2.2 Cooper T45-Climax 4	*2 laps behind*	14/25

1959 Championship position: Unplaced

	Race	Circuit	No	Entrant	Tyres	Capacity/Car/Engine	Comment	Q Pos/Entries
ret	MONACO GP	Monte Carlo	38	High Efficiency Motors	D	2.5 Cooper T45-Maserati 4	*transmisssion/17 laps behind*	8/24

The landscape at Eau Rouge has changed remarkably little over the 50-plus years since this photo was taken, showing Roy Salvadori's Cooper leading the BRM of Harry Schell. One obstacle long removed, however, is the metal bus stop positioned a mere yard or so from the track.

ret	DUTCH GP	Zandvoort	4	David Brown Corporation	A	2.5 Aston Martin DBR4/250 6	overheating	13/15
ret	FRENCH GP	Reims	16	High Efficiency Motors	D	2.5 Cooper T45-Maserati 4	engine	16/22
6	BRITISH GP	Aintree	2	David Brown Corporation	A	2.5 Aston Martin DBR4/250 6	1 lap behind	2/30
6	PORTUGUESE GP	Monsanto	10	David Brown Corporation	A	2.5 Aston Martin DBR4/250 6	3 laps behind	12/16
ret	ITALIAN GP	Monza	24	David Brown Corporation	A	2.5 Aston Martin DBR4/250 6	engine	17/21
ret	US GP	Sebring	12	High Efficiency Motors	D	2.5 Cooper T45-Maserati 4	transmission	11/19

1960 Championship position: Unplaced

ret	MONACO GP	Monte Carlo	14	High Efficiency Motors	D	2.5 Cooper T51-Climax 4	overheating	12/24
dns	DUTCH GP	Zandvoort	17	David Brown Corporation	D	2.5 Aston Martin DBR4/250 6	dispute over starting money	(20)/21
ret	BRITISH GP	Silverstone	18	David Brown Corporation	D	2.5 Aston Martin DBR4/250 6	steering	13/25
8	US GP	Riverside	14	High Efficiency Motors	D	2.5 Cooper T51-Climax 4	2 laps behind	15/23

1961 Championship position: 17th   Wins: 0   Pole positions: 0   Fastest laps: 0   Points scored: 2

8	FRENCH GP	Reims	42	Yeoman Credit Racing Team	D	1.5 Cooper T53-Climax 4	1 lap behind	15/26
6	BRITISH GP	Aintree	36	Yeoman Credit Racing Team	D	1.5 Cooper T53-Climax 4		13/30
10	GERMAN GP	Nürburgring	19	Yeoman Credit Racing Team	D	1.5 Cooper T53-Climax 4		15/27
6	ITALIAN GP	Monza	40	Yeoman Credit Racing Team	D	1.5 Cooper T53-Climax 4	1 lap behind	=17/33
ret	US GP	Watkins Glen	19	Yeoman Credit Racing Team	D	1.5 Cooper T53-Climax 4	engine when 2nd	12/19

1962 Championship position: Unplaced

ret	DUTCH GP	Zandvoort	20	Bowmaker Racing Team	D	1.5 Lola Mk4-Climax V8	withdrawn after Surtees' crash	17/20
ret	MONACO GP	Monte Carlo	26	Bowmaker Racing Team	D	1.5 Lola Mk4-Climax V8	suspension	12/21
ret	FRENCH GP	Rouen	20	Bowmaker Racing Team	D	1.5 Lola Mk4-Climax V8	oil pressure	14/17
ret	BRITISH GP	Aintree	26	Bowmaker Racing Team	D	1.5 Lola Mk4-Climax V8	battery	=11/21
ret	GERMAN GP	Nürburgring	15	Bowmaker Racing Team	D	1.5 Lola Mk4-Climax V8	gearbox	9/30
ret	ITALIAN GP	Monza	44	Bowmaker Racing Team	D	1.5 Lola Mk4-Climax V8	engine	13/30
dns	US GP	Watkins Glen	19	Bowmaker Racing Team	D	1.5 Lola Mk4-Climax V8	Surtees drove car	(11)/20
ret	SOUTH AFRICAN GP	Kyalami	7	Bowmaker Racing Team	D	1.5 Lola Mk4-Climax V8	fuel leak –split tank	11/17

GP Starts: 47   GP Wins: 0   Pole positions: 0   Fastest laps: 0   Points: 19

SANESI, Consalvo (I) b 28/3/1911, Terranuova Bracciolini, Arezzo – d 28/7/1998 Milan

1950 Championship position: Championship position: 4th   Wins: 0   Pole positions: 0   Fastest laps: 0   Points scored: 15

	Race	Circuit	No	Entrant	Tyres	Capacity/Car/Engine	Comment	Q Pos/Entries
ret	ITALIAN GP	Monza	46	Scuderia Alfa Romeo SpA	P	1.5 s/c Alfa Romeo 158 8	engine	4/27

1951 Championship position: 10th=   Wins: 0   Pole positions: 0   Fastest laps: 0   Points scored: 3

4	SWISS GP	Bremgarten	28	Scuderia Alfa Romeo SpA	P	1.5 s/c Alfa Romeo 159 8	1 lap behind	4/21
ret	BELGIAN GP	Spa	6	Scuderia Alfa Romeo SpA	P	1.5 s/c Alfa Romeo 159 8	radiator	6/13
10	FRENCH GP	Reims	6	Scuderia Alfa Romeo SpA	P	1.5 s/c Alfa Romeo 159 8	pushed car to finish/19 laps behind	5/23
6	BRITISH GP	Silverstone	3	Scuderia Alfa Romeo SpA	P	1.5 s/c Alfa Romeo 159 8	6 laps behind	6/20

GP Starts: 5   GP Wins: 0   Pole positions: 0   Fastest laps: 0   Points: 3

CONSALVO SANESI

A MODEST and retiring man, Consalvo Sanesi joined Alfa Romeo as first an engineer and then a travelling mechanic, before being promoted to the role of test driver. He carried out his duties assiduously before finally taking the wheel in competition.

After the Second World War, Sanesi returned to his main role as a test driver for Alfa Romeo, but he was also given numerous opportunities to drive the superb Tipo 158/159-series cars in races. In 1946, he won his heat and finished third in the Milan GP, while in 1947 he was second to Achille Varzi at Bari and third in the Italian GP held at Sempione Park, after claiming pole position.

The following year saw Consalvo take second place in the French GP and third with fastest lap at the Monza Autodrome GP. In 1949, Alfa Corse did not compete in Formula 1, although Sanesi finished second in the touring car class in the Mille Miglia with an Alfa. When the team returned in 1950, he drove in only one grand prix, but won the Coppa Inter Europa sports car race at Monza.

Consalvo had his most active grand prix season in 1951, scoring points in two of his four starts, but after Alfa's withdrawal from grand prix racing at the end of the year, he concentrated fully on sports cars, winning his class in the 1954 Carrera Panamericana. A testing accident later that year with the Disco Volante left him with serious injuries, but he returned to competition in 1955, taking second place in the Verminico hill-climb with a 1.9 Alfa.

In 1964, when aged nearly 53, Sanesi shared a Scuderia Sant Ambroeuse Alfa Romeo 1600TZ with Roberto Businello and was very fortunate to escape with his life. In the middle of the night, his car was running slowly past the pits with no rear lights when he was hit from behind by a faster Cobra driven by Dick Johnson. The Alfa slammed into a concrete wall and exploded into flames. Luckily, Consalvo was swiftly rescued by Jocko Maggiocommo, a brave member of the Renault team, who pulled him from the inferno. Both received burns, but made full recoveries. Sanesi never raced again.

STÉPHANE SARRAZIN

WINNING the Pilote Elf award for the 1993 season was the launch pad for Stéphane Sarrazin to swiftly climb the French motorsport ladder. He won the Formule Renault title in 1995, and then made his mark in French F3 during 1996 and, in particular, 1997, when he finished second in the final standings, behind Patrice Gay. His performances earned him a seat in the Apomatox-run Prost Junior Team for 1998, and he kicked off his F3000 career with a superb win in the wet at Oschersleben. Unfortunately, his season slid away somewhat after that, but nonetheless he retained his place for 1999.

Before the series got under way, Sarrazin was elevated to the grand prix ranks when Minardi called him up at short notice to deputise for the injured Luca Badoer. With no testing, the Frenchman acquitted himself extremely well on his grand prix debut, but his race ended dramatically when his car suffered a stuck throttle.

Back in F3000, Stéphane took a single win at the Hungaroring, but it was series champion Nick Heidfeld who was given the nod for the vacant Prost Grand Prix seat for 2000. It had been thought that the Frenchman was being groomed for this place, and a disappointed Sarrazin elected to take over Heidfeld's prized West Competition drive to compete for a third year in the FIA F3000 series. This move failed to work for both parties and they soon parted company, Stéphane taking up testing duties back with Prost in 2001 and then with Toyota the following year. He had another crack at single-seater racing in 2003 in the Nissan World Series, achieving two victories, and also joined up with Pescarolo Sport to win the Spa 1000km.

Sarrazin then chose the unusual step of moving into rallying, initially in the French series, which he won at the first attempt with Subaru. He also took part in three WRC events, taking a stage win in the Rally of Catalunya, and finished as top privateer in all of them. His performances brought a works Impreza drive for 2005, when the Frenchman took a fourth overall on the Rally of Corsica, but he also found time to join Aston Martin for three races, taking a third in the GT class at Le Mans.

In 2006, Stéphane restricted his rally appearances to just four asphalt events, allowing him to concentrate on a full ALMS season with Aston Martin. Taking three GT1 class wins, he was second overall in that class of the drivers' championship and was awarded the Rookie of the Year title. For 2007, he and Aston Martin partner Pedro Lamy joined the powerful works Peugeot squad to win the Le Mans Series and take second place in the Le Mans 24-hours. The following year, Sarrazin and Lamy gained another two wins, at Monza and the Nürburgring, but could not prevent Audi from taking the title. The versatile Frenchman continued his successful rally exploits by taking third place in the 2009 Monte Carlo Rally in a Peugeot 207, while at Le Mans he had to settle for second place once again, behind the sister car after Audi were toppled at last.

SARRAZIN, Stéphane (F) b 2/11/1974, Alès

1999 Championship position: Unplaced									
	Race	Circuit	No	Entrant	Tyres	Capacity/Car/Engine	Comment		Q Pos/Entries
ret	BRAZILIAN GP	Interlagos	20	Fondmetal Minardi Ford	B	3.0 Minardi M01-Ford Zetec R V10	accident – stuck throttle		17/22
GP Starts: 1 GP Wins: 0 Pole positions: 0 Fastest laps: 0 Points: 0									

SATO, Takuma (J) b 28/1/1977, Tokyo

	Race	Circuit	No	Entrant	Tyres	Capacity/Car/Engine	Comment	Q Pos/Entries
2002 Championship position: 15th= Wins: 0 Pole positions: 0 Fastest laps: 0 Points scored: 2								
ret	AUSTRALIAN GP	Melbourne	10	DHL Jordan Honda	B	3.0 Jordan EJ12-Honda V10	*outside 107% time/electronics	*22/22
9	MALAYSIAN GP	Sepang	10	DHL Jordan Honda	B	3.0 Jordan EJ12-Honda V10	1 lap behind	15/22
9	BRAZILIAN GP	Interlagos	10	DHL Jordan Honda	B	3.0 Jordan EJ12-Honda V10	2 laps behind	19/22
ret	SAN MARINO GP	Imola	10	DHL Jordan Honda	B	3.0 Jordan EJ12-Honda V10	gearbox	14/22
ret	SPANISH GP	Barcelona	10	DHL Jordan Honda	B	3.0 Jordan EJ12-Honda V10	spun off	18/21
ret	AUSTRIAN GP	A1-Ring	10	DHL Jordan Honda	B	3.0 Jordan EJ12-Honda V10	hit by Heidfeld	18/22
ret	MONACO GP	Monte Carlo	10	DHL Jordan Honda	B	3.0 Jordan EJ12-Honda V10	accident – hit barrier	16/22
10	CANADIAN GP	Montreal	10	DHL Jordan Honda	B	3.0 Jordan EJ12-Honda V10	1 lap behind	15/22
16	EUROPEAN GP	Nürburgring	10	DHL Jordan Honda	B	3.0 Jordan EJ12-Honda V10	2 laps behind	14/22
ret	BRITISH GP	Silverstone	10	DHL Jordan Honda	B	3.0 Jordan EJ12-Honda V10	engine	14/22
ret	FRENCH GP	Magny Cours	10	DHL Jordan Honda	B	3.0 Jordan EJ12-Honda V10	spun off	14/21
8	GERMAN GP	Hockenheim	10	DHL Jordan Honda	B	3.0 Jordan EJ12-Honda V10	1 lap behind	12/22
10	HUNGARIAN GP	Hungaroring	10	DHL Jordan Honda	B	3.0 Jordan EJ12-Honda V10	1 lap behind	14/20
11	BELGIAN GP	Spa	10	DHL Jordan Honda	B	3.0 Jordan EJ12-Honda V10	1 lap behind	16/20
12	ITALIAN GP	Monza	10	DHL Jordan Honda	B	3.0 Jordan EJ12-Honda V10	1 lap behind	18/20
11	UNITED STATES GP	Indianapolis	10	DHL Jordan Honda	B	3.0 Jordan EJ12-Honda V10	1 lap behind	15/20
5	JAPANESE GP	Suzuka	10	DHL Jordan Honda	B	3.0 Jordan EJ12-Honda V10		7/20
2003 Championship position: 18th Wins: 0 Pole positions: 0 Fastest laps: 0 Points scored: 3								
6	JAPANESE GP	Suzuka	16	Lucky Strike BAR Honda	B	3.0 BAR 005-Honda V10	replaced Villeneuve	13/22

TAKUMA SATO

DESPITE the claims made by those who preceded him into the top flight, Takuma Sato was probably the most naturally talented – and spectacular – Japanese driver to reach Formula 1. His impetuosity counted against him too many times, however, and his big chance to join the elite passed by, leaving him to try to resurrect his career in the USA.

Uniquely, Sato's journey to the pinnacle of motorsport started on two wheels, but on pedal cycles rather than motorbikes. From what could have been a successful career as a bike racer, he deviated on to four wheels, scraping together enough money to buy a kart and, the following year, to enter Honda's Suzuka Racing School scholarship. Incredibly, given his lack of experience, he won the prize of a fully paid drive in the 1998 All-Japan Formula 3 Championship, but curiously decided to pass on the offer to pursue his dream of reaching Formula 1 via European competition.

Sato arrived in the UK to contest a part-season of Formula Vauxhall Junior and made enough of an impression to graduate to the Formula Opel Euroseries. In 1999, his first full year of car racing, he took sixth place in the hotly contested EFDA-run championship, before stepping up again to compete in Class B at the last few rounds of the British F3 championship. Having proved his ability to handle an F3 car, he joined the crack Carlin Motorsport squad to contest the full 2000 British F3 championship. Unfazed by the step up in standards, and by the level of competition, he won a total of five races and eventually claimed third overall in the championship. This earned him his first F1 tests with Jordan and British American Racing. The latter reacted first and signed him as a test driver, leaving him to gain further valuable experience with Carlin in Formula 3 for 2001. Starting the season as a clear favourite, the Japanese driver dominated

proceedings. He broke the record for the number of wins in a season, 12 from a possible 13 victories going his way, as well as first place in the Marlboro Masters at Zandvoort and the international race that supported the British Grand Prix. Sato ended his F3 career on a high when he won the Macau Grand Prix in November that year, taking victory in both the preliminary qualifying event and the main race.

After his impressive test outings for BAR, and courtesy of Honda, Sato ended the year with a seat in the top flight, alongside Giancarlo Fisichella at Jordan Grand Prix for 2002.

It proved to be a dramatic first year in the premier category, a series of stellar performances often punctuated by accidents, including notable incidents at Monaco and the A1-Ring, the latter putting him in hospital after his car was harpooned by Nick Heidfeld's Sauber. With the pressure on to produce something tangible from the year, however, he delivered on home ground, scoring his first F1 points for fifth place in a sensational race at Suzuka.

With Jordan reverting to Ford power in 2003, BAR reclaimed Sato as its third driver, and he proved central to the development of the Honda-powered 005 and 006 race cars. At the final race of the year, however, he was back in the limelight, having replaced the departed Jacques Villeneuve for his home race at Suzuka, and again scoring points, this time after a strong drive to sixth place.

When Honda took a bigger role in the team, Sato was assured of a full race seat alongside Jenson Button for 2004, and he enjoyed perhaps BAR's most competitive season to date. While the more experienced Button began to harvest podiums for the team, he set about diligently collecting points, and occasionally outperforming the Briton. He claimed his first podium at Indianapolis in the US GP, and added fourth places in both Italy and Japan for good measure, eventually racking up 34 points and eighth overall in the standings.

Sato remained with BAR and Honda into 2005, when expectations again proved high after a strong winter of testing. In the event, the first half of the year proved to be a major let-down. Having missed one race through illness, he was forced to stand on the sidelines for another two events following BAR's post-Imola ban. His confidence seemed to wane as teammate Button's smooth and flowing style garnered the points. The season reached a low-ebb in front of his home fans at Suzuka, where he ran Jarno Trulli's Toyota off the track and eventually was excluded from the results.

After taking fierce criticism in Japan, Honda agreed to Sato being replaced for 2006 by Rubens Barrichello, but offered an olive branch by agreeing to supply engines to the hastily formed Super Aguri Racing Team, which threw Sato the lifeline his Formula 1 career required. The year became one huge development exercise, with the expanding team in a state of constant flux, but Takuma was the lynchpin of the driving personnel. Although always a back-marker, he set about his difficult task with typical relish, helping to make the fledgling team's first year more than credible.

With the benefit of winter testing, and a solid engine and gearbox package, the Super Aguri put in some eye-opening early-season performances in 2007, Takuma taking a sixth place in Canada. As the season wore on, however, the development slowed and the team slipped back down the grid. By the end of the year, Honda had lost interest in supporting the team further and, with no other major sponsorship, survival became the order of the day. Sadly, after four races of the 2008 season, the team was forced to close, and for Sato the F1 dream was over.

After a year's enforced sabbatical, the personable Japanese driver pitched up in the USA, intent on forging a new career in the Indy Racing League. His first season with KV Racing in 2010 was only notable for a long list of accidents, but things improved in 2011, when he managed three top-six finishes. He switched camps for 2012 to come under the watchful eye of Bobby Rahal, who has all the experience that anyone would need to guide the Japanese driver to a breakthrough.

2004 Championship position: 8th Wins: 0 Pole positions: 0 Fastest laps: 0 Points scored: 34

9	AUSTRALIAN GP	Melbourne	10	Lucky Strike BAR Honda	B	3.0 BAR 006-Honda V10	collision with Trulli/1 lap behind	7/20
15/ret	MALAYSIAN GP	Sepang	10	Lucky Strike BAR Honda	B	3.0 BAR 006-Honda V10	*no time set/engine/4 laps behind	*20/20
5	BAHRAIN GP	Bahrain Circuit	10	Lucky Strike BAR Honda	B	3.0 BAR 006-Honda V10		5/20
ret	SAN MARINO GP	Imola	10	Lucky Strike BAR Honda	B	3.0 BAR 006-Honda V10	gearbox problems/engine failure	7/20
5	SPANISH GP	Barcelona	10	Lucky Strike BAR Honda	B	3.0 BAR 006-Honda V10		3/20
ret	MONACO GP	Monte Carlo	10	Lucky Strike BAR Honda	B	3.0 BAR 006-Honda V10	blown engine	7/20
ret	EUROPEAN GP	Nürburgring	10	Lucky Strike BAR Honda	B	3.0 BAR 006-Honda V10	engine	2/20
ret	CANADIAN GP	Montreal	10	Lucky Strike BAR Honda	B	3.0 BAR 006-Honda V10	engine	17/20
3	U S GP	Indianapolis	10	Lucky Strike BAR Honda	B	3.0 BAR 006-Honda V10	first podium	3/20
ret	FRENCH GP	Magny Cours	10	Lucky Strike BAR Honda	B	3.0 BAR 006-Honda V10	engine	7/20
11	BRITISH GP	Silverstone	10	Lucky Strike BAR Honda	B	3.0 BAR 006-Honda V10		9/20
8	GERMAN GP	Hockenheim	10	Lucky Strike BAR Honda	B	3.0 BAR 006-Honda V10	spin	8/20
6	HUNGARIAN GP	Hungaroring	10	Lucky Strike BAR Honda	B	3.0 BAR 006-Honda V10		3/20
ret	BELGIAN GP	Spa	10	Lucky Strike BAR Honda	B	3.0 BAR 006-Honda V10	collision with Webber on lap 1	15/20
4	ITALIAN GP	Monza	10	Lucky Strike BAR Honda	B	3.0 BAR 006-Honda V10		5/20
6	CHINESE GP	Shanghai	10	Lucky Strike BAR Honda	B	3.0 BAR 006-Honda V10	*10 place drop – engine change	*19/20
4	JAPANESE GP	Suzuka	10	Lucky Strike BAR Honda	B	3.0 BAR 006-Honda V10		4/20
6	BRAZILIAN GP	Interlagos	10	Lucky Strike BAR Honda	B	3.0 BAR 006-Honda V10		6/20

2005 Championship position: 14th Wins: 0 Pole positions: 0 Fastest laps: 0 Points scored: 1

14/ret	AUSTRALIAN GP	Melbourne	4	BAR Lucky Strike Honda	M	3.0 BAR 007-Honda V10	*no practice time set/2 laps behind	*19/20
dns	MALAYSIAN GP	Sepang	4	BAR Lucky Strike Honda	M	3.0 BAR 007-Honda V10	unwell after free practice	– /–
ret	BAHRAIN GP	Sakhir Circuit	4	BAR Lucky Strike Honda	M	3.0 BAR 007-Honda V10	worn brakes	13/20
dsq*	SAN MARINO GP	Imola	4	BAR Lucky Strike Honda	M	3.0 BAR 007-Honda V10	5th on road/*dsq – car underweight	6/20
12	EUROPEAN GP	Nürburgring	4	BAR Lucky Strike Honda	M	3.0 BAR 007-Honda V10	collision Massa/1 lap behind	16/20
ret	CANADIAN GP	Montreal	4	BAR Lucky Strike Honda	M	3.0 BAR 007-Honda V10	collision-long stop/gearbox – spun off	6/20
ret/dns*	U S GP	Indianapolis	4	BAR Lucky Strike Honda	M	3.0 BAR 007-Honda V10	*withdrawn after parade lap	8/20
11	FRENCH GP	Magny Cours	4	BAR Lucky Strike Honda	M	3.0 BAR 007-Honda V10	spin/1 lap behind	5/20
16	BRITISH GP	Silverstone	4	BAR Lucky Strike Honda	M	3.0 BAR 007-Honda V10	killed engine on grid/2 laps behind	8/20
12	GERMAN GP	Hockenheim	4	BAR Lucky Strike Honda	M	3.0 BAR 007-Honda V10	2 separate collisions/1 lap behind	8/20
8	HUNGARIAN GP	Hungaroring	4	BAR Lucky Strike Honda	M	3.0 BAR 007-Honda V10	1 lap behind	10/20
9	TURKISH GP	Hungaroring	4	BAR Lucky Strike Honda	M	3.0 BAR 007-Honda V10	started from pitlane	14/20
16	ITALIAN GP	Monza	4	BAR Lucky Strike Honda	M	3.0 BAR 007-Honda V10	fuel-rig problem – extra pit stop/-1 lap	5/20
ret	BELGIAN GP	Spa	4	BAR Lucky Strike Honda	M	3.0 BAR 007-Honda V10	collision with Michael Schumacher	11/20
10	BRAZILIAN GP	Interlagos	4	BAR Lucky Strike Honda	M	3.0 BAR 007-Honda V10	*no time set/grid penalty from Spa/-1 lap	*19/20
13/dsq*	JAPANESE GP	Suzuka	4	BAR Lucky Strike Honda	M	3.0 BAR 007-Honda V10	ran Trulli off track/disqualfied post-race	5/20
ret	CHINESE GP	Shanghai	4	BAR Lucky Strike Honda	M	3.0 BAR 007-Honda V10	gearbox	17/20

2006 Championship position: Unplaced

18	BAHRAIN GP	Bahrain	22	Super Aguri F1 Team	B	2.4 Super Aguri SA05-Honda V8	4 laps behind	20/22
14	MALAYSIAN GP	Sepang	22	Super Aguri F1 Team	B	2.4 Super Aguri SA05-Honda V8	3 laps behind	21/22
12	AUSTRALIAN GP	Melbourne	22	Super Aguri F1 Team	B	2.4 Super Aguri SA05-Honda V8	2 laps behind	21/22
ret	SAN MARINO GP	Imola	22	Super Aguri F1 Team	B	2.4 Super Aguri SA05-Honda V8	spun off	21/22
ret	EUROPEAN GP	Nürburgring	22	Super Aguri F1 Team	B	2.4 Super Aguri SA05-Honda V8	hydraulics	21/22
17	SPANISH GP	Barcelona	22	Super Aguri F1 Team	B	2.4 Super Aguri SA05-Honda V8	4 laps behind	20/22
ret	MONACO GP	Monte Carlo	22	Super Aguri F1 Team	B	2.4 Super Aguri SA05-Honda V8	electrics	20/22
17	BRITISH GP	Silverstone	22	Super Aguri F1 Team	B	2.4 Super Aguri SA05-Honda V8	3 laps behind	20/22
ret	CANADIAN GP	Montreal	22	Super Aguri F1 Team	B	2.4 Super Aguri SA05-Honda V8	accident	21/22
ret	U S GP	Indianapolis	22	Super Aguri F1 Team	B	2.4 Super Aguri SA05-Honda V8	accident – hit Monteiro	18/22
ret	FRENCH GP	Magny Cours	22	Super Aguri F1 Team	B	2.4 Super Aguri SA05-Honda V8	clutch at start	22/22
ret	GERMAN GP	Hockenheim	22	Super Aguri F1 Team	B	2.4 Super Aguri SA05-Honda V8	gearbox oil leak	19/22
13	HUNGARIAN GP	Hungaroring	22	Super Aguri F1 Team	B	2.4 Super Aguri SA05-Honda V8	5 laps behind	19/22
nc	TURKISH GP	Istanbul	22	Super Aguri F1 Team	B	2.4 Super Aguri SA05-Honda V8	collision – pit stop – new floor, etc/-17 laps	22/22
16	ITALIAN GP	Monza	22	Super Aguri F1 Team	B	2.4 Super Aguri SA05-Honda V8	2 laps behind	21/22
dsq*	CHINESE GP	Shanghai	22	Super Aguri F1 Team	B	2.4 Super Aguri SA05-Honda V8	14th – but*dsq for blocking faster drivers	21/22
15	JAPANESE GP	Suzuka	22	Super Aguri F1 Team	B	2.4 Super Aguri SA05-Honda V8	1 lap behind	20/22
10	BRAZILIAN GP	Interlagos	22	Super Aguri F1 Team	B	2.4 Super Aguri SA05-Honda V8	1 lap behind	20/22

2007 Championship position: 17th Wins: 0 Pole positions: 0 Fastest laps: 0 Points scored: 4

12	AUSTRALIAN GP	Melbourne	22	Super Aguri F1 Team	B	2.4 Super Aguri SA07-Honda V8	1 lap behind	10/22
13	MALAYSIAN GP	Sepang	22	Super Aguri F1 Team	B	2.4 Super Aguri SA07-Honda V8	incident with Liuzzi/1 lap behind	14/22
ret	BAHRAIN GP	Bahrain	22	Super Aguri F1 Team	B	2.4 Super Aguri SA07-Honda V8	engine	17/22
8	SPANISH GP	Barcelona	22	Super Aguri F1 Team	B	2.4 Super Aguri SA07-Honda V8	1 lap behind	13/22
17	MONACO GP	Monte Carlo	22	Super Aguri F1 Team	B	2.4 Super Aguri SA07-Honda V8	2 laps behind	21/22
6	CANADIAN GP	Montreal	22	Super Aguri F1 Team	B	2.4 Super Aguri SA07-Honda V8	good race strategy	11/22
ret	U S GP	Indianapolis	22	Super Aguri F1 Team	B	2.4 Super Aguri SA07-Honda V8	spun off	18/22
16	FRENCH GP	Magny Cours	22	Super Aguri F1 Team	B	2.4 Super Aguri SA07-Honda V8	2 laps behind	19/22
14	BRITISH GP	Silverstone	22	Super Aguri F1 Team	B	2.4 Super Aguri SA07-Honda V8	2 laps behind	00/22
ret	EUROPEAN GP	Nürburgring	22	Super Aguri F1 Team	B	2.4 Super Aguri SA07-Honda V8	hydraulics	16/22
15	HUNGARIAN GP	Hungaroring	22	Super Aguri F1 Team	B	2.4 Super Aguri SA07-Honda V8	1 lap behind	19/22
18	TURKISH GP	Istanbul	22	Super Aguri F1 Team	B	2.4 Super Aguri SA07-Honda V8	lost time avoiding Trulli spin/1 lap behind	19/22
16	ITALIAN GP	Monza	22	Super Aguri Racing	B	2.4 Super Aguri SA07-Honda V8	1 lap behind	17/22
15	BELGIAN GP	Spa	22	Super Aguri Racing	B	2.4 Super Aguri SA07-Honda V8	1 lap behind	19/22
15/ret	JAPANESE GP	Fuji Speedway	22	Super Aguri Racing	B	2.4 Super Aguri SA07-Honda V8	hit Button/damaged tyre/2 laps behind	21/22
14	CHINESE GP	Shanghai	22	Super Aguri Racing	B	2.4 Super Aguri SA07-Honda V8	1 lap behind	20/22
12	BRAZILIAN GP	Interlagos	22	Super Aguri Racing	B	2.4 Super Aguri SA07-Honda V8	2 laps behind	21/22

2008 Championship position: Unplaced

ret	AUSTRALIAN GP	Melbourne	22	Super Aguri Racing	B	2.4 Super Aguri SA08A-Honda V8	transmission	20/22
16	MALAYSIAN GP	Sepang	22	Super Aguri Racing	B	2.4 Super Aguri SA08A-Honda V8	ran off track/2 laps behind	20/22
17	BAHRAIN GP	Bahrain	22	Super Aguri Racing	B	2.4 Super Aguri SA08A-Honda V8	1 lap behind	20/22
13	SPANISH GP	Barcelona	22	Super Aguri Racing	B	2.4 Super Aguri SA08A-Honda V8	1 lap behind	22/22

GP Starts: 90 GP Wins: 0 Pole positions: 0 Fastest laps: 0 Points: 44

LUDOVICO SCARFIOTTI

A GREAT all-rounder who wasn't out of the top drawer, Ludovico Scarfiotti nevertheless had his moment of glory in 1966, taking the 3-litre Ferrari to a momentous victory in front of the rapturous 'tifosi' at Monza on a glorious September afternoon. It was the zenith of a career that had started a decade earlier in a far more modest Fiat 1100 saloon. The winner of his class in the Mille Miglia in 1956 and 1957, Scarfiotti originally had raced just for fun, which he could afford to do, being related to the wealthy Agnelli family who, of course, controlled the FIAT empire. He tested a works Ferrari sports car as early as 1958, but had to be content with campaigning a little 2-litre OSCA, taking second place in the Naples Grand Prix at Posillipo.

Ludovico finally joined the Scuderia's sports car team in 1960, sharing the fourth-place car with Giulio Cabianca and Willy Mairesse in the Targa Florio. His first real success came in 1962, when he took the European mountain-climb championship in Ferrari's 2-litre V6 car, and this confirmed his place in the works team for 1963, alongside John Surtees and Mairesse, when the rest of the Scuderia's drivers were being shown the door.

Scarfiotti's early-season sports car outings were encouraging. Sharing the 250P with Surtees, he won at Sebring, and later he won at Le Mans, this time with Lorenzo Bandini. Impressed with his efforts, Ferrari rewarded him with his grand prix debut at Zandvoort, and after a steady drive he took sixth place, enough to earn another opportunity at Reims. Unfortunately, he crashed and hit a telegraph pole in practice, which left him with leg injuries serious enough not only to keep him out for some time, but also to prompt him to announce his retirement from Formula 1.

However, Scarfiotti was back in action in 1964, winning the Nürburgring 1000km with Nino Vaccarella in the works Ferrari 275P and finishing second at Mosport in the 330P. Contrary to his earlier intentions, he was back in a Ferrari single-seater at Monza, but mostly was employed by the Scuderia in sports cars the following year. Driving the lovely 1.6-litre Ferrari Dino, he took his second mountain-climb championship, and he was also second in the Monza 1000km with Surtees.

The 1966 season was his best, but only courtesy of his famous Italian GP victory, as little else was achieved bar a second place in the Nürburgring 1000km. Indeed, he was rather lucky to escape injury after being involved in accidents at both Le Mans and the Targa Florio.

Scarfiotti was one of four drivers (the others were Bandini, Mike Parkes and newcomer Chris Amon) who represented Ferrari in 1967, and the season started well with second places with the Ferrari P4 sports car at Daytona and in the Monza 1000km. Then came a fifth place in the Race of Champions and a staged dead-heat with Parkes to win the Syracuse Grand Prix, before the first disaster. Bandini was killed at Monaco and soon Parkes – with whom Scarfiotti had just taken a second place at Le Mans – was badly injured at Spa. 'Lulu' seemed to lose heart and, after a dispute with the management, took his leave, appearing briefly in Dan Gurney's Eagle at Monza.

For 1968, Scarfiotti found a berth in the declining Cooper team. The cars were slow, but reliable, and he managed to pick up a couple of distant fourth-place finishes. Although he had forsaken Ferrari, his first-class sports car talents were not allowed to go to waste, since he signed for Porsche to race their prototypes alongside another mountain-climb specialist, Gerhard Mitter. A second place in the BOAC 500 at Brands Hatch was his best placing for the Stuttgart firm, for while practising for the Obersalzberg hillclimb at Rossfeld in June, 1968, inexplicably he failed to brake at a corner, ran straight on and crashed into a clump of trees. He was thrown from his car, suffering multiple fractures, and died in the ambulance.

SCARFIOTTI, Ludovico (I) b 18/10/1933, Turin – d 8/6/1968, Rossfeld, Germany

1963 Championship position: 15th=   Wins: 0   Pole positions: 0   Fastest laps: 0   Points scored: 1

	Race	Circuit	No	Entrant	Tyres	Capacity/Car/Engine	Comment	Q Pos/Entries
6	DUTCH GP	Zandvoort	4	Scuderia Ferrari SpA SEFAC	D	1.5 Ferrari 156 V6	2 laps behind	11/19
dns	FRENCH GP	Reims	14	Scuderia Ferrari SpA SEFAC	D	1.5 Ferrari 156 V6	practice accident	(14)/21

1964 Championship position: Unplaced

	Race	Circuit	No	Entrant	Tyres	Capacity/Car/Engine	Comment	Q Pos/Entries
9	ITALIAN GP	Monza	6	Scuderia Ferrari SpA SEFAC	D	1.5 Ferrari 156 V6	1 lap behind	=16/25

1965 Championship position: Unplaced

	Race	Circuit	No	Entrant	Tyres	Capacity/Car/Engine	Comment	Q Pos/Entries
dns	MEXICAN GP	Mexico City	24	Scuderia Ferrari SpA SEFAC	D	1.5 Ferrari 1512 F12	car driven by Rodriguez	- / -

1966 Championship position: 10th   Wins: 0   Pole positions: 0   Fastest laps: 1   Points scored: 9

	Race	Circuit	No	Entrant	Tyres	Capacity/Car/Engine	Comment	Q Pos/Entries
ret	GERMAN GP	Nürburgring	11	Scuderia Ferrari SpA SEFAC	D	2.4 Ferrari Dino 246 V6	electrics	4/30
1	ITALIAN GP	Monza	6	Scuderia Ferrari SpA SEFAC	F	3.0 Ferrari 312/66 V12	FL	2/22

1967 Championship position: 19th=   Wins: 0   Pole positions: 0   Fastest laps: 0   Points scored: 1

	Race	Circuit	No	Entrant	Tyres	Capacity/Car/Engine	Comment	Q Pos/Entries
6	DUTCH GP	Zandvoort	22	Scuderia Ferrari SpA SEFAC	F	3.0 Ferrari 312/67 V12	1 lap behind	15/17
nc	BELGIAN GP	Spa	2	Scuderia Ferrari SpA SEFAC	F	3.0 Ferrari 312/67 V12	pit stop – hydraulic pipe/4 laps behind	9/18
ret	ITALIAN GP	Monza	10	Anglo American Racers	G	3.0 Eagle T1G-Weslake V12	engine	10/18

1968 Championship position: 13th=   Wins: 0   Pole positions: 0   Fastest laps: 0   Points scored: 6

	Race	Circuit	No	Entrant	Tyres	Capacity/Car/Engine	Comment	Q Pos/Entries
ret	SOUTH AFRICAN GP	Kyalami	15	Cooper Car Co	F	3.0 Cooper T86-Maserati V12	accident – broken brake line	15/23
4	SPANISH GP	Jarama	15	Cooper Car Co	F	3.0 Cooper T86B-BRM V12	1 lap behind	12/14
4	MONACO GP	Monte Carlo	6	Cooper Car Co	F	3.0 Cooper T86B-BRM V12	pit stop – wheel change/4 laps behind	=17/18

GP Starts: 10   GP Wins: 1   Pole positions: 0   Fastest laps: 1   Points: 17

GIORGIO SCARLATTI

A SOLID, dependable, but not too quick Italian sports car driver, Giorgio Scarlatti raced a Maserati T200S in 1954/55, his best finishes being a second in class in the Tour of Sicily, and third places at Bari and Caserta. At this time, he bought a Ferrari 500 to race in Formula 1, but after a fourth place in the 1956 Naples Grand Prix, he proved to be hopelessly slow in his efforts to qualify at Monaco.

For 1957, Giorgio aligned himself with the works Maserati team and shared a point with Harry Schell for their fifth place in the Italian Grand Prix, taking another fifth at the non-championship Modena GP and sixth at Pescara, although he was ten minutes behind the winner, Stirling Moss.

After the works team had closed their doors, Scarlatti soldiered on with the 250F, sharing fourth place in the Buenos Aires City GP after Jean Behra took over the car, and earned third place (and a class win) in the Targa Florio, where he partnered Behra in the Frenchman's Porsche. Jean was of the opinion that outright victory had been possible, but Scarlatti was not able to drive quickly enough.

In 1959, Giorgio again raced the outdated Maserati, but disappointed when entrusted with the third works Cooper at Monza in place of the injured Masten Gregory. He continued to race various ill-prepared single-seaters without success until 1961, although he did a little better in sports cars, winning that year's Pescara four-hours with a young Lorenzo Bandini in a Ferrari 246 V6. Scarlatti continued to race Ferrari GTs occasionally thereafter, taking fourth (and another class win) in the 1962 Targa Florio. A year later, back at the Madonnie circuit, he took the Scuderia Venezia Ferrari to sixth place with Juan Manuel Bordeu.

SCARLATTI, Giorgio (I) b 2/10/1921, Rome – d 26/7/1990, Rome

1956 Championship position: Unplaced

	Race	Circuit	No	Entrant	Tyres	Capacity/Car/Engine	Comment	Q Pos/Entries
dnq	MONACO GP	Monte Carlo	36	Giorgio Scarlatti	P	2.0 Ferrari 500 4		17/19
ret	GERMAN GP	Nürburgring	14	Scuderia Centro Sud	P	2.0 Ferrari 500 4	engine	17/21

1957 Championship position: 16th=   Wins: 0   Pole positions: 0   Fastest laps: 0   Points scored: 1

	Race	Circuit	No	Entrant	Tyres	Capacity/Car/Engine	Comment	Q Pos/Entries
ret*	MONACO GP	Monte Carlo	34	Officine Alfieri Maserati	P	2.5 Maserati 250F 6	*Schell took over/oil pressure	14/21
10	GERMAN GP	Nürburgring	4	Officine Alfieri Maserati	P	2.5 Maserati 250F 6	1 lap behind	13/24
6	PESCARA GP	Pescara	8	Officine Alfieri Maserati	P	2.5 Maserati 250F 6	1 lap behind	10/16
5*	ITALIAN GP	Monza	8	Officine Alfieri Maserati	P	2.5 Maserati 250F 6	*Schell took over car/3 laps behind	12/19

1958 Championship position: Unplaced

	Race	Circuit	No	Entrant	Tyres	Capacity/Car/Engine	Comment	Q Pos/Entries
ret	MONACO GP	Monte Carlo	46	Giorgio Scarlatti	P	2.5 Maserati 250F 6	engine – con rod	14/28
ret	DUTCH GP	Zandvoort	10	Giorgio Scarlatti	P	2.5 Maserati 250F 6	rear axle	16/17

1959 Championship position: Unplaced

	Race	Circuit	No	Entrant	Tyres	Capacity/Car/Engine	Comment	Q Pos/Entries
dnq	MONACO GP	Monte Carlo	54	Scuderia Ugolini	D	2.5 Maserati 250F 6		18/24
8*	FRENCH GP	Reims	40	Scuderia Ugolini	D	2.5 Maserati 250F 6	*8th placed car disqualified/-9 laps	21/22
12	ITALIAN GP	Monza	10	Cooper Car Co	D	2.5 Cooper T51-Climax 4	4 laps behind	12/21

	1960 Championship position: Unplaced								
ret	ARGENTINE GP	Buenos Aires	8	Giorgio Scarlatti	D	2.5 Maserati 250F 6		*overheating*	18/22
dnq	MONACO GP	Monte Carlo	30	Scuderia Castellotti	D	2.5 Cooper T51-Ferrari 4			22/24
ret	ITALIAN GP	Monza	36	Scuderia Castellotti	D	2.5 Cooper T51-Maserati 4		*throttle cable*	5/16
	1961 Championship position: Unplaced								
ret	FRENCH GP	Reims	34	Scuderia Serenissima	D	1.5 de Tomaso F1-OSCA 4		*engine*	– / –
dns	"	"	32	Scuderia Serenissima	D	1.5 Cooper T51-Maserati 4		*car raced by Trintignant*	26/26

GP Starts: 12   GP Wins: 0   Pole positions: 0   Fastest laps: 0   Points: 1

IAN SCHECKTER

THE elder brother of world champion Jody, Ian Scheckter followed his sibling to Europe in mid-1972 after winning the domestic South African Formula Ford series with a Merlyn. It was a brief stay, during which he proved his competitiveness. He returned to South Africa to contest the national championship in a Team Gunston Chevron and attempt to break Dave Charlton's long stranglehold on the title.

Ian made his grand prix debut at Kyalami in 1974 and had a handful of Formula 1 outings over the next couple of years, but it was only after he had finally clinched the South African championship (by then for Formula Atlantic cars) in 1976 that he took up the offer of a full-time grand prix drive with March in 1977.

The season was an utter shambles, as the new 771 chassis was not ready until mid-season, and when it raced it proved to be no improvement on the earlier model. The bewildered Scheckter, who managed just two finishes from 13 starts, found that his Formula 1 career had been buried. The final ignominy came in Japan, where he was deported for having only a tourist visa. His car remained unused in the pit lane.

Scheckter returned home to continue his association with Lexington Racing and achieve success once more, winning the Atlantic titles in 1977/78 and 1978/79. Then he switched to saloon car racing with BMW South Africa's 535i, but in 1983 he returned to Atlantic with a March 832-Mazda. This combination was potent enough for him to claim another two titles. He briefly raced Sarel van der Merve's March-Porsche in IMSA in 1984 and early 1985, but then was out of the cockpit until tempted to return to the South African Modified V8 Championship early in 1989. His return came to a swift end, however, after a tragic incident at Killarney, where his Ford Sapphire was in a collision with another competitor, Hannes Grobler. The cars were launched over a barrier into the pit lane, killing two bystanders and injuring many others. Both drivers escaped unhurt, but in shock. Scheckter never raced again, but he still gets behind the wheel on occasion for demonstrations, hill-climbs and historic racing. His son, Jaki, followed in the family tradition, racing successfully in junior single-seaters and winning the 1995 Barber Dodge Series – he beat Juan Pablo Montoya – before a lack of funds stalled his progress.

SCHECKTER, Ian (ZA) b 22/8/1947, East London

	1974 Championship position: Unplaced							
	Race	*Circuit*	*No*	*Entrant*	*Tyres*	*Capacity/Car/Engine*	*Comment*	*Q Pos/Entries*
13	SOUTH AFRICAN GP	Kyalami	29	Team Gunston	G	3.0 Lotus 72E-Cosworth V8	*2 laps behind*	22/27
dnq	AUSTRIAN GP	Österreichring	31	Hesketh Racing	F	3.0 Hesketh 308-Cosworth V8		26/31
	1975 Championship position: Unplaced							
ret	SOUTH AFRICAN GP	Kyalami	32	Lexington Racing	G	3.0 Tyrrell 007-Cosworth V8	*spun off*	17/28
ret	SWEDISH GP	Anderstorp	21	Frank Williams Racing Cars	G	3.0 Williams FW04-Cosworth V8	*burst tyre – spun off*	20/26
12	DUTCH GP	Zandvoort	20	Frank Williams Racing Cars	G	3.0 Williams FW03-Cosworth V8	*5 laps behind*	19/25
	1976 Championship position: Unplaced							
ret	SOUTH AFRICAN GP	Kyalami	15	Lexington Racing	G	3.0 Tyrrell 007-Cosworth V8	*collision with Leclère*	16/25
	1977 Championship position: Unplaced							
ret	ARGENTINE GP	Buenos Aires	10	Team Rothmans International	G	3.0 March 761B-Cosworth V8	*battery terminal*	17/21
ret	BRAZILIAN GP	Interlagos	10	Team Rothmans International	G	3.0 March 761B-Cosworth V8	*transmission*	17/22
11	SPANISH GP	Jarama	10	Team Rothmans International	G	3.0 March 761B-Cosworth V8	*3 laps behind*	17/31
dnq	MONACO GP	Monte Carlo	10	Team Rothmans International	G	3.0 March 761B-Cosworth V8	*injured in practice accident*	26/26
ret	BELGIAN GP	Zolder	10	Team Rothmans International	G	3.0 March 761B-Cosworth V8	*spun off*	21/32
dns	"	"	10	Team Rothmans International	G	3.0 March 771-Cosworth V8	*practice only*	– / –
ret	SWEDISH GP	Anderstorp	10	Team Rothmans International	G	3.0 March 761B-Cosworth V8	*driveshaft – c.v. joint*	21/31
nc	FRENCH GP	Dijon	10	Team Rothmans International	G	3.0 March 761B-Cosworth V8	*11 laps behind*	20/30
ret	BRITISH GP	Silverstone	10	Team Rothmans International	G	3.0 March 761B-Cosworth V8	*spun off*	24/36
ret	GERMAN GP	Hockenheim	10	Team Rothmans International	G	3.0 March 761B-Cosworth V8	*clutch*	18/30
ret	AUSTRIAN GP	Österreichring	10	Team Rothmans International	G	3.0 March 761B-Cosworth V8	*spun off*	24/30
10	DUTCH GP	Zandvoort	10	Team Rothmans International	G	3.0 March 771-Cosworth V8	*2 laps behind*	25/34
ret	ITALIAN GP	Monza	10	Team Rothmans International	G	3.0 March 771-Cosworth V8	*transmission*	17/34
ret	US GP EAST	Watkins Glen	10	Team Rothmans International	G	3.0 March 771-Cosworth V8	*crashed at chicane*	21/27
ret	CANADIAN GP	Mosport Park	10	Team Rothmans International	G	3.0 March 771-Cosworth V8	*engine*	18/27

GP Starts: 18   GP Wins: 0   Pole positions: 0   Fastest laps: 0   Points: 0

JODY SCHECKTER

A PRODIGY, Jody Scheckter burst upon the motor racing scene in much the same manner as Ricardo Rodriguez had done a decade earlier. Immensely talented, brave almost to the point of being foolhardy and blindingly quick in any car he chose to drive, somehow he managed to avoid the 'Grim Reaper' in those wild early days to become a dry-humoured, somewhat world-weary elder statesman who felt he could manage the inherent risks to control his own destiny.

Jody started his racing early, running a kart at 12 before moving on to motorcycles and then saloons by the age of 18. The youngster achieved tremendous success in his home-built Renault, and he scored numerous victories before his racing took a back seat to a spell of national service. Towards the end of 1970, Team Lawson entrusted their Mazda to him in the Springbok series; he finished fifth in the Bulawayo three-hours and won his class in the Goldfields nine-hours. His immediate ambition, though, was to do well in the Formula Ford Sunshine series and thus win the 'driver to Europe' prize that went with it. Sure enough, young Jody did exactly that in his Lola T200 Formula Ford, and he was on his way to England early in 1971.

The headstrong Scheckter got himself into a Merlyn at Brands Hatch and sensationally led the race until he spun. This set the pattern for his short Formula Ford career. Spin or win seemed to be the order of the day until, after a few races, he felt he needed the tougher challenge of Formula 3, jumping in at the deep end with an EMC and then a works Merlyn. By the end of the year, he was winning at this level, in addition to hustling a Ford Escort Mexico indecently quickly. McLaren were first in with their pen, Jody being signed to race for their Formula 2 team in 1972.

Generally, Jody's luck was out with the McLaren M21, but he did manage one win in the Greater London Trophy at Crystal Palace. As a bonus, the team gave him his grand prix debut at Watkins Glen, where he kept the lid on things and finished a creditable ninth. McLaren kept him on for the 1973 season, although with Peter Revson and Denny Hulme on board they didn't really have room to accommodate him. Perhaps they wished they hadn't when his 1973 grand prix season turned into a succession of accidents, the most serious being his infamous spin at the beginning of the British Grand Prix, which not only halted the race, but also wiped out a good proportion of the field. Ever the paradox at this stage of his career, he also raced for Sid Taylor in America, winning the L & M F5000 series in a Trojan, and competed in Can-Am with a Porsche 917 – completely without mishap.

With McLaren unable to offer Jody a firm deal for 1974, Ken Tyrrell stepped in and signed the South African to head his team, newly shorn of the retired Jackie Stewart and deceased François Cevert. He proved an inspired choice, the still relatively inexperienced charger taking two grand prix wins (at Anderstorp and Brands Hatch) and finishing third in the championship table, only ten points adrift of the champion, Enmerson Fittipaldi.

Jody found it hard to maintain his scintillating form the following season, but he did have the wonderful bonus of winning the South African Grand Prix, becoming the only native driver to win his home event. In 1976, Tyrrell launched the bizarre, but effective six-wheel P34 car. In Scheckter's hands, this became a serious machine: he took it to a historic victory in Sweden and racked up the points regularly elsewhere to finish a very creditable third in the world championship, behind James Hunt and Niki Lauda. That was also the year when Scheckter achieved another ambition by winning the Wynn's 1000km at Kyalami in a BMW, with Gunnar Nilsson and Harold Grohs.

Feeling out of sync with the Tyrrell six-wheel philosophy, Jody took a big gamble by joining Wolf for 1977, but it paid off immediately when he gave the restructured team a winning debut in the Argentine Grand Prix. The car wasn't consistently good at every circuit, but Jody never let that become a problem. Two more wins followed, and second place to Lauda in the championship was his reward. His 1978 season was not so productive, the new Wolf chassis, struggling to come to terms with ground-effect, being far more troublesome than the relatively straightforward machine of the previous year. Seventh place in the final standings masked a year when the driver certainly delivered more than the car was perhaps capable of doing.

An offer from Ferrari for 1979 was too good to refuse, and by then the wild man of the early days was but a distant memory. Indeed, incredible though it may seem, Jody was driving almost conservatively. Certainly he had everything weighed up and his performances were the model of economy: he did just enough and no more. Early-season wins in Belgium and Monaco gave him a platform to build on, and fittingly he was able to clinch the world championship in style, with a third win of the season at Monza.

His ambition realised, Jody planned just one more year. As it happened, it was easily the worst of his career, leaving him frustrated and a little bemused. The ultimate humiliation came at Montreal, where he failed to qualify; he knew it was just one of those things, that circumstances had conspired against him, but it hurt his pride nonetheless. Scheckter had come in with a bang, but went out with a whimper. He walked away unhurt, however, and there were a few people who didn't believe that possible in 1973.

Ever his own man, after retiring, Jody settled in the United States and began a new life without even mentioning his achievements. Most of his new acquaintances knew nothing of Scheckter the Formula 1 world champion, and that's exactly the way he wanted it as he built a highly successful business manufacturing firearms training simulators.

Meanwhile, Jody was able to help his sons from his first marriage, Tomas and Toby, to taste competition for themselves in the junior single-seater formulas. In Formula 1, Tomas managed to secure a role as test driver for Jaguar, before building a worthy career for himself in the IRL. Proving particularly fast on ovals, he has won two races, and claimed seven pole positions from more than 100 starts.

Jody has since returned to the United Kingdom and embarked upon a new venture. He purchased Laverstoke Park Farm in Hampshire and developed a highly successful organic foods business. His links with Formula 1 no doubt proved invaluable, as the company was chosen to supply his products to the exclusive Formula 1 Paddock Club.

SCHECKTER, Jody (ZA) b 29/1/1950, East London

1972 Championship position: Unplaced

	Race	Circuit	No	Entrant	Tyres	Capacity/Car/Engine	Comment	Q Pos/Entries
9	US GP	Watkins Glen	21	Yardley Team McLaren	G	3.0 McLaren M19A-Cosworth V8	*1 lap behind*	8/32

1973 Championship position: Unplaced

	Race	Circuit	No	Entrant	Tyres	Capacity/Car/Engine	Comment	Q Pos/Entries
9/ret	SOUTH AFRICAN GP	Kyalami	7	Yardley Team McLaren	G	3.0 McLaren M19C-Cosworth V8	*engine/4 laps behind*	3/25
ret	FRENCH GP	Paul Ricard	8	Yardley Team McLaren	G	3.0 McLaren M23-Cosworth V8	*collision – Fittipaldi/suspension*	2/25
ret/dns	BRITISH GP	Silverstone	30	Yardley Team McLaren	G	3.0 McLaren M23-Cosworth V8	*caused multiple accident at 1st start*	6/29
ret	CANADIAN GP	Mosport Park	0	Yardley Team McLaren	G	3.0 McLaren M23-Cosworth V8	*accident with Cevert*	3/26
ret	US GP	Watkins Glen	0	Yardley Team McLaren	G	3.0 McLaren M23-Cosworth V8	*suspension*	11/28

1974 Championship position: 3rd   Wins: 2   Pole positions: 0   Fastest laps: 2   Points scored: 45

	Race	Circuit	No	Entrant	Tyres	Capacity/Car/Engine	Comment	Q Pos/Entries
ret	ARGENTINE GP	Buenos Aires	3	Elf Team Tyrrell	G	3.0 Tyrrell 006-Cosworth V8	*cylinder head gasket*	12/26
13	BRAZILIAN GP	Interlagos	3	Elf Team Tyrrell	G	3.0 Tyrrell 006-Cosworth V8	*1 lap behind*	14/25
8	SOUTH AFRICAN GP	Kyalami	3	Elf Team Tyrrell	G	3.0 Tyrrell 006-Cosworth V8		8/27
5	SPANISH GP	Jarama	3	Elf Team Tyrrell	G	3.0 Tyrrell 007-Cosworth V8	*2 laps behind*	- / -
dns	"	"	3	Elf Team Tyrrell	G	3.0 Tyrrell 006-Cosworth V8	*brake problems – set grid time*	9/28
3	BELGIAN GP	Nivelles	3	Elf Team Tyrrell	G	3.0 Tyrrell 007-Cosworth V8		2/32
2	MONACO GP	Monte Carlo	3	Elf Team Tyrrell	G	3.0 Tyrrell 007-Cosworth V8		=4/28
1	SWEDISH GP	Anderstorp	3	Elf Team Tyrrell	G	3.0 Tyrrell 007-Cosworth V8		2/28
5	DUTCH GP	Zandvoort	3	Elf Team Tyrrell	G	3.0 Tyrrell 007-Cosworth V8		5/27
4	FRENCH GP	Dijon	3	Elf Team Tyrrell	G	3.0 Tyrrell 007-Cosworth V8	FL	7/30
1	BRITISH GP	Brands Hatch	3	Elf Team Tyrrell	G	3.0 Tyrrell 007-Cosworth V8		3/34
2	GERMAN GP	Nürburgring	3	Elf Team Tyrrell	G	3.0 Tyrrell 007-Cosworth V8	FL	4/32
ret	AUSTRIAN GP	Österreichring	3	Elf Team Tyrrell	G	3.0 Tyrrell 007-Cosworth V8	*engine*	5/31
3	ITALIAN GP	Monza	3	Elf Team Tyrrell	G	3.0 Tyrrell 007-Cosworth V8		12/31
ret	CANADIAN GP	Mosport Park	3	Elf Team Tyrrell	G	3.0 Tyrrell 007-Cosworth V8	*accident – brake failure*	3/30
ret	US GP	Watkins Glen	3	Elf Team Tyrrell	G	3.0 Tyrrell 007-Cosworth V8	*fuel pipe*	6/30

1975 Championship position: 7th=   Wins: 1   Pole positions: 0   Fastest laps: 0   Points scored: 20

	Race	Circuit	No	Entrant	Tyres	Capacity/Car/Engine	Comment	Q Pos/Entries
11	ARGENTINE GP	Buenos Aires	3	Elf Team Tyrrell	G	3.0 Tyrrell 007-Cosworth V8	*1 lap behind*	9/23
ret	BRAZILIAN GP	Interlagos	3	Elf Team Tyrrell	G	3.0 Tyrrell 007-Cosworth V8	*oil tank*	8/23
1	SOUTH AFRICAN GP	Kyalami	3	Elf Team Tyrrell	G	3.0 Tyrrell 007-Cosworth V8		3/28
ret	SPANISH GP	Montjuich Park	3	Elf Team Tyrrell	G	3.0 Tyrrell 007-Cosworth V8	*engine*	13/26
7	MONACO GP	Monte Carlo	3	Elf Team Tyrrell	G	3.0 Tyrrell 007-Cosworth V8	*1 lap behind*	7/26
2	BELGIAN GP	Zolder	3	Elf Team Tyrrell	G	3.0 Tyrrell 007-Cosworth V8		9/24
7	SWEDISH GP	Anderstorp	3	Elf Team Tyrrell	G	3.0 Tyrrell 007-Cosworth V8	*1 lap behind*	8/26
16/ret	DUTCH GP	Zandvoort	3	Elf Team Tyrrell	G	3.0 Tyrrell 007-Cosworth V8	*engine/8 laps behind*	4/25
9	FRENCH GP	Paul Ricard	3	Elf Team Tyrrell	G	3.0 Tyrrell 007-Cosworth V8		2/26
3/ret	BRITISH GP	Silverstone	3	Elf Team Tyrrell	G	3.0 Tyrrell 007-Cosworth V8	*spun off in rainstorm/1 lap behind*	6/28
ret	GERMAN GP	Nürburgring	3	Elf Team Tyrrell	G	3.0 Tyrrell 007-Cosworth V8	*accident – tyre failure*	3/26
8	AUSTRIAN GP	Österreichring	3	Elf Team Tyrrell	G	3.0 Tyrrell 007-Cosworth V8	*1 lap behind*	10/30
8	ITALIAN GP	Monza	3	Elf Team Tyrrell	G	3.0 Tyrrell 007-Cosworth V8	*1 lap behind*	4/28
6	US GP	Watkins Glen	3	Elf Team Tyrrell	G	3.0 Tyrrell 007-Cosworth V8		10/24

1976 Championship position: 3rd   Wins: 1   Pole positions: 1   Fastest laps: 1   Points scored: 49

	Race	Circuit	No	Entrant	Tyres	Capacity/Car/Engine	Comment	Q Pos/Entries
5	BRAZILIAN GP	Interlgos	3	Elf Team Tyrrell	G	3.0 Tyrrell 007-Cosworth V8		13/22
4	SOUTH AFRICAN GP	Kyalami	3	Elf Team Tyrrell	G	3.0 Tyrrell 007-Cosworth V8		12/25
ret	US GP WEST	Long Beach	3	Elf Team Tyrrell	G	3.0 Tyrrell 007-Cosworth V8	*suspension*	11/27
ret	SPANISH GP	Jarama	3	Elf Team Tyrrell	G	3.0 Tyrrell 007-Cosworth V8	*oil pump belt*	14/30
4	BELGIAN GP	Zolder	3	Elf Team Tyrrell	G	3.0 Tyrrell P34-Cosworth V8		7/29
2	MONACO GP	Monte Carlo	3	Elf Team Tyrrell	G	3.0 Tyrrell P34-Cosworth V8		5/25
1	SWEDISH GP	Anderstorp	3	Elf Team Tyrrell	G	3.0 Tyrrell P34-Cosworth V8		1/27
6	FRENCH GP	Paul Ricard	3	Elf Team Tyrrell	G	3.0 Tyrrell P34-Cosworth V8		9/30
2*	BRITISH GP	Brands Hatch	3	Elf Team Tyrrell	G	3.0 Tyrrell P34-Cosworth V8	**1st place car disqualified*	8/30
dns	"	"	3	Elf Team Tyrrell	G	3.0 Tyrrell 007-Cosworth V8	*practice only*	- / -
2	GERMAN GP	Nürburgring	3	Elf Team Tyrrell	G	3.0 Tyrrell P34-Cosworth V8	FL	8/28
ret	AUSTRIAN GP	Österreichring	3	Elf Team Tyrrell	G	3.0 Tyrrell P34-Cosworth V8	*suspension/accident*	10/25
5	DUTCH GP	Zandvoort	3	Elf Team Tyrrell	G	3.0 Tyrrell P34-Cosworth V8		8/27
5	ITALIAN GP	Monza	3	Elf Team Tyrrell	G	3.0 Tyrrell P34-Cosworth V8		2/29
4	CANADIAN GP	Mosport Park	3	Elf Team Tyrrell	G	3.0 Tyrrell P34-Cosworth V8		7/27
2	US GP EAST	Watkins Glen	3	Elf Team Tyrrell	G	3.0 Tyrrell P34-Cosworth V8		2/27
ret	JAPANESE GP	Mount Fuji	3	Elf Team Tyrrell	G	3.0 Tyrrell P34-Cosworth V8	*overheating*	5/27

1977 Championship position: 2nd   Wins: 3   Pole positions: 1   Fastest laps: 2   Points scored: 55

	Race	Circuit	No	Entrant	Tyres	Capacity/Car/Engine	Comment	Q Pos/Entries
1	ARGENTINE GP	Buenos Aires	20	Walter Wolf Racing	G	3.0 Wolf WR1-Cosworth V8		11/21
ret	BRAZILIAN GP	Interlagos	20	Walter Wolf Racing	G	3.0 Wolf WR1-Cosworth V8	*engine*	15/22
2	SOUTH AFRICAN GP	Kyalami	20	Walter Wolf Racing	G	3.0 Wolf WR1-Cosworth V8		5/23
dns	"	"	20	Walter Wolf Racing	G	3.0 Wolf WR2-Cosworth V8	*practice only*	- / -
3	US GP WEST	Long Beach	20	Walter Wolf Racing	G	3.0 Wolf WR2-Cosworth V8	*puncture when leading*	3/22
3	SPANISH GP	Jarama	20	Walter Wolf Racing	G	3.0 Wolf WR2-Cosworth V8		5/31
1	MONACO GP	Monte Carlo	20	Walter Wolf Racing	G	3.0 Wolf WR1-Cosworth V8	FL	2/26
dns	"	"	20	Walter Wolf Racing	G	3.0 Wolf WR3-Cosworth V8	*practice only*	- / -
ret	BELGIAN GP	Zolder	20	Walter Wolf Racing	G	3.0 Wolf WR3-Cosworth V8	*engine*	4/32
dns	"	"	20	Walter Wolf Racing	G	3.0 Wolf WR2-Cosworth V8	*practice only*	- / -
ret	SWEDISH GP	Anderstorp	20	Walter Wolf Racing	G	3.0 Wolf WR1-Cosworth V8	*hit Watson*	4/31
dns	"	"	20	Walter Wolf Racing	G	3.0 Wolf WR2-Cosworth V8	*practice only*	- / -
ret	FRENCH GP	Dijon	20	Walter Wolf Racing	G	3.0 Wolf WR3-Cosworth V8	*hit by Regazzoni*	8/30
ret	BRITISH GP	Silverstone	20	Walter Wolf Racing	G	3.0 Wolf WR1-Cosworth V8	*engine*	4/36
2	GERMAN GP	Hockenheim	20	Walter Wolf Racing	G	3.0 Wolf WR1-Cosworth V8		1/30
ret	AUSTRIAN GP	Österreichring	20	Walter Wolf Racing	G	3.0 Wolf WR3-Cosworth V8	*spun off*	8/30
dns	"	"	20	Walter Wolf Racing	G	3.0 Wolf WR1-Cosworth V8	*practice only*	- / -

3	DUTCH GP	Zandvoort	20	Walter Wolf Racing	G	3.0 Wolf WR2-Cosworth V8	1 lap behind	15/34
ret	ITALIAN GP	Monza	20	Walter Wolf Racing	G	3.0 Wolf WR1-Cosworth V8	engine	3/34
3	US GP EAST	Watkins Glen	20	Walter Wolf Racing	G	3.0 Wolf WR2-Cosworth V8		9/27
1	CANADIAN GP	Mosport Park	20	Walter Wolf Racing	G	3.0 Wolf WR1-Cosworth V8		9/27
10	JAPANESE GP	Mount Fuji	20	Walter Wolf Racing	G	3.0 Wolf WR3-Cosworth V8	pit stop – tyres/FL/2 laps behind	6/23

1978 Championship position: 7th   Wins: 0   Pole positions: 0   Fastest laps: 0   Points scored: 24

10	ARGENTINE GP	Buenos Aires	20	Walter Wolf Racing	G	3.0 Wolf WR4-Cosworth V8		- / -
dns	"	" "	20	Walter Wolf Racing	G	3.0 Wolf WR1-Cosworth V8	set grid time in car	15/26
ret	BRAZILIAN GP	Rio	20	Walter Wolf Racing	G	3.0 Wolf WR1-Cosworth V8	collision with Tambay/suspension	12/28
ret	SOUTH AFRICAN GP	Kyalami	20	Walter Wolf Racing	G	3.0 Wolf WR1-Cosworth V8	engine cut out – accident	5/30
dns	"	" "	20	Walter Wolf Racing	G	3.0 Wolf WR3-Cosworth V8	practice only	- / -
ret	US GP WEST	Long Beach	20	Walter Wolf Racing	G	3.0 Wolf WR3-Cosworth V8	hit by Tambay	10/30
dns	"	" "	20	Walter Wolf Racing	G	3.0 Wolf WR1-Cosworth V8	practice only	- / -
3	MONACO GP	Monte Carlo	20	Walter Wolf Racing	G	3.0 Wolf WR1-Cosworth V8		9/30
dns	"	" "	20	Walter Wolf Racing	G	3.0 Wolf WR5-Cosworth V8	practice only	- / -
ret	BELGIAN GP	Zolder	20	Walter Wolf Racing	G	3.0 Wolf WR1-Cosworth V8	spun off	5/30
4	SPANISH GP	Jarama	20	Walter Wolf Racing	G	3.0 Wolf WR5-Cosworth V8		=9/29
ret	SWEDISH GP	Anderstorp	20	Walter Wolf Racing	G	3.0 Wolf WR5-Cosworth V8	overheating	6/27
6	FRENCH GP	Paul Ricard	20	Walter Wolf Racing	G	3.0 Wolf WR5-Cosworth V8		7/29
ret	BRITISH GP	Brands Hatch	20	Walter Wolf Racing	G	3.0 Wolf WR5-Cosworth V8	gearbox	3/30
dns	"	" "	20	Walter Wolf Racing	G	3.0 Wolf WR6-Cosworth V8	practice only	- / -
2	GERMAN GP	Hockenheim	20	Walter Wolf Racing	G	3.0 Wolf WR5-Cosworth V8		4/30
ret	AUSTRIAN GP	Österreichring	20	Walter Wolf Racing	G	3.0 Wolf WR5-Cosworth V8	spun off in first part of race	7/31
12	DUTCH GP	Zandvoort	20	Walter Wolf Racing	G	3.0 Wolf WR6-Cosworth V8	handling problems/2 laps behind	15/33
dns	"	"	20	Walter Wolf Racing	G	3.0 Wolf WR5-Cosworth V8	practice only	- / -
12	ITALIAN GP	Monza	20	Walter Wolf Racing	G	3.0 Wolf WR5-Cosworth V8	did not practice this car/1 lap behind	- / -
dns	"	"	20	Walter Wolf Racing	G	3.0 Wolf WR6-Cosworth V8	car damaged at first start	9/32
3	US GP EAST	Watkins Glen	20	Walter Wolf Racing	G	3.0 Wolf WR6-Cosworth V8		11/27
2	CANADIAN GP	Montreal	20	Walter Wolf Racing	G	3.0 Wolf WR6-Cosworth V8		2/28

1979 WORLD CHAMPION   Wins: 3   Pole positions: 1   Fastest laps: 0   Points scored: 60

ret/dns*	ARGENTINE GP	Buenos Aires	11	Scuderia Ferrari SpA SEFAC	M	3.0 Ferrari 312T3 F12	*hurt wrist in first start	5/26
6	BRAZILIAN GP	Interlagos	11	Scuderia Ferrari SpA SEFAC	M	3.0 Ferrari 312T3 F12	1 lap behind	6/26
2	SOUTH AFRICAN GP	Kyalami	11	Scuderia Ferrari SpA SEFAC	M	3.0 Ferrari 312T4 F12	pit stop – tyres when leading	2/26
2	US GP WEST	Long Beach	11	Scuderia Ferrari SpA SEFAC	M	3.0 Ferrari 312T4 F12		3/26
4	SPANISH GP	Jarama	11	Scuderia Ferrari SpA SEFAC	M	3.0 Ferrari 312T4 F12		5/27
1	BELGIAN GP	Zolder	11	Scuderia Ferrari SpA SEFAC	M	3.0 Ferrari 312T4 F12		=6/28
1	MONACO GP	Monte Carlo	11	Scuderia Ferrari SpA SEFAC	M	3.0 Ferrari 312T4 F12		1/25
7	FRENCH GP	Dijon	11	Scuderia Ferrari SpA SEFAC	M	3.0 Ferrari 312T4 F12	pit stop – tyres/1 lap behind	5/27
5	BRITISH GP	Silverstone	11	Scuderia Ferrari SpA SEFAC	M	3.0 Ferrari 312T4 F12	1 lap behind	11/26
4	GERMAN GP	Hockenheim	11	Scuderia Ferrari SpA SEFAC	M	3.0 Ferrari 312T4 F12		5/26
4	AUSTRIAN GP	Österreichring	11	Scuderia Ferrari SpA SEFAC	M	3.0 Ferrari 312T4 F12		9/26
2	DUTCH GP	Zandvoort	11	Scuderia Ferrari SpA SEFAC	M	3.0 Ferrari 312T4 F12		5/26
1	ITALIAN GP	Monza	11	Scuderia Ferrari SpA SEFAC	M	3.0 Ferrari 312T4 F12		3/28

Zoom shots were all the fashion way back when. Jody Scheckter's Ferrari is given the artistic treatment to spice up a mundane shot taken at Monaco in 1979.

4	CANADIAN GP	Montreal	11	Scuderia Ferrari SpA SEFAC	M	3.0 Ferrari 312T4 F12	*pit stop – tyres/1 lap behind*		9/29
ret	US GP EAST	Watkins Glen	11	Scuderia Ferrari SpA SEFAC	M	3.0 Ferrari 312T4 F12	*tyre failure – suspension*		16/30

1980 Championship position: 19th   Wins: 0   Pole positions: 0   Fastest laps: 0   Points scored: 2

ret	ARGENTINE GP	Buenos Aires	1	Scuderia Ferrari SpA SEFAC	M	3.0 Ferrari 312T5 F12	*engine*	11/28
ret	BRAZILIAN GP	Interlagos	1	Scuderia Ferrari SpA SEFAC	M	3.0 Ferrari 312T5 F12	*engine*	8/28
ret	SOUTH AFRICAN GP	Kyalami	1	Scuderia Ferrari SpA SEFAC	M	3.0 Ferrari 312T5 F12	*engine – electrics*	9/28
5	US GP WEST	Long Beach	1	Scuderia Ferrari SpA SEFAC	M	3.0 Ferrari 312T5 F12	*pit stop – tyres/1 lap behind*	16/27
8	BELGIAN GP	Zolder	1	Scuderia Ferrari SpA SEFAC	M	3.0 Ferrari 312T5 F12	*2 laps behind*	14/27
ret	MONACO GP	Monte Carlo	1	Scuderia Ferrari SpA SEFAC	M	3.0 Ferrari 312T5 F12	*handling*	17/27
12	FRENCH GP	Paul Ricard	1	Scuderia Ferrari SpA SEFAC	M	3.0 Ferrari 312T5 F12	*2 pit stops – tyres*	19/27
10	BRITISH GP	Brands Hatch	1	Scuderia Ferrari SpA SEFAC	M	3.0 Ferrari 312T5 F12	*pit stop – nose cone/3 laps behind*	23/26
13	GERMAN GP	Hockenheim	1	Scuderia Ferrari SpA SEFAC	M	3.0 Ferrari 312T5 F12	*pit stop – tyres/1 lap behind*	21/26
13	AUSTRIAN GP	Österreichring	1	Scuderia Ferrari SpA SEFAC	M	3.0 Ferrari 312T5 F12	*pit stop – tyres/1 lap behind*	22/25
9	DUTCH GP	Zandvoort	1	Scuderia Ferrari SpA SEFAC	M	3.0 Ferrari 312T5 F12	*2 pit stops – tyres/1 lap behind*	12/28
8	ITALIAN GP	Imola	1	Scuderia Ferrari SpA SEFAC	M	3.0 Ferrari 312T5 F12	*1 lap behind*	16/28
dnq	CANADIAN GP	Montreal	1	Scuderia Ferrari SpA SEFAC	M	3.0 Ferrari 312T5 F12		26/28
11	US GP EAST	Watkins Glen	1	Scuderia Ferrari SpA SEFAC	M	3.0 Ferrari 312T5 F12	*3 laps behind*	23/27

GP Starts: 110 (112)   GP Wins: 10   Pole positions: 3   Fastest laps: 5   Points: 255

SCHELL, Harry (F/USA) b 29/6/1921, Paris, France – d 13/5/1960, Silverstone Circuit, Northamptonshire, England

1950 Championship position: Unplaced

	Race	Circuit	No	Entrant	Tyres	Capacity/Car/Engine	Comment	Q Pos/Entries
ret	MONACO GP	Monte Carlo	8	Horschell Racing Corp	D	1.1 Cooper T12-JAP V2	*multiple accident*	20/21
8	SWISS GP	Bremgarten	44	Ecurie Bleue	D	4.5 Lago-Talbot T26C 6	*3 laps behind*	18/18

1951 Championship position: Unplaced

12	SWISS GP	Bremgarten	32	Enrico Platé	P	1.5 s/c Maserati 4CLT/48 4	*4 laps behind*	17/21
ret	FRENCH GP	Reims	20	Enrico Platé	P	1.5 s/c Maserati 4CLT/48 4	*overheating engine*	22/23

1952 Championship position: Unplaced

ret	SWISS GP	Bremgarten	40	Enrico Platé	P	2.0 Maserati 4CLT/Platé 4	*engine*	18/21
ret	FRENCH GP	Rouen	18	Enrico Platé	P	2.0 Maserati 4CLT/Platé 4	*gearbox*	12/20
ret	"	"	16	Enrico Platé	P	2.0 Maserati 4CLT/Platé 4	*took over de Graffenried's car/brakes*	– / –
17	BRITISH GP	Silverstone	33	Enrico Platé	P	2.0 Maserati 4CLT/Platé 4	*7 laps behind*	32/32

1953 Championship position: Unplaced

7*	ARGENTINE GP	Buenos Aires	28	Equipe Gordini	E	2.0 Gordini Type 16 6	*took over Trintignant's car/6 laps behind*	– / –
ret	DUTCH GP	Zandvoort	20	Equipe Gordini	E	2.0 Gordini Type 16 6	*transmission*	10/20
7	BELGIAN GP	Spa	20	Equipe Gordini	E	2.0 Gordini Type 16 6	*3 laps behind*	12/22
ret	FRENCH GP	Reims	6	Equipe Gordini	E	2.0 Gordini Type 16 6	*engine*	20/25
ret	BRITISH GP	Silverstone	28	Equipe Gordini	E	2.0 Gordini Type 16 6	*magneto*	9/29
ret	GERMAN GP	Nürburgring	11	Equipe Gordini	E	2.0 Gordini Type 16 6	*head gasket*	10/35
9	ITALIAN GP	Monza	38	Equipe Gordini	E	2.0 Gordini Type 16 6	*5 laps behind*	15/30

1954 Championship position: Unplaced

6	ARGENTINE GP	Buenos Aires	28	Harry Schell	P	2.5 Maserati A6GCM/250F 6	*3 laps behind*	11/18
ret	FRENCH GP	Reims	48	Harry Schell	P	2.5 Maserati A6GCM/250F 6	*fuel pump*	21/22
12	BRITISH GP	Silverstone	3	Harry Schell	P	2.5 Maserati A6GCM/250F 6	*7 laps behind*	16/31
7	GERMAN GP	Nürburgring	15	Harry Schell	P	2.5 Maserati A6GCM/250F 6	*1 lap behind*	14/23
ret	SWISS GP	Bremgarten	34	Officine Alfieri Maserati	P	2.5 Maserati 250F 6	*oil pump*	13/16
ret	SPANISH GP	Pedralbes	24	Harry Schell	P	2.5 Maserati 250F 6	*transmission – rear axle*	4/22

1955 Championship position: Unplaced

6*	ARGENTINE GP	Buenos Aires	28	Officine Alfieri Maserati	P	2.5 Maserati 250F 6	*Behra took over/5 laps behind*	7/22
7*	"	"	"	22	Officine Alfieri Maserati	P	2.5 Maserati 250F 6	*Mantovani/Musso co-drove/13 laps behind*	– / –
ret*	"	"	"	26	Officine Alfieri Maserati	P	2.5 Maserati 250F 6	*Bucci/Menditéguy co-drove/*fuel starvation*	– / –
ret	MONACO GP	Monte Carlo	46	Scuderia Ferrari	E	2.5 Ferrari 555 4	*engine*	18/22
dns	BELGIAN GP	Spa	4	Scuderia Ferrari	E	2.5 Ferrari 555 4	*Trintignant drove car*	– / –
ret	BRITISH GP	Aintree	30	Vandervell Products Ltd	P	2.5 Vanwall 4	*broken throttle pedal*	7/25
9	"	"	28	Vandervell Products Ltd	P	2.5 Vanwall 4	*took over Wharton's car/18 laps behind*	– / –
ret	ITALIAN GP	Monza	42	Vandervell Products Ltd	P	2.5 Vanwall 4	*suspension*	13/22

1956 Championship position: 12th=   Wins: 0   Pole positions: 0   Fastest laps: 0   Points scored: 3

ret	MONACO GP	Monte Carlo	16	Vandervell Products Ltd	P	2.5 Vanwall 4	*spun off avoiding Fangio*	5/19
4	BELGIAN GP	Spa	10	Vandervell Products Ltd	P	2.5 Vanwall 4	*1 lap behind*	6/16
ret	FRENCH GP	Reims	22	Vandervell Products Ltd	P	2.5 Vanwall 4	*engine*	4/20
10*	"	"	24	Vandervell Products Ltd	P	2.5 Vanwall 4	*took over Hawthorn's car/5 laps behind*	– / –
ret	BRITISH GP	Silverstone	16	Vandervell Products Ltd	P	2.5 Vanwall 4	*fuel pipe*	5/28
ret	GERMAN GP	Nürburgring	12	Scuderia Centro Sud	P	2.5 Maserati 250F 6	*overheating*	12/21
ret	ITALIAN GP	Monza	18	Vandervell Products Ltd	P	2.5 Vanwall 4	*transmission*	10/26

1957 Championship position: 7th=   Wins: 0   Pole positions: 0   Fastest laps: 0   Points scored: 8

4	ARGENTINE GP	Buenos Aires	22	Scuderia Centro Sud	P	2.5 Maserati 250F 6	*2 laps behind*	9/16
ret*	MONACO GP	Monte Carlo	38	Officine Alfieri Maserati	P	2.5 Maserati 250F 6	*king pins*	8/21
ret	"	"	"	34	Officine Alfieri Maserati	P	2.5 Maserati 250F 6	*took over Scarlatti's car/mechanical*	– / –
5	FRENCH GP	Rouen	6	Officine Alfieri Maserati	P	2.5 Maserati 250F 6	*7 laps behind*	4/15
ret	BRITISH GP	Aintree	6	Officine Alfieri Maserati	P	2.5 Maserati 250F 6	*water pump*	7/19
7	GERMAN GP	Nürburgring	3	Officine Alfieri Maserati	P	2.5 Maserati 250F 6		6/24
3	PESCARA GP	Pescara	6	Officine Alfieri Maserati	P	2.5 Maserati 250F 6		5/16
ret	ITALIAN GP	Monza	4	Officine Alfieri Maserati	P	2.5 Maserati 250F 6	*fuel pump*	6/19
5*	"	"	8	Officine Alfieri Maserati	P	2.5 Maserati 250F 6	*took over Scarlatti's car/3 laps behind*	– / –

HARRY SCHELL

BORN in Paris, but of American parents, Harry O'Reilly Schell was a fun-loving extrovert who was one of the great characters of the 1950s motor racing scene. His childhood during the 1930s was filled by racing, for his father, Laury, was the patron of Ecurie Bleue, a team that raced Delahayes and Talbots. His mother, Lucy, took over the running of the team following the death of her husband in a road accident and ran René Dreyfus at Indianapolis just before the Second World War. Young Harry was on that trip, and resolved to race himself once old enough.

During the war, Harry served in the US military in Finland, and by the late 1940s he was taking his first steps in racing. In 1949, he managed a second place with a Talbot in the Coupe du Salon at Montlhéry, but it was the following year, when he raced a Cooper-JAP, that brought him success. He handled the little car with great verve, frequently embarrassing Formula 2 opposition. At the Circuit du Lac, in Aix-les-Bains, he succeeded in beating the works Ferrari in his heat and comfortably led the final before being forced into retirement. He managed to gain an entry for the Monaco GP that year, but was eliminated in the first-lap multiple crash. At Bremgarten, however, he enjoyed his first taste of a real grand prix machine, taking a Talbot into eighth place.

In the main, Schell raced Maseratis entered by Ecurie Platé in 1951 and 1952, but he started to gain solid results only when he joined forces with Simca Gordini. A second place in the Cadours GP of 1952 encouraged both parties to continue together the following year, when Harry was out of luck in the championship grands prix, but took a string of good finishes in the French championship rounds. Schell ran his own Maserati A6GCM in 1954, taking second place at Castelfusano, and thirds at Pescara and Aintree, but by the end-of-season Spanish GP, he had his own Maserati 250F and caused something of a stir by driving off into the distance at the start. He only lost the lead to Juan Fangio after a spin, but eventually retired with transmission failure. There was talk of the American having run on half-tanks to break up the opposition, but certainly he had made his mark, for both Vanwall and Ferrari employed his services in 1955, and he won some minor events for Tony Vandervell. Schell showed the green machines' startling potential in 1956, when he put on a marvellous show at Reims, snapping at the heels of the works Ferraris, and scored a win in the Caen GP, before taking his leave to join the works Maserati team in 1957.

Harry fulfilled a useful subordinate role to Fangio, recording a number of good results, including a fine if distant third place at Pescara. He also took second place at Pau and third at Modena, before arranging to join BRM for the 1958 and 1959 seasons. He proved an excellent acquisition for the Bourne team, but his second place at Zandvoort was the closest the American would ever get to that elusive grand prix win. At the end of the 1959 season, he purchased a Cooper-Climax, which he raced under the Ecurie Bleue banner as a privateer. He also raced the car at the beginning of 1960, before joining the Yeoman Credit team. It was while practising with one of their cars for the International Trophy in the wet at Silverstone that he lost his life, crashing after the Cooper got away from him on one of the circuit's fast bends. Harry was an immensely popular character, and his death was a great loss to the racing scene as it moved into a new era.

	1958 Championship position: 5th=	Wins: 0	Pole positions: 0	Fastest laps: 0	Points scored: 14				
6	ARGENTINE GP	Buenos Aires	8	Joakim Bonnier	P	2.5 Maserati 250F 6	3 laps behind	8/10
5	MONACO GP	Monte Carlo	8	Owen Racing Organisation	D	2.5 BRM P25 4	9 laps behind	11/28
2	DUTCH GP	Zandvoort	15	Owen Racing Organisation	D	2.5 BRM P25 4		7/17
5	BELGIAN GP	Spa	10	Owen Racing Organisation	D	2.5 BRM P25 4	1 lap behind	7/20
ret	FRENCH GP	Reims	16	Owen Racing Organisation	D	2.5 BRM P25 4	overheating	3/21
5	BRITISH GP	Silverstone	20	Owen Racing Organisation	D	2.5 BRM P25 4		2/21
ret	GERMAN GP	Nürburgring	6	Owen Racing Organisation	D	2.5 BRM P25 4	brakes	8/26
6	PORTUGUESE GP	Oporto	10	Owen Racing Organisation	D	2.5 BRM P25 4	1 lap behind	7/15
ret	ITALIAN GP	Monza	10	Owen Racing Organisation	D	2.5 BRM P25 4	collision with Von Trips on grid	9/21
5	MOROCCAN GP	Casablanca	16	Owen Racing Organisation	D	2.5 BRM P25 4		10/25

	1959 Championship position: 10th=	Wins: 0	Pole positions: 0	Fastest laps: 0	Points scored: 5				
ret	MONACO GP	Monte Carlo	16	Owen Racing Organisation	D	2.5 BRM P25 4	crash – damaged radiator	9/24
ret	DUTCH GP	Zandvoort	6	Owen Racing Organisation	D	2.5 BRM P25 4	gearbox	6/15
7	FRENCH GP	Reims	6	Owen Racing Organisation	D	2.5 BRM P25 4	3 laps behind	9/22
4	BRITISH GP	Aintree	8	Owen Racing Organisation	D	2.5 BRM P25 4	1 lap behind	3/30
nc	GERMAN GP	AVUS	10	Owen Racing Organisation	D	2.5 BRM P25 4	5th heat 1/nc heat 2/11 laps behind	8/16
5	PORTUGUESE GP	Monsanto	6	Owen Racing Organisation	D	2.5 BRM P25 4	3 laps behind	9/16
7	ITALIAN GP	Monza	2	Owen Racing Organisation	D	2.5 BRM P25 4	2 laps behind	7/21
ret	US GP	Sebring	19	Ecurie Bleue	D	2.2 Cooper T51-Climax 4	clutch	3/19

	1960 Championship position: Unplaced							
ret	ARGENTINE GP	Buenos Aires	34	Ecurie Bleue	D	2.2 Cooper T51-Climax 4	fuel pump	9/22

GP Starts: 56   GP Wins: 0   Pole positions: 0   Fastest laps: 0   Points: 32

SCHENKEN, Tim (AUS) b 26/9/1943, Gordon, Sydney, New South Wales

	1970 Championship position: Unplaced							
	Race	Circuit	No	Entrant	Tyres	Capacity/Car/Engine	Comment	Q Pos/Entries
ret	AUSTRIAN GP	Österreichring	26	Frank Williams Racing Cars	D	3.0 de Tomaso 505-Cosworth V8	engine	18/24
ret	ITALIAN GP	Monza	54	Frank Williams Racing Cars	D	3.0 de Tomaso 505-Cosworth V8	engine	22/27
nc	CANADIAN GP	St Jovite	10	Frank Williams Racing Cars	D	3.0 de Tomaso 505-Cosworth V8	pit stop – shock absorber/-11 laps	17/20
ret	US GP	Watkins Glen	30	Frank Williams Racing Cars	D	3.0 de Tomaso 505-Cosworth V8	rear suspension	20/27

	1971 Championship position: 14th=	Wins: 0	Pole positions: 0	Fastest laps: 0	Points scored: 5				
9	SPANISH GP	Montjuich Park	8	Motor Racing Developments	G	3.0 Brabham BT33-Cosworth V8	3 laps behind	21/22
10	MONACO GP	Monte Carlo	8	Motor Racing Developments	G	3.0 Brabham BT33-Cosworth V8	pit stop – wheel change/-4 laps	18/23
ret	DUTCH GP	Zandvoort	25	Motor Racing Developments	G	3.0 Brabham BT33-Cosworth V8	collision with Pescarolo	19/24
12/ret	FRENCH GP	Paul Ricard	8	Motor Racing Developments	G	3.0 Brabham BT33-Cosworth V8	engine – oil pressure/5 laps behind	14/24
12/ret	BRITISH GP	Silverstone	8	Motor Racing Developments	G	3.0 Brabham BT33-Cosworth V8	gearbox/5 laps behind	7/24
6	GERMAN GP	Nürburgring	25	Motor Racing Developments	G	3.0 Brabham BT33-Cosworth V8		9/23
3	AUSTRIAN GP	Österreichring	8	Motor Racing Developments	G	3.0 Brabham BT33-Cosworth V8		7/22
ret	ITALIAN GP	Monza	11	Motor Racing Developments	G	3.0 Brabham BT33-Cosworth V8	rear subframe	9/24
ret	CANADIAN GP	Mosport Park	8	Motor Racing Developments	G	3.0 Brabham BT33-Cosworth V8	transistor box	17/27
ret	US GP	Watkins Glen	23	Motor Racing Developments	G	3.0 Brabham BT33-Cosworth V8	valve	16/32

	1972 Championship position: 19th=	Wins: 0	Pole positions: 0	Fastest laps: 0	Points scored: 2				
5	ARGENTINE GP	Buenos Aires	19	Brooke Bond Oxo/Rob Walker/Team Surtees	F	3.0 Surtees TS9B-Cosworth V8		11/22
ret	SOUTH AFRICAN GP	Kyalami	16	Brooke Bond Oxo/Rob Walker/Team Surtees	F	3.0 Surtees TS9B-Cosworth V8	engine	=8/27
8	SPANISH GP	Jarama	12	Brooke Bond Oxo/Rob Walker/Team Surtees	F	3.0 Surtees TS9B-Cosworth V8	2 laps behind	18/26
ret	MONACO GP	Monte Carlo	10	Team Surtees	F	3.0 Surtees TS9B-Cosworth V8	hit barrier	13/25
ret	BELGIAN GP	Nivelles	35	Team Surtees	F	3.0 Surtees TS9B-Cosworth V8	engine	21/26
17	FRENCH GP	Clermont Ferrand	27	Flame Out-Team Surtees	F	3.0 Surtees TS9B-Cosworth V8	pit stop – fuel pressure/-2 laps	5/29
ret	BRITISH GP	Brands Hatch	22	Flame Out-Team Surtees	F	3.0 Surtees TS9B-Cosworth V8	rear suspension mounting	5/27
14	GERMAN GP	Nürburgring	15	Team Surtees	F	3.0 Surtees TS9B-Cosworth V8	pit stops – tyre – electrical/-1 lap	12/27
11	AUSTRIAN GP	Österreichring	24	Team Surtees	F	3.0 Surtees TS9B-Cosworth V8	pit stops – tyres/2 laps behind	8/26
ret	ITALIAN GP	Monza	8	Team Surtees	F	3.0 Surtees TS9B-Cosworth V8	hit chicane	22/27
7	CANADIAN GP	Mosport Park	22	Team Surtees	F	3.0 Surtees TS9B-Cosworth V8	1 lap behind	=12/25
ret	US GP	Watkins Glen	22	Team Surtees	F	3.0 Surtees TS14-Cosworth V8	oil leak	32/32

	1973 Championship position: Unplaced							
14	CANADIAN GP	Mosport Park	26	Frank Williams Racing Cars	F	3.0 Iso Marlboro 1R-Cosworth V8	pit stop – tyres/5 laps behind	24/26

	1974 Championship position: Unplaced							
14/ret	SPANISH GP	Jarama	23	Trojan-Tauranac Racing	F	3.0 Trojan T103-Cosworth V8	spun off/8 laps behind	26/28
10	BELGIAN GP	Nivelles	41	Trojan-Tauranac Racing	F	3.0 Trojan T103-Cosworth V8	2 laps behind	23/32
ret	MONACO GP	Monte Carlo	23	Trojan-Tauranac Racing	F	3.0 Trojan T103-Cosworth V8	multiple accident	24/28
dnq	DUTCH GP	Zandvoort	23	Trojan-Tauranac Racing	F	3.0 Trojan T103-Cosworth V8		26/27
ret	BRITISH GP	Brands Hatch	23	Trojan-Tauranac Racing	F	3.0 Trojan T103-Cosworth V8	suspension	=25/34
dnq	GERMAN GP	Nürburgring	23	Trojan-Tauranac Racing	F	3.0 Trojan T103-Cosworth V8		28/32
10	AUSTRIAN GP	Österreichring	23	Trojan-Tauranac Racing	F	3.0 Trojan T103-Cosworth V8	4 laps behind	19/31
ret	ITALIAN GP	Monza	29	Trojan-Tauranac Racing	F	3.0 Trojan T103-Cosworth V8	gear selection	20/31
dsq*	US GP	Watkins Glen	31	John Player Team Lotus	G	3.0 Lotus 76-Cosworth V8	*started unofficially – 2nd reserve	27/30

GP Starts: 34   GP Wins: 0   Pole positions: 0   Fastest laps: 0   Points: 7

SCHERRER, Albert (CH) b 28/2/1908, Riehen – d 5/7/1986, Basel

	1953 Championship position: Unplaced							
	Race	Circuit	No	Entrant	Tyres	Capacity/Car/Engine	Comment	Q Pos/Entries
8	SWISS GP	Bremgarten	18	HW Motors	D	2.0 HWM-Alta 4	16 laps behind	18/23

GP Starts: 1   GP Wins: 0   Pole positions: 0   Fastest laps: 0   Points: 0

TIM SCHENKEN

WITH 42 wins in Formula Ford and a Grovewood Award in 1968, Tim Schenken was obviously a man to watch, and in 1969 he continued the good work in Rodney Bloor's Sports Motors Formula 3 Brabham at home and abroad, winning the French Craven A title.

For 1970, Tim and the Sports Motors team took the step up to Formula 2 and had an up-and-down season, the best results being second at Paul Ricard, and third at both Pau and Mantorp Park. Schenken also made his grand prix debut, joining a Williams team that was still reeling from the loss of Piers Courage, but he could do nothing with the de Tomaso.

The following season, Schenken appeared to have made the big breakthrough. Signed as number two to Graham Hill in the Brabham team, he was restricted to the old BT33 (possibly an advantage, as it was easier to set up than the 'lobster-claw' BT34), but overshadowed the former world champion for much of the year. His two points finishes were not really just reward for his efforts, although in non-title races he took third place in the International Trophy and fourth in the Race of Champions.

In 1972, Tim made what turned out to be the biggest mistake of his career, joining Team Surtees for a season that effectively sabotaged his long-term grand prix ambitions. There was some solace, however, for he had been leading the Rondel Formula 2 outfit with distinction and was invited to join the Ferrari sports car team, for whom he scored a win in the Buenos Aires 1000km and the Nürburgring 1000km, in addition to four second places, all paired with Ronnie Peterson.

After ambitious plans to race a Formula 1 Rondel failed to materialise in 1973 and the Trojan project with his old Brabham boss, Ron Tauranac, turned into an embarrassing failure in 1974, poor Tim must have thought things couldn't get any worse, but they did when he was invited to handle a Lotus 76 in the 1974 US GP. He found the car almost undriveable, and his one race for the Hethel team ended in non-qualification.

Schenken then embarked on a programme of sports car and GT racing for George Loos, racing his stable of Porsches during 1975–77, and winning the Nürburgring 100kKm with Toine Hezemans and Rolf Stommelen in 1977. He also shared a Jaguar XJ12C with John Fitzpatrick in the 1977 European GT championship, before retiring to concentrate on his successful Tiga racing car business with partner Howden Ganley. After the company was wound up in 1989,

Tim returned to Australia, where now he became the representative to the FIA for the Confederation of Australian Motor Sport. In addition, he has acted as the race director for the Australian V8 Supercar series and served as clerk of the course for the Formula 1 grand prix in Melbourne.

ALBERT SCHERRER

AN amateur Swiss national racer, Albert Scherrer competed from the late 1940s through to the mid-1950s. His Jaguar XK120 provided some top-three finishes, either outright or in class, at such circuits as Bremgarten and Geneva. He was also a stalwart of the well-supported and popular Swiss hill-climbs of that period.

Scherrer's only major race was in the 1953 Swiss Grand Prix, for which he hired one of John Heath's HWM-Altas. Despite a shunt, he made it to the finish, but did not complete enough laps to be classified.

Subsequently, Scherrer competed domestically in a Mercedes 300SL, winning the over-2600cc production sports class in the 1956 Ollon-Villars hill-climb.

DOMENICO 'MIMMO' SCHIATTARELLA

ANOTHER driver to have found his way on to the grand prix grid in the 1990s by dint of finance rather than a track record of major successes, Domenico 'Mimmo' Schiattarella began racing in Italian Formula 4 in 1985. He won that championship the following term and graduated to Italian Formula 3, where he spent the next three years. By 1991, he was a leading runner along with the likes of Luca Badoer and Jacques Villeneuve, but he threw away his chance of becoming the champion in the final round at Vallelunga, where he pushed his title rival Giambattista Busi off the circuit and was black-flagged.

Schiattarella spent part of the next year in the Sud-Am championship, before making an end-of-year appearance in the Macau F3 race, where he finished fifth.

A couple of outings in the Project Indy Lola tested the Indy car waters, but the chance to drive for Simtek at the end of the 1994 season whetted Domenico's appetite for more in 1995. Apparently, his contract was for the first half of the year only, Hideki Noda having laid down his wedge of cash for the balance of the season. In the event, 'Mimmo' failed to get past round five at Monaco: despite possessing a very promising car, Simtek were in such financial difficulties that they could no longer carry on.

Subsequently, in the main, Schiattarella concentrated on sports car racing. In 1996, he won the Vallelunga six-hours in a Ferrari F40 against moderate opposition, and he shared a Lotus GT1 with Badoer on a couple of occasions the following year. The 1998 season saw the briefest of returns to single-seaters in CART with Project Indy, after Roberto Moreno quit the team.

'Mimmo' found a competitive ride at last in 1999, driving Team Rafanelli's Riley & Scott MkII sports car in the American Le Mans Series. Teamed with Eric van de Poele, he won the opening round at Road Atlanta and placed well elsewhere. The likeable Italian also joined Alex Caffi and Andrea Montermini at Le Mans, where the Italian trio took a Courage-Nissan into a fine sixth place.

Between 2000 and 2003, Schiattarella competed in North America, firstly in a Ferrari 333SP and a Lola, before settling into a partnership with Emanuele Naspetti in a Ferrarai 550 Maranello.

HEINZ SCHILLER

A SWISS speedboat champion before turning to four-wheeled sport, Heinz Schiller made a good start in a 1500cc Porsche GT and RS sports. He took numerous placings and wins with the car in the mid-1950s, including second in class in the 1957 Mille Miglia. Early in 1958, he was allowed to race his Porsche RS at the Formula 2 Pau GP, circulating steadily to earn a distant sixth place.

After hill-climbing in the Porsche Carrera Abarth in 1961, the Schiller tasted some real single-seater competition with Ecurie Filipinetti in 1962, partnering Jo Siffert. He mainly handled the team's Porsche 718, but had a single chance in the more competitive Lotus 24-BRM V8 at the German GP.

Schiller made just one more open-wheeled appearance for the team, back in the old Porsche at Pau in 1963, when he finished third, albeit five laps behind the Lotus duo of Jim Clark and Trevor Taylor. He continued to race Filipinetti's GT cars, taking second in class at the Nürburgring 1000km and also a class win at the Ollon-Villars hill-climb in the Porsche Carrera Abarth.

In 1964, Schiller raced his Porsche 904 in long-distance events with Jo Siffert, and took tenth place (and third in class) at Le Mans in the works car with Gerhard Koch.

SCHIATTARELLA, Domenico 'Mimmo' (I) b 17/11/1967, Milan

	1994 Championship position: Unplaced							
	Race	Circuit	No	Entrant	Tyres	Capacity/Car/Engine	Comment	Q Pos/Entries
19	EUROPEAN GP	Jerez	32	MTV Simtek Ford	G	3.5 Simtek S941-Ford HB V8	5 laps behind	26/28
ret	AUSTRALIAN GP	Adelaide	32	MTV Simtek Ford	G	3.5 Simtek S941-Ford HB V8	gear selection	26/28
	1995 Championship position: Unplaced							
ret	BRAZILIAN GP	Interlagos	11	MTV Simtek Ford	G	3.0 Simtek S195-Ford ED V8	steering box	26/26
9	ARGENTINE GP	Buenos Aires	11	MTV Simtek Ford	G	3.0 Simtek S195-Ford ED V8	4 laps behind	20/26
ret	SAN MARINO GP	Imola	11	MTV Simtek Ford	G	3.0 Simtek S195-Ford ED V8	suspension	23/26
15	SPANISH GP	Barcelona	11	MTV Simtek Ford	G	3.0 Simtek S195-Ford ED V8	4 laps behind	22/26
ret/dns*	MONACO GP	Monte Carlo	11	MTV Simtek Ford	G	3.0 Simtek S195-Ford ED V8	*accident at first start	(20)/26

GP Starts: 6 (7)   GP Wins: 0   Pole positions: 0   Fastest laps: 0   Points: 0

SCHILLER, Heinz (CH) b 25/1/1930, Frauenfeld – d 26/3/2007, Geneva

	1962 Championship position: Unplaced							
	Race	Circuit	No	Entrant	Tyres	Capacity/Car/Engine	Comment	Q Pos/Entries
ret	GERMAN GP	Nürburgring	28	Ecurie Filipinetti	D	1.5 Lotus 24-BRM V8	oil pressure	20/30

GP Starts: 1   GP Wins: 0   Pole positions: 0   Fastest laps: 0   Points: 0

SCHLESSER, Jean-Louis (F) b 12/9/1948, Nancy

1983	Championship position: Unplaced							
	Race	Circuit	No	Entrant	Tyres	Capacity/Car/Engine	Comment	Q Pos/Entries
dnq	FRENCH GP	Paul Ricard	18	RAM Automotive Team March	P	3.0 March-RAM 01-Cosworth V8		29/29
	1988	Championship position: Unplaced						
11	ITALIAN GP	Monza	5	Canon Williams Team	G	3.5 Williams FW12-Judd V8	collided with Senna/2 laps behind	22/31

GP Starts: 1   GP Wins: 0   Pole positions: 0   Fastest laps: 0   Points: 0

JEAN-LOUIS SCHLESSER

A NEPHEW of the late Jo Schlesser, Jean-Louis Schlesser is a driver who missed the Formula 1 boat. Unfortunately, the immensely popular Frenchman will be best remembered for inadvertently tangling with Ayrton Senna near the end of the 1988 Italian GP as the Brazilian was about to lap his Williams.

A graduate of Formule Renault, Schlesser became bogged down in French Formula 3 and production racing, before turning to the European F3 championship in 1981. His Martini was saddled with the wrong brand of tyres, however, and the undoubted high spot of the year was a terrific second place at Le Mans, sharing a Rondeau with Jacky Haran and Philippe Streiff. Still determined to succeed in single-seaters, Jean-Louis joined the Maurer F2 team alongside Stefan Bellof in 1982, but it was another season of frustration, as he did not enjoy the best of equipment.

In 1983, Schlesser began work as a test driver for Williams and attempted to qualify the RAM for the French GP. Then he returned to production cars, winning the French championship in 1985, before Tom Walkinshaw signed him for the TWR Jaguar sports car team in 1986. Disappointingly, finishes were thin on the ground and he was released, ultimately joining the Kouros Sauber team, which became the official representative of the Mercedes factory in 1988.

Schlesser scored two wins and finished second to Martin Brundle in the points standings that year, and the following season he made no mistake, winning five rounds (Suzuka, Jarama, the Nürburgring, Donington and Mexico City) to claim the World Sports Car Championship, a feat he repeated in 1990, when he shared the title with Mauro Baldi.

Since the 1990s, Jean-Louis has been tackling another branch of the sport, the gruelling cross-desert marathons. In 1999, at the 11th attempt, he finally won the Granada–Dakar Rally, driving his own Schlesser-buggy. Subsequently, he repeated the feat in 2000 on the Paris–Dakar–Cairo.

JO SCHLESSER

A TRUE all-rounder and as brave as they come, Jo Schlesser loved every form of motorsport and competed in as many of them as he possibly could during a career that started in 1952, when he rallied a Panhard. He tried the contemporary French vogue of Monomill racing in 1954, but then his serious competition activities were put on hold for three years while he worked in Madagascar.

Back in Europe in 1957, Schlesser finished second in the Liège–Rome–Liège Rally with a Mercedes, which he soon replaced with a Ferrari 250GT, but success did not really come until 1960 when he took second in class at the Nürburgring 1000km and second overall in the Rouen GP. This was in contrast to his rather disappointing year in a Formula 2 Cooper, a sixth place at Syracuse being his only result worth mentioning. Jo's 1961 season was curtailed by a very big accident during practice at Le Mans, which left him with a badly broken arm and leg, but he was back in action the following year with a Formula Junior Brabham, putting in some superb drives to become one of the formula's leading protagonists.

The advent of the 1-litre Formula 2 in 1964 gave Jo the chance to pit himself against some of racing's top names. He became a respected member of the Continental F2 fraternity, joining the Matra works team in 1966 and running the same car under the Ford France banner the following season, before setting up a team with great friend Guy Ligier to race McLarens in 1968. Since 1965, Schlesser had also made something of name for himself at the wheel of powerful sports cars, including a Shelby Cobra and then the Ford France GT40, winning the Reims 12-hour race in 1967, paired with Guy Ligier.

Schlesser's grand prix experience was limited to just two outings, however, in the Formula 2 class of the German GP and when he was invited to race the totally unproven air-cooled Honda in the 1968 French GP – it must be said, much against the wishes of John Surtees. In the opening laps of the race, Schlesser lost control of the car in pouring rain, crashing it into an earth bank, whereupon it burst into flames, swiftly claiming the life of its 41-year-old driver.

SCHLESSER, Jo (F) b 18/5/1928, Liouville, nr Nancy – d 7/7/1968, Rouen Circuit

	1966 Championship position: Unplaced							
	Race	Circuit	No	Entrant	Tyres	Capacity/Car/Engine	Comment	Q Pos/Entries
10*	GERMAN GP (F2)	Nürburgring	33	Matra Sports	D	1.0 Matra MS5-Cosworth 4 F2	*3rd in F2 class/1 lap behind	20/30
	1967 Championship position: Unplaced							
ret	GERMAN GP (F2)	Nürburgring	23	Ecurie Ford-France	D	1.6 Matra MS5-Cosworth 4 F2	clutch	18/25
	1968 Championship position: Unplaced							
ret	FRENCH GP	Rouen	18	Honda Racing (France)	F	3.0 Honda RA302 V8	crashed – fatal accident	17/18

GP Starts: 3   GP Wins: 0   Pole positions: 0   Fastest laps: 0   Points: 0

BERND SCHNEIDER

A MULTIPLE karting champion, and then a graduate of Formula Ford 1600 and FF2000, Bernd Schneider finished equal third in his first year of German F3 in 1986, but when he came back to slaughter the opposition in 1988, winning seven of the eight rounds he contested, many watchers were convinced that here at last was a German with a big future. Little did they realise that it would be at the wheel of Mercedes touring and sports cars that he would taste success, rather than in grand prix racing, where two miserable seasons with Zakspeed and a couple of drives with Arrows unfairly left him washed up as a GP driver at the age of 26.

Bernd drove a Kremer Porsche in Interserie racing in 1990 and then raced in IMSA for the Joest team, before reviving his career in the DTM with a Zakspeed Mercedes. He switched to an AMG works car for 1992 and soon was considered the fastest driver in the Mercedes squad, but the scintillating form of Nicola Larini and the Alfas in 1993 meant his quest for the championship would have to wait a little longer. After enduring the frustration of often leading, but hitting mechanical problems in 1994, Bernd's luck changed and everything came together a year on. In the AMG Mercedes, the German regularly blitzed the opposition, taking 11 wins from 23 starts to claim both the DTM and ITC titles. Nobody could have deserved his success more, and he rightly became the key driver in the Stuttgart giant's racing programme. The final year of the ITC in 1996 yielded only four wins, but his consistent finishes earned him second in the final standings, behind Manuel Reuter's Opel.

The high-tech formula having been scrapped, Mercedes unleashed their CLK-GTR on the FIA GT series, and Bernd shared in six wins from the 11 races to emerge as the clear drivers' champion. Despite five wins from ten starts, the German had to settle for second place in 1998, behind AMG team-mates Klaus Ludwig and Ricardo Zonta.

Since Mercedes concentrated solely on Le Mans for 1999, Bernd was without a regular racing schedule, but with the revised DTM series in place for 2000, he relished the chance to fight for the championship once again, winning six races and the series in the stunning new V8-engined CLK. He was crowned champion again in 2001 with three wins in a shortened programme, but lost out to Laurent Aiello's Audi the following season. In 2003, the 'Schneidermeister' was back on top, but only after a thrilling battle with newcomer Christijan Albers had gone to the final round at Hockenheim.

After a couple of seasons when Bernd was fighting to keep the DTM newcomers at bay, and perhaps he was no longer the quickest man around, Mercedes' favourite son still remained a competitive force in the series. After sixth and fourth places respectively, the veteran had enough speed and guile to clinch a record fifth title in 2006. He would race on competitvely for another two seasons, before taking honourable retirement at the end of the 2008 season, having scored more than 40 wins in the class where he had driven with such distinction.

SCHNEIDER, Bernd (D) b 20/7/1964, Saarbrücken

	1988 Championship position: Unplaced							
	Race	Circuit	No	Entrant	Tyres	Capacity/Car/Engine	Comment	Q Pos/Entries
dnq	BRAZILIAN GP	Rio	10	West Zakspeed Racing	G	1.5 t/c Zakspeed 881 4		30/31
dnq	SAN MARINO GP	Imola	10	West Zakspeed Racing	G	1.5 t/c Zakspeed 881 4		30/31
dnq	MONACO GP	Monte Carlo	10	West Zakspeed Racing	G	1.5 t/c Zakspeed 881 4		28/30
ret	MEXICAN GP	Mexico City	10	West Zakspeed Racing	G	1.5 t/c Zakspeed 881 4	engine	15/30
dnq	CANADIAN GP	Montreal	10	West Zakspeed Racing	G	1.5 t/c Zakspeed 881 4		30/31
dnq	US GP (DETROIT)	Detroit	10	West Zakspeed Racing	G	1.5 t/c Zakspeed 881 4		29/31
ret	FRENCH GP	Paul Ricard	10	West Zakspeed Racing	G	1.5 t/c Zakspeed 881 4	gearbox	21/31
dnq	BRITISH GP	Silverstone	10	West Zakspeed Racing	G	1.5 t/c Zakspeed 881 4		30/31
12	GERMAN GP	Hockenheim	10	West Zakspeed Racing	G	1.5 t/c Zakspeed 881 4	1 lap behind	22/31
dnq	HUNGARIAN GP	Hungaroring	10	West Zakspeed Racing	G	1.5 t/c Zakspeed 881 4		28/31
13/ret	BELGIAN GP	Spa	10	West Zakspeed Racing	G	1.5 t/c Zakspeed 881 4	gearbox/5 laps behind	25/31
ret	ITALIAN GP	Monza	10	West Zakspeed Racing	G	1.5 t/c Zakspeed 881 4	engine	15/31
dnq	PORTUGUESE GP	Estoril	10	West Zakspeed Racing	G	1.5 t/c Zakspeed 881 4		30/31
dnq	SPANISH GP	Jerez	10	West Zakspeed Racing	G	1.5 t/c Zakspeed 881 4		27/31
ret	JAPANESE GP	Suzuka	10	West Zakspeed Racing	G	1.5 t/c Zakspeed 881 4	unwell after practice accident	25/31
dnq	AUSTRALIAN GP	Adelaide	10	West Zakspeed Racing	G	1.5 t/c Zakspeed 881 4		30/31

1989 Championship position: Unplaced

	Race	Circuit	No	Entrant		Tyres	Capacity/Car/Engine	Comment	Q Pos/Entries
ret	BRAZILIAN GP	Rio	34	West Zakspeed Racing		P	3.5 Zakspeed 891-Yamaha V8	collision with Cheever	25/38
dnpq	SAN MARINO GP	Imola	34	West Zakspeed Racing		P	3.5 Zakspeed 891-Yamaha V8		38/39
dnpq	MONACO GP	Monte Carlo	34	West Zakspeed Racing		P	3.5 Zakspeed 891-Yamaha V8		33/38
dnpq	MEXICAN GP	Mexico City	34	West Zakspeed Racing		P	3.5 Zakspeed 891-Yamaha V8		35/39
dnpq	US GP (PHOENIX)	Phoenix	34	West Zakspeed Racing		P	3.5 Zakspeed 891-Yamaha V8		37/39
dnpq	CANADIAN GP	Montreal	34	West Zakspeed Racing		P	3.5 Zakspeed 891-Yamaha V8		35/39
dnpq	FRENCH GP	Paul Ricard	34	West Zakspeed Racing		P	3.5 Zakspeed 891-Yamaha V8		34/39
dnpq	BRITISH GP	Silverstone	34	West Zakspeed Racing		P	3.5 Zakspeed 891-Yamaha V8		36/39
dnpq	GERMAN GP	Hockenheim	34	West Zakspeed Racing		P	3.5 Zakspeed 891-Yamaha V8		39/39
dnpq	HUNGARIAN GP	Hungaroring	34	West Zakspeed Racing		P	3.5 Zakspeed 891-Yamaha V8		34/39
dnpq	BELGIAN GP	Spa	34	West Zakspeed Racing		P	3.5 Zakspeed 891-Yamaha V8		35/39
dnpq	ITALIAN GP	Monza	34	West Zakspeed Racing		P	3.5 Zakspeed 891-Yamaha V8		34/39
dnpq	PORTUGUESE GP	Estoril	34	West Zakspeed Racing		P	3.5 Zakspeed 891-Yamaha V8		38/39
dnpq	SPANISH GP	Jerez	34	West Zakspeed Racing		P	3.5 Zakspeed 891-Yamaha V8		34/38
ret	JAPANESE GP	Suzuka	34	West Zakspeed Racing		P	3.5 Zakspeed 891-Yamaha V8	engine on lap 1	21/39
dnpq	AUSTRALIAN GP	Adelaide	34	West Zakspeed Racing		P	3.5 Zakspeed 891-Yamaha V8		33/39

1990 Championship position: Unplaced

	Race	Circuit	No	Entrant		Tyres	Capacity/Car/Engine	Comment	Q Pos/Entries
12	US GP (PHOENIX)	Phoenix	10	Footwork Arrows Racing		G	3.5 Arrows A11-Cosworth V8	2 laps behind	20/35
dnq	SPANISH GP	Jerez	10	Footwork Arrows Racing		G	3.5 Arrows A11B-Cosworth V8		29/33

GP Starts: 9   GP Wins: 0   Pole positions: 0   Fastest laps: 0   Points: 0

SCHOELLER, Rudolf (CH) b 27/4/1902, Düren, Germany – d 7/3/1978, Grabs

1952 Championship position: Unplaced

	Race	Circuit	No	Entrant	Tyres	Capacity/Car/Engine	Comment	Q Pos/Entries
ret	GERMAN GP	Nürburgring	118	Ecurie Espadon	P	2.0 Ferrari 212 V12	shock absober	24/32

GP Starts: 1   GP Wins: 0   Pole positions: 0   Fastest laps: 0   Points: 0

SCHROEDER, Rob (USA) b 11/5/1926, El Dorado, Arkansas – d 3/12/2012, Dallas, Texas

1962 Championship position: 0   Wins: 0   Pole positions: 0   Fastest laps: 0   Points scored: 0

	Race	Circuit	No	Entrant	Tyres	Capacity/Car/Engine	Comment	Q Pos/Entries
10	US GP	Watkins Glen	26	John Mecom	D	1.5 Lotus 24-Climax V8	hired Rob Walker's car/-7 laps	17/20

GP Starts: 1   GP Wins: 0   Pole positions: 0   Fastest laps: 0   Points: 0

RUDOLF SCHOELLER

A SWISS veteran, Rudolf Schoeller tagged along with Rudi Fischer's Espadon team in 1952. Apart from his one German Grand Prix drive, he was a reserve entry (but not employed) at non-championship Formula 2 races at both Rouen and AVUS. At the end of the year, apparently he bought the team's old 212 car to race in minor events at home.

ROB SCHROEDER

A VETERAN of the Second World War, Rob Schroeder began racing sports cars in the Mid-West and on the West Coast in the early 1950s. He sampled a variety of machines, such as a Kurtis-Buick in 1957, and then a Lotus and a Lister owned by Jim Hall, before really making a mark in 1960 when he began racing and maintaining a Maserati Tipo 61 entered by Dick Hall.

After some success in the car the following year, Rob was given the opportunity to race John Mecom's Chevrolet Corvette at the beginning of 1962, before taking over the Texas oil millionaire's de Tomaso single-seater and sports cars. With his vast family wealth, 'Little John' Mecom was able to indulge in any hobby that took his fancy and, having exhausted his pursuit of animals as a big-game hunter, he had assembled a menagerie of racing machines to indulge his new-found passion. The only problem was that as the only male heir, racing the machines was strictly off-limits, so he hired rising talent, such as Roger Penske and A.J. Foyt no less, to drive his machines.

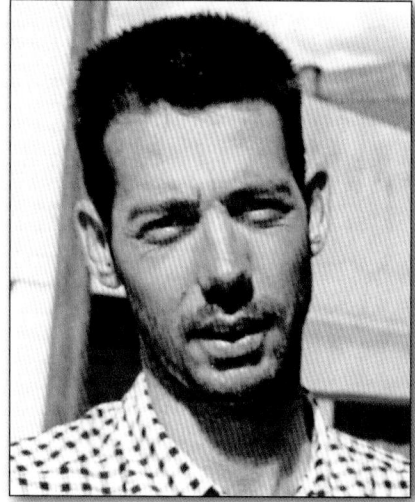

Schroeder was the right man at the right time, however, to race in Mecom's Lotus 24-Climax V8, which had been hired from Rob Walker for the 1962 United States Grand Prix. He drove sensibly to take a distant tenth and also took part in the non-championship Mexican Grand Prix that followed. There, to give some idea of his level, he qualified some 4.8 seconds off the similar car handled by Roger Penske.

Nonetheless, Schroeder stayed the course in the race to finish sixth, albeit three laps down on the winning car shared by Jim Clark and Trevor Taylor. The tragic death of Ricardo Rodriguez at this event may have influenced his decision to retire at the end of that year, after which he set up a Goodyear tyre dealership in Dallas.

MICHAEL SCHUMACHER

WHEN Michael Schumacher burst upon the grand prix stage with a sensational qualifying performance on his debut for Jordan at Spa, the hype machine went into overdrive, billing this young 'unknown' as the next Ayrton Senna. In truth, his racing career had been very carefully planned before he ever stepped into an F1 car, and he had the comforting prospect of major manufacturer and commercial backing with which to develop his top-level career. However, he has since proved beyond all doubt that he was the supreme driver of his time; statistically, he is the greatest of all time.

A former karting star, with a year in German F3 behind him, Michael was recruited to the Mercedes junior driver scheme and was placed in the Sauber-Mercedes Group C programme for two seasons, where he was schooled in the art of handling big, powerful cars in a very disciplined and professional framework. In parallel with his sports car drives, he returned to German Formula 3, winning the series comfortably. Then he was offered the now famous Jordan drive at Spa, which soon made him a very hot property and, after much legal wrangling, the somewhat bemused driver was whisked off to join the Benetton team in time for the next race at Monza. Three points-scoring finishes in his first three races were more than enough evidence for Flavio Briatore to plan the team's future around the German star, who would not disappoint.

In his first full grand prix season, Michael proved to be not only very quick, but also remarkably consistent, rarely making costly mistakes and putting in some scintillating performances. The supreme moment was his fully deserved win at Spa, where he made his own luck and reaped the rewards.

The 1993 season provided more evidence of Schumacher's increasing maturity. Only Williams' dominance stood between him and the top step of the podium on numerous occasions, and he took a superbly thought-out win at Estoril. Much work was done over the winter months, and when the new Benetton B194 was placed in his hands he left Senna and Williams struggling in his wake in the opening two races. It seemed as though the balance of power might be about to shift, and tragically it did so at Imola with the death of Ayrton Senna, leaving Michael to chase a world championship that he felt would be much devalued by the loss of the Brazilian. From then on, his season was surrounded by controversy. Amid rumblings that the team were running some form of traction control, he won six of the first seven grands prix, but he was excluded at Silverstone for ignoring the black flag, which earned him a two-race ban. This, together with the loss of his win at Spa after he was disqualified for having an illegal skid-block, left the door open for Damon Hill to make a late challenge for the title. When the pair 'collided' in Adelaide, Schumacher became Germany's first world champion, but the manner of his triumph was tarnished and can have brought him little inner satisfaction.

The following season was a different matter entirely as Schumacher ruthlessly exposed the shortcomings of both the Williams team and their drivers, delivering a succession of brilliant performances. His dominant wins in Monaco, France and Germany looked almost routine, especially when compared with his extraordinary displays at Spa and in the European GP at the Nürburgring where, quite frankly, the rest of the field, Jean Alesi apart, were made to look like novices.

It was natural that Ferrari, so long in the doldrums, looked to Schumacher to return them to the top, and they were prepared to stump up a massive retainer to capture his signature. His immediate championship prospects for 1996 were not deemed bright, but the German still produced drives of genius, such as in the wet in Spain, and later in the season at Spa and Monza. It was much the same story the following year as he took the fight to the superior Williams of Jacques Villeneuve, brilliant wins in the wet at Monaco and Spa, and on slicks on a treacherous track at Magny-Cours emphasising his mesmeric car control. His refusal to concede defeat led to an inglorious end to his title challenge in a Jerez gravel trap after an outrageous manoeuvre on his title rival. Subsequently, he was stripped of his points and his second place in the championship.

With the slate wiped clean for 1998, Ferrari was still the underdog, as McLaren Mercedes now boasted the fastest machine on the track. Again, however, Michael ruthlessly took advantage of any weakness shown by his rivals. In the end, stalling the Ferrari on the grid at Suzuka effectively stymied his title chances for the third time in as many years, but it would be churlish to criticise the German too harshly for his error, as it was only his brilliance that had extended the title fight to the end.

Schumacher and Ferrari were left facing a fourth attempt to clinch a championship that by now must have seemed like the Holy Grail. Dominant performances at Imola and in Monaco provided a satisfactory start, but a relatively low-speed shunt on the first lap of the British Grand Prix left the unlucky German with a broken leg. His title chances were gone for another season.

The 2000 season was when it all went right for the Scuderia. A record-equalling nine wins, clinched that first Ferrari drivers' title since 1979, and Schumacher's third since his impressive entry to F1. For 2001, Ferrari dominated the season as once again their challengers self-destructed. Another nine wins were chalked up and the title was sewn up by mid-summer in Hungary; further successes saw the now four-time champion surpass Alain Prost's records for career wins and total points. Sadly for the rest of the field, much the same occurred in 2002. Indeed, Michael romped to his fifth world title in record breaking time, clinching the crown at the French GP on 21st July. In all, the German would win on 11 occasions – another new record.

In 2003, Ferrari triumphed again, although only just. Despite another six wins, it was by no means an easy year, Kimi Räikkönen threatening to prevent the German from winning a record breaking sixth drivers' title right up to the final race of the season. The following year was all about Schumacher and Ferrari again, as they stormed to both titles with little or no opposition. Michael took his seventh crown at Spa at the end of August, eventually racking up victories in 13 of the 18 races.

After five seasons at the top, rule changes instigated by the FIA and the progress made by Michelin had brought the opposition much closer to Schumacher and Ferrari. When Renault chalked up four successive victories, Michael's title chances started to look very doubtful. Despite a couple of exceptional performances to make the podium and an easy ten points taken in the farcical US Grand Prix, his task in overhauling Fernando Alonso was impossible. Even so, the German fought tenaciously for every track position like a young charger.

For 2006, Ferrari provided Michael with machinery that could win an eighth title, and how close he came – only a rare engine failure at Suzuki finally crushed his championship hopes as Alonso and Renault prevailed. Although his brilliant performances had brought seven wins, once again his flagrant disregard for the ethics of racing, after blocking the track during practice at Monaco, cast a long shadow upon his reputation.

Seemingly worn out by the pressures of being at the very top in every one of his 15 full seasons, Michael then retired to become a consultant with Ferrari, but inevitably perhaps for such a competitive individual, he was tempted back by Mercedes to spearhead their F1 return in 2010.

At the age of 41, Schumacher faced a massive challenge in his attempt to rekindle his former glories. Thus far, the jury has been out on the wisdom of his return. While often outpaced by his younger team-mate, Nico Rosberg, he has still been canny enough to garner points when they were on offer. The 2012 season sees the third and final year of his contract, and he must be hoping that Ross Brawn and his team can finally produce a winning car to make his comeback a fairy tale rather than just a fascinating postscript.

SCHUMACHER Michael (D) b 3/1/1969, Hürth-Hermühlheim

	Race	Circuit	No	Entrant	Tyres	Capacity/Car/Engine	Comment	Q Pos/Entries
	1991 Championship position: 12th=		Wins: 0	Pole positions: 0		Fastest laps: 0	Points scored: 4	
ret	BELGIAN GP	Spa	32	Team 7UP Jordan	G	3.5 Jordan 191-Ford HB V8	clutch at start	7/34
5	ITALIAN GP	Monza	19	Camel Benetton Ford	P	3.5 Benetton B191-Ford HB V8		7/34
6	PORTUGUESE GP	Estoril	19	Camel Benetton Ford	P	3.5 Benetton B191-Ford HB V8		10/34
6	SPANISH GP	Barcelona	19	Camel Benetton Ford	P	3.5 Benetton B191-Ford HB V8		5/33
ret	JAPANESE GP	Suzuka	19	Camel Benetton Ford	P	3.5 Benetton B191-Ford HB V8	engine	9/31
ret	AUSTRALIAN GP	Adelaide	19	Camel Benetton Ford	P	3.5 Benetton B191-Ford HB V8	collision with Alesi	6/32
	1992 Championship position: 3rd		Wins: 1	Pole positions: 0		Fastest laps: 2	Points scored: 53	
4	SOUTH AFRICAN GP	Kyalami	19	Camel Benetton Ford	G	3.5 Benetton B191B-Ford HB V8		6/30
3	MEXICAN GP	Mexico City	19	Camel Benetton Ford	G	3.5 Benetton B191B-Ford HB V8		3/30
3	BRAZILIAN GP	Interlagos	19	Camel Benetton Ford	G	3.5 Benetton B191B-Ford HB V8	1 lap behind	5/31
2	SPANISH GP	Barcelona	19	Camel Benetton Ford	G	3.5 Benetton B192-Ford HB V8		2/32
ret	SAN MARINO GP	Imola	19	Camel Benetton Ford	G	3.5 Benetton B192-Ford HB V8	spun – suspension damage	5/32
4	MONACO GP	Monte Carlo	19	Camel Benetton Ford	G	3.5 Benetton B192-Ford HB V8		6/32
2	CANADIAN GP	Montreal	19	Camel Benetton Ford	G	3.5 Benetton B192-Ford HB V8		5/32
ret	FRENCH GP	Magny Cours	19	Camel Benetton Ford	G	3.5 Benetton B192-Ford HB V8	accident – collision with Senna	5/30
4	BRITISH GP	Silverstone	19	Camel Benetton Ford	G	3.5 Benetton B192-Ford HB V8		4/32
3	GERMAN GP	Hockenheim	19	Camel Benetton Ford	G	3.5 Benetton B192-Ford HB V8		6/32
ret	HUNGARIAN GP	Hungaroring	19	Camel Benetton Ford	G	3.5 Benetton B192-Ford HB V8	collision – lost rear wing/spun off	4/31
1	BELGIAN GP	Spa	19	Camel Benetton Ford	G	3.5 Benetton B192-Ford HB V8	FL	3/30
3	ITALIAN GP	Monza	19	Camel Benetton Ford	G	3.5 Benetton B192-Ford HB V8	clutch	6/28
7	PORTUGUESE GP	Estoril	19	Camel Benetton Ford	G	3.5 Benetton B192-Ford HB V8	started from back/puncture/-2 laps	5/26
ret	JAPANESE GP	Suzuka	19	Camel Benetton Ford	G	3.5 Benetton B192-Ford HB V8	gearbox	5/26
2	AUSTRALIAN GP	Adelaide	19	Camel Benetton Ford	G	3.5 Benetton B192-Ford HB V8	FL	5/26
	1993 Championship position: 4th		Wins: 1	Pole positions: 0		Fastest laps: 5	Points scored: 52	
ret	SOUTH AFRICAN GP	Kyalami	5	Camel Benetton Ford	G	3.5 Benetton B192B-Ford HB V8	collision with Senna	3/26
3	BRAZILIAN GP	Interlagos	5	Camel Benetton Ford	G	3.5 Benetton B192B-Ford HB V8	FL	4/26
ret	EUROPEAN GP	Donington	5	Camel Benetton Ford	G	3.5 Benetton B193B-Ford HB V8		3/26
2	SAN MARINO GP	Imola	5	Camel Benetton Ford	G	3.5 Benetton B193B-Ford HB V8		3/26
3	SPANISH GP	Barcelona	5	Camel Benetton Ford	G	3.5 Benetton B193B-Ford HB V8	FL	4/26
ret	MONACO GP	Monte Carlo	5	Camel Benetton Ford	G	3.5 Benetton B193B-Ford HB V8	active hydraulics/fire	2/26
2	CANADIAN GP	Montreal	5	Camel Benetton Ford	G	3.5 Benetton B193B-Ford HB V8	FL	3/26
3	FRENCH GP	Magny Cours	5	Camel Benetton Ford	G	3.5 Benetton B193B-Ford HB V8	FL	7/26
2	BRITISH GP	Silverstone	5	Camel Benetton Ford	G	3.5 Benetton B193B-Ford HB V8		3/26
2	GERMAN GP	Hockenheim	5	Camel Benetton Ford	G	3.5 Benetton B193B-Ford HB V8	FL	3/26
ret	HUNGARIAN GP	Hungaroring	5	Camel Benetton Ford	G	3.5 Benetton B193B-Ford HB V8	fuel pump drive	3/26
2	BELGIAN GP	Spa	5	Camel Benetton Ford	G	3.5 Benetton B193B-Ford HB V8		3/25
ret	ITALIAN GP	Monza	5	Camel Benetton Ford	G	3.5 Benetton B193B-Ford HB V8	engine	5/26
1	PORTUGUESE GP	Estoril	5	Camel Benetton Ford	G	3.5 Benetton B193B-Ford HB V8		6/26
ret	JAPANESE GP	Suzuka	5	Camel Benetton Ford	G	3.5 Benetton B193B-Ford HB V8	collision with Hill/suspension	4/24
ret	AUSTRALIAN GP	Adelaide	5	Camel Benetton Ford	G	3.5 Benetton B193B-Ford HB V8	engine	4/24
	1994 WORLD CHAMPION		Wins: 8	Pole positions: 6		Fastest laps: 9	Points scored: 92	
1	BRAZILIAN GP	Interlagos	5	Mild Seven Benetton Ford	G	3.5 Benetton B194-Ford Zetec-R V8	FL	2/28
1	PACIFIC GP	T.I. Circuit	5	Mild Seven Benetton Ford	G	3.5 Benetton B194-Ford Zetec-R V8	FL	2/28
1	SAN MARINO GP	Imola	5	Mild Seven Benetton Ford	G	3.5 Benetton B194-Ford Zetec-R V8	FL	2/28
1	MONACO GP	Monte Carlo	5	Mild Seven Benetton Ford	G	3.5 Benetton B194-Ford Zetec-R V8	FL	1/24
2	SPANISH GP	Barcelona	5	Mild Seven Benetton Ford	G	3.5 Benetton B194-Ford Zetec-R V8	car stuck in 5th gear/FL	1/27
1	CANADIAN GP	Montreal	5	Mild Seven Benetton Ford	G	3.5 Benetton B194-Ford Zetec-R V8	FL	1/27
1	FRENCH GP	Magny Cours	5	Mild Seven Benetton Ford	G	3.5 Benetton B194-Ford Zetec-R V8		3/28
2/dsq*	BRITISH GP	Silverstone	5	Mild Seven Benetton Ford	G	3.5 Benetton B194-Ford Zetec-R V8	*later disqualified for ignoring black flag	2/28
ret	GERMAN GP	Hockenheim	5	Mild Seven Benetton Ford	G	3.5 Benetton B194-Ford Zetec-R V8	engine	4/28
1	HUNGARIAN GP	Hungaroring	5	Mild Seven Benetton Ford	G	3.5 Benetton B194-Ford Zetec-R V8	FL	1/28
1/dsq*	BELGIAN GP	Spa	5	Mild Seven Benetton Ford	G	3.5 Benetton B194-Ford Zetec-R V8	*later dsq – excess skidblock wear	2/28
1	EUROPEAN GP	Jerez	5	Mild Seven Benetton Ford	G	3.5 Benetton B194-Ford Zetec-R V8	FL	1/28
2	JAPANESE GP	Suzuka	5	Mild Seven Benetton Ford	G	3.5 Benetton B194-Ford Zetec-R V8		1/28
ret	AUSTRALIAN GP	Adelaide	5	Mild Seven Benetton Ford	G	3.5 Benetton B194-Ford Zetec-R V8	collision with Hill/FL	2/28
	1995 WORLD CHAMPION		Wins: 9	Pole positions: 4		Fastest laps: 8	Points scored: 102	
1	BRAZILIAN GP	Interlagos	1	Mild Seven Benetton Renault	G	3.0 Benetton B195-Renault V10	FL	2/26
3	ARGENTINE GP	Buenos Aires	1	Mild Seven Benetton Renault	G	3.0 Benetton B195-Renault V10	FL	3/26
ret	SAN MARINO GP	Imola	1	Mild Seven Benetton Renault	G	3.0 Benetton B195-Renault V10	accident – crashed	1/26
1	SPANISH GP	Barcelona	1	Mild Seven Benetton Renault	G	3.0 Benetton B195-Renault V10		1/26
1	MONACO GP	Monte Carlo	1	Mild Seven Benetton Renault	G	3.0 Benetton B195-Renault V10		2/26
5	CANADIAN GP	Montreal	1	Mild Seven Benetton Renault	G	3.0 Benetton B195-Renault V10	led race – gearbox/throttle trouble/FL	1/24
1	FRENCH GP	Magny Cours	1	Mild Seven Benetton Renault	G	3.0 Benetton B195-Renault V10	FL	2/24
ret	BRITISH GP	Silverstone	1	Mild Seven Benetton Renault	G	3.0 Benetton B195-Renault V10	collision with Hill	2/24
1	GERMAN GP	Hockenheim	1	Mild Seven Benetton Renault	G	3.0 Benetton B195-Renault V10	FL	2/24
11/ret	HUNGARIAN GP	Hungaroring	1	Mild Seven Benetton Renault	G	3.0 Benetton B195-Renault V10	fuel pump/4 laps behind	3/24
1	BELGIAN GP	Spa	1	Mild Seven Benetton Renault	G	3.0 Benetton B195-Renault V10		16/24
ret	ITALIAN GP	Monza	1	Mild Seven Benetton Renault	G	3.0 Benetton B195-Renault V10	run into by Hill	2/24
2	PORTUGUESE GP	Estoril	1	Mild Seven Benetton Renault	G	3.0 Benetton B195-Renault V10		3/24
1	EUROPEAN GP	Nürburgring	1	Mild Seven Benetton Renault	G	3.0 Benetton B195-Renault V10	FL	3/24
1	PACIFIC GP	T.I. Circuit	1	Mild Seven Benetton Renault	G	3.0 Benetton B195-Renault V10	FL	3/24
1	JAPANESE GP	Suzuka	1	Mild Seven Benetton Renault	G	3.0 Benetton B195-Renault V10	FL	1/24
ret	AUSTRALIAN GP	Adelaide	1	Mild Seven Benetton Renault	G	3.0 Benetton B195-Renault V10	collision with Alesi	3/24

1996 Championship position: 3rd Wins: 3 Pole positions: 4 Fastest laps: 2 Points scored: 59

Pos	GP	Circuit	No	Team	Tyre	Engine	Notes	Grid
ret	AUSTRALIAN GP	Melbourne	1	Scuderia Ferrari	G	3.0 Ferrari F310-V10	brakes	4/22
3	BRAZILIAN GP	Interlagos	1	Scuderia Ferrari	G	3.0 Ferrari F310-V10	1 lap behind	4/22
ret	ARGENTINE GP	Buenos Aires	1	Scuderia Ferrari	G	3.0 Ferrari F310-V10	debris damage to rear wing	2/22
2	EUROPEAN GP	Nürburgring	1	Scuderia Ferrari	G	3.0 Ferrari F310-V10		3/22
2	SAN MARINO GP	Imola	1	Scuderia Ferrari	G	3.0 Ferrari F310-V10		1/22
ret	MONACO GP	Monte Carlo	1	Scuderia Ferrari	G	3.0 Ferrari F310-V10	crashed on lap 1	1/22
1	SPANISH GP	Barcelona	1	Scuderia Ferrari	G	3.0 Ferrari F310-V10	FL	3/22
ret	CANADIAN GP	Montreal	1	Scuderia Ferrari	G	3.0 Ferrari F310-V10	driveshaft	3/22
ret/dns*	FRENCH GP	Magny Cours	1	Scuderia Ferrari	G	3.0 Ferrari F310-V10	*engine on parade lap	1/22
ret	BRITISH GP	Silverstone	1	Scuderia Ferrari	G	3.0 Ferrari F310-V10	hydraulic leak	3/22
4	GERMAN GP	Hockenheim	1	Scuderia Ferrari	G	3.0 Ferrari F310-V10		3/20
9/ret	HUNGARIAN GP	Hungaroring	1	Scuderia Ferrari	G	3.0 Ferrari F310-V10	throttle/7 laps behind	1/20
1	BELGIAN GP	Spa	1	Scuderia Ferrari	G	3.0 Ferrari F310-V10		3/20
1	ITALIAN GP	Monza	1	Scuderia Ferrari	G	3.0 Ferrari F310-V10	FL	3/20
3	PORTUGUESE GP	Estoril	1	Scuderia Ferrari	G	3.0 Ferrari F310-V10		4/20
2	JAPANESE GP	Suzuka	1	Scuderia Ferrari	G	3.0 Ferrari F310-V10		3/20

1997 Championship position: Unplaced* Wins: 5 Pole positions: 3 Fastest laps: 2 Points scored: 0 (*78 points scored subsequently disallowed by FIA)

Pos	GP	Circuit	No	Team	Tyre	Engine	Notes	Grid
2	AUSTRALIAN GP	Melbourne	5	Scuderia Ferrari Marlboro	G	3.0 Ferrari F310B-V10		3/24
5	BRAZILIAN GP	Interlagos	5	Scuderia Ferrari Marlboro	G	3.0 Ferrari F310B-V10	lack of grip	2/22
ret	ARGENTINE GP	Buenos Aires	5	Scuderia Ferrari Marlboro	G	3.0 Ferrari F310B-V10	collision with Barrichello	4/22
2	SAN MARINO GP	Imola	5	Scuderia Ferrari Marlboro	G	3.0 Ferrari F310B-V10		3/22
1	MONACO GP	Monte Carlo	5	Scuderia Ferrari Marlboro	G	3.0 Ferrari F310B-V10	FL	2/22
4	SPANISH GP	Barcelona	5	Scuderia Ferrari Marlboro	G	3.0 Ferrari F310B-V10		7/22
1	CANADIAN GP	Montreal	5	Scuderia Ferrari Marlboro	G	3.0 Ferrari F310B-V10	race shortened after Panis crash	1/22
1	FRENCH GP	Magny Cours	5	Scuderia Ferrari Marlboro	G	3.0 Ferrari F310B-V10	FL	1/22
ret	BRITISH GP	Silverstone	5	Scuderia Ferrari Marlboro	G	3.0 Ferrari F310B-V10	wheel bearing	4/22
2	GERMAN GP	Hockenheim	5	Scuderia Ferrari Marlboro	G	3.0 Ferrari F310B-V10		4/22
4	HUNGARIAN GP	Hungaroring	5	Scuderia Ferrari Marlboro	G	3.0 Ferrari F310B-V10		1/22
1	BELGIAN GP	Spa	5	Scuderia Ferrari Marlboro	G	3.0 Ferrari F310B-V10		3/22
6	ITALIAN GP	Monza	5	Scuderia Ferrari Marlboro	G	3.0 Ferrari F310B-V10		9/22
6	AUSTRIAN GP	A1-Ring	5	Scuderia Ferrari Marlboro	G	3.0 Ferrari F310B-V10	stop & go penalty	9/22
ret	LUXEMBOURG GP	Nürburgring	5	Scuderia Ferrari Marlboro	G	3.0 Ferrari F310B-V10	collision damage	5/22
1	JAPANESE GP	Suzuka	5	Scuderia Ferrari Marlboro	G	3.0 Ferrari F310B-V10		2/22
ret	EUROPEAN GP	Jerez	5	Scuderia Ferrari Marlboro	G	3.0 Ferrari F310B-V10	collision with Villeneuve	2/22

1998 Championship position: 2nd Wins: 6 Pole positions: 3 Fastest laps: 6 Points scored: 86

Pos	GP	Circuit	No	Team	Tyre	Engine	Notes	Grid
ret	AUSTRALIAN GP	Melbourne	3	Scuderia Ferrari Marlboro	G	3.0 Ferrari F300-V10	engine	3/22
3	BRAZILIAN GP	Interlagos	3	Scuderia Ferrari Marlboro	G	3.0 Ferrari F300-V10		4/22
1	ARGENTINE GP	Buenos Aires	3	Scuderia Ferrari Marlboro	G	3.0 Ferrari F300-V10		2/22
2	SAN MARINO GP	Imola	3	Scuderia Ferrari Marlboro	G	3.0 Ferrari F300-V10	FL	3/22
3	SPANISH GP	Barcelona	3	Scuderia Ferrari Marlboro	G	3.0 Ferrari F300-V10		3/22
10	MONACO GP	Monte Carlo	3	Scuderia Ferrari Marlboro	G	3.0 Ferrari F300-V10	collision with Würz/2 laps behind	4/22
1	CANADIAN GP	Montreal	3	Scuderia Ferrari Marlboro	G	3.0 Ferrari F300-V10	FL	3/22
1	FRENCH GP	Magny Cours	3	Scuderia Ferrari Marlboro	G	3.0 Ferrari F300-V10		2/22
1	BRITISH GP	Silverstone	3	Scuderia Ferrari Marlboro	G	3.0 Ferrari F300-V10	stop & go penalty/FL	2/22
3	AUSTRIAN GP	A1-Ring	3	Scuderia Ferrari Marlboro	G	3.0 Ferrari F300-V10		4/22
5	GERMAN GP	Hockenheim	3	Scuderia Ferrari Marlboro	G	3.0 Ferrari F300-V10	lack of grip	9/22
1	HUNGARIAN GP	Hungaroring	3	Scuderia Ferrari Marlboro	G	3.0 Ferrari F300-V10	FL	3/22
ret	BELGIAN GP	Spa	3	Scuderia Ferrari Marlboro	G	3.0 Ferrari F300-V10	collision with Coulthard/FL	4/22
1	ITALIAN GP	Monza	3	Scuderia Ferrari Marlboro	G	3.0 Ferrari F300-V10		1/22
2	LUXEMBOURG GP	Nürburgring	3	Scuderia Ferrari Marlboro	G	3.0 Ferrari F300-V10		1/22
ret	JAPANESE GP	Suzuka	3	Scuderia Ferrari Marlboro	G	3.0 Ferrari F300-V10	started from back of grid/puncture/FL	1/22

1999 Championship position: 5th Wins: 2 Pole positions: 3 Fastest laps: 5 Points scored: 44

Pos	GP	Circuit	No	Team	Tyre	Engine	Notes	Grid
8	AUSTRALIAN GP	Melbourne	3	Scuderia Ferrari Marlboro	B	3.0 Ferrari F399-V10	started from back/puncture/-1 lap/FL	3/22
2	BRAZILIAN GP	Interlagos	3	Scuderia Ferrari Marlboro	B	3.0 Ferrari F399-V10r		4/22
1	SAN MARINO GP	Imola	3	Scuderia Ferrari Marlboro	B	3.0 Ferrari F399-V10r	FL	3/22
1	MONACO GP	Monte Carlo	3	Scuderia Ferrari Marlboro	B	3.0 Ferrari F399-V10		2/22
3	SPANISH GP	Barcelona	3	Scuderia Ferrari Marlboro	B	3.0 Ferrari F399-V10	FL	4/22
ret	CANADIAN GP	Montreal	3	Scuderia Ferrari Marlboro	B	3.0 Ferrari F399-V10	crashed	1/22
5	FRENCH GP	Magny Cours	3	Scuderia Ferrari Marlboro	B	3.0 Ferrari F399-V10		6/22
ret/dns*	BRITISH GP	Silverstone	3	Scuderia Ferrari Marlboro	B	3.0 Ferrari F399-V10	broken leg in 1st start – did not restart	2/22
2	MALAYSIAN GP	Sepang	3	Scuderia Ferrari Marlboro	B	3.0 Ferrari F399-V10	allowed Irvine to win/FL	1/22
2	JAPANESE GP	Suzuka	3	Scuderia Ferrari Marlboro	B	3.0 Ferrari F399-V10	FL	1/22

2000 WORLD CHAMPION Wins: 9 Pole positions: 9 Fastest laps: 2 Points scored: 108

Pos	GP	Circuit	No	Team	Tyre	Engine	Notes	Grid
1	AUSTRALIAN GP	Melbourne	3	Scuderia Ferrari Marlboro	B	3.0 Ferrari F1-2000-V10		3/22
1	BRAZILIAN GP	Interlagos	3	Scuderia Ferrari Marlboro	B	3.0 Ferrari F1-2000-V10	FL	3/22
1	SAN MARINO GP	Imola	3	Scuderia Ferrari Marlboro	B	3.0 Ferrari F1-2000-V10		2/22
3	BRITISH GP	Silverstone	3	Scuderia Ferrari Marlboro	B	3.0 Ferrari F1-2000-V10		5/22
5	SPANISH GP	Barcelona	3	Scuderia Ferrari Marlboro	B	3.0 Ferrari F1-2000-V10	slow puncture	1/22
1	EUROPEAN GP	Nürburgring	3	Scuderia Ferrari Marlboro	B	3.0 Ferrari F1-2000-V10	FL	2/22
ret	MONACO GP	Monte Carlo	3	Scuderia Ferrari Marlboro	B	3.0 Ferrari F1-2000-V10	broken rear suspension when in lead	1/22
1	CANADIAN GP	Montreal	3	Scuderia Ferrari Marlboro	B	3.0 Ferrari F1-2000-V10	despite wheel bearing problem	1/22
ret	FRENCH GP	Magny Cours	3	Scuderia Ferrari Marlboro	B	3.0 Ferrari F1-2000-V10	engine	1/22
ret	AUSTRIAN GP	A1-Ring	3	Scuderia Ferrari Marlboro	B	3.0 Ferrari F1-2000-V10	pushed off by Zonta on lap 1	4/22
ret	GERMAN GP	Hockenheim	3	Scuderia Ferrari Marlboro	B	3.0 Ferrari F1-2000-V10	collision with Fisichella at start	2/22
2	HUNGARIAN GP	Hungaroring	3	Scuderia Ferrari Marlboro	B	3.0 Ferrari F1-2000-V10		1/22

2	BELGIAN GP	Spa	3	Scuderia Ferrari Marlboro	B	3.0 Ferrari F1-2000-V10		4/22
1	ITALIAN GP	Monza	3	Scuderia Ferrari Marlboro	B	3.0 Ferrari F1-2000-V10		1/22
1	U S GP	Indianapolis	3	Scuderia Ferrari Marlboro	B	3.0 Ferrari F1-2000-V10		1/22
1	JAPANESE GP	Suzuka	3	Scuderia Ferrari Marlboro	B	3.0 Ferrari F1-2000-V10		1/22
1	MALAYSIAN GP	Sepang	3	Scuderia Ferrari Marlboro	B	3.0 Ferrari F1-2000-V10		1/22

2001 WORLD CHAMPION Wins: 9 Pole positions: 11 Fastest laps: 3 Points scored: 123

1	AUSTRALIAN GP	Melbourne	1	Scuderia Ferrari Marlboro	B	3.0 Ferrari F2001-V10	FL	1/22
1	MALAYSIAN GP	Sepang	1	Scuderia Ferrari Marlboro	B	3.0 Ferrari F2001-V10		1/22
2	BRAZILIAN GP	Interlagos	1	Scuderia Ferrari Marlboro	B	3.0 Ferrari F2001-V10	survived trip into gravel trap	1/22
ret	SAN MARINO GP	Imola	1	Scuderia Ferrari Marlboro	B	3.0 Ferrari F2001-V10	faulty front brake caliper	4/22
1	SPANISH GP	Barcelona	1	Scuderia Ferrari Marlboro	B	3.0 Ferrari F2001-V10	inherited lead on last lap/FL	1/22
2	AUSTRIAN GP	A1-Ring	1	Scuderia Ferrari Marlboro	B	3.0 Ferrari F2001-V10	given second place by Barrichello	1/22
1	MONACO GP	Monte Carlo	1	Scuderia Ferrari Marlboro	B	3.0 Ferrari F2001-V10		2/22
2	CANADIAN GP	Montreal	1	Scuderia Ferrari Marlboro	B	3.0 Ferrari F2001-V10	beaten by brother Ralf	1/22
1	EUROPEAN GP	Nürburgring	1	Scuderia Ferrari Marlboro	B	3.0 Ferrari F2001-V10		1/22
1	FRENCH GP	Magny Cours	1	Scuderia Ferrari Marlboro	B	3.0 Ferrari F2001-V10		2/22
2	BRITISH GP	Silverstone	1	Scuderia Ferrari Marlboro	B	3.0 Ferrari F2001-V10	car not well balanced	1/22
ret	GERMAN GP	Hockenheim	1	Scuderia Ferrari Marlboro	B	3.0 Ferrari F2001-V10	fuel pressure	4/22
1	HUNGARIAN GP	Hungaroring	1	Scuderia Ferrari Marlboro	B	3.0 Ferrari F2001-V10		1/22
1	BELGIAN GP	Spa	1	Scuderia Ferrari Marlboro	B	3.0 Ferrari F2001-V10	FL	3/22
4	ITALIAN GP	Monza	1	Scuderia Ferrari Marlboro	B	3.0 Ferrari F2001-V10		3/22
2	U S GP	Indianapolis	1	Scuderia Ferrari Marlboro	B	3.0 Ferrari F2001-V10		1/22
1	JAPANESE GP	Suzuka	1	Scuderia Ferrari Marlboro	B	3.0 Ferrari F2001-V10		1/22

2002 WORLD CHAMPION Wins: 11 Pole positions: 7 Fastest laps: 7 Points scored: 144

1	AUSTRALIAN GP	Melbourne	1	Scuderia Ferrari Marlboro	B	3.0 Ferrari F2001-V10		2/22
3	MALAYSIAN GP	Sepang	1	Scuderia Ferrari Marlboro	B	3.0 Ferrari F2001-V10	collision with Montoya – new nose cone	1/22
1	BRAZILIAN GP	Interlagos	1	Scuderia Ferrari Marlboro	B	3.0 Ferrari F2002-V10		2/22
1	SAN MARINO GP	Imola	1	Scuderia Ferrari Marlboro	B	3.0 Ferrari F2002-V10		1/22
1	SPANISH GP	Barcelona	1	Scuderia Ferrari Marlboro	B	3.0 Ferrari F2002-V10	FL	1/21
1	AUSTRIAN GP	A1-Ring	1	Scuderia Ferrari Marlboro	B	3.0 Ferrari F2002-V10	allowed to win by Barrichello/FL	3/22
2	MONACO GP	Monte Carlo	1	Scuderia Ferrari Marlboro	B	3.0 Ferrari F2002-V10		3/22
1	CANADIAN GP	Montreal	1	Scuderia Ferrari Marlboro	B	3.0 Ferrari F2002-V10		2/22
2	EUROPEAN GP	Nürburgring	1	Scuderia Ferrari Marlboro	B	3.0 Ferrari F2002-V10	FL	3/22
1	BRITISH GP	Silverstone	1	Scuderia Ferrari Marlboro	B	3.0 Ferrari F2002-V10	60th Grand Prix win	3/22
1	FRENCH GP	Magny Cours	1	Scuderia Ferrari Marlboro	B	3.0 Ferrari F2002-V10		2/21
1	GERMAN GP	Hockenheim	1	Scuderia Ferrari Marlboro	B	3.0 Ferrari F2002-V10	FL	1/22
2	HUNGARIAN GP	Hungaroring	1	Scuderia Ferrari Marlboro	B	3.0 Ferrari F2002-V10	FL	2/20
1	BELGIAN GP	Spa	1	Scuderia Ferrari Marlboro	B	3.0 Ferrari F2002-V10	FL	1/20
2	ITALIAN GP	Monza	1	Scuderia Ferrari Marlboro	B	3.0 Ferrari F2002-V10	content with 2nd place to Barrichello	2/20
2	U S GP	Indianapolis	1	Scuderia Ferrari Marlboro	B	3.0 Ferrari F2002-V10	bungled finish – lost win to Barrichello	1/20
1	JAPANESE GP	Suzuka	1	Scuderia Ferrari Marlboro	B	3.0 Ferrari F2002-V10	FL	1/20

2003 WORLD CHAMPION Wins: 6 Pole positions: 5 Fastest laps: 5 Points scored: 93

4	AUSTRALIAN GP	Melbourne	1	Scuderia Ferrari Marlboro	B	3.0 Ferrari F2002-V10	damaged barge-board	1/20
6	MALAYSIAN GP	Sepang	1	Scuderia Ferrari Marlboro	B	3.0 Ferrari F2002-V10	hit Trulli – damage/1 lap behind/FL	3/20
ret	BRAZILIAN GP	Interlagos	1	Scuderia Ferrari Marlboro	B	3.0 Ferrari F2002-V100	accident spun off in wet	7/20
1	SAN MARINO GP	Imola	1	Scuderia Ferrari Marlboro	B	3.0 Ferrari F2002-V10	FL	1/20
1	SPANISH GP	Barcelona	1	Scuderia Ferrari Marlboro	B	3.0 Ferrari F2003-GA-V10		1/20
1	AUSTRIAN GP	A1-Ring	1	Scuderia Ferrari Marlboro	B	3.0 Ferrari F2003-GA-V10	despite refuelling drama/FL	1/20
3	MONACO GP	Monte Carlo	1	Scuderia Ferrari Marlboro	B	3.0 Ferrari F2003-GA-V10	bottled up behind Trulli	5/19
1	CANADIAN GP	Montreal	1	Scuderia Ferrari Marlboro	B	3.0 Ferrari F2003-GA-V10	nursed brake problem	3/20
5	EUROPEAN GP	Nürburgring	1	Scuderia Ferrari Marlboro	B	3.0 Ferrari F2003-GA-V10	collision with Montoya – spun	2/20
3	FRANCE GP	Magny Cours	1	Scuderia Ferrari Marlboro	B	3.0 Ferrari F2003-GA-V10		3/20
4	BRITISH GP	Silverstone	1	Scuderia Ferrari Marlboro	B	3.0 Ferrari F2003-GA-V10	unlucky with delayed pit stops	5/20
7	GERMAN GP	Hockenheim	1	Scuderia Ferrari Marlboro	B	3.0 Ferrari F2003-GA-V10	puncture when 2nd/1 lap behind	6/20
8	HUNGARIAN GP	Hungaroring	1	Scuderia Ferrari Marlboro	B	3.0 Ferrari F2003-GA-V10	lapped by winner	8/20
1	ITALIAN GP	Monza	1	Scuderia Ferrari Marlboro	B	3.0 Ferrari F2003-GA-V10	FL	1/20
1	U S GP	Indianapolis	1	Scuderia Ferrari Marlboro	B	3.0 Ferrari F2003-GA-V10	FL	7/20
8	JAPANESE GP	Suzuka	1	Scuderia Ferrari Marlboro	B	3.0 Ferrari F2003-GA-V10	two separate collisions and a spin	14/20

2004 WORLD CHAMPION Wins: 13 Pole positions: 8 Fastest laps: 10 Points scored: 148

1	AUSTRALIAN GP	Melbourne	1	Scuderia Ferrari Marlboro	B	3.0 Ferrari F2004-V10	FL	1/20
1	MALAYSIAN GP	Sepang	1	Scuderia Ferrari Marlboro	B	3.0 Ferrari F2004-V10		1/20
1	BAHRAIN GP	Bahrain Circuit	1	Scuderia Ferrari Marlboro	B	3.0 Ferrari F2004-V10	FL	1/20
1	SAN MARINO GP	Imola	1	Scuderia Ferrari Marlboro	B	3.0 Ferrari F2004-V10	FL	2/20
1	SPANISH GP	Barcelona	1	Scuderia Ferrari Marlboro	B	3.0 Ferrari F2004-V10	FL	1/20
ret	MONACO GP	Monte Carlo	1	Scuderia Ferrari Marlboro	B	3.0 Ferrari F2004-V10	hit Montoya-suspension damage/FL	4/20
1	EUROPEAN GP	Nürburgring	1	Scuderia Ferrari Marlboro	B	3.0 Ferrari F2004-V10	FL	1/20
1	CANADIAN GP	Montreal	1	Scuderia Ferrari Marlboro	B	3.0 Ferrari F2004-V10		6/20
1	U S GP	Indianapolis	1	Scuderia Ferrari Marlboro	B	3.0 Ferrari F2004-V10		2/20
1	FRENCH GP	Magny Cours	1	Scuderia Ferrari Marlboro	B	3.0 Ferrari F2004-V10	FL	2/20
1	BRITISH GP	Silverstone	1	Scuderia Ferrari Marlboro	B	3.0 Ferrari F2004-V10	FL	4/20
1	GERMAN GP	Hockenheim	1	Scuderia Ferrari Marlboro	B	3.0 Ferrari F2004-V10		1/20
1	HUNGARIAN GP	Hungaroring	1	Scuderia Ferrari Marlboro	B	3.0 Ferrari F2004-V10	FL	1/20
2	BELGIAN GP	Spa	1	Scuderia Ferrari Marlboro	B	3.0 Ferrari F2004-V10		2/20
2	ITALIAN GP	Monza	1	Scuderia Ferrari Marlboro	B	3.0 Ferrari F2004-V10	recovered after spin on lap 1	3/20
12	CHINESE GP	Shanghai	1	Scuderia Ferrari Marlboro	B	3.0 Ferrari F2004-V10	*no time set/spin/puncture/-1 lap/FL	*18/20
1	JAPANESE GP	Suzuka	1	Scuderia Ferrari Marlboro	B	3.0 Ferrari F2004-V10		1/20
7	BRAZILIAN GP	Interlagos	1	Scuderia Ferrari Marlboro	B	3.0 Ferrari F2004-V10	*10 place drop-engine change/spin	*18/20

2005 Championship position: 3rd   Wins: 1   Pole positions: 1   Fastest laps: 3   Points scored: 62

ret	AUSTRALIAN GP	Melbourne	1	Scuderia Marlboro Ferrari	B	Ferrari F2004M-3.0 Ferrari V10	accident with Heidfeld	18/20
7	MALAYSIAN GP	Sepang	1	Scuderia Marlboro Ferrari	B	Ferrari F2004M-3.0 Ferrari V10	struggled with tyres	13/20
ret	BAHRAIN GP	Bahrain	1	Scuderia Marlboro Ferrari	B	Ferrari F2005-3.0 Ferrari V10	hydraulics problem caused spin	6/20
2	SAN MARINO GP	Imola	1	Scuderia Marlboro Ferrari	B	Ferrari F2005-3.0 Ferrari V10	FL	13/20
ret	SPANISH GP	Barcelona	1	Scuderia Marlboro Ferrari	B	Ferrari F2005-3.0 Ferrari V10	punctured tyre	8/18
6	MONACO GP	Monte Carlo	1	Scuderia Marlboro Ferrari	B	Ferrari F2005-3.0 Ferrari V10	collision with Coulthard/FL	8/18
5	EUROPEAN GP	Nürburgring	1	Scuderia Marlboro Ferrari	B	Ferrari F2005-3.0 Ferrari V10	lack of grip	10/20
2	CANADIAN GP	Montreal	1	Scuderia Marlboro Ferrari	B	Ferrari F2005-3.0 Ferrari V10		2/20
1	U S GP	Indianapolis	1	Scuderia Marlboro Ferrari	B	Ferrari F2005-3.0 Ferrari V10	tyre safety issue – only 6 cars started/FL	5/20
3	FRENCH GP	Magny Cours	1	Scuderia Marlboro Ferrari	B	Ferrari F2005-3.0 Ferrari V10		4/20
6	BRITISH GP	Silverstone	1	Scuderia Marlboro Ferrari	B	Ferrari F2005-3.0 Ferrari V10	car not fast enough	10/20
5	GERMAN GP	Hockenheim	1	Scuderia Marlboro Ferrari	B	Ferrari F2005-3.0 Ferrari V10	lack of grip	5/20
2	HUNGARIAN GP	Hungaroring	1	Scuderia Marlboro Ferrari	B	Ferrari F2005-3.0 Ferrari V10		1/20
ret	TURKISH GP	Hungaroring	1	Scuderia Marlboro Ferrari	B	Ferrari F2005-3.0 Ferrari V10	*no time set/collision with Webber	*17/20
10	ITALIAN GP	Monza	1	Scuderia Marlboro Ferrari	B	Ferrari F2005-3.0 Ferrari V10	off-track excursion at Lesmo 2	7/20
ret	BELGIAN GP	Spa	1	Scuderia Marlboro Ferrari	B	Ferrari F2005-3.0 Ferrari V10	shunted off by Sato	7/20
4	BRAZILIAN GP	Interlagos	1	Scuderia Marlboro Ferrari	B	Ferrari F2005-3.0 Ferrari V10		7/20
7	JAPANESE GP	Suzuka	1	Scuderia Marlboro Ferrari	B	Ferrari F2005-3.0 Ferrari V10		14/20
ret	CHINESE GP	Shanghai	1	Scuderia Marlboro Ferrari	B	Ferrari F2005-3.0 Ferrari V10	worn tyres –spun out	6/20

2006 Championship position: 2nd   Wins: 7   Pole positions: 4   Fastest laps: 7   Points scored: 00

2	BAHRAIN GP	Bahrain	5	Scuderia Ferrari Marlboro	B	2.4 Ferrari 248F1-V8	just pipped by Alonso	1/22
6	MALAYSIAN GP	Sepang	5	Scuderia Ferrari Marlboro	B	2.4 Ferrari 248F1-V8	lack of grip from tyres	4/22
ret	AUSTRALIAN GP	Melbourne	5	Scuderia Ferrari Marlboro	B	2.4 Ferrari 248F1-V8	ran wide –hit wall	11/22
1	SAN MARINO GP	Imola	5	Scuderia Ferrari Marlboro	B	2.4 Ferrari 248F1-V8		1/22
1	EUROPEAN GP	Nürburgring	5	Scuderia Ferrari Marlboro	B	2.4 Ferrari 248F1-V8	FL	2/22
2	SPANISH GP	Barcelona	5	Scuderia Ferrari Marlboro	B	2.4 Ferrari 248F1-V8		3/22
5	MONACO GP	Monte Carlo	5	Scuderia Ferrari Marlboro	B	2.4 Ferrari 248F1-V8	*penalty – blocking – started from pitlane/FL	*1/22
2	BRITISH GP	Silverstone	5	Scuderia Ferrari Marlboro	B	2.4 Ferrari 248F1-V8		3/22
2	CANADIAN GP	Montreal	5	Scuderia Ferrari Marlboro	B	2.4 Ferrari 248F1-V8		5/22
1	U S GP	Indianapolis	5	Scuderia Ferrari Marlboro	B	2.4 Ferrari 248F1-V8	FL	1/22
1	FRENCH GP	Magny Cours	5	Scuderia Ferrari Marlboro	B	2.4 Ferrari 248F1-V8	FL	1/22
1	GERMAN GP	Hockenheim	5	Scuderia Ferrari Marlboro	B	2.4 Ferrari 248F1-V8	FL	2/22
8/ret	HUNGARIAN GP	Hungaroring	5	Scuderia Ferrari Marlboro	B	2.4 Ferrari 248F1-V8	broken track rod/2 laps behind	12/22
3	TURKISH GP	Istanbul	5	Scuderia Ferrari Marlboro	B	2.4 Ferrari 248F1-V8	ran off track/FL	2/22
1	ITALIAN GP	Monza	5	Scuderia Ferrari Marlboro	B	2.4 Ferrari 248F1-V8	90th Grand Prix win	2/22
1	CHINESE GP	Shanghai	5	Scuderia Ferrari Marlboro	B	2.4 Ferrari 248F1-V8		6/22
ret	JAPANESE GP	Suzuka	5	Scuderia Ferrari Marlboro	B	2.4 Ferrari 248F1-V8	engine	2/22
4	BRAZILIAN GP	Interlagos	5	Scuderia Ferrari Marlboro	B	2.4 Ferrari 248F1-V8	collision – Fisichella – puncture/FL	10/22

2010 Championship position: 9th   Wins: 0   Pole positions: 0   Fastest laps: 0   Points scored: 72

6	BAHRAIN GP	Sakhir Circuit	3	Mercedes GP Petronas F1 Team	B	2.4 Mercedes MGP W01-V8		7/24
10	AUSTRALIAN GP	Melbourne	3	Mercedes GP Petronas F1 Team	B	2.4 Mercedes MGP W01-V8	lap 1 collision – wing damage	7/24
ret	MALAYSIAN GP	Sepang	3	Mercedes GP Petronas F1 Team	B	2.4 Mercedes MGP W01-V8	rear wheel nut	8/24
10	CHINESE GP	Shanghai Circuit	3	Mercedes GP Petronas F1 Team	B	2.4 Mercedes MGP W01-V8	poor tyre strategy	9/24
4	SPANISH GP	Barcelona	3	Mercedes GP Petronas F1 Team	B	2.4 Mercedes MGP W01-V8		6/24
12*	MONACO GP	Monte Carlo	3	Mercedes GP Petronas F1 Team	B	2.4 Mercedes MGP W01-V8	*6th but given 20-sec penalty after race	7/24
4	TURKISH GP	Istanbul Park	3	Mercedes GP Petronas F1 Team	B	2.4 Mercedes MGP W01-V8		5/24
11	CANADIAN GP	Montreal	3	Mercedes GP Petronas F1 Team	B	2.4 Mercedes MGP W01-V8	1 lap behind	13/24
15	EUROPEAN GP	Valencia	3	Mercedes GP Petronas F1 Team	B	2.4 Mercedes MGP W01-V8	held up at pitlane exit under safety car	15/24
9	BRITISH GP	Silverstone	3	Mercedes GP Petronas F1 Team	B	2.4 Mercedes MGP W01-V8		10/24
9	GERMAN GP	Hockenheim	3	Mercedes GP Petronas F1 Team	B	2.4 Mercedes MGP W01-V8	1 lap behind	11/24
11	HUNGARIAN GP	Hungaroring	3	Mercedes GP Petronas F1 Team	B	2.4 Mercedes MGP W01-V8	incident with Barrichello/1 lap behind	14/24
7	BELGIAN GP	Spa	3	Mercedes GP Petronas F1 Team	B	2.4 Mercedes MGP W01-V8		11/24
9	ITALIAN GP	Monza	3	Mercedes GP Petronas F1 Team	B	2.4 Mercedes MGP W01-V8		12/24
13	SINGAPORE GP	Marina Bay Circuit	3	Mercedes GP Petronas F1 Team	B	2.4 Mercedes MGP W01-V8	1 lap behind	9/24
6	JAPANESE GP	Suzuka	3	Mercedes GP Petronas F1 Team	B	2.4 Mercedes MGP W01-V8		10/24
4	KOREAN GP	Yeongam	3	Mercedes GP Petronas F1 Team	B	2.4 Mercedes MGP W01-V8		9/24
7	BRAZILIAN GP	Interlagos	3	Mercedes GP Petronas F1 Team	B	2.4 Mercedes MGP W01-V8		8/24
ret	ABU DHABI GP	Yas Marina Circuit	4	Mercedes GP Petronas F1 Team	B	2.4 Mercedes MGP W01-V8	spun – hit by Liuzzi	8/24

2011 Championship position: 8th   Wins: 0   Pole positions: 0   Fastest laps: 0   Points scored: 76

ret	AUSTRALIAN GP	Melbourne	7	Mercedes GP Petronas F1 Team	P	2.4 Mercedes MGP W02-V8	hit by Alguersuari – damaged floor	11/24
9	MALAYSIAN GP	Sepang	7	Mercedes GP Petronas F1 Team	P	2.4 Mercedes MGP W02-V8		11/24
8	CHINESE GP	Shanghai Circuit	7	Mercedes GP Petronas F1 Team	P	2.4 Mercedes MGP W02-V8		14/24
12	TURKISH GP	Istanbul Park	7	Mercedes GP Petronas F1 Team	P	2.4 Mercedes MGP W02-V8	collision with Petrov – needed new wing	8/24
6	SPANISH GP	Barcelona	7	Mercedes GP Petronas F1 Team	P	2.4 Mercedes MGP W02-V8		10/24
ret	MONACO GP	Monte Carlo	7	Mercedes GP Petronas F1 Team	P	2.4 Mercedes MGP W02-V8	air box fire – killed engine	5/24
4	CANADIAN GP	Montreal	7	Mercedes GP Petronas F1 Team	P	2.4 Mercedes MGP W02-V8	collision with Petrov – needed new wing	8/24
17	EUROPEAN GP	Valencia	7	Mercedes GP Petronas F1 Team	P	2.4 Mercedes MGP W02-V8		11/24
9	BRITISH GP	Silverstone	7	Mercedes GP Petronas F1 Team	P	2.4 Mercedes MGP W02-V8	collision – Kobayashi – needed new wing	8/24
8	GERMAN GP	Hockenheim	7	Mercedes GP Petronas F1 Team	P	2.4 Mercedes MGP W02-V8	spin/1 lap behind	10/24
ret	HUNGARIAN GP	Hungaroring	7	Mercedes GP Petronas F1 Team	P	2.4 Mercedes MGP W02-V8	gearbox	9/24
5	BELGIAN GP	Spa	7	Mercedes GP Petronas F1 Team	P	2.4 Mercedes MGP W02-V8	*no time set	*24/24
5	ITALIAN GP	Monza	7	Mercedes GP Petronas F1 Team	P	2.4 Mercedes MGP W02-V8		8/24
ret	SINGAPORE GP	Marina Bay Circuit	7	Mercedes GP Petronas F1 Team	P	2.4 Mercedes MGP W02-V8	accident – ran into Pérez	8/24
6	JAPANESE GP	Suzuka	7	Mercedes GP Petronas F1 Team	P	2.4 Mercedes MGP W02-V8		7/24
ret	KOREAN GP	Yeongam	7	Mercedes GP Petronas F1 Team	P	2.4 Mercedes MGP W02-V8	hit from behind by Petrov – lost rear wheel	7/24
5	INDIAN GP	Buddh Circuit	7	Mercedes GP Petronas F1 Team	P	2.4 Mercedes MGP W02-V8		12/24
7	ABU DHABI GP	Yas Marina Circuit	7	Mercedes GP Petronas F1 Team	P	2.4 Mercedes MGP W02-V8		8/24
15	BRAZILIAN GP	Interlagos	7	Mercedes GP Petronas F1 Team	P	2.4 Mercedes MGP W02-V8	collision –Senna – puncture/1 lap behind	10/24

GP Starts: 287 (289)   GP Wins: 91   Pole positions: 68   Fastest laps: 76   Points: 1439 *(not incuding 1997 total of 78 points which were disallowed from championship)*

RALF SCHUMACHER

AS the younger brother of the prodigiously talented Michael Schumacher, it would have been perfectly understandable if Ralf had opted for a profession as diametrically opposed to his sibling's as could be found. He had other ideas, however, and despite being in the shadow of the most successful grand prix driver of all time, he managed to make his own considerable mark in Formula 1. Six wins, six pole positions and eight fastest laps from 180 races is a record of which many drivers would be proud.

The younger Schumacher first made an impression in German Formula 3 during the 1994 season, when he scored a single victory, but posted an additional nine top-three finishes to claim third place in the final standings. The following year, he became embroiled in a battle with Norberto Fontana for the crown, but despite a run of three wins in mid-season, eventually he was beaten into second place by the Argentinian.

Although courted by Opel for a drive in the ITC series in 1996, Ralf and his manager, Willy Weber, decided that he should race in Formula Nippon in Japan as the next stage of his career development. It was a successful move for the young German, who posted three victories to take the title. In addition, he shared a Toyota Supra with Naoki Hattori in the All-Japan GT championship.

Ralf's year in Japan was crucial to his progress, as he stepped up to F1 with Jordan in 1997. He was paired with Giancarlo Fisichella, and the two young turks slugged it out in a battle for supremacy within the team, which was counter-productive for everyone. Ralf simply over-drove in his attempts to impress. A podium finish in Argentina should have been cause for major celebration, but it was tainted by his crassness in pushing his team-mate into premature retirement. The German was joined by Damon Hill in 1998, and both drivers spent the first part of the season vainly looking for an answer to seemingly insoluble problems. Ralf's superb drive into sixth place in the wet at Silverstone, however, proved to be the turning point for the team. He seemed to grow in confidence race by race and was deeply frustrated to have to hold station behind Hill at Spa, where Jordan's first grand prix win was achieved. By then, though, he had already decided to accept an offer from Williams for 1999.

If the 1999 season buried the reputation – and F1 career – of the popular Alex Zanardi, then it was the making of the previously unfancied Ralf Schumacher who, by the end of the year, had earned a respect that went far beyond mere acceptance that he was on the grand prix grid on his own merits. Nobody expected fireworks with the team consigned to running Supertec-engined cars, but a surprise was in store. Schumacher was the revelation of the season, and could have won both the Italian and European grands prix if circumstances had played into his hands. More than anything, however, he had finally proved that he didn't need his big brother at all. He was very much his own man.

In 2000, Schumacher was the undisputed team leader and Williams had BMW power, although the engines were not expected to set the world alight on their debut, but this was enough to allow the German to shine. It was not all plain sailing, though, as he struggled to hold sway over his young team-mate, Jenson Button. As the Briton gained in confidence, experience and points, so Schumacher's demeanour changed; the already quiet driver became even more withdrawn.

With the mercurial Juan Pablo Montoya on board for 2001, interest centred on how the German would fare against, if anything, an even more unpredictable talent. He took advantage of Montoya's learning curve by winning his first grand prix at Imola in April and taking a second win in Canada, following a head-to-head with brother Michael. Then he inherited a victory in his homeland when Montoya again fell foul of me-

chanical troubles, but as the stoic Colombian began to get the breaks, Ralf's game became shaky. By the time Montoya won in Italy, Schumacher was looking more like the Williams number two and went into 2002 with much to prove.

However, Ralf was back on form by the time of the Australian GP, taking third on the grid, but becoming caught up in a massive crash at the start, which claimed nearly half the field. He continued his form at the next race, the Malaysian GP, notching up his, and BMW WilliamsF1's, only win of the season. Two strong finishes in the next two races followed – second in Brazil and third at the San Marino GP – but the rest of the season was overshadowed by Montoya's performances, particularly in qualifying.

The following year, Ralf appeared to be a contender for the championship at the mid-point of the campaign, and his final position of fifth could and should have been higher. Like Montoya, he started slowly and didn't manage to get on to the podium until Montreal. By then, Williams had found a turn of speed and he took back-to-back wins in the European and French races to head into contention for the drivers' crown. Somehow, though, it all went wrong for the German, and the final six races of the season yielded little as he fell away badly. His cause wasn't helped by an accident during testing at Monza that led to him missing the Italian GP with concussion.

The 2004 campaign would be Ralf's final effort with Williams, and his relationship with the team, especially bosses Frank Williams and Patrick Head, became troubled; talks on renewing his contract led to little but frustration. It was reported that he was heading to Toyota, but all discussions were put on hold after he suffered a high-speed crash at the US GP, which left him with two broken vertebrae and sidelined from six races.

Despite his season's tally of just six points finishes and a best of second in Japan, Toyota decided to take up its option on Schumacher for 2005. However, he took some time to gel with the team and was slow to make an impression. Things were not helped when he suffered another nasty crash at Indianapolis after a tyre deflated, which triggered a mass boycott by the Michelin runners. He bounced back, though, with a run of points-scoring finishes, culminating with a podium in Hungary. Indeed, he could have won the rain-affected Belgian Grand Prix but for a disastrously called pit stop for dry tyres when the track was still too wet for them. By the end of the year, he was much more confident with the revised Toyota 105B and just edged team-mate Jarno Trulli for sixth place in the final standings.

The following year, 2006, turned out to be one of deep disappointment, and it was only after the mid-season introduction of the TF106B that results picked up. However, an underpowered engine left Ralf fighting in the main for the minor points-scoring places. Toyota were still committed to winning in Formula 1, but the team had made little progress, and as Schumacher entered the final year of a very lucrative contract, the feeling was that he was a luxury they could ill afford. He was not helped by the inherent understeer that the T107 possessed, and he struggled to adapt his driving style accordingly. Although the car was capable of performing strongly on occasion, more often than not it was let down by niggling problems that undermined the driver's efforts. A paltry total of five world championship points by the time the season closed led to Schumacher looking elsewhere for employment in Formula 1.

After a disappointing test for Force India, Ralf decided to take up the opportunity of racing in the DTM series for Mercedes, for whom he has competed since 2008. Thus far, he has failed to take a victory, but seems sanguine about not joining the front-runners. He appears more than happy to look forward to a different challenge, having become involved in the yachting business.

SCHUMACHER, Ralf (D) b 30/6/1975, Hürth-Hermühlheim

	1997 Championship position: 11th	Wins: 0		Pole positions: 0		Fastest laps: 0	Points scored: 13	
	Race	Circuit	No	Entrant	Tyres	Capacity/Car/Engine	Comment	Q Pos/Entries
ret	AUSTRALIAN GP	Melbourne	11	B&H Total Jordan Peugeot	G	3.0 Jordan 197 Peugeot V10	gearbox	12/24
ret	BRAZILIAN GP	Interlagos	11	B&H Total Jordan Peugeot	G	3.0 Jordan 197 Peugeot V10	electrics	10/22
3	ARGENTINE GP	Buenos Aires	11	B&H Total Jordan Peugeot	G	3.0 Jordan 197 Peugeot V10	collision with Fisichella	6/22
ret	SAN MARINO GP	Imola	11	B&H Total Jordan Peugeot	G	3.0 Jordan 197 Peugeot V10	driveshaft	5/22
ret	MONACO GP	Monte Carlo	11	B&H Total Jordan Peugeot	G	3.0 Jordan 197 Peugeot V10	crashed	6/22
ret	SPANISH GP	Barcelona	11	B&H Total Jordan Peugeot	G	3.0 Jordan 197 Peugeot V10	engine	9/22
ret	CANADIAN GP	Montreal	11	B&H Total Jordan Peugeot	G	3.0 Jordan 197 Peugeot V10	accident	7/22
6	FRENCH GP	Magny Cours	11	B&H Total Jordan Peugeot	G	3.0 Jordan 197 Peugeot V10		3/22
5	BRITISH GP	Silverstone	11	B&H Total Jordan Peugeot	G	3.0 Jordan 197 Peugeot V10		5/22
5	GERMAN GP	Hockenheim	11	B&H Total Jordan Peugeot	G	3.0 Jordan 197 Peugeot V10		7/22
5	HUNGARIAN GP	Hungaroring	11	B&H Total Jordan Peugeot	G	3.0 Jordan 197 Peugeot V10		14/22
ret	BELGIAN GP	Spa	11	B&H Total Jordan Peugeot	G	3.0 Jordan 197 Peugeot V10	started from pits/spun off	6/22
ret	ITALIAN GP	Monza	11	B&H Total Jordan Peugeot	G	3.0 Jordan 197 Peugeot V10	hit Herbert – collision damage	8/22
5	AUSTRIAN GP	A1-Ring	11	B&H Total Jordan Peugeot	G	3.0 Jordan 197 Peugeot V10		11/22
ret	LUXEMBOURG GP	Nürburgring	11	B&H Total Jordan Peugeot	G	3.0 Jordan 197 Peugeot V10	collision with Fisichella on lap 1	8/22
9*	JAPANESE GP	Suzuka	11	B&H Total Jordan Peugeot	G	3.0 Jordan 197 Peugeot V10	*5th place car disqualified	13/22
ret	EUROPEAN GP	Jerez	11	B&H Total Jordan Peugeot	G	3.0 Jordan 197 Peugeot V10	alternator	16/22

	1998 Championship position: 10th	Wins: 0		Pole positions: 0		Fastest laps: 0	Points scored: 14	
ret	AUSTRALIAN GP	Melbourne	10	B&H Jordan Mugen Honda	G	3.0 Jordan 198-Mugen Honda V10	collision with Magnussen on lap 1	9/22
ret	BRAZILIAN GP	Interlagos	10	B&H Jordan Mugen Honda	G	3.0 Jordan 198-Mugen Honda V10	spun off	8/22
ret	ARGENTINE GP	Buenos Aires	10	B&H Jordan Mugen Honda	G	3.0 Jordan 198-Mugen Honda V10	suspension failure – spun off	5/22
7	SAN MARINO GP	Imola	10	B&H Jordan Mugen Honda	G	3.0 Jordan 198-Mugen Honda V10	low air valve pressure/1 lap behind	9/22
11	SPANISH GP	Barcelona	10	B&H Jordan Mugen Honda	G	3.0 Jordan 198-Mugen Honda V10	2 laps behind	11/22
ret	MONACO GP	Monte Carlo	10	B&H Jordan Mugen Honda	G	3.0 Jordan 198-Mugen Honda V10	collision damage after shunt	16/22
ret	CANADIAN GP	Montreal	10	B&H Jordan Mugen Honda	G	3.0 Jordan 198-Mugen Honda V10	clutch	5/22
ret	FRENCH GP	Magny Cours	10	B&H Jordan Mugen Honda	G	3.0 Jordan 198-Mugen Honda V10	collision damage/3 laps behind	6/22
6	BRITISH GP	Silverstone	10	B&H Jordan Mugen Honda	G	3.0 Jordan 198-Mugen Honda V10	1 lap behind	10/22
5	AUSTRIAN GP	A1-Ring	10	B&H Jordan Mugen Honda	G	3.0 Jordan 198-Mugen Honda V10		9/22
6	GERMAN GP	Hockenheim	10	B&H Jordan Mugen Honda	G	3.0 Jordan 198-Mugen Honda V10		4/22
9	HUNGARIAN GP	Hungaroring	10	B&H Jordan Mugen Honda	G	3.0 Jordan 198-Mugen Honda V10	1 lap behind	10/22
2	BELGIAN GP	Spa	10	B&H Jordan Mugen Honda	G	3.0 Jordan 198-Mugen Honda V10		8/22
3	ITALIAN GP	Monza	10	B&H Jordan Mugen Honda	G	3.0 Jordan 198-Mugen Honda V10		6/22
ret	LUXEMBOURG GP	Nürburgring	10	B&H Jordan Mugen Honda	G	3.0 Jordan 198-Mugen Honda V10	brake disc	6/22
ret	JAPANESE GP	Suzuka	10	B&H Jordan Mugen Honda	G	3.0 Jordan 198-Mugen Honda V10	engine	7/22

	1999 Championship position: 6th	Wins: 0		Pole positions: 0		Fastest laps: 1	Points scored: 35	
3	AUSTRALIAN GP	Melbourne	6	Winfield Williams	B	3.0 Williams FW21-Supertec V10		8/22
4	BRAZILIAN GP	Interlagos	6	Winfield Williams	B	3.0 Williams FW21-Supertec V10	1 lap behind	11/22
ret	SAN MARINO GP	Imola	6	Winfield Williams	B	3.0 Williams FW21-Supertec V10	throttle	9/22
ret	MONACO GP	Monte Carlo	6	Winfield Williams	B	3.0 Williams FW21-Supertec V10	accident	16/22
5	SPANISH GP	Barcelona	6	Winfield Williams	B	3.0 Williams FW21-Supertec V10		10/22
4	CANADIAN GP	Montreal	6	Winfield Williams	B	3.0 Williams FW21-Supertec V10		13/22
4	FRENCH GP	Magny Cours	6	Winfield Williams	B	3.0 Williams FW21-Supertec V10		16/22
3	BRITISH GP	Silverstone	6	Winfield Williams	B	3.0 Williams FW21-Supertec V10		8/22
ret	AUSTRIAN GP	A1-Ring	6	Winfield Williams	B	3.0 Williams FW21-Supertec V10	spun off on lap 1	8/22
4	GERMAN GP	Hockenheim	6	Winfield Williams	B	3.0 Williams FW21-Supertec V10		11/22
9	HUNGARIAN GP	Hungaroring	6	Winfield Williams	B	3.0 Williams FW21-Supertec V10	1 lap behind	16/22
5	BELGIAN GP	Spa	6	Winfield Williams	B	3.0 Williams FW21-Supertec V10		5/22
2	ITALIAN GP	Monza	6	Winfield Williams	B	3.0 Williams FW21-Supertec V10	FL	5/22
4	EUROPEAN GP	Nürburgring	6	Winfield Williams	B	3.0 Williams FW21-Supertec V10	puncture – led race	4/22
ret	MALAYSIAN GP	Sepang	6	Winfield Williams	B	3.0 Williams FW21-Supertec V10	spun off	8/22
5	JAPANESE GP	Suzuka	6	Winfield Williams	B	3.0 Williams FW21-Supertec V10		9/22

	2000 Championship position: 5th	Wins: 0		Pole positions: 0		Fastest laps: 0	Points scored: 24	
3	AUSTRALIAN GP	Melbourne	9	BMW WilliamsF1 Team	B	3.0 Williams FW22-BMW V10		11/22
5*	BRAZILIAN GP	Interlagos	9	BMW WilliamsF1 Team	B	3.0 Williams FW22-BMW V10	*2nd place car disqualified/-1 lap	11/22
ret	SAN MARINO GP	Imola	9	BMW WilliamsF1 Team	B	3.0 Williams FW22-BMW V10	fuel pick-up	7/22
4	BRITISH GP	Silverstone	9	BMW WilliamsF1 Team	B	3.0 Williams FW22-BMW V10	despite broken exhaust	7/22
4	SPANISH GP	Barcelona	9	BMW WilliamsF1 Team	B	3.0 Williams FW22-BMW V10		5/22
ret	EUROPEAN GP	Nürburgring	9	BMW WilliamsF1 Team	B	3.0 Williams FW22-BMW V10	collision with Irvine	5/22
ret	MONACO GP	Monte Carlo	9	BMW WilliamsF1 Team	B	3.0 Williams FW22-BMW V10	crashed – suffered cut leg	9/22
14/ret	CANADIAN GP	Montreal	9	BMW WilliamsF1 Team	B	3.0 Williams FW22-BMW V10	punted off by Villeneuve/5 laps behind	12/22
5	FRENCH GP	Magny Cours	9	BMW WilliamsF1 Team	B	3.0 Williams FW22-BMW V10	slight overheating problem	5/22
ret	AUSTRIAN GP	A1-Ring	9	BMW WilliamsF1 Team	B	3.0 Williams FW22-BMW V10	brakes	19/22
7	GERMAN GP	Hockenheim	9	BMW WilliamsF1 Team	B	3.0 Williams FW22-BMW V10	diffuser damage after collision	14/22
5	HUNGARIAN GP	Hungaroring	9	BMW WilliamsF1 Team	B	3.0 Williams FW22-BMW V10		4/22
3	BELGIAN GP	Spa	9	BMW WilliamsF1 Team	B	3.0 Williams FW22-BMW V10		6/22
3	ITALIAN GP	Monza	9	BMW WilliamsF1 Team	B	3.0 Williams FW22-BMW V10		7/22
ret	UNITED STATES GP	Indianapolis	9	BMW WilliamsF1 Team	B	3.0 Williams FW22-BMW V10	engine	10/22
ret	JAPANESE GP	Suzuka	9	BMW WilliamsF1 Team	B	3.0 Williams FW22-BMW V10	handling – spun off	6/22
ret	MALAYSIAN GP	Sepang	9	BMW WilliamsF1 Team	B	3.0 Williams FW22-BMW V10	engine	8/22

	2001 Championship position: 4th	Wins: 3		Pole positions: 1		Fastest laps: 5	Points scored: 49	
ret	AUSTRALIAN GP	Melbourne	5	BMW WilliamsF1 Team	M	3.0 Williams FW23-BMW V10	hit from behind by Villeneuve	5/22
5	MALAYSIAN GP	Sepang	5	BMW WilliamsF1 Team	M	3.0 Williams FW23-BMW V10	understeer problems	3/22
ret	BRAZILIAN GP	Interlagos	5	BMW WilliamsF1 Team	M	3.0 Williams FW23-BMW V10	collision – Barrichello/later spun off/FL	2/22
1	SAN MARINO GP	Imola	5	BMW WilliamsF1 Team	M	3.0 Williams FW23-BMW V10	FL	3/22
ret	SPANISH GP	Barcelona	5	BMW WilliamsF1 Team	M	3.0 Williams FW23-BMW V10	spun off	5/22

ret	AUSTRIAN GP	A1-Ring	5	BMW WilliamsF1 Team	M	3.0 Williams FW23-BMW V10	overheating brakes	3/22
ret	MONACO GP	Monte Carlo	5	BMW WilliamsF1 Team	M	3.0 Williams FW23-BMW V10	hydraulics	5/22
1	CANADIAN GP	Montreal	5	BMW WilliamsF1 Team	M	3.0 Williams FW23-BMW V10	FL	2/22
4	EUROPEAN GP	Nürburgring	5	BMW WilliamsF1 Team	M	3.0 Williams FW23-BMW V10	10 sec stop & go penalty – pit exit	2/22
2	FRENCH GP	Magny Cours	5	BMW WilliamsF1 Team	M	3.0 Williams FW23-BMW V10		1/22
ret	BRITISH GP	Silverstone	5	BMW WilliamsF1 Team	M	3.0 Williams FW23-BMW V10	engine	10/22
1	GERMAN GP	Hockenheim	5	BMW WilliamsF1 Team	M	3.0 Williams FW23-BMW V10		2/22
4	HUNGARIAN GP	Hungaroring	5	BMW WilliamsF1 Team	M	3.0 Williams FW23-BMW V10		4/22
7	BELGIAN GP	Spa	5	BMW WilliamsF1 Team	M	3.0 Williams FW23-BMW V10	started from back of grid	2/22
3	ITALIAN GP	Monza	5	BMW WilliamsF1 Team	M	3.0 Williams FW23-BMW V10	FL	4/22
ret	UNITED STATES GP	Indianapolis	5	BMW WilliamsF1 Team	M	3.0 Williams FW23-BMW V10	spun off	3/22
6	JAPANESE GP	Suzuka	5	BMW WilliamsF1 Team	M	3.0 Williams FW23-BMW V10	missed chicane – stop & go penalty/FL	3/22

2002 Championship position: 4th   Wins: 1   Pole positions: 0   Fastest laps: 0   Points scored: 42

ret	AUSTRALIAN GP	Melbourne	5	BMW WilliamsF1 Team	M	3.0 Williams FW24-BMW V10	ran into Barrichello at first corner	3/22
1	MALAYSIAN GP	Sepang	5	BMW WilliamsF1 Team	M	3.0 Williams FW24-BMW V10		4/22
2	BRAZILIAN GP	Interlagos	5	BMW WilliamsF1 Team	M	3.0 Williams FW24-BMW V10		3/22
3	SAN MARINO GP	Imola	5	BMW WilliamsF1 Team	M	3.0 Williams FW24-BMW V10		3/22
11/ret	SPANISH GP	Barcelona	5	BMW WilliamsF1 Team	M	3.0 Williams FW24-BMW V10	engine/2 laps behind	3/21
4	AUSTRIAN GP	A1-Ring	5	BMW WilliamsF1 Team	M	3.0 Williams FW24-BMW V10		2/22
3	MONACO GP	Monte Carlo	5	BMW WilliamsF1 Team	M	3.0 Williams FW24-BMW V10	additional pit stop for tyre change	4/22
7	CANADIAN GP	Montreal	5	BMW WilliamsF1 Team	M	3.0 Williams FW24-BMW V10	refuelling delay at pit stop	4/22
4	EUROPEAN GP	Nürburgring	5	BMW WilliamsF1 Team	M	3.0 Williams FW24-BMW V10	handling problems	2/22
8	BRITISH GP	Silverstone	5	BMW WilliamsF1 Team	M	3.0 Williams FW24-BMW V10	refuelling delay at pit stop/1 lap behind	4/22
5	FRENCH GP	Magny Cours	5	BMW WilliamsF1 Team	M	3.0 Williams FW24-BMW V10	wrong tyre choice	5/21
3	GERMAN GP	Hockenheim	5	BMW WilliamsF1 Team	M	3.0 Williams FW24-BMW V10		2/22
3	HUNGARIAN GP	Hungaroring	5	BMW WilliamsF1 Team	M	3.0 Williams FW24-BMW V10		3/20
5	BELGIAN GP	Spa	5	BMW WilliamsF1 Team	M	3.0 Williams FW24-BMW V10		4/20
ret	ITALIAN GP	Monza	5	BMW WilliamsF1 Team	M	3.0 Williams FW24-BMW V10	engine	4/20
16	UNITED STATES GP	Indianapolis	5	BMW WilliamsF1 Team	M	3.0 Williams FW24-BMW V10	hit Montoya – lost wing/2 laps behind	5/20
11/ret	JAPANESE GP	Suzuka	5	BMW WilliamsF1 Team	M	3.0 Williams FW24-BMW V10	engine/5 laps behind	5/20

2003 Championship position: 5th   Wins: 2   Pole positions: 3   Fastest laps: 1   Points scored: 58

8	AUSTRALIAN GP	Melbourne	4	BMW WilliamsF1 Team	M	3.0 Williams FW25-BMW V10	delayed pit stop – locking wheel nut	9/20
4	MALAYSIAN GP	Sepang	4	BMW WilliamsF1 Team	M	3.0 Williams FW25-BMW V10	good drive from rear of grid	17/20
7	BRAZILIAN GP	Interlagos	4	BMW WilliamsF1 Team	M	3.0 Williams FW25-BMW V10	race stopped due to accident	6/20
4	SAN MARINO GP	Imola	4	BMW WilliamsF1 Team	M	3.0 Williams FW25-BMW V10		2/20
5	SPANISH GP	Barcelona	4	BMW WilliamsF1 Team	M	3.0 Williams FW25-BMW V10	ran off circuit – diffuser damage/-1 lap	7/20
6	AUSTRIAN GP	A1-Ring	4	BMW WilliamsF1 Team	M	3.0 Williams FW25-BMW V10		10/20
4	MONACO GP	Monte Carlo	4	BMW WilliamsF1 Team	M	3.0 Williams FW25-BMW V10	lost time running off circuit	1/20
2	CANADIAN GP	Montreal	4	BMW WilliamsF1 Team	M	3.0 Williams FW25-BMW V10		1/20
1	EUROPEAN GP	Nürburgring	4	BMW WilliamsF1 Team	M	3.0 Williams FW25-BMW V10		3/20
1	FRANCE GP	Magny Cours	4	BMW WilliamsF1 Team	M	3.0 Williams FW25-BMW V10		1/20

Ralf Schumacher wins the 2003
French Grand Prix for Williams-
BMW at Magny-Cours. The
German took a total of six wins
for the team before moving to
Toyota on a three-year contract.

9	BRITISH GP	Silverstone	4	BMW WilliamsF1 Team	M	3.0 Williams FW25-BMW V10	guide vane adrift – blocked airflow	4/20
ret	GERMAN GP	Hockenheim	4	BMW WilliamsF1 Team	M	3.0 Williams FW25-BMW V10	ran into Barrichello at start	2/20
4	HUNGARIAN GP	Hungaroring	4	BMW WilliamsF1 Team	M	3.0 Williams FW25-BMW V10	recovered from early spin	2/20
dns	ITALIAN GP	Monza	4	BMW WilliamsF1 Team	M	3.0 Williams FW25-BMW V10	unwell – pulled out after first practice	- / -
ret	U S GP	Indianapolis	4	BMW WilliamsF1 Team	M	3.0 Williams FW25-BMW V10	spun off in wet	5/20
12	JAPANESE GP	Suzuka	4	BMW WilliamsF1 Team	M	3.0 Williams FW25-BMW V10	*no practice time/1 lap behind/FL	*19/20

2004 Championship position: 9th=   Wins: 0   Pole positions: 0   Fastest laps: 0   Points scored: 23

4	AUSTRALIAN GP	Melbourne	4	BMW WilliamsF1 Team	M	3.0 Williams FW26-BMW V10		8/20
ret	MALAYSIAN GP	Sepang	4	BMW WilliamsF1 Team	M	3.0 Williams FW26-BMW V10	engine	7/20
7	BAHRAIN GP	Sakhir Circuit	4	BMW WilliamsF1 Team	M	3.0 Williams FW26-BMW V10	collision with Sato – spin	4/20
7	SAN MARINO GP	Imola	4	BMW WilliamsF1 Team	M	3.0 Williams FW26-BMW V10	collision with Alonso – spin	5/20
6	SPANISH GP	Barcelona	4	BMW WilliamsF1 Team	M	3.0 Williams FW26-BMW V10		6/20
10/ret	MONACO GP	Monte Carlo	4	BMW WilliamsF1 Team	M	3.0 Williams FW26-BMW V10	gearbox/8 laps behind	12/20
ret	EUROPEAN GP	Nürburgring	4	BMW WilliamsF1 Team	M	3.0 Williams FW26-BMW V10	accident with da Matta on lap 1	9/20
dsq*	CANADIAN GP	Montreal	4	BMW WilliamsF1 Team	M	3.0 Williams FW26-BMW V10	2nd - but *dsq for brake duct infringement	1/20
ret	U S GP	Indianapolis	4	BMW WilliamsF1 Team	M	3.0 Williams FW26-BMW V10	tyre deflated – heavy accident	6/20
ret	CHINESE GP	Shanghai	4	BMW WilliamsF1 Team	M	3.0 Williams FW26-BMW V10	accident damage	5/20
2	JAPANESE GP	Suzuka	4	BMW WilliamsF1 Team	M	3.0 Williams FW26-BMW V10		2/20
5	BRAZILIAN GP	Interlagos	4	BMW WilliamsF1 Team	M	3.0 Williams FW26-BMW V10		7/20

2005 Championship position: 6th   Wins: 0   Pole positions: 1   Fastest laps: 1   Points scored: 45

12	AUSTRALIAN GP	Melbourne	17	Panasonic Toyota Racing	M	3.0 Toyota TF105- V10		15/20
5	MALAYSIAN GP	Sepang	17	Panasonic Toyota Racing	M	3.0 Toyota TF105- V10	vibration and tyre wear	5/20
4	BAHRAIN GP	Sakhir Circuit	17	Panasonic Toyota Racing	M	3.0 Toyota TF105- V10		6/20
9*	SAN MARINO GP	Imola	17	Panasonic Toyota Racing	M	3.0 Toyota TF105- V10	*6th but given 25-sec penalty – pit violation	10/20
4	SPANISH GP	Barcelona	17	Panasonic Toyota Racing	M	3.0 Toyota TF105- V10		4/18
6	MONACO GP	Monte Carlo	17	Panasonic Toyota Racing	M	3.0 Toyota TF105- V10	*no practice time	*18/18
ret	EUROPEAN GP	Nürburgring	17	Panasonic Toyota Racing	M	3.0 Toyota TF105- V10	spun off	8/20
6	CANADIAN GP	Montreal	17	Panasonic Toyota Racing	M	3.0 Toyota TF105- V10	1 lap behind	10/20
dns	U S GP	Indianapolis	17	Panasonic Toyota Racing	M	3.0 Toyota TF105- V10	injured in free practice accident	- / -
7	FRENCH GP	Magny Cours	17	Panasonic Toyota Racing	M	3.0 Toyota TF105- V10	3-stop strategy/1 lap behind	12/20
8	BRITISH GP	Silverstone	17	Panasonic Toyota Racing	M	3.0 Toyota TF105- V10	poor handling	9/20
6	GERMAN GP	Hockenheim	17	Panasonic Toyota Racing	M	3.0 Toyota TF105- V10		12/20
3	HUNGARIAN GP	Hungaroring	17	Panasonic Toyota Racing	M	3.0 Toyota TF105- V10		5/20
12	TURKISH GP	Istanbul	17	Panasonic Toyota Racing	M	3.0 Toyota TF105- V10	1 lap behind	9/20
6	ITALIAN GP	Monza	17	Panasonic Toyota Racing	M	3.0 Toyota TF105- V10		10/20
7	BELGIAN GP	Spa	17	Panasonic Toyota Racing	M	3.0 Toyota TF105- V10	switched to wrong tyres in wet/FL	6/20
8	BRAZILIAN GP	Interlagos	17	Panasonic Toyota Racing	M	3.0 Toyota TF105- V10	1 lap behind	11/20
8	JAPANESE GP	Suzuka	17	Panasonic Toyota Racing	M	3.0 Toyota TF105- V10	strategy spoiled by safety-car intervention	1/20
3	CHINESE GP	Shanghai	17	Panasonic Toyota Racing	M	3.0 Toyota TF105- V10		9/20

2006 Championship position: 10th   Wins: 0   Pole positions: 0   Fastest laps: 0   Points scored: 20

14	BAHRAIN GP	Bahrain	7	Panasonic Toyota Racing-	B	2.4 Toyota TF106-V8	tyre temperature problems/1 lap behind	17/22
8	MALAYSIAN GP	Sepang	7	Panasonic Toyota Racing-	B	2.4 Toyota TF106-V8	*engine penalty – started from back of grid	*10/22
3	AUSTRALIAN GP	Melbourne	7	Panasonic Toyota Racing-	B	2.4 Toyota TF106-V8	despite drive-thru penalty – pitlane speeding	6/22
9	SAN MARINO GP	Imola	7	Panasonic Toyota Racing-	B	2.4 Toyota TF106-V8		6/22
ret	EUROPEAN GP	Nürburgring	7	Panasonic Toyota Racing-	B	2.4 Toyota TF106-V8	engine	11/22
ret	SPANISH GP	Barcelona	7	Panasonic Toyota Racing-	B	2.4 Toyota TF106-V8	electronics	6/22
8	MONACO GP	Monte Carlo	7	Panasonic Toyota Racing-	B	2.4 Toyota TF106B-V8		11/22
ret	BRITISH GP	Silverstone	7	Panasonic Toyota Racing-	B	2.4 Toyota TF106B-V8	hit by Speed – collided with Webber	7/22
ret	CANADIAN GP	Montreal	7	Panasonic Toyota Racing-	B	2.4 Toyota TF106B-V8	handling	14/22
ret	U S GP	Indianapolis	7	Panasonic Toyota Racing-	B	2.4 Toyota TF106B-V8	wheel bearing	8/22
4	FRENCH GP	Magny Cours	7	Panasonic Toyota Racing-	B	2.4 Toyota TF106B-V8		5/22
9	GERMAN GP	Hockenheim	7	Panasonic Toyota Racing-	B	2.4 Toyota TF106B-V8	drive-thru pen – pitlane speeding	8/22
6	HUNGARIAN GP	Hungaroring	7	Panasonic Toyota Racing-	B	2.4 Toyota TF106B-V8	1 lap behind	7/22
7	TURKISH GP	Istanbul	7	Panasonic Toyota Racing-	B	2.4 Toyota TF106B-V8		5/22
15	ITALIAN GP	Monza	7	Panasonic Toyota Racing-	B	2.4 Toyota TF106B-V8	1 lap behind	13/22
ret	CHINESE GP	Shanghai	7	Panasonic Toyota Racing-	B	2.4 Toyota TF106B-V8	engine – oil pressure	17/22
7	JAPANESE GP	Suzuka	7	Panasonic Toyota Racing-	B	2.4 Toyota TF106B-V8	held up by team mate Trulli	3/22
ret	BRAZILIAN GP	Interlagos	7	Panasonic Toyota Racing-	B	2.4 Toyota TF106B-V8	rear suspension failure	7/22

2007 Championship position: 16th   Wins: 0   Pole positions: 0   Fastest laps: 0   Points scored: 5

8	AUSTRALIAN GP	Melbourne	11	Panasonic Toyota Racing-	B	2.4 Toyota TF107-V8		9/22
15	MALAYSIAN GP	Sepang	11	Panasonic Toyota Racing-	B	2.4 Toyota TF107-V8	extra stop - slow puncture /1 lap behind	9/22
12	BAHRAIN GP	Bahrain	11	Panasonic Toyota Racing-	B	2.4 Toyota TF107-V8	bogged down in traffic/1 lap behind	14/22
ret	SPANISH GP	Barcelona	11	Panasonic Toyota Racing-	B	2.4 Toyota TF107-V8	hit by Wurz – later retired – loose nose section	17/22
16	MONACO GP	Monte Carlo	11	Panasonic Toyota Racing-	B	2.4 Toyota TF107-V8	2 laps behind	20/22
8	CANADIAN GP	Montreal	11	Panasonic Toyota Racing-	B	2.4 Toyota TF107-V8		18/22
ret	U S GP	Indianapolis	11	Panasonic Toyota Racing-	B	2.4 Toyota TF107-V8	multiple collision on lap 1	12/22
10	FRENCH GP	Magny Cours	11	Panasonic Toyota Racing-	B	2.4 Toyota TF107-V8	1 lap behind	11/22
ret	BRITISH GP	Silverstone	11	Panasonic Toyota Racing-	B	2.4 Toyota TF107-V8	front wheel worked loose	6/22
ret	EUROPEAN GP	Nürburgring	11	Panasonic Toyota Racing-	B	2.4 Toyota TF107-V8	accident – colision with Heidfeld	9/22
6	HUNGARIAN GP	Hungaroring	11	Panasonic Toyota Racing-	B	2.4 Toyota TF107-V8		6/22
12	TURKISH GP	Istanbul	11	Panasonic Toyota Racing-	B	2.4 Toyota TF107-V8	one stop strategy/1 lap behind	18/22
15	ITALIAN GP	Monza	11	Panasonic Toyota Racing-	B	2.4 Toyota TF107-V8	1 lap behind	18/22
10	BELGIAN GP	Spa	11	Panasonic Toyota Racing-	B	2.4 Toyota TF107-V8		12/22
ret	JAPANESE GP	Suzuka	11	Panasonic Toyota Racing-	B	2.4 Toyota TF107-V8	wet electronics and puncture	16/22
ret	CHINESE GP	Shanghai	11	Panasonic Toyota Racing-	B	2.4 Toyota TF107-V8	spun off	6/22
11	BRAZILIAN GP	Interlagos	11	Panasonic Toyota Racing-	B	2.4 Toyota TF107-V8	1 lap behind	15/22

GP Starts: 180   GP Wins: 6   Pole positions: 6   Fastest laps: 8   Points: 329

VERN SCHUPPAN

AFTER a few successful years in karting in Australia, Vern Schuppan travelled to Britain in 1969 to race in Formula Ford, a series where he made a good impression the following year in a Palliser. This led to a works drive for Hugh Dibley's marque in Formula Atlantic in 1971, when he proceeded to win the Yellow Pages championship. After a Tyrrell test, Vern was contracted as a junior driver for BRM, but his dream of a grand prix debut at Spa was snatched away when his car was taken by Peter Gethin. This meant his opportunities were restricted to a couple of non-title events, in which he did well, taking fifth place in the Oulton Park Gold Cup and fourth in the John Player Challenge at Brands Hatch. He found backing from Singapore Airlines to run a March 722-BDA in a couple of F2 events and more in Formula Atlantic

At the top level, it was much the same the following year, Vern kicking his heels in F1 and being restricted to appearances in the Race of Champions and the International Trophy. He accepted an offer to join the Gulf/Wyer team, initially to replace the injured John Watson, taking second place in the Spa 1000km with Howden Ganley and fifth at Dijon with Mike Hailwood

For 1974, Schuppan settled into an F5000 programme with Sid Taylor and Theodore Racing, which produced little by way of results in either a Trojan or a Lola. Ironically, when he drove a one-off race for the VDS team at Brands Hatch in the Rothmans series' final round, he took the Chevron to victory. At last a grand prix chance came with Ensign, courtesy of sponsorship from Teddy Yip, but he dropped out after a few unproductive races, preferring to race the Gulf sports cars. He ended the season on a high note, however, taking a win in the Macau Grand Prix with his trusty March.

In 1975, Schuppan was back with Theodore for more F5000, before heading across the Atlantic to race for Dan Gurney's Eagle team. He picked up another F1 outing with Graham Hill, deputising for the injured Rolf Stommelen in Sweden, but he was already concentrating on building a career Stateside. In 1976, Vern hit the USAC trail with AAR, won a race at Elkhart Lake and earned the Rookie of the Year award at Indianapolis. His best finish at the 'Brickyard', however, was third in the disputed 1981 race, a lap behind Bobby Unser and Mario Andretti

In 1997, Schuppan took time out of his busy F5000 and USAC schedule to replace fellow countryman Larry Perkins at Surtees for a few races. He nearly scored a point at Hockenheim, but was forced to drop out when paying drivers were drafted into the team.

The following season began with Vern recording second place to Warwick Brown in the four-race Australian F5000 championship, before taking his Elfin to race in Can-Am. He continued to drive in this category and the newly formed CART single-seater series, but by the early 1980s he had become heavily involved in endurance racing, winning the Le Mans 24-hours in 1983 for the powerful Rothmans Porsche factory team with Al Holbert and Hurley Haywood. Thereafter, Vern became a successful Porsche entrant in the FIA and Japanese sports car series, developing the basic 962 design on behalf of customers around the world. Later he became a partner in Stefan Johansson's successful Indy Lights team, which was hoping to move up to the CART series, but ultimately they failed to find the necessary budget.

SCHUPPAN, Vern (AUS) b 19/3/1943, Booleroo, Whyalla, South Australia

	Race	Circuit	No	Entrant	Tyres	Capacity/Car/Engine	Comment	Q Pos/Entries
	1972 Championship position: Unplaced							
dns	BELGIAN GP	Nivelles	26	Marlboro BRM	F	3.0 BRM P153B V12	Marko raced car	(26)/26
	1974 Championship position: Unplaced							
15	BELGIAN GP	Nivelles	22	Team Ensign	F	3.0 Ensign N174-Cosworth V8	pit stop – fuel feed/3 laps behind	14/32
ret	MONACO GP	Monte Carlo	22	Team Ensign	F	3.0 Ensign N174-Cosworth V8	spun off	25/28
dsq*	SWEDISH GP	Anderstorp	22	Team Ensign	F	3.0 Ensign N174-Cosworth V8	*started unofficially	27/28
ret/dsq*	DUTCH GP	Zandvoort	22	Team Ensign	F	3.0 Ensign N174-Cosworth V8	fuel line/*tyre change outside pits	17/27
dnq	FRENCH GP	Dijon	22	Team Ensign	F	3.0 Ensign N174-Cosworth V8		23/30
dnq	BRITISH GP	Brands Hatch	22	Team Ensign	F	3.0 Ensign N174-Cosworth V8		30/34
ret	GERMAN GP	Nürburgring	22	Team Ensign	F	3.0 Ensign N174-Cosworth V8	transmission	22/32
	1975 Championship position: Unplaced							
ret	SWEDISH GP	Anderstorp	22	Embassy Racing with Graham Hill	G	3.0 Hill GH1-Cosworth V8	driveshaft	– / –
dns	"	"	22T	Embassy Racing with Graham Hill	G	3.0 Lola T370-Cosworth V8	set grid time in this car	26/26
	1977 Championship position: Unplaced							
12	BRITISH GP	Silverstone	18	Team Surtees	G	3.0 Surtees TS19-Cosworth V8	2 laps behind	23/36
7	GERMAN GP	Hockenheim	18	Team Surtees	G	3.0 Surtees TS19-Cosworth V8	1 lap behind	19/30
16	AUSTRIAN GP	Österreichring	18	Team Surtees	G	3.0 Surtees TS19-Cosworth V8	pit stop – tyres/2 laps behind	25/30
dnq	DUTCH GP	Zandvoort	18	Team Surtees	G	3.0 Surtees TS19-Cosworth V8		29/34

GP Starts: 9   GP Wins: 0   Pole positions: 0   Fastest laps: 0   Points: 0

ADOLFO J SCHWELM-CRUZ

AN enthusiastic Argentinian, Adolfo Schwelm-Cruz was more popularly known as 'Teddy'. He had added his mother's name, Cruz, to his surname after journalists complained that they could not pronounce it. He was educated in England and was mainly based in Europe, so despite his frequent appearances in Argentina, he was not so well known in the country of his birth.

Adolfo began racing in 1949 in a Jaguar XK120, followed by an Alfa Romeo Monza, in sports car and road races at home. In addition, he joined a large contingent of his fellow countrymen for a limited programme of miscellaneous events from 1949 through to 1951, when he scored his best result on foreign soil, taking sixth in the Gran Premio di Roma at Caracalla at the wheel of a Maserati A6G.

In 1950 at the Targa Florio, Adolfo had himself driven around the circuit in a saloon car and made notes about each corner. Later he handed these to his co-driver, Fabio Colonna, and drove the race taking instructions. In his Alfa Romeo, he was eighth and production class winner for cars above 1.5 litres.

At the beginning of 1953, Adolfo made his only grand prix appearance in one of the works Cooper-Bristols, which broke a stub axle and then shed a wheel. He fared no better in the Buenos Aires City Libre GP, where the same car suffered a broken camshaft.

Subsequently, Schwelm-Cruz returned to competition in his ancient Alfa and was seen later in a Maserati sports. After retiring from competition, he lived in Italy and ran a car importing business.

ARCHIE SCOTT-BROWN

A TINY Scot, Archie Scott-Brown made light of the disabilities caused by his mother having contracted German measles when he was in the womb. As a baby, he had undergone no fewer than 22 operations to repair and add as much function as possible to his partly formed right arm, and badly deformed legs and feet. Determined to lead as full a life as the next man, he was always bursting with vitality and exuberance. He worked as a travelling salesman to fund his motorsport ambitions.

Scott-Brown began racing in 1950 in a minor way in an MG TD, but it was 1954 before he began to make his mark, forming a great partnership with Brian Lister to race his Lister-Bristol. Soon he began winning club and national events all over the country with the car, and he earned himself a chance in the Connaught F1 team for 1956, taking part in the British Grand Prix and finishing second in the International Trophy race. His performances drew admiration from everyone for the amazing way he handled any type of machinery – Juan Fangio for one thought his car control was phenomenal.

In 1957, Archie had the opportunity to race the works BRM in the British GP, but after a brake problem in testing and discussions with friends, he was persuaded to decline the offer. He continued to race in sports cars, however, and returned to Lister, handling the ferocious Lister-Jaguar.

By this time, Scott-Brown was greatly frustrated by his inability to gain an international licence, which stopped him from competing abroad. He did obtain permission to race in New Zealand early in 1958, when he won the Lady Wigram Trophy. The following May, when competing in a big sports car race at Spa, he lost control of his Lister on a section of damp track while dicing with Masten Gregory. He crashed into a field and the car burst into flames; the brave and luckless Scot died from his injuries the following day.

SCHWELM-CRUZ, Adolfo J (RA) b 28/6/1923, Buenos Aires – d 10/2/2010, Buenos Aires

1953 Championship position: Unplaced

	Race	Circuit	No	Entrant	Tyres	Capacity/Car/Engine	Comment	Q Pos/Entries
ret	ARGENTINE GP	Buenos Aires	24	Cooper Car Co	D	2.0 Cooper T20-Bristol 6	*broken stub axle – lost wheel*	13/16

GP Starts: 1 GP Wins: 0 Pole positions: 0 Fastest laps: 0 Points: 0

SCOTT-BROWN, Archie (GB) b 13/5/1927, Paisley, Renfrewshire, Scotland – d 19/5/1958, Heusy, Belgium

1956 Championship position: Unplaced

	Race	Circuit	No	Entrant	Tyres	Capacity/Car/Engine	Comment	Q Pos/Entries
ret	BRITISH GP	Silverstone	19	Connaught Engineering	P	2.5 Connaught B Type-Alta 4	*stub axle – lost wheel*	10/28

GP Starts: 1 GP Wins: 0 Pole positions: 0 Fastest laps: 0 Points: 0

PIERO SCOTTI

AN Italian businessman in the import-export trade, Piero Scotti financed his racing on the back of a mineral water bottling company. He began racing in the late 1940s with a Cisitalia, before making his mark with third place in the 1950 Targa Florio in an Ermini. In 1951, he graduated to a Ferrari 212, taking third place in that year's Mille Miglia. Then he ran a succession of machines from Maranello, sharing a works car with Giuseppe Farina to win the Casablanca 12-hours. He continued to find success in minor events in 1954 with a powerful Ferrari 375MMM, before trying his hand at Formula 1 in 1956.

Scotti bought an F1 Connaught on hire purchase to race with works assistance and had it painted red. He retired the car on his debut at the Syracuse Grand Prix and then recorded seventh in the International Trophy, some seven laps down on the winner. He took the car to Spa-Francorchamps for his only world championship start, but after retiring from the Belgian Grand Prix, he returned the car to the factory and gave up racing.

WOLFGANG SEIDEL

AN enthusiastic garage owner from Dusseldorf, Wolfgang Seidel raced intermittently in grands prix for a decade without any success, despite campaigning some quite decent machinery on occasion.

Seidel began racing in the early 1950s with a Veritas, before sharing an OSCA to take fourth in class in the 1954 Reims 12-hours. After a relatively successful run in his Porsche 1500GT, he bought a Ferrari 250GT, and his second place in the 1957 Reims 12-hours with Phil Hill helped to secure some occasional drives with a number of sports car teams. Most notable of these was Ferrari, with whom he scored third places in the 1957 Venezuelan Grand Prix and the Sebring 12-hours in 1958. His best ever result, however, was a victory in the 1959 Targa Florio, sharing a works Porsche 1500cc with Eddie Barth.

Wolfgang's main thrust in single-seaters came in 1961, when he ran a Lotus 18 with little reward. Second in the poorly supported Pries von Wien race, behind Stirling Moss, was easily his best finish. In 1962, he raced a Porsche 718, which naturally was reliable, but he was not quick enough to achieve much. He replaced it with a Lotus 24-BRM V8 in mid-season, but was no more convincing in this machine either, and he retired from competition at the end of the year.

SCOTTI, Piero (I) b 11/11/1909, Florence – d 14/2/1976, Samedan, Switzerland

1956 Championship position: Unplaced

	Race	Circuit	No	Entrant	Tyres	Capacity/Car/Engine	Comment	Q Pos/Entries
ret	BELGIAN GP	Spa	28	Piero Scotti	P	2.5 Connaught B Type-Alta 4	oil pressure	12/16

GP Starts: 1   GP Wins: 0   Pole positions: 0   Fastest laps: 0   Points: 0

SEIDEL, Wolfgang (D) b 4/7/1926, Düsseldorf – d 1/3/1987, Munich

1953 Championship position: Unplaced

	Race	Circuit	No	Entrant	Tyres	Capacity/Car/Engine	Comment	Q Pos/Entries
16	GERMAN GP	Nürburgring	22	Wolfgang Seidel	–	2.0 Veritas RS 6	4 laps behind	29/35
1958 Championship position: Unplaced								
ret	BELGIAN GP	Spa	32	Scuderia Centro Sud	P	2.5 Maserati 250F 6	rear axle	17/20
ret	GERMAN GP (F2)	Nürburgring	22	R R C Walker Racing Team	D	1.5 Cooper T43-Climax 4 F2	suspension	22/26
ret	MOROCCAN GP	Casablanca	26	Scuderia Centro Sud	P	2.5 Maserati 250F 6	accident	20/25
1960 Championship position: Unplaced								
9	ITALIAN GP	Monza	10	Wolfgang Seidel	D	1.5 Cooper T45-Climax 4		13/16
1961 Championship position: Unplaced								
dns	BELGIAN GP	Spa	48	Scuderia Colonia	D	1.5 Lotus 18-Climax 4	car raced by Bianchi	(21)/25
17	BRITISH GP	Aintree	52	Scuderia Colonia	D	1.5 Lotus 18-Climax 4	17 laps behind	22/30
ret	GERMAN GP	Nürburgring	26	Scuderia Colonia	D	1.5 Lotus 18-Climax 4	steering	23/27
ret	ITALIAN GP	Monza	56	Scuderia Colonia	D	1.5 Lotus 18-Climax 4	engine	28/33
1962 Championship position: Unplaced								
nc	DUTCH GP	Zandvoort	16	Ecurie Maarsbergen	D	1.5 Emeryson 1006-Climax 4	28 laps behind	20/20
ret	BRITISH GP	Aintree	44	Autosport Team Wolfgang Seidel	D	1.5 Lotus 24-BRM V8	brakes/overheating	21/21
dnq	GERMAN GP	Nürburgring	34	Autosport Team Wolfgang Seidel	D	1.5 Lotus 24-BRM V8		28/30

GP Starts: 10   GP Wins: 0   Pole positions: 0   Fastest laps: 0   Points: 0

THE wonder of the age, Ayrton Senna's colossal talent bestrode grand prix racing for a decade. He had virtually made it his own personal fiefdom (in the widest sense) with a frightening intensity and commitment that could be viewed as bordering on arrogance. Yet his creed was simplicity itself: his innate talent, just like that of a great musician, was to be continually developed day by day, year after year. To achieve this goal, everything else had to match his expectations: the machine and organisation at his disposal had to perform to his exacting standards, otherwise they served no useful purpose. Toleman, Lotus and then McLaren were blessed by his gifts, but immediately discarded when no longer of use. At the beginning of 1994, having finally landed the Williams-Renault drive he had long coveted, Ayrton stood poised on the brink of another period of success. Then, with the new partnership having barely begun, came that blackest of weekends at Imola...

From a well-to-do Brazilian family, Ayrton began racing karts from a very early age and had amassed eight seasons of experience before travelling to Britain to make his Formula Ford debut in 1981. Twelve wins ensured the FF1600 title was his, and the Brazilian returned the following year to continue his climb to fame and fortune in the FF2000 series. A tally of 21 wins from 27 starts tells its own story. In 1983, he joined the West Surrey Racing F3 team and became embroiled in a fabulous tussle for the Marlboro championship with Martin Brundle. In the end, his early-season run of wins kept him in front when the title was decided, and after testing for both Williams and McLaren he agreed to drive for Toleman in Formula 1 in 1984.

The phenomenal talent was soon in evidence, his drive in the wet at Monaco being outstanding. He was poised to challenge Alain Prost for the lead when the race was controversially stopped, but he had made his mark on an event he would win for a staggering sixth time in 1993. When it became clear that Toleman were not able to provide him with the means to win, the Brazilian engineered his way out of his contract and joined Lotus. Almost immediately, his first grand prix victory arrived, his skills in the wet at Estoril provoking memories of the great Jacky Ickx. Over the next three seasons, he proved to be the fastest man around, certainly in qualifying, where he amassed 16 pole positions, but he scored only six wins, due in part to the fragility of the Lotus. It was crystal clear to him that to win the championship, he needed a Honda engine, but definitely not a Lotus, so for 1988 he joined the McLaren team to partner Prost.

Senna was supremely confident in his ability to out-drive the Frenchman and was as good as his word. In a season when McLaren took victory in all bar one of the 16 races, he emerged triumphant in a manner more convincing than the eight-to-seven-wins margin suggests. Relationships between the two superstars were never more than cordial at best, and they broke down completely in 1989 as both drivers waged war within the confines of the team. This time, the championship battle ended in Prost's favour when the Brazilian was deftly taken out by the Frenchman at the Suzuka chicane. By then, of course, Prost had nothing to lose, having already decided to take his leave of McLaren, although he and Senna would be embroiled in further controversy during the following season. With Prost needing points at Suzuka to maintain Ferrari's challenge, Ayrton seemed to take his revenge, driving into the back of the Frenchman's car at the first corner. It was an unworthy way for the title to be decided, wiping away the memory of some great performances earlier in the season.

In many ways, 1991 was Senna's finest championship triumph. Initially, the new V12 Honda was not markedly superior to its lighter predecessor, despite the impression given by Ayrton's four straight wins from the start of the season. In fact, these had been extremely hard-won triumphs that had demanded every ounce of the Brazilian's skill and guile. The following season found him in the unusual position of underdog, Williams and Renault finally having found the edge and the ability to sustain it. Predictably, he gave his all, winning at Monaco, Hungary and Monza, but perceived shortcomings at McLaren were already irking him, and his frustration was probably not helped by his inability to muscle into a Williams drive alongside Prost in 1993.

During the winter months, McLaren had to come to terms with the loss of Honda power and hoped that the replacement Ford engine would be sufficiently promising to tempt the unhappy Brazilian to continue. In the event, Senna deigned to drive – initially on a race-by-race basis for a reported fee of $1 million per race. Luckily for us lesser beings, he served up a number of superb performances, which can seldom have been bettered at any time in the history of motor racing. Brazil, Donington and Adelaide showed us all why he was truly one of the sport's all-time greats.

When it was announced that Senna would be joining the all-conquering Williams-Renault team for 1994, it was difficult to see how anybody would be able to beat him, Nigel Mansell and Prost having taken the previous two titles with comparative ease. Things did not start well for the Brazilian, however, the latest FW16 car proving troublesome to sort, although somehow he managed to assert his authority in practice, exploring the outer edges of the car's performance to take pole position.

In the first two races, he struggled to match Michael Schumacher's Benetton, however, and in the third at Imola his lead in the early stages of the restarted race looked extremely tenuous. Then came disaster. Possibly the steering column on the Williams sheared or perhaps the car became unsettled on the bumpy track surface, but the Brazilian appeared helpless as it speared into the concrete wall at the Tamburello corner. As fate would have it, part of the suspension flew back and struck poor Senna, who then stood no chance of survival, being officially pronounced dead in a Bologna hospital later that afternoon.

The aftermath of Senna's death caused shock waves to ripple through the sport. Additional safety measures, some sound and others less so, were introduced as grand prix racing tried to come to terms with the loss of its premier talent. For his legion of fans, he was irreplaceable and things would never be the same again. For the sport at large, that awful day ushered in a new era, but although time would heal the wounds, the scars would always remain.

SENNA, Ayrton (BR) b 21/3/1960, São Paulo – d 1/5/1994, Bologna, Italy

1984 Championship position: 9th=   Wins: 0   Pole positions: 0   Fastest laps: 1   Points scored: 13

	Race	Circuit	No	Entrant	Tyres	Capacity/Car/Engine	Comment	Q Pos/Entries
ret	BRAZILIAN GP	Rio	19	Toleman Group Motorsport	P	1.5 t/c Toleman TG183B-Hart 4	turbo boost pressure	17/27
6	SOUTH AFRICAN GP	Kyalami	19	Toleman Group Motorsport	P	1.5 t/c Toleman TG183B-Hart 4	3 laps behind	13/27
6*	BELGIAN GP	Spa	19	Toleman Group Motorsport	P	1.5 t/c Toleman TG183B-Hart 4	*6th place car disqualified/2 laps behind	19/27
dnq	SAN MARINO GP	Imola	19	Toleman Group Motorsport	P	1.5 t/c Toleman TG183B-Hart 4	tyre problems	28/28
ret	FRENCH GP	Dijon	19	Toleman Group Motorsport	M	1.5 t/c Toleman TG184-Hart 4	turbo	13/27
2*	MONACO GP	Monte Carlo	19	Toleman Group Motorsport	M	1.5 t/c Toleman TG184-Hart 4	race stopped – rain/FL/*half points	13/27
7	CANADIAN GP	Montreal	19	Toleman Group Motorsport	M	1.5 t/c Toleman TG184-Hart 4	2 laps behind	9/26
ret	US GP (DETROIT)	Detroit	19	Toleman Group Motorsport	M	1.5 t/c Toleman TG184-Hart 4	accident – broken wishbone	7/27
ret	US GP (DALLAS)	Dallas	19	Toleman Group Motorsport	M	1.5 t/c Toleman TG184-Hart 4	driveshaft	6/27
3	BRITISH GP	Brands Hatch	19	Toleman Group Motorsport	M	1.5 t/c Toleman TG184-Hart 4		7/27
ret	GERMAN GP	Hockenheim	19	Toleman Group Motorsport	M	1.5 t/c Toleman TG184-Hart 4	accident – rear wing failure	9/27
ret	AUSTRIAN GP	Österreichring	19	Toleman Group Motorsport	M	1.5 t/c Toleman TG184-Hart 4	oil pressure	10/28
ret	DUTCH GP	Zandvoort	19	Toleman Group Motorsport	M	1.5 t/c Toleman TG184-Hart 4	engine	13/27
ret	EUROPEAN GP	Nürburgring	19	Toleman Group Motorsport	M	1.5 t/c Toleman TG184-Hart 4	hit Rosberg	12/26
3	PORTUGUESE GP	Estoril	19	Toleman Group Motorsport	M	1.5 t/c Toleman TG184-Hart 4		3/27

1985 Championship position: 4th   Wins: 2   Pole positions: 7   Fastest laps: 3   Points scored: 38

	Race	Circuit	No	Entrant	Tyres	Capacity/Car/Engine	Comment	Q Pos/Entries
ret	BRAZILIAN GP	Rio	12	John Player Special Team Lotus	G	1.5 t/c Lotus 97T-Renault V6	electrics	4/25
1	PORTUGUESE GP	Estoril	12	John Player Special Team Lotus	G	1.5 t/c Lotus 97T-Renault V6	FL	1/26
7/ret	SAN MARINO	Imola	12	John Player Special Team Lotus	G	1.5 t/c Lotus 97T-Renault V6	out of fuel	1/26
ret	MONACO GP	Monte Carlo	12	John Player Special Team Lotus	G	1.5 t/c Lotus 97T-Renault V6	engine	1/26
16	CANADIAN GP	Montreal	12	John Player Special Team Lotus	G	1.5 t/c Lotus 97T-Renault V6	pit stop – turbo pipe loose/FL/-5 laps	2/25
ret	US GP (DETROIT)	Detroit	12	John Player Special Team Lotus	G	1.5 t/c Lotus 97T-Renault V6	hit wall/FL	1/25
ret	FRENCH GP	Paul Ricard	12	John Player Special Team Lotus	G	1.5 t/c Lotus 97T-Renault V6	engine – accident	2/26
10/ret	BRITISH GP	Silverstone	12	John Player Special Team Lotus	G	1.5 t/c Lotus 97T-Renault V6	fuel injection problems/5 laps behind	4/26
ret	GERMAN GP	Nürburgring	12	John Player Special Team Lotus	G	1.5 t/c Lotus 97T-Renault V6	driveshaft c.v. joint	5/27
2	AUSTRIAN GP	Österreichring	12	John Player Special Team Lotus	G	1.5 t/c Lotus 97T-Renault V6		14/27
3	DUTCH GP	Zandvoort	12	John Player Special Team Lotus	G	1.5 t/c Lotus 97T-Renault V6		4/27
3	ITALIAN GP	Monza	12	John Player Special Team Lotus	G	1.5 t/c Lotus 97T-Renault V6		1/26
1	BELGIAN GP	Spa	12	John Player Special Team Lotus	G	1.5 t/c Lotus 97T-Renault V6		2/24
2	EUROPEAN GP	Brands Hatch	12	John Player Special Team Lotus	G	1.5 t/c Lotus 97T-Renault V6		1/27
ret	SOUTH AFRICAN GP	Kyalami	12	John Player Special Team Lotus	G	1.5 t/c Lotus 97T-Renault V6	engine	4/21
ret	AUSTRALIAN GP	Adelaide	12	John Player Special Team Lotus	G	1.5 t/c Lotus 97T-Renault V6	engine	1/25

1986 Championship position: 4th   Wins: 2   Pole positions: 8   Fastest laps: 0   Points scored: 55

	Race	Circuit	No	Entrant	Tyres	Capacity/Car/Engine	Comment	Q Pos/Entries
2	BRAZILIAN GP	Rio	12	John Player Special Team Lotus	G	1.5 t/c Lotus 98T-Renault V6	incident with Mansell	1/25
1	SPANISH GP	Jerez	12	John Player Special Team Lotus	G	1.5 t/c Lotus 98T-Renault V6		1/25
ret	SAN MARINO GP	Imola	12	John Player Special Team Lotus	G	1.5 t/c Lotus 98T-Renault V6	wheel bearing	1/26
3	MONACO GP	Monte Carlo	12	John Player Special Team Lotus	G	1.5 t/c Lotus 98T-Renault V6		3/26
2	BELGIAN GP	Spa	12	John Player Special Team Lotus	G	1.5 t/c Lotus 98T-Renault V6		4/25
5	CANADIAN GP	Montreal	12	John Player Special Team Lotus	G	1.5 t/c Lotus 98T-Renault V6	1 lap behind	2/25
1	US GP (DETROIT)	Detroit	12	John Player Special Team Lotus	G	1.5 t/c Lotus 98T-Renault V6		1/26
ret	FRENCH GP	Paul Ricard	12	John Player Special Team Lotus	G	1.5 t/c Lotus 98T-Renault V6	spun off on oil	1/26
ret	BRITISH GP	Brands Hatch	12	John Player Special Team Lotus	G	1.5 t/c Lotus 98T-Renault V6	gearbox	3/26
2	GERMAN GP	Hockenheim	12	John Player Special Team Lotus	G	1.5 t/c Lotus 98T-Renault V6		3/26
2	HUNGARIAN GP	Hungaroring	12	John Player Special Team Lotus	G	1.5 t/c Lotus 98T-Renault V6		1/26
ret	AUSTRIAN GP	Österreichring	12	John Player Special Team Lotus	G	1.5 t/c Lotus 98T-Renault V6	engine misfire	8/26
ret	ITALIAN GP	Monza	12	John Player Special Team Lotus	G	1.5 t/c Lotus 98T-Renault V6	transmission at start	5/27
4/ret	PORTUGUESE GP	Estoril	12	John Player Special Team Lotus	G	1.5 t/c Lotus 98T-Renault V6	out of fuel/1 lap behind	1/27
3	MEXICAN GP	Mexico City	12	John Player Special Team Lotus	G	1.5 t/c Lotus 98T-Renault V6		1/26
ret	AUSTRALIAN GP	Adelaide	12	John Player Special Team Lotus	G	1.5 t/c Lotus 98T-Renault V6	engine	3/26

1987 Championship position: 3rd   Wins: 2   Pole positions: 1   Fastest laps: 3   Points scored: 57

	Race	Circuit	No	Entrant	Tyres	Capacity/Car/Engine	Comment	Q Pos/Entries
ret	BRAZILIAN GP	Rio	12	Camel Team Lotus Honda	G	1.5 t/c Lotus 99T-Honda V6	engine	3/23
2	SAN MARINO GP	Imola	12	Camel Team Lotus Honda	G	1.5 t/c Lotus 99T-Honda V6		1/27
ret	BELGIAN GP	Spa	12	Camel Team Lotus Honda	G	1.5 t/c Lotus 99T-Honda V6	accident with Mansell	3/26
1	MONACO GP	Monte Carlo	12	Camel Team Lotus Honda	G	1.5 t/c Lotus 99T-Honda V6	FL	2/26
1	US GP (DETROIT)	Detroit	12	Camel Team Lotus Honda	G	1.5 t/c Lotus 99T-Honda V6	FL	2/26
4	FRENCH GP	Paul Ricard	12	Camel Team Lotus Honda	G	1.5 t/c Lotus 99T-Honda V6	1 lap behind	3/26
3	BRITISH GP	Silverstone	12	Camel Team Lotus Honda	G	1.5 t/c Lotus 99T-Honda V6	1 lap behind	3/26
3	GERMAN GP	Hockenheim	12	Camel Team Lotus Honda	G	1.5 t/c Lotus 99T-Honda V6	1 lap behind	2/26
2	HUNGARIAN GP	Hungaroring	12	Camel Team Lotus Honda	G	1.5 t/c Lotus 99T-Honda V6		6/26
5	AUSTRIAN GP	Österreichring	12	Camel Team Lotus Honda	G	1.5 t/c Lotus 99T-Honda V6	2 laps behind	7/26
2	ITALIAN GP	Monza	12	Camel Team Lotus Honda	G	1.5 t/c Lotus 99T-Honda V6	FL	4/28
7	PORTUGUESE GP	Estoril	12	Camel Team Lotus Honda	G	1.5 t/c Lotus 99T-Honda V6	pit stop – throttle/2 laps behind	5/27
5	SPANISH GP	Jerez	12	Camel Team Lotus Honda	G	1.5 t/c Lotus 99T-Honda V6	tyre problems	5/28
ret	MEXICAN GP	Mexico City	12	Camel Team Lotus Honda	G	1.5 t/c Lotus 99T-Honda V6	clutch – spun off	7/27
2	JAPANESE GP	Suzuka	12	Camel Team Lotus Honda	G	1.5 t/c Lotus 99T-Honda V6		8/27
dsq*	AUSTRALIAN GP	Adelaide	12	Camel Team Lotus Honda	G	1.5 t/c Lotus 99T-Honda V6	2nd – but dsq*for oversize brake ducts	4/27

1988 WORLD CHAMPION   Wins: 8   Pole positions: 13   Fastest laps: 3   Points scored: 94

	Race	Circuit	No	Entrant	Tyres	Capacity/Car/Engine	Comment	Q Pos/Entries
dsq*	BRAZILIAN GP	Rio	12	Honda Marlboro McLaren	G	1.5 t/c McLaren MP4/4-Honda V6	*illegally changed cars at start	1/31
1	SAN MARINO GP	Imola	12	Honda Marlboro McLaren	G	1.5 t/c McLaren MP4/4-Honda V6		1/31
ret	MONACO GP	Monte Carlo	12	Honda Marlboro McLaren	G	1.5 t/c McLaren MP4/4-Honda V6	hit barrier when leading/FL	1/30
2	MEXICAN GP	Mexico City	12	Honda Marlboro McLaren	G	1.5 t/c McLaren MP4/4-Honda V6		1/30
1	CANADIAN GP	Montreal	12	Honda Marlboro McLaren	G	1.5 t/c McLaren MP4/4-Honda V6	FL	1/31
1	US GP (DETROIT)	Detroit	12	Honda Marlboro McLaren	G	1.5 t/c McLaren MP4/4-Honda V6		1/31
2	FRENCH GP	Paul Ricard	12	Honda Marlboro McLaren	G	1.5 t/c McLaren MP4/4-Honda V6		2/31
1	BRITISH GP	Silverstone	12	Honda Marlboro McLaren	G	1.5 t/c McLaren MP4/4-Honda V6		3/31

1	GERMAN GP	Hockenheim	12	Honda Marlboro McLaren	G	1.5 t/c McLaren MP4/4-Honda V6		1/31
1	HUNGARIAN GP	Hungaroring	12	Honda Marlboro McLaren	G	1.5 t/c McLaren MP4/4-Honda V6		1/31
1	BELGIAN GP	Spa	12	Honda Marlboro McLaren	G	1.5 t/c McLaren MP4/4-Honda V6		1/31
10/ret	ITALIAN GP	Monza	12	Honda Marlboro McLaren	G	1.5 t/c McLaren MP4/4-Honda V6	*collision with Schlesser/2 laps behind*	1/31
6	PORTUGUESE GP	Estoril	12	Honda Marlboro McLaren	G	1.5 t/c McLaren MP4/4-Honda V6	*collision with Mansell/pitstop*	2/31
4	SPANISH GP	Jerez	12	Honda Marlboro McLaren	G	1.5 t/c McLaren MP4/4-Honda V6	*pit stop – tyres*	1/31
1	JAPANESE GP	Suzuka	12	Honda Marlboro McLaren	G	1.5 t/c McLaren MP4/4-Honda V6	*FL*	1/31
2	AUSTRALIAN GP	Adelaide	12	Honda Marlboro McLaren	G	1.5 t/c McLaren MP4/4-Honda V6		1/31

1989 Championship position: 2nd   Wins: 5   Pole positions: 13   Fastest laps: 3   Points scored: 60

11	BRAZILIAN GP	Rio	1	Honda Marlboro McLaren	G	3.5 McLaren MP4/5-Honda V10	*lap 1 collision/4 pit stops/2 laps behind*	1/38
1	SAN MARINO GP	Imola	1	Honda Marlboro McLaren	G	3.5 McLaren MP4/5-Honda V10	*aggregate of two parts*	1/39
1	MONACO GP	Monte Carlo	1	Honda Marlboro McLaren	G	3.5 McLaren MP4/5-Honda V10		1/38
1	MEXICAN GP	Mexico City	1	Honda Marlboro McLaren	G	3.5 McLaren MP4/5-Honda V10		1/39
ret	US GP (PHOENIX)	Phoenix	1	Honda Marlboro McLaren	G	3.5 McLaren MP4/5-Honda V10	*electrics/FL*	1/39
7/ret	CANADIAN GP	Montreal	1	Honda Marlboro McLaren	G	3.5 McLaren MP4/5-Honda V10	*engine/3 laps behind*	2/39
ret	FRENCH GP	Paul Ricard	1	Honda Marlboro McLaren	G	3.5 McLaren MP4/5-Honda V10	*transmission at start*	2/39
ret	BRITISH GP	Silverstone	1	Honda Marlboro McLaren	G	3.5 McLaren MP4/5-Honda V10	*gearbox – spun off*	1/39
1	GERMAN GP	Hockenheim	1	Honda Marlboro McLaren	G	3.5 McLaren MP4/5-Honda V10	*FL*	1/39
2	HUNGARIAN GP	Hungaroring	1	Honda Marlboro McLaren	G	3.5 McLaren MP4/5-Honda V10		2/39
1	BELGIAN GP	Spa	1	Honda Marlboro McLaren	G	3.5 McLaren MP4/5-Honda V10		1/39
ret	ITALIAN GP	Monza	1	Honda Marlboro McLaren	G	3.5 McLaren MP4/5-Honda V10	*engine*	1/39
ret	PORTUGUESE GP	Estoril	1	Honda Marlboro McLaren	G	3.5 McLaren MP4/5-Honda V10	*collision with Mansell*	1/39
1	SPANISH GP	Jerez	1	Honda Marlboro McLaren	G	3.5 McLaren MP4/5-Honda V10	*FL*	1/38
dsq*	JAPANESE GP	Suzuka	1	Honda Marlboro McLaren	G	3.5 McLaren MP4/5-Honda V10	**1st – but disqualified for push start*	1/39
ret	AUSTRALIAN GP	Adelaide	1	Honda Marlboro McLaren	G	3.5 McLaren MP4/5-Honda V10	*collision with Brundle*	1/39

1990 WORLD CHAMPION   Wins: 6   Pole positions: 10   Fastest laps: 2   Points scored: 78

1	US GP (PHOENIX)	Phoenix	27	Honda Marlboro McLaren	G	3.5 McLaren MP4/5B-Honda V10		5/35
3	BRAZILIAN GP	Interlagos	27	Honda Marlboro McLaren	G	3.5 McLaren MP4/5B-Honda V10	*pit stop – collision with Nakajima*	1/35
ret	SAN MARINO GP	Imola	27	Honda Marlboro McLaren	G	3.5 McLaren MP4/5B-Honda V10	*wheel rim damage – spun off*	1/34
1	MONACO GP	Monza	27	Honda Marlboro McLaren	G	3.5 McLaren MP4/5B-Honda V10	*FL*	1/35
1	CANADIAN GP	Montreal	27	Honda Marlboro McLaren	G	3.5 McLaren MP4/5B-Honda V10		1/35
20/ret	MEXICAN GP	Mexico City	27	Honda Marlboro McLaren	G	3.5 McLaren MP4/5B-Honda V10	*puncture/6 laps behind*	3/35
3	FRENCH GP	Paul Ricard	27	Honda Marlboro McLaren	G	3.5 McLaren MP4/5B-Honda V10		3/35
3	BRITISH GP	Silverstone	27	Honda Marlboro McLaren	G	3.5 McLaren MP4/5B-Honda V10		2/35
1	GERMAN GP	Hockenheim	27	Honda Marlboro McLaren	G	3.5 McLaren MP4/5B-Honda V10		1/35
2	HUNGARIAN GP	Hungaroring	27	Honda Marlboro McLaren	G	3.5 McLaren MP4/5B-Honda V10	*pit stop – puncture*	4/35
1	BELGIAN GP	Spa	27	Honda Marlboro McLaren	G	3.5 McLaren MP4/5B-Honda V10		1/33
1	ITALIAN GP	Monza	27	Honda Marlboro McLaren	G	3.5 McLaren MP4/5B-Honda V10	*FL*	1/33
2	PORTUGUESE GP	Estoril	27	Honda Marlboro McLaren	G	3.5 McLaren MP4/5B-Honda V10	*pit stop – tyres*	3/33
ret	SPANISH GP	Jerez	27	Honda Marlboro McLaren	G	3.5 McLaren MP4/5B-Honda V10	*punctured radiator/engine*	1/33
ret	JAPANESE GP	Suzuka	27	Honda Marlboro McLaren	G	3.5 McLaren MP4/5B-Honda V10	*collision with Prost*	1/30
ret	AUSTRALIAN GP	Adelaide	27	Honda Marlboro McLaren	G	3.5 McLaren MP4/5B-Honda V10	*missed 2nd gear – crashed*	1/30

Senna took eight wins with the McLaren MP4/4-Honda in the 1988 season, to claim the first of his three world championship titles.

1991 WORLD CHAMPION   Wins: 6   Pole positions: 8   Fastest laps: 2   Points scored: 96

	Race	Circuit	No	Entrant	Tyres	Capacity/Car/Engine	Comment	Q Pos/Entries
1	US GP (PHOENIX)	Phoenix	1	Honda Marlboro McLaren	G	3.5 McLaren MP4/6-Honda V12		1/34
1	BRAZILIAN GP	Interlagos	1	Honda Marlboro McLaren	G	3.5 McLaren MP4/6-Honda V12	lost 3rd-5th gears	1/34
1	SAN MARINO GP	Imola	1	Honda Marlboro McLaren	G	3.5 McLaren MP4/6-Honda V12		1/34
1	MONACO GP	Monte Carlo	1	Honda Marlboro McLaren	G	3.5 McLaren MP4/6-Honda V12		1/34
ret	CANADIAN GP	Montreal	1	Honda Marlboro McLaren	G	3.5 McLaren MP4/6-Honda V12	electrics/alternator	3/34
3	MEXICAN GP	Mexico City	1	Honda Marlboro McLaren	G	3.5 McLaren MP4/6-Honda V12		3/34
3	FRENCH GP	Magny Cours	1	Honda Marlboro McLaren	G	3.5 McLaren MP4/6-Honda V12		3/34
4/ret	BRITISH GP	Silverstone	1	Honda Marlboro McLaren	G	3.5 McLaren MP4/6-Honda V12	out of fuel/1 lap behind	2/34
7/ret	GERMAN GP	Hockenheim	1	Honda Marlboro McLaren	G	3.5 McLaren MP4/6-Honda V12	out of fuel/1 lap behind	2/34
1	HUNGARIAN GP	Hungaroring	1	Honda Marlboro McLaren	G	3.5 McLaren MP4/6-Honda V12		1/34
1	BELGIAN GP	Spa	1	Honda Marlboro McLaren	G	3.5 McLaren MP4/6-Honda V12		1/34
2	ITALIAN GP	Monza	1	Honda Marlboro McLaren	G	3.5 McLaren MP4/6-Honda V12	FL	1/34
2	PORTUGUESE GP	Estoril	1	Honda Marlboro McLaren	G	3.5 McLaren MP4/6-Honda V12		3/34
5	SPANISH GP	Barcelona	1	Honda Marlboro McLaren	G	3.5 McLaren MP4/6-Honda V12	spin	3/33
2	JAPANESE GP	Suzuka	1	Honda Marlboro McLaren	G	3.5 McLaren MP4/6-Honda V12	allowed Berger to win/FL	2/31
1*	AUSTRALIAN GP	Adelaide	1	Honda Marlboro McLaren	G	3.5 McLaren MP4/6-Honda V12	rain shortened race/*half points	1/32

1992   Championship position: 4th   Wins: 3   Pole positions: 1   Fastest laps: 1   Points scored: 50

	Race	Circuit	No	Entrant	Tyres	Capacity/Car/Engine	Comment	Q Pos/Entries
3	SOUTH AFRICAN GP	Kyalami	1	Honda Marlboro McLaren	G	3.5 McLaren MP4/6B-Honda V12		2/30
ret	MEXICAN GP	Mexico City	1	Honda Marlboro McLaren	G	3.5 McLaren MP4/6B-Honda V12	transmission	6/30
ret	BRAZILIAN GP	Interlagos	1	Honda Marlboro McLaren	G	3.5 McLaren MP4/7A-Honda V12	electrics	3/31
dns	"	"	1	Honda Marlboro McLaren	G	3.5 McLaren MP4/6B-Honda V12	practice only	-/-
9/ret	SPANISH GP	Barcelona	1	Honda Marlboro McLaren	G	3.5 McLaren MP4/7A-Honda V12	spun off/3 laps behind	3/32
3	SAN MARINO GP	Imola	1	Honda Marlboro McLaren	G	3.5 McLaren MP4/7A-Honda V12		3/32
1	MONACO GP	Monte Carlo	1	Honda Marlboro McLaren	G	3.5 McLaren MP4/7A-Honda V12		3/32
ret	CANADIAN GP	Montreal	1	Honda Marlboro McLaren	G	3.5 McLaren MP4/7A-Honda V12	electrics	1/32
ret	FRENCH GP	Magny Cours	1	Honda Marlboro McLaren	G	3.5 McLaren MP4/7A-Honda V12	collision damage on lap 1	3/30
ret	BRITISH GP	Silverstone	1	Honda Marlboro McLaren	G	3.5 McLaren MP4/7A-Honda V12	transmission	3/32
2	GERMAN GP	Hockenheim	1	Honda Marlboro McLaren	G	3.5 McLaren MP4/7A-Honda V12		3/32
1	HUNGARIAN GP	Hungaroring	1	Honda Marlboro McLaren	G	3.5 McLaren MP4/7A-Honda V12		3/31
5	BELGIAN GP	Spa	1	Honda Marlboro McLaren	G	3.5 McLaren MP4/7A-Honda V12	gambled to stay on slicks	2/30
1	ITALIAN GP	Monza	1	Honda Marlboro McLaren	G	3.5 McLaren MP4/7A-Honda V12		2/28
3	PORTUGUESE GP	Estoril	1	Honda Marlboro McLaren	G	3.5 McLaren MP4/7A-Honda V12	pit stops – handling/1 lap behind/FL	3/26
ret	JAPANESE GP	Suzuka	1	Honda Marlboro McLaren	G	3.5 McLaren MP4/7A-Honda V12	engine	3/26
ret	AUSTRALIAN GP	Adelaide	1	Honda Marlboro McLaren	G	3.5 McLaren MP4/7A-Honda V12	ran into the back of Mansell	2/26

1993   Championship position: 2nd   Wins: 5   Pole positions: 1   Fastest laps: 1   Points scored: 73

	Race	Circuit	No	Entrant	Tyres	Capacity/Car/Engine	Comment	Q Pos/Entries
2	SOUTH AFRICAN GP	Kyalami	8	Marlboro McLaren	G	3.5 McLaren MP4/8-Ford HB V8		2/26
1	BRAZILIAN GP	Interlagos	8	Marlboro McLaren	G	3.5 McLaren MP4/8-Ford HB V8		3/26
1	EUROPEAN GP	Donington	8	Marlboro McLaren	G	3.5 McLaren MP4/8-Ford HB V8	*FL *(set via pit lane)	4/26
ret	SAN MARINO GP	Imola	8	Marlboro McLaren	G	3.5 McLaren MP4/8-Ford HB V8	hydraulic failure	4/26
2	SPANISH GP	Barcelona	8	Marlboro McLaren	G	3.5 McLaren MP4/8-Ford HB V8		3/26
1	MONACO GP	Monte Carlo	8	Marlboro McLaren	G	3.5 McLaren MP4/8-Ford HB V8		3/26
18/ret	CANADIAN GP	Montreal	8	Marlboro McLaren	G	3.5 McLaren MP4/8-Ford HB V8	electrics/7 laps behind	8/26
4	FRENCH GP	Magny Cours	8	Marlboro McLaren	G	3.5 McLaren MP4/8-Ford HB V8		5/26
5/ret	BRITISH GP	Silverstone	8	Marlboro McLaren	G	3.5 McLaren MP4/8-Ford HB V8	out of fuel on last lap/1 lap behind	4/26
4	GERMAN GP	Hockenheim	8	Marlboro McLaren	G	3.5 McLaren MP4/8-Ford HB V8	collision and spin on lap 1	4/26
ret	HUNGARIAN GP	Hungaroring	8	Marlboro McLaren	G	3.5 McLaren MP4/8-Ford HB V8	throttle	4/26
4	BELGIAN GP	Spa	8	Marlboro McLaren	G	3.5 McLaren MP4/8-Ford HB V8		5/25
ret	ITALIAN GP	Monza	8	Marlboro McLaren	G	3.5 McLaren MP4/8-Ford HB V8	ran into back of Brundle	4/26
ret	PORTUGUESE GP	Estoril	8	Marlboro McLaren	G	3.5 McLaren MP4/8-Ford HB V8	engine	4/26
1	JAPANESE GP	Suzuka	8	Marlboro McLaren	G	3.5 McLaren MP4/8-Ford HB V8		2/24
1	AUSTRALIAN GP	Adelaide	8	Marlboro McLaren	G	3.5 McLaren MP4/8-Ford HB V8		1/24

1994   Championship position: Unplaced   Pole positions: 3

	Race	Circuit	No	Entrant	Tyres	Capacity/Car/Engine	Comment	Q Pos/Entries
ret	BRAZILIAN GP	Interlagos	2	Rothmans Williams Renault	G	3.5 Williams FW16-Renault V10	spun off and stalled	1/28
ret	PACIFIC GP	T.I. Circuit	2	Rothmans Williams Renault	G	3.5 Williams FW16-Renault V10	hit by Häkkinen – spun out	1/28
ret	SAN MARINO GP	Imola	2	Rothmans Williams Renault	G	3.5 Williams FW16-Renault V10	fatal race accident	1/28

GP Starts: 161   GP Wins: 41   Pole positions: 65   Fastest laps: 19   Points: 614

SENNA, Bruno (Bruno Senna Lalli) (BR) b 15/10/1983 São Paulo

2010   Championship position: Unplaced

	Race	Circuit	No	Entrant	Tyres	Capacity/Car/Engine	Comment	Q Pos/Entries
ret	BAHRAIN GP	Sakhir Circuit	21	HRT F1 Team	B	2.4 HRT F110-Cosworth V8	radiator/engine overheating	23/24
ret	AUSTRALIAN GP	Melbourne	21	HRT F1 Team	B	2.4 HRT F110-Cosworth V8	hydraulics	23/24
16	MALAYSIAN GP	Sepang	21	HRT F1 Team	B	2.4 HRT F110-Cosworth V8	4 laps behind	23/24
16	CHINESE GP	Shanghai Circuit	21	HRT F1 Team	B	2.4 HRT F110-Cosworth V8	2 laps behind	23/24
ret	SPANISH GP	Barcelona	21	HRT F1 Team	B	2.4 HRT F110-Cosworth V8	accident – crashed on lap 1	24/24
ret	MONACO GP	Monte Carlo	21	HRT F1 Team	B	2.4 HRT F110-Cosworth V8	hydraulics	22/24
ret	TURKISH GP	Istanbul Park	21	HRT F1 Team	B	2.4 HRT F110-Cosworth V8	fuel pressure	22/24
ret	CANADIAN GP	Montreal	21	HRT F1 Team	B	2.4 HRT F110-Cosworth V8	gearbox	22/24
20	EUROPEAN GP	Valencia	21	HRT F1 Team	B	2.4 HRT F110-Cosworth V8	2 laps behind	24/24
19	GERMAN GP	Hockenheim	21	HRT F1 Team	B	2.4 HRT F110-Cosworth V8	4 laps behind	21/24
17	HUNGARIAN GP	Hungaroring	21	HRT F1 Team	B	2.4 HRT F110-Cosworth V8	3 laps behind	23/24
ret	BELGIAN GP	Spa	21	HRT F1 Team	B	2.4 HRT F110-Cosworth V8	rear suspension	21/24
ret	ITALIAN GP	Monza	21	HRT F1 Team	B	2.4 HRT F110-Cosworth V8	hydraulics	23/24
ret	SINGAPORE GP	Marina Bay Circuit	21	HRT F1 Team	B	2.4 HRT F110-Cosworth V8	accident damage	23/24
15	JAPANESE GP	Suzuka	21	HRT F1 Team	B	2.4 HRT F110-Cosworth V8	2 laps behind	23/24
14	KOREAN GP	Yeongam	21	HRT F1 Team	B	2.4 HRT F110-Cosworth V8	2 laps behind	24/24

| 21 | BRAZILIAN GP | Interlagos | 21 | HRT F1 Team | B | 2.4 HRT F110-Cosworth V8 | *2 laps behind* | 24/24 |
| 19 | ABU DHABI GP | Yas Marina Circuit | 21 | HRT F1 Team | B | 2.4 HRT F110-Cosworth V8 | *2 laps behind* | 23/24 |

2011 Championship position: 18th Wins: 0 Pole positions: 0 Fastest laps: 0 Points scored: 2								
dns	HUNGARIAN GP	Hungaroring	9	Renault F1 Team	P	2.4 Renault R31-V8	*free practice 1 only – no time set*	- / -
13	BELGIAN GP	Spa	9	Renault F1 Team	P	2.4 Renault R31-V8	*collision – wing damage – drive thru penalty*	10/24
9	ITALIAN GP	Monza	9	Renault F1 Team	P	2.4 Renault R31-V8	*1 lap behind*	10/24
15	SINGAPORE GP	Marina Bay Circuit	9	Renault F1 Team	P	2.4 Renault R31-V8	*spin – new front wing/2 laps behind*	16/24
16	JAPANESE GP	Suzuka	9	Renault F1 Team	P	2.4 Renault R31-V8	*2 laps behind*	8/24
13	KOREAN GP	Yeongam	9	Renault F1 Team	P	2.4 Renault R31-V8	*1 lap behind*	15/24
12	INDIAN GP	Buddh Circuit	9	Renault F1 Team	P	2.4 Renault R31-V8	*1 lap behind*	15/24
16	ABU DHABI GP	Yas Marina Circuit	9	Renault F1 Team	P	2.4 Renault R31-V8	*drive thru pen-ignoring blue flags/-1 lap*	14/24
17	BRAZILIAN GP	Interlagos	9	Renault F1 Team	P	2.4 Renault R31-V8	*collision – Schumacher – drive-thru/-2 laps*	9/24

GP Starts: 26   GP Wins: 0   Pole positions: 0   Fastest laps: 0   Points: 2

BRUNO SENNA

MODEST, polite and personable, Bruno Senna outwardly possesses none of the often frightening intensity of his late uncle, but following in the footsteps of one of the sport's greatest talents requires its own kind of determination, and that has carried him on a gentle upward curve as he seeks to make his own place in the grand prix history books.

The young Bruno was only 12 years old when the tragedy of Imola fell upon his family in May, 1994, and although he had driven go-karts on the family farm, any sporting aspirations were quashed with immediate effect. Having overcome another tragedy when his father, Flávio, was killed in a motorcycling accident in 1996, Senna had to wait until 2004 before finally he was given the opportunity to race when, under the watchful eye of Carlin Motorsport, he briefly tried his hand in the UK Formula BMW series, before taking the plunge into the British F3 series with Räikkönen Robertson Racing. Given his lack of experience, tenth in his debut year was satisfactory; in 2006, he stayed on board, and upped his game to take five victories and third in the final standings. A successful trip to Australia at the end of the year saw him win three F3 races before he returned to Europe to take up a seat at Arden Racing in the GP2 series.

An early-season win at Barcelona, where he skilfully nursed his car to the finish on worn tyres, was a great boost to his confidence and proved that he was not out of place against some experienced campaigners. Eighth place was a good platform when he switched teams to iSport for 2008, and he was immediately at the sharp end of the grid. An emotional victory at Monaco, which brought obvious pride to the Senna family, and another win at Silverstone were the high points of a year when he suffered some unlucky breaks, and in the end he was runner-up to Giorgio Pantano. Nevertheless, he handled his triumphs and misfortunes with great equanimity to prove a tough and resilient competitor.

A hoped-for opportunity to graduate to Formula 1 with Honda in 2009 came to nought after the manufacturer withdrew, so Senna kept his hand in with selected drives for Team Oreca in the Le Mans Series, where he took third places at Barcelona and Portimao.

In 2010, Bruno finally achieved his ambition of reaching Formula 1, but only after a worrying couple of months when the original Campos Meta project was taken over and renamed Hispania Racing. The new owners kept him on board for their 'seat of the pants' introduction to F1. He drove in all but one of the season's races, the driver line-up shifting due mainly to monetary pressures. None of them could achieve anything noteworthy, however, and the team strategy seemed to be based on minimising the time lost in obeying the blue flags!

Having gained a foothold on the grid, Senna needed to move to a better team, but the only option was a place at Lotus-Renault, originally as reserve and test driver. Following the pre-season injury to Robert Kubica, it might have been expected that he would have gained promotion, but in the end the experienced Nick Heidfeld was drafted in. Bruno bided his time and was given a run in free practice in Hungary. His assured performance convinced the team to drop the German, who had failed to meet expectations, leaving him to seize his chance to impress at Spa.

Scoring his first points in the next race, at Monza, ticked another box on the Brazilian's CV, but rather patchy performances thereafter counted against his chances of retaining the seat for 2012.

Having first sought his family's blessing, Bruno entered negotiations with Williams for the 2012 season and, after extensive testing and evaluations, he was confirmed as the partner of his old GP2 rival, Pastor Maldonado.

SERAFINI, Dorino (I) b 22/7/1909, Pesaro – d 5/7/2000, Pesaro

1950 Championship position: Unplaced

	Race	Circuit	No	Entrant	Tyres	Capacity/Car/Engine	Comment	Q Pos/Entries
2*	ITALIAN GP	Monza	48	Scuderia Ferrari	P	4.5 Ferrari 375F1 V12	*car taken over by Ascari	6/27

GP Starts: 1   GP Wins: 0   Pole positions: 0   Fastest laps: 0   Points: 3

DORINO SERAFINI

A TOP-NOTCH motorcycle racer on home soil in the 1930s, Dorino Serafini took both the Italian 175cc and 500cc championships before accepting a ride on the works Gilera, with which he won the 500cc European motorcycle championship in 1939.

Dorino's two-wheeled exploits came to a halt with the outbreak of the Second World War. When racing resumed, he was 37 years old and opted for competition on four wheels. His prospects were spoilt by a very serious accident in the 1947 Comminges Grand Prix, however, when the steering column failed on his Maserati 4CL. That put him into the trees and out of action for some time, with multiple fractures and burns. He returned to racing at the end of 1948 and went on to drive an OSCA in the following year. Subsequently, he was never quite the same prospect. He had forged a good friendship with Alberto Ascari and Luigi Villoresi, and they recommended that he join them in the Ferrari team for 1950.

Serafini shared the second-place Ferrari with Ascari in his only grand prix start and took a number of other second places – notably at Pedralbes, in the F1 car, and in the Eva Perón Cup race at Buenos Aires and the Circuit of Garda with the F2 T166.

It was much the same story in 1951, with second places again in both the Syracuse and San Remo GPs, before another big accident – this time in the Mille Miglia – left Serafini with a broken arm and leg. Thereafter, he raced less frequently, but he returned to contest the 1954 Brescia–Rome–Brescia classic, taking seventh place overall and first in the GT class with his Lancia.

SERRA, Chico (Francisco) (BR) b 3/2/1957, São Paulo

1981 Championship position: Unplaced

	Race	Circuit	No	Entrant	Tyres	Capacity/Car/Engine	Comment	Q Pos/Entries
7	US GP WEST	Long Beach	21	Fittipaldi Automotive	M	3.0 Fittipaldi F8C-Cosworth V8	2 laps behind	18/29
ret	BRAZILIAN GP	Rio	21	Fittipaldi Automotive	M	3.0 Fittipaldi F8C-Cosworth V8	startline collision	22/30
ret	ARGENTINE GP	Buenos Aires	21	Fittipaldi Automotive	M	3.0 Fittipaldi F8C-Cosworth V8	gearbox	20/29
dnq	SAN MARINO GP	Imola	21	Fittipaldi Automotive	A	3.0 Fittipaldi F8C-Cosworth V8		28/30
ret	BELGIAN GP	Zolder	21	Fittipaldi Automotive	M	3.0 Fittipaldi F8C-Cosworth V8	engine	20/31
dnq	MONACO GP	Monte Carlo	21	Fittipaldi Automotive	A/M	3.0 Fittipaldi F8C-Cosworth V8		24/31
11	SPANISH GP	Jarama	21	Fittipaldi Automotive	M	3.0 Fittipaldi F8C-Cosworth V8	1 lap behind	21/30
dns	FRENCH GP	Dijon	21	Fittipaldi Automotive	M	3.0 Fittipaldi F8C-Cosworth V8	accident in warm-up	(24)/29
dnq	BRITISH GP	Silverstone	21	Fittipaldi Automotive	M	3.0 Fittipaldi F8C-Cosworth V8		25/30
dnq	GERMAN GP	Hockenheim	21	Fittipaldi Automotive	M	3.0 Fittipaldi F8C-Cosworth V8		30/30
dnq	DUTCH GP	Zandvoort	21	Fittipaldi Automotive	P	3.0 Fittipaldi F8C-Cosworth V8		28/30
dnq	ITALIAN GP	Monza	21	Fittipaldi Automotive	P	3.0 Fittipaldi F8C-Cosworth V8		30/30
dnq	CANADIAN GP	Montreal	21	Fittipaldi Automotive	P	3.0 Fittipaldi F8C-Cosworth V8		26/30
dnq	CAESARS PALACE GP	Las Vegas	21	Fittipaldi Automotive	P	3.0 Fittipaldi F8C-Cosworth V8		26/30

1982 Championship position: 26th   Wins: 0   Pole positions: 0   Fastest laps: 0   Points scored: 1

	Race	Circuit	No	Entrant	Tyres	Capacity/Car/Engine	Comment	Q Pos/Entries
17	SOUTH AFRICAN GP	Kyalami	20	Fittipaldi Automotive	P	3.0 Fittipaldi F8D-Cosworth V8	5 laps behind	25/30
ret	BRAZILIAN GP	Rio	20	Fittipaldi Automotive	P	3.0 Fittipaldi F8D-Cosworth V8	spun off	25/31
dnq	US GP WEST	Long Beach	20	Fittipaldi Automotive	P	3.0 Fittipaldi F8D-Cosworth V8		29/31
6	BELGIAN GP	Zolder	20	Fittipaldi Automotive	P	3.0 Fittipaldi F8D-Cosworth V8	3 laps behind	25/32
dnpq	MONACO GP	Monte Carlo	20	Fittipaldi Automotive	P	3.0 Fittipaldi F8D-Cosworth V8		30/31
11	US GP (DETROIT)	Detroit	20	Fittipaldi Automotive	P	3.0 Fittipaldi F8D-Cosworth V8	3 laps behind	26/28
dnq	CANADIAN GP	Montreal	20	Fittipaldi Automotive	P	3.0 Fittipaldi F8D-Cosworth V8		29/29
ret	DUTCH GP	Zandvoort	20	Fittipaldi Automotive	P	3.0 Fittipaldi F8D-Cosworth V8	fuel pump	19/31
ret	BRITISH GP	Brands Hatch	20	Fittipaldi Automotive	P	3.0 Fittipaldi F8D-Cosworth V8	accident with Jarier	21/30
dnq	FRENCH GP	Paul Ricard	20	Fittipaldi Automotive	P	3.0 Fittipaldi F9-Cosworth V8		29/30
11	GERMAN GP	Hockenheim	20	Fittipaldi Automotive	P	3.0 Fittipaldi F9-Cosworth V8	2 laps behind	26/30
7	AUSTRIAN GP	Österreichring	20	Fittipaldi Automotive	P	3.0 Fittipaldi F9-Cosworth V8	2 laps behind	20/29
dnq	SWISS GP	Dijon	20	Fittipaldi Automotive	P	3.0 Fittipaldi F9-Cosworth V8		27/29
11	ITALIAN GP	Monza	20	Fittipaldi Automotive	P	3.0 Fittipaldi F9-Cosworth V8	3 laps behind	26/30
dnq	CAESARS PALACE GP	Las Vegas	20	Fittipaldi Automotive	P	3.0 Fittipaldi F9-Cosworth V8		30/30

1983 Championship position: Unplaced

	Race	Circuit	No	Entrant	Tyres	Capacity/Car/Engine	Comment	Q Pos/Entries
9	BRAZILIAN GP	Rio	30	Arrows Racing Team	G	3.0 Arrows A6-Cosworth V8	1 lap behind	23/27
ret	FRENCH GP	Paul Ricard	30	Arrows Racing Team	G	3.0 Arrows A6-Cosworth V8	gearbox	26/29
8	SAN MARINO GP	Imola	30	Arrows Racing Team	G	3.0 Arrows A6-Cosworth V8	2 laps behind	20/28
7	MONACO GP	Monte Carlo	30	Arrows Racing Team	G	3.0 Arrows A6-Cosworth V8	2 laps behind	15/28

GP Starts: 18   GP Wins: 0   Pole positions: 0   Fastest laps: 0   Points: 1

CHICO SERRA

A CONTEMPORARY and bitter rival of fellow countryman Nelson Piquet, Chico Serra enjoyed an outstanding Formula Ford season in 1977, winning the Townsend Thoresen FF1600 championship, before stepping into Formula 3 with the Ron Dennis-run Project Four March. It was a strong year, with Piquet and Derek Warwick among the opposition, but Chico was unflustered, escaping a huge accident at Mallory Park to finish third in the Vandervell series and joint second with Warwick in the BP championship.

Back in Formula 3 in 1979, Serra made no mistake, winning the 20-round Vandervell championship, taking five victories and seven second places and putting his Project Four March on the front row no fewer than 16 times. Moving into Formula 2 along with the team, he found the going tough, being very much the number-two driver to Andrea de Cesaris.

Having joined Emerson Fittipaldi to race his fading team's cars in grands prix, Serra struggled again, but when he managed to get the car on to the grid, more often than not he brought it home to the finish, gaining his only championship point at Zolder in 1982. After the team closed its doors, he briefly raced the Arrows while Alan Jones prevaricated over the prospect of a grand prix comeback with the team, before losing out to Thierry Boutsen.

In 1985, Chico ventured out of Brazil to appear in his only CART race, for Theodore at Portland, which ended in retirement due to an engine failure.

Serra returned to his homeland, but far from turning his back on the sport, he continued to race saloons, breaking the dominance of Ingo Hoffmann by taking the Brazilian stock car championship in three consecutive seasons between 1999 and 2001. He continued to race stock cars, GT3s and trucks in his native land throughout the rest of the decade.

DOUG SERRURIER

A MAINSTAY of the South African motor racing scene as driver, constructor and later entrant, Doug Serrurier – a former grass track and speedway rider both at home and abroad – began his circuit racing career driving a Triumph TR2 in 1956, before starting work on the first of his home-built LDS specials, the initials being derived from his full name (Louis Douglas Serrurier).

A trip to Europe saw Doug initially purchase a Cooper T51 from Alan Brown, while further machines soon followed from the factory, including the 'low-line' T53, which provided the inspiration for his own LDS Mk2 of 1961. Powered by an Alfa Romeo engine, this was just one of a gradually evolving series of cars that were developed during the early 1960s, later models being based upon Brabham designs (much to the chagrin of Jack Brabham). For the most part, they were driven by Serrurier himself and another veteran, Rhodesian star Sam Tingle.

By 1966, it was becoming increasingly impractical to compete with the major constructors so, after sharing Roy Pierpoint's Lola T70 to take second place in the Cape Town three-hours, Serrurier decided to buy one of these cars, which he shared with Jackie Pretorious, winning the Roy Hesketh three-hours in 1967. After more or less retiring from racing at the end of 1969, he entered Pretorious in the South African F1 series with a Surtees, but still had occasional road and rally outings himself as well as trying his hand at powerboat racing.

Until well into his seventies, Serrurier continued to build and rebuild fast cars, such as the AC Cobra and Ferrari Daytona to his usual superb standards in his backyard workshop near Johannesburg, often incorporating his own suspension designs.

SERRURIER, Doug (ZA) b 9/12/1920, Germiston, Transvaal – d 4/7/2006, Alberton, Johannesburg, South Africa

	1962 Championship position: Unplaced							
	Race	Circuit	No	Entrant	Tyres	Capacity/Car/Engine	Comment	Q Pos/Entries
ret	SOUTH AFRICAN GP	East London	21	Otelle Nucci	D	1.5 LDS Mk2-Alfa Romeo 4	radiator leak	=13/17
	1963 Championship position: Unplaced							
11	SOUTH AFRICAN GP	East London	16	Otelle Nucci	D	1.5 LDS Mk2-Alfa Romeo 4	7 laps behind	18/21
	1965 Championship position: Unplaced							
dnq	SOUTH AFRICAN GP	East London	21	Otelle Nucci	D	1.5 LDS Mk2-Climax 4		23/25
	GP Starts: 2 GP Wins: 0 Pole positions: 0 Fastest laps: 0 Points: 0							

GEORGES 'JOHNNY' SERVOZ-GAVIN

A HANDSOME, blond playboy racer, Georges 'Johnny' Servoz-Gavin loved the good life, but significantly he also possessed a great deal of natural talent.

After being thrown out of the Winfield driving school in 1963, 'Johnny' did a little rallying in 1964, before spending all his money on a Brabham for 1965. He was wild, but fast, taking fourth place in the French F3 series to earn a lucrative contract to drive with Matra in 1966. He duly won the title and thus was promoted to the Matra Formula 2 team for 1967. His results were moderate, and only a splendid fourth in the F1/F2 non-title Spanish GP kept him on board.

An accident suffered by Jackie Stewart at a Formula 2 meeting early in 1968 brought the Frenchman a glorious opportunity to show his ability on the grand prix stage. Having taken over the Scotsman's Tyrrell Matra, 'Johnny' led the early laps of the Monaco GP in sensational style, but clipped a barrier and broke a driveshaft. Later in the season, he redeemed himself somewhat with a superb second place in the Italian GP, but this performance did not lead to a full-time grand prix ride. For 1969, he concentrated on the European F2 championship and, with victory in the Rome GP, took the title of top non-graded driver. In grands prix, he was mainly entrusted with the Matra MS84 and succeeded in gaining a point with it at Mosport, the only time any 4WD car has achieved this feat.

The following season saw a full-time promotion to Formula 1 when 'Johnny' was paired with Stewart in the Tyrrell team, running the difficult March 701. He finished fifth in the Spanish GP, but then after hitting the chicane and failing to qualify for the Monaco Grand Prix, he suddenly announced his retirement from racing.

Ultimately, perhaps, 'Johnny' had decided that the risks inherent in racing at the time were not worthwhile, but apparently he also had a problem with his vision. The Frenchman had suffered a minor injury to his eye when a tree branch had struck him in the face while driving off road the previous winter, and this may have been the deciding factor.

Subsequently, Servoz-Gavin sustained burns in two separate boating fires, and after a period of ill-health, he died from a pulmonary embolism in 2006, aged just 64.

SERVOZ-GAVIN, 'Johnny' (Georges) (F) b 18/1/1942, Grenoble – d 29 May 2006, Grenoble

	Race	Circuit	No	Entrant	Tyres	Capacity/Car/Engine	Comment	Q Pos/Entries
	1967 Championship position: Unplaced							
ret	MONACO GP	Monte Carlo	2	Matra Sports	D	1.6 Matra MS7-Cosworth 4 F2	fuel injection unit drive	11/18
	1968 Championship position: 12th=	Wins: 0	Pole positions: 0	Fastest laps: 0	Points scored: 6			
ret	MONACO GP	Monte Carlo	11	Matra International	D	3.0 Matra MS10-Cosworth V8	hit chicane – broken driveshaft	=2/18
ret	FRENCH GP	Rouen	32	Cooper Car Co	F	3.0 Cooper T86B-BRM V12	spun off – hit tree	16/18
2	ITALIAN GP	Monza	5	Matra International	D	3.0 Matra MS10-Cosworth V8		14/24
ret	CANADIAN GP	St Jovite	15	Matra International	D	3.0 Matra MS10-Cosworth V8	spun off	13/22
ret	MEXICAN GP	Mexico City	23	Matra International	D	3.0 Matra MS10-Cosworth V8	engine – ignition/8 laps behind	16/21
	1969 Championship position: 16th=	Wins: 0	Pole positions: 0	Fastest laps: 0	Points scored: 1			
ret	GERMAN GP (F2)	Nürburgring	27	Matra International	D	1.6 Matra MS7-Cosworth 4 F2	engine/FL (F2 class)	11/26
6	CANADIAN GP	Mosport Park	19	Matra International	D	3.0 Matra MS84-Cosworth V8 4WD	6 laps behind	15/20
nc	US GP	Watkins Glen	16	Matra International	D	3.0 Matra MS84-Cosworth V8 4WD	2 pitstops – wheel bearing/-16 laps	15/18
8	MEXICAN GP	Mexico City	16	Matra International	D	3.0 Matra MS84-Cosworth V8 4WD	2 laps behind	14/17
	1970 Championship position: 19th=	Wins: 0	Pole positions: 0	Fastest laps: 0	Points scored: 2			
ret	SOUTH AFRICAN GP	Kyalami	2	Tyrrell Racing Organisation	D	3.0 March 701-Cosworth V8	engine	17/24
5	SPANISH GP	Jarama	16	Tyrrell Racing Organisation	D	3.0 March 701-Cosworth V8		17/22
dnq	MONACO GP	Monte Carlo	20	Tyrrell Racing Organisation	D	3.0 March 701-Cosworth V8	car not seeded	14/21
	GP Starts: 12 GP Wins: 0 Pole positions: 0 Fastest laps: 0 Points: 9							

SETTEMBER, Tony (USA) b 10/7/1926, Manila. Philippines

1962 Championship position: Unplaced

	Race	Circuit	No	Entrant	Tyres	Capacity/Car/Engine	Comment	Q Pos/Entries
11	BRITISH GP	Aintree	40	Emeryson Cars	D	1.5 Emeryson 1004-Climax 4	4 laps behind	19/21
ret	ITALIAN GP	Monza	48	Emeryson Cars	D	1.5 Emeryson 1004-Climax 4	cylinder head gasket	21/30

1963 Championship position: Unplaced

	Race	Circuit	No	Entrant	Tyres	Capacity/Car/Engine	Comment	Q Pos/Entries
8/ret	BELGIAN GP	Spa	24	Scirocco Powell (Racing Cars)	D	1.5 Scirocco SP-BRM V8	accident/5 laps behind	19/20
ret	FRENCH GP	Reims	38	Scirocco Powell (Racing Cars)	D	1.5 Scirocco SP-BRM V8	rear hub bearing	20/21
ret	BRITISH GP	Silverstone	15	Scirocco Powell (Racing Cars)	D	1.5 Scirocco SP-BRM V8	ignition	18/23
ret	GERMAN GP	Nürburgring	23	Scirocco Powell (Racing Cars)	D	1.5 Scirocco SP-BRM V8	accident	22/26
dnq	ITALIAN GP	Monza	34	Scirocco Powell (Racing Cars)	D	1.5 Scirocco SP-BRM V8		23/28

GP Starts: 6   GP Wins: 0   Pole positions: 0   Fastest laps: 0   Points: 0

TONY SETTEMBER

A CALIFORNIAN of Italian descent, Tony Settember initially raced an MG in SCCA in 1955, before building a reputation on the West Coast with a Mercedes 300SL and then a Corvette. In 1959, he travelled to Europe where, initially driving a WRE-Maserati sports car, he took a win in the Naples GP at Posillipo, but he achieved little else before returning home.

Back in California, Tony continued his winning ways with the Corvette. In 1960, he became the guardian of Hugh Powell, a fabulously wealthy teenager with money to burn, and he persuaded his young charge to join him a Formula 1 adventure.

Settember commissioned Emeryson to build a chassis for the 1962 season, but he did not fit the car properly and relationships in the team became strained when no success was achieved. In the event, Paul Emery departed before the season was out, and the two Americans formed the Scirocco-Powell team for 1963, using BRM power. Their car was attractive, but slow, although Settember was flattered by an inherited second-place finish in the non-championship Austrian Grand Prix, some five laps down.

Aside from their F1 travails, Powell and Settember entered a 5-litre Corvette for the 1962 Le Mans 24-hours. With the largest engine displacement, it was given the honour of carrying race number 1 and was given a place at the head of the field for the start. Thus Settember was photographed leading the pack towards the Dunlop Bridge, before inevitably being overwhelmed by faster machines.

When Powell finally called a halt to proceedings, Settember continued his racing activities back in the USA with Lotus 23 and 30 sports cars, and then an AC Cobra, before trying his hand at Can-Am in the late 1960s with a Lola T70.

Settember appeared intermittently in the L & M F5000 series between 1972 and 1974, with a McLaren M10B and then a Lola T330, but he never seriously threatened the front-runners.

JAMES 'HAP' SHARP

A TEXAN involved in the oil drilling business, James R. Sharp was an SCCA racer who drove a Chevrolet Corvette and then a Cooper Monaco to success between 1958 and 1963. A long-time associate of Jim Hall, he became the co-owner of Chaparral and began racing their first machine in 1962, taking the honours at the Road America 500-miler with Hall. Mainly racing in the USRRC series, in 1964, 'Hap' was fifth overall in the championship and he also won the Nassau Trophy teamed with Roger Penske.

Improving on this the following year, 'Hap' took third overall in the series and won the Sebring 12-hours with Hall. He also recorded six other big wins and a string of second places, including another Nassau victory. He raced less frequently thereafter, a win with the Chaparral 2E in the Governor's Trophy at Nassau in late 1966 being his last outright victory. 'Hap' joined Phil Hill in the classic 2E wing car at the Targa Florio in 1967, but the machine was sidelined by a puncture. His last race was at Sebring in 1968, when he shared a Corvette to take a sixth pace overall and win the GT class.

A great Formula 1 enthusiast, Sharp had the wherewithal to arrange a succession of grand prix drives on the North American continent in the early 1960s, at first with a hired Cooper and then Reg Parnell's Lotus-BRM, with which he came close to scoring a point in Mexico City in 1963.

After retiring from the sport, Sharp suffered from personal problems in later life and, after being diagnosed with cancer, he committed suicide in Argentina in May, 1993.

SHARP, 'Hap' (James R Sharp) (USA) b 1/1/1928, Tulsa – d 11/5/1992, San Martin de los Andes, Argentina

1961 Championship position: Unplaced

	Race	Circuit	No	Entrant	Tyres	Capacity/Car/Engine	Comment	Q Pos/Entries
10	US GP	Watkins Glen	3	'Hap' Sharp	D	1.5 Cooper T53-Climax 4	3rd works car/7 laps behind	17/19

1962 Championship position: Unplaced

	Race	Circuit	No	Entrant	Tyres	Capacity/Car/Engine	Comment	Q Pos/Entries
11	US GP	Watkins Glen	24	'Hap' Sharp	D	1.5 Cooper T53-Climax 4	9 laps behind	15/20

1963 Championship position: Unplaced

	Race	Circuit	No	Entrant	Tyres	Capacity/Car/Engine	Comment	Q Pos/Entries
ret	US GP	Watkins Glen	22	Reg Parnell (Racing)	D	1.5 Lotus 24-BRM V8	engine	18/21
7	MEXICAN GP	Mexico City	22	Reg Parnell (Racing)	D	1.5 Lotus 24-BRM V8	4 laps behind	16/21

1964 Championship position: Unplaced

	Race	Circuit	No	Entrant	Tyres	Capacity/Car/Engine	Comment	Q Pos/Entries
nc	US GP	Watkins Glen	23	Rob Walker Racing Team	D	1.5 Brabham BT11-BRM V8	long pit stop – engine/45 laps behind	18/19
13	MEXICAN GP	Mexico City	23	Rob Walker Racing Team	D	1.5 Brabham BT11-BRM V8	5 laps behind	19/19

GP Starts: 6   GP Wins: 0   Pole positions: 0   Fastest laps: 0   Points: 0

BRIAN SHAWE-TAYLOR

A GARAGE proprietor from Gloucestershire, Brian Shawe-Taylor gained some success before the Second World War, winning the 1939 Nuffield Trophy. After the hostilities had ceased, he reappeared with a B-Type ERA. When his entry for the 1950 British GP was refused on the grounds that his car was too old, he shared Joe Fry's Maserati instead. He was developing a reputation as a very quick driver, and in 1951 he practised with Tony Vandervell's Ferrari at Reims, but in the event Reg Parnell raced the car after his BRM failed to show.

Having scored some good placings with the ERA at Goodwood (second in both the Richmond Trophy and the Chichester Cup), Brian was granted an entry for the British GP and succeeded in finishing eighth, the first privateer home. He shared a works Aston Martin with George Abecassis at Le Mans and finished fifth, before his progress was halted by an accident in the Daily Graphic Trophy at Goodwood, where he spun the ERA and was hit by Toni Branca's car. Seriously injured, this promising driver recovered, but never raced again.

SHAWE-TAYLOR, Brian (GB) b 29/1/1915, Dublin, Republic of Ireland – d 1/5/1999, Dowdeswell, nr Cheltenham, Gloucestershire

1950 Championship position: Unplaced

	Race	Circuit	No	Entrant	Tyres	Capacity/Car/Engine	Comment	Q Pos/Entries
10*	BRITISH GP	Silverstone	10	Joe Fry	D	1.5 s/c Maserati 4CL 4	*took over car from Fry/6 laps behind	– / –

1951 Championship position: Unplaced

	Race	Circuit	No	Entrant	Tyres	Capacity/Car/Engine	Comment	Q Pos/Entries
dns	FRENCH GP	Reims	26	G A Vandervell	P	4.5 Ferrari T375/Thinwall Spl V12	Reg Parnell drove car	– / –
8	BRITISH GP	Silverstone	9	Brian Shawe-Taylor	D	1.5 s/c ERA B Type 6	6 laps behind	12/20

GP Starts: 2   GP Wins: 0   Pole positions: 0   Fastest laps: 0   Points: 0

SHELBY, Carroll (USA) b 11/1/1923, Leesburg, Texas

1958 Championship position: Unplaced

	Race	Circuit	No	Entrant	Tyres	Capacity/Car/Engine	Comment	Q Pos/Entries
ret	FRENCH GP	Reims	28	Scuderia Centro Sud	P	2.5 Maserati 250F 6	engine	17/21
9	BRITISH GP	Silverstone	5	Scuderia Centro Sud	P	2.5 Maserati 250F 6	3 laps behind	15/21
ret	PORTUGUESE GP	Oporto	28	Temple Buell	P	2.5 Maserati 250F 6	crashed – brakes	10/15
ret	ITALIAN GP	Monza	34	Temple Buell	P	2.5 Maserati 250F 6	engine	17/21
4*	"	"	32	Scuderia Centro Sud	P	2.5 Maserati 250F 6	Gregory's car/*no points awarded	– / –

1959 Championship position: Unplaced

	Race	Circuit	No	Entrant	Tyres	Capacity/Car/Engine	Comment	Q Pos/Entries
ret	DUTCH GP	Zandvoort	5	David Brown Corporation	A	2.5 Aston-Martin DBR4/250 6	engine	10/15
ret	BRITISH GP	Aintree	4	David Brown Corporation	A	2.5 Aston-Martin DBR4/250 6	magneto	6/30
8	PORTUGUESE GP	Monsanto	9	David Brown Corporation	A	2.5 Aston-Martin DBR4/250 6	4 laps behind	13/16
10	ITALIAN GP	Monza	26	David Brown Corporation	A	2.5 Aston-Martin DBR4/250 6	2 laps behind	19/21

GP Starts: 8   GP Wins: 0   Pole positions: 0   Fastest laps: 0   Points: 0

SHELLY, Tony (NZ) b 2/2/1937, Wellington – d 4/10/1998, Taupo

1962 Championship position: Unplaced

	Race	Circuit	No	Entrant	Tyres	Capacity/Car/Engine	Comment	Q Pos/Entries
ret	BRITISH GP	Aintree	48	John Dalton	D	1.5 Lotus 18/21-Climax 4	cylinder head gasket	18/21
dnq	GERMAN GP	Nürburgring	29	John Dalton	D	1.5 Lotus 18/21-Climax 4		27/30
dnq	ITALIAN GP	Monza	60	Autosport Team Wolfgang Seidel	D	1.5 Lotus 24-BRM V8		22/30

GP Starts: 1   GP Wins: 0   Pole positions: 0   Fastest laps: 0   Points: 0

CARROLL SHELBY

THIS HARD-BITTEN Texan began racing in 1952 with an MG TC, winning his first event. He soon progressed to more potent machinery in the shape of an Allard-Cadillac and a Ferrari in 1953, and the following season he competed abroad for the first time, racing in Argentina before travelling to Europe to drive David Brown's Aston Martin DB3S.

In 1955, Shelby continued to race in sports car events, sharing a Ferrari with Phil Hill to take second place in the Sebring 12-hours, and also made his F1 debut for Maserati with a sixth place in the Syracuse GP. Staying in the USA for 1956, he virtually swept the board in SCCA circles, winning 27 races – 19 of them consecutively – in his Ferrari. Then, in 1957, driving a Ferrari for John Edgar, he finished second to Juan Fangio in the Cuban GP. He also continued his winning ways in SCCA, overcoming a nasty crash at Riverside in which he sustained facial injuries.

Tempted back to Europe in 1958, Shelby raced the outdated Maserati 250F, and was unfortunate to be stripped of his points at Monza after taking over Masten Gregory's car to earn a fourth-place finish. He also renewed his association with Aston Martin, finishing third with Stuart Lewis-Evans in the Tourist Trophy at Goodwood to set up a full season in both Formula 1 and sports cars in 1959.

The grand prix project was a huge disappointment. Although the front-engined cars were beautifully made, their reliability was suspect and they were unable to compete with the fleet little Coopers. In direct contrast, the sports car programme went well and the Feltham team eventually took the World Sports Car Championship, Carroll playing his part by winning the Le Mans 24-hours with Roy Salvadori, and the Tourist Trophy at Goodwood with Stirling Moss and Jack Fairman.

In 1960, Shelby competed in SCCA events once more, but by then he was suffering from heart trouble and retired at season's end. It was the beginning of a new chapter, though, and he would gain even greater fame, first developing the AC Cobra, and then overseeing Ford's massive and ultimately successful assault on the Le Mans 24-hour race, which culminated in victory in 1966.

After many years of failing health, Carroll was literally given a new lease of life in 1990, after receiving a successful heart transplant. This has since offered him the freedom to travel the world once more, and relive his racing days with many old friends and acquaintances.

Shelby started the Carroll Shelby Heart Fund to help finance organ transplants for children. His tireless fundraising has led to countless successful life-saving operations over the past two decades.

In the meantime, the iconic Shelby brand has been marketed through a number of special and limited-edition variants in partnership with Ford.

In 2008, Carroll celebrated his 85th birthday with 800 of his closest friends at the Las Vegas Shelby Bash. The following year, the octogenarian was presented with a lifetime achievement award, as the Automotive Executive of the Year, in Detroit.

TONY SHELLY

A POPULAR New Zealander who made a promising start to his career by winning the first big race he contested at Teretonga with a Cooper in 1958, Tony Shelly became a leading driver 'down-under' before travelling to Europe in 1962 to race for John Dalton, mainly in non-championship events.

Considering his unfamiliarity with the tracks, Tony acquitted himself very well, taking his four-cylinder Lotus 18 into fifth place in the Lombank Trophy and following that with a third in the Lavant Cup.

Tony went back to New Zealand at the end of the season and never returned to compete in Europe. He continued racing 'down-under' in 1963/64, before retiring to concentrate on his thriving car dealerships, although he did have occasional outings in later years.

JO SIFFERT

ALTHOUGH he could be a wild and hairy driver, the fans loved Jo Siffert, perhaps because he was a man who chanced his arm a little more than most. Now some 40 years on, he is chiefly remembered for the 1968 British Grand Prix where, in Rob Walker's dark-blue Lotus 49, he resisted all of Chris Amon's attempts to pass in the Ferrari to take a fairy-tale victory. 'Seppi' was a very underrated grand prix driver, having spent the bulk of his career without complaint in second-rank equipment.

Siffert had the heart of a lion and, despite his frail appearance, was an immensely tough and doughty competitor – no doubt born of his motorcycling career, during which he won the 350cc Swiss championship on a Gilera and

acted as passenger for Edgar Strub in the 1959 sidecar world championship.

Jo's first competition on four wheels came in 1960, when he raced in Formula Junior, but he really came to prominence the following year when, driving a Lotus 21, he won the Eifelrennen race among others to emerge as joint European Formula Junior champion with Tony Maggs. For 1962, he decided to step up to Formula 1 with Ecurie Filipinetti. Although no results of note were achieved, he plugged away into 1963, buying the Filipinetti Lotus 24-BRM to run as an independent.

He was finally rewarded with a championship point at the French Grand Prix at Reims. In addition, he won his first F1 race, the Syracuse

Grand Prix, and took second place, behind Jim Clark, in the Imola Grand Prix.

Purchasing a Brabham for 1964 increased Siffert's grand prix competitiveness, and he scored a superb win in the Mediterranean Grand Prix, where even the great Jim Clark had to take second best, the final margin being a tenth of a second. Amazingly, 'Seppi' repeated the victory in 1965, when again he saw off the great Scot, this time by the huge margin of three-tenths of a second! He had joined the Walker team at the beginning of that year and struck up a wonderful relationship with Rob that saw them through the many tough times that followed.

The 1966 and '67 seasons were a period of struggle, when Siffert scraped the occasional point, but top-three finishes were achieved only in non-title races. Hopes were high for 1968, however, when Walker persuaded Colin Chapman to provide him with a Lotus 49, and after the team's wonderful day at Brands Hatch, 'Seppi' was a front-runner for the rest of the year; sometimes he was quicker than the works car of Graham Hill. He remained with Walker for one more season, but after a bright start, it faded disappointingly. By then, Siffert had established himself as a star of the Porsche sports car team, having won five major races in the 1969 season alone. A tempting offer from Ferrari was dangled in front of him, but Porsche, desperate not to lose his services, paid for him to join the STP March team for 1970.

It was an absolutely disastrous grand prix year for 'Seppi', only partly salvaged by success in Formula 2 with the works BMW and in sports car racing with the Gulf Porsche team. For the latter, he won the Targa Florio, the Spa 1000km and the Österreichring 1000km, all with Brian Redman.

Siffert set out on a hectic racing programme in 1971. He joined the BRM Formula 1 team, purchased a Chevron to race in F2 and a Porsche 917 for Can-Am, and continued to race the works Porsche with the Gulf/John Wyer outfit. The season was very successful. Apart from his dominant BRM triumph in the Austrian Grand Prix, he took plenty of top-three finishes in the other formulas, and the popular Swiss had much to look forward to in 1972 when he arrived at Brands Hatch for the season's finale, the Rothmans Victory Race.

During the race, however, a suspension failure sent the BRM P160 hurtling into a bank, where it burst into flames. Poor Siffert was trapped in the wreckage and when he was finally extricated was found to have died of asphyxia, having survived the initial impact with a broken leg.

Coming so soon after the loss of Pedro Rodriguez, the death of another of the sport's great 'tigers' was a further dreadful blow to the BRM team.

SIFFERT, Jo (CH) b 7/7/1936, Fribourg – d 24/10/1971, Brands Hatch Circuit, Kent, England

1962 Championship position: Unplaced

	Race	Circuit	No	Entrant	Tyres	Capacity/Car/Engine	Comment	Q Pos/Entries
dnq*	MONACO GP	Monte Carlo	46	Ecurie Nationale Suisse	D	1.5 Lotus 21-Climax 4	*faster than 5 seeded drivers	13/21
10	BELGIAN GP	Spa	22	Ecurie Filipinetti	D	1.5 Lotus 21-Climax 4	3 laps behind	17/20
ret	FRENCH GP	Rouen	40	Ecurie Filipinetti	D	1.5 Lotus 24-BRM V8	clutch	15/17
dns	"	"	40	Ecurie Filipinetti	D	1.5 Lotus 21-Climax 4	practice only	– / –
12	GERMAN GP	Nürburgring	19	Ecurie Filipinetti	D	1.5 Lotus 21-Climax 4		17/30
dnq	ITALIAN GP	Monza	42	Ecurie Filipinetti	D	1.5 Lotus 24-BRM V8		26/30

1963 Championship position: 15th   Wins: 0   Pole positions: 0   Fastest laps: 0   Points scored: 1

	Race	Circuit	No	Entrant	Tyres	Capacity/Car/Engine	Comment	Q Pos/Entries
ret	MONACO GP	Monte Carlo	25	Siffert Racing Team	D	1.5 Lotus 24-BRM V8	engine	12/17
ret	BELGIAN GP	Spa	28	Siffert Racing Team	D	1.5 Lotus 24-BRM V8	crashed in rain storm	14/20
7	DUTCH GP	Zandvoort	36	Siffert Racing Team	D	1.5 Lotus 24-BRM V8	3 laps behind	=17/19
6	FRENCH GP	Reims	36	Siffert Racing Team	D	1.5 Lotus 24-BRM V8	1 lap behind	10/21
ret	BRITISH GP	Silverstone	25	Siffert Racing Team	D	1.5 Lotus 24-BRM V8	gearbox	15/23
9/ret	GERMAN GP	Nürburgring	18	Siffert Racing Team	D	1.5 Lotus 24-BRM V8	differential/5 laps behind	9/26
ret	ITALIAN GP	Monza	54	Siffert Racing Team	D	1.5 Lotus 24-BRM V8	oil pressure	16/28
ret	US GP	Watkins Glen	14	Siffert Racing Team	D	1.5 Lotus 24-BRM V8	gearbox	=13/21
9	MEXICAN GP	Mexico City	14	Siffert Racing Team	D	1.5 Lotus 24-BRM V8	6 laps behind	9/21

1964 Championship position: 10th   Wins: 0   Pole positions: 0   Fastest laps: 0   Points scored: 7

	Race	Circuit	No	Entrant	Tyres	Capacity/Car/Engine	Comment	Q Pos/Entries
8	MONACO GP	Monte Carlo	24	Siffert Racing Team	D	1.5 Lotus 24-BRM V8	pit stops – misfire, etc/22 laps behind	16/20
nc	DUTCH GP	Zandvoort	36	Siffert Racing Team	D	1.5 Brabham BT11-BRM V8	pit stops – misfire/25 laps behind	18/18
ret	BELGIAN GP	Spa	17	Siffert Racing Team	D	1.5 Brabham BT11-BRM V8	engine	13/20
ret	FRENCH GP	Rouen	30	Siffert Racing Team	D	1.5 Brabham BT11-BRM V8	clutch	17/17
11	BRITISH GP	Brands Hatch	20	Siffert Racing Team	D	1.5 Brabham BT11-BRM V8	4 laps behind	=16/25
4	GERMAN GP	Nürburgring	19	Siffert Racing Team	D	1.5 Brabham BT11-BRM V8		10/24
ret	AUSTRIAN GP	Zeltweg	20	Siffert Racing Team	D	1.5 Brabham BT11-BRM V8	accident	12/20
7	ITALIAN GP	Monza	12	Siffert Racing Team	D	1.5 Brabham BT11-BRM V8	1 lap behind	6/25
3	US GP	Watkins Glen	22	Rob Walker Racing Team	D	1.5 Brabham BT11-BRM V8	1 lap behind	12/19
ret	MEXICAN GP	Mexico City	22	Rob Walker Racing Team	D	1.5 Brabham BT11-BRM V8	fuel pump	13/19

1965 Championship position: 11th   Wins: 0   Pole positions: 0   Fastest laps: 0   Points scored: 5

	Race	Circuit	No	Entrant	Tyres	Capacity/Car/Engine	Comment	Q Pos/Entries
7	SOUTH AFRICAN GP	East London	12	Rob Walker Racing Team	D	1.5 Brabham BT11-BRM V8	2 laps behind	14/25
6	MONACO GP	Monte Carlo	14	Rob Walker Racing Team	D	1.5 Brabham BT11-BRM V8	2 laps behind	=10/17
8	BELGIAN GP	Spa	21	Rob Walker Racing Team	D	1.5 Brabham BT11-BRM V8	1 lap behind	8/21
6	FRENCH GP	Clermont Ferrand	36	Rob Walker Racing Team	D	1.5 Brabham BT11-BRM V8	1 lap behind	14/17
9	BRITISH GP	Silverstone	16	Rob Walker Racing Team	D	1.5 Brabham BT11-BRM V8	2 laps behind	18/23
13	DUTCH GP	Zandvoort	28	Rob Walker Racing Team	D	1.5 Brabham BT11-BRM V8	pit stop – fuel feed/25 laps behind	=10/17
ret	GERMAN GP	Nürburgring	17	Rob Walker Racing Team	D	1.5 Brabham BT11-BRM V8	engine	11/22
ret	ITALIAN GP	Monza	44	Rob Walker Racing Team	D	1.5 Brabham BT11-BRM V8	gearbox	10/23
11	US GP	Watkins Glen	16	Rob Walker Racing Team	D	1.5 Brabham BT11-BRM V8	pit stop – clutch slip/11 laps behind	11/18
4	MEXICAN GP	Mexico City	16	Rob Walker Racing Team	D	1.5 Brabham BT11-BRM V8		11/18

1966 Championship position: 14th   Wins: 0   Pole positions: 0   Fastest laps: 0   Points scored: 3

	Race	Circuit	No	Entrant	Tyres	Capacity/Car/Engine	Comment	Q Pos/Entries
ret	MONACO GP	Monte Carlo	14	Rob Walker Racing Team	D	2.0 Brabham BT11-BRM V8	clutch	13/16
ret	BELGIAN GP	Spa	21	Rob Walker Racing Team	D	3.0 Cooper T81-Maserati V12	engine	14/18
ret	FRENCH GP	Reims	38	Rob Walker Racing Team	D	3.0 Cooper T81-Maserati V12	overheating	6/17
nc	BRITISH GP	Brands Hatch	20	Rob Walker Racing Team	D	3.0 Cooper T81-Maserati V12	pit stop – overheating/10 laps behind	11/20
ret	DUTCH GP	Zandvoort	28	Rob Walker Racing Team	D	3.0 Cooper T81-Maserati V12	engine	11/18
ret	ITALIAN GP	Monza	36	Rob Walker Racing Team	D	3.0 Cooper T81-Maserati V12	engine	17/22
4	US GP	Watkins Glen	19	Rob Walker Racing Team	D	3.0 Cooper T81-Maserati V12	3 laps behind	13/19
ret	MEXICAN GP	Mexico City	19	Rob Walker Racing Team	F	3.0 Cooper T81-Maserati V12	suspension bolt	11/19

1967 Championship position: 11th   Wins: 0   Pole positions: 0   Fastest laps: 0   Points scored: 6

	Race	Circuit	No	Entrant	Tyres	Capacity/Car/Engine	Comment	Q Pos/Entries
ret	SOUTH AFRICAN GP	Kyalami	12	Rob Walker/Jack Durlacher Racing	F	3.0 Cooper T81-Maserati V12	engine	16/18
ret	MONACO GP	Monte Carlo	17	Rob Walker/Jack Durlacher Racing	F	3.0 Cooper T81-Maserati V12	engine	=9/18
10	DUTCH GP	Zandvoort	20	Rob Walker/Jack Durlacher Racing	F	3.0 Cooper T81-Maserati V12	pit stop – overheating/7 laps behind	16/17
7	BELGIAN GP	Spa	34	Rob Walker/Jack Durlacher Racing	F	3.0 Cooper T81-Maserati V12	1 lap behind	16/18
4	FRENCH GP	Le Mans	18	Rob Walker/Jack Durlacher Racing	F	3.0 Cooper T81-Maserati V12	3 laps behind	11/15
ret	BRITISH GP	Silverstone	17	Rob Walker/Jack Durlacher Racing	F	3.0 Cooper T81-Maserati V12	engine	18/21
ret	GERMAN GP	Nürburgring	14	Rob Walker/Jack Durlacher Racing	F	3.0 Cooper T81-Maserati V12	fuel pump	13/25
dns	CANADIAN GP	Mosport Park	14	Rob Walker/Jack Durlacher Racing	F	3.0 Cooper T81-Maserati V12	starter ring on way to grid	(13)/19
ret	ITALIAN GP	Monza	6	Rob Walker/Jack Durlacher Racing	F	3.0 Cooper T81-Maserati V12	crashed – puncture	13/18
4	US GP	Watkins Glen	15	Rob Walker/Jack Durlacher Racing	F	3.0 Cooper T81-Maserati V12	2 laps behind	12/18
12/ret	MEXICAN GP	Mexico City	15	Rob Walker/Jack Durlacher Racing	F	3.0 Cooper T81-Maserati V12	engine – no water/6 laps behind	10/19

1968 Championship position: 7th   Wins: 1   Pole positions: 1   Fastest laps: 3   Points scored: 12

	Race	Circuit	No	Entrant	Tyres	Capacity/Car/Engine	Comment	Q Pos/Entries
7	SOUTH AFRICAN GP	Kyalami	19	Rob Walker/Jack Durlacher Racing	F	3.0 Cooper T81-Maserati V12	3 laps behind	16/23
ret	SPANISH GP	Jarama	16	Rob Walker/Jack Durlacher Racing	F	3.0 Lotus 49-Cosworth V8	transmission vibration	=9/14
ret	MONACO GP	Monte Carlo	17	Rob Walker/Jack Durlacher Racing	F	3.0 Lotus 49-Cosworth V8	transmission	=2/18
7/ret	BELGIAN GP	Spa	3	Rob Walker/Jack Durlacher Racing	F	3.0 Lotus 49-Cosworth V8	oil pressure/3 laps behind	9/18
ret	DUTCH GP	Zandvoort	21	Rob Walker/Jack Durlacher Racing	F	3.0 Lotus 49-Cosworth V8	gear selectors	13/19
11	FRENCH GP	Rouen	34	Rob Walker/Jack Durlacher Racing	F	3.0 Lotus 49-Cosworth V8	6 laps behind	12/18
1	BRITISH GP	Brands Hatch	22	Rob Walker/Jack Durlacher Racing	F	3.0 Lotus 49B-Cosworth V8	FL	4/20
ret	GERMAN GP	Nürburgring	16	Rob Walker/Jack Durlacher Racing	F	3.0 Lotus 49B-Cosworth V8	wet ignition	9/20
ret	ITALIAN GP	Monza	20	Rob Walker/Jack Durlacher Racing	F	3.0 Lotus 49B-Cosworth V8	shock absorber mounting	9/24
ret	CANADIAN GP	St Jovite	12	Rob Walker/Jack Durlacher Racing	F	3.0 Lotus 49B-Cosworth V8	oil leak/FL	=3/22
5	US GP	Watkins Glen	16	Rob Walker/Jack Durlacher Racing	F	3.0 Lotus 49B-Cosworth V8	pit stop – fuel/3 laps behind	12/21
6	MEXICAN GP	Mexico City	16	Rob Walker/Jack Durlacher Racing	F	3.0 Lotus 49B-Cosworth V8	pit stop – throttle/FL/1 lap behind	1/21

1969 Championship position: 9th Wins: 0 Pole positions: 0 Fastest laps: 0 Points scored: 15

4	SOUTH AFRICAN GP	Kyalami	4	Rob Walker/Jack Durlacher Racing	F	3.0 Lotus 49B-Cosworth V8		=12/18
ret	SPANISH GP	Montjuich Park	10	Rob Walker/Jack Durlacher Racing	F	3.0 Lotus 49B-Cosworth V8	engine	6/14
3	MONACO GP	Monte Carlo	9	Rob Walker/Jack Durlacher Racing	F	3.0 Lotus 49B-Cosworth V8		6/16
2	DUTCH GP	Zandvoort	10	Rob Walker/Jack Durlacher Racing	F	3.0 Lotus 49B-Cosworth V8		10/15
9	FRENCH GP	Clermont Ferrand	3	Rob Walker/Jack Durlacher Racing	F	3.0 Lotus 49B-Cosworth V8	pit stop – damaged nose/4 laps behind	9/13
8	BRITISH GP	Silverstone	10	Rob Walker/Jack Durlacher Racing	F	3.0 Lotus 49B-Cosworth V8	pit stop – fuel/3 laps behind	9/17
5*/ret	GERMAN GP	Nürburgring	11	Rob Walker/Jack Durlacher Racing	F	3.0 Lotus 49B-Cosworth V8	accident/*11th on road/2 laps behind	4/26
8/ret	ITALIAN GP	Monza	30	Rob Walker/Jack Durlacher Racing	F	3.0 Lotus 49B-Cosworth V8	engine/4 laps behind	8/15
ret	CANADIAN GP	Mosport Park	9	Rob Walker/Jack Durlacher Racing	F	3.0 Lotus 49B-Cosworth V8	driveshaft	=8/20
ret	US GP	Watkins Glen	10	Rob Walker/Jack Durlacher Racing	F	3.0 Lotus 49B-Cosworth V8	fuel metering unit drive belt	5/18
ret	MEXICAN GP	Mexico City	10	Rob Walker/Jack Durlacher Racing	F	3.0 Lotus 49B-Cosworth V8	collision with Courage	5/17

1970 Championship position: Unplaced

10	SOUTH AFRICAN GP	Kyalami	16	March Engineering	F	3.0 March 701-Cosworth V8	pit stop – broken exhaust/5 laps behind	9/24
dnq*	SPANISH GP	Jarama	14	March Engineering	F	3.0 March 701-Cosworth V8	*not seeded driver	16/22
8	MONACO GP	Monte Carlo	19	March Engineering	F	3.0 March 701-Cosworth V8	engine – misfire/4 laps behind	11/21
7	BELGIAN GP	Spa	9	March Engineering	F	3.0 March 701-Cosworth V8	engine – fuel feed/2 laps behind	10/18
ret	DUTCH GP	Zandvoort	9	March Engineering	F	3.0 March 701-Cosworth V8	engine	17/24
ret	FRENCH GP	Clermont Ferrand	12	March Engineering	F	3.0 March 701-Cosworth V8	accident – locked brakes	16/23
ret	BRITISH GP	Brands Hatch	15	March Engineering	F	3.0 March 701-Cosworth V8	rear suspension bracket	21/25
8/ret	GERMAN GP	Hockenheim	12	March Engineering	F	3.0 March 701-Cosworth V8	engine/3 laps behind	4/25
9	AUSTRIAN GP	Österreichring	3	March Engineering	F	3.0 March 701-Cosworth V8	1 lap behind	19/24
ret	ITALIAN GP	Monza	50	March Engineering	F	3.0 March 701-Cosworth V8	engine	7/27
ret	CANADIAN GP	St Jovite	21	March Engineering	F	3.0 March 701-Cosworth V8	engine	14/20
9	US GP	Watkins Glen	11	March Engineering	F	3.0 March 701-Cosworth V8	pit stop – tyre/3 laps behind	23/27
ret	MEXICAN GP	Mexico City	11	March Engineering	F	3.0 March 701-Cosworth V8	engine	16/18

1971 Championship position: 4th= Wins: 1 Pole positions: 1 Fastest laps: 1 Points scored: 19

ret	SOUTH AFRICAN GP	Kyalami	17	Yardley-BRM	F	3.0 BRM P153 V12	overheating	=16/25
ret	SPANISH GP	Montjuich Park	15	Yardley-BRM	F	3.0 BRM P160 V12	gear linkage	10/22
ret	MONACO GP	Monte Carlo	14	Yardley-BRM	F	3.0 BRM P160 V12	engine – oil line	=3/23
6	DUTCH GP	Zandvoort	9	Yardley-BRM	F	3.0 BRM P160 V12	2 laps behind	8/24
4	FRENCH GP	Paul Ricard	14	Yardley-BRM	F	3.0 BRM P160 V12		6/24
9	BRITISH GP	Silverstone	16	Yardley-BRM	F	3.0 BRM P160 V12	2 pit stops – condenser/2 laps behind	2/24
ret	GERMAN GP	Nürburgring	21	Yardley-BRM	F	3.0 BRM P160 V12	coil failure	3/23
1	AUSTRIAN GP	Österreichring	14	Yardley-BRM	F	3.0 BRM P160 V12	FL	1/22
9	ITALIAN GP	Monza	20	Yardley-BRM	F	3.0 BRM P160 V12	stuck in gear for final laps/2 laps behind	3/24
9	CANADIAN GP	Mosport Park	14	Yardley-BRM	F	3.0 BRM P160 V12	pit stop – dirt in nose of car/-3 laps	2/27
2	US GP	Watkins Glen	14	Yardley-BRM	F	3.0 BRM P160 V12		7/32

GP Starts: 96 GP Wins: 2 Pole positions: 2 Fastest laps: 4 Points: 68

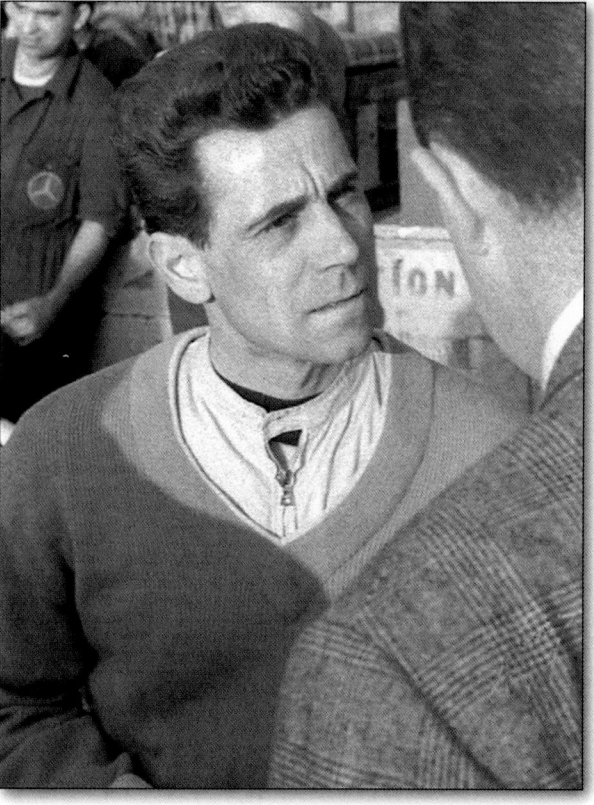

ANDRÉ SIMON

NOW a somewhat forgotten figure, André Simon was a key member of the Simca-Gordini team in 1950, winning at the Circuit de Médoc and taking a string of second-place finishes that year (German Grand Prix, Aix-les-Bains, Angoulême, Reims, Geneva and Périgueux). He continued to race the light blue cars in both grands prix and Formula 2 the following season, winning at Les Sables d'Olonne. For 1952, he joined Ferrari, but raced in only a few events, although he did share the winning T500 after Alberto Ascari had taken over his machine at the Comminges Grand Prix. He also took second place in both the Paris GP and the Autodrome GP at Monza, and fourth in the Monaco GP held for sports cars that year.

From 1953 on, André raced intermittently as an independent in both grands prix and sports car events, taking a third for Gordini in the 1954 International Trophy. In 1955, he replaced the injured Hans Herrmann in the Mercedes at short notice at Monaco and also raced the German team's sports cars, taking third in the Tourist Trophy. Driving a Maserati 250F, he won the Albi Grand Prix in 1955, but by then it was a much less important event than in previous years. He raced in a few more grands prix without success, his last decent placing being second in the rain-soaked 1956 Caen GP in a Gordini.

Turning to sports car and GT racing, Simon was third in the Paris 1000km at Montlhéry in Jean-Louis Schlesser's Ferrari, and third in the Auvergne Trophy and Coupe de la Marne Debouteville at Rouen in 1961, also in a Ferrari. In 1962, he won the Tour de France with co-driver Maurice Dupeyron – his last major win, although he continued racing until 1965, when he finished 12th in the Nürburgring 1000km in a Ford France AC Cobra with old friend Jo Schlesser.

Simon then returned to his family garage business, which he had inherited on the death of his father when only a youngster.

SIMON, André (F) b 5/1/1920, Paris

1951 Championship position: Unplaced

	Race	Circuit	No	Entrant	Tyres	Capacity/Car/Engine	Comment	Q Pos/Entries
ret	FRENCH GP	Reims	34	Equipe Gordini	E	1.5 s/c Simca-Gordini Type 15 4	engine	21/23
ret	GERMAN GP	Nürburgring	83	Equipe Gordini	E	1.5 s/c Simca-Gordini Type 15 4	engine	12/23
6	ITALIAN GP	Monza	48	Equipe Gordini	E	1.5 s/c Simca-Gordini Type 15 4	6 laps behind	11/22
ret	SPANISH GP	Pedralbes	16	Equipe Gordini	E	1.5 s/c Simca-Gordini Type 15 4	engine	10/20

1952 Championship position: Unplaced

	Race	Circuit	No	Entrant	Tyres	Capacity/Car/Engine	Comment	Q Pos/Entries
ret*	SWISS GP	Bremgarten	32	Scuderia Ferrari	P	2.0 Ferrari 500 4	*Farina took over/magneto	4/21
6	ITALIAN GP	Monza	8	Scuderia Ferrari	P	2.0 Ferrari 500 4	1 lap behind	7/35

1955 Championship position: Unplaced

	Race	Circuit	No	Entrant	Tyres	Capacity/Car/Engine	Comment	Q Pos/Entries
ret	MONACO GP	Monte Carlo	4	Daimler Benz AG	C	2.5 Mercedes-Benz W196 8	drove the injured Herrmann's car/valve	10/22
dns	" " "	16	Ecurie Rosier	P	2.5 Maserati 250F 6	practice only – drove Mercedes	– / –
ret	BRITISH GP	Aintree	8	Officine Alfieri Maserati	P	2.5 Maserati 250F 6	gearbox	8/25

1956 Championship position: Unplaced

	Race	Circuit	No	Entrant	Tyres	Capacity/Car/Engine	Comment	Q Pos/Entries
ret	FRENCH GP	Reims	42	André Simon	P	2.5 Maserati 250F 6	engine	20/20
9	ITALIAN GP	Monza	12	Equipe Gordini	E	2.5 Gordini Type 16 6	5 laps behind	25/26

1957 Championship position: Unplaced

	Race	Circuit	No	Entrant	Tyres	Capacity/Car/Engine	Comment	Q Pos/Entries
dnq	MONACO GP	Monte Carlo	4	Scuderia Centro Sud	P	2.5 Maserati 250F 6		19/21
nc*	ITALIAN GP	Monza	28	Ottorino Volonterio	P	2.5 Maserati 250F 6	*Volonterio took over/15 laps behind	16/19

GP Starts: 11   GP Wins: 0   Pole positions: 0   Fastest laps: 0   Points: 0

MOISES SOLANA

A NATURAL athlete who excelled at a number of sports, Moises Solana was first and foremost an expert exponent of the sport of jai-alai, and so good was he that it provided him with the means to go motor racing.

Solana raced at the early age of 18, in 1954, in the Carrera Panamericana, and by the end of the decade was rated on a par with the famous Rodriguez brothers. While they ventured abroad to find fame and fortune, however, he preferred to stay at home and combine his dual sporting activities, which saw him handling a incredible variety of machinery in many different classes of racing.

In 1962, Solana arranged to drive a Bowmaker Lola in the non-championship Mexican F1 race, but he rejected the car in practice, claiming that it was not satisfactory. In reality, he withdrew out of respect for Ricardo Rodriguez, who had been killed in a practice crash. After running a tired Centro Sud BRM in the following year's race, from 1964 through to 1968 he came to an arrangement to run a third works Lotus in Mexico and the USA when available. Despite some excellent qualifying performances, which included seventh fastest for the 1967 US Grand Prix, he was unable to score any worthwhile results, as the cars always seemed to fail him. After the wing failed on his final appearance, he vowed never to drive for Colin Chapman again.

Sadly, Solana would never get the opportunity to race a Formula 1 car for anyone else. He was killed in 1969 while competing in the Valle de Bravo hill-climb after losing control of his McLaren M6B. He clipped a kerb and crashed over a bridge into a ravine, the car catching fire; the 33-year-old perished in the inferno.

SOLANA, Moises (MEX) b 25/12/1935, Mexico City – d 27/7/1969, Valle de Bravo, nr Mexico City

1963 Championship position: Unplaced

	Race	Circuit	No	Entrant	Tyres	Capacity/Car/Engine	Comment	Q Pos/Entries
11/ret	MEXICAN GP	Mexico City	13	Scuderia Centro Sud	D	1.5 BRM P57 V8	cam follower/8 laps behind	11/21

1964 Championship position: Unplaced

	Race	Circuit	No	Entrant	Tyres	Capacity/Car/Engine	Comment	Q Pos/Entries
10	MEXICAN GP	Mexico City	17	Team Lotus	D	1.5 Lotus 33-Climax V8	2 laps behind	14/19

1965 Championship position: Unplaced

	Race	Circuit	No	Entrant	Tyres	Capacity/Car/Engine	Comment	Q Pos/Entries
12	US GP	Watkins Glen	18	Team Lotus	D	1.5 Lotus 25-Climax V8	15 laps behind	=15/18
ret	MEXICAN GP	Mexico City	18	Team Lotus	D	1.5 Lotus 25-Climax V8	ignition	9/18

1966 Championship position: Unplaced

	Race	Circuit	No	Entrant	Tyres	Capacity/Car/Engine	Comment	Q Pos/Entries
ret	MEXICAN GP	Mexico City	9	Cooper Car Co	F	3.0 Cooper T81-Maserati V12	overheating	16/19

1967 Championship position: Unplaced

	Race	Circuit	No	Entrant	Tyres	Capacity/Car/Engine	Comment	Q Pos/Entries
ret	US GP	Watkins Glen	18	Team Lotus	F	3.0 Lotus 49-Cosworth V8	electrics – ignition	7/18
ret	MEXICAN GP	Mexico City	18	Team Lotus	F	3.0 Lotus 49-Cosworth V8	front suspension	9/19

1968 Championship position: Unplaced

	Race	Circuit	No	Entrant	Tyres	Capacity/Car/Engine	Comment	Q Pos/Entries
ret	MEXICAN GP	Mexico City	12	Gold Leaf Team Lotus	F	3.0 Lotus 49B-Cosworth V8	collapsed wing	11/21

GP Starts: 8   GP Wins: 0   Pole positions: 0   Fastest laps: 0   Points: 0

ALEX SOLER-ROIG

A SOPHISTICATED Spaniard from a wealthy background, Alex Soler-Roig had the means to try his hand at Formula 1 over a three-year period, but it was obvious that he lacked the hunger or speed to be truly competitive.

Soler-Roig won his first event in 1958 at Montjuich and continued to race in his own country, usually with a Porsche, until he joined the European Formula 2 circus in 1968 for his first sustained attempt at professional racing. His season with a Lola was not very successful, so in 1969 he switched full time to sports car and GT racing, winning the Jarama six-hours with close friend Jochen Rindt and finishing fourth in the Sebring 12-hours with Rudi Lins, on both occasions in Porsches.

Alex finished second in the Buenos Aires 1000km in 1970 with his Porsche 908, again teamed with Rindt, and cleaned up in Spanish G5/6 races with his Porsche 917. It was through his connection with the Lotus driver that he bought himself a ride in the third works car in the middle of the season. The Spaniard was not helped by having to make do with whatever chassis Colin Chapman could cobble together for him; it was a complete waste of time and money for the inexperienced Spaniard.

There was talk of an Alex joining a new F1 team for 1971, to be led by Rindt, but this idea had come to nought even before the Austrian was killed at Monza. Instead, Soler-Roig joined March for the 1971 season. However, although he made the grids, he felt dissatisfied with the engines he was given and quit in mid-season, preferring to concentrate on his drive in the European touring car championship with Ford Germany, which yielded two excellent victories in the Capri, co-driving with Dieter Glemser.

Alex's short spell in the Marlboro BRM team at the beginning of 1972 was another Formula 1 disaster, the team being over-extended in trying to run up to five cars, so once again he returned to touring cars with the Capri along with Glemser, Jochen Mass and Gérard Larrousse, The move brought further wins at Zandvoort and Jarama, the latter victory being his final race, for he called it a day at the end of the season.

SOLER-ROIG, Alex (E) b 29/10/1932, Barcelona

	Race	Circuit	No	Entrant	Tyres	Capacity/Car/Engine	Comment	Q Pos/Entries
	1970 Championship position: Unplaced							
dnq	SPANISH GP	Jarama	23	Garvey Team Lotus	F	3.0 Lotus 49C-Cosworth V8		21/22
dnq	BELGIAN GP	Spa	22	World Wide Racing	F	3.0 Lotus 72C-Cosworth V8	insufficient practice	18/18
dnq	FRENCH GP	Clermont Ferrand	9	World Wide Racing	F	3.0 Lotus 49C-Cosworth V8		23/23
	1971 Championship position: Unplaced							
ret	SOUTH AFRICAN GP	Kyalami	26	STP March	F	3.0 March 711-Cosworth V8	engine	25/25
ret	SPANISH GP	Montjuich Park	19	STP March	F	3.0 March 711-Cosworth V8	fuel line	20/22
dnq	MONACO GP	Monte Carlo	18	STP March	F	3.0 March 711-Cosworth V8		22/23
ret	DUTCH GP	Zandvoort	19	STP March	F	3.0 March 711-Cosworth V8	engine	17/24
ret	FRENCH GP	Paul Ricard	18	STP March	F	3.0 March 711-Cosworth V8	fuel pump	22/24
	1972 Championship position: Unplaced							
ret	ARGENTINE GP	Buenos Aires	6	España Marlboro BRM	F	3.0 BRM P160B V12	accident – stuck throttle	21/22
ret	SPANISH GP	Jarama	28	España Marlboro BRM	F	3.0 BRM P160B V12	accident – no gears	22/26

GP Starts: 6 GP Wins: 0 Pole positions: 0 Fastest laps: 0 Points: 0

SOMMER, Raymond (F) b 31/8/1906, Paris – d 10/9/1950, Cadours Circuit, nr Toulouse

	Race	Circuit	No	Entrant	Tyres	Capacity/Car/Engine	Comment	Q Pos/Entries
	1950 Championship position: 10= Wins: 0 Pole positions: 0 Fastest laps: 0 Points scored: 3							
4	MONACO GP	Monte Carlo	42	Scuderia Ferrari	P	1.5 s/c Ferrari 125 V12	3 laps behind	9/21
ret	SWISS GP	Bremgarten	20	Scuderia Ferrari	P	2.0 Ferrari 166 V12 F2	suspension	13/18
ret	BELGIAN GP	Spa	6	Raymond Sommer	D	4.5 Lago-Talbot T26C 6	engine	5/14
ret	FRENCH GP	Reims	12	Automobiles Talbot-Darracq	D	4.5 Lago-Talbot T26C-GS 6	engine	17/20
ret	ITALIAN GP	Monza	12	Raymond Sommer	D	4.5 Lago-Talbot T26C 6	gearbox	8/27

GP Starts: 5 GP Wins: 0 Pole positions: 0 Fastest laps: 0 Points: 3

'SPARKEN, Mike' (Michel Poberejsky) (F) b 16/6/1930, Neuilly sur Seine, nr Paris

	Race	Circuit	No	Entrant	Tyres	Capacity/Car/Engine	Comment	Q Pos/Entries
	1955 Championship position: Unplaced							
7	BRITISH GP	Aintree	26	Equipe Gordini	E	2.5 Gordini Type 16 6	9 laps behind	23/25

GP Starts: 1 GP Wins: 0 Pole positions: 0 Fastest laps: 0 Points: 0

RAYMOND SOMMER

GIVEN the format of this book, Raymond Sommer's entry is brief, and unfortunately lack of space prevents me from writing more fully about this truly exceptional individual, who surely epitomised all that is good about motor racing – courage, tenacity, enthusiasm, persistence and sportsmanship.

The son of a rich carpet manufacturer in the Ardennes, Sommer first came to fame by defeating the works Alfas in his private machine at Le Mans in 1932, driving for all but three of the 24 hours because his co-driver, Luigi Chinetti, was unwell. The following year, he won again, this time with the legendary Tazio Nuvolari. In fact, Sommer made a big impression at the Sarthe track in the ensuing years, leading every race at some point until 1938.

Raymond also went grand prix racing, usually as an independent, for he could not bear the constraints that a team might impose. Thus he had to make do with whatever machinery was available, but he always drove it to its limit, taking great delight when he managed to beat a car from the mighty Scuderia Ferrari or Mercedes teams. In this context, his record of successes was remarkable, even if he failed to win a monoposto grand prix outright before the Second World War, although he did win the French sports car grand prix with Jean-Pierre Wimille in 1936.

During the war, Sommer served as a private in the French army and then as a member of the resistance, before serving time as a prisoner of war. Once he was released, he was eager to get back into racing action. In 1946, he enjoyed his best season, which included a famous victory in the Grand Prix of St Cloud after Wimille's Alfa failed; additional victories at Montlhéry, Forez, Lille and Marseilles ensured that he was crowned the champion of France for the third time.

In 1947, Sommer was a major player in his Scuderia Milano Maserati 4CL. He led the Pau Grand Prix until he crashed after a chaotic pit stop, during which he was covered in fuel. For the rest of the season, he was the main threat to the Alfas of Wimille and Carlo Felice Trossi, but more often than not some mechanical gremlin would conspire to ruin his chances. He drove a semi-works Ferrari the following year, winning the F2 Coupe des Petites Cylindrées at Reims and the GP of Florence, and taking third place in the Italian Grand Prix in Turin.

Having equipped himself with a big Talbot, Sommer was like a cat among the pigeons in 1949, hammering the car for all it was worth and frequently mixing it with the Italians, who viewed his on-the-edge, no-quarter-asked-or-given style with some concern. His only success came at the end of the year, however, in the Coupe de Salon at Montlhéry, where he was the beneficiary of a first-lap mêlée that eliminated some of the favourites.

Sommer was driving as well as ever in 1950, scoring a fourth place at Monaco in his nimble Formula 2 Ferrari, with which he also took F2 wins at Roubaix, Aix-les-Bains and Bremgarten. He reverted to his Talbot for the later championship grands prix, where power was all, but no points were gained. It came as a huge shock when the motor racing world learned of his death while competing in a minor end-of-season 500cc race at Cadours. It is thought that a wheel bearing seized on his Cooper, causing it to crash. As was his normal practice, he was only wearing a linen helmet, which offered no protection.

A year after his death, a superb monument was unveiled to Sommer the 'Coeur de Lion' at the Circuit de Cadours in the Midi Pyrenees, while another is situated in his home village of Mouzon in the Ardennes, where he was laid to rest.

'MIKE SPARKEN'

THIS Frenchman, real name Michael Poberejsky, was a great amateur enthusiast who raced sports cars under the pseudonym 'Mike Sparken'. In 1952, he ran an Aston Martin DB2 and won his class at the Coupe d'Autumne meeting at Montlhéry, but much of his success came in North African events. He won the 1955 sports car race at Agadir in his 3-litre Ferrari T750S, which he shipped to England and drove impressively in the British Empire Trophy before the clutch failed, and at Goodwood, where he placed second. His only single-seater drive of any note was at the wheel of the works Gordini at the British Grand Prix that year.

Subsequently, Sparken became involved in the world of classic cars, owning some very desirable machines. One of these was a Ferrari 275GTB, which he acquired in 1971. Subsequently, it was sold in April, 1995, for US$450,000 as part of a divorce settlement. A month later, the car went to auction at Coys and sold for a cool US$1 million. Ouch!

SCOTT SPEED

HE fitted Red Bull's requirements. He was an American, he had the name, the looks and the talk, but could Scott Speed walk the walk? In the end, the answer was no, and the USA must wait a while longer to unearth a 'real deal' that has been missing since the days of Mario Andretti. The young Speed was quite convincing in his early career, rising through the usual karting and junior car classes, and doing well enough to win the Red Bull American Driver Search. This earned the American the chance to compete in selected races in the 2003 British F3 series, but in the event illness curtailed his season and he had to wait until the following year to start his European racing in earnest. Despite still being in great discomfort from ulcerative colitis, he competed in both the Formula Renault and Eurocup series, and he became the first American to win a European Formula Junior title.

In March 2005, Scott impressed at an F1 Barcelona test to win a role with Red Bull Racing, assuming the third driver duties in both the US and Canadian grands prix. Meanwhile, the personable Californian was honing his racing skills in the very competitive GP2 series. Although he failed to win in this category, he was often a front-runner and finished a solid third in the final placings.

The long absence of a US driver from Formula 1 came to an end in 2006, when Scott took up a seat in the newly created Toro Rosso team alongside Vitantonio Liuzzi. The American thought he had bagged a vital point in just his third race, but he had overtaken David Coulthard under a yellow flag. The subsequent penalty denied the driver his hard-fought prize. Enraged, the normally easy-going Speed was further punished with a $5,000 fine for directing foul and abusive language at the stewards. Thereafter, his season was spent keeping his nose clean, trying to learn the circuits, and attempting to wrest the best from a largely undistinguished car and engine package. He did little wrong, but crucially perhaps failed to add a vital spark to the team with a drive of extra-special quality.

Scott's second season was spent running under constant speculation that his seat was under threat, and it was punctuated by a number of collisions that culminated in him spinning out of the European Grand Prix. Team principal Franz Tost had seen enough and drafted in a young Sebastian Vettel. The American's relations with Red Bull remained intact, however, and they set about preparing him for a potential drive in their NASCAR team. He negotiated the feeder ARCA and Craftsman Truck series with flying colours in 2008, and his performances in the Nationwide second-tier showed that he had distinct promise in the discipline. His two seasons in the Sprint Cup failed to bring the results everyone was looking for, however, and Speed was 'let go' at the end of 2010, without a ride initially. He has since found drives with a couple of the smaller teams. Still only 29, he has plenty of time to prove that he can make a mark in this 'take no prisoners' environment.

SPEED, Scott (USA) b 24/1/1983, Manteca, California

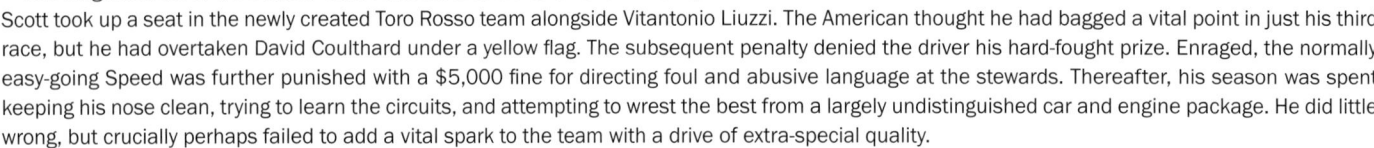

	Race	Circuit	No	Entrant	Tyres	Capacity/Car/Engine	Comment	Q Pos/Entries
	2005 Championship position: Unplaced							
app	CANADIAN GP	Montreal	37	Scuderia Toro Rosso	M	3.0 Toro Rosso STR01-Cosworth V10	*ran as 3rd driver in practice only*	– / –
app	U S GP	Indianapolis	37	Scuderia Toro Rosso	M	3.0 Toro Rosso STR01-Cosworth V10	*ran as 3rd driver in practice only*	– / –

	Race	Circuit	No	Entrant	Tyres	Capacity/Car/Engine	Comment	Q Pos/Entries
	2006 Championship position: Unplaced							
13	BAHRAIN GP	Sakhir Circuit	21	Scuderia Toro Rosso	M	3.0 Toro Rosso STR01-Cosworth V10	*1 lap behind*	16/22
ret	MALAYSIAN GP	Sepang	21	Scuderia Toro Rosso	M	3.0 Toro Rosso STR01-Cosworth V10	*clutch*	17/22
9*	AUSTRALIAN GP	Melbourne	21	Scuderia Toro Rosso	M	3.0 Toro Rosso STR01-Cosworth V10	*8th – but*25 sec penalty added*	19/22
15	SAN MARINO GP	Imola	21	Scuderia Toro Rosso	M	3.0 Toro Rosso STR01-Cosworth V10	*1 lap behind*	18/22
11	EUROPEAN GP	Nürburgring	21	Scuderia Toro Rosso	M	3.0 Toro Rosso STR01-Cosworth V10	*1 lap behind*	19/22
ret	SPANISH GP	Barcelona	21	Scuderia Toro Rosso	M	3.0 Toro Rosso STR01-Cosworth V10	*engine*	17/22
13	MONACO GP	Monte Carlo	21	Scuderia Toro Rosso	M	3.0 Toro Rosso STR01-Cosworth V10	*1 lap behind*	19/22
ret	BRITISH GP	Silverstone	21	Scuderia Toro Rosso	M	3.0 Toro Rosso STR01-Cosworth V10	*collision – accident damage*	15/22
10	CANADIAN GP	Montreal	21	Scuderia Toro Rosso	M	3.0 Toro Rosso STR01-Cosworth V10	*1 lap behind*	18/22
ret	U S GP	Indianapolis	21	Scuderia Toro Rosso	M	3.0 Toro Rosso STR01-Cosworth V10	*multiple accident on lap 1*	13/22
10	FRENCH GP	Magny Cours	21	Scuderia Toro Rosso	M	3.0 Toro Rosso STR01-Cosworth V10	*1 lap behind*	15/22
12	GERMAN GP	Hockenheim	21	Scuderia Toro Rosso	M	3.0 Toro Rosso STR01-Cosworth V10	*no time set/1 lap behind*	*22/22
11	HUNGARIAN GP	Hungaroring	21	Scuderia Toro Rosso	M	3.0 Toro Rosso STR01-Cosworth V10	*extra tyre stop/1 lap behind*	20/22
13	TURKISH GP	Istanbul	21	Scuderia Toro Rosso	M	3.0 Toro Rosso STR01-Cosworth V10	*1 lap behind*	18/22
13	ITALIAN GP	Monza	21	Scuderia Toro Rosso	M	3.0 Toro Rosso STR01-Cosworth V10	*1 lap behind*	15/22
14	CHINESE GP	Shanghai	21	Scuderia Toro Rosso	M	3.0 Toro Rosso STR01-Cosworth V10	*1 lap behind*	11/22
18/ret	JAPANESE GP	Suzuka	21	Scuderia Toro Rosso	M	3.0 Toro Rosso STR01-Cosworth V10	*steering/5 laps behind*	19/22
11	BRAZILIAN GP	Interlagos	21	Scuderia Toro Rosso	M	3.0 Toro Rosso STR01-Cosworth V10	*1 lap behind*	17/22
	2007 Championship position: Unplaced							
ret	AUSTRALIAN GP	Melbourne	19	Scuderia Toro Rosso	B	2.4 Toro Rosso STR02-Ferrari V8	*tyres*	18/22
14	MALAYSIAN GP	Sepang	19	Scuderia Toro Rosso	B	2.4 Toro Rosso STR02-Ferrari V8	*1 lap behind*	17/22
ret	BAHRAIN GP	Sakhir Circuit	19	Scuderia Toro Rosso	B	2.4 Toro Rosso STR02-Ferrari V8	*collision with Button on lap 1*	19/22
ret	SPANISH GP	Barcelona	19	Scuderia Toro Rosso	B	2.4 Toro Rosso STR02-Ferrari V8	*no time set/rear tyre*	*22/22
9	MONACO GP	Monte Carlo	19	Scuderia Toro Rosso	B	2.4 Toro Rosso STR02-Ferrari V8	*1 lap behind*	18/22
ret	CANADIAN GP	Montreal	19	Scuderia Toro Rosso	B	2.4 Toro Rosso STR02-Ferrari V8	*accident – front suspension*	16/22
13	U S GP	Indianapolis	19	Scuderia Toro Rosso	B	2.4 Toro Rosso STR02-Ferrari V8	*2 laps behind*	20/22
ret	FRENCH GP	Magny Cours	19	Scuderia Toro Rosso	B	2.4 Toro Rosso STR02-Ferrari V8	*hydraulics*	15/22
ret	BRITISH GP	Silverstone	19	Scuderia Toro Rosso	B	2.4 Toro Rosso STR02-Ferrari V8	*collision with Wurz*	15/22
ret	EUROPEAN GP	Nürburgring	19	Scuderia Toro Rosso	B	2.4 Toro Rosso STR02-Ferrari V8	*spun off on flooded track*	18/22

GP Starts: 28   GP Wins: 0   Pole positions: 0   Fastest laps: 0   Points: 0

MIKE SPENCE

HAVING overcome polio as a child with no ill effects, from a young age Mike Spence harboured dreams of becoming a racing driver. After his army service, he took up club racing in 1958 with a Turner, before moving into Formula Junior in 1960 with a Cooper-Austin. He made his Formula 1 debut the following year with an Emeryson-Climax at Solitude and won the minor Commander York Trophy at Silverstone in the same car. For 1962, he entered his own Formula Junior Lotus under the wing of Ian Walker's team, preparing the car himself in the evenings after his day job was done. He had only one big win – at Reims – but scored many placings and was taken on by Lotus on a three-year contract in 1963.

The fair-haired Englishman drove in the Formula Junior team, but the car proved difficult to handle and Mike's confidence dropped. Things gradually came around when the car was made more competitive, however, and he enjoyed a late-season boost when he stood in for the injured Trevor Taylor at Monza. In 1964, he was planning a season of Formula 2 and the occasional grand prix when he was thrust into the F1 team after Peter Arundell's accident.

For one so inexperienced, Spence coped well, especially as Arundell had made such a big impression in his few starts. Colin Chapman had no hesitation in keeping him in the team with Jim Clark for 1965, and he soon repaid that faith by winning the Race of Champions and performing well on other occasions. With Arundell fit to return for 1966, Mike was out of a drive, but he bade farewell by winning the non-championship South African GP on New Year's Day, before spending the rest of the year marking time with Tim Parnell's team. Joining the works BRM line-up for 1967 was a step back up, but he was given the task of sorting the troublesome BRM H16 and did superbly to take it to five points finishes. He also raced the fabulous winged Chaparral with Phil Hill. The car was quick, but fragile, suffering repeated transmission failures, but at Brands Hatch in the BOAC 500 it had its great day, crushing the Ferraris.

In 1968, Mike Spence had been racing for ten years; it had been a long haul to the top, but suddenly his talent had begun to flower and he was about to take his rightful place among the very top echelon of his profession. Yet fate would decree otherwise. The shadow of Jim Clark, which perhaps inevitably had held him back throughout his years at Lotus, passed over him once more as (after Jackie Stewart was sidelined with a wrist injury) he took over the late Scotsman's Lotus for the forthcoming Indianapolis 500.

In qualifying, everything had gone well, but when he took a team-mate's car out for a few shakedown laps, he lost control and crashed into the wall. The right front wheel flew back and struck him on the head, and poor Spence died in hospital a few hours later.

SPENCE, Mike (GB) b 30/12/1936, Croydon, Surrey – d 7/5/1968, Indianapolis Speedway, Indiana, USA

	Race	Circuit	No	Entrant	Tyres	Capacity/Car/Engine	Comment	Q Pos/Entries
	1963 Championship position: Unplaced							
13/ret	ITALIAN GP	Monza	6	Team Lotus	D	1.5 Lotus 25-Climax V8	*oil pressure/13 laps behind*	9/28
	1964 Championship position: 12th= Wins: 0 Pole positions: 0 Fastest laps: 0 Points scored: 4							
9	BRITISH GP	Brands Hatch	2	Team Lotus	D	1.5 Lotus 25-Climax V8	*3 laps behind*	=12/25
8	GERMAN GP	Nürburgring	2	Team Lotus	D	1.5 Lotus 33-Climax V8	*1 lap behind*	17/24
dns	"	"	23	Team Lotus	D	1.5 Lotus 25-Climax V8	*practice only – Mitter's car*	– / –
ret	AUSTRIAN GP	Zeltweg	2	Team Lotus	D	1.5 Lotus 33-Climax V8	*driveshaft*	8/20
6	ITALIAN GP	Monza	10	Team Lotus	D	1.5 Lotus 33-Climax V8	*1 lap behind*	8/25
7/ret	US GP	Watkins Glen	2	Team Lotus	D	1.5 Lotus 33-Climax V8	*fuel feed/Clark took over car/-8 laps*	6/19
ret	"	"	1	Team Lotus	D	1.5 Lotus 25-Climax V8	*fuel injection/given Clark's car*	– / –
4	MEXICAN GP	Mexico City	2	Team Lotus	D	1.5 Lotus 25-Climax V8		5/19
dns	"	" "	1	Team Lotus	D	1.5 Lotus 33-Climax V8	*practice only*	– / –

1965 Championship position: 8th   Wins: 0   Pole positions: 0   Fastest laps: 0   Points scored: 10

4	SOUTH AFRICAN GP	East London	6	Team Lotus	D	1.5 Lotus 33-Climax V8		=3/25
7	BELGIAN GP	Spa	18	Team Lotus	D	1.5 Lotus 33-Climax V8	1 lap behind	12/21
7	FRENCH GP	Clermont Ferrand	8	Team Lotus	D	1.5 Lotus 33-Climax V8	1 lap behind	=10/17
4	BRITISH GP	Silverstone	6	Team Lotus	D	1.5 Lotus 33-Climax V8		6/23
dns	"	"	77	Team Lotus	D	1.5 Lotus 25-Climax V8	practice only	- / -
8	DUTCH GP	Zandvoort	8	Team Lotus	D	1.5 Lotus 25-Climax V8	1 lap behind	8/17
ret	GERMAN GP	Nürburgring	2	Team Lotus	D	1.5 Lotus 33-Climax V8	driveshaft	6/22
11/ret	ITALIAN GP	Monza	26	Team Lotus	D	1.5 Lotus 33-Climax V8	alternator/13 laps behind	8/23
dns	"	"	28	Team Lotus	D	1.5 Lotus 25-Climax V8	practice only – Geki's car	- / -
ret	US GP	Watkins Glen	6	Team Lotus	D	1.5 Lotus 33-Climax V8	engine	4/18
dns	"	"	18	Team Lotus	D	1.5 Lotus 25-Climax V8	practice only – Solana's car	- / -
3	MEXICAN GP	Mexico City	6	Team Lotus	D	1.5 Lotus 33-Climax V8		6/18

1966 Championship position: 12th=   Wins: 0   Pole positions: 0   Fastest laps: 0   Points scored: 4

ret	MONACO GP	Monte Carlo	6	Reg Parnell Racing Ltd	F	2.0 Lotus 25-BRM V8	rear suspension	12/16
ret	BELGIAN GP	Spa	16	Reg Parnell Racing Ltd	F	2.0 Lotus 25-BRM V8	accident in rain storm	7/18
ret	FRENCH GP	Reims	32	Reg Parnell Racing Ltd	F	2.0 Lotus 25-BRM V8	clutch	10/17
ret	BRITISH GP	Brands Hatch	17	Reg Parnell Racing Ltd	F	2.0 Lotus 25-BRM V8	oil leak	9/20
5	DUTCH GP	Zandvoort	32	Reg Parnell Racing Ltd	F	2.0 Lotus 25-BRM V8	3 laps behind	12/18
ret	GERMAN GP	Nürburgring	15	Reg Parnell Racing Ltd	F	2.0 Lotus 25-BRM V8	electrics	14/30
5	ITALIAN GP	Monza	(42) 32	Reg Parnell Racing Ltd	F	2.0 Lotus 25-BRM V8	1 lap behind	14/22
ret	US GP	Watkins Glen	18	Reg Parnell Racing Ltd	F	2.0 Lotus 25-BRM V8	electrics	12/19
dns	MEXICAN GP	Mexico City	18	Reg Parnell Racing Ltd	F	2.0 Lotus 25-BRM V8	accident in practice	(12)/19

1967 Championship position: 10th   Wins: 0   Pole positions: 0   Fastest laps: 0   Points scored: 9

ret	SOUTH AFRICAN GP	Kyalami	6	Owen Racing Organisation	D	3.0 BRM P83 H16	oil pipe	13/18
6	MONACO GP	Monte Carlo	5	Owen Racing Organisation	D	3.0 BRM P83 H16	4 laps behind	=12/18
8	DUTCH GP	Zandvoort	10	Owen Racing Organisation	F	3.0 BRM P83 H16	gearbox problems/3 laps behind	12/17
5	BELGIAN GP	Spa	12	Owen Racing Organisation	G	3.0 BRM P83 H16	1 lap behind	11/18
dns	"	"	14	Owen Racing Organisation	G/D	2.1 BRM P261 V8	practice only	- / -
ret	FRENCH GP	Le Mans	11	Owen Racing Organisation	G	3.0 BRM P83 H16	driveshaft	12/15
ret	BRITISH GP	Silverstone	4	Owen Racing Organisation	D	3.0 BRM P83 H16	ignition	11/21
ret	GERMAN GP	Nürburgring	12	Owen Racing Organisation	G	3.0 BRM P83 H16	transmission	12/25
5	CANADIAN GP	Mosport Park	16	Owen Racing Organisation	G	3.0 BRM P83 H16	3 laps behind	10/19
5	ITALIAN GP	Monza	36	Owen Racing Organisation	G	3.0 BRM P83 H16	1 lap behind	12/18
ret	US GP	Watkins Glen	8	Owen Racing Organisation	G	3.0 BRM P83 H16	engine	13/18
5	MEXICAN GP	Mexico City	8	Owen Racing Organisation	G	3.0 BRM P83 H16	2 laps behind	11/19

1968 Championship position: Unplaced

ret	SOUTH AFRICAN GP	Kyalami	12	Owen Racing Organisation	G	3.0 BRM P115 H16	boiling fuel	13/23
dns	"	"	11	Owen Racing Organisation	G	3.0 BRM P126 V12	Rodriguez this raced car	- / -

GP Starts: 36   GP Wins: 0   Pole positions: 0   Fastest laps: 0   Points: 27

ALAN STACEY

HAVING made his competition debut in 1955, Alan Stacey spent three years in club racing, almost exclusively at the wheel of Lotus XI sports cars. He won seven races with his own car in 1956, before being invited to drive for the works during the following season.

Alan had the handicap of an artificial lower right leg, but this proved no obstacle to his racing, nor did it seem to limit his competitiveness, otherwise Colin Chapman certainly would not have signed him to race his sports cars full time for 1958. He won the Farningham Trophy at Brands Hatch and scored another victory at Crystal Palace, also taking third place in the Rouen GP. He made his grand prix debut at Silverstone that year, but in common with team-mates Innes Ireland and Graham Hill, he suffered a frustrating 1959 season as a lack of reliability undermined the Lotus team's efforts in F1, F2 and sports car racing.

Hill having departed for BRM, Stacey was promoted to the position of Ireland's number two in 1960, and once the European season started he was given one of Chapman's stunning rear-engined Lotus 18s to drive. He finished fourth in the International Trophy race, but retired at both Monaco and Zandvoort, where he had lain in third place before transmission trouble. During the Belgian GP at Spa, however, it is thought that the luckless Stacey was hit full in the face by a bird. Stunned, he lost control and suffered fatal injuries after being flung from the car when it hit a bank.

STACEY, Alan (GB) b 29/8/1933, Broomfield, nr Chelmsford, Essex – d 19/6/1960, Spa-Francorchamps Circuit, Belgium

	1958 Championship position: Unplaced							
	Race	Circuit	No	Entrant	Tyres	Capacity/Car/Engine	Comment	Q Pos/Entries
ret	BRITISH GP	Silverstone	18	Team Lotus	D	2.0 Lotus 16-Climax 4	overheating	20/21
	1959 Championship position: Unplaced							
8	BRITISH GP	Aintree	30	Team Lotus	D	2.5 Lotus 16-Climax 4	4 laps behind	12/30
ret	US GP	Sebring	11	Team Lotus	D	2.5 Lotus 16-Climax 4	clutch	12/31
	1960 Championship position: Unplaced							
ret	ARGENTINE GP	Buenos Aires	22	Team Lotus	D	2.5 Lotus 16-Climax 4	driver exhaustion – sunstroke	14/22
ret	MONACO GP	Monte Carlo	24	Team Lotus	D	2.5 Lotus 18-Climax 4	engine mountings	13/24
ret	DUTCH GP	Zandvoort	5	Team Lotus	D	2.5 Lotus 18-Climax 4	transmission	8/21
ret	BELGIAN GP	Spa	16	Team Lotus	D	2.5 Lotus 18-Climax 4	fatal accident	17/18

GP Starts: 7   GP Wins: 0   Pole positions: 0   Fastest laps: 0   Points: 0

STARRABBA, Prince Gaetano (I) b 3/12/1932, Palermo, Sicily

	1961 Championship position: Unplaced							
	Race	Circuit	No	Entrant	Tyres	Capacity/Car/Engine	Comment	Q Pos/Entries
ret	ITALIAN GP	Monza	72	Prince Gaetano Starrabba	D	1.5 Lotus 18-Maserati 4	engine	30/33

GP Starts: 1   GP Wins: 0   Pole positions: 0   Fastest laps: 0   Points: 0

STEWART, Ian (GB) b 15/7/1929, Edinburgh, Scotland

	1953 Championship position: Unplaced							
	Race	Circuit	No	Entrant	Tyres	Capacity/Car/Engine	Comment	Q Pos/Entries
ret	BRITISH GP	Silverstone	15	Ecurie Ecosse	D	2.0 Connaught A Type-Lea Francis 4	engine	20/29

GP Starts: 1   GP Wins: 0   Pole positions: 0   Fastest laps: 0   Points: 0

GAETANO STARRABBA

AN Italian nobleman, Gaetano Starrabba enjoyed a long competition career, mainly within the confines of his home shores. In the mid-1950s, the count raced a 2-litre Maserati sports car, before replacing it with a Ferrari Testa Rossa 500, which he drove into seventh place in the 1957 Targa Florio.

With the 1.5 litre formula in full swing by mid-1961 and plenty of races in which to take part, Gaetano purchased a Lotus 18 chassis powered by a four-cylinder Maserati unit. His best finishes with the car came in 1963, when he took sixth place at Syracuse and fifth in the Rome GP.

After a brief spell with the F3 Giannini-Brabham in 1964, Starrabba returned to sports cars and GTs, taking 13th and a class win in the 1966 Targa Florio with a Ferrari 250LM. Subsequently, he raced both a Porsche Carrera '6' and a 911.

IAN STEWART

NOT related to the brothers Jackie and Jimmy, young Scot Ian Stewart mainly raced his Jaguar XK120 north of the border in 1951, before coming to prominence as a founder member of the Ecurie Ecosse team in 1952. That year, he won the Jersey Road Race, the Wakefield Trophy and other sports car events in their Jaguar C-Type.

For 1953, the team laid more ambitious plans, running a Formula 2 Connaught, which Ian handled in the British GP and Libre events. They also contested Continental sports car races, Stewart finishing second in the Nürburgring 1000km, with Roy Salvadori, and fourth at Le Mans, with Peter Whitehead.

The following season began with an accident in the Buenos Aires 1000km in the team's D-Type, from which Ian escaped with minor injuries. When he got married shortly afterwards, he decided to retire from the sport and concentrate on his business interests.

JACKIE STEWART was the driving force behind the transformation of motor racing from a sport where death was almost routine to one where driver safety is of prime concern. When he began racing, the risks were blithely accepted with a shrug of the shoulders as an occupational hazard. However, the determined little Scot, who saw many of his friends and colleagues perish, pursued his campaign with remarkable fervour long into his retirement. He, more than any other individual, is responsible for the emergence of the highly organised and remarkably safe sport we know today. As if this weren't enough, Stewart was also a truly great racing driver, a triple world champion who was more than a worthy successor to his great idol, Jim Clark.

Motor racing was a familiar activity when young Jackie was growing up, for his brother, Jimmy – eight years his senior – was a driver for Ecurie Ecosse. However, Jackie was more interested in clay pigeon shooting. He was an excellent shot, winning many tournaments at home and abroad, and he was hoping to take part in the 1960 Rome Olympics, but missed the team when he had an 'off day' at the final trials. That was the biggest disappointment of his sporting life, worse than anything that he ever suffered during his racing days. His circuit career began in a casual way, at the wheel of a Healey Sprite and a Marcos, before he joined Ecurie Ecosse in 1963. Driving the team's GT and touring cars, he virtually swept the board. While still racing for them, he came under the guidance of Ken Tyrrell and drove a Cooper-BMC in Formula 3, where he set about thrashing the opposition. Colin Chapman tried him in his Ron Harris Formula 2 team and liked what he saw, putting the Scot into a Formula 1 Lotus for the Rand GP at Kyalami, where he retired in the first heat, but won the second.

Offered a seat alongside Jim Clark for 1965, Stewart wisely declined, preferring to join BRM, where he could learn his trade with Graham Hill and not face the pressure of being compared directly with his fellow Scot. A second place in the Race of Champions and a win in the International Trophy gave fair notice that here was a special talent, and his grand prix performances went from strength to strength, culminating in his first world championship win at Monza. In the 1966 Tasman series, he took the BRM to four victories, and then he won the opening grand prix of the year at Monaco in the 2-litre car. After that his luck changed. Victory seemed certain at the Indianapolis 500 until an engine failure close to the finish, and on his return to Europe he crashed the BRM in a rainstorm at Spa. Lying trapped in the car for some time, soaked in petrol and with a cracked collarbone, was an experience the Scot would never forget, and no doubt it acted as the catalyst for his subsequent safety crusade.

Jackie stayed with BRM for a third season in 1967, but it was a disappointing year, the H16 car proving woefully unreliable. His second place with it in Belgium was a remarkable achievement, especially as he had been obliged to hold it in gear for much of the race. The only compensation was a drive for Ferrari in the BOAC 500 at Brands Hatch, where he shared a P4 with Chris Amon, the pair taking second place and clinching the championship for Maranello. Of greater importance, however, was the development of his working partnership with Ken Tyrrell and Matra, Jackie taking the French Formula 2 car to victory in four of the last five races of the season as a prelude to a Formula 1 effort in 1968.

At last Stewart was in a competitive car, and following the death of Jim Clark he appeared to be the favourite to take the title. Unfortunately, his season was interrupted by a crash in a Formula 2 race, which sidelined him with a wrist injury. Although he missed only two grands prix, it was enough to crucially blunt his title challenge. A feature of the year was his brilliant win in the German GP in the most appalling conditions, truly one of his greatest drives, and there was no stopping him in 1969 as he swept to his first championship with six grand prix wins in the Matra MS80, a car he loved to drive.

For the 1970 season, Tyrrell was forced to resort to a March chassis, for Matra were running their own operation once more. Despite a promising start with wins in the Race of Champions and the Spanish GP, and a second place in the International Trophy, however, all was not well. The car was not up to the expectations of a world champion and therefore not of the required standard, and Tyrrell secretly set Derek Gardner to work on building his own grand prix challenger at the greatest possible speed. The new car was unveiled at the Canadian GP, where Stewart took pole position. The future was now clear and henceforth Tyrrell built his own cars. The 1971 season saw Jackie back at his brilliant best, using the new Tyrrell to devastating effect; he won six grands prix and easily took his second world championship. He was much in demand that year and undertook the ten-round Can-Am series for Carl Haas, winning two rounds in the Lola. The strain of transatlantic travel, however, was already taking its toll.

Jackie's health suffered in 1972 due to an ulcer, which caused him to miss six weeks of the season, enough for his title chances to disappear as an ebullient Emerson Fittipaldi made the most of his opportunities with the Lotus 72. Not that Stewart was about to let the title slip away without a fight. He won the French GP on his return and finished the year on a winning note with back-to-back victories at Mosport and Watkins Glen to sound a warning that he would not be so easy to beat in 1973. And so it proved. By then, Stewart was the complete driver, mentally and physically prepared to cope with every eventuality. He won as he pleased at Kyalami, Monte Carlo, Zandvoort and the Nürburgring, thus passing the late Jim Clark's number of wins to set a new record total of 27. His last race in Europe was one of his greatest. As he climbed through the field after a puncture at Monza (to take fourth place), it was a stirring sight to see him forced to drive at the limit lap after lap, picking off one car after another.

Jackie had decided to retire after the US GP at Watkins Glen and what would have been his 100th grand prix start, but the weekend was clouded by tragedy when his team-mate, François Cevert, was killed in practice. The Tyrrell team withdrew their cars, and the wonderful career of John Young Stewart was over.

Having stepped out of the cockpit for good, Jackie has laboured harder than ever, working in the corporate sector for such motorsport giants as Ford and Bridgestone. Eventually, he was persuaded to return to the front line to support his son, Paul, who raced with some success before setting up his own team, Paul Stewart Racing. The near-dominance of the operation in the junior formulas during the early 1990s led to an ambitious move into Formula 1 in 1997. With a five-year engine deal from Ford, and Jackie's business acumen and vast experience, Stewart Grand Prix was clearly going to be a serious force. Having the necessary funding to compete properly was a crucial factor in persuading the Stewarts to take the plunge.

Without doubt, 1999 was a momentous year for Jackie, who reached his 60th birthday, saw Stewart Grand Prix achieve their maiden victory at the European Grand Prix and took the decision to sell the Formula 1 team he had built up to Ford. Timing is everything, and in retrospect it turned out to be a very wise decision to sell before the costs of running a Formula 1 team became ruinous for all bar the elite.

In 2001, Jackie joined Sir Jack Brabham and Sir Stirling Moss as a knight of the realm. Freed of the day-to-day duties of running a team, he launched back into his entrepreneurial activities with all the vim and vigour of a man half his age. Happily, the bouncy Scot, replete with his trademark tartan cap and trews, is a regular fixture in the F1 paddock.

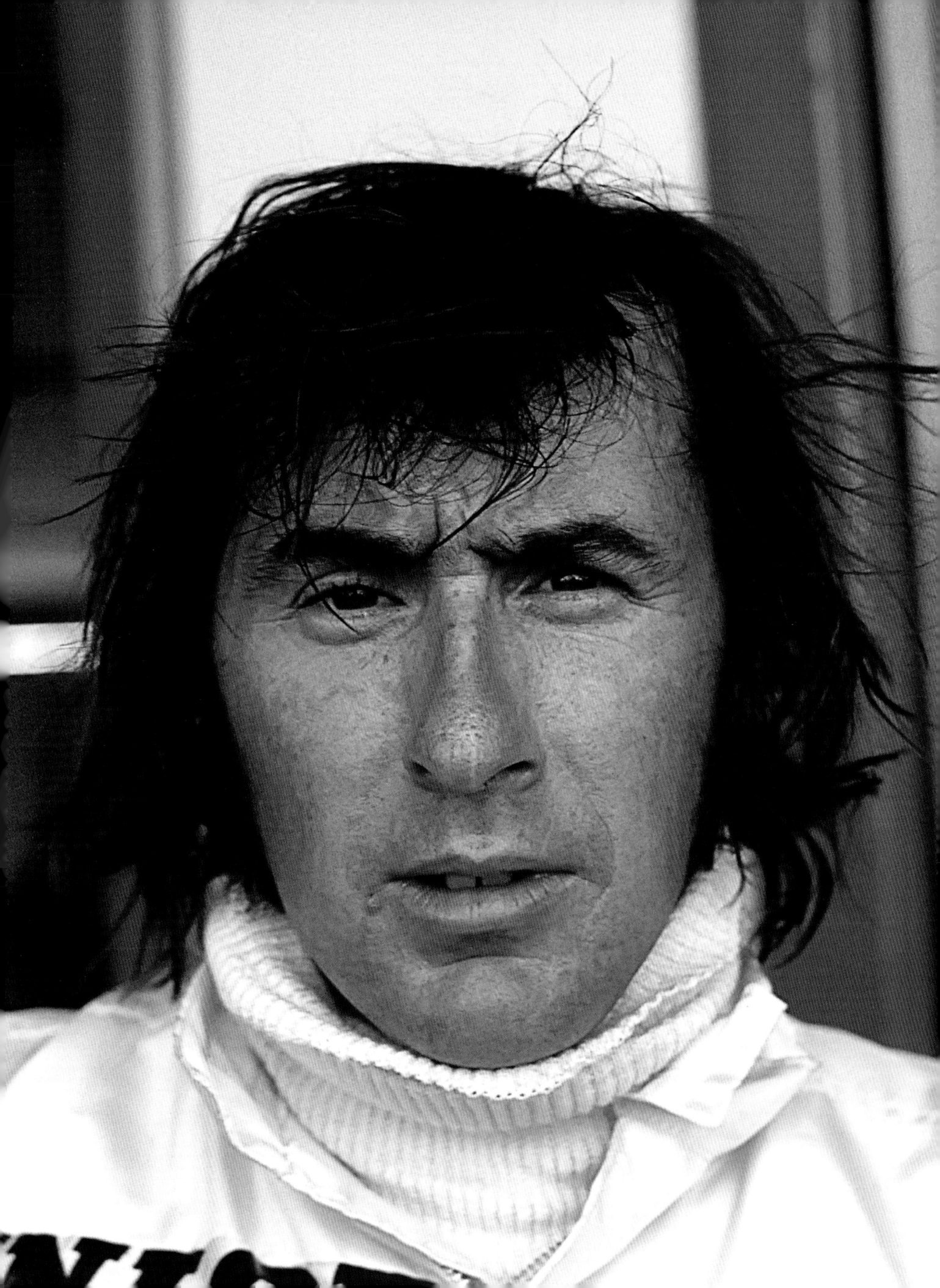

STEWART, Jackie (John Young) (GB) b 11/6/1939, Dumbuck, Dunbartonshire, Scotland

1965 Championship position: 3rd   Wins: 1   Pole positions: 0   Fastest laps: 0   Points scored: 34

	Race	Circuit	No	Entrant	Tyres	Capacity/Car/Engine	Comment	Q Pos/Entries
6	SOUTH AFRICAN GP	East London	4	Owen Racing Organisation	D	1.5 BRM P261 V8	2 laps behind	11/25
3	MONACO GP	Monte Carlo	4	Owen Racing Organisation	D	1.5 BRM P261 V8		3/17
2	BELGIAN GP	Spa	8	Owen Racing Organisation	D	1.5 BRM P261 V8		3/21
2	FRENCH GP	Clermont Ferrand	12	Owen Racing Organisation	D	1.5 BRM P261 V8		2/17
5	BRITISH GP	Silverstone	4	Owen Racing Organisation	D	1.5 BRM P261 V8		=3/23
2	DUTCH GP	Zandvoort	12	Owen Racing Organisation	D	1.5 BRM P261 V8		6/17
ret	GERMAN GP	Nürburgring	10	Owen Racing Organisation	D	1.5 BRM P261 V8	suspension	2/22
1	ITALIAN GP	Monza	32	Owen Racing Organisation	D	1.5 BRM P261 V8		3/23
ret	US GP	Watkins Glen	4	Owen Racing Organisation	D	1.5 BRM P261 V8	suspension	6/18
ret	MEXICAN GP	Mexico city	4	Owen Racing Organisation	D	1.5 BRM P261 V8	clutch	8/18

1966 Championship position: 7th   Wins: 1   Pole positions: 0   Fastest laps: 0   Points scored: 14

	Race	Circuit	No	Entrant	Tyres	Capacity/Car/Engine	Comment	Q Pos/Entries
1	MONACO GP	Monte Carlo	12	Owen Racing Organisation	D	2.0 BRM P261 V8		3/16
ret	BELGIAN GP	Spa	15	Owen Racing Organisation	D	2.0 BRM P261 V8	spun off in rainstorm – injured	3/18
dns	"	"	15	Owen Racing Organisation	G/D	3.0 BRM P83 H16	practice only	- / -
ret	BRITISH GP	Brands Hatch	4	Owen Racing Organisation	D	2.0 BRM P261 V8	engine	8/20
4	DUTCH GP	Zandvoort	14	Owen Racing Organisation	G	2.0 BRM P261 V8	2 laps behind	8/18
5	GERMAN GP	Nürburgring	6	Owen Racing Organisation	D	2.0 BRM P261 V8		3/30
ret	ITALIAN GP	Monza	28	Owen Racing Organisation	G	3.0 BRM P83 H16	fuel leak	9/22
ret	US GP	Watkins glen	4	Owen Racing Organisation	G	3.0 BRM P83 H16	engine	6/19
ret	MEXICAN GP	Mexico City	4	Owen Racing Organisation	G	3.0 BRM P83 H16	oil leak	10/19

1967 Championship position: 9th   Wins: 0   Pole positions: 0   Fastest laps: 0   Points scored: 10

	Race	Circuit	No	Entrant	Tyres	Capacity/Car/Engine	Comment	Q Pos/Entries
ret	SOUTH AFRICAN GP	Kyalami	5	Owen Racing Organisation	D	3.0 BRM P83 H16	engine	9/18
ret	MONACO GP	Monte Carlo	4	Owen Racing Organisation	F	2.1 BRM P261 V8	transmission	6/18
dns	"	"	4T	Owen Racing Organisation	F	3.0 BRM P83 H16	practice only	- / -
ret	DUTCH GP	Zandvoort	9	Owen Racing Organisation	G	3.0 BRM P83 H16	brakes	11/17
2	BELGIAN GP	Spa	14	Owen Racing Organisation	G	3.0 BRM P83 H16		6/18
dns	"	"	12	Owen Racing Organisation	G/D	2.1 BRM P261 V8	practice only	- / -
3	FRENCH GP	Le Mans	10	Owen Racing Organisation	G	2.1 BRM P261 V8	1 lap behind	10/15
dns	"	"	10	Owen Racing Organisation	G/D/F	3.0 BRM P83 H16	practice only	- / -
ret	BRITISH GP	Silverstone	3	Owen Racing Organisation	G	3.0 BRM P83 H16	transmission	12/21
ret	GERMAN GP	Nürburgring	11	Owen Racing Organisation	G	3.0 BRM P115 H16	transmission	4/25
dns	"	"	11	Owen Racing Organisation	G/D	3.0 BRM P83 H16	practice only	- / -
ret	CANADIAN GP	Mosport Park	15	Owen Racing Organisation	G	3.0 BRM P115 H16	throttle slides – spun off	9/19
ret	ITALIAN GP	Monza	34	Owen Racing Organisation	G	3.0 BRM P115 H16	engine	7/18
ret	US GP	Watkins Glen	7	Owen Racing Organisation	G	3.0 BRM P115 H16	fuel metering unit belt	10/18
ret	MEXICAN GP	Mexico City	7	Owen Racing Organisation	G	3.0 BRM P115 H16	engine vibration	12/19

1968 Championship position: 2   Wins: 3   Pole positions: 0   Fastest laps: 2   Points scored: 36

	Race	Circuit	No	Entrant	Tyres	Capacity/Car/Engine	Comment	Q Pos/Entries
ret	SOUTH AFRICAN GP	Kyalami	16	Matra International	D	3.0 Matra MS9-Cosworth V8	engine	3/23
dns	"	"	26	Matra International	D	1.6 Matra MS7-Cosworth 4	practice only	- / -
4	BELGIAN GP	Spa	7	Matra International	D	3.0 Matra MS10-Cosworth V8	pit stop – fuel/1 lap behind	2/18
1	DUTCH GP	Zandvoort	8	Matra International	D	3.0 Matra MS10-Cosworth V8		5/19
3	FRENCH GP	Rouen	28	Matra International	D	3.0 Matra MS10-Cosworth V8	pit stop – tyres/1 lap behind	2/18
6	BRITISH GP	Brands Hatch	14	Matra International	D	3.0 Matra MS10-Cosworth V8	2 laps behind	=6/20
1	GERMAN GP	Nürburgring	6	Matra International	D	3.0 Matra MS10-Cosworth V8	FL	6/20
ret	ITALIAN GP	Monza	4	Matra International	D	3.0 Matra MS10-Cosworth V8	engine	6/24
6	CANADIAN GP	St Jovite	14	Matra International	D	3.0 Matra MS10-Cosworth V8	pit stop – suspension/7 laps behind	=10/22
1	US GP	Watkins Glen	15	Matra International	D	3.0 Matra MS10-Cosworth V8	FL	2/21
7	MEXICAN GP	Mexico City	15	Matra International	D	3.0 Matra MS10-Cosworth V8	fuel feed problems/1 lap behind	7/21

1969 WORLD CHAMPION   Wins: 6   Pole positions: 2   Fastest laps: 5   Points scored: 63

	Race	Circuit	No	Entrant	Tyres	Capacity/Car/Engine	Comment	Q Pos/Entries
1	SOUTH AFRICAN GP	Kyalami	7	Matra International	D	3.0 Matra MS10-Cosworth V8	FL	4/18
dns	"	"	20	Matra International	D	3.0 Matra MS80-Cosworth V8	practice only	- / -
1	SPANISH GP	Montjuich Park	7	Matra International	D	3.0 Matra MS80-Cosworth V8		4/14
ret	MONACO GP	Monte Carlo	7	Matra International	D	3.0 Matra MS80-Cosworth V8	driveshaft/FL	1/16
1	DUTCH GP	Zandvoort	4	Matra International	D	3.0 Matra MS80-Cosworth V8	FL	2/15
dns	"	"	4T	Matra International	D	3.0 Matra MS84-Cosworth V8 4WD	practice only	- / -
1	FRENCH GP	Clermont Ferrand	2	Matra International	D	3.0 Matra MS80-Cosworth V8	FL	1/13
dns	"	"	2T	Matra International	D	3.0 Matra MS84-Cosworth V8 4WD	practice only	- / -
1	BRITISH GP	Silverstone	3	Matra International	D	3.0 Matra MS80-Cosworth V8	FL	2/17
dns	"	"	30	Matra International	D	3.0 Matra MS84-Cosworth V8 4WD	practice only	- / -
2	GERMAN GP	Nürburgring	7	Matra International	D	3.0 Matra MS80-Cosworth V8		2/26
dns	"	"	7T	Matra International	D	3.0 Matra MS84-Cosworth V8 4WD	practice only	- / -
1	ITALIAN GP	Monza	20	Matra International	D	3.0 Matra MS80-Cosworth V8		3/15
dns	"	"	24	Matra International	D	3.0 Matra MS84-Cosworth V8 4WD	practice only	- / -
ret	CANADIAN GP	Mosport Park	17	Matra International	D	3.0 Matra MS80-Cosworth V8	hit by Ickx	=2/20
ret	US GP	Watkins Glen	3	Matra International	D	3.0 Matra MS80-Cosworth V8	engine	3/18
dns	"	"	3	Matra International	D	3.0 Matra MS84-Cosworth V8 4WD	practice only	- / -
4	MEXICAN GP	Mexico City	3	Matra International	D	3.0 Matra MS80-Cosworth V8		3/17

1970 Championship position: 5th=   Wins: 1   Pole positions: 4   Fastest laps: 0   Points scored: 25

	Race	Circuit	No	Entrant	Tyres	Capacity/Car/Engine	Comment	Q Pos/Entries
3	SOUTH AFRICAN GP	Kyalami	1	Tyrrell Racing Organisation	D	3.0 March 701-Cosworth V8		1/24
1	SPANISH GP	Jarama	1	Tyrrell Racing Organisation	D	3.0 March 701-Cosworth V8		3/22
ret	MONACO GP	Monte Carlo	21	Tyrrell Racing Organisation	D	3.0 March 701-Cosworth V8	engine	1/21
ret	BELGIAN GP	Spa	11	Tyrrell Racing Organisation	D	3.0 March 701-Cosworth V8	engine	1/18
2	DUTCH GP	Zandvoort	5	Tyrrell Racing Organisation	D	3.0 March 701-Cosworth V8		2/24
9	FRENCH GP	Clermont Ferrand	1	Tyrrell Racing Organisation	D	3.0 March 701-Cosworth V8	pit stop – ignition	4/23

ret	BRITISH GP	Brands Hatch	1	Tyrrell Racing Organisation	D	3.0 March 701-Cosworth V8	melted clutch line – fire	8/25
ret	GERMAN GP	Hockenheim	1	Tyrrell Racing Organisation	D	3.0 March 701-Cosworth V8	engine	7/25
ret	AUSTRIAN GP	Österreichring	1	Tyrrell Racing Organisation	D	3.0 March 701-Cosworth V8	split fuel line	4/24
2	ITALIAN GP	Monza	18	Tyrrell Racing Organisation	D	3.0 March 701-Cosworth V8		4/27
dns	"	"	18	Tyrrell Racing Organisation	D	3.0 Tyrrell 001-Cosworth V8	practice only	– / –
ret	CANADIAN GP	St Jovite	3	Tyrrell Racing Organisation	D	3.0 Tyrrell 001-Cosworth V8	broken stub axle	1/20
dns	"	" "	1	Tyrrell Racing Organisation	D	3.0 March 701-Cosworth V8	practice only	– / –
ret	US GP	Watkins Glen	1	Tyrrell Racing Organisation	D	3.0 Tyrrell 001-Cosworth V8	engine – oil leak	2/27
dns	"	"	33	Tyrrell Racing Organisation	D	3.0 Tyrrell 001-Cosworth V8	practice only	– / –
ret	MEXICAN GP	Mexico City	1	Tyrrell Racing Organisation	D	3.0 Tyrrell 001-Cosworth V8	steering – hit dog	2/18

1971 WORLD CHAMPION Wins: 6 Pole positions: 6 Fastest laps: 3 Points scored: 62

2	SOUTH AFRICAN GP	Kyalami	9	Elf Team Tyrrell	G	3.0 Tyrrell 001-Cosworth V8		1/25
dns	" "	"	10	Elf Team Tyrrell	G	3.0 Tyrrell 002-Cosworth V8	practice only – Cevert's car	– / –
1	SPANISH GP	Montjuich Park	11	Elf Team Tyrrell	G	3.0 Tyrrell 003-Cosworth V8		3/22
dns	" "	" " "	11T	Elf Team Tyrrell	G	3.0 Tyrrell 001-Cosworth V8	practice only	– / –
1	MONACO GP	Monte Carlo	11	Elf Team Tyrrell	G	3.0 Tyrrell 003-Cosworth V8	FL	1/23
dns	"	" "	11T	Elf Team Tyrrell	G	3.0 Tyrrell 001-Cosworth V8	practice only	– / –
11	DUTCH GP	Zandvoort	5	Elf Team Tyrrell	G	3.0 Tyrrell 003-Cosworth V8	spin in rain/5 laps behind	3/24
dns	"	"	5T	Elf Team Tyrrell	G	3.0 Tyrrell 001-Cosworth V8	practice only	– / –
1	FRENCH GP	Paul Ricard	11	Elf Team Tyrrell	G	3.0 Tyrrell 003-Cosworth V8	FL	1/24
dns	"	"	11T	Elf Team Tyrrell	G	3.0 Tyrrell 001-Cosworth V8	practice only	– / –
1	BRITISH GP	Silverstone	12	Elf Team Tyrrell	G	3.0 Tyrrell 003-Cosworth V8	FL	=1/24
1	GERMAN GP	Nürburgring	2	Elf Team Tyrrell	G	3.0 Tyrrell 003-Cosworth V8		1/23
dns	"	"	2T	Elf Team Tyrrell	G	3.0 Tyrrell 001-Cosworth V8	practice only	– / –
ret	AUSTRIAN GP	Österreichring	11	Elf Team Tyrrell	G	3.0 Tyrrell 003-Cosworth V8	lost wheel	2/22
dns	"	"	11T	Elf Team Tyrrell	G	3.0 Tyrrell 001-Cosworth V8	practice only	– / –
ret	ITALIAN GP	Monza	30	Elf Team Tyrrell	G	3.0 Tyrrell 003-Cosworth V8	engine	7/24
1	CANADIAN GP	Mosport Park	11	Elf Team Tyrrell	G	3.0 Tyrrell 003-Cosworth V8		1/27
dns	"	" "	11T	Elf Team Tyrrell	G	3.0 Tyrrell 001-Cosworth V8	practice only	– / –
5	US GP	Watkins Glen	8	Elf Team Tyrrell	G	3.0 Tyrrell 003-Cosworth V8	chunking tyres	1/32

1972 Championship position: 2nd Wins: 4 Pole positions: 2 Fastest laps: 4 Points scored: 45

1	ARGENTINE GP	Buenos Aires	21	Elf Team Tyrrell	G	3.0 Tyrrell 003-Cosworth V8	FL	2/22
ret	SOUTH AFRICAN GP	Kyalami	1	Elf Team Tyrrell	G	3.0 Tyrrell 003-Cosworth V8	gearbox	1/27
dns	" "	"	1T	Elf Team Tyrrell	G	3.0 Tyrrell 004-Cosworth V8	practice only	– / –
ret	SPANISH GP	Jarama	1	Elf Team Tyrrell	G	3.0 Tyrrell 003-Cosworth V8	spun – holed radiator	4/26
dns	"	"	1T	Elf Team Tyrrell	G	3.0 Tyrrell 004-Cosworth V8	practice only	– / –
4	MONACO GP	Monte Carlo	1	Elf Team Tyrrell	G	3.0 Tyrrell 004-Cosworth V8	2 spins/misfire/2 laps behind	=8/25
dns	"	" "	1T	Elf Team Tyrrell	G	3.0 Tyrrell 003-Cosworth V8	practice only	– / –
1	FRENCH GP	Clermont Ferrand	4	Elf Team Tyrrell	G	3.0 Tyrrell 003-Cosworth V8		3/29
2	BRITISH GP	Brands Hatch	1	Elf Team Tyrrell	G	3.0 Tyrrell 003-Cosworth V8	FL	4/27
dns	"	" "	1	Elf Team Tyrrell	G	3.0 Tyrrell 005-Cosworth V8	accident in practice	– / –
11/ret	GERMAN GP	Nürburgring	1	Elf Team Tyrrell	G	3.0 Tyrrell 003-Cosworth V8	collision – Regazzoni/1 lap behind	2/27
7	AUSTRIAN GP	Österreichring	1	Elf Team Tyrrell	G	3.0 Tyrrell 005-Cosworth V8	handling problems	3/26
ret	ITALIAN GP	Monza	1	Elf Team Tyrrell	G	3.0 Tyrrell 005-Cosworth V8	transmission	3/27
dns	"	"	1T	Elf Team Tyrrell	G	3.0 Tyrrell 004-Cosworth V8	practice only	– / –
1	CANADIAN GP	Mosport Park	1	Elf Team Tyrrell	G	3.0 Tyrrell 005-Cosworth V8	FL	=4/25
dns	"	" "	1T	Elf Team Tyrrell	G	3.0 Tyrrell 004-Cosworth V8	practice only	– / –
dns	"	" "	2T	Elf Team Tyrrell	G	3.0 Tyrrell 006-Cosworth V8	practice only	– / –
1	US GP	Watkins Glen	1	Elf Team Tyrrell	G	3.0 Tyrrell 005-Cosworth V8	FL	1/32

Jackie Stewart takes his Tyrrell 006 to victory in the 1973 Monaco Grand Prix. Pole position and fastest race lap merely emphasised the Scot's dominance as he secured his third win on the Monte Carlo street circuit.

	1973 WORLD CHAMPION	Wins: 5	Pole positions: 3	Fastest laps: 1	Points scored: 71				
3	ARGENTINE GP	Buenos Aires	6	Elf Team Tyrrell	G	3.0 Tyrrell 005-Cosworth V8	*slow puncture*	4/19
2	BRAZILIAN GP	Rio	3	Elf Team Tyrrell	G	3.0 Tyrrell 005-Cosworth V8		8/20
1	SOUTH AFRICAN GP	Kyalami	(4) 3	Elf Team Tyrrell	G	3.0 Tyrrell 006-Cosworth V8		16/25
dns	" "	"	4	Elf Team Tyrrell	G	3.0 Tyrrell 005-Cosworth V8	*practice crash – brake failure*	(3)/25
ret	SPANISH GP	Montjuich Park	3	Elf Team Tyrrell	G	3.0 Tyrrell 006-Cosworth V8	*disc brake mounting*	4/22
dns	"	" "	3T	Elf Team Tyrrell	G	3.0 Tyrrell 005-Cosworth V8	*practice only*	– / –
1	BELGIAN GP	Zolder	5	Elf Team Tyrrell	G	3.0 Tyrrell 006-Cosworth V8		6/23
1	MONACO GP	Monte Carlo	5	Elf Team Tyrrell	G	3.0 Tyrrell 006-Cosworth V8		1/26
dns	"	" "	5T	Elf Team Tyrrell	G	3.0 Tyrrell 005-Cosworth V8	*practice only*	– / –
5	SWEDISH GP	Anderstorp	5	Elf Team Tyrrell	G	3.0 Tyrrell 006-Cosworth V8	*brake problems*	3/22
dns	"	"	5T	Elf Team Tyrrell	G	3.0 Tyrrell 005-Cosworth V8	*practice only*	– / –
4	FRENCH GP	Paul Ricard	5	Elf Team Tyrrell	G	3.0 Tyrrell 006-Cosworth V8		1/25
dns	"	" "	5T	Elf Team Tyrrell	G	3.0 Tyrrell 005-Cosworth V8	*practice only*	– / –
10	BRITISH GP	Silverstone	5	Elf Team Tyrrell	G	3.0 Tyrrell 006-Cosworth V8	*pit stop to remove debris/1 lap behind*	=4/29
dns	"		42	Elf Team Tyrrell	G	3.0 Tyrrell 005-Cosworth V8	*practice only*	– / –
1	DUTCH GP	Zandvoort	5	Elf Team Tyrrell	G	3.0 Tyrrell 006-Cosworth V8		2/24
dns	"	"	5T	Elf Team Tyrrell	G	3.0 Tyrrell 005-Cosworth V8	*practice only*	– / –
1	GERMAN GP	Nürburgring	5	Elf Team Tyrrell	G	3.0 Tyrrell 006-Cosworth V8		1/23
dns	"	"	5T	Elf Team Tyrrell	G	3.0 Tyrrell 005-Cosworth V8	*practice only*	– / –
2	AUSTRIAN GP	Österreichring	5	Elf Team Tyrrell	G	3.0 Tyrrell 006-Cosworth V8		7/25
4	ITALIAN GP	Monza	5	Elf Team Tyrrell	G	3.0 Tyrrell 006-Cosworth V8	*pit stop – tyres/FL*	6/25
5	CANADIAN GP	Mosport Park	5	Elf Team Tyrrell	G	3.0 Tyrrell 006-Cosworth V8	*1 lap behind*	9/26
dns	US GP	Watkins Glen	5	Elf Team Tyrrell	G	3.0 Tyrrell 006-Cosworth V8	*withdrawn after Cevert's death*	(6)/28

GP Starts: 99   GP Wins: 27   Pole positions: 17   Fastest laps: 15   Points: 360

JIMMY STEWART

AFTER cutting his teeth on hill-climbs and scratch races with a Healey in 1951/52, Jimmy Stewart became an integral part of the Ecurie Ecosse team the following year, racing both the Jaguar C-Type and XK120 with great success. Then he was given the chance to race the team's Cooper-Bristol in that year's British GP and ran in sixth place, going very quickly indeed, before spinning out.

Back with the Ecosse C-Type in 1954, Stewart continued to build a reputation as a very fast and fearless driver. He won three races in one meeting at Goodwood, but his season was soon cut short by injury when he was involved in a collision at Le Mans and thrown from the car, suffering a fractured elbow.

He was back in 1955, but another crash in practice for a major sports car race at Silverstone left him badly injured. This time he retired, but later could enjoy the many fabulous successes of his younger brother, Jackie.

STEWART, Jimmy (GB) b 6/3/1931, Dumbuck, Dunbartonshire, Scotland – d 3/1/2008, Glasgow, Scotland

	1953 Championship position: Unplaced							
	Race	Circuit	No	Entrant	Tyres	Capacity/Car/Engine	Comment	Q Pos/Entries
ret	BRITISH GP	Silverstone	18	Ecurie Ecosse	D	2.0 Cooper T20-Bristol 6	*spun off*	15/29

GP Starts: 1   GP Wins: 0   Pole positions: 0   Fastest laps: 0   Points: 0

STOHR, Siegfried (I) b 10/10/1952, Rimini

	1981 Championship position: Unplaced							
	Race	Circuit	No	Entrant	Tyres	Capacity/Car/Engine	Comment	Q Pos/Entries
dnq	US GP WEST	Long Beach	30	Arrows Racing Team	M	3.0 Arrows A3-Cosworth V8		28/29
ret	BRAZILIAN GP	Rio	30	Arrows Racing Team	M	3.0 Arrows A3-Cosworth V8	*collision with Tambay*	21/30
9	ARGENTINE GP	Buenos Aires	30	Arrows Racing Team	M	3.0 Arrows A3-Cosworth V8	*1 lap behind*	19/29
dnq	SAN MARINO GP	Imola	30	Arrows Racing Team	M	3.0 Arrows A3-Cosworth V8		25/30
ret/dns*	BELGIAN GP	Zolder	30	Arrows Racing Team	M	3.0 Arrows A3-Cosworth V8	*ran into Patrese at first start	13/31
ret	MONACO GP	Monte Carlo	30	Arrows Racing Team	M	3.0 Arrows A3-Cosworth V8	*electrics*	14/31
ret	SPANISH GP	Jarama	30	Arrows Racing Team	M	3.0 Arrows A3-Cosworth V8	*engine*	23/30
dnq	FRENCH GP	Dijon	30	Arrows Racing Team	M	3.0 Arrows A3-Cosworth V8		25/29
ret	BRITISH GP	Silverstone	30	Arrows Racing Team	P	3.0 Arrows A3-Cosworth V8	*collision with Rebaque*	18/30
12	GERMAN GP	Hockenheim	30	Arrows Racing Team	P	3.0 Arrows A3-Cosworth V8	*1 lap behind*	24/30
ret	AUSTRIAN GP	Österreichring	30	Arrows Racing Team	P	3.0 Arrows A3-Cosworth V8	*spun off – could not restart*	24/28
7	DUTCH GP	Zandvoort	30	Arrows Racing Team	P	3.0 Arrows A3-Cosworth V8	*3 laps behind*	21/30
dnq	ITALIAN GP	Monza	30	Arrows Racing Team	P	3.0 Arrows A3-Cosworth V8		28/30

GP Starts: 8 (9)   GP Wins: 0   Pole positions: 0   Fastest laps: 0   Points: 0

SIEGFRIED STOHR

BORN in Rimini of an Italian mother and a German father, Siegfried Stohr was successful in both karts and the junior Formula Italia championship, which he won in 1977 on the back of several excellent performances. Then he moved up to take the 1978 Italian F3 championship with a Chevron-Toyota, a title that was very much secondary to the European crown at the time. Nevertheless, he jumped straight into Formula 2 for 1979, taking second places at Vallelunga and Pau with a Chevron, before switching less successfully to a March.

Hoping to build on his satisfactory first season, Stohr joined the Alan Docking team to race a Toleman in 1980 and did a very sound job, scoring a win at Enna and a second place at Pau, and earning fourth place in the European F2 championship, won by Brian Henton.

Having taken his Beta sponsorship to Arrows the following season, Stohr never really got to grips with things in his one shot at grand prix racing. Initially, he was very much the number two to his big pal, Riccardo Patrese, and his confidence took a serious knock when he ran into the back of his team-mate's car on a chaotic grid at Zolder, seriously injuring a team mechanic.

The mid-season switch to Pirelli tyres was another factor in Stohr's disappointing year, although he did come close to a championship point with a seventh place at Zandvoort. However, failure to qualify for his home race at Monza was the final straw for the sensitive Stohr who, having been replaced by Jacques Villeneuve for the North American races, decided to retire from racing. Subsequently, he set up a very successful racing school known as Guidare Pilotare, which is based at the Misano circuit, near his birthplace of Rimini.

ROLF STOMMELEN

ALTHOUGH both Kurt Ahrens and Gerhard Mitter promised much, they failed to make a permanent mark on grand prix racing. Rolf Stommelen, however, became the first German driver since Wolfgang von Trips to appear regularly on the F1 starting grids.

After campaigning his private Porsche 904 GTS in 1964/65, Rolf was invited to join the works team for endurance racing. He soon became a key member of the team, winning the 1967 Targa Florio with Paul Hawkins, and the Daytona 24-hours and Paris 1000km in 1968, as well as taking many placings. He was also successfully involved in Porsche's European mountain-climb programme with the 2-litre Bergspyder.

After dipping his toe into the water by competing in the 1969 German GP with a hired F2 Lotus, Stommelen gained sponsorship for a full F1 season in 1970 with a works Brabham and showed distinct promise, highlighted by a brilliant drive in Austria, where he drove from 18th to finish third. He was also busy making his mark in Formula 2 with the Eifelland Caravans-backed Brabham, and was a works driver for the Alfa Romeo sports car team, for whom he drove until 1974.

For 1971, Stommelen took his sponsorship money to Surtees, but the partnership produced little and relations were strained, so it was no surprise when he branched out on his own for 1972 with the curious-looking March-based Eifelland-Ford, which performed even more lamely than its appearance promised. Temporarily on the Formula 1 sidelines after this fiasco, he grabbed the lifeline of a Brabham drive after Andrea de Adamich's accident at Silverstone in 1973 and then was called up to replace Guy Edwards in the Embassy Hill Lola in mid-1974.

Rolf got on well with Hill and secured a seat for 1975, but his first race in the new Hill GH1 at the trouble-torn Spanish GP ended in disaster when a wing stay failed while he was leading the race. The car was pitched into the crowd, killing four spectators and seriously injuring the driver. Happily, Rolf soon recovered and returned later in the year, but by then Tony Brise had emerged as Hill's prize asset.

For 1976, Stommelen returned to sports car racing with Martini Porsche, winning at Enna and Watkins Glen, which helped him to a couple of rides in the works Brabham that season. The following year, he won the Nürburgring 1000km for Porsche and also took the German national touring car title in the Gelo Racing 935 turbo.

With Warsteiner backing the Arrows team in 1978, Rolf was given the second seat and a chance to renew his grand prix career, but the season was a severe disappointment, and he returned to sports car and GT racing, where he was still a competitive runner. In 1980, he won the Daytona 24-hours and the Nürburgring 1000km in a Porsche, and he continued to race for such top endurance teams as Porsche, Lancia and Rondeau, as well as trying his hand at IMSA.

While racing a Porsche 'replica' 935 in the last category, he lost his life after crashing in a race at Riverside in April, 1983.

STOMMELEN, Rolf (D) b 11/7/1943, Siegen – d 24/4/1983, Riverside Circuit, California, USA

1969 Championship position: Unplaced

	Race	Circuit	No	Entrant	Tyres	Capacity/Car/Engine	Comment	Q Pos/Entries
8*	GERMAN GP (F2)	Nurburging	22	Roy Winkelmann Racing Ltd	F	1.6 Lotus 59B-Ford 4 F2	*4th in F2 class	22/26

1970 Championship position: 11th Wins: 0 Pole positions: 0 Fastest laps: 0 Points scored: 10

	Race	Circuit	No	Entrant	Tyres	Capacity/Car/Engine	Comment	Q Pos/Entries
ret	SOUTH AFRICAN GP	Kyalami	14	Auto Motor Und Sport	G	3.0 Brabham BT33-Cosworth V8	engine	15/24
ret	SPANISH GP	Jarama	24	Auto Motor Und Sport	G	3.0 Brabham BT33-Cosworth V8	engine	20/22
dnq	MONACO GP	Monte Carlo	6	Auto Motor Und Sport	G	3.0 Brabham BT33-Cosworth V8	car not seeded	15/21
5	BELGIAN GP	Spa	19	Auto Motor Und Sport	G	3.0 Brabham BT33-Cosworth V8		7/18
dnq	DUTCH GP	Zandvoort	19	Auto Motor Und Sport	G	3.0 Brabham BT33-Cosworth V8		22/24
7	FRENCH GP	Clermont Ferrand	22	Auto Motor Und Sport	G	3.0 Brabham BT33-Cosworth V8		14/23
dns	BRITISH GP	Brands Hatch	18	Auto Motor Und Sport	G	3.0 Brabham BT33-Cosworth V8	accident in practice	(10)/25
5	GERMAN GP	Hockenheim	21	Auto Motor Und Sport	G	3.0 Brabham BT33-Cosworth V8	1 lap behind	11/25
3	AUSTRIAN GP	Österreichring	11	Auto Motor Und Sport	G	3.0 Brabham BT33-Cosworth V8		16/24
5	ITALIAN GP	Monza	46	Auto Motor Und Sport	G	3.0 Brabham BT33-Cosworth V8		20/27
ret	CANADIAN GP	St Jovite	12	Auto Motor Und Sport	G	3.0 Brabham BT33-Cosworth V8	steering	18/20
12	US GP	Watkins Glen	16	Auto Motor Und Sport	G	3.0 Brabham BT33-Cosworth V8	pit stop – brakes/-4 laps	19/27
ret	MEXICAN GP	Mexico City	16	Auto Motor Und Sport	G	3.0 Brabham BT33-Cosworth V8	fuel system	17/18

1971 Championship position: 18th= Wins: 0 Pole positions: 0 Fastest laps: 0 Points scored: 3

	Race	Circuit	No	Entrant	Tyres	Capacity/Car/Engine	Comment	Q Pos/Entries
12	SOUTH AFRICAN GP	Kyalami	21	Auto Motor Und Sport-Team Surtees	F	3.0 Surtees TS7-Cosworth V8	2 laps behind	15/25
ret	SPANISH GP	Montjuich Park	25	Auto Motor Und Sport-Team Surtees	F	3.0 Surtees TS9-Cosworth V8	fuel pressure release valve	19/22
6	MONACO GP	Monte Carlo	24	Auto Motor Und Sport-Team Surtees	F	3.0 Surtees TS9-Cosworth V8	1 lap behind	=15/23
dsq	DUTCH GP	Zandvoort	29	Auto Motor Und Sport-Team Surtees	F	3.0 Surtees TS9-Cosworth V8	spun off – push start	10/24
11	FRENCH GP	Paul Ricard	24	Auto Motor Und Sport-Team Surtees	F	3.0 Surtees TS9-Cosworth V8	2 laps behind	10/24
5	BRITISH GP	Silverstone	24	Auto Motor Und Sport-Team Surtees	F	3.0 Surtees TS9-Cosworth V8	1 lap behind	12/24
10	GERMAN GP	Nürburgring	12	Auto Motor Und Sport-Team Surtees	F	3.0 Surtees TS9-Cosworth V8	handling problems/-1 lap	12/23
7	AUSTRIAN GP	Österreichring	24	Auto Motor Und Sport-Team Surtees	F	3.0 Surtees TS9-Cosworth V8		12/22
dns	ITALIAN GP	Monza	8	Auto Motor Und Sport-Team Surtees	F	3.0 Surtees TS9-Cosworth V8	accident in practice	(23)/24
ret	CANADIAN GP	Mosport Park	24	Auto Motor Und Sport-Team Surtees	F	3.0 Surtees TS9-Cosworth V8	oil pressure	23/27

1972 Championship position: Unplaced

	Race	Circuit	No	Entrant	Tyres	Capacity/Car/Engine	Comment	Q Pos/Entries
13	SOUTH AFRICAN GP	Kyalami	25	Team Eifelland Caravans	G	3.0 Eifelland 21/March 721-Cosworth V8	2 laps behind	25/27
ret	SPANISH GP	Jarama	16	Team Eifelland Caravans	G	3.0 Eifelland 21/March 721-Cosworth V8	spun – hit barrier	17/26
10	MONACO GP	Monte Carlo	27	Team Eifelland Caravans	G	3.0 Eifelland 21/March 721-Cosworth V8	poor handling in rain/-3 laps	25/25
11	BELGIAN GP	Nivelles	6	Team Eifelland Caravans	G	3.0 Eifelland 21/March 721-Cosworth V8	2 laps behind	20/26
16	FRENCH GP	Clermont Ferrand	10	Team Eifelland Caravans	G	3.0 Eifelland 21/March 721-Cosworth V8	pit stop – puncture/-1 lap	=17/29
10	BRITISH GP	Brands Hatch	33	Team Eifelland Caravans	G	3.0 Eifelland 21/March 721-Cosworth V8	5 laps behind	25/27
ret	GERMAN GP	Nürburgring	22	Team Eifelland Caravans	G	3.0 Eifelland 21/March 721-Cosworth V8	electrics	14/27
15	AUSTRIAN GP	Österreichring	27	Team Eifelland Caravans	G	3.0 Eifelland 21/March 721-Cosworth V8	pit stops – bodywork /-6 laps	=17/26

1973 Championship position: Unplaced

	Race	Circuit	No	Entrant	Tyres	Capacity/Car/Engine	Comment	Q Pos/Entries
11	GERMAN GP	Nürburgring	9	Ceramica Pagnossin Team MRD	G	3.0 Brabham BT42-Cosworth V8		16/23
ret	AUSTRIAN GP	Österreichring	9	Ceramica Pagnossin Team MRD	G	3.0 Brabham BT42-Cosworth V8	front wheel bearing	17/25
12	ITALIAN GP	Monza	9	Ceramica Pagnossin Team MRD	G	3.0 Brabham BT42-Cosworth V8		9/25
12	CANADIAN GP	Mosport Park	9	Ceramica Pagnossin Team MRD	G	3.0 Brabham BT42-Cosworth V8	4 laps behind	18/26

1974 Championship position: Unplaced

	Race	Circuit	No	Entrant	Tyres	Capacity/Car/Engine	Comment	Q Pos/Entries
ret	AUSTRIAN GP	Österreichring	27	Embassy Racing with Graham Hill	F	3.0 Lola T370-Cosworth V8	tyre punctured – accident	13/31
ret	ITALIAN GP	Monza	27	Embassy Racing with Graham Hill	F	3.0 Lola T370-Cosworth V8	suspension mounting plate	14/31
11	CANADIAN GP	Mosport Park	27	Embassy Racing with Graham Hill	F	3.0 Lola T370-Cosworth V8	2 laps behind	11/30
12	US GP	Watkins Glen	27	Embassy Racing with Graham Hill	F	3.0 Lola T370-Cosworth V8	2 pit stops – tyres/-5 laps	21/30

1975 Championship position: Unplaced

	Race	Circuit	No	Entrant	Tyres	Capacity/Car/Engine	Comment	Q Pos/Entries
13	ARGENTINE GP	Buenos Aires	23	Embassy Racing with Graham Hill	G	3.0 Lola T370-Cosworth V8	pit stop – tyre/2 laps behind	19/23
14	BRAZILIAN GP	Interlagos	23	Embassy Racing with Graham Hill	G	3.0 Lola T370-Cosworth V8	1 lap behind	23/23
7	SOUTH AFRICAN GP	Kyalami	23	Embassy Racing with Graham Hill	G	3.0 Lola T371-Cosworth V8		14/28
ret	SPANISH GP	Montjuich Park	22	Embassy Racing with Graham Hill	G	3.0 Hill GH1-Cosworth V8	accident – lost rear wing	9/26
16	AUSTRIAN GP	Österreichring	22	Embassy Racing with Graham Hill	G	3.0 Hill GH1-Cosworth V8	2 laps behind	26/30
ret	ITALIAN GP	Monza	22	Embassy Racing with Graham Hill	G	3.0 Hill GH1-Cosworth V8	accident at chicane	23/28

1976 Championship position: 19th= Wins: 0 Pole positions: 0 Fastest laps: 0 Points scored: 1

	Race	Circuit	No	Entrant	Tyres	Capacity/Car/Engine	Comment	Q Pos/Entries
6	GERMAN GP	Nürburgring	77	Martini Racing	G	3.0 Brabham BT45-Alfa Romeo F12		15/28
dns	"	"	32	RAM Racing	G	3.0 Brabham BT44B-Cosworth V8	practice only	– / –
12	DUTCH GP	Zandvoort	25	Hesketh Racing with Rizla/Penthouse	G	3.0 Hesketh 308D-Cosworth V8	3 laps behind	25/27
ret	ITALIAN GP	Monza	7	Martini Racing	G	3.0 Brabham BT45-Alfa Romeo F12	engine – fuel system	11/29

1978 Championship position: Unplaced

	Race	Circuit	No	Entrant	Tyres	Capacity/Car/Engine	Comment	Q Pos/Entries
9	SOUTH AFRICAN GP	Kyalami	36	Arrows Racing Team	G	3.0 Arrows FA1-Cosworth V8	pit stop – fuel/1 lap behind	22/30
9	US GP WEST	Long Beach	36	Arrows Racing Team	G	3.0 Arrows FA1-Cosworth V8	1 lap behind	18/30
ret	MONACO GP	Monte Carlo	36	Arrows Racing Team	G	3.0 Arrows FA1-Cosworth V8	driver unwell – rib injury	=18/30
ret	BELGIAN GP	Zolder	36	Arrows Racing Team	G	3.0 Arrows FA1-Cosworth V8	accident	17/30
14	SPANISH GP	Jarama	36	Arrows Racing Team	G	3.0 Arrows FA1-Cosworth V8	2 pit stops/4 laps behind	19/29
14	SWEDISH GP	Anderstorp	36	Arrows Racing Team	G	3.0 Arrows FA1-Cosworth V8	3 laps behind	24/27
15	FRENCH GP	Paul Ricard	36	Arrows Racing Team	G	3.0 Arrows FA1-Cosworth V8	1 lap behind	21/29
dnq	BRITISH GP	Brands Hatch	36	Arrows Racing Team	G	3.0 Arrows FA1-Cosworth V8		27/30
dsq	GERMAN GP	Hockenheim	36	Arrows Racing Team	G	3.0 Arrows FA1-Cosworth V8	took back entrance to pits	17/30
dnpq	AUSTRIAN GP	Österreichring	36	Arrows Racing Team	G	3.0 Arrows A1-Cosworth V8		31/31
dnpq	DUTCH GP	Zandvoort	36	Arrows Racing Team	G	3.0 Arrows A1-Cosworth V8		33/33
dnpq	ITALIAN GP	Monza	36	Arrows Racing Team	G	3.0 Arrows A1-Cosworth V8		31/33
16	US GP EAST	Watkins Glen	36	Arrows Racing Team	G	3.0 Arrows A1-Cosworth V8	pit stop – brakes/-5 laps	22/27
dnq	CANADIAN GP	Montreal	36	Arrows Racing Team	G	3.0 Arrows A1-Cosworth V8		27/28

GP Starts: 54 GP Wins: 0 Pole positions: 0 Fastest laps: 0 Points: 14

PHILIPPE STREIFF

A TALL, intense French driver, Philippe Streiff came to the fore in 1980, when an acrimonious Formula 3 season ended with a splendid win at the final European round at Zolder. The following year, he concentrated on winning the French F3 championship in his Martini and took fourth in the European series, joining the two-car AGS Formula 2 team for 1982. His season was up and down, however, due in part to arguments that raged over the technical regulations, but he finished the year strongly to take sixth place in the final standings.

In 1983, AGS and Streiff really got to work, despite the team's chronic shortage of funds. The Frenchman carried the fight to the dominant Ralts, although he had to wait until the very end of the 1984 season before scoring a long overdue and well-earned win. However, he did have the fillip of a grand prix outing for Renault in the 1984 Portuguese GP. His F3000 campaign with AGS in 1985 was well funded yet strewn with mechanical failures, but by then he had been elevated to the grand prix ranks, taking over the Ligier of Andrea de Cesaris in mid-season and scoring a fine third place in the end-of-year Australian GP. With Ligier missing the South African GP because of the political situation, Philippe drove for Tyrrell, and he joined the Ockham team full time in 1986 to handle their Renault-engined cars. He drove well enough on occasion during the next two seasons, but generally was outpaced by team-mates Martin Brundle and Jonathan Palmer, the latter claiming the non-turbo honours after a switch to Cosworth power in 1987.

Streiff took a gamble when he joined the tiny AGS GP team for 1988, but at least it was an environment with which he was familiar. Early in the season, he caught the eye with some spirited performances, most notably at Imola, where he qualified and raced superbly, only for engine problems to intervene. He was looking forward to another season with the team in 1989, but in a pre-season test at Rio he crashed heavily, sustaining serious back injuries. Perhaps due to a lack of prompt medical assistance, these resulted in him becoming a tetraplegic.

Happily, Streiff has since kept himself involved with the sport as a commentator and as the organiser of the annual Elf Kart Masters at Bercy.

STREIFF, Philippe (F) b 26/6/1955, La Tronche, nr Grenoble

	Race	Circuit	No	Entrant	Tyres	Capacity/Car/Engine	Comment	Q Pos/Entries
	1984 Championship position: Unplaced							
ret	PORTUGUESE GP	Estoril	33	Equipe Renault Elf	M	1.5 t/c Renault RE50 V6	driveshaft	13/27
	1985 Championship position: 15th= Wins: 0 Pole positions: 0 Fastest laps: 0 Points scored: 4							
10	ITALIAN GP	Monza	25	Equipe Ligier Gitanes	P	1.5 t/c Ligier JS25-Renault V6	2 laps behind	19/26
9	BELGIAN GP	Spa	25	Equipe Ligier Gitanes	P	1.5 t/c Ligier JS25-Renault V6	1 lap behind	18/24
8	EUROPEAN GP	Brands Hatch	25	Equipe Ligier Gitanes	P	1.5 t/c Ligier JS25-Renault V6	2 laps behind	5/27
ret	SOUTH AFRICAN GP	Kyalami	4	Tyrrell Racing Organisation	G	1.5 t/c Tyrrell 014-Renault V6	accident	18/21
3	AUSTRALIAN GP	Adelaide	25	Equipe Ligier Gitanes	P	1.5 t/c Ligier JS25-Renault V6		18/25
	1986 Championship position: 13th Wins: 0 Pole positions: 0 Fastest laps: 0 Points scored: 3							
7	BRAZILIAN GP	Rio	4	Data General Team Tyrrell	G	1.5 t/c Tyrrell 014-Renault V6	2 laps behind	18/25
ret	SPANISH GP	Jerez	4	Data General Team Tyrrell	G	1.5 t/c Tyrrell 014-Renault V6	engine – lost oil	20/25
ret	SAN MARINO GP	Imola	4	Data General Team Tyrrell	G	1.5 t/c Tyrrell 014-Renault V6	transmission	22/26
11	MONACO GP	Monte Carlo	4	Data General Team Tyrrell	G	1.5 t/c Tyrrell 015-Renault V6	hit by Jones – spin/4 laps behind	13/26
12	BELGIAN GP	Spa	4	Data General Team Tyrrell	G	1.5 t/c Tyrrell 015-Renault V6	3 laps behind	18/25
11	CANADIAN GP	Montreal	4	Data General Team Tyrrell	G	1.5 t/c Tyrrell 014-Renault V6	4 laps behind	17/25
9	US GP (DETROIT)	Detroit	4	Data General Team Tyrrell	G	1.5 t/c Tyrrell 015-Renault V6		18/26
dns	"	"	4	Data General Team Tyrrell	G	1.5 t/c Tyrrell 014-Renault V6	practice only	– / –
ret	FRENCH GP	Paul Ricard	4	Data General Team Tyrrell	G	1.5 t/c Tyrrell 015-Renault V6	fuel leak – fire	17/26
6	BRITISH GP	Brands Hatch	4	Data General Team Tyrrell	G	1.5 t/c Tyrrell 015-Renault V6	3 laps behind	16/26
ret	GERMAN GP	Hockenheim	4	Data General Team Tyrrell	G	1.5 t/c Tyrrell 015-Renault V6	engine	18/26
8	HUNGARIAN GP	Hungaroring	4	Data General Team Tyrrell	G	1.5 t/c Tyrrell 015-Renault V6	2 laps behind	18/26
ret	AUSTRIAN GP	Österreichring	4	Data General Team Tyrrell	G	1.5 t/c Tyrrell 015-Renault V6	engine	20/26
9	ITALIAN GP	Monza	4	Data General Team Tyrrell	G	1.5 t/c Tyrrell 015-Renault V6	2 laps behind	23/27
ret	PORTUGUESE GP	Estoril	4	Data General Team Tyrrell	G	1.5 t/c Tyrrell 015-Renault V6	engine	23/27
ret	MEXICAN GP	Mexico City	4	Data General Team Tyrrell	G	1.5 t/c Tyrrell 015-Renault V6	turbo	19/26
5/ret	AUSTRALIAN GP	Adelaide	4	Data General Team Tyrrell	G	1.5 t/c Tyrrell 015-Renault V6	out of fuel/2 laps behind	10/26
	1987 Championship position: 14th Wins: 0 Pole positions: 0 Fastest laps: 0 Points scored: 4							
11*	BRAZILIAN GP	Rio	4	Data General Team Tyrrell	G	3.5 Tyrrell DG 016-Cosworth V8	*2nd non-turbo/4 laps behind	20/23
8*	SAN MARINO GP	Imola	4	Data General Team Tyrrell	G	3.5 Tyrrell DG 016-Cosworth V8	*1st non-turbo/2 laps behind	22/27

9*	BELGIAN GP	Spa	4	Data General Team Tyrrell	G	3.5 Tyrrell DG 016-Cosworth V8	*2nd non-turbo/4 laps behind	23/26
ret	MONACO GP	Monte Carlo	4	Data General Team Tyrrell	G	3.5 Tyrrell DG 016-Cosworth V8	hit barrier	23/26
ret	US GP (DETROIT)	Detroit	4	Data General Team Tyrrell	G	3.5 Tyrrell DG 016-Cosworth V8	lost wheel – hit wall	14/26
6*	FRENCH GP	Paul Ricard	4	Data General Team Tyrrell	G	3.5 Tyrrell DG 016-Cosworth V8	*1st non-turbo/4 laps behind	25/26
ret	BRITISH GP	Silverstone	4	Data General Team Tyrrell	G	3.5 Tyrrell DG 016-Cosworth V8	engine	23/26
4*	GERMAN GP	Hockenheim	4	Data General Team Tyrrell	G	3.5 Tyrrell DG 016-Cosworth V8	*1st non-turbo/1 lap behind	22/26
9*	HUNGARIAN GP	Hungaroring	4	Data General Team Tyrrell	G	3.5 Tyrrell DG 016-Cosworth V8	*2nd non-turbo/2 laps behind	14/26
ret/dns	AUSTRIAN GP	Österreichring	4	Data General Team Tyrrell	G	3.5 Tyrrell DG 016-Cosworth V8	accident in first start	25/26
12*	ITALIAN GP	Monza	4	Data General Team Tyrrell	G	3.5 Tyrrell DG 016-Cosworth V8	*1st non-turbo/3 laps behind	24/28
12*	PORTUGUESE GP	Estoril	4	Data General Team Tyrrell	G	3.5 Tyrrell DG 016-Cosworth V8	*3rd non-turbo/4 laps behind	21/27
7*	SPANISH GP	Jerez	4	Data General Team Tyrrell	G	3.5 Tyrrell DG 016-Cosworth V8	*2nd non-turbo/1 lap behind	15/28
8*	MEXICAN GP	Mexico City	4	Data General Team Tyrrell	G	3.5 Tyrrell DG 016-Cosworth V8	*3rd non-turbo/3 laps behind	25/27
12*	JAPANESE GP	Suzuka	4	Data General Team Tyrrell	G	3.5 Tyrrell DG 016-Cosworth V8	*2nd non-turbo/2 laps behind	26/27
ret	AUSTRALIAN GP	Adelaide	4	Data General Team Tyrrell	G	3.5 Tyrrell DG 016-Cosworth V8	spun off	18/27

1988 Championship position: Unplaced

ret	BRAZILIAN GP	Rio	14	Automobiles Gonfaronaise Sportive	G	3.5 AGS JH23-Cosworth V8	brakes – spun off	19/31
10	SAN MARINO GP	Imola	14	Automobiles Gonfaronaise Sportive	G	3.5 AGS JH23-Cosworth V8	2 laps behind	13/31
ret/dns*	MONACO GP	Monte Carlo	14	Automobiles Gonfaronaise Sportive	G	3.5 AGS JH23-Cosworth V8	*throttle cable on parade lap	12/30
12	MEXICAN GP	Mexico City	14	Automobiles Gonfaronaise Sportive	G	3.5 AGS JH23-Cosworth V8	4 laps behind	19/30
ret	CANADIAN GP	Monteal	14	Automobiles Gonfaronaise Sportive	G	3.5 AGS JH23-Cosworth V8	rear suspension	10/31
ret	US GP (DETROIT)	Detroit	14	Automobiles Gonfaronaise Sportive	G	3.5 AGS JH23-Cosworth V8	suspension	11/31
ret	FRENCH GP	Paul Ricard	14	Automobiles Gonfaronaise Sportive	G	3.5 AGS JH23-Cosworth V8	fuel leak	17/31
ret	BRITISH GP	Silverstone	14	Automobiles Gonfaronaise Sportive	G	3.5 AGS JH23-Cosworth V8	broken rear wing – crashed	16/31
ret	GERMAN GP	Hockenheim	14	Automobiles Gonfaronaise Sportive	G	3.5 AGS JH23-Cosworth V8	throttle cable	16/31
ret	HUNGARIAN GP	Hungaroring	14	Automobiles Gonfaronaise Sportive	G	3.5 AGS JH23-Cosworth V8	lost wheel	23/31
10*	BELGIAN GP	Spa	14	Automobiles Gonfaronaise Sportive	G	3.5 AGS JH23-Cosworth V8	*3rd & 4th cars dsq/-1 lap	18/31
ret	ITALIAN GP	Monza	14	Automobiles Gonfaronaise Sportive	G	3.5 AGS JH23-Cosworth V8	gearbox	23/31
9	PORTUGUESE GP	Estoril	14	Automobiles Gonfaronaise Sportive	G	3.5 AGS JH23-Cosworth V8	2 laps behind	21/31
ret	SPANISH GP	Jerez	14	Automobiles Gonfaronaise Sportive	G	3.5 AGS JH23-Cosworth V8	engine	13/31
8	JAPANESE GP	Suzuka	14	Automobiles Gonfaronaise Sportive	G	3.5 AGS JH23-Cosworth V8	1 lap behind	18/31
11/ret	AUSTRALIAN GP	Adelaide	14	Automobiles Gonfaronaise Sportive	G	3.5 AGS JH23-Cosworth V8	electrics	16/31

GP Starts: 52 (54)   GP Wins: 0   Pole positions: 0   Fastest laps: 0   Points: 11

STUCK, Hans (A) b 27/12/1900, Warsaw, Poland – d 8/2/1978, Grainau, nr Garmisch-Partenkirchen, Germany

1951 Championship position: Unplaced

	Race	Circuit	No	Entrant	Tyres	Capacity/Car/Engine	Comment	Q Pos/Entries
dns	ITALIAN GP	Monza	32	BRM Ltd	D	1.5 s/c BRM P15 V16	tried car in practice only	– / –
	1952	Championship position: Unplaced						
ret	SWISS GP	Bremgarten	2	AFM	–	2.0 AFM 4-Küchen V8	engine	14/21
dnq	ITALIAN GP	Monza	20	Ecurie Espadon	P	2.0 Ferrari 212 V12		33/35
	1953	Championship position: Unplaced						
ret	GERMAN GP	Nürburgring	21	Hans Stuck	–	2.0 AFM-Bristol 6		23/35
nc	ITALIAN GP	Monza	48	Hans Stuck	–	2.0 AFM-Bristol 6	23 laps behind winner	29/30

GP Starts: 3   GP Wins: 0   Pole positions: 0   Fastest laps: 0   Points: 0

HANS STUCK

WITH a competition career that spanned some 39 years – from 1924 to 1963 – Hans Stuck took part in more than 700 events. Most of his success was gained in hill-climbs, of which he became the undisputed master during the 1920s in his Austro-Daimlers. He remained dominant in the early 1930s with a Mercedes SSK sports, by which time he was also winning on the circuits, taking the 1931 Rio de Janeiro GP. In 1934, he joined the Auto Union team, winning the German, Swiss and Czech GPs. He added the Italian GP to his tally in 1935, as well as an unending run of hill-climb successes.

After the Second World War, Stuck got back into action with a little 1100cc Cisitalia, before racing the AFM Formula 2 car, which was fast, but fragile. He took a third place in the 1950 Solitude GP and won a minor race at Grenzlandring in 1951, but on the hills, of course, he was still a regular winner. By the end of the 1952 season, the AFM was totally outclassed and he briefly raced an Ecurie Espadon Ferrari, taking fifth at AVUS and ninth at Modena.

Later Stuck joined BMW and raced their cars successfully until the early 1960s.

HANS-JOACHIM STUCK

AS the son of the famous pre-war Auto Union ace, it was perhaps natural that Hans-Joachim Stuck followed his father into a career in motor racing, especially as he had driven karts and small-capacity BMWs long before he was eligible for a racing licence. After driving a BMW 2002 in national hill-climbs, he graduated to the works European touring car championship team, winning the Nürburgring 24-hour race in 1969. Then he took over from Jochen Mass in the Ford Germany Capri in the national series for 1972 and won the Spa 24-hours with Mass as co-driver.

Stuck's single-seater career began properly in 1973, when he raced the works March in Formula 2, graduating to the grand prix team the following year, but he proved to be somewhat inconsistent, very quick on some occasions, but mysteriously lacklustre on others. He did well in F2, however, finishing second in the championship with four wins, at Barcelona, Hockenheim, Rouen and Enna.

Having been dropped initially from the March grand prix team for 1975, Stuck made a successful sortie into IMSA with BMW, but then was recalled to the Bicester ranks to replace the out-of-favour Lella Lombardi. He remained with the team in 1976, but again it was the same infuriating mixture of the brilliant and the banal. At Watkins Glen, he finished fifth, after being 23rd on the first lap; occasional Formula 2 outings with the 762 produced three wins in only five starts.

Given the chance to race the Brabham-Alfa in 1977, following the death of Carlos Pace in an air crash, Hans-Joachim scored superb third places in Germany and Austria, and led the US GP at Watkins Glen before blotting his copybook by sliding off the circuit. From then on, it was downhill all the way as far as Formula 1 was concerned, a season with Shadow bringing only one points finish, and an even more dispiriting year with ATS yielding the same return.

Hans then turned his back on F1, but certainly not on motorsport, for soon he became immersed in a huge schedule of sports, GT and touring car racing. He joined the Rothmans Porsche team in 1985, sharing the drivers' crown with Derek Bell in both 1985 and 1986, and won Le Mans with Bell and Al Holbert in 1986 and '87. After a switch to Audi, his presence spiced up IMSA's GTO class in 1989; back at home, he won the 1990 DTM championship in the awesome 3.6-litre V8 Quattro.

As the 1990s unfolded, Stuck was still racing competitively in German Super Touring for Audi and was a Le Mans regular. In 1994, he finished third with Danny Sullivan and Thierry Boutsen in a Dauer Porsche 962LM, and the following year he was placed sixth, this time in a Kremer Porsche with Boutsen and Christophe Bouchut.

Just as Stuck's career seemed to be winding down came the surprise news that he was forsaking Audi to join Opel's squad to contest the Class 1 ITC series in 1996. Driving the Team Rosberg car, he could still show the youngsters a thing or two, winning both rounds in Helsinki. He was also part of the factory Porsche team, taking second at Le Mans with Boutsen and Bob Wollek in the 911 GT1. In 1997, he teamed up with Boutsen to contest the FIA GT championship in one of the works cars, but despite a number of top-six placings, the experienced duo were deemed too old and dropped at season's end. The immensely popular Stuck was not prepared to hang up his helmet, however, and remained a quick and spectacular driver, mainly racing a BMW M3 in the GT3 class in the American Le Mans Series. In 2004, he returned to Europe and shared the winning BMW M3 GTR to win the Nürburgring 24-hour race for a third time, and in 2005 he was one of many ex-F1 drivers tempted back into single-seater action in the GP Masters series, where he took a sixth place at Kyalami. In 2008, he was appointed by Volkswagen to represent them on motorsport matters, and he was still an occasional competitor, mainly on home soil, racing the VW Scirocco and Audi R8, often with old colleagues such as Emanuele Pirro and Frank Biela.

In 2011, Stuck took part in the Nürburgring 24-hours for the 20th and final time – he had first raced in the event in 1970 – before announcing his retirement from driving. He raced a Lamborghini Gallardo GT3, along with his two sons, Johannes and Ferdinand, to a 15th place at the finish

STUCK, Hans-Joachim (D) b 1/1/1951, Grainau, nr Garmisch-Partenkirchen

	1974 Championship position: 16th=		Wins: 0	Pole positions: 0	Fastest laps: 0	Points scored: 5			
	Race	Circuit	No	Entrant	Tyres	Capacity/Car/Engine	Comment		Q Pos/Entries
ret	ARGENTINE GP	Buenos Aires	9	March Engineering	G	3.0 March 741-Cosworth V8	transmission		23/26
ret	BRAZILIAN GP	Interlagos	9	March Engineering	G	3.0 March 741-Cosworth V8	seized c.v. joint		13/25
5	SOUTH AFRICAN GP	Kyalami	9	March Engineering	G	3.0 March 741-Cosworth V8			7/27
4	SPANISH GP	Jarama	9	March Engineering	G	3.0 March 741-Cosworth V8	2 laps behind		14/28
ret	BELGIAN GP	Nivelles	9	March Engineering	G	3.0 March 741-Cosworth V8	clutch		10/32
ret	MONACO GP	Monte Carlo	9	March Engineering	G	3.0 March 741-Cosworth V8	collision with Hunt		9/28
ret	DUTCH GP	Zandvoort	9	March Engineering	G	3.0 March 741-Cosworth V8	collision while braking		22/27
dnq	FRENCH GP	Dijon	9	March Engineering	G	3.0 March 741-Cosworth V8			26/30
ret	BRITISH GP	Brands Hatch	9	March Engineering	G	3.0 March 741-Cosworth V8	spun off		9/34
7	GERMAN GP	Nürburgring	9	March Engineering	G	3.0 March 741-Cosworth V8			20/32

	Race	Circuit	No.	Team		Car	Comment	Pos.
11/ret	AUSTRIAN GP	Österreichring	9	March Engineering	G	3.0 March 741-Cosworth V8	suspension – spun off/-6 laps	15/31
ret	ITALIAN GP	Monza	9	March Engineering	G	3.0 March 741-Cosworth V8	engine mounting bolts	18/31
ret	CANADIAN GP	Mosport Park	9	March Engineering	G	3.0 March 741-Cosworth V8	engine – fuel pressure	23/30
dnq	US GP	Watkins Glen	9	March Engineering	G	3.0 March 741-Cosworth V8		28/30

1975 Championship position: Unplaced

ret	BRITISH GP	Silverstone	10	Lavazza March	G	3.0 March 751-Cosworth V8	spun off in rain – hit barrier	14/28
ret	GERMAN GP	Nürburgring	10	Lavazza March	G	3.0 March 751-Cosworth V8	engine	7/26
ret	AUSTRIAN GP	Österreichring	10	Lavazza March	G	3.0 March 751-Cosworth V8	spun off in rain – hit barrier	4/30
ret	ITALIAN GP	Monza	10	Lavazza March	G	3.0 March 751-Cosworth V8	hit chicane	16/28
8	US GP	Watkins Glen	10	Lavazza March	G	3.0 March 751-Cosworth V8	puncture – took flag in pits/-1 lap	13/24

1976 Championship position: 13th Wins: 0 Pole positions: 0 Fastest laps: 0 Points scored: 8

4	BRAZILIAN GP	Interlagos	34	March Racing	G	3.0 March 761-Cosworth V8		14/22
12	SOUTH AFRICAN GP	Kyalami	34	March Racing	G	3.0 March 761-Cosworth V8	2 laps behind	17/25
ret	US GP WEST	Long Beach	34	Theodore Racing	G	3.0 March 761-Cosworth V8	collision with Fittipaldi	18/27
ret	SPANISH GP	Jarama	34	March Racing	G	3.0 March 761-Cosworth V8	gearbox	17/30
ret	BELGIAN GP	Zolder	34	March Racing	G	3.0 March 761-Cosworth V8	suspension	15/29
4	MONACO GP	Monte Carlo	34	March Racing	G	3.0 March 761-Cosworth V8	1 lap behind	6/25
ret	SWEDISH GP	Anderstorp	34	March Racing	G	3.0 March 761-Cosworth V8	engine	20/27
7	FRENCH GP	Paul Ricard	34	March Racing	G	3.0 March 761-Cosworth V8		17/30
ret	BRITISH GP	Brands Hatch	34	March Racing	G	3.0 March 761-Cosworth V8	collision – Peterson & Depailler	17/30
ret/dns	GERMAN GP	Nürburgring	34	March Racing	G	3.0 March 761-Cosworth V8	clutch in first start	4/28
ret	AUSTRIAN GP	Österreichring	34	March Racing	G	3.0 March 761-Cosworth V8	fuel pressure	11/25
ret	DUTCH GP	Zandvoort	34	March Racing	G	3.0 March 761-Cosworth V8	engine	18/27
ret	ITALIAN GP	Monza	34	March Racing	G	3.0 March 761-Cosworth V8	collision with Andretti	6/29
ret	CANADIAN GP	Mosport Park	34	March Racing	G	3.0 March 761-Cosworth V8	handling	8/27
5	US GP EAST	Watkins Glen	34	March Racing	G	3.0 March 761-Cosworth V8		6/27
ret	JAPANESE GP	Mount Fuji	34	March Racing	G	3.0 March 761-Cosworth V8	electrics	18/27

1977 Championship position: 11th Wins: 0 Pole positions: 0 Fastest laps: 0 Points scored: 12

ret	SOUTH AFRICAN GP	Kyalami	10	Team Rothmans International	G	3.0 March 761B-Cosworth V8	engine	18/23
ret	US GP WEST	Long Beach	8	Martini Racing	G	3.0 Brabham BT45B-Alfa Romeo F12	brakes	17/22
6	SPANISH GP	Jarama	8	Martini Racing	G	3.0 Brabham BT45B-Alfa Romeo F12	1 lap behind	13/31
ret	MONACO GP	Monte Carlo	8	Martini Racing	G	3.0 Brabham BT45B-Alfa Romeo F12	fire – electrical fault	5/26
6	BELGIAN GP	Zolder	8	Martini Racing	G	3.0 Brabham BT45B-Alfa Romeo F12	1 lap behind	18/32
10	SWEDISH GP	Anderstorp	8	Martini Racing	G	3.0 Brabham BT45B-Alfa Romeo F12	1 lap behind	5/31
ret	FRENCH GP	Dijon	8	Martini Racing	G	3.0 Brabham BT45B-Alfa Romeo F12	collision with Laffite	13/30
5	BRITISH GP	Silverstone	8	Martini Racing	G	3.0 Brabham BT45B-Alfa Romeo F12		7/36
3	GERMAN GP	Hockenheim	8	Martini Racing	G	3.0 Brabham BT45B-Alfa Romeo F12		5/30
3	AUSTRIAN GP	Österreichring	8	Martini Racing	G	3.0 Brabham BT45B-Alfa Romeo F12		4/30
7	DUTCH GP	Zandvoort	8	Martini Racing	G	3.0 Brabham BT45B-Alfa Romeo F12	2 laps behind	19/34
ret	ITALIAN GP	Monza	8	Martini Racing	G	3.0 Brabham BT45B-Alfa Romeo F12	engine	11/34
ret	US GP EAST	Watkins Glen	8	Martini Racing	G	3.0 Brabham BT45B-Alfa Romeo F12	car jumped out of gear – crashed	2/27
ret	CANADIAN GP	Mosport Park	8	Martini Racing	G	3.0 Brabham BT45B-Alfa Romeo F12	engine	13/27
7	JAPANESE GP	Mount Fuji	8	Martini Racing	G	3.0 Brabham BT45B-Alfa Romeo F12	1 lap behind	4/23

1978 Championship position: 18th Wins: 0 Pole positions: 0 Fastest laps: 0 Points scored: 2

17	ARGENTINE GP	Buenos Aires	16	Shadow Racing Team	G	3.0 Shadow DN8-Cosworth V8	handling problems/2 laps behind	18/27
ret	BRAZILIAN GP	Rio	16	Shadow Racing Team	G	3.0 Shadow DN8-Cosworth V8	fuel pump	9/28
dnq	SOUTH AFRICAN GP	Kyalami	16	Shadow Racing Team	G	3.0 Shadow DN8-Cosworth V8		30/30
dns	US GP WEST	Long Beach	16	Shadow Racing Team	G	3.0 Shadow DN9-Cosworth V8	practice accident	(23)/30
ret	MONACO GP	Monte Carlo	16	Shadow Racing Team	G	3.0 Shadow DN9-Cosworth V8	collision with Keegan – steering	17/30
ret	BELGIAN GP	Zolder	16	Shadow Racing Team	G	3.0 Shadow DN9-Cosworth V8	spun off – stalled	20/30
ret	SPANISH GP	Jarama	16	Shadow Racing Team	G	3.0 Shadow DN9-Cosworth V8	broken rear suspension	24/29
11	SWEDISH GP	Anderstorp	16	Shadow Racing Team	G	3.0 Shadow DN9-Cosworth V8	2 laps behind	20/27
11	FRENCH GP	Paul Ricard	16	Shadow Racing Team	G	3.0 Shadow DN9-Cosworth V8	1 lap behind	20/29
5	BRITISH GP	Brands Hatch	16	Shadow Racing Team	G	3.0 Shadow DN9-Cosworth V8	1 lap behind	18/30
ret	GERMAN GP	Hockenheim	16	Shadow Racing Team	G	3.0 Shadow DN9-Cosworth V8	collision with Mass	24/30
ret	AUSTRIAN GP	Österreichring	16	Shadow Racing Team	G	3.0 Shadow DN9-Cosworth V8	spun off in rain	23/31
ret	DUTCH GP	Zandvoort	16	Shadow Racing Team	G	3.0 Shadow DN9-Cosworth V8	differential	18/33
ret/dns	ITALIAN GP	Monza	16	Shadow Racing Team	G	3.0 Shadow DN9-Cosworth V8	crash at first start – concussion	17/32
ret	US GP EAST	Watkins Glen	16	Shadow Racing Team	G	3.0 Shadow DN9-Cosworth V8	fuel pump	14/27
ret	CANADIAN GP	Montreal	16	Shadow Racing Team	G	3.0 Shadow DN9-Cosworth V8	hit by Fittipaldi	8/28

1979 Championship position: 19th= Wins: 0 Pole positions: 0 Fastest laps: 0 Points scored: 2

dns	ARGENTINE GP	Buenos Aires	9	ATS Wheels	G	3.0 ATS D2-Cosworth V8	car unprepared	26/26
ret	BRAZILIAN GP	Interlagos	9	ATS Wheels	G	3.0 ATS D2-Cosworth V8	broken steering wheel	24/26
ret	SOUTH AFRICAN GP	Kyalami	9	ATS Wheels	G	3.0 ATS D2-Cosworth V8	spun off	24/26
dsq	US GP WEST	Long Beach	9	ATS Wheels	G	3.0 ATS D2-Cosworth V8	push start after spin	23/26
14	SPANISH GP	Jarama	9	ATS Wheels	G	3.0 ATS D2-Cosworth V8	2 pitstops – tyres/6 laps behind	21/27
8	BELGIAN GP	Zolder	9	ATS Wheels	G	3.0 ATS D2-Cosworth V8	pitstop – puncture/1 lap behind	20/28
ret	MONACO GP	Monte Carlo	9	ATS Wheels	G	3.0 ATS D2-Cosworth V8	broken wheel	12/26
dns	FRENCH GP	Dijon	9	ATS Wheels	G	3.0 ATS D2-Cosworth V8	tyre dispute – car withdrawn	(23)/27
dnq	BRITISH GP	Silverstone	9	ATS Wheels	G	3.0 ATS D2-Cosworth V8		25/26
ret	GERMAN GP	Hockenheim	9	ATS Wheels	G	3.0 ATS D2-Cosworth V8	broken suspension	23/26
ret	AUSTRIAN GP	Österreichring	9	ATS Wheels	G	3.0 ATS D3-Cosworth V8	engine	18/26
dns	"	"	9	ATS Wheels	G	3.0 ATS D3-Cosworth V8	practice only	– / –
ret	DUTCH GP	Zandvoort	9	ATS Wheels	G	3.0 ATS D3-Cosworth V8	driveshaft	15/26
11	ITALIAN GP	Monza	9	ATS Wheels	G	3.0 ATS D3-Cosworth V8	1 lap behind	15/28
ret	CANADIAN GP	Montreal	9	ATS Wheels	G	3.0 ATS D3-Cosworth V8	accident with Arnoux	12/29
5	US GP	Watkins Glen	9	ATS Wheels	G	3.0 ATS D3-Cosworth V8		14/30

GP Starts: 72 (74) GP Wins: 0 Pole positions: 0 Fastest laps: 0 Points: 29

DANNY SULLIVAN

THANKS to his fabulous success in Indy car racing, Danny Sullivan became a multi-millionaire, but it wasn't always that way, for the kid from Kentucky spent a good few hard seasons in England, climbing the ladder towards a top-line career.

Without any financial help, Danny took on numerous menial jobs to help realise his dream of being a racing driver, and his tenacity somehow helped him to cling on in various junior formulas where, despite scoring the occasional success, frequently he seemed to be knocked back by some misfortune. Eventually, he went back to the States to get his career moving again, making a good impression in Can-Am with an old Lola in 1980. He returned the following year, winning a race at Las Vegas and taking fourth in the championship. Suddenly the momentum was building; an Indy car debut for Forsythe-Newman at Atlanta in 1982 brought third place, but after he had been bumped from the team by Héctor Rebaque and his bank balance, Danny returned to Can-Am to finish third in the standings.

For 1983, Danny took the plunge into Formula 1 with Tyrrell, a fifth place at Monaco and a very impressive second in the Race of Champions showing what he could do. Running Cosworth engines against the turbo brigade put him at a disadvantage, but while he rarely made many mistakes, he didn't deliver anything out of the ordinary in the eyes of F1's movers and shakers, and he was passed over for rides in 1984

Having already looked the part in his two 1982 CART drives, the lure of a competitive drive in Indy cars took Danny back across the Atlantic. In Doug Shierson's team, he took three wins in 1984 (Cleveland, Pocono and Sanair), before hitting it big after joining Roger Penske's crack team for 1985. It was there that he made himself a household name in the USA with his famous victory in the Indianapolis 500, surviving a 360-degree spin to catch and pass Mario Andretti in a dramatic race.

In 1986, Sullivan won two more races (Meadowlands and Cleveland) to take third place in the standings, but the following year was not so successful and he slumped to ninth with no wins. He was back with a bang in 1988, however, taking the Indy car title with four wins (Portland, Michigan, Nazareth and Laguna Seca) and eight pole positions, before joining the ultimately unsuccessful Patrick Racing Alfa Romeo effort. Then he moved to the Galles team with substantial backing from Molson, taking his total of wins to 17 by the end of the 1993 season.

Danny was out of an Indy car drive at the start of 1994, but he did quite well in a couple of guest outings for Alfa Romeo in the 'DTM on tour' rounds at Donington and Mugello. He also took third place at Le Mans in a Dauer Porsche with Thierry Boutsen and Hans Stuck, before the chance came to resurrect his Indy car career with the fledgling PacWest team. His experience was invaluable when he tested the car late in the year, and he was taken on for a full-time ride in 1995. Apart from a bright performance in the opening round at Miami, the season was largely unrewarding, however, and was cut short when he suffered a nasty crash at Michigan, which left him suffering from a broken pelvis.

Happily, Danny made a full recovery, but there was no realistic prospect of him making another return to Indy car competition. Having become a commentator for ABC TV, he continued to make selected appearances in sports car events, posting an eighth place at Le Mans in 1998 in the Team Bigazzi McLaren F1 GTR with Nelson Piquet and Johnny Cecotto.

Danny has been involved in the sport in various capacities, including acting as drivers' representative on the FIA stewards' panel in F1 on occasion. He also has many business interests, particularly within the media and automotive industries in the United States.

SULLIVAN, Danny (USA) b 9/3/1950, Louisville, Kentucky

	1983 Championship position: 17th		Wins: 0	Pole positions: 0	Fastest laps: 0	Points scored: 2		
	Race	Circuit	No	Entrant	Tyres	Capacity/Car/Engine	Comment	Q Pos/Entries
11	BRAZILIAN GP	Rio	4	Benetton Tyrrell Team	G	3.0 Tyrrell 011-Cosworth V8	1 lap behind	21/27
8	US GP WEST	Long Beach	4	Benetton Tyrrell Team	G	3.0 Tyrrell 011-Cosworth V8	severe tyre vibration/2 laps behind	9/28
ret	FRENCH GP	Paul Ricard	4	Benetton Tyrrell Team	G	3.0 Tyrrell 011-Cosworth V8	clutch	24/29
ret	SAN MARINO GP	Imola	4	Benetton Tyrrell Team	G	3.0 Tyrrell 011-Cosworth V8	spun off	22/28
5	MONACO GP	Monte Carlo	4	Benetton Tyrrell Team	G	3.0 Tyrrell 011-Cosworth V8	2 laps behind	20/28
12	BELGIAN GP	Spa	4	Benetton Tyrrell Team	G	3.0 Tyrrell 011-Cosworth V8	1 lap behind	23/28
ret	US GP (DETROIT)	Detroit	4	Benetton Tyrrell Team	G	3.0 Tyrrell 011-Cosworth V8	electrics	16/27
dsq*	CANADIAN GP	Montreal	4	Benetton Tyrrell Team	G	3.0 Tyrrell 011-Cosworth V8	9th on road/*car underweight	22/28
14	BRITISH GP	Silverstone	4	Benetton Tyrrell Team	G	3.0 Tyrrell 011-Cosworth V8	2 laps behind	23/29
12	GERMAN GP	Hockenheim	4	Benetton Tyrrell Team	G	3.0 Tyrrell 011-Cosworth V8	2 laps behind	21/29
ret	AUSTRIAN GP	Österreichring	4	Benetton Tyrrell Team	G	3.0 Tyrrell 011-Cosworth V8	multiple collision on lap 1	23/29
ret	DUTCH GP	Zandvoort	4	Benetton Tyrrell Team	G	3.0 Tyrrell 011-Cosworth V8	engine	26/29
ret	ITALIAN GP	Monza	4	Benetton Tyrrell Team	G	3.0 Tyrrell 011-Cosworth V8	fuel pump drive	22/29
ret	EUROPEAN GP	Brands Hatch	4	Benetton Tyrrell Team	G	3.0 Tyrrell 012-Cosworth V8	fire – broken fuel line	20/29
7	SOUTH AFRICAN GP	Kyalami	4	Benetton Tyrrell Team	G	3.0 Tyrrell 012-Cosworth V8	2 laps behind	19/26

GP Starts: 15　GP Wins: 0　Pole positions: 0　Fastest laps: 0　Points: 2

MARC SURER

SOMETHING of a late starter in motor racing, Marc Surer graduated from karts and Super Vee to the German F3 championship with the KWS team, taking the runner-up slot in 1976. The following year, he made the move into Formula 2, gathering valuable experience. He had also been signed by Jochen Neerpasch to race a BMW 320i in the up-to-2-litre division of the German touring car championship for BMW's 'junior team', but his season was somewhat overshadowed by a clash with Hans Heyer, which saw him suspended for two months.

Despite this unfortunate incident, Marc was promoted to the BMW Team Polifac Formula 2 squad for 1978, as number two to Bruno Giacomelli, who went on to dominate proceedings. Surer backed his team-mate superbly, however, taking a clear second in the championship with six second-place finishes. In 1979, he was promoted to team leader and duly took the honours, but serious doubts over his pedigree were already being voiced, as he seemed unable to stamp his authority on races in the manner of a true champion.

Nevertheless, Marc had already been given his grand prix baptism by Ensign, and he signed to drive for ATS in 1980, but his season had barely begun when he crashed in practice for the South African GP, sustaining broken ankles that sidelined him until mid-season. For 1981, he joined the little Ensign team and really began to come out of his shell, taking a superb fourth place and fastest lap in Brazil, and sixth at Monaco, before moving to Teddy Yip's Theodore set-up.

In 1982, Marc's progress was halted once more by injury, when a crash at Kyalami left him with leg injuries that delayed his Arrows debut. When fit again, he was somewhat overshadowed by the emerging Thierry Boutsen and his chances to shine were restricted by the late development of the turbo car in 1984. When François Hesnault quit the Brabham team early in 1985, Marc finally got the opportunity to show his ability, and he enjoyed his best ever season as team-mate to Nelson Piquet. In 1986, the tough Swiss driver was back with Arrows, but while taking part in a German rally, he crashed his Ford into a tree; his co-driver was killed, and he sustained serious injuries and burns that ended his competitive racing career.

In 1998, Surer began an association with BMW, looking after their young driver programme until he was appointed head of motorsport, where he was responsible for overseeing both Johnny Cecotto and Joachim Winkelhock in their respective championship winning seasons of 1994 and 1995.

Since then, Marc has maintained close links with the sport on a number of fronts. Not only has he acted as a commentator and presenter for German and Swiss TV, but also he set up his own race driving school in Switzerland; more recently, he has taken over the running of a karting facility in Ondara, Spain. He still enjoys racing, taking on the youngsters in karts, making selective appearances in historics events and guesting as a legend driver in the Scirocco Cup.

SURER, Marc (CH) b 18/9/1951, Aresdorf

1979 Championship position: Unplaced

	Race	Circuit	No	Entrant	Tyres	Capacity/Car/Engine	Comment	Q Pos/Entries
dnq	ITALIAN GP	Monza	22	Team Ensign	G	3.0 Ensign N179-Cosworth V8		26/28
dnq	CANADIAN GP	Montreal	22	Team Ensign	G	3.0 Ensign N179-Cosworth V8		26/29
ret	US GP EAST	Watkins Glen	22	Team Ensign	G	3.0 Ensign N179-Cosworth V8	engine	21/30

1980 Championship position: Unplaced

	Race	Circuit	No	Entrant	Tyres	Capacity/Car/Engine	Comment	Q Pos/Entries
ret	ARGENTINE GP	Buenos Aires	9	Team ATS	G	3.0 ATS D3-Cosworth V8	fire – brake fluid on disc	21/28
7	BRAZILIAN GP	Interlagos	9	Team ATS	G	3.0 ATS D3-Cosworth V8	1 lap behind	20/28
dnq	SOUTH AFRICAN GP	Kyalami	9	Team ATS	G	3.0 ATS D4-Cosworth V8	practice crash – broken ankle	26/28
ret	FRENCH GP	Paul Ricard	9	Team ATS	G	3.0 ATS D4-Cosworth V8	gearbox	11/27
ret	BRITISH GP	Brands Hatch	9	Team ATS	G	3.0 ATS D4-Cosworth V8	engine	15/27
12	GERMAN GP	Hockenheim	9	Team ATS	G	3.0 ATS D4-Cosworth V8	1 lap behind	13/26
12	AUSTRIAN GP	Österreichring	9	Team ATS	G	3.0 ATS D4-Cosworth V8	1 lap behind	16/25
10	DUTCH GP	Zandvoort	9	Team ATS	G	3.0 ATS D4-Cosworth V8	pit stop – fuel/3 laps behind	20/28
ret	ITALIAN GP	Imola	9	Team ATS	G	3.0 ATS D4-Cosworth V8	engine	23/28
dnq	CANADIAN GP	Montreal	9	Team ATS	G	3.0 ATS D4-Cosworth V8		25/28
8	US GP EAST	Watkins Glen	9	Team ATS	G	3.0 ATS D4-Cosworth V8	2 laps behind	17/27

1981 Championship position: 16th   Wins: 0   Pole positions: 0   Fastest laps: 1   Points scored: 4

	Race	Circuit	No	Entrant	Tyres	Capacity/Car/Engine	Comment	Q Pos/Entries
ret	US GP WEST	Long Beach	14	Ensign Racing	M	3.0 Ensign N180B-Cosworth V8	electrics	19/29
4	BRAZILIAN GP	Rio	14	Ensign Racing	M	3.0 Ensign N180B-Cosworth V8	FL	18/30

ret	ARGENTINE GP	Buenos Aires	14	Ensign Racing	M	3.0 Ensign N180B-Cosworth V8	engine	16/29
9	SAN MARINO GP	Imola	14	Ensign Racing	M	3.0 Ensign N180B-Cosworth V8	pit stop – tyres/1 lap behind	21/30
11	BELGIAN GP	Zolder	14	Ensign Racing	M	3.0 Ensign N180B-Cosworth V8	2 laps behind	15/31
6	MONACO GP	Monte Carlo	14	Ensign Racing	M	3.0 Ensign N180B-Cosworth V8	2 laps behind	19/31
12	FRENCH GP	Paul Ricard	33	Theodore Racing Team	M	3.0 Theodore TY01-Cosworth V8	2 laps behind	21/29
11/ret	BRITISH GP	Silverstone	33	Theodore Racing Team	A	3.0 Theodore TY01-Cosworth V8	fuel pressure/7 laps behind	24/30
14/ret	GERMAN GP	Hockenheim	33	Theodore Racing Team	A	3.0 Theodore TY01-Cosworth V8	spun off last corner/2 laps behind	22/30
ret	AUSTRIAN GP	Österreichring	33	Theodore Racing Team	A	3.0 Theodore TY01-Cosworth V8	distributor	23/28
8	DUTCH GP	Zandvoort	33	Theodore Racing Team	A	3.0 Theodore TY01-Cosworth V8	3 laps behind	20/30
dnq	ITALIAN GP	Monza	33	Theodore Racing Team	A	3.0 Theodore TY01-Cosworth V8		25/30
9	CANADIAN GP	Montreal	33	Theodore Racing Team	A	3.0 Theodore TY01-Cosworth V8	2 laps behind	19/30
ret	CAESARS PALACE GP	Las Vegas	33	Theodore Racing Team	A	3.0 Theodore TY01-Cosworth V8	rear suspension	23/30

1982 Championship position: 20= Wins: 0 Pole positions: 0 Fastest laps: 0 Points scored: 3

7*	BELGIAN GP	Zolder	29	Arrows Racing Team	P	3.0 Arrows A4-Cosworth V8	*3rd place car dsq/4 laps behind	24/32
9	MONACO GP	Monte Carlo	29	Arrows Racing Team	P	3.0 Arrows A4-Cosworth V8	6 laps behind	19/31
8	US GP (DETROIT)	Detroit	29	Arrows Racing Team	P	3.0 Arrows A4-Cosworth V8	1 lap behind	19/28
5	CANADIAN GP	Montreal	29	Arrows Racing Team	P	3.0 Arrows A4-Cosworth V8	1 lap behind	16/29
10	DUTCH GP	Zandvoort	29	Arrows Racing Team	P	3.0 Arrows A4-Cosworth V8	pit stop – tyres/1 lap behind	17/31
ret	BRITISH GP	Brands Hatch	29	Arrows Racing Team	P	3.0 Arrows A4-Cosworth V8	engine	22/30
13	FRENCH GP	Paul Ricard	29	Arrows Racing Team	P	3.0 Arrows A4-Cosworth V8	2 laps behind	20/30
6	GERMAN GP	Hockenheim	29	Arrows Racing Team	P	3.0 Arrows A4-Cosworth V8	1 lap behind	27/30
ret	AUSTRIAN GP	Österreichring	29	Arrows Racing Team	P	3.0 Arrows A4-Cosworth V8	air lock in fuel system	21/29
15	SWISS GP	Dijon	29	Arrows Racing Team	P	3.0 Arrows A5-Cosworth V8	pit stop – tyres/4 laps behind	14/29
ret	ITALIAN GP	Monza	29	Arrows Racing Team	P	3.0 Arrows A4-Cosworth V8	engine	19/30
7	CAESARS PALACE GP	Las Vegas	29	Arrows Racing Team	P	3.0 Arrows A5-Cosworth V8	1 lap behind	17/30

1983 Championship position: 15th Wins: 0 Pole positions: 0 Fastest laps: 0 Points scored: 4

6	BRAZILIAN GP	Rio	29	Arrows Racing Team	G	3.0 Arrows A6-Cosworth V8		20/27
5	US GP WEST	Long Beach	29	Arrows Racing Team	G	3.0 Arrows A6-Cosworth V8	1 lap behind	16/28
10	FRENCH GP	Paul Ricard	29	Arrows Racing Team	G	3.0 Arrows A6-Cosworth V8	1 lap behind	21/29
6	SAN MARINO GP	Imola	29	Arrows Racing Team	G	3.0 Arrows A6-Cosworth V8	1 lap behind	12/28
ret	MONACO GP	Monte Carlo	29	Arrows Racing Team	G	3.0 Arrows A6-Cosworth V8	accident with Warwick	12/28
11	BELGIAN GP	Spa	29	Arrows Racing Team	G	3.0 Arrows A6-Cosworth V8	started from pitlane/1 lap behind	10/28
11	US GP (DETROIT)	Detroit	29	Arrows Racing Team	G	3.0 Arrows A6-Cosworth V8	2 laps behind	5/27
ret	CANADIAN GP	Montreal	29	Arrows Racing Team	G	3.0 Arrows A6-Cosworth V8	transmission	14/28
17	BRITISH GP	Silverstone	29	Arrows Racing Team	G	3.0 Arrows A6-Cosworth V8	3 laps behind	19/29
7	GERMAN GP	Hockenheim	29	Arrows Racing Team	G	3.0 Arrows A6-Cosworth V8	1 lap behind	20/29
ret	AUSTRIAN GP	Österreichring	29	Arrows Racing Team	G	3.0 Arrows A6-Cosworth V8	accident – Ghinzani & Laffite	22/29
8	DUTCH GP	Zandvoort	29	Arrows Racing Team	G	3.0 Arrows A6-Cosworth V8	2 laps behind	14/29
10	ITALIAN GP	Monza	29	Arrows Racing Team	G	3.0 Arrows A6-Cosworth V8	1 lap behind	20/29
ret	EUROPEAN GP	Brands Hatch	29	Arrows Racing Team	G	3.0 Arrows A6-Cosworth V8	engine	17/29
8	SOUTH AFRICAN GP	Kyalami	29	Arrows Racing Team	G	3.0 Arrows A6-Cosworth V8	2 laps behind	22/26

1984 Championship position: 20th Wins: 0 Pole positions: 0 Fastest laps: 0 Points scored: 1

7*	BRAZILIAN GP	Rio	17	Barclay Nordica Arrows BMW	G	3.0 Arrows A6-Cosworth V8	*5th place car dsq/-2 laps	25/27
*9	SOUTH AFRICAN GP	Kyalami	17	Barclay Nordica Arrows BMW	G	3.0 Arrows A6-Cosworth V8	4 laps behind	23/27
8*	BELGIAN GP	Zolder	17	Barclay Nordica Arrows BMW	G	3.0 Arrows A6-Cosworth V8	*6th place car dsq/-2 laps	24/27
ret	SAN MARINO GP	Imola	17	Barclay Nordica Arrows BMW	G	1.5 t/c Arrows A7-BMW 4	turbo	16/28
ret	FRENCH GP	Dijon	17	Barclay Nordica Arrows BMW	G	3.0 Arrows A6-Cosworth V8	accident with Warwick	20/27
dnq	MONACO GP	Monte Carlo	17	Barclay Nordica Arrows BMW	G	3.0 Arrows A6-Cosworth V8		21/27
ret	CANADIAN GP	Montreal	17	Barclay Nordica Arrows BMW	G	3.0 Arrows A6-Cosworth V8	engine	23/26
ret/dns*	US GP (DETROIT)	Detroit	17	Barclay Nordica Arrows BMW	G	3.0 Arrows A6-Cosworth V8	hit Piquet – 1st start/did not restart	22/27
ret	US GP (DALLAS)	Dallas	17	Barclay Nordica Arrows BMW	G	1.5 t/c Arrows A7-BMW 4	hit wall	22/27
11*	BRITISH GP	Brands Hatch	17	Barclay Nordica Arrows BMW	G	1.5 t/c Arrows A7-BMW 4	*11th place car dsq/4 laps behind	15/27
ret	GERMAN GP	Hockenheim	17	Barclay Nordica Arrows BMW	G	1.5 t/c Arrows A7-BMW 4	turbo	14/27
6	AUSTRIAN GP	Österreichring	17	Barclay Nordica Arrows BMW	G	1.5 t/c Arrows A7-BMW 4	1 lap behind	19/28
ret	DUTCH GP	Zandvoort	17	Barclay Nordica Arrows BMW	G	1.5 t/c Arrows A7-BMW 4	wheel bearing	19/27
ret	ITALIAN GP	Monza	17	Barclay Nordica Arrows BMW	G	1.5 t/c Arrows A7-BMW 4	engine	15/27
ret	EUROPEAN GP	Nürburgring	17	Barclay Nordica Arrows BMW	G	1.5 t/c Arrows A7-BMW 4	accident with Berger, Fabi & Ghinzani	16/26
ret	PORTUGUESE GP	Estoril	17	Barclay Nordica Arrows BMW	G	1.5 t/c Arrows A7-BMW 4	electrics	16/27

1985 Championship position: 13= Wins: 0 Pole positions: 0 Fastest laps: 0 Points scored: 5

15	CANADIAN GP	Montreal	8	Motor Racing Developments Ltd	P	1.5 t/c Brabham BT54-BMW 4	3 laps behind	20/25
8	US GP (DETROIT)	Detroit	8	Motor Racing Developments Ltd	P	1.5 t/c Brabham BT54-BMW 4	1 lap behind	11/25
8	FRENCH GP	Paul Ricard	8	Motor Racing Developments Ltd	P	1.5 t/c Brabham BT54-BMW 4	1 lap behind	14/26
6	BRITISH GP	Silverstone	8	Motor Racing Developments Ltd	P	1.5 t/c Brabham BT54-BMW 4	2 laps behind	15/26
ret	GERMAN GP	Nürburgring	8	Motor Racing Developments Ltd	P	1.5 t/c Brabham BT54-BMW 4	engine	11/27
6	AUSTRIAN GP	Österreichring	8	Motor Racing Developments Ltd	P	1.5 t/c Brabham BT54-BMW 4	1 lap behind	11/27
10/ret	DUTCH GP	Zandvoort	8	Motor Racing Developments Ltd	P	1.5 t/c Brabham BT54-BMW 4	exhaust/5 laps behind	9/27
4	ITALIAN GP	Monza	8	Motor Racing Developments Ltd	P	1.5 t/c Brabham BT54-BMW 4		9/26
8	BELGIAN GP	Spa	8	Motor Racing Developmetns Ltd	P	1.5 t/c Brabham BT54-BMW 4	1 lap behind	12/24
ret	EUROPEAN GP	Brands Hatch	8	Motor Racing Developments Ltd	P	1.5 t/c Brabham BT54-BMW 4	turbo	7/27
ret	SOUTH AFRICAN GP	Kyalami	8	Motor Racing Developments Ltd	P	1.5 t/c Brabham BT54-BMW 4	engine	5/21
ret	AUSTRALIAN GP	Adelaide	8	Motor Racing Developments Ltd	P	1.5 t/c Brabham BT54-BMW 4	engine	6/25

1986 Championship position: Unplaced

ret	BRAZILIAN GP	Rio	17	Barclay Arrows BMW	G	1.5 t/c Arrows A8-BMW 4	engine	20/25
ret	SPANISH GP	Jerez	17	Barclay Arrows BMW	G	1.5 t/c Arrows A8-BMW 4	fuel system	22/25
9/ret	SAN MARINO GP	Imola	17	Barclay Arrows BMW	G	1.5 t/c Arrows A8-BMW 4	out of fuel/3 laps behind	15/26
9	MONACO GP	Monte Carlo	17	Barclay Arrows BMW	G	1.5 t/c Arrows A8-BMW 4	3 laps behind	17/26
9	BELGIAN GP	Spa	17	Barclay Arrows BMW	G	1.5 t/c Arrows A8-BMW 4	2 laps behind	21/25

GP Starts: 81 (82) GP Wins: 0 Pole positions: 0 Fastest laps: 1 Points: 17

JOHN SURTEES, MBE, OBE

JOHN SURTEES is widely honoured as the only world champion on both two wheels and four, a remarkable achievement of which he can be justly proud. That tag tends to be used so often, however, that it is easy to forget what a brilliant all-round racing driver he really was. Born into a motorcycling background – his father, Jack, was an amateur racer – the young Surtees began racing on two wheels seriously in 1951, becoming a star on Nortons through to the mid-1950s, when he switched to the Italian MV Agusta concern. From 1956 to 1960, he was the outstanding rider of the day, winning seven world titles in the 350cc and 500cc classes. He had some promising trials with both Vanwall and Aston Martin in 1959 and, when his bike commitments allowed, embarked on his car racing career early in 1960.

A win first time out at Goodwood in Ken Tyrrell's Cooper Formula Junior marked Surtees down as a special talent. No sooner had he purchased his own F2 Cooper than he received an invitation from Lotus to race their Formula 1 Lotus 18. At this point, Colin Chapman was adroitly juggling a number of drivers, a situation of which John was unaware. Nevertheless, he proved staggeringly quick for one so inexperienced. In his second grand prix, he was second only to Jack Brabham, and he led in Portugal before an error cost him dear. Not so worldly wise in those early days, he shied away from signing to drive alongside Jim Clark for the 1961 season, unhappy with Chapman's somewhat cavalier attitude towards his contract with Innes Ireland. In the short term at least, it proved to be the wrong decision.

Having joined the Yeoman Credit-backed team running off-the-shelf Coopers for 1961, Surtees recorded only mediocre results, the sole minor success being a win in the Glover Trophy. Things improved when the team, now under the Bowmaker banner, aligned themselves with Lola. Surtees became deeply involved in the development of the car and came close to a grand prix victory. He did win a non-title race at Mallory Park, but at the end of the year could resist the overtures of Ferrari no longer.

John had a galvanising effect on the team, not only as a driver, but also as a source of technical input, particularly in the development of the monocoque chassis. Prior to his arrival at Maranello, Ferrari had completely lost their way, but by mid-1963 Surtees had won both the German GP and Mediterranean GP to re-establish the Scuderia as a potent force once more. When the team introduced the 158 V8 engine early in 1964, he at last found the car in which he could make a realistic championship bid. Mid-season victories in Germany and Italy enabled him to travel to the final round in Mexico with a chance of the title, and luck was on his side when his two rivals, Clark and Graham Hill, both hit trouble. It may not have been one of the most convincing championship wins, but in a year when all the cars were evenly matched, it was still thoroughly deserved.

The 1965 season found Ferrari bogged down with their flat-12 engine project, and most of Surtees' success came in the older 158 V8 at the beginning of the season. Apart from his sports car commitments for the Scuderia, which brought victory in the Nürburgring 1000km, he was also running his own Lola T70 on the North American sports car scene, but in practice for a race at Mosport he suffered a massive accident, which he was very lucky to survive. As it was, he lay in hospital with serious back injuries for many weeks before making a brave comeback the following spring. Ironically, 1966 was probably his finest year, despite the bitter disagreement that caused him to leave Ferrari in mid-term. Before the split, he had won the Belgian GP, the Syracuse GP and the Monza 1000km sports car race, but afterwards he scored victories in the Mexican GP for Cooper and a whole succession of sports car races in his Lola.

The 1967 season was another busy one. Surtees joined the Honda F1 effort, but development proved to be a slow and painful process, although some reward came when the hastily prepared Lola-based 'Hondola' won a sensational Italian GP by a hair's breadth from Brabham. John's involvement with Lola was deep. Running their Formula 2 car, he broke the Brabham dominance on occasion, which was a not inconsiderable feat, but the Lola-Aston Martin sports car project was best forgotten. Meanwhile, his transatlantic journeys to bag some of the lucrative purse money on offer in Can-Am continued unhindered.

With little headway being made during the second year of the Surtees-Honda alliance, the project was abandoned at the end of the season. For 1969, John joined BRM, but it became a nightmarish season for both parties. His Can-Am drives for Chaparral that year were also less than satisfactory when the narrow 2H car proved to be the most difficult machine he had ever handled.

The logical decision was to follow the example of fellow drivers Brabham and Bruce McLaren, and build his own Formula 1 car. John was obliged to run a McLaren while his own challenger was being prepared, but a superb drive and fastest lap in South Africa proved he could still cut it behind the wheel. There was even a brief and successful return to Ferrari for three sports car races, before development of the Surtees TS7 took over, an aggregate win in the end-of-season Gold Cup race at Oulton Park boosting his morale. The 1971 season proved tougher than expected, however, as the new TS9 made only an occasional impression on the grand prix elite. In the less rarefied atmosphere of non-championship races, he scored some useful placings, again winning the Gold Cup, but there was no denying it had been a disappointing season for a man who had been used to much greater things.

Mike Hailwood's drive at Monza, coupled with a realisation that he could no longer fulfill all the roles in his team effectively, saw Surtees take a back seat in 1972. His third place in the International Trophy was his last Formula 1 success, while in Formula 2 he signed off his racing career with wins in the Japanese GP at Mount Fuji and the Shell GP at Imola. Thereafter, he concentrated on running his team, a succession of drivers – good, bad and indifferent – filling the cockpit, depending on the exigencies of the times. Certainly few of them could meet the exacting standards required by this hardest of taskmasters. When suitable sponsorship dried up and medical problems that had dogged him intermittently as a result of his 1965 Mosport accident resurfaced, Surtees quit the racing scene somewhat disillusioned. Happily, having remarried and become a contented family man, he re-emerged to enjoy the historic racing scene in both cars and bikes, where he is a major attraction, demonstrating many of the machines he handled with such brilliance in the past.

In 2005/06, he was tempted back to the circuits to head up the Team GB entry in the A1GP series, as well as to help advance the careers of Robbie Kerr and Oliver Jarvis.

Then he concentrated fully on guiding the promising career of his son, Henry, who had risen through the ranks of Formula BMW and Formula Renault to compete in the newly created Formula 2 championship in 2009. Tragedy soon befell the popular youngster, however, when he was killed in a freak accident at Brands Hatch after an errant wheel from another car struck him full on the head. The 18-year-old was pronounced brain dead in hospital and permission was given by the closely-knit Surtees family for his organs to be used to help others. There could be no recompense for such a loss, but at least they had the satisfaction of knowing that in death he had saved many other lives.

SURTEES, John (GB) b 11/2/1934, Tatsfield, Surrey

1960 Championship position: 11th= Wins: 0 Pole positions: 1 Fastest laps: 1 Points scored: 6

	Race	Circuit	No	Entrant	Tyres	Capacity/Car/Engine	Comment	Q Pos/Entries
ret	MONACO GP	Monte Carlo	26	Team Lotus	D	2.5 Lotus 18-Climax 4	transmission	15/24
2	BRITISH GP	Silverstone	9	Team Lotus	D	2.5 Lotus 18-Climax 4		11/25
ret	PORTUGUESE GP	Oporto	18	Team Lotus	D	2.5 Lotus 18-Climax 4	radiator/FL	1/16
ret	US GP	Riverside	11	Team Lotus	D	2.5 Lotus 18-Climax 4	spun – hit by Clark	6/23

1961 Championship position: 11th= Wins: 0 Pole positions: 0 Fastest laps: 0 Points scored: 4

	Race	Circuit	No	Entrant	Tyres	Capacity/Car/Engine	Comment	Q Pos/Entries
ret	MONACO GP	Monte Carlo	22	Yeoman Credit Racing Team	D	1.5 Cooper T53-Climax 4	head gasket	=12/21
7	DUTCH GP	Zandvoort	12	Yeoman Credit Racing Team	D	1.5 Cooper T53-Climax 4		9/17
5	BELGIAN GP	Spa	24	Yeoman Credit Racing Team	D	1.5 Cooper T53-Climax 4		4/25
ret	FRENCH GP	Reims	40	Yeoman Credit Racing Team	D	1.5 Cooper T53-Climax 4	suspension – accident	=6/26
ret	BRITISH GP	Aintree	34	Yeoman Credit Racing Team	D	1.5 Cooper T53-Climax 4	transmission	10/30
5	GERMAN GP	Nürburgring	18	Yeoman Credit Racing Team	D	1.5 Cooper T53-Climax 4		10/27
ret	ITALIAN GP	Monza	42	Yeoman Credit Racing Team	D	1.5 Cooper T53-Climax 4	accident	19/33
ret	US GP	Watkins Glen	18	Yeoman Credit Racing Team	D	1.5 Cooper T53-Climax 4	engine	=9/19
dns	"	" "	26	Frank J Harrison	D	1.5 Lotus 18-Climax 4	Lloyd Ruby's car – practice only	– / –

1962 Championship position: 4th Wins: 0 Pole positions: 1 Fastest laps: 0 Points scored: 19

	Race	Circuit	No	Entrant	Tyres	Capacity/Car/Engine	Comment	Q Pos/Entries
ret	DUTCH GP	Zandvoort	19	Bowmaker Racing Team	D	1.5 Lola 4-Climax V8	suspension	1/20
4	MONACO GP	Monte Carlo	28	Bowmaker Racing Team	D	1.5 Lola 4-Climax V8	1 lap behind	11/21
5	BELGIAN GP	Spa	5	Bowmaker Racing Team	D	1.5 Lola 4-Climax V8	1 lap behind	11/20
5	FRENCH GP	Rouen	18	Bowmaker Racing Team	D	1.5 Lola 4-Climax V8	3 laps behind	5/17
2	BRITISH GP	Aintree	24	Bowmaker Racing Team	D	1.5 Lola 4-Climax V8		2/21
dns	"	"	24	Bowmaker Racing Team	D	1.5 Lola 4A-Climax V8	practice only	– / –
2	GERMAN GP	Nürburgring	14	Bowmaker Racing Team	D	1.5 Lola 4-Climax V8		4/30
dns	"	"	14	Bowmaker Racing Team	D	1.5 Lola 4A-Climax V8	practice only	– / –
ret	ITALIAN GP	Monza	46	Bowmaker Racing Team	D	1.5 Lola 4A-Climax V8	engine	8/30
dns	"	"	46	Bowmaker Racing Team	D	1.5 Lola 4-Climax V8	practice only	– / –
ret	US GP	Watkins Glen	18	Bowmaker Racing Team	D	1.5 Lola 4-Climax V8	crankcase plug	20/20
ret	SOUTH AFRICAN GP	East London	6	Bowmaker Racing Team	D	1.5 Lola 4-Climax V8	engine	5/17

1963 Championship position: 4th Wins: 1 Pole positions: 1 Fastest laps: 3 Points scored: 22

	Race	Circuit	No	Entrant	Tyres	Capacity/Car/Engine	Comment	Q Pos/Entries
4	MONACO GP	Monte Carlo	21	Scuderia Ferrari SpA SEFAC	D	1.5 Ferrari 156 V6	FL	=3/17
ret	BELGIAN GP	Spa	9	Scuderia Ferrari SpA SEFAC	D	1.5 Ferrari 156 V6	fuel injection pipe	10/20
3	DUTCH GP	Zandvoort	2	Scuderia Ferrari SpA SEFAC	D	1.5 Ferrari 156 V6	1 lap behind	5/19
ret	FRENCH GP	Reims	16	Scuderia Ferrari SpA SEFAC	D	1.5 Ferrari 156 V6	fuel pump	=4/21
2	BRITISH GP	Silverstone	10	Scuderia Ferrari SpA SEFAC	D	1.5 Ferrari 156 V6	FL	5/23
1	GERMAN GP	Nürburgring	7	Scuderia Ferrari SpA SEFAC	D	1.5 Ferrari 156 V6	FL	2/26
ret	ITALIAN GP	Monza	4	Scuderia Ferrari SpA SEFAC	D	1.5 Ferrari 156 V6	engine	1/28
9/ret	US GP	Watkins Glen	23	Scuderia Ferrari SpA SEFAC	D	1.5 Ferrari 156 V6	engine – valve spring/-28 laps	3/21
dsq	MEXICAN GP	Mexico City	23	Scuderia Ferrari SpA SEFAC	D	1.5 Ferrari 156 V6	push start at pitstop	2/21
ret	SOUTH AFRICAN GP	East London	3	Scuderia Ferrari SpA SEFAC	D	1.5 Ferrari 156 V6	engine	4/21

1964 WORLD CHAMPION Wins: 2 Pole positions: 2 Fastest laps: 2 Points scored: 40

	Race	Circuit	No	Entrant	Tyres	Capacity/Car/Engine	Comment	Q Pos/Entries
ret	MONACO GP	Monte Carlo	21	Scuderia Ferrari SpA SEFAC	D	1.5 Ferrari 158 V8	gearbox	=3/20
dns	"	" "	21	Scuderia Ferrari SpA SEFAC	D	1.5 Ferrari 156 V6	practice only	– / –
2	DUTCH GP	Zandvoort	2	Scuderia Ferrari SpA SEFAC	D	1.5 Ferrari 158 V8		4/18
ret	BELGIAN GP	Spa	10	Scuderia Ferrari SpA SEFAC	D	1.5 Ferrari 158 V8	engine	5/20
ret	FRENCH GP	Rouen	24	Scuderia Ferrari SpA SEFAC	D	1.5 Ferrari 158 V8	oil pipe	3/17
3	BRITISH GP	Brands Hatch	7	Scuderia Ferrari SpA SEFAC	D	1.5 Ferrari 158 V8		5/25
dns	"	" " "	7	Scuderia Ferrari SpA SEFAC	D	1.5 Ferrari 156 V6	practice only	– / –
1	GERMAN GP	Nürburgring	7	Scuderia Ferrari SpA SEFAC	D	1.5 Ferrari 158 V8	FL	1/24
ret	AUSTRIAN GP	Zeltweg	7	Scuderia Ferrari SpA SEFAC	D	1.5 Ferrari 158 V8	rear suspension	2/20
1	ITALIAN GP	Monza	2	Scuderia Ferrari SpA SEFAC	D	1.5 Ferrari 158 V8	FL	1/25
2	US GP	Watkins Glen	7	North American Racing Team	D	1.5 Ferrari 158 V8		2/19
dns	"	" " "	7T	North American Racing Team	D	1.5 Ferrari 156 V6	practice only	– / –
dns	"	" " "	8T	North American Racing Team	D	1.5 Ferrari 1512 F12	practice only	– / –
2	MEXICAN GP	Mexico City	7	North American Racing Team	D	1.5 Ferrari 158 V8		4/19

1965 Championship position: 5th Wins: 0 Pole positions: 0 Fastest laps: 0 Points scored: 17

	Race	Circuit	No	Entrant	Tyres	Capacity/Car/Engine	Comment	Q Pos/Entries
2	SOUTH AFRICAN GP	East London	1	Scuderia Ferrari SpA SEFAC	D	1.5 Ferrari 158 V8		2/25
4/ret	MONACO GP	Monte Carlo	18	Scuderia Ferrari SpA SEFAC	D	1.5 Ferrari 158 V8	out of fuel/1 lap behind	5/17
ret	BELGIAN GP	Spa	1	Scuderia Ferrari SpA SEFAC	D	1.5 Ferrari 158 V8	engine	6/21
3	FRENCH GP	Clermont Ferrand	2	Scuderia Ferrari SpA SEFAC	D	1.5 Ferrari 158 V8		=3/17
3	BRITISH GP	Silverstone	1	Scuderia Ferrari SpA SEFAC	D	1.5 Ferrari 1512 F12		=3/23
dns	"	"	71	Scuderia Ferrari SpA SEFAC	D	1.5 Ferrari 158 V8	practice only	– / –
7	DUTCH GP	Zandvoort	2	Scuderia Ferrari SpA SEFAC	D	1.5 Ferrari 1512 F12	1 lap behind	=2/17
dns	"	"	2	Scuderia Ferrari SpA SEFAC	D	1.5 Ferrari 158 V8	practice only	– / –
ret	GERMAN GP	Nürburgring	7	Scuderia Ferrari SpA SEFAC	D	1.5 Ferrari 1512 F12	gearbox	4/22
ret	ITALIAN GP	Monza	8	Scuderia Ferrari SpA SEFAC	D	1.5 Ferrari 1512 F12	clutch	2/23

1966 Championship position: 2 Wins: 2 Pole positions: 2 Fastest laps: 3 Points scored: 28

	Race	Circuit	No	Entrant	Tyres	Capacity/Car/Engine	Comment	Q Pos/Entries
ret	MONACO GP	Monte Carlo	17	Scuderia Ferrari SpA SEFAC	D	3.0 Ferrari 312/66 V12	transmission	2/16
1	BELGIAN GP	Spa	6	Scuderia Ferrari SpA SEFAC	D	3.0 Ferrari 312/66 V12	FL	1/18
ret	FRENCH GP	Reims	10	Cooper Car Co	D	3.0 Cooper T81-Maserati V12	overheating	2/17
ret	BRITISH GP	Brands Hatch	12	Cooper Car Co	D	3.0 Cooper T81-Maserati V12	transmission	6/20

	GP	Circuit	No	Entrant	Tyre	Car/Engine	Notes	Grid
ret	DUTCH GP	Zandvoort	24	Cooper Car Co	D	3.0 Cooper T81-Maserati V12	*electrics*	10/18
2	GERMAN GP	Nürburgring	7	Cooper Car Co	D	3.0 Cooper T81-Maserati V12	*FL*	2/30
ret	ITALIAN GP	Monza	14	Cooper Car Co	F	3.0 Cooper T81-Maserati V12	*fuel leak*	4/22
3	US GP	Watkins Glen	7	Cooper Car Co	F	3.0 Cooper T81-Maserati V12	*spin – pit stop/FL/1 lap behind*	4/19
1	MEXICAN GP	Mexico City	7	Cooper Car Co	F	3.0 Cooper T81-Maserati V12		1/19

1967 Championship position: 4th Wins: 1 Pole positions: 0 Fastest laps: 0 Points scored: 20

	GP	Circuit	No	Entrant	Tyre	Car/Engine	Notes	Grid
3	SOUTH AFRICAN GP	Kyalami	11	Honda Racing	G	3.0 Honda RA273 V12	*tyre problems/1 lap behind*	6/18
ret	MONACO GP	Monte Carlo	7	Honda Racing	F	3.0 Honda RA273 V12	*engine*	3/18
ret	DUTCH GP	Zandvoort	7	Honda Racing	F	3.0 Honda RA273 V12	*sticking throttle slides*	=6/17
ret	BELGIAN GP	Spa	7	Honda Racing	F	3.0 Honda RA273 V12	*engine*	10/18
6	BRITISH GP	Silverstone	7	Honda Racing	F	3.0 Honda RA273 V12	*2 laps behind*	7/21
4	GERMAN GP	Nürburgring	7	Honda Racing	F	3.0 Honda RA273 V12		7/25
1	ITALIAN GP	Monza	14	Honda Racing	F	3.0 Honda RA300 V12	*Lola developed chassis*	9/18
ret	US GP	Watkins Glen	3	Honda Racing	F	3.0 Honda RA300 V12	*alternator – flat battery*	11/18
4	MEXICAN GP	Mexico City	3	Honda Racing	F	3.0 Honda RA300 V12	*1 lap behind*	7/19

1968 Championship position: 7th Wins: 0 Pole positions: 1 Fastest laps: 1 Points scored: 12

	GP	Circuit	No	Entrant	Tyre	Car/Engine	Notes	Grid
8	SOUTH AFRICAN GP	Kyalami	7	Honda Racing	F	3.0 Honda RA300 V12	*2 pit stops – misfire/5 laps behind*	6/23
ret	SPANISH GP	Jarama	7	Honda Racing	F	3.0 Honda RA301 V12	*gearbox*	7/14
ret	MONACO GP	Monte Carlo	8	Honda Racing	F	3.0 Honda RA301 V12	*gearbox*	4/18
ret	BELGIAN GP	Spa	20	Honda Racing	F	3.0 Honda RA301 V12	*rear suspension/FL*	4/18
ret	DUTCH GP	Zandvoort	7	Honda Racing	F	3.0 Honda RA301 V12	*alternator drive – flat battery*	9/19
2	FRENCH GP	Rouen	16	Honda Racing	F	3.0 Honda RA301 V12	*pit stop – tyres*	7/18
5	BRITISH GP	Brands Hatch	7	Honda Racing	F	3.0 Honda RA301 V12	*rear wing fell off/2 laps behind*	9/20
ret	GERMAN GP	Nürburgring	7	Honda Racing	F	3.0 Honda RA301 V12	*overheating – ignition*	7/20
ret	ITALIAN GP	Monza	14	Honda Racing	F	3.0 Honda RA301 V12	*crashed avoiding Amon*	1/24
ret	CANADIAN GP	St Jovite	8	Honda Racing	F	3.0 Honda RA301 V12	*transmission*	=6/22
3	US GP	Watkins Glen	5	Honda Racing	F	3.0 Honda RA301 V12	*1 lap behind*	9/21
ret	MEXICAN GP	Mexico City	5	Honda Racing	F	3.0 Honda RA301 V12	*overheating*	6/21

1969 Championship position: 11th Wins: 0 Pole positions: 0 Fastest laps: 0 Points scored: 6

	GP	Circuit	No	Entrant	Tyre	Car/Engine	Notes	Grid
ret	SOUTH AFRICAN GP	Kyalami	10	Owen Racing Organisation	D	3.0 BRM P138 V12	*engine*	=9/18
5	SPANISH GP	Montjuich Park	14	Owen Racing Organisation	D	3.0 BRM P138 V12	*2 pit stops – fuel feed/6 laps behind*	9/14
ret	MONACO GP	Monte Carlo	14	Owen Racing Organisation	D	3.0 BRM P138 V12	*gearbox – accident with Brabham*	7/16
9	DUTCH GP	Zandvoort	14	Owen Racing Organisation	D	3.0 BRM P138 V12	*pit stop – fuel/3 laps behind*	12/15
dns	"	"	14T	Owen Racing Organisation	D	3.0 BRM P139 V12	*practice only*	–/–
ret	BRITISH GP	Silverstone	14	Owen Racing Organisation	D	3.0 BRM P139 V12	*collapsed front suspension*	6/17
dns	GERMAN GP	Nürburgring	14	Owen Racing Organisation	D	3.0 BRM P139 V12	*suspension problems*	(12)/26
11	ITALIAN GP	Monza	14	Owen Racing Organisation	D	3.0 BRM P139 V12	*2 pit stops – various/8 laps behind*	10/15
ret	CANADIAN GP	Mosport Park	14	Owen Racing Organisation	D	3.0 BRM P139 V12	*engine*	14/20
3	US GP	Watkins Glen	14	Owen Racing Organisation	D	3.0 BRM P139 V12	*2 laps behind*	11/18
ret	MEXICAN GP	Mexico City	14	Owen Racing Organisation	D	3.0 BRM P139 V12	*gearbox*	10/17

1970 Championship position: 17th Wins: 0 Pole positions: 0 Fastest laps: 1 Points scored: 3

	GP	Circuit	No	Entrant	Tyre	Car/Engine	Notes	Grid
ret	SOUTH AFRICAN GP	Kyalami	7	Team Surtees	F	3.0 McLaren M7C-Cosworth V8	*engine/FL*	=7/24
ret	SPANISH GP	Jarama	8	Team Surtees	F	3.0 McLaren M7C-Cosworth V8	*gearbox*	14/22
ret	MONACO GP	Monte Carlo	14	Team Surtees	F	3.0 McLaren M7C-Cosworth V8	*oil pressure*	16/21
6	DUTCH GP	Zandvoort	16	Team Surtees	F	3.0 McLaren M7C-Cosworth V8	*1 lap behind*	14/24
ret	BRITISH GP	Brands Hatch	20	Team Surtees	F	3.0 Surtees TS7-Cosworth V8	*oil pressure*	20/25
9/ret	GERMAN GP	Hockenheim	7	Team Surtees	F	3.0 Surtees TS7-Cosworth V8	*engine/4 laps behind*	15/25
ret	AUSTRIAN GP	Österreichring	15	Team Surtees	F	3.0 Surtees TS7-Cosworth V8	*engine*	=11/24
ret	ITALIAN GP	Monza	14	Team Surtees	F	3.0 Surtees TS7-Cosworth V8	*electrics*	=10/27
5	CANADIAN GP	St Jovite	4	Team Surtees	F	3.0 Surtees TS7-Cosworth V8	*pit stop – misfire/1 lap behind*	=5/20
ret	US GP	Watkins Glen	17	Team Surtees	F	3.0 Surtees TS7-Cosworth V8	*flywheel*	8/27
8	MEXICAN GP	Mexico City	17	Team Surtees	F	3.0 Surtees TS7-Cosworth V8	*1 lap behind*	15/18

1971 Championship position: 18th Wins: 0 Pole positions: 0 Fastest laps: 0 Points scored: 3

	GP	Circuit	No	Entrant	Tyre	Car/Engine	Notes	Grid
ret	SOUTH AFRICAN GP	Kyalami	20	Brooke Bond Oxo/R. Walker/Team Surtees	F	3.0 Surtees TS9-Cosworth V8	*gearbox*	=5/25
dns	"	"	20T	Brooke Bond Oxo/R. Walker/Team Surtees	F	3.0 Surtees TS7-Cosworth V8	*practice only*	–/–
11	SPANISH GP	Montjuich Park	24	Brooke Bond Oxo/R. Walker/Team Surtees	F	3.0 Surtees TS9-Cosworth V8	*2 pit stops – body damage/-8 laps*	22/22
7	MONACO GP	Monte Carlo	22	Brooke Bond Oxo/R. Walker/Team Surtees	F	3.0 Surtees TS9-Cosworth V8	*1 lap behind*	=9/23
5	DUTCH GP	Zandvoort	23	Brooke Bond Oxo/R. Walker/Team Surtees	F	3.0 Surtees TS9-Cosworth V8	*2 laps behind*	7/24
8	FRENCH GP	Paul Ricard	22	Brooke Bond Oxo/R. Walker/Team Surtees	F	3.0 Surtees TS9-Cosworth V8		13/24
6	BRITISH GP	Silverstone	23	Brooke Bond Oxo/R. Walker/Team Surtees	F	3.0 Surtees TS9-Cosworth V8	*1 lap behind*	18/24
7	GERMAN GP	Nürburgring	7	Brooke Bond Oxo/R. Walker/Team Surtees	F	3.0 Surtees TS9-Cosworth V8		15/23
ret	AUSTRIAN GP	Österreichring	22	Brooke Bond Oxo/R. Walker/Team Surtees	F	3.0 Surtees TS9-Cosworth V8	*engine*	18/22
ret	ITALIAN GP	Monza	7	Brooke Bond Oxo/R. Walker/Team Surtees	F	3.0 Surtees TS9-Cosworth V8	*engine*	15/24
11	CANADIAN GP	Mosport Park	22	Brooke Bond Oxo/R. Walker/Team Surtees	F	3.0 Surtees TS9-Cosworth V8	*4 laps behind*	14/27
17	US GP	Watkins Glen	18	Brooke Bond Oxo/R. Walker/Team Surtees	F	3.0 Surtees TS9-Cosworth V8	*pit stop – ignition/5 laps behind*	14/32

1972 Championship position: Unplaced

	GP	Circuit	No	Entrant	Tyre	Car/Engine	Notes	Grid
ret	ITALIAN GP	Monza	7	Team Surtees	F	3.0 Surtees TS14-Cosworth V8	*fuel vaporisation*	19/27
dns	US GP	Watkins Glen	24	Team Surtees	F	3.0 Surtees TS14-Cosworth V8	*engine shortage*	(25)/32

GP Starts: 111 GP Wins: 6 Pole positions: 8 Fastest laps: 11 Points: 180

ADRIAN SUTIL

A FRACAS in a Shanghai nightclub, where Adrian Sutil assaulted a senior member of the Lotus-Renault team with a champagne glass, has cast a long shadow over the German's Formula 1 career, which could prove to have a terminal effect. In the resulting court case, he was found guilty of grievous bodily harm, and he escaped with a suspended gaol sentence and a hefty fine, which went to charity. But the damage had been done, and the normally placid and good-natured driver lost his seat in the Force India team at the end of 2011, ironically following his best ever season.

Sutil's father is a concert violinist, and the young Adrian spent his tender years engrossed in the study of the piano, but by the time he had reached his teens, his career ambitions lay in a more fast-moving discipline. The German began his career, like most, in karts, first getting behind the wheel at the age of 14, before moving up to the Swiss Formula Ford 1800 championship in 2002. He dominated the series, winning all ten races en route to taking his first title. Bolstered by his success, he graduated to the German Formula BMW championship in 2003, and then the Formula 3 Euroseries for the following year. He continued to learn and did enough to make an impression on the HBR team boss, Colin Kolles, for the future.

In the 2005 F3 Euroseries, Sutil was partnered in the ASM squad by Lewis Hamilton, who cut a swathe through the opposition. The German was left with the crumbs, but did take two wins and second place in the championship to continue his upward path. With Kolles as his mentor, he gained a test role at Midland F1 and three Friday appearances that caught the eye. Meanwhile, he continued to race successfully in Japan and with the TOMS Dallara, taking five wins on his way to the title.

Sutil's big break came when he was chosen by Spyker to race for the 2007 season, and the 23-year-old German soon began to make a good impression, particularly in practice. A rain-hit session in Monaco saw him at the very top of the time-sheets, marking him down as one to watch. Subsequently, there were a few incidents as the young driver perhaps overreached himself to compensate for the lack of speed in his car. However, he did have the satisfaction of claiming his first world championship point in the Japanese Grand Prix.

The 2008 season was a long hard slog for the team and, on the one occasion when points seemed a real probability, there was heartache. Sutil was truly outstanding in the wet at Monaco, holding a secure fourth place with only nine laps remaining, but then his Force India was punted into retirement by Kimi Räikkönen. Sutil's main aim then was to outperform his team-mate, Giancarlo Fisichella, and after a mid-season upgrade to the car, things improved on that score, as he kept his vastly more experienced partner on his toes.

While things looked up for 2009 when the team received Mercedes engines, Sutil was unable to make much of an impression until the Italian Grand Prix at Monza, where he put the car on the front row and set the fastest race lap, before finishing a slightly disappointing fourth. Real progress came the following year, when at last he had a car that was capable of scoring points, and a mid-season burst from Barcelona to Silverstone helped him on his way to a respectable 11th place in the standings.

For 2011, the German faced a fresh challenge in new team-mate Paul di Resta, and he had to raise his game accordingly. He emerged as a more polished performer, the silly errors that had previously proved costly largely having been eradicated. His efforts put him at the top of all the runners outside the top four teams, so to lose his seat to Nico Hülkenberg must have come as a bitter blow. Now he must wait to see if he can find a way back into Formula 1.

SUTIL, Adrian (D) b 11/1/1983, Gräfeling

	Race	Circuit	No	Entrant	Tyres	Capacity/Car/Engine	Comment	Q Pos/Entries
	2006 Championship position: Unplaced							
app	EUROPEAN GP	Nürburgring	39	MF1 Racing	B	2.4 Midland M16-Toyota V8	ran as 3rd driver in practice only	– /–
app	FRENCH GP	Magny Cours	39	MF1 Racing	B	2.4 Midland M16-Toyota V8	ran as 3rd driver in practice only	– /–
app	JAPANESE GP	Suzuka	39	MF1 Racing	B	2.4 Midland M16-Toyota V8	ran as 3rd driver in practice only	– /–
	2007 Championship position: 19th Wins: 0 Pole positions: 0 Fastest laps: 0 Points scored: 1							
2	AUSTRALIAN GP	Melbourne	20	Etihad Aldar Spyker F1 Team	B	2.4 Spyker F8 VII-Ferrari V8	2 laps behind	21/22
ret	MALAYSIAN GP	Sepang	20	Etihad Aldar Spyker F1 Team	B	2.4 Spyker F8 VII-Ferrari V8	accident on lap 1	22/22
15	BAHRAIN GP	Sakhir Circuit	20	Etihad Aldar Spyker F1 Team	B	2.4 Spyker F8 VII-Ferrari V8	4 laps behind	20/22
13	SPANISH GP	Barcelona	20	Etihad Aldar Spyker F1 Team	B	2.4 Spyker F8 VII-Ferrari V8	2 laps behind	20/22
ret	MONACO GP	Monte Carlo	20	Etihad Aldar Spyker F1 Team	B	2.4 Spyker F8 VII-Ferrari V8	accident	19/22
ret	CANADIAN GP	Montreal	20	Etihad Aldar Spyker F1 Team	B	2.4 Spyker F8 VII-Ferrari V8	accident	21/22
14	U S GP	Indianapolis	20	Etihad Aldar Spyker F1 Team	B	2.4 Spyker F8 VII-Ferrari V8	2 laps behind	21/22
17	FRENCH GP	Magny Cours	20	Etihad Aldar Spyker F1 Team	B	2.4 Spyker F8 VII-Ferrari V8	2 laps behind	22/22
ret	BRITISH GP	Silverstone	20	Etihad Aldar Spyker F1 Team	B	2.4 Spyker F8 VII-Ferrari V8	engine	20/22
ret	EUROPEAN GP	Nürburgring	20	Etihad Aldar Spyker F1 Team	B	2.4 Spyker F8 VII-Ferrari V8	accident	21/22
17	HUNGARIAN GP	Hungaroring	20	Etihad Aldar Spyker F1 Team	B	2.4 Spyker F8 VII-Ferrari V8	2 laps behind	21/22
21/ret	TURKISH GP	Istanbul	20	Etihad Aldar Spyker F1 Team	B	2.4 Spyker F8 VII-Ferrari V8	fuel pressure/5 laps behind	21/22
19	ITALIAN GP	Monza	20	Etihad Aldar Spyker F1 Team	B	2.4 Spyker F8 VII-Ferrari V8	1 lap behind	21/22

14	BELGIAN GP	Spa	20	Etihad Aldar Spyker F1 Team	B	2.4 Spyker F8 VII-Ferrari V8		20/22
8*	JAPANESE GP	Suzuka	20	Etihad Aldar Spyker F1 Team	B	2.4 Spyker F8 VII-Ferrari V8	*8th car penalized 25 secs/-1 lap	20/22
ret	CHINESE GP	Shanghai	20	Etihad Aldar Spyker F1 Team	B	2.4 Spyker F8 VII-Ferrari V8	accident	21/22
ret	BRAZILIAN GP	Interlagos	20	Etihad Aldar Spyker F1 Team	B	2.4 Spyker F8 VII-Ferrari V8	brakes	21/22

2008 Championship position: Unplaced

ret	AUSTRALIAN GP	Melbourne	20	Force India F1 Team	B	2.4 Force India VJM01-Ferrari V8	hydraulic pressure	19/22
ret	MALAYSIAN GP	Sepang	20	Force India F1 Team	B	2.4 Force India VJM01-Ferrari V8	hydraulics	21/22
19	BAHRAIN GP	Sakhir Circuit	20	Force India F1 Team	B	2.4 Force India VJM01-Ferrari V8	2 laps behind	20/22
ret	SPANISH GP	Barcelona	20	Force India F1 Team	B	2.4 Force India VJM01-Ferrari V8	accident – spun rammed by Vettel	20/22
16	TURKISH GP	Istanbul	20	Force India F1 Team	B	2.4 Force India VJM01-Ferrari V8	collision with Vettel – pitstop/-1 lap-	20/20
ret	MONACO GP	Monte Carlo	20	Force India F1 Team	B	2.4 Force India VJM01-Ferrari V8	hit by Räikkönen – accident damage	19/20
ret	CANADIAN GP	Montreal	20	Force India F1 Team	B	2.4 Force India VJM01-Ferrari V8	gearbox	17/20
19	FRENCH GP	Magny Cours	20	Force India F1 Team	B	2.4 Force India VJM01-Ferrari V8	1 lap behind	20/20
ret	BRITISH GP	Silverstone	20	Force India F1 Team	B	2.4 Force India VJM01-Ferrari V8	spun off	19/20
15	GERMAN GP	Hockenheim	20	Force India F1 Team	B	2.4 Force India VJM01-Ferrari V8		19/20
ret	HUNGARIAN GP	Hungaroring	20	Force India F1 Team	B	2.4 Force India VJM01-Ferrari V8	brakes/puncture	20/20
ret	EUROPEAN GP	Valencia	20	Force India F1 Team	B	2.4 Force India VJM01-Ferrari V8	accident – crashed into wall	20/20
13	BELGIAN GP	Spa	20	Force India F1 Team	B	2.4 Force India VJM01-Ferrari V8	1 lap behind	18/20
19	ITALIAN GP	Monza	20	Force India F1 Team	B	2.4 Force India VJM01-Ferrari V8	2 laps behind	20/20
ret	SINGAPORE GP	Singapore Circuit	20	Force India F1 Team	B	2.4 Force India VJM01-Ferrari V8	hit tyres avoiding Massa	19/20
ret	JAPANESE GP	Suzuka	20	Force India F1 Team	B	2.4 Force India VJM01-Ferrari V8	rear tyre failure	19/20
ret	CHINESE GP	Shanghai	20	Force India F1 Team	B	2.4 Force India VJM01-Ferrari V8	gearbox	19/20
16	BRAZILIAN GP	Interlagos	20	Force India F1 Team	B	2.4 Force India VJM01-Ferrari V8	1 lap behind	20/20

2009 Championship position: 17th Wins: 0 Pole positions: 0 Fastest laps: 1 Points scored: 5

9	AUSTRALIAN GP	Melbourne	20	Force India F1 Team	B	2.4 Force India VJM02-Mercedes V8	pit stop – debris damage	19/20
17	MALAYSIAN GP	Sepang	20	Force India F1 Team	B	2.4 Force India VJM02-Mercedes V8	rain-shortened race/1 lap behind	10/20
ret	CHINESE GP	Shanghai	20	Force India F1 Team	B	2.4 Force India VJM02-Mercedes V8	accident	19/20
16	BAHRAIN GP	Sakhir Circuit	20	Force India F1 Team	B	2.4 Force India VJM02-Mercedes V8	1 lap behind	16/20
ret	SPANISH GP	Barcelona	20	Force India F1 Team	B	2.4 Force India VJM02-Mercedes V8	ran into Trulli on lap 1	19/20
14	MONACO GP	Monte Carlo	20	Force India F1 Team	B	2.4 Force India VJM02-Mercedes V8	changed tyre strategy/1 lap behind	15/20
17	TURKISH GP	Istanbul	20	Force India F1 Team	B	2.4 Force India VJM02-Mercedes V8	1 lap behind	15/20
17	BRITISH GP	Silverstone	20	Force India F1 Team	B	2.4 Force India VJM02-Mercedes V8	started from pitlane/1 lap behind	18/20
15	GERMAN GP	Hockenheim	20	Force India F1 Team	B	2.4 Force India VJM02-Mercedes V8	collision Raikkonen – wing damage	7/20
ret	HUNGARIAN GP	Hungaroring	20	Force India F1 Team	B	2.4 Force India VJM02-Mercedes V8	water temperature	18/20
10	EUROPEAN GP	Valencia	20	Force India F1 Team	B	2.4 Force India VJM02-Mercedes V8		12/20
11	BELGIAN GP	Spa	20	Force India F1 Team	B	2.4 Force India VJM02-Mercedes V8		11/20
4	ITALIAN GP	Monza	20	Force India F1 Team	B	2.4 Force India VJM02-Mercedes V8	FL	2/20
ret	SINGAPORE GP	Singapore Circuit	20	Force India F1 Team	B	2.4 Force India VJM02-Mercedes V8	brakes	16/20
13	JAPANESE GP	Suzuka	20	Force India F1 Team	B	2.4 Force India VJM02-Mercedes V8	collision with Kovailainen – spin	4/20
ret	BRAZILIAN GP	Interlagos	20	Force India F1 Team	B	2.4 Force India VJM02-Mercedes V8	hit bt Trulli on on lap 1	3/20
17	ABU DHABI GP	Yas Marina Circuit	20	Force India F1 Team	B	2.4 Force India VJM02-Mercedes V8	1 lap behind	18/20

2010 Championship position: 11th Wins: 0 Pole positions: 0 Fastest laps: 0 Points scored: 47

12	BAHRAIN GP	Sakhir Circuit	14	Force India F1 Team	B	2.4 Force India VJM03-Mercedes V8	collision with Kubica on lap 1	10/24
ret	AUSTRALIAN GP	Melbourne	14	Force India F1 Team	B	2.4 Force India VJM03-Mercedes V8	engine	10/24
5	MALAYSIAN GP	Sepang	14	Force India F1 Team	B	2.4 Force India VJM03-Mercedes V8		4/24
11	CHINESE GP	Shanghai Circuit	14	Force India F1 Team	B	2.4 Force India VJM03-Mercedes V8		10/24
7	SPANISH GP	Barcelona	14	Force India F1 Team	B	2.4 Force India VJM03-Mercedes V8		11/24
8	MONACO GP	Monte Carlo	14	Force India F1 Team	B	2.4 Force India VJM03-Mercedes V8		12/24
9	TURKISH GP	Istanbul Park	14	Force India F1 Team	B	2.4 Force India VJM03-Mercedes V8		11/24
10	CANADIAN GP	Montreal	14	Force India F1 Team	B	2.4 Force India VJM03-Mercedes V8	delayed by puncture/1 lap behind	9/24
6	EUROPEAN GP	Valencia	14	Force India F1 Team	B	2.4 Force India VJM03-Mercedes V8		13/24
8	BRITISH GP	Silverstone	14	Force India F1 Team	B	2.4 Force India VJM03-Mercedes V8		14/24
17*	GERMAN GP	Hockenheim	14	Force India F1 Team	B	2.4 Force India VJM03-Mercedes V8	ran off track – extra pit stop/-2 laps	14/24
ret	HUNGARIAN GP	Hungaroring	14	Force India F1 Team	B	2.4 Force India VJM03-Mercedes V8	pitlane collision with Kubica	13/24
5	BELGIAN GP	Spa	14	Force India F1 Team	B	2.4 Force India VJM03-Mercedes V8		8/24
16	ITALIAN GP	Monza	14	Force India F1 Team	B	2.4 Force India VJM03-Mercedes V8	nose damage/1 lap behind	11/24
9*	SINGAPORE GP	Marina Bay Circuit	14	Force India F1 Team	B	2.4 Force India VJM03-Mercedes V8	*8th but given 20-sec penalty	16/24
ret	JAPANESE GP	Suzuka	14	Force India F1 Team	B	2.4 Force India VJM03-Mercedes V8	oil leak	15/24
ret	KOREAN GP	Yeongam	14	Force India F1 Team	B	2.4 Force India VJM03-Mercedes V8	collision Kobayashi – penalty for Brazil	12/24
12	BRAZILIAN GP	Interlagos	14	Force India F1 Team	B	2.4 Force India VJM03-Mercedes V8		18/24
13	ABU DHABI GP	Yas Marina Circuit	14	Force India F1 Team	B	2.4 Force India VJM03-Mercedes V8		13/24

2011 Championship position: 9th Wins: 0 Pole positions: 0 Fastest laps: 0 Points scored: 42

9	AUSTRALIAN GP	Melbourne	14	Force India F1 Team	P	2.4 Force India VJM04-Mercedes V8	11th but 7 & 8th cars dsq/-1 lap	16/24
11	MALAYSIAN GP	Sepang	14	Force India F1 Team	P	2.4 Force India VJM04-Mercedes V8	collision Barrichello – extra pit stop	17/24
15	CHINESE GP	Shanghai Circuit	14	Force India F1 Team	P	2.4 Force India VJM04-Mercedes V8	1 lap behind	8/24
13	TURKISH GP	Istanbul Park	14	Force India F1 Team	P	2.4 Force India VJM04-Mercedes V8	1 lap behind	12/24
13	SPANISH GP	Barcelona	14	Force India F1 Team	P	2.4 Force India VJM04-Mercedes V8	1 lap behind	17/24
7	MONACO GP	Monte Carlo	14	Force India F1 Team	P	2.4 Force India VJM04-Mercedes V8	1 lap behind	15/24
ret	CANADIAN GP	Montreal	14	Force India F1 Team	P	2.4 Force India VJM04-Mercedes V8	gambled on slicks – spun off	14/24
9	EUROPEAN GP	Valencia	14	Force India F1 Team	P	2.4 Force India VJM04-Mercedes V8	1 lap behind	10/24
11	BRITISH GP	Silverstone	14	Force India F1 Team	P	2.4 Force India VJM04-Mercedes V8	1 lap behind	11/24
6	GERMAN GP	Hockenheim	14	Force India F1 Team	P	2.4 Force India VJM04-Mercedes V8		8/24
7	HUNGARIAN GP	Hungaroring	14	Force India F1 Team	P	2.4 Force India VJM04-Mercedes V8	2 laps behind	11/24
7	BELGIAN GP	Spa	14	Force India F1 Team	P	2.4 Force India VJM04-Mercedes V8		15/24
ret	ITALIAN GP	Monza	14	Force India F1 Team	P	2.4 Force India VJM04-Mercedes V8	hydraulics	12/24
8	SINGAPORE GP	Marina Bay Circuit	14	Force India F1 Team	P	2.4 Force India VJM04-Mercedes V8	1 lap behind	9/24
11	JAPANESE GP	Suzuka	14	Force India F1 Team	P	2.4 Force India VJM04-Mercedes V8		11/24
ret	KOREAN GP	Yeongam	14	Sahara Force India F1 Team	P	2.4 Force India VJM04-Mercedes V8		10/24
9	INDIAN GP	Buddh Circuit	14	Sahara Force India F1 Team	P	2.4 Force India VJM04-Mercedes V8	1 lap behind	8/24
8	ABU DHABI GP	Yas Marina Circuit	14	Sahara Force India F1 Team	P	2.4 Force India VJM04-Mercedes V8		9/24
6	BRAZILIAN GP	Interlagos	14	Sahara Force India F1 Team	P	2.4 Force India VJM04-Mercedes V8	1 lap behind	8/24

GP Starts: 90 GP Wins: 0 Pole positions: 0 Fastest laps: 1 Points: 95

AGURI SUZUKI

WITH a father who had founded the Japanese karting association, the young Aguri Suzuki naturally became involved in the sport, winning the title in 1981. Then he moved into F3 and finished second in the 1983 championship, which brought an offer to race for Nissan in sports and touring cars; he duly took the 1986 Group A championship. Single-seaters were still his first priority, however, and in 1987 he went into the All-Japan F3000 series, becoming runner-up in the championship, before finishing the job the following year by taking the title.

Suzuki's eyes were now on grand prix racing, and he spent a brief period in Europe racing the Footwork-backed March in the F3000 series, before being given a race in the Japanese GP with the Larrousse team in place of the indisposed Yannick Dalmas. Having previously been associated with Yamaha, he joined the Zakspeed team, which was running the Japanese manufacturer's engines for 1989, but he drew a complete blank, failing even to pre-qualify the hopeless device at any of the 16 grands prix.

This could have sunk many a driver's career, but luckily Aguri was able to find a drive with Larrousse in 1990, when he became a points scorer on three occasions, including his splendid drive at Suzuka, which cemented his future. Unfortunately, the precarious financial position at Larrousse, and consequent lack of testing and development, blunted his progress the following year, and for 1992 he joined the Footwork team, which was regrouping and armed with the Mugen Honda V10. His season was disappointing, his form not helped by the problems he had in fitting into the cockpit, and he was completely overshadowed by team-mate Michele Alboreto. For 1993, he remained with the team, paired with Derek Warwick, but once again finishes in the points eluded him. The year was punctuated by a worryingly high number of spins and collisions, and apart from sixth place on the grid at Spa, which seemed to suit the Footwork's active suspension system, there was precious little to cheer the Japanese driver, who lost his drive when the restructured Arrows team under Jack Oliver were no longer in receipt of finance from the Far East.

Aguri returned home to race for Nissan, perhaps thinking his F1 career was behind him, but with Eddie Irvine suspended, he was called into the Jordan team at the Pacific GP. He was uneasy about this because of his lack of preparation and fitness, and he was proved right when he spun out. However, it did not hurt his long-term plans and, with Mugen Honda's backing, he signed to race for Ligier in 1995 in a season shared with Martin Brundle. Sixth place at Hockenheim apart, the Japanese driver looked less than convincing when compared with his team-mates. He had already decided to retire from Formula 1 after the Japanese GP, but a practice accident at Suzuka left him with a neck injury and cracked ribs, and he was unable to take any further part in proceedings.

For 1996, Suzuki signed a contract with Nissan to return to the All-Japan GT championship to race their revised Skyline, and he was a member of the crew of the TWR-run Nissan R390 that finished third at Le Mans in 1998. By then, he had formed his own team, Autobacs Racing Team Aguri (ARTA), which competed in Super GT racing in Japan with a Nissan Skyline, before switching to a Honda for 2000, which was the last season that he would race. He also fielded a team in Formula Nippon between 1997 and 2002, before joining forces with Adrian Fernandez to found an Indy Racing League team, running Japanese hopeful Kosuki Matsuura, before switching camps to Panther Racing.

His dream of running a Formula 1 team was finally realised in 2006, when he launched the Super Aguri F1 Team with major backing from Honda, who wanted to keep Takuma Sato on the grid. The team was always under-funded during its short existence, but the professionalism and determination shown by all concerned deserved more than sudden extinction early in 2008, when Honda finally withdrew their support.

Aguri returned to Japan to contest the 2010 All-Japan GT500 championship, where his cars were always a factor, but not championship winners.

SUZUKI, Aguri (J) b 8/9/1960, Tokyo

	1988 Championship position: Unplaced							
	Race	Circuit	No	Entrant	Tyres	Capacity/Car/Engine	Comment	Q Pos/Entries
16	JAPANESE GP	Suzuka	29	Larrousse Calmels	G	3.5 Lola LC88-Cosworth V8	3 laps behind	20/31
	1989 Championship position: Unplaced							
dnpq	BRAZILIAN GP	Rio	35	West Zakspeed Racing	P	3.5 Zakspeed 891-Yamaha V8		36/38
dnpq	SAN MARINO GP	Imola	35	West Zakspeed Racing	P	3.5 Zakspeed 891-Yamaha V8		37/39
dnpq	MONACO GP	Monte Carlo	35	West Zakspeed Racing	P	3.5 Zakspeed 891-Yamaha V8		37/38
dnpq	MEXICAN GP	Mexico City	35	West Zakspeed Racing	P	3.5 Zakspeed 891-Yamaha V8		36/39
dnpq	US GP (PHOENIX)	Phoenix	35	West Zakspeed Racing	P	3.5 Zakspeed 891-Yamaha V8		38/39
dnpq	CANADIAN GP	Montreal	35	West Zakspeed Racing	P	3.5 Zakspeed 891-Yamaha V8		38/39
dnpq	FRENCH GP	Paul Ricard	35	West Zakspeed Racing	P	3.5 Zakspeed 891-Yamaha V8		37/39
dnpq	BRITISH GP	Silverstone	35	West Zakspeed Racing	P	3.5 Zakspeed 891-Yamaha V8		38/39
dnpq	GERMAN GP	Hockenheim	35	West Zakspeed Racing	P	3.5 Zakspeed 891-Yamaha V8		38/39
dnpq	HUNGARIAN GP	Hungaroring	35	West Zakspeed Racing	P	3.5 Zakspeed 891-Yamaha V8		38/39
dnpq	BELGIAN GP	Spa	35	West Zakspeed Racing	P	3.5 Zakspeed 891-Yamaha V8		36/39
dnpq	ITALIAN GP	Monza	35	West Zakspeed Racing	P	3.5 Zakspeed 891-Yamaha V8		36/39
dnpq	PORTUGUESE GP	Estoril	35	West Zakspeed Racing	P	3.5 Zakspeed 891-Yamaha V8		37/39
dnpq	SPANISH GP	Jerez	35	West Zakspeed Racing	P	3.5 Zakspeed 891-Yamaha V8		36/38
dnpq	JAPANESE GP	Suzuka	35	West Zakspeed Racing	P	3.5 Zakspeed 891-Yamaha V8		34/39
dnpq	AUSTRALIAN GP	Adelaide	35	West Zakspeed Racing	P	3.5 Zakspeed 891-Yamaha V8		36/39

1990 Championship position: 10th=   Wins: 0   Pole positions: 0   Fastest laps: 0   Points scored: 6

Result	GP	Circuit	No	Team	Tyre	Car	Notes	Grid
ret	US GP (PHOENIX)	Phoenix	30	Espo Larrousse F1	G	3.5 Lola LC89-Lamborghini V12	brakes	18/35
ret	BRAZILIAN GP	Rio	30	Espo Larrousse F1	G	3.5 Lola LC89-Lamborghini V12	suspension	18/35
ret	SAN MARINO GP	Imola	30	Espo Larrousse F1	G	3.5 Lola 90-Lamborghini V12	clutch	16/34
ret	MONACO GP	Monte Carlo	30	Espo Larrousse F1	G	3.5 Lola 90-Lamborghini V12	electrics	15/35
12	CANADIAN GP	Montreal	30	Espo Larrousse F1	G	3.5 Lola 90-Lamborghini V12	collision with Martini – pit stop/-4 laps	18/35
ret	MEXICAN GP	Mexico City	30	Espo Larrousse F1	G	3.5 Lola 90-Lamborghini V12	collision with Nakajima	19/35
7	FRENCH GP	Paul Ricard	30	Espo Larrousse F1	G	3.5 Lola 90-Lamborghini V12	1 lap behind	14/35
6	BRITISH GP	Silverstone	30	Espo Larrousse F1	G	3.5 Lola 90-Lamborghini V12	1 lap behind	9/35
ret	GERMAN GP	Hockenheim	30	Espo Larrousse F1	G	3.5 Lola 90-Lamborghini V12	clutch	11/35
ret	HUNGARIAN GP	Hungaroring	30	Espo Larrousse F1	G	3.5 Lola 90-Lamborghini V12	engine	19/35
ret/dns*	BELGIAN GP	Spa	30	Espo Larrousse F1	G	3.5 Lola 90-Lamborghini V12	crash at first start/*did not restart	11/33
ret	ITALIAN GP	Monza	30	Espo Larrousse F1	G	3.5 Lola 90-Lamborghini V12	electrics	18/33
14/ret	PORTUGUESE GP	Estoril	30	Espo Larrousse F1	G	3.5 Lola 90-Lamborghini V12	collision with Caffi/3 laps behind	11/33
6	SPANISH GP	Jerez	30	Espo Larrousse F1	G	3.5 Lola 90-Lamborghini V12		15/33
3	JAPANESE GP	Suzuka	30	Espo Larrousse F1	G	3.5 Lola 90-Lamborghini V12		10/30
ret	AUSTRALIAN GP	Adelaide	30	Espo Larrousse F1	G	3.5 Lola 90-Lamborghini V12	differential	24/30

1991 Championship position: 18th=   Wins: 0   Pole positions: 0   Fastest laps: 0   Points scored: 1

Result	GP	Circuit	No	Team	Tyre	Car	Notes	Grid
6	US GP (PHOENIX)	Phoenix	30	Larrousse F1	G	3.5 Lola L91-Cosworth V8	2 laps behind	21/34
dns	BRAZILIAN GP	Interlagos	30	Larrousse F1	G	3.5 Lola L91-Cosworth V8	no fuel pressure on dummy grid	17/34
ret	SAN MARINO GP	Imola	30	Larrousse F1	G	3.5 Lola L91-Cosworth V8	spun off	20/34
ret	MONACO GP	Monte Carlo	30	Larrousse F1	G	3.5 Lola L91-Cosworth V8	brake problems – crashed	19/34
ret	CANADIAN GP	Montreal	30	Larrousse F1	G	3.5 Lola L91-Cosworth V8	fire – broken fuel line	22/34
ret	MEXICAN GP	Mexico City	30	Larrousse F1	G	3.5 Lola L91-Cosworth V8	gearbox	19/34
ret	FRENCH GP	Magny Cours	30	Larrousse F1	G	3.5 Lola L91-Cosworth V8	clutch	22/34
ret	BRITISH GP	Silverstone	30	Larrousse F1	G	3.5 Lola L91-Cosworth V8	collision with Alesi	22/34
ret	GERMAN GP	Hockenheim	30	Larrousse F1	G	3.5 Lola L91-Cosworth V8	started from pitlane/engine	22/34
ret	HUNGARIAN GP	Hungaroring	30	Larrousse F1	G	3.5 Lola L91-Cosworth V8	engine	22/34
dnq	BELGIAN GP	Spa	30	Larrousse F1	G	3.5 Lola L91-Cosworth V8		27/34
dnq	ITALIAN GP	Monza	30	Larrousse F1	G	3.5 Lola L91-Cosworth V8		30/34
ret	PORTUGUESE GP	Estoril	30	Larrousse F1	G	3.5 Lola L91-Cosworth V8	gearbox	25/34
dnq	SPANISH GP	Barcelona	30	Larrousse F1	G	3.5 Lola L91-Cosworth V8		27/33
ret	JAPANESE GP	Suzuka	30	Larrousse F1	G	3.5 Lola L91-Cosworth V8	engine	25/31
dnq	AUSTRALIAN GP	Adelaide	30	Larrousse F1	G	3.5 Lola L91-Cosworth V8		27/32

1992 Championship position: Unplaced

Result	GP	Circuit	No	Team	Tyre	Car	Notes	Grid
8	SOUTH AFRICAN GP	Kyalami	10	Footwork Mugen Honda	G	3.5 Footwork FA13-Mugen Honda V10	2 laps behind	16/30
dnq	MEXICAN GP	Mexico City	10	Footwork Mugen Honda	G	3.5 Footwork FA13-Mugen Honda V10		27/30
ret	BRAZILIAN GP	Interlagos	10	Footwork Mugen Honda	G	3.5 Footwork FA13-Mugen Honda V10	oil system	22/31
7	SPANISH GP	Barcelona	10	Footwork Mugen Honda	G	3.5 Footwork FA13-Mugen Honda V10	2 laps behind	19/32
10	SAN MARINO GP	Imola	10	Footwork Mugen Honda	G	3.5 Footwork FA13-Mugen Honda V10	2 laps behind	11/32
11	MONACO GP	Monte Carlo	10	Footwork Mugen Honda	G	3.5 Footwork FA13-Mugen Honda V10	2 laps behind	19/32
dnq	CANADIAN GP	Montreal	10	Footwork Mugen Honda	G	3.5 Footwork FA13-Mugen Honda V10		27/32
ret	FRENCH GP	Magny Cours	10	Footwork Mugen Honda	G	3.5 Footwork FA13-Mugen Honda V10	slid off avoiding Grouillard	15/30
12	BRITISH GP	Silverstone	10	Footwork Mugen Honda	G	3.5 Footwork FA13-Mugen Honda V10	2 laps behind	17/32
ret	GERMAN GP	Hockenheim	10	Footwork Mugen Honda	G	3.5 Footwork FA13-Mugen Honda V10	spun off lap 1	15/32
ret	HUNGARIAN GP	Hungaroring	10	Footwork Mugen Honda	G	3.5 Footwork FA13-Mugen Honda V10	collision with Gachot	14/31
9	BELGIAN GP	Spa	10	Footwork Mugen Honda	G	3.5 Footwork FA13-Mugen Honda V10	1 lap behind	25/30
ret	ITALIAN GP	Monza	10	Footwork Mugen Honda	G	3.5 Footwork FA13-Mugen Honda V10	spun off	19/28
10	PORTUGUESE GP	Estoril	10	Footwork Mugen Honda	G	3.5 Footwork FA13-Mugen Honda V10	started from pitlane/3 laps behind	17/26
8	JAPANESE GP	Suzuka	10	Footwork Mugen Honda	G	3.5 Footwork FA13-Mugen Honda V10	1 lap behind	16/26
8	AUSTRALIAN GP	Adelaide	10	Footwork Mugen Honda	G	3.5 Footwork FA13-Mugen Honda V10	2 laps behind	18/26

1993 Championship position: Unplaced

Result	GP	Circuit	No	Team	Tyre	Car	Notes	Grid
ret	SOUTH AFRICAN GP	Kyalami	10	Footwork Mugen Honda	G	3.5 Footwork FA13B-Mugen Honda V10	ran into Barbazza – suspension	20/26
ret	BRAZILIAN GP	Rio	10	Footwork Mugen Honda	G	3.5 Footwork FA13B-Mugen Honda V10	crashed in rainstorm	19/26
ret	EUROPEAN GP	Donington	10	Footwork Mugen Honda	G	3.5 Footwork FA14-Mugen Honda V10	gearbox	23/26
9	SAN MARINO GP	Imola	10	Footwork Mugen Honda	G	3.5 Footwork FA14-Mugen Honda V10	stop & go penalty/brakes/-7 laps	21/26
10	SPANISH GP	Barcelona	10	Footwork Mugen Honda	G	3.5 Footwork FA14-Mugen Honda V10	2 laps behind	19/26
ret	MONACO GP	Monte Carlo	10	Footwork Mugen Honda	G	3.5 Footwork FA14-Mugen Honda V10	spun off	18/26
13	CANADIAN GP	Montreal	10	Footwork Mugen Honda	G	3.5 Footwork FA14-Mugen Honda V10	gearbox trouble – spin/3 laps behind	16/26
12	FRENCH GP	Magny Cours	10	Footwork Mugen Honda	G	3.5 Footwork FA14-Mugen Honda V10	stalled at pit stop/2 laps behind	13/26
ret	BRITISH GP	Silverstone	10	Footwork Mugen Honda	G	3.5 Footwork FA14-Mugen Honda V10	spun off	10/26
ret	GERMAN GP	Hockenheim	10	Footwork Mugen Honda	G	3.5 Footwork FA14-Mugen Honda V10	gearbox	8/26
ret	HUNGARIAN GP	Hungaroring	10	Footwork Mugen Honda	G	3.5 Footwork FA14-Mugen Honda V10	spun off	10/26
ret	BELGIAN GP	Spa	10	Footwork Mugen Honda	G	3.5 Footwork FA14-Mugen Honda V10	hydraulic failure	6/25
ret	ITALIAN GP	Monza	10	Footwork Mugen Honda	G	3.5 Footwork FA14-Mugen Honda V10	collision with Warwick spun off on lap 1	8/26
ret	PORTUGUESE GP	Estoril	10	Footwork Mugen Honda	G	3.5 Footwork FA14-Mugen Honda V10	spin/gearbox	16/26
ret	JAPANESE GP	Suzuka	10	Footwork Mugen Honda	G	3.5 Footwork FA14-Mugen Honda V10	spun off	9/24
7	AUSTRALIAN GP	Adelaide	10	Footwork Mugen Honda	G	3.5 Footwork FA14-Mugen Honda V10	1 lap behind	10/24

1994 Championship position: Unplaced

Result	GP	Circuit	No	Team	Tyre	Car	Notes	Grid
ret	PACIFIC GP	T.I. Circuit	15	Sasol Jordan	G	3.5 Jordan 194-Hart V10	steering problem – crashed	20/28

1995 Championship position: 17th=   Wins: 0   Pole positions: 0   Fastest laps: 0   Points scored: 1

Result	GP	Circuit	No	Team	Tyre	Car	Notes	Grid
8	BRAZILIAN GP	Interlagos	25	Ligier Gitanes Blondes	G	3.0 Ligier JS41-Mugen Honda V10	2 laps behind	15/26
ret	ARGENTINE GP	Buenos Aires	25	Ligier Gitanes Blondes	G	3.0 Ligier JS41-Mugen Honda V10	collision with Salo	19/26
11	SAN MARINO GP	Imola	25	Ligier Gitanes Blondes	G	3.0 Ligier JS41-Mugen Honda V10	3 laps behind	16/26
6	GERMAN GP	Hockenheim	25	Ligier Gitanes Blondes	G	3.0 Ligier JS41-Mugen Honda V10	1 lap behind	18/24
ret	PACIFIC GP	T.I. Circuit	25	Ligier Gitanes Blondes	G	3.0 Ligier JS41-Mugen Honda V10	spun off	13/24
dns	JAPANESE GP	Suzuka	25	Ligier Gitanes Blondes	G	3.0 Ligier JS41-Mugen Honda V10	accident in practice	(13)/24

GP Starts: 63 (64)   GP Wins: 0   Pole positions: 0   Fastest laps: 0   Points: 8

TOSHIO SUZUKI

IN 1993, Toshio Suzuki took part in a grand prix for the first time, at the age of 38, having arranged a two-race deal with Larrousse in place of Philippe Alliot. His aim was to finish, and in that he succeeded, but just to compete at this level must have been a source of great satisfaction for this very popular driver, who had been Japanese Formula 3 champion as far back as 1979. He raced in Europe during 1980/81, and was a leading contender in the Japanese F2 and F3000 series for more than a decade. He enjoyed little luck, however, until the 1995 season, when at last things went his way and he won the All-Japan F3000 series at the last gasp for Hoshino Racing.

It was in sports car racing that Toshio found his greatest success. After driving Toyotas, he joined Nissan to team up with Kazuyoshi Hoshino, the pair becoming a formidable combination not only at home, but also on the international stage. Their proudest triumph was in the 1992 Daytona 24-hours when, with Masahiro Hasemi, they became the first all-Japanese crew to win a major endurance race.

The veteran Suzuki became a regular in the All-Japan GT championship, racing a Toyota Supra, and a member of the driver line-up for the Japanese giant's Le Mans assault. After finishing ninth in the 1998 Le Mans 24-hours with the Toyota GT-One, he teamed up again with Ukyo Katayama and Keiichi Tsuchiya to finish a fine second a year later.

Suzuki returned to domestic competition and for a while took over the running of the R & D team in the GT300 class. As Nissan's chief test driver, he is also known for his almost obsessive development work for the Nissan GT-R. The Japanese ace has pounded around the Nürburgring's Nordschleife developing the GT-R V-Spec, setting a time of 7 minutes, 24.2 seconds in semi-wet conditions in 2010, but inevitably more will come as the beast is refined and tamed.

JACQUES SWATERS

A GREAT enthusiast, Jacques Swaters made his racing debut in the 1948 Spa 24-hours in an MG shared with his friend, Paul Frère. In 1950, he was one of the founders of Ecurie Belgique and initially handled a Veritas, but when André Pilette was injured in the team's Talbot at the 1951 Dutch GP, he stepped in to take his place.

For 1952, the team bought a Ferrari T500, which was mainly raced by Charles de Tornaco, but Swaters drove it in two grands prix the following year and also won the AVUS F2 race. For 1954, he raced the Ferrari fitted with a 625 engine, but found greater success in sports car events with the team's recently acquired Jaguar C-Type, taking fourth at Le Mans and third in the Reims 12-hours with Roger Laurent. Swaters then concentrated on sports cars, taking the team's D-Type to third place at Le Mans with Johnny Claes in 1955, and finishing fourth in 1956 with the same car, partnered by Freddy Rousselle.

By then, Swaters was busy with the management of Ecurie Francorchamps and his thriving Ferrari concession; he retired from racing after a final appearance in the Sarthe classic in 1957.

SUZUKI, Toshio (J) b 10/3/1955, Saitama

1993 Championship position: Unplaced

	Race	Circuit	No	Entrant	Tyres	Capacity/Car/Engine	Comment	Q Pos/Entries
12	JAPANESE GP	Suzuka	19	Larrousse F1	G	3.5 Larrousse LH93-Lamborghini V12	spin/2 laps behind	23/24
14	AUSTRALIAN GP	Adelaide	19	Larrousse F1	G	3.5 Larrousse LH93-Lamborghini V12	5 laps behind	24/24

GP Starts: 2   GP Wins: 0   Pole positions: 0   Fastest laps: 0   Points: 0

SWATERS, Jacques (B) b 30/10/1926, Woluwe-Saint-Lambert, Brussels – d 10/12/2010, Brussels

1951 Championship position: Unplaced

	Race	Circuit	No	Entrant	Tyres	Capacity/Car/Engine	Comment	Q Pos/Entries
10	GERMAN GP	Nürburgring	93	Ecurie Belgique	D	4.5 Lago-Talbot T26C 6	2 laps behind	22/23
ret	ITALIAN GP	Monza	28	Ecurie Belgique	D	4.5 Lago-Talbot T26C 6	overheating	22/22

1953 Championship position: Unplaced

dns	BELGIAN GP	Spa	42	Ecurie Francorchamps	E	2.0 Ferrari 500 4	practised only	- / -
7	GERMAN GP	Nürburgring	18	Ecurie Francorchamps	E	2.0 Ferrari 500 4	1 lap behind	19/35
ret	SWISS GP	Bremgarten	2	Ecurie Francorchamps	E	2.0 Ferrari 500 4	crashed	13/23

1954 Championship position: Unplaced

ret	BELGIAN GP	Spa	2	Ecurie Francorchamps	E	2.5 Ferrari 500/625 4	engine	14/15
8	SWISS GP	Bremgarten	2	Ecurie Francorchamps	E	2.5 Ferrari 500/625 4	8 laps behind	16/16
ret	SPANISH GP	Pedralbes	30	Ecurie Francorchamps	E	2.5 Ferrari 500/625 4	engine	19/22

GP Starts: 7   GP Wins: 0   Pole positions: 0   Fastest laps: 0   Points: 0

TORANOSUKE TAKAGI

A PROTÉGÉ of Satoru Nakajima, Toranosuke Takagi has an apt forename, since in part it means 'tiger' in Japanese, which fits this aggressive hard charger's racing style. Conversely, off the track, he is low-key, and is of a retiring and shy disposition.

After a brilliant karting career and a season in Formula Toyota, Takagi was picked by TOM'S to succeed Jacques Villeneuve in their F3 squad when he was aged just 18 in 1993. He caught the eye of Nakajima, who gave him a chance to race in his F3000 team late the following year.

Then three seasons were spent in Formula Nippon, where Takagi was a regular top-six runner and an occasional winner. The 1997 campaign also saw the Japanese driver clock up over 2000km of testing in preparation for his inclusion in the Tyrrell line-up the following year. Unfortunately, he stepped into a team that was going through the motions, having been purchased by British American Racing. However, the year gave him a useful opportunity to learn the circuits and provided a good platform to build on when he took his sponsorship to Arrows for 1999. As at Tyrrell, he impressed with a fair turn of speed, but as often as not was found wanting when it came to putting everything together in the races.

On the basis of two years spent in admittedly poor cars, Takagi proved to be just the latest in a long line of Japanese hopefuls, and he returned to Formula Nippon with the Nakajima team in 2000, where he found immediate success by taking the championship crown. Having failed to make the grade in Formula 1, he tried his hand at the Champ Car series with Walker Racing and then the IRL for Mo Nunn Racing.

Takagi's best year was 2003, when he placed tenth in the final IRL standings (despite a 23-point deduction for unacceptable driving at Texas) and took a very good fifth place in the Indianapolis 500, which won him the prestigious Rookie of the Year honour. Things swiftly turned sour in 2004, however, after he crashed heavily in a pre-season test at Motegi. Seemingly lacking confidence in his Dallara chassis thereafter, 'Tiger' tamely ran in a conservative manner as he wound down a season to forget.

In 2005, Takagi was back in Japan and had taken on part ownership of the front-running Cerumo team in the All-Japan (Super) GT series. He won both races held at Fuji and shared the championship with his driving partner, Yuji Tachikawa, in a Lexus SC430. In 2006, he dropped down to 11th in the final placings, but such was the level of competition that he was only 12 points adrift of the championship winning score. Less happy was his return to Formula Nippon, where the former champion failed to score even a single point in his two seasons in the category.

Takagi raced on in Super GTs until the end of the 2008 season, before acting as director of his team, Lexus Team Zent Cerumo, running a Lexus 430C.

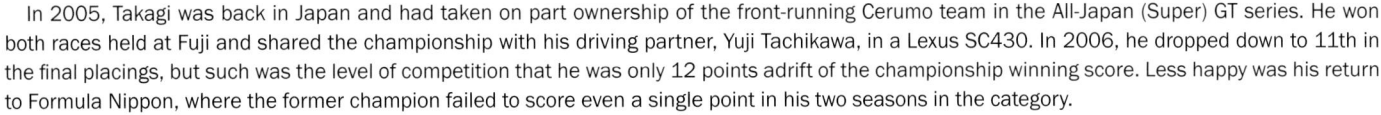

TAKAGI, Toranosuke (J) b 12/2/1972, Shizouka

	Race	Circuit	No	Entrant	Tyres	Capacity/Car/Engine	Comment	Q Pos/Entries
	1998 Championship position: Unplaced							
ret	AUSTRALIAN GP	Melbourne	21	Tyrrell Ford	G	3.0 Tyrrell 026-Ford Zetec-R V10	collision on first lap	13/22
ret	BRAZILIAN GP	Interlagos	21	Tyrrell Ford	G	3.0 Tyrrell 026-Ford Zetec-R V10	engine	17/22
12	ARGENTINE GP	Buenos Aires	21	Tyrrell Ford	G	3.0 Tyrrell 026-Ford Zetec-R V10	2 laps behind	13/22
ret	SAN MARINO GP	Imola	21	Tyrrell Ford	G	3.0 Tyrrell 026-Ford Zetec-R V10	engine	15/22
13	SPANISH GP	Barcelona	21	Tyrrell Ford	G	3.0 Tyrrell 026-Ford Zetec-R V10	2 laps behind	21/22
11	MONACO GP	Monte Carlo	21	Tyrrell Ford	G	3.0 Tyrrell 026-Ford Zetec-R V10	2 laps behind	20/22
ret	CANADIAN GP	Montreal	21	Tyrrell Ford	G	3.0 Tyrrell 026-Ford Zetec-R V10	transmission	16/22
ret	FRENCH GP	Magny Cours	21	Tyrrell Ford	G	3.0 Tyrrell 026-Ford Zetec-R V10	engine	20/22
9	BRITISH GP	Silverstone	21	Tyrrell Ford	G	3.0 Tyrrell 026-Ford Zetec-R V10	4 laps behind	19/22
ret	AUSTRIAN GP	A1-Ring	21	Tyrrell Ford	G	3.0 Tyrrell 026-Ford Zetec-R V10	spun off on first corner	20/22
13	GERMAN GP	Hockenheim	21	Tyrrell Ford	G	3.0 Tyrrell 026-Ford Zetec-R V10	1 lap behind	15/22
14	HUNGARIAN GP	Hungaroring	21	Tyrrell Ford	G	3.0 Tyrrell 026-Ford Zetec-R V10	3 laps behind	18/22
ret	BELGIAN GP	Spa	21	Tyrrell Ford	G	3.0 Tyrrell 026-Ford Zetec-R V10	spun off	19/22
9	ITALIAN GP	Monza	21	Tyrrell Ford	G	3.0 Tyrrell 026-Ford Zetec-R V10	1 lap behind	19/22
16	LUXEMBOURG GP	Nürburgring	21	Tyrrell Ford	G	3.0 Tyrrell 026-Ford Zetec-R V10	3 laps behind	19/22
ret	JAPANESE GP	Suzuka	21	Tyrrell Ford	G	3.0 Tyrrell 026-Ford Zetec-R V10	collision with Tuero	17/22
	1999 Championship position: Unplaced							
7	AUSTRALIAN GP	Melbourne	15	Arrows	B	3.0 Arrows A20-V10		17/22
8	BRAZILIAN GP	Interlagos	15	Arrows	B	3.0 Arrows A20-V10	3 laps behind	19/22
ret	SAN MARINO GP	Imola	15	Arrows	B	3.0 Arrows A20-V10	fuel pressure	20/22
ret	MONACO GP	Monte Carlo	15	Arrows	B	3.0 Arrows A20-V10	engine	19/22
12	SPANISH GP	Barcelona	15	Arrows	B	3.0 Arrows A20-V10	3 laps behind	20/22
ret	CANADIAN GP	Montreal	15	Arrows	B	3.0 Arrows A20-V10	transmission	19/22
11/dsq*	FRENCH GP	Magny Cours	15	Arrows	B	3.0 Arrows A20-V10	*used illegal spec tyres	22/22
16	BRITISH GP	Silverstone	15	Arrows	B	3.0 Arrows A20-V10	2 laps behind	19/22
ret	AUSTRIAN GP	A1-Ring	15	Arrows	B	3.0 Arrows A20-V10	engine	20/22

ret	GERMAN GP	Hockenheim	15	Arrows	B	3.0 Arrows A20-V10	*engine*	22/22
ret	HUNGARIAN GP	Hungaroring	15	Arrows	B	3.0 Arrows A20-V10	*gearbox*	21/22
ret	BELGIAN GP	Spa	15	Arrows	B	3.0 Arrows A20-V10	*clutch*	19/22
ret	ITALIAN GP	Monza	15	Arrows	B	3.0 Arrows A20-V10	*spun off*	22/22
ret	EUROPEAN GP	Nürburgring	15	Arrows	B	3.0 Arrows A20-V10	*spun off*	21/22
ret	MALAYSIAN GP	Sepang	15	Arrows	B	3.0 Arrows A20-V10	*driveshaft*	22/22
ret	JAPANESE GP	Suzuka	15	Arrows	B	3.0 Arrows A20-V10	*gearbox*	19/22

GP Starts: 32   GP Wins: 0   Pole positions: 0   Fastest laps: 0   Points: 0

NORITAKE TAKAHARA

ALTHOUGH not as fast a driver in the 1970s as his rivals, Masahiro Hasemi and Kazuyoshi Hoshi-no, Noritake Takahara nevertheless achieved the results that mattered, winning the Japanese F2 title and the Grand Champion sports car series – for the third time – in 1976.

Takahara began racing in 1969 in a Honda S800 coupé and was a successful March driver in Japan in the early 1970s. In 1973, he appeared very briefly in European Formula 2 with a GRD, and the following season saw him race a works March 741 in the International Trophy, where he drove steadily and sensibly into 11th place. His ninth-place finish in a rented Surtees at Fuji in 1976 earned him the distinction of being the first Japanese driver to finish a world championship grand prix.

Much to the chagrin of Hasemi, Takahara took over his seat in the Kojima team in 1977, racing in that year's grand prix. He was a leading contender in the Japanese Formula 2 series for the rest of the decade, driving Nova, Martini and March chassis, and like his aforementioned rivals continued to race, although much less regularly, throughout the 1980s.

KUNIMITSU TAKAHASHI

HAVING begun his career on two wheels as a motorcycle racer, Kunimitsu Takahashi gained the distinction of being the first Japanese rider to win a world championship grand prix on a 250cc Honda in 1961, when aged just 21. A serious accident in 1962 during the Isle of Man TT races halted his progress, however, and eventually he switched to four wheels.

Takahashi soon began racing Datsuns with some verve, using his exciting trademark drifting style through the corners. He won the Japanese Grand Prix for sports cars in 1966 and 1971.

A regular competitor in the Japanese sports car series in the 1970s, he raced the old Tyrrell that had been used by Kazuyoshi Hoshino the previous year in the 1977 Japanese GP and took a distant ninth place, although satisfyingly he was ahead of the Kojima driven by Hoshino.

Subsequently, he joined the Kojima team for the domestic Formula 2 series and later also ran a Toleman TG280 with backing from Yokohama tyres.

Takahashi was Japanese sports car champion four times in the 1980s: 1985 and '86 (with Kenji Takahashi), 1987 (with Kenneth Acheson) and 1989 (with Stanley Dickens). He also took a class win at Le Mans in 1995 with a Honda NSX.

Subsequently, Takahashi competed regularly in the Japanese F3000 championship and formed his own GT team to successfully race a Honda NSX GT2 in the All-Japan GT championship. After retirement from competition in 2000, he became the chairman of the Super GT series from 2003 to 2007.

TAKAHARA, Noritake (J) b 6/6/1951, Tokyo

1976 Championship position: Unplaced								
	Race	Circuit	No	Entrant	Tyres	Capacity/Car/Engine	Comment	Q Pos/Entries
9	JAPANESE GP	Mount Fuji	18	Team Surtees	G	3.0 Surtees TS19-Cosworth V8	*3 laps behind*	24/27
1977 Championship position: Unplaced								
ret	JAPANESE GP	Mount Fuji	51	Kojima Engineering	B	3.0 Kojima KE009-Cosworth V8	*crashed avoiding Andretti's wheel*	19/23

GP Starts: 2   GP Wins: 0   Pole positions: 0   Fastest laps: 0   Points: 0

TAKAHASHI, Kunimitsu (J) b 29/1/1940, Tokyo

1977 Championship position: Unplaced								
	Race	Circuit	No	Entrant	Tyres	Capacity/Car/Engine	Comment	Q Pos/Entries
9	JAPANESE GP	Mount Fuji	50	Meiritsu Racing Team	D	3.0 Tyrrell 007-Cosworth V8	*2 laps behind*	22/23

GP Starts: 1   GP Wins: 0   Pole positions: 0   Fastest laps: 0   Points: 0

PATRICK TAMBAY

EASY-GOING and impeccably mannered, by general consensus Patrick Tambay was just too nice a guy to succeed in the cut-throat world of grand prix racing. Certainly the cosmopolitan Frenchman had a lot of talent, but perhaps he lacked the single-minded determination that is a crucial part of any true champion's armoury.

Patrick's career got off to the brightest of starts when he won the Pilote Elf scheme, which was the passport to Formule Renault in 1973. Having finished as runner-up in the series, he leapfrogged straight into the European F2 championship with the Elf team for 1974 and won a round at Nogaro to cap a consistent first season at this level. A seat in the Elf-backed works March team the following year should have brought him more success than a singleton victory. Although he scored four second places to take the runner-up position in the series, worryingly he was involved in a series of silly accidents. Competing in the series with Elf backing for a third year in 1976, but this time running a Martini chassis, he once again scored just a single victory – remarkably, like his two previous wins, it came at Nogaro – but finishing third in the championship was regarded as a failure by the French oil company, who dropped him in favour of Didier Pironi.

Tambay's career was in limbo at the start of 1977 until he was offered the Carl Haas/Jim Hall Can-Am car in place of the badly injured Brian Redman. Although in the main the opposition was modest, he made the most of the opportunity and won six of the seven rounds in which he competed to take the championship easily. His luck had changed for the better; after a fiasco at Dijon, where he was dumped into a Surtees at short notice in a desperate attempt to get him into the race, he finally made his grand prix debut in Teddy Yip's Ensign at Silverstone. Given the previous poor reliability record of the N177, the inexperienced Tambay did well to score points in three races, and even a massive practice crash at Monza failed to dent the Frenchman's new-found confidence.

Joining the McLaren team in 1978 should have led to Patrick making the big breakthrough, but unfortunately their star was temporarily on the wane, and although he took five points-scoring finishes that year, his second season was something of a disaster. Failing to qualify at both Zolder and Monaco was the nadir of a year in which McLaren plumbed the depths. So in 1980, Tambay was back across 'the pond', making hay in Can-Am once more and taking a second title in the Carl Haas Lola T530.

Teddy Yip still had faith in the Frenchman and signed him for his Theodore F1 outfit for 1981. A sixth place in the US GP first time out was way beyond the little team's expectations, but Patrick performed so well in the car subsequently that he was an obvious candidate to replace Jean-Pierre Jabouille when he decided to retire from Ligier in mid-season. However, Tambay's short stay with the French team was a desperately unhappy one, ending in a string of accidents that could have beached his grand prix career for good.

In motor racing, one man's misfortune is another's opportunity, however, and in the saddest of circumstances Patrick was brought into the Ferrari line-up in place of the late Gilles Villeneuve. He soon found his feet and after yet another dreadful setback for the team at Hockenheim, when Pironi was injured

so terribly in practice, he rose to the occasion magnificently by winning the race. For the rest of the season, he carried the weight of the team manfully, despite a painful back problem that caused him to miss two races. He was joined by René Arnoux for 1983, when the two Frenchmen had the equipment to launch a championship assault. Although Arnoux came closer in terms of results, Tambay's all-round performances were more convincing, and it was a major surprise when he was released at the end of the year to make way for Michele Alboreto.

Moving to Renault for the 1984 season, Tambay failed to find any sort of continuity, as minor problems constantly undermined his efforts. This led to an inconsistency that was scarcely helped by the introduction of the disappointing RE60 in 1985. He made a solid start, but the car could never be persuaded to offer a truly satisfactory level of performance on a regular basis, which must have driven both Patrick and Derek Warwick to distraction as they gave their all. At the end of the year, the Renault factory team closed their doors to lick their wounds, leaving Tambay seeking employment once more. He found it with the Haas Lola team, who were embarking on a full season with the Ford turbo engine. As an exercise in wasting money, this was as good as any, and both he and Alan Jones were forced to spend the season in midfield mediocrity before the team folded.

Subsequently, Patrick joined the TWR Jaguar team for the 1989 season, gaining some good placings with Jan Lammers. Then he returned to grand prix racing once more, as a TV commentator and, briefly during 1994, in a PR role with the now defunct Larrousse team.

Tambay's son, Adrien, has been making his way in the sport, winning in both the GP3 and Auto GP single-seater classes, before lining up a drive with Audi in the DTM series.

TAMBAY, Patrick (F) b 25/6/1949, Paris

1977 Championship position: 17th= Wins: 0 Pole positions: 0 Fastest laps: 0 Points scored: 5

	Race	Circuit	No	Entrant	Tyres	Capacity/Car/Engine	Comment	Q Pos/Entries
dnq	FRENCH GP	Dijon	18	Team Surtees	G	3.0 Surtees TS19-Cosworth V8	Ensign not ready/ran 1 session only	29/30
ret	BRITISH GP	Silverstone	23	Theodore Racing Hong Kong	G	3.0 Ensign N177-Cosworth V8	electrics	16/36
6	GERMAN GP	Hockenheim	23	Theodore Racing Hong Kong	G	3.0 Ensign N177-Cosworth V8		11/30
ret	AUSTRIAN GP	Österreichring	23	Theodore Racing Hong Kong	G	3.0 Ensign N177-Cosworth V8		7/30
5/ret	DUTCH GP	Zandvoort	23	Theodore Racing Hong Kong	G	3.0 Ensign N177-Cosworth V8	out of fuel/2 laps behind	12/34
ret	ITALIAN GP	Monza	23	Theodore Racing Hong Kong	G	3.0 Ensign N177-Cosworth V8	engine	21/34
dnq	US GP EAST	Watkins Glen	23	Theodore Racing Hong Kong	G	3.0 Ensign N177-Cosworth V8	engine problems in practice	27/27
5	CANADIAN GP	Mosport Park	23	Theodore Racing Hong Kong	G	3.0 Ensign N177-Cosworth V8		16/27
ret	JAPANESE GP	Mount Fuji	23	Theodore Racing Hong Kong	G	3.0 Ensign N177-Cosworth V8	engine	16/23

1978 Championship position: 13th= Wins: 0 Pole positions: 0 Fastest laps: 0 Points scored: 8

	Race	Circuit	No	Entrant	Tyres	Capacity/Car/Engine	Comment	Q Pos/Entries
6	ARGENTINE GP	Buenos Aires	8	Marlboro Team McLaren	G	3.0 McLaren M26-Cosworth V8		9/27
ret	BRAZILIAN GP	Rio	8	Marlboro Team McLaren	G	3.0 McLaren M26-Cosworth V8	hit by Scheckter – spun off	5/28
ret	SOUTH AFRICAN GP	Kyalami	8	Marlboro Team McLaren	G	3.0 McLaren M26-Cosworth V8	spun – radiator and rear wing damage	4/30
12/ret	US GP WEST	Long Beach	8	Marlboro Team McLaren	G	3.0 McLaren M26-Cosworth V8	hit by Laffite/6 laps behind	11/30
7	MONACO GP	Monte Carlo	8	Marlboro Team McLaren	G	3.0 McLaren M26-Cosworth V8	1 lap behind	11/30
ret	SPANISH GP	Jarama	8	Marlboro Team McLaren	G	3.0 McLaren M26-Cosworth V8	spun off	14/29
4	SWEDISH GP	Anderstorp	8	Marlboro Team McLaren	G	3.0 McLaren M26-Cosworth V8	1 lap behind	15/27
9	FRENCH GP	Paul Ricard	8	Marlboro Team McLaren	G	3.0 McLaren M26-Cosworth V8	pit stop – rear end problems	6/29
6	BRITISH GP	Brands Hatch	8	Marlboro Team McLaren	G	3.0 McLaren M26-Cosworth V8	1 lap behind	20/30
ret	GERMAN GP	Hockenheim	8	Marlboro Team McLaren	G	3.0 McLaren M26-Cosworth V8	puncture – crashed	11/30
ret	AUSTRIAN GP	Österreichring	8	Marlboro Team McLaren	G	3.0 McLaren M26-Cosworth V8	spun off	14/31
9	DUTCH GP	Zandvoort	8	Marlboro Team McLaren	G	3.0 McLaren M26-Cosworth V8	1 lap behind	14/33
5	ITALIAN GP	Monza	8	Marlboro Team McLaren	G	3.0 McLaren M26-Cosworth V8		19/32
6	US GP EAST	Watkins Glen	8	Marlboro Team McLaren	G	3.0 McLaren M26-Cosworth V8		18/27
8	CANADIAN GP	Montreal	8	Marlboro Team McLaren	G	3.0 McLaren M26-Cosworth V8		17/28

1979 Championship position: Unplaced

	Race	Circuit	No	Entrant	Tyres	Capacity/Car/Engine	Comment	Q Pos/Entries
ret/dns*	ARGENTINE GP	Buenos Aires	8	Marlboro Team McLaren	G	3.0 McLaren M28-Cosworth V8	accident at first start/*did not restart	9/26
ret	BRAZILIAN GP	Interlagos	8	Marlboro Team McLaren	G	3.0 McLaren M28-Cosworth V8	accident with Regazzoni	18/26
dns	"	"	8	Marlboro Team McLaren	G	3.0 McLaren M28-Cosworth V8	crashed in practice	- / -
10	SOUTH AFRICAN GP	Kyalami	8	Marlboro Team McLaren	G	3.0 McLaren M28-Cosworth V8	pit stop – tyres/2 laps behind	17/26
ret	US GP WEST	Long Beach	8	Löwenbräu Team McLaren	G	3.0 McLaren M28-Cosworth V8	accident with Lauda	19/26
13	SPANISH GP	Jarama	8	Marlboro Team McLaren	G	3.0 McLaren M28-Cosworth V8	pit stop – fuel/3 laps behind	20/27
dnq	BELGIAN GP	Zolder	8	Marlboro Team McLaren	G	3.0 McLaren M28-Cosworth V8		25/28
dnq	MONACO GP	Monte Carlo	8	Marlboro Team McLaren	G	3.0 McLaren M28-Cosworth V8		22/25
10	FRENCH GP	Dijon	8	Marlboro Team McLaren	G	3.0 McLaren M28-Cosworth V8	2 laps behind	20/27
7/ret	BRITISH GP	Silverstone	8	Marlboro Team McLaren	G	3.0 McLaren M28-Cosworth V8	out of fuel/2 laps behind	18/26
ret	GERMAN GP	Hockenheim	8	Marlboro Team McLaren	G	3.0 McLaren M29-Cosworth V8	broken rear suspension	15/26
10	AUSTRIAN GP	Österreichring	8	Marlboro Team McLaren	G	3.0 McLaren M29-Cosworth V8	1 lap behind	14/26
ret	DUTCH GP	Zandvoort	8	Marlboro Team McLaren	G	3.0 McLaren M29-Cosworth V8	engine	14/26
ret	ITALIAN GP	Monza	8	Marlboro Team McLaren	G	3.0 McLaren M29-Cosworth V8	engine	14/28
ret	CANADIAN GP	Montreal	8	Marlboro Team McLaren	G	3.0 McLaren M29-Cosworth V8	engine	20/29
ret	US GP EAST	Watkins Glen	8	Marlboro Team McLaren	G	3.0 McLaren M29-Cosworth V8	engine	22/30

1981 Championship position: 18th= Wins: 0 Pole positions: 0 Fastest laps: 0 Points scored: 1

	Race	Circuit	No	Entrant	Tyres	Capacity/Car/Engine	Comment	Q Pos/Entries
6	US GP WEST	Long Beach	33	Theodore Racing Team	M	3.0 Theodore TY01-Cosworth V8	1 lap behind	17/29
10	BRAZILIAN GP	Rio	33	Theodore Racing Team	M	3.0 Theodore TY01-Cosworth V8	1 lap behind	19/30
ret	ARGENTINE GP	Buenos Aires	33	Theodore Racing Team	M	3.0 Theodore TY01-Cosworth V8	engine – lost oil	14/29
11	SAN MARINO GP	Imola	33	Theodore Racing Team	M	3.0 Theodore TY01-Cosworth V8	pit stop – tyres/2 laps behind	16/30
dnq	BELGIAN GP	Zolder	33	Theodore Racing Team	M	3.0 Theodore TY01-Cosworth V8		28/31
7	MONACO GP	Monte Carlo	33	Theodore Racing Team	M	3.0 Theodore TY01-Cosworth V8	4 laps behind	16/31
13	SPANISH GP	Jarama	33	Theodore Racing Team	M	3.0 Theodore TY01-Cosworth V8	2 laps behind	16/30
ret	FRENCH GP	Dijon	25	Equipe Talbot Gitanes	M	3.0 Ligier JS17-Matra V12	seized rear wheel bearing	16/29
ret	BRITISH GP	Silverstone	25	Equipe Talbot Gitanes	M	3.0 Ligier JS17-Matra V12	ignition	15/30
ret	GERMAN GP	Hockenheim	25	Equipe Talbot Gitanes	M	3.0 Ligier JS17-Matra V12	rear wheel bearing	11/30
ret	AUSTRIAN GP	Österreichring	25	Equipe Talbot Gitanes	M	3.0 Ligier JS17-Matra V12	engine	17/28
ret	DUTCH GP	Zandvoort	25	Equipe Talbot Gitanes	M	3.0 Ligier JS17-Matra V12	accident with Pironi	11/30

In 1982, having been drafted into the Ferrari team in place of Gilles Villeneuve, Tambay was thrust into the leadership of the team following the practice accident suffered by Didier Pironi in the German Grand Prix at Hockenheim. The Frenchman responded magnificently by taking victory in the race.

ret	ITALIAN GP	Monza	25	Equipe Talbot Gitanes	M	3.0 Ligier JS17-Matra V12	*puncture*	15/30
ret	CANADIAN GP	Montreal	25	Equipe Talbot Gitanes	M	3.0 Ligier JS17-Matra V12	*spun off*	17/30
ret	CAESARS PALACE GP	Las Vegas	25	Equipe Talbot Gitanes	M	3.0 Ligier JS17-Matra V12	*crashed*	7/30

1982 Championship position: 7th   Wins: 1   Pole positions: 0   Fastest laps: 0   Points scored: 25

8	DUTCH GP	Zandvoort	27	Scuderia Ferrari SpA SEFAC	G	1.5 t/c Ferrari 126C2 V6	*tyre problems/1 lap behind*	6/31
3	BRITISH GP	Brands Hatch	27	Scuderia Ferrari SpA SEFAC	G	1.5 t/c Ferrari 126C2 V6		13/30
4	FRENCH GP	Paul Ricard	27	Scuderia Ferrari SpA SEFAC	G	1.5 t/c Ferrari 126C2 V6		5/30
1	GERMAN GP	Hockenheim	27	Scuderia Ferrari SpA SEFAC	G	1.5 t/c Ferrari 126C2 V6		5/30
4	AUSTRIAN GP	Österreichring	27	Scuderia Ferrari SpA SEFAC	G	1.5 t/c Ferrari 126C2 V6	*pit stop – tyre/1 lap behind*	4/29
dns	SWISS GP	Dijon	27	Scuderia Ferrari SpA SEFAC	G	1.5 t/c Ferrari 126C2 V6	*bad back – withdrawn on Sunday a.m.*	(10)/29
2	ITALIAN GP	Monza	27	Scuderia Ferrari SpA SEFAC	G	1.5 t/c Ferrari 126C2 V6		3/30
dns	CAESARS PALACE GP	Las Vegas	27	Scuderia Ferrari SpA SEFAC	G	1.5 t/c Ferrari 126C2 V6	*bad back – withdrawn on Sunday a.m.*	(8)/30

1983 Championship position: 4th   Wins: 1   Pole positions: 4   Fastest laps: 1   Points scored: 40

5	BRAZILIAN GP	Rio	27	Scuderia Ferrari SpA SEFAC	G	1.5 t/c Ferrari 126C2/B V6		3/27
ret	US GP WEST	Long Beach	27	Scuderia Ferrari SpA SEFAC	G	1.5 t/c Ferrari 126C2/B V6	*accident with Rosberg*	1/28
4	FRENCH GP	Paul Ricard	27	Scuderia Ferrari SpA SEFAC	G	1.5 t/c Ferrari 126C2/B V6	*pit stop – tyres*	11/29
1	SAN MARINO GP	Imola	27	Scuderia Ferrari SpA SEFAC	G	1.5 t/c Ferrari 126C2/B V6		3/28
4	MONACO GP	Monte Carlo	27	Scuderia Ferrari SpA SEFAC	G	1.5 t/c Ferrari 126C2/B V6		4/28
2	BELGIAN GP	Spa	27	Scuderia Ferrari SpA SEFAC	G	1.5 t/c Ferrari 126C2/B V6		2/28
ret	US GP (DETROIT)	Detroit	27	Scuderia Ferrari SpA SEFAC	G	1.5 t/c Ferrari 126C2/B V6	*stalled at start*	3/27
3	CANADIAN GP	Montreal	27	Scuderia Ferrari SpA SEFAC	G	1.5 t/c Ferrari 126C2/B V6	*FL*	4/28
3	BRITISH GP	Silverstone	27	Scuderia Ferrari SpA SEFAC	G	1.5 t/c Ferrari 126C3 V6		2/29
ret	GERMAN GP	Hockenheim	27	Scuderia Ferrari SpA SEFAC	G	1.5 t/c Ferrari 126C3 V6	*engine*	1/29
ret	AUSTRIAN GP	Österreichring	27	Scuderia Ferrari SpA SEFAC	G	1.5 t/c Ferrari 126C3 V6	*engine*	1/29
2	DUTCH GP	Zandvoort	27	Scuderia Ferrari SpA SEFAC	G	1.5 t/c Ferrari 126C3 V6		2/29
4	ITALIAN GP	Monza	27	Scuderia Ferrari SpA SEFAC	G	1.5 t/c Ferrari 126C3 V6		2/29
ret	EUROPEAN GP	Brands Hatch	27	Scuderia Ferrari SpA SEFAC	G	1.5 t/c Ferrari 126C3 V6	*fluid leak, lost brakes – accident*	6/29
ret	SOUTH AFRICAN GP	Kyalami	27	Scuderia Ferrari SpA SEFAC	G	1.5 t/c Ferrari 126C3 V6	*turbo*	1/26

1984 Championship position: 11th   Wins: 0   Pole positions: 1   Fastest laps: 0   Points scored: 11

5*/ret	BRAZILIAN GP	Rio	15	Equipe Renault Elf	M	1.5 t/c Renault RE50 V6	**5th place car dsq/out of fuel*	8/27
ret	SOUTH AFRICAN GP	Kyalami	15	Equipe Renault Elf	M	1.5 t/c Renault RE50 V6	*fuel metering unit/FL*	4/27
7*	BELGIAN GP	Zolder	15	Equipe Renault Elf	M	1.5 t/c Renault RE50 V6	*spin/*6th place car dsq/2 laps behind*	12/27
ret	SAN MARINO GP	Imola	15	Equipe Renault Elf	M	1.5 t/c Renault RE50 V6	*hit by Cheever*	14/28
2	FRENCH GP	Dijon	15	Equipe Renault Elf	M	1.5 t/c Renault RE50 V6		1/27
ret	MONACO GP	Monte Carlo	15	Equipe Renault Elf	M	1.5 t/c Renault RE50 V6	*collision with Warwick – hurt leg*	6/27
dns	CANADIAN GP	Montreal	15	Equipe Renault Elf	M	1.5 t/c Renault RE50 V6	*unfit – withdrew after untimed practice*	– / –
ret	US GP (DETROIT)	Detroit	15	Equipe Renault Elf	M	1.5 t/c Renault RE50 V6	*transmission*	9/27
ret	US GP (DALLAS)	Dallas	15	Equipe Renault Elf	M	1.5 t/c Renault RE50 V6	*hit wall*	10/27
8/ret	BRITISH GP	Brands Hatch	15	Equipe Renault Elf	M	1.5 t/c Renault RE50 V6	*turbo*	10/27
5	GERMAN GP	Hockenheim	15	Equipe Renault Elf	M	1.5 t/c Renault RE50 V6		4/27
ret	AUSTRIAN GP	Österreichring	15	Equipe Renault Elf	M	1.5 t/c Renault RE50 V6	*engine*	5/28
6	DUTCH GP	Zandvoort	15	Equipe Renault Elf	M	1.5 t/c Renault RE50 V6	*1 lap behind*	5/27
ret	ITALIAN GP	Monza	15	Equipe Renault Elf	M	1.5 t/c Renault RE50 V6	*throttle cable*	8/27
ret	EUROPEAN GP	Nürburgring	15	Equipe Renault Elf	M	1.5 t/c Renault RE50 V6	*fuel feed*	3/26
7	PORTUGUESE GP	Estoril	15	Equipe Renault Elf	M	1.5 t/c Renault RE50 V6	*1 lap behind*	7/27

1985 Championship position: 11th=   Wins: 0   Pole positions: 0   Fastest laps: 0   Points scored: 11

5	BRAZILIAN GP	Rio	15	Equipe Renault Elf	G	1.5 t/c Renault RE60 V6	*2 laps behind*	11/25
3	PORTUGUESE GP	Estoril	15	Equipe Renault Elf	G	1.5 t/c Renault RE60 V6	*1 lap behind*	12/26
3	SAN MARINO GP	Imola	15	Equipe Renault Elf	G	1.5 t/c Renault RE60 V6	*1 lap behind*	11/26
ret	MONACO GP	Monte Carlo	15	Equipe Renault Elf	G	1.5 t/c Renault RE60 V6	*hit Johansson on lap 1*	17/26
7	CANADIAN GP	Montreal	15	Equipe Renault Elf	G	1.5 t/c Renault RE60 V6	*1 lap behind*	10/25
ret	US GP (DETROIT)	Detroit	15	Equipe Renault Elf	G	1.5 t/c Renault RE60 V6	*spun off*	15/25
6	FRENCH GP	Paul Ricard	15	Equipe Renault Elf	G	1.5 t/c Renault RE60B V6		10/26
ret	BRITISH GP	Silverstone	15	Equipe Renault Elf	G	1.5 t/c Renault RE60B V6	*spun – hit by Johansson*	13/26
ret	GERMAN GP	Nürburgring	15	Equipe Renault Elf	G	1.5 t/c Renault RE60B V6	*spun off*	16/27
10/ret	AUSTRIAN GP	Österreichring	15	Equipe Renault Elf	G	1.5 t/c Renault RE60B V6	*engine/6 laps behind*	8/27
ret	DUTCH GP	Zandvoort	15	Equipe Renault Elf	G	1.5 t/c Renault RE60B V6	*started from pitlane/transmission*	6/27
7	ITALIAN GP	Monza	15	Equipe Renault Elf	G	1.5 t/c Renault RE60B V6	*1 lap behind*	8/26
ret	BELGIAN GP	Spa	15	Equipe Renault Elf	G	1.5 t/c Renault RE60B V6	*gearbox*	13/24
12	EUROPEAN GP	Brands Hatch	15	Equipe Renault Elf	G	1.5 t/c Renault RE60B V6	*3 laps behind*	17/27
ret	AUSTRALIAN GP	Adelaide	15	Equipe Renault Elf	G	1.5 t/c Renault RE60B V6	*transmission*	8/25

1986 Championship position: 15th=   Wins: 0   Pole positions: 0   Fastest laps: 0   Points scored: 2

ret	BRAZILIAN GP	Rio	16	Team Haas (USA) Ltd	G	1.5 t/c Lola THL1-Hart 4	*flat battery*	13/25
8	SPANISH GP	Jerez	16	Team Haas (USA) Ltd	G	1.5 t/c Lola THL1-Hart 4	*6 laps behind*	18/25
ret	SAN MARINO GP	Imola	16	Team Haas (USA) Ltd	G	1.5 t/c Lola THL1-Hart 4	*engine*	11/26
ret	MONACO GP	Monte Carlo	16	Team Haas (USA) Ltd	G	1.5 t/c Lola THL2-Cosworth V6	*accident with Brundle*	8/26
ret	BELGIAN GP	Spa	16	Team Haas (USA) Ltd	G	1.5 t/c Lola THL2-Cosworth V6	*accident with Fabi*	10/25
dns	CANADIAN GP	Montreal	16	Team Haas (USA) Ltd	G	1.5 t/c Lola THL2-Cosworth V6	*accident in Sunday a.m. warm-up*	(14)/25
ret	FRENCH GP	Paul Ricard	16	Team Haas (USA) Ltd	G	1.5 t/c Lola THL2-Cosworth V6	*brakes*	13/26
ret	BRITISH GP	Brands Hatch	16	Team Haas (USA) Ltd	G	1.5 t/c Lola THL2-Cosworth V6	*gearbox*	17/26
8	GERMAN GP	Hockenheim	16	Team Haas (USA) Ltd	G	1.5 t/c Lola THL2-Cosworth V6	*1 lap behind*	13/26
7	HUNGARIAN GP	Hungaroring	16	Team Haas (USA) Ltd	G	1.5 t/c Lola THL2-Cosworth V6	*2 laps behind*	6/26
5	AUSTRIAN GP	Österreichring	16	Team Haas (USA) Ltd	G	1.5 t/c Lola THL2-Cosworth V6	*2 laps behind*	13/26
ret	ITALIAN GP	Monza	16	Team Haas (USA) Ltd	G	1.5 t/c Lola THL2-Cosworth V6	*accident with Patrese*	15/27
nc	PORTUGUESE GP	Estoril	16	Team Haas (USA) Ltd	G	1.5 t/c Lola THL2-Cosworth V6	*3 pit stops – brakes/8 laps behind*	14/27
ret	MEXICAN GP	Mexico City	16	Team Haas (USA) Ltd	G	1.5 t/c Lola THL2-Cosworth V6	*hit by Arnoux on lap 1*	8/26
nc	AUSTRALIAN GP	Adelaide	16	Team Haas (USA) Ltd	G	1.5 t/c Lola THL2-Cosworth V6	*hit Dumfries/gearbox/12 laps behind*	17/26

GP Starts: 113 (114)   GP Wins: 2   Pole positions: 5   Fastest laps: 2   Points: 103

GABRIELE TARQUINI

A PLEASANT and underrated Italian, Gabriele Tarquini caused quite a stir in 1985 when, as reigning karting world champion and with almost no Formula 3 experience to speak of, he became an instant front-runner in F3000. He finished his first year a very creditable sixth in the standings, but his 1986 season was less startling as the newly formed Coloni team struggled to find its feet, although he did score third places at Enna and the Österreichring.

Joining Lamberto Leoni's FIRST racing ream for 1987, Gabriele was once again a 'nearly-man' in terms of ultimate success. He made his Formula 1 debut for Osella at Imola, however, and then rejoined Enzo Coloni for a testing first grand prix season for the Italian squad in 1988.

With poor Philippe Streiff gravely injured in a Brazilian testing accident, Tarquini joined the AGS line-up for the 1989 San Marino GP, soon gaining a priceless point for the little team in Mexico. Over the next three seasons, the ever-cheerful Italian plugged away against insurmountable odds as the debt-ridden team headed towards extinction, but before the end came he was allowed to sign for Fondmetal (formerly Osella). With Ford HB engines at his disposal for 1992, he had easily his best opportunity to shine, but the team was hampered by a lack of adequate funding – the Italian was under strict instructions to conserve the car at all costs – and any promise it had possessed soon evaporated, resulting in the outfit's withdrawal before the season was out.

Tarquini then joined the horde of famous names in the Italian touring car championship in 1993, taking third place in the series with a works Alfa Romeo. He was chosen to spearhead the Italian manufacturer's move into the BTCC series in 1994 and enjoyed a highly successful season, winning eight of the 21 rounds to take the championship crown. He also gained well-earned plaudits from all for his off-track demeanour, and was a credit to the series and his sport.

It looked like following this success would be tough in 1995, and so it proved when Alfa lost their advantage. Initially, Gabriele was racing in Italy, but the company's sudden decision to withdraw from their domestic championship saw him back in Britain for the balance of the year. The sudden transition from being the dominant force to midfield strugglers was quite a shock, but he always gave his best.

Partly due to his links with Fondmetal, Tarquini had been an occasional test driver for Tyrrell, and he was drafted in to deputise for the indisposed Ukyo Katayama at the Nürburgring, although this one-off return to F1 was not particularly distinguished.

In 1996, Gabriele stepped up to the high-profile International touring car series as a works driver alongside the experienced Nicola Larini and Alessandro Nannini in the Alfa 155 V6 TI and scored a big win at Silverstone, but he endured a thin time of it otherwise. So it was back to the Super Touring category in 1997, the Italian switching his allegiance to Honda. Although his six seasons driving the Accord in the BTCC, the German and the European Super Touring series produced no more than the occasional win, he was still regarded as one of the class's most accomplished performers.

Having returned to Alfa Romeo for 2002, Gabriele was back on top as European touring car champion the following year, and he still remained a key member of the Autodelta team until they withdrew their works support at the end of 2005. The ever-durable Tarquini soon found a berth with the ambitious SEAT squad for 2006, taking an emotional first win for the marque at Istanbul on his way to fifth place in series.

In 2007, Tarquini took only a single win, but the following year he bounced back to finish second only to his SEAT team mate, Yvan Muller, in the final standings. He became the oldest driver ever to win an FIA championship in 2009, when he turned the tables on the Frenchman. In 2010, the roles were reversed again. Having moved to Chevrolet, Muller gained the upper hand, and Gabriele had to be content with being runner-up, despite taking five race wins to his rival's three.

TARQUINI, Gabriele (I) b 2/3/1962, Giulianova Lido, nr Pescara, Teramo

	1987 Championship position: Unplaced							
	Race	Circuit	No	Entrant	Tyres	Capacity/Car/Engine	Comment	Q Pos/Entries
ret	SAN MARINO GP	Imola	22	Osella Squadra Corse	G	1.5 t/c Osella FA1G-Alfa Romeo V8	gearbox	27/27
	1988 Championship position: Unplaced							
ret	BRAZILIAN GP	Rio	31	Coloni SpA	G	3.5 Coloni FC188-Cosworth V8	rear upright bearing	25/31
ret	SAN MARINO GP	Imola	31	Coloni SpA	G	3.5 Coloni FC188-Cosworth V8	throttle cable	17/31
ret	MONACO GP	Monte Carlo	31	Coloni SpA	G	3.5 Coloni FC188-Cosworth V8	suspension	24/30
14	MEXICAN GP	Mexico City	31	Coloni SpA	G	3.5 Coloni FC188-Cosworth V8	5 laps behind	21/30
8	CANADIAN GP	Montreal	31	Coloni SpA	G	3.5 Coloni FC188-Cosworth V8	2 laps behind	26/31
dnpq	US GP (DETROIT)	Detroit	31	Coloni SpA	G	3.5 Coloni FC188-Cosworth V8		31/31
dnpq	FRENCH GP	Paul Ricard	31	Coloni SpA	G	3.5 Coloni FC188-Cosworth V8		31/31
dnpq	BRITISH GP	Silverstone	31	Coloni SpA	G	3.5 Coloni FC188-Cosworth V8		31/31

dnpq	GERMAN GP	Hockenheim	31	Coloni SpA	G	3.5 Coloni FC188-Cosworth V8		31/31
13	HUNGARIAN GP	Hungaroring	31	Coloni SpA	G	3.5 Coloni FC188-Cosworth V8	*rear suspension/5 laps behind*	22/31
nc	BELGIAN GP	Spa	31	Coloni SpA	G	3.5 Coloni FC188-Cosworth V8	*steering rack problem/7 laps behind*	22/31
dnq	ITALIAN GP	Monza	31	Coloni SpA	G	3.5 Coloni FC188B-Cosworth V8		29/31
11	PORTUGUESE GP	Estoril	31	Coloni SpA	G	3.5 Coloni FC188B-Cosworth V8	*5 laps behind*	26/31
dnpq	SPANISH GP	Jerez	31	Coloni SpA	G	3.5 Coloni FC188B-Cosworth V8		31/31
dnpq	JAPANESE GP	Suzuka	31	Coloni SpA	G	3.5 Coloni FC188B-Cosworth V8		31/31
dnq	AUSTRALIAN GP	Adelaide	31	Coloni SpA	G	3.5 Coloni FC188B-Cosworth V8		27/31

1989 Championship position: 26th= Wins: 0 Pole positions: 0 Fastest laps: 0 Points scored: 1

8	SAN MARINO GP	Imola	40	Automobiles Gonfaronaise Sportive	G	3.5 AGS JH23B-Cosworth V8	*1 lap behind*	18/39
ret	MONACO GP	Monte Carlo	40	Automobiles Gonfaronaise Sportive	G	3.5 AGS JH23B-Cosworth V8	*electrics*	13/38
6	MEXICAN GP	Mexico City	40	Automobiles Gonfaronaise Sportive	G	3.5 AGS JH23B-Cosworth V8	*1 lap behind*	17/39
7/ret	US GP (PHOENIX)	Phoenix	40	Automobiles Gonfaronaise Sportive	G	3.5 AGS JH23B-Cosworth V8	*engine on last lap/2 laps behind*	24/39
ret	CANADIAN GP	Montreal	40	Automobiles Gonfaronaise Sportive	G	3.5 AGS JH23B-Cosworth V8	*collision with Arnoux*	25/39
ret	FRENCH GP	Paul Ricard	40	Automobiles Gonfaronaise Sportive	G	3.5 AGS JH23B-Cosworth V8	*engine*	21/39
dns	"	"	40		G	3.5 AGS JH24-Cosworth V8	*practice only – new car*	– / –
dnq	BRITISH GP	Silverstone	40	Automobiles Gonfaronaise Sportive	G	3.5 AGS JH24-Cosworth V8		29/39
dnpq	GERMAN GP	Hockenheim	40	Automobiles Gonfaronaise Sportive	G	3.5 AGS JH23B-Cosworth V8		33/39
dnpq	HUNGARIAN GP	Hungaroring	40	Automobiles Gonfaronaise Sportive	G	3.5 AGS JH24-Cosworth V8		35/39
dnpq	BELGIAN GP	Spa	40	Automobiles Gonfaronaise Sportive	G	3.5 AGS JH23B-Cosworth V8		– / –
dnpq	"	"	40		G	3.5 AGS JH24-Cosworth V8		34/39
dnq	ITALIAN GP	Monza	40	Automobiles Gonfaronaise Sportive	G	3.5 AGS JH24-Cosworth V8	*brake problems*	31/39
dnpq	PORTUGUESE GP	Estoril	40	Automobiles Gonfaronaise Sportive	G	3.5 AGS JH24-Cosworth V8		36/39
dnpq	SPANISH GP	Jerez	40	Automobiles Gonfaronaise Sportive	G	3.5 AGS JH24-Cosworth V8		30/38
dnpq	JAPANESE GP	Suzuka	40	Automobiles Gonfaronaise Sportive	G	3.5 AGS JH24-Cosworth V8		37/39
dnpq	AUSTRALIAN GP	Adelaide	40	Automobiles Gonfaronaise Sportive	G	3.5 AGS JH24-Cosworth V8		38/39

1990 Championship position: Unplaced

dnpq	US GP (PHOENIX)	Phoenix	17	Automobiles Gonfaronaise Sportive	G	3.5 AGS JH24-Cosworth V8		31/35
dnpq	BRAZILIAN GP	Interlagos	17	Automobiles Gonfaronaise Sportive	G	3.5 AGS JH24-Cosworth V8		31/35
dnpq	SAN MARINO GP	Imola	17	Automobiles Gonfaronaise Sportive	G	3.5 AGS JH25-Cosworth V8	*no time recorded*	– /34
dnpq	MONACO GP	Monte Carlo	17	Automobiles Gonfaronaise Sportive	G	3.5 AGS JH25-Cosworth V8		31/35
dnpq	CANADIAN GP	Montreal	17	Automobiles Gonfaronaise Sportive	G	3.5 AGS JH25-Cosworth V8		31/35
dnpq	MEXICAN GP	Mexico City	17	Automobiles Gonfaronaise Sportive	G	3.5 AGS JH25-Cosworth V8		32/35
dnq	FRENCH GP	Paul Ricard	17	Automobiles Gonfaronaise Sportive	G	3.5 AGS JH25-Cosworth V8		28/35
ret	BRITISH GP	Silverstone	17	Automobiles Gonfaronaise Sportive	G	3.5 AGS JH25-Cosworth V8	*engine*	26/35
dnpq	GERMAN GP	Hockenheim	17	Automobiles Gonfaronaise Sportive	G	3.5 AGS JH25-Cosworth V8		31/35
13	HUNGARIAN GP	Hungaroring	17	Automobiles Gonfaronaise Sportive	G	3.5 AGS JH25-Cosworth V8	*pit stop – tyres/3 laps behind*	24/35
dnq	BELGIAN GP	Spa	17	Automobiles Gonfaronaise Sportive	G	3.5 AGS JH25-Cosworth V8		28/33
dnq	ITALIAN GP	Monza	17	Automobiles Gonfaronaise Sportive	G	3.5 AGS JH25-Cosworth V8		27/33
dnq	PORTUGUESE GP	Estoril	17	Automobiles Gonfaronaise Sportive	G	3.5 AGS JH25-Cosworth V8		29/33
ret	SPANISH GP	Jerez	17	Automobiles Gonfaronaise Sportive	G	3.5 AGS JH25-Cosworth V8	*electrics*	22/33
dnq	JAPANESE GP	Suzuka	17	Automobiles Gonfaronaise Sportive	G	3.5 AGS JH25-Cosworth V8		28/30
ret	AUSTRALIAN GP	Adelaide	17	Automobiles Gonfaronaise Sportive	G	3.5 AGS JH25-Cosworth V8	*oil fire*	26/30

1991 Championship position: Unplaced

8	US GP (PHOENIX)	Phoenix	17	Automobiles Gonfaronaise Sportive	G	3.5 AGS JH25-Cosworth V8	*pit stop – tyres/misfire/4 laps behind*	22/34
ret	BRAZILIAN GP	Interlagos	17	Automobiles Gonfaronaise Sportive	G	3.5 AGS JH25-Cosworth V8	*spun off on first lap*	24/34
dnq	SAN MARINO GP	Imola	17	Automobiles Gonfaronaise Sportive	G	3.5 AGS JH25-Cosworth V8		27/34
ret	MONACO GP	Monte Carlo	17	Automobiles Gonfaronaise Sportive	G	3.5 AGS JH25-Cosworth V8	*gearbox*	20/34
dnq	CANADIAN GP	Montreal	17	Automobiles Gonfaronaise Sportive	G	3.5 AGS JH25-Cosworth V8		28/34
dnq	MEXICAN GP	Mexico City	17	Automobiles Gonfaronaise Sportive	G	3.5 AGS JH25-Cosworth V8		28/34
dnq	FRENCH GP	Paul Ricard	17	Automobiles Gonfaronaise Sportive	G	3.5 AGS JH25B-Cosworth V8		29/34
dnq	BRITISH GP	Silverstone	17	Automobiles Gonfaronaise Sportive	G	3.5 AGS JH25B-Cosworth V8		30/34
dnq	GERMAN GP	Hockenheim	17	Automobiles Gonfaronaise Sportive	G	3.5 AGS JH25B-Cosworth V8		29/34
dnpq	HUNGARIAN GP	Hungaroring	17	Automobiles Gonfaronaise Sportive	G	3.5 AGS JH25B-Cosworth V8		31/34
dnpq	BELGIAN GP	Spa	17	Automobiles Gonfaronaise Sportive	G	3.5 AGS JH25B-Cosworth V8		32/34
dnpq	ITALIAN GP	Monza	17	Automobiles Gonfaronaise Sportive	G	3.5 AGS JH27-Cosworth V8		32/34
dnpq	"	"	17	Automobiles Gonfaronaise Sportive	G	3.5 AGS JH25B-Cosworth V8		– / –
dnq	PORTUGUESE GP	Estoril	17	Automobiles Gonfaronaise Sportive	G	3.5 AGS JH27-Cosworth V8		28/34
12	SPANISH GP	Barcelona	14	Fondmetal F1 SpA	G	3.5 Fomet F1-Cosworth V8	*2 laps behind*	22/33
11	JAPANESE GP	Suzuka	14	Fondmetal F1 SpA	G	3.5 Fomet F1-Cosworth V8	*3 laps behind*	24/31
dnpq	AUSTRALIAN GP	Adelaide	14	Fondmetal F1 SpA	G	3.5 Fomet F1-Cosworth V8		31/32

1992 Championship position: Unplaced

ret	SOUTH AFRICAN GP	Kyalami	15	Fondmetal F1 SpA	G	3.5 Fondmetal GR01-Ford HB V8	*engine*	15/30
ret	MEXICAN GP	Mexico City	15	Fondmetal F1 SpA	G	3.5 Fondmetal GR01-Ford HB V8	*clutch*	14/30
ret	BRAZILIAN GP	Interlagos	15	Fondmetal F1 SpA	G	3.5 Fondmetal GR01-Ford HB V8	*radiator overheating*	19/31
ret	SPANISH GP	Barcelona	15	Fondmetal F1 SpA	G	3.5 Fondmetal GR01-Ford HB V8	*spun off*	18/32
ret	SAN MARINO GP	Imola	15	Fondmetal F1 SpA	G	3.5 Fondmetal GR01-Ford HB V8	*overheating*	22/32
ret	MONACO GP	Monte Carlo	15	Fondmetal F1 SpA	G	3.5 Fondmetal GR01-Ford HB V8	*overheating*	25/32
ret	CANADIAN GP	Montreal	15	Fondmetal F1 SpA	G	3.5 Fondmetal GR02-Ford HB V8	*gearbox failed at start*	18/32
ret	FRENCH GP	Magny Cours	15	Fondmetal F1 SpA	G	3.5 Fondmetal GR02-Ford HB V8	*throttle cable*	23/30
14	BRITISH GP	Silverstone	15	Fondmetal F1 SpA	G	3.5 Fondmetal GR02-Ford HB V8	*2 laps behind*	15/32
ret	GERMAN GP	Hockenheim	15	Fondmetal F1 SpA	G	3.5 Fondmetal GR02-Ford HB V8	*engine*	19/32
ret	HUNGARIAN GP	Hungaroring	15	Fondmetal F1 SpA	G	3.5 Fondmetal GR02-Ford HB V8	*collision with van de Poele on lap 1*	12/31
ret	BELGIAN GP	Spa	15	Fondmetal F1 SpA	G	3.5 Fondmetal GR02-Ford HB V8	*engine*	11/30
ret	ITALIAN GP	Monza	15	Fondmetal F1 SpA	G	3.5 Fondmetal GR02-Ford HB V8	*gearbox*	20/28

1995 Championship position: Unplaced

14	EUROPEAN GP	Nürburgring	3	Nokia Tyrrell Yamaha	G	3.0 Tyrrell 023-Yamaha V10	*6 laps behind*	19/24

GP Starts: 38 GP Wins: 0 Pole positions: 0 Fastest laps: 0 Points: 1

PIERO TARUFFI

ORIGINALLY a successful motorcycle racer, Piero Taruffi won the 1932 500cc European motorcycling championship on a Norton. He had first tasted four-wheel competition as a 17-year-old in the family Fiat way back in 1923, but he raced motorcycles until he returned to cars for the 1930 Mille Miglia and soon began to show promise with his 2-litre Itala. That brought him to the attention of Ferrari, who provided him with a 2.3 Alfa Romeo to beat Clemente Biondetti in the Coppa Frigo hill-climb. He was still racing on two wheels, but took second place in the 1932 Rome GP, behind Luigi Fagioli in an Alfa Monza, and third in the 1933 Eifelrennen. Ironically, after beating the Ferrari works rider in a motorcycling event, he was dropped from the car team, but friends rallied round to help him purchase a private 8C Maserati, in which he impressed enough to be offered a works drive in 1934. His season was curtailed when he crashed badly at Tripoli in the 16-cylinder W5.

In 1935, Taruffi moved to the Bugatti team, taking a third at Turin. He was still involved in motorcycling, and although he stopped racing in

1937, he continued to manage the Gilera team both before and after the Second World War.

Between 1947 and 1949, Piero drove Dusio's Cisitalias with great success and was crowned Italian 1500cc champion. Guesting for Alfa Romeo, he took fourth in the Monza Grand Prix in 1948 with the 158. Having joined Scuderia Ferrari in 1949, he took second place in the Rome Grand Prix at Caracalla with the Tipo 166 Formula 2 car. At the same time, he continued to race the Cisitalia, which earned him the Italian F2 championship.

In 1950, he occasionally represented both Alfa Romeo and Ferrari. For the former, he took third in the Grand Prix of Nations in Geneva, and for the latter, his third in the end-of-year Penya Rhin Grand Prix at Barcelona brought an invitation to join the works team on a regular basis in 1951. This was the final year of Alfa's dominance, but Piero finished second in the Swiss Grand Prix at the daunting Bremgarten circuit and third in the non-title Bari Grand Prix at Lungomare. In sports cars, he took second place in the Tour of Sicily and, sharing a 4.1-litre with Lu-

igi Chinetti, won the Carrera Panamericana road race run between Mexico City and Léon.

Taruffi enjoyed his finest year in 1952. The Ferrari Tipo 500 having become the car to beat, he backed the brilliant Alberto Ascari superbly, winning the Swiss Grand Prix at Bremgarten, and with some other excellent drives he finished third in the drivers' championship. In other important single-seater races, he won the Paris GP at Montlhéry, and was second at both Syracuse and Naples, while in the big-capacity cars he took second in Turin and won the Daily Express Formula Libre Silverstone race in Tony Vandervell's Ferrari 'Thinwall Special'. For 1953, he returned to Gilera to run their motorcycling team, but also joined the Lancia team, racing their sports cars without great success, although he did finish second in the Carrera Panamericana in a 3.3 litre Lancia. He also established two 500cc speed records with his twin-boom Gilera at Montlhéry.

Things improved in 1954 with Lancia, as victories in the Targa Florio and the Tour of Sicily demonstrate, the latter success being repeated the following year, this time at the wheel of a Ferrari. Taruffi also returned to grand prix action with Ferrari, in a fourth car, to strengthen their driving team; he did his usual reliable job to bring the car home in sixth place. He had shown he was still an occasional grand prix driver who could be relied upon, and Mercedes called him into their team after Hans Herrmann had put himself out of action. He drove the silver car to excellent finishes in his two outings.

For 1956, Taruffi joined Maserati's sports car team, sharing the winning car with Stirling Moss, Harry Schell and Jean Behra in the Nürburgring 1000km, and taking second in the Targa Florio, the Circuit of Sicily and the Pescara Grand Prix. His final F1 race was the 1957 Syracuse Grand Prix where, driving a Scuderia Centro Sud Maserati 250F, he finished fourth, despite a broken shock absorber. Soon after, and at his 13th attempt, he achieved his great ambition by nursing his sick Ferrari to victory in the ill-fated Mille Miglia. After the disaster that had befallen the event, in which Alphonse de Portago and Edmund Nelson were killed along with 11 spectators, he announced his retirement from racing and set up a racing drivers' school. In 1959, he published The Technique of Motor Racing, which became the standard by which other driving texts were measured.

Taruffi also did some important work as a designer, being involved with the circuit of Misano Adriatica, while the expansion of the Vallelunga track also benefited from his expertise.

There is a Piero Taruffi museum in Bagnoregio, a small town between Viterbo and Orvieto in central Italy, which has vintage cars and motorbikes, and many items of memorabilia of his era.

TARUFFI, Piero (I) b 12/10/1906, Albone Laziale, Rome – d 12/1/1988, Rome

1950 Championship position: Unplaced

	Race	Circuit	No	Entrant	Tyres	Capacity/Car/Engine	Comment	Q Pos/Entries
ret	ITALIAN GP	Monza	54	Alfa Romeo SpA	P	1.5 s/c Alfa Romeo 158 8	*Fangio took over/engine	7/27

1951 Championship position: 6th=   Wins: 0   Pole positions: 0   Fastest laps: 0   Points scored: 10

	Race	Circuit	No	Entrant	Tyres	Capacity/Car/Engine	Comment	Q Pos/Entries
2	SWISS GP	Bremgarten	44	Scuderia Ferrari	P	4.5 Ferrari 375F1 V12		6/21
ret	BELGIAN GP	Spa	12	Scuderia Ferrari	P	4.5 Ferrari 375F1 V12	transmission	5/13
5	GERMAN GP	Nürburgring	73	Scuderia Ferrari	P	4.5 Ferrari 375F1 V12		6/23
5	ITALIAN GP	Monza	8	Scuderia Ferrari	P	4.5 Ferrari 375F1 V12	2 laps behind	6/22
ret	SPANISH GP	Pedralbes	8	Scuderia Ferrari	P	4.5 Ferrari 375F1 V12	lost wheel	7/20

1952 Championship position: 3rd   Wins: 1   Pole positions: 0   Fastest laps: 1   Points scored: 22

	Race	Circuit	No	Entrant	Tyres	Capacity/Car/Engine	Comment	Q Pos/Entries
1	SWISS GP	Bremgarten	30	Scuderia Ferrari	P	2.0 Ferrari 500 4	FL	2/21
ret	BELGIAN GP	Spa	6	Scuderia Ferrari	P	2.0 Ferrari 500 4	spun – hit by Behra	3/22
3	FRENCH GP	Rouen	12	Scuderia Ferrari	P	2.0 Ferrari 500 4	2 laps behind	3/20
2	BRITISH GP	Silverstone	17	Scuderia Ferrari	P	2.0 Ferrari 500 4	1 lap behind	3/32
4	GERMAN GP	Nürburgring	103	Scuderia Ferrari	E	2.0 Ferrari 500 4	1 lap behind	5/32
7	ITALIAN GP	Monza	14	Scuderia Ferrari	P	2.0 Ferrari 500 4	3 laps behind	6/35

1954 Championship position: Unplaced

	Race	Circuit	No	Entrant	Tyres	Capacity/Car/Engine	Comment	Q Pos/Entries
6	GERMAN GP	Nürburgring	4	Scuderia Ferrari	P	2.5 Ferrari 625 4	1 lap behind	13/23

1955   Championship position: 6th   Wins: 0   Pole positions: 0   Fastest laps: 0   Points scored: 9

	Race	Circuit	No	Entrant	Tyres	Capacity/Car/Engine	Comment	Q Pos/Entries
8*	MONACO GP	Monte Carlo	48	Scuderia Ferrari	E	2.5 Ferrari 555 4	*Frere took over car/14 laps behind	15/22
4	BRITISH GP	Aintree	50	Daimler Benz AG	C	2.5 Mercedes Benz-W196 8	1 lap behind	5/25
2	ITALIAN GP	Monza	14	Daimler Benz AG	C	2.5 Mercedes Benz-W196 8		9/22

1956 Championship position: Unplaced

	Race	Circuit	No	Entrant	Tyres	Capacity/Car/Engine	Comment	Q Pos/Entries
ret	FRENCH GP	Reims	8	Officine Alfieri Maserati	P	2.5 Maserati 250F 6	engine	16/20
ret	ITALIAN GP	Monza	16	Vandervell Products Ltd	P	2.5 Vanwall 4	suspension	4/26

GP Starts: 18   GP Wins: 1   Pole positions: 0   Fastest laps: 1   Points: 41

HENRY TAYLOR

A FARMER by profession, Henry Taylor entered club racing in 1954 with a Cooper-Vincent, taking the Autosport championship the following year. He added to his experience by racing a Jaguar D-Type, taking third in the 1957 Belgian sports car GP, but it was 1958 before he began to make his mark in single-seaters, winning the GP de Paris in a Cooper. He continued to make good progress in Formula 2, taking a superb second place at the 1959 Auvergne Trophy, ahead of McLaren's works car, and second in class at the British GP at Aintree.

For 1960, Taylor signed to race Ken Tyrrell's Cooper-Austin in Formula Junior, winning the prestigious Monaco race, and made his debut in the Yeoman Credit Cooper, scoring a morale boosting fourth place at Reims for a team still reeling from Chris Bristow's fatal accident at Spa. He continued under the UDT Laystall banner in 1961, racing the team's Lotus 18/21 F1 car as well as a Lotus 19 in sports car events. He gained a few minor placings outside grands prix, until a nasty crash in the British GP left him injured and trapped in his car. He recovered to compete again at the ill-fated Monza race where, perhaps with the tragic events of the day in mind, he decided to retire from circuit racing to concentrate on farming.

Taylor was soon back in action, however, rallying for Ford and becoming the first man to compete in the Cortina. Later he returned to the tracks occasionally in 1963 and 1964, when he finished second at both Zolder and Brands Hatch, and third at the Nürburgring in Alan Mann's Lotus-Cortina. After finally retiring in 1966, he became competitions manager at Ford.

TAYLOR, Henry (GB) b 16/12/1932, Shefford, Bedfordshire

1959 Championship position: Unplaced

	Race	Circuit	No	Entrant	Tyres	Capacity/Car/Engine	Comment	Q Pos/Entries
11*	BRITISH GP (F2)	Aintree	58	R H H Parnell	D	1.5 Cooper T51-Climax 4 F2	*2nd in F2 class/6 laps behind	21/30

1960 Championship position: 16th=   Wins: 0   Pole positions: 0   Fastest laps: 0   Points scored: 3

	Race	Circuit	No	Entrant	Tyres	Capacity/Car/Engine	Comment	Q Pos/Entries
7	DUTCH GP	Zandvoort	10	Yeoman Credit Racing Team	D	2.5 Cooper T51-Climax 4	5 laps behind	14/21
4	FRENCH GP	Reims	46	Yeoman Credit Racing Team	D	2.5 Cooper T51-Climax 4	1 lap behind	12/23
8	BRITISH GP	Silverstone	15	Yeoman Credit Racing Team	D	2.5 Cooper T51-Climax 4	3 laps behind	16/25
dns	PORTUGUESE GP	Oporto	10	Yeoman Credit Racing Team	D	2.5 Cooper T51-Climax 4	practice accident – injured	– /16
14	US GP	Riverside	8	Yeoman Credit Racing Team	D	2.5 Cooper T51-Climax 4	pit stop/7 laps behind	14/23

1961 Championship position: Unplaced

	Race	Circuit	No	Entrant	Tyres	Capacity/Car/Engine	Comment	Q Pos/Entries
dnq	MONACO GP	Monte Carlo	34	UDT-Laystall Racing Team	D	1.5 Lotus 18-Climax 4		17/21
dnp	BELGIAN GP	Spa	16	UDT-Laystall Racing Team	D	1.5 Lotus 18/21-Climax 4	car crashed by Allison	– / –
10	FRENCH GP	Reims	30	UDT-Laystall Racing Team	D	1.5 Lotus 18/21-Climax 4	3 laps behind	25/26
ret	BRITISH GP	Aintree	30	UDT-Laystall Racing Team	D	1.5 Lotus 18/21-Climax 4	accident in rain	17/30
11	ITALIAN GP	Monza	20	UDT-Laystall Racing Team	D	1.5 Lotus 18/21-Climax 4	4 laps behind	23/33

GP Starts: 8   GP Wins: 0   Pole positions: 0   Fastest laps: 0   Points: 3

JOHN TAYLOR

A PROTÉGÉ of Bob Gerard, John Taylor raced extensively in Formula Junior during 1962/63 with the Midlander's Cooper-Ford, gaining quite a bit of success, mainly at club level. He also took part in the British non-championship Formula 1 races of the period. In 1964, he was fifth in the Aintree 200 with a four-cylinder car and seventh in the Mediterranean Grand Prix at Enna in Gerard's Cooper-Climax V8, which he drove in three more non-championship races in 1965.

Having finished sixth in the 1966 International Trophy at Silverstone, Taylor took David Bridges' Brabham-BRM to the French Grand Prix and, despite his limited experience, scored a priceless point. However, in the German Grand Prix, on a greasy track, he spun on the first lap and was involved in a collision with Jacky Ickx's Formula 2 Matra. His car crashed off the track and burst into flames, leaving the poor driver badly burned. Although he seemed to be making a slow recovery, he died in hospital a few weeks later.

MIKE TAYLOR

A N amateur racer who showed a great deal of skill in the Lotus XI sports car in 1958, winning a number of club races, Mike Taylor continued to race the car in 1959, taking victory in the GP des Frontières at Chimay. He also campaigned a Formula 2 Cooper-Climax and won the BARC 200 at Aintree against moderate opposition, before making his GP debut at the same venue in July. Late in the season, he planned to compete in the US GP, but had to stand down after contracting jaundice.

For the 1960 season, Mike's syndicate bought one of Colin Chapman's latest Lotus 18s, which – after an outing in the International Trophy – he took to Spa for the Belgian GP. In a meeting that saw Stirling Moss badly injured, and Alan Stacey and Chris Bristow killed, the car careered off the track into the woods during practice after the steering column failed, leaving Taylor with multiple injuries, but lucky to have survived. He successfully sued Lotus for damages, but never raced again, turning instead to a business in property speculation.

TAYLOR, John (GB) b 23/3/1933, Leicester – d 8/9/1966, Koblenz, Germany

	1964 Championship position: Unplaced								
	Race	Circuit	No	Entrant	Tyres	Capacity/Car/Engine	Comment		Q Pos/Entries
14	BRITISH GP	Brands Hatch	22	Bob Gerard Racing	D	1.0 Cooper T73-Ford 4	long pit stop – gearbox/-24 laps		20/25
	1966 Championship position: 17th=	Wins: 0	Pole positions: 0	Fastest laps: 0	Points scored: 1				
6	FRENCH GP	Reims	44	David Bridges	G	2.0 Brabham BT11-BRM V8	3 laps behind		15/17
8	BRITISH GP	Brands Hatch	22	David Bridges	G	2.0 Brabham BT11-BRM V8	4 laps behind		16/20
8	DUTCH GP	Zandvoort	38	David Bridges	G	2.0 Brabham BT11-BRM V8	6 laps behind		18/18
ret	GERMAN GP	Nürburgring	16	David Bridges	G	2.0 Brabham BT11-BRM V8	accident – later proved to be fatal		26/30
	GP Starts: 5	GP Wins: 0	Pole positions: 0	Fastest laps: 0	Points: 1				

TAYLOR, Mike (GB) b 24/4/1934, London

	1959 Championship position: Unplaced								
	Race	Circuit	No	Entrant	Tyres	Capacity/Car/Engine	Comment		Q Pos/Entries
ret	BRITISH GP (F2)	Aintree	50	Alan Brown Equipe	D	1.5 Cooper T45-Climax 4 F2	transmission		24/30
	1960 Championship position: Unplaced								
dns	BELGIAN GP	Spa	20	Taylor-Crawley Racing Team	D	2.5 Lotus 18-Climax 4	broken steering – crashed		– / –
	GP Starts: 1	GP Wins: 0	Pole positions: 0	Fastest laps: 0	Points: 0				

TREVOR TAYLOR

EVEN the gritty and determined Yorkshireman Trevor Taylor was eventually battered into submission by a catalogue of crashes that would have frightened a lesser man from the cockpit of a racing car forever. As it was, he returned from a bombed-out Formula 1 career to establish himself later as a top-line F5000 campaigner, which says a lot for the qualities he possessed.

The son of a garage proprietor, Trevor was given much encouragement in his early racing days by his father, who bought a Triumph TR2 for him to race in 1955. This was soon replaced by a succession of 500cc F3 cars, one of them the ex-Stuart Lewis-Evans Cooper-Norton. Progress was slow initially, but by 1958 Taylor was good enough to take the British F3 championship. The garage purchased an F2 Cooper for him to race in 1959, but apart from a minor Libre win at Rufforth, little of note was achieved. Colin Chapman offered to run him as part of his junior team in 1960 if he purchased a Lotus 18, and it proved to be a sound decision for both parties. Taylor shared the championship that year with Jim Clark and was taken into the team proper for 1961, when again he won the title, this time on his own. With Innes Ireland injured at Monaco, he was given his grand prix debut at Zandvoort, where he finished 13th and last, in a race unique for its complete lack of a pit stop or retirement.

There were a few other Formula 1 outings that year, Taylor's best results being a second place in the Rand GP at Kyalami, followed by a win in the Cape GP at Killarney early in 1962. By then, Chapman had placed his faith in the youngster, putting him into the Formula 1 team at the expense of Ireland. A second place at Zandvoort was a great start, but he was shaken up at Spa, where a duel with Willy Mairesse left both cars wrecked and the Belgian in hospital. This was followed by an 80mph crash-test into the back of Maurice Trintignant's stalled car at Rouen, which left him bruised from head to foot, while at the Nürburgring he was the victim of an engine malady that sent him through a hedge. His confidence was restored at the end of the year, however, when he shared the winning car in the Mexican GP with Clark and then won the Natal GP at Westmead.

Having been retained for 1963, Taylor took second places at Pau and Karlskoga, but apart from a single point at Monaco he was out of luck in championship events. The Mediterranean GP at Enna supplied perhaps his most astounding escape, after he was pitched from his Lotus at over 100mph, rolling some 50 yards down the track as his car hurtled to destruction. Amazingly, he emerged with just grazes and bruising. With Peter Arundell knocking at the door, he was released to join the BRP team in 1964, but apart from a sixth place at Watkins Glen, there was little to enthuse about in the performances of the pale green cars.

Trevor raced a Brabham in Formula 2 during 1965/66, and was briefly involved in the amateurish Shannon project, which represented the nadir of his career. From 1967, he went back to basics, first running a Lotus 47 with encouraging results, before moving up to a Lola T70 to win the 1969 Tourist Trophy at Oulton Park. This was the inaugural year of F5000, and he took his Surtees TS5 right to the brink of a championship win, before losing out to Peter Gethin after the pair collided in the final round at Brands Hatch. He continued in the formula throughout the next three seasons, always a competitive proposition, but never quite the force of that first year. At the end of 1972, he brought the curtain down on a sometimes unlucky career, but the fact that he had emerged intact after some of those early mishaps was probably cause enough for him to count his blessings.

TAYLOR, Trevor (GB) b 26/12/1936, Gleadless, nr Sheffield, Yorkshire – d 27/9/2010, Wickersley, nr Rotherham, South Yorkshire

	Race	Circuit	No	Entrant	Tyres	Capacity/Car/Engine	Comment	Q Pos/Entries
	1959 Championship position: Unplaced							
dnq	BRITISH GP (F2)	Aintree	44	Ace Garage (Rotherham)	D	1.5 Cooper T51-Climax 4		– /30
	1961 Championship position: Unplaced							
13	DUTCH GP	Zandvoort	16	Team Lotus	D	1.5 Lotus 18-Climax 4	2 laps behind	16/17
	1962 Championship position: 10th Wins: 0 Pole positions: 0 Fastest laps: 0 Points scored: 6							
2	DUTCH GP	Zandvoort	5	Team Lotus	D	1.5 Lotus 24-Climax V8		10/20
dns	"	"	5	Team Lotus	D	1.5 Lotus 24-Climax 4	practice only	– / –
ret	MONACO GP	Monte Carlo	20	Team Lotus	D	1.5 Lotus 24-Climax V8	oil leak	17/21

dns	"	" "	20	Team Lotus	D	1.5 Lotus 24-BRM V8	*practice only*	– / –
ret	BELGIAN GP	Spa	17	Team Lotus	D	1.5 Lotus 24-Climax V8	*accident with Mairesse*	3/20
8	FRENCH GP	Rouen	14	Team Lotus	D	1.5 Lotus 25-Climax V8	*hit Trintignant at finish/6 laps behind*	12/17
8	BRITISH GP	Aintree	22	Team Lotus	D	1.5 Lotus 24-Climax V8	*1 lap behind*	10/21
ret	GERMAN GP	Nürburgring	6	Team Lotus	D	1.5 Lotus 24-Climax V8	*engine problems – accident*	26/30
ret	ITALIAN GP	Monza	22	Team Lotus	D	1.5 Lotus 25-Climax V8	*gearbox*	16/30
12	US GP	Watkins Glen	9	Team Lotus	D	1.5 Lotus 25-Climax V8	*pit stop – oil pressure/15 laps behind*	8/20
ret	SOUTH AFRICAN GP	East London	2	Team Lotus	D	1.5 Lotus 25-Climax V8	*gearbox*	9/17

1963 Championship position: 15th=   Wins: 0   Pole positions: 0   Fastest laps: 0   Points scored: 1

6	MONACO GP	Monte Carlo	10	Team Lotus	D	1.5 Lotus 25-Climax V8	*gearchange problems/2 laps behind*	9/17
ret	BELGIAN GP	Spa	2	Team Lotus	D	1.5 Lotus 25-Climax V8	*leg injury after practice accident*	11/20
10	DUTCH GP	Zandvoort	8	Team Lotus	D	1.5 Lotus 25-Climax V8	*pit stop – misfire/14 laps behind*	10/19
13/ret	FRENCH GP	Reims	20	Team Lotus	D	1.5 Lotus 25-Climax V8	*transmission/12 laps behind*	7/21
ret/dsq*	BRITISH GP	Silverstone	5	Team Lotus	D	1.5 Lotus 25-Climax V8	*fuel pump/*push start at pitstop*	=10/23
8	GERMAN GP	Nürburgring	4	Team Lotus	D	1.5 Lotus 25-Climax V8	*1 lap behind*	18/26
ret	US GP	Watkins Glen	9	Team Lotus	D	1.5 Lotus 25-Climax V8	*transistor box*	=7/21
ret	MEXICAN GP	Mexico City	9	Team Lotus	D	1.5 Lotus 25-Climax V8	*engine*	12/21
8	SOUTH AFRICAN GP	East London	2	Team Lotus	D	1.5 Lotus 25-Climax V8	*spin/pit stop – gearchange/-4 laps*	=7/21

1964 Championship position: 197h=   Wins: 0   Pole positions: 0   Fastest laps: 0   Points scored: 1

ret	MONACO GP	Monte Carlo	15	British Racing Partnership	D	1.5 BRP Mk1-BRM V8	*fuel leak*	14/20
7	BELGIAN GP	Spa	4	British Racing Partnership	D	1.5 BRP Mk2-BRM V8	*1 lap behind*	12/20
ret	FRENCH GP	Rouen	18	British Racing Partnership	D	1.5 BRP Mk2-BRM V8	*brakes – accident*	12/17
ret	BRITISH GP	Brands Hatch	12	British Racing Partnership	D	1.5 Lotus 24-BRM V8	*unwell after practice crash*	=16/25
dns	"	" "	12	British Racing Partnership	D	1.5 BRP Mk2-BRM V8	*practice accident*	– / –
ret	AUSTRIAN GP	Zeltweg	15	British Racing Partnership	D	1.5 BRP Mk1-BRM V8	*rear suspension*	16/20
dnq	ITALIAN GP	Monza	44	British Racing Partnership	D	1.5 BRP Mk1-BRM V8		22/25
6	US GP	Watkins Glen	12	British Racing Partnership	D	1.5 BRP Mk2-BRM V8	*4 laps behind*	15/19
ret	MEXICAN GP	Mexico City	12	British Racing Partnership	D	1.5 BRP Mk2-BRM V8	*overheating*	18/19

1966 Championship position: Unplaced

ret	BRITISH GP	Brands Hatch	23	Aiden Jones/Paul Emery	D	3.0 Shannon-Climax Godiva V8	*split fuel tank*	18/20

GP Starts: 27   GP Wins: 0   Pole positions: 0   Fastest laps: 0   Points: 8

MIKE THACKWELL

IN 1980, at the age of 19, Mike Thackwell became the then youngest ever starter in a world championship grand prix when he left the grid at Montreal, only to be involved in a multiple collision that halted the race. His car was hors de combat and the race restarted without him. So there's the conundrum: technically, did he start or not? In the event, it would be nearly four years before another grand prix opportunity came his way, and by then his career had lost momentum – and perhaps he had lost the necessary determination.

Mike's early career was meteoric. In 1979, aged just 18, he contested the Vandervell F3 series in a works March, finishing third in the championship with five wins. In 1980, he raced the ICI March 802, putting in some brilliant drives without gaining the reward he deserved, turned down the chance to race the works Ensign, practised an Arrows at Zandvoort and then joined the Tyrrell team for Montreal.

A hot favourite for the Formula 2 title in 1981, Thackwell started the season with a win at Silverstone, but a heavy crash at Thruxton left him on crutches and his title hopes evaporated. Ron Tauranac, unconvinced about Mike's fitness, dropped him from the F2 team just before the start of the 1982 season, and his confused driver was left in the lurch, eventually scraping a deal together that saw him living from race to race. Fortunately, the New Zealander was back in the Ralt fold for 1983, although a slowish start meant he had to play second fiddle to team-mate and champion-elect Jonathan Palmer. However, 1984 was to be his year and, showing a new resolve, he dominated proceedings, winning seven of the 11 rounds, taking six poles and nine fastest laps, and leading an incredible 408 of the 580 laps run.

Still without a Formula 1 ride and eyeing Indy car racing, Thackwell moved somewhat unwillingly into F3000 with Ralt in 1985. Having proved beyond doubt that he was the best driver in the series, but failed to clinch the title through sheer bad luck, understandably he felt dissatisfied with his lot and refused to commit himself to a full season in 1986. When he did compete, notably at Pau, he showed what talent was being wasted, subsequently running around – albeit quite successfully – in endurance racing with Sauber and Brun before a brief reunion with Ralt in F3000 in 1988. Disillusioned, he walked away from the sport before the age of 30.

Having cut his motor racing links, Thackwell dropped out of sight and has been reported to have done a number of jobs, including a special needs teacher, and running both a pub and surfboard shop in Cornwall.

THACKWELL, Mike (NZ) b 30/3/1961, Auckland

	1980 Championship position: Unplaced							
	Race	Circuit	No	Entrant	Tyres	Capacity/Car/Engine	Comment	Q Pos/Entries
dnq	DUTCH GP	Zandvoort	30	Warsteiner Arrows Racing Team	G	3.0 Arrows A3-Cosworth V8		27/28
ret/dns*	CANADIAN GP	Montreal	43	Candy Tyrrell Team	G	3.0 Tyrrell 010-Cosworth V8	accident at first start/*did not restart	(24)/28
dnq	US GP EAST	Watkins Glen	43	Candy Tyrrell Team	G	3.0 Tyrrell 010-Cosworth V8		26/27
	1984 Championship position: Unplaced							
ret	CANADIAN GP	Montreal	10	Skoal Bandit Formula 1 Team	P	1.5 t/c RAM 02-Hart 4	broken turbo wastegate	25/26
dnq	GERMAN GP	Hockenheim	4	Tyrrell Racing Organisation	G	3.0 Tyrrell 012-Cosworth V8		27/27

GP Starts: 1 (2)   GP Wins: 0   Pole positions: 0   Fastest laps: 0   Points: 0

THIELE, Alfonso (I/USA) b 5/4/1922, Istanbul, Turkey – d 15/7/1986, Novara, Italy

	1960 Championship position: Unplaced							
	Race	Circuit	No	Entrant	Tyres	Capacity/Car/Engine	Comment	Q Pos/Entries
ret	ITALIAN GP	Monza	34	Scuderia Centro Sud	D	2.5 Cooper T51-Maserati 4	gearbox	9/16

GP Starts: 1   GP Wins: 0   Pole positions: 0   Fastest laps: 0   Points: 0

THOMPSON, Eric (GB) b 4/11/1919, Ditton Hill, Surbiton, Surrey

	1952	Championship position: 11th=		Wins: 0	Pole positions: 0	Fastest laps: 0	Points scored: 2	
	Race	Circuit	No	Entrant	Tyres	Capacity/Car/Engine	Comment	Q Pos/Entries
5	BRITISH GP	Silverstone	5	Connaught Engineering	D	2.0 Connaught A Type-Lea Francis 4	3 laps behind	9/32

GP Starts: 1   GP Wins: 0   Pole positions: 0   Fastest laps: 0   Points: 2

ALFONSO THIELE

WITH the exception of his single-seater drive in the 1960 Italian GP, Alfonso Thiele was exclusively a sports car pilot, and a pretty good one at that.

Thiele spent most of the late 1950s campaigning the little Fiat Abarth (taking a 750cc class win in the 1957 Mille Miglia), before graduating to a more potent proposition with the Ferrari 250GT. In 1959, he emerged victorious in the first ever Monza 'Lottery Grand Prix'. Subsequently, this race was run for single-seaters.

In the early 1960s, he was a works driver for both the Fiat Abarth and Alfa Romeo teams. With the latter, he took a fine fourth place in the 1964 Targa Florio, just behind team-mate Roberto Businello.

LESLIE THORNE

A CHARTERED accountant by profession, Leslie Thorne raced extensively in trials and hill-climbs both before and after the Second World War.

After some impressive performances in a Formula 3 Cooper-Norton during 1953, Thorne's friend, David Murray (the owner of Ecurie Ecosse), persuaded him to try his hand with the team's Formula 2 Connaught in 1954. He raced the car in that year's British Grand Prix, but otherwise drove mainly in Formula Libre events, his best finish being sixth in the Chichester Cup at Goodwood.

ERIC THOMPSON

LIFE as a Lloyd's broker left Eric Thompson with less time to race than he would have liked, but he still managed to make his mark as a member of the Aston Martin sports car team between 1949 and 1953. He enjoyed some excellent results with David Brown's équipe, finishing third at Le Mans in 1951 with Lance Macklin and second at Dundrod in the 1953 Tourist Trophy, and winning the BARC nine-hours at Goodwood with Reg Parnell.

Thompson's single-seater outings were largely confined to minor Formula Libre events in Rob Walker's Connaught. Given a works machine for the 1952 British GP, however, he did extremely well to bring the car home in fifth place and secure two championship points in his only grand prix appearance.

THORNE, Leslie (GB) b 23/6/1916, Greenock, Renfrewshire, Scotland – d 13/7/1993, Troon, Ayrshire, Scotland

1954 Championship position: Unplaced

	Race	Circuit	No	Entrant	Tyres	Capacity/Car/Engine	Comment	Q Pos/Entries
nc	BRITISH GP	Silverstone	26	Ecurie Ecosse	D	2.0 Connaught A Type-Lea Francis 4	*12 laps behind*	23/31

GP Starts: 1   GP Wins: 0   Pole positions: 0   Fastest laps: 0   Points: 0

TINGLE, Sam (RSR) b 24/8/1921, Manchester, England – d 19/12/2008, Somerset West, South Africa

1963 Championship position: Unplaced

	Race	Circuit	No	Entrant	Tyres	Capacity/Car/Engine	Comment	Q Pos/Entries
ret	SOUTH AFRICAN GP	East London	20	Sam Tingle	D	1.5 LDS Mk1-Alfa Romeo 4	*driveshaft*	17/21
	1965 Championship position: Unplaced							
13	SOUTH AFRICAN GP	East London	25	Sam Tingle	D	1.5 LDS Mk1-Alfa Romeo 4	*12 laps behind*	20/25
	1967 Championship position: Unplaced							
ret	SOUTH AFRICAN GP	Kyalami	18	Sam Tingle	F	2.7 LDS Mk3B-Climax 4	*burst tyre – accident*	14/18
	1968 Championship position: Unplaced							
ret	SOUTH AFRICAN GP	Kyalami	18	Team Gunston	F	3.0 LDS Mk3B-Repco V8	*ignition/fuel*	22/23
	1969 Championship position: Unplaced							
8	SOUTH AFRICAN GP	Kyalami	17	Team Gunston	F	3.0 Brabham BT24-Repco V8	*7 laps behind*	18/18

GP Starts: 5   GP Wins: 0   Pole positions: 0   Fastest laps: 0   Points: 0

TITTERINGTON, Desmond (GB) b 1/5/1928, Cultra, nr Holywood, Co Down, Northern Ireland – d 13/4/2002, Dundee, Scotland

1956 Championship position: Unplaced

	Race	Circuit	No	Entrant	Tyres	Capacity/Car/Engine	Comment	Q Pos/Entries
ret	BRITISH GP	Silverstone	20	Connaught Engineering	P	2.5 Connaught B Type-Alta 4	*engine*	11/28

GP Starts: 1   GP Wins: 0   Pole positions: 0   Fastest laps: 0   Points: 0

SAM TINGLE

A GREAT enthusiast, Rhodesian Sam Tingle began racing in his homeland in 1947, at the wheel of an old Bentley. This was replaced with a succession of cars, mainly MGs, before he acquired the ex-Johnny Claes, ex-Dick Gibson Connaught, which earned him the Rhodesian championship.

Sam contested the South African championship with great verve throughout the 1960s in one of Doug Serrurier's Cooper-based LDS-Alfas, scoring his first big win in the 1966 Border Trophy at East London, although he took many other good placings.

By 1968, Sam was perhaps past his prime, but he still managed to stay competitive in his final seasons in the sport by getting his hands on an ex-works Brabham BT24-Repco entered by Team Gunston.

DESMOND TITTERINGTON

A LTHOUGH Ulsterman Desmond Titterington drove in only a single grand prix, he was a very fine driver indeed and, had he not chosen suddenly to retire from competition at the end of the 1956 season, quite probably he would have become a household name. Having gained experience in an Allard in novice trials and handicaps from 1951, he joined Ecurie Ecosse for the 1953 Tourist Trophy at Dundrod, finishing sixth with Bob Dickson in an Aston Martin. Early the following year, he showed his versatility by taking sixth place in the Monte Carlo Rally in a Jaguar and then raced his own Triumph TR2, before receiving an invitation to rejoin Ecurie Ecosse, who had lost the services of the injured Jimmy Stewart. Racing the Scottish team's Jaguar, he was second in the BARC nine-hours at Goodwood in 1955; he also won a number of national events for them. In addition, he drove for Mercedes in the 1955 Targa Florio, finishing fourth with John Fitch. So impressed were Jaguar that they signed him as a works driver for major sports car races; he took third place at Reims in 1956.

In Formula 1, Titterington scored a superb third at Oulton Park in 1955 on his debut for Vanwall and also took third in the 1956 International Trophy for Connaught, for whom he drove in that year's British GP. What a pity that business and family reasons deprived the racing world of the chance to witness how his career might have developed.

MAURICE TRINTIGNANT

THE youngest of the five sons of a prosperous vineyard owner, Maurice Trintignant followed three of his brothers into racing. Despite the death of one of them, Louis, at Péronne in 1933, he could not resist the urge to try his hand at the sport five years later at the wheel of the Bugatti driven by his unfortunate sibling. He took it to fifth place in the Pau GP and won the 1939 GP des Frontières at Chimay, before the Second World War caused the cessation of racing activities. When the first post-war motor race was held in the Bois de Boulogne, Trintignant was there with his trusty Bugatti. Unfortunately, his car suffered fuel starvation, caused by rat droppings (les petoules) left in the tank from its wartime lay-up. This was the cause of much merriment, and henceforth Maurice was given the sobriquet 'Le Petoulet', which he accepted in fine spirit.

Maurice soon replaced the Bugatti with an Amilcar, winning at Avignon in 1947, and after half a season in the Gersac team's Delage, he joined the Simca Gordini team. The 1948 season started well with wins at Perpignan and Montlhéry, but he was seriously injured in the tragic Swiss GP at Bremgarten, where three drivers were killed. Maurice was more fortunate. He had spun his car and been flung into the middle of the track, and only the split-second reactions by the approaching Giuseppe Farina, Bira and Robert Manzon enabled them to miss his unconscious body, the avoiding action eliminating the three brave pilots. In hospital, Trintignant's life hung by a thread as he lay in a coma for eight days. At one stage, he was pronounced dead, but his pulse returned and a slow recovery began. He was back in action at the beginning of 1949 for Simca, winning the Circuit des Ramparts at Angoulême. Showing no ill effects from his accident, he remained with Gordini to the end of the 1953 season, taking the little pale blue car to victories at Geneva in 1950, Albi and Cadours in 1951, and Cadours again in 1953, the year he was crowned racing champion of France. The Gordinis, of course, were notorious for their fragility, and in world championship grands prix, he could achieve no better than three fifth places.

After winning the Buenos Aires GP in Louis Rosier's Ferrari, Trintignant joined the works team for the bulk of 1954, which brought an immediate improvement in results. Regularly placing in world championship events, he won F1 races at Caen and Rouen, and was second at Syracuse and Bari. He also shared the winning 4.9-litre Ferrari with Froilán González to win the Le Mans 24-hour race. In 1955, a steady drive at Monaco brought him his first ever world championship win, and in sports cars he won the Messina ten-hours with Eugenio Castellotti. He continued to race the Scuderia's sports cars successfully in 1956, winning the Agadir, Dakar and Swedish GPs. In Formula 1, however, the situation was less happy; he had a dismal time in the Vanwall and the ambitious, but ill-fated Bugatti. He drove less frequently in 1957, but won the F2 Coupe de Vitesse at Reims in Ferrari's Dino V6 and took third in the Moroccan GP in BRM's P25.

Maurice was back at the forefront again in 1958 when, with Rob Walker's little Cooper, he won the Monaco GP once more, and also took victories at Pau and Clermont-Ferrand. He would enjoy his two-year association with the Walker équipe and, despite being number two to Stirling Moss, provided them with some excellent grand prix results in 1959, as well as another victory at Pau. After he finished second at Le Mans in the Aston Martin that year, his outings with David Brown's Formula 1 team in 1960 were restricted by the project's myriad problems, and he was forced to find rides with Centro Sud. He also ran his own Cooper in Formula 2 that season, plenty of solid placings gaining excellent remuneration. He was also awarded the Légion d'honneur for his services to French motor racing, but he had no intention of resting on his laurels. After a thin time in 1961, he was back with Rob Walker in 1962 following the Goodwood accident that ended the career of Stirling Moss. Although now past his best, Trintignant could still teach Jim Clark a thing or two, as he demonstrated when he took a third win at Pau.

Maurice raced very little in 1963 and retirement seemed imminent, but he purchased a BRM V8 for 1964 and drove exceedingly well in the German GP to be classified fifth, thus taking two championship points at the age of 47. Although this was his final season in grands prix, his final farewell came at Le Mans in 1965, ending a remarkable career during which – his Bremgarten crash apart – he had perhaps been one of the safest drivers in the sport. He was rarely involved in accidents and his mechanical sympathy ensured a great many finishes, which was much appreciated by team managers.

In his final race, 'Le Petoulet' drove a Ford GT, which was quite a long way down the chain of motor racing evolution from a Type 35 GP Bugatti, and the cause of his retirement from the 24-hour race certainly wasn't rat droppings!

TRINTIGNANT, Maurice (F) b 30/10/1917, Sainte Cécile-les-Vignes, Vaucluse – d 13/2/2005, Nimes, Gard, France

1950 Championship position: Unplaced

	Race	Circuit	No	Entrant	Tyres	Capacity/Car/Engine	Comment	Q Pos/Entries
ret	MONACO GP	Monte Carlo	12	Equipe Gordini	E	1.5 s/c Simca Gordini T15 4	multiple accident	13/21
ret	ITALIAN GP	Monza	42	Equipe Gordini	E	1.5 s/c Simca Gordini T15 4	water pipe	12/27

1951 Championship position: Unplaced

	Race	Circuit	No	Entrant	Tyres	Capacity/Car/Engine	Comment	Q Pos/Entries
ret	FRENCH GP	Reims	32	Equipe Gordini	E	1.5 s/c Simca Gordini T15 4	engine	18/23
ret	GERMAN GP	Nürburgring	81	Equipe Gordini	E	1.5 s/c Simca Gordini T15 4	engine	14/23
dns*	ITALIAN GP	Monza	50	Equipe Gordini	E	1.5 s/c Simca Gordini T15 4	*indisposed – Behra drove car in race	12/22
ret	SPANISH GP	Pedralbes	12	Equipe Gordini	E	1.5 s/c Simca Gordini T15 4	engine	11/20

1952 Championship position: 11th= Wins: 0 Pole positions: 0 Fastest laps: 0 Points scored: 2

	Race	Circuit	No	Entrant	Tyres	Capacity/Car/Engine	Comment	Q Pos/Entries
dns	SWISS GP	Bremgarten	14	Ecurie Rosier	P	2.0 Ferrari 166 V12 F2	engine trouble	- / -
5	FRENCH GP	Rouen	30	Equipe Gordini	E	1.5 Simca Gordini T15 4	5 laps behind	6/20
ret	BRITISH GP	Silverstone	25	Equipe Gordini	E	2.0 Gordini T16 6	gearbox	21/32
ret	GERMAN GP	Nürburgring	109	Equipe Gordini	E	2.0 Gordini T16 6	brakes/suspension	3/32
6	DUTCH GP	Zandvoort	12	Equipe Gordini	E	2.0 Gordini T16 6	3 laps behind	5/18
ret	ITALIAN GP	Monza	4	Equipe Gordini	E	2.0 Gordini T16 6	engine	4/35

1953 Championship position: 9th= Wins: 0 Pole positions: 0 Fastest laps: 0 Points scored: 4

	Race	Circuit	No	Entrant	Tyres	Capacity/Car/Engine	Comment	Q Pos/Entries
7*	ARGENTINE GP	Buenos Aires	28	Equipe Gordini	E	2.0 Gordini T16 6	*Schell took over car/6 laps behind	7/16
6	DUTCH GP	Zandvoort	24	Equipe Gordini	E	2.0 Gordini T16 6	3 laps behind	12/20
5	BELGIAN GP	Spa	18	Equipe Gordini	E	2.0 Gordini T16 6	1 lap behind	8/22
ret	FRENCH GP	Reims	4	Equipe Gordini	E	2.0 Gordini T16 6	transmission	23/25
ret	BRITISH GP	Silverstone	29	Equipe Gordini	E	2.0 Gordini T16 6	transmission	8/29
ret	GERMAN GP	Nürburgring	10	Equipe Gordini	E	2.0 Gordini T16 6	differential	5/35
ret	SWISS GP	Bremgarten	8	Equipe Gordini	E	2.0 Gordini T16 6	transmission	4/23
5	ITALIAN GP	Monza	36	Equipe Gordini	E	2.0 Gordini T16 6	1 lap behind	8/30

1954 Championship position: 4th Wins: 0 Pole positions: 0 Fastest laps: 0 Points scored: 17

	Race	Circuit	No	Entrant	Tyres	Capacity/Car/Engine	Comment	Q Pos/Entries
4	ARGENTINE GP	Buenos Aires	26	Ecurie Rosier	P	2.5 Ferrari 625 4	1 lap behind	5/18
2	BELGIAN GP	Spa	8	Scuderia Ferrari	P	2.5 Ferrari 625 4		6/18
dns	"	"	8	Scuderia Ferrari	P	2.5 Ferrari 553 4	practice only	- / -
ret	FRENCH GP	Reims	4	Scuderia Ferrari	P	2.5 Ferrari 625 4	engine	9/22
5	BRITISH GP	Silverstone	10	Scuderia Ferrari	P	2.5 Ferrari 625/555 4	3 laps behind	8/31
3	GERMAN GP	Nürburgring	2	Scuderia Ferrari	P	2.5 Ferrari 625 4		7/23
ret	SWISS GP	Bremgarten	26	Scuderia Ferrari	P	2.5 Ferrari 625/555 4	engine	4/16
5	ITALIAN GP	Monza	30	Scuderia Ferrari	P	2.5 Ferrari 625/555 4	5 laps behind	11/21
ret	SPANISH GP	Pedralbes	40	Scuderia Ferrari	P	2.5 Ferrari 625/555 4	gearbox	8/22

1955 Championship position: 4th Wins: 1 Pole positions: 0 Fastest laps: 0 Points scored: 11.33

	Race	Circuit	No	Entrant	Tyres	Capacity/Car/Engine	Comment	Q Pos/Entries
ret	ARGENTINE GP	Buenos Aires	14	Scuderia Ferrari	E	2.5 Ferrari 625/555 4	engine	14/22
2*	"	"	12	Scuderia Ferrari	E	2.5 Ferrari 625/555 4	*González/Farina also drove car	- / -
3*	"	"	10	Scuderia Ferrari	E	2.5 Ferrari 625/555 4	*Farina/Maglioli co-drove car/-2 laps	- / -
1	MONACO GP	Monte Carlo	44	Scuderia Ferrari	E	2.5 Ferrari 625/555 4		9/22
6	BELGIAN GP	Spa	4	Scuderia Ferrari	E	2.5 Ferrari 555 4	1 lap behind	10/14
ret	DUTCH GP	Zandvoort	4	Scuderia Ferrari	E	2.5 Ferrari 555 4	gearbox	8/16
dns	"		4	Scuderia Ferrari	E	2.5 Ferrari 625 4	practice only	- / -
ret	BRITISH GP	Aintree	18	Scuderia Ferrari	P	2.5 Ferrari 625/555 4	overheating	13/25
8	ITALIAN GP	Monza	8	Scuderia Ferrari	E	2.5 Ferrari 555 4	3 laps behind	15/22

1956 Championship position: Unplaced

	Race	Circuit	No	Entrant	Tyres	Capacity/Car/Engine	Comment	Q Pos/Entries
ret	MONACO GP	Monte Carlo	14	Vandervell Products Ltd	P	2.5 Vanwall 4	overheating after accident	6/19
ret	BELGIAN GP	Spa	12	Vandervell Products Ltd	P	2.5 Vanwall 4	fuel pipe	7/16
ret	FRENCH GP	Reims	28	Automobiles Bugatti	E	2.5 Bugatti 251 8	throttle pedal	18/20
ret	BRITISH GP	Silverstone	17	Vandervell Products Ltd	P	2.5 Vanwall 4	fuel line	16/28
ret	ITALIAN GP	Monza	20	Vandervell Products Ltd	P	2.5 Vanwall 4	rear suspension	=11/26

1957 Championship position: 10th= Wins: 0 Pole positions: 0 Fastest laps: 0 Points scored: 5

	Race	Circuit	No	Entrant	Tyres	Capacity/Car/Engine	Comment	Q Pos/Entries
5	MONACO GP	Monte Carlo	30	Scuderia Ferrari	E	2.5 Lancia-Ferrari 801 V8	5 laps behind	6/21
ret	FRENCH GP	Rouen	16	Scuderia Ferrari	E	2.5 Lancia-Ferrari 801 V8	magneto	8/15
4*	BRITISH GP	Aintree	16	Scuderia Ferrari	E	2.5 Lancia-Ferrari 801 V8	*Collins took over car/2 laps behind	9/19

1958 Championship position: 7th Wins: 1 Pole positions: 0 Fastest laps: 0 Points scored: 12

	Race	Circuit	No	Entrant	Tyres	Capacity/Car/Engine	Comment	Q Pos/Entries
1	MONACO GP	Monte Carlo	20	R R C Walker Racing Team	D	2.0 Cooper T45-Climax 4		5/28
9	DUTCH GP	Zandvoort	9	R R C Walker Racing Team	D	2.0 Cooper T45-Climax 4	3 laps behind	8/17
7	BELGIAN GP	Spa	28	Scuderia Centro Sud	P	2.5 Maserati 250F 6	1 lap behind	16/20
ret	FRENCH GP	Reims	18	Owen Racing Organisation	D	2.5 BRM P25 4	broken camshaft gear	7/21
8	BRITISH GP	Silverstone	4	R R C Walker Racing Team	D	2.0 Cooper T43-Climax 4	2 laps behind	12/21
3	GERMAN GP	Nürburgring	11	R R C Walker Racing Team	D	2.2 Cooper T45-Climax 4		7/26
8	PORTUGUESE GP	Oporto	12	R R C Walker Racing Team	D	2.0 Cooper T43-Climax 4	2 laps behind	9/15
ret	ITALIAN GP	Monza	2	R R C Walker Racing Team	D	2.2 Cooper T45-Climax 4	gearbox	13/21
dns	"	"	2	R R C Walker Racing Team	D	2.0 Cooper T43-Climax 4	practice only	- / -
ret	MOROCCAN GP	Casablanca	38	R R C Walker Racing Team	D	2.2 Cooper T45-Climax 4	engine	9/25

1959 Championship position: 5th Wins: 0 Pole positions: 0 Fastest laps: 1 Points scored: 19

	Race	Circuit	No	Entrant	Tyres	Capacity/Car/Engine	Comment	Q Pos/Entries
3	MONACO GP	Monte Carlo	32	R R C Walker Racing Team	D	2.5 Cooper T51-Climax 4	2 laps behind	6/24
8	DUTCH GP	Zandvoort	10	R R C Walker Racing Team	D	2.5 Cooper T51-Climax 4	2 laps behind	11/15
nc	FRENCH GP	Reims	14	R R C Walker Racing Team	D	2.5 Cooper T51-Climax 4	spun and stalled/14 laps behind	8/22
5	BRITISH GP	Aintree	18	R R C Walker Racing Team	D	2.5 Cooper T51-Climax 4	1 lap behind	4/30
4*	GERMAN GP	AVUS	8	R R C Walker Racing Team	D	2.5 Cooper T51-Climax 4	*6th Heat 1/4th Heat 2/1 lap behind	12/16
4	PORTUGUESE GP	Monsanto	5	R R C Walker Racing Team	D	2.5 Cooper T51-Climax 4	2 laps behind	4/16
9	ITALIAN GP	Monza	16	R R C Walker Racing Team	D	2.5 Cooper T51-Climax 4	2 laps behind	13/21

2	US GP	Sebring	6	R R C Walker Racing Team	D	2.5 Cooper T51-Climax 4	*FL*		5/19

1960		Championship position: Unplaced						
3*	ARGENTINE GP	Buenos Aires	38	R R C Walker Racing Team	D	2.5 Cooper T51-Climax 4	*Moss took over car – no points allowed*	8/22
ret	MONACO GP	Monte Carlo	44	Scuderia Centro Sud	D	2.5 Cooper T51-Maserati 4	*gearbox*	16/24
ret	DUTCH GP	Zandvoort	18	Scuderia Centro Sud	D	2.5 Cooper T51-Maserati 4	*transmission*	17/21
ret	FRENCH GP	Reims	38	Scuderia Centro Sud	D	2.5 Cooper T51-Maserati 4	*hit by Graham Hill on grid*	18/23
11	BRITISH GP	Silverstone	19	David Brown Corporation	D	2.5 Aston Martin DBR5/250 6	*5 laps behind*	21/25
15	US GP	Riverside	18	Scuderia Centro Sud	D	2.5 Cooper T51-Maserati 4	*9 laps behind*	19/23

1961	Championship position: Unplaced							
7	MONACO GP	Monte Carlo	42	Scuderia Serenissima	D	1.5 Cooper T51-Maserati 4	*5 laps behind*	16/21
ret	BELGIAN GP	Spa	26	Scuderia Serenissima	D	1.5 Cooper T51-Maserati 4	*gearbox*	19/25
dns	"	"	26	Scuderia Serenissima	D	1.5 Cooper T43-Climax 4	*practice only*	– / –
13	FRENCH GP	Reims	32	Scuderia Serenissima	D	1.5 Cooper T51-Maserati 4	*11 laps behind*	23/26
dns	"	"	34	Scuderia Serenissima	D	1.5 de Tomaso F1-OSCA 4	*practice only*	– / –
ret	GERMAN GP	Nürburgring	20	Scuderia Serenissima	D	1.5 Cooper T51-Maserati 4	*engine*	21/27
9	ITALIAN GP	Monza	48	Scuderia Serenissima	D	1.5 Cooper T51-Maserati 4	*2 laps behind*	22/33

1962	Championship position: Unplaced							
ret	MONACO GP	Monte Carlo	30	Rob Walker Racing Team	D	1.5 Lotus 24-Climax V8	*first corner accident*	7/21
8	BELGIAN GP	Spa	18	Rob Walker Racing Team	D	1.5 Lotus 24-Climax V8	*2 laps behind*	16/20
7	FRENCH GP	Rouen	28	Rob Walker Racing Team	D	1.5 Lotus 24-Climax V8	*hit by Trevor Taylor after finish*	13/17
ret	GERMAN GP	Nürburgring	17	Rob Walker Racing Team	D	1.5 Lotus 24-Climax V8	*gearbox*	11/30
ret	ITALIAN GP	Monza	36	Rob Walker Racing Team	D	1.5 Lotus 24-Climax V8	*electrics*	19/30
ret	US GP	Watkins Glen	6	Rob Walker Racing Team	D	1.5 Lotus 24-Climax V8	*brakes – fluid leak*	19/20

1963	Championship position: Unplaced							
ret	MONACO GP	Monte Carlo	17	Reg Parnell (Racing)	D	1.5 Lola Mk4A-Climax V8	*raced in Amon's car/clutch*	– / –
dns	"	" "	17	Reg Parnell (Racing)	D	1.5 Lola Mk4-Climax V8	*practice only – blown engine*	14/17
8	FRENCH GP	Reims	28	Reg Parnell (Racing)	D	1.5 Lola Mk4-Climax V8	*3 laps behind*	15/21
9	ITALIAN GP	Monza	66	Scuderia Centro Sud	D	1.5 BRM P57 V8	*3 laps behind*	20/28

1964	Championship position: 16th=	Wins: 0	Pole positions: 0	Fastest laps: 0	Points scored: 2			
ret	MONACO GP	Monte Carlo	4	Maurice Trintignant	D	1.5 BRM P57 V8	*overheating*	13/20
11	FRENCH GP	Rouen	28	Maurice Trintignant	D	1.5 BRM P57 V8	*5 laps behind*	16/17
dnq	BRITISH GP	Brands Hatch	25	Maurice Trintignant	D	1.5 BRM P57 V8		25/25
5/ret	GERMAN GP	Nürburgring	22	Maurice Trintignant	D	1.5 BRM P57 V8	*flat battery/1 lap behind*	14/24
ret	ITALIAN GP	Monza	48	Maurice Trintignant	D	1.5 BRM P57 V8	*fuel injection*	21/25

GP Starts: 80 (81)   GP Wins: 2   Pole positions: 0   Fastest laps: 1   Points: 72.33

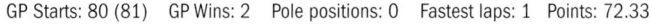

The waiting game. Trintignant scored a surprise win in the 1958 Monaco Grand Prix with Rob Walker's 2-litre Cooper-Climax after more fancied runners dropped out. The little Frenchman passes the front of the old station, long since demolished and replaced by a 1970s hotel complex.

AT the end of the 2011 season, Jarno Trulli had amassed more than 250 grand prix starts, placing him fourth in the all-time list and poised to overtake his compatriot, Riccardo Patrese. Just before the 2012 season was about to start, however, the pleasant driver was shuffled out of the grand prix pack and left to reflect on a front-line career that had promised so much, yet delivered so little. A single brilliant win at Monaco in 2004 and a further ten podium visits were scant reward for someone with a career that spanned 15 seasons.

Trulli had been a star in karting from 1983, and by the time he moved into cars, the slightly-built Italian had racked up successes all around the world. His mid-1995 debut in German F3 was sensational; in his half-season, he amassed enough points to place fourth in the final rankings, signing off the year with wins in the last two rounds at Hockenheim.

It is not surprising, therefore, that Trulli was the hot favourite for the title with his KMS Motorsport Dallara in 1996. The little Italian delivered with six wins, and it was only the late-season appearance of Nick Heidfeld that gave him cause for concern.

Benetton boss Flavio Briatore put the Formula 3 star under contract and duly found him a seat in the Minardi team for 1997. Paired with the experienced Ukyo Katayama, Jarno soon proved the faster driver, and his already astonishing rise towards the top was further fast-tracked when he was moved into the Prost line-up to replace the injured Olivier Panis.

Sixth place on the grid on Jarno's debut for the team at the French Grand Prix was a sign of good things in the offing, and a fourth-place finish in Germany was followed by a brilliant performance in Austria, where he led the race until his engine failed.

Naturally impatient for success, Trulli had to endure a largely barren season in 1998, when his car was overweight and unreliable. The frustrated driver hardly enjoyed a decent run throughout the year, and his motivation was given another searching examination at the beginning of 1999, when the Prost was still a midfield runner at best. It is fair to say that the Prost team was not the happiest of ships during the year, both drivers having their differences with the demanding proprietor. Not unnaturally, Jarno grabbed his big chance by signing for Jordan for 2000, and subsequently the relationship soured to the point that his second place in the European Grand Prix was dismissed by Alain Prost as lucky.

Paired with a resurgent Heinz-Harald Frentzen, young Trulli had his work cut out in dealing with the less than successful EJ10, but he featured at the front on several occasions when the car allowed, including an appearance on the front row at Monaco after an inspired qualifying lap. Tenth in the race was poor reward for his efforts, however, and he could not better the fourth-place finish he achieved at round two in Brazil. The Italian remained at Jordan for 2001, convinced that the now Honda-powered EJ11 could only be an improvement over the 2000 car. Testing times showed both car and driver to be close to the leading midfield pace, but he would be frustrated once again when the season started in earnest.

Still an occasional flyer in qualifying, the Italian seemed to lose his momentum in races, clocking a best finish of fourth on two occasions (Spain and USA), but again failing to break on to the podium. Good for top-six finishes when he wasn't retiring, however, Trulli ended the season in ninth overall and was still a target for envious eyes.

This led to an end-of-season 'struggle' for his services, after manager Briatore exercised an option on the Italian on behalf of Renault. Although initially Trulli was reluctant to leave Jordan for what, on 2001 form, was a lower-ranking team, he still appeared in a different set of overalls for 2002.

Given Renault's pedigree in F1, and the rate at which the company was known to develop its programmes in the formula, the move proved to be

a good one. While the Jordan team struggled, Renault finished the 2002 season with 23 points, although Trulli failed to find a podium to top his best performances of fourth at Monaco and Monza. His true form was again seen in qualifying, and it was there that he consistently outperformed team-mate Jenson Button 12–5.

For 2003, Trulli had a new team-mate in the form of Fernando Alonso, and although both got on well, the more experienced Italian found himself overshadowed. Alonso scored the team's first win since it had been re-formed, while Trulli notched up just 33 points – 22 less than the Spaniard – with a best of third place at the German GP.

Despite the disappointment, Trulli continued with Renault in 2004, initially doing well and notching up a lot of points, before eventually taking his first pole and race win convincingly at Monte Carlo. After that, however, his season went downhill, leaving team boss Briatore increasingly frustrated. The result was that the two went their separate ways with three grands prix still to go; Trulli switched to the Toyota team for the races in Japan and Brazil.

With the challenge of new team-mate Ralf Schumacher to deal with in 2005, Jarno certainly stamped his authority, proving to be the pacesetter at a number of races and scoring Toyota's first ever podium with a superb second place in Malaysia, a result that he matched in Bahrain. As the season wore on, however, the Italian struggled to match his early-season promise, despite regularly picking up points. Nevertheless, he felt very comfortable with his team, despite a hugely disappointing 2006 campaign. That year, his car was rarely a contender, and it was only at Monaco, where he held a superb third place, that a podium place beckoned.

Toyota still had great faith in the Italian, however, signing him up until 2009 to spearhead their continued drive for success. After another moribund year in 2007, when the team completely lost their way, Trulli's drive seemed in danger when Fernando Alonso was approached following his acrimonious departure from McLaren.

In the end, the Italian remained as Toyota's team leader, the promising Timo Glock acting as support. Having failed so dismally to impress in the two previous years, it came as a surprise when the team's 2008 season started in anger in Australia. Suddenly, the Toyota TF108 was possessed of more than a fair turn of speed, and Trulli's immediate prospects were buoyed by a splendid fourth place in Malaysia. Indeed, things had picked up for the Japanese team, and the consistent driver posted ten points-paying finishes, the highlight of which was a superb third place in the French Grand Prix, behind the dominant Ferraris of Felipe Massa and Kimi Räikkönen.

Toyota reaffirmed their commitment to Formula 1 in 2009, but Trulli was under pressure as the hitherto underperforming team demanded a breakthrough grand prix win at the very least. He delivered a second place in Japan, but this was too little, too late, as the Japanese giant followed Honda out of the sport.

Left with few options, the veteran Trulli threw in his lot with the hastily formed Team Lotus for 2010. He was already familiar with many of the personnel, who had come from Toyota, and his considerable experience was seen as being vital to a team so hastily assembled. It must have come as a real shock to be consigned to the lower reaches of the grid, and it didn't get any better in 2011, when the Italian complained endlessly about his inability to come to terms with the Lotus T128's power steering.

Jarno's long tenure in F1 came to a sudden end when the well-sponsored Vitaly Petrov swooped to take his seat away at the beginning of 2012. It may be that he will race on elsewhere, before perhaps devoting his full-time attention to his beloved vineyards and developing his already successful range of wines.

TRULLI, Jarno (I) b Pescara, Italy 13/7/1974

1997 Championship position: 15th Wins: 0 Pole positions: 0 Fastest laps: 0 Points scored: 3

	Race	Circuit	No	Entrant	Tyres	Capacity/Car/Engine	Comment	Q Pos/Entries
9	AUSTRALIAN GP	Melbourne	21	Minardi Team	B	3.0 Minardi M197-Hart V8	3 laps behind	17/24
12	BRAZILIAN GP	Interlagos	21	Minardi Team	B	3.0 Minardi M197-Hart V8	1 lap behind	17/22
9	ARGENTINE GP	Buenos Aires	21	Minardi Team	B	3.0 Minardi M197-Hart V8	1 lap behind	18/22
ret/dns*	SAN MARINO GP	Imola	21	Minardi Team	B	3.0 Minardi M197-Hart V8	*hydraulic pump on parade lap	20/22
ret	MONACO GP	Monte Carlo	21	Minardi Team	B	3.0 Minardi M197-Hart V8	accident – slid off	18/22
15	SPANISH GP	Barcelona	21	Minardi Team	B	3.0 Minardi M197-Hart V8	2 laps behind	18/22
ret	CANADIAN GP	Montreal	21	Minardi Team	B	3.0 Minardi M197-Hart V8	engine	20/22
10	FRENCH GP	Magny Cours	14	Prost Gauloise Blondes	B	3.0 Prost JS45-Mugen Honda V10	2 laps behind	6/22
8	BRITISH GP	Silverstone	14	Prost Gauloise Blondes	B	3.0 Prost JS45-Mugen Honda V10	1 lap behind	13/22
4	GERMAN GP	Hockenheim	14	Prost Gauloise Blondes	B	3.0 Prost JS45-Mugen Honda V10	collision with Villeneuve/1 lap behind	11/22
7	HUNGARIAN GP	Hungaroring	14	Prost Gauloise Blondes	B	3.0 Prost JS45-Mugen Honda V10		12/22
15	BELGIAN GP	Spa	14	Prost Gauloise Blondes	B	3.0 Prost JS45-Mugen Honda V10	started in spare car from pits/-2 laps	14/22
10	ITALIAN GP	Monza	14	Prost Gauloise Blondes	B	3.0 Prost JS45-Mugen Honda V10		16/22
ret	AUSTRIAN GP	A1-Ring	14	Prost Gauloise Blondes	B	3.0 Prost JS45-Mugen Honda V10	engine – led race	3/22

1998 Championship position: 15th= Wins: 0 Pole positions: 0 Fastest laps: 0 Points scored: 1

	Race	Circuit	No	Entrant	Tyres	Capacity/Car/Engine	Comment	Q Pos/Entries
ret	AUSTRALIAN GP	Melbourne	12	Gauloises Prost Peugeot	B	3.0 Prost AP01-Peugeot V10	gearbox	15/22
ret	BRAZILIAN GP	Interlagos	12	Gauloises Prost Peugeot	B	3.0 Prost AP01-Peugeot V10	fuel pressure	12/22
11	ARGENTINE GP	Buenos Aires	12	Gauloises Prost Peugeot	B	3.0 Prost AP01-Peugeot V10	2 laps behind	16/22
ret	SAN MARINO GP	Imola	12	Gauloises Prost Peugeot	B	3.0 Prost AP01-Peugeot V10	throttle	16/22
9	SPANISH GP	Barcelona	12	Gauloises Prost Peugeot	B	3.0 Prost AP01-Peugeot V10	2 laps behind	16/22
ret	MONACO GP	Monte Carlo	12	Gauloises Prost Peugeot	B	3.0 Prost AP01-Peugeot V10	gearbox	10/22
ret	CANADIAN GP	Montreal	12	Gauloises Prost Peugeot	B	3.0 Prost AP01-Peugeot V10	multiple collision on lap 1	14/22
ret	FRENCH GP	Magny Cours	12	Gauloises Prost Peugeot	B	3.0 Prost AP01-Peugeot V10	spun off	12/22
ret	BRITISH GP	Silverstone	12	Gauloises Prost Peugeot	B	3.0 Prost AP01-Peugeot V10	spun off	15/22
10	AUSTRIAN GP	A1-Ring	12	Gauloises Prost Peugeot	B	3.0 Prost AP01-Peugeot V10	1 lap behind	16/22
12	GERMAN GP	Hockenheim	12	Gauloises Prost Peugeot	B	3.0 Prost AP01-Peugeot V10	1 lap behind	14/22
ret	HUNGARIAN GP	Hungaroring	12	Gauloises Prost Peugeot	B	3.0 Prost AP01-Peugeot V10	electronics	16/22
6	BELGIAN GP	Spa	12	Gauloises Prost Peugeot	B	3.0 Prost AP01-Peugeot V10	2 laps behind	13/22
13	ITALIAN GP	Monza	12	Gauloises Prost Peugeot	B	3.0 Prost AP01-Peugeot V10	3 laps behind	10/22
ret	LUXEMBOURG GP	Nürburgring	12	Gauloises Prost Peugeot	B	3.0 Prost AP01-Peugeot V10	gearbox	14/22
12/ret	JAPANESE GP	Suzuka	12	Gauloises Prost Peugeot	B	3.0 Prost AP01-Peugeot V10	engine/3 laps behind	14/22

1999 Championship position: 11th= Wins: 0 Pole positions: 0 Fastest laps: 0 Points scored: 7

	Race	Circuit	No	Entrant	Tyres	Capacity/Car/Engine	Comment	Q Pos/Entries
ret	AUSTRALIAN GP	Melbourne	19	Gauloises Prost Peugeot	B	3.0 Prost AP02-Peugeot V10	collision with Gené	12/22
ret	BRAZILIAN GP	Interlagos	19	Gauloises Prost Peugeot	B	3.0 Prost AP02-Peugeot V10	gearbox	13/22
ret	SAN MARINO GP	Imola	19	Gauloises Prost Peugeot	B	3.0 Prost AP02-Peugeot V10	collision – broken suspension	14/22
7	MONACO GP	Monte Carlo	19	Gauloises Prost Peugeot	B	3.0 Prost AP02-Peugeot V10	1 lap behind	7/22
6	SPANISH GP	Barcelona	19	Gauloises Prost Peugeot	B	3.0 Prost AP02-Peugeot V10	1 lap behind	9/22
ret	CANADIAN GP	Montreal	19	Gauloises Prost Peugeot	B	3.0 Prost AP02-Peugeot V10	collision with Alesi on lap 1	9/22
7	FRENCH GP	Magny Cours	19	Gauloises Prost Peugeot	B	3.0 Prost AP02-Peugeot V10		8/22
9	BRITISH GP	Silverstone	19	Gauloises Prost Peugeot	B	3.0 Prost AP02-Peugeot V10		14/22
7	AUSTRIAN GP	A1-Ring	19	Gauloises Prost Peugeot	B	3.0 Prost AP02-Peugeot V10	1 lap behind	13/22
ret	GERMAN GP	Hockenheim	19	Gauloises Prost Peugeot	B	3.0 Prost AP02-Peugeot V10	engine	9/22
8	HUNGARIAN GP	Hungaroring	19	Gauloises Prost Peugeot	B	3.0 Prost AP02-Peugeot V10	1 lap behind	13/22
12	BELGIAN GP	Spa	19	Gauloises Prost Peugeot	B	3.0 Prost AP02-Peugeot V10		12/22
ret	ITALIAN GP	Monza	19	Gauloises Prost Peugeot	B	3.0 Prost AP02-Peugeot V10	gearbox	12/22
2	EUROPEAN GP	Nürburgring	19	Gauloises Prost Peugeot	B	3.0 Prost AP02-Peugeot V10		10/22
ret/dns*	MALAYSIAN GP	Sepang	19	Gauloises Prost Peugeot	B	3.0 Prost AP02-Peugeot V10	*engine failure on parade lap	(18)/22
ret	JAPANESE GP	Suzuka	19	Gauloises Prost Peugeot	B	3.0 Prost AP02-Peugeot V10	engine	7/22

2000 Championship position: 10th= Wins: 0 Pole positions: 0 Fastest laps: 0 Points scored: 6

	Race	Circuit	No	Entrant	Tyres	Capacity/Car/Engine	Comment	Q Pos/Entries
ret	AUSTRALIAN GP	Melbourne	6	Benson & Hedges Jordan	B	3.0 Jordan EJ10-Mugen Honda V10	exhaust	6/22
4*	BRAZILIAN GP	Interlagos	6	Benson & Hedges Jordan	B	3.0 Jordan EJ10-Mugen Honda V10	*2nd place car disqualified	12/22
15/ret	SAN MARINO GP	Imola	6	Benson & Hedges Jordan	B	3.0 Jordan EJ10-Mugen Honda V10	gearbox/4 laps behind	8/22
6	BRITISH GP	Silverstone	6	Benson & Hedges Jordan	B	3.0 Jordan EJ10-Mugen Honda V10		11/22
12	SPANISH GP	Barcelona	6	Benson & Hedges Jordan	B	3.0 Jordan EJ10-Mugen Honda V10	stalled at first pit stop/1 lap behind	7/22
ret	EUROPEAN GP	Nürburgring	6	Benson & Hedges Jordan	B	3.0 Jordan EJ10-Mugen Honda V10	hit from behind by Fisichella on lap 1	6/22
ret	MONACO GP	Monte Carlo	6	Benson & Hedges Jordan	B	3.0 Jordan EJ10-Mugen Honda V10	gearbox	2/22
6	CANADIAN GP	Montreal	6	Benson & Hedges Jordan	B	3.0 Jordan EJ10-Mugen Honda V10		7/22
6	FRENCH GP	Magny Cours	6	Benson & Hedges Jordan	B	3.0 Jordan EJ10-Mugen Honda V10		9/22
ret	AUSTRIAN GP	A1-Ring	6	Benson & Hedges Jordan	B	3.0 Jordan EJ10-Mugen Honda V10	multiple collision on lap 1	5/22
9	GERMAN GP	Hockenheim	6	Benson & Hedges Jordan	B	3.0 Jordan EJ10-Mugen Honda V10	stop & go penalty – impeded Barrichello	6/22
7	HUNGARIAN GP	Hungaroring	6	Benson & Hedges Jordan	B	3.0 Jordan EJ10-Mugen Honda V10	1 lap behind	12/22
ret	BELGIAN GP	Spa	6	Benson & Hedges Jordan	B	3.0 Jordan EJ10-Mugen Honda V10	hit by Button	2/22
ret	ITALIAN GP	Monza	6	Benson & Hedges Jordan	B	3.0 Jordan EJ10-Mugen Honda V10	multiple accident on lap 1	6/22
ret	U S GP	Indianapolis	6	Benson & Hedges Jordan	B	3.0 Jordan EJ10-Mugen Honda V10	engine	5/22
13	JAPANESE GP	Suzuka	6	Benson & Hedges Jordan	B	3.0 Jordan EJ10-Mugen Honda V10	car bottoming due to fuel load/-1 lap	15/22
12	MALAYSIAN GP	Sepang	6	Benson & Hedges Jordan	B	3.0 Jordan EJ10-Mugen Honda V10	collision damage/1 lap behind	9/22

2001 Championship position: 7th= Wins: 0 Pole positions: 0 Fastest laps: 0 Points scored: 12

	Race	Circuit	No	Entrant	Tyres	Capacity/Car/Engine	Comment	Q Pos/Entries
ret	AUSTRALIAN GP	Melbourne	12	B & H Jordan Honda	B	3.0 Jordan EJ11-Honda V10	misfire	7/22
8	MALAYSIAN GP	Sepang	12	B & H Jordan Honda	B	3.0 Jordan EJ11-Honda V10	accident damage – handling/-1 lap	5/22
5	BRAZILIAN GP	Interlagos	12	B & H Jordan Honda	B	3.0 Jordan EJ11-Honda V10	1 lap behind	7/22
5	SAN MARINO GP	Imola	12	B & H Jordan Honda	B	3.0 Jordan EJ11-Honda V10		5/22
4	SPANISH GP	Barcelona	12	B & H Jordan Honda	B	3.0 Jordan EJ11-Honda V10		6/22
dsq*	AUSTRIAN GP	A1-Ring	12	B & H Jordan Honda	B	3.0 Jordan EJ11-Honda V10	*exited pitlane under red light	5/22
ret	MONACO GP	Monte Carlo	12	B & H Jordan Honda	B	3.0 Jordan EJ11-Honda V10	hydraulics	8/22
11/ret	CANADIAN GP	Montreal	12	B & H Jordan Honda	B	3.0 Jordan EJ11-Honda V10	brakes/6 laps behind	4/22

ret	EUROPEAN GP	Nürburgring	12	B & H Jordan Honda	B	3.0 Jordan EJ11-Honda V10	gearbox hydraulics	7/22
5	FRENCH GP	Magny Cours	12	B & H Jordan Honda	B	3.0 Jordan EJ11-Honda V10		5/22
ret	BRITISH GP	Silverstone	12	B & H Jordan Honda	B	3.0 Jordan EJ11-Honda V10	suspension – hit by Coulthard on lap1	4/22
ret	GERMAN GP	Hockenheim	12	B & H Jordan Honda	B	3.0 Jordan EJ11-Honda V10	hydraulics	10/22
ret	HUNGARIAN GP	Hungaroring	12	B & H Jordan Honda	B	3.0 Jordan EJ11-Honda V10	hydraulics	5/22
ret	BELGIAN GP	Spa	12	B & H Jordan Honda	B	3.0 Jordan EJ11-Honda V10	engine	16/22
ret	ITALIAN GP	Monza	12	B & H Jordan Honda	B	3.0 Jordan EJ11-Honda V10	punted off by Button on lap 1	5/22
4*	UNITED STATES GP	Indianapolis	12	B & H Jordan Honda	B	3.0 Jordan EJ11-Honda V10	*dsq – but re-instated on appeal	8/22
8	JAPANESE GP	Suzuka	12	B & H Jordan Honda	B	3.0 Jordan EJ11-Honda V10	1 lap behind	8/22

2002 Championship position: 8th   Wins: 0   Pole positions: 0   Fastest laps: 0   Points scored: 9

ret	AUSTRALIAN GP	Melbourne	14	Mild Seven Renault F1 Team	M	3.0 Renault R202-V10	accident – lost control of car	7/22
ret	MALAYSIAN GP	Sepang	14	Mild Seven Renault F1 Team	M	3.0 Renault R202-V10	overheating	12/22
ret	BRAZILIAN GP	Interlagos	14	Mild Seven Renault F1 Team	M	3.0 Renault R202-V10	engine	6/22
9	SAN MARINO GP	Imola	14	Mild Seven Renault F1 Team	M	3.0 Renault R202-V10	oversteer/1 lap behind	8/22
10/ret	SPANISH GP	Barcelona	14	Mild Seven Renault F1 Team	M	3.0 Renault R202-V10	engine/2 laps behind	9/21
ret	AUSTRIAN GP	A1-Ring	14	Mild Seven Renault F1 Team	M	3.0 Renault R202-V10	fuel pressure	16/22
4	MONACO GP	Monte Carlo	14	Mild Seven Renault F1 Team	M	3.0 Renault R202-V10	1 lap behind	7/22
6	CANADIAN GP	Montreal	14	Mild Seven Renault F1 Team	M	3.0 Renault R202-V10		10/22
8	EUROPEAN GP	Nürburgring	14	Mild Seven Renault F1 Team	M	3.0 Renault R202-V10	misfiring engine/1 lap behind	7/22
ret	BRITISH GP	Silverstone	14	Mild Seven Renault F1 Team	M	3.0 Renault R202-V10	electronics	7/22
ret	FRENCH GP	Magny Cours	14	Mild Seven Renault F1 Team	M	3.0 Renault R202-V10	engine	8/21
ret	GERMAN GP	Hockenheim	14	Mild Seven Renault F1 Team	M	3.0 Renault R202-V10	spun off	8/22
8	HUNGARIAN GP	Hungaroring	14	Mild Seven Renault F1 Team	M	3.0 Renault R202-V10	1 lap behind	6/20
ret	BELGIAN GP	Spa	14	Mild Seven Renault F1 Team	M	3.0 Renault R202-V10	engine	7/20
4	ITALIAN GP	Monza	14	Mild Seven Renault F1 Team	M	3.0 Renault R202-V10	started from back of grid	11/20
5	U S GP	Indianapolis	14	Mild Seven Renault F1 Team	M	3.0 Renault R202-V10		8/20
ret	JAPANESE GP	Suzuka	14	Mild Seven Renault F1 Team	M	3.0 Renault R202-V10	engine	11/20

2003 Championship position: 8th   Wins: 0   Pole positions: 0   Fastest laps: 0   Points scored: 33

5	AUSTRALIAN GP	Melbourne	7	Mild Seven Renault F1 Team	M	3.0 Renault R3-V10		12/20
5	MALAYSIAN GP	Sepang	7	Mild Seven Renault F1 Team	M	3.0 Renault R3-V10	spun by M Schumacher/1 lap behind	2/20
8	BRAZILIAN GP	Interlagos	7	Mild Seven Renault F1 Team	M	3.0 Renault R3-V10		5/20
13	SAN MARINO GP	Imola	7	Mild Seven Renault F1 Team	M	3.0 Renault R3-V10	drove Alonso's spare car/1 lap behind	16/20
ret	SPANISH GP	Barcelona	7	Mild Seven Renault F1 Team	M	3.0 Renault R3-V10	hit by Coulthard on lap 1	4/20
8	AUSTRIAN GP	A1-Ring	7	Mild Seven Renault F1 Team	M	3.0 Renault R3-V10	1 lap behind	6/20
6	MONACO GP	Monte Carlo	7	Mild Seven Renault F1 Team	M	3.0 Renault R3-V10		4/19
ret	CANADIAN GP	Montreal	7	Mild Seven Renault F1 Team	M	3.0 Renault R3-V10	hit by Pizzonia – collision damage	8/20
ret	EUROPEAN GP	Nürburgring	7	Mild Seven Renault F1 Team	M	3.0 Renault R3-V10	fuel pump	6/20
ret	FRANCE GP	Magny Cours	7	Mild Seven Renault F1 Team	M	3.0 Renault R3-V10	engine	6/20
6	BRITISH GP	Silverstone	7	Mild Seven Renault F1 Team	M	3.0 Renault R3-V10	lack of grip	2/20
3	GERMAN GP	Hockenheim	7	Mild Seven Renault F1 Team	M	3.0 Renault R3-V10		4/20
7	HUNGARIAN GP	Hungaroring	7	Mild Seven Renault F1 Team	M	3.0 Renault R3-V10	1 lap behind	6/20
ret	ITALIAN GP	Monza	7	Mild Seven Renault F1 Team	M	3.0 Renault R3-V10	throttle failure on lap 1	6/20
4	U S GP	Indianapolis	7	Mild Seven Renault F1 Team	M	3.0 Renault R3-V10		10/20
5	JAPANESE GP	Suzuka	7	Mild Seven Renault F1 Team	M	3.0 Renault R3-V10	*no time set/great drive in race	*20/22

2004 Championship position: 6th   Wins: 1   Pole positions: 2   Fastest laps: 0   Points scored: 46

7	AUSTRALIAN GP	Melbourne	7	Mild Seven Renault F1 Team	M	3.0 Renault R24-V10	1 lap behind	9/20
5	MALAYSIAN GP	Sepang	7	Mild Seven Renault F1 Team	M	3.0 Renault R24-V10		8/20
4	BAHRAIN GP	Sakhir Circuit	7	Mild Seven Renault F1 Team	M	3.0 Renault R24-V10		7/20
5	SAN MARINO GP	Imola	7	Mild Seven Renault F1 Team	M	3.0 Renault R24-V10	brake problems	9/20
3	SPANISH GP	Barcelona	7	Mild Seven Renault F1 Team	M	3.0 Renault R24-V10		4/20
1	MONACO GP	Monte Carlo	7	Mild Seven Renault F1 Team	M	3.0 Renault R24-V10	first Grand Prix win	1/20
4	EUROPEAN GP	Nürburgring	7	Mild Seven Renault F1 Team	M	3.0 Renault R24-V10		3/20
ret	CANADIAN GP	Montreal	7	Mild Seven Renault F1 Team	M	3.0 Renault R24-V10	suspension	3/20
4	UNITED STATES GP	Indianapolis	7	Mild Seven Renault F1 Team	M	3.0 Renault R24-V10	*no time set/great drive in race	*20/20
4	FRANCE GP	Magny Cours	7	Mild Seven Renault F1 Team	M	3.0 Renault R24-V10		5/20
ret	BRITISH GP	Silverstone	7	Mild Seven Renault F1 Team	M	3.0 Renault R24-V10	accident	5/20
11	GERMAN GP	Hockenheim	7	Mild Seven Renault F1 Team	M	3.0 Renault R24-V10	hit debris – new nosecone	6/20
ret	HUNGARIAN GP	Hungaroring	7	Mild Seven Renault F1 Team	M	3.0 Renault R24-V10	engine	9/20
9	BELGIAN GP	Spa	7	Mild Seven Renault F1 Team	M	3.0 Renault R24-V10	spun by Montoya/poor handling	1/20
10	ITALIAN GP	Monza	7	Mild Seven Renault F1 Team	M	3.0 Renault R24-V10	poor grip	9/20
11	JAPANESE GP	Suzuka	17	Pansonic Toyota Racing	M	3.0 Toyota TF104-V10	tyre problems/1 lap behind	6/20
12	BRAZILIAN GP	Interlagos	17	Pansonic Toyota Racing	M	3.0 Toyota TF104-V10	1 lap behind	10/20

2005 Championship position: 7th   Wins: 0   Pole positions: 1   Fastest laps: 0   Points scored: 43

9	AUSTRALIAN GP	Melbourne	16	Panasonic Toyota Racing	M	3.0 Toyota TF105-V10	grip problems with rear tyres	2/20
2	MALAYSIAN GP	Sepang	16	Panasonic Toyota Racing	M	3.0 Toyota TF105-V10	first podium for Toyota	2/20
2	BAHRAIN GP	Sakhir Circuit	16	Panasonic Toyota Racing	M	3.0 Toyota TF105-V10		3/20
5*	SAN MARINO GP	Imola	16	Panasonic Toyota Racing	M	3.0 Toyota TF105-V10	*3rd & 5th placed cars disqualified	5/20
3	SPANISH GP	Barcelona	16	Panasonic Toyota Racing	M	3.0 Toyota TF105-V10		5/18
10	MONACO GP	Monte Carlo	16	Panasonic Toyota Racing	M	3.0 Toyota TF105-V10	extra pit stop/1 lap behind	5/18
8	EUROPEAN GP	Nürburgring	16	Panasonic Toyota Racing	M	3.0 Toyota TF105-V10	drive-through penalty	4/20
ret	CANADIAN GP	Montreal	16	Panasonic Toyota Racing	M	3.0 Toyota TF105-V10	brake disc exploded	9/20
ret/dns*	U S GP	Indianapolis	16	Panasonic Toyota Racing	M	3.0 Toyota TF105-V10	*withdrawn after parade lap	1/20
5	FRENCH GP	Magny Cours	16	Panasonic Toyota Racing	M	3.0 Toyota TF105-V10	1 lap behind	2/20
9	BRITISH GP	Silverstone	16	Panasonic Toyota Racing	M	3.0 Toyota TF105-V10	1 lap behind	5/20
14/ret	GERMAN GP	Hockenheim	16	Panasonic Toyota Racing	M	3.0 Toyota TF105-V10	engine pneumatics	9/20
4	HUNGARIAN GP	Hungaroring	16	Panasonic Toyota Racing	M	3.0 Toyota TF105-V10	collision – damaged diffuser	3/20
6	TURKISH GP	Hungaroring	16	Panasonic Toyota Racing	M	3.0 Toyota TF105-V10		5/20
5	ITALIAN GP	Monza	16	Panasonic Toyota Racing	M	3.0 Toyota TF105-V10		6/20
ret	BELGIAN GP	Spa	16	Panasonic Toyota Racing	M	3.0 Toyota TF105-V10	spun off	4/20

13	BRAZILIAN GP	Interlagos	16	Panasonic Toyota Racing	M	3.0 Toyota TF105-V10	2 laps behind	8/20
ret	JAPANESE GP	Suzuka	16	Panasonic Toyota Racing	M	3.0 Toyota TF105-V10	*no time set/taken off by Sato	*19/20
15	CHINESE GP	Shanghai	16	Panasonic Toyota Racing	M	3.0 Toyota TF105-V10	lost out in due to safety car/-1 lap	12/20

2006 Championship position: 12th　　Wins: 0　　Pole positions: 0　　Fastest laps: 0　　Points scored: 15

16	BAHRAIN GP	Sakhir Circuit	8	Panasonic Toyota Racing-	B	2.4 Toyota TF106-V8	tyre problems/1 lap behind	14/22
9	MALAYSIAN GP	Sepang	8	Panasonic Toyota Racing-	B	2.4 Toyota TF106-V8	collision damage – diffuser/-1 lap	13/22
ret	AUSTRALIAN GP	Melbourne	8	Panasonic Toyota Racing-	B	2.4 Toyota TF106-V8	collision with Coulthard	10/22
ret	SAN MARINO GP	Imola	8	Panasonic Toyota Racing-	B	2.4 Toyota TF106-V8	steering column	9/22
9	EUROPEAN GP	Nürburgring	8	Panasonic Toyota Racing-	B	2.4 Toyota TF106-V8	lack of balance/1 lap behind	7/22
10	SPANISH GP	Barcelona	8	Panasonic Toyota Racing-	B	2.4 Toyota TF106-V8	collision with Ralf Schumacher/-1 lap	7/22
17/ret	MONACO GP	Monte Carlo	8	Panasonic Toyota Racing-	B	2.4 Toyota TF106-V8	hydraulics/6 laps behind	8/22
11	BRITISH GP	Silverstone	8	Panasonic Toyota Racing-	B	2.4 Toyota TF106-V8	*no time set/1 lap behind	*22/22
6	CANADIAN GP	Montreal	8	Panasonic Toyota Racing-	B	2.4 Toyota TF106-V8	engine misfire/1 lap behind	4/22
4	U S GP	Indianapolis	8	Panasonic Toyota Racing-	B	2.4 Toyota TF106-V8	started from pitlane	20/22
ret	FRENCH GP	Magny Cours	8	Panasonic Toyota Racing-	B	2.4 Toyota TF106-V8	brakes	4/22
7	GERMAN GP	Hockenheim	8	Panasonic Toyota Racing-	B	2.4 Toyota TF106-V8		13/22
12/ret	HUNGARIAN GP	Hungaroring	8	Panasonic Toyota Racing-	B	2.4 Toyota TF106-V8	engine/5 laps behind	9/22
9	TURKISH GP	Istanbul	8	Panasonic Toyota Racing-	B	2.4 Toyota TF106-V8	1 lap behind	13/22
7	ITALIAN GP	Monza	8	Panasonic Toyota Racing-	B	2.4 Toyota TF106-V8		11/22
ret	CHINESE GP	Shanghai	8	Panasonic Toyota Racing-	B	2.4 Toyota TF106-V8	engine – pneumatic pressure loss	18/22
6	JAPANESE GP	Suzuka	8	Panasonic Toyota Racing-	B	2.4 Toyota TF106-V8	tyre graining	4/22
ret	BRAZILIAN GP	Interlagos	8	Panasonic Toyota Racing-	B	2.4 Toyota TF106-V8	rear suspension failure	3/22

2007 Championship position: 13th　　Wins: 0　　Pole positions: 0　　Fastest laps: 0　　Points scored: 8

9	AUSTRALIAN GP	Melbourne	12	Panasonic Toyota Racing-	B	2.4 Toyota TF107-V8	1 lap behind	8/22
7	MALAYSIAN GP	Sepang	12	Panasonic Toyota Racing-	B	2.4 Toyota TF107-V8		8/22
7	BAHRAIN GP	Sakhir Circuit	12	Panasonic Toyota Racing-	B	2.4 Toyota TF107-V8		9/22
ret	SPANISH GP	Barcelona	12	Panasonic Toyota Racing-	B	2.4 Toyota TF107-V8	fuel line	6/22
15	MONACO GP	Monte Carlo	12	Panasonic Toyota Racing-	B	2.4 Toyota TF107-V8	2 laps behind	14/22
ret	CANADIAN GP	Montreal	12	Panasonic Toyota Racing-	B	2.4 Toyota TF107-V8	puncture – pit stop/later crashed	10/22
6	U S GP	Indianapolis	12	Panasonic Toyota Racing-	B	2.4 Toyota TF107-V8		8/22
ret	FRENCH GP	Magny Cours	12	Panasonic Toyota Racing-	B	2.4 Toyota TF107-V8	hit Kovalainen – suspension damage	8/22
ret	BRITISH GP	Silverstone	12	Panasonic Toyota Racing-	B	2.4 Toyota TF107-V8	handling – tyres	10/22
13	EUROPEAN GP	Nürburgring	12	Panasonic Toyota Racing-	B	2.4 Toyota TF107-V8	1 lap behind	8/22
10	HUNGARIAN GP	Hungaroring	12	Panasonic Toyota Racing-	B	2.4 Toyota TF107-V8	1 lap behind	9/22
16	TURKISH GP	Istanbul	12	Panasonic Toyota Racing-	B	2.4 Toyota TF107-V8	collision with Fisichella/1 lap behind	9/22
11	ITALIAN GP	Monza	12	Panasonic Toyota Racing-	B	2.4 Toyota TF107-V8		9/22
11	BELGIAN GP	Spa	12	Panasonic Toyota Racing-	B	2.4 Toyota TF107-V8		9/22
13	JAPANESE GP	Fuji Speedway	12	Panasonic Toyota Racing-	B	2.4 Toyota TF107-V8	spin/1 lap behind	14/22
13	CHINESE GP	Shanghai	12	Panasonic Toyota Racing-	B	2.4 Toyota TF107-V8	1 lap behind	13/22
8	BRAZILIAN GP	Interlagos	12	Panasonic Toyota Racing-	B	2.4 Toyota TF107-V8	1 lap behind	8/22

2008 Championship position: 9th　　Wins: 0　　Pole positions: 0　　Fastest laps: 0　　Points scored: 31

ret	AUSTRALIAN GP	Melbourne	12	Panasonic Toyota Racing	B	2.4 Toyota TF108-V8	battery	6/22
4	MALAYSIAN GP	Sepang	12	Panasonic Toyota Racing	B	2.4 Toyota TF108-V8		5/22
6	BAHRAIN GP	Sakhir Circuit	12	Panasonic Toyota Racing	B	2.4 Toyota TF108-V8		7/22
8	SPANISH GP	Barcelona	12	Panasonic Toyota Racing	B	2.4 Toyota TF108-V8	lost 6th – wrongly called in for pit stop	8/22
10	TURKISH GP	Istanbul	12	Panasonic Toyota Racing	B	2.4 Toyota TF108-V8		8/20
13	MONACO GP	Monte Carlo	12	Panasonic Toyota Racing	B	2.4 Toyota TF108-V8	1 lap behind	8/20
6	CANADIAN GP	Montreal	12	Panasonic Toyota Racing	B	2.4 Toyota TF108-V8		14/20
3	FRENCH GP	Magny Cours	12	Panasonic Toyota Racing	B	2.4 Toyota TF108-V8		5/20
7	BRITISH GP	Silverstone	12	Panasonic Toyota Racing	B	2.4 Toyota TF108-V8	1 lap behind	14/20
9	GERMAN GP	Hockenheim	12	Panasonic Toyota Racing	B	2.4 Toyota TF108-V8		4/20
7	HUNGARIAN GP	Hungaroring	12	Panasonic Toyota Racing	B	2.4 Toyota TF108-V8		9/20
5	EUROPEAN GP	Valencia	12	Panasonic Toyota Racing	B	2.4 Toyota TF108-V8		7/20
16	BELGIAN GP	Spa	12	Panasonic Toyota Racing	B	2.4 Toyota TF108-V8	collision with Bourdais/1 lap behind	11/20
13	ITALIAN GP	Monza	12	Panasonic Toyota Racing	B	2.4 Toyota TF108-V8		7/20
ret	SINGAPORE GP	Marina Bay Circuit	12	Panasonic Toyota Racing	B	2.4 Toyota TF108-V8	hydraulics	11/20
5	JAPANESE GP	Suzuka	12	Panasonic Toyota Racing	B	2.4 Toyota TF108-V8		7/20
ret	CHINESE GP	Shanghai	12	Panasonic Toyota Racing	B	2.4 Toyota TF108-V8	accident damage	9/20
8	BRAZILIAN GP	Interlagos	12	Panasonic Toyota Racing	B	2.4 Toyota TF108-V8		2/20

2009 Championship position: 8th　　Wins: 0　　Pole positions: 1　　Fastest laps: 1　　Points scored: 32.5

3	AUSTRALIAN GP	Melbourne	9	Panasonic Toyota Racing	B	2.4 Toyota TF109-V8		8/20
4	MALAYSIAN GP	Sepang	9	Panasonic Toyota Racing	B	2.4 Toyota TF109-V8	rain-shortened race	2/20
ret	CHINESE GP	Shanghai	9	Panasonic Toyota Racing	B	2.4 Toyota TF109-V8	hit by Kubica – accident damage	6/20
3	BAHRAIN GP	Sakhir Circuit	9	Panasonic Toyota Racing	B	2.4 Toyota TF109-V8	FL	1/20
ret	SPANISH GP	Barcelona	9	Panasonic Toyota Racing	B	2.4 Toyota TF109-V8	spun and hit by Sutil on lap 1	7/20
13	MONACO GP	Monte Carlo	9	Panasonic Toyota Racing	B	2.4 Toyota TF109-V8	1 lap behind	19/20
4	TURKISH GP	Istanbul	9	Panasonic Toyota Racing	B	2.4 Toyota TF109-V8		5/20
7	BRITISH GP	Silverstone	9	Panasonic Toyota Racing	B	2.4 Toyota TF109-V8		4/20
17	GERMAN GP	Hockenheim	9	Panasonic Toyota Racing	B	2.4 Toyota TF109-V8	collision – Nakajima/pit stop new nose	14/20
8	HUNGARIAN GP	Hungaroring	9	Panasonic Toyota Racing	B	2.4 Toyota TF109-V8		12/20
13	EUROPEAN GP	Valencia	9	Panasonic Toyota Racing	B	2.4 Toyota TF109-V8	one-stop strategy	18/20
ret	BELGIAN GP	Spa	9	Panasonic Toyota Racing	B	2.4 Toyota TF109-V8	brakes	2/20
14	ITALIAN GP	Monza	9	Panasonic Toyota Racing	B	2.4 Toyota TF109-V8	1 lap behind	11/20
12	SINGAPORE GP	Marina Bay Circuit	9	Panasonic Toyota Racing	B	2.4 Toyota TF109-V8		15/20
2	JAPANESE GP	Suzuka	9	Panasonic Toyota Racing	B	2.4 Toyota TF109-V8		2/20
ret	BRAZILIAN GP	Interlagos	9	Panasonic Toyota Racing	B	2.4 Toyota TF109-V8	collision with Sutil on lap 1	4/20
7	ABU DHABI GP	Yas Marina Circuit	9	Panasonic Toyota Racing	B	2.4 Toyota TF109-V8		6/20

2010 Championship position: Unplaced

17/ret	BAHRAIN GP	Sakhir Circuit	18	Lotus Racing	B	2.4 Lotus T127 Cosworth V8	clutch/hydraulics/3 laps behind	20/24

dns	AUSTRALIAN GP	Melbourne	18	Lotus Racing	B	2.4 Lotus T127 Cosworth V8	*hydraulic failure before start*	20/24
17	MALAYSIAN GP	Sepang	18	Lotus Racing	B	2.4 Lotus T127 Cosworth V8	*5 laps behind*	18/24
ret	CHINESE GP	Shanghai Circuit	18	Lotus Racing	B	2.4 Lotus T127 Cosworth V8	*hydraulics*	20/24
17	SPANISH GP	Barcelona	18	Lotus Racing	B	2.4 Lotus T127 Cosworth V8	*3 laps behind*	19/24
15/ret	MONACO GP	Monte Carlo	18	Lotus Racing	B	2.4 Lotus T127 Cosworth V8	*accident – ran into Chandhok*	19/24
ret	TURKISH GP	Istanbul Park	18	Lotus Racing	B	2.4 Lotus T127 Cosworth V8	*hydraulics*	19/24
ret	CANADIAN GP	Montreal	18	Lotus Racing	B	2.4 Lotus T127 Cosworth V8	*brakes/vibration*	20/24
21	EUROPEAN GP	Valencia	18	Lotus Racing	B	2.4 Lotus T127 Cosworth V8	*2 laps behind*	19/24
16	BRITISH GP	Silverstone	18	Lotus Racing	B	2.4 Lotus T127 Cosworth V8	*1 lap behind*	21/24
ret	GERMAN GP	Hockenheim	18	Lotus Racing	B	2.4 Lotus T127 Cosworth V8	*gearbox*	18/24
15	HUNGARIAN GP	Hungaroring	18	Lotus Racing	B	2.4 Lotus T127 Cosworth V8	*3 laps behind*	21/24
19	BELGIAN GP	Spa	18	Lotus Racing	B	2.4 Lotus T127 Cosworth V8	*spin/1 lap behind*	18/24
ret	ITALIAN GP	Monza	18	Lotus Racing	B	2.4 Lotus T127 Cosworth V8	*gearbox*	18/24
ret	SINGAPORE GP	Marina Bay Circuit	18	Lotus Racing	B	2.4 Lotus T127 Cosworth V8	*hydraulics*	21/24
13	JAPANESE GP	Suzuka	18	Lotus Racing	B	2.4 Lotus T127 Cosworth V8	*2 laps behind*	19/24
ret	KOREAN GP	Yeongam	18	Lotus Racing	B	2.4 Lotus T127 Cosworth V8	*hydraulics*	19/24
19	BRAZILIAN GP	Interlagos	18	Lotus Racing	B	2.4 Lotus T127 Cosworth V8	*2 laps behind*	20/24
21/ret	ABU DHABI GP	Yas Marina Circuit	18	Lotus Racing	B	2.4 Lotus T127 Cosworth V8	*rear wing/4 laps behind*	19/24

2011 Championship position: Unplaced

13	AUSTRALIAN GP	Melbourne	21	Lotus Racing	P	2.4 Lotus T128 Renault V8	*2 laps behind*	20/24
ret	MALAYSIAN GP	Sepang	21	Lotus Racing	P	2.4 Lotus T128 Renault V8	*clutch sensor*	20/24
19	CHINESE GP	Shanghai Circuit	21	Lotus Racing	P	2.4 Lotus T128 Renault V8	*1 lap behind*	20/24
18	TURKISH GP	Istanbul Park	21	Lotus Racing	P	2.4 Lotus T128 Renault V8	*1 lap behind*	19/24
18	SPANISH GP	Barcelona	21	Lotus Racing	P	2.4 Lotus T128 Renault V8	*2 laps behind*	18/24
13	MONACO GP	Monte Carlo	21	Lotus Racing	P	2.4 Lotus T128 Renault V8	*2 laps behind*	19/24
16	CANADIAN GP	Montreal	21	Lotus Racing	P	2.4 Lotus T128 Renault V8	*1 lap behind*	19/24
20	EUROPEAN GP	Valencia	21	Lotus Racing	P	2.4 Lotus T128 Renault V8	*2 laps behind*	20/24
ret	BRITISH GP	Silverstone	21	Lotus Racing	P	2.4 Lotus T128 Renault V8	*oil leak*	21/24
ret	HUNGARIAN GP	Hungaroring	21	Lotus Racing	P	2.4 Lotus T128 Renault V8	*water leak*	20/24
14	BELGIAN GP	Spa	21	Lotus Racing	P	2.4 Lotus T128 Renault V8	*1 lap behind*	19/24
14	ITALIAN GP	Monza	21	Lotus Racing	P	2.4 Lotus T128 Renault V8	*2 laps behind*	19/24
ret	SINGAPORE GP	Marina Bay Circuit	21	Lotus Racing	P	2.4 Lotus T128 Renault V8	*gearbox*	9/24
19	JAPANESE GP	Suzuka	21	Lotus Racing	P	2.4 Lotus T128 Renault V8		19/24
17	KOREAN GP	Yeongam	21	Lotus Racing	P	2.4 Lotus T128 Renault V8	*1 lap behind*	20/24
19	INDIAN GP	Buddh Circuit	21	Lotus Racing	P	2.4 Lotus T128 Renault V8	*5 laps behind*	20/24
18	ABU DHABI GP	Yas Marina Circuit	21	Lotus Racing	P	2.4 Lotus T128 Renault V8	*2 laps behind*	19/24
18	BRAZILIAN GP	Interlagos	21	Lotus Racing	P	2.4 Lotus T128 Renault V8	*2 laps behind*	20/24

GP Starts: 252   GP Wins: 1   Pole positions: 4   Fastest laps: 1   Points: 246.5

ESTEBAN TUERO

WAS Esteban Tuero a case of too much too soon? He was a young Argentinian who was assiduously groomed for stardom. Sent around the world at huge expense, he was found a place in a grand prix car, only to end up back in his homeland racing a 2-litre VW Polo within a year.

After an apprenticeship in the Sud-Am F3 series, Esteban travelled to Italy in 1996 to race in the national Formula 3 championship, but before long he had been elevated to F3000 with Draco. Plans had already been laid for his graduation to F1 with Minardi, and the following season he headed off to Japan to compete in Formula Nippon alongside Norberto Fontana. Precious little was achieved by way of results, but this did not stop the still inexperienced driver from gaining the super licence required to take up a grand prix drive with the Italian team in 1998.

Tuero's one season in the big time went well enough. Having proved to be a quick learner, he was evenly matched with team-mate Shinji Nakano, but in the last race of the year in Japan he tangled with Toranosuke Takagi's Tyrrell, injuring vertebrae in his neck. He went home to convalesce and never returned. Later he announced his retirement from Formula 1 on 'irrevocable personal grounds', mysteriously adding that he was sworn to secrecy about his reasons for taking such a decision.

Rumours circulated that his retirement was due to the critical press he had been receiving at home; another suggestion was that sponsorship problems and disagreements over money between his manager and Minardi were the reason the young driver had decided to opt out of the F1 rat race.

So Tuero settled into the popular Argentine TC2000 touring car series with the aforementioned VW Polo. Subsequently, he also raced Chevrolet, Peugeot and Renault cars in search of success. While Fontana has managed to win the series outright, however, Tuero has recorded only two race wins and just a single pole position in more than a decade of competition.

TUERO, Esteban (RA) b 22/4/1978, Buenos Aires

1998 Championship position: Unplaced

	Race	Circuit	No	Entrant	Tyres	Capacity/Car/Engine	Comment	Q Pos/Entries
ret	AUSTRALIAN GP	Melbourne	23	Fondmetal Minardi Ford	B	3.0 Minardi M198-Ford Zetec R V10	engine	17/22
ret	BRAZILIAN GP	Interlagos	23	Fondmetal Minardi Ford	B	3.0 Minardi M198-Ford Zetec R V10	gearbox	19/22
ret	ARGENTINE GP	Buenos Aires	23	Fondmetal Minardi Ford	B	3.0 Minardi M198-Ford Zetec R V10	accident	20/22
8	SAN MARINO GP	Imola	23	Fondmetal Minardi Ford	B	3.0 Minardi M198-Ford Zetec R V10	2 laps behind	19/22
15	SPANISH GP	Barcelona	23	Fondmetal Minardi Ford	B	3.0 Minardi M198-Ford Zetec R V10	2 laps behind	19/22
ret	MONACO GP	Monte Carlo	23	Fondmetal Minardi Ford	B	3.0 Minardi M198-Ford Zetec R V10	crashed on lap 1	21/22
ret	CANADIAN GP	Montreal	23	Fondmetal Minardi Ford	B	3.0 Minardi M198-Ford Zetec R V10	electrics	21/22
ret	FRENCH GP	Magny Cours	23	Fondmetal Minardi Ford	B	3.0 Minardi M198-Ford Zetec R V10	hydraulics	22/22
ret	BRITISH GP	Silverstone	23	Fondmetal Minardi Ford	B	3.0 Minardi M198-Ford Zetec R V10	spun off	20/22
ret	AUSTRIAN GP	A1-Ring	23	Fondmetal Minardi Ford	B	3.0 Minardi M198-Ford Zetec R V10	spun off	19/22
16	GERMAN GP	Hockenheim	23	Fondmetal Minardi Ford	B	3.0 Minardi M198-Ford Zetec R V10	2 laps behind	21/22
ret	HUNGARIAN GP	Hungaroring	23	Fondmetal Minardi Ford	B	3.0 Minardi M198-Ford Zetec R V10	gearbox	21/22
ret	BELGIAN GP	Spa	23	Fondmetal Minardi Ford	B	3.0 Minardi M198-Ford Zetec R V10	electrics	22/22
11	ITALIAN GP	Monza	23	Fondmetal Minardi Ford	B	3.0 Minardi M198-Ford Zetec R V10	2 laps behind	22/22
nc	LUXEMBOURG GP	Nürburgring	23	Fondmetal Minardi Ford	B	3.0 Minardi M198-Ford Zetec R V10	11 laps behind	21/22
ret	JAPANESE GP	Suzuka	23	Fondmetal Minardi Ford	B	3.0 Minardi M198-Ford Zetec R V10	collision with Takagi – injured neck	21/22

GP Starts: 16   GP Wins: 0   Pole positions: 0   Fastest laps: 0   Points: 0

GUY TUNMER

A SOUTH African amateur racer, Guy Tunmer began competing in Minis in the late 1960s, then raced an Alfa with brother Derek before turning to single-seaters more regularly in 1973 with a March 722, although his season was disrupted by a broken wrist. For 1974, after acquiring a Chevron,

he cleaned up in the domestic Formula Atlantic championship and earned himself a drive in the Team Gunston Lotus 72E for 1975, alongside Eddie Keizan.

In his only grand prix appearance, Guy did very well to finish in 11th place, ahead of works driver Jacky Ickx and team-mate Keizan in similar cars. In the local F1 series, he managed a singleton victory by winning the False Bay 100 at Killarney.

Guy also ventured to race in Europe in John Lepp's March at the Monza 1000km.

When the premier domestic single-seater class switched to Formula Atlantic, Tunmer raced his own front-running Chevron B34 in 1976, before switching to touring cars

Tunmer died at the age of 50 in 1999, from injuries he had received a week earlier in a motorcycle accident.

TONI ULMEN

THE outstanding Veritas driver, Toni Ulmen was the German F2 champion in 1949 and always posed a real threat in his Veritas-Meteor. In 1950, he was third at Erlen, less than ten seconds behind two Ferraris led by Luigi Villoresi, second in the Eifelrennen and fourth in the German Grand Prix.

In 1951, Ulmen took second place and fastest lap at AVUS, and third at the ultrafast and dangerous Grenzlandring circuit.

For 1952, Toni entered his sports-bodied Veritas in two world championship events without success, but he took a fifth place at the Eifelrennen, and won the Formula 2 high-speed thrash at Grenzlandring and a 2-litre sports car race at the Nürburgring.

Despite having announced his retirement in early 1953, Ulmen was soon back, albeit briefly, sharing Herman Roosdorp's Jaguar in sports car events and finishing third in the Spa 24-hours.

Ulmen had been involved in the family business in the motor trade and although he sold out in 1966, his name is carried by a successful dealership group in Germany to this day.

TUNMER, Guy (ZA) b Fricksburg, Transvaal 1/12/1948 – d 22/6/1999, Sandton, Johannesburg

1975 Championship position: Unplaced

	Race	Circuit	No	Entrant	Tyres	Capacity/Car/Engine	Comment	Q Pos/Entries
11	SOUTH AFRICAN GP	Kyalami	34	Team Gunston	G	3.0 Lotus 72E-Cosworth V8	2 laps behind	25/28

GP Starts: 1   GP Wins: 0   Pole positions: 0   Fastest laps: 0   Points: 0

ULMEN, Toni (D) b Düsseldorf 12/1/1906 – d 4/11/1976, Düsseldorf

1952 Championship position: Unplaced

	Race	Circuit	No	Entrant	Tyres	Capacity/Car/Engine	Comment	Q Pos/Entries
ret	SWISS GP	Bremgarten	4	Toni Ulmen	–	2.0 Veritas-Meteor 6 sports	fuel tank	16/21
8	GERMAN GP	Nürburgring	125	Toni Ulmen	–	2.0 Veritas-Meteor 6 sports	2 laps behind	15/32

GP Starts: 2   GP Wins: 0   Pole positions: 0   Fastest laps: 0   Points: 0

BOBBY UNSER

THE exploits of the Unser racing dynasty are legendary. Bobby's uncle, Louis, won the famous Pikes Peak hill-climb nine times, and his younger brother, Al, and nephew, Al Junior, have also achieved enormous success in USAC/Indy car racing, both having become champions and Indy 500 winners.

Bobby enjoyed an equally illustrious racing career: twice the USAC champion (1968 and 1974) and three times the Indianapolis 500 winner (1968, 1975 and 1981), he easily stands among the all-time greats with a total of 35 Indy car victories and 49 pole positions to his credit. In addition, he surpassed his uncle by winning the Pikes Peak event no fewer than 13 times.

Never slow to give his opinion, Unser has been a controversial TV pundit who took no prisoners. He has also worked as a public speaker and made thousands of personal appearances.

Bobby's grand prix experience with the works BRM team in 1968 could hardly have been less auspicious: not allowed to race at Monza due to clashing race schedules, he managed to crash his car in practice at Watkins Glen and also blew a couple of engines. All in all, an expensive exercise best forgotten.

ALBERTO URIA

LIKE many other local drivers, Alberto Uria helped make up the numbers in the international events held in the Argentine in 1955/56.

A Uruguayan, Alberto crossed the River Plate with his elderly Maserati A6GCM fitted with a 250F engine, but could only manage a distant 14th on aggregate in the 1955 Buenos Aires City Grand Prix. The following season, he shared the car with Oscar González, trailing home sixth on the road. The pair were not classified, however, being ten laps adrift.

UNSER, Bobby (USA) b 20/2/1934, Colorado Springs, Colorado

1968 Championship position: Unplaced

	Race	Circuit	No	Entrant	Tyres	Capacity/Car/Engine	Comment	Q Pos/Entries
dns	ITALIAN GP	Monza	25	Owen Racing Organisation	G	3.0 BRM P126 V12	racing in USAC event within 24 hours	(20)/24
ret	US GP	Watkins Glen	9	Owen Racing Organisation	G	3.0 BRM P138 V12	engine	– / –
dns	"	" "	9	Owen Racing Organisation	G	3.0 BRM P126 V12	accident in practice – set time in car	19/21

GP Starts: 1   GP Wins: 0   Pole positions: 0   Fastest laps: 0   Points: 0

URIA, Alberto (U) b 11/7/1924, Montivideo – d 4/12/1988 Montevideo

1955 Championship position: Unplaced

	Race	Circuit	No	Entrant	Tyres	Capacity/Car/Engine	Comment	Q Pos/Entries
ret	ARGENTINE GP	Buenos Aires	30	Alberto Uria	–	2.5 Maserati A6GCM/250F 6	fuel starvation	21/22

1956 Championship position: Unplaced

	Race	Circuit	No	Entrant	Tyres	Capacity/Car/Engine	Comment	Q Pos/Entries
6*	ARGENTINE GP	Buenos Aires	16	Alberto Uria	–	2.5 Maserati A6GCM/250F 6	*shared with Oscar González/-10 laps	13/15

GP Starts: 2   GP Wins: 0   Pole positions: 0   Fastest laps: 0   Points: 0

NINO VACCARELLA

A SICILIAN with a law degree and the principal of a private school inherited from his father, Nino Vaccarella was almost deified by the local fans after some superb drives in the Targa Florio, a race that he won three times – and it could have been more. His first victory came in 1965 in a works Ferrari 275 P2 shared with Lorenzo Bandini, the next in 1971, this time driving an Alfa Romeo T33/3 with Toine Hezemans. He came out of retirement in 1975 to record his third triumph, although this time the Alfa T33 T12 he shared with Arturo Merzario was pitted against poor opposition.

After early competition in a Fiat and then a Lancia Aurelia, Vaccarella stepped up to a Maserati sports in 1959. This led to him joining Count Volpi's Scuderia Serenissima team in 1961 to gain experience in Formula 1, sports and GT cars

Third place in the 1962 Targa Florio, sharing a works Porsche with Jo Bonnier, helped establish Nino as a top sports car driver, and he soon became in demand. He also won Le Mans in 1964 for Ferrari with Jean Guichet, the 1964 Nürburgring 1000km with Ludovico Scarfiotti and the 1970 Sebring 12-hours with Mario Andretti and Ignazio Giunti. He scored many other placings, too, and was a very reliable practitioner, rarely damaging the car and enjoying a remarkable ratio of finishes in this punishing category.

Vaccarella's Formula 1 career started brightly with Scuderia Serenissima in 1961, when he took a third in the Coppa Italia at Vallelunga and finished sixth in the 1962 Pau Grand Prix, but that was as far as it went. His ties to his school in Sicily prevented him from committing fully to an offer from Ferrari for 1963, and he ended up with just a one-off Ferrari drive at Monza in 1965 as reward for his sports car success for the Prancing Horse.

VACCARELLA, Nino (I) b 4/3/1933, Palermo, Sicily

	Race	Circuit	No	Entrant	Tyres	Capacity/Car/Engine	Comment	Q Pos/Entries
	1961 Championship position: Unplaced							
ret	ITALIAN GP	Monza	50	Scuderia Serenissima	D	1.5 de Tomaso F1-Alfa Romeo 4	engine	20/33
	1962 Championship position: Unplaced							
dnq	MONACO GP	Monte Carlo	42	Scuderia SSS Republica di Venezia	D	1.5 Lotus 18/21-Climax 4		21/21
15	GERMAN GP	Nürburgring	26	Scuderia SSS Republica di Venezia	D	1.5 Porsche 718 F4		15/30
9	ITALIAN GP	Monza	24	Scuderia SSS Republica di Venezia	D	1.5 Lotus 24-Climax V8	2 laps behind	14/30
	1965 Championship position: Unplaced							
12/ret	ITALIAN GP	Monza	6	Scuderia Ferrari SpA SEFAC	D	1.5 Ferrari 158 V8	engine/8 laps behind	15/23

GP Starts: 4   GP Wins: 0   Pole positions: 0   Fastest laps: 0   Points: 0

van de POELE, Eric (B) b 30/9/1961, Verviers, nr Spa

	Race	Circuit	No	Entrant	Tyres	Capacity/Car/Engine	Comment	Q Pos/Entries
	1991 Championship position: Unplaced							
dnpq	US GP (PHOENIX)	Phoenix	35	Modena Team SpA	G	3.5 Lambo 291-Lamborghini V12		34/34
dnpq	BRAZILIAN GP	Interlagos	35	Modena Team SpA	G	3.5 Lambo 291-Lamborghini V12		31/34
9/ret	SAN MARINO GP	Imola	35	Modena Team SpA	G	3.5 Lambo 291-Lamborghini V12	fuel pump/4 laps behind	21/34
dnpq	MONACO GP	Monte Carlo	35	Modena Team SpA	G	3.5 Lambo 291-Lamborghini V12		32/34
dnpq	CANADIAN GP	Montreal	35	Modena Team SpA	G	3.5 Lambo 291-Lamborghini V12		33/34
dnpq	MEXICAN GP	Mexico City	35	Modena Team SpA	G	3.5 Lambo 291-Lamborghini V12		32/34
dnpq	FRENCH GP	Magny Cours	35	Modena Team SpA	G	3.5 Lambo 291-Lamborghini V12		33/34
dnpq	BRITISH GP	Silverstone	35	Modena Team SpA	G	3.5 Lambo 291-Lamborghini V12		33/34
dnq	GERMAN GP	Hockenheim	35	Modena Team SpA	G	3.5 Lambo 291-Lamborghini V12		30/34
dnq	HUNGARIAN GP	Hungaroring	35	Modena Team SpA	G	3.5 Lambo 291-Lamborghini V12		29/34
dnq	BELGIAN GP	Spa	35	Modena Team SpA	G	3.5 Lambo 291-Lamborghini V12		30/34
dnq	ITALIAN GP	Monza	35	Modena Team SpA	G	3.5 Lambo 291-Lamborghini V12		29/34
dnq	PORTUGUESE GP	Estoril	35	Modena Team SpA	G	3.5 Lambo 291-Lamborghini V12		30/34
dnq	SPANISH GP	Barcelona	35	Modena Team SpA	G	3.5 Lambo 291-Lamborghini V12		30/33
dnq	JAPANESE GP	Suzuka	35	Modena Team SpA	G	3.5 Lambo 291-Lamborghini V12		29/31
dnq	AUSTRALIAN GP	Adelaide	35	Modena Team SpA	G	3.5 Lambo 291-Lamborghini V12		29/32
	1992 Championship position: Unplaced							
13	SOUTH AFRICAN GP	Kyalami	7	Motor Racing Developments Ltd	G	3.5 Brabham BT60B-Judd V10	4 laps behind	26/30
dnq	MEXICAN GP	Mexico City	7	Motor Racing Developments Ltd	G	3.5 Brabham BT60B-Judd V10		28/30
dnq	BRAZILIAN GP	Interlagos	7	Motor Racing Developments Ltd	G	3.5 Brabham BT60B-Judd V10		29/31
dnq	SPANISH GP	Barcelona	7	Motor Racing Developments Ltd	G	3.5 Brabham BT60B-Judd V10		28/32
dnq	SAN MARINO GP	Imola	7	Motor Racing Developments Ltd	G	3.5 Brabham BT60B-Judd V10		30/32
dnq	MONACO GP	Monte Carlo	7	Motor Racing Developments Ltd	G	3.5 Brabham BT60B-Judd V10		27/32
dnq	CANADIAN GP	Montreal	7	Motor Racing Developments Ltd	G	3.5 Brabham BT60B-Judd V10		28/32
dnq	FRENCH GP	Magny Cours	7	Motor Racing Developments Ltd	G	3.5 Brabham BT60B-Judd V10		29/30
dpq	BRITISH GP	Silverstone	7	Motor Racing Developments Ltd	G	3.5 Brabham BT60B-Judd V10		30/32
dnq	GERMAN GP	Hockenheim	7	Motor Racing Developments Ltd	G	3.5 Brabham BT60B-Judd V10		28/32
ret	HUNGARIAN GP	Hungaroring	14	Fondmetal	G	3.5 Fondmetal GR02-Ford HB V8	multiple collision – spun off	18/31
10	BELGIAN GP	Spa	14	Fondmetal	G	3.5 Fondmetal GR02-Ford HB V8	1 lap behind	15/30
ret	ITALIAN GP	Monza	14	Fondmetal	G	3.5 Fondmetal GR02-Ford HB V8	clutch	25/28

GP Starts: 5   GP Wins: 0   Pole positions: 0   Fastest laps: 0   Points: 0

ERIC van de POELE

A POPULAR Belgian driver, Eric van de Poele began his career in French Formula 3 in 1984, before a season in Belgian Group N and the Benelux Formula Ford championships. Then he briefly sampled the German F3 series, but really made an impression in the Zakspeed BMW junior team, winning the German championship, with the added highlight of a victory in the Spa 24-hours with Didier Theys and Jean-Michel Martin. After another season of touring cars with Schnitzer BMW, Eric made the break into single-seaters at last with an F3000 drive with GA Motorsports in 1989. He enjoyed two happy years with the team, taking second place in the 1990 championship after three wins (Pau, Birmingham and Nogaro).

With long-time sponsors Lease Plan behind him, Eric joined the newly formed Lambo team for a crack at grands prix in 1991. Although the car was never a competitive proposition, mysteriously it ran very well at Imola, where van de Poele held a secure fifth place until a fuel pump failure on the last lap. For 1992, he threw in his lot with the, by then, distinctly shaky Brabham team for another frustrating string of non-qualifications, before jumping out of the frying pan and into the fire with Fondmetal, a team also facing imminent extinction.

Eric was on the sidelines for much of 1993, but landed a deal to lead the Nissan Primera challenge in the 1994 British touring car championship. It was a tough season as the team struggled to optimise the car. Frustrated at the lack of progress, he quit the series in mid-season.

Early in 1995, sharing a Ferrari 333SP with Fermin Velez, Eric won the Sebring 12-hours (he also took a stint in the Mauro Baldi/Michele Alboreto fourth-place car). When the season got into full swing, he was back behind the wheel of a Primera, this time in the Spanish touring car championship. With the car being a much more serious contender, he enjoyed two competitive seasons in the series, but another win at Sebring (this time with a Riley & Scott) left him itching for a return to the more potent prototype classes.

The Belgian joined Wayne Taylor in the Doyle Risi Racing Ferrari 333SP to contest the Professional Racing Series in America in 1998, and won rounds at Las Vegas and the Petit Le Mans at Road Atlanta. Teaming up with Mimo Schiattarella at Team Rafanelli for 1999, Eric won the opening round of the ALMS Series at Atlanta, but then his season was dealt a serious blow when a jammed throttle caused a heavy crash while testing the works Nissan in preparation for the Le Mans 24-hour race, which sidelined him for three months with cracked vertebrae.

After making a full recovery, Eric continued to race regularly in the Grand-Am, ALMS and FIA GT championships, handling myriad sports and GT machines on an ad-hoc basis, including a Cadillac, Lister, Porsche, Ferrari and Maserati. In 2006, he made an impressive return to single-seaters in the Grand Prix Masters series, taking a third place at Losail and then second spot in the next race at Silverstone.

Eric celebrated his 50th birthday in 2011, and he was still as keen as ever to get behind the wheel. He won the Spa 12-hour race in the Belgian touring car series with a Volvo S60.

ANDRÉ van der LOF

K NOWN popularly as 'Dries', André van der Lof was a Dutch industrialist who amassed his wealth in the manufacture of electrical cable. He raced as a hobby, and was a lively and enthusiastic competitor who took part in both circuit racing and rallies in the Netherlands in the early 1950s.

When the inaugural Dutch Grand Prix was given championship status in 1952, the organisers arranged for 'Dries' and compatriot Jan Flinterman to take part at the expense of regular runners. Van der Lof was found a place in one of John Heath's HWMs, but much of his race was spent visiting the pits with magneto trouble.

'Dries' continued to take an active interest in motorsport thereafter and was still competing occasionally in historic events into his early sixties, driving a Maserati 250F and the ex-Chico Landi Ferrari T375.

Continuing the family racing tradition, André's granddaughter, Shirley, proved to be a promising racer, taking fourth place in the ATS Formula 3 Trophy in 2008.

van der LOF, André (NL) b 23/8/1919, Emmen – d 24/5/1990 Enschede

	1952 Championship position: Unplaced							
	Race	Circuit	No	Entrant	Tyres	Capacity/Car/Engine	Comment	Q Pos/Entries
nc	DUTCH GP	Zandvoort	30	HW Motors Ltd	D	2.0 HWM-Alta 4	pit stop/20 laps behind	14/18
	GP Starts: 1 GP Wins: 0 Pole positions: 0 Fastest laps: 0 Points: 0							

GIJS van LENNEP

A MUCH respected driver, Gijs van Lennep always gave a good account of himself whenever his occasional grand prix opportunities arose; he scored a point for both Williams and Ensign when their cars were hardly at their most competitive.

Having started in Formula Vee in 1965, van Lennep soon took up sports car racing to such effect that he was in the Porsche factory team in 1967, taking third place with Vic Elford in the Circuit of Mugello. After concentrating on Formula 3 in 1968, he returned to sports cars and scored some good placings in the Racing For Holland Abarth. He was awarded the Porsche Cup for the best private entrant in 1970, when he finished second in the Interserie Championship with a Porsche 917.

The 1971 season found Gijs much in demand. He won the Le Mans 24-hours with Helmut Marko for Martini Porsche and the Paris 1000km for Gulf/Wyer. He also took second place in the Targa Florio for Alfa Romeo, as well as hiring a Surtees to make his GP debut.

Adding F5000 to his already hectic schedule, van Lennep won the 1972 Rothmans title in a Surtees TS11 and enjoyed continued sports car success with Martini Racing, winning the 1973 Targa Florio with Herbert Muller and the 1976 Le Mans 24-hours partnering Jacky Ickx, after which he announced his retirement from racing,

BASIL van ROOYEN

H AVING shown his talent as early as 1963, when he beat Lotus Cortina ace John Whitmore in an identical machine, Basil van Rooyen was a dominant force in saloons in South Africa for many years, handling a variety of cars, including Ford Mustangs and Alfa Romeo GTs. With backing from STP, he also moved into national single-seaters in 1968 with a Brabham BT24, although he had to make do with John Love's old Cooper for the 1968 grand prix. The following year, he raised a few eyebrows by qualifying the much more competitive McLaren M7A comfortably in the middle of the grid.

With the McLaren at his disposal, van Rooyen took wins at Killarney and Roy Hesketh, but then wrote it off in a big way at Kyalami, suffering slight facial injuries.

Basil decided that he was better off returning to the more comfortable environment of saloon cars, racing an Alfa Romeo, a Mazda and a Vauxhall until 1973, when he virtually retired from racing. However, when Formula Atlantic was introduced in 1975, he was tempted back into single-seaters with a Chevron B34-BDA for a couple of seasons in 1976/77. He was called back into action with Team Gunston for a one-off drive in 1978, taking a third at Kyalami.

van LENNEP, Gijs (NL) b 16/3/1942, Bloemendaal

1971 Championship position: Unplaced

	Race	Circuit	No	Entrant	Tyres	Capacity/Car/Engine	Comment	Q Pos/Entries
8	DUTCH GP	Zandvoort	30	Stichting Autoraces Nederland	F	3.0 Surtees TS7-Cosworth V8	5 laps behind	21/24
dns	US GP	Watkins Glen	19	Team Surtees	F	3.0 Surtees TS9-Cosworth V8	Posey drove car	(29)/32

1973 Championship position: 19th= Wins: 0 Pole positions: 0 Fastest laps: 0 Points scored: 1

	Race	Circuit	No	Entrant	Tyres	Capacity/Car/Engine	Comment	Q Pos/Entries
6	DUTCH GP	Zandvoort	26	Frank Williams Racing Cars	F	3.0 Iso Marlboro 1R-Cosworth V8	2 laps behind	20/24
9	AUSTRIAN GP	Österreichring	26	Frank Williams Racing Cars	F	3.0 Iso Marlboro 1R-Cosworth V8	2 laps behind	24/25
ret	ITALIAN GP	Monza	26	Frank Williams Racing Cars	F	3.0 Iso Marlboro 1R-Cosworth V8	overheating	23/25

1974 Championship position: Unplaced

	Race	Circuit	No	Entrant	Tyres	Capacity/Car/Engine	Comment	Q Pos/Entries
14	BELGIAN GP	Nivelles	21	Frank Williams Racing Cars	F	3.0 Williams FW02-Cosworth V8	3 laps behind	30/32
dnq	DUTCH GP	Zandvoort	21	Frank Williams Racing Cars	F	3.0 Williams FW01-Cosworth V8		27/27

1975 Championship position: 19th= Wins: 0 Pole positions: 0 Fastest laps: 0 Points scored: 1

	Race	Circuit	No	Entrant	Tyres	Capacity/Car/Engine	Comment	Q Pos/Entries
10	DUTCH GP	Zandvoort	31	HB Bewaking Team Ensign	G	3.0 Ensign N174-Cosworth V8	pit stop – tyres/4 laps behind	22/25
15	FRENCH GP	Paul Ricard	31	HB Bewaking Team Ensign	G	3.0 Ensign N175-Cosworth V8	1 lap behind	22/26
6	GERMAN GP	Nürburgring	19	HB Bewaking Team Ensign	G	3.0 Ensign N175-Cosworth V8		24/26

GP Starts: 8 GP Wins: 0 Pole positions: 0 Fastest laps: 0 Points: 2

van ROOYEN, Basil (ZA) b 19/4/1939, Johannesburg

1968 Championship position: Unplaced

	Race	Circuit	No	Entrant	Tyres	Capacity/Car/Engine	Comment	Q Pos/Entries
ret	SOUTH AFRICAN GP	Kyalami	25	John Love	F	2.7 Cooper T79-Climax 4	head gasket	20/23

1969 Championship position: Unplaced

	Race	Circuit	No	Entrant	Tyres	Capacity/Car/Engine	Comment	Q Pos/Entries
ret	SOUTH AFRICAN GP	Kyalami	18	Team Lawson	D	3.0 McLaren M7A-Cosworth V8	brakes	=9/18

GP Starts: 2 GP Wins: 0 Pole positions: 0 Fastest laps: 0 Points: 0

VERSTAPPEN, Jos (NL) b 4/3/1972, Montfort

1994 Championship position: 10th Wins: 0 Pole positions: 0 Fastest laps: 0 Points scored:10

	Race	Circuit	No	Entrant	Tyres	Capacity/Car/Engine	Comment	Q Pos/Entries
ret	BRAZILIAN GP	Interlagos	6	Mild Seven Benetton Ford	G	3.5 Benetton B194-Ford Zetec-R V8	hit by Irvine – multiple accident	9/28
ret	PACIFIC GP	T.I. Circuit	6	Mild Seven Benetton Ford	G	3.5 Benetton B194-Ford Zetec-R V8	spun off after making pit stop	10/28
ret	FRENCH GP	Magny Cours	6	Mild Seven Benetton Ford	G	3.5 Benetton B194-Ford Zetec-R V8	spun off – brake trouble	8/28
8*	BRITISH GP	Silverstone	6	Mild Seven Benetton Ford	G	3.5 Benetton B194-Ford Zetec-R V8	*2nd place car disqualified/-1 lap	10/28
ret	GERMAN GP	Hockenheim	6	Mild Seven Benetton Ford	G	3.5 Benetton B194-Ford Zetec-R V8	car caught fire in refuelling	19/28
3	HUNGARIAN GP	Hungaroring	6	Mild Seven Benetton Ford	G	3.5 Benetton B194-Ford Zetec-R V8		12/28
3*	BELGIAN GP	Spa	6	Mild Seven Benetton Ford	G	3.5 Benetton B194-Ford Zetec-R V8	*1st place car disqualified	6/28
ret	ITALIAN GP	Monza	6	Mild Seven Benetton Ford	G	3.5 Benetton B194-Ford Zetec-R V8	puncture on lap 1	10/28
5	PORTUGUESE GP	Estoril	6	Mild Seven Benetton Ford	G	3.5 Benetton B194-Ford Zetec-R V8		10/28
ret	EUROPEAN GP	Jerez	6	Mild Seven Benetton Ford	G	3.5 Benetton B194-Ford Zetec-R V8	spun off	12/28

1995 Championship position: Unplaced

	Race	Circuit	No	Entrant	Tyres	Capacity/Car/Engine	Comment	Q Pos/Entries
ret	BRAZILIAN GP	Interlagos	12	MTV Simtek Ford	G	3.0 Simtek S195-Ford ED V8	clutch	24/26
ret	ARGENTINE GP	Buenos Aires	12	MTV Simtek Ford	G	3.0 Simtek S195-Ford ED V8	gearbox	14/26
ret	SAN MARINO GP	Imola	12	MTV Simtek Ford	G	3.0 Simtek S195-Ford ED V8	gearbox	17/26
12	SPANISH GP	Barcelona	12	MTV Simtek Ford	G	3.0 Simtek S195-Ford ED V8	2 laps behind	16/26
ret/dns	MONACO GP	Monte Carlo	12	MTV Simtek Ford	G	3.0 Simtek S195-Ford ED V8	gearbox at first start	(23)/26

1996 Championship position: 16th Wins: 0 Pole positions: 0 Fastest laps: 0 Points scored: 1

	Race	Circuit	No	Entrant	Tyres	Capacity/Car/Engine	Comment	Q Pos/Entries
ret	AUSTRALIAN GP	Melbourne	17	TWR Arrows	G	3.0 Footwork FA17-Hart V8	engine	12/22
ret	BRAZILIAN GP	Interlagos	17	TWR Arrows	G	3.0 Footwork FA17-Hart V8	engine	13/22
6	ARGENTINE GP	Buenos Aires	17	TWR Arrows	G	3.0 Footwork FA17-Hart V8		7/22
ret	EUROPEAN GP	Nürburgring	17	TWR Arrows	G	3.0 Footwork FA17-Hart V8		13/22
ret	SAN MARINO GP	Imola	17	TWR Arrows	G	3.0 Footwork FA17-Hart V8	refuelling accident	14/22
ret	MONACO GP	Monte Carlo	17	TWR Arrows	G	3.0 Footwork FA17-Hart V8	slid into barrier on lap 1	12/22
ret	SPANISH GP	Barcelona	17	TWR Arrows	G	3.0 Footwork FA17-Hart V8	spun off	13/22
ret	CANADIAN GP	Montreal	17	TWR Arrows	G	3.0 Footwork FA17-Hart V8	engine	13/22
ret	FRENCH GP	Magny Cours	17	TWR Arrows	G	3.0 Footwork FA17-Hart V8	detached steering arm	16/22
10	BRITISH GP	Silverstone	17	TWR Arrows	G	3.0 Footwork FA17-Hart V8	1 lap behind	15/22
ret	GERMAN GP	Hockenheim	17	TWR Arrows	G	3.0 Footwork FA17-Hart V8	ran into Katayama on lap 1	17/20
ret	HUNGARIAN GP	Hungaroring	17	TWR Arrows	G	3.0 Footwork FA17-Hart V8	spun off	17/20
ret	BELGIAN GP	Spa	17	TWR Arrows	G	3.0 Footwork FA17-Hart V8	crashed – broken stub axle	16/20
8	ITALIAN GP	Monza	17	TWR Arrows	G	3.0 Footwork FA17-Hart V8	1 lap behind	15/20
ret	PORTUGUESE GP	Estoril	17	TWR Arrows	G	3.0 Footwork FA17-Hart V8	engine	16/20
11	JAPANESE GP	Suzuka	17	TWR Arrows	G	3.0 Footwork FA17-Hart V8	1 lap behind	17/20

1997 Championship position: Unplaced

	Race	Circuit	No	Entrant	Tyres	Capacity/Car/Engine	Comment	Q Pos/Entries
ret	AUSTRALIAN GP	Melbourne	18	Tyrrell	G	3.0 Tyrrell 025-Ford ED4 V8	incident with Katayama – crashed	21/24
15	BRAZILIAN GP	Interlagos	18	Tyrrell	G	3.0 Tyrrell 025-Ford ED4 V8	2 laps behind	21/22
ret	ARGENTINE GP	Buenos Aires	18	Tyrrell	G	3.0 Tyrrell 025-Ford ED4 V8	fuel pressure	16/22
10	SAN MARINO GP	Imola	18	Tyrrell	G	3.0 Tyrrell 025-Ford ED4 V8	2 laps behind	21/22
8	MONACO GP	Monte Carlo	18	Tyrrell	G	3.0 Tyrrell 025-Ford ED4 V8	2 laps behind	22/22
11	SPANISH GP	Barcelona	18	Tyrrell	G	3.0 Tyrrell 025-Ford ED4 V8	1 lap behind	19/22

ret	CANADIAN GP	Montreal	18	Tyrrell	G	3.0 Tyrrell 025-Ford ED4 V8	air valve	14/22
ret	FRENCH GP	Magny Cours	18	Tyrrell	G	3.0 Tyrrell 025-Ford ED4 V8	stuck throttle – crashed	18/22
ret	BRITISH GP	Silverstone	18	Tyrrell	G	3.0 Tyrrell 025-Ford ED4 V8	engine	20/22
10	GERMAN GP	Hockenheim	18	Tyrrell	G	3.0 Tyrrell 025-Ford ED4 V8	1 lap behind	20/22
ret	HUNGARIAN GP	Hungaroring	18	Tyrrell	G	3.0 Tyrrell 025-Ford ED4 V8	pneumatic leak	18/22
ret	BELGIAN GP	Spa	18	Tyrrell	G	3.0 Tyrrell 025-Ford ED4 V8	spun off	21/22
ret	ITALIAN GP	Monza	18	Tyrrell	G	3.0 Tyrrell 025-Ford ED4 V8	engine	20/22
12	AUSTRIAN GP	A1-Ring	18	Tyrrell	G	3.0 Tyrrell 025-Ford ED4 V8	2 laps behind	20/22
ret	LUXEMBOURG GP	Nürburgring	18	Tyrrell	G	3.0 Tyrrell 025-Ford ED4 V8	engine	21/22
13*	JAPANESE GP	Suzuka	18	Tyrrell	G	3.0 Tyrrell 025-Ford ED4 V8	*5th place car disqualfied/-1 lap	21/22
16	EUROPEAN GP	Jerez	18	Tyrrell	G	3.0 Tyrrell 025-Ford ED4 V8	1 lap behind	22/22

1998 Championship position: Unplaced

12	FRENCH GP	Magny Cours	19	Stewart Ford	B	3.0 Stewart SF2-Ford Zetec-R V10	2 laps behind	15/22
ret	BRITISH GP	Silverstone	19	Stewart Ford	B	3.0 Stewart SF2-Ford Zetec-R V10	engine	17/22
ret	AUSTRIAN GP	A1-Ring	19	Stewart Ford	B	3.0 Stewart SF2-Ford Zetec-R V10	engine	12/22
ret	GERMAN GP	Hockenheim	19	Stewart Ford	B	3.0 Stewart SF2-Ford Zetec-R V10	transmission	19/22
13	HUNGARIAN GP	Hungaroring	19	Stewart Ford	B	3.0 Stewart SF2-Ford Zetec-R V10	3 laps behind	17/22
ret	BELGIAN GP	Spa	19	Stewart Ford	B	3.0 Stewart SF2-Ford Zetec-R V10	engine	17/22
ret	ITALIAN GP	Monza	19	Stewart Ford	B	3.0 Stewart SF2-Ford Zetec-R V10	gearbox	17/22
13	LUXEMBOURG GP	Nürburgring	19	Stewart Ford	B	3.0 Stewart SF2-Ford Zetec-R V10	2 laps behind	18/22
ret	JAPANESE GP	Suzuka	19	Stewart Ford	B	3.0 Stewart SF2-Ford Zetec-R V10	gearbox	19/22

2000 Championship position: 12th Wins: 0 Pole positions: 0 Fastest laps: 0 Points scored: 5

ret	AUSTRALIAN GP	Melbourne	19	Arrows Supertec	B	3.0 Arrows A21-Supertec V10	track-rod failure – retired by team	13/22
7	BRAZILIAN GP	Interlagos	19	Arrows Supertec	B	3.0 Arrows A21-Supertec V10	1 lap behind	10/22
14	SAN MARINO GP	Imola	19	Arrows Supertec	B	3.0 Arrows A21-Supertec V10	3 laps behind	16/22
ret	BRITISH GP	Silverstone	19	Arrows Supertec	B	3.0 Arrows A21-Supertec V10	electrics	8/22
ret	SPANISH GP	Barcelona	19	Arrows Supertec	B	3.0 Arrows A21-Supertec V10	gearbox	12/22
ret	EUROPEAN GP	Nürburgring	19	Arrows Supertec	B	3.0 Arrows A21-Supertec V10	collision with Irvine – crashed	14/22
ret	MONACO GP	Monte Carlo	19	Arrows Supertec	B	3.0 Arrows A21-Supertec V10	accident	15/22
5	CANADIAN GP	Montreal	19	Arrows Supertec	B	3.0 Arrows A21-Supertec V10		13/22
ret	FRENCH GP	Magny Cours	19	Arrows Supertec	B	3.0 Arrows A21-Supertec V10	gearbox	20/22
rer	AUSTRIAN GP	A1-Ring	19	Arrows Supertec	B	3.0 Arrows A21-Supertec V10	engine	10/22
ret	GERMAN GP	Hockenheim	19	Arrows Supertec	B	3.0 Arrows A21-Supertec V10	spun off	11/22
13	HUNGARIAN GP	Hungaroring	19	Arrows Supertec	B	3.0 Arrows A21-Supertec V10	2 laps behind	20/22
15	BELGIAN GP	Spa	19	Arrows Supertec	B	3.0 Arrows A21-Supertec V10	1 lap behind	20/22
4	ITALIAN GP	Monza	19	Arrows Supertec	B	3.0 Arrows A21-Supertec V10		11/22
ret	UNITED STATES GP	Indianapolis	19	Arrows Supertec	B	3.0 Arrows A21-Supertec V10	slid off track	13/22
ret	JAPANESE GP	Suzuka	19	Arrows Supertec	B	3.0 Arrows A21-Supertec V10	gearbox	14/22
10	MALAYSIAN GP	Sepang	19	Arrows Supertec	B	3.0 Arrows A21-Supertec V10	1 lap behind	14/22

2001 Championship position: 18th Wins: 0 Pole positions: 0 Fastest laps: 0 Points scored: 1

10	AUSTRALIAN GP	Melbourne	14	Orange Arrows Asiatech	B	3.0 Arrows A22-Asiatech V10	1 lap behind	15/22
7	MALAYSIAN GP	Sepang	14	Orange Arrows Asiatech	B	3.0 Arrows A22-Asiatech V10	ran light fuel load strategy at start	18/22
ret	BRAZILIAN GP	Interlagos	14	Orange Arrows Asiatech	B	3.0 Arrows A22-Asiatech V10	ran into Montoya – $15.000 fine	17/22
ret	SAN MARINO GP	Imola	14	Orange Arrows Asiatech	B	3.0 Arrows A22-Asiatech V10	broken exhaust	17/22
12	SPANISH GP	Barcelona	14	Orange Arrows Asiatech	B	3.0 Arrows A22-Asiatech V10	2 laps behind	16/22
6	AUSTRIAN GP	A1-Ring	14	Orange Arrows Asiatech	B	3.0 Arrows A22-Asiatech V10	ran light fuel strategy at start/-1 lap	16/22
8	MONACO GP	Monte Carlo	14	Orange Arrows Asiatech	B	3.0 Arrows A22-Asiatech V10	1 lap behind	19/22
ret	CANADIAN GP	Montreal	14	Orange Arrows Asiatech	B	3.0 Tyrrell A22-Asiatech V10	brakes	13/22
ret	EUROPEAN GP	Nürburgring	14	Orange Arrows Asiatech	B	3.0 Arrows A22-Asiatech V10	engine	19/22
13	FRENCH GP	Magny Cours	14	Orange Arrows Asiatech	B	3.0 Arrows A22-Asiatech V10	fuel rig problem at first stop/-2 laps	18/22
10	BRITISH GP	Silverstone	14	Orange Arrows Asiatech	B	3.0 Arrows A22-Asiatech V10	2 laps behind	17/22
9	GERMAN GP	Hockenheim	14	Orange Arrows Asiatech	B	3.0 Arrows A22-Asiatech V10	1 lap behind	20/22
12	HUNGARIAN GP	Hungaroring	14	Orange Arrows Asiatech	B	3.0 Arrows A22-Asiatech V10	3 laps behind	21/22
10	BELGIAN GP	Spa	14	Orange Arrows Asiatech	B	3.0 Arrows A22-Asiatech V10	*outside 107% time/1 lap behind	*19/22
ret	ITALIAN GP	Monza	14	Orange Arrows Asiatech	B	3.0 Arrows A22-Asiatech V10	electrics	19/22
ret	UNITED STATES GP	Indianapolis	14	Orange Arrows Asiatech	B	3.0 Arrows A22-Asiatech V10	engine	20/22
15	JAPANESE GP	Suzuka	14	Orange Arrows Asiatech	B	3.0 Arrows A22-Asiatech V10	2 laps behind	21/22

2003 Championship position: Unplaced

11	AUSTRALIAN GP	Melbourne	19	European Minardi Cosworth	B	3.0 Minardi PS03-Cosworth V10	*no time/started from pitlane/-1 lap	*19/20
13	MALAYSIAN GP	Sepang	19	European Minardi Cosworth	B	3.0 Minardi PS03-Cosworth V10	4 laps behind	18/20
ret	BRAZILIAN GP	Interlagos	19	European Minardi Cosworth	B	3.0 Minardi PS03-Cosworth V10	started from pitlane/spun off	19/20
ret	SAN MARINO GP	Imola	19	European Minardi Cosworth	B	3.0 Minardi PS03-Cosworth V10	*no time/started from pits/electrics	*20/20
12	SPANISH GP	Barcelona	19	European Minardi Cosworth	B	3.0 Minardi PS03-Cosworth V10	3 laps behind	19/20
ret	AUSTRIAN GP	A1-Ring	19	European Minardi Cosworth	B	3.0 Minardi PS03-Cosworth V10	*no time set/launch control failure	*20/20
ret	MONACO GP	Monte Carlo	19	European Minardi Cosworth	B	3.0 Minardi PS03-Cosworth V10	fuel pick-up	18/19
9	CANADIAN GP	Montreal	19	European Minardi Cosworth	B	3.0 Minardi PS03-Cosworth V10	2 laps behind	15/20
14	EUROPEAN GP	Nürburgring	19	European Minardi Cosworth	B	3.0 Minardi PS03-Cosworth V10	3 laps behind	18/20
16	FRANCE GP	Magny Cours	19	European Minardi Cosworth	B	3.0 Minardi PS03-Cosworth V10	4 laps behind	19/20
15	BRITISH GP	Silverstone	19	European Minardi Cosworth	B	3.0 Minardi PS03-Cosworth V10	2 laps behind	19/20
ret	GERMAN GP	Hockenheim	19	European Minardi Cosworth	B	3.0 Minardi PS03-Cosworth V10	hydraulics	19/20
12	HUNGARIAN GP	Hungaroring	19	European Minardi Cosworth	B	3.0 Minardi PS03-Cosworth V10	3 laps behind	18/20
ret	ITALIAN GP	Monza	19	European Minardi Cosworth	B	3.0 Minardi PS03-Cosworth V10	oil leak	17/20
10	UNITED STATES GP	Indianapolis	19	European Minardi Cosworth	B	3.0 Minardi PS03-Cosworth V10	4 laps behind	19/20
15	JAPANESE GP	Suzuka	19	European Minardi Cosworth	B	3.0 Minardi PS03-Cosworth V10	2 laps behind	17/20

GP Starts: 106 (107)   GP Wins: 0   Pole positions: 0   Fastest laps: 0   Points: 17

JOS VERSTAPPEN

DUTCHMAN Jos Verstappen has certainly seen plenty of highs and lows in his intermittent grand prix career. He might have blossomed into a major talent had he found an environment where his undoubted abilities were nurtured and a long-term relationship with a team was established. As it turned out, his career has been largely unfulfilled. It is a case of 'what might have been' for his adoring Dutch supporters.

The young Jos might not have pursued the path of motorsport at all after being hospitalised following a bad crash in his first ever kart race as a ten-year-old. Soon, however, the passion to compete was all consuming, and he quickly became one of Europe's outstanding kart racers, before moving to Formula Opel Lotus in 1992. He demolished the opposition in the Benelux series and then turned his attention to the Euroseries, immediately putting the cat among the pigeons with his forceful and often brilliant driving.

Naturally much sought after, Jos opted to race a WTS Dallara-Opel in the German F3 championship in 1993 and cut a swathe through the opposition in this class as well, winning eight races on his way to the title. Victory in the Marlboro Masters at Zandvoort helped attract the Formula 1 teams to his door, and Benetton immediately moved to sign him on a long-term contract.

An injury to JJ Lehto meant that Verstappen's debut was not long in coming. Being thrown in at the deep end as number two to Michael Schumacher could not be considered the easiest way to start a grand prix career, but the Dutchman did well in his first two appearances before Lehto returned. After the Finn's confidence had been quickly sapped, Verstappen was called back into the team and soon made headline news worldwide after escaping from an inferno when his Benetton caught fire at a refuel-ling stop during the German Grand Prix. Luckily, he suffered only minor burns and, in the next race, scored his first podium finish. His meteoric rise came to an abrupt halt, however, when Benetton decided that a proper learning season with Simtek was in order, but again he caught the eye with some impressive qualifying performances in his short spell with the team before it folded.

In 1996, the young Dutchman restarted his grand prix career at TWR Arrows, causing quite a stir in the early-season races when he took the unfancied car into the top half of the timing sheets. Inevitably, as the year wore on, he struggled to impress, as the chassis lacked development, and he was overhauled by others. A move to Tyrrell should have brought more reward, but the team was clearly uncompetitive in 1997, and the hard-charging Verstappen could only take satisfaction in mostly being the equal of his team-mate, Mika Salo. Ken Tyrrell wanted to retain his services, having sold out to Craig Pollock, but Jos was passed over in favour of paying driver Ricardo Rosset.

Luckily, another F1 chance soon presented itself when Verstappen replaced the out-of-favour Jan Magnussen in the Stewart line-up in mid-1998. In his half-season with the outfit, he fared little better than his hapless predecessor, however, and it seems that there was more than a little friction with team owner Jackie Stewart. Harvey Postlethwaite certainly thought highly of his talents and employed him to help in the development of Honda's grand prix challenger. Sadly, the former Tyrrell guru's untimely death brought proceedings to a halt and contributed to an about-face by the Japanese car giant, which took the project to British American Racing. For Verstappen, it was a return to his father's karting centre in Holland, where he was left tinkering with his beloved machines and waiting for the phone call that might resurrect his career.

A very late deal with former employer Arrows rescued the Dutchman for 2000, but accidents and mechanical unreliability combined to thwart much of Verstappen's season. Two scrapping points finishes – in the wet in Canada and at the Italian GP – hinted at his untapped ability, but for 2001, it looked as though he would be left in the wilderness again. In the end, however, it was Pedro de la Rosa who got the bullet in favour of Brazilian Enrique Bernoldi, which left Jos as undoubted team leader for the year. Most surprising, though, was his inability to out-qualify his rookie team-mate, and his year was spent scrapping among the lower orders, with just a single point as his only reward for a season's toil. Eventually, he was dropped from the team, and in the following season little was seen of 'Jos the Boss', the Dutchman being on the sidelines.

In January 2003, Verstappen returned to the grand prix scene, courtesy of a drive at Minardi-Cosworth. Given their minimal budget, Paul Stoddart's team were very much bottom of the pile, and the Dutchman could not drag the PS03 higher than the ninth place he managed in Canada. Thus his F1 days were over, but a new opportunity to display his talents opened up in the cockpit of the orange liveried Team Netherlands car in the A1GP Series. The temperamental driver was involved in his fair share of incidents, but his brilliance shone in Durban, where he snatched victory in the feature race on the final lap from Neel Jani's brakeless Team Switzerland car.

Jos then fell out with team boss Jan Lammers over their financial arrangements and subsequently failed to reach an agreement with former boss Paul Stoddart in negotiations to race for Minardi in Champ Cars for 2007. That left him to find a berth in sports car racing. Driving a privately entered Porsche Spyder in 2008 proved to be a very rewarding experience, and he took class victories at Le Mans, Barcelona and Spa on the way to LMP2 championship honours. This success perhaps could have led to a future in the category, but apart from a works drive at Le Mans with Aston Martin in 2009, no more racing opportunities seem to have arisen for the Dutchman, whose troubled personal life appears to be of more interest to the press than his sporting activities.

SEBASTIAN VETTEL

EVERY sport has its giants and legendary figures, those who stand at the head of the pantheon of greats. Football reveres such players as Pele, Maradona, and the holy trinity of Best, Law and Charlton. Lately these titans of the game have been joined by Lionel Messi, a player whose wizardry and outrageous skills could eventually place him on a different plane altogether. Today, in Formula 1, where such immortals as Juan Manuel Fangio, Jackie Stewart, Ayrton Senna and Michael Schumacher have written themselves into the record books with their magnificent feats, there is perhaps a parallel. Along has come a boyish-looking young German driver who, in just over four seasons, has re-written the record books in an astonishing manner. Apart from the matter of mere statistics and in addition to his skills, Sebastian Vettel seems to have a massive mental capacity that allows him to assimilate and process all the data he requires to produce stunning performances on the track.

Being the son of an enthusiastic hill-climb and karting competitor, Sebastian took to the wheel of karts as a toddler, and he made his competition debut aged just seven. In 1997, he took his first German title, and after moving up to the European series, he was crowned champion in both the Junior and Senior classes, before taking the big step into cars for 2003. Vettel's talent was immediately in evidence in the Formula BMW series, where he ended his debut year in second place overall, taking the top rookie honours in the process. The following year, the German youngster was totally dominant in winning 18 of the 20 races, and this naturally ensured his promotion to the F3 Euroseries for 2005. Although Lewis Hamilton was the runaway champion, the German made a great impression once again in his rookie year, taking fifth overall. Staying in the F3 Euroseries for 2006, he went head to head with his slightly older team-mate, Paul di Resta, in the battle for the title, just being edged out by the Scot in the final standings. Further evidence of his talent came in his handling of the more powerful cars in the World Series by Renault, where he scored a win and a second place on his debut for Carlin Motorsport at Misano. Towards the end of the year, the slightly-built Vettel cut a childlike figure in the high-octane Formula 1 paddock as he fulfilled the third-driver role at BMW-Sauber. In taking the wheel in the first practice session in Istanbul, when just 19 years, 53 days old, he became the youngest driver to appear at a grand prix meeting, and that was just for starters.

Vettel then was scheduled to take part in a full season in the World Series by Renault in 2007, but he was pulled from the series early, when holding a comfortable lead in the championship, to take over from the indisposed Robert Kubica, following the Pole's frightening accident in Montreal.

The mop-haired German teenager proved to be a formidable talent with a maturity beyond his years. On his grand prix debut at the 2007 US Grand Prix, he became the sport's youngest ever points scorer at just 19 years and 349 days, when he took eighth place at the Indianapolis Motor Speedway. Having made such a great impression, it was impossible to keep his career on hold, and he was soon found a place in the Toro Rosso team, under fatherly influence of Gerhard Berger.

Given the chance to show his worth, the youngster grabbed it with both hands. An astonishing drive in the rain at Mount Fuji saw Sebastian in a potential podium position, until he blotted his copybook big style by ramming Mark Webber's Red Bull. Distraught at his gaffe, he was in tears after the race, but he soon showed his mettle a week later in China, where he made amends by recording a superb fourth place, Toro Rosso's highest ever finish at the time.

In 2008, the German competed in a full season for the first time, but had to wait until Monaco before he could race the STR3; he immediately turned heads with a brilliant fifth-place finish in the rain. More points-paying finishes followed, but no one could have predicted the events of a rain-hit Monza in early September. Not only did he take pole position (the youngest ever, naturally), but also on race day he managed to drive away from the field in the wet, before controlling the race as the track dried out. Thus the history books were in need of further revision as he became the youngest ever grand prix winner at the tender age of 21 years, 72 days. His stunning Italian Grand Prix win aside, Sebastian also notched another 25 world championship points in the Toro Rosso, to place him an impressive eighth in the overall standings.

Not surprisingly, Vettel's elevation to the Red Bull team came in short order, and in the rain in Shanghai, once again he showed his mastery of wet weather to lead the team to a 1-2 finish. With Red Bull gathering momentum, he scored a famous win in the dry at Silverstone and appeared to be mounting a championship challenge until retirements in Hungary and Valencia halted his progress. Thereafter, he scored two more outstanding wins in the remaining six races, scoring 37 points to champion Jenson Button's 23, but he had to be content with being the sport's youngest ever runner-up.

Vettel had served good warning to his rivals that he would be a very strong contender in 2010, especially when he sped away from the opposition in Bahrain. Fortunately for his rivals, a faulty sparking plug dropped him to fourth, while retirement in Melbourne when leading comfortably left him trailing in the points. However, a win in Malaysia put his championship chase back on track. Thereafter, he had the machinery advantage to make a straight run for the title, along with team-mate Mark Webber, but crucial errors contrived to make his bid much more difficult. His collision with his team-mate in Turkey, when disputing the lead, and then clumsily taking out Jenson Button at Spa were the aberrations. He also lost a potential haul of points after a tardy start at Silverstone left him with contact and a first-lap puncture. Otherwise, his end-of-season run was the stuff of champions. Overcoming the disappointment of losing a win in Korea due to an engine failure, Sebastian's three victories from the last four races proved to be just enough for a thrilling finale in Abu Dhabi. Tick another box: youngest ever world champion at 23 years, 135 days.

Vettel was on a roll, and in 2011 the opposition felt the full force of his talents. By the halfway point in the season, at Silverstone, he had taken five wins and three second-place finishes to lead team-mate Webber by the huge margin of 80 points. Strangely off the pace in his home race at the Nürburgring, he still managed to salvage fourth, before stamping his authority on proceedings once again with three straight poles, and wins in Belgium, Italy and Singapore. A third place in Japan was sufficient for the German to celebrate his second consecutive championship, and there were still four races left of the season!

There was still unfinished personal business for Sebastian, however, as he chased down more records. Wins in Korea and India brought his tally to 11 for the season, but left him two short of Michael Schumacher's 13 wins in 2004. Even so, he did set a number of new records for a season: taking 15 pole positions and the most front-row starts (17); posting the most laps led (739); and scoring the highest number of points (392). It is interesting to compare the last figure with Schumacher's runaway 2004 season. Using the scoring system in place at that time, the Ferrari driver's 148 points from 18 starts yielded an average of 8.222 points per race. Vettel's tally, based on the same system, would have been 161 points from 19 starts, giving a better average of 8.473 per race.

VETTEL, Sebastian (D) b 3/7/1987, Heppenheim

2006 Championship position: Unplaced

	Race	Circuit	No	Entrant	Tyres	Capacity/Car/Engine	Comment	Q Pos/Entries
app	TURKISH GP	Istanbul	38	BMW Sauber F1 Team	B	2.4 BMW Sauber F1.06-V8	ran as 3rd driver in practice only	– / –
app	ITALIAN GP	Monza	38	BMW Sauber F1 Team	B	2.4 BMW Sauber F1.06-V8	ran as 3rd driver in practice only	– / –
app	CHINESE GP	Shanghai Circuit	38	BMW Sauber F1 Team	B	2.4 BMW Sauber F1.06-V8	ran as 3rd driver in practice only	– / –
app	JAPANESE GP	Suzuka	38	BMW Sauber F1 Team	B	2.4 BMW Sauber F1.06-V8	ran as 3rd driver in practice only	– / –
app	BRAZILIAN GP	Interlagos	38	BMW Sauber F1 Team	B	2.4 BMW Sauber F1.06-V8	ran as 3rd driver in practice only	– / –

2007 Championship position: 14th   Wins: 0   Pole positions: 0   Fastest laps: 0   Points scored: 6

	Race	Circuit	No	Entrant	Tyres	Capacity/Car/Engine	Comment	Q Pos/Entries
app	AUSTRALIAN GP	Melbourne	35	BMW Sauber F1 Team	B	2.4 BMW Sauber F1.07-V8	ran as 3rd driver in practice only	– / –
app	MALAYSIAN GP	Indianapolis	35	BMW Sauber F1 Team	B	2.4 BMW Sauber F1.07-V8	ran as 3rd driver in practice only	– / –
8	U S GP	Indianapolis	10	BMW Sauber F1 Team	B	2.4 BMW Sauber F1.07-V8	scored point on Grand Prix debut	7/22
16	HUNGARIAN GP	Hungaroring	19	Scuderia Toro Rosso	B	2.4 Toro Rosso STR02-Ferrari V8	1 lap behind	20/22
19	TURKISH GP	Istanbul	19	Scuderia Toro Rosso	B	2.4 Toro Rosso STR02-Ferrari V8	1 lap behind	20/22
18	ITALIAN GP	Monza	19	Scuderia Toro Rosso	B	2.4 Toro Rosso STR02-Ferrari V8	1 lap behind	16/22
ret	BELGIAN GP	Spa	19	Scuderia Toro Rosso	B	2.4 Toro Rosso STR02-Ferrari V8	steering	17/22
ret	JAPANESE GP	Fuji Speedway	19	Scuderia Toro Rosso	B	2.4 Toro Rosso STR02-Ferrari V8	ran into Webber behind safety car	00/22
4	CHINESE GP	Shanghai	19	Scuderia Toro Rosso	B	2.4 Toro Rosso STR02-Ferrari V8	*5 place penalty – blocking	*12/22
ret	BRAZILIAN GP	Interlagos	19	Scuderia Toro Rosso	B	2.4 Toro Rosso STR02-Ferrari V8	hydraulics	13/22

2008 Championship position: 8th   Wins: 1   Pole positions: 1   Fastest laps: 0   Points scored: 35

	Race	Circuit	No	Entrant	Tyres	Capacity/Car/Engine	Comment	Q Pos/Entries
ret	AUSTRALIAN GP	Melbourne	15	Scuderia Toro Rosso	B	2.4 Toro Rosso STR02B-Ferrari V8	multiple collision on lap 1	10/22
ret	MALAYSIAN GP	Sepang	15	Scuderia Toro Rosso	B	2.4 Toro Rosso STR02B-Ferrari V8	exhaust/fire	15/22
ret	BAHRAIN GP	Sakhir Circuit	15	Scuderia Toro Rosso	B	2.4 Toro Rosso STR02B-Ferrari V8	accident damage	19/22
ret	SPANISH GP	Barcelona	15	Scuderia Toro Rosso	B	2.4 Toro Rosso STR02B-Ferrari V8	multiple collision on lap 1	18/22
17	TURKISH GP	Istanbul	15	Scuderia Toro Rosso	B	2.4 Toro Rosso STR02B-Ferrari V8	pit stop after collision with Sutil/-1 lap	14/20
5	MONACO GP	Monte Carlo	15	Scuderia Toro Rosso	B	2.4 Toro Rosso STR03-Ferrari V8	one-stop strategy	18/20
8	CANADIAN GP	Montreal	15	Scuderia Toro Rosso	B	2.4 Toro Rosso STR03-Ferrari V8	*no time set	*20/20
12	FRENCH GP	Magny Cours	15	Scuderia Toro Rosso	B	2.4 Toro Rosso STR03-Ferrari V8		13/20
ret	BRITISH GP	Silverstone	15	Scuderia Toro Rosso	B	2.4 Toro Rosso STR03-Ferrari V8	hit by Coulthard on lap 1	11/20
8	GERMAN GP	Hockenheim	15	Scuderia Toro Rosso	B	2.4 Toro Rosso STR03-Ferrari V8		9/20
ret	HUNGARIAN GP	Hungaroring	15	Scuderia Toro Rosso	B	2.4 Toro Rosso STR03-Ferrari V8	overheating engine	11/20
6	EUROPEAN GP	Valencia	15	Scuderia Toro Rosso	B	2.4 Toro Rosso STR03-Ferrari V8		6/20
5	BELGIAN GP	Spa	15	Scuderia Toro Rosso	B	2.4 Toro Rosso STR03-Ferrari V8		10/20
1	ITALIAN GP	Monza	15	Scuderia Toro Rosso	B	2.4 Toro Rosso STR03-Ferrari V8		1/20
5	SINGAPORE GP	Singapore Circuit	15	Scuderia Toro Rosso	B	2.4 Toro Rosso STR03-Ferrari V8		7/20
6*	JAPANESE GP	Suzuka	15	Scuderia Toro Rosso	B	2.4 Toro Rosso STR03-Ferrari V8	*6th place car penalised	9/20
9	CHINESE GP	Shanghai	15	Scuderia Toro Rosso	B	2.4 Toro Rosso STR03-Ferrari V8	delayed at pit stop	8/20
4	BRAZILIAN GP	Interlagos	15	Scuderia Toro Rosso	B	2.4 Toro Rosso STR03-Ferrari V8		7/20

2009 Championship position: 2nd   Wins: 4   Pole positions: 4   Fastest laps: 3   Points scored: 84

	Race	Circuit	No	Entrant	Tyres	Capacity/Car/Engine	Comment	Q Pos/Entries
ret	AUSTRALIAN GP	Melbourne	15	Red Bull Racing	B	2.4 Red Bull RB5-Renault V8	accident with Kubica – given penalty	3/20
ret	MALAYSIAN GP	Sepang	15	Red Bull Racing	B	2.4 Red Bull RB5-Renault V8	*10-place penalty from Oz/spun-off	*3/20
1	CHINESE GP	Shanghai	15	Red Bull Racing	B	2.4 Red Bull RB5-Renault V8		1/20
2	BAHRAIN GP	Sakhir Circuit	15	Red Bull Racing	B	2.4 Red Bull RB5-Renault V8		3/20
4	SPANISH GP	Barcelona	15	Red Bull Racing	B	2.4 Red Bull RB5-Renault V8		2/20
ret	MONACO GP	Monte Carlo	15	Red Bull Racing	B	2.4 Red Bull RB5-Renault V8	accident – locked up brakes	4/20
3	TURKISH GP	Istanbul	15	Red Bull Racing	B	2.4 Red Bull RB5-Renault V8	ran wide on lap 1 – lost lead	1/20
1	BRITISH GP	Silverstone	15	Red Bull Racing	B	2.4 Red Bull RB5-Renault V8	FL	1/20
2	GERMAN GP	Nürburgring	15	Red Bull Racing	B	2.4 Red Bull RB5-Renault V8		4/20

Vettel's remarkable win for Toro Rosso in the 2008 Italian Grand Prix marked him out as a special talent. The German youngster has since gone on to prove himself a truly formidable competitor with Red Bull Racing.

Sebastian Vettel streaks away from the field at the start of the 2011 European Grand Prix in Valencia. The remarkable young driver would make it his sixth win of a season in which he would be the dominant force, taking a record 11 wins and 15 pole positions.

ret	HUNGARIAN GP	Hungaroring	15	Red Bull Racing	B	2.4 Red Bull RB5-Renault V8	collison – suspension damage	2/20
ret	EUROPEAN GP	Valencia	15	Red Bull Racing	B	2.4 Red Bull RB5-Renault V8	engine	4/20
3	BELGIAN GP	Spa	15	Red Bull Racing	B	2.4 Red Bull RB5-Renault V8	lost time early in race/FL	8/20
8	ITALIAN GP	Monza	15	Red Bull Racing	B	2.4 Red Bull RB5-Renault V8	poor grip	9/20
4	SINGAPORE GP	Marina Bay Circuit	15	Red Bull Racing	B	2.4 Red Bull RB5-Renault V8		2/20
1	JAPANESE GP	Suzuka	15	Red Bull Racing	B	2.4 Red Bull RB5-Renault V8		1/20
4	BRAZILIAN GP	Interlagos	15	Red Bull Racing	B	2.4 Red Bull RB5-Renault V8		16/20
1	ABU DHABI GP	Yas Marina Circuit	15	Red Bull Racing	B	2.4 Red Bull RB5-Renault V8	FL	2/20

2010 WORLD CHAMPION Wins: 5 Pole positions: 10 Fastest laps: 3 Points scored: 256

4	BAHRAIN GP	Sakhir Circuit	5	Red Bull Racing	B	2.4 Red Bull RB6-Renault V8	led race until sparking plug problem	1/24
ret	AUSTRALIAN GP	Melbourne	5	Red Bull Racing	B	2.4 Red Bull RB6-Renault V8	led race – wheel problem – spun off	1/24
1	MALAYSIAN GP	Sepang	5	Red Bull Racing	B	2.4 Red Bull RB6-Renault V8		3/24
6	CHINESE GP	Shanghai	5	Red Bull Racing	B	2.4 Red Bull RB6-Renault V8	wing damage after collision with Sutil	1/24
3	SPANISH GP	Barcelona	5	Red Bull Racing	B	2.4 Red Bull RB6-Renault V8	pit stop – brake disc faiure	2/24
2	MONACO GP	Monte Carlo	5	Red Bull Racing	B	2.4 Red Bull RB6-Renault V8	FL	3/24
ret	TURKISH GP	Istanbul	5	Red Bull Racing	B	2.4 Red Bull RB6-Renault V8	collision with Webber	3/24
4	CANADIAN GP	Montreal	5	Red Bull Racing	B	2.4 Red Bull RB6-Renault V8	transmission ol leak	3/24
1	EUROPEAN GP	Valencia	5	Red Bull Racing	B	2.4 Red Bull RB6-Renault V8		1/24
7	BRITISH GP	Silverstone	5	Red Bull Racing	B	2.4 Red Bull RB6-Renault V8	ran wide on 1st lap	1/24
3	GERMAN GP	Hockenheim	5	Red Bull Racing	B	2.4 Red Bull RB6-Renault V8	FL	1/24
3	HUNGARIAN GP	Hungaroring	5	Red Bull Racing	B	2.4 Red Bull RB6-Renault V8	drive-thru – too slow behind safety car/FL	1/24
ret	BELGIAN GP	Spa	5	Red Bull Racing	B	2.4 Red Bull RB6-Renault V8	crashed into Button	5/24
4	ITALIAN GP	Monza	5	Red Bull Racing	B	2.4 Red Bull RB6-Renault V8		6/24
2	SINGAPORE GP	Marina Bay Circuit	5	Red Bull Racing	B	2.4 Red Bull RB6-Renault V8		2/24
1	JAPANESE GP	Suzuka	5	Red Bull Racing	B	2.4 Red Bull RB6-Renault V8		1/24
ret	KOREAN GP	Yeongam	5	Red Bull Racing	B	2.4 Red Bull RB6-Renault V8	led race until engine failure	1/24
1	BRAZILIAN GP	Interlagos	5	Red Bull Racing	B	2.4 Red Bull RB6-Renault V8		2/24
1	ABU DHABI GP	Yas Marina Circuit	5	Red Bull Racing	B	2.4 Red Bull RB6-Renault V8		1/24

2011 WORLD CHAMPION Wins: 11 Pole positions: 15 Fastest laps: 3 Points scored: 392

1	AUSTRALIAN GP	Melbourne	1	Red Bull Racing	P	2.4 Red Bull RB7-Renault V8		1/24
1	MALAYSIAN GP	Sepang	1	Red Bull Racing	P	2.4 Red Bull RB7-Renault V8		1/24
2	CHINESE GP	Shanghai Circuit	1	Red Bull Racing	P	2.4 Red Bull RB7-Renault V8		1/24
1	TURKISH GP	Istanbul Park	1	Red Bull Racing	P	2.4 Red Bull RB7-Renault V8		1/24
1	SPANISH GP	Barcelona	1	Red Bull Racing	P	2.4 Red Bull RB7-Renault V8		2/24
1	MONACO GP	Monte Carlo	1	Red Bull Racing	P	2.4 Red Bull RB7-Renault V8		1/24
2	CANADIAN GP	Montreal	1	Red Bull Racing	P	2.4 Red Bull RB7-Renault V8		1/24
1	EUROPEAN GP	Valencia	1	Red Bull Racing	P	2.4 Red Bull RB7-Renault V8	FL	1/24
2	BRITISH GP	Silverstone	1	Red Bull Racing	P	2.4 Red Bull RB7-Renault V8		2/24
4	GERMAN GP	Hockenheim	1	Red Bull Racing	P	2.4 Red Bull RB7-Renault V8		3/24
2	HUNGARIAN GP	Hungaroring	1	Red Bull Racing	P	2.4 Red Bull RB7-Renault V8		1/24
1	BELGIAN GP	Spa	1	Red Bull Racing	P	2.4 Red Bull RB7-Renault V8		1/24
1	ITALIAN GP	Monza	1	Red Bull Racing	P	2.4 Red Bull RB7-Renault V8		1/24
1	SINGAPORE GP	Marina Bay Circuit	1	Red Bull Racing	P	2.4 Red Bull RB7-Renault V8		1/24
3	JAPANESE GP	Suzuka	1	Red Bull Racing	P	2.4 Red Bull RB7-Renault V8		1/24
1	KOREAN GP	Yeongam	1	Red Bull Racing	P	2.4 Red Bull RB7-Renault V8	FL	2/24
1	INDIAN GP	Buddh Circuit	1	Red Bull Racing	P	2.4 Red Bull RB7-Renault V8	FL	1/24
ret	ABU DHABI GP	Yas Marina Circuit	1	Red Bull Racing	P	2.4 Red Bull RB7-Renault V8	rear tyre puncture on lap 1 – suspension	1/24
2	BRAZILIAN GP	Interlagos	1	Red Bull Racing	P	2.4 Red Bull RB7-Renault V8	1 lap behind	1/24

GP Starts: 81   GP Wins: 21   Pole positions: 30   Fastest laps: 9   Points: 773

EVEN to this day, opinions are sharply divided about Gilles Villeneuve. To many, he was simply what motor racing was all about. To the more dispassionate, he was an accident waiting to happen, and when the end came, well, they were proved right, weren't they?

In soccer, if the ball goes to a player like Pele or George Best, or today Lionel Messi, there is a collective sense of anticipation, a feeling that something special could be about to happen. It was like that with Gilles. As an ordinary punter, denied access to the inner sanctum of pit or paddock, you could stand on any corner, at any circuit and wait for his Ferrari to scream into view. Then came the reward. With a glint of wildness in his eyes, and the car at some wicked angle – more often than not at its very limit and then some – he would pass and you could sense the thrill.

Gilles raced snowmobiles for several years and tried drag racing with a modified Ford Mustang, before turning to Formula Ford in the Quebec region in 1973. Winning seven out of ten races seemed to indicate that a move into Formula Atlantic would be needed to test his powers, but he was soon sidelined, albeit only for a month, by a fractured leg sustained in an accident at Mosport. Once back in the groove, he started to be noticed at home in 1975, when he and Bobby Rahal were seen as the men most likely to go far.

Villeneuve made an interesting short trip to Europe and ran in the Formula 2 Pau Grand Prix for Ron Dennis. This was the first sight of the French-Canadian on European soil, and he soon began throwing his March-Hart around the track with typical abandon. After qualifying a very respectable tenth, his race ended early with an overheating engine, but he had made an impression for sure, and even more so after a race at Trois Rivières in 1976, when James Hunt, Alan Jones and Vittorio Brambilla no less were soundly thrashed.

When Hunt returned to Britain, he told McLaren to sign up Gilles as soon as possible. He would dominate the Atlantic season with his March 76B in both the USA and Canada, despite losing his sponsor, which curtailed his activities.

Without the finance to pursue Formula 2, Villeneuve continued in Atlantics in 1977, when he clinched the championship once more. He also tried his hand briefly at Can-Am with Walter Wolf's team.

When his big break finally came in July of that year, the French-Canadian was in a works McLaren – at Silverstone – but for only one race. He made the most of it, however, indulging in countless spins, which to most onlookers seemed to indicate that he was in over his head. Gilles knew better: he was just finding the limits of a grand prix car, and the only way to do that was to go up to and beyond the point of adhesion. Amazingly, Teddy Mayer, ever the perfectionist, felt that he could pass on the feisty Villeneuve, whom he believed would cost the team a huge amount of money in repair bills!

Walter Wolf then recommended Villeneuve to Ferrari, and the 'Commendatore' immediately took a liking to the French-Canadian who, in physique at least, reminded him of the great Tazio Nuvolari. After a satisfactory test, he was soon pitched into action as a replacement for Niki Lauda, who had walked out immediately after clinching the title at Watkins Glen. It all could have ended after just two races, however, for at Fuji he ran into the Tyrrell of Ronnie Peterson and his car somersaulted wildly into a prohibited area, killing two spectators. This time, Gilles walked away...

Villeneuve was involved in a string of shunts at the start of 1978, some of his own making, some not. He was undoubtedly very quick, however, and as the year wore on he became faster still. At Monza, he and Mario Andretti battled for the win, only for both drivers to be penalised for jumping the start. The last race of 1978 was in Canada and, fittingly perhaps, Gilles finally scored his first grand prix win, but only after Jean-Pierre Jarier's Lotus had hit trouble. He felt that his win was somewhat devalued by that – not having won the race on merit took the gloss off the victory. In statistical terms, 1979 was the season when he could have won the world championship, but instead it went to team-mate Jody Scheckter, and Gilles supported the South African all the way. There were, of course, thrilling moments, such as his battle with René Arnoux at Dijon, or flashes of genius in his qualifying performance at Watkins Glen in the rain, when he was 11 seconds quicker than team-mate Jody Scheckter. There was also controversy, such as his notorious return to the pits at Zandvoort with the rear wheel hanging off the Ferrari following a blown tyre and spin. Pure Gilles!

In 1980, Villeneuve's efforts were handicapped by the truly awful handling of the Ferrari 312T5, which even his matchless skill could do little to tame, but the new 126CK V6 car was a different proposition. Certainly the chassis still needed to be refined, but the turbo power gave him a chance to compete on more equal terms with the Williamses and Brabhams. He took only two wins that year, but both were memorable. At Monaco, he pounced on Alan Jones' faltering Williams to take an unlikely win when many would have long given up the race for lost. Then came an unforgettable performance at Jarama, where he kept the snarling pack of cars in his wake for the bulk of the race to take a win one would not have believed possible.

Certainly the cars of the period did a driver like Villeneuve no favours, and by the time the 1982 season came around, he hated ground-effect and all it stood for. But he was being paid to drive, so he got on with the job in typical fashion. At Imola, the Ferraris had it all their own way and he had the race under control, until team-mate Didier Pironi 'stole' the victory from him on the last lap. He was shocked and outraged, suffering every other conceivable hurt over the Frenchman's underhand tactics. He would not speak to him again – ever.

Two weeks later at Zolder, Gilles was hardly any less anguished. He went out for practice, 100 per cent committed as usual, but this time he did not return, for having touched the March of Jochen Mass, his Ferrari cart-wheeled across the track in an accident of sickening ferocity. The hapless driver was thrown from the car, receiving terrible injuries. There was no hope of survival, but while the little man had gone, the legend he left behind would never die.

VILLENEUVE, Gilles (CDN) b 18/1/1950, Saint-Jean-sur-Richelieu, Chambly, Quebec – d 8/5/1982, Zolder Circuit, Belgium

1977 Championship position: Unplaced

	Race	Circuit	No	Entrant	Tyres	Capacity/Car/Engine	Comment	Q Pos/Entries
11	BRITISH GP	Silverstone	40	Marlboro Team McLaren	G	3.0 McLaren M23-Cosworth V8	faulty temperature gauge/2 laps behind	9/36
12/ret	CANADIAN GP	Mosport Park	21	Scuderia Ferrari SpA SEFAC	G	3.0 Ferrari 312T2 F12	driveshaft	17/27
ret	JAPANESE GP	Mount Fuji	11	Scuderia Ferrari SpA SEFAC	G	3.0 Ferrari 312T2 F12	collision with Peterson – crashed	20/23

1978 Championship position: 9th   Wins: 1   Pole positions: 0   Fastest laps: 1   Points scored: 17

	Race	Circuit	No	Entrant	Tyres	Capacity/Car/Engine	Comment	Q Pos/Entries
8	ARGENTINE GP	Buenos Aires	12	Scuderia Ferrari SpA SEFAC	M	3.0 Ferrari 312T2 F12	FL	7/27
ret	BRAZILIAN GP	Rio	12	Scuderia Ferrari SpA SEFAC	M	3.0 Ferrari 312T2 F12	spun off	6/28
ret	SOUTH AFRICAN GP	Kyalami	12	Scuderia Ferrari SpA SEFAC	M	3.0 Ferrari 312T3 F12	oil leak	8/30
ret	US GP WEST	Long Beach	12	Scuderia Ferrari SpA SEFAC	M	3.0 Ferrari 312T3 F12	collision with Regazzoni	2/30
ret	MONACO GP	Monte Carlo	12	Scuderia Ferrari SpA SEFAC	M	3.0 Ferrari 312T3 F12	tyre failure – accident	8/30
4	BELGIAN GP	Zolder	12	Scuderia Ferrari SpA SEFAC	M	3.0 Ferrari 312T3 F12		4/30
10	SPANISH GP	Jarama	12	Scuderia Ferrari SpA SEFAC	M	3.0 Ferrari 312T3 F12	pit stop – tyres/1 lap behind	5/29
9	SWEDISH GP	Anderstorp	12	Scuderia Ferrari SpA SEFAC	M	3.0 Ferrari 312T3 F12	pit stop – tyres/1 lap behind	7/27
12	FRENCH GP	Paul Ricard	12	Scuderia Ferrari SpA SEFAC	M	3.0 Ferrari 312T3 F12	pit stops – tyres/1 lap behind	9/29
ret	BRITISH GP	Brands Hatch	12	Scuderia Ferrari SpA SEFAC	M	3.0 Ferrari 312T3 F12	driveshaft	13/30
8	GERMAN GP	Hockenheim	12	Scuderia Ferrari SpA SEFAC	M	3.0 Ferrari 312T3 F12	pit stop – tyres	15/30
3	AUSTRIAN GP	Österreichring	12	Scuderia Ferrari SpA SEFAC	M	3.0 Ferrari 312T3 F12		11/31
6	DUTCH GP	Zandvoort	12	Scuderia Ferrari SpA SEFAC	M	3.0 Ferrari 312T3 F12		5/33
7*	ITALIAN GP	Monza	12	Scuderia Ferrari SpA SEFAC	M	3.0 Ferrari 312T3 F12	*2nd but – 1 min penalty – jumped start	2/32
ret	US GP EAST	Watkins Glen	12	Scuderia Ferrari SpA SEFAC	M	3.0 Ferrari 312T3 F12	engine	4/27
1	CANADIAN GP	Montreal	12	Scuderia Ferrari SpA SEFAC	M	3.0 Ferrari 312T3 F12		3/28

1979 Championship position: 2nd   Wins: 3   Pole positions: 1   Fastest laps: 6   Points scored: 53

	Race	Circuit	No	Entrant	Tyres	Capacity/Car/Engine	Comment	Q Pos/Entries
12/ret	ARGENTINE GP	Buenos Aires	12	Scuderia Ferrari SpA SEFAC	M	3.0 Ferrari 312T3 F12	engine/5 laps behind	10/26
5	BRAZILIAN GP	Interlagos	12	Scuderia Ferrari SpA SEFAC	M	3.0 Ferrari 312T3 F12	1 lap behind	5/26
1	SOUTH AFRICAN GP	Kyalami	12	Scuderia Ferrari SpA SEFAC	M	3.0 Ferrari 312T4 F12	FL	3/26
1	US GP WEST	Long Beach	12	Scuderia Ferrari SpA SEFAC	M	3.0 Ferrari 312T4 F12	FL	1/26
7	SPANISH GP	Jarama	12	Scuderia Ferrari SpA SEFAC	M	3.0 Ferrari 312T4 F12	pit stop – tyres/FL	3/27
7/ret	BELGIAN GP	Zolder	12	Scuderia Ferrari SpA SEFAC	M	3.0 Ferrari 312T4 F12	out of fuel/FL/1 lap behind	=6/28
ret	MONACO GP	Monte Carlo	12	Scuderia Ferrari SpA SEFAC	M	3.0 Ferrari 312T4 F12	transmission	2/25
2	FRENCH GP	Dijon	12	Scuderia Ferrari SpA SEFAC	M	3.0 Ferrari 312T4 F12		3/27
14/ret	BRITISH GP	Silverstone	12	Scuderia Ferrari SpA SEFAC	M	3.0 Ferrari 312T4 F12	fuel vaporisation/5 laps behind	13/26
8	GERMAN GP	Hockenheim	12	Scuderia Ferrari SpA SEFAC	M	3.0 Ferrari 312T4 F12	pit stop – rear wing/FL/1 lap behind	9/26
2	AUSTRIAN GP	Österreichring	12	Scuderia Ferrari SpA SEFAC	M	3.0 Ferrari 312T4 F12		5/26
ret	DUTCH GP	Zandvoort	12	Scuderia Ferrari SpA SEFAC	M	3.0 Ferrari 312T4 F12	blown tyre – suspension damage/FL	6/26
2	ITALIAN GP	Monza	12	Scuderia Ferrari SpA SEFAC	M	3.0 Ferrari 312T4 F12		5/28
2	CANADIAN GP	Montreal	12	Scuderia Ferrari SpA SEFAC	M	3.0 Ferrari 312T4 F12		2/29
1	US GP EAST	Watkins Glen	12	Scuderia Ferrari SpA SEFAC	M	3.0 Ferrari 312T4 F12		3/30

1980 Championship position: 10th=   Wins: 0   Pole positions: 0   Fastest laps: 0   Points scored: 6

	Race	Circuit	No	Entrant	Tyres	Capacity/Car/Engine	Comment	Q Pos/Entries
ret	ARGENTINE GP	Buenos Aires	2	Scuderia Ferrari SpA SEFAC	M	3.0 Ferrari 312T5 F12	accident – suspension/steering	8/28
16/ret	BRAZILIAN GP	Interlagos	2	Scuderia Ferrari SpA SEFAC	M	3.0 Ferrari 312T5 F12	jammed throttle/4 laps behind	3/28
ret	SOUTH AFRICAN GP	Kyalami	2	Scuderia Ferrari SpA SEFAC	M	3.0 Ferrari 312T5 F12	transmission	10/28

Gilles Villeneuve made his grand prix debut at the 1977 British Grand Prix in a one-off race for McLaren. However, he failed to impress team boss Teddy Mayer after his somewhat wild and enthusiastic performance at Silverstone. Then the rookie found his way into a seat at Ferrari, replacing newly crowned champion Niki Lauda, who had quit Maranello part way through the season.

Farewell Gilles. A typically committed Villeneuve gives his all during practice for the 1982 Belgian Grand Prix at Zolder, where he would lose his life after a collision with Jochen Mass.

ret	US GP WEST	Long Beach	2	Scuderia Ferrari SpA SEFAC	M	3.0 Ferrari 312T5 F12	driveshaft	10/27
6	BELGIAN GP	Zolder	2	Scuderia Ferrari SpA SEFAC	M	3.0 Ferrari 312T5 F12	1 lap behind	12/27
5	MONACO GP	Monte Carlo	2	Scuderia Ferrari SpA SEFAC	M	3.0 Ferrari 312T5 F12	pit stop – tyre/1 lap behind	6/27
8	FRENCH GP	Paul Ricard	2	Scuderia Ferrari SpA SEFAC	M	3.0 Ferrari 312T5 F12	pit stop – tyres/1 lap behind	17/27
ret	BRITISH GP	Brands Hatch	2	Scuderia Ferrari SpA SEFAC	M	3.0 Ferrari 312T5 F12	engine	19/27
6	GERMAN GP	Hockenheim	2	Scuderia Ferrari SpA SEFAC	M	3.0 Ferrari 312T5 F12	pit stop – tyres	16/26
8	AUSTRIAN GP	Österreichring	2	Scuderia Ferrari SpA SEFAC	M	3.0 Ferrari 312T5 F12	pit stop – tyres/1 lap behind	15/25
7	DUTCH GP	Zandvoort	2	Scuderia Ferrari SpA SEFAC	M	3.0 Ferrari 312T5 F12	pit stop – tyres/1 lap behind	7/28
ret	ITALIAN GP	Imola	2	Scuderia Ferrari SpA SEFAC	M	3.0 Ferrari 312T5 F12	puncture – accident	8/28
5	CANADIAN GP	Montreal	2	Scuderia Ferrari SpA SEFAC	M	3.0 Ferrari 312T5 F12		22/28
ret	US GP EAST	Watkins Glen	2	Scuderia Ferrari SpA SEFAC	M	3.0 Ferrari 312T5 F12	hit chicane	18/27

1981 Championship position: 7th   Wins: 2   Pole positions: 1   Fastest laps: 1   Points scored: 25

ret	US GP WEST	Long Beach	27	Scuderia Ferrari SpA SEFAC	M	1.5 t/c Ferrari 126CK V6	driveshaft	5/29
ret	BRAZILIAN GP	Rio	27	Scuderia Ferrari SpA SEFAC	M	1.5 t/c Ferrari 126CK V6	turbo wastegate	7/30
ret	ARGENTINE GP	Buenos Aires	27	Scuderia Ferrari SpA SEFAC	M	1.5 t/c Ferrari 126CK V6	driveshaft	7/29
7	SAN MARINO GP	Imola	27	Scuderia Ferrari SpA SEFAC	M	1.5 t/c Ferrari 126CK V6	pit stop – tyres/FL	1/30
4	BELGIAN GP	Zolder	27	Scuderia Ferrari SpA SEFAC	M	1.5 t/c Ferrari 126CK V6		7/31
1	MONACO GP	Monte Carlo	27	Scuderia Ferrari SpA SEFAC	M	1.5 t/c Ferrari 126CK V6		2/31
1	SPANISH GP	Jarama	27	Scuderia Ferrari SpA SEFAC	M	1.5 t/c Ferrari 126CK V6		7/30
ret	FRENCH GP	Dijon	27	Scuderia Ferrari SpA SEFAC	M	1.5 t/c Ferrari 126CK V6	electrics	11/29
ret	BRITISH GP	Silverstone	27	Scuderia Ferrari SpA SEFAC	M	1.5 t/c Ferrari 126CK V6	spun off	8/30
10	GERMAN GP	Hockenheim	27	Scuderia Ferrari SpA SEFAC	M	1.5 t/c Ferrari 126CK V6	pit stop – tyres/1 lap behind	8/30
ret	AUSTRIAN GP	Österreichring	27	Scuderia Ferrari SpA SEFAC	M	1.5 t/c Ferrari 126CK V6	accident	3/28
ret	DUTCH GP	Zandvoort	27	Scuderia Ferrari SpA SEFAC	M	1.5 t/c Ferrari 126CK V6	accident – Giacomelli & Patrese	16/30
ret	ITALIAN GP	Monza	27	Scuderia Ferrari SpA SEFAC	M	1.5 t/c Ferrari 126CK V6	turbo	9/30
3	CANADIAN GP	Montreal	27	Scuderia Ferrari SpA SEFAC	M	1.5 t/c Ferrari 126CK V6		11/30
dsq*	CAESARS PALACE GP	Las Vegas	27	Scuderia Ferrari SpA SEFAC	M	1.5 t/c Ferrari 126CK V6	*started from wrong grid position	3/30

1982 Championship position: 15th=   Wins: 0   Pole positions: 0   Fastest laps: 0   Points scored: 6

ret	SOUTH AFRICAN GP	Kyalami	27	Scuderia Ferrari SpA SEFAC	G	1.5 t/c Ferrari 126C2 V6	turbo	3/30
ret	BRAZILIAN GP	Rio	27	Scuderia Ferrari SpA SEFAC	G	1.5 t/c Ferrari 126C2 V6	spun off	2/31
dsq*	US GP WEST	Long Beach	27	Scuderia Ferrari SpA SEFAC	G	1.5 t/c Ferrari 126C2 V6	3rd on road/*wing infringement	7/31
2	SAN MARINO GP	Imola	27	Scuderia Ferrari SpA SEFAC	G	1.5 t/c Ferrari 126C2 V6	overtaken by Pironi on last lap	3/14
dns	BELGIAN GP	Zolder	27	Scuderia Ferrari SpA SEFAC	G	1.5 t/c Ferrari 126C2 V6	fatal practice accident	(8)/32

GP Starts: 67   GP Wins: 6   Pole positions: 2   Fastest laps: 8   Points: 107

THE modern-day racing driver is an incredibly glamorous figure in a sport where image is everything. Yet perhaps F1's corporate culture and the hawkish nature of some sections of the media have turned these superstars into comparatively bland individuals, whose thoughts and opinions are screened and shaped before being made public via non-controversial press releases or media conferences. Whether naturally or by intention, Jacques Villeneuve was one man who stood out as an exception to this rule. The Canadian's 'grunge' look, complete with sporadically bleached hair, aimed to appeal to the younger pop-culture generation, and his outspoken views on Formula 1 often caused agitation within the portals of the FIA.

Being the son of such a legendary father naturally helped Jacques to get his fledgling career off the ground, but after a none-too-impressive three seasons spent in Italian F3 between 1989 and 1991, it seemed that his name was greater than his talent. He soon proved the doubters wrong, however, when a move to Japan to race in F3 saw him score three victories and take second place in the series. Luck can play a huge part in the shaping of any driver's career, and in Villeneuve's case it came in the form of an invitation to compete in the 1992 Player's Trois Rivières race in Quebec. Then an unknown quantity, he took a fine third place, and his new mentor, Craig Pollock, set in motion a deal for him to race in Formula Atlantic full time in 1993.

The young French-Canadian fought a three-way battle for the title, and although he came up short. Jerry Forsythe and Barry Green decided that he was the driver to stick with when they made the move to the Indy car championship in 1994. Villeneuve took to the series like a duck to water; winning a race at Elkhart Lake and finishing a very close second in the Indy 500 contributed to an impressive sixth place in the final standings. Things were even better the following year, when Jacques not only became the youngest ever PPG Cup champion, but also scooped the Indy 500, despite being two laps down at one stage. His stock was at its highest and, astutely, he and Pollock decided that the chance of a dream move to Formula 1 with Williams-Renault for 1996 was much too good to pass up.

Jacques blew into the new F1 season like a full-force gale. He could easily have won his maiden race in Australia and, as the season progressed, he grew into an ever stronger threat to Damon Hill. In fact, he came closer to beating his more experienced team-mate than the final points table showed. His performances convinced the Williams management that they could dispense with the services of their loyal stalwart and put their faith in the bouncy, self-assured enfant terrible.

Villeneuve duly delivered in 1997 when, with a cocktail of brilliance and some notable gaffes – both on and off track – he squared up to the challenge of Michael Schumacher and Ferrari, slugging it out right up to the thrilling finale at Jerez, where the German attempted his outrageous blocking manoeuvre. To win the world championship is hard enough in itself, but to achieve such a feat in only his second year in F1 was a truly remarkable performance. He had to win the title that season for, with Renault pulling their works supported engine out of racing, Williams would no longer be the leading force of yore.

In 1998, Jacques hustled the garishly liveried Mecachrome-engined Williams FW20 for all it was worth, often placing it above quicker cars, but after spending the previous two seasons eyeing up the silverware, the French-Canadian's expectations were lowered to a scramble for points-scoring finishes and the odd podium place. If nothing else, it proved his calibre as a top-notch performer.

Certainly Patrick Head would have liked to hold on to Jacques for a fourth year, but the attraction of the British American Racing project, headed by mentor Pollock, was irresistible. Of course, history now records that the first year for the cocksure new team was one of self-inflicted hu-

miliation, as the acquisition of even a single world championship point proved beyond them. There were rumours that Villeneuve was set to return to Williams, but he honoured his BAR contract in 2000. The BAR 002 was a whole lot more reliable than its predecessor, and some strong-arm drives allowed him to pick up points on a regular basis during the year. There were no podiums, however, and a mid-season slump again brought renewed rumours of a move elsewhere, but once more he decided to stay loyal to BAR and Pollock for 2001.

Partnered with Frenchman Olivier Panis, Villeneuve came out on top, taking the team's first podium finish in Spain and adding another at Hockenheim. The 003 was another disappointing car, however, but the French-Canadian remained loyal to the cause and inked another extension to his contract. All seemed well, until mentor and team boss Pollock announced his resignation on the eve of the official 2002 launch, leaving Prodrive boss David Richards to take charge. Jacques stayed on, despite being visibly upset by the news, only to find that the Honda-powered 004 was again well off the pace. The team didn't score a point until mid-season, stoking further gossip that he might move on, but instead it was Panis who was eased aside by the arrival of Jenson Button. However, Villeneuve's place on the team was not favoured by Richards, who felt that some of his massive retainer could have been better used on research and development; before the end of the season, BAR announced that they wouldn't be retaining the former world champion. On receiving the news, he got his final punch in early, quitting before the Japanese Grand Prix.

The 2004 season was spent mostly on the sidelines as Villeneuve sought to recharge his batteries and secure a comeback for 2005. The opportunity to return came sooner than expected, however, and when Renault fell out with Jarno Trulli, he was able to make his comeback three races early. His short time with the team was pretty uninspiring, though, but Sauber had already committed to running the French-Canadian by that point, and he was back on the grid full time in 2005, having signed a two-year deal. Certainly his early drives were tentative to say the least, as he struggled to come to grips with a machine that was not to his liking. Despite persistent rumours that he would be replaced, he retained the confidence of Peter Sauber and had begun to perform with more confidence by mid-season. In truth, though, his performances indicated that he was really a shadow of his former self.

When Sauber sold out to BMW, Jacques retained a seat alongside Nick Heidfeld for 2006. Many thought that this was due to the considerable pay-off required if BMW had opted to look elsewhere, but that is open to conjecture. Clearly, however, the longevity of Villeneuve's grand prix career rested soundly on his performances in 2006. Generally he matched the pace of his younger team-mate, but a heavy crash in the German GP ultimately brought the curtain down early on the former champion's grand prix career. Robert Kubica had stepped into his seat for the Hungarian Grand Prix and did well enough to be promised further outings. This made Villeneuve feel that he was being squeezed out by the BMW hierarchy, so he chose to walk away from Formula 1.

Jacques then joined Peugeot in an attempt to win the Le Mans 24-hour race and match the 'triple crown' achieved by Graham Hill back in 1972. He was unlucky, just missing out by finishing in second place in 2008. Then, rather like Juan Pablo Montya, he looked towards NASCAR as a possible platform for his racing career, but despite some promise in sporadic appearances, a lack of sponsorship largely curtailed his activities.

After flirting with a return to Formula 1 with the Stefan and his own Villeneuve teams, both of which failed to materialise, Jacques, now past 40, seems to be destined to take part in celebrity races or assume guest roles, having committed to the Indian-based i1 Super Series, which has already been postponed to 2013.

VILLENEUVE, Jacques (CDN) b 9/4/1971, Saint-Jean-sur-Richelieu, Chambly, Quebec

1996 Championship position: 2nd   Wins: 4   Pole positions: 3   Fastest laps: 6   Points scored: 78

	Race	Circuit	No	Entrant	Tyres	Capacity/Car/Engine	Comment	Q Pos/Entries
2	AUSTRALIAN GP	Melbourne	6	Rothmans Williams Renault	G	3.0 Williams FW18-Renault V10	led debut race until oil leak/FL	1/22
ret	BRAZILIAN GP	Interlagos	6	Rothmans Williams Renault	G	3.0 Williams FW18-Renault V10	spun off	3/22
2	ARGENTINE GP	Buenos Aires	6	Rothmans Williams Renault	G	3.0 Williams FW18-Renault V10		3/22
1	EUROPEAN GP	Nürburgring	6	Rothmans Williams Renault	G	3.0 Williams FW18-Renault V10		2/22
11/ret	SAN MARINO GP	Imola	6	Rothmans Williams Renault	G	3.0 Williams FW18-Renault V10	broken suspension/6 laps behind	3/22
ret	MONACO GP	Monte Carlo	6	Rothmans Williams Renault	G	3.0 Williams FW18-Renault V10	collision with Badoer	10/22
3	SPANISH GP	Barcelona	6	Rothmans Williams Renault	G	3.0 Williams FW18-Renault V10		2/22
2	CANADIAN GP	Montreal	6	Rothmans Williams Renault	G	3.0 Williams FW18-Renault V10	FL	2/22
2	FRENCH GP	Magny Cours	6	Rothmans Williams Renault	G	3.0 Williams FW18-Renault V10	FL	6/22
1	BRITISH GP	Silverstone	6	Rothmans Williams Renault	G	3.0 Williams FW18-Renault V10	FL	2/22
3	GERMAN GP	Hockenheim	6	Rothmans Williams Renault	G	3.0 Williams FW18-Renault V10		3/20
1	HUNGARIAN GP	Hungaroring	6	Rothmans Williams Renault	G	3.0 Williams FW18-Renault V10		3/20
2	BELGIAN GP	Spa	6	Rothmans Williams Renault	G	3.0 Williams FW18-Renault V10		1/20
7	ITALIAN GP	Monza	6	Rothmans Williams Renault	G	3.0 Williams FW18-Renault V10	suspension damage/1 lap behind	2/20
1	PORTUGUESE GP	Estoril	6	Rothmans Williams Renault	G	3.0 Williams FW18-Renault V10	FL	2/20
ret	JAPANESE GP	Suzuka	6	Rothmans Williams Renault	G	3.0 Williams FW18-Renault V10	lost wheel after pit stop/FL	1/20

1997 WORLD CHAMPION   Wins: 7   Pole positions: 10   Fastest laps: 3   Points scored: 81

	Race	Circuit	No	Entrant	Tyres	Capacity/Car/Engine	Comment	Q Pos/Entries
ret	AUSTRALIAN GP	Melbourne	3	Rothmans Williams Renault	G	3.0 Williams FW19-Renault V10	collision with Irvine and Herbert	1/24
1	BRAZILIAN GP	Interlagos	3	Rothmans Williams Renault	G	3.0 Williams FW19-Renault V10	FL	1/22
1	ARGENTINE GP	Buenos Aires	3	Rothmans Williams Renault	G	3.0 Williams FW19-Renault V10		1/22
ret	SAN MARINO GP	Imola	3	Rothmans Williams Renault	G	3.0 Williams FW19-Renault V10	gear selection	1/22
ret	MONACO GP	Monte Carlo	3	Rothmans Williams Renault	G	3.0 Williams FW19-Renault V10	accident damage	3/22
1	SPANISH GP	Barcelona	3	Rothmans Williams Renault	G	3.0 Williams FW19-Renault V10		1/22
ret	CANADIAN GP	Montreal	3	Rothmans Williams Renault	G	3.0 Williams FW19-Renault V10	hit wall	2/22
4	FRENCH GP	Magny Cours	3	Rothmans Williams Renault	G	3.0 Williams FW19-Renault V10		4/22
1	BRITISH GP	Silverstone	3	Rothmans Williams Renault	G	3.0 Williams FW19-Renault V10		1/22
ret	GERMAN GP	Hockenheim	3	Rothmans Williams Renault	G	3.0 Williams FW19-Renault V10	tangled with Trulli – spun off	9/22
1	HUNGARIAN GP	Hungaroring	3	Rothmans Williams Renault	G	3.0 Williams FW19-Renault V10		2/22
5*	BELGIAN GP	Spa	3	Rothmans Williams Renault	G	3.0 Williams FW19-Renault V10	*3rd place car dsq/FL	1/22
5	ITALIAN GP	Monza	3	Rothmans Williams Renault	G	3.0 Williams FW19-Renault V10		4/22
1	AUSTRIAN GP	A1-Ring	3	Rothmans Williams Renault	G	3.0 Williams FW19-Renault V10	FL	1/22
1	LUXEMBOURG GP	Nürburgring	3	Rothmans Williams Renault	G	3.0 Williams FW19-Renault V10		2/22
dsq*	JAPANESE GP	Suzuka	3	Rothmans Williams Renault	G	3.0 Williams FW19-Renault V10	*5th on road – dsq after appeal	1/22
3	EUROPEAN GP	Jerez	3	Rothmans Williams Renault	G	3.0 Williams FW19-Renault V10		1/22

1998 Championship position: 5th   Wins: 0   Pole positions: 0   Fastest laps: 0   Points scored: 21

	Race	Circuit	No	Entrant	Tyres	Capacity/Car/Engine	Comment	Q Pos/Entries
5	AUSTRALIAN GP	Melbourne	1	Winfield Williams	G	3.0 Williams FW20-Mechachrome V10	1 lap behind	4/22
7	BRAZILIAN GP	Interlagos	1	Winfield Williams	G	3.0 Williams FW20-Mechachrome V10	1 lap behind	10/22
ret	ARGENTINE GP	Buenos Aires	1	Winfield Williams	G	3.0 Williams FW20-Mechachrome V10	collision with Coulthard	7/22
4	SAN MARINO GP	Imola	1	Winfield Williams	G	3.0 Williams FW20-Mechachrome V10		6/22
6	SPANISH GP	Barcelona	1	Winfield Williams	G	3.0 Williams FW20-Mechachrome V10	1 lap behind	10/22
5	MONACO GP	Monte Carlo	1	Winfield Williams	G	3.0 Williams FW20-Mechachrome V10	1 lap behind	13/22
10	CANADIAN GP	Montreal	1	Winfield Williams	G	3.0 Williams FW20-Mechachrome V10	collision – lost rear wing/6 laps behind	6/22
4	FRENCH GP	Magny Cours	1	Winfield Williams	G	3.0 Williams FW20-Mechachrome V10		5/22
7	BRITISH GP	Silverstone	1	Winfield Williams	G	3.0 Williams FW20-Mechachrome V10	1 lap behind	3/22
6	AUSTRIAN GP	A1-Ring	1	Winfield Williams	G	3.0 Williams FW20-Mechachrome V10		11/22
3	GERMAN GP	Hockenheim	1	Winfield Williams	G	3.0 Williams FW20-Mechachrome V10		3/22
3	HUNGARIAN GP	Hungaroring	1	Winfield Williams	G	3.0 Williams FW20-Mechachrome V10		6/22
ret	BELGIAN GP	Spa	1	Winfield Williams	G	3.0 Williams FW20-Mechachrome V10	spun off	6/22
ret	ITALIAN GP	Monza	1	Winfield Williams	G	3.0 Williams FW20-Mechachrome V10	spun off	2/22
8	LUXEMBOURG GP	Nürburgring	1	Winfield Williams	G	3.0 Williams FW20-Mechachrome V10	1 lap behind	9/22
6	JAPANESE GP	Suzuka	1	Winfield Williams	G	3.0 Williams FW20-Mechachrome V10		6/22

1999 Championship position: Unplaced

	Race	Circuit	No	Entrant	Tyres	Capacity/Car/Engine	Comment	Q Pos/Entries
ret	AUSTRALIAN GP	Melbourne	22	British American Racing	B	3.0 BAR 001-Supertec V10	lost rear wing	11/22
ret	BRAZILIAN GP	Interlagos	22	British American Racing	B	3.0 BAR 001-Supertec V10	*practice time disallowed/hydraulics	*21/21
ret	SAN MARINO GP	Imola	22	British American Racing	B	3.0 BAR 001-Supertec V10	transmission	5/22
ret	MONACO GP	Monte Carlo	22	British American Racing	B	3.0 BAR 001-Supertec V10	oil leak	8/22
ret	SPANISH GP	Barcelona	22	British American Racing	B	3.0 BAR 001-Supertec V10	transmission	6/22
ret	CANADIAN GP	Montreal	22	British American Racing	B	3.0 BAR 001-Supertec V10	accident	16/22
ret	FRENCH GP	Magny Cours	22	British American Racing	B	3.0 BAR 001-Supertec V10	spun off	12/22
ret	BRITISH GP	Silverstone	22	British American Racing	B	3.0 BAR 001-Supertec V10	gearbox	9/22
ret	AUSTRIAN GP	A1-Ring	22	British American Racing	B	3.0 BAR 001-Supertec V10	broken driveshaft	9/22
ret	GERMAN GP	Hockenheim	22	British American Racing	B	3.0 BAR 001-Supertec V10	collision with Diniz	12/22
ret	HUNGARIAN GP	Hungaroring	22	British American Racing	B	3.0 BAR 001-Supertec V10	clutch	9/22
15	BELGIAN GP	Spa	22	British American Racing	B	3.0 BAR 001-Supertec V10r	1 lap behind	9/22
8	ITALIAN GP	Monza	22	British American Racing	B	3.0 BAR 001-Supertec V10		11/22
10/ret	EUROPEAN GP	Nürburgring	22	British American Racing	B	3.0 BAR 001-Supertec V10	clutch/5 laps behind	8/22
ret	MALAYSIAN GP	Sepang	22	British American Racing	B	3.0 BAR 001-Supertec V10	hydraulics	10/22
9	JAPANESE GP	Suzuka	22	British American Racing	B	3.0 BAR 001-Supertec V10	1 lap behind	11/22

2000 Championship position: 7th   Wins: 0   Pole positions: 0   Fastest laps: 0   Points scored: 17

	Race	Circuit	No	Entrant	Tyres	Capacity/Car/Engine	Comment	Q Pos/Entries
4	AUSTRALIAN GP	Melbourne	22	Lucky Strike BAR Honda	B	3.0 BAR 002-Honda V10		8/22
ret	BRAZILIAN GP	Interlagos	22	Lucky Strike BAR Honda	B	3.0 BAR 002-Honda V10	gearbox	10/22
5	SAN MARINO GP	Imola	22	Lucky Strike BAR Honda	B	3.0 BAR 002-Honda V10	1 lap behind	9/22
16/ret	BRITISH GP	Silverstone	22	Lucky Strike BAR Honda	B	3.0 BAR 002-Honda V10	gearbox/4 laps behind	10/22
ret	SPANISH GP	Barcelona	22	Lucky Strike BAR Honda	B	3.0 BAR 002-Honda V10	engine	6/22
ret	EUROPEAN GP	Nürburgring	22	Lucky Strike BAR Honda	B	3.0 BAR 002-Honda V10	engine	9/22
7	MONACO GP	Monte Carlo	22	Lucky Strike BAR Honda	B	3.0 BAR 002-Honda V10	1 lap behind	17/22

15/ret	CANADIAN GP	Montreal	22	Lucky Strike BAR Honda	B	3.0 BAR 002-Honda V10	*ran into Ralf Schumacher/5 laps behind*	6/22
4	FRENCH GP	Magny Cours	22	Lucky Strike BAR Honda	B	3.0 BAR 002-Honda V10		7/22
4	AUSTRIAN GP	A1-Ring	22	Lucky Strike BAR Honda	B	3.0 BAR 002-Honda V10	*lost time in 1st lap melée/1 lap behind*	7/22
8	GERMAN GP	Hockenheim	22	Lucky Strike BAR Honda	B	3.0 BAR 002-Honda V10	*collision with Zonta*	9/22
12	HUNGARIAN GP	Hungaroring	22	Lucky Strike BAR Honda	B	3.0 BAR 002-Honda V10	*2 laps behind*	16/22
7	BELGIAN GP	Spa	22	Lucky Strike BAR Honda	B	3.0 BAR 002-Honda V10		7/22
ret	ITALIAN GP	Monza	22	Lucky Strike BAR Honda	B	3.0 BAR 002-Honda V10	*electrics*	4/22
4	UNITED STATES GP	Indianapolis	22	Lucky Strike BAR Honda	B	3.0 BAR 002-Honda V10		8/22
6	JAPANESE GP	Suzuka	22	Lucky Strike BAR Honda	B	3.0 BAR 002-Honda V10	*1 lap behind*	9/22
5	MALAYSIAN GP	Sepang	22	Lucky Strike BAR Honda	B	3.0 BAR 002-Honda V10		6/22

2001 Championship position: 7th=   Wins: 0   Pole positions: 0   Fastest laps: 0   Points scored: 12

ret	AUSTRALIAN GP	Melbourne	10	Lucky Strike BAR Honda	B	3.0 BAR 003-Honda V10	*ran into Ralf Schumacher at start*	8/22
ret	MALAYSIAN GP	Sepang	10	Lucky Strike BAR Honda	B	3.0 BAR 003-Honda V10	*spun off on wet track*	7/22
7	BRAZILIAN GP	Interlagos	10	Lucky Strike BAR Honda	B	3.0 BAR 003-Honda V10	*1 lap behind*	12/22
ret	SAN MARINO GP	Imola	10	Lucky Strike BAR Honda	B	3.0 BAR 003-Honda V10	*engine*	11/22
3	SPANISH GP	Barcelona	10	Lucky Strike BAR Honda	B	3.0 BAR 003-Honda V10		7/22
8	AUSTRIAN GP	A1-Ring	10	Lucky Strike BAR Honda	B	3.0 BAR 003-Honda V10	*stop & go pen – speeding in pits/-1 lap*	12/22
4	MONACO GP	Monte Carlo	10	Lucky Strike BAR Honda	B	3.0 BAR 003-Honda V10		9/22
ret	CANADIAN GP	Montreal	10	Lucky Strike BAR Honda	B	3.0 BAR 003-Honda V10	*driveshaft*	9/22
9	EUROPEAN GP	Nürburgring	10	Lucky Strike BAR Honda	B	3.0 BAR 003-Honda V10	*1 lap behind*	11/22
ret	FRENCH GP	Magny Cours	10	Lucky Strike BAR Honda	B	3.0 BAR 003-Honda V10	*electrics*	10/22
8	BRITISH GP	Silverstone	10	Lucky Strike BAR Honda	B	3.0 BAR 003-Honda V10	*1 lap behind*	12/22
3	GERMAN GP	Hockenheim	10	Lucky Strike BAR Honda	B	3.0 BAR 003-Honda V10		12/22
9	HUNGARIAN GP	Hungaroring	10	Lucky Strike BAR Honda	B	3.0 BAR 003-Honda V10	*2 laps behind*	10/22
8	BELGIAN GP	Spa	10	Lucky Strike BAR Honda	B	3.0 BAR 003-Honda V10		6/22
6	ITALIAN GP	Monza	10	Lucky Strike BAR Honda	B	3.0 BAR 003-Honda V10	*short of fuel*	15/22
ret	U S GP	Indianapolis	10	Lucky Strike BAR Honda	B	3.0 BAR 003-Honda V10	*collision damage*	18/22
10	JAPANESE GP	Suzuka	10	Lucky Strike BAR Honda	B	3.0 BAR 003-Honda V10	*1 lap behind*	14/22

2002 Championship position: 12th=   Wins: 0   Pole positions: 0   Fastest laps: 0   Points scored: 4

ret	AUSTRALIAN GP	Melbourne	11	Lucky Strike BAR Honda	B	3.0 BAR 004-Honda V10	*spun off*	13/22
8	MALAYSIAN GP	Sepang	11	Lucky Strike BAR Honda	B	3.0 BAR 004-Honda V10	*1 lap behind*	13/22
10/ret	BRAZILIAN GP	Interlagos	11	Lucky Strike BAR Honda	B	3.0 BAR 004-Honda V10	*engine/3 laps behind*	15/22
7	SAN MARINO GP	Imola	11	Lucky Strike BAR Honda	B	3.0 BAR 004-Honda V10	*1 lap behind*	10/22
7	SPANISH GP	Barcelona	11	Lucky Strike BAR Honda	B	3.0 BAR 004-Honda V10	*1 lap behind*	15/21
10	AUSTRIAN GP	A1-Ring	11	Lucky Strike BAR Honda	B	3.0 BAR 004-Honda V10	*1 lap behind*	17/22
ret	MONACO GP	Monte Carlo	11	Lucky Strike BAR Honda	B	3.0 BAR 004-Honda V10	*started from pitlane/engine*	14/22
ret	CANADIAN GP	Montreal	11	Lucky Strike BAR Honda	B	3.0 BAR 004-Honda V10	*engine*	9/22
12	EUROPEAN GP	Nürburgring	11	Lucky Strike BAR Honda	B	3.0 BAR 004-Honda V10	*1 lap behind*	19/22
4	BRITISH GP	Silverstone	11	Lucky Strike BAR Honda	B	3.0 BAR 004-Honda V10	*1 lap behind*	9/22
ret	FRENCH GP	Magny Cours	11	Lucky Strike BAR Honda	B	3.0 BAR 004-Honda V10	*engine*	13/21
ret	GERMAN GP	Hockenheim	11	Lucky Strike BAR Honda	B	3.0 BAR 004-Honda V10	*gearbox*	11/22
ret	HUNGARIAN GP	Hungaroring	11	Lucky Strike BAR Honda	B	3.0 BAR 004-Honda V10	*transmission failure*	13/20
8	BELGIAN GP	Spa	11	Lucky Strike BAR Honda	B	3.0 BAR 004-Honda V10	*frustrated by a slower Fisichella*	12/20
9	ITALIAN GP	Monza	11	Lucky Strike BAR Honda	B	3.0 BAR 004-Honda V10	*ran too much wing*	9/20
6	UNITED STATES GP	Indianapolis	11	Lucky Strike BAR Honda	B	3.0 BAR 004-Honda V10		7/20
ret	JAPANESE GP	Suzuka	11	Lucky Strike BAR Honda	B	3.0 BAR 004-Honda V10	*engine*	9/20

2003 Championship position: 14th=   Wins: 0   Pole positions: 0   Fastest laps: 0   Points scored: 6

9	AUSTRALIAN GP	Melbourne	16	Lucky Strike BAR Honda	B	3.0 BAR 005-Honda V10	*radio and tyre problems*	6/20
dns	MALAYSIAN GP	Sepang	16	Lucky Strike BAR Honda	B	3.0 BAR 005-Honda V10	*electronics/gearbox before start*	12/20
6	BRAZILIAN GP	Interlagos	16	Lucky Strike BAR Honda	B	3.0 BAR 005-Honda V10	*race stopped after accident*	13/20
ret	SAN MARINO GP	Imola	16	Lucky Strike BAR Honda	B	3.0 BAR 005-Honda V10	*oil fire*	7/20
ret	SPANISH GP	Barcelona	16	Lucky Strike BAR Honda	B	3.0 BAR 005-Honda V10	*engine*	11/20
12	AUSTRIAN GP	A1-Ring	16	Lucky Strike BAR Honda	B	3.0 BAR 005-Honda V10	*major electronic problems/1 lap behind*	12/20
ret	MONACO GP	Monte Carlo	16	Lucky Strike BAR Honda	B	3.0 BAR 005-Honda V10	*engine*	11/19
ret	CANADIAN GP	Montreal	16	Lucky Strike BAR Honda	B	3.0 BAR 005-Honda V10	*brakes*	14/20
ret	EUROPEAN GP	Nürburgring	16	Lucky Strike BAR Honda	B	3.0 BAR 005-Honda V10	*transmission*	17/20
9	FRANCE GP	Magny Cours	16	Lucky Strike BAR Honda	B	3.0 BAR 005-Honda V10	*1 lap behind*	12/20
10	BRITISH GP	Silverstone	16	Lucky Strike BAR Honda	B	3.0 BAR 005-Honda V10		9/20
9	GERMAN GP	Hockenheim	16	Lucky Strike BAR Honda	B	3.0 BAR 005-Honda V10	*early colllision with Wilson/-2 laps*	13/20
ret	HUNGARIAN GP	Hungaroring	16	Lucky Strike BAR Honda	B	3.0 BAR 005-Honda V10	*hydraulic leak*	16/20
6	ITALIAN GP	Monza	16	Lucky Strike BAR Honda	B	3.0 BAR 005-Honda V10	*1 lap behind*	10/20
ret	U S GP	Indianapolis	16	Lucky Strike BAR Honda	B	3.0 BAR 005-Honda V10	*engine*	12/20

2004 Championship position: Unplaced

11	CHINESE GP	Shanghai	7	Mild Seven Renault F1 Team	M	3.0 Renault R24-V10	*1 lap behind*	12/20
10	JAPANESE GP	Suzuka	7	Mild Seven Renault F1 Team	M	3.0 Renault R24-V10	*1 lap behind*	9/20
10	BRAZILIAN GP	Interlagos	7	Mild Seven Renault F1 Team	M	3.0 Renault R24-V10	*1 lap behind*	14/20

2005 Championship position: 14th=   Wins: 0   Pole positions: 0   Fastest laps: 0   Points scored: 9

13	AUSTRALIAN GP	Melbourne	11	Sauber Petronas	M	3.0 Sauber C24-Petronas V10	*poor grip*	4/20
ret	MALAYSIAN GP	Sepang	11	Sauber Petronas	M	3.0 Sauber C24-Petronas V10	*locked brakes and spun off*	16/20
11/ret	BAHRAIN GP	Bahrain	11	Sauber Petronas	M	3.0 Sauber C24-Petronas V10	*collision with Coulthard/3 laps behind*	16/20
4*	SAN MARINO GP	Imola	11	Sauber Petronas	M	3.0 Sauber C24-Petronas V10	**3rd & 5th placed cars disqualified*	11/20
ret	SPANISH GP	Barcelona	11	Sauber Petronas	M	3.0 Sauber C24-Petronas V10	*engine*	12/18
11	MONACO GP	Monte Carlo	11	Sauber Petronas	M	3.0 Sauber C24-Petronas V10	*collision with Massa/1 lap behind*	9/20
13	EUROPEAN GP	Nürburgring	11	Sauber Petronas	M	3.0 Sauber C24-Petronas V10	*off track at start*	15/20
9	CANADIAN GP	Montreal	11	Sauber Petronas	M	3.0 Sauber C24-Petronas V10	*collision with Sato/1 lap behind*	8/20
dns*	U S GP	Indianapolis	11	Sauber Petronas	M	3.0 Sauber C24-Petronas V10	**withdrawn after parade lap*	12/20
8	FRENCH GP	Magny Cours	11	Sauber Petronas	M	3.0 Sauber C24-Petronas V10	*1 lap behind*	10/20
14	BRITISH GP	Silverstone	11	Sauber Petronas	M	3.0 Sauber C24-Petronas V10	*bungled pit stop/1 lap behind*	11/20
15	GERMAN GP	Hockenheim	11	Sauber Petronas	M	3.0 Sauber C24-Petronas V10	*hit by Barrichello/3 laps behind*	14/20

ret	HUNGARIAN GP	Hungaroring	11	Sauber Petronas	M	3.0 Sauber C24-Petronas V10	engine fire	15/20
11	TURKISH GP	Istanbul	11	Sauber Petronas	M	3.0 Sauber C24-Petronas V10	*no time set/1 lap behind	*18/20
11	ITALIAN GP	Monza	11	Sauber Petronas	M	3.0 Sauber C24-Petronas V10	1 lap behind	12/20
6	BELGIAN GP	Spa	11	Sauber Petronas	M	3.0 Sauber C24-Petronas V10	survived collision with Karthikeyan	14/20
12	BRAZILIAN GP	Interlagos	11	Sauber Petronas	M	3.0 Sauber C24-Petronas V10	1 lap behind	12/20
12*	JAPANESE GP	Suzuka	11	Sauber Petronas	M	3.0 Sauber C24-Petronas V10	*11th but 25-sec pen – forced Trulli off	8/20
10	CHINESE GP	Shanghai	11	Sauber Petronas	M	3.0 Sauber C24-Petronas V10		12/20

2006 Championship position: 15th   Wins: 0   Pole positions: 0   Fastest laps: 0   Points scored: 7

ret	BAHRAIN GP	Bahrain	17	BMW Sauber F1 Team	M	2.4 BMW Sauber F1.06-BMW V8	engine	11/22
7	MALAYSIAN GP	Sepang	17	BMW Sauber F1 Team	M	2.4 BMW Sauber F1.06-BMW V8		14/22
6	AUSTRALIAN GP	Melbourne	17	BMW Sauber F1 Team	M	2.4 BMW Sauber F1.06-BMW V8		9/22
12	SAN MARINO GP	Imola	17	BMW Sauber F1 Team	M	2.4 BMW Sauber F1.06-BMW V8		12/22
8	EUROPEAN GP	Nürburgring	17	BMW Sauber F1 Team	M	2.4 BMW Sauber F1.06-BMW V8		8/22
12	SPANISH GP	Barcelona	17	BMW Sauber F1 Team	M	2.4 BMW Sauber F1.06-BMW V8	1 lap behind	14/22
14	MONACO GP	Monte Carlo	17	BMW Sauber F1 Team	M	2.4 BMW Sauber F1.06-BMW V8	1 lap behind	15/22
8	BRITISH GP	Silverstone	17	BMW Sauber F1 Team	M	2.4 BMW Sauber F1.06-BMW V8		10/22
ret	CANADIAN GP	Montreal	17	BMW Sauber F1 Team	M	2.4 BMW Sauber F1.06-BMW V8	crashed out lapping Ralf Schumacher	11/22
ret	U S GP	Indianapolis	17	BMW Sauber F1 Team	M	2.4 BMW Sauber F1.06-BMW V8	engine	6/22
11	FRENCH GP	Magny Cours	17	BMW Sauber F1 Team	M	2.4 BMW Sauber F1.06-BMW V8	1 lap behind	18/22
ret	GERMAN GP	Hockenheim	17	BMW Sauber F1 Team	M	2.4 BMW Sauber F1.06-BMW V8	hit Heidfeld – new nose/later crashed out	14/22

GP Starts: 163   GP Wins: 11   Pole positions: 13   Fastest laps: 9   Points: 235

LUIGI VILLORESI

SUCCESS and tragedy in equal measure marked the 25-year career of 'Gigi' Villoresi, the silver-haired Italian who was at his zenith in the immediate post-war era. He began racing in 1931 with Fiats, before turning to the marque that would make his name, Maserati. That was in 1936, and by then he and his brother, Emilio, had established a reputation as a pretty wild pair. Nevertheless, Luigi won the voiturette Brno GP in Czechoslovakia in 1937 to earn promotion to the Maserati grand prix team. He became the 1500cc Italian champion in 1938 and 1939, and took wins in the Albi, Pescara and South African GPs. He also won the Targa Florio in both 1939 and 1940, again in a Maserati, but the period was clouded by the death of Emilio, who by then was racing as a rival in the Alfa Romeo team.

During the Second World War, Villoresi was held as a prisoner of war, but immediately upon his release he was looking to race again. He and Giuseppe Farina soon vied for the title of Italy's fastest driver, and with Jean-Pierre Wimille he was regarded as the world's best. In 1946, he scored victories in Nice and the Circuit of Voghera with his Maserati, and took a 3-litre 8CL to Indianapolis, where he finished seventh. The following season, he notched up wins at Buenos Aires, Mar del Plata, Nimes, Nice, Strasbourg and Luxembourg. The 1948 season saw him suffer a major crash at Bremgarten, which he was lucky to survive, although he would triumph as Italian champion for the second successive year. Wins were recorded at Buenos Aires in two races, Comminges, Albi, Silverstone (the first post-war British GP) and Barcelona. After winning the Libre races at Interlagos and Gavea, Villoresi finally forsook his beloved Maserati to join Ferrari along with Alberto Ascari, to whom he passed on much of his racecraft. He was soon winning races for the Scuderia at Zandvoort in the supercharged car, and in Formula 2 at Brussels, Luxembourg, Rome and Garda.

The 1950 and 1951 seasons were spent chasing the Alfa Romeos, but Villoresi still found success aplenty; wins at Buenos Aires and Rosario were followed by more success at Marseilles, Erlen and Monza in 1950, while the following year saw a very consistent championship campaign with the Type 375, which he took to victory at Syracuse and Pau in non-title events. It was a good year for 'Gigi', for he won the Mille Miglia and was second in the Carrera Panamericana, and he shared a Lancia with Ascari to win the Sestrieres Rally. During 1952/53, he was forced to sit in the shadow of his brilliant pupil, Ascari, but could still do the job when required, taking wins at Turin and Modena.

Villoresi signed for Lancia for the 1954 season along with Ascari, but they were forced to wait for their Formula 1 car, which failed to appear until the last grand prix of the season. 'Gigi' raced for Maserati in the interim, but a crash in the Mille Miglia had dulled his edge. He continued with the Lancia concern in 1955, but after the death of Ascari and the subsequent amalgamation of the team with Ferrari, he found himself out of a works drive when the 1956 season began. By then well past his best, he drove privateer Maseratis and the works OSCA in sports car events. It was in this form of racing, driving a Maserati, that he suffered yet another serious injury when he crashed at Castelfusano and broke his leg very badly. Begged by his family to retire, he deferred to their wishes, but couldn't resist taking part in the 1958 Acropolis Rally, which he won in a Lancia.

VILLORESI, Luigi (I) b 16/5/1909, Milan – d 24/8/1997, Modena

	1950 Championship position: Unplaced							
	Race	Circuit	No	Entrant	Tyres	Capacity/Car/Engine	Comment	Q Pos/Entries
ret	MONACO GP	Monte Carlo	38	Scuderia Ferrari	P	1.5 s/c Ferrari 125 V12	transmission/rear axle	6/21
ret	SWISS GP	Bremgarten	22	Scuderia Ferrari	P	1.5 s/c Ferrari 125 V12	transmission	4/18
6	BELGIAN GP	Spa	2	Scuderia Ferrari	P	1.5 s/c Ferrari 125 V12	2 laps behind	4/14
dns	FRENCH GP	Reims	8	Scuderia Ferrari	P	1.5 s/c Ferrari 125/275 V12	withdrawn to race in F2 support	- / -
	1951 Championship position: 5th		Wins: 0	Pole positions: 0	Fastest laps: 0	Points scored: 18		
ret	SWISS GP	Bremgarten	18	Scuderia Ferrari	P	4.5 Ferrari 375F1 V12	crashed in rain	3/21
3	BELGIAN GP	Spa	10	Scuderia Ferrari	P	4.5 Ferrari 375F1 V12		3/13
3	FRENCH GP	Reims	10	Scuderia Ferrari	E	4.5 Ferrari 375F1 V12	3 laps behind	4/23
3	BRITISH GP	Silverstone	10	Scuderia Ferrari	P	4.5 Ferrari 375F1 V12	2 laps behind	5/20
4	GERMAN GP	Nürburgring	72	Scuderia Ferrari	P	4.5 Ferrari 375F1 V12		5/25
4	ITALIAN GP	Monza	4	Scuderia Ferrari	P	4.5 Ferrari 375F1 V12	1 lap behind	5/22
ret	SPANISH GP	Pedralbes	4	Scuderia Ferrari	P	4.5 Ferrari 375F1 V12	ignition	5/20
	1952 Championship position: 7th=		Wins: 0	Pole positions: 0	Fastest laps: 0	Points scored: 8		
3	DUTCH GP	Zandvoort	6	Scuderia Ferrari	P	2.0 Ferrari 500 4		4/18
3	ITALIAN GP	Monza	16	Scuderia Ferrari	P	2.0 Ferrari 500 4		2/35
	1953 Championship position: 5th		Wins: 0	Pole positions: 0	Fastest laps: 1	Points scored: 17		
2	ARGENTINE GP	Buenos Aires	14	Scuderia Ferrari	P	2.0 Ferrari 500 4	1 lap behind	3/16
ret	DUTCH GP	Zandvoort	4	Scuderia Ferrari	P	2.0 Ferrari 500 4	throttle cable/FL	4/20
2	BELGIAN GP	Spa	8	Scuderia Ferrari	P	2.0 Ferrari 500 4		5/22
6	FRENCH GP	Reims	12	Scuderia Ferrari	P	2.0 Ferrari 500 4		3/25
ret	BRITISH GP	Silverstone	7	Scuderia Ferrari	P	2.0 Ferrari 500 4	transmission	6/29
ret*	GERMAN GP	Nürburgring	4	Scuderia Ferrari	P	2.0 Ferrari 500 4	*Ascari took over car/engine	6/35
8*	“	“	1	Scuderia Ferrari	P	2.0 Ferrari 500 4	*took over Ascari's car/1 lap behind	- / -
6	SWISS GP	Bremgarten	28	Scuderia Ferrari	P	2.0 Ferrari 500 4	3 laps behind	6/23
3	ITALIAN GP	Monza	2	Scuderia Ferrari	P	2.0 Ferrari 500 4	1 lap behind	5/30
	1954 Championship position: 15th=		Wins: 0	Pole positions: 0	Fastest laps: 0	Points scored: 2		
5	FRENCH GP	Reims	14	Officine Alfieri Maserati	P	2.5 Maserati 250F 6	on loan from Lancia/3 laps behind	14/22
ret*	BRITISH GP	Silverstone	32	Officine Alfieri Maserati	P	2.5 Maserati 250F 6	*Ascari took over/oil pressure	27/31
dns	GERMAN GP	Nürburgring	5	Officine Alfieri Maserati	P	2.5 Maserati 250F 6	withdrawn after Marimón's death	(10)/23
ret	ITALIAN GP	Monza	22	Officine Alfieri Maserati	P	2.5 Maserati 250F 6	clutch	6/21
ret	SPANISH GP	Pedralbes	36	Scuderia Lancia	P	2.5 Lancia D50 V8	brakes	5/22
	1955 Championship position: 12th=		Wins: 0	Pole positions: 0	Fastest laps: 0	Points scored: 2		
ret	ARGENTINE GP	Buenos Aires	34	Scuderia Lancia	P	2.5 Lancia D50 V8	fuel pump	11/22
ret	“	“	36	Scuderia Lancia	P	2.5 Lancia D50 V8	took Castellotti's car – crashed	- / -
5	MONACO GP	Monte Carlo	28	Scuderia Lancia	P	2.5 Lancia D50 V8	1 lap behind	7/22
dns	ITALIAN GP	Monza	10	Scuderia Ferrari	P	2.5 Lancia D50 V8	tyre problems in practice	(8)/22
	1956 Championship position: 15th=		Wins: 0	Pole positions: 0	Fastest laps: 0	Points scored: 2		
5	BELGIAN GP	Spa	22	Scuderia Centro Sud	P	2.5 Maserati 250F 6	2 laps behind	11/16
ret	FRENCH GP	Reims	38	Luigi Piotti	P	2.5 Maserati 250F 6	brakes	10/20
6	BRITISH GP	Silverstone	11	Luigi Piotti	P	2.5 Maserati 250F 6	5 laps behind	19/28
ret	GERMAN GP	Nürburgring	18	Luigi Piotti	P	2.5 Maserati 250F 6	engine	- /20
ret*	ITALIAN GP	Monza	34	Officine Alfieri Maserati	P	2.5 Maserati 250F 6	*Bonnier took over car/engine	8/26

GP Starts: 31   GP Wins: 0   Pole positions: 0   Fastest laps: 1   Points: 49

Luigi Villoresi, in the beautiful Lancia D50 (28), jostles for position with the Maserati of Cesare Perdisa as they round the old Gasometer hairpin at the start of the 1955 Monaco Grand Prix.

OTTORINO VOLONTERIO

A LAWYER from Locarno, Ottorino Volonterio raced a Maserati sports car with a modicum of success, taking second place in the Coupe de Paris at Montlhéry in 1955. He shared Baron de Graffenried's Maserati at Pedralbes in 1954, but when he acquired the car for 1955 he was usually slow, sometimes hopelessly so.

In 1957, Volonterio purchased a Maserati 250F, but in the main he wisely left it to others to race; Herbert Mackay-Fraser practised the car for the GP de Reims, but was killed in the F2 supporting race. Ottorino did make one final appearance, at Monza, where he shared the car with André Simon, the pair trailing home some 15 laps behind.

RIKKY von OPEL

A N heir to the Opel automobile fortune, Rikky von Opel began his racing career under the pseudonym 'Antonio Bronco', but soon reverted to his true name after a successful introduction to Formula Ford in 1970.

Rikky jumped staight into Formula 3 the following year with a Lotus and showed much promise, which was realised in 1972 when, driving the Iberia-sponsored works F3 Ensign, he took the Lombard North Central title. He was so impressed with Mo Nunn's little team that he commissioned a Formula 1 car to go grand prix racing in 1973.

Inevitably with such an inexperienced pairing, success was thin on the ground, and von Opel was damned as a playboy racer, which was unfair, as he took the whole project very seriously indeed. When the opportunity arose to drive a pukka works Brabham at the beginning of the European season in 1974, he grabbed it, reasoning that he could learn much in this established team.

After he was unable qualify the car at Dijon for the French Grand Prix, von Opel turned his back on the sport, having tried, but failed to make the grade. He returned to his society lifestyle and pursued more leisurely interests.

VOLONTERIO, Ottorino (CH) b 7/12/1917, Orselina – d 10/3/2003, Lugano

1954 Championship position: Unplaced

	Race	Circuit	No	Entrant	Tyres	Capacity/Car/Engine	Comment	Q Pos/Entries
ret*	SPANISH GP	Pedralbes	22	Baron de Graffenried	P	2.5 Maserati A6GCM/250F 6	*took over de Graffenried's car/engine	– /22

1956 Championship position: Unplaced

	Race	Circuit	No	Entrant	Tyres	Capacity/Car/Engine	Comment	Q Pos/Entries
nc	GERMAN GP	Nürburgring	22	Ottorino Volonterio	P	2.5 Maserati A6GCM/250F 6	6 laps behind	19/21

1957 Championship position: Unplaced

	Race	Circuit	No	Entrant	Tyres	Capacity/Car/Engine	Comment	Q Pos/Entries
nc*	ITALIAN GP	Monza	28	Ottorino Volonterio	P	2.5 Maserati 250F 6	*shared with Simon/15 laps behind	– /19

GP Starts: 3   GP Wins: 0   Pole positions: 0   Fastest laps: 0   Points: 0

von OPEL, Rikky (FL) b 14/10/1947, New York, USA

1973 Championship position: Unplaced

	Race	Circuit	No	Entrant	Tyres	Capacity/Car/Engine	Comment	Q Pos/Entries
15	FRENCH GP	Paul Ricard	29	Team Ensign	F	3.0 Ensign N173-Cosworth V8	3 laps behind	25/25
13	BRITISH GP	Silverstone	28	Team Ensign	F	3.0 Ensign N173-Cosworth V8	pit stop – temperature gauge/-6 laps	21/29
dns	DUTCH GP	Zandvoort	28	Team Ensign	F	3.0 Ensign N173-Cosworth V8	suspension pick up failure	(14)/24
ret	AUSTRIAN GP	Österreichring	28	Team Ensign	F	3.0 Ensign N173-Cosworth V8	fuel pressure	19/25
ret	ITALIAN GP	Monza	28	Team Ensign	F	3.0 Ensign N173-Cosworth V8	overheating	17/25
nc	CANADIAN GP	Mosport Park	28	Team Ensign	F	3.0 Ensign N173-Cosworth V8	2 pit stops – ran off road/12 laps behind	26/26
ret	US GP	Watkins Glen	28	Team Ensign	F	3.0 Ensign N173-Cosworth V8	stuck throttle	28/28

1974 Championship position: Unplaced

	Race	Circuit	No	Entrant	Tyres	Capacity/Car/Engine	Comment	Q Pos/Entries
dns	ARGENTINE GP	Buenos Aires	22	Team Ensign	F	3.0 Ensign N174-Cosworth V8	handling problems in practice	26/26
ret	SPANISH GP	Jarama	8	Motor Racing Developments	F	3.0 Brabham BT44-Cosworth V8	oil leak	25/28
ret	BELGIAN GP	Nivelles	8	Motor Racing Developments	F	3.0 Brabham BT44-Cosworth V8	oil pressure	22/32
dnq	MONACO GP	Monte Carlo	8	Motor Racing Developments	F	3.0 Brabham BT44-Cosworth V8		28/28
9	SWEDISH GP	Anderstorp	8	Motor Racing Developments	F	3.0 Brabham BT44-Cosworth V8	1 lap behind	20/28
9	DUTCH GP	Zandvoort	8	Motor Racing Developments	F	3.0 Brabham BT44-Cosworth V8	2 laps behind	23/27
dnq	FRENCH GP	Dijon	8	Motor Racing Developments	F	3.0 Brabham BT44-Cosworth V8		28/30

GP Starts: 10   GP Wins: 0   Pole positions: 0   Fastest laps: 0   Points: 0

WOLFGANG von TRIPS

A DASHING, handsome and immensely popular German aristocrat, Wolfgang von Trips stood on the verge of the drivers' world championship at Monza on a sunny September day in 1961. Everything was going to plan: his red Ferrari sat on pole position at the head of a two-by-two grid, cunningly arranged by the organisers to help reduce the chances of any fast non-Italian machines gaining the all-important tow. When the flag dropped, however, von Trips was not the quickest away and was enmeshed in the leading bunch, which hammered around the banking to complete the first lap. The German was under pressure from the Lotus of Jim Clark, and when the young Scot pulled out of the Ferrari's slipstream in an attempt to pass, von Trips moved over too...

Clipping the front wheel of the Lotus sent the number four Ferrari out of control, and it crashed up a bank and along a fence packed with spectators before rolling back down to the track. The driver lay on the circuit, having been flung there like a rag doll; Jim Clark was wandering around unhurt, but in shock as the cars sped past on their third lap; and one driver and 14 spectators would pay the sport's ultimate price. The race went on, and von Trips' team-mate, Phil Hill, was crowned world champion, but the German was dead. Such were the stark realities of motor racing.

Von Trips had always lived on the edge and already had had two lucky escapes at the Monza track before he met his fate. On his first grand prix appearance in 1956, his participation was ended by a practice crash when the steering failed on his Lancia-Ferrari, but he escaped serious injury. In 1958, he collided with Harry Schell on the opening lap of the Italian Grand Prix and ended up with a broken leg.

Returning to action at the start of 1959, von Trips spun the works Formula 2 Porsche at Monaco and eliminated the rest of his class. This sorry tally makes him seem a liability, but that was far from the case, for from the earliest days, when he took a third place in the 1955 Tourist Trophy in a Mercedes 300SLR at Dundrod, he was a fearless and skilled driver, particularly in sports cars.

In 1956, Wolfgang was a doughty campaigner in the works Porsche, winning the 1.5-litre classes at Sebring with Hans Herrmann and the Nürburgring 1000km with Umberto Maglioli, and the Berlin Grand Prix outright.

In 1957, von Trips joined Ferrari to race their sports cars, taking a third place in the Buenos Aires 1000km and second place to Piero Taruffi in the Mille Miglia. He was also given a chance to handle the works Ferrari in three grand prix races; by finishing a fine third at Monza, he cemented his place on the team for the following season.

The 1958 season was one of tragedy for the Scuderia, with the deaths of Luigi Musso and Peter Collins, but von Trips scored valuable placings that helped Mike Hawthorn to become the world champion. In addition, he enjoyed success in Ferrari sports cars again and was the European hill-climb champion in a works Porsche RSK.

Von Trips was dropped from the Ferrari roster for 1959 and returned to competition with Porsche, driving their Formula 2 car and sharing the sports machine with Joakim Bonnier. They took class wins at Sebring and the Nürburgring, and 'Taffy' drove a brilliant race in the Tourist Trophy at Goodwood to finish second, ahead of Tony Brooks' more powerful Ferrari.

Back with Ferrari in 1960, von Trips was emerging as a trusty and reliable single-seater exponent. Apart from his solid placings in the championship races, with the ageing front-engined 246 Dino, he won at Syracuse and Solitude in the new T156 rear-engined car. In addition, he took a fine second place in the Formula 2-only German Grand Prix for Porsche, behind on-form team-mate Bonnier.

Wolfgang's work with the rear-engined prototype car set him up for the 1961 season and, with the new 156 'sharknose' Ferrari, he took his first grand prix win at Zandvoort in masterly style, followed by a solid second in the Belgian Grand Prix at Spa in a Ferrari 1-2-3-4 walk-over. In sports cars, the Targa Florio was won with Olivier Gendebien, and then back in Formula 1 he coped with the early wet conditions at Aintree to extend his championship lead. Even a second place behind genius Stirling Moss in the German Grand Prix seemed to be sufficient, for the next race was at Monza and surely the title would be his...

von TRIPS, Wolfgang (D) b 4/5/1928, Horrem, nr Cologne – d 10/9/1961, Monza Circuit, Italy

1956 Championship position: Unplaced

	Race	Circuit	No	Entrant	Tyres	Capacity/Car/Engine	Comment	Q Pos/Entries
dns	ITALIAN GP	Monza	50	Scuderia Ferrari	E	2.5 Lancia-Ferrari D50 V8	accident in practice	(=11)/26

1957 Championship position: 12th= Wins: 0 Pole positions: 0 Fastest laps: 0 Points scored: 4

	Race	Circuit	No	Entrant	Tyres	Capacity/Car/Engine	Comment	Q Pos/Entries
6*	ARGENTINE GP	Buenos Aires	18	Scuderia Ferrari	E	2.5 Lancia-Ferrari D50A V8	*Perdisa & Collins co-drove/2 laps behind	- /16
7/ret*	MONACO GP	Monte Carlo	24	Scuderia Ferrari	E	2.5 Lancia-Ferrari 801 V8	engine/*Hawthorn drove car for 4 laps	9/21
3	ITALIAN GP	Monza	36	Scuderia Ferrari	E	2.5 Lancia-Ferrari 801 V8	2 laps behind	8/19

1958 Championship position: 10th Wins: 0 Pole positions: 0 Fastest laps: 0 Points scored: 9

	Race	Circuit	No	Entrant	Tyres	Capacity/Car/Engine	Comment	Q Pos/Entries
ret	MONACO GP	Monte Carlo	40	Scuderia Ferrari	E	2.4 Ferrari Dino 246 V6	engine	12/28
3	FRENCH GP	Reims	6	Scuderia Ferrari	E	2.4 Ferrari Dino 246 V6		21/21
ret	BRITISH GP	Silverstone	3	Scuderia Ferrari	E	2.4 Ferrari Dino 246 V6	engine	11/21
4	GERMAN GP	Nürburgring	4	Scuderia Ferrari	E	2.4 Ferrari Dino 246 V6		5/26
5	PORTUGUESE GP	Oporto	24	Scuderia Ferrari	E	2.4 Ferrari Dino 246 V6	1 lap behind	6/15
ret	ITALIAN GP	Monza	16	Scuderia Ferrari	E	2.4 Ferrari Dino 246 V6	collision with Schell – broken leg	6/21

1959 Championship position: Unplaced

	Race	Circuit	No	Entrant	Tyres	Capacity/Car/Engine	Comment	Q Pos/Entries
ret	MONACO GP (F2)	Monte Carlo	6	Dr Ing hcf Porsche KG	D	1.5 Porsche 718 F4 F2	multiple accident	12/24
dns	GERMAN GP (F2)	AVUS	14	Dr Ing hcf Porsche KG	D	1.5 Porsche 718 F4 F2	withdrawn after Behra's accident	- / -
6	US GP	Sebring	4	Scuderia Ferrari	D	2.4 Ferrari Dino 246 V6	4 laps behind	6/19

1960 Championship position: 6th= Wins: 0 Pole positions: 0 Fastest laps: 0 Points scored: 10

	Race	Circuit	No	Entrant	Tyres	Capacity/Car/Engine	Comment	Q Pos/Entries
5	ARGENTINE GP	Buenos Aires	30	Scuderia Ferrari	D	2.4 Ferrari Dino 246 V6	1 lap behind	5/22
8/ret	MONACO GP	Monte Carlo	38	Scuderia Ferrari	D	2.4 Ferrari Dino 246 V6	clutch/39 laps behind	8/24
5	DUTCH GP	Zandvoort	2	Scuderia Ferrari	D	2.4 Ferrari Dino 246 V6	1 lap behind	15/21
dns	"	"	2	Scuderia Ferrari	D	2.4 Ferrari Dino 246P V6	practice only	- / -
ret	BELGIAN GP	Spa	26	Scuderia Ferrari	D	2.4 Ferrari Dino 246 V6	transmission	11/18
11/ret	FRENCH GP	Reims	4	Scuderia Ferrari	D	2.4 Ferrari Dino 246 V6	transmission/19 laps behind	5/23
6	BRITISH GP	Silverstone	11	Scuderia Ferrari	D	2.4 Ferrari Dino 246 V6	2 laps behind	7/25
4	PORTUGUESE GP	Oporto	28	Scuderia Ferrari	D	2.4 Ferrari Dino 246 V6		9/16
5	ITALIAN GP	Monza	22	Scuderia Ferrari	D	2.5 Ferrari Dino 246MP V6 F2	2 laps behind/1st in F2 class	6/16
9	US GP	Riverside	26	Scuderia Centro Sud	D	2.5 Cooper T51-Maserati 4	3 laps behind	16/23

1961 Championship position: 2nd Wins: 2 Pole positions: 1 Fastest laps: 0 Points scored: 33

	Race	Circuit	No	Entrant	Tyres	Capacity/Car/Engine	Comment	Q Pos/Entries
4/ret	MONACO GP	Monte Carlo	40	Scuderia Ferrari SpA SEFAC	D	1.5 Ferrari 156 V6	engine failed – crashed/2 laps behind	6/21
1	DUTCH GP	Zandvoort	3	Scuderia Ferrari Spa SEFAC	D	1.5 Ferrari 156 V6		2/17
2	BELGIAN GP	Spa	2	Scuderia Ferrari SpA SEFAC	D	1.5 Ferrari 156 V6		2/25
ret	FRENCH GP	Reims	20	Scuderia Ferrari SpA SEFAC	D	1.5 Ferrari 156 V6	engine	2/26
1	BRITISH GP	Aintree	4	Scuderia Ferrari SpA SEFAC	D	1.5 Ferrari 156 V6		=1/30
2	GERMAN GP	Nürburgring	3	Scuderia Ferrari SpA SEFAC	D	1.5 Ferrari 156 V6		5/27
ret	ITALIAN GP	Monza	4	Scuderia Ferrari SpA SEFAC	D	1.5 Ferrari 156 V6	collision with Clark – fatal accident	1/33

GP Starts: 27   GP Wins: 2   Pole positions: 1   Fastest laps: 0   Points: 56

Wolfgang von Trips takes the 'shark nose' Ferrari 156 V6 to victory in the 1961 Dutch Grand Prix at Zandvoort. The German aristocrat seemed set to win the world championship that year until his tragic fatal accident at Monza.

JO VONLANTHEN

A CAR trader from Frauenfeld in Switzerland, Jo Vonlanthen began racing in Formula Vee in 1968, before moving up to Formula 3 the following year, competing mostly in Germany due to the ban on motorsport in Switzerland. Hill-climbs were still allowed in his homeland, however, and this is where he found some success, before breaking out on to the circuits with a GRD. His performances won the 1972 Swiss Formula 3 championship.

Vonlanthen went into Formula 2 in 1973, also with a GRD, taking a third place in the Rome Grand Prix, but this was easily his best result until he came second behind Jacques Laffite in the opening round of the 1975 series at Estoril in a March 742-BMW, when most of the front-runners fell by the wayside.

His brief Formula 1 career lasted just two races in 1975, Jo obtaining private funding to buy a seat with Williams. He made the grid for the Austrian Grand Prix only because both Brian Henton and Wilson Fittipaldi had suffered practice mishaps, and Mark Donohue had crashed heavily on race morning. After taking a distant 14th place in the non-championship Swiss Grand Prix, held at the French Dijon circuit a week later, his budget was spent and his Formula 1 dream over.

Jo returned to Formula 2 on an irregular basis with a March 752 in 1976, but never really featured among the front-runners. His passion for the sport did not diminish, however, and he has built a very successful business based on his private collection of F1 cars, which he demonstrates at the many historic festivals around the globe.

FRED WACKER Jnr

A LTHOUGH deemed a socialite due to his fun-filled lifestyle, which included playing in two Jazz bands in the 1950s and 1960s, Fred Wacker, Jr was first and foremost a successful businessman who had made his fortune at the helm of Ammco Tools Inc, an automotive parts manufacturer. He was also a skilled SCCA racer and founder member of the Chicago branch, who competed regularly at the wheel of an Allard-Cadillac; he was a member of the Cunningham team that competed at Le Mans in 1951.

In 1952, Wacker was involved in an unfortunate accident with John Fitch at Watkins Glen, which in those days was a street course. A youngster sitting near the track was killed and a number of others badly injured when his Allard sideswiped the unprotected crowd. This led to a ban on open street racing in the United States thereafter.

The wealthy Wacker raced for Gordini on a number of occasions, taking a third place at Chimay in 1953 and fourth in the minor Cadours Grand Prix the following season.

In world championship grands prix, he was extremely lucky to escape with a lightly fractured skull after crashing the Gordini in practice for the 1953 Swiss Grand Prix. After his European adventures, he continued racing Allard sports cars at home, but had wound down his appearances by the end of the 1956 season.

VONLANTHEN, Jo (CH) b 31/5/1942, St Ursen

1975 Championship position: Unplaced

	Race	Circuit	No	Entrant	Tyres	Capacity/Car/Engine	Comment	Q Pos/Entries
ret	AUSTRIAN GP	Österreichring	20	Frank Williams Racing Cars	G	3.0 Williams FW03-Cosworth V8	engine	29/30

GP Starts: 1   GP Wins: 0   Pole positions: 0   Fastest laps: 0   Points: 0

WACKER Jnr, Frederick G. (USA) b 10/7/1918, Chicago, Illinois – d 16/7/1998, Lake Bluff, Illinois

1953 Championship position: Unplaced

	Race	Circuit	No	Entrant	Tyres	Capacity/Car/Engine	Comment	Q Pos/Entries
dns	DUTCH GP	Zandvoort	40	Equipe Gordini	E	2.0 Gordini Type 16 6	engine needed by Schell	– /20
9	BELGIAN GP	Spa	38	Equipe Gordini	E	2.0 Gordini Type 16 6	4 laps behind	15/22
dns	SWISS GP	Bremgarten	44	Equipe Gordini	E	2.0 Gordini Type 16 6	practice crash – fractured skull	– /23

1954 Championship position: Unplaced

	Race	Circuit	No	Entrant	Tyres	Capacity/Car/Engine	Comment	Q Pos/Entries
ret	SWISS GP	Bremgarten	14	Equipe Gordini	E	2.5 Gordini Type 16 6	transmission	15/16
6	ITALIAN GP	Monza	42	Equipe Gordini	E	2.5 Gordini Type 16 6	5 laps behind	18/21

GP Starts: 3   GP Wins: 0   Pole positions: 0   Fastest laps: 0   Points: 0

DAVE WALKER

A RUGGED Australian, Dave Walker had trained to be an accountant until a chance meeting with some motorsport enthusiasts took him hill-climbing. He travelled to Britain in 1962, dreaming of emulating the likes of Jack Brabham, but soon realised that he was too inexperienced to make it at this stage and hitch-hiked home to go racing in a more serious manner.

By 1966, Walker had returned to begin an on-off Formula 3 career, which saw him slowly climb the ladder. In 1967, he took the European trail in a Merlyn, winning a race at Ojatia, but during 1968 he was back in Formula Ford in the works Alexis. The following year saw him in a Lotus at the head of the field, which led to a dream move to the works Lotus F3 team in 1970, when he won the Lombank F3 championship. In 1971, he was back for more, securing both the Shell and Forward Trust titles.

Walker's grand prix debut in the Lotus turbine would set the tone for his unhappy F1 career, however; he crashed the car when a points finish was possible on the day. Nevertheless, he was chosen to partner Emerson Fittipaldi in 1972, but apart from a fifth place in the non-title Brazilian Grand Prix, the year was a personal disaster for him. While his Brazilian team-mate stormed to his first world championship, the Australian failed to score even a single point.

Set to race for GRD in Formula 2 in 1973, Dave's career never really got off the ground thereafter, as he suffered two separate road accidents, breaking a leg in one and badly injuring an arm in the other. He came back to race in 2-litre sports car events and Formula 2, and then had a brief stab at F5000 in 1975, before trying his hand at Canadian Formula Atlantic.

PETER WALKER

H AVING gained a certain notoriety for his aggressive, sliding style in Peter Whitehead's ERA before the Second World War, Peter Walker became one of the few drivers to glean much success in the E-Type ERA in the late 1940s, both on the circuits and on the hills, where he put in some stunning performances in 1948. He raced the ERA at the 1950 British GP with Tony Rolt, but it soon failed. He did well to finish the race the following year, however, when he took the hitherto unreliable BRM into seventh place, despite extreme discomfort from a burning-hot exhaust.

Signed by Jaguar in 1951 to race their sports cars, Walker shared his greatest triumphs with old friend Whitehead, the pair winning Le Mans and finishing second at Dundrod in the Tourist Trophy. In addition, he took second place at Le Mans in 1953, this time with Stirling Moss.

Having moved to Aston Martin, Peter won the Goodwood nine-hours with Dennis Poore in 1955, and raced single-seaters once more at Zandvoort (for Moss) and Aintree (for Rob Walker). After escaping a nasty accident at Le Mans in 1956 relatively lightly, he decided to retire, although he was tempted back one more time, to race Rob Walker's Connaught at Syracuse in 1957.

HEINI WALTER

A SWISS amateur, Heini Walter had developed a passion for racing while working in his parents' motorcycle and bicycle workshop. He had trained to be a driving instructor before eventually going into the restaurant business, but also owned a small garage that was used for the preparation of his racing cars. He began competing in hill-climbs in 1947 with a pre-war Bugatti, and he was only seen intermittently due to the pressures of the family businesses. The purchase of a Merkel-Porsche for the 1955 season put him on the map for the wrong reasons. He was a runaway winner of the 1100cc class, but his car was found to be illegal and he was disqualified from the results.

In 1957, Heini bought a Porsche Spyder and immediately began to find success, particularly when he acquired an RSK model to race on both circuits and in hill-climbs. He was an extremely able driver who became European mountain-climb champion in both 1960 and 1961, and he drove sensibly in the Filipinetti Porsche at the German Grand Prix, his only major appearance in a single-seater.

Later Walter concentrated on hill-climbs with a Porsche 904, taking the GT class in the 1964 European hill-climb championship. For a while, he raced a Ferrari 250LM, before returning to his beloved Porsche marque with an ex-works 910, with which he finished his career in 1967.

WALKER, Dave (AUS) b 10/6/1941, Sydney, New South Wales

1971 Championship position: Unplaced

	Race	Circuit	No	Entrant	Tyres	Capacity/Car/Engine	Comment	Q Pos/Entries
ret	DUTCH GP	Zandvoort	15	Gold Leaf Team Lotus	F	Turbine Lotus 56B-Pratt & Witney	crashed in the rain	22/24
dns	"	"	12	Gold Leaf Team Lotus	F	3.0 Lotus 72D-Cosworth V8	practice only	– / –

1972 Championship position: Unplaced

	Race	Circuit	No	Entrant	Tyres	Capacity/Car/Engine	Comment	Q Pos/Entries
dsq	ARGENTINE GP	Buenos Aires	12	John Player Team Lotus	F	3.0 Lotus 72D-Cosworth V8	outside assistance	20/22
10	SOUTH AFRICAN GP	Kyalami	9	John Player Team Lotus	F	3.0 Lotus 72D-Cosworth V8	1 lap behind	=18/27
9/ret	SPANISH GP	Jarama	21	John Player Team Lotus	F	3.0 Lotus 72D-Cosworth V8	out of fuel/3 laps behind	24/26
14	MONACO GP	Monte Carlo	9	John Player Team Lotus	F	3.0 Lotus 72D-Cosworth V8	pit stop – handling/5 laps behind	14/25
14	BELGIAN GP	Nivelles	33	John Player Team Lotus	F	3.0 Lotus 72D-Cosworth V8	2 pit stops – tyres-oil pressure/-6 laps	12/26
18/ret	FRENCH GP	Clermont Ferrand	6	John Player Team Lotus	F	3.0 Lotus 72D-Cosworth V8	gearbox/4 laps behind	26/29
ret	BRITISH GP	Brands Hatch	9	John Player Team Lotus	F	3.0 Lotus 72D-Cosworth V8	rear suspension	=14/27
ret	GERMAN GP	Nürburgring	25	John Player Team Lotus	F	3.0 Lotus 72D-Cosworth V8	oil tank	23/27
ret	AUSTRIAN GP	Österreichring	21	John Player Team Lotus	F	3.0 Lotus 72D-Cosworth V8	engine	19/26
ret	US GP	Watkins Glen	11	John Player Team Lotus	F	3.0 Lotus 72D-Cosworth V8	engine	31/32

GP Starts: 11   GP Wins: 0   Pole positions: 0   Fastest laps: 0   Points: 0

WALKER, Peter (GB) b 7/12/1912, Leeds, Yorkshire – d 1/3/1984, Newtown, Worcester

1950 Championship position: Unplaced

	Race	Circuit	No	Entrant	Tyres	Capacity/Car/Engine	Comment	Q Pos/Entries
ret*	BRITISH GP	Silverstone	9	Peter Walker	D	1.5 s/c ERA E Type 6	*shared car with Rolt/gearbox	10/21

1951 Championship position: Unplaced

	Race	Circuit	No	Entrant	Tyres	Capacity/Car/Engine	Comment	Q Pos/Entries
7	BRITISH GP	Silverstone	7	BRM Ltd	D	1.5 s/c BRM P15 V16	burnt by exhaust/6 laps behind	19/20

1955 Championship position: Unplaced

	Race	Circuit	No	Entrant	Tyres	Capacity/Car/Engine	Comment	Q Pos/Entries
ret	DUTCH GP	Zandvoort	26	Stirling Moss Ltd	D	2.5 Maserati 250F 6	wheel bearing	10/16
ret	BRITISH GP	Silverstone	36	R R C Walker Racing Team	D	2.5 Connaught B-Alta 4	*shared car with Rolt/throttle cable	– /25

GP Starts: 4   GP Wins: 0   Pole positions: 0   Fastest laps: 0   Points: 0

WALTER, Heini (CH) b 28/7/1927, Alpthal – d 12/5/2009, Aesch

1962 Championship position: Unplaced

	Race	Circuit	No	Entrant	Tyres	Capacity/Car/Engine	Comment	Q Pos/Entries
14	GERMAN GP	Nürburgring	32	Ecurie Filipinetti	D	1.5 Porsche 718 F4	1 lap behind	14/30

GP Starts: 1   GP Wins: 0   Pole positions: 0   Fastest laps: 0   Points: 0

WARD, Rodger (USA) b 10/1/1921, Beloit, Kansas – d 5/7/2004, Anaheim, California

1959 Championship position: Unplaced

	Race	Circuit	No	Entrant	Tyres	Capacity/Car/Engine	Comment	Q Pos/Entries
ret	US GP	Sebring	1	Leader Cards Incorporated	–	1.75 Kurtis Kraft-Offenhauser 4	clutch/ran midget car – outclassed	19/19
	1963	Championship position: Unplaced						
ret	US GP	Watkins Glen	18	Reg Parnell (Racing)	D	1.5 Lotus 24-BRM V8	gear selection	17/21

GP Starts: 2   GP Wins: 0   Pole positions: 0   Fastest laps: 0   Points: 0

RODGER WARD

HAVING learned about cars at his father's scrapyard, Rodger Ward soon built himself a hot rod, which might have got him into trouble if the Second World War hadn't taken him into the air force, where he was trained as a pilot. He was stationed in Wichita Falls, Texas, and the local midget track proved an irresistible attraction. His daredevil style won him many fans, and after a breakthrough race in 1950 at Gilmore, where he beat the Offys with his Ford, and winning the 1951 AAA stock car title, he felt he was ready to tackle Indianapolis.

For a number of years, Ward's luck was out. Indeed, he was fortunate to escape serious injury in a fatal accident involving his close friend, Bill Vukovitch, during the 1955 race. He seriously thought about quitting, but eventually began to rebuild his career, winning three USAC races in 1957 while his bad luck at Indy continued. It all changed in 1959, however, when he finally won the Indianapolis 500, starting a run of successes at the 'Brickyard' (first/second/third/first/fourth/second) that extended through to 1964. With a total of 26 USAC career victories, he is one of Indy car racing's all-time greats.

Rodger perhaps holds the unwanted distinction of having raced the most unsuitable machine ever to appear in a Formula 1 grand prix when he ran a Kurtis Midget at the first ever US Grand Prix at Sebring in 1959. Sometimes he stepped away from his USAC programme to race in sports cars with a Cooper Monaco, and in 1963 he made his second F1 appearance, at Walkins Glen in the US Grand Prix, this time with more suitable machinery – a Lotus 24-BRM V8.

SOMETIMES there seems to be no justice in motor racing. For a driver as committed and talented as Derek Warwick to have toiled for more than a decade and taken part in nearly 150 grands prix without even a single victory must be particularly galling. Yet there is no bitterness from the down-to-earth Hampshireman who, in the early days of his Formula 1 career, looked a likelier prospect than Nigel Mansell.

After the hurly-burly of stock car racing, where he was crowned world champion in 1973, Derek funded his own early career in Formula Ford. He took second place in the 1976 DJM championship in a Hawke, before moving into Formula 3 the following year with a Chevron, when he did very well in his privateer car, taking numerous second places, but not quite cracking a win at this level

That changed in 1978 when Warwick became embroiled in a terrific three-way battle with Nelson Piquet and Chico Serra, winning the Vandervell F3 championship and emerging as runner-up to the former in the BP series. In total, he won ten races with his Ralt RT1-Toyota.

Moving to Formula 2 in 1979 with a Theodore Racing-entered March brought little cheer, a fifth place at Mugello being Derek's only worthwhile finish, but a switch to Toleman for 1980 signalled the start of a great relationship with the emerging team. That first year was in Formula 2, and he won two races (at Silverstone and Monza) as his more experienced team-mate, Brian Henton, took the coveted European title. Flushed with their success, Toleman made the jump to Formula 1 the following year, but it proved to be a tough baptism for Warwick, who managed to qualify only at the season's final race.

Things could only get better, and they did. In 1982 and 1983, Warwick battled away in the Pirelli-shod turbo car, scrapping ferociously for every place, no matter how far down the field. No doubt this fighting spirit helped to earn him his chance when the call came from Renault to race for them in 1984. He would never get closer to that elusive grand prix win than on his debut for the team at Rio, where he was leading comfortably when the suspension collapsed. Somehow the blow seemed to set the tone for a season that failed to meet expectations of both the car and driver.

Then came the worst decision of Warwick's career – to stay with Renault in 1985. The year was a personal disaster, and the offer of a seat at Williams, which he rejected and was taken by Mansell instead, must always haunt him. When the French team pulled the plug on their Formula 1 effort, and with Ayrton Senna blocking his move to Lotus, Derek became an out-of-work grand prix driver. A Jaguar sports car ride was his only realistic option for 1986, but he did a fine job for the team, missing the drivers' championship by just one point.

However, the tragic death of Elio de Angelis led to his swift return to the grand prix scene with the difficult 'lowline' Brabham BT55, a car with which nobody could have found success.

Warwick then joined Arrows who, like their new driver, were still looking for their first grand prix victory, and this was their tenth season of trying. In the three years he was with the team, a few worthwhile results were achieved, but the cars were mediocrity personified. A switch to the well-funded, but disorganised Lotus team in 1990 was probably the bottom of the barrel for poor Derek, who showed incredible bravery at Monza, where he crashed spectacularly at the exit of the Parabolica, only to calmly walk back to the pits to take the spare car for the inevitable restart, and then at Jerez, where he raced despite Martin Donnelly's disturbing accident in practice.

Derek took another Formula 1 sabbatical to return to sports car racing, first with Jaguar in 1991 and then the following year with Peugeot, with whom he enjoyed the sweet taste of victory at Le Mans and also shared the drivers' championship with team-mate Yannick Dalmas. His cheery presence could be found in the Formula 1 paddocks yet again in 1993, however, as he teamed up with Jackie Oliver once more in the renamed Footwork team. The year was better than the team had experienced for some time, but even with the expensive acquisition of the TAG/McLaren active suspension system, the cars were top-six runners at best.

At the end of the season, rightly no longer interested in Formula 1 if he could not have a competitive car, Warwick stepped back to consider his options, which as it turned out were none, or none that excited him. So he took a year out before signing to drive for Alfa Romeo in the 1995 BTCC. Unfortunately, once again it was the story of Derek's career: right car, wrong time.

Apart from sharing a Courage at Le Mans with Jan Lammers and Mario Andretti, Warwick then took another sabbatical to set up his own BTCC team, Triple Eight Race Engineering, which would run the works Vauxhall Vectras. Two seasons of driving one of the cars brought more frustration than success, although a win at Knockhill in 1998 gave him the satisfaction of claiming a BTCC victory before standing down from driving duties to continue in a management role with his team.

Derek then stepped away from the sport to concentrate on his car dealership in St Helier, Jersey, where he resides. In 2011, he was asked to take over the role of president of the BRDC at Silverstone from Damon Hill. He received a ringing endorsement from the membership, who appreciate to a man the sound practical qualities that he possesses to help drive forward the redevelopment of the circuit complex in the 21st century.

WARWICK, Derek (GB) b 27/8/1954, Alresford, Hampshire

1981 Championship position: Unplaced

	Race	Circuit	No	Entrant	Tyres	Capacity/Car/Engine	Comment	Q Pos/Entries
dnq	SAN MARINO GP	Imola	36	Candy Toleman Motorsport	M	1.5 t/c Toleman TG181-Hart 4		29/30
dnq	BELGIAN GP	Zolder	36	Candy Toleman Motorsport	P	1.5 t/c Toleman TG181-Hart 4		29/31
dnpq	MONACO GP	Monte Carlo	36	Candy Toleman Motorsport	P	1.5 t/c Toleman TG181-Hart 4		31/31
dnq	SPANISH GP	Jarama	36	Candy Toleman Motorsport	P	1.5 t/c Toleman TG181-Hart 4		29/30
dnq	FRENCH GP	Dijon	36	Candy Toleman Motorsport	P	1.5 t/c Toleman TG181-Hart 4		29/29
dnq	BRITISH GP	Silverstone	36	Candy Toleman Motorsport	P	1.5 t/c Toleman TG181-Hart 4		29/30
dnq	GERMAN GP	Hockenheim	36	Candy Toleman Motorsport	P	1.5 t/c Toleman TG181-Hart 4		28/30
dnq	AUSTRIAN GP	Österreichring	36	Candy Toleman Motorsport	P	1.5 t/c Toleman TG181-Hart 4		26/28
dnq	DUTCH GP	Zandvoort	36	Candy Toleman Motorsport	P	1.5 t/c Toleman TG181-Hart 4		30/30
dnq	ITALIAN GP	Monza	36	Candy Toleman Motorsport	P	1.5 t/c Toleman TG181-Hart 4		27/30
dnq	CANADIAN GP	Montreal	36	Candy Toleman Motorsport	P	1.5 t/c Toleman TG181-Hart 4		29/30
ret	CAESARS PALACE GP	Las Vegas	36	Candy Toleman Motorsport	P	1.5 t/c Toleman TG181-Hart 4	gearbox	22/30

1982 Championship position: Unplaced   Fastest laps: 1

	Race	Circuit	No	Entrant	Tyres	Capacity/Car/Engine	Comment	Q Pos/Entries
ret	SOUTH AFRICAN GP	Kyalami	35	Candy Toleman Motorsport	P	1.5 t/c Toleman TG181C-Hart 4	accident	14/30

dnq	BRAZILIAN GP	Rio	35	Candy Toleman Motorsport	P	1.5 t/c Toleman TG181C-Hart 4		30/31
dnpq	US GP WEST	Long Beach	35	Candy Toleman Motorsport	P	1.5 t/c Toleman TG181C-Hart 4		31/31
ret/dns*	SAN MARINO GP	Imola	35	Toleman Group Motorsport	P	1.5 t/c Toleman TG181C-Hart 4	*electrics on parade lap	(8)/14
ret	BELGIAN GP	Zolder	35	Toleman Group Motorsport	P	1.5 t/c Toleman TG181C-Hart 4	driveshaft	21/32
dnq	MONACO GP	Monte Carlo	35	Toleman Group Motorsport	P	1.5 t/c Toleman TG181C-Hart 4		24/31
ret	DUTCH GP	Zandvoort	35	Toleman Group Motorsport	P	1.5 t/c Toleman TG181C-Hart 4	engine/FL	13/31
ret	BRITISH GP	Brands Hatch	35	Toleman Group Motorsport	P	1.5 t/c Toleman TG181C-Hart 4	driveshaft – c.v. joint	16/30
15	FRENCH GP	Paul Ricard	35	Toleman Group Motorsport	P	1.5 t/c Toleman TG181C-Hart 4	pit stop/4 laps behind	14/30
10	GERMAN GP	Hockenheim	35	Toleman Group Motorsport	P	1.5 t/c Toleman TG181C-Hart 4	pit stop/2 laps behind	15/30
ret	AUSTRIAN GP	Österreichring	35	Toleman Group Motorsport	P	1.5 t/c Toleman TG181C-Hart 4	rear suspension	15/29
ret	SWISS GP	Dijon	35	Toleman Group Motorsport	P	1.5 t/c Toleman TG181C-Hart 4	engine	21/29
ret	ITALIAN GP	Monza	35	Toleman Group Motorsport	P	1.5 t/c Toleman TG183-Hart 4	spin – hit by Henton	16/30
ret	CAESARS PALACE GP	Las Vegas	35	Toleman Group Motorsport	P	1.5 t/c Toleman TG183-Hart 4	misfire – sparking plugs	10/30

1983 Championship position: 14th   Wins: 0   Pole positions: 0   Fastest laps: 0   Points scored: 9

8	BRAZILIAN GP	Rio	35	Candy Toleman Motorsport	P	1.5 t/c Toleman TG183B-Hart 4	1 lap behind	5/27
ret	US GP WEST	Long Beach	35	Candy Toleman Motorsport	P	1.5 t/c Toleman TG183B-Hart 4	tyre failure – accident	6/28
ret	FRENCH GP	Paul Ricard	35	Candy Toleman Motorsport	P	1.5 t/c Toleman TG183B-Hart 4	split water pipe – engine	9/29
ret	SAN MARINO GP	Imola	35	Candy Toleman Motorsport	P	1.5 t/c Toleman TG183B-Hart 4	spun off	14/28
ret	MONACO GP	Monte Carlo	35	Candy Toleman Motorsport	P	1.5 t/c Toleman TG183B-Hart 4	accident with Surer	10/28
7	BELGIAN GP	Spa	35	Candy Toleman Motorsport	P	1.5 t/c Toleman TG183B-Hart 4	2 pit stops – tyre – fuel	22/28
ret	US GP (DETROIT)	Detroit	35	Candy Toleman Motorsport	P	1.5 t/c Toleman TG183B-Hart 4	water leak – engine	9/27
ret	CANADIAN GP	Montreal	35	Candy Toleman Motorsport	P	1.5 t/c Toleman TG183B-Hart 4	engine – turbo	12/28
ret	BRITISH GP	Silverstone	35	Candy Toleman Motorsport	P	1.5 t/c Toleman TG183B-Hart 4	gearbox	10/29
ret	GERMAN GP	Hockenheim	35	Candy Toleman Motorsport	P	1.5 t/c Toleman TG183B-Hart 4	engine	9/29
ret	AUSTRIAN GP	Österreichring	35	Candy Toleman Motorsport	P	1.5 t/c Toleman TG183B-Hart 4	turbo	10/29
4	DUTCH GP	Zandvoort	35	Candy Toleman Motorsport	P	1.5 t/c Toleman TG183B-Hart 4	pit stop – fuel	7/29
6	ITALIAN GP	Monza	35	Candy Toleman Motorsport	P	1.5 t/c Toleman TG183B-Hart 4	pit stop – fuel	12/29
5	EUROPEAN GP	Brands Hatch	35	Candy Toleman Motorsport	P	1.5 t/c Toleman TG183B-Hart 4	pit stop – fuel	11/29
4	SOUTH AFRICAN GP	Kyalami	35	Candy Toleman Motorsport	P	1.5 t/c Toleman TG183B-Hart 4	pit stop – fuel/1 lap behind	13/26

1984 Championship position: 7th   Wins: 0   Pole positions: 0   Fastest laps: 1   Points scored: 23

ret	BRAZILIAN GP	Rio	16	Equipe Renault Elf	M	1.5 t/c Renault RE50 V6	hit by Lauda – suspension	3/27
3	SOUTH AFRICAN GP	Kyalami	16	Equipe Renault Elf	M	1.5 t/c Renault RE50 V6	1 lap behind	9/27
2	BELGIAN GP	Zolder	16	Equipe Renault Elf	M	1.5 t/c Renault RE50 V6		4/27
4	SAN MARINO GP	Imola	16	Equipe Renault Elf	M	1.5 t/c Renault RE50 V6	1 lap behind	4/28
ret	FRENCH GP	Dijon	16	Equipe Renault Elf	M	1.5 t/c Renault RE50 V6	accident with Surer	7/27
ret	MONACO GP	Monte Carlo	16	Equipe Renault Elf	M	1.5 t/c Renault RE50 V6	accident with Tambay	5/27
ret	CANADIAN GP	Montreal	16	Equipe Renault Elf	M	1.5 t/c Renault RE50 V6	loose underbody	4/26
ret	US GP (DETROIT)	Detroit	16	Equipe Renault Elf	M	1.5 t/c Renault RE50 V6	gearbox/FL	6/27
ret	US GP (DALLAS)	Dallas	16	Equipe Renault Elf	M	1.5 t/c Renault RE50 V6	spun off	3/27
2	BRITISH GP	Brands Hatch	16	Equipe Renault Elf	M	1.5 t/c Renault RE50 V6		6/27
3	GERMAN GP	Hockenheim	16	Equipe Renault Elf	M	1.5 t/c Renault RE50 V6		3/27
ret	AUSTRIAN GP	Österreichring	16	Equipe Renault Elf	M	1.5 t/c Renault RE50 V6	engine	6/28
ret	DUTCH GP	Zandvoort	16	Equipe Renault Elf	M	1.5 t/c Renault RE50 V6	spun off on oil	4/27
ret	ITALIAN GP	Monza	16	Equipe Renault Elf	M	1.5 t/c Renault RE50 V6	oil pressure	12/27
11/ret	EUROPEAN GP	Nürburgring	16	Equipe Renault Elf	M	1.5 t/c Renault RE50 V6	engine/6 laps behind	7/26
ret	PORTUGUESE GP	Estoril	16	Equipe Renault Elf	M	1.5 t/c Renault RE50 V6	gearbox	9/27

1985 Championship position: 13th=   Wins: 0   Pole positions: 0   Fastest laps: 0   Points scored: 5

10	BRAZILIAN GP	Rio	16	Equipe Renault Elf	G	1.5 t/c Renault RE60 V6	2 pit stops – plugs – tyres/-4 laps	10/25
7	PORTUGUESE GP	Estoril	16	Equipe Renault Elf	G	1.5 t/c Renault RE60 V6	2 laps behind	6/26
10	SAN MARINO GP	Imola	16	Equipe Renault Elf	G	1.5 t/c Renault RE60 V6	spin/pit stop – electrics/4 laps behind	14/26
5	MONACO GP	Monte Carlo	16	Equipe Renault Elf	G	1.5 t/c Renault RE60 V6	1 lap behind	10/26
ret	CANADIAN GP	Montreal	16	Equipe Renault Elf	G	1.5 t/c Renault RE60 V6	accident	6/25
ret	US GP (DETROIT)	Detroit	16	Equipe Renault Elf	G	1.5 t/c Renault RE60 V6	transmission	6/25
7	FRENCH GP	Paul Ricard	16	Equipe Renault Elf	G	1.5 t/c Renault RE60 V6		11/26
5	BRITISH GP	Silverstone	16	Equipe Renault Elf	G	1.5 t/c Renault RE60B V6	1 lap behind	12/26
ret	GERMAN GP	Nürburgring	16	Equipe Renault Elf	G	1.5 t/c Renault RE60B V6	ignition	20/27
ret	AUSTRIAN GP	Österreichring	16	Equipe Renault Elf	G	1.5 t/c Renault RE60B V6	engine	13/27
ret	DUTCH GP	Zandvoort	16	Equipe Renault Elf	G	1.5 t/c Renault RE60B V6	gearbox	12/27
ret	ITALIAN GP	Monza	16	Equipe Renault Elf	G	1.5 t/c Renault RE60B V6	transmission	12/26
6	BELGIAN GP	Spa	16	Equipe Renault Elf	G	1.5 t/c Renault RE60B V6	1 lap behind	14/24
ret	EUROPEAN GP	Brands Hatch	16	Equipe Renault Elf	G	1.5 t/c Renault RE60B V6	fuel injection	8/27
ret	AUSTRALIAN GP	Adelaide	16	Equipe Renault Elf	G	1.5 t/c Renault RE60B V6	transmission	12/25

1986 Championship position: Unplaced

ret	CANADIAN GP	Montreal	8	Motor Racing Developments Ltd	P	1.5 t/c Brabham BT55-BMW 4	engine	10/25
10	US GP (DETROIT)	Detroit	8	Motor Racing Developments Ltd	P	1.5 t/c Brabham BT55-BMW 4	pit stop – tyres/3 laps behind	15/26
9	FRENCH GP	Paul Ricard	8	Motor Racing Developments Ltd	P	1.5 t/c Brabham BT55-BMW 4	gearbox trouble/3 laps behind	14/26
8	BRITISH GP	Brands Hatch	8	Motor Racing Developments Ltd	P	1.5 t/c Brabham BT55-BMW 4	2 pit stops – tyres/3 laps behind	9/26
7	GERMAN GP	Hockenheim	8	Motor Racing Developments Ltd	P	1.5 t/c Brabham BT55-BMW 4	1 lap behind	20/26
ret	HUNGARIAN GP	Hungaroring	8	Motor Racing Developments Ltd	P	1.5 t/c Brabham BT55-BMW 4	accident with Alboreto	19/26
dns	AUSTRIAN GP	Österreichring	8	Motor Racing Developments Ltd	P	1.5 t/c Brabham BT55-BMW 4	Patrese took over car for race	(10)/26
ret	ITALIAN GP	Monza	8	Motor Racing Developments Ltd	P	1.5 t/c Brabham BT55-BMW 4	brakes – spun off	7/27
ret	PORTUGUESE GP	Estoril	8	Motor Racing Developments Ltd	P	1.5 t/c Brabham BT55-BMW 4	electrics	12/27
ret	MEXICAN GP	Mexico City	8	Motor Racing Developments Ltd	P	1.5 t/c Brabham BT55-BMW 4	engine	7/26
ret	AUSTRALIAN GP	Adelaide	8	Motor Racing Developments Ltd	P	1.5 t/c Brabham BT55-BMW 4	brakes	20/26

1987 Championship position: 16th=   Wins: 0   Pole positions: 0   Fastest laps: 0   Points scored: 3

ret	BRAZILIAN GP	Rio	17	USF&G Arrows Megatron	G	1.5 t/c Arrows A10-Megatron 4	engine	8/23
11/ret	SAN MARINO GP	Imola	17	USF&G Arrows Megatron	G	1.5 t/c Arrows A10-Megatron 4	out of fuel/4 laps behind	11/27
ret	BELGIAN GP	Spa	17	USF&G Arrows Megatron	G	1.5 t/c Arrows A10-Megatron 4	water hose	12/26
ret	MONACO GP	Monte Carlo	17	USF&G Arrows Megatron	G	1.5 t/c Arrows A10-Megatron 4	gear linkage	11/26

ret	US GP (DETROIT)	Detroit	17	USF&G Arrows Megatron	G	1.5 t/c Arrows A10-Megatron 4	hit wall	10/26
ret	FRENCH GP	Paul Ricard	17	USF&G Arrows Megatron	G	1.5 t/c Arrows A10-Megatron 4	turbo	10/26
5	BRITISH GP	Silverstone	17	USF&G Arrows Megatron	G	1.5 t/c Arrows A10-Megatron 4		13/26
ret	GERMAN GP	Hockenheim	17	USF&G Arrows Megatron	G	1.5 t/c Arrows A10-Megatron 4	turbo	13/26
6	HUNGARIAN GP	Hungaroring	17	USF&G Arrows Megatron	G	1.5 t/c Arrows A10-Megatron 4	2 laps behind	9/26
ret	AUSTRIAN GP	Österreichring	17	USF&G Arrows Megatron	G	1.5 t/c Arrows A10-Megatron 4	engine	11/26
ret	ITALIAN GP	Monza	17	USF&G Arrows Megatron	G	1.5 t/c Arrows A10-Megatron 4	electrics	12/28
13	PORTUGUESE GP	Estoril	17	USF&G Arrows Megatron	G	1.5 t/c Arrows A10-Megatron 4	2 spins/4 laps behind	12/27
10	SPANISH GP	Jerez	17	USF&G Arrows Megatron	G	1.5 t/c Arrows A10-Megatron 4	2 laps behind	12/28
ret	MEXICAN GP	Mexico City	17	USF&G Arrows Megatron	G	1.5 t/c Arrows A10-Megatron 4	hit by Nakajima	11/27
10	JAPANESE GP	Suzuka	17	USF&G Arrows Megatron	G	1.5 t/c Arrows A10-Megatron 4	1 lap behind	14/27
ret	AUSTRALIAN GP	Adelaide	17	USF&G Arrows Megatron	G	1.5 t/c Arrows A10-Megatron 4	transmission	12/27

1988 Championship position: 17th=   Wins: 0   Pole positions: 0   Fastest laps: 0   Points scored: 17

4	BRAZILIAN GP	Rio	17	USF&G Arrows Megatron	G	1.5 t/c Arrows A10B-Megatron 4		11/31
9	SAN MARINO GP	Imola	17	USF&G Arrows Megatron	G	1.5 t/c Arrows A10B-Megatron 4	2 laps behind	14/31
4	MONACO GP	Monte Carlo	17	USF&G Arrows Megatron	G	1.5 t/c Arrows A10B-Megatron 4	1 lap behind	7/30
5	MEXICAN GP	Mexico City	17	USF&G Arrows Megatron	G	1.5 t/c Arrows A10B-Megatron 4	1 lap behind	9/30
7	CANADIAN GP	Montreal	17	USF&G Arrows Megatron	G	1.5 t/c Arrows A10B-Megatron 4	2 laps behind	16/31
ret	US GP (DETROIT)	Detroit	17	USF&G Arrows Megatron	G	1.5 t/c Arrows A10B-Megatron 4	stuck throttle – crashed	9/31
ret	FRENCH GP	Paul Ricard	17	USF&G Arrows Megatron	G	1.5 t/c Arrows A10B-Megatron 4	spun off avoiding Nakajima	11/31
6	BRITISH GP	Silverstone	17	USF&G Arrows Megatron	G	1.5 t/c Arrows A10B-Megatron 4	1 lap behind	9/31
7	GERMAN GP	Hockenheim	17	USF&G Arrows Megatron	G	1.5 t/c Arrows A10B-Megatron 4	1 lap behind	12/31
ret	HUNGARIAN GP	Hungaroring	17	USF&G Arrows Megatron	G	1.5 t/c Arrows A10B-Megatron 4	brakes	12/31
5*	BELGIAN GP	Spa	17	USF&G Arrows Megatron	G	1.5 t/c Arrows A10B-Megatron 4	*3rd & 4th place cars disqualified	10/31
4	ITALIAN GP	Monza	17	USF&G Arrows Megatron	G	1.5 t/c Arrows A10B-Megatron 4		6/31
4	PORTUGUESE GP	Estoril	17	USF&G Arrows Megatron	G	1.5 t/c Arrows A10B-Megatron 4	severe vibration problems	10/31
ret	SPANISH GP	Jerez	17	USF&G Arrows Megatron	G	1.5 t/c Arrows A10B-Megatron 4	slid over kerb – chassis damage	17/31
ret	JAPANESE GP	Suzuka	17	USF&G Arrows Megatron	G	1.5 t/c Arrows A10B-Megatron 4	spun off	7/31
ret	AUSTRALIAN GP	Adelaide	17	USF&G Arrows Megatron	G	1.5 t/c Arrows A10B-Megatron 4	engine	7/31

1989 Championship position: 10th   Wins: 0   Pole positions: 0   Fastest laps: 0   Points scored: 7

5	BRAZILIAN GP	Rio	9	Arrows Grand Prix International	G	3.5 Arrows A11-Cosworth V8		8/38
5	SAN MARINO GP	Imola	9	Arrows Grand Prix International	G	3.5 Arrows A11-Cosworth V8	1 lap behind	12/39
ret	MONACO GP	Monte Carlo	9	Arrows Grand Prix International	G	3.5 Arrows A11-Cosworth V8	electrical short-circuit	6/38
ret	MEXICAN GP	Mexico City	9	Arrows Grand Prix International	G	3.5 Arrows A11-Cosworth V8	electrics	10/39
ret	US GP (PHOENIX)	Phoenix	9	Arrows Grand Prix International	G	3.5 Arrows A11-Cosworth V8	ran into de Cesaris – suspension	10/39
ret	CANADIAN GP	Montreal	9	Arrows Grand Prix International	G	3.5 Arrows A11-Cosworth V8	engine	12/39
9	BRITISH GP	Silverstone	9	Arrows Grand Prix International	G	3.5 Arrows A11-Cosworth V8	2 laps behind	19/39
6	GERMAN GP	Hockenheim	9	Arrows Grand Prix International	G	3.5 Arrows A11-Cosworth V8	no clutch/1 lap behind	17/39
10	HUNGARIAN GP	Hungaroring	9	Arrows Grand Prix International	G	3.5 Arrows A11-Cosworth V8	collision – Nakajima/1 lap behind	9/39
6	BELGIAN GP	Spa	9	Arrows Grand Prix International	G	3.5 Arrows A11-Cosworth V8		10/39
ret	ITALIAN GP	Monza	9	Arrows Grand Prix International	G	3.5 Arrows A11-Cosworth V8	fuel flow – engine cut out	16/39
ret	PORTUGUESE GP	Estoril	9	Arrows Grand Prix International	G	3.5 Arrows A11-Cosworth V8	accident	22/39
9	SPANISH GP	Jerez	9	Arrows Grand Prix International	G	3.5 Arrows A11-Cosworth V8	despite collisions/2 laps behind	16/38
6*	JAPANESE GP	Suzuka	9	Arrows Grand Prix International	G	3.5 Arrows A11-Cosworth V8	*1st place car dsq/1 lap behind	25/39
ret	AUSTRALIAN GP	Adelaide	9	Arrows Grand Prix International	G	3.5 Arrows A11-Cosworth V8	engine cut in and out – crashed	20/39

1990 Championship position: 14th   Wins: 0   Pole positions: 0   Fastest laps: 0   Points scored: 3

ret	US GP (PHOENIX)	Phoenix	11	Camel Team Lotus	G	3.5 Lotus 102-Lamborghini V12	rear suspension	24/35
ret	BRAZILIAN GP	Rio	11	Camel Team Lotus	G	3.5 Lotus 102-Lamborghini V12	electrics	24/35
7	SAN MARINO GP	Imola	11	Camel Team Lotus	G	3.5 Lotus 102-Lamborghini V12	1 lap behind	11/34
ret	MONACO GP	Monte Carlo	11	Camel Team Lotus	G	3.5 Lotus 102-Lamborghini V12	brakes/spun – stalled	13/35
6	CANADIAN GP	Montreal	11	Camel Team Lotus	G	3.5 Lotus 102-Lamborghini V12	partly detached undertray/-2 laps	11/35
10	MEXICAN GP	Mexico City	11	Camel Team Lotus	G	3.5 Lotus 102-Lamborghini V12	low on revs/1 lap behind	11/35
11	FRENCH GP	Paul Ricard	11	Camel Team Lotus	G	3.5 Lotus 102-Lamborghini V12	1 lap behind	16/35
ret	BRITISH GP	Silverstone	11	Camel Team Lotus	G	3.5 Lotus 102-Lamborghini V12	engine	16/35
8	GERMAN GP	Hockenheim	11	Camel Team Lotus	G	3.5 Lotus 102-Lamborghini V12	severe vibration/1 lap behind	16/35
5	HUNGARIAN GP	Hungaroring	11	Camel Team Lotus	G	3.5 Lotus 102-Lamborghini V12		11/35
11	BELGIAN GP	Spa	11	Camel Team Lotus	G	3.5 Lotus 102-Lamborghini V12	misfire/1 lap behind	18/33
ret	ITALIAN GP	Monza	11	Camel Team Lotus	G	3.5 Lotus 102-Lamborghini V12	clutch	12/33
ret	PORTUGUESE GP	Estoril	11	Camel Team Lotus	G	3.5 Lotus 102-Lamborghini V12	throttle jammed	22/33
ret	SPANISH GP	Jerez	11	Camel Team Lotus	G	3.5 Lotus 102-Lamborghini V12	gearbox	10/33
ret	JAPANESE GP	Suzuka	11	Camel Team Lotus	G	3.5 Lotus 102-Lamborghini V12	gearbox	12/30
ret	AUSTRALIAN GP	Adelaide	11	Camel Team Lotus	G	3.5 Lotus 102-Lamborghini V12	gearbox	11/30

1993 Championship position: 15th=   Wins: 0   Pole positions: 0   Fastest laps: 0   Points scored: 4

7/ret	SOUTH AFRICAN GP	Kyalami	9	Footwork Mugen Honda	G	3.5 Footwork FA13B-Mugen Honda V10	spun off/3 laps behind	22/26
9	BRAZILIAN GP	Interlagos	9	Footwork Mugen Honda	G	3.5 Footwork FA13B-Mugen Honda V10	2 laps behind	18/26
ret	EUROPEAN GP	Donington	9	Footwork Mugen Honda	G	3.5 Footwork FA14-Mugen Honda V10	gearbox	14/26
ret	SAN MARINO GP	Imola	9	Footwork Mugen Honda	G	3.5 Footwork FA14-Mugen Honda V10	spun off	15/26
13	SPANISH GP	Barcelona	9	Footwork Mugen Honda	G	3.5 Footwork FA14-Mugen Honda V10	2 spins/3 laps behind	16/26
ret	MONACO GP	Monte Carlo	9	Footwork Mugen Honda	G	3.5 Footwork FA14-Mugen Honda V10	throttle failure	12/26
16	CANADIAN GP	Montreal	9	Footwork Mugen Honda	G	3.5 Footwork FA14-Mugen Honda V10	poor handling/4 laps behind	18/26
13	FRENCH GP	Magny Cours	9	Footwork Mugen Honda	G	3.5 Footwork FA14-Mugen Honda V10	2 laps behind	15/26
6	BRITISH GP	Silverstone	9	Footwork Mugen Honda	G	3.5 Footwork FA14-Mugen Honda V10	1 lap behind	8/26
17	GERMAN GP	Hockenheim	9	Footwork Mugen Honda	G	3.5 Footwork FA14-Mugen Honda V10	spin – wing damage/3 laps behind	11/26
4	HUNGARIAN GP	Hungaroring	9	Footwork Mugen Honda	G	3.5 Footwork FA14-Mugen Honda V10	1 lap behind	9/26
ret	BELGIAN GP	Spa	9	Footwork Mugen Honda	G	3.5 Footwork FA14-Mugen Honda V10	electrical failure	7/25
ret	ITALIAN GP	Monza	9	Footwork Mugen Honda	G	3.5 Footwork FA14-Mugen Honda V10	collision with Suzuki on lap 1	11/26
15/ret	PORTUGUESE GP	Estoril	9	Footwork Mugen Honda	G	3.5 Footwork FA14-Mugen Honda V10	taken off by Patrese/8 laps behind	9/26
14/ret	JAPANESE GP	Suzuka	9	Footwork Mugen Honda	G	3.5 Footwork FA14-Mugen Honda V10	hit by Irvine – spun off/5 laps behind	7/24
10	AUSTRALIAN GP	Adelaide	9	Footwork Mugen Honda	G	3.5 Footwork FA14-Mugen Honda V10	driver unwell/spin/2 laps behind	17/24

GP Starts: 146 (147)   GP Wins: 0   Pole positions: 0   Fastest laps: 2   Points: 71

JOHN WATSON, MBE

IT is possible that John Watson, 'Wattie', has been denied the credit that is his due, which may sound strange when you consider that he holds the MBE. Because his successes in grand prix racing were not concentrated into one great spell, however, his long and in the main very successful career, which spanned more than 20 years, tends to be overlooked.

In fact, Watson started racing way back in 1963/64 in his native Northern Ireland with an Austin Healey Sprite, before graduating to single-seaters. Outstanding in Irish Formula Libre in 1968/69 with his Brabham BT16 and then a LolaT100, he soon crossed the water to try his hand against sterner opposition.

In 1970, 'Wattie' took his Brabham BT30 into the European Formula 2 championship, but a patchy start to his career at this level ended in a heavy crash in practice at Rouen, which left him with a broken arm and leg. Undaunted, he was back the following year and, competing as a privateer in his elderly car, put to shame many more vaunted names. His persistence was about to bring rewards, for in 1972 a sixth place in the John Player Trophy race at Brands Hatch in a March 721, plus some excellent drives in Alan McCall's F2 Tui, caught the eye of both Brabham and Gulf, who gave the then bearded Ulsterman his first real breaks. However, the 'luck of the Irish' deserted him when, in the Race of Champions early in 1973, he broke his leg once more after the throttle stuck open on the new Brabham BT42.

With typical quiet determination, he was back in time to make his grand prix debut at Silverstone in the old BT37, and by the end of the year he had set up a full Formula 1 season with Hexagon Racing's private Brabham. A great drive to sixth place at Monaco was followed by some terrific performances, especially once he had the use of the BT44 chassis, headed by a brilliant drive into fourth in Austria after a pit stop had left him down in 21st place.

Sadly, the team were unable to continue in 1975 and, having previously driven in a few Formula 2 races for Surtees, Watson joined 'Big John's' outfit. A second place in the Race of Champions and fourth in the International Trophy were as good as it was going to get in a year fraught with mechanical difficulties. Just before the end of the season, Surtees withdrew to regroup his efforts, leaving 'Wattie' unemployed save for guest appearance with Lotus who, at that time, were in disarray. Fortunately, he soon picked up a ride in the Penske team at Watkins Glen and, after taking ninth place with a car not set up for the track, he was offered a contract for the 1976 season. The team suffered something of an up-and-down year, but John's magnificent victory in Austria gave him the confidence that comes from being a winner. The only thing he lost that day was his famous beard, as a result of a wager with Roger Penske!

When Penske decided to call it a day at the end of the year, Bernie Ecclestone lost no time in signing John to join Carlos Pace in his Brabham-

Alfa team for 1977. Tragically, the Brazilian was soon killed in an air crash, leaving Watson to carry the burden of development in an unproven car. He nearly won at Paul Ricard until fuel pick-up problems took away his last-lap lead, but the season ended as a major disappointment after beginning with so much promise.

Things improved in 1978, when Watson was teamed with Niki Lauda and at least was a regular points scorer, although his performances seemed a trifle erratic. However, he still finished sixth in the championship. When James Hunt became disillusioned with McLaren, he was chosen to take his place. Initially, it seemed to be a disastrous move, for the team were at a low ebb under the declining Teddy Mayer regime. The season was frustrating, with points scraped here and there in a difficult car, and 1980 brought even less cheer, John being out-driven in the early part of the year by newcomer Alain Prost. Some observers were tempted to write him off, but he fought back, and his confidence and speed began to return – particularly when he was installed in the John Barnard-designed MP4 under McLaren's new Ron Dennis regime in 1981. He scored a somewhat lucky win at Silverstone when René Arnoux's Renault faltered, and generally re-established his standing as one of the leading drivers, which had seemed under threat.

Joined by Niki Lauda in 1982, Watson answered the Austrian's Long Beach challenge with a well-taken win at Zolder, but overall his season was hampered by unpredictable lapses in form that led to some lacklustre showings. In 1983, he came through the field to take an unexpected win at Long Beach, but generally was handicapped by the lack of turbo power until late in the season.

Watson fully expected to remain paired with Lauda for a third year in 1984, but protracted negotiations worked against him when Alain Prost suddenly became available after being released by Renault. With no other options open, 'Wattie' was left to find a seat in sports car racing, driving occasionally for Rothmans Porsche over the next couple of years and taking a win at Fuji in 1984 with Stefan Bellof. A last-minute call-up by McLaren to deputise for the injured Lauda in the end-of-season European Grand Prix merely emphasised how two seasons out can take away the edge; there would be no more Formula 1.

Instead, Watson returned to endurance racing, having won the 1984 Fuji 1000km with Bellof in a Rothmans Porsche. Then he joined the Silk Cut Jaguar team in 1987. Sharing the XJR-8 with Jan Lammers, he took victories at Jarama, Monza, and Fuji to enable the pair to finish second to Roel Boesel in the drivers' standings. He briefly raced a TOMS Toyota in 1988, before retiring from the track to concentrate on his Silverstone-based Performance Driving School. For more than 15 years, 'Wattie' has settled into a role of commentator and presenter, covering a huge number of championships from Formula 1 through to touring and GT cars.

WATSON, John (GB) b 4/5/1946, Belfast, Northern Ireland

1973 Championship position: Unplaced

	Race	Circuit	No	Entrant	Tyres	Capacity/Car/Engine	Comment	Q Pos/Entries
ret	BRITISH GP	Silverstone	29	Ceramica Pagnossin-Team MRD	G	3.0 Brabham BT37-Cosworth V8	*seized fuel metering unit*	=23/29
ret	US GP	Watkins Glen	9	Ceramica Pagnossin-Team MRD	G	3.0 Brabham BT42-Cosworth V8	*engine*	25/28

1974 Championship position: 14th=   Wins: 0   Pole positions: 0   Fastest laps: 0   Points scored: 6

	Race	Circuit	No	Entrant	Tyres	Capacity/Car/Engine	Comment	Q Pos/Entries
12	ARGENTINE GP	Buenos Aires	28	John Goldie Racing with Hexagon	F	3.0 Brabham BT42-Cosworth V8	*pit stop – new nose cone/-4 laps*	20/26
ret	BRAZILIAN GP	Interlagos	28	John Goldie Racing with Hexagon	F	3.0 Brabham BT42-Cosworth V8	*clutch*	15/25
ret	SOUTH AFRICAN GP	Kyalami	28	John Goldie Racing with Hexagon	F	3.0 Brabham BT42-Cosworth V8	*fuel union*	13/27
11	SPANISH GP	Jarama	28	John Goldie Racing with Hexagon	F	3.0 Brabham BT42-Cosworth V8	*pit stop – tyres/4 laps behind*	16/28
11	BELGIAN GP	Nivelles	28	John Goldie Racing with Hexagon	F	3.0 Brabham BT42-Cosworth V8	*pit stop – tyres/2 laps behind*	19/32
6	MONACO GP	Monte Carlo	28	John Goldie Racing with Hexagon	F	3.0 Brabham BT42-Cosworth V8	*1 lap behind*	=21/28
11	SWEDISH GP	Anderstorp	28	John Goldie Racing with Hexagon	F	3.0 Brabham BT42-Cosworth V8	*3 laps behind*	14/28
7	DUTCH GP	Zandvoort	28	John Goldie Racing with Hexagon	F	3.0 Brabham BT42-Cosworth V8		13/27
16	FRENCH GP	Dijon	28	John Goldie Racing with Hexagon	F	3.0 Brabham BT42-Cosworth V8	*pit stop – exhaust/4 laps behind*	14/30

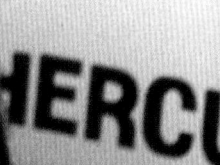

	Grand Prix	Circuit	No	Team	Tyre	Car/Engine	Notes	Grid/Fin
11	BRITISH GP	Brands Hatch	28	Goldie Hexagon Racing	F	3.0 Brabham BT42-Cosworth V8	pit stop – puncture/2 laps behind	13/34
ret	GERMAN GP	Nürburgring	28	Goldie Hexagon Racing	F	3.0 Brabham BT44-Cosworth V8	accident damage	14/32
dns	"	"	28	Goldie Hexagon Racing	F	3.0 Brabham BT42-Cosworth V8	practice only	– / –
4	AUSTRIAN GP	Österreichring	28	Goldie Hexagon Racing	F	3.0 Brabham BT44-Cosworth V8		11/31
7	ITALIAN GP	Monza	28	Goldie Hexagon Racing	F	3.0 Brabham BT44-Cosworth V8	1 lap behind	4/31
ret	CANADIAN GP	Mosport Park	28	Goldie Hexagon Racing	F	3.0 Brabham BT44-Cosworth V8	broken suspension – accident	15/30
5	US GP	Watkins Glen	28	Goldie Hexagon Racing	F	3.0 Brabham BT44-Cosworth V8		7/30

1975 Championship position: Unplaced

	Grand Prix	Circuit	No	Team	Tyre	Car/Engine	Notes	Grid/Fin
dsq*	ARGENTINE GP	Buenos Aires	18	Team Surtees	G	3.0 Surtees TS16-Cosworth V8	*repairs on car outside of pit area	15/23
10	BRAZILIAN GP	Interlagos	18	Team Surtees	G	3.0 Surtees TS16-Cosworth V8	slow puncture	13/23
ret	SOUTH AFRICAN GP	Kyalamia	18	Team Surtees	G	3.0 Surtees TS16-Cosworth V8	clutch	10/28
8	SPANISH GP	Montjuich Park	18	Team Surtees	G	3.0 Surtees TS16-Cosworth V8	pit stop – flat spotted tyre/3 laps behind	6/26
ret	MONACO GP	Monte Carlo	18	Team Surtees	G	3.0 Surtees TS16-Cosworth V8	spun off	17/26
10	BELGIAN GP	Zolder	18	Team Surtees	G	3.0 Surtees TS16-Cosworth V8	collision – new nose cone/-2 laps	18/24
16	SWEDISH GP	Anderstorp	18	Team Surtees	G	3.0 Surtees TS16-Cosworth V8	3 laps behind	10/26
ret	DUTCH GP	Zandvoort	18	Team Surtees	G	3.0 Surtees TS16-Cosworth V8	severe vibration	14/25
13	FRENCH GP	Paul Ricard	18	Team Surtees	G	3.0 Surtees TS16-Cosworth V8	1 lap behind	14/26
11/ret	BRITISH GP	Silverstone	18	Team Surtees	G	3.0 Surtees TS16-Cosworth V8	spun off in rainstorm/2 laps behind	18/28
ret	GERMAN GP	Nürburgring	6	John Player Team Lotus	G	3.0 Lotus 72F-Cosworth V8	broken front suspension	14/26
10	AUSTRIAN GP	Österreichring	18	Team Surtees	G	3.0 Surtees TS16-Cosworth V8	1 lap behind	18/30
9	US GP	Watkins Glen	28	Penske Cars	G	3.0 Penske PC1-Cosworth V8	went off at chicane/2 laps behind	– / –
dns	"	" "	28	Penske Cars	G	3.0 Penske PC3-Cosworth V8	practice only – set grid time in car	12/24

1976 Championship position: 7th Wins: 1 Pole positions: 0 Fastest laps: 0 Points scored: 20

	Grand Prix	Circuit	No	Team	Tyre	Car/Engine	Notes	Grid/Fin
ret	BRAZILIAN GP	Interlagos	28	Citibank Team Penske	G	3.0 Penske PC3-Cosworth V8	fire – broken fuel line	8/22
5	SOUTH AFRICAN GP	Kyalami	28	Citibank Team Penske	G	3.0 Penske PC3-Cosworth V8	1 lap behind	3/25
nc	US GP WEST	Long Beach	28	Citibank Team Penske	G	3.0 Penske PC3-Cosworth V8	pit stops – nose cone – exhaust/-11 laps	9/27
ret	SPANISH GP	Jarama	28	Citibank Team Penske	G	3.0 Penske PC3-Cosworth V8	engine	13/30
7	BELGIAN GP	Zolder	28	Citibank Team Penske	G	3.0 Penske PC3-Cosworth V8	1 lap behind	17/29
10	MONACO GP	Monte Carlo	28	Citibank Team Penske	G	3.0 Penske PC3-Cosworth V8	2 laps behind	17/25
ret	SWEDISH GP	Anderstorp	28	Citibank Team Penske	G	3.0 Penske PC3-Cosworth V8	accident – throttle stuck open	17/27
3*	FRENCH GP	Paul Ricard	28	Citibank Team Penske	G	3.0 Penske PC4-Cosworth V8	*dsq – but reinstated on appeal	8/30
3	BRITISH GP	Brands Hatch	28	Citibank Team Penske	G	3.0 Penske PC4-Cosworth V8	1 lap behind	11/30
7	GERMAN GP	Nürburgring	28	Citibank Team Penske	G	3.0 Penske PC4-Cosworth V8		19/28
1	AUSTRIAN GP	Österreichring	28	Citibank Team Penske	G	3.0 Penske PC4-Cosworth V8		2/25
ret	DUTCH GP	Zandvoort	28	Citibank Team Penske	G	3.0 Penske PC4-Cosworth V8	gearbox	4/27
11	ITALIAN GP	Monza	28	Citibank Team Penske	G	3.0 Penske PC4-Cosworth V8		29/29
10	CANADIAN GP	Mosport Park	28	Citibank Team Penske	G	3.0 Penske PC4-Cosworth V8	1 lap behind	14/27
6	US GP EAST	Watkins Glen	28	Citibank Team Penske	G	3.0 Penske PC4-Cosworth V8		8/27
ret	JAPANESE GP	Mount Fuji	28	Citibank Team Penske	G	3.0 Penske PC4-Cosworth V8	engine	4/27

1977 Championship position: 13th= Wins: 0 Pole positions: 1 Fastest laps: 2 Points scored: 9

	Grand Prix	Circuit	No	Team	Tyre	Car/Engine	Notes	Grid/Fin
ret	ARGENTINE GP	Buenos Aires	7	Martini Racing	G	3.0 Brabham BT45-Alfa Romeo F12	sheared suspension mounting	2/21
ret	BRAZILIAN GP	Interlagos	7	Martini Racing	G	3.0 Brabham BT45-Alfa Romeo F12	crashed	7/22
6	SOUTH AFRICAN GP	Kyalami	7	Martini Racing	G	3.0 Brabham BT45-Alfa Romeo F12	FL	11/23
dsq	US GP WEST	Long Beach	7	Martini Racing	G	3.0 Brabham BT45B-Alfa Romeo F12	outside assistance	6/22
ret	SPANISH GP	Jarama	7	Martini Racing	G	3.0 Brabham BT45B-Alfa Romeo F12	fuel metering unit	6/31
ret	MONACO GP	Monte Carlo	7	Martini Racing	G	3.0 Brabham BT45B-Alfa Romeo F12	gearbox	1/26
ret	BELGIAN GP	Zolder	7	Martini Racing	G	3.0 Brabham BT45B-Alfa Romeo F12	hit by Andretti	2/32
5	SWEDISH GP	Anderstorp	7	Martini Racing	G	3.0 Brabham BT45B-Alfa Romeo F12		2/31
2	FRENCH GP	Dijon	7	Martini Racing	G	3.0 Brabham BT45B-Alfa Romeo F12	low of fuel on last lap when leading	4/30
ret	BRITISH GP	Silverstone	7	Martini Racing	G	3.0 Brabham BT45B-Alfa Romeo F12	engine – fuel feed	2/36
ret	GERMAN GP	Hockenheim	7	Martini Racing	G	3.0 Brabham BT45B-Alfa Romeo F12	engine	2/30
8	AUSTRIAN GP	Österreichring	7	Martini Racing	G	3.0 Brabham BT45B-Alfa Romeo F12	FL/1 lap behind	12/30
ret	DUTCH GP	Zandvoort	7	Martini Racing	G	3.0 Brabham BT45B-Alfa Romeo F12	engine – lost oil – damaged sump	8/34
ret	ITALIAN GP	Monza	7	Martini Racing	G	3.0 Brabham BT45B-Alfa Romeo F12	accident – hit kerb	14/34
12	US GP EAST	Watkins Glen	7	Martini Racing	G	3.0 Brabham BT45B-Alfa Romeo F12	3 pit stops – tyres/2 laps behind	3/27
ret	CANADIAN GP	Mosport Park	7	Martini Racing	G	3.0 Brabham BT45B-Alfa Romeo F12	hit Peterson	10/27
ret	JAPANESE GP	Mount Fuji	7	Martini Racing	G	3.0 Brabham BT45B-Alfa Romeo F12	gearbox	3/23

1978 Championship position: 6th Wins: 0 Pole positions: 1 Fastest laps: 0 Points scored: 25

	Grand Prix	Circuit	No	Team	Tyre	Car/Engine	Notes	Grid/Fin
ret	ARGENTINE GP	Buenos Aires	2	Parmalat Racing Team	G	3.0 Brabham BT45C-Alfa Romeo F12	engine	4/27
8	BRAZILIAN GP	Rio	2	Parmalat Racing Team	G	3.0 Brabham BT45C-Alfa Romeo F12	2 laps behind	21/28
3	SOUTH AFRICAN GP	Kyalami	2	Parmalat Racing Team	G	3.0 Brabham BT46-Alfa Romeo F12		10/30
dns	" "	"	2	Parmalat Racing Team	G	3.0 Brabham BT45C-Alfa Romeo F12	practice only	– / –
ret	US GP WEST	Long Beach	2	Parmalat Racing Team	G	3.0 Brabham BT46-Alfa Romeo F12	oil tank	5/30
4	MONACO GP	Monte Carlo	2	Parmalat Racing Team	G	3.0 Brabham BT46-Alfa Romeo F12		2/30
ret	BELGIAN GP	Zolder	2	Parmalat Racing Team	G	3.0 Brabham BT46-Alfa Romeo F12	spun – damaged chassis	9/30
5	SPANISH GP	Jarama	2	Parmalat Racing Team	G	3.0 Brabham BT46-Alfa Romeo F12		7/29
ret	SWEDISH GP	Anderstorp	2	Parmalat Racing Team	G	3.0 Brabham BT46B-Alfa Romeo F12	fan car/stuck throttle after spin	2/27
4	FRENCH GP	Paul Ricard	2	Parmalat Racing Team	G	3.0 Brabham BT46-Alfa Romeo F12		1/29
3	BRITISH GP	Brands Hatch	2	Parmalat Racing Team	G	3.0 Brabham BT46-Alfa Romeo F12		9/30
7	GERMAN GP	Hockenheim	2	Parmalat Racing Team	G	3.0 Brabham BT46-Alfa Romeo F12		5/30
7	AUSTRIAN GP	Österreichring	2	Parmalat Racing Team	G	3.0 Brabham BT46-Alfa Romeo F12	pit stop-tyres/1 lap behind	10/31
4	DUTCH GP	Zandvoort	2	Parmalat Racing Team	G	3.0 Brabham BT46-Alfa Romeo F12		8/33
2*	ITALIAN GP	Monza	2	Parmalat Racing Team	G	3.0 Brabham BT46-Alfa Romeo F12	*after 1st & 2nd cars given 1 min pen	7/32
ret	US GP EAST	Watkins Glen	2	Parmalat Racing Team	G	3.0 Brabham BT46-Alfa Romeo F12	engine	7/27
ret	CANADIAN GP	Montreal	2	Parmalat Racing Team	G	3.0 Brabham BT46-Alfa Romeo F12	collision with Andretti	4/28

1979 Championship position: 9th= Wins: 0 Pole positions: 0 Fastest laps: 0 Points scored: 15

	Grand Prix	Circuit	No	Team	Tyre	Car/Engine	Notes	Grid/Fin
3	ARGENTINE GP	Buenos Aires	7	Marlboro Team McLaren	G	3.0 McLaren M28-Cosworth V8		6/26
8	BRAZILIAN GP	Interlagos	7	Marlboro Team McLaren	G	3.0 McLaren M28-Cosworth V8	1 lap behind	14/26
ret	SOUTH AFRICAN GP	Kyalami	7	Marlboro Team McLaren	G	3.0 McLaren M28-Cosworth V8	ignition	=14/26

WATSON

ret	US GP WEST	Long Beach	7	Löwenbräu Team McLaren	G	3.0 McLaren M28-Cosworth V8	fuel injection unit	18/26
ret	SPANISH GP	Jarama	7	Marlboro Team McLaren	G	3.0 McLaren M28-Cosworth V8	engine	18/27
6	BELGIAN GP	Zolder	7	Marlboro Team McLaren	G	3.0 McLaren M28-Cosworth V8		19/28
4	MONACO GP	Monte Carlo	7	Marlboro Team McLaren	G	3.0 McLaren M28-Cosworth V8		=13/25
11	FRENCH GP	Dijon	7	Marlboro Team McLaren	G	3.0 McLaren M28-Cosworth V8	pit stop – tyres/2 laps behind	15/27
4	BRITISH GP	Silverstone	7	Marlboro Team McLaren	G	3.0 McLaren M29-Cosworth V8	1 lap behind	7/26
5	GERMAN GP	Hockenheim	7	Marlboro Team McLaren	G	3.0 McLaren M29-Cosworth V8		12/26
9	AUSTRIAN GP	Österreichring	7	Marlboro Team McLaren	G	3.0 McLaren M29-Cosworth V8	1 lap behind	16/26
ret	DUTCH GP	Zandvoort	7	Marlboro Team McLaren	G	3.0 McLaren M29-Cosworth V8	engine	12/26
ret	ITALIAN GP	Monza	7	Marlboro Team McLaren	G	3.0 McLaren M29-Cosworth V8	accident with Jarier	19/28
6	CANADIAN GP	Montreal	7	Marlboro Team McLaren	G	3.0 McLaren M29-Cosworth V8	pit stop – fuel/2 laps behind	17/29
6	US GP EAST	Watkins Glen	7	Marlboro Team McLaren	G	3.0 McLaren M29-Cosworth V8	pit stop – tyres/1 lap behind	13/30

1980 Championship position: 10th=   Wins: 0   Pole positions: 0   Fastest laps: 0   Points scored: 6

ret	ARGENTINE GP	Buenos Aires	7	Marlboro Team McLaren	G	3.0 McLaren M29-Cosworth V8	gearbox oil leak	17/28
11	BRAZILIAN GP	Interlagos	7	Marlboro Team McLaren	G	3.0 McLaren M29-Cosworth V8	1 lap behind	23/28
11	SOUTH AFRICAN GP	Kyalami	7	Marlboro Team McLaren	G	3.0 McLaren M29-Cosworth V8	2 laps behind	21/28
4	US GP WEST	Long Beach	7	Marlboro Team McLaren	G	3.0 McLaren M29-Cosworth V8	1 lap behind	21/27
nc	BELGIAN GP	Zolder	7	Marlboro Team McLaren	G	3.0 McLaren M29-Cosworth V8	2 pit stops – brakes/11 laps behind	20/27
dnq	MONACO GP	Monte Carlo	7	Marlboro Team McLaren	G	3.0 McLaren M29-Cosworth V8		21/27
7	FRENCH GP	Paul Ricard	7	Marlboro Team McLaren	G	3.0 McLaren M29-Cosworth V8	1 lap behind	13/27
8	BRITISH GP	Brands Hatch	7	Marlboro Team McLaren	G	3.0 McLaren M29-Cosworth V8	pit stop – tyres/2 laps behind	12/27
ret	GERMAN GP	Hockenheim	7	Marlboro Team McLaren	G	3.0 McLaren M29-Cosworth V8	engine	20/26
ret	AUSTRIAN GP	Österreichring	7	Marlboro Team McLaren	G	3.0 McLaren M29-Cosworth V8	engine	21/25
ret	DUTCH GP	Zandvoort	7	Marlboro Team McLaren	G	3.0 McLaren M29-Cosworth V8	engine	9/28
ret	ITALIAN GP	Imola	7	Marlboro Team McLaren	G	3.0 McLaren M29-Cosworth V8	brakes/wheel bearing	14/28
4	CANADIAN GP	Montreal	7	Marlboro Team McLaren	G	3.0 McLaren M29-Cosworth V8		7/28
nc	US GP EAST	Watkins Glen	7	Marlboro Team McLaren	G	3.0 McLaren M29-Cosworth V8	pit stop – shock absorber/9 laps behind	9/27

1981 Championship position: 6th   Wins: 1   Pole positions: 0   Fastest laps: 1   Points scored: 27

ret	US GP WEST	Long Beach	7	McLaren International	M	3.0 McLaren M29F-Cosworth V8	engine	23/29
8	BRAZILIAN GP	Rio	7	McLaren International	M	3.0 McLaren M29F-Cosworth V8	1 lap behind	15/30
ret	ARGENTINE GP	Buenos Aires	7	McLaren International	M	3.0 McLaren M29F-Cosworth V8	transmission	11/29
10	SAN MARINO GP	Imola	7	McLaren International	M	3.0 McLaren MP4-Cosworth V8	pit stop – new nose cone/2 laps behind	7/30
7	BELGIAN GP	Zolder	7	McLaren International	M	3.0 McLaren MP4-Cosworth V8	gearbox problems	5/31
ret	MONACO GP	Monte Carlo	7	McLaren International	M	3.0 McLaren MP4-Cosworth V8	engine	10/31
3	SPANISH GP	Jarama	7	McLaren International	M	3.0 McLaren MP4-Cosworth V8		4/30
2	FRENCH GP	Dijon	7	McLaren International	M	3.0 McLaren MP4-Cosworth V8		2/29
1	BRITISH GP	Silverstone	7	McLaren International	M	3.0 McLaren MP4-Cosworth V8		5/30
6	GERMAN GP	Hockenheim	7	McLaren International	M	3.0 McLaren MP4-Cosworth V8	1 lap behind	9/30
6	AUSTRIAN GP	Österreichring	7	McLaren International	M	3.0 McLaren MP4-Cosworth V8		12/28
ret	DUTCH GP	Zandvoort	7	McLaren International	M	3.0 McLaren MP4-Cosworth V8	electrics	8/30
ret	ITALIAN GP	Monza	7	McLaren International	M	3.0 McLaren MP4-Cosworth V8	crashed	7/30
2	CANADIAN GP	Montreal	7	McLaren International	M	3.0 McLaren MP4-Cosworth V8	FL	9/30
7	CAESARS PALACE GP	Las Vegas	7	McLaren International	M	3.0 McLaren MP4-Cosworth V8	pit stop – tyres	6/30

1982 Championship position: 2nd=   Wins: 2   Pole positions: 0   Fastest laps: 1   Points scored: 39

6	SOUTH AFRICAN GP	Kyalami	7	Marlboro McLaren International	M	3.0 McLaren MP4B-Cosworth V8		9/30
2*	BRAZILIAN GP	Rio	7	Marlboro McLaren International	M	3.0 McLaren MP4B-Cosworth V8	*1st & 2nd place cars disqualified	12/31
6	US GP WEST	Long Beach	7	Marlboro McLaren International	M	3.0 McLaren MP4B-Cosworth V8	1 lap behind	11/31
1	BELGIAN GP	Zolder	7	Marlboro McLaren International	M	3.0 McLaren MP4B-Cosworth V8	FL	12/32
ret	MONACO GP	Monte Carlo	7	Marlboro McLaren International	M	3.0 McLaren MP4B-Cosworth V8	oil leak/battery	10/31
1	US GP (DETROIT)	Detroit	7	Marlboro McLaren International	M	3.0 McLaren MP4B-Cosworth V8		17/28
3	CANADIAN GP	Montreal	7	Marlboro McLaren International	M	3.0 McLaren MP4B-Cosworth V8		6/29
9	DUTCH GP	Zandvoort	7	Marlboro McLaren International	M	3.0 McLaren MP4B-Cosworth V8	pit stop – tyres/1 lap behind	11/31
ret	BRITISH GP	Brands Hatch	7	Marlboro McLaren International	M	3.0 McLaren MP4B-Cosworth V8	spun off avoiding Jarier and Serra	12/30
ret	FRENCH GP	Paul Ricard	7	Marlboro McLaren International	M	3.0 McLaren MP4B-Cosworth V8	battery lead	12/30
ret	GERMAN GP	Hockenheim	7	Marlboro McLaren International	M	3.0 McLaren MP4B-Cosworth V8	front suspension	11/30
ret	AUSTRIAN GP	Österreichring	7	Marlboro McLaren International	M	3.0 McLaren MP4B-Cosworth V8	engine – split water hose	18/29
13	SWISS GP	Dijon	7	Marlboro McLaren International	M	3.0 McLaren MP4B-Cosworth V8	pit stop – broken skirt/3 laps behind	11/29
4	ITALIAN GP	Monza	7	Marlboro McLaren International	M	3.0 McLaren MP4B-Cosworth V8		12/30
2	CAESARS PALACE GP	Las Vegas	7	Marlboro McLaren International	M	3.0 McLaren MP4B-Cosworth V8		9/30

1983 Championship position: 6th=   Wins: 1   Pole positions: 0   Fastest laps: 1   Points scored: 22

ret	BRAZILIAN GP	Rio	7	Marlboro McLaren International	M	3.0 McLaren MP4/1C-Cosworth V8	engine	16/27
1	US GP WEST	Long Beach	7	Marlboro McLaren International	M	3.0 McLaren MP4/1C-Cosworth V8		22/28
ret	FRENCH GP	Paul Ricard	7	Marlboro McLaren International	M	3.0 McLaren MP4/1C-Cosworth V8	throttle linkage	14/29
5	SAN MARINO GP	Imola	7	Marlboro McLaren International	M	3.0 McLaren MP4/1C-Cosworth V8	1 lap behind	24/28
dnq	MONACO GP	Monte Carlo	7	Marlboro McLaren International	M	3.0 McLaren MP4/1C-Cosworth V8		23/28
ret	BELGIAN GP	Spa	7	Marlboro McLaren International	M	3.0 McLaren MP4/1C-Cosworth V8	accident with Jarier	20/28
3	US GP (DETROIT)	Detroit	7	Marlboro McLaren International	M	3.0 McLaren MP4/1C-Cosworth V8	FL	21/27
6	CANADIAN GP	Montreal	7	Marlboro McLaren International	M	3.0 McLaren MP4/1C-Cosworth V8	pit stop – tyres/1 lap behind	20/28
9	BRITISH GP	Silverstone	7	Marlboro McLaren International	M	3.0 McLaren MP4/1C-Cosworth V8	pit stop – tyres/1 lap behind	24/29
5	GERMAN GP	Hockenheim	7	Marlboro McLaren International	M	3.0 McLaren MP4/1C-Cosworth V8	pit stop – tyres/1 lap behind	23/29
9	AUSTRIAN GP	Österreichring	7	Marlboro McLaren International	M	3.0 McLaren MP4/1C-Cosworth V8	pit stop – tyres/2 laps behind	17/29
3	DUTCH GP	Zandvoort	7	Marlboro McLaren International	M	3.0 McLaren MP4/1C-Cosworth V8	pit stop – tyres	15/29
ret	ITALIAN GP	Monza	7	Marlboro McLaren International	M	1.5 t/c McLaren MP4/1E-TAG V6	engine	15/29
ret	EUROPEAN GP	Brands Hatch	7	Marlboro McLaren International	M	1.5 t/c McLaren MP4/1E-TAG V6	accident – rear wing failure	10/29
dsq*	SOUTH AFRICAN GP	Kyalami	7	Marlboro McLaren International	M	1.5 t/c McLaren MP4/1E-TAG V6	*overtook cars on warm-up lap	15/26

1985 Championship position: Unplaced

7	EUROPEAN GP	Brands Hatch	1	Marlboro McLaren International	G	1.5 t/c McLaren MP4/2B-TAG V6	2 laps behind	21/27

GP Starts: 152   GP Wins: 5   Pole positions: 2   Fastest laps: 5   Points: 169

MARK WEBBER

IT has been a long haul for the perennially unlucky Mark Webber. After well over a century of grand prix starts with four different teams, however, at last he found a home at Red Bull where he could realise his full potential by not only taking his maiden grand prix win at the 147th attempt, but also going on to become a serious world championship challenger.

Having been born in the country outside Canberra, Webber's first attraction was to motorbikes – a hobby helped by his father's position as the local dealer – before he turned his attention to four wheels with a spell in karting. It took a few years, however, for the bug to bite. Then, having won the state kart title, he moved immediately into Formula Ford, recording fourth overall in a strong category in Australia, before taking the big step to Europe with the help of his long-term partner, Anne, who now acts as his business manager.

Offered a works Van Diemen for the annual FFord Festival in 1995, Mark duly finished third and was retained to spearhead the team's challenge for the full 1996 championship. He came second overall before a winning return to the FFord Festival. The Australian then moved into Formula 3, but the year was beset by financial struggles. He soldiered on, however, and eventually won a round of the series at Brands Hatch before going on to take fourth overall.

Webber's performances had not gone unnoticed, and he was approached by Mercedes-Benz to join their band of young guns in the 1998 FIA GT Championship. Not having to provide sponsorship to land the seat, he agreed and was paired with Germany's Bernd Schneider in the CLK GT machine. The first season passed successfully, the pair taking five race wins, but a return to the Mercedes fold for 1999 almost proved Webber's undoing when he endured two harrowing moments during the build-up to the annual Le Mans 24-hour race. The car's aerodynamics caused it to flip on the flat-out Mulsanne Straight with potentially calamitous consequences. His lucky escape prompted him to return to single-seaters, having already picked up the occasional test outing with the Arrows team in F1 and attracted the backing of Paul Stoddart, who was looking to break into motorsport on the back of his lucrative airline parts business. The pair hit it off immediately, Webber becoming a key part of Stoddart's fledgling FIA F3000 team for 2000. Despite their general inexperience, he managed to finish third overall that year, with a win at Silverstone, and his performances were enough for him to be snapped up by the Super Nova team for 2001. Despite wins at Imola, Monaco and Magny-Cours, he was well beaten to the title by Justin Wilson.

Mark's big break came when Paul Stoddart took over the Minardi team for 2002. The Aussie pair made an emotional debut together in Melbourne, where Webber benefited from a mass pile-up at the start to bring his car home in fifth place, scoring rare points for Minardi and joining an elite band of drivers to have scored on their F1 debut. Although there was never any chance of repeating that result, Webber had showcased his abilities, and it gained him a move up the grid to Jaguar Racing, where he spent a largely frustrating 2003 season. However, the revised scoring system allowed him to rack up 17 points for tenth in the championship, and to stamp his authority on team-mate Antonio Pizzonia and former F3000 rival Wilson.

Continuing with Jaguar in 2004, Webber endured another frustrating campaign and only managed seven points all year, but his fighting displays – and a front-row start in Malaysia – were sufficient to make him a target for Williams. The team saw his no-nonsense approach to F1 as being in the same mould as their own, and he made an intriguing pairing with the quietly-spoken Nick Heidfeld. It was an exasperating first season for him, however, and in spite of some excellent qualifying performances, and a first podium at Monaco, he saw the performance of his car slipping further behind that of his competitors.

The loss of BMW engines was another hammer blow to the team's standing, but being under contract, Webber was obliged to stick with the team for 2006 and try to get the best from a car running a Cosworth engine package. In the event, a tawdry tally of seven points was accrued as a catalogue of retirements blighted his year. Most notably, a possible third place at Monaco was lost when an exhaust problem affected the car's wiring loom; it was a dispiriting year for the beleaguered team.

After two seasons and little tangible success, it was hardly surprising that Webber decided to seek pastures new, and he jumped at the opportunity to join David Coulthard at the better funded – if still unproven – Red Bull Racing for 2007. He had a mixed season, the car being beset by numerous technical maladies that restricted his chances of points-scoring finishes. However, he did use his wet-weather prowess to grab a podium place in the European Grand Prix. In another rain-affected race in Japan, he seemed set for a career-best second place until he was rammed inadvertently from behind by Sebastian Vettel while under safety car rules.

For 2008, Mark had the prospect of a potentially competitive car in the Adrian Newey-designed RB4, as proved in Malaysia by his feisty performance in both qualifying and the race. Indeed, he surprised many doubters with some formidable performances and a run of points-paying finishes, highlighted by a fourth place at Monaco. Thereafter, it was something of an anticlimax, as only six points were gained from the remaining 12 races of the season. His preparations for 2009 were hampered by an unfortunate accident back home in Australia, where he suffered a broken leg while competing in a cycle race. Happily, he recovered in time for the start of the season and, armed with an ultra-competitive car in the shape of Newey's Red Bull RB05, he looked set to challenge at the sharp end of the grid.

New team-mate Vettel took Red Bull's maiden victory in China, Mark having to settle for second place, but after another podium in Spain, the Australian began to gather momentum, which peaked with his emotional first win at the Nürburgring. That was followed by another win in Brazil and second place in Abu Dhabi, behind Vettel, which left the team looking like strong title contenders for 2010.

So it would prove as Newey and his team supplied the two drivers with a car to challenge for the championship. In a roller-coaster ride of a season, Mark put in some tremendous drives to win flawlessly in Spain and at Monaco, before surviving unscathed after running into the back of Heikki Kovalainen at Valencia. Undeterred, he bounced back to win both the British and Hungarian grands prix, and headed into the mid-season break at the top of the championship table. When racing resumed, a four-way battle for the title ensued, with Mark still holding the advantage after a second place in the Japanese Grand Prix. It all unravelled at the next race in Korea, however, when he crashed out to surrender his championship lead.

On the back foot thereafter, Webber brought his extraordinary season to a close in Abu Dhabi, where the luckless driver had to pit early, a move that was covered by Ferrari on behalf of Fernando Alonso. This bottled up the pair in the midfield while Vettel took the opportunity to snatch the title at the 11th hour. It was a bitter pill for Webber, who might have seen his best ever chance of the title disappear. It certainly looked that way in 2011, when the Australian was somewhat overwhelmed by the stunning displays of Vettel. Poor Mark must have been bemused by the scorching pace of the German and could only take consolation from a massive haul of points that helped Red Bull take the constructors' title, topped off by a dominant victory in the end-of-season Brazilian Grand Prix.

With just a one-year contract extension in his pocket, Webber may now be looking over his shoulder at such young chargers as Daniel Ricciardo and Jean-Éric Vergne, who are chasing his place at Red Bull Racing.

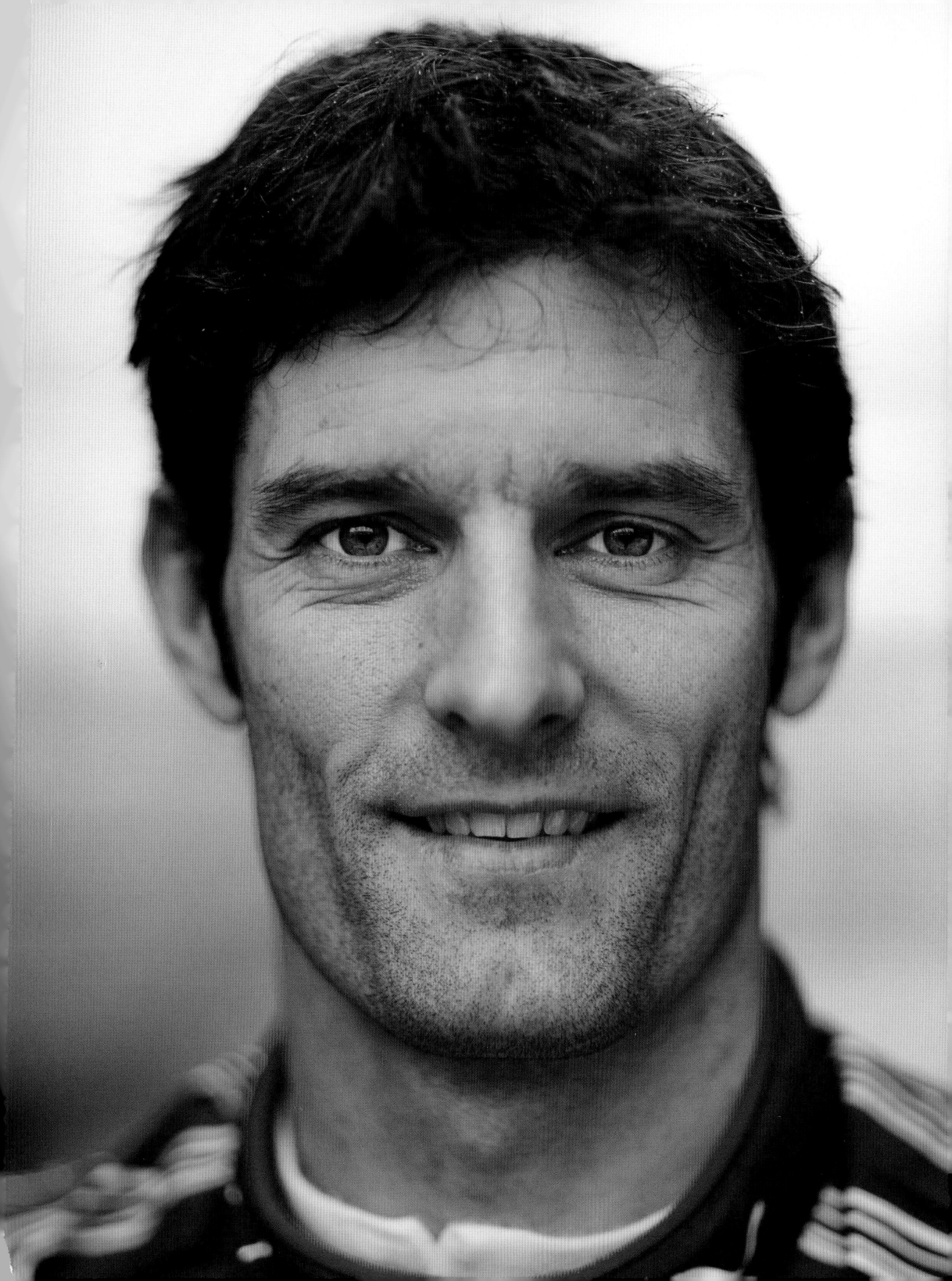

WEBBER, Mark (AUS) b 28/7/1976, Queanbeyan, New South Wales

2002 Championship position: 15th= Wins: 0 Pole positions: 0 Fastest laps: 0 Points scored: 2

	Race	Circuit	No	Entrant	Tyres	Car/Engine	Comment	Q Pos/Entries
5	AUSTRALIAN GP	Melbourne	23	KL Minardi Asiatech	M	3.0 Minardi PS02-Asiatech V10	2 laps behind	18/22
ret	MALAYSIAN GP	Sepang	23	KL Minardi Asiatech	M	3.0 Minardi PS02-Asiatech V10	electrics	21/22
11	BRAZILIAN GP	Interlagos	23	KL Minardi Asiatech	M	3.0 Minardi PS02-Asiatech V10	collision with Massa/3 laps behind	20/22
11	SAN MARINO GP	Imola	23	KL Minardi Asiatech	M	3.0 Minardi PS02-Asiatech V10	1 lap behind	19/22
dns	SPANISH GP	Barcelona	23	KL Minardi Asiatech	M	3.0 Minardi PS02-Asiatech V10	structural failure – car withdrawn	(21)/22
12	AUSTRIAN GP	A1-Ring	23	KL Minardi Asiatech	M	3.0 Minardi PS02-Asiatech V10	2 laps behind	21/22
11	MONACO GP	Monte Carlo	23	KL Minardi Asiatech	M	3.0 Minardi PS02-Asiatech V10	2 laps behind	19/22
11	CANADIAN GP	Montreal	23	KL Minardi Asiatech	M	3.0 Minardi PS02-Asiatech V10	1 lap behind	21/22
15	EUROPEAN GP	Nürburgring	23	KL Minardi Asiatech	M	3.0 Minardi PS02-Asiatech V10	2 laps behind	20/22
ret	BRITISH GP	Silverstone	23	KL Minardi Asiatech	M	3.0 Minardi PS02-Asiatech V10	spun off	20/22
8	FRENCH GP	Magny Cours	23	KL Minardi Asiatech	M	3.0 Minardi PS02-Asiatech V10	slight misfire & oversteer/1 lap behind	18/22
ret	GERMAN GP	Hockenheim	23	KL Minardi Asiatech	M	3.0 Minardi PS02-Asiatech V10	hydraulics	21/22
16	HUNGARIAN GP	Hungaroring	23	KL Minardi Asiatech	M	3.0 Minardi PS02-Asiatech V10	2 laps behind	19/20
ret	BELGIAN GP	Spa	23	KL Minardi Asiatech	M	3.0 Minardi PS02-Asiatech V10	gearbox	19/20
ret	ITALIAN GP	Monza	23	KL Minardi Asiatech	M	3.0 Minardi PS02-Asiatech V10	electrics	19/20
ret	UNITED STATES GP	Indianapolis	23	KL Minardi Asiatech	M	3.0 Minardi PS02-Asiatech V10	steering	18/20
10	JAPANESE GP	Suzuka	23	KL Minardi Asiatech	M	3.0 Minardi PS02-Asiatech V10	2 laps behind	19/20

2003 Championship position: 9th= Wins: 0 Pole positions: 0 Fastest laps: 0 Points scored: 17

	Race	Circuit	No	Entrant	Tyres	Car/Engine	Comment	Q Pos/Entries
ret	AUSTRALIAN GP	Melbourne	14	Jaguar Racing	M	3.0 Jaguar R4-Cosworth V10	broken suspension	14/20
ret	MALAYSIAN GP	Sepang	14	Jaguar Racing	M	3.0 Jaguar R4-Cosworth V10	oil system	16/20
9/ret	BRAZILIAN GP	Interlagos	14	Jaguar Racing	M	3.0 Jaguar R4-Cosworth V10	accident	3/20
ret	SAN MARINO GP	Imola	14	Jaguar Racing	M	3.0 Jaguar R4-Cosworth V10	driveshaft	5/20
7	SPANISH GP	Barcelona	14	Jaguar Racing	M	3.0 Jaguar R4-Cosworth V10	1 lap behind	14/20
7	AUSTRIAN GP	A1-Ring	14	Jaguar Racing	M	3.0 Jaguar R4-Cosworth V10	1 lap behind	17/20
ret	MONACO GP	Monte Carlo	14	Jaguar Racing	M	3.0 Jaguar R4-Cosworth V10	engine	9/19
7	CANADIAN GP	Montreal	14	Jaguar Racing	M	3.0 Jaguar R4-Cosworth V10	slight oversteer/1 lap behind	6/20
6	EUROPEAN GP	Nürburgring	14	Jaguar Racing	M	3.0 Jaguar R4-Cosworth V10	1 lap behind	11/20
6	FRENCH GP	Magny Cours	14	Jaguar Racing	M	3.0 Jaguar R4-Cosworth V10	1 lap behind	9/20
14	BRITISH GP	Silverstone	14	Jaguar Racing	M	3.0 Jaguar R4-Cosworth V10	1 lap behind	11/20
11/ret	GERMAN GP	Hockenheim	14	Jaguar Racing	M	3.0 Jaguar R4-Cosworth V10	spun off/3 laps behind	11/20
6	HUNGARIAN GP	Hungaroring	14	Jaguar Racing	M	3.0 Jaguar R4-Cosworth V10		3/20
7	ITALIAN GP	Monza	14	Jaguar Racing	M	3.0 Jaguar R4-Cosworth V10	1 lap behind	11/20
ret	UNITED STATES GP	Indianapolis	14	Jaguar Racing	M	3.0 Jaguar R4-Cosworth V10	spun off in wet	14/20
11	JAPANESE GP	Suzuka	14	Jaguar Racing	M	3.0 Jaguar R4-Cosworth V10		6/20

2004 Championship position: 13th Wins: 0 Pole positions: 0 Fastest laps: 0 Points scored: 7

	Race	Circuit	No	Entrant	Tyres	Car/Engine	Comment	Q Pos/Entries
ret	AUSTRALIAN GP	Melbourne	14	Jaguar Racing	M	3.0 Jaguar R5-Cosworth V10	gearbox	6/20
ret	MALAYSIAN GP	Sepang	14	Jaguar Racing	M	3.0 Jaguar R5-Cosworth V10	spun off	2/20
8	BAHRAIN GP	Sakhir Circuit	14	Jaguar Racing	M	3.0 Jaguar R5-Cosworth V10	1 lap behind	14/20
13	SAN MARINO GP	Imola	14	Jaguar Racing	M	3.0 Jaguar R5-Cosworth V10	1 lap behind	8/20
12	SPANISH GP	Barcelona	14	Jaguar Racing	M	3.0 Jaguar R5-Cosworth V10	slow pit stop/lack of grip/1 lap behind	9/20
ret	MONACO GP	Monte Carlo	14	Jaguar Racing	M	3.0 Jaguar R5-Cosworth V10	electrics	12/20
7	EUROPEAN GP	Nürburgring	14	Jaguar Racing	M	3.0 Jaguar R5-Cosworth V10		14/20
ret	CANADIAN GP	Montreal	14	Jaguar Racing	M	3.0 Jaguar R5-Cosworth V10	collision damage	14/20
ret	UNITED STATES GP	Indianapolis	14	Jaguar Racing	M	3.0 Jaguar R5-Cosworth V10	engine	10/20
9	FRANCE GP	Magny Cours	14	Jaguar Racing	M	3.0 Jaguar R5-Cosworth V10		12/20
8	BRITISH GP	Silverstone	14	Jaguar Racing	M	3.0 Jaguar R5-Cosworth V10		10/20
6	GERMAN GP	Hockenheim	14	Jaguar Racing	M	3.0 Jaguar R5-Cosworth V10		12/20
10	HUNGARIAN GP	Hungaroring	14	Jaguar Racing	M	3.0 Jaguar R5-Cosworth V10	1 lap behind	11/20
ret	BELGIAN GP	Spa	14	Jaguar Racing	M	3.0 Jaguar R5-Cosworth V10	multiple collision on lap 1	7/20
9	ITALIAN GP	Monza	14	Jaguar Racing	M	3.0 Jaguar R5-Cosworth V10		11/20
10	CHINESE GP	Shanghai	14	Jaguar Racing	M	3.0 Jaguar R5-Cosworth V10	1 lap behind	12/20
ret	JAPANESE GP	Suzuka	14	Jaguar Racing	M	3.0 Jaguar R5-Cosworth V10	cockpit overheated with scalding air	3/20
ret	BRAZILIAN GP	Interlagos	14	Jaguar Racing	M	3.0 Jaguar R5-Cosworth V10	collision with Klien	12/20

2005 Championship position: 11th Wins: 0 Pole positions: 1 Fastest laps: 0 Points scored: 28

	Race	Circuit	No	Entrant	Tyres	Car/Engine	Comment	Q Pos/Entries
5	AUSTRALIAN GP	Melbourne	7	BMW WilliamsF1 Team	M	3.0 Williams FW27-BMW V10		3/20
ret	MALAYSIAN GP	Sepang	7	BMW WilliamsF1 Team	M	3.0 Williams FW27-BMW V10	collision with Fisichella	4/20
6	BAHRAIN GP	Bahrain	7	BMW WilliamsF1 Team	M	3.0 Williams FW27-BMW V10		5/20
7*	SAN MARINO GP	Imola	7	BMW WilliamsF1 Team	M	3.0 Williams FW27-BMW V10	*3rd & 5th place cars disqualified	4/20
6	SPANISH GP	Barcelona	7	BMW WilliamsF1 Team	M	3.0 Williams FW27-BMW V10	changed pit stop strategy	2/18
3	MONACO GP	Monte Carlo	7	BMW WilliamsF1 Team	M	3.0 Williams FW27-BMW V10		3/18
ret	EUROPEAN GP	Nürburgring	7	BMW WilliamsF1 Team	M	3.0 Williams FW27-BMW V10	first corner collision	3/20
5	CANADIAN GP	Montreal	7	BMW WilliamsF1 Team	M	3.0 Williams FW27-BMW V10		14/20
dns*	U S GP	Indianapolis	7	BMW WilliamsF1 Team	M	3.0 Williams FW27-BMW V10	*withdrawn after parade lap	9/20
12	FRENCH GP	Magny Cours	7	BMW WilliamsF1 Team	M	3.0 Williams FW27-BMW V10	overheated cockpit/2 laps behind	13/20
11	BRITISH GP	Silverstone	7	BMW WilliamsF1 Team	M	3.0 Williams FW27-BMW V10	poor aerodynamics/1 lap behind	12/20
nc	GERMAN GP	Hockenheim	7	BMW WilliamsF1 Team	M	3.0 Williams FW27-BMW V10	suspension damage/12 laps behind	6/20
7	HUNGARIAN GP	Hungaroring	7	BMW WilliamsF1 Team	M	3.0 Williams FW27-BMW V10	1 lap behind	16/20
ret	TURKISH GP	Istanbul	7	BMW WilliamsF1 Team	M	3.0 Williams FW27-BMW V10	tyre failure against undertray	7/20
14	ITALIAN GP	Monza	7	BMW WilliamsF1 Team	M	3.0 Williams FW27-BMW V10	collison – new front wing/1 lap behind	14/20
4	BELGIAN GP	Spa	7	BMW WilliamsF1 Team	M	3.0 Williams FW27-BMW V10		10/20
nc	BRAZILIAN GP	Interlagos	7	BMW WilliamsF1 Team	M	3.0 Williams FW27-BMW V10	long stop – collision damage/-26 laps	14/20
4	JAPANESE GP	Suzuka	7	BMW WilliamsF1 Team	M	3.0 Williams FW27-BMW V10		7/20
7	CHINESE GP	Shanghai Circuit	7	BMW WilliamsF1 Team	M	3.0 Williams FW27-BMW V10		10/20

2006 Championship position: 14th Wins: 0 Pole positions: 0 Fastest laps: 0 Points scored: 7

	Race	Circuit	No	Entrant	Tyres	Car/Engine	Comment	Q Pos/Entries
6	BAHRAIN GP	Bahrain	9	WilliamsF1Team	B	2.4 Williams FW28-Cosworth V8		7/22

ret	MALAYSIAN GP	Sepang	9	WilliamsF1Team	B	2.4 Williams FW28-Cosworth V8	hydraulics	5/22
ret	AUSTRALIAN GP	Melbourne	9	WilliamsF1Team	B	2.4 Williams FW28-Cosworth V8	gearbox	7/22
6	SAN MARINO GP	Imola	9	WilliamsF1Team	B	2.4 Williams FW28-Cosworth V8		10/22
ret	EUROPEAN GP	Nürburgring	9	WilliamsF1Team	B	2.4 Williams FW28-Cosworth V8	hydraulics	10/22
9	SPANISH GP	Barcelona	9	WilliamsF1Team	B	2.4 Williams FW28-Cosworth V8	1 lap behind	11/22
ret	MONACO GP	Monte Carlo	9	WilliamsF1Team	B	2.4 Williams FW28-Cosworth V8	exhaust/fire	3/22
ret	BRITISH GP	Silverstone	9	WilliamsF1Team	B	2.4 Williams FW28-Cosworth V8	collision – taken out by Ralf Schumacher	17/22
12	CANADIAN GP	Montreal	9	WilliamsF1Team	B	2.4 Williams FW28-Cosworth V8	1 lap behind	17/22
ret	U S GP	Indianapolis	9	WilliamsF1Team	B	2.4 Williams FW28-Cosworth V8	multiple collsion on lap 1	12/22
ret	FRENCH GP	Magny Cours	9	WilliamsF1Team	B	2.4 Williams FW28-Cosworth V8	tyre failure/spin/wheel rim damage	11/22
ret	GERMAN GP	Hockenheim	9	WilliamsF1Team	B	2.4 Williams FW28-Cosworth V8	engine	11/22
ret	HUNGARIAN GP	Hungaroring	9	WilliamsF1Team	B	2.4 Williams FW28-Cosworth V8	accident on lap 1 – broken front wing	6/22
10	TURKISH GP	Istanbul	9	WilliamsF1Team	B	2.4 Williams FW28-Cosworth V8	1 lap behind	10/22
10	ITALIAN GP	Monza	9	WilliamsF1Team	B	2.4 Williams FW28-Cosworth V8	hit kerb	19/22
8	CHINESE GP	Shanghai	9	WilliamsF1Team	B	2.4 Williams FW28-Cosworth V8		15/22
ret	JAPANESE GP	Suzuka	9	WilliamsF1Team	B	2.4 Williams FW28-Cosworth V8	handling problems – crashed	00/22
ret	BRAZILIAN GP	Interlagos	9	WilliamsF1Team	B	2.4 Williams FW28-Cosworth V8	hit by Rosberg – rear wing damage	11/22

2007 Championship position: 12th   Wins: 0   Pole positions: 0   Fastest laps: 0   Points scored: 10

13	AUSTRALIAN GP	Melbourne	15	Red Bull Racing	B	2.4 Red Bull RB3-Renault V8	1 lap behind	7/22
10	MALAYSIAN GP	Sepang	15	Red Bull Racing	B	2.4 Red Bull RB3-Renault V8		10/22
ret	BAHRAIN GP	Sakhir Circuit	15	Red Bull Racing	B	2.4 Red Bull RB3-Renault V8	gearbox	8/22
ret	SPANISH GP	Barcelona	15	Red Bull Racing	B	2.4 Red Bull RB3-Renault V8	transmission	19/22
ret	MONACO GP	Monte Carlo	15	Red Bull Racing	B	2.4 Red Bull RB3-Renault V8	misfire/gearbox	6/22
9	CANADIAN GP	Montreal	15	Red Bull Racing	B	2.4 Red Bull RB3-Renault V8		6/22
7	U S GP	Indianapolis	15	Red Bull Racing	B	2.4 Red Bull RB3-Renault V8		9/22
12	FRENCH GP	Magny Cours	15	Red Bull Racing	B	2.4 Red Bull RB3-Renault V8	1 lap behind	14/22
ret	BRITISH GP	Silverstone	15	Red Bull Racing	B	2.4 Red Bull RB3-Renault V8	hydraulics	11/22
3	EUROPEAN GP	Nürburgring	15	Red Bull Racing	B	2.4 Red Bull RB3-Renault V8		6/22
9	HUNGARIAN GP	Hungaroring	15	Red Bull Racing	B	2.4 Red Bull RB3-Renault V8		10/22
ret	TURKISH GP	Istanbul	15	Red Bull Racing	B	2.4 Red Bull RB3-Renault V8	differential/hydraulics	12/22
9	ITALIAN GP	Monza	15	Red Bull Racing	B	2.4 Red Bull RB3-Renault V8		11/22
7	BELGIAN GP	Spa	15	Red Bull Racing	B	2.4 Red Bull RB3-Renault V8		8/22
ret	JAPANESE GP	Fuji Speedway	15	Red Bull Racing	B	2.4 Red Bull RB3-Renault V8	accident – rammed by Vettel	8/22
10	CHINESE GP	Shanghai	15	Red Bull Racing	B	2.4 Red Bull RB3-Renault V8	extra pit stop for tyres	7/22
ret	BRAZILIAN GP	Interlagos	15	Red Bull Racing	B	2.4 Red Bull RB3-Renault V8	transmission	5/22

2008 Championship position: 11th   Wins: 0   Pole positions: 0   Fastest laps: 0   Points scored: 21

ret	AUSTRALIAN GP	Melbourne	10	Red Bull Racing	B	2.4 Red Bull RB4-Renault V8	1 lap collision with Davidson	15/22
7	MALAYSIAN GP	Sepang	10	Red Bull Racing	B	2.4 Red Bull RB4-Renault V8		8/22
7	BAHRAIN GP	Sakhir Circuit	10	Red Bull Racing	B	2.4 Red Bull RB4-Renault V8		11/22
5	SPANISH GP	Barcelona	10	Red Bull Racing	B	2.4 Red Bull RB4-Renault V8		7/22
7	TURKISH GP	Istanbul	10	Red Bull Racing	B	2.4 Red Bull RB4-Renault V8		6/20
4	MONACO GP	Monte Carlo	10	Red Bull Racing	B	2.4 Red Bull RB4-Renault V8		9/20
12	CANADIAN GP	Montreal	10	Red Bull Racing	B	2.4 Red Bull RB4-Renault V8		10/20
6	FRENCH GP	Magny Cours	10	Red Bull Racing	B	2.4 Red Bull RB4-Renault V8	brake balance problems	8/20
10	BRITISH GP	Silverstone	10	Red Bull Racing	B	2.4 Red Bull RB4-Renault V8	spun on opening lap	2/20
ret	GERMAN GP	Hockenheim	10	Red Bull Racing	B	2.4 Red Bull RB4-Renault V8	oil cooler and leak	8/20
9	HUNGARIAN GP	Hungaroring	10	Red Bull Racing	B	2.4 Red Bull RB4-Renault V8	lack of grip	8/20
12	EUROPEAN GP	Valencia	10	Red Bull Racing	B	2.4 Red Bull RB4-Renault V8	collision damage/1 lap behind	14/20
8*	BELGIAN GP	Spa	10	Red Bull Racing	B	2.4 Red Bull RB4-Renault V8	*9th on road but 8th placed car penalized	7/20
8	ITALIAN GP	Monza	10	Red Bull Racing	B	2.4 Red Bull RB4-Renault V8	spin and also collision with Hamilton	3/20
ret	SINGAPORE GP	Singapore Circuit	10	Red Bull Racing	B	2.4 Red Bull RB4-Renault V8	gearbox	13/20
8	JAPANESE GP	Suzuka	10	Red Bull Racing	B	2.4 Red Bull RB4-Renault V8	*9th on road but 6th placed car penalized	6/20
14	CHINESE GP	Shanghai	10	Red Bull Racing	B	2.4 Red Bull RB4-Renault V8	race tactics hampered by grid penalty	12/20
9	BRAZILIAN GP	Interlagos	10	Red Bull Racing	B	2.4 Red Bull RB4-Renault V8	struggled with heavily-fuelled car	

2009 Championship position: 4th   Wins: 2   Pole positions: 1   Fastest laps: 3   Points scored: 69.5

12	AUSTRALIAN GP	Melbourne	14	Red Bull Racing	B	2.4 Red Bull RB5-Renault V8	pit stop – collision damage/1 lap behind	10/22
6	MALAYSIAN GP	Sepang	14	Red Bull Racing	B	2.4 Red Bull RB5-Renault V8	rain-shortended race – half points	7/22
2	CHINESE GP	Shanghai	14	Red Bull Racing	B	2.4 Red Bull RB5-Renault V8		3/22
11	BAHRAIN GP	Sakhir Circuit	14	Red Bull Racing	B	2.4 Red Bull RB5-Renault V8		19/22
3	SPANISH GP	Barcelona	14	Red Bull Racing	B	2.4 Red Bull RB5-Renault V8		5/22
5	MONACO GP	Monte Carlo	14	Red Bull Racing	B	2.4 Red Bull RB5-Renault V8		8/22
2	TURKISH GP	Istanbul	14	Red Bull Racing	B	2.4 Red Bull RB5-Renault V8		4/22
2	BRITISH GP	Silverstone	14	Red Bull Racing	B	2.4 Red Bull RB5-Renault V8	bodywork damage from debris	3/22
1	GERMAN GP	Nürburgring	14	Red Bull Racing	B	2.4 Red Bull RB5-Renault V8		1/22
3	HUNGARIAN GP	Hungaroring	14	Red Bull Racing	B	2.4 Red Bull RB5-Renault V8	delay at pit stop and wrong tyre chice/FL	3/22
9	EUROPEAN GP	Valencia	14	Red Bull Racing	B	2.4 Red Bull RB5-Renault V8		9/22
9	BELGIAN GP	Spa	14	Red Bull Racing	B	2.4 Red Bull RB5-Renault V8	drive-thru' pen - rejoined in unsafe manner	9/22
ret	ITALIAN GP	Monza	14	Red Bull Racing	B	2.4 Red Bull RB5-Renault V8	accident – lap 1 collision with Rosberg	10/22
ret	SINGAPORE GP	Marina Bay Circuit	14	Red Bull Racing	B	2.4 Red Bull RB5-Renault V8	brakes – accident	4/22
17	JAPANESE GP	Suzuka	14	Red Bull Racing	B	2.4 Red Bull RB5-Renault V8	*no time set/2 laps behind/FL	*22/22
1	BRAZILIAN GP	Interlagos	14	Red Bull Racing	B	2.4 Red Bull RB5-Renault V8	FL	2/22
2	ABU DHABI GP	Yas Marina Circuit	14	Red Bull Racing	B	2.4 Red Bull RB5-Renault V8		3/22

2010 Championship position: 3rd   Wins: 4   Pole positions: 5   Fastest laps: 3   Points scored: 242

8	BAHRAIN GP	Sakhir Circuit	6	Red Bull Racing	B	2.4 Red Bull RB6-Renault V8		6/24
9	AUSTRALIAN GP	Melbourne	6	Red Bull Racing	B	2.4 Red Bull RB6-Renault V8	strategy spoiled by safety car period/FL	2/24
2	MALAYSIAN GP	Sepang	6	Red Bull Racing	B	2.4 Red Bull RB6-Renault V8	FL	1/24
8	CHINESE GP	Shanghai Circuit	6	Red Bull Racing	B	2.4 Red Bull RB6-Renault V8	delayed at pit stop/wing tweaked	2/24
1	SPANISH GP	Barcelona	6	Red Bull Racing	B	2.4 Red Bull RB6-Renault V8		1/24
1	MONACO GP	Monte Carlo	6	Red Bull Racing	B	2.4 Red Bull RB6-Renault V8		1/24

3	TURKISH GP	Istanbul Park	6	Red Bull Racing	B	2.4 Red Bull RB6-Renault V8	*survived collision with Vettel*	1/24
5	CANADIAN GP	Montreal	6	Red Bull Racing	B	2.4 Red Bull RB6-Renault V8	*5-place grid penalty – gearbox change*	2/24
ret	EUROPEAN GP	Valencia	6	Red Bull Racing	B	2.4 Red Bull RB6-Renault V8	*accident – ran into Kovalainen*	2/24
1	BRITISH GP	Silverstone	6	Red Bull Racing	B	2.4 Red Bull RB6-Renault V8		2/24
6	GERMAN GP	Hockenheim	6	Red Bull Racing	B	2.4 Red Bull RB6-Renault V8		4/24
1	HUNGARIAN GP	Hungaroring	6	Red Bull Racing	B	2.4 Red Bull RB6-Renault V8		2/24
2	BELGIAN GP	Spa	6	Red Bull Racing	B	2.4 Red Bull RB6-Renault V8		1/24
6	ITALIAN GP	Monza	6	Red Bull Racing	B	2.4 Red Bull RB6-Renault V8	*battled with Hulkenberg*	4/24
3	SINGAPORE GP	Marina Bay Circuit	6	Red Bull Racing	B	2.4 Red Bull RB6-Renault V8		5/24
2	JAPANESE GP	Suzuka	6	Red Bull Racing	B	2.4 Red Bull RB6-Renault V8	*FL*	2/24
ret	KOREAN GP	Yeongam	6	Red Bull Racing	B	2.4 Red Bull RB6-Renault V8	*accident- crashed*	2/24
2	BRAZILIAN GP	Interlagos	6	Red Bull Racing	B	2.4 Red Bull RB6-Renault V8		3/24
8	ABU DHABI GP	Yas Marina Circuit	6	Red Bull Racing	B	2.4 Red Bull RB6-Renault V8	*glanced barrier– early pit stop*	5/24

2011 Championship position: 3rd   Wins: 1   Pole positions: 2   Fastest laps: 7   Points scored: 258

5	AUSTRALIAN GP	Melbourne	2	Red Bull Racing	P	2.4 Red Bull RB7-Renault V8		3/24
4	MALAYSIAN GP	Sepang	2	Red Bull Racing	P	2.4 Red Bull RB7-Renault V8	*poor start – KERS problem/FL*	3/24
2	CHINESE GP	Shanghai Circuit	2	Red Bull Racing	P	2.4 Red Bull RB7-Renault V8	*great drive from 18th on grid/FL*	18/24
2	TURKISH GP	Istanbul Park	2	Red Bull Racing	P	2.4 Red Bull RB7-Renault V8	*FL*	2/24
4	SPANISH GP	Barcelona	2	Red Bull Racing	P	2.4 Red Bull RB7-Renault V8		1/24
4	MONACO GP	Monte Carlo	2	Red Bull Racing	P	2.4 Red Bull RB7-Renault V8	*FL*	3/24
3	CANADIAN GP	Montreal	2	Red Bull Racing	P	2.4 Red Bull RB7-Renault V8		4/24
3	EUROPEAN GP	Valencia	2	Red Bull Racing	P	2.4 Red Bull RB7-Renault V8		2/24
3	BRITISH GP	Silverstone	2	Red Bull Racing	P	2.4 Red Bull RB7-Renault V8		1/24
3	GERMAN GP	Hockenheim	2	Red Bull Racing	P	2.4 Red Bull RB7-Renault V8		1/24
5	HUNGARIAN GP	Hungaroring	2	Red Bull Racing	P	2.4 Red Bull RB7-Renault V8		6/24
2	BELGIAN GP	Spa	2	Red Bull Racing	P	2.4 Red Bull RB7-Renault V8	*FL*	3/24
ret	ITALIAN GP	Monza	2	Red Bull Racing	P	2.4 Red Bull RB7-Renault V8	*collision – Massa/lost front wing crashed*	5/24
9	SINGAPORE GP	Marina Bay Circuit	2	Red Bull Racing	P	2.4 Red Bull RB7-Renault V8		2/24
4	JAPANESE GP	Suzuka	2	Red Bull Racing	P	2.4 Red Bull RB7-Renault V8		6/24
3	KOREAN GP	Yeongam	2	Red Bull Racing	P	2.4 Red Bull RB7-Renault V8		4/24
4	INDIAN GP	Buddh Circuit	1	Red Bull Racing	P	2.4 Red Bull RB7-Renault V8		3/24
4	ABU DHABI GP	Yas Marina Circuit	2	Red Bull Racing	P	2.4 Red Bull RB7-Renault V8	*FL*	4/24
1	BRAZILIAN GP	Interlagos	2	Red Bull Racing	P	2.4 Red Bull RB7-Renault V8	*FL*	2/24

GP Starts: 176   GP Wins: 7   Pole positions: 9   Fastest laps: 13   Points: 699.5

Webber scored a brilliant win for Red Bull in the 2010 Monaco Grand Prix. The popular Australian was just edged out of the championship that year by team-mate Vettel in a thrilling finale at Abu Dhabi.

KARL WENDLINGER

RACING was in Karl Wendlinger's blood, for both his father and grandfather had competed in the past, and naturally he followed suit. After some karting experience, the Austrian was helped greatly by Gerhard Berger (an old family friend) to get started in FF1600 in 1987. Assisted by former grand prix driver Dr Helmut Marko, Karl came to the fore in the 1989 German F3 championship with some excellent drives in a Ralt and took the title, edging out Michael Schumacher and Heinz-Harald Frentzen after the closest of battles.

This trio of young talent was selected by Mercedes-Benz to be groomed in their Group C programme as possible candidates for a future Formula 1 return. Paired with Jochen Mass, the best possible tutor, the young Austrian learned quickly and helped the company achieve its goal of winning the teams' championship with a win at Spa, and second places at Suzuka and Monza. The necessity of having top-class equipment at his disposal was brought home, however, when he endured a rather lacklustre time in Formula 3000 that year with a Marko-run Lola, taking only two championship points.

The 1991 season saw the two star pupils, Wendlinger and Schumacher, paired together in the same Mercedes, and they performed splendidly in the somewhat less than previously dominant silver cars. A win at Autopolis was the high point of the season, and Karl was found a place in the Leyton House team for the final two races of the year. All eyes were really opened in South Africa at the beginning of 1992, when he qualified the largely unregarded car in seventh place on the grid. A brilliant fourth place in Canada gave some indication of his potential, but the season was largely inconclusive due to reliability problems with the Ilmor V10. It had been a useful preparatory year for him, though, and for 1993 he moved to the new Sauber team as Mercedes had foreseen. In its first season, the Swiss entrant made excellent progress and Wendlinger scored points on four occasions, although unfortunately he was involved in a number of on-track incidents that blotted his copybook somewhat.

The 1994 season saw Karl partnered by his ex-Mercedes Group C team-mate, Frentzen, and it was immediately apparent that the newcomer meant business. Everything started satisfactorily for him, with points-scoring finishes in Brazil and at Imola, but then he was involved in a relatively low-speed crash during practice for the Monaco GP, the impact resulting in a brain contusion and swelling. He was immediately hospitalised and kept in a stable condition by means of a medically induced coma for almost three weeks, but thankfully he was soon on the road to recovery, although it was not until near the end of the season that he returned to the cockpit. Unfortunately, after testing in Barcelona, he was not well enough to race and had to wait until the beginning of 1995 to resume his career. Somehow the old spark was missing, and he struggled visibly to come to terms with the sheer speed of Frentzen. Eventually, Sauber took the tough decision to rest him from the team in favour of Jean-Christophe Boullion, and it was only at season's end, when the Frenchman's star had waned in the wake of some poor performances, that Karl was brought back for a final chance to show he could still do the business. Sadly, it seems that when he withdrew from the Australian Grand Prix, suffering the effects of a practice crash, his fate was sealed.

Instead of looking back on a lost career, Karl started to build a new one. A two-year contract with Audi saw him compete in both the German and Italian Super Touring series, before he was invited to join the ORECA team for 1998 to drive their Chrysler Viper. A win in the GT2 class with Justin Bell at the A1-Ring brought his first victory of any kind since his Group C Mercedes days in 1991 and, after he teamed up with Olivier Beretta for 1999, the Viper pair stormed to the newly formed Sports Racing World Cup, winning six of the nine rounds. This included a class win at Le Mans, which he repeated the following year with Beretta and Dominique Dupuy.

In 2001, Wendlinger raced the problematic Chrysler LMP prototype. Even with a best result of fourth place at Le Mans (with Beretta and Pedro Lamy), he failed to convince the Chrysler Corporation that it was worth continuing and they cancelled the programme, leaving him to find employment with Audi in the DTM for 2002/03. In truth, he was overshadowed by his team-mates, Laurent Aïello and Mathias Ekstöm, and relished the chance to return to GT racing in 2004 with JMB, driving a Ferrari 575 Maranello and taking a fine win in the Donington 500km with Jaime Melo.

Wendlinger continued to compete in the GT classes of the FIA GT series. In 2005, he won the Magny-Cours 500km in a Maserati with Andrea Bertolini, and the following year, after switching to an Aston Martin DBR9, he took victory in the Mugello 500km. More success followed with the car in 2007, when he recorded three wins (at Monza, Adria and Zolder) with Ryan Sharp.

Their winning partnership continued in 2008, when victory in the Tourist Trophy at Silverstone was followed by wins at Oschersleben and Brno. Wendlinger and Sharp then switched camps to race a Saleen in 2009, immediately replicating their Silverstone triumph, before the season turned sour for the Czech outfit after their victory in Hungary was denied them following exclusion over a technical issue. Wendlinger soon began looking for alternative employment and found a berth with the Swiss Racing Team, driving a Nissan GTR in 2010 and a Lamborghini Murciélago in 2011. Unfortunately, the Austrian's season ended early after both team cars were severely damaged at Sachsenring.

WENDLINGER, Karl (A) b 20/12/1968, Kufstein

1991 Championship position: Unplaced

	Race	Circuit	No	Entrant	Tyres	Capacity/Car/Engine	Comment	Q Pos/Entries
ret	JAPANESE GP	Suzuka	16	Leyton House Racing	G	3.5 Leyton House CG911-Ilmor V10	multiple collision on lap 1	22/32
20	AUSTRALIAN GP	Adelaide	16	Leyton House Racing	G	3.5 Leyton House CG911-Ilmor V10	rain-shortened race/2 laps behind	26/31

1992 Championship position: 12th — Wins: 0 — Pole positions: 0 — Fastest laps: 0 — Points scored: 3

	Race	Circuit	No	Entrant	Tyres	Capacity/Car/Engine	Comment	Q Pos/Entries
ret	SOUTH AFRICAN GP	Kyalami	16	March F1	G	3.5 March CG 911-Ilmor V10	overheating	7/30
ret	MEXICAN GP	Mexico City	16	March F1	G	3.5 March CG 911-Ilmor V10	collision with Capelli on lap 1	19/30
ret	BRAZILIAN GP	Interlagos	16	March F1	G	3.5 March CG 911-Ilmor V10	clutch	9/31
8	SPANISH GP	Barcelona	16	March F1	G	3.5 March CG 911-Ilmor V10	2 laps behind	9/32
12	SAN MARINO GP	Imola	16	March F1	G	3.5 March CG 911-Ilmor V10	3 laps behind	12/32
ret	MONACO GP	Monte Carlo	16	March F1	G	3.5 March CG 911-Ilmor V10	gearbox	16/32
4	CANADIAN GP	Montreal	16	March F1	G	3.5 March CG 911-Ilmor V10	1 lap behind	12/32
ret	FRENCH GP	Magny Cours	16	March F1	G	3.5 March CG 911-Ilmor V10	gearbox	21/30
ret	BRITISH GP	Silverstone	16	March F1	G	3.5 March CG 911-Ilmor V10	gearbox	21/32
16	GERMAN GP	Hockenheim	16	March F1	G	3.5 March CG 911-Ilmor V10	3 laps behind	10/32
ret	HUNGARIAN GP	Hungaroring	16	March F1	G	3.5 March CG 911-Ilmor V10	collision with Grouillard	23/31
11	BELGIAN GP	Spa	16	March F1	G	3.5 March CG 911-Ilmor V10	1 lap behind	18/30
10	ITALIAN GP	Monza	16	March F1	G	3.5 March CG 911-Ilmor V10	3 laps behind	17/28
ret	PORTUGUESE GP	Estoril	16	March F1	G	3.5 March CG 911-Ilmor V10	oil cooler/gearbox	22/26

1993 Championship position: 11th= — Wins: 0 — Pole positions: 0 — Fastest laps: 0 — Points scored: 7

	Race	Circuit	No	Entrant	Tyres	Capacity/Car/Engine	Comment	Q Pos/Entries
ret	SOUTH AFRICAN GP	Kyalami	29	Sauber	G	3.5 Sauber C12-Ilmor V10	electronics	10/26
ret	BRAZILIAN GP	Interlagos	29	Sauber	G	3.5 Sauber C12-Ilmor V10	overheating	8/26
ret	EUROPEAN GP	Donington	29	Sauber	G	3.5 Sauber C12-Ilmor V10	hit by Michael Andretti on lap 1	5/26
ret	SAN MARINO GP	Imola	29	Sauber	G	3.5 Sauber C12-Ilmor V10	engine	5/26
ret	SPANISH GP	Barcelona	29	Sauber	G	3.5 Sauber C12-Ilmor V10	engine	6/26
13	MONACO GP	Monte Carlo	29	Sauber	G	3.5 Sauber C12-Ilmor V10	collision with Lehto – pit stop/-4 laps	8/26
6	CANADIAN GP	Montreal	29	Sauber	G	3.5 Sauber C12-Ilmor V10	1 lap behind	9/26
ret	FRENCH GP	Magny Cours	29	Sauber	G	3.5 Sauber C12-Ilmor V10	gearbox	11/26
ret	BRITISH GP	Silverstone	29	Sauber	G	3.5 Sauber C12-Ilmor V10	spun off	18/26
9	GERMAN GP	Hockenheim	29	Sauber	G	3.5 Sauber C12-Ilmor V10	1 lap behind	14/26
6	HUNGARIAN GP	Hungaroring	29	Sauber	G	3.5 Sauber C12-Ilmor V10	1 lap behind	17/26
ret	BELGIAN GP	Spa	29	Sauber	G	3.5 Sauber C12-Ilmor V10	engine	12/26
4	ITALIAN GP	Monza	29	Sauber	G	3.5 Sauber C12-Ilmor V10	1 lap behind	15/26
5	PORTUGUESE GP	Estoril	29	Sauber	G	3.5 Sauber C12-Ilmor V10	1 lap behind	13/26
ret	JAPANESE GP	Suzuka	29	Sauber	G	3.5 Sauber C12-Ilmor V10	stuck throttle	16/24
15/ret	AUSTRALIAN GP	Adelaide	29	Sauber	G	3.5 Sauber C12-Ilmor V10	brake disc – spun off/5 laps behind	11/24

1994 Championship position: 18th= — Wins: 0 — Pole positions: 0 — Fastest laps: 0 — Points scored: 4

	Race	Circuit	No	Entrant	Tyres	Capacity/Car/Engine	Comment	Q Pos/Entries
6	BRAZILIAN GP	Interlagos	29	Sauber Mercedes	G	3.5 Sauber C13-Mercedes Benz V10	2 laps behind	7/28
ret	PACIFIC GP	T.I. Circuit	29	Sauber Mercedes	G	3.5 Sauber C13-Mercedes Benz V10	accident – hit by Alboreto	19/28
4	SAN MARINO GP	Imola	29	Sauber Mercedes	G	3.5 Sauber C13-Mercedes Benz V10	broken exhaust	10/28
dns	MONACO GP	Monte Carlo	29	Sauber Mercedes	G	3.5 Sauber C13-Mercedes Benz V10	practice accident – seriously injured	- / -

1995 Championship position: Unplaced

	Race	Circuit	No	Entrant	Tyres	Capacity/Car/Engine	Comment	Q Pos/Entries
ret	BRAZILIAN GP	Interlagos	29	Red Bull Sauber Ford	G	3.0 Sauber C14-Ford Zetec-R V8	electrics	19/26
ret	ARGENTINE GP	Buenos Aires	29	Red Bull Sauber Ford	G	3.0 Sauber C14-Ford Zetec-R V8	collision with Gachot	21/26
ret	SAN MARINO GP	Imola	29	Red Bull Sauber Ford	G	3.0 Sauber C14-Ford Zetec-R V8	stuck wheel nut	21/26
13	SPANISH GP	Barcelona	29	Red Bull Sauber Ford	G	3.0 Sauber C14-Ford Zetec-R V8	2 laps behind	20/26
10	JAPANESE GP	Suzuka	29	Red Bull Sauber Ford	G	3.0 Sauber C14-Ford Zetec-R V8	2 laps behind	16/24
ret	AUSTRALIAN GP	Adelaide	29	Red Bull Sauber Ford	G	3.0 Sauber C14-Ford Zetec-R V8	withdrew – driver unwell	18/24

GP Starts: 41   GP Wins: 0   Pole positions: 0   Fastest laps: 0   Points: 14

PETER WESTBURY

PETER WESTBURY'S career fell neatly into two halves, the first as a top-notch hill-climber, the second as a true circuit racer. He took to the hills in 1962 with a Cooper-Daimler and, when the V8 was dropped into his own Felday chassis in 1963, his first British hill-climb championship was duly attained. For the following year, he got his hands on the Ferguson 4WD, which proved almost unbeatable.

Although Wesbury continued to compete in 1965, he was busy building up his Felday Engineering firm. He made a successful transition to Formula 3 in 1967, however, with a Brabham BT21. He won races at Silverstone, Chimay and Clermont-Ferrand, and took further victories at Chimay again and Reims in 1968.

That year saw a couple of Formula 2 drives, before a full season in 1969 with his own Brabham BT30, which yielded second place in the Lottery GP at Monza and fifth in the F2 class of the German Grand Prix.

Peter was given a chance to try a pukka F1 machine when he joined BRM for the 1970 US Grand Prix, but the car suffered a blown engine and the disappointed driver failed to qualify. He was a consistent top-six finisher in Formula 2 during 1970/71, but results sagged the following year, and early in 1973 he announced his retirement.

WESTBURY, Peter (GB) b 26/5/1938, South London

1969 Championship position: Unplaced

	Race	Circuit	No	Entrant	Tyres	Capacity/Car/Engine	Comment	Q Pos/Entries
9*	GERMAN GP (F2)	Nürburgring	31	Felday Engineering Ltd	F	1.6 Brabham BT30-Cosworth 4 F2	*5th in F2 class/1 lap behind	18/26

1970 Championship position: Unplaced

	Race	Circuit	No	Entrant	Tyres	Capacity/Car/Engine	Comment	Q Pos/Entries
dnq	US GP	Watkins Glen	32	Yardley Team BRM	D	3.0 BRM P153 V12		25/27

GP Starts: 1   GP Wins: 0   Pole positions: 0   Fastest laps: 0   Points: 0

WHARTON, Ken (GB) b 21/3/1916, Smethwick, Worcestershire – d 12/1/1957, Ardmore Circuit, New Zealand

1952 Championship position: 10=   Wins: 0   Pole positions: 0   Fastest laps: 0   Points scored: 3

	Race	Circuit	No	Entrant	Tyres	Capacity/Car/Engine	Comment	Q Pos/Entries
4	SWISS GP	Bremgarten	22	Scuderia Franera	D	2.0 Frazer Nash FN48-Bristol 6	2 laps behind	13/21
ret	BELGIAN GP	Spa	36	Scuderia Franera	D	2.0 Frazer Nash FN48-Bristol 6	spun off	7/22
ret	DUTCH GP	Zandvoort	34	Scuderia Franera	D	2.0 Frazer Nash 421-Bristol 6	transmission	7/18
9	ITALIAN GP	Monza	40	Scuderia Franera	D	2.0 Cooper T20-Bristol 6	4 laps behind	15/35

1953 Championship position: Unplaced

	Race	Circuit	No	Entrant	Tyres	Capacity/Car/Engine	Comment	Q Pos/Entries
ret	DUTCH GP	Zandvoort	32	Ken Wharton	D	2.0 Cooper T23-Bristol 6	rear suspension	18/20
ret	FRENCH GP	Reims	40	Ken Wharton	D	2.0 Cooper T23-Bristol 6	engine	14/25
8	BRITISH GP	Silverstone	16	Ken Wharton	D	2.0 Cooper T23-Bristol 6	10 laps behind	11/29
7	SWISS GP	Bremgarten	20	Ken Wharton	D	2.0 Cooper T23-Bristol 6	3 laps behind	9/23
nc	ITALIAN GP	Monza	30	Ken Wharton	D	2.0 Cooper T23-Bristol 6	23 laps behind	19/30

1954 Championship position: Unplaced

	Race	Circuit	No	Entrant	Tyres	Capacity/Car/Engine	Comment	Q Pos/Entries
ret	FRENCH GP	Reims	42	Owen Racing Organisation	D	2.5 Maserati 250F 6	transmission	16/22
8	BRITISH GP	Silverstone	8	Owen Racing Organisation	D	2.5 Maserati 250F 6	4 laps behind	9/31
dns	GERMAN GP	Nürburgring	17	Owen Racing Organisation	D	2.5 Maserati 250F 6	withdrawn during practice	– /23
6	SWISS GP	Bremgarten	18	Owen Racing Organisation	D	2.5 Maserati 250F 6	2 laps behind	8/16
8	SPANISH GP	Pedralbes	28	Owen Racing Organisation	D	2.5 Maserati 250F 6	6 laps behind	14/22

1955 Championship position: Unplaced

	Race	Circuit	No	Entrant	Tyres	Capacity/Car/Engine	Comment	Q Pos/Entries
nc*	BRITISH GP	Aintree	28	Vandervell Products Ltd	P	2.5 Vanwall 4	*Schell took over car/18 laps behind	15/25
ret	ITALIAN GP	Monza	44	Vandervell Products Ltd	P	2.5 Vanwall 4	fuel injection pump mounting	17/22

GP Starts: 15   GP Wins: 0   Pole positions: 0   Fastest laps: 0   Points: 3

KEN WHARTON

A GARAGE owner from Smethwick, near Birmingham, Ken Wharton was a versatile all-rounder who began racing immediately before the Second World War in an Austin 7 special, but it was not until the late 1940s that he began to make his mark in a number of motorsport arenas. In trials, he won successive RAC championships, and his special was much copied by his competitors, while in rallies he campaigned a Ford Pilot, winning the Tulip Rally on three occasions.

In 1950, Wharton won at Zandvoort with a Cooper-JAP, while in 1951 he went hill-climbing, winning the first of four successive championships. Meanwhile, he had taken up circuit racing in a big way, initially competing in grands prix with a large and old-fashioned Frazer-Nash. It ran reliably on its debut at Bremgarten in 1952, and he took it to fourth place, his best ever world championship finish.

This car had been replaced by a more competitive Cooper-Bristol by the end of the season, but Ken could gain no major success with it the following season. He was kept busy by BRM, however, who were still racing their V16 car in Libre events, and he joined the Owen team for 1954 to handle their Maserati 250F in grands prix and their V16 in Libre races, winning the Glover Trophy.

As if he wasn't already sufficiently stretched by his commitments, Wharton also tried his hand at sports car racing with the works Jaguar, winning the 1954 Reims 12-hours with Peter Whitehead. For 1955, he joined the Vanwall team, suffering a nasty accident in the International Trophy at Silverstone, which resulted in burns to his arms and neck. Generally, it was an unproductive year, and he freelanced in 1956, taking a third place in the Australian Tourist Trophy in Melbourne with a Ferrari Monza. However, early in 1957 he was killed after crashing this car in a sports car race at Ardmore, New Zealand.

GRAHAM WHITEHEAD

HAVING begun racing in half-brother Peter's ERA in 1951, Graham Whitehead drove his Formula 2 Alta in the 1952 British Grand Prix, which was his only grand prix start. Although he raced single-seaters on occasion, his appearances tended to be restricted to Libre events in an ERA. He embarked on a long and generally successful period when he competed in his Jaguar and Aston Martin sports cars, often paired with Peter, or with Tony Gaze in his Aston DB3 or HWM.

The Whiteheads' greatest success together was second place in the 1958 Le Mans 24-hours, only weeks before the crash in the Tour de France that killed Peter. Graham escaped serious injury, however, and returned to competition, racing his Aston Martin DBR1 and then a Ferrari 250GT in smaller GT races until the end of the 1961 season.

PETER WHITEHEAD

A THROWBACK to the age of the truly amateur driver, wealthy businessman Peter Whitehead had the means with which to indulge his passion for motorsport in the best possible fashion. He began racing in 1934 and soon began making a name for himself in an ERA. He took the car to Australia in 1938 and won the grand prix at the Bathurst circuit.

Peter's trusty ERA was back in action after the Second World War and took second place in the 1947 British Empire Trophy at the Isle of Man. The following year, he was seriously injured – not when racing, but in an air crash at Croydon Aerodrome when preparing to fly to Milan to arrange the purchase of a Ferrari 125. It was the 1949 season before he was able to put the green machine through its paces in competition. He looked set to win the French GP at Reims, until gearbox problems dropped him to third place, but he did triumph in Czechoslovakia, becoming the first Briton to win a major race abroad since Dick Seaman in 1938. His successes with the Ferrari continued into the 1950 season, when he took the Jersey Road Race and the Ulster Trophy. Despite his amateur status, Peter was certainly no slouch as a driver and he scored some excellent Continental placings in the 1951 season with the Ferrari, but undoubtedly the highlight of his year was a glorious Le Mans win with Peter Walker for Jaguar.

The 1952 and 1953 seasons saw Whitehead campaigning an Alta and a Cooper-Alta in addition to his Ferrari, but by then he was finding it more rewarding to race sports cars, where the chances of success were greater. In 1953, with a D-Type Jaguar, he won the Reims 12-hours with Stirling Moss and the Hyères 12-hours with Tom Cole. He triumphed again in the Reims 12-hours the following year, sharing a works Jaguar with Ken Wharton, but after his last British GP appearance, little was seen of him in Formula 1. He preferred to concentrate on his newly acquired Cooper-Jaguar sports car and Libre events with his Ferrari 3-litre – particularly in the Antipodes, where he often raced during the British winter.

Peter's last great performance came in the 1958 Le Mans 24-hours, when he shared the second-placed Aston Martin with his half-brother, Graham. Just a couple of months later, during the Tour de France, the pair's Jaguar, with Graham at the wheel, crashed over a bridge parapet into a ravine, injuring the driver, but killing his unfortunate passenger.

BILL WHITEHOUSE

ONE of the top 500cc F3 Cooper drivers of the early 1950s, 'Big Bill' Whitehouse raced Gordon Watson's Formula 2 Alta briefly in 1951, before breaking out of the tiddler class in 1954 with his own Formula 2 Connaught. Sensibly, he kept to Libre and national events, with the exception of the British Grand Prix at Silverstone.

After an accident, Bill retired from competition, but once he was fit the lure of the track proved too great for this enthusiast. In 1957, he bought an F2 Cooper-Climax, which he raced at the Syracuse Grand Prix, and when his car suffered engine trouble at Reims, he was delighted to be loaned the works Bobtail 'streamliner' for the race. Tragically, he met his death when a tyre appeared to blow as he approached Thillois; the car somersaulted into a field and burst into flames. Poor Whitehouse was thrown out, suffering burns and serious internal injuries, from which he had no chance of survival. Soon after, in the same race, Herbert Mackay-Fraser was also killed when he crashed his Lotus.

Bill's son and racing companion, Brian, continued to compete in club events.

WHITEHEAD, Graham (GB) b 15/4/1922, Harrogate, Yorkshire – d 15/1/1981, Lower Basildon, nr Reading, Berkshire

1952 Championship position: Unplaced

	Race	Circuit	No	Entrant	Tyres	Capacity/Car/Engine	Comment	Q Pos/Entries
12	BRITISH GP	Silverstone	1	Peter Whitehead	D	2.0 Alta F2 4	5 laps behind	12/32

GP Starts: 1   GP Wins: 0   Pole positions: 0   Fastest laps: 0   Points: 0

WHITEHEAD, Peter (GB) b 12/11/1914, Menstone, nr Ilkley, Yorkshire – d 21/9/1958, Lasalle, nr Nimes, France

1950 Championship position: 9=   Wins: 0   Pole positions: 0   Fastest laps: 0   Points scored: 4

	Race	Circuit	No	Entrant	Tyres	Capacity/Car/Engine	Comment	Q Pos/Entries
dns	MONACO GP	Monte Carlo	28	Peter Whitehead	D	1.5 s/c Ferrari 125 V12	3 engine failures in practice	(21)/21
3	FRENCH GP	Reims	14	Peter Whitehead	D	1.5 s/c Ferrari 125 V12	3 laps behind	19/20
7	ITALIAN GP	Monza	8	Peter Whitehead	D	1.5 s/c Ferrari 125 V12	8 laps behind	18/27

1951 Championship position: Unplaced

ret	SWISS GP	Bremgarten	16	Scuderia Ferrari	D	1.5 s/c Ferrari 125 V12	crashed – cut face	9/21
ret	FRENCH GP	Reims	24	Graham Whitehead	D	1.5 s/c Ferrari 125 V12	cylinder head gasket	20/23
9	BRITISH GP	Silverstone	14	G A Vandervell	P	4.5 Thinwall Ferrari 375F1 V12	7 laps behind	8/20
ret	ITALIAN GP	Monza	16	Peter Whitehead	D	1.5 s/c Ferrari 125 V12	engine	19/22

1952 Championship position: Unplaced

ret	FRENCH GP	Rouen	26	Peter Whitehead	D	2.0 Alta F2 4	clutch	13/20
10	BRITISH GP	Silverstone	21	Peter Whitehead	D	2.0 Ferrari 125 V12 F2	4 laps behind	20/32
dnq	ITALIAN GP	Monza	68	Peter Whitehead	D	2.0 Ferrari 125 V12 F2		29/35

1953 Championship position: Unplaced

9	BRITISH GP	Silverstone	20	Atlantic Stable	D	2.0 Cooper T24-Alta 4	brake problems/11 laps behind	14/29

1954 Championship position: Unplaced

ret	BRITISH GP	Silverstone	21	Peter Whitehead	D	2.5 Cooper T24-Alta 4	engine	24/31

GP Starts: 10   GP Wins: 0   Pole positions: 0   Fastest laps: 0   Points: 4

WHITEHOUSE, Bill (GB) b 1/4/1909, London – d 14/7/1957, Reims Circuit, France

1954 Championship position: Unplaced

	Race	Circuit	No	Entrant	Tyres	Capacity/Car/Engine	Comment	Q Pos/Entries
ret	BRITISH GP	Silverstone	22	Bill Whitehouse	D	2.0 Connaught A Type-Lea Francis 4	fuel system	19/31

GP Starts: 1   GP Wins: 0   Pole positions: 0   Fastest laps: 0   Points: 0

WIDDOWS, Robin (GB) b 27/5/1942, Cowley, nr Uxbridge, Middlesex

1968 Championship position: Unplaced

	Race	Circuit	No	Entrant	Tyres	Capacity/Car/Engine	Comment	Q Pos/Entries
ret	BRITISH GP	Brands Hatch	16	Cooper Car Co	F	3.0 Cooper T86-BRM V12	ignition	18/20

GP Starts: 1   GP Wins: 0   Pole positions: 0   Fastest laps: 0   Points: 0

ROBIN WIDDOWS

AN Olympic-standard bobsleigh rider, Robin Widdows represented Great Britain in Sapporo in 1964 and Grenoble in 1968. He also raced an MG Midget and a then Lotus 23, winning the Autosport Class C championship in 1965, before successfully moving up to Formula 3 the following year. A group of friends financed a season of Formula 2 under the Whitley Racing Syndicate banner in 1967 in a Brabham BT23, the highlight of a 19-race schedule being a surprise win in the Rhine Cup at Hockenheim.

For 1968, Widdows joined the Chequered Flag team to drive a McLaren M4A and took second place at Pau with a superb display, backing this up with a third in the Lottery Grand Prix at Monza. The ailing Cooper team gave him his only grand prix outing at that year's British Grand Prix at Brands Hatch, and although the car was hardly a world-beater, Robin acquitted himself well before retiring mid-way through the race. Mysteriously, there were no further calls to race in Formula 1, so it was back to Formula 2 with Bob Gerard in 1969.

Widdows did well once more, winning the Lottery Grand Prix at Monza and taking second in a slipstreamer fest at Reims. He also raced sports cars for Matra, finishing seventh at Le Mans with Nanni Galli. In addition, he raced Ulf Norinder's Lola T70 and took an end-of-year trip to South Africa to share Alistair Walker's Ferrari P4, the pair taking second place in the Lourenço Marques three-hour race. In 1970, he raced Alistair Walker's Brabham BT30, again in Formula 2, until suddenly retiring from competition in mid-season after deciding that he was not going to make any further progress. Subsequently, he returned to F1 as the representative of Moët & Chandon between 1992 and 1998.

EPPIE WIETZES

ONE of Canada's most enduring and successful drivers at national level, Eppie Wietzes began racing as far back as 1958, and by the early 1960s he was a leading sports and GT contender with such diverse cars as AC Cobras, Ford Mustangs and a Ford GT40.

In 1967, Wietzes hired the third works Lotus to race alongside Jim Clark (pictured) and Graham Hill in the first World Championship Canadian GP. Switching to single-seaters, he was Canadian FA champion with a Lola T142 in 1969, and again the following year, this time with a McLaren M10. Then he became one of the leading privateers on the US F5000 circuit in the early 1970s.

Wietzes won a round at Donnybrooke in 1972 in his Lola T300 and drove superbly in 1974, generally being beaten only by Mario Andretti and Brian Redman. He ran a hired Brabham in the 1974 grand prix, without success and, after the demise of F5000 Stateside, he re-appeared in Trans-Am. In 1981, he took the CRC championship with some stylish drives in Garretson Enterprises' Chevrolet Corvette.

MIKE WILDS

A FORMER Firestone employee, Mike Wilds spent seven years in club racing before hitting the Formula 3 trail in 1972. With backing from a loyal sponsor, Dempster Developments, he was a leading runner and occasional winner in F3 before opting to race in F5000 in 1974. In mid-season, however, he was given the chance to race in Formula 1, initially with a March and then with Ensign. Invited to lead the BRM team for 1975, poor Wilds only lasted two races before the Stanley axe fell.

Shortly afterwards, Mike split from his long-time sponsor and went back to F5000, racing an ex-works Shadow in 1976. Driving a Ralt, he took the F2 class championship in the 1978 Aurora AFX series, and later he became a star of club racing once more, enjoying himself immensely in historics and sports cars. In 1994, he was invited to demonstrate the ex-Gilles Villeneuve Ferrari 312T3 at the Goodwood Festival of Speed. Unfortunately, he crashed the car quite heavily, sustaining a broken leg and other serious injuries. Undeterred, he was back on the tracks once more in 1995 and since has been a champion in historic racing events, driving a Chevron B31/36 sports car.

Nowadays, Mike offers hands-on driving tuition, passing on the wealth of experience he has gained by racing at all levels for more than 45 years.

WIETZES, Eppie (CDN) b 28/5/1938, Assen, Netherlands

1967 Championship position: Unplaced

	Race	Circuit	No	Entrant	Tyres	Capacity/Car/Engine	Comment	Q Pos/Entries
ret	CANADIAN GP	Mosport Park	5	Team Lotus/Comstock Racing Team	F	3.0 Lotus 49-Cosworth V8	wet ignition	17/19

1974 Championship position: 0 Unplaced

	Race	Circuit	No	Entrant	Tyres	Capacity/Car/Engine	Comment	Q Pos/Entries
ret	CANADIAN GP	Mosport Park	50	Team Canada Formula 1 Racing	G	3.0 Brabham BT42-Cosworth V8	transmission	26/30

GP Starts: 2 GP Wins: 0 Pole positions: 0 Fastest laps: 0 Points: 0

WILDS, Mike (GB) b 7/1/1946, Chiswick, London

1974 Championship position: Unplaced

	Race	Circuit	No	Entrant	Tyres	Capacity/Car/Engine	Comment	Q Pos/Entries
dnq	BRITISH GP	Brands Hatch	35	Dempster International Racing Team	F	3.0 March 731-Cosworth V8		33/34
dnq	AUSTRIAN GP	Österreichring	22	Team Ensign	F	3.0 Ensign N174-Cosworth V8		29/31
dnq	ITALIAN GP	Monza	25	Team Ensign	F	3.0 Ensign N174-Cosworth V8		29/31
dnq	CANADIAN GP	Mosport Park	22	Team Ensign	F	3.0 Ensign N174-Cosworth V8		28/30
nc	US GP	Watkins Glen	22	Team Ensign	F	3.0 Ensign N174-Cosworth V8	pit stop – fuel pump/9 laps behind	22/30

1975 Championship position: Unplaced

	Race	Circuit	No	Entrant	Tyres	Capacity/Car/Engine	Comment	Q Pos/Entries
ret	ARGENTINE GP	Buenos Aires	14	Stanley BRM	G	3.0 BRM P201 V12	oil scavenge pump drive belt	22/23
ret	BRAZILIAN GP	Interlagos	14	Stanley BRM	G	3.0 BRM P201 V12	electrics – damaged by loose nut	22/23

1976 Championship position: Unplaced

	Race	Circuit	No	Entrant	Tyres	Capacity/Car/Engine	Comment	Q Pos/Entries
dnq	BRITISH GP	Brands Hatch	40	Team P R Reilly	G	3.0 Shadow DN3-Cosworth V8		29/30

GP Starts: 3 GP Wins: 0 Pole positions: 0 Fastest laps: 0 Points: 0

WILLIAMS, Jonathan (GB) b 26/10/1942, Cairo, Egypt

1967 Championship position: Unplaced

	Race	Circuit	No	Entrant	Tyres	Capacity/Car/Engine	Comment	Q Pos/Entries
8	MEXICAN GP	Mexico City	12	Scuderia Ferrari SpA SEFAC	F	3.0 Ferrari 312/67 V12	2 laps behind	16/19

GP Starts: 1 GP Wins: 0 Pole positions: 0 Fastest laps: 0 Points: 0

JONATHAN WILLIAMS

AFTER racing Minis and then impressively in an Austin A40, Jonathan Williams graduated to Formula Junior in 1963, basing himself in Europe. He was soon joined by his old pal, Piers Courage, and they lived a hand-to-mouth existence, racing their F3 Lotus 22-Fords from their base in Lausanne. The following year, Charles Lucas took both of them on board with a pair of Brabhams, and it was a highly successful year all round, Jonathan taking wins at Monza and Zolder. When Courage returned to the UK to develop his career, Williams stayed on the Continent to take a works Formula 3 drive with de Sanctis. It was a good move for the diminutive driver, who recorded eight wins that plucked him from relative obscurity to a seat with Ferrari in 1967.

It was a season that promised much, but delivered little. When the Formula 2 car proved to be uncompetitive (it was withdrawn after just one outing at Rouen), Williams was left with a few sports car and Can-Am outings until he was the surprise choice for the end-of-season Mexican Grand Prix. It was a daunting debut for the driver, being thrown at the last minute into a car he did not fit properly. In the end, he did the best he could and soldiered on to take a distant eighth place, before being discarded as casually as he seemed to have been signed.

A Formula 1 project for Abarth proved abortive, leaving Jonathan scratching for rides thereafter, although he took a thrilling win for Frank Williams at the Monza Lottery in 1968 to show that he still had the talent. In 1969, he teamed up with Paul Hawkins, but this partnership ended when the Australian was killed at Oulton Park. Thereafter, he hooked up with de Tomaso to briefly race their F2 car and test the ill-fated grand prix car driven by Piers Courage. At that stage, his career had lost any focus and he took occasional sports car drives, the last of which was in the 1971 Targa Florio in old friend Antonio Nicodemi's Lola, the pair finishing seventh. By then, having qualified as a pilot, he was flying private jets out of the South of France, before settling on a new lifestyle to pursue his new found passion for writing and photography.

ROGER WILLIAMSON

REMEMBERED as a smashing bloke, completely without pretension, and a terrific talent, Roger Williamson needlessly paid the ultimate price in front of millions of TV viewers on a tragic day at Zandvoort in 1973.

Roger had a successful karting career behind him when, with encouragement from his father, he took up circuit racing in an 850 Mini, winning 14 races in 1968. Having decided to try single-seaters, he purchased a Cooper T71, which unfortunately was burnt out in a garage fire. He took the engine and fitted it to a Ford Anglia, however, and it proved to be a potent combination. In 1970, he won the 1000cc class of the Hepolite Glacier championship with ease and decided to try Formula 3 the following year. Despite his inexperience, he soon became a front-runner, his spectacular driving in a March 713 catching the eye. He was fortunate at this time to be helped financially by local businessman and racing enthusiast Tom Wheatcroft; they became firm friends, and Tom guided his rise towards the top.

Having won the Lombank F3 championship, Williamson stayed in the formula for a further year and convincingly took both the major F3 titles that season. His foray into Formula 2 was not so happy, but it was good experience for a planned season in 1973 with GRD. The car turned out to be no match for the dominant March chassis, so Wheatcroft swiftly provided his charge with the equipment he needed. Almost immediately, Roger won the Lottery GP at Monza, and would have taken another victory at Misano but for engine problems, establishing himself as a truly serious talent.

A season in Formula 1 was the goal in 1974, and to this end Wheatcroft hired an STP March for a couple of races so that Williamson could become acclimatised. At Silverstone, he was eliminated in the now notorious Jody Scheckter-induced carnage, and then came Zandvoort. It is thought that a tyre failed, sending his car into an inadequately secured barrier, which launched it across the track. The March came to rest upside down and on fire, with poor Roger trapped in the cockpit. Scandalously, nobody came to his aid, apart from the brave David Purley, who single-handedly attempted to right the inverted machine. Then the fire caught hold and a truly nightmarish scene was complete. For Williamson, it was a cruel and gruesome end.

WILLIAMSON, Roger (GB) b 2/2/1948, Leicester – d 29/7/1973, Zandvoort Circuit, Netherlands

1973 Championship position: Unplaced

	Race	Circuit	No	Entrant	Tyres	Capacity/Car/Engine	Comment	Q Pos/Entries
ret/dns	BRITISH GP	Silverstone	14	STP March Racing/Wheatcroft Racing	G	3.0 March 731-Cosworth V8	*multiple accident at first start*	22/29
ret	DUTCH GP	Zandvoort	14	STP March Racing Team	G	3.0 March 731-Cosworth V8	*fatal accident*	18/24

GP Starts: 1 (2) GP Wins: 0 Pole positions: 0 Fastest laps: 0 Points: 0

JUSTIN WILSON

ALTHOUGH he doesn't necessarily look like a racing driver, the tall and gangly Justin Wilson proved that he has plenty of talent during his fleeting spell in Formula 1 – and since – despite the problems of having to squeeze his 6ft 4in frame into a single-seater racing car.

Wilson started racing karts at the age of eight and managed to be competitive in almost every series he contested. He moved up to Formula Vauxhall Junior and, taking victory on his debut, became the first ever 16-year-old to win a motor race. He spent two more years in the class, before deciding to join the brand-new Formula Palmer Audi championship in 1998. After a slow start to the year, his fortunes picked up, and six wins from the last seven races eventually secured the title. This was his big break, as series organiser Jonathan Palmer not only took the Briton under his wing, but also arranged an F3000 seat as first prize. Grasping the opportunity, Justin was one of only seven drivers to qualify for all ten rounds in the 1999 season, scoring twice with the Astromega team.

Eventually, Wilson opted for a seat at Nordic Racing, and the 2000 season yielded fifth in points, two podiums and an improved knowledge of the circuits. The following year, he was the first British driver to succeed in F3000, on the back of wins at Interlagos, the A1-Ring and Hungaroring, as well as seven further podiums. Wilson's consistency allowed him to break Juan Montoya's records for points accumulated and podium finishes

Although F1 was the natural progression, there were no viable seats available for 2002, so Wilson was forced to bide his time in the Telefónica World Series by Nissan championship, where he claimed two wins and six podium finishes to claim fourth overall.

That result was enough to convince Minardi boss Paul Stoddart that Wilson was the right man for his team, and the Briton duly signed to race alongside F1 veteran Jos Verstappen. Although the Minardi remained a back-of-the-grid car, both drivers caused eyebrows to be raised by often making up a lot of places on the opening laps of grands prix. Wilson's rookie performances eventually led to him being transferred to Jaguar to replace the under-performing Antonio Pizzonia. Running alongside former F3000 rival Mark Webber proved to be a tricky experience, however, as the Aussie was more established in the team. Wilson plugged away under the weight of greater expectations, however, eventually scoring a maiden world championship point for eighth place at the US Grand Prix.

Despite targeting several teams the following season, Wilson stumbled over the usual obstacle facing British drivers – lack of sponsorship. As a result of being unable to raise the funds to secure a seat in the top flight, he looked at alternative offers of employment for 2004 and plumped for the Champ Car series with Mi-Jack Conquest Racing. He acquitted himself extremely well, battling for Rookie of the Year honours with rising American star A.J. Allmendinger; a best finish of fourth in the season's Mexican finale saw him finish 11th overall, and runner-up in the rookie standings.

Wilson moved to the RuSPORT team for 2005, becoming a strong contender as the season progressed. He was the class of the field at Portland, where an engine let go while he had a comfortable lead, but a maiden victory was finally achieved in Toronto. Another followed in the Mexico City finale, and he finished third in the final standings. Remaining in situ for 2006, despite missing a race at Surfers Paradise due to a broken wrist, he moved up to finish in second place in the championship, even though he had won just one race, at Edmonton. Justin decided to stay with the team for a third year, and despite the upheaval caused by changes of ownership, he finished second once more, but still was unable to break the vice-like grip that Sébastien Bourdais exerted on the series.

After the open-wheel merger in 2008, Wilson took the French champion's place at Newman/Haas/Lanigan Racing, but could only manage a win at Detroit. With top rides now out of reach, he was forced to race for smaller teams, such as Dale Coyne, to whom he delivered their first ever Champ Car win after 23 years of trying, on an emotional day at Watkins Glen in 2009.

Subsequently, Justin moved to Dryer and Reinbold with mixed results, before suffering a serious back injury at New Hampshire, which curtailed his 2011 season. The Briton was fit for the start of the 2012 campaign, however, and started the year with his first win in the Rolex 24-hour sports car race at Daytona, before announcing his return to Coyne for the IRL season.

WILSON, Justin (GB) b 31/7/1978, Sheffield, South Yorkshire

2003 Championship position: 19th=   Wins: 0   Pole positions: 0   Fastest laps: 0   Points scored: 1

	Race	Circuit	No	Entrant	Tyres	Car/Engine	Comment	Q Pos/Entries
ret	AUSTRALIAN GP	Melbourne	18	European Minardi Cosworth	B	3.0 Minardi PS03-Cosworth V10	*no time set/radiator	*20/20
ret	MALAYSIAN GP	Sepang	18	European Minardi Cosworth	B	3.0 Minardi PS03-Cosworth V10	withdrew – cramped by HANS system	19/20
ret	BRAZILIAN GP	Interlagos	18	European Minardi Cosworth	B	3.0 Minardi PS03-Cosworth V10	spun off	20/20
ret	SAN MARINO GP	Imola	18	European Minardi Cosworth	B	3.0 Minardi PS03-Cosworth V10	refuelling problem/lost coolant	18/20
11	SPANISH GP	Barcelona	18	European Minardi Cosworth	B	3.0 Minardi PS03-Cosworth V10	2 laps behind	18/20
13	AUSTRIAN GP	A1-Ring	18	European Minardi Cosworth	B	3.0 Minardi PS03-Cosworth V10	2 laps behind	18/20
ret	MONACO GP	Monte Carlo	18	European Minardi Cosworth	B	3.0 Minardi PS03-Cosworth V10	fuel pick-up	19/19
ret	CANADIAN GP	Montreal	18	European Minardi Cosworth	B	3.0 Minardi PS03-Cosworth V10	transmission	18/20
13	EUROPEAN GP	Nürburgring	18	European Minardi Cosworth	B	3.0 Minardi PS03-Cosworth V10	2 laps behind	19/20

14	FRENCH GP	Magny Cours	18	European Minardi Cosworth	B	3.0 Minardi PS03-Cosworth V10	*3 laps behind*	20/20
16	BRITISH GP	Silverstone	18	European Minardi Cosworth	B	3.0 Minardi PS03-Cosworth V10	*2 laps behind*	18/20
ret	GERMAN GP	Hockenheim	15	Jaguar Racing	M	3.0 Jaguar R4-Cosworth V10	*stuck in gear*	16/20
ret	HUNGARIAN GP	Hungaroring	15	Jaguar Racing	M	3.0 Jaguar R4-Cosworth V10	*engine*	12/20
ret	ITALIAN GP	Monza	15	Jaguar Racing	M	3.0 Jaguar R4-Cosworth V10	*gearbox*	15/20
8	UNITED STATES GP	Indianapolis	15	Jaguar Racing	M	3.0 Jaguar R4-Cosworth V10	*2 laps behind*	16/20
13	JAPANESE GP	Suzuka	15	Jaguar Racing	M	3.0 Jaguar R4-Cosworth V10	*1 lap behind*	10/20

GP Starts: 16   GP Wins: 0   Pole positions: 0   Fastest laps: 0   Points: 1

WILSON, Vic (GB) b 14/4/1931, Drypool, Kingston-upon-Hull – d 14/10/2001, Gerrards Cross, Buckinghamshire

	1960 Championship position: Unplaced							
	Race	Circuit	No	Entrant	Tyres	Capacity/Car/Engine	Comment	Q Pos/Entries
ret	ITALIAN GP	Monza	30	Equipe Prideaux/Dick Gibson	D	1.5 Cooper T43-Climax 4	*engine – oil sump*	16/16
	1966 Championship position: Unplaced							
dns	BELGIAN GP	Spa	8	Team Chamaco-Collect	G	2.0 BRM P261-V8	*practice only – Bondurant raced car*	(17)/18

GP Starts: 1   GP Wins: 0   Pole positions: 0   Fastest laps: 0   Points: 0

VIC WILSON

HAVING been born in England, Vic Wilson spent his teens living in South Africa. He began racing in Rhodesia in the late 1950s, finding success with a variety of MGs and then a Lotus XI. Plans to race a Lotus in England went awry when the car was written off, but then he approached Dick Gibson, who was languishing in hospital after recently crashing his nearly-new Cooper.

Wilson repaired the machine and went racing along with Bruce Halford and Keith Ballisat, taking the wheel of the Cooper in the boycotted Italian Grand Prix of 1960.

After settling in Yorkshire, Vic did not race at all between 1961 and 1963, but at the behest of his wealthy cousin, Bernard White, he returned late in 1964, before a busy season racing a Lotus 30 with a 4.7-litre Ford engine and a Ferrari 250LM in 1965. Team Chamaco Collect then planned a full season of grands prix in 1966 with a couple of old BRMs, but after Vic took a distant fourth at the Syracuse Grand Prix and practised briefly at Spa, Bob Bondurant became the team's sole driver, leaving Wilson out in the cold.

MANFRED WINKELHOCK

MANFRED WINKELHOCK was a likeable man, friendly and unassuming, for whom Formula 1 was not the be-all-and-end-all of his life. He was quite content to enjoy his racing in sports prototypes and touring cars, happy to be part of the grand prix scene while it wanted him.

Having started racing in the Scirocco Cup in 1976, Winkelhock soon began a long and happy association with BMW, which saw him progress rapidly through their junior team from saloons to Formula 2. He would spend three seasons in the formula, coming close to victory at Hockenheim in 1981, when his troubled Ralt was overhauled almost within sight of the finish.

An abortive drive for Arrows apart, Manfred's grand prix career began with the ATS team at the start of 1982. There were those who thought his style harsh and crude, but there was no doubting either his commitment or bravery as he manhandled the cars for all they were worth. Unfortunately, as the statistics show, his Formula 1 efforts were largely frustrated by a catalogue of retirements, and no doubt he was glad to be able to go racing properly in the Kremer Porsche – particularly in 1985, when the season had started so brightly with a second place at Mugello and then a win at Monza, with Marc Surer.

Tragedy struck at Mosport, however, when in an unexplained accident, Manfred's Porsche left the track at high speed. He was eventually freed from the wreckage and taken to hospital critically injured. Although no bones were broken, his head injuries were severe, and he died some 24 hours later.

WINKELHOCK, Manfred (D) b 6/10/1951, Waiblingen, nr Stuttgart – d 12/8/1985, Toronto, Canada

1980 Championship position: Unplaced

	Race	Circuit	No	Entrant	Tyres	Capacity/Car/Engine	Comment	Q Pos/Entries
dnq	ITALIAN GP	Imola	30	Warsteiner Arrows Racing Team		3.0 Arrows A3-Cosworth V8		26/28

1982 Championship position: 22nd= Wins: 0 Pole positions: 0 Fastest laps: 0 Points scored: 2

	Race	Circuit	No	Entrant	Tyres	Capacity/Car/Engine	Comment	Q Pos/Entries
10	SOUTH AFRICAN GP	Kyalami	9	Team ATS	A	3.0 ATS D5-Cosworth V8	2 laps behind	20/30
5*	BRAZILIAN GP	Rio	9	Team ATS	A	3.0 ATS D5-Cosworth V8	*1st & 2nd cars dsq/1 lap behind	15/31
ret	US GP WEST	Long Beach	9	Team ATS	A	3.0 ATS D5-Cosworth V8	collision with Borgudd	25/31
dsq	SAN MARINO GP	Imola	9	Team ATS	A	3.0 ATS D5-Cosworth V8	car under weight limit	12/14
ret	BELGIAN GP	Zolder	9	Team ATS	A	3.0 ATS D5-Cosworth V8	clutch	14/32
ret	MONACO GP	Monte Carlo	9	Team ATS	M	3.0 ATS D5-Cosworth V8	differential	14/31
ret	US GP (DETROIT)	Detroit	9	Team ATS	M	3.0 ATS D5-Cosworth V8	steering arm – accident	5/28
dnq	CANADIAN GP	Montreal	9	Team ATS	M	3.0 ATS D5-Cosworth V8		27/29
12	DUTCH GP	Zandvoort	9	Team ATS	M	3.0 ATS D5-Cosworth V8	delayed start/2 laps behind	18/31
dnq	BRITISH GP	Brands Hatch	9	Team ATS	M	3.0 ATS D5-Cosworth V8		27/30
11	FRENCH GP	Paul Ricard	9	Team ATS	M	3.0 ATS D5-Cosworth V8	2 laps behind	18/30
ret	GERMAN GP	Hockenheim	9	Team ATS	M	3.0 ATS D5-Cosworth V8	clutch/gearbox	17/30
ret	AUSTRIAN GP	Österreichring	9	Team ATS	M	3.0 ATS D5-Cosworth V8	spun off	25/29
ret	SWISS GP	Dijon	9	Team ATS	M	3.0 ATS D5-Cosworth V8	engine mounting	20/29
dnq	ITALIAN GP	Monza	9	Team ATS	M	3.0 ATS D5-Cosworth V8		28/30
nc	CAESARS PALACE GP	Las Vegas	9	Team ATS	M	3.0 ATS D5-Cosworth V8	2 pit stops – misfire/13 laps behind	22/30

1983 Championship position: Unplaced

	Race	Circuit	No	Entrant	Tyres	Capacity/Car/Engine	Comment	Q Pos/Entries
15*	BRAZILIAN GP	Rio	9	Team ATS	G	1.5 t/c ATS D6-BMW 4	*13th placed car dsq/fuel feed/-4 laps	25/27
ret	US GP WEST	Long Beach	9	Team ATS	G	1.5 t/c ATS D6-BMW 4	mechanical breakage – hit wall	24/28
ret	FRENCH GP	Paul Ricard	9	Team ATS	G	1.5 t/c ATS D6-BMW 4	exhaust – engine	10/29
11	SAN MARINO GP	Imola	9	Team ATS	G	1.5 t/c ATS D6-BMW 4	3 laps behind	7/28
ret	MONACO GP	Monte Carlo	9	Team ATS	G	1.5 t/c ATS D6-BMW 4	accident with Boesel	16/28
ret	BELGIAN GP	Spa	9	Team ATS	G	1.5 t/c ATS D6-BMW 4	lost rear wheel	7/28
ret	US GP (DETROIT)	Detroit	9	Team ATS	G	1.5 t/c ATS D6-BMW 4	hit wall	22/27
9*/ret	CANADIAN GP	Montreal	9	Team ATS	G	1.5 t/c ATS D6-BMW 4	*9th placed car dsq/2 pitstops/-3 laps	7/28
ret	BRITISH GP	Silverstone	9	Team ATS	G	1.5 t/c ATS D6-BMW 4	overheating	8/29
dnq	GERMAN GP	Hockenheimq	9	Team ATS	G	1.5 t/c ATS D6-BMW 4		29/29
ret	AUSTRIAN GP	Österreichring	9	Team ATS	G	1.5 t/c ATS D6-BMW 4	overheating	13/29
dsq*	DUTCH GP	Zandvoort	9	Team ATS	G	1.5 t/c ATS D6-BMW 4	*overtook cars on parade lap	9/29
ret	ITALIAN GP	Monza	9	Team ATS	G	1.5 t/c ATS D6-BMW 4	broken exhaust	9/29
8	EUROPEAN GP	Brands Hatch	9	Team ATS	G	1.5 t/c ATS D6-BMW 4	pit stop – tyres/1 lap behind	9/29
ret	SOUTH AFRICAN GP	Kyalami	9	Team ATS	G	1.5 t/c ATS D6-BMW 4	engine	8/26

1984 Championship position: Unplaced

	Race	Circuit	No	Entrant	Tyres	Capacity/Car/Engine	Comment	Q Pos/Entries
excl	BRAZILIAN GP	Rio	14	Team ATS	P	1.5 t/c ATS D7-BMW 4	push started against regulations	(15)/27
ret	SOUTH AFRICAN GP	Kyalami	14	Team ATS	P	1.5 t/c ATS D7-BMW 4	engine/battery	12/27
ret	BELGIAN GP	Zolder	14	Team ATS	P	1.5 t/c ATS D7-BMW 4	electrics/exhaust	6/27
ret	SAN MARINO GP	Imola	14	Team ATS	P	1.5 t/c ATS D7-BMW 4	turbo	7/28
ret	FRENCH GP	Dijon	14	Team ATS	P	1.5 t/c ATS D7-BMW 4	clutch	8/27
ret	MONACO GP	Monte Carlo	14	Team ATS	P	1.5 t/c ATS D7-BMW 4	spun off	12/27
8	CANADIAN GP	Montreal	14	Team ATS	P	1.5 t/c ATS D7-BMW 4	2 laps behind	12/26
ret	US GP (DETROIT)	Detroit	14	Team ATS	P	1.5 t/c ATS D7-BMW 4	accident	14/27
8	US GP (DALLAS)	Dallas	14	Team ATS	P	1.5 t/c ATS D7-BMW 4	3 laps behind	13/27
ret	BRITISH GP	Brands Hatch	14	Team ATS	P	1.5 t/c ATS D7-BMW 4	spun off	11/27
ret	GERMAN GP	Hockenheim	14	Team ATS	P	1.5 t/c ATS D7-BMW 4	turbo boost/gearbox	13/27
dns	AUSTRIAN GP	Österreichring	14	Team ATS	P	1.5 t/c ATS D7-BMW 4	gearbox in Sunday a.m.warm-up	(14)/28
ret	DUTCH GP	Zandvoort	14	Team ATS	P	1.5 t/c ATS D7-BMW 4	spun off	16/27
ret/dns*	ITALIAN GP	Monza	14	Team ATS	P	1.5 t/c ATS D7-BMW 4	*gearbox on parade lap	(21)/27
10	PORTUGUESE GP	Estoril	2	MRD International	M	1.5 t/c Brabham BT53-BMW 4	1 lap behind	19/27

1985 Championship position: Unplaced

	Race	Circuit	No	Entrant	Tyres	Capacity/Car/Engine	Comment	Q Pos/Entries
13	BRAZILIAN GP	Rio	9	Skoal Bandit Formula 1 Team	P	1.5 t/c RAM 03-Hart 4	4 laps behind	16/25
nc	PORTUGUESE GP	Estoril	9	Skoal Bandit Formula 1 Team	P	1.5 t/c RAM 03-Hart 4	tyre problems/17 laps behind	15/26
ret	SAN MARINO GP	Imola	9	Skoal Bandit Formula 1 Team	P	1.5 t/c RAM 03-Hart 4	engine	23/26
dnq	MONACO GP	Monte Carlo	9	Skoal Bandit Formula 1 Team	P	1.5 t/c RAM 03-Hart 4		24/26
ret	CANADIAN GP	Montreal	9	Skoal Bandit Formula 1 Team	P	1.5 t/c RAM 03-Hart 4	hit by de Cesaris – hit wall	14/25
ret	US GP (DETROIT)	Detroit	9	Skoal Bandit Formula 1 Team	P	1.5 t/c RAM 03-Hart 4	turbo	20/25
12	FRENCH GP	Paul Ricard	9	Skoal Bandit Formula 1 Team	P	1.5 t/c RAM 03-Hart 4	3 laps behind	20/26
ret	BRITISH GP	Silverstone	9	Skoal Bandit Formula 1 Team	P	1.5 t/c RAM 03-Hart 4	turbo	18/26
ret	GERMAN GP	Nürburgring	9	Skoal Bandit Formula 1 Team	P	1.5 t/c RAM 03-Hart 4	engine	22/27

GP Starts: 46 (47) GP Wins: 0 Pole positions: 0 Fastest laps: 0 Points: 2

WINKELHOCK, Markus (D) b 13/6/1980, Bad Cannstatt, nr Stuttgart

2006 Championship position: Unplaced

	Race	Circuit	No	Entrant	Tyres	Capacity/Car/Engine	Comment	Q Pos/Entries
app	BAHRAIN GP	Sakhir Circuit	39	MF1 Racing	B	2.4 Midland M16-Toyota V8	ran as 3rd driver in practice only	–/–
app	AUSTRALIAN GP	Melbourne	39	MF1 Racing	B	2.4 Midland M16-Toyota V8	ran as 3rd driver in practice only	–/–
app	GERMAN GP	Hockenheim	39	MF1 Racing	B	2.4 Midland M16-Toyota V8	ran as 3rd driver in practice only	–/–
app	HUNGARIAN GP	Hungaroring	39	MF1 Racing	B	2.4 Midland M16-Toyota V8	ran as 3rd driver in practice only	–/–

2007 Championship position: Unplaced

	Race	Circuit	No	Entrant	Tyres	Capacity/Car/Engine	Comment	Q Pos/Entries
ret	EUROPEAN GP	Nürburgring	21	Etihad Aldar Spyker Team	B	2.4 Spyker F8 VII-Ferrari V8	briefly led race on lap 1/electronics	22/22

GP Starts: 1 GP Wins: 0 Pole positions: 0 Fastest laps: 0 Points: 0

MARKUS WINKELHOCK

WHEN Markus Winkelhock woke up on the morning of his first race start for Spyker, at the Nürburgring in 2007, no doubt he had been dreaming about emulating his late father, Manfred, in becoming a fully-fledged grand prix driver. Little can he have expected that he would lead the opening laps of the European Grand Prix following a freak downpour of rain just after the race got under way. The team's inspired decision to begin the race from the pit lane on full wets enabled him to take his back-marker car through the floods as other competitors slid off the track or headed to the pits. Unfortunately, the proceedings were red-flagged and his moment of glory was brought to a sudden halt.

The cheery German was handed his opportunity to shine after 18 months of patiently fulfilling his test and development role at both Midland and then Spyker, following the sudden dismissal of Christijan Albers. His tenure seemed unlikely to last, however, as paying drivers were poised to take the second seat on a more permanent basis.

The young Winkelhock often proved to be a front-runner when contesting the German F3 Euroseries between 2001 and 2004, when he notched up a total of six victories over the three seasons. He was generally overshadowed by the performances of faster drivers, however, such as Christian Klien, Timo Glock and Ryan Briscoe, and his best championship placing was fourth overall in his final year. Helped in no small part by Mercedes motorsport supremo Norbert Haug (a great family friend), Markus was found a place in the DTM series for the 2004 season. But unfortunately his Original-Telle CLK was not the most competitive of machines and, despite showing glimpses of outright speed in the older-spec car, he ended his season without scoring as much as a single point.

Opting to resume his single-seater career led Markus to the World Series by Renault championship for the 2005 season, when he managed to take three wins and a third place overall behind the stand-out driver, Robert Kubica. His spirited performances were enough for Colin Kolles to offer him a chance to test for the Jordan team at the end of the year, and also they earned him the opportunity to join the roster of hopefuls on the Midland testing and reserve driver crew in 2006. While adding a grand prix start to his racing CV was a big plus, his competition future was destined to be back in the DTM series. Having already made occasional appearances as a replacement driver for Audi in 2007, he was found a place in the Team Rosberg squad. Despite the disadvantage of handling a year-old-spec Audi A4, Marcus performed creditably in his three seasons in the class, fourth places being his best finishes.

In 2011, Winkelhock switched to the FIA GT series to drive a Lamborghini with Marc Basseng. The Germans took both race wins at Zolder and a further win at Navarra on their way to fifth overall in the standings.

WISELL, Reine (S) b 30/9/1941, Motala, nr Linköping

1970 Championship position: 15th= Wins: 0 Pole positions: 0 Fastest laps: 0 Points scored: 4

	Race	Circuit	No	Entrant	Tyres	Capacity/Car/Engine	Comment	Q Pos/Entries
3	US GP	Watkins Glen	23	Gold Leaf Team Lotus	F	3.0 Lotus 72C-Cosworth V8		9/27
nc	MEXICAN GP	Mexico City	23	Gold Leaf Team Lotus	F	3.0 Lotus 72C-Cosworth V8	3 pit stops – oil line/9 laps behind	12/18

1971 Championship position: 9th= Wins: 0 Pole positions: 0 Fastest laps: 0 Points scored: 9

	Race	Circuit	No	Entrant	Tyres	Capacity/Car/Engine	Comment	Q Pos/Entries
4	SOUTH AFRICAN GP	Kyalami	3	Gold Leaf Team Lotus	F	3.0 Lotus 72C-Cosworth V8		=13/25
nc	SPANISH GP	Montjuich Park	3	Gold Leaf Team Lotus	F	3.0 Lotus 72C-Cosworth V8	pit stop – gearbox/17 laps behind	=16/22
ret	MONACO GP	Monte Carlo	2	Gold Leaf Team Lotus	F	3.0 Lotus 72C-Cosworth V8	rear hub bearing	12/23
dsq	DUTCH GP	Zandvoort	14	Gold Leaf Team Lotus	F	3.0 Lotus 72D-Cosworth V8	reversed into pits	6/24
6	FRENCH GP	Paul Ricard	2	Gold Leaf Team Lotus	F	3.0 Lotus 72D-Cosworth V8		15/24
nc	BRITISH GP	Silverstone	3	Gold Leaf Team Lotus	F	Turbine Lotus 56B-Pratt & Whitney	2 pitstops/11 laps behind	19/24
8	GERMAN GP	Nürburgring	9	Gold Leaf Team Lotus	F	3.0 Lotus 72D-Cosworth V8	left on grid – fuel pressure	17/23
4	AUSTRIAN GP	Österreichring	3	Gold Leaf Team Lotus	F	3.0 Lotus 72D-Cosworth V8		10/22
5	CANADIAN GP	Mosport Park	3	Gold Leaf Team Lotus	F	3.0 Lotus 72D-Cosworth V8	1 lap behind	=7/27
ret	US GP	Watkins Glen	3	Gold Leaf Team Lotus	F	3.0 Lotus 72D-Cosworth V8	brakes – hit barrier	10/32

1972 Championship position: Unplaced

	Race	Circuit	No	Entrant	Tyres	Capacity/Car/Engine	Comment	Q Pos/Entries
ret	ARGENTINE GP	Buenos Aires	4	Marlboro BRM	F	3.0 BRM P153 V12	water leak	=16/22
ret	SPANISH GP	Jarama	10	Austria Marlboro BRM	F	3.0 BRM P160B V12	went off at end of straight	10/26
ret	MONACO GP	Monte Carlo	28	Marlboro BRM	F	3.0 BRM P160B V12	engine	16/25
ret	FRENCH GP	Clermont Ferrand	24	Marlboro BRM	F	3.0 BRM P160B V12	gear linkage	=19/29
ret	GERMAN GP	Nürburgring	18	Marlboro BRM	F	3.0 BRM P160C V12	seized engine	17/27
12	ITALIAN GP	Monza	24	Marlboro BRM	F	3.0 BRM P160C V12	pit stop – gearbox/4 laps behind	10/27
ret	CANADIAN GP	Mosport Park	6	John Player Team Lotus	F	3.0 Lotus 72C-Cosworth V8	engine	16/25
10	US GP	Watkins Glen	12	John Player Team Lotus	F	3.0 Lotus 72C-Cosworth V8	2 laps behind	16/32

1973 Championship position: Unplaced

	Race	Circuit	No	Entrant	Tyres	Capacity/Car/Engine	Comment	Q Pos/Entries
ret/dns*	SWEDISH GP	Anderstorp	27	Team Pierre Robert	G	3.0 March 731-Cosworth V8	suspension on parade lap	(14)/22
ret	FRENCH GP	Paul Ricard	15	Clarke-Mordaunt-Guthrie-Durlacher	G	3.0 March 731-Cosworth V8	engine – fuel vaporisation	22/25

1974 Championship position: Unplaced

	Race	Circuit	No	Entrant	Tyres	Capacity/Car/Engine	Comment	Q Pos/Entries
ret	SWEDISH GP	Anderstorp	9	March Engineering	G	3.0 March 741-Cosworth V8	suspension	16/28

GP Starts: 22 (23) GP Wins: 0 Pole positions: 0 Fastest laps: 0 Points: 13

REINE WISELL

A CONTEMPORARY and rival of Ronnie Peterson in Scandinavian Formula 3, Reine Wisell did not quite have the talent to make a top-line career, despite a most promising start in 1970 when, thrust into the Lotus team at Watkins Glen, he took the 72C into third place.

Wisell's career had begun as far back as 1962 with an unreliable Mini Cooper and then he switched to an Anglia, which was similarly troublesome, but he plugged away, returning to a Mini in 1965 to take the runner-up position in the Swedish Group 5 championship. Early in 1966, he swapped his saloon for a Cooper F3 car and soon began to show a great deal of flair. By the end of that season, he had done well enough to progress to a Brabham, bought from his experienced rival, Picko Troberg. He soon became the man to watch in 1967, comfortably taking the Swedish F3 title, but more importantly making an impression in his occasional appearances in European events. Now was the time to spread his wings and compete outside Scandinavia on a regular basis. He travelled to Bologna with Ronnie Peterson, the two Swedes ordering themselves a new F3 Tecno each for the 1968 season. Reine gained valuable experience racing abroad that year and scored 11 wins in total, while his younger rival concentrated on racing at home and took the Swedish crown.

In 1969, Wisell took up an offer to race F3 and GT cars for Chevron, but generally endured a disappointing time. Feeling that he needed to find a more challenging arena, he was persuaded to join Jo Bonnier's sports car team in 1970, and also he took over the Sid Taylor F5000 McLaren with great success, winning three of the final four rounds towards the end of the year. By then, his big chance had arrived, his performance and that of Emerson Fittipaldi earning them places in the Lotus team for 1971. It was a hectic year for the Swede, who did a full Formula 2 programme, highlighted by a splendid win in the Pau GP. His performances in Formula 1 were solid, but not inspired, however, and Chapman decided to promote his current hotshot, Dave Walker, into the team for 1972.

Wisell moved to BRM, who were running a multi-car squad that spread the available resources too thinly. Nothing worthwhile was achieved, and he even made a brief return to Lotus in place of the luckless Walker for the Canadian GP. No longer considered to have sufficient grand prix potential, he drifted into other forms of the sport, and his superb win in the F2 Eifelrennen was a timely reminder of the talent that still lurked. However, his subsequent occasional grand prix appearances brought no joy.

After sharing a Gulf/John Wyer GR7 with Vern Schuppan in 1974, but gaining little success, Wisell drove a Porsche Carrera with distinction in 1975, before racing in European and Swedish championships with a Group 2 Chevrolet Camaro. Later he raced in historics, along with David Piper, and did some driver instruction in Sweden in the summer months and Spain in the winter. Currently he divides his time between Sweden and Thailand, and when recently quizzed on his current activities, he replied, "As little as possible!"

ROELOF WUNDERINK

HAVING begun his racing career in a Simca in 1970, Roelof Wunderink progressed to Formula Ford and won the Dutch championship in 1972. Already having the benefit of strong sponsorship from HB Alarm Systems, he rushed through Formula 3 and into F5000 for the 1974 season. He had Teddy Pilette's championship winning Chevron B24 at his disposal, but failed to register anything but a fifth at Mugello and a sixth at Zolder.

Somehow, Wunderink found himself in a works-backed Ensign for 1975 without having demonstrated anything like the form to justify such a chance. Nevertheless, he bravely got on with the job, hampered at first by having to make do with the 1974 car, and then being sidelined with a broken cheekbone and concussion after a testing accident in the F5000 car. At the end of the season, having tried, but failed, the quiet Dutchman stepped out of the racing limelight.

WUNDERINK, Roelof (NL) b 12/12/1948, Eindhoven

	Race	Circuit	No	Entrant	Tyres	Capacity/Car/Engine	Comment	Q Pos/Entries
	1975 Championship position: Unplaced							
ret	SPANISH GP	Montjuich Park	31	HB Bewaking Team Ensign	G	3.0 Ensign N174-Cosworth V8	driveshaft c.v. joint	19/26
dnq	MONACO GP	Monte Carlo	31	HB Bewaking Team Ensign	G	3.0 Ensign N174-Cosworth V8		23/26
dnq	BRITISH GP	Silverstone	31	HB Bewaking Team Ensign	G	3.0 Ensign N175-Cosworth V8		27/28
nc	AUSTRIAN GP	Österreichring	33	HB Bewaking Team Ensign	G	3.0 Ensign N174-Cosworth V8	pit stop – tyres/4 laps behind	28/30
dnq	ITALIAN GP	Monza	31	HB Bewaking Team Ensign	G	3.0 Ensign N175-Cosworth V8		27/28
ret	US GP	Watkins Glen	31	HB Bewaking Team Ensign	G	3.0 Ensign N175-Cosworth V8	gearbox	22/24
	GP Starts: 3 GP Wins: 0 Pole positions: 0 Fastest laps: 0 Points: 0							

ALEX WURZ

A BMX cycling champion and kart graduate, Alex Wurz made a big impression in the 1994 German Formula 3 championship when he took the runner-up slot, behind Jörg Müller, and finished ahead of both Ralf Schumacher and Norberto Fontana.

Results dipped somewhat the following season, but the Austrian's abilities were appreciated by the management at Team Joest, who gave him a chance in their Opel Calibra for the 1996 ITC season. This provided the opportunity for him to gain experience in a high-profile environment, and his career received an unexpected, but massive boost when he shared Joest's Porsche WSC95 at Le Mans with Manuel Reuter and Davy Jones, becoming the youngest-ever winner of the Sarthe classic.

Then Wurz not only gained a foothold on the grand prix ladder with a testing contract with Benetton in 1997, but also was given a seat in the works Mercedes squad to race their CLK-GTR alongside Bernd Schneider in the FIA GT championship.

When the lanky Austrian unexpectedly stepped into the big time, replacing sinusitis victim Gerhard Berger in Montreal, he was still largely an unknown quantity, but his three-race stint, which culminated in a fine third place in the British Grand Prix, no doubt sealed a full-time drive for 1998. Teamed with Italian hotshot Giancarlo Fisichella, the quiet, but tough Wurz showed he was no soft touch as he banged wheels with Michael Schumacher in Monaco and emerged from a roll into the gravel in Montreal seemingly completely unperturbed.

A string of solid drives into the points increased Alex's credibility, but his inexorable rise to the top was about to come to an end in 1999, when the Austrian found the inherent characteristics of the Benetton B199 at odds with his particular driving style. He stayed on board for another season, hoping that the simpler B200 would return him to the top six on a regular basis. It was not to be, however, and he was forced to endure a trying season that yielded just one points scoring finish (fifth in Italy) before being ousted in favour of the then latest rising star, Jenson Button.

Alex remained much in demand as a talented test driver and slotted easily into the McLaren Mercedes fold, despite having no glimpse of a race seat with Ron Dennis' team. His fifth term on the reserves bench finally brought a call to action, however when Juan Pablo Montoya's shoulder injury sidelined him for the San Marino Grand Prix. The Austrian answered the call and delivered a solid fourth place (which was elevated to third following Jenson Button's exclusion). Eager for more race action, he accepted an offer from Williams to take his testing and development expertise to Grove with the promise of a race drive in 2007.

Given his lack of racing action for such a long time, Wurz did a sound enough job and even grabbed a podium in Canada after a canny drive. With the team being forced to run Kazuki Nakajima as part of the Toyota engine deal, however, he moved back to a test role at Honda and joined Peugeot to race their 908 HDi sport cars, victory at Le Mans being their holy grail. Their prayers were

answered when Alex took his second Le Mans win in 2009, teamed with Marc Gené and David Brabham. He also recorded victories with the silver and blue machines in the Spa 1000km in both 2010 and 2011, with Anthony Davidson and Gené, before signing off the French car giant's sporting involvement with a big win in the Petit Le Mans at Road Atlanta (with Stéphane Sarrazin and Franck Montagny), before announcing his intention to join Toyota for their new asasult on Le Mans in 2012. Alex has also been hired by Williams to act as a driver coach to their less experienced Formula 1 chargers, Pastor Maldonado and Bruno Senna.

WURZ, Alexander (A) b 15/2/1974, Waidhofen

	Race	Circuit	No	Entrant	Tyres	Capacity/Car/Engine	Comment	Q Pos/Entries
	1997 Championship position: 14th		Wins: 0	Pole positions: 0	Fastest laps: 0	Points scored: 4		
ret	CANADIAN GP	Montreal	8	Mild Seven Benetton Renault	G	3.0 Benetton B197-Renault V10	transmission	11/22
ret	FRENCH GP	Magny Cours	8	Mild Seven Benetton Renault	G	3.0 Benetton B197-Renault V10	spun off	7/22
3	BRITISH GP	Silverstone	8	Mild Seven Benetton Renault	G	3.0 Benetton B197-Renault V10		8/22
	1998 Championship position: 7th=		Wins: 0	Pole positions: 0	Fastest laps: 1	Points scored: 17		
7	AUSTRALIAN GP	Melbourne	6	Mild Seven Benetton Playlife	B	3.0 Benetton B199-Playlife V10	1 lap behind	11/22
4	BRAZILIAN GP	Interlagos	6	Mild Seven Benetton Playlife	B	3.0 Benetton B199-Playlife V10		5/22

Pos	GP	Circuit	No	Team	T	Car/Engine	Notes	Grid
4	ARGENTINE GP	Buenos Aires	6	Mild Seven Benetton Playlife	B	3.0 Benetton B199-Playlife V10	*FL*	8/22
ret	SAN MARINO GP	Imola	6	Mild Seven Benetton Playlife	B	3.0 Benetton B199-Playlife V10	*engine*	5/22
4	SPANISH GP	Barcelona	6	Mild Seven Benetton Playlife	B	3.0 Benetton B199-Playlife V10		5/22
ret	MONACO GP	Monte Carlo	6	Mild Seven Benetton Playlife	B	3.0 Benetton B199-Playlife V10	*accident*	6/22
4	CANADIAN GP	Montreal	6	Mild Seven Benetton Playlife	B	3.0 Benetton B199-Playlife V10	*rolled car at first start*	11/22
5	FRENCH GP	Magny Cours	6	Mild Seven Benetton Playlife	B	3.0 Benetton B199-Playlife V10	*1 lap behind*	10/22
4	BRITISH GP	Silverstone	6	Mild Seven Benetton Playlife	B	3.0 Benetton B199-Playlife V10	*1 lap behind*	12/22
9	AUSTRIAN GP	A1-Ring	6	Mild Seven Benetton Playlife	B	3.0 Benetton B199-Playlife V10	*1 lap behind*	17/22
11	GERMAN GP	Hockenheim	6	Mild Seven Benetton Playlife	B	3.0 Benetton B199-Playlife V10		7/22
ret	HUNGARIAN GP	Hungaroring	6	Mild Seven Benetton Playlife	B	3.0 Benetton B199-Playlife V10	*gearbox*	9/22
ret	BELGIAN GP	Spa	6	Mild Seven Benetton Playlife	B	3.0 Benetton B199-Playlife V10	*collision with Coulthard*	11/22
ret	ITALIAN GP	Monza	6	Mild Seven Benetton Playlife	B	3.0 Benetton B199-Playlife V10	*gearbox*	7/22
7	EUROPEAN GP	Nürburgring	6	Mild Seven Benetton Playlife	B	3.0 Benetton B199-Playlife V10		8/22
9	JAPANESE GP	Suzuka	6	Mild Seven Benetton Playlife	B	3.0 Benetton B199-Playlife V10	*1 lap behind*	9/22

1999 Championship position: 13th=   Wins: 0   Pole positions: 0   Fastest laps: 0   Points scored: 3

Pos	GP	Circuit	No	Team	T	Car/Engine	Notes	Grid
ret	AUSTRALIAN GP	Melbourne	10	Mild Seven Benetton Playlife	B	3.0 Benetton B199-Playlife V10	*suspension*	10/22
7	BRAZILIAN GP	Interlagos	10	Mild Seven Benetton Playlife	B	3.0 Benetton B199-Playlife V10	*1 lap behind*	9/21
ret	SAN MARINO GP	Imola	10	Mild Seven Benetton Playlife	B	3.0 Benetton B199-Playlife V10	*collision with de la Rosa*	17/22
6	MONACO GP	Monte Carlo	10	Mild Seven Benetton Playlife	B	3.0 Benetton B199-Playlife V10	*1 lap behind*	10/22
10	SPANISH GP	Barcelona	10	Mild Seven Benetton Playlife	B	3.0 Benetton B199-Playlife V10	*1 lap behind*	18/22
ret	CANADIAN GP	Montreal	10	Mild Seven Benetton Playlife	B	3.0 Benetton B199-Playlife V10	*driveshaft on lap 1*	11/22
ret	FRENCH GP	Magny Cours	10	Mild Seven Benetton Playlife	B	3.0 Benetton B199-Playlife V10	*spun off*	13/22
10	BRITISH GP	Silverstone	10	Mild Seven Benetton Playlife	B	3.0 Benetton B199-Playlife V10		18/22
5	AUSTRIAN GP	A1-Ring	10	Mild Seven Benetton Playlife	B	3.0 Benetton B199-Playlife V10		10/22
7	GERMAN GP	Hockenheim	10	Mild Seven Benetton Playlife	B	3.0 Benetton B199-Playlife V10		13/22
7	HUNGARIAN GP	Hungaroring	10	Mild Seven Benetton Playlife	B	3.0 Benetton B199-Playlife V10		7/22
14	BELGIAN GP	Spa	10	Mild Seven Benetton Playlife	B	3.0 Benetton B199-Playlife V10		7/22
ret	ITALIAN GP	Monza	10	Mild Seven Benetton Playlife	B	3.0 Benetton B199-Playlife V10	*electrics*	14/22
ret	EUROPEAN GP	Nürburgring	10	Mild Seven Benetton Playlife	B	3.0 Benetton B199-Playlife V10	*collision with Diniz*	11/22
8	MALAYSIAN GP	Sepang	10	Mild Seven Benetton Playlife	B	3.0 Benetton B199-Playlife V10		7/22
10	JAPANESE GP	Suzuka	10	Mild Seven Benetton Playlife	B	3.0 Benetton B199-Playlife V10	*1 lap behind*	15/22

2000 Championship position: 15th=   Wins: 0   Pole positions: 0   Fastest laps: 0   Points scored: 2

Pos	GP	Circuit	No	Team	T	Car/Engine	Notes	Grid
7*	AUSTRALIAN GP	Melbourne	12	Mild Seven Benetton Playlife	B	3.0 Benetton B200-Playlife V10	*6th placed car disqualified	14/22
ret	BRAZILIAN GP	Interlagos	12	Mild Seven Benetton Playlife	B	3.0 Benetton B200-Playlife V10	*gearbox*	13/22
9	SAN MARINO GP	Imola	12	Mild Seven Benetton Playlife	B	3.0 Benetton B200-Playlife V10	*1 lap behind*	11/22
9	BRITISH GP	Silverstone	12	Mild Seven Benetton Playlife	B	3.0 Benetton B200-Playlife V10	*1 lap behind*	20/22
10	SPANISH GP	Barcelona	12	Mild Seven Benetton Playlife	B	3.0 Benetton B200-Playlife V10	*wheel problem at 2nd pitstop/-1 lap*	19/22
12/ret	EUROPEAN GP	Nürburgring	12	Mild Seven Benetton Playlife	B	3.0 Benetton B200-Playlife V10	*collision with Herbert/6 laps behind*	15/22
ret	MONACO GP	Monte Carlo	12	Mild Seven Benetton Playlife	B	3.0 Benetton B200-Playlife V10	*started in spare from pits/accident*	12/22
9	CANADIAN GP	Montreal	12	Mild Seven Benetton Playlife	B	3.0 Benetton B200-Playlife V10		14/22
ret	FRENCH GP	Magny Cours	12	Mild Seven Benetton Playlife	B	3.0 Benetton B200-Playlife V10	*spun off*	17/22
10	AUSTRIAN GP	A1-Ring	12	Mild Seven Benetton Playlife	B	3.0 Benetton B200-Playlife V10	*1 lap behind*	14/22
ret	GERMAN GP	Hockenheim	12	Mild Seven Benetton Playlife	B	3.0 Benetton B200-Playlife V10	*gearbox*	7/22
11	HUNGARIAN GP	Hungaroring	12	Mild Seven Benetton Playlife	B	3.0 Benetton B200-Playlife V10	*1 lap behind*	11/22
13	BELGIAN GP	Spa	12	Mild Seven Benetton Playlife	B	3.0 Benetton B200-Playlife V10	*1 lap behind*	19/22
5	ITALIAN GP	Monza	12	Mild Seven Benetton Playlife	B	3.0 Benetton B200-Playlife V10	*1 lap behind*	13/22
10	UNITED STATES GP	Indianapolis	12	Mild Seven Benetton Playlife	B	3.0 Benetton B200-Playlife V10		11/22
ret	JAPANESE GP	Suzuka	12	Mild Seven Benetton Playlife	B	3.0 Benetton B200-Playlife V10	*spun off*	11/22
7	MALAYSIAN GP	Sepang	12	Mild Seven Benetton Playlife	B	3.0 Benetton B200-Playlife V10	*brake problems late in race*	5/22

2005 Championship position: 17th=   Wins: 0   Pole positions: 0   Fastest laps: 0   Points scored: 6

Pos	GP	Circuit	No	Team	T	Car/Engine	Notes	Grid
app	BAHRAIN GP	Sakhir Circuit	35	West McLaren Mercedes	M	3.0 McLaren MP4/20-Mercedes V10	*ran as 3rd driver in practice only*	– /–
3*	SAN MARINO GP	Imola	10	West McLaren Mercedes	M	3.0 McLaren MP4/20-Mercedes V10	*3rd & 5th placed cars disqualified	7/20
app	MONACO GP	Monte Carlo	35	West McLaren Mercedes	M	3.0 McLaren MP4/20-Mercedes V10	*ran as 3rd driver in practice only*	– /–
app	EUROPEAN GP	Nürburgring	35	West McLaren Mercedes	M	3.0 McLaren MP4/20-Mercedes V10	*ran as 3rd driver in practice only*	– /–
app	GERMAN GP	Hockenheim	35	West McLaren Mercedes	M	3.0 McLaren MP4/20-Mercedes V10	*ran as 3rd driver in practice only*	– /–
app	BELGIAN GP	Spa	35	West McLaren Mercedes	M	3.0 McLaren MP4/20-Mercedes V10	*ran as 3rd driver in practice only*	– /–
app	BRAZILIAN GP	Interlagos	35	West McLaren Mercedes	M	3.0 McLaren MP4/20-Mercedes V10	*ran as 3rd driver in practice only*	– /–

2006 Championship position: Unplaced

Pos	GP	Circuit	No	Team	T	Car/Engine	Notes	Grid
app	BAHRAIN GP	Sakhir Circuit	35	WilliamsF1Team	B	2.4 Williams FW28-Cosworth V8	*ran as 3rd driver in practice only*	– /–
app	MALAYSIAN GP	Sepang	35	WilliamsF1Team	B	2.4 Williams FW28-Cosworth V8	*ran as 3rd driver in practice only*	– /–
app	AUSTRALIAN GP	Melbourne	35	WilliamsF1Team	B	2.4 Williams FW28-Cosworth V8	*ran as 3rd driver in practice only*	– /–
app	SAN MARINO GP	Imola	35	WilliamsF1Team	B	2.4 Williams FW28-Cosworth V8	*ran as 3rd driver in practice only*	– /–
app	EUROPEAN GP	Nürburgring	35	WilliamsF1Team	B	2.4 Williams FW28-Cosworth V8	*ran as 3rd driver in practice only*	– /–
app	SPANISH GP	Barcelona	35	WilliamsF1Team	B	2.4 Williams FW28-Cosworth V8	*ran as 3rd driver in practice only*	– /–
app	MONACO GP	Monte Carlo	35	WilliamsF1Team	B	2.4 Williams FW28-Cosworth V8	*ran as 3rd driver in practice only*	– /–
app	BRITISH GP	Silverstone	35	WilliamsF1Team	B	2.4 Williams FW28-Cosworth V8	*ran as 3rd driver in practice only*	– /–
app	CANADIAN GP	Montreal	35	WilliamsF1Team	B	2.4 Williams FW28-Cosworth V8	*ran as 3rd driver in practice only*	– /–
app	U S GP	Indianapolis	35	WilliamsF1Team	B	2.4 Williams FW28-Cosworth V8	*ran as 3rd driver in practice only*	– /–
app	FRENCH GP	Magny Cours	35	WilliamsF1Team	B	2.4 Williams FW28-Cosworth V8	*ran as 3rd driver in practice only*	– /–
app	GERMAN GP	Hockenheim	35	WilliamsF1Team	B	2.4 Williams FW28-Cosworth V8	*ran as 3rd driver in practice only*	– /–
app	HUNGARIAN GP	Hungaroring	35	WilliamsF1Team	B	2.4 Williams FW28-Cosworth V8	*ran as 3rd driver in practice only*	– /–
app	TURKISH GP	Istanbul	35	WilliamsF1Team	B	2.4 Williams FW28-Cosworth V8	*ran as 3rd driver in practice only*	– /–
app	ITALIAN GP	Monza	35	WilliamsF1Team	B	2.4 Williams FW28-Cosworth V8	*ran as 3rd driver in practice only*	– /–
app	CHINESE GP	Shanghai	35	WilliamsF1Team	B	2.4 Williams FW28-Cosworth V8	*ran as 3rd driver in practice only*	– /–
app	JAPANESE GP	Suzuka	35	WilliamsF1Team	B	2.4 Williams FW28-Cosworth V8	*ran as 3rd driver in practice only*	– /–
app	BRAZILIAN GP	Interlagos	35	WilliamsF1Team	B	2.4 Williams FW28-Cosworth V8	*ran as 3rd driver in practice only*	– /–

2007 Championship position: 11th   Wins: 0   Pole positions: 0   Fastest laps: 0   Points scored: 13

Pos	GP	Circuit	No	Team	T	Car/Engine	Notes	Grid
ret	AUSTRALIAN GP	Melbourne	17	AT&T WilliamsF1 Team	B	2.4 Williams FW29-Toyota V8	*accident – hit by Coulthard*	15/22

9	MALAYSIAN GP	Sepang	17	AT&T WilliamsF1 Team	B	2.4 Williams FW29-Toyota V8		20/22
11	BAHRAIN GP	Bahrain	17	AT&T WilliamsF1 Team	B	2.4 Williams FW29-Toyota V8	1 lap behind	11/22
ret	SPANISH GP	Barcelona	17	AT&T WilliamsF1 Team	B	2.4 Williams FW29-Toyota V8	accident – ran into Ralf Schumacher	18/22
7	MONACO GP	Monte Carlo	17	AT&T WilliamsF1 Team	B	2.4 Williams FW29-Toyota V8	1 lap behind	12/22
3	CANADIAN GP	Montreal	17	AT&T WilliamsF1 Team	B	2.4 Williams FW29-Toyota V8	despite wing damage from collision	20/22
10	U S GP	Indianapolis	17	AT&T WilliamsF1 Team	B	2.4 Williams FW29-Toyota V8	1 lap behind	17/22
14	FRENCH GP	Magny Cours	17	AT&T WilliamsF1 Team	B	2.4 Williams FW29-Toyota V8	1 lap behind	18/22
13	BRITISH GP	Silverstone	17	AT&T WilliamsF1 Team	B	2.4 Williams FW29-Toyota V8	1 lap behind	13/22
4	EUROPEAN GP	Nürburgring	17	AT&T WilliamsF1 Team	B	2.4 Williams FW29-Toyota V8		12/22
14	HUNGARIAN GP	Hungaroring	17	AT&T WilliamsF1 Team	B	2.4 Williams FW29-Toyota V8	1 lap behind	13/22
11	TURKISH GP	Istanbul	17	AT&T WilliamsF1 Team	B	2.4 Williams FW29-Toyota V8		16/22
13	ITALIAN GP	Monza	17	AT&T WilliamsF1 Team	B	2.4 Williams FW29-Toyota V8	1 lap behind	13/22
ret	BELGIAN GP	Spa	17	AT&T WilliamsF1 Team	B	2.4 Williams FW29-Toyota V8	fuel pressure	16/22
ret	JAPANESE GP	Suzuka	17	AT&T WilliamsF1 Team	B	2.4 Williams FW29-Toyota V8	accident – hit by Sato and ran into Massa	18/22
12	CHINESE GP	Shanghai	17	AT&T WilliamsF1 Team	B	2.4 Williams FW29-Toyota V8	1 lap behind	19/22

GP Starts: 69   GP Wins: 0   Pole positions: 0   Fastest laps: 1   Points: 45

SAKON YAMAMOTO

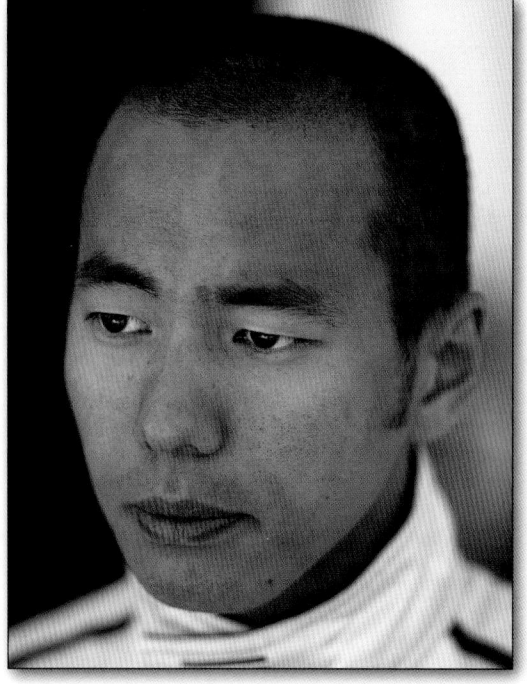

THAT Sakon Yamamoto found a berth with three Formula 1 teams must be due almost entirely to his personal sponsorship, as his racing resumé outside Japan hardly bears close scrutiny.

Having taken up karting at the age of 12, Sakon developed his skills eventually to take the local FA Class in 1999. After sampling the European karting scene, the young Japanese driver graduated to the Formula 3 class and, having joined the TOM'S team for the 2001 season, he placed fourth overall in his debut year at home.

To progress his career, Sakon opted to compete in both German F3 and the Formula 3 Euro Series, but he found the competition too hot and retreated to his homeland for 2004. He scored a win and eighth overall in F3, before his career really took off in 2005, when he graduated to the premier Japanese single-seater series, Formula Nippon. Wins at Sugo, Suzuka and Motegi, plus strong finishes at Fuji and Mine, saw him crowned the series champion, ironically well ahead of runner-up Yuichi Ide.

Sakon also competed successfully in the Super GT series, taking a Nissan to victory with Richard Lyons at Sepang and sharing the winning Toyota Supra GT at Sugo with Tetsuya Kataoka. With his intimate knowledge of the Suzuka circuit, he was drafted into the Jordan team as their third driver for the 2005 Japanese Grand Prix, and he impressed onlookers with his brief performance in the Friday practice.

After being overlooked initially by Super Aguri, Yamamoto continued to race in Formula Nippon until he was finally called into the squad as the third driver at Silverstone, before being promoted to a race seat at Hockenheim. The 24-year-old enjoyed a seven-race spell through to the end of the season, but was discarded for 2007 as Honda's choice; Anthony Davidson took his place. The Japanese driver moved into GP2 instead, but his 11 races yielded nothing in terms of results, which made it almost laughable that he was hired by Spyker to see out the season.

For 2008, Yamamoto bought a seat in the top ART Grand Prix team for both the GP2 and the winter GP2 Asia series. He only managed a single fourth place in the former, but at least made some impression in the latter, finishing ninth overall.

One might have thought that Yamamoto would have given up the ghost by this stage, but in 2010 he was back in Formula 1 with tail-enders HRT. Having taken on the third driver role in Turkey, he was drafted into the team for a seven-race stint in a shifting driver line-up.

For 2011, Yamamoto hooked up with Virgin Racing for the first three races of the season, but this time his services were definitely not required.

YAMAMOTO, Sakon (J) b 9/7/1982, Toyohashi City, Aichi

	2005 Championship position: Unplaced							
	Race	Circuit	No	Entrant	Tyres	Capacity/Car/Engine	Comment	Q Pos/Entries
app	JAPANESE GP	Suzuka	39	Jordan Toyota	B	3.0 Jordan EJ15B-Toyota V10	ran as 3rd driver in practice only	- /-
	2006 Championship position: Unplaced							
app	BRITISH GP	Silverstone	41	Super Aguri F1Team	B	2.4 Super Aguri SA05-Honda V8	ran as 3rd driver in practice only	- /-
app	CANADIAN GP	Montreal	41	Super Aguri F1Team	B	2.4 Super Aguri SA05-Honda V8	ran as 3rd driver in practice only	- /-
app	U S GP	Indianapolis	41	Super Aguri F1Team	B	2.4 Super Aguri SA05-Honda V8	ran as 3rd driver in practice only	- /-
app	FRENCH GP	Magny Cours	41	Super Aguri F1Team	B	2.4 Super Aguri SA05-Honda V8	ran as 3rd driver in practice only	- /-
ret	GERMAN GP	Hockenheim	23	Super Aguri F1Team	B	2.4 Super Aguri SA05-Honda V8	driveshaft	21/22
ret	HUNGARIAN GP	Hungaroring	23	Super Aguri F1Team	B	2.4 Super Aguri SA05-Honda V8	engine	22/22
ret	TURKISH GP	Istanbul	23	Super Aguri F1Team	B	2.4 Super Aguri SA05-Honda V8	spun off	21/22
ret	ITALIAN GP	Monza	23	Super Aguri F1Team	B	2.4 Super Aguri SA05-Honda V8	hydraulics	22/22
16	CHINESE GP	Shanghai	23	Super Aguri F1Team	B	2.4 Super Aguri SA05-Honda V8	4 laps behind	22/22
17	JAPANESE GP	Suzuka	23	Super Aguri F1Team	B	2.4 Super Aguri SA05-Honda V8	4 laps behind	22/22
16	BRAZILIAN GP	Interlagos	23	Super Aguri F1Team	B	2.4 Super Aguri SA05-Honda V8	2 laps behind	21/22

2007 Championship position: Unplaced

ret	HUNGARIAN GP	Hungaroring	21	Etihad Aldar Spyker F1 Team	B	2.4 Spyker F8 VII-Ferrari V8	*spun off*		22/22
20	TURKISH GP	Istanbul	21	Etihad Aldar Spyker F1 Team	B	2.4 Spyker F8 VII-Ferrari V8	*1 lap behind*		22/22
20	ITALIAN GP	Monza	21	Etihad Aldar Spyker F1 Team	B	2.4 Spyker F8 VII-Ferrari V8	*1 lap behind*		22/22
17	BELGIAN GP	Spa	21	Etihad Aldar Spyker F1 Team	B	2.4 Spyker F8 VII-Ferrari V8	*1 lap behind*		22/22
12	JAPANESE GP	Suzuka	21	Etihad Aldar Spyker F1 Team	B	2.4 Spyker F8 VII-Ferrari V8	*1 lap behind*		18/22
17	CHINESE GP	Shanghai	21	Etihad Aldar Spyker F1 Team	B	2.4 Spyker F8 VII-Ferrari V8	*3 laps behind*		22/22
ret	BRAZILIAN GP	Interlagos	21	Etihad Aldar Spyker F1 Team	B	2.4 Spyker F8 VII-Ferrari V8	*accident – hit by Fisichella*		22/22

2010 Championship position: Unplaced

app	TURKISH GP	Istanbul	21	HRT F1 Team	B	2.4 HRT F110-Cosworth V8	*ran as 3rd driver in practice only*		–/–
20	BRITISH GP	Silverstone	21	HRT F1 Team	B	2.4 HRT F110-Cosworth V8	*2 laps behind*		24/24
ret	GERMAN GP	Hockenheim	20	HRT F1 Team	B	2.4 HRT F110-Cosworth V8	*gearbox*		23/24
19	HUNGARIAN GP	Hungaroring	20	HRT F1 Team	B	2.4 HRT F110-Cosworth V8	*4 laps behind*		24/24
20	BELGIAN GP	Spa	21	HRT F1 Team	B	2.4 HRT F110-Cosworth V8	*2 laps behind*		21/24
19	ITALIAN GP	Monza	21	HRT F1 Team	B	2.4 HRT F110-Cosworth V8	*2 laps behind*		24/24
16	JAPANESE GP	Suzuka	21	HRT F1 Team	B	2.4 HRT F110-Cosworth V8	*3 laps behind*		24/24
15	KOREAN GP	Yeongam	21	HRT F1 Team	B	2.4 HRT F110-Cosworth V8	*2 laps behind*		23/24

GP Starts: 21   GP Wins: 0   Pole positions: 0   Fastest laps: 0   Points: 0

ALEX YOONG

DESPITE making history as the first Malaysian to break into Formula 1, Alex Yoong never looked like making his stay long-term. Eventually, he turned his hand to other disciplines within the sport, none of which seemed to lead to a permanent tenure.

Alex had the means to make a start in racing in his homeland and did well enough to get the opportunity to venture to Europe, where he raced in Formula Renault and Formula 3 without notable success before his funding dried up.

By then, the Malaysian government had decided that Yoong could act as an ambassador for the country and offered to help back his racing ambitions. The personable driver tried his hand at various F3000 series in Italy, Europe and Japan, but they yielded little in the way of success. However, his funding was attractive to struggling F1 outfits and, with three races remaining in the 2001 season, he was drafted into the second Minardi seat alongside Fernando Alonso. Despite not shining, Yoong was retained in the Italian team for 2002. A full season alongside Mark Webber was in prospect, but the Malaysian's performances were so hit and miss that he was 'rested' for two races in mid-season. Even though his pace picked up a little on his return, he was not retained by the team at the end of the year.

That effectively spelt the end of Yoong's F1 involvement, and he has since flitted from Champ Car to Australian V8 to sports cars to the GP2 Asia Series. He did find some success in the A1GP, representing Malaysia and scoring four wins for the team, of which he was the franchise holder. In 2010, he won the GTC class of the Zuhai 1000km in an Audi R8 LMS, and he intends to continue his career in the Indian Super Series planned for 2013.

YOONG, Alex (MAL) b 20/7/1976, Kuala Lumpur

2001 Championship position: Unplaced

	Race	Circuit	No	Entrant	Tyres	Car/Engine	Comment	Q Pos/Entries
ret	ITALIAN GP	Monza	20	European Minardi F1	M	3.0 Minardi PS01-European V10	*spun off*	22/22
ret	UNITED STATES GP	Indianapolis	20	European Minardi F1	M	3.0 Minardi PS01-European V10	*gearbox*	22/22
16	JAPANESE GP	Suzuka	20	European Minardi F1	M	3.0 Minardi PS01-European V10	*3 laps behind*	22/22

2002 Championship position: Unplaced

7	AUSTRALIAN GP	Melbourne	22	KL Minardi Asiatech	M	3.0 Minardi PS02-Asiatech V10	*2 laps behind*	21/22
ret	MALAYSIAN GP	Sepang	22	KL Minardi Asiatech	M	3.0 Minardi PS02-Asiatech V10	*gearbox*	22/22
13	BRAZILIAN GP	Interlagos	22	KL Minardi Asiatech	M	3.0 Minardi PS02-Asiatech V10	*4 laps behind*	22/22
dnq	SAN MARINO GP	Imola	22	KL Minardi Asiatech	M	3.0 Minardi PS02-Asiatech V10	*failed to make 107% time*	22/22
dns	SPANISH GP	Barcelona	22	KL Minardi Asiatech	M	3.0 Minardi PS02-Asiatech V10	*structural failure – car withdrawn*	(21)/22
ret	AUSTRIAN GP	A1-Ring	22	KL Minardi Asiatech	M	3.0 Minardi PS02-Asiatech V10	*engine*	22/22
ret	MONACO GP	Monte Carlo	22	KL Minardi Asiatech	M	3.0 Minardi PS02-Asiatech V10	*accident*	22/22
14	CANADIAN GP	Montreal	22	KL Minardi Asiatech	M	3.0 Minardi PS02-Asiatech V10	*2 laps behind*	22/22
ret	EUROPEAN GP	Nürburgring	22	KL Minardi Asiatech	M	3.0 Minardi PS02-Asiatech V10	*hydraulics*	22/22
dnq	BRITISH GP	Silverstone	22	KL Minardi Asiatech	M	3.0 Minardi PS02-Asiatech V10	*failed to make 107% time*	22/22
10	FRENCH GP	Magny Cours	22	KL Minardi Asiatech	M	3.0 Minardi PS02-Asiatech V10	*4 laps behind*	19/22
dnq	GERMAN GP	Hockenheim	22	KL Minardi Asiatech	M	3.0 Minardi PS02-Asiatech V10	*failed to make 107% time*	22/22
13	ITALIAN GP	Monza	22	KL Minardi Asiatech	M	3.0 Minardi PS02-Asiatech V10	*5 laps behind*	20/20
ret	UNITED STATES GP	Indianapolis	22	KL Minardi Asiatech	M	3.0 Minardi PS02-Asiatech V10	*engine*	20/20
ret	JAPANESE GP	Suzuka	22	KL Minardi Asiatech	M	3.0 Minardi PS02-Asiatech V10	*spun off*	20/20

GP Starts: 14   GP Wins: 0   Pole positions: 0   Fastest laps: 0   Points: 0

ALESSANDRO 'ALEX' ZANARDI

A TREMENDOUSLY popular driver, who dazzled in Champ Car and disappointed in Formula 1, Alex Zanardi lost his legs in horrific fashion at the Lausitz-ring, and then staged a brave and remarkable comeback to win races in both the European Touring Car Championship and then the World Touring Car Championship.

The first chapter in the career of this quiet and unassuming Italian began with seven seasons spent racing karts before he contested the national Formula 3 series in 1988. His promise shone through the following year, but his Racing for Italy Ralt RT33 was handicapped when a change to unleaded fuel in mid-season hobbled the Toyota engine and inevitably his results suffered. After switching to a Dallara chassis in 1990, however, he finished second in the championship, just three points adrift of Roberto Colciago, winning two of the series' 12 rounds.

Having made an inauspicious debut in F3000 at the tail end of the 1989 season, nothing much was expected of Zanardi when he took his place in the new Il Barone Rampante team for the start of the 1991 campaign. Extensive pre-season testing gave the Italian an early advantage, but despite vic-tories at Vallelunga and Mugello, eventually he lost the championship to the more consistent finishing record of Christian Fittipaldi. Not that it re-ally mattered, for by that time he had been chosen to fill the Jordan seat vacated by Michael Schumacher for the final three races of the season.

Zanardi's hopes of a place in the Tyrrell line-up for 1992 were dashed when the team opted for Andrea de Cesaris, but he secured a testing contract with Benetton and ultimately made three unhappy appearances for Minardi in place of his former F3000 adversary, Fittipaldi, who had injured his back.

Alessandro was offered a chance to prove himself in 1993 when Mika Häkkinen left Lotus for McLaren, and team boss Peter Collins was pleased with the Italian's early form. He drove a storming race at Mona-co, where he was unlucky to miss the points, and his contribution to the development of the team's highly complex active-suspension programme drew warm praise, but his season came to a premature end after an ex-tremely violent 150mph accident at Spa's notorious Eau Rouge. The car was destroyed and Zanardi ended up in hospital with severe concussion.

While he recovered from this shaking, he was rested in favour of Pedro Lamy for the remaining grands prix. The Portuguese hotshot retained the ride for the 1994 season, although Zanardi was kept on in the role of test driver. As fate would have it, Lamy was badly injured in a testing accident at Silverstone, putting Alessandro back in for the balance of a dispiriting season as the once great Team Lotus heaved its dying breath.

Alex was forced to sit out the 1995 season, save for an occasional Lotus GT drive, but at the end of the year he secured a deal to com-pete in the Indy car series with Target/Chip Ganassi Racing after glowing recommendations from Adrian Reynard and Rick Gorne. He adapted to CART in a sensational manner. The brilliant Italian won 15 races from his 51 starts and claimed successive PPG Cup championships in 1997 and 1998.

Zanardi's success in Champ Car meant that he came into Formula 1 focus once more and he signed to drive for Williams, partnering Ralf Schumacher for the 1999 season. Finding that the cars differed quite dramatically from those he'd left behind, he struggled to adapt

With an inexperienced engineer for much of the season and more than his fair share of unreliability, Zanardi failed to score a single point, while team-mate Schumacher took some 35. His best performance came at Monza, where he qualified in fourth and finished seventh, but he was dropped from the Williams squad at the end of the year, giving British driver Jenson Button the chance of a lifetime with a drive for the 2000 season.

Zanardi was still under contract and being paid by Williams in 2000, so he sat out the season and enjoyed life away from the track. In 2001, the Ital-ian returned to Champ Cars with his former engineer, Mo Nunn, now a team owner in his own right. With a new team, it took time for Alex to get fully up to speed, and just when it looked like everything was coming good, he suffered his horrific accident at the German Lausitzring, losing the lower half of each leg. Having cheated death, he fought back in remarkable fashion, learning to walk on the artificial limbs he consistently modified and improved. Some 20 months after that fateful day in Germany, he was back in the Champ Car cockpit, and before an emotional crowd he completed 13 laps to symbolically complete his unfinished 2001 race.

In 2004, Alex made a real return to racing, driving for BMW in the European Touring Car Championship, where he took a sixth place in the final race of the year at Dubai. The following year, after a win in the Italian Touring Car Championship at Mugello, he scored his first ever WTCC victory at Oschersle-ben. A huge crowd favourite in the category, he proceeded to take another win, at Istanbul, in 2006, and remained an integral part of the BMW family. He recorded further victories at Brno in both 2008 and 2009, before bringing a close to his track career.

Having participated successfully as a disabled competitor the 2007 New York Marathon, Alex began to take the sport of paracycling very seriously. He has already won a number of important events in this discipline and is on course to fulfill his ambition of representing Italy in the 2012 London Paralympic Games.

ZANARDI, Alessandro (I) b 23/10/1966, Bologna

1991 Championship position: Unplaced

	Race	Circuit	No	Entrant	Tyres	Capacity/Car/Engine	Comment	Q Pos/Entries
9	SPANISH GP	Barcelona	32	Team 7UP Jordan	G	3.5 Jordan 191-FordHB V8	1 lap behind	20/33
ret	JAPANESE GP	Suzuka	32	Team 7UP Jordan	G	3.5 Jordan 191-FordHB V8	gearbox	13/31
9	AUSTRALIAN GP	Adelaide	32	Team 7UP Jordan	G	3.5 Jordan 191-FordHB V8	race stopped after 14 laps – rain	16/32

1992 Championship position: Unplaced

	Race	Circuit	No	Entrant	Tyres	Capacity/Car/Engine	Comment	Q Pos/Entries
dnq	BRITISH GP	Silverstone	23	Minardi Team	G	3.5 Minardi M192-Lamborghini V12		27/32
ret	GERMAN GP	Hockenheim	23	Minardi Team	G	3.5 Minardi M192-Lamborghini V12	clutch on first lap	24/32
dnq	HUNGARIAN GP	Hungaroring	23	Minardi Team	G	3.5 Minardi M192-Lamborghini V12		29/31

1993 Championship position: 20th Wins: 0 Pole positions: 0 Fastest laps: 0 Points scored: 1

	Race	Circuit	No	Entrant	Tyres	Capacity/Car/Engine	Comment	Q Pos/Entries
ret	SOUTH AFRICAN GP	Kyalami	11	Team Lotus	G	3.5 Lotus 107B-Ford HB V8	collision with Hill	16/26
6	BRAZILIAN GP	Interlagos	11	Team Lotus	G	3.5 Lotus 107B-Ford HB V8	1 lap behind	15/26
8	EUROPEAN GP	Donington	11	Team Lotus	G	3.5 Lotus 107B-Ford HB V8	4 laps behind	13/26
ret	SAN MARINO GP	Imola	11	Team Lotus	G	3.5 Lotus 107B-Ford HB V8	lost wheel – spun into wall	20/26
14/ret	SPANISH GP	Barcelona	11	Team Lotus	G	3.5 Lotus 107B-Ford HB V8	engine/5 laps behind	15/26
7	MONACO GP	Monte Carlo	11	Team Lotus	G	3.5 Lotus 107B-Ford HB V8	2 laps behind	20/26
11	CANADIAN GP	Montreal	11	Team Lotus	G	3.5 Lotus 107B-Ford HB V8	spin/2 laps behind	21/26
ret	FRENCH GP	Magny Cours	11	Team Lotus	G	3.5 Lotus 107B-Ford HB V8	active suspension failure	17/26
ret	BRITISH GP	Silverstone	11	Team Lotus	G	3.5 Lotus 107B-Ford HB V8	lost body panel – spun off	14/26
ret	GERMAN GP	Hockenheim	11	Team Lotus	G	3.5 Lotus 107B-Ford HB V8	spun off	15/26
ret	HUNGARIAN GP	Hungaroring	11	Team Lotus	G	3.5 Lotus 107B-Ford HB V8	gearbox failure	21/26
dns	BELGIAN GP	Spa	11	Team Lotus	G	3.5 Lotus 107B-Ford HB V8	accident in Friday a.m. practice	– / –

1994 Championship position: Unplaced

	Race	Circuit	No	Entrant	Tyres	Capacity/Car/Engine	Comment	Q Pos/Entries
9	SPANISH GP	Barcelona	11	Team Lotus	G	3.5 Lotus 107C-Mugen Honda V10	3 laps behind	23/27
15/ret	CANADIAN GP	Montreal	11	Team Lotus	G	3.5 Lotus 107C-Mugen Honda V10	7 laps behind/engine	23/27
ret	FRENCH GP	Magny Cours	11	Team Lotus	G	3.5 Lotus 109-Mugen Honda V10	engine on fire	23/28
ret	BRITISH GP	Silverstone	11	Team Lotus	G	3.5 Lotus 109-Mugen Honda V10	started from pitlane/engine	19/28
ret	GERMAN GP	Hockenheim	11	Team Lotus	G	3.5 Lotus 109-Mugen Honda V10	multiple accident at start	21/28
13	HUNGARIAN GP	Hungaroring	11	Team Lotus	G	3.5 Lotus 109-Mugen Honda V10	5 laps behind	22/28
ret	ITALIAN GP	Monza	11	Team Lotus	G	3.5 Lotus 109-Mugen Honda V10	collision with Morbidelli on lap 1	13/28
16	EUROPEAN GP	Jerez	12	Team Lotus	G	3.5 Lotus 109-Mugen Honda V10	2 laps behind	21/28
13	JAPANESE GP	Suzuka	12	Team Lotus	G	3.5 Lotus 109-Mugen Honda V10	2 laps behind	17/28
ret	AUSTRALIAN GP	Adelaide	12	Team Lotus	G	3.5 Lotus 109-Mugen Honda V10	throttle	14/28

1999 Championship position: Unplaced

	Race	Circuit	No	Entrant	Tyres	Capacity/Car/Engine	Comment	Q Pos/Entries
ret	AUSTRALIAN GP	Melbourne	5	Winfield Williams	B	3.0 Williams FW21-Supertec V10	accident	15/22
ret	BRAZILIAN GP	Interlagos	5	Winfield Williams	B	3.0 Williams FW21-Supertec V10	transmission	16/21
11/ret	SAN MARINO GP	Imola	5	Winfield Williams	B	3.0 Williams FW21-Supertec V10	spun off/4 laps behind	10/22
8	MONACO GP	Monte Carlo	5	Winfield Williams	B	3.0 Williams FW21-Supertec V10	2 laps behind	11/22
ret	SPANISH GP	Barcelona	5	Winfield Williams	B	3.0 Williams FW21-Supertec V10	transmission	17/22
ret	CANADIAN GP	Montreal	5	Winfield Williams	B	3.0 Williams FW21-Supertec V10	accident	12/22
ret	FRENCH GP	Magny Cours	5	Winfield Williams	B	3.0 Williams FW21-Supertec V10	engine	15/22
11	BRITISH GP	Silverstone	5	Winfield Williams	B	3.0 Williams FW21-Supertec V10		13/22
ret	AUSTRIAN GP	A1-Ring	5	Winfield Williams	B	3.0 Williams FW21-Supertec V10	out of fuel	14/22
ret	GERMAN GP	Hockenheim	5	Winfield Williams	B	3.0 Williams FW21-Supertec V10	differential	14/22
ret	HUNGARIAN GP	Hungaroring	5	Winfield Williams	B	3.0 Williams FW21-Supertec V10	differential	15/22
8	BELGIAN GP	Spa	5	Winfield Williams	B	3.0 Williams FW21-Supertec V10		15/22
7	ITALIAN GP	Monza	5	Winfield Williams	B	3.0 Williams FW21-Supertec V10	loose undertray	4/22
ret	EUROPEAN GP	Nürburgring	5	Winfield Williams	B	3.0 Williams FW21-Supertec V10	transmission	18/22
10	MALAYSIAN GP	Sepang	5	Winfield Williams	B	3.0 Williams FW21-Supertec V10	1 lap behind	16/22
ret	JAPANESE GP	Suzuka	5	Winfield Williams	B	3.0 Williams FW21-Supertec V10	electrics	16/22

GP Starts: 41 GP Wins: 0 Pole positions: 0 Fastest laps: 0 Points: 1

Following spectacular success in Champ Car racing, Zanardi returned to Formula 1 with Williams in 1999. Sadly, the Italian failed to get to grips with the car and its tyre characteristics, and his brief reappearance in grand prix racing was a great disappointment for all concerned.

RICARDO ZONTA

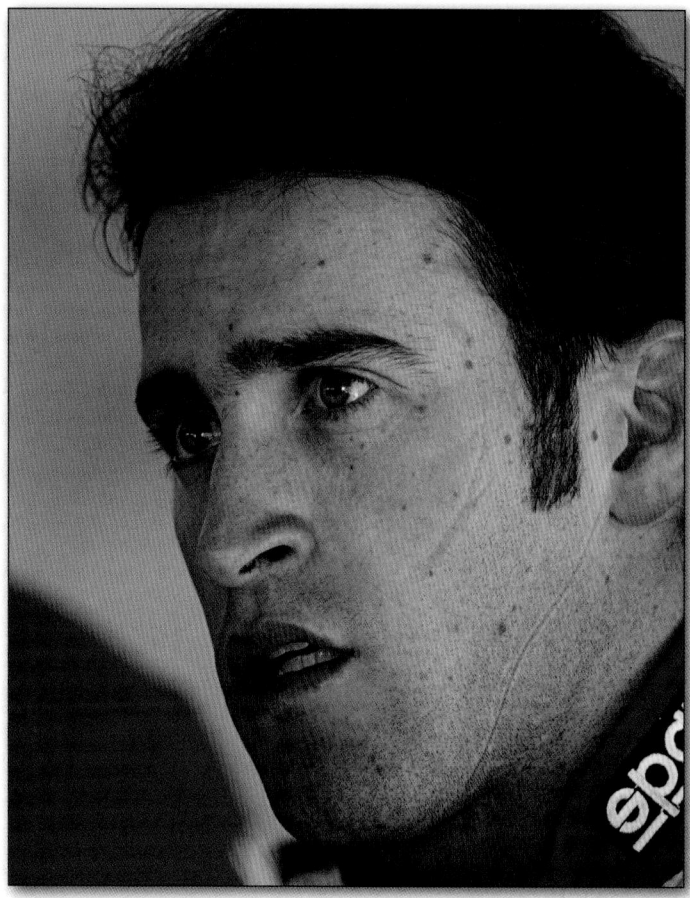

WHEN British American Racing launched their new challenger at the beginning of 1999, quite naturally all eyes were on Jacques Villeneuve, and Ricardo Zonta's grand prix debut in the second car went largely unheralded. The disastrous season that BAR endured provided the Brazilian with the toughest of baptisms in the big time. He was injured in a practice crash at his home track, which forced him to miss three races, and then emerged unscathed from a massive off at Eau Rouge during practice for the Belgian Grand Prix at Spa later in the year. Through all this, his self-confidence remained unshakeable, for the ambitious driver has been a champion in every major category in which he has competed.

Zonta's father was a racer on the local dirt tracks around his native Curitiba, and the young Ricardo soon began making his mark in karts following his debut in 1987. By 1991, he was Brazilian champion and, after a season in Formula Chevrolet, he moved up to Formula 3 in the Sud-Am series. Six victories in the 1995 season brought him the South American F3 championship and with it the opportunity to travel to Europe and race in the F3000 series with the Italian Draco Engineering team.

Wins at Mugello and Estoril marked Zonta as a man to watch. After switching to the top-ranking Super Nova team for 1997, he had the equipment, and the talent, to score three wins on his way to the F3000 title after a tremendous battle with team-mate Juan Pablo Montoya. It was no surprise when he was offered a testing contract with McLaren in 1998, and Mercedes placed him alongside the experienced Klaus Ludwig in their CLK-GTR to contest the FIA GT championship. The pair duly shared the drivers' crown after five wins in the ten-round series.

That success led to him being invited to partner Villeneuve in BAR's high-profile debut season, but it wasn't until the start of the 2000 campaign that things began to improve for the Brazilian, as he inherited sixth spot in Melbourne after Mika Salo's Sauber was disqualified for a technical infringement. Similar finishes in Italy and the USA followed, but that wasn't enough to keep his seat safe. No longer regarded as quite the hot property of 1998, he was forced to take the test-driver role with Jordan, but his time with the team didn't go well. Despite standing in for Heinz-Harald Frentzen twice, he didn't impress and found himself in the F1 wilderness again.

In an effort to kick-start his reputation, Zonta started competing in a new championship, the Telefónica World Series by Nissan. The result was impressive: he won eight races and the series to put himself back in Formula 1 with Toyota as test driver. Although not yielding a race seat, the testing role continued in 2004, when the Brazilian was able to get extra running as one of the third/reserve drivers allowed into Friday practice sessions. He did enough during these brief outings to impress the team and, from the Hungarian Grand Prix onwards, he was drafted in to replace the out-of-favour Cristiano da Matta. In his five race appearances, however, he failed to finish higher than tenth, and with Ralf Schumacher also being snapped up by Toyota for 2005, he returned to a testing and development role once more, which continued until the end of 2006, when he accepted the same job for Renault.

That position allowed Zonta to return to racing action in the Brazilian stock car series, but he continued to race abroad. In 2008, he finished third at Le Mans for Peugeot (with Franck Montagny and Christian Klien) and successfully raced a Lola for Krohn Racing in the ALMS. In the 2010 FIA GT series, driving a Lamborghini, he was the winner at both Spa and Navarra, but his outings for Nissan in 2011 were less rewarding and he cut short his GT season. He returned to stock cars in Brazil, where he has since formed his own team and will race a Chevrolet in 2012.

ZONTA, Ricardo (BR) b 23/3/1976, Curitiba

	Race	Circuit	No	Entrant	Tyres	Capacity/Car/Engine	Comment	Q Pos/Entries
	1999 Championship position: Unplaced							
ret	AUSTRALIAN GP	Melbourne	23	British American Racing	B	3.0 BAR 001-Supertec V10	engine	19/22
dns	BRAZILIAN GP	Interlagos	23	British American Racing	B	3.0 BAR 001-Supertec V10	practice accident – injured foot	– / –
ret	CANADIAN GP	Montreal	23	British American Racing	B	3.0 BAR 001-Supertec V10	accident	17/22
9	FRENCH GP	Magny Cours	23	British American Racing	B	3.0 BAR 001-Supertec V10		10/22
ret	BRITISH GP	Silverstone	23	British American Racing	B	3.0 BAR 001-Supertec V10	suspension	16/22
15/ret	AUSTRIAN GP	A1-Ring	23	British American Racing	B	3.0 BAR 001-Supertec V10	clutch/ 8 laps behind	15/22
ret	GERMAN GP	Hockenheim	23	British American Racing	B	3.0 BAR 001-Supertec V10	engine	18/22
13	HUNGARIAN GP	Hungaroring	23	British American Racing	B	3.0 BAR 001-Supertec V10	2 laps behind	17/22
ret	BELGIAN GP	Spa	23	British American Racing	B	3.0 BAR 001-Supertec V10	gearbox	17/22
ret	ITALIAN GP	Monza	23	British American Racing	B	3.0 BAR 001-Supertec V10	wheel bearing	18/22
8	EUROPEAN GP	Nürburgring	23	British American Racing	B	3.0 BAR 001-Supertec V10	1 lap behind	17/22
ret	MALAYSIAN GP	Sepang	23	British American Racing	B	3.0 BAR 001-Supertec V10	engine	13/22
12	JAPANESE GP	Suzuka	23	British American Racing	B	3.0 BAR 001-Supertec V10	1 lap behind	18/22

2000 Championship position: 14th   Wins: 0   Pole positions: 0   Fastest laps: 0   Points scored: 3

	Race	Circuit	No	Entrant	Tyres	Capacity/Car/Engine	Comment	Q Pos/Entries
6*	AUSTRALIAN GP	Melbourne	23	Lucky Strike BAR Honda	B	3.0 BAR 002-Honda V10	*6th place car disqualified	16/22
9*	BRAZILIAN GP	Interlagos	23	Lucky Strike BAR Honda	B	3.0 BAR 002-Honda V10	*2nd place car dsq/2 laps behind	8/22
12	SAN MARINO GP	Imola	23	Lucky Strike BAR Honda	B	3.0 BAR 002-Honda V10	1 lap behind	14/22
ret	BRITISH GP	Silverstone	23	Lucky Strike BAR Honda	B	3.0 BAR 002-Honda V10	spun off	16/22
8	SPANISH GP	Barcelona	23	Lucky Strike BAR Honda	B	3.0 BAR 002-Honda V10	1 lap behind	17/22
ret	EUROPEAN GP	Nürburgring	23	Lucky Strike BAR Honda	B	3.0 BAR 002-Honda V10	spun off	19/22
ret	MONACO GP	Monte Carlo	23	Lucky Strike BAR Honda	B	3.0 BAR 002-Honda V10	restarted in spare car/accident	20/22
8	CANADIAN GP	Montreal	23	Lucky Strike BAR Honda	B	3.0 BAR 002-Honda V10		8/22
ret	FRENCH GP	Magny Cours	23	Lucky Strike BAR Honda	B	3.0 BAR 002-Honda V10	brakes	19/22
ret	AUSTRIAN GP	A1-Ring	23	Lucky Strike BAR Honda	B	3.0 BAR 002-Honda V10	engine	6/22
ret	GERMAN GP	Hockenheim	23	Lucky Strike BAR Honda	B	3.0 BAR 002-Honda V10	spun off	12/22
14	HUNGARIAN GP	Hungaroring	23	Lucky Strike BAR Honda	B	3.0 BAR 002-Honda V10	2 laps behind	18/22
12	BELGIAN GP	Spa	23	Lucky Strike BAR Honda	B	3.0 BAR 002-Honda V10	1 lap behind	13/22
6	ITALIAN GP	Monza	23	Lucky Strike BAR Honda	B	3.0 BAR 002-Honda V10	early puncture	17/22
6	UNITED STATES GP	Indianapolis	23	Lucky Strike BAR Honda	B	3.0 BAR 002-Honda V10		12/22
9	JAPANESE GP	Suzuka	23	Lucky Strike BAR Honda	B	3.0 BAR 002-Honda V10	1 lap behind	18/22
ret	MALAYSIAN GP	Sepang	23	Lucky Strike BAR Honda	B	3.0 BAR 002-Honda V10	engine	11/22

2001 Championship position: Unplaced

	Race	Circuit	No	Entrant	Tyres	Capacity/Car/Engine	Comment	Q Pos/Entries
7	CANADIAN GP	Montreal	11	B & H Jordan Honda	B	3.0 Jordan EJ11-Honda V10	1 lap behind	12/22
ret	GERMAN GP	Hockenheim	11	B & H Jordan Honda	B	3.0 Jordan EJ11-Honda V10	tagged Verstappen – damaged car	15/22

2004 Championship position: Unplaced

	Race	Circuit	No	Entrant	Tyres	Capacity/Car/Engine	Comment	Q Pos/Entries
app	AUSTRALIAN GP	Melbourne	38	Pansonic Toyota Racing	M	3.0 Toyota TF104-V10	ran as 3rd driver in practice only	- /-
app	MALAYSIAN GP	Sepang	38	Pansonic Toyota Racing	M	3.0 Toyota TF104-V10	ran as 3rd driver in practice only	- /-
app	BAHRAIN GP	Sakhir Circuit	38	Pansonic Toyota Racing	M	3.0 Toyota TF104-V10	ran as 3rd driver in practice only	- /-
app	SAN MARINO GP	Imola	38	Pansonic Toyota Racing	M	3.0 Toyota TF104-V10	ran as 3rd driver in practice only	- /-
app	SPANISH GP	Barcelona	38	Pansonic Toyota Racing	M	3.0 Toyota TF104-V10	ran as 3rd driver in practice only	- /-
app	MONACO GP	Monte Carlo	38	Pansonic Toyota Racing	M	3.0 Toyota TF104-V10	ran as 3rd driver in practice only	- /-
app	EUROPEAN GP	Nürburgring	38	Pansonic Toyota Racing	M	3.0 Toyota TF104-V10	ran as 3rd driver in practice only	- /-
app	CANADIAN GP	Montreal	38	Pansonic Toyota Racing	M	3.0 Toyota TF104-V10	ran as 3rd driver in practice only	- /-
app	UNITED STATES GP	Indianapolis	38	Pansonic Toyota Racing	M	3.0 Toyota TF104-V10	ran as 3rd driver in practice only	- /-
app	FRENCH GP	Magny Cours	38	Pansonic Toyota Racing	M	3.0 Toyota TF104-V10	ran as 3rd driver in practice only	- /-
app	BRITISH GP	Silverstone	38	Pansonic Toyota Racing	M	3.0 Toyota TF104-V10	ran as 3rd driver in practice only	- /-
ret	HUNGARIAN GP	Hungaroring	16	Pansonic Toyota Racing	M	3.0 Toyota TF104-V10	electronics	15/20
10/ret	BELGIAN GP	Spa	16	Pansonic Toyota Racing	M	3.0 Toyota TF104-V10	engine failure when 4th/3 laps behind	20/20
11	ITALIAN GP	Monza	16	Pansonic Toyota Racing	M	3.0 Toyota TF104-V10	poor grip	11/20
ret	CHINESE GP	Shanghai	16	Pansonic Toyota Racing	M	3.0 Toyota TF104-V10	gearbox	14/20
13	BRAZILIAN GP	Interlagos	17	Pansonic Toyota Racing	M	3.0 Toyota TF104-V10	1 lap behind	14/20

2005 Championship position: Unplaced

	Race	Circuit	No	Entrant	Tyres	Capacity/Car/Engine	Comment	Q Pos/Entries
app	AUSTRALIAN GP	Melbourne	38	Pansonic Toyota Racing	M	3.0 Toyota TF105-V10	ran as 3rd driver in practice only	- /-
app	MALAYSIAN GP	Sepang	38	Pansonic Toyota Racing	M	3.0 Toyota TF105-V10	ran as 3rd driver in practice only	- /-
app	BAHRAIN GP	Sakhir Circuit	38	Pansonic Toyota Racing	M	3.0 Toyota TF105-V10	ran as 3rd driver in practice only	- /-
app	SAN MARINO GP	Imola	38	Pansonic Toyota Racing	M	3.0 Toyota TF105-V10	ran as 3rd driver in practice only	- /-
app	SPANISH GP	Barcelona	38	Pansonic Toyota Racing	M	3.0 Toyota TF105-V10	ran as 3rd driver in practice only	- /-
app	MONACO GP	Monte Carlo	38	Pansonic Toyota Racing	M	3.0 Toyota TF104-V10	ran as 3rd driver in practice only	- /-
app	EUROPEAN GP	Nürburgring	38	Pansonic Toyota Racing	M	3.0 Toyota TF104-V10	ran as 3rd driver in practice only	- /-
app	CANADIAN GP	Montreal	38	Pansonic Toyota Racing	M	3.0 Toyota TF104-V10	ran as 3rd driver in practice only	- /-
dns	UNITED STATES GP	Indianapolis	17	Pansonic Toyota Racing	M	3.0 Toyota TF104-V10	withdrawn after parade lap	13/20
app	BRITISH GP	Silverstone	38	Pansonic Toyota Racing	M	3.0 Toyota TF104-V10	ran as 3rd driver in practice only	- /-
app	GERMAN GP	Hockenheim	38	Pansonic Toyota Racing	M	3.0 Toyota TF104-V10	ran as 3rd driver in practice only	- /-
app	HUNGARIAN GP	Hungaroring	38	Pansonic Toyota Racing	M	3.0 Toyota TF104-V10	ran as 3rd driver in practice only	- /-
app	TURKISH GP	Istanbul	38	Pansonic Toyota Racing	M	3.0 Toyota TF104-V10	ran as 3rd driver in practice only	- /-
app	ITALIAN GP	Monza	38	Pansonic Toyota Racing	M	3.0 Toyota TF104-V10	ran as 3rd driver in practice only	- /-
app	BELGIAN GP	Spa	38	Pansonic Toyota Racing	M	3.0 Toyota TF104-V10	ran as 3rd driver in practice only	- /-
app	BRAZILIAN GP	Interlagos	38	Pansonic Toyota Racing	M	3.0 Toyota TF104-V10	ran as 3rd driver in practice only	- /-
app	JAPANESE GP	Suzuka	38	Pansonic Toyota Racing	M	3.0 Toyota TF104-V10	ran as 3rd driver in practice only	- /-
app	CHINESE GP	Shanghai Circuit	38	Pansonic Toyota Racing	M	3.0 Toyota TF104-V10	ran as 3rd driver in practice only	- /-

GP Starts: 36   GP Wins: 0   Pole positions: 0   Fastest laps: 0   Points: 3

ZORZI, Renzo (I) b 12/12/1946, Ziano di Fiemme, nr Turin

1975 Championship position: Unplaced

	Race	Circuit	No	Entrant	Tyres	Capacity/Car/Engine	Comment	Q Pos/Entries
14	ITALIAN GP	Monza	20	Frank Williams Racing Cars	G	3.0 Williams FW03-Cosworth V8	6 laps behind	22/28

1976 Championship position: Unplaced

	Race	Circuit	No	Entrant	Tyres	Capacity/Car/Engine	Comment	Q Pos/Entries
9	BRAZILIAN GP	Interlagos	21	Frank Williams Racing Cars	G	3.0 Williams FW04-Cosworth V8	1 lap behind	17/22

1977 Championship position: Unplaced

	Race	Circuit	No	Entrant	Tyres	Capacity/Car/Engine	Comment	Q Pos/Entries
ret	ARGENTINE GP	Buenos Aires	17	Shadow Racing Team	G	3.0 Shadow DN5-Cosworth V8	gearbox	21/21
6	BRAZILIAN GP	Interlagos	17	Shadow Racing Team	G	3.0 Shadow DN5-Cosworth V8	1 lap behind	18/22
ret	SOUTH AFRICAN GP	Kyalami	17	Shadow Racing Team	G	3.0 Shadow DN8-Cosworth V8	engine	20/23
ret	US GP WEST	Long Beach	16	Shadow Racing Team	G	3.0 Shadow DN8-Cosworth V8	gearbox	20/22
ret	SPANISH GP	Jarama	16	Shadow Racing Team	G	3.0 Shadow DN8-Cosworth V8	engine	24/31

GP Starts: 7   GP Wins: 0   Pole positions: 0   Fastest laps: 0   Points: 1

RENZO ZORZI

ALTHOUGH he has the same date of birth as Emerson Fittipaldi, Renzo Zorzi does not have the same racing pedigree. A graduate of Italian Formula 3 while acting as a test driver at Pirelli, he shot to prominence with a surprise win in the 1975 Monaco Formula 3 support race, but only after Conny Andersson had been given a one-minute penalty and the other front-runners had eliminated each other.

Zorzi's immediate reward was a Williams seat for the Italian Grand Prix, where he drove sensibly to the finish. He started the 1976 season in the newly constituted Wolf-Williams équipe, but was dropped after just one grand prix, being replaced by Michel Leclère. For Renzo, it was back to Formula 3 in a Modus while he waited for a further opportunity, which came in 1977, when Francesco Ambrosio sponsored his drive in the Shadow team. A sixth place in the Brazilian Grand Prix was achieved mainly because of a high rate of attrition, and soon he would become a Formula 1 casualty himself, losing his drive after falling out with Ambrosio. He reappeared towards the end of the decade in occasional rounds of the World Championship of Makes, and then in the 1980 Aurora AFX Monza Lottery Grand Prix in Charles Clowes' Arrows A1B, retiring after a collision.

Subsequently, Zorzi went on to run a driving school in Italy.

RICARDO ZUNINO

HAVING begun racing in 1969, Ricardo Zunino soon progressed to the national scene in touring cars with a Fiat. Helped by sponsorship from the Automobile Club of Argentina, he was lucky enough to be given the chance to travel to Europe to take a shot at the big time.

During two seasons with a March-BMW in Formula 2 (1977/78), however, Zunino's performances were nothing more than thoroughly ordinary, despite having access to very competitive machinery. A lacklustre start to his third year in the formula convinced him that a switch to the less demanding world of the Aurora F1 championship would be beneficial, and he was right. Racing an Arrows in the final nine rounds of the series, he won one race and finished five others in the top six.

Somewhat ambitiously, the quiet and pleasant Argentinian managed to step into grand prix racing at the end of 1979, when Niki Lauda suddenly quit racing during practice in Montreal. He started 1980 still driving the second Brabham BT49, but was eased out of the team in mid-season when the well-funded Hector Rebaque took his place. Ricardo was back with Brabham at the start of 1981, but only for the non-championship South African Grand Prix, in which he finished eighth.

Zunino then joined Tyrrell to contest the two South American rounds, before giving way to a shining new talent by the name of Michele Alboreto. He returned home to find that Argentina had become embroiled in the Falklands War, which had a severe effect on the country's economy and, by extension, sponsorship funding for Formula 1 hopefuls such as himself and his contemporary, Miguel Guerra.

ZUNINO, Ricardo (RA) b 13/4/1949, Buenos Aires

1979 Championship position: Unplaced

	Race	Circuit	No	Entrant	Tyres	Capacity/Car/Engine	Comment	Q Pos/Entries
7	CANADIAN GP	Montreal	5	Parmalat Racing Team	G	3.0 Brabham BT49-Cosworth V8	pit stop – gear linkage/4 laps behind	19/29
ret	US GP EAST	Watkins Glen	5	Parmalat Racing Team	G	3.0 Brabham BT49-Cosworth V8	spun off	9/30

1980 Championship position: Unplaced

	Race	Circuit	No	Entrant	Tyres	Capacity/Car/Engine	Comment	Q Pos/Entries
7	ARGENTINE GP	Buenos Aires	6	Parmalat Racing Team	G	3.0 Brabham BT49-Cosworth V8	2 laps behind	16/28
8	BRAZILIAN GP	Interlagos	6	Parmalat Racing Team	G	3.0 Brabham BT49-Cosworth V8	1 lap behind	18/28
10	SOUTH AFRICAN GP	Kyalami	6	Parmalat Racing Team	G	3.0 Brabham BT49-Cosworth V8	1 lap behind	17/28
ret	US GP WEST	Long Beach	6	Parmalat Racing Team	G	3.0 Brabham BT49-Cosworth V8	hit wall avoiding Mass	18/27
ret	BELGIAN GP	Zolder	6	Parmalat Racing Team	G	3.0 Brabham BT49-Cosworth V8	clutch/gearbox	22/27
dnq	MONACO GP	Monte Carlo	6	Parmalat Racing Team	G	3.0 Brabham BT49-Cosworth V8		25/27
ret	FRENCH GP	Paul Ricard	6	Parmalat Racing Team	G	3.0 Brabham BT49-Cosworth V8	clutch	22/27

1981 Championship position: Unplaced

	Race	Circuit	No	Entrant	Tyres	Capacity/Car/Engine	Comment	Q Pos/Entries
13	BRAZILIAN GP	Rio	4	Tyrrell Racing	M	3.0 Tyrrell 010-Cosworth V8	5 laps behind	24/30
13*	ARGENTINE GP	Buenos Aires	4	Tyrrell Racing	M	3.0 Tyrrell 010-Cosworth V8	*1 lap pen – overshot chicane/-2 laps	24/29

GP Starts: 10 GP Wins: 0 Pole positions: 0 Fastest laps: 0 Points: 0

GIOVANNA AMATI   MICHAEL AMMERMÜLLER   MICHAEL BARTELS   ASDRÚBAL FONTES BAYARDO   ENRICO BERTAGGIA   GARY BRABHAM

TINO BRAMBILLA   GIANFRANCO BRANCATELLI   RYAN BRISCOE   COLIN CHAPMAN   JAN CHAROUX   PEDRO CHAVES

KEVIN COGAN   ALBERTO COLOMBO   ALBERTO CRESPO   ALAIN DE CHANGY   BERNARD DE DRIVER   PIERO DUSIO

BERNIE ECCLESTONE   CARLO FACETTI   FAIRUZ FAUZY   WILLIE FERGUSON   GIORGIO FRANCIA   HIROSHI FUSHIDA

DIVINA GALICA   HELM GLÖCKLER   BRIAN GUBBY   NAOKI HATTORI   NEIL JANI   JUAN JOVER

KEN KAVANAGH   DAVID KENNEDY   BRUCE KESSLER   MIKKA KOZAROWITSKY   MASAMI KUWASHIMA   CLAUDIO LANGES

BAS LEINDERS

JEAN LUCIENBONNET

PERRY McCARTHY

BRIAN MAGUIRE

HARRY MERKEL

GIORGIO MONDINI

BILL MOSS

SATOSHI MOTOYAMA

JAC NELLEMAN

CHANOCH NISSANY

ALFREDO PIÁN

ALEXANDRE PRÉMAT

ERNESTO PRINOTH

CLIVE PUZEY

LUIS RAZIA

KEN RICHARDSON

ALAN ROLLINSON

JEAN-CLAUDE RUDAZ

VINCENTE SOSPIRI

STEPHEN SOUTH

OTTO STUPPACHER

ANDY SUTCLIFFE

LUIGI TARAMAZZO

DENNIS TAYLOR

ENRICO TOCCACELO

TONY TRIMMER

DAVIDE VALSECCHI

JEAN-ÉRIC VERGNE

JACQUES VILLENUEVE

ERNESTO VISO

VOLKER WEIDLER

ROBERT WICKENS

DESIRÉ WILSON

JOACHIM WINKELHOCK

BJÖRN WIRDHEIM

EMILIO ZAPICO

AMATI, Giovanna (I) b 20/7/1962, Rome

1992

	Race	Circuit	No	Entrant	Tyres	Capacity/Car/Engine	Comment	Pos/Entries
dnq	SOUTH AFRICAN GP	Kyalami	8	Motor Racing Developments Ltd	G	3.5 Brabham BT60B-Judd V10		30/30
dnq	MEXICAN GP	Mexico City	8	Motor Racing Developments Ltd	G	3.5 Brabham BT60B-Judd V10		30/30
dnq	BRAZILIAN GP	Interlagos	8	Motor Racing Developments Ltd	G	3.5 Brabham BT60B-Judd V10		30/31

Lady driver who competed regularly in Italian national racing before reaching the limit of her abilities in European F3000

AMMERMÜLLER, Michael, (D) b 14/2/1986, Pocking

2006

	Race	Circuit	No	Entrant	Tyres	Capacity/Car/Engine	Comment	Pos/Entries
app	CHINESE GP	Shanghai	37	Red Bull Racing	M	2.4 Red Bull RB2-Ferrari V8	ran as 3rd driver in practice only	– /–
app	JAPANESE GP	Suzuka	37	Red Bull Racing	M	2.4 Red Bull RB2-Ferrari V8	ran as 3rd driver in practice only	– /–
app	BRAZILIAN GP	Interlagos	37	Red Bull Racing	M	2.4 Red Bull RB2-Ferrari V8	ran as 3rd driver in practice only	– /–

Runner-up in Formula Renault series in both Germany and Italy led to him sgning as Red Bull Junior driver. He took a single win (at Valencia) in GP2 in 2006 for Arden. A wrist injury hampered his progress in 2007 and he was dropped by Red Bull. Subsequently raced in the A1GP series, taking a sprint race win for Germany in Zuhai.

BARTELS, Michael (D) b 8/3/1968, Plettenberg

1991

	Race	Circuit	No	Entrant	Tyres	Capacity/Car/Engine	Comment	Q Pos/Entries
dnq	GERMAN GP	Hockenheim	12	Team Lotus	G	3.5 Lotus 102B-Judd V8		28/34
dnq	HUNGARIAN GP	Hungaroring	12	Team Lotus	G	3.5 Lotus 102B-Judd V8		30/34
dnq	ITALIAN GP	Monza	12	Team Lotus	G	3.5 Lotus 102B-Judd V8		28/34
dnq	SPANISH GP	Barcelona	12	Team Lotus	G	3.5 Lotus 102B-Judd V8		29/33

Star of German F3 in the late eighties, but subsequently left in the shadows of Schumacher and Wendlinger. He successfully competed in the saloon car DTM/ITC series and latterly has been a star in Sports and GT Championships. Driving a Vitaphone Maserati MC12 with Andrea Bertolini he was FIA GT champion in 2006 and 2008-2010.

BAYARDO, Asdrúbal Fontes (U) b 26/12/1922, Pan de Azucar – d 9/7/2006, Montivideo

1959

	Race	Circuit	No	Entrant	Tyres	Capacity/Car/Engine	Comment	Q Pos/Entries
dnq	FRENCH GP	Reims	36	Scuderia Centro Sud	D	2.5 Maserati 250F 6	no practice time recorded	– / –

Star of the mid 1950's Argentine Formula Libre series with a Chevrolet-engined Maserati 4CLT, who subsequently took part in endurance events

BERTAGGIA, Enrico (I) b 19/9/1964, Noale, nr Venice

1989

	Race	Circuit	No	Entrant	Tyres	Capacity/Car/Engine	Comment	Q Pos/Entries
dnpq	BELGIAN GP	Spa	32	Coloni SpA	P	3.5 Coloni FC189-Cosworth V8		39/39
dnpq	ITALIAN GP	Monza	32	Coloni SpA	P	3.5 Coloni FC189-Cosworth V8		38/39
dnpq	PORTUGUESE GP	Estoril	32	Coloni SpA	P	3.5 Coloni FC189-Cosworth V8		39/39
dnpq	SPANISH GP	Jerez	32	Coloni SpA	P	3.5 Coloni FC189-Cosworth V8		38/38
dnpq	JAPANESE GP	Suzuka	32	Coloni SpA	P	3.5 Coloni FC189-Cosworth V8	no practice time recorded	– / 39
dnpq	AUSTRALIAN GP	Adelaide	32	Coloni SpA	P	3.5 Coloni FC189-Cosworth V8		39/39

1992

	Race	Circuit	No	Entrant	Tyres	Capacity/Car/Engine	Comment	Q Pos/Entries
dnp	SOUTH AFRICAN GP	Kyalami	35	Andrea Moda Formula	G	3.5 Coloni C4B-Judd V10	team excluded from meeting	– / –
dnp	MEXICAN GP	Mexico City	35	Andrea Moda Formula	G	3.5 Moda S921-Judd V10	cars not ready – entry withdrawn	– / –

1987 Italian F3 Champion who failed to make the grade in F3000. Replaced Raphanel at Coloni and then resurfaced with Andrea Moda – opting out after just two races.

BOBBI, Matteo (I) b 2/7/1978, Milan

2003

	Race	Circuit	No	Entrant	Tyres	Capacity/Car/Engine	Comment	Q Pos/Entries
app	SAN MARINO GP	Imola	39	European Minardi Cosworth	M	3.0 Minardi PS03-Ford Cosworth V10	ran as 3rd driver in practice only	– /–

Minardi test driver between 2001-2003. Successful in Formula Renualt and Spanish Formula Nissan. Won the 2003 GT title (with Biagi) in a BMS Scuderia Italia Ferrari. With Jaime Melo he won the 2006 FIA GT2 championship in a Ferrari 430GT

BRABHAM, Gary (AUS) b 29/3/1961, Wimbledon, London, England

1990

	Race	Circuit	No	Entrant	Tyres	Capacity/Car/Engine	Comment	Q Pos/Entries
dnpq	US GP (PHOENIX)	Phoenix	39	Life Racing Engines	P	3.5 Life L190 W12		34/35
dnpq	BRAZILIAN GP	Interlagos	39	Life Racing Engines	P	3.5 Life L190 W12		35/35

Second son of Sir Jack. After an excellent British F3 record, he found his career blighted after the Life fiasco. Gary shared the winning Nissan NPT-90 with brother Geoff and Derek Daly in the 1991 Sebring 12-hour race. Had a one-off drive in CART (at Surfers Paradise) in 1994, and followed this with touring car appearances (also down-under).

BRAMBILLA, Tino (Ernesto) (I) b 31/1/1934, Monza

1963

	Race	Circuit	No	Entrant	Tyres	Capacity/Car/Engine	Comment	Q Pos/Entries
dnq	ITALIAN GP	Monza	62	Scuderia Centro Sud	D	1.5 Cooper T53-Maserati 4		26/28

1969

dns	ITALIAN GP	Monza	10	Scuderia Ferrari SpA SEFAC	F	3.0 Ferrari 312/68/69 V12	*Pedro Rodriguez raced car*	– / –

Notoriously hard racer and elder brother of Vittorio. Tino raced works Formula 2 Ferraris with some success, but he was never given a real F1 chance.

BRANCATELLI, Gianfranco (I) b 18/1/1950, Torino

1979

	Race	Circuit	No	Entrant	Tyres	Capacity/Car/Engine	Comment	Q Pos/Entries
dnq	SPANISH GP	Jarama	36	Willi Kauhsen Racing Team	G	3.0 Kauhsen WK-Cosworth V8		27/27
dnq	BELGIAN GP	Zolder	36	Willi Kauhsen Racing Team	G	3.0 Kauhsen WK-Cosworth V8		28/28
dnpq	MONACO GP	Monte Carlo	24	Team Merzario	G	3.0 Merzario A2-Cosworth V8		25/25

1970s Formula Italia and F3 star who, after his unhappy failures in F1, turned to a solid career in touring cars and Group C racing

BRISCOE, Ryan (AUS) b 24/9/1981, Sydney, New South Wales

2004

	Race	Circuit	No	Entrant	Tyres	Capacity/Car/Engine	Comment	Q Pos/Entries
app	HUNGARIAN GP	Hungarorong	38	Panasonic Toyota Racing	M	3.0 Toyota TF104-V10	*ran as 3rd driver in practice only*	– /–
app	BELGIAN GP	Spa	38	Panasonic Toyota Racing	M	3.0 Toyota TF104-V10	*ran as 3rd driver in practice only*	– /–
app	ITALIAN GP	Monza	38	Panasonic Toyota Racing	M	3.0 Toyota TF104-V10	*ran as 3rd driver in practice only*	– /–
app	CHINESE GP	Shanghai	38	Panasonic Toyota Racing	M	3.0 Toyota TF104-V10	*ran as 3rd driver in practice only*	– /–
app	JAPANESE GP	Suzuka	38	Panasonic Toyota Racing	M	3.0 Toyota TF104-V10	*ran as 3rd driver in practice only*	– /–
app	BRAZILIAN GP	Interlagos	38	Panasonic Toyota Racing	M	3.0 Toyota TF104-V10	*ran as 3rd driver in practice only*	– /–

Successful in karting, Briscoe was also the 2003 EuroSeries F3 Champion. Testing for Toyota led to his move to the US with Ganassi for 2005, but his debut season ended in serious injury at Chicagoland. Subsequently, the talented Australian has established himself at Penske, winning 6 IRL races between 2008 and 2010.

CADE, Phil (USA) b 12/7/1916, Charles City, Iowa – d 28/8/2001, Winchester, Massachusetts

1959

	Race	Circuit	No	Entrant	Tyres	Capacity/Car/Engine	Comment	Q Pos/Entries
dns	US GP	Sebring	22	Phil Cade	D	2.5 Maserati 250F 6	*engine problems*	(18)/19

Amateur enthusiast who raced a Chrysler-engined 1936 Maserati in SCCA events during the 1950s

CHAPMAN, Colin (GB) b 19/5/1928, Richmond, Surrey – d 16/12/1982, East Carelton, nr Norwich, Norfolk

1956

	Race	Circuit	No	Entrant	Tyres	Capacity/Car/Engine	Comment	Q Pos/Entries
dns	FRENCH GP	Reims	26	Vandervell Products Ltd	P	2.5 Vanwall 4	*practice accident – car damaged*	(5)/20

Founder of Lotus, a true innovator whose designs changed the shape of Formula 1. Chapman was a very good sports car driver, who could mix it with the best

CHAROUZ, Jan (CZ) b 17/7/1987, Prague

2011

	Race	Circuit	No	Entrant	Tyres	Capacity/Car/Engine	Comment	Q Pos/Entries
dns	BRAZILIAN GP	Interlagos	23	HRT F1 Team	P	2.4 HRT F111-Cosworth V8	*ran as 3rd driver in practice 1 only*	– / –

Son of Czech team owner Antonin Charouz. Running in his father's team, Jan won the 2006 F3000 International Masters crown and was the 2009 Le Mans Series champion in works-backed Aston Martin (with Thomas Enge and Stefan Mucke). One of a number of Renault F1 test drivers in 2010.

CHAVES Pedro (P) b 27/2/65, Porto

1991

	Race	Circuit	No	Entrant	Tyres	Capacity/Car/Engine	Comment	Q Pos/Entries
dnpq	US GP (PHOENIX)	Phoenix	31	Coloni Racing Srl	G	3.5 Coloni C4-Cosworth V8		32/34
dnpq	BRAZILIAN GP	Interlagos	31	Coloni Racing Srl	G	3.5 Coloni C4-Cosworth V8		33/34
dnpq	SAN MARINO GP	Imola	31	Coloni Racing Srl	G	3.5 Coloni C4-Cosworth V8		34/34
dnpq	MONACO GP	Monte Carlo	31	Coloni Racing Srl	G	3.5 Coloni C4-Cosworth V8		33/34
dnpq	CANADIAN GP	Montreal	31	Coloni Racing Srl	G	3.5 Coloni C4-Cosworth V8		34/34
dnpq	MEXICAN GP	Mexico City	31	Coloni Racing Srl	G	3.5 Coloni C4-Cosworth V8		33/34
dnpq	FRENCH GP	Magny Cours	31	Coloni Racing Srl	G	3.5 Coloni C4-Cosworth V8		34/34
dnpq	BRITISH GP	Silverstone	31	Coloni Racing Srl	G	3.5 Coloni C4-Cosworth V8		34/34
dnpq	GERMAN GP	Hockenheim	31	Coloni Racing Srl	G	3.5 Coloni C4-Cosworth V8		34/34
dnpq	HUNGARIAN GP	Hungaroring	31	Coloni Racing Srl	G	3.5 Coloni C4-Cosworth V8		34/34
dnpq	BELGIAN GP	Spa	31	Coloni Racing Srl	G	3.5 Coloni C4-Cosworth V8		33/34
dnpq	ITALIAN GP	Monza	31	Coloni Racing Srl	G	3.5 Coloni C4-Cosworth V8	*no time recorded*	*34/34
dnpq	PORTUGUESE GP	Estoril	31	Coloni Racing Srl	G	3.5 Coloni C4-Cosworth V8		34/34

The 1990 British F3000 champion, who competed successfully in Indy Lights for three seasons after his moribund 1991 season with Coloni. In Spain he was was runner-up in their 1996 Touring Car series with a BMW and took the 2002 GT crown with Miguel Ramos in a Saleen. Pedro was also a Rally Champion in Portugal in 1999 and 2000.

COGAN, Kevin (USA) b 31/3/1956, Culver City, California

1980

	Race	Circuit	No	Entrant	Tyres	Capacity/Car/Engine	Comment	Q Pos/Entries
dnq	CANADIAN GP	Montreal	51	RAM/Rainbow Jeans Racing	G	3.0 Williams FW07B-Cosworth V8		28/28

1981

dnq	US GP WEST	Long Beach	4	Tyrrell Racing	M	3.0 Tyrrell 010-Cosworth V8		25/29

One-time IndyCar winner (at Phoenix in 1986) but his later career was blighted by injury after a succession of major accidents.

COLOMBO, Alberto (I) b 23/2/1946, Veredo, nr Milan

1978

	Race	Circuit	No	Entrant	Tyres	Capacity/Car/Engine	Comment	Q Pos/Entries
dnq	BELGIAN GP	Zolder	10	ATS Racing Team	G	3.0 ATS HS1-Cosworth V8		28/30
dnq	SPANISH GP	Jarama	10	ATS Racing Team	G	3.0 ATS HS1-Cosworth V8		28/29
dnpq	ITALIAN GP	Monza	34	Team Merzario	G	3.0 Merzario A1-Cosworth V8		32/32

The 1974 Italian F3 champion who raced competitvely in Formula 2 (1974-80) His best year was 1977, when he finished seventh overall, with eight top-six finishes.

CRESPO, Alberto (RA) b 16/1/1930 Buenos Aires – d 14/8/1991 Buenos Aires

1952

	Race	Circuit	No	Entrant	Tyres	Capacity/Car/Engine	Comment	Q Pos/Entries
dnq	ITALIAN GP	Monza	58	Enrico Platé	P	2.0 Maserati 4CLT/48-Maserati Platé 4		26/35

Came briefly to Europe as a youngster in 1952, and raced a works Talbot to fourth place in the Albi GP. Later took Enrico Plate's Maserati to sixth place at La Baule.

de CHANGY, Alain (B) b 5/2/1922, Brussels – d 5/8/1994, Etterbeek, Brussels

1959

	Race	Circuit	No	Entrant	Tyres	Capacity/Car/Engine	Comment	Q Pos/Entries
dnq	MONACO GP	Monte Carlo	12	Equipe Nationale Belge	D	1.5 Cooper T51-Climax 4		19/24

Sports car driver whose best International result was a 6th place at Le Mans in 1958, sharing a Ferrari 250 Testa Rossa with 'Beurlys'.

de DRYVER, Bernard (B) b 19/9/1952, Brussels

1977

	Race	Circuit	No	Entrant	Tyres	Capacity/Car/Engine	Comment	Q Pos/Entries
dnq	BELGIAN GP	Zolder	38	British Formula 1 Racing	G	3.0 March 761-Cosworth V8		31/32

1978

dnpq	BELGIAN GP	Zolder	23	Bernard de Dryver	G	3.0 Ensign N177-Cosworth V8	did not qualify for official practice	

Drove a full season in the Aurora F1 series in 1979 with a Fittipaldi F5A, taking fourth in the championship. Raced occcasionaly thereafter in sports cars

de RIU, Giovanni (I) b 10/3/1925 Macomer, Nuoro, Sardega – d 11/12/2008, Stresa, Lake Maggiore

1954

	Race	Circuit	No	Entrant	Tyres	Capacity/Car/Engine	Comment	Q Pos/Entries
dnq	ITALIAN GP	Monza	2	Giovanni de Riu	P	2.5 Maserati A6GCM/250F 6	too slow	21/21

After retirement from racing he was a member the CSAI (Commissione Sportiva Automobilistica Italiana)

DOCHNAL, Frank J. (USA) b 8/10/1920, St Louis, Missouri – d 7/7/2010, St Louis, Missouri

1963

	Race	Circuit	No	Entrant	Tyres	Capacity/Car/Engine	Comment	Q Pos/Entries
dns	MEXICAN GP	Mexico City	20	Frank J Dochnal	D	1.5 Cooper T53-Climax 4	crashed in unofficial practice	– / –

Dochnal was a racing mechanic who had some success locally, whose fleeting appearance above seems to be the "high point "of his career. Also acted as a technical official for USAC.

DUSIO, Piero (I) b 13/10/1899, Scurzolengo d'Asti – d 7/11/1975, Victoria, Buenos Aires, Argentina

1952

	Race	Circuit	No	Entrant	Tyres	Capacity/Car/Engine	Comment	Q Pos/Entries
dnq	ITALIAN GP	Monza	44	Piero Dusio	P	Cisitalia D46	engine – no time set	– / –

Italian amateur pre-war champion who built the little Cisitalia D46 racers which found wide favour – unlike the later Porsche-based Tipo 360 Grand Prix car

ECCLESTONE, Bernie (GB) b 28/10/1930, St Peters, Suffolk

1958

	Race	Circuit	No	Entrant	Tyres	Capacity/Car/Engine	Comment	Q Pos/Entries
dnq	MONACO GP	Monte Carlo	12	B C Ecclestone	A	2.5 Connaught B-Alta 4	not seen as a serious attempt	28/28
dnq	BRITISH GP	Silverstone	14	B C Ecclestone	D	2.5 Connaught B-Alta 4	car driven by Fairman	21/21

Subsequently owned the Brabham team and, in his capacities with FOCA and the FIA, has shaped the development of modern-day Grand Prix racing.

FACETTI, Carlo (I) b 26/6/1935, Cormano, Milan

1974

	Race	Circuit	No	Entrant	Tyres	Capacity/Car/Engine	Comment	Q Pos/Entries
dnq	ITALIAN GP	Monza	31	Scuderia Finotto	G	3.0 Brabham BT42-Cosworth V8		27/31

1979 European Touring Car Champion with Martino Finotto in a 3.2 litre BMW CSL clocking up 5 wins.

FAUZY, Fairuz (MAL) b 24/10/1982, Kuala Lumpur

2010

	Race	Circuit	No	Entrant	Tyres	Capacity/Car/Engine	Comment	Q Pos/Entries
app	MALAYSIAN GP	Sepang	19	Lotus Racing	B	2.4 Lotus T127-Cosworth V8	ran as 3rd driver in practice 1 only	– /–
app	BRITISH GP	Silverstone	18	Lotus Racing	B	2.4 Lotus T127-Cosworth V8	ran as 3rd driver in practice 1 only	– /–
app	GERMAN GP	Hockenheim	19	Lotus Racing	B	2.4 Lotus T127-Cosworth V8	ran as 3rd driver in practice 1 only	– /–
app	SINGAPORE GP	Marina Bay Circuit	18	Lotus Racing	B	2.4 Lotus T127-Cosworth V8	ran as 3rd driver in practice 1 only	– /–
app	ABU DHABI GP	Yas Marina Circuit	19	Lotus Racing	B	2.4 Lotus T127-Cosworth V8	ran as 3rd driver in practice 1 only	– /–

A single win across the GP2 Asia, A1 GP and Formula Renualt 3.5 series during 2008-09 for the Malaysian who switched to a reserve role at Lotus-Renault in 2011 after leaving rivals Lotus Racing.

FERGUSON, Willie (ZA) b 6/3/1940, Johannesburg – d 19/5/2007, Durban

1972

	Race	Circuit	No	Entrant	Tyres	Capacity/Car/Engine	Comment	Q Pos/Entries
dns	SOUTH AFRICAN GP	Kyalami	28	Team Gunston	F	3.0 Brabham BT33-Cosworth V8	engine in practice	27/27
dns	" "	"	27T	Team Gunston	F	3.0 Surtees TS9-Cosworth V8	car driven by Love in race	– / –

Early seventies South African F1 series mainstay with his Lola, who was unlucky to miss out on his only Grand Prix start when his locally rebuilt engine failed.

FISCHER, Ludwig (D) b 17/12/1915, Straubling – d 8/3/1991 Bad Reichenhall

1952

	Race	Circuit	No	Entrant	Tyres	Capacity/Car/Engine	Comment	Q Pos/Entries
dns	GERMAN GP	Nürburgring	131	Ludwig Fischer	–	2.0 AFM BMW 6		31/32

Raced in German F2 in the early fifties, before running, mainly in national events and hillclimbs, with a Porsche RS. Fischer continued to compete well into the following decade with a Mecedes Benz 230SL

FRANCIA, Giorgio (I) b 8/11/1947, Bologna

1977

	Race	Circuit	No	Entrant	Tyres	Capacity/Car/Engine	Comment	Q Pos/Entries
dnq	ITALIAN GP	Monza	21	Martini Racing	G	3.0 Brabham BT45B-Alfa Romeo F12	withdrawn after first practice	34/34

1981

	Race	Circuit	No	Entrant	Tyres	Capacity/Car/Engine	Comment	Q Pos/Entries
dnq	SPANISH GP	Jarama	32	Osella Squadra Corse	M	3.0 Osella FA1B-Cosworth V8		30/30

1974 German F3 Champion in a March-Toyota, and then successful in both Osella and latterly Alfa Romeos. Raced for well over two decades in most categories.

FUSHIDA, Hiroshi (J) b 10/3/1946, Kyoto

1975

	Race	Circuit	No	Entrant	Tyres	Capacity/Car/Engine	Comment	Q Pos/Entries
dns	DUTCH GP	Zandvoort	35	Maki Engineering	G	3.0 Maki F101C-Cosworth V8	blown engine in practice	(25)/25
dnq	BRITISH GP	Silverstone	35	Maki Engineering	G	3.0 Maki F101C-Cosworth V8		28/28

An early Toyota works driver who often raced away from his home country, Fushida raced in F5000 in the US, at Le Mans for Mazda in 1973 and Bathurst in 1975, taking a class win. He ran the TOMS F3 Team for more than a decade and later was the General Manager of Bentley's Racing Technology

GALICA, Divina (GB) b 13/8/1946, Bushey Heath nr Watford, Hertfordshire

1976

	Race	Circuit	No	Entrant	Tyres	Capacity/Car/Engine	Comment	Q Pos/Entries
dnq	BRITISH GP	Brands Hatch	13	Shellsport/Whiting	G	3.0 Surtees TS16-Cosworth V8		28/30

1978

	Race	Circuit	No	Entrant	Tyres	Capacity/Car/Engine	Comment	Q Pos/Entries
dnq	ARGENTINE GP	Buenos Aires	24	Olympus Cameras with Hesketh	G	3.0 Hesketh 308E-Cosworth V8		27/27
dnq	BRAZILIAN GP	Rio	24	Olympus Cameras with Hesketh	G	3.0 Hesketh 308E-Cosworth V8		28/28

Determined lady racer and international skier who made her mark in the mid-seventies Shellsport G8 series

'GIMAX' (FRANCHI, Carlo) (I) b 1/12/1938, Lainate, nr Milan

1978

	Race	Circuit	No	Entrant	Tyres	Capacity/Car/Engine	Comment	Q Pos/Entries
dnq	ITALIAN GP	Monza	18	Team Surtees	G	3.0 Surtees TS20-Cosworth V8		28/32

Veteran Italian racer who managed to get his hands on works Surtees, and managed nothing more than to get in the way of everyone else. For the record, his pseudonym 'Gimax' stemmed from the abrieviations of the names of his sons Gigi and Massimo.

GLÖCKLER, Helmut (D) b 13/1/1909, Frankfurt – d 18/12/1993, Frankfurt

1953

	Race	Circuit	No	Entrant	Tyres	Capacity/Car/Engine	Comment	Q Pos/Entries
dns	GERMAN GP	Nürburgring	39	Equipe Anglaise	D	2.0 Cooper T23-Bristol 6	engine threw rod in practice	– /35

Helm was very successful with a Veritas sports and a single seater Deutsch-Bonnet before he drove his brother Walter's Glockler-Porsche special to win the German championship in 1952. He drove the first works Porsche 550 Coupé at Le Mans in 1953 and won the German sports car title for a second time the following year.

GUBBY, Brian (GB) b 17/4/1934, Epsom, Surrey

1965

	Race	Circuit	No	Entrant	Tyres	Capacity/Car/Engine	Comment	Q Pos/Entries
dnq	BRITISH GP	Silverstone	26	Brian Gubby	D	1.5 Lotus 24-Climax V8	*gearbox failure*	23/23

A promising driver who graduated from Formula Junior to race briefly in F1 on a shoestring budget. Survived a big crash at Enna in 1964 and after a gearbox problem nearly caused him to crash in practice for the 1965 Britsh GP he retired on the spot. Subsequently built up a car dealership and has been a successful race horse trainer.

HATTORI, Naoki (J) b 13/6/1966, Yokkaichi, Mie

1991

	Race	Circuit	No	Entrant	Tyres	Capacity/Car/Engine	Comment	Q Pos/Entries
dnpq	JAPANESE GP	Suzuka	31	Coloni Racing Srl	G	3.5 Coloni C4-Cosworth V8		31/31
dnpq	AUSTRALIAN GP	Adelaide	31	Coloni Racing Srl	G	3.5 Coloni C4-Cosworth V8		32/32

Japanese F3 champion in 1990 and a front-runner in the All-Japan F3000 championship. Made an abortive attempt to find success in CART in 1999

HEYER, Hans (D) b 16/3/1943, Mönchengladbach *(also included in main statistics)*

1977

	Race	Circuit	No	Entrant	Tyres	Capacity/Car/Engine	Comment	Q Pos/Entries
dnq/ret	GERMAN GP	Hockenheim	35	ATS Racing Team	G	3.0 Penske PC4-Cosworth V8	*started illegally/gear linkage*	27/30

Started the above race illegally and subsequently disqualified.

JONES, Tom (CDN) b 26/4/1943, Dallas, Texas

1967

	Race	Circuit	No	Entrant	Tyres	Capacity/Car/Engine	Comment	Q Pos/Entries
dnq	CANADIAN GP	Mosport Park	41	Tom Jones	-	2.0 Cooper T82-Climax V8	*too slow – not allowed to start*	19/19

A group of enthusiasts from Cleveland, Ohio entered the unknown Jones, but unfotunately the inexperienced pilot was 20 seconds off the pace of Mike Fisher

JANI, Neel (CH) b 8/12/1983, Rorschach

2006

	Race	Circuit	No	Entrant	Tyres	Capacity/Car/Engine	Comment	Q Pos/Entries
app	BAHRAIN GP	Sakhir Circuit	40	Scuderia Toro Rosso	M	3.0 Toro Rosso STR01-Cosworth V10	*ran as 3rd driver in practice only*	- /-
app	MALAYSIAN GP	Sepang	40	Scuderia Toro Rosso	M	3.0 Toro Rosso STR01-Cosworth V10	*ran as 3rd driver in practice only*	- /-
app	AUSTRALIAN GP	Melbourne	40	Scuderia Toro Rosso	M	3.0 Toro Rosso STR01-Cosworth V10	*ran as 3rd driver in practice only*	- /-
app	SAN MARINO GP	Imola	40	Scuderia Toro Rosso	M	3.0 Toro Rosso STR01-Cosworth V10	*ran as 3rd driver in practice only*	- /-
app	EUROPEAN GP	Nürburgring	40	Scuderia Toro Rosso	M	3.0 Toro Rosso STR01-Cosworth V10	*ran as 3rd driver in practice only*	- /-
app	SPANISH GP	Barcelona	40	Scuderia Toro Rosso	M	3.0 Toro Rosso STR01-Cosworth V10	*ran as 3rd driver in practice only*	- /-
app	MONACO GP	Monte Carlo	40	Scuderia Toro Rosso	M	3.0 Toro Rosso STR01-Cosworth V10	*ran as 3rd driver in practice only*	- /-
app	BRITISH GP	Silverstone	40	Scuderia Toro Rosso	M	3.0 Toro Rosso STR01-Cosworth V10	*ran as 3rd driver in practice only*	- /-
app	CANADIAN GP	Montreal	40	Scuderia Toro Rosso	M	3.0 Toro Rosso STR01-Cosworth V10	*ran as 3rd driver in practice only*	- /-
app	U S GP	Indianapolis	40	Scuderia Toro Rosso	M	3.0 Toro Rosso STR01-Cosworth V10	*ran as 3rd driver in practice only*	- /-
app	FRENCH GP	Magny Cours	40	Scuderia Toro Rosso	M	3.0 Toro Rosso STR01-Cosworth V10	*ran as 3rd driver in practice only*	- /-
app	GERMAN GP	Hockenheim	40	Scuderia Toro Rosso	M	3.0 Toro Rosso STR01-Cosworth V10	*ran as 3rd driver in practice only*	- /-
app	HUNGARIAN GP	Hungaroring	40	Scuderia Toro Rosso	M	3.0 Toro Rosso STR01-Cosworth V10	*ran as 3rd driver in practice only*	- /-
app	TURKISH GP	Istanbul	40	Scuderia Toro Rosso	M	3.0 Toro Rosso STR01-Cosworth V10	*ran as 3rd driver in practice only*	- /-
app	ITALIAN GP	Monza	40	Scuderia Toro Rosso	M	3.0 Toro Rosso STR01-Cosworth V10	*ran as 3rd driver in practice only*	- /-
app	CHINESE GP	Shanghai	40	Scuderia Toro Rosso	M	3.0 Toro Rosso STR01-Cosworth V10	*ran as 3rd driver in practice only*	- /-
app	JAPANESE GP	Suzuka	40	Scuderia Toro Rosso	M	3.0 Toro Rosso STR01-Cosworth V10	*ran as 3rd driver in practice only*	- /-
app	BRAZILIAN GP	Interlagos	40	Scuderia Toro Rosso	M	3.0 Toro Rosso STR01-Cosworth V10	*ran as 3rd driver in practice only*	- /-

A Swiss national of Indian origin, Jani was a very quick driver who made his mark in GP2, A1GP and the Champ Car series and was unlucky not to have been given a chance in F1.

JOVER, Juan (E) b 23/11/1923, Barcelona, – d 28/6/1960, Sitges, Catalunya

1951

	Race	Circuit	No	Entrant	Tyres	Capacity/Car/Engine	Comment	Q Pos/Entries
dns	SPANISH GP	Pedralbes	46	Scuderia Milano	-	1.5 s/c Maserati 4CLT/48 4	*engine in practice*	18/20

Famous Spanish 'gentleman' racer, on bikes and in cars, from the early 1920's. In the immediate post war era, his most notable result being 2nd at Le Mans in 1949 with Louveau in a Delage. He continued throughout the 1950's, surviving a serious practice accident at Le Mans in 1954. Jover lost his life in a road accident near Barcelona.

KAVANAGH, Ken (AUS) b 12/12/1923, Melbourne, Victoria

1958

	Race	Circuit	No	Entrant	Tyres	Capacity/Car/Engine	Comment	Q Pos/Entries
dnq	MONACO GP	Monte Carlo	50	Ken Kavanagh	-	2.5 Maserati 250F 6		19/28
dns	BELGIAN GP	Spa	34	Ken Kavanagh	-	2.5 Maserati 250F 6	*engine in practice*	(20)/28

Very successful Norton and Moto-Guzzi motor cycle racer, who dabbled briefly with four-wheeled competition.

KENNEDY, David (IRL) b 15/1/1953, Sligo

1980

	Race	Circuit	No	Entrant	Tyres	Capacity/Car/Engine	Comment	Q Pos/Entries
dnq	ARGENTINE GP	Buenos Aires	18	Shadow Cars	G	3.0 Shadow DN11-Cosworth V8		25/28
dnq	BRAZILIAN GP	Interlagos	18	Shadow Cars	G	3.0 Shadow DN11-Cosworth V8		26/28
dnq	SOUTH AFRICAN GP	Kyalami	18	Shadow Cars	G	3.0 Shadow DN11-Cosworth V8		27/28
dnq	US GP WEST	Long Beach	18	Shadow Cars	G	3.0 Shadow DN11-Cosworth V8		25/27
dnq	BELGIAN GP	Zolder	18	Shadow Cars	G	3.0 Shadow DN11-Cosworth V8		26/27
dnq	MONACO GP	Monte Carlo	18	Theodore Shadow	G	3.0 Shadow DN11-Cosworth V8		27/27
dnq	FRENCH GP	Paul Ricard	18	Theodore Shadow	G	3.0 Shadow DN12-Cosworth V8		27/27

1976-77 Formula Ford champion who switched to sports cars after his brief F1 career failed to take off. Qualified and raced in 1980 Spanish GP – subsequently deprived of championship status. Raced regularly with Mazda in the late eighties

KESSLER, Bruce (USA) b 23/3/1936, Seattle, Washington

1958

	Race	Circuit	No	Entrant	Tyres	Capacity/Car/Engine	Comment	Q Pos/Entries
dnq	MONACO GP	Monte Carlo	12	B C Ecclestone	A	2.5 Connaught B Type-Alta 4		21/28

SCCA Sports car driver who briefly dabbled with F1. Retired after a sports car crash at Ponoma in 1959 left him in a coma. Later became a successful TV and movie director.

KOZAROWITSKY, Mikko (SF) b 17/5/1948, Helsinki

1977

	Race	Circuit	No	Entrant	Tyres	Capacity/Car/Engine	Comment	Q Pos/Entries
dnq	SWEDISH GP	Anderstorp	32	RAM Racing/F & S Properties	G	3.0 March 761-Cosworth V8		31/31
dnpq	BRITISH GP	Silverstone	32	RAM Racing/F & S Properties	G	3.0 March 761-Cosworth V8	injured hand in accident	36/36

More than decent rival of Keke Rosberg in Super Vee, who raced for Fred Opert in Formula Atlantic. Saddled with a hopeless RAM March which torpedoed his career.

KRAKAU, Willi (D) b 4/12/1911 Schonebeck- Felgeleben – d 26/4/1995, Peine

1952

	Race	Circuit	No	Entrant	Tyres	Capacity/Car/Engine	Comment	Q Pos/Entries
dns	GERMAN GP	Nürburgring	133	Willi Krakau	–	2.0 AFM 6		28/32

Former Olympic rower, who raced his home built BMW based specials in the late forties and early fifties.

KUHNKE, Kurt (D) b 13/4/1912, Stettin (Szczecin, Poland) – d 8/2/1969, Braunschweig

1963

	Race	Circuit	No	Entrant	Tyres	Capacity/Car/Engine	Comment	Q Pos/Entries
dnq	GERMAN GP	Nürburgring	27	Kurt Kuhnke	D	1.5 BKL Lotus 18-Borgward 4		26/26

Successful with his 500cc Cooper in Germany in the early and mid-fifties, but was uncompetetive with his F1 car in non-championship events in 1962 and 1963.

KUWASHIMA, Masami (J) b 14/9/1950, Kumagaya

1976

	Race	Circuit	No	Entrant	Tyres	Capacity/Car/Engine	Comment	Q Pos/Entries
dns	JAPANESE GP	Mount Fuji	21	Walter Wolf Racing	G	3.0 Williams FW05-Cosworth V8	sponsors withdrew – Binder raced	(26)/27

Promising in European Formula 3 in 1972-73, Kuwashima graduated to Formula 2 in 1974, where showed considerable promise, before returning to Japan. He successfully raced in domestic F2000 and Formula 2 competition before retiring at the end of 1979.

LANGES, Claudio (I) b 20/7/1960, Brescia

1990

	Race	Circuit	No	Entrant	Tyres	Capacity/Car/Engine	Comment	Q Pos/Entries
dnpq	US GP (PHOENIX)	Phoenix	34	EuroBrun Racing	P	3.5 EuroBrun ER189-Judd V8		33/35
dnpq	BRAZILIAN GP	Interlagos	34	EuroBrun Racing	P	3.5 EuroBrun ER189-Judd V8		34/35
dnpq	SAN MARINO GP	Imola	34	EuroBrun Racing	P	3.5 EuroBrun ER189B-Judd V8		32/34
dnpq	MONACO GP	Monte Carlo	34	EuroBrun Racing	P	3.5 EuroBrun ER189B-Judd V8		33/35
dnpq	CANADIAN GP	Montreal	34	EuroBrun Racing	P	3.5 EuroBrun ER189B-Judd V8		34/35
dnpq	MEXICAN GP	Mexico City	34	EuroBrun Racing	P	3.5 EuroBrun ER189B-Judd V8		34/35
dnpq	FRENCH GP	Paul Ricard	34	EuroBrun Racing	P	3.5 EuroBrun ER189B-Judd V8		33/35
dnpq	BRITISH GP	Silverstone	34	EuroBrun Racing	P	3.5 EuroBrun ER189B-Judd V8		33/35
dnpq	GERMAN GP	Hockenheim	34	EuroBrun Racing	P	3.5 EuroBrun ER189B-Judd V8		34/35
dnpq	HUNGARIAN GP	Hungaroring	34	EuroBrun Racing	P	3.5 EuroBrun ER189B-Judd V8		34/35
dnpq	BELGIAN GP	Spa	34	EuroBrun Racing	P	3.5 EuroBrun ER189B-Judd V8		32/33
dnpq	ITALIAN GP	Monza	34	EuroBrun Racing	P	3.5 EuroBrun ER189B-Judd V8		32/33
dnpq	PORTUGUESE GP	Estoril	34	EuroBrun Racing	P	3.5 EuroBrun ER189B-Judd V8		32/33
dnpq	SPANISH GP	Jerez	34	EuroBrun Racing	P	3.5 EuroBrun ER189B-Judd V8		32/33

Gave a number of good performances in junior formulae and F3000, but his task with the EuroBrun was hopeless. Moved on to succesfully race touring cars

LEINDERS, Bas (B) b 16/7/1975, Bree

2004

	Race	Circuit	No	Entrant	Tyres	Capacity/Car/Engine	Comment	Q Pos/Entries
app	MALAYSIAN GP	Sepang	40	European Minardi Cosworth	M	3.0 Minardi PS04B-Ford Cosworth V10	ran as 3rd driver in practice only	–/–
app	BAHRAIN GP	Sakhir Circuit	40	European Minardi Cosworth	M	3.0 Minardi PS04B-Ford Cosworth V10	ran as 3rd driver in practice only	–/–
app	SAN MARINO GP	Imola	40	European Minardi Cosworth	M	3.0 Minardi PS04B-Ford Cosworth V10	ran as 3rd driver in practice only	–/–

	Race	Circuit	No	Entrant		Tyres	Capacity/Car/Engine	Comment	Q Pos/Entries
app	SPANISH GP	Barcelona	40	European Minardi Cosworth		M	3.0 Minardi PS04B-Ford Cosworth V10	*ran as 3rd driver in practice only*	- /-
app	MONACO GP	Monte Carlo	40	European Minardi Cosworth		M	3.0 Minardi PS04B-Ford Cosworth V10	*ran as 3rd driver in practice only*	- /-
app	EUROPEAN GP	Nürburgring	40	European Minardi Cosworth		M	3.0 Minardi PS04B-Ford Cosworth V10	*ran as 3rd driver in practice only*	- /-
app	CANADIAN GP	Montreal	40	European Minardi Cosworth		M	3.0 Minardi PS04B-Ford Cosworth V10	*ran as 3rd driver in practice only*	- /-
app	US GP	Indianapolis	40	European Minardi Cosworth		M	3.0 Minardi PS04B-Ford Cosworth V10	*ran as 3rd driver in practice only*	- /-
app	FRENCH GP	Magny Cours	40	European Minardi Cosworth		M	3.0 Minardi PS04B-Ford Cosworth V10	*ran as 3rd driver in practice only*	- /-
app	BRITISH GP	Silverstone	40	European Minardi Cosworth		M	3.0 Minardi PS04B-Ford Cosworth V10	*ran as 3rd driver in practice only*	- /-
app	GERMAN GP	Hockenheim	40	European Minardi Cosworth		M	3.0 Minardi PS04B-Ford Cosworth V10	*ran as 3rd driver in practice only*	- /-
app	HUNGARIAN GP	Hungaroring	40	European Minardi Cosworth		M	3.0 Minardi PS04B-Ford Cosworth V10	*ran as 3rd driver in practice only*	- /-
app	BELGIAN GP	Spa	40	European Minardi Cosworth		M	3.0 Minardi PS04B-Ford Cosworth V10	*ran as 3rd driver in practice only*	- /-
app	ITALIAN GP	Monza	40	European Minardi Cosworth		M	3.0 Minardi PS04B-Ford Cosworth V10	*ran as 3rd driver in practice only*	- /-
app	CHINESE GP	Shanghai Circuit	40	European Minardi Cosworth		M	3.0 Minardi PS04B-Ford Cosworth V10	*ran as 3rd driver in practice only*	- /-
app	JAPANESE GP	Suzuka	40	European Minardi Cosworth		M	3.0 Minardi PS04B-Ford Cosworth V10	*ran as 3rd driver in practice only*	- /-
app	BRAZILIAN GP	Interlagos	40	European Minardi Cosworth		M	3.0 Minardi PS04B-Ford Cosworth V10	*ran as 3rd driver in practice only*	- /-

Belgian driver who enjoyed a strong early career in Formula 3 and F3000, but after failing to break into F1 full-time, built a solid career in sports and GT racing.

LONDOÑO-BRIDGE, Ricardo (CO) b 8/8/1949, Medelin – d 18/7/2009, Boca Tinajones

1981

	Race	Circuit	No	Entrant	Tyres	Capacity/Car/Engine	Comment	Q Pos/Entries
excl	BRAZILIAN GP	Rio de Janeiro	14	Ensign	P	3.0 Ensign N180B-Cosworth V8	*refused entry – no super licence*	- /-

Took part in unofficial Wednesday practice session and managed to blot his copybook by hitting Rosberg's Fittipaldi. Denied his super licence he then raced briefly in Europe in Formula 2 in 1981. Subsequently raced in IMSA, before retiring to Colombia where he was reputedly involved in drugs and firearms trafficking. Murdered in 2009.

'LUCIENBONNET', (BONNET, Jean Lucien) (F) b 7/1/1923 Nice – d 19/8/1962, Enna, Sicily, Italy

1959

	Race	Circuit	No	Entrant	Tyres	Capacity/Car/Engine	Comment	Q Pos/Entries
dnq	MONACO GP	Monte Carlo	14	Jean Lucienbonnet	D	2.0 Cooper T45-Climax 4 F2		23/24

A motor and motorboat dealer by trade, 'Lucienbonnet' rallied Alfa Romeos, and raced in GT and Formula Junior formulae. Killed in a Formula Junior race in Sicily

McCARTHY, Perry (GB) b 3/3/1963, Stepney, London

1992

	Race	Circuit	No	Entrant	Tyres	Capacity/Car/Engine	Comment	Q Pos/Entries
dnpq	SPANISH GP	Barcelona	35	Andrea Moda Formula	G	3.5 Moda S921-Judd V10	*did not practice*	- /32
dnpq	SAN MARINO GP	Imola	35	Andrea Moda Formula	G	3.5 Moda S921-Judd V10		32/32
dnpq	MONACO GP	Monte Carlo	35	Andrea Moda Formula	G	3.5 Moda S921-Judd V10	*did not practice*	- /32
dnpq	CANADIAN GP	Montreal	35	Andrea Moda Formula	G	3.5 Moda S921-Judd V10	*did not practice*	- /32
dnpq	BRITISH GP	Silverstone	35	Andrea Moda Formula	G	3.5 Moda S921-Judd V10		32/32
excl*	GERMAN GP	Hockenheim	35	Andrea Moda Formula	G	3.5 Moda S921-Judd V10	*missed car weight check	32/32
dnpq	HUNGARIAN GP	Hungaroring	35	Andrea Moda Formula	G	3.5 Moda S921-Judd V10	*no time recorded*	- /31
dnq	BELGIAN GP	Spa	35	Andrea Moda Formula	G	3.5 Moda S921-Judd V10		29/30

Ever enthusiatic but impecunious racer, whose tilt at F1 was mainly confined to the pitlane.

McGUIRE, Brian (AUS) b 13/12/1945, Melbourne, Victoria – d 29/8/1977, Brands Hatch Circuit, Kent, England

1976

	Race	Circuit	No	Entrant	Tyres	Capacity/Car/Engine	Comment	Q Pos/Entries
dnc	BRITISH GP	Brand Hatch	41	Brian McGuire	G	3.0 Williams FW04-Cosworth V8	*reserve entry – not allowed to compete*	

1977

dnpq	BRITISH GP	Silverstone	45	Brian McGuire	G	McGuire BM1-Cosworth V8		35/36

Travelled over from Australia with Alan Jones to seek fame and fortune, but killed practising his own car during a national meeting at Brands Hatch.

MERKEL, Harry (D) b 10/1/1918, Taucha, Leipzig – d /11/2/1995, Killarney Vale, NSW, Australia

1952

	Race	Circuit	No	Entrant	Tyres	Capacity/Car/Engine	Comment	Q Pos/Entries
dns	GERMAN GP	Nürburgring	134	Willi Krakau	-	2.0 BMW-Eigenbau 6	*no time set*	- / -

A former motor cycle racer who defected from the DDR to Western Germany, drove mainly in sports car races into the sixties, before retiring to set up a car dealership

MONDINI, Giorgio (I) b 19/7/1980, Genoa, Italy

2006

	Race	Circuit	No	Entrant	Tyres	Capacity/Car/Engine	Comment	Q Pos/Entries
app	MALAYSIAN GP	Sepang	39	MF1 Racing	M	2.4 Midland M16-Toyota V8	*ran as 3rd driver in practice only*	- /-
app	SAN MARINO GP	Imola	39	MF1 Racing	M	2.4 Midland M16-Toyota V8	*ran as 3rd driver in practice only*	- /-
app	SPANISH GP	Barcelona	39	MF1 Racing	M	2.4 Midland M16-Toyota V8	*ran as 3rd driver in practice only*	- /-
app	MONACO GP	Monte Carlo	39	MF1 Racing	M	2.4 Midland M16-Toyota V8	*ran as 3rd driver in practice only*	- /-
app	BRITISH GP	Silverstone	39	MF1 Racing	M	2.4 Midland M16-Toyota V8	*ran as 3rd driver in practice only*	- /-
app	CANADIAN GP	Montreal	39	MF1 Racing	M	2.4 Midland M16-Toyota V8	*ran as 3rd driver in practice only*	- /-
app	US GP	Indianapolis	39	MF1 Racing	M	2.4 Midland M16-Toyota V8	*ran as 3rd driver in practice only*	- /-
app	TURKISH GP	Istanbul	39	MF1 Racing	M	2.4 Midland M16-Toyota V8	*ran as 3rd driver in practice only*	- /-
app	ITALIAN GP	Monza	39	Spyker MF1 Racing	M	2.4 Spyker M16-Toyota V8	*ran as 3rd driver in practice only*	- /-

A graduate of Formula Renault, who made little impression in either GP2 or A1GP. Later tested for HRT F1 team in 2011.

MOSS, Bill (GB) b 4/12/1933, Luton, Bedfordshire – d 13/1/2010, Dorchester

1959

	Race	Circuit	No	Entrant	Tyres	Capacity/Car/Engine	Comment	Q Pos/Entries
dnq	BRITISH GP (F2)	Aintree	56	United Racing Stable	D	1.5 Cooper T51-Climax 4 F2		– /30

British Formula Junior runner who won the 1961 John Davy Trophy series with a Gemini.

MOTOYAMA, Satoshi (J) b 4/3/1971, Tokyo

2003

	Race	Circuit	No	Entrant	Tyres	Capacity/Car/Engine	Comment	Q Pos/Entries
app	JAPANESE GP	Suzuka	36	Jordan Ford	B	3.0 Jordan EJ13-Ford Cosworth V8	ran as 3rd driver in practice only	– /–

Failed to get a break into F1, despite his impressive record in winning the Formula Nippon titles in 1998, 2001, 2003, and 2005. Also three-time All-Japan GT champion.

NELLEMAN, Jac (DK) b 19/4/1944, Copenhagen

1976

	Race	Circuit	No	Entrant	Tyres	Capacity/Car/Engine	Comment	Q Pos/Entries
dnq	SWEDISH GP	Anderstorp	33	RAM Racing	G	3.0 Brabham BT42-Cosworth V8		27/27
dnq	"	"	33	RAM Racing	G	3.0 Brabham BT44B-Cosworth V8		– / –

Danish karting and Formula Ford champion, who later raced in Formula 3 and F5000. Retired in 1979 to build a successful business career, but returned to race historics.

NISSANY, Chanoch (IL) b 29/7/1963, Tel Aviv

2005

	Race	Circuit	No	Entrant	Tyres	Capacity/Car/Engine	Comment	Q Pos/Entries
dns	HUNGARIAN GP	Hungaroring	40	European Minardi Cosworth	B	3.0 Minardi PS05-Cosworth V10	ran as 3rd driver in practice only	– /–

An Israeli businessman, based in Hungary, who started his motor sport career at the age of 38. Three F3000 starts for Coloni in 2004 got him a super licence.

OPPITZHAUSER, Karl (A) b 4/10/1941, Bruck an der Leitha

1976

	Race	Circuit	No	Entrant	Tyres	Capacity/Car/Engine	Comment	Q Pos/Entries
dnp	AUSTRIAN GP	Österreichring	40	Sports Cars of Austria	G	3.0 March 761-Cosworth V8	not allowed to compete	

Having no previous F1 experience stymied this Formula Vee and sports car racer's attempt to join the GP ranks. Later enjoyed a lengthy career in touring cars and GTs.

PIÀN, Alfredo (RA) b 21/10/1912, Las Rosas, nr Santa Fe – d 25/7/1990, Las Rosas, nr Santa Fe

1950

	Race	Circuit	No	Entrant	Tyres	Capacity/Car/Engine	Comment	Q Pos/Entries
dns	MONACO GP	Monte Carlo		Scuderia Achille Varzi	–	1.5 s/c Maserati 4CLT/48 4	injured in practice accident	(18)/21

This Argentine had a fine reputation at home in endurance races, but his intended debut at Monaco ended with leg injuries, when he spun on oil and crashed in practice.

PRÉMAT, Alexandre (F) b 5/4/1982, Juvisy-sur-Orge

2006

	Race	Circuit	No	Entrant	Tyres	Capacity/Car/Engine	Comment	Q Pos/Entries
app	CHINESE GP	Hungaroring	39	MF1 Racing	M	2.4 Midland M16-Toyota V8	ran as 3rd driver in practice only	– /–

Fast Frenchman who failed to break into F1, but enjoyed much success in the F3, A1GP and GP2 series. Later a works Audi driver in their DTM and sports cars.

PRINOTH, Ernesto (I) b 15/4/1923 Ortisei, Bolzano – d 26/11/1981 Innsbruck, Austria

1962

	Race	Circuit	No	Entrant	Tyres	Capacity/Car/Engine	Comment	Q Pos/Entries
dnq	ITALIAN GP	Monza	54	Scuderia Jolly Club	D	1.5 Lotus 18-Climax 4		27/30

In 1961 he finished a very distant third to Stirling Moss and Seidel in the Vienna GP, and second to Baghetti's Porsche in the Coppa Italia, in a decent national field.

PUZEY, Clive (RSR) b 11/7/1941, Bulawayo

1965

	Race	Circuit	No	Entrant	Tyres	Capacity/Car/Engine	Comment	Q Pos/Entries
dnpq	SOUTH AFRICAN GP	East London	24	Clive Puzey Motors	D	1.5 Lotus 18-Climax 4		– / –

Rhodesian national who raced competitively in the South African Formula 1 series in the 1960s. Later ran a garage in his home town before emigrating to Australia.

RAZIA, Luis (BR) b 4/4/1989, Barreiras

2011

	Race	Circuit	No	Entrant	Tyres	Capacity/Car/Engine	Comment	Q Pos/Entries
app	CHINESE GP	Shanghai	21	Team Lotus	P	2.4 Lotus T128-Renault V8	ran as 3rd driver in practice 1 only	– /–

2006 South American F3 Champion, who has had some good performances in various single seater categories since coming to Europe, the highlight being a GP2 series victory at Monza in 2009. Overshadowed by Rapax team mate and 2010 GP2 Champion Pastor Maldonado, Razia continued in the category in 2011 with Team Air Asia.

RICHARDSON, Ken (GB) b 21/8/1911, Bourne, Lincolnshire – d 27/6/1997 Bourne, Lincolnshire

1951

	Race	Circuit	No	Entrant	Tyres	Capacity/Car/Engine	Comment	Q Pos/Entries
dns	ITALIAN GP	Monza	32	BRM Ltd	D	1.5 s/c BRM P15 V16	did not possess correct licence	(10)/22

Test and development driver on the drawn-out and largely unsuccessful BRM V16 project of the early fifties.

ROLLINSON, Alan (GB) b 15/5/1943, Walsall, Staffordshire

1965

	Race	Circuit	No	Entrant	Tyres	Capacity/Car/Engine	Comment	Q Pos/Entries
dnq	BRITISH GP	Silverstone	25	Gerard Racing	D	1.5 Cooper T71/73-Ford 4		22/23

British F5000 front-runner who never made a Grand Prix start, but enjoyed a long and successful career in other formulae.

RUDAZ, Jean-Claude (CH) b 7/7/1942, La Grande Dixence, Sion

1964

	Race	Circuit	No	Entrant	Tyres	Capacity/Car/Engine	Comment	Q Pos/Entries
dns	ITALIAN GP	Monza	60	Fabre Urbain	D	1.5 Cooper T60-Climax V8	engine in practice	(20)/25

The young Swiss qualified for the above race but non-started with a blown engine. Drove a Renault Gordini for René Bonnet at Le Mans in 1964.

SEIFFERT, Günther (D) b 18/10/1937, Oldenberg

1962

	Race	Circuit	No	Entrant	Tyres	Capacity/Car/Engine	Comment	Q Pos/Entries
dnq	GERMAN GP	Nürburgring	34	Autosport Team Wolfgang Seidel	D	1.5 Lotus 24-BRM V8	shared car with Seidel	30/30

Slow coach German driver who trailed around at the back of a number of non-championship F1 races in 1962-63.

SOSPIRI, Vincenzo (I) b 7/10/1966, Italy

1997

	Race	Circuit	No	Entrant	Tyres	Capacity/Car/Engine	Comment	Q Pos/Entries
dnq	AUSTRALIAN GP	Melbourne	25	Mastercard Lola F1 Team	B	3.0 Lola T/97/30-Ford Zetec R V8	not within 107% of pole	24/24
dnp	BRAZILIAN GP	Interlagos	25	Mastercard Lola F1 Team	B	3.0 Lola T/97/30-Ford Zetec R V8	cars did not practice	- / -

1995 F3000 champion caught up in the Lola F1 fiasco. Found success in sportscars, and the IRL, but failed to impress in a brief CART foray.

SOUTH, Stephen (GB) b 19/2/1952, Harrow, Middlesex

1980

	Race	Circuit	No	Entrant	Tyres	Capacity/Car/Engine	Comment	Q Pos/Entries
dnq	US GP WEST	Long Beach	8	Marlboro Team McLaren	G	3.0 McLaren M29-Cosworth V8		27/27

Looked to have a big future until a Can-Am accident in 1980 which resulted in the amputation of part of his leg.

STUPPACHER, Otto (A) b 3/3/1947, Vienna

1976

	Race	Circuit	No	Entrant	Tyres	Capacity/Car/Engine	Comment	Q Pos/Entries
dns	ITALIAN GP	Monza	39	OASC Racing Team	G	3.0 Tyrrell 007-Cosworth V8	left circuit after practice	(26)/29
dnq	CANADIAN GP	Mosport Park	39	OASC Racing Team	G	3.0 Tyrrell 007-Cosworth V8		27/27
dnq	US GP EAST	Watkins Glen	39	OASC Racing Team	G	3.0 Tyrrell 007-Cosworth V8		27/27

Hill-climber and Porsche sports car exponent of no great pedigree. Stuppacher missed his big chance to compete in a Grand Prix when at Monza he left the circuit having failed to qualify. However, front-runners Hunt, Mass and Watson had their times disallowed due to fuel irregularities which would have allowed the Austrian into the race. The luckless Otto was back already in Vienna and unable to return in time to take up a place on the grid which was gratefully taken by World Champion to be James Hunt.

SUTCLIFFE, Andy (GB) b 9/5/1947, Mildenhall, Suffolk

1977

	Race	Circuit	No	Entrant	Tyres	Capacity/Car/Engine	Comment	Q Pos/Entries
dnpq	BRITISH GP	Silverstone	33	RAM Racing	G	3.0 March 761-Cosworth V8		32/36

British Formula 3 flyer who failed to meet his expectations in Formula 2 with a privateer March

TARAMAZZO, Luigi (I) b 5/5/1932, Ceva – d 15/2/2004, Vallecrosia

1958

	Race	Circuit	No	Entrant	Tyres	Capacity/Car/Engine	Comment	Q Pos/Entries
dnq	MONACO GP	Monte Carlo	50	Ken Kavanagh	-	2.5 Maserati 250F	shared Kavanah's car	- / -

Sports and GT racer who had a career which lasted more than twenty years. Raced mainly in Italy, most notably in a Ferrari 250 GTO.

TAYLOR, Dennis (GB) b 12/6/1921, Sidcup, Kent – d 2/6/1962 Monte Carlo, Monaco

1959

	Race	Circuit	No	Entrant	Tyres	Capacity/Car/Engine	Comment	Q Pos/Entries
dnq	BRITISH GP (F2)	Aintree	62	Dennis Taylor	D	1.5 Lotus 12-Climax 4 F2		- /30

Enthusiastic sports and Formula Junior racer who was sadly killed when he crashed in the Monaco Formula Junior support race in 1962.

TESTUT, André (MC) b 13/4/1926, Lyon, France – d 24/9/2005

1958

	Race	Circuit	No	Entrant	Tyres	Capacity/Car/Engine	Comment	Q Pos/Entries
dnq	MONACO GP	Monte Carlo	56	André Testut	D	2.5 Maserati 250F 6		24/28

1959

	Race	Circuit	No	Entrant	Tyres	Capacity/Car/Engine	Comment	Q Pos/Entries
dnq	MONACO GP	Monte Carlo	56	Monte Carlo Auto Sport	D	2.5 Maserati 250F 6		24/24

Monegasque who achieved little in his occasional sports and GT appearances, mainly with the Porsche and Osca marques.

TOCCACELO, Enrico (I) b 12/12/1978, Rome

2005

	Race	Circuit	No	Entrant	Tyres	Capacity/Car/Engine	Comment	Q Pos/Entries
app	TURKISH GP	Istanbul	40	European Minardi Cosworth	B	3.0 Minardi PS05-Cosworth V10	ran as 3rd driver in practice only	– / –
app	ITALIAN GP	Monza	40	European Minardi Cosworth	B	3.0 Minardi PS05-Cosworth V10	ran as 3rd driver in practice only	– / –
app	BELGIAN GP	Spa	40	European Minardi Cosworth	B	3.0 Minardi PS05-Cosworth V10	ran as 3rd driver in practice only	– / –

Race winner, and runner-up to Vitantoni Liuzzi in the 2004 FIA F3000 series. Also won a race for Italy in A1GP in 2006. Subsequently raced in the Superleague Formula.

TRIMMER, Tony (GB) b 24/1/1943, Maidenhead, Berkshire

1975

	Race	Circuit	No	Entrant	Tyres	Capacity/Car/Engine	Comment	Q Pos/Entries
dnq	GERMAN GP	Nürburgring	35	Maki Engineering	G	3.0 Maki F101C-Cosworth V8		26/26
dnq	AUSTRIAN GP	Österreichring	35	Maki Engineering	G	3.0 Maki F101C-Cosworth V8		30/30
dnq	ITALIAN GP	Monza	35	Maki Engineering	G	3.0 Maki F101C-Cosworth V8		28/28

1976

	Race	Circuit	No	Entrant	Tyres	Capacity/Car/Engine	Comment	Q Pos/Entries
dnq	JAPANESE GP	Mount Fuji	54	Maki Engineering	G	3.0 Maki F102A-Cosworth V8		27/27

1977

	Race	Circuit	No	Entrant	Tyres	Capacity/Car/Engine	Comment	Q Pos/Entries
dnpq	BRITISH GP	Silverstone	44	Melchester Racing	G	3.0 Surtees TS19-Cosworth V8		34/36

1978

	Race	Circuit	No	Entrant	Tyres	Capacity/Car/Engine	Comment	Q Pos/Entries
dnq	BRITISH GP	Brands Hatch	40	Melchester Racing	G	3.0 McLaren M23-Cosworth V8		30/30

Formula Ford star and 1970 British Formula 3 champion, whose career lost its way after he ended up in succession of uncompetitive cars.

VALSECCHI, Davide (I) b 24/1/1987, Eupilio

2011

	Race	Circuit	No	Entrant	Tyres	Capacity/Car/Engine	Comment	Q Pos/Entries
app	MALAYSIAN GP	Sepang	20	Team Lotus	P	2.4 Lotus T128-Renault V8	ran as 3rd driver in practice 1 only	– / –

GP2 sprint race winner at Monza in 2008, Valsecchi was the 2009-10 GP2 Asia series champion with three wins.

VERGNE, Jean-Éric (F) b 25/4/1999, Pontoise

2011

	Race	Circuit	No	Entrant	Tyres	Capacity/Car/Engine	Comment	Q Pos/Entries
app	KOREAN GP	Yeongam	19	Scuderia Toro Rosso	P	2.4 Toro Rosso STR6-Ferrari V8	ran as 3rd driver in practice 1 only	– / –
app	ABU DHABI GP	Yas Marina Circuit	20	Scuderia Toro Rosso	P	2.4 Toro Rosso STR6-Ferrari V8	ran as 3rd driver in practice 1 only	– / –
app	BRAZILIAN GP	Interlagos	20	Scuderia Toro Rosso	P	2.4 Toro Rosso STR6-Ferrari V8	ran as 3rd driver in practice 1 only	– / –

Red Bull star graduate, was the 2010 British Formula 3 champion and 2011 runner-up in the Formula Renault 3.5 Series, fast-tracked into an F1 seat with Toro Rosso.

VILLENEUVE, Jacques (CDN) b 4/11/1953, Saint-Jean-sur-Richelieu, Chambly, Quebec

1981

	Race	Circuit	No	Entrant	Tyres	Capacity/Car/Engine	Comment	Q Pos/Entries
dnq	CANADIAN GP	Montreal	30	Arrows Racing Team	P	3.0 Arrows A3-Cosworth V8		28/30
dnq	CAESARS PALACE GP	Las Vegas	30	Arrows Racing Team	P	3.0 Arrows A3-Cosworth V8		27/28

1983

	Race	Circuit	No	Entrant	Tyres	Capacity/Car/Engine	Comment	Q Pos/Entries
dnq	CANADIAN GP	Montreal	17	RAM Automotive Team March	P	3.0 March RAM 01-Cosworth V8		28/30

Younger brother of the great Gilles, and, of course, uncle of his son Jacques. The elder Jacques' F1 career never took off, but he did win an Indy Car race in 1985

VISO, Ernesto José (YV) b 19/3/1985, Caracas

2006

	Race	Circuit	No	Entrant	Tyres	Capacity/Car/Engine	Comment	Q Pos/Entries
app	BRAZILIAN GP	Interlagos	39	MF1 Racing	M	2.4 Midland M16-Toyota V8	ran as 3rd driver in practice only	– / –

Known as E.J. in the US, this 2006 GP2 winner, is now a regular competitor in the Indy Racing League, where his best finish is a third place at Iowa in 2010.

WEIDLER, Volker (D) b 18/3/1962, Weinheim, nr Mannheim

1989

	Race	Circuit	No	Entrant	Tyres	Capacity/Car/Engine	Comment	Q Pos/Entries
dnpq	BRAZILIAN GP	Rio	39	Rial Racing	G	3.5 Rial ARC2-Cosworth V8		33/38
dnpq	SAN MARINO GP	Imola	39	Rial Racing	G	3.5 Rial ARC2-Cosworth V8		39/39
dnpq	MONACO GP	Monte Carlo	39	Rial Racing	G	3.5 Rial ARC2-Cosworth V8		36/38
dnpq	MEXICAN GP	Mexico City	39	Rial Racing	G	3.5 Rial ARC2-Cosworth V8		34/39
dnpq	US GP (PHOENIX)	Phoenix	39	Rial Racing	G	3.5 Rial ARC2-Cosworth V8		36/39

dnpq	CANADIAN GP	Montreal	39	Rial Racing		G	3.5 Rial ARC2-Cosworth V8		37/39
dnpq	FRENCH GP	Paul Ricard	39	Rial Racing		G	3.5 Rial ARC2-Cosworth V8		33/39
dnpq	BRITISH GP	Silverstone	39	Rial Racing		G	3.5 Rial ARC2-Cosworth V8		39/39
excl*	GERMAN GP	Hockenheim	39	Rial Racing		G	3.5 Rial ARC2-Cosworth V8	*received outside assistance	30/39
dnq	HUNGARIAN GP	Hungaroring	39	Rial Racing		G	3.5 Rial ARC2-Cosworth V8		30/39

F3000 graduate whose time with Rial put paid to any further F1 chances. Won Le Mans with Mazda in 1991, and then went to race in F3000 in Japan, but an ear problem forced him into premature retirement when his career was back on the up.

WICKENS, Robert (CDN) b 13/3/1989, Toronto

2011

	Race	Circuit	No	Entrant	Tyres	Capacity/Car/Engine	Comment	Q Pos/Entries
app	ABU DHABI GP	Yas Marina Circuit	25	Marussia Virgin Racing	P	2.4 Virgin MVR-02-Cosworth V8	ran as 3rd driver in practice 1 only	- / -

A very talented driver who has shone in every junior single seater category, including A1GP and GP3. Crowned Formula Renault 3.5 Series Champion in 2011.

WHITEAWAY, Ted (GB) b 1/11/1928, Feltham, Middlesex – d 18/10/1995, Perth, Western Australia, Australia

1955

	Race	Circuit	No	Entrant	Tyres	Capacity/Car/Engine	Comment	Q Pos/Entries
dnq	MONACO GP	Monte Carlo	24	E N Whiteaway	D	2.5 HWM-Alta 4		22/22

British amateur who briefly raced his outdated HWM on the continent early in 1955. His best lap at Monaco was some 16 seconds of the pace of pole sitter Fangio.

WILSON, Desiré (ZA) b 26/11/1953, Johannesburg

1980

	Race	Circuit	No	Entrant	Tyres	Capacity/Car/Engine	Comment	Q Pos/Entries
dnq	BRITISH GP	Brands Hatch	43	Brands Hatch Racing	G	3.0 Williams FW07-Cosworth V8		27/27

Became the first woman ever to win a Formula 1 race of any kind at a round of the Aurora F1 series at Brands Hatch in 1980. Finished an excellent sixth in the 1981 South African GP racing for Tyrrell, sadly for Desiré, the race was subsequently deprived of championship status.

WINKELHOCK, Joachim (D) b 24/10/1960, Waiblingen, nr Stuttgart

1989

	Race	Circuit	No	Entrant	Tyres	Capacity/Car/Engine	Comment	Q Pos/Entries
dnpq	BRAZILIAN GP	Rio	41	Automobiles Gonfaronaise Sportive	G	3.5 AGS JH23B-Cosworth V8		35/38
dnpq	SAN MARINO GP	Imola	41	Automobiles Gonfaronaise Sportive	G	3.5 AGS JH23B-Cosworth V8		35/39
dnpq	MONACO GP	Monte Carlo	41	Automobiles Gonfaronaise Sportive	G	3.5 AGS JH23B-Cosworth V8		38/38
dnpq	MEXICAN GP	Mexico City	41	Automobiles Gonfaronaise Sportive	G	3.5 AGS JH23B-Cosworth V8		38/39
dnpq	US GP (PHOENIX)	Phoenix	41	Automobiles Gonfaronaise Sportive	G	3.5 AGS JH23B-Cosworth V8		35/39
dnpq	CANADIAN GP	Montreal	41	Automobiles Gonfaronaise Sportive	G	3.5 AGS JH23B-Cosworth V8		36/39
dnpq	FRENCH GP	Paul Ricard	41	Automobiles Gonfaronaise Sportive	G	3.5 AGS JH23B-Cosworth V8		39/39

1988 German F3 champion who had a disastrous F1 spell with AGS before turning to touring cars with BMW. BTCC champion in 1993, and a Le Mans winner in 1999 sharing a BMW with Pierluigi Martini and Yannick Dalmas.

WIRDHEIM, Björn (S) b 4/4/1980, Växjö

2003

	Race	Circuit	No	Entrant	Tyres	Capacity/Car/Engine	Comment	Q Pos/Entries
app	US GP	Indianapolis	36	Jordan Ford	B	3.0 Jordan EJ13-Ford Cosworth V8	ran as 3rd driver in practice only	- /-

2004

	Race	Circuit	No	Entrant	Tyres	Capacity/Car/Engine	Comment	Q Pos/Entries
app	AUSTRALIAN GP	Melbourne	37	Jaguar Racing	M	3.0 Jaguar R5-Ford Cosworth V10	ran as 3rd driver in practice only	- /-
app	MALAYSIAN GP	Sepang	37	Jaguar Racing	M	3.0 Jaguar R5-Ford Cosworth V10	ran as 3rd driver in practice only	- /-
app	BAHRAIN GP	Sakhir Circuit	37	Jaguar Racing	M	3.0 Jaguar R5-Ford Cosworth V10	ran as 3rd driver in practice only	- /-
app	SAN MARINO GP	Imola	37	Jaguar Racing	M	3.0 Jaguar R5-Ford Cosworth V10	ran as 3rd driver in practice only	- /-
app	SPANISH GP	Barcelona	37	Jaguar Racing	M	3.0 Jaguar R5-Ford Cosworth V10	ran as 3rd driver in practice only	- /-
app	MONACO GP	Monte Carlo	37	Jaguar Racing	M	3.0 Jaguar R5-Ford Cosworth V10	ran as 3rd driver in practice only	- /-
app	EUROPEAN GP	Nürburgring	37	Jaguar Racing	M	3.0 Jaguar R5-Ford Cosworth V10	ran as 3rd driver in practice only	- /-
app	CANADIAN GP	Montreal	37	Jaguar Racing	M	3.0 Jaguar R5-Ford Cosworth V10	ran as 3rd driver in practice only	- /-
app	US GP	Indianapolis	37	Jaguar Racing	M	3.0 Jaguar R5-Ford Cosworth V10	ran as 3rd driver in practice only	- /-
app	FRENCH GP	Magny Cours	37	Jaguar Racing	M	3.0 Jaguar R5-Ford Cosworth V10	ran as 3rd driver in practice only	- /-
app	BRITISH GP	Silverstone	37	Jaguar Racing	M	3.0 Jaguar R5-Ford Cosworth V10	ran as 3rd driver in practice only	- /-
app	GERMAN GP	Hockenheim	37	Jaguar Racing	M	3.0 Jaguar R5-Ford Cosworth V10	ran as 3rd driver in practice only	- /-
app	HUNGARIAN GP	Hungaroring	37	Jaguar Racing	M	3.0 Jaguar R5-Ford Cosworth V10	ran as 3rd driver in practice only	- /-
app	BELGIAN GP	Spa	37	Jaguar Racing	M	3.0 Jaguar R5-Ford Cosworth V10	ran as 3rd driver in practice only	- /-
dns	ITALIAN GP	Monza	37	Jaguar Racing	M	3.0 Jaguar R5-Ford Cosworth V10	ran as 3rd driver in practice only	- /-
app	CHINESE GP	Shanghai Circuit	37	Jaguar Racing	M	3.0 Jaguar R5-Ford Cosworth V10	ran as 3rd driver in practice only	- /-
app	BRAZILIAN GP	Interlagos	37	Jaguar Racing	M	3.0 Jaguar R5-Ford Cosworth V10	ran as 3rd driver in practice only	- /-

2003 F3000 Champion who lost his way in the struggling Jaguar team. Subsequently forged a successful long-term career in Japan.

ZAPICO, Emilio (E) b 21/5/1944, Léon – d 6/8/1996, Huete

1976

	Race	Circuit	No	Entrant	Tyres	Capacity/Car/Engine	Comment	Q Pos/Entries
dnq	SPANISH GP	Jarama	25	Mapfre-Williams	G	3.0 Williams FW04-Cosworth V8	third works car	27/30

A more than decent touring and sports car driver in Europe for more than a decade, who failed to make his home race with a year-old Williams. Died after a road accident.